A LEXICON OF
GREEK PERSONAL
NAMES

THE BRITISH ACADEMY

# A LEXICON OF GREEK PERSONAL NAMES

EDITED BY

P. M. FRASER

AND

E. MATTHEWS

WITH THE COLLABORATION OF MANY SCHOLARS

VOLUME IIIA

THE PELOPONNESE
WESTERN GREECE
SICILY AND MAGNA GRAECIA

CLARENDON PRESS · OXFORD

# OXFORD

UNIVERSITY PRESS

Great Clarendon Street, Oxford OX2 6DP
Oxford University Press is a department of the University of Oxford.
It furthers the University's objective of excellence in research, scholarship,
and education by publishing worldwide in
Oxford New York

Auckland Cape Town Dar es Salaam Hong Kong Karachi
Kuala Lumpur Madrid Melbourne Mexico City Nairobi
New Delhi Shanghai Taipei Toronto

With offices in
Argentina Austria Brazil Chile Czech Republic France Greece
Guatemala Hungary Italy Japan Poland Portugal Singapore
South Korea Switzerland Thailand Turkey Ukraine Vietnam

Oxford is a registered trade mark of Oxford University Press
in the UK and in certain other countries

Published in the United States
by Oxford University Press Inc., New York

ISBN 13: 978-0-19-815229-3
ISBN 10: 0-19-815229-9

4 6 5 3

Printed in Great Britain
on acid-free paper by
Antony Rowe Ltd,
Chippenham, Wiltshire

## ACKNOWLEDGMENTS

In the preparation of this Volume we have incurred many debts to scholars at home and abroad, whose contribution of material has made our task easier and the published Volume more complete than it could otherwise have been.

We have to thank, for the *Peloponnese*: Dr Ch. Kritzas, Director of the Epigraphical Museum, Athens; Dr A. D. Rizakis, Institute for Greek and Roman Antiquity (KERA) in Athens; Professor P. Siewert, University of Vienna; Dr A. J. S. Spawforth, University of Newcastle; Professor R. Stroud, Mellon Professor of Classical Studies at the American School of Classical Studies in Athens; for *W. Greece and Illyria*: Dr C. Antonetti, University of Venice; Professor P. Cabanes, University of Paris X, Nanterre; Dr D. Strauch, Berlin-Brandenburgische Akademie der Wissenschaften; for *Dalmatia*: Dr E. Marin, Director of the Archaeological Museum, Split; for *S. Italy*: Professor M. Lazzarini, University, 'La Sapienza', Rome; Professor E. Miranda, University of Naples; Dr N. K. Rutter, University of Edinburgh; Professor H. Solin, University of Helsinki; for *Sicily*: Professor F. Cordano, University of Macerata, Professor G. Manganaro, University of Catania; Professor R. J. A. Wilson, University of Nottingham.

J. A. W. Warren (Mrs Cargill Thompson) undertook responsibility for the numismatic evidence from the Peloponnese and from the Ionian Islands, Aetolia and Acarnania, and in addition gave valuable assistance on some of the coinage of Epirus and Illyria. We are deeply grateful for her expert contribution in an area beyond our capability. M. D. Mulliez, University of Reims, and M. J. Oulhen, University of Rennes II, informed us of new readings arising from their revisions of, respectively, the manumission documents of Delphi and the Delphic list of 'Theorodokoi'. Dr B. Petrakos, General Secretary of the Archaeological Society at Athens, made available to us the indexes of his unpublished Corpus of the inscriptions of Oropos.

The foundations of the *Lexicon* were laid many years ago, and the work of many of the contributors listed in Volume I forms part of this Volume also, particularly the archaeological material provided by Dr A. W. Johnston, and the research, especially for the Peloponnese, carried out by Dr S. M. Sherwin-White and Dr A. Griffin.

The Council of the British Academy wishes to place on record its deep obligation to the Council of the Archaeological Society at Athens for substantial annual grants to the *Lexicon* since 1992. For specific grants for this Volume, thanks are due to the Marc Fitch Trust, and to the Craven Committee and the Hulme University Fund (Oxford University), the Jowett Copyright Trustees of Balliol College, and All Souls College. Grants have also been received from the following Greek societies in the U.K.: the Hellenic Foundation, the London Hellenic Society, and the Hellenic Society of Professional People.

We must express our appreciation of the work of the *Lexicon* staff in bringing this challenging Volume to completion: especially that of Richard Catling, for his skilful handling of material from the Peloponnese, and his work in the difficult area of S. Italy; and of Heather Baker for her skill and patience in the management of the data. Ilias Arnaoutoglou, engaged in the preparation of the material from Thrace and Macedonia for Volume IV, also assisted in the final stages of this Volume. Jonathan Moffett continued to manage our database programs, and Sebastian Rahtz to advise on typesetting. Yannis Kharalambous adapted and corrected the Monotype Porson and Greek Sans Serif fonts.

We thank all these for their contributions to an enterprise which is now of international dimensions. Finally, we must record our sadness at the death of Professor O. Masson, with whom over the years we have had many lively and fruitful exchanges, and whose unique knowledge of onomastics will be greatly missed.

P. M. F.
E. M.

# INTRODUCTION

This Volume contains personal names from the Peloponnese, W. Greece (Aetolia, Acarnania, the Ionian Islands, Epirus, Illyria and the Corinthian colonial sites in Dalmatia), and Sicily and Magna Graecia. Our original intention had been to include within the same volume Central Greece (Locris, Phocis and Boeotia with Megara) and Thessaly, but considerations of bulk made us decide to divide the Volume and to defer this large area to a second part (IIIB), each of approximately equal size, representing recognisable historical and linguistic areas. Since the two parts have been prepared in parallel, it is hoped that IIIB will be published after only a short interval. The numeration of the following volumes will remain unchanged.

This dichotomy apart, Volume III follows, except for a few very insignificant modifications, the pattern of its predecessors, and it is not necessary to repeat the basic information provided in the Preface to Volume I concerning the categories of persons included, the method used in the entries and other details. We have seen no reason to change these features, which seem to have served a wide spectrum of users. Nonetheless, as we progress through the regions of the ancient Greek world new features are encountered which require special treatment within the framework of the *Lexicon*, and merit some explanation, both in general terms and region by region.

The inhabitants of each region of Greece spoke, and largely wrote, a dialect different in some degree from their neighbours, and it is *Lexicon* practice to retain these dialect-forms as independent names (see *LGPN* I xii). In the onomastic field, however, especially in the archaic period of epichoric scripts, it is frequently difficult to determine the correct prime (nominative) forms of proper names, and dialectologists may disagree with some of those we have extrapolated from inflected cases, for disagreement is inevitable over personal names in a way that does not arise within the stereotyped framework of common nouns. The uncertainties are not explicable purely on linguistic grounds. In every type of text, epichoric alphabets reveal an unhappy propensity to be inconsistent in usage and adherence to a single accepted form, and names are frequently isolated without any linguistic context to give assistance. In addition, many of the texts are of uncertain interpretation, and may be based on early and unreliable copies. By comparison, the dialect-forms of the period of the Ionic alphabet, such as the intervocalic consonantal aspirate, the intervocalic sigma and the terminal rho, are straightforward; they, too, have been retained as separate forms. It is to be remembered that, particularly in the Imperial period, a taste for archaism led to the re-introduction of archaic forms.

The task, both for the editors in deciding how to treat such variants, and for the reader in negotiating the results, would be facilitated by a system of cross-reference between different forms of the same name, though we do not underestimate the dangers that lurk in such linguistic equations, especially in inscriptions of Hellenistic and Imperial date, in which simple etacism and dialectal variations may easily be confused, and in some cases cannot indeed be distinguished. It had been our intention to introduce such a system in this Volume, but unfortunately, for technical reasons, this has not proved possible. We hope to introduce it in Volume IIIB, where the heavily dialectal character of the material should make it a valuable aid.

It is the aim of the *Lexicon* to provide a regional onomastic picture; but there may be radical demographic changes which alter onomastic foundations. We may contrast the social stability of cities such as Athens and Rhodes, where onomastic changes do, of course, occur, but where there is also a basic onomastic continuity, with the situation in Magna Graecia and Sicily and, in a different way, in the Peloponnese. The establishment of Roman power in S. Italy in the later fourth century and in Sicily at the end of the third could only open the door eventually to new onomastic developments. On a smaller scale, the sack of Corinth in 146 B.C., and the establishment of a Roman colony there in 46 B.C., and at Patrai in 14 B.C., of which the former at least was largely settled with Italian freedmen, meant a new population, and therefore new onomastic features based on Roman foundations, be it in Greek or in Latin. Greek names in Latin, in Italy particularly, a widespread and complicated phenomenon, feature largely in this Volume.

The List of Abbreviations has grown considerably, mainly because of the need, in the absence of corpora, to cite local journals and guides, especially for Sicily. We continue to use the abbreviations for ancient sources established by Liddell and Scott and the *Diccionario griego-español*; but readers will appreciate that, with the passage of time, newer editions of texts have become available. We have, for example, made use of the recent volumes in the series of the Loeb Hippocrates (for *Epid.* 2, 4, 5-7), particularly on points of dating, though continuing to use Littré where necessary for points of detail for manuscript readings; similarly, the later volumes of the Loeb Plutarch, *Moralia*; the edition by M. Davies of Alcman, Stesichorus and Ibycus, *Poetarum Melicorum Graecorum Fragmenta*, in place of D. L. Page's *Poetae Melici Graeci*; and Kassel-Austin's *Poetae Comici Graeci*.

Continuing the practice begun in Volume II, we include a Reverse Index of names occurring in this Volume; a limited 'market research' exercise persuaded us that it would be helpful to readers if we retained the accents, even though the correct accentuation may be in doubt, especially in cases of non-Greek names recorded in Greek.

The Peloponnese and W. Greece do not stand as regional headings except in cases where no more precise location can be assigned. The various regions which make up this Volume are listed in alphabetical order, irrespective of geographical location. An exception was made for the regions of S. Italy (Apulia, Bruttium etc.) which it was felt should not be dispersed by the alphabetical arrangement. They have been kept together with the formula 'S. Italy (Apulia)', 'S. Italy (Bruttium)' etc.

A wide range of civic and ethnic subdivisions will be found in this Volume, from the tribes, phratries and κῶμαι of Argos and the ἔθνη of Epirus to the civic units (many existing as no more than two- or three-letter abbreviations) which occur in the lists of magistrates at Epizephyrian Locri, Syracuse, Tauromenium and elsewhere.[1] As previously (see *LGPN* I xi), all these units have been recorded, not only because of their intrinsic interest but because they enable us to distinguish between homonyms in communities where particular names are very common (e.g. Νυμφόδωρος, Ὀλυμπίς and Φρῦνις at Tauromenium). In the numerous cases where they exist in very abbreviated form, we have retained the Greek letters; in other cases, for example in Epirus, the numerous ethnic groups of this type are given in transliteration. In all cases, they appear on the third line of the location-hierarchy, after region and, where appropriate, city.

The formula first devised to embrace within *LGPN* I the many individuals of uncertain status attested on Delos over a long period (I xi) has been used extensively in this Volume. Thus, dedicants at the major cult centres of Dodona and Olympia who do not have a specific ethnic appear as Dodona* and Olympia* ('attested at' Dodona, Olympia), in preference to their being held over, in the absence of any indication of citizenship, to the final Volume of 'Others'. The principle has been stretched to the limit by the inclusion of the many freedmen in S. Italy, particularly at Pompeii and Herculaneum, with Greek names (mostly in Latin), about whose origins we can have no certainty, but who were clearly active members of their communities. It has not, however, been extended to slaves, even though their names at manumission (the situation in which we most often come across them) often indicate a strong local influence. Slaves without ethnics, including those 'born in the house', will, as always planned, appear in the final Volume.

Names from vases, which featured so largely in *LGPN* II, occur here primarily from Corinth and from Rhegium ('Chalcidian vases'). In a *Lexicon* confining itself to the historical period, names on vases present the particular difficulty of deciding whether or not to treat those depicted and named as historical. Where the context is heroic, we have assigned the status 'heroic'; in generic scenes involving fighting, horses, chariots etc., we have assigned

'heroic?'; and 'fictitious?' to all other individuals, unless there is good reason to think they are historical people, for example if the name occurs as part of a dedication. It may be noted that if the source of a name is an artefact, we now indicate this by adding after the reference '(vase)', '(tile)', '(loomweight)' etc.

The numismatic material for the Peloponnese and for much of W. Greece has been edited by Jennifer Warren, who contributes the following note: 'Concerning personal names on coins, readers should be alerted to the fact that while the coverage will be reliable for coinages that have been researched in detail and in recent years (for example, those of Epirus, Laconia, the Duoviral coinage of Corinth, and the bronze coinage of the Achaean League), for some other series, especially in northwest Greece, this cannot be so. For these coinages, where an exhaustive search through unpublished collections - beyond the scope of *LGPN* - has been wanting, it has sometimes been necessary to rely on references in Münsterberg to citations of unillustrated *unica* in early catalogues, which it has not been possible to confirm. It should further be appreciated that it is on late Hellenistic bronze coins that names are often found most plentifully, but have not always been exhaustively collected.

Personal names often appear on coins in abbreviated form. The full form has been cited in *LGPN* either when the expansion seemed reasonably certain, or, occasionally, when the abbreviation suggests a rare name specific to the locality. The extent of the restoration has been indicated as necessary.'

## 1 The Peloponnese

We must express our thanks to Dr Ch. Kritzas, Director of the Epigraphical Museum of Athens, formerly Ephor of the Greek Archaeological Service for Argolido-Korinthia, for providing unpublished material from that region, and to G. Kavvadias and Dr A. Oikonomou-Laniado for providing unpublished material from the same area; to Dr A. D. Rizakis for scrutinizing our Achaea file and making material available to us in advance of publication; to Dr P. Siewert for scrutinizing and adding to our file of Elis; to Dr A. J. S. Spawforth for advising us on the bulky and complicated material from Imperial Laconia; to Professor R. Stroud for putting at our disposal long ago his unpublished prosopography of Corinthia; and to Professor P. Themeles, Director of the excavations at Messene, for keeping us well supplied with offprints of his preliminary publications of newly-discovered inscriptions there.

The Peloponnese has perhaps been the most straightforward of all the major regions covered in this volume; nevertheless some additional explanations are called for.

---

[1] see N. F. Jones, *Public Organization in Ancient Greece* (Mem. of the American Philosophical Society 176, Philadelphia, 1987.)

## 1.1 Argolis

The fragmentary manumission texts from the neighbour-hood of Argos,[2] in which names are listed in pairs, one in the nominative and the other in the genitive, do not specify the identity of either party. We have followed the view of Baunack and others, that the name in the nomin-ative is that of the slave, while that in the genitive is the name of the owner or the guarantor. However, because of the uncertainty that exists, those taken to be the emancip-ated slaves are included under the rhubric 'Argos*'.

## 1.2 Elis

The abbreviations found in lists of cult-officials at Elis (*IvOl* 62; 64 etc.) have not been treated as civic units, since they never appear in a civic context, but as 'statuses' and as such are given at the end of the entry, in Greek, in the form in which they appear in the documents.

## 1.3 Laconia

The reference to 'Wade-Gery' is to manuscript marginalia in Professor H. T. Wade-Gery's copy of 'Poralla', made available to us by Dr S. Hornblower.

## 2  Western Greece

### 2.1 Aetolia

We are grateful to Dr C. Antonetti for reading our file of Aetolia and for making helpful comments; we have also taken advantage of Dr Antonetti's published topograph-ical studies to identify settlements whose exact location is disputed.

### 2.2 Ionian Islands

With regard to the Ionian Islands (in which we have in-cluded Leukas, in spite of its later role as head of the Acarnanian League), we owe much to Dr D. Strauch, who is preparing an edition of the inscriptions of these islands for the new series of *Inscriptiones Graecae*. He has made available to us material collected by G. Klaffenbach on his travels there in the 1930s. We indicate these as 'Unp. (*IG* Archive)'. In addition, many of the names described as 'Unp. (Leukas Mus.)' are those of tombstones seen by Fraser in the early 1950s and later, which to the best of our knowledge remain unpublished.

### 2.3 Epirus and Illyria

We are fortunate to have had the closest collaboration over the years with Professor P. Cabanes, who has undertaken, with N. Ceka and F. Drini, the publication of the Greek inscriptions of Epirus and Southern Illyria.[3] The next volume in the series will contain the epigraphical material from the notable site of Bouthrotos, consisting, first and foremost, of the remarkable series of manumission docu-ments, which, though fewer in number, equal those of Delphi in complexity and wealth of information. Through the generosity of Professor Cabanes, the *Lexicon* has been able to incorporate all the material (much of it unpub-lished) from this *Corpus*. Though it is unlikely to be pub-lished for some time, we have cited the *Corpus* number, adding, in the case of texts already published, a reference to the existing publication.[4]

This whole region poses the problem of the relation-ship of *ethne* and *koina* to cities, and of the interdepend-ence of larger and smaller *ethne*. The numerous tribal units attested in literary and epigraphical sources range from the large and well-attested Molossoi and Thesprotoi down to small federated units with shifting affiliations and, often, no ascertainable location. Normally, we have sub-sumed them directly under Epirus, and have not tried to reflect their affiliations. At Bouthrotos, however, where more than seventy five are attested, almost all operating within the *koinon* of the Prasaiboi, it seemed important to indicate their cohesion by subsuming them as 'demes' under the heading 'Bouthrotos (Prasaiboi)'.

### 2.4  Coinage of Apollonia and Epidamnos-Dyrrhachion

Some explanation is required of our treatment of the names which appear on the silver and bronze coinage of these two cities after about 250 B.C.. There are usually two names, one in the genitive on the reverse, tradition-ally (but not necessarily accurately) regarded as the magis-trate, the 'prytanis', and the other in the nominative on the obverse, taken to be the 'moneyer'. Difficulties arise as regards the citation of references, the dating and the related problem of the identification of homonyms.

For the silver coinage, we cite the catalogues published by A. Maier in the *Numismatische Zeitschrift* for 1908, and by H. Ceka in his *Questions de numismatique illyrienne*; additional material is given mainly by reference to vari-ous articles by R. Münsterberg. Unfortunately, neither Maier nor Ceka in *Questions* covered the bronze coinage, of which there is no single published catalogue. We have tried to track down references in the standard collections, but where we failed, we have been obliged to cite Ceka's *Probleme* (in Albanian), in which he lists the names on the bronze, but gives no detailed references.

The overall chronological limits of the coinage have been disputed, but current opinion is that it ran from, approximately, the middle of the third to the middle of

---

[2]Texts: *IG* IV (1) 530, with *BCH* 33 (1909) p. 183 n. 2; ib. p. 456 f. no. 23; *JÖAI* 14 (1911) Beibl. p. 146 no. 4; *SEG* XLII 279.

[3]This Franco-Albanian collaboration has produced the *Corpus* of the inscriptions of Epidamnos-Dyrrhachion (1995), and of Apollonia (in press), both of which were made available to us ahead of publication.

[4]The texts from the Theatre are most easily accessible in *SEG*

XXXVIII 465-517, where the readings made by L. Morricone in the 1930s (published by G. Pugliese-Carratelli in *PdelP* 41 (1986) pp. 383 ff.) are given, with comments by P. Cabanes.

[5]see M. Beauregard, *Grecs et Illyriens* pp. 95 ff. for a preliminary study identifying some individuals on the coins with homonyms in other contexts, for example on tiles.

the first century B.C.. Within that broad span, hoard-evidence offers the basis for assigning coins to more precisely defined periods,[5] but unfortunately no study of this kind has been carried out comprehensively.

In the absence of an established internal chronology, we have no sound basis for distinguishing between the different instances of the same name, which may recur frequently. Δαμήν, for example, occurs in the genitive ('prytanis') in combination with seventeen different 'moneyers', and Ἀλκαῖος in the nominative with twenty-six different 'prytaneis'. These are extreme cases, but the problem recurs many times in less extreme forms. We have adopted a schematic presentation of the evidence: all examples of a name in the genitive are subsumed under one entry, and similarly all those of a name in the nominative; we have kept the names on silver coinage separate from those on bronze, even though some names are very distinctive and identity correspondingly more probable.

We must express our gratitude to Dr P. Kinns, a member of our Committee, who put at our disposal his preliminary studies of this coinage; to Professor Cabanes for making available to us the numismatic appendix, edited by Marc Beauregard, to appear in the forthcoming *Corpus* of the inscriptions of Apollonia; to the late Professor O. Masson, to Professor O. Picard and to Mme H. Nicolet for valuable exchanges of views and information at a late stage. It goes without saying that they cannot be held in any way responsible for the schematic way in which we have been obliged to treat this onomastically rich material within the framework of the *Lexicon*.

There remains one matter for regret regarding the Epirus file, namely the absence from it of many names that will appear in the unpublished lead plaques on which were inscribed the oracular enquiries at Dodona. The numerous publications of C. Carapanos, D. Evangelides and S. Dakaris have been the main source of our material. The publication of the subscription-list on a leaden tablet by Dr A. Antoniou, Δωδώνη, is an indication of how many onomastic surprises may be expected from the shrine.

## 2.5  Dalmatian islands and coast

Although this Adriatic region lies well to the north of, and distinct from, the original regional boundaries of this Volume, it seemed desirable that the material from the Corinthian and other colonies of the Dalmatian coast and islands should be accommodated here, alongside Illyria. Historical considerations led us to separate off this part of the later Roman province of Illyricum, where the onomastic features are of a different nature, and form a natural part of Volume IV. We have been helped throughout this part of our work by the assiduous collaboration of Dr E. Marin, Director of the Archaeological Museum of Split.[6] Fraser particularly wishes to thank Dr Marin for accompanying him on a trip to the Dalmatian Islands, which enabled him to study the material there.

## 3  Magna Graecia and Sicily

In Magna Graecia, and to a lesser extent in Sicily, a unique onomastic situation existed. Sicily became a Roman province in 241 B.C., and the Oscan- and Messapian-speaking Italian provinces from Campania southward to the Straits had become increasingly subject to Roman influence since the end of the fourth century. While, however, the old colonial cities of Sicily retained their predominantly Greek, or native, way of life, in spite of Roman exploitation and administration, as illustrated in Cicero's *Verrine Orations*, in the cities of S. Italy Latin colonies took the place of Greek cities as the principal urban unit, and a predominantly libertine population, of Italian and Oriental origin, replaced the descendants of the Greek colonists. The process, begun long before, was not completed until the Social War in 89 B.C., but the Greek cities from Brundisium to Rhegium were wholly under Roman influence, politically, economically and socially, from long before that date. The Greek *cognomina* of *liberti* cannot be regarded as a reflection of traditional local nomenclature, but in due course they and their descendants came to form the stock of the region.

It did not seem to us a practicable proposition to pursue Greek names in their various Latin forms up to the gates of Rome. On historical as well as practical grounds a compromise was clearly necessary (not least because of the comprehensive onomastic work of Professor H. Solin), and our solution has been to restrict our published file, on the Adriatic side, to the northern border of Apulia, roughly on the same latitude as southern Campania, omitting the Samnite hinterland. In Campania, the line of demarcation has been drawn along the forty-first parallel, thus including the whole of the Bay of Naples, with Puteoli and Misenum, but omitting the cities of the hinterland, notably Capua. Our slogan has been δεῖ που στῆναι

A similar decision had to be taken as regards chronology, for to have kept to our usual later limit of the mid.-seventh century A.D. would have been to stray into the new world that followed the barbarian inroads into Italy and Sicily, when nomenclature underwent changes that could not be accommodated to a *Lexicon* of Greek personal names. Similarly we have not exploited the names of martyrs etc. contained in the *Martyrologium Hieronymianum* and similar texts.

We have included in S. Italy the few natives of the area who appear in inscriptions abroad with the ethnics Βρύ(έ)ττιος, Λευκανός, Μεσσάπιος, Ἰᾶπυξ, Καμπανός, but have regarded the epichoric inscriptions of these Italic regions as beyond our brief.

In Sicily, more especially at Syracuse and Catana, both the reading and the chronology of the numerous texts from the Christian catacombs, which have been intensively (and sometimes unsuccessfully) studied over generations, present serious problems. The graffiti were badly written, and many have now disappeared, while the cursive style of writing and lack of orthography make many of the texts

---

[6]The epigraphical fruits of Dr Marin's excavations at Salona and Narona will appear in Volume IV, for which he prepared our Dalmatia file, with the assistance of Dr I. Britvić.

difficult to decipher and to date. We hope that we have collected most of this material, and, if we have, we and users of this Volume owe much to the epigraphical skills and tireless labours of the Revd. Professor S. A. Agnello, S. J., and the Revd. Professor A. Ferrua, S. J. We have in general adopted the chronology set forth by Agnello in *Scritti in onore di Guido Libertini* (Ist. di arch. dell' Università di Catania, Florence 1958), pp. 65-82, 'Probleme di datazione delle Catacombe di Siracusa', who especially casts doubt on the existence of pre-Constantinian burials. We have used the wide bracket 'iii-v A.D.' in the large majority of cases in which a consular date is not given. On the textual side we have been greatly indebted to Ferrua's 'Epigrafia sicula, pagana e christiana' (*RAC* 18 (1941) pp. 151-243), and to his detailed scrutiny of texts in his monograph, *Note e Giunte*.

Our debts to scholars in this area where difficult texts, of both the archaic and the late Roman periods, have been published and re-published several times, and where new texts are regularly discovered, are particularly great. We owe a long-standing debt to Professor Solin, who prepared our original file of Greek names at Pompeii, and since then has provided us with a list of Greek names from his current work on the revision of *CIL* X, and has generally kept us abreast of his many researches, and stimulated us by lively debate. Professor E. Miranda made available to us her *Corpus* of the inscriptions of Naples before publication; Professor M. Lazzarini cast a critical eye on the Greek material in our S. Italian file; Professor F. Cordano, Professor G. Manganaro and Professor R. J. A. Wilson kept us informed of current epigraphical work and new discoveries in Sicily; we were helped at a late stage by receiving a copy of the onomasticon of Sicily prepared by Dr J. Curbera.

P. M. F.
E. M.

Abbreviations of Greek and Latin authors used are not included in this list, except that editions of fragments (*FGrH, FVS* etc.) have been retained. The conventions followed are those of Liddell and Scott, *A Greek-English Lexicon* (9th edn., and Supplements) and of the *Diccionario griego-español* (Madrid, 1980-).

| | |
|---|---|
| *AA* | *Archäologischer Anzeiger. Beiblatt zum Jahrbuch des (Kaiserlichen) Deutschen Archäologischen Instituts* (Berlin, 1890–1962); from 1963 published separately as *Archäologischer Anzeiger* |
| *AAA* | Ἀρχαιολογικὰ Ἀνάλεκτα ἐξ Ἀθηνῶν, *Athens Annals of Archaeology*, 1– (Athens, 1968– ) |
| *AbhBerlAk* | *Abhandlungen der (Königlich Preussischen) Deutschen Akademie der Wissenschaften zu Berlin*, phil.-hist. Kl. (Berlin, 1804– ) |
| *AbhMainzAk* | *Abhandlungen der Geistes- und Sozialwissenschaftlichen Klasse, Akademie der Wissenschaften und der Literatur in Mainz*, 1– (Mainz, 1950– ) |
| *ABME* | Ἀρχεῖον τῶν Βυζαντινῶν Μνημείων τῆς Ἑλλάδος, ed. A. K. Orlandos, 1–12 (Athens, 1946–73) |
| *ABV* | J. D. Beazley, *Attic Black-Figure Vase-Painters* (Oxford, 1956) |
| *Achaean Grave Stelai* | J. A. Papapostolou, *Achaean Grave Stelai*, with epigraphical notes by A. Rizakis (Βιβλ. Ἀθ. Ἀρχ. Ἑτ., 135 [Athens, 1993]) |
| *Achaïe* | A. D. Rizakis, *Achaïe*. I, *Sources textuelles et histoire régionale* (*Meletemata*, 20 [Athens, 1995]); II, *Inscriptions de Patras* [forthcoming] |
| *Achaia und Elis* | *Achaia und Elis in der Antike. Akten des 1. Internationalen Symposiums, Athen, 19–21 Mai 1989*, ed. A. D. Rizakis (*Meletemata*, 13 [Athens, 1991]) |
| *Acragas Graeca* | J. R. de Waele, *Acragas Graeca. Die historische Topographie des griechischen Akragas auf Sizilien*. I, *Historischer Teil* (The Hague, 1971) |
| *AD* | Ἀρχαιολογικὸν Δελτίον, 1– (Athens, 1915– ) |
| *AE* | Ἀρχαιολογικὴ Ἐφημερίς. Περιοδικὸν τῆς ἐν Ἀθήναις Ἀρχαιολογικῆς Ἑταιρείας (Athens, 1910– ) (for earlier vols. see *EA*) |
| *Aegyptus* | *Aegyptus. Rivista Italiana di Egittologia e di Papirologia*, 1– (Milan, 1920– ) |
| *AEMÖ* | *Archaeologisch-epigraphische Mittheilungen aus Oesterreich(-Ungarn)*, 1–20 (Vienna, 1877–97) |
| *AEp* | *L'Année épigraphique* (Paris, 1888– ); 1888–1961 published separately and in *RA*; 1962– separately |
| *Ag.* | *The Athenian Agora. Results of Excavations conducted by the American School of Classical Studies at Athens*, 1– (Princeton, 1953– ) |
| Ag. Inv. | Agora Inventory. V. Grace's inventory of amphora stamps (Athens, Agora Museum) |
| Agnello | S. L. Agnello, *Silloge di iscrizioni paleocristiane della Sicilia* (Rome, 1953) |
| *AJA* | *American Journal of Archaeology*, 1–11 (Boston, 1885–96); 2nd ser. 1– (1897– ) |
| *AJPh* | *American Journal of Philology*, 1– (Baltimore, 1879– ) |
| *Akrai* | L. Bernabò Brea, *Akrai* (Catania, 1956) |
| *Albania* | *Albania. Revue d'archéologie, d'histoire, d'art et des sciences appliquées en Albanie et dans les Balkans*, 1–5 (Paris, 1925–35); subsequently *Cahiers d'archéologie, d'histoire et d'art en Albanie et dans les Balkans*, 6 (Paris, 1939) |
| *Alt-Ägina* | *Alt-Ägina*, 1– (Mainz, 1974– ) |
| *Alt-Ithaka* | W. Dörpfeld, *Alt-Ithaka. Ein Beitrag zur Homer-Frage. Studien und Ausgrabungen auf der Insel Leukas-Ithaka*, 2 vols. (Munich, 1927) |
| *AM* | *Mitteilungen des Deutschen Archäologischen Instituts, Athenische Abteilung*, 1– (Athens, 1876–1939; Berlin, 1951– ) |
| Amandry | M. Amandry, *Le monnayage des duovirs corinthiens* (*BCH* Suppl., 15 [Athens, 1988]) |
| *AMGR* | *Annuario del Museo Greco-Romano*, ed. A. Adriani, 1 vol.; subsequently *Annuaire du Musée Gréco-Romain*, 3 vols. (Alexandria, 1934–52) |
| *AMSMG* | *Atti e Memorie della Società Magna Grecia* (Rome, 1925–32); NS 1–25 (1954–84); 3rd ser. 1– (1992– ) |
| Amyx | D. A. Amyx, *Corinthian Vase-Painting of the Archaic Period*. II, *Commentary: The Study of Corinthian Vases* (Berkeley, Los Angeles and London, 1988), Chapter 6, 'Inscriptions', pp. 547-615 |
| *Anc. Soc.* | *Ancient Society*, 1– (Louvain, 1970– ) |
| *Ancient Art in Bowdoin College* | K. Herbert, *Ancient Art in Bowdoin College. A Descriptive Catalogue of the Warren and other Collections* (Cambridge, Mass., 1964) |
| *Ancient Macedonia* | *Ancient Macedonia* (Ἀρχαία Μακεδονία). *Papers read at the International Symposia held in Thessaloniki, 1968– (Institute for Balkan Studies*, 122, 155, 193, 204, 240 [Thessaloniki, 1970– ]) |
| *Anfore da trasporto* | M. A. Rizzo, *Le Anfore da trasporto e il commercio etrusco arcaico*. I, *Complessi tombali dell'Etruria meridionale* (Soprintendenza archeologica per l'Etruria meridionale, *Studi di archeologia*, 3 [Rome, 1990]) |
| *Ann. Fac. Lett. Fil. Bari* | *Annali della Facoltà di Lettere e Filosofia di Bari*, 1– (Bari, 1954– ) |
| *Ann. S. Chiara* | *Annali del Pontificio Istituto Superiore di Scienze e Lettere 'S. Chiara' dell'Ordine dei Frati Minori*, 1– (Naples, 1948/9– ) |
| *Ann. Univ. Lecce* | *Annali dell'Università di Lecce. Facoltà di Lettere e Filosofia e Magistero*, 1– (Lecce, 1963/4– ) |

Anon. Med. Lond.                *Anonymi Londiniensis ex Aristotelis Iatricis Menoniis et aliis Medicis Eclogae*, ed. H. Diels
                                (*Supplementum Aristotelicum*, 3 (1) [Berlin, 1893])

Anthemonte–Kalindoia            M. B. Hatzopoulos and L. D. Loukopoulou, *Recherches sur les marches orientales des Temenides
                                (Anthemonte - Kalindoia)*, I (*Meletemata*, 11 [Athens, 1992])

Antike Helme                    *Antike Helme. Sammlung Lipperheide und andere Bestände des Antikenmuseums Berlin*
                                (*Römisch-Germanisches Zentralmuseum, Forschungsinstitut für Vor- und Frühgeschichte,
                                Monographien*, 14 [Mainz, 1988])

Antiken Terracotten             R. Kekulé von Stradonitz, *Die Antiken Terracotten*, 7 vols. (Berlin and Stuttgart, 1880-1911)

Antonetti, *Les Étoliens*       C. Antonetti, *Les Étoliens. Image et Religion* (*Annales Littéraires de l'Université de Besançon*, 405
                                [Paris, 1990])

Antoniou, *Dodone*              A. I. Antoniou, Δωδώνη. Συμβολὴ Ἠπειρωτῶν στὴν ἀνοικοδόμηση κτισμάτων τοῦ Ἱεροῦ τῆς Δωδώνης
                                (μετὰ τὸ 219 π.Χ.) (Athens, 1991)

Anz. Wien                       *Anzeiger der (Österreichisches) Akademie der Wissenschaften in Wien*, phil.-hist. Kl. (Vienna,
                                1864– )

APF                             J. K. Davies, *Athenian Propertied Families 600–300 B.C.* (Oxford, 1971)

Apollo                          *Apollo. Bollettino dei Musei Provinciali del Salernitano*, 1– (Salerno, 1961– )

AR                              *Archaeological Reports* (Society for the Promotion of Hellenic Studies/Managing Committee of the
                                British School at Athens [London, 1955– ])

Arch. Class.                    *Archeologia Classica*, 1– (Rome, 1949– )

Arch. Coll. *Johns Hopkins*     E. R. Williams, *The Archaeological Collection of the Johns Hopkins University* (Baltimore and
Univ.                           London, 1984)

Arch. Miss. scient.             *Archives des Missions scientifiques et littéraires*, 1– (Ministère de l'Instruction Publique [Paris,
                                1850–90])

Arch. Pap.                      *Archiv für Papyrusforschung und verwandte Gebiete*, 1– (Leipzig, 1901–1990; Stuttgart and
                                Leipzig, 1991– )

Arch. Sicilia sud-orient.       *Archeologia nella Sicilia sud-orientale*, edd. P. Pelagatti and G. Voza (Centre Jean Bérard [Naples,
                                1973])

Arch. Subacquea                 *Archeologia Subacquea*. II, *Le Isole Eolie* (*BdA* Suppl. to no. 29 [Rome, 1985]) pp. 7-127

Archaeology                     *Archaeology*, 1– (Cambridge, Mass., 1948– )

Arctos                          *Arctos. Acta Philologica Fennica*, 1–2 (Helsinki, 1930–1); NS 1– (1954– )

Arena, *Iscr. Cor.*             R. Arena, *Le iscrizioni corinzie su vasi* (*Mem. Linc.* ser. 8, 13 (2) [Rome, 1968])

Arena, *Iscr. Sic.*             R. Arena, *Iscrizioni greche arcaiche di Sicilia e Magna Grecia*. I, *Iscrizioni di Megara Iblea e
                                Selinunte* (Milan, 1989); II, *Iscrizioni di Gela e Agrigento* (Milan, 1992); III, *Iscrizioni delle
                                Colonie Euboiche* (Pisa, 1994); IV, *Iscrizioni delle Colonie Achee* (Alessandria, 1996)

Argive Heraeum                  C. Waldstein, *The Argive Heraeum*, 2 vols. (Boston, 1902–5)

Arndt, *Vasenkunde*             P. Arndt, *Studien zur Vasenkunde* (Leipzig, 1887)

Artemis Orthia                  *The Sanctuary of Artemis Orthia at Sparta*, ed. R. M. Dawkins (*Society for the Promotion of
                                Hellenic Studies*, Suppl. Paper, 5 [London, 1929])

ASAA                            *Annuario della (Reg.) Scuola Archeologica di Atene e delle Missioni Italiane in Oriente*, 1–16
                                (Bergamo etc., 1914–42); NS 1– (Rome, 1942– )

ASCL                            *Archivio Storico per la Calabria e la Lucania*, 1– (Rome, 1931– )

ASNP                            *Annali della Scuola Normale Superiore di Pisa, Classe di lettere e filosofia*, ser. 1, 1–30 (Pisa,
                                1873–1929); ser. 2, 1–39 (1932–1970); ser. 3, 1– (1971– )

ASP                             *Archivio Storico Pugliese*, 1– (Bari, 1948– )

ASSicilia                       *Archivio Storico per la Sicilia*, see *Archivio Storico Siciliano*

ASSiciliano                     *Archivio Storico Siciliano*, 1– (Società Siciliana per la Storia Patria [Palermo, 1876– ]); from
                                1935-1943 published as *Archivio Storico per la Sicilia* (R. Deputazione di Storia Patria per la
                                Sicilia, Palermo)

ASSiciliaOrientale              *Archivio Storico per la Sicilia Orientale*, 1– (Società di Storia Patria per la Sicilia Orientale
                                [Catania, 1904– ])

ASSiracusano                    *Archivio Storico Siracusano*, 1– (Società Siracusana di Storia Patria [Syracuse, 1955– ])

Athenaeum                       *Athenaeum. Studi di Letteratura e Storia dell'Antichità*, NS 1– (Pavia, 1923– )

Athenian Democratic Accounts    *Ritual, Finance, Politics: Athenian Democratic Accounts presented to David Lewis*, edd. R. Osborne
                                and S. Hornblower (Oxford, 1994)

Atti Acc. Arch. Napoli          *Atti dell'Accademia di Archeologia, Lettere e Belle Arti*, 1–25 (Naples, 1865–1908); NS 1–15
                                (1910–36)

Atti Acc. Palermo               *Atti dell'Accademia di Scienze, Lettere e Arti di Palermo*, ser. 4, 1–26 (Palermo, 1941–66)

Atti Acc. Pontan.               *Atti dell'Accademia Pontaniana*, 1– (Naples, 1952– )

Atti Caserta                    *Atti della Commissione Conservatrice dei Monumenti ed Oggetti di Antichità e Belle Arti nella
                                Provincia di Terra di Lavoro*, 1–27 (Caserta, 1880–96)

Atti Centro Studi               *Centro Studi e Documentazione sull'Italia Romana, Atti*, 1–9 (Milan and Varese, 1967–1977);
Documentazione                  *Centro Ricerche e Documentazione sull'Antichità Classica, Atti*, 10– (Milan, 1978– )

Atti Conv. Taranto              *Atti dei Convegni di Studi sulla Magna Grecia, Taranto*, 1– (Naples/Taranto, 1962– )

Atti VII Congr. Naz. Arch.      *Atti del VII Congresso Nazionale di Archeologia Cristiana, Cassino 1987* [forthcoming]
Crist.

Audollent, *Defix. Tab.*        A. Audollent, *Defixionum Tabellae* (Paris, 1904)

| | |
|---|---|
| *Ausonia* | *Ausonia. Rivista della Società Italiana di Archeologia e Storia dell'Arte*, 1–10 (Rome, 1906–1921) |
| Babelon, *Traité* | E. Babelon, *Traité des monnaies grecques et romaines*, 3 vols. in 9 (Paris, 1901–32) |
| *BABesch* | *Bulletin Antieke Beschaving (Annual papers on classical archeology)*, 1– (Leiden, 1926– ) |
| *Bakërr Hoard* | H. Ceka, 'Le trésor numismatique de Bakërr', *Stud. Alb.* 9 (1972) pp. 49-68 |
| Barbieri, *L'albo senatorio* | G. Barbieri, *L'albo senatorio da Settimio Severo a Carino (193-285)* (*Studi pubblicati dall'Istituto Italiano per la Storia Antica*, 6 [Rome, 1952]) |
| Barreca | C. Barreca, *Le Catacombe di Siracusa alla luce degli ultimi scavi e recenti scoperte* (2nd edn. Rome, 1934) |
| *Basilicata Antica* | D. Adamesteanu, *La Basilicata Antica, Storia e Monumenti* (Cava dei Tirreni, 1974) |
| *BCH* | *Bulletin de correspondance hellénique*, 1– (Paris, 1877– ) |
| *BdA* | *Bollettino d'Arte*, 1– (Rome, 1907– ); temporarily published as *Le Arti*, 1–5 (Milan, 1938–43) |
| *BE* | J. and L. Robert et al., *Bulletin épigraphique* (in *REG* 1938– ) |
| Becatti, *Oreficerie Antiche* | G. Becatti, *Oreficerie Antiche dalle Minoiche alle Barbariche* (Rome, 1955) |
| Bechtel, *KOS* | F. Bechtel, *Kleine onomastische Studien. Aufsätze zur griechischen Eigennamenforschung* (*Beiträge zur klassischen Philologie*, 125 [Königstein/Ts., 1981]) |
| Bees | N. A. Bees, *Die griechisch-christlichen Inschriften des Peloponnes*, I. *Isthmos-Korinthos* (Christlich-Archäologische Gesellschaft zu Athen [Athens, 1941]) |
| Beloch, *GG* | J. Beloch, *Griechische Geschichte*, 4 vols., 2nd edn., 1–2 (Strasbourg, 1912–16); 3–4 (Berlin and Leipzig, 1922–7) |
| Bernabò Brea, *Isole Eolie* | L. Bernabò Brea, *Le Isole Eolie dal tardo antico ai Normanni* (Ravenna, 1988) |
| Bernabò Brea–Cavalier, *Castello di Lipari* | L. Bernabò Brea and M. Cavalier, *Il Castello di Lipari e il Museo Eoliano* (Palermo, 1958) |
| Bernand, *El-Kanaïs* | A. Bernand, *Le Paneion d'El-Kanaïs. Les inscriptions grecques* (Leiden, 1972) |
| Bernardini, *Rudiae* | M. Bernardini, *La Rudiae Salentina* (Lecce, 1955) |
| Berve | H. Berve, *Das Alexanderreich auf prosopographischer Grundlage*, 2 vols. (Munich, 1926) |
| Bidez, *Biographie d'Empédocle* | J. M. A. Bidez, *La Biographie d'Empédocle* (Université de Gand, *Recueil de travaux publiées par la faculté de philosophie et lettres*, 12 [Ghent, 1894]) |
| Bilabel | F. Bilabel, *Die Kleineren Historikerfragmente auf Papyrus* (*Kleine Texte für Vorlesungen und Übungen*, 149 [Bonn, 1923]) |
| *Bion of Borysthenes* | J. F. Kindstrand, *Bion of Borysthenes. A Collection of the Fragments with Introduction and Commentary* (*Studia Graeca Upsaliensia*, 11 [Uppsala, 1976]) |
| *BM Bronzes* | H. B. Walters, *Catalogue of the Bronzes, Greek, Roman, and Etruscan in the Department of Greek and Roman Antiquities, British Museum* (London, 1899) |
| BM Hawkins | British Museum coins register - E. Hawkins, *Greek Acquisitions prior to 1837* |
| *BM Lamps* | D. M. Bailey, *A Catalogue of the Lamps in the British Museum*, 4 vols. (British Museum Publications [London, 1975–1996]) |
| *BM Terracottas* | H. B. Walters, *Catalogue of the Terracottas in the Department of Greek and Roman Antiquities, British Museum* (London, 1903) |
| *BM Vases* | E. J. Forsdyke, H. B. Walters and C. H. Smith, *Catalogue of the Greek and Etruscan Vases in the British Museum*, 4 vols. in 5 (London, 1893–1925) |
| *BMC Corinth* | B. V. Head, *A Catalogue of the Greek Coins in the British Museum. Corinth, Colonies of Corinth etc.* (London, 1889) |
| *BMC Italy* | R. S. Poole, *A Catalogue of the Greek Coins in the British Museum. Italy* (London, 1873) |
| *BMC Pelop.* | P. Gardner, *A Catalogue of the Greek Coins in the British Museum. Peloponnesus (excluding Corinth)* (London, 1887) |
| *BMC Sicily* | B. V. Head, P. Gardner and R. S. Poole, *A Catalogue of the Greek Coins in the British Museum. Sicily* (London, 1876) |
| *BMC Thessaly* | P. Gardner, *A Catalogue of the Greek Coins in the British Museum. Thessaly to Aetolia* (London, 1883) |
| *BMI* | *The Collection of Ancient Greek Inscriptions in the British Museum*, edd. E. L. Hicks, C. T. Newton et al., 4 vols. (London, 1874–1916) |
| Boardman, *Archaic Greek Gems* | J. Boardman, *Archaic Greek Gems. Schools and Artists in the Sixth and Early Fifth Centuries BC* (London, 1968) |
| Boardman, *Gems* | J. Boardman, *Greek Gems and Finger Rings, Early Bronze Age to Late Classical* (London, 1970) |
| *Boll. Arch.* | *Bollettino di Archeologia*, 1– (Ministero per i Beni Culturali e Ambientali [Rome, 1990– ]) |
| *Boston Bronzes* | M. Comstock and C. Vermeule, *Greek, Etruscan, and Roman Bronzes in the Museum of Fine Arts, Boston* (Boston, 1971) |
| *Boston Coins* | A. B. Brett, *Catalogue of Greek Coins* (Museum of Fine Arts, Boston [Boston, 1955]) |
| *Boston Mus. Rep.* | *Museum of Fine Arts, Boston, Annual Report*, 1– (Boston, 1873– ); 1965– renamed *The Museum Year: Museum of Fine Arts Boston* |
| Bove, *Documenti finanziarie* | L. Bove, *Documenti di operazioni finanziarie dall'archivio dei Sulpici. Tabulae Pompeianae di Murecine* (Naples, 1984) |
| Bove, *Documenti processuali* | L. Bove, *Documenti processuali dalle Tabulae Pompeianae di Murecine* (Naples, 1979) |
| *Bovino* | *Bovino. Studi per la storia della città antica. La collezione Museale*, edd. M. Mazzei and S. M. Casano (*Archeologia del Mediterraneo Antico*, 1 [Taranto, 1995]) |

| | |
|---|---|
| *BPW* | *Berliner philologische Wochenschrift*, 1–64 (Berlin, 1881–1944); 41 (1921)–64 (1944) *Philologische Wochenschrift* |
| Bradford | A. S. Bradford jnr., *A Prosopography of Lacedaemonians from the death of Alexander the Great 323 B.C., to the sack of Sparta by Alaric, A.D. 396* (*Vestigia*, 27 [Munich, 1977]) |
| Breccia, *Iscriz.* | E. Breccia, *Catalogue général des antiquités égyptiennes du Musée d'Alexandrie, Nos. 1–568, Iscrizioni greche e latine* (Cairo, 1911) |
| Breccia, *Monum.* | E. Breccia, *Monuments de l'Égypte Gréco-Romaine*, 2 vols. (Société archéologique d'Alexandrie [Bergamo, 1926]) |
| *Bronzes grecs et romains (Madrid)* | R. Thouvenot, *Catalogue des figurines et objets de bronze du Musée Archéologique de Madrid. I, Bronzes grecs et romains* (Paris, 1927) |
| *Brooklyn Mus. Ann.* | *The Brooklyn Museum Annual*, 1– (Brooklyn, 1959/60– ) |
| Brown, *Ptolemaic Paintings* | B. R. Brown, *Ptolemaic Paintings and Mosaics and the Alexandrian Style* (*Monographs on Archaeology and Fine Arts*, 6 [Cambridge, Mass., 1957]) |
| Brunšmid | J. Brunšmid, *Die Inschriften und Münzen der griechischen Städte Dalmatiens* (*Abhandlungen des archäologisch-epigraphischen Seminares der Universität Wien*, 13 [Vienna, 1898]) |
| *BSA* | *Annual of the British School at Athens*, 1– (London, 1894/5– ) |
| *BSAAlex* | *Bulletin de la Société (Royale) Archéologique d'Alexandrie*, 1–5 (Alexandria, 1898–1902); NS 1– (1904– ) |
| *BTCGI* | *Bibliografia topografica della colonizzazione greca in Italia e nelle isole tirreniche*, edd. G. Nenci and G. Vallet, 1– (Pisa and Rome, 1977– ) |
| *Bull. Arch. Crist.* | *Bullettino di Archeologia Cristiana*, 5 series (Rome, 1863–94) |
| *Bull. Mus. Hongr.* | *Bulletin du Musée Hongroise des Beaux-Arts*, 1– (Budapest, 1947– ) |
| *Bull. Mus. Imp. Rom.* | *Bullettino del Museo dell'Impero Romano*, 1–14, in *Bullettino della Commissione Archeologica Communale di Roma*, 58–71 (Rome, 1930–45) |
| *BUST* | *Buletin i Universitetit Shtetëror të Tiranës. Reviste Shkencore, Seria Shkencat Shoqerore*, 1– (Tirana, 1948– ) |
| *BZ* | *Byzantinische Zeitschrift*, 1– (Leipzig, 1892–1941; Munich, 1943–1990; Stuttgart and Leipzig, 1991/2– ) |
| Cabanes, *L'Épire* | P. Cabanes, *L'Épire de la mort de Pyrrhos à la conquête romaine (272–167)* (*Annales Littéraires de l'Université de Besançon*, 186, *Centre de Recherches d'Histoire Ancienne*, 19 [Paris, 1976]) |
| *CAF* | *Comicorum Atticorum Fragmenta*, ed. T. Kock, 3 vols. (Leipzig, 1880–8) |
| *CAG* | *Commentaria in Aristotelem Graeca*, 23 vols. (Berlin, 1882–1909) |
| Callipolitis-Feytmans, *Plats* | D. Callipolitis-Feytmans, *Les Plats attiques à figures noires* (École française d'Athènes, *Travaux et Mémoires*, 19 [Paris, 1974]) |
| Cambi, *Stobreč* | N. Cambi, *Starokršćanska bazilika i benediktinski samostanski kompleks u Stobreču* (Split, 1974) |
| Camodeca, *L'Archivio Puteolano* | G. Camodeca, *L'Archivio Puteolano dei Sulpicii*, I (*Pubblicazioni del Dipartimento di Diritto Romano e Storia della Scienza Romanistica dell'Università degli Studi 'Federico II'*, 4 [Naples, 1992]) |
| Carapanos, *Dodone* | C. Carapanos, *Dodone et ses ruines* (Paris, 1878) |
| Cartledge, *Agesilaos* | P. Cartledge, *Agesilaos and the Crisis of Sparta* (London, 1987) |
| Cartledge–Spawforth | P. Cartledge and A. Spawforth, *Hellenistic and Roman Sparta: A Tale of Two Cities* (London, 1989) |
| Castrèn | P. Castrèn, *Ordo Populusque Pompeianus. Polity and Society in Roman Pompeii* (*Acta Instituti Romani Finlandiae*, 8 [Rome, 1975]) |
| *CE* | *Chronique d'Égypte*, 1– (Brussels, 1925– ) |
| *CEG* | P. A. Hansen, *Carmina Epigraphica Graeca*. [I], *Saeculorum VIII–V a.Chr.n.*; II, *Saeculi IV a.Chr.n.* (Berlin, 1983, 1989) |
| Ceka | H. Ceka, *Questions de numismatique illyrienne avec un catalogue des monnaies d'Apollonie et de Dyrrhachium* (Tirana, 1972) |
| Ceka, *Probleme* | H. Ceka, *Probleme të numismatikës ilire* (Tirana, 1967) |
| *CGF* | *Comicorum Graecorum Fragmenta*, I. fasc. prior, *Doriensium Comoedia Mimi Phlyaces*, ed. G. Kaibel (*Poetarum Graecorum Fragmenta*, 4 (1) [Berlin, 1899]) |
| *CGFP* | *Comicorum Graecorum fragmenta in papyris reperta*, ed. C. Austin (Berlin and New York, 1973) |
| *Chiron* | *Chiron. Mitteilungen der Kommission für alte Geschichte und Epigraphik des Deutschen Archäologischen Instituts*, 1– (Munich, 1971– ) |
| *CIA* | *Corpus Inscriptionum Atticarum*, edd. A. Kirchhoff et al. (Berlin, 1873– ). III (1–2), *Inscriptiones Atticae aetatis Romanae*, ed. W. Dittenberger (1878–82). *Appendix. Defixionum tabellae in Attica regione repertae*, ed. R. Wuensch (1897) |
| *CID* | *Corpus des Inscriptions de Delphes*. I, *Lois sacrées et règlements religieux*, ed. G. Rougemont; II, *Les comptes du quatrième et du troisième siècle*, ed. J. Bousquet; III, *Les Hymnes à Apollon*, ed. A. Bélis (Paris, 1977– ) |
| *CIG* | *Corpus Inscriptionum Graecarum*, edd. A. Boeckh, J. Franz et al., 4 vols. (Berlin, 1825–77) |
| *CIJ* | *Corpus Inscriptionum Judaicarum. Recueil des inscriptions juives qui vont du III^e siècle avant Jésus-Christ au VII^e siècle de notre ère*, ed. J.-B. Frey, 2 vols. (Pontificio Istituto di Archeologia Cristiana, *Sussidi allo Studio della Antichità Cristiane*, 1, 3 [Vatican City, 1936–52]) |

| | |
|---|---|
| *CIL* | *Corpus Inscriptionum Latinarum*, edd. Th. Mommsen et al., 17 vols. with supplements (Berlin, 1863– ) |
| *Cinquant' Anni Lic. Class.* | *I Cinquant' Anni d'un Liceo Classico, Comune di Sala Consilina*, ed. V. Bracco (Salerno, 1984) |
| *CIRB* | *Corpus Inscriptionum Regni Bosporani*, edd. V. V. Struve et al. (Moscow and Leningrad, 1965) |
| *Cl. Rh.* | *Clara Rhodos. Studi e materiali pubblicati a cura dell'Istituto storico-archeologico di Rodi*, 10 vols. (Rhodes, 1928–41) |
| *Classical Heritage* | *Classical Heritage. Greek and Roman Art from Cambridge College Collections. An Exhibition at the Fitzwilliam Museum, Cambridge, 1 August - 17 September, 1978* (Cambridge, 1978) |
| *Classical Vases* | A. H. Ashmead and K. M. Philips jnr., *Catalogue of the Classical Collection, Museum of Art, the Rhode Island School of Design: Classical Vases* (Providence, Rhode Island, 1976) |
| Clerk, *Coins Ach. League* | M. G. Clerk, *Catalogue of the Coins of the Achaean League* (London, 1895) |
| *Coll. Alex.* | J. U. Powell, *Collectanea Alexandrina* (Oxford, 1925) |
| *Coll. Bunbury* | *Catalogue of the Bunbury Collection of Greek Coins*, 2 vols., Sotheby, Wilkinson and Hodge sales, 15th June and 7th December 1896 (London, 1896) |
| *Coll. de Luynes* | J. Babelon, *Catalogue de la Collection de Luynes. Monnaies grecques*, 4 vols. (Paris, 1924–36) |
| *Coll. Hunter* | G. Macdonald, *Catalogue of the Greek Coins in the Hunterian Collection, University of Glasgow*, 3 vols. (Glasgow, 1899–1905) |
| *Coll. McClean* | S. W. Grose, *Fitzwilliam Museum. Catalogue of the McClean Collection of Greek Coins*, 3 vols. (Cambridge, 1923–29) |
| *Coll. Philipsen* | *Sammlung Gustav Philipsen in Copenhagen. Antike Münzen*, Hirsch sale no. 25, 29th November 1909 (Munich, 1909) |
| *Coll. Photiades* | *Collection Photiadès Pacha, Monnaies Grecques*, Hoffmann sale, 19th May 1890 (Paris, 1890) |
| *Coll. Rhousopoulos* | *Auctions-Catalog einer hochbedeutenden Sammlung griechischer Münzen aus dem Nachlasse eines bekannten Archäologen*, Hirsch sale no. 13, 15th May 1905 (Munich, 1905) |
| *Coll. Santangelo* | G. Fiorelli, *Catalogo del Museo Nazionale di Napoli, Medagliere. I, Monete Greche* (Naples, 1870) |
| *Coll. Walcher* | *Catalogue de la collection des médailles grecques de M. le Chevalier Léopold Walcher de Molthein* (Paris and Vienna, 1895) |
| *Coll. Weber* | L. Forrer, *The Weber Collection. Descriptive Catalogue of the Collection of Greek Coins formed by Sir Hermann Weber*, 3 vols. in 7 (London, 1922–9) |
| *Colosse de Memnon* | A. and E. Bernand, *Les Inscriptions grecques et latines du Colosse de Memnon* (*Institut Français d'Archéologie Orientale, Bibliothèque d'Étude*, 31 [Paris, 1960]) |
| *Comptes et Inventaires* | *Comptes et inventaires dans la cité grecque. Actes du colloque internationale d'épigraphie tenu à Neuchâtel du 23 au 26 septembre 1986 en l'honneur de Jacques Tréheux*, ed. D. Knoepfler (Neuchâtel and Geneva, 1988) |
| *Congr. Int. Num.* | *Congrès International de Numismatique, Paris, 6-11 juillet, 1953*, 2 vols. (Commission Internationale de Numismatique [Paris, 1953–7]) |
| *Contr. Ist. Fil. Class.* | *Contributi dell'Istituto di Filologia Classica*, sezione di Storia Antica, 1– (Milan, 1963– ) |
| Cook, *Hadra Vases* | B. F. Cook, *Inscribed Hadra Vases in the Metropolitan Museum of Art* (*The Metropolitan Museum of Art Papers*, 12 [New York, 1966]) |
| *Copenhagen NM Guides* | *Guides to the National Museum, Department of Oriental and Classical Antiquities. Greece, Italy and the Roman Empire* (Copenhagen, 1968) |
| Cordano, *Tessere Pubbliche* | F. Cordano, *Le Tessere Pubbliche dal Tempio di Atena a Camarina* (*Studi pubblicati dall'Istituto Italiano per la Storia Antica*, 50 [Rome, 1992]) |
| Cordano, 'Camarina VII' | F. Cordano, 'Camarina VII. Alcuni documenti iscritti importanti per la storia della città', *BdA* 69 (1984) pp. 31-54; 'Appendice: Elenco degli Antroponimi' pp. 52-4 |
| *Corinth* | *Corinth. Results of Excavations conducted by the American School of Classical Studies at Athens*, 1– (Cambridge, Mass., 1929–43; Princeton, 1948– ) |
| *Corolla Num.* | *Corolla Numismatica. Numismatic Essays in honour of Barclay V. Head* (Oxford, 1906) |
| Costabile, *Ist. Bruzio* | F. Costabile, *Istituzioni e forme costituzionali nelle città del Bruzio in età Romana. Civitates foederatae, coloniae e municipia in Italia meridionale attraverso i documenti epigrafici* (*Pubblicazioni della Facoltà di Giurisprudenza di Catanzaro*, 2 [Naples, 1984]) |
| Costabile, *Municipium Locrensium* | F. Costabile, *Municipium Locrensium. Istituzioni ed organizzazione sociale di Locri romana* (Naples, 1976) |
| *CPh.* | *Classical Philology*, 1– (Chicago, 1906– ) |
| *CPR* | *Corpus Papyrorum Raineri*, 1– (Vienna, 1895– ) |
| *CQ* | *Classical Quarterly*, 1– (London, 1907–38; Oxford, 1939– ) |
| *CRAI* | *Comptes-rendus de l'Académie des Inscriptions et Belles-lettres*, 4th ser. (Paris, 1874– ) |
| *Cron. Arch.* | *Cronache di Archeologia e di Storia dell'Arte*, 1– (Catania, 1962– ) |
| *Cron. Erc.* | *Cronache Ercolanesi. Bollettino del Centro Internazionale per lo Studio dei Papiri Ercolanesi*, 1– (Naples, 1971– ) |
| *Cron. Pomp.* | *Cronache Pompeiane. Rivista dell'Associazione Internazionale 'Amici di Pompei'*, 1– (Naples, 1975– ) |
| *CSCA* | *California Studies in Classical Antiquity*, 1–12 (Berkeley, 1968–1979) |
| *Culte des divinités orientales en Campanie* | V. Tram Tam Tinh, *Le culte des divinités orientales en Campanie en dehors de Pompei, de Stabies et d'Herculanum* (*Études préliminaires aux religions orientales dans l'empire romain*, 27 [Leiden, 1972]) |

| | |
|---|---|
| *CVA* | *Corpus Vasorum Antiquorum*, various places and dates of publication. See T. H. Carpenter, *Summary Guide to Corpus Vasorum Antiquorum* (Oxford, 1984) |
| *CVA Adolphseck* 1 | *Germany* 11, ed. F. Brommer (Munich, 1956) |
| *CVA Genova* 1 | *Italy* 19, ed. L. Bernabò Brea (Rome, 1942) |
| *CVA London* 7 | *Great Britain* 10, ed. F. N. Pryce (London, 1932) |
| *CVA Robinson* 3 | *USA* 7, ed. D. M. Robinson (Cambridge, Mass., 1938) |
| *CVA Taranto* 3 | *Italy* 35, ed. C. Drago (Rome, 1962) |
| D'Isanto | G. D'Isanto, *Capua Romana. Ricerche di Prosopografia e Storia Sociale* (*Vetera*, 9 [Rome, 1993]) |
| Dakaris, *Kassope* | S. I. Dakaris, Κασσώπη. Νεώτερες Ἀνασκαφές 1977-1983 (Ioannina, 1984) |
| *Das Heroon von Kalydon* | E. Dyggve, F. Poulsen and K. Rhomaios, *Das Heroon von Kalydon* (*Det Kongelige Danske Videnskabernes Selskabs Skrifter*, 7 Raekke, Historisk og Filosofisk Afd., 4 (4) [Copenhagen, 1934]) |
| Daux | G. Daux, *Chronologie delphique* (Paris, 1943) |
| Daux, *Delphes* | G. Daux, *Delphes au II^e et au I^er siècle depuis l'abaissement de l'Étolie jusqu'à la paix romaine 191-31 av. J.-C.* (Paris, 1936) |
| Daux, *Paus. à Delphes* | G. Daux, *Pausanias à Delphes* (Diss. Paris [Paris, 1936]) |
| *DCB* | *Dictionary of Christian Biography*, edd. W. Smith and H. Wace, 4 vols. (London, 1877–87) |
| de Cadalvène, *Recueil* | E. de Cadalvène, *Recueil de médailles grecques inédites* (Paris, 1828) |
| De Falco, *L'Epicureo Demetrio Lacone* | V. De Falco, *L'Epicureo Demetrio Lacone* (*Bibl. Filol. Class.*, 11 [Naples, 1923]) |
| De Franciscis | A. De Franciscis, *Stato e Società in Locri Epizefiri (L'Archivio dell'Olympieion Locrese)* (*Pubblicazioni a cura del Centro Studi della Magna Grecia della Università di Napoli*, NS 3 [Naples, 1972]) |
| De Franciscis, *Sacello Augustali* | A. De Franciscis, *Il Sacello degli Augustali a Miseno* (Naples, 1991) |
| Deichgräber, *Griech. Empirikerschule* | K. Deichgräber, *Die griechische Empirikerschule. Sammlung der Fragmente und Darstellung der Lehre* (Berlin, 1930; repr. Berlin and Zurich, 1965) |
| Delatte, *VP* | A. Delatte, *La Vie de Pythagore de Diogène Laerce* (*Academie royale de Belgique. Classe des lettres et des science morales et politiques, Mémoires*, 17 (2) [Brussels, 1922]) |
| *Demetrias* | *Demetrias*, 1– (*Die Deutschen archäologischen Forschungen in Thessalien* [Bonn, 1976– ]) |
| Demitsas | M. G. Demitsas, Ἡ Μακεδονία ἐν λίθοις φθεγγομένοις καὶ μνημείοις σωζομένοις (Athens, 1896) |
| Desy, *Timbres amphoriques* | P. Desy, *Les timbres amphoriques de l'Apulie républicaine: documents pour une histoire économique et sociale* (*BAR International Series*, 554 [Oxford, 1989]) |
| *Deutsch. Lit.* | *Deutsches Litteraturzeitung*, 1– (Berlin, 1880– ) |
| *DGE* | *Dialectorum Graecarum exempla epigraphica potiora*, ed. E. Schwyzer (3rd edn. Leipzig, 1923) |
| *Di Terra in Terra* | *Di Terra in Terra. Nuove scoperte archeologiche nella provincia di Palermo* (Palermo, 1991) |
| *DIEEE* | Δελτίον τῆς Ἱστορικῆς καὶ Ἐθνολογικῆς Ἑταιρείας τῆς Ἑλλάδος, 1– (Athens, 1883– ) |
| Diehl, *Hydria* | E. Diehl, *Die Hydria. Formgeschichte und Verwendung im Kult des Altertums* (Mainz, 1964) |
| Diels, *DG* | H. Diels, *Doxographi Graeci* (Berlin, 1879) |
| *Dionysiaca* | *Dionysiaca. Nine Studies in Greek Poetry by former pupils, presented to Sir Denys Page on his seventieth birthday*, edd. R. D. Dawe, J. Diggle and P. E. Easterling (Cambridge, 1978) |
| Dito, *Velia* | O. Dito, *Velia, Colonia Focese. Contributo per la Storia della Magna Grecia (con epigrafe inedite)* (Rome, 1891) |
| Donderer | M. Donderer, *Die Mosaizisten der Antike und ihre wirtschaftliche und soziale Stellung: eine Quellenstudie* (*Erlanger Forschungen, Reihe A, Geisteswissenschaften*, 48 [Erlangen, 1989]) |
| Dubois, *IGDGG* | L. Dubois, *Inscriptions Grecques Dialectales de Grand Grèce. I, Colonies eubéennes. Colonies ioniennes. Emporia* (*École Pratique des Hautes Études, IV^e Section, Sciences Historiques et Philologiques. III. Hautes Études du Monde Gréco-Romain*, 21 [Geneva, 1995]) |
| Dubois, *IGDS* | L. Dubois, *Inscriptions Grecques Dialectales de Sicile. Contribution à l'Étude du Vocabulaire Grec Colonial* (*Collection de l'école française de Rome*, 119 [Rome, 1989]) |
| Dubois, *RDA* | L. Dubois, *Recherches sur le dialecte arcadien*, 3 vols. (*Bibliothèque des Cahiers de l'Institut de Linguistique de Louvain*, 33–35 [Louvain, 1988]) |
| Durrbach, *Choix* | F. Durrbach, *Choix d'Inscriptions de Délos*, I (Paris, 1921) |
| Dyson, *Roman Villas of Buccino* | S. L. Dyson, *The Roman Villas of Buccino. Wesleyan University Excavation in Buccino, Italy 1969-1972* (*BAR International Series*, 187 [Oxford, 1983]) |
| *Ét. Thas.* | *Études thasiennes*, 1– (Paris, 1944– ) |
| *EA* | Ἐφημερὶς Ἀρχαιολογική (Athens, 1837–1909); for later vols. see *AE* |
| *EAD* | *Exploration archéologique de Délos*, 1– (Paris, 1909– ) |
| Ebert, *Gr. Sieg.* | J. Ebert, *Griechische Epigramme auf Sieger an gymnischen und hippischen Agonen* (*Abh. Akad. Leipzig*, 63 (2) [Berlin, 1972]) |
| *EILakArk* | W. Peek, *Epigramme und andere Inschriften aus Lakonien und Arkadien* (*SBHeidAk* 1971 (2) [Heidelberg, 1971]) |
| *Entella* | *Entella*, ed. G. Nenci, 1– (Pisa, 1995– ) |
| *Ep. Chron.* | Ἠπειρωτικὰ Χρονικά, 1–16 (Ioannina, 1926–41); 17– (1973– ) |
| *Eph. Ep.* | *Ephemeris Epigraphica. Corporis Inscriptionum Latinarum Supplementum*, 1–9 (Rome, 1872–1913) |
| *Epig. Rom. di Canosa* | *Le Epigrafi Romane di Canosa*, edd. M. Chelotti, R. Gaeta, V. Morizio and M. Silvestrini, 2 vols. (Dipartimento di Scienze dell'Antichità dell'Università di Bari, sezione storica, *Documenti e Studi*, 7 [Bari, 1990]) |

| | |
|---|---|
| *Epigrafia del Villaggio* | *L'Epigrafia del Villaggio*, edd. A. Calbi, A. Donati and G. Poma (*Epigrafia e Antichità*, 12 [Faenza, 1993]) |
| *Epigrafia e Territorio* | *Epigrafia e Territorio: Politicà e Società. Temi di Antichità Romane*, 1– (Dipartimento di Scienze dell'Antichità dell'Università di Bari, sezione storica, *Documenti e Studi*, 1, 5, 17 [Bari, 1983– ]) |
| *Epigraphica* | *Epigraphica. Rivista Italiana di Epigrafia*, 1– (Milan, 1937– ) |
| *Epistolographi* | *Epistolographi Graeci*, ed. R. Hercher (Paris, 1873) |
| *Eretria* | *Eretria. Fouilles et recherches*, 1–7 (Berne, 1968–85); 8– (Lausanne, 1993– ) |
| *Ergon* | Τὸ Ἔργον τῆς ἐν Ἀθήναις Ἀρχαιολογικῆς Ἑταιρείας (Athens, 1955– ) |
| *Essays M. Thompson* | *Greek Numismatics and Archaeology. Essays in honor of Margaret Thompson*, edd. O. Morkholm and N. M. Waggoner (Wetteren, 1979) |
| *Essays S. Robinson* | *Essays in Greek Coinage presented to Stanley Robinson*, edd. C. M. Kraay and G. K. Jenkins (Oxford, 1968) |
| Evans, *Horsemen* | A. J. Evans, 'The "Horsemen" of Tarentum. A Contribution towards the Numismatic History of Great Greece', NC 1889, pp. 1-342; also published separately with indexes etc. (London, 1889) |
| *Evemero di Messene* | G. Vallauri, *Evemero di Messene* (*Università di Torino, Pubblicazioni della Facoltà di Lettere e Filosofia*, 8 (3) [Turin, 1956]) |
| *FD* | *Fouilles de Delphes*, 1– (Paris, 1909– ) |
| *Felix Ravenna* | *Felix Ravenna. Rivista di Antichità Ravennati, Cristiane, Bizantine*, 1– (Ravenna/Bologna, 1911– ) |
| Ferrua, *NG* | A. Ferrua, *Note e Giunte alle Iscrizioni Cristiane Antiche della Sicilia* (Pontificio Istituto di Archeologia Cristiana, *Sussidi allo Studio delle Antichità Cristiane*, 9 [Vatican City, 1989]) |
| *Festschr. Neutsch* | *Forschungen und Funde. Festschrift Bernhard Neutsch*, edd. F. Krinzinger et al. (*Innsbrucker Beiträge zur Kulturwissenschaft*, 21 [Innsbruck, 1980]) |
| Feyel, *Polybe* | M. Feyel, *Polybe et l'histoire de Béotie au III$^e$ siècle de notre ère* (Paris, 1942) |
| *FGrH* | F. Jacoby, *Die Fragmente der griechischen Historiker*, I–III C (Berlin/Leiden, 1926–58) |
| Flacelière | R. Flacelière, *Les Aitoliens à Delphes. Contribution à l'histoire de la Grèce centrale au III$^e$ siècle av. J.-C.* (*BEFAR*, 143 [Paris, 1937]) |
| *Forma Italiae* | *Forma Italiae* (Unione Accademica Nazionale [Rome/Florence, 1926– ]) |
| Franke, *Münz. v. Epirus* | P. R. Franke, *Die antiken Münzen von Epirus. I, Poleis, Stämme und Epirotischer Bund bis 27 v. Chr. Katalog und Untersuchungen* (Deutsch. Arch. Inst./Kommission für alte Geschichte und Epigraphik [Wiesbaden, 1961]) |
| Franklin | J. L. Franklin jr, *Pompeii: The Electoral Programmata, Campaigns and Politics, A.D. 71-79* (*Papers and Monographs of the American Academy in Rome*, 28 [Rome, 1980]) |
| Fraser, *Ptol. Alex.* | P. M. Fraser, *Ptolemaic Alexandria*, 3 vols. (Oxford, 1972) |
| Fraser, *RFM* | P. M. Fraser, *Rhodian Funerary Monuments* (Oxford, 1977) |
| Fraser–Rönne, *BWGT* | P. M. Fraser and T. Rönne, *Boeotian and West Greek Tombstones* (*Acta Instituti Atheniensis Regni Sueciae*, 6 [Lund, 1957]) |
| Frazer, *Paus. Descr. of Greece* | J. G. Frazer, *Pausanias's Description of Greece*, 6 vols. (2nd edn. London, 1913) |
| Frenz | H. G. Frenz, *Römische Grabreliefs in Mittel- und Süditalien* (*Archaeologica*, 37 [Rome, 1985]) |
| *FSA* | *Die Fragmente der Sikelischer Ärzte, Akron, Philistion und des Diokles von Karystos*, ed. M. Wellmann (*Fragmentsammlung der griechischen Ärzte*, 1 [Berlin, 1901]) |
| Führer | J. Führer, *Forschungen zur Sicilia Sotterranea* (*AbhBayerAk*, philosoph.-philolog. Cl., 20 (3) [Munich, 1897]) |
| Führer–Schultze | J. Führer and V. Schultze, *Die altchristlichen Grabstätten Siziliens* (*JDAI* Ergänzungsheft, 8 [Berlin, 1907]) |
| Furtwängler, *Gemmen* | A. Furtwängler, *Die Antiken Gemmen. Geschichte der Steinschneidekunst im klassischen Altertum*, 3 vols. in 4 (Leipzig and Berlin, 1900) |
| *FVS* | *Die Fragmente der Vorsokratiker*, ed. H. Diels, 6th revised edn. by W. Kranz, 3 vols. (Berlin, 1951–2) |
| Gallatin, *Euainetos* | A. Gallatin, *Syracusan dekadrachms of the Euainetos type* (Cambridge, Mass., 1930) |
| Garrucci, *Monete dell'Italia Antica* | R. Garrucci, *Le Monete dell'Italia Antica, Raccolta Generale. I, Monete Fuse; II, Monete Coniate* (Rome, 1885) |
| *Getty Mus. Journ.* | *The J. Paul Getty Museum Journal*, 1– (The J. Paul Getty Museum, Malibu, California, 1974– ) |
| Giannakopoulou, *Gytheion* | P. E. Giannakopoulos, Τὸ Γύθειον. Ἀρχαιολογικὴ καὶ Ἱστορικὴ Ἄποψις ἀπὸ τῆς Προϊστορικῆς ἐποχῆς μέχρι τοῦ Μεγάλου Κωνσταντίνου (Athens, 1987) |
| Giannini, *Parad. Gr.* | A. Giannini, *Paradoxographorum Graecorum Reliquiae* (*Classici Greci e Latini. Sezione Testi e Commenti*, 3 [Milan, 1966]) |
| *Glotta* | *Glotta. Zeitschrift für griechische und lateinische Sprache*, 1– (Göttingen, 1909– ) |
| *Gnomon* | *Gnomon. Kritische Zeitschrift für die gesamte klassische Altertumswissenschaft*, 1– (Berlin, 1925–45; Munich, 1949– ) |
| *God. Balk. Isp.* | *Godišnjak*, 1– (Akademija Nauka i Umjetnosti Bosne i Hercegovine, Centar za balkanoloska ispitivanja [Sarajevo, 1956– ]) |
| Gow, *Theocritus* | *Theocritus*, ed. A. S. F. Gow, 2 vols. (Cambridge, 1950) |
| *GP* | *The Greek Anthology, The Garland of Philip*, edd. A. S. F. Gow and D. L. Page, 2 vols. (Cambridge, 1968) |
| *Gr. Gr.* | W. Peek, *Griechische Grabgedichte* (*Schriften und Quellen der alten Welt*, 7 [Berlin, 1960]) |

| | |
|---|---|
| *GRBS* | *Greek, Roman and Byzantine Studies*, 1– (San Antonio, Texas, 1956; Cambridge, Mass., 1957–9; Durham, N. Carolina, 1960– ) |
| *Grecs et Illyriens* | *Grecs et Illyriens dans les inscriptions en langue grecque d'Épidamne-Dyrrhachion et d'Apollonia d'Illyrie. Actes de la Table ronde internationale (Clermont-Ferrand, 19-21 octobre 1989)*, ed. P. Cabanes (Paris, 1993) |
| *Griech. Epigr. Kreta* | A. Wilhelm, *Griechische Epigramme aus Kreta* (*Symb. Osl.* Suppl., 13 [Oslo, 1950]) |
| Guarducci, *Ep. Gr.* | M. Guarducci, *Epigrafia greca*, 4 vols. (Rome, 1967–78) |
| *Guida Pompeii* | E. La Rocca, M. de Vos and A. de Vos, *Guida Archeologica di Pompei* (Milan, 1976) |
| *GVI* | W. Peek, *Griechische Vers-Inschriften*. I, *Grab-Epigramme* (Berlin, 1955) |
| Habicht, *Athen hell. Zeit* | C. Habicht, *Athen in hellenistischer Zeit* (Munich, 1994) |
| Hammond, *Epirus* | N. G. L. Hammond, *Epirus* (Oxford, 1967) |
| *Harmonia* | Ἁρμονία. Ἐπιστημονικὸν Περιοδικόν, 1–3 (Athens, 1900–2) |
| *HCT* | A. W. Gomme, A. Andrewes and K. J. Dover, *A Historical Commentary on Thucydides*, 5 vols. (Oxford, 1945–1981) |
| *HE* | *The Greek Anthology, Hellenistic Epigrams*, edd. A. S. F. Gow and D. L. Page, 2 vols. (Cambridge, 1965) |
| Heckel, *Last Days* | W. Heckel, *The Last Days and Testament of Alexander the Great: a Prosopographic Study* (*Historia* Einzelschrift, 56 [Stuttgart, 1988]) |
| Heitsch | *Die griechischen Dichterfragmente der römischen Kaiserzeit*, ed. E. Heitsch, 2 vols. (*Abhandlungen der Akademie der Wissenschaften in Göttingen*, phil.-hist. Kl., ser. 3, 49, 58 [Göttingen, 1961–4]) |
| *Helikon* | *Helikon. Rivista di Tradizione e Cultura Classica dell'Università di Messina*, 1– (Naples/Messina/Rome, 1961– ) |
| *Hellenika* | Ἑλληνικά, 1–11 (Athens, 1928–39); 12– (Ἑταιρεία Μακεδονικῶν Σπουδῶν [Thessaloniki, 1952– ]) |
| Helly, *Gonnoi* | B. Helly, *Gonnoi*. I, *La cité et son histoire*. II, *Les inscriptions* (Amsterdam, 1973) |
| *Hermes* | *Hermes. Zeitschrift für Klassische Philologie*, 1– (Berlin, 1866–1944; Wiesbaden, 1952–83; Stuttgart, 1984– ) |
| Herzfelder, *Monnaies de Rhégion* | H. Herzfelder, *Les Monnaies d'argent de Rhégion frappées entre 461 et le milieu du IV$^e$ siécle av. J.-C.* (Paris, 1957) |
| *Hesp.* | *Hesperia*, 1– (American School of Classical Studies [Princeton, 1932– ]) |
| Heuzey, *Excursion* | L. A. Heuzey, *Excursion dans la Thessalie turque en 1858 par Léon Heuzey* (*Collection de l'Institut Néo-hellénique de l'Université de Paris*, 5 [Paris, 1927]) |
| Heuzey, *Le Mont Olympe* | L. Heuzey, *Le Mont Olympe et l'Acarnanie* (Paris, 1860) |
| *HG* | R. Herzog, *Heilige Gesetze von Kos* (*AbhBerlAk* 1928 (6) [Berlin, 1928]) |
| *Himera* | *Himera*. II, *Campagne di scavo 1966-1973* (Rome, 1976) |
| *Hist. Rom. Rel.* | *Historicorum Romanorum Reliquiae*, I, ed. H. Peter (2nd edn. Leipzig, 1916) |
| *Historia* | *Historia. Zeitschrift für alte Geschichte*, 1– (Wiesbaden, 1950– ) |
| *HN*$^2$ | B. V. Head, *Historia Numorum. A Manual of Greek Numismatics* (2nd edn. Oxford, 1911) |
| Holm, *Gesch. Sic.* | A. Holm, *Geschichte Siciliens im Alterthum*, 3 vols. (Leipzig, 1870–1898) |
| *Horos* | Ὅρος, 1– (Athens, 1983– ) |
| *HSCP* | *Harvard Studies in Classical Philology*, 1– (Cambridge, Mass., 1890– ) |
| *HSCP* Suppl. | *Harvard Studies in Classical Philology* Suppl. 1 (1940). Athenian Studies presented to W. S. Ferguson |
| *Hyettos* | R. Étienne and D. Knoepfler, *Hyettos de Béotie et la chronologie des archontes fédéraux entre 250 et 171 avant J.-C.* (*BCH* Suppl., 3 [Paris, 1976]) |
| *Hyperboreus* | *Hyperboreus. Studia Classica*, 1– (Bibliotheca Classica Petropolitana [St. Petersburg, 1994– ]) |
| *IApoll* | *Corpus des inscriptions grecques d'Illyrie méridionale et d'Épire*. I, *Inscriptions d'Épidamne-Dyrrhachion et d'Apollonia*. 2 A, *Inscriptions d'Apollonia d'Illyrie*, edd. P. Cabanes and N. Ceka; 2 B, *Listes des noms de monétaires d'Apollonia et Épidamne-Dyrrhachion*, ed. H. Ceka and M. Beauregard (Paris, forthcoming) |
| *IAquil* | *Inscriptiones Aquileiae*, ed. J. B. Brusin, 3 vols. (*Pubblicazioni della Deputazione di Storia Patria per il Friuli*, 20 [Udine, 1991–3]) |
| *IBouthrot* | *Corpus des inscriptions grecques d'Illyrie méridionale et d'Épire*. II, *Inscriptions de Bouthrotos*, edd. P. Cabanes and F. Drini [forthcoming] |
| *IC* | *Inscriptiones Creticae*, ed. M. Guarducci, 4 vols. (Rome, 1935–50) |
| *ICI* | *Inscriptiones Christianae Italiae septimo saeculo antiquiores*, 1– (Bari, 1985– ) |
| *ICos* | *Iscrizioni di Cos*, ed. M. Segre (*Monografie della Scuola Archeologica di Atene e delle Missioni Italiane in Oriente*, 6 [Rome, 1993]) |
| *ICUR* | *Inscriptiones Christiani Urbis Romae septimo saeculo antiquiores*, edd. A. Silvagni, A. Ferrua, D. Mazzolini and C. Carletti, NS 1– (Vatican City, 1900– ) |
| *ID* | *Inscriptions de Délos*, edd. A. Plassart, J. Coupry, F. Durrbach, P. Roussel and M. Launey, 7 vols. and Index I, ed. J. Tréheux (Paris, 1926–1992) |
| *IDidyma* | *Didyma*. II, *Die Inschriften*, edd. A. Rehm and R. Harder (Berlin, 1958) |
| *IDyrrh* | *Corpus des inscriptions grecques d'Illyrie méridionale et d'Épire*. I, *Inscriptions d'Épidamne-Dyrrhachion et d'Apollonie*. 1, *Inscriptions d'Épidamne-Dyrrhachion*, edd. P. Cabanes and F. Drini (*Études Epigraphiques*, 2 [Paris, 1995]) |

| | |
|---|---|
| *IEG* | *Iambi et Elegi Graeci ante Alexandrum cantati*, ed. M. L. West, 2 vols. (2nd edn. Oxford, 1989–92) |
| *IEK* | *Die Inschriften von Erythrai und Klazomenai*, edd. H. Engelmann and R. Merkelbach, 2 vols. (*IGSK*, 1–2 [Bonn, 1972–3]) |
| *IEph* | *Die Inschriften von Ephesos*, edd. R. Merkelbach, J. Nollé et al., 7 vols. in 8 (*IGSK*, 11–17 [Bonn, 1979–81]) |
| *IFayoum* | *Recueil des inscriptions grecques du Fayoum*, ed. E. Bernand, 3 vols. (vol. I, Leiden, 1975; vols. II–III, *Institut Français d'Archéologie Orientale du Caire, Bibliothèque d'Étude*, 79–80 [Paris, 1981]) |
| *IG* | *Inscriptiones Graecae* (Berlin, 1877– ); [2] (Berlin, 1913– ); [3] Vol. I (1–2) (Berlin, 1981–94), various editors |
| *IGA* | *Inscriptiones Graecae antiquissimae praeter Atticas in Attica repertas*, ed. H. Roehl (Berlin, 1882) |
| *IGB* | *Inscriptiones Graecae in Bulgaria repertae*, ed. G. Mihailov, 4 vols. in 5 (Sofia, 1951–66; 1[2] 1970) |
| *IGLMP* | M. T. Manni Piraino, *Iscrizioni greche lapidarie del museo di Palermo* (Σικελικά, 6 [Palermo, 1973]) |
| *IGR* | *Inscriptiones Graecae ad res Romanas pertinentes*, edd. R. Cagnat, G. Lafaye et al., vols. I, II and IV (Paris, 1906–27) |
| *IGSI* | *Inscriptiones Graecae Siciliae et Infimae Italiae ad Ius pertinentes*, edd. V. Arangio-Ruiz and A. Olivieri (Milan, 1925) |
| *IGUR* | L. Moretti, *Inscriptiones Graecae Urbis Romae*, 4 vols. in 5 (*Studi pubblicati dall'Istituto Italiano per la Storia Antica*, 17, 22 (1-2), 28, 47 [Rome, 1968–1990]) |
| *IIasos* | *Die Inschriften von Iasos*, ed. W. Blümel, 2 vols. (*IGSK*, 28 (1–2) [Bonn, 1985]) |
| *IItal* | *Inscriptiones Italiae*, 1– (Unione Accademica Nazionale [Rome, 1931– ]) |
| Ijsewijn | J. Ijsewijn, *De sacerdotibus sacerdotiisque Alexandri Magni et Lagidarum eponymis* (*Verhandelingen van de Koninklijke Vlaamse Academie voor Wetenschappen, Letteren en Schone Kunsten van België, Klasse de Letteren*, 42 [Brussels, 1961]) |
| *IKourion* | *The Inscriptions of Kourion*, ed. T. B. Mitford (*Memoirs of the American Philosophical Society*, 83 [Philadelphia, 1971]) |
| *IKyz* | *Die Inschriften von Kyzikos u. Umgebung*, ed. E. Schwertheim, 2 vols. (*IGSK*, 18, 26 [Bonn, 1980, 1983]) |
| *ILat. Palermo* | L. Bivona, *Iscrizioni Latine Lapidarie del Museo di Palermo* (Σικελικά, 5 [Palermo, 1970]) |
| *ILat. Term. Imer.* | L. Bivona, *Iscrizioni Latine Lapidarie del Museo Civico di Termini Imerese* (Σικελικά, 8 [Rome, 1994]) |
| *ILGR* | *Inscriptiones Latinae in Graecia Repertae. Additamenta ad CIL III*, ed. M. Šašel Kos (*Epigrafia e Antichità. Studi a cura dell'Istituto di Storia Antica dell'Università di Bologna*, 5 [Faenza, 1979]) |
| *ILind* | *Lindos. Fouilles et recherches 1902–1914*. II, *Inscriptions*, ed. C. Blinkenberg, 2 vols. (Berlin and Copenhagen, 1941) |
| *Iliria* | *Iliria. Studime dhe Materiale Arkeologjike*, 1– (Tirana, 1971– ) |
| *ILS* | *Inscriptiones Latinae selectae*, ed. H. Dessau, 3 vols. in 4 (Berlin, 1892–1916) |
| Imhoof-Blümer, *MGr* | F. Imhoof-Blümer, *Monnaies grecques* (Paris and Leipzig, 1883) |
| *IMM* | *Die Inschriften von Magnesia am Maeander*, ed. O. Kern (Berlin, 1900) |
| *Impegno per Pompeii* | *Un Impegno per Pompeii. Fotopiano e Documentazione della Necropoli di Porta Nocera*, edd. A. D'Ambrosio and S. De Caro (Touring Club Italiano [Milan, 1983]) |
| *INap* | *Iscrizioni Greche d'Italia. Napoli*, ed. E. Miranda, 2 vols. (Unione Accademica Nazionale [Rome, 1990, 1995]) |
| *Index Hipp.* | *Index Hippocraticus*, edd. J.-H. Kühn, U. Fleischer et al. (Göttingen, 1989) |
| *IOlbia* | *Nadpisi Olbii (1917-1965) (Inscriptions of Olbia)*, ed. E. I. Levi (Leningrad, 1968) |
| *IOrop* | *Inscriptions d'Oropos*, ed. B. Ch. Petrakos [forthcoming] |
| *IPArk* | G. Thür and H. Taeuber, *Prozessrechtliche Inschriften der Griechischen Poleis: Arkadien* (*Sitzungberichte der Österreichische Akademie der Wissenschaften*, 607, *Veröffentlichungen der Kommission für antike Rechtsgeschichte*, 8 [Vienna, 1994]) |
| *IPerg* | *Die Inschriften von Pergamon*, ed. M. Fraenkel, 2 vols. (*Altertümer von Pergamon*, 8 [Berlin, 1890–5]) |
| *IPhilae* | *Les inscriptions grecques de Philae*, edd. A. and E. Bernand, 2 vols. (Paris, 1969) |
| *IPr* | *Die Inschriften von Priene*, ed. F. Hiller von Gaertringen (Berlin, 1906) |
| *IPrusa* | *Die Inschriften von Prusa ad Olympum*, ed. T. Corsten, 2 vols. (*IGSK*, 39–40 [Bonn, 1991, 1993]) |
| *IRhamnous* | B. Ch. Petrakos, *Inscriptions of Rhamnous* [forthcoming] |
| *IRhodPer* | *Die Inschriften der Rhodischen Peraia*, ed. W. Blümel (*IGSK*, 38 [Bonn, 1991]) |
| *Iscr. Gr. Verona* | T. Ritti, *Iscrizioni e rilievi greci del Museo Maffeiano di Verona* (*Collezione e Musei Archeologici del Veneto*, 21 [Rome, 1981]) |
| *Iscr. Trebula Caiatia Cubulteria* | *Le iscrizioni antiche di Trebula, Caiatia e Cubulteria*, ed. H. Solin (Caserta, 1993) |
| *ISmyrna* | *Die Inschriften von Smyrna*, ed. G. Petzl, 2 vols. (*IGSK*, 23 (1), 24 (1) [Bonn, 1982, 1987]) |
| *Istros* | *Istros. Revue Roumaine d'archéologie et d'histoire ancienne*, 1–2 (Bucharest, 1934–1935/6) |
| *Italic Dialects* | R. S. Conway, *The Italic Dialects*, 2 vols. (Cambridge, 1897) |
| *ITrall* | *Die Inschriften von Tralleis und Nysa*. I, *Die Inschriften von Tralleis*, ed. F. B. Poljakov (*IGSK*, 36 (1) [Bonn, 1989]) |
| *IvOl* | *Die Inschriften von Olympia*, edd. W. Dittenberger and K. Purgold (*Olympia*, 5 [Berlin, 1896]) |
| Jenkins, *Coins of Greek Sicily* | G. K. Jenkins, *Coins of Greek Sicily* (2nd edn. London, 1976) |

*JHS*                          *Journal of Hellenic Studies*, 1– (Society for the Promotion of Hellenic Studies [London, 1881– ])
*JIAN*                         *Journal international d'archéologie numismatique*, ed. I. N. Svoronos, 1–21 (Athens, 1898–1927)
*JIWE*                         D. Noy, *Jewish Inscriptions of Western Europe*. I, *Italy (excluding the city of Rome)*, *Spain and Gaul* (Cambridge, 1993)
*JNG*                          *Jahrbuch für Numismatik und Geldgeschichte*, 1– (Bayerisches Numismatisches Gesellschaft [Munich, 1949–51, 1986– ; Kallmünz, 1952–85])
*JÖAI*                         *Jahreshefte des Österreichischen Archäologischen Institutes in Wien*, 1– (Vienna, 1898– )
Johnston, *Trademarks*         A. W. Johnston, *Trademarks on Greek Vases* (Warminster, 1979)
*Journ. Glass Stud.*           *Journal of Glass Studies*, 1– (The Corning Museum of Glass [Corning, N.Y., 1959– ])
*Jubice Hoard*                 H. Ceka, 'Thesari i Jubicës, hallkë tjetër me rëndësi për rënditjen kronologjike të drahmeve ilire (Le trésor numismatique de Jubice [Koplik-Shkodër]', *Iliria* 1 (1971) pp. 83–101
*Kafizin*                      T. B. Mitford, *The Nymphaeum of Kafizin: the Inscribed Pottery* (*Kadmos* Suppl., 2 [Berlin and New York, 1980])
Keil, *Analecta Epigr.*        C. Keil, *Analecta Epigraphica et Onomatologica* (Leipzig, 1842)
*Kenchreai*                    *Kenchreai, Eastern Port of Corinth. Results of Investigations by the University of Chicago and Indiana University for the American School of Classical Studies at Athens*, 1– (Leiden, 1976– )
*KF*                           R. Herzog, *Koische Forschungen und Funde* (Leipzig, 1899)
King, *Engraved Gems*          C. W. King, *Handbook of Engraved Gems* (2nd edn. London, 1885)
*Kl. Pauly*                    *Der Kleine Pauly. Lexikon der Antike auf der Grundlage von Pauly's Realencyclopädie*, edd. K. Ziegler, W. Sontheimer and H. Gärtner, 5 vols. (Stuttgart, 1964–75)
Klaffenbach, *Var. Epigr.*     G. Klaffenbach, *Varia Epigraphica* (*AbhBerlAk*, 1958 (2) [Berlin, 1958])
*Klearchos*                    *Klearchos. Bollettino dell'Associazione Amici del Museo Nazionale di Reggio Calabria*, 1– (Naples, 1959– )
Klee                           T. Klee, *Zur Geschichte der gymnischen Agone an griechischen Festen* (Leipzig and Berlin, 1918)
*Klio*                         *Klio. Beiträge zur Alten Geschichte*, 1– (Leipzig, 1901–44; Berlin, 1959– )
Kockel                         V. Kockel, *Die Grabbauten vor dem Herkulaner Tor in Pompeji* (*Beiträge zur Erschliessung hellenistischer und kaiserzeitlicher Skulptur und Architektur*, 1 [Mainz, 1983])
*Kokalos*                      Κώκαλος. *Studi pubblicati dall'Istituto di Storia Antica dell'Università di Palermo*, 1– (Palermo, 1955– )
*Korkyra*                      *Korkyra. Archaische Bauten und Bildwerke*, ed. G. Rodenwaldt, 2 vols. (Deutsch. Arch. Inst. [Berlin, 1939–40])
Kraay, *Greek Coins and History*   C. M. Kraay, *Greek Coins and History: some current problems* (London, 1969)
Kramolisch                     H. Kramolisch, *Demetrias*. II, *Die Strategen des thessalischen Bundes vom Jahr 196 v. Chr. bis zum Ausgang der römischen Republik* (*Beiträge zur ur- und frühgeschichtlichen Archäologie des Mittelmeer-Kulturraumes*, 18 [Bonn, 1978])
Kretschmer                     P. Kretschmer, *Die griechische Vaseninschriften, ihrer Sprache nach untersucht* (Gütersloh, 1894)
*Kythera*                      *Kythera, Excavations and Studies conducted by the University of Pennsylvania Museum and the British School at Athens*, edd. G. L. Huxley and J. N. Coldstream (London, 1972)
*L'Illyrie mérid.*             *L'Illyrie méridionale et l'Épire dans l'Antiquité*. I, *Actes du colloque international de Clermont-Ferrand (22–25 octobre, 1984)*. II, *Actes du colloque international de Clermont Ferrand (25–27 octobre, 1990)*, ed. P. Cabanes [Clermont-Ferrand, 1987; Paris, 1993])
*L'Incidenza dell'Antico*      *L'Incidenza dell'Antico. Studi in memoria di Ettore Lepore*. I, *Atti del Convegno Internazionale, Anacapri 24-28 marzo 1991*, ed. A. Storchi Marino (Naples, 1995)
*Laconia Survey*               *Continuity and Change in a Greek Rural Landscape: The Laconia Survey*, edd. W. Cavanagh, J. Crouwel, R. W. V. Catling and G. Shipley, 2 vols. (*BSA* Suppl., 27 [London, 1996])
*Lampes antiques BN*           M.-C. Hellmann, *Lampes Antiques de la Bibliothèque Nationale*. I, *Collection Froehner*. II, *Fonds General: Lampes pré-romaines et romaines* (Paris, 1985, 1987)
*Lampes d'Argos*               A. Bovon, *Lampes d'Argos* (*Études Péloponnésiennes*, 5 [Paris, 1966])
Landi, *DISMG*                 A. Landi, *Dialetti e interazione sociale in Magna Grecia. Lineamenti di una storia linguistica attraverso la documentazione epigrafica* (*Università di Napoli, Centro di Studi per la Magna Grecia*, 4 [Naples, 1979])
*Laos*                         *Laos*. II, *La tomba a camera di Marcellina*, edd. E. Greco and P. G. Guzzo (Istituto per la storia e l'archeologia della Magna Grecia, *Magna Grecia*, 7 [Taranto, 1992])
Laum, *Stiftungen*             B. Laum, *Stiftungen in der griechischen und römischen Antike. Ein Beitrag zur antiken Kulturgeschichte*, 2 vols. (Berlin, 1914)
Launey                         M. Launey, *Recherches sur les armées hellénistiques*, 2 vols. (*BEFAR*, 169 [2nd edn. Paris, 1949–50])
Lazzarini                      M. L. Lazzarini, *Le formule delle dediche votive nella Grecia arcaica* (*Mem. Linc.*, ser. 8, 19 (2) [Rome, 1976])
*LCS*                          A. D. Trendall, *The Red-figured Vases of Lucania, Campania, and Sicily*, 2 vols. (*Oxford Monographs on Classical Archaeology* [Oxford, 1967])
*Le Arti*                      see *BdA*
Le Rider, *Monnaies crétoises*  G. Le Rider, *Monnaies crétoises du Vᵉ au Iᵉʳ siècle av. J.-C.* (*Études Crétoises*, 15 [Paris, 1966])
Leake, *Northern Greece*       W. M. Leake, *Travels in Northern Greece*, 4 vols. (London, 1835)
Leiwo                          M. Leiwo, *Neapolitana. A Study of Population and Language in Graeco-Roman Naples* (Societas Scientiarum Fennica, *Commentationes Humanarum Litterarum*, 102 [Helsinki, 1994])

| | |
|---|---|
| *Lex Sacra from Selinous* | M. H. Jameson, D. R. Jordan and R. D. Kotansky, *A Lex Sacra from Selinous* (*GRBS* Monographs, 11 [Durham, North Carolina, 1993]) |
| *LGPN* | *A Lexicon of Greek Personal Names.* I, *The Aegean Islands, Cyprus, Cyrenaica*, edd. P. M. Fraser and E. Matthews; II, *Attica*, edd. M. J. Osborne and S. G. Byrne (Oxford, 1987, 1994) |
| Libertini, *Isole Eolie* | G. Libertini, *Le Isole Eolie nell'antichità greca e romana: ricerche storiche ed archeologiche* (*Pubblicazioni del R. Instituto di studi superiori practici e di perfezionamento in Firenze, sezione di filologia e filosofia*, NS 3 [Florence, 1921]) |
| Libertini, *Mus. Arch. Sirac.* | G. Libertini, *Il Regio Museo Archeologico di Siracusa* (Rome, 1929) |
| Libertini, *Museo Biscari* | G. Libertini, *Il Museo Biscari*, I (Milan and Rome, 1930) |
| Liegle, *Euainetos* | J. Liegle, *Euainetos. Eine Werkfolge nach Originalen des Stäatlichen Münzkabinetts zu Berlin* (*Winckelmannsprogramm der archäologischen Gesellschaft zu Berlin*, 101 [Berlin, 1941]) |
| *Lilibeo* | *Lilibeo. Testimonianze Archeologiche dal IV sec. a.c. al V sec. d.c.*, Marsala, Chiesa del Collegio dal 3 dicembre 1984 (Palermo, 1984) |
| Lindgren, *AGBC* | H. C. Lindgren, *Ancient Greek Bronze Coins: European Mints from the Lindgren Collection* (San Mateo, California, 1989) |
| Lo Porto, *Civ. indig. nella Lucania orientale* | F. G. Lo Porto, *Civiltà indigena e penetrazione greca nella Lucania orientale* (*Mon. Ant.*, Serie Miscellanea, 1 (3) [Rome, 1973]) |
| *Locri Epizefiri 2* | M. Barra Bagnasco et al., *Locri Epizefiri*, II. *Gli isolati I2 e I3 dell'area Centocamere* (*Università degli Studi di Torino, Studi e Materiali di Archeologia*, 1 [Florence, 1989]) |
| Loewy | E. Loewy, *Inschriften griechischer Bildhauer* (Leipzig, 1885; repr. Osnabrück, 1965) |
| Lorber | F. Lorber, *Inschriften auf korinthischen Vasen. Archäologisch-epigraphische Untersuchungen zur korinthischen Vasenmalerei im 7. und 6. Jh. v. Chr.* (Deutsch. Arch. Inst., *Archäologische Forschungen*, 6 [Berlin, 1979]) |
| *LSAG*[2] | L. H. Jeffery, *The Local Scripts of Archaic Greece* (2nd edn. with Supplement by A. W. Johnston [Oxford, 1990]) |
| *Lucera Romana* | *Lucera Romana*, ed. V. A. Sirago (Lucera, 1980) |
| Maier | A. Maier, 'Die Silverprägung von Apollonia und Dyrrhachion', in *NZ* NS 1 (1908) pp. 1-33 |
| Maiuri, *Nuovi Scavi* | A. Maiuri, *Ercolano. I Nuovi Scavi (1927-1958)*, I (Rome, 1958) |
| Manganaro, *PdelP* | G. Manganaro, 'Nuove tavolette di piombo inscritte siceliote', *PdelP* forthcoming |
| Manganaro, *QUCC* | G. Manganaro, 'Sikelika II', *QUCC* forthcoming |
| Marcadé | J. Marcadé, *Recueil des signatures de sculpteurs grecs*, 2 vols. (Paris, 1953–7) |
| Masson, *OGS* | O. Masson, *Onomastica Graeca Selecta*, edd. C. Dobias and L. Dubois, 2 vols. (Paris, 1990) |
| *Master Bronzes from the Classical World* | D. G. Mitten and S. F. Doeringer, *Master Bronzes from the Classical World* (Mainz, 1967) |
| Mayer, *Apulien* | M. Mayer, *Apulien vor und während der Hellenisirung* (Leipzig and Berlin, 1914) |
| *MChr* | L. Mitteis and U. Wilcken, *Grundzüge und Chrestomathie der Papyruskunde.* II, *Juristische Teil*, ed. L. Mitteis, 2 vols. (Leipzig and Berlin, 1912) |
| *Mél. Daux* | *Mélanges helléniques offerts à Georges Daux* (Paris, 1974) |
| *Mél. Nicole* | *Mélanges Nicole. Recueil de mémoires de philologie classique et d'archéologie offerts à Jules Nicole* (Geneva, 1905) |
| *Mél. Vatin* | Εὔκρατα. *Mélanges offerts à Claude Vatin*, edd. M.-Cl. Amouretti and P. Villard (*Travaux du Centre Camille Jullian*, 17 [Aix-en-Provence, 1994]) |
| *MEFRA* | *Mélanges de l'École Française de Rome, Antiquité*, 83– (1971–), formerly *Mélanges d'Archéologie et d'Histoire*, 1–82 (1881–1970) |
| Meineke, *Anal. Alex.* | A. Meineke, *Analecta Alexandrina* (Berlin, 1843) |
| *Meligunis-Lipara* | L. Bernabò Brea and M. Cavalier, *Meligunis-Lipára*, 1– (*Pubblicazioni del Museo Eoliano di Lipari* [Palermo, 1960– ]) |
| Mello–Voza | M. Mello and G. Voza, *Le Iscrizioni Latine di Paestum*, 2 vols. (Naples, 1968–9) |
| *Mem. Accad. Arch. Napoli* | *Memorie dell'Accademia di Archeologia, Lettere e (Belle) Arti di Napoli*, 1–6 (Naples, 1911–42); NS 1– (1951– ) |
| *Mem. Linc.* | *Atti della (Reale) Accademia Nazionale dei Lincei, Classe di scienze morali, storiche e filologiche, Memorie*, ser. 3–8 (Rome, 1877– ) |
| *Mem. Pont.* | *Atti della Pontificia Accademia Romana di Archeologia*, ser. 3, *Memorie*, 1– (Rome, 1923– ) |
| *Memnonion* | P. Perdrizet and G. Lefebvre, *Les graffites grecs du Memnonion d'Abydos* (Nancy, Paris, and Strasbourg, 1919) |
| Michel | C. Michel, *Recueil d'inscriptions grecques* (Brussels, 1900; Supplément 1912–27) |
| *Milet* | *Milet. Ergebnisse der Ausgrabungen und Untersuchungen seit dem Jahre 1899*, edd. Th. Wiegand et al., 1– (Berlin, 1906– ) |
| Mionnet | T. E. Mionnet, *Description de médailles antiques grecques et romaines*, with 15 supplements (Paris, 1807–37) |
| *Misc. Etrusco-Italica* | *Miscellanea Etrusco-Italica*, I, ed. M. Cristofani (*Quaderni di Archeologia Etrusco-Italica*, 22 [Rome, 1993]) |
| *Misc. Gr. Rom.* | *Miscellanea Greca e Romana*, 1– (*Studi pubblicati dall'Istituto Italiano per la Storia Antica* [Rome, 1965– ]) |
| *Miscellanea* | *Miscellanea* (*Pubblicazioni dell'Istituto di Epigrafia e Antichità Greche e Romane dell'Università di Roma, Tituli*, 2 [Rome, 1980]) |

Mitsos     M. Th. Mitsos, Ἀργολικὴ Προσωπογραφία (Βιβλ. Ἀθ. Ἀρχ. Ἑτ., 36 [Athens, 1952])

*MkB*     Μουσεῖον καὶ Βιβλιοθήκη τῆς Εὐαγγελικῆς Σχολῆς ἐν Σμύρνηι, 1–5 (2) (Smyrna, 1873/5–1885/6)

ML     R. Meiggs and D. Lewis, *A Selection of Greek Historical Inscriptions to the end of the fifth century B.C.* (Oxford, 1969; revised edn., 1988)

*Mnem.*     *Mnemosyne. Biblioteca Classica Batava*, 1– (Leiden, 1852– )

*Mon. Ant.*     *Monumenti Antichi*, 1– ((Reale) Accademia Nazionale dei Lincei [Milan, 1890– ])

*Mon. Piot*     *Monuments et Mémoires. Fondation Eugène Piot*, 1– (Academie des Inscriptions et Belles-Lettres [Paris, 1894– ])

*Monte Sannace*     A. Ciancio, E. M. de Juliis, A. Riccardi and F. Rossi, *Monte Sannace: gli scavi dell'acropoli (1978-1983)* (*Università di Lecce, Dipartimento di Scienze dell'Antichità, settore storico-archeologico*, 3 [Galatina, 1989])

Monti, *Ischia*     P. Monti, *Ischia. Archeologia e Storia* (Naples, 1980)

Moretti, *IAG*     L. Moretti, *Iscrizioni agonistiche greche* (*Studi pubblicati dall'Istituto Italiano per la Storia Antica*, 12 [Rome, 1953])

Moretti, *ISE*     L. Moretti, *Iscrizioni storiche ellenistiche*, 2 vols. (*Biblioteca di studi superiori*, 53, 62 [Florence, 1967–76])

Moretti, *Olymp.*     L. Moretti, *Olympionikai, i vincitori negli antichi agoni olimpici* (*Mem. Linc.*, 8th ser., 8 (2) [Rome, 1957]) [Addenda, *Klio* 52 (1970) pp. 295 ff.; *Misc. Gr. Rom.* 12 (1987) pp. 67-91; *Proc. Sympos. Olympic Games* pp. 119-28]

Morkholm, *EHC*     O. Morkholm, *Early Hellenistic coinage from the accession of Alexander to the Peace of Apamea (336-188 B.C.)*, edd. P. Grierson and U. Westermark (Cambridge, 1991)

Mouritsen     H. Mouritsen, *Elections, Magistrates and Municipal Élite. Studies in Pompeian Epigraphy*, (*Analecta Romana Instituti Danici* Suppl., 15 [Rome, 1988])

Münsterberg     R. Münsterberg, 'Die Beamtennamen auf den griechischen Münzen', *NZ* NS 4–20 (1911–27); repr. Hildesheim, Zurich and New York, 1985

*Münzpr. der Laked.*     S. Grunauer-von Hoerschelmann, *Die Münzprägung der Lakedaimonier* (Deutsch. Arch. Inst., *Antike Münzen und geschnittene Steine*, 7 [Berlin, 1978])

*Mus. Arch. di Bari*     *Il Museo Archeologico di Bari*, ed. E. M. de Juliis (Bari, 1983)

*Mus. Arch. Taranto*     R. Belli Pasqua, *Catalogo del Museo Nazionale Archeologico di Taranto. IV (1), Taranto. La scultura in marmo e in pietra* (Taranto, 1995)

*Mus. Naz. Reggio*     *Il Museo Nazionale di Reggio Calabria*, ed. E. Lattanzi (Rome, 1987)

*Musée de Mariemont*     *Les Antiquités égyptiennes, grecques, étrusques, romaines et gallo-romaines du Musée de Mariemont* (Brussels, 1952)

*Museo di Venosa*     *Il Museo Archeologico Nazionale di Venosa*, ed. M. Salvatore (Ministero per i Beni Culturali e Ambientali, Soprintendenza Archeologica della Basilicata [Matera, 1991])

*Museo Ribezzo*     *Ricerche e Studi. Museo 'Francesco Ribezzo' - Brindisi. Quaderni*, 1– (Fasano, 1964– )

Nachtergael, *Les Galates*     G. Nachtergael, *Les Galates en Grèce et les Sôtéria de Delphes. Recherches d'histoire et d'épigraphie hellénistiques* (*Académie Royale de Belgique, Mémoires de la Classe des Lettres*, 63 (1) [Brussels, 1977]) Appendix, 'Corpus des actes relatifs aux Sôtéria de Delphes', pp. 391-495

*Napoli Antica*     *Napoli Antica* (Soprintendenza Archeologica per le province di Napoli e Caserta [Naples, 1985])

Naville sale     Naville and Co., sale catalogues 1–14 (Geneva, 1920–9); subsequently *Ars Classica* sale catalogues 15–18 (1930–8)

*NC*     *Numismatic Chronicle*, 1– (London, 1839– )

*Neapolis*     *Neapolis. Rivista di Archeologia, Epigrafica e Numismatica*, 1–2 (Naples, 1913–14)

*Necropoli via Cappuccini*     *La Necropoli di via Cappuccini a Brindisi*, edd. A. Cocchiaro and G. Andreassi (Fasano, 1988)

*Nemea*     D. E. Birge, L. H. Kraynak and S. G. Miller, *Excavations at Nemea. I, Topographical and Architectural Studies: the Sacred Square, the Xenon, and the Bath* (Berkeley, Los Angeles and Oxford, 1992)

*Nemea Guide*     *Nemea. A Guide to the Site and Museum*, ed. S. G. Miller (Berkeley, Los Angeles and Oxford, 1990)

*Neos Hellenomnemon*     Νέος Ἑλληνομνήμων, ed. S. P. Lambros, 1–21 (Athens, 1904–1930)

Neratzoulis     P. Neratzoulis, Ἀχαιῶν δωδεκαπόλεως ἐρείπια καὶ μνημεῖα (Athens, 1938)

*Neue Forsch. in Pompeji*     *Neue Forschungen in Pompeji und den anderen vom Vesuvausbruch 79 n.Chr. verschütteten Städten*, edd. B. Andreae and H. Kyrieleis (Deutsch. Arch. Inst. [Recklinghausen, 1975])

Noe, *Thurian Di-Staters*     S. P. Noe, *The Thurian Di-Staters* (American Numismatic Society, *Numismatic Notes and Monographs*, 71 [New York, 1935])

Noll, *Inschr. Wien.*     R. Noll, *Griechische und lateinische Inschriften der Wiener Antikensammlung* (Vienna, 1962)

Novak, *Vis*     G. Novak, *Vis*, I (Zagreb, 1961)

*NS*     A. Maiuri, *Nuova silloge epigrafica di Rodi e Cos* (Florence, 1925)

*NScav*     *Notizie degli Scavi di Antichità* ((Reale) Accademia Nazionale dei Lincei [Rome, 1876– ])

*Nuovo Didask.*     *Nuovo Didaskaleion*, 1– (Centro di Studi di Storia Arte e Lett. Crist. Antica/Centro di Studi sull'Antico Cristianesimo, Università di Catania [Catania, 1947– ])

*N Y Bronzes*     G. M. A. Richter, *Greek, Etruscan and Roman Bronzes* (Metropolitan Museum of Art [New York, 1915])

*NZ*     *Numismatische Zeitschrift*, 1– (Vienna, 1869– )

*OGIS*     *Orientis Graeci Inscriptiones Selectae*, ed. W. Dittenberger, 2 vols. (Leipzig, 1903–5)

| | |
|---|---|
| *Oikoumene* | *Oikoumene. Studi paleocristiani pubblicati in onore del Concilio Ecumenico Vaticano II* (Catania, 1964) |
| *Ol. Ber.* | *Bericht über die Ausgrabungen in Olympia*, 1– (Deutsch. Arch. Inst. [Berlin, 1936– ]) |
| *Ol. Forsch.* | *Olympische Forschungen*, 1– (Deutsch. Arch. Inst. [Berlin, 1944– ]) |
| *Op. Ath.* | *Opuscula Atheniensia (Acta Instituti Atheniensis Regni Sueciae)* 1–9 (Lund, 1953–69); 10– (Stockholm, 1971– ) |
| *Ordona* | J. Mertens et al., *Ordona*, 1– (Brussels and Rome, 1965– ) |
| Orlandos, *Alipheira* | A. K. Orlandos, Ἡ Ἀρκαδικὴ Ἀλιφείρα καὶ τὰ Μνημεῖα της (Βιβλ. Ἀθ. Ἀρχ. Ἑτ., 58 [Athens, 1967–8]) |
| Orsi, *Le necropoli di Passo Marinaro* | P. Orsi, *Le necropoli di Passo Marinaro a Camarina. Campagne di scavo, 1904-1909*, ed. M. T. Lanza (*Mon. Ant.*, Serie Miscellanea, 4 [Rome, 1990]) |
| Osborne, *Naturalization* | M. J. Osborne, *Naturalization in Athens (Verhandelingen van der Koninklijke Academie voor Wetenschappen, Letteren en Schone Kunsten van België, Klasse der Letteren*, 98, 101, 109 [Brussels, 1981–83]) |
| *Ostraka* | *Ostraka. Rivista di Antichità*, 1– (Naples, 1992– ) |
| Overbeck | J. Overbeck, *Die antiken Schriftquellen zur Geschichte der bildenden Künste bei den Griechen* (Leipzig, 1868) |
| *PA* | *Prosopographia Attica*, ed. J. Kirchner, 2 vols. (Berlin, 1901–3) |
| Pace, *Camarina* | B. Pace, *Camarina. Topografia - Storia - Archeologia* (Sicilia Antiqua, Collezione di Monografie Storico-Archeologiche [Catania 1927]) |
| *PAE* | Πρακτικὰ τῆς ἐν Ἀθήναις Ἀρχαιολογικῆς Ἑταιρείας (Athens, 1889– ) |
| Page, *FGE* | D. L. Page, *Further Greek Epigrams*, edd. R. D. Dawe and J. Diggle (Cambridge, 1981) |
| Pagenstecher, *Calen. Reliefkeramik* | R. Pagenstecher, *Die Calenische Reliefkeramik (JDAI* Ergänzungsheft, 8 [Berlin, 1909]) |
| Pagenstecher, *Nekrop.* | R. Pagenstecher, *Nekropolis. Untersuchungen über Gestalt und Entwicklung der alexandrinischen Grabanlagen und ihrer Malereien* (Leipzig, 1919) |
| *Palinuro* | R. Naumann and B. Neutsch, *Palinuro. Ergebnisse der Ausgrabungen*. II, *Nekropole, Terrassenzone und Einzelfunde (Röm. Mitt.* Ergänzungsheft, 4 [Heidelberg, 1960]) |
| *PAmh* | *The Amhurst Papyri*, edd. B. P. Grenfell and A. S. Hunt, 2 vols. (London, 1900–1) |
| Pantos, *Sphragismata* | P. A. Pantos, Τὰ Σφραγίσματα τῆς Αἰτωλικῆς Καλλιπόλεως (Diss. Athens, 1985) |
| Papaefthimiou | W. Papaefthimiou, *Grabreliefs späthellenistischer und römischer Zeit aus Sparta und Lakonien (Quellen und Forschungen zur antiken Welt*, 13 [Munich, 1992]) |
| Parlangèli, *Studi Messapici* | O. Parlangèli, *Studi Messapici (Memorie dell'Istituto Lombardo – Accademia di Scienze e Lettere, Classe di Lettere – Scienze Morali e Storiche*, 26 [Milan, 1960]) |
| *Parnassos* | Παρνασσός, 1–17 (Φιλολογικὸς Σύλλογος Παρνασσός [Athens, 1877–1895]); NS 1– (1959– ); from 1896–1939 published as Ἐπετηρὶς τοῦ Φιλολογικοῦ Συλλόγου Παρνασσός |
| Patsch, *Narona* | C. Patsch, *Zur Geschichte und Topographie von Narona (Kaiserliche Akademie der Wissenschaften, Schriften der Balkankommission, Antiquarische Abt.*, 5 [Vienna, 1907]) |
| Patsch, *Sandschak Berat* | C. Patsch, *Das Sandschak Berat in Albanien (Kaiserliche Akademie der Wissenschaften, Schriften der Balkankommission, Antiquarische Abt.*, 3 [Vienna, 1904]) |
| *Pausilypon* | R. T. Günther, *Pausilypon. The Imperial Villa near Naples* (Oxford, 1913) |
| *PBSR* | *Papers of the British School at Rome*, 1– (London, 1902– ) |
| *PCG* | *Poetae Comici Graeci*, edd. R. Kassel and C. Austin, vols. 2, 3(2), 4, 5, 7, 8 (Berlin and New York, 1983– ) |
| *PCZ* | *Catalogue général des antiquités égyptiennes du Musée du Caire, Zenon Papyri*, ed. C. C. Edgar, 5 vols. (Cairo, 1925–40) |
| *PdelP* | *La Parola del Passato. Rivista di studi antichi*, 1– (Naples, 1946– ) |
| Peek, *AG* | W. Peek, *Attische Grabschriften*, 2 vols. (*AbhBerlAk*, Kl. Spr., Lit., Kunst, 1953 (4); 1956 (3) [Berlin, 1954, 1957]) |
| Peek, *IAEpid* | W. Peek, *Inschriften aus dem Asklepieion von Epidauros (Abh. Akad. Leipzig*, 60 (2) [Berlin, 1969]) |
| Peek, *NIEpid* | W. Peek, *Neue Inschriften aus Epidauros (Abh. Akad. Leipzig*, 63 (5) [Berlin, 1972]) |
| *PEG* | *Poetae Epici Graeci. Testimonia et fragmenta*, I, ed. A. Bernabé (Leipzig, 1987) |
| *PEleph* | *Elephantine-Papyri*, ed. O. Rubensohn (*Ägyptische Urkunden aus den Königlichen Museen in Berlin, Sonderheft* [Berlin, 1907]) |
| *Peloponnesiaka* | Πελοποννησιακά, 1– (Ἑταιρεία Πελοποννησιακῶν Σπουδῶν [Athens, 1956– ]) |
| *PEnt* | Ἐντεύξεις. *Requêtes et plaintes addressées au roi d'Égypte au III*e *siècle avant J.-C.*, ed. O. Guéraud (*Publications de la Société Royale Égyptienne de Papyrologie, Textes et Documents*, 1 [Cairo, 1931]) |
| Perlman | P. J. Perlman, *The 'Theorodokia' in the Peloponnese* (Diss. Berkeley, 1984; UMI, Ann Arbor, 1989) |
| Petrakos, *Oropos* | B. Ch. Petrakos, Ὁ Ὠρωπὸς καὶ τὸ ἱερὸν τοῦ Ἀμφιαράου (Βιβλ. Ἀθ. Ἀρχ. Ἑτ., 63 [Athens, 1968]) |
| *PFrankf* | *Griechische Papyri aus dem Besitz des Rechtswissenschaftlichen Seminars der Universität Frankfurt*, ed. H. Lewald (*SBHeidAk*, phil.-hist. Kl., 14 [Heidelberg, 1920]) |
| PH | W. R. Paton and E. L. Hicks, *The Inscriptions of Cos* (Oxford, 1891) |
| *Phegos* | Φηγός. Τιμητικὸς τόμος γιὰ τὸν καθηγητὴ Σωτήρη Δάκαρη (Ioannina, 1994) |
| *Philia Epi* | Φίλια Ἔπη εἰς Γεώργιον Ἐ. Μυλωνᾶν διὰ τὰ 60 ἔτη τοῦ ἀνασκαφικοῦ ἔργου, 4 vols. (Βιβλ. Ἀθ. Ἀρχ. Ἑτ., 103 [Athens, 1986–89]) |
| *Philol.* | *Philologus*, 1– (Stolberg, 1846; Göttingen, 1847–96; Leipzig, 1897–1944; Berlin, 1954– ) |

| | |
|---|---|
| *Philolakon* | *Φιλολάκων. Laconian Studies in honour of Hector Catling*, ed. J. Motyka Sanders (London, 1992) |
| *Phlyax Vases* | A. D. Trendall, *Phlyax Vases (Second edition, revised and enlarged)* (*BICS* Suppl., 19 [London, 1967]) |
| *PIR*[2] | *Prosopographia Imperii Romani saec.* I. II. III[2], edd. E. Groag, A. Stein, L. Petersen, I–V(3) (A–O) (Berlin and Leipzig, 1933–87); [*PIR*[1] vol. III (P–Z), edd. E. Klebs, H. Dessau, P. von Rohden (Berlin, 1897)] |
| *PKöln* | *Kölner Papyri*, 1– (*Abhandlungen der Rheinisch-Westfälische Akademie der Wissenschaften, Papyrologica Coloniensia*, 7 [Cologne, 1976– ]) |
| *Platon* | *Πλάτων*, 1– (*Εταιρεία Ἑλλήνων Φιλολόγων* [Athens, 1949– ]) |
| *PLitLond* | *Catalogue of the Literary Papyri in the British Museum*, ed. H. J. M. Milne (London, 1927) |
| *PLRE* | *Prosopography of the Later Roman Empire*. I, A.D. 260–395, edd. A. H. M. Jones, J. R. Martindale and J. Morris (Cambridge, 1971); II, A.D. 395–527, ed. J. R. Martindale (1980); IIIA-B, A.D. 527–641, ed. J. R. Martindale (1992) |
| *PM* | E. Pfuhl and H. Möbius, *Die östgriechischen Grabreliefs*, 2 vols. (Deutsch. Arch. Inst. [Mainz, 1977–9]) |
| *PMG* | *Poetae Melici Graeci*, ed. D. L. Page (Oxford, 1962) |
| *PMGF* | *Poetarum Melicorum Graecorum Fragmenta*. I, *Alcman, Stesichorus, Ibycus, post D. L. Page*, ed. M. Davies (Oxford, 1991) |
| *PMich* | *Michigan Papyri*, 1– (I–VIII, *University of Michigan Studies, Humanistic Series*, 24, 28, 40, 42-3, 47-8, 50 [Ann Arbor, 1931–51]; X–XII, XIV, XVI, *American Studies in Papyrology*, 6, 9, 14, 22, 30 [Toronto/Ann Arbor/Atlanta, 1970– ]; IX [Case Western Reserve University, 1971]; XIII, XV [Zutphen, 1977– ]) |
| *Polemon* | *Πολέμων. Ἀρχαιολογικὸν Περιοδικόν*, 1–8 (Athens, 1929–66) |
| *Poralla*[2] | P. Poralla, *A Prosopography of Lacedaemonians from the Earliest Times to the death of Alexander the Great (X-323 B.C.)* (2nd edn. with Introduction, Addenda and Commentary by A. S. Bradford [Chicago, 1985]) |
| Postolakas | A. Postolakas, *Κατάλογος τῶν ἀρχαίων νομισμάτων τῶν νήσων Κερκύρας, Λευκάδος, Ἰθάκης, Κεφαλληνίας, Ζακύνθου καὶ Κυθήρων* (Athens, 1866) |
| Pouilloux, *Forteresse* | J. Pouilloux, *La forteresse de Rhamnonte (Étude de topographie et d'histoire)* (*BEFAR*, 179 [Paris, 1954]) |
| *POxy* | *The Oxyrhynchus Papyri*, 1– (Egypt Exploration Society [London, 1898– ]) |
| *PP* | *Prosopographia Ptolemaica*, edd. W. Peremans, E. van 't Dack et al., 9 vols. (*Studia Hellenistica*, 6, 8, 11–13, 17, 20–21, 25 [Louvain, 1950–81]) |
| *PPC* | I. Michaelidou-Nicolaou, *Prosopography of Ptolemaic Cyprus* (*Studies in Mediterranean Archaeology*, 44 [Göteborg, 1976]) |
| *PPetr* | *The Flinders Petrie Papyri*, edd. J. P. Mahaffy and J. G. Smyly, 3 vols. (Royal Irish Academy, *Cunningham Memoirs*, 8, 9, 11 [Dublin, 1891–1905]) |
| *PPetr*[2] | *The Petrie Papyri, Second Edition*. I, *The Wills*, ed. W. Clarysse (*Collectanea Hellenistica*, 2 [Brussels, 1991]) |
| *PRain Cent.* | *Papyrus Erzherzog Rainer. Festschrift zum 100-Jährigen Bestehen der Papyrussammlung der Österreichischen Nationalbibliothek*, 2 vols. (Vienna, 1983) |
| Praschniker–Schober | C. Praschniker and A. Schober, *Archäologische Forschungen in Albanien und Montenegro* (*Akademie der Wissenschaften in Wien, Schriften der Balkankommission, Antiquarische Abt.*, 8 [Vienna, 1919]) |
| *PRein* | *Papyrus grecs et démotiques*, ed. Th. Reinach (Paris, 1905); *Les Papyrus Th. Reinach*, 2nd edn., ed. P. Collart (*Bibliothèque de l'Institut Français d'Archéologie Orientale*, 39 [Cairo, 1940]) |
| Pritchett, *Topography* | W. K. Pritchett, *Studies in Ancient Greek Topography*, 1–6 (*University of California Publications, Classical Studies*, 1, 4, 22, 28, 31, 33 [Berkeley and Los Angeles, 1965–89]); 7– (Amsterdam, 1991– ) |
| *Proc. Sympos. Olympic Games* | *Proceedings of an International Symposium on the Olympic Games, 5-9 September 1988*, edd. W. Coulson and H. Kyrieleis (Athens, 1992) |
| *PSI* | *Papiri greci e latini*, 15 vols. (*Pubblicazioni della Società Italiana per la ricerca dei Papiri greci e latini in Egitto* [Florence, 1912–79]) |
| *PSorb* | *Papyrus de la Sorbonne, nos. 1 à 68*, ed. H. Cadell (*Travaux de l'Institut de Papyrologie de Paris*, 4 [Paris, 1966]) |
| *PTeb* | *The Tebtunis Papyri*, edd. B. P. Grenfell, A. S. Hunt, J. G. Smyly et al., 3 vols. in 4 (London, 1902–38); vol. IV, edd. J. G. Keenan and J. C. Shelton (*Graeco-Roman Memoirs*, 64 [London, 1976]) |
| *PUG* | *Papiri dell'Università di Genova*, 1– (vol. I, *Università di Genova, Fondazione Nobile Agostino Poggi*, 10 [Milan, 1974]; vols. II–III, *Papyrologica Florentina*, 6, 20 [Florence, 1980–91]) |
| *Puglia Paleocrist. Altomed.* | *Puglia Paleocristiana e Altomedievale*, 1– (*Sezione Apuliae Res* di *Vetera Christianorum*, 1– [Gallatina/Bari, 1970– ]) |
| *Puteoli* | *Puteoli. Studi di Storia Antica*, 1– (Pozzuoli, 1977– ) |
| *Quad. di Storia* | *Quaderni di Storia*, 1– (Bari, 1975– ) |
| *QUCC* | *Quaderni Urbinati di Cultura Classica*, 1– (Urbino, 1966– ) |
| *RA* | *Revue archéologique*, 6 series in 2 fasc. 1844–1957, annually 1958– (Paris, 1844– ) |

RAAN  *Rendiconti della Accademia di Archeologia, Lettere e Belle Arti*, 1– (Società Nazionale di Scienze, Lettere ed Arti, Napoli [Naples 1862– ])

Raffeiner, *Sklaven*  H. Raffeiner, *Sklaven und Freigelassen. Eine soziologische Studie auf der Grundlage des griechischen Grabepigramms* (*Commentationes Aenipontanae* 22, *Philologie und Epigraphik*, 2 [Innsbruck, 1977])

Ramagli, *Cuore del Sud*  N. Ramagli, *Nel Cuore del Sud* (Naples, 1952)

Rass. Stor. Salern.  *Rassegna Storica Salernitana*, 1–28 (Società Salernitana di Storia Salernitana [Salerno, 1937–68]); NS 1– (1984– )

Ravel, *Colts of Ambracia*  O. Ravel, *The 'Colts' of Ambracia* (American Numismatic Society, *Numismatic Notes and Monographs*, 37 [New York, 1928])

RE  *Real-Encyclopädie der classischen Altertumswissenschaft*, edd. A. F. Pauly, G. Wissowa, W. Kroll et al., 66 vols. with 15 supplements (Stuttgart, 1894–1980)

RÉnip  J.-Cl. Decourt, *La vallée de l'Énipeus en Thessalie. Études de topographie et de géographie antique* (*BCH* Suppl., 21 [Paris, 1990])

REA  *Revue des études anciennes*, 1– (Bordeaux, 1899– )

REG  *Revue des études grecques*, 1– (Paris, 1888– )

Regling, *Terina*  K. L. Regling, *Terina* (*Programm zum Winckelmannsfeste der archäologischen Gesellschaft zu Berlin*, 66 [Berlin, 1906])

Rend. Linc.  *Atti della (Reale) Accademia Nazionale dei Lincei, Rendiconti*, 1– (Rome, 1885– )

Rend. Pont.  *Atti della Pontificia Accademia Romana di Archeologia, Rendiconti*, 3rd ser., 1– (Rome/Vatican City, 1923– )

Rend. Torn. Acc. Arch. Napoli  *Rendiconto delle Tornate e dei Lavori dell'Accademia di Archeologia, Lettere e Belle Arti*, NS 1–48 (Naples, 1887–1934)

Rev. Épig.  *Revue épigraphique*, edd. E. Espérandieu and A. Reinach, 1–2 (Paris, 1913–14)

Rh. Mus.  *Rheinisches Museum für Philologie*, 1–9 (Bonn, 1827–39); NS 1– (Frankfurt, 1842– )

Richter, *Engraved Gems*  G. M. A. Richter, *The Engraved Gems of the Greeks, Etruscans and Romans*, 2 vols. (London, 1968–71)

RIJG  *Recueil des inscriptions juridiques grecques*, edd. R. Dareste, B. Haussoullier and T. Reinach, 2 vols. (Paris, 1891–8)

Riv. Arch. Crist.  *Rivista di Archeologia Cristiana*, 1– (Pontificia Commissione di Archeologia Sacra, Pontificio Istituto di Archeologia Cristiana [Rome/Vatican City, 1924– ])

Riv. Fil.  *Rivista di Filologia e di Istruzione Classica*, 1– (Turin, 1873– )

Riv. Ist. Naz. Arch. Stor. d'Arte  *Rivista dell'Istituto Nazionale d'Archeologia e Storia dell'Arte*, 1–9 (Rome, 1929–42); NS 1–24 (1952–77); 3rd ser. 1– (1978– )

Riv. It. Num.  *Rivista Italiana di Numismatica e Scienze affini*, 1– (Società Numismatica Italiana [Milan, 1888– ])

Riv. Stor. Antica  *Rivista di Storia Antica*, 1–13 (Messina/Padua, 1895–1910)

Riv. Stor. Antichità  *Rivista Storica dell'Antichità*, 1– (Bologna, 1971– )

Riv. Stor. Calab.  *Rivista Storica Calabrese*, NS 1– (Reggio di Calabria, 1980– )

Riv. Stud. Pomp.  *Rivista di Studi Pompeiani*, 1– (Associazione Internazionale Amici di Pompeii [Rome, 1987– ])

Röm. Mitt.  *Mitteilungen des (Kaiserlich) Deutschen Archäologischen Instituts, Roemische Abteilung*, 1– (Rome, 1886– )

Römische Gräberstrassen  *Römische Gräberstrassen: Selbstdarstellung - Status - Standard. Kolloquium in München vom 28. bis 30. Oktober 1985*, edd. H. von Hesberg and P. Zanker (*Abh. Bayer. Akad.*, phil.-hist. Kl., NS 96 [Munich, 1987])

Robert, *Coll. Froehner*  L. Robert, *Collection Froehner*. I, *Inscriptions grecques* (Paris, 1936)

Robert, *Ét. Num. Gr.*  L. Robert, *Études de numismatique grecque* (Paris, 1951)

Robert, *EEP*  L. Robert, *Études épigraphiques et philologiques* (*Bibliothèque de l'École des Hautes Études*, 278 [Paris, 1938])

Robert, *Gladiateurs*  L. Robert, *Les gladiateurs dans l'Orient grec* (2nd. edn. Amsterdam, 1971)

Robert, *Hell.*  L. Robert, *Hellenica. Recueil d'épigraphie, de numismatique, et d'antiquités grecques*, 13 vols. (vol. 1, Limoges, 1940; vols. 2-13, Paris, 1946–65)

Robert, *Noms indigènes*  L. Robert, *Noms indigènes dans l'Asie Mineure gréco-romaine*, I (*Bibliothèque archéologique et historique de l'Institut Français d'Archéologie d'Istanbul*, 13 [Paris, 1963])

Robert, *OMS*  L. Robert, *Opera minora selecta. Épigraphie et antiquités grecques*, 7 vols. (Amsterdam, 1969–90)

Roesch, *Ét. Béot.*  P. Roesch, *Études béotiennes* (Institut Fernand Courby, Lyon [Paris, 1982])

Roesch, *Thespies*  P. Roesch, *Thespies et la confédération béotienne* (Institut Fernand Courby, Lyon [Paris, 1965])

Roma Medio Repubblicana  *Roma Medio Repubblicana. Aspetti culturali di Roma e del Lazio nei secoli IV e III a. c.* (Rome, 1973)

Romans in N. Campania  P. Arthur, *Romans in Northern Campania* (*Archaeological Monographs of the British School at Rome*, 1 [London, 1991])

RPC  A. M. Burnett, M. Amandry and P. Rippolès, *Roman Provincial Coinage*. I, *From the Death of Caesar to the Death of Vitellius (44 BC-AD 69)* (London and Paris, 1992)

RPh  *Revue de philologie, de littérature et d'histoire anciennes*, 1– (Paris, 1877– )

RQ  *Römische Quartalschrift für Christliche Alterthumskunde und für Kirchengeschichte*, 1– (Rome, 1887– )

Rumpf, *Chalkid. Vas.*  A. Rumpf, *Chalkidische Vasen* (Deutsch. Arch. Inst. [Berlin and Leipzig, 1927])

*Rupes loquentes*   *Rupes loquentes. Atti del Convegno internazionale di studio sulle iscrizioni rupestri di età romana in Italia, Roma-Bomarzo, 13-15. X. 1989*, ed. L. Gasperini (*Studi pubblicati dall'Istituto Italiano per la Storia Antica*, 53 [Rome, 1992])

Russu   I. I. Russu, *Illirii. Istoria - Limba şi Onomastica - Romanizarea* (Bucharest, 1969)

*RVAp*   A. D. Trendall and A. Cambitoglou, *The Red-Figured Vases of Apulia*, 2 vols. (*Oxford Monographs on Classical Archaeology* [Oxford, 1978–82])

*RVP*   A. D. Trendall, *The Red-Figured Vases of Paestum* (British School at Rome, 1987)

Sambon   A. Sambon, *Les Monnaies antiques de l'Italie*. I, *Étrurie–Ombrie–Picenum–Samnium–Campanie (Cumes et Naples)* (Paris, 1903)

*Samml. Ludwig*   H. A. Cahn, L. Mildenberg et al., *Antikenmuseum Basel und Sammlung Ludwig. Griechische Münzen aus Grossgriechenland und Sizilien* (Basel, 1988)

Sandberg, *Euploia*   N. Sandberg, Εὔπλοια. *Études épigraphiques* (*Acta Universitatis Gotoburgensis*, 1954 (8) [Göteborg, 1954])

Santoro, *NSM*   C. Santoro, *Nuovi Studi Messapici*, 2 vols. (*Saggi e Testi*, 24-25 [Galatina, 1982-3])

Sarikakis   Th. Ch. Sarikakis, ʿΠροσωπογραφία τῆς Ἀκτίας Νικοπόλεωςʾin *AE* 1970, pp. 66-85

*SB*   *Sammelbuch griechischer Urkunden aus Ägypten*, edd. F. Preisigke, F. Bilabel et al., 1– (Strasbourg/Berlin/Leipzig etc., 1915– )

*SBBerlAk*   *Sitzungsberichte der (Preussischen) Deutschen Akademie der Wissenschaften zu Berlin*, phil.-hist. Kl. (Berlin, 1882–1938)

Schlosser   J. von Schlosser, *Beschreibung der altgriechischen Münzen*. I, *Thessalien, Illyrien, Dalmatien und die Inseln des adriatischen Meeres, Epeiros* (Vienna, 1893)

Schöne, *Mus. Bocchi*   R. Schöne, *Le Antichità del Museo Bocchi di Adria* (Rome, 1878)

Schwartz, *ACO*   E. Schwartz, *Acta Conciliorum Oecumenicorum* (Berlin, 1914–40)

*Schweizer Münzblätter*   *Schweizer Münzblätter. Gazette numismatique suisse*, 1– (Schweizerisches Numismatisches Gesellschaft [Basel, 1949– ])

*Scritti Degrassi*   A. Degrassi, *Scritti Vari di Antichità*, 4 vols. (Rome/Venice/Trieste, 1962-71)

*Scritti Montevecchi*   *Scritti in onore di Orsolina Montevecchi*, edd. E. Bresciani, G. Geraci, S. Pernigotti and G. Susini (Bologna, 1981)

*Scritti Sciarra Bardaro*   *Scritti di Antichità in memoria di Benita Sciarra Bardaro*, edd. C. Marangio and A. Nitti (Fasano, 1994)

*Scritti Zambelli*   *Scritti storico-epigrafici in memoria di Marcello Zambelli*, ed. L. Gasperini (*Università di Macerata, Pubblicazioni della Facoltà di Lettere e Filosofia*, 5 [Rome, 1978])

*Sculpture from Arcadia and Laconia*   *Sculpture from Arcadia and Laconia. Proceedings of an International Conference held at the American School of Classical Studies at Athens, April 10-14, 1992*, edd. O. Palagia and W. Coulson (*Oxbow Monographs*, 30 [Oxford, 1993])

*Second Suppl. RVAp*   A. D. Trendall and A. Cambitoglou, *Second Supplement to the Red-Figured Vases of Apulia*, 3 vols. (*BICS* Suppl., 60 [London, 1991-2])

Seeck, *Libanius*   O. Seeck, *Die Briefe des Libanius* (*Texte und Untersuchungen*, NS 15 [Leipzig, 1906]; repr. Hildesheim, 1966)

*SEG*   *Supplementum Epigraphicum Graecum*, edd. J. J. E. Hondius, A. G. Woodhead, 1–25 (Leiden, 1923–71); edd. H. W. Pleket and R. S. Stroud, 26–7 (Alphen, 1979–80), 28– (Amsterdam, 1982– )

Seltman, *Temple Coins of Olympia*   C. T. Seltman, *The Temple Coins of Olympia*, 2 vols. (repr. from *Nomisma* 8, 9 and 11 [Cambridge, 1921])

*Semitica*   *Semitica. Cahiers publiées par l'Institut d'études sémitiques de l'Université de Paris*, 1– (Paris, 1948– )

Serricchio, *Iscrizioni di Siponto*   C. Serricchio, *Iscrizioni romani-paleocristiani e medievali di Siponto* (Manfredonia, 1978)

Sestieri, *ILat. Albania*   P. C. Sestieri, 'Iscrizioni Latine d'Albania', *Studi e Testi*, ser. 2, *Archeologica*, 1 (Reale Istituto di Studi Albanesi [Tirana, 1943]) pp. 1–118

*SGDI*   *Sammlung der griechischen Dialekt-Inschriften*, edd. H. Collitz, F. Bechtel et al., 4 vols. (Göttingen, 1884–1915)

Sherk   R. K. Sherk, *Roman Documents from the Greek East. Senatus Consulta and Epistulae to the Age of Augustus* (Baltimore, 1969)

*Sic. Arch.*   *Sicilia Archeologica. Rassegna periodica di studi, notizie e documentazione*, 1– (Trapani, 1968– )

*Sic. Gymn.*   *Siculorum Gymnasium*, 1– (Rassegna Semestrale della Facoltà di Lettera e Filosofia dell'Università di Catania [Catania, 1948– ])

Siebert, *Ateliers*   G. Siebert, *Recherches sur les ateliers de bols à reliefs du Péloponnèse à l'époque hellénistique* (*BEFAR*, 233 [Paris, 1978])

*Silver Coinage of Velia*   R. T. Williams, *The Silver Coinage of Velia* (Royal Numismatic Society, *Special Publication*, 25 [London, 1992])

*Silver for the Gods*   A. Oliver jnr., *800 Years of Greek and Roman Silver*, The Toledo Museum of Art, Toledo, Ohio (*Oct. 8 - Nov. 20, 1977*) (Toledo, Ohio, 1977)

Sinn, *Stadtröm. Marmorurnen*   F. Sinn, *Stadtrömische Marmorurnen* (*Beiträge zur Erschliessung hellenistischen und kaiserzeitlichen Skulptur und Architekten*, 8 [Mainz, 1987])

*SIRIS*   L. Vidman, *Sylloge inscriptionum religionis Isiacae et Sarapiacae* (*Religiongeschichtliche Versuche und Vorarbeiten*, 28 [Berlin, 1969])

| | |
|---|---|
| Siviero, *Ori e Ambre* | R. Siviero, *Gli Ori e le Ambre del Museo Nazionale di Napoli* (*Le Opere d'Arte Recuperate*, 2 [Florence, 1954]) |
| Skalet | C. H. Skalet, *Ancient Sicyon, with a prosopographia Sicyonia* (*The Johns Hopkins University Studies in Archaeology*, 3 [Baltimore, 1928]) Chapter 12, 'Prosopographia Sicyonia', pp. 181-214 |
| *SLG* | *Supplementum Lyricis Graecis. Poetarum lyricorum graecorum fragmenta quae recens innotuerunt*, ed. D. L. Page (Oxford, 1974) |
| Smutny, *Gk. Lat. Inscr. at Berkeley* | R. J. Smutny, *Greek and Latin Inscriptions at Berkeley* (*University of California Publications, Classical Studies*, 2 [Berkeley and Los Angeles, 1966]) |
| *SNG ANS Etruria–Calabria* | *Sylloge Nummorum Graecorum. The Collection of the American Numismatic Society*. I, *Etruria–Calabria* (New York, 1969) |
| *SNG Berry* | *Sylloge Nummorum Graecorum. The Burton Y. Berry Collection* (New York, 1961-2) |
| *SNG Cop. Aetolia–Euboea* | *Sylloge Nummorum Graecorum. The Royal Collection of Coins and Medals, Danish National Museum. Aetolia–Euboea* (Copenhagen, 1944) |
| *SNG Cop. Apulia–Lucania* | *Sylloge Nummorum Graecorum. The Royal Collection of Coins and Medals, Danish National Museum. Italy*. II, *Apulia–Lucania: Metapontum* (Copenhagen, 1942) |
| *SNG Cop. Argolis–Aegean Islands* | *Sylloge Nummorum Graecorum. The Royal Collection of Coins and Medals, Danish National Museum. Argolis–Aegean Islands* (Copenhagen, 1944) |
| *SNG Cop. Epirus–Acarnania* | *Sylloge Nummorum Graecorum. The Royal Collection of Coins and Medals, Danish National Museum. Epirus–Acarnania* (Copenhagen, 1943) |
| *SNG Cop. Phliasia–Laconia* | *Sylloge Nummorum Graecorum. The Royal Collection of Coins and Medals, Danish National Museum. Phliasia–Laconia* (Copenhagen, 1944) |
| *SNG Cop. Thessaly–Illyricum* | *Sylloge Nummorum Graecorum. The Royal Collection of Coins and Medals, Danish National Museum. Thessaly–Illyricum* (Copenhagen, 1943) |
| *SNG Delepierre* | *Sylloge Nummorum Graecorum. France, Bibliothèque Nationale. Cabinet des Médailles, Collection Jean et Marie Delepierre* (Paris, 1983) |
| *SNG Evelpidis* | *Sylloge Nummorum Graecorum. Grèce. Collection Réna H. Evelpidis, Athènes*. II, *Macédoine–Thessalie–Illyrie–Épire–Corcyre* (Louvain, 1975) |
| *SNG Fitz. Macedonia–Acarnania* | *Sylloge Nummorum Graecorum. Fitzwilliam Museum: Leake and General Collections*. III, *Macedonia–Acarnania* (Oxford, 1951) |
| *SNG Lloyd* | *Sylloge Nummorum Graecorum. The Lloyd Collection* (London, 1933-37) |
| *SNG Lockett* | *Sylloge Nummorum Graecorum*. III, *The Lockett Collection* (London, 1938-49) |
| *SNG Oxford* | *Sylloge Nummorum Graecorum. Ashmolean Museum, Oxford* (London, 1962) |
| *SNR* | *Revue Suisse de numismatique*, 1–23 (Geneva, 1891–1923); subsequently published as *Schweizerische Numismatische Rundschau*, 24– (Bern, 1928– ) |
| Sokolowski | F. Sokolowski, (I) *Lois sacrées de l'Asie Mineure*; (II) *Lois sacrées des cités grecques, Supplément*; (III) *Lois sacrées des cités grecques* (École Française d'Athènes, *Travaux et Mémoires*, 9, 11, 18 [Paris, 1955–69]) |
| Solin, *Lukan. Inschr.* | H. Solin, *Zu lukanischen Inschriften* (*Commentationes Humanarum Litterarum*, 69 [Helsinki, 1981]) |
| *SP* | *Select Papyri*. I, *Private Affairs*, edd. A. S. Hunt and C. C. Edgar (Loeb [London and New York, 1932]); II, *Official Documents*, edd. A. S. Hunt and C. C. Edgar (London and Cambridge, Mass., 1934); III, *Literary Papyri, Poetry*, ed. D. L. Page (1950) |
| *Sp.* | *Spomenik*, 1– (Srpska Kralevska Akademija [Belgrade, 1888–1942]; Srpska Akademija Nauka [1948– ]) |
| *St. Etr.* | *Studi Etruschi*, 1– (Florence, 1927– ) |
| *St. Rom.* | *Studi Romani. Rivista di Archeologia e Storia*, 1–2 (Rome, 1913–14) |
| Stählin | F. Stählin, *Das Hellenistische Thessalien. Landeskundliche und geschichtliche Beschreibung Thessaliens in der hellenischen und römischen Zeit* (Stuttgart, 1924) |
| Stephanis | I. E. Stephanis, Διονυσιακοὶ Τεχνῖται. Συμβολὲς στὴν Προσωπογραφία τοῦ Θεάτρου καὶ τῆς Μουσικῆς τῶν Ἀρχαίων Ἑλλήνων (Herakleion, 1988) |
| Stibbe, *Lakonische Vasenmaler* | C. M. Stibbe, *Lakonische Vasenmaler des sechsten Jahrhunderts v. Chr.*, 2 vols. (*Studies in Ancient Civilization*, NS 1 [Amsterdam and London, 1972]) |
| *Storia di Napoli* | *Storia di Napoli*, 11 vols. (Naples, 1967-78) |
| Strazzulla | V. Strazzulla, *Museum Epigraphicum seu Inscriptionum Christianarum quae in Syracusanis Catacumbis repertae sunt Corpusculum* (Società Siciliana per la Storia Patria, *Documenti per servire alla storia di Sicilia*, 3rd ser. - epigrafia, 3 [Palermo, 1897]) |
| *Stud. Alb.* | *Studia Albanica*, 1– (Université d'État de Tirana, Institut d'histoire et de linguistique [Tirana, 1964– ]) |
| *Stud. D. M. Robinson* | *Studies presented to David Moore Robinson on his seventieth birthday*, edd. G. E. Mylonas and D. Raymond, 2 vols. (St. Louis, 1951-3) |
| *Studi Adriani* | *Alessandria e il mondo ellenistico-romano: studi in onore di Achille Adriani*, edd. N. Bonacasa and A. Di Vita, 3 vols. (*Studi e Materiali*, 4–6 [Rome, 1983–4]) |
| *Studi di Antichità* | *Studi di Antichità*, 1– (Quaderni dell'Istituto di Archeologia e Storia antica, Università di Lecce [Lecce, 1980– ]) |
| *Studi Merid.* | *Studi Meridionali. Rivista trimestrale di studi sull'Italia Centro-meridionale*, 1– (Rome, 1968– ) |
| *Studi Ribezzo* | *Studi storico-linguistici in onore di Francesco Ribezzo*, edd. C. Santoro and C. Marangio (*Testi e Monumenti*, 11 [Mesagne, 1978]) |

| | |
|---|---|
| *Studi Storici* | *Studi Storici per l'Antichità Classica*, 1–5 (Pisa, 1908–12) |
| *Summa Gall. Auction I* | *The Summa Galleries Inc. Auction I, Friday, September 18, 1981* (Beverly Hills, California) |
| *Suppl. Cir.* | G. Oliverio, G. Pugliese Carratelli, and D. Morelli, 'Supplemento epigrafico cirenaico', *ASAA* NS 23–4 (1961–2) pp. 219–375 |
| *Suppl. Hell.* | *Supplementum Hellenisticum*, edd. H. J. Lloyd-Jones and P. J. Parsons (Berlin and New York, 1983) |
| *Suppl. It.* | *Supplementa Italica, Nuova Serie*, 1– (Unione Accademica Nazionale [Rome, 1981– ]) |
| *Suppl. Rod.* | G. Pugliese Carratelli, 'Supplemento epigrafico rodio', *ASAA* NS 14–16 (1952–4) pp. 247–316; 'Nuovo supplemento epigrafico rodio', ib. NS 17–18 (1957) pp. 157-181 |
| Susini, *Fonti Salento* | G. Susini, *Fonti per la storia greca e romana del Salento* (Accademia delle Scienze dell'Istituto di Bologna, Classe di Scienze Morali [Bologna, 1962]) |
| *SVF* | *Stoicorum veterum fragmenta*, ed. J. von Arnim, 4 vols. (Leipzig, 1903–24) |
| *Syll*[3] | *Sylloge Inscriptionum Graecarum*, ed. W. Dittenberger, 4 vols. (3rd edn., ed. F. Hiller v. Gaertringen [Leipzig, 1915–24]) |
| *Synedrio Archaia Thessalia* | Διεθνὲς Συνέδριο γιὰ τὴν Ἀρχαία Θεσσαλία στὴ μνήμη τοῦ Δημήτρη Ρ. Θεοχάρη (Δημοσιεύματα τοῦ Ἀρχαιολογικοῦ Δελτίου, 48 [Athens, 1992]) |
| *Syringes* | J. Baillet, *Inscriptions grecques et latines des Tombeaux des Rois ou Syringes*, 3 vols. (*Mémoires de l'Institut Français d'Archéologie Orientale de Caire*, 42 [Cairo, 1920–26]) |
| *TAPA* | *Transactions of the American Philological Association*, 1– (various places of pubn., 1869– ) |
| *Taras* | *Taras. Rivista di archeologia*, 1– (Galatina, 1981– ) |
| *TCal* | M. Segre, 'Tituli Calymnii', *ASAA* NS 6–7 (1944–5, publ. 1952) |
| *TCam* | M. Segre and I. Pugliese Carratelli, 'Tituli Camirenses', *ASAA* NS 11–13 (1947–51) pp. 141–318; 'Tituli Camirenses, Supplementum', ibid. NS 14–16 (1952–4) pp. 211–46 |
| *Ténos* | R. Étienne, *Ténos. II, Ténos et les Cyclades du milieu du IV^e siècle av. J.-C. au milieu du III^e siècle ap. J.-C.* (*BEFAR*, 263 bis [Paris, 1990]) |
| *Teanum Apulum* | A. Russi, *Teanum Apulum. Le Iscrizioni e la Storia del Municipio* (*Studi pubblicati dall'Istituto Italiano per la Storia Antica*, 25 [Rome, 1976]) |
| *Territorio Flegreo* | G. Camodeca, 'Le iscrizioni di Quarto' in *Materiali per lo studio storico-archeologico del territorio flegreo. Quarto Flegreo* (Naples, 1980) pp. 87-99 |
| *Thess. Hemerol.* | Θεσσαλικὸ Ἡμερολόγιο. Ἱστορικόν, Λαογραφικόν, Λογοτεχνικὸν περιοδικόν, 1– (Larisa, 1980– ) |
| *Thess. Mnem.* | A. S. Arvanitopoullos, Θεσσαλικὰ Μνημεία. Περιγραφὴ τῶν ἐν τῶι Ἀθανασακείωι Μουσείωι Βόλου γραπτῶν στηλῶν τῶν Παγασῶν (Athens, 1909) |
| Thomopoulos, *Hist. Patr.* | S. N. Thomopoulos, Ἱστορία τῆς πόλεως τῶν Πατρῶν ἀπὸ ἀρχαιοτάτων χρόνων μέχρι τοῦ 1821 (Athens, 1887; 2nd edn. Patras, 1950) |
| Thompson, *Agrinion* | M. Thompson, *The Agrinion Hoard* (American Numismatic Society, *Numismatic Notes and Monographs*, 159 [New York, 1968]) |
| *TMByz* | *Travaux et Mémoires*, 1– (Centre de recherche d'histoire et de civilisation byzantines [Paris, 1965– ]) |
| Tölle-Kastenbein, *Peplosfiguren* | R. Tölle-Kastenbein, *Frühklassische Peplosfiguren - Originale* (Mainz, 1980) |
| Tod, *GHI* | M. N. Tod, *Greek Historical Inscriptions*, 2 vols. (Oxford, 1933–48; 1² 1946) |
| Trendall, *Early S. It. Vase-painting* | A. D. Trendall, *Early South Italian Vase-painting (revised 1973)* (*Forschungen zur antiken Keramik. I. Reihe - Bilder Griechischer Vasen*, 12 [Mainz, 1974]) |
| *TrGF* | *Tragicorum Graecorum Fragmenta*, edd. B. Snell, R. Kannicht and S. Radt, 4 vols. (Göttingen, 1971–8) |
| Troisi, *Epigrafi mobili* | F. Ferrandini Troisi, *Epigrafi "mobili" del Museo Archeologico di Bari* (Dipartimento di Scienze dell'Antichità dell'Università di Bari, sezione storica, *Documenti e Studi*, 12 [Bari, 1992]) |
| *Tyche* | *Tyche. Beiträge zur alten Geschichte, Papyrologie und Epigraphik*, 1– (Vienna, 1986– ) |
| Ugolini, *Alb. Ant.* | L. M. Ugolini, *Albania Antica*, 3 vols. (Rome, 1927–42) |
| Uguzzoni–Ghinatti | A. Uguzzoni and F. Ghinatti, *Le Tavole Greche di Eraclea* (*Università degli studi di Padova, Pubblicazioni dell'Istituto di Storia Antica*, 7 [Rome, 1968]) |
| Unp. | Unpublished material. [Cited sparingly, with an indication of the source given in the following brackets] |
| Urban, *Wachstum* | R. Urban, *Wachstum und Krise des achäischen Bundes. Quellenstudien zur Entwicklung des Bundes von 280 bis 222 v. Chr.* (*Historia* Einzelschriften, 35 [Wiesbaden, 1979]) |
| Usener, *Kl. Schr.* | H. Usener, *Kleiner Schriften*, 4 vols. (Stuttgart, 1912-13; repr. Osnabrück, 1965) |
| *VAHD* | *Vjesnik za Arheologiju i Historiju Dalmatinsku*, 1– (Split, 1878– ); originally published as *Bullettino di Archeologia e Storia Dalmata* |
| *VAMZ* | *Vjesnik Arheološkog Muzeja u Zagrebu*, 3rd series, 1– (Zagreb, 1958– ) |
| van Keuren, *Coinage of Heraclea* | F. van Keuren, *The Coinage of Heraclea Lucaniae* (*Archaeologica*, 110 [Rome, 1994]) |
| Vandermersch | C. Vandermersch, *Vins et Amphores de Grande Grèce et de Sicile, IV^e-III^e s. avant J.-C.* (Centre Jean Bérard, *Études*, 1 [Naples, 1994]) |
| Vatin, *Delph. à l'ép. imp.* | C. Vatin, *Delphes à l'époque imperiale* (Unpublished Diss., Sorbonne, 1965) |
| Vélissaropoulos, *Nauclères* | J. Vélissaropoulos, *Les Nauclères grecs. Recherches sur les institutions maritimes en Grèce et dans l'Orient hellénisé* (*Hautes Études du Monde Gréco-Romain*, 9 [Geneva and Paris, 1980]) |

*Vetera Christianorum*  *Vetera Christianorum*, 1– (Università di Bari, Istituto di Letteratura Cristiana Antica [Bari, 1964– ])

Vial  C. Vial, *Délos Indépendante (314–167 av. J.-C.). Étude d'une communauté civique et ses institutions* (*BCH* Suppl., 10 [Paris, 1984])

Vlasto  O. E. Ravel, *Descriptive Catalogue of the Collection of Tarentine Coins formed by M. P. Vlasto* (London, 1947)

Vollenweider,  M.-L. Vollenweider, *Die Steinschneidekunst und ihre Künstler in spätrepublikanischer und*
*Steinschneidekunst*  *Augusteischer Zeit* (Baden-Baden, 1966)

Šašel, *IL*  A. and J. Šašel, *Inscriptiones Latinae quae in Iugoslavia inter annos MCMXL et MCMLX, inter annos MCMLX et MCMLXX, et inter annos MCMII et MCMXL repertae et editae sunt*, 3 vols. (*Situla, Dissertationes Musei Nationalis Labacensis*, 5, 19, 25 [Ljubljana, 1963–86])

Walbank  F. W. Walbank, *A Historical Commentary on Polybius*, 3 vols. (Oxford, 1957–79)

Wehrli, *Schule Arist.*  F. Wehrli, *Die Schule des Aristoteles, Texte und Kommentar*, 10 fasc. and supplement (Basel and Stuttgart, 1944–59; 2nd edns. of 2 and 4, 1967–8)

Weinreich, *Menekrates Zeus u.*  O. Weinreich, *Menekrates Zeus und Salmoneus. Religionsgeschichtliche Studien zur Psychopathologie*
*Salmoneus*  *des Gottmenschentums in Antike und Neuzeit* (*Tübinger Beiträge zur Altertumswissenschaft*, 18 [Stuttgart, 1933]); repr. in O. Weinreich, *Religionsgeschichtliche Studien* (Darmstadt, 1968) pp. 299–434

Welles, *RC*  C. B. Welles, *Royal Correspondence in the Hellenistic Period, A Study in Greek Epigraphy* (New Haven, 1934)

Welzl  *Catalogue de la grande collection de monnaies et médailles de M. Léopold Welzl de Wellenheim*, 2 vols. (Vienna, 1909)

Wessel  *Inscriptiones Graecae Christianae Veteres Occidentis*, ed. C. Wessel (*Inscriptiones Christianae Italiae, Subsidia*, 1 [Bari, 1989])

Westermark–Jenkins  U. Westermark and K. Jenkins, *The Coinage of Kamarina* (Royal Numismatic Society, *Special Publication*, 9 [London, 1980])

Whitehead, *Aineias*  D. Whitehead, *Aineias the Tactician. How to Survive under Siege* (*Clarendon Ancient History Series* [Oxford, 1990])

*Wien. Stud.*  *Wiener Studien. Zeitschrift für klassische Philologie*, 1– (Vienna, 1879– )

Wilhelm, *Beitr.*  A. Wilhelm, *Beiträge zur griechischen Inschriftenkunde* (*Sonderschriften des Österreichischen Archäologischen Institutes in Wien*, 7 [Vienna, 1909])

Wilhelm, *Neue Beitr.*  A. Wilhelm, *Neue Beiträge zur griechischen Inschriftenkunde*, 6 parts (*SBWienAk*, phil.-hist. Kl., 166 (1) (3), 175 (1), 179 (6), 183 (3), 214 (4) [Vienna, 1911–32])

Wilson, *Sicily*  R. J. A. Wilson, *Sicily under the Roman Empire: the Archaeology of a Roman Province, 36BC-AD535* (Warminster, 1990)

*Wiss. Mitth. Bosn.*  *Wissenschaftliche Mittheilungen aus Bosnien und der Hercegovina*, 1–12 (Bosnisch-Hercegovinischen Landesmuseum in Sarajevo [Vienna, 1893–1912]); NS 1–6 (Sarajevo, 1971–9)

Work, *Earlier Staters of*  E. Work, *The Earlier Staters of Heraclea Lucaniae* (American Numismatic Society, *Numismatic*
*Heraclea*  *Notes and Monographs*, 91 [New York, 1940])

Wuilleumier, *Tarente*  P. Wuilleumier, *Tarente des origines à la conquête romaine* (*BEFAR*, 148 [Paris, 1939])

*ZA*  *Živa Antika*, 1– (Skopje, 1951– )

Zeller  E. Zeller, *Die Philosophie der Griechen in ihrer geschichtlichen Entwicklung*, 3 vols. in 6 (5th edn. Leipzig, 1919–23; repr. Hildesheim, 1963)

*ZfN*  *Zeitschrift für Numismatik*, 1–42 (Berlin, 1874–1935)

*ZPE*  *Zeitschrift für Papyrologie und Epigraphik*, 1– (Bonn, 1967– )

## Other Abbreviations

| | | | | | |
|---|---|---|---|---|---|
| acc. | accusative | fem. | feminine | *νεώτ.* | *νεώτερος* |
| ad. | adoptive | fict. | fictitious | n. gent. | nomen gentilicium |
| amph. | amphora | fr(r). | fragment(s) | n. pr. | nomen proprium |
| ap. | apud | freed. | freedman/woman | no(s). | number(s) |
| apogr. | apographon | gen. | genitive | nom. | nominative |
| attr. | attribution | her. | heroic | NS | New Series |
| biling. | bilingual | het. | hetaira | pap. | papyrus |
| bp. | bishop | ident. | identification | patr. adj. | patronymic adjective |
| codd. | codices | Ital. | Italicus | pl(l). | plate(s) |
| d. | daughter | koin. | koinon | *πρεσβύτ.* | *πρεσβύτερος* |
| dat. | dative | lap. | lapis | pryt. | prytanis |
| dem. | demotic | Lat. | Latin | s. | son |
| dub. | dubious | locn. | location | Suppl. | Supplement |
| ed(d). | editor(es) | m. | mother | t.e. | *τῆς ἐπιγονῆς* |
| ed(d). pr(r). | editor(es) prior(es) | maj. | majuscule | tab. | tabula |
| emp. | emperor | masc. | masculine | unp. | unpublished |
| ethn. | ethnic | money. | moneyer | voc. | vocative |
| f. | father | ms(s). | manuscript(s) | | |
| fals. | falsum | n. | note | | |

# A

Ἄβα
ILLYRIA:
—EPIDAMNOS-DYRRHACHION: (1) hell.-imp. IDyrrh 66 (d. Ἀφροδίσιος); (2) ~ ib. 67 (d. Σθενίων)

Ἀβαία
ILLYRIA:
—EPIDAMNOS-DYRRHACHION: (1) hell.-imp. ib. 65 (ABA ABAIA—lap.); (2) ~ ib. 68 (d. Λυσανίας); (3) ~ ib. 69 (d. Μάννικος)

Ἄβαιος
ILLYRIA:
—BALAIITAI*: (1) ii BC SEG XXXVIII 521, 26; cf. CRAI 1991, pp. 197 ff.; L'Illyrie mérid. 2 p. 204 f. (f. Βοῦλος)

Ἀβαντίδας
KORINTHIA:
—SIKYON: (1) f. iii BC RE (-) (Skalet 1) (s. Πασέας: tyrant)

Ἀβασκάντη
S. ITALY (LUCANIA):
—COSILINUM: (1) f. iii AD Suppl. It. 3 p. 46 no. 1 (Lat. Helvia Abascante)

Ἀβασκάντιλλα
S. ITALY (CAMPANIA):
—DIKAIARCHIA-PUTEOLI: (1) ?ii AD Puteoli 3 (1979) p. 154 no. 1 (CIL X 1884) (Lat. Cornelia Abasc[an]tilla)

Ἀβάσκαντος
ARGOLIS:
—EPIDAUROS: (1) i-ii AD IG IV (1)² 507 (f. Ἀσκληπᾶς); (2) 184 AD ib. 393, 5 (f. Παραμόνη)
DALMATIA:
—TRAGURION: (3) imp. CIL III 2691 (Lat. Abascant(us))
ELIS: (4) 245-249 AD IvOl 121, 9 (Αὐρ. Ἀ.: s. Ζωῖλος)
KORINTHIA:
—KORINTH: (5) ii/iii AD BM Lamps 3 pp. 404 no. Q3252; 405 no. Q3255; SEG XXVII 35. 1 (lamps)
LAKONIA:
—SPARTA: (6) 116 or 117 AD IG V (1) 380, 7 (Bradford (2)) (Ἀ. Παρθένιος); (7) f. iii AD IG V (1) 303, 7 (Artemis Orthia pp. 327-8 no. 57); BSA 79 (1984) p. 283 (Bradford (1)) (Κλ. [Ἀβ]άσκαντος)
S. ITALY (APULIA):
—CANUSIUM*: (8) imp. Epig. Rom. di Canosa 94 (CIL IX 363) (Lat. Abascantus: slave?)
—LARINUM: (9) imp. Contr. Ist. Fil. Class. 1 (1963) p. 254 no. 16 (Lat. [Aba]scantus)
S. ITALY (CALABRIA):
—TARAS-TARENTUM: (10) imp. NScav 1894, p. 67 no. 41 (Eph. Ep. VIII 63) (Lat. C. Iulius Abascantus)
S. ITALY (CAMPANIA):
—ATELLA*: (11) imp. CIL X 3734 (Lat. M. Verrius Abascantus: f. M. Verrius Celsus, M. Verrius Flaccus: freed.)
—DIKAIARCHIA-PUTEOLI: (12) imp. ib. 1869 (Lat. Abas[cantus]); (13) ~ ib. 2022 (Lat. P. Aemilius Abascantus); (14) ~ ib. 2914 (Lat. Abascantus)
—DIKAIARCHIA-PUTEOLI?: (15) imp. ib. 1833; cf. Puteoli 11 (1987) p. 42 (Lat. Abascantus)
—DIKAIARCHIA-PUTEOLI*: (16) imp. CIL X 2289 (Lat. Abascantus: freed.); (17) ~ ib. 2871 (Lat. C. Pomponius Abascantus: freed.)
—HERCULANEUM: (18) m. i AD PdelP 3 (1948) p. 171 no. 16; 8 (1953) p. 463 no. 57, 3; 58; 10 (1955) p. 453 no. 79 (Lat. C. Novius Aba[sc]a[n]tus); (19) ~ ib. 3 (1948) p. 182 no. 30 (Lat. M. Nonius Abascantus); (20) ~ CIL IV 10720 b (Lat. [Ab]ascantus); (21) 63 AD PdelP 9 (1954) p. 55 no. 61 (Lat. Q. Granius Abascan[tus]); (22) ~ ib. (Lat. P. Cornelius Abascantus)
—HERCULANEUM*: (23) i BC-i AD CIL X 1403 g I, 9 (Lat. Q. Maecius Abascantus: freed.); (24) c. 50-75 AD ib. 1403 a III, 1 (Lat. D. Lucilius Abascantus: freed.)
—MISENUM: (25) ?ii AD ib. 3334 (Lat. P. Aelius Abascantus: f. P. Aelius Rufinus)
—POMPEII: (26) i BC-i AD ib. IV 2363 (Lat. Abascantus); (27) ~ ib. 4319 (Lat. Abascantus); (28) ~ ib. 4916 (Castrèn 245. 1) (Lat. C. Mateius Abas(cantus)); (29) ~ Neue Forsch. in Pompeji p. 266 no. 70 (Lat. Abascantus); (30) c. 51-62 AD CIL IV 3340. 92, 7 (Castrèn 375. 4) (Lat. L. Sextilius Aba[sc]antus); (31) 56 AD CIL IV 3340. 19, 21; 22, 21 (Castrèn 22. 2) (Lat. A. Alfius Abascantus); (32) ~ CIL IV 3340. 25, 17 (Castrèn 205. 3) (Lat. Ti. Iulius Abascantus); (33) 57 AD CIL IV 3340. 30, 6, 20 (Lat. Abasc[antus])
—SALERNUM: (34) imp. IItal 1 (1) 138 (CIL X 588) (Lat. P. Aurelius Abasscant(us))
—SURRENTUM: (35) imp. NScav 1928, p. 210 no. 14 (Lat. Claudius Abascantus); (36) ~ ib. p. 210 no. 15 (Lat. Claudius Abascanthus); (37) ~ St. Rom. 2 (1914) p. 346 no. 2 = NScav 1928, p. 211 no. 21 (Lat. Abascantus)
SICILY:
—SYRACUSE: (38) iii-v AD ib. 1920, p. 327; (39) ~ Strazzulla 263 (Wessel 1158)
—SYRACUSE?: (40) iii-v AD Strazzulla 189 (ASSicilia 1938-9, p. 24; Wessel 972); cf. Riv. Arch. Crist. 18 (1941) p. 192 no. 60 (T. Μαρούλλιος Ἀ.)

Ἀβεύριος
MESSENIA:
—MESSENE: (1) ?i BC SEG XXIII 203, 4; PAE 1960, p. 213

Ἀβιάνιος
SICILY:
—KATANE: (1) imp. GVI 1936 (MEFRA 106 (1994) p. 94 no. 6)

Ἀβίαντος
AIGINA: (1) hell.? IG VII 162 (Ἀ(μ)ίαντος?: f. Τιμέας)

Ἀβλάβιος
SICILY:
—SYRACUSE: (1) iii-v AD NScav 1947, p. 211 no. 1

Ἀβλίων
AIGINA: (1) ?c. 475-450 BC IG IV (1) 6 (Lazzarini 265); LSAG² p. 113 no. 17 (date); cf. Alt-Ägina II (2) pp. 46-7 (ηαβλίον: s. Ἀλτιλλος)

Ἀβοζίκα
ILLYRIA:
—EPIDAMNOS-DYRRHACHION: (1) hell.-imp. IDyrrh 70

Ἀβόλητος
LAKONIA:
—SPARTA: (1) s. i BC IG V (1) 135, 7; 260, 1; 261, 3; 465, 4; 578, 10 (Bradford (-)) (f. Δάμιππος)
MESSENIA:
—THOURIA: (2) s. iii BC IG V (1) 1386, 16 (s. Ἀρ—)

Ἀβολίδας
MESSENIA:
—MESSENE: (1) f. iii BC PAE 1991, p. 99 no. 7, 18

Ἀβουλήνη
S. ITALY (CAMPANIA):
—SUESSULA: (1) imp. CIL X 3766 (Lat. Abulene)

Ἀβουνδαντία
SICILY:
—SYRACUSE: (1) iii-v AD IG XIV 172 (Strazzulla 72; Agnello 11; Wessel 872); cf. Ferrua, NG 174 (Ἀβου(ν)δαντία)

Ἄβρα
ARGOLIS:
—ARGOS: (1) i BC/i AD IG IV (1) 647 (Μαινία Ἀ.)

Ἄβρακος
EPIROS:
—NIKOPOLIS: (1) imp. Wiss. Mitth. Bosn. 4 (1896) p. 386 no. 1 (Sarikakis 1)

Ἀβρίας
LAKONIA:
—KYTHERA: (1) hell.-imp. IG V (1) 942, 3 and Add. p. 306 (f. Ἐπικράτης)
—SPARTA: (2) ii/i BC ib. XII (3) Suppl. 1299, 25; 1625 (Bradford (3)) (f. Ἀντίβιος); (3) c. 76 BC IG VII 417, 32 (IOrop 525; Bradford (1)) (s. Ἀντίβιος); (4) c. 25-1 BC IG V (1) 212, 43 (Bradford (2)) (f. Γοργώπας)

Ἄβρον
ARGOLIS:
—HERMIONE: (1) i AD IG II² 8497 (d. Ταυρίων)

Ἄβρος
ELIS:
—KEPIDES: (1) iii AD CIG 9294 b, 4 (f. Αὐρ. Ζωσίμη)

Ἀβροσύνα
ACHAIA:
—AIGION: (1) ii BC IG IV (1)² 628 (d. Θέοξις)

Ἀβροτέλεια
S. ITALY (CALABRIA):
—TARAS-TARENTUM: (1) iv BC Iamb., VP 267 (FVS I p. 448) (d. Ἀβροτέλης)

Ἀβροτέλης
S. ITALY (CALABRIA):
—TARAS-TARENTUM: (1) iv BC Iamb., VP 267 (FVS I p. 446); FVS I p. 448 (f. Ἀβροτέλεια)

Ἀβρότονον
KORINTHIA:
—KORINTH: (1) iv/iii BC Men., Pk. 476, 482 (het./fict.)

Ἄβρων
AKARNANIA:
—THYRREION: (1) iii BC IG IX (1)² (2) 257; Fraser–Rönne, BWGT pl. 24
ARGOLIS:
—ARGOS: (2) viii BC Plu., Mor. 772 E; RE Supplbd. 4 (1a) (f. Μέλισσος (Korinth): fict.?); (3) ?v-iv BC ib. (2) (fict.?)
EPIROS:
—ARGOS (AMPHILOCH.): (4) c. 305-295 BC BMC Corinth p. 123 nos. 14-15; SNG Cop. Epirus–Acarnania 314-15 (coins); SNR 56 (1977) pp. 97-8; p. 111 (date) (Ἄβρ(ων))
ILLYRIA:
—APOLLONIA: (5) c. 321-315 BC IApoll 310 (ηάβ-: f. Ἀμφαλκίδας); (6) c. 250-50 BC Maier 9 (Ceka 128); cf. IApoll Ref. Bibl. n. 1 (coin) (pryt.)

## Ἀγαθάγγελος

LAKONIA:
—SPARTA:
—Pitana: (1) s. ii AD IG v (1) 472, 2; 663, 1 (Bradford (-)) (Γ. Ἀβίδιος Ἀ., Ἀγαθάνγελος—663)
S. ITALY (APULIA):
—CANUSIUM: (2) 223 AD Epig. Rom. di Canosa 35 III, 35 (CIL IX 338) (Lat. P. Carinatius Agathangelus)
S. ITALY (CALABRIA):
—BRENTESION-BRUNDISIUM: (3) ii/iii AD Studi Ribezzo p. 64 no. 8 (Lat. Agathangelus)
—TARAS-TARENTUM*: (4) f. ii AD Misc. Gr. Rom. 3 p. 197 no. T9 (Lat. M. Ulpius Agathagelus: imp. freed.?)
S. ITALY (CAMPANIA):
—DIKAIARCHIA-PUTEOLI*: (5) imp. NScav 1927, p. 333 no. 9 (Lat. [Ag]athangelus: freed.)
—HERCULANEUM*: (6) i BC-i AD CIL x 1403 g III, 66 (Lat. C. Calvisius Agatangelus: freed.)
—KYME*: (7) imp. Eph. Ep. VIII 446 (Lat. Agathangelus: freed.)

## Ἀγαθάμερος

AIGINA: (1) ?i BC IG IV (1) 126 (f. Κλεισταινέτη)
ARKADIA:
—MEGALOPOLIS: (2) ii/i BC ib. v (2) 442, 20 (s. Καλλίβιος)
LAKONIA:
—SPARTA: (3) i BC/i AD? ib. v (1) 177, 3 (Bradford (-)) (f. Ἀριστοκράτης)
MESSENIA:
—THOURIA: (4) ii/i BC IG v (1) 1384, 6 (f. Φιλόξενος)

## Ἀγαθανδρίδας

KORINTHIA:
—KORINTH: (1) a. 191 BC SEG XXVI 392, 9 (f. Τιμοσθένης)

## Ἀγαθάνωρ

LAKONIA:
—SPARTA: (1) hell.-imp. IG v (1) 195, 3 (Bradford (-))
SICILY:
—SYRACUSE: (2) 332 BC SEG XLI 107, 11

## Ἀγαθάριν

LAKONIA:
—TEUTHRONE: (1) ii-i BC IG v (1) 1219 = Mél. Daux pp. 303-7 (Ἀγαθάριν)

## Ἀγαθαρχίδας

KORINTHIA:
—KORINTH: (1) 429 BC Th. ii 83. 4

## Ἀγαθαρχίς

S. ITALY (CAMPANIA):
—POMPEII*: (1) m. i BC CIL I² 3134 (Impegno per Pompeii 31 OS; Castrèn 395. 4) (Lat. Stronnia Agatarchis: freed.)

## Ἀγάθαρχος

ACHAIA:
—AIGEIRA: (1) c. 266 BC IG XII (9) 1187, 34; Robert, Ét. Num. Gr. p. 179 ff. (date) (s. Δαμόκριτος)
ARKADIA:
—MANTINEIA-ANTIGONEIA: (2) c. 300-221 BC IG v (2) 323. 100 (tessera) (s. Στέφανος)
—TEGEA: (3) iii BC ib. 30, 2 ([Ἀ]γ[ά]θαρχος: f. —οτος); (4) f. ii BC ib. 44, 27 (Ἀγάθαρχο[ς])
KERKYRA: (5) 536 BC RE (3); Moretti, Olymp. 118
KORINTHIA:
—KORINTH: (6) ?vi BC SEG XXIX 344
S. ITALY (BRUTTIUM):
—PETELIA: (7) ?c. 475 BC IGSI 19, 6 (Landi, DISMG 171); LSAG² p. 261 no. 28 (date)

## Ἀγαθᾶς

S. ITALY (CALABRIA):
—TARAS-TARENTUM: (8) c. 272-235 BC Vlasto 852-4 (coins) (Evans, Horsemen p. 178 VIII B.1; p. 182 no. 7)
SICILY:
—AKRAI: (9) ?iii BC SGDI 3243 (Akrai p. 155 no. 5) (?s. Ἀρτέμων)
—GELA-PHINTIAS: (10) f. ii BC IG XIV 256, 40 (Dubois, IGDS 161); cf. SEG XL 804 (f. Πολύξενος)
—HALOUNTION: (11) i BC-i AD? IG XIV 369 (s. Ἡράκλειος)
—KENTORIPA: (12) i BC-i AD IGLMP 29 (f. Εὐβουλίδας)
—LIPARA: (13) imp. NScav 1947, p. 218 no. 6 (Ἀγάθαρ.—apogr.)
—MEGARA HYBLAIA: (14) f. v BC SEG XXVI 1093 (s. Πολι—)
—MORGANTINA: (15) ?iv/iii BC ib. XXXIX 1009, 6 (f. Ἱάρων)
—SYRACUSE: (16) 413 BC RE (5); (17) 214 BC Plb. vii 4. 1, 7
—SYRACUSE?:
—(Νητ.): (18) hell. Manganaro, PdelP forthcoming no. 4 II, 8 (f. Φιντίας)
—TAUROMENION: (19) c. 239-216 BC IG XIV 421 an. 2; 421 an. 25 (SGDI 5219) (s. Εὔανδρος); (20) c. 195 BC IG XIV 421 an. 46 (SGDI 5219) (s. Κλεόδωρος); (21) c. 172-162 BC IG XIV 421 an. 69; 421 an. 79 (SGDI 5219) (s. Διονύσιος); (22) c. 168-155 BC IGSI 4 III (IV), 4 an. 86; SGDI 2610, 3 (s. Μένων); (23) 155-151 BC IG XIV 421 an. 86; 421 an. 88 (SGDI 5219); IGSI 4 III (IV), 1 an. 86, 35 an. 90 (II s. Ἀγάθαρχος I); (24) c. 155-151 BC IG XIV 421 an. 88 (SGDI 5219); IGSI 4 III (IV), 1 an. 86, 35 an. 90 (I f. Ἀγάθαρχος II); (25) c. 148 BC ib. l. 55 an. 93 (f. Γοργίας)
—(Χαλκ.): (26) ?ii/i BC IG XIV 421 D an. 12 (SGDI 5219) (s. Διονύσιος)
—THERMAI HIMERAIAI: (27) i AD IG XIV 331; cf. Kokalos 20 (1974) p. 234 no. 7 (Ὤλος Πάπιος Ἀ.)

## Ἀγαθάς

S. ITALY (CALABRIA):
—RUDIAE: (1) imp. NScav 1897, p. 405 no. 12 (Bernardini, Rudiae p. 87; Susini, Fonti Salento p. 122 no. 66) (Lat. Agathas)
S. ITALY (CAMPANIA):
—DIKAIARCHIA-PUTEOLI: (2) 196 AD CIL x 1786 (Lat. M. Octavius Agatha)
—POMPEII: (3) i BC-i AD ib. IV 2005 (Lat. Agathas)

## Ἀγαθέας

AKARNANIA:
—THYRREION: (1) ii/i BC IG IX (1)² (2) 341
S. ITALY (CALABRIA):
—TARAS-TARENTUM: (2) iii/ii BC ASP 22 (1969) pp. 89-90 no. 2 (loomweight)

## Ἀγάθεια

S. ITALY (CALABRIA):
—BRENTESION-BRUNDISIUM: (1) ii/i BC Studi Ribezzo p. 77 no. 16 + Arctos 15 (1981) pp. 106-7 (Lat. Vettia Agathea)
S. ITALY (CAMPANIA):
—ATELLA*: (2) imp. CIL x 3739 (Lat. Arria Agathea: freed.)
—POMPEII*: (3) i BC Impegno per Pompeii 7 OS (Castrèn 169. 4) (Lat. Flavia Agathea: freed.)

## Ἀγάθη

AITOLIA:
—CHALKIS: (1) iii-iv AD SEG XXXVIII 430 (tile)
ARGOLIS:
—ARGOS: (2) byz. BCH 28 (1904) p. 420 no. 4; cf. TMByz 9 (1985) p. 370 no. 112
S. ITALY (APULIA):
—VIBINUM*: (3) i BC/i AD Taras 12 (1992) pp. 154-5 no. 1 (Lat. Vibia Agatha: freed.)

## Ἀγαθήμερος

S. ITALY (CALABRIA):
—BRENTESION-BRUNDISIUM*: (4) ii AD Epigraphica 27 (1965) p. 164 (Lat. Agathe: m. Δαμᾶς: freed.?)
S. ITALY (CAMPANIA):
—CAPREAE: (5) imp. ZPE 71 (1988) p. 196 no. 5 (Lat. Agathe)
—DIKAIARCHIA-PUTEOLI: (6) imp. CIL x 1996 (Lat. Silicia Agathe); (7) ?i-ii AD ib. 2580 (Lat. Iulia Agathe: m. Μοσχίων, Ἑρμογένης)
—NEAPOLIS: (8) imp. NScav 1892, p. 55; cf. Leiwo p. 112 no. 85 (Lat. Corn. Agathe: d. Ἀγάθων, Velia Rufina)
—POMPEII: (9) i BC-i AD CIL IV 10061; cf. Gnomon 45 (1973) p. 269 (Lat. Acate); (10) ~ NScav 1916, p. 303 no. 111 (Castrèn 158. 9) (Lat. Epidia Agathe)
SICILY: (11) iii-v AD Riv. Arch. Crist. 18 (1941) p. 236 no. 131
—AKRAI: (12) iii-v AD Epigraphica 5-6 (1943-4) p. 99; (13) ~ ib. pp. 98-9
—KATANE: (14) iii-v AD IG XIV 457; (15) ~ ib. 523 (Wessel 1379); (16) ~ IG XIV 524 (Agnello 46; Wessel 479); cf. SEG XXXI 831; (17) ~ IG XIV 552 (Agnello 56; Wessel 861); cf. Riv. Arch. Crist. 18 (1941) p. 239 no. 134; (18) ~ Libertini, Museo Biscari p. 318 no. 9; (19) iv-v AD SEG XXXI 830 (Agnello 106; Wessel 1042)
—LICODIA EUBEA (MOD.): (20) ?vi AD IG XIV 254 (IGLMP 18; Wessel 614); cf. Riv. Arch. Crist. 18 (1941) p. 208 no. 82 (Λανθάνουσα (ἡ) καὶ Ἀ.)
—MOTYKA: (21) iii-v AD Agnello 70
—SYRACUSE: (22) iii-v AD IG XIV 62 (Strazzulla 3; Wessel 1322); (23) ~ ASSiracusano 1956, p. 48; (24) ~ Rend. Pont. 22 (1946-7) p. 237 no. 44; (25) ~ NScav 1907, p. 765 no. 28; (26) ~ Strazzulla 299 (Wessel 192); (27) ~ Strazzulla 341; cf. Ferrua, NG 124 (Ἀ)γάθη); (28) ~ Mem. Pont. 1 (1923) p. 115 no. 4; Riv. Arch. Crist. 32 (1956) p. 19 fig. 7 (Lat. Agathe)
—TAUROMENION: (29) iii-v AD Wessel 1055 (Ferrua, NG 474) (Ἰαγάθη)
—USTICA: (30) iii-v AD IG XIV 592; cf. Riv. Arch. Crist. 18 (1941) p. 237 no. 133

## Ἀγαθημερίς

S. ITALY (APULIA):
—CANUSIUM: (1) i-ii AD Epig. Rom. di Canosa 64 (Lat. Agathemeris)
S. ITALY (CAMPANIA):
—DIKAIARCHIA-PUTEOLI: (2) imp. CIL x 2850 (Lat. Babbia Agathemeris); (3) ~ ib. 3087 (Lat. Verria Agathemeris)
—SALERNUM: (4) s. i AD IItal 1 (1) 124 (Lat. Flavia Agathemeris)

## Ἀγαθήμερος

ARKADIA:
—TEGEA: (1) 165 AD IG v (2) 50, 83
ELIS: (2) 57-61 AD IvOl 79, 7 (Ἀγαθή[μερος])
—OLYMPIA*: (3) 36-24 BC ib. 62, 19 (?s. Ἀρχιάδας: Δου.)
ILLYRIA:
—EPIDAMNOS-DYRRHACHION: (4) ?ii-i BC IDyrrh 14 (f. Ἀριστόδαμος); (5) hell.-imp. ib. 72 (s. Νικόπολις)
LAKONIA:
—OITYLOS: (6) imp. IG v (1) 1307
S. ITALY (APULIA):
—CANNAE*: (7) m. i AD Epig. Rom. di Canosa 195 a (Lat. Q. Eppius Agatemer: freed.)
S. ITALY (CAMPANIA):
—DIKAIARCHIA-PUTEOLI: (8) ?i-ii AD CIL x 2259 (Lat. Ti. Claudius Agathemerus); (9) 51 AD Bove, Documenti finanziarie p. 102 T.P. 20 pag. 2, 9; pp. 102-3 pag. 2, 5 (Lat. L. Marius Agathemer)
—DIKAIARCHIA-PUTEOLI*: (10) imp. CIL x 1737 (Lat. Agathemerus: freed.?)

**Ἀγαθητύχη**

—POMPEII: (**11**) i BC-i AD ib. IV 8565, 5 (Lat. Agathemer); (**12**) ~ ib. x 927 (Lat. Agathemer)
—SALERNUM: (**13**) ?ii AD IItal 1 (1) 29 (CIL x 547) (Lat. P. Aelius Agathemerus)
SICILY:
—KATANE: (**14**) iii-v AD IG XIV 485 (Κορνήλιος Ἀ.) ?= (**15**); (**15**) ~ ib. 492 (Κορνήλιος Ἀ.) ?= (14)

**Ἀγαθητύχη**
S. ITALY (CAMPANIA):
—DIKAIARCHIA-PUTEOLI: (**1**) imp. CIL x 3088 (Lat. Verria Agatetyche)

**Ἀγαθία**
S. ITALY (CAMPANIA):
—POMPEII*: (**1**) i BC-i AD Römische Gräberstrassen p. 205 a (Lat. Caecilia Agathia: freed.)
SICILY:
—THERMAI HIMERAIAI: (**2**) imp. CIL x 7432 (ILat. Term. Imer. 135) (Lat. Publicia Agathia)

**Ἀγαθιάδας**
LAKONIA:
—SPARTA: (**1**) s. viii BC D.S. viii fr. 21 (Poralla² 1)

**Ἀγαθιανός**
S. ITALY (CAMPANIA):
—POMPEII: (**1**) i BC-i AD CIL IV 8345 (Lat. Agathianus)

**Ἀγαθίας**
AITOLIA:
—KALYDON: (**1**) 192 BC IG IX (1)² (1) 31, 26 (s. Νικάνωρ)
ARKADIA: (**2**) 316 BC ib. v (2) 549, 31 (f. Αἰσαγένης)
—PALLANTION: (**3**) a. 316 BC SEG XI 1084, 37 (Perlman A.3) (f. Δαΐμαχος)
—TEGEA: (**4**) iii BC IG v (2) 40, 35 (s. Ἀ—); (**5**) f. ii BC ib. 44, 18 (Ἀγαθί[ας]?: f. Καλλίμαχος)
——(Krariotai): (**6**) iii BC ib. 40, 44; (**7**) f. iii BC ib. 36, 64 (f. Δαμαίνετος)
LAKONIA:
—SPARTA: (**8**) c. 130-140 AD ib. v (1) 66, 15; 67, 4 (Bradford (4)) (Φούρνιος Ἀ.); (**9**) c. 140-160 AD IG v (1) 115, 4 (Bradford (3)) (Τ. Ὀκτ. Ἀ.); (**10**) ~ IG v (1) 156 a, 3 (Bradford (1)) (s. Σωσίνικος)
—Limnai: (**11**) a. 212 AD IG v (1) 682, 9 (Bradford (2)) (Αὐρ. Ἀ.)
MESSENIA: (**12**) ii AD AD 2 (1916) p. 117 no. 82 (f. Τιμοκράτις)
—PHARAI: (**13**) 30 AD IG v (1) 1359, 4 (f. Στεφανίς)
—THOURIA: (**14**) f. ii BC SEG XI 972, 63 (s. Εὐδαμίδας); (**15**) 182 BC IvOl 46, 9 (IPArk 31 IIB) (Ἀ[γ]αθίας: f. Σωκράτης)
SICILY:
—TAUROMENION: (**16**) c. 203 BC IG XIV 421 an. 38 (SGDI 5219) (s. Ἀπολλώνιος)

**Ἀγαθίδας**
EPIROS:
—AMBRAKIA: (**1**) ii-i BC CIG 1800, 9 (s. Καλλικράτης)

**Ἀγαθιν**
SICILY:
—KENTORIPA: (**1**) ii AD MEFRA 106 (1994) p. 85 (Πουβλειλία Ἀ.)

**Ἀγαθῖνος**
ARGOLIS:
—EPIDAUROS: (**1**) c. 370 BC IG IV (1)² 102, 103
ELIS: (**2**) ?iii BC Paus. vi 13. 11; cf. Moretti, Olymp. p. 184 (s. Θρασύβουλος: Iamidai)

KORINTHIA:
—KORINTH: (**3**) 393 BC X., HG iv 8. 10; (**4**) 217 BC Plb. v 95. 3
—SIKYON: (**5**) ?254 BC Nachtergael, Les Galates 9, 9 (Stephanis 18) (s. Κριτόδαμος)
LAKONIA:
—SPARTA: (**6**) s. i AD RE (8); Supplbd. 1 (Bradford (-)) (Κλ. Ἀ.: doctor)
LEUKAS: (**7**) iv/iii BC Unp. (IG arch.); (**8**) hell.? IG IX (1) 552
S. ITALY (CAMPANIA):
—POMPEII: (**9**) 54 AD CIL IV 3340. 5, 4; 91, 4; 151, 10 (Castrèn 161. 3) (Lat. M. Fabius Agathinus)
S. ITALY (LUCANIA):
—HYELE-VELIA: (**10**) imp. PdelP 21 (1966) p. 336 no. 4 (-θεῖ-: f. Σωφρόνα)
—METAPONTION: (**11**) hell.? IG XIV 2406. 7
SICILY:
—THERMAI HIMERAIAI: (**12**) f. i BC Cic., In Verr. II ii 89; 92; 94; 116 (Lat. Agathinus: f. Καλλιδάμα); (**13**) imp. Kokalos 20 (1974) p. 235 no. 8 (f. Ἀττίκων)

**Ἀγάθιος**
SICILY:
—SYRACUSE: (**1**) iii-v AD Riv. Arch. Crist. 36 (1960) p. 26 no. 14 ([Ἀ]γάθι[ος]?); (**2**) ~ Strazzulla 333 (Wessel 944)

**Ἀγάθιππος**
ARGOLIS:
—EPIDAUROS: (**1**) ii AD AE 1975, pp. 26-7 no. 19 (Ἀγάθ[ιππ]ος)

**Ἀγαθις**
KORINTHIA:
—SIKYON: (**1**) ii/i BC SEG XI 251, 1 (f. Ἀριστόμαχος)

**Ἀγαθίων**
AITOLIA: (**1**) iv BC BCH 52 (1928) p. 205 n. 1, 3 (f. —ίων); (**2**) ?b. 280 BC Klio 15 (1918) p. 48 no. 67, 2 (f. —ων)
EPIROS:
—AMBRAKIA: (**3**) ii BC SEG XLII 542 (s. Νικίας)
ILLYRIA:
—APOLLONIA: (**4**) imp. IApoll 326 (s. Τρίτος)
——(Po.): (**5**) iii/ii BC ib. 7; cf. L'Illyrie mérid. 2 p. 207 (f. Σώστρατος)
—EPIDAMNOS-DYRRHACHION: (**6**) c. 250-50 BC Ceka, Probleme p. 151 no. 1; cf. Münsterberg p. 37 (coin) (pryt.) ?= (7); (**7**) ~ Maier 91-2; Münsterberg Nachtr. p. 14 (coin) (Ceka 316; 353; 421) (pryt.) ?= (6); (**8**) hell.-imp. IDyrrh 74 (s. Ἐπίκαδος); (**9**) ~ ib. 242 (f. Θεοδωρίδας); (**10**) ~ ib. 376 (f. Στρατονίκα); (**11**) imp. ib. 73 (s. Δαναός)

**Ἀγαθόα**
KORINTHIA:
—KORINTH: (**1**) v BC SEG XI 242

**Ἀγαθοκλέα**
ARGOLIS:
—TROIZEN: (**1**) imp. IG IV (1) 814
EPIROS:
—NIKOPOLIS: (**2**) imp. Hellenika 22 (1969) p. 71 no. 8 (Sarikakis 2)
ILLYRIA:
—EPIDAMNOS-DYRRHACHION: (**3**) hell.-imp. IDyrrh 75 (d. Ἀγαθοκλῆς); (**4**) ~ ib. 76 (d. Νεσίων)
MESSENIA:
—MESSENE: (**5**) ?iv BC SEG XLI 359 ([Ἀγα]θοκλέ[α])

**Ἀγαθόκλεια**
AKARNANIA:
—ALYZIA: (**1**) iii BC Plb. xv 31. 9 (d. Ἀριστομένης)

ARGOLIS:
—HERMIONE: (**2**) ?ii-i BC IG IV (1) 731 I, 9 (m. Ἀπολλωνία)
—PHLEIOUS: (**3**) iv BC ib. 452 (m. Μελιθήριος)
ARKADIA:
—TEGEA: (**4**) ii-iii AD ib. v (2) 187 (-κλια: m. Ἀλεξάνδρα)
KORINTHIA:
—KORINTH: (**5**) byz. Corinth VIII (3) 532, 6; cf. TMByz 9 (1985) p. 363 no. 41 (-κλια); (**6**) ~ Corinth VIII (3) 659 (-κλια)
LAKONIA:
—GYTHEION: (**7**) ii BC IG v (1) 1152 (d. Σωσικράτης)
S. ITALY (CALABRIA):
—BRENTESION-BRUNDISIUM: (**8**) imp. NScav 1892, p. 353 ff (Lat. Seia Agathoclea)
S. ITALY (CAMPANIA):
—MISENUM*: (**9**) imp. CIL x 3563 (Lat. F(u)lvia Agathoclea: m. Claudia)

**Ἀγαθοκλείδας**
LEUKAS: (**1**) hell. Ep. Chron. 31 (1994) p. 49 no. 4 (AD 45 (1990) Chron. p. 254 no. 3)

**Ἀγαθοκλῆς**
ACHAIA:
—PELLENE: (**1**) m. iii BC IG v (2) 368, 101
AIGINA: (**2**) ?f. i BC Alt-Ägina I (2) p. 43 no. 4, 1 (s. Ἐρατοκλῆς)
AIGINA?: (**3**) ?i BC EAD xxx p. 356 no. 19 (I f. Ἀγαθοκλῆς II); (**4**) ~ ib. (II s. Ἀγαθοκλῆς I)
AITOLIA:
—KALLION/KALLIPOLIS: (**5**) byz. BCH 98 (1974) p. 635 (f. Ἀλέξανδρος)
—KONOPE-ARSINOE?: (**6**) s. iii BC IG IX (1)² (1) 24, 2 (or Korinthia Korinth?)
ARGOLIS:
—ARGOS: (**7**) iii BC Mnem. NS 47 (1919) p. 166 no. 14; (**8**) ii BC IG II² 8361 a, 2 (f. Γλαῦκον); (**9**) m. ii BC Siebert, Ateliers pp. 18; 171 (date) (Ἀγαθοκλέ(ος) (gen.): potter); (**10**) c. 146-32 BC BMC Pelop. p. 144 no. 110 (coin)
—EPIDAUROS: (**11**) i-iii AD IG IV (1)² 727; cf. Peek, IAEpid 313 (f. Νικοστράτη)
—HERMIONE: (**12**) hell.? IG IV (1) 737 (I f. Ἀγαθοκλῆς II); (**13**) ~ ib. (II s. Ἀγαθοκλῆς I); (**14**) ii-i BC ib. 732 IV, 10 (f. Φίλων); (**15**) c. 135-130 BC FD III (4) 169, 2, 9 (f. Σωσθένης)
—MYKENAI: (**16**) hell.? IG IV (1) 504
ARKADIA:
—TEGEA: (**17**) m. iv BC ib. v (2) 6, 68, 85; (**18**) s. iii BC ib. 116, 5 (Ἀγαθ[οκ]λῆς: f. Φίλιππος); (**19**) ii BC ib. 43, 12 (s. Ὀλυμπ—); (**20**) ~ ib. 199; (**21**) ~ SEG XI 1058, 7 (Ἀγα[θ]οκλῆς); (**22**) ii-i BC IG v (2) 163; (**23**) i BC ib. 45, 8; (**24**) ii AD ib. 55, 56 (s. Ὀνήσυλος); (**25**) f. ii AD ib. 124; 125 (Π. Μέμμιος Ἀ.); (**26**) a. 212 AD ib. 132. 2 (Μ. Αὐρ. Ἀγαθοκλ[ῆς]: s. Ὀνήσιμος)
——(Athaneatai): (**27**) m. iii BC ib. 36, 85 (s. Ἐπιτέλης)
ELIS: (**28**) 20-16 BC IvOl 65, 11 (s. Θρασυμήδης); (**29**) 85 AD EA 1905, p. 255 no. 1, 7 (Ἀ. ὁ καὶ Να—)
EPIROS:
—ANTIGONEIA: (**30**) v-vi AD Iliria 1977-8, p. 234 pl. V a + BE 1980, no. 303 (mosaic)
—BOUTHROTOS (PRASAIBOI): (**31**) a. 163 BC IBouthrot 18, 19; 33, 16 (SEG XXXVIII 475; 492) (s. Ἐργοτέλης) ?= (33); (**32**) ~ IBouthrot 31, 94 (SEG XXXVIII 490) IBouthrot 51, 24 (s. Ἀγάθων); (**33**) ~ ib. 78, 11; 79, 10; 80, 9; 81, 9; 82, 9; 83, 9; 84, 9; 85, 9; 86, 11; 87, 10; 88, 8 (BCH 118 (1994) pp. 122 f. nos. 1-11) (s. Ἐργοτέλης) ?= (31); (**34**) ~ IBouthrot 113, 13
——Bouthrotioi: (**35**) a. 163 BC ib. 105, 6 (f. Ἀν..ίδας, Ἀνοχίδας?)
EPIROS?:
—APOMP(H)OS: (**36**) f. ii BC BCH 45 (1921) p. 22 IV, 38 (s. Λυ—)

ILLYRIA:
—EPIDAMNOS-DYRRHACHION: (37) c. 250-50 BC BMC Thessaly p. 76 nos. 158-9; Unp. (Paris, BN) 265 (coin) (pryt.) ?= (38); (38) ~ Münsterberg p. 37 (coin) (Ceka 1) (pryt.) ?= (37); (39) ii-i BC IDyrrh 530 (tile); (40) hell.-imp. ib. 75 (f. Ἀγαθοκλέα); (41) ~ ib. 248 (f. Θεύδοτος)

KEPHALLENIA:
—PALE: (42) 132 AD IG II² 3301, 6 (f. Ἀρνούφιλος)

KERKYRA: (43) iv/iii BC ib. IX (1) 976, 1 (f. Σθένιππος)

KORINTHIA:
—KORINTH: (44) f. iii BC Thess. Mnem. 194 (GVI 1572; Gr. Gr. 208) (s. Ἀγαθώνυμος); (45) m. iii BC Corinth VIII (3) 33 a, 5 (Ἀγαθοκλ[ῆς]); (46) v-vi AD ib. 531, 4; cf. TMByz 9 (1985) p. 365 no. 54 (s. Ἀφοβία)
—SIKYON: (47) c. 200-172 BC IG VII 1724, 2 (-κλεῖς: s. Ἀμύντας)

LAKONIA:
—EPIDAUROS LIMERA: (48) iii AD ib. v (1) 934 (Papaefthimiou p. 158 no. 33)
—GYTHEION: (49) f. ii AD IG v (1) 1171, 11 = II² 3596 (f. Δαμονικίδας)
—HIPPOLA: (50) ?ii-i BC ib. v (1) 1277 d
—SPARTA: (51) ii/i BC ib. 966, 2, 19 (s. Φιλοκλεΐδας); (52) i BC-i AD? SEG XLII 332 ([Ἀγα]θοκλῆς: s. [—σ]τρατος); (53) s. i BC IG v (1) 93, 33 (Bradford (42)) ([Ἀγα]θοκλῆς); (54) c. 30-20 BC IG v (1) 141, 4; SEG XXXV 329 (date) (Bradford (36)) (f. Μουσαῖος); (55) c. 25-1 BC IG v (1) 210, 19 (Bradford (30)) (f. Ἀρχίδαμος); (56) ~ IG v (1) 210, 39 (Bradford (30)) (f. Χαίρων); (57) i BC/i AD IG v (1) 48, 17 (Bradford (39)) (f. Σωτηρίδας); (58) c. 1-10 AD IG v (1) 209, 27; SEG XXXV 331 (date) (Bradford (33)) (f. Δάμιππος); (59) c. 70-100 AD IG v (1) 676, 1 (Bradford (16)) (s. Κλεόφαντος); (60) c. 80-100 AD SEG XI 608, 2 (Bradford (8)) (s. Εὐδαιμονίδας); (61) c. 90-110 AD SEG XI 569, 16; 609, 5; BSA 75 (1980) pp. 214-19 (ident., stemma) (Bradford (13); (32)) (Γ. Ἰούλ. Ἀ.: s. Γ. Ἰούλ. Πολύευκτος, f. Γ. Ἰούλ. Δαμάρης, ?f. Γ. Ἰούλ. Ἱπποθράης); (62) c. 100 AD SEG XI 515, 3 (Bradford (27)) (I f. Ἀγαθοκλῆς II); (63) ~ SEG XI 515, 3 (Bradford (4)) (Τ. Κλ. Ἀ.: II s. Ἀγαθοκλῆς I); (64) ~ SEG XI 534, 2 (Bradford (16)) (s. Στέφανος) ?= (73); (65) c. 100-105 AD SEG XI 515, 7; 534, 7 (Bradford (25); (26)) (I f. Ἀγαθοκλῆς II) ?= (75); (66) ~ SEG XI 515, 7; 534, 7 (Bradford (2); (3)) (II s. Ἀγαθοκλῆς I) ?= (76); (67) ~ SEG XI 537 a, 8; 537 b, 4 (Bradford (18)) (Ἀγαθοκ[λῆς]); (68) c. 100-120 AD IG v (1) 99, 4; 137, 22 (Bradford (28)) (I f. Ἀγαθοκλῆς II); (69) ~ IG v (1) 99, 4; 137, 22 (Bradford (5)) (II s. Ἀγαθοκλῆς II); (70) ~ SEG XI 610, 5 (Bradford (34)) (Ἀγα[θο]κλῆς: f. Εὐδαμίδας); (71) c. 100-125 AD IG v (1) 40, 8 (Bradford (7)) (s. Ἀριστοκλῆς); (72) ii AD IG v (1) 178, 1 (Bradford (22)) (Ἀγαθοκλ[ῆς]); (73) f. ii AD IG v (1) 32 A, 1; 62, 5; SEG XI 547 a, [9]; 547 b, 5; 547 c, [2]; 579, [8] (Bradford (15)) (s. Στέφανος) ?= (64); (74) c. 105-110 AD IG v (1) 20 B, 3; BSA 26 (1923-5) p. 168 C 6/7, 8 (Bradford (14)) (s. Σωσίδαμος); (75) c. 105-115 AD IG v (1) 99, 4; 137, 22 (Bradford (28)) (I f. Ἀγαθοκλῆς II) ?= (65); (76) ~ IG v (1) 99, 4; 137, 22 (Bradford (5)) (II s. Ἀγαθοκλῆς I) ?= (66); (77) ~ IG v (1) 103, 2 (Bradford (41)); (78) c. 110 AD SEG XI 516, 4 (Bradford (24)) (I f. Ἀγαθοκλῆς II); (79) ~ SEG XI 516, 4 (Bradford (1)) (Ἀγαθοκ[λ]ῆς: II s. Ἀγαθοκλῆς I); (80) ~ SEG XI 542, 4 (Bradford (17)) (s. Ξενοκράτης); (81) m. ii AD IG v (1) 71 II, 16; 113, 6; 161, 5 (Bradford (37)) (f. Φιλοκράτης); (82) ~ IG v (1) 71 III, 45; 86, 23; 108, 3; 966, 3 and add. (Bradford (12)) (s. Φιλοκλεΐδας); (83)

~ IG v (1) 87, 3; 113, 5; 160, 7; 446, 4 (Bradford (11)) (s. Φίλιππος); (84) c. 130 AD IG v (1) 60, 3 (Bradford (31)) (Ἀ<α>[γα]θοκλῆς: f. Ἀριστονικίδας ὁ καὶ Διόσκορος); (85) c. 137-140 AD IG v (1) 59, 4; 65, 14; SEG XI 521 b, 3; 549, 4 (Bradford (20)) (Μ. Κλ. Ἀ., Μ. Κλώδιος Ἀ.—SEG XI 521 b); (86) c. 150-160 AD SEG XI 552, 7 (Bradford (21)) (Ἀγαθο[κλῆς]?); (87) c. 150-175 AD IG v (1) 116, 3; SEG XI 530, [5] (Bradford (38)) (f. Φιλοκρατίδας); (88) s. ii AD IG v (1) 46, 7; 534, 3; 591, 6; BSA 75 (1980) p. 219 (stemma); 80 (1985) pp. 194; p. 208 (Bradford (9); (23)) (Γ. Ἰούλ. Ἀ.: s. Ἱπποθράης, f. Ἰουλ. Ἐτυμοκλήδεια); (89) f. iii AD IG v (1) 170, 2; BSA 80 (1985) p. 245 (date) (Bradford (35)) (f. Αὐρ. Καλήμερος); (90) ~ IG v (1) 535, 3 (Bradford (40)) (f. Σέξ. Πομπ. Σπάταλος); (91) c. 230-260 AD IG v (1) 556, 8 (Bradford (29)) (I f. Μ. Αὐρ. Ἀγαθοκλῆς II); (92) ~ IG v (1) 556, 8 (Bradford (6)) (Μ. Αὐρ. Ἀ.: II s. Ἀγαθοκλῆς I)
—TEUTHRONE: (93) imp. IG v (1) 1220 b (Ἀγαθοκ[λῆς])

LEUKAS: (94) hell. ib. IX (1) 537; cf. AM 27 (1902) p. 355 (Ἀ[γα]θοκλῆς]: I f. Ἀγαθοκλῆς II); (95) ~ IG IX (1) 537; cf. AM 27 (1902) p. 355 (II s. Ἀγαθοκλῆς I); (96) ?iii BC Unp. (IG arch.)

MESSENIA:
—KORONE: (97) ii BC IG v (1) 1397, 7
—MESSENE: (98) s. ii BC SEG XLI 341, 10 (f. Πάνθηρος)
—THOURIA: (99) ii-i BC IG v (1) 1385, 18 (s. Χηρικράτης); (100) f. ii BC SEG XI 972, 68 (f. Ἀρήσιππος); (101) ~ ib. l. 118 (s. Φίλων)

PELOPONNESE?: (102) ii AD PAE 1992, p. 72 B, 17 (f. Πομπώνιος)

S. ITALY (BRUTTIUM):
—LOKROI EPIZEPHYRIOI: (103) iv BC Mus. Naz. Reggio p. 34
—(Γαψ.): (104) iv/iii BC De Franciscis 4, 2; 5, 2; 22, 2 (f. Διογένης) ?= (106); (105) ~ ib. 6, 6 (s. Διογένης) ?= (106); (106) ~ ib. 29, 5 ?= (105) (104)
—(Λογ.): (107) iv/iii BC ib. 2, 4 (s. Ἀγαθόλας)
—RHEGION: (108) hell. Kokalos 32 (1986) p. 217 no. 1 (tiles); (109) imp. IG XIV 626 (Klearchos 22 (1980) pp. 111-15) (Lat. Sallustis Agathocles o kae Rodios)

S. ITALY (CAMPANIA):
—DIKAIARCHIA-PUTEOLI: (110) ii-iii AD IG XIV 834 (s. Τρύφων) ?= (111); (111) ~ ib. 835 (f. Ἀνδρόνικος) ?= (110)
—DIKAIARCHIA-PUTEOLI*: (112) i BC CIL I² 1616 (CIL X 1550) (Lat. L. Galonius Agathocl(es): freed.)
—NEAPOLIS: (113) c. 80 BC IG VII 416, 14 (IOrop 523; Stephanis 26) (s. Θεοδόσιος)
—POMPEII: (114) 57 AD CIL IV 3340. 31, 19 (Castrèn 205. 4) (Lat. C. Iulius Agat[hocles])

S. ITALY (LUCANIA):
—HYELE-VELIA: (115) c. 140 BC ID 1965 a, 1; 1965 b, 2; 2004, 3; 2595, 8; Athenaeum 63 (1985) p. 496 (stemma) (s. Ἕρμων, f. Ἕρμων); (116) 119 BC ID 2598, 27 (?s. Ἕρμων)
—POSEIDONIA-PAESTUM: (117) s. i BC Mello-Voza 24 (Lat. [Ag]athoc[les])

S. ITALY?: (118) hell. Memnonion 55 (Ἀγαθω-: f. Κρίτων?)

SICILY: (119) iv-iii BC D.L. viii 90 (f. Εὔδοξος)
—LEONTINOI: (120) 433 BC IG I³ 54, 4 (f. Τιμήνωρ)
—MORGANTINA: (121) ?iv/iii BC SEG XXXIX 1009, 3-5
—SYRACUSE: (122) vii BC RE Supplbd. 1 (14 b); (123) v BC CGF p. 152 T 1 (f. Σώφρων); (124) 361-289 BC RE (15) (I s. Καρκῖνος (Rhegion), f. Ἀγαθοκλῆς II, Ἀρχάγαθος, Ἡρακλείδας, Θεοξένα, Λάνασσα: tyrant); (125) c. 290 BC ib. (16) (II s. Ἀγαθοκλῆς I)

—THERMAI HIMERAIAI: (126) f. iv BC D.S. xix 2. 5 (f. Ἡρακλείδης)
—THERMAI HIMERAIAI*: (127) i-ii AD CIL X 7409 (ILat. Term. Imer. 102) (Lat. C. Haterius Agatocles: freed.)

Ἀγαθόλας
ARGOLIS:
—HERMIONE: (1) iii BC IG IV (1) 729 I, 13 (f. Εὔφρων)
LAKONIA:
—SPARTA: (2) c. 140 AD ib. v (1) 65, 15; SEG XI 549, 5 (Bradford (-)) (f. Ἀριστέας)
S. ITALY (BRUTTIUM):
—LOKROI EPIZEPHYRIOI:
——(Λογ.): (3) iv/iii BC De Franciscis 2, 4 (f. Ἀγαθοκλῆς)

Ἀγαθονίκα
ARGOLIS:
—EPIDAUROS: (1) i BC-i AD? Peek, NIEpid 57 A ([Ἀ]γαθονίκα)

Ἀγαθονίκη
ILLYRIA:
—APOLLONIA: (1) ?iii AD IApoll 273 (-νεί-)
S. ITALY (CAMPANIA):
—NEAPOLIS: (2) iii-iv AD IG XIV 826. 1 (INap 217) (-νή-)

Ἀγαθόνικος
LAKONIA:
—SPARTA:
——Limnai: (1) c. 70-100 AD IG v (1) 676, 13 (Bradford (1)) (f. Νίκαρχος) ?= (2); (2) ~ IG v (1) 676, 16 (Bradford (2)) (f. Ζῆλος) ?= (1)
SICILY:
—SYRACUSE: (3) iii-v AD Riv. Arch. Crist. 30 (1954) p. 22; cf. Ferrua, NG 350 (-νη-)

Ἀγαθόξενος
S. ITALY (CALABRIA):
—TARAS-TARENTUM: (1) ?iv BC IG XIV 671 (Landi, DISMG 192) (Ἀγαθ[ό]ξεν[ος])

Ἀγαθόπους
AIGINA: (1) 173-177 AD Moretti, Olymp. 876; 879 ?= (2); (2) ii/iii AD SEG XXXVII 251 (Μ. Αὐρ. Ἀγ[αθόπους]) ?= (1)
ARKADIA:
—TEGEA: (3) ii-iii AD IG v (2) 178
EPIROS:
—NIKOPOLIS: (4) imp. SEG XXIV 431 (Sarikakis 10) (Ἀντ. Ἀγαθόπο[υς])
KORINTHIA:
—KORINTH: (5) ?ii/iii AD SEG XL 303 (Ὀκτ. Ἀ.); (6) byz. Bees 44; cf. TMByz 9 (1985) p. 359 no. 5 (Ἀγαθόπ[ους])
LAKONIA:
—GYTHEION: (7) f. ii AD IG v (1) 1170, 5 (f. Ἐπίκτητος)
—SPARTA: (8) m. iii AD ib. 565, 3, 9; SEG XI 633, 9; 740, [2]; BSA 79 (1984) p. 284 (date) (Bradford (3); (4)) (I f. Μ. Αὐρ. Φίλητος, Μ. Αὐρ. Ἀγαθόπους II); (9) ~ IG v (1) 565, 8; SEG XI 740, 1; BSA 79 (1984) p. 284 (date) (Bradford (1)) (Μ. Αὐρ. Ἀ.: II s. Ἀγαθόπους I)
—Konosoura: (10) c. 212-230 AD IG v (1) 684, 15 (Bradford (2)) (Αὐρ. Ἀγαθόπο[υς])
S. ITALY (APULIA):
—LARINUM: (11) imp. CIL IX 744; cf. Forma Italiae 36 p. 97 no. 18 (Lat. Agathopus: I f. Ἀγαθόπους II); (12) ~ CIL IX 744; cf. Forma Italiae 36 p. 97 no. 18 (Lat. Agathopus: II s. Ἀγαθόπους I, Severa)
S. ITALY (BRUTTIUM):
—RHEGION*: (13) imp. IG XIV 620, 8 ([Ἀγαθό]πους: slave?)
S. ITALY (CALABRIA):
—BRENTESION-BRUNDISIUM: (14) imp. CIL IX 68 (Lat. Agathopus); (15) ~ ib. 159 (Lat. P. Pacilius Agathopus); (16) ~ NScav 1895, p. 267 b = Epigraphica 25 (1963) p. 65 no. 60; cf. 42 (1980) p. 155 (Lat. L. Tranquillus Agatopus)

S. Italy (Campania):
—DIKAIARCHIA-PUTEOLI: (17) imp. *CIL* x 2697 a (Lat. M. Marcius Agathopus: s. Marcius Faustus); (18) ~ ib. 8366 (Lat. A. Aelius Agathopus); (19) ~ *NScav* 1897, p. 529 (Audollent, *Defix. Tab.* 200 (terracotta)); (20) ?i-ii AD *CIL* x 3036, 12 (Lat. Caninius Agathop(us)); (21) 41 AD ib. 2792 (Lat. C. Octavius Agathop(us) minor); (22) 53 AD Camodeca, *L'Archivio Puteolano* 1 pp. 229-30 (Lat. N. Castricius Agathopus); (23) ii AD *AJA* 77 (1973) p. 164 no. 15 (Lat. Agathopus)
—DIKAIARCHIA-PUTEOLI*: (24) imp. *CIL* x 1723 (Lat. Agathopus: freed.)
—MISENUM*: (25) imp. ib. 3371 (Lat. Agathopus: freed.)
—NUCERIA ALFATERNA: (26) imp. *NScav* 1932, p. 318 (Lat. C. Flavonius Agathopus)
Sicily:
—KATANE: (27) imp. *IG* xiv 458
—SYRACUSE: (28) iii-v AD *ASSiracusano* 1956, p. 48; (29) ~ *Riv. Arch. Crist.* 18 (1941) p. 212 no. 87 (Ἀγα[θό]που[ς]); (30) ~ *NScav* 1912, p. 299
—TAUROMENION: (31) i-ii AD ib. 1920, pp. 340-1 (Lat. M. Marcius Agathopus: I f. Ἀγαθόπους II); (32) ~ ib. (Lat. Q. Marcius Agathopus: II s. Ἀγαθόπους I, Λαΐς)
—THERMAI HIMERAIAI: (33) i AD *Epigraphica* 3 (1941) p. 261 no. 20 (*ILat. Term. Imer.* 162) (Lat. Agathopus); (34) iv AD *Epigraphica* 3 (1941) p. 261 no. 19 (*ILat. Term. Imer.* 81) (Lat. Cornelius Acathobus)

**Ἄγαθος**
Illyria:
—EPIDAMNOS-DYRRHACHION: (1) imp. *IDyrrh* 71
Korinthia:
—KORINTH: (2) iii BC *SEG* xxxi 306, 11 (f. Ἀγαθώνυμος)
Lakonia:
—SPARTA: (3) ii/iii AD *IG* v (1) 526, 2 (Bradford (-)) (M. Αὐρ. Ἀ.)
Messenia: (4) ii AD *AD* 2 (1916) p. 117 no. 82
—MESSENE: (5) ?35-44 AD *IG* v (1) 1432, 1; cf. *SEG* xxix 396
S. Italy (Campania):
—DIKAIARCHIA-PUTEOLI?: (6) imp. *IG* xiv 2405. 1 (lamp)

**Ἀγάθυλλος**
Arkadia: (1) ?ii-i BC *RE* (-); *Suppl. Hell.* pp. 5-6
Sicily:
—SELINOUS:
——(Ἡρακλείδας): (2) m. v BC Dubois, *IGDS* 36, 6 (Arena, *Iscr. Sic.* 1 69) (s. Ξένις)

**Ἀγάθυμος**
Aitolia:
—KALYDON: (1) c. 143 BC *IG* ix (1)² (1) 137, 37 (s. Λέων)
Epiros:
—AMBRAKIA: (2) hell.? *BCH* 79 (1955) p. 267 (s. Δαμαίνετος)

**Ἀγάθυρσος**
S. Italy (Campania):
—DIKAIARCHIA-PUTEOLI: (1) imp. *CIL* x 2198 (Lat. P. Caesonius Agatursus); (2) ~ ib. 2746 (Lat. C. Modestius Agathyrsus)

**Ἀγάθων**
Achaia: (1) 146 BC *IG* iv (1)² 28, 128 (s. Τηρεύς: synoikos); (2) ~ ib. l. 133 (s. Διόφαντος: synoikos)
—DYME: (3) ii-i BC *SGDI* 1617 c (f. Στρατονίκα)
Aitolia: (4) 185 BC *IG* ix (1)² (1) 32, 4
—TRICHONION: (5) ?160 BC *SGDI* 1702, 14

Akarnania:
—ECHINOS?: (6) ii BC *IG* ix (1)² (2) 371
—THYRREION: (7) ii BC ib. 250, 12
Argolis:
—ARGOS: (8) iii BC ib. iv (1) 527, 15; cf. *BCH* 37 (1913) p. 309; (9) c. 295-288 BC *IG* vii 2, 5 (s. Ἀρχίας)
—ARGOS*: (10) f. iii BC ib. iv (1) 529, 15 ([Ἀ]γάθων: slave/freed.?); (11) ii-i BC ib. 530, 15; cf. *BCH* 33 (1909) p. 183 n. 2 (katoikos?)
—HERMIONE: (12) iv BC *IG* iv (1) 742, 16; (13) iii BC ib. 728, 16; (14) ~ ib. l. 20; (15) ~ ib. l. 24; (16) ~ ib. l. 26; (17) ~ ib. l. 28; (18) ii-i BC ib. 732 IV, 20 (s. Νουμήνιος); (19) imp. ib. 730 III, 5 (s. Κλειναγόρας)
—PHLEIOUS: (20) iv BC *SEG* xxvi 416, 4
Arkadia:
—LOUSOI*: (21) ?iii BC *IG* v (2) 406 (Robert, *Coll. Froehner* 28 (bronze))
—TEGEA: (22) hell.? *AP* xvi 280; (23) i BC *IG* v (2) 45, 3 ([Ἀ]γάθων)
——(Apolloniatai): (24) s. iv BC ib. 41, 16 (Ἀ[γ]άθων)
Dalmatia:
—ISSA: (25) hell. Brunšmid p. 27 no. 18, 1, 2-4 (*SEG* xl 514; *VAHD* 84 (1991) p. 253 no. 3) (s. Μενητίδας, f. Θεογένης, Ἡραΐς, Ἄδυλα) ?= (27); (26) ~ Brunšmid p. 27 no. 18, 7 (*SEG* xl 514; *VAHD* 84 (1991) p. 253 no. 3) (II s. Ἀγάθων I); (27) ~ Brunšmid p. 27 no. 18, 6-7 (*SEG* xl 514; *VAHD* 84 (1991) p. 253 no. 3) (I f. Ἀπολλωνίδας, Ἀγάθων II) ?= (25); (28) ~ Brunšmid p. 28 no. 20, 3; (29) iii-ii BC ib. l. 1 (f. Δάμων)
—ISSA?: (30) iii-ii BC ib. p. 34 no. 32 (s. Διονύσιος)
Epiros:
—BOUTHROTOS (PRASAIBOI): (31) a. 163 BC *IBouthrot* 31, 94 (*SEG* xxxviii 490); *IBouthrot* 51, 24 (f. Ἀγαθοκλῆς)
—DODONA*: (32) iv-iii BC *SGDI* 1598; (33) hell. *SEG* xix 426 b
—NIKOPOLIS: (34) i BC-i AD ib. xxiv 428 (biling.) (*ILGR* 161) (Σεξ. Ποπίλλιος Ἀ.)
Illyria:
—EPIDAMNOS-DYRRHACHION: (35) hell.-imp. *IDyrrh* 77; (36) ~ ib. 78 (s. Δαμόξενος); (37) ~ ib. 173 (f. Διοφάνης)
Korinthia:
—KORINTH: (38) m. iii BC *Corinth* viii (3) 33 a, 4 (Ἀγάθω[ν]); (39) f. ii BC ib. viii (1) 66; cf. *SEG* xi 70 (Ἀγάθ[ων]: f. Σώστρατος); (40) imp. *Corinth* viii (3) 285, 3 (Lat. [Scri]bonius Agatho); (41) i BC/i AD *AE* 1977, p. 78 no. 24, 3 (Lat. Heius Agathon: s. Γ. Ἥιος Κορίνθιος, Λικινία Φιλίστα)
—KROMNA: (42) c. 325-280 BC *SEG* xxii 219 (or Paphlagonia Kromna)
Lakonia:
—SPARTA: (43) imp. *IG* v (1) 772 (Bradford (-))
Messenia:
—KORONE: (44) ii BC *IG* v (1) 1397, 1
—MESSENE: (45) s. ii BC *BCH* 95 (1971) p. 544, 4, 18 (f. Ἀριστέας)
S. Italy (Apulia):
—CANUSIUM: (46) ii-iii AD *Epig. Rom. di Canosa* 102 (Lat. Agatho)
S. Italy (Bruttium):
—PETELIA: (47) c. 200-175 BC *IG* xi (4) 1244-6 (s. Νύμφιος)
S. Italy (Calabria):
—BRENTESION-BRUNDISIUM: (48) imp. *CIL* ix 158 (Lat. C. Oppius Agatho)
S. Italy (Campania):
—KYME: (49) hell.? *IG* xiv 860 (Ἀγάθ(ω)ν: f. Ζωΐλος)
—NEAPOLIS: (50) imp.? ib. 2412. 1 (seal); (51) imp. *NScav* 1892, p. 55; cf. Leiwo p. 112 no. 85 (Lat. Cornelius Agatho: f. Ἀγάθη)
—NEAPOLIS?: (52) imp.? *IG* xiv 2404. 1 (tile)

—POMPEII: (53) i BC-i AD *CIL* iv 97 (Lat. Agatho); (54) ~ ib. x 805, 3 (Lat. A[ga]tho); (55) ~ *NScav* 1898, p. 499 (Castrèn 119. 7) (Lat. M. Clodius Agatho); (56) 25 BC *CIL* x 884 (Castrèn 389. 1) (Lat. P. Stallius Agatho)
—SALERNUM: (57) imp. *IItal* i (1) 204 (*CIL* x 603) (Lat. M. Annaeus Agatho)
—SALERNUM*: (58) imp. *IItal* i (1) 86 (*CIL* x 634) (Lat. A. Sergius Agatho: s. A. Sergius Amoenus: freed.); (59) ?i AD *IItal* i (1) 238 II, 13 (*CIL* x 557) (Lat. L. Appuleius Agatho: freed.)
S. Italy (Lucania):
—COSILINUM: (60) imp. *IItal* iii (1) 219 (*CIL* x 327) (Lat. [A]gathon)
—POSEIDONIA-PAESTUM*: (61) i BC-i AD Mello–Voza 11 (Lat. P. Tirienus Agatho: freed.)
Sicily:
—ADRANON: (62) iii-ii BC *PdelP* 16 (1961) p. 127 (s. Εὔδαμος)
—AKRAI: (63) ?iii BC *SGDI* 3240, 4 (*Akrai* p. 156 no. 7) (f. Ἡράκλειος); (64) ii BC ib. p. 156 no. 6, 8 (f. Ἀπολλώνιος)
—KATANE: (65) ii-iii AD *Epigraphica* 51 (1989) p. 173 no. 44 (Lat. Seius Agatho); (66) iv-v AD *SEG* xxxi 830 (Agnello 106; Wessel 1042)
—LIPARA: (67) hell.? *IG* xiv 383 (Libertini, *Isole Eolie* p. 218 no. 1)
—SYRACUSE: (68) imp. *IG* xiv 18; (69) iii-v AD Strazzulla 170 (Wessel 826); cf. Ferrua, *NG* 11 a (Ἀγά(θ)ων); (70) ~ Strazzulla 276 (Agnello 22; Wessel 727) ([Ἀ]γάθων); (71) 410 AD Strazzulla 4 (Agnello 100; *GVI* 448; Wessel 1036)
—TAUROMENION: (72) c. 237-203 BC *IG* xiv 421 an. 4; 421 an. 12; 421 an. 24; 421 an. 38 (*SGDI* 5219) (s. Ἀρέσανδρος, f. Ἀρέσανδρος); (73) c. 233 BC *IG* xiv 421 an. 8 (*SGDI* 5219); (74) c. 147-144 BC *IG* xiv 421 an. 97 (*SGDI* 5219); *IGSI* 4 III (IV), 66 an. 94 (f. Νικόστρατος); (75) ?ii/i BC *IG* xiv 421 D an. 11 (*SGDI* 5219) (f. Ξένετος); (76) 411 AD *IG* xiv 444 (Wessel 354); cf. Ferrua, *NG* 483
——(Ἰδομ.): (77) ?ii/i BC *IG* xiv 421 D an. 10 (*SGDI* 5219) (f. Εὐκλείδας); (78) ~ *IG* xiv 421 D an. 13 (*SGDI* 5219) (s. Εὐκλείδας)
——(Σπαρ.): (79) ?ii/i BC *IGSI* 10 I, 1 (f. Ἀμμώνιος); (80) f. i BC *Cron. Arch.* 3 (1964) p. 44 III, 15 (f. —δωρος)
——(Σπαρτ.): (81) ?ii/i BC *IG* xiv 421 D an. 4 (*SGDI* 5219) (f. Σωτέλης)
—THERMAI HIMERAIAI: (82) i-ii AD *Eph. Ep.* VIII 700 (*ILat. Term. Imer.* 51) (Lat. Aquillius Agathon)
—ZANKLE-MESSANA: (83) ?ii BC *IG* xiv 401, 9 (f. Πείσανδρος)
Zakynthos: (84) iv BC Carapanos, *Dodone* p. 39 no. 1, 4 (s. Ἐχέφυλος)

**Ἀγαθωνίς**
S. Italy (Campania):
—DIKAIARCHIA-PUTEOLI: (1) ?ii AD *Puteoli* 3 (1979) p. 154 no. 1 (*CIL* x 1884) (Lat. Cornelia Agathonis)

**Ἀγαθώνυμος**
Elis: (1) ?f. ii AD *IvOl* 126, 5 ([Ἀγα]θώνυμος)
Korinthia:
—KORINTH: (2) 343 BC *CID* ii 31, 98; 34 II, 80; (3) iii BC *SEG* xxxi 306, 11 (s. Ἄγαθος); (4) f. iii BC *Thess. Mnem.* 194 (*GVI* 1572; *Gr. Gr.* 208) (f. Ἀγαθοκλῆς)

**Ἀγαῖος**
Argolis:
—ARGOS: (1) a. 303 BC *CEG* II 816, 14; (2) i AD *SEG* xxvi 429, 10 (s. Θρασέας)
—KLEONAI: (3) 191-146 BC *BMC Pelop.* p. 14 no. 157; *SNG Cop. Phliasia–Laconia* 337 (coin)
—OINOE?: (4) s. vi BC *SEG* xxxviii 314, 2 (f. Ἀμυντις)

ELIS: **(5)** c. 575 BC Hdt. vi 127. 3 (f. Ὀνόμαστος)

**Ἀγακλείδας**
ILLYRIA:
—AULON: **(1)** hell. *Iliria* 1977-8, p. 292 pl. IV.5 (*SEG* XXXII 621 (tile)) (-κλί-)

**Ἀγακλῆς**
ARGOLIS:
—EPIDAUROS*: **(1)** c. 370 BC *IG* IV (1)² 102, 170 + *SEG* XXV 383, 145
LAKONIA:
—BOIAI: **(2)** ii AD *IG* V (1) 955 (Π. Μέμμιος Ἀ. Πολωνιανός)

**Ἀγακλυτός**
S. ITALY (CAMPANIA):
—DIKAIARCHIA-PUTEOLI: **(1)** imp. *CIL* X 2488 (Lat. Agaclytus)

**Ἀγαλίδας**
ARGOLIS:
—ARGOS: **(1)** ii BC *SEG* XLII 279, 22 (f. Σωπάτρα)

**Ἀγαλλῆς**
ARKADIA:
—PHIGALEIA: **(1)** s. i BC *IvOl* 402 (f. Ἄρχιππος)

**Ἀγαλλίας**
ARKADIA:
—TEGEA:
——(Krariotai): **(1)** s. iv BC *IG* V (2) 41, 50 (Ἀγαλλίας: s. Κάλλις)

**Ἀγαλλίδας**
ARKADIA:
—MT. KYLLENE*: **(1)** iv-iii BC ib. 362

**Ἀγαλλίς**
KERKYRA: **(1)** iii/ii BC *RE* (1); *PP* 16814

**Ἀγαλλομένη**
AIGINA: **(1)** imp. *IG* IV (1) 109

**Ἀγαλματίς**
SICILY:
—SYRACUSE*: **(1)** ?iii AD ib. XIV 19; cf. Ferrua, *NG* 356 (slave?)

**Ἀγαμέμνων**
AKARNANIA:
—KOMBOTI (MOD.): **(1)** iii/ii BC *IG* IX (1)² (2) 385
KORINTHIA:
—KORINTH: **(2)** c. 590-570 BC Amyx 33. 1 (vase) (Lorber 52) (-νōν: her.?)

**Ἀγαμήδης**
KORINTHIA:
—SIKYON: **(1)** c. 225-200 BC *SEG* XIX 80, 15 (s. Ἀπολλᾶς)

**Ἀγαμήστωρ**
ACHAIA: **(1)** c. 325-300 BC *IG* IV (1)² 257 + Peek, *IAEpid* 108 (f. —μ—ίας)
ARKADIA: **(2)** 168 BC Phld., *Acad. Ind.* 28, 4-5 (s. Πολύξενος)

**Ἀγαμήτωρ**
ARKADIA:
—MANTINEIA-ANTIGONEIA: **(1)** ?vi/v BC Moretti, *Olymp.* 163 (Ἀγαμή(σ)τωρ?)

**Ἀγανίς**
S. ITALY (CAMPANIA):
—DIKAIARCHIA-PUTEOLI: **(1)** imp. *CIL* X 2721 (Lat. Maticia Aganis)

**Ἀγανορίδας**
ACHAIA:
—PATRAI: **(1)** c. 210-207 BC *IG* IV (1)² 73, 19; *SEG* XXXV 303 (date) (s. Τιμανορίδας)

ARGOLIS:
—EPIDAUROS: **(2)** c. 370-365 BC Peek, *IAEpid* 52 A, 33 (Ἀγα[νορί]δας)

**Ἀγανώ**
ARKADIA:
—STYMPHALOS: **(1)** hell.? *PAE* 1929, p. 92

**Ἀγάνωρ**
AKARNANIA:
—ANAKTORION: **(1)** iv/iii BC *IG* IX (1)² (2) 212, 3 (s. Λαγίσκος)
EPIROS:
—DODONA: **(2)** iii BC Antoniou, *Dodone* Aa, 24
KORINTHIA:
—KORINTH: **(3)** c. 570-550 BC Amyx 85. 3 (vase) (Lorber 145) (-νōρ: her.?)

**Ἀγαπάνωρ**
AKARNANIA:
—PHOITIAI: **(1)** iv BC *IG* IX (1)² (2) 602, 3
—THYRREION: **(2)** 216 BC ib. 583, 18 (s. Πύρριχος)

**Ἀγαπᾶς**
AIGINA: **(1)** ?f. iii AD *Alt-Ägina* I (2) p. 49 no. 44 (f. Ἱλαρος)

**Ἀγαπάτις**
ARGOLIS:
—HERMIONE: **(1)** ii-i BC *IG* IV (1) 732 III, 14, 16 (m. Σωτηρίς, Ζώπυρος)

**Ἀγάπη**
AKARNANIA:
—ALYZIA: **(1)** byz. ib. IX (1)² (2) 446 b
S. ITALY (CAMPANIA):
—DIKAIARCHIA-PUTEOLI: **(2)** ?ii AD *CIL* X 2505 (Lat. Flavia Agape)
—MISENUM*: **(3)** imp. ib. 3674 (Lat. Aemilia Agape)
—NEAPOLIS: **(4)** iii-iv AD *IG* XIV 826. 2 (*INap* 218); **(5)** ~ ib. 219
SICILY:
—SYRACUSE: **(6)** iii-v AD Ferrua, *NG* 197

**Ἀγαπήτα**
ARKADIA:
—TEGEA: **(1)** ?iv BC *IG* V (2) 92

**Ἀγαπητός**
LAKONIA:
—SPARTA: **(1)** c. 125-150 AD *SEG* XI 578, 2 (Bradford (-)) (s. Χαρίξενος)
MESSENIA:
—MESSENE: **(2)** i AD *IG* V (1) 1467, 3 (I f. Ἀγαπητός II); **(3)** ~ ib. l. 3, 5-6 (II s. Ἀγαπητός I, f. —ώνιος, —μενος)
S. ITALY (CALABRIA):
—BRENTESION-BRUNDISIUM: **(4)** ii-iii AD *Taras* 11 (1991) p. 289 (*Epigraphica* 57 (1995) p. 53) (Lat. [P.] Gerellanus Agapetus)
SICILY:
—SYRACUSE: **(5)** iii-v AD *NScav* 1893, p. 285 (Strazzulla 70) (Ἀ[γ]απιτός)

**Ἀγάπιος**
SICILY:
—SYRACUSE: **(1)** iii-v AD *IG* XIV 64 (Strazzulla 5; Wessel 337)

**Ἀγαπωμένη**
KORINTHIA:
—KORINTH: **(1)** iii-iv AD *Corinth* VIII (3) 136, 1-2; cf. *TMByz* 9 (1985) p. 360 no. 10
S. ITALY (CALABRIA):
—VALETIUM: **(2)** imp. Susini, *Fonti Salento* p. 165 no. 130 (*CIL* IX 28) (Lat. Terraea Agapomene)

**Ἀγαπωμενός**
KORINTHIA:
—KORINTH: **(1)** iii-iv AD *Corinth* VIII (3) 136, 3; cf. *TMByz* 9 (1985) p. 360 no. 10
S. ITALY (BRUTTIUM):
—RHEGION: **(2)** ii AD *IGUR* 1165 (*GVI* 1025) (f. Ἀτίμητος)
S. ITALY (CAMPANIA):
—POMPEII: **(3)** c. 51-62 AD *CIL* IV 3340. 73, 11 (Castrèn 324. 1) (Lat. C. Proculeius Agapomenus)
SICILY:
—KATANE*: **(4)** imp. *CIL* X 7063 (Lat. Decimius Agapomenus: freed.)

**Ἀγάριν**
LAKONIA:
—OITYLOS: **(1)** imp. *IG* V (1) 1303

**Ἀγαρίστα**
KORINTHIA:
—SIKYON: **(1)** f. vi BC *RE* (1) (Skalet 4) (and Athens: d. Κλεισθένης, m. Κλεισθένης (Athens), Ἀριστώνυμος (Athens), ?m. Μεγακλῆς (Athens), Ἱπποκράτης (Athens))

**Ἀγᾶς**
ILLYRIA:
—EPIDAMNOS-DYRRHACHION: **(1)** c. 250-50 BC Maier 93 (Münsterberg Nachtr. p. 14; Ceka 354); cf. *IApoll Ref. Bibl.* n. 2 (coin) (Ἀγᾶτος (gen.): pryt.)
S. ITALY (LUCANIA):
—METAPONTION: **(2)** ?v-iv BC *JNG* 33 (1983) p. 13 (coin graffito)

**Ἀγάσαρχος**
SICILY:
—SELINOUS: **(1)** vi/v BC Manganaro, *PdelP* forthcoming no. 18, 8, 10 (ha-: f. Χάρων, Ἀθανις)

**Ἀγασέας**
ARKADIA:
—TEGEA:
——(Krariotai): **(1)** m. iii BC *IG* V (2) 36, 88 (s. Ἀριστοφάνης)

**Ἀγασία**
S. ITALY (CALABRIA):
—BRENTESION-BRUNDISIUM: **(1)** imp. *CIL* IX 6103 (Lat. Agasia)

**Ἀγασίας**
ACHAIA:
—PATRAI: **(1)** m. ii BC *IG* IX (1)² (2) 208, 9 (s. Ὀλυμπίων)
ARKADIA:
—MANTINEIA-ANTIGONEIA: **(2)** c. 425-385 BC ib. V (2) 323. 4 (tessera) (Ἀγασί[ας]: f. Σίμων)
—STYMPHALOS: **(3)** 401 BC *RE* (1)
SICILY:
—SELINOUS: **(4)** s. vi BC Dubois, *IGDS* 75 (Arena, *Iscr. Sic.* I 29; *IGLMP* 84) (s. Καρίας)

**Ἀγασιγράτις**
ARGOLIS:
—KALAURIA: **(1)** iii BC *IG* IV (1) 840 I, 1, 13 (d. Τεισίας, m. Σωσιφάνης, Νικαγόρα, Ἀριστόκλεια)

**Ἀγασίδαμος**
EPIROS:
—AMBRAKIA: **(1)** ii-i BC *CIG* 1798 (f. Βίος)
S. ITALY (LUCANIA):
—HERAKLEIA: **(2)** 280-270 BC *BMC Italy* p. 231 no. 46 (coin) (van Keuren, *Coinage of Heraclea* p. 84 no. 110) (Ἀγασίδαμ(ος))

**Ἀγασικλείδας**
ARGOLIS:
—TROIZEN: **(1)** ?192 AD *IG* IV (1) 782, 2 (I f. Ἀγασικλείδας II); **(2)** ~ ib. l. 2 (II s. Ἀγασικλείδας I: doctor)

## Ἀγασικλῆς
ARGOLIS:
—HERMIONE: (1) iv BC SEG XI 382, 25 (s. Σωσι—, f. Θηβαΐς)
—KALAURIA: (2) iii BC IG IV (1) 841, [8], 13; (3) imp. ib. 846 (s. Σωσιφάνης)
—TROIZEN: (4) ?146 BC ib. 757 B, 17
KORINTHIA:
—SIKYON: (5) ?v BC Paus. ii 10. 3 (Skalet 5) (s. Νικαγόρα)

## Ἀγασίλαος
KERKYRA: (1) c. 166 BC IG II² 2316, 7-8 (s. Φιλόξενος)

## Ἀγασίληϝος
S. ITALY (CAMPANIA):
—KYME?: (1) c. 650 BC Dubois, IGDGG I 22 (vase) (Arena, Iscr. Sic. III A 3); LSAG² p. 83 (-λεϝος: f. Πύρρος)

## Ἀγασιμένης
KORINTHIA:
—SIKYON: (1) c. 405 BC Paus. x 9. 10; cf. CEG II 819 (Skalet 6) (Ἀγεμένης, Ἀγεσιμένης—mss.: name—Dindorf)

## Ἀγάσιον
LAKONIA:
—SPARTA: (1) i-ii AD IG V (1) 785 (Bradford (-))

## Ἀγάσιππος
ELIS:
—OLYMPIA*: (1) hell. IvOl 721 (Ἀγάσιπ(πος))
LAKONIA:
—KARDAMYLE: (2) i BC-i AD IG V (1) 1334 (Ἀγάσιππ[ος]: f. Ξενόστρατος)
—SPARTA: (3) f. iii AD SEG XLII 320, 2 (f. Αὐρ. Ἀρτέμων)

## Ἀγασισθένης
LAKONIA:
—SPARTA: (1) 149 BC Paus. vii 12. 7 (Bradford (-))

## Ἀγασίων
DALMATIA:
—ISSA: (1) iii BC Brunšmid p. 9 fr. G, 15 (Ἀγασίων: s. Ἀρχέβιος)
EPIROS:
—DODONA*: (2) iv-iii BC SEG XV 408 a (Ἀγ[α]σίων)

## Ἀγασώ
ARKADIA:
—TEGEA: (1) ii BC IG IV (1)² 226 (d. Πολίας); (2) ~ ib. v (2) 145; (3) ?ii BC ib. 200

## Ἀγάτας
SICILY:
—LIPARA: (1) hell.? BTCGI 9 p. 86

## Ἄγβωρ
SICILY:
—LILYBAION: (1) ii-i BC SEG XXXIV 953, 3 (Ἀ. Βούκιος?)

## Ἀγγάριος
KORINTHIA:
—KORINTH: (1) vii/vi BC Amyx Gr 5 a. 3 (vase) (Lorber 2 a) (Ἀνγά-)

## Ἄγγειλις
SICILY:
—SELINOUS: (1) s. vi BC Dubois, IGDS 31, 3 (Arena, Iscr. Sic. I 60); cf. SEG XXXVIII 962 (Ἀνγ-)

## Ἀγγελῆς
LAKONIA:
—EPIDAUROS LIMERA: (1) m. ii BC ib. XIII 259, [1], 16, 25 (s. Ζήνων)

## Ἄγγελος
EPIROS:
—MOLOSSOI: (1) iv BC Plu., Pyrr. 2. 1

## Ἀγγενίδας
LAKONIA:
—SPARTA: (1) 426 BC X., HG ii 3. 10 (Poralla² 3)

## Ἀγγίφρακτος
SICILY:
—SYRACUSE: (1) iii-v AD IG XIV 65 with Add. p. 686 (Strazzulla 6) (Ἀγφίρακτος—apogr.)

## Ἀγέας
ACHAIA:
—ASCHEION: (1) c. 230-200 BC BCH 45 (1921) p. 12 II, 63 (s. Εὔοχος)
—PELLENE: (2) c. 315-280 BC FD III (1) 426, 3 (Ἀγέ[α] (gen.): f. Φίλλις)
—PELLENE?: (3) ?263-261 BC ib. III (3) 190, 7 (s. Ἀγίων)
AITOLIA: (4) ?209 or 205 BC Flacelière p. 407 no. 38 b, 5; Nachtergael, Les Galates 68, 3
—KALLION/KALLIPOLIS: (5) f. iii BC IG IX (1)² (1) 8, 14; Das Heroon von Kalydon p. 293, 11
ARGOLIS:
—EPIDAUROS: (6) c. 365-335 BC IG IV (1)² 103, 17-18, [19], 31, 37, 56, 81, 83, 99 + SEG XXV 386, [33]
ARKADIA:
—TEGEA: (7) m. iv BC IG V (2) 6, 69; (8) c. 240-229 BC ib. 11, 19; 13, 10
EPIROS:
—AMBRAKIA: (9) m. iii BC ib. 368, 25 (f. —μων)
—MOLOSSOI: (10) iii/ii BC Syll³ 1206, 9; cf. Cabanes, L'Épire p. 583 no. 60 (?f. Μολοσσός)
MESSENIA:
—ABIA: (11) ii BC IG V (1) 1351 (s. Ἄρχιππος)
S. ITALY (BRUTTIUM):
—KROTON: (12) iv BC Iamb., VP 267 (FVS 1 p. 446)
S. ITALY (CALABRIA):
—TARAS-TARENTUM: (13) c. 272-235 BC Vlasto 822 (coin) (Evans, Horsemen p. 177 VIII A.4) (ha-)
SICILY:
—AKRAI: (14) ii BC Akrai p. 156 no. 6, 7 (I f. Ἀγέας II); (15) ~ ib. l. 7 (II s. Ἀγέας I)
—SYRACUSE: (16) hell.? IG XIV 10 (SGDI 3235) (Ἀγέας: f. Ἐπικράτης)
—TAUROMENION: (17) c. 219-198 BC IG XIV 421 an. 22; 421 an. 31; 421 an. 43 (SGDI 5219) (s. Μένων); (18) c. 177-167 BC IG XIV 421 an. 64; 421 an. 74 (SGDI 5219) (f. Φιλιστίων)
——(Σπαρτ.): (19) ?ii/i BC IG XIV 421 D an. 3; 421 D an. 13 (SGDI 5219); IGSI 10 II, 26 (s. Φιλιστίων, f. Φιλιστίων)

## Ἀγέδαμος
MESSENIA:
—KALAMAI: (1) i AD IG V (1) 1370, 1

## Ἀγεδᾶς
ELIS:
—OLYMPIA*: (1) ?c. 475-450 BC IvOl 12, 6 (DGE 416); LSAG² p. 220 no. 13 (date) (f. Πιτθώ)

## Ἀγελάδας
ARGOLIS:
—ARGOS: (1) vi/v BC RE s.v. Hageladas; GP 579; Overbeck 388 f. (s. Ἀργεῖος: sculptor)
LEUKAS: (2) hell.? IG IX (1) 541 (tile) ([Ἀγ]ελάδας)

## Ἀγελαΐδας
ARGOLIS:
—ARGOS: (1) c. 480-460 BC CEG I 380. iii (f. Ἀργειάδας)

## Ἀγέλαιος
EPIROS:
—DODONA: (1) c. 330 BC Cabanes, L'Épire p. 580 no. 55, 6 (Ἀγί-)
—KOLPAIOI: (2) f. ii BC ib. p. 580 no. 54, 7 (s. Ἀνίκατος)
LAKONIA:
—EPIDAUROS LIMERA: (3) ?ii-i BC IG V (1) 1005 (s. Ἀριστοκράτης); (4) ~ ib. 1007 (Ἀγέ[λαιος]: f. Ἀριστοκράτης)

## Ἀγέλαος
AITOLIA: (1) c. 260 BC FD III (4) 178, 2; (2) ?253 BC Nachtergael, Les Galates 10, 4
—APERANTOI: (3) iii BC SBBerlAk 1936, p. 388 no. 2, 2 (L'Illyrie mérid. 1 p. 110 fig. 7) (f. Λαώ); (4) iii/ii BC SEG XVII 275, 2 (L'Illyrie mérid. 1 p. 110 fig. 8)
—BOUKATION: (5) m. ii BC IG IX (1)² (1) 107, 7
—KALLION/KALLIPOLIS: (6) 175 BC SGDI 1987, 12 (s. Ἀγχέμαχος)
—KALYDON: (7) c. 142 BC IG IX (1)² (1) 137, 46 (f. Φίλων); (8) a. 142 BC ib. l. 58 (Ἀ[γέ]λαος)
—KONOPE-ARSINOE: (9) c. 225-200 BC ib. 31, 2, 146; (10) f. ii BC REG 62 (1949) p. 28 B, 15
AKARNANIA:
—PALAIROS: (11) ii BC IG IX (1)² (2) 451, 12 (f. Λέων)
—STRATOS: (12) 263-262 BC ib. IX (1)² (1) 3 A, 25 (Ἀγέ[λ]αος); (13) a. 167 BC ib. IX (2) 6 a, 4; cf. Stählin p. 220 (date) (f. Ἐπίγνητος)
—THYRREION: (14) iii-ii BC SEG XXVII 159, 7; cf. PAE 1977, p. 483 with pl. 244 a (s. Σ—); (15) i BC/i AD IG IX (1)² (2) 349
ARKADIA:
—TEGEA: (16) 554 BC Paus. x 7. 7 (Stephanis 35)
EPIROS: (17) iv-iii BC Cabanes, L'Épire p. 585 no. 68, 11 (Ἀγέλ[αος])
—AMBRAKIA: (18) ii BC SEG XLII 542 (s. Πυρρίας)
—BOUTHROTOS (PRASAIBOI): (19) a. 163 BC IBouthrot 102, 3
—KOLPAIOI: (20) f. ii BC Cabanes, L'Épire p. 580 no. 54, 6 (s. Ἀντίοχος)
—MOLOSSOI: (21) hell. ib. p. 581 no. 56, 8
—TRIPHYLAI: (22) 370-368 BC ib. p. 534 no. 1, 16
—TRIPOLISSIOI?: (23) hell. SGDI 1360; cf. Cabanes, L'Épire p. 584 no. 64
—VOTONOSI (MOD.): (24) f. iii BC SEG XXIV 457 a (s. Νικόλαος)
KERKYRA: (25) ?ii BC IG IX (1) 708 (Ἀ[γ]έλαος: f. Σίμακος)
SICILY:
—SYRACUSE?:
——(Λακυν.): (26) hell. Mem. Linc. 8 (1938) p. 127 no. 35. 4 (bullet); cf. L'Incidenza dell'Antico pp. 420 ff. (s. Πυρρίας)

## Ἀγέλας
KORINTHIA:
—KORINTH: (1) her. FGrH 244 F 331. 3 (s. Ἰξίων, f. Πρύμνις: king); (2) ~ ib. (s. Βάκχις, f. Εὐδάμων: king)
S. ITALY (BRUTTIUM):
—KROTON: (3) iv BC Iamb., VP 267 (FVS 1 p. 446)

## Ἀγέλη
S. ITALY (CAMPANIA):
—DIKAIARCHIA-PUTEOLI: (1) imp. AJA 2 (1898) p. 387 no. 35 (Lat. Egnatia Agele)
—POMPEII: (2) i BC-i AD CIL IV 8191 (Lat. Agele)
—STABIAE: (3) imp. PBSR 40 (1972) p. 128 no. 3 (Lat. Pontia Agele)

## Ἀγέλλυς
EPIROS:
—DODONA: (1) iii BC Antoniou, Dodone Ab, 11; (2) ~ ib. l. 45

**Ἀγελόχεια**
LAKONIA:
—SPARTA?: (**1**) ?iii BC *HE* 1905 (d. Δαμάρετος)

**Ἀγέλοχος**
AITOLIA: (**1**) 244 or 240 BC *SGDI* 2512, 2 (Flacelière p. 402 no. 28 a); Nachtergael, *Les Galates* 59, [2]; (**2**) 213 or 205 BC ib. 66, 4
—KONOPE-ARSINOE: (**3**) 163 BC *IG* IX (1)² (1) 101, 12
—PHILOTAIEIS: (**4**) c. 162 BC ib. 105, 7
AKARNANIA:
—STRATOS: (**5**) 169 or 168 BC ib. p. LII, s.a. 169-168 BC; cf. 100, 1 ([Ἀγ]έλοχος: s. Τριχᾶς, ?f. Τριχᾶς)
ARGOLIS:
—EPIDAUROS: (**6**) c. 370-360 BC *BSA* 61 (1966) p. 272 no. 4 A, 28 (Ἀγέλοχ[ος])
DALMATIA:
—ISSA:
——(Pamphyloi): (**7**) iv/iii BC Brunšmid p. 8, 34 (s. Θεόδωρος)
ELIS:
—LASION: (**8**) c. 230-200 BC *BCH* 45 (1921) p. 14 II, 126 (Ἀγέλ[ο]χος: f. Ἴερις)
EPIROS:
—AMBRAKIA: (**9**) iv BC *Op. Ath.* 10 (1971) p. 64 no. 7 (f. Εὐβούλα)
ILLYRIA:
—APOLLONIA: (**10**) 318 BC Osborne, *Naturalization* D39; cf. *IDyrrh* 513 ([Ἀγ]έλοχος)
ITHAKE: (**11**) hell. *Rev. Épig.* 1 (1913) p. 47 no. 9
LAKONIA:
—SPARTA: (**12**) m. v BC Paus. iii 11 .5 (Poralla² 4) (s. Τεισαμενός (Elis), f. Ἁγίας: mantis)
S. ITALY (BRUTTIUM):
—LOKROI EPIZEPHYRIOI: (**13**) iv/iii BC De Franciscis 36, 4
——(Τηλ.): (**14**) iv/iii BC ib. 33, 2 (s. Ἀλεξίδαμος)
S. ITALY (CALABRIA):
—TARAS-TARENTUM: (**15**) c. 411 BC *IG* XII (9) 187 (*Syll*³ 105) (Ἡγέ-)
SICILY:
—KAMARINA: (**16**) ?iv/iii BC *SEG* XXXIX 1002, 2 ([Ἀ]γέλοχος: f. —αρχος)
—SYRACUSE?:
——(Περ.): (**17**) hell. Manganaro, *PdelP* forthcoming no. 4 I, 3 (s. Νικόλοχος)
——(Πλε.): (**18**) hell. *NScav* 1961, p. 349 (bullet); cf. *BE* 1965, no. 502; *L'Incidenza dell'Antico* pp. 420 ff. (f. Κάνθαρος)

**Ἀγεμάχα**
AITOLIA:
—KALYDON: (**1**) m. ii BC *IG* IX (1)² (1) 137, 2, 7, 9, 41 (d. Ἀνδρομένης, ?m. Διονύσιος, m. Ἀνδρόνικος (Proscheion), Ἀνδρομένης (Proscheion))

**Ἀγέμαχος**
AIGINA: (**1**) iv BC ib. IV (1) 41 (f. Κλεόδικος)
AITOLIA: (**2**) ?247 BC *Syll*³ 444 A, 3; *CID* II 139, 2; (**3**) c. 232-228 BC *Syll*³ 499, 3; Nachtergael, *Les Galates* 62, [3]
—PHOLANTIOI: (**4**) s. iii BC *IG* IX (1)² (1) 24, 11, [13]; 25, 60 (s.p.) (Ἀγέ(μ)αχος—l. 11: s. Ἐπίνικος)
AKARNANIA:
—PALAIROS: (**5**) s. iii BC ib. IX (1)² (2) 520
—STRATOS: (**6**) ?153 BC ib. IX (1)² (1) 109, 7; (**7**) s. ii BC ib. 36, 14 (Ἀγέμ[αχος], Ἀγεμ[ος?]: f. Ὑβρίστας)
ARGOLIS:
—ARGOS: (**8**) c. 60 BC ib. VII 420, 52 (*IOrop* 528) (f. Πολυκράτης)
——(Pamphyloi-Olisseidai): (**9**) c. 400 BC *SEG* XXIX 361, 9 (ha-)
—EPIDAUROS:
——Pierias (Hysminatai): (**10**) c. 335-325 BC *IG* IV (1)² 108, 143

ARKADIA:
—TEGEA: (**11**) 165 AD ib. v (2) 50, 13 (f. Ἀπολλώνιος)
——(Hippothoitai): (**12**) iii BC ib. 40, 38 (s. Κλεώνομος)
——(Krariotai): (**13**) f. iii BC ib. 36, 48 (s. Ἀγίας: metic)
ELIS: (**14**) ?i BC *IvOl* 728 (tile); (**15**) i/ii AD Plu., *Mor.* 664 B-D; (**16**) iii AD *SEG* XV 259, 6
ELIS?: (**17**) imp. *NY Bronzes* pp. 295-6 no. 859 (bronze)
EPIROS:
—AMBRAKIA: (**18**) ii-i BC *CIG* 1799 (f. Ἀριστόλας)
ITHAKE: (**19**) hell. *IG* IX (1) 659
PELOPONNESE: (**20**) s. iii BC *SEG* XIII 278, 14 (s. Σάων)
S. ITALY (CALABRIA):
—TARAS-TARENTUM: (**21**) s. iii BC *FD* III (1) 444, 1 (s. Δεινοκράτης)
SICILY:
—LIPARA*: (**22**) ii/i BC *Meligunis-Lipara* 5 p. 72 T. 2006 (tile); cf. *Kokalos* 32 (1986) p. 219 no. 3
—NEAITON: (**23**) iii BC Dubois, *IGDS* 101 (s. Πολύαρχος)

**Ἀγεμόνα**
ILLYRIA:
—EPIDAMNOS-DYRRHACHION: (**1**) hell.-imp. *IDyrrh* 79

**Ἀγεμονεύς**
TRIPHYLIA:
—MAKISTOS: (**1**) 399-369 BC *SEG* XXXV 389, 11

**Ἀγεμος**
ACHAIA:
—PELLENE: (**1**) m. iii BC *IG* v (2) 368, 113 (Ἀγεμος)
AITOLIA:
—KALLION/KALLIPOLIS: (**2**) 153-144 BC *SGDI* 2279, 11
AKARNANIA:
—STRATOS: (**3**) ii BC *IG* IX (1)² (2) 408 (*Gr. Gr.* 213) (f. Πανταλέων)

**Ἀγεμώ**
ARKADIA:
—ASEA: (**1**) ?c. 525 BC *IG* v (2) 559 (Lazzarini 410); *LSAG*² p. 215 no. 6 (date) (-μό)

**Ἀγέμων**
ARGOLIS:
—EPIDAUROS: (**1**) c. 370 BC *IG* IV (1)² 102, 7, 48, [91], 107
—PHLEIOUS: (**2**) 359 BC *SEG* XXVII 16, 4 (Stephanis 1051) (Ἡγέ-)

**Ἀγένομος**
ARKADIA:
—MEGALOPOLIS: (**1**) hell.? *IG* v (2) 448, 9 ([Ἀγ]ένομος)

**Ἀγέπολις**
ARKADIA:
—MEGALOPOLIS: (**1**) c. 250-175 BC *IC* 4 p. 282 no. 206 E (s. Κάλλιππος)

**Ἀγεσίλαος**
ACHAIA:
—PATRAI: (**1**) iii-ii BC *Achaean Grave Stelai* 65 (f. Ξενοκλέα)

**Ἀγεσίλας**
DALMATIA:
—ISSA: (**1**) iii BC Brunšmid p. 9 fr. G, 3 (Ἀγεσί[λας])

**Ἀγεστος**
AITOLIA:
—KALLION/KALLIPOLIS: (**1**) f. iii BC *IG* IX (2) 216, 2 + *SEG* III 471 (s. Ἀγρολέων)

**Ἀγέστρατος**
AITOLIA:
—OPHIEIS: (**1**) 194 BC *SGDI* 1978, 3, 7 etc.
ARGOLIS:
—ARGOS: (**2**) iii BC *SEG* XVII 152 (f. Λάτροπος)
ARKADIA:
—MEGALOPOLIS: (**3**) s. ii BC *IG* v (2) 439, 83 ([Ἀγ]έστρατος)
—TEGEA:
——(Krariotai): (**4**) s. iv BC ib. 41, 52 ([Ἀγέ]σστρατος: s. Λα—)
EPIROS:
—DODONA*: (**5**) ii BC *SEG* XXXIII 477 (tile)
ILLYRIA:
—APOLLONIA: (**6**) iii BC *IApoll* 5 (f. Λύσων)
KORINTHIA:
—KORINTH: (**7**) 3 AD *Corinth* VIII (1) 14, 33; cf. *SEG* XI 61 (f. —μων)
SICILY:
—SELINOUS: (**8**) s. vi BC Dubois, *IGDS* 31, 5 (Arena, *Iscr. Sic.* I 60); cf. *SEG* XXXVIII 962 (hαγέ-)
—SYRACUSE: (**9**) c. 350-320 BC ib. XVIII 772 (s. Μοσχίων)
—TAUROMENION: (**10**) c. 195-181 BC *IG* XIV 421 an. 46; 421 an. 60 (*SGDI* 5219) (f. Θάρριππος)

**Ἀγέτας**
MESSENIA:
—MESSENE: (**1**) iii BC *IG* v (1) 1441 b

**Ἀγεύς**
ARGOLIS:
—ARGOS: (**1**) s. iv BC ib. v (2) 550, 13; Moretti, *Olymp.* 464 (s. Ἀριστοκλῆς)

**Ἀγήανδρος**
ARGOLIS:
—ARGOS: (**1**) 228-146 BC BM coin 1925 1-15-8 to 10; *NC* 1924, p. 319 (coins) (Ἀγήάν(δρος))

**Ἀγηΐδαμος**
ARGOLIS:
—ARGOS: (**1**) iii BC *IG* IV (1) 618 II, 6 (Ἀγη[ΐ]δαμος: s. Κριθέας)

**Ἀγηικράτης**
ARGOLIS:
—ARGOS: (**1**) v BC ib. 552, 10 (hαγῆhικρ[άτης])

**Ἀγηΐλας**
LAKONIA:
—AMYKLAI*: (**1**) iv BC *SEG* XI 695 (Bradford s.v. Ἀγησίλαος (5)) (hαγῆhί-)

**Ἀγηΐξενος**
LAKONIA:
—SPARTA: (**1**) ii BC *IG* v (1) 965, 1, 5; *REG* 99 (1986) p. 139 (name) (Bradford s.v. Ἀγήξενος (-)) (Ἀγήξενος—lap., Ἀγη(ΐ)ξενος—Masson: f. Ἀρισταγόρας)

**Ἀγηΐπολις**
LAKONIA:
—GERENIA: (**1**) v BC *IG* v (1) 1338 (Poralla² 13) ([h]αγῆhίπολις)

**Ἀγήιππα**
ARGOLIS:
—ARGOS: (**1**) iii BC *IG* IV (1) 571

**Ἀγηιππία**
LAKONIA:
—SPARTA: (**1**) i BC/i AD *SEG* XI 677, 2 (Bradford s.v. Ἀγησιππία (2)) (-hιπ-: d. Ἵππαρχος)

**Ἁγηΐς**
ARGOLIS:
—ARGOS: (**1**) c. 475-450 BC *SEG* XXIX 362; *LSAG*² p. 444 no. C (date) (hαγῆhίς)

**Ἀγηΐστρατος**
LAKONIA:
—SPARTA: (1) 427 BC X., *HG* ii 3. 10; *IG* v (1) 1231, 8 (Poralla² 17) (*ḫαγηηΐστρατος—IG*, Ἀγησίστρατος—X.); (2) iv BC *SEG* XI 639, 7 (*ḫαγηηΐσστ*[*ρατος*]: ?f. —*μίδας*)

**Ἀγήμαχος**
MESSENIA:
—MESSENE: (1) f. i BC Polyaen. ii 35

**Ἀγημονίδας**
ACHAIA:
—DYME: (1) 170-164 BC *OGIS* 252 (*SEG* XIV 368); cf. *SEG* XVII 207; XIV 369, 2; cf. XVII 207; *Historia* 7 (1958) pp. 376-8 (date) (s. Ζέφυρος)
ITHAKE: (2) hell. *IG* IX (1) 668
KERKYRA: (3) c. 500 BC *SEG* XXX 520 (*ḫαγḗμονίδαι* (dat.))

**Ἀγήμων**
ACHAIA:
—PATRAI: (1) iv BC *Achaean Grave Stelai* 14 (Ἀγήμω[ν], Ἀγημώ?)
AITOLIA: (2) ?a. 246 BC *SGDI* 2509, 3; (3) c. 225-200 BC *FD* III (4) 366, 3
AKARNANIA: (4) c. 400-350 BC *NZ* 10 (1878) p. 14 no. 2 (coin)
—KOMBOTI (MOD.): (5) iv BC *IG* IX (1)² (2) 384
—THYRREION: (6) iii-ii BC *SEG* XXVII 159, 9; cf. *PAE* 1977, pl. 244 a (f. Ἀριστόμαχος); (7) ii BC *IG* IX (1)² (2) 249, 8
ARKADIA:
—MANTINEIA-ANTIGONEIA: (8) c. 300-221 BC ib. v (2) 323. 102 (tessera) (f. Δίαιος)
ELIS: (9) 72 BC Moretti, *Olymp.* 694
KERKYRA: (10) c. 340-335 BC *CID* II 20, 6 ([Ἀ]γήμων)
KORINTHIA:
—KORINTH: (11) inc. *Corinth* VIII (1) 36; cf. *SEG* XI 67 (Ἀγήμω[ν]); (12) s. ix BC *FGrH* 244 F 331 ?= (13); (13) viii BC Polem. fr. 76 (f. Ἀλκυόνη) ?= (12); (14) f. ii AD *Lampes d'Argos* 251; *Corinth* IV (2) p. 188 no. 561 (lamp)
LAKONIA:
—SPARTA: (15) hell.-imp. *IG* v (1) 195, 9 (Bradford (4)); (16) s. i BC *IG* v (1) 93, [25]; 211, 41 (Bradford (1)) (s. Περικλῆς); (17) i/ii AD *IG* v (1) 58, 2; 667, 10; *SEG* XI 563, 2 (Bradford (2); (3)) (Τιβ. Κλ. Ἀ.)
—TEUTHRONE: (18) iii/ii BC *SEG* XXII 304, 1 (date—*LGPN*)
LEUKAS: (19) c. 167-50 BC *BMC Thessaly* p. 179 no. 78; *SNG Cop. Epirus-Acarnania* 377 (coins); (20) f. i BC *IG* IX (1) 534, 10 (*Iscr. Gr. Verona* p. 24) (s. Τελέσων)

**Ἀγήν**
EPIROS: (1) 234-168 BC *BMC Thessaly* p. 90 no. 36; Franke, *Münz. v. Epirus* p. 183 II ser. 53 (coins)
ILLYRIA:
—APOLLONIA: (2) hell. *IApoll* 345 (tile) (f. Αἰσχρίων); (3) c. 250-50 BC Münsterberg Nachtr. p. 54 [13]; Maier 11; *NZ* 20 (1927) p. 53 (coin) (Ceka 47; 65) (pryt.); (4) i BC Maier 129 (coin) (s. Παρμήν: money.)
—EPIDAMNOS-DYRRHACHION: (5) 318 BC Osborne, *Naturalization* D39; cf. *IDyrrh* 513 ([Ἀ]γήν); (6) c. 250-50 BC Ceka, *Probleme* p. 151 no. 3; cf. *IApoll Ref. Bibl.* s.v. (coin) (pryt.); (7) ?ii BC *IDyrrh* 116 (f. Ἀριστήν)
ILLYRIA?: (8) iv BC *TrGF* 1 p. 260; cf. Fraser-Rönne, *BWGT* p. 168 n. 68; *Sic. Gymn.* 26 (1973) pp. 97 ff. (fict.)
KERKYRA: (9) hell. *Syll³* 1174, 7; (10) iii/ii BC *GVI* 1511, 7; cf. Fraser-Rönne, *BWGT* p. 112 no. 3 (f. Φιλίστιον)

**Ἀγήνωρ**
EPIROS:
—DODONA: (1) iii BC Antoniou, *Dodone* Ab, 33 (Ἀγήνωρ)
LAKONIA: (2) 109-105 BC *PRein* 1 15, 29; 16, [36]; 20, 35; 23, 27; *PP* 3777 (Bradford (-)) (s. Βαρκαῖος)
S. ITALY (CAMPANIA):
—DIKAIARCHIA-PUTEOLI: (3) imp. *AJA* 2 (1898) p. 378 no. 10 (Lat. M. Caecilius Agenor)

**Ἀγησαγόρα**
KORINTHIA:
—KORINTH: (1) hell. *IG* VII 2113 (-γει-)

**Ἀγησαγόρας**
AITOLIA:
—BOUKATION: (1) c. 164 BC ib. IX (1)² (1) 99, 4 (f. Ἀντίοχος)

**Ἀγησανδρίδας**
KORINTHIA:
—KORINTH: (1) 472 BC Moretti, *Olymp.* 229 ([Ἀγη]σανδρίδας)
LAKONIA:
—SPARTA: (2) s. v BC *RE* (-) (Poralla² 5) (s. Ἀγήσανδρος)

**Ἀγήσανδρος**
ACHAIA:
—DYME: (1) s. iii BC *SEG* XIII 278, 17 (s. Ἀριστόδαμος)
AITOLIA:
—BOUKATION: (2) c. 164 BC *IG* IX (1)² (1) 99, 8-9
—KALLION/KALLIPOLIS: (3) 170 BC *SGDI* 1740, 11 (s. Ἀρίσταρχος)
—PHISTYON: (4) 204-190 BC *IG* IX (1)² (1) 95, 9; 97, 12; (5) s. ii BC *SBBerlAk* 1936, p. 364 no. 1, 3 ?= (7); (6) ~ ib. l. 4; (7) c. 125-100 BC ib. p. 367 no. 2, 2 (*SEG* XII 303) ?= (5)
—PROSCH(E)ION: (8) m. ii BC *SBBerlAk* 1936, p. 371 a, 1 (*SEG* XLI 528 A) (f. Λάμιος)
AKARNANIA:
—DERION: (9) c. 325-315 BC *Hesp.* 57 (1988) p. 148 A, 42 (*SEG* XXXVI 331); cf. *Hesp.* 48 (1979) pp. 78 f. with pl. 22 c (f. Τελένικος)
ARGOLIS:
—EPIDAUROS: (10) c. 350-200 BC *SEG* XXVI 452. 1
ARKADIA: (11) 401 BC X., *An.* vi 3. 5 (Ἡ-)
—MANTINEIA-ANTIGONEIA: (12) f. iii BC *IG* v (2) 278, 3; *EILakArk* 17 (date)
EPIROS:
—AMBRAKIA: (13) hell. *SEG* XXXIX 523 (f. Φρυνίων)
—BOUTHROTOS (PRASAIBOI):
——Bouthrotioi: (14) f. ii BC *IBouthrot* 1, 9; 76, 7; 97, 6 (s. Λαμίσκος, f. Λαμίσκος); (15) a. 163 BC ib. 92, 6; 100, 8; 133, 4 (f. Ζώϊλος)
——Telaioi: (16) a. 163 BC ib. 104, 14 (Ἀγ[ήσαν]δρος: s. Σίμακος)
KEPHALLENIA:
—SAME: (17) hell. *IG* IX (1) 635 ([Ἀ]γήσαν[δρος])
KERKYRA: (18) hell. ib. 735-6 (*BM Terracottas* E 131); *BM Terracottas* E 191; *Korkyra* 1 p. 166 no. 1 (tiles)
KORINTHIA:
—KORINTH: (19) c. 225-200 BC *BCH* 23 (1899) p. 93 no. 3, 15 (-γεί-: s. Δωρόθεος)
LAKONIA:
—SPARTA: (20) 423 BC Th. iv 132. 3 (Poralla² 6) (Ἡ-: f. Πασιτελίδας) ?= (21); (21) 411-409 BC Th. viii 91. 2 (Poralla² 6) (f. Ἀγησανδρίδας) ?= (20)
LEUKAS: (22) f. i BC *IG* IX (1) 534, 5 (*Iscr. Gr. Verona* p. 24) (f. Βάθυος)
S. ITALY (BRUTTIUM):
—LOKROI EPIZEPHYRIOI:
——(Ἀστ.): (23) iv/iii BC De Franciscis 21, 5

SICILY:
—KAMARINA: (24) ?iv/iii BC *SEG* XXXIX 1001, 10 (s. Δάμαρχος)
—MORGANTINA: (25) iv/iii BC ib. 1013, 7 (s. Ἁλίαρχος)
—SELINOUS: (26) f. v BC Dubois, *IGDS* 44 (Arena, *Iscr. Sic.* 1 49; *IGLMP* 67) (ḫαγέ-)

**Ἀγησαρέτα**
AKARNANIA:
—PALAIROS: (1) iv/iii BC *IG* IX (1)² (2) 457

**Ἀγήσαρχος**
ACHAIA:
—TRITAIA: (1) ?120 BC Moretti, *Olymp.* 649 (s. Αἱμόστρατος)
AKARNANIA:
—ASTAKOS: (2) ii BC *IG* IX (1)² (2) 435, 16 (f. Σώτων) ?= (3); (3) m. ii BC ib. 209, 2 (f. Εὐρύλοχος) ?= (2)
ARKADIA:
—MEGALOPOLIS: (4) iii BC *RE* Supplbd. 1 (2) (f. Πτολεμαῖος)
—MT. KYLLENE*: (5) iv-iii BC *IG* v (2) 363
ELIS: (6) 113 AD *IvOl* 90, 6 (f. Ἀριστόδημος)
PELOPONNESE?: (7) s. iii BC *IG* IV (1) 727 B, 10 (Perlman H.2) (Ἀγήσα[ρχος])
S. ITALY (LUCANIA):
—METAPONTION: (8) iv BC Iamb., *VP* 267 (*FVS* 1 p. 446)
SICILY:
—SABUCINA (MOD.): (9) m. v BC Dubois, *IGDS* 173 (vase) (Arena, *Iscr. Sic.* II 110) ([ḫ]αγέσαρχος)

**Ἀγησιάναξ**
DALMATIA:
—ISSA:
——(Dymanes): (1) iv/iii BC Brunšmid p. 9, 54 (s. Θεμίστιος)

**Ἀγησίας**
ACHAIA: (1) 167 BC Plb. xxx 13. 3
—AIGION: (2) m. iii BC Peek, *IAEpid* 42, 24 (Perlman E.3); Perlman p. 63 f. (date) (s. Αἰσανορίδας)
ARGOLIS:
—EPIDAUROS: (3) iv/iii BC *IG* IV (1)² 202 (s. Ἀριστομήδης)
——(Azantioi): (4) 146 BC ib. 28, 36 (f. Χάριππος)
—HERMIONE: (5) ?ii-i BC ib. IV (1) 733, 6 (Ἀγησιά[δας]?: f. Θεάρης)
ARKADIA: (6) 308 BC ib. v (2) 550, 5
—MANTINEIA-ANTIGONEIA: (7) c. 300-221 BC ib. 323. 36 (tessera) (s. Ἄσινις); (8) ~ ib. 323. 37-8 (tesserae) (s. Ἀλκίας)
—PHIGALEIA: (9) i BC/i AD *SEG* XXIII 248 (Ἀγησίας)
—TEGEA:
——(Athaneatai): (10) s. iv BC *IG* v (2) 41, 34 (f. Εὐθύδαμος)
EPIROS:
—AMBRAKIA: (11) hell.? *SEG* XXIV 419 (s. Τιμόδαμος)
SICILY:
—SYRACUSE: (12) 472 or 468 BC *RE* s.v. Agesias (1); Moretti, *Olymp.* 248 (s. Σώστρατος)

**Ἀγησιβούλα**
SICILY:
—LIPARA: (1) hell.? *IG* XIV 384 (Libertini, *Isole Eolie* p. 218 no. 2)

**Ἀγησίδαμος**
ARKADIA:
—MANTINEIA-ANTIGONEIA: (1) c. 300-221 BC *IG* v (2) 323. 78 (tessera) (f. Θεοχάρης)
—MEGALOPOLIS: (2) 359 BC *CID* II 5 I, 26
—TEGEA: (3) iv/iii BC *IG* v (2) 115 (s. Ἀγησίστρατος)
DALMATIA:
—ISSA: (4) hell.? Brunšmid p. 24 no. 13 (*VAHD* 84 (1991) p. 258 no. 9) (s. Δωρικλῆς); (5) ~

Brunšmid p. 24 no. 13 (*VAHD* 84 (1991) p. 258 no. 9) (s. Φιλήσιος); (**6**) ~ Brunšmid p. 24 no. 13 (*VAHD* 84 (1991) p. 258 no. 9) (I f. Ἀγησίδαμος II); (**7**) ~ Brunšmid p. 24 no. 13 (*VAHD* 84 (1991) p. 258 no. 9) (II s. Ἀγησίδαμος I); (**8**) iii BC *SEG* XXXI 597 (s. Εὐάρης); (**9**) ii BC Brunšmid p. 27 no. 19 (*SEG* XL 515) + *VAHD* 84 (1991) p. 254 no. 4 (s. Κλήνετος)

LAKONIA:
—ASOPOS: (**10**) imp. *IG* V (1) 996 (s. Σωτηρικλῆς)
—SPARTA: (**11**) s. vii BC *PMGF* 1 10 b, 3, 11, 19 (s. Δαμότιμος)

MESSENIA:
—MESSENE: (**12**) f. iii BC *PAE* 1991, p. 99 no. 7, 28; (**13**) a. 221 BC Moretti, *Olymp.* 580

S. ITALY (BRUTTIUM):
—LOKROI EPIZEPHYRIOI: (**14**) 476 BC ib. 218 (s. Ἀρχέστρατος); (**15**) iv/iii BC De Franciscis 36, 2 (Ἀγησ[ίδα]μος)
——(Εὐρ.): (**16**) iv/iii BC ib. 12, 2 (s. Ἰηρίας)
——(Θρα.): (**17**) iv/iii BC ib. 22, 8 (s. Αἰνησίδαμος)
—TERINA: (**18**) c. 356-355 BC *IG* IV (1)² 95, 45 (Perlman E.2); Perlman pp. 46-9 (date) (f. Μέγων)

S. ITALY (LUCANIA):
—METAPONTION: (**19**) iv BC Iamb., *VP* 267 (*FVS* 1 p. 446)

SICILY:
—GELA-PHINTIAS: (**20**) vi/v BC Pi., *N.* i 29; ix 42 (f. Χρόμιος)

TRIPHYLIA: (**21**) 399-369 BC *SEG* XXXV 389, 9

## Ἀγησίδας
LAKONIA:
—SPARTA: (**1**) s. vii BC Arist. fr. 611. 9 (Poralla² 7) (Ἀγησίδα(μο)ς?—Huxley)

## Ἀγησικλείδας
LAKONIA:
—SPARTA: (**1**) c. 100 AD *SEG* XI 513, 8 (Bradford (-)) (s. Δαμοκράτης)

## Ἀγησικλῆς
ARGOLIS:
—HERMIONE?: (**1**) iv BC *IG* IV (1) 747 A, 3 (s. Ἀγίας)
LAKONIA:
—SPARTA: (**2**) f. vi BC *RE* (1) (Poralla² 2) (Ἀγασικλῆς—Poralla: ?s. Ἀρχίδαμος, Ἱπποκρατίδας, f. Ἀρίστων: king)

## Ἀγησικράτης
ARGOLIS:
—TROIZEN: (**1**) iv BC *IG* IV (1) 764, 7 (s. Μνασίας)

## Ἀγησίλαος
ACHAIA: (**1**) s. iv BC *IMM* 258 (s. Ἐράσιππος)
—KALLISTAI: (**2**) c. 230-200 BC *BCH* 45 (1921) p. 12 II, 62 (s. Νεοκράτης)
—PATRAI: (**3**) c. 146-32 BC *SNG Cop. Phliasia-Laconia* 156 (coin) (f. Δαμασίας)
—PELLENE: (**4**) c. 315-280 BC *FD* III (4) 403 IV, 1 ([Ἀγη]σίλαος)
LAKONIA: (**5**) arch.? *PLitLond* 114, 18 (Ἡ-)
—SPARTA: (**6**) her. *RE* (2) (Poralla² 8) (s. Δορυσσός, f. Ἀρχέλαος: king/dub.); (**7**) m. vi BC Hdt. viii 131. 2; cf. vi 65. 1 (Poralla² 10) (Ἡγησίλεως, Ἆγις—Hdt. vi 65: s. Ἱπποκρατίδας, f. Μενάρης); (**8**) vi/v BC *FGrH* 287 F 4; cf. Poralla² p. 9 (dub.); (**9**) c. 444-360 BC *RE* (4) (Poralla² 9) (s. Ἀρχίδαμος, Εὐπωλία, f. Ἀρχίδαμος, Εὔπωλία, Προαύγα: king) ?= (19); (**10**) iv-iii BC *SEG* XI 457, 9 (Poralla² 12) (ἁγησιλα(ο)[ς]); (**11**) 333 BC Arr., *An.* ii 13. 6 (Poralla² 11) (s. Ἀρχίδαμος, Δεινίχα); (**12**) m. iii BC *RE* (6) (Bradford (2)) (s. Εὐδαμίδας, ?s. Ἀρχιδάμεια, f. Ἱππομέδων); (**13**) c. 50-75 AD *IG* V (1) 278, 4 (Bradford (3)) (s. Νεόλας); (**14**) c. 90-110 AD *IG* V (1) 19, 7, 10, 11, 16; 667, 4; *SEG* XI

559, 1; 567? (Bradford (4)) (Γ. Ἰούλ. Ἀ.); (**15**) c. 100 AD *IG* V (1) 79, 13 (Bradford (7)) (I f. Ἀγησίλαος II); (**16**) ~ *IG* V (1) 79, 13 (Bradford (1)) (II s. Ἀγησίλαος I); (**17**) ii AD *IG* V (1) 378 b (Bradford (4)) (Ἰούλ. Ἀ.); (**18**) ~ *IG* V (1) 378 b (Bradford (6)) (Φλ. Ἀγησί[λαος])
—SPARTA?: (**19**) 396-394 BC *IEph* 133 ([Ἀ]γησίλα[ο]s) ?= (9)

S. ITALY (CAMPANIA):
—DIKAIARCHIA-PUTEOLI: (**20**) imp. *CIL* X 3037 (Lat. M. Val. Agesilaus)

## Ἀγησίλας
ARKADIA:
—LOUSOI: (**1**) 546 BC Paus. viii 18. 8
—MEGALOPOLIS: (**2**) s. ii BC *IG* V (2) 439, 67 (Ἀγησίλα[ς])
SICILY:
—SYRACUSE: (**3**) i BC-i AD? *NScav* 1892, p. 359

## Ἀγήσιλλα
AIGINA: (**1**) hell. *IG* II² 7949 (Ἀγή[σιλ]λα)

## Ἀγησίλοχος
ARKADIA:
—MANTINEIA-ANTIGONEIA: (**1**) c. 185 BC *Milet* 1 (3) 148, 20; *Chiron* 19 (1989) pp. 279 ff. (date) (f. Διοκλῆς)
ARKADIA?: (**2**) c. 230-200 BC *BCH* 45 (1921) p. 13 II, 109 (s. Ἀμφίδαμος)

## Ἀγησίμαχος
AIGINA: (**1**) s. vii BC Pi., *N.* vi, 22 (f. Σαοκλείδας)
ARKADIA:
—ALEA: (**2**) m. iii BC *BCH* 38 (1914) p. 466 no. 9, 2 (Ἀγη[σί]μαχος: s. Π—)

## Ἀγησίνικος
LAKONIA:
—SPARTA: (**1**) s. i BC *IG* V (1) 95, 8 (Bradford (1)) (s. Καλλ—); (**2**) ~ *IG* V (1) 95, 10; 135, 1; *SEG* XI 505, 2 (Bradford (4); (5)) (s. Σωκλείδας); (**3**) c. 25-1 BC *IG* V (1) 210, 16 (Bradford (2)) (s. Λαχάρης); (**4**) c. 90-100 AD *SEG* XI 558, 7 (Bradford (3)) (s. Νεόλας); (**5**) c. 105-110 AD *SEG* XI 569, 9 (Bradford (6)) (f. Καλλικρατίδας)

## Ἀγησίνοος
ARKADIA:
—MANTINEIA-ANTIGONEIA:
——(Posoidaia): (**1**) m. iv BC *IG* V (2) 271, 17 (f. Θωρακίδας)

## Ἀγησίπολις
ACHAIA:
—DYME: (**1**) 218 BC Plb. v 17. 4
AITOLIA:
—BOUKATION: (**2**) 190 BC *IG* IX (1)² (1) 97, 6
—TRICHONION: (**3**) 190 BC Sherk 37 B, 70; cf. *SEG* XXVII 123 (Ἀγησιπόλιος (fem. gen.))
—TRIKORPHOS (MOD.): (**4**) iv BC ib. XXV 624 (Ἀγησιπόλιος (gen.): f. Ἀγώ)
ARGOLIS:
—ARGOS: (**5**) f. i BC Unp. (Ch. Kritzas) (f. Αἴσχις)
LAKONIA:
—SPARTA: (**6**) c. 410-380 BC *RE* (1) (Poralla² 14) (s. Παυσανίας: king); (**7**) c. 390-370 BC *RE* (2) (Poralla² 15) (s. Κλεόμβροτος: king); (**8**) s. iii BC Plb. iv 35. 10 (Bradford (1)) (I s. Κλεόμβροτος, Χιλωνίς, f. Ἀγησίπολις II); (**9**) c. 225-184 BC Plb. iv 35. 10, 12; xxiii 6. 1; Liv. xxxiv 26. 14 (Bradford (2)) (II s. Ἀγησίπολις I: king)

## Ἀγησιππία
LAKONIA:
—SPARTA: (**1**) m. ii AD *IG* V (1) 502, 9 (Bradford (1)) (d. Ὀνασίων, m. Κλέων)

## Ἀγησιππίδας
LAKONIA:
—SPARTA: (**1**) 419 BC Th. v 52. 1; 56. 1 (Poralla² 16)

## Ἀγήσιππος
ACHAIA:
—AIGION: (**1**) m. iii BC Peek, *IAEpid* 42, 17, 22 (Perlman E.3); Perlman p. 63 f. (date) (s. Ἐράσιππος)
AITOLIA:
—THERMOS*: (**2**) hell. *IG* IX (1)² (1) 85. 5 (tile) (Ἀγήσιπ[πος])
AKARNANIA: (**3**) iii BC ib. IX (1)² (2) 580 (f. Ἀγησίστρατος)
ARKADIA:
—MEGALOPOLIS: (**4**) ii/i BC ib. V (2) 442, 12 (f. Βαθυκλῆς)
LAKONIA:
—GYTHEION: (**5**) 211 AD ib. V (1) 1163, 11 (f. Ἀριστοκράτης)
—SPARTA: (**6**) c. 25-1 BC ib. 212, 20 (Bradford (2)) (f. Πολυνίκης); (**7**) c. 90-100 AD *SEG* XI 560, 4; 609, 2 (Bradford (1)) (Ἀγ[ήσι]ππος—560: s. Ὀνασίων); (**8**) c. 125-150 AD *IG* V (1) 114, 11 (Bradford s.v. Ἀγησίππιος (-)) (Ἀγήσιππ<ι>ος: f. Νίκιππος)
S. ITALY (BRUTTIUM):
—RHEGION: (**9**) 84-80 BC *SEG* I 418, 4 (*Suppl. It.* 5 p. 59 no. 11) (f. Ὀνόμαστος)
S. ITALY (CALABRIA):
—TARAS-TARENTUM: (**10**) iv BC *RE* (5)

## Ἄγησις
AKARNANIA:
—THYRREION: (**1**) ?iii BC *SEG* XL 463
ILLYRIA:
—EPIDAMNOS-DYRRHACHION: (**2**) hell. *IDyrrh* 24 (s./d. Νικήν); (**3**) hell.-imp. ib. 80 (s./d. Ἑρμάφιλος)
KEPHALLENIA:
—SAME: (**4**) iv/iii BC *Op. Ath.* 10 (1971) p. 66 no. 14

## Ἀγησισθένης
ARKADIA?: (**1**) c. 230-200 BC *BCH* 45 (1921) p. 13 II, 111 (Ἀγησισθέν[ης]: f. Ἀστοφάνης)
LAKONIA:
—SPARTA: (**2**) c. 30-20 BC *IG* V (1) 142, 17 (Bradford (-)) (Ἀγησισθένης: s. Ἀλκιμένης)

## Ἀγησιστράτα
LAKONIA:
—SPARTA: (**1**) c. 295-241 BC Plu., *Agis* 4; 18; 20 (Bradford (-)) (d. Εὐδαμίδας, Ἀρχιδάμεια, m. Ἆγις, Ἀρχίδαμος)

## Ἀγησίστρατος
AKARNANIA: (**1**) iii BC *IG* IX (1)² (2) 580 (s. Ἀγήσιππος)
—THYRREION: (**2**) ii BC ib. 247, 8 (s. Μνασίστρατος)
ARGOLIS:
—ARGOS: (**3**) ?320 BC ib. V (2) 549, 17 (s. Περίλας); (**4**) ?272 BC *FD* III (1) 82 (s. Φίλιππος)
ARKADIA:
—MEGALOPOLIS: (**5**) 308 BC *IG* V (2) 550, 7; (**6**) ?145 BC ib. 439, 40 (f. Κερκίδας)
—TEGEA: (**7**) iv/iii BC ib. 115 (f. Ἀγησίδαμος); (**8**) hell. ib. 186; (**9**) iii-ii BC ib. 223
ELIS: (**10**) vi/v BC *RE* s.v. Hegesistratos (2) (Ἡγησίστρατος—Hdt.: mantis/Telliadai)

## Ἀγησιφῶν
ACHAIA:
—PATRAI: (**1**) m. i BC *IPhilae* 55, 7 (f. Θεόδοτος)

## Ἀγησιχόρα
LAKONIA:
—SPARTA: (**1**) s. vii BC *PMGF* 1 1, 53, 57, 77, 79, 90 (Poralla² 18)

## Ἀγησίων
ARKADIA:
—TEGEA: (1) iii/ii BC *IG* v (2) 97 (Ἀγησίω[ν])
KORINTHIA:
—KORINTH: (2) s. iii BC ib. IX (1)² (1) 24, 3 (s. Διοκλῆς)

## Ἀγησόι
LEUKAS: (1) hell. ib. IX (1) 574

## Ἀγησύλις
SICILY:
—LIPARA: (1) s. iv BC *SEG* XXXII 920 (XXXIV 957. 1); *Chiron* 22 (1992) p. 385 (name) (ἁγη-)

## Ἀγησώ
ACHAIA:
—DYME?: (1) iv BC *SEG* XXIV 340 (Ἀγήσω(ν)— ed.: d. Εὐβολλεύς)

## Ἀγήσων
AITOLIA:
—BOUKATION: (1) 190 BC *IG* IX (1)² (1) 97, 13, 14?
—DEXIEIS: (2) c. 263 BC ib. 3 A, 21; 18, 8
—KALYDON: (3) 129 BC ib. 137, 93 (f. Λύκωπος)
—PHILOTAIEIS: (4) f. ii BC ib. 96, 22 (f. Στόμας)
—PHISTYON: (5) ii BC ib. 110 a, 5; (6) ~ ib. l. 6; (7) f. ii BC ib. 111, 4 (f. Σκορπίων) ?= (9); (8) 190 BC ib. 97, 3 ?= (9); (9) ~ ib. l. 11 (s. Φαλακρίων) ?= (7) (8); (10) c. 164 BC ib. 99, 13 ?= (12); (11) 163 BC ib. 103, 10; (12) 161 BC ib. 100, 3 ?= (13) (10); (13) ~ ib. l. 9 ?= (12)
—PHISTYON?: (14) f. ii BC ib. 104, 9
AKARNANIA:
—ANAKTORION: (15) hell. *AD* 44 (1989) Chron. p. 145
—STRATOS: (16) 263-262 BC *IG* IX (1)² (1) 3 A, 23

## Ἀγήτα
LAKONIA:
—SPARTA: (1) c. 25-1 BC ib. v (1) 212, 46 (Bradford (3)); (2) i BC/i AD? *IG* v (1) 177, 5; *SEG* XI 634 (ident.) (Bradford (4)); (3) s. ii AD *SEG* XI 811, 2 + XXXV 324, 2; *BSA* 80 (1985) pp. 194; p. 225; pp. 228-9 (ident., stemma) (Bradford (2)) (Μεμμία Ἀ.: d. Π. Μέμμιος Πρατόλας, m. Τιβ. Κλ. Ἀντίπατρος, Τιβ. Κλ. Πρατόλας) ?= (5); (4) ii/iii AD *IG* v (1) 249; *BSA* 80 (1985) pp. 225; 230-1 (ident., stemma) (Bradford (1)) (Κλ. Ἀ.: d. Κλ. Ἀντίπατρος); (5) ~ *IG* v (1) 1399, 9; *BSA* 80 (1985) pp. 213-15 (ident.) (and Messenia Messene: m. Π. Αἰλ. Ἁρμόνικος (Messene)) ?= (3)

## Ἀγήτας
AITOLIA:
—BOUKATION: (1) 190 BC *IG* IX (1)² (1) 97, 11 (s. Ψυλλίων); (2) 163 BC ib. 103, 8 (f. Λυκόφρων)
—KALLION/KALLIPOLIS: (3) 218-190 BC *RE* (-); *IG* IX (1)² (1) 59 a with n.; p. L, s.a. 218 BC, 201 BC; IX (1)² (3) 614, [1]; *SGDI* 2049, 1; Sherk 37 B, 72-3; cf. *SEG* XXVII 123; *Syll*³ 636, 12; *SGDI* 1856, 16 (s. Λόχαγος, f. Λόχαγος) ?= (5); (4) ?165 BC ib. 1765, 1 (s.p.) (?s. Λόχαγος); (5) 153-144 BC ib. 2279, 2 (f. Λόχαγος) ?= (3)
AKARNANIA:
—ALYZIA: (6) m. ii BC *IG* IX (1)² (2) 208, 2, [32] (s. Νικίας)

## Ἀγητορίδας
LAKONIA:
—GERONTHRAI: (1) ii BC *SEG* 11 163 (Ἀγητο[ρίδας]?, Ἀγήτω[ρ]?: f. —ρ)
—OITYLOS: (2) iii/ii BC *IG* v (1) 1295, 8 (Bradford (4)) ([Ἀγ]ητορίδα[ς])

---

—SPARTA: (3) f. iv BC Plu., *Mor.* 578 F (Poralla² 19); (4) i BC/i AD? *IG* v (1) 177, 2; *SEG* XI 634 (name) (Bradford (1)) ([Ἀγη]τορίδας: s. Δαμοκρατίδας); (5) s. ii AD *IG* v (1) 531, 12 (Bradford (2)) (Γ. Ἰούλ. Ἀ.); (6) c. 160 AD *IG* v (1) 39, 28, 36; 71 III, 40; 86, 18 (Bradford (3))

## Ἀγητος
LAKONIA:
—SPARTA: (1) s. vi BC Hdt. vi 61-2 (Poralla² 20) (s. Ἀλκίδας)

## Ἀγήτωρ
AKARNANIA: (1) ii BC BM coin 1920 8-5-182 (coin)
ARKADIA: (2) 388 BC *RE* (3); cf. Moretti, *Olymp.* sub 384
LAKONIA:
—SPARTA: (3) s. iii BC Ath. 482a; (4) f. ii BC *IC* 4 p. 284 no. 208 A, 6 (Bradford (-)) (f. Πεδέστρατος); (5) 170 BC *SEG* XLI 115 I, 34 (f. Ὀλυμπιώ)

## Ἀγιάδας
ARGOLIS:
—EPIDAUROS: (1) hell.-imp. *IG* IV (1)² 731, 1, 5 (f. Λαμέδων, Κλειφαντίς)
——(Azantioi): (2) 146 BC ib. 28, 38 (f. Ἀριστόβιος)
ARKADIA:
—MEGALOPOLIS: (3) 263 BC ib. IX (1)² (1) 17, 12 (s. Κλεόδαμος)
ELIS: (4) vi/v BC Moretti, *Olymp.* 183
—PISA: (5) 365-363 BC *IvOl* 36, 5 (Perlman O.1)
EPIROS:
—BOUTHROTOS (PRASAIBOI):
——Opatai: (6) a. 163 BC *IBouthrot* 93, 7 (s. Στράταγος)
—PANDOSIA: (7) 168-148 BC *BMC Thessaly* p. 109 no. 1; Franke, *Münz. v. Epirus* p. 110 I ser. 2 (coin); p. 109 (name) (Ἀγιά(δας))
KORINTHIA:
—SIKYON: (8) s. iii BC *SEG* III 348, 2 (Ἀγιάδας: s. Ἀγις)
LAKONIA:
—GYTHEION: (9) ii-iii AD *IG* v (1) 1196
—SPARTA: (10) s. i BC ib. 124, 16 (Bradford (3)) (s. Φιλισ—); (11) c. 90-120 AD *IG* v (1) 31, 2 + *SEG* XI 483; *IG* v (1) 79, 11; *SEG* XI 539, 6; 641, 1 (Bradford (2)) (f. Δαμοκρατίδας); (12) c. 105-110 AD *IG* v (1) 97, 11; *SEG* XI 564, 18; 569, 5 (Bradford (2)) (s. Δαμοκρατίδας); (13) c. 130 AD *IG* v (1) 60, 2 (Bradford (5)) (Ἀ<ι>γιάδας: f. Δείναρχος); (14) 137 AD *IG* v (1) 59, 3; *SEG* XI 521 b, 2 (Bradford (1)) (Ἀγι(ά)δας—59: s. Ἀριστοκράτης); (15) c. 140-150 AD *IG* v (1) 64, 13 (Bradford (6)) (f. Δικαίαρχος)

## Ἀγίας
ACHAIA: (1) m. iii BC *TCal* 32, 5, 17 (f. Λύσιππος)
—AIGION: (2) c. 271 BC *IG* IX (1)² (1) 12, 15 (s. Κλεοσθένης)
—DYME: (3) ?iii-ii BC *SGDI* 1619 (f. Κληνίς)
—PATRAI: (4) ii/i BC *SEG* XIX 400, 1 (f. Τιμανορίδας); (5) 32-31 BC *BMC Pelop.* p. 23 nos. 14-15; *RPC* I p. 259 no. 1245 (coin) (s. Λύσων)
AITOLIA: (6) ?262 or 258 BC Nachtergael, *Les Galates* 5, 8
—NEOPOLIS: (7) 213 BC *IG* IX (1)² (1) 96, 15-16
—PROSCH(E)ION: (8) 250 BC ib. XI (2) 287 B, 127; XI 1075 (f. Νικόλαος)
AKARNANIA:
—THYRREION: (9) iii BC ib. IX (1)² (2) 245, 16 (Ἀγ[ίας]); (10) ~ ib. 597 (s. Νίκανδρος)
AKARNANIA?: (11) c. 325-315 BC *Hesp.* 57 (1988) p. 148 B, 4 (*SEG* XXXVI 331); cf. *Hesp.*

---

48 (1979) pp. 78 f. with pl. 22; cf. Perlman p. 174 (locn.) (s. Κλε—)
ARGOLIS:
—ARGOS: (12) ?s. iv BC *FGrH* 305; cf. Fraser, *Ptol. Alex.* 2 p. 1010 n. 42 and n. 63; (13) c. 235 BC Plu., *Arat.* 29; (14) ?125 BC *FD* III (2) 69, 8 = *IG* II² 1134, 13; *FD* III (4) 277 B, [10] (f. Ἐμπεδοσθένης)
—HERMIONE?: (15) iv BC *IG* IV (1) 747 A, 4 (f. Ἀγησικλῆς)
—TROIZEN: (16) vii-vi BC *RE* s.v. Hagias (1)
ARKADIA: (17) 401 BC X., *An.* ii 5. 31
—HERAIA: (18) 369-361 BC *IG* v (2) 1, 62; Tod, *GHI* II 132 (date)
—KLEITOR: (19) 331-328 BC *Syll*³ 291 (f. Χαρίδαμος); (20) c. 230-200 BC *BCH* 45 (1921) p. 12 II, 69 + *SEG* XXX 494 (s. Ἀνάξιππος)
—LYKOSOURA*: (21) f. ii AD *IG* v (2) 520 (f. Τιμοκρατέα)
—MAINALIOI: (22) 369-361 BC ib. 1, 17; Tod, *GHI* II 132 (date)
—MANTINEIA-ANTIGONEIA: (23) 362 BC *CID* II 1 II, 24
—MEGALOPOLIS: (24) 316 BC *IG* v (2) 549, 23
—ORCHOMENOS: (25) ?ii BC ib. 345, 8 (f. Δαμόξενος: date—LGPN)
—PHENEOS: (26) m. iii BC ib. IX (1)² (1) 22, 2 (f. Λάαλκος)
—TEGEA:
——(Krariotai): (27) f. iii BC ib. v (2) 36, 48 (f. Ἀγέμαχος: metic)
—THELPHOUSA: (28) s. iii BC *FD* III (4) 15 (f. Φιλίσκος)
ELIS: (29) 479 BC Hdt. ix 33. 5 (Poralla² 21) (and Lakonia Sparta: Ἡγίης: s. Ἀντίοχος: mantis/Iamidai); (30) i BC/i AD *IvOl* 74, 3 (Ἀγί[ας]: f. Σωσιμένης); (31) i AD ib. 77, 6; 82, 4; 86, 4; 432, 3; 433, 3; 434, 3 (Τιβ. Κλ. Ἀ.: s. Λύσων, f. Τιβ. Κλ. Λύσων Κοσμόπολις: Π.)
ILLYRIA:
—APOLLONIA: (32) c. 250-50 BC Maier 38 (coin) (Münsterberg Nachtr. p. 53; Ceka 1-3) (money.)
—EPIDAMNOS-DYRRHACHION: (33) hell. *IDyrrh* 81 (s. Ἀριστοφάνης)
KORINTHIA:
—KORINTH: (34) 329 BC *IG* II² 1672, 157, 170 (Ἡγίας—l. 170)
—SIKYON: (35) c. 365-330 BC BM coin 1893 6-4-28; *Coll. McClean* 6251 (coin) (Ἀγία[s], Ἀγιά[δας]?)
LAKONIA:
—GYTHEION: (36) i-ii AD *IG* v (1) 1176, 1 (f. Εὔτυχος)
—SPARTA: (37) 405 BC Paus. iii 11. 5; x 9. 7 (Poralla² 22) (Ἄβας—Paus. x: s. Ἀγέλοχος: mantis); (38) 352 BC *CID* II 31, 65 (Poralla² 23)
MESSENIA:
—MESSENE: (39) ii/i BC *IvOl* 397, 5; 398, 4 (f. Ἀριστομένης: sculptor); (40) i BC ib. 399, 5; 400, 4; cf. *SEG* XL 388 (s. Ἀριστομένης, f. Πυρίλαμπος: sculptor)
—THOURIA: (41) s. iii BC *IG* v (1) 1386, 1 (Ἀγιά[δας]?—IG)
S. ITALY (LUCANIA):
—METAPONTION: (42) m. iii BC *SEG* XXX 1175, 14 (doctor)
SICILY:
—MEGARA HYBLAIA: (43) vi/v BC Guarducci, *Ep. Gr.* 1 pp. 315-16 no. 6 (Dubois, *IGDS* 27; Arena, *Iscr. Sic.* I 7) (ha-: f. Καπρόγονον)
—SELINOUS: (44) vi/v BC Manganaro, *PdelP* forthcoming no. 18, 9 (ἁγί[ας]: f. Σιλανός); (45) ~ ib. l. 11 (ha-: s. Φιλόδαμος)
TRIPHYLIA:
—MAKISTOS: (46) 399-369 BC *SEG* XXXV 389, 10

ZAKYNTHOS: (47) ?iii BC *Memnonion* 443

**Ἀγιᾶτις**
LAKONIA:
—SPARTA: (1) c. 260-224 BC Plu., *Cleom.* 1; 22 (Bradford (-)) (d. Γύλιππος, m. Εὐρυδαμίδας)

**Ἀγίδαμος**
MESSENIA:
—ABIA: (1) i AD *IG* V (1) 1354 (I f. Ἀγίδαμος II); (2) ~ ib. (II s. Ἀγίδαμος I)

**Ἀγιδώ**
LAKONIA:
—SPARTA: (1) s. vii BC *PMGF* 1 1, 40, 42, 58, 80 (Poralla² 24)

**Ἀγίεια**
LAKONIA:
—GERONTHRAI: (1) iii-ii BC *IG* V (1) 1127, 2; (2) ~ ib. l. 3

**Ἀγιεύς**
ARGOLIS:
—ARGOS?: (1) v BC ib. IV (1) 533, 5
—MYKENAI: (2) iii/ii BC *SEG* III 312, 6 (Ἀγ[ι]εύς)

**Ἄγιλλος**
AIGINA: (1) v/iv BC *IG* IV (1)² 236 (Lazzarini 748) (háγι-: f. Ἀνδρόκριτος)

**Ἀγίλοχος**
ELIS: (1) i BC Moretti, *Olymp.* 711; *IvOl* 191 (s. Νικέας) ?= (2); (2) m. i BC ib. 412, 2 (f. Νικέας) ?= (1)

**Ἀγιμένης**
KORINTHIA:
—SIKYON: (1) ?255 BC Nachtergael, *Les Galates* 8, 57 (Stephanis 40) (s. Φιλομένης)

**Ἄγιον**
LAKONIA:
—SPARTA: (1) c. 220 AD *IG* V (1) 653 b, 11 (*Artemis Orthia* p. 356-8 no. 143); *BSA* 79 (1984) pp. 279-82 (ident., date) (Bradford (-)) (Αὐρ. Ἀ.: d. Εὔδαμος, m. Σέξ. Πομπ. Γόργιππος, ?m. Σέξ. Πομπ. Εὔδαμος, Σέξ. Πομπ. Ὀνασικράτης)
MESSENIA:
—ABIA: (2) i AD *IG* V (1) 1354 (Ἰουλ. Ἀ.)

**Ἄγιος**
S. ITALY (CAMPANIA):
—SALERNUM: (1) imp. *IItal* I (1) 42 (*CIL* X 567) (Lat. C. Caesonius Hagius: s. Ὕμνος)

**Ἀγιππία**
LAKONIA:
—SPARTA: (1) ?ii-i BC *IG* V (1) 714 (Bradford (-))

**Ἀγιππίδας**
LAKONIA:
—SPARTA: (1) ?i AD *IG* V (1) 337; *Artemis Orthia* p. 341 no. 89 (date) (Bradford (-)) (f. Θευ—)

**Ἄγιππος**
LAKONIA:
—KARDAMYLE: (1) i AD *SEG* XI 948, 18 (f. Πρατόνικος)
—OITYLOS: (2) iii/ii BC *IG* V (1) 1295, 4 (Bradford (2))
—SPARTA: (3) c. 110-150 AD *IG* V (1) 114, 10; *SEG* XI 516, [2]; 543, 4 (Bradford (1)) ([Ἄ]γ[ι]ππος—*SEG* XI 543: s. Πωλλίων)
MESSENIA:
—MESSENE: (4) imp. *PAE* 1970, p. 139 (Ἀγιππ[ος])
ZAKYNTHOS: (5) c. 245-236 BC *IG* IX (1)² (1) 25, 67 (f. Τιμοκράτης)

**Ἆγις**
AITOLIA:
—BOUKATION?: (1) c. 162 BC ib. 106, 11 (Ἀγ(ι)ς)
—DEXIEIS: (2) c. 245-236 BC ib. 25, 71 (Ἀγ[ις])
ARGOLIS:
—ARGOS: (3) ?c. 575-550 BC *SEG* XI 314, 9; *LSAG*² p. 168 no. 8 (date) (háγι[ς]?); (4) c. 458 BC *IG* I³ 1149, 29 ([Ἆ]γις); (5) s. iv BC *RE* (8); Berve 16; Stephanis 4
ARKADIA:
—MEGALOPOLIS: (6) 208 BC *IMM* 38, 26; (7) ii/i BC *IG* V (2) 442, 14 (s. Ξε—)
—THELPHOUSA: (8) s. iii BC *FD* III (4) 20 + *SEG* XXXI 540 (Ἀγιφιλέας—*FD*: s. Φιλέας)
ELIS: (9) 572 BC Moretti, *Olymp.* 93
EPIROS:
—DODONA*: (10) iv-iii BC *SGDI* 1586
KERKYRA: (11) hell. *IG* IX (1) 894, 1 (s. Ἀμφίαλος)
KORINTHIA:
—SIKYON: (12) s. iii BC *SEG* III 348, 2 ([Ἆγι]δος (gen.): f. Ἀγιάδας)
LAKONIA:
—SPARTA: (13) arch.? *IPr* 316, 9 ?= (16); (14) her. *RE* (1); cf. Bilabel 13 IV verso (Poralla² 25) ([Αἰ]γεύς—Bilabel: s. Εὐρυσθένης, f. Ἐχέστρατος, Ἀμφικλῆς, ?f. Λυκοῦργος: king/dub.); (15) ?viii-vii BC *HE* 2717 (Poralla² 28) (s. Ἰφικρατίδας, Ἀλεξίππα: fict.?); (16) c. 460-400 BC *RE* (2) (Poralla² 26) (s. Ἀρχίδαμος, Λαμπιτώ, f. Λατυχίδας: king) ?= (13); (17) c. 375-330 BC *RE* (3) (Poralla² 27) (s. Ἀρχίδαμος, Δεινίχα: king); (18) c. 275-241 BC *RE* (4) (Bradford (1)) (s. Εὐδαμίδας, Ἀγησιστράτα, f. Εὐρυδαμίδας: king); (19) ii BC *SEG* XI 856, 3 (Bradford (3)) (Ἆγις: s. Ἀριστοκλῆς); (20) c. 30-20 BC *IG* V (1) 211, 29 (Bradford (5)) (s. Στράτιος); (21) c. 25-1 BC *IG* V (1) 210, 31 (Bradford (8)) (f. Κληνικίδας); (22) ?i AD *IG* V (1) 588 (Bradford (9)) (f. Ἰουλ. Παντιμία); (23) ?s. i AD *IG* V (1) 358; *SEG* XI 485, 3 (Bradford (4)); (24) ~ *SEG* XI 532, 1 (Bradford (6)); (25) c. 70-100 AD *IG* V (1) 281, 5 (*Artemis Orthia* pp. 314-15 no. 34; Bradford (4)) (s. Κλέανδρος); (26) m. ii AD *IG* V (1) 71 II, 14; 71 III, 51; 86, 29; 494, 2; *BSA* 80 (1985) p. 242 (stemma) (Bradford (2)) (Γ. Πομπώνιος Ἀ.: s. Ἀλκαστος)
LAKONIA?: (27) ?c. 550 BC *Ét. Thas.* 9 pp. 25-6 fig. 32; *LSAG*² p. 447 no. B (—αγις?)
S. ITALY (CALABRIA):
—TARAS-TARENTUM: (28) iv/iii BC *IG* XIV 668 I, 12 (Landi, *DISMG* 194) (hᾶ-); (29) 281 BC *RE* (6)

**Ἀγίς**
LAKONIA:
—SPARTA: (1) c. 110-130 AD *BSA* 89 (1994) pp. 437-8 no. 10, 2 (Ὀκτ. Ἀ.: d. Ὀκτ. Λογγῖνος, Ἰουλ. Νίκιον)

**Ἀγιστέα**
S. ITALY (LUCANIA):
—METAPONTION: (1) iv BC Landi, *DISMG* 150 (hαγιστέα (gen.?))

**Ἀγιτέλης**
LAKONIA:
—SPARTA: (1) c. 25-1 BC *IG* V (1) 210, 56; 212, 62 (Bradford (-))
MESSENIA:
—THOURIA: (2) f. ii BC *SEG* XI 972, 84 (f. Χηρικράτης)

**Ἀγίων**
ACHAIA:
—PELLENE?: (1) ?263-261 BC *FD* III (3) 190, 7 (f. Ἀγέας)
ARKADIA:
—LOUSOI: (2) c. 230-200 BC *BCH* 45 (1921) p. 12 II, 68 (f. Ἀλκέτας)
—MEGALOPOLIS: (3) 191-146 BC *BMC Pelop.* p. 14 no. 166 (coin) (Ἀγίω[ν])

ILLYRIA:
—EPIDAMNOS-DYRRHACHION: (4) c. 250-50 BC Maier 94; 96 (Ceka 355; 395); *Iliria* 1971, p. 97 nos. 41-2 (coin) (pryt.)
LAKONIA:
—SPARTA: (5) hell.-imp. *IG* V (1) 195, 7 (Bradford (5)); (6) i BC/i AD? *IG* V (1) 177, 1 (Bradford (3)) (f. Μουσαῖος); (7) c. 95-145 AD *SEG* XI 490, 1, 7; 544, 4; 574, 6; 579, [1] (Bradford (1)) (s. Ἀρτεμίσιος); (8) c. 150-160 AD *SEG* XI 585, 12; XXX 410, [18] (Bradford (4)) (f. Φιλωνίδας); (9) c. 175-200 AD *SEG* XI 503, 23 (Bradford (2)) (Γ. Ἰούλ. Ἀ.: s. Φιλωνίδας)
MESSENIA:
—MESSENE?: (10) ii/i BC *SEG* XI 979, 56
S. ITALY (BRUTTIUM):
—LOKROI EPIZEPHYRIOI:
——(Κοβ.): (11) iv/iii BC De Franciscis 32, 5 (s. Χαρίξενος)

**Ἀγκαίδας**
LAKONIA:
—SPARTA: (1) f. vi BC *SEG* XXXV 319 (Ἀν-, Ἀγκαίδας?: date—R.W.V.C.)

**Ἀγκαῖος**
S. ITALY (CAMPANIA):
—DIKAIARCHIA-PUTEOLI*: (1) imp. *CIL* X 1963 (Lat. Ancaeus: slave?)

**Ἀγλαΐς**
S. ITALY (CALABRIA):
—TARAS-TARENTUM: (1) imp. *NScav* 1893, p. 254 no. 3 (Lat. Aglai[s])

**Ἀγλαΐων**
ELIS:
—OLYMPIA*: (1) s. v BC *Ol. Forsch.* 5 p. 150 no. 1

**Ἄγλαος**
ARGOLIS:
—EPIDAUROS: (1) ?iv AD *IG* IV (1)² 517 + Peek, *IAEpid* 211 ([Ἄ]γλαος: s. Μηνογένης)
ARKADIA:
—PSOPHIS: (2) 685-657 BC *RE* (3) (fict.?)
LAKONIA:
—SPARTA: (3) c. 105 AD *SEG* XI 546 a, 6; 546 b, 6 (Bradford (-)) (f. Γ. Ἀντ. Ὠφελίων)
S. ITALY (CALABRIA):
—RUDIAE: (4) i AD *NScav* 1957, p. 197 (Susini, *Fonti Salento* p. 111 no. 48) (Lat. M. Caprius Aglaus)

**Ἀγλαοτέλης**
ITHAKE: (1) 208 BC *IMM* 36, 2 ([Ἀ]γλαοτέλης)

**Ἀγλαόφαμος**
ARGOLIS:
—METHANA-ARSINOE: (1) ?i BC *IG* IV (1) 853, 2 ([Ἀγλ]αόφαμος)

**Ἀγλάων**
ITHAKE: (1) hell. *BCH* 29 (1905) p. 164 no. 5 (reading—Strauch)

**Ἀγλωκράτης**
ARGOLIS:
—TROIZEN: (1) ?146 BC *IG* IV (1) 757 B, 7 (Ἀγλωκρά[της]: s. —λισ—)

**Ἀγλώμαχος**
ARKADIA:
—TEGEA?: (1) m. iii BC ib. V (2) 368, 4 (Ἀγ(λ)ώμαχος)

**Ἀγλωτέλης**
ARGOLIS:
—EPIDAUROS:
——Melkidon: (1) c. 335-325 BC ib. IV (1)² 106 I, 11, 16 (Ἀ[γλ]ωτέλης)

**Ἀγλωτρόφης**
DALMATIA:
—ISSA: (1) iii BC Brunšmid p. 9 fr. G, 14
(Ἀγλωτρόφ[ης]: f. —οτο[ς])
——(Hylleis): (2) iv/iii BC ib. p. 8, 31 (s. —τος);
(3) ~ ib. l. 48 (s. Μνάστηρ); (4) ~ ib. p. 9, 57
([Ἀ]γλωτρόφης: s. Δαφναῖος)

**Ἀγλωφάνης**
ARGOLIS:
—HERMIONE: (1) ?ii-i BC IG IV (1) 733, 5
(Ἀγλωφ[άνης]: f. Λύσων)

**Ἀγναγόρα**
MESSENIA: (1) vii BC RE (-) (?d. Νικομήδης,
Πύρρος, d. Νικοτέλεια: fict.)

**Ἀγναγόρας**
ARKADIA:
—TEGEA: (1) ii BC IG V (2) 43, 7 (Ἀγναγ[όρας]:
f. Πασιτέλης)

**Ἀγναμπτος**
ARGOLIS:
—EPIDAUROS*: (1) c. 370-360 BC Peek, IAEpid
52 A, 4; BSA 61 (1966) p. 271 no. 4 A, 7 +
Peek, IAEpid 48

**Ἀγνείας**
ARGOLIS:
—EPIDAUROS*: (1) c. 370-365 BC ib. 52 A, 73
(Ἀγνε[ί]α[ς])

**Ἀγνη**
KORINTHIA:
—KORINTH: (1) ii AD Corinth VIII (3) 182 (Lat.
Hagne)
LAKONIA:
—SPARTA: (2) iii AD IG V (1) 733, 2 (GVI 1054;
Bradford (-)) (m. Φαῦστος)
S. ITALY (CAMPANIA):
—BAIAI*: (3) s. i AD Puteoli 3 (1979) p. 160 no.
4 (Lat. Acilia Hagne: freed.?)
—DIKAIARCHIA-PUTEOLI: (4) ?ii AD CIL X 1933
(Lat. Coelia Hagne)
SICILY:
—KATANE: (5) iii-v AD Agnello 59 (Wessel 353);
cf. Ferrua, NG 417
—ZANKLE-MESSANA: (6) imp. CIL X 6980 (Lat.
Numitoria Hagne)

**Ἀγνίας**
S. ITALY (CAMPANIA):
—DIKAIARCHIA-PUTEOLI: (1) imp. CIL X 2031
(Lat. Agnia: s. Ἀγνος, Sucessa)

**Ἀγνόθεμις**
AIGINA: (1) i BC-i AD IG IV (1) 44 + AD 31
(1976) Chron. p. 7 (f. Εὐάμερος)

**Ἀγνος**
S. ITALY (CAMPANIA):
—DIKAIARCHIA-PUTEOLI: (1) imp. CIL X 2031
(Lat. Agnos: f. Ἀγνίας)
—DIKAIARCHIA-PUTEOLI*: (2) imp. NScav
1885, p. 169 (Lat. C. Geminius Hagnus:
freed.)
SICILY:
—KAMARINA: (3) s. v BC Dubois, IGDS 121,
22 (Arena, Iscr. Sic. II 143; SEG XXXVIII
940; Cordano, 'Camarina VII' 9) (—ραγνος—
Arena)

**Ἀγνώ**
EPIROS:
—NIKOPOLIS: (1) imp. SEG XXXIX 543 (Ἀγνω
Σ—lap.)

**Ἀγνων**
ARGOLIS:
—PHLEIOUS: (1) ii BC IG IV (1) 453

---

S. ITALY (CALABRIA):
—TARAS-TARENTUM?: (2) f. iii BC HE 2178 (s.
Εὐάνθης)

**Ἀγοραῖος**
AITOLIA:
—APERANTOI: (1) ?ii BC IG IX (1)² (1) 164 (f.
Τελένικος)

**Ἀγόραισος**
ARGOLIS:
—HERMIONE: (1) iii-ii BC ib. IV (1) 679, 36
(Perlman H.3) (s. Πραξίας)

**Ἀγοράσιος**
SICILY:
—SYRACUSE: (1) iii-v AD Strazzulla 215; cf. Fer-
rua, NG 282 (n. pr.?)

**Ἀγοράστη**
SICILY:
—ZANKLE-MESSANA: (1) ii/iii AD Epigraphica 3
(1941) p. 257 no. 12 (Riv. Arch. Crist. 18
(1941) p. 232 no. 125) (Αὐρ. Ἀ. Ἰλαριτάς)

**Ἀγόρατος**
EPIROS:
—AMBRAKIA: (1) m. iii BC IG V (2) 368, 21
(Ἀ[γό]ρατος: f. Πυθόδωρος)

**Ἀγουσία**
KEPHALLENIA: (1) s. ii AD SEG XXX 516 (Οὐλπία Ἀ.)

**Ἀγραπτος**
ELIS?: (1) ?i AD RE (-)

**Ἀγρέας**
ARKADIA:
—TEGEA: (1) iv/iii BC IG V (2) 32, 11

**Ἀγριος**
AITOLIA: (1) ?253 BC Nachtergael, Les Galates
10, 4
—PSOLOUNTIOI: (2) s. ii BC SEG XXV 621, 10
(s. Κλεόξενος)
S. ITALY (CAMPANIA):
—POMPEII: (3) c. 51-62 AD CIL IV 3340. 82, 1
(Castrèn 118. 2) (Lat. Claudius Agrius)
SICILY:
—HALAISA: (4) ii BC IGSI 2 A II, 38 (Dubois,
IGDS 196)

**Ἀγρίππας**
EPIROS:
—NIKOPOLIS: (1) imp. Hellenika 22 (1969) p.
70 no. 7 (Sarikakis 46) (Ἀγρή-: f. Εὐάρεστος)

**Ἀγριππιανή**
ACHAIA:
—PATRAI: (1) iv-v AD SEG XXIX 425, 2

**Ἀγριππῖνος**
SICILY:
—ZANKLE-MESSANA: (1) imp. IG XIV 403 (-πεῖ-)

**Ἀγρίτας**
AIGINA: (1) ?c. 475-450 BC CEG I 129; LSAG²
p. 113 no. 18 (date) (n. pr.?: ?f. Κυδόνικος)

**Ἀγροίτας**
AITOLIA:
—KONOPE-ARSINOE: (1) c. 200 BC SBBerlAk
1936, p. 362 no. 2

**Ἀγροίτης**
SICILY:
—CALTANISSETA (MOD.): (1) s. iv BC Guarducci, Ep. Gr. 3 p. 482 (vase) (Dubois, IGDS
170)

---

**Ἀγρολέων**
AITOLIA:
—KALLION/KALLIPOLIS: (1) f. iii BC IG IX (2)
216, 2 (f. Ἀγεστος)

**Ἀγρων**
ILLYRIA:
—APOLLONIA: (1) ?ii BC IApoll 126 (f. Νικαία)
—ARDIAIOI: (2) iii BC RE (3) (s. Πλευράτος, f.
Πίννης: king)

**Ἀγυλαῖος**
LAKONIA:
—SPARTA: (1) c. 227 BC Plu., Cleom. 8 (Brad-
ford (-))

**Ἀγυλίδας**
KORINTHIA:
—KORINTH: (1) iii-ii BC IG XII (3) 832 (f. Φιλ-
ήρατος)

**Ἀγυλις**
SICILY:
—KAMARINA: (1) ?f. iii BC SEG XXXIV 947
(vase) (Cordano, 'Camarina VII' 66) (Ἀγύλιος
(gen.), ἀγύλιος (adj.?)—Cordano)

**Ἀγυλλος**
ACHAIA:
—PATRAI: (1) m. iii BC IG V (2) 368, 61
([Ἀ]γυλλος: s. Κλεομένης)
TRIPHYLIA:
—PHRIXA: (2) c. 230-200 BC BCH 45 (1921) p.
13 II, 87 (f. Πύρριχος, Ξενόδοκος, Μορφίων)

**Ἀγύλος**
LAKONIA: (1) m. vi BC Paus. v 17. 2; vi 19. 8
(Poralla² 348) (Ἡ-: f. Θεοκλῆς: sculptor)
S. ITALY (BRUTTIUM):
—KROTON: (2) iv BC Iamb., VP 267 (FVS I p.
446)
S. ITALY (LUCANIA):
—HERAKLEIA: (3) iv/iii BC SEG XXX 1163

**Ἀγύρανος**
SICILY:
—KAMARINA: (1) f. v BC Cordano, Tessere Pub-
bliche 29 ([Ἀ]γύρανος: f. Ἀλίας)

**Ἀγυρις**
SICILY:
—AGYRION: (1) v/iv BC D.S. xiv 9. 2; 78. 7; 95.
4 ff.; cf. RE s.v. Agyrion (-) (tyrant)

**Ἀγυς**
ACHAIA:
—PATRAI: (1) c. 146-32 BC BMC Pelop. p. 22
no. 1 (coin) (s. Αἰσχρίων)

**Ἀγχέμαχος**
AITOLIA:
—KALLION/KALLIPOLIS: (1) 175 BC SGDI
1987, 12 (f. Ἀγέλαος)
SICILY:
—AKRAGAS: (2) vi/v BC Acragas Graeca 1 p. 30
no. 1 (Dubois, IGDS 178; Arena, Iscr. Sic. II
89) (Ἀνχέ-: f. —τό)

**Ἀγχίαλος**
ARKADIA:
—TEGEA: (1) ii AD IG V (2) 123 (Ἀν-)

**Ἀγχίβιος**
LAKONIA:
—GERONTHRAI: (1) c. 500 BC ib. V (1) 1134,
3; LSAG² p. 201 no. 45 (date) (Poralla² 29)
(Ἀν-)

**Ἀγχιθέα**
LAKONIA:
—SPARTA: (1) vi/v BC Suda Π 820 (Poralla² p.
13) (?m. Παυσανίας, Νικομήδης)

**Ἀγχίμαχος**
ILLYRIA:
—BYLLIONES BYLLIS: (1) imp. Iliria 1987 (2),
p. 105 no. 64 (Lat. Anchimachi (gen.?))

## Ἀγχίμολος
LAKONIA:
—SPARTA: (1) 511 BC Hdt. v 63; Arist., *Ath.* 19. 5; Schol. Ar., *Lys.* 1153 (Poralla² 30) (Ἀγχιμόλιος—Hdt.: s. Ἀστήρ)

## Ἀγχίπυλος
ELIS: (1) iv BC D.L. ii 126; Ath. 44c (Ἀρχίπυλος—D.L. cod. D, Ἀγχίμολος—Ath.)

## Ἀγχίτας
SICILY:
—GELA-PHINTIAS: (1) v BC *FVS* I p. 308 F 1 + Page, *FGE* 550; cf. Iamb., *VP.* 113 (Ἀγχίτος—Iamb.: f. Παυσανίας)

## Ἀγώ
AITOLIA:
—TRIKORPHOS (MOD.): (1) iv BC *SEG* XXV 624 (d. Ἀγησίπολις)
ARGOLIS:
—HERMIONE: (2) ?ii-i BC *IG* IV (1) 731 III, 9 (m. Νικοβούλα)
ARKADIA:
—MANTINEIA-ANTIGONEIA: (3) ii-i BC ib. II² 9279 (*Ag.* XVII 538) (d. Εὐήρης)
—MEGALOPOLIS: (4) i BC *IG* V (2) 466; (5) ii AD ib. 465
EPIROS:
—ARGOS (AMPHILOCH.): (6) iv/iii BC *AD* 42 (1987) Chron. p. 184 (*SEG* XLII 483) (Ἀγώς (gen.))
ILLYRIA:
—EPIDAMNOS-DYRRHACHION: (7) hell.-imp. *IDyrrh* 82

## Ἄγων
SICILY:
—THERMAI HIMERAIAI: (1) i-ii AD *CIL* X 7398 a (*ILat. Term. Imer.* 88) (Lat. Caninius Agon)

## Ἀγωνίππα
AITOLIA:
—KALLION/KALLIPOLIS: (1) iii/ii BC *IG* IX (1)² (1) 155

## Ἀγώνιππος
AITOLIA: (1) ?225 BC Nachtergael, *Les Galates* 63, 2
ARKADIA:
—HERAIA: (2) m. iii BC *IG* IV (1)² 96, 43 (Perlman E.3); Perlman p. 63 f. (date) (f. Ἀριστοκράτης)
EPIROS:
—BOUTHROTOS (PRASAIBOI): (3) a. 163 BC *IBouthrot* 36, 14 (*SEG* XXXVIII 495) (s. Εὐαλκίδας)
ILLYRIA:
—APOLLONIA: (4) i BC Maier 137 (coin) (money.); (5) ~ ib. 162 (coin) (I f. Ἀγώνιππος II); (6) ~ ib. (coin) (II s. Ἀγώνιππος I: money.); (7) ~ ib. 123-5 (coin) (pryt.)
SICILY:
—TAUROMENION: (8) c. 238 BC *IG* XIV 421 an. 3 (*SGDI* 5219) (f. Ἡράκλητος)

## Ἀγωνίς
AKARNANIA:
—STRATOS: (1) iv/iii BC *SEG* XXIX 476
ARKADIA:
—MANTINEIA-ANTIGONEIA: (2) ii BC *IG* V (2) 286
SICILY:
—LILYBAION*: (3) f. i BC Cic., *In Caecil.* 55-6 (Lat. Agonis: freed.)

## Ἀγώνυμος
ARKADIA: (1) s. iv BC Unp. (Tripolis Mus.)

## Ἀδάη
S. ITALY: (1) ?iii-iv AD *IG* VII 2543, 4 (*GVI* 2035) (m. Νήδυμος (Boiotia, Thebes): Ital.)

## Ἀδαμάντιος
KORINTHIA:
—KORINTH: (1) byz. *Corinth* VIII (3) 582, 3; cf. *TMByz* 9 (1985) p. 363 no. 42

## Ἀδάμας
ARGOLIS:
—ARGOS: (1) f. iii BC *CID* II 122 I, 10 (s. Ὁρμασίλας)
—HERMIONE: (2) iii BC *IG* IV (1) 729 II, 9 (f. Ἀντίοχος)
ARKADIA:
—MANTINEIA-ANTIGONEIA: (3) c. 300-221 BC ib. v (2) 323. 101 (tessera) (s. Αἰσαγένης)

## Ἀδάμαστος
AKARNANIA:
—THYRREION: (1) ii BC ib. IX (1)² (2) 251, 9 (s. Φίλιππος)

## Ἀδαμάτας
EPIROS:
—VOTONOSI (MOD.): (1) ?iii BC *SEG* XXIV 465 (Ἀδα[μ]άτας: s. Νίκανδρος)
ILLYRIA:
—EPIDAMNOS-DYRRHACHION: (2) imp. *IDyrrh* 83 (Ἀδαμά[τας], Ἀδαμά[του], Ἀδάμα[ντος]? (gen.))
S. ITALY (CALABRIA):
—TARAS-TARENTUM: (3) vi BC Paus. vi 14. 11 (f. Ἄνοχος)

## Ἀδάματος
ILLYRIA:
—SKODRAI: (1) a. 168 BC *Iliria* 1972, p. 403; *God. Balk. Isp.* 13. 11 (1976) p. 225 no. 5 (coin)

## Ἀδέας
KORINTHIA:
—SIKYON: (1) f. iv BC X., *HG* vii 1. 45; *IG* II² 448 7, 13, 41 (Skalet 10) (s. Εὔφρων, f. Εὔφρων)

## Ἀδείμαντος
ACHAIA:
—DYME*: (1) c. 219 BC *SGDI* 1612, 24 (*Tyche* 5 (1990) p. 124) (f. Θρασύβουλος)
AKARNANIA:
—TYRBEION/TORYBEIA?: (2) m. iv BC *BCH* 63 (1939) p. 145 inv. 4000, 2; cf. *CID* II sub 26 (ident.) (II s. Ἀδείμαντος I) ?= (4); (3) ~ *BCH* 63 (1939) p. 145 inv. 4000, 3; cf. *CID* II sub 26 (I f. Ἀδείμαντος II); (4) c. 334 BC ib. 26, 20 ([Ἀδε]ίμαντος: s. Ἀ—) ?= (2)
ARGOLIS:
—EPIDAUROS: (5) inc. *IG* IV (1)² 738 (Ἀδείμα[ντος])
KORINTHIA:
—KORINTH: (6) f. v BC *RE* (2); Plu., *Mor.* 871 A; Page, *FGE* 718 with comm. (s. Ὤκυτος, f. Ἀριστεύς, Ναυσινίκα, Ἀκροθίνιον, Ἀλεξιβία)
LAKONIA:
—SPARTA: (7) 220 BC Plb. iv 22. 7, 9; 23. 5, 8 (Bradford (-))
SICILY:
—LIPARA: (8) hell.? *IG* XIV 385; cf. *SEG* XXXIV 958 (Ἀδείμαν[τος]: s. Φρίξος)
—SELINOUS: (9) v BC Dubois, *IGDS* 35, 3 (Arena, *Iscr. Sic.* I 64)
—SELINOUS?: (10) vi/v BC *SEG* XXXIX 1020 A, 1 (f. Εὐκλῆς)

## Ἀδειστίδας
ARGOLIS:
—EPIDAUROS: (1) iii/ii BC *IG* IV (1)² 243 (s. Ἱαρώνυμος, Ἀρισταγόρα)

## Ἀδελφία
SICILY:
—SYRACUSE: (1) iii-v AD *CIL* X 7123 (Strazzulla 418; Agnello 71); cf. Führer-Schultze p. 316; Ferrua, *NG* 154 (Lat. Adelfia)

## Ἀδέσποτος
S. ITALY (CAMPANIA):
—HERCULANEUM: (1) m. i AD *PdelP* 3 (1948) p. 170 no. 15 (Lat. Sex. Cloelius Ad[es]potus)

## Ἀδίστα
EPIROS:
—BOUTHROTOS (PRASAIBOI): (1) a. 163 BC *IBouthrot* 29, 13 (*SEG* XXXVIII 487); *IBouthrot* 136, 8 ?= (4); (2) ~ ib. 40, 7 (*SEG* XXXVIII 499); (3) ~ *IBouthrot* 46, 4; (4) ~ ib. 47, 9 ?= (1)
ILLYRIA:
—BYLLIONES BYLLIS: (5) imp. *SEG* II 365
—EPIDAMNOS-DYRRHACHION: (6) imp. *IDyrrh* 84 (d. Δάζιος)

## Ἀδμάτα
ARGOLIS:
—ARGOS: (1) ?iii BC *IG* IV (1) 531

## Ἄδματος
AKARNANIA:
—STRATOS: (1) c. 325-315 BC *Hesp.* 57 (1988) p. 148 A, 39 (*SEG* XXXVI 331); cf. *Hesp.* 48 (1979) pp. 78 f. with pl. 22 c (Ἀδμάτο(υ) (gen.): f. Αἰσχρίων)
EPIROS:
—BOUTHROTOS (PRASAIBOI): (2) a. 163 BC *IBouthrot* 29, 36 (*SEG* XXXVIII 487); (3) ~ *IBouthrot* 30, 16 (*SEG* XXXVIII 488); (4) ~ *IBouthrot* 30, 37 (*SEG* XXXVIII 488) (Ἀ[δ]ματος—ed. pr., Ἀ[ἴ]νατος—*IBouthrot*) ?= (5); (5) ~ *IBouthrot* 33, 18 (*SEG* XXXVIII 492) (f. Λαμία) ?= (4); (6) ~ *IBouthrot* 48, 9
——Aigidorioi: (7) iii/ii BC Cabanes, *L'Épire* p. 574 no. 48, [2] (s. Ἀμφίνους) ?= (8); (8) a. 163 BC *IBouthrot* 39, 1 (*SEG* XXXVIII 498); *IBouthrot* 97, 2 (s.p.) (s. Ἀμφίνους) ?= (7)
——Lyktennoi: (9) a. 163 BC ib. 56, 2 (*SEG* XXXVIII 507); *IBouthrot* 89, 4; 114, 3; 115, 3, 10 (s. Νίκαιος)
——MOLOSSOI: (10) f. v BC *RE* (3) s.v. Admetus (f. Φθία)
——PASSARON: (11) ii BC *AE* 1914, p. 239 no. 19 (f. Λαμία)
——PHOINIKE: (12) f. ii BC *BCH* 45 (1921) p. 23 IV, 53 (Ἀδμα[τος])
——POIONOS: (13) 356-355 BC *IG* IV (1)² 95, 27 (Perlman E.2); Perlman p. 40 f. (date); Hammond, *Epirus* p. 518 (locn.)
KORINTHIA:
—SIKYON: (14) 263 BC *IG* IX (1)² (1) 17, 86; (15) 176 BC *Syll*³ 585, 271 (s. Ἀριστομένης)

## Ἀδμητίς
S. ITALY (CAMPANIA):
—DIKAIARCHIA-PUTEOLI: (1) imp. *CIL* X 1909 (Lat. Admetis)

## Ἄδμητος
LAKONIA:
—SPARTA: (1) c. 100 AD *SEG* XI 626, 5 (Bradford (2)) (I f. Ἄδμητος II); (2) ~ *SEG* XI 626, 5 (Bradford (1)) (II s. Ἄδμητος I)
S. ITALY (APULIA):
—BARION: (3) imp. *Suppl. It.* 8 p. 38 no. 6 (Lat. Calv[ius] [A]dme[tus])
S. ITALY (CAMPANIA):
—POMPEII: (4) i BC-i AD *CIL* IV 3996 (Lat. Admetus); (5) ~ ib. 8209 (Castrèn 241. 1) (Lat. Atimetus—*CIL*, Admetus—Solin); (6) ~ *CIL* IV 10098 c; 10083 c (Castrèn 82. 1); *Gnomon* 45 (1973) p. 269 (Lat. C. Caecina Admetus); (7) ~ *CIL* IV 10189 (Castrèn 106. 2) (Lat. M. Castricius Admetus Syrus)

**Ἄδορπος?**
ITHAKE?: (1) iv BC Unp. (*IG* arch.) (tile)

**Ἀδρανίων**
SICILY:
—AKRAGAS: (1) s. ii BC *Acragas Graeca* 1 p. 34 no. 5, 7 (*IGUR* 2; Dubois, *IGDS* 185) (s. Ἀλέξανδρος)

**Ἀδρανόδωρος**
SICILY:
—SYRACUSE: (1) 215-214 BC *RE* (-)

**Ἄδραστος**
ARGOLIS:
—ARGOS: (1) ?c. 575-550 BC *SEG* XI 336, 7; *LSAG*² p. 168 no. 7 (date)
S. ITALY (CAMPANIA):
—DIKAIARCHIA-PUTEOLI: (2) imp. *CIL* X 2342 (Lat. Adrastus)
—SURRENTUM*: (3) imp. ib. 741 (Lat. M. Livius Adrastus: freed.)

**Ἄδρησις**
SICILY:
—SYRACUSE: (1) iii-v AD *Nuovo Didask.* 4 (1950) p. 62 no. 19 (Ἰουλ. Ἄ.)

**Ἀδριανός**
SICILY:
—KATANE: (1) iii-v AD *IG* XIV 526 (Wessel 241)
—SYRACUSE: (2) iii-v AD *IG* XIV 67 (Strazzulla 8; Wessel 1352) (Ἀδριαν[ός], Ἀδριαν[ή]?); (3) ~ Strazzulla 332 (Wessel 1268); cf. Ferrua, *NG* 115 (Ἀδρια[νός], Ἀδρια[νή]?)

**Ἀδρίσκος**
SICILY:
—SELINOUS?: (1) v BC *SEG* XXXIX 1021 III, 1 (Ἀ(ν)δρίσκος?)

**Ἄδυλα**
DALMATIA:
—ISSA: (1) hell. Brunšmid p. 27 no. 18, 4 (*SEG* XL 514; *VAHD* 84 (1991) p. 253 no. 3) (d. Ἀγάθων)

**Ἄδυλος**
EPIROS:
—BOUTHROTOS (PRASAIBOI): (1) a. 163 BC *IBouthrot* 19, 3 (*SEG* XXXVIII 476); (2) ~ *IBouthrot* 101, 5 (f. Ἄτταλος)
ILLYRIA:
—AMANTIA: (3) ii-i BC Cabanes, *L'Épire* p. 562 no. 38 (*SEG* XXVI 723) (s. Ἀρχέλαος)
—OLYMPE: (4) s. iii BC ib. XXXV 697 (f. Νίκανδρος)

**Ἀδυλώ**
EPIROS:
—BOUTHROTOS (PRASAIBOI): (1) a. 163 BC *IBouthrot* 17, 11; 21, 30 (*SEG* XXXVIII 474; 478) (?m. Μελισσώς); (2) ~ *IBouthrot* 17, 25 (*SEG* XXXVIII 474); (3) ~ *IBouthrot* 21, 3 (*SEG* XXXVIII 478); (4) ~ *IBouthrot* 30, 32 (*SEG* XXXVIII 488) (d. Μυρτίλος); (5) ~ *IBouthrot* 39, 3 (*SEG* XXXVIII 498); *IBouthrot* 51, 28 (d. Στέφανος)

**Ἀδύμμας**
EPIROS:
—DODONA: (1) iii BC Antoniou, *Dodone* Bb, 2

**Ἀδώνιος**
S. ITALY (CAMPANIA):
—POMPEII: (1) i BC-i AD *CIL* IV 2462

**Ἀέθιος**
ARKADIA:
—MEGALOPOLIS: (1) 304 BC *IG* V (2) 550, 14 (Ἀέθ(λ)ιος?)

**Ἀείμναστος**
LAKONIA:
—SPARTA: (1) 479-464 BC Hdt. ix 64. 2; *FGrH* 104 F 1 2. 5; Plu., *Arist.* 19 (Poralla² 31) (-μνη-, Ἀρίμνηστος—Plu.)
SICILY:
—HENNA: (2) 403 BC *RE* Supplbd. 1 (-); Diod. xiv 14 (-μνη-)

**Ἀέριος**
SICILY:
—AKRAGAS: (1) ii-iii AD *SEG* XXVI 1058 + XXXVIII 922 (Ἀέρι (voc.))
—SYRACUSE: (2) iii-v AD *IG* XIV 83 (Strazzulla 24; Wessel 867); cf. Ferrua, *NG* 157 (Ἀέ(τ)ιος?—*IG* and Strazzulla, Ἀ(γ)ριος?—*IG*)

**Ἀέροπος**
EPIROS: (1) iii/ii BC Liv. xxix 12. 11 (Lat. Aeropus)
—AMBRAKIA: (2) c. 200 BC *IG* IX (1)² (1) 31, 127 (s. Εὔαλκος)
—BOUTHROTOS (PRASAIBOI): (3) a. 163 BC *IBouthrot* 19, 5 (*SEG* XXXVIII 476)
——Kestrinoi: (4) a. 163 BC *IBouthrot* 16, 2 (*SEG* XXXVIII 473) (s. Μύρτων)
—MOLOSSOI: (5) iv/iii BC Plu., *Pyrr.* 8. 9
—PHOTIKE (NR.): (6) hell. *SEG* XXVII 228 (s. Μενέδαμος)

**Ἀεσχυλῖνος**
KORINTHIA:
—KORINTH: (1) f. vi BC Amyx 47 (vase) (Lorber 77) (-ρυ-: ?s. Πετάλας)

**Ἀέτιος**
S. ITALY (CAMPANIA):
—POMPEII: (1) i BC-i AD *CIL* IV 2159 (Castrèn 416. 1) (Lat. Travius Aetius)

**Ἀετίων**
KORINTHIA:
—KORINTH: (1) f. vii BC *RE* s.v. Eetion (6); cf. *FGrH* 90 F 57 (Ἠ-: s. Ἐχεκράτης, f. Κύψελος)

**Ἀετός**
ARGOLIS:
—EPIDAUROS: (1) f. ii BC *IG* IV (1)² 359 (Peek, *IAEpid* 153. 7); (2) c. 195-146 BC BM coin 1920 5-15-28; Unp. (Vienna, Münzkabinett); cf. Clerk, *Coins Ach. League* p. 10 no. 165 (coins)

**Ἀζαρία**
S. ITALY (CALABRIA):
—TARAS-TARENTUM*: (1) byz. *JIWE* 1 118 (*CIJ* 1 627) (f. Δαυδᾶτος: Jew)

**Ἀθάμας**
S. ITALY (LUCANIA):
—POSEIDONIA-PAESTUM: (1) vi BC *RE* (6); (2) hell.? ib. (2); Clem. Al., *Strom.* vi 17. 3

**Ἀθαναγόρας**
SICILY:
—SYRACUSE: (1) 415 BC *RE* s.v. Athenagoras (2) (-θη-)

**Ἀθανάδας**
ACHAIA: (1) iv/iii BC *Ét. Thas.* 3 p. 321 no. 116 (-θη-: f. Πυθίων)
—DYME: (2) c. 270 BC *IG* IX (1)² (1) 13, 35 (-θη-: f. Τίμων); (3) s. iii BC *SEG* XIII 278, 19 (s. Μεθίκων)
—DYME*: (4) c. 219 BC *SGDI* 1612, 16 (*Tyche* 5 (1990) p. 124) (s. Ἔπευκτος)
AKARNANIA:
—ECHINOS: (5) iv/iii BC *SEG* XXIX 472
—PALAIROS: (6) hell. *IG* IX (1)² (2) 561 ([Ἀ]θανάδ[ας]); (7) s. iii BC ib. 525
—THYRREION: (8) ii BC ib. 248, 18 (s. Εὔαλκος)

**Ἀθάνιππος**
ARGOLIS:
—EPIDAUROS*: (9) c. 370-335 BC ib. IV (1)² 103, 18, 48; Peek, *IAEpid* 52 A, 6
—TROIZEN: (10) iii BC *IG* IV (1) 772, 1 (f. Ἀπολλόδωρος); (11) ~ ib. 824, 4 (f. Ἀπολλόδωρος)
ELIS: (12) ?i AD *EA* 1905, p. 259 no. 2, 4 (f. Εὐφρόσυνος)
EPIROS:
—AMBRAKIA?: (13) ?iv/iii BC *RE* (-); *FGrH* 303
ILLYRIA:
—APOLLONIA: (14) c. 250-50 BC *Bakërr Hoard* p. 65 no. 135; Münsterberg p. 36; Nachtr. p. 12 (Ceka 4-6) (money.)
KORINTHIA:
—SIKYON: (15) 399 BC X., *HG* iii 1. 18 (Skalet 12) (-θη-)
MESSENIA:
—MESSENE: (16) m. ii BC *IG* II² 986, 13 (Ἀθηνάδης: f. Νεοκλῆς); (17) s. ii BC ib. V (1) 1445 (n. pr.?)
S. ITALY (BRUTTIUM):
—RHEGION: (18) m. ii BC Nachtergael, *Les Galates* 70, 4, 8 (Stephanis 55) (s. Ζώπυρος)

**Ἀθάναιος**
AKARNANIA:
—ASTAKOS: (1) ii BC *IG* IX (1)² (2) 434, 4 (f. Κράτιππος)
LAKONIA:
—SPARTA: (2) 422 BC Th. iv 119. 2; 122. 1 (Poralla² 32) (-θή-: s. Περικλείδας)
PELOPONNESE: (3) s. iii BC *SEG* XIII 278, 8 (s. Δαμα—)

**Ἀθαναΐς**
SICILY:
—THERMAI HIMERAIAI: (1) imp. *Eph. Ep.* VIII 705 (*ILat. Term. Imer.* 107) (Lat. Ignatia Athanais)

**Ἀθάνας**
S. ITALY (APULIA): (1) iv/iii BC Pagenstecher, *Calen. Reliefkeramik* p. 120 n. 1

**Ἀθανασία**
SICILY:
—SYRACUSE: (1) iii-v AD *Riv. Arch. Crist.* 36 (1960) p. 29 no. 25

**Ἀθανάσιος**
S. ITALY (APULIA):
—CANUSIUM: (1) iii AD *Epig. Rom. di Canosa* 38 (*CIL* IX 339) (Lat. L. Annius Rufus Athenasius)
SICILY:
—SYRACUSE: (2) iii-v AD *IG* XIV 72 (Strazzulla 13 (brick)); (3) ~ ib. 312 (Wessel 1159) (Ἀτανά[σιος]); (4) ~ *Nuovo Didask.* 6 (1956) p. 61 no. 20 (Ἀθανά[σιος])

**Ἀθάνασις**
S. ITALY (CAMPANIA):
—NEAPOLIS: (1) iii-iv AD *IG* XIV 826. 3 (*INap* 220)

**Ἀθανίππη**
ARKADIA:
—STYMPHALOS: (1) hell.? *PAE* 1929, p. 92

**Ἀθάνιππος**
ACHAIA:
—PELLENE: (1) 191-146 BC *BMC Pelop.* p. 12 nos. 143-4 (coin)
ARGOLIS:
—ARGOS: (2) ?iii BC *Memnonion* 381
—EPIDAUROS*: (3) iv/iii BC Peek, *NIEpid* 39, 1, 3 (Ἀθά[νι]ππος)
KORINTHIA:
—KORINTH: (4) f. iii BC ib. l. 1, 3 (Ἀθά[νι]ππος)
S. ITALY (BRUTTIUM):
—LOKROI EPIZEPHYRIOI:
——(Μνα.): (5) iv/iii BC De Franciscis 9, 4 ?= (6); (6) ~ ib. 28, 6 (f. Σωσίλας) ?= (5)
SICILY:
—TYNDARIS: (7) imp. *IG* II² 10293 (f. Ἕρμων)

## Ἄθανις
SICILY:
—ECHETLA: (1) vi/v BC Manganaro, *PdelP* forthcoming 10
—KAMARINA: (2) f. v BC Cordano, *Tessere Pubbliche* 53 (Ἀθα[ν]ις: f. Ἵππαρχος); (3) s. v BC Dubois, *IGDS* 121, 14 (Arena, *Iscr. Sic.* II 143; *SEG* XXXVIII 940) ([Ἀθ]ανις—Dubois, [Μεσσ]άνιος—Arena: f. Ὀνάσιμος); (4) ?ii BC ib. XXXIX 996, 5 (Dubois, *IGDS* 126; Cordano, 'Camarina VII' 67) (s. Βασίας)
—SELINOUS: (5) vi/v BC Manganaro, *PdelP* forthcoming no. 18, 7 (s. Ἄντανδρος); (6) ~ ib. l. 10 (Ἄθαν[ις]: s. Ἀγάσαρχος)
——(Ἡρακλείδας): (7) m. v BC Dubois, *IGDS* 36, 3 (Arena, *Iscr. Sic.* I 69) (s. Τάμμαρος)
—SYRACUSE: (8) m. iv BC *RE* (2); *FGrH* 562 (Ἀθάνας—Diod. Sic.)
—TAUROMENION: (9) c. 236-210 BC *IG* XIV 421 an. 5; 421 an. 31 (*SGDI* 5219) (f. Ἀρτεμίδωρος); (10) c. 233-213 BC *IG* XIV 421 an. 8; 421 an. 14; 421 an. 28 (*SGDI* 5219) (f. Φιλιστίων); (11) c. 189-154 BC *IG* XIV 421 an. 52; 421 an. 64; 421 an. 77; 421 an. 87 (*SGDI* 5219); *IGSI* 4 II (III), 16 an. 71 (s. Ἀρτεμίδωρος, f. Ἀρτεμίδωρος)
——(Σπαρ.): (12) ?ii/i BC *IG* XIV 421 D an. 14 (*SGDI* 5219) (f. Ἀρτεμίδωρος) ?= (13); (13) ~ *IG* XIV 421 [D] an. 1 (*SGDI* 5219) (f. Ἐπιγένης) ?= (12); (14) f. i BC *Cron. Arch.* 3 (1964) p. 45 III, 30 (f. Διογένης)

## Ἀθανίων
ACHAIA:
—BOURA: (1) hell. *IG* V (1) 1367 (Ἀθαπτων—apogr., Ἀθα(νί)ων—ed.)
AITOLIA: (2) 217 BC Nachtergael, *Les Galates* 65, 4 (Ἀθ[α]νίων)
AKARNANIA:
—THYRREION: (3) m. iii BC *SEG* XL 464 II side 1, 9 ([Ἀθ]ανίων)
ARGOLIS:
—HERMIONE: (4) ii BC *IG* IV (1) 738 (f. Κάλλις)
ARKADIA:
—KLEITOR: (5) m. iii BC ib. IV (1)² 96, 46 (Perlman E.3); Perlman p. 63 f. (date) (f. Τιμίας)
—MANTINEIA-ANTIGONEIA: (6) f. iii BC *IG* V (2) 278, 4; *EILakArk* 17 (date)
ILLYRIA:
—APOLLONIA: (7) ?i BC *IApoll* 154 (f. Σωτηρίχα); (8) imp. ib. 45
—DIMALE: (9) hell. *Iliria* 1982 (1), p. 120 no. 2 (tile); cf. p. 122
—EPIDAMNOS-DYRRHACHION: (10) hell.-imp. *IDyrrh* 127 (f. Ἀρκασία)

## Ἀθανόδωρος
ACHAIA: (1) ?c. 480-460 BC *CEG* I 380 ii (-δōρος: sculptor)
—AIGION: (2) i AD Moretti, *Olymp.* 773, 778, 786 (Lat. Athenodorus)
ARKADIA:
—KLEITOR: (3) c. 400 BC *RE* (25) (-θη-: sculptor)
LAKONIA:
—SPARTA?: (4) c. 500 BC Paus. iii 16. 4 (Poralla² 33) (name—Madvig)
SICILY:
—SYRACUSE: (5) iii/ii BC *RE* (-)
—TAUROMENION: (6) ?ii/i BC *IG* XIV 421 III (*SGDI* 5219 III, 10)

## Ἀθανοκλῆς
ACHAIA: (1) 189 BC *SEG* XXV 445, 12 + *IPArk* 18; Polyaen. vi 3

## Ἀθανώ
SICILY:
—MENAI: (1) imp. *NScav* 1920, p. 337

## Ἄθας
S. ITALY (BRUTTIUM):
—SYBARIS-THOURIOI-COPIAE: (1) iv BC Landi, *DISMG* 121 (Ἀθα—?: f. —ασέας)

## Ἀθαύμαντος
ARGOLIS:
—EPIDAUROS: (1) iv BC Peek, *NIEpid* 35 ([Ἀ]θαύμαντος) ?= (2); (2) iv-iii BC *IG* IV (1)² 163 ?= (1)

## Ἀθερίων
LAKONIA:
—AMYKLAI: (1) her. Paus. vii 20. 7 (and Achaia Patrai: s. Πρευγένης: oikist/dub.)

## Ἄθετος
S. ITALY (CAMPANIA):
—POMPEII: (1) i BC-i AD *CIL* IV 3934; 3938 (Lat. Athetus)

## Ἀθηναγόρας
ACHAIA: (1) 146 BC *IG* IV (1)² 28, 72 (s. Ἕρμων: synoikos)
ARGOLIS:
—ARGOS: (2) inc. *An. Ox.* iii 411 (fict.)
DALMATIA:
—ISSA:
——(Dymanes): (3) iv/iii BC Brunšmid p. 9, 61 (s. Κλεόμηλος)
EPIROS:
—BOUTHROTOS: (4) ii AD *IBouthrot* 185 (Ugolini, *Alb. Ant.* 3 p. 223 a) (Φλάβιος Ἀ.)

## Ἀθήναιος
AIGINA: (1) imp. Unp. (Kolonna Acropolis Wall) (or Athens?: Γ. Π.—ιος Φίρμος Ἀθήναιος (n. pr.?))
ARGOLIS:
—EPIDAUROS: (2) ii-iii AD *IG* IV (1)² 581; 740 (n. pr.?)
—HERMIONE: (3) i BC-i AD? ib. IV (1) 734, 12
EPIROS:
—NIKOPOLIS: (4) imp. *Hellenika* 22 (1969) p. 72 no. 11 (Sarikakis 4) (f. Λεοντίσκος)
ILLYRIA:
—EPIDAMNOS-DYRRHACHION: (5) hell.-imp. *IDyrrh* 134 (Ἀθ[ήν]αιος)
—KORCA (MOD.): (6) hell. *Iliria* 1983 (2), p. 221 no. 3; cf. *SEG* XXXIII 487 (pithos) (Ἀθήνα[ιος]: name—A.W.J.)
KORINTHIA:
—KORINTH: (7) imp. *Corinth* VIII (2) 139 (Lat. -lius Athenaeus); (8) byz. ib. VIII (3) 553; cf. *TMByz* 9 (1985) p. 363 no. 43 (-νε-)
MESSENIA:
—MESSENE: (9) ii AD *IvOl* 465, 2 (Ἰούλ. Ἀ.: s. Ἰούλιος Νεοπολιτανός)
S. ITALY (CALABRIA):
—OSTUNI (MOD.): (10) hell.? Parlangèli, *Studi Messapici* p. 238 O. 34
S. ITALY (CAMPANIA):
—HERCULANEUM: (11) i BC-i AD *Ann. S. Chiara* 13 (1963) p. 233 (Lat. Athenaeus)
—NEAPOLIS: (12) hell. *SEG* XXXV 1059 (s. Διονύσιος)
S. ITALY (LUCANIA):
—HYELE-VELIA: (13) imp. *Eph. Ep.* VIII 847 (Lat. Athenaeus)
SICILY:
—SEGESTA: (14) i BC *RPC* I p. 648 (coin)

## Ἀθηναΐς
ARGOLIS:
—HERMIONE: (1) iii BC *IG* IV (1) 728, 32 (d. Ἀθηνόδωρος)
ILLYRIA:
—EPIDAMNOS-DYRRHACHION: (2) hell.-imp. *IDyrrh* 86 (d. Ἡρακλείδας)
S. ITALY (BRUTTIUM):
—HIPPONION-VIBO VALENTIA: (3) imp. *CIL* X 64 (Lat. Athenais)

—RHEGION: (4) 79 AD ib. 7, 12 (Lat. Terentia Athenais)
S. ITALY (CAMPANIA):
—DIKAIARCHIA-PUTEOLI: (5) imp. ib. 1816 (Lat. Aquilleia Athenais); (6) ~ ib. 2081 (Lat. Ant. Athenais); (7) ~ ib. 2116 (Lat. Athenais: d. Ἀθηνίων); (8) ~ *Röm. Mitt.* 19 (1904) p. 187 no. 4 (Lat. Gessia Athenais)
—NEAPOLIS*: (9) i BC/i AD *NScav* 1926, p. 235; cf. Leiwo p. 97 no. 46 (Lat. Fuficia Athenais: freed.)
—POMPEII: (10) i BC-i AD *CIL* IV 4150 (Lat. Atenais)
S. ITALY (LUCANIA):
—METAPONTION*: (11) i BC-i AD Landi, *DISMG* 158 (slave?)
SICILY:
—SYRACUSE: (12) ?iii-v AD Ferrua, *NG* 253 (Ἀθηναΐδαν (acc.))
—THERMAI HIMERAIAI: (13) i-ii AD *CIL* X 7378 (*ILat. Term. Imer.* 53) (Lat. Athe[nais])

## Ἀθηνᾶς
DALMATIA:
—PHAROS: (1) iii/ii BC *SEG* XXIII 489, 20, [32]; cf. XLI 545 (s. Διονυσσο—)

## Ἀθηνήσιον
SICILY:
—PANORMOS: (1) imp. *CIL* X 7302 (Lat. Ath(e)nision)

## Ἀθήνιος
S. ITALY (LUCANIA):
—POSEIDONIA-PAESTUM: (1) ii-i BC *NScav* 1950, p. 137 (Γ. Ἀ.: s. Γάϊος)

## Ἀθηνίων
ILLYRIA:
—EPIDAMNOS-DYRRHACHION: (1) iii-ii BC *IDyrrh* 473 (?s. Ἐρ—)
KERKYRA*: (2) ?i BC *GVI* 1288, 3 (f. Μνασέας)
KORINTHIA:
—KORINTH: (3) 178 BC *Syll*³ 585, 244 (II s. Ἀθηνίων I); (4) ~ ib. l. 245 (I f. Ἀθηνίων II)
—TENEA: (5) i BC *SEG* XIII 248, 5 (f. Βάκχιος)
S. ITALY (CAMPANIA):
—DIKAIARCHIA-PUTEOLI: (6) imp. *CIL* X 2116 (Lat. Athenio: f. Ἀθηναΐς)
—KYME: (7) ii-iii AD *IG* XIV 868 (*GVI* 367)
—NOLA*: (8) imp. *RAAN* 30 (1955) p. 200 (Lat. D. Septumuleius Athenio: freed.)
ZAKYNTHOS: (9) 156 BC *ID* 1417 A II, 147

## Ἀθηνογένης
ARGOLIS:
—ARGOS: (1) s. iii BC Cabanes, *L'Épire* p. 546 nos. 14-15 (sculptor) ?= (2); (2) iii/ii BC *IG* IV (1)² 205, 4; 208, 4; 243, 4; 696; 697 (s. Ἀριστομένης: sculptor) ?= (1)
LEUKAS: (3) 216 BC ib. IX (1)² (2) 583, 2-3, 63 (s. Διογένης); (4) c. 167-50 BC *Coll. Weber* 3095 (coin)

## Ἀθηνόδοτος
ARGOLIS:
—EPIDAUROS: (1) iii BC Peek, *IAEpid* 43, 28 ([Ἀ]θηνόδοτος: s. Ἁλιειός)

## Ἀθηνοδώρα
ILLYRIA:
—LYCHNIDOS: (1) ii-iii AD *Sp.* 71 (1931) p. 107 no. 256
S. ITALY (CAMPANIA):
—ATELLA: (2) imp. *CIL* X 3740 (Lat. Athenodora)
—NEAPOLIS: (3) i BC-i AD *IG* XIV 761 (*INap* 89); cf. Leiwo p. 117 no. 97 (d. Ἀντίοχος)

## Ἀθηνόδωρος
AITOLIA:
—KONOPE-ARSINOE: (1) 250-150 BC Fraser-Rönne, *BWGT* p. 144 no. 4

Ἀργολις:
—HERMIONE: (2) iii BC *IG* IV (1) 728, 32 (f. Ἀθηναΐς)
ARKADIA:
—TEGEA: (3) ii AD ib. V (2) 55, 26 (f. Ἐπαφρόδιτος)
KORINTHIA:
—KORINTH: (4) ii/iii AD Philostr., *Ep.* 41; (5) byz. *Corinth* VIII (1) 161; cf. *TMByz* 9 (1985) p. 359 no. 3
LAKONIA:
—SPARTA: (6) c. 25-1 BC *SEG* XI 505, 7 (Bradford (-)) (f. Δαμοκράτης)
S. ITALY: (7) imp. *NScav* 1895, p. 326 (seal) (Lat. C. Caelius Athenodorus)
S. ITALY (CALABRIA):
—TARAS-TARENTUM: (8) i-ii AD *Misc. Gr. Rom.* 3 p. 197 no. T7 (Lat. Athenodorus); (9) ii-iii AD *IG* XIV 680; cf. *SEG* XXVI 909 ([Ἀθ]ηνόδωρος)
S. ITALY (CAMPANIA):
—BAIAI: (10) imp. *Eph. Ep.* VIII 385 (Lat. Iulius Atenororus)
—DIKAIARCHIA-PUTEOLI: (11) imp. *AJA* 2 (1898) p. 379 no. 13 (Lat. C. Ducenius Athenodorus); (12) ?i-ii AD *Eph. Ep.* VIII 396 (Lat. Athenodorus)
—MISENUM*: (13) imp. *CIL* X 3373 (Lat. Iulius Athenodorus)
—NEAPOLIS*: (14) ii AD *INap* 87; cf. *SEG* XLI 860 (Πομπ. Ἀ.: freed.)
—POMPEII: (15) i BC-i AD *CIL* IV 2017
S. ITALY (LUCANIA):
—ATINA LUCANA: (16) imp. *IItal* III (1) 145 (*CIL* X 347) (Lat. Athenodorus)
—HERAKLEIA: (17) i BC *SEG* XXIV 552 (biling.) (s. Λέων)
SICILY:
—SYRACUSE: (18) iv/v AD *Riv. Arch. Crist.* 36 (1960) p. 32 no. 29 (Lat. Atinodorus: s. Mucianus)

Ἀθηνοφάνης
AIGINA: (1) imp. *IG* IV (1) 82 (Ἀ[θη]νο[φ]ά[νης]?: f. Ἀριστοκλῆς)

Ἀθηράδας
LAKONIA:
—SPARTA: (1) 700 BC Moretti, *Olymp.* 24 (Poralla² 34)

Ἄθικτα
S. ITALY (LUCANIA):
—GRUMENTUM: (1) imp. *CIL* X 217 (Lat. Aticta)

Ἄθικτος
S. ITALY (CAMPANIA):
—DIKAIARCHIA-PUTEOLI*: (1) imp. ib. 2679 (Lat. Athictus: freed.?)
—HERCULANEUM*: (2) c. 50-75 AD ib. 1403 a III, 3 (Lat. C. Noleius Athictus: freed.)
—POMPEII: (3) i BC-i AD ib. IV 6894 (Lat. Athictus); (4) ~ ib. 7523; 7545 (Lat. Athictus); (5) c. 51-62 AD ib. 3340. 106, 5 (Castrèn 99. 4) (Lat. D. Caprasius Atictus); (6) 56 AD *CIL* IV 3340. 26, 21 (Castrèn 443. 1) (Lat. N. Veratius Atiktus)
—SURRENTUM: (7) imp. *NScav* 1928, p. 208 no. 5 (Lat. Athictus)

Ἄθλος
ARGOLIS:
—NAUPLIA: (1) ii BC *SEG* XI 373

Αἰακίδας
AITOLIA: (1) ?247 BC *Syll*³ 444 A, 1; *CID* II 139, 2 ?= (2)
—KALLION/KALLIPOLIS: (2) c. 245-236 BC *IG* IX (1)² (1) 25, 56, 66 ?= (1)

EPIROS:
—MOLOSSOI: (3) s. iv BC *RE* (4); Plu., *Pyrrh.* 1. 5 (-δης: s. Ἀρύββας, Τρωιάς, f. Πύρρος, Δηιδάμεια, Τρωιάς)
KEPHALLENIA:
—PRONNOI: (4) c. 210 BC *IG* IX (1)² (1) 31, 95 (s. Σωτίων)

Αἰακός
S. ITALY (CAMPANIA):
—POMPEII: (1) i BC-i AD *CIL* IV 1327 (Lat. Aeacus)

Αἰβάτιος
ILLYRIA:
—APOLLONIA: (1) c. 250-50 BC Maier 120; 108; Münsterberg Nachtr. p. 13 (coin) (Ceka 7) (money.); (2) i BC Maier 150 (coin) (?s. Λυσα—: money.)
—EPIDAMNOS-DYRRHACHION: (3) c. 250-50 BC Münsterberg Nachtr. p. 14 (Ceka 16); cf. *IApoll Ref. Bibl.* n. 5 (coin) ((Αἰβ)άτιος: money.)

Αἰγεία
SICILY:
—SYRACUSE: (1) iii-v AD *IG* XIV 68 (Strazzulla 9; Agnello 36; Wessel 791) ((Λ)ίγεια?, (Ἀρ)γεία?—*IG*)

Αἰγεύς
AITOLIA:
—THERMOS*: (1) s. iii BC *IG* IX (1)² (1) 60 VI, 2
LAKONIA:
—SPARTA: (2) her. *RE* (2) (s. Οἰόλυκος, f. Ὑραῖος: dub.)
S. ITALY (CAMPANIA):
—POMPEII: (3) i BC-i AD *CIL* IV 5070 (Lat. Aeceus)

Αἰγιαλεύς
ACHAIA: (1) 242-238 BC *IG* IV (1)² 71, 1
—AIGION: (2) c. 230-200 BC *BCH* 45 (1921) p. 11 II, 59 (s. Κριτόβουλος)
LAKONIA:
—SPARTA: (3) ii-iii AD X. Eph. V 1. 2 ff. (and Sicily: fict.)

Αἰγιάλη
DALMATIA:
—EPETION: (1) imp. *CIL* III 12826 (Lat. Laelia Aegiale)

Αἰγιαλός
S. ITALY (CAMPANIA):
—DIKAIARCHIA-PUTEOLI*: (1) imp. ib. X 1999 (Lat. Aegialus: slave?)
—HERCULANEUM*: (2) m. i AD *Cron. Erc.* 7 (1977) p. 118 D, 9 (Lat. [M.] [H]erennius Aegialus: freed.)
—POMPEII*: (3) m. i AD *Impegno per Pompeii* 5 OS (Castrèn 119. 6) (Lat. A. Clodius Aegialus: freed.)

Αἰγίας
KORINTHIA:
—SIKYON: (1) 243 BC Plu., *Arat.* 18-19; Polyaen. vi 5 (Skalet 13) (Αἰσίας—Polyaen.)

Αἰγιεύς
S. ITALY (CALABRIA):
—TARAS-TARENTUM: (1) iv BC *ASP* 22 (1969) pp. 90-1 no. 3 (loomweight)

Αἰγικλῆς
ARKADIA:
—MANTINEIA-ANTIGONEIA: (1) c. 300-221 BC *IG* V (2) 323. 22 (tessera) (s. Αὐτόνοος)

Αἰγίλεια
EPIROS:
—NIKOPOLIS: (1) imp. *CIG* 1814 (Sarikakis 5) (Αἰγιλε[ία]—Sarikakis, Αἰγιλε[ῖνα?]—*CIG*)

Αἰγίμιος
ELIS: (1) v-iv BC *RE* (3); Supplbd. 1 (doctor)

Αἴγιμος
ILLYRIA:
—APOLLONIA: (1) hell. *IApoll* 344 (tile)

Αἰγινήτας
KORINTHIA:
—SIKYON: (1) iii/ii BC Plin., *NH* XXXV 145 (Skalet 14) (Lat. Aeginetas: painter)

Αἴγινος
PELOPONNESE: (1) s. iii BC *SEG* XIII 278, 9 (f. Ἀλεξίδαμος)

Αἰγιπᾶς
S. ITALY (CAMPANIA):
—DIKAIARCHIA-PUTEOLI: (1) imp. *CIL* X 1996 (Lat. M. Acutius Aegipas)

Αἰγίων
AIGINA: (1) imp. *IG* IV (1) 76

Αἰγλαῖος
S. ITALY (CAMPANIA):
—HERCULANEUM*: (1) i BC-i AD *Ann. S. Chiara* 13 (1963) pp. 251-4 (Lat. Erennius Aeglaius: freed.)

Αἰγλαπιός
ARKADIA:
—STYMPHALOS: (1) ?iv BC *SNG Berry* 871; cf. *ASNP* 20 (1990) p. 420 f. (coin graffito)

Αἰγλάτας
ARKADIA:
—MANTINEIA-ANTIGONEIA:
——(Posoidaia): (1) c. 425-400 BC *SEG* XXXI 348, 21
LAKONIA:
—SPARTA: (2) c. 530-500 BC Moretti, *IAG* 9 (Lazzarini 849; *CEG* I 374; Poralla² 37)

Αἴγλη
EPIROS:
—DODONA*: (1) iv-iii BC *SGDI* 1561 (*Syll*³ 1160) (Α[ἴ]γλη)
S. ITALY (CAMPANIA):
—NEAPOLIS: (2) i BC-i AD *IG* XIV 762 (*INap* 90); cf. Leiwo p. 117 no. 98 (d. Ζωίλος)
—POMPEII: (3) 70-79 AD *CIL* IV 7862; Mouritsen p. 110 (date) (Lat. Aegle)

Αἰγύπιος
ARGOLIS:
—ARGOS: (1) iii BC *BCH* 38 (1914) p. 467 no. 9, 3 ([Αἰ]γύπιος: f. Πάννις)
ARKADIA:
—ORCHOMENOS: (2) iii/ii BC ib. p. 465 no. 8, 13

Αἰγυπτία
EPIROS:
—DODONA*: (1) ?iv BC *SEG* XXIII 473 (Αἰγυπτ[ί]α (n. pr.?))

Αἰγύπτιος
PELOPONNESE?: (1) s. iii BC *IG* V (1) 1426, 13 (f. Θρασύβουλος)

Αἴγυπτος
ELIS: (1) c. 400-365 BC Paus. vi 12. 6 (f. Τίμων); (2) ~ Moretti, *Olymp.* 365; *RE* s.v. Timon (3-4) (Αἴσυπος, Αἴσιπος, Αἴγυπος—mss., Αἴσηπος—Dindorf and Moretti, Ἀ.—*RE*: s. Τίμων); (3) ii BC *IvOl* 189; cf. Moretti, *Olymp.* 639
S. ITALY (CAMPANIA):
—POMPEII: (4) i BC-i AD *CIL* IV 2107 (Lat. Aegyptus)

Αἴγων
ARGOLIS:
—ARGOS: (1) ?vi BC *RE* (-) (king)

**Αἰδήμων**
S. Italy (Bruttium):
—kroton: (2) iv bc Iamb., *VP* 267 (*FVS* I p. 446)

**Αἰδήμων**
S. Italy (Campania):
—dikaiarchia-puteoli: (1) imp. *CIL* x 1834, 5 (Lat. Aedemo)

**Αἰετός**
Aigina: (1) c. 470 bc *SEG* xlii 258 (Lazzarini 264)

**Αἴϝας**
Elis:
—olympia*: (1) v bc *SEG* xi 1228

**Αἰθάλης**
S. Italy (Campania):
—surrentum: (1) imp. *Forma Italiae* 2 p. 163 no. 45 (Lat. Aeitales)
Sicily:
—motyka (hortensiana): (2) iv/v ad Agnello 93

**Αἰθήρ**
Argolis:
—argos: (1) c. 458 bc *IG* I³ 1149, 13 (-θέρ)

**Αἰθίδας**
Messenia:
—messene: (1) ii/iii ad *SEG* xl 367 (xli 376 E) (θηρυλοσενικαιθιδας—lap., Νικαιθίδας?, (Σ)αιθίδας?)

**Αἰθίοψ**
Korinthia:
—korinth: (1) s. viii bc *IEG* I p. 98 fr. 293

**Αἴθρα**
Lakonia:
—sparta: (1) viii/vii bc Paus. x 10. 8 (Poralla² 38) (dub.)
S. Italy (Calabria):
—brentesion-brundisium: (2) i bc/i ad *Necropoli via Cappuccini* p. 287 no. E43 (Lat. Audia Etrhe)

**Αἰθρία**
Akarnania:
—phoitiai: (1) iii-ii bc *IG* ix (1)² (2) 389

**Αἰθύρας**
S. Italy (Lucania):
—herakleia: (1) ?iv bc Landi, *DISMG* 215 (—αιθύρα—, Διθύρα[ς]?—ed.)

**Αἴθων**
Arkadia:
—mantineia-antigoneia: (1) 64 or 62 bc *IG* v (2) 265, 50 (s. Φιλοσθένης)
—phigaleia: (2) v bc ib. 425, 4 (-θῶν)
S. Italy (Campania):
—pompeii: (3) 57 ad *CIL* iv 3340. 38, 14 (Castrèn 454. 38) (Lat. L. Vettius Aethon)

**Αἰκισθένης**
Argolis:
—argos:
——(Hyrnathioi-Temenidai): (1) c. 400 bc *SEG* xxix 361, 21 (-νἕς)

**Αἰλία**
Epiros:
—nikopolis: (1) imp. *Parnassos* 9 (1885) p. 67 (Sarikakis 7)

**Αἰλιανή**
Sicily:
—katane: (1) imp. *IG* xiv 478 (Ἰουλ. Α(ἰ)λιαν[ή]: d. Αἰλιανός)

**Αἰλιανός**
S. Italy (Apulia):
—venusia: (1) v ad *JIWE* I 77 (*CIJ* I 578) (Ἠλι-: f. Ἀσελλα: Jew)
Sicily:
—katane: (2) imp. *IG* xiv 478 (f. Ἰουλ. Αἰλιανή)
—syracuse: (3) iii-v ad Strazzulla 336 (Wessel 1059); cf. Ferrua, *NG* 119 ((A)ιλιανός—Wessel, [Αἰ]διλιανός—Strazzulla, [Σεκουν]διλιανός—Ferrua)

**Αἰμιλιανός**
Aitolia:
—klauseion (mod.): (1) byz. *PAE* 1958, p. 62; cf. *BCH* 83 (1959) p. 664 (Αἰμε[ιλ]ιανός: bp.)
Sicily:
—syracuse: (2) 393 ad Strazzulla 350 (Wessel 716)

**Αἰμίλιος**
S. Italy (Bruttium):
—sybaris-thourioi-copiae: (1) arch. *FGrH* 292 F 2 (fict.)

**Αἰμονίδας**
Elis:
—thraistos: (1) f. iv bc *IG* ix (1)² (1) 138, 2

**Αἶμος**
Aitolia:
—thermos*: (1) s. iii bc ib. 60 VII, 6

**Αἰμόστρατος**
Achaia:
—tritaia: (1) ?120 bc Paus. vi 12. 8 (f. Ἀγήσαρχος)

**Αἰμύλος**
Arkadia:
—mantineia-antigoneia: (1) c. 300-221 bc *IG* v (2) 323. 9 (tessera) (Α[ἰ]μύλ[ος]: f. Αὖτοπις)

**Αἴμων**
S. Italy (Bruttium):
—kroton: (1) iv bc Iamb., *VP* 267 (*FVS* I p. 446)
S. Italy (Lucania):
—tegianum (nr.): (2) ?iii ad *Rupes loquentes* p. 438 (Lat. Aur. Aemo)

**Αἶνα?**
S. Italy (Calabria):
—taras-tarentum: (1) imp. *CIL* ix 6163 (Lat. Domitia Aina?)

**Αἰνέας**
Argolis:
—epidauros: (1) ii-i bc *IG* iv (1)² 734
——Politas: (2) c. 370-335 bc ib. 102, 101 + *SEG* xxv 383, 122; *IG* iv (1)² 103, 47
—nemea*: (3) s. iv bc *SEG* xxx 353, 2, 11 (f. Εὐβούλα)
—troizen: (4) iv bc *IG* iv (1) 764, 7 (f. Αἰνησίδαμος)
Arkadia: (5) ?c. 500 bc *SEG* xi 1043 (bronze) (Lazzarini 359); *LSAG²* p. 215 no. 8 (date)
—stymphalos: (6) 366 bc *RE* (6) ?= (Αἰνείας (3))
Elis: (7) f. iii bc Paus. vi 2. 4; viii 10. 5 (f. Θρασύβουλος: Iamidai)
Epiros:
—thesprotoi: (8) i bc *SEG* xiii 248, 8 (f. Φίλων)
Illyria:
—apollonia: (9) c. 250-50 bc Münsterberg Nachtr. p. 12; Maier 12 (Ceka 1; 24); cf. *IApoll Ref. Bibl.* n. 6 (coin) (pryt.)
Korinthia:
—korinth: (10) 423 bc Th. iv 119. 2 (s. Ὠκυτος)

—sikyon: (11) c. 146-32 bc *NC* 1984, p. 17 Group 11 no. 1 (coin) ?= (12); (12) i bc ib. p. 18 Group 12 no. 1 (coin) ?= (11)
Messenia:
—thouria: (13) f. ii bc *SEG* xi 972, 38 (s. Τεταρτίδας)
Peloponnese?: (14) 11 ad *PAE* 1992, p. 71 A, 34 (Σέξ. Καλπούρνιος Ἀ.)
S. Italy (Bruttium):
—lokroi epizephyrioi: (15) iii-ii bc *SEG* xxix 953 (?s. Ὀνα—)
——(Ἀνξ.): (16) iv/iii bc De Franciscis 2, 5 (s. Αἰνείδας)
S. Italy (Calabria):
—brentesion-brundisium: (17) imp. *Epigraphica* 25 (1963) p. 76 no. 77 (Lat. Ti. Iulius Aeneas)
S. Italy (Lucania):
—metapontion: (18) iv bc Iamb., *VP* 267 (*FVS* I p. 446)
Sicily:
—halaisa: (19) f. i bc Cic., *In Verr.* II iii 170 (Lat. Aeneas)
—selinous: (20) vi/v bc Dubois, *IGDS* 43 (Arena, *Iscr. Sic.* I 45; *IGLMP* 63)

**Αἰνείας**
Achaia:
—pellene: (1) m. iii bc *IG* v (2) 368, 95 (s. Κ—)
Arkadia:
—stymphalos: (2) 401 bc X., *An.* iv 7. 13; (3) f. iv bc *RE* (3); Whitehead, *Aineias* pp. 10-13 (locn.) ?= (Αἰνέας (6))

**Αἰνείδας**
S. Italy (Bruttium):
—lokroi epizephyrioi:
——(Ἀνξ.): (1) iv/iii bc De Franciscis 2, 5 (f. Αἰνέας)

**Αἰνέλαος**
Aitolia:
—lechoioi: (1) 163 bc *IG* ix (1)² (1) 102, 7 (Αἰνέλαος)

**Αἰνεσίδημος**
Sicily:
—leontinoi: (1) ?v bc Paus. v 22. 7; cf. *RE* (2) (tyrant)

**Αἰνέστρατος**
Argolis:
—methana-arsinoe: (1) i bc *IG* iv (1) 853, 7 (Αἰνε(σί)στρατος—IG)

**Αἰνέτα**
Korinthia:
—korinth: (1) c. 610-590 bc Amyx 18. 1 (vase) (Lorber 28); *LSAG²* p. 131 no. 9 (date) (het.?)

**Αἴνετος**
Argolis:
—hermione: (1) iii bc *IG* iv (1) 729 II, 10 (f. Ἀρίστιππος)
Epiros:
—ambrakia: (2) vi bc *EA* 1897, p. 164 (Ἐπ]αίνετος?)
Korinthia:
—sikyon: (3) iv/iii bc *CID* II 120 A, 46 (f. —ος)
Lakonia: (4) c. 431-403 bc *IG* v (1) 701; *LSAG²* p. 201 no. 57 (date) (Poralla² 42) (Αἴνητος—Poralla)
Sicily:
—kamarina: (5) ?iv/iii bc *SEG* xxxix 1000 ([—]αίνετος?)

**Αἰνηΐας**
Lakonia: (1) ?f. iv bc *IG* v (1) 703 (Poralla² 40) (-νηhί-)

**Αἰνηΐδας**
LAKONIA:
—SPARTA: (**1**) iv/iii BC *SEG* XI 654 (Poralla²
38d)

**Αἰνήσανδρος**
ARKADIA:
—MEGALOPOLIS: (**1**) s. iii BC *BCH* 38 (1914) p.
464 no. 7, 1 (Αἰνήσαν[δρος]?)

**Αἰνησίας**
ARKADIA:
—MEGALOPOLIS: (**1**) iv/iii BC *RE* Supplbd. 3 (2)
LAKONIA:
—SPARTA: (**2**) 432 BC Th. ii 2; X., *HG* ii 3. 10
(Poralla² 39)
MESSENIA:
—MESSENE: (**3**) s. ii BC *SEG* XLI 341, 12 (s. Σόϊ-
ξις); (**4**) c. 146-32 BC *BMC Pelop.* p. 110 no.
16 (coin)

**Αἰνησίβιος**
ARGOLIS:
—EPIDAUROS*: (**1**) c. 370-365 BC Peek, *IAEpid*
52 A, 37 (Αἰνη[σίβ]ιος)

**Αἰνησίδαμος**
ACHAIA:
—DYME: (**1**) 198 BC *RE* s.v. Ainesidemos (7)
(Lat. Aenesidemus)
ARGOLIS:
—EPIDAUROS: (**2**) s. iv BC *SEG* XVII 182 = Peek,
*NIEpid* 93 (?s. Αἰ—)
——(Hysminatai): (**3**) 146 BC *IG* IV (1)² 28, 11
(f. Μηνόφιλος)
—TROIZEN: (**4**) iv BC ib. IV (1) 764, 7 (Αἰνη-
σίδ[αμος]: s. Αἰνέας)
ARKADIA:
—TEGEA: (**5**) m. iv BC ib. V (2) 6, 114 (Αἰ-
νησα(ίδαμ)ος?, Αἰνήσα(ανδρ)ος?)
S. ITALY (BRUTTIUM):
—LOKROI EPIZEPHYRIOI:
——(Θρα.): (**6**) iv/iii BC De Franciscis 22, 8 (f.
Ἀγησίδαμος)
SICILY:
—AKRAGAS: (**7**) s. vi BC *RE* (1) (s. Ἐμμενίδας, f.
Θήρων, Ξενοκράτης, ?f. Πράξανδρος)
—GELA-PHINTIAS: (**8**) s. vi BC Hdt. vii 154. 1
(-δη-: s. Πάταικος); (**9**) c. 525-500 BC Dubois,
*IGDS* 142 a (vase) (Arena, *Iscr. Sic.* II 30)
(-νε̄-)
—KAMARINA: (**10**) f. v BC Cordano, *Tessere Pub-
bliche* 80 (Arena, *Iscr. Sic.* II 141 A) (-νε̄-:
s. Πάσιλλος); (**11**) ?ii BC *SEG* XXXIX 996, 11
(Dubois, *IGDS* 126) + *BE* 1979, no. 676
(Cordano, 'Camarina VII' 68) (Αἰνησί[δ]αμος,
Αἴνησι[ς] [Θ]άλλου—Dubois: f. —ων)

**Αἰνησιμβρότα**
LAKONIA:
—SPARTA: (**1**) s. vii BC *PMGF* 1 1, 73 (Poralla²
41)

**Αἴνησις**
SICILY:
—MORGANTINA: (**1**) iv/iii BC *SEG* XXXIX 1012,
6 ([Αἴν]ησις: s. Θέων)
—TAUROMENION: (**2**) c. 221 BC *IG* XIV 421 an.
20 (*SGDI* 5219) (s. Μένανδρος)

**Αἰνησίων**
PELOPONNESE: (**1**) c. 192 BC *SEG* XIII 327, 13
(s. Ξένων)

**Αἰνησώ**
ARKADIA:
—LYKOSOURA*: (**1**) i BC *IG* V (2) 521 (d. Ἐρά-
σιππος)
S. ITALY (BRUTTIUM):
—RHEGION:

——(Τεισ.): (**2**) s. ii BC ib. XIV 615, 8; *Klearchos*
21 (1979) pp. 83-96 (date) (Αἰνησοῦς?—
Lazzarini: d. Νίκων)
SICILY:
—LIPARA: (**3**) ?iv-iii BC Libertini, *Isole Eolie* p.
223 no. 38 + *SEG* XXXIV 958

**Αἰνητίδας**
LAKONIA:
—SPARTA: (**1**) c. 50-25 BC *IG* V (1) 208, 3 (Brad-
ford (-)) (f. Ἀντίλας)

**Αἴνητος**
LAKONIA:
—AMYKLAI: (**1**) imp.? Moretti, *Olymp.* 945 (Po-
ralla² 43)

**Αἰνίας**
ARKADIA:
—TEGEA: (**1**) m. iv BC *IG* V (2) 6, 104

**Αἰνίππα**
KORINTHIA:
—KORINTH: (**1**) c. 570-550 BC Amyx 66. 3
(vase) (Lorber 122) (her.)

**Αἴνιππος**
S. ITALY (BRUTTIUM):
—RHEGION: (**1**) iii-ii BC Guarducci, *Ep. Gr.* 2
p. 496 (Landi, *DISMG* 33)

**Αἴνιχος**
AITOLIA:
—APERANTOI: (**1**) hell. *IG* IX (1)² (1) 163 (Αἴ-
νι(κ)ος?—ed.: f. Εὐρύνομος)

**Αἰνώι**
KORINTHIA:
—KORINTH: (**1**) c. 570-550 BC Amyx 70. 4
(vase) (Lorber 126) (-νόϊ: her.)

**Αἴνων**
SICILY:
—SELINOUS: (**1**) m. v BC Dubois, *IGDS* 36, 2
(Arena, *Iscr. Sic.* I 69) (-νōν: s. Βλέπων)

**Αἰόλαος**
ARGOLIS:
—ARGOS: (**1**) ?iii BC *SEG* XI 332; cf. Masson,
*OGS* 2 p. 390 no. 24

**Αἰόλας**
KORINTHIA:
—KORINTH: (**1**) c. 615-600 BC Amyx 4. 5 (vase)
(Lorber 24) (her.)

**Αἰόλη**
S. ITALY (CAMPANIA):
—POMPEII: (**1**) i BC-i AD *CIL* IV 4830 (Lat.
Aeole)

**Αἴολος**
SICILY:
—LIPARA: (**1**) ?f. v BC *Chiron* 22 (1992) p. 388
no. 6 (vase) (Αἴο[λος]?)

**Αἴπολος**
AIGINA: (**1**) imp. *IG* IV (1) 127 (*REG* 15 (1902)
p. 138 no. 1) (n. pr.?: f. Κότυς)

**Αἴπυτος**
ILLYRIA:
—EPIDAMNOS-DYRRHACHION: (**1**) hell. *IDyrrh*
87 (s. Πανάνδριος); (**2**) hell.-imp. ib. 171 (f.
Διονύσιος)

**Αἰρήιππος**
LAKONIA: (**1**) c. 431-403 BC *IG* V (1) 702;
*LSAG*² p. 201 no. 59 (date) (Poralla² 44)
(ḥαιρή[ιππος])

**Αἴροπος**
EPIROS:
—GENOAIOI: (**1**) ?c. 370-344 BC Cabanes,
*L'Épire* p. 536 no. 2, 10

**Αἶσα**
SICILY:
—KASMENAI: (**1**) vi BC *Arch. Class.* 17 (1965) p.
193 + *ZPE* 99 (1993) pp. 123-4 (d. Νουνφίων,
m. Καλικράτης)

**Αἰσαγένης**
ARKADIA: (**1**) 316 BC *IG* V (2) 549, 30 (s. Ἀγαθίας)
—MANTINEIA-ANTIGONEIA: (**2**) c. 300-221 BC
ib. 323. 101 (tessera) (f. Ἀδάμας)
—TEGEA: (**3**) ii/i BC ib. 22 ([Α]ἰσαγένης: s. Βαθυκλῆς); (**4**) i BC ib. 45, 6

**Αἰσανορίδας**
ACHAIA:
—AIGION: (**1**) m. iii BC Peek, *IAEpid* 42, 25
(Perlman E.3); Perlman p. 63 f. (date) (f. Ἀγη-
σίας)

**Αἰσάνωρ**
ARGOLIS:
—EPIDAUROS*: (**1**) c. 370-365 BC Peek, *IAEpid*
52 B, 58, 65, 68

**Αἰσιμέλης**
KORINTHIA:
—KORINTH: (**1**) vi BC *IG* IV (1) 303 (pinax) (Αἰ-
σιμέλ(ε̄)ς)

**Αἰσιμίδας**
KERKYRA: (**1**) 433 BC Th. i 47. 1 (-δης)

**Αἴσιμος**
AITOLIA:
—THERMOS*: (**1**) s. iii BC *IG* IX (1)² (1) 60 VII,
13

**Αἰσχένας**
ARGOLIS:
—HERMIONE: (**1**) iii BC ib. IV (1) 728, 11 (f. Πυθόδωρος) ?= (2); (**2**) ~ ib. l. 22 (f. Πυθόδωρος)
?= (1)

**Αἰσχίναρ**
ELIS: (**1**) iii/ii BC *IvOl* 39, 34 (Perlman O.2)

**Αἰσχίνας**
ACHAIA:
—PATRAI: (**1**) hell.? *SGDI* 1627 (f. Σάτυρος)
ACHAIA?: (**2**) 193 BC *IG* V (2) 293, 10 (s. Μναί-
στρατος)
AKARNANIA: (**3**) 401 BC X., *An.* iv 8. 18; cf. iv
3. 22
—MEDION: (**4**) 216 BC *IG* IX (1)² (2) 583, 21 (s.
Τελέστας)
ARGOLIS:
—ARGOS: (**5**) 369 BC Paus. iv 26. 7 (f. Ἐπιτέλης);
(**6**) iii BC *IG* IV (1) 618 II, 3 (s. Κρηθεύς); (**7**)
c. 220-200 BC *SEG* XI 414, 30 (Perlman E.5)
(s. Εὐέτης)
—EPIDAUROS: (**8**) c. 370 BC *IG* IV (1)² 102, 268
——Naupheis: (**9**) iv BC ib. 54, 10 (Αἰσ[χ]ίνας)
—HERMIONE: (**10**) iii BC ib. IV (1) 728, 21 (f.
Πυθόδωρος)
—HERMIONE?: (**11**) iv BC ib. 747 A, 8 (f. Νικο-
κλῆς)
—TROIZEN: (**12**) i BC *SEG* XXXVII 309
([Αἰ]σχίν[α] (voc.), [Αἰ]σχίν[η]—ed.)
ARKADIA: (**13**) iv BC *RE* (17) (-νης); (**14**) iii/ii
BC *IG* XII (9) 843 (-νης: f. —λων: date—
Knoepfler)
DALMATIA:
—ISSA: (**15**) iii BC Brunšmid p. 9 fr. H, 8 (Αἰ-
σχ[ίνας?]: f. Σάλλας); (**16**) f. ii BC ib. p. 23 no.
10, 11 (f. Φίλων)
——(Pamphyloi): (**17**) iv/iii BC ib. p. 7, 22 (s.
Σάλλας)
ELIS: (**18**) 760 BC Moretti, *Olymp.* 5
ILLYRIA:
—APOLLONIA: (**19**) hell. *IApoll* 21; (**20**) c. 250-
50 BC Münsterberg Nachtr. p. 13 (Ceka 9);
*IApoll Ref. Bibl.* n. 7 (coin) (money.); (**21**) ~

*Bakërr Hoard* p. 63 no. 8 (coin) (Ceka 32) (pryt.); **(22)** imp. *IApoll* 73 (f. Ἕσπερος)
—OLYMPE: **(23)** s. iii BC *SEG* XXXV 697 (s. Σιμίας)

KORINTHIA:
—SIKYON: **(24)** vi BC Plu., *Mor.* 859 D; *FGrH* 105 F 1 (-νης: tyrant); **(25)** m. v BC *IG* IV (1) 425, 6

SICILY:
—SELINOUS?: **(26)** vi/v BC *SEG* XXXIX 1020 B, 8 (f. Ἀρχέστρατος)

**Αἰσχίνης**
ELIS: **(1)** hell.-imp. Moretti, *Olymp.* 946-947
S. ITALY (APULIA):
—CANUSIUM*: **(2)** i AD *Epig. Rom. di Canosa* 126 (*CIL* IX 375) (Lat. -isius Aeschinus: freed.)
S. ITALY (CAMPANIA):
—NEAPOLIS: **(3)** s. ii BC *RE* (20)

**Αἰσχις**
ARGOLIS:
—ARGOS: **(1)** 228-146 BC *BMC Pelop.* p. 147 nos. 144-5 (coin); **(2)** f. i BC Unp. (Ch. Kritzas) (s. Ἀγησίπολις)

**Αἰσχίων**
ARGOLIS:
—HERMIONE: **(1)** iii BC *IG* IV (1) 685

**Αἴσχρα**
EPIROS:
—BOUTHROTOS (PRASAIBOI): **(1)** a. 163 BC *IBouthrot* 18, 9 (*SEG* XXXVIII 475) (d. Λέων); **(2)** ~ *IBouthrot* 38, 17 (*SEG* XXXVIII 497) (d. Μενοίτας)

**Αἰσχρία**
LEUKAS: **(1)** iv/iii BC Unp. (Leukas Mus., inscr.)

**Αἰσχρίας**
ACHAIA:
—AIGION: **(1)** 214 BC *IG* IX (1)² (1) 31, 175 (f. Κλέων)
EPIROS:
—KASSOPE: **(2)** iv/iii BC *SEG* XXXIV 589 (s. Ἱππαρχος)

**Αἰσχρίς**
AITOLIA:
—AGRINION: **(1)** 190 BC Sherk 37 B, 75; cf. *SEG* XXVII 123
KEPHALLENIA: **(2)** iii-ii BC *Op. Ath.* 10 (1971) p. 65 no. 10

**Αἰσχρίων**
ACHAIA:
—DYME: **(1)** iii BC *AJPh* 31 (1910) p. 399 no. 74 c, 6 (I f. Αἰσχρίων II); **(2)** ~ ib. l. 6 (II s. Αἰσχρίων I, Σατύρα); **(3)** s. iii BC *SEG* XIII 278, 18 (s. Ἄνδριος); **(4)** ~ ib. l. 21 (s. Φίλων)
—PATRAI: **(5)** hell.? *SGDI* 1628 (f. Ξένις); **(6)** m. iii BC *Achaean Grave Stelai* 17 (f. Εὐφάνης); **(7)** c. 146-32 BC *BMC Pelop.* p. 22 no. 1 (coin) (f. Ἄγυς); **(8)** ~ BM coin 1887 6-6-11 (coin) (s. Λυσίας)
—TRITAIA: **(9)** hell.-imp. Neratzoulis p. 22 no. 8 (*Achaie* II 318) (f. Ξενώ)
AITOLIA: **(10)** iii BC *SEG* XVIII 244, 4 (Αἰσχρίων[ος] (gen.), Αἰσχριών[δα?] (gen.)—ed.)
—KALYDON: **(11)** c. 210 BC *IG* IX (1)² (1) 31, 96 (Αἰσκ-: f. Λυκίσκος); **(12)** a. 142 BC ib. 137, 57
—LYSIMACHEIA: **(13)** hell. ib. 128 ([Αἰσ]χρίων: f. —χιδα—)
—PHISTYON: **(14)** f. ii BC ib. 98, 9; 100, 2 (s.p.) (Αἰσκρίων—no. 98); **(15)** imp. ib. 113, 2 (Αἰσσ-: f. Καλλίστρατος)
—TRICHONION: **(16)** s. iii BC ib. 117, 6

AKARNANIA: **(17)** c. 250-167 BC *BMC Thessaly* p. 169 no. 11; *Coll. Weber* 1472? (coins) (I f. Αἰσχρίων II); **(18)** ~ *BMC Thessaly* p. 169 no. 11; *Coll. Weber* 1472? (coins) (II s. Αἰσχρίων I); **(19)** c. 170 BC Plb. xxviii 5. 1
—ANAKTORION: **(20)** iv BC *IG* IX (1)² (2) 217 (Α(ἰ)σχρίων)
—KORONTA: **(21)** iii/ii BC ib. 603 (f. Πολέμαρχος)
—STRATOS: **(22)** c. 325-315 BC *Hesp.* 57 (1988) p. 148 A, 39 (*SEG* XXXVI 331); cf. *Hesp.* 48 (1979) pp. 78 f. with pl. 22 c (s. Ἄδματος); **(23)** hell. *IG* IX (1) 594 (f. Φάλαρις); **(24)** ii BC ib. IX (1)² (2) 394, 14 (f. Ἐπίγνητος)
—THYRREION: **(25)** 216 BC ib. 583, 18 (s. Κλεώνυμος); **(26)** 167 BC *Klio* 75 (1993) p. 132, 3-4 (s. Κλεώνυμος)
ARKADIA:
—MEGALOPOLIS: **(27)** ii/i BC *IG* V (2) 442, 19 (Αἰσ[χ]ρίων: f. Φιλόνικος)
—TEGEA: **(28)** m. iv BC ib. 6, 105 (Αἰσ[χ]ρ[ί]ων); **(29)** iv/iii BC ib. 32, 6
DALMATIA:
—ISSA:
——(Hylleis): **(30)** iv/iii BC Brunšmid p. 8, 39 (f. Πρώταρχος)
EPIROS:
—AMBRAKIA: **(31)** a. 167 BC *SEG* XXXV 665 A, 7 (s. Αἴσχρων)
EPIROS?: **(32)** ?427 BC *IG* V (1) 1231, 2; cf. Cabanes, *L'Épire* p. 446 (locn.); cf. *SEG* XL 356 (-ōν)
ILLYRIA: **(33)** ii-i BC ib. XXXIV 820 (f. Μοσχίων)
—APOLLONIA: **(34)** hell. *IApoll* 345 (tile) (s. Ἀγήν); **(35)** imp. ib. 46
—BYLLIONES NIKAIA (KLJOS (MOD.)): **(36)** iii/ii BC *SEG* XXXV 696; cf. XXXVIII 569 (?f. Χρήσιμος (Other): slave?)
—EPIDAMNOS-DYRRHACHION: **(37)** hell.-imp. *IDyrrh* 311 (f. Μενίσκα)
KERKYRA: **(38)** s. iv BC *IG* II² 9010; **(39)** c. 330-315 BC *SEG* XXIII 189 I, 13; *Hesp.* 57 (1988) p. 148 B, 7 (*SEG* XXXVI 331); cf. *Hesp.* 48 (1979) pp. 78 f. with pl. 22 (s. Τεύθρας); **(40)** iv/iii BC *IG* IX (1) 706 (Κορκυρα 1 p. 163 no. 1) (f. Φιλόξενος)
KORINTHIA:
—KORINTH: **(41)** s. iii BC *IG* II² 9052, 2, 4; cf. Osborne, *Naturalization* T97 (f. Ἀριστόκλεια)
LAKONIA:
—SPARTA: **(42)** ii BC *IG* V (1) 8, 5 (Bradford (-)) (s. Αἴσχρων)
MESSENIA:
—MESSENE: **(43)** 316-309 BC *IG* II² 1956, 64; *Ancient Macedonia* 5 p. 445 with n. 10 (date); **(44)** c. 223 BC *IG* IX (1)² (1) 31, 34 (f. Καλλικράτης)
—MESSENE?: **(45)** ii/i BC *SEG* XI 979, 18 ([Α]ἰσχρίων)
S. ITALY (CALABRIA):
—TARAS-TARENTUM: **(46)** c. 160 BC *ID* 1716, 5 (s. Ἡρακλείδας, Μυραλλίς (Syracuse))
S. ITALY (LUCANIA):
—HYELE-VELIA: **(47)** iv BC *IG* XIV 656 (Landi, *DISMG* 48) (s. Διονύσιος); **(48)** 188 BC *Syll³* 585, 132 (f. Εὔδοξος)
SICILY: **(49)** hell.? *QUCC* 78 (1995) pp. 132-3 (bronze); **(50)** iii-ii BC *IG* XIV 2398. 1; *Meligunis-Lipara* 2 p. 62 T. 186; 5 p. 72 T. 2003; cf. *Kokalos* 32 (1986) pp. 219-20 nos. 4-11 (tiles)
—MENAI: **(51)** hell.? *Riv. Stor. Antica* 5 (1900-1) p. 56 no. 31 ([Αἰ]σχρίων: s. Βομβυλῖνος)
—MORGANTINA: **(52)** ii BC *SEG* XXVII 655, 8 (Dubois, *IGDS* 194); cf. *PdelP* 44 (1989) p. 205 (s. Ὅλτος); **(53)** ~ *SEG* XXVII 655, 4-5, 7 (Dubois, *IGDS* 194); cf. *PdelP* 44 (1989) p. 205 (s. Στράτιος, f. Στράτιος)
—SYRACUSE: **(54)** iv/iii BC Ugolini, *Alb. Ant.* 2 p. 154 no. 6 (s. Φιλῖνος); **(55)** f. i BC *RE* (6) (Lat. Aeschrio)
—SYRACUSE?: **(56)** 307 BC D.S. xx 60. 1-3

——(Μακ.): **(57)** hell. Manganaro, *PdelP* forthcoming no. 4 II, 7 (s. Ἕρμων)
—ZANKLE-MESSANA: **(58)** c. 316-309 BC *IG* II² 1956, 64; *Ancient Macedonia* 5 p. 445 with n. 10 (date)

**Αἴσχρων**
AITOLIA?: **(1)** 288 BC *IG* II² 652, [20]; Flacelière p. 90 n. 2 ([Αἴσχ]ρων: s. Πρόξενος); **(2)** 204 BC *IG* II² 845, 12 (s. Πρόξενος)
AKARNANIA:
—STRATOS?: **(3)** c. 300 BC *SEG* XIV 475
ARGOLIS:
—ARGOS: **(4)** iii BC *IG* IV (1) 772, 3 (f. Ἀκέστωρ)
—(Polatheis): **(5)** ii-i BC ib. 530, 8; cf. *BCH* 33 (1909) p. 183 n. 2
—MYKENAI: **(6)** ?c. 500-480 BC *IG* IV (1) 492, 7; *LSAG²* p. 174 no. 2 (date)
ARKADIA:
—TEGEA:
——(Krariotai): **(7)** s. iii BC *IG* V (2) 36, 123 (Αἴσχρω[ν]?: f. Καράνιος)
DALMATIA:
—ISSA:
——(Dymanes): **(8)** iv/iii BC Brunšmid p. 8, 32 + Wilhelm, *Neue Beitr.* 3 p. 17 ([Αἴσ]χρων: s. Ἀριστήν)
EPIROS:
—AMBRAKIA: **(9)** 238-168 BC *SNG Cop. Epirus-Acarnania* 35; *SNG Evelpidis* 11 1783 (coins); **(10)** a. 167 BC *SEG* XXXV 665 A, 7 (f. Αἰσχρίων)
—BOUTHROTOS (PRASAIBOI): **(11)** a. 163 BC *IBouthrot* 21, 13 (*SEG* XXXVIII 478) (f. Φιλίστιον)
LAKONIA:
—SPARTA: **(12)** ii BC *IG* V (1) 8, 5 (Bradford (-)) (f. Αἰσχρίων)
S. ITALY (CALABRIA):
—TARAS-TARENTUM: **(13)** iv/iii BC *IG* XIV 668 I, 2 (Landi, *DISMG* 194)
SICILY:
—KAMARINA: **(14)** f. v BC Cordano, *Tessere Pubbliche* 37 (-χρον-: f. Δόξξος)
—MEGARA HYBLAIA: **(15)** c. 500 BC *IvOl* 22 ab, 17 (Dubois, *IGDS* 28; Arena, *Iscr. Sic.* I 52) (or Sicily Selinous: [Α]ἴσχρον)

**Αἰσχυλίδας**
ARGOLIS:
—EPIDAUROS: **(1)** c. 340-320 BC Peek, *NIEpid* 19 B, 20 (Αἰσ[χυλ]ίδας)

**Αἰσχυλῖνος**
EPIROS:
—DODONA*: **(1)** iv BC *Ep. Chron.* 10 (1935) p. 252 no. 9

**Αἰσχύλιος**
ARGOLIS:
—ARGOS: **(1)** iv-iii BC *BCH* 27 (1903) p. 264 no. 8 (gen.?)

**Αἰσχύλις**
SICILY:
—PETRA:
——(Σάννειος): **(1)** f. iii BC *SEG* XXX 1121, 25 (Dubois, *IGDS* 208); *SEG* XL 785 (name) (s. Πράτων)

**Αἰσχυλίς**
SICILY:
—SELINOUS: **(1)** 361 BC *CID* II 4 I, 46

**Αἰσχυλίσκος**
KERKYRA: **(1)** ?s. i BC *IG* IX (1) 737-42 (tiles)

**Αἰσχυλίων**
ARGOLIS:
—NEMEA*: **(1)** v BC *Hesp.* 44 (1975) p. 149 (vase) (-ōν)

## Αἰσχύλος

ACHAIA:
—PELLENE: (1) c. 210-207 BC *IG* IV (1)² 73, 15; *SEG* XXXV 303 (date) (s. Ἀρχιμήδης)
AIGINA: (2) s. v BC *IG* IV (1) 1590 (s. Περίλος)
AKARNANIA: (3) 375 BC Tod, *GHI* II 126, 26
—ASTAKOS: (4) ii BC *IG* IX (1)² (2) 435, 17 (f. Δημῶναξ)
ARGOLIS:
—ARGOS: (5) ?c. 500-480 BC ib. IV (1) 561; cf. *SEG* XI 328; *LSAG*² p. 169 no. 17 (date) (-λλος: s. Θίοψ); (6) c. 458 BC *IG* I³ 1149, 79 ([Α]ἰσχύλος); (7) iii BC ib. IV (1) 618 I, 8 (f. —ίων); (8) ~ ib. 632 (s. Ἀν—); (9) ~ *SEG* XVII 150, 1 (f. Πρατέας); (10) ~ ib. l. 8 (s. Πρατέας); (11) 242 BC Plu., *Arat.* 25; (12) c. 146-32 BC BM coin 1887 6-6-13 (coin); cf. *NC* 1888, p. 10
——(Arachnadai): (13) m. iv BC *SEG* XVII 146, 4
—EPIDAUROS: (14) 364 AD Peek, *NIEpid* 55 (f. Νίκων)
—NEMEA*: (15) f. v BC *SEG* XXIX 353 a
—PHLEIOUS: (16) s. v BC *RE* (10)
ARKADIA:
—MANTINEIA-ANTIGONEIA: (17) c. 300-221 BC *IG* V (2) 323. 88 (tessera) ([Α]ἰσχύλος: s. Πλειστίας)
DALMATIA:
—ISSA:
——(Pamphyloi): (18) iv/iii BC Brunšmid p. 9, 51 (Αἰσχύλο[ς])
ELIS: (19) v/iv BC Paus. vi 1. 3 (f. Σύμμαχος); (20) iii/ii BC *IvOl* 39, 3 (Perlman O.2)
EPIROS:
—ARGOS (AMPHILOCH.): (21) iv/iii BC *SEG* XXXII 563 (f. Κοσσύφα)
ILLYRIA:
—APOLLONIA: (22) c. 250-50 BC Maier 43 (coin) (Ceka 10) (money.)
—EPIDAMNOS-DYRRHACHION: (23) hell.-imp. *IDyrrh* 88 (s. Θεότιμος)
KERKYRA: (24) ?iii BC *IG* IX (1) 695, 6 (Α(ἰ)σχύλος: f. Φιλωνίδας); (25) ii/i BC ib. 876 (Αἰ[σχύλος?]); (26) hell.-imp. ib. 587 + Unp. (*IG* arch.) (locn.)
KORINTHIA:
—KORINTH: (27) f. iv BC Plu., *Tim.* 4
MESSENIA:
—MESSENE: (28) iii BC *SEG* XXIII 209, 11
S. ITALY (BRUTTIUM):
—KROTON: (29) ?c. 500-475 BC ib. XXXIII 768 (bronze); cf. *LSAG*² p. 457 no. R (date) (Ἀ.—edd. and M.L., Ἡἰσχύλος—A.W.J.: s. Ἐχεσθένης)
—LOKROI EPIZEPHYRIOI:
——(Κυλ.): (30) iv/iii BC De Franciscis 6, 2 (f. Τελέδαμος)
—RHEGION: (31) ?iii BC *BCH* 23 (1899) p. 540 no. 27, 2
S. ITALY (CAMPANIA):
—NEAPOLIS: (32) i BC/i AD *INap* 126 ter, 2 (f. Καλλινίκη) ?= (33); (33) ~ ib. l. 5 (Αἰσ[χ]ύ[λος]: f. Καλλινίκη) ?= (32)
—POMPEII: (34) i BC-i AD *IG* XIV 2414. 4-6 (tesserae)
S. ITALY (LUCANIA):
—HERAKLEIA: (35) s. iv BC *BCH* 23 (1899) p. 501 no. 17, 2; 62 (1938) p. 342 n. 1 (date) (f. Γοργέας)
SICILY:
—ADRANON: (36) i BC-i AD? *IG* XIV 567 (s. Χρύσων)
—AKRAI: (37) ii-i BC *SGDI* 3246, 28 (*Akrai* pp. 152-3 no. 2, 28; Dubois, *IGDS* 109) (s. Διονύσιος)
—HALAISA: (38) inc. Manganaro, *QUCC* forthcoming no. 49 (Αἰσχύ[λος])
—KALE AKTE: (39) i BC *IG* II² 10291 (s. Ἀπολλόδωρος)
—KAMARINA: (40) f. v BC Cordano, *Tessere Pubbliche* 1 a (Arena, *Iscr. Sic.* II 125 A) (s. Ἀριστις); (41) iv/iii BC Dubois, *IGDS* 122, 4 (Cordano, 'Camarina VII' 69) (Α(ἰ)σχύλος: f. Νάρων)
—SELINOUS: (42) ?s. iii BC *IG* XIV 271 (Dubois, *IGDS* 56; *IGLMP* 55) (f. Ἀρκεσώι)
—SYRACUSE: (43) 341 BC *CID* II 12 II, 20 ([Αἰ]σχύλος)
—TAUROMENION: (44) c. 159 BC *IG* XIV 421 an. 82 (*SGDI* 5219)
—TYNDARIS: (45) f. i BC Cic., *In Verr.* II iv 48 (Lat. Aeschylus)

## Αἰσχύτης

ARKADIA:
—KLEITOR: (1) 369-361 BC *IG* V (2) 1, 55; Tod, *GHI* II 132 (date)

## Αἴσχυτος

ACHAIA:
—PHARAI: (1) iii-ii BC *Achaean Grave Stelai* 60 (s. Σῖμος)

## Αἴσων

ARGOLIS:
—ARGOS: (1) 420 BC Th. v 40. 3
—EPIDAUROS: (2) c. 365-335 BC *IG* IV (1)² 103, 134

## Αἰσώνιος

ARGOLIS:
—ARGOS: (1) ?i AD Unp. (Argos, Kavvadias)

## Αἰσωπίδας

EPIROS:
—AMBRAKIA: (1) a. 167 BC *SEG* XXXV 665 A, 10 (f. Χαιρέας)

## Αἴσωπος

EPIROS: (1) s. iv BC *IG* II² 8855; cf. *AM* 67 (1942) p. 228 no. 56
S. ITALY (CALABRIA):
—BRENTESION-BRUNDISIUM: (2) imp. *NScav* 1893, p. 443 no. 5 (Lat. C. Caesius Aesopus)
SICILY:
—SYRACUSE: (3) iii-v AD ib. p. 290 no. 46 + Ferrua, *NG* 16 ([Αἴσ]ωπος: s. Καρποκρᾶς)

## Αἰτωλίων

AITOLIA: (1) 217 BC Nachtergael, *Les Galates* 65, 4 ([Αἰ]τωλίων)

## Αἰχμαγόρας

ARGOLIS:
—ARGOS: (1) s. iv BC Unp. (Argos, Kavvadias)

## Αἰχμαῖος

ARKADIA:
—MANTINEIA-ANTIGONEIA: (1) c. 300-221 BC *IG* V (2) 323. 72 (tessera) (s. Ἀλκιππος)

## Αἰχμάνωρ

ELIS:
—SALMONE: (1) ?c. 425 BC *IvOl* 18, 2; *LSAG*² p. 221 no. 20 (date)

## Αἰχμιάδας

KEPHALLENIA:
—PALE: (1) iii/ii BC Unp. (*IG* arch.)

## Αἰχμίας

AKARNANIA:
—PALAIROS: (1) iii/ii BC *IG* IX (1)² (2) 546

## Αἶχμις

ARGOLIS:
—ARGOS: (1) f. iii BC *CID* II 120 A, 11; 121 II, 18 (f. —νων)
ARKADIA:
—ORCHOMENOS: (2) viii BC Paus. viii 5. 10 (s. Βριάκας, ?f. Ἀριστοκράτης: king)

## Αἰχμύλος

ELIS: (1) ?257 BC *FD* III (3) 196, 1 (s. Πυθίων)

## Ἄκα

SICILY:
—HERBESSOS: (1) vi/v BC Dubois, *IGDS* 166 a-b (vase) (Arena, *Iscr. Sic.* II 120)

## Ἀκάκιος

MESSENIA:
—MESSENE: (1) byz. *ABME* 11 (1969) p. 147
S. ITALY (APULIA):
—CANUSIUM: (2) c. 484-519 AD *Epig. Rom. di Canosa* 69 (*CIL* IX 410) (Lat. Acacius)

## Ἀκαμαντία

LAKONIA:
—SPARTA: (1) c. 1-10 AD *IG* V (1) 209, 32; *SEG* XXXV 331 (date) (Bradford (1))

## Ἀκάμας

EPIROS:
—AMBRAKIA: (1) m. iii BC *IG* V (2) 368, 23 ([Ἀ]κάμας)
KORINTHIA:
—KORINTH: (2) c. 570-550 BC Amyx 87. 1 (vase) (Lorber 107) (her.?)

## Ἀκανθίς

LEUKAS: (1) hell.? *IG* IX (1) 553

## Ἄκανθος

LAKONIA:
—SPARTA: (1) 720 BC Moretti, *Olymp.* 17 (Poralla² 46); (2) 421 BC Th. v 19. 2; 24 (Poralla² 47)
S. ITALY (CAMPANIA):
—POMPEII: (3) i BC-i AD *CIL* IV 8565, 7; 8585; 8588 (Lat. Acanthus)
SICILY:
—AKRAGAS: (4) vi BC Luc., *Phal.* 1 9 (fict.)

## Ἀκάνθρωπος

S. ITALY (BRUTTIUM):
—KROTON: (1) ?c. 475 BC *SEG* XXXIII 767 (bronze); cf. XXXIX 1046; *LSAG*² p. 456 no. 23a (date) (Ἀράνθρō-, Ἀρ. Ἄνθρōπος?—Dubois: s. Θέογνις)

## Ἀκαρνάν

AKARNANIA:
—OINIADAI: (1) ?iv-iii BC *IG* IX (1)² (2) 426. 5 (tile)

## Ἀκᾶς

SICILY:
—SYRACUSE:
——(Τῦος): (1) iv BC Manganaro, *PdelP* forthcoming no. 3, 5 (f. Βιδεύς)

## Ἄκαστος

S. ITALY (APULIA):
—LUCERIA: (1) imp. *CIL* IX 857 (Lat. C. Gavius Acastus: freed.)
S. ITALY (CAMPANIA):
—POMPEII: (2) i BC-i AD ib. IV 2449 (Lat. Acastus); (3) ~ ib. 2925 (Lat. Acastus)
—POMPEII*: (4) i BC *Impegno per Pompeii* 7 OS (Castrèn 169. 3) (Lat. Acastus: freed.)

## Ἀκεστίας

S. ITALY (CALABRIA):
—TARAS-TARENTUM: (1) ?iii-ii BC Guarducci, *Ep. Gr.* 3 p. 358 (Landi, *DISMG* 208)

## Ἀκεστόδωρος

ARKADIA:
—MEGALOPOLIS: (1) hell. *RE* (-)

## Ἀκεστορίδας

ARKADIA:
—MEGALOPOLIS: (1) ?iii BC ib.; *FGrH* 28 (-δης)

KORINTHIA:
—KORINTH: (2) 337 BC D.S. xix 5. 1 (-δης); (3) iii BC Peek, *NIEpid* 13, 5 (Ἀκεστορίδ[ας]: f. Δαμοφάνης)

Ἀκέστωρ
ARGOLIS:
—ARGOS: (1) iii BC *IG* IV (1) 772, 3 (s. Αἴσχρων: sculptor)
—HERMIONE: (2) iii BC ib. 729 II, 5 (f. Μάργος)
ARKADIA: (3) iii BC *SEG* XXXVII 352

Ἀκήρατος
ACHAIA:
—PELLENE: (1) iv BC *Eretria* VI 180 (Ἀκήρατος: f. Φραστορίδας)
EPIROS:
—AMBRAKIA: (2) f. ii BC *AD* 39 (1984) Chron. p. 190 + pl. 77 γ (f. Πυθόδωρος); (3) a. 167 BC *SEG* XXXV 665 A, 8 (s. Πυθόδωρος)

Ἀκίνδυνος
ACHAIA:
—AIGEIRA: (1) ii-iii AD *JÖAI* 19-20 (1919) Beibl. p. 40 (f. Σεβῆρος)
LAKONIA:
—SPARTA: (2) ii-iii AD *IG* V (1) 803, 1 (Bradford s.v. Ἀκίνδοινος (-)) (-δοι-); (3) c. 145-150 AD *IG* V (1) 55, 5; 119, 7 (Bradford (-)) (Λ. Ἀπρώνιος Ἀ., [Ἀ]κίν[δυνος]?—119)
S. ITALY (CALABRIA):
—BRENTESION-BRUNDISIUM: (4) imp. *CIL* IX 6123 (Lat. P. Gerellanus Acindynus)
S. ITALY (CAMPANIA):
—DIKAIARCHIA-PUTEOLI: (5) imp. ib. X 1995 (Lat. Acindynus)

Ἄκκα
SICILY:
—TERRAVECCHIA DI CUTI (MOD.): (1) vi/v BC Dubois, *IGDS* 175 c (loomweight) (Arena, *Iscr. Sic.* II 115; *Di Terra in Terra* p. 55 nos. 66-7)

Ἀκμάζων
ARKADIA:
—TEGEA: (1) ii AD *IG* V (2) 55, 52 (s. Ζώσιμος)

Ἀκμαντίδας
KORINTHIA:
—SIKYON: (1) vi/v BC *SEG* XI 244, 65

Ἀκματίδας
LAKONIA:
—SPARTA: (1) s. vi BC Moretti, *Olymp.* 160 (*CEG* I 372; Lazzarini 832; Poralla² 47a; Ebert, *Gr. Sieg.* 9)

Ἀκμονίδας
S. ITALY (CALABRIA):
—TARAS-TARENTUM: (1) iv BC Iamb., *VP* 267 (*FVS* I p. 446) (Ἀχμονίδας—ms.: name—C. Keil)

Ἄκνη
ILLYRIA:
—APOLLONIA: (1) imp. *IApoll* 243

Ἀκόντιος
S. ITALY (CAMPANIA):
—DIKAIARCHIA-PUTEOLI?: (1) imp. *CIL* X 1833; cf. *Puteoli* 11 (1987) p. 42 (Lat. -ntius Acontius)

Ἀκουβία
SICILY:
—SYRACUSE: (1) iii-v AD *IG* XIV 69 (Strazzulla 10; *ASSicilia* 1938-9, p. 26; Wessel 1002)

Ἀκούης
ARKADIA:
—TEGEA: (1) arch. Polyaen. i 11

Ἀκουσιλάδας
S. ITALY (CALABRIA):
—TARAS-TARENTUM: (1) vi BC Iamb., *VP* 267 (*FVS* I p. 446)

Ἀκουσίλαος
ARGOLIS:
—ARGOS:
——Kerkas: (1) v BC *RE* (3) (*FGrH* 2; *FVS* 9) (s. Κάβας)

Ἀκουσίλας
DALMATIA:
—ISSA: (1) iii BC Brunšmid p. 9 fr. H, 6 (Ἀκοσ[ίλας], Ἀκ[ο]ύσ[ιλας]?: f. Διοκλῆς)
——(Hylleis): (2) iv/iii BC ib. p. 9, 54 (f. Μνησίπολις)

Ἀκράγας
ARKADIA:
—LOUSOI: (1) c. 210-207 BC *IG* IV (1)² 73, 24; *SEG* XXXV 303 (date) (s. Κλέϊς)

Ἄκραντος
ARKADIA:
—MANTINEIA-ANTIGONEIA: (1) c. 475-450 BC *IG* V (2) 262, 10 (*IPArk* 8); *LSAG*² p. 216 no. 29 (date) (Ἄδραντος—*IPArk*)

Ἀκράτητος
MESSENIA:
—MESSENE: (1) iv/iii BC *IG* V (1) 1435, 8

Ἀκρατίδας
LAKONIA:
—SPARTA: (1) 334-324 BC *CID* II 79 A I, [20]; 95, [15]; 97, 26; 102 II B, 34; 120 A, 22 (Poralla² 49)

Ἄκρατος
S. ITALY (APULIA):
—BARION*: (1) i BC-i AD *Mus. Arch. di Bari* p. 151 no. 5 (*CIL* IX 301) (Lat. Acratus: freed.?)
S. ITALY (CAMPANIA):
—HERCULANEUM: (2) m. i AD *Cron. Erc.* 7 (1977) p. 116 B a, 13 (Lat. M. Calatorius Acratus)
—POMPEII: (3) i BC-i AD *CIL* IV 3908 (Lat. Acratus); (4) ~ ib. 6783 (Lat. Acratus)

Ἀκρίβεα
ARKADIA:
—THELPHOUSA: (1) imp. *SEG* XXII 325 (-ρεί-)

Ἀκριοκώι
SICILY:
—SELINOUS: (1) m. v BC Dubois, *IGDS* 34 (Arena, *Iscr. Sic.* I 70) (-κόι, Ἀκροικόι—Dubois, Ἀκιδοκόι—Arena)

Ἀκρίς
S. ITALY (CAMPANIA):
—POMPEII: (1) i BC-i AD *Impegno per Pompeii* 15 ES no. 2 (Lat. Acris)

Ἀκρίσιος
KORINTHIA:
—SIKYON: (1) 367 BC X., *HG* vii 1. 45 (Skalet 19); (2) ii-i BC *IG* IV (1) 431 (Ἀκρίσ[ιος])

Ἀκρίφιος
ARKADIA:
—KLEITOR: (1) c. 369 BC Paus. viii 27. 2 (and Arkadia Megalopolis: oikist)

Ἀκροθίνιον
KORINTHIA:
—KORINTH: (1) a. 480 BC Plu., *Mor.* 871 A (d. Ἀδείμαντος)

Ἀκρόπολις
EPIROS:
—NIKOPOLIS: (1) imp. Unp. (Nikopolis Mus.) (Φαωνία Ἀκρόπολεις)

Ἄκρος
SICILY:
—AKRAGAS: (1) f. v BC Dubois, *IGDS* 180 a, 3 (Arena, *Iscr. Sic.* II 90)

Ἀκρότατος
ARGOLIS:
—NEMEA*: (1) iv/iii BC *SEG* XXIX 349 i; *Nemea Guide* pp. 37; 188 (ident.) (kalos) ?= (-/)
EPIROS:
—BOUTHROTOS (PRASAIBOI): (2) a. 163 BC *IBouthrot* 50, 8
LAKONIA:
—SPARTA: (3) c. 350-310 BC *RE* (1) (Bradford (1)) (s. Κλεομένης, f. Ἀρεύς); (4) c. 300-262 BC *RE* (2); *FD* III (4) 418 (Bradford (2)) (s. Ἀρεύς, f. Ἀρεύς: king) ?= (1); (5) 210 BC *IG* IX (1)² (1) 29, 11 (Bradford (3)) (f. —ας)

Ἀκρυπτίδας
ARGOLIS:
—EPIDAUROS: (1) iii/ii BC *IG* IV (1)² 243 (Ἀκρυπτίδας: f. Ἱαρώνυμος); (2) ~ ib. (s. Ἱαρώνυμος, Ἀρισταγόρα)

Ἄκρων
AITOLIA: (1) c. 225-200 BC *FD* III (4) 366, 5
ARGOLIS:
—EPIDAUROS: (2) ii BC Peek, *IAEpid* 153. 20 (s. Εὔαινος)
MESSENIA:
—THOURIA: (3) f. ii BC *SEG* XI 972, 54 (s. Φιλόδαμος)
S. ITALY (CALABRIA):
—LUPIAE: (4) imp. *Ann. Univ. Lecce* 8-9 (1977-80) p. 212 a (Lat. Tut. Acro)
S. ITALY (CAMPANIA):
—HERCULANEUM*: (5) i BC-i AD *CIL* X 1403 g III, 16 (Lat. Acro: freed.)
SICILY:
—AKRAGAS: (6) s. v BC *RE* (3); Supplbd. 1; *FSA* pp. 108 ff.; Page, *FGE* 554 (s. Ξένων: doctor)
—KAMARINA: (7) m. v BC Pi., *O.* v 8 (Cordano, 'Camarina VII' 10) (f. Ψαῦμις)
—SELINOUS: (8) ?c. 425-400 BC Marcadé 1 2; Dubois, *IGDS* 83; *LSAG*² p. 277 no. 44 (date) (s. Πράτων: sculptor)

Ἀκρωνίδας
MESSENIA:
—MESSENE: (1) iii BC *SEG* XXIII 210, 7 (Ἀκρωνί[δ]ας)

Ἀκταῖος
KORINTHIA:
—KORINTH: (1) ii AD *Ag.* VII p. 94 no. 257; *SEG* XXVII 35. 2 (lamps) (Ἀλταῖος—*Ag.*)

Ἀκταίων
KORINTHIA:
—KORINTH: (1) s. viii BC *RE* (3) (s. Μέλισσος)

Ἀκτή
ARGOLIS:
—ARGOS: (1) i BC *SEG* XI 345, 2, 5
ELIS: (2) imp. ib. XLI 390
ILLYRIA:
—APOLLONIA: (3) ii AD *IApoll* 209 (m. Ἰουλ. Φοίβη)
LAKONIA:
—TAINARON-KAINEPOLIS: (4) ?ii BC *IG* V (1) 1252 (d. Ὁμόνοια)
S. ITALY (APULIA):
—RUBI*: (5) i-ii AD *Epigrafia e Territorio* 2 p. 81 no. 18 (*CIL* IX 314) (Lat. Acte: freed.)
S. ITALY (CAMPANIA):
—DIKAIARCHIA-PUTEOLI: (6) imp. ib. X 2865 (Lat. Pompeia Acte: d. Ἀφροδισία)
—HERCULANEUM: (7) 60 AD *PdelP* 1 (1946) p. 382 no. 5, 5 (Lat. Livia Acte)

—POMPEII: (**8**) i BC-i AD *CIL* IV 2057 (Lat. Acte)

**Ἀκτιακή**
SICILY:
—KATANE: (**1**) imp. *IG* XIV 487

**Ἀκτιακός**
KORINTHIA:
—KORINTH: (**1**) m. ii AD ib. VII 1773, 18 (Stephanis 97) (Φάβ. Ἀ.)
LAKONIA:
—SPARTA: (**2**) m. ii AD *IG* v (1) 108, 7 (Bradford (-)) (Τιβ. [Κλ]. Ἀ.)

**Ἀκτιάς**
AKARNANIA:
—PALAIROS: (**1**) hell.-imp. *IG* IX (1)² (2) 562 ([Ἀ]κτιάς (n. pr.?))

**Ἀκτιος**
EPIROS:
—DODONA*: (**1**) hell. *SEG* XIX 428 (n. pr.?)
—NIKOPOLIS: (**2**) imp. *PAE* 1913, p. 97 no. 7 (Sarikakis 74) (Τιβ. Κλ. Ἀ.)

**Ἀκύλας**
ELIS: (**1**) ii/iii AD *IvOl* 106, 8 ([Ἀ]κύλας: I f. Ἀκύλας II); (**2**) ~ ib. l. 8 (II s. Ἀκύλας I)
S. ITALY (BRUTTIUM):
—LOKROI EPIZEPHYRIOI: (**3**) i BC-i AD? Landi, *DISMG* 244, 9

**Ἀκυλίνη**
ARGOLIS:
—EPIDAUROS: (**1**) ii-iii AD *IG* IV (1)² 569 (Αἰλ. Ἀκυλείνη: d. Π. Αἰλ. Εὔτυχος)

**Ἀκύλιος**
MESSENIA:
—ASINE: (**1**) i/ii AD ib. v (1) 1410 (Γάιος Ἀ.)

**Ἀλαθίων**
AITOLIA: (**1**) ?a. 246 BC *SGDI* 2508, 3

**Ἀλάστωρ**
KORINTHIA:
—KORINTH: (**1**) c. 570-550 BC Amyx 66. 16 (vase) (Lorber 122) (-στōρ: her.)

**Ἄλβιος**
SICILY:
—SYRACUSE: (**1**) iii-v AD *IG* XIV 70 (Strazzulla 11)

**Ἄλγαλσος**
ILLYRIA:
—PARTHINI: (**1**) 168 BC Liv. xliv 30. 13 (Lat. Algalsus)

**Ἀλεᾶτις**
ARGOLIS:
—NEMEA*: (**1**) c. 368 BC *SEG* XI 292

**Ἀλείδας**
SICILY:
—SEGESTA: (**1**) iv/iii BC ib. XXX 1119, 7 (Dubois, *IGDS* 206); *SEG* XL 785 (name) (f. Ἀπέλλιχος); (**2**) ~ ib. XLI 827

**Ἀλειός**
ARKADIA:
—KLEITOR: (**1**) c. 230-200 BC *BCH* 45 (1921) p. 12 II, 70 + *SEG* XXX 494 (f. Δαμοτάγης)
—MEGALOPOLIS: (**2**) hell.? *IG* v (2) 448, 8 ([Ἀ]λειός)

**Ἀλέκιος?**
KORINTHIA:
—KORINTH: (**1**) ii-iii AD *SEG* XXVII 35. 3 (lamp) (Ἀλέκιος)

**Ἀλεκτορίων**
ARGOLIS:
—ARGOS: (**1**) ii-iii AD ib. XLI 285 I, 10; cf. *BCH* 115 (1991) p. 322 (n. pr.?)

**Ἀλεκτρύων**
LAKONIA: (**1**) hell.-imp.? *Bronzes grecs et romains (Madrid)* 563 (?f. Ἀντιγόνη)

**Ἄλεξα**
KERKYRA: (**1**) ii BC *AM* 27 (1902) p. 371 no. 54 (*SEG* XXXIII 444)

**Ἀλεξαμενός**
AITOLIA: (**1**) ?278-277 BC *FD* III (1) 87, 3; 88, 2; (**2**) ?240-228 BC ib. III (3) 218 A, 2

**Ἀλεξάνδρα**
ARKADIA:
—TEGEA: (**1**) ii-iii AD *IG* v (2) 187 (d. Ἀγαθόκλεια)
LAKONIA:
—SPARTA: (**2**) i-ii AD ib. v (1) 770 (Bradford (-)) (m. Ἀλκιδάμα)
LEUKAS: (**3**) imp. *IG* IX (1) 596 (Ἰουλ. Ἀ.)
S. ITALY (APULIA):
—VENUSIA: (**4**) v-vi AD *CIL* IX 6231 (ЯIWE I 63) (Lat. Alexan(d)ra, Alexan(d)r(i)a—ЯIWE: Jew)
SICILY:
—SYRACUSE: (**5**) 179 BC *PRein* III 29 a; (**6**) iii-v AD Barreca 18 (Wessel 848); cf. Ferrua, *NG* 91 (Ἀλεκαξά(ν)δρα)

**Ἀλεξάνδρεια**
ARGOLIS:
—EPIDAUROS: (**1**) hell. *IG* IV (1)² 30 (-ρεα)
DALMATIA:
—RIZON (NR.): (**2**) imp. Šašel, *IL* 1855 (Lat. Alexandria)
ILLYRIA:
—EPIDAMNOS-DYRRHACHION: (**3**) i BC-i AD *CIL* III 617 (Sestieri, *ILat. Albania* 34) (Lat. Fregan[i]a Alexandr[e]a: d. Εὐνομία)
KEPHALLENIA:
—SAME?: (**4**) ?ii AD Clem. Al., *Strom.* iii 5. 2 (m. Ἐπιφάνης: fict.)
KORINTHIA:
—KORINTH: (**5**) imp. *Corinth* VIII (2) 181 (Lat. [A]lexandria); (**6**) byz. ib. VIII (3) 678 ([Ἀλ]εξάνδρια)
S. ITALY (CAMPANIA): (**7**) imp. *IG* XIV 890 (fals.?)
—DIKAIARCHIA-PUTEOLI: (**8**) imp. *CIL* X 2038 (Lat. Alexandria: d. Πελάγιος); (**9**) ~ *NScav* 1902, p. 398 (Lat. Marcia Alexandria: d. Ὀνήσιμος)
—MISENUM: (**10**) imp. *Eph. Ep.* VIII 425 (Lat. Alexandria: d. Ἀλέξανδρος)
—STABIAE: (**11**) 535 AD *CIL* X 786 (Lat. Alexandria)
SICILY:
—KATANE: (**12**) imp. ib. 7080 (Lat. Numonia Alexandrea)
—SYRACUSE: (**13**) iii-v AD *ASSiracusano* 1956, p. 63 = Ferrua, *NG* 339 b; (**14**) ~ Strazzulla 460 (Lat. Alexsandria); (**15**) iv-v AD *IG* XIV 71 (Strazzulla 12); (**16**) ~ Führer–Schultze p. 289 a (Wessel 851 a); (**17**) ~ Führer–Schultze p. 289 b (Wessel 851 b)

**Ἀλεξανδρίδας**
LAKONIA:
—SPARTA: (**1**) 316 BC *IG* v (2) 549, 31 (Poralla² 49b; Bradford (-)) (f. Σελείδας)

**Ἀλέξανδρος**
ACHAIA: (**1**) 146 BC *IG* IV (1)² 28, 88 (f. Ἡρακλείδας: synoikos); (**2**) ~ ib. l. 100 (f. Διονύσιος: synoikos); (**3**) ~ ib. l. 142 (s. Ὀφέλων: synoikos); (**4**) iii AD *SEG* XIII 480; cf. *BE* 1955, no. 95 (Μ. Αὐρ. Ἀ.)

—PATRAI: (**5**) 185 BC *IG* IX (1)² (1) 32, 44 (f. Δορκίας, Στράτων)
AIGINA: (**6**) ii BC *SEG* XI 8, 1; (**7**) ii/i BC *Alt-Ägina* I (2) p. 43 no. 3, 1 (f. Πόσσιτος); (**8**) imp. ib. p. 46 no. 25 (I f. Ἀλέξανδρος II); (**9**) ~ ib. (II s. Ἀλέξανδρος I); (**10**) ?i-ii AD ib. p. 46 no. 21 ([Ἀλ]έξανδρος: I f. Ἀλέξανδρος II); (**11**) ~ ib. ([Ἀλέξ]ανδρος: II s. Ἀλέξανδρος I); (**12**) ?f. iii AD ib. p. 49 no. 43 (Αὐρ. Ἀ.: s. Ἐπικλῆς)
AIGINA?: (**13**) hell.? *EAD* XXX p. 357 no. 23 (f. Κέρδων)
AITOLIA: (**14**) 322 BC D.S. xviii 38. 1; cf. *IG* IX (1)² (1) p. XIII, 106; (**15**) ?316 BC *FD* III (4) 387, 3 (s. Φυρταῖος); (**16**) c. 260 BC ib. 178, 2 ([Ἀλέξ]ανδρος); (**17**) ?257 BC Nachtergael, *Les Galates* 7, 4; (**18**) ?254 BC *Syll*³ 436, 3; Nachtergael, *Les Galates* 9, 5; (**19**) ?a. 246 BC *SGDI* 2508, 2; (**20**) ~ ib. 2509, 3; (**21**) 244 or 240 BC ib. 2512, 2 (Flacelière p. 402 no. 28 a); Nachtergael, *Les Galates* 59, [3]; (**22**) ?225 BC ib. 63, 3; (**23**) iii/ii BC Pantos, *Sphragismata* p. 130 no. 105; p. 437; (**24**) 219 BC *RE* (30); Plb. iv 57. 2; 58. 9; (**25**) 217 BC Nachtergael, *Les Galates* 65, 4; (**26**) 193 BC *Syll*³ 603, 4
—AGRAIOI: (**27**) ?ii-i BC *IG* IX (1)² (1) 167
—BOUKATION?: (**28**) c. 162 BC ib. 106, 13
—KALLION/KALLIPOLIS: (**29**) byz. *BCH* 98 (1974) p. 635 (s. Ἀγαθοκλῆς, Ἰλαρία)
—KALYDON: (**30**) 210-185 BC *IG* IX (1)² (1) pp. L f., s.a. 204 BC, 196 BC, 185 BC; 29, 22; 30, 10, 14; 31, 16 (s. Νικίας); (**31**) 178 BC *Syll*³ 636, 12 (f. Νικίας); (**32**) 154 BC *IG* IX (1)² (1) p. LII, s.a. 154 BC; IX (1)² (3) 638 9, 1, 2, 20 (s. Νικίας)
—KONOPE-ARSINOE: (**33**) 184 BC ib. IX (1)² (1) 131, 11 (f. Ἀλεξομενός)
—PLEURON: (**34**) iv/iii BC *RE* (84); *Coll. Alex.* pp. 121 ff. (s. Σάτυρος, Στρατόκλεια)
—POTIDANIA: (**35**) m. ii BC *SBBerlAk* 1936, p. 371 b, 13 (*SEG* XLI 528 B) (f. Φίλιππος)
—THERMOS: (**36**) 163 BC *IG* IX (1)² (1) 102, 7 (f. Φαλακρίων)
—THYRISKAIOI: (**37**) 217-207 BC *FD* III (3) 221, 5 + *BCH* 73 (1949) p. 268 no. 19 (Ἀλέ[ξαν]δρος)
—TRICHONION: (**38**) iii BC *IG* IX (1)² (1) 68 (s. Ἀλέξων) ?= (**40**); (**39**) c. 272-245 BC ib. pp. XLIX ff., s.a. 261 BC, 253 BC, 245 BC; cf. 13, 4 n.; (**40**) 218 BC Plb. v 13 ?= (**38**); (**41**) 203-173 BC *IG* IX (1)² (1) 30, 15; cf. Liv. xxxv 12. 6 (family) (f. Δικαίαρχος, Θόας); (**42**) ii BC *IG* IX (1)² (1) 76 (s. Θόας); (**43**) c. 141 BC ib. 34, 22; 137, 28 (s. Ἀλέξων)
AITOLIA?: (**44**) hell. *SBBerlAk* 1936, p. 386 no. 3 b (bullet) ([Ἀ]λέξανδρος); (**45**) c. 215-205 BC *FD* III (4) 362, 5 (Ἀλέξανδρος]); (**46**) 139-122 BC ib. III (6) 83, 4 (s. Ἀμφίλοχος, Κλεαρέτα)
AKARNANIA: (**47**) iii/ii BC *RE* (59); *Syll*³ 585, 32 (s. Ἀντίοχος, f. Φίλιππος, Ἀντίγονος)
—ALYZIA: (**48**) ?353 BC Tod, *GHI* II 160, 19 ([Ἀ]λέξανδρος: f. Θεο—)
—ANAKTORION (NR.): (**49**) iv-iii BC *SEG* XXXVI 534 (Ἀλέξαν[δρος])
—ANAKTORION: (**50**) hell. *AD* 44 (1989) Chron. p. 145 (f. Πυστάκα)
—STRATOS: (**51**) s. iii BC *IG* IX (1)² (2) 404; Fraser–Rönne, *BWGT* pl. 25 ([Ἀλ]έξανδρος); (**52**) c. 169 BC *IG* IX (1)² (1) 69 (s. Πολεμαῖος); (**53**) i BC/i AD? Heuzey, *Le Mont Olympe* p. 490 no. 62
—THYRREION: (**54**) 216 BC *IG* IX (1)² (2) 583, 18 (f. Σωτίων); (**55**) ii BC ib. 248, 10 (f. Ἀλκαίνετος)
AKARNANIA?: (**56**) ii BC Unp. (Agrinion Mus.)
ARGOLIS:
—ARGOS: (**57**) ii BC *IG* II² 8374, 2 (f. Σωσικράτεια); (**58**) ~ *BCH* 33 (1909) pp. 456-7 no. 23, 8; (**59**) 70-79 AD *IG* IV (1) 584, 4 (f. —ης); (**60**) ii AD *SEG* XVI 253, 9 (Γ. Φλ. Ἀ.)

—EPIDAUROS: (61) iii-ii BC Peek, *IAEpid* 312 ([Ἀ]λέξανδρος: f. Δωρόθεος); (62) ii-iii AD *IG* IV (1)² 497; 498

—HERMIONE: (63) ii-i BC ib. IV (1) 732 I, 15 (f. Σαμβατεύς); (64) i BC-i AD? ib. 730 III, 6 (f. Ἀσία); (65) ~ ib. 734, 8

—KLEONAI: (66) imp. ib. 490, 10 (Δομίτιος Ἀ.)

—KLEONAI?: (67) imp. *CIL* III 545, 1 (Lat. Alexander)

—METHANA-ARSINOE: (68) i BC *IG* IV (1) 853, 2 (Ἀλέξα[νδρος])

—VOURVOURA (MOD.): (69) ii-iii AD *BCH* 66-7 (1942-3) p. 326

ARKADIA: (70) iv/iii BC *IG* II² 9973 (s. Ἀλεξίμαχος); (71) 308 BC ib. V (2) 550, 1; (72) ?257 BC Nachtergael, *Les Galates* 7, 10; cf. Stephanis 2106 (f. Πολύμναστος)

—KLEITOR: (73) a. 212 AD *IG* V (2) 369, 24 + *SEG* XXXI 347, 17 (Ἰούλ. Ἀ.); (74) ~ *IG* V (2) 369, 27 + *SEG* XXXI 347, 20 (I f. Αὐρ. Ἀλέξανδρος II); (75) ~ *IG* V (2) 369, 27 + *SEG* XXXI 347, 20 (Αὐρ. Ἀ.: II s. Ἀλέξανδρος I)

—MANTINEIA-ANTIGONEIA: (76) i BC *IG* V (2) 332

—TEGEA: (77) m. iv BC ib. 6, 117 (Ἀλ[έξ]εαν[δρος]?); (78) c. 240-229 BC ib. 11, 14; (79) ii AD ib. 55, 29 (f. Ζώσιμος); (80) 165 AD ib. 50, 15 (s. Θεογείτων); (81) ~ ib. l. 52 (f. Ἀριστοκλῆς); (82) ~ ib. l. 64 (f. Αὐτόλυκος); (83) ~ ib. l. 79 (f. Ἐπίκτητος)

DALMATIA:

—TRAGURION: (84) imp. *CIL* III 2689 (Lat. L. Iul. Alexander)

ELIS: (85) 36-24 BC *IvOl* 62, 17 (I f. Ἀλέξανδρος II: Iamidai); (86) ~ ib. l. 17 (II s. Ἀλέξανδρος I); (87) ii-iii AD ib. 568 (s. —φῶν); (88) f. ii AD ib. 92, 25 (f. Ἄνθος); (89) ii/iii AD ib. 103, 15; 107, 8; 110, 14; 112, [2] (Αὐ(ρ). Ἀ.—110: II s. Ἀλέξανδρος I: mantis/Iamidai); (90) ~ ib. 103, [15]; 107, 8; 110, 14; 112, [2] (I f. Αὐρ. Ἀλέξανδρος II); (91) iii AD *SEG* XV 259, 7; (92) m. iii AD *IvOl* 120, 9 ([Ἀλέξα]νδρος: f. Βιβούλλιος Φαυστινιανός)

EPIROS: (93) iii/ii BC Liv. xxxii 10. 2 (Lat. Alexander); (94) m. ii BC *Thess. Mnem.* 46 (f. Παρμενίσκος)

—ANTIGONEIA: (95) v-vi AD *Iliria* 1977-8, p. 234 pl. V c + *BE* 1980, no. 303 (mosaic)

—BOUTHROTOS (PRASAIBOI): (96) a. 163 BC *IBouthrot* 25, 10; 31, 90 (*SEG* XXXVIII 483; 490) (s. Ἀριστοκλῆς); (97) ~ *IBouthrot* 31, 87 (*SEG* XXXVIII 490) (f. Ἀριστοκλῆς); (98) ~ *IBouthrot* 42, 14 (*SEG* XXXVIII 501); (99) ~ *IBouthrot* 45, 8 (s. Πύρρος); (100) ~ ib. 158

——Kestrinoi: (101) a. 163 BC ib. 25, 1 (*SEG* XXXVIII 483) (f. Δείνων)

——Pullieioi: (102) a. 163 BC *IBouthrot* 115, 11 (s. Ἀνεροίτας)

—DODONA: (103) iii BC Antoniou, *Dodone* Ba, 7; (104) ~ ib. l. 24 (Ἀλέξανδρος)

—DODONA*: (105) ii BC *PAE* 1968, p. 52 no. 6; cf. *BE* 1995, no. 292 (Ἀλέξα[νδρος?]: Ἀνδρ—); (106) ~ *PAE* 1968, p. 52 no. 6; cf. *BE* 1995, no. 292 (Ἀλέξαν[δρος?]: s. Ἀνδρομ—)

—KASSOPE: (107) 234-168 BC Dakaris, *Kassope* p. 23 (*SEG* XXXV 671) (Ἀλεξά[νδρος]); (108) i BC Cabanes, *L'Épire* p. 564 no. 42, 9 (*SEG* XXVI 718)

—KOILOPOI: (109) ?iv/iii BC *SGDI* 1354, 6; cf. Cabanes, *L'Épire* p. 582 no. 58

—MOLOSSOI: (110) iv BC *RE* (19) (s. Ἀλκέτας); (111) m. iv BC ib. (6); Berve 38; Cabanes, *L'Épire* index s.v. (s. Νεοπτόλεμος, f. Νεοπτόλεμος, Κάδμεια: king I); (112) ~ ib. p. 539 no. 3, 14; (113) f. iii BC *RE* (7) (s. Πύρρος, Λάνασσα (Syracuse): king II)

—NIKOPOLIS: (114) imp. *SEG* XLII 546 (?s. —όβουλος); (115) ~ Unp. (Nikopolis Mus.) (Ἀλέσ-); (116) ~ ib. (s. Θράσων)

—TEPELENE (MOD.): (117) hell.-imp. *Iliria* 1976, p. 320 with pl. 7 (f. Κόσμιλλα)

—THESPROTOI: (118) m. iv BC Cabanes, *L'Épire* p. 576 no. 49, 2 (*SEG* XXVI 717)

—TIAIOI: (119) c. 330 BC Cabanes, *L'Épire* p. 580 no. 55, 9

—VOTONOSI (MOD.): (120) ?m. iii BC *SEG* XXIV 464 (f. Θεύδοτος)

ILLYRIA:

—AMANTIA: (121) ii BC Ugolini, *Alb. Ant.* 1 p. 191 no. 9 (f. Φίντων); (122) ii-i BC *SEG* I 265 (Guarducci, *Ep. Gr.* 1 p. 372) (f. Ἀριστώ)

—APOLLONIA: (123) i BC Maier 128 (coin) (pryt.); (124) imp. *IApoll* 27 (Ἀλέξαν[δρος])

—BYLLIONES: (125) iii/ii BC *SEG* XXXV 696; cf. XXXVIII 569 (f. Βοῦλος)

—EPIDAMNOS-DYRRHACHION: (126) c. 250-50 BC Maier 149; 161; 257; 289; 293; Münsterberg p. 39; Nachtr. p. 16 (coin) (Ceka 21 with *IApoll Ref. Bibl.* n. 9; 22-7) (money.); (127) hell.-imp. *IDyrrh* 390 (f. Σωτήριχος)

—LYCHNIDOS: (128) ?i-ii AD *ZA* 6 (1956) p. 169 no. 4 (f. Ἀμύντας); (129) ii-iii AD *Sp.* 71 (1931) p. 110 no. 266 (*SEG* XXXIX 603) (f. Ἀρίστων); (130) ~ *Sp.* 71 (1931) p. 110 no. 266 (*SEG* XXXIX 603) (s. Ἀρίστων, Ἀννία); (131) ~ *Sp.* 77 (1934) p. 51 no. 45

—OLYMPE: (132) s. iii BC *SEG* XXXV 697 (f. Ἀρχέλαος)

ILLYRIA?:

—APOLLONIA: (133) iv-iii BC *IG* IX (2) 1174 (*IApoll* 312) (f. Σίμα)

KEPHALLENIA: (134) i BC-i AD *IRhodPer* 471, 1

KERKYRA: (135) b. 227 BC *GVI* 922, 2 (*Gr. Gr.* 140) (s. Σάτυρος, Καλλιόπα)

KORINTHIA:

—KORINTH: (136) viii BC *FGrH* 244 F 331. 3 (king); (137) imp. *CIL* III 7272, 2 (Lat. Antonius Alexander: s. Ἀντ. Τιμόθεος); (138) ?ii AD *IG* VII 3431; (139) iii/iv AD *Ag.* VII p. 90 no. 249; *SEG* XXXVI 323 (lamps) ([Ἀλ]έξανδρος—*Ag.*); (140) ~ *Corinth* VIII (3) 305, 4 (*GVI* 592) (f. Νικίας); (141) byz. *Corinth* VIII (3) 526 (Ἀλέξαν[δρος]); (142) ~ ib. 650 (Ἀλέξ[ανδρος]?); (143) vii-viii AD *SEG* XXIX 307

—KORINTH*: (144) i BC/i AD ib. XI 214 a

—SIKYON: (145) b. 356 BC *CID* II 8 II, 12; (146) f. iii BC *Mnem.* NS 44 (1916) p. 65 (Skalet 20) (I f. Ἀλέξανδρος II); (147) ~ *Mnem.* NS 44 (1916) p. 65 (Skalet 21) (II s. Ἀλέξανδρος I)

LAKONIA:

—EPIDAUROS LIMERA: (148) ii AD *SEG* XI 894 a, 4, 7 = XLI 311 (s. Ὀνήσιμος)

—HYPERTELEATON*: (149) imp. *IG* V (1) 1030

—KARYAI: (150) imp. *SEG* XI 891

—KYTHERA: (151) inc. *FGrH* 275 F 83; *RE* (69) (Poralla² 49c; Stephanis 105)

—SPARTA: (152) 370 BC D.S. xv 64. 2 (Poralla² 51); (153) c. 175-200 AD *IG* V (1) 468, 3; *SEG* XI 784 (date) (Bradford (1)) (Ἀλέξανδ[ρος]: II s. Ἀλέξανδρος I); (154) ~ *IG* V (1) 468, 5; *SEG* XI 784 (date) (Bradford (4)) (I f. Ἀλέξανδρος II); (155) iii AD *SEG* XI 854 (Bradford (3))

MESSENIA:

—KORONE: (156) 246 AD *IG* V (1) 1398, 95 (Αὐρ. Ἀ.)

—MESSENE: (157) hell.-imp. *PAE* 1991, p. 106 no. 8, 9; (158) ?f. i AD ib. 1992, p. 79, 10

—MESSENE*: (159) 343 AD *ABME* 11 (1969) p. 88 (bp.)

—PHARAI?: (160) imp. *IG* V (1) 1365; cf. PM 1684 (f. Θεόφιλος)

—PROTE*: (161) ?i AD *IG* V (1) 1535; (162) iii AD *SEG* XI 1009 (f. Γαλατίας)

S. ITALY (APULIA):

—CANUSIUM: (163) 223 AD *Epig. Rom. di Canosa* 35 II, 18 (*CIL* IX 338) (Lat. Q. Iunius Alexander); (164) ~ *Epig. Rom. di Canosa* 35 IV, 2 (*CIL* IX 338) (Lat. T. Pompeius Alexander); (165) byz. *Riv. Arch. Crist.* 69 (1993) p. 113 (Lat. Alexander)

—HERDONIA: (166) ?ii/i BC *Taras* 9 (1989) p. 224 (Lat. Pilipus Cepalo Faber Alexsand(er))

—LUCERIA: (167) imp. *ASP* 34 (1981) p. 34 no. 44 (Lat. Alexander)

—LUCERIA*: (168) imp. *CIL* IX 885 (Lat. L. Saenius Alexander: freed.)

S. ITALY (APULIA)?: (169) f. i BC Desy, *Timbres amphoriques* 44; 119; 133-4; 151; 321-3; 1178; 1240 (amph.) (Lat. Alex(ander))

S. ITALY (BRUTTIUM):

—HIPPONION-VIBO VALENTIA: (170) imp. *CIL* X 82 (Lat. C. Segulius Alexander)

—HIPPONION-VIBO VALENTIA*: (171) imp. ib. (Lat. Alexander: freed.)

—SYBARIS-THOURIOI-COPIAE: (172) f. i AD *NScav* 1970, Suppl. 3 p. 551 (Lat. M. Caninius Al[exan]der)

—TAURIANA: (173) imp. *Rend. Linc.* 19 (1964) p. 141 no. 25 (Lat. [A]lexsande(r))

S. ITALY (CALABRIA):

—BRENTESION-BRUNDISIUM: (174) imp. *NScav* 1893, p. 444 no. 8 (Lat. [Ale]xsande[r])

—TARAS-TARENTUM: (175) c. 302-280 BC Vlasto 697 (coin) (Evans, *Horsemen* p. 134 VI D.4) (Ἀλέξαν(δρος))

S. ITALY (CAMPANIA):

—DIKAIARCHIA-PUTEOLI: (176) imp. *AJA* 2 (1898) p. 378 no. 12 (Lat. C. Calvius Alexander); (177) ~ *IG* XIV 850 (Γ. Νυμφ(ίδιος) Ἀλέξα(νδρος)?); (178) ~ *CIL* X 1723 (Lat. L. Iulius Alexander); (179) ~ ib. 2036 (Lat. Alexander: ?f. Primigenia); (180) ~ ib. 2037 (Lat. —ius Alexander); (181) ~ ib. 2125 (Lat. T. Aufid. Alexander); (182) ~ ib. 2296 (Lat. Clodius Alexander); (183) ~ ib. 3092 (Lat. T. Vestorius Alexander); (184) m. i AD Camodeca, *L'Archivio Puteolano* I p. 196 (Lat. A. —utius Alexander)

—DIKAIARCHIA-PUTEOLI*: (185) imp. *CIL* X 1962 (Lat. L. Faenius Alexand(e)r: freed.); (186) ~ ib. 2402 (Lat. P. Fabius Alexander: freed.); (187) ~ ib. 3019 (Lat. C. Trebius Alexander: freed.); (188) ~ ib. 3028 (Lat. M. Tullius Alexander: freed.); (189) i/ii AD ib. 1740 (*Puteoli* 7-8 (1983-4) p. 295 no. 1) (Lat. Alexander: s. Ὀρόντης: imp. freed.)

—HERCULANEUM: (190) i BC-i AD *CIL* X 1403 c I, 2 (Lat. C. Iulius Alexander); (191) m. i AD *PdelP* 6 (1951) p. 224 no. 1 (Lat. Q. Granius Alexander); (192) 41-79 AD *Cron. Erc.* 7 (1977) p. 115 A c, 14 (Lat. C. Brinnius Alexander)

—KYME: (193) imp. *AJA* 2 (1898) p. 397 no. 62 (Lat. C. Laecanius Alexander); (194) ~ *Eph. Ep.* VIII 443 (Lat. L. Valerius Alexa[nder]); (195) ii-iii AD *SEG* XXIX 948 (f. Λεωνίδης)

—LITERNUM: (196) imp. *CIL* X 3719 (Lat. C. Cassius Alexander: f. Cassia Spes)

—MISENUM: (197) imp. *Eph. Ep.* VIII 425 (Lat. L. Aemilius Alexand(er): f. Ἀλεξάνδρεια)

—MISENUM*: (198) imp. *CIL* X 3394 (Lat. L. Aelius Alexander); (199) ~ ib. 3447 (Lat. L. Crispius Alexander); (200) ~ ib. 3675 (Lat. M. Antonius Alexander: freed.); (201) ?i-ii AD ib. 3582 (Lat. C. Iulius Alexander); (202) 246 AD *NScav* 1909, p. 210 (*ILS* 9221) (Lat. C. Iulius Alexander); (203) 247 AD *CIL* X 3335 (Lat. T. Fl. Alexander: I f. Ἀλέξανδρος II, Fl. Marcus, Ulp. Sabinus, Aurel. Fausta); (204) ~ ib. (Lat. Marc. Alexander: II s. Ἀλέξανδρος I)

—NEAPOLIS: (205) c. 100 BC *ID* 1755, 4; 1931, 2 (f. Σαραπίων); (206) 203 AD *CIL* VI 220, 11 (Lat. T. Flavius Alexander)

—PITHEKOUSSAI-AENARIA: (207) imp. ib. X 6796 (Lat. M. Octavius Alexander)

—POMPEII: (208) i BC-i AD ib. IV 1397, 5 (Castrèn 155. 2) (Lat. Domitius Alexander); (209) ~ *CIL* IV 1593 (Lat. A[lex]ander); (210) ~ ib. 2432; (211) ~ ib. 4535 (Lat. Alexan[der]); (212) ~ ib. 4698 (Lat. Alexander);

**(213)** ~ ib. 5128 (Lat. Alexander); **(214)** ~ ib. 9258; cf. *Gnomon* 45 (1973) p. 275 (Castrèn 35. 4) (Lat. M. Anton. Alexander: freed.); **(215)** ~ *CIL* x 8058. 8 (seal) (Castrèn 65. 2) (Lat. Ti. Babinius Alexan(der)); **(216)** 32 AD *CIL* x 900, 4 (*Eph. Ep.* VIII 853) (Lat. Alexander); **(217)** ?33-34 AD *CIL* x 909 (Lat. Alexand[er])
—POMPEII*: **(218)** i AD ib. 8042. 44 (tiles) (Lat. Domitius Alexan(der))
—SALERNUM: **(219)** imp. *IItal* I (I) 139 (Lat. Q. Messius Alexander)
—SALERNUM*: **(220)** imp. ib. 81 (*CIL* x 627) (Lat. C. Proculeius Alexander: f. Proculeius Magnus: freed.); **(221)** i/ii AD *IItal* I (I) 15 (Sinn, *Stadtröm. Marmorurnen* 460) (Lat. C. Iulius Alexander); **(222)** ~ *IItal* I (I) 15 (Sinn, *Stadtröm. Marmorurnen* 460) (Lat. L. Lucretius Alexander)
—STABIAE (NR.): **(223)** i AD *Riv. Ist. Naz. Arch. Stor. d'Arte* 10 (1987) p. 83 nos. 197-202 (Lat. Domitius Alexan(der))
S. ITALY (LUCANIA):
—HYELE-VELIA: **(224)** c. 50 BC *IG* VII 1765, 9; cf. *BSA* 70 (1975) pp. 132-3 (date) (f. Ζωῖλος)
SICILY:
—AKRAGAS: **(225)** s. ii BC *Acragas Graeca* 1 p. 34 no. 5, 7 (*IGUR* 2; Dubois, *IGDS* 185) (f. Ἀδρανίων)
—SYRACUSE: **(226)** iii-v AD *IG* XIV 72 (Strazzulla 13); **(227)** ~ *IG* XIV 2406. 8 (seal); **(228)** ~ *Riv. Arch. Crist.* 36 (1960) p. 29 no. 24; **(229)** ~ Strazzulla 305 (Agnello 24; Wessel 860); **(230)** ~ ib. 714 (Barreca 17)
—TAUROMENION: **(231)** c. 148 BC *IGSI* 4 III (IV), 57 an. 93 (s. Ξένων)
——(Ἱππ.): **(232)** ?ii/i BC *IG* XIV 421 D an. 5; 421 D an. 9 (*SGDI* 5219) ([Ἀλέξανδρ]ος—an. 5: s. Ξάνθιππος, f. Ξάνθιππος)
——(Σιπποκ.): **(233)** f. i BC *Cron. Arch.* 3 (1964) p. 45 IV, 7 (s. Ξάνθιππος)
SICILY?: **(234)** iv-v AD *SEG* XVI 568 (lamp)

**Ἀλεξάνωρ**
ACHAIA:
—AIGION: **(1)** f. ii BC *Corinth* VIII (I) 2, 2, 7 (f. Νικάδας)
ARKADIA:
—MEGALOPOLIS: **(2)** ?145 BC *IG* v (2) 439, 37 (f. Θεότιμος)
EPIROS:
—AMBRAKIA: **(3)** f. ii BC *AD* 39 (1984) Chron. p. 190 + pl. 77 γ (f. Ἀντίβουλος)
—BOUTHROTOS (PRASAIBOI): **(4)** a. 163 BC *IBouthrot* 28, 36; 29, 37; 36, 17 (*SEG* XXXVIII 486; 487; 495); *IBouthrot* 139, 6 (s. Ἀρχίδαμος); **(5)** ~ ib. 34, 1 (*SEG* XXXVIII 493)
—DODONA: **(6)** iii BC Antoniou, *Dodone* Aa, 14
—MOLOSSOI: **(7)** iii/ii BC *Syll*³ 1206, 5; cf. Cabanes, *L'Épire* p. 583 no. 60
KEPHALLENIA:
—SAME: **(8)** 293-168 BC *PAE* 1912, p. 188 no. 148 (s. Λαμίσκος)
LAKONIA:
—SPARTA: **(9)** i BC/i AD *IG* v (1) 146, 8 (Bradford (2)) ([Ἀλε]ξάνωρ); **(10)** ii AD *IG* v (1) 726, 3 (*GVI* 646; Bradford (1))
PELOPONNESE?: **(11)** iii BC *IG* v (1) 1426, 31 (f. Αὐτόλοχος) ?= (*12*); **(12)** s. iii BC ib. l. 16 (s. Λυσίων) ?= (*11*)

**Ἀλέξαρχος**
ACHAIA: **(1)** 146 BC ib. IV (1)² 28, 77 (f. Δεινίας: synoikos)
ARKADIA:
—TEGEA:
——(Athaneatai): **(2)** s. iv BC ib. v (2) 41, 31 (Ἀλέξαρ[χος]: f. —λας)
KORINTHIA:
—KORINTH: **(3)** 413 BC Th. vii 19. 4

**Ἀλεξᾶς**
ACHAIA:
—AIGION: **(1)** s. i AD *FD* III (4) 100, 3 (Π. Κορνήλιος Ἀ.)
ARGOLIS:
—ARGOS: **(2)** 135 AD Peek, *IAEpid* 154, 4 (and Argolis Epidauros: [Ἀλ]εξᾶς: s. Διόδοτος)
—EPIDAUROS: **(3)** iii AD *SEG* XXXIX 358, 6 (f. Σπόρος)
ELIS:
—OLYMPIA*: **(4)** 28-24 BC *IvOl* 64, 27 (?s. Σόφων: Δου.); **(5)** ~ ib. l. 34 (?s. Λύκος: Δου.)
KORINTHIA:
—KORINTH: **(6)** imp. *Corinth* VIII (3) 361 (Ἀλεξᾶς)
LAKONIA:
—SPARTA: **(7)** c. 134-145 AD *IG* v (1) 62, 9; 63, 19; *SEG* XI 550, 12 (Bradford (3)) (Γ. Ἰούλ. Ἀ.: I f. Ἀλεξᾶς II); **(8)** c. 140-145 AD *SEG* XI 550, 12 (Bradford (1)) (II s. Ἀλεξᾶς I); **(9)** a. 212 AD *IG* v (1) 562, 11 (Πετρ(ώνιος) Ἀλεξᾶ[ς])
——Pitana: **(10)** c. 105 AD ib. 675, 6 (Bradford (2)) (s. Χρυσέρως)
PELOPONNESE?: **(11)** 11 AD *PAE* 1992, p. 72 B, 6 (s. Τίμων)
S. ITALY (CAMPANIA):
—LITERNUM: **(12)** imp. *CIL* x 3718 (Lat. Q. Hortensius Alexa)
—POMPEII: **(13)** i BC-i AD ib. IV 2964 (Castrèn 297. 2) (Lat. Paccius Alexa); **(14)** ~ *CIL* IV 8029 (Lat. Alexa)
S. ITALY (LUCANIA):
—SERRA DI VAGLIO (MOD.): **(15)** f. v BC *ASCL* 40 (1972) p. 41 (vase)

**Ἀλεξεινίδας**
ELIS: **(1)** ?272-271 BC *FD* III (3) 185, 5, 8; 187, 2; cf. *SEG* XL 419 (-δης: s. Φιλωνίδας)

**Ἀλεξεύς**
ARGOLIS:
—ARGOS: **(1)** a. 303 BC *CEG* II 816, 9

**Ἀλεξήν**
ILLYRIA:
—EPIDAMNOS-DYRRHACHION: **(1)** hell.-imp. *IDyrrh* 90 (s. Κλέων); **(2)** ~ ib. 407 (f. Τευταία)

**Ἀλεξῆς**
AITOLIA: **(1)** c. 220 BC *ILind* 130, 4 (f. Πασίων)

**Ἀλεξία?**
SICILY:
—SYRACUSE: **(1)** iii-v AD *IG* XIV 192 (Strazzulla 136; Agnello 105; Wessel 773) (Ἀλεσχιη—lap.)

**Ἀλεξιάδας**
ARKADIA:
—TEGEA:
——(Apolloniatai): **(1)** f. iii BC *IG* v (2) 36, 52 (f. Ἱππιχος)
EPIROS:
—AMBRAKIA: **(2)** a. 167 BC *SEG* XXXV 665 A, 12 (f. Διοκλῆς)
KORINTHIA:
—KORINTH: **(3)** i BC/i AD *Corinth* VIII (2) 65; 66 (f. P. Caninius Agrippa)
PELOPONNESE?: **(4)** s. iii BC *IG* IV (1) 727 B, 9 (Perlman H.2) (s. Ἀνδρότιμος)

**Ἀλεξιάδης**
KORINTHIA:
—KORINTH: **(1)** imp. *Corinth* VIII (3) 351 b (Lat. Alexia[des])

**Ἀλεξιανός**
S. ITALY (CALABRIA):
—LUPIAE: **(1)** i-ii AD *NScav* 1957, p. 193 (Susini, *Fonti Salento* p. 147 no. 96) (Lat. [Ale]xianus)

**Ἀλεξίας**
AITOLIA:
—TRICHONION: **(1)** iv/iii BC *IG* IX (1)² (1) 123
ARGOLIS:
—HERMIONE: **(2)** ?c. 460-450 BC ib. IV (1) 683 (Lazzarini 74); cf. *SEG* XI 378; *LSAG*² p. 181 no. 8 (date) (s. Λύων); **(3)** ~ *IG* IV (1) 684 (Lazzarini 75); cf. *SEG* XI 379; *LSAG*² p. 181 no. 9 (date) (f. Ἀριστομένης)
—KALAURIA: **(4)** iii BC *IG* IV (1) 850, 7
ARKADIA: **(5)** ?278 BC *FD* III (1) 29, 1 (s. N—); **(6)** ?255 BC Nachtergael, *Les Galates* 8, 53 (Stephanis 121) (s. Ἀσκλάπιχος)
—MANTINEIA-ANTIGONEIA: **(7)** c. 300-221 BC *IG* v (2) 323. 73 (tessera) (s. Μενάλκης)
—MANTINEIA-ANTIGONEIA?: **(8)** v-iv BC Thphr., *HP* ix 16. 8
—PSOPHIS: **(9)** 191-146 BC BM coin 1920 8-5-1225; cf. *NC* 1921, p. 172 (coin) ([Ἀ]λεξίας)
—THELPHOUSA: **(10)** 369-361 BC *IG* v (2) 1, 66; Tod, *GHI* II 132 (date)
ILLYRIA:
—APOLLONIA: **(11)** ii AD *IApoll* 209
SICILY:
—SELINOUS: **(12)** m. v BC *SEG* XXXIV 971 (Dubois, *IGDS* 55; Arena, *Iscr. Sic.* I 38; Lazzarini 955) (Ἀ[λε]ξίας, Ἀ[λε]ξέας—Lazzarini: s. Ξένων)

**Ἀλεξιβία**
KORINTHIA:
—KORINTH: **(1)** a. 480 BC Plu., *Mor.* 871 A (d. Ἀδείμαντος)

**Ἀλεξίβιος**
ARGOLIS:
—HERMIONE: **(1)** f. ii BC *IC* 2 p. 24 no. 7 B, 2 (f. Εὔθυμος)
ARKADIA: **(2)** 304 BC *IG* v (2) 550, 18 ?= (*3*)
—HERAIA: **(3)** ?s. iv BC Moretti, *Olymp.* 483 ?= (*2*)
—MEGALOPOLIS: **(4)** iv/iii BC *IG* v (2) 479, 2; **(5)** s. iii BC ib. l. 8

**Ἀλεξίδαμος**
AKARNANIA:
—PHOITIAI: **(1)** iv BC ib. IX (1)² (2) 602, 13 (Ἀλεξίδ[αμος])
ARGOLIS:
—ARGOS: **(2)** 105 BC *JÖAI* 14 (1911) Beibl. p. 146 no. 4, 20 (f. —οινίς, —ίς)
PELOPONNESE: **(3)** s. iii BC *SEG* XIII 278, 9 (s. Αἴγινος)
S. ITALY (BRUTTIUM):
—LOKROI EPIZEPHYRIOI:
——(Τηλ.): **(4)** iv/iii BC De Franciscis 33, 2 (Ἀλε[ξί]δαμος: f. Ἀγέλοχος)
S. ITALY (LUCANIA):
—METAPONTION: **(5)** ?m. v BC B. xi tit.; 18 (s. Φαῖσκος)
S. ITALY?: **(6)** ?iv BC *BM Vases* F 606

**Ἀλεξίδας**
ARGOLIS:
—EPIDAUROS: **(1)** iv BC *IG* IV (1)² 322 (f. Ἀλεξικλῆς)

**Ἀλεξικίσκος?**
KERKYRA: **(1)** ?ii-i BC ib. IX (1) 745 (tile) (Ἀλεξικίσκου (gen.)—apogr., Ἀλεξικ(λέους)?)

**Ἀλεξικλῆς**
ACHAIA:
—DYME: **(1)** ii-i BC *CIG* 1550 (*SEG* XI 1262) (Δεξικλῆς—SEG: f. Σωτίων, Νικοστράτα)
ARGOLIS:
—EPIDAUROS: **(2)** iv BC *IG* IV (1)² 322 (s. Ἀλεξίδας, f. Θέαρις); **(3)** c. 365-335 BC ib. 103, 142, 157 ?= (*5*); **(4)** iv/iii BC ib. 156
——Kolonaia: **(5)** 335-325 BC ib. 108, 151 ?= (*3*)
KERKYRA: **(6)** ?iii/ii BC ib. IX (1) 743-4 (tiles); **(7)** 208 BC *IMM* 44, 40 (f. Κλείδικος)

## Ἀλεξικράτης

ARKADIA:
—HERAIA: (1) 369-361 BC *IG* v (2) 1, 59; Tod, *GHI* II 132 (date)

EPIROS:
—MOLOSSOI: (2) iv/iii BC Plu., *Pyrr.* 5. 8

LAKONIA:
—SPARTA: (3) ?i AD *IG* v (1) 327 (Bradford (2)) (s. Πολύξενος); (4) c. 100-125 AD *IG* v (1) 51, 29; 52, 6; *SEG* XI 538, 2; *BSA* 27 (1925-6) p. 219 (ident.) (Bradford (1)) (II s. (nat.) Λύσιππος, s. (ad.) Ἀλεξικράτης I); (5) ~ *IG* v (1) 51, [29]; 52, 6; *SEG* XI 538, 2; *BSA* 27 (1925-6) p. 219 (ident.) (Bradford (1 f. (ad.) Ἀλεξικράτης II); (6) ii AD *IG* v (1) 178, 2 (Bradford (3)) (Ἀλεξικρά[της])

MESSENIA:
—MESSENE?: (7) ii/i BC *SEG* XI 979, 44

## Ἀλεξίκων

ARGOLIS:
—EPIDAUROS*: (1) c. 360-350 BC *IG* IV (1)² 113, 4

## Ἀλέξιλα

ARGOLIS:
—EPIDAUROS: (1) iv/iii BC ib. 728

## Ἀλεξίλαος

ITHAKE: (1) hell. *SEG* XVII 256; (2) ?ii BC Unp. (*IG* arch.) ([Ἀ]λεξίλαος, Δεξίλαος?: s. Κυδωνίας)

## Ἀλεξίλας

AKARNANIA:
—DERION: (1) m. iii BC *IG* IV (1)² 96, 61, 64 (Perlman E.3); cf. *IG* IX (1)² (2) p XIX; cf. Perlman p. 63 f. (date); p. 168 (locn.) (f. Ἀρισταρχίδας)

ARGOLIS:
—ARGOS: (2) inc. *SEG* XXXVIII 309 (Ἀλεξιλα (masc. gen./fem. nom.?))

## Ἀλεξίλοχος

ARKADIA:
—KLEITOR: (1) c. 230-200 BC *BCH* 45 (1921) p. 12 II, 71 (f. Δείναρχος: name—Oulhen)

## Ἀλεξίμαχος

ACHAIA:
—DYME: (1) iii BC *AJPh* 31 (1910) p. 399 no. 74 a, 3 (s. Ἀρχίας, f. Πλειστιάς)
—TRITAIA?: (2) m. iii BC *IG* v (2) 368, 79 with index (Ἀλεξίμ[αχος]: f. Ἀρκαδίων)

AIGINA: (3) ?s. ii BC *Alt-Ägina* I (2) p. 46 no. 18 (Ἀλεξίμα[χος]); (4) i BC-i AD ib. p. 45 no. 12, 6 (Ἀλεξίμ[αχος])

AITOLIA: (5) hell. *ZPE* 108 (1995) p. 91 no. 5 (f. Δαμόφιλος); (6) ?262 BC *FD* III (4) 358, 4
—KALYDON: (7) m. ii BC *IG* IX (1)² (1) 137, 21, 45 (s. Στρόμβιχος)

AKARNANIA:
—LIMNAIA: (8) m. ii BC *Syll*³ 669, 9 (*IG* v (1) 29, 9) (s. Καρδαμίων)

ARGOLIS:
—ARGOS: (9) v BC *SEG* XI 339, 8 (Ἀλεξίμ[αχος]: f. Φιλέας); (10) imp. *IG* IV (1) 605
—EPIDAUROS: (11) c. 335-325 BC ib. IV (1)² 108, 160 (Ἀλε[ξ]ίμ[α]χος)

ARKADIA: (12) iv/iii BC ib. II² 9973 (f. Ἀλέξανδρος)
—STYMPHALOS: (13) iii BC *SEG* XI 1109, 4 (f. Ἔργιππος)

ELIS: (14) f. iv BC ib. xv 241, 7
ELIS?: (15) ?ii/i BC *IvOl* 192 (f. Ἀριστόδαμος)

EPIROS: (16) c. 330 BC Cabanes, *L'Épire* p. 580 no. 55, 2
—BOUTHROTOS (PRASAIBOI): (17) a. 163 BC *IBouthrot* 17, 25 (*SEG* XXXVIII 474); (18) ~ *IBouthrot* 28, 33; 33, 1; 35, 1 (s.p.) (*SEG* XXXVIII 486; 492; 494); *IBouthrot* 48, 7 (s. Σίμακος); (19) ~ ib. 31, 97 (*SEG* XXXVIII 490) (f. Λέων) ?= (22); (20) ~ *IBouthrot* 32, 25 (*SEG* XXXVIII 491); (21) ~ *IBouthrot* 60, 5 (*SEG* XXXVIII 511)
——Opatai: (22) a. 163 BC *IBouthrot* 139, 10 (f. Λέων) ?= (19)
—CHARADROS: (23) a. 167 BC *SEG* XXXV 665 A, 15 (f. Μενέλαος)
—DODONA*: (24) iv-iii BC *SGDI* 1593 ([Ἀ]λεξίμαχος, Δεξίμαχος?)
—KLATHRIOI: (25) f. ii BC Cabanes, *L'Épire* p. 589 no. 75, 13 (*SEG* XXXVII 510) (f. Ἀντίνους)

KORINTHIA:
—KORINTH: (26) c. 570-550 BC Amyx 121. 1 (vase) (Ἀλεξ(ί)μαρος: fict.?)

LAKONIA:
—SPARTA: (27) f. ii BC *IC* 2 p. 244 no. 4 B, 1 (Bradford (1)) (s. Σωίδαμος); (28) s. i BC *IG* v (1) 93, 14 (Bradford (4)) (f. Δάμαρχος); (29) ?i AD *IG* v (1) 180, 11 (Bradford (3)) (Ἀλεξίμ[αχος]); (30) c. 100-120 AD *IG* v (1) 97, 16; *SEG* XI 564, 10; 565, 5; 642, 1 (Bradford (2)) (s. Σωτήριχος)

MESSENIA:
—MESSENE: (31) iii BC *IG* v (1) 1441 a, 1

## Ἀλεξιμένης

AITOLIA:
—PAPHANOI: (1) 263 BC ib. IX (1)² (1) 17, 13

ARKADIA:
—LOUSOI?: (2) iii BC *SEG* XI 1122, 6 (*IPArk* 22)
—MEGALOPOLIS: (3) c. 225 BC *SEG* XI 414, 27 (Perlman E.5) (s. Ἡσίοδος)

ELIS: (4) ?308 BC *IG* v (2) 550, 10 (f. Δαμόλυτος)

## Ἀλεξίνικος

ARKADIA:
—MANTINEIA-ANTIGONEIA: (1) 64 or 62 BC ib. 265, 46 (s. Ἀλέξων)

ELIS: (2) f. iii BC Moretti, *Olymp.* 544

## Ἀλέξινος

ELIS: (1) iv/iii BC *RE* (-); cf. *SVF* 4 p. 175 s.v.

## Ἀλέξιος

S. ITALY (CAMPANIA):
—DIKAIARCHIA-PUTEOLI: (1) 61 AD *Puteoli* 9-10 (1985-6) p. 31 no. 5 (Lat. T—lius Alecsus)

## Ἀλεξίπολις

MESSENIA:
—MESSENE: (1) 39 BC *IG* II² 1043 III, 116; *SEG* XXII 112 (locn.) (Ἀξίπολις—*IG* per err.)

## Ἀλεξίππα

AKARNANIA:
—PALAIROS: (1) f. iii BC *IG* IX (1)² (2) 454

EPIROS:
—AMBRAKIA: (2) hell.? *SEG* XVII 306 (d. Ἀλκίας)

LAKONIA:
—SPARTA: (3) ?viii-vii BC *HE* 2721 (Poralla² 52) (m. Ἑρπυλίδας, Ἐράτων, Χαίρις, Λύκος, Ἄγις, Ἀλέξων, Γύλιππος: fict.?)

## Ἀλεξιππίδας

LAKONIA:
—SPARTA: (1) 412 BC Th. viii 58. 1; X., *HG* ii 3. 10 (Poralla² 53)

## Ἀλέξιππος

ARGOLIS:
—ARGOS: (1) 363-361 BC *IG* II² 3067; *SEG* XXVII 12, 4; 14, 4 (Stephanis 123)

ARKADIA: (2) 360 BC *CID* II 4 III, 7
—KYNAITHA: (3) ?253 BC Nachtergael, *Les Galates* 10, 34 (Stephanis 124) (s. Δεινομένης)

DALMATIA:
—ISSA:
——(Hylleis): (4) iv/iii BC Brunšmid p. 9, 53 (f. Ἀριστήν)

PELOPONNESE?: (5) s. iii BC *IG* v (1) 1426, 29 (f. Κλεοσθένης)

## Ἀλεξις

ARKADIA:
—KLEITOR: (1) i BC *SEG* XXXIII 291, 4 (Stephanis 128) (s. Κλεινίας)
—TEGEA: (2) imp. *IG* v (2) 188 (Ἀλεξι (voc.?), Ἀλεξίω(ν)?—*IG*)

EPIROS:
—DODONA: (3) iii BC Antoniou, *Dodone* Ab, 21

KORINTHIA:
—SIKYON: (4) f. iii BC Paus. vi 3. 6 (Skalet 22) (f. Κάνθαρος)

LAKONIA:
—SPARTA: (5) c. 100-125 AD *IG* v (1) 51, 8; 52, 2; *SEG* XI 562, [5] (Bradford (-)) (s. Φιλοκράτης)

S. ITALY (BRUTTIUM):
—SYBARIS-THOURIOI-COPIAE: (6) iv BC *RE* (19); *PCG* 2 pp. 21 ff. (and Athens)

S. ITALY (CALABRIA):
—TARAS-TARENTUM: (7) 324 BC Berve 44 (Stephanis 127)

S. ITALY (CAMPANIA):
—DIKAIARCHIA-PUTEOLI: (8) ?ii AD *CIL* X 3122 (Lat. M. Ulpius Alexis)

SICILY:
—SYRACUSE: (9) vi/v BC Guarducci, *Ep. Gr.* 1 p. 344 no. 3 (Dubois, *IGDS* 88)
—SYRACUSE?:
——(Λογ.): (10) hell. Manganaro, *PdelP* forthcoming no. 4 V, 5 (s. Τηλέγονος)

## Ἀλεξίων

ACHAIA:
—DYME*: (1) c. 219 BC *SGDI* 1612, 33 (*Tyche* 5 (1990) p. 124) (f. Κλέων)
—PELLENE: (2) m. iv BC *CID* II 19, 5 (s. Θυρσιάδας)

AKARNANIA:
—ANAKTORION: (3) c. 325-315 BC *Hesp.* 57 (1988) p. 148 A, 21 (*SEG* XXXVI 331); cf. *Hesp.* 48 (1979) pp. 78 f. with pl. 22 c (s. Ἀνδρόμαχος)

ARGOLIS:
—ARGOS: (4) iii BC *Mnem.* NS 43 (1915) p. 372 C, 14 (Perlman A.22) (s. X—)
—EPIDAUROS*: (5) c. 370-365 BC Peek, *IAEpid* 52 B, 9 ([Ἀλ]εξίων)

ARKADIA: (6) iii BC *IG* v (2) 415, 13 (*IPArk* 23) (Ἀλεξίω[ν])
—GORTYS: (7) iii-ii BC *SEG* XI 1166 (*BCH* 75 (1951) p. 132 (tile))
—STYMPHALOS: (8) c. 315-280 BC *FD* III (1) 38, 3 (*Syll*³ 516); Daux sub F11 (ident.) (f. Ἔργιππος, Δρομεύς); (9) c. 230-200 BC *BCH* 45 (1921) p. 13 II, 117 (Ἀλεξίων: f. Ἔργιππος, ?f. Τηλεφάνης, Σέανθος)

ELIS: (10) 16-12 BC *IvOl* 65, 3, 9 (s. Προξενίδης, f. Τιμόλαος); (11) ?i AD ib. 427 (Ἀ.); (12) c. 5 AD ib. 69, 20; 76, [3]; 77, [8] (s. Μικκίας, f. Μικκίας); (13) m. i AD ib. 426, 2; 429, 4 (M. Ἀντ. Ἀ.: s. M. Ἀντ. Πισανός, f. Ἀντ. Κλεοδίκη); (14) 69-73 AD ib. 84, 17 ([Ἀντ.] Ἀ.) ?= (15); (15) i/ii AD ib. 283, [4] (Γ. [Ἀντ.] [Ἀλεξίων]: s. M. Ἀντ. Κάλλιππος Πισανός) ?= (14)

EPIROS:
—AMBRAKIA: (16) iii-ii BC *Op. Ath.* 10 (1971) p. 64 no. 11 (f. Δάμων)

ILLYRIA:
—APOLLONIA: (17) ii BC *IApoll* 13; (18) ii-i BC ib. 379; (19) imp. ib. 47 (Ἀλε(ξ)ίων: s. Χόρτας); (20) ~ ib. 48; (21) ~ ib. 195 (f. Ἀνδρόνικος)
—EPIDAMNOS-DYRRHACHION: (22) c. 250-50 BC Ceka, *Probleme* p. 151 no. 4 (coin) (pryt.); (23) ~ Maier 100-3; cf. *IApoll Ref. Bibl.* n. 11 (coin) (Ceka 2; 317; 334) (pryt.); (24) hell.-imp. *IDyrrh* 91; (25) ~ ib. 92; (26) ~ ib. 164 (f. Δάζιος)

KERKYRA: (27) iii-ii BC *AE* 1914, p. 235 no. 5 (f. Ἀρίστων)

KORINTHIA:
—SIKYON: (28) 314 BC D.S. xix 67. 1 (Skalet 23); (29) ?254 BC Nachtergael, *Les Galates* 9, 13 (Stephanis 129) (s. Ἀλκ—ος); (30) c. 146-32 BC *BMC Pelop.* p. 51 nos. 191-2; *NC* 1984, p. 15 Group 10 no. 4 (coins)
LAKONIA:
—SPARTA: (31) ?m. ii AD *IG* v (1) 161, 2 (Bradford (2)) (I f. Ἀλεξίων II); (32) ~ *IG* v (1) 161, 2 (Bradford (1)) (II s. Ἀλεξίων I)
MESSENIA:
—THOURIA: (33) f. ii BC *SEG* XI 972, 28 (f. Ἀρίστων); (34) ~ ib. l. 39 (s. Γλαῦκος)
PELOPONNESE: (35) s. iii BC ib. XIII 278, 11 (Ἀλεξ[ίω]ν: s. Ἀριστέας)
S. ITALY (CALABRIA):
—RUDIAE: (36) i AD *NScav* 1897, p. 405 no. 11 (Susini, *Fonti Salento* p. 125 no. 69) (Lat. Alexio)

**Ἀλεξομενός**
AITOLIA:
—BOUKATION: (1) c. 162 BC *IG* IX (1)² (1) 106, 3 ?= (2); (2) 161 BC ib. 100, 6 ?= (1)
—KALYDON: (3) 197-193 BC *RE* (1); *IG* IX (1)² (1) p. LI, s.a. 197 BC; *Syll*³ 603, 2
—KONOPE-ARSINOE: (4) 184 BC *IG* IX (1)² (1) 131, 11 (s. Ἀλέξανδρος)
—KONOPE-ARSINOE?: (5) 184 BC ib. l. 10; (6) ~ ib. l. 12
—PLEURON: (7) c. 202-190 BC ib. 30, 1, 4; Sherk 37 B, 71; cf. *SEG* XXVII 123
—TRICHONION: (8) 185 BC *IG* IX (1)² (1) 32, 3, 14

**Ἀλεξόμμας**
ILLYRIA:
—BYLLIONES: (1) iii/ii BC *SEG* XXXV 679 (XXXVIII 524)

**Ἄλεξος**
ARGOLIS:
—EPIDAUROS*: (1) c. 370 BC *IG* IV (1)² 102, 86

**Ἄλεξυς**
AKARNANIA:
—THYRREION: (1) iii BC ib. IX (1)² (2) 245, 15
EPIROS:
—DODONA: (2) iii BC Antoniou, *Dodone* Aa, 15
LAKONIA:
—SPARTA: (3) c. 190-220 AD *IG* v (1) 817 (Papaefthimiou p. 142 no. 16); *BSA* 79 (1984) pp. 268-9 (date) (Bradford (-)) (M. Αὐρ. Ἄ.: s. Θέων)

**Ἀλεξώ**
ILLYRIA:
—APOLLONIA: (1) imp. *IApoll* 186 (Φουρία Ἀ.)

**Ἀλέξων**
ACHAIA: (1) 250 BC Plb. i 43. 2 ff.
AITOLIA: (2) ?255 BC Nachtergael, *Les Galates* 8, 5; 19, 3; Flacelière p. 398 no. 21 c, 3; (3) 244 or 240 BC *SGDI* 2512, 3 (Flacelière p. 402 no. 28 a); Nachtergael, *Les Galates* 59, [3]; (4) ?228-215 BC *FD* III (4) 364, 3; *SGDI* 2525, 3; (5) 224 or 221 BC ib. 2524, 3; Nachtergael, *Les Galates* 64, 2
—BOUKATION: (6) c. 162 BC *IG* IX (1)² (1) 106, 3
—HERMATTIOI: (7) c. 213 BC ib. 188, 35
—KALYDON: (8) m. ii BC ib. 137, 24
—KONOPE-ARSINOE: (9) 184 BC ib. 131, 7 (s. Στράταγος)
—MAKYNEIS: (10) s. ii BC *SEG* XXV 621, 11 (f. Ξενίας)
—PHILOTAIEIS: (11) f. ii BC *IG* IX (1)² (1) 96, 22 (s. Ἀρίσταρχος)
—POTANA: (12) 177 BC *SGDI* 2058, 6 (f. Νικόστρατος)
—PROSCH(E)ION: (13) c. 245 BC *IG* IX (1)² (1) 11, 49 (f. Ταυρίσκος); (14) c. 157 BC ib. 108, 4

—TRICHONION: (15) iii BC ib. 68 (f. Ἀλέξανδρος); (16) c. 141 BC ib. 34, 22; 137, 28 (?f. Νίκανδρος, f. Ἀλέξανδρος, ?f. Δωρίμαχος)
AITOLIA?: (17) ?228-215 BC *FD* III (4) 364, 5; *SGDI* 2525, 4
AKARNANIA:
—PALAIROS: (18) ii BC *IG* IX (1)² (2) 451, 16 (f. Δορκύλος)
—STRATOS: (19) a. 167 BC ib. IX (2) 6 a, 3; cf. Stählin p. 220 (date) (s. Πολέμαρχος)
—THYRREION: (20) ii BC *IG* IX (1)² (2) 248, 20 (s. Λέων)
ARGOLIS:
—TROIZEN: (21) 153-144 BC *SGDI* 2295, 17 (f. Ἀρίστων)
ARKADIA:
—MANTINEIA-ANTIGONEIA: (22) 64 or 62 BC *IG* v (2) 265, 47 (f. Ἀλεξίνικος)
EPIROS:
—BOUTHROTOS (PRASAIBOI): (23) a. 163 BC *IBouthrot* 32, 25 (*SEG* XXXVIII 491)
LAKONIA:
—GYTHEION?: (24) ?ii BC *RA* 1904, p. 8 no. 5
—SPARTA: (25) ?viii-vii BC *HE* 2717 (Poralla² 54) (s. Ἰφικρατίδας, Ἀλεξίππα: fict.?)

**Ἄλεος**
ARKADIA:
—TEGEA: (1) 165 AD *IG* v (2) 50, 14 (f. Ἄμυκος)

**Ἀλέως**
ARKADIA:
—LOUSOI: (1) m. iii BC *BCH* 38 (1914) p. 457 no. 3, 2 (f. Θέοξις)
—TEGEA: (2) m. iii BC *IG* v (2) 368, 73 (Ἀλέω (gen.): f. Δάμαρχος)

**Ἀλήθεια**
S. ITALY (CAMPANIA):
—DIKAIARCHIA-PUTEOLI*: (1) imp. *CIL* x 2536 (Lat. Instania Aletheia: freed.)

**Ἀλήτης**
KORINTHIA:
—KORINTH: (1) her. *RE* (5) (f. Ἰξίων: king)

**Ἀλθαιμένης**
ARGOLIS:
—ARGOS: (1) her. ib. (2) (s. Κίσσος)

**Ἀλίαρχος**
SICILY:
—MORGANTINA: (1) iv/iii BC *SEG* XXXIX 1013, 7 (Ἀλίαρ[χος]: f. Ἀγήσανδρος)

**Ἀλίας**
SICILY:
—KAMARINA: (1) f. v BC Cordano, *Tessere Pubbliche* 29 ([Ἀ]λίας: s. Ἀγύρανος)

**Ἀλιειός**
ARGOLIS:
—EPIDAUROS: (1) iii BC Peek, *IAEpid* 43, 28 (f. Ἀθηνόδοτος)

**Ἀλικέα**
EPIROS:
—ELATREIA: (1) ?v BC Hammond, *Epirus* p. 53; p. 427 (locn.)

**Ἁλικεύς**
ARGOLIS:
—ARGOS: (1) iii BC *IG* IV (1) 618 I, 2 (f. —έας)

**Ἁλικός**
ACHAIA:
—AIGION: (1) s. iii BC ib. 727 A, 10 (Perlman H.1) (Ἁδικος—Perlman: f. —ος)

**Ἁλιμήδης**
KORINTHIA:
—KORINTH: (1) c. 570-550 BC Amyx 66. 9 (vase) (Lorber 122) (hαλιμέδēς: her.)

**Ἁλίνη**
S. ITALY (APULIA):
—CANUSIUM*: (1) m. i BC *Epig. Rom. di Canosa* 75 (*CIL* I² 1707; *CIL* IX 352) (Lat. Livia Haline: freed.)
—SPINAZZOLA (MOD.): (2) ?i BC *Epigraphica* 46 (1984) pp. 194 ff. (*SEG* XXXIII 759) (Lat. Haline: freed.)

**Ἅλινος**
S. ITALY (APULIA):
—AECAE: (1) imp. *Scritti Zambelli* p. 338 (Lat. Halinus)

**Ἁλιόδωρος**
ARKADIA:
—MEGALOPOLIS: (1) ii/i BC *IG* v (2) 443, 5 (*IPArk* 32) (f. Φιλίσκος)

**Ἁλίπων**
EPIROS:
—MOLOSSOI: (1) c. 343-330 BC Cabanes, *L'Épire* p. 588 no. 74, 11 (*SEG* XXVI 700) (f. Νικάνωρ)

**Ἁλιστίων**
LAKONIA:
—SPARTA: (1) iii BC ib. XL 348 B, 10

**Ἄλκα**
ACHAIA:
—DYME: (1) iii BC *AJPh* 31 (1910) p. 399 no. 74 a, 5 (d. Πλειστιάς)
KORINTHIA:
—KORINTH: (2) c. 590-570 BC Amyx 33. 2 (vase) (Lorber 52) (her.?)

**Ἀλκάδας**
SICILY:
—SYRACUSE: (1) 343 BC D.S. xvi 70. 6 (f. Καλλιμένης)

**Ἀλκάδης**
ARGOLIS:
—TROIZEN: (1) ?146 BC *IG* IV (1) 757 B, 13 (s. —ιος)

**Ἀλκαθόα**
LAKONIA:
—SPARTA: (1) vi/v BC Schol. Ar., *Eq.* 84 (Poralla² 55) (?m. Παυσανίας, Νικομήδης)

**Ἀλκάθους**
KORINTHIA:
—SIKYON: (1) 359 BC *SEG* XXVII 16, 5

**Ἀλκαινέτη**
ACHAIA:
—AIGION: (1) ii-iii AD *EA* 1884, p. 89, 1 (Ἀλκαιν[έτη]: d. Στύραξ)

**Ἀλκαίνετος**
ACHAIA?: (1) 193 BC *IG* v (2) 293, 7 ([Ἀ]λκαίνετος: s. Εὔβουλος)
AKARNANIA:
—THYRREION: (2) iii BC ib. IX (1)² (2) 245, 8; (3) ii BC ib. 248, 10 (s. Ἀλέξανδρος); (4) ~ ib. 251, 8 ([Ἀλ]καίνετος: s. Ἀνδροτέλης)
ARGOLIS:
—PHLEIOUS: (5) iii BC ib. IV (1) 454 (Ἀλκα[ί]νετο[ς])
ARKADIA:
—ALEA: (6) 370-367 BC ib. v (2) 2, 3 (Ἀλκαίνε[τος])
TRIPHYLIA:
—LEPREON: (7) m. v BC *RE* (-); Moretti, *Olymp.* 276; 309 (s. Θέαντος, f. Ἑλλάνικος, Θέαντος)

**Ἀλκαῖος**
AKARNANIA:
—THYRREION: (1) ii BC *IG* IX (1)² (2) 251, 4 (s. Μενοίτιος)

ARKADIA:
—MANTINEIA-ANTIGONEIA: (2) c. 300-221 BC ib. v (2) 323. 39-40 (tesserae) (s. Ἀλκίβιος)
—TEGEA: (3) f. iii BC ib. 35, 16 (s. Δαμάγητος)
EPIROS:
—BOUTHROTOS: (4) ?i AD IBouthrot 200 (SEG XXXVII 509) (T. Πομπώνιος Ἀ.)
ILLYRIA:
—APOLLONIA: (5) c. 250-50 BC Maier 96 (coin) (Ceka 11) (money.)
——(Litai): (6) iii BC Robert, Hell. 10 p. 283 ff.; cf. CRAI 1991, p. 197 ff.; L'Illyrie mérid. 2 p. 204 f. (f. Ἀπελλέας)
—EPIDAMNOS-DYRRHACHION: (7) c. 250-50 BC Maier 137-8; 160; 162; 169; 252; 274; 284; 307; 314; 320; 330; 346; 355-6; 360; 375; 403; Münsterberg p. 38; Nachtr. p. 14; p. 16 (Ceka 28-52); IApoll Ref. Bibl. n. 12 (coin) (money.)
KERKYRA: (8) ?i BC IG IX (1) 746; Korkyra 1 pp. 166-7 nos. 2-3 (tiles)
KORINTHIA:
—KORINTH: (9) 246-221 BC BGU 1978, 3
—SIKYON: (10) iv BC TCal 1 C, 21 (f. Νικόμαχος)
MESSENIA:
—MESSENE: (11) iii/ii BC RE (13); HE 14 ff.
SICILY:
—SYRACUSE: (12) ii BC IG II² 10399 (Ἀλκ[αῖ]ος: f. Φιλωνίδας)

Ἀλκαμένης
ACHAIA: (1) 146 BC Plb. xxxviii 17. 9; Paus. vii 15. 8; 15. 10
ARGOLIS:
—ARGOS:
——(Hylleis): (2) ?c. 460-450 BC IG IV (1) 517, 5 (Lazzarini 937); LSAG² p. 170 no. 32 (date) ([Ἀ]λκαμένης)
ARKADIA:
—MANTINEIA-ANTIGONEIA: (3) 64 or 62 BC IG v (2) 265, 49 (s. Μανδρηκίδας)
ILLYRIA:
—EPIDAMNOS-DYRRHACHION: (4) c. 250-50 BC Münsterberg p. 38 (coin) (Ceka 248) (pryt.)
KORINTHIA:
—SIKYON: (5) c. 250 BC IG IX (1)² (1) 24, 4 (f. Σωσικράτης)
LAKONIA:
—SPARTA: (6) s. viii BC RE (1) (Poralla² 56) (s. Τήλεκλος, f. Πολύδωρος: king); (7) 412 BC Th. viii 5. 1-2; 8. 2; 10. 2, 4; 11. 3 (Poralla² 57) (s. Σθενελαΐδας); (8) 220 BC Plb. iv 22. 11 (Bradford (1)); (9) ii BC IG v (1) 29, 16 (Syll³ 669; Bradford (2)) (f. Γόργις); (10) i BC/i AD IG v (1) 49, 3; 95, 18; 212, 17 (Bradford (3)) (f. Κλέανδρος)
SICILY:
—AKRAGAS: (11) ?vi BC RE (3) (tyrant)

Ἀλκανδρίδας
LAKONIA:
—SPARTA: (1) c. 140-145 AD SEG XI 550, 16; BSA 80 (1985) pp. 246-7 (ident., stemma) (Bradford (4)) ([Π.] [Αἰλ.] Ἀλκ[ανδ]ρίδας: ?f. Π. Αἴλ. Νικανδρίδας); (2) s. ii AD IG v (1) 305, 8 (Artemis Orthia pp. 333-4 no. 69); IG v (1) 553, 3; 554, 2; 555 a-b, 11; SEG XI 499, 9; 802, [3]; 831, [11]; BSA 80 (1985) pp. 246-7 (ident., stemma) (Bradford (6)) ([Π.] Αἴλ. Ἀ.: ?s. Π. Αἴλ. Νικανδρίδας, f. Π. Αἴλ. Δαμοκρατίδας); (3) f. iii AD Moretti, Olymp. 917; 920; IG v (1) 304 (Artemis Orthia pp. 330-1 no. 64); IG v (1) 556, 2; SEG XI 740, 7; 803, 2; 831, [1]; 844, 2; BSA 79 (1984) pp. 273-4; pp. 279-83 (date); 80 (1985) pp. 246-8 (ident., stemma) (Bradford (2)) (Π. Αἴλ. Ἀ.: s. Π. Αἴλ. Δαμοκρατίδας); (4) c. 250-260 AD IG v (1) 593, 10; BSA 80 (1985) pp. 225; 243-4 (ident., stemma) (Bradford (3)) (Κλ. Ἀ.: ?s.

Τιβ. Κλ. Πρατόλαος ὁ καὶ Δαμοκρατίδας, s. Ἰουλ. Ἐτεαρχίς)

Ἀλκανδρος
ARGOLIS:
—ARGOS: (1) m. v BC SEG XXXVI 340 (sherd)
ILLYRIA:
—EPIDAMNOS-DYRRHACHION: (2) c. 250-50 BC Maier 104 (coin) (Ceka 3) (pryt.)
LAKONIA:
—SPARTA: (3) ?viii-vii BC Plu., Lyc. 11; Paus. iii 18. 2 (Poralla² 58) (dub.)
MESSENIA:
—THOURIA: (4) f. ii BC SEG XI 972, 21 (s. Ἀριστοκράτης)
SICILY:
—AKRAGAS: (5) ?vi/v BC RE (4) (tyrant)

Ἀλκάνωρ
ARGOLIS:
—ARGOS: (1) m. vi BC Hdt. i 82. 4; Paus. ii 20. 7; FGrH 287 F 2b (Ἀγήνωρ—FGrH 287: f. Περίλαος)
EPIROS:
—KASSOPE: (2) i BC Cabanes, L'Épire p. 564 no. 42, 11 (SEG XXVI 718) (f. Φίλανδρος)
KORINTHIA:
—KORINTH*: (3) iv BC ib. XI 52 f (amph.)
TRIPHYLIA:
—LEPREON: (4) f. v BC ib. xv 253 (Lazzarini 866) (f. Κόρδαφος)

Ἀλκαστος
LAKONIA:
—SPARTA: (1) ii AD IG IV (1)² 511 (Bradford (5)) (f. Σέξ. Πομπ. Ἰλαριανός); (2) f. ii AD IG v (1) 32 A, 15; 37, 5; 65, 2; 116, 14; 128, 3; 289, 6; 290, 1; 494, 2; 495, 2; SEG XI 495, 1; 523, 4; 548, 9; 587, [6]; 780, 2; [843]; BSA 80 (1985) pp. 241-2 (ident., stemma) (Bradford (3)) (Γ. Πομπώνιος Ἀ.: f. Γ. Πομπώνιος Ἀριστέας, Γ. Πομπώνιος Ἆγις); (3) c. 105-110 AD IG v (1) 97, 17; SEG XI 564, 11 (Bradford (1)) (s. Τιμόκριτος); (4) s. ii AD IG v (1) 494, 9; BSA 80 (1985) pp. 241-2 (ident., stemma) (Bradford (4)) (Γ. Πομπώνιος Ἀ.: ?s. Γ. Πομπώνιος Ἀριστέας); (5) ~ SEG XI 817, 4; XXXVI 353, 14; BSA 80 (1985) pp. 194; 206-8 (stemma) (Bradford (2)) (s. Μεμμία Ξενοκράτεια)

Ἀλκέμαχος
EPIROS: (1) ?198 BC IG II² 2313, 24; SEG XLI 113; Habicht, Athen hell. Zeit p. 134 (date) ([Ἀ]λκέμαχος: s. Χάροψ)

Ἀλκέσιππος
AITOLIA: (1) c. 200-182 BC IG II² [4931]; Syll³ 631, 1, 4 (s. Βουθήρας)

Ἀλκέτας
AKARNANIA:
—PHOITIAI: (1) 263-262 BC IG IX (1)² (1) 3 A, 23
—THYRREION: (2) c. 325-315 BC Hesp. 57 (1988) p. 148 A, 27 (SEG XXXVI 331); cf. Hesp. 48 (1979) pp. 78 f. with pl. 22 c (s. Ἀντίμαχος); (3) iii BC IG IX (1)² (2) 245, 15; (4) ?iii/ii BC ib. 311
ARGOLIS:
—HALIEIS: (5) s. iv BC ib. IV (1)² 121, 120
ARKADIA:
—LOUSOI: (6) c. 230-200 BC BCH 45 (1921) p. 12 II, 68 (s. Ἀγίων)
ELIS: (7) m. iii BC IG v (2) 368, 56 (s. Νικοκράτης)
EPIROS:
—MOLOSSOI: (8) c. 420-370 BC RE (3); Cabanes, L'Épire p. 534 no. 1; cf. p. 537 sub no. 2 (s. Θαρύπας, f. Νεοπτόλεμος, Ἀρύββας: king I); (9) c. 365-306 BC RE (4); cf.

D.S. xix 88. 3; 89. 3 (s. Ἀρύββας, f. Ἀλέξανδρος, Τεῦκρος, Ἠϊονεύς, Νῖσος: king II)
LAKONIA:
—SPARTA: (10) 377 BC X., HG v 4. 56; Polyaen. ii 7 (Poralla² 59) (-της)
MESSENIA:
—THOURIA: (11) f. ii BC SEG XI 972, 60 (f. Λέων)

Ἀλκέτις
S. ITALY (BRUTTIUM):
—LOKROI EPIZEPHYRIOI?: (1) iv/iii BC HE 2837

Ἀλκετος
ARGOLIS:
—ARGOS: (1) f. iii BC IG IV (1) 529, 24 ([Ἀλ]κετος)
ARKADIA:
—KLEITOR: (2) c. 400-375 BC Moretti, Olymp. 395 (s. Ἀλκίνους)

Ἀλκη
S. ITALY (CAMPANIA):
—POMPEII: (1) i BC-i AD Atti Acc. Pontan. 39 (1990) p. 294 no. 77 (Lat. Alce)
SICILY:
—THERMAI HIMERAIAI: (2) ?ii AD CIL x 7372 (ILat. Term. Imer. 41) (Lat. Aelia Alce)

Ἀλκήν
EPIROS:
—AMPHILOCHOI: (1) iii BC GVI 2017 (Ἀλκη—apogr.)

Ἀλκηστις
AITOLIA:
—PHISTYON: (1) 163 BC IG IX (1)² (1) 103, 4, 10

Ἀλκία
SICILY:
—SYRACUSE: (1) 309 BC D.S. xx 33. 5; cf. Beloch, GG IV (2) pp. 255-6 (?m. Λάνασσα)

Ἀλκιάδας
AITOLIA: (1) ?271 BC Syll³ 419, 2
ARGOLIS:
—ARGOS: (2) a. 324 BC CID II 120 A, 6 (f. —ης)
MESSENIA:
—KOLONIDES: (3) ii BC IG v (1) 1402, 5 ([Ἀ]λκιάδας: f. Δεξίων)
SICILY:
—GELA-PHINTIAS?: (4) f. v BC Dubois, IGDS 134 b, 8 (Arena, Iscr. Sic. II 47)

Ἀλκιάδης
SICILY:
—SYRACUSE: (1) ?f. iv BC IG XIV 5 (vase)

Ἀλκίας
ACHAIA:
—PHARAI: (1) iii BC Achaean Grave Stelai 3 (f. Τελέσαρχος)
AITOLIA:
—RHADEOI: (2) f. ii BC IG IX (1)² (1) 96, 23 (s. Λυκίσκος)
ARGOLIS:
—ARGOS: (3) 337-328 BC CID II 74 I, 74; 76 II, 23; 120 A, 2; 121 III, 15 (f. Γάψων); (4) 327-324 BC ib. 97, 27; 102 II B, [29] (f. Φίλλις)
ARKADIA:
—KLEITOR: (5) ?262-253 BC Nachtergael, Les Galates 5, 18?; 10, 32 (Stephanis 132) (s. Δαΐφαντος)
—MANTINEIA-ANTIGONEIA: (6) c. 300-221 BC IG v (2) 323. 37-8 (tesserae) (f. Ἀγησίας); (7) ?iii BC ib. 318, 21; (8) f. iii BC ib. 272, 6
——(Enyalia): (9) m. iv BC ib. 271, 7 (s. Ἀριστόξενος)
—PALLANTION: (10) a. 316 BC SEG XI 1084, 35 (Perlman A.3) (f. Τιμόστρατος)
—TEGEA*: (11) f. iii BC IG v (2) 36, 25 (f. —σος)
ELIS: (12) 334 BC Berve 46; (13) ?i AD IvOl 413 (s. Δαμάρετος, Θεοξένα) ?= (14); (14) ~ ib. 414 (f. Δαμάρετος) ?= (13)

EPIROS:
—AMBRAKIA: (15) hell.? *SEG* XVII 306 (f. Ἀλεξίππα)
S. ITALY (BRUTTIUM):
—LOKROI EPIZEPHYRIOI:
——(Σκα.): (16) iv/iii BC De Franciscis 3, 13; 27, 5 (s. Ἄλκιμος)
S. ITALY (LUCANIA):
—METAPONTION: (17) iv BC Iamb., *VP* 267 (*FVS* 1 p. 446)
—METAPONTION*: (18) f. ii BC Landi, *DISMG* 159 (amph.) (Vandermersch p. 161) (Ἀλκία[s])
SICILY:
—GELA-PHINTIAS: (19) f. v BC Dubois, *IGDS* 131. 7 (Arena, *Iscr. Sic.* II 45)
—SYRACUSE?: (20) hell. Manganaro, *PdelP* forthcoming no. 4 V, 11 (f. Ἑρμῶναξ)

## Ἀλκιβία
ARGOLIS:
—EPIDAUROS: (1) iv/iii BC Peek, *NIEpid* 95 (d. Λαρχίδας)
LAKONIA:
—SPARTA: (2) s. i BC *IG* V (1) 141, 5; 465, 5; 578, 2 (Bradford (-)) (d. Τεισαμενός, m. Τεισαμενός: mantis?)

## Ἀλκιβιάδας
KORINTHIA:
—SIKYON: (1) iv BC *Suda* M 141 (?f. Μέναιχμος)
LAKONIA:
—SPARTA: (2) 413 BC Th. viii 6. 3 (Poralla² 60) (f. Ἔνδιος); (3) iii/ii BC Plb. xxii 1. 9; 11. 7; xxiii 4. 3; Liv. xxxix 35. 7; 36. 2, 14; 37. 21; Paus. vii 9. 2-4 (Ἀλκιβιάδης—Plb.)
—SPARTA?: (4) ?c. 525-500 BC *SEG* XXVII 135 (Lazzarini 857); *LSAG*² p. 447 no. 47a (Poralla² 59a) ([Ἀλ]κιβιάδ[ας])

## Ἀλκιβιάδης
S. ITALY: (1) imp. *CIL* X 8059. 26 (seal) (Lat. Alcibiades)
S. ITALY (CAMPANIA):
—NEAPOLIS: (2) s. ii AD *IG* XIV 763 (*INap* 91); cf. Leiwo p. 126 no. 114 (-κει-)
S. ITALY?: (3) 218-222 AD *IG* XIV 2416. 14
SICILY:
—SYRACUSE: (4) ii-iii AD *CIL* X 7127 (*ILat. Palermo* 45) (Lat. Iunius Alcibiades)

## Ἀλκίβιος
ARGOLIS:
—EPIDAUROS: (1) c. 365-335 BC *IG* IV (1)² 103, 143, 157, 158
ARKADIA:
—MANTINEIA-ANTIGONEIA: (2) c. 300-221 BC ib. V (2) 323. 39-40 (tesserae) (f. Ἀλκαῖος)
KORINTHIA:
—SIKYON: (3) iv BC *Suda* M 141 (?f. Μέναιχμος)

## Ἀλκιδάμα
LAKONIA:
—SPARTA: (1) i-ii AD *IG* V (1) 770 (Bradford s.v. Ἀλκιλάδας (-)) (Ἀλκιδάδα—apogr.: d. Ἀλεξάνδρα)
ZAKYNTHOS: (2) hell. *IG* IX (1) 600 (d. Ἀρχικλῆς, m. Κληνίππα)

## Ἀλκιδαμίδας
MESSENIA:
—MESSENE: (1) viii BC Paus. iv 23. 6

## Ἀλκίδαμος
ACHAIA:
—PELLENE: (1) m. iii BC *IG* V (2) 368, 109 (s. M—)
AITOLIA: (2) ?247 BC *Syll*³ 444 A, 3; *CID* II 139, 2
ARGOLIS:
—EPIDAUROS*: (3) hell.? Peek, *NIEpid* 76 ([Ἀ]λκίδαμος: s. Ξενοκλ—)

KORINTHIA:
—KORINTH: (4) f. ii BC *Corinth* VIII (1) 73, 3 (sculptor)

## Ἀλκίδας
AKARNANIA:
—ANAKTORION: (1) ?iii BC *IG* IX (1)² (2) 594 (Ἀλκίδ[α]ς)
LAKONIA:
—SPARTA: (2) s. vi BC Hdt. vi 61. 5 (Poralla² 61) (-κείδης: f. Ἄγητος); (3) s. v BC *RE* (1) (Poralla² 62) (and Thessaly Herakleia Trachinia: oikist); (4) 374 BC D.S. xv 46. 2 (Poralla² 63); (5) 244 BC Moretti, *Olymp.* 566 (Bradford (-))
S. ITALY (BRUTTIUM):
—LOKROI EPIZEPHYRIOI:
——(Γαγ.): (6) iv/iii BC De Franciscis 28, 3 (Ἀλ<ι>κίδας: s. Εὐκλείδας)

## Ἀλκίδημος
S. ITALY (CAMPANIA):
—POMPEII: (1) i BC-i AD *CIL* IV 1383; cf. p. 463 (Lat. Alcidemus)

## Ἀλκίδης
S. ITALY: (1) imp. ib. x 8059. 27 (seal) (Lat. Alcides)
S. ITALY (CAMPANIA):
—DIKAIARCHIA-PUTEOLI: (2) ?i-ii AD ib. 2581 (Lat. C. Iulius Alcides: f. Ἀντιοχίς)
—DIKAIARCHIA-PUTEOLI*: (3) ?ii AD ib. 1571 (Lat. Alcides: freed.)
SICILY:
—AKRAGAS: (4) hell.-imp.? *Cron. Arch.* 16 (1977) p. 150 n. 15

## Ἀλκιδώ
LAKONIA:
—HYPERTELEATON*: (1) ?c. 500 BC *SEG* XXXII 391; *LSAG*² p. 447 no. D (date)

## Ἀλκιθοΐδας
ARGOLIS:
—ARGOS?: (1) v BC *IG* IV (1) 553, 4 (Ἀλκιτθίδας—ed., Ἀλκιτοΐδας—Boeckh)
ARKADIA:
—TEGEA:
——(Apolloniatai): (2) iv/iii BC ib. V (2) 38, 38 (Ἀλκιθο[ΐδα]ς: s. Νικόστρατος)

## Ἄλκιθοος
ACHAIA:
—AIGION: (1) m. ii BC ib. IX (1)² (3) 721 B, 4 (f. Κλεογένης)

## Ἄλκιθος
ACHAIA:
—AIGION: (1) 169 BC Plb. xxviii 12. 9; 19. 3 (s. Ξενοφῶν)

## Ἀλκίμαχος
ACHAIA:
—AIGION: (1) m. iii BC *IG* IV (1)² 96, 18 (Perlman E.3); Perlman p. 63 f. (date) (I f. Ἀλκίμαχος II); (2) ~ *IG* IV (1)² 96, 18 (Perlman E.3); Perlman p. 63 f. (date) (II s. Ἀλκίμαχος I)
AITOLIA:
—THESTIEIS: (3) 213 BC *IG* IX (1)² (1) 96, 13
ARGOLIS:
—ARGOS: (4) 345-324 BC *CID* II 31, 77; 97, 28; 102 II B, 29 (s. Ἀντίμαχος)
ARKADIA:
—MANTINEIA-ANTIGONEIA: (5) c. 300-221 BC *IG* V (2) 323. 23 (tessera) (s. Ἱππαῖος)
EPIROS:
—MOLOSSOI: (6) ii/i BC *GVI* 1063 (*SEG* XII 340) (s. Νεόπτολεμος)
ILLYRIA:
—APOLLONIA?: (7) 321-319 BC Osborne, *Naturalization* D37; cf. *IApoll* 311 (I f. Ἀλκίμαχος II); (8) ~ Osborne, *Naturalization* D37; cf. *IApoll* 311 (II s. Ἀλκίμαχος I)

KORINTHIA:
—KORINTH: (9) ii BC *IG* II² 9068 (f. Ζωπύρα)
—SIKYON: (10) v BC ib. IX (2) 209; (11) m. iv BC *AE* 1925-6, p. 185

## Ἀλκιμέδων
AIGINA: (1) 460 BC Moretti, *Olymp.* 264 (s. Ἰφίων)
ARKADIA:
—MEGALOPOLIS: (2) s. ii BC *IG* V (2) 436, 4 (f. —της) ?= (3); (3) ~ ib. 439, 73 (f. Ξενοκράτης) ?= (2)

## Ἀλκιμένεια
AKARNANIA:
—THYRREION: (1) iii BC ib. IX (1)² (2) 258

## Ἀλκιμένης
ACHAIA: (1) m. iv BC Plu., *Dion* 23
ARGOLIS:
—EPIDAUROS:
——(Hysminatai): (2) 146 BC *IG* IV (1)² 28, 16 (f. Ἀλκίφρων)
—HERMIONE: (3) iii BC ib. IV (1) 729 II, 16 (f. Καραῖος)
KORINTHIA:
—KORINTH: (4) 392 BC X., *HG* iv 4. 7
LAKONIA:
—SPARTA: (5) c. 30-20 BC *IG* V (1) 142, 17 (Bradford (-)) (Ἀλκιμένης: f. Ἀγησισθένης)
MESSENIA:
—MESSENE: (6) i BC/i AD *IG* V (1) 1438 a, 9 ([Ἀλκ]ιμένης)

## Ἀλκιμίδας
AIGINA: (1) f. v BC Pi., *N.* vi, 8, 60; cf. Klee p. 102 no. 114
SICILY:
—GELA-PHINTIAS: (2) c. 525-500 BC Dubois, *IGDS* 150 (vase) (Arena, *Iscr. Sic.* II 16); (3) vi/v BC Dubois, *IGDS* 144 e (vase) (Arena, *Iscr. Sic.* II 21)

## Ἀλκιμίων
S. ITALY (CAMPANIA):
—NOLA?: (1) m. i AD *IItal* 1 (1) 23* (or S. Italy (Campania) Nuceria Alfaterna: Lat. Ti. Claudius Alcimio)

## Ἄλκιμος
ACHAIA:
—DYME: (1) s. iii BC *SEG* XIII 278, 20
AITOLIA:
—THERMOS*: (2) s. iii BC *IG* IX (1)² (1) 60 IV, 13
ARKADIA:
—MEGALOPOLIS: (3) ii/i BC ib. V (2) 443, 7 (*IPArk* 32) (Ἀλκ[ι]μος: s. Λυκῖνος)
—TEGEA: (4) ii AD *IG* V (2) 55, 69 (f. Ἀπολλώνις)
DALMATIA:
—ISSA: (5) imp. *CIL* III 13285 (Lat. C. Reius Alcimo)
EPIROS: (6) 304 BC *RE* (11)
—BOUTHROTOS (PRASAIBOI): (7) a. 163 BC *IBouthrot* 31, 100, 108 (*SEG* XXXVIII 490) (I s. Λυσανίας, f. Ἄλκιμος II); (8) ~ *IBouthrot* 31, 103 (*SEG* XXXVIII 490) (II ~ Ἄλκιμος I)
——De{lioi): (9) a. 163 BC *IBouthrot* 67, 5 (s. Πύρρος)
—THESPROTOI: (10) s. iii BC *FD* III (2) 83, 1 (s. Νίκανδρος)
ILLYRIA:
—EPIDAMNOS-DYRRHACHION: (11) hell. *IDyrrh* 93 (s. Μνασέας)
KERKYRA:
——(Hylleis): (12) ii BC *IG* IX (1) 694, 5, 40 (*RIJG* XXV B); cf. *SEG* XXV 609 (f. Ψύλλα)
KORINTHIA:
—KORINTH: (13) imp. *CIL* III 6100, 1 (Lat. L. Rutilius Alcimus: f. L. Rutilius Martialis); (14) ~ ib. 7268 (Lat. Alcimus)
—SIKYON: (15) vi/v BC *SEG* XI 244, 27

LAKONIA:
—SPARTA: (16) 362-358 BC *CID* II 1 I, 36; 4 II, 54; 5 II, 31 (Poralla² 64); (17) c. 30 BC-46 AD *IG* V (1) 141, 25 (*SEG* XXXV 329 (date)); *IG* V (1) 299; *SEG* XI 717; *FD* III (2) 160, 1 (Bradford (2)) (s. Σωκλείδας); (18) c. 100-105 AD *SEG* XI 561, 3 (Bradford (3)) (I f. Ἄλκιμος II); (19) ~ *SEG* XI 561, 3 (Bradford (1)) (Ἀλκιμος: II s. Ἄλκιμος I)
LEUKAS: (20) 167 BC *Klio* 75 (1993) p. 132, 2 (s. Σώσανδρος)
MESSENIA: (21) 153 AD *SEG* XI 995 (Φλ. Ἀ.)
S. ITALY (BRUTTIUM):
—LOKROI EPIZEPHYRIOI:
——(Σκα.): (22) iv/iii BC De Franciscis 3, 13; 27, 5 (f. Ἀλκίας)
—PETELIA: (23) 102-114 AD *Klearchos* 3 (1961) p. 68 (*CIL* X 112) (Lat. Q. Fidubius Alcimus)
S. ITALY (CAMPANIA):
—DIKAIARCHIA-PUTEOLI: (24) ?i-ii AD ib. 2946 (Lat. Ti. Claudius Alcimus)
—HERCULANEUM: (25) i BC-i AD ib. IV 10508 b (Lat. Alcimus); (26) m. i AD *PdelP* 3 (1948) p. 173 no. 18; p. 176 no. 21 (Lat. M. Caesius Alcimus); (27) ~ *CIL* IV 10722; 10784-8 (amph.); 10857-9 (vases) (Lat. M. Livius Alcimus)
—HERCULANEUM*: (28) m. i AD *Cron. Erc.* 7 (1977) p. 117 C b, 15 (Lat. C. Iulius Alcimus: freed.)
—PITHEKOUSSAI-AENARIA: (29) imp. *CIL* X 6786 (Lat. C. Metilius Alcimus)
—POMPEII: (30) i BC-i AD ib. IV 1289; (31) ~ ib. 1785 (Lat. Alcimus); (32) ~ ib. 1901; (33) ~ ib. 1934 (Lat. Alcimus) ?= (34); (34) ~ ib. 1944 (Lat. Alcimus) ?= (33); (35) ~ ib. 9999 (Lat. Alcimus); (36) 57 AD ib. 3340. 40, 21 (Castrèn 457. 3) (Lat. C. Vibius Alcimus)
SICILY: (37) iv BC *RE* (18); *FGrH* 560
—AKRAGAS?: (38) iv BC *SEG* XXVIII 761 (sculptor)

**Ἀλκινάδας**
LAKONIA:
—SPARTA: (1) c. 550-525 BC ib. XXXII 399; *LSAG*² p. 447 no. C (date) (Ἀλκινάδας); (2) 421 BC Th. V 19. 2; 24 (Poralla² 65)

**Ἀλκινόα**
ELIS: (1) 53 AD *IvOl* 435, 2; *ZPE* 99 (1993) p. 232 (stemma) (Κλ. Ἀλκιν[ό]α: d. Κλ. Θεογένης, Ἰουλ. Χρυσαρέτα, ?m. Λ. Βετληνὸς Λαῖτος)
EPIROS:
—AVARICE (MOD.): (2) ii BC *SEG* XXIV 468 (d. Γλαυκίας)
ZAKYNTHOS: (3) ?iv BC ib. XL 507

**Ἀλκινόϝα**
KORINTHIA:
—KORINTH: (1) c. 615-600 BC Amyx 4. 2 (vase) (Lorber 24) (her.)

**Ἀλκίνοος**
ELIS: (1) 372-368 BC *IvOl* 166, 4 (*CEG* II 828); Paus. VI 1. 4 (Ἀλκινόο (gen.): f. Τρωῖλος)
EPIROS:
—DODONA*: (2) iv BC *PAE* 1932, p. 52 no. 5

**Ἀλκίνος**
AKARNANIA:
—THYRREION: (1) 263-262 BC *IG* IX (1)² (1) 3 A, 23; (2) ii/i BC ib. IX (1)² (2) 256, 7
ARKADIA:
—MEGALOPOLIS: (3) c. 279-248 BC Nachtergael, *Les Galates* 3, 7; 8, 22; 17, 1; cf. Stephanis 851 (f. Ἐπήρατος)

**Ἀλκίνους**
ARKADIA:
—KLEITOR: (1) c. 400-375 BC Paus. VI 9. 2 (f. Ἄλκετος)

KERKYRA: (2) iii/ii BC *IG* IX (1) 683, 13

**Ἀλκίνων**
SICILY:
—KENTORIPA: (1) iii-v AD *NScav* 1907, p. 494 (Λαμνα Κορνηλι. Ἀ.)

**Ἀλκίππα**
S. ITALY (BRUTTIUM):
—SYBARIS-THOURIOI-COPIAE: (1) iii BC Theoc., *Id.* V 132 (fict.)

**Ἀλκιππος**
AITOLIA:
—PHILOTAIEIS: (1) c. 157 BC *IG* IX (1)² (1) 108, 9
ARKADIA:
—MANTINEIA-ANTIGONEIA: (2) c. 300-221 BC ib. V (2) 323. 72 (tessera) (f. Ἀ[λ]χμαῖος)
——(Hoplodmia): (3) m. iv BC ib. 271, 13 (f. Τιμόφαντος)
KORINTHIA:
—KORINTH: (4) iv-iii BC *SEG* XXIX 338, 5
LAKONIA:
—SPARTA: (5) c. 500 BC ib. XI 638, 8; *LSAG*² p. 201 no. 44 (date) (-ιπος); (6) f. v BC Plu., *Mor.* 775 C (Poralla² 66); (7) iii BC *SEG* XL 348 B, 6; (8) c. 25-1 BC *IG* V (1) 210, 34 (Bradford (1)) ([Ἀλ]κιππος: s. Σήριππος); (9) ~ *IG* V (1) 212, 13 (Bradford (3)) (f. Σίων); (10) ?s. i AD *IG* V (1) 282; *Artemis Orthia* pp. 313-14 no. 31 (date) (Bradford (2))
SICILY:
—CASTEL DI IUDICA (MOD.): (11) ?iii BC Manganaro, *PdelP* forthcoming no. 6, 2 (s. Πύρριχος); (12) ~ ib. l. 3 (f. Ὄνασος)

**Ἄλκις**
ARGOLIS:
—ARGOS: (1) iii BC *IG* IV (1) 618 I, 5 (f. Δαμοσθένης)
MESSENIA: (2) viii BC Paus. IV 9. 3 (f. Τεῖσις)

**Ἀλκισθένης**
ACHAIA:
—PATRAI: (1) 122 BC *SEG* XV 254, 8 (f. Δάμων)
ARGOLIS:
—ARGOS:
——(Hylleis): (2) c. 458 BC *IG* I³ 1149, 5 ([Ἀλ]κισθένες, [Αἰ]κισθένες?)
ARKADIA:
—TEGEA: (3) f. ii BC ib. V (2) 44, 17 (s. Εὐξενίδας)
——(Athaneatai): (4) s. iv BC ib. 41, 30 (f. —ος)
——(Krariotai): (5) f. iii BC ib. 36, 62 (s. Λυσίστρατος) ?= (6); (6) s. iii BC ib. l. 121 (Ἀλκισθέν[ης]: f. Νικίας) ?= (5)
KERKYRA: (7) c. 500 BC *SEG* XXX 524
KORINTHIA:
—SIKYON: (8) ?253 BC Nachtergael, *Les Galates* 10, 48 (Stephanis 143) (s. Ἀριστογένης)
LAKONIA:
—SPARTA:
——Limnai: (9) c. 225 AD *IG* V (1) 547, 17; 682, [9]; 683, 6 (Bradford (-)) (M. Αὐρ. Ἀ.: s. Εὐέλπιστος)
S. ITALY (BRUTTIUM):
—SYBARIS-THOURIOI-COPIAE: (10) vi BC *RE* (4) (Ἀλκιμένης, Ἀντιμένης, Ἀντισθένης—al.)

**Ἀλκισοΐδας**
LAKONIA:
—SPARTA: (1) c. 30-20 BC *IG* V (1) 211, 38 (Bradford (-)) (s. Ἱππόδαμος)

**Ἀλκίστρατος**
AKARNANIA:
—THYRREION: (1) iii-ii BC *SEG* XXVII 159, 4; cf. *PAE* 1977, pl. 244 a (s. Ζώπυρος)
ARKADIA:
—TEGEA: (2) ii BC *SEG* XI 1058, 1 (Ἀλκίστ[ρ]ατος)

**Ἀλκιφρονίδας**
ARGOLIS:
—EPIDAUROS: (1) c. 335-325 BC *IG* IV (1)² 106 III, 101 (Ἀλκιφρονί[δας])

**Ἀλκίφρων**
ARGOLIS:
—ARGOS: (1) 418 BC Th. V 59. 5; *RE* (2)
—EPIDAUROS:
——(Hysminatai): (2) 146 BC *IG* IV (1)² 28, 16 (s. Ἀλκιμένης)
——Erilais: (3) m. iii BC Peek, *IAEpid* 42, 29 (Perlman E.3); Perlman p. 63 f. (date)
SICILY:
—SELINOUS: (4) s. vi BC Dubois, *IGDS* 31, 4 (Arena, *Iscr. Sic.* I 60); cf. *SEG* XXXVIII 962 (Ἀλκ[ί]φρων)

**Ἀλκιφῶν**
AKARNANIA:
—THYRREION: (1) ii BC *IG* IX (1)² (2) 248, 8, 19 (s. Κλεομένης, f. Κλεομένης)

**Ἀλκίων**
ILLYRIA:
—APOLLONIA: (1) imp. *IApoll* 49
—EPIDAMNOS-DYRRHACHION: (2) imp. *IDyrrh* 15 (f. —ερως); (3) ~ ib. 205 (f. Εὐλίμενος)

**Ἀλκμαίων**
S. ITALY (BRUTTIUM):
—KROTON: (1) vi/v BC *RE* (6); Supplbd. I; 12 cols. 22 ff.; *FVS* I pp. 210-216 no. 24 (s. Πείριθος: doctor)

**Ἀλκμάν**
ARKADIA:
—KLEITOR: (1) 369-361 BC *IG* V (2) 1, 54; Tod, *GHI* II 132 (date)
LAKONIA:
—SPARTA:
——Mesoa: (2) s. vii BC *RE* (-); Supplbd. 11; *PMGF* I testimonia; *CQ* NS 15 (1965) p. 188 f. (date) (Poralla² 67) (or Lydia Sardis: ?s. Δάμας, Τίταρος)

**Ἀλκμανίδας**
ILLYRIA:
—EPIDAMNOS-DYRRHACHION: (1) c. 250-50 BC Münsterberg p. 38; Nachtr. p. 14 (coin) (Ceka 267) (pryt.)

**Ἀλκυόνη**
KORINTHIA:
—KORINTH: (1) ix BC Polem. fr. 76 (d. Ἀγήμων) ?= (2); (2) viii BC Arist., *Pol.* 1274a 35 (m. Διοκλῆς) ?= (1)
S. ITALY (CAMPANIA):
—POMPEII: (3) i BC-i AD *CIL* IV 9917 (Lat. Alcyone)

**Ἀλκύσων**
EPIROS:
—NIKOPOLIS?: (1) v-vi AD *PAE* 1925-6, p. 129 (mosaic)

**Ἀλκύων**
LEUKAS: (1) hell. *IG* IX (1) 554

**Ἄλκων**
ACHAIA:
—PELLENE: (1) f. iii BC ib. II² 1957, 21 ([Ἄ]λ[κω]ν?)
ARKADIA:
—MT. KYLLENE*: (2) iv-iii BC ib. V (2) 362
EPIROS:
—MOLOSSOI: (3) vi BC Hdt. VI 127. 4
ILLYRIA:
—APOLLONIA: (4) c. 250-50 BC Münsterberg Nachtr. p. 12 (Ceka 85); *Bakërr Hoard* p. 64 no. 88 (coin) (pryt.)
—EPIDAMNOS-DYRRHACHION: (5) c. 250-50 BC Maier 120; 152; 158; 209; 230; 301; 337; 377 (coin) (Ceka 53-62) (money.)

KEPHALLENIA:
—PALE: (6) iii/ii BC *IG* VII 377, 3, 8 (*IOrop* 80) (s. *Λακράτης*)
S. ITALY (APULIA)?: (7) f. i BC Desy, *Timbres amphoriques* 181 (amph.) (Lat. Alco: slave?/potter)
S. ITALY (CAMPANIA):
—POMPEII: (8) i BC-i AD *CIL* IV 10240 (Lat. Alco)

**Ἀλμένας**
SICILY:
—HIMERA (NR.): (1) m. v BC *SEG* XXXVI 833 (n. pr.?)

**Ἀλογίωσος?**
S. ITALY (CAMPANIA):
—POMPEII: (1) i BC-i AD *CIL* IV 8098 (Lat. Alogiosus)

**Ἁλος**
S. ITALY (CAMPANIA):
—POMPEII: (1) i BC/i AD *Impegno per Pompeii* 3 ES (Lat. Halus)
SICILY:
—SELINOUS: (2) f. v BC Dubois, *IGDS* 38, 11, 17 (Arena, *Iscr. Sic.* I 63) (ἁ-: s. *Πυκέλειος*) ?= (*3*); (3) ~ Dubois, *IGDS* 38, 3-4 (Arena, *Iscr. Sic.* I 63) (ἁ-: f. *Λυκῖνος, Ναύερος*) ?= (*2*)

**Ἁλτιλλος**
AIGINA: (1) ?c. 475-450 BC *IG* IV (1) 6 (Lazzarini 265); cf. *Alt-Ägina* II (2) pp. 46-7 (ἡάλ-: f. *Ἀβλίων*)

**Ἀλύγας?**
ARKADIA:
—MANTINEIA-ANTIGONEIA:
——(Posoidaia): (1) m. iv BC *IG* V (2) 271, 18 ([Ἀ]λύγας—Hoffmann, [Ὀ]λύγας?— *IG*, [Π]λύγας?)

**Ἀλύπης**
SICILY:
—SYRACUSE: (1) 156 BC *ID* 1417 A II, 114

**Ἀλύπητος**
EPIROS:
—BOUTHROTOS: (1) ii BC *IBouthrot* 15, 21 (*SEG* XXXVIII 472); (2) ~ *IBouthrot* 190 (s. *Χρήσιμος*)
—PEUKESTOI: (3) iii BC *IG* IX (1)² (2) 243, 2 ([Ἀλύ]πητος: f. *Κλεοφάνης*)
KERKYRA: (4) c. 315-280 BC *FD* III (4) 406, 3 (Ἀ[λ]ύπητος: f. *Χλεμύτας*)
KORINTHIA:
—KORINTH: (5) 334 BC *CID* II 79 A I, 27 (Ἀλύ[πητος])
LAKONIA:
—SPARTA: (6) 377 BC X., *HG* V 4. 52 (Poralla² 68)

**Ἀλυπιάς**
S. ITALY (CAMPANIA):
—DIKAIARCHIA-PUTEOLI: (1) ?i-ii AD *CIL* X 2283 (Lat. Claudia Alypias)

**Ἀλυπίς**
SICILY:
—SYRACUSE: (1) c. 166 BC *ID* 1403 B b, II 86; 1412 a, 66

**Ἀλυπις**
SICILY:
—SYRACUSE: (1) iii-v AD *Riv. Arch. Crist.* 17 (1940) p. 47 (masc./fem.)

**Ἁλυπος**
AITOLIA:
—KALYDON: (1) c. 142 BC *IG* IX (1)² (1) 137, 48 (f. *Ἀριστόδαμος*)
—KONOPE-ARSINOE: (2) hell. *SBBerlAk* 1936, p. 364 no. 7 d (tile)

ARGOLIS:
—EPIDAUROS*: (3) c. 335-325 BC Peek, *IAEpid* 50, 13, 15
ARKADIA:
—PHIGALEIA: (4) c. 100-90 BC *SEG* XXXIII 290 A, 6; *BSA* 70 (1975) pp. 129-31 (date); cf. Stephanis 576 (f. *Δαμοκράτης*)
—TEGEA: (5) 191 AD *IG* V (2) 52, 5 (*Κλαυ. Ἀ.*)
EPIROS:
—AMBRAKIA: (6) iii/ii BC Plb. xxi 25. 11 ?= (7); (7) ~ *Demetrias* 1 pp. 175 ff. (*SEG* XXVI 688, 13) ?= (6)
KERKYRA: (8) imp. *IG* IX (1) 896
KORINTHIA:
—SIKYON: (9) v/iv BC *RE* (2); Marcadé 1 3 (Skalet 29) (sculptor)
S. ITALY (CAMPANIA):
—DIKAIARCHIA-PUTEOLI: (10) imp. *NScav* 1924, p. 84 (Lat. A. Egnatius Alypus); (11) ?iv AD *Puteoli* 6 (1982) p. 150 no. 5 (Lat. Valerius Alypus)
—HERCULANEUM*: (12) c. 72-79 AD *CIL* X 1403 i + *Cron. Erc.* 7 (1977) p. 117 C b, 20 (Lat. Q. Sallustius Alypus: freed.)
—POMPEII: (13) i BC-i AD *CIL* IV 1548 (Castrèn 119. 8) (Lat. L. Clodius Alypus); (14) ~ *CIL* IV 3377 (Lat. Halypus); (15) ~ ib. 7694 (Lat. Alipus); (16) ~ ib. 8420 b (Lat. Alypus)
SICILY:
—LILYBAION: (17) imp. ib. X 7224 (Lat. Alypus)

**Ἀλυπώ**
EPIROS:
—BOUTHROTOS: (1) i BC-i AD? *IBouthrot* 171 (Ugolini, *Alb. Ant.* 3 p. 121)
—BOUTHROTOS (PRASAIBOI): (2) a. 163 BC *IBouthrot* 31, 12 (*SEG* XXXVIII 490) (d. Ἀνδρων); (3) ~ *IBouthrot* 31, 78 (*SEG* XXXVIII 490); (4) ~ *IBouthrot* 31, 103 (*SEG* XXXVIII 490); (5) ~ *IBouthrot* 32, 7 (*SEG* XXXVIII 491) ?= (6); (6) ~ *IBouthrot* 35, 5 (*SEG* XXXVIII 494) ?= (5)

**Ἁλυς**
S. ITALY (CAMPANIA):
—POMPEII*: (1) i BC-i AD *CIL* X 981 (Lat. Halys: freed.)

**Ἀλφειόδωρος**
ARGOLIS:
—TROIZEN: (1) ?146 BC *IG* IV (1) 757 B, 28 (-φιό-: f. *Λύσων*)

**Ἀλφειός**
ELIS: (1) c. 201-213 AD *IvOl* 107, [13]; 110, 21 (Αὐ(ρ). Ἀ.: s. *Σόφων*)
LAKONIA:
—SPARTA: (2) 480 BC Hdt. vii 227; Paus. iii 12. 9 (Poralla² 69) (Ἀλφεός—Hdt.: s. *Ὀρσίφαντος*)

**Ἀλφησιδώ**
ARGOLIS:
—EPIDAUROS: (1) ii BC Peek, *IAEpid* 153. 26 ((Ἀ)λφησιδώ)

**Ἁλφις**
SICILY:
—AKRAI: (1) imp. *SEG* XLII 834 (Ἀ. *Λοῦκις*)

**Ἁλων**
ELIS: (1) iii BC *Ag.* XVII 455 (f. *Ἀρκεσίλαος*)

**Ἀλώπεκος**
LAKONIA:
—SPARTA: (1) her. Paus. iii 16. 9 (Poralla² 70) (s. *Ἱρβος*?: dub.)
S. ITALY (LUCANIA):
—METAPONTION: (2) iv BC Iamb., *VP* 267 (*FVS* 1 p. 446)

**Ἀμάδας**
ARKADIA:
—MANTINEIA-ANTIGONEIA: (1) c. 300-221 BC *IG* V (2) 323. 105 (tessera) (f. *Δᾶμις*)

**Ἀμαζονίς**
SICILY:
—LILYBAION: (1) ?iii AD *NScav* 1905, p. 217 (Lat. Amazonis)

**Ἀμαζών**
S. ITALY (CAMPANIA):
—MISENUM: (1) imp. *Eph. Ep.* VIII 429 (Lat. Didia Amazon)

**Ἀμαθώι**
KORINTHIA:
—KORINTH: (1) c. 570-550 BC Amyx 77. 4 (vase) (Lorber 111) (ἁμαθόι: her.)

**Ἀμάνιτος**
S. ITALY (BRUTTIUM):
—LOKROI EPIZEPHYRIOI:
——(Τηλ.): (1) iv/iii BC De Franciscis 32, 6 (s. *Φιλόμηλος*)

**Ἁμαξος?**
ILLYRIA:
—EPIDAMNOS-DYRRHACHION: (1) c. 250-50 BC Welzl 3245; cf. *IApoll Ref. Bibl.* n. 16 (coin) (pryt.)

**Ἀμαρανθίς**
S. ITALY (BRUTTIUM):
—SYBARIS-THOURIOI-COPIAE: (1) f. i AD *NScav* 1970, Suppl. 3 p. 551 (Lat. Cossutia Amaranthis)

**Ἀμάρανθος**
S. ITALY (CAMPANIA):
—DIKAIARCHIA-PUTEOLI: (1) imp. *CIL* X 2910 (Lat. T. Rasidius Amaranthus); (2) 46 AD Bove, *Documenti finanziarie* p. 162 T.P. 49, 3 (Lat. C. Iulius Amarantus); (3) ?ii AD *CIL* X 2014 (Lat. Cl. Amaranthus)
—HERCULANEUM*: (4) i BC-i AD ib. 1403 f I, 11 (Lat. A. Ofillius Amarantus: freed.)
—POMPEII: (5) i BC-i AD ib. IV 1174 (Lat. Amarantus); (6) ~ ib. 1213 (Lat. Amarantus); (7) ~ ib. 1547 (Lat. Amarantus); (8) ~ ib. 4295; 4296 (Lat. Amaranthus); (9) ~ ib. 4863 (Lat. Amaranthus); (10) ~ ib. 5098 (Lat. Amarantus); (11) ~ ib. 9055 (Lat. Amaranthus); (12) ~ ib. 9179 (Lat. Amarantus); (13) ~ ib. 10008 (Lat. Amaranthus); (14) c. 51-62 AD ib. 3340. 100, 7 (Castrèn 42. 8) (Lat. C. Arrius Amarantus); (15) 55 AD *CIL* IV 3340. 12, 16; 43, 20; 48, 18; 49, 20; 71, 6; 76, 7; 101, 5; 109, 6 (Castrèn 318. 8) (Lat. N. Popidius Amarantus); (16) 70-79 AD *CIL* IV 9829 a; Mouritsen p. 111 (date) (Lat. Amarantus Pompeianus)
SICILY:
—ZANKLE-MESSANA: (17) imp. *Mon. Ant.* 24 (1916) p. 173 (Lat. Stellius Nove— Amaranthus: f. *Κύτισος*)

**Ἀμαράντιν**
S. ITALY (CAMPANIA):
—DIKAIARCHIA-PUTEOLI*: (1) imp. *CIL* X 1725 (Lat. Septimia Amarantin: freed.)

**Ἀμάραντος**
ACHAIA: (1) iii AD *SEG* XIII 480; cf. *BE* 1955, no. 95; Barbieri, *L'albo senatorio* p. 795 (*M. Αὐρ. Ἀ.*: s. *Νίκανδρος*)
AIGINA: (2) f. iii AD *Alt-Ägina* I (2) p. 48 no. 37 (I f. *Αὐρ. Ἀμάραντος* II); (3) ~ ib. (*Αὐρ. Ἀ.*: II s. *Ἀμάραντος* I)
ARGOLIS:
—HERMIONE: (4) imp. *IG* IV (1) 699, 1 (*Αὐρ. Ἀ.*: f. *Ἰωτάπη*)
LAKONIA:
—SPARTA: (5) f. ii AD ib. V (1) 40, 3; 57, 8; 65, 16; 112, 1; 118, 4; *SEG* XI 514, [3]; 549, 6 (Bradford (1); (2)) (s. *Δημέας*, f. *Δημέας*) ?=

(6); (6) c. 120-125 AD *IG* V (1) 1315, 28; *SEG*
XI 596, 4 (Bradford (3)) (f. Εὐθυμοκλῆς) ?= (5)

**Ἀμαρυλλίς**
S. ITALY (CALABRIA):
—BRENTESION-BRUNDISIUM: (1) imp. *Epi-
graphica* 25 (1963) p. 62 no. 54 (Lat. Mamia
Amarillis)
—BRENTESION-BRUNDISIUM*: (2) imp. *CIL* IX
6136 (Lat. Sileia Amaryllis: freed.)
S. ITALY (CAMPANIA):
—ABELLA: (3) imp. ib. X 1209 (Lat. Critonia
Amaryllis)
—POMPEII: (4) i BC-i AD ib. IV 1507, 3 (Lat.
Amarillis) ?= (5); (5) ~ ib. 1510 (Lat. Ama-
ryllis) ?= (4)

**Ἄμασις**
ELIS: (1) ?v-iv BC Thphr., *Fr.* 108

**Ἀμάχιος**
KERKYRA:
—KASSIOPA: (1) imp. *AAA* 4 (1971) p. 204 fig.
1; cf. *AD* 26 (1971) Chron. p. 348
SICILY:
—KATANE: (2) ?iii-v AD *SEG* XXVI 1173 (f. Ἰοῦ-
στος)

**Ἀμβρακίας**
EPIROS:
—AMBRAKIA: (1) vi BC ib. XLI 540; cf. *BE* 1994,
no. 38 (Ἀνβρακίας (n. pr.?))

**Ἀμβρακίς**
EPIROS:
—AMBRAKIA?: (1) iv BC D.L. V 14 (n. pr.?:
slave/freed.)

**Ἀμβροσία**
S. ITALY (CAMPANIA):
—NEAPOLIS*: (1) imp. *IG* XIV 809 (*INap* 160);
cf. Leiwo p. 129 no. 116 (Lat. Servilia Am-
brosia: freed.)

**Ἀμβρόσιος**
S. ITALY (CAMPANIA):
—DIKAIARCHIA-PUTEOLI: (1) i BC/i AD? *RE* (3)
(Ἀ. Ῥουστικός)

**Ἀμέθυστος**
ARKADIA:
—TEGEA: (1) 165 AD *IG* V (2) 50, 68 (f. Ἐπαφρῦς)
KORINTHIA:
—KORINTH: (2) imp. *AE* 1977, p. 80 no. 28, 5
(Lat. [Am]ethys[tus]); (3) ~ *SEG* XI 138 f
S. ITALY (APULIA):
—LUCERIA: (4) imp. *Rend. Linc.* 24 (1969) p. 29
no. 11 (Lat. L. Luccius Amethystus)
S. ITALY (CALABRIA):
—BRENTESION-BRUNDISIUM*: (5) i AD *Taras* 6
(1986) p. 125 (*NScav* 1899, p. 451) (Lat. Cn.
Pomponiu[s] Amethust[us]: freed.)
S. ITALY (CAMPANIA):
—HERCULANEUM: (6) i BC-i AD *CIL* IV 10649
(Lat. Amethystus)
—HERCULANEUM*: (7) c. 50-75 AD ib. X 1403 a
I, 8 (Lat. Q. Novius Amethystus: freed.)
—POMPEII: (8) i BC-i AD ib. IV 4858 (Lat.
Amethystus); (9) 45 AD ib. X 825 (Castrèn
314. 4) (Lat. Q. Pompeius Amethystus)
S. ITALY (LUCANIA):
—VOLCEI: (10) imp. *IItal* III (1) 118 (Lat. Ama-
tistus: f. Ianuarius)
SICILY:
—SYRACUSE: (11) iii-v AD Wessel 138 + *Nuovo
Didask.* 6 (1956) p. 58 no. 15

**Ἀμεινίας**
ACHAIA:
—DYME: (1) ii BC *ICos* ED 232, 13 ([Ἀμε]ινίας:
s. Δίων)

**AKARNANIA:**
—ECHINOS: (2) c. 80 BC *IG* VII 416, 16 (*IOrop*
523); *IG* VII 542, 5 (Ἀμιν-: s. Χαιρήμων)
KORINTHIA:
—KORINTH: (3) imp. ib. IV (1) 399 (Ἀμιν-)
—SIKYON: (4) c. 146-32 BC *BMC Pelop.* p. 51
no. 193 (coin)
LAKONIA:
—KYTHERA: (5) hell.-imp. *IG* V (1) 942, 5
—SPARTA: (6) 423 BC Th. iv 132. 3 (Poralla² 71)
S. ITALY (CAMPANIA):
—NEAPOLIS: (7) i BC *IG* II² 9990 ([Ἀ]μεινίας: f.
—ένης)
SICILY:
—SELINOUS: (8) s. v BC *IGLMP* 69 + *SEG*
XXXIV 972 (name—Manganaro)

**Ἀμείνιππος**
LAKONIA:
—SPARTA: (1) c. 30-20 BC *IG* V (1) 211, 16
(Bradford (-)) (s. Δαμοκράτης)

**Ἀμεινοκλῆς**
KORINTHIA:
—KORINTH: (1) viii/vii BC *RE* (2)
S. ITALY (BRUTTIUM):
—LOKROI EPIZEPHYRIOI:
——(Πυρ.): (2) iv/iii BC De Franciscis 24, 7; 38,
5 (s. Χαιρεσίλας) ?= (3); (3) ~ ib. 29, 8 ?= (2)

**Ἀμεινόκριτος**
S. ITALY (BRUTTIUM):
—LOKROI EPIZEPHYRIOI:
——(Τιω.): (1) iv/iii BC ib. 2, 2; 3, 3 (s. Πρωτο-
γένης, f. Πρωτογένης) ?= (2); (2) ~ ib. 10, 3 ?=
(1)

**Ἀμείνων**
SICILY:
—KAMARINA: (1) ?ii BC *SEG* XXXIX 996, 7
(Dubois, *IGDS* 126; Cordano, 'Camarina
VII' 71) (s. Δαμάτριος)

**Ἄμεμπτον**
KERKYRA: (1) imp. *IG* IX (1) 944 (Κλ. Ἄμε-
μπ(τ)ον)

**Ἄμεμπτος**
ARKADIA:
—TEGEA: (1) ii AD ib. V (2) 54, 24 ([Ἄμε]νπτος)
S. ITALY (CAMPANIA):
—POMPEII: (2) i BC-i AD *CIL* IV 4004 (Lat.
Amempt(u)s)

**Ἀμέντα**
ILLYRIA:
—EPIDAMNOS-DYRRHACHION: (1) hell.-imp.
*IDyrrh* 94 (Ἀμέντας (fem. gen./masc. nom.?):
?m. Ἀμεντάν)

**Ἀμεντάν**
ILLYRIA:
—EPIDAMNOS-DYRRHACHION: (1) hell.-imp. ib.
(?s. Ἀμέντα)

**Ἀμέριμνος**
S. ITALY (APULIA):
—VIBINUM: (1) f. i AD *Bovino* p. 144 no. 196
(*Quad. di Storia* 35 (1992) p. 85) (Lat. C.
Pontidius Amerimnus)
S. ITALY (CAMPANIA):
—DIKAIARCHIA-PUTEOLI: (2) imp. *CIL* X 2177
(Lat. Q. Brittius Amerimnus Charitiosus)
—HERCULANEUM*: (3) imp. ib. X 1403 g I, 20
(Lat. C. Opsius Amerimnus: freed.)
—POMPEII: (4) i BC-i AD ib. IV 2139 (Lat.
Amerimnus); (5) ~ ib. 4839; (6) ~ ib. 5402
(Lat. Ameri(m)nus); (7) ~ ib. 8245 (Castrèn
205. 5) (Lat. C. Iulius Amerimnus)

**Ἀμέρτας**
ELIS: (1) s. v BC Moretti, *Olymp.* 337

**Ἀμετέρα**
ARKADIA:
—MEGALOPOLIS: (1) ii BC *IG* V (2) 536 (d. Ἀρ-
χικλῆς, m. Ἀριστώ)

**Ἀμετερός**
MESSENIA:
—MESSENE: (1) iii BC ib. V (1) 1441 a, 1

**Ἀμεύιππος**
LAKONIA:
—MALEA?: (1) c. 500 BC *SEG* XXXV 357;
*LSAG*² p. 447 no. F (-ἱππος)

**Ἄμη**
S. ITALY (CAMPANIA):
—PITHEKOUSSAI-AENARIA: (1) viii/vii BC
Dubois, *IGDGG* 1 7 (vase) (Arena, *Iscr.
Sic.* III 8) (Ἀμέ)

**Ἀμιάδας**
AIGINA: (1) hell.? *IG* IV (1) 185

**Ἀμιαντίς**
S. ITALY (LUCANIA):
—POSEIDONIA-PAESTUM: (1) imp. *CIL* X 500
(Mello–Voza 210) (Lat. Vinnia Amiantis: d.
Lucia Herria)

**Ἀμίαντος**
ARKADIA:
—TEGEA: (1) 165 AD *IG* V (2) 50, 69 (I f. Ἀμίαν-
τος II); (2) ~ ib. l. 69 (II s. Ἀμίαντος I); (3) ~
ib. l. 72 (s. Ἀντίοχος)
—TRAPEZOUS: (4) c. 575 BC Hdt. vi 127. 3 (s.
Λυκοῦργος)
ILLYRIA:
—APOLLONIA: (5) i BC Maier 159 (coin) (s. Σω-
σίλοχος: money.)
LAKONIA:
—SPARTA: (6) c. 30-20 BC *IG* V (1) 211, 17
(Bradford (-)) (s. Ἀριστόνικος)
S. ITALY (APULIA):
—VENUSIA: (7) imp. *CIL* IX 575 (Lat. L. Stae-
dius Amianthus)
S. ITALY (CAMPANIA):
—HERCULANEUM*: (8) i BC-i AD ib. X 1403 g
II, 13 (Lat. A. Troilus Amiantus: freed.)
—POMPEII: (9) i BC-i AD ib. IV 1786; cf. p.
212 (Lat. Amianth[us]); (10) ~ ib. 1809; 1844;
1859; 1905; 1936; 1942; 1942 a, b (Lat. Ami-
anth[us]); (11) ~ ib. 4005 (Lat. Amianth[us]);
(12) ~ ib. 5163 (Lat. Amiantus); (13) ~ ib.
10196 (Lat. Amiantus)
—SALERNUM: (14) imp. *IItal* I (1) 160 (*CIL* X
647) (Lat. P. Vetilius Amiantus)
—SURRENTUM: (15) imp. *Rend. Torn. Acc.
Arch. Napoli* 1 (1887) p. 9 no. 3 (Lat. Ami-
antus)
S. ITALY (LUCANIA):
—POSEIDONIA-PAESTUM: (16) imp. *CIL* X 500
(Mello–Voza 210) (Lat. Vinnius Amiantus: s.
Lucia Herria)
SICILY:
—DREPANON?: (17) f. iii AD *IG* XIV 283 (*IGR* I
502) (Ἀσίννιος Ἀ.)

**Ἄμιλλα**
S. ITALY (CAMPANIA):
—DIKAIARCHIA-PUTEOLI: (1) imp. *CIL* X 2622
(Lat. Iunia Amile: m. Ἄμιλλος)

**Ἄμιλλος**
S. ITALY (BRUTTIUM):
—HIPPONION-VIBO VALENTIA: (1) imp. ib. 82
(Lat. C. Segulius Amillus)
S. ITALY (CAMPANIA):
—DIKAIARCHIA-PUTEOLI: (2) imp. ib. 2622
(Lat. M. Iunius Hamillus: s. Ἄμιλλα) ?= (3);
(3) ~ ib. 2630 (Lat. M. Iunius Hamillus) ?=
(2)
—POMPEII: (4) i BC-i AD ib. IV 3710-11 (Lat.
Hamillus (sinistr.))

**Ἀμίμητος**
Lakonia:
—sparta: (1) c. 140-160 AD *IG* v (1) 74, 8 (Bradford (-)) (-μεί-: s. Ὀνάσιμος)

**Ἀμίσκος**
S. Italy (Bruttium):
—rhegion: (1) hell.? *IG* xiv 2400 add. (p. 706) ([Λ]αμίσκος?—ed.)

**Ἀμισσός**
Arkadia:
—megalopolis: (1) s. iv BC Berve 53 (Lat. Amissus: dub.)

**Ἀμίτιος**
Epiros:
—ambrakia: (1) ii-i BC *CIG* 1798 (s. Φιλιστίων)

**Ἀμμαῖος**
Argolis:
—epidauros: (1) ii-iii AD *IG* iv (1)² 566 (Ἀμμ[ώνι]ος?)

**Ἀμμάλα**
Illyria: (1) hell.-imp. *L'Illyrie mérid.* 1 p. 117 (Masson, *OGS* 2 p. 581) (d. Σερδελαΐδας)

**Ἄμμασα**
Illyria:
—epidamnos-dyrrhachion: (1) hell.-imp. *IDyrrh* 95 (Ἄμμασα: d. Ἀγαθ—)

**Ἄμμη**
S. Italy (Apulia):
—spinazzola (mod.): (1) f. i AD *Epigrafia e Territorio* 1 p. 19 no. 1 (Lat. Amme)

**Ἀμμία**
Argolis:
—hermione: (1) ?ii-i BC *IG* iv (1) 731 I, 10 (d. Σωσικράτης); (2) ~ ib. l. 13 (d. Στράτων); (3) ~ ib. 731 II, 1 (d. Ἀφροδισία); (4) ii-i BC ib. 732 II, 10 (d. Ἀσκληπιόδωρος)
Epiros:
—bouthrotos (prasaiboi): (5) a. 163 BC *IBouthrot* 17, 29 (*SEG* xxxviii 474) (I m. Ἀμμία II); (6) ~ *IBouthrot* 17, 29 (*SEG* xxxviii 474) (II d. Ἀμμία I); (7) ~ *IBouthrot* 45, 15; (8) imp. Ugolini, *Alb. Ant.* 3 p. 214 (Lat. Iunia Ammia)
—orikos: (9) hell.-imp. *Klio* 40 (1962) p. 290
Illyria: (10) 167 BC *SGDI* 1854, 6, 8 etc. (slave/freed.)
—bylliones byllis: (11) imp. *SEG* II 370
S. Italy (Apulia):
—canusium*: (12) s. i BC *Epig. Rom. di Canosa* 197 (*CIL* ix 402) (Lat. Tutoria Ammia: freed.)
S. Italy (Campania):
—pompeii: (13) i BC-i AD ib. iv 2345 (Castrèn 457. 4) (Lat. Vibia Ammia)
Sicily:
—thermai himeraiai*: (14) imp. *CIL* x 7441 (*ILat. Term. Imer.* 150) (Lat. [Vi]bia Ammia: freed.)

**Ἀμμιανή**
Korinthia:
—korinth: (1) byz. *Corinth* viii (3) 588 ([Ἀμ]μιανή)

**Ἀμμιάς**
S. Italy (Campania):
—misenum*: (1) imp. *CIL* x 3611 (Lat. Naevia Ammias: d. Naevius Sentianus, Καρπίμη)

**Ἀμμίκα**
Illyria:
—epidamnos-dyrrhachion: (1) hell.-imp. *IDyrrh* 398 (m. Τατώ)

**Ἄμμιλα**
Illyria:
—apollonia: (1) ?i BC *IApoll* 14; Robert, *Hell.* 9 p. 72 (locn.)

**Ἀμμιλώ**
Epiros:
—ioannina (mod.): (1) iii/ii BC *BCH* 118 (1994) p. 727 (d. Σιμίας)

**Ἄμμινα**
Illyria:
—apollonia: (1) imp. *IApoll* 50 ([Ἄ]μμινα)
—epidamnos-dyrrhachion: (2) hell.-imp. *IDyrrh* 96 (d. Φίλων)

**Ἀμμωνιανός**
S. Italy (Campania):
—misenum*: (1) imp. *CIL* x 3612 (Lat. Ammonius Ammonianus)

**Ἀμμώνιος**
Achaia:
—dyme*: (1) c. 219 BC *SGDI* 1612, 79 (*Tyche* 5 (1990) p. 124) (s. Πεισίας)
Dalmatia:
—issa: (2) iii/ii BC Brunšmid p. 21 no. 8; *Istros* 2 (1935-6) pp. 18 ff. (date)
Elis: (3) 36-24 BC *IvOl* 62, 14 (I f. Ἀμμώνιος II); (4) ~ ib. l. 14 (II s. Ἀμμώνιος I: doctor/Φ.); (5) c. 5 AD ib. 69, 25 (Ἀμμώ[νιος]: f. —ων)
Korinthia:
—korinth: (6) ii BC *ZPE* 1 (1967) p. 230; cf. Stephanis 1786 (f. Νειλεύς)
Messenia:
—messene: (7) hell.-imp. *PAE* 1991, p. 106 no. 8, 4 (f. —ιθίων); (8) i BC-i AD *SEG* xxiii 218 (s. Δαματρία)
S. Italy (Calabria):
—brentesion-brundisium: (9) imp. *NScav* 1892, p. 353 y (Lat. P. Saeius Ammonius)
Sicily:
—syracuse: (10) ii-i BC *IG* xiv 8, 4 (*IGLMP* 105)
—tauromenion:
——(Ἀρεθ.): (11) ii/i BC *IGSI* 8 II 9 (s. Σαραπίων)
——(Σπαρ.): (12) ii/i BC ib. 10 I, 1 (s. Ἀγάθων)

**Ἀμμωνόδοτος**
Sicily:
—tauromenion: (1) c. 236-232 BC *IG* xiv 421 an. 5; 421 an. 9 (*SGDI* 5219) (f. Μόσχος, Νεμήνιος)

**Ἀμομφάρετος**
Lakonia:
—sparta: (1) c. 600 BC Plu., *Sol.* 10 (Poralla² 72)
——Pitana: (2) c. 505-479 BC Hdt. ix 53-7; 71. 2; 85. 1; Plu., *Arist.* 17 (Poralla² 73) (s. Πολιάδας)

**Ἀμπελίδας**
Lakonia:
—sparta: (1) 421 BC Th. v 22. 2 (Poralla² 74)

**Ἀμπέλιον**
S. Italy (Apulia):
—luceria: (1) imp. *CIL* ix 785 (Lat. Terentia Ampelium)
S. Italy (Campania):
—atella*: (2) imp. ib. x 3738 (Lat. Ampelium: freed.)

**Ἀμπέλιος**
S. Italy (Campania):
—neapolis?: (1) ii-iii AD *Gnomon* 45 (1973) pp. 270-1 (Lat. Ampelius)
—pompeii: (2) i BC-i AD *CIL* iv 10217 (Lat. Ampelius)

**Ἀμπελίς**
S. Italy (Calabria):
—hyria: (1) ?i/ii AD ib. ix 228 (Lat. Flavia Ampelis)
S. Italy (Campania):
—dikaiarchia-puteoli: (2) imp. ib. x 2166 (Lat. Ampelis); (3) ~ ib. 2999 (Lat. Terentia Ampelis);
—surrentum: (4) imp. ib. 750 (Lat. Pompeia Ampelis); (5) ~ *Rend. Torn. Acc. Arch. Napoli* 1 (1887) p. 8 no. 1 (Lat. Messia Ampelis)

**Ἄμπελος**
S. Italy (Campania):
—pompeii: (1) i BC-i AD *CIL* iv 10003 (Lat. Anpelus); (2) ~ ib. 10181 e (Lat. Anpelus); (3) ~ *Römische Gräberstrassen* p. 217 + *Arctos* 26 (1992) p. 120 (Lat. L. Calventius Ampelus)

**Ἀμπλιᾶτος**
S. Italy (Campania):
—neapolis: (1) iii-iv AD *INap* 221

**Ἄμπλις**
Sicily:
—rosolini (mod.): (1) ?iii-v AD *SEG* xxvi 1117

**Ἀμύκη**
S. Italy (Campania):
—pompeii: (1) i BC-i AD *CIL* x 1009 (Castrèn 246. 6) (Lat. Melissaea Amyce)

**Ἄμυκλα**
Lakonia: (1) s. v BC Plu., *Alc.* 1; *Lyc.* 16 (Poralla² 75)

**Ἀμυκλαῖος**
Korinthia:
—korinth: (1) vi/v BC Paus. x 13. 7 (sculptor)

**Ἄμυκλας**
Lakonia:
—sparta: (1) s. i BC *IG* v (1) 136, 3 (Bradford (-)) ([Ἄ]μύκλας: s. Τ—)

**Ἄμυκος**
Arkadia:
—tegea: (1) ii AD *IG* v (2) 55, 53 (f. Στράτυλλος); (2) 165 AD ib. 50, 3-4 (Τιβ. Κλ. Ἀ.: f. Δαμακίων); (3) ~ ib. l. 14 (s. Ἄλεος); (4) ~ ib. l. 17 (s. Ὀρειβάτης)
S. Italy (Campania):
—herculaneum*: (5) i BC-i AD *CIL* x 1403 g II, 8 (Lat. A. Tetteius Amycus: freed.)

**Ἀμύμων**
Illyria:
—skodrai: (1) a. 168 BC *Iliria* 1972, p. 403 (coin)
Korinthia:
—sikyon: (2) iii BC *TrGF* 1 p. 284

**Ἀμύνα**
S. Italy (Campania):
—misenum*: (1) imp. *CIL* x 3646 (Lat. Amyna)

**Ἀμύνανδρος**
Aitolia: (1) ?252-248 BC *Syll*³ 422, 4; (2) 224 or 221 BC *SGDI* 2524, 5; Nachtergael, *Les Galates* 64, 3
—aperantoi: (3) iii BC *AD* 22 (1967) Chron. p. 322 (s. Πολεμαῖος)
—thermos: (4) m. iii BC *IG* ix (1)² (1) 22, 6
Akarnania: (5) 316 BC ib. v (2) 549, 29 (*Syll*³ 314) (s. Περίανδρος)
Epiros:
—argos (amphiloch.): (6) iv BC *SNG Cop. Epirus–Acarnania* 320; *NZ* 10 (1878) p. 95 nos. 55-6 (coins); Franke, *Münz. v. Epirus* p. 17 n. 5 (locn.)

**Ἀμύνας**

—ATHAMANES: (7) 220-189 BC RE (2); BCH 45 (1921) p. 16 III, 34; Welles, RC 35 (SEG XXXVIII 1227) (king) ?= (Ἀμύνας (1))
—ATHAMANES?: (8) s. iii BC IG IX (2) 208 + Moretti, ISE 2 94 (s. Μάχαος) ?= (Ἀμύνας (1))
—DODONA: (9) c. 330 BC Cabanes, L'Épire p. 580 no. 55, 7; (10) iii BC Antoniou, Dodone Aa, 25; (11) ~ ib. Ab, 55 (Ἀμύνα[νδρος])
—MOLOSSOI: (12) c. 343-330 BC Cabanes, L'Épire p. 588 no. 74, 9 (SEG XXVI 700) (s. Ἔρυξις); (13) ~ Cabanes, L'Épire p. 588 no. 74, 10 (SEG XXVI 700) (s. Ἴνων); (14) c. 237-232 BC SGDI 1348, 2; Hammond, Epirus p. 593 (date); (15) ii BC SGDI 1357, 7-8; cf. Cabanes, L'Épire p. 583 no. 61
—PEIALES: (16) 370-368 BC ib. p. 534 no. 1, 14, 30
S. ITALY (BRUTTIUM):
—LOKROI EPIZEPHYRIOI:
——(Mνα.): (17) iv/iii BC De Franciscis 2, 4 (f. Θεστορίδας) ?= (18); (18) 278 BC ib. 28, 2 (f. Εὐφρονίσκος) ?= (17)

**Ἀμύνας**
EPIROS:
—ATHAMANES: (1) 219 BC Plb. iv 16. 9 (king) ?= (Ἀμύνανδρος (8) Ἀμύνανδρος (7))

**Ἀμυνόμαχος**
ARKADIA:
—TEGEA: (1) i BC-i AD IG V (2) 201

**Ἀμύντας**
AIGINA: (1) ?i BC Alt-Ägina I (2) p. 44 no. 11, 4 (f. Μειδίας)
AITOLIA:
—BOUKATION?: (2) c. 162 BC IG IX (1)² (1) 106, 10 (Ἀμύντ(ας))
AKARNANIA:
—PALAIROS: (3) f. iii BC ib. IX (1)² (2) 466
—THYRREION: (4) c. 200 BC ib. 294
ARGOLIS:
—EPIDAUROS: (5) iii/ii BC Peek, NIEpid 15, 13 (s. Δημήτριος); (6) ii BC Peek, IAEpid 130 ([Ἀ]μύντας: s. Δημήτριος)
ARKADIA:
—ORCHOMENOS: (7) 369-361 BC IG V (2) 1, 48; Tod, GHI II 132 (date)
EPIROS:
—ATERARGOI: (8) iii/ii BC Cabanes, L'Épire p. 561 no. 35, 3 (f. —δρος)
—BOUTHROTOS (PRASAIBOI): (9) a. 163 BC IBouthrot 28, 24 (SEG XXXVIII 486)
—DODONA*: (10) iv-iii BC SGDI 1588
ILLYRIA:
—APOLLONIA: (11) imp. IApoll 43 (?f. Φίλιππος); (12) ~ ib. 51 (I f. Ἀμύντας II); (13) ~ ib. (II s. Ἀμύντας I)
—DIMALE*: (14) hell. Iliria 1982 (1), p. 120 no. 5 (tile)
—EPIDAMNOS-DYRRHACHION: (15) c. 250-50 BC Maier 105-11; 466-9; Münsterberg p. 38; Nachtr. p. 14 (coin) (Ceka 69; 162; 168; 231; 266; 275; 286; 356; 411; 423; 432; 445) (pryt.)
—LYCHNIDOS: (16) ?i-ii AD ZA 6 (1956) p. 169 no. 4 (s. Ἀλέξανδρος)
ITHAKE: (17) hell. IG IX (1) 666
KORINTHIA:
—KORINTH: (18) vii/vi BC Amyx Gr 5 a. 5 (vase) (Lorber 2 a); (19) m. iii BC Corinth VIII (3) 33 b, 2; cf. SEG XXV 330 ([Ἀ]μύντ[ας])
—SIKYON: (20) c. 200-172 BC IG VII 1724, 2 (-μού-: f. Ἀγαθοκλῆς)
MESSENIA:
—MESSENE: (21) ii BC SEG XLI 347 (I s. Φίλων, ?f. Ἀμύντας II); (22) ~ ib. (II ?s. Ἀμύντας I, ?f. Ἀμύντας III); (23) ~ ib. ([Ἀ]μύντ]ας: III ?s. Ἀμύντας II)
S. ITALY (CAMPANIA):
—DIKAIARCHIA-PUTEOLI: (24) imp. CIL X 1871 (Lat. Amyntas)

**Ἀμυντῖνος**
S. ITALY (CAMPANIA):
—POMPEII: (1) i BC-i AD ib. IV 3200 g (Lat. Amuntinus)

**Ἀμυντίς**
ARGOLIS:
—OINOE?: (1) s. vi BC SEG XXXVIII 314, 1 (s. Ἀγαῖος)

**Ἀμύντωρ**
ARGOLIS:
—EPIDAUROS: (1) iii BC Peek, IAEpid 43, 30 (s. Νικέας)
KORINTHIA:
—KORINTH: (2) iii BC IG II² 9053 (s. Ξένων)

**Ἀμύρα**
ILLYRIA:
—APOLLONIA: (1) imp. IApoll 236

**Ἀμύριος**
ARKADIA:
—MANTINEIA-ANTIGONEIA: (1) ?iii BC IG V (2) 319, 19

**Ἀμυρις**
S. ITALY (LUCANIA):
—SIRIS: (1) f. vi BC RE (-) (f. Δάμασος)

**Ἀμφαίνετος**
ARGOLIS:
—HERMIONE: (1) c. 210-207 BC IG IV (1)² 73, 5; SEG XXXV 303 (date) (s. Μνάμων)
ARKADIA: (2) 316 BC IG V (2) 549, 35 (s. Πεδάρετος)

**Ἀμφάλκης**
ARKADIA: (1) vii/vi BC Call. dieg. vi 9; fr. 191 (s. Βαθυκλῆς)
—TEGEA: (2) ?218 BC IG V (2) 16, 1

**Ἀμφαλκίδας**
ILLYRIA:
—APOLLONIA: (1) c. 321-315 BC IApoll 310 (s. Ἄβρων)
—SKODRAI: (2) a. 168 BC Iliria 1972, p. 401 (coin)

**Ἀμφαρείδας**
ARKADIA:
—KLEITOR: (1) ?253 BC Nachtergael, Les Galates 10, 36 (Stephanis 163) (s. Δεινίας)

**Ἀμφάρης**
LAKONIA:
—SPARTA: (1) 241 BC Plu., Agis 19-21 (Bradford (-))
ZAKYNTHOS: (2) c. 230-200 BC BCH 45 (1921) p. 15 II, 144 (f. Ξοῦθος)

**Ἀμφία**
KERKYRA: (1) iii BC SEG XXV 614

**Ἀμφίαλος**
KERKYRA: (1) hell. IG IX (1) 894, 2 (Ἀμυραλος—apogr., Ἀμ(φί)αλος—ed.: f. Ἄγις)

**Ἀμφιάναξ**
ARGOLIS:
—HERMIONE: (1) m. iv BC Unp. (Ch. Kritzas)
ARKADIA: (2) s. iv BC IG II² 8379 (date—M.J.O.)

**Ἀμφιάρης**
LAKONIA:
—SPARTA: (1) 296 BC Moretti, Olymp. 515 (Bradford (-))

**Ἀμφίας**
ACHAIA: (1) 146 BC IG IV (1)² 28, 70 (s. Ἀμφίστρατος: synoikos)

AITOLIA:
—THESTIEIS: (2) 213 BC ib. IX (1)² (1) 96, 12, 15
ARGOLIS:
—ARGOS: (3) ii-i BC BCH 33 (1909) p. 447 no. 6 (f. —ος)
—EPIDAUROS: (4) 423 BC Th. iv 119. 2; Schol. Ar., Eq. 794 (s. Εὐπαΐδας)
ARKADIA:
—MANTINEIA-ANTIGONEIA: (5) c. 300-221 BC IG V (2) 323. 24 (tessera) (s. Ἀριστόκριτος)
—TEGEA: (6) iv BC ib. 31, 4 (f. Εὐκράτης)
ILLYRIA:
—APOLLONIA: (7) c. 250-50 BC Maier 44; 118 (Ceka 12-13); IApoll Ref. Bibl. n. 15 (coin) (money.); (8) i BC Maier 129-30 (coin) (s. Σώπολις: pryt.)

**Ἀμφιδάμα**
ARGOLIS:
—TROIZEN: (1) ?c. 550-525 BC CEG 1 138 (m. Δαμότιμος)

**Ἀμφιδάμας**
LAKONIA:
—SPARTA: (1) i BC/i AD BSA 89 (1994) pp. 433-4 no. 2, 10 (Ἀμφιδάμα[ς]: f. Ἀριστοδάμας)

**Ἀμφίδαμος?**: (1) c. 230-200 BC BCH 45 (1921) p. 13 II, 109 (f. Ἀγησίλοχος)
ELIS: (2) 219 BC Plb. iv 75. 6; 84. 2, 4, 8; 86. 3, 5, 7

**Ἀμφιθάλης**
MESSENIA:
—MESSENE: (1) iii BC SEG XXIII 209, 9

**Ἀμφίθεος**
ARKADIA:
—ORCHOMENOS: (1) m. iii BC BCH 38 (1914) p. 462 no. 6, 11 (Ἀμφ[ίθε]ος)

**Ἀμφικλῆς**
ARGOLIS:
—HERMIONE: (1) ii-i BC IG IV (1) 732 V, 2 (f. Δάμας)
ARKADIA:
—TEGEA: (2) m. iv BC ib. V (2) 6, 116
ILLYRIA:
—EPIDAMNOS-DYRRHACHION: (3) ?iii BC IDyrrh 250 (f. Ἱερήν); (4) hell.-imp. ib. 400 (f. Τιμᾶς)
LAKONIA:
—SPARTA: (5) her. Paus. iii 16. 9 (Poralla² 76) (s. Ἆγις, f. Ἀμφισθένης: dub.)

**Ἀμφικόριος**
EPIROS:
—ARKTANES: (1) 370-368 BC Cabanes, L'Épire p. 534 no. 1, 9, 26

**Ἀμφικράτηρ**
ELIS: (1) c. 85-93 AD IvOl 86, 6, 15 (Ἀν-: s. Ἀσκληπιάδηρ)

**Ἀμφικράτης**
ARGOLIS:
—EPIDAUROS:
——Dexelis: (1) c. 365-335 BC IG IV (1)² 103, 61
ELIS: (2) c. 57-93 AD IvOl 79, 4; 83, [3]; 84, 19; 85, [13]; 86, 10 (Ἀνφικράτηρ—86: I f. Ἀμφικράτης II); (3) ~ ib. 79, 4; 83, 3; 84, 19; 85, [13]; 86, 10 (Ἀνφικράτηρ—86: II s. Ἀμφικράτης I: M.); (4) c. 85-93 AD ib. l. 9 (Ἀν-: I f. Ἀμφικράτης II: Klytiadai); (5) ~ ib. l. 9 (Ἀν-: II s. Ἀμφικράτης I: mantis/Klytiadai/M.)
S. ITALY (LUCANIA):
—HYELE-VELIA: (6) ii-i BC IG II² 8481 a (Ag. XVII 448) (s. Ἀριστομένης)

**Ἀμφίκριτος**
ARGOLIS:
—ARGOS:

**Ἀμφιλαΐδας**
——(Pamphyloi): (**1**) ?c. 460-450 BC *IG* IV (1) 517, 7 (Lazzarini 937); *LSAG*² p. 170 no. 32 (date)

**Ἀμφιλαΐδας**
AKARNANIA:
—THYRREION: (**1**) ?i BC *IG* IX (1)² (2) 343

**Ἀμφιλῖνος**
ARGOLIS:
—EPIDAUROS*: (**1**) c. 290-270 BC *SEG* XXV 401 B, 103

**Ἀμφίλοχος**
ACHAIA:
—OLENOS: (**1**) ?iv BC Thphr., *Fr.* 109; cf. Ael., *NA* v 29 (fict.?)
AITOLIA?: (**2**) 139-122 BC *FD* III (6) 83, 3 (f. Ἀλέξανδρος)
ARKADIA:
—TEGEA: (**3**) iii BC *IG* v (2) 30, 17 (Ἀμφίλοχος)
SICILY:
—THERMAI HIMERAIAI*: (**4**) imp. *Epigraphica* 3 (1941) p. 265 no. 31 (pithos) (Lat. Ampilochus)

**Ἀμφίλυτος**
AKARNANIA: (**1**) 539 BC *RE* (1); *IG* IX (1)² (2) p. X, s.a. 539 BC
ARGOLIS:
—EPIDAUROS: (**2**) c. 350-200 BC *SEG* XXVI 452. 3; (**3**) iv/iii BC *IG* IV (1)² 161
KORINTHIA:
—KORINTH: (**4**) ?viii BC Paus. ii 1. 1 (f. Εὔμηλος); (**5**) i BC/i AD *Corinth* XIII p. 319 no. X-116

**Ἀμφίμαχος**
ARKADIA:
—PHIGALEIA: (**1**) c. 240 BC *IG* v (2) 419, 7 (*IPArk* 28) (Ἀνφίμα[χος])
ARKADIA?: (**2**) hell. *Syringes* 649 (?s. Δαΐμαχος)
LAKONIA:
—GERONTHRAI: (**3**) iv BC *IG* v (1) 1121 (Poralla² 77) (Ἀμφίμαχος)

**Ἀμφιμέδων**
KERKYRA: (**1**) ii-i BC *AA* 1940, p. 203

**Ἀμφιμενίδας**
LAKONIA: (**1**) ?c. 525-500 BC *SEG* XI 955 (Lazzarini 102); *LSAG*² p. 200 no. 33 (date) (Poralla² 106a) (Ἀν-)

**Ἀμφιμήδης**
ARGOLIS:
—HERMIONE: (**1**) iii BC *IG* IV (1) 729 II, 22 (s. Πασκάλας)

**Ἀμφίμναστος**
ILLYRIA:
—EPIDAMNOS-DYRRHACHION: (**1**) vi BC Hdt. vi 127. 2 (s. Ἐπίστροφος)

**Ἀμφίνομος**
S. ITALY (BRUTTIUM):
—SYBARIS-THOURIOI-COPIAE: (**1**) vii-vi BC *ILind* 2 B XXVI
S. ITALY (CAMPANIA):
—POMPEII: (**2**) i BC-i AD *NScav* 1916, p. 302 no. 5 (Castrèn 158. 10) (Lat. M. Epidius Ampinomus)
SICILY:
—KATANE: (**3**) arch.? *RE* (5) (dub.)

**Ἀμφίνους**
EPIROS:
—BOUTHROTOS (PRASAIBOI):
——Aigidorioi: (**1**) iii/ii BC Cabanes, *L'Épire* p. 574 no. 48, 3 ([Ἀ]μφίνους: f. Ἄδματος) ?= (2); (**2**) a. 163 BC *IBouthrot* 39, 1 (*SEG* XXXVIII 498) (f. Ἄδματος) ?= (1)

**Ἀμφισθένης**
KERKYRA: (**1**) iv/iii BC *IG* IX (1) 976, 3 (f. Θερσίων)
LAKONIA:
—SPARTA: (**2**) her. Paus. iii 16. 9 (Poralla² 78) (s. Ἀμφικλῆς, f. Ἴρβος?: dub.)

**Ἀμφίστρατος**
ACHAIA: (**1**) 146 BC *IG* IV (1)² 28, 70 (-σστρα-: f. Ἀμφίας: synoikos)
ARKADIA:
—MANTINEIA-ANTIGONEIA: (**2**) c. 300-221 BC ib. v (2) 323. 42 (tessera) (s. Νέαρχος)
—TEGEA:
——(Hippothoitai): (**3**) iv/iii BC ib. 38, 43 (f. Ἀριστόμαχος)
ILLYRIA:
—BYLLIONES: (**4**) iii BC *SEG* XXXVIII 559

**Ἀμφίτιμος**
LEUKAS: (**1**) 190 BC *Syll*³ 585, 99 (f. Ἐράτων)

**Ἀμφιτρύων**
S. ITALY (CAMPANIA):
—POMPEII: (**1**) i BC-i AD *CIL* IV 4514, 11 (Lat. Ampit(r)uo)

**Ἀμφίων**
KORINTHIA:
—KORINTH: (**1**) viii/vii BC Hdt. v 92 (f. Λάβδα)
S. ITALY (CALABRIA):
—BRENTESION-BRUNDISIUM: (**2**) imp. *CIL* IX 6112 (Lat. Calavius Amphio)
S. ITALY (CAMPANIA):
—ABELLA*: (**3**) imp. ib. x 1221 (Lat. A. Fuficius Amphio: freed.)
—DIKAIARCHIA-PUTEOLI: (**4**) ?i-ii AD ib. 2541 (Lat. C. Iulius Amphio)
—NEAPOLIS: (**5**) iii AD *IG* XIV 2412. 5 (seal) (Αὐρ. Ἀνφίο(νος) (gen.), Ἄμφιος?)
—OPLONTIS: (**6**) i BC-i AD *Guida Pompeii* p. 346 no. 2 (Lat. L. Arrianus Amphio)
—POMPEII: (**7**) i BC-i AD *CIL* IV 1353 b; cf. p. 206 (Lat. Amphio); (**8**) ~ ib. 3007 (Lat. Amphio); (**9**) ~ ib. 4096 (Lat. Amphio); (**10**) ~ *NScav* 1896, p. 228 (Castrèn 367. 2) (Lat. L. Sepunius Amphio); (**11**) ~ *Röm. Mitt.* 13 (1894) p. 357 = *NScav* 1895, p. 211 (seal) (Castrèn 118. 3) (Lat. Ti. Claudius Amphio); (**12**) 2 BC *CIL* x 890, 3 (Castrèn 249. 3) (Lat. T. Mescinius Amphio)
—POMPEII*: (**13**) i BC-i AD *CIL* IV 3864 (Lat. Lucius [Decius]? [Amp]hio: freed.)
—SALERNUM*: (**14**) ?i AD *IItal* I (1) 238 III, 10 (*CIL* x 557) (Lat. L. Appuleius Amphio: freed.)
SICILY: (**15**) imp. ib. 8059. 419 (seal) (Lat. L. Valerius Amphio)

**Ἀμφώνυμος**
AITOLIA: (**1**) f. iii BC *Das Heroon von Kalydon* p. 293, 12 (f. Γάστρων)

**Ἀμώμητος**
KERKYRA: (**1**) ?i BC *IG* IX (1) 747 (*BM Terracottas* E 186 (tile))

**Ἀμωμίς**
S. ITALY (CAMPANIA):
—DIKAIARCHIA-PUTEOLI: (**1**) imp. *IG* XIV 859, 13 (Audollent, *Defix. Tab.* 208)

**Ἄμωμος**
EPIROS:
—BOUTHROTOS (PRASAIBOI): (**1**) a. 163 BC *IBouthrot* 132, 9 (Ἄμωμος: s. Τρυ—)
S. ITALY (APULIA):
—LARINUM: (**2**) imp. *CIL* IX 745 (Lat. Amomus)

S. ITALY (CAMPANIA):
—DIKAIARCHIA-PUTEOLI: (**3**) imp. ib. x 2220 (Lat. C. Calvius Amomus); (**4**) ~ ib. 2380 (Lat. Egnatius Amomus: s. Κύνναμος)
—DIKAIARCHIA-PUTEOLI*: (**5**) imp. ib. 1965 (Lat. Lic. Amomus: s. Licinia Primigenia: freed.?)
—POMPEII: (**6**) i BC-i AD ib. IV 8897 (Lat. Amomus)

**Ἄμων**
KORINTHIA:
—KORINTH?: (**1**) m. v BC *IG* IV (1) 357 (bronze) (Lazzarini 348) (-μōν: s. Σώνοος)

**Ἄνα**
ILLYRIA: (**1**) 188 BC *SGDI* 2014, 2, 3, 5, 6, 9, 11 (slave/freed.)
—SKODRAI: (**2**) byz. *SEG* XVIII 265
S. ITALY (APULIA):
—VENUSIA: (**3**) v AD *JIWE* I 72 (*CIJ* I 575) (Jew)
S. ITALY (LUCANIA):
—PALINURUM: (**4**) iv BC *Apollo* 2 (1962) pp. 3-7

**Ἀναγαλλίς**
KERKYRA: (**1**) hell.-imp.? *Suda* A 1817

**Ἀνάκλητος**
S. ITALY (CALABRIA):
—RUDIAE: (**1**) imp. *NScav* 1897, p. 407 no. 16 = Bernardini, *Rudiae* p. 87 (Susini, *Fonti Salento* p. 123 no. 67) (Lat. Anacletus)

**Ἄνακος**
ARKADIA:
—PHIGALEIA: (**1**) ?iv BC *FGrH* 387 F 1 (Stephanis 172)

**Ἀνάκτωρ**
ARGOLIS:
—ARGOS: (**1**) f. i BC Unp. (Ch. Kritzas) (I f. Ἀνάκτωρ II); (**2**) ~ ib. (II s. Ἀνάκτωρ I)

**Ἄνανθος**
ARGOLIS:
—ARGOS: (**1**) iv-iii BC *Argive Heraeum* 2 p. 186 no. 12 and pl. 69 (sherd) (Ἀναν[θος]?)
—HERMIONE: (**2**) iii BC *IG* IV (1) 729 II, 11 (s. Τρεῦθος)

**Ἀνανίας**
MESSENIA:
—MESSENE: (**1**) byz. *ABME* 11 (1969) p. 100 no. 2 = *PAE* 1969, p. 119 no. 7, 1; cf. *TMByz* 9 (1985) p. 372 no. 148 (Ἀνανίου (gen.))

**Ἀναξαγόρα**
SICILY:
—SYRACUSE: (**1**) s. v BC *IG* I³ 1371 (Dubois, *IGDS* 96)

**Ἀναξαγόρας**
AIGINA: (**1**) vi/v BC *RE* (6); Overbeck 433-6; Page, *FGE* 511; *Alt-Ägina* II (2) pp. 33-4 (sculptor)
SICILY:
—GELA-PHINTIAS: (**2**) c. 321-300 BC Michel 368, 5 (f. Διοκλῆς)

**Ἀναξάνδρα**
KORINTHIA:
—SIKYON: (**1**) s. iii BC Clem. Al., *Str.* iv 124 (Overbeck 2104; Skalet 32) (d. Νεάλκης: painter)

**Ἀναξανδρίδας**
LAKONIA:
—SPARTA: (**1**) f. vii BC Hdt. viii 131. 2 (Poralla² 80) (-δης: s. Θεόπομπος, ?s. Χιλωνίς, f. Ἀρχίδαμος: king); (**2**) c. 575-520 BC *RE* (1) (Poralla² 81) (s. Λέων, f. Κλεομένης, Δωριεύς, Λεωνίδας, Κλεόμβροτος: king)

## Ἀνάξανδρος

AITOLIA:
—APEIRIKOI: (1) 178 BC Syll³ 636, 17 (s. Τελέσαρχος)

ARGOLIS:
—HERMIONE: (2) i BC-i AD? IG IV (1) 730 I, 5 (s. Πασι—); (3) ~ ib. 734, 8

EPIROS: (4) iii BC Cabanes, L'Épire p. 587 no. 73, 11 ([Ἀν]άξανδρος)
—AKRALESTOI: (5) iii/ii BC ib. p. 561 no. 35, 6; Robert, Hell. I pp. 95 ff. (locn.) (f. Ἀνδρόνικος)
—BOUTHROTOS (PRASAIBOI):
—Kammeoi: (6) a. 163 BC IBouthrot 90, 8 (s. Κέφαλος)
—CHAONES: (7) s. iii BC ib. 6, 15 (SEG XXXVIII 468) (s. Κέφαλος)
—DODONA: (8) iii BC Antoniou, Dodone Aa, 4
—ENCHESTOI: (9) c. 200 BC IG IX (1)² (1) 31, 133 (f. Ἀνδρόνικος)
—MOLOSSOI: (10) m. iv BC Cabanes, L'Épire p. 539 no. 3, 11
—PHARGANAIOI: (11) f. ii BC ib. p. 589 no. 75, 9 (SEG XXXVII 510) (s. Γέλων)

LAKONIA:
—SPARTA: (12) m. vii BC RE (1) (Poralla² 82) (s. Εὐρυκράτης, f. Εὐρυκρατίδας: king); (13) ?s. v BC Moretti, Olymp. 327 (Poralla² 83); (14) 352 BC D.S. xvi 39. 6 (Poralla² 84)

## Ἀναξίβιος

ARKADIA:
—MEGALOPOLIS: (1) ?358 BC CID II 6 A, 9; (2) 134 or 130 BC FD III (3) 120, 9, 15 (f. Ἀναξίδαμος)

LAKONIA:
—SPARTA: (3) c. 435-388 BC RE (-) (Poralla² 86)

S. ITALY (CALABRIA):
—BRENTESION-BRUNDISIUM: (4) i AD Athenaeum 45 (1967) pp. 155-7 (Lat. Anaxibius)

## Ἀναξιδαμίδας

ARGOLIS:
—TROIZEN*: (1) iv BC IG IV (1) 823, 68, 73

## Ἀναξίδαμος

ACHAIA: (1) 207 BC Plb. xi 18. 1

ARKADIA:
—MEGALOPOLIS: (2) m. iii BC IG IV (1)² 96, 34 (Perlman E.3); Perlman p. 63 f. (date) (s. Εὔστρατος); (3) 164-156 BC Plb. xxx 30. 1; xxxiii 3. 2; (4) 134 or 130 BC FD III (3) 120, 8, 15 (s. Ἀναξίβιος)

LAKONIA:
—SPARTA: (5) ?m. vii BC Paus. iii 7. 6; iv 15. 3 (Poralla² 87) (s. Ζευξίδαμος, f. Ἀρχίδαμος: king/dub.)

## Ἀναξίδωρος

ARGOLIS:
—EPIDAUROS: (1) s. v BC IG IV (1)² 148 + Peek, IAEpid 66 (Lazzarini 283) (f. Ἄναξις); (2) iv/iii BC IG IV (1)² 197 (Ἀναξ[ί]δ[ωρος]: f. Θιάρης)
—EPIDAUROS?: (3) s. iv BC SEG XI 375 (f. Ἀναξίων)

## Ἀναξικλέα

ILLYRIA:
—EPIDAMNOS-DYRRHACHION: (1) hell.-imp. IDyrrh 97 (d. Φαλίος)

## Ἀναξικράτης

ARGOLIS:
—ARGOS?: (1) ?iv-iii BC RE (8); Supplbd. 14; FGrH 307

ARKADIA: (2) 308 BC IG V (2) 550, 4

## Ἀναξιλαΐδας

PELOPONNESE: (1) c. 230-200 BC BCH 45 (1921) p. 11 II, 40 (Ἀναξ[ι]λαΐδας—Oulhen)

## Ἀναξίλαος

ACHAIA:
—DYME: (1) 215 BC PP 14996; cf. Brooklyn Mus. Ann. 10 (1968-9) p. 138 no. 26 (s. Ἀριστεύς)
ITHAKE: (2) 208 BC IMM 36, 2 (s. Κλεομήδης)

KORINTHIA:
—KORINTH: (3) 54-68 AD Corinth VIII (2) 54, 6; VIII (3) 212, 4; Amandry pp. 221-6; RPC I p. 256 nos. 1207-9 (coin) (Lat. Ti. Claudius Anaxilaus/Anaxilas); (4) s. ii AD Corinth VIII (1) 15, 7; VIII (3) 223, 7 (Τιβ. Ἀππαληνὸς Ἀ., Ἀνάξιλλος—15)

## Ἀναξίλας

AIGINA: (1) ?268 BC FD III (3) 200 (f. Λύανδρος, Ὀνυμακλῆς)

ARGOLIS:
—EPIDAUROS: (2) c. 365-335 BC IG IV (1)² 103, 139
—EPIDAUROS*: (3) c. 370 BC ib. 102, 51

ARKADIA:
—MANTINEIA-ANTIGONEIA: (4) ?272 BC FD III (1) 30, 1 (s. Πολλίας)

LAKONIA:
—SPARTA: (5) inc. Plu., Mor. 217 C ?= (6); (6) ?vii BC Hdt. viii 131 (Poralla² 88) (Ἀναξίλεως—Hdt.: s. Ἀρχίδαμος, f. Λατυχίδας: king) ?= (5); (7) c. 600 BC Plu., Sol. 10 (Poralla² 89)

S. ITALY (BRUTTIUM):
—RHEGION: (8) vi/v BC RE s.v. Anaxilaos (1); Moretti, Olymp. 208 (and Sicily Zankle-Messana: s. Κρητίνης, f. Κλεόφρων: tyrant)

SICILY:
—SELINOUS: (9) c. 500 BC SEG XXIX 403

## Ἀναξιμένης

SICILY:
—KAMARINA: (1) m. v BC Dubois, IGDS 118

## Ἀναξίπολις

AKARNANIA:
—ECHINOS?: (1) ii BC IG IX (1)² (2) 372

## Ἀνάξιππος

ARKADIA:
—KLEITOR: (1) c. 230-200 BC BCH 45 (1921) p. 12 II, 69 + SEG XXX 494 (f. Ἁγίας)

EPIROS:
—DODONA*: (2) iv-iii BC PAE 1956, p. 155 no. 12

LAKONIA:
—SPARTA: (3) iii BC SEG XL 348 B, 6 (Ἀνάξιππ[ος])

PELOPONNESE?: (4) s. iii BC ib. xxv 449, 44 (IPArk 26) (Ἀνάξιππ[ος])

ZAKYNTHOS: (5) c. 350-250 BC BMC Pelop. p. 97 no. 37 (coin) (Ἀνάξι(ππος), Ἀναξί(πολις)?)

## Ἄναξις

ARGOLIS:
—EPIDAUROS: (1) s. v BC IG IV (1)² 148 + Peek, IAEpid 66 (Lazzarini 283) (s. Ἀναξίδωρος)

## Ἀναξίς

KORINTHIA:
—KORINTH: (1) ?ii BC Corinth VIII (3) 299, 1 (Ἀναξικλῆ[ς]—ed., Ἄναξι χαῖρε—LGPN)

## Ἀναξίων

AITOLIA: (1) c. 240 BC Marcadé I 97, 2 (f. Σώνικος)

ARGOLIS:
—ARGOS: (2) c. 80 BC IG VII 416, 42, 52 (IOrop 523) (I f. Ἀναξίων II); (3) ~ IG VII 416, 42, 52 (IOrop 523) (II s. Ἀναξίων I); (4) imp. IG IV (1) 581 (f. Μ. Ἀντ. Ἀριστοκράτης)
—EPIDAUROS?: (5) s. iv BC SEG XI 375 (s. Ἀναξίδωρος)
—EPIDAUROS*: (6) c. 370 BC IG IV (1)² 102, 202

## Ἀναξώ

SICILY:
—SYRACUSE: (1) ?ii-i BC NScav 1920, p. 325 (Ἀ[ν]αξώ: d. Φιλιστίων)

## Ἀνάπαυμα

S. ITALY (CALABRIA):
—BRENTESION-BRUNDISIUM: (1) imp. CIL IX 72 (Lat. Ana(u)pauma)

## Ἀναπίας

SICILY:
—KATANE: (1) arch.? RE (-) (dub.)

## Ἀνάριστος

S. ITALY (CAMPANIA):
—POMPEII: (1) i BC-i AD CIL IV 4923 (Lat. Anaristus)

## Ἀναστασία

KORINTHIA:
—KORINTH: (1) byz. Corinth VIII (3) 561, 5; cf. TMByz 9 (1985) p. 363 no. 38 (d. Ἀνδρέας, Εὐγένεια); (2) ~ Corinth VIII (3) 671, 6; cf. TMByz 9 (1985) p. 360 no. 7

SICILY: (3) iii-v AD IG XIV 599 (Wessel 641); cf. Riv. Arch. Crist. 18 (1941) p. 225 n. 1
—SYRACUSE: (4) iii-v AD IG XIV 73 (Strazzulla 14) (Ἀνα(σ)τασέα)

## Ἀναστάσιος

ILLYRIA:
—EPIDAMNOS-DYRRHACHION: (1) c. 431-518 AD RE (1); PLRE II (4) (Φλ. Ἀ. ὁ ἐπικαλ. Δίκορος: emp.)

KORINTHIA:
—KORINTH: (2) s. iv AD Corinth VIII (3) 530, 5, 7; cf. TMByz 9 (1985) p. 362 no. 34

S. ITALY (CAMPANIA):
—NEAPOLIS?: (3) byz.? IG XIV 2419. 11 (Ἀννα-)

S. ITALY (LUCANIA):
—TEGIANUM: (4) ?iii AD CIL X 375 (Lat. Aurelius Anastasius)

SICILY:
—SYRACUSE: (5) iii-v AD ib. 7169 (Strazzulla 421; Ferrua, NG 358) (Lat. [An]astasius: f. An—); (6) ?vi AD Agnello 84 (Lat. Anastasius)

## Ἀνάστασις

S. ITALY (APULIA):
—VENUSIA: (1) v AD JIWE I 52 (CIJ I 576) (-σης: Jew)

SICILY:
—SYRACUSE: (2) iii-v AD Riv. Arch. Crist. 32 (1956) p. 24 i; (3) ~ Rend. Pont. 22 (1946-7) p. 234 no. 25

## Ἀναστασώ

SICILY: (1) byz. BZ 19 (1910) p. 470 (ring)

## Ἀνατολή

ACHAIA:
—PHARAI: (1) i BC/i AD ILGR 43, 2 (Lat. Vibia Anatole)

S. ITALY (APULIA):
—CANUSIUM*: (2) i AD Epig. Rom. di Canosa 81 (Lat. Atania Anatole: freed.)

S. ITALY (CALABRIA):
—BRENTESION-BRUNDISIUM: (3) imp. CIL IX 71 (Lat. Anatole)

S. ITALY (CAMPANIA):
—POMPEII: (4) i BC-i AD ib. IV 8809 (Lat. Anatolii—CIL, Anatile—Solin)

## Ἀνατόλης

SICILY:
—NEAITON (NR.): (1) vi AD NScav 1891, p. 355 + Ferrua, NG 496 (Wessel 312) (-τώ-)

**Ἀνατολικός**
KORINTHIA:
—KORINTH: (**1**) s. iv AD *Corinth* VIII (3) 522, 2;
cf. *TMByz* 9 (1985) p. 362 no. 35 (n. pr.?: ?f.
*Εὐσέβιος*)

**Ἀνατόλιος**
KORINTHIA:
—KORINTH: (**1**) s. v AD Cyr. S., *V. Cyriac* 4
S. ITALY (CALABRIA):
—TARAS-TARENTUM: (**2**) ?vii-viii AD *CIL* IX
6400 (*JIWE* I 120) (Lat. Anatoli(us): s. Ius-
tus: Jew)
S. ITALY (CAMPANIA):
—DIKAIARCHIA-PUTEOLI: (**3**) imp. *CIL* x 2069
(Lat. Anatolius: f. C. Antistius Respectus)

**Ἀναυχίδας**
ELIS: (**1**) hell.? Moretti, *Olymp.* 948-949 (s. *Φίλυς*); (**2**) ii BC *SEG* XLI 387

**Ἀνδήνα**
ILLYRIA:
—EPIDAMNOS-DYRRHACHION: (**1**) hell.-imp.
*IDyrrh* 98

**Ἄνδοκος**
LAKONIA:
—SPARTA: (**1**) 362-361 BC *CID* II I II, 10; 4 I,
33 (Poralla² 90)

**Ἀνδραγαθιανός**
S. ITALY (CAMPANIA):
—DIKAIARCHIA-PUTEOLI: (**1**) ?ii AD *Puteoli* 12-
13 (1988-9) p. 213 no. 2 (Lat. Andragathi-
anus: s. *Ζώσιμος*)

**Ἀνδράγαθος**
AKARNANIA:
—PALAIROS: (**1**) ii/i BC *IG* IX (1)² (2) 560
([Ἀν]δράγα[θε] (voc.), [Ἀν]δραγά[θα]?)
ARGOLIS:
—ARGOS: (**2**) iii-ii BC ib. IV (1) 654 (f. Ἄτταλος)
ILLYRIA:
—APOLLONIA: (**3**) imp. *IApoll* 274
PELOPONNESE: (**4**) s. iii BC *SEG* XIII 278, 16

**Ἀνδρέα**
S. ITALY (LUCANIA):
—HYELE-VELIA: (**1**) imp. *CIL* x 466 (Lat. Pub-
lilia Andrea: m. L. Valerius Susceptus)

**Ἀνδρέας**
ACHAIA: (**1**) 146 BC *IG* IV (1)² 28, 92 (s. *Νικο-
κράτης*: synoikos)
AITOLIA: (**2**) 244 or 240 BC *SGDI* 2511, 2
(Flacelière p. 402 no. 29)
ARGOLIS:
—ARGOS: (**3**) f. v BC *Argive Heraeum* 2 p. 186
no. 11 and pl. 69 (sherd) (Ἀνδρέ[ας]); (**4**) f. ii
BC *RE* (12); *IvOl* 318, 5; *IG* XIV 1232; Paus.
vi 16. 7; cf. Moretti, *Olymp.* 621 (and Caria
Kaunos: sculptor); (**5**) imp. *IvOl* 657, 2
—PHLEIOUS: (**6**) 327-324 BC *CID* II 32, 35; 97,
27; 102 II B, [36]; 120 A, 50 (s. *Μιλτιάδας*)
ARKADIA:
—METHYDRION: (**7**) 191-146 BC *Coll. McClean*
6503; Unp. (Athens, NM) (coins)
—TEGEA: (**8**) 263 BC *IG* XI (2) 113, 22
(Stephanis 175)
DALMATIA:
—ISSA: (**9**) f. ii BC Brunšmid p. 23 no. 10, 7 (s.
*Νίκων*)
ELIS:
—OLYMPIA*: (**10**) byz. *IvOl* 657
ILLYRIA:
—EPIDAMNOS-DYRRHACHION: (**11**) ?vi AD *AEp*
1984, no. 816 (Lat. Andreas)
KORINTHIA:
—KORINTH: (**12**) arch. Plu., *Mor.* 1137 F; (**13**)
byz. *Hesp.* 41 (1972) p. 41 no. 30 ([Ἀν]δρέας);
(**14**) ~ *Corinth* VIII (1) 154; cf. *TMByz* 9

(1985) p. 360 no. 15 (s. *Πυρόμαλλος*); (**15**)
~ *Corinth* VIII (1) 164; (**16**) ~ ib. 206; cf.
*TMByz* 9 (1985) p. 361 no. 21; (**17**) ~ *Corinth* VIII (3) 547; cf. *TMByz* 9 (1985) p. 363
no. 44 (Ἀνδρέ[ας]); (**18**) ~ *Corinth* VIII (3) 551,
2; cf. *TMByz* 9 (1985) p. 362 no. 36; (**19**) ~
*Corinth* VIII (3) 552, 4; cf. *TMByz* 9 (1985)
p. 362 no. 37; (**20**) ~ *Corinth* VIII (3) 558 a, 2;
558 b, 2; cf. *TMByz* 9 (1985) p. 363 no. 39;
(**21**) ~ *Corinth* VIII (3) 561, 2; cf. *TMByz* 9
(1985) p. 363 no. 38 (f. *Ἀναστασία*); (**22**) ?581
AD *SEG* XXIX 319, 6
—KORINTH*: (**23**) byz. *AP* vii 672 (*TMByz* 9
(1985) p. 283 no. 20); *PLRE* II (8)
—SIKYON: (**24**) vii BC Hdt. vi 26. 1; *FGrH* 105
F 2 (Skalet 33) (f. *Ὀρθαγόρας, Μύρων*)
LAKONIA:
—SPARTA: (**25**) 64 BC Moretti, *Olymp.* 702
(Bradford (-))
MESSENIA:
—MESSENE: (**26**) f. iii BC *PAE* 1991, p. 100 no.
8; cf. 1989, p. 96; (**27**) byz. *DIEEE* 6 (1901)
p. 390 no. 13 (Ἀντρέας); (**28**) vi/vii AD Mosch.,
*Prat. Spir.* 116-17, 176?
S. ITALY (APULIA):
—BARION: (**29**) vi AD *Puglia Paleocrist. Altomed.*
4 p. 145 (mosaic) (Lat. Andrea)
—VENUSIA: (**30**) imp. *CIL* IX 569 (Lat. L.
Scutarius Andrea)
SICILY:
—GELA-PHINTIAS: (**31**) s. vi BC Arena, *Iscr. Sic.*
II 6 (vase)
—IAITON*: (**32**) hell. *AA* 1994, p. 241 no. 5 a-b
(bullet) (?s. *Φίλιος*)
—KAMARINA: (**33**) hell. *SEG* XXXIX 1001, 9 (f.
—ων)
—KATANE: (**34**) iii-v AD Ferrua, *NG* 427
([Ἀν]δρέου (gen.))
—PANORMOS: (**35**) ?ii BC *RE* (10); *FGrH* 571
—SYRACUSE: (**36**) ?ii BC *Milet* I (3) 79, 8 (f. *Ἀρί-
βαζος*)
—SYRACUSE?:
——(Πλη.): (**37**) hell. Manganaro, *PdelP* forth-
coming no. 4 I, 5 (s. *Θέων*)
—ZANKLE-MESSANA: (**38**) iii-ii BC *NScav* 1942,
p. 82 (brick)

**Ἄνδρεια**
KERKYRA: (**1**) hell. *IG* IX (1) 894, 3

**Ἀνδρείας**
ILLYRIA:
—EPIDAMNOS-DYRRHACHION: (**1**) iv/iii BC
*IDyrrh* 25 (s. *Ἀριστώ*)

**Ἀνδρεύς**
AKARNANIA:
—OINIADAI: (**1**) v/iv BC Hp., *Epid.* v 4; *Abh-
MainzAk* 1982 (9) p. 35 (locn.) (or Thessaly?)

**Ἀνδρίας**
ACHAIA: (**1**) 146 BC *IG* IV (1)² 28, 66 (s. *Ἀρι-
στοπάμων*: synoikos)
ARKADIA:
—MEGALOPOLIS: (**2**) c. 315-280 BC *FD* III (1)
45, 2
—TEGEA:
——(Krariotai): (**3**) iii BC *IG* v (2) 40, 25 (s.
*Ἀριστογείτων*)
ELIS:
—THRAISTOS: (**4**) f. iv BC ib. IX (1)² (1) 138, 2
(Ἀ[ν]δρίας)
LAKONIA:
—SPARTA: (**5**) hell.? ib. v (1) 811; (**6**) iii BC ib.
1317, 5 (Bradford (2)); (**7**) s. i BC *IG* v (1)
208, 4; 212, 27-8 (Bradford (1); (3)) (s. *Ἀν-
δρίων*, f. *Πολυκλείδας, Φίλων*)
TRIPHYLIA:
—LEPREON: (**8**) c. 230-200 BC *BCH* 45 (1921)
p. 12 II, 81 (f. *Λιμναῖος*)

**Ἀνδρικός**
ACHAIA: (**1**) 146 BC *IG* IV (1)² 28, 84 (s. *Μέ-
νανδρος*: synoikos); (**2**) ~ ib. l. 91 (I f. *Ἀνδρικός*
II: synoikos); (**3**) ~ ib. l. 91 (II s. *Ἀνδρικός* I:
synoikos)
ARGOLIS:
—ARGOS: (**4**) ii-i BC ib. IV (1) 530, 6; cf. *BCH*
33 (1909) p. 183 n. 2

**Ἀνδρῖνος**
ARGOLIS:
—EPIDAUROS*: (**1**) c. 370-360 BC *BSA* 61
(1966) p. 272 no. 4 B II, 11
LAKONIA:
—SPARTA: (**2**) c. 125 AD *SEG* XI 575, 15 (Brad-
ford (-)) (*Τιβ. Κλ. Ἀνδρεῖνος*)

**Ἀνδριος**
ACHAIA:
—DYME: (**1**) s. iii BC *SEG* XIII 278, 18 (f. *Αἰ-
σχρίων*)
PELOPONNESE: (**2**) s. iii BC ib. l. 9 (Ἀ. *Βρε*.)

**Ἀνδρίσκος**
EPIROS:
—BOUTHROTOS (PRASAIBOI): (**1**) a. 163 BC
*IBouthrot* 25, 11; 31, 91 (*SEG* XXXVIII 483;
490)
——Sakaronoi: (**2**) a. 163 BC *IBouthrot* 114, 9;
120, 8 (s. *Κέφαλος*)
ILLYRIA:
—APOLLONIA: (**3**) c. 250-50 BC Maier 13 (coin)
(Ceka 83) (pryt.)
SICILY:
—TAUROMENION: (**4**) c. 226-178 BC *IG* XIV 421
an. 15; 421 an. 63 (*SGDI* 5219) (s. *Νυμφόδω-
ρος*, f. *Νυμφόδωρος*); (**5**) c. 173 BC *IG* XIV 421
an. 68 (*SGDI* 5219); (**6**) c. 160 BC *IG* XIV 421
an. 81 (*SGDI* 5219) (s. *Φιλιστίων*)
——(Σπαρ.): (**7**) f. i BC *Cron. Arch.* 3 (1964) p.
44 III, 1

**Ἀνδρίων**
ACHAIA:
—PELLENE: (**1**) m. iii BC Peek, *IAEpid* 42, 60,
64 (Perlman E.3); Perlman p. 63 f. (date) (f.
*Παυσανίας*)
AITOLIA:
—BOUKATION: (**2**) 190 BC *IG* IX (1)² (1) 97, 13;
(**3**) 164 BC ib. 99, 4
—DAIANES: (**4**) 161 BC ib. 100, 7
—PHISTYON: (**5**) ii BC ib. 110 a, 1
ILLYRIA:
—APOLLONIA: (**6**) c. 250-50 BC Maier 14; *BMC
Thessaly* p. 57 no. 19 (coin) (Ceka 36) (pryt.);
(**7**) ~ Maier 47 (coin) (Ceka 14) (money.); (**8**)
imp.? *IApoll* 190; cf. *SEG* XXXVII 533 (s. *Πο-
δᾶς*)
—EPIDAMNOS-DYRRHACHION: (**9**) hell.-imp.
*IDyrrh* 122 (f. *Ἀριστώ*); (**10**) ~ ib. 208 (f. *Εὔ-
νους*)
LAKONIA:
—SPARTA: (**11**) c. 50-25 BC *IG* v (1) 208, 4
(Bradford (2)) (f. *Ἀνδρίας*); (**12**) c. 125 AD *IG*
v (1) 1314, 9 (Bradford (1)) (s. *Νικόστρατος*);
(**13**) 197 or 198 AD *IG* v (1) 448, 11 (Bradford
(3)) (f. *Δαμάριστος*)

**Ἀνδρόβιος**
ARGOLIS:
—ARGOS: (**1**) c. 315 BC *SEG* XXXII 370, 7 (Ἀν-
δρόβ[ιος], Ἀνδρόβ[ολος]?)
—TROIZEN: (**2**) iv BC *IG* IV (1) 764, 2 (s. *Νίκις*)
ARKADIA:
—TEGEA: (**3**) c. 315-280 BC *FD* III (1) 37, 2 (f.
*Θεόδωρος*)
EPIROS:
—BOUTHROTOS (PRASAIBOI): (**4**) a. 163 BC
*IBouthrot* 21, 45 (*SEG* XXXVIII 478)
LAKONIA:
—SPARTA?: (**5**) 316 BC *IG* v (2) 549, 28 (Brad-
ford (-)) (s. *Εὐδαμίδας*)

**Ἀνδρόβολος**
AITOLIA:
—PHILOTAIEIS: (**1**) 161 BC *IG* IX (1)² (1) 100, 7
LAKONIA:
—SPARTA: (**2**) ii BC ib. v (1) 29, 16 (*Syll*³ 669; Bradford (-)) (f. Δαμαισίδας)

**Ἀνδρόβουλος**
AITOLIA: (**1**) f. iii BC *Das Heroon von Kalydon* p. 293, 13 (f. Κλέανδρος)

**Ἀνδροδάμας**
S. ITALY (BRUTTIUM):
—RHEGION: (**1**) vii BC Arist., *Pol.* 1274 b, 23

**Ἀνδροίτας**
ARKADIA:
—KLEITOR: (**1**) ?253 BC Nachtergael, *Les Galates* 10, 33; cf. Stephanis 2412 (f. Τίμαρχος)

**Ἀνδροκάδης**
EPIROS:
—ARKTANES EURYMENAI: (**1**) 370-368 BC Cabanes, *L'Épire* p. 534 no. 1, 10, 27
—BOUTHROTOS (PRASAIBOI): (**2**) a. 163 BC *IBouthrot* 15, 18 (*SEG* XXXVIII 472)

**Ἀνδρόκκας**
EPIROS:
—DODONA: (**1**) c. 330 BC Cabanes, *L'Épire* p. 580 no. 55, 4; (**2**) iii BC Antoniou, *Dodone* Aa, 5; (**3**) ~ ib. l. 27 ([Ἀν]δρ[ό]κκας); (**4**) ~ ib. Ab, 20 (Ἀνδρ[όκκ]ας); (**5**) ~ ib. Ba, 37

**Ἀνδροκλέα**
EPIROS:
—BOUTHROTOS (PRASAIBOI): (**1**) a. 163 BC *IBouthrot* 26, 16; 29, 11; 32, 19, 23 (*SEG* XXXVIII 484; 487; 491)

**Ἀνδροκλείδας**
EPIROS:
—MOLOSSOI: (**1**) iv BC Plu., *Pyrr.* 2. 1 (-δης)
LAKONIA: (**2**) hell.? ib. *Mor.* 217 C (Poralla² 91) (Μανδροκλείδας?—Wade-Gery)
—SPARTA: (**3**) iv BC *SEG* XI 639, 5 ([Ἀνδ]ροκλείδας: ?s. Ἐπικ—)

**Ἀνδροκλείων**
EPIROS:
—MOLOSSOI: (**1**) iv BC Plu., *Pyrr.* 2. 2

**Ἀνδροκλῆς**
AKARNANIA: (**1**) 197 BC *RE* Supplbd. 11 (11) (Lat. Androcles)
ARGOLIS:
—EPIDAUROS: (**2**) ?iii BC Peek, *IAEpid* 226, 4 (Ἀ[ν]δ[ρ]οκλῆς: f. Τιμοκλῆς)
—EPIDAUROS*: (**3**) c. 370-365 BC ib. 52 A, 9 (Ἀνδ[ροκλῆ[s])
—HERMIONE: (**4**) iii BC *IG* IV (1) 729 II, 15 (f. Φιλόξενος); (**5**) ?iii-ii BC ib. 735, 2 (s. Νῖκις); (**6**) ii-i BC ib. 732 I, 4 ([Ἀ]νδροκλῆς: f. Δημήτριος)
—METHANA-ARSINOE: (**7**) ?c. 600 BC *CEG* 1 137; cf. Guarducci, *Ep. Gr.* 1 p. 362 f. (s. Εὐμάρης)
ARKADIA:
—LOUSOI?: (**8**) iii BC *SEG* XI 1122, 10 (*IPArk* 22) (Ἀνδροκλ[ῆς])
—MANTINEIA-ANTIGONEIA: (**9**) iv/iii BC *IG* v (2) 279 ([Ἀν]δροκλῆς: f. Ἑρμίας); (**10**) ~ ib. (s. Εὐαίνετος); (**11**) ?253 BC *FD* III (1) 20, 1 (f. Ἐργοίτας)
—MEGALOPOLIS: (**12**) hell.? *IG* v (2) 448, 5 ([Ἀν]δροκλῆ[ς])
KERKYRA: (**13**) i BC-i AD ib. IX (1) 897
KORINTHIA:
—KORINTH: (**14**) c. 336-324 BC *CID* II 75 II, 49; 79 A I, 18; 97, 32; 99 A, [4]; 102 II B, 33; 120 A, 35 (s. Ἀνδρότιμος)

LAKONIA:
—SPARTA: (**15**) ii-iii AD X. Eph. v 1. 6 (fict.)
MESSENIA: (**16**) viii BC *RE* (1) (s. Φίντας: king) ?= (Ἀνδροκλος (*1*)); (**17**) vii BC ib. (2)
TRIPHYLIA: (**18**) s. iv BC *IG* II² 10461, 2 (f. Μαρσύας)

**Ἀνδροκλίς**
ARGOLIS:
—HERMIONE: (**1**) iii BC ib. IV (1) 728, 29

**Ἀνδροκλος**
MESSENIA: (**1**) 768 BC Moretti, *Olymp.* 3; *RE* (3) ?= (Ἀνδροκλῆς (*16*))

**Ἀνδροκος**
EPIROS:
—TALAONOI/TALAIANES: (**1**) iii-ii BC *SGDI* 1349, 9; cf. Cabanes, *L'Épire* p. 580 no. 53 (s. Νικόμαχος)

**Ἀνδρόκριτος**
AIGINA: (**1**) v/iv BC *IG* IV (1)² 236 (Lazzarini 748) (s. Ἄγιλλος)

**Ἀνδροκύδης**
ARGOLIS:
—ARGOS: (**1**) c. 370 BC *SEG* XI 379 b, 3 (sculptor)
—EPIDAUROS?: (**2**) m. v BC ib. XXIV 274 (Lazzarini 941) (Ἀνδροκύδ[η]s)

**Ἀνδρόλαος**
AITOLIA:
—RHADEOI: (**1**) f. ii BC *IG* IX (1)² (1) 96, 21 (s. Λυκίσκος)
AKARNANIA:
—ANAKTORION: (**2**) c. 325-315 BC *Hesp.* 57 (1988) p. 148 A, 23 (*SEG* XXXVI 331); cf. *Hesp.* 48 (1979) pp. 78 f. with pl. 22 c (s. Ἀνδρόμαχος)

**Ἀνδρόλοχος**
ELIS: (**1**) 217 BC Plb. v 94. 6

**Ἀνδρομάχα**
AITOLIA:
—KLAUSEION (MOD.): (**1**) byz. *PAE* 1958, p. 61; cf. *BCH* 83 (1959) p. 664
EPIROS: (**2**) s. iv BC *IG* IV (1)² 122, 60

**Ἀνδρόμαχος**
AITOLIA: (**1**) ?254 BC *Syll*³ 436, 3; Nachtergael, *Les Galates* 9, 5
—THERMOS*: (**2**) s. iii BC *IG* IX (1)² (1) 60 V, 4
AKARNANIA:
—ALYZIA: (**3**) iv BC Peek, *NIEpid* 73
—ANAKTORION: (**4**) c. 325-315 BC *Hesp.* 57 (1988) p. 148 A, 21-23 (*SEG* XXXVI 331); cf. *Hesp.* 48 (1979) p. 78-9 + pl. 22 c (f. Ἀλεξίων, Δαμότιμος, Ἀνδρόλαος)
ARKADIA:
—TEGEA: (**5**) c. 225 BC Peek, *IAEpid* 331, 22 (Perlman E.5) ([Ἀ]νδρόμαχος: s. Ἰαροκλῆς)
ELIS: (**6**) 364 BC X., *HG* vii 4. 19; (**7**) ?320 BC *IG* v (2) 549, 18 (s. Λυσιάναξ)
EPIROS:
—AMBRAKIA: (**8**) 60 BC Moretti, *Olymp.* 704; cf. Bradford (-) (or Lakonia Sparta)
—THESPROTOI: (**9**) ?s. ii BC Cabanes, *L'Épire* p. 551 no. 26 ([Ἀν]δρόμαχος)
—TOSKESI (MOD.): (**10**) iv BC *AD* 23 (1968) Chron. p. 292 (f. Πουλάδας)
ILLYRIA:
—APOLLONIA: (**11**) i BC Maier 141; 144 (coin) (money.)
KORINTHIA:
—KORINTH: (**12**) 360 BC *CID* II 4 II, 61
SICILY:
—TAUROMENION: (**13**) iv BC *RE* (3) (f. Τίμαιος)

—(Δεξ.): (**14**) ?ii/i BC *IG* XIV 421 D an. 3 (*SGDI* 5219); *IGSI* 4 III (IV), 101 D an. 6 (s. Ἀπολλωνίδας)

**Ἀνδρομέδα**
KORINTHIA:
—KORINTH: (**1**) c. 615-550 BC Amyx 4. 3 (vase) (Lorber 24) (her.)

**Ἀνδρομέδης**
LAKONIA:
—SPARTA: (**1**) 420 BC Th. v 42. 1 (Poralla² 92); (**2**) c. 400-375 BC *IG* v (1) 1232, 8 (Poralla² 93)

**Ἀνδρομένης**
ACHAIA: (**1**) iii BC Robert, *EEP* 114, 12
—PELLENE: (**2**) m. iii BC *IG* v (2) 368, 112 (f. Μνάσων)
AITOLIA: (**3**) 290-280 BC *FD* III (1) 149, 1 (s. Κλεώνυμος)
—KALYDON: (**4**) m. ii BC *IG* IX (1)² (1) 137, 2, 41 (f. Ἀγεμάχα)
—PROSCH(E)ION: (**5**) 143 BC ib. l. 42 (s. Ἀγεμάχα (Kalydon))
ARGOLIS:
—EPIDAUROS:
——Selegeis: (**6**) m. iii BC Peek, *IAEpid* 42, 9, 15 (Perlman E.3); Perlman p. 63 f. (date)
EPIROS:
—KASSOPE: (**7**) ii BC *AE* 1914, p. 238 no. 16 (f. Φιλωτέρα); (**8**) f. ii BC Cabanes, *L'Épire* p. 564 no. 41, 2
KORINTHIA:
—KORINTH: (**9**) 304 BC Moretti, *Olymp.* 493
LAKONIA:
—SPARTA: (**10**) s. i BC *IG* v (1) 127, [4]; 211, 34 (Bradford (-)) (f. Κραταιμένης)
MESSENIA:
—MESSENE:
——(Aristomachidai): (**11**) 11 AD *PAE* 1992, p. 71 A, 11 (Α(ν)δρομένης: f. Νίκαρχος)

**Ἀνδρομήδης**
AIGINA: (**1**) iii BC *SEG* XXVI 919, 25 (s. Δαμαγόρας)
KEPHALLENIA:
—SAME: (**2**) 208 BC *IMM* 35, 2 (Ἀν[δρ]ομήδης: f. Φιλίσκος)

**Ἀνδρόνικος**
ACHAIA: (**1**) 146 BC *IG* IV (1)² 28, 145 (f. Δαμάτριος: synoikos)
AITOLIA: (**2**) 167 BC Liv. xlv 31. 15 (Lat. Andronicus: I f. Ἀνδρόνικος II); (**3**) ~ ib. (Lat. Andronicus: II s. Ἀνδρόνικος I)
—AGRINION: (**4**) 143 BC *IG* IX (1)² (1) 34, [7]; 137, 26 (f. Σάτυρος)
—KALLION/KALLIPOLIS: (**5**) 157 BC *FD* III (3) 9, 26
—KONOPE-ARSINOE: (**6**) c. 143 BC *IG* IX (1)² (1) 34, [8]; 137, 27 (f. Μενέλαος)
—PHILOTAIEIS: (**7**) m. ii BC ib. 107, 3
—PHISTYON: (**8**) f. ii BC ib. 98, 7 (Ἀνδ[ρ]όνικ[ος])
—PHISTYON?: (**9**) i BC ib. 110 b, 13 (s. Νικίας)
—PROSCH(E)ION: (**10**) m. ii BC ib. 137, 8 (s. Ἀγεμάχα (Kalydon))
—THERMOS: (**11**) 214 BC ib. 177, 18 (s. Βίττος)
—THESTIEIS: (**12**) 213 BC ib. 96, 14
—TRICHONION: (**13**) hell. ib. 127
AKARNANIA:
—OINIADAI: (**14**) iii/ii BC ib. IX (1)² (2) 419. 1; 419. 3
—STRATOS: (**15**) hell.? ib. 414 b (s. Τέλων)
—THYRREION: (**16**) iii BC ib. 596, 6
ARGOLIS:
—ARGOS: (**17**) c. 100-90 BC *SEG* XXXIII 290 A, 7; *BSA* 70 (1975) pp. 129-31 (date); cf. Stephanis 181 (I f. Ἀνδρόνικος II); (**18**) ~ *SEG* XXXIII 290 A, 7; *BSA* 70 (1975) pp. 129-31 (date) (Stephanis 181) (II s. Ἀνδρόνικος I)
—EPIDAUROS*: (**19**) c. 370-365 BC Peek, *IAEpid* 52 B, 55 ([Ἀν]δρ[ό]νικος)
ARKADIA:
—ORCHOMENOS: (**20**) iii BC *BCH* 39 (1915) p. 116

—PHENEOS: (21) i-ii AD *IG* II² 10478 (f. Κλέων)
ELIS: (22) s. ii BC ib. IX (1)² (3) 721 C, 2 (f. Κλεογένης)
EPIROS:
—AKRALESTOI: (23) iii/ii BC Cabanes, *L'Épire* p. 561 no. 35, 6; Robert, *Hell.* 1 pp. 95 ff. (locn.) (s. Ἀνάξανδρος)
—AMBRAKIA: (24) ii-i BC *CIG* 1797 (s. Γοργίας); (25) ~ ib. 1799 (f. Γοργίας) ?= (26); (26) ~ ib. (f. Ἀριστίων) ?= (25)
—ARGOS (AMPHILOCH.): (27) hell.? *IG* IX (1) 532 (s. Τέλων)
—BOUTHROTOS (PRASAIBOI): (28) a. 163 BC *IBouthrot* 14, 15 (*SEG* XXXVIII 471) (s. Κλεότιμος); (29) ~ *IBouthrot* 14, 22; 18, 3; 21, 41; 31, 25 (*SEG* XXXVIII 471; 475; 478; 490); cf. Cabanes, *L'Épire* p. 406 (s. Ταυρίσκος, ?f. Μεγανίκα); (30) ~ *IBouthrot* 14, 30; 21, 22 (*SEG* XXXVIII 471; 478) (s. Φίλιππος, f. Φίλιππος); (31) ~ *IBouthrot* 15, 19 (*SEG* XXXVIII 472); (32) ~ *IBouthrot* 21, 39 (*SEG* XXXVIII 478); (33) ~ *IBouthrot* 27, 9 (*SEG* XXXVIII 485); (34) ~ *IBouthrot* 29, 56 (*SEG* XXXVIII 487); (35) ~ *IBouthrot* 33, 3 (*SEG* XXXVIII 492); (36) ~ *IBouthrot* 43, 29 (*SEG* XXXVIII 502) (s. Λέων); (37) ~ *IBouthrot* 48, 10; (38) ~ ib. 52, 7 (*SEG* XXXVIII 517) (f. Πατροκλῆς); (39) ~ *IBouthrot* 55, 8 (*SEG* XXXVIII 506); (40) ~ *IBouthrot* 64 (*SEG* XXXVIII 515) (Ἀνδρόνι[κος]); (41) ~ *IBouthrot* 128, 11 (f. Νικόλαος)
——Cherrioi: (42) a. 163 BC ib. 59, 1 (*SEG* XXXVIII 510) (f. Νικάνωρ); (43) ~ *IBouthrot* 90, 5 (f. Λυσίμαχος); (44) ~ ib. 111, 12; 112, 13 (s. Ταυρίσκος)
——Optasinoi: (45) a. 163 BC ib. 141, 7 (s. Ταυρίσκος)
——Polleioi: (46) ii-i BC ib. 52, 1; 53, 1; 55, 2 (*SEG* XXXVIII 504; 506; 517) ?= (47); (47) a. 163 BC *IBouthrot* 69, 17; 70, 12; 71, 10 (*BCH* 118 (1994) pp. 129 f. B 1-3); *IBouthrot* 102, 4 (s. Ἄνδρων) ?= (46)
—CHAONES:
——Myonoi: (48) iii/ii BC ib. 7 (*SEG* XXXVIII 470) ([Ἀ]νδρόν[ικος]: s. Φίλιππος)
—DODONA: (49) iii BC Antoniou, *Dodone* Aa, 17
—ENCHESTOI: (50) iii-ii BC *SGDI* 1349, 2; cf. Cabanes, *L'Épire* p. 580 no. 53 with p. 365 ?= (51); (51) c. 200 BC *IG* IX (1)² (1) 31, 133 (s. Ἀνάξανδρος) ?= (50)
ILLYRIA:
—APOLLONIA: (52) ii BC *IApoll* 12 (f. Ἀριστόμαχος); (53) ii-i BC ib. 150 (f. Στρατονίκη); (54) imp. ib. 195 (-νει-: s. Ἀλεξίων)
—EPIDAMNOS-DYRRHACHION: (55) c. 250-50 BC Münsterberg Nachtr. p. 14 (Ceka 64); *IApoll Ref. Bibl.* n. 17 (coin) (money.); (56) hell.-imp. *IDyrrh* 252 (f. Ἱέρων)
—LISSOS?: (57) ?iii AD *Albania* 5 (1935) p. 95 no. 4
ILLYRIA?:
—APOLLONIA: (58) f. ii BC *Thess. Mnem.* 130 (s. Χαιρήμων)
KEPHALLENIA:
—PRONNOI: (59) hell.-imp. Unp. (*IG* arch.) (Ἀνδρονίκη, Ἀνδρόνικε (voc.)—apogr.)
LAKONIA:
—SPARTA: (60) s. i BC *IG* V (1) 93, 19 (Bradford (10)) (f. Πασιτέλης); (61) ~ *IG* V (1) 124, 2, 6 (Bradford (1)) (s. Ἀριστοκλῆς); (62) ~ *IG* V (1) 124, 8 (Bradford (1)) ([Ἀ]νδρόνικος: s. Ἀρίστων); (63) ~ *IG* V (1) 133, 6 (Bradford (9)) (f. Κιθαιρών); (64) i BC/i AD *IG* V (1) 48, 1 (Bradford (8)) (f. Καβωνίδας); (65) c. 1-10 AD *IG* V (1) 209, 25; *SEG* XXXV 331 (date) (Bradford (3)) (s. Νικοκλῆς); (66) c. 105-110 AD *SEG* XI 569, 7 (Bradford (4)) (s. Πολύγνωτος); (67) c. 140-145 AD *IG* V (1) 63, 18 (Bradford (5)) (-νει-: s. Ξενοκράτης); (68) ~ *SEG* XI 550, 6 (Bradford (7)) ([Ἀ]νδρόνεικος: f. Φῆλιξ); (69) c. 150-160 AD *SEG* XI 552, 3 (Bradford (6)) ([Ἀ]νδρόν[ικος]); (70) c. 180-210 AD *IG* V (1)

306 (*Artemis Orthia* p. 328 no. 59); *BSA* 79 (1984) p. 283 (date) (Bradford (11)) (Ἀνδρόνι[κος]: f. —εος)
MESSENIA:
—MESSENE: (71) iv/iii BC *IG* V (1) 1435, 14
PELOPONNESE: (72) 112 BC *FD* III (2) 70 A, 35
PELOPONNESE?: (73) s. iii BC *IG* V (1) 1426, 15 (f. Φυσαλίων)
S. ITALY (APULIA):
—VENUSIA: (74) v AD *CIL* IX 6219 (*JIWE* 1 85) (Lat. Andronicus: s. Bonus: Jew)
S. ITALY (CALABRIA):
—TARAS-TARENTUM: (75) ?205-203 BC *FD* III (4) 427 III, 1 (s. Φίλιππος, f. Φιλιππίς, Φίλιππος, [—]ρίας)
S. ITALY (CAMPANIA):
—DIKAIARCHIA-PUTEOLI: (76) 51 BC Cic., *ad Att.* v 15. 3 (freed.?); (77) ?ii AD *IG* XIV 835 (-νει-: s. Ἀγαθοκλῆς)
—HERCULANEUM*: (78) i BC-i AD *CIL* X 1403 l II, 15; cf. *Cron. Erc.* 7 (1977) p. 116 c, 15 (Lat. C. Caesetius Andronicu(s): freed.)
—NEAPOLIS: (79) f. iii AD *ILS* 6453 (*Napoli Antica* p. 389 no. 115. 3); cf. Leiwo p. 157 no. 127 (Lat. C. Iu[liu]s Andronicus)
S. ITALY (LUCANIA):
—POSEIDONIA-PAESTUM: (80) imp. Mello–Voza 80 (Lat. M. Suitius [A]ndronic[us])
SICILY:
—LIPARA: (81) imp. Libertini, *Isole Eolie* p. 222 no. 28 ([Ἀν]δρόνι[κος])

## Ἀνδροπείθης
ARGOLIS:
—EPIDAUROS: (1) f. iii BC Peek, *IAEpid* 87 ([Ἀ]νδροπείθης)
ARKADIA:
—MEGALOPOLIS: (2) ?i BC *IG* V (2) 469. 11 (tile) ([Ἀν]δροπείθης)

## Ἀνδροσθένης
AIGINA: (1) iv BC *RE* (10) (s. Ὀνασίκριτος)
ARGOLIS:
—ARGOS: (2) s. iv BC Peek, *NIEpid* 16, 30 (Perlman E.6) (f. Φάλακρος)
ARKADIA:
—MAINALIOI: (3) ?420-416 BC *RE* (1); Moretti, *Olymp.* 336; 343 (s. Λοχαῖος)
—TEGEA: (4) ii BC *IG* V (2) 176 (*GVI* 2080)
——(Krariotai): (5) s. iv BC *IG* V (2) 41, 44 (Ἀνδροσ[θένης]: f. Ἄνδρων)
EPIROS:
—BOUTHROTOS (PRASAIBOI): (6) a. 163 BC *IBouthrot* 29, 13; 40, 8 (*SEG* XXXVIII 487; 499); *IBouthrot* 136, 7; (7) ~ ib. 47, 6 ([Ἀνδ]ρόνικος: ?s. Σωσίπατρος); (8) ~ ib. 128, 8 (s. Λέων); (9) ~ ib. 136, 8
KORINTHIA:
—KORINTH: (10) c. 315-280 BC *FD* III (1) 178, 2; 179, 2 (f. —ένης, Ἑρμοκράτης)
LEUKAS: (11) ii BC *AM* 27 (1902) p. 370 no. 50
SICILY:
—SYRACUSE?: (12) 394 BC *IG* II² 18, 5 f.

## Ἀνδροσθενίδας
AITOLIA: (1) 224 or 221 BC *SGDI* 2524, 3; Nachtergael, *Les Galates* 64, 2

## Ἀνδρόσκυλος
SICILY:
—KAMARINA: (1) f. v BC Cordano, *Tessere Pubbliche* 33 (Ἀνδρόσκ[υλος]?: f. Πρατόλας)

## Ἀνδροτέλεια
LAKONIA:
—SPARTA: (1) ii-i BC *SEG* XI 677 c, 2 (Bradford (2)) (-λια: m. Ἐτυμοκλήδεια)

## Ἀνδροτέλης
AKARNANIA:
—THYRREION: (1) iii BC *IG* IX (1)² (2) 598 (s. Λέων); (2) s. iii BC ib. 282; (3) ii BC ib. 251, 8 (f. Ἀλκαίνετος)

ARGOLIS:
—HERMIONE: (4) iv BC ib. IV (1) 742, 5
—HERMIONE*: (5) iv BC ib. l. 16
KEPHALLENIA:
—SAME: (6) f. iii BC *Op. Ath.* 10 (1971) p. 66 no. 12 (*BCH* 83 (1959) p. 658)

## Ἀνδρότιμος
ACHAIA:
—KARYNEIA: (1) 134 or 130 BC *FD* III (3) 119, 3, 6 (s. Δεξίων)
ARKADIA:
—STYMPHALOS: (2) iii BC *IG* V (2) 356, 6
KORINTHIA:
—KORINTH: (3) c. 327-324 BC *CID* II 97, 32; 99 A, [4]; 102 II B, [33]; 120 A, 35 (f. Ἀνδροκλῆς)
—SIKYON: (4) c. 146-32 BC *NC* 1984, p. 15 Group 10 no. 5; p. 17 Group 11 no. 2 (coins)
PELOPONNESE?: (5) s. iii BC *IG* IV (1) 727 B, 9 (Perlman H.2) (Ἀν[δρό]τιμος: f. Ἀλεξιάδας)

## Ἄνδρυς
AITOLIA:
—PROSCH(E)ION: (1) 356-354 BC *IG* IV (1)² 95, 38 (Perlman E.2); Perlman p. 40 f. (date)

## Ἀνδρύτας
KORINTHIA:
—KORINTH: (1) c. 590-570 BC Amyx 33. 5 (vase) (Lorber 52) (her.?)

## Ἄνδρων
ACHAIA: (1) 146 BC *IG* IV (1)² 28, 134 (s. Δημήτριος: synoikos)
—PATRAI: (2) c. 146-32 BC *Coll. Hunter* 2 p. 126 no. 3 (coin) (s. Λυσίξενος)
—PELLENE: (3) ?255-253 BC Nachtergael, *Les Galates* 8, 16; 10, 15 (s. Πολύξενος)
AITOLIA:
—BOUKATION?: (4) c. 162 BC *IG* IX (1)² (1) 106, 11
—KALYDON: (5) 129 BC ib. 137, 97 (s. Νικόβουλος)
—THERMOS*: (6) s. iii BC ib. 60 III, 10; (7) ~ ib. 60 VII, 12
—THESTIEIS: (8) 213 BC ib. 96, 14
—TRICHONION: (9) s. iii BC ib. 117, 3
AITOLIA?:
—PROENNIOI: (10) ?153 BC ib. 109, 10
AKARNANIA: (11) iv/iii BC *Thess. Mnem.* 160 (*IG* IX (1)² (2) 584) (s. Καλλίας)
—ANAKTORION: (12) iii BC ib. 227
—ASTAKOS: (13) ii BC ib. 434, 14 (s. Φιλήμων) ?= (14); (14) ~ ib. 435, 19 (f. Νικόμαχος) ?= (13)
—OINIADAI: (15) m. ii BC ib. 209, 17 (f. Γάστρος)
—THYRREION: (16) iii-ii BC *SEG* XXVII 159, 3; cf. *PAE* 1977, pl. 244 a (s. Αἰδ—)
ARGOLIS:
—ARGOS: (17) ?iv BC *RE* (13)
—EPIDAUROS: (18) 151 AD *IG* IV (1)² 388, 5 + Peek, *IAEpid* 158 (name)
—EPIDAUROS*: (19) c. 370-365 BC ib. 52 B, 7 ([Ἀ]νδρων)
—HERMIONE: (20) ii BC *IG* IV (1)² 259 (f. Ἀριστώ)
ARKADIA:
—TEGEA:
——(Krariotai): (21) s. iv BC ib. V (2) 41, 44 (s. Ἀνδροσθένης)
ELIS: (22) ?i AD *EA* 1905, p. 259 no. 2, 10 (f. Ἀπολλώνιος)
EPIROS:
—ANTIGONEIA: (23) imp. *AE* 1914, p. 238 no. 15; Cabanes, *L'Épire* p. 234 n. 96 (locn.) (s. Λυσήν)
—BOUTHROTOS (PRASAIBOI): (24) a. 163 BC *IBouthrot* 31, 12 (*SEG* XXXVIII 490) (f. Ἀλυπώ)

——Polleioi: (25) a. 163 BC *IBouthrot* 69, 17; 70, 12; 71, 10 (*BCH* 118 (1994) pp. 129 f. B 1-3); *IBouthrot* 102, 4 (f. Ἀνδρόνικος)
—DELVINE (MOD.): (26) iii BC *AE* 1914, p. 237 no. 12 (s. Διονύσιος)
—DODONA: (27) iii BC Antoniou, *Dodone* Ba, 30; (28) ~ ib. l. 34 (Ἄνδρων)
—IKADOTOI: (29) m. iv BC Cabanes, *L'Épire* p. 576 no. 49, 9 (*SEG* XXVI 717) (s. Νικάνωρ)
ILLYRIA:
—APOLLONIA: (30) i BC Maier 131; 163 (coin) (pryt.)
ITHAKE: (31) hell. *Rev. Épig.* 1 (1913) p. 47 no. 14
KERKYRA: (32) ?i BC *IG* IX (1) 748 (tile)
KORINTHIA:
—SIKYON: (33) iv/iii BC *SEG* XII 218 (f. Νίκων)
LEUKAS: (34) f. i BC *IG* IX (1) 534, 7, 11 (*Iscr. Gr. Verona* p. 24) (s. Σωτίων)
MESSENIA:
—MESSENE: (35) 31 BC–14 AD *SEG* XXIII 207, 18 (Π. Οὐαλ. Ἀ.)
——(Aristomachidai): (36) 11 AD *PAE* 1992, p. 71 A, 10 (s. Ἀπολλώνιος)
——(Daiphontidai): (37) 11 AD ib. l. 21 (s. Ἀπολλώνιος)
S. ITALY: (38) iv-iii BC *Misc. Etrusco-Italica* 1 p. 194 no. A3 (bronze) (Ἀν[δρ]ων)
S. ITALY (BRUTTIUM):
—RHEGION: (39) ii-i BC *IG* XIV 613 (s. Θρασίας) ?= (43)
S. ITALY (LUCANIA):
—HYELE-VELIA: (40) ii/i BC *EAD* XXX 332 (s. Ἀρίστων)
SICILY: (41) iii BC Vandermersch p. 162 (amph.) (or S. Italy); (42) f. iii BC ib. p. 161 (amph.) (or S. Italy: Ἄνδρ(ων))
—APOLLONIA: (43) ii BC *IG* XIV 359; cf. *Kokalos* 17 (1971) p. 179 (s. Θρασίας) ?= (39)
—KAMARINA: (44) ?ii BC *SEG* XXXIX 996, 10 (Dubois, *IGDS* 126; Cordano, 'Camarina VII' 72) (f. Μύσκων)
—KATANE: (45) ?v BC *RE* (9) (Stephanis 187)
—KENTORIPA: (46) f. i BC Cic., *In Verr.* II ii 156; *In Verr.* II iii 108 (Lat. Andro)
—SYRACUSE: (47) 361 BC Polyaen. v 2. 4
—SYRACUSE?:
——(Δυν.): (48) hell. *Mem. Linc.* 8 (1938) p. 128 no. 35. 9 (bullet) (s. Ἡρακλείδας)
—TAUROMENION: (49) c. 229 BC *IG* XIV 421 an. 12 (*SGDI* 5219); (50) c. 225 BC *IG* XIV 421 an. 16 (*SGDI* 5219) (s. Λυκῖνος); (51) c. 221 BC *IG* XIV 421 an. 20 (*SGDI* 5219) (f. Διόδωρος)
SICILY?: (52) iii/ii BC Vandermersch p. 162 (amph.) (or S. Italy: Ἀνδ[ρ]ω(ν))

**Ἀνδρωνίδας**
ACHAIA: (1) ii BC *RE* (-)
ARGOLIS:
—HERMIONE: (2) iii-ii BC *IG* IV (1) 687 (f. Νίκις)
KORINTHIA:
—SIKYON: (3) c. 146-32 BC BM coin 1920 5-15-135 (coin)
LEUKAS: (4) c. 167-50 BC *BMC Thessaly* p. 183 nos. 132-3; p. 186 nos. 171-2 (coins)

**Ἀνδρωφέλης**
ARGOLIS:
—EPIDAUROS: (1) ii-iii AD Peek, *IAEpid* 201 ([Ἀνδ]ρωφέλης)

**Ἀνέγκλητος**
LAKONIA:
—SPARTA: (1) c. 150-160 AD *IG* V (1) 53, 13, 23; 54, [4] (Bradford (-)) (s. Εὐπόριστος, f. Στέφανος)
S. ITALY (CAMPANIA):
—DIKAIARCHIA-PUTEOLI: (2) imp. *NScav* 1888, p. 197 no. 1 (Lat. D. Rupilius Anencletus)

**Ἀνερείας**
EPIROS:
—DODONA: (1) iii BC Antoniou, *Dodone* Ab, 49
—TRIPOLITAI: (2) ?c. 370-344 BC Cabanes, *L'Épire* p. 536 no. 2, 12
—VOTONOSI (MOD.): (3) ?f. iii BC *SEG* XXIV 459 (-ρή-: s. Δέξανδρος)

**Ἀνεροίτας**
EPIROS:
—ARKTANES: (1) ?c. 370-344 BC Cabanes, *L'Épire* p. 536 no. 2, 11
—BOUTHROTOS (PRASAIBOI):
——Opatai: (2) a. 163 BC *IBouthrot* 69, 18; 70, 13; 71, 11 (*BCH* 118 (1994) pp. 129 f. B 1-3) (f. Θεύδοτος)
——Pullieoi: (3) a. 163 BC *IBouthrot* 115, 11 (f. Ἀλέξανδρος)
—MOLOSSOI: (4) c. 210 BC *IG* IX (1)² (1) 29, 23 (f. Λυκίσκος)
—TALAONOI/TALAIANES: (5) iii-ii BC *SGDI* 1349, 5; cf. Cabanes, *L'Épire* p. 580 no. 53 (f. Νίκανδρος)

**Ἀνήριστος**
LAKONIA:
—SPARTA: (1) vi/v BC Hdt. vii 134. 2 (Poralla² 94) (f. Σπερθίας); (2) c. 480-430 BC Hdt. vii 137. 2; Th. ii 67. 1 (Poralla² 95) (s. Σπερθίας)

**Ἀνθᾶς**
ARGOLIS:
—EPIDAUROS: (1) v/iv BC Peek, *IAEpid* 116

**Ἀνθέας**
ARGOLIS:
—EPIDAUROS: (1) iii/ii BC ib. 153. 9 (Ἀνθέ[ας])

**Ἄνθεια**
MESSENIA:
—MESSENE: (1) ?i AD *IG* V (1) 1482

**Ἀνθείας**
KERKYRA: (1) c. 500 BC *SEG* XXX 520 (Ἀνθε[ί]ας)

**Ἄνθεμα**
KORINTHIA:
—KORINTH: (1) c. 575-550 BC Amyx Gr 16 (vase) (Arena, *Iscr. Cor.* 84) (Ἀνθ(ε)μα)

**Ἀνθεμίδης**
EPIROS:
—BOUTHROTOS (PRASAIBOI): (1) a. 163 BC *IBouthrot* 46, 5

**Ἀνθέμιον**
S. ITALY (CAMPANIA):
—DIKAIARCHIA-PUTEOLI*: (1) imp. *CIL* X 3117 (Lat. Trolia Anthemium: m. Χρῆστος: freed.)

**Ἀνθεμίς**
SICILY:
—LIPARA: (1) inc. *BTCGI* 9 p. 93

**Ἀνθεμίων**
ARGOLIS:
—HERMIONE: (1) iii BC *IG* IV (1) 728, 5 (f. Πόλις)

**Ἀνθεμόκριτος**
ARGOLIS:
—ARGOS: (1) iii BC *RE* (1)
ARKADIA:
—MANTINEIA-ANTIGONEIA: (2) 64 or 62 BC *IG* V (2) 265, 48 (f. Σιμίας)
SICILY:
—GELA-PHINTIAS?: (3) f. v BC Dubois, *IGDS* 134 a, 2 (Arena, *Iscr. Sic.* II 80) ([Ἀνθ]εμόκριτος?, [Πολ]εμόκριτος?)

**Ἀνθεμώ**
AITOLIA:
—KALLION/KALLIPOLIS: (1) a. 166 BC *IG* IX (1)² (3) 676, 12, [14], 15 ff.

**Ἀνθέμων**
ELIS:
—OLYMPIA*: (1) s. v BC *Ol. Forsch.* 5 p. 150 no. 2 ([Ἀ]νθέμων)

**Ἀνθεσίλαος**
ARKADIA:
—STYMPHALOS: (1) iii BC *IG* V (2) 389, 16 (Perlman L.1)

**Ἀνθεσίλας**
KORINTHIA:
—KORINTH: (1) c. 510-500 BC Amyx Gr 17 (vase) (Arena, *Iscr. Cor.* 93); *LSAG*² p. 132 no. 28 (date)

**Ἀνθεστία**
ILLYRIA:
—APOLLONIA: (1) imp. *IApoll* 380
LAKONIA:
—SPARTA: (2) i BC-i AD *IG* V (1) 756 (Bradford (-))

**Ἀνθεστίων**
ARGOLIS:
—ARGOS: (1) 52 BC Moretti, *Olymp.* 708

**Ἀνθεσφόρος**
ARKADIA:
—TEGEA: (1) 78 AD *IG* V (2) 49, 3 (f. Ἄτταλος)
LAKONIA:
—SPARTA: (2) i BC/i AD ib. V (1) 207 (Ἀνσεσ[φόρος]?); (3) c. 140 AD ib. 65, 1; *SEG* XI 523, 3; [636]? (Bradford (-)) (f. Τελεσφόρος)
S. ITALY (CAMPANIA):
—DIKAIARCHIA-PUTEOLI: (4) imp. *CIL* X 2542 (Lat. Iulius Antisphorus)
S. ITALY (LUCANIA):
—COSILINUM: (5) i BC/i AD *IItal* III (1) 226 (Lat. [A]ntesphor: f. Pedo)

**Ἀνθεύς**
ARGOLIS:
—TROIZEN: (1) ?146 BC *IG* IV (1) 757 B, 40 (s. Ὀνυμακλῆς)
DALMATIA:
—ISSA:
——(Dymanes): (2) iv/iii BC Brunšmid p. 9, 59 ([Ἀ]νθεύς: s. Ποσειδαῖος)

**Ἄνθη**
SICILY:
—KENTORIPA: (1) i-ii AD *Epigraphica* 51 (1989) pp. 166-7 no. 30 (Lat. Alfia Anthe: m. Rustia Festa); (2) ii-iii AD *Sic. Gymn.* 2 (1949) p. 95 no. 1 (Στατία Ἀ.)

**Ἀνθηδώ**
ARGOLIS:
—TROIZEN: (1) ii-i BC *IG* IV (1) 818

**Ἀνθήδων**
KERKYRA: (1) imp. ib. IX (1) 898

**Ἄνθης**
KYNOURIA:
—ANTHANA: (1) her. St. Byz. s.v. Ἀνθάνα (Poralla² 96) (oikist/dub.)

**Ἀνθιάδας**
ARGOLIS:
—ARGOS: (1) f. iii BC Moretti, *ISE* 41, 26 (Perlman A.24)

**Ἀνθιάνιλλα**
S. ITALY (CALABRIA):
—BRENTESION-BRUNDISIUM: (1) ?s. ii AD *NScav* 1910, p. 146 (Lat. Clodia Anthianilla: d. L. Clodius Pollio, Seia Quintilia)

**Ἀνθιανός**
S. ITALY (CAMPANIA):
—DIKAIARCHIA-PUTEOLI: (1) ?iii AD ib. 1909, p. 215 (Lat. T. Caesius Anthianus)

**Ἄνθιμος**
S. ITALY (APULIA):
—CANUSIUM: (1) 223 AD Epig. Rom. di Canosa 35 IV, 14 (CIL IX 338) (Lat. M. Ulpius Anthimus)
S. ITALY (CAMPANIA):
—DIKAIARCHIA-PUTEOLI*: (2) imp. ib. x 2814 (Lat. C. Ostorius Anthimus: freed.)
SICILY:
—AKRAI: (3) iii-v AD BZ 19 (1910) p. 470 (ring)
—SYRACUSE: (4) iii-v AD CIL x 7143 (Lat. Annius Anthimus)

**Ἀνθίνα**
ILLYRIA:
—EPIDAMNOS-DYRRHACHION: (1) hell.-imp. IDyrrh 100 (d. Ἱέρων)

**Ἄνθινος**
ARGOLIS:
—ARGOS?: (1) v BC IG IV (1) 552, 8 (Ἄνθινο[ς])

**Ἀνθίππα**
AITOLIA:
—TRICHONION: (1) ?ii BC ib. IX (1)² (1) 119
ARGOLIS:
—ARGOS*: (2) 105 BC JÖAI 14 (1911) Beibl. p. 146 no. 4, 23 (slave/freed.?)

**Ἄνθιππος**
ARGOLIS:
—ARGOS: (1) c. 366-338 BC Petrakos, Oropos pp. 196-7 no. 47, 13, 29 (IOrop 520); (2) iii BC IG IV (1) 528, 4 (Ἄνθιπ[πος])
DALMATIA:
—ISSA:
——(Dymanes): (3) iv/iii BC Brunšmid p. 9, 57 (Ἀνφιππος?: f. Εὔξενος)
LAKONIA:
—SPARTA: (4) c. 110-115 AD SEG XI 540, 5 (Bradford (-)) (f. Φίλιππος)
S. ITALY (BRUTTIUM):
—LOKROI EPIZEPHYRIOI:
——(Προ.): (5) iv/iii BC De Franciscis 38, 3 (f. Ἀνθίων)

**Ἀνθίς**
AIGINA: (1) iii/ii BC IG II² 7950
AKARNANIA:
—THYRREION: (2) ?i BC ib. IX (1)² (2) 344
ARGOLIS:
—ARGOS*: (3) f. iii BC ib. IV (1) 529, 6 (slave/freed.?)
S. ITALY (APULIA):
—VENUSIA: (4) imp. CIL IX 486 (Lat. Babullia Anthis)
S. ITALY (BRUTTIUM):
—TERINA: (5) iv-iii BC SEG XVI 583 (Ἀ[νθ]ίς?, Ἀ[τθ]ίς—ed.)
S. ITALY (CALABRIA):
—BRENTESION-BRUNDISIUM: (6) imp. Epigraphica 25 (1963) p. 36 no. 7 (Lat. Antonia Anthis)
—BRENTESION-BRUNDISIUM*: (7) i AD NScav 1892, p. 352 o = Epigraphica 25 (1963) p. 33 no. 2 (Lat. Mercellia Anthis: freed.)
S. ITALY (CAMPANIA):
—DIKAIARCHIA-PUTEOLI: (8) imp. CIL x 2032 (Lat. Agria Anthis); (9) m. i AD Camodeca, L'Archivio Puteolano 1 p. 220 (Lat. Pom[pe]ia Anthis)
—HERCULANEUM: (10) 59 AD Ostraka 2 (1993) pp. 201-3 (Lat. Pompeia Anthis)
—POMPEII: (11) i BC-i AD CIL IV 8218 (Lat. Anthis)

SICILY:
—LIPARA: (12) iv/v AD Bernabò Brea, Isole Eolie p. 90 with fig. 44

**Ἀνθίσκος**
ILLYRIA:
—EPIDAMNOS-DYRRHACHION: (1) c. 200-172 BC RA 1948, p. 826 no. 1, 5 (IDyrrh 523) (s. Ἀπελλέας)

**Ἀνθίων**
S. ITALY (BRUTTIUM):
—LOKROI EPIZEPHYRIOI:
——(Προ.): (1) iv/iii BC De Franciscis 38, 3 (s. Ἄνθιππος)
S. ITALY (CAMPANIA):
—SALERNUM: (2) imp. IItal I (1) 175 (CIL x 590) (Lat. Anthio)

**Ἄνθος**
AKARNANIA:
—ANAKTORION (NR.): (1) ?iii-iv AD AAA 4 (1971) p. 193 (s. Ῥουφίων)
ARKADIA:
—TEGEA: (2) ii AD IG v (2) 55, 35 (s. Ἔρως)
ELIS: (3) f. ii AD IvOl 92, 25 (Ἀνθ[ο]ς: s. Ἀλέξανδρος); (4) ~ ib. 93, 4
ILLYRIA:
—APOLLONIA: (5) iv/iii BC IApoll 8
—EPIDAMNOS-DYRRHACHION: (6) 52 AD CIL x (1) 769 (Lat. C. Dyrrachinius Anthus)
KORINTHIA:
—KORINTH: (7) ii-iii AD SEG XI 140 b
LAKONIA:
—GYTHEION: (8) imp. IG v (1) 1206 (Γ. Ἰούλ. Ἀ.)
—SPARTA: (9) c. 175-200 AD ib. 129, 3 (Bradford (-)) (Π. Μέμμιος Ἀ.)
—TAINARON-KAINEPOLIS: (10) imp. IG v (1) 1251
S. ITALY (APULIA):
—CANUSIUM: (11) 223 AD Epig. Rom. di Canosa 35 II, 12 (CIL IX 338) (Lat. C. Silius Anthus)
—LARINUM: (12) ?i/ii AD ib. 763 (Lat. L. Plotius Anthus)
S. ITALY (BRUTTIUM):
—KROTON: (13) imp. ib. x 109 (Lat. C. Iulius Anthus)
—RHEGION*: (14) i BC/i AD SEG XXXIX 1062 B (slave?)
S. ITALY (CALABRIA):
—TARAS-TARENTUM: (15) imp. NScav 1894, p. 68 no. 44 (Lat. C. Memmius Anthu(s)); (16) ~ Misc. Gr. Rom. 3 p. 176 (Lat. Cn. Publicius Anthus)
S. ITALY (CAMPANIA):
—ATELLA: (17) imp. CIL x 3734 (Lat. M. Verrius Anthus)
—DIKAIARCHIA-PUTEOLI: (18) imp. ib. 2426 (Lat. Fl. Anthus Maximianus); (19) ~ ib. 2490 (Lat. Anthus: f. Γραφική); (20) ~ ib. 2529 (Lat. Anthus); (21) ~ NScav 1885, p. 145 (Eph. Ep. VIII 411) (Lat. Anthus); (22) 35 AD Camodeca, L'Archivio Puteolano 1 p. 99 no. 1 (Lat. A. Titinius Anthus); (23) 48 AD Puteoli 7-8 (1983-4) p. 76 no. 3 (Lat. L. Cocceius Anth[us])
—HERCULANEUM: (24) i BC-i AD CIL x 1403 d II, 3 (Lat. Sex. Pompeius Anthus)
—HERCULANEUM: (25) m. i AD Cron. Erc. 7 (1977) p. 117 C b, 9 (Lat. –ttius Anthus: freed.); (26) c. 50-75 AD CIL x 1403 a II, 2 (Lat. M. Nonius Anthus: freed.)
—POMPEII: (27) i BC-i AD ib. IV 3184 (Lat. Anthus); (28) ~ ib. 8021 (Lat. Anthus); (29) ~ ib. 8108 (Lat. Anthus); (30) ~ ib. 8691 (Lat. Antus); (31) c. 51-62 AD ib. 3340. 80, 6 (Castrèn 281. 2) (Lat. C. Numitorius Anthus); (32) ~ CIL IV 3340. 93, 1 (Lat. Anthus); (33) 55 AD ib. 3340. 12, 19; 91, 5 (Castrèn 191. 7) (Lat. N. Herennius Anthus)

—POMPEII*: (34) i BC-i AD CIL IV 8760 (Lat. Anthus: slave?)
—SURRENTUM: (35) imp. ib. x 692 (Lat. Anthus: imp. freed.)
S. ITALY (CAMPANIA)*: (36) imp. ib. 8042. 107 (tile) (Lat. M. Vetronius Anthus)
SICILY:
—LIPARA: (37) iv/v AD Bernabò Brea, Isole Eolie p. 90 with fig. 44 (Σκριβώνιος Ἄνθ[ος])
—THERMAI HIMERAIAI: (38) imp. Himera 2 p. 701 no. 300 (brick)
—THERMAI HIMERAIAI*: (39) imp. CIL x 7300 (ILat. Term. Imer. p. 261 no. A1) (Lat. M. Aemilius Anthus: freed.)

**Ἀνθοῦσα**
ARGOLIS:
—ARGOS: (1) v-vi AD Unp. (Oikonomou-Laniado)
ILLYRIA:
—LYCHNIDOS: (2) ?s. ii AD ZA 6 (1956) p. 167 no. 3 + BE 1958, no. 301 (d. Δρυπέτης)
KORINTHIA:
—KORINTH: (3) byz. Corinth VIII (3) 578; cf. TMByz 9 (1985) p. 363 no. 45
LAKONIA:
—SPARTA: (4) ?ii AD IG v (1) 248 (Bradford (-)) (d. Δαμαίνετος)
—TAINARON-KAINEPOLIS: (5) imp. IG v (1) 1251
S. ITALY (APULIA):
—TEANUM APULUM*: (6) imp. Teanum Apulum p. 83 no. 26 (Lat. [Thuri]dia Anthusa: freed.?)
S. ITALY (CALABRIA):
—RUDIAE*: (7) i BC/i AD NScav 1897, p. 405 no. 10 = Bernardini, Rudiae p. 88 (Susini, Fonti Salento p. 109 no. 45) (Lat. Attia Ant[hu]sa: freed.)
S. ITALY (CAMPANIA):
—POMPEII: (8) i BC-i AD CIL IV 141 (Lat. Anthusa); (9) ~ ib. 1230 (Lat. Anthusa)
—SALERNUM: (10) s. i AD IItal I (1) 151 (CIL x 555) (Lat. Anthusa: d. Φιλόχορος, Ἀρέσκουσα)

**Ἀνθρακίς**
S. ITALY (CAMPANIA):
—DIKAIARCHIA-PUTEOLI: (1) 43 AD Puteoli 12-13 (1988-9) p. 4 no. 1 (Lat. Titinia Antracis)

**Ἄνθραξ**
S. ITALY (CAMPANIA):
—DIKAIARCHIA-PUTEOLI: (1) imp. CIL x 3282 (Lat. Antrax)

**Ἀνθρωπία**
ILLYRIA:
—APOLLONIA: (1) imp. IApoll 25 ([Ἀ]νθρωπία: d. Ζώπυρος)

**Ἀνθρωπίδας**
ACHAIA:
—PATRAI?: (1) hell. AJA 54 (1950) p. 122

**Ἀνθρώπινος**
SICILY:
—APOLLONIA: (1) f. i BC Cic., In Verr. II v 90 (Lat. Anthropinus)
—SYRACUSE: (2) 317 BC Polyaen. v 3. 8

**Ἀνθρωπίσκος**
ILLYRIA:
—BYLLIONES: (1) c. 200-198 BC SEG XXXV 680, 3; cf. XXXVIII 541 (f. Πάτων); (2) f. ii BC ib. 534 (f. Μελάνθιος)
KERKYRA: (3) 208 BC IMM 44, 2
S. ITALY (CALABRIA):
—TARAS-TARENTUM: (4) iv/iii BC IG XIV 668 II, 10 (Landi, DISMG 194) (Ἀνθρωπίσ(κ)ος—apogr.)

**Ἀνθρωπίων**
ILLYRIA:
—EPIDAMNOS-DYRRHACHION: (1) hell.-imp. IDyrrh 101 (s. Εὔανδρος)

## Ἄνθρωπος

S. ITALY (APULIA):
—RUBI?: (1) ?iv BC Kretschmer p. 4 n. 4 (vase)
S. ITALY (CALABRIA):
—TARAS-TARENTUM: (2) c. 302-280 BC Evans, *Horsemen* p. 134 VI D.1; cf. *NC* 1930, p. 122 n. 22 (coin) (Ἄνθρωπ.—coins, Ἄνθρωπ(ος), Ἀνθρωπ(ίσκος)?)
S. ITALY?: (3) 456 BC Moretti, *Olymp.* 272

## Ἀνίας

KORINTHIA:
—KORINTH: (1) v AD *Corinth* VIII (3) 542, 4; cf. *TMByz* 9 (1985) p. 365 no. 59 (s. Παῦλος)
SICILY:
—AKRAI: (2) imp. *SEG* XLII 830

## Ἀνίκατος

EPIROS:
—AMBRAKIA: (1) iii/ii BC Unp. (Arta Mus., inscr.) (s. Θεύδοτος)
—CHARADROS: (2) a. 167 BC *SEG* XXXV 665 A, 14
—DODONA: (3) ii BC *SGDI* 1358, 7; cf. Cabanes, *L'Épire* p. 583 no. 62
—KASSOPE: (4) iii-ii BC *SEG* XVII 309 (s. Κέφαλος)
—KOLPAIOI: (5) f. ii BC Cabanes, *L'Épire* p. 580 no. 54, 7 (f. Ἀγέλαιος)
ILLYRIA:
—APOLLONIA: (6) c. 250-50 BC Münsterberg Nachtr. p. 12 (Ceka 15) (Ἀνί[κα]τος: pryt.)

## Ἀνίκητος

ACHAIA:
—AIGION?: (1) i AD *Achaean Grave Stelai* 42 (-νεί-)
—KARYNEIA: (2) ii AD ib. 26 (-νεί-)
ARGOLIS:
—HERMIONE: (3) iii-ii BC *IG* IV (1) 712, 1, 4 (Ἀνεί[κητος]: f. Ἀριστις)
ARKADIA:
—TEGEA: (4) hell.-imp.? ib. v (2) 256
ELIS:
—OLYMPIA*: (5) 245-265 AD *IvOl* 121, 28; 122, 23 (-νεί-)
LAKONIA:
—SPARTA: (6) c. 120 AD *IG* V (1) 1315, 29 (Bradford (1)) (Κλ. Ἀνείκητος: s. Πανκ—); (7) c. 140-150 AD *SEG* XI 497, 1 (Bradford (2)) (-νεί-: f. Σιδηρᾶς)
S. ITALY: (8) imp. *CIL* X 8059. 147 (seal) (Lat. C. Sex. Anicetus); (9) ~ ib. 8059. 273 (seal) (Lat. Neratius Anicetus)
S. ITALY (APULIA):
—LUCERIA: (10) imp. ib. IX 827 (Lat. C. Lusius Anicetus); (11) ~ ib. 873 (Lat. M. Arrius Anicetus)
—VENUSIA: (12) v AD *JIWE* I 50 (*CIJ* I 577) (-νή-: f. Ἐρ—: Jew); (13) ~ *JIWE* I 50 (*CIJ* I 577) (-νή-: s. Ἐρ—: Jew)
S. ITALY (CAMPANIA):
—DIKAIARCHIA-PUTEOLI: (14) imp. *CIL* IV 3891; X 1946 (Lat. C. Ummidius Actius Anicetus); (15) ~ ib. 2051 (Lat. Anicetus); (16) ~ ib. 2052 (Lat. Anicetus); (17) ~ ib. 3098, 3 (Lat. Veturius Anicetus: II s. Ἀνίκητος I, Χάρις); (18) ~ ib. l. 4 (Lat. C. Veturius Anicetus: I f. Ἀνίκητος II, Κιτιάς I, Κιτιάς II, Veturia Severa); (19) ~ ib. 8203 (Lat. M. Vibius Anicetus)
—HERCULANEUM: (20) i BC-i AD ib. IV 10535 (Lat. Anicetus); (21) ~ *Cron. Erc.* 18 (1988) p. 199 (Lat. Mamius Anicetus); (22) m. i AD *PdelP* 10 (1955) p. 459 no. 82 (Lat. [L.] [An]nius Ani[c]etus)
—POMPEII: (23) i BC-i AD *CIL* IV 2150 (Lat. Anicet[us]); (24) ~ ib. 2310 f (Lat. Anicetus); (25) ~ ib. 2994 (Lat. Anice[t]us); (26) ~ ib. 4148 (Lat. Anicetus); (27) ~ ib. 4698 (Lat. Anicetus); (28) ~ ib. 5374 (Lat. Anicetus);

(29) ~ ib. 9189 (Castrèn 118. 5) (Lat. Ti. Claudius Ani[ce]t[us])
S. ITALY (LUCANIA):
—VOLCEI: (30) imp. *IItal* III (1) 20 (*CIL* X 410) (Lat. C. Coelius Anicetus: s. Coelia Prima)
SICILY:
—HALOUNTION: (31) imp. *NScav* 1902, p. 473 (*ILat. Palermo* 42) (Lat. Cn. Caninius Anicetus: f. Tertius)
—SYRACUSE: (32) iii-v AD *Riv. Arch. Crist.* 18 (1941) p. 214 no. 91 (Ἀνεί-)
—THERMAI HIMERAIAI: (33) imp. *IG* XIV 338 (Σουλπίκιος Ἀ.)

## Ἀντιοχίδας

KORINTHIA:
—KORINTH: (1) c. 570-550 BC Amyx 89. 3 (vase) (Lorber 108) ((Ἀ)ντιοχίδας: her.?)
LAKONIA: (2) c. 550 BC *Cl. Rh.* 8 p. 86; *LSAG²* p. 199 no. 16 a

## Ἀντίοχος

ACHAIA:
—PELLENE: (1) m. iii BC *IG* V (2) 368, 106 (Ἀντίοχος?: s. Νεοσ—)
KORINTHIA:
—KORINTH: (2) 127 AD *Colosse de Memnon* 25 (Lat. C. Maenius Haniochus)
S. ITALY (LUCANIA):
—METAPONTION: (3) iv BC Iamb., *VP* 267 (*FVS* 1 p. 446) (Ἀλίοχος—ms.: name—C. Keil)

## Ἄνιππος?

ARGOLIS:
—NEMEA*: (1) iv/iii BC *SEG* XXXVIII 300 (Ἀνιππος (n. pr.?))

## Ἀνκίσκος

SICILY:
—KAMARINA: (1) s. v BC ib. 934 (Arena, *Iscr. Sic.* II 146) (-σσκος)

## Ἄννα

KORINTHIA:
—KORINTH: (1) byz. *SEG* XXIX 309 (Jew); (2) ~ *Corinth* VIII (3) 613; (3) ~ ib. 625 ([Ἄ]ννα)

## Ἀνναία

ILLYRIA:
—EPIDAMNOS-DYRRHACHION: (1) hell.-imp. *BUST* 1962 (2), p. 132 (*Stud. Alb.* 1965, p. 98) (Lat. Annea); (2) ~ *IDyrrh* 103 (d. Ἐπίκαδος); (3) ~ ib. 104 (d. Κάλσος); (4) ~ ib. 105 (d. Μενέστρατος); (5) imp. ib. 102 (d. Γλαυκίας)

## Ἀνναῖος

DALMATIA:
—ISSA: (1) iii/ii BC *SEG* XXXV 689-90 (s. Θεύδοτος, f. Θεύδοτος)
ILLYRIA:
—EPIDAMNOS-DYRRHACHION: (2) hell.-imp. *BUST* 1962 (2), p. 132 (*Stud. Alb.* 1965, p. 98) (Lat. Annaius)

## Ἀννία

ILLYRIA:
—LYCHNIDOS: (1) ii-iii AD *Sp.* 71 (1931) p. 110 no. 266 (*SEG* XXXIX 603) (d. Πλάτωρ, m. Ἀλέξανδρος, Νικόπολις)
S. ITALY (CAMPANIA):
—NEAPOLIS: (2) iv-v AD *IG* XIV 826. 4 (*INap* 244)

## Ἀννίκα

ILLYRIA:
—AMANTIA (NR.): (1) ii BC *SEG* XXXIX 553
—EPIDAMNOS-DYRRHACHION: (2) hell.-imp. *IDyrrh* 106 (d. Πρεύρατος)

## Ἄννος

ILLYRIA:
—EPIDAMNOS-DYRRHACHION: (1) hell.-imp. ib. 107 (s. Ἀντίγονος)

## Ἀννουλα

ILLYRIA:
—APOLLONIA: (1) ?iii AD *IApoll* 279

## Ἀννυλα

EPIROS:
—DODONA*: (1) iii/ii BC *Syll³* 1163
ILLYRIA:
—APOLLONIA: (2) hell.-imp. *BUST* 1962 (2), p. 132 (*Stud. Alb.* 1965, p. 98) (Lat. Annula)
—EPIDAMNOS-DYRRHACHION: (3) ?ii AD ib. p. 72 no. 46 (Lat. Annula: d. Εὔπορος)

## Ἀννώ

ILLYRIA:
—EPIDAMNOS-DYRRHACHION: (1) hell.-imp. *IDyrrh* 108 (Ἀννὼ Πομπηία)

## Ἄνοιστος

ARKADIA:
—TEGEA: (1) c. 369-362 BC *IG* V (2) 173, 7

## Ἀνόπτης

S. ITALY (APULIA):
—CANUSIUM*: (1) i AD *Epig. Rom. di Canosa* 89 (Lat. A. Baebius Anoptes: freed.)
—LUCERIA*: (2) imp. *CIL* IX 876 (Lat. P. Pilius Anoptes: freed.)
S. ITALY (CAMPANIA):
—DIKAIARCHIA-PUTEOLI: (3) imp. ib. X 2035 (Lat. C. Albius Anoptes)
—DIKAIARCHIA-PUTEOLI*: (4) i BC/i AD *Puteoli* 6 (1982) p. 146 no. 3 (Lat. Q. Calavius Anoptes: freed.)
—HERCULANEUM*: (5) i BC-i AD *CIL* X 1403 f I, 6 (Lat. Q. Iunius Anoptes: freed.)
—KYME: (6) ii-iii AD *IG* XIV 868 (*GVI* 367)
—SALERNUM*: (7) ?i AD *IItal* I (1) 238 II, 18 (*CIL* X 557) (Lat. L. Appuleius Anoptes: freed.)

## Ἀνοχίδας

AITOLIA:
—KALYDON: (1) f. iv BC *IG* IX (1)² (1) 138, 12

## Ἄνοχις

ARGOLIS:
—ARGOS: (1) m. iv BC ib. II² 8368 (f. Καλλικράτης)

## Ἄνοχος

S. ITALY (CALABRIA):
—TARAS-TARENTUM: (1) c. 520 BC Moretti, *Olymp.* 130-1 (s. Ἀδαμάτας)
SICILY:
—SELINOUS: (2) c. 500 BC *SEG* XXIX 403

## Ἀντάγορος

ARKADIA:
—TEGEA: (1) s. iii BC *IG* V (2) 116, 3 (Ἀντάγ[ο]ρος: f. Ἰμπεδις)

## Ἄνταγρος

AITOLIA:
—BOUKATION: (1) 163 BC ib. IX (1)² (1) 101, 7 (Ἀντάγ(ο)ρος?—ed.: f. Εὔαρχος)

## Ἀνταῖος

AKARNANIA:
—STRATOS: (1) f. iii BC ib. IX (1)² (2) 400 (s. Σίννος)
ARKADIA:
—TEGEA: (2) ?i BC ib. V (2) 202
S. ITALY (APULIA):
—CANUSIUM*: (3) i AD *Epig. Rom. di Canosa* 121 (*CIL* IX 373) (Lat. P. Dasimius Antaeus: freed.)
S. ITALY (CAMPANIA):
—SALERNUM*: (4) imp. *IItal* I (1) 154 (*CIL* X 579) (Lat. A. Clodius Antaeus: freed.)

## Ἀντάλκης

ILLYRIA:
—APOLLONIA: (**1**) c. 250-50 BC Münsterberg
Nachtr. p. 12 (Ceka 15) (money.)

## Ἀνταλκίδας

LAKONIA:
—SPARTA: (**1**) c. 425-367 BC RE (-) (Poralla²
97); cf. Did., in D. vii 13 (Ἀντιαλκίδας—Did.:
s. Λέων, ?s. Τελευτία)

## Ἀνταλλίδας

ARGOLIS:
—EPIDAUROS: (**1**) iv BC IG IV (1)² 329 (f. Ταῖς)

## Ἀνταλλίς

S. ITALY (LUCANIA):
—HERAKLEIA: (**1**) iv/iii BC Festschr. Neutsch p.
408

## Ἄνταλλος

DALMATIA:
—ISSA: (**1**) hell. Brunšmid p. 26 no. 17 (SEG
XL 513) + VAHD 84 (1991) p. 252 no. 2 (f.
Θεύδοτος); (**2**) ~ ib. p. 26 no. 17 (SEG XL 513)
+ VAHD 84 (1991) p. 252 no. 2 (s. Ἀριστήν)
——(Dymanes): (**3**) iv/iii BC Brunšmid p. 7, 24
([Ἄν]ταλλος: s. Ἀρίσταρχος); (**4**) ~ ib. l. 26 (s.
Σώπατρος); (**5**) ~ ib. p. 8, 41 ([Ἀντα]λλος: s.
Ἀριστήν)
——(Hylleis): (**6**) iv/iii BC ib. p. 8, 37 (s. Μενε-
κράτης)
ILLYRIA:
—EPIDAMNOS-DYRRHACHION (NR.)?: (**7**) ii BC
SEG XXXVIII 572, 3; cf. CRAI 1991, p. 197
ff.; L'Illyrie mérid. 2 p. 206 ([Ἄν]ταλλος)
S. ITALY (BRUTTIUM):
—SYBARIS-THOURIOI-COPIAE: (**8**) 196 BC IG IX
(1)² (1) 31, 18 (f. Λέων)
S. ITALY (LUCANIA):
—HYELE-VELIA: (**9**) 188 BC Syll³ 585, 128 (f.
Χαροπῖνος)
SICILY: (**10**) hell. SEG XXXIII 455 (Ἀντα[λλος:
f. Ζώπυρος); (**11**) iii-ii BC Vandermersch p.
162 (amph.) (or S. Italy: Ἄνταλ(λ)ος))
—GELA-PHINTIAS: (**12**) f. ii BC IG XIV 256, 39
(Dubois, IGDS 161); cf. SEG XL 804 (I f.
Ἄνταλλος II); (**13**) ~ IG XIV 256, 39 (Dubois,
IGDS 161); cf. SEG XL 804 (II s. Ἄνταλλος
I)
—KAMARINA: (**14**) ?iv/iii BC ib. XXXIX 1002, 5
(Ἄνταλ[λος]: f. Δικαιαγόρα); (**15**) hell. ib. 1001,
9 (f. Φύλαρχος)
—MORGANTINA: (**16**) iv/iii BC ib. 1013, 4
(Ἀντ[αλλος]?: s. Χάρων); (**17**) ~ ib. l. 8 (s. Ἡρα-
κλείδας); (**18**) iii BC Dubois, IGDS 192 (vase);
cf. Guarducci, Ep. Gr. 3 p. 346
—NEAITON: (**19**) iii/ii BC NScav 1897, p. 86; cf.
Rupes loquentes p. 455
—SOLOUS: (**20**) s. ii BC SEG XLI 836 ([Ἄν]ταλλος
Ὁ[ρνιχᾶ]ς: s. Ἀσκλαπος); (**21**) ?i BC IGLMP
114, 4; cf. SEG XXXVIII 964 (II s. Ἄνταλλος I,
f. Ἄνταλλος III Ὀρνιχᾶς); (**22**) ~ IGLMP 114,
4; cf. SEG XXXVIII 964 (A. Ὀρνιχᾶς: III s.
Ἄνταλλος II); (**23**) ~ IGLMP 114, 5; cf. SEG
XXXVIII 964 (I f. Ἄνταλλος II)
—SYRACUSE?:
——(Ἑρμ.): (**24**) hell. Manganaro, PdelP forth-
coming no. 4 I, 11 (s. Σώπατρος)
—TAUROMENION: (**25**) c. 174-160 BC IG XIV
421 an. 67; 421 an. 81 (SGDI 5219) (f. Φάλακρος)
—THERMAI HIMERAIAI: (**26**) ?ii/i BC ib. 3248;
cf. Kokalos 20 (1974) p. 219 no. 1 (s. Νύμφων)

## Ἀνταμένης

LAKONIA:
—SPARTA: (**1**) iii BC SEG XL 348 A, 1
—THALAMAI: (**2**) i BC-i AD IG V (1) 1321 a

## Ἀντάνδρα

ARGOLIS:
—ARGOS: (**1**) hell.? SEG XI 356 (Ἀντάνδρα)

## Ἄντανδρος

ACHAIA:
—AIGEIRA: (**1**) c. 100-90 BC ib. XIX 335, 3, 23;
BSA 70 (1975) pp. 127 ff. (date) (s. Ἐρέδαμος)
—DYME: (**2**) s. iii BC SEG XIII 278, 30; (**3**) 143
BC IG IX (1)² (1) 34, 19
—KALLISTAI: (**4**) 191-146 BC Coll. McClean
6456 (coin)
AITOLIA: (**5**) 224 or 221 BC SGDI 2524, 3;
Nachtergael, Les Galates 64, 2
—KONOPE-ARSINOE: (**6**) ?ii BC SEG XXXIV 467
AITOLIA?: (**7**) iii BC Marcadé I 4 (sculptor)
AKARNANIA:
—TYRBEION/TORYBEIA: (**8**) 356-354 BC IG IV
(1)² 95, 18 (Perlman E.2); Perlman p. 40 f.
(date); cf. BCH 90 (1966) pp. 174 f. (locn.)
ARGOLIS:
—PHLEIOUS: (**9**) iii BC IG IV (1) 446, 1
([Ἄ]ντανδ[ρ]ος)
ELIS: (**10**) iii-ii BC ib. 429, 9 (Stephanis 194) (s.
Εὐώνυμος); (**11**) i BC/i AD IG XII (8) 176, 4 (s.
Θεόδωρος)
EPIROS:
—PHOINIKE: (**12**) iii-ii BC AE 1914, p. 236 no.
8 (s. Κεφαλῖνος)
ILLYRIA:
—APOLLONIA: (**13**) ii-i BC IApoll 120 (Ἄν-
τα(ν)δρ(ο)ς: f. Μενήν)
KORINTHIA:
—KORINTH: (**14**) a. 191 BC SEG XXVI 392, 8
(Ἄνταν[δρ]ο[ς])
MESSENIA: (**15**) viii BC RE (5)
SICILY:
—KAMARINA: (**16**) v BC QUCC 78 (1995) p. 127
no. 2 (bronze) (s. Πύθις)
—KAMARINA?: (**17**) ?v/iv BC Manganaro, PdelP
forthcoming no. 14 (Ἀντανδ[ρο]ς)
—SELINOUS: (**18**) vi/v BC ib. no. 18, 7 (f. Ἄθανις)
—SYRACUSE: (**19**) s. iv BC RE (6); FGrH 565 (s.
Καρκίνος (Rhegion))

## Ἀντάνωρ

ELIS: (**1**) 217 BC Plb. v 94. 6
EPIROS: (**2**) c. 200 BC IG IX (1)² (1) 31, 129 (f.
Κλέαρχος, Νικάνωρ)
—BOUTHROTOS (PRASAIBOI): (**3**) a. 163 BC
IBouthrot 92, 5; (**4**) ~ ib. 134, 12
—CHAONES: (**5**) c. 300 BC FD III (4) 409, 8 (Ἀν-
τάνω[ρ]: s. Εὐθυμίδας)
ILLYRIA:
—OLYMPE: (**6**) s. iii BC SEG XXXV 697 (f. Ζωΐ-
λος)

## Ἄνταρχος

EPIROS:
—AMBRAKIA: (**1**) 263 BC IG IX (1)² (1) 17, 42
(Ἄνταρχος: s. Θεόπομπος)

## Ἀντέας

ARKADIA: (**1**) iii BC PP s.v. 15628 (f. Στράταγος)

## Ἄντεια

ARKADIA:
—ORCHOMENOS: (**1**) ?ii BC IG V (2) 345, 9
([Ἄν]τεια?: d. Δαμόξενος, m. Δαμόξενος: date—
LGPN)

## Ἀντέρως

AIGINA: (**1**) imp. Alt-Ägina I (2) p. 47 no. 27,
2 (I f. Ἀντέρως II); (**2**) ~ ib. l. 2 (II s. Ἀντέρως
I); (**3**) ?iii AD ib. p. 50 no. 47 (f. Αὐρ. Εὔδημος)
ARGOLIS:
—ARGOS: (**4**) ii/i BC IG IV (1) 539 (f. Εὔπορος)
—EPIDAUROS: (**5**) iii-iv AD Peek, IAEpid 227 (s.
Τιμοκλῆς)
ARKADIA:
—TEGEA: (**6**) ii AD IG V (2) 55, 82 (s. Τυχέας)

## Ἀντίας

EPIROS:
—NIKOPOLIS: (**7**) imp. SEG XXXIX 532 (s. Φιλ-
έρως)
KORINTHIA:
—KORINTH: (**8**) ?i AD IG IV (1) 853, 10, 12, 18
etc. (Λ. Λικίννιος Ἀ.); (**9**) iii AD SEG XXXVIII
294
S. ITALY (APULIA):
—AECAE: (**10**) imp. CIL IX 955 (Lat. Anteros)
—AUSCULUM: (**11**) imp. ib. 682 (Lat. Anteros)
—BARION: (**12**) f. i AD Suppl. It. 8 p. 42 no. 10
(Lat. P. Petius Anteros)
—GNATHIA-EGNATIA: (**13**) i AD ib. 11 p. 40 no.
19 (Lat. Anteros)
—RUBI: (**14**) m. ii AD Epigrafia e Territorio 2 p.
73 no. 14 (CIL IX 6183) (Lat. M. Arrecinus
Anteros)
S. ITALY (CALABRIA):
—BRENTESION-BRUNDISIUM*: (**15**) imp. ib.
6112 (Lat. P. Calavius Anteros: freed.)
—TARAS-TARENTUM: (**16**) imp. ib. 254 + Misc.
Gr. Rom. 3 p. 202 no. T22 (Lat. D. Veturius
Anteros)
S. ITALY (CAMPANIA): (**17**) i AD CIL X 8047.
2 (pithos) (Lat. Anteros)
—CAPREAE: (**18**) imp. Eph. Ep. VIII 672 (Lat.
C. Fannius Anteros)
—DIKAIARCHIA-PUTEOLI: (**19**) imp. CIL X
2039 (Lat. P. Alfenius Anteros); (**20**) ~ ib.
2941 (Lat. Anteros)
—DIKAIARCHIA-PUTEOLI*: (**21**) imp. ib. 2367
(Lat. Cn. Domitius Anteros: freed.)
—POMPEII: (**22**) i BC-i AD ib. IV 3991 (Lat.
Anteros); (**23**) ~ ib. 4869 (Lat. Anteros); (**24**)
~ ib. 4925 (Lat. Anteros); (**25**) ~ ib. 8962
(Lat. Antiros—Solin); (**26**) ~ ib. X 865 (Lat.
Anteros); (**27**) ~ Atti Acc. Pontan. 39 (1990)
p. 301 no. 131 (Lat. Anteros); (**28**) 32 AD CIL
X 899, 6 (Castrèn 197. 8) (Lat. Holconius
Anteros)
—POMPEII*: (**29**) 7 BC CIL X 924, 3 (Lat.
Anteros: freed.?)
—STABIAE: (**30**) i AD ib. 773 (Lat. Anteros)
S. ITALY (LUCANIA):
—GRUMENTUM*: (**31**) imp. ib. 274 (Lat. Gn.
Vettius Anteros: freed.)
SICILY:
—TYNDARIS*: (**32**) imp. ib. 7483 (Lat. C. Iulius
Ante[ros]: f. Ἔρως: freed.?)

## Ἀντήνωρ

ILLYRIA:
—APOLLONIA: (**1**) hell. IApoll 346 (tile) (-τένορ)
—SKAMPIS: (**2**) imp. BUST 1961 (1), p. 123 no.
22 (Lat. Antenor)
KEPHALLENIA: (**3**) her. RE (3)
S. ITALY (CALABRIA):
—BRENTESION-BRUNDISIUM: (**4**) 32 or 33 AD
Athenaeum 42 (1964) pp. 299-306; cf. Scritti
Degrassi 3 p. 278 (Lat. Antenor)
S. ITALY (CAMPANIA):
—POMPEII: (**5**) i BC-i AD CIL IV 1531 (Lat.
Antenor); (**6**) ~ ib. 4101 (Lat. Antenor); (**7**)
~ ib. 8944 (Lat. Antenor); (**8**) ~ Neue Forsch.
in Pompeji p. 263 no. 11 (Lat. Antenor)
SICILY?: (**9**) v BC Plu., Numa 8 (fict.?)

## Ἀντιάλκης

LAKONIA:
—SPARTA: (**1**) c. 25-1 BC IG V (1) 212, 6 (Bradford (-)) (f. Νικάσιππος)

## Ἀντιαλκίδας

LAKONIA:
—SPARTA: (**1**) s. i BC IG V (1) 93, 15 (Bradford
(-)) (s. Φάνης)

## Ἀντίας

AITOLIA:
—KALYDON: (**1**) a. 142 BC IG IX (1)² (1) 137,
80 (Ἀντία[ς])
ARGOLIS:
—ARGOS: (**2**) ?444 BC Pi., N. x, 40; (**3**) ii BC
SEG XLII 279, 21 (s. Ἀντίμαχος)

## Ἀντιβία

—MYKENAI: (4) ?c. 500-480 BC IG IV (1) 492, 5, 6; LSAG² p. 174 no. 2 (date)
ARKADIA:
—TEGEA: (5) ?s. iv BC IG v (2) 39, 4 (f. —ας)
ELIS: (6) 28-16 BC IvOl 64, 12; 65, 13; 69, [13] (f. Κάλλιτος: mantis/Klytiadai)
KORINTHIA:
—KORINTH: (7) c. 570-550 BC Amyx 58. 2 (vase) (Ἀντίας: her.?)
MESSENIA:
—THOURIA: (8) s. iii BC IG v (1) 1386, 13 (s. Πρατόνικος)

## Ἀντιβία

ARKADIA?: (1) iv/iii BC HE 684

## Ἀντίβιος

LAKONIA:
—SPARTA: (1) ii/i BC IG VII 521, 32 (IOrop 525); IG XII (3) Suppl. 1299, 25; 1625 (Bradford (1)) (s. Ἀβρίας, f. Ἀβρίας); (2) c. 80-90 AD IG v (1) 674, 16 (Bradford (2)) (f. Ξενάκων)

## Ἀντίβολος

AITOLIA:
—KALYDON: (1) s. iii BC FD III (1) 519, 2 (f. Θεόδοτος)
ARKADIA:
—TEGEA: (2) m. iv BC IG v (2) 6, 75
EPIROS:
—DODONA: (3) iii BC Antoniou, Dodone Ab, 24
—DOIESSTOI: (4) f. ii BC Cabanes, L'Épire p. 580 no. 54, 4 (s. Νικάνωρ)

## Ἀντίβουλος

EPIROS:
—AMBRAKIA: (1) f. ii BC AD 39 (1984) Chron. p. 190 + pl. 77 γ (s. Ἀλεξάνωρ)

## Ἀντιγένης

ACHAIA:
—DYME: (1) s. iii BC SEG XIII 278, 26 (s. Ξενότιμος)
AITOLIA: (2) c. 232-228 BC Syll³ 499, 3; Nachtergael, Les Galates 62, [4]
ARGOLIS:
—ARGOS:
——(Naupliadai): (3) ii/i BC BCH 33 (1909) p. 176 no. 2, 8 (s. Πολυκράτης)
ARKADIA:
—TEGEA: (4) c. 365-335 BC IG IV (1)² 103, 45, 61; (5) iv/iii BC ib. v (2) 32, 10
ELIS: (6) ii/i BC Moretti, Olymp. 663 (s. Ἰάσων)
—OLYMPIA*: (7) i BC-i AD IvOl 936, 2 (I s. Ἀρ—, f. Ἀντιγένης II); (8) ~ ib. l. 2 (II s. Ἀντιγένης I)
ILLYRIA:
—EPIDAMNOS-DYRRHACHION: (9) c. 250-50 BC Maier 224; 322; Münsterberg Nachtr. p. 15 (coin) (Ceka 66-7) (money.)
KORINTHIA:
—KORINTH: (10) v BC Corinth VIII (3) 14
MESSENIA:
—THOURIA: (11) f. ii BC SEG XI 972, 106 (f. Δεξίας)
SICILY:
—GELA-PHINTIAS: (12) i BC/i AD GP 191 (fict.?)
—HENNA: (13) c. 135 BC D.S. xxxiv-v 2. 5, 8, 15 (?s. Πύθων)

## Ἀντιγόνα

EPIROS:
—AMBRAKIA: (1) ii BC Unp. (Arta Mus., inscr.) (Ἀντιγόνα: ?d. Μελ—)
—BOUTHROTOS (PRASAIBOI): (2) a. 163 BC IBouthrot 22, 14 (SEG XXXVIII 479); (3) ~ IBouthrot 29, 61 (SEG XXXVIII 487)
—MOLOSSOI: (4) hell.? IG II² 9972 (-γόνη)
MESSENIA:
—MESSENE: (5) imp. SEG XLI 368 (Ἀντιγονία-ed.)

## Ἀντιγόνη

LAKONIA: (1) hell.-imp.? Bronzes grecs et romains (Madrid) 563 (-τυγώ-: ?d. Δάμων, Ἀλεκτρύων)
SICILY: (2) i BC/i AD GP 1311; 1363; 1366; 1491; 1494 (het.)

## Ἀντίγονος

ACHAIA:
—PHARAI*: (1) i-ii AD CIL III 14203. 13 (Lat. Antigonus: freed.)
AIGINA: (2) imp. IG IV (1) 110
AITOLIA:
—AGRAIOI: (3) ii-i BC ib. IX (1)² (1) 198 (s. Πυρρανοίδας)
AKARNANIA: (4) iii/ii BC RE (7); Syll³ 585, 33 (s. Ἀλέξανδρος)
—ASTAKOS: (5) ii BC IG IX (1)² (2) 434, 5 (s. Πτολεμαῖος)
—KECHRINIA (MOD.): (6) hell.? AD 26 (1971) Chron. p. 325
ARGOLIS:
—ARGOS: (7) imp. SEG XXVIII 396, 6 (Τιβ. Κλ. Ἀ.) ?= (8); (8) ~ ib. 397 (Τι[β.] Κλ. Ἀ.) ?= (7); (9) c. 45 AD FD III (1) 534, 6
—HERMIONE: (10) imp. IG IV (1) 724, 1 (I f. Ἀντίγονος II); (11) ~ ib. l. 1 (II s. Ἀντίγονος I); (12) iii AD ib. 726, 8 (Αὐρ. Ἀ.: s. Αὐρ. Σώστρατος, Αὐρ. Λουκία)
ARKADIA:
—TEGEA: (13) m. ii AD ib. v (2) 48, 22
EPIROS:
—BOUTHROTOS (PRASAIBOI): (14) a. 163 BC IBouthrot 14, 22 (SEG XXXVIII 471); IBouthrot 135, 5 (f. Σίμακος) ?= (23); (15) ~ ib. 36, 2 (SEG XXXVIII 495) (I f. Ἀντίγονος II); (16) ~ IBouthrot 36, 2 (SEG XXXVIII 495) (II s. Ἀντίγονος I); (17) ~ IBouthrot 78, 10; 79, [9]; 80, 9; 81, 9; 82, 8; 83, 8; 84, 9; 85, 9; 86, 10; 87, 9; 88, 7; 156, 9; 157, 5 (BCH 118 (1994) pp. 122 f. nos. 1-13) (f. Ἀππoίτας) ?= (20); IBouthrot 99, 4 (BCH 118 (1994) p. 121 B); (19) ~ IBouthrot 127, 5 (s. Λυκόφρων) ?= (21)
——Kydestoi: (20) f. ii BC REG 62 (1949) p. 28, 12; IBouthrot 69, 2, 10-11; 70, [2], 8-9; 71, 1, 7 (BCH 118 (1994) p. 129 B 1-3); IBouthrot 77, 7 (s. Λυκόφρων, f. Λυκόφρων, Ἀππoίτας) ?= (17)
——Opatai: (21) a. 163 BC ib. 118, 5 (f. Λυκόφρων) ?= (19); (22) ~ ib. 119; 120, 1; (23) ~ ib. 127, 7 (BCH 118 (1994) p. 128 A); IBouthrot 135, 2 (f. Ἀππoίτας) ?= (14)
ILLYRIA:
—EPIDAMNOS-DYRRHACHION: (24) c. 250-50 BC Maier 236 (Ceka 68); Maier 338 (coin) (money.); (25) hell.-imp. IDyrrh 107 (f. Ἄντος); (26) imp. ib. 4
—KORCA (MOD.): (27) hell. SEG XXXIII 487 (pithoi)
—LYCHNIDOS: (28) ii-iii AD Demitsas 341 (s. Ναύτης)
LAKONIA:
—ASOPOS: (29) imp. IG v (1) 997
—GYTHEION: (30) ii-iii AD ib. 1182
—SPARTA: (31) s. i BC ib. 124, 7 (Bradford (1)) (s. Ἀντιμένης); (32) imp. IG v (1) 204 (Bradford (2)) ([Ἀν]τίγονος)
S. ITALY (APULIA):
—CANUSIUM*: (33) imp. Epig. Rom. di Canosa 153 (CIL IX 388) (Lat. M. Licinius Antigonus: freed.)
S. ITALY (CALABRIA):
—TARAS-TARENTUM: (34) ii-i BC SEG XXX 1217
S. ITALY (CAMPANIA):
—DIKAIARCHIA-PUTEOLI: (35) ii/iii AD Puteoli 4-5 (1980-1) p. 283 no. 15 (Lat. Apuleius Antigonus)
—DIKAIARCHIA-PUTEOLI*: (36) ?ii AD CIL x 2453 (Lat. T. Flavius Antigonus: freed.)
—HERCULANEUM: (37) m. i AD ib. IV 10802 (amph.) (Lat. L. R. Antigonus)
—POMPEII: (38) i BC-i AD ib. 2362; cf. p. 220 (Lat. C. A. Antigonus)
SICILY:
—KAMARINA: (39) f. v BC Cordano, Tessere Pubbliche 85 (f. Θρίπαινος)

## Ἀντίδικος

AITOLIA:
—APERANTOI: (1) hell.? IG IX (1)² (1) 165 (f. Ἀντικράτεια)

## Ἀντίδωρος

ILLYRIA:
—APOLLONIA: (1) s. iii BC IApoll 176; cf. SEG XXXIX 550 (f. Σιμίας)
S. ITALY (BRUTTIUM):
—LOKROI EPIZEPHYRIOI:
——(Ἀγκ.): (2) iv/iii BC De Franciscis 15, 5; 30, 7 (s. Κράτων)

## Ἀντιδώτας

AITOLIA:
—KALLION/KALLIPOLIS: (1) 195 BC SGDI 2119, 8

## Ἀντίκκας

EPIROS:
—ETHNESTAI: (1) ?c. 370-344 BC Cabanes, L'Épire p. 536 no. 2, 7 (Ἀντίκκας)

## Ἀντικλείδας

LAKONIA:
—SPARTA: (1) s. v BC Schol. E., Hipp. 230; cf. Ebert, Gr. Sieg. 28 (Poralla² 98) (f. Λέων)

## Ἀντικλῆς

LAKONIA:
—SPARTA: (1) c. 50-25 BC IG v (1) 208, 2 (Bradford (-)) (f. Παντίας)
MESSENIA: (2) 748 BC Moretti, Olymp. 8 (RE (2))

## Ἀντικράτεια

AITOLIA:
—APERANTOI: (1) hell.? IG IX (1)² (1) 165 (d. Ἀντίδικος)

## Ἀντικράτης

AKARNANIA:
—ASTAKOS: (1) 167 BC Klio 75 (1993) p. 132, 7-8 (Ἀντι[κρά]της: f. Ἑσπερίων)
—THYRREION: (2) ii BC IG IX (1)² (2) 327 (f. Μόσχιον)
ARGOLIS:
—ARGOS: (3) f. iii BC CID II 120 A, 15 (s. Πολύστρατος)
—EPIDAUROS: (4) 600 BC Moretti, Olymp. 77
——(Azantioi): (5) 146 BC IG IV (1)² 28, 34 (s. Κλεισθένης)
ARKADIA:
—MEGALOPOLIS: (6) ii/i BC ib. v (2) 443, 8; 444, 6 (IPArk 32) (f. Ἱέρων)
ELIS:
—OLYMPIA*: (7) ii/i BC IvOl 397, 1 (Ἀντικράτη[ς])
EPIROS:
—AMBRAKIA: (8) iv/iii BC Unp. (Arta Mus., inscr.) (Ἀντικρ[άτης]: f. —σιος)
LAKONIA:
—SPARTA: (9) 362 BC Plu., Ages. 35 (Poralla² 99); cf. RE s.v. Machairion (or Arkadia Mantineia-Antigoneia: Ἀ. ὁ ἐπικαλ. Μαχαιρίων?—RE)
MESSENIA:
—MESSENE: (10) iii/ii BC SEG XLI 365 (f. Διοσκουρίδας); (11) ?f. ii AD ib. 335, 11
S. ITALY (CALABRIA):
—TARAS-TARENTUM: (12) f. iii BC Eretria VI 184
SICILY:
—AKRAI: (13) iii-ii BC SGDI 3242, 9 (Akrai p. 157 no. 8) (s. Ἀρτέμων)

**Ἀντικρατίδας**
ARGOLIS:
—TROIZEN: (1) i BC/i AD? *IG* IV (1) 808
([Ἀν]τικρ[α]τίδας)

**Ἀντίκριτος**
ARGOLIS:
—EPIDAUROS: (1) c. 370 BC ib. IV (1)² 102, 67
—EPIDAUROS*: (2) c. 365-335 BC ib. 103, 159
ARKADIA:
—MANTINEIA-ANTIGONEIA: (3) f. iii BC ib. v
(2) 278, 8; *EILakArk* 17 (date)

**Ἀντιλαΐδας**
AKARNANIA:
—PALAIROS: (1) iii BC *IG* IX (1)² (2) 475
ARGOLIS:
—HERMIONE: (2) m. iv BC Unp. (Ch. Kritzas)
(f. Ἐρατοκλῆς)
ARKADIA:
—MANTINEIA-ANTIGONEIA: (3) c. 475-450 BC
*IG* v (2) 262, 11 (*IPArk* 8); *LSAG*² p. 216
no. 29 (date)
—TEGEA:
——(Athaneatai): (4) s. iv BC *IG* v (2) 174 a, 8

**Ἀντίλας**
LAKONIA:
—SPARTA: (1) iii/ii BC *SEG* XI 468, 5 (Bradford
(2)) (Ἀντίλα[ς]: s. Ἀριστομένης); (2) c. 50-25 BC
*IG* v (1) 208, 3 (Bradford (1)) (s. Αἰνητίδας)

**Ἀντιλέων**
AITOLIA: (1) ?265-259 BC Nachtergael, *Les Ga-
lates* 4, 3 ([Ἀντ]ιλέων); (2) ?252-248 BC *Syll*³
422, 4; (3) ?a. 246 BC *SGDI* 2508, 3
—DAIANES: (4) 161 BC *IG* IX (1)² (1) 100, 8
—KONOPE-ARSINOE: (5) 139-122 BC *FD* III (4)
170, 3 (I f. Ἀντιλέων II); (6) ~ ib. l. 3 (II s.
Ἀντιλέων I)
—PHISTYON: (7) c. 125-100 BC *SBBerlAk* 1936,
p. 367 no. 2, 3 (*SEG* XII 303) (f. Λέων)
—TAPHEIEIS: (8) 272 BC *IG* IX (1)² (1) 13, 18
AKARNANIA:
—KORONTA: (9) iv/iii BC *SEG* XXIX 476 (f. Τι-
μολέων)
ILLYRIA:
—AULON: (10) hell. *Iliria* 1977-8, p. 292 pl.
IV.5 (*SEG* XXXII 621 (tile))
LAKONIA:
—SPARTA: (11) 362-360 BC *CID* II 1 I, 36; 4 II,
54 (Poralla² 100)
S. ITALY (LUCANIA):
—HERAKLEIA: (12) v-iv BC Wehrli, *Schule Ar-
ist.* ix Phainias fr. 16; cf. Plu., *Mor.* 770 C (or
S. Italy (Lucania) Metapontion)
—METAPONTION: (13) c. 262 BC *IG* IX (1)² (1)
17 A, 75 (Ἀντιλέων: f. Λέων)

**Ἀντίλοχος**
ARGOLIS:
—EPIDAUROS*: (1) c. 370 BC ib. IV (1)² 102, 270
ILLYRIA:
—APOLLONIA: (2) ii-i BC *IApoll* 162 (Ἀν-
τίλ[ο]χος: f. Φίλιππος)
—EPIDAMNOS-DYRRHACHION: (3) c. 250-50 BC
Maier 112-3 (coin) (Ceka 192; 446) (pryt.);
(4) ii-i BC *IDyrrh* 531 (tile) (Ἀντίλ[οχος?]:
pryt.)
SICILY: (5) c. 250 BC *PSI* 626 I, 9-11 (f. Διονυ-
σόδωρος, Ἑρμογένης)

**Ἀντιμαχίδας**
KORINTHIA:
—KORINTH: (1) 575-550 BC Amyx 119. 6 (vase)
(Lorber 99) (her.?)

**Ἀντίμαχος**
AITOLIA: (1) ?269 BC *FD* III (4) 415, 8
—KALYDON: (2) hell. *IG* IX (1)² (1) 146

AKARNANIA:
—THYRREION: (3) c. 325-315 BC *Hesp.* 57
(1988) p. 148 A, 27 (*SEG* XXXVI 331); cf.
*Hesp.* 48 (1979) pp. 78 f. with pl. 22 c (f.
Ἀλκέτας)
ARGOLIS:
—ARGOS: (4) c. 370 BC *IG* IV (1)² 102, 7, 11 ?=
(7); (5) 327-324 BC *CID* II 97, 28; 102 II B,
[29] (f. Ἀλκίμαχος); (6) ii BC *SEG* XLII 279,
21 (f. Ἀντίας)
—EPIDAUROS*: (7) c. 370 BC *IG* IV (1)² 102,
137, 143, 274, 290 ?= (4)
ARKADIA:
—LOUSOI: (8) 191-146 BC *BMC Pelop.* p. 14 no.
165 (coin)
—TEGEA: (9) m. iii BC *IG* v (2) 368, 71 (s. Νικ—)
DALMATIA:
—ISSA:
——(Dymanes): (10) iv/iii BC Brunšmid p. 8, 43
(f. Εὐάρης)
ELIS:
—DYSPONTION: (11) 772 BC Moretti, *Olymp.* 2
EPIROS:
—BOUTHROTOS: (12) i BC-i AD *IBouthrot* 177
(Ugolini, *Alb. Ant.* 3 p. 125)
—DODONA*: (13) iv BC *Ep. Chron.* 10 (1935) p.
256 no. 18 A
EPIROS?:
—ARRONOS?: (14) 370-368 BC Cabanes, *L'Épire*
p. 534 no. 1, 3
ILLYRIA:
—APOLLONIA: (15) i BC Ceka, *Probleme* p. 139
no. 1 (coin) (pryt.); (16) imp. *IApoll* 37; (17)
~ ib. 55 (f. Λύσων)
—EPIDAMNOS-DYRRHACHION: (18) c. 250-50
BC Ceka, *Probleme* p. 151 no. 6 (coin) (pryt.);
(19) ~ Maier 150; 155; 163; Münsterberg
Nachtr. p. 14 (coin) (Ceka 69-72) (money.)
LAKONIA:
—SPARTA: (20) iii BC *IG* v (1) 145, 3 (Bradford
(2)) (s. Τάσκος); (21) s. i BC *IG* v (1) 93, 20
(Bradford (1)) (s. Πασίμαχος)
S. ITALY (CAMPANIA):
—HERCULANEUM*: (22) i BC-i AD *CIL* x 1403 g
I, 27 + *Arctos* 19 (1985) pp. 203 ff. (Lat. C.
Iulius Antimachus—Solin: freed.)
SICILY:
—TAUROMENION: (23) c. 234 BC *IG* XIV 421 an.
7 (*SGDI* 5219) (s. Θρασύμαχος); (24) c. 185 BC
*IG* XIV 421 an. 56 (*SGDI* 5219) (s. Νικόστρα-
τος); (25) c. 182 BC *IG* XIV 421 an. 59 (*SGDI*
5219)
—TYNDARIS: (26) ?i BC *Arch. Class.* 17 (1965)
p. 203 (s. Φίλων)

**Ἀντιμέδων**
S. ITALY (BRUTTIUM):
—KROTON: (1) iv BC Iamb., *VP* 267 (*FVS* I p.
446)

**Ἀντιμένης**
ARKADIA:
—TEGEA: (1) iv BC *SEG* XXXVI 382, 3
KORINTHIA:
—SIKYON: (2) vi/v BC ib. XI 244, 76 (-νẽς); (3)
s. iii BC ib. III 346, 2 (-νεις: s. Σωχαρίδας)
LAKONIA:
—SPARTA: (4) s. i BC *IG* v (1) 124, 7 (Bradford
(-)) (f. Ἀντίγονος)
S. ITALY (LUCANIA):
—METAPONTION: (5) iv BC Iamb., *VP* 267
(*FVS* I p. 446)

**Ἀντιμενίδας**
LAKONIA:
—SPARTA: (1) 420 BC Th. v 42. 1 (Poralla² 101)

**Ἀντιμώ?**
EPIROS:
—BOUTHROTOS (PRASAIBOI): (1) a. 163 BC
*IBouthrot* 158 (Ἀντιμώ)

**Ἀντίνομος**
ACHAIA:
—PELLENE: (1) ?263-261 BC *FD* III (3) 190, 8
(s. Τεισι—)

**Ἀντίνοος**
EPIROS:
—KLATHRIOI: (1) f. ii BC Cabanes, *L'Épire* p.
553 no. 32; p. 554 no. 33, 2 (*SEG* XXXVII
511) ?= (Ἀντίνους (5))

**Ἀντίνους**
EPIROS: (1) ii BC Cabanes, *L'Épire* p. 585 no.
69; (2) ~ ib. p. 590 no. 76, 7 (*SEG* XXVI 704)
(s. Ἀντίπατρος)
—DODONA: (3) iii BC Antoniou, *Dodone* Ba, 27
(Ἀ[ντίν]ους)
—KLATHRIOI: (4) f. ii BC Cabanes, *L'Épire* p.
589 no. 75, 12 (*SEG* XXXVII 510) (s. Ἀλεξίμαχος)
—MOLOSSOI: (5) ii BC Plb. xxvii 15. 7; xxx 7. 2
?= (Ἀντίνοος (1)); (6) f. ii BC Cabanes, *L'Épire*
p. 589 no. 75, 14 (*SEG* XXXVII 510) (s. Νικόμαχος)
—ORESTOI: (7) ?164 BC Cabanes, *L'Épire* p. 586
no. 71, 8 (s. Δόκιμος)

**Ἀντιομάχα**
EPIROS:
—BOUTHROTOS (PRASAIBOI): (1) a. 163 BC
*IBouthrot* 151, 8

**Ἀντιόχεια**
SICILY:
—SYRACUSE: (1) iii-v AD *IG* XIV 74 (Strazzulla
15; Führer–Schultze p. 23; Wessel 503); cf.
Ferrua, *NG* 156 (-χια)

**Ἀντιοχιανή**
SICILY:
—SYRACUSE: (1) imp. *SEG* IV 9 (Wessel 1015);
cf. *Riv. Arch. Crist.* 18 (1941) p. 167 no. 28
(Ἰουλ. Ἀ. (n. pr.?))

**Ἀντιοχίς**
ACHAIA:
—PATRAI: (1) i-ii AD *ILGR* 49, 1 (Lat. Marcia
Antiochis: m. Alliatius Probus)
ILLYRIA:
—EPIDAMNOS-DYRRHACHION: (2) hell.-imp.
*IDyrrh* 26
KORINTHIA:
—KORINTH?: (3) imp. *CIL* III 544, 5 (Lat. An-
tiochis)
KYNOURIA:
—EUA?: (4) m. ii AD *SEG* XXXV 292 (d. Φορτου-
νᾶτος)
MESSENIA:
—MESSENE: (5) iii-iv AD *IG* v (1) 1494, 2; cf.
*TMByz* 9 (1985) p. 372 no. 145
S. ITALY (APULIA):
—CANUSIUM*: (6) i-ii AD *Epig. Rom. di Canosa*
167 (Lat. Pacilia Antiochis: freed.)
S. ITALY (BRUTTIUM):
—HIPPONION-VIBO VALENTIA: (7) imp. *CIL* x
83 (Lat. Titiria Antiochis)
S. ITALY (CAMPANIA):
—DIKAIARCHIA-PUTEOLI: (8) imp. *SEG* XXXII
1031; (9) ?i-ii AD *CIL* x 2284 (Lat. Claudia
Antiochis); (10) ~ ib. 2581 (Lat. Iulia Anti-
ochis: d. Ἀλκίδης)
—POMPEII: (11) i BC-i AD ib. 926 (Castrèn 89.
1) (Lat. Calidia Antiochis: m. Σκύλαξ); (12)
56 AD *CIL* IV 3340. 23, 4; 24, 5, 16 (Castrèn
424. 1) (Lat. Umbricia Antiochis)
—SALERNUM: (13) ?ii AD *IItal* I (1) 31 (*CIL* x
550) (Lat. Sep. Antiochis); (14) ~ *IItal* I (1)
31 (*CIL* x 550) (Lat. Aelia Antiochis)

**Ἀντίοχος**
ACHAIA: (1) ii BC *BGU* 1939 fr. C, 3 (f. Νικά-
νωρ)
ACHAIA?: (2) c. 300 BC *SEG* XIV 375, 6
([Ἀντ]ίοχος)

**AIGINA: (3)** ?i BC *Alt-Ägina* 1 (2) p. 44 no. 8 (Ἀντίῳ[χος])

**AITOLIA: (4)** c. 280-275 BC Flacelière p. 414 no. 47; *SEG* XV 338; **(5)** 137 BC *IG* IX (1)² (3) 634, 1; 677, 16

—BOUKATION: **(6)** c. 164 BC ib. IX (1)² (1) 99, 3 (s. Ἀγησαγόρας)

—KALYDON: **(7)** s. ii BC *SEG* XXV 621, 3 (s. Μενεκλῆς)

—KONOPE-ARSINOE: **(8)** m. ii BC *SBBerlAk* 1936, p. 371 b, 1 (*SEG* XLI 528 B)

—THESTIEIS: **(9)** f. ii BC *BCH* 45 (1921) p. 24 IV, 75; Unp. (Oulhen) small list face B, 4 (reading—Oulhen)

AKARNANIA: **(10)** 194 BC *Syll*³ 585, 32 (f. Ἀλέξανδρος)

AKARNANIA?: **(11)** s. iii BC *IG* XI (4) 519, 11 (f. Ῥάχας)

ARGOLIS:

—EPIDAUROS: **(12)** imp. ib. IV (1)² 445 (Ἀντίῳ[χο]ς: s. Φίλων); **(13)** i-ii AD *SEG* XXX 394 (Ἀντίοχ(ο)ς); **(14)** ii AD *IG* IV (1)² 480 (f. Π. Αἰλ. Διονύσιος); **(15)** c. 160 AD ib. 126, 1 (Π. Αἰλ. Ἀ.)

—HERMIONE: **(16)** iii BC ib. IV (1) 729 II, 9 (s. Ἀδάμας)

—PHLEIOUS: **(17)** c. 400-375 BC ib. II² 10479 (s. Ἑρμογένης)

ARKADIA:

—MEGALOPOLIS: **(18)** s. iv BC ib. V (2) 450

—TEGEA: **(19)** i/ii AD ib. 63; **(20)** m. ii AD ib. 48, 3 (Ἀντίοχ[ος]); **(21)** 165 AD ib. 50, 72 (f. Ἀμίαντος)

ELIS: **(22)** vi/v BC Hdt. ix 33. 1 (f. Τεισαμενός, Ἠλίας); **(23)** 36-24 BC *IvOl* 61, [6]; 62, 8 (f. Δαμάρετος); **(24)** 28-24 BC ib. 64, 8 (I f. Ἀντίοχος II); **(25)** ~ ib. l. 8, 29 (II s. Ἀντίοχος I, ?f. Ἴλαρος); **(26)** c. 177-189 AD ib. 102, 17; 103, 21; 104, 20 ([Ἀ]ντίοχος: f. Θεοδόσιος, —ας)

EPIROS: **(27)** c. 240-220 BC *PP* 15180; *IKourion* 60 (s. Νικάνωρ, Πράϋλα)

—AMPHILOCHOI: **(28)** c. 208 BC *FD* III (4) 135, 22 (s. Φυλλίδας)

—BOUTHROTOS (PRASAIBOI): **(29)** a. 163 BC *IBouthrot* 22, 20 (*SEG* XXXVIII 479) (?s. Νίκανδρος); **(30)** ~ *IBouthrot* 117, 10

—DODONA: **(31)** ?v BC *BCH* 53 (1929) p. 506; **(32)** iii BC Antoniou, *Dodone* Ab, 40

—DODONA*: **(33)** iv-iii BC *SGDI* 1587

—IOANNINA (MOD.): **(34)** iii-ii BC *Op. Ath.* 10 (1971) p. 65 no. 3 (*SEG* XXXVII 516) (s. Μενέφυλος) ?= (*37*)

—KODRION: **(35)** iii-ii BC *Iliria* 1972, p. 38 (pithos)

—KOLPAIOI: **(36)** f. ii BC Cabanes, *L'Épire* p. 580 no. 54, 6-7 (Ἀτίοχος—l. 6: f. Ἀγέλαος, Λυκόφρων)

—TALAONOI/TALAIANES: **(37)** iii-ii BC *SGDI* 1349, 8; cf. Cabanes, *L'Épire* p. 580 no. 53 (s. Μενέφυλος) ?= (*34*); **(38)** c. 200 BC *IG* IX (1)² (1) 31, 126 (f. Δόκιμος)

ILLYRIA:

—APOLLONIA: **(39)** i BC Maier 136; cf. 153 (coin) (s. Βακχίδης: pryt.)

—EPIDAMNOS-DYRRHACHION: **(40)** c. 250-50 BC ib. 170; 280; 294; Münsterberg Nachtr. p. 16 (coin) (Ceka 65; 73-6) (Ἀντίοχος—Ceka 65: money.); **(41)** hell.-imp. *IDyrrh* 158 (f. Γοργίς); **(42)** ~ ib. 260 (f. Καλλικράτης); **(43)** ~ ib. 374 (f. Στρατονίκα); **(44)** iii-iv AD ib. 60 (f. Περπέτουα)

KORINTHIA:

—KORINTH: **(45)** inc. *Corinth* VIII (1) 64; cf. *SEG* XI 69 (Ἀντίοχ[ος]); **(46)** hell.? *SB* 4375; **(47)** c. 160 AD *SEG* III 334, 40, 46, 52 (Stephanis 212) (Λ. Μάριος Ἀ.)

LAKONIA:

—SPARTA: **(48)** 338 BC Plu., *Mor.* 217 F (*RE* (19); Poralla² 102); **(49)** s. i BC *IG* V (1) 896 (tiles) (Bradford (3)); **(50)** f. ii AD *IG* V (1) 162, 7 (Bradford (5)) (I f. Ἀντίοχος II) ?= (*52*)

**(51)** ~ *IG* V (1) 162, 7 (Bradford (1)) (II s. Ἀντίοχος I) ?= (*53*); **(52)** c. 105-110 AD *IG* V (1) 97, 14; *SEG* XI 564, 8 (Bradford (4)) (I f. Ἀντίοχος II) ?= (*50*); **(53)** ~ *IG* V (1) 97, 14; *SEG* XI 564, 8 (Bradford (2)) (II s. Ἀντίοχος I) ?= (*51*)

MESSENIA: **(54)** viii BC Paus. iv 4. 4; 5. 8; *RE* (14) (s. Φίντας, f. Εὐφάης: king)

PELOPONNESE?: **(55)** ii AD *PAE* 1992, p. 72 B, 15 (I f. Ἀντίοχος II); **(56)** ~ ib. l. 15 (II s. Ἀντίοχος I)

S. ITALY (APULIA):

—CANNAE: **(57)** 355-360 AD *Epig. Rom. di Canosa* 18 (*CIL* IX 318) (Lat. Annius Antiochus)

—SIPONTUM*: **(58)** ?i BC ib. 6242; cf. Serricchio, *Iscrizioni di Siponto* 1 (Lat. T. Tremeliu(s) Antioch(us): freed.)

—VENUSIA: **(59)** ii-iii AD *GVI* 1218 (*SEG* XXX 1226) (Lat. [Anti]ochus)

—VENUSIA*: **(60)** imp. *CIL* IX 590 (Lat. L. Tullianus Antiochus: freed.)

S. ITALY (APULIA)?: **(61)** f. i BC Desy, *Timbres amphoriques* 167; 182; 241; 303 (amph.) (Lat. Antioc(hus): slave?/potter)

S. ITALY (BRUTTIUM):

—LOKROI EPIZEPHYRIOI:

——(Τιω.): **(62)** 278 BC De Franciscis 30, 2 (f. Σιμίας)

—RHEGION*: **(63)** m. vi BC Rumpf, *Chalkid. Vas.* p. 47 no. 8 (vase) (Arena, *Iscr. Sic.* III p. 105 no. 12) (her.?)

S. ITALY (CALABRIA):

—BRENTESION-BRUNDISIUM*: **(64)** i BC Desy, *Timbres amphoriques* 380-3; 869 (amph.) (slave/potter)

S. ITALY (CAMPANIA):

—ATELLA*: **(65)** imp. *CIL* X 3738 (Lat. L. Naevius Antiochus: freed.); **(66)** ~ ib. 3743 (Lat. L. Caesius Antiochus: freed.)

—DIKAIARCHIA-PUTEOLI: **(67)** imp. ib. 1577 (Lat. Iulius Antiochus)

—MISENUM*: **(68)** ?i-ii AD ib. 3582 (Lat. Cassius Antiochus)

—NEAPOLIS: **(69)** i BC-i AD *IG* XIV 761 (*INap* 89); cf. Leiwo p. 117 no. 97 (Ἀντ[ίο]χος: f. Ἀθηνοδώρα); **(70)** i BC/i AD *INap* 168, 5; cf. Leiwo p. 78 no. 23

—NOLA: **(71)** imp. *CIL* X 1329 (Lat. A. Spurius Antiochus)

—NUCERIA ALFATERNA*: **(72)** i AD *Boll. Arch.* 1-2 (1990) p. 243 (Lat. M. Nassius Antiochus: freed.)

—POMPEII: **(73)** i BC-i AD *CIL* IV 1221 (Castrèn 129. 10) (Lat. Cornelius Antio[chu]s); **(74)** ~ *CIL* IV 1427 (Lat. Antiocus); **(75)** ~ ib. 1802 (Lat. Antiocus); **(76)** ~ ib. 3645 (3272) (Lat. Antiochus); **(77)** ~ ib. 8792 (Lat. Antiochus); **(78)** ~ ib. 863 (Lat. Antiochus); **(79)** ?i AD *NScav* 1961, p. 200 no. 3 (Lat. Q. Stnippius Antiochus)

—POMPEII*: **(80)** i BC-i AD *CIL* X 1048 (Castrèn 89. 2) (Lat. M. Caledius Antiochus: freed.); **(81)** s. i BC *Impegno per Pompeii* 27 OS (Castrèn 94. 1) (Lat. A. Campius Antiochus: freed.)

—SALERNUM?: **(82)** imp. *IItal* I (1) 4 (*CIL* X 454) (Lat. M. Marci[us] Antioch[us])

—SALERNUM*: **(83)** ?i AD *IItal* I (1) 238 II, 6 (*CIL* X 557) (Lat. L. Appuleius Antiochus: freed.)

S. ITALY (CAMPANIA)*: **(84)** imp. ib. 8042. 86 (tiles) (Lat. L. Pontius Antiochus)

S. ITALY (LUCANIA):

—POSEIDONIA-PAESTUM*: **(85)** i BC-i AD Mello—Voza 14 (Lat. [L.] [Fla]vius Antio[chus]: freed.)

SICILY:

—HERBESSOS*: **(86)** imp. *Epigraphica* 51 (1989) p. 186 no. 71 (Lat. L. Clodius Antiochus)

—KAMARINA: **(87)** f. v BC Cordano, *Tessere Pubbliche* 29 (Ἀντ[ίο]χος: f. Κυλωΐδας)

—LIPARA: **(88)** iii AD *Epigraphica* 3 (1941) p. 270 no. 46 (Αὐρ. Ἀ.)

—LIPARA*: **(89)** imp.? Libertini, *Isole Eolie* p. 227 no. 57 (Κορνήλιος Ἀ.: freed.?)

—SYRACUSE: **(90)** v BC *RE* (60); *FGrH* 555 (s. Ξενοφάνης); **(91)** ?ii/iii AD *CIL* X 7130. 6 + *Epigraphica* 51 (1989) p. 184 (Lat. Roscianus Antiocus); **(92)** iii-v AD Strazzulla 251 (-ωχος); **(93)** ~ ib. 268 (Wessel 1364) (-ωχος); **(94)** ~ Ferrua, *NG* 377

TRIPHYLIA:

—LEPREON: **(95)** f. iv BC *RE* (12); cf. (6); Moretti, *Olymp.* 360

**Ἀντιπᾶς**

MESSENIA:

—PYLOS: **(1)** imp.? *Harmonia* 2 (1901) p. 202 (f. Ξοανικός)

S. ITALY (CALABRIA):

—BRENTESION-BRUNDISIUM: **(2)** imp. *NScav* 1900, p. 245 no. 2 (*Rend. Linc.* 24 (1969) p. 172 no. 4)

**Ἀντιπάτρα**

ARGOLIS:

—ARGOS*: **(1)** ii-i BC *IG* IV (1) 530, 9; cf. *BCH* 33 (1909) p. 183 n. 2 (slave/freed.?)

ARKADIA:

—STYMPHALOS: **(2)** iv-iii BC *SEG* XLII 355 (Ἀ[ν]τιπάτ[ρ]α)

EPIROS:

—BOUTHROTOS (PRASAIBOI): **(3)** a. 163 BC *IBouthrot* 14, 19; 22, 25 (*SEG* XXXVIII 471; 479); **(4)** ~ *IBouthrot* 31, 30; 32, 27 (*SEG* XXXVIII 490-1); **(5)** ~ *IBouthrot* 38, 14 (*SEG* XXXVIII 497); **(6)** ~ *IBouthrot* 47, 28; **(7)** ~ ib. 137, 9

S. ITALY (CAMPANIA):

—DIKAIARCHIA-PUTEOLI: **(8)** imp. *CIL* X 2070 (Lat. Antipatra)

**Ἀντίπατρος**

ACHAIA:

—PATRAI: **(1)** c. 100 AD *ILGR* 73 (Lat. Ti. Cl. Antipater)

AIGINA: **(2)** imp. *IG* IV (1) 20

AITOLIA:

—THERMOS*: **(3)** s. iii BC ib. IX (1)² (1) 60 III, 20

AKARNANIA:

—PALAIROS: **(4)** ii BC ib. IX (1)² (2) 451, 5 (Ἀντίπατ[ρος]: s. Ὀφέλανδρος)

—THYRREION: **(5)** ?ii-i BC *SEG* XXIX 480

ARGOLIS:

—ARGOS?: **(6)** m. iii BC Peek, *IAEpid* 42, 61 (Perlman E.3); Perlman p. 63 f. (date) (Ἀντίπα[τρος]: f. Φαντίας)

—EPIDAUROS*: **(7)** ii-i BC Peek, *NIEpid* 44

ARKADIA: **(8)** 284 BC *PEleph* 3, 2, etc.

—ALIPHEIRA: **(9)** iii BC Orlandos, *Alipheira* p. 225

—KYNAITHA: **(10)** i AD *Achaean Grave Stelai* 48 (Τι. Κλ. Ἀ.); **(11)** ~ ib. 69 (Lat. Ti. Claudius Antipater)

DALMATIA:

—ISSA:

——(Pamphyloi): **(12)** iv/iii BC Brunšmid p. 7, 25 (s. Σάλλας)

—PHAROS: **(13)** iii/ii BC *SEG* XXIII 489, 21, 32; cf. XLI 545 (s. Νικᾶς)

ELIS: **(14)** 181-185 AD *IvOl* 102, 9, 25 (Μ. Ἀντ. Ἀ.: f. Ζώσιμος)

EPIROS: **(15)** 274 BC *IG* XI (2) 199 B, 15; 287 B, 57 (s. Βάλαγρος); **(16)** ii BC Cabanes, *L'Épire* p. 590 no. 76, 8 (*SEG* XXVI 704) (Ἀντίπ[ατρος]: f. Ἀντίνους); **(17)** 136 BC Moretti, *Olymp.* 643 ?= (*19*)

—AMBRAKIA: **(18)** ii-i BC *CIG* 1800, 5 (s. Πασίων)

—BOUTHROTOS (PRASAIBOI): (**19**) a. 163 BC *IBouthrot* 9, 5, 7 (*SEG* XXXVIII 489) (s. Ἀρχίας) ?= (*17*); (**20**) ~ *IBouthrot* 19, 6 (*SEG* XXXVIII 476); (**21**) ~ *IBouthrot* 30, 37 (*SEG* XXXVIII 488) (Ἀντίπ[ατρος]); (**22**) ~ *IBouthrot* 40, 11 (*SEG* XXXVIII 499); (**23**) ~ *IBouthrot* 41, 12 (*SEG* XXXVIII 500); (**24**) ~ *IBouthrot* 101, 2 (s. Ἐπικράτης); (**25**) ~ ib. 148; (**26**) ~ ib. 153, 8 (s. —μένης)
KERKYRA: (**27**) ii-iii AD *IG* IX (1) 946 (Ἰούλ. Ἀ.)
KORINTHIA:
—KORINTH: (**28**) 181 BC *Syll*[3] 585, 215 (s. Μενέδαμος)
LAKONIA:
—SPARTA: (**29**) c. 100 AD *SEG* XI 513, 4; 515, 3 (Bradford (1)); (**30**) ii AD *SEG* XI 869 (Bradford (5)) ?= (*34*); (**31**) ii-iii AD *IG* V (1) 819 (Bradford (5)); (**32**) c. 120 AD *SEG* XI 490, 5; 544, 2 (Bradford (1)) (Γ. Ἰούλ. Ἀ.) ?= (*34*); (**33**) ?c. 140 AD *IG* V (1) 291, 3 (*Artemis Orthia* p. 322 no. 47 (date); Bradford (4)) (Ἀντίπα[τρος]); (**34**) c. 150-160 AD *IG* V (1) 53, 37 (Ἰούλ. Ἀ.) ?= (*30*) (*32*); (**35**) s. ii AD ib. 249, 1; *SEG* XI 811, 7; *BSA* 80 (1985) pp. 225; 228-9 (ident., stemma) (Bradford (2); (3)) ((Τιβ.) Κλ. Ἀ.: ?s. Τιβ. Κλ. Βρασίδας, s. Μεμμία Ἀγήτα, f. Κλ. Ἀγήτα); (**36**) c. 175-200 AD *IG* V (1) 663, 6; *SEG* XI 503, 2 (Γ. Ἰούλ. Ἀ.: s. Λυσικράτης)
S. ITALY (CAMPANIA):
—DIKAIARCHIA-PUTEOLI: (**37**) imp. *CIL* X 1577 (Lat. Antipater); (**38**) ?ii AD ib. 1571 (Lat. T. Flavius Antipater)
—HERCULANEUM: (**39**) m. i AD *PdelP* 8 (1953) p. 461 no. 50, 7; 16 (1961) p. 72 no. 102, 7 (Lat. Q. Iunius Antipater)
SICILY:
—GELA-PHINTIAS: (**40**) m. v BC Dubois, *IGDS* 144 b (vase) (Arena, *Iscr. Sic.* II 65) ([Ἀ]ντίπατρος)
—TAUROMENION: (**41**) c. 230 BC *IG* XIV 421 an. 11 (*SGDI* 5219) (f. Θεόδωρος)

**Ἄντιππος**
LAKONIA:
—SPARTA: (**1**) 421 BC Th. v 19. 2; 24 (Poralla[2] 103)

**Ἀντιρήδας**
KERKYRA: (**1**) 356-354 BC *IG* IV (1)[2] 95, 28 (Perlman E.2); Perlman p. 40 f. (date)

**Ἄντις**
ILLYRIA:
—EPIDAMNOS-DYRRHACHION: (**1**) imp. *IDyrrh* 110; cf. *BE* 1970, no. 351 (s./d. Ἐπίκαδος)

**Ἀντισθένης**
AITOLIA:
—KALLION/KALLIPOLIS: (**1**) m. ii BC *IG* IX (1)[2] (3) 639. 8, 5; *SBBerlAk* 1936, p. 371 a, 2 (*SEG* XLI 528 A) (f. Ἑλλάνικος)
ARGOLIS:
—ARGOS: (**2**) ii-i BC *Mnem*. NS 47 (1919) p. 164 no. 9, 5 (Ἀντισθέ[νης]: f. Λυσίας)
—EPIDAUROS: (**3**) c. 370 BC *IG* IV (1)[2] 102, 108; (**4**) ii-i BC ib. 11[2] 8488 (f. Ἱερώνυμος)
——Tenias: (**5**) c. 335-325 BC ib. IV (1)[2] 108, 141
—EPIDAUROS*: (**6**) c. 370-365 BC Peek, *IAEpid* 52 B, 39 (Ἀντισθ[ένης])
—TROIZEN: (**7**) imp. *IG* IV (1) 792 (f. Ἀρίστων)
LAKONIA:
—SPARTA: (**8**) 412 BC Th. viii 39; 61. 2 (Poralla[2] 104) ?= (*9*); (**9**) 398 BC X., *HG* iii 2. 6 ?= (*8*)
MESSENIA:
—MESSENE: (**10**) iii/ii BC *SEG* XXIII 228; *Klio* 52 (1970) p. 298; *SEG* XXXVII 334 (date) (s. Πολύστρατος); (**11**) ii BC *Ergon* 1995, p. 29
SICILY:
—AKRAGAS: (**12**) 406 BC D.S. xiii 84. 1, 4 (Ἀ. ὁ ἐπικαλ. Ῥόδος)

—KAMARINA: (**13**) f. v BC Cordano, *Tessere Pubbliche* 1b (Arena, *Iscr. Sic.* II 126 A) (-νες: s. Παρμένων)

**Ἀντίστιος**
ARKADIA:
—MANTINEIA-ANTIGONEIA: (**1**) ii AD *IG* V (2) 313 (Λ. Ἀ.)

**Ἀντιφάης**
ARKADIA: (**1**) 308 BC ib. 550, 3
—TEGEA:
——(Athaneatai): (**2**) m. iii BC ib. 36, 84 (f. Ἀριστοπάμων)

**Ἀντιφάνης**
ARGOLIS:
—ARGOS: (**1**) c. 435-365 BC *RE* (21); Marcadé 1 5 f. (sculptor)
—EPIDAUROS: (**2**) iv/iii BC *IG* IV (1)[2] 258 (f. Φαίνιππος)
—EPIDAUROS*: (**3**) c. 370 BC ib. 102, 301; (**4**) c. 370-365 BC Peek, *IAEpid* 52 B, 44, 57; (**5**) iv/iii BC Peek, *NIEpid* 20, 14 (*SEG* XXV 404, 11)
ARKADIA:
—MANTINEIA-ANTIGONEIA: (**6**) iv/iii BC *Thess. Mnem.* 164
—MEGALOPOLIS: (**7**) i BC-i AD? *RE* (18); *GP* 725-782
—TEGEA: (**8**) arch.? Paus. viii 48. 1; (**9**) c. 230-200 BC *BCH* 45 (1921) p. 13 II, 112
ELIS: (**10**) f. i BC *IvOl* 202; 203 (f. Φίλιστος, Θεοδότα); (**11**) ~ ib. 406, 1; (**12**) i BC/i AD *IG* XII (8) 176, 5 (f. Ἀριστοκράτης)
KORINTHIA:
—KORINTH: (**13**) m. iii BC *Corinth* VIII (3) 33 f, 6 (s. —ανδρίδας)
—SIKYON?: (**14**) iii-ii BC *IG* IV (1) 429, 8 (Stephanis 222) (s. Δάμαρχος)

**Ἀντιφανίδας**
PELOPONNESE?: (**1**) s. iii BC *IG* V (1) 1426, 18 (s. Ἀριστοκράτης)

**Ἀντίφας**
ARKADIA:
—MANTINEIA-ANTIGONEIA: (**1**) c. 300-221 BC ib. V (2) 323. 54 (tessera) (s. Τελεσῖνος)

**Ἀντιφάτας**
ACHAIA:
—PELLENE: (**1**) c. 338-300 BC *SEG* XXXII 476, 3; Roesch, *Ét. Béot.* pp. 271-2 (date); cf. *SEG* XXXVIII 385 (f. Οἰκλῆς)
KORINTHIA:
—KORINTH: (**2**) c. 570-550 BC Amyx 104 A. 2 (vase) (Lorber 92) (her.?)

**Ἀντίφιλος**
AITOLIA: (**1**) iii/ii BC *IG* IX (1) 272, 3 (s. Θρασυμήδης)
—ORIBATOI: (**2**) m. ii BC ib. IX (1)[2] (1) 137, 25
ARGOLIS:
—EPIDAUROS: (**3**) iv BC *CEG* II 818
—EPIDAUROS*: (**4**) c. 370 BC *IG* IV (1)[2] 102, 250
EPIROS:
—ARGOS (AMPHILOCH.): (**5**) iv BC *BMC Thessaly* p. 172 no. 2; *NZ* 10 (1878) p. 94 no. 53 (coins) (Ἀντίφι(λος))
PELOPONNESE: (**6**) c. 192 BC *SEG* XIII 327, 14 (s. Διοκκῆς)
SICILY:
—SYRACUSE?: (**7**) ?s. vi BC *RE* (5)

**Ἀντιφῶν**
EPIROS:
—BOUTHROTOS (PRASAIBOI): (**1**) a. 163 BC *IBouthrot* 25, 15; 30, 48; cf. *SEG* XXXVIII 483; 499, 27; (**2**) ~ *IBouthrot* 58, 7, 8, 10

(*SEG* XXXVIII 509); *IBouthrot* 105, 4-5 (s. Βοΐσκος, f. Κλῆτις, Λέαινα) ?= (*3*)
——Bouthrotioi: (**3**) a. 163 BC ib. 115, 14; 118, 6 (s. Βοΐσκος) ?= (*2*)
MESSENIA:
—MESSENE: (**4**) c. 225 BC *SEG* XI 414, 17 (Perlman E.5) ([Ἀν]τιφῶν: s. Πασιφάνης)

**Ἀντίων**
ARGOLIS:
—ARGOS: (**1**) 336-324 BC *CID* II 76 II, 23; 95, [12]; 97, 23; 102 II B, 28; 120 A, 1; 121 III, 14 (f. Πολυκράτης); (**2**) f. iii BC ib. 122 I, 9 (s. Πολυκράτης)
——(Pamphyloi-Olisseidai): (**3**) c. 400 BC *SEG* XXIX 361, 10 (-ōν)

**Ἀντίωρος**
LAKONIA:
—SPARTA: (**1**) her. Plu., *Lyc.* 31 (Poralla[2] 105) (s. Λυκοῦργος: dub.)

**Ἄντοχος**
AITOLIA: (**1**) s. iii BC *FD* III (4) 166 a, 1 (*IG* IX (1)[2] (1) 182 b)
—THERMOS*: (**2**) hell. ib. 85. 7 (tile)
AKARNANIA:
—THYRREION: (**3**) ii BC ib. IX (1)[2] (2) 249, 2 (s. Νικίας)

**Ἀντωνία**
ARKADIA:
—TEGEA: (**1**) imp. ib. V (2) 218
ILLYRIA:
—APOLLONIA: (**2**) imp. *IApoll* 253
SICILY:
—MOTYKA (NR.): (**3**) imp. *IG* XIV 243 (-νεία)

**Ἀντωνῖνος**
ARGOLIS:
—EPIDAUROS: (**1**) ii-iii AD *PAE* 1990, p. 47 (-νεῖ-)
SICILY:
—AKRAI?: (**2**) ?ii-iii AD *IG* XIV 2413. 17, 3 (-νεῖ-)
—SYRACUSE: (**3**) iii-iv AD *SEG* XVIII 402; (**4**) iii-v AD *IG* XIV 75 (Strazzulla 16; Wessel 1378)

**Ἀντώνιος**
ARGOLIS:
—ARGOS: (**1**) i BC-i AD *RE* (10) ?= (Ἀριστοκράτης (*14*)); (**2**) f. i AD *GP* 3584 tit.
KORINTHIA:
—KORINTH: (**3**) f. ii AD *Ag.* VII p. 93 no. 255; *SEG* XXVII 35. 4 (lamps)

**Ἀντῶνις**
ARKADIA:
—TEGEA: (**1**) ii AD *IG* V (2) 55, 78 (s. Ἡρακλᾶς)
S. ITALY (CAMPANIA):
—NEAPOLIS: (**2**) ii-iii AD ib. XIV 767 (*INap* 92); cf. Leiwo p. 108 no. 73 (Ἀντώνι (voc.))

**Ἀνυίλας**
LAKONIA:
—SPARTA: (**1**) c. 25-1 BC *IG* V (1) 210, 33; Masson, *OGS* 2 p. 510 (name) (Bradford (-)) ([Ἀ]νυίλας, Ἀνυΐλας?—Masson: s. Ἀριστομένης)

**Ἄνυστις**
LAKONIA: (**1**) s. iv BC Plin., *NH* vii 84; Masson, *OGS* 2 p. 510 (name) (Poralla[2] 106) (Lat. Anystis)

**Ἀνύτη**
ARKADIA:
—TEGEA: (**1**) f. iii BC *RE* (-); *HE* 664-759

**Ἀξιανός**
S. ITALY: (**1**) imp. *CIL* X 8059. 192 (seal) (Lat. L. Herennius Axianus)

**Ἀξιοθέα**
ARGOLIS:
—PHLEIOUS: (**1**) iv BC *RE* (2)

**Ἀξιόνικος**
ACHAIA:
—PELLENE: (1) c. 405 BC Paus. x 9. 10; cf. CEG II 819

**Ἀξιόπιστος**
ARKADIA:
—MEGALOPOLIS: (1) m. iii BC Peek, IAEpid 42, 3 (Perlman E.3); Perlman p. 63 f. (date) ([Ἀξι]όπιστος: s. Πολίας)
S. ITALY (BRUTTIUM):
—LOKROI EPIZEPHYRIOI?: (2) iii/ii BC RE (-) (or Korinthia Sikyon?)

**Ἄξιος**
S. ITALY (CAMPANIA):
—DIKAIARCHIA-PUTEOLI: (1) imp. CIL x 2871 (Lat. Pomponius Axius)

**Ἀξίοχος**
AITOLIA: (1) 224 or 221 BC SGDI 2524, 4; Nachtergael, Les Galates 64, 3
AKARNANIA:
—KORONTA: (2) 356-354 BC IG IV (1)² 95, 12 (Perlman E.2); Perlman p. 40 f. (date)
—PALAIROS: (3) ?s. iv BC IG IX (1)² (2) 465
ARGOLIS:
—EPIDAUROS:
——Isarnia: (4) m. iii BC ib. IV (1)² 96, 36, 38 (Perlman E.3); Perlman p. 63 f. (date)
—EPIDAUROS*: (5) c. 370 BC IG IV (1)² 102, 56
EPIROS:
—AMBRAKIA: (6) 238-168 BC SNG Cop. Epirus–Acarnania 36; SNG Evelpidis II 1782 (coins)
S. ITALY (CAMPANIA):
—POMPEII: (7) 57 AD CIL IV 3340. 40, 19, 24; 73, 8; x 8058. 68 (seal) (Castrèn 314. 2) (Lat. Sex. Pompeius Axiochus)

**Ἀξίωμα**
SICILY:
—LIPARA: (1) hell.-imp. NScav 1929, p. 71 fig. 30

**Ἀπάλη**
S. ITALY (CAMPANIA):
—NUCERIA ALFATERNA: (1) s. i BC Riv. Stud. Pomp. 3 (1989) p. 22 (Lat. Egnatia Apal[e])

**Ἀπάμα**
ARKADIA:
—MEGALOPOLIS: (1) iii/ii BC RE (6) (d. Ἀλέξανδρος (Macedon))

**Ἀπαρκέας**
ILLYRIA: (1) byz.? AR 1983-4, p. 116 (n. pr.?)

**Ἀπατάριον**
LAKONIA:
—SPARTA: (1) i/ii AD IG v (1) 607, 27; BSA 75 (1980) pp. 214-19 (ident., stemma) (Bradford (-)) (Ἰουλ. Ἀ.: ?m. Τιβ. Κλ. Δαμοκράτης, Τιβ. Κλ. Σιμήδης)

**Ἀπάτη**
AIGINA: (1) imp. IG IV (1) 78 (d. Ἐπίκτησις)
S. ITALY (APULIA):
—LUCERIA: (2) ?i AD CIL IX 861 (Lat. Iulia Apate: m. Λαμύρα)
S. ITALY (CALABRIA):
—HYRIA: (3) i/ii AD Misc. Gr. Rom. 3 p. 220 (Lat. Avia Apate: m. C. Avius Rufus)
S. ITALY (CAMPANIA):
—DIKAIARCHIA-PUTEOLI: (4) imp. CIL x 2208 (Lat. Apate); (5) ?i-ii AD ib. 2300 (Lat. Clodia Apate)

**Ἀπελλαῖος**
ELIS: (1) 540 BC Moretti, Olymp. 114

**Ἀπελλάκων**
LAKONIA:
—SPARTA: (1) m. ii AD IG v (1) 37, 12 (Bradford (-)) (f. Καλλικράτης)

**Ἀπελλᾶς**
EPIROS:
—KASSOPE: (1) c. 342-325 BC BMC Thessaly p. 99 no. 13; Franke, Münz. v. Epirus p. 75 II ser. 21 (coin) (Ἀπελλᾶ(s))
ILLYRIA:
—EPIDAMNOS-DYRRHACHION: (2) hell.-imp. IDyrrh 113 (f. Ἀπολλώνιος)
KORINTHIA:
—KORINTH: (3) ii-iii AD SEG XI 132, 3; 135 (s. Νήψις)
S. ITALY (CAMPANIA):
—AEQUANA*: (4) i AD NScav 1896, p. 332 (Lat. Apella: f. Ἄρατος: imp. freed.)
—SALERNUM: (5) imp. IItal I (1) 87 (CIL x 638) (Lat. A. Servilius Apellas)

**Ἀπελλέας**
ARGOLIS:
—TROIZEN*: (1) iv BC IG IV (1) 823, 74
ILLYRIA:
—APOLLONIA:
——(Litai): (2) iii BC Robert, Hell. 10 p. 283 ff.; cf. CRAI 1991, p. 197 ff.; L'Illyrie mérid. 2 p. 204 f. (s. Ἀλκαῖος)
—EPIDAMNOS-DYRRHACHION: (3) c. 200-172 BC RA 1948, p. 826 no. 1, 5 (IDyrrh 523) (f. Ἀνθίσκος)
ITHAKE: (4) hell. Rev. Épig. 1 (1913) p. 47 no. 1

**Ἀπελλῆς**
ACHAIA: (1) 146 BC IG IV (1)² 28, 113 (s. Εὐάλκης: synoikos)
AIGINA: (2) m. ii BC ib. II² 981, 7 (f. [..]ήσιππος)
ARGOLIS:
—HERMIONE: (3) iii-ii BC ib. IV (1) 679, 22, 35 (Perlman H.3)
—TROIZEN: (4) imp. IG IV (1) 836 B, 5; (5) f. ii AD ib. 758, 17 (s. Σωσίβιος)
KORINTHIA:
—KORINTH?: (6) iii BC NScav 1891, p. 383 (or Kerkyra?)
S. ITALY (APULIA):
—LUCERIA: (7) imp. CIL IX 834 (Lat. Apelles)
S. ITALY (CALABRIA):
—BRENTESION-BRUNDISIUM*: (8) i BC Desy, Timbres amphoriques 34; 389-99; 697-8; 1030; 1078; 1099; 1105 (amph.) (Ἀ., Ἀπηλλῆς, Ἀπελέας—var. Lat. Apellas, Apelaes, Apellais)
S. ITALY (CAMPANIA):
—HERCULANEUM*: (9) i BC-i AD CIL IV 10677-8 (Lat. Apelles: imp. slave?); (10) ~ ib. x 1403 g III, 62 (Lat. C. Lusius Apelles: freed.)
S. ITALY (LUCANIA):
—HERAKLEIA: (11) c. 125-100 BC EAD xxx 297 (s. Θεμίσων)
SICILY:
—SYRACUSE: (12) 453 BC D.S. xi 88. 5

**Ἀπελλίας**
ARKADIA:
—HERAIA: (1) m. iii BC SEG XI 413, 28 (Perlman E.4) (s. Λάνομος)

**Ἀπέλλικος**
ILLYRIA:
—APOLLONIA: (1) c. 250-50 BC NZ 20 (1927) p. 54 (coin) (Ceka 53) (pryt.)

**Ἄπελλις**
ARKADIA:
—MEGALOPOLIS: (1) s. ii BC IG v (2) 438, 18 (f. Ἄψιππος); (2) ~ ib. l. 19 (s. Ἄψιππος)
SICILY:
—AKRAI: (3) ii BC Akrai p. 154 no. 3, 12 (?s. Διονύσιος)
——(Ἀν.): (4) ii BC ib. l. 7 (Ἀπελ[λ]ις: s. Ἀρτεμᾶς)
—GELA-PHINTIAS?: (5) f. v BC Dubois, IGDS 134 a, 2 (Arena, Iscr. Sic. II 80) (Ἀπελ(λ)ις); (6) ~ Dubois, IGDS 134 b, 1, 7 (Arena, Iscr. Sic. II 47)

**Ἀπελλίχος**
AKARNANIA:
—LEKKA (MOD.): (1) hell.? IG IX (1)² (2) 240
ARKADIA:
—ALIPHEIRA: (2) iii BC EILakArk 11 = Orlandos, Alipheira p. 218 no. 3 (s. Τελέας); (3) ?273 BC SEG XXV 447, 9 (IPArk 24); Chiron 3 (1973) pp. 85-93 (date) (Ἀπέλ(λ)ιχος)
—MEGALOPOLIS: (4) iv/iii BC IG v (2) 468 (terracotta) (s. Πολεμαρχίδας)
SICILY:
—SEGESTA: (5) iv/iii BC SEG XXX 1119, 7 (Dubois, IGDS 206) (s. Ἀλείδας)

**Ἀπελλίων**
ARGOLIS:
—ARGOS: (1) iii BC IG IV (1) 772, 3; IV (1)² 228, 1; 698 (f. Τόρων)
ARKADIA:
—KLEITOR: (2) i AD ib. v (2) 374
MESSENIA:
—MESSENE: (3) 80 AD ib. v (1) 1468, 6; cf. SEG XL 366 (s. Φίλιππος)
SICILY:
—KAMARINA: (4) f. v BC Cordano, Tessere Pubbliche 55 ([Ἀπ]ελλίōν: f. Σικανός)

**Ἀπελλόδωρος**
KERKYRA: (1) c. 500 BC SEG XXX 521 + L'Illyrie mérid. 2 p. 205 (Ἀπελλόδōρο[s])

**Ἀπέλλων**
ILLYRIA:
—APOLLONIA?: (1) imp. IApoll 255 (Ἀπ[έλ]λων, Ἀπ[όλ]λων—ed.: f. —ερήν)
PELOPONNESE?: (2) s. iii BC SEG XXV 449, 45 (IPArk 26) (Ἀπέλλω[ν])

**Ἄπελος**
SICILY:
—SELINOUS: (1) f. v BC Dubois, IGDS 38, 1, 16 (Arena, Iscr. Sic. I 63) (s. Λυκῖνος) ?= (2); (2) ~ Dubois, IGDS 38, 6 (Arena, Iscr. Sic. I 63) ?= (1); (3) ~ Dubois, IGDS 38, 18 (Arena, Iscr. Sic. I 63) (s. Φοῖνιξ)

**Ἀπεταῖος**
ARGOLIS:
—NEMEA*: (1) f. v BC SEG XXIX 353 c

**Ἀπῆγα**
LAKONIA:
—SPARTA: (1) iii/ii BC Plb. xiii 7. 6 (Bradford (-)); Anz. Wien 58 (1921) pp. 70-3 (ident.) (queen) ?= (Ἀπία (2))

**Ἀπήμαντος**
MESSENIA:
—THOURIA: (1) f. ii BC SEG XI 972, 43-4 (f. —ις)
S. ITALY (BRUTTIUM):
—LOKROI EPIZEPHYRIOI:
——(Λακ.): (2) iv/iii BC De Franciscis 27, 7 (f. Σωσικράτης)
—RHEGION: (3) ii BC Mus. Naz. Reggio p. 159 no. 28 (Ἀπέ-)

**Ἀπήμων**
MESSENIA:
—THOURIA: (1) f. ii BC SEG XI 972, 35 (f. Ἀρίστιππος)

**Ἀπία**
AKARNANIA:
—PALAIROS: (1) s. iii BC IG IX (1)² (2) 521 (Ἀπιας (nom./gen.?))

**Ἀπιάδας**

ARGOLIS:
—ARGOS: (2) s. iii BC ib. IV (1)² 621 A (d. Ἀρίστιππος) ?= (Ἀπῆγα (1))
SICILY:
—AKRAI: (3) 35 AD SEG XLII 833, 13

**Ἀπιάδας**
S. ITALY (BRUTTIUM):
—LOKROI EPIZEPHYRIOI:
——(Δυσ.): (1) iv/iii BC De Franciscis 32, 3 (s. Ἀριστείδας)

**Ἄπιος**
S. ITALY (BRUTTIUM):
—LOKROI EPIZEPHYRIOI:
——(Ἀγκ.): (1) iv/iii BC ib. 27, 6 (f. Λεωνίδας)

**Ἀπίων**
S. ITALY (CAMPANIA):
—DIKAIARCHIA-PUTEOLI: (1) ii AD Atti Acc. Arch. Napoli 41 (1924) pp. 43-79

**Ἄπλα**
ELIS: (1) i/ii AD IvOl 470, 14 (Ἰουλ. Ἄ.: ?d. Γ. Ἰούλ. Σώστρατος, m. Π. Μέμμιος Φιλόδαμος)

**Ἄπλος**
S. ITALY (CAMPANIA):
—DIKAIARCHIA-PUTEOLI: (1) imp. IG XIV 859, 8 (Audollent, Defix. Tab. 208)
—POMPEII: (2) i BC-i AD Neue Forsch. in Pompeji p. 266 no. 70 (Lat. Aplus)

**Ἀποκίας**
AITOLIA: (1) ?271 BC Syll³ 419, 3

**Ἀπολαύστη**
SICILY:
—THERMAI HIMERAIAI: (1) i-ii AD CIL X 7428 (ILat. Term. Imer. 127) (Lat. Apolauste: m. Τέχνη)

**Ἀπόλαυστος**
S. ITALY (APULIA):
—TEANUM APULUM: (1) ?ii AD CIL IX 709 (Teanum Apulum p. 152 no. 3a) (or S. Italy (Apulia) Luceria: Lat. M. Ulpius Apolaustus)
S. ITALY (CAMPANIA):
—DIKAIARCHIA-PUTEOLI: (2) imp. CIL X 1886 (Lat. Sex. Patulcius Apolaustus)
—DIKAIARCHIA-PUTEOLI*: (3) imp. ib. 3062 (Lat. L. Plotius Apolaustus: s. Εὐπραξία: freed.)
—NEAPOLIS: (4) 194 AD INap 44 col. I, 3 (M. Αὐρ. Ἀ. νεώτ.)
—SARNUM: (5) s. i AD NScav 1932, p. 319 (Sinn, Stadtröm. Marmorurnen 193) (Lat. Sex. Avonius A[polau]stus)

**Ἀπολλᾶς**
ACHAIA:
—TRITAIA: (1) ii-i BC Achaean Grave Stelai 72 (f. Σωτηρίχα)
AIGINA?: (2) f. v BC LSAG² p. 113 no. 22
ARGOLIS:
—EPIDAUROS: (3) ?iii AD Peek, NIEpid 108 ([Ἀπο]λλᾶς: s. Ἀπολλώνιος)
ARKADIA:
—PHENEOS: (4) 145-125 BC Nachtergael, Les Galates 80, 15 (Stephanis 237); (5) ii/i BC IG IV (1)² 100, 3 (Stephanis 238) ([Ἀπ]ολλᾶς: s. Βίων)
—TEGEA: (6) 165 AD IG V (2) 50, 38 (f. Ἀφροδᾶς)
——(Krariotai): (7) f. iii BC ib. 36, 37 ([Ἀπο]λλᾶς: s. Πυθάγγελος)
ILLYRIA:
—APOLLONIA: (8) i BC IApoll Ref. Bibl. n. 50 (coin)
KORINTHIA:
—KORINTH?: (9) iii BC IG IV (1)² 97, 17 (Ἀπολλ[ᾶς])

—SIKYON: (10) c. 225-200 BC SEG XIX 80, 22 (s. Θαρρύνων, f. Θαρρύνων, Ἀγαμήδης)

**Ἀπολλινάριος**
S. ITALY (CAMPANIA):
—KYME: (1) imp. CIL X 3684 (Lat. Apollinarius)

**Ἀπολλινάρις**
EPIROS:
—NIKOPOLIS: (1) 148 AD ILS 2104 (Sarikakis 6) (Lat. P. Aelius Apollin(aris))
S. ITALY (APULIA):
—CANUSIUM: (2) 223 AD Epig. Rom. di Canosa 35 II, 38 (CIL IX 338) (Lat. L. Triccius Apollinaris); (3) ~ Epig. Rom. di Canosa 35 IV, 26 (CIL IX 338) (Lat. L. Triccius Apollinaris iun(ior))
—LUCERIA: (4) imp. ib. 815 (Lat. Apollinaris)
S. ITALY (CAMPANIA):
—DIKAIARCHIA-PUTEOLI: (5) imp. ib. X 2087 (Lat. Apollinaris); (6) ~ ib. 2207 (Lat. Apollinaris)
—DIKAIARCHIA-PUTEOLI*: (7) imp. ib. 3110 (Lat. [V]icrius Apollinaris: freed.)
—MISENUM*: (8) imp. ib. 3523 (Lat. L. Iulius Apollinaris); (9) ~ ib. 3533 (Lat. C. Arris Apollinaris: f. Domitius); (10) ~ ib. 3595 (Lat. Iulius Apollinaris); (11) ~ ib. 3635 (Lat. Iulius Apollinaris); (12) ~ ib. 3651 (Lat. Valerius Apollinaris: freed.); (13) ~ ib. 8374 (Lat. Q. Mettius Apollinaris); (14) ~ ib. (Lat. C. Maximius Apollinaris); (15) ?i-ii AD ib. 3596 (Lat. Iulius Apollinaris: f. Σεραπιάς)
—NEAPOLIS: (16) 71 AD INap 84 col. I, 5 (Ἰουλ. Ἄ.)
—SURRENTUM: (17) ?i/ii AD Cinquant' Anni Lic. Class. p. 280 no. 1 (Lat. T. Flavius Apollinaris)

**Ἀπολλογένης**
ARKADIA: (1) ?255 BC Nachtergael, Les Galates 8, 51 (Stephanis 239) (s. Ὀρθαγόρας)
KORINTHIA:
—KORINTH: (2) byz. Thphyl., Q. Nat. p. 17 (dub.)

**Ἀπολλόδοτος**
KERKYRA: (1) ?ii BC IG IX (1) 708 (f. Ἀπολλόδωρος)
KORINTHIA:
—KORINTH: (2) m. ii AD Corinth VIII (3) 170, [9]; 226, 6 (Π. Αἴλ. Ἄ.: f. Π. Αἴλ. Σῶπις)
—OINOE: (3) ?iv BC IG IV (1) 1561 (fals.?)
SICILY:
—KAMARINA: (4) iv/iii BC Dubois, IGDS 122, 5 (Cordano, 'Camarina VII' 73) (Ἀπολλόδο[τ]ος: s. Ἀριστόμαχος)
—SYRACUSE: (5) i BC-i AD? IG XIV 13 (Sic. Gymn. 16 (1963) p. 59) (s. Λεύκιος)

**Ἀπολλόδωρος**
ACHAIA: (1) ii BC IG XII (9) 1127 (s. Λέων); (2) 146 BC ib. IV (1)² 28, 95 (s. Δωρόθεος: synoikos); (3) ~ ib. l. 115 (f. Εὔπορος: synoikos); (4) ~ ib. l. 124 (s. Γαλάτας: synoikos)
AIGINA: (5) ?i BC Alt-Ägina I (2) p. 44 no. 10 (I f. Ἀπολλόδωρος II); (6) ~ ib. (II s. Ἀπολλόδωρος I)
AITOLIA:
—THERMOS*: (7) s. iii BC IG IX (1)² (1) 60 VII, 9
AKARNANIA: (8) iii BC Breccia, Iscriz. 293 (f. Μενέμαχος)
ARGOLIS:
—ARGOS: (9) ii BC SEG XLII 279, 3 (Ἀπολλόδ[ωρος]); (10) 105 BC JÖAI 14 (1911) Beibl. p. 146 no. 4, 10 (f. Φιλαγόρας)
—ARGOS*: (11) ii BC SEG XLII 279, 17 (f. Θεανώ: katoikos)

—EPIDAUROS: (12) i-ii AD IG IV (1)² 486 (s. Ταυρίων)
—EPIDAUROS*: (13) c. 370 BC ib. 102, 226, 296
—HERMIONE: (14) i BC-i AD? ib. IV (1) 730 II, 4 (s. Δα.ο.μου (gen.))
—METHANA-ARSINOE: (15) i BC ib. 853, 4 (Ἀπολλόδωρ[ος])
—TROIZEN: (16) c. 405 BC FD III (1) 64; Paus. x 9. 10; cf. CEG II 819 (s. Καλλιφῶν); (17) iii BC IG IV (1) 772, 1 (f. Εὐτυχίς); (18) ~ ib. l. 1 (Ἀπ[ολ]λόδωρος: s. Ἀθανάδας, f. Δαμοσθένεια); (19) ~ ib. 824, 4 (s. Ἀθανάδας)
ARKADIA: (20) iii BC BSAAlex 15 (1914) p. 89 (s. Λέων)
—MEGALOPOLIS: (21) m. iv BC SEG XX 716, 21 (Suppl. Cir. 103)
—ORCHOMENOS: (22) ?ii BC IG V (2) 345, 11 (Ἀπολλόδω[ρος]: date—LGPN)
DALMATIA:
—ISSA:
——(Dymanes): (23) iv/iii BC Brunšmid p. 9, 51
——(Hylleis): (24) iv/iii BC ib. p. 8, 38 (s. Ποσειδαῖος)
EPIROS:
—AMBRAKIA: (25) hell.? BCH 17 (1893) p. 632 no. 1 (-ολό-); (26) s. iii BC SEG XVII 307 a (f. Λῆνα)
—BOUTHROTOS (PRASAIBOI):
——Bouthrotioi: (27) f. ii BC IBouthrot 1, 10 (f. Ἀρχέδαμος); (28) a. 163 BC ib. 120, 9 (s. Ἀριστοκλῆς)
—DODONA*: (29) iv-iii BC Carapanos, Dodone p. 111 no. 6 (tile)
ILLYRIA:
—APOLLONIA: (30) imp. IApoll 52
KERKYRA: (31) ?iii-ii BC IG IX (1) 749-51; PAE 1966, p. 87; SEG XXXIX 488 (tiles); (32) ?ii BC IG IX (1) 708 (s. Ἀπολλόδοτος); (33) ?i AD Diels, DG p. 383, 24; cf. Clem. Al., Strom. v 48. 4 n. ad loc.
KORINTHIA:
—KORINTH: (34) iii/ii BC Hesp. 41 (1972) p. 200 no. 2, 2; (35) c. 221 BC IG IV (1)² 42, 24 (f. Ὀλύμπιχος); (36) i BC AD 22 (1967) Chron. p. 538 ([Ἀ]πολλόδωρο[ς])
—SIKYON: (37) c. 100-90 BC SEG XXXIII 290 A, 17; BSA 70 (1975) pp. 129-31 (date); cf. Stephanis 272 (f. Ἀπολλώνιος)
LEUKAS: (38) hell.? IG IX (1) 555
MESSENIA:
—MESSENE: (39) s. ii BC SEG XLI 341, 11 (f. Κάλλων)
—THOURIA: (40) f. ii BC ib. XI 972, 97 (s. Σάτυρος)
PELOPONNESE: (41) c. 230-200 BC BCH 45 (1921) p. 11 II, 33 (s. Ṃ—ος: reading—Oulhen)
S. ITALY: (42) s. iv BC Boston Bronzes 612 (bronze); SEG XXX 1149 bis (date); Misc. Etrusco-Italica 1 p. 196 no. A8 (Ἀπολλό(δ)ωρος)
S. ITALY (CALABRIA):
—BRENTESION-BRUNDISIUM?: (43) i BC Desy, Timbres amphoriques 1005 (amph.) (Lat. Apolod(orus): slave?/potter)
—TARAS-TARENTUM: (44) hell. RE (70) (doctor)
S. ITALY (CAMPANIA):
—FRATTE DI SALERNO (MOD.): (45) f. v BC SEG XXXVII 817 A (vase) (Arena, Iscr. Sic. IV 33) (-δο-)
—KYME: (46) ii/iii AD Clem. Al., Strom. xvi 79. 3
—NEAPOLIS: (47) i BC/i AD INap 93; cf. Leiwo p. 74 no. 17 (s. Μᾶμος)
—POMPEII: (48) i BC-i AD CIL IV 2462 (-πολό-)
S. ITALY (LUCANIA):
—HYELE-VELIA: (49) ii/i BC ID 2631, 17 (s. Διονύσιος); (50) imp. PdelP 21 (1966) p. 336 no. 3 (f. Ὄνησος)

—PADULA (MOD.): (**51**) vi/v BC *Apollo* 9 (1993) pp. 5-6 (Arena, *Iscr. Sic.* IV 32) (*Δυ.* Ἀπολλόδορος)

SICILY: (**52**) m. i BC *RE* Supplbd. 3 (26a) (*PP* 14586)

—AGYRION: (**53**) f. i BC Cic., *In Verr.* II iii 74; *In Verr.* II iv 50 (Lat. Apollodorus Pyragrus)

—AKRAI: (**54**) ?iii BC *SGDI* 3240, 3 (*Akrai* p. 156 no. 7) (f. Ἡρακλείδας); (**55**) iii-ii BC *SGDI* 3242, 3 (*Akrai* p. 157 no. 8) (s. Νυμφόδωρος)

—GELA-PHINTIAS: (**56**) s. iv BC Peek, *IAEpid* 41, 85-6 (Perlman E.2); Perlman pp. 46-9 (date) (Ἀπολλών[ι]ος—Perlman); (**57**) iv/iii BC *PCG* 2 pp. 502 ff.; *RE* (57) + Supplbd. 1 (*PA* 1383)

—HALAISA: (**58**) f. i BC Cic., *In Verr.* II ii 19 (*RE* (47)) (Lat. Apollodorus Laphiro)

——(Σαλ.): (**59**) ii-i BC *SEG* XXXVII 759 (f. Λαπίρων)

—HERAKLEIA MINOA?: (**60**) iii BC ib. IX 821 (s. Ἱκέτας)

—IAITON: (**61**) iv BC ib. XXXIV 937 (pithos)

—KALE AKTE: (**62**) i BC *IG* II² 10291 (f. Αἰσχύλος)

—LIPARA: (**63**) imp.? *BTCGI* 9 p. 92

—MENAI: (**64**) hell. *Riv. Stor. Antica* 5 (1900-1) p. 57 no. 35 (f. Θεόδωρος)

—MORGANTINA: (**65**) iv/iii BC *SEG* XXXIX 1013, 6 (-λί-: s. Δράκων)

—SYRACUSE: (**66**) ?137 BC *SGDI* 2098, 4 (s. Φίλιππος)

—SYRACUSE?:

——(Φελ.): (**67**) hell. Manganaro, *PdelP* forthcoming no. 4 V, 7 (s. Νεμήνιος)

——(Κρα.): (**68**) hell. ib. no. 4 I, 13 (f. Ἀριστόξενος)

—TAUROMENION: (**69**) c. 235 BC *IG* XIV 421 an. 6 (*SGDI* 5219) (f. Ἐράτων); (**70**) c. 217 BC *IG* XIV 421 an. 24 (*SGDI* 5219); (**71**) c. 212 BC *IG* XIV 421 an. 29 (*SGDI* 5219); (**72**) c. 207 BC *IG* XIV 421 an. 34 (*SGDI* 5219) (s. Σωσιφάνης); (**73**) c. 201 BC *IG* XIV 421 an. 40 (*SGDI* 5219); (**74**) c. 197 BC *IG* XIV 421 an. 44 (*SGDI* 5219) (Ἀπολλόδ[ωρος]: s. Νυμφόδωρος); (**75**) c. 192 BC *IG* XIV 421 an. 49 (*SGDI* 5219) (f. Πολέμαρχος); (**76**) c. 184-152 BC *IG* XIV 421 an. 57; 421 an. 89 (*SGDI* 5219); *IGSI* 4 III (IV), 43 an. 91 (s. Ἐράτων, f. Ἐράτων); (**77**) c. 182 BC *IG* XIV 421 an. 59 (*SGDI* 5219) (s. Ἀρτεμίδωρος) ?= (79); (**78**) c. 181-161 BC *IG* XIV 421 an. 60; 421 an. 80 (*SGDI* 5219) (f. Φρῦνις); (**79**) c. 169 BC *IG* XIV 421 an. 72 (*SGDI* 5219) (f. Ἀρτεμίδωρος) ?= (77); (**80**) c. 163 BC *IG* XIV 421 an. 78 (*SGDI* 5219) (f. Σώπατρος); (**81**) c. 154-140 BC *IG* XIV 421 an. 87; 421 an. 101 (*SGDI* 5219); *IGSI* 4 III (IV), 42 an. 91 (s. Ἀρτεμίδωρος); (**82**) c. 151-149 BC *IG* XIV 421 an. 90 (*SGDI* 5219); *IGSI* 4 III (IV), 50 an. 92 (s. Φρῦνις); (**83**) c. 149 BC ib. l. 50 an. 92 (f. Ἡράκλητος); (**84**) ?ii/i BC *IG* XIV 421 D an. 1 (*SGDI* 5219) (s. Νεμήνιος)

——(Ἀλκ.): (**85**) ?ii/i BC *IG* XIV 421 D an. 13 (*SGDI* 5219) (s. Μενεκράτης)

——(Ἀρεθ.): (**86**) ?ii/i BC *IG* XIV 421 D an. 4 (*SGDI* 5219); *IGSI* 12 I, 1 (I f. Ἀπολλόδωρος II); (**87**) ~ *IG* XIV 421 D an. 4 (*SGDI* 5219); *IGSI* 12 I, 1 (II s. Ἀπολλόδωρος I); (**88**) ~ *IG* XIV 421 D an. 10 (*SGDI* 5219) (f. Διονύσιος); (**89**) ~ *IG* XIV 421 D an. 12 (*SGDI* 5219) (f. Ἀρτεμίδωρος)

——(Δαμ.): (**90**) ?ii/i BC *IGSI* 4 III (IV), 138 D an. 8 (s. Φρῦνις)

——(Πιπρε.): (**91**) ii/i BC ib. 12 II, 1 (f. Ἡράκλητος)

—THERMAI HIMERAIAI: (**92**) ?ii/i BC *SGDI* 3248; cf. *Kokalos* 20 (1974) p. 219 no. 1 (s. Φάλακρος)

—ZANKLE-MESSANA: (**93**) ?ii BC *IG* XIV 401, 11 (s. Ἀρχέδαμος)

**Ἀπολλόθεμις**

AIGINA: (**1**) hell. ib. IV (1) 152 (f. Ῥοδοκλέα)

**Ἀπολλοκράτης**

SICILY:

—SYRACUSE: (**1**) m. iv BC *RE* (-); cf. Plu., *Mor.* 559 E; Beloch, *GG* III (2) pp. 102-7 (s. Διονύσιος, Σωφροσύνα)

**Ἀπολλοῦς**

ARKADIA:

—TEGEA: (**1**) ii AD *IG* V (2) 54, 18

**Ἀπολλοφάνης**

ACHAIA:

—DYME*: (**1**) c. 219 BC *SGDI* 1612, 76 (*Tyche* 5 (1990) p. 124) (f. Δαμάτριος)

ARGOLIS:

—EPIDAUROS: (**2**) imp. Peek, *NIEpid* 61, 3-4 ([Ἀπ]ολλοφάνης); (**3**) 111 AD *SEG* XXXIX 358, 10 (f. Σωτήριχος)

ARKADIA: (**4**) ?a. 370 BC Paus. ii 26. 7

—MEGALOPOLIS: (**5**) ?i BC *IG* V (2) 481

ELIS: (**6**) f. ii AD *IvOl* 92, 9, 21 (s. Ἀρίστων, ?f. Ἐπιτυχίων); (**7**) 181-185 AD ib. 102, 5 ([Τ.] [Φ]λ. Ἀ.: Χ.)

EPIROS:

—AMBRAKIA: (**8**) ii-i BC *CIG* 1800, 6 (f. Εὔνους)

—BOUTHROTOS (PRASAIBOI): (**9**) a. 163 BC *IBouthrot* 45, 7 (f. Σωτήριχος)

KORINTHIA:

—KORINTH: (**10**) i/ii AD *Ag.* VII p. 91 no. 230; *SEG* XXIII 175 a (lamps)

LAKONIA:

—GYTHEION: (**11**) m. ii AD *IG* V (1) 1174, 12 (s. Ἀπολλώνιος)

MESSENIA:

—KYPARISSIA: (**12**) 72 BC Moretti, *Olymp.* 690

S. ITALY (CAMPANIA):

—NEAPOLIS: (**13**) imp. *IG* XIV 816 (*INap* 179) (Ἀπο(λλ)οφάνης: f. Φόρνιος)

ZAKYNTHOS: (**14**) i BC/i AD *IvOl* 224, 2 (f. Πολύξενος)

**Ἀπολλωνία**

AIGINA: (**1**) ii BC *IG* II² 7951 (d. Ἀπολλωνίδας)

AIGINA?: (**2**) ii-i BC ib. IV (1) 80 (d. Ἀπολλώνιος)

ARGOLIS:

—HERMIONE: (**3**) ?ii-i BC ib. 731 I, 9 (d. Ἀγαθόκλεια); (**4**) ~ ib. l. 14 (m. Λυκῖνος); (**5**) i BC-i AD? ib. 730 III, 7 (m. Φιλοκρατέα)

EPIROS: (**6**) imp. *CIG* 1828 (Ἀπολλώνιος-apogr.)

—BOUTHROTOS (PRASAIBOI): (**7**) a. 163 BC *IBouthrot* 17, 21; 31, 85 (*SEG* XXXVIII 474; 490) ?= (8); (**8**) ~ *IBouthrot* 147, [5], 7; cf. 19, 2 (Ἀπολλ[ωνία]) ?= (7)

KORINTHIA:

—KORINTH: (**9**) iii-iv AD *Corinth* VIII (1) 133 (-πωλ-)

—KROMMYON: (**10**) imp. *IG* IV (1) 195 (Αἰ-)

S. ITALY (APULIA):

—CANUSIUM: (**11**) imp.? *Epig. Rom. di Canosa* 77 (*CIL* IX 355) (Lat. Arruntia Apollonia)

S. ITALY (CAMPANIA):

—DIKAIARCHIA-PUTEOLI: (**12**) imp. ib. X 2665 (Lat. Otacilia Apollonia: m. Εὐσέβιος); (**13**) ~ ib. 2815 (Lat. Otacilia Apollonia Marcella)

—MISENUM*: (**14**) ?ii AD ib. 3541 (Lat. Flavia Apollonia)

—NEAPOLIS: (**15**) 110 BC *ID* 2265 (d. Ἀπολλώνιος)

S. ITALY (LUCANIA):

—ATINA LUCANA: (**16**) imp. *IItal* III (1) 189 (*CIL* X 314) (Lat. Antonia Apollonia)

—GRUMENTUM: (**17**) imp. ib. 249 (Lat. Bruttia Apollonia)

—VOLCEI: (**18**) imp. *IItal* III (1) 89 (Lat. Otacilia Apollonia: m. Δωρίς)

SICILY:

—SYRACUSE: (**19**) iii-v AD *NScav* 1918, p. 279

**Ἀπολλωνιάδης**

S. ITALY: (**1**) inc. *SB* 8078

SICILY:

—AGYRION: (**2**) 339 BC D.S. xvi 82. 4 (tyrant)

**Ἀπολλωνίδας**

ACHAIA:

—ASCHEION: (**1**) c. 230-200 BC *BCH* 45 (1921) p. 12 II, 63 (f. Εὔανδρος)

—AIGINA: (**2**) ii BC *IG* II² 7951 (f. Ἀπολλωνία)

ARGOLIS:

—EPIDAUROS: (**3**) i BC ib. IV (1)² 227 (f. Ἀσκλαπιάς)

—EPIDAUROS*: (**4**) c. 370 BC ib. 102, 75; (**5**) c. 365-335 BC ib. 103, 166, 168

—HERMIONE: (**6**) iii BC ib. IV (1) 728, 19

ARKADIA:

—TEGEA: (**7**) 308 BC *RE* (18); Moretti, *Olymp.* 486

——(Apolloniatai): (**8**) m. iii BC *IG* V (2) 36, 103 (f. Δαμοκλῆς)

——(Krariotai): (**9**) iii BC ib. 40, 16 ([Ἀ]πολλωνίδας); (**10**) f. iii BC ib. 36, 43 (f. Δαμάτριος: metic)

DALMATIA:

—ISSA: (**11**) hell. Brunšmid p. 27 no. 18, 6 (*SEG* XL 514; *VAHD* 84 (1991) p. 253 no. 3) (s. Ἀγάθων); (**12**) iii/ii BC *SEG* XXXV 681 ([Ἀ]πολλωνίδ[ας]); (**13**) ~ ib. 688 (Ἀπολλωνίδ<ι>ας); (**14**) f. ii BC Brunšmid p. 23 no. 10, 9 (f. Τιμασίων)

KORINTHIA:

—KORINTH: (**15**) m. iv BC *CEG* II 874 ii, 3

—SIKYON: (**16**) 185-169 BC *RE* (21) (Skalet 41)

LAKONIA:

—SPARTA: (**17**) 181 or 180 BC Plb. xxiv 7. 6-7 (Bradford (1)); (**18**) c. 100-125 AD *IG* V (1) 137, 1 (Bradford (2)) (s. Πασικλῆς)

MESSENIA:

—MESSENE: (**19**) c. 146-32 BC *BMC Pelop.* p. 110 no. 17 (coin); (**20**) c. 140 BC *IvOl* 52, 5 (s. Νίκανδρος)

—THOURIA: (**21**) ii-i BC *IG* V (1) 1385, 29 (s. Ἀπολλώνιος)

SICILY:

—GELA-PHINTIAS: (**22**) iii BC *SEG* VIII 611 (-δης: s. Ἱππίας)

—KAMARINA: (**23**) f. v BC Cordano, *Tessere Pubbliche* 129 (Ἀπολλῶ[νίδας]—ed., Ἀπολλό[δωρος]?: f. Κόρειος); (**24**) iv/iii BC Dubois, *IGDS* 122, 3 (Cordano, 'Camarina VII' 74) (s. Φρῦνος); (**25**) hell. *SEG* XXXIX 1001, 6 (f. Σωσιγένης); (**26**) iii BC Manganaro, *PdelP* forthcoming no. 1, 8 (s. Σώσανδρος)

—MORGANTINA: (**27**) iv/iii BC *SEG* XXXIX 1008, 10 (f. Φιλίαρχος)

—SYRACUSE: (**28**) 214 BC Liv. xxiv 28. 1 (Lat. Apollonides)

—TAUROMENION: (**29**) c. 228 BC *IG* XIV 421 an. 13 (*SGDI* 5219) (f. Φιλόδαμος); (**30**) c. 40 BC *Cron. Arch.* 3 (1964) p. 54 I, 23 (s. —ις)

——(Δεξ.): (**31**) ?ii/i BC *IG* XIV 421 D an. 3 (*SGDI* 5219); *IGSI* 4 III (IV), 101 D an. 6 (f. Ἀνδρόμαχος)

**Ἀπολλωνίδης**

AITOLIA:

—THERMOS*: (**1**) s. iii BC *IG* IX (1)² (1) 60 II, 21; (**2**) ~ ib. 60 III, 9 (-ολω-); (**3**) ~ ib. l. 18; (**4**) ~ ib. l. 21; (**5**) ~ ib. l. 24; (**6**) ~ ib. 60 IV, 2 (-ολω-); (**7**) ~ ib. l. 21; (**8**) ~ ib. 60 V, 17

ARGOLIS:

—ARGOS: (**9**) imp. ib. IV (1) 649, 3 (Π. Ἀ.); (**10**) ?iii AD ib. l. 1 (Αὐ[ρ]. Ἀ.)

—HERMIONE: (**11**) ?ii-i BC ib. 731 I, 1 (Ἀπ[ολ]λωνίδης: f. Δημώ)

—TROIZEN: (**12**) f. ii AD ib. 758, 18 (f. Διόγνητος)

ILLYRIA:

—EPIDAMNOS-DYRRHACHION: (**13**) hell.-imp. *IDyrrh* 441 (f. Φιλουμένη)

S. Italy (Bruttium):
—lokroi epizephyrioi?: (14) 178 bc Syll³ 585, 240 (or Cilicia Zephyrion: s. Ἀσκληπιόδωρος)
S. Italy (Campania):
—dikaiarchia-puteoli: (15) ?ii ad CIL x 3149 (Lat. Aelius Apollonides)
S. Italy (Lucania):
—hyele-velia: (16) hell.? PdelP 25 (1970) p. 264 no. 7 (f. Ζήνων)
Sicily: (17) f. iv bc IG II² 10287 (s. Εὐαίνετος)

Ἀπολλώνιος
Achaia:
—aigeira: (1) c. 83-60 bc FD III (1) 223, 2, 5 (s. Διονύσιος)
—patrai: (2) iii-iv ad SEG xxxiv 340
Achaia?: (3) 193 bc IG v (2) 293, 13 (f. Χάρης)
Aigina: (4) ii-i bc ib. iv (1) 138 a (f. Νήνη); (5) hell.-imp. ib. 105; (6) ?f. i ad Alt-Ägina I (2) p. 46 no. 20, 2 (-λώνιος); (7) ?iii-iv ad ib. p. 48 no. 33 (Ἀπολλώνι[ος])
Aigina?: (8) ii-i bc IG iv (1) 80 (f. Ἀπολλωνία)
Aitolia: (9) c. 235 bc ib. II² 1299, 112; (10) 214 bc ib. ix (1)² (1) 31, 169 (-ολώ-: s. Νικόστρατος)
—thermos*: (11) s. iii bc ib. 60 II, 6 (-ολώ-); (12) ~ ib. 60 III, 3; (13) ~ ib. l. 22; (14) ~ ib. 60 IV, 3; (15) ~ ib. l. 5; (16) ~ ib. l. 9; (17) ~ ib. l. 10; (18) ~ ib. l. 17; (19) ~ ib. l. 19; (20) ~ ib. 60 V, 12; (21) ~ ib. 60 VI, 5
Akarnania:
—echinos?: (22) ii bc ib. ix (1)² (2) 373
—stratos: (23) ii bc ib. 394, 14 (s. Ξένων)
—thyrreion: (24) ii bc ib. 250, 14 (s. Ἐχετέρμων)
Argolis:
—argos: (25) 255 bc PCZ 59182, 11 (f. Στύραξ); (26) ii bc SEG xlii 279, 10 ([Ἀπο]λλώνιος); (27) f. ii bc IG xi (4) 1236 (f. Πρόμαχος); (28) 105 bc JÖAI 14 (1911) Beibl. p. 146 no. 4, 13 (Ἀπολλώ[νι]ος); (29) imp. IG iv (1) 620, 5 (Μαίνιος Ἀπολλώνιος); (30) i-ii ad ib. 587, 6
—epidauros: (31) ii bc ib. iv (1)² 376 (Peek, IAEpid 153. 23) (Ἀπολλώ[ν]ιος); (32) ii/i bc IG iv (1)² 64, 2 (s. Σάτυρος); (33) ~ ib. 629, 2 (f. Σωκράτης); (34) imp. Peek, IAEpid 341 ([Ἀπολλ]ών[ι]ος); (35) ~ IG iv (1)² 448 (s. Βρομιοκλῆς); (36) i ad ib. 642, 3; 643 (f. Ἰσίων); (37) 32 ad Peek, IAEpid 45, 43 ([Ἀπ]ολλώνιος: s. Ἐπίδαμος); (38) 33 ad Moretti, Olymp. 758; (39) ?iii ad Peek, NIEpid 108 ([Ἀπολ]λώνιος: f. Ἀπολλᾶς); (40) 231 ad IG iv (1)² 408 (s. Δωρᾶς); (41) 237 ad ib. + Peek, IAEpid 167 (f. Δωρᾶς)
—hermione: (42) ii-i bc IG iv (1) 732 I, 17 (s. Ἀριστοκλῆς); (43) ~ ib. 732 II, 12 (s. Δαμάρετος); (44) i bc-i ad? ib. 730 II, 3 (s. Ὀνάσων); (45) ~ ib. l. 5 (s. Συρτόνικος); (46) ~ ib. 730 III, 11
—methana-arsinoe: (47) i bc ib. 853, 7 (s. Τίμαιος)
Arkadia: (48) ii bc ASAA 2 (1916) p. 171 no. 138 = BCH 34 (1910) pp. 247-8 no. 40; cf. Fraser, RFM pp. 107 n. 124; 108 n. 132; (49) ii/iii ad IG II² 3758, 5
—kleitor: (50) ?262-255 bc Nachtergael, Les Galates 5, 39, 41, 42; 8, 32; cf. Stephanis 1799; 2810-12 ([Ἀ]πολλώνιος: f. Νέων)
—mantineia-antigoneia: (51) iii bc IG v (2) 273 ([Ἀπολ]λώνιος); (52) iii-ii bc ib. 319, 38; (53) ?16 ad ib. 274, 2
—megalopolis: (54) f. ii bc ib. 19 (f. Τιμοκλῆς)
—psophis: (55) ii-iii ad Achaean Grave Stelai 23
—tegea: (56) s. iv bc SEG xxxvi 383, 9 (s. Ξενίας); (57) i ad IG v (2) 46, 6 ([Ἀ]πολλώνιο[ς]: f. Νικάνωρ); (58) 165 ad ib. 50, 13 (s. Ἀγέμαχος)
——(Athaneatai): (59) iv/iii bc ib. 38, 21

Dalmatia:
—issa: (60) iii/ii bc SEG xxxi 601 (VAHD 84 (1991) p. 258 no. 8) (f. Πάμφιλος)
Elis: (61) c. 146-32 bc BMC Pelop. p. 6 no. 68 (coin); (62) s. i bc IvOl [289]; 290, 2 (s. Λάδοκος: sculptor); (63) 20-16 bc ib. 65, 6 (f. Βάργος); (64) c. 20 bc-i ad ib. 220, 6; 369, 3; 424, 2 (I f. Ἀπολλώνιος II ὁ καὶ Τιβέριος Κλαύδιος); (65) ~ ib. 220, 6; 369, 3; 424, 2 (Ἀπολλ[ώ]νιος ὁ καὶ Τιβέριος [Κλ]αύδιος— 220, Τι[βέριος] [Κλ]αύδιος ὁ καὶ Ἀπολλών[ιος]— 369, Ἀ. ὁ καὶ Τιβέριος—424: II s. Ἀπολλώνιος I); (66) ?i ad EA 1905, p. 259 no. 2, 10 ([Ἀπ]ολλώνιος: s. Ἄνδρων)
—olympia*: (67) 113-117 ad IvOl 91, 18 (?s. Μουσαῖος: slave?)
Epiros:
—ambrakia: (68) ii-i bc CIG 1798; (69) ~ ib. (s. Πολύστρατος); (70) hell.-imp. BCH 17 (1893) p. 632 no. 3 (-ολώ-); (71) imp.? SEG xxiv 417 (-ολώ-)
—bouthrotos (prasaiboi): (72) a. 163 bc IBouthrot 41, 21; 43, 25-7 (SEG xxxviii 500; 502) (s. Διογένης, f. Διογένης, Θεανώ) ?= (73); (73) ~ IBouthrot 158 ?= (72)
——Ancheropaioi: (74) a. 163 bc ib. 90, 7; 96, 5 (s. Νικόμαχος)
——Cherrioi: (75) a. 163 bc ib. 98, 8 (s. Εὐρίοπος)
——Trallianoi: (76) a. 163 bc ib. 29, 46 (SEG xxxviii 487)
—nikopolis: (77) s. i ad FD III (6) 132, 4 (Sarikakis 11) (f. Σεύθης)
Illyria:
—amantia: (78) hell.? BUST 1958 (2), p. 107 (BE 1967, no. 338) (Ἀπολλωος—ed. p. 107, Ἀπολλωνος—p. 103, Ἀπολλών(ι)ος?—BE)
—apollonia: (79) c. 250-50 bc Maier 68 (coin) (Ceka 16) (money.); (80) imp. IApoll 197
—epidamnos-dyrrhachion: (81) hell.-imp. IDyrrh 113 (s. Ἀπελλᾶς); (82) ~ ib. 114 (s. Δείνων); (83) ~ ib. 161 (f. Δαζαῖος); (84) ~ ib. 169 (f. Διανόμα); (85) ~ ib. 241 (-λλό-: f. Θεοδώρα)
Korinthia:
—korinth: (86) iii bc ITrall I 33 B, 9 (f. Λέων)
—sikyon: (87) c. 100-90 bc SEG xxxiii 290 A, 17; BSA 70 (1975) pp. 129-31 (date) (Stephanis 272) (s. Ἀπολλόδωρος); (88) i bc NC 1984, p. 19 Group 12 no. 7 (coin); (89) i ad SEG xi 254
Lakonia:
—epidauros limera: (90) imp. IG v (1) 1006
—gytheion: (91) m. ii ad ib. 1174, 12 (f. Ἀπολλοφάνης)
—hyperteleaton*: (92) imp. ib. 1046 ([Ἀπολλ]ώνιος?)
—sparta: (93) i-ii ad ib. 196 (Bradford (10)) ([Ἀπο]λλώνιο[ς]); (94) f. ii ad IG v (1) 162, 6 (Bradford (11)) (I f. Ἀπολλώνιος II); (95) ~ IG v (1) 162, 6 (Bradford (1)) (II s. Ἀπολλώνιος I); (96) c. 140-160 ad IG v (1) 37, 9; 64, 5; SEG xi 587, [3] (Bradford (14)) (f. Μητρόδωρος); (97) c. 150-160 ad IG v (1) 69, 29; 70, 6; 71 III, 20; SEG xi 622, 1 (Bradford (3)) (s. Ἔραστος); (98) c. 170-190 ad SEG xi 627, 5 (Bradford (5)) (s. Ζώσιμος) ?= (100); (99) c. 175-200 ad IG v (1) 129, 4 (Bradford (7)) (Π. Μέμμιος Ἀ.); (100) f. iii ad IG v (1) 170, 17; BSA 80 (1985) p. 245 (date) (Bradford (6)) (Αὐρ. Ἀ.: s. Ζώσιμος) ?= (98); (101) c. 217-230 ad SEG xi 616 a, 5 (Bradford (13)) (Ἀπολλώνι[ος]); (102) c. 230-260 ad IG v (1) 556, 10 (Bradford (8)) (Αὐ. Ἀ.); (103) ~ SEG xi 633, 3 (Bradford (4)) (Αὐρ. Ἀ.: s. Καμινᾶς); (104) ~ SEG xi 633, 11; 844, [7] (Bradford (12)) (I f. Αὐρ. Ἀπολλώνιος II); (105) ~ SEG xi 633, 11 (Bradford (2)) (Αὐρ. Ἀ.: II s. Ἀπολλώνιος I); (106) a. 230 ad SEG xi 844, 7 (Αὐρ. Ἀπ[ολλ]ώνιος?)

Leukas: (107) hell.? IG ix (1) 556
Messenia:
—asine: (108) ii ad ib. v (1) 1408 (f. Ἐπίγονος)
—messene: (109) hell.-imp. Schol. Dion. Thr. p. 183, 31; (110) 31 bc-14 ad SEG xxiii 207, 20 (f. Καλλίας)
——(Aristomachidai): (111) 11 ad PAE 1992, p. 71 A, 10 (Ἀπολλώ[νιος]: f. Ἄνδρων)
——(Daiphontidai): (112) 11 ad ib. l. 21 (f. Ἄνδρων)
——(Kleolaidai): (113) 11 ad ib. l. 29 (s. Ἀρτέμων)
—thouria: (114) ii-i bc IG v (1) 1385, 29 (f. Ἀπολλωνίδας)
S. Italy (Apulia):
—luceria: (115) imp. CIL ix 851 (Lat. Domitius Apollonius); (116) ~ ib. 896 (Lat. C. Valvennius Apollonius)
—venusia: (117) imp. ib. 548 (Lat. Apollonius: f. Πυραλλίς)
S. Italy (Calabria):
—kallipolis: (118) ?ii-iii ad NScav 1957, p. 411 (Lat. Apollonius)
—taras-tarentum: (119) c. 280-272 bc Vlasto 762; 767; 789-96; 798-802 (coins) (Evans, Horsemen p. 159 VII C.5-7; p. 160 VII F.1-5); (120) c. 272-235 bc Vlasto 894-8 (Evans, Horsemen p. 180 VIII H.1); cf. NC 1930, p. 122 (coins)
—taras-tarentum?: (121) inc. Wuilleumier, Tarente p. 710 s.v. (terracotta) ([Ἀπο]λλώνιος)
S. Italy (Campania):
—dikaiarchia-puteoli: (122) imp. CIL x 1752 (Lat. Apollonius); (123) ~ ib. 8059. 287 (seal) (Lat. M. Obul. Apollonius); (124) ?i-ii ad Eph. Ep. viii 370 (Lat. C. Iulius Apollonius)
—dikaiarchia-puteoli*: (125) imp. CIL x 1953 (Lat. Apollonius: slave?)
—neapolis: (126) 110 bc ID 2126; 2265 (s. Διοσκουρίδης, f. Ἀρτεμῶ, Ἀπολλωνία)
—neapolis*: (127) imp. CIL x 1497 (Lat. D. Servilius Apollonius: doctor/freed.)
—nola*: (128) imp. ib. 1292 (Lat. C. Cavilius Apollonius: freed.)
—pompeii: (129) i bc-i ad ib. iv 2462 (-λώ-); (130) ~ ib. 8961 (Lat. Apollo[nius]); (131) i bc/i ad ib. x 907 (Castrèn 68. 2) (Lat. Apollonius); (132) c. 51-62 ad CIL iv 3340. 95, 7 (Castrèn 402. 4) (Lat. P. Terentius Apollonius); (133) 57 ad CIL iv 3340. 32, 18; 40, 16; 43, 21; 48, 23; 59, 10; 69, 10; 116, 6 (Castrèn 190. 9) (Lat. Cn. Aelius Apollonius)
—pompeii*: (134) i bc-i ad CIL iv 6889 (Lat. Apollonius: freed.); (135) ~ ib. x 1069 (Lat. P. Minicius Apollonius: freed.)
—salernum: (136) imp. IItal I (1) 218 (CIL x 626) (Lat. P. Popilio Apolloni (dat.))
S. Italy (Lucania):
—herakleia: (137) imp. SEG xxvi 1132 (I f. Ἀπολλώνιος II); (138) ~ ib. (II s. Ἀπολλώνιος I)
——(Fε. ἄνθεμον): (139) iv/iii bc IGSI I I, 96 (DGE 62; Uguzzoni–Ghinatti I) (I f. Ἀπολλώνιος II); (140) ~ IGSI I I, 96 (DGE 62; Uguzzoni–Ghinatti I) (II s. Ἀπολλώνιος I)
——(Πε. καρυκείον): (141) iv/iii bc IGSI I I, 4, 9, 97, 186 (DGE 62; Uguzzoni–Ghinatti I); IGSI I II, 4, 8 (DGE 63; Uguzzoni–Ghinatti II) (s. Ἡράκλητος)
—volcei: (142) imp. IItal III (1) 286; cf. Solin, Lukan. Inschr. p. 59 (Lat. Steius Ap(o)llonius)
Sicily:
—agyrion: (143) i bc-i ad? IG xiv 588 (f. Διόδωρος)
—akrai: (144) ii bc Akrai p. 156 no. 6, 8 (s. Ἀγάθων); (145) ~ ib. l. 9 (f. Ἔλωρις); (146) ii-i bc SGDI 3246, 48 (Akrai pp. 152-3 no. 2, 48; Dubois, IGDS 109) (s. Ἀρχάγαθος)
—drepanon: (147) f. i bc RE (59) (Lat. A. Clodius Apollonius: s. Νίκων)

—GELA-PHINTIAS: (148) f. ii BC IG XIV 256, 46 (Dubois, IGDS 161); cf. SEG XL 804 (s. Σάτυρος)
—HALAISA: (149) ii BC IGSI 2 A II, 73 (Dubois, IGDS 196) (f. Ἡρακλείδας)
—KAMARINA: (150) hell. SEG XXXIX 1001, 7 (s. Φιντίας)
—KATANE: (151) ii-i BC ISmyrna 689 III, 32 (s. Πόπλιος)
—KENTORIPA: (152) i BC-i AD? IG XIV 577
—LIPARA: (153) imp. Libertini, Isole Eolie p. 225 no. 46 ([Ἀπολ]λ(ώ)νιος)
—MENAI: (154) hell. Riv. Stor. Antica 5 (1900-1) p. 57 no. 35
—PANORMOS: (155) f. i BC Cic., In Verr. II v 16 ff. (Lat. Apollonius Geminus: s. Διοκλῆς)
—SOLOUS: (156) iii/ii BC Kokalos 9 (1963) pp. 186-7 (s. Ἀρίστων, f. Ἀρίστων, Φίλων); (157) ~ ib. (s. Ἀρίστων); (158) ?i BC IGLMP 114, 2; cf. SEG XXXVIII 964 (II s. Ἀπολλώνιος I); (159) ~ IGLMP 114, 3; cf. SEG XXXVIII 964 (I f. Ἀπολλώνιος II)
—SYRACUSE: (160) ii-i BC IG XIV 8, 11 (IGLMP 105) (Ἀπολλώ[νιος]); (161) ~ SEG XXXIV 974, 3 (IGLMP 106; Stephanis 269); (162) ?s. i BC Sic. Gymn. 16 (1963) p. 61 (Ἀπολλώ[νιος]: f. Δωνᾶτος)
—TAUROMENION: (163) c. 203 BC IG XIV 421 an. 38 (SGDI 5219) (f. Ἀγαθίας); (164) c. 141 BC IG XIV 421 an. 100 (SGDI 5219); (165) ?ii/i BC IG XIV 421 D an. 3 (SGDI 5219) (I f. Ἀπολλώνιος II); (166) ~ IG XIV 421 D an. 3 (SGDI 5219) (II s. Ἀπολλώνιος I); (167) ii/i BC IGSI 5 IV, 4
——(Χαλκ.): (168) ii/i BC ib. 7 II, 33 (f. Φιλιστίων)

**Ἀπολλώνις**
ARKADIA:
—TEGEA: (1) ii AD IG V (2) 55, 69 (s. Ἄλκιμος); (2) ii-iii AD ib. 178 (GVI 960) (s. Σωτηρώι)

**Ἀπολλωνίς**
AIGINA?: (1) i BC-i AD EAD XXX p. 356 no. 21 (?d. Εὐκλῆς)
ARGOLIS:
—ARGOS: (2) i-ii AD IG IV (1) 645, 1; (3) ~ ib. l. 3
ILLYRIA:
—EPIDAMNOS-DYRRHACHION: (4) hell.-imp. IDyrrh 115 (Ἀπολλώνιε? (masc. voc.)—ed.: d. Λύκος)
KORINTHIA:
—KORINTH: (5) ii-iii AD Corinth VIII (1) 134, 4; cf. SEG XI 91 (Δομετία Σατορνῖλα Ἀ.: d. Φιλίππα, Λ. Δομέτιος)

**Ἀπολλῶς**
S. ITALY (LUCANIA):
—HERAKLEIA: (1) imp. ib. XXVI 1132 (Ἀπολλώ[ς]: s. Νικόλαος)

**Ἄπονος**
SICILY:
—TAUROMENION: (1) iii-v AD IG XIV 445 (Ferrua, NG 484)

**Ἄποντις**
SICILY:
—SELINOUS:
——(Ἡρακλείδας): (1) m. v BC Dubois, IGDS 36, 3 (Arena, Iscr. Sic. I 69) (Ἀπόντιος (nom./gen.?): f. Ξένιος)

**Ἀππειραῖος**
SICILY:
—SEGESTA: (1) ?ii BC IG XIV 287 (Dubois, IGDS 213) (Διόδωρος Ἀ.: s. Τίττελος)

**Ἀπποίτας**
EPIROS:
—BOUTHROTOS (PRASAIBOI): (1) a. 163 BC IBouthrot 37, 8 (SEG XXXVIII 496); (2) ~

IBouthrot 78, 10; 79, 9; 80, 8; 81, 9; 82, 8; 83, 8; 84, 8; 85, 9; 86, 10; 87, 9; 88, 7; 156, 9; 157, 5 (BCH 118 (1994) pp. 122 ff. nos. 1-13) (s. Ἀντίγονος) ?= (6) (4)
——Hermiatoi: (3) a. 163 BC IBouthrot 116, 9 (BCH 118 (1994) p. 121 A)
——Kydestoi: (4) a. 163 BC REG 62 (1949) p. 28 B, 12; IBouthrot 69, 10; 70, 8; 71, 7; 99, 6 (BCH 118 (1994) p. 129 ff. B 1-3) (s. Ἀντίγονος) ?= (2)
——Opatai: (5) a. 163 BC IBouthrot 127, 7 (BCH 118 (1994) p. 128 A); IBouthrot 135, 2 (s. Ἀντίγονος)
——PRASAIBOI: (6) ?m. ii BC ib. 123-5; 155 (BCH 118 (1994) p. 120 nos. 2-5) ?= (2)

**Ἄπρα**
SICILY:
—KATANE: (1) 435 AD Agnello 96; cf. Ferrua, NG 405 (d. Γεντιανός, Ἀσκληπιοδότη)

**Ἄπρυλλα**
S. ITALY (APULIA):
—LUCERIA: (1) imp. CIL IX 854 (Lat. Erucua Aprylla)

**Ἀπταραῖος**
ARGOLIS:
—HERMIONE: (1) iii BC IG IV (1) 729 I, 14 (s. Εὐθυμίδας)

**Ἀπτοίατος?**
ILLYRIA:
—APOLLONIA: (1) c. 250-50 BC Maier 15; Bakërr Hoard p. 64 no. 89 (coin) (Ceka 86) (pryt.)

**Ἀπτυρίς**
ILLYRIA:
—LYCHNIDOS: (1) ii-iii AD GVI 1943, 5, 15 (d. Νικόλεως, Ζηνωΐς)

**Ἀπύρηνος**
S. ITALY (APULIA):
—GNATHIA-EGNATIA: (1) imp. CIL IX 6078. 37 (tile) (Lat. Apyrenus)

**Ἀπφη**
S. ITALY (CAMPANIA):
—POMPEII*: (1) m. i AD Impegno per Pompeii 21 OS no. 1 (Castrèn 389. 3) (Lat. Stallia Aphe: freed.)

**Ἀπφιάς**
S. ITALY (APULIA):
—BARION: (1) imp. CIL IX 290 (Lat. Apphias: m. Φοῖβος)
S. ITALY (CAMPANIA):
—DIKAIARCHIA-PUTEOLI: (2) imp. ib. X 2943; cf. Puteoli 11 (1987) p. 56 (Lat. Seia Affias)

**Ἀπφῦς**
KORINTHIA:
—KORINTH: (1) imp. IG IV (1) 207

**Ἀπώνιος**
SICILY:
—GELA-PHINTIAS: (1) ii/i BC SEG XXXI 837, 7

**Ἀράβαννα**
ARGOLIS:
—ARGOS: (1) byz. BCH 31 (1907) p. 184; cf. TMByz 9 (1985) p. 370 no. 113 (Jew)

**Ἀραθθίων**
EPIROS:
—AMBRAKIA: (1) vi BC SEG XLI 540; cf. BE 1994, no. 38 (-ōν); (2) a. 167 BC SEG XXXV 665 A, 9 (Ἀραθθίων (m): f. Μνασιλαΐδας)

**Ἀραῖνος**
ARGOLIS:
—ARGOS: (1) f. v BC ib. XI 329 (Ἀραhῖνος (n. pr.?))

**Ἄρακος**
LAKONIA:
—SPARTA: (1) c. 440-365 BC RE (1) (Poralla² 107)

**Ἀραότης**
SICILY:
—TERRAVECCHIA DI CUTI (MOD.): (1) vi/v BC Arena, Iscr. Sic. II 117 A (Dubois, IGDS 176 a 2) (-τε̄ς, Ἀδράστη—Dubois)

**Ἀραπία**
ARGOLIS:
—HERMIONE: (1) ?ii/i BC IG IV (1) 732 IV, 15

**Ἀρασίδαμος**
MESSENIA:
—THOURIA: (1) ii/i BC ib. V (1) 1384, 5 (s. Δαμοτέλης)

**Ἀράτα**
LAKONIA: (1) s. iv BC ib. IV (1)² 122, 1 (Bradford (2))
—SPARTA: (2) i-ii AD IG V (1) 579 (Bradford (1)) (d. Τυχάρετος)

**Ἀράτιος?**
SICILY:
—KAMARINA: (1) s. v BC Dubois, IGDS 119, 5; Arena, Iscr. Sic. II 145 (Ἀρατιο (nom./gen.?))

**Ἀρατίων**
ARGOLIS:
—EPIDAUROS: (1) c. 340-330 BC SEG XXV 387 A, 16 (Ἀ[ρ]ατίων)

**Ἄρατος**
AITOLIA:
—THESTIEIS: (1) f. iii BC IG IX (1)² (1) 9, 12 (Ἄρατος)
ARGOLIS:
—ARGOS: (2) 364 BC ib. II² 3038 (Stephanis 291)
KORINTHIA:
—SIKYON: (3) 271-214 BC RE (2); FGrH 231; Moretti, Olymp. 574 (Skalet 44) (I s. Κλεινίας, Ἀριστοδάμα, f. Ἄρατος II); (4) c. 250-214 BC RE (3) (Skalet 45) (II s. Ἄρατος I, f. Ἄρατος III); (5) c. 230-200 BC BCH 45 (1921) p. 11 II, 34 (Ἄρατ[ος]); (6) 181-179 BC Plb. xxiv 6. 3; 10. 8 (Skalet 46) (III s. Ἄρατος II)
LAKONIA:
—SPARTA: (7) viii/vii BC Just. iii 4. 8 (Poralla² 109) (f. Φάλανθος: dub.); (8) s. iii BC SEG XI 668 (vase); BSA 30 (1928-30) p. 245 fig. 3, 15-18 (Poralla² 109a); (9) ii BC IG V (1) 961, 1, 9 (Bradford (3)) (s. Νικίας); (10) s. i BC IG V (1) 94, 2 (Bradford (3)) (Ἀρα[τος]: f. Λυκομήδης); (11) c. 30-20 BC IG V (1) 211, 14 (Bradford (1)) (s. Δεξικράτης)
S. ITALY (CAMPANIA):
—AEQUANA*: (12) i AD NScav 1896, p. 332 (Lat. Aratus: s. Ἀπελλᾶς: freed.)
SICILY:
—KAMARINA: (13) f. v BC Cordano, Tessere Pubbliche 84 (Ἄρατο[ς]: s. Ἐκφαντίδας)

**Ἀργαῖος**
ARGOLIS:
—HERMIONE*: (1) ?i AD IG IV (1) 690, 4 (s. Ἀριστόνικος)

**Ἀργεάδης**
EPIROS:
—DODONA: (1) 168-148 BC BMC Thessaly p. 93 nos. 68-71; Franke, Münz. v. Epirus pp. 37-9; pp. 308 ff. (coin) (Μενέδημος Ἀ. (n. pr.?))

## Ἀργεία
ARKADIA:
—TEGEA: (1) ii-iii AD *EILakArk* 9, 1 (?m. Ἰού-λιος)
EPIROS:
—BOUTHROTOS (PRASAIBOI): (2) a. 163 BC *IBouthrot* 20, 3; 26, 11; 29, 4 (*SEG* XXXVIII 477; 484; 487) (Ἀργέα—29: d. Πολέμων)

## Ἀργειάδας
ARGOLIS:
—ARGOS: (1) c. 480-460 BC *CEG* I 380. iii (s. Ἀγελαΐδας)

## Ἀργεῖος
ACHAIA:
—AIGEIRA?: (1) c. 252-248 BC *FD* III (4) 419, 1 (s. Πραξίων)
AIGINA: (2) f. v BC *IG* IV (1) 57; *LSAG²* p. 113 no. 10 (date) (s. Ἐπαίνετος)
AIGINA?: (3) iii/ii BC Breccia, *Iscriz.* 232
AITOLIA:
—KALYDON: (4) c. 213 BC *IG* IX (1)² (1) 188, 2
AKARNANIA:
—ALYZIA: (5) s. iv BC ib. IV (1)² 95, 70 (Perlman E.2); Perlman pp. 46-9 (date) (s. Γόργος)
ELIS: (6) 368-365 BC X., *HG* vii 1. 33; vii 4. 15-16; (7) 265 BC *IG* II² 686, 12 (s. Κλεινίας); (8) 141-145 AD *IvOl* 95, 8 (f. Φιλουμενός)
EPIROS:
—DODONA*: (9) iv-iii BC *SEG* XV 407 (Ἀρ-γεῖ(ος))
LAKONIA:
—SPARTA: (10) c. 100-125 AD *IG* V (1) 152, 7 (Bradford (-)) (-γί-: s. Ἔρως)
SICILY:
—AKRAGAS: (11) 406 BC D.S. xiii 87. 5

## Ἀργέννη
S. ITALY (CAMPANIA):
—PITHEKOUSSAI-AENARIA*: (1) imp. *CIL* x 6787 (Lat. Argenne: imp. freed.)

## Ἄργεννος
LAKONIA:
—ASOPOS: (1) c. 100-137 AD *IG* V (1) 971, 15

## Ἀργέντις
SICILY:
—SYRACUSE: (1) iii-v AD *SEG* IV 17 (Barreca 383)

## Ἀργιλεωνίς
LAKONIA:
—SPARTA: (1) c. 480-420 BC Plu., *Mor.* 219 D; 240 C (Poralla² 110) (m. Βρασίδας)

## Ἀργῖνα
ILLYRIA:
—APOLLONIA: (1) imp. *IApoll* 327 (-γεῖ-)

## Ἀργολικός
LAKONIA:
—SPARTA: (1) f. i AD Tac., *Ann.* vi 18.2; *PIR²* I 174 (Bradford (-)) (Lat. Argolicus: s. Γ. Ἰούλ. Λάκων)

## Ἄργος
S. ITALY (CALABRIA):
—BRENTESION-BRUNDISIUM*: (1) imp. *Epigraphica* 25 (1963) p. 60 no. 49 (Lat. Argus: s. Εὔοδος: freed.)

## Ἀργόφιλος
KORINTHIA:
—SIKYON: (1) vi/v BC *SEG* XI 244, 51

## Ἄργυλος
ARGOLIS:
—HERMIONE: (1) ii-iii AD *IG* II² 8498

## Ἄργυρις
SICILY:
—SYRACUSE: (1) iii-v AD ib. XIV 76 (Strazzulla 17) (Ἀ.?, Ἀργυρίς?)

## Ἄργυρος
S. ITALY (APULIA):
—CANUSIUM: (1) ii AD *Epig. Rom. di Canosa* 118 (*CIL* IX 372) (Lat. P. Curtius Argyr(us))
S. ITALY (BRUTTIUM):
—HIPPONION-VIBO VALENTIA: (2) imp. ib. x 8059. 50 (seal) (Lat. Argyrus)
S. ITALY (CAMPANIA):
—POMPEII: (3) i BC-i AD ib. IV 1407 (Lat. Argyrus)

## Ἄρδαλος
ARGOLIS:
—TROIZEN: (1) ?vi BC Plu., *Mor.* 1133a; Paus. ii 31. 3; Plin., *NH* vii 204 (Stephanis 294)

## Ἀρέας
PELOPONNESE: (1) c. 192 BC *SEG* XIII 327, 18 (Ἀγέας?: s. Πευθέας)

## Ἀρέθουσα
ILLYRIA:
—EPIDAMNOS-DYRRHACHION*: (1) imp. *AEp* 1978, no. 761 (Lat. Arethusa: d. Χρυσίς: threpte)
S. ITALY (APULIA):
—VENUSIA: (2) imp. *CIL* IX 520 (Lat. Arethusa)
S. ITALY (CAMPANIA):
—DIKAIARCHIA-PUTEOLI: (3) imp. ib. x 2901 (Lat. Pullia Arethusa)

## Ἀρέθων
S. ITALY (CALABRIA):
—TARAS-TARENTUM: (1) c. 302-280 BC Vlasto 666-7 (coin) (Evans, *Horsemen* p. 132 VI A.1)
SICILY:
—SYRACUSE?:
——(Μακ.): (2) hell. Manganaro, *PdelP* forthcoming no. 4 V, 10 (f. Μουσαῖος)

## Ἀρειάδας
SICILY:
—SELINOUS: (1) v BC Dubois, *IGDS* 35, 1 (Arena, *Iscr. Sic.* I 64)

## Ἀρείας
EPIROS:
—DODONA: (1) iii BC Antoniou, *Dodone* Ab, 42 (Ἀρείας)

## Ἄρειος
ACHAIA: (1) s. iii BC *PTeb* 815 fr. 3 recto, 2 (s. Θέων: t.e.)

## Ἄρειφος?
EPIROS:
—DODONA: (1) iii BC Antoniou, *Dodone* Ab, 46

## Ἀρέσανδρος
S. ITALY (LUCANIA):
—LEUKANOI: (1) iv BC Iamb., *VP* 267 (*FVS* I p. 447; *RE* s.v. Aresas (-)) (Ὀρέσανδρος—ms.: name—Nauck)
SICILY:
—TAUROMENION: (2) c. 237-218 BC *IG* XIV 421 an. 4; 421 an. 12; 421 an. 24 (*SGDI* 5219) (f. Ἀγάθων); (3) c. 203 BC *IG* XIV 421 an. 38 (*SGDI* 5219) (s. Ἀγάθων)

## Ἀρέσκιος
S. ITALY (CAMPANIA):
—DIKAIARCHIA-PUTEOLI: (1) imp. *CIL* x 2027 (Lat. Arescius)

## Ἄρεσκος
S. ITALY (APULIA):
—GNATHIA-EGNATIA: (1) imp. ib. IX 6175 (Lat. Ariscus)

## Ἀρέσκουσα
ACHAIA:
—PATRAI*: (1) i AD *ILGR* 60, 4 (Lat. Arescusa: freed.)
LAKONIA:
—BOIAI: (2) ii-iii AD *IG* V (1) 960, [1], 16
S. ITALY (APULIA):
—AECAE: (3) imp. *CIL* IX 956 (Lat. Gavia Arescusa: d. P. Gavius Iucundus, Gavia Iucunda)
—CANUSIUM: (4) ?f. i AD *Epig. Rom. di Canosa* 62 (*CIL* IX 351) (Lat. Trebellia Arescusa)
S. ITALY (CALABRIA):
—BRENTESION-BRUNDISIUM*: (5) imp. ib. 161 (Lat. Pacilia Arescusa: freed.)
S. ITALY (CAMPANIA):
—DIKAIARCHIA-PUTEOLI: (6) imp. ib. x 2379 (Lat. Ducenia Arescusa); (7) ?i-ii AD ib. 2583 (Lat. Iulia Arescusa); (8) ?ii AD *NScav* 1901, p. 20 (Lat. Aelia Arescusa)
—DIKAIARCHIA-PUTEOLI*: (9) imp. *CIL* x 2367 (Lat. Domitia Arescusa: freed.); (10) ~ ib. 2527 (Lat. Arescusa: freed.); (11) ?i-ii AD ib. 2557 (Lat. Iulia Arescusa: m. Iulia Primigenia: freed.)
—HERCULANEUM: (12) m. i AD *PdelP* 6 (1951) p. 229 no. 15; 16 (Lat. Arescusa) ?= (13); (13) ~ ib. 9 (1954) p. 57 no. 63 (Lat. Arescu[sa]) ?= (12)
—MISENUM*: (14) imp. *CIL* x 3554 (Lat. Octabia Arescusa); (15) ii AD ib. VI 8684 (*Puteoli* 12-13 (1988-9) p. 65 no. 1) (Lat. Claudia Arescusa: m. Αὔξιμος)
—POMPEII: (16) i BC-i AD *CIL* IV 1940; cf. p. 704 (Lat. Arescusa)
—PRETURO (MOD.): (17) imp. *NScav* 1928, p. 228 (Lat. Arescusa: freed.)
—SALERNUM: (18) s. i AD *IItal* I (1) 151 (*CIL* x 555) (Lat. Arescusa: m. Ἀνθοῦσα)
—SURRENTUM*: (19) imp. *Cinquant' Anni Lic. Class.* p. 281 no. 3 (Lat. Livia Arescusa: freed.)
SICILY:
—SYRACUSE?: (20) ?iii-v AD *Riv. Arch. Crist.* 18 (1941) p. 214 no. 92 (Οὐεργιλία Ἀ.)

## Ἀρεσκουσιανός
S. ITALY (APULIA):
—CANUSIUM: (1) 223 AD *Epig. Rom. di Canosa* 35 II, 26 (*CIL* IX 338) (Lat. L. Herennius Arescusianus)

## Ἀρέσκων
ARKADIA:
—TEGEA: (1) m. ii AD *IG* V (2) 48, 11 (Ἀρέσ[κων])
MESSENIA:
—KORONE: (2) 246 AD ib. v (1) 1398, 24 (Αὐρ. Ἀ.)
S. ITALY (LUCANIA):
—VOLCEI: (3) imp. *IItal* III (1) 117 (Lat. D. Dinnius Arisco)

## Ἀρεστίων
S. ITALY (CAMPANIA):
—POMPEII: (1) i BC-i AD *CIL* IV 8327-8 c (Lat. C. M. Arestion)

## Ἄρεστος
ELIS:
—OLYMPIA*: (1) 36-24 BC *IvOl* 62, 18 (?s. Μολοσσός: Δου.)

## Ἀρέτα
KORINTHIA:
—KORINTH: (1) ii BC *IG* II² 9054 (-τη: d. Σύμμαχος)
LAKONIA:
—SPARTA: (2) s. vii BC *PMGF* I 1, 71 (Poralla² 111)
SICILY:
—AKRAGAS: (3) f. v BC Dubois, *IGDS* 180 b, 5 (Arena, *Iscr. Sic.* II 90)
—SYRACUSE: (4) f. iv BC *RE* (2); cf. Beloch, *GG* III (2) pp. 102-7 (-τη: d. Διονύσιος, Ἀριστομάχα, m. Ἀρεταῖος, Ἱππαρῖνος)

**Ἀρεταβίων**
KERKYRA: (1) ii-i BC Unp. (*IG* arch.)

**Ἀρεταῖος**
KORINTHIA:
—KORINTH: (1) ii AD Luc., *Tox.* 22-3 (fict.)
SICILY:
—SYRACUSE: (2) 357 BC *FGrH* 566 F 114 (s. Δίων, Ἀρέτα)

**Ἀρετακλῆς**
ARKADIA:
—MEGALOPOLIS: (1) iii BC *SEG* XVII 141, 5 ([Ἀρ]ετακλῆς: s. Ἄρετις)

**Ἀρετάφιλος**
EPIROS: (1) hell. *SGDI* 1361; cf. Cabanes, *L'Épire* p. 584 no. 65 ([Ἀρ]ετάφιλος)

**Ἀρέτη**
ARGOLIS:
—EPIDAUROS: (1) imp.? *IG* IV (1)² 739 (Ἀρέτης (fem. gen./masc. nom.?))
ILLYRIA:
—EPIDAMNOS-DYRRHACHION: (2) imp. *CIL* III 603 (Sestieri, *ILat. Albania* 80) (Lat. Arete)
KERKYRA: (3) imp. *IG* IX (1) 899
KORINTHIA:
—KORINTH: (4) v AD *SEG* XI 142
LAKONIA:
—SPARTA: (5) ii/iii AD *IG* v (1) 547, 8 (Bradford (-)) (Πομπωνία Καλλιστονίκη ἡ καὶ Ἀ.: d. Πομπώνιος Πανθάλης Διογένης Ἀριστέας, Μεμμία Λογγῖνα)
S. ITALY (CAMPANIA):
—NEAPOLIS: (6) i-ii AD *CIL* x 1506; cf. Leiwo p. 91 (Lat. Fulvia Arete: m. L. Furius Furianus)
SICILY:
—KATANE: (7) imp. *Sic. Gymn.* 14 (1961) p. 183 (Lat. Vibia Arete)
—SYRACUSE: (8) iii-v AD Strazzulla 302 (Wessel 781)

**Ἀρέτης**
ILLYRIA:
—EPIDAMNOS-DYRRHACHION: (1) imp.? *RE* (2) (dub.)

**Ἀρέτιππος**
LAKONIA:
—SPARTA: (1) c. 60-20 BC *IG* v (1) 211, 48; VII 420, 42, 54 (*IOrop* 528; Bradford (-)) (s. Λύσιππος)

**Ἄρετις**
ARKADIA:
—MEGALOPOLIS: (1) iii BC *SEG* XVII 141, 5 (f. Ἀρετακλῆς)

**Ἀρετώ**
MESSENIA:
—MESSENE?: (1) imp. *IG* v (1) 1500 (Ἀρετοῖ (voc.))

**Ἀρέτων**
ACHAIA: (1) 138 AD *IvOl* 382, 8 (Λ. Γέλλιος Ἀ.)
LAKONIA:
—SPARTA: (2) m. ii AD *SEG* XI 622, 2 (Bradford (1)) (Λ. Ἀρέτω[ν]: s. Φιλαθήναιος) ?= (3); (3) c. 140-160 AD *IG* v (1) 71 III, 33 (Bradford (2)) ?= (2); (4) c. 225-250 AD *IG* v (1) 529, 14 (I f. Μ. Αὐρ. Ἀρέτων); (5) ~ ib. l. 14 (Bradford (3)) (Μ. Αὐρ. Ἀ.: II s. Ἀρέτων I)
MESSENIA:
—KORONE: (6) 246 AD *IG* v (1) 1398, 71 (Αὐρ. Ἀ.); (7) ~ ib. l. 96 (Αὐρ. Ἀ.)

**Ἀρεύς**
LAKONIA: (1) inc. Ant. Lib. xii lemma; *RE* Supplbd. 1 (5) (Poralla² 113) (dub.)
—SPARTA: (2) ?v BC Plu., *Mor.* 217 F (Poralla² 112) (Ἀρηγεύς—mss.); (3) iv BC *SEG* XI 639,

2; (4) c. 330-265 BC *RE* (1); *IC* 2 p. 250 no. 12 A; *IvOl* 308; *SEG* XXV 444; *Münzpr. der Laked.* p. 112 Group 1 (coins) (Bradford (1)) (s. Ἀκρότατος, f. Ἀκρότατος: king); (5) f. iii BC *SEG* XI 668 (vase); *BSA* 30 (1928-30) pp. 244-5 fig. 2, 14; (6) c. 262-254 BC Paus. iii 6. 6; *FD* III (4) 418 (Bradford (2)) (s. Ἀκρότατος, Χιλωνίς: king); (7) iii/ii BC *RE* (3) (Bradford (3)); (8) c. 80-100 AD *SEG* XI 511, 3; 608, 6 (Bradford (4)) (f. Τ. Τρεβελληνὸς Μενεκλῆς); (9) c. 105-110 AD *IG* v (1) 20 B, 7 (Bradford (4)) (Τ. Τρεβελληνὸς Ἀ.: s. Πολέμαρχος)

**Ἀρεφίων?**
ARGOLIS:
—ARGOS: (1) ?c. 460-450 BC *SEG* XVI 244, 4 (Lazzarini 939); *LSAG*² p. 170 no. 36 (name, date) ([Ἀ]ρεφίōν—*LSAG*, [Β]ρεφίων?, [Ε]ρεφίων?)

**Ἀρήγων**
ARGOLIS:
—EPIDAUROS:
——Pleiatios (Hylleis): (1) m. iii BC Peek, *IA-Epid* 42, 59 (Perlman E.3); Perlman p. 63 f. (date) (f. Ἀριστοκράτης)
KORINTHIA:
—KORINTH: (2) arch. *RE* (-) (painter)

**Ἀρηξίδαμος**
ARKADIA:
—LOUSOI: (1) iv/iii BC *SEG* XXXVI 375 = XL 370 (bronze) (Ἀρē-)
LAKONIA:
—SPARTA?: (2) 207 BC Plb. xi 18. 3-5 (Bradford (-))

**Ἀρήξιππος**
LAKONIA:
—SPARTA: (1) f. iii BC *IG* v (1) 255 (*CEG* II 821; Moretti, *IAG* 18; Poralla² 114) (Ἀρ[ή]ξιππος: date—*LGPN*); (2) s. i BC *IG* v (1) 94, 22 (Bradford (4)) (Ἀρή[ξιππος]: f. Εὐάγγελος); (3) c. 25-1 BC *IG* v (1) 210, 5 (Bradford (1)) (s. Δαμοκράτης); (4) ~ *IG* v (1) 210, 29 (Bradford (2)) (s. Εὐάγγελος)

**Ἀρηξίων**
ARKADIA:
—PARRHASIOI: (1) 401 BC *RE* Supplbd. 4 (-) (mantis)
—TEGEA: (2) f. iii BC *IG* v (2) 35, 14 (f. —νθίας)

**Ἄρης**
MESSENIA:
—MESSENE: (1) 33 AD *SEG* XLI 335, 4 (s. Ἀρχέδαμος)
S. ITALY (CAMPANIA):
—DIKAIARCHIA-PUTEOLI: (2) m. i AD Camodeca, *L'Archivio Puteolano* 1 p. 125 no. 5 (Lat. Ambivius Ares)

**Ἀρήσιππος**
MESSENIA:
—THOURIA: (1) f. ii BC *SEG* XI 972, 68 (s. Ἀγαθοκλῆς)

**Ἀρητάδας**
KORINTHIA:
—KORINTH: (1) ?vi BC *IG* IV (1) 304 (pinax) (Ἀρētάδ[ας])

**Ἀρθέταυρος**
ILLYRIA: (1) ii BC *RE* Supplbd. 1 (-); Russu s.v.

**Ἀρθμιάδας**
LAKONIA:
—SPARTA: (1) ?viii-vii BC Plu., *Lyc.* 5 (Poralla² 115) (dub.)

**Ἀριάγνη**
KORINTHIA:
—KORINTH: (1) byz. *Hesp.* 41 (1972) p. 41 no. 32, 4
SICILY:
—SYRACUSE: (2) iii-v AD *SEG* IV 15 (Agnello 41; Wessel 396); (3) ~ *Nuovo Didask.* 6 (1956) p. 64 no. 34 (Ἀριάγν[η])

**Ἀριάδνη**
ARGOLIS:
—ARGOS (NR.): (1) byz. *SEG* XXIX 372, 2; cf. *TMByz* 9 (1985) p. 370 no. 121
S. ITALY (APULIA):
—TEANUM APULUM: (2) i-ii AD *CIL* IX 706 (*Teanum Apulum* pp. 100-103 no. 38) (Lat. Claudia Ariad(i)ne: m. Ἐλπίς)

**Ἀρίαιθος**
ARKADIA:
—TEGEA: (1) hell. *FGrH* 316; *RE* s.v. Araithos

**Ἀριάνθης**
ARGOLIS:
—ARGOS: (1) v BC *PMG* 738

**Ἀρίανθος**
ACHAIA:
—PELLENE: (1) m. iii BC *IG* v (2) 368, 102 (Ἀρίανθος?—*IG*)
ILLYRIA:
—EPIDAMNOS-DYRRHACHION: (2) hell.-imp. *IDyrrh* 280 (f. Λαήν)

**Ἀρίβαζος**
SICILY:
—SYRACUSE: (1) ?ii BC *Milet* 1 (3) 79, 8 (and Caria Miletos: Ἄμβατος?—ed.: s. Ἀνδρέας, f. Ματροφάνης)

**Ἀρίγνωτος**
LAKONIA:
—SPARTA: (1) iv/iii BC *CID* II 120 A, 29 (Poralla² 116) (f. —ας)

**Ἀριδείκης**
KORINTHIA:
—KORINTH: (1) arch. Plin., *NH* xxxv 16 (Lat. Aridices, Ardices—mss.: painter)

**Ἀρίδηλος**
S. ITALY (CAMPANIA):
—DIKAIARCHIA-PUTEOLI: (1) imp. *CIL* x 2377 (Lat. Aridelus)

**Ἀριεύς**
KORINTHIA:
—KORINTH: (1) viii BC Paus. ii 4. 4

**Ἀρίζηλος**
EPIROS:
—DODONA*: (1) iv BC *SEG* XV 405 a

**Ἀρίκκας**
EPIROS:
—DODONA: (1) iii BC Antoniou, *Dodone* Aa, 32; (2) ~ ib. l. 38 ([Ἀρί?]κκας); (3) ~ ib. Ab, 5

**Ἀρικράτης**
LAKONIA:
—SPARTA: (1) s. i BC *IG* v (1) 254 (*Artemis Orthia* p. 355 no. 141; Bradford (-)) (f. Σοίξιάδας)

**Ἀρίμναστος**
ILLYRIA:
—EPIDAMNOS-DYRRHACHION: (1) c. 250-50 BC Maier 114-9; *Bakërr Hoard* p. 66 no. 2; Münsterberg Nachtr. p. 14 (coin) (Ceka 82; 109; 204; 208; 219; 257; 268; 291; 302; 350; 447) (pryt.); (2) ~ Patsch, *Narona* p. 97 no. 4; cf. *IApoll Ref. Bibl.* n. 22 (coin) (pryt.)
SICILY:
—PETRA: (3) f. iii BC *SEG* XXX 1121, 26 (Dubois, *IGDS* 208) (s. Σῖμος)

## Ἀρίουσα

LAKONIA:
—SPARTA: (1) i-ii AD *IG* V (1) 767 (Bradford (-))

## Ἀρισαμίδας

AIGINA: (1) iii BC *IG* IV (1)² 256 ([Ἀ]ρισαμίδας: s. Λαδάμας)
ARKADIA:
—LOUSOI?: (2) iii BC *SEG* XI 1122, 6 + *IPArk* 22 ([Ἀ]ρισαμίδας)

## Ἀρίσαμος

ARKADIA: (1) iii BC *IG* V (2) 415, 6 (*IPArk* 23) (f. Τιμοσθένης)

## Ἀρίστα

EPIROS:
—BOUTHROTOS (PRASAIBOI): (1) a. 163 BC *IBouthrot* 21, 35; 28, 22; 29, 31; 36, 4 (*SEG* XXXVIII 478; 486-7; 495) (I m. Λύκος, Ἀρίστα II, Μελισσίς); (2) ~ *IBouthrot* 21, 35 (*SEG* XXXVIII 478) (II d. Σωσίπατρος, Ἀρίστα I)
KERKYRA: (3) s. ii AD *IG* IX (1) 730-1 (Ἀ[ρ]ίστα: d. Λυσανίας)
S. ITALY (CALABRIA):
—TARAS-TARENTUM: (4) hell.? ib. XIV 2406. 10 (loomweight) (*RA* 1932 (1), p. 37 no. 3)
S. ITALY (LUCANIA):
—HYELE-VELIA: (5) hell.? *PdelP* 25 (1970) p. 263 no. 4 (-σστα: d. Φιλικός)

## Ἀρισταγόρα

ARGOLIS:
—EPIDAUROS: (1) iii/ii BC *IG* IV (1)² 243 (d. Δωριεύς, m. Ἀκρυπτίδας, Ἀδεισιτίδας)
—TROIZEN: (2) s. iv BC ib. 122, 10, 16
EPIROS:
—AMBRAKIA: (3) iv/iii BC Unp. (Arta Mus., inscr.) (d. Καλλικράτης)
KORINTHIA:
—KORINTH: (4) m. iv BC *IG* II² 9056; (5) m. iii BC *RE* (2)
—KORINTH?: (6) m. iv BC ib. (1)
MESSENIA:
—MESSENE: (7) iii BC *IG* V (1) 1444 (d. Νικαγόρας)
SICILY:
—SYRACUSE: (8) hell. *NScav* 1892, p. 359

## Ἀρισταγόρας

AITOLIA: (1) ?228-215 BC *FD* III (4) 364, 3 (Ἀριστα[α]γ[όρ]ας)
ARGOLIS:
—ARGOS:
——(Pamphyloi-Olisseidai): (2) c. 400 BC *SEG* XXIX 361, 8
—EPIDAUROS*: (3) c. 370-365 BC Peek, *IAEpid* 52 B, 11 (Ἀ[ρι]σ[τ]αγό[ρας])
ARKADIA:
—MANTINEIA-ANTIGONEIA: (4) hell. *IG* II² 9280 (f. Θεαρίς)
EPIROS:
—AMBRAKIA: (5) s. iii BC *HE* 1393 (Ἀρηϊμένης—*AP* vii post 438: s. Θεύπομπος)
KORINTHIA:
—KORINTH: (6) hell. Peek, *AG* 2 p. 57 no. 201; (7) ?iii-ii BC *IG* IV (1) 199 (Ἀρισταγόρα?)
LAKONIA:
—SPARTA: (8) ii BC ib. V (1) 965, 1, 5 (Bradford (1)) (s. Ἀγηΐξενος); (9) c. 100 AD *SEG* XI 515, 5 (Bradford (2)) (f. Δεινοκρατίδας)
LEUKAS: (10) hell.? *IG* IX (1) 557 (Ἀρισταγό[ρας?])

## Ἀρισταγόρη

S. ITALY (CAMPANIA):
—NEAPOLIS: (1) i BC/i AD *INap* 94; cf. Leiwo p. 77 no. 22 (d. Χαιρέας)

## Ἀριστάγορος

ARGOLIS:
—ARGOS: (1) c. 63 BC *Mnem.* NS 47 (1919) pp. 260-1 no. 27, 5 ([Ἀ]ρισ[τ]άγορος: s. Χ—)

LAKONIA:
—KYTHERA: (2) c. 250 BC *IG* XI (4) 636, 3, 9 (s. Σωτηρίσκος)

## Ἀρισταινέτα

AITOLIA?: (1) iii BC *FD* III (4) 130; [131] ([Ἀρισ]ται[ν]έτα—no. 130, [Τιμαρ]έτα?, [Ἐπαιν]έτα?—ed.: d. Τιμόλαος, m. Τιμόλαος)

## Ἀρισταίνετος

ACHAIA:
—DYME*: (1) c. 219 BC *SGDI* 1612, 13 (*Tyche* 5 (1990) p. 124) (f. Λύκων)
ARGOLIS:
—EPIDAUROS: (2) iv BC *IG* IV (1)² 173
—KLEONAI: (3) hell. *SEG* XXVI 422

## Ἀρίσταινος

ACHAIA: (1) f. ii BC *IC* 2 p. 23 no. 6 F, 3 (s. Δαμοκάδης) ?= (2)
—DYME: (2) c. 210-180 BC *RE* (2); *FD* III (3) 122, 2 with n.; *SEG* XXII 214, 2; cf. Walbank 2 pp. 287; 550 (Ἀρισταίνετος—mss. Plb.: s. Τιμοκάδης) ?= (1)
AKARNANIA:
—THYRREION: (3) ii BC *IG* IX (1)² (2) 250, 7 (f. Ἀριστόφιλος)
ARGOLIS:
—EPIDAUROS:
——Politas: (4) c. 365-335 BC ib. IV (1)² 103, 106 (Ἀρίστα(ι)νος)
——HERMIONE: (5) i BC/i AD ib. IV (1) 722, 3 (s. Τίμαρχος); (6) ~ ib. l. 5 (I f. Ἀρίσταινος II); (7) ~ ib. l. 5 (II s. Ἀρίσταινος I)
ARKADIA:
—HERAIA: (8) m. iii BC ib. IV (1)² 96, 35 (Perlman E.3); Perlman p. 63 f. (date) (f. Θεόκτας)

## Ἀρισταῖος

ARGOLIS:
—ARGOS: (1) iv-iii BC Unp. (Ch. Kritzas)
—EPIDAUROS: (2) c. 350-200 BC *SEG* XXVI 452. 1
—EPIDAUROS*: (3) inc. *IG* IV (1)² 717 (tile) ?= (4); (4) c. 370-360 BC ib. 102, 255, 275-7, 280, 287, 289, 292-3, 295-8, 300, 304-5; 743, 5; Peek, *IAEpid* 52 A, 8, 10, 14, 17, 21; *BSA* 61 (1966) p. 271 no. 4 A, 11, 18 ?= (3)
ARKADIA:
—MANTINEIA-ANTIGONEIA: (5) c. 300-221 BC *IG* V (2) 323. 89 (tessera) ([Ἀρισ]ταῖος: f. Ἀριστόδαμος)
——TEGEA: (6) m. iv BC ib. 6, 68; (7) ~ ib. l. 79; (8) ~ ib. l. 112 ([Ἀρι]σταῖος); (9) hell.? ib. 170. 10 (tile) (Ἀρισταῖ(ος)?); (10) f. iii BC ib. 35, 23 (s. Ἀριστίων)
——(Hippothoitai): (11) iv/iii BC ib. 38, 48 (f. Τιμοκρέτης); (12) f. iii BC ib. 36, 71 (s. Τιμόστρατος)
LAKONIA:
—SPARTA: (13) 243-240 BC *PP* 2538 (Bradford (-))
MESSENIA:
—THOURIA: (14) f. ii BC *SEG* XI 972, 29 (f. Εὐεργέτας)
S. ITALY (BRUTTIUM):
—KROTON: (15) s. vi BC *RE* (7) (Ἀρισταίων: s. Δαμοφῶν)
S. ITALY (CAMPANIA):
—NEAPOLIS: (16) her. *IG* XIV 759, 4, 9 (*INap* 43; Laum, *Stiftungen* II 212) (Ἀρισταῖοι (n. gent.)); (17) i BC/i AD *INap* 113, 7 (Ἀρισταῖο(ς))

## Ἀρίσταιχμος

ARGOLIS:
—EPIDAUROS: (1) ?iv BC Peek, *IAEpid* 72, 2 (Ἀρί[σ]τ[α]ιχμο[ς]); (2) c. 370-365 BC ib. 52 B, 32 (Ἀρίστ᾽αιχμος) ?= (3); (3) c. 365-335 BC *IG* IV (1)² 103, 42, 69, 78 ?= (2)
—TROIZEN: (4) ?146 BC ib. IV (1) 757 B, 37 (Ἀρίσταιχμος: f. Φρουρίδας)

ARKADIA:
—ALEA: (5) f. iii BC ib. IX (1)² (1) 9, 3 (f. Καλλιστώ)
—HELISSON: (6) c. 221 BC ib. IV (1)² 42, 3 + Peek, *IAEpid* 8 (Ἀρίστα[ι](χ)μος?, Ἀρίστ..μος—*IG*, Ἀρίστ[αρ]μος—Peek)
—STYMPHALOS?: (7) iii BC *IG* V (2) 352, 8 (f. —λας)
ELIS: (8) c. 343 BC D. xviii 295

## Ἀρίστακος

S. ITALY (CALABRIA):
—TARAS-TARENTUM: (1) iv/iii BC *IG* XIV 668 II, 18 (Landi, *DISMG* 194) (Ἀρίστα(ρχ)ος?, Ἀρίστα[ι]ος?—*IG*); (2) c. 160 BC *ID* 1716, 6 (s. Ἡρακλείδας, Μυραλλίς (Syracuse))

## Ἀριστάναξ

ACHAIA: (1) 146 BC *IG* IV (1)² 28, 118 (f. Σκόπας: synoikos)

## Ἀριστανδρίδας

PELOPONNESE: (1) c. 230-200 BC *BCH* 45 (1921) p. 11 II, 44 (Ἀρισ[τ]ανδρίδας)

## Ἀρίστανδρος

ACHAIA:
—AIGION: (1) c. 230-200 BC ib. l. 57 (s. Ξενομένης); (2) ~ ib. p. 12 II, 60 (s. Εὐρύας)
AIGINA: (3) s. iii BC *SEG* XI 413, 29 (Perlman E.4) (Ἀρίσ[τ]ανδρος: s. Πασίων); (4) ?i BC *Alt-Ägina* I (2) p. 44 no. 11, 2 (Ἀρίστανδρ[ος]: f. Δημήτριος)
AITOLIA?: (5) c. 220-150 BC *SNG Cop.* Aetolia-Euboea 41 (coin)
AKARNANIA:
—THYRREION: (6) m. ii BC *Syll*³ 669, 8 (*IG* V (1) 29, 8) (s. Ἀρχέστρατος)
ARGOLIS:
—ARGOS: (7) s. v BC *BCH* 33 (1909) p. 450 no. 20 (-σστα-); (8) hell. *IG* VII 1563 (Ἀρί[σ]τανδ[ρ]ος: f. Σωσιγένης)
——Ἐλαιόν (Dymmadai): (9) s. iii BC *Mnem.* NS 43 (1915) p. 366 A, 3 (Perlman A.17); *Mnem.* NS 43 (1915) pp. 366-7 B, 3 (Perlman A.18); *SEG* XVI 247, 3 (Perlman A.19) (s. Ἀριστεύς)
—EPIDAUROS: (10) c. 370 BC *IG* IV (1)² 102, 16 ?= (12)
——(Hylleis): (11) 146 BC ib. 28, 55 (f. Καλλικράτης)
——Naupheis: (12) c. 365-335 BC ib. 103, 80 ?= (10)
——Pagasina (Azantioi): (13) m. iii BC ib. 96, 47 (Perlman E.3); Perlman p. 63 f. (date) (Ἀρ[ίσταν]δρος)
ARKADIA:
—HERAIA: (14) s. iv BC Peek, *NIEpid* 16, 27 (Perlman E.6) (Ἀρ[ίστ]ανδρο[ς]: f. Ἀριστοκράτης)
—MEGALOPOLIS: (15) a. 369 BC Paus. viii 30. 10; (16) iii BC *SEG* XXIII 226 = *PAE* 1988, p. 59 no. α (f. Ἀρχίδαμος); (17) s. ii BC *IG* V (2) 439, 71 (s. Νικολαΐδας); (18) ii/i BC ib. 443, 24; 444, 5; 445, 10 (*IPArk* 32) (f. Πολύξενος)
—ORCHOMENOS: (19) iv BC *IOlbia* 4 (s. Μέλισσος)
—TEGEA: (20) 356-345 BC *CID* II 31, 15; 34 I, 40; *SEG* XXXI 560, 2 (Ἀ[ρί]σ[τ]α[ν]δρος—*SEG*)
ELIS: (21) m. iv BC *IvOl* 44, 8 ([Ἀ]ρί[σ]τανδρ[ος])
ILLYRIA:
—EPIDAMNOS-DYRRHACHION: (22) c. 250-50 BC Münsterberg p. 38 (coin) (Ceka 448) (pryt.)
KERKYRA: (23) iii/ii BC *GVI* 1511, 5; cf. Fraser-Rönne, *BWGT* p. 112 no. 3
LAKONIA:
—SPARTA: (24) hell.? *IG* V (1) 651 (Bradford (2)); (25) c. 143 BC *IG* IX (1)² (1) 137, 31 (Bradford (5)) (f. Ἀριστοκράτης); (26) s. i BC *IG* V (1) 124, 3 (Bradford (4)); (27) ~ *IG* V (1) 124, 11 (Bradford (7)) (f. Πολυαινίδας); (28) c.

48-31 BC *Münzpr. der Laked.* p. 134 Group 14 series 21; p. 140 Group 15 series 26; p. 146 Group 16 series 12; p. 155-6 Group 18 (coin) (Bradford (3)); **(29)** c. 25-1 BC *IG* v (1) 212, 37 (Bradford (1)) (s. Πολυαινίδας)

TRIPHYLIA:
—PYRGOI: **(30)** c. 230-200 BC *BCH* 45 (1921) p. 12 II, 84 (locn.—Oulhen)

### Ἀριστάνωρ
AKARNANIA:
—THYRREION: **(1)** iv/iii BC *SEG* xxv 630
ARKADIA:
—ORCHOMENOS: **(2)** ?c. 378 BC *BCH* 102 (1978) p. 335, 96 (*IPArk* 15)

### Ἀρισταρέτα
ACHAIA:
—PELLENE: **(1)** ii-i BC *SEG* XI 1277

### Ἀριστάρχη
S. ITALY (CAMPANIA):
—NOLA: **(1)** imp. *CIL* x 1297 (Lat. Titia Aristarche)

### Ἀρισταρχίδας
AKARNANIA:
—DERION: **(1)** m. iii BC Peek, *IAEpid* 42, 61, 64 (Perlman E.3); cf. *IG* IX (1)² (2) p. XIX; cf. Perlman p. 63 f. (date); p. 168 (locn.) (s. Ἀλεξίλας)
LAKONIA:
—SPARTA: **(2)** s. i BC *IG* v (1) 897 (tiles) (Bradford (-))

### Ἀρισταρχίς
AITOLIA:
—KALYDON: **(1)** ii BC *IG* IX (1)² (1) 145 (d. Εὐρυδίκα)

### Ἀρίσταρχος
ACHAIA:
—LEONTION?: **(1)** 263 BC ib. 17, 55 (s. Ἀριστείδας)
—PATRAI: **(2)** c. 146-32 BC *BMC Pelop.* p. 22 no. 5; *Coll. Hunter* 2 p. 125 no. 2 (coin) (s. Δάμων)
AIGINA: **(3)** v BC *SEG* XXXVII 262 (?s. Εὔθοινος); **(4)** ii BC ib. XI 9, 1; **(5)** iii AD ib. 15 (Ἀρίσταρχ[ος])
AITOLIA: **(6)** ?228-215 BC *FD* III (4) 364, 2; *SGDI* 2525, 2
—BOUKATION: **(7)** 164-163 BC *IG* IX (1)² (1) 99, 10, 13; 103, 9
—BOUKATION?: **(8)** c. 162 BC ib. 106, 11, 13
—EIDAIOI: **(9)** m. ii BC ib. 107, 4
—ERTAIOI: **(10)** 263-262 BC ib. 3 A, 18
—KALLION/KALLIPOLIS: **(11)** 170 BC *SGDI* 1740, 11 (f. Ἀγήσανδρος)
—KONOPE-ARSINOE: **(12)** 184 BC *IG* IX (1)² (1) 131, 6
—PHILOTAIEIS: **(13)** f. ii BC ib. 96, 22 (f. Ἀλέξων)
—THERMOS*: **(14)** s. iii BC ib. 60 VII, 7
—THESTIEIS: **(15)** iii/ii BC *SBBerlAk* 1936, p. 386 no. 2 b
ARGOLIS:
—ARGOS: **(16)** v BC *SEG* XI 339, 6 (Ἀρίσταρ[χος]: f. Κίκος); **(17)** f. iii BC *CID* II 122 I, 14 (f. Δαμοσθένης); **(18)** 102 BC *FD* III (1) 227, [3], 7 (s. Εὔφρων)
—EPIDAUROS: **(19)** c. 370 BC *IG* IV (1)² 102, 38 ?= (20); **(20)** ~ ib. l. 266 ?= (19); **(21)** c. 340-330 BC *SEG* xxv 387 A, [9], 16; **(22)** iv/iii BC *IG* IV (1)² 235; 254; 254 a; 289; Peek, *IAEpid* 142. 1; 142. 3-5 (s. Ἐργῖλος, f. Ἀρίσταρχος, Κλεαρίστα, Ἐργῖλος) ?= (23); **(23)** ~ *IG* IV (1)² 238; 239 (I f. Ἀρίσταρχος II, Κλεαρίστα) ?= (22); **(24)** ~ ib. 238 (II s. Ἀρίσταρχος I); **(25)** iii BC ib. 168, 4; *SEG* XVII 178, 2; **(26)** ~ *IG* IV (1)² 304

—(Hylleis): **(27)** 146 BC ib. 28, 53 (s. Διόδωρος)
—(Hysminatai): **(28)** 146 BC ib. l. 19 ([Ἀρί]σταρχος: f. Σθενείδας)
—Pagasina (Azantioi): **(29)** m. iii BC ib. 96, 47 (Perlman E.3); Perlman p. 63 f. (date)
—HERMIONE: **(30)** iii BC *IG* IV (1) 728, 12; **(31)** ?268-255 BC Nachtergael, *Les Galates* 2 bis, [4-5]; 3, [4], 15; 4, 7; 5, 9; 8, 30-1; 15, 1; 15 bis, 16; cf. Stephanis 1993; 2174 (f. Πυθοκλῆς, Παντακλῆς)
—TROIZEN: **(32)** ?146 BC *IG* IV (1) 757 B, 34 (Ἀρί[σ]ταρχος: s. Ἀριστόνικος)
ARKADIA:
—MANTINEIA-ANTIGONEIA: **(33)** 64 or 62 BC ib. v (2) 265, 48 (s. Μένιππος)
—ORCHOMENOS: **(34)** iii BC *SEG* XXXIII 319, 18 (Ἀρίσταρ[χο]s)
—TEGEA: **(35)** v BC *RE* (21); *TrGF* 1 pp. 89-92; **(36)** f. iii BC *IG* v (2) 35, 17 (s. Θεόδωρος)
DALMATIA:
—ISSA: **(37)** iv/iii BC *VAHD* NS 8 (1905) p. 97 (*VAMZ* 1970, p. 33 f. frr. I-J); **(38)** f. ii BC Brunšmid p. 22 no. 9, 11 (['Ἀρί]σταρχος)
——(Dymanes): **(39)** iv/iii BC ib. p. 7, 20 (f. Δαμάτριος); **(40)** ~ ib. l. 24 (f. Ἄνταλλος); **(41)** ~ ib. p. 9, 64 (Ἀ[ρί]σταρχος: f. —τίων)
ELIS: **(42)** inc. *IvOl* 208; cf. Moretti, *Olymp.* 992 ([Ἀ]ρίσταρχ[ος]); **(43)** ~ Paus. vi 16. 7; **(44)** 36-24 BC *IvOl* 59, 19; 62, 6 (s. Κῦρος: mantis/Iamidai/Ξ.); **(45)** 28-16 BC ib. 64, 19; 65, 16 (s. Ἀριστοκλῆς: Μ.); **(46)** ?i AD *EA* 1905, p. 259 no. 2, 5 (I f. Ἀρίσταρχος II); **(47)** ~ ib. l. 5 ([Ἀ]ρίσταρχος: II s. Ἀρίσταρχος I); **(48)** ?i-ii AD *FGrH* 412; **(49)** iii AD *SEG* XV 259, 14 ([Ἀρίσ]ταρχος)
EPIROS:
—AMBRAKIA: **(50)** m. iv BC *RE* (6); **(51)** hell.? *CIG* 1802 (s. Λυκίσκος); **(52)** 225-205 BC *FD* III (3) 220, 7; **(53)** a. 167 BC *SEG* XXXV 665 A, 10 (f. Λαμίσκος)
—KASSOPE: **(54)** f. ii BC Cabanes, *L'Épire* p. 564 no. 41, 10 (s. Ἀριστομένης)
ILLYRIA:
—AMANTIA (NR.): **(55)** ii BC *SEG* XXXIX 553 (s. Κλεάνωρ)
—APOLLONIA: **(56)** c. 250-50 BC Münsterberg p. 36; Maier 16 (Ceka 5; ; 51; 124) (pryt.); **(57)** i BC Maier 142; cf. *IApoll Ref. Bibl.* Addenda (1) (coin) (?s. Ἱππο—: money.); **(58)** ~ Maier 154 (coin) (money.); **(59)** imp. *IApoll* 53
—EPIDAMNOS-DYRRHACHION: **(60)** c. 250-50 BC Ceka, *Probleme* p. 151 no. 8 (coin) (pryt.) ?= (61); **(61)** ~ Maier 120-4; Münsterberg Nachtr. p. 14 (coin) (Ceka 53; 181; 187; 220; 303; 385; 442) (pryt.) ?= (60); **(62)** hell.-imp. *IDyrrh* 312 (f. Μενίσκα)
KORINTHIA:
—SIKYON: **(63)** m. iv BC *An. Ox.* iv 117; **(64)** hell.? Plin., *NH* i index lib. v (Skalet 47)
LAKONIA:
—SPARTA: **(65)** 400 BC Poralla² 117
MESSENIA:
—MESSENE: **(66)** iii BC *SEG* XXIII 209, 1; **(67)** ~ ib. l. 6
—MESSENE?: **(68)** ii/i BC ib. XI 979, 51
—THOURIA: **(69)** f. ii BC ib. 972, 59 (f. Νόμας)
PELOPONNESE?: **(70)** a. 164 BC *IvOl* 47, 3 (*Syll*³ 665)
S. ITALY (BRUTTIUM):
—LOKROI EPIZEPHYRIOI: **(71)** hell.? De Franciscis p. 102 (s. Μένων)
——(Γαγ.): **(72)** iv/iii BC ib. 16, 2 (f. Φιλοκράτης)
——(Σωτ.): **(73)** iv/iii BC ib. 18, 2 (s. Ἀριστεύς)
S. ITALY (CAMPANIA):
—NEAPOLIS: **(74)** i BC *IG* II² 9990 a = *Ag.* XVII 634 ([Ἀρ]ίσταρχ[ος]: f. Ἀριστο—)

S. ITALY (LUCANIA):
—HERAKLEIA: **(75)** iv/iii BC *IGSI* 1 I, 1, 165 (*DGE* 62; Uguzzoni–Ghinatti I) (s. Ἡρακλείδας); **(76)** f. iii BC *Festschr. Neutsch* p. 141
SICILY: **(77)** ii/i BC *IG* XIV 2398. 2; *Meligunis-Lipara* 5 p. 183 T. 2181; cf. *Kokalos* 32 (1986) p. 221 no. 12 (tiles)
—GELA-PHINTIAS: **(78)** c. 500-475 BC Dubois, *IGDS* 149 d (vase) (Arena, *Iscr. Sic.* II 31)
—KAMARINA: **(79)** ?264 BC *FD* III (3) 202, 3 (s. Σιληνός)
—MORGANTINA: **(80)** ii BC *SEG* XXVII 655, 5, 8 (Dubois, *IGDS* 194); cf. *PdelP* 44 (1989) p. 205 (Ἀρίσταρ[χος]: ?s. Φιλιστίων, ?f. Φίλων)
—SYRACUSE:
——(Ἑρμεῖος): **(81)** ?iv BC Manganaro, *PdelP* forthcoming no. 3, 2 (f. Δίων)
—TAUROMENION: **(82)** c. 218 BC *IG* XIV 421 an. 23 (*SGDI* 5219) (s. Εὔθυμος); **(83)** c. 158-145 BC *IG* XIV 421 an. 83; 421 an. 93; 421 an. 96 (*SGDI* 5219) (s. Θεόκριτος); **(84)** c. 155 BC *IG* XIV 421 an. 86 (*SGDI* 5219) (s. Ἡράκλητος); **(85)** c. 142 BC *IGSI* 4 II (III), 63 an. 77 (f. —ος)
——(Δαμ.): **(86)** c. 153 BC ib. 4 III (IV), 20 an. 88 (s. Θεόδωρος)
——(Δεξ.): **(87)** ?ii/i BC *IG* XIV 421 D an. 14 (*SGDI* 5219) (s. Ζώπυρος)

### Ἀρίσταρχυρ
ELIS?: **(1)** ?iv-iii BC Robert, *Coll. Froehner* 32 ([Ἀ]ρίσταρχυρ)

### Ἀρίστας
AKARNANIA:
—THYRREION: **(1)** iii BC *IG* IX (1)² (2) 245, 15
ARGOLIS:
—EPIDAUROS: **(2)** iv/iii BC Peek, *IAEpid* 142. 1 (s. Ἀρίσταρχος)
—EPIDAUROS*: **(3)** ii/i BC *IG* IV (1)² 100, 9 (Stephanis 312)
ILLYRIA:
—APOLLONIA: **(4)** imp. *IApoll* 54

### Ἀριστέας
ACHAIA: **(1)** 231 BC *CPR* XVIII 16, 337; **(2)** ii AD *IvOl* 472, 5 (Μ. Ἀντ. Ἀ.: s. Δάμων); **(3)** 119-138 AD *IG* v (1) 1352, 11 (f. Δάμων)
—AIGION: **(4)** 399 BC *SEG* XL 54, 3, 7
—DYME: **(5)** s. iii BC ib. XIII 278, 25 (s. Τίμαιος)
—TRITAIA: **(6)** c. 210-207 BC *IG* IV (1)² 73, 23; *SEG* XXXV 303 (date) (s. Ἀριστεύς)
ACHAIA?: **(7)** 193 BC *IG* v (2) 293, 20 (s. Μενέδαμος)
AIGINA: **(8)** iv/iii BC *FD* III (4) 398 (s. Ἡρακλε—)
AITOLIA:
—ANDREATAI: **(9)** 163 BC *IG* IX (1)² (1) 101, 10
AKARNANIA:
—THYRREION: **(10)** ii BC ib. IX (1)² (2) 251, 11 (f. Λύκος)
ARGOLIS:
—ARGOS: **(11)** v BC Unp. (Ch. Kritzas) (-σστέ-); **(12)** hell. *FGrH* 317; **(13)** hell.? *SEG* XXXVIII 307; **(14)** ?iii BC Clem. Al., *Strom.* ii 68. 22 ?= (15); **(15)** 272 BC *RE* (3) (Ἀριστεύς—Polyaen.) ?= (14); **(16)** ii BC *Mnem.* NS 47 (1919) p. 168 no. 18
—EPIDAUROS: **(17)** i BC *SEG* XI 451 (s. Σωτάκων)
—EPIDAUROS*: **(18)** c. 370-360 BC *BSA* 61 (1966) p. 272 no. 4 B II, 21; cf. Peek, *IAEpid* 48
ARKADIA:
—ALIPHEIRA: **(19)** iii BC Orlandos, *Alipheira* p. 218 no. 2
—LOUSOI: **(20)** iv/iii BC *IG* v (2) 390, 5 (Perlman L.3)
—MANTINEIA-ANTIGONEIA: **(21)** c. 300-221 BC *IG* v (2) 323. 43 (tessera) (s. Ἀριστόδαμος)

—MEGALOPOLIS: (22) ii BC *IvOl* 396 (Loewy 271) (s. Νίκανδρος: sculptor)
—PHIGALEIA: (23) ii/i BC *IG* v (2) 426 (Ἀριστέα[ς])
ELIS: (24) s. i AD *IvOl* 430, 4 (Τιβ. Κλ. Ἀ.: f. Τιβ. Κλ. Πέλοψ)
ILLYRIA:
—APOLLONIA: (25) c. 250-50 BC Münsterberg Nachtr. p. 13; Maier 98; Ceka 17-18; cf. *IApoll Ref. Bibl.* n. 25 (locn.) (coin) (money.)
—EPIDAMNOS-DYRRHACHION: (26) c. 250-50 BC Maier 419; Münsterberg Nachtr. p. 15 (Ceka 79-80); cf. *IApoll Ref. Bibl.* n. 23 (coin) (money.); (27) hell.-imp. *IDyrrh* 165 (f. Δάζιος)
KERKYRA: (28) iii BC *Korkyra* 1 p. 164 no. 2 (f. —εντις (fem.)); (29) ?iii-ii BC *IG* IX (1) 752; *Korkyra* 1 p. 167 no. 4 (tiles); (30) c. 229-48 BC *BMC Thessaly* p. 146 nos. 488-98; *SNG Cop. Epirus-Acarnania* 227-9 (coins) (s. Ἀρίστων)
KORINTHIA:
—KORINTH: (31) ii AD Luc., *DMort* 11. 1 (fict.)
—SIKYON: (32) 224 or 221 BC Nachtergael, *Les Galates* 64, 9 (Stephanis 314) (s. Ἀριστίας)
LAKONIA: (33) i BC *IG* II² 9146 (f. Ἀρίστιον)
—SPARTA: (34) m. ii AD ib. v (1) 495, 2; *SEG* XI [843]; *BSA* 80 (1985) pp. 241-2 (ident., stemma) (Bradford (2)) (Γ. Πομπώνιος Ἀ.: s. Γ. Πομπώνιος Ἀλκαστος, f. Π. Πομπώνιος Ἀλκαστος); (35) c. 140 AD *IG* v (1) 65, 15; *SEG* XI 549, 5 (Bradford (1)) (s. Ἀγαθόλας); (36) c. 140-145 AD *IG* v (1) 1314, 34 (Bradford (5)); (37) ~ *IG* v (1) 1314, 39 (Bradford (3)) (s. Σωσίδαμος); (38) c. 175-200 AD *IG* v (1) 89, 6; 129, 1 (Bradford (4)) ([Γ.] Ἰούλ. Ἀ.); (39) ii/iii AD *IG* v (1) 546, 6; 547, 2; 684, 3; *BSA* 79 (1984) pp. 281-3 (ident.; 80 (1985) pp. 241-2 (ident., stemma) (Bradford s.v. Πανθάλης (2)) (Γ. Πομπώνιος Πανθάλης Διογένης Ἀ.: f. Πομπώνιος Πανθάλης ὁ καὶ Ἀριστοκλῆς, Πομπωνία Καλλιστονίκη ἡ καὶ Ἀρέτη); (40) f. iii AD *IG* v (1) 602, 2; *SEG* XXXV 337, 8; *BSA* 80 (1985) pp. 225; 239-43 (ident., stemma) (Bradford (6)) (Γ. Πομπώνιος Ἀ. ὁ καὶ Περικλῆς: s. Πομπώνιος Πανθάλης ὁ καὶ Ἀριστοκλῆς, f. Πομπωνία Καλλιστονίκη)
LEUKAS: (41) ii BC *AM* 27 (1902) p. 371 no. 52 (Ἀριστέα (masc. nom./gen.?))
MESSENIA:
—ABIA: (42) ?i/ii AD *IG* v (1) 1358, 4 (f. Ἀρχίππα)
—KYPARISSIA: (43) iii BC ib. 1424 (s. Θαλίαρχος)
—MESSENE: (44) iv/iii BC ib. 1435, 5; (45) s. ii BC *BCH* 95 (1971) p. 544, 4, 18 (s. Ἀγάθων)
—THOURIA: (46) ii-i BC *IG* v (1) 1385, 22 (f. Διόδωρος); (47) f. ii BC *SEG* XI 972, 27 (f. Γοργίδας); (48) ~ ib. l. 115 (f. Τίμων)
PELOPONNESE: (49) s. iii BC ib. XIII 278, 11 (f. Ἀλεξίων)
PELOPONNESE?: (50) s. iii BC ib. XXV 449, 42 (*IPArk* 26) (Ἀριστέα[ς])
S. ITALY (BRUTTIUM):
—RHEGION:
——(Ἀμφιμ.): (51) ii BC *IG* XIV 616, 4, 9 with Add. p. 688 (*Mus. Naz. Reggio* p. 159 no. 29) (s. Ἀριστόμαχος, f. Ἀριστόμαχος)
S. ITALY (CALABRIA):
—TARAS-TARENTUM: (52) c. 650-625 BC *Antike Helme* p. 396 no. 18 (bronze)
S. ITALY (LUCANIA):
—METAPONTION: (53) iv BC Iamb., *VP* 267 (*FVS* 1 p. 446)
SICILY:
—ABAKAINON: (54) hell. *IGLMP* 124 (f. Ὀλτίσκος)
—AKRAI: (55) ?iii BC *SGDI* 3240, 8 (*Akrai* p. 156 no. 7) (f. Ξένων); (56) ii BC ib. p. 156 no. 6, 12 (s. Ξένων)

—LIPARA*: (57) ii/i BC *Meligunis-Lipara* 2 p. 82 T. 237; cf. *Kokalos* 32 (1986) p. 221 no. 13 (tile)
—SYRACUSE:
——(Κραταιμείος): (58) iv BC Manganaro, *PdelP* forthcoming no. 3, 9 (s. Στράτων)
—SYRACUSE?:
——(Πλη.): (59) hell. ib. no. 4 I, 8 (s. Νίκων)
—TAUROMENION: (60) c. 239 BC *IG* XIV 421 an. 2 (*SGDI* 5219) (s. Ἀρτεμίδωρος) ?= (61); (61) c. 238 BC *IG* XIV 421 an. 3 ?= (60); (62) c. 209 BC ib. 421 an. 32 (*SGDI* 5219); (63) c. 146 BC *IG* XIV 421 an. 95 (*SGDI* 5219) (f. Μόσχος)

**Ἀρίστεια**
ARGOLIS:
—ARGOS: (1) ?c. 550-525 BC *SEG* XXVI 423 (Lazzarini 275 b); *LSAG²* p. 168 no. 12 (?d. Ἐκεθαῖος)

**Ἀριστείας**
ARKADIA:
—MEGALOPOLIS: (1) f. iii BC *EILakArk* 20 (f. Τιμανορίδας)
—TEGEA: (2) m. iv BC *IG* v (2) 6, 93

**Ἀριστείδας**
ACHAIA:
—LEONTION?: (1) 263 BC ib. IX (1)² (1) 17, 55 (f. Ἀρίσταρχος)
—PATRAI: (2) c. 185 BC *Milet* 1 (3) 148, 21; *Chiron* 19 (1989) pp. 279 ff. (date)
ACHAIA?: (3) 193 BC *IG* v (2) 293, 8 (s. Ἡράκλειτος)
ARGOLIS:
—EPIDAUROS: (4) iii BC ib. IV (1)² 278 (s. Ἀριστοκράτης); (5) ii-i BC Peek, *IAEpid* 33, 1 (-στί-: s. Καλλικλῆς) ?= (6); (6) i BC-i AD *IG* IV (1)² 645 (-στί-: f. Καλλικλῆς) ?= (5); (7) i AD ib. 644 (-στί-: s. Καλλικλῆς)
——(Azantioi): (8) 146 BC ib. 28, 26 (f. Σωσικράτης)
ARKADIA: (9) ?265-253 BC Nachtergael, *Les Galates* 4, 12; 7, 11; 8, 10; 10, 8-9; cf. Stephanis 1429 (-δης: f. Κλειτόριος)
—MANTINEIA-ANTIGONEIA: (10) f. iii BC *IG* v (2) 272, 4 (Ἀριστείδα[ς])
—TEGEA:
——(Apolloniatai): (11) s. iv BC ib. 41, 12 (Ἀριστεί[δ]ας)
——(Athaneatai): (12) s. iii BC ib. 36, 114 (s. Δίων: metic)
EPIROS:
—BOUTHROTOS (PRASAIBOI): (13) a. 163 BC *IBouthrot* 14, 13 (*SEG* XXXVIII 471) (f. Δαίδαλος); (14) ~ *IBouthrot* 78, 7, 9; 79, 6, 8; 80, 6-7; 81, 6, 8; 82, 6-7; 83, 5-6; 84, 6-7; 85, 6-7; 86, 7-8; 87, [6], 8; 88, 5-6 (*BCH* 118 (1994) pp. 122 f. nos. 1-11); cf. *IBouthrot* 5, 5
—PHOTIKE: (15) imp. *ILGR* 165 (Lat. Aristides)
ILLYRIA:
—EPIDAMNOS-DYRRHACHION: (16) iv BC *IDyrrh* 34 (-στεί-: f. Ἧαις)
LAKONIA: (17) iii BC *IG* II² 9152 = *AM* 67 (1942) p. 109 no. 210 (Bradford (8)) (f. Παρθένιον)
—GYTHEION: (18) ?ii BC *RA* 1904 (2), p. 8 no. 5 (Bradford (7)) (Ἀριστ[είδας], Ἀριστ[ων]?— Bradford I f. Ἀριστείδας II); (19) ~ *RA* 1904 (2), p. 8 no. 5 (Bradford (1); *PP* 15338) (Ἀριστεί[δας]: II s. Ἀριστείδας I)
—SPARTA: (20) c. 450-434 BC *IG* v (1) 1229, 8 (Poralla² 119) (-στί-); (21) c. 30-20 BC *IG* v (1) 211, 13 (Bradford (3)) (-στεί-: s. Κλεόδαμος); (22) c. 100-105 AD *SEG* XI 537 b, 7 (Bradford (6)) (-στί-: I f. Ἀριστείδας II); (23) ~ *SEG* XI 537 b, 7 (Bradford (2)) (-στί-: II s. Ἀριστείδας I); (24) c. 125 AD *IG* v (1) 1314, 10 (Bradford (5)) (Ἀριστε[ί]δ[ας]: f. Ἀρίων); (25) c.

140-150 AD *IG* v (1) 64, 16; 289, 4 (*Artemis Orthia* p. 321 no. 46; Bradford s.v. Εὐδόκιμος (2)) (Εὐδόκιμος ὁ καὶ Ἀ., Ἀριστείδαρ—289: s. Δαμοκράτης)
MESSENIA:
—THOURIA: (26) ii-i BC *IG* v (1) 1385, 17 (f. Νικομήδης); (27) ii/i BC ib. 1384, 22 (s. Κρατιππίδας)
S. ITALY (BRUTTIUM):
—LOKROI EPIZEPHYRIOI: (28) s. v BC *RE* (21); cf. Supplbd. 3 col. 158
——(Ἀστ.): (29) iv/iii BC De Franciscis 20, 9 (f. Ἀρχιππος)
——(Δυσ.): (30) iv/iii BC ib. 32, 4 (f. Ἀπιάδας)
——(Λογ.): (31) 277 BC ib. 8, 2; 31, 2 (s. Ἀρκεσίλας)
——(Πυρ.): (32) iv/iii BC ib. 16, 5 (f. Κλήσαρχος)
S. ITALY (CALABRIA):
—TARAS-TARENTUM: (33) c. 302-280 BC Vlasto 910-12 (Evans, *Horsemen* p. 180 VIII L.2); *NC* 1918, p. 145 (coins) (Ἀριστείδ(ας))

**Ἀριστείδης**
ARKADIA:
—TEGEA: (1) 165 AD *IG* v (2) 50, 25 (-στί-: s. Ἀριστίων)
ELIS: (2) ?ii AD *RE* (15); Moretti, *Olymp.* 951
S. ITALY (BRUTTIUM):
—RHEGION: (3) iv BC Iamb., *VP* 267 (*FVS* 1 p. 447)
S. ITALY (LUCANIA):
—HYELE-VELIA: (4) f. iv BC Polyaen. vi 11; *RE* (14)
S. ITALY?: (5) hell. Desy, *Timbres amphoriques* 1179 (amph.) (Lat. Iulius Aristides)

**Ἀρίστεον**
ARGOLIS:
—ARGOS: (1) a. 303 BC *CEG* II 816, 14

**Ἀριστερῖνος**
KORINTHIA:
—KORINTH?: (1) ?iii BC *IG* IV (1)² 261 (f. —ατος)

**Ἀρίστερμις**
KORINTHIA:
—KORINTH: (1) inc. *Syringes* 705 (s. Χάρμος)

**Ἀριστεύς**
ACHAIA:
—DYME: (1) 215 BC *PP* 14996; cf. *Brooklyn Mus. Ann.* 10 (1968-9) p. 138 no. 26 (f. Ἀναξίλαος)
—TRITAIA: (2) c. 210-207 BC *IG* IV (1)² 73, 23; *SEG* XXXV 303 (date) (f. Ἀριστέας)
AIGINA: (3) i BC-i AD *Alt-Ägina* 1 (2) p. 46 no. 21
ARGOLIS:
—ARGOS: (4) s. v BC *RE* (2); Moretti, *Olymp.* 335 (s. Χείμων); (5) iv-iii BC Unp. (Argos, Kavvadias); (6) iv/iii BC ib.; (7) ?320 BC *IG* v (2) 549, 16 (f. Ἀριστομένης); (8) iii BC ib. IV (1)² 238; 239; 240; *Mnem.* NS 47 (1919) p. 163 no. 8 b (f. Καλλικράτης); (9) m. iii BC *IG* IV (1)² 96, 24 (Peek, *IAEpid* 42; Perlman E.3); Perlman p. 63 f. (date) (I f. Ἀριστεύς II); (10) ~ *IG* IV (1)² 96, 24 (Peek, *IAEpid* 42; Perlman E.3); Perlman p. 63 f. (date) (II s. Ἀριστεύς I)
——(Sphyreidai): (11) m. iv BC *SEG* XVII 146, 2
——Elaion (Dymmadai): (12) s. iii BC *Mnem.* NS 43 (1915) p. 366 A, 3 (Perlman A.17); *Mnem.* NS 43 (1915) pp. 366-7 B, 3 (Perlman A.18); *SEG* XVI 247, 3 (Perlman A.19) (f. Ἀρίστανδρος)
——Mykenai (Daiphonteis): (13) iii/ii BC *IG* IV (1) 498, 11; *SEG* XI 303 a (locn.)
——Pallas (Heraieis): (14) s. iii BC ib. XVII 144, 4 (Perlman A.20) (s. Μναίτιμος)
—EPIDAUROS*: (15) c. 290-270 BC *SEG* XXV 402, 75

ARKADIA:
—TEGEA: (16) m. iii BC *IG* IV (1)² 96, 70 (Perlman E.3); Perlman p. 63 f. (date) (s. Φίλιππος)

EPIROS:
—BOUTHROTOS (PRASAIBOI): (17) a. 163 BC *IBouthrot* 30, 21 (*SEG* XXXVIII 488) (f. Ἀριστόμαχος) ?= (18)
——Phonidatoi: (18) a. 163 BC *IBouthrot* 144, 7 (f. Ἀριστόμαχος) ?= (17)

KORINTHIA:
—KORINTH: (19) c. 475-430 BC *RE* (3) (Ἀριστέας—Hdt. vii 137. 3: s. Ἀδείμαντος); (20) 435 BC Th. i 29. 2 (s. Πέλλιχος)

LAKONIA:
—SPARTA: (21) c. 450-434 BC *IG* v (1) 213, 81; 1230, 5; *LSAG*² p. 201 no. 54 (date) (Poralla² 118) ?= (22); (22) 423 BC Th. iv 132. 3 ?= (21); (23) s. i BC *IG* v (1) 92, 8 (Bradford (3)) (f. Ἀριστόνικος); (24) c. 30-20 BC *IG* v (1) 142, 13 (Bradford (1)) (s. Ἀριστόνικος); (25) c. 120 AD *SEG* XI 545, 3; cf. Bradford (2); (26) ?m. ii AD *IG* v (1) 47, 2; cf. Bradford (2)

MESSENIA:
—ASINE: (27) ?316 BC *SEG* XII 219 (s. Νεοκλῆς)
—MESSENE: (28) 54-68 AD *IG* v (1) 1449, 6 (f. Κλεόφατος)

S. ITALY (BRUTTIUM):
—LOKROI EPIZEPHYRIOI:
——(Γαψ.): (29) iv/iii BC De Franciscis 16, 5; 38, 6 (f. Ἀριστόμαχος)
——(Δυσ.): (30) 279 BC ib. 13, 5 (f. Ἐμμενίδας)
——(Κοβ.): (31) iv/iii BC ib. 3, 4; 38, 4 (f. Εὐχέλας)
——(Σκι.): (32) iv/iii BC ib. 20, 18 (s. Σίμων)
——(Σωτ.): (33) iv/iii BC ib. 18, 2 (f. Ἀρίσταρχος)

SICILY:
—TYNDARIS: (34) f. i BC Cic., *In Verr.* II v 110 (Lat. Aristeus: s. Δέξων)

**Ἀρίστη**
SICILY:
—ZANKLE-MESSANA: (1) imp. *CIL* x 6981 (Lat. Claudia Ariste: m. Ἀρίστων)

**Ἀριστήδεια**
LAKONIA:
—TEUTHRONE: (1) i BC/i AD *IG* v (2) 538 (d. Νικίας, m. Σωτιμίδας)

**Ἀριστηίδας**
S. ITALY (CALABRIA):
—TARAS-TARENTUM: (1) iii BC *SEG* XVI 579 (Landi, *DISMG* 204)

**Ἀριστηϝίς**
S. ITALY (BRUTTIUM):
—SYBARIS-THOURIOI-COPIAE: (1) vii/vi BC *SEG* XXXVI 941 (Arena, *Iscr. Sic.* IV 1); cf. *BE* 1987, no. 746 (-στεϝίς)

**Ἀριστήν**
DALMATIA:
—ISSA: (1) hell. Brunšmid p. 26 no. 17 (*SEG* XL 513) + *VAHD* 84 (1991) p. 252 no. 2 (f. Θεύδετος, Σώπατρος, Ἄνταλλος)
——(Dymanes): (2) iv/iii BC Brunšmid p. 8, 28 (f. Μητρικῶν); (3) ~ ib. l. 32 (f. Αἴσχρων); (4) ~ ib. l. 41 (f. Ἄνταλλος) ?= (5); (5) ~ ib. l. 42 (f. —ων) ?= (4)
——(Hylleis): (6) iv/iii BC ib. p. 9, 53 ([Ἀ]ριστήν: s. Ἀλέξιππος)

ILLYRIA:
—APOLLONIA: (7) hell. *IApoll* 111 (f. Κτήσων); (8) ~ ib. 347 (tile); (9) ~ ib. 359 (tile) (Ἀριστ[η]ν[ος] (gen.): f. Ἱέρων); (10) c. 250-50 BC *Bakërr Hoard* p. 165 no. 135; Münsterberg Nachtr. p. 12; Maier 17 (coin) (Ceka 4; 6; 70) (pryt.); (11) ~ Maier 22; 56; 73; 103 (coin) (Ceka 19-22) (money.); (12) iii/ii BC *IApoll* 7; cf. *L'Illyrie mérid.* 2 p. 207 (f. Ψύλλος); (13) ii-i BC *IApoll* 122 (f. Μνασήν); (14) imp. ib. 55 (Ἀρίστην ὁ καὶ Λύσων Ἀντιμάχου: s. Παρμενίσκος); (15) ~ ib. 56
—BALAIITAI: (16) ii BC *SEG* XXXVIII 521, 2; cf. *CRAI* 1991, pp. 197 ff.; *L'Illyrie mérid.* 2 p. 204 f. (s. Ἐξάκιος)
—BALAIITAI*: (17) ii BC *SEG* XXXVIII 521, 9, 12; cf. *CRAI* 1991, pp. 197 ff.; *L'Illyrie mérid.* 2 p. 204 f. (s. Παρμήν)
—EPIDAMNOS-DYRRHACHION: (18) hell. *IDyrrh* 328 (f. Νικήν); (19) c. 250-50 BC *BMC Thessaly* p. 76 nos. 160-1 (coin) (pryt.) ?= (21); (20) ~ Münsterberg Nachtr. p. 14 (Ceka 81); cf. *IApoll Ref. Bibl.* n. 24 (coin) (money.); (21) ~ Maier 125-32; 471-2; Münsterberg Nachtr. p. 14; *SNG Cop. Thessaly-Illyricum* 452 (Ceka 16; 28; 77; 83; 152; 169; 188; 251; 264; 269; 346; 376; 378; 404; 415; 424; 433; 460); cf. *IApoll Ref. Bibl.* n. 5 (coin) (pryt.) ?= (19); (22) ~ ib. *IDyrrh* 116 (s. Ἀγήν); (23) ii-i BC ib. 532 (tiles); (24) f. ii BC *SEG* XXXVIII 558; (25) hell.-imp. *IDyrrh* 117 (s. Ἀφροδίσιος); (26) ~ ib. 118 (s. Σκυρθάνας); (27) ~ ib. 159 (f. Γοργις); (28) ~ ib. 181 (f. Ἐννεάτωρ); (29) hell.-imp.? ib. 239 (f. Θάρνα?)

**Ἀριστίας**
ARGOLIS:
—PHLEIOUS: (1) v BC *RE* (2); *TrGF* 1 pp. 85-7 (s. Πρατίνας)
ILLYRIA:
—APOLLONIA: (2) imp. *IApoll* 57
—EPIDAMNOS-DYRRHACHION: (3) iii BC *IDyrrh* 19 (Ἀριστία[ς]: s. Σώστρατος)
KORINTHIA:
—SIKYON: (4) 224 or 221 BC Nachtergael, *Les Galates* 64, 10; cf. Stephanis 314 (f. Ἀριστέας)
S. ITALY (CALABRIA):
—TARAS-TARENTUM: (5) c. 302-280 BC Vlasto 706 (coin) (Evans, *Horsemen* p. 135 VI F.2); *JIAN* 4 (1901) p. 98

**Ἀριστῖνος**
ARGOLIS:
—ARGOS:
——Lyrkeion (Dmaihippidai): (1) c. 316-222 BC *SEG* XVII 143, 2 (Perlman A.15)

**Ἀρίστιον**
LAKONIA: (1) i BC *IG* II² 9146 (d. Ἀριστέας)
LEUKAS: (2) ii BC *AM* 27 (1902) p. 370 no. 49
MESSENIA:
—MESSENE: (3) ii-i BC *SEG* XXXIX 385 + XLI 364

**Ἀριστίππα**
ARGOLIS:
—ARGOS: (1) ii BC ib. XLII 279, 18 (d. Διοκλῆς)
KORINTHIA:
—KORINTH: (2) ?f. v BC *Hesp.* 41 (1972) p. 212 no. 12
—SIKYON: (3) iv-iii BC Unp. (Sikyon Mus.)

**Ἀρίστιππος**
AITOLIA: (1) ?255 BC Nachtergael, *Les Galates* 8, 4; 19, 3; Flacelière p. 398 no. 21 c, [2]; (2) ?254-237 BC Nachtergael, *Les Galates* 9, 17; 60, [5?] (Stephanis 323) (s. Κάλλων)
AKARNANIA:
—STRATOS: (3) iii BC *SEG* XXV 634 (I f. Λυκίνος, Ἀρίστιππος II); (4) ~ ib. (II s. Ἀρίστιππος I)
ARGOLIS:
—ARGOS: (5) a. 316 BC ib. XIII 243, 6 (Perlman A.6) (Ἀρίστιππος); (6) ?277 BC *FD* III (1) 88, 5 (s. Ἀ—ος); (7) 272 BC Plu., *Pyrrh.* 30; *RE* (4) (?f. Ἀριστόμαχος); (8) c. 270-234 BC ib. (5); *IG* IV (1)² 621 A; Plu., *Mor.* 781 E (Ἀριστόδημος—Plu.: ?s. Ἀριστόμαχος, f. Ἀπία: tyrant)
—HERMIONE: (9) iii BC *IG* IV (1) 729 II, 10 (s. Αἴνετος)
ARKADIA: (10) 320-316 BC ib. v (2) 549, 12, 24 (s. Ἀριστοκλῆς)
—MANTINEIA-ANTIGONEIA: (11) c. 300-221 BC ib. 323. 75 (tessera) (s. Κλεόθοινος)
—PHENEOS: (12) c. 230-200 BC *BCH* 45 (1921) p. 13 II, 118 (Ἀρίστ[ιπ]πος: s. Ἀρίωδος: name—Oulhen)
—TEGEA: (13) s. iv BC *IG* v (2) 41, 61 (Ἀρίστιππο[ς]); (14) iii/ii BC ib. 142 (f. Δαμάτριος)
ARKADIA?: (15) ii BC *RE* (7); *FGrH* 317
EPIROS:
—KASSOPE: (16) i BC Cabanes, *L'Épire* p. 564 no. 42, 2 (*SEG* XXVI 71) ([Ἀρ]ίστιππος)
ILLYRIA:
—APOLLONIA: (17) c. 250-50 BC Maier 19 (coin) (Ceka 89) (pryt.); (18) ~ Maier 90; Münsterberg Nachtr. p. 13 (Ceka 23) (money.); (19) f. ii BC *BCH* 45 (1921) p. 22 IV, 36 (f. Λαμίσκος)
KORINTHIA:
—KORINTH: (20) ii BC *IG* II² 9059 (f. Ἀριστομένης)
LAKONIA:
—SPARTA: (21) inc. Front., *Strat.* iii 2. 8 (Poralla² 120) (Lat. Aristippus); (22) i BC *IG* v (1) 126, 7 (Bradford (-)) (f. Πεισίστρατος)
MESSENIA:
—MESSENE: (23) ?iii BC *FD* III (1) 517, 1 ([Ἀ]ρίστιππος: s. Ποίμανδρος)
—THOURIA: (24) f. ii BC *SEG* XI 972, 35 (s. Ἀπήμων); (25) ii/i BC *IG* v (1) 1384, 13 (s. Δαμοθέρσης)
S. ITALY (BRUTTIUM):
—LOKROI EPIZEPHYRIOI:
——(Κοβ.): (26) iv/iii BC De Franciscis 7, 2 (s. Γλαύκιππος)
——(Κρα.): (27) iv/iii BC ib. 26, 7 (f. Εὔθυμος)
——(Ὀμβ.): (28) 277 BC ib. 8, 7 (f. Ἀριστόδαμος)
——(Φαω.): (29) iv/iii BC ib. 2, 3 (f. Κάλλιππος); (30) ~ ib. 22, 18 (s. Ἀριστοτέλης)
S. ITALY (CALABRIA):
—LUPIAE (NR.): (31) iv BC Troisi, *Epigrafi mobili* 97
—TARAS-TARENTUM: (32) ?vi BC Iamb., *VP* 267 (*FVS* 1 p. 446); (33) c. 280-272 BC Vlasto 710-12; 732-8 (coin) (Evans, *Horsemen* p. 157 VII A.1; p. 158 VII B.1) (Ἀρίστιπ(πος)); (34) c. 235-228 BC Vlasto 947-9 (coins) (Evans, *Horsemen* p. 195 IX E.1)

**Ἀριστίς**
ARGOLIS:
—HERMIONE: (1) iii/ii BC *IG* IV (1) 712, 1 (s. Ἀνίκητος); (2) ~ ib. l. 3 (s. Γέρυλλος)
—KLEONAI: (3) ?c. 560 BC *SEG* XI 290, 1 (Ebert, *Gr. Sieg.* 2; Lazzarini 847; *Nemea* 1 p. 277 no. 25); *LSAG*² p. 150 no. 5 (date) (s. Φείδων)
ARKADIA: (4) 232 BC *CPR* XVIII 12, 239 (Ἀριστις: s. Εὐήνωρ)
MESSENIA:
—MESSENE: (5) f. ii BC *SEG* XLI 331, 2 (s. Τιμογένης)
S. ITALY (CALABRIA):
—TARAS-TARENTUM: (6) iii BC ib. XVI 579 (Landi, *DISMG* 204); (7) c. 272-235 BC Vlasto 820-1 (coins) (Evans, *Horsemen* p. 176 VIII A.1; p. 182 no. 4); cf. Evans, *Horsemen* p. 147 n. 183
SICILY:
—ECHETLA: (8) vi/v BC Manganaro, *PdelP* forthcoming 7
—KAMARINA: (9) f. v BC Cordano, *Tessere Pubbliche* 1 a (Arena, *Iscr. Sic.* II 125 A) (f. Αἰσχύλος)
—SELINOUS: (10) s. v BC Dubois, *IGDS* 60 (Arena, *Iscr. Sic.* I 24; *IGLMP* 98) (f. Ἀριστόδαμος)

**Ἀριστίς**
ARGOLIS:
—EPIDAUROS: (1) ii/i BC *IG* IV (1)² 248 (Ἀριστίν (acc.): d. Ἀριστοκράτης)

MESSENIA: (2) iv BC ib. II² 9340

**Ἀρίστιχος**

ARKADIA:
—PHIGALEIA: (1) m. iii BC SEG XXIII 243
MESSENIA:
—KOLONIDES: (2) ii BC IG v (1) 1402, 8
—MESSENE: (3) iii BC SEG XXIII 210, 14

**Ἀριστίων**

ACHAIA:
—DYME: (1) ii BC Achaean Grave Stelai 43 (s. Εὐθυνίων)
AIGINA: (2) s. v BC Alt-Ägina II (1) 68 (or Athens?); (3) s. iii BC IG IV (1) 727 A, 8 (Perlman H.1) (s. Ἑρμοκλῆς); (4) ?s. i BC Alt-Ägina I (2) p. 43 no. 5
AITOLIA:
—KALLION/KALLIPOLIS: (5) hell. IG IX (1)² (1) 158
AKARNANIA:
—ANAKTORION: (6) 356-354 BC ib. IV (1)² 95, 22 (Perlman E.2); Perlman pp. 46-9 (date) (s. Περίανδρος)
—MEDION: (7) c. 356-330 BC IG IV (1)² 95, 13 (Perlman E.2); Perlman p. 40 f. (date); SEG XXIII 189 I, 2
—OINIADAI?: (8) hell.-imp. IG IX (1)² (2) 425
—PALAIROS: (9) iii BC ib. 476
ARGOLIS:
—ARGOS: (10) c. 458 BC ib. I³ 1149, 18 ([Ἀ]ριστίōν); (11) ii-i BC ib. IV (1) 611 (Nachtergael, Les Galates 79)
——(Dymanes-Doriadai): (12) 105 BC JÖAI 14 (1911) Beibl. p. 146 no. 4, 4 (I f. Ἀριστίων II); (13) ~ ib. l. 4 (II s. Ἀριστίων I)
—EPIDAUROS: (14) m. iv BC Moretti, Olymp. 415 (s. Θεοφίλης); (15) iv/iii BC IG IV (1)² 162; (16) hell.? SEG XL 224 (f. Τίμαιος); (17) f. iii BC ib. XXX 395
——Erilais: (18) c. 323-309 BC IG IV (1)² 49, 14 (Perlman E.8)
—HERMIONE: (19) ii/i BC SEG XVII 162 (f. Κλεώ)
ARKADIA:
—MANTINEIA-ANTIGONEIA: (20) ?iii BC IG v (2) 319, 42
—MEGALOPOLIS: (21) ?145 BC ib. 439, 30 (ś. Φιλογένης)
—ORCHOMENOS: (22) 322 BC SGDI 2661, 2; cf. IG v (2) p. 146 s.v. Orchomenus (s. Πολύφραστος)
—TEGEA: (23) iv BC ib. 31, 9 (s. Ἐχεμένης); (24) f. iii BC ib. 35, 5 ([Ἀρισ]τίων?); (25) ~ ib. l. 23 (f. Ἀρισταῖος); (26) ~ ib. l. 31 (s. Τολμίδας); (27) s. iii BC ib. 116, 4 (s. Ἰσχόμαχος); (28) ii-i BC ib. 203; (29) ii AD ib. 252; (30) 165 AD ib. 50, 25 (f. Ἀριστείδης); (31) ~ ib. l. 59 (I f. Ἀριστίων II); (32) ~ ib. l. 59 (II s. Ἀριστίων I); (33) ~ ib. l. 74 (f. Βουδᾶς); (34) ~ ib. l. 77 (Σουλπίκιος Ἀ.)
——(Apolloniatai): (35) iv/iii BC ib. 38, 29 (f. Φιλοκλῆς)
——(Krariotai): (36) f. iii BC ib. 36, 38 (f. Ξενόφαντος)
DALMATIA:
—ISSA: (37) iii BC Brunšmid p. 9 fr. G, 6 + VAMZ 1970, p. 37 frr. G and M (s. Μάμαρχος); (38) f. ii BC Brunšmid p. 23 no. 10, 10 (f. Μίνατος)
—PHAROS: (39) imp. CIL III 3094 (Lat. Aristio)
EPIROS:
—AMBRAKIA: (40) v/iv BC BCH 79 (1955) p. 267 (f. Ἀριστόι); (41) ii-i BC CIG 1799, 5 (s. Ἀνδρόνικος); (42) i BC-i AD ib. 1806 (f. Πουβλιώι)
ILLYRIA:
—APOLLONIA: (43) iii-ii BC IApoll 33; (44) imp. ib. 58 (Ἀρισστίω[ν]: s. Δωρίων)

—EPIDAMNOS-DYRRHACHION: (45) hell. IDyrrh 2; (46) hell.-imp. ib. 123 (f. Ἀριστώ); (47) ~ ib. 392 (Ἀρίσ(τί)ωνο[ς] (gen.): f. Τάτα)
KERKYRA: (48) iii/ii BC IG XI (4) 1241 (f. Ἀρίστων)
KORINTHIA:
—KORINTH: (49) vi BC SEG XLI 540 B ([Ἀρι]στίων?); (50) imp. IG II² 9055 (f. Ἀριστ—)
—SIKYON: (51) vi/v BC SEG XI 244, 49 (-ōν)
LAKONIA:
—SPARTA: (52) iii BC ib. XL 348 B, 8; (53) c. 25-1 BC IG v (1) 261; Artemis Orthia p. 303 no. 12 (name, date) (Bradford (11)) (Ἀρίστων—IG: f. Ἀριστοκράτης)
LEUKAS: (54) ii BC AM 27 (1902) p. 370 no. 48 b (Ἀριστίω[ν])
MESSENIA:
—MESSENE: (55) ii BC PAE 1969, p. 106, 13
—THOURIA: (56) f. ii BC SEG XI 972, 2, 17 (f. Ἀριστομένης); (57) ~ ib. l. 125 (Ἀρίστων—ed.: s. Ἀριστομήδης)
PELOPONNESE?: (58) 11 AD PAE 1992, p. 72 B, 1 (s. Θεόδωρος)
S. ITALY (CALABRIA):
—TARAS-TARENTUM: (59) c. 160 BC ID 1716, 1 (f. Ἡρακλείδας); (60) ~ ib. l. 4 (s. Ἡρακλείδας, Μυραλλίς (Syracuse))
S. ITALY (LUCANIA):
—HERAKLEIA: (61) iv/iii BC IGSI 1 I, 95, 122, 165 (DGE 62; Uguzzoni-Ghinatti I)
SICILY:
—GELA-PHINTIAS: (62) f. ii BC IG XIV 256, 1 (Dubois, IGDS 161); cf. SEG XL 804 (s. Ἰστιεῖος); (63) ~ IG XIV 256, 43 (Dubois, IGDS 161); cf. SEG XL 804 (s. Νυμφόδωρος)
—KAMARINA: (64) f. v BC Cordano, Tessere Pubbliche 15 (-ōν: s. Δεινίας); (65) iii BC Manganaro, PdelP forthcoming no. 1, 7 (s. Διοκλῆς)
—MEGARA HYBLAIA: (66) f. vi BC Dubois, IGDS 19 (Arena, Iscr. Sic. I 2) (-ōν: s. Νίσις)
—NEAITON: (67) iii/ii BC SGDI 5260 (Sic. Gymn. 16 (1963) p. 55); cf. Rupes loquentes p. 454 (s. Ἀγαθ—)
TRIPHYLIA:
—LEPREON: (68) ?475-450 BC SEG XXV 472; LSAG² p. 450 no. 15 a (date) (-ōν)

**Ἀριστόβιος**

ARGOLIS:
—ARGOS: (1) c. 458 BC IG I³ 1149, 11 (Ἀριστόβι[ος])
—EPIDAUROS:
——(Azantioi) (2) 146 BC ib. IV (1)² 28, 38 (s. Ἀγιάδας)
—EPIDAUROS*: (3) c. 370-360 BC BSA 61 (1966) p. 272 no. 4 B II, 12
ARKADIA:
—TEGEA:
——(Apolloniatai): (4) f. iii BC IG v (2) 36, 55 (s. Εὐπράκτας: metic)
ELIS: (5) c. 177-209 AD IvOl 102, 21; 103, 23; 104, 23; 105, [12]; 107, [17] (II s. Ἀριστόβιος I); (6) 181-189 AD ib. 102, 21; 104, 23 (I f. Ἀριστόβιος II)
EPIROS:
—AMBRAKIA: (7) a. 167 BC SEG XXXV 665 A, 8 (s. Αὐτόλυκος)
LAKONIA:
—SPARTA: (8) c. 105-110 AD IG v (1) 97, 10; SEG XI 564, 17 (Bradford (2)) (I f. Ἀριστόβιος II); (9) c. 105-115 AD IG v (1) 97, 10; SEG XI 564, 17 (Bradford (1)) (II s. Ἀριστόβιος I)

**Ἀριστοβούλα**

ARGOLIS:
—METHANA-ARSINOE: (1) ii-i BC IG II² 9328 (-λη: d. Σωσιγένης)

EPIROS:
—MOLOSSOI: (2) ?iv/iii BC SGDI 1353, 2; cf. Cabanes, L'Épire p. 582 no. 57
SICILY:
—SYRACUSE (NR.): (3) ii-i BC IG XIV 4 (SGDI 3233); cf. Rupes loquentes p. 451 no. 2 (d. Θεόδωρος)

**Ἀριστόβουλος**

ACHAIA:
—AIGION: (1) m. ii BC IG IX (1)² (3) 667, 3; cf. Walbank 3 p. 707 (s. Εὐαγόρας, f. Εὐαγόρας)
—ASCHEION: (2) c. 210-207 BC IG IV (1)² 73, 28; SEG XXXV 303 (date) (Ἀριστόβου[λος]: s. Λεόντιχος); (3) 188 BC Syll³ 585, 150 (f. Λεόντιχος)
AITOLIA: (4) ?a. 246 BC SGDI 2508, 2; (5) 213 or 205 BC Nachtergael, Les Galates 66, 3
—APERANTOI: (6) ?iii BC L'Illyrie mérid. 1 p. 108 no. 4; cf. p. 98 (locn.) (SEG XXXVII 434) (f. Θαύμανδρος)
ARGOLIS:
—EPIDAUROS: (7) iii/ii BC IG IV (1)² 356 (Peek, IAEpid 153. 4); (8) ii/i BC IG IV (1)² 65, 4, 15, 19, 22-3; 630, 2 (s. Ξενόδοκος); (9) ii-iii AD ib. 532 (f. Ἐπαφρόδιτος)
—EPIDAUROS*: (10) c. 370-365 BC Peek, IAEpid 52 A, 28
—PHLEIOUS: (11) ii-i BC IG IV (1) 461 (f. Ζώπυρος)
—TROIZEN: (12) f. ii AD ib. 758, 19 (I f. Ἀριστόβουλος II); (13) ~ ib. l. 19 (II s. Ἀριστόβουλος I)
ARKADIA:
—PAOS: (14) c. 230-200 BC BCH 45 (1921) p. 12 II, 72
ELIS:
—OLYMPIA*: (15) f. v BC SEG XXIV 321 (-βō-)
KORINTHIA:
—SIKYON: (16) vi/v BC ib. XI 244, 61
LAKONIA:
—SPARTA: (17) c. 110-135 AD IG v (1) 32 A, 7; 32 B, 32; 34, 11; 139, 1; 487, 4; SEG XI 490, 6; 496, 2; 579, 1 (Bradford (1)) (Τιβ. Κλ. Ἀ.); (18) c. 150-160 AD IG v (1) 69, 32; 71 III, 28; SEG XI 554, 4 (Bradford (2)) (Ἀριστόβου(λος)—69: f. Νικηφόρος)
MESSENIA:
—MESSENE: (19) 126 AD IG v (1) 1469, 5; cf. SEG XL 366 (I f. Ἀριστόβουλος II); (20) ~ IG v (1) 1469, 5; cf. SEG XL 366 (II s. Ἀριστόβουλος I)
—PHARAI: (21) i AD IG v (1) 1364 (Ἰούλ. Ἀ.)
S. ITALY (CAMPANIA):
—DIKAIARCHIA-PUTEOLI: (22) imp. CIL x 2973 (Lat. Aristobulus)
—NEAPOLIS: (23) i BC/i AD INap 174, 3; cf. Leiwo p. 60 no. 1 (Ἀρ[ισ]τόβουλο[ς])
SICILY:
—SYRACUSE?: (24) hell. IG XIV 2407. 17; cf. L'Incidenza dell'Antico pp. 420 ff. (bullet) (f. Κρίθων)
—TAUROMENION: (25) c. 147 BC IGSI 4 III (IV), 63 an. 94 (f. Δαμάτριος)

**Ἀριστόγειτος**

EPIROS:
—DODONA*: (1) v-iv BC SEG XV 391 a (Ἀριστογειτοσα—lap., Ἀριστογείτων?—SEG index)
KORINTHIA:
—KORINTH: (2) 274 BC IG XI (2) 199 A, 89
SICILY:
—AKRAI: (3) ?iii BC SGDI 3239, 5 (Akrai p. 157 no. 9) (s. Παυσανίας); (4) ii BC ib. p. 156 no. 6, 17 (f. Πύρριχος); (5) ii-i BC SGDI 3246, 21 (Akrai pp. 152-3 no. 2; Dubois, IGDS 109) (s. Παυσανίας)
—SELINOUS: (6) ?f. vi BC ib. 73 (Arena, Iscr. Sic. 1 18; IGLMP 80); cf. Guarducci, Ep. Gr. 3 pp. 171-2 (s. Ἀρκαδίων)

## Ἀριστογείτων

ARKADIA:
—TEGEA: **(1)** s. iii BC *IG* IV (1) 727 B, 7 (Perlman H.2) (Ἀριστ[ο]γείτων: f. Ἀριστόξενος)
——(Krariotai): **(2)** iii BC *IG* v (2) 40, 25 (f. Ἀνδρίας)
ELIS: **(3)** 217 BC Plb. v 94. 6
KORINTHIA:
—KORINTH: **(4)** s. iv BC *Corinth* VIII (1) 11, 14; cf. *SEG* XI 60 (Ἀριστογε[ίτων]—*SEG*, Ἀριστογέ[νης]—*Corinth*)
—SIKYON: **(5)** vi/v BC ib. 244, 66 (-τōν)

## Ἀριστογένης

ACHAIA: **(1)** 146 BC *IG* IV (1)² 28, 78 (f. Φιλόδαμος: synoikos); **(2)** ~ ib. l. 107 (f. Ἐργασίων: synoikos)
EPIROS:
—BOUTHROTOS (PRASAIBOI): **(3)** a. 163 BC *IBouthrot* 99, 3 (*BCH* 118 (1994) p. 121 B)
KORINTHIA:
—SIKYON: **(4)** ?253 BC Nachtergael, *Les Galates* 10, 25 (Stephanis 325) (s. Εὐφράνωρ); **(5)** ~ Nachtergael, *Les Galates* 10, 48; cf. Stephanis 143 (f. Ἀλκισθένης)
LAKONIA:
—SPARTA: **(6)** c. 30-20 BC *IG* v (1) 211, 8 (Bradford (-)) (s. Ἀριστοκλῆς)
S. ITALY (LUCANIA):
—HERAKLEIA: **(7)** c. 275 BC *SNG ANS Etruria-Calabria* no. 870; van Keuren, *Coinage of Heraclea* p. 90 no. 130 (coin) (Ἀριστογέ[νης])
SICILY:
—KAMARINA: **(8)** ?ii BC *SEG* XXXIX 996, 8 (Dubois, *IGDS* 126; Cordano, 'Camarina VII' 75) (f. Θεόδωρος)
—SYRACUSE: **(9)** 409 BC X., *HG* i 2. 8 (f. Ἡρακλείδας); **(10)** 208 BC *IMM* 72, 8 (Dubois, *IGDS* 97) ([Ἀρι]στογένης)

## Ἀριστογενίδας

LAKONIA:
—SPARTA: **(1)** 403-399 BC *ID* 87 b, 11 (Poralla² 121)

## Ἀριστοδάμα

ARGOLIS:
—ARGOS: **(1)** iv-iii BC *BCH* 27 (1903) p. 265 no. 14 (Ἀριστοδ[άμ]α, Ἀριστοδ[ίκ]α?)
KORINTHIA:
—SIKYON: **(2)** f. iii BC Paus. ii 10. 3; iv 14. 7 (Skalet 52) (m. Ἄρατος)

## Ἀριστοδάμας

KERKYRA: **(1)** ?iii BC *IG* IX (1) 695, 1, 4
LAKONIA:
—SPARTA: **(2)** i BC/i AD *BSA* 89 (1994) pp. 433-4 no. 2, 9 (s. Ἀμφιδάμας); **(3)** c. 100-120 AD *IG* v (1) 99, 2; 147, 2; *SEG* XI 562, 4; 569, 8 (Bradford (-)) (f. Φιλοξενίδας)

## Ἀριστοδαμίδας

ARGOLIS:
—ARGOS: **(1)** ?vii BC *FGrH* 115 F 393 (s. Μέροψ, f. Φείδων: king)
LAKONIA:
—SPARTA: **(2)** ?s. i AD *IG* v (1) 678, 1 (Bradford (-)) (Ἀριστοδαμί[δας])

## Ἀριστόδαμος

ACHAIA: **(1)** 236 BC *PPetr*² I *Wills* 18, 15 (-δη-); **(2)** 167 BC Plb. XXX 13. 3
—AIGEIRA: **(3)** c. 225-200 BC *BCH* 23 (1899) p. 93 no. 3, 11 + *SEG* III 362 (f. Λαπομπίδας)
—AIGION: **(4)** c. 146-32 BC *BMC Pelop.* p. 3 nos. 24-5 (coin)
—DYME: **(5)** s. iii BC *SEG* XIII 278, 17 (f. Ἀγήσανδρος)
—DYME*: **(6)** c. 219 BC *SGDI* 1612, 22 (*Tyche* 5 (1990) p. 124) (s. Μεγακλῆς)

—PATRAI: **(7)** ?ii BC *Achaean Grave Stelai* 20 (f. Νοστία); **(8)** c. 146-32 BC *SNG Cop. Phliasia-Laconia* 157; *Coll. Photiades* 1012 (coin) (f. Ἀριστομένης); **(9)** ii/i BC *FD* III (4) 52, 2, 8; *SEG* XIX 400, 1 (s. Λυκῖνος, f. Λυκῖνος)
AITOLIA: **(10)** ii AD *IG* IX (1)² (1) 92, 4 (s. Βίων)
—KALYDON: **(11)** c. 142 BC ib. 137, 48 (s. Ἄλυπος)
—POTIDANIA: **(12)** m. ii BC *SBBerlAk* 1936, p. 371 a, 11 (*SEG* XLI 528 A); *SBBerlAk* 1936, p. 371 b, 12 (*SEG* XLI 528 B) (s. Σιμιάδας)
AKARNANIA:
—KOMBOTI (MOD.): **(13)** ii BC *IG* IX (1)² (2) 386
ARGOLIS:
—ARGOS: **(14)** f. vi BC *SEG* XXXV 266 bis; **(15)** ?316 BC *IG* v (2) 549, 26 (s. Ἀριστόμαχος); **(16)** ?304 BC ib. 550, 23; **(17)** ii AD *SEG* XVI 253, 10 (s. Γάιος)
——(Hyrnathioi): **(18)** ?c. 460-450 BC *IG* IV (1) 517, 6 (Lazzarini 937); *LSAG*² p. 170 no. 32 (date) ([Ἀ]ριστόδαμος)
—EPIDAUROS: **(19)** iv BC *IG* IV (1)² 174; **(20)** f. ii BC Peek, *IAEpid* 153. 8 (s. Ἀρίστων); **(21)** ii-iii AD *IG* IV (1)² 688 (f. Θία?ος)
——(Azantioi): **(22)** 146 BC ib. 28, 30 (I f. Ἀριστόδαμος II); **(23)** ~ ib. l. 30 (II s. Ἀριστόδαμος I)
——Erilais: **(24)** c. 365-335 BC ib. 103, 89
—EPIDAUROS*: **(25)** c. 290-270 BC ib. 109 II, 100, 102 (Ἀριστόδ[αμος]); **(26)** c. 200-175 BC Peek, *NIEpid* 80 (s. Νικοκράτης)
—HERMIONE: **(27)** ?ii-i BC *IG* IV (1) 731 III, 14 (f. Νίκαιος)
—LERNA: **(28)** i-iii AD ib. 664; **(29)** ~ ib. 665
—METHANA-ARSINOE: **(30)** ii-i BC ib. 855, 1 (f. Καλλίμαχος); **(31)** ~ ib. l. 3 (s. Καλλίμαχος, Ξενοφάντα); **(32)** i BC ib. 853, 4 (Ἀριστόδ[α]μος)
—TROIZEN: **(33)** iii BC ib. 774, 4 (s. Εὐρυτίδας); **(34)** ~ ib. 775 (f. Ἀρχέστρατος)
ARKADIA: **(35)** 236 BC *PPetr*² I Wills 18, 21 (-δη-)
—ALIPHEIRA: **(36)** s. iii BC *SEG* XXV 448, 1, [4], 8 + *IPArk* 25
—LOUSOI?: **(37)** iii BC *SEG* XI 1122, 7 (*IPArk* 22) (Ἀριστόδαμ[ος])
—MANTINEIA-ANTIGONEIA: **(38)** c. 300-221 BC *IG* v (2) 323. 41 (tessera) (s. Μενεκράτης); **(39)** ~ ib. 323. 43 (tessera) (f. Ἀριστέας); **(40)** ~ ib. 323. 89 (tessera) ([Ἀρισ]τόδαμος: s. Ἀρισταῖος); **(41)** iii BC ib. 368, 116 ?= (42); **(42)** m. iii BC ib. l. 76 ?= (41)
—MEGALOPOLIS: **(43)** c. 235 BC ib. II² 1299, 104; **(44)** ii/i BC ib. v (2) 443, 8; 444, 6; 445, 11 (*IPArk* 32) (f. Πρόξενος); **(45)** ~ *IG* v (2) 444, 14 (*IPArk* 32) (Ἀριστόδα[μος]); **(46)** i BC *IG* v (2) 466
—MEGALOPOLIS?: **(47)** hell.? *Platon* 26 (1974) p. 10 no. 53
—ORCHOMENOS?: **(48)** s. vii BC Wehrli, *Schule Arist.* vii fr. 144; *IG* v (2) p. xii, 116ff. (stemma) (Ἀριστομηδης?: s. Ἀριστοκράτης)
—PHIGALEIA: **(49)** f. iii BC *RE* (24) (-δη-: s. (nat.) Ἀρτύλας, s. (ad.) Τριταῖος (Megalopolis): tyrant); **(50)** i/ii AD *IvOl* 442 (f. Τιβ. Ὄππιος Τίμανδρος)
—TEGEA: **(51)** m. iv BC *IG* v (2) 6, 65; **(52)** f. iii BC ib. 42, 6 ([Ἀρι]στόδαμ[ος]); **(53)** ii-i BC ib. 165, 2; **(54)** i BC ib. 164; **(55)** imp.? ib. 565 (Ἀριστόδαμο[ς])
——(Athaneatai): **(56)** iv/iii BC ib. 38, 3 (f. —ας) ?= (57); **(57)** ~ ib. l. 55 (f. Δαμέας) ?= (56)
—THELPHOUSA: **(58)** a. 228 BC ib. IV (1)² 72 B, 29 (s. Δ—)
ELIS: **(59)** c. 400-388 BC Moretti, *Olymp.* 383; Page, *FGE* 899; cf. Ebert, *Gr. Sieg.* 34 (Ἀριστόδημος—Paus.: s. Θράσυς); **(60)** ?ii BC *RE* (27) (*FGrH* 414)
—OLYMPIA*: **(61)** v BC *SEG* XI 1228; **(62)** ii/i BC *IvOl* 397, 1

ELIS?: **(63)** ii/i BC Moretti, *Olymp.* 664 (s. Ἀλεξίμαχος)
EPIROS: **(64)** s. iv BC *IG* IV (1)² 95, 77 (Perlman E.2); Perlman pp. 46-9 (date) (f. Γέρων)
—AMBRAKIA: **(65)** ii BC *SEG* XLII 543 (s. Ξένων)
—KASSOPE: **(66)** 356-354 BC *IG* IV (1)² 95, 25 (Perlman E.2); Perlman p. 40 f. (date)
ILLYRIA:
—EPIDAMNOS-DYRRHACHION: **(67)** c. 250-50 BC Münsterberg p. 38 (coin) (pryt.); **(68)** ? *Jubice Hoard* p. 96 no. 3 (coin) (Ceka 84) (pryt.); **(69)** ~ Maier 125; 156; 323; 347; 359; *Bakërr Hoard* p. 66 no. 2; 15; *Jubice Hoard* p. 96 nos. 3-4; p. 96 no. 13 (Ceka 82-93); cf. Ceka 77 (coin) (money.); **(70)** ?ii-i BC *IDyrrh* 14 (s. Ἀγαθήμερος); **(71)** ii-i BC ib. 565 (tiles)
KEPHALLENIA:
—PRONNOI: **(72)** c. 215-205 BC *FD* III (4) 362, 10
KORINTHIA:
—KORINTH: **(73)** her. *FGrH* 244 F 331; Paus. ii 4. 4 (Ἀριστόδημος—Paus., Ἀριστομήδης—Sync.: s. Εὐδάμων, f. Τελέστας: king)
—SIKYON: **(74)** vi/v BC *SEG* XI 244, 71; **(75)** ?255 BC Nachtergael, *Les Galates* 8, 13 (Stephanis 334) (-δη-: s. Εὐτέλης); **(76)** i BC *IG* II² 10310 (-δη-: f. Ῥόδιον)
LAKONIA:
—SPARTA: **(77)** ?vi BC *RE* s.v. Aristodemos (2) (Poralla² 122) (?s. Ἀριστόβουλος); **(78)** 480 BC Hdt. vii 229-31; ix 71 (Poralla² 124) (-δη-); **(79)** ?v/iv BC Plu., *Mor.* 773 F (Poralla² 126) (-δη-); **(80)** 394 BC X., *HG* iv 2. 9; Paus. iii 5. 7 (Poralla² 125) (-δη-); **(81)** f. ii BC *IC* 2 p. 244 no. 4 B, 2 (Bradford (2)) (s. Αὐτίας); **(82)** c. 143 BC *IG* IX (1)² (1) 137, 30 (Bradford (2)); **(83)** s. i BC *IG* v (1) 92, 5 (Bradford (5)) (s. Πασίμαχος); **(84)** ~ *IG* v (1) 95, 17 (Bradford (16)) (f. Πασικλῆς); **(85)** ~ *IG* v (1) 124, 5; 212, 3, 26 (Bradford (1)) ([Ἀρι]στόδαμος—212: s. Ἀριστοκλείδας, f. Ἀριστοκλείδας); **(86)** ~ *IG* v (1) 266 (*Artemis Orthia* pp. 304-5 no. 15; Bradford (12)) ([Ἀρι]στόδ[αμος]?: f. Ἀριστοκράτης); **(87)** c. 30-20 BC *IG* v (1) 211, 24 (Bradford (17)) (f. Σίπομπος); **(88)** ~ *IG* v (1) 211, 49 (Bradford (9); Stephanis 327); **(89)** c. 25-1 BC *IG* v (1) 210, 23 (Bradford (6)) (s. Σαλίαρχος); **(90)** ~ *IG* v (1) 212, 19 (Bradford (4)) (s. Νικοκλῆς); **(91)** ~ *IG* v (1) 212, 44 (Bradford (7)) (s. Ξενοχάρης); **(92)** ?i AD *IG* v (1) 180, 12 (Ἀριστόδ[αμος]?); **(93)** s. i AD ib. 508; *SEG* XI 776, 3 (Bradford (13)) (Ἰούλ. Ἀ.: f. Γ. Ἰούλ. Χαρίξενος); **(94)** c. 80-100 AD *SEG* XI 511, 6 (Bradford (15)) (Ἀριστόδ[α]μος: f. Λάμπις); **(95)** c. 100 AD *SEG* XI 513, 1 (Bradford (8)); **(96)** ~ *SEG* XI 515, 4 (Bradford (14)) (f. Εὔθυμος); **(97)** c. 100-120 AD *SEG* XI 842 a ([Ἀρι]στόδα[μος]); **(98)** m. ii AD ib. 643, 2 (Bradford (11)) (Ἀριστόδαμο[ς]); **(99)** c. 160-170 AD *IG* v (1) 109, 11 (Bradford (3)) (s. Νικα—)
MESSENIA:
—ABIA: **(100)** ?c. 500-475 BC *IG* v (1) 1356, 2 (Poralla² 123); *LSAG*² p. 206 no. 6 (date) (-σστό-)
—MESSENE: **(101)** i AD *IG* v (1) 1436, 23 (Ἀριστόδ[αμος])
—THOURIA: **(102)** ii-i BC ib. 1385, 24 (f. Νικίας); **(103)** f. ii BC *SEG* XI 972, 66 (s. Εὔμναστος); **(104)** ~ ib. l. 72 (s. Δάμων); **(105)** ~ ib. l. 126 (s. Ἀριστοφάνης)
S. ITALY (APULIA-CALABRIA): **(106)** c. 425-400 BC *Second Suppl. RVAp* I p. 6 no. 46a (vase) (-σστό-)
S. ITALY (BRUTTIUM):
—LOKROI EPIZEPHYRIOI: **(107)** iv/iii BC De Franciscis 34, 2
——(Λακ.): **(108)** 277 BC ib. 9, 4
——(Ὀμβ.): **(109)** 277 BC ib. 8, 7 (s. Ἀρίστιππος)

S. ITALY (CALABRIA):
—TARAS-TARENTUM: (110) iv/iii BC IG XIV 668
II, 19 (Landi, DISMG 194); (111) f. iii BC
SEG XL 901 (vase)
S. ITALY (LUCANIA):
—HERAKLEIA: (112) ?iv BC NC 1917, p. 174 no.
5 e-f (coin); van Keuren, Coinage of Heraclea
p. 78 no. 93
——(Κν. σφαιρωτῆρες): (113) iv/iii BC IGSI 1 I,
184 (DGE 62; Uguzzoni–Ghinatti I)
—METAPONTION: (114) f. vi BC IG I³ 1006
(Landi, DISMG 145) (Ἀριστόδα[μος]); (115)
iv BC RE (10) (Stephanis 332); cf. Osborne,
Naturalization PT134 (and Athens: Ἀ. ὁ ἐπι-
καλ. Στεμφύλιος)
S. ITALY(LUCANIA):
—HERAKLEIA:
——(Fε. γυῖον): (116) iv/iii BC IGSI 1 I, 187
(DGE 62; Uguzzoni–Ghinatti I) (s. Σύμμα-
χος)
SICILY:
—AKRAI: (117) hell.? SGDI 3244 (Akrai p. 158
no. 12) (s. Σωσίβιος); (118) ii-i BC SGDI 3246,
46 (Akrai pp. 152-3 no. 2; Dubois, IGDS
109) (s. Σῶσις)
—APOLLONIA: (119) f. i BC Cic., In Verr. II v
15 (Lat. Aristodamus)
—KAMARINA: (120) m. v BC Dubois, IGDS 120,
2 (Arena, Iscr. Sic. II 142 A; SEG XXXVIII
939; Cordano, 'Camarina VII' 11) (s. Χαίριππος)
—SELINOUS: (121) s. v BC Dubois, IGDS 60
(Arena, Iscr. Sic. I 24; IGLMP 98) (s. Ἀριστις)
—THERMAI HIMERAIAI: (122) ?ii-i BC IG XIV
316, 3 (Dubois, IGDS 203) (s. Σιμίας); (123)
ii-iii AD IG XIV 329 (Kokalos 20 (1974) p. 230
no. 5) (f. Νεμηνίδας)
—ZANKLE-MESSANA: (124) ?ii BC IG XIV 401, 6
(s. Εὔβιος)
TRIPHYLIA:
—SAMIKON: (125) c. 230-200 BC BCH 45 (1921)
p. 13 II, 89 (Ἀριστόδα[μος])

**Ἀριστόδημος**
ACHAIA:
—AIGION: (1) i/ii AD RE (33)
ELIS: (2) s. i BC IvOl 216, [1]; 217 (s. Λυκο-
μήδης, f. Λυκομήδης); (3) 36-24 BC ib. 62, 3
(Ἀ[ριστόδη]μος?: f. Κλέϊππος); (4) 67 AD ib. 82,
5 (I f. Ἀριστόδημος II); (5) ~ ib. l. 5 (II s.
Ἀριστόδημος I, ?f. Ἀριστόδημος III); (6) ~ ib.
l. [9], 14 (III ?s. Ἀριστόδημος II, ?f. —ος); (7)
113 AD ib. 90, 6 (s. Ἀγήσαρχος)
—OLYMPIA*: (8) s. v BC Ol. Forsch. 5 p. 150
no. 3 (-δε̄-)
MESSENIA: (9) viii BC RE (7) (king)
PELOPONNESE: (10) c. 230-200 BC BCH 45
(1921) p. 11 II, 41
S. ITALY (CAMPANIA):
—KYME: (11) vi/v BC RE (8) (Ἀ. ὁ ἐπικαλ. Μα-
λακός: s. Ἀριστοκράτης: tyrant)
SICILY:
—SYRACUSE: (12) 46 BC Sic. Gymn. 16 (1963) p.
60 no. 2, 2 (f. Ἀθ—)
—THERMAI HIMERAIAI: (13) ?ii-i BC IG XIV
316, 1 (Dubois, IGDS 203) (Ἀ. Πέρσιος: s.
Νεμηνίδας)

**Ἀριστοδίκα**
EPIROS:
—BOUTHROTOS (PRASAIBOI): (1) ii-i BC IBouth-
rot 55, 7 (SEG XXXVIII 506); (2) a. 163 BC
IBouthrot 40, 5 (SEG XXXVIII 499); (3) ~
IBouthrot 40, 17 (SEG XXXVIII 499)

**Ἀριστόδικος**
ARGOLIS:
—TROIZEN: (1) iv BC IG IV (1) 764, 6 (s. Ἐπαί-
νετος)

LAKONIA:
—SPARTA: (2) c. 25-1 BC ib. v (1) 212, 35 (Brad-
ford (-)) (s. Ἀριστόκριτος)
PELOPONNESE: (3) c. 192 BC SEG XIII 327, 14
(Ἀ[ρισ]τόδικος: f. Δαμοτίων)
S. ITALY (CAMPANIA):
—KYME: (4) inc. Porph., Abst. iii 16. 2

**Ἀριστόδοκος**
KORINTHIA:
—KORINTH: (1) s. iv BC Peek, NIEpid 16, 21
(Ἀρ[ιστ]όδοκος: f. Ἀριστομήδης)

**Ἀριστόδωρος**
ARGOLIS:
—EPIDAUROS*: (1) c. 365-335 BC IG IV (1)²
103, 62
MESSENIA:
—MESSENE: (2) i AD ib. v (1) 1436, 7
(Ἀρ[ισ]τ[όδ]ωρος)
SICILY:
—SYRACUSE: (3) f. iv BC [Pl.], Ep. 358 B

**Ἀριστόθεμις**
ARKADIA:
—MEGALOPOLIS?: (1) ii AD IG v (2) 495 (f. Νι-
κομάχη)

**Ἀριστόθεος**
ARGOLIS:
—TROIZEN: (1) c. 130 BC FD III (3) 124 (FGrH
835; Stephanis 337) (s. Νικόθεος)

**Ἀριστόι**
EPIROS:
—AMBRAKIA: (1) v/iv BC BCH 79 (1955) p.
267 (d. Ἀριστίων); (2) iv-iii BC CIG 1803; cf.
Fraser–Rönne, BWGT pp. 169 ff. (Ἀριστοι—
apogr.: d. Νίκαρχος)

**Ἀριστοκλέας**
ACHAIA: (1) imp.? IG II² 8401 (s. Καρπόδωρος)
EPIROS:
—NIKOPOLIS: (2) imp. SEG XXVII 239 (Μαν.
Ἀριστοκλίας—mosaic)

**Ἀριστόκλεια**
ARGOLIS:
—KALAURIA: (1) iii BC IG IV (1) 840, 4 (d. Σω-
φάνης, Ἀγασιγράτις)
—PHLEIOUS: (2) iii BC ib. 455
ARKADIA:
—MEGALOPOLIS: (3) ii/iii AD ib. v (2) 517, 23
(d. Σάων)
EPIROS?: (4) i BC ib. II² 8532; SEG XIII 144, 1
([Ἀρ]ιστόκλεα: d. Ἀριστοτέλης)
KORINTHIA:
—KORINTH: (5) s. iii BC IG II² 9052, 4; cf. Os-
borne, Naturalization T97 (d. Αἰσχρίων, m.
Φιλοκράτης (Sikyon and Athens, Hamaxan-
teia))
LAKONIA:
—TAINARON-KAINEPOLIS: (6) ii-iii AD IG v (1)
1249, 20 (GVI 2028); (7) c. 220-240 AD IG
v (1) 601, 5; BSA 79 (1984) p. 265 (ident.,
date); p. 284 (stemma) (Bradford (-)) (Αὐρ.
Ἀ.: d. Χαρτηρίς, m. Αὐρ. Χαρτηρίς)
SICILY:
—HALOUNTION: (8) i BC-i AD IG XIV 368 (IG-
LMP 41) (d. Φιλ—)
—KAMARINA: (9) hell. SEG XXXIV 943
—SELINOUS: (10) s. vi BC Arena, Iscr. Sic. I 57
(vase) (Dubois, IGDS 81)

**Ἀριστοκλείδας**
AIGINA: (1) ?475 BC Pi., N. iii, 15, 67; cf. Klee
p. 101 no. 47 (s. Ἀριστοφάνης)
ARKADIA:
—ORCHOMENOS: (2) ?m. iii BC RE Supplbd. 1
(4a) (tyrant) ?= (Ἀριστομηλίδας (1))

ILLYRIA:
—APOLLONIA: (3) 361 BC CID II 4 II, 21; cf.
IApoll 305
KORINTHIA:
—SIKYON: (4) vi/v BC SEG XI 244, 64
LAKONIA:
—SPARTA: (5) f. iii BC CID II 122 I, 6 (Bradford
(3)) (s. Ἐμπεδίας); (6) c. 80 BC IG VII 416, 60
(IOrop 523; Bradford (2)) (s. Σωκράτης); (7)
s. i BC IG v (1) 124, 5; 212, 3 (Bradford (4))
(f. Ἀριστόδαμος); (8) c. 25-1 BC IG v (1) 212,
26 (Bradford (1)) (s. Ἀριστόδαμος)
MESSENIA:
—THOURIA: (9) ii-i BC IG v (1) 1385, 34 (f. Ἀρι-
στοκλῆς)
S. ITALY (CALABRIA):
—TARAS-TARENTUM: (10) vi BC Iamb., VP 267
(FVS 1 p. 446)
SICILY:
—TAUROMENION:
——(Σπαρ.): (11) f. i BC Cron. Arch. 3 (1964) p.
46 IV, 24 (s. Φιλαίνετος)

**Ἀριστοκλείδης**
AIGINA: (1) ii BC IG IV (1) 13 (f. Χαρίκλεια)
EPIROS:
—NIKOPOLIS: (2) f. ii AD FD III (4) 83, 2
(Sarikakis 14) (s. Διογένης)

**Ἀριστοκλῆς**
ACHAIA: (1) 146 BC IG IV (1)² 28, 117 (f. Ἀρι-
στοτέλης: synoikos)
—DYME*: (2) c. 219 BC SGDI 1612, 81 (Tyche
5 (1990) p. 124) (f. Ἄφαιστος)
ACHAIA?: (3) 193 BC IG v (2) 293, 12
([Ἀρ]ιστοκλῆς)
AIGINA: (4) imp. ib. IV (1) 82
(ΑΡΙΣ[.]ΣΠΛΗΣ—apogr., Ἀρισ[τοκ]λῆς—ed.,
Ἀρισ[τ]ε[ίδης?—LGPN: s. Ἀθηνοφάνης)
AITOLIA:
—KONOPE-ARSINOE: (5) 173 BC SGDI 1853, 10
AKARNANIA:
—ASTAKOS: (6) m. ii BC IG IX (1)² (2) 208, 3,
[33] (f. Ναυσίμαχος)
ARGOLIS:
—ARGOS: (7) s. iv BC ib. v (2) 550, 13; cf. Mo-
retti, Olymp. 464 (f. Ἀγεύς); (8) iii-ii BC IG IV
(1) 630 c; (9) ii BC ib. II² 8372 (f. Μνάσιππος);
(10) f. i BC Unp. (Ch. Kritzas) (Ἀριστο[κλῆ]ς:
s. Νικίας)
—ARGOS?: (11) ?114 BC IG IV (1) 558, 36
(Stephanis 341)
—EPIDAUROS: (12) c. 335-325 BC IG IV (1)²
108, 160, 166; (13) iv/iii BC SEG XIV 327;
(14) iii BC IG IX (2) 362 (f. Σωσίκλεια); (15)
iii/ii BC ib. IV (1)² 281 (Ἀρισ[τοκλῆς]: f. Σω-
σικλῆς); (16) ii BC ib. 99, 15 (f. Κλεαιχμίδας);
(17) ii/i BC ib. 231; cf. Peek, IAEpid 99 (s.
Σωσικράτης)
——(Azantioi): (18) 146 BC IG IV (1)² 28, 35 (f.
Ἀριστοκράτης)
—HERMIONE: (19) ii-i BC ib. IV (1) 732 I, 18
(-σστο-: f. Ἀπολλώνιος); (20) ~ ib. 732 II, 6 (f.
Καλλίας); (21) ~ ib. l. 20 (f. Ὀνάσιμος)
—PHLEIOUS: (22) s. iv BC Peek, NIEpid 16, 24
(Perlman E.6) (f. Νεοκλῆς)
—TROIZEN: (23) ?146 BC IG IV (1) 757 B, 15 (f.
Λύσις)
ARKADIA: (24) 320-316 BC ib. v (2) 549, 12, 24
(f. Ἀρίστιππος)
—MANTINEIA-ANTIGONEIA: (25) c. 425-385 BC
ib. 323. 18 (tessera) (s. Λοβίας)
—MT. LYKAION*: (26) hell.? ib. p. 146 no. 553
(6-7) (tile)
—TEGEA: (27) iv BC ib. 31, 2 (Ἀριστοκλῆ[s]); (28)
m. iv BC ib. 6, 56 (f. —τος); (29) ~ ib. l. 66;
(30) iii BC ib. 30, 6 ([Ἀρι]στοκλῆς: s. Λύσιπ-
πος); (31) ~ ib. l. 20 ([Ἀρ]ι[στ]οκλῆς?); (32) f.
iii BC ib. 35, 33 (f. Ἔσφαντος); (33) ii BC SEG
XI 1058; (34) 165 AD IG v (2) 50, 52 (s. Ἀλέξανδρος)

——(Apolloniatai): (35) iv/iii BC ib. 38, 31 (Ἀριστο[κλ]ῆς: s. Ἀριστόλας)

DALMATIA:

—ISSA:

——(Hylleis): (36) iv/iii BC Brunšmid p. 8, 29 (Ἀρ[ιστοκλ]ῆς?: f. Ἀρίστων)

ELIS: (37) 28-16 BC IvOl 64, 19; 65, [16] (f. Ἀρίσταρχος)

EPIROS:

—BOUTHROTOS (PRASAIBOI): (38) a. 163 BC IBouthrot 25, 10; 31, 87 (SEG XXXVIII 483; 490) (s. Ἀλέξανδρος, f. Ἀλέξανδρος); (39) ~ IBouthrot 106 (s. Νίκων)

——Bouthrotioi: (40) a. 163 BC ib. 120, 9 (f. Ἀπολλόδωρος)

—DODONA*: (41) v BC SEG XV 385

—NIKOPOLIS: (42) imp. FD III (4) 440, 1 (Sarikakis 15) ([Ἀρισ?]τοκλῆς)

ILLYRIA:

—APOLLONIA: (43) c. 250-50 BC Maier 21 (coin) (Ceka 37) (pryt.); (44) ii BC IApoll 39; (45) ii-i BC ib. 140 (f. Παρμήν); (46) imp. ib. 198

—DIVJAKA (MOD.): (47) hell. Iliria 1982 (1), p. 111 no. 52 = p. 120 no. 7 (tile)

—EPIDAMNOS-DYRRHACHION: (48) iii BC IDyrrh 19 (f. Θεανώ)

ITHAKE: (49) v/iv BC Unp. (IG arch.) (vase) (-κλῆς)

KERKYRA: (50) iv/iii BC IG IX (1) 976, 5 (f. —άδας); (51) ?iii-ii BC ib. 753 (tile); (52) ?ii-i BC ib. 754 (tile) (s. Εὐπόλεμος)

KORINTHIA:

—KORINTH: (53) 172 BC PMich III 190, 15, 19, 24, 25, 27, 30, 33, 38 (s. Ἡρακλείδας, f. Ἡρακλείδας: t.e.); (54) v AD SEG XXIX 308, 2; cf. XXXI 291 ([Ἀρι]στοκλῆς—SEG XXIX, [Θε-μι]στοκλῆς—SEG XXXI)

—SIKYON: (55) s. vi BC RE (22) (Skalet 55) (sculptor)

LAKONIA: (56) iii BC PSI 626 recto I, 3 (Bradford (6)) (s. Νίκανδρος)

—AMYKLAI*: (57) ?iv/iii BC IG v (1) 1574 b (Bradford (16))

—GYTHEION: (58) 211 AD IG v (1) 1163, 12 (f. Σωσίνικος)

—HYPERTELEATON*: (59) imp. ib. 1017

—KARYAI?: (60) i-ii AD ib. 925

—SPARTA: (61) 422 BC Th. v 16. 2; HCT 4 p. 120 (locn.) (Poralla² 127) (or Phokis Delphi: s. Παυσανίας) ?= (62); (62) 418 BC Th. v 71. 3; 72. 1 (Poralla² 127) ?= (61); (63) ii BC SEG XI 856, 3 (Bradford (19)) (Ἀ[ρ]ιστοκλῆς: f. Ἆγις); (64) ?161 BC Daux, Delphes p. 679, 5 (Bradford (10)); (65) s. i BC IG v (1) 124, 2, 6 (Bradford (20)) (f. Ἀνδρόνικος); (66) c. 30-20 BC IG v (1) 141, 3; SEG XXXV 329 (date) (Bradford (24)) (f. Καλλικράτης); (67) ~ IG v (1) 141, 14; SEG XXXV 329 (date) (Bradford (2)) (s. Καλλικράτης); (68) ~ IG v (1) 211, 8 (Bradford (22)) (f. Ἀριστογένης); (69) ~ IG v (1) 211, 22 (Bradford (7)) (s. Φιλέας); (70) ~ IG v (1) 211, 45 (Bradford (21)) (f. Ἀρχίτας); (71) c. 25-1 BC IG v (1) 210, 12 (Bradford (23)) (I f. Ἀριστοκλῆς II); (72) ~ IG v (1) 210, 12 (Bradford (1)) (II s. Ἀριστοκλῆς I); (73) ~ IG v (1) 210, 45 (Bradford (8)) (s. Φιλονικίδας); (74) ~ IG v (1) 212, 36 (Bradford (9)) (s. Πολυστρατίδας); (75) i AD IG v (1) 274 (Bradford (13)); (76) i-ii AD IG v (1) 242 (Bradford (15)); (77) ~ IG v (1) 746 (Bradford (17)) (Ἀ. ὁ καὶ Ζῆθος); (78) c. 100-125 AD IG v (1) 40, 8 (Bradford (18)) (f. Ἀγαθοκλῆς); (79) ?ii AD SEG XI 624, 2 ([Ἀρισ?]τοκλῆς); (80) c. 105-110 AD IG v (1) 97, 12; SEG XI 564, 19 (Bradford (3)) (Ἀριστοκράτης—SEG: s. Καλλικράτης) ?= (84); (81) ~ IG v (1) 97, 24; SEG XI 564, 24 (Bradford (4)) (νεώτ.: s. Καλλικράτης); (82) c. 105-115 AD IG v (1) 20 B, 8; 51, 37; 52, 8; SEG XI 538, [6] (Bradford (5)) (s. Λύσιππος); (83) c. 115-120 AD SEG XI 481, 5; 490, 4; 571, [1] (Bradford (14)); (84) c. 130-150 AD

IG v (1) 71 II, 3; 71 [III]; SEG XI 579, 2 (Bradford (25)) (f. Καλλικράτης) ?= (80); (85) c. 150-225 AD IG v (1) 311, [4]; 541, 11; 542, 5 (Artemis Orthia pp. 360-1 no. 146); IG v (1) 543, 8; 544, 15 (Artemis Orthia pp. 358-9 no. 145); IG v (1) 547, 9, 11, 14; 592, 9; BSA 79 (1984) pp. 270-3 (date); 80 (1985) pp. 194; pp. 209-11 (Bradford s.v. Πρατόλαος (4)) (Π. Μέμμιος Πρατόλαος ὁ καὶ Ἀ.: s. Π. Μέμμιος Δαμάρης, f. Π. Μέμμιος Δαμάρης, Μεμμία Λογγῖνα); (86) c. 160 AD IG v (1) 71 III, 57; 86, 35 (Bradford (26)) (f. Φιλοξενίδας); (87) ii/iii AD IG v (1) 547, 7 (Bradford s.v. Πανθάλης (1)) (Πομπώνιος Πανθάλης ὁ καὶ Ἀ.: s. Πομπώνιος Πανθάλης Διογένης Ἀριστέας, Μεμμία Λογγῖνα)

LEUKAS: (88) c. 167-50 BC BMC Thessaly p. 179 nos. 79-80; SNG Cop. Epirus–Acarnania 378 (coins)

MESSENIA:

—MESSENE: (89) ?ii BC IG v (1) 1477; (90) i AD ib. 1436, 32; (91) ?35-44 AD ib. 1432, 2 etc. (s. Καλλικράτης); (92) ii/iii AD SEG XXIII 216 (f. Καλλίς)

—THOURIA: (93) ii-i BC IG v (1) 1385, 34 (s. Ἀριστοκλείδας); (94) f. ii BC SEG XI 972, 101 (f. Πρατόνικος)

S. ITALY (BRUTTIUM):

—LOKROI EPIZEPHYRIOI:

——(Ἀγκ.): (95) iv/iii BC De Franciscis 18, 4 (s. Θέων)

S. ITALY (CALABRIA):

—TARAS-TARENTUM: (96) f. iii BC IG II² 3779, 9; cf. Stephanis 1839 (f. Νικοκλῆς); (97) c. 272-235 BC Vlasto 877-82 (coins) (Evans, Horsemen p. 179 VIII D.1)

—TARAS-TARENTUM?: (98) iii BC D.L. vii 13; Ath. 603 e (Stephanis 340)

SICILY:

—AKRAI: (99) ?iii BC SGDI 3243 (Akrai p. 155 no. 5) (f. Σῶσις); (100) ii BC IG XIV 214 a, 5 (Akrai p. 155 no. 4); cf. IGLMP 30 ([Ἀρι]στοκλῆς)

—SYRACUSE?:

——(Πλη.): (101) hell. Manganaro, PdelP forthcoming no. 4 II, 9 (f. Τιμασίων)

——(Τηλ.): (102) hell. ib. no. 4 V, 6 (f. Καλλίας)

—TAUROMENION: (103) ?ii/i BC IG XIV 421 D an. 1 (SGDI 5219) (I f. Ἀριστοκλῆς II); (104) ~ IG XIV 421 D an. 1 (SGDI 5219) (II s. Ἀριστοκλῆς I)

—ZANKLE-MESSANA: (105) ii AD RE (15)

## Ἀριστοκράτεια

ARGOLIS:

—ARGOS*: (1) f. iii BC IG IV (1) 529, 17 ([Ἀρι]στοκράτεια: slave/freed.?)

EPIROS:

—KASSOPE: (2) ii BC GVI 1078, 2 (IG IX (1)² (2) 312 a) (m. Ἐχενίκα)

KORINTHIA:

—KORINTH: (3) c. 400-375 BC ib. II² 9057

—SIKYON?: (4) iii BC HE 2635 (fict.?)

TRIPHYLIA:

—LEPREON: (5) iii/ii BC SEG XXII 360, 3

## Ἀριστοκράτης

ACHAIA: (1) 146 BC IG IV (1)² 28, 127 (f. Σωτηρίδας: synoikos); (2) ~ ib. l. 135 (f. Σωτηρίδας); (3) ~ ib. l. 162 (s. Νικοκράτης: synoikos)

—PATRAI: (4) 171 BC SGDI 261, 3 (f. Ἀρίων)

ACHAIA?: (5) c. 300 BC SEG XIV 375, 7

AIGINA: (6) vi/v BC Hdt. vi 73 (f. Κάσαμβος)

AKARNANIA: (7) ?254 BC Nachtergael, Les Galates 9, 54 (Stephanis 350) (s. Σωτίων)

—THYRREION: (8) iii BC IG IX (1)² (2) 245, 1

ARGOLIS:

—ARGOS: (9) iii/ii BC BCH 27 (1903) p. 260 no. 1 (f. Φαηνός); (10) ?ii BC IG IV (1) 661 (tile) (Ἀριστοκρά[της]); (11) ii-i BC ib. 530, 2; cf. BCH 33 (1909) p. 183 n. 2 (s. Τιμαγόρας); (12) f. i BC Unp. (Ch. Kritzas) (f. Κλεαίνετος);

(13) imp. IG IV (1) 599, 2; 600, 2; (14) i BC/i AD ib. II² 3889; IV (1) 581; cf. SEG XXX 155 (M. Ἀντ. Ἀ.: s. Ἀναξίων) ?= (Ἀντώνιος (1))

—ARGOS?: (15) f. i BC ib. XXIII 180, 2 ([Ἀρι]στοκράτης: s. Δαμ—: date—Kritzas)

—EPIDAUROS: (16) c. 370 BC IG IV (1)² 102, 43 ?= (29); (17) c. 350-250 BC AD 28 (1973) Chron. pl. 84 α; (18) iii BC IG IV (1)² 165, 2 (Ἀριστ[οκράτ]ης?); (19) ~ ib. 278 (f. Ἀριστείδας); (20) iii/ii BC Peek, IAEpid 129, 1 (s. Λάκριτος, f. Ἀριστόφιλος); (21) c. 221 BC IG IV (1)² 42, 14; (22) ii BC ib. 370 (Peek, IAEpid 153. 17); (23) ii/i BC IG IV (1)² 232, 1 (s. Δαμύλος, f. Δαμύλος, Δαμώ); (24) ~ ib. 248 (f. Ἀριστίς); (25) 135 AD Peek, IAEpid 154, 3 (f. Τιμοκλῆς)

——(Azantioi): (26) 146 BC IG IV (1)² 28, 33 (f. Τίμαρχος); (27) ~ ib. l. 35 (s. Ἀριστοκλῆς)

——(Hysminatai): (28) 146 BC ib. l. 18 (s. Θεόφιλος)

—Aphylonia (Azantioi): (29) c. 365-335 BC ib. 103, 82 ?= (16)

——Miltias (Azantioi): (30) m. iii BC ib. 96, 72 (Perlman E.3); Perlman p. 63 f. (date)

——Mysias: (31) m. iii BC IG IV (1)² 96, 44 (Perlman E.3); Perlman p. 63 f. (date) (Ἀριστοκρά[της]: f. Ἀριστόλας)

——Pleiatios (Hylleis): (32) m. iii BC IG IV (1)² 96, 69 + Peek, IAEpid 42, 59, 62 (Perlman E.3); Perlman p. 63 f. (date) (s. Ἀρήγων)

—METHANA-ARSINOE: (33) iv BC IG IV (1) 861

—TROIZEN: (34) iv BC ib. 764, 4 (f. Τιμοκράτης)

ARKADIA:

—HERAIA: (35) s. iv BC Peek, NIEpid 16, 27 (Perlman E.6) (s. Ἀρίστανδρος); (36) m. iii BC IG IV (1)² 96, 42 (Perlman E.3); Perlman p. 63 f. (date) (s. Ἀγώνιππος)

—MEGALOPOLIS: (37) imp.? IG v (2) 482

—ORCHOMENOS: (38) viii BC RE (1) (or Arkadia Trapezous: s. Αἴχμις, f. Ἱκέτας: dub.); (39) m. vii BC ib.; FGrH 124 F 23; 244 F 334 (or Arkadia Trapezous: s. Ἱκέτας, f. Ἀριστόδαμος, Ἐρισθένεια: king)

—TEGEA: (40) 369-361 BC IG v (2) 1, 12; Tod, GHI II 132 (date); (41) ii BC IG v (2) 141 (Ἀριστοκράτης: s. Θῆρις)

ELIS: (42) 36-24 BC IvOl 59, [23]; 62, 16; 64, 21 (f. Πολυχάρης); (43) i BC/i AD IG XII (8) 176, 5 (s. Ἀντιφάνης)

KERKYRA: (44) iv/iii BC ib. IX (1) 976, 6 (f. Καλλίας); (45) ?168 BC Klee p. 16 II C, 91 (f. Στράτων)

KORINTHIA:

—KORINTH: (46) hell.? SEG XXVIII 292 (s. Θέρσανδρος); (47) imp. IG II² 9058; (48) f. ii AD Corinth VIII (3) 106, 5 (Lat. M. Antonius Aristocra[tes]) ?= (49); (49) ~ ib. 221 (Lat. [Ant]onius Aristocra[tes]) ?= (48)

—SIKYON: (50) ?253 BC Nachtergael, Les Galates 10, 38; cf. Stephanis 1288 (f. Ἵππων)

LAKONIA:

—EPIDAUROS LIMERA: (51) ?ii-i BC IG v (1) 1005 (f. Ἀγέλαιος); (52) ~ ib. 1007 (s. Ἀγέλαιος)

—GYTHEION: (53) 211 AD ib. 1163, 10 (s. Ἀγήσιππος)

—HYPERTELEATON*: (54) imp. ib. 1028

—SPARTA: (55) 374 BC D.S. xv 45. 4 (Poralla² 128); (56) m. iii BC IG IV (1)² 96, 70 (Perlman E.3); Perlman p. 63 f. (date) (Bradford (31)) (f. Ἀρίστων); (57) c. 143 BC IG IX (1)² (1) 137, 31 (Bradford (2)) (s. Ἀρίστανδρος); (58) 101-60 BC Klio 15 (1918) p. 33 no. 54, [2], 7; (59) i BC IG v (1) 126, 4 (Bradford (7)) (s. Ἀριστόνικος); (60) hell.-imp. IG v (1) 195, 5 (Bradford (37)); (61) s. i BC IG v (1) 96, 3 (Bradford (21)) (Ἀριστοκρά[της]); (62) i AD IG v (1) 266 (Artemis Orthia pp. 304-5 no. 15; Bradford (3)) (Ἀριστοκρ[άτης]: s. Ἀριστόδαμος); (63) 43-31 BC Münzpr. der Laked. p. 154 Group 17 series 13; pp. 159-60 Group 21 series 2 (coin); BSA 80 (1985) pp. 215-16 (ident., stemma)

(Bradford (23)) (s. Δαμάρης, ?f. Δαμάρης); (64)
c. 30-20 BC *IG* v (1) 211, 6 (Bradford (21));
(65) c. 25-1 BC *IG* v (1) 261 (*Artemis Orthia*
p. 303 no. 12; Bradford (6)) (s. Ἀριστίων); (66)
i BC/i AD *IG* v (1) 48, 11 (Bradford (12)) (s.
Εὐτελίδας); (67) ~ *IG* v (1) 49, 4; 210, 26;
*SEG* XI 676, 1 (Bradford (34)) (f. Δαμοκλῆς);
(68) i BC/i AD? *IG* v (1) 177, 3 (Bradford (1))
([Ἀρι]στοκράτης: s. Ἀγαθάμερος); (69) i BC/i AD
*RE* (25); *FGrH* 591; Cartledge–Spawforth p.
177 (date) (Bradford (16)) (s. Ἵππαρχος); (70)
c. 1-10 AD *IG* v (1) 209, 31; *SEG* XXXV 331
(date) (Bradford (21)); (71) f. i AD *IG* IV (1)²
85, 5; 86, 23, 31 + Peek, *IAEpid* 36; *IG* IV
(1)² 681, 4; *BSA* 80 (1985) pp. 215-9 (ident.,
stemma) (Bradford (9)) (Λ. Οὐολοσσηνὸς Ἀ.: s.
Δαμάρης, ?f. Λ. Οὐολοσσηνὸς Δαμάρης); (72) i/ii
AD *IG* v (1) 469, 2; 607, 18; *BSA* 75 (1980)
pp. 214-19 (ident., stemma) (Bradford (26))
(Τιβ. Κλ. Ἀ.: f. Τιβ. Κλ. Δαμοκράτης, ?f. Τιβ.
Κλ. Σιμήδης); (73) c. 80-100 AD *SEG* XI 608, 3
(Bradford (20)) (s. Τιμοκράτης); (74) c. 90-100
AD *SEG* XI 558, 6 (Bradford (11)) (s. Δαμοκρατίδας); (75) c. 90-105 AD *SEG* XI 512, 2;
562, 2 (Bradford (15)) (s. Ἡρᾶς); (76) c. 90-
125 AD *IG* v (1) 32 B, 6; 82, 3; 477, 3; v (2)
544, 7; *SEG* XI 516, 1; 542, [2]; 545, 3; 559,
5; 569, 1; 605, 7; 63, 2; *BSA* 80 (1985) pp.
215; 219-24 (ident., stemma) (Bradford (10);
(24)) (Λ. Οὐολοσσηνὸς Ἀ.: s. Λ. Οὐολοσσηνὸς
Δαμάρης, Μεμμία Δαμοκρατία, ?f. Οὐολοσσηνὴ
Ἰοῦστα); (77) c. 100-120 AD *IG* v (1) 103, 5
+ *SEG* XI 568; 537 a, 3 (Bradford (35)) (f.
Λουϊάδας); (78) c. 100-125 AD *IG* v (1) 103,
7; 483, 2; *SEG* XI 537 a, 5; 569, 25 (Bradford (19)) (s. Κάμιλλος); (79) ii AD *IG* v (1)
159, 22 (Bradford (27)); (80) c. 105-110 AD
*IG* v (1) 20 B, 7 (Bradford (29)) (I f. Ἀριστοκράτης II); (81) ~ *IG* v (1) 20 B, 7 (Bradford (4)) (II s. Ἀριστοκράτης I); (82) c. 120 AD
*SEG* XI 518, 6 (Bradford (18)) (Ἀριστοκρατίδης:
s. Καλλικράτης); (83) c. 134 AD *IG* v (1) 287,
1 (Bradford (17)) (Μ. Οὔλπ. Ἀ.: s. Καλλικράτης); (84) 137 AD *IG* v (1) 59, 3; *SEG* XI
521 b, 2 (Bradford (28)) (f. Ἀγιάδας); (85) c.
140-145 AD *SEG* XI 524, 24 (Bradford (5))
([Ἀρι]στοκράτης: II s. Ἀριστοκράτης I); (86) ~
*SEG* XI 524, [24] (Bradford (30)) (I f. Ἀριστοκράτης II); (87) c. 150-155 AD *IG* v (1) 71 III,
16; *BSA* 75 (1980) p. 216 (ident.) (Bradford
(25)) ?= (88); (88) c. 150-175 AD *SEG* XXX
407, 2-3; *BSA* 75 (1980) pp. 210-20 (ident.,
stemma) (Κλ. [Ἀριστο]κράτης: s. Τιβ. Κλ. Σιμήδης, f. Κλ. Σιμήδης) ?= (87); (89) s. ii AD *IG* v
(1) 46, 10 (Bradford (13)) (Μ. Ἀ.: s. Φίρμος);
(90) ~ *IG* v (2) 543; *BSA* 80 (1985) pp. 215;
223-4 (ident., locn., date, stemma); 89 (1994)
pp. 437-8 no. 10, 11 (Πομπ. Ἀ.: s. Πομπ. Ἀ.: f.
Δαμαίνετος, Οὐολοσσηνὴ Ἰοῦστα); (91) c. 175 AD
*IG* v (1) 680, 8; *BSA* 79 (1984) pp. 266-7
(ident., stemma) (Bradford (33)) (?s. Δαμαίνετος, f. Δαμαίνετος); (92) c. 225-250 AD *IG* v
(1) 529, 2; 530, 8; 653 a, 5 (*Artemis Orthia*
p. 356 no. 142); *BSA* 79 (1984) pp. 266-7
(ident., stemma) (Bradford (8)) (Μ. Αὐρ. Ἀ.,
Ἀριστοκράτηρ—*IG* v 653 a: s. Δαμαίνετος); (93)
c. 230-260 AD *IG* v (1) 556, 8 (Bradford (14))
(Αὐρ. Ἀ.: s. Ἡρακλᾶς)
——Amyklai: (94) ii/i BC *IG* v (1) 26, 2 (Bradford (36)) (f. Νηκλῆς)
——SPARTA?: (95) ii AD *SEG* XI 839, 3 (Bradford
(22)) ([Ἀ]ριστοκράτης)
MESSENIA:
——MESSENE: (96) c. 223 BC *IG* IX (1)² (1) 31, 36
(f. Σοφοκλῆς); (97) ?i AD *PAE* 1969, p. 100 a,
8; (98) 84 AD *SEG* XLI 334, 5
——MESSENE?: (99) ii/i AD ib. XI 979, 36
——THOURIA: (100) f. ii BC ib. 972, 21 (f. Ἄλκαν-
δρος)
PELOPONNESE?: (101) s. iii BC *IG* v (1) 1426,
19 (f. Ἀντιφανίδας); (102) 11 AD *PAE* 1992, p.

72 B, 20 (f. Ὀνησιφόρος)
S. ITALY (BRUTTIUM):
——LOKROI EPIZEPHYRIOI:
——(Κοβ.): (103) iv/iii BC De Franciscis 21, 4,
9
——(Προ.): (104) iv/iii BC ib. 11, 4 (s. Μένων)
——RHEGION: (105) vii-vi BC *RE* (26)
S. ITALY (CALABRIA):
——TARAS-TARENTUM: (106) c. 272-235 BC Vlasto
908-9; 1088 (coins) (Evans, *Horsemen* p. 180
VIII L.1; p. 182 no. 1)
S. ITALY (CAMPANIA):
——KYME: (107) vi BC *RE* (4) (f. Ἀριστόδημος)
SICILY: (108) iii-ii BC *Meligunis-Lipara* 2 p.
332; cf. *Kokalos* 32 (1986) p. 221 no. 14
——AKRAI: (109) ii BC *Akrai* p. 156 no. 6, 6 (f.
Δαμοκράτης)
——LIPARA: (110) hell.? Libertini, *Isole
Eolie* p. 221 no. 24 (Ἀριστοκιχ—apogr.,
Ἀριστοκρά[της]—*LGPN*, Ἀριστόκλεος (gen.)—
ed.)
——TAUROMENION: (111) c. 209 BC *IG* XIV 421
an. 32 (*SGDI* 5219) (f. Ἐπιγένης); (112) c. 190
BC *IG* XIV 421 an. 51 (*SGDI* 5219); (113) c.
152 BC *IGSI* 4 III (IV), 27 an. 89 (f. Ἐπιγέ-
νης); (114) c. 146 BC *IG* XIV 421 an. 95 (*SGDI*
5219); *IGSI* 4 III (IV), 71 an. 95 (s. Ζώπυ-
ρος); (115) c. 40 BC *Cron. Arch.* 3 (1964) p. 55
I, 37 f. Ἀριστομένης)
——(Ταυ.): (116) c. 145 BC *IGSI* 4 III (IV), 88
an. 97 (f. Φάλακρος)
——(Χαλ.): (117) ?ii/i BC *IG* XIV 421 D an. 5;
421 [D] an. 2 (*SGDI* 5219) (s. Ἀριστομένης, f.
Ἀριστομένης)

**Ἀριστοκρατίδας**
LAKONIA:
——SPARTA: (1) c. 30-20 BC *IG* v (1) 141, 1;
211, 1; *SEG* XXXV 329 (date) (Bradford (1))
(Ἀριστοκρατίδ[ας]—141); (2) c. 1-10 AD *IG* v
(1) 209, 12; *SEG* XXXV 331 (date) (Bradford
(2)) (Ἀρισ[το]κρατίδας: f. Δαμοκράτης); (3) c.
80-100 AD *SEG* XI 511, 2 (Bradford (3)) (f.
Νικίας)

**Ἀριστοκρέτης**
ARKADIA:
——TEGEA:
——(Krariotai): (1) s. iv BC *IG* v (2) 41, 47
(Ἀριστοκρέτης: s. Δαμο—)
S. ITALY (BRUTTIUM):
——TERINA: (2) c. 325-300 BC *IGSI* 21, 4 (*SEG*
IV 73; Landi, *DISMG* 170) (?s. Ἱστιαῖος)

**Ἀριστοκρίτα**
AITOLIA:
——KALLION/KALLIPOLIS: (1) iii/ii BC *AD* 26
(1971) Chron. p. 283

**Ἀριστόκριτος**
ARGOLIS:
——ARGOS: (1) ii/i BC *SEG* XXVIII 1246, 24-5 (s.
Χαρίξενος)
——EPIDAUROS:
——Rhopitais: (2) c. 370-335 BC *IG* IV (1)² 102,
76, 80; 103, 84
——HALIEIS: (3) s. iv BC ib. 122, 19
——HERMIONE: (4) m. iv BC Unp. (Ch. Kritzas)
(s. Μεγακλῆς)
——TROIZEN: (5) 333 BC *SEG* XXXIV 122, 57
ARKADIA:
——MANTINEIA-ANTIGONEIA: (6) c. 300-221 BC
*IG* v (2) 323. 24 (tessera) (f. Ἀμφίας)
——PHIGALEIA: (7) m. iii BC *SEG* XXIII 239, 1
——TEGEA: (8) ii-i BC *IG* v (2) 170. 11 (tile) (Ἀρι-
στόκριτ(ος))
KORINTHIA:
——SIKYON: (9) ?254-253 BC Nachtergael, *Les
Galates* 9, 76; 10, 71; cf. Stephanis 429 (f.
Ἀρχεδάμας)

LAKONIA:
——SPARTA: (10) s. v BC *RE* (3) (Poralla² 129);
cf. Plu., *Lys.* 2 (Ἀριστόκλειτος—Plu.: f. Λύσαν-
δρος, Λίβυς); (11) ii/i BC *IG* v (1) 256 (Brad-
ford (3)) (f. Ξενοκλῆς); (12) c. 25-1 BC *IG* v (1)
212, 15 (Bradford (1)) (s. Ξενόστρατος); (13) ~
*IG* v (1) 212, 35 (Bradford (2)) (f. Ἀριστόδι-
κος)
S. ITALY (BRUTTIUM):
——LOKROI EPIZEPHYRIOI:
——(Ψαθ.): (14) iv/iii BC De Franciscis 3, 2; 28,
5 (f. Σάτυρος)
SICILY:
——SYRACUSE: (15) f. iv BC [Pl.], *Ep.* 319 A; 363
D

**Ἀριστόλα**
ARGOLIS:
——ARGOS: (1) iii BC *IG* IV (1) 527, 6; cf. *BCH*
37 (1913) p. 308 (Ἀριστόλ[α])
——HERMIONE: (2) ii-i BC *IG* IV (1) 732 I, 11 (m.
Ξένων)

**Ἀριστολαΐδας**
ACHAIA:
——DYME: (1) c. 219 BC *SGDI* 1612, 1 (*Tyche* 5
(1990) p. 124)
AIGINA: (2) f. v BC *IG* IV (1) 62; *LSAG*² p. 113
no. 10 (date)
ARGOLIS:
——EPIDAUROS: (3) f. iv BC Peek, *IAEpid* 1; (4)
c. 370 BC *IG* IV (1)² 102, 62; (5) c. 350-200
BC *SEG* XXVI 452. 2; (6) c. 335-325 BC *IG*
IV (1)² 106 I, 2, 7; cf. *SEG* XXV 389 ([Ἀρι-
στ]ολαΐδας); (7) c. 324-315 BC *CID* II 120 A,
54 (f. Ἀστυλαΐδας); (8) c. 300-275 BC ib. l. 53;
122 I, 15 (s. Ἀστυλαΐδας)
ARKADIA:
——MANTINEIA-ANTIGONEIA:
——(Posoidaia): (9) c. 425-400 BC *SEG* XXXI
348, 19
——MEGALOPOLIS: (10) 359 BC *CID* II 5 I, 41
([Ἀρι]στολα[α]ΐδας); (11) m. iii BC *IG* IV (1)²
96, 67 (Perlman E.3); Perlman p. 63 f. (date)
(f. Καλλιπάτας)
ELIS:
——LASION: (12) vi BC *SEG* XI 1173 a, 3
KERKYRA: (13) hell. *IG* IX (1) 890 (f. Θεομήδης)
——(Hylleis): (14) ii BC ib. 694, 2 (*RIJG* XXV
B); cf. *SEG* XXV 609 (f. Ἀριστομένης)

**Ἀριστόλαος**
AITOLIA: (1) ?240-228 BC *FD* III (3) 218 A, 2
(-σστό-)
AKARNANIA:
——LIMNAIA: (2) s. iv BC *IG* IV (1)² 95, 56-7
(Perlman E.2); Perlman pp. 46-9 (date) (f.
Θωπίνας)
ARGOLIS:
——EPIDAUROS: (3) c. 370 BC *IG* IV (1)² 102, 14
EPIROS:
——DODONA*: (4) iv-iii BC *SGDI* 1578, 3, 6
(Ἀρισ[τό]λαος)
ILLYRIA:
——EPIDAMNOS-DYRRHACHION: (5) hell.-imp.
*IDyrrh* 119 (s. Ξενήν)
KORINTHIA:
——SIKYON: (6) m. iv BC *RE* (-) (Skalet 59) (Lat.
Aristolaus: s. Παυσίας: painter)
MESSENIA:
——MESSENE?: (7) c. 223 BC *IG* IX (1)² (1) 31, 39
(f. Ἀρίστων)

**Ἀριστόλας**
AKARNANIA:
——THYRREION: (1) m. iii BC *SEG* XL 464 II side
1, 8 ([Ἀριστ?]όλας: ?s. Ὀρσικράτης); (2) ii BC
*IG* IX (1)² (2) 315
ARGOLIS:
——EPIDAUROS: (3) 191-146 BC *ZfN* 9 (1882) p.
255 no. 11 (coin)
——Mysias: (4) m. iii BC *IG* IV (1)² 96, 44
(Perlman E.3); Perlman p. 63 f. (date) (?s.

Δαμοκλῆς); (5) ~ IG IV (1)² 96, 44 (Perlman E.3); Perlman p. 63 f. (date) (s. Ἀριστοκράτης)
—TROIZEN: (6) iii BC IG IV (1) 825, 6
ARKADIA:
—MEGALOPOLIS: (7) ii BC ib. v (2) 536 (f. Ἀριστώ)
—TEGEA: (8) iv BC ib. 54 ([Ἀρισ]τόλας?: s. Δαμ—)
——(Apolloniatai): (9) iv/iii BC ib. 38, 31 (f. Ἀριστοκλῆς)
——(Hippothoitai): (10) m. iii BC ib. 36, 82 (f. Δαμόστρατος)
EPIROS:
—AMBRAKIA: (11) ii-i BC CIG 1799 (Ἀριστό[λ]ας: s. Ἀγέμαχος)
KEPHALLENIA:
—SAME: (12) f. iii BC Op. Ath. 10 (1971) p. 66 no. 12 (BCH 83 (1959) p. 658)
LAKONIA:
—SPARTA: (13) c. 225 BC SEG XI 414, 39 (Perlman E.5; Bradford (3)) (f. Ἱππότας); (14) c. 30-20 BC IG v (1) 211, 18 (Bradford (4)) (f. Κρατιστόλας); (15) c. 25-1 BC IG v (1) 210, 53; 212, 51 (Bradford (1)); (16) i BC/i AD SEG XI 676, 2 (Bradford (2)) (Ἀριστό[λας]: f. Γοργώι)
MESSENIA:
—ABIA: (17) i BC/i AD IG v (1) 1353 (f. Βίων)
—MESSENE: (18) iv/iii BC SEG XI 1037, 19 (Ἀριστόλα[ς])
SICILY:
—TAUROMENION: (19) c. 228 BC IG XIV 421 an. 13 (SGDI 5219) (I f. Ἀριστόλας II); (20) ~ IG XIV 421 an. 13 (SGDI 5219) (II s. Ἀριστόλας I)

**Ἀριστόλη**
S. ITALY (CAMPANIA):
—NEAPOLIS: (1) i BC/i AD SEG IV 96 (INap 152) (d. Ἐπίλυτος)

**Ἀριστόλοχος**
ELIS: (1) ?c. 475 BC SEG XXXI 358, 4; LSAG² p. 450 no. E (date); (2) 72 BC Moretti, Olymp. 693
ILLYRIA:
—APOLLONIA: (3) i BC Ceka, Probleme p. 139 no. 2 (coin) (pryt.); (4) ~ Maier 165 (coin) (money.)
LAKONIA:
—SPARTA: (5) 378 BC X., HG v 4. 22 (Poralla² 130)

**Ἀριστόμαντις**
ELIS: (1) c. 95-105 AD IvOl 431, 5-6 (Κλ. Ἀ.: m. Κλ. Λουκηνὸς Σαίκλαρος)
KEPHALLENIA:
—PALE: (2) ii-iii AD IG IX (1) 645, 2-3 (Βι. Ἀ. (masc.))

**Ἀριστομάχα**
ARGOLIS:
—ARGOS: (1) 470-450 BC ib. I³ 858 (Ἀρισ[το]μάχη: d. Γλαυκῖνος)
EPIROS:
—BOUTHROTOS (PRASAIBOI): (2) a. 163 BC IBouthrot 29, 63 (SEG XXXVIII 487) (Ἀρι[στο]μάχα); (3) ~ IBouthrot 30, 22, 25; 40, 9 (SEG XXXVIII 488; 499); (4) ~ IBouthrot 32, 4 (SEG XXXVIII 491)
KORINTHIA:
—KORINTH?: (5) c. 490-470 BC Tölle-Kastenbein, Peplosfiguren pp. 235-6 no. 42 a (BM Bronzes 188) (or Argolis Hermione?)
LAKONIA:
—SPARTA: (6) v BC IG v (1) 1345 a (Lazzarini 103; Poralla² 131)
SICILY:
—SYRACUSE: (7) v/iv BC RE (3); cf. Beloch, GG III (2) pp. 102-7 (-χη: d. Ἱππαρῖνος, m. Ἱππαρῖνος, Νυσαῖος, Ἀρέτα, Σωφροσύνα)

**Ἀριστομαχίδας**
ARKADIA:
—TEGEA: (1) s. iv BC IG v (2) 66

LAKONIA:
—GERONTHRAI: (2) c. 500 BC ib. v (1) 1134, 4; LSAG² p. 201 no. 45 (date) (Poralla² 132)

**Ἀριστόμαχος**
ACHAIA:
—AIGION: (1) c. 230-200 BC BCH 45 (1921) p. 11 II, 58 (s. Ἀρχύλος)
ACHAIA?: (2) 193 BC IG v (2) 293, 24 (f. Δαμοκλῆς)
—AIGINA: (3) ii BC SEG XI 17
AITOLIA: (4) 224 or 221 BC SGDI 2524, 5; Nachtergael, Les Galates 64, 4; (5) 217 BC ib. 65, 3
—KALYDON: (6) s. ii BC SEG XXV 621,. 2 (f. Ἀρίστων)
—THERMOS*: (7) s. iii BC IG IX (1)² (1) 60 III, 11
AKARNANIA:
—ANAKTORION: (8) hell.? AD 42 (1987) Chron. p. 184 (SEG XLII 484)
—LIMNAIA: (9) c. 325-315 BC Hesp. 57 (1988) p. 148 A, 32-3 (SEG XXXVI 331); cf. Hesp. 48 (1979) pp. 78 f. with pl. 22 c (f. Δρωξίας, Φίλιστος)
—THYRREION: (10) iii-ii BC SEG XXVII 159, 9; cf. PAE 1977, pl. 244 a (s. Ἀγήμων)
ARGOLIS:
—ARGOS: (11) inc. SEG XXVIII 399 ([Ἀρι]στόμαχος); (12) ?c. 575-550 BC ib. XI 336, 10; LSAG² p. 168 no. 7 (date); (13) ?316 BC IG v (2) 549, 26 (f. Ἀριστόδαμος); (14) c. 280-240 BC RE (16); IG IV (1)² 621 B; v (2) 9, 2 (I ?s. Ἀρίστιππος, f. Ἀριστόμαχος II); (15) c. 260-222 BC RE (17); IG IV (1)² 621 B; v (2) 9, 2 (II s. Ἀριστόμαχος I: tyrant); (16) 253 BC ib. II² 774, 8, 10; (17) s. iii BC ib. IV (1)² 621 B (Ἀριστό[μαχος]: I f. Ἀριστόμαχος II); (18) ~ ib. (II s. Ἀριστόμαχος I); (19) f. ii BC IvOl 318; IG XIV 1232; RE (21) (and Caria Kaunos: sculptor); (20) f. i BC ASAA NS 1-2 (1939-40) p. 168 no. 21 B I, 12; (21) ~ Unp. (Ch. Kritzas) (f. Πίστων)
—EPIDAUROS: (22) c. 335-325 BC IG IV (1)² 106 I, 91 (Ἀριστόμαχος)
—EPIDAUROS*: (23) c. 370 BC ib. 102, 57
—HERMIONE: (24) iii BC ib. IV (1) 729 I, 16 (Ἀρισ[τ]όμ[α]χος: s. Σήραμβος)
—KLEONAI: (25) ?c. 229 BC SEG XXIII 178, 25 (or Argolis Argos)
ARKADIA:
—MANTINEIA-ANTIGONEIA: (26) c. 475-450 BC IG v (2) 262, 6 (IPArk 8); LSAG² p. 216 no. 29 (date) (-στό-); (27) ?iii BC IG v (2) 318, 10
—TEGEA:
——(Athaneatai): (28) iv/iii BC ib. 38, 17 ([Ἀρι]στόμαχος: s. Μιλτιάδας); (29) ~ ib. l. 20 (f. —ας)
——(Hippothoitai): (30) iv/iii BC ib. l. 43 (s. Ἀμφίστρατος)
ELIS: (31) ?i AD IvOl 414 (f. Δαμώ)
EPIROS:
—BOUTHROTOS (PRASAIBOI): (32) a. 163 BC IBouthrot 17, 31; 25, 29 (SEG XXXVIII 474; 483); (33) ~ IBouthrot 21, 39 (SEG XXXVIII 478); (34) ~ IBouthrot 22, 13 (SEG XXXVIII 479); (35) ~ IBouthrot 30, 21 (SEG XXXVIII 488) (s. Ἀριστεύς) ?= (47); (36) ~ IBouthrot 31, 74 (SEG XXXVIII 490) (f. Λυσανίας) ?= (38); (37) ~ IBouthrot 107 (s. Βοΐσκος); (38) ~ ib. 110, 8 (f. Λυσανίας) ?= (43) (36); (39) ~ ib. l. 8 (s. Νίκανδρος); (40) ~ ib. 116, 6 (BCH 118 (1994) p. 121 A) (Ἀρι[στό]μαχος]); (41) ~ IBouthrot 143, 8
——Aixonioi: (42) a. 163 BC ib. 57 (SEG XXXVIII 508); IBouthrot 60, 3 (SEG XXXVIII 511); IBouthrot 117, 3; 118, 2, 5; 168, 3 (SEG XXXVIII 469); (43) ~ IBouthrot 111, 11; 112, 12; 122, 7 (f. Λυσανίας) ?= (38)

—Dionioi: (44) a. 163 BC ib. 68, 12 (s. Νικόμαχος)
—Kestrinoi Barrioi: (45) a. 163 BC ib. 41, 1 (SEG XXXVIII 500) (s. Νικόλαος)
—Pelmatioi: (46) a. 163 BC IBouthrot 127, 9 (BCH 118 (1994) p. 128 A) (s. Δρωπύλος)
—Phonidatoi: (47) a. 163 BC IBouthrot 144, 7 (s. Ἀριστεύς) ?= (35)
—OMPHALES: (48) ?342-326 BC Cabanes, L'Épire p. 540 no. 4, 5 (IApoll 308); Cabanes, L'Épire p. 541 no. 5, 3; p. 541 no. 6, 4 (SEG XXVI 699)
ILLYRIA:
—APOLLONIA: (49) ii BC IApoll 12 (s. Ἀνδρόνικος)
—EPIDAMNOS-DYRRHACHION: (50) c. 250-50 BC Maier 133-7 (Ceka 29; 205; 304; 347; 386?); cf. IApoll Ref. Bibl. n. 26 (coin) (pryt.)
KORINTHIA:
—KORINTH: (51) 216 BC Plb. vii 5. 3
—SIKYON: (52) m. iii BC Syll³ 458 (Skalet 62) (s. Σώσανδρος) ?= (53); (53) c. 264-251 BC Plu., Arat. 5 (Skalet 61) ?= (52); (54) ii/i BC SEG XI 251, 1 ([Ἀρ]ιστόμ[α]χος: s. Ἀγαθις)
LAKONIA:
—SPARTA: (55) iii BC ib. XL 348 B, 9 (Ἀριστόμαχ[ος]); (56) c. 206 BC IG IX (1)² (1) 28, 3 (Bradford (1)) (s. Λυσίμαχος); (57) c. 30-20 BC IG v (1) 211, 33 (Bradford (2)) (s. Πασικλῆς); (58) c. 25-1 BC IG v (1) 212, 2 (Bradford (3))
MESSENIA:
—MESSENE: (59) 192 BC IG IX (1)² (1) 31, 23 (f. Φίλιππος)
—THOURIA: (60) ii/i BC ib. v (1) 1384, 14 (s. Θεόφιλος)
PELOPONNESE: (61) c. 230-200 BC BCH 45 (1921) p. 11 II, 37 (Ἀ[ρι]στόμαχος)
S. ITALY (BRUTTIUM):
—KROTON: (62) 215 BC Liv. xxiv 2. 9, 11; 3. 11, 13 (Lat. Aristomachus)
—LOKROI EPIZEPHYRIOI:
——(Γαψ.): (63) iv/iii BC De Franciscis 16, 5; 38, 6 (s. Ἀριστεύς)
—RHEGION:
——(Ἀμφιμ.): (64) ii BC IG XIV 616, 4 with Add. p. 688 (Mus. Naz. Reggio p. 159 no. 29) (f. Ἀριστέας); (65) ~ IG XIV 616, 9 with Add. p. 688 (Mus. Naz. Reggio p. 159 no. 29) (s. Ἀριστέας)
S. ITALY (LUCANIA):
—HYELE-VELIA: (66) iv/iii BC IG IV (1)² 258 ([Ἀρι]στόμαχος: s. Ἀρκέσας)
SICILY:
—AKRAI: (67) ?iii BC SGDI 3240, 6 (Akrai p. 156 no. 7) (s. Διονυσόδωρος); (68) iii-ii BC SGDI 3242, 2 (Akrai p. 157 no. 8)
—KAMARINA: (69) iv/iii BC Dubois, IGDS 122, 2 (Ἀ[ρι]στόμαχος: f. —δας) ?= (70); (70) ~ ib. l. 5-7, 9 (Cordano, 'Camarina VII' 76) (f. Νεμέρατος, Ἀπολλόδοτος) ?= (69)
—KENTORIPA: (71) imp.? IG XIV 2397. 1 (tile)
—SYRACUSE: (72) s. iv BC ib. IV (1)² 95, 64 (Perlman E.2); Perlman pp. 46-9 (date)
ZAKYNTHOS: (73) ?257-253 BC Nachtergael, Les Galates 7, 2, 48; 8, 2; 9, 2; 10, 2; cf. Stephanis 2568 (f. Φιλωνίδας)

**Ἀριστομέδα**
ARKADIA:
—KYNAITHA: (1) c. 230-200 BC BCH 45 (1921) p. 12 II, 65; p. 27 V, 4 (d. Πελοπίδας)
ELIS:
—LETRINOI?: (2) ii BC SEG XI 1174 a (Ἀριστομέδαρ (fem. gen.))

**Ἀριστομέδων**
ARGOLIS:
—ARGOS: (1) iv-iii BC Unp. (Ch. Kritzas); (2) ?s. iv BC Paus. x 1. 10; cf. Daux, Paus. à Delphes pp. 136-140; FD III (3) pp. 123 ff. (sculptor)
—TROIZEN: (3) iii BC IG IV (1) 774, 11

ILLYRIA:
—EPIDAMNOS-DYRRHACHION: (4) hell.-imp. *IDyrrh* 120 (s. *Πύρων*)
KERKYRA: (5) hell. *IG* IX (1) 589, 2, 4 (f. *Φιλιστίς*, *Ἡράκλεια*)
SICILY:
—TAUROMENION: (6) c. 188 BC ib. XIV 421 an. 53 (*SGDI* 5219) (f. *Εὐκλείδας*)

**Ἀριστομένεια**
ILLYRIA:
—EPIDAMNOS-DYRRHACHION: (1) hell.-imp. *IDyrrh* 61 (*Ἀριστομένεạ*); (2) ~ ib. 121 (-νεα: d. *Ἱππίας*)

**Ἀριστομένης**
ACHAIA:
—AIGION: (1) 157 BC *FD* III (3) 125, 4, 6; cf. Stephanis 375 (f. *Ἄριστυς*)
—PATRAI: (2) c. 146-32 BC *SNG Cop. Phliasia-Laconia* 157; *Coll. Photiades* 1012 (coin) (s. *Ἀριστόδαμος*)
—AIGINA: (3) 446 BC Pi., *P.* viii, 5, 80; cf. Klee p. 83 no. 68 (s. *Ξενάρκης*)
AKARNANIA:
—ALYZIA: (4) iii/ii BC *PP* 14592; *IG* IX (1)² (2) 583, 21, 64; *Hermes* 85 (1957) pp. 501 ff. (ident.) (s. *Μεννείας*, f. *Ἀγαθόκλεια*); (5) i BC *IG* IX (1)² (2) 446 b (s. *Μεννέας*)
ARGOLIS:
—ARGOS: (6) ?320 BC ib. V (2) 549, 16 (s. *Ἀριστεύς*); (7) iii BC ib. IV (1) 736 ?= (8); (8) iii/ii BC ib. IV (1)² 205, 4; 208, 4; 243, 4; 696; 697 (f. *Ἀθηνογένης*) ?= (7)
—HERMIONE: (9) ?c. 460-450 BC ib. IV (1) 684 (Lazzarini 75); cf. *SEG* XI 379; *LSAG*² p. 181 no. 9 (date) (-νε̄ς: s. *Ἀλεξίας*)
ARKADIA:
—MEGALOPOLIS: (10) iii BC *IG* V (2) 478, 8
—TEGEA: (11) f. iii BC ib. 35, 30 (f. *Μενέας*); (12) iii-iv AD ib. 156 (f. *Εὔτυχος*)
ELIS: (13) s. i AD *IvOl* 429, 8 (*Τιβ. Κλ. Ἀ.*: *Ἀντ. Κλεοδίκη*)
EPIROS:
—AMBRAKIA: (14) m. iii BC *IG* V (2) 368, 22 (*[Ἀρι]στομένης*); (15) ~ ib. l. 24 (*[Ἀρι]στομένης*); (16) 238-168 BC *JIAN* 12 (1909-10) p. 45 no. 13 (coin) (*Ἀριστομέν(ης)*)
—KASSOPE: (17) f. ii BC Cabanes, *L'Épire* p. 564 no. 41, 11 (f. *Ἀρίσταρχος*)
ILLYRIA:
—APOLLONIA: (18) 208 BC *IMM* 45, 2 (*IApoll* 315)
—EPIDAMNOS-DYRRHACHION: (19) iii-ii BC *IDyrrh* 62 (f. *Ἀριστώ*); (20) c. 250-50 BC *BMC Thessaly* p. 76 no. 162 (coin); cf. *Iliria* 1992, p. 164 no. 3 (tile) (pryt.) ?= (21); (21) ~ Maier 136; 138; 473; Münsterberg Nachtr. p. 14 (Ceka 18; 30; 132; 386?; 387); cf. *IApoll Ref. Bibl.* nn. 17 and 26 (coin) (pryt.) ?= (20); (22) hell.-imp. *IDyrrh* 27 (s. *Καλλικράτης*)
—GUREZEZE (MOD.): (23) hell. *Iliria* 1982 (1), p. 104 no. 3 = p. 120 no. 8 (tile)
—KERKYRA: (24) ?iii-ii BC *IG* IX (1) 755 = *BM Terracottas* E 188; *Korkyra* 1 p. 167 no. 5? (tiles)
——(Hylleis): (25) ii BC *IG* IX (1) 694, 1, 2, 35 etc. (*RIJG* XXV B); cf. *SEG* XXV 609 (s. *Ἀριστολαΐδας*)
KORINTHIA:
—KORINTH: (26) ii BC *IG* II² 9059 (s. *Ἀρίστιππος*); (27) imp.? *Syringes* 1030; (28) ii AD *SEG* XLI 273 B, 6 (III s. *Ἀριστομένης* II); (29) ~ ib. l. 4-5 (I s. *Μένανδρος*, *Φλαβιανή*, f. *Ἀριστομένης* II); (30) ~ ib. l. 5-6 (II s. *Ἀριστομένης* I, f. *Ἀριστομένης* III); (31) a. 212 AD *IG* IX (1) 12, 19 (*Γέλλιος Ἀ.*)
—SIKYON: (32) 176 BC *Syll*³ 585, 271 (f. *Ἄδματος*)

LAKONIA:
—SPARTA: (33) iii/ii BC *SEG* XI 468, 5 (Bradford (5)) (*[Ἀριστ]ομένης?*: f. *Ἀντίλας*); (34) c. 25-1 BC *IG* V (1) 210, 33 (Bradford (6)) (f. *Ἀννίλας*); (35) c. 1-10 AD *IG* V (1) 209, 8; *SEG* XXXV 331 (date) (Bradford (7)) (I f. *Ἀριστομένης* II); (36) ~ *IG* V (1) 209, 8; *SEG* XXXV 331 (date) (Bradford (1)) (II s. *Ἀριστομένης* I); (37) i/ii AD *IG* V (1) 97, 4; 674, 5 + *SEG* XI 842; 524, [4]; 564, 4; 597, [7] (Bradford (4)) (I s. *Ἐπίκτητος*, f. *Ἀριστομένης* II); (38) c. 105-115 AD *IG* V (1) 103, 8 (Bradford (8)) (*[Ἀρ]ιστομένης*: II s. *Ἀριστομένης* II); (39) ~ *IG* V (1) 103, 8 (Bradford (2)) (*[Ἀρ]ιστομένης*: II s. *Ἀριστομένης* I); (40) c. 140-145 AD *SEG* XI 524, [4]; 597, 7 (*[Ἀριστομένη]ς*: II s. *Ἀριστομένης* I)
—SPARTA?: (41) c. 400-375 BC Polyaen. ii 31. 1 (Poralla² 133)
LEUKAS: (42) c. 167-50 BC *BMC Thessaly* p. 179 no. 81; *SNG Cop. Epirus-Acarnania* 379; *Coll. McClean* 5364 (coins) (*Ἱππομένης—Coll. McClean* per err.); (43) f. i BC *IG* IX (1) 534, 10 (*Iscr. Gr. Verona* p. 24) (s. *Λέων*)
MESSENIA: (44) viii/vii BC *RE* (1) (?s. *Νικομήδης*, *Πύρρος*, s. *Νικοτέλεια*, f. *Γόργος*: fict.?)
—MESSENE: (45) ?i BC *PAE* 1969, p. 100 a, 12; (46) i BC *IvOl* 397-399 (s. *Ἀγίας*, f. *Ἀγίας*: sculptor); (47) ?i BC *SEG* XXIII 203, 7 (*[Ἀρ]ιστομένης*); (48) 31 BC-14 AD ib. 207, 27 (f. *Διονύσιος*); (49) i BC/i AD *IG* V (1) 1438 a, 3 (*Ἀριστομέ[νης]*); (50) i AD ib. 1479 (f. *Δαμοκλῆς*, *Μενεστράτα*); (51) 54-68 AD ib. 1450, 10 (*Τ. Κλ. Ἀ.*: *Διονύσιος*); (52) ?ii AD *SEG* XLI 335, 17; (53) 126 AD *IG* V (1) 1469, 3; cf. *SEG* XL 366 (*Τιβ. Κλ. Ἀ.*: s. *Τιβ. Κλ. Κρισπιανός*)
—THOURIA: (54) f. ii BC ib. XI 972, 1, 17; *IvOl* 46, 3, 15 (s. *Ἀριστίων*)
PELOPONNESE?: (55) 182 BC ib. l. [3], 14, 67 (fict.?)
S. ITALY (LUCANIA):
—HYELE-VELIA: (56) ii-i BC *IG* II² 8481 a (*Ag.* XVII 448) (f. *Ἀμφικράτης*)
—METAPONTION: (57) iv BC Iamb., *VP* 267 (*FVS* 1 p. 446)
SICILY:
—AKRAI: (58) ii BC *Akrai* p. 156 no. 6, 21 (s. *Ζώπυρος*)
—SYRACUSE?: (59) iv BC D.L. iii 19
—TAUROMENION: (60) ?ii/i BC *IG* XIV 421 [D] an. 2 (*SGDI* 5219) (s. *Ἀριστοκράτης*); (61) c. 40 BC *Cron. Arch.* 3 (1964) p. 53 I, 7, 13, 30, 37 (s. *Ἀριστοκράτης*)
——(Οἰ̄.): (62) ?ii/i BC *IG* XIV 421 D an. 11 (*SGDI* 5219) (f. *Ἀρτεμίδωρος*)
——(Χαλ.): (63) ?ii/i BC *IG* XIV 421 D an. 5 (*SGDI* 5219) (f. *Ἀριστοκράτης*)
ZAKYNTHOS: (64) iv/iii BC *IG* V (1) 1425, 5 (f. *Μέναλκος*); (65) hell. ib. IX (1) 600 (f. *Ἀρχικλῆς*)

**Ἀριστομενίδας**
LAKONIA:
—SPARTA: (1) 427-396 BC Paus. iii 9. 3 (Poralla² 134) (*Ἀριστομηνίδας—*Paus., *Ἀριστομηλίδας—*Keil: ?f. *Κλεόρα*, *Πείσανδρος*); (2) ii BC *SEG* XI 681 (Bradford (3)) (f. *—ργενίδας*); (3) s. i BC *IG* V (1) 134, 5 (Bradford (2)) (s. *Νίκανδρος*); (4) c. 120-130 AD *SEG* XI 518, 5; 544, 7; 579, 6 (Bradford (1)) (*Ἀριστομενείδας—*579: s. *Κλεόμαχος*)

**Ἀριστομήδα**
ARGOLIS:
—HERMIONE?: (1) ?iii BC *IG* IV (1) 746

**Ἀριστομήδης**
AITOLIA: (1) iii BC *AEMÖ* 4 (1880) p. 61
ARGOLIS:
—ARGOS: (2) ii/i BC *SEG* XXII 266, 3, 5, 21, [26] (f. *Αὖγις*)

—EPIDAUROS: (3) c. 370 BC *IG* IV (1)² 102, 55 ?= (4); (4) c. 365-335 BC ib. 103, 33, 72-3, 76, 81 ?= (3); (5) c. 340-320 BC Peek, *NIEpid* 19 C, 24 (*Ἀρισ[τ]ομή[δης]*); (6) iv/iii BC *IG* IV (1)² 202 (f. *Ἀγησίας*)
——(Azantioi): (7) 146 BC ib. 28, 29 (s. *Λυσίμαχος*)
——Pagasina (Azantioi): (8) m. iii BC ib. 96, 47 (Perlman E.3); Perlman p. 63 f. (date)
ARKADIA:
—PHENEOS: (9) m. iii BC *IG* IV (1)² 96, 70 (Perlman E.3); Perlman p. 63 f. (date) (*Ἀριστο[μή]δης*: f. *Κλεαῖος*)
—TEGEA: (10) iv BC *IG* V (2) 31, 11 (s. *Σάστρατος*)
EPIROS:
—AMBRAKIA: (11) a. 167 BC *SEG* XXXV 665 A, 6 (s. *Δαμαίνετος*); (12) ~ ib. l. 11 (s. *Δαμίων*)
KORINTHIA:
—KORINTH: (13) ?c. 600-575 BC ib. XXII 243 c (*[Ἀρι]στομέ̄δε̄[ς]*); (14) s. iv BC Peek, *NIEpid* 16, 21 (s. *Ἀριστόδοκος*)
—SIKYON: (15) 326-325 BC *CID* II 32, 44; 99 B, 15; 100, 4
MESSENIA:
—MESSENE: (16) 293-168 BC *PAE* 1912, p. 189 no. 224
—THOURIA: (17) f. ii BC *SEG* XI 972, 125 (f. *Ἀριστίων*)

**Ἀριστομηλίδας**
ARKADIA:
—ORCHOMENOS: (1) ?m. iii BC Paus. viii 47. 6 (tyrant) ?= (*Ἀριστοκλείδας* (2))

**Ἀριστον**
ARGOLIS:
—HERMIONE: (1) ii-i BC *IG* IV (1) 732 II, 3 (d. *Σάφις*)

**Ἀριστονίκα**
ACHAIA:
—DYME: (1) iii BC *AJPh* 31 (1910) p. 399 no. 74 a, 13 (d. *Λυσίας*)
AITOLIA:
—APERANTOI: (2) iii/ii BC *SEG* XVII 275, 3 (*L'Illyrie mérid.* 1 p. 110 fig. 8)
ARGOLIS:
—ARGOS: (3) hell.? *SEG* XXXV 169 A, 1 (*Ἀριστον[ί]κη*: d. *Πλειστίας*)
—TROIZEN: (4) iv BC *IG* IV (1) 763 (d. *Τελλίας*)
LAKONIA:
—SPARTA: (5) iii/ii BC *SEG* XLII 329, 5; (6) c. 30-20 BC *IG* V (1) 141, 16; *SEG* XXXV 329 (date) (Bradford (-)) (d. *Νικοκράτης*)
—TEUTHRONE: (7) hell.-imp. *IG* V (1) 1221

**Ἀριστονίκη**
ZAKYNTHOS: (1) iii-ii BC *AA* 1932, p. 155 no. 4 (d. *Κλέων*)

**Ἀριστονικίδας**
LAKONIA:
—SPARTA: (1) c. 90-110 AD *IG* V (1) 97, 5; *SEG* XI 561, 5; 564, 5; 605, 3 (Bradford (2)) (*Ἀριστονεικίδας—SEG* XI 564: s. *Εὐτυχίδας*); (2) c. 100-125 AD *IG* V (1) 20 B, 4; *SEG* XI 517, 6; 540, 2; 611, 4; XXXVI 361, 28; *BSA* 26 (1923-5) p. 168 C 7, 4 (Bradford (3)) (*Ἀριστονεικίδας—SEG* XI 517 and XXXVI 361: s. *Μουσαῖος*); (3) c. 130 AD *IG* V (1) 60, 3 (Bradford (1)) (*Ἀ. ὁ καὶ Διόσκορος*: *Ἀγαθοκλῆς*); (4) c. 135 AD *IG* V (1) 32 A, 14 (Bradford (5)); (5) c. 137-170 AD *IG* V (1) 116, 7; *SEG* XI 548, 20 (Bradford (4)) (*Ἀριστο<σ>νικίδας—IG*, *[Ἀρι]στονεικί[δας]—SEG*: s. *Νικηφόρος*)

**Ἀριστόνικος**
AITOLIA:
—PLEURON: (1) f. iii BC *IG* IX (1)² (1) 9, 9 (*[Ἀρισ?]τόνικος*)
AKARNANIA:
—THYRREION: (2) iii/ii BC ib. IX (1)² (2) 306 (*Ἀριστόνικ[ος]*, *Ἀριστονίκ[α?]*); (3) ii BC ib. 316 (-νει-)

ARGOLIS:
—ARGOS: (4) ?vii BC RE (15); FGrH 131 F 5 (Stephanis 366)
—EPIDAUROS*: (5) c. 335-325 BC IG IV (1)² 106 II, 131 ?= (6); (6) c. 330-310 BC SEG XXV 395, 8-9 ([Ἀρι]στόνικος) ?= (5); (7) c. 290-270 BC IG IV (1)² 109 III, 90
—HERMIONE*: (8) ?i AD ib. IV (1) 690, 4 (Ἀριστόν[ικος]: f. Ἀργαῖος)
—TROIZEN: (9) ?146 BC ib. 757 B, 34 (Ἀριστό[ν]ικος: f. Ἀρίσταρχος)
ARKADIA:
—MANTINEIA-ANTIGONEIA: (10) c. 300-221 BC ib. v (2) 323. 74 (tessera) (s. Δαμοτέλης)
—MEGALOPOLIS: (11) 143 BC ID 2593, 40 (Ἀριστόνικ[ος])
DALMATIA:
—ISSA: (12) iii BC SEG XXXV 691, 5 (VAHD 84 (1991) p. 256 no. 6) (s. Ξενοκλῆς); (13) ~ SEG XXXV 691, 8 (VAHD 84 (1991) p. 256 no. 6) (-νει-: s. Ξενοκλῆς)
ELIS:
—OLYMPIA*: (14) f. ii AD IvOl 92, 23 (Ἀρισ[τ]όνεικος: ?s. Ποσείδιππος: slave?)
KORINTHIA:
—KORINTH: (15) iii-ii BC Hesp. 41 (1972) p. 204 no. 6 ([Ἀρ]ιστόνικος, [Καλλ]ιστόνικος, [Πλε]ιστόνικος); (16) ii AD SEG XXXVI 344; Corinth IV (2) p. 205 no. 702 (lamps) (-νει-)
LAKONIA:
—SPARTA: (17) ii-i BC IG IX (2) 518 (Bradford (2)) ([Ἀρισ]τό[ν]ικος: s. Εὐαμέριος); (18) i BC IG v (1) 126, 5 (Bradford (6)) (f. Ἀριστοκράτης); (19) s. i BC IG v (1) 92, 8; 142, 13 (Bradford (1); (5)) (s. Ἀριστεύς, f. Ἀριστεύς); (20) c. 30-20 BC IG v (1) 142, 18 (Bradford (8)) (Ἀριστόνικος: f. —ρος); (21) ~ IG v (1) 211, 17 (Bradford (4)) (f. Ἀμίαντος); (22) c. 140-160 AD IG v (1) 53, 33; 154, 5 (Bradford (3); (7)) (Κανίνιος Ἀ.: f. Κανίνιος Εὔπορος)
MESSENIA:
—KYPARISSIA: (23) m. iii BC IG IV (1)² 96, 68 (Perlman E.3); Perlman p. 63 f. (date) (s. Σόφων)
—THOURIA: (24) ii/i BC IG v (1) 1384, 18 (f. Κάλλιππος)
S. ITALY (CALABRIA):
—TARAS-TARENTUM: (25) inc. FGrH 57; RE (16)
SICILY:
—KENTORIPA: (26) hell. IG XIV 574, 2 (Dubois, IGDS 188) (Ἡράκλειος Ἀ.: s. Ἀ—)
ZAKYNTHOS: (27) ?205 BC IG VII 296, 5, 8 (IOrop 177) (s. Διόφαντος)

**Ἀριστονόα**
AITOLIA: (1) inc. FD III (1) 575 (IG IX (1)² (1) 200) (her.?)
EPIROS:
—NIKOPOLIS: (2) i AD SEG XXXVII 528

**Ἀριστονόη**
AIGINA: (1) imp. IG IV (1) 83, 1 (d. Ποσειδώνιος)

**Ἀριστόνοθος**
S. ITALY?: (1) m. vii BC Guarducci, Ep. Gr. 3 pp. 477-8 (Arena, Iscr. Sic. III p. 116 no. A2); cf. SEG XXVII 664 + XXIX 946; LGPN I (1) (or Euboia: Ἀριστόνοφος—vase: potter)

**Ἀριστόνοος**
AITOLIA:
—TRICHONION: (1) s. iii BC IG IX (1)² (1) 117, 8
ARGOLIS:
—ARGOS: (2) iii BC ib. v (2) 34, 29
KORINTHIA:
—KORINTH: (3) c. 334 BC FD III (2) 190-2 (Syll³ 449); cf. Coll. Alex. pp. 162 ff.; Kl. Pauly s.v. Aristonoos (s. Νικοσθένης)

**Ἀριστόνους**
AIGINA: (1) vi/v BC RE (9); Overbeck 439; Alt-Ägina II (2) p. 34 (sculptor)
ARGOLIS:
—EPIDAUROS*: (2) c. 370 BC IG IV (1)² 102, 254, 261
SICILY:
—GELA-PHINTIAS: (3) c. 580 BC Th. vi 4. 4 (and Sicily Akragas: oikist); (4) vi/v BC FGrH 566 F 21

**Ἀριστοξένα**
ARGOLIS:
—HERMIONE: (1) ?i AD IG IV (1) 690, 2 (d. Περικλείδης)

**Ἀριστοξενίδας**
ARKADIA:
—MANTINEIA-ANTIGONEIA: (1) c. 300-221 BC ib. v (2) 323. 55 (tessera) (Ἀριστοξεν[ί]δας: s. Καλλισθένης)

**Ἀριστόξενος**
ACHAIA:
—AIGION: (1) c. 245-236 BC ib. IX (1)² (1) 25, 54 (I f. Ἀριστόξενος II); (2) ~ ib. l. 54 (II s. Ἀριστόξενος I)
ARKADIA: (3) ?255 BC Nachtergael, Les Galates 8, 27; cf. Stephanis 1337 (Ἀριστόξ[εν]ος: f. Καλλικράτης)
—MANTINEIA-ANTIGONEIA:
——(Enyalia): (4) m. iv BC IG v (2) 271, 7 (f. Ἀλκίας)
—TEGEA: (5) s. iii BC ib. IV (1) 727 B, 7 (Perlman H.2) (s. Ἀριστογείτων)
ARKADIA?: (6) ?255 BC Nachtergael, Les Galates 8, 26 (Stephanis 370) (Ἀριστ[ό]ξεν[ος])
DALMATIA:
—ISSA: (7) hell. Brunšmid p. 30 no. 25 ([Ἀρι]στόξενο[ς]?: f. Νικασώ)
——(Dymanes): (8) iv/iii BC ib. p. 9, 63 (f. Σώσανδρος)
KERKYRA: (9) s. v BC AD 19 (1964) Chron. p. 325
LAKONIA:
—BOIAI: (10) imp. IG v (1) 954 ([Ἀρι]στόξενος: f. Ἀγακλ—)
—SPARTA: (11) c. 100-125 AD ib. 152, 8 (Bradford (-)) (f. Φιλοκλῆς)
LEUKAS: (12) iii BC SEG XXXIX 485
MESSENIA:
—MESSENE: (13) i AD IG v (1) 1436, 16
—THOURIA: (14) f. ii BC SEG XI 972, 23 (s. Κλέαρχος)
S. ITALY: (15) v/iv BC RE (10); Evans, Horsemen pp. 54 ff.; Work, Earlier Staters of Heraclea p. 20 no. 19; SNG ANS Etruria-Calabria 325; Samml. Ludwig 140; van Keuren, Coinage of Heraclea p. 23 and pp. 54-5 nos. 8-10 (coins)
S. ITALY (CALABRIA):
—TARAS-TARENTUM: (16) iv BC RE (7); cf. Wehrli, Schule Arist. ii pp. 10 ff. (s. Σπίνθαρος); (17) c. 280-272 BC Vlasto 818 (coin) (Ἀριστόξ(ενος))
SICILY:
—AKRAI: (18) ?iii BC SGDI 3240, 2 (Akrai p. 156 no. 7) (f. Δαϊκράτης)
—SELINOUS: (19) ?vi BC RE (5); IEG 2 pp. 45-6; CGF p. 87
—SYRACUSE?:
——(Κρα.): (20) hell. Manganaro, PdelP forthcoming no. 4 I, 13 (s. Ἀπολλόδωρος)
—ZANKLE-MESSANA: (21) ?ii BC IG XIV 401, 14 (f. —χρων)

**Ἀριστοπάμων**
ACHAIA: (1) 146 BC ib. IV (1)² 28, 66-7 (f. Ἀνδρίας, Πολυκλῆς: synoikos)

ARKADIA:
—MEGALOPOLIS: (2) c. 230-200 BC SEG XXXVI 379 (Ἀριστοπά[μ]ων: s. Λυδιάδας); (3) 208 BC IMM 38, 26
—TEGEA: (4) iv BC IG v (2) 31, 3 (s. Ξενοκλῆς)
——(Athaneatai): (5) m. iii BC ib. 36, 84 (s. Ἀντιφάης)

**Ἀριστοπείθης**
AIGINA: (1) ii/i BC ib. IV (1) 40 (s. Εὐηθίδας)

**Ἀριστόπολις**
ARGOLIS:
—ARGOS:
——(Kerkadai): (1) f. iii BC ib. 529, 23
——(Naupliadai): (2) iii BC ib. 527, 5; cf. BCH 37 (1913) p. 308
ARKADIA:
—KLEITOR: (3) i-ii AD IG v (2) 372 (f. Στατία)
—TEGEA: (4) iii BC ib. IV (1)² 265
LAKONIA: (5) 41 AD SEG XIII 258, 8
—SPARTA: (6) c. 1-10 AD IG v (1) 209, 21; SEG XXXV 331 (date) (Bradford (-)) (s. (ad.) Δαμόχαρις)
SICILY:
—TAUROMENION: (7) c. 196 BC IG XIV 421 an. 45 (SGDI 5219) (f. Περικλῆς) ?= (8); (8) c. 183 BC IG XIV 421 an. 58 (SGDI 5219) ?= (7); (9) c. 151 BC IG XIV 421 an. 90 (SGDI 5219) (s. Δαμάτριος); (10) ~ IGSI 4 III (IV), 36 an. 90 (f. Φιλόδαμος)
——(Ἀλκ.): (11) ?ii/i BC IG XIV 421 D an. 9; 421 [D] an. 1 (SGDI 5219); IGSI 4 III (IV), 156 D an. 9 (s. Φιλόδαμος)

**Ἀριστος**
LAKONIA:
—SPARTA: (1) 404 BC D.S. xiv 10. 2; 70. 3 (Poralla² 135) (Ἀρέτης—D.S. xiv 70)
MESSENIA:
—MESSENE: (2) hell.-imp. SEG XLI 369 (n. pr.?); (3) ii-iii AD ib. 366 E
S. ITALY (CAMPANIA):
—NEAPOLIS: (4) s. i BC IG XIV 741 (INap 30); cf. Leiwo p. 152 (Λ. Ἑρέννιος Ἀ.: s. Πύθων)
SICILY:
—LEONTINOI: (5) m. v BC QUCC 78 (1995) p. 124 (vase) (Ἀριστō (gen.): f. Ἀρίστων)
—PANORMOS: (6) f. i BC Cic., In Verr. II iv 29 (Lat. Aristus)

**Ἀριστοτέλης**
ACHAIA: (1) 146 BC IG IV (1)² 28, 117 (s. Ἀριστοκλῆς: synoikos)
AKARNANIA:
—PALAIROS: (2) iii BC ib. IX (1)² (2) 477; Fraser–Rönne, BWGT pl. 24
ARGOLIS:
—ARGOS: (3) 224 BC RE (12); (4) 196 BC IG IX (1)² (1) 30, 20 ([Ἀ]ριστοτέλης: s. Π—)
—EPIDAUROS: (5) 38 AD ib. IV (1)² 600, 4 (f. Αὐτονόη)
——Dorimachis: (6) c. 365-335 BC ib. 103, 52
—TROIZEN: (7) 153-144 BC SGDI 2295, 15 (s. Νίκανδρος); (8) 150-140 BC ib. l. 16 (f. Θεαρίων)
ARKADIA:
—KLEITOR: (9) ?iv/iii BC HE 670 (II s. Ἀριστοτέλης I); (10) ~ ib. 671 (I f. Ἀριστοτέλης II)
—TEGEA: (11) m. iv BC IG v (2) 6, 105 ([Ἀρισ]τ[ο]τέλης?); (12) iv/iii BC ib. 32, 2; (13) iii BC ib. 30, 16 ([Ἀρι]στοτέλης?); (14) ii-i BC ib. 166 ([Ἀρισ]τοτέλης?)
——(Athaneatai): (15) iii BC ib. 40, 7 ([Ἀρισ]τοτέλης?); (16) s. iii BC ib. 36, 109 (f. Φίλων)
——(Krariotai): (17) iii BC ib. 40, 27 (s. Περικλῆς)
ELIS:
—OLYMPIA*: (18) ii-i BC IvOl 190
EPIROS:
—BOUTHROTOS (PRASAIBOI): (19) iii/ii BC IBouthrot 2, 3-4; 3, 3-5; 4, 2, 4 (s. Ἀρχίας) ?= (20); (20) a. 163 BC ib. 101, 1 (s. Ἀρχίας) ?= (19)

Ἐπιρος?: **(21)** i BC *IG* II² 8532; *SEG* XIII 144, 2 (['Ἀρι]στοτέλης: f. Ἀριστόκλεια)

LAKONIA:

—HIPPOLA: **(22)** iii-ii BC *IG* v (1) 1527 (['Ἀρ]ισστοτέ[λης])

—SPARTA: **(23)** c. 450-434 BC ib. 1230, 5; *LSAG*² p. 201 no. 54 (date) (Poralla² 136) (-λὲς); **(24)** iv BC *SEG* XI 639, 6 (Ἀρισστοτέ[λης]: ?f. —μων); **(25)** 396 BC D.S. xiv 78. 1 (Poralla² 137); **(26)** i BC *IG* v (1) 27, 21, 31 (Bradford (7)); **(27)** i BC/i AD? *IG* v (1) 264 (*Artemis Orthia* p. 298 no. 4; Bradford (5)); **(28)** i-ii AD *IG* v (1) 836 (Bradford (2)) (?s. Καλλικράτης); **(29)** ii-iii AD *IG* v (1) 695 (Bradford (8)); **(30)** c. 133 AD *IG* v (1) 286, 2 (*Artemis Orthia* p. 319 no. 43; Bradford (10)) (-λῆρ: ?f. Φλ. Λάκων); **(31)** c. 140-145 AD *SEG* XI 550, 11; *BSA* 80 (1985) pp. 210-11 (ident.); cf. Bradford (4) (Κλ. Ἀ.: II ?s. Τιβ. Κλ. Ἀριστοτέλης I) ?= (*34*); **(32)** c. 150-175 AD *IG* v (1) 68, 14; 109, 3; *SEG* XI 493, 6; 528, 4; *BSA* 80 (1985) p. 210 (ident.); cf. Bradford (4) (Τιβ. Κλ. Ἀ.: I ?f. Κλ. Ἀριστοτέλης II); **(33)** ii/iii AD *IG* v (1) 527, 12; 547, 13; 591, 3; 592, 3; *BSA* 80 (1985) pp. 225; 238 (ident., stemma) (Bradford (4)) (Τιβ. Κλ. Ἀ.: s. Τιβ. Κλ. Σπαρτιατικός, f. Κλ. Φιλοκράτεια); **(34)** ~ *IG* v (1) 592, 3; *BSA* 80 (1985) pp. 210-11 (ident.); cf. Bradford (4) (Ἀριστοτ[έλης]: f. Κλ. Λογγῖνα) ?= (*31*); **(35)** f. iii AD *IG* v (1) 303, 5 (*Artemis Orthia* pp. 327-8 no. 57); *BSA* 79 (1984) p. 283 (Bradford (3)) (Πομπ. ['Ἀρ]ιστοτέληρ: s. Μηνοφάνης); **(36)** ~ *IG* v (1) 528, 2; 529, 7; *BSA* 80 (1985) pp. 210-11 (ident.); cf. Bradford (4) (Τιβ. Κλ. Ἀ.); **(37)** a. 212 AD *BSA* 89 (1994) p. 435 no. 6, 3

—TAINARON-KAINEPOLIS: **(38)** imp.? *IG* v (1) 1236 (f. Πρυαῖος, Δαμαρμενίδας); **(39)** ii/iii AD ib. 601, 4; 1240, 12; *BSA* 79 (1984) pp. 265-6 (ident., date); p. 284 (stemma) (Bradford (1)) (Αὐρ. Ἀ., Ἀρ[ιστοτέ]λης—1240: s. Ἑλλάνικος, f. Αὐρ. Χαρτηρίς)

S. ITALY (BRUTTIUM):

—HIPPONION-VIBO VALENTIA*: **(40)** imp. *CIL* x 8041. 5 (tile) (Lat. Aristotel(es))

—KROTON?: **(41)** m. iii BC *IG* XII Suppl. p. 138 no. 313, 4 (f. —ων)

—LOKROI EPIZEPHYRIOI:

——(Φαω.): **(42)** iv/iii BC De Franciscis 22, 18 (f. Ἀρίστιππος)

S. ITALY (CALABRIA):

—S. PANCRAZIO SALENTINO (MOD.): **(43)** c. 500 BC *SEG* XXXIII 807 (vase) (Arena, *Iscr. Sic.* IV 87) (-λὲς—*SEG*, -λὲς?—ed. and Arena)

SICILY: **(44)** iv BC D.L. v 35

—MELITA: **(45)** m. i BC Cic., *ad Fam.* xiii 52 (Lat. A. Licinius Aristoteles)

## Ἀριστότιμος

ACHAIA: **(1)** iii-ii BC *Achaean Grave Stelai* 62 (f. Σατυρίων)

ELIS: **(2)** 272 BC *RE* (2) (s. Δαμάρετος, f. Μυρώ: tyrant)

ΕΡΙRΟS:

—KASSOPE: **(3)** hell. *SEG* XXIV 438 (s. Ἀρμόδιος)

LAKONIA:

—SPARTA: **(4)** s. i BC *IG* v (1) 93, 23; 211, 25 (Bradford (4)) (-τει-: f. Πρατόλας); **(5)** m. ii AD *IG* v (1) 109, 12; cf. *SEG* XI 614; **(6)** c. 130-140 AD *IG* v (1) 65, 13; 66, [14]; 67, [3]; *SEG* XI [614] (Bradford (3)) (-τει-: I f. Ἀριστότιμος II); **(7)** ~ *IG* v (1) 65, 13; 66, 14; 67, 3; *SEG* XI 549, 3; 614 (Bradford (1)) (-τει-: II s. Ἀριστότιμος I); **(8)** c. 160-170 AD *IG* v (1) 109, 12 (Bradford (2)) (-τει-: s. Εὐδαιμοκλῆς)

## Ἀριστοῦχος

ARGOLIS:

—EPIDAUROS: **(1)** iv BC *IG* IV (1)² 187 (-στόχ-)

## Ἀριστόφαμος

S. ITALY (CALABRIA):

—TARAS-TARENTUM: **(1)** c. 210 BC ib. IX (1)² (1) 31, 82 (s. Λύκων)

## Ἀριστοφάνης

ACHAIA:

—DYME: **(1)** c. 270 BC ib. 13, 35 (f. Φιλοκράτης)

AIGINA: **(2)** ?475 BC Pi., *N.* iii, 20 (f. Ἀριστοκλείδας)

AKARNANIA:

—KORONTA: **(3)** hell. *AD* 25 (1970) Chron. p. 297 no. γ (s. Νικοφάνης)

ARGOLIS:

—EPIDAUROS*: **(4)** c. 370-365 BC Peek, *IAEpid* 52 A, 37 ?= (*5*); **(5)** c. 365-335 BC *IG* IV (1)² 103, 49 ?= (*4*)

—HERMIONE: **(6)** iii BC ib. IV (1) 685

—LYRKEIA (MOD.): **(7)** inc. *SEG* XXII 261

ARKADIA:

—HERAIA: **(8)** iii BC *IG* v (2) 415, 10 (*IPArk* 23) (f. Ἀστέας)

—KLEITOR: **(9)** ?ii BC *IG* v (2) 376

—TEGEA: **(10)** f. ii BC ib. 44, 4 (s. Βιαῖος)

——(Krariotai): **(11)** c. 369-362 BC ib. 173, 31; cf. *CEG* II 657 (['Ἀρι]στοφάνης); **(12)** m. iii BC *IG* v (2) 36, 88 (f. Ἀγασέας)

ARKADIA?: **(13)** c. 200 BC *SEG* XVII 829, 2, 5, 11

DALMATIA:

—ISSA?: **(14)** iii/ii BC Brunšmid p. 31 no. 27; *Istros* 2 (1935-6) pp. 18 ff. (or Dalmatia Tragurion)

ΕΡΙRΟS:

—BOUTHROTOS (PRASAIBOI): **(15)** a. 163 BC *IBouthrot* 14, 28; 28, 17 (*SEG* XXXVIII 471; 486) (s. Μαχάτας, f. Μαχάτας) ?= (*16*); **(16)** ~ *IBouthrot* 15, 13 (*SEG* XXXVIII 472) ?= (*15*); **(17)** ~ *IBouthrot* 48, 9; **(18)** ~ ib. 159

ILLYRIA:

—EPIDAMNOS-DYRRHACHION: **(19)** hell. *IDyrrh* 81 (f. Ἀγίας)

KORINTHIA:

—KORINTH: **(20)** iv AD Seeck, *Libanius* pp. 88-90 (s. Μένανδρος)

LAKONIA:

—OITYLOS: **(21)** f. ii BC *IG* v (1) 1296, 2 (['Ἀρι]στοφάνης: s. Πολυκράτης, Φιλωνυμία)

—SPARTA: **(22)** c. 30-20 BC ib. 142, 12 (Bradford (-)) (Ἀριστ[ο]φάνης: s. Εὔτυχος)

MESSENIA:

—THOURIA: **(23)** f. ii BC *SEG* XI 972, 24 (s. Φιλόξενος); **(24)** ~ ib. l. 41 (['Ἀρι]τοφάνης: s. Τιμοκράτης); **(25)** ~ ib. l. 103 (f. Φιλόξενος); **(26)** ~ ib. l. 126 (f. Ἀριστόδαμος)

S. ITALY (BRUTTIUM):

—LOKROI EPIZEPHYRIOI:

——(Ἀγκ.): **(27)** iv/iii BC De Franciscis 20, 14 (f. Σώσιππος)

SICILY:

—AKRAI: **(28)** ii BC *Akrai* p. 156 no. 6, 10 (s. Ἀρχάγαθος)

—LIPARA: **(29)** hell.? Libertini, *Isole Eolie* p. 220 no. 19

—SELINOUS: **(30)** s. vi BC Dubois, *IGDS* 31, 2, 7 (Arena, *Iscr. Sic.* I 60); cf. *SEG* XXXVIII 962

—SYRACUSE: **(31)** iii BC ib. XL 516 (I f. Ἀριστοφάνης II); **(32)** ~ ib. (II s. Ἀριστοφάνης I)

## Ἀριστόφαντος

AKARNANIA: **(1)** 218 BC Plb. v 6. 1

—THYRREION: **(2)** ii BC *IG* IX (1)² (2) 321; cf. *AbhBerlAk* 1958 (2), pp. 29 f. (name) (['Ἀριστ?]όφαντος)

ARGOLIS:

—EPIDAUROS: **(3)** inc. *SEG* XXXVIII 322 (?s. Ἀρχαγέτας); **(4)** iv-iii BC *IG* IV (1)² 8; **(5)** 115 BC ib. 63, 1, 10 (f. Ἀρχέλοχος)

——(Hylleis): **(6)** 146 BC ib. 28, 48 (f. Λαδαμίδας)

——Alamais: **(7)** c. 310-300 BC ib. 114, 12-13 (Ἀρι[σ]τ[όφ]αντος)

——Tenias: **(8)** c. 335-325 BC ib. 108, 110, 142

KORINTHIA:

—KORINTH: **(9)** 405 BC Paus. x 9. 10; cf. *CEG* II 819

## Ἀριστοφιλίδας

S. ITALY (CALABRIA):

—TARAS-TARENTUM: **(1)** s. vi BC Hdt. iii 136. 2 (-δης: king)

## Ἀριστόφιλος

AKARNANIA:

—THYRREION: **(1)** ii BC *IG* IX (1)² (2) 250, 7 (['Ἀρι]στόφιλος: s. Ἀρίσταινος)

ARGOLIS:

—EPIDAUROS: **(2)** iii/ii BC Peek, *IAEpid* 129, 1 (['Ἀρ]ιστόφιλος: s. Ἀριστοκράτης)

ARKADIA:

—TEGEA: **(3)** f. iii BC *IG* v (2) 42, 7 (['Ἀρ]ιστόφιλ[ος])

KORINTHIA:

—KORINTH: **(4)** vi BC ib. IV (1) 306 (pinax); **(5)** iii BC ib. XI 1173, 4; cf. Marcadé II 24 (s. Εὐσθένης: sculptor)

## Ἀριστόφρων

ARGOLIS:

—ARGOS: **(1)** a. 316 BC *SEG* XIII 243, 2 (Perlman A.6) (?s. Δαμ—)

## Ἀριστόφυλος

AITOLIA: **(1)** iii/ii BC Pantos, *Sphragismata* p. 151 no. 121; p. 447 f.

—KALLION/KALLIPOLIS: **(2)** 153-144 BC *SGDI* 2279, 11, 13 (s. Λάδικος)

AKARNANIA:

—ANAKTORION: **(3)** c. 305-295 BC *NZ* 10 (1878) p. 68 no. 42; p. 68 no. 45 (coin); *SNR* 56 (1977) pp. 97-8; p. 111 (date)

ARGOLIS:

—EPIDAUROS: **(4)** c. 370 BC *IG* IV (1)² 102, 64, 67

SICILY:

—KENTORIPA: **(5)** ?i BC ib. XIV 575 (f. Ἡράκλειος)

## Ἀριστοφῶν

AKARNANIA:

—THYRREION: **(1)** ii BC ib. IX (1)² (2) 252, 7 (Ἀριστόφωνος (gen.): f. Ἐπιχάρης)

ARGOLIS:

—EPIDAUROS: **(2)** v BC Peek, *NIEpid* 69 (['Ἀρι]στοφõ[ν])

S. ITALY (BRUTTIUM):

—RHEGION: **(3)** s. iv BC *IG* II² 10133 (s. Εὔνικος)

## Ἀριστρᾶς

ARGOLIS:

—EPIDAUROS: **(1)** c. 370 BC ib. IV (1)² 102, 82; 109 III, 20?

## Ἀρίστρατος

ACHAIA:

—PELLENE: **(1)** m. iii BC ib. v (2) 368, 96 (Ἀρίστρα[τος])

ARGOLIS:

—EPIDAUROS: **(2)** c. 340-330 BC *SEG* XXV 387 A, 21 (Ἀρίστρατ[ος])

KORINTHIA:

—SIKYON: **(3)** m. iv BC *RE* (2) (Skalet 64) (tyrant)

## Ἀριστύλις

SICILY:

—LIPARA: **(1)** inc. *Chiron* 22 (1992) p. 386; **(2)** imp. *Meligunis-Lipara* 5 p. 184 T. 2181; cf. *SEG* XLI 818

## Ἀρίστυλλος

ILLYRIA:

—APOLLONIA: **(1)** ?iii BC *IApoll* 378 (['Ἀρ]ίστυλλος: f. Πεντικός)

**Ἀρίστυλος**

S. ITALY (LUCANIA):
—HERAKLEIA: (**1**) iii BC Landi, *DISMG* 214 (f. Ἰστιειός)

SICILY:
—SELINOUS: (**2**) f. vi BC Dubois, *IGDS* 84 (Arena, *Iscr. Sic.* I 35; Lazzarini 209; *IGLMP* 35) (s. —ίας)

**Ἄριστυς**

ACHAIA:
—AIGION: (**1**) 157 BC *FD* III (3) 125, 4, 5; 126, 5 (Stephanis 375) (s. Ἀριστομένης)

**Ἀριστώ**

ACHAIA:
—DYME: (**1**) ii BC *Achaean Grave Stelai* 32 (d. Ξενόφιλος)

AIGINA: (**2**) hell.-imp. *IG* IV (1) 42 (d. Δικαιογένης)

AITOLIA:
—TRICHONION: (**3**) iii BC ib. IX (1)² (1) 120

ARGOLIS:
—ARGOS: (**4**) iii BC *SEG* XI 371, 9 (*GVI* 1328)
—ARGOS*: (**5**) ii-i BC *IG* IV (1) 530, 17; cf. *BCH* 33 (1909) p. 183 n. 2 (slave/freed.?)
—EPIDAUROS: (**6**) imp. Peek, *IAEpid* 341 ([Ἀ]ριστώ)
—HERMIONE: (**7**) ii BC *IG* IV (1)² 259 (d. Ἄνδρων, m. Μέλισσα)

ARKADIA:
—MEGALOPOLIS: (**8**) ii BC ib. V (2) 536 (d. Ἀριστόλας, Ἀμετέρα, m. Δαμάρης)
—TEGEA: (**9**) iv/iii BC ib. 74; (**10**) i BC-i AD ib. 204

ILLYRIA:
—AMANTIA: (**11**) ii-i BC *SEG* I 265 (Guarducci, *Ep. Gr.* I p. 372) (d. Ἀλέξανδρος)
—APOLLONIA: (**12**) imp. *IApoll* 38 (Ἀ. Φονδανία); (**13**) ~ ib. 59
—EPIDAMNOS-DYRRHACHION: (**14**) iv/iii BC *IDyrrh* 25 (Ἀριστοῦς (gen.): m. Ἀνδρείας); (**15**) iii-ii BC ib. 62 (d. Ἀριστομένης); (**16**) hell.-imp. ib. 122 (d. Ἀνδρίων); (**17**) ~ ib. 123 (d. Ἀριστίων); (**18**) ~ ib. 124 (d. Παλμίων)

LEUKAS: (**19**) hell.? *IG* IX (1) 545

S. ITALY (LUCANIA):
—HERAKLEIA: (**20**) iii BC Landi, *DISMG* 216. 3 (loomweight)

**Ἀριστώι**

ARGOLIS:
—ARGOS: (**1**) a. 303 BC *CEG* II 816, 21

SICILY:
—KAMARINA: (**2**) s. v BC *SEG* XXXVIII 935, 1 (Arena, *Iscr. Sic.* II 147) (-στόι: ?d. Φάϋλλος); (**3**) ~ *SEG* XXXVIII 935, 5 (Arena, *Iscr. Sic.* II 147) ([Ἀ]ριστόι)

**Ἀρίστων**

ACHAIA: (**1**) 146 BC *IG* IV (1)² 28, 144 (s. Ἀρμένιος: synoikos)
—DYME: (**2**) iii BC *AJPh* 31 (1910) p. 399 no. 74 b, 3 (s. Φίντων)
—DYME*: (**3**) c. 219 BC *SGDI* 1612, 26 (*Tyche* 5 (1990) p. 124) (f. Σάτυρος)
—PELLENE: (**4**) m. iii BC *IG* V (2) 368, 103 (s. Ξεν—)

ACHAIA?: (**5**) 193 BC ib. 293, 5 (s. Σωτίων)

AIGINA: (**6**) 183 BC *FD* III (3) 240, 9, 31 (*IG* IX (1)² (1) 179) (f. Θεόλυτος)

AITOLIA: (**7**) ?269 BC *CID* II 129 A, 2; (**8**) 244 or 240 BC *SGDI* 2512, 2 (Flacelière p. 402 no. 28 a); Nachtergael, *Les Galates* 59, 3 ?= (*14*)
—DAIANES: (**9**) 263-262 BC *IG* IX (1)² (1) 3 A, 20
—HERMATTIOI: (**10**) 175 BC *SGDI* 1843, 4 (f. Λύκος)
—KALYDON: (**11**) s. ii BC *SEG* XXV 621, 2 (s. Ἀριστόμαχος)
—POTIDANIA: (**12**) m. ii BC *SBBerlAk* 1936, p. 371 a, 12 (*SEG* XLI 528 A) (s. Εὐβουλίδας)
—RHADEOI: (**13**) f. ii BC *IG* IX (1)² (1) 96, 23 (f. Νικόστρατος)
—TRICHONION: (**14**) b. 238 BC ib. 31, 184 ?= (*8*) (*15*)
—TRICHONION?: (**15**) 221 BC ib. p. L, s.a. 221 BC; Plb. iv 5. 1; 9. 9; 17. 1 ?= (*14*)

AKARNANIA:
—ASTAKOS: (**16**) m. iii BC *SEG* XXVII 153, 5; cf. *PAE* 1977, pl. 244 b (f. Νικιάδας)
—ECHINOS?: (**17**) ii BC *IG* IX (1)² (2) 378
—PALAIROS: (**18**) iii BC ib. 478
—STRATOS: (**19**) 193 BC *Syll*³ 603, 3; (**20**) 154 BC *SGDI* 1908, 15, 19 (s. Πύρρος)
—THYRREION: (**21**) iii BC *IG* IX (1)² (2) 245, 16; (**22**) ii BC ib. 316

ARGOLIS:
—ARGOS: (**23**) v BC *RE* (42); Page, *FGE* 39; Stephanis 379; (**24**) ?c. 480 BC *IG* IV (1) 554, 2; *LSAG*² p. 169 no. 17 (date) (-σστων); (**25**) s. v BC *FGrH* 84 F 21 a; 260 F 13; (**26**) iv BC *IG* IV (1) 629; (**27**) s. iii BC *SEG* XI 440 a b, 4; *Corinth* VIII (1) 60 (I f. Ἀρίστων II); (**28**) ~ *SEG* XI 440 a b, 4; *Corinth* VIII (1) 60 (II s. Ἀρίστων I: sculptor); (**29**) ii BC *SEG* XLII 279, 20 (f. Δημήτριος)
—EPIDAUROS: (**30**) c. 350-250 BC *AD* 28 (1973) Chron. pl. 81 γ; (**31**) f. ii BC Peek, *IAEpid* 153. 8 (f. Ἀριστόδαμος); (**32**) 151 AD *IG* IV (1)² 388, 4 (f. Ἐπιτυγχάνων)
——(Azantioi): (**33**) 146 BC ib. 28, 41 ([Ἀρί]στων: s. Κλεισθένης)
—EPIDAUROS*: (**34**) c. 370 BC ib. 102, 252; (**35**) c. 370-365 BC ib. l. 200; 743, 4; Peek, *IAEpid* 52 A, 38, 49; (**36**) c. 335-325 BC *IG* IV (1)² Addenda 106 II, 136, 139-40
—HERMIONE: (**37**) iii BC ib. IV (1) 729 I, 3 (f. Ἀριστώνυμος); (**38**) ~ ib. l. 8 (f. Σωσίων)
—TROIZEN: (**39**) iii BC ib. 753, [3], 5 with Add. (f. Ἀ—); (**40**) 153-144 BC *SGDI* 2295, 17 (s. Ἀλέξων); (**41**) ?146 BC *IG* IV (1) 757 B, 37 (s. Κομᾶς); (**42**) imp. ib. 792 (s. Ἀντισθένης)

ARKADIA: (**43**) iii BC ib. V (2) 415, 13 (*IPArk* 23)
—MEGALOPOLIS: (**44**) 369-361 BC *IG* V (2) 1, 24; Tod, *GHI* II 132 (date); (**45**) iii BC *IG* V (2) 478, 7; (**46**) ~ ib. 483 ([Ἀρ]ίστων); (**47**) ?274 BC *FD* III (1) 46, 1 (Ἀρίσ[τω]ν: f. Πύρρανθος); (**48**) 170-168 BC Plb. xxviii 6. 2, 8; xxix 25. 6; (**49**) i BC *IG* II² 9299 (I f. Ἀρίστων II); (**50**) ~ ib. (II s. Ἀρίστων I)
—ORCHOMENOS: (**51**) i BC/i AD ib. V (2) 350
—PHIGALEIA: (**52**) ii BC ib. 420 (Ἀρίστων: f. Προκλείδας)
—TEGEA: (**53**) iii BC ib. 40, 3 ([Ἀρ]ίστων); (**54**) iii-ii BC ib. 205; (**55**) ii-i BC ib. 165, 4; (**56**) f. ii BC ib. 44, 15 (s. Νίκις); (**57**) ii AD ib. 55, 59 (f. Νίκων); (**58**) m. ii AD ib. 48, 7
——(Hippothoitai): (**59**) iv/iii BC ib. 38, 52 (f. Κύμβαλος)
——(Krariotai): (**60**) f. iii BC ib. 36, 41 (f. Καλλίας); (**61**) ~ ib. l. 66 (I f. Ἀρίστων II: metic); (**62**) ~ ib. l. 66 (II s. Ἀρίστων I: metic)

DALMATIA:
—ISSA:
——(Hylleis): (**63**) iv/iii BC Brunšmid p. 8, 29 (s. Ἀριστοκλῆς)

ELIS: (**64**) f. ii AD *IvOl* 92, 5 (I f. Ἀρίστων II); (**65**) ~ ib. l. 5, 9 (II s. Ἀρίστων I, f. Ἀπολλοφάνης)

EPIROS:
—AMBRAKIA?: (**66**) ?iv BC *PAE* 1957, p. 87 (vase)
—BOUTHROTOS (PRASAIBOI): (**67**) a. 163 BC *IBouthrot* 14, 11; 17, 15; 21, 7, 15; 31, 34; 40, 15 (*SEG* XXXVIII 471; 474; 478; 490; 499) (s. Φίλιππος) ?= (69); (**68**) ~ *IBouthrot* 22, 9 (*SEG* XXXVIII 479) ?= (70); (**69**) ~ *IBouthrot* 22, 16 (*SEG* XXXVIII 479) ?= (67); (**70**) ~ *IBouthrot* 45, 5 (f. Φιλώτας) ?= (68)
—KASSOPE: (**71**) iii-ii BC *SEG* XXXV 670 (f. Νίκανδρος)

ILLYRIA:
—APOLLONIA: (**72**) c. 250-50 BC Maier 12; 28; 63; 94; 102; Münsterberg Nachtr. p. 13 (Ceka 24-29); *IApoll Ref. Bibl.* n. 28 (coin) (money.); (**73**) ~ Maier 22-24 + Münsterberg Nachtr. p. 12 (coin) (Ceka 19; 84) (pryt.); (**74**) i BC Maier 133 (coin) (s. Λυσήν: money.)
—BYLLIONES BYLLIS (NR.): (**75**) hell. *Iliria* 1982 (1), p. 108 no. 24 = p. 120 no. 9 (tile)
—EPIDAMNOS-DYRRHACHION: (**76**) hell. *IDyrrh* 125 (I f. Ἀρίστων II); (**77**) ~ ib. (II s. Ἀρίστων I); (**78**) ~ ib. 126 (s. Μοσχίων); (**79**) c. 250-50 BC Maier 141 (coin) (Ceka 250) (pryt.); (**80**) ~ Maier 171; 259; 275; 378; Münsterberg Nachtr. p. 17 (Ceka 94-7); *IApoll Ref. Bibl.* n. 28 (coin) (money.)
—LYCHNIDOS: (**81**) ii-iii AD *Sp.* 71 (1931) p. 110 no. 266 (*SEG* XXXIX 603), f. Νικόπολις, Ἀλέξανδρος

KEPHALLENIA:
—KRANIOI: (**82**) c. 230-200 BC *BCH* 45 (1921) p. 14 II, 138 (s. Δαμοφῶν)
—PALE: (**83**) ?iv BC *IG* I² 1070. 2 (-σστων)

KERKYRA: (**84**) iii-ii BC *AE* 1914, p. 235 no. 5 (s. Ἀλεξίων); (**85**) c. 229-48 BC *BMC Thessaly* p. 146 nos. 493-8; *SNG Cop. Epirus–Acarnania* 227-8 (coins) (f. Ἀριστέας); (**86**) iii/ii BC *IG* XI (4) 1241 (s. Ἀρίστων) ?= (87)

KERKYRA?: (**87**) iii/ii BC ib. 1227, 3 ?= (86); (**88**) c. 200 BC *IBouthrot* 10; cf. *SEG* XXXVIII 464 (s. Μοσχίδας, Λυσώ)

KORINTHIA:
—KORINTH: (**89**) 413 BC *RE* (25) (s. Πύρριχος); (**90**) m. iii BC *Corinth* VIII (1) 60 (sculptor); (**91**) i BC/i AD ib. VIII (3) 151 (Lat. C. Heius Arist[o]); (**92**) i AD ib. XII p. 103 no. 650; (**93**) ii-iii AD ib. VIII (3) 493 ([Ἀ]ρίστων)
—SIKYON: (**94**) vi/v BC *SEG* XI 244, 20 (-τὸν); (**95**) m. iv BC *IG* II² 10303 (f. Εὐκράτεια)

LAKONIA: (**96**) vi-v BC Paus. v 23. 7; *RE* (60) (Poralla² 139)
—SPARTA: (**97**) m. vi BC *RE* (1) (Poralla² 138) (s. Ἀγησικλῆς, f. Δαμάρατος: king); (**98**) m. iii BC *IG* IV (1)² 96, 70 (Perlman E.3); Perlman p. 63 f. (date) (Bradford (1)) (s. Ἀριστοκράτης); (**99**) ii BC *IG* V (1) 898 (tiles) (Bradford (6)); (**100**) s. i BC *IG* V (1) 124, 1 (Bradford (3)) (s. Ἀριστ—); (**101**) ~ *IG* V (1) 124, 3 (Bradford (16)) (f. Θελξίνοος); (**102**) ~ *IG* V (1) 124, 8 (Bradford (9)) (f. Ἀνδρόνικος); (**103**) i BC/i AD *IG* V (1) 146, 6 (Bradford (18)) ([Ἀρ]ίστων?); (**104**) i AD *SEG* XXVI 462, 2 (?s. Ἐ—); (**105**) f. i AD *IG* V (1) 268; *Artemis Orthia* pp. 305-6 no. 18 (date) (Bradford (15)) (f. Πρατιάδας); (**106**) c. 80-100 AD *IG* V (1) 147, 15 (Bradford (7)) (Γ. Ἰούλ. Ἀ.); (**107**) c. 100 AD *SEG* XI 626, 3 (Bradford (1)) (s. Ἀφροδίσιος); (**108**) f. ii AD *SEG* XXXI 340, 9 (f. Σῖμος); (**109**) m. ii AD *IG* V (1) 72, 2 (Bradford (12)); (**110**) ~ *IG* V (1) 160, 5 (Bradford (4)) (s. Δαμόλας); (**111**) c. 170 AD *IG* V (1) 116, 4 (Bradford (8)) (Τιβ. Κλ. Ἀ.); (**112**) ~ *IG* V (1) 116, 12 (Bradford (13)) (f. Διογένης); (**113**) a. 212 AD *IG* V (1) 597, 11 (Bradford (14)) (f. Αὐρ. Νικαφορίς); (**114**) c. 230-260 AD *SEG* XI 633, 4 (Bradford (5)) ([Α]ὐρ. Ἀ.: s. Δαμόνικος)
—Limnai: (**115**) c. 70-100 AD *IG* V (1) 676, 15 (Bradford (10)) (f. Ἀφροδίσιος)

LEUKAS: (**116**) hell.? *IG* IX (1) 558; (**117**) ~ ib. 559; (**118**) iii BC *SEG* XXXIV 473

MESSENIA:
—KORONE: (**119**) 246 AD *IG* V (1) 1398, 59 (Αὐρ. Ἀ.)
—MESSENE: (**120**) iv/iii BC ib. 1435, 3; (**121**) ii BC *PAE* 1969, p. 106, 7; (**122**) ~ ib. l. 12; (**123**) i BC *SEG* XIII 248, 11; Stephanis 389 (s. Εὐκλείδης); (**124**) i AD *IG* XII Suppl. p. 167 no. 449 (f. Γάϊος); (**125**) ?f. i AD *PAE* 1992, p. 79, 6 (f. Θάλιππος) ?= (*130*); (**126**) 11 AD ib.

p. 71 A, 5 (f. Εὐδαιμοκλῆς); (127) ii AD IvOl 459, 3 (Π. Αἰλ. Ἀ.: II s. Π. Αἰλ. Ἀρίστων I) ?= (129); (128) ~ ib. l. 5 (Π. Αἰλ. Ἀ.: I f. Π. Αἰλ. Ἀρίστων II); (129) ii/iii AD IG v (1) 1399, 6 (f. Ἁρμόνικος) ?= (127)

——(Kleolaidai): (130) 11 AD PAE 1992, p. 71 A, 24 (f. Θάλιππος) ?= (125)

—MESSENE?: (131) c. 223 BC IG IX (1)² (1) 31, 39 (s. Ἀριστόλαος); (132) ii/i BC SEG XI 979, 48; (133) ~ ib. l. 62

—THOURIA: (134) f. ii BC ib. 972, 28 (s. Ἀλεξίων); (135) ~ ib. l. 62 (s. Νίκων); (136) ii/i BC IG v (1) 1384, 10 (s. Καλλισθένης)

PELOPONNESE: (137) s. iii BC SEG XIII 278, 14 (s. Δάμαρχος)

S. ITALY: (138) f. ii BC Desy, Timbres amphoriques 4-5; 14; 16-17 (amph.) (IG XIV 2393. 136 a) (Γάιος Ἀ., Lat. C. Aristo)

S. ITALY (BRUTTIUM):

—LOKROI EPIZEPHYRIOI: (139) i AD NScav 1890, p. 266 (pithos); cf. Costabile, Municipium Locrensium p. 74 (date) (Ἀρίστω[ν])

——(Ἀλχ.): (140) iv/iii BC De Franciscis 32, 4 (s. Μνάσων)

——(Βοω.): (141) iv/iii BC ib. 27, 8 (s. Φίλων)

——(Κρα.): (142) iv/iii BC ib. 24, 3; 38, 7 (f. Ἐπίγονος)

——(Θρα.): (143) iv/iii BC ib. 21, 5

—RHEGION: (144) ?vi-v BC RE (44) (Stephanis 382)

—SYBARIS-THOURIOI-COPIAE: (145) 40-32 BC Moretti, Olymp. 717; 721

S. ITALY (CALABRIA):

—TARAS-TARENTUM: (146) c. 272-235 BC Vlasto 927-33 (coins) (Evans, Horsemen p. 181 VIII M.1-2); (147) ii/i BC IG II² 10413

—TARAS-TARENTUM?: (148) iv-iii BC Wuilleumier, Tarente p. 430 (terracotta)

S. ITALY (CAMPANIA):

—DIKAIARCHIA-PUTEOLI: (149) ?i-ii AD CIL x 2582 (Lat. L. Antonius Aristo iunior: s. Ἀφροδισία)

—NEAPOLIS: (150) i BC/i AD IG XIV 759, 1 (INap 43; Dubois, IGDGG 1 29); (151) i AD IG XIV 769 (INap 95); cf. Leiwo p. 122 no. 108; (152) 71 AD IG XIV 760, 17 (INap 85) (s. Βύκκος)

—NUCERIA ALFATERNA: (153) m. vi BC Dubois, IGDGG 1 30 (vase) (-στōν)

—POMPEII: (154) i BC-i AD CIL IV 8619 a (Lat. Aristo)

—POMPEII*: (155) m. i AD Impegno per Pompeii 22 EN (Castrèn 8. 1) (Lat. L. Aebius Aristo: f. Aebia Fausta: freed.)

S. ITALY (LUCANIA):

—HERAKLEIA: (156) c. 125-100 BC EAD XXX 295 (f. Θεόφιλος)

—HYELE-VELIA: (157) hell.? PdelP 21 (1966) p. 336 no. 3 (?f. Ὄνησος); (158) ~ ib. p. 337 no. 14; (159) ii/i BC EAD XXX 332 (f. Ἄνδρων); (160) i AD SEG XXXVIII 1020. 2; PdelP 25 (1970) p. 262 (οὐλις Ἀρίστωνος: doctor)

—VILLA POTENZA (MOD.): (161) f. i AD BdA 69 (1984) pp. 40-3 (Lat. Q. Petrusidius Aristo: I f. Ἀρίστων II, Q. Petrusidius Verus: freed.); (162) ~ ib. (Lat. Q. Petrusidius Aristo: II s. Ἀρίστων I: freed.)

S. ITALY (?): (163) c. 365-340 BC IG II² 8942 (f. Δημητρία)

SICILY: (164) iii-ii BC Vandermersch p. 163 (amph.) (Desy, Timbres amphoriques 4, 14)Desy, Timbres amphoriques 4, 16 (or S. Italy: Lat. C. Aristo) ?= (165); (165) iii/ii BC Vandermersch p. 163 (amph.) (Desy, Timbres amphoriques 5, 17; IG XIV 2393. 136) (or S. Italy: Γάιος Ἀ.) ?= (164); (166) i-ii AD Kokalos 32 (1986) p. 222 no.s 15-16 (tiles)

—AKRAI: (167) ii BC Akrai p. 158 no. 11

—KAMARINA: (168) ?iv/iii BC SEG XXXIV 940, 6 (Dubois, IGDS 124; PdelP 44 (1989) p. 192

no. 3; Cordano, 'Camarina VII' 77) (s. Ἐμμενίδας); (169) iv/iii BC Dubois, IGDS 122, 6, 9 (Cordano, 'Camarina VII' 78) (s. Ἐπίγονος); (170) hell. SEG XXXIX 1001, 5, 6 (s. Ζωῖλος)

—KATANE: (171) imp. CIL x 7049 (Lat. Aristo); (172) iii-v AD IG XIV 538 (Agnello 50; Wessel 862); cf. Riv. Arch. Crist. 18 (1941) p. 240 no. 137

—LEONTINOI: (173) m. v BC QUCC 78 (1995) p. 124 (vase) (-τōν: s. Ἄριστος)

—MORGANTINA: (174) ?iv/iii BC SEG XXXIX 1009, 3 ([Ἀρί]στων: f. Κληναγόρας); (175) ~ ib. 1010, 4 (f. Σάτυρος); (176) iv/iii BC ib. 1012, 8 (f. Παυσανίας)

—MT. ERYX*: (177) imp. IG XIV 281 (f. Κάρπιμος)

—PETRA: (178) f. iii BC SEG XXX 1121, 27 (Dubois, IGDS 208) (f. Σώσανδρος)

—SOLOUS: (179) iii/ii BC Kokalos 9 (1963) pp. 186-7 (f. Ἀπολλώνιος); (180) ~ ib. (I s. Ἀπολλώνιος, f. Ἀπολλώνιος, Φίλων, Ἀρίστων II); (181) ~ ib. (II s. Ἀρίστων I)

—SYRACUSE: (182) hell.? IG XII (2) 310 (f. Εὐβουλία); (183) ~ ib. XIV 205; (184) ~ KF 95; (185) 214 BC Liv. xxiv. 2 (Stephanis 383) (Lat. Aristo); (186) ii-i BC IG XIV 8, 3 (IGLMP 105) ([Ἀ]ρίστων); (187) ii/i BC SEG XXXIII 639, 7, 12; (188) ~ Unp. (Rhodes Mus., tit. sep.); (189) imp. IG XIV 5 (1 ([Ἀρί]στων); (190) i-ii AD Charito i 1. 3 (f. Χαιρέας: fict.)

—SYRACUSE?:

——(Ἀρχ.): (191) hell. Manganaro, PdelP forthcoming no. 4 I, 10 (s. Λέων)

—TAUROMENION: (192) c. 168 BC IG XIV 421 an. 73 (SGDI 5219) (s. Ὄνασος); (193) c. 150 BC IGSI 4 III (IV), 40 an. 91 (f. Ἄρχας); (194) ?ii/i BC IG XIV 421 D an. 10 (SGDI 5219) (f. Ἄρχας); (195) ii/i BC IGSI 11 I, 23; 12 I, 9, 18; 12 II, 11, 15 etc.; 12 III, 13, 14

——(Ταυ.): (196) ii/i BC ib. 5 II, 10 (s. Ἄρχας)

—ZANKLE-MESSANA: (197) imp. CIL x 6981 (Lat. Aristo: s. Ἀρίστη)

## Ἀριστώνεια

AKARNANIA:

—THYRREION: (1) ii BC IG IX (1)² (2) 317

## Ἀριστωνίδας

ILLYRIA:

—APOLLONIA: (1) 14-29 AD IApoll 173 (Ἀριστωνί̣δ̣[ας])

## Ἀριστωνύμα

ARGOLIS:

—HERMIONE: (1) iii BC IG IV (1) 693 (d. Καλλιστώ)

## Ἀριστώνυμος

ACHAIA:

—PATRAI: (1) ii BC Achaean Grave Stelai 34 (f. Παμφίλα)

AITOLIA:

—KONOPE-ARSINOE: (2) 184 BC IG IX (1)² (1) 131, 9 (f. Δείνων)

AKARNANIA:

—PALAIROS: (3) hell.? ib. IX (1)² (2) 569, 1

—TYRBEION/TORYBEIA: (4) c. 330 BC SEG XXIII 189 I, 7; cf. BCH 90 (1966) pp. 174 f. (locn.)

ARGOLIS:

—ARGOS: (5) ?304 BC IG v (2) 550, 25; (6) m. iii BC ib. IV (1)² 96, 24 (Perlman E.3); Perlman p. 63 f. (date) (f. Νίκιππος)

—HERMIONE: (7) iii BC IG IV (1) 729 I, 3 (s. Ἀρίστων)

ARKADIA:

—MEGALOPOLIS: (8) s. ii BC ib. v (2) 437, 21; 443, 25; 444, 5; 445, 11 (IPArk 32) (s. Πάσων)

—METHYDRION: (9) 401 BC RE (3)

KORINTHIA:

—KORINTH: (10) 431-423 BC Th. ii 33. 1; iv 119. 2 (f. Εὐφαμίδας)

—SIKYON: (11) s. vii BC RE (1) (Skalet 66) (s. Μύρων, f. Κλεισθένης, ?f. Μύρων, Ἰσόδαμος: tyrant?)

LAKONIA:

—HYPERTELEATON*: (12) iii BC IG v (1) 977, 12 (Bradford (1)); (13) imp. IG v (1) 1060 (Bradford (2)) (f. Πολύνικος)

MESSENIA:

—THOURIA: (14) f. ii BC SEG XI 972, 93 (f. Φιλόστρατος)

S. ITALY (BRUTTIUM):

—LOKROI EPIZEPHYRIOI:

——(Σκι.): (15) 280 BC De Franciscis 35, 2 (f. Ζώιππος)

S. ITALY (LUCANIA):

—HYELE-VELIA: (16) hell.? IG XIV 661 (Landi, DISMG 49) (?f. Σώσανδρος)

## Ἀρίφαντος

SICILY:

—AKRAGAS: (1) f. vi BC Epistolographi p. 427 no. 72; FGrH 577 F 3 (Ἀριστόφαντος—FGrH: fict.)

## Ἀρίφιλος

SICILY:

—LIPARA: (1) ?s. iii BC Kokalos 13 (1967) p. 198 no. 2

## Ἀρίφρων

KORINTHIA:

—SIKYON: (1) f. iv BC RE (2); PMG 813; cf. IG II² 4533, 9-18; IV (1)² 132 (Skalet 67)

## Ἀριώ?

S. ITALY (CAMPANIA):

—POMPEII: (1) i BC-i AD CIL IV 1410 (Lat. Ario (fem.))

## Ἀρίωδος

ARKADIA:

—PHENEOS: (1) c. 230-200 BC BCH 45 (1921) p. 13 II, 118 (f. Ἀρίστιππος)

## Ἀριώμων

SICILY:

—GELA-PHINTIAS: (1) m. v BC Dubois, IGDS 140 (vase) (Arena, Iscr. Sic. II 53) (-ό̣μōν?)

## Ἀρίων

ACHAIA:

—PATRAI: (1) 171 BC SGDI 2611, 3 (s. Ἀριστοκράτης)

LAKONIA:

—SPARTA: (2) c. 450-434 BC IG v (1) 1228, 7; LSAG² p. 201 no. 53 (date) (Poralla² 140) (Ἀρίō(ν)); (3) s. i BC IG v (1) 127, 8 ([Ἀρ]ίων: s. Ἀλ—); (4) ?ii AD EILakArk 3 (f. Γενέθλιος); (5) c. 105-110 AD IG v (1) 20 B, 1 (Bradford (12)) (f. Εὐάμερος); (6) c. 125 AD IG v (1) 1314, 4 (Bradford (8)) (Ἰούλ. Ἀ.); (7) ~ IG v (1) 1314, 8 (Bradford (11)) (f. Δαμόνικος); (8) ~ IG v (1) 1314, 10 (Bradford (3)) (s. Ἀριστείδας); (9) c. 140 AD IG v (1) 65, 29 (Bradford (14)) (f. Ζωσᾶς); (10) c. 140-145 AD IG v (1) 1314, 36 (Bradford (4)) (?s. Εὐθ.); (11) c. 140-160 AD IG v (1) 112, 9 (Bradford (5)) (-ρεί-: s. Εὔτυχος); (12) ~ IG v (1) 112, 13 (Bradford (5)) (-ρεί-: f. Νικάρων); (13) c. 140-180 AD SEG XI 501, 1; 582, 11 (Bradford (9)) (Γ. Ἰούλ. Ἀ.); (14) c. 175-205 AD IG v (1) 473, 2; SEG XXXVI 360, 5; BSA 81 (1986) p. 324 no. 2 (ident., date) (Bradford (13)) (-ρεί-: f. Σωκράτης); (15) c. 230-260 AD SEG XI 633, 2 (Bradford (10)) (I f. Αὐρ. Ἀρίων II); (16) ~ SEG XI 633, 2 (Bradford (2)) (Αὐρ. Ἀ.: II s. Ἀρίων I)

MESSENIA:

—MESSENE: (17) iv/iii BC IG v (1) 1435, 4; (18) hell.? ib. 1464; cf. SEG XLI 373 + Proc. Sympos. Olympic Games p. 90

## Ἀρκαδία
S. Italy (Bruttium):
—lokroi epizephyrioi: (19) v/iv bc *RE* (6); *FVS* i p. 443 no. 53 fr. 4 (Lat. Arion)
Sicily:
—syracuse: (20) imp. *NScav* 1912, pp. 293-4 (Lat. Sex. Alfius Arion)

## Ἀρκαδία
Arkadia:
—tegea: (1) i-ii ad *IG* v (2) 206

## Ἀρκάδιον
Lakonia:
—sparta: (1) imp. ib. v (1) 790 (Bradford (-))

## Ἀρκαδίων
Achaia: (1) iv bc *RE* Supplbd. 1 (-); cf. Page, *FGE* 1624
—tritaia?: (2) m. iii bc *IG* v (2) 368, 79 with index (s. Ἀλεξίμαχος)
Arkadia:
—kleitor: (3) a. 212 ad ib. 369, 20; *SEG* xxxi 347, 13 (Αὐρ. Ἀ.: s. Σωτάδης)
Korinthia:
—sikyon: (4) ii-iii ad ib. xi 256, 1 (f. Σωσικράτης)
Lakonia:
—sparta: (5) c. 140-145 ad *IG* v (1) 1314, 46 (Bradford (-)); (6) a. 212 ad *BSA* 89 (1994) p. 435 no. 6, 6 (I f. Αὐρ. Ἀρκαδίων II); (7) ~ ib. l. 6 ([Α]ὐρ. Ἀ.: II s. Ἀρκαδίων I)
Sicily:
—selinous: (8) ?f. vi bc Dubois, *IGDS* 73 (Arena, *Iscr. Sic.* I 18; *IGLMP* 73); cf. Guarducci, *Ep. Gr.* 3 pp. 121-2 (-ōν: f. Ἀριστόγειτος)

## Ἀρκάς
Elis:
—olympia*: (1) ?iv bc *IvOl* 843 (n. pr.?)
S. Italy (Apulia):
—venusia: (2) imp. *NScav* 1916, p. 184 (Lat. Ti. Iulius Arcas)
S. Italy (Campania):
—dikaiarchia-puteoli: (3) imp. *CIL* x 1834, 1 (Lat. Arka)
S. Italy (Lucania):
—herakleia:
——(Με. κιβώτιον): (4) iv/iii bc *IGSI* 1 I, 181 (*DGE* 62; Uguzzoni–Ghinatti I) (s. Φιλώτας)

## Ἀρκασία
Illyria:
—epidamnos-dyrrhachion: (1) hell.-imp. *IDyrrh* 127 (d. Ἀθανίων)

## Ἀρκάτις
Sicily:
—syracuse: (1) iii-v ad Strazzulla 375 + Ferrua, *NG* 138 (Barreca 13) (Ἀκράτις—Strazzulla)

## Ἀρκέας
S. Italy (Calabria):
—taras-tarentum: (1) vi bc Iamb., *VP* 267 (*FVS* 1 p. 446)

## Ἀρκείδας
S. Italy (Bruttium):
—lokroi epizephyrioi:
——(Βοω.): (1) iv/iii bc De Franciscis 15, 6 (f. Δαμοκλῆς)
——(Δυσ.): (2) iv/iii bc ib. 17, 8 (f. Φιλιστίων)
——(Πυρ.): (3) 276 bc ib. 23, 4 (s. Σώσιππος)
——(Στρ.): (4) iv/iii bc ib. 22, 20 (f. Ὀνάσιμος)

## Ἀρκείλας
Argolis:
—argos: (1) ?c. 460-450 bc *IG* iv (1)² 137 (Lazzarini 402); *LSAG*² p. 170 no. 37 (date) (-κεhίλ-)

## Ἀρκεσα
Argolis:
—epidauros: (1) iii/ii bc *IG* iv (1)² 228, 4 (m. Νικαρέτα)

## Ἀρκέσας
S. Italy (Lucania):
—hyele-velia: (1) iv/iii bc ib. 258 (f. Ἀριστόμαχος)

## Ἀρκεσίλαϝος
S. Italy (Apulia): (1) vi bc *Glotta* 4 (1913) p. 201 (vase) (Arena, *Iscr. Sic.* IV 94)

## Ἀρκεσίλαος
Argolis:
—epidauros:
——Koleis: (1) c. 310-300 bc *IG* iv (1)² 114, 5-6
Arkadia:
—lykosoura*: (2) arch. Paus. viii 10. 10
—megalopolis: (3) 188 bc *RE* (13); Moretti, *Olymp.* 608; (4) 168-160 bc *RE* (15)
Elis: (5) iii bc *Ag.* xvii 455 (s. Ἅλων)
Korinthia:
—korinth: (6) ?254 bc Nachtergael, *Les Galates* 9, 56 (Stephanis 400) (s. Ἱέρων)
—sikyon: (7) s. iii bc *RE* (2) (Overbeck 1768-9; Skalet 68) (s. Τεισικράτης: painter)
Lakonia:
—sparta: (8) m. v bc Moretti, *Olymp.* 305; 311 (Poralla² 141) (f. Λίχας); (9) 241 bc Plu., *Agis* 18 (Bradford (1)); (10) 184 bc Plb. xxiii 6. 1 (Bradford (2))
Sicily:
—katane: (11) 403 bc D.S. xiv 15. 1
—syracuse: (12) 307 bc Just. xxii 8. 14 (Lat. Arcesilaus)

## Ἀρκεσίλας
Arkadia:
—megalopolis: (1) 208 bc *IMM* 38, 54 (f. Νικήρατος)
Illyria:
—apollonia: (2) i bc Ceka, *Probleme* p. 139 no. 3 (coin) (pryt.)
Lakonia:
—sparta: (3) m. iii bc Peek, *IAEpid* 42, 63 (Perlman E.3); Perlman p. 63 f. (date) (Bradford (3)) (f. Πολύφαντος)
Messenia:
—messene: (4) m. iv bc *AM* 67 (1942) p. 111 no. 216 (s. Σάτυρος)
S. Italy (Bruttium):
—lokroi epizephyrioi:
——(Λογ.): (5) 277 bc De Franciscis 8, 2; 31, 2 (f. Ἀριστείδας)
——(Ὀμβ.): (6) iv/iii bc ib. 2, 3 (f. Θήρων)
Sicily:
—syracuse?:
——(Και.): (7) hell. *Mem. Linc.* 8 (1938) p. 128 no. 35. 8 (bullet) (f. Πολύξενος)

## Ἀρκέσιλλος
Argolis:
—epidauros: (1) iii bc *IG* iv (1)² 159

## Ἀρκεσος
Elis: (1) 36-24 bc *IvOl* 62, 11; 64, 15; 65, 19 (s. Ἁρμόδιος: T.)
Lakonia:
—sparta: (2) 379 bc Plu., *Pelop.* 13; *Mor.* 586 E; 598 F (Poralla² 142) (Ἀρκισσος—*Pelop.* 13)

## Ἀρκεσώι
Sicily:
—selinous: (1) ?s. iii bc *IG* xiv 271 (Dubois, *IGDS* 56; *IGLMP* 55) (d. Αἰσχύλος)

## Ἀρκετος
Arkadia:
—kleitor: (1) ?274 bc *FD* iii (1) 83, 17

## Ἀρκεφῶν
Aitolia:
—prosch(e)ion: (1) c. 157 bc *IG* ix (1)² (1) 108, 4

## Ἄρκισα
Aitolia:
—phistyon?: (1) i bc ib. 110 b, 12 (d. Ἀρκίσων)
Epiros:
—ambrakia: (2) iii bc *SEG* xxiv 413 (d. Ἔπανδρος)

## Ἀρκίσας
Aitolia:
—aperantoi: (1) iii/ii bc *SBBerlAk* 1936, p. 388 no. 2, 7 (*L'Illyrie mérid.* 1 p. 110 fig. 7); cf. *L'Illyrie mérid.* 1 p. 98 (locn.)

## Ἀρκίσων
Aitolia: (1) 264 bc *IG* ix (1)² (1) p. XLIX, s.a. 264 bc ?= (2); (2) c. 255 bc ib. 173, 1; cf. *FD* iii (3) 144, 1; cf. *BCH* 102 (1978) p. 478 (Ἀρκ[ί]σων—Pomtow, Ἀρκ[ίσων]—FD) ?= (1); (3) ?m. ii bc *IG* ix (1)² (1) 74 (Ἀρκίσ[ων])
—kalydon: (4) 150 bc ib. ix (1)² (3) 633, 1
—kasilioi: (5) s. ii bc *SEG* xxv 621, 7 (s. Ἐπίνικος)
—phistyon?: (6) i bc *IG* ix (1)² (1) 110 b, 13 (f. Ἄρκισα)
—trichonion: (7) s. iii bc ib. 117, 5

## Ἀρκίων
Aitolia:
—kalydon: (1) 129 bc ib. 137, 84 (s. Λυσ—)
Leukas: (2) f. i bc ib. ix (1) 534, 9 (*Iscr. Gr. Verona* p. 24) (I f. Ἀρκίων II); (3) ~ *IG* ix (1) 534, 9 (*Iscr. Gr. Verona* p. 24) (II s. Ἀρκίων I)

## Ἀρκοίας
Arkadia:
—tegea: (1) s. v bc *IG* v (2) 175, 2

## Ἀρκολέων
Akarnania:
—palairos: (1) ii bc ib. ix (1)² (2) 451, 20 (f. Εὔνικος)
Epiros:
—bouthrotos (prasaiboi): (2) a. 163 bc *IBouthrot* 18, 7-8; 26, 13; 30, 6 (*SEG* xxxviii 475; 484; 488) (s. Σώσανδρος, f. Σώσανδρος)

## Ἀρκολύκα
Lakonia:
—tainaron-kainepolis: (1) ?ii-i bc *IG* v (1) 1266

## Ἄρκος
Akarnania:
—anaktorion: (1) ?354 bc Tod, *GHI* ii 160, 8 (s. Τηρεύς)
—medion: (2) m. ii bc *IG* ix (1)² (2) 209, 3 (f. Φίλων)

## Ἀρκύλη
Sicily: (1) vi/v bc Dubois, *IGDS* 17 b (vase) (Arena, *Iscr. Sic.* II 79; Lazzarini 752 b); cf. *LSAG*² pp. 247-8 nos. 21-2 (Ἀρφύλε, Ἀρ(ι)φύλε—LSAG, Ἀρφύλε—Orlandini)

## Ἀρμάτης
Sicily:
—syracuse?:
——(Λαβ.): (1) hell. Manganaro, *PdelP* forthcoming no. 4 I, 4 (f. Παγχαρίων)

## Ἀρματίδας
Korinthia:
—korinth: (1) c. 570-550 bc Amyx 74. 8 (vase) (Lorber 129) (hαρ-: her.)

**Ἀρμένας**
LAKONIA:
—SPARTA: (1) iii/ii BC *RE* (-) (Bradford (-)) (s. *Νάβις*, ?s. *Ἀπία* (Argos))

**Ἀρμένιος**
ACHAIA: (1) 146 BC *IG* IV (1)² 28, 144 (f. Ἀρί-στων: synoikos)

**Ἄρμενος**
EPIROS:
—KOILOPOI: (1) ?iv/iii BC *SGDI* 1354, 6; cf. Cabanes, *L'Épire* p. 582 no. 58

**Ἀρμινίδας**
ARKADIA:
—THELPHOUSA: (1) f. v BC *SEG* XI 1123

**Ἀρμίς**
KEPHALLENIA:
—SAME: (1) iv/iii BC Fraser–Rönne, *BWGT* p. 117 no. 2. 4

**Ἀρμίων**
MESSENIA:
—MESSENE: (1) hell.? *PAE* 1993, p. 63

**Ἀρμόδικος**
LAKONIA:
—KYTHERA: (1) c. 230-200 BC *BCH* 45 (1921) p. 19 III, 101

**Ἀρμόδιος**
AITOLIA: (1) c. 225-200 BC *FD* III (4) 366, 2 ([Ἀρ]μόδιος)
—TRICHONION: (2) s. iii BC *IG* IX (1)² (1) 117, 4
ARGOLIS:
—ARGOS: (3) ii BC ib. IV (1)² 627 (f. Φιλοκλῆς)
ARKADIA:
—MEGALOPOLIS?: (4) ii/iii AD ib. V (2) 519
—TEGEA: (5) iv/iii BC ib. 32, 4
ELIS: (6) iv/iii BC Paus. vi 12. 6 (f. Κάλλων); (7) m. iii BC *Cl. Rh.* 2 p. 169 no. 1, 17; (8) 36-24 BC *IvOl* 62, 11; 64, 15; 65, [19] (f. Ἀρκεσος); (9) i BC/i AD ib. 74, 9 (Ἀρμ[ό]διος: ?f. Πριμίων); (10) 229-232 AD *SEG* XV 258, 4 (Φλ. Ἀ.)
EPIROS:
—KASSOPE: (11) hell. ib. XXIV 438 (f. Ἀριστότι-μος)
KEPHALLENIA:
—PANORMOS: (12) iii-v AD *IG* XIV 895 (*SEG* XXXVII 790)
KORINTHIA:
—SIKYON: (13) m. v BC *IG* IV (1) 425, 4; (14) i BC *SEG* XIII 248, 9; cf. Stephanis 1664 (f. Μενίσκος)
LAKONIA:
—KOTYRTA: (15) hell.? *SEG* II 173 (Ἀρμόδ(ι)ος)
MESSENIA:
—ASINE: (16) hell.-imp. *IG* V (1) 1407 (f. Δημό-νικος)
—KORONE: (17) ii BC ib. 1397, 6
SICILY:
—GELA-PHINTIAS: (18) f. v BC Dubois, *IGDS* 149 b (vase) (Arena, *Iscr. Sic.* II 149 b) (hαρ-)
—KAMARINA: (19) f. v BC Cordano, *Tessere Pubbliche* 140 (f. —ν)
TRIPHYLIA:
—LEPREON: (20) hell. *RE* (3); *FGrH* 319; Page, *FGE* p. 85

**Ἀρμοδίσκος**
S. ITALY (BRUTTIUM):
—RHEGION (NR.): (1) iv-iii BC Landi, *DISMG* 33. 2 (brick); *Klearchos* 18 (1976) p. 105 (date) (Ἀρμοδίσ(κ)ος)

**Ἀρμονία**
ARGOLIS:
—ARGOS*: (1) ii-i BC *IG* IV (1) 530, 10; cf. *BCH* 33 (1909) p. 183 n. 2 (Ἀρμον[ία], Ἀρμόν[ικος]?: slave/freed.?)

ILLYRIA:
—EPIDAMNOS-DYRRHACHION: (2) ii-i BC *Neos Hellenomnemon* 16 (1922) p. 343 no. 12
LAKONIA:
—SPARTA?: (3) 196 BC *SGDI* 1993, 4, 5 (slave/freed.)
S. ITALY (CAMPANIA):
—KYME: (4) imp. *Eph. Ep.* VIII 451 (Lat. Harmonia: m. Ὑγῖνος, Ὄνειρος, Ἡρακλείδας II, Φαῦστος)
—NUCERIA ALFATERNA*: (5) i AD *SEG* XXXII 1023 (biling.) (Lat. Harmonia: freed.)
SICILY:
—SYRACUSE: (6) 214 BC *RE* (2) (Lat. Harmonia: d. Γέλων)

**Ἀρμονικία**
LAKONIA:
—SPARTA: (1) c. 30-20 BC *IG* V (1) 142, 24 (Bradford (-)) (d. Σικλείδας)

**Ἀρμόνικος**
LAKONIA:
—SPARTA: (1) 80-70 BC *IG* IX (2) 534, 21; Kramolisch p. 116 n. 74 (date) (Bradford (1)) (s. Εὐδαμίδας); (2) s. i BC *IG* V (1) 92, 6 (Bradford (3)) (f. Εὐδαμίδας); (3) s. i AD *IG* V (1) 79, 15, 17; 275, 8 (*Artemis Orthia* pp. 312-13 no. 30 (date)); *IG* V (1) 480, 2; *SEG* XI 546 a, 7; 546 b, 7; 632, 2 (Bradford (2); (5)) (Τιβ. Κλ. Ἀρμόνεικος: f. Τιβ. Κλ. Ξενοφάνης, Πλειστόξε-νος); (4) c. 105-135 AD *IG* V (1) 97, 15; 485, 2; *SEG* XI 563, 4; 564, 9; 565, 3; XXXI 340, 4 (Bradford (2)) (Τιβ. Κλ. Ἀρμόνεικος: s. Πλει-στόξενος); (5) c. 125-133 AD *SEG* XI 547 a, [10]; 547 b, 6; 547 c, [2]; 575, [1]? (Bradford (4)) (-νει-, Ἀρμόν[ικ]ο[ς]—547 b: f. Νικόμαχος)
MESSENIA:
—MESSENE: (6) ii-iii AD *IvOl* 446 (Π. Αἴλ. Ἀρ-μόνεικος) ?= (7); (7) ii/iii AD *IG* V (1) 1399, 19; *BSA* 80 (1985) pp. 213-5 (ident.) (-νει-: s. Ἀρίστων, Ἀγήτα (Sparta)) ?= (6)

**Ἀρμονόα**
EPIROS:
—AMBRAKIA: (1) hell.? *SEG* XVII 303

**Ἀρμόξενος**
AKARNANIA:
—STRATOS: (1) 154 BC *SGDI* 1908, 11, 14 (s. Πολυπείθης)
MESSENIA:
—MESSENE: (2) ii/i BC *IG* V (1) 1437, 9 ([Ἀ](ρ)μ(όξ)εν(ο)[ς]—ed., ΒΜΦΕΕΝΟ—apogr.)

**Ἀρμοξίδαμος**
S. ITALY (BRUTTIUM):
—PETELIA: (1) ?c. 475 BC *IGSI* 19, 6 (Landi, *DISMG* 171); *LSAG*² p. 261 no. 28 (date)

**Ἄρμος**
LAKONIA:
—AMYKLAI*: (1) c. 510-500 BC *IG* V (1) 832 B; *LSAG*² p. 200 no. 32 (date)

**Ἄρμοστος**
LAKONIA:
—SPARTA: (1) c. 220 AD *IG* V (1) 544, 7 (*Artemis Orthia* pp. 358-9 no. 145; Bradford (-)) (f. M. Αὐρ. Εὔπορος)

**Ἀρνέας**
ILLYRIA:
—DIMALE: (1) i BC-i AD? *Iliria* 1986 (1), p. 102 no. 3 (?s. Πραουγουν— (gen.))

**Ἀρνήσιος**
KORINTHIA:
—KORINTH: (1) ?vi BC *IG* IV (1) 322 (pinax) ([Ἀ]ρνέσιος)

**Ἀρνιάδας**
KERKYRA: (1) c. 600 BC *CEG* I 145; cf. *SEG* XXXVI 541

**Ἀρνιόπα**
AKARNANIA:
—STRATOS: (1) ii BC ib. XXIX 477
AKARNANIA?: (2) ?f. iv BC Unp. (Agrinion Mus.)

**Ἀρνίοπος**
AKARNANIA:
—STRATOS: (1) iv/iii BC *IG* IX (1)² (2) 395, 16 ([Ἀρ]νίοπος—LGPN, [Ἀ]ν(τ)ίοπος?—ed.: s. Φι-λόξενος)

**Ἀρνίσκος**
ELIS: (1) inc. Paus. vi 16. 7 (f. Λάμπος)
ILLYRIA:
—EPIDAMNOS-DYRRHACHION: (2) c. 250-50 BC Münsterberg p. 260; Nachtr. p. 14 (coin) (Ceka 31) (pryt.)
ITHAKE: (3) 208 BC *IMM* 36, 1
LEUKAS: (4) hell.? *IG* IX (1) 546

**Ἀρνούφιλος**
KEPHALLENIA:
—PALE: (1) 132 AD ib. II² 3301, 6-7 (s. Ἀγαθο-κλῆς)

**Ἀρξιάδας**
MESSENIA:
—MESSENE: (1) f. iii BC *PAE* 1991, p. 100 no. 8, 7; cf. 1989, p. 96

**Ἀρξιλαΐδας**
LAKONIA:
—SPARTA?: (1) inc. Polyaen. ii 8 (Poralla² 144)

**Ἀρξίλας**
SICILY:
—LIPARA: (1) v-iv BC *BTCGI* 4 p. 15

**Ἀρουάνδη**
KEPHALLENIA:
—SAME: (1) imp. *SEG* XXXIV 475

**Ἀρούρα**
SICILY:
—HALAISA: (1) imp. *CIL* X 7460 (Lat. Helvia Arura)

**Ἀρπαγίων**
AITOLIA:
—KALYDON: (1) c. 117 BC *BCH* 74 (1950) p. 33 no. 1, 14, 20 (f. Πολεμαῖος)

**Ἀρπαλίς**
KERKYRA: (1) iii/ii BC *GVI* 1511, 4; cf. Fraser–Rönne, *BWGT* p. 112 no. 3 (m. Φιλίστιον)

**Ἅρπαξ**
S. ITALY (CAMPANIA):
—POMPEII: (1) imp. *Mon. Ant.* 33 (1929) p. 238 no. 20 (Lat. Harpax)

**Ἀρποκρᾶς**
S. ITALY (CALABRIA):
—BRENTESION-BRUNDISIUM: (1) imp. *CIL* IX 136 (Lat. M. Lollius Arphocras)
S. ITALY (CAMPANIA):
—DIKAIARCHIA-PUTEOLI: (2) 38 AD Camodeca, *L'Archivio Puteolano* I p. 143 no. 1 (Lat. T. Vestorius Arpocra minor)
—POMPEII: (3) i BC-i AD *CIL* IV 2192 (Lat. Arphokras); (4) ~ ib. 2193; 2400 (Lat. Arpocras); (5) ~ ib. 2481 a

**Ἀρποκρατίων**
ARGOLIS:
—ARGOS: (1) ii AD *RE* (2)
S. ITALY (CAMPANIA):
—DIKAIARCHIA-PUTEOLI: (2) ?ii AD *CIL* X 2593 (Lat. Ulpius Arpocration)

**Ἀρραχίων**
ARKADIA:
—PHIGALEIA: (1) 572-564 BC Moretti, *Olymp.* 95; 99; 102

**Ἀρρηνιανή**
EPIROS:
—NIKOPOLIS: (1) imp. *Ep. Chron.* 31 (1994) p. 42 no. 8 (*AD* 45 (1990) Chron. p. 257 no. 5)

**Ἀρριδαῖος**
KORINTHIA:
—KORINTH: (1) s. ii AD *Corinth* VIII (1) 15, 50 (*Λ. Κλώδιος Ἀ.*)

**Ἀρριφῶν**
AITOLIA:
—TRICHONION: (1) ii AD Paus. ii 37. 3

**Ἄρροπος**
EPIROS:
—VOTONOSI (MOD.): (1) f. iii BC *SEG* XXIV 462 (*Ἄρροπος*: s. *Κόρραγος*)

**Ἀρσενίδας**
ACHAIA: (1) 146 BC *IG* IV (1)² 28, 87 (f. *Θεόδωρος*: synoikos)

**Ἀρσένιος**
SICILY:
—SYRACUSE: (1) iii-v AD ib. XIV 77 (Strazzulla 18; Wessel 1188) (*Ἀρσέν[ιος]?, Ἀρσεν[ία]?*)

**Ἀρσινέα**
LAKONIA:
—HYPERTELEATON*: (1) imp. *IG* V (1) 1024 (m. *Εὔτυχᾶς*)

**Ἀρσινόα**
EPIROS:
—BOUTHROTOS (PRASAIBOI): (1) a. 163 BC *IBouthrot* 39, 2; 42, 18 (*SEG* XXXVIII 498; 501) (I m. *Ἀρσινόα* II); (2) ~ *IBouthrot* 39, 2; 42, 17 (501) (II d. *Δέξιππος, Ἀρσινόα* I)

**Ἀρσινόη**
ILLYRIA:
—APOLLONIA: (1) imp. *IApoll* 246 (d. *Διοσκ—*)
S. ITALY (APULIA):
—VENUSIA: (2) i AD *Rend. Linc.* 29 (1974) p. 616 no. 15 (Lat. Arsino[e])
S. ITALY (CAMPANIA):
—DIKAIARCHIA-PUTEOLI: (3) imp. *CIL* X 2760 (Lat. Naevia Arsinoe)
—MISENUM: (4) imp. *AJA* 2 (1898) p. 395 no. 56 (Lat. Valeria Arsenoe)
—POMPEII: (5) i BC-i AD *CIL* IV 10097 a (Lat. Arsynoe); (6) m. i AD *Impegno per Pompeii* 9 ES no. 6 (Lat. Arsinoe)
SICILY:
—ZANKLE-MESSANA: (7) imp. *SEG* IV 47 (*Βαλερία Ἀ.*)

**Ἀρταμίδωρος**
SICILY:
—KAMARINA: (1) ?iv/iii BC ib. XXXIV 940, 7 (Dubois, *IGDS* 124; *PdelP* 44 (1989) p. 192 no. 3; Cordano, 'Camarina VII' 80) (s. *Ἡρακλείδας*); (2) ?ii BC *SEG* XXXIX 996, 9 (Dubois, *IGDS* 126; Cordano, 'Camarina VII' 81) (s. *Θεοδόσιος*)
—SYRACUSE?:
——(Ὑπα.): (3) hell. Manganaro, *PdelP* forthcoming no. 4 V, 1 (s. *Σωτάδας*)
——(Μακ.): (4) hell. ib. l. 2 (s. *Φιλωνίδας*)
——(Πλη.): (5) hell. ib. no. 4 II, 2 (f. *Σώσανδρος*)

**Ἄρτας**
S. ITALY (CALABRIA):
—MESSAPIOI: (1) s. v BC *RE* (1); Th. vii 33. 4; *PCG* 5 p. 8 fr. 1, 3; cf. Polem. fr. 89 (*Ἀ.—*Th., *Ἄρτος*—alii: tyrant)

**Ἀρτάφαν**
SICILY:
—LILYBAION: (1) iii-iv AD *IGLMP* 26 (*Ἀρτάφαντος* (gen.): f. *Ἰάσων*)

**Ἀρτεμᾶς**
ARGOLIS:
—EPIDAUROS: (1) c. 370 BC *IG* IV (1)² 102, 219 (*Ἀ[ρτ]εμᾶς*)
—METHANA-ARSINOE: (2) ii-i BC ib. IV (1) 871
ARKADIA:
—TEGEA: (3) ii AD ib. V (2) 55, 91 (f. *Χρυσῆς*); (4) 165 AD ib. 50, 20 (I f. *Ἀρτεμᾶς* II); (5) ~ ib. l. 20 (II s. *Ἀρτεμᾶς* I)
EPIROS:
—PHOINIKE: (6) imp. Ugolini, *Alb. Ant.* 2 p. 156 no. 12 (s. *Ἀρτεμίδωρος*)
LAKONIA:
—HYPERTELEATON*: (7) imp. *IG* V (1) 1065 (f. *Χαιρᾶς*)
—SPARTA: (8) c. 170-190 AD *SEG* XI 627, 8 (Bradford (1)) (s. *Ῥουφίων*); (9) a. 212 AD *IG* V (1) 596, 3 (Bradford (2)) (f. *Ἀντ. Εὐδαμία*)
LEUKAS: (10) c. 167-50 BC *BMC Thessaly* p. 181 no. 105; p. 182 nos. 121-2; p. 183 nos. 134-5 (coins)
S. ITALY (CAMPANIA):
—BAIAI: (11) imp. *CIL* X 1762 (Lat. Artema)
SICILY:
—AKRAI:
——(Ἀν.): (12) ii BC *Akrai* p. 154 no. 3, 8 (*Ἀρτεμ[ας]*: f. *Ἀπελλις*)

**Ἀρτεμίδοτος**
SICILY:
—KAMARINA: (1) iii BC Pace, *Camarina* p. 160 no. 3 (Cordano, 'Camarina VII' 82) (f. *Ἀρτεμώ*)

**Ἀρτεμιδώρα**
AKARNANIA:
—PALAIROS: (1) hell.-imp. *SEG* XXVII 158 (καλεισαρτεμιορας—lap.: ?m. *Καλεῖς*: name—*LGPN*)
ARGOLIS:
—ARGOS*: (2) ii BC ib. XLII 279, 23 (*[Ἀρ]τε[μ]ιδώρα*: slave/freed.?)
ILLYRIA:
—LYCHNIDOS: (3) ii-iii AD Demitsas 340 (m. *Δημητριάς*)
S. ITALY (CAMPANIA):
—DIKAIARCHIA-PUTEOLI: (4) imp. *CIL* X 2623 (Lat. Iunia Artemidora)
SICILY:
—LIPARA: (5) hell.? Libertini, *Isole Eolie* p. 225 no. 48
—SEGESTA: (6) iv/iii BC *SEG* XLI 827 (*[Ἀρ]τε]μιδώρα*: d. *Νύμφων*)

**Ἀρτεμίδωρος**
ACHAIA: (1) 146 BC *IG* IV (1)² 28, 108 (f. *Διονύσιος*: synoikos)
AITOLIA:
—THERMOS: (2) hell.-imp. *AD* 44 (1989) Chron. p. 141
—THERMOS*: (3) s. iii BC *IG* IX (1)² (1) 60 III, 12; (4) ~ ib. l. 17; (5) ~ ib. 60 IV, 7; (6) ~ ib. l. 15
AKARNANIA:
—THYRREION: (7) ii BC ib. IX (1)² (2) 320
ARGOLIS:
—ARGOS: (8) hell. *Cl. Rh.* 2 p. 242 no. 166
—ARGOS*: (9) ii BC *SEG* XLII 279, 8 (katoikos) ?= (10); (10) ~ ib. l. 16 (katoikos) ?= (9)
—EPIDAUROS: (11) imp. *IG* IV (1)² 449; 450 (f. *Διογένης*)
—TROIZEN: (12) f. ii BC ib. IV (1) 752, 9 + IV (1)² 77, 15
ARKADIA:
—NONAKRIS: (13) c. 250 BC Peek, *IAEpid* 330, 15

DALMATIA:
—ISSA: (14) f. ii BC Brunšmid p. 23 no. 10, 1; (15) ~ ib. l. 12 (f. —*τυλος*)
——(Dymanes): (16) iv/iii BC ib. p. 8, 33 (f. —*s*)
EPIROS:
—PHOINIKE: (17) imp. Ugolini, *Alb. Ant.* 2 p. 156 no. 12 (*[Ἀρ]τεμίδωρος*: f. *Ἀρτεμᾶς*) ?= (18); (18) ~ ib. (*[Ἀρτ]εμίδωρος*) ?= (17)
ILLYRIA:
—BYLLIONES NIKAIA (KLJOS (MOD.)): (19) iii/ii BC *SEG* XXXV 696 (*[Κλ]εόδωρος*—ed.: f. *Πραΰλλας*: name—*LGPN*)
KORINTHIA:
—KORINTH (NR.): (20) hell.? *IG* IV (1) 1559 (fals.?)
—KORINTH: (21) a. 212 AD ib. VII 1776, 20 (Stephanis 412) (*Μ. Αὐφίδ. Ἀ.*)
LAKONIA:
—SPARTA: (22) c. 230-260 AD *IG* V (1) 556, 11 (Bradford (-)) (*Αὐρ. Ἀ.*: s. *Λύκος*)
S. ITALY (BRUTTIUM):
—RHEGION: (23) imp. *IG* XIV 621, 2 (*Ἀρτεμίδω[ρος]*); (24) imp.? ib. 2400. 8 (tile)
S. ITALY (CALABRIA):
—BRENTESION-BRUNDISIUM: (25) imp. *CIL* IX 64 (Lat. L. Acceratius Artemidorus)
—TARAS-TARENTUM: (26) iv BC *SEG* XXX 1218 (Landi, *DISMG* 191) (s. *Κριτόλας*); (27) imp. *NScav* 1894, p. 67 no. 42 (Lat. Artemidorus)
—TARAS-TARENTUM*: (28) f. iii AD *Studi Adriani* 3 pp. 476-9 (sculptor)
S. ITALY (CAMPANIA):
—DIKAIARCHIA-PUTEOLI: (29) ?i AD *CIL* X 2500 (Lat. L. Iulius A(r)temidorus); (30) ?ii-iii AD ib. 8187 (Lat. Aurelius Artemidorus)
—MISENUM*: (31) ?i-ii AD ib. 3359 (Lat. Artemidorus)
—NEAPOLIS: (32) iv/iii BC Sambon 463 (coin) (*Ἀρτεμίδ(ωρος)*)
—NOLA: (33) ?ii AD *CIL* X 1300 (Lat. T. Flavius Artemidorus)
S. ITALY (LUCANIA):
—HERAKLEIA: (34) c. 250-175 BC *SEG* XXXII 810 (f. *Μένιππος*)
—LEUKANOI: (35) c. 208 BC *FD* III (4) 135, 11 (f. *Θεόδωρος*)
—POSEIDONIA-PAESTUM: (36) imp. Mello—Voza 177 (Lat. Q. Geminius Artemidorus); (37) ?ii AD ib. 89 (Lat. L. Dic. Artemidorus)
—POSEIDONIA-PAESTUM*: (38) imp. ib. 174 (Lat. L. Venedius Artem[idorus]: freed.)
SICILY:
—AKRAI: (39) ii-i BC *SGDI* 3246, 9, 11 (*Akrai* pp. 152-3 no. 2; Dubois, *IGDS* 109) (s. *Ἡράκλειος*, f. *Ζώπυρος*); (40) ~ *SGDI* 3246, 13 (*Akrai* pp. 152-3 no. 2; Dubois, *IGDS* 109) (s. *Πολύξενος*)
—ENTELLA: (41) f. iii BC *SEG* XXX 1121, 2 (Dubois, *IGDS* 208); *SEG* XXX 1123, 2 (Dubois, *IGDS* 211); *SEG* XXXV 999, 2 (Dubois, *IGDS* 212) (s. *Εἴελος*)
—HALAISA: (42) ii BC *IGSI* 2 B II, 15 (Dubois, *IGDS* 196) (*Ἀρτεμίδωρ[ος]*)
—INESSA-AITNA: (43) f. i BC Cic., *In Verr.* II iii 105 (Lat. Artemidorus)
—KATANE: (44) imp. *Sic. Gymn.* 14 (1961) p. 190 (s. *Κλήμης*)
—LIPARA*: (45) i-ii AD *Meligunìs-Lipára* 2 p. 101 T. 290; cf. *Kokalos* 32 (1986) p. 223 nos. 18-19 (tiles)
—SEGESTA: (46) f. iii BC *IG* XIV 291 (Dubois, *IGDS* 216); *SEG* XLI 825 (date) (f. *Τίττελος*); (47) m. iii BC *NScav* 1931, p. 398; cf. *SEG* XLI 825 (s. *Δόσσις Γραδαναῖος*)
—SYRACUSE: (48) c. 275 BC Plb. i 8. 3; (49) s. iii BC *Arch. Class.* 17 (1965) p. 186 no. 2 (f. —*χος*); (50) 208 BC *IMM* 72, 4 (Dubois, *IGDS* 97) (*Ἀρτεμίδ[ωρος]*); (51) iii-v AD Ferrua, *NG* 335 (*Ἀρτεμί[δωρ]ος*)
—TAUROMENION: (52) c. 239 BC *IG* XIV 421 an. 2 (*SGDI* 5219) (f. *Ἀριστέας*); (53) c. 236-177

BC *IG* XIV 421 an. 5; 421 an. 31; 421 an. 52; 421 an. 64 (*SGDI* 5219) (s. Ἄθανις, f. Ἄθανις); **(54)** c. 233 BC *IG* XIV 421 an. 8 (*SGDI* 5219) (f. Διονύσιος); **(55)** c. 203 BC *IG* XIV 421 an. 38 (*SGDI* 5219); **(56)** c. 200 BC *IG* XIV 421 an. 41 (*SGDI* 5219); **(57)** c. 194 BC *IG* XIV 421 an. 47 (*SGDI* 5219); **(58)** c. 182 BC *IG* XIV 421 an. 59 (*SGDI* 5219) (f. Ἀπολλόδωρος); **(59)** c. 178 BC *IG* XIV 421 an. 63 (*SGDI* 5219) (f. Κρίθων); **(60)** c. 173 BC *IG* XIV 421 an. 68 (*SGDI* 5219) (f. Νεμήνιος); **(61)** c. 170-154 BC *IG* XIV 421 an. 77; 421 an. 87 (*SGDI* 5219); *IGSI* 4 II (III), 16 an. 71 (s. Ἄθανις); **(62)** c. 169 BC *IG* XIV 421 an. 72 (*SGDI* 5219) (s. Ἀπολλόδωρος) ?= (**65**); **(63)** c. 166 BC *IGSI* 4 II (III), 47 an. 75; **(64)** c. 165 BC *IG* XIV 421 an. 76 (*SGDI* 5219) (f. Ἀρχάγαθος); **(65)** c. 154-140 BC *IG* XIV 421 an. 87; 421 an. 101 (*SGDI* 5219); *IGSI* 4 III (IV), 42 an. 91 (f. Ἀπολλόδωρος) ?= (**62**); **(66)** c. 149 BC ib. l. 50 an. 92 (s. Φιλωνίδας); **(67)** c. 145 BC *IG* XIV 421 an. 96 (*SGDI* 5219); *IGSI* 4 III (IV), 78 an. 96 (s. Ἀ—); **(68)** c. 143 BC *IG* XIV 421 an. 98 (*SGDI* 5219); **(69)** c. 140 BC *IG* XIV 421 an. 101 (*SGDI* 5219) (s. Εὔφορος); **(70)** ?ii/i BC *IG* XIV 421 D an. 2 (*SGDI* 5219) (I f. Ἀρτεμίδωρος II); **(71)** ~ *IG* XIV 421 D an. 2 (*SGDI* 5219) (II s. Ἀρτεμίδωρος I); **(72)** c. 40 BC *Cron. Arch.* 3 (1964) p. 54 I, 24 (f. Νικασίων); **(73)** ~ ib. p. 56 I, 10 ——(Ἀρεθ.): **(74)** ?ii/i BC *IG* XIV 421 D an. 12 (*SGDI* 5219) (s. Ἀπολλόδωρος) ——(Κ.): **(75)** c. 146 BC *IGSI* 4 III (IV), 74 an. 95 (s. Θεόφιλος) ——(Καλ.): **(76)** ?ii/i BC *IG* XIV 421 D an. 3; 421 D an. 9 (*SGDI* 5219) (f. Ζώπυρος) ——(Οἰν.): **(77)** ?ii/i BC *IG* XIV 421 D an. 11 (*SGDI* 5219) (s. Ἀριστομένης) ——(Οἰτ.): **(78)** ?ii/i BC *IG* XIV 421 D an. 8 (*SGDI* 5219) (s. Ὄνασος) ——(Σπαρ.): **(79)** ?ii/i BC *IG* XIV 421 D an. 14 (*SGDI* 5219) (s. Ἄθανις) —TYNDARIS: **(80)** imp. Manganaro, *QUCC* forthcoming no. 21 (s. Νικίας)

**Ἀρτέμιν**
ACHAIA:
—PATRAI?: **(1)** ii-i BC *GVI* 530 (d. Ἑρμόδωρος)

**Ἀρτέμιος**
S. ITALY (CAMPANIA):
—NEAPOLIS: **(1)** 375-250 BC *SNG ANS Etruria–Calabria* 348 (coin)

**Ἄρτεμις**
LAKONIA:
—SPARTA: **(1)** ?ii-i BC *IG* V (1) 760 (Bradford (-))
S. ITALY (CAMPANIA):
—NOLA: **(2)** ?i AD *CIL* X 1308 (Lat. Iulia Apusia Artemis)
—PITHEKOUSSAI-AENARIA: **(3)** imp. ib. 6805 (Lat. Artemis: m. Salluvia Naevilla)

**Ἀρτεμισία**
AIGINA: **(1)** hell. *IG* IV (1) 86; **(2)** ii BC *SEG* XI 8, 2
ARGOLIS:
—HERMIONE: **(3)** ii-i BC *IG* IV (1) 732 III, 15 (d. Σωσθένης)
S. ITALY (APULIA):
—CANUSIUM: **(4)** ii-iii AD *Epig. Rom. di Canosa* 82 (*CIL* IX 357) (Lat. Attia Artemisia)
S. ITALY (CAMPANIA):
—DIKAIARCHIA-PUTEOLI: **(5)** imp. ib. X 2636 (Lat. Laecania Artemisia: m. Laecanius Venerianus); **(6)** ~ ib. 8372 (Lat. Terentia Artemisia); **(7)** ~ *NScav* 1885, p. 500 (Lat. Valeria Artemisia); **(8)** ?ii AD *CIL* X 1571 (Lat. Flavia Artemisia)

SICILY:
—SYRACUSE: **(9)** iii-v AD Strazzulla 390 (Agnello 29; Wessel 859); cf. Ferrua, *NG* 144 (m. Εὐτύχης)
—THERMAI HIMERAIAI: **(10)** i-ii AD *CIL* X 7374 (*ILat. Term. Imer.* 44) (Lat. Artemisia: m. Ἀσιατικός)

**Ἀρτεμίσιος**
LAKONIA:
—SPARTA: **(1)** c. 95-145 AD *SEG* XI 490, 1, 7; 544, 4; 574, [6]; 579, [2] (Bradford (-)) (f. Ἀγίων)
MESSENIA:
—KORONE: **(2)** 246 AD *IG* V (1) 1398, 33 (Κλ. Ἀ.); **(3)** ~ ib. l. 86 (Ὀπ(πιος) Ἀ.)
S. ITALY (CAMPANIA):
—DIKAIARCHIA-PUTEOLI: **(4)** imp. *CIL* X 2138 (Lat. Ti. Aurel. Artemisius)
SICILY:
—LIPARA: **(5)** imp. *Epigraphica* 3 (1941) p. 270 no. 45 (f. Κύϊντος Βαλέριος Νίγερ)

**Ἀρτεμίσκος**
SICILY:
—KENTORIPA: **(1)** hell. *IG* XIV 574, 4 (Dubois, *IGDS* 188) ([Ἀρτ]εμίσκος Κάβαλλος: s. Νύμφων)

**Ἀρτεμίων**
SICILY:
—SAMPIERI (MOD.): **(1)** iii-v AD *Riv. Arch. Crist.* 18 (1941) p. 216 no. 94 (Αὐτεμειονlap., Ἀ., Ἀνθεμίων?—ed.)

**Ἀρτεμοκλέα**
KERKYRA: **(1)** imp. *IG* IX (1) 900

**Ἀρτεμώ**
ARGOLIS:
—ARGOS: **(1)** ii AD *SEG* XXVIII 223, 9 (Κλ. [Ἀ]ρτ[ε]μώ: m. Βηδία Ἰώ)
ARKADIA:
—TEGEA: **(2)** ii AD *IG* V (2) 252
EPIROS:
—BOUTHROTOS (PRASAIBOI): **(3)** a. 163 BC *IBouthrot* 19, 7 (*SEG* XXXVIII 476)
LAKONIA: **(4)** ii-iii AD *IG* XIV 1420 (*GVI* 613; Bradford (-))
S. ITALY (CAMPANIA):
—NEAPOLIS: **(5)** 110 BC *ID* 2265 (d. Ἀπολλώνιος)
SICILY:
—KAMARINA: **(6)** ?iii BC Pace, *Camarina* p. 160 no. 3 (Cordano, 'Camarina VII' 83) (d. Ἀρτεμίδοτος)
—SYRACUSE: **(7)** hell.-imp. *AM* 23 (1898) p. 393 no. 62

**Ἀρτέμων**
AITOLIA:
—THERMOS*: **(1)** s. iii BC *IG* IX (1)² (1) 60 II, 22; **(2)** ~ ib. l. 25; **(3)** ~ ib. 60 VI, 19
ARGOLIS:
—ARGOS: **(4)** ii AD *SEG* XVI 253, 2 (Ἀρτ[έμ]ων)
ARKADIA:
—MANTINEIA-ANTIGONEIA: **(5)** 27 BC-15 AD *IG* V (2) 268 (f. Ἐπιγόνη); **(6)** ii-iii AD ib. 275, 9 (I f. Ἀρτέμων II); **(7)** ~ ib. l. 9 (II s. Ἀρτέμων I)
—TEGEA: **(8)** i AD ib. 47, 9 ([Ἀρ]τέμων)
ELIS: **(9)** c. 85-93 AD *IvOl* 86, 2, 5, 7 (I s. Ἀρχέλαος, f. Ἀρχέλαος, Ἀρτέμων II) ?= (**11**); **(10)** ~ ib. l. 7 (II s. Ἀρτέμων I); **(11)** ~ ib. l. 16 ([Ἀρτ]έμων) ?= (**9**); **(12)** 225-229 AD ib. 114, 4 ([Αὐρ.] Ἀ.: I ?f. Αὐρ. Ἀρτέμων II: F.); **(13)** ~ ib. l. 7 (Αὐρ. Ἀ[ρτ]έμων: II ?s. Αὐρ. Ἀρτέμων I)
EPIROS:
—BOUTHROTOS (PRASAIBOI): **(14)** a. 163 BC *IBouthrot* 19, 7 (*SEG* XXXVIII 476) ——Bouthrotioi: **(15)** a. 163 BC *IBouthrot* 92, 7; 93, 7; 105, 6 (s. Ἀρχέλαος)

KORINTHIA:
—KORINTH: **(16)** v-vi AD Bees 41; cf. *TMByz* 9 (1985) p. 359 no. 6
—SIKYON: **(17)** i BC-i AD *IG* II² 10307 (f. Κλεοπάτρα)
LAKONIA:
—SPARTA: **(18)** f. iii AD *SEG* XLII 320, 1 (Αὐρ. Ἀ.: s. Ἀγάσιππος)
MESSENIA:
—MESSENE:
——(Kleolaidai): **(19)** ii AD *PAE* 1992, p. 71 A, 29 (f. Ἀπολλώνιος)
S. ITALY (CAMPANIA):
—DIKAIARCHIA-PUTEOLI: **(20)** imp. *RAAN* 42 (1967) pp. 4-6 (Lat. L. Annius Artemo); **(21)** i/ii AD *Puteoli* 4-5 (1980-1) p. 286 no. 17 (Lat. C. Iulius Artemo: f. C. Iulius Optatus)
S. ITALY (LUCANIA):
—HYELE-VELIA: **(22)** imp. *IG* II² 8483 (f. Δίφιλος)
SICILY:
—AKRAI: **(23)** ?iii BC *SGDI* 3239, 6 (*Akrai* p. 157 no. 9) (s. Παυσανίας); **(24)** ~ *SGDI* 3240, 3 (*Akrai* p. 156 no. 7) (f. Νικασίων); **(25)** ~ *SGDI* 3243 (*Akrai* p. 155 no. 5) (f. Δαμοκλῆς, ?f. Ἀγάθαρχος); **(26)** iii-ii BC *SGDI* 3242, 9 (*Akrai* p. 157 no. 8) (f. Ἀντικράτης); **(27)** ii BC ib. p. 154 no. 3, 4 (f. Θεόδωρος); **(28)** ~ ib. l. 9 (I f. Ἀρτέμων II); **(29)** ~ ib. l. 10 (II s. Ἀρτέμων I)
—ASSOROS (NR.): **(30)** imp.? Manganaro, *QUCC* forthcoming no. 18 ([Ἀρ]τέμων)
—ENTELLA: **(31)** f. i BC Cic., *In Verr.* II iii 200 (Lat. Artemo)
—GELA-PHINTIAS: **(32)** f. ii BC *IG* XIV 256, 38 (Dubois, *IGDS* 161); cf. *SEG* XL 804 (s. Εὔθυμος)
—HELOROS: **(33)** ii-i BC Dubois, *IGDS* 100, 4 (Ἀρτέμω[ν]: s. Ἀρχωνίδας)
—KATANE: **(34)** imp. *IG* XIV 452 + Ferrua, *NG* 428 (Ἀρτέμ[ων]: f. Εὔπλους)
—KENTORIPA: **(35)** hell.? *IG* XIV 2397. 2 (tile); **(36)** f. i BC Cic., *In Verr.* II ii 156; *In Verr.* II iii 108 (Lat. Artemo)
—KEPHALOIDION: **(37)** f. i BC ib. *In Verr.* II ii 128 (Lat. Artemo Climachias)
—SEGESTA: **(38)** ?ii BC *IG* XIV 287 (Dubois, *IGDS* 213) (f. Μινύρα)
—SYRACUSE: **(39)** iii-v AD Ferrua, *NG* 191
—TAUROMENION: **(40)** c. 144 BC *IG* XIV 421 an. 97 (*SGDI* 5219); *IGSI* 4 III (IV), 85 an. 97 (s. Ἱπποκράτης)
—THERMAI HIMERAIAI: **(41)** ?i BC *IG* XIV 340 (f. Ζώπυρος Ὠκιδίας); **(42)** i-ii AD *CIL* X 7435 (*ILat. Term. Imer.* 141) (Lat. C. Sabidius Artemo)

**Ἀρτεμωνίς**
S. ITALY (CAMPANIA):
—SALERNUM*: **(1)** imp. *IItal* 1 (1) 87 (*CIL* X 638) (Lat. Servilia Artemonis: freed.)

**Ἀρτίπους**
ARGOLIS:
—EPIDAUROS: **(1)** ?iii AD Peek, *IAEpid* 232, 1 (f. Ὀνάσων)

**Ἄρτος**
S. ITALY (APULIA):
—RUBI: **(1)** ii BC Troisi, *Epigrafi mobili* 99 (bronze) (s. Ἄτοτος)

**Ἀρτύας**
ARKADIA:
—MANTINEIA-ANTIGONEIA:
——(Posoidaia): **(1)** c. 425-400 BC *SEG* XXXI 348, 5

**Ἀρτυκλῆς**
ARGOLIS:
—EPIDAUROS*: **(1)** c. 370-365 BC Peek, *IAEpid* 52 A, 25, 27, 46 (Ἀρ[τυ]κλῆς)

**Ἀρτύλας**
ARKADIA:
—PHIGALEIA: (**1**) f. iii BC Paus. viii 27. 11 (f. (nat.) Ἀριστόδαμος)

**Ἀρύββας**
ARKADIA:
—TEGEA: (**1**) s. iv BC SEG XXXVI 383, 5 (-ύβας: f. Κλέανδρος)
EPIROS: (**2**) s. iv BC IG IV (1)² 122, 63
—DODONA*: (**3**) ?iv/iii BC SEG XXIII 476 b
—MOLOSSOI: (**4**) c. 390-323 BC RE (1); Moretti, Olymp. 450; Osborne, Naturalization D14 (and Athens: Ἀρύμβας—D. S. xvi 72 and xix 88: s. Ἀλκέτας, f. Αἰακίδης, Ἀλκέτας: king I)
—MOLOSSOI?: (**5**) s. iv BC RE (2); Berve 156

**Ἀρύστας**
ARKADIA: (**1**) 401 BC X., An. vii 3. 23-4

**Ἀρυτάμας**
LAKONIA:
—SPARTA: (**1**) 636 BC Moretti, Olymp. 57 (Poralla² 145)

**Ἀρχάγαθος**
ILLYRIA:
—EPIDAMNOS-DYRRHACHION: (**1**) hell.-imp. IDyrrh 286 (f. Λαΐς)
PELOPONNESE: (**2**) s. iii BC RE (7) (Lat. Archagathus: s. Λυσανίας: doctor)
SICILY:
—AKRAI: (**3**) ?iii BC SGDI 3243 (Akrai p. 155 no. 5) (s. Ἡρακλείδας); (**4**) iii-ii BC SGDI 3242, 6 (Akrai p. 157 no. 8) (I f. Ἀρχάγαθος II); (**5**) ~ SGDI 3242, 6 (Akrai p. 157 no. 8) (II s. Ἀρχάγαθος I); (**6**) ii BC ib. p. 156 no. 6, 10 (f. Ἀριστοφάνης); (**7**) ii-i BC SGDI 3246, 48 (Akrai pp. 152-3 no. 2; Dubois, IGDS 109) (f. Ἀπολλώνιος)
—HALAISA: (**8**) m. i BC Cic., ad Fam. xiii 32. 1 (Lat. M. Clodius Archagathus)
—HALOUNTION: (**9**) f. i BC ib. In Verr. II iv 51; 53 (Lat. Archagathus)
—KALE AKTE*: (**10**) i BC/i AD RE s.v. Caecilius (2); PIR² s.v. Caecilius 14 (A. Καικίλιος Ἀ.: freed.?)
—KAMARINA: (**11**) ?ii BC SEG XXXIX 996, 1 (Dubois, IGDS 126; Cordano, 'Camarina VII' s.v. Ἀρχάγαθος (A.—SEG, Ἀρκάγαθος—Cordano and Dubois)
—SYRACUSE: (**12**) 310-307 BC RE (1); cf. Walbank 2 pp. 32-3 (Ἀγάθαρχος—Plb. and D.S.: I s. Ἀγαθοκλῆς, f. Ἀρχάγαθος II); (**13**) 289 BC RE (2) (II s. Ἀρχάγαθος I); (**14**) f. ii BC Iasos 177, 14 (f. Νύμφων)
—TAUROMENION: (**15**) c. 165 BC IG XIV 421 an. 76 (SGDI 5219) (s. Ἀρτεμίδωρος)
—TYNDARIS: (**16**) hell.-imp. IG XIV 376

**Ἀρχαγέτας**
ARGOLIS:
—EPIDAUROS: (**1**) inc. SEG XXXVIII 322 (n. pr.?: ?f. Ἀριστόφαντος)

**Ἀρχαγόρας**
ARGOLIS:
—ARGOS: (**1**) 401 BC X., An. iv 2. 13; iv 2. 17
ARKADIA:
—TEGEA: (**2**) f. iii BC IG v (2) 35, 22 (f. Καλλίας) ?= (3); (**3**) ~ ib. IX (2) 430 (GVI 1460) (Ἀ[ρ]χαγόρας—Peek, Σ[τ]ασαγόρας—IG: f. Καλλίας) ?= (2)
LAKONIA:
—KYTHERA: (**4**) ii BC IG v (1) 963, 1, 7 (I f. Ἀρχαγόρας II); (**5**) ~ ib. l. 1, 7 (II s. Ἀρχαγόρας I)

**Ἀρχάδας**
EPIROS:
—AMBRAKIA: (**1**) ?ii BC AD 10 (1926) p. 67 fig. 4

**Ἀρχαιώι**
ARGOLIS:
—EPIDAUROS: (**1**) iii BC Peek, IAEpid 308

**Ἀρχανδρος**
ARKADIA:
—TEGEA: (**1**) c. 240-229 BC IG v (2) 12
LEUKAS: (**2**) f. i BC ib. IX (1) 534, 11 (Iscr. Gr. Verona p. 24) (f. Κάρμων)

**Ἀρχαρέτα**
AITOLIA:
—KALYDON: (**1**) iii BC IG IX (2) 458, 3 (d. Λεπτίνας)

**Ἀρχας**
SICILY:
—TAUROMENION: (**1**) c. 150 BC ib. XIV 421 an. 91 (SGDI 5219); IGSI 4 III (IV), 40 an. 91 (s. Ἀρίστων); (**2**) ?ii/i BC IG XIV 421 D [an. 10?] (SGDI 5219) (s. Ἀρίστων) ?= (3)
——(Tav.): (**3**) ii/i BC IGSI 5 II, 10 (f. Ἀρίστων) ?= (2)

**Ἀρχάς**
S. ITALY (CAMPANIA):
—HERCULANEUM: (**1**) i BC-i AD CIL X 1440 (Lat. [Vi]ciria Archas: m. Balbus)

**Ἀρχέας**
ARGOLIS:
—PHLEIOUS: (**1**) c. 210-207 BC IG IV (1)² 73, 13; SEG XXXV 303 (date) (s. Εὐτελίδας)
ARKADIA:
—MANTINEIA-ANTIGONEIA: (**2**) iv BC IG v (2) 331
—TEGEA: (**3**) iv/iii BC ib. 38, 60; (**4**) ?218 BC ib. 16, 14
——(Athaneatai): (**5**) iv/iii BC ib. 38, 5
——(Krariotai): (**6**) iv/iii BC ib. l. 27 (f. Γόργιππος)
MESSENIA:
—MESSENE: (**7**) ii-i BC SEG XLI 343, 7 ([Ἀρ]χέας)
SICILY:
—KAMARINA: (**8**) f. v BC Cordano, Tessere Pubbliche 76 (s. Μένανδρος)

**Ἀρχέβιος**
DALMATIA:
—ISSA: (**1**) iii BC Brunšmid p. 9 fr. G, 15 (f. Ἀγασίων)
——(Hylleis): (**2**) iv/iii BC ib. p. 8, 35 (Ἀ[ρ]χέβιος: s. Διονύσιος)
—ISSA?: (**3**) hell.? ib. p. 32 no. 29 (s. Κλεόδικος)
EPIROS:
—DODONA*: (**4**) v BC SEG XV 385 (s. Ἀρχωνίδας)

**Ἀρχεβούλα**
SICILY:
—THERMAI HIMERAIAI: (**1**) imp. SGDI 3250 (Kokalos 20 (1974) pp. 246-7 no. 17) (m. Δημοσθένης)

**Ἀρχέγονος**
EPIROS:
—DODONA: (**1**) ?iv-iii BC SEG XIX 434 (s. Δαμασιάδας: date—A.W.J.)

**Ἀρχεδάμας**
KORINTHIA:
—SIKYON: (**1**) ?254-253 BC Nachtergael, Les Galates 9, 76; 10, 71 (Skalet 71; Stephanis 429) (s. Ἀριστόκριτος)

**Ἀρχέδαμος**
ACHAIA:
—BOURA: (**1**) c. 271 BC IG IX (1)² (1) 12, 27 (s. Καλλίδαμος)
ACHAIA?: (**2**) 193 BC ib. v (2) 293, 23 (s. Παμφάης)

AIGINA: (**3**) i BC-i AD Alt-Ägina I (2) p. 46 no. 22 ([Ἀρ]χέδαμος: s. Ἐργασίων)
AITOLIA:
—KALYDON: (**4**) iii/ii BC IG IX (1)² (1) 136, 11
—PHOLAI: (**5**) 191-174 BC RE (5); IG IX (1)² (1) p. LI, s.a. 191 BC, 188 BC, 182 BC, 175 BC; IX (1)² (3) 629, 1; BCH 58 (1934) p. 157, 1
—PROSCH(E)ION: (**6**) c. 215-205 BC FD III (4) 362, 9 ([Ἀρ]χέδαμος)
AKARNANIA:
—DERION: (**7**) c. 325-315 BC Hesp. 57 (1988) p. 148 A, 43 (SEG XXXVI 331); cf. Hesp. 48 (1979) pp. 78 f. with pl. 22 c (f. Βραχύμηλος)
—PHOITIAI: (**8**) iv BC IG IX (1)² (2) 602, 9 (s. Γλαυ—)
—THYRREION: (**9**) iii-ii BC SEG XXVII 159, 10; cf. PAE 1977, pl. 244 a (Ἀρχέδαμος, Ἐχέδαμος?: f. Ἡρακλείδας)
ARGOLIS:
—ARGOS: (**10**) ?316 BC IG v (2) 549, 27 (s. Ἀρχίας); (**11**) ii/i BC SEG XXII 266, 2 (Ἀρχέδ[α]μος)
—EPIDAUROS: (**12**) m. iii BC IG VII 13, 7 (f. Νικάτας); (**13**) iii/ii BC ib. IV (1)² 221; 222 (s. Εὐάνθης, f. Εὐάνθης)
—EPIDAUROS*: (**14**) c. 370 BC ib. 102, 50
ELIS: (**15**) v/iv BC Moretti, Olymp. 369 (s. Ξενίας)
EPIROS:
—BOUTHROTOS (PRASAIBOI):
——Bouthrotioi: (**16**) f. ii BC IBouthrot 1, 10 (s. Ἀπολλόδωρος)
ILLYRIA:
—EPIDAMNOS-DYRRHACHION: (**17**) iii BC IDyrrh 19 (f. Φιλωτία)
KORINTHIA:
—KORINTH: (**18**) c. 337-335 BC CID II 56 III, [5]?, 15; 63, [11]; cf. p. 90
MESSENIA:
—MESSENE: (**19**) c. 220 BC SEG XXXVIII 339; cf. PAE 1971, p. 166 nos. 6-7; (**20**) 31 BC-14 AD SEG XXIII 207, 12; PAE 1992, p. 71 A, 1 (f. Κράτων); (**21**) 33 AD SEG XLI 335, 4 (f. Ἄρης)
S. ITALY (BRUTTIUM):
—LOKROI EPIZEPHYRIOI:
——(Δυσ.): (**22**) iv/iii BC De Franciscis 11, 1
——(Τυν.): (**23**) iv/iii BC ib. 18, 2 (f. Ἀρχιππος)
—RHEGION: (**24**) s. iv BC IG IV (1)² 95, 47 + Peek, IAEpid 41, 47 (name) (Perlman E.2); Perlman pp. 46-9 (date) (Ἀλκέδαμος—IG and Perlman: s. Ἱππίων); (**25**) hell. IG XIV 2400. 1 (tile)
SICILY:
—AKRAGAS: (**26**) f. v BC Dubois, IGDS 180 b, 1 (Arena, Iscr. Sic. II 90)
—AKRAI: (**27**) ?iii BC SGDI 3245, 4 (Akrai p. 158 no. 10; IGLMP 31) (Ἀρχέδαμ[ος]: ?s. Νυμφόδωρος); (**28**) ii-i BC SGDI 3246, 36 (Akrai pp. 152-3 no. 2; Dubois, IGDS 109) (s. Φίλων)
——(Καννεύς): (**29**) ii-i BC SGDI 3246, 40 (Akrai pp. 152-3 no. 2; Dubois, IGDS 109) (I f. Ἀρχέδαμος II); (**30**) ~ SGDI 3246, 40 (Akrai pp. 152-3 no. 2; Dubois, IGDS 109) (II s. Ἀρχέδαμος I)
—ERGETION: (**31**) f. ii BC BCH 45 (1921) p. 25 IV, 107 (SEG XXII 455); cf. Sic. Gymn. 17 (1964) pp. 47 f.
—KAMARINA: (**32**) m. v BC Dubois, IGDS 120, 1 (Arena, Iscr. Sic. II 142 A; SEG XXXVIII 939; Cordano, 'Camarina VII' 12) (f. Ἐ—εἴδας)
—SELINOUS: (**33**) ?c. 525-500 BC Dubois, IGDS 67 (Arena, Iscr. Sic. I 33; GVI 1670); LSAG² p. 277 no. 33 (date) (Ἀρχέδ[α]μος: s. Πυθέας); (**34**) vi/v BC Dubois, IGDS 82; cf. LSAG² p. 277 no. 34
—SYRACUSE: (**35**) iii BC IG IX (2) 370 (-δημος)

—ZANKLE-MESSANA: (36) ?ii BC ib. XIV 401, 11 (f. Ἀπολλόδωρος)

**Ἀρχεθάλης**
SICILY:
—KAMARINA: (1) m. v BC Dubois, *IGDS* 120, 2 (Arena, *Iscr. Sic.* II 142 A; *SEG* XXXVIII 939; Cordano, 'Camarina VII' 13) (Ἀ[ρχ]εθάλες?: s. Χίρων)

**Ἀρχεκράτης**
ARGOLIS:
—ARGOS: (1) ?c. 460-450 BC *SEG* XVI 244, 3 (Lazzarini 939); *LSAG²* p. 170 no. 36 (date) ([Ἀ]ρχεκράτες); (2) f. iii BC *IG* IV (1) 529, 12 (Ἀρχεκρ[άτης])

**Ἀρχελάα**
ELIS:
—OLYMPIA*: (1) ?iv BC *IvOl* 844 (Ἀρ[χ]ελάα)

**Ἀρχελαΐδας**
ARGOLIS:
—EPIDAUROS: (1) c. 365-335 BC *IG* IV (1)² 103, 146
KERKYRA: (2) ii BC ib. IX (1) 901
LAKONIA:
—SPARTA: (3) ?397 BC *Hell. Oxy.* ix 2; fr. 2? (Poralla² 146) (Ἀρχελ[αΐδας]—fr. 2)

**Ἀρχελαΐς**
AKARNANIA:
—OINIADAI: (1) iii/ii BC *IG* IX (1)² (2) 419. 2
LAKONIA:
—SPARTA: (2) byz. ib. V (1) 822 (Bradford (-)) (-λαεΐς)

**Ἀρχέλαος**
ACHAIA:
—AIGION: (1) ?228-215 BC *SGDI* 2525, 7 (f. Κλεόμαχος)
—DYME: (2) iv BC *FGrH* 115 F 194; (3) ii/i BC *Achaean Grave Stelai* 55 (Ἀρχέδαος—lap.: s. Σωσίστρατος)
—PHARAI: (4) iv BC ib. 13; (5) ii BC ib. 66
AIGINA: (6) ?i BC *Alt-Ägina* I (2) p. 45 no. 13 (Ἀρχέλ[αος])
AITOLIA: (7) s. iii BC *IG* IX (1)² (1) 27, 5; cf. *SEG* XXXVI 532 (or Lokris (Opuntian) Opous); (8) m. ii BC *IG* IX (1)² (3) 681, 3
—KONOPE-ARSINOE: (9) 263 BC ib. IX (1)² (1) 17, 57
—KONOPE-ARSINOE?: (10) 184 BC ib. 131, 16 (Ἀρχέλ[αος])
AKARNANIA: (11) 197 BC *RE* Supplbd. 11 (10a) (Lat. Archelaus)
ARGOLIS:
—EPIDAUROS: (12) ii BC *IG* IV (1)² 246, 2 (Ἀρχέλα[ος]: f. Εὔνομος)
DALMATIA:
—ISSA:
——(Dymanes): (13) iv/iii BC Brunšmid p. 7, 19 ([Ἀρ]χ[έ]λαος: s. Μεσόδαμος)
ELIS: (14) a. 85-93 AD *IvOl* 86, 2 (Ἀρχέλ[αος]: f. Ἀρτέμων); (15) 245-249 AD ib. 121, 5 (I f. Τ. Φλ. Ἀρχέλαος II); (16) 245-265 AD ib. l. 5, 21; 122, 4, 8, 18; 483, 3; 484, 3; 485, 4; 515, [2]?; cf. *PIR²* 213 (Τ. Φλ. Ἀ.: II s. Ἀρχέλαος I, f. Φλ. Ἀρχέλαος III, ?f. Σκίπας, Σωτηρίδας; (17) 265 AD *IvOl* 122, 8 (Φλ. Ἀ.: III s. Τ. Φλ. Ἀρχέλαος II)
EPIROS:
—BOUTHROTOS (PRASAIBOI): (18) a. 163 BC *IBouthrot* 18, 5 (*SEG* XXXVIII 475); (19) ~ *IBouthrot* 18, 6 (*SEG* XXXVIII 475); (20) ~ *IBouthrot* 101, 3 (s. Ἀρχίλλος)
——Bouthrotioi: (21) a. 163 BC ib. 92, 8; 93, 7; 105, 6 (f. Ἀρτέμων)
—POLICAN (MOD.): (22) hell.? *SEG* XXIV 473 (Ἀρχ[έλ]αος: f. Ξένυς)

ILLYRIA:
—AMANTIA: (23) ii-i BC Cabanes, *L'Épire* p. 562 no. 38 (*SEG* XXVI 723) (f. Ἀδύλος)
—APOLLONIA: (24) i BC Maier 133 (coin) (pryt.)
—BYLLIONES: (25) c. 200 BC *SEG* XXXV 680, 7; cf. XXXVIII 541 ([Ἀρ]χέλα[ος]: f. Νικάσιος)
—EPIDAMNOS-DYRRHACHION: (26) hell.-imp. *IDyrrh* 128 ([Ἀρ]χέλαος, [Ε]χέλαος?)
—OLYMPE: (27) s. iii BC *SEG* XXXV 697 (s. Ἀλέξανδρος)
LAKONIA:
—SPARTA: (28) ?ix/viii BC *RE* (5) (Poralla² 147) (s. Ἀγησίλαος, f. Τήλεκλος: king/dub.)
LEUKAS: (29) f. i BC *IG* IX (1) 534, 9 (*Iscr. Gr. Verona* p. 24) (f. Εὐφράνωρ)
S. ITALY (CAMPANIA):
—KYME: (30) 251 AD *CIL* X 3699 II, 4 (Lat. T. Flavius Archelaus)
—MISENUM*: (31) imp. *NScav* 1928, p. 196 no. 5 (Lat. Iulius Archelaus)

**Ἀρχέλαρ**
ELIS: (1) c. 85-93 AD *IvOl* 86, 5, 14 (s. Ἀρτέμων)

**Ἀρχέλας**
AKARNANIA:
—THYRREION: (1) ii BC *IG* IX (1)² (2) 318; Fraser-Rönne, *BWGT* pl. 24
S. ITALY (BRUTTIUM):
—LOKROI EPIZEPHYRIOI:
——(Ἀστ.): (2) iv/iii BC De Franciscis 33, 5 (s. Κλέανδρος)
——(Φαω.): (3) iv/iii BC ib. 15, 7 (s. Εὐθυμίσκος) ?= (4); (4) ~ ib. 29, 6 ?= (3)
SICILY:
—MORGANTINA: (5) iv/iii BC Dubois, *IGDS* 191 (s. Εὔκλείδας)

**Ἀρχέλοχος**
ARGOLIS:
—EPIDAUROS: (1) iv BC *IG* IV (1)² 317 (s. Ἐπίστρατος) ?= (7); (2) s. iv BC *SEG* XI 438 (s. Εὐεργίδας, ?s. Ἀρχενίκα); (3) c. 210-207 BC *IG* IV (1)² 73, 4; *SEG* XXXV 303 (date) (s. Τιμαΐδας); (4) f. ii BC *IG* IV (1)² 359 (Peek, *IAEpid* 153. 7); (5) 115 BC *IG* IV (1)² 63, 1, 10 (s. Ἀριστόφαντος); (6) 32 AD ib. 101, 3 (s. Σώδαμος)
——Politas: (7) c. 365-335 BC ib. 103, 71 ?= (1)
—PHLEIOUS: (8) ?s. v BC ib. IV (1) 451 (f. Συμάδας)

**Ἀρχέμανδρος**
ARGOLIS:
—EPIDAUROS: (1) iv BC Peek, *IAEpid* 162 ?= (2); (2) c. 335-325 BC ib. 50, 12, 17, 21 ?= (1)
—EPIDAUROS*: (3) c. 370-360 BC *BSA* 61 (1966) p. 273 no. 4 B III, 2; cf. Peek, *IAEpid* 48 (Ἀρχέμα[νδρος]); (4) c. 335-325 BC *IG* IV (1)² 106 I, 70 (Ἀρ[χέμ]ανδρ[ος])

**Ἀρχεμαχίδας**
ACHAIA:
—PELLENE: (1) 336-334 BC ib. VII 3055, 10 + *CID* II 102 I n. on l. 7; *JHS* 91 (1971) pp. 15 ff. (date) (s. Δαμέας); (2) 191-146 BC *SNG Cop. Phliasia–Laconia* 329; *Coll. McClean* 6414 (coin) (Ἀρχεμαχί[δας])
KORINTHIA:
—KORINTH: (3) a. 191 BC *SEG* XXVI 392, 8 (s. Φίλαιθος)

**Ἀρχέμαχος**
AITOLIA:
—TRICHONION: (1) ?c. 220 BC Flacelière p. 416 no. 51, 3
ARGOLIS:
—ARGOS: (2) iii BC *IG* IV (1) 527, 3; cf. *BCH* 37 (1913) p. 308 (?s. Ἀρχε—)
——Keramis: (3) iii BC *SEG* XIII 241, 8 (s. Σωφάνης)
—EPIDAUROS: (4) iii/ii BC *IG* IV (1)² 228, 4

KORINTHIA:
—KORINTH: (5) a. 191 BC *SEG* XXVI 392, 10 (s. Πειθίδαμος)
S. ITALY (CALABRIA):
—TARAS-TARENTUM: (6) vi BC Iamb., *VP* 267 (*FVS* 1 p. 446)

**Ἀρχέμβροτος**
KEPHALLENIA:
—SAME: (1) c. 230-200 BC *BCH* 45 (1921) p. 14 II, 136 (Ἀρ[χέ]μβροτο[s]: f. Καλλίλας)
LAKONIA:
—SPARTA: (2) f. vii BC *Suda T* 1205 (*IEG* 2 p. 149); cf. Stephanis 2443 (Poralla² 148) (f. Τυρταῖος)

**Ἀρχεμένης**
LEUKAS: (1) vi/v BC *AD* 24 (1969) Chron. p. 278 (Ἀρχεμέ[νēς])

**Ἀρχεναύτας**
KORINTHIA:
—KORINTH?: (1) vi/v BC Page, *FGE* 827 (-της)

**Ἀρχενίκα**
ARGOLIS:
—EPIDAUROS: (1) s. iv BC *SEG* XI 438 (?m. Ἀρχέλοχος)
ARKADIA:
—MEGALOPOLIS: (2) ?131 BC *IG* V (2) 440, 9 (d. Ξένανδρος, m. Φιλοκλῆς)

**Ἀρχένοος**
KORINTHIA:
—SIKYON: (1) vi/v BC *SEG* XI 244, 43

**Ἀρχένους**
ARGOLIS:
—ARGOS: (1) imp. *IG* IV (1) 589, 2 ([Ἀρ]χένους: s. Εὐκράτης, Καλλίστιον)

**Ἀρχέπολις**
AITOLIA:
—BOUKATION: (1) 190 BC ib. IX (1)² (1) 97, 6
ARGOLIS:
—HERMIONE: (2) iii-ii BC *SEG* XVII 172 (Ἀρχέπολις: f. Λυσίξενος)
ARKADIA: (3) iv BC *IG* V (2) p. xxii l. 9 (f. Κρίθων)
—TEGEA: (4) iii/ii BC ib. IV (1)² 318 (f. Λυσίξενος)

**Ἀρχεσίλας**
ARGOLIS:
—ARGOS: (1) ?c. 575-550 BC *SEG* XI 336, 6; *LSAG²* p. 168 no. 7 (date) (f. Χάρων)

**Ἀρχεστράτα**
ARGOLIS:
—EPIDAUROS: (1) iv BC *IG* IV (1)² 317

**Ἀρχέστρατος**
AIGINA: (1) f. v BC ib. IV (1) 65; *LSAG²* p. 113 no. 10 (date)
AKARNANIA:
—THYRREION: (2) m. ii BC *Syll³* 669, 8 (*IG* V (1) 29, 8) (f. Ἀρίστανδρος)
ARGOLIS:
—EPIDAUROS: (3) c. 315-280 BC *FD* III (1) 95, 2 (Ἀρχέσ[τρα]τος: f. Ναυκράτης); (4) c. 127-94 BC *IG* IV (1)² 591, 3 (Ἀρχέστρα[τος]: I f. Ἀρχέστρατος II); (5) ~ ib. l. 3 ([Ἀρχέσ]τρατος: II s. Ἀρχέστρατος I)
—EPIDAUROS*: (6) c. 370 BC ib. 102, 37
—TROIZEN: (7) iii BC ib. IV (1) 775 (s. Ἀριστόδαμος)
KORINTHIA:
—SIKYON: (8) ?315 BC *BCH* 62 (1938) pp. 343-4 no. 8, 3 (f. Σώστρατος)
S. ITALY (BRUTTIUM):
—LOKROI EPIZEPHYRIOI: (9) 476 BC Pi., *O.* x, 2, 99; xi, 11 (f. Ἀγησίδαμος)
SICILY:
—GELA-PHINTIAS: (10) iv BC *RE* (16); *Suppl. Hell.* pp. 46 ff. (or Sicily Syracuse)

—SELINOUS?: (11) vi/v BC SEG XXXIX 1020 B, 7 (s. Αἰσχίνας)

### Ἀρχέτιμος
ARKADIA: (1) ?253 BC Nachtergael, Les Galates 10, 26; cf. Stephanis 1900 (f. Ξεννίας)
KORINTHIA:
—KORINTH: (2) 435 BC Th. i 29. 2 (s. Εὐρύτιμος); (3) 343 BC CID II 31, 101
SICILY:
—GELA-PHINTIAS: (4) iv BC IG II² 8459 (f. Κλεοπάμων)
—SYRACUSE: (5) inc. D.L. i 40; (6) vii BC RE (4); (7) ?265-259 BC Nachtergael, Les Galates 4, 13; cf. Stephanis 1325 (f. Καλλίας)

### Ἀρχέτιος
SICILY:
—SELINOUS: (1) vi/v BC Arena, Iscr. Sic. I 58 (Ἀρχέτιος: s. Εὐκλῆς)

### Ἀρχεύς
AIGINA: (1) c. 425-400 BC Ag. XVII 392 (?s. Ἀλ—)
ARGOLIS:
—HERMIONE: (2) m. iv BC Unp. (Ch. Kritzas) (s. Δαμόκριτος)

### Ἀρχεφῶν
EPIROS:
—DODONA*: (1) iii BC Cabanes, L'Épire p. 550 no. 23; cf. L'Illyrie mérid. 2 p. 64

### Ἀρχέψιος
ARKADIA:
—MEGALOPOLIS: (1) 369-361 BC IG v (2) 1, 26; Tod, GHI II 132 (date)

### Ἀρχη
S. ITALY (APULIA):
—ARGYRIPPA-ARPI*: (1) imp. CIL IX 934 (Lat. Arche: ?d. Εὔανθος: freed.)
S. ITALY (CAMPANIA):
—NOLA: (2) imp. ib. X 1267 (Lat. Caesia Arche)

### Ἀρχήν
EPIROS:
—BOUTHROTOS (PRASAIBOI):
——Bouthrotioi: (1) f. ii BC IBouthrot 1, 5, 8 (s. Ἀρχιάδας)
ILLYRIA:
—APOLLONIA: (2) c. 250-50 BC Maier 25; 26; 27 (coin) (Ceka 57; 61; 76) (pryt.); (3) ~ Maier 58 (coin) (Ceka 30) (money.); (4) i BC Maier 127 (coin) (s. Ὀλυμπιόδωρος: money.); (5) ~ ib. 134 (coin) (pryt.); (6) imp. IApoll 207 (f. Λεοντίων)
—EPIDAMNOS-DYRRHACHION: (7) hell. IDyrrh 22; (8) c. 250-50 BC Maier 142-3; Bakërr Hoard p. 66 nos. 40-41 (coin) (Ceka 4; 270) (pryt.); (9) hell.-imp. IDyrrh 129 (s. Νικήρατος); (10) ~ ib. 443 (f. Φιλώ); (11) ~ ib. 446 (f. Φίλων)

### Ἀρχιάδας
ELIS: (1) i BC-i AD IvOl 218 (f. Τιμόλας); (2) ~ ib. (Moretti, Olymp. 741) (s. Τιμόλας) ?= (3); (3) 36-24 BC IvOl 62, 2, 20 (Ἀρχιάδ[ας]: ?f. Ἀγαθήμερος: Δ.) ?= (2)
EPIROS:
—AMBRAKIA: (4) 238-168 BC Schlosser 30 (coin)
—BOUTHROTOS (PRASAIBOI):
——Bouthrotioi: (5) f. ii BC IBouthrot 1, 5 (f. Ἀρχήν)
LAKONIA:
—SPARTA: (6) ?m. ii BC IG v (1) 887 (Bradford (2)); (7) ?i AD IG v (1) 180, 13 (Bradford (5)); (8) c. 90-100 AD IG v (1) 80, 4; SEG XI 558, 1; 559, 7 (Bradford (6)) (f. Δαμέας); (9) c. 110-115 AD SEG XI 540, 4 (Bradford (7)) (f. Νεόλας); (10) s. ii AD IG v (1) 331 (Artemis


Orthia p. 337 no. 75; Bradford (3)) (-δαρ: s. —δας); (11) ~ IG v (1) 473, 3; BSA 81 (1986) p. 324 no. 2 (ident.) (Bradford (1)) (s. Νεόλας); (12) 359 AD SEG XI 464, 4 (Bradford (4))
SICILY:
—TYNDARIS: (13) ?ii AD IGUR 823 (Ἀρχι(ά)δ[ας]: f. Ξένων)

### Ἀρχιάναξ
SICILY:
—LIPARA: (1) ?iii BC NScav 1929, p. 71 fig. 30; p. 78

### Ἀρχίας
ACHAIA:
—BOURA: (1) iv BC Tz., Chil. vi 176, 182 (fict.?)
—DYME: (2) iii BC AJPh 31 (1910) p. 399 no. 74 a, 3 (f. Ἀλεξίμαχος)
AIGINA: (3) ?253 BC Nachtergael, Les Galates 10, 56 (Stephanis 438)
AITOLIA: (4) iii BC ITrall I 33 B, 1 (f. Νίκων)
—KONOPE-ARSINOE: (5) hell. SBBerlAk 1936, p. 364 no. 7 e (tile) ([Ἀ]ρχίας)
AKARNANIA: (6) ?204 BC IG VII 303, 62 (Petrakos, Oropos pp. 188-91 no. 45; IOrop 324)
ARGOLIS:
—ARGOS: (7) iv-iii BC Unp. (Ch. Kritzas); (8) ?316 BC IG v (2) 549, 27 (f. Ἀρχέδαμος); (9) a. 303 BC CEG II 816, 8; (10) iii-ii BC BCH 27 (1903) pp. 264-5 no. 12 (Ἀρχία[ς]); (11) c. 295-288 BC IG VII 2, 5 (f. Ἀγάθων)
—EPIDAUROS: (12) iv/iii BC ib. IV (1)² 728; (13) ~ Peek, NIEpid 40 ([Ἀ]ρχίας)
——Koleis: (14) c. 365-335 BC IG IV (1)² 103, 140
—EPIDAUROS*: (15) c. 370-365 BC Peek, IAEpid 52 A, 27; 52 B, 56; (16) c. 340-330 BC SEG XXV 387 A, 18; (17) iv/iii BC Peek, NIEpid 20, 31 (SEG XXV 404, 27)
ARKADIA: (18) iv/iii BC D.L. iv 38
—KLEITOR: (19) imp. IG v (2) 371 (s. Φίλιππος)
—MANTINEIA-ANTIGONEIA: (20) c. 300-221 BC ib. 323. 56 (tessera) (s. Ἡρωίδας)
ELIS: (21) m. iv BC IvOl 44, 9; (22) m. iii BC IG v (2) 368, 133 (s. Φιλλίας); (23) ~ ib. l. 134
EPIROS:
—AMBRAKIA: (24) hell.? SEG XXIV 416 (-χεί-: f. Κλεώ)
—BOUTHROTOS (PRASAIBOI): (25) iii/ii BC IBouthrot 2, 3; 3, 3; 4, 3 (f. Ἀριστοτέλης) ?= (27); (26) a. 163 BC ib. 38, 10 (SEG XXXVIII 497); (27) ~ IBouthrot 101, 1 (f. Ἀριστοτέλης) ?= (25); (28) ~ ib. 117, 11 ?= (29)
——Essyrioi: (29) f. ii BC ib. 2, 6; 3, 6; 4, 5; 13, [6?]; cf. Ugolini, Alb. Ant. 3 p. 120; IBouthrot 54, 6; 58, 3; 59, [3], 6; 64 (SEG XXXVIII 505; 515; 509; 510); IBouthrot 69, 16; 70, 12, 71, 10 (BCH 118 (1994) p. 129 B 1-3); IBouthrot 102, 4; 105, 6 (s. Γλαυκίας) ?= (28)
—KHOSEPSI (MOD.): (30) imp. SEG XXIV 415 (Π. Ρόβριος Ἀ.: f. Θραικίδας, Τερτία)
—PRASAIBOI: (31) a. 163 BC IBouthrot 9, 5 (SEG XXXVIII 489) (f. Ἀντίπατρος)
KERKYRA: (32) ii/i BC IG IX (1) 756; Korkyra I p. 167 no. 6 (tiles)
KORINTHIA:
—KORINTH: (33) s. viii BC RE (2); Plu., Mor. 773 B (and Sicily Syracuse: s. Εὐάγητος, ?f. Ὀρτυγία (Syracuse), Συράκουσα (Syracuse), Κόσσα: oikist); (34) iii BC RE (23); FGrH 575 F 2
LAKONIA:
—GERONTHRAI: (35) c. 500 BC IG v (1) 1134, 8; LSAG² p. 201 no. 45 (date) (Poralla² 149)
—SPARTA:
——Pitana: (36) c. 525 BC Hdt. iii 55; Plu., Mor. 860 C (Poralla² 150) (Ἀρχίης—Hdt.: f. Σάμιος); (37) m. v BC Hdt. iii 55. 2 (Poralla² 151) (-ης: s. Σάμιος, ?f. Σάμιος)


S. ITALY (APULIA):
—VENUSIA: (38) ?ii BC Museo di Venosa p. 121 no. 39 with pl. 8 (vase) ([Ἀ]ρχίας)
S. ITALY (BRUTTIUM):
—KROTON: (39) s. vi BC JNG 33 (1983) p. 12 (coin graffito)
—SYBARIS-THOURIOI-COPIAE: (40) iv/iii BC RE (10); Supplbd. 10 (17b) (Stephanis 439)
S. ITALY (CAMPANIA):
—NEAPOLIS: (41) i BC IG XIV 776 (INap 106) (f. Δημήτριος)
S. ITALY (LUCANIA):
—HERAKLEIA: (42) iv/iii BC SEG XXX 1170; (43) c. 280 BC SNG Oxford 632; NC 1918, p. 141 no. 76 (van Keuren, Coinage of Heraclea p. 79 no. 96 (coins))
SICILY:
—HYBLA: (44) m. iv BC Moretti, Olymp. 422; 429; 435; Page, FGE 1552 (Stephanis 440) (s. Εὐκλῆς)
—KAMARINA: (45) m. v BC Dubois, IGDS 120 (Arena, Iscr. Sic. II 142 A; SEG XXXVIII 939, 5; Cordano, 'Camarina VII' 15) (f. Σωσίας); (46) 425 BC Th. iv 25. 7 (Cordano, 'Camarina VII' 14)
TRIPHYLIA:
—PYRGOI: (47) c. 230-200 BC BCH 45 (1921) p. 12 II, 84 (locn.—Oulhen)

### Ἀρχίβιος
ILLYRIA:
—APOLLONIA: (1) c. 250-50 BC Maier 28-30 (Ceka 25; 50; 95) (pryt.)
LEUKAS: (2) ii-iii AD RE (7) (or Egypt Alexandria: s. Πτολεμαῖος)
S. ITALY (CAMPANIA):
—MISENUM*: (3) m. ii AD Puteoli 11 (1987) p. 137 no. 5 (Lat. L. Archibius Magnus)

### Ἀρχιδάμεια
LAKONIA:
—AIGILA*: (1) m. vii BC Paus. iv 17. 1 (Poralla² 152) (dub.)
—SPARTA: (2) c. 310-241 BC Plu., Pyrrh. 27; Agis 4; 20; Polyaen. viii 47 (Bradford (-)) (-μια, Ἀρχίδαμις—Polyaen.: m. Ἀγησιστράτα, ?m. Ἀγησίλαος, Ἀρχίδαμος)

### Ἀρχιδαμίδας
LAKONIA:
—SPARTA: (1) ?vi/v BC Plu., Lyc. 20; Mor. 218 B (Poralla² 153)

### Ἀρχίδαμος
AITOLIA:
—CHOLEOI: (1) f. iii BC IG IX (1)² (1) 9, 10 (Ἀρ[χί]δαμος)
—KALLION/KALLIPOLIS: (2) 225-205 BC FD III (3) 220, 5
—PLEURON: (3) s. iii BC IG IX (1)² (1) 57 ?= (4); (4) 220 BC RE (7); Plb. iv 57. 7; 58. 9; cf. IG IX (1)² (1) p. LI, s.a. 186 BC, 180 BC, 174 BC (s. Πανταλέων, ?f. Πανταλέων) ?= (3)
AITOLIA?: (5) 165 BC ZPE 101 (1994) p. 128, 7
ARGOLIS:
—EPIDAUROS: (6) iv/iii BC Peek, IAEpid 142. 6; 142. 7 (s. Ἐργῖλος, f. Ἐργῖλος); (7) ~ SEG XIV 328 (f. Φιλικός)
ARKADIA:
—HERAIA: (8) iii BC IG v (2) 415, 10 (IPArk 23) (Ἀρχ[ί]δαμος: s. Τιμάνωρ)
—MEGALOPOLIS: (9) iii BC SEG XXIII 226 = PAE 1988, p. 59 no. α (s. Ἀρίστανδρος: sculptor)
ELIS: (10) m. iv BC X., HG vii 1. 33, 38; (11) 296 BC Moretti, Olymp. 522
EPIROS:
—BOUTHROTOS (PRASAIBOI): (12) a. 163 BC IBouthrot 28, 35; 29, 37; 36, 16 (SEG XXXVIII 486; 487; 495) ?= (13); (13) ~ IBouthrot 114, 6; 116, 6 (BCH 118 (1994) p. 121 A) ?= (15) (12); (14) ~ IBouthrot 132, 8; (15) ~ ib. 139, 6 (f. Ἀλεξάνωρ) ?= (13)

——Bouthrotioi: (16) a. 163 BC ib. l. 10 (f. Θύρμαξ)

KORINTHIA:
—KORINTH: (17) ?iii BC IG II² 9060 (s. Σωτέλης)

LAKONIA:
—SPARTA: (18) viii/vii BC Paus. iii 7. 5 (Poralla² 155) (s. Θεόπομπος, f. Ζευξίδαμος: king/dub.); (19) f. vii BC Hdt. viii 131. 2 (Poralla² 154) (-δη-: s. Ἀναξανδρίδας, f. Ἀναξίλας: king); (20) ?m. vii BC Hdt. viii 131. 2 (Poralla² 154) (-δη-); (21) s. vii BC Paus. iii 7. 6 (Poralla² 156) (s. Ἀναξίδαμος, f. Ἀγησικλῆς, Ἀναξίλας: king/dub.); (22) c. 490-427 BC RE (3) (Poralla² 157) (s. Ζευξίδαμος ὁ ἐπικαλ. Κυνίσκος, f. Ἀγις, Ἀγησίλαος, Κυνίσκα: king); (23) c. 400-338 BC RE (4) (Poralla² 158) (s. Ἀγησίλαος, Κλεόρα, f. Εὐδαμίδας, Ἀγις, Ἀγησίλαος: king); (24) iv/iii BC Plu., Agis 3; Dem. 35 (Bradford (2)) (s. Εὐδαμίδας, ?s. Ἀρχιδάμεια, f. Εὐδαμίδας: king); (25) m. iii BC RE (6) (Bradford (3)) (s. Εὐδαμίδας, Ἀγησιστράτα: king?); (26) c. 25-1 BC IG V (1) 210, 19 (Bradford (1)) (s. Ἀγαθοκλῆς)

## Ἀρχιδώ
MESSENIA:
—ASINE: (1) ii AD IG V (1) 1414 (d. Χρύσιππος)

## Ἀρχικλείδας
ARGOLIS:
—PHLEIOUS: (1) iii BC ib. IV (1) 462 (f. Θωμάντα)

## Ἀρχικλῆς
ARKADIA:
—MEGALOPOLIS: (1) ii BC ib. V (2) 536 (f. Ἀμετέρα)
KORINTHIA:
—KORINTH: (2) c. 370 BC ib. IV (1)² 102, 16
LAKONIA:
—SPARTA: (3) ?i BC BSA 15 (1908-9) p. 113
SICILY:
—NAXOS: (4) vi/v BC Arena, Iscr. Sic. III 73 (vase) (Ἀρχ(ι)κλῆς)
ZAKYNTHOS: (5) hell. IG IX (1) 600 (f. Ἀλκιδάμα); (6) ~ ib. (s. Ἀριστομένης, f. Κληνίππα)

## Ἀρχικράτης
ACHAIA: (1) 146 BC Plb. xxxviii 17. 9
—PATRAI: (2) c. 146-32 BC BMC Pelop. p. 23 no. 7; Mionnet 2 p. 191 no. 320 (coin) (s. Δικαίαρχος)
ARGOLIS:
—EPIDAUROS*: (3) c. 370-360 BC Peek, IAEpid 52 A, 6; BSA 61 (1966) p. 271 no. 4 A, 19
—TROIZEN: (4) iii BC IG IV (1) 825, 3

## Ἀρχιλέων
ARGOLIS:
—EPIDAUROS: (1) iii BC ib. IV (1)² 348 (f. Τείσις)

## Ἄρχιλλος
ARGOLIS:
—HERMIONE: (1) ?ii-i BC ib. IV (1) 733, 4 (s. Ἀμ—)
EPIROS:
—BOUTHROTOS (PRASAIBOI): (2) a. 163 BC IBouthrot 101, 3 (s. Φιλόδαμος, f. Φιλόδαμος, Ἀρχέλαος)
KORINTHIA:
—KORINTH: (3) s. iv BC Corinth VIII (1) 11, 5 (f. Ἀρχιτέλης); (4) ?262 or 258 BC Nachtergael, Les Galates 5, 7 + BCH 101 (1977) p. 335; (5) s. iii BC FD III (4) 365, 1 + BCH 101 (1977) p. 335 (Ἀγ[υ]λλος—FD)
MESSENIA:
—MESSENE?: (6) ii/i BC SEG XI 979, 30

## Ἄρχιλος
ARGOLIS:
—EPIDAUROS: (1) iv BC IG IV (1)² 183

## Ἀρχιλοχίδας
LAKONIA: (1) c. 550 BC Cl. Rh. 8 pp. 85 ff. with pl. 4; LSAG² p. 199 no. 16a

## Ἀρχίλοχος
ARGOLIS:
—EPIDAUROS: (1) 138 AD Peek, IAEpid 230, 5; Peek, NIEpid 83, 2 (Τιβ. Κοΐντος Ἀ.)
KERKYRA: (2) 544 BC Moretti, Olymp. 111

## Ἀρχιμήδης
ACHAIA:
—PELLENE: (1) c. 210-207 BC IG IV (1)² 73, 15; SEG XXXV 303 (date) (f. Αἰσχύλος)
ARGOLIS:
—EPIDAUROS: (2) 184-207 AD IG IV (1)² 393, 2, 6; 400, 4 (s. Ἴλαρος, f. Ἴλαρος)
ILLYRIA:
—EPIDAMNOS-DYRRHACHION: (3) c. 250-50 BC Maier 191; 285; 321; 339; 379; 395 (Ceka 98-105); cf. IApoll Ref. Bibl. n. 32 (coin) (money.)
KERKYRA: (4) i BC-i AD? IG IX (1) 727 (f. Μνασίλας); (5) i BC-i AD ib. 902
SICILY:
—SYRACUSE: (6) c. 287-212 BC RE (3) + Supplbd. 3 (PP 16528) (s. Φειδίας)

## Ἀρχίμυθος
S. ITALY (CALABRIA):
—TARAS-TARENTUM?: (1) c. 315-280 BC FD III (1) 132 + SEG XXIII 306 (s. Κλέανδρος)

## Ἀρχινίδας
SICILY:
—SELINOUS: (1) m. v BC Dubois, IGDS 68 (Arena, Iscr. Sic. I 32; IGLMP 95) (f. Εὐρυφῶν)

## Ἀρχίνικος
ARKADIA:
—PHIGALEIA: (1) iii BC IG V (2) 427 (Ἀρχίνικο[ς])
S. ITALY (CALABRIA):
—TARAS-TARENTUM: (2) hell.? ib. XIV 2406. 86 (Ἀρχίνικ(ος): ?f. Φειδίας)

## Ἄρχιννυς
EPIROS:
—VOTONOSI (MOD.): (1) f. iii BC SEG XXIV 461 (f. Φερένικος)

## Ἀρχίνομος
SICILY:
—AKRAGAS: (1) vi/v BC D.L. viii 53; Suda E 1002; cf. Bidez, Biographie d'Empédocle p. 55 (?f. Ἐμπεδοκλῆς, Καλλικρατίδας: fict.)

## Ἄρχινος
ACHAIA:
—DYME: (1) s. iii BC SEG XIII 278, 20 (s. Σατυρίων)
ARGOLIS:
—ARGOS: (2) ?f. iii BC Polyaen. iii 8; Schol. Pi., O. vii, 152d (king/tyrant)
—EPIDAUROS*: (3) c. 335-325 BC IG IV (1)² 108, 112 (Ἀρχ[ῖ]νος)
—HERMIONE: (4) ?ii-i BC ib. IV (1) 731 III, 10 (-χεῖ-: f. Τρύφαινα)
ARKADIA:
—MEGALOPOLIS: (5) hell. BCH 84 (1960) p. 695 (tile); (6) ?iii-ii BC IG V (2) 469 (12-13) (tile)
EPIROS:
—AMBRAKIA: (7) vi BC RE (1)
—KELAITHOI: (8) c. 230-200 BC BCH 45 (1921) p. 16 III, 28 (f. Νικόλαος: reading—Oulhen)

## Ἄρχιον
KORINTHIA:
—SIKYON: (1) hell. IG II² 10294

LAKONIA: (2) hell. ib. XII (9) 794 (Bradford (-))

## Ἀρχίππα
ARGOLIS:
—ARGOS:
——(Paionidai): (1) iii BC IG IV (1) 527, 17; cf. BCH 37 (1913) p. 309 ([Ἀρ]χίππα)
—HERMIONE: (2) ii-i BC IG IV (1) 732 I, 13 (m. Διονύσιος); (3) i BC-i AD? ib. 734, 10 (Ἀρ[χ]ίππα: d. Σ—)
MESSENIA:
—ABIA: (4) ?i/ii AD ib. V (1) 1358, 3 (d. Ἀριστέας)

## Ἄρχιππος
ACHAIA: (1) 146 BC Plb. xxxviii 18. 4
—AIGION: (2) 191-146 BC BM coin 1926 2-4-9; SNG Fitz. Macedonia–Acarnania 3658 (coin) (Ἀρχιπ[πος])
ARGOLIS:
—ARGOS: (3) 327-324 BC CID II 97, 33; 99 A, 6; 102 II B, [30]; 120 A, 5 (f. Δαΐμαχος); (4) f. iii BC ib. 121 II, 15 (f. Θιόκριτος); (5) iii/ii BC IG IV (1) 580 (Ἀρχιππ[ος]: f. Δεξίστρατος); (6) 195 BC Liv. xxxiv 40. 6 (Lat. Archippus)
—HERMIONE: (7) iii BC IG IV (1) 697 (Λάρχιππος—apogr.)
—KALAURIA: (8) iii BC ib. 850, 1
—KLEONAI: (9) c. 230-200 BC BCH 45 (1921) p. 15 II, 147 (f. Μέντωρ)
ARKADIA:
—MANTINEIA-ANTIGONEIA: (10) 359 BC CID II 5 I, 4; (11) i BC IG V (2) 332
—PHIGALEIA: (12) s. i BC IvOl 402 (s. Ἀγαλλῆς, f. Φιλόθηρος)
—TEGEA: (13) iv/iii BC IG V (2) 38, 71; (14) 165 AD ib. 50, 56 (s. Εὐτυχᾶς)
——(Krariotai): (15) s. iv BC ib. 41, 53 (Ἀρχιππ[ος]: f. —τόνικος)
ELIS: (16) m. iii BC ib. 368, 132 (f. Ἄρχων)
ILLYRIA:
—EPIDAMNOS-DYRRHACHION: (17) c. 250-50 BC Maier 144 (coin) (Ceka 318) (pryt.)
LAKONIA: (18) ?i AD IG V (1) 1360, 7
—SPARTA: (19) c. 143 BC ib. IX (1)² (1) 137, 31 (Bradford (2)) (s. Ἁρμ—); (20) ?i BC IG V (1) 611 (Bradford (9)) (Ἀρχιπ[πος]: f. Ἱππ—); (21) s. i BC IG V (1) 96, 5 (Bradford (3)) (s. Νικ—); (22) ~ IG V (1) 899 a-b (tiles) (Bradford (5)); (23) c. 30-20 BC IG V (1) 211, 36 (Bradford (8)) (f. Ἱέραρχος); (24) c. 25-1 BC IG V (1) 50, 25; 95, 19; 127, 7 (Bradford (4)) (s. Φιλωνυμίδας); (25) c. 90-100 AD SEG XI 570, 7 (Bradford (7)) (f. Εὔδαμος); (26) c. 95-105 AD SEG XI 562, 7 (Bradford (11)); (27) c. 100-120 AD SEG XI 610, 6 (Bradford (10)) (f. Καλλικράτης); (28) c. 120 AD SEG XI 545, 2 (Bradford (6))
MESSENIA:
—ABIA: (29) ii BC IG V (1) 1351 (f. Ἀγέας)
—MESSENE: (30) c. 223 BC ib. IX (1)² (1) 31, 35 (s. Ἀρχίων)
PELOPONNESE: (31) c. 192 BC SEG XIII 327, 21 (s. Ἀριστ—)
S. ITALY (BRUTTIUM):
—LOKROI EPIZEPHYRIOI:
——(Ἀστ.): (32) iv/iii BC De Franciscis 20, 9 (s. Ἀριστοκλείδας)
——(Κοβ.): (33) iv/iii BC ib. 34, 12
——(Πυρ.): (34) iv/iii BC ib. 12, 3 (s. Ὀναῖος)
——(Στρ.): (35) iv/iii BC ib. 3, 5 (s. Εὐκέλαδος)
——(Τυν.): (36) iv/iii BC ib. 18, 2 (s. Ἀρχέδαμος)
S. ITALY (CALABRIA):
—TARAS-TARENTUM: (37) v/iv BC RE (12); FVS 46
S. ITALY (CAMPANIA):
—NEAPOLIS: (38) i BC INap 101; cf. Leiwo p. 83 no. 29 (f. Βίβιος)
SICILY:
—SYRACUSE: (39) 266 BC IG XII (9) 1187, 15; Robert, Ét. Num. Gr. pp. 179 ff. (date) (s. Εὔξενος)
—TAUROMENION: (40) c. 224 BC IG XIV 421 an. 17 (SGDI 5219) (s. Εὔανδρος)

## Ἀρχίς
ARGOLIS:
—ARGOS: (1) iv-iii BC Mitsos p. 48 s.v. Ἀρχίς 1; (2) ii-i BC IG IV (1) 530, 9; cf. BCH 33 (1909) p. 183 n. 2 (slave/freed.)
KORINTHIA:
—KORINTH: (3) iv-iii BC SEG XXII 237 c (loom-weight)
LEUKAS: (4) iii/ii BC ib. XXVII 174

## Ἀρχίστας
LAKONIA:
—SPARTA: (1) 403-399 BC ID 87 b, 12 (Poralla² 159)

## Ἀρχίστρατος
ARGOLIS:
—ARGOS:
——(Lykophronidai): (1) c. 450 BC ML 42 B, 45

## Ἀρχίτας
LAKONIA:
—SPARTA: (1) c. 30-20 BC IG V (1) 211, 45 (Bradford (-)) (s. Ἀριστοκλῆς)

## Ἀρχιτέλης
ACHAIA:
—PATRAI: (1) hell.? SGDI 1628 (f. Στρατοκλῆς)
ARGOLIS:
—ARGOS: (2) ?c. 460-450 BC IG IV (1)² 139 (Lazzarini 76); LSAG² p. 170 no. 38 (date) (Ἀρχιτέλη[s]: f. Θιαῖος); (3) a. 303 BC CEG II 816, 19; (4) ii-i BC Mnem. NS 47 (1919) p. 164 no. 9, 3
—EPIDAUROS: (5) c. 335-325 BC IG IV (1)² 108, 156, 160, 167 ?= (6); (6) c. 290-270 BC SEG XXV 400, 22 ?= (5)
—EPIDAUROS*: (7) c. 370-360 BC BSA 61 (1966) p. 272 no. 4 B I, 5 + Peek, IAEpid 48 (Ἀρχιτέλ[ης])
DALMATIA:
—ISSA: (8) iii BC Brunšmid p. 9 fr. H, 7 (Ἀρχιτ[έλης], Ἀρχίτ[ιμος]?: f. Εὐάγορος)
ILLYRIA:
—EPIDAMNOS-DYRRHACHION: (9) hell.-imp. IDyrrh 255 (f. Ἵππων)
KORINTHIA:
—KORINTH: (10) f. v BC FGrH 115 F 193; (11) s. iv BC Corinth VIII (1) 11, 5 (s. Ἀρχίλλος); (12) ii BC BGU 1222, 12
LAKONIA:
—SPARTA: (13) s. i BC IG V (1) 133, 3 (Bradford (-)) (f. Πρατόνικος)
MESSENIA:
—ABIA: (14) ii AD GVI 1555 (f. Θεοφάνης, Ἱλαρος)

## Ἀρχιφάης
AKARNANIA?: (1) iv/iii BC IG IX (1)² (2) 576; cf. Arch. Class. 25-6 (1973-4) p. 273 (or Thessaly Eretria?: Ἀρχιφάω (gen.))
ARKADIA:
—ORCHOMENOS: (2) f. iii BC BCH 38 (1914) p. 461 no. 5, 5

## Ἀρχίων
MESSENIA:
—MESSENE: (1) c. 223 BC IG IX (1)² (1) 31, 35 (f. Ἀρχιππος)

## Ἀρχόι
MESSENIA:
—MESSENE: (1) iii/ii BC ib. V (1) 1442

## Ἀρχομενίδας
SICILY:
—SYRACUSE: (1) v BC Paus. v 23. 6 (f. Φίλιστος)

## Ἄρχος
ILLYRIA: (1) m. iii BC Thess. Mnem. 170 (f. Ῥόδων)

## Ἄρχυλις
SICILY:
—HENNA: (2) ?iii BC Arch. Class. 17 (1965) p. 188 (?s. Δαμάτριος)

## Ἀρχύλις
SICILY:
—LIPARA: (1) inc. Chiron 22 (1992) p. 386; (2) ~ ib.; (3) hell. Libertini, Isole Eolie p. 226 no. 52; (4) hell.-imp. Epigraphica 11 (1949) pp. 52-3 no. 2 (f. Ἡδυχρώ)

## Ἀρχυλίς
MESSENIA:
—MESSENE: (1) ii/i BC SEG XXIII 224 + PAE 1988, p. 59 ([Βακ]χυλίς—SEG, [Ἀ]ρχυλίς—PAE: d. Δαμάτριος, m. Εὔφορβος)

## Ἀρχυλίς
SICILY:
—SELINOUS: (1) s. v BC Dubois, IGDS 40, 1

## Ἄρχυλλος
ARKADIA:
—MANTINEIA-ANTIGONEIA:
——(Epalea): (1) m. iv BC IG V (2) 271, 4 (s. Γλαυκίδας)

## Ἀρχύλος
ACHAIA:
—AIGION: (1) c. 230-200 BC BCH 45 (1921) p. 11 II, 58 (f. Ἀριστόμαχος)
S. ITALY (BRUTTIUM):
—SYBARIS-THOURIOI-COPIAE: (2) 397 BC D.S. xiv 52. 5; 53. 4

## Ἀρχύτας
LAKONIA:
—SPARTA: (1) 405 BC X., HG ii 3. 10 (Poralla² 160)
S. ITALY (CALABRIA):
—TARAS-TARENTUM: (2) f. iv BC RE (3); FVS 47 (?s. Μνασαγόρας, Μνάσαρχος, Μνασαγέτας, Ἑστιαῖος)
SICILY:
—KENTORIPA: (3) i BC-i AD? IG XIV 576; Sic. Gymn. 16 (1963) pp. 53-4 (Ἀ. Σάντρα, Αὐχυταυ (gen.)—apogr.: s. Ἑστιόδωρος)

## Ἀρχώ
AITOLIA: (1) ii BC IG II² 7987
ARGOLIS:
—EPIDAUROS: (2) ii/i BC ib. IV (1)² 212 (d. Ἀστυλαίδας, Ἐχεκράτεια, ?m. Δαμοκλῆς, Ἀστυλαίδας)
EPIROS:
—BOUTHROTOS (PRASAIBOI): (3) a. 163 BC IBouthrot 22, 12 (SEG XXXVIII 479)
SICILY:
—LIPARA: (4) inc. Chiron 22 (1992) p. 386

## Ἄρχων
ACHAIA:
—AIGEIRA: (1) c. 187-169 BC RE (6); PP 14806; SGDI 1774, 1; IG IV (1)² 625 (s. Φιλοκλῆς)
ACHAIA?: (2) ?170-168 BC AM 33 (1908) p. 109 VI no. 1
ARGOLIS:
—HERMIONE: (3) ?ii-i BC IG IV (1) 731 I, 5 (s. Κλεομήδης)
ARKADIA:
—MEGALOPOLIS: (4) ?262-255 BC Nachtergael, Les Galates 5, [19]; 6, [2]; 8, 23; cf. Stephanis 1355 (f. Καλλισθένης)
ELIS: (5) m. iii BC IG V (2) 368, 132 (s. Ἀρχιππος)
LAKONIA:
—SPARTA: (6) c. 25-1 BC ib. V (1) 210, 22 (Bradford (2)) (f. Δαμάρης)
SICILY:
—LIPARA: (7) hell. Libertini, Isole Eolie p. 227 no. 56
—TERRAVECCHIA DI CUTI (MOD.): (8) s. v BC SEG XXVII 657, 1, 6-7, 10 (Dubois, IGDS

## Ἀρχωνίδας
EPIROS:
—DODONA*: (1) v BC SEG XV 385 (f. Ἀρχέβιος)
KORINTHIA:
—KORINTH: (2) iii-ii BC Hesp. 41 (1972) p. 204 no. 6 ([Ἀρ]χωνίδ[ας], [Ἐρ]χωνίδας)
—SIKYON: (3) 263 BC IG IX (1)² (1) 17, 80 (s. Εὐκλείδας)
LAKONIA:
—SPARTA: (4) c. 520 BC Ael., VH xii 8 (Poralla² 161)
SICILY: (5) ?v BC CGF p. 165 fr. 61; (6) 356 BC Plu., Dio 42 (-δης)
—AKRAI: (7) ii BC IGLMP 30, 3 (Akrai p. 155 no. 4) ([Ἀρ]χωνίδας)
—HELOROS: (8) ii-i BC Dubois, IGDS 100, 4 (f. Ἀρτέμων); (9) f. i BC Cic., In Verr. II iii 129; In Verr. II iv 59 (Lat. Archonidas)
—HERBITA: (10) c. 446-414 BC RE (1) (I ?f. Δήμων, Ἀρχωνίδας II: king); (11) v/iv BC ib. (2) (II ?s. Ἀρχωνίδας I) ?= (12)
—HERBITA?: (12) 385 BC IG I³ 228, [6], 21, 23, 25 (-δης) ?= (11)
—KAMARINA: (13) f. v BC Cordano, Tessere Pubbliche 5 (Arena, Iscr. Sic. II 127 A) (-χō-: f. Ἡρακλείδας); (14) ~ Cordano, Tessere Pubbliche 23 (Arena, Iscr. Sic. II 131 A) (-χō-: f. Σικανός); (15) m. v BC Dubois, IGDS 120, 4 (Arena, Iscr. Sic. II 142 A; SEG XXXVIII 939) (f. Σωσίας); (16) iv/iii BC Manganaro, PdelP forthcoming no. 2, 4 ([Ἀρχω]νίδας: f. Ξενικράτης)
—LIPARA: (17) i AD Epigraphica 3 (1941) p. 259 no. 14

## Ἀρωμάτιον
ILLYRIA:
—APOLLONIA: (1) imp. IApoll 261
LAKONIA:
—GYTHEION: (2) 41 AD SEG XIII 258, 60, 61 (Φαινί[α] Ἀ(ρ)ωμάτιον)

## Ἀσάλατος
ARKADIA:
—PALLANTION: (1) 359 BC CID II 5 I, 21

## Ἀσάμων
ELIS: (1) ii BC Moretti, Olymp. 452; SEG XXXIII 329; XXXVII 361 (date) (s. Ἵππαρχος)

## Ἄσανδρος
EPIROS:
—MOLOSSOI: (1) iv/iii BC Unp. (Arta Mus., inscr.) (f. Δόκιμος)
—VOTONOSI (MOD.): (2) ?f. iii BC SEG XXIV 459 (s. Πολύνικος)
MESSENIA:
—THOURIA: (3) ii-i BC IG V (1) 1385, 26 (f. Σώταιρος)

## Ἄσαρος
SICILY:
—KAMARINA: (1) f. v BC Cordano, Tessere Pubbliche 26 (f. Εὐκλήτας)

## Ἄσβεστος
S. ITALY (APULIA):
—CANUSIUM: (1) ii-iii AD Epig. Rom. di Canosa 53 (Lat. Asbestus)
—CANUSIUM*: (2) ii-iii AD ib. (Lat. L. Annius Asbestus: freed.)
—LUCERIA*: (3) imp. ASP 34 (1981) p. 17 no. 18 (Lat. Asbestus: freed.)
S. ITALY (CAMPANIA):
—ATELLA*: (4) imp. CIL X 3750 (Lat. A. Plautius Asbestus: freed.)
—HERCULANEUM*: (5) i BC-i AD ib. 1403 l II, 9; cf. Cron. Erc. 7 (1977) p. 116 c, 9 (Lat. T. Quinctius Asbestus: freed.)
—POMPEII: (6) i BC-i AD CIL IV 2222 (Lat. Asbestus); (7) ~ ib. 761-3 (Lat. Asbestus)

## Ἀσέας
ARGOLIS:
—EPIDAUROS*: (1) c. 365-335 BC *IG* IV (1)²
103, 55

## Ἀσελλα
S. ITALY (APULIA):
—VENUSIA: (1) v AD *JIWE* I 77 (*CIJ* I 578) (d.
*Αἰλιανός*: Jew)
SICILY:
—LIPARA: (2) 369 AD Libertini, *Isole Eolie* p.
221 no. 27 (*SEG* XXXVI 848); cf. Ferrua, *NG*
530

## Ἀσία
ARGOLIS:
—ARGOS: (1) a. 303 BC *CEG* II 816, 12
—HERMIONE: (2) i BC-i AD? *IG* IV (1) 730 III,
6 (d. *Ἀλέξανδρος*)
LAKONIA: (3) ii BC ib. II² 9147 (Bradford (-))
(d. *Δίων*)
S. ITALY (APULIA):
—CANUSIUM: (4) ii AD *Epig. Rom. di Canosa* 78
(Lat. Arruntia Asia: m. *Ἀσιατικός*)
S. ITALY (CAMPANIA):
—LITERNUM: (5) imp. *CIL* X 3720 (Lat.
Cossinia Asia)
—POMPEII: (6) i BC-i AD *Römische
Gräberstrassen* p. 222 (Lat. Asia)
—POMPEII*: (7) i BC-i AD *CIL* X 1010 (Castrèn
246. 8) (Lat. Melissaea Asia: freed.)

## Ἀσιάδας
LAKONIA:
—SPARTA: (1) iii BC *SEG* XL 348 B, 10

## Ἀσιατική
S. ITALY (CAMPANIA):
—POMPEII: (1) i BC-i AD *CIL* IV 10011 (Lat.
Asiatice)
—POMPEII*: (2) i BC-i AD ib. X 1011 (Castrèn
246. 9) (Lat. Melissea Asiatice: freed.)

## Ἀσιατικός
AIGINA?: (1) imp. *EAD* XXX p. 356 no. 16 with
n. 1 (s. *Νικηφᾶς*)
S. ITALY (APULIA):
—CANUSIUM: (2) ii AD *Epig. Rom. di Canosa* 78
(Lat. M. Arruntius Asiaticus: s. *Ἴσσος*, *Ἀσία*)
S. ITALY (CALABRIA):
—BRENTESION-BRUNDISIUM: (3) ?i AD *Necro-
poli via Cappuccini* p. 276 no. E24 (Lat. Ti.
Latinius Asiaticus)
—LUPIAE: (4) i-ii AD *CIL* IX 25 (Susini, *Fonti
Salento* p. 139 no. 88) (Lat. Q. Volumnius
Asiaticus)
S. ITALY (CAMPANIA):
—DIKAIARCHIA-PUTEOLI*: (5) imp. *Territorio
Flegreo* 1 p. 92 no. 8 (Lat. L. Octavius Asia-
ticus: freed.)
—HERCULANEUM: (6) m. i AD *PdelP* 16 (1961)
p. 70 no. 94 (Lat. Asiaticus)
—NEAPOLIS: (7) 71 AD *INap* 84 col. I, 5 (*Δομί-
τιος* *Ἀ.*); (8) 194 AD ib. 44 col. I, 4 (*Καίλ(ιος)*
*Ἀ.*)
—POMPEII: (9) i BC-i AD *CIL* IV 1657; cf. p. 210
(Lat. Asiaticus); (10) ~ ib. 3991 (Lat. Asiati-
cus); (11) ~ ib. 2393-4 (Lat. Dapnus Asiati-
cus)
—SALERNUM: (12) imp. *IItal* I (1) 209 (*CIL* X
613) (Lat. L. Iuventius Asiaticus)
S. ITALY (LUCANIA):
—EBURUM?: (13) imp. *IItal* III (1) 282 (Lat.
Bruttius Asiaticus)
—VOLCEI?: (14) imp. ib. 10 (*CIL* X 446) (or
Italy (Hirpini) Compsa: Lat. C. Spedius Asi-
aticus: s. *Ἀτίμητος*, Allidia Statuta)
SICILY:
—THERMAI HIMERAIAI: (15) i-ii AD ib. 7374
(*ILat. Term. Imer.* 44) (Lat. M. Albius Asiati-
cus: s. *Φιλόκαλος*, *Ἀρτεμισία*)

## Ἀσίκα
S. ITALY (CALABRIA):
—VALETIUM: (1) c. 500 BC *SEG* XXXIII 808
(bronze); *LSAG*² p. 457 no. S

## Ἄσιμος
EPIROS:
—PHOTIKE: (1) imp. *BCH* 16 (1892) p. 175 no.
3 (Lat. Asimus)

## Ἀσινις
ARKADIA:
—MANTINEIA-ANTIGONEIA: (1) c. 300-221 BC
*IG* V (2) 323. 36 (tessera) (f. *Ἀγησίας*)

## Ἄσιντος
LAKONIA:
—SPARTA?: (1) 316 BC ib. 549, 36 (Bradford (-))
(*Ἄ[σ]ιντος*: f. *Πασικλῆς*)

## Ἄσιος
KERKYRA: (1) imp. *IG* IX (1) 862 (tile)

## Ἀσκαύλης
S. ITALY (CAMPANIA):
—POMPEII: (1) i BC-i AD *CIL* IV 636 (Lat. As-
caules)

## Ἀσκλαπιάδας
ACHAIA: (1) 146 BC *IG* IV (1)² 28, 97 (I f.
*Ἀσκλαπιάδας* II: synoikos); (2) ~ ib. l. 97 (II s.
*Ἀσκλαπιάδας* I: synoikos); (3) ~ ib. l. 125 (I f.
*Ἀσκλαπιάδας* II: synoikos); (4) ~ ib. l. 125 (II
s. *Ἀσκλαπιάδας* I: synoikos); (5) ~ ib. l. 131 (s.
*Φιλοκράτης*: synoikos)
—DYME: (6) iii BC *AJPh* 31 (1910) p. 399 no.
74 b, 2 (s. *Κλέων*); (7) iii-ii BC *Syll*³ 530, 14;
cf. *Achaia und Elis* p. 115 (s. *Δρόμας*)
AITOLIA: (8) ?225 BC Nachtergael, *Les Galates*
63, 4
AKARNANIA:
—THYRREION: (9) iii-ii BC *SEG* XXVII 159, 8;
cf. *PAE* 1977, pl. 244 a (f. *Νεαγένης*)
ARGOLIS:
—ARGOS: (10) ?277 BC *FD* III (1) 88, 5 (s. *Μενέ-
στρατος*); (11) i BC-i AD *Mnem.* NS 47 (1919)
p. 167 no. 16
—ARGOS?: (12) iv BC *SEG* XI 368
—EPIDAUROS: (13) c. 370-360 BC *BSA* 61
(1966) p. 272 no. 4 B II, 7, 13, 15, 18-19;
(14) c. 365-335 BC *IG* IV (1)² 103, 10
—METHANA-ARSINOE: (15) i BC ib. II² 9329
(*[Ἀσ]κληπιάδης*: f. *Σωτηρίς*); (16) ~ ib. IV (1)
853, 5 (*Ἀσκλαπιάδας* I f. *Ἀσκλαπιάδας* II); (17)
~ ib. l. 5 (*Ἀσκλαπιάδας* II s. *Ἀσκλαπιάδας* I)
—PHLEIOUS: (18) iv/iii BC *RE* s.v. Asklepiades
(33)
—TROIZEN: (19) ?146 BC *IG* IV (1) 757 B, 10 (f.
*Ἀσκλαπιόδωρος*)
ARKADIA: (20) s. iii BC *PP* 2444; cf. Launey I
p. 125 n. 2 (*Ἀσκ[λ]η[πιάδης]*?: s. *Θεόδωρος*)
—LYKOSOURA*: (21) ii-i BC *IG* V (2) 546, 5 (tile)
(*Ἀσκλα[π]ιάδας*)
—MANTINEIA-ANTIGONEIA: (22) m. iii BC ib.
368, 117 (*[Ἀσ]κλαπιάδας*)
—TEGEA: (23) iii BC ib. 30, 4 (f. *—χίδης*); (24)
ii-i BC ib. 165, 7
ILLYRIA:
—APOLLONIA: (25) c. 250-50 BC Maier 91 (coin)
(Ceka 31) (money.)
KORINTHIA:
—KORINTH: (26) m. iii BC *Corinth* VIII (3) 33
d, 8; cf. *SEG* XXV 330 (*[Ἀσκλα]πιάδας*); (27)
iii/ii BC *Milet* I (3) 78, 1 (*Ἀσκληπιάδης*: f. *Νί-
κανδρος*)
—SIKYON: (28) iii BC *Mél. Daux* p. 136 no. 6 c
= *AD* 43 (1988) Chron. p. 503 (*Ἀσκληπιάδης*)
LAKONIA: (29) imp.? *Syringes* 216 (Bradford
(-)) (*-δης*: ?s. *Πεύκετος*)
—SPARTA: (30) c. 100-110 AD *IG* V (1) 58, 3; cf.
*SEG* XI 509 (Bradford (-)) (*[Ἀ]σκλ[α]πιάδας*)

## SICILY:
—GELA-PHINTIAS: (31) f. ii BC *IG* XIV 256,
37 (Dubois, *IGDS* 161); cf. *SEG* XL 804 (I
f. *Ἀσκλαπιάδας* II); (32) ~ *IG* XIV 256, 37
(Dubois, *IGDS* 161); cf. *SEG* XL 804 (II s.
*Ἀσκλαπιάδας* I)
—SELINOUS: (33) s. v BC Dubois, *IGDS* 83 (n.
pr.)
—SYRACUSE: (34) ii BC *IG* II² 10396
(*[Ἀσκ]ληπιάδης*—lap.: f. *Τύχων*)

## Ἀσκλαπιάς
AKARNANIA:
—THYRREION: (1) iii BC ib. IX (1)² (2) 245, 9
(*[Ἀσ]κλαπιάδι* (dat.))
ARGOLIS:
—ARGOS*: (2) 105 AD *JÖAI* 14 (1911) Beibl. p.
146 no. 4, 26 (slave/freed.?)
—EPIDAUROS: (3) i BC *IG* IV (1)² 227 (d.
*Ἀπολλωνίδας*, m. *Μένανδρος*); (4) i-ii AD Peek,
*NIEpid* 49, 3 (d. *Χάρης*)
ELIS: (5) hell. *IG* II² 8527 (*-κλη-*: d. *Θεόδωρος*)

## Ἀσκλαπιόδωρος
ACHAIA:
—DYME*: (1) c. 219 BC *SGDI* 1612, 68, 70
(*Tyche* 5 (1990) p. 124) (*[Ἀσ]κλαπιόδωρος*: f.
*Εὔμηλος*, *Μηνόδωρος*)
ARGOLIS:
—EPIDAUROS: (2) iii BC *IG* IV (1)² 338
—TROIZEN: (3) ?146 BC ib. IV (1) 757 B, 8, 10
(s. *Ἀσκλαπιάδας*)
MESSENIA: (4) iii BC *SEG* XI 980 b = *AD* 25
(1970) Chron. p. 174; cf. *SEG* XXXIV 322
S. ITALY (CALABRIA):
—TARAS-TARENTUM: (5) c. 80-70 BC *IG* VII
3195, 22; *AE* 1925-6, pp. 35-6 no. 149, 17,
[21] (*IOrop* 524); *BSA* 70 (1975) pp. 121-2
(date) (Stephanis 462) (s. *Πυθέας*)

## Ἀσκλάπιχος
ARKADIA: (1) ?255 BC Nachtergael, *Les Galates*
8, 53; cf. Stephanis 121 (f. *Ἀλεξίας*)

## Ἀσκλαπίων
EPIROS:
—AMBRAKIA: (1) ii-i BC *CIG* 1800 + Leake,
*Northern Greece* 4 plate XXXV no. 170, 26
(*[Ἀσ]κλαπίων*)

## Ἀσκλάπος
ILLYRIA:
—EPIDAMNOS-DYRRHACHION: (1) c. 250-50 BC
Unp. (Paris, BN) 266; cf. Münsterberg p.
260 = Nachtr. p. 14 (coin) (pryt.) ?= (2);
(2) ~ Maier 145-7; 474; Münsterberg p. 260
= Nachtr. p. 14 (coin) (Ceka 193; 245; 365;
444) (pryt.) ?= (1); (3) hell.-imp. *IDyrrh* 202
(*Ἀσσ-*: f. *Εὐκλέα*)
LAKONIA:
—SPARTA: (4) c. 100-105 AD *SEG* XI 546 a,
4; 546 b, [4] (I f. *Ἀσκλαπος* II) ?= (7); (5)
~ ib. 546 a, 4; 546 b, 4 (II s. *Ἀσκλαπος* I)
?= (8); (6) c. 105-122 AD ib. 569, 23; 574,
4 (Bradford (3)) (*[Ἀσ]κλαπος*—574: f. *Ἑρμογένης*); (7) c. 125-150 AD *IG* V (1) 114, 2 (Bradford (2)) (*Ἀσκλαπ[ιό]s*—*IG*: I f. *Ἀσκλαπος* II)
?= (4); (8) ~ *IG* V (1) 114, 2 (Bradford (1))
(*Ἀσκλαπ[ιό]s*—*IG*: II s. *Ἀσκλαπος* I) ?= (5)
SICILY:
—AKRAGAS: (9) s. iii BC *BMC Sicily* p. 22 no.
154 (coin) (*Ἀσκλαπιός*—*BMC*)
—GELA-PHINTIAS (NR.): (10) i BC *SEG* XLI 843
—SOLOUS: (11) s. ii BC ib. 836 (f. *Ἄνταλλος* *Ὀρνιχᾶς*)

## Ἀσκλάπων
ACHAIA: (1) 146 BC *IG* IV (1)² 28, 79 (f. *Ἀχαιός*:
synoikos)
—PATRAI: (2) m. i BC Cic., *Ad Fam.* xiii 20; *Ad
Fam.* xvi 9. 2 (Lat. Asclapo: doctor) ?= (3)
—PATRAI?: (3) hell.-imp. *RE* s.v. Asklation (1);
Erot. 103 (*Ἀσκλατίων*—mss.: doctor: name—
*LGPN*) ?= (2)

—PHARAI: (4) ii BC *Achaean Grave Stelai* 71 ([Ἀσ]κλᾶπων: s. Λυκίσκος)

AITOLIA:
—THERMOS*: (5) s. iii BC *IG* IX (1)² (1) 60 II, 2; (6) ~ ib. 60 VII, 3

ARKADIA:
—TEGEA: (7) f. ii BC ib. v (2) 44, 13 (s. Σαώτας)

LAKONIA:
—SPARTA: (8) s. i BC ib. v (1) 92, 2 (Bradford (-)) (f. Φιλοκλῆς)

MESSENIA:
—ASINE: (9) hell.-imp. *IG* v (1) 1407 (f. Μύρων)
—MESSENE: (10) 31 BC-14 AD *SEG* XXIII 207, 31 (s. Τιμοκράτης)

## Ἀσκλᾶς

S. ITALY (CAMPANIA):
—DIKAIARCHIA-PUTEOLI: (1) imp. *CIL* x 2326 (Lat. L. Cornelius Ascla: s. Ἰσιδώρα)
—DIKAIARCHIA-PUTEOLI*: (2) imp. ib. 2162 (Lat. T. Barbius Ascla: freed.)
—POMPEII: (3) i BC-i AD ib. IV 7295 (Lat. Ascla); (4) ~ ib. 8194 (Lat. Ascula)

## Ἀσκληπᾶς

ARGOLIS:
—EPIDAUROS: (1) i-ii AD *IG* IV (1)² 507 (s. Ἀβάσκαντος); (2) 135 AD Peek, *NIEpid* 8, 1 (s. Παράμονος)
PELOPONNESE: (3) c. 230-200 BC *BCH* 45 (1921) p. 11 II, 39 (Ἀσκλη[πᾶ]ς)
S. ITALY (CAMPANIA):
—POMPEII: (4) 55 AD *CIL* IV 3340. 13, [6], 9 (Castrèn 261. 2) (Lat. L. Murtius Asclepa)

## Ἀσκληπία

S. ITALY (CAMPANIA):
—DIKAIARCHIA-PUTEOLI: (1) imp. *CIL* x 2367 (Lat. Gessia Asclepia)

## Ἀσκληπιάδηρ

ELIS: (1) c. 85-93 AD *IvOl* 86, 3 (Ἀσκλη[πιάδηρ]: I f. Ἀσκληπιάδηρ II); (2) ~ ib. l. 3, 6 (II s. Ἀσκληπιάδηρ I, f. Ἀμφικράτηρ)

## Ἀσκληπιάδης

ACHAIA: (1) iii BC *SEG* XXVI 919, 64 (s. Διο—)
AIGINA: (2) c. 100-60 BC *IG* VII 419, 8 (*IOrop* 526); *IG* VII 2448, 2; 3196, 3; *BSA* 70 (1975) p. 121 (date) (Stephanis 454) (s. Θεόφραστος, f. Θεόφραστος); (3) ?f. i BC *Alt-Ägina* I (2) p. 43 no. 4, 3 (f. Κλέων); (4) iii AD *SEG* XI 4 b, 1 (I f. Αὐρ. Ἀσκληπιάδης II); (5) ~ ib. l. 1 (Αὐρ. Ἀ.: II s. Ἀσκληπιάδης I); (6) ~ *Alt-Ägina* I (2) p. 47 no. 31 (Αὐρ. Ἀσκληπιάδ[ης]); (7) ?iii-iv AD ib. p. 48 no. 33
AITOLIA:
—THERMOS*: (8) s. iii BC *IG* IX (1)² (1) 60 III, 16; (9) ~ ib. 60 V, 13; (10) ~ ib. l. 14; (11) ~ ib. l. 16; (12) ~ ib. 60 VI, 1
ARGOLIS:
—EPIDAUROS: (13) ?i AD Peek, *NIEpid* 48, 2-3 (Ἀ[σ]κληπιά[δης])
—TROIZEN: (14) ?287 BC *IG* IV (1) 750, 16, [41]; (15) imp. ib. 816
ARKADIA: (16) ii/i BC *SEG* XLI 1635, 5-6 (f. Μηνόδωρος, Καλλίστρατος)
ELIS: (17) f. i AD *IvOl* 74, 5; 80, 7 ([Ἀσ]κληπιάδης: s. Σωσιμένης)
EPIROS:
—NIKOPOLIS: (18) imp. *AEMÖ* 15 (1892) p. 127 no. 1 (Sarikakis 17); (19) i BC/i AD *SEG* XXXVII 526 (Sarikakis 46) (s. Νικάνωρ)
ILLYRIA:
—APOLLONIA: (20) imp. *IApoll* 60 (Ἀ. Λαίλιος)
KORINTHIA:
—KORINTH: (21) 241 AD Moretti, *Olymp.* 930; cf. *SEG* XXXVII 362 (Π. Ἀ.)
LAKONIA:
—HYPERTELEATON*: (22) imp. *IG* v (1) 1042 (f. Φιλόκαλος)

—SPARTA: (23) ii AD ib. 159, 31 (Bradford (2)); (24) ?a. 212 AD *IG* v (1) 606, 3 (Bradford (3)) (f. Αὐρ. Τιμοκράτεια)
MESSENIA:
—MESSENE (NR.): (25) f. ii AD *SEG* XI 982 (s. Μνασίστρατος)
S. ITALY (CAMPANIA): (26) imp. *CIL* x 8059. 279 (seal) (Lat. T. Novius Asclepi(ades))
S. ITALY (CAMPANIA):
—DIKAIARCHIA-PUTEOLI: (27) imp. ib. 1587 (Lat. Asclepiades)
—MISENUM*: (28) imp. ib. 3391 (Lat. M. Naevius Asclepiades); (29) ~ ib. 3502 (Lat. Iulius Asclepiades); (30) ~ ib. 3644 (Lat. Q. Valerius Asclepiades)
—NEAPOLIS*: (31) ii AD ib. 1769 (Lat. Aelius Asclepiades)
—POMPEII: (32) i BC-i AD ib. IV 7855 (Lat. Asclepiades)
S. ITALY (CAMPANIA)*: (33) i BC-i AD ib. x 8042. 76; *Kokalos* 32 (1986) pp. 260-1 nos. 144-5 (tiles) (Lat. Q. Mucius Asclepiad(es))

## Ἀσκληπιάς

SICILY:
—KATANE: (1) imp. *IG* XIV 460

## Ἀσκληπιοδότη

SICILY:
—KATANE: (1) 435 AD Agnello 96; cf. Ferrua, *NG* 405 (m. Ἄπρα)

## Ἀσκληπιοδοτιανός

S. ITALY (APULIA):
—CANUSIUM: (1) 223 AD *Epig. Rom. di Canosa* 35 III, 22 (*CIL* IX 338) (Lat. L. Ceius Asclepiodotianus)

## Ἀσκληπιόδοτος

AIGINA: (1) i BC-i AD *Alt-Ägina* I (2) p. 45 no. 15 (I f. Ἀσκληπιόδοτος II); (2) ~ ib. ([Ἀσ]κληπιόδοτος: II s. Ἀσκληπιόδοτος I)
S. ITALY (CAMPANIA):
—DIKAIARCHIA-PUTEOLI: (3) iii AD *IG* XIV 837 (Σεουηριανὸς Ἀ.)
—NEAPOLIS: (4) 536 AD *PLRE* III A (2)

## Ἀσκληπιόδωρος

ARGOLIS:
—HERMIONE: (1) ii-i BC *IG* IV (1) 732 II, 11 (f. Ἀμμία)
KERKYRA: (2) ?s. i BC ib. IX (1) 757 (tile)
KERKYRA?: (3) hell. ib. 833 (bullet) (Ἀσσκληπιόδω[ρος])
LAKONIA:
—AKRIAI: (4) iii AD *SEG* XLII 297, 1 (Ἀσκληπιόδ[ωρος], Ἀσκληπιόδ[οτος])
S. ITALY (BRUTTIUM):
—LOKROI EPIZEPHYRIOI?: (5) 178 BC *Syll*³ 585, 240 (or Cilicia Zephyrion: f. Ἀπολλωνίδης)

## Ἀσκληπιός

DALMATIA:
—PHAROS: (1) imp. Šašel, *IL* 2930 (Lat. Leucius As[cle]pi[us]: I f. Λ. Ἀσκληπιός II: doctor); (2) ~ ib. (Lat. Leuci[us] Asclepi[us]: II s. Λ. Ἀσκληπιός I)
S. ITALY (APULIA):
—CANUSIUM: (3) 223 AD *Epig. Rom. di Canosa* 35 IV, 32 (*CIL* IX 338) (Lat. T. Pompeius Asclepius)
S. ITALY (CAMPANIA):
—DIKAIARCHIA-PUTEOLI: (4) imp. ib. x 2405 (Lat. Cl. Asclepius); (5) ?i AD ib. 2500 (Lat. M. Helvius Asclepius)

## Ἀσκληπίων

EPIROS:
—AMBRAKIA: (1) ?ii BC *AD* 10 (1926) p. 67 fig. 4 (s. Δικαῖος)

## Ἀσκληπώ

ARKADIA:
—MANTINEIA-ANTIGONEIA: (1) ii AD *IG* v (2) 310 (Μεμμία Ἀ.)

## Ἀσκλήπων

ARGOLIS:
—TROIZEN: (1) imp. ib. IV (1) 835 A, 1, 5
ELIS: (2) c. 181 AD *IvOl* 100, 7

## Ἀσκυλῖνα

LAKONIA:
—HIPPOLA: (1) imp. *SEG* XXVI 455 (Poralla² 161a) (Ἀσκυλῖνα<ι>)

## Ἄσμενος

ARGOLIS:
—ARGOS: (1) ?iii BC *SB* 4046 (Ἀσμ[ενος])
S. ITALY (CAMPANIA):
—POMPEII: (2) i BC-i AD *CIL* IV 6791 (Lat. Asmenus)

## Ἄσπαρ

ARGOLIS:
—ARGOS: (1) iv AD *SEG* XI 350, 1; cf. *TMByz* 9 (1985) p. 370 no. 114 (Jew)

## Ἀσπασία

ACHAIA:
—DYME: (1) hell. *BCH* 4 (1880) p. 521 no. 3 (d. Θέων); (2) iii-ii BC *Achaean Grave Stelai* 74 (Ἀσπασία: d. Μοσχίων)
ARKADIA:
—THISOA?: (3) ?iii BC *IG* v (2) 499
MESSENIA:
—MESSENE: (4) i BC-i AD? *PAE* 1991, p. 98 no. 5
S. ITALY (APULIA):
—GNATHIA-EGNATIA: (5) imp. *CIL* IX 263 (Lat. Helvia Haspasia)
S. ITALY (CAMPANIA):
—POMPEII: (6) i BC-i AD ib. IV 9237; (7) ~ ib. 10129 (Lat. Aspasia)
SICILY:
—SYRACUSE: (8) iii-v AD Barreca 385 (Ἀσπασ(ί)α)

## Ἀσπάσιος

ARGOLIS:
—HERMIONE: (1) iii BC *IG* IV (1) 729 II, 14 (f. Κίτος)
ELIS: (2) 217 BC Plb. v 94. 6; (3) c. 50 BC *SEG* XXXVII 388, 6 (f. —ρωπος)
S. ITALY (CAMPANIA):
—DIKAIARCHIA-PUTEOLI*: (4) imp. *CIL* x 3039 (Lat. Q. Valerius Aspasius: freed.)

## Ἀσπασίς

ARKADIA: (1) m. ii BC Unp. (Tripolis Mus.) ([Ἀ]σπασίς: d. Πάσιππος)

## Ἀσπίμμας

ILLYRIA:
—BYLLIONES: (1) i BC Cabanes, *L'Épire* p. 562 no. 36 (*SEG* XXXVIII 570) (s. Πραΰλος)

## Ἀσπίς

MESSENIA:
—MESSENE: (1) ii/iii AD *IG* v (1) 1487
SICILY:
—KATANE: (2) imp. *Helikon* 2 (1962) pp. 488-9 (-πεί[ς])

## Ἄσπονδος

EPIROS:
—DODONA: (1) iii BC Antoniou, *Dodone* Ab, 31

## Ἀσπριανός

SICILY:
—SYRACUSE: (1) iii-v AD Strazzulla 322 (Wessel 1358)

## Ἄσπρων?

S. ITALY (CAMPANIA):
—KYME: (1) ?c. 450-425 BC Dubois, *IGDGG* I 20 (Arena, *Iscr. Sic.* III 29); *LSAG*² p. 240

no. 16 (date) (Ἀσ[π]ρōν—Arena, Ἄσ(τ)ρōν— Jeffery and Landi, Ἀ[..]ο[..]—Dubois)

**Ἀσσινοκλῆς**
SICILY:
—TAUROMENION: (1) c. 40 BC *Cron. Arch.* 3 (1964) p. 54 I, 8, 31

**Ἄσσινος**
SICILY:
—AGYRION: (1) i BC Manganaro, *PdelP* forthcoming no. 5, 7 (s. Φιλώτας)

**Ἀσταφίς**
LAKONIA:
—SPARTA: (1) s. vii BC *PMGF* I 1, 74 (Poralla² 162)

**Ἀστέας**
ARKADIA:
—ALEA: (1) 421 BC *IG* I³ 80, 8
—HERAIA: (2) iii BC ib. v (2) 415, 9 (*IPArk* 23) (Ἀσ[τέ]ας: s. Ἀριστοφάνης)
—TEGEA:
——(Athaneatai): (3) iv/iii BC *IG* v (2) 38, 13
——(Hippothoitai): (4) c. 369-362 BC ib. 173, 35; cf. *CEG* II 657 ([Ἀσ]τέας)
PELOPONNESE?: (5) s. iii BC *SEG* XXV 449, 46 (*IPArk* 26)
S. ITALY (CALABRIA):
—TARAS-TARENTUM: (6) vi BC Iamb., *VP* 267 (*FVS* I p. 446)
S. ITALY (LUCANIA):
—POSEIDONIA-PAESTUM: (7) m. iv BC *RE* (2); *RVP* p. 84 f. (Ἀσσ-)

**Ἄστεια**
ELIS:
—PISA: (1) ii BC *GVI* 453 (d. Φιλήτωρ)
ILLYRIA:
—APOLLONIA: (2) imp. *IApoll* 61 (-τηα)

**Ἀστειός**
ARGOLIS:
—PHLEIOUS: (1) iv BC *SEG* XXVI 416, 5
S. ITALY (CAMPANIA):
—HERCULANEUM*: (2) i BC-i AD *CIL* x 1403 l II, 10; cf. *Cron. Erc.* 7 (1977) p. 116 c, 10 (Lat. M. Volusius Astius: freed.)
—POMPEII: (3) i BC-i AD *CIL* IV 1299 (Lat. Astius)

**Ἄστεκτος**
EPIROS:
—NIKOPOLIS: (1) imp. *SEG* XXIV 432 (Sarikakis 49) (Γ. Κέστιος Ἀ.)

**Ἀστερίδας**
ITHAKE: (1) hell. *SEG* XVII 261 ([Ἀ]στερίδας)

**Ἀστέριν**
SICILY:
—THERMAI HIMERAIAI: (1) iii AD *Epigraphica* 3 (1941) p. 260 no. 16 (*ILat. Term. Imer.* 140) (Lat. Rustia Asterin)

**Ἀστερῖνος**
KORINTHIA:
—KORINTH: (1) iv/iii BC Peek, *IAEpid* 110 (f. —ατος)

**Ἀστέρις**
SICILY:
—KATANE: (1) imp. *IG* XIV 461

**Ἀστερίς**
S. ITALY (CAMPANIA):
—DIKAIARCHIA-PUTEOLI: (1) imp. *CIL* x 2285 (Lat. Claudia Asteris)
—DIKAIARCHIA-PUTEOLI*: (2) s. i AD ib. 2314 (Sinn, *Stadtröm. Marmorurnen* 185) (Lat. Coelia Asteris: freed.)

**Ἀστερόπα**
EPIROS:
—ATHAMANES: (1) 175 BC *SGDI* 1987, 7-8 (slave/freed.)

**Ἀστεροπαῖος**
S. ITALY (CAMPANIA):
—POMPEII: (1) i BC-i AD *CIL* IV 9258 (Lat. M. Diocles A[st]eropeus)
—POMPEII*: (2) i BC-i AD ib. 1422 (Lat. Asteropaeus)

**Ἀστερωπός**
LAKONIA:
—SPARTA: (1) vii/vi BC Plu., *Cleom.* 10; *RE* (-) (Poralla² 164)

**Ἄστη**
S. ITALY (CAMPANIA):
—NEAPOLIS: (1) ?i AD *GVI* 182 (*INap* 98); cf. Leiwo p. 121 no. 107

**Ἀστήρ**
LAKONIA:
—AIGILIA: (1) i-ii AD *IG* v (1) 950 a (fals.?)
—SPARTA: (2) s. vi BC Hdt. v 63. 2 (Poralla² 165) (f. Ἀγχίμολος)
S. ITALY: (3) imp. *CIL* x 8059. 9 (seal) (Lat. P. Acutius Aster)

**Ἀστίας**
ARGOLIS:
—EPIDAUROS: (1) c. 358-345 BC *CID* II 7 A, 3; 31, 35, 39, 60 ?= (2)
—EPIDAUROS*: (2) c. 370-365 BC Peek, *IAEpid* 52 A, 49; 52 B, 59, 64 ?= (1) (3); (3) c. 370-335 BC *IG* IV (1)² 102, 111; 103, 38 ?= (2)

**Ἀστίδας**
ARKADIA:
—MANTINEIA-ANTIGONEIA: (1) iv-iii BC *SEG* XI 347 (f. Θιγγωνίδας)

**Ἀστικός**
S. ITALY (CAMPANIA):
—POMPEII: (1) i BC-i AD *CIL* IV 1091 (Lat. Asticus)

**Ἀστομάχις**
SICILY:
—ZANKLE-MESSANA: (1) f. iv AD *Epigraphica* 3 (1941) p. 253 no. 2 (Ἀ(ρι)στομάχις?)

**Ἀστορίδης**
ACHAIA:
—AIGEIRA: (1) iv BC *JÖAI* 19-20 (1919) Beibl. p. 39 (s. —δης)

**Ἄστος**
S. ITALY (CAMPANIA):
—NEAPOLIS: (1) i BC/i AD *INap* 113, 2 (Ἀσσ-); (2) ~ ib. l. 3 (Ἀσ(το)ς?: f. Ἰσιάς); (3) ~ ib. l. 5 (Ἀσσ-: s. Ἡρακλείδης); (4) ~ ib. 151, 1; cf. Leiwo p. 104 no. 61 (Π. Οὐικίριος Ἀ.?: s. Χαρίλης) ?= (6); (5) ~ *INap* 151, 3 (?f. Κοκκήϊος); (6) ~ ib. 177 (Π. Οὐικίριος Ἀ.) ?= (4)
—POMPEII: (7) i BC-i AD *CIL* IV 1771; cf. p. 211 (Lat. Astus); (8) ~ ib. 1851 (Castrèn 33. 1) (Lat. Anteius Astus); (9) ~ *CIL* IV 2508, 34 (Lat. Astus); (10) ~ ib. 10181 a (Lat. Astus)

**Ἀστοφάνης**
ARKADIA?: (1) c. 230-200 BC *BCH* 45 (1921) p. 13 II, 111 (Ἀσ[τ]οφάνης: s. Ἀγησισθένης)

**Ἀστράβακος**
LAKONIA:
—SPARTA: (1) her. Hdt. vi 69. 3; Paus. iii 16. 6, 9 (Poralla² 166) (s. Ἴρβος?: fict.)

**Ἀστράγαλος**
S. ITALY (CAMPANIA):
—POMPEII: (1) 37 BC *CIL* IV 2437 (Castrèn 11. 3) (Lat. C. Aelius Astraga[l]us)

**Ἀστυάναξ**
ARGOLIS:
—HERMIONE: (1) iii BC *IG* IV (1) 729 I, 20 (s. Στράτων)
ARKADIA: (2) her. Paus. viii 38. 5 (dub.)

**Ἄστυδος**
AITOLIA:
—ARAKYNEIS: (1) 263 BC *IG* IX (1)² (1) 17, 81 (Ἀστύ(λ)ος?—ed.: s. Ταυρίσκος)

**Ἀστυκλῆς**
ARKADIA:
—TEGEA: (1) m. iv BC ib. v (2) 6, 62 ([Ἀσ]τυκλῆς)
S. ITALY (BRUTTIUM):
—LOKROI EPIZEPHYRIOI: (2) vi/v BC *IvOl* 144, 1 (Lazzarini 853; Landi, *DISMG* 235; Ebert, *Gr. Sieg.* 16; *CEG* I 399); Paus. vi 6. 4 (f. Εὔθυμος)

**Ἀστυκράτης**
ARKADIA:
—MEGALOPOLIS: (1) iii BC *IG* v (2) 478, 3; (2) ~ ib. l. 5

**Ἀστυκρατίδας**
LAKONIA:
—SPARTA: (1) 331 BC Plu., *Mor.* 219 B (Poralla² 168)

**Ἀστυλαΐδας**
ARGOLIS:
—EPIDAUROS: (1) iv-iii BC *IG* IV (1)² 9; (2) iv/iii BC ib. 249 = *SEG* XXXII 386; Peek, *IAEpid* 85; 324; cf. *PdelP* 48 (1993) pp. 394-5; (3) ~ *CID* II 120 A, 53-4; 122 I, 15; *IG* IV (1)² 128, 32 (s. Ἀριστολαΐδας, f. Ἀριστολαΐδας); (4) ii/i BC ib. 212; 234, 4 (f. Πατροκλείδας, Ἀρχώ) ——(Azantioi?): (5) ii/i BC ib. l. 1 (s. Θιοκλείδας, ?s. Ἀρχώ)

**Ἄστυλλος**
ARKADIA:
—TEGEA: (1) m. iv BC ib. v (2) 6, 96, 100

**Ἄστυλος**
ARKADIA: (1) s. iv BC *RE* (2)
S. ITALY (BRUTTIUM):
—KROTON: (2) vi/v BC ib. (3); Moretti, *Olymp.* 178-9; 186-7
S. ITALY (CAMPANIA):
—POMPEII: (3) i BC-i AD *CIL* IV 423; 7243; 7248; 7464; 7525; 9831 (Lat. Astylus)
S. ITALY (LUCANIA):
—METAPONTION: (4) iv BC Iamb., *VP* 267 (*FVS* I p. 446); Pl., *Lg.* 840 A

**Ἀστυμέλοισα**
LAKONIA:
—SPARTA: (1) s. vii BC *PMGF* I 3 fr. 3, 64, 73

**Ἀστυόχεια**
ARGOLIS:
—ARGOS: (1) iv BC *IG* IV (1) 568 (Ἀστ[υ]όχε[ι]α: d. Τελέστας)

**Ἀστυοχίδας**
ELIS: (1) ?257 BC *FD* III (3) 195, 1 (f. Χάροψ)

**Ἀστύοχος**
ARKADIA?: (1) ?264 BC ib. III (1) 24, 2; *BCH* 102 (1978) p. 600 ([Ἀσ]τύοχος)
LAKONIA:
—SPARTA: (2) 412 BC *RE* (3) (Poralla² 169)

**Ἀστύτιμος**
LEUKAS: (1) imp.? *IG* IX (1) 597 (-τει-)

**Ἀστυφάνης**
ARGOLIS:
—EPIDAUROS*: (1) c. 365-335 BC ib. IV (1)² 103, 65

**Ἀστύφιλος**
S. ITALY (LUCANIA):
—POSEIDONIA-PAESTUM: (1) f. v BC Plu., *Cim.*
18 (mantis)

**Ἀστώ**
AITOLIA:
—KALLION/KALLIPOLIS: (1) iii/ii BC *IG* IX (1)²
(1) 155

**Ἄστων**
AITOLIA: (1) ?255-254 BC Nachtergael, *Les Ga-
lates* 8, 66; 9, 68; cf. Stephanis 489 (f. Αὐτό-
λυκος)
S. ITALY (BRUTTIUM):
—KROTON: (2) vi-v BC *RE* (-)

**Ἀστώχος**
ARGOLIS:
—HERMIONE: (1) iii BC *IG* IV (1) 729 I, 10 (f.
Θαρσίας)

**Ἀσυγκρίτη**
S. ITALY (APULIA):
—HERDONIA: (1) f. iii AD *ZPE* 103 (1994) p.
162 no. 4 (Lat. Asyncrite)

**Ἀσύγκριτος**
S. ITALY (CALABRIA):
—BRENTESION-BRUNDISIUM: (1) imp. *CIL* IX
114 (Lat. C. Falerius Asyncritus)
—HYRIA*: (2) imp. ib. 224 (Lat. P. Gerellanus
Asyncritus: I f. Ἀσύγκριτος II: freed.); (3) ~
ib. (Lat. P. Gerellanus Asyncritus: II s. Ἀσύγ-
κριτος I: freed.)

**Ἀσύλλιος**
SICILY:
—SYRACUSE: (1) iii-v AD Strazzulla 218; cf. Fer-
rua, *NG* 285

**Ἀσυλλις**
SICILY:
—HERBITA: (1) iii-v AD *Arch. Class.* 17 (1965)
p. 200

**Ἀσφάλιος**
ARGOLIS:
—EPIDAUROS*: (1) c. 370-365 BC Peek, *IAEpid*
52 A, 13 (Ἀσ[φά]λιος) ?= (Ἀσφαλτος (1))
ARKADIA:
—TEGEA:
——(Hippothoitai): (2) f. iii BC *IG* V (2) 36, 74
(Ἀσφά[λιος]: f. Νικάσιππος: metic)

**Ἄσφαλτος**
ARGOLIS:
—EPIDAUROS: (1) c. 370 BC ib. IV (1)² 102, 248
(Ἀσφάλ(ι)ος?) ?= (Ἀσφάλιος (1))

**Ἀσχία**
S. ITALY (APULIA):
—LARINUM: (1) imp. *Riv. Stor. Antica* 5 (1900-
1) p. 620 no. 3 (Lat. Freia Aschia)

**Ἀσωνίδας**
AIGINA: (1) 480 BC Hdt. vii 181 (-δης)

**Ἀσωπόδωρος**
ARGOLIS:
—ARGOS: (1) c. 480-460 BC *CEG* I 380. ii; *RE*
(6) (Ἀσōπόδōρος: sculptor)
—ARGOS?: (2) s. v BC Plin., *NH* xxxiv 50; cf. *RE*
s.v. Argeios (18) (Lat. Asopodorus: sculptor)
—PHLEIOUS: (3) ?iv-iii BC ib. (5); *IEG* 2 p. 46
(Stephanis 468)
KORINTHIA:
—KORINTH: (4) vi BC *IG* IV (1) 225 (pinax)
(Ἀσōπόδōρος)


**Ἄσωπος**
KORINTHIA:
—KORINTH: (1) iv-iii BC *AR* 1962-3, p. 11 (n.
pr.?)
LAKONIA:
—HYPERTELEATON*: (2) imp. *IG* V (1) 1018;
(3) ~ ib. 1037

**Ἀταιτυκας?**
SICILY:
—HYKKARA (NR.): (1) s. v BC *Di Terra in Terra*
p. 201 (vase) (Ἀταιτυκαι (gen.?))

**Ἀταλάντη**
S. ITALY (CAMPANIA):
—NEAPOLIS: (1) s. ii AD *IG* XIV 763 (*INap* 91);
cf. Leiwo p. 126 no. 114 (Αὐρ. Ἀ.)
—POMPEII: (2) i BC-i AD *CIL* IV 2411; (3) ~
*NScav* 1897, p. 275 (Castrèn 145. 3) (Lat.
Curvia Atalante)

**Ἄταρβος**
AITOLIA: (1) c. 200-150 BC *CSCA* 6 (1973) p.
75 nos. 68-9 (coins) (Ἀταρ(βος), Ἀταρ(βίων)?)

**Ἀτείριος**
ILLYRIA:
—EPIDAMNOS-DYRRHACHION: (1) ?ii-i BC *IG*
XII (8) 196, 6; cf. *IDyrrh* 515 (f. —χρη—)

**Ἀτέκμαρτος**
ARKADIA:
—ORCHOMENOS: (1) ?c. 369-361 BC *BCH* 102
(1978) p. 348, 31 (*IPArk* 14)

**Ἀτέλης**
ARKADIA:
—MANTINEIA-ANTIGONEIA: (1) imp. *IG* V (2)
337

**Ἀτθικός**
ARGOLIS:
—ARGOS?: (1) c. 365-335 BC ib. IV (1)² 103, 13

**Ἀτθίς**
S. ITALY (CAMPANIA):
—STABIAE*: (1) imp. *RAAN* 19 (1938-9) p. 124
(Lat. Clodia Atthis: freed.)

**Ἀτιλιανός**
ARGOLIS:
—EPIDAUROS: (1) ii-iii AD *IG* IV (1)² 516, 3 (Π.
Ἀ.)

**Ἀτίλιος**
LAKONIA:
—GYTHEION: (1) f. ii AD ib. V (1) 1171, 8 = II²
3596 (-τεί-: s. Δαμονικίδας)

**Ἀτιμητιανός**
S. ITALY (CAMPANIA):
—MISENUM*: (1) imp. *CIL* X 3382 (Lat. M.
Meus. Atimetianus)

**Ἀτίμητος**
ARGOLIS:
—ARGOS: (1) imp. *IG* IV (1) 648 (-τεί-: s. Ἥρων)
KORINTHIA:
—KORINTH: (2) ii AD *Ag.* VII pp. 92 no. 236;
94 no. 265; 96 no. 289; *Lampes antiques BN*
I 31 (lamps) (Ἀτεί-); (3) f. ii AD *Corinth*
VIII (3) 237, 5 (Lat. [P.] [Ae]ficius Atimetus
[Lic]inianus: II s. Π. Αἰφίκιος Ἀτίμητος I,
—νία Γαλήνη, f. P. Aeficius Firmus Statianus);
(4) ~ ib. l. 7 (Lat. [P.] [Aef]icius Atimetus: I
f. Π. Αἰφίκιος Ἀτίμητος II Λικινιανός)
LAKONIA:
—SPARTA: (5) c. 105-110 AD *IG* V (1) 20 B, 10;
194, 3 (Bradford (-)) (Τιβ. Κλ. Ἀτείματος)
MESSENIA:
—MESSENE: (6) ii/iii AD *IG* V (1) 1483 (Γ. Πομ-
πώνιος Ἀτείμητος)


S. ITALY (APULIA):
—VIBINUM: (7) iii AD *Bovino* p. 148 no. 200
(Lat. Atimetus: slave?)
S. ITALY (BRUTTIUM):
—RHEGION: (8) ii AD *IGUR* 1165 (*GVI* 1025)
(-τεί-: s. Ἀγαπωμενός, Κούιντα)
S. ITALY (CALABRIA):
—BRENTESION-BRUNDISIUM: (9) imp. *CIL* IX
90 (Lat. D. Camianus Atimetus)
S. ITALY (CAMPANIA):
—DIKAIARCHIA-PUTEOLI: (10) imp. ib. X 1783
(Lat. M. Laelius Atimetus); (11) ~ ib. 2651
(Lat. L. Licinius Atimetus: f. Ζωΐλος, Ὡραία);
(12) m. i AD Camodeca, *L'Archivio Puteolano*
I p. 93 no. 21 (Lat. C. Novius Atimetus); (13)
52 AD ib. p. 120 no. 4 (Lat. A. Attiolenus Ati-
metus)
—DIKAIARCHIA-PUTEOLI*: (14) imp. *CIL* X
1945 (Lat. Cn. Cossutius Atimetus: freed.?);
(15) ~ ib. 2386 (Lat. M. Epidius Atimetus:
freed.)
—HERCULANEUM: (16) i BC-i AD ib. IV 2509, 5
(5449) (Lat. Atimetus); (17) ~ ib. X 1403 l I,
4; cf. *Cron. Erc.* 7 (1977) p. 116 b, 10 (Lat.
Atimetus); (18) m. i AD *PdelP* 3 (1948) p. 173
no. 18; p. 176 no. 21 (Lat. Iulius Atimetus);
(19) ~ ib. p. 182 no. 27 (Lat. C. Petronius
Atimetus)
—HERCULANEUM*: (20) i BC-i AD *CIL* X 1403 e,
6 (Lat. C. Vibius Atime[tus]: freed.); (21) c.
50-75 AD ib. 1403 a I, 24 (Lat. C. Messenius
Atimetus: freed.); (22) c. 72-79 AD ib. 1403 i
+ *Cron. Erc.* 7 (1977) p. 117 C b, 21 (Lat. C.
Messienus Atimetus: freed.)
—MISENUM: (23) 97 AD De Franciscis, *Sacello
Augustali* p. 24 no. 4 (Lat. C. Volusius Ati-
metus)
—NOLA: (24) ?i AD *CIL* X 1307 (Lat. Sex. Iulius
Atimetus: s. Εὐήμερος, Ῥοδόπη)
—POMPEII: (25) i BC-i AD ib. IV 1725; 1728;
1729 (Lat. Atimetus); (26) ~ ib. 4234 (Lat.
Atimetus); (27) ~ ib. 4683 (Lat. Atimetus);
(28) ~ ib. 8145; (29) ~ ib. 9839 a (Castrèn
32. 2) (Lat. Annius Atimetus); (30) ~ *NScav*
1916, p. 303 no. 81 (*Apollo* 6 (1985-88) p.
247) (Lat. Atimetus: s. Χρυσέρως, Urbana);
(31) m. i AD *CIL* X 1031 (Castrèn 259. 1);
Kockel p. 106 (date) (Lat. C. Munatius Atimetus); (32) ~ *Impegno per Pompeii* 9 ES no. 8
(Lat. Atimetus); (33) 57 AD *CIL* IV 3340. 37,
20; 38, 16 (Castrèn 246. 10) (Lat. L. Melissaeus Atimetus)
—STABIAE: (34) imp. *PBSR* 40 (1972) p. 128
no. 6 (Lat. L. Paccius Atimetus)
—SURRENTUM: (35) imp. *CIL* X 717 a (Lat. Ati-
metus: s. Ἐλευθερίς)
S. ITALY (LUCANIA):
—ATINA LUCANA: (36) imp. *IItal* III (1) 191
(Lat. A[ti]metus)
—MURO LUCANO (MOD.): (37) imp. *NScav*
1886, p. 282 (*Eph. Ep.* VIII 279) (Lat. Ati-
metus)
—POTENTIA: (38) imp. *CIL* X 155 (Lat. Figelius
Atimetus)
—VOLCEI?: (39) imp. *IItal* III (1) 10 (*CIL* X
446) (or Italy (Hirpini) Compsa: Lat. C. Spe-
dius Atimetus: f. Ἀσιατικός) ?= (40); (40) ~
*IItal* III (1) 12 (or Italy (Hirpini) Compsa:
Lat. Spedius Atimetus) ?= (39)
SICILY:
—KEPHALOIDION: (41) imp. *CIL* X 7456 (Lat.
Panius Atimetus)

**Ἀτις**
ARGOLIS:
—NEMEA*: (1) inc. *SEG* XXIX 349 b

**Ἀτίτα?**
SICILY:
—TERRAVECCHIA DI CUTI (MOD.): (1) vi/v BC
Dubois, *IGDS* 175 d (loomweight) (Arena,
*Iscr. Sic.* II 116) (Ἀ. (gen.?)—ed.)

## Ἀτλατίδας

ARGOLIS:
—EPIDAUROS: (1) c. 370 BC *IG* IV (1)² 102, 53, 101

## Ἆτος

SICILY:
—SELINOUS: (1) f. v BC Dubois, *IGDS* 38, 18 (Arena, *Iscr. Sic.* I 63) (s. Ναυεριάδας)

## Ἄτοτος

S. ITALY (APULIA):
—RUBI: (1) ii BC Troisi, *Epigrafi mobili* 99 (bronze) (f. Ἄρτος)

## Ἀτόφδας

SICILY:
—SELINOUS?: (1) v BC *SEG* XXXIX 1021 III, 4 (Ἀτόφδας)

## Ἀτρεστίδας

ARKADIA: (1) 348 BC D. xix 305
—MANTINEIA-ANTIGONEIA: (2) ?iv BC *PCG* 6 p. 702 fr. 3
—MEGALOPOLIS: (3) 369-361 BC *IG* v (2) 1, 27; Tod, *GHI* II 132 (date)

## Ἄττα

ILLYRIA:
—APOLLONIA: (1) imp. *IApoll* 240

## Ἄτταλος

AKARNANIA: (1) 250 BC *Brooklyn Mus. Ann.* 10 (1968-9) p. 135 no. 6
—THYRREION: (2) imp. *IG* IX (1)² (2) 350 (Ἄτα-)
ARGOLIS:
—ARGOS: (3) iii-ii BC ib. IV (1) 654 (s. Ἀνδράγαθος)
—HERMIONE: (4) ii-i BC ib. 732 IV, 23 (s. Σώφρων)
ARKADIA:
—TEGEA: (5) 78 AD ib. v (2) 49, 3 (s. Ἀνθεσφόρος); (6) m. ii AD ib. 48, 1 (Ἀτταλο[ς])
EPIROS:
—AMBRAKIA: (7) iii/ii BC ib. IX (1) 686, 2, 17 (f. Παυσανίας)
—BOUTHROTOS (PRASAIBOI): (8) a. 163 BC *IBouthrot* 101, 5 (s. Ἀδύλος)
KORINTHIA:
—KORINTH: (9) imp. *Corinth* VIII (3) 364 d (Lat. Attalus); (10) ?iii AD ib. VIII (2) 173 (Lat. [Aur]elius Attalus)
LAKONIA:
—GYTHEION: (11) f. i BC *IG* v (1) 1186, 2, 4, 7, 11, 18 (*GVI* 2003) (s. Τύχη)
—KARDAMYLE: (12) i AD *SEG* XI 948, 4 (f. Ποσείδιππος)
S. ITALY: (13) imp. *Epig. Rom. di Canosa* Instr. 20 (amph.) (Lat. L. Attalus)
S. ITALY (APULIA):
—CANUSIUM: (14) 223 AD ib. 35 IV, 8 (*CIL* IX 338) (Lat. T. Pompeius Attalus)
—VENUSIA: (15) i BC/i AD *Museo di Venosa* p. 213 no. 16 (Lat. C. Volteius Attalus: f. C. Volteius Maximus)
S. ITALY (CAMPANIA):
—DIKAIARCHIA-PUTEOLI: (16) ?ii AD *CIL* x 8059. 42 (seal) (Lat. M. Antonius Attalus Ulpianus)
—NOLA*: (17) imp. *Atti Acc. Pontan.* 21 (1971-2) pp. 392-7 (Lat. M. [–] Attalus: freed.)
—POMPEII: (18) 54 AD *CIL* IV 3340. 7, 16; 48, 20; 93, 10 (Castrèn 81. 8) (Lat. Q. Caecilius Attalus); (19) 70-79 AD *CIL* IV 3718; Mouritsen p. 111 (date)
SICILY:
—NEAITON: (20) f. i BC Cic., *In Verr.* II iv 59 (Lat. Attalus)

## Ἀττᾶς

S. ITALY (CAMPANIA):
—HERCULANEUM*: (1) m. i AD *Cron. Erc.* 7 (1977) p. 117 C b, 11 (Lat. [Q.] Maecius Atta: freed.)

## Ἀττέα

EPIROS:
—BOUTHROTOS (PRASAIBOI): (1) a. 163 BC *IBouthrot* 14, 8; 21, 21, 26 (*SEG* XXXVIII 471; 478) (m. Λυκίσκος, Πρωτόμαχος)

## Ἀττία

S. ITALY (LUCANIA): (1) f. iv BC *RA* 1979, pp. 249 f. (vase) (Ἀτ(τ)ία)

## Ἀττική

EPIROS:
—NIKOPOLIS: (1) imp. *PAE* 1913, p. 97 no. 11 (Sarikakis 18)
KEPHALLENIA:
—PANORMOS: (2) imp. *CIL* x 7318 + *Eph. Ep.* VIII 697 (Lat. Caecilia Attica)
S. ITALY (APULIA):
—LUCERIA*: (3) imp. *ASP* 34 (1981) p. 7 no. 5 (Lat. [Se]stilia Attica: freed.)
S. ITALY (CAMPANIA):
—DIKAIARCHIA-PUTEOLI: (4) imp. *CIL* x 2124 (Lat. Attica); (5) ~ ib. 2408 (Lat. Fabricia Attice)
—POMPEII: (6) i BC-i AD ib. IV 8191 (Lat. Attice)
S. ITALY (LUCANIA):
—GRUMENTUM: (7) imp. ib. x 232 (Lat. Turcia Attica)

## Ἀττικιανός

S. ITALY (CAMPANIA):
—DIKAIARCHIA-PUTEOLI: (1) imp. *AJA* 2 (1898) p. 386 no. 33 (Γ. Πομπ. Ἀ.: I ?f. Γ. Πομπ. Ἀττικιανός II); (2) ~ ib. (Γ. Πομπ. Ἀττικιαν<ων>ός: II ?s. Γ. Πομπ. Ἀττικιανός I)

## Ἀττίκιλλα

S. ITALY (CALABRIA):
—PORTO CESAREO (MOD.): (1) imp. *CIL* IX 11 (Susini, *Fonti Salento* p. 92 no. 24) (Lat. Claudia Atticilla)
S. ITALY (CAMPANIA):
—DIKAIARCHIA-PUTEOLI: (2) imp. *CIL* x 2617 (Lat. Iunia Atticilla: d. Ἀττικός, Πρέπουσα)
SICILY:
—SYRACUSE: (3) iii-v AD *ASSiracusano* 1956, p. 63 (Κλωδεία Ἀ.)

## Ἀττικός

ARGOLIS:
—EPIDAUROS: (1) 205 AD *IG* IV (1)² 399, 1 + Peek, *IAEpid* 159
—TROIZEN: (2) imp. *IG* IV (1) 835 C, 6 (—υλλήϊος Ἀ.)
PELOPONNESE?: (3) 11 AD *PAE* 1992, p. 72 B, 5 (I f. Ἀττικός II); (4) ~ ib. l. 5 (II s. Ἀττικός I)
S. ITALY: (5) imp. *CIL* x 8059. 106 (seal) (Lat. L. Cerrinius Atticus)
S. ITALY (APULIA):
—LUCERIA: (6) imp. ib. IX 810 (Lat. C. Marius Atticus); (7) ?s. ii AD *Rend. Linc.* 24 (1969) p. 28 no. 10 (Lat. C. Iunius Atticus)
S. ITALY (CALABRIA):
—RUDIAE: (8) imp. Susini, *Fonti Salento* p. 134 no. 80 (Lat. Atticus)
S. ITALY (CAMPANIA):
—DIKAIARCHIA-PUTEOLI: (9) imp. *CIL* x 1783 (Lat. Q. Granius Atticus); (10) ~ ib. 1816 (Lat. M. Val. Atticus); (11) ~ ib. 2220 (Lat. Atticus); (12) ~ ib. 2617 (Lat. M. Iunius Atticus: f. Ἵλαρος, Ἀττίκιλλα, Iunia Sperata); (13) ~ ib. 2834 (Lat. A. Paxeus Atticus)

—DIKAIARCHIA-PUTEOLI?: (14) c. 70-200 AD ib. 2192; cf. D'Isanto 68. 1 (Lat. A. Caesellius Atticus)
—DIKAIARCHIA-PUTEOLI*: (15) imp. *CIL* x 1887 (Lat. Atticus: freed.); (16) ~ ib. 2220 (Lat. C. Iunius Atticus: freed.); (17) ~ ib. 2234 (Lat. Atticus: freed.)
—NEAPOLIS: (18) i BC Ath. 14 f; (19) imp. *CIL* x 1486 (Lat. Iulius Atticus); (20) i-ii AD *IG* XIV 808 (*INap* 159); cf. Leiwo p. 106 no. 70 (Σέργιος Ἀ.)
—NOLA: (21) 33 AD *CIL* x 1233 (Lat. L. Ippellius Atticus)
—NOLA*: (22) imp. *RAAN* 30 (1955) p. 200 (Lat. D. Septumuleius Atticus: freed.)
—POMPEII: (23) i BC-i AD *CIL* IV 2508, 22 (Lat. Atticus); (24) ~ ib. 6801 (Lat. Atticus); (25) ~ *Römische Gräberstrassen* p. 223 a (Lat. P. Cluvius Atticus); (26) c. 51-62 AD *CIL* IV 3340. 81, 9 (Castrèn 255. 2) (Lat. [L.] Minicius Atticus); (27) 56 AD *CIL* IV 3340. 22, 16; 35, 17; 49, 15; 67; 99; 115; *Impegno per Pompeii* 11 ES no. 1 (Castrèn 434. 5) (Lat. A. Veius Atticus)
SICILY:
—KATANE: (28) imp. *CIL* x 7101 (Lat. Vipsanius Atticus)
—SEGESTA: (29) iv/iii BC *SEG* XXX 1119, 7 (Dubois, *IGDS* 206) (s. Πίστων)
—ZANKLE-MESSANA: (30) imp. *Mon. Ant.* 24 (1916) p. 196 (Lat. M. Sellius Atticus)
—ZANKLE-MESSANA*: (31) ?i AD *Epigraphica* 3 (1941) p. 258 no. 13 (Lat. Atticus)

## Ἀττίκων

SICILY:
—THERMAI HIMERAIAI: (1) i AD *Kokalos* 20 (1974) p. 235 no. 8 (s. Ἀγαθῖνος)

## Ἀττινᾶς

AITOLIA:
—THERMOS*: (1) s. iii BC *IG* IX (1)² (1) 60 IV, 18 (Ἀτ(τ)ινᾶς)

## Ἀττίνη

S. ITALY (CAMPANIA):
—POMPEII: (1) i BC-i AD *CIL* IV 2258 (Lat. Attine)

## Ἀττίνις

SICILY:
—PHILOSOPHIANA: (1) byz. *JIWE* I 157 (*SEG* XV 599)

## Ἄττος

S. ITALY (CAMPANIA):
—NEAPOLIS: (1) 41-54 AD *IG* XIV 728 (*INap* 16); cf. Leiwo p. 161 no. 135 (Ναούϊος Ἀ.)
SICILY:
—IAITON*: (2) ?iv/iii BC *Kokalos* 17 (1971) p. 174 (*AA* 1994, p. 239 no. 1 (bullet)) ((Τ)αίτου?—*AA*: ?f. Δαμάτριος)

## Ἄτωτος

ARGOLIS:
—ARGOS: (1) c. 480-460 BC *CEG* I 380. iii (-τō-: sculptor)

## Αὐγάζων

S. ITALY (CALABRIA):
—RUDIAE: (1) f. ii AD *CIL* IX 23 (Susini, *Fonti Salento* p. 103 no. 38) (Lat. M. Tuccius Augazo: f. M. Tuccius Cerialis)

## Αὐγᾶς?

S. ITALY (BRUTTIUM):
—SYBARIS-THOURIOI-COPIAE: (1) ?iv BC *JNG* 33 (1983) p. 14 (coin graffito) (Μισαυγα—graff.)

## Αὐγέας

LAKONIA:
—SPARTA?: (1) arch.? *IPr* 316, 3

## Αὐγείας
ARGOLIS:
—ARGOS: (1) iii BC *IG* IV (1) 527, 6 + *Hesp.* 16 (1947) p. 86 no. 9; cf. *BCH* 37 (1913) p. 308 (Αὐγει(α)s—*Hesp.*, Λύριs—*BCH*: f. Λακώ)

## Αὔγη
EPIROS:
—NIKOPOLIS: (1) imp. *SEG* XXIV 430 (Sarikakis 81) (Κλ. Ά.)
LAKONIA:
—PYRRHICHOS: (2) imp.? *IG* V (1) 1287 b
S. ITALY (APULIA):
—TEANUM APULUM*: (3) i-ii AD *Teanum Apulum* p. 72 no. 18 (Lat. Cluentia Auge: m. M. Plotius Placidus: freed.); (4) ii/iii AD ib. p. 71 no. 16 (Lat. Muttiena Auge: freed.)
S. ITALY (BRUTTIUM):
—HIPPONION-VIBO VALENTIA: (5) imp. *CIL* X 61 (Lat. Mettia Auge)
S. ITALY (CALABRIA):
—BRENTESION-BRUNDISIUM: (6) imp. ib. IX 121 (Lat. Gavinia Auge)
—HYRIA: (7) imp. ib. 229 (Lat. Auce)
S. ITALY (CAMPANIA):
—DIKAIARCHIA-PUTEOLI: (8) imp. ib. X 2495 (Lat. Hammonia Auge); (9) ~ ib. 3006 (Lat. Thoria Auge); (10) ?i-ii AD ib. 2549 (Lat. Iulia Auge)
—DIKAIARCHIA-PUTEOLI*: (11) ?i-ii AD ib. 2269 (Lat. Iulia Auge: freed.?); (12) ~ ib. 2585 (Lat. Iulia Auge: freed.)
—POMPEII: (13) i BC-i AD ib. IV 1547 c (Lat. Auge); (14) ~ ib. 1808 (Lat. Auge); (15) c. 70 AD ib. X 1025, 7 (Castrèn 241. 3); Kockel p. 84 (date) (Lat. Marcia Auge)
—POMPEII*: (16) i BC-i AD *Römische Gräberstrassen* p. 227 (Lat. Popidia Auge: freed.)
—SALERNUM*: (17) ?i AD *IItal* I (1) 238 III, 17 (*CIL* X 557) (Lat. Appuleia Auge: freed.)
S. ITALY (LUCANIA):
—ATINA LUCANA: (18) imp. *IItal* III (1) 196 (Lat. Auge: m. Luxilius Pedo)
SICILY:
—PARTHENIKON: (19) imp. *CIL* X 7264 (Lat. Aelia Aug[e])
—THERMAI HIMERAIAI: (20) i AD *ILat. Term. Imer.* 128 (Lat. Patulcia Auge)

## Αὐγῆς
S. ITALY (CAMPANIA):
—NEAPOLIS: (1) imp. *IG* XIV 772 (*INap* 99); cf. Leiwo p. 108 no. 76 (Αὐγῆδος (gen.))

## Αὔγις
ARGOLIS:
—ARGOS: (1) ii/i BC *SEG* XXII 266, 1, 3, 5, 20, [26] (s. Ἀριστομήδης)

## Αὐγουρῖνα
S. ITALY (CAMPANIA):
—NEAPOLIS: (1) iii-iv AD *IG* XIV 826. 5 (*INap* 222) (-ρεί-)

## Αὐγουστιανός
LAKONIA:
—SPARTA: (1) s. ii AD *IG* V (1) 144 a (Bradford (2)) (f. Χαρμόσυνος); (2) c. 212-235 AD *IG* V (1) 144 b (Bradford (1)) (Αὐρ. Ά.: s. Χαρμόσυνος)

## Αὐδαός
MESSENIA:
—MESSENE: (1) ii-iii AD *SEG* XLI 366 A

## Αὐδᾶτα
ILLYRIA: (1) iv BC *RE* (-); Berve s.v. Κυννάνη; cf. *RE* s.v. Eurydike (15) (also known as Εὐρυδίκη: m. Κυννάνη (Macedon))

## Αὖκτος
LAKONIA:
—TAINARON-KAINEPOLIS: (1) imp. *IG* V (1) 1251

## Αὔλη
S. ITALY (CAMPANIA):
—SALERNUM: (1) imp. *IItal* I (1) 76 (Lat. Sittia Aule)

## Αὐλία
SICILY:
—AKRAI: (1) 35 AD *SEG* XLII 833, 10 (Αὐλί[α]: d. Τίτος, Φαβία, m. Φάβιλλα)

## Αὐλίσκος
ARGOLIS:
—TROIZEN: (1) arch.? Paus. ii 31. 6

## Αὖλος
AIGINA?: (1) imp. *IG* IV (1) 88
ARGOLIS:
—ARGOS: (2) i BC *SEG* XI 344, 1, 4 (*GVI* 104); (3) imp. *IG* II² 8378 (f. Φιλουμένη); (4) ii AD *SEG* XVI 253, 15 (f. Ἱερώνυμος)
—EPIDAUROS: (5) imp. *IG* IV (1)² 512 (I f. Αὖλος II); (6) ~ ib. (II s. Αὖλος I)
EPIROS:
—BOUTHROTOS (PRASAIBOI): (7) a. 163 BC *IBouthrot* 37, 3 (*SEG* XXXVIII 496)

## Αὐλών
S. ITALY (CALABRIA):
—TARAS-TARENTUM: (1) ?ii-i BC Landi, *DISMG* 202 ((n. pr.?): f. Αὖλος Τιτίνιος)

## Αὐξάνιος
S. ITALY (APULIA):
—VENUSIA: (1) iv-v AD *JIWE* I 115-16 (Αὐξάνειος—115: Jew)

## Αὐξάνων
SICILY:
—SYRACUSE: (1) iii-v AD *IG* XIV 78 (Strazzulla 19; Agnello 1; Wessel 504); cf. Barreca 25 (Αὔξαντος—Barreca per err.); (2) ~ *SEG* XXXIX 1027 (Αὐχξά-)
—TAUROMENION: (3) iii-v AD *IG* XIV 166 (Strazzulla 107); Ferrua, *NG* 481 (locn.) (s. Σαβῖνος)

## Αὐξέντιος
SICILY:
—KATANE: (1) imp. *IG* XIV 462

## Αὔξησις
S. ITALY (APULIA):
—CANUSIUM*: (1) imp. *Epig. Rom. di Canosa* 94 (*CIL* IX 363) (Lat. Baebia Auxesis: freed.)
—VIBINUM: (2) imp. *Bovino* p. 146 no. 197 (Lat. Flavia Auxesis)
S. ITALY (CAMPANIA):
—MISENUM*: (3) ?i-ii AD *CIL* X 3564 (Lat. Claudia Auxesis)
—POMPEII*: (4) i BC-i AD *Impegno per Pompeii* 15 OS (Castrèn 34. 3) (Lat. Antistia Auxesis: freed.)

## Αὔξητος
SICILY:
—THERMAI HIMERAIAI: (1) imp. *CIL* X 7415 (*ILat. Term. Imer.* 111) (Lat. C. Laesanius Auxetus)

## Αὔξιμος
S. ITALY (CAMPANIA):
—MISENUM*: (1) ii AD *CIL* VI 8684 (*Puteoli* 12-13 (1988-9) p. 65 no. 1) (Lat. Auximus: s. Κάρπος, Ἀρέσκουσα)

## Αὔρα
S. ITALY (CAMPANIA):
—DIKAIARCHIA-PUTEOLI: (1) ?ii AD *CIL* X 2438 (Lat. Marcia Aura)

## Αὐρηλιανός
SICILY:
—SYRACUSE: (1) iii-v AD Strazzulla 383 (Wessel 700)

## Αὐρήλιος
SICILY:
—SYRACUSE: (1) iii-v AD Strazzulla 155 (Wessel 877); (2) ~ Strazzulla 231 (Αὐρ[ή]λ[ιος])

## Αὐσόνιος
LAKONIA:
—SPARTA: (1) m. iv AD Seeck, *Libanius* p. 92 (*PLRE* I (4)?; Bradford (-)) (Αὐσώνιος?)

## Αὐσωνεύς
SICILY:
—LIPARA: (1) s. i BC *BMC Sicily* p. 264 nos. 81-84; *RPC* I p. 168 no. 626 (coins) (Γ. Ά. (dub.))

## Αὐταγαθίδας
EPIROS:
—DODONA*: (1) iv BC Carapanos, *Dodone* p. 44 no. 12

## Αὐτάγαθος
KERKYRA:
—(Amphineis): (1) c. 500 BC *SEG* XXX 521 + *L'Illyrie mérid.* 2 p. 205

## Αὐτάρετος
LAKONIA:
—SPARTA: (1) vii/vi BC *Artemis Orthia* p. 370 no. 169. 26 with pl. 161. 4 (Lazzarini 404); *LSAG*² pp. 189 n. 1 (name); 198 no. 3 (date) (Αὐτάρετος)

## Αὐτάριστος
ARKADIA:
—MANTINEIA-ANTIGONEIA: (1) c. 425-385 BC *IG* V (2) 323. 8 (tessera) (Αὐτάριστ[ος]: f. Κοσμίερος)

## Αὐτέας
ARKADIA:
—MANTINEIA-ANTIGONEIA: (1) c. 300-221 BC ib. 323. 99 (tessera) (s. Νῖκις)

## Αὐτεσίων
ACHAIA?: (1) iii/ii BC *RE* (2); *FGrH* 298

## Αὐτή
S. ITALY (CAMPANIA):
—NUCERIA ALFATERNA: (1) imp. *CIL* X 1981 (Lat. Iulia Aute)

## Αὐτίας
ARKADIA:
—MANTINEIA-ANTIGONEIA: (1) c. 300-221 BC *IG* V (2) 323. 29 (tessera) (f. Θεοφιλίδας)
LAKONIA:
—SPARTA: (2) f. ii BC *IC* 2 p. 244 no. 4 B, 3 (Bradford (-)) (f. Ἀριστόδαμος)

## Αὐτόβιος
KORINTHIA:
—KORINTH: (1) m. iii BC *Corinth* VIII (3) 33 a, 6 (s. Ἐπ—)

## Αὐτόβουλος
ILLYRIA:
—APOLLONIA: (1) c. 250-50 BC Maier 31-4; Münsterberg Nachtr. p. 12 (coin) (Ceka 2; 88; 92; 98; 103) (pryt.)

## Αὐτόδαμος
ACHAIA:
—PELLENE: (1) m. iii BC *IG* V (2) 368, 98

## Αὐτοδίκη
S. ITALY (CAMPANIA):
—SALERNUM: (1) imp. *IItal* I (1) 77 (Lat. Ovia Autodice)

**Αὐτοκλείδας**
LAKONIA:
—SPARTA: (1) iii BC *IG* v (1) 145, 2 (Bradford
(-)) (Α[ὐτ]οκλε[ί]δας: s. Αὐτοκλῆς)

**Αὐτοκλῆς**
ARKADIA:
—TEGEA: (1) c. 240-229 BC *IG* v (2) 11, 18
LAKONIA:
—SPARTA: (2) iii BC ib. v (1) 145, 3 (Bradford
(-)) (Αὐτοκλίος (gen.): f. Αὐτοκλείδας)
MESSENIA:
—THOURIA: (3) f. ii BC *SEG* XI 972, 80 (f. Πυ-
θόδωρος)

**Αὐτοκράτης**
ACHAIA?: (1) ?iii/ii BC *RE* (5); *FGrH* 297
AKARNANIA:
—MEDION: (2) hell.? *SEG* XL 463
LAKONIA:
—SPARTA: (3) c. 450-434 BC *IG* v (1) 1229, 10
(Poralla² 170) (Αὐτοκράτε̄[s], Αὐτοκρατί[δας]?);
(4) c. 160-180 AD *IG* v (1) 666, 5; Cartledge–
Spawforth p. 232 no. 11 (date) (Bradford (-))
(Γ. Ἰούλ. Ἀ., Λυ(σι)κράτης?—Spawforth)

**Αὐτοκρατίδας**
EPIROS:
—DODONA*: (1) iv BC Carapanos, *Dodone* p. 44
no. 12

**Αὐτοκρέτης**
ARKADIA:
—TEGEA: (1) iv/iii BC *IG* v (2) 38, 68 (Αὐτο-
κρέτ[ης])

**Αὐτολαΐδας**
MESSENIA:
—THOURIA: (1) ii-i BC ib. v (1) 1385, 20 (s. Ξε-
νόστρατος)

**Αὐτόλοχος**
PELOPONNESE?: (1) s. iii BC ib. 1426, 30 (s. Ἀλεξάνωρ)

**Αὐτόλυκος**
AITOLIA: (1) ?255-254 BC Nachtergael, *Les Ga-
lates* 8, 66; 9, 68 (Stephanis 489) (s. Ἄστων)
?= (2)
AITOLIA?: (2) c. 278 BC *IG* II² 2325, 213 (s.e.)
?= (1)
AKARNANIA:
—THYRREION: (3) ii BC ib. IX (1)² (2) 251, 5 (s.
Καλλικράτης)
ARKADIA:
—TEGEA: (4) 165 AD ib. v (2) 50, 64 (s. Ἀλέξαν-
δρος)
EPIROS:
—AMBRAKIA: (5) a. 167 BC *SEG* XXXV 665 A, 8
(f. Ἀριστόβιος)
KORINTHIA:
—KORINTH: (6) m. v BC Schol. Pi., *O*. xiii, 58
b-c; *Dionysiaca* pp. 1-16 (ident.) (?s. Ναμερ-
τίδας); (7) imp. *SEG* XXXII 377 (lamp) (Αὐ-
τό(λ)υκος?)

**Αὐτόματος**
S. ITALY (CAMPANIA):
—MISENUM*: (1) ?i-ii AD *CIL* x 3357 (Lat. C.
Iulius Automatus: imp. freed.)

**Αὐτομέδα**
KEPHALLENIA:
—SAME: (1) hell. *IG* IX (1) 629
S. ITALY (LUCANIA): (2) ?c. 475-450 BC *Clas-
sical Vases* 65 (vase) (Arena, *Iscr. Sic.* IV 88);
cf. *LSAG*² p. 458 no. W

**Αὐτόμεδος**
LAKONIA:
—SPARTA: (1) her. Poralla² p. 35 (Lat.
Automedus: dub.)

**Αὐτομέδουσα**
KORINTHIA:
—KORINTH: (1) c. 600-575 BC Amyx 24. 5
(vase) (Lorber 44) (her.)

**Αὐτομέδων**
AITOLIA?: (1) i BC/i AD *GP* 1509 ff. with comm.
(locn.)

**Αὐτόμεια**
MESSENIA:
—MESSENE: (1) ?35-44 AD *IG* v (1) 1433, 26;
*SEG* XXIX 396 (d. Νεμέριος)

**Αὐτομένης**
KORINTHIA:
—KORINTH: (1) viii BC *FGrH* 244 F 331. 3
(king)

**Αὐτομήδης**
ARGOLIS:
—PHLEIOUS: (1) v BC B. ix 25 (s. Τιμόξενος)
KERKYRA: (2) her. Wehrli, *Schule Arist.* iv fr.
192

**Αὐτόμολος**
LAKONIA:
—OITYLOS: (1) iii/ii BC *IG* v (1) 1295, 2 (n. pr.?)

**Αὐτονόη**
ARGOLIS:
—EPIDAUROS: (1) 38 AD ib. IV (1)² 600, 4 (d.
Ἀριστοτέλης)
ILLYRIA:
—SKAMPIS: (2) imp. *BUST* 1961 (1), p. 122 no.
21 (Lat. Autonoe Itia)
S. ITALY (APULIA):
—LUCERIA: (3) imp. *ASP* 34 (1981) p. 23 no.
25 (Lat. Autonoe)

**Αὐτόνοος**
ARKADIA:
—MANTINEIA-ANTIGONEIA: (1) c. 300-221 BC
*IG* v (2) 323. 22 (tessera) (f. Αἰγικλῆς)
—TEGEA: (2) c. 225 BC Peek, *IAEpid* 331, 22
(Perlman E.5) ([Αὐ]τόνοος: s. Ἰσχέμαχος)

**Αὐτόπας**
ARKADIA:
—TEGEA:
——(Athaneatai): (1) s. iv BC *IG* v (2) 41, 38 (s.
Λάκων)

**Αὔτοπις**
ARKADIA:
—MANTINEIA-ANTIGONEIA: (1) c. 300-221 BC
ib. 323. 9 (tessera) (s. Αἰμύλος)

**Αὐτοσθένης**
ACHAIA:
—PELLENE: (1) ?a. 247 BC *FD* III (4) 403 III, 3
(s. Ἀχαιός)
AIGINA: (2) imp. *Arch. Class.* 17 (1965) pp.
306-9 (Α(ὐ)τοσθένης?, Lat. Athoste(nes))

**Αὐτοσθενίδας**
S. ITALY (CALABRIA):
—TARAS-TARENTUM: (1) inc. *NScav* 1894, p. 61
no. 5 (Αὐτοσθεν[ίδας]?)

**Αὐτόστολος**
S. ITALY (CAMPANIA):
—POMPEII: (1) i BC-i AD *CIL* IV 5400; 10226;
10246 b, g (Lat. Autostolus)

**Αὐτόφιλος**
KORINTHIA:
—KORINTH: (1) s. vi BC Amyx Gr 18 (vase)
(Arena, *Iscr. Cor.* 94) (Αὐτόφιλ[ος])

**Αὐτοχαρίδας**
LAKONIA: (1) v BC Iamb., *VP* 267 (*FVS* I p.
447; Poralla² 172)

—SPARTA: (2) 422 BC Th. v 12. 1 (Poralla² 171)

**Αὐφίδιος**
ACHAIA:
—PATRAI: (1) 20 AD Moretti, *Olymp.* 727

**Ἀφαίστιος**
AKARNANIA:
—STRATOS (NR.): (1) ?vi-v BC *AD* 22 (1967)
Chron. p. 323

**Ἀφαιστίων**
ACHAIA:
—DYME: (1) iii BC *AJPh* 31 (1910) p. 399 no.
74 b, 3 (f. Φίντων)
S. ITALY (CALABRIA):
—TARAS-TARENTUM: (2) 267 BC *SEG* XXVII
1114 A, 8 (*PP* 17003 a; Stephanis 1124)
(Ἥφαι-: s. Δαμέας)
SICILY:
—SELINOUS: (3) vi/v BC Manganaro, *PdelP*
forthcoming no. 18, 1 (-ōν: s. -σαιτας)

**Ἀφαιστος**
ACHAIA:
—DYME*: (1) c. 219 BC *SGDI* 1612, 81 (*Tyche*
5 (1990) p. 124) ([Ἅ]φαιστος: s. Ἀριστοκλῆς)

**Ἀφάρη**
S. ITALY (CAMPANIA):
—ATELLA: (1) imp. *CIL* x 3755 (Lat. Apare)

**Ἀφέλεια**
S. ITALY (APULIA):
—CANUSIUM*: (1) imp. *Epig. Rom. di Canosa*
Add. 11 (Lat. Atania Apheli[a]: freed.)
—LARINUM*: (2) imp. *CIL* IX 6247 (Lat. Li-
cinia Aphelea: freed.)

**Ἀφθόνητος**
AIGINA: (1) ?f. i AD *Alt-Ägina* I (2) p. 46 no.
20, 5 (s. Ἑρ—)
AIGINA?: (2) imp. *EAD* XXX p. 356 no. 17 with
n. 1 (s. Σωτηρίων)
ARGOLIS:
—EPIDAUROS: (3) iii-ii BC Le Rider, *Monnaies
crétoises* p. 258 I, 6, 8 (s. Σωτιμίδας, f. Σωτι-
μίδας, Κλεόμαχος)
—METHANA-ARSINOE: (4) i BC *IG* IV (1) 853,
10 (Ἀφθόνητος: s. Μένανδρος)
ARKADIA:
—MEGALOPOLIS: (5) 274 BC ib. XI (2) 199 B, 14
KEPHALLENIA:
—KRANIOI: (6) iii/ii BC ib. IX (1) 276, 2
LAKONIA: (7) ii-i BC ib. v (1) 975, 1 (Bradford
(3))
—SPARTA: (8) c. 133 AD *IG* v (1) 32 A, 8; 34,
12; 61, 1; 112, 11; 286, 6 (*Artemis Orthia* p.
319 no. 43 (date)); *SEG* XI 492, 9; 547 b, 2;
580, 2 (Bradford (2)) (Μ. Οὔλπ. Ἀ.); (9) 144
AD *SEG* XLI 317, 2 (f. Σωσικράτης); (10) s. ii
AD *IG* v (1) 323; *Artemis Orthia* p. 319 no. 43
(date) (Bradford (1)) (Μ. Οὐαλέριος Οὐλπιανὸς
Ἀ.: s. Σωσικράτης)
SICILY:
—KENTORIPA: (11) imp. *Riv. Stor. Antica* 5
(1900-1) p. 48 no. 14 (Lat. L. Calpurnius
[Aph]thonetus); (12) i-ii AD *NScav* 1953, pp.
364-5 (Lat. L. Calpurnius Apthonetus)

**Ἀφνειος**
MESSENIA:
—MESSENE (NR.): (1) ii AD *SEG* XI 983

**Ἀφοβία**
KORINTHIA:
—KORINTH: (1) v-vi AD *Corinth* VIII (3) 531, 7;
cf. *TMByz* 9 (1985) p. 365 no. 54 (name) (m.
Ἰωάννης, Ἀγαθοκλῆς)

**Ἀφόβιος**
ARGOLIS:
—ARGOS: (1) v-vi AD Unp. (Oikonomou-
Laniado); (2) ~ ib.

**Ἄφοβος**
S. ITALY (LUCANIA):
—HYELE-VELIA: (1) 157 BC *ID* 1416 B I, 64-5
([Ἄ]φοβος)

**Ἀφρικανός**
ARGOLIS:
—EPIDAUROS: (1) imp. *IG* IV (1)² 457; 471; 472
SICILY:
—SYRACUSE: (2) iii-v AD *NScav* 1907, p. 758

**Ἀφροδᾶς**
ARKADIA:
—LYKOSOURA*: (1) imp. *IG* V (2) 547. 1 (terracotta)
—TEGEA: (2) ii AD ib. 55, 41 (f. Ἀφροδίων); (3) ~
ib. l. 57 (s. Λουκᾶς); (4) ~ ib. l. 61 (s. Εὐφρόσυνος); (5) ~ ib. l. 90 (s. Ὀνησᾶς); (6) 165 AD ib.
50, 37 (f. Διογένης); (7) ~ ib. l. 38 (s. Ἀπολλᾶς);
(8) ~ ib. l. 44-5 (f. Τέρτιος, Σωτηρᾶς)
ELIS: (9) 265 AD *IvOl* 122, 7 (s. Αὐρ. Εὐτύχης)

**Ἀφρόδειος?**
MESSENIA:
—MESSENE: (1) ii-iii AD *SEG* XLI 366 D (Φ. Μ.
Θηρίππου καὶ Ἀφροδεί[ο]υ? (gen.))

**Ἀφροδισία**
AIGINA: (1) iii BC *IG* IV (1) 91; (2) imp. ib. 83,
4; (3) ~ ib. 93
AKARNANIA:
—ANAKTORION: (4) hell. *AD* 44 (1989) Chron.
p. 145
ARGOLIS:
—HERMIONE: (5) ?ii-i BC *IG* IV (1) 731 II, 2 (m.
Ἀμμία, Δινία, Τλανώ, Ζώτιχος); (6) ii-i BC ib.
732 II, 9; (7) ~ ib. 732 III, 4; (8) ~ ib. l. 20
(d. Ξένων); (9) ~ ib. l. 24 (m. Σωτηρίων); (10)
ii AD *SEG* XVII 163, 8 (-δει-)
—METHANA-ARSINOE: (11) imp. *IG* IV (1) 867
+ *SEG* XXXVII 317
—PHLEIOUS: (12) imp. *IG* IV (1) 473 (-δει-)
EPIROS: (13) iii BC *Thess. Mnem.* 28 (-δει-: d.
Θεύδοτος)
—BOUTHROTOS (PRASAIBOI): (14) a. 163 BC
*IBouthrot* 19, 7 (*SEG* XXXVIII 476)
—PHOINIKE: (15) ii-iii AD Ugolini, *Alb. Ant.* 2
p. 155 no. 8 (Ἀφροδε[ι]σία: Jew?)
ILLYRIA:
—APOLLONIA: (16) imp. *IApoll* 62; (17) ~ ib. 63
—EPIDAMNOS-DYRRHACHION: (18) hell.-imp.
*IDyrrh* 130 (-δει-); (19) ~ ib. 131 (-δει-); (20)
imp. ib. 132 (d. Ὅρος)
KERKYRA: (21) i BC-i AD *IG* IX (1) 903
KORINTHIA:
—SIKYON: (22) ii-iii AD *SEG* XI 256, 12 (-δει-:
d. Σωσικράτης)
LAKONIA:
—GYTHEION: (23) i BC-i AD *IG* V (1) 1204 (-δει-)
—SPARTA: (24) f. iii AD ib. 549, 12 (Bradford
(-)) (Αὐρ. Ἀφροδεισία: d. Νοήμων)
S. ITALY (APULIA):
—LARINUM: (25) imp. *CIL* IX 6244 (Lat. Coelia
Afrodisia)
—VENUSIA: (26) imp. ib. 594 (Lat. Aprodisia:
m. Ἀφροδίσιος)
—VIBINUM: (27) ii AD *Taras* 12 (1992) p. 156
no. 3 (Lat. Aphrodisia: ?d. Θάλλος)
S. ITALY (CALABRIA):
—BRENTESION-BRUNDISIUM: (28) i BC *IG* II²
8432 (d. Γάϊος); (29) imp. *CIL* IX 203 (Lat.
Vibia Ap[h]rodisia)
—BRENTESION-BRUNDISIUM*: (30) imp. *Epi-
graphica* 25 (1963) p. 78 no. 81; cf. *Scritti De-
grassi* 3 p. 73 (Lat. Tutoria Aprodisia: freed.);
(31) ~ *CIL* IX 201 (Lat. Veratia Aphrodisia:
freed.)
S. ITALY (CAMPANIA):
—CAPREAE: (32) ?i-ii AD *Eph. Ep.* VIII 671 (Lat.
Iulia Aphrodisia: imp. freed.)
—DIKAIARCHIA-PUTEOLI: (33) imp. *CIL* X
2093 (Lat. Afrodisia); (34) ~ ib. 2094 with

Add. p. 972 (Lat. Aprodisia); (35) ~ ib. 2865
(Lat. Pompeia Aphrodisia: m. Ἀκτή); (36) ~
ib. 3086 b (Lat. Claudia Afrodisia); (37) ~
*NScav* 1897, p. 530 (Audollent, *Defix. Tab.*
201 (terracotta)) (-δει-); (38) ?i-ii AD *CIL* X
2582 (Lat. Iulia Aphrodisia: m. Ἀρίστων); (39)
?ii-iii AD ib. 3058 (Lat. Valeria Afrodisia)
—DIKAIARCHIA-PUTEOLI*: (40) imp. ib. 2101
(Lat. Arria Aphrodisia: freed.); (41) ~ ib.
2123 (Lat. Attia Afrodisia: freed.)
—MISENUM*: (42) imp. ib. 3573 (Lat. Afro-
disia: freed.)
—SALERNUM: (43) imp. *IItal* I (1) 150 (*CIL* X
554) (Lat. Annia Aphrodisia)
SICILY:
—KATANE: (44) imp. *SGDI* 5237 (*IGLMP* 7)
([Ἀφρο]δισία)
—LIPARA: (45) imp. *Epigraphica* 11 (1949) p. 52
no. 1 (Ἀ. Κλωδία); (46) imp.? Libertini, *Isole
Eolie* p. 223 no. 37
—SYRACUSE: (47) iii-v AD *IG* XIV 79 (Strazzulla
20; Wessel 205); (48) ~ *IG* XIV 80
(Strazzulla 248; Wessel 711); cf. Ferrua,
*NG* 313 (Ἀφρο(δι)σία—Strazzulla and Fer-
rua, Ἀφροσία—Wessel); (49) ~ *SEG* XVIII 398
(Ἀφροδ[ισία]—ed., Ἀφροδ[ίτη]?—*LGPN*); (50)
~ Strazzulla 220 (Wessel 1187) (Ἀφροδ(ι)σ(ί)α)

**Ἀφροδισιάς**
SICILY:
—SYRACUSE: (1) imp. *IG* XIV 23 (d. Διονύσιος,
Φιλίστα)

**Ἀφροδίσιος**
ACHAIA: (1) 146 BC ib. IV (1)² 28, 80 (s. Ξενότι-
μος: synoikos)
AIGINA: (2) imp. ib. IV (1) 92; (3) i-ii AD *Alt-
Ägina* I (2) p. 47 no. 27, 5 (Ἀφρο[δίσιος]: f.
Θεοφάνης)
ARGOLIS:
—ARGOS: (4) iii/ii BC *IG* V (2) 263, 1, 15 (s.
Κύδιμος)
—ARGOS*: (5) ii BC *SEG* XLII 279, 15
(katoikos); (6) ~ ib. l. 16 (slave/freed.?)
—EPIDAUROS: (7) i-ii AD *IG* IV (1)² 549 (-δεί-: f.
Ἱεροκλῆς); (8) ii-iii AD ib. 532 (Ἀφ[ρο]δείσιος: I
f. Ἀφροδίσιος II); (9) ~ ib. ([Ἀ]φροδε[ί]σιος: II
s. Ἀφροδίσιος I); (10) f. ii AD ib. 381, 4; 382, 6
(f. Ὀνησιφόρος); (11) 232 AD ib. 410, 9 (-δεί-:
f. Διόδοτος)
—HERMIONE: (12) ?ii-i BC ib. IV (1) 731 II, 9
(s. Ζεύξιλα); (13) ii-i BC ib. 732 IV, 24 (s. Σω-
σίδας)
—TROIZEN: (14) i BC ib. II² 10462 (s. Εὔτυχος);
(15) 198-211 AD ib. IV (1) 793, 9 (f. Γέλλιος)
ARKADIA:
—KLEITOR: (16) m. iii AD *SEG* XXXV 350 I, 2
(f. Αὐρ. Ἐπαφρόδιτος)
—TEGEA: (17) ii AD *IG* V (2) 131 (Ἀφρο[δείσι]ος);
(18) 165 AD ib. 50, 6 (s. Φορτουνᾶτος)
ELIS: (19) 28-24 BC *IvOl* 64, 6, 30 (-δεί-: s. Εὔ-
πορος, ?f. Ἐπίκτητος: Γ.); (20) 53 AD Moretti,
*Olymp.* 781; *IvOl* 226 (Τιβ. Κλ. Ἀφροδείσιος);
(21) c. 77 or 81 AD ib. 85, 4 (Ἀφροδείσιο[ς])
EPIROS:
—BOUTHROTOS (PRASAIBOI): (22) a. 163 BC
*IBouthrot* 21, 9, 11 (*SEG* XXXVIII 478);
*IBouthrot* 184 (I s. Μᾶρκος, f. Ἀφροδίσιος II);
(23) ~ ib. 21, 9, 11 (*SEG* XXXVIII 478);
*IBouthrot* 184 (II s. Ἀφροδίσιος I)
ILLYRIA:
—EPIDAMNOS-DYRRHACHION: (24) c. 250-50
BC Maier 114; 192; 212; 232; 238; 310; 319;
331; 489; 491; Münsterberg p. 39; Nachtr.
pp. 15-17 (Ceka 107-22); cf. *IApoll Ref. Bibl.*
nn. 34-5 (coin); (25) hell.-imp. *IDyrrh* 66 (f.
Ἄβα); (26) ~ ib. 117 (f. Ἀριστήν); (27) ~ ib. 144
([Ἀφ]ροδίσιος: f. Βρύγος)
KORINTHIA:
—KORINTH: (28) imp. *IG* IV (1) 374 (tile)
([Ἀ]φροδείσ[ιος]) ?= (29); (29) ~ *Corinth* IV (1)

p. 16; *Hesp.* 34 (1965) p. 20; 41 (1972) p. 313
no. 20 (tile) (-δεί-) ?= (28); (30) ii-iii AD *Ken-
chreai* V App. I (lamp)
—SIKYON: (31) iii-ii BC *SEG* XI 252; (32) ?ii-i
BC Unp. (Sikyon Mus.) (Ἀφροδίσι[ος])
LAKONIA: (33) imp. *Syringes* 1469 (Bradford
(4))
—HYPERTELEATON*: (34) imp. *IG* V (1) 1068
([Ἀφρο]δείσιος)
—LEUKTRA: (35) imp. *SEG* XXII 312 (f. Φειδίας)
—SPARTA: (36) ?m. ii BC *IG* V (1) 887 (Bradford
(7)); (37) c. 25-1 BC *IG* V (1) 210, 13 (Brad-
ford (9)) (f. Δαμοκράτης); (38) c. 100 AD *SEG*
XI 626, 3 (Bradford (8)) (f. Ἀρίστων) ?= (42);
(39) c. 125-150 AD *IG* V (1) 114, 7 (Bradford
(10)) (f. Εὐήμερος); (40) c. 212-220 AD *IG* V
(1) 527, 2 (Bradford (3)) (Μ. Αὐρ. Ἀφροδείσιος:
s. Σωσίπολις); (41) c. 225-250 AD *SEG* XXXIV
308, 11 (Bradford (2)) ([Ἀφ]ροδείσιος: s. Εὐκα-
τάλλακτος)
—Limnai: (42) c. 70-100 AD *IG* V (1) 676, 15
(Bradford (1)) (-δεί-: s. Ἀρίστων) ?= (38)
MESSENIA:
—MESSENE: (43) imp. *SEG* XLI 375 F
([Ἀ]φροδείσιος)
PELOPONNESE?: (44) 11 AD *PAE* 1992, p. 72 B,
18 (f. Καλλίστρατος)
S. ITALY: (45) ?i BC *Epig. Rom. di Canosa* Instr.
19 (amph.) (Lat. Aprodi(sius)); (46) imp. *CIL*
X 8059. 161 (seal) (Lat. M. Felsonius Afrodi-
sius); (47) ~ ib. 8059. 208 (seal) (Lat. Iulius
Aphrodisius)
S. ITALY (APULIA):
—VENUSIA: (48) imp. ib. IX 594 (Lat. Veidius
Aprodisius: s. Ἀφροδισία)
S. ITALY (BRUTTIUM):
—PETELIA: (49) ii AD *Klearchos* 14 (1972) p. 127
no. 15 (Lat. M(anius) Meconi(us) Aphrodi-
si(us))
S. ITALY (CALABRIA):
—NERETUM: (50) 341 AD *CIL* IX 10 (Susini,
*Fonti Salento* p. 89 no. 23) (Lat. C. Gem.
Afrodisius)
—TARAS-TARENTUM*: (51) i-ii AD *Misc. Gr.
Rom.* 3 p. 195 no. T3 (Lat. C. Carrinas
Aphrodisius: freed.)
S. ITALY (CAMPANIA): (52) s. i AD *BM Lamps*
2 p. 300 no. Q1214 (Ἀφροδείσι(ος))
—DIKAIARCHIA-PUTEOLI: (53) imp. *CIL* X
2092 (Lat. Afrodisius); (54) ?i-ii AD ib. 2614
(Lat. Iulius Afrodisius: s. Διονύσιος, Τύχη);
(55) m. i AD *RAAN* 47 (1972) p. 312 no. 2
(Lat. Aphrodisius)
—POMPEII:
—(Boscoreale): (56) i BC-i AD *NScav* 1895, p.
211 (seal) (Castrèn 81. 7) (Lat. L. Caecilius
Aphrodisius)
SICILY:
—KATANE: (57) imp. *IG* XIV 504 (-δει-)

**Ἀφροδίσις**
ARKADIA:
—TEGEA: (1) ii AD ib. V (2) 55, 38 (-δεί-: s. Δα-
μάτριος); (2) ~ ib. 207
ILLYRIA:
—APOLLONIA: (3) imp. *IApoll* 199 (s. Λύκα)
SICILY:
—SYRACUSE: (4) 416 AD Strazzulla 393 (Wessel
946); cf. Ferrua, *NG* 145 (-σης)

**Ἀφροδίτα**
ARGOLIS:
—HERMIONE: (1) ?ii-i BC *IG* IV (1) 731 II, 19
(d. Σ—δης)

**Ἀφροδίτη**
S. ITALY (APULIA):
—VENUSIA*: (1) imp. *NScav* 1908, p. 443 +
*Misc. Gr. Rom.* 4 p. 293 (Lat. Severia Aph-
rodite: freed.); (2) m. ii AD *Epig. Rom. di
Canosa* 215 (Lat. Aphrodite: freed.?)

S. Italy (Campania):
—dikaiarchia-puteoli: (3) ?ii-iii ad *CIL* x 2154 (Lat. Aurelia Afrodite: m. Aurelia Puteolana)
—kyme: (4) imp. *AJA* 2 (1898) p. 397 no. 61 (Lat. Livia Prodite)
—salernum: (5) imp. *IItal* 1 (1) 161 (*CIL* x 650) (Lat. Vibia Aphrodite)
Sicily:
—akrillai: (6) iii-v ad *Epigraphica* 12 (1950) p. 96 no. 2; cf. Ferrua, *NG* 503
—syracuse: (7) iii-v ad Strazzulla 157 ([Ἀφ]ροδίτη)

**Ἀφροδιτία**
Argolis:
—argos*: (1) f. iii bc *IG* iv (1) 529, 10 (slave/freed.?)
S. Italy (Calabria):
—taras-tarentum: (2) imp. *NScav* 1894, p. 68 no. 45 (Lat. Artimia Aprhoditia)
S. Italy (Lucania):
—herakleia: (3) iv/iii bc *IG* xiv 646, 3 (Landi, *DISMG* 212)
Sicily:
—lipara: (4) ?ii-i bc *Epigraphica* 11 (1949) p. 50 no. 1

**Ἀφροδιτώ**
Sicily:
—katane: (1) imp. *CIL* x 7046 (Lat. Aphrodito Mimas)

**Ἀφροδίων**
Arkadia:
—tegea: (1) ii ad *IG* v (2) 55, 41 (s. Ἀφροδᾶς)
Korinthia:
—korinth: (2) imp. *SEG* xxxv 396 (lamp)

**Ἀφροδώ**
Aigina?: (1) imp. *EAD* xxx p. 357 no. 26 (d. Ζώπυρος)
Arkadia:
—tegea: (2) imp. *IG* v (2) 208; (3) ii-iii ad ib. 179, 1 (-εδώ)
Lakonia:
—sparta:
——Konosoura: (4) c. 212 ad ib. v (1) 566, 7 (Bradford (-)) (Αὐρ. Ἀ.)
—tainaron-kainepolis: (5) ?iii ad *IG* v (1) 1267 (Ἀφροδώ)

**Ἀφρώ**
S. Italy (Apulia):
—lavello (mod.): (1) ii-iii ad *Rend. Linc.* 29 (1974) p. 628 no. 36 (Lat. Aphro)
—venusia*: (2) ii-iii ad ib. p. 627 no. 36 (Lat. Aphro: slave?)
S. Italy (Bruttium):
—petelia: (3) i/ii ad *Klearchos* 22 (1980) p. 33 (Lat. Philicia Aphro)
S. Italy (Campania):
—pithekoussai-aenaria: (4) imp. Monti, *Ischia* p. 224 n. 43 (Lat. Aphro)

**Ἀχαΐς**
Sicily:
—gela-phintias: (1) i bc/i ad *GP* 195 (n. pr.?: fict.?)

**Ἀχαϊκή**
Argolis:
—phleious: (1) ii-i bc *SEG* xxvi 417

**Ἀχαϊκός**
Argolis:
—argos*: (1) ii ad ib. xvi 258 b, 8 (M. Ἀντ. Ἀ.) ?= (6)

Arkadia:
—teuthis?: (2) ii-i bc ib. xxxv 347 B
—thisoa: (3) iv bc ib. xxxvii 336; *Hyperboreus* 1994 (1), p. 151 f. (date)
Elis: (4) c. 65-75 ad *IvOl* 83, 5 (Λ. Σαίνιος Ἀχα[ϊκός]); (5) 197-201 ad ib. 106, 9 (f. Μοντανός)
Korinthia:
—korinth: (6) i/ii ad *Corinth* viii (3) 134, [10]; 224, 2; *BCH* 28 (1904) p. 425 no. 7, 14 (*ILS* 8863) (M. Ἀντ. Ἀ., Lat. M. Antonius Achaicus) ?= (1); (7) ii ad *Corinth* viii (3) 357 (Lat. [Ac]haicu[s])
—korinth?: (8) c. 50 ad *1 Ep. Cor.* 16. 17
Lakonia:
—sparta: (9) c. 105-115 ad *IG* v (1) 103, 6 (Bradford (-))
Messenia:
—asine: (10) ii ad *IG* v (1) 1408 (Ἀντ. Ἀ.)
Peloponnese?: (11) ii ad *PAE* 1992, p. 71 A, 31 (Σέξ. Κοίλιος Ἀχαϊκός)
S. Italy (Calabria):
—brentesion-brundisium: (12) imp. *CIL* ix 44 (Lat. C. Antonius Achaicus)
S. Italy (Campania):
—dikaiarchia-puteoli: (13) imp. ib. x 2539 (Lat. Ti. Iulius Achaicus)

**Ἀχαιός**
Achaia: (1) ii bc D.S. xxxiv-v 2. 16; 2. 42; (2) 146 bc *IG* iv (1)² 28, 79 (s. Ἀσκλάπων: synoikos)
—pellene: (3) c. 279-247 bc *FD* iii (4) 403 II, 1; III, 4 (s. Ταλθύβιος); (4) ?a. 247 bc ib. 403 III, 2 (s. Ξέναρχος, f. Ξέναρχος, Αὐτοσθένης)
Argolis:
—hermione: (5) iii bc *IG* iv (1) 729 II, 8 (f. Σῶσος)
Sicily:
—syracuse: (6) s. iv bc *RE* (7) + Supplbd. 9

**Ἀχελῷος**
S. Italy (Campania):
—surrentum: (1) imp. *CIL* x 740 (Lat. M. Livius Achelous)

**Ἀχένατος**
Sicily:
—gela-phintias?: (1) ?c. 430 bc *Ancient Art in Bowdoin College* 196 (Johnston, *Trademarks* p. 167 and fig. 13 m (vase)) (n. pr.?)

**Ἀχιλλᾶς**
S. Italy (Campania):
—misenum*: (1) imp. *CIL* x 3515 (Lat. Pison. Acillas)

**Ἀχιλλεύς**
Achaia:
—patrai: (1) ii-iii ad *IG* II² 10046 a (f. Θεόξενος)
Elis: (2) c. 221-230 ad *IvOl* 113, 14 ([Ἀχι]λλεύς)
—olympia*: (3) v bc ib. 837, 2 (?f. Πολυκλ—)
Illyria: (4) f. iii bc Plu., *Pyrr.* 2. 7
Korinthia:
—korinth: (5) m. ii ad *IG* vii 1773, 29 (Stephanis 499) (Ἀ. Κλ. Ἀ.)
S. Italy (Campania):
—atella*: (6) s. iii ad *Epigraphica* 29 (1967) p. 22 (Lat. Caesonius Achilleus: freed.)
Sicily:
—katane: (7) imp. *CIL* x 7025 (*Epigraphica* 51 (1989) p. 168 no. 33) (Lat. Achilleus)
—lilybaion: (8) ?ii-i bc *SEG* xxxiv 955; cf. xxxix 1005 (s. Πρόθυμος)

—syracuse: (9) iii-v ad *IG* xiv 81 (Strazzulla 22; Wessel 1052) (-λεούς); (10) ~ *IG* xiv 82 (Strazzulla 23; Wessel 652); cf. Ferrua, *NG* 314 (-λεούς); (11) ~ *Nuovo Didask.* 4 (1950) p. 64 no. 24 (-λέους)

**Ἀχιλλῆς**
Illyria:
—bylliones byllis: (1) imp. *Iliria* 1987 (2), p. 107 no. 66 (Lat. M. Insteius Agiles)
S. Italy (Campania):
—salernum: (2) ?ii ad *IItal* 1 (1) 31 (*CIL* x 550) (Lat. L. Sep. Achilles)
S. Italy (Lucania):
—volcei (nr.): (3) ?i bc Dyson, *Roman Villas of Buccino* p. 34 no. 2 (pithos) (Lat. Aciles)

**Ἀχιλλιανός**
S. Italy (Campania):
—dikaiarchia-puteoli: (1) ii ad *NScav* 1927, p. 332 no. 5; cf. *Puteoli* 3 (1979) p. 156 no. 2 (Lat. M. Laecanius Achillianus)

**Ἀχλαδαῖος**
Korinthia:
—korinth: (1) vii bc Paus. iv 19. 2

**Ἄχυρις**
Sicily: (1) iv/iii bc *SEG* xxxix 1034 (?f. Δάμαρχος)

**Ἀχώρητος**
Arkadia:
—mantineia-antigoneia: (1) ?c. 350 bc *Klio* 15 (1918) p. 56 no. 78, 1

**Ἀχώριστος**
S. Italy (Apulia):
—venusia: (1) imp. *CIL* ix 509 (*NScav* 1939, p. 149 no. 2) (Lat. P. Antonius Achoristus)
—vibinum: (2) f. i ad *Bovino* p. 144 no. 196; *Quad. di Storia* 35 (1992) p. 85 (Lat. M. Vibius Achoristus)

**Ἀψέφης**
Achaia:
—aigeira: (1) s. iv bc *BCH* 62 (1938) p. 341 (Ἀψέφεος (gen.): f. Μανίδας)

**Ἀψίνης**
Lakonia:
—sparta: (1) s. iii ad *PLRE* I (1); Cartledge–Spawforth p. 182 (ident.) (f. Ὀνάσιμος); (2) f. iv ad *PLRE* I (2); Cartledge–Spawforth p. 182 (ident.) (Bradford (-)) (s. Ὀνάσιμος)

**Ἄψιππος**
Arkadia:
—megalopolis: (1) s. ii bc *IG* v (2) 438, 18 (s. Ἀπελλις, f. Ἀπελλις)

**Ἄψυρτος**
S. Italy (Campania):
—dikaiarchia-puteoli: (1) imp. *CIL* x 1949 (Lat. Poblicius Apsyrtus)
—herculaneum: (2) m. i ad *PdelP* 3 (1948) p. 182 no. 30; 8 (1953) p. 463 no. 56, 6 (Lat. Iunius Apsyrtus); (3) 41-79 ad *Cron. Erc.* 7 (1977) p. 115 A c, 12 (Lat. Q. Annius Apsyrtus)
—pompeii: (4) i bc-i ad *CIL* iv 8535; 8540 (Lat. Apsyrtus).

**Ἄψψος**
Illyria:
—apollonia: (1) imp. *IApoll* 264 (f. Πλαῖος)

# B

**Βαβελύκα**
ARGOLIS:
—ARGOS: (**1**) v-iv BC Iamb., *VP* 267 (*FVS* I p. 447)

**Βάβις**
ARKADIA:
—MANTINEIA-ANTIGONEIA: (**1**) c. 425-385 BC *IG* V (2) 323. 12 (tessera)

**Βάβος**
AKARNANIA:
—ASTAKOS: (**1**) ii BC ib. IX (I)² (**2**) 434, 19 (s. Δελμάτας)

**Βαβύρτας**
AITOLIA: (**1**) 290-280 BC *FD* III (I) 150, I (f. Πιττίας)
MESSENIA:
—MESSENE: (**2**) 221 BC Plb. iv 4. 5, 7; *RE* Supplbd. I (-)

**Βαδηΐας**
LAKONIA:
—OITYLOS: (**1**) iii/ii BC *IG* V (I) 1295, 3 (Bradford (-)) (B(ϝ)αδηΐας)

**Βάδιμος**
ARKADIA:
—PHIGALEIA: (**1**) m. iii BC *SEG* XXIII 239, 2; (**2**) ~ ib. l. 3; (**3**) s. iii BC ib. 242

**Βάδυλα**
ILLYRIA:
—EPIDAMNOS-DYRRHACHION: (**1**) hell.-imp. *IDyrrh* 136 = 85 (B(ϝ)άδυλα: d. Γοργήν)

**Βαθέας**
ARKADIA:
—KLEITOR: (**1**) c. 330 BC *SEG* XXIII 189 II, 22
KORINTHIA:
—SIKYON: (**2**) vi/v BC ib. XI 244, 6

**Βαθυκλῆς**
ARGOLIS:
—EPIDAUROS:
——(Dymanes): (**1**) 146 BC *IG* IV (I)² 28, 7 (f. Πολυκράτης)
—HERMIONE: (**2**) iv/iii BC *HE* 2357 (f. Φίντων)
ARKADIA: (**3**) vii/vi BC Ath. 781d; Call. dieg. vi 9; fr. 191, 32-5; D.L. i 28 (f. Ἀμφάλκης, Θυρίων)
—MEGALOPOLIS: (**4**) ii/i BC *IG* V (2) 442, 13 (s. Ἀγήσιππος)
—TEGEA: (**5**) f. iii BC ib. 42, 5 ([Βα]θυκλῆς); (**6**) ii BC ib. 141; (**7**) ii/i BC ib. 22 (f. Αἰσαγένης)
——(Apolloniatai): (**8**) iv/iii BC ib. 38, 39 ([Β]αθυκλῆς: s. —ίδας)
—THISOA: (**9**) 359 BC *CID* II 5 I, 23 (and Arkadia Megalopolis); (**10**) c. 230-200 BC *BCH* 45 (1921) p. 15 III, 6 (B[α]θυκλῆ[s]—Oulhen)
MESSENIA:
—PROTE*: (**11**) imp. *SEG* XI 1021 (f. Ἐρατοσθένης)

**Βαθυλλίς**
EPIROS:
—BOUTHROTOS: (**1**) imp. *IBouthrot* 191 (*SEG* XXXII 624)

**Βάθυλλος**
ELIS:
—PISA: (**1**) 365-363 BC *IvOl* 36, 7 (Perlman O.1) (Βάθυλ[λος]: s. Κλεόμαχος)
S. ITALY (CALABRIA):
—BRENTESION-BRUNDISIUM*: (**2**) imp. *CIL* IX 6395 (Lat. C. Octavius Bathyllus: freed.)

S. ITALY (CAMPANIA):
—DIKAIARCHIA-PUTEOLI: (**3**) imp. ib. X 1889 (Lat. Sex. Publicius Bathyllus)
—PITHEKOUSSAI-AENARIA*: (**4**) imp. ib. 6804 (Lat. M. Antonius Bathyllus: imp. freed.)
S. ITALY (LUCANIA):
—POSEIDONIA-PAESTUM: (**5**) vi/v BC Iamb., *VP* 267 (*FVS* I p. 447); D.L. viii 83 (Βαθύλαος—Iamb.)

**Βαθύλος**
ARKADIA:
—TEGEA: (**1**) s. iv BC *SEG* XXXVI 383, 9 ([Β]α[θ]ύλος)
LAKONIA:
—SPARTA: (**2**) c. 140-160 AD *IG* V (I) 154, 4 (Bradford (-)) (f. Πίστος)

**Βάθυος**
AKARNANIA: (**1**) c. 250-167 BC *NZ* 10 (1878) p. 28 no. 25 (coins) (Βάθυς—no. 25 c: s. Νικίας)
—KORONTA: (**2**) m. ii BC *IG* IX (I)² (2) 209, 19 (f. Νικίας)
LEUKAS: (**3**) c. 167-50 BC *BMC Thessaly* p. 179 nos. 82-3; *SNG Cop. Epirus-Acarnania* 380 (coins); (**4**) f. i BC *IG* IX (I) 534, 5 (*Iscr. Gr. Verona* p. 24) (s. Ἀγήσανδρος)

**Βάθυς**
AITOLIA: (**1**) c. 315-280 BC *FD* III (I) 142, I (f. Εὔδικος)

**Βαΐς**
SICILY:
—SYRACUSE: (**1**) iii-v AD *NScav* 1907, p. 760 no. 18; cf. Ferrua, *NG* 83 a (-ής)

**Βαιστίρων**
DALMATIA:
—ISSA: (**1**) iii-ii BC Brunšmid p. 29 no. 24 (Βαιστίρωνο[s] (gen.), Ϙαιστίρων?: f. Νικαία)

**Βάκχεια**
EPIROS:
—NIKOPOLIS: (**1**) imp. *Ep. Chron.* 31 (1994) p. 41 no. 3 (Βάκχε[ι]α)
SICILY:
—SYRACUSE: (**2**) v-vi AD Strazzulla 204; cf. Ferrua, *NG* 27 b (date) (Βάχια (nom.))

**Βακχεῖος**
S. ITALY (CAMPANIA):
—MAMERTINOI: (**1**) hell. *SB* 417 f (Βακεῖ-: f. Μαραῖος)

**Βακχιάδας**
KORINTHIA:
—SIKYON: (**1**) hell. *FGrH* 387 (Skalet 74) (Βακχίδας—ms., *B.*—Meineke)

**Βακχίδης**
ILLYRIA:
—APOLLONIA: (**1**) i BC Maier 136; cf. 153 (coin) (f. Ἀντίοχος)

**Βάκχιος**
AITOLIA:
—THERMOS*: (**1**) s. iii BC *IG* IX (I)² (I) 60 III, 7; (**2**) ~ ib. 60 VII, I; (**3**) ~ ib. l. 22 (Βά[κ]χιος)
ARKADIA:
—TEGEA: (**4**) hell.? ib. V (2) 171 (Βάκχι(ος)?: ?f. Ἐπήρατος); (**5**) f. ii BC ib. 44, 19 (s. Νικόλας)
KORINTHIA:
—TENEA: (**6**) i BC *SEG* XIII 248, 5 (Βάκχιος: s. Ἀθηνίων)
S. ITALY (LUCANIA):
—LEUKANOI: (**7**) c. 316-309 BC *IG* II² 1956, 48; *Ancient Macedonia* 5 p. 445 with n. 10 (date)

**Βάκχις**
KORINTH: (**1**) her. *RE* (2) (s. Πρύμνις, f. Ἀγέλας: king)

**Βακχίς**
EPIROS:
—BOUTHROTOS (PRASAIBOI): (**1**) a. 163 BC *IBouthrot* 22, 14 (*SEG* XXXVIII 479)
KORINTHIA:
—SIKYON: (**2**) ii BC *AD* 18 (1963) Mel. p. 21 no. 35
S. ITALY (CAMPANIA):
—POMPEII: (**3**) i BC-i AD *CIL* IV 8238; 8246 (Lat. Bacchis)

**Βακχιώ**
AKARNANIA:
—THYRREION: (**1**) hell. *SEG* XXXIX 483

**Βακχίων**
SICILY:
—THERMAI HIMERAIAI: (**1**) imp. *CIL* X 7373 (*ILat. Term. Imer.* 42) (Lat. C. Aemil. Bacchio)

**Βάκχος**
S. ITALY (CAMPANIA):
—POMPEII: (**1**) i BC-i AD *CIL* IV 3508 (Lat. Bacchus (n.pr.?))

**Βακχυλίδης**
SICILY:
—SYRACUSE: (**1**) iii-v AD *Riv. Arch. Crist.* 18 (1941) p. 202 no. 75 (-χιλλ-)

**Βάκχυλλος**
S. ITALY (CAMPANIA):
—DIKAIARCHIA-PUTEOLI: (**1**) ?i AD *CIL* X 2260 + *Puteoli* 11 (1987) p. 46 (Lat. Ti. Claudius Baccyllus)

**Βακχύλος**
LAKONIA:
—SPARTA: (**1**) ii AD *IG* V (I) 118, 6; *SEG* XI 589 (name) (Bradford (1)) ([Αἰσ]χύλος—*IG*, [Βακ]χύλος—*SEG*: s. Ἀ—); (**2**) c. 125-150 AD *SEG* XI 578, I (Bradford (3)) (I f. Βακχύλος II); (**3**) ~ *SEG* XI 578, I (Bradford (2)) (Τιβ. Κλ. Β.: II s. Βακχύλος I)
S. ITALY (CAMPANIA)?: (**4**) imp.? *IG* XIV 2414. 14 (tessera) (Βα(κ)χύλος)

**Βάλαγρος**
EPIROS: (**1**) 274 BC ib. XI (2) 287 B, 57 (f. Ἀντίπατρος)

**Βάλακρος**
EPIROS:
—MOLOSSOI: (**1**) f. iii BC *FGrH* 703 F 9 (s. Νίκανδρος)

**Βαλεντία**
SICILY:
—SYRACUSE: (**1**) iii-v AD *NScav* 1918, p. 278 (Barreca 58)

**Βαλεντῖνος**
SICILY:
—SYRACUSE: (**1**) iii-v AD Strazzulla 169 (Wessel 1114); cf. Ferrua, *NG* 10 a ([Β]αλεντῖνος)

**Βαλερία**
SICILY:
—SYRACUSE: (**1**) iii-v AD Strazzulla 186 (Wessel 875) (-ρία)

**Βαλεριανός**
KORINTHIA:
—KORINTH: (**1**) byz. *PAE* 1961, p. 132; cf. *TMByz* 9 (1985) p. 367 no. 83

**Βαλέριος**
KORINTHIA:
—KORINTH: (1) ii/iii AD *Corinth* IV (2) p. 207 no. 716; *Lampes antiques BN* 1 26 (lamps)

**Βαλέρις**
SICILY:
—SYRACUSE: (1) iii-v AD Wessel 1367 (Barreca 61)

**Βαλλαῖος**
ILLYRIA: (1) f. ii BC Brunšmid pp. 78 ff. nos. 1-27; pp. 82 ff. nos. 28-47; *BMC Thessaly* p. 81 nos. 1-11 (coin); cf. *Schweizer Münzblätter* 162 (1991) pp. 25-30 (date) (king)

**Βᾶλος**
ARGOLIS:
—ARGOS: (1) ?c. 494-468 BC *SEG* XI 329 a, 1 (Lazzarini 747); *SEG* XIII 246 (name); *LSAG*² p. 169 no. 25 (date) (s. Πρατέας)

**Βαναξεύς**
LAKONIA:
—SPARTA: (1) iii/ii BC *SEG* XXIV 281 (Bradford (-)) (B(ϝ)αναξεύς: date—*LGPN*)

**Βάννιος**
S. ITALY: (1) s. iv BC *SEG* XXIX 1026 (Νούιος B.)

**Βάντιος**
ILLYRIA:
—EPIDAMNOS-DYRRHACHION: (1) hell.-imp. *IDyrrh* 235 (f. Ἡρακλείδης); (2) ~ ib. 263 (f. Κλέα)

**Βαπτίς**
S. ITALY (CAMPANIA):
—POMPEII: (1) i BC-i AD *CIL* IV 1507, 12; cf. p. 208 (Lat. Baptis)

**Βάρβαρος**
KERKYRA?: (1) hell. *RAAN* 21 (1941) p. 276 no. 1 + *BE* 1944, no. 119 a; cf. *IBouthrot* 186
LAKONIA:
—SPARTA: (2) c. 220 AD *SEG* XXXIV 311, 9; *BSA* 79 (1984) pp. 267-9 (date) (Bradford (-)) (Αὐρ. B.)
S. ITALY (APULIA):
—GNATHIA-EGNATIA: (3) imp. *CIL* IX 264 (Lat. Barbarus)
S. ITALY (CAMPANIA):
—NEAPOLIS: (4) imp. *Mem. Accad. Arch. Napoli* 2 (1913) pp. 236-45 (Lat. Barbarus: s. Cumanus)
—POMPEII*: (5) i AD *CIL* X 8048. 44 (vases) (Lat. A. Tettius Barbarus)

**Βάργος**
ELIS: (1) 20-16 BC *IvOl* 65, 6 (s. Ἀπολλώνιος: T.)
ILLYRIA:
—EPIDAMNOS-DYRRHACHION: (2) hell.-imp. *IDyrrh* 299 (f. Μάξιμα)

**Βάρδυλλις**
ILLYRIA: (1) v/iv BC *RE* (1) (f. Κλεῖτος); (2) iv BC ib. (2) (?s. Κλεῖτος, f. Βίρκεννα)

**Βάρηξ**
SICILY:
—LIPARA: (1) i BC *SEG* XLII 855 ([Σ]ήιος Βάρηξ)

**Βάρις**
ARGOLIS:
—HERMIONE: (1) iii BC *IG* IV (1) 729 II, 3 (s. Μάργος)

**Βαρίς**
S. ITALY (CAMPANIA):
—SALERNUM: (1) i BC/i AD *IItal* I (1) 130 (Lat. Acilia Baris)

**Βαρκαῖος**
LAKONIA: (1) 109-105 BC *PRein* I 15, 29; 16, [36]; 20, 35; 23, 27 (Bradford (-)) (f. Ἀγήνωρ)

**Βαρναῖος**
ILLYRIA:
—EPIDAMNOS-DYRRHACHION: (1) hell.-imp. *IDyrrh* 360 (f. Πορτία)

**Βαρνᾶς**
SICILY:
—PRIOLO (MOD.): (1) iii-v AD *Riv. Arch. Crist.* 18 (1941) p. 216 no. 95 (Ἀνναῖος B.: Jew?)

**Βαρτώ**
SICILY:
—SYRACUSE: (1) iii-v AD *NScav* 1893, p. 303 no. 90 (Barreca 54)

**Βάρχιλλα**
S. ITALY (CAMPANIA):
—POMPEII: (1) i BC/i AD *Impegno per Pompeii* 3 ES (Lat. Veia Barchilla: d. Numerus)

**Βασίας**
ARKADIA: (1) 401 BC X., *An.* iv 1. 18
ELIS: (2) 400 BC ib. vii 8. 10
SICILY:
—KAMARINA: (3) ?ii BC *SEG* XXXIX 996, 5 (Dubois, *IGDS* 126; Cordano, 'Camarina VII' 84) (f. Ἀθανις)

**Βασίλα**
KORINTHIA:
—KORINTH KENCHREAI: (1) inc. *ILGR* 125, 6 (Lat. Iulia Basila)
S. ITALY (APULIA):
—SOLETUM: (2) i BC Susini, *Fonti Salento* p. 96 no. 31 (Lat. Basila)

**Βασίλεια**
MESSENIA:
—MESSENE: (1) i BC/i AD *PAE* 1969, p. 118 no. 6
S. ITALY (CAMPANIA):
—MISENUM: (2) imp. *AJA* 96 (1992) pp. 82-4 (Lat. Fulvia Basilia)

**Βασιλείδας**
LAKONIA:
—SPARTA: (1) c. 100-125 AD *IG* V (1) 137, 20 (Bradford (-)) (-λί-: f. Δαμονικίδας)

**Βασιλείδης**
ELIS: (1) 245-249 AD *IvOl* 121, 4, 8, 20 (Αὐρ. B.: f. Αὐρ. Νεοκλῆς, ?f. Ζώσιμος)
SICILY: (2) imp. *IG* XIV 301 (*IGLMP* 107) (T. Νασίδις B.)
—TAUROMENION: (3) ii-iii AD *Epigraphica* 3 (1941) p. 267 no. 36 (*ILat. Palermo* 52) (Lat. P. Edusius Basilides)
—THERMAI HIMERAIAI: (4) imp. *ILat. Term. Imer.* 153 (Lat. L. Vecil[ius] Basilides)

**Βασίλειος**
ACHAIA:
—PATRAI: (1) iv-v AD *SEG* XIII 277, 2 (-λι-: I f. Βασίλειος II); (2) ~ ib. l. 2 (-λι-: II s. Βασίλειος I)
S. ITALY (APULIA):
—LUCERIA: (3) imp. *CIL* IX 842 (Lat. Basilius)
SICILY: (4) byz. *BZ* 19 (1910) p. 470 (ring)
—HALOUNTION: (5) byz. *IG* XIV 2395. 1 (tile) (Βασήλης)
—KENTORIPA: (6) ?iii-iv AD *Sic. Gymn.* 2 (1949) p. 96 no. 3 (Βασί[λιος]?)

**Βασιλεύς**
S. ITALY (CAMPANIA):
—DIKAIARCHIA-PUTEOLI: (1) imp. *CIL* X 1997 (Lat. Acutius Basileus: s. Θέων)

**Βασιλίς**
S. ITALY (CAMPANIA):
—DIKAIARCHIA-PUTEOLI: (1) 53 AD Camodeca, *L'Archivio Puteolano* I pp. 229-30 (Lat. Titinia Basilis)
SICILY:
—KATANE: (2) imp. *IG* XIV 450; cf. *SEG* XXXVIII 942; (3) ?iv-v AD *MEFRA* 106 (1994) pp. 88-9 no. 6

**Βασιλίσκος**
SICILY:
—LIPARA: (1) imp. *Epigraphica* 51 (1989) p. 194 no. 89 (Lat. Basiliscus)
—ZANKLE-MESSANA: (2) f. i BC Cic., *In Verr.* II iv 25 (Lat. Cn. Pompeius Basiliscus)

**Βάσσα**
S. ITALY (CAMPANIA):
—DIKAIARCHIA-PUTEOLI: (1) imp. *CIL* X 3187 + *Puteoli* 11 (1987) p. 61

**Βάσσιλα**
S. ITALY (CAMPANIA):
—DIKAIARCHIA-PUTEOLI: (1) imp. *CIL* X 2810 (Lat. Oppia Bassilla)

**Βάσσος**
AIGINA: (1) her. *RE* (-) (Βασσίδαι (n. gent.)—Pi., Βασσιάδαι—Schol. Pi.); (2) ?f. i AD *Alt-Ägina* I (2) p. 48 no. 38 (f. Αὐρ. Ἡρακλᾶς)
ARKADIA:
—TEGEA: (3) imp. *SEG* XXIII 234
KORINTHIA:
—KORINTH: (4) i AD Ap. Ty., *Ep.* 36; 37; 74
SICILY:
—KATANE: (5) iii-v AD *NScav* 1918, p. 63 no. 7 (Wessel 140) (doctor)

**Βαστίας**
LAKONIA: (1) hell. *IG* V (1) 707 (Poralla² 341) (B(ϝ)αστίας)

**Βάτινα**
ILLYRIA:
—EPIDAMNOS-DYRRHACHION: (1) hell.-imp. *BUST* 1962 (2), p. 132 (*Stud. Alb.* 1965, p. 98) (Lat. Batina); (2) ~ *IDyrrh* 137

**Βάτουνα**
ILLYRIA:
—EPIDAMNOS-DYRRHACHION: (1) hell.-imp. ib. 138 (d. Ἐπίκτησις)

**Βάτραχος**
ILLYRIA:
—APOLLONIA: (1) c. 250-50 BC Münsterberg Nachtr. p. 12; cf. *IApoll Ref. Bibl.* n. 36 (coin) ([Βά]τραλ[χ]ος?: money.)
LAKONIA: (2) ?ii BC Plin., *NH* xxxvi 42; *RE* (2) (Lat. Batrachus: sculptor/dub.)

**Βάτταλος**
AITOLIA: (1) ?228-215 BC *FD* III (4) 364, 2

**Βάττος**
KORINTHIA:
—KORINTH: (1) 425 BC Th. iv 43. 1

**Βάτων**
AKARNANIA:
—PHOITIAI: (1) iv BC *IG* IX (1)² (2) 602, 7 (s. Κι—)
ILLYRIA:
—APOLLONIA: (2) c. 250-50 BC *Bakërr Hoard* p. 63 no. 8; *Jubice Hoard* p. 98 no. 1 (coin) (Ceka 32-3) (money.)
—DARDANIOI: (3) 200 BC Liv. xxxi 28. 1-2 (Lat. Bato: s. Λόγγαρος: king)
—EPIDAMNOS-DYRRHACHION: (4) hell.-imp. *IDyrrh* 139 (s. Νεστίων)
—EPIDAMNOS-DYRRHACHION (NR.)?: (5) ii BC *SEG* XXXVIII 572, 6; cf. *CRAI* 1991, p. 197 ff.; *L'Illyrie mérid.* 2 p. 206 (f. Ὄλαπος)

**Βαυκιδίων**
ILLYRIA:
—LYCHNIDOS: (1) ii-iii AD BSA 18 (1911-12) p. 176 no. 18 (s. Κάλλιστος)

**Βαῦκις**
ARGOLIS:
—TROIZEN: (1) v/iv BC Paus. vi 8. 4; Moretti, Olymp. 358

**Βεβαῖος**
SICILY:
—KENTORIPA: (1) c. 60 BC IG VII 420, 46, 56, 62 (IOrop 528) (f. Ἐμμενίδας)

**Βέβρυξ**
S. ITALY (CAMPANIA):
—POMPEII: (1) i BC-i AD Impegno per Pompeii 21 OS no. 2 (Lat. Bebrix)

**Βέγετος**
ELIS: (1) 185-189 AD IvOl 104, 18 (s. K—)

**Βέγος**
LAKONIA:
—SPARTA?: (1) f. iii BC BSA 45 (1950) p. 271

**Βείδιππος**
LAKONIA:
—SPARTA: (1) c. 25-1 BC IG v (1) 210, 10 (Bradford (2)) (B(ϝ)είδιππος: I f. Βείδιππος II); (2) ~ IG v (1) 210, 10 (Bradford (1)) (B(ϝ)είδιππος: II s. Βείδιππος I)

**Βέλλος**
ILLYRIA: (1) c. 168 BC Liv. xliv 31. 9 (Lat. Bellus)

**Βέλλων**
LAKONIA:
—SPARTA: (1) i/ii AD IG v (1) 490, 11 (Bradford (3)) (f. Ἰλάρα); (2) m. ii AD IG v (1) 89, 12; 129, 2; 490, 2 (Bradford (1); (2)) (s. Εὐκλείδας, Ἰλάρα, f. Δαμίων)

**Βελτίς**
ARGOLIS:
—HERMIONE: (1) i BC-i AD? IG IV (1) 730 I, 4 (d. Κλεοπάτρα)

**Βενδίς**
S. ITALY (LUCANIA):
—POSEIDONIA-PAESTUM*: (1) 160 AD Mello-Voza 66 (Lat. Bendis: d. Βίθυς (Philippopolis), Actia Secunda)

**Βένετος**
ILLYRIA:
—APOLLONIA: (1) imp. Sestieri, ILat. Albania p. 111 no. 8 (amph.) (Lat. Venet[us])
—EPIDAMNOS-DYRRHACHION: (2) hell.-imp. IDyrrh 207 (f. Εὔνοια)

**Βένιγνα**
SICILY:
—SYRACUSE: (1) 428 AD Strazzulla 178 (Wessel 655); cf. BZ 8 (1899) p. 109

**Βενοῦστα**
SICILY:
—MORGANTINA*: (1) ?i BC SEG XXIX 931-3 (slave?)

**Βενουστίων**
SICILY:
—AUGUSTA (MOD.): (1) iii-v AD Riv. Arch. Crist. 18 (1941) p. 195 no. 63

**Βενοῦστος**
SICILY:
—SYRACUSE: (1) ?335 AD Strazzulla 377 (Wessel 1210) (Β[ενο]ύστος)

**Βερενίκα**
AITOLIA:
—KASILIOI: (1) s. ii BC SEG XXV 621, 7 (d. Σωτηρίδας)

**Βερενίκη**
EPIROS: (1) iv/iii BC Ag. XVII 456 ([Βερ]ενίκη)
—AMBRAKIA: (2) imp. Ep. Chron. 1 (1926) p. 116 (Βερο-)
S. ITALY (APULIA):
—LARINUM: (3) ?i-ii AD Riv. Stor. Antica 5 (1900-1) p. 621 (CIL IX 774) (Lat. Iulia Beronice)
—VENUSIA: (4) imp. ib. 535 (Lat. Antonia Berenice); (5) v AD JIWE I 42 (CIJ I 580) (Βερον[ίκ]η: Jew); (6) ~ JIWE I 59 (CIJ I 581) (-ρο-: d. Ἰωσῆς: Jew)
S. ITALY (BRUTTIUM):
—RHEGION: (7) ii-iii AD Suppl. It. 5 p. 67 no. 20 (SEG XL 857) (Βερνίκη)
S. ITALY (CALABRIA):
—BRENTESION-BRUNDISIUM: (8) i AD Epigraphica 25 (1963) p. 82 no. 92 (Lat. [Va]leria Beronice)
S. ITALY (CAMPANIA):
—DIKAIARCHIA-PUTEOLI: (9) imp. CIL X 2420 (Lat. Beronice); (10) ?ii AD ib. 3132 (Lat. Ulpia Beronice)
—NEAPOLIS: (11) imp. Mon. Ant. 8 (1898) p. 228 (-νεί- Ἰουνία)
—POMPEII: (12) i BC-i AD CIL IV 2198; 2256 (Lat. Beronice)
SICILY:
—THERMAI HIMERAIAI: (13) imp. ib. X 7445 (ILat. Term. Imer. 157) (Lat. Veronice: d. Δαματρία)

**Βερνικιανός**
MESSENIA:
—KORONE: (1) 246 AD IG v (1) 1398, 81 (Αὐρ. Βερνεικιανός)

**Βερόη**
EPIROS:
—MOLOSSOI: (1) iv/iii BC RE s.v. Beroe (6) (Lat. Beroe)
S. ITALY (CAMPANIA):
—POMPEII: (2) i BC-i AD CIL IV 4189

**Βέρσαντος**
ILLYRIA:
—EPIDAMNOS-DYRRHACHION: (1) hell.-imp. IDyrrh 184 (B(ϝ)έρσαντος: f. Ἐπίκαδος)

**Βέρσας**
ILLYRIA:
—EPIDAMNOS-DYRRHACHION: (1) hell.-imp. ib. 140 (B(ϝ)έρσας: s. Τρίτος)

**Βέσσων**
SICILY:
—SYRACUSE: (1) iii-v AD NScav 1912, p. 299

**Βετούριος**
ARKADIA:
—MANTINEIA-ANTIGONEIA: (1) c. 130 AD BMC Pelop. p. 177 nos. 89-90 (coin)

**Βημαῖος**
EPIROS:
—DODONA*: (1) v-iv BC Carapanos, Dodone p. 44 no. 13 (s. Φυλλεύς)

**Βήρυλλος**
S. ITALY (APULIA):
—RUBI: (1) ii AD Epigrafia e Territorio 2 p. 63 no. 7 (CIL IX 653) (Lat. Beryllus: s. Aurelia Donata)
S. ITALY (CAMPANIA):
—DIKAIARCHIA-PUTEOLI: (2) imp. ib. X 2596 (Lat. Herennius Beryllus); (3) ~ ib. 3050 (Lat. M. Valerius Beryllus: f. M. Valerius Lupus)

**Βήρυτία**
ILLYRIA:
—EPIDAMNOS-DYRRHACHION: (1) ?i AD AEp 1978, no. 742 (Lat. Iulia Berytia)

**Βηρύτιος**
S. ITALY (CAMPANIA):
—POMPEII: (1) i BC-i AD CIL IV 4862 (Lat. Berutius)

**Βιάδας**
LAKONIA: (1) ii BC IG v (1) 965, 18; (2) 73 BC ib. 1145, 28, 45; 1146, 15
—GYTHEION: (3) b. 19 AD SEG XI 932; (4) c. 15 AD ib. 923, 34 (Τερέντιος B.)
—OITYLOS: (5) f. ii BC IG v (1) 935, 8 ([B]ιάδας)
—SPARTA: (6) c. 150-160 AD ib. 71 III, 8-9, 24; 294, 3 (Artemis Orthia p. 325 no. 52); SEG XI 493, 7; 528, 1; 553, 3; 585, 1 (Bradford (-)) (Γ. Ἀβίδιος B.)

**Βιαῖος**
AITOLIA:
—APEIRIKOI?: (1) m. ii BC SBBerlAk 1936, p. 371 b, 14 (SEG XLI 528 B) (f. Εὔαρχος)
ARKADIA:
—TEGEA: (2) f. ii BC IG v (2) 44, 4 (f. Ἀριστοφάνης)

**Βιάνωρ**
AKARNANIA: (1) s. iv BC RE (5); Berve 214; (2) 197 BC RE Supplbd. 11 (5a) (Lat. Bianor) ?= (6)
—PHOITIAI: (3) iv BC IG IX (1)² (2) 602, 10 (Βιά[νωρ?]: f. Ϝοινίδας)
LAKONIA:
—SPARTA?: (4) ?iii AD ib. v (1) 569, 2; cf. Cartledge-Spawforth p. 210 (Bradford (-)) (Γ. Ῥούβριος B.: s. Σερᾶς)
LEUKAS: (5) ?256 BC SGDI 2659, 3 + ZPE 101 (1994) pp. 223 f. ([Βι]άνωρ: s. Τίμων); (6) 216 BC IG IX (1)² (2) 583, 20 (s. Θάλων) ?= (2)

**Βίας**
KORINTHIA:
—KORINTH: (1) f. vi BC Corinth XV (3) p. 359 no. 5 (pinax) ?= (2); (2) c. 590-570 BC Amyx 28. 1 (pinax) (Lorber 41) (f. Τιμωνίδας) ?= (1)
LAKONIA:
—SPARTA: (3) f. iv BC Plu., Mor. 192 C (Poralla² 173)
S. ITALY (CALABRIA):
—TARAS-TARENTUM: (4) iv/iii BC IG XIV 668 I, 6 (Landi, DISMG 194)

**Βιβία**
S. ITALY?: (1) 191 BC SGDI 1985, 3-4 (slave/freed.); (2) 189 BC ib. 1960, 3 (slave/freed.)

**Βίβιος**
ARKADIA:
—MEGALOPOLIS: (1) hell. IG v (2) 469 (25) (tile)
S. ITALY (CAMPANIA):
—NEAPOLIS: (2) i BC INap 101; cf. Leiwo p. 83 no. 29 (s. Ἄρχιππος) ?= (8); (3) s. ii BC INap 185 (f. M—); (4) i BC/i AD SEG IV 97 (INap 102); cf. Leiwo p. 62 no. 3 (s. Ἐπίλυτος); (5) ~ SEG IV 99 (INap 115) (s. Ἐπίλυτος); (6) ~ SEG IV 100 (INap 114) (f. Ἐπίλυτος); (7) ~ ib. 103; cf. Leiwo p. 104 no. 60 (s. Χάρμας); (8) ~ INap 107; cf. Leiwo p. 83 no. 30 (f. Δίκα) ?= (2); (9) ~ INap 134; cf. Leiwo p. 78 no. 24 (Βείβι[ος])
S. ITALY (LUCANIA):
—LEUKANOI: (10) c. 208 BC FD III (4) 134, 20 (I f. Βίβιος II); (11) ~ ib. l. 20 (II s. Βίβιος I)

**Βιγιλαντία**
SICILY:
—SYRACUSE: (**1**) iii-v AD Strazzulla 280 (Wessel 947)

**Βιδεύς**
SICILY:
——(Τυ̂ος): (**1**) iv BC Manganaro, *PdelP* forthcoming no. 3, 5 (Βειδεύς (n. pr.?): s. Ἀκα̂ς)

**Βιδώ**
ILLYRIA:
—EPIDAMNOS-DYRRHACHION: (**1**) hell.-imp. *IDyrrh* 141 (B(ϝ)ιδου̂ (gen.?))

**Βιζάτιος?**
S. ITALY (APULIA):
—BUTUNTUM: (**1**) ?iv BC *SEG* XXXVI 892 (Troisi, *Epigrafi mobili* 66 (loomweight)) (or S. Italy (Calabria) Taras-Tarentum)

**Βιθυνικός**
EPIROS:
—NIKOPOLIS: (**1**) ii AD *SEG* XXIV 426 (Sarikakis 177) (Τ. Φλ. Βειθυνικός: s. Ἰουλ. Μάγνα)
S. ITALY (CAMPANIA):
—POMPEII: (**2**) i BC-i AD *CIL* IV 1108 (Lat. Bithynicus)

**Βιθυνός**
S. ITALY (APULIA):
—VENUSIA*: (**1**) imp. ib. IX 671 (Lat. L. Aurelius Bithynus: freed.)

**Βίθυς**
AIGINA: (**1**) iii AD *AE* 1913, p. 96 no. 8 (Βεί-)
S. ITALY (APULIA):
—AUSCULUM: (**2**) imp. *CIL* X 1885; cf. *Puteoli* 11 (1987) p. 44 (locn.) (Lat. C. Minatius Bithus)
—LUCERIA: (**3**) imp. *CIL* IX 815 (Lat. C. Sescenius Bithus: freed.)
S. ITALY (BRUTTIUM):
—TAURIANA: (**4**) ii-iii AD *Rend. Linc.* 19 (1964) p. 133 no. 2 (Lat. Bithus: f. Ἡδίστη)
S. ITALY (CAMPANIA):
—CAPREAE*: (**5**) f. iii *Epigraphica* 29 (1967) p. 59 (Lat. Aur. Bitus)
—HERCULANEUM*: (**6**) i BC-i AD *CIL* X 1403 g III, 52 (Lat. Q. Novius Bithus: freed.)
—KYME*: (**7**) i BC *CIL* I² 3129, 4 (Audollent, *Defix. Tab.* 199) (Lat. C. Blossius Bithus: freed.)
—MISENUM*: (**8**) ?ii AD *NScav* 1928, p. 196 no. 4 + *Puteoli* 11 (1987) p. 139 no. 6 (Lat. Flavius Bithus: II s. Βίθυς I (Thrace, Bessoi))
—POMPEII: (**9**) i BC-i AD *CIL* IV 1667 (Castrèn 221. 4) (Lat. M. Lollius Bithus)
S. ITALY (LUCANIA):
—POSEIDONIA-PAESTUM*: (**10**) 160 AD Mello-Voza 66 (Lat. Bithus: II s. Βίθυς I (Thrace, Philippopolis), Actia Secunda)

**Βι̂ππος**
ARGOLIS:
—ARGOS: (**1**) ?ii BC Unp. (Ch. Kritzas) ?= (Βίππος (*1*))

**Βίκτωρ**
SICILY:
—SYRACUSE: (**1**) iii-v AD *IG* XIV 83 (Strazzulla 24; Wessel 867); cf. Ferrua, *NG* 157 (Βίκτων—*IG* maj., Βίκτω(ρ)—edd., Βίντων—Ferrua)

**Βικτωρία**
SICILY:
—COMISO (MOD.): (**1**) iii-v AD *NScav* 1937, p. 467 (*Helikon* 2 (1962) p. 500); cf. *Riv. Arch. Crist.* 18 (1941) p. 199 no. 72

—SYRACUSE: (**2**) ii-iii AD ib. p. 171 no. 32; (**3**) iii-v AD *IG* XIV 84 (Strazzulla 25) (Βει-); (**4**) ~ ib. 185 (Wessel 1319); (**5**) ~ Strazzulla 239 (Wessel 151); (**6**) ~ Strazzulla 292 (Βη-); (**7**) ~ ib. 372 (Wessel 690); (**8**) ~ Strazzulla 373 (Wessel 653) (Βικκτω-); (**9**) ~ Ferrua, *NG* 255 (Βικτωριαν[ή]?—Ferrua); (**10**) 433 AD *IG* XIV 85 (Strazzulla 26; Wessel 1366)

**Βικτωρι̂νος**
KORINTHIA:
—KORINTH?: (**1**) m. vi AD *RE* (10); Bees 1-2
SICILY:
—AKRAI: (**2**) iii-v AD Ferrua, *NG* 200
—SYRACUSE: (**3**) imp. *IG* XIV 87 (Strazzulla 28; Wessel 195); cf. Ferrua, *NG* 159 ([Βι]κτορι̂νος); (**4**) iii-v AD *IG* XIV 86 (Strazzulla 27; Wessel 1104) (Βει-: ?s. Ἐπιφάνιος); (**5**) byz. *SEG* IV 10

**Βινκόμαλος**
S. ITALY (APULIA):
—VENUSIA: (**1**) iv-v AD *JIWE* I 111 (*CIJ* I 593) (Βιν[κ]όμαλο[ς]: f. Φαυστι̂νος: Jew)

**Βιόδαμος**
LAKONIA:
—GERONTHRAI: (**1**) iii-ii BC *IG* V (1) 1127, 5
—SPARTA: (**2**) s. i BC ib. 93, 18 (Bradford (1)) (B(ϝ)ιόδαμος: s. —φάνης); (**3**) c. 90-100 AD *SEG* XI 558, 2 (Bradford (2)) (f. Πασικλείδας)

**Βιόλα**
ARGOLIS:
—ARGOS: (**1**) byz. *SEG* XXVI 436, 6; cf. *TMByz* 9 (1985) p. 370 no. 117

**Βιόλας**
LAKONIA:
—SPARTA: (**1**) c. 25-1 BC *IG* V (1) 210, 21 (Bradford (1)) (s. Νίκανδρος)

**Βίος**
EPIROS:
—AMBRAKIA: (**1**) ii-i BC *CIG* 1798 (s. Ἀγασίδαμος: mantis)

**Βιότη**
SICILY:
—THERMAI HIMERAIAI: (**1**) imp. *IG* XIV 323 (Κανυληΐα [Βι]ότη)

**Βίοτος**
S. ITALY (BRUTTIUM):
—RHEGION: (**1**) inc. *NScav* 1888, p. 593 no. 7 (Lat. T. Biotus)
S. ITALY (CAMPANIA):
—KYME: (**2**) ?c. 450 BC Dubois, *IGDGG* I 21 b (vase) (Arena, *Iscr. Sic.* III 22); *LSAG²* p. 240 no. 15 (date)
SICILY:
—GELA-PHINTIAS: (**3**) f. v BC Dubois, *IGDS* 131. 8 (Arena, *Iscr. Sic.* II 45)

**Βίππος**
ARGOLIS:
—ARGOS: (**1**) 182-181 BC Plb. xxiii 18. 3; xxiv 1. 6; 2. 4 (Βήιπος, Βέϊπο(s), Βίππων, Βήππων—mss.) ?= (Βι̂ππος (*1*))

**Βίρκεννα**
ILLYRIA: (**1**) iv/iii BC *RE* (-) (d. Βάρδυλλις, m. Ἔλενος)

**Βιτάλα**
SICILY:
—AKRAGAS: (**1**) iii AD *IGLMP* 2

**Βιτάλιος**
SICILY:
—SYRACUSE: (**1**) iii-v AD *IG* XIV 141 (Strazzulla 81; Wessel 876); (**2**) ~ *NScav* 1893, p. 278 no. 3 + Ferrua, *NG* 2 a (Βιτ[άλιο]s?)

**Βι̂τις**
AITOLIA:
—LITHOVOUNI (MOD.) (AKRAI?): (**1**) v/iv BC *SEG* XXXIV 466 (vase) (Βίτιος (nom./gen.?))

**Βίτος**
ARGOLIS:
—TROIZEN: (**1**) ii/i BC *IG* IV (1) 790 (s. Θεύδωρος)
S. ITALY (APULIA):
—VENUSIA: (**2**) iv-v AD *JIWE* I 111 (*CIJ* I 593) (B[ί]τος: f. Σάρα: Jew)

**Βίττος**
AITOLIA: (**1**) ?263-261 BC *FD* III (3) 184, 1; [190]; *Syll³* 498, 2; Nachtergael, *Les Galates* 3, 1
—THERMOS: (**2**) 214 BC *IG* IX (1)² (1) 177, 18 (f. Ἀνδρόνικος)
—TRICHONION: (**3**) 190-178 BC ib. 97, 2; 131, 1; *Syll³* 636, 16 (f. Νίκανδρος)

**Βίτων**
ARGOLIS:
—ARGOS: (**1**) s. vii BC *RE* (1) (s. Κυδίππα)
ARKADIA: (**2**) f. iii BC *HE* 2555; *GP* 3370
S. ITALY (CALABRIA):
—BRENTESION-BRUNDISIUM: (**3**) imp. *CIL* IX 85 (Lat. Biton: ?s. Σωκράτης)
S. ITALY (CAMPANIA):
—DIKAIARCHIA-PUTEOLI: (**4**) ?i-ii AD ib. X 2261 (Lat. Ti. Claudius Bito)
SICILY:
—SYRACUSE: (**5**) 397 BC D.S. xiv 53. 5

**Βιύσθιος?**
SICILY: (**1**) hell. Manganaro, *PdelP* forthcoming no. 9 (Βειυσθιώι (masc./dat.?, fem./nom.?)—ed.)

**Βιώ**
AITOLIA:
—KALYDON: (**1**) a. 142 BC *IG* IX (1)² (1) 137, 66, 74

**Βίων**
AITOLIA: (**1**) ?253 BC Nachtergael, *Les Galates* 10, 4; (**2**) ii AD *IG* IX (1)² (1) 92, 4 (f. Νικίας, Ἀριστόδαμος)
—THERMOS*: (**3**) s. iii BC ib. 60 II, 9
ARGOLIS:
—EPIDAUROS: (**4**) iii BC Peek, *IAEpid* 43, 34 (f. Ποσειδαι̂ος)
—EPIDAUROS*: (**5**) c. 370-365 BC ib. 52 B, 62
ARKADIA:
—PHENEOS: (**6**) ii/i BC *IG* IV (1)² 100, 3; cf. Stephanis 238 (f. Ἀπολλα̂ς)
ILLYRIA:
—APOLLONIA: (**7**) ii-i BC *IApoll* 134 (f. Νικώ); (**8**) i BC Ceka, *Probleme* p. 139 no. 5; cf. *IApoll Ref. Bibl.* n. 37 (coin) (pryt.); (**9**) ~ Maier 155; 157; 161 (coin) (money.); (**10**) ~ ib. 137-9 (coin) (pryt.)
—BALAIITAI: (**11**) ii BC *SEG* XXXVIII 521, 1; cf. *CRAI* 1991, pp. 197 ff.; *L'Illyrie mérid.* 2 p. 204 f. (s. Κλειγένης)
—EPIDAMNOS-DYRRHACHION: (**12**) c. 250-50 BC Maier 148 (coin) (Ceka 5) (pryt.)
KORINTHIA:
—KORINTH: (**13**) c. 570-550 BC Amyx 103. 1 (vase) (Lorber 96) (-ōv: her.?)
—SIKYON: (**14**) ?254 BC Nachtergael, *Les Galates* 9, 32; cf. Stephanis 1329 (f. Καλλίβιος)
LAKONIA: (**15**) ii-i BC *IG* II² 9150 (f. Ἰατρόκλεια)
—SPARTA?: (**16**) 400 BC X., *An.* viii 8. 6 (Poralla² 174)
MESSENIA:
—ABIA: (**17**) i BC/i AD *IG* V (1) 1353 (s. Ἀριστόλας)
SICILY:
—SYRACUSE: (**18**) ?f. iv BC *RE* (12)

**Βιωνίδας**
LAKONIA:
—SPARTA: (1) 220 BC Plb. iv 22. 11 (Bradford (-))

**Βιωτική**
KORINTHIA:
—KORINTH: (1) ii-iii AD SEG XXXI 565 (Βει-)

**Βίωτος**
S. ITALY (LUCANIA):
—LAOS*: (1) iv-iii BC AMSMG 1929, p. 169 (terracotta)
—MONTESCAGLIOSO (MOD.): (2) iii BC St. Etr. 52 (1984) p. 479 (tiles)
SICILY: (3) f. iii BC Vandermersch p. 164; Arch. Subacquea 2 p. 62 (amph.) (or S. Italy)
—HALOUNTION: (4) ii-i BC IG XIV 366 (IG-LMP 43) ([Β]ίωτος: s. Τίμανδρος)

**Βιωτώ**
S. ITALY (CALABRIA):
—TARAS-TARENTUM (NR.): (1) iii BC Atti Conv. Taranto 22 (1982) p. 457 (Λεοντὶς B.)

**Βλαῖσος**
S. ITALY (CAMPANIA):
—CAPREAE: (1) iii-ii BC RE (4)

**Βλάστη**
S. ITALY (CAMPANIA):
—STABIAE*: (1) imp. RAAN 19 (1938-9) p. 124 (Lat. Clodia Blaste: freed.)
SICILY:
—KATANE: (2) iii-v AD ASSiciliaOrientale 1931, pp. 39-41 no. 11 (d. Καιλία Ἑόρτη)
—SYRACUSE: (3) iii-v AD Strazzulla 274 (Wessel 1353) (Βλάσθ[η])

**Βλάστιος**
DALMATIA:
—ISSA: (1) iii/ii BC Brunšmid p. 24 no. 12; BCH 114 (1990) p. 506 fig. 4 (Βλάτιος—ed., Βλάστιο[s]—BCH: s. Κα—)

**Βλάστος**
ARGOLIS:
—EPIDAUROS: (1) iii AD IG IV (1)² 693 (T. Aἴλ. B.)
ARKADIA:
—TEGEA: (2) m. ii AD ib. v (2) 48, 2 (Βλάστ[ος])
EPIROS:
—NIKOPOLIS: (3) imp. CIG 1821 b addenda (Sarikakis 72) (Κλ. B.)
KORINTHIA:
—KALA NESIA (MOD.): (4) ?ii AD SEG XXVIII 386 (M. Ἀντ. B.)
—KORINTH: (5) ii AD ib. XVII 130 (mantis)
LAKONIA:
—TAINARON-KAINEPOLIS: (6) imp. IG v (1) 1263
—TEUTHRONE: (7) ii-i BC ib. 1219; Mél. Daux pp. 303-7 (name) ([Β]λάστος, Βλάστη—IG)
S. ITALY (CALABRIA):
—TARAS-TARENTUM*: (8) ii AD Arch. Class. 31 (1979) p. 136 no. 3 (Lat. P. Aelius Blastus: imp. freed.)
S. ITALY (CAMPANIA):
—DIKAIARCHIA-PUTEOLI: (9) 53 AD Camodeca, L'Archivio Puteolano 1 pp. 229-30 (Lat. Cn. Pollius Blastus)
—DIKAIARCHIA-PUTEOLI*: (10) imp. IG XIV 856 (Π. Φουλούϊος B.: freed.); (11) ~ CIL x 2234 (Lat. Blastus: freed.); (12) ~ NScav 1891, p. 340 (Lat. A. Nonius Blastus: freed.); (13) 41 AD Camodeca, L'Archivio Puteolano 1 p. 238 (Lat. Cn. Pompeius Blastus: freed.)
—MISENUM*: (14) imp. CIL x 3463 (Lat. Blastus: freed.)
—POMPEII: (15) i BC-i AD ib. IV 2436 (Lat. Blastus); (16) ~ ib. 8115 (Lat. Blastus)

——(Boscoreale): (17) i BC-i AD NScav 1895, p. 211 (terracotta) (Lat. Blastus)
—SALERNUM: (18) m. i BC IItal I (1) 125 (CIL x 566) (Lat. Blastus)
—STABIAE: (19) i BC-i AD Riv. Stud. Pomp. 1 (1987) p. 185 fig. 65 left (Lat. Q. Poppaeus Blastus)
—STABIAE*: (20) i BC-i AD ib. p. 185 fig. 65 right (Lat. Blastus: ?f. Poppaea Fausta: freed.)
—SURRENTUM: (21) imp. St. Rom. 2 (1914) p. 346 no. 12 = NScav 1928, p. 208 no. 4 (Lat. Blastus)
S. ITALY (LUCANIA):
—POTENTIA*: (22) i-ii AD CIL x 8340 a + ZPE 106 (1995) p. 284 no. 3 (Lat. P. Campulaeus Blastus: freed.)
SICILY:
—KATANE: (23) imp. CIL x 7076 (Lat. L. Luscius Blast[us]: s. Prima)

**Βλάττος**
S. ITALY (APULIA):
—CANUSIUM: (1) 195 BC Syll³ 585, 13 (s. Μάτουρος)

**Βλέπων**
SICILY:
—SELINOUS: (1) m. v BC Dubois, IGDS 36, 2 (Arena, Iscr. Sic. 1 69) (Βλέπōν—Arena, Ναεπōν—Dubois: f. Aἴνων)

**Βλεψίας**
AIGINA: (1) her. Pi., O. viii, 75 (Βλεψιάδαι (n. gent.))
ELIS:
—PISA: (2) ii AD Luc., DMort 27. 7

**Βλόσων**
S. ITALY (BRUTTIUM):
—KROTON: (1) inc. MkB 2 (1876-8) p. 13 (f. Δαμοκήδης)
SICILY:
—SYRACUSE?:
——(Μακ.): (2) hell. Manganaro, PdelP forthcoming no. 4 II, 3 (Βλόσων: s. Φίλων)
SICILY?: (3) iv BC AD 19 (1964) Chron. p. 315 + Manganaro, QUCC forthcoming no. 57 (Ἀρβλόσωνος—AD, [Π]ὰρ Βλόσωνος—Manganaro)

**Βλύας**
ARKADIA:
—MEGALOPOLIS: (1) 369-361 BC IG v (2) 1, 25; Tod, GHI II 132 (date)

**Βοάθοος**
ARKADIA:
—MANTINEIA-ANTIGONEIA: (1) c. 300-221 BC IG v (2) 323. 57 (tessera) (s. Γοργίλος)

**Βόηθος**
ARGOLIS:
—ARGOS: (1) hell.-imp.? SEG XXV 371
ARKADIA:
—ORCHOMENOS: (2) imp. IG v (2) 348 (Βόι-)
—TEGEA: (3) ?ii-i BC ib. 190 ([Β]όηθος?)
S. ITALY (CAMPANIA):
—HERCULANEUM*: (4) i BC-i AD CIL x 1403 l II, 12; cf. Cron. Erc. 7 (1977) p. 116 c, 12 (Lat. M. Volusius Boethus: freed.)
—POMPEII: (5) i BC-i AD CIL IV 10066 (Lat. Boetus)
SICILY:
—MELITA: (6) iv-v AD JIWE 1 167 (Jew)

**Βοίδας**
KORINTHIA:
—SIKYON: (1) iv/iii BC RE s.v. Boedas (Skalet 76) (Lat. Boedas: s. Λύσιππος: sculptor)

**Βοικήν**
ILLYRIA:
—EPIDAMNOS-DYRRHACHION: (1) c. 250-50 BC Ceka, Probleme p. 151 no. 13; IApoll Ref. Bibl. n. 38 (coin) (Β(ϝ)οικήν: pryt.) ?= (2); (2) ~ Maier 149-51 (coin) (Ceka 22; 70; 170) (Β(ϝ)οικήν: pryt.) ?= (1); (3) ii-i BC IDyrrh 533 (tiles) (Β(ϝ)οικήν)

**Βόϊλλα**
EPIROS:
—BOUTHROTOS (PRASAIBOI): (1) a. 163 BC IBouthrot 28, 30 (SEG XXXVIII 486) (d. Νικόλαος, ?m. Νικόλαος, Νικάδας); (2) ~ IBouthrot 40, 13 (SEG XXXVIII 499)
—PRASAIBOI: (3) ii-i BC IBouthrot 52, 7 (SEG XXXVIII 517) (d. Λύκος)
KERKYRA: (4) i BC-i AD IG IX (1) 904 (BOI-ΛΛΑ—apogr., Βόϊλ(λ)α—ed.)

**Βοινέας**
LAKONIA:
—SPARTA: (1) c. 450-434 BC ib. v (1) 1229, 7 (Poralla² 342) (Β(ϝ)οινέ[ας], Βοινε[ύς]?)

**Βοῖσκα**
EPIROS:
—BOUTHROTOS (PRASAIBOI): (1) a. 163 BC IBouthrot 14, 20; 22, 26 (SEG XXXVIII 471; 479); (2) ~ IBouthrot 29, 16 (SEG XXXVIII 487); (3) ~ IBouthrot 29, 42 (SEG XXXVIII 487); (4) ~ IBouthrot 29, 42 (SEG XXXVIII 487); (5) ~ IBouthrot 103, 5; (6) ~ ib. 136, 8; (7) ~ ib. 145, 8
KORINTHIA:
—KORINTH: (8) 146 BC HE 656 (m. Ῥοδόπα)

**Βοῖσκος**
EPIROS: (1) iv BC Cabanes, L'Épire p. 586 no. 70, 1; (2) 316-309 BC IG II² 1956, 190; Ancient Macedonia 5 p. 445 with n. 10 (date)
—BOUTHROTOS (PRASAIBOI): (3) a. 163 BC IBouthrot 13, 9; cf. Ugolini, Alb. Ant. 3 p. 120 (f. —s); (4) ~ IBouthrot 14, 17; 18, 4-5; 22, 17; 23, 5; 26, 10; 29, 4, 51; 30, 12, 28; 31, 81; 33, 20; 38, 8; 43, 17-18 (SEG XXXVIII 471; 475; 479; 481; 484; 487-8; 490; 492; 497; 502; IBouthrot 48, 6 (s. Πολέμων, f. Πολέμων) ?= (15); (5) ~ ib. 14, 24 (SEG XXXVIII 471) (s. Θερσίλοχος, ?s. Θεοδότα); (6) ~ IBouthrot 18, 15 (SEG XXXVIII 475) (f. Λυκίσκος) ?= (14); (7) ~ IBouthrot 21, 24 (SEG XXXVIII 478); (8) ~ IBouthrot 23, 3 (SEG XXXVIII 481); (9) ~ IBouthrot 25, 23 (SEG XXXVIII 483); (10) ~ IBouthrot 36, 6 (SEG XXXVIII 495); (11) ~ IBouthrot 37, 7 (SEG XXXVIII 496) ?= (15); (12) ~ IBouthrot 41, 12 (SEG XXXVIII 500) (s. ΒΩΔΥΚΟΣ); (13) ~ IBouthrot 43, 22 (SEG XXXVIII 502) (s. Πολέμων); (14) ~ IBouthrot 52, 10 (SEG XXXVIII 517) (f. Λυκίσκος) ?= (6); (15) ~ IBouthrot 54, 6 (SEG XXXVIII 505); IBouthrot 145, 13; 152, 6 (f. Πολέμων) ?= (11) (4), (16) ~ ib. 103, 8; 156, 10; 157, 7 (BCH 118 (1994) p. 127 nos. 12-13) (f. Φαλακρίων) ?= (41); (17) ~ IBouthrot 104, 15 (Βοῖσκος]: s. —δρος); (18) ~ ib. 107 (f. Ἀριστόμαχος); (19) ~ ib. 135, 13; 143, 8; 152, 5 (f. Μενοίτας) ?= (32); (20) ~ ib. 143, 10 (s. Ὕβριμος); (21) ~ ib. 145, 9
——Bouthrotioi: (22) a. 163 BC ib. 115, 14; 118, 6 (f. Ἀντιφῶν) ?= (40); (23) ~ ib. 149, 10 (f. —os)
——Datonioi: (24) a. 163 BC ib. 66, 9 (f. Νικάνωρ) ?= (25); (25) ~ ib. 75, 8 (s. Νικάνωρ) ?= (24)
——Eschatioi: (26) a. 163 BC ib. 98, 7 (s. Νικίας) ?= (27); (27) ~ ib. 99, 6 (BCH 118 (1994) p. 121 B) ?= (26)
——Kestrinoi: (28) a. 163 BC IBouthrot 31, 6 (SEG XXXVIII 490) (f. Μενέδαμος)
——Kolonoi: (29) a. 163 BC IBouthrot 146, 8 (f. —ους)
——Loigyphioi: (30) a. 163 BC ib. 121, 4, 11; 122, 4 (s.e.)

——Messaneoi: (31) f. ii BC ib. 6, 2 (*SEG* XXXVIII 468) ?= (*32*); (32) a. 163 BC *IBouthrot* 14, 9; 18, 1; 21, 17; 26, 5; 27, 6; 38, 12; 41, 7, 10 (*SEG* XXXVIII 471; 475; 478; 484-5; 497; 500); *IBouthrot* 146, 3 (f. *Μενοίτας*) ?= (*19*) (*31*); (33) ~ ib. 14, 9; 17, [3], 5; 19, 8; 21, 17; 38, 13; 41, 6, 10 (*SEG* XXXVIII 471; 476; 478; 497; 500) (s. *Μενοίτας, Δεινομάχα*)
——Sakaronoi: (34) a. 163 BC *IBouthrot* 136, 4
—CHARADROS: (35) a. 167 BC *SEG* XXXV 665 A, 14 (s. *Χάροψ*)
—DODONA: (36) hell. *IG* IX (1) 688, 2, 18 (s. *Λυκόφρων*)
—DODONA*: (37) hell. Cabanes, *L'Épire* p. 584 no. 63, 1 (*SEG* XXVI 705) (*Βο*[*ίσκ*]*ος*: f. *Φορμίσκος*)
—OPOUOI: (38) iii-ii BC *SGDI* 1349, 10; cf. Cabanes, *L'Épire* p. 580 no. 53 (s. *Νίκανδρος*)
—PRASAIBOI: (39) ii-i BC *IBouthrot* 53, 7 (*SEG* XXXVIII 504) (s. *Κλεόμαχος*); (40) a. 163 BC *IBouthrot* 58, 7 (*SEG* XXXVIII 509); *IBouthrot* 105, 4 (f. *Ἀντιφῶν*) ?= (*22*); (41) ~ ib. 67, 6 (s. *Φαλακρίων*) ?= (*16*); (42) ~ ib. 132, 4 (s. *Λυσανίας*)
—TALAONOI/TALAIANES: (43) iii-ii BC *SGDI* 1349, 7; cf. Cabanes, *L'Épire* p. 580 no. 53 (f. *Δόκιμος*)
ILLYRIA:
—BYLLIONES (RABIJE (MOD.)): (44) ?s. ii BC *SEG* XXXII 626, 6; cf. XXXVIII 520; cf. *CRAI* 1991, p. 197 ff. (*Βοῖ*[*σκος*]: f. *Πραυγίμμας*)
KERKYRA: (45) ?iii BC *IG* IX (1) 758-9 (tiles)
KORINTHIA:
—KORINTH: (46) m. iii BC *Corinth* VIII (3) 33 f, 10 (*Βοίσκ*[*ος*])
PELOPONNESE: (47) c. 192 BC *SEG* XIII 327, 20 ([*B*]*οΐσκος*: s. *Ὀνάσιμος*)
S. ITALY (BRUTTIUM):
—KROTON: (48) 400-375 BC *SNG ANS Etruria–Calabria* 347 (coin)

**Βοιτώ**
ILLYRIA:
—APOLLONIA: (1) ?iii-ii BC *IApoll* 20

**Βοιώ**
ARGOLIS:
—ARGOS: (1) v-iv BC Iamb., *VP* 267 (*FVS* 1 p. 447)

**Βοιωτιανός**
S. ITALY (BRUTTIUM):
—RHEGION: (1) ii-iii AD *Suppl. It.* 5 p. 71 no. 27 (Lat. Valerius Boeotianus)

**Βοιώτιος**
LAKONIA:
—SPARTA: (1) 409 BC X., *HG* i 4. 2 (Poralla² 175); (2) c. 147-165 AD *SEG* XI 498, 1; 629 (Bradford (-)) (*Γ. Ἰούλ. Β.*)

**Βοιωτός**
ARKADIA:
—MEGALOPOLIS: (1) s. ii BC *IG* V (2) 439, 74 (s. *Τίμανδρος*)
KORINTHIA:
—SIKYON: (2) 124 BC Moretti, *Olymp.* 647 (Skalet 77)
SICILY:
—SYRACUSE: (3) iv/iii BC *RE* (10) (Stephanis 530)

**Βόλιχος**
S. ITALY (APULIA):
—MONTE SANNACE (MOD.): (1) v/iv BC *Mon. Ant.* 45 (1961) p. 325

**Βόλκων**
SICILY:
—SYRACUSE: (1) 451 BC D.S. xi 91

**Βόλων**
S. ITALY (CAMPANIA):
—SALERNUM*: (1) ?i AD *IItal* 1 (1) 238 III, 15 (*CIL* X 557) (Lat. L. Appuleius Bolo: freed.)

**Βομβύκιον**
S. ITALY (CAMPANIA):
—HERCULANEUM: (1) i BC-i AD ib. IV 10628 (Lat. Bombycion)

**Βομβυλῖνος**
SICILY:
—MENAI: (1) hell.? *Riv. Stor. Antica* 5 (1900-1) p. 56 no. 32 (f. *Αἰσχρίων, Νυμφόδωρος*)

**Βονιφᾶς**
SICILY:
—KATANE: (1) iii-v AD *IG* XIV 531 (Agnello 47; Wessel 634); cf. Ferrua, *NG* 438
—TAUROMENION: (2) iii-v AD *IG* XIV 143 (Strazzulla 83; Wessel 1315; *ASSicilia* 1938-9, p. 52); Ferrua, *NG* 477 (name, locn.) (f. *Κωνστάντις*)

**Βονιφατία**
SICILY:
—SYRACUSE: (1) iii-v AD *IG* XIV 134 (Strazzulla 242; Agnello 38; Wessel 178); (2) ~ Strazzulla 339 (Wessel 226)

**Βονιφάτιος**
SICILY:
—SYRACUSE: (1) iii-v AD *IG* XIV 88 (Strazzulla 29; Wessel 160); cf. *ASSicilia* 1938-9, p. 29 (-*φάτις*: s. *Εὐσέβιος*); (2) ~ Strazzulla 339 (Wessel 226); cf. Ferrua, *NG* 123 (-*της*); (3) ~ Strazzulla 340 (Barreca 83) (-*νυ*-); (4) ~ Wessel 1313 (Barreca 82) (-*νυ*-)

**Βοριάδης**
AITOLIA:
—EURYTANES: (1) 426 BC Th. iii 100. 1

**Βορμίων**
S. ITALY (LUCANIA):
—HERAKLEIA:
——(*Με. κιβώτιον*): (1) iv/iii BC *IGSI* 1 I, 180 (*DGE* 62; Uguzzoni–Ghinatti I) (s. *Φιλώτας*)

**Βορυσθένης**
S. ITALY (CAMPANIA):
—DIKAIARCHIA-PUTEOLI: (1) ?ii AD *CIL* X 2013 (Lat. T. Aelius Borysthenes)

**Βοσκασία**
SICILY:
—SYRACUSE: (1) iii-v AD Strazzulla 161; cf. Ferrua, *NG* 6 ([*τύμ*]*βος Κασία*—Ferrua)

**Βοστρύχα**
EPIROS:
—DODONA*: (1) iv BC *SEG* XV 400 (d. *Δόρκων*)

**Βοστρώ**
ILLYRIA:
—APOLLONIA: (1) iii-ii BC *IApoll* 33

**Βοτιάδας**
LEUKAS: (1) ?vi-v BC Unp. (*IG* arch.)

**Βότιχος**
ILLYRIA:
—BYLLIONES: (1) c. 200 BC *SEG* XXXV 679 (XXXVIII 524) (s. *Λυκίσκος*)

**Βότριχος**
ARKADIA: (1) iii/ii BC *IG* V (1) 724, 1

**Βότρυς**
ACHAIA: (1) 146 BC ib. IV (1)² 28, 138 (s. *Δαμοχάρης*: synoikos)
ARKADIA:
—TEGEA: (2) iii/ii BC ib. V (2) 191

**Βότρυς**
S. ITALY (CALABRIA):
—TARAS-TARENTUM: (3) iv/iii BC ib. XIV 668 II, 2 (Landi, *DISMG* 194) (*Βότ*[*ρυς*])
S. ITALY (LUCANIA):
—LEUKANOI: (4) ?ii BC *IG* XII (1) 106, 4 (sculptor)
SICILY:
—ZANKLE-MESSANA: (5) ?v BC *RE* (3)

**Βοτρύων**
S. ITALY (CAMPANIA):
—HERCULANEUM*: (1) f. i AD *CIL* X 1403 g I, 11 (Lat. M. Caninius Botrio: freed.) ?= (2)
—NEAPOLIS: (2) ?i AD ib. 1501; cf. Leiwo p. 110 (Lat. M. Caninius Botryo: f. M. Caninius Severus) ?= (*1*)

**Βόττος**
SICILY:
—HYKKARA: (1) imp. *IG* XIV 294 (f. *Δόμνα*)

**Βότυρος**
S. ITALY (CALABRIA):
—TARAS-TARENTUM: (1) iv/iii BC ib. 668 II, 16 (Landi, *DISMG* 194)

**Βουβάλιον**
EPIROS:
—BOUTHROTOS (PRASAIBOI):
——Messaneoi: (1) a. 163 BC *IBouthrot* 17, 3, 5; 38, 12 (*SEG* XXXVIII 474; 497); *IBouthrot* 48, 12; 50, 12 (d. *Μενοίτας, Δεινομάχα*)

**Βουβαλίς**
AKARNANIA:
—ANAKTORION: (1) iii BC *IG* IX (1)² (2) 227
EPIROS:
—BOUTHROTOS (PRASAIBOI): (2) a. 163 BC *IBouthrot* 22, 28 (*SEG* XXXVIII 479); (3) ~ *IBouthrot* 43, 36 (*SEG* XXXVIII 502); (4) ~ *IBouthrot* 93, 5
LEUKAS: (5) i BC-i AD? *IG* IX (1) 595 (d. *Ἐπιγένης*)

**Βούβαλος**
DALMATIA:
—PHAROS: (1) imp. *CIL* III 3095 (Lat. Iul. Bubalus)
KERKYRA: (2) ?ii BC *IG* IX (1) 760-1; cf. *BM Terracottas* E 190 (tiles) (*Βούβανος*—*BM Terracottas*)

**Βουδᾶς**
ARKADIA:
—TEGEA: (1) ii AD *IG* V (2) 55, 62 (f. *Εὐτυχιανός*); (2) 165 AD ib. 50, 74 (s. *Ἀριστίων*)
SICILY:
—SYRACUSE: (3) iii-v AD Ferrua, *NG* 392 (-*δδ*-)

**Βούδιος**
KORINTHIA:
—KORINTH: (1) byz. *Corinth* VIII (1) 207; cf. *TMByz* 9 (1985) p. 361 no. 22 (-*δις*)

**Βουδίων**
AIGINA: (1) her. *RE* s.v. Budion (-); cf. s.v. Budidai (-) (*Βουδίδαι* (n. gent.))

**Βουδόρκα**
AITOLIA:
—PROSCH(E)ION: (1) c. 157 BC *IG* IX (1)² (1) 108, 3 (masc. nom.)

**Βοῦζος**
S. ITALY (APULIA):
—CANUSIUM: (1) ?c. 241-232 BC ib. XI (4) 642, 3 (s. *Ὀρτείρας*)

**Βουθήρας**
AITOLIA: (1) c. 271 BC ib. IX (1)² (1) 12, 40 ?= (2) (5); (2) ?271 BC *Syll*³ 419, 2 ?= (*1*); (3) c. 200 BC *IG* II² 4931; *Syll*³ 631, 2 (f. *Ἀλκέσιππος*)
—KONOPE-ARSINOE: (4) ?205-203 BC *FD* III (2) 134 b, 5 (*Syll*³ 564)

**Βοῦθος**

—TITRAI: (5) c. 265-260 BC FD III (3) 199, 1
(s. Εὐάνθιος) ?= (1):
S. ITALY (BRUTTIUM):
—RHEGION: (6) iv/iii BC RE s.v. Lykos (50); PP
16931; FGrH 570 (Λύκος ὁ καὶ Β.: ?f. (ad.) Λυκόφρων (Chalkis))

**Βοῦθος**
S. ITALY (BRUTTIUM):
—KROTON: (1) iv BC Iamb., VP 267 (FVS 1 p.
446) (Ξοῦθος?—Diels)

**Βουθύων**
ACHAIA:
—DYME*: (1) c. 219 BC SGDI 1612, 48, 52
(Tyche 5 (1990) p. 124) (s. Πρόκριτος, f. Λέων)

**Βουκολέων**
ARGOLIS:
—ARGOS: (1) a. 303 BC CEG II 816, 12

**Βουκολίων**
S. ITALY (APULIA): (1) s. iv BC RVAp p. 510
no. 131 (vase) (SEG XL 908 b)

**Βουκόλος**
S. ITALY (CAMPANIA):
—DIKAIARCHIA-PUTEOLI: (1) imp. CIL X 2544
(Lat. C. Iulius Bucolus); (2) ?ii AD ib. 2448
(Lat. Bucolus)
—HERCULANEUM: (3) i BC-i AD ib. IV 10620
(Lat. Bucolus)
—POMPEII: (4) i BC-i AD Neue Forsch. in Pom-
peji p. 263 no. 2 (Lat. Bucolus); (5) c. 51-62
AD CIL IV 3340. 84, 8; 89, 9 (Castrèn 158.
12) (Lat. M. Epidius Bucolus)

**Βουλαγόρας**
DALMATIA:
—ISSA:
——(Pamphyloi): (1) iv/iii BC Brunšmid p. 7, 20
(s. Φιλέας); (2) ~ ib. p. 8, 29 (f. Σωσίμαχος);
(3) ~ ib. l. 49 (Βου[λαγόρας?]: f. Ἡρωίδας)
S. ITALY (BRUTTIUM):
—KROTON?: (4) f. iv BC Iamb., VP 265

**Βούλαρχος**
AITOLIA:
—AGRINION: (1) 165-143 BC SGDI 1818; IG IX
(1)² (3) 639. 8, 1 (f. Ὑβρίστας)

**Βουληϊανός**
KORINTHIA:
—KORINTH: (1) imp. IEph 1116, 1; BE 1971,
no. 307 (Ἀ. Λικίννιος Β., Βουλτιανός—BE)

**Βουλήκριτος**
ARGOLIS:
—PHLEIOUS: (1) iii BC IG IV (1) 456

**Βουλιάδας**
LEUKAS: (1) v BC AM 27 (1902) p. 369 no. 33

**Βοῦλις**
LAKONIA:
—SPARTA: (1) f. v BC RE s.v. Bulis (3); Poralla²
176 (Βοῦρις—Plu., Βούλης—Stob.: s. Νικόλαος,
f. Νικόλαος)

**Βοῦλος**
ILLYRIA:
—BALAIITAI*: (1) ii BC SEG XXXVIII 521, 25;
cf. CRAI 1991, pp. 197 ff.; L'Illyrie mérid. 2
p. 204 f. (s. Ἀβαῖος)
—BYLLIONES: (2) iii/ii BC SEG XXXV 696; cf.
XXXVIII 569 (s. Ἀλέξανδρος)
S. ITALY (LUCANIA):
—VOLCEI (NR.): (3) ?i BC Dyson, Roman Villas
of Buccino p. 34 no. 3 (pithos) (Lat. Bulos)

**Βούμας**
ARKADIA:
—LOUSOI: (1) iv/iii BC IG V (2) 389, 15 (Perl-
man L.1)

**Βοῦς**
SICILY:
—MOTYKA: (1) ii-iii AD MEFRA 106 (1994) pp.
107-8 no. 20 (m. Οὐέττιος)

**Βούσιρις**
SICILY:
—SYRACUSE: (1) 513 AD Agnello 98 (Barreca
459) (Lat. Busiris)
SICILY?: (2) s. v AD PLRE II (-) (Lat. Fl.
Gelasius Busiris)

**Βουτάδας**
KORINTHIA:
—SIKYON: (1) ?vii BC RE (-) (Skalet 78) (Lat.
Butades: potter)

**Βουτακίδας**
S. ITALY (BRUTTIUM):
—KROTON: (1) vi BC Hdt. v 47. 1 (-δης: f. Φίλ-
ιππος)

**Βούτας**
ARGOLIS:
—ARGOS: (1) ?c. 460-450 BC Mnem. NS 47
(1919) p. 161 no. 6, 4; LSAG² p. 170 no.
31 (date) (Βούτα[ς])

**Βραζώ**
ILLYRIA:
—EPIDAMNOS-DYRRHACHION: (1) hell.-imp.
IDyrrh 142

**Βρασίδας**
ARGOLIS:
—EPIDAUROS: (1) iii AD IG IV (1)² 455, 1; cf.
SEG XXII 290, 8 (?f. Γεώργιος)
LAKONIA:
—SPARTA: (2) c. 465-422 BC RE (1); IPr 316,
8 (Poralla² 177) (s. Τέλλις, Ἀργιλεωνίς); (3) f. i
BC Anthemonte-Kalindoia p. 53 no. A8 (SEG
XLII 557) (Βρασίδας: f. Λυκοῦργος); (4) s. i BC
IG V (1) 95, 6 (Bradford (9)) (Βρα[σίδας]: f.
Μεναλκίδας); (5) c. 115-175 AD RE (2); PIR²
C 818; IG V (1) 46, 6; 161, 1; 312, 11; 472, 9;
496; 497, 3; 498; 500-1; 525, 10; 526, 10; FD
III (1) 543, 5; SEG XI 530, 1; 683, 4; BSA 80
(1985) pp. 224-30 (ident., stemma) (Bradford
(4); (5); (8); (10); (11)) (Κλ. Β.: f. Κλ. Ἀντί-
πατρος, Τιβ. Κλ. Πρατόλαος, Τιβ. Κλ. Σπαρτια-
τικός, Τιβ. Κλ. Βρασίδας II); (6) c. 145-155 AD
IG V (1) 71 III, 21; SEG XI 529, 2 (Bradford
(3)) (Σέξ. Πομπ. Β.); (7) c. 160-240 AD IG V
(1) 302, 4 (Artemis Orthia p. 327 no. 56); IG
V (1) 312, 11 (Artemis Orthia p. 333 no. 68);
IG V (1) 332 (Artemis Orthia p. 337 no. 76);
IG V (1) 501, 5; BSA 79 (1984) pp. 283 no. 4;
pp. 284-5 no. 15; 80 (1985) pp. 225; pp. 236-
8 (ident., stemma) (Bradford (1)) (Τιβ. Κλ. Β.:
II s. Τιβ. Κλ. Βρασίδας I)
S. ITALY (CAMPANIA):
—DIKAIARCHIA-PUTEOLI: (8) imp. CIL X 2173
(Lat. Brasidas)

**Βρασιδία**
S. ITALY (CAMPANIA):
—SURRENTUM: (1) imp. ib. 721 (Lat. Brasidia)

**Βράχας**
ARGOLIS:
—ARGOS: (1) c. 458 BC IG I³ 1149, 69 ([Β]ράχας)
——(Kleodaidai): (2) a. 316 BC SEG XIII 240,
2 (Perlman A.4) (Βράχας: f. Παναίτιος)

**Βραχίδας**
SICILY:
—AKRAI: (1) s. vi BC Akrai p. 161 no. 19
(Dubois, IGDS 106) (Βραχίδας, Βραχύλας—
Akrai)

**Βράχυλλος**
ACHAIA: (1) 126 AD SEG XI 1198 (Π. Ἐγνάτιος
Βράχυ[λλος])
ARKADIA:
—TEGEA: (2) m. iv BC IG V (2) 6, 93 (f. Θίβρων);
(3) hell.? ib. 255 (f. Κλεαινέτα)
SICILY:
—KAMARINA: (4) f. v BC Cordano, Tessere Pub-
bliche 24 (Arena, Iscr. Sic. II 132 A) (f. Θεα-
ρίδας)

**Βραχύμηλος**
AKARNANIA:
—DERION: (1) c. 325-315 BC Hesp. 57 (1988)
p. 148 A, 43 (SEG XXXVI 331); cf. Hesp. 48
(1979) pp. 78 f. with pl. 22 c (s. Ἀρχέδαμος)

**Βρέμουσα**
S. ITALY (CAMPANIA):
—DIKAIARCHIA-PUTEOLI: (1) ?ii AD CIL X 2215
(Lat. Calpurnia Braemusa: m. Θυμέλη)

**Βρέμων**
LAKONIA:
—SPARTA: (1) c. 240-200 BC SEG XI 413, 27
(Perlman E.4; Bradford (-)) (f. Δαμαρμενίδας)

**Βρεῦκος**
ILLYRIA:
—EPIDAMNOS-DYRRHACHION: (1) imp.? IDyrrh
143 (s. -ίων)

**Βρεφύλος**
ARGOLIS:
—ARGOS: (1) iv-iii BC Unp. (Ch. Kritzas)

**Βριάκας**
ARKADIA:
—ORCHOMENOS: (1) viii BC Paus. viii 5. 10 (s.
Αἰγινήτης, f. Αἴχμις: king)

**Βριζῖνος**
S. ITALY (APULIA):
—CANUSIUM*: (1) c. 346-393 AD Epig. Rom. di
Canosa 103 (CIL IX 6192) (Lat. Brizinus)

**Βριμίας**
ELIS: (1) hell.? Moretti, Olymp. 952

**Βρισηΐς**
ARGOLIS:
—ARGOS: (1) v-vi AD Unp. (Oikonomou-
Laniado) (Βρησε<ε>ΐδος (gen.): m. Πέτρος)
S. ITALY (APULIA):
—LUCERIA: (2) imp. CIL IX 899 (Lat. Vitoria
Briseis: m. L. Vitorius Fortunatus)
S. ITALY (CAMPANIA):
—KYME: (3) imp. AJA 2 (1898) p. 396 no. 60
(Lat. Briseis)
—NEAPOLIS: (4) iii-iv AD IG XIV 826. 6 (INap
223) (Βρει-)

**Βρόκχος**
S. ITALY (BRUTTIUM):
—SYBARIS-THOURIOI-COPIAE: (1) f. i AD
NScav 1970, Suppl. 3 p. 60 nos. 193; 197;
199; p. 496 nos. 698; 704; p. 497 no. 705
(tiles); cf. Atti Conv. Taranto 32 (1992) pp.
413 ff. (date) (Lat. L. Vinuleius Brocchus)
SICILY:
—THERMAI HIMERAIAI: (2) i-ii AD CIL X 7377
(ILat. Term. Imer. 52) (Lat. M. Arrunti[us]
Brocc[hus])

**Βρομιοκλῆς**
ARGOLIS:
—EPIDAUROS: (1) imp. IG IV (1)² 448 (f. Ἀπολ-
λώνιος)

**Βρόμιος**
ACHAIA: (1) 146 BC ib. 28, 137 (I f. Βρόμιος
II: synoikos); (2) ~ ib. l. 137 (II s. Βρόμιος I:
synoikos)

**Βροντῖνος**
S. ITALY (CAMPANIA):
—DIKAIARCHIA-PUTEOLI: (3) imp. *CIL* x 1914 (Lat. Bromius)
—POMPEII: (4) i BC-i AD ib. IV 8460 (Lat. Bromius); (5) ~ ib. 10146 (Lat. Bromius)

**Βροντῖνος**
S. ITALY (LUCANIA):
—METAPONTION: (1) vi/v BC *RE* (-); *FVS* 17 (*Βροτῖνος*—D.L.)

**Βρόχυς**
ARKADIA:
—TEUTHIS?: (1) iv BC *IG* v (2) 500 (*Βρόχυ*[ς])

**Βρύανθος**
S. ITALY (BRUTTIUM):
—RHEGION*: (1) imp. ib. XIV 618, 5 (slave?)

**Βρύας**
ARGOLIS:
—ARGOS: (1) ?417 BC *RE* (2); (2) ?278-277 BC *FD* III (1) 87, 5; 88, 4-5 (s. *Μενέστρατος*)
KORINTHIA:
—SIKYON: (3) f. iv BC Plin., *NH* xxxv 123 (Skalet 79) (Lat. Bryes: f. *Παυσίας*: painter)
S. ITALY (BRUTTIUM):
—KROTON: (4) iv BC Iamb., *VP* 267 (*FVS* I p. 446) ?= (5)
S. ITALY (CALABRIA):
—TARAS-TARENTUM: (5) iv BC Iamb., *VP* 267 (*FVS* I p. 446) ?= (4)

**Βρῦγος**
ILLYRIA:
—EPIDAMNOS-DYRRHACHION: (1) hell.-imp. *IDyrrh* 144 (s. *Ἀφροδίσιος*); (2) ~ ib. 408 (*Βρεῖ*-: f. *Τευταία*)

**Βρύουσα**
EPIROS:
—NIKOPOLIS: (1) imp. *CIG* 1818; cf. *BE* 1972, no. 242

**Βρύσων**
ACHAIA: (1) iv BC *RE* (3)
AKARNANIA:
—STRATOS: (2) c. 425-400 BC *IG* IX (1)² (2) 390, 8 (*Βρ*[ύ]*σων*)

**Βρύττιος**
S. ITALY (LUCANIA):
—HYELE-VELIA: (1) iv/iii BC *PdelP* 25 (1970) p. 263 no. 5

**Βρύων**
KERKYRA: (1) c. 500 BC *SEG* xxx 523; cf. *L'Illyrie mérid.* 2 p. 202 (-ōν)
S. ITALY (CAMPANIA):
—DIKAIARCHIA-PUTEOLI*: (2) imp. *IG* XIV 847 (*Κ. Καλπούρν*(*ιος*) *B*.: freed.)

**Βυβλώ**
ILLYRIA:
—APOLLONIA: (1) imp. *IApoll* 247 (d. *Σωσιπά-τρα*)

**Βύβων**
ELIS:
—OLYMPIA*: (1) vi BC *IvOl* 717; cf. *Syll*³ 1071 (-βōν: s. *Φόρυς*)

**Βυζάνιος**
LAKONIA:
—SPARTA: (1) c. 90-100 AD *SEG* XI 558, 12 (Bradford (-)) (*Βυζάν*(*τ*)*ιος*?: f. *Γάιος*)

**Βυζαντία**
S. ITALY (CAMPANIA):
—POMPEII: (1) i BC-i AD *Neue Forsch. in Pompeji* p. 266 no. 60 (Lat. Byzantia (n.pr./ethn.?))

**Βύκελος**
KORINTHIA:
—SIKYON: (1) v/iv BC Moretti, *Olymp.* 370 (Skalet 80)

**Βύκκος**
S. ITALY (CAMPANIA):
—NEAPOLIS: (1) 71 AD *IG* XIV 760, 17 (*INap* 85) (f. *Ἀρίστων*)

**Βύνδακος**
S. ITALY (BRUTTIUM):
—KROTON: (1) iv BC Iamb., *VP* 267 (*FVS* I p. 448) (s. *Θέοφρις*)

**Βύνθαρος**
AKARNANIA:
—OINIADAI: (1) 263-262 BC *IG* IX (1)² (1) 3 A, 22

**Βύρος?**
S. ITALY (LUCANIA):
—METAPONTION: (1) ?c. 550-525 BC Lazzarini 883 (Landi, *DISMG* 134); *LSAG*² p. 260 no. 14 (name, date) (*Βύρο*[ς]—*LSAG*², *Ρυπό*[ς]—*SGDI* 1644, *Βύρθ*[ος]—Lazzarini: ?f. *Θεάγης*)

**Βύτιος**
ARGOLIS:
—MYKENAI: (1) ?c. 475 BC *SEG* XI 298, 3 (Lazzarini 936); *LSAG*² p. 174 no. 3 (date)
S. ITALY (BRUTTIUM):
—LOKROI EPIZEPHYRIOI: (2) c. 356-355 BC *IG* IV (1)² 95, 41 (Perlman E.2); Perlman p. 40 f. (date)

**Βύτις**
LAKONIA:
—SPARTA: (1) 336 BC *CID* II 24 II, 8; cf. *REG* 99 (1988) p. 136 (Poralla² 178)

**Βύττιν**
S. ITALY (CALABRIA):
—BRENTESION-BRUNDISIUM: (1) imp. *CIL* IX 147 (Lat. Eutychia quae et Buttin: d. *Ἔρως*, *Μυρρίνη*)

**Βυττίς**
S. ITALY (CAMPANIA):
—DIKAIARCHIA-PUTEOLI*: (1) imp. ib. x 2481 (Lat. Antonia Buttis: freed.)

**Βυχχύλος**
SICILY:
—MOTYKA (NR.): (1) iv-v AD *IG* XIV 250 (*SEG* XXXIX 994); cf. *BE* 1991, no. 762 (*Σόσιος B.*, *Βαχχύλος*—BE)

**Βῶθις**
ARKADIA:
—MANTINEIA-ANTIGONEIA: (1) c. 475-450 BC *IG* v (2) 262, 12 (*IPArk* 8); *LSAG*² p. 216 no. 29 (date) (*Βō*-, *Βοῦθις*—IG index)

**Βῶκυς**
SICILY:
—SYRACUSE: (1) iii-v AD *SEG* IV 12 (Wessel 977); cf. Ferrua, *NG* 273 (*Εὐσταχὶς ἡ κὲ B.*)

**Βωλαγόρας**
ARGOLIS:
—HERMIONE: (1) iii BC *IG* IV (1) 729 I, 17 (f. *Εὔθυμος*); (2) ~ ib. 729 II, 6 (f. *Ἐμπύλος*)

**Βωρθίας**
LAKONIA:
—SPARTA: (1) s. i BC ib. v (1) 94, 5 (Bradford s.v. *Βωρθιάδας* (2)) (*B*(*ϝ*)*ωρθί*[*ας*]: f. *Εὐμωλίων*)

**Βώτακος**
SICILY:
—GELA-PHINTIAS (NR.): (1) iv/iii BC Dubois, *IGDS* 159 (bronze)

**Βῶτος**
SICILY:
—KAMARINA: (1) f. vi BC *SEG* XXXII 918 A (vase) (*Βō*-)

**Βώτων**
ACHAIA: (1) 146 BC *IG* IV (1)² 28, 132 (s. *Σώστρατος*: synoikos)

**Βῶχυς**
SICILY:
—SYRACUSE: (1) iii-v AD *Nuovo Didask.* 4 (1950) pp. 58-9 no. 10

# Γ

**Γᾶ**
EPIROS:
—TREN (MOD.): (1) hell.? *Iliria* 1971, p. 44 (loomweight) (*Γᾶς* (gen.)—ed., *Ἰάς*?: ?d. *Μηνόδοτος*)
S. ITALY: (2) imp. *CIL* x 8059. 11 (seal) (Lat. L. Aelius Gaa)
S. ITALY (APULIA):
—CANUSIUM: (3) imp. *Epig. Rom. di Canosa* 207 (*CIL* IX 408) (Lat. A. Graecidius Ga)

—VENUSIA: (4) i AD *Museo di Venosa* p. 214 no. 18 (Lat. P. Annius Ga: f. P. Annius Gavianus)
S. ITALY (CAMPANIA):
—DIKAIARCHIA-PUTEOLI*: (5) i AD *CIL* x 3114 (Lat. M. Vinicius Gaha: freed.)

**Γαβιανός**
S. ITALY (CAMPANIA):
—NEAPOLIS: (1) iii-iv AD *IG* XIV 826. 7 (*INap* 226); (2) ~ *IG* XIV 826. 8 (*INap* 224-5) (-βει-)

**Γαδαῖος**
SICILY: (1) c. 100 BC D.S. xxxvi 3. 5; cf. *Arch. Class.* 17 (1965) p. 201 n. 82 (*Γ. Τιτίνιος ἐπικαλ. Γ.*, *Γαλαῖος*?—Manganaro)

**Γάϝρων**
KORINTHIA:
—KORINTH: (1) c. 570-550 BC Lorber 105, 2 (*Γάϝρō*[ν])

**Γάζα**
S. Italy (Campania):
—salernum*: (1) imp. IItal I (1) 75 (Lat. Numonia Gaza: freed.)
Sicily:
—syracuse: (2) ?ii-i bc SEG xvi 538 ii; cf. BE 1974, no. 731 (name)

**Γάϊα**
Sicily:
—syracuse: (1) iii-v ad Rend. Pont. 22 (1946-7) p. 237 no. 46; cf. Strazzulla 417 (Γαλήν[η]?—Strazzulla)

**Γαιανή**
Sicily:
—syracuse: (1) iii-iv ad Agnello 23 + Ferrua, NG 46 (Γα[λήνη]—Agnello, Γα[ιαν]ή—Ferrua)
Sicily?: (2) iii-v ad IG xiv 598; cf. Riv. Arch. Crist. 18 (1941) p. 203 no. 76; cf. Ferrua, NG 528

**Γαΐζατος**
Illyria:
—apollonia: (1) imp. IApoll 64

**Γαιόμαχος**
Aitolia:
—daianes: (1) 161 bc IG ix (1)² (1) 100, 7

**Γάϊος**
Achaia:
—patrai: (1) ii ad Luc., Asin. 55 (fict.)
Argolis:
—argos: (2) ii ad SEG xvi 253, 10 (f. Ἀριστόδαμος)
—epidauros: (3) ii ad IG iv (1)² 560; 571
Arkadia:
—kleitor: (4) a. 212 ad ib. v (2) 369, 2 (Ἰούλ. Γ.)
Elis: (5) 113-117 ad IvOl 91, 4, 8, 9; 95, [9] (I s. Μουσαῖος, f. Μουσαῖος, Γάϊος II: Δ.); (6) 113-145 ad ib. 91, 9, 19; 95, 9 (II s. Γάϊος I, ?f. Πολύκαρπος)
Illyria:
—apollonia: (7) i bc Ceka, Probleme p. 139 no. 7 (coin)
—epidamnos-dyrrhachion: (8) c. 250-50 bc BMC Thessaly p. 78 no. 185; Unp. (Paris, BN) 270; Schlosser 63; cf. IApoll Ref. Bibl. n. 39 (coin) (pryt.); (9) ii-i bc IDyrrh 534 (tile); (10) hell.-imp. ib. 278 (f. Λαβία); (11) ~ ib. 416 (f. Τραύζινα); (12) ~ ib. 417 (f. Τραύζινα); (13) imp. ib. 147; (14) ~ ib. 149 (Γά[ϊος]: I f. Γάϊος II); (15) ~ ib. 150 (Γάϊ[ος]: II s. Γάϊος I); (16) ~ ib. 150 (I f. Γάϊος II); (17) ~ ib. (II s. Γάϊος I)
Kephallenia:
—same: (18) c. 230-200 bc BCH 45 (1921) p. 15 II, 146 (f. Μάαρκος Κορνήλιος)
Korinthia:
—korinth: (19) f. ii ad Ag. vii p. 96 no. 290; Corinth iv (2) pp. 206-7 nos. 706, 717 (lamps)
—korinth?: (20) m. i ad Ep. Rom. 16. 23; 1 Ep. Cor. 1. 14
Lakonia:
—sparta: (21) c. 25-1 bc IG v (1) 212, 12 (Bradford (3)) (f. Ποσείδιππος); (22) c. 90-100 ad SEG xi 558, 12 (Bradford (1)) (s. Βυζάνιος); (23) c. 100-120 ad IG v (1) 80, 5; SEG xi 571 (Bradford (2)) (f. Λύσιππος)
Messenia:
—messene: (24) i ad IG xii Suppl. p. 167 no. 449 (s. Ἀρίστων); (25) ?i/ii ad SEG xli 338
Peloponnese: (26) ii ad PAE 1992, p. 72 B, 8 (s. Πόπλιος)
S. Italy (Calabria):
—brentesion-brundisium: (27) i bc IG ii² 8432 ([Γ]άϊος: f. Ἀφροδισία)
—taras-tarentum?: (28) iii-ii bc Atti Conv. Taranto 15 (1975) p. 558 (terracotta)

S. Italy (Campania):
—dikaiarchia-puteoli: (29) imp. IG xiv 856
—neapolis: (30) inc. Gal. xii pp. 746; 751; 755; 763; 986 etc. (doctor); (31) ?131 bc ID 2601, 19 (I f. Γάϊος II); (32) ~ ib. l. 19 (II s. Γάϊος I)
S. Italy (Lucania):
—poseidonia-paestum: (33) ii-i bc NScav 1950, p. 137 (f. Γ. Ἀθήνιος)
Sicily:
—syracuse: (34) iii-v ad ib. 1918, p. 277 (Barreca 85) (Γάϊς)

**Γαισύλος**
Lakonia:
—sparta: (1) c. 356 bc Plu., Dion 49 (Poralla² 180)

**Γαιϋλος**
Lakonia:
—thalamai*: (1) v bc IG v (1) 1316, 6 (Poralla² 179) (Γαιηύλος)

**Γάλαιθος**
Epiros: (1) c. 330 bc Cabanes, L'Épire p. 580 no. 55, 3; cf. SGDI 1351, 3 (Γάλαιθος—SGDI)
—kassope: (2) iv/iii bc Thess. Mnem. 74 (Γάλλιθος—ed.: s. Ξένων)

**Γάλαισος**
Lakonia:
—tainaron-kainepolis: (1) 198-211 ad SEG xxiii 199, 20 (Τιβ. Κλ. Γ.)
S. Italy (Campania):
—herculaneum*: (2) i bc-i ad CIL x 1403 k, 8 (Lat. Galaesus: freed.)

**Γαλαίστας**
Epiros:
—athamanes: (1) m. ii bc RE (1); PP 2155 (Γαλαίστης—Diod.: s. Ἀμύνανδρος)
—dodona: (2) iii bc Antoniou, Dodone Ba, 3 (Γαλ(α)ίστας)

**Γαλάτας**
Achaia: (1) 146 bc IG iv (1)² 28, 124 (f. Ἀπολλόδωρος: synoikos)

**Γαλάτεια**
Aitolia:
—ophioneis: (1) imp.? ib. ix (1)² (1) 161

**Γαλάτης**
S. Italy (Campania):
—pompeii: (1) i bc-i ad CIL iv 8819 (Lat. Galata)
—surrentum: (2) ?ii ad NScav 1928, p. 212 no. 2 (Lat. Flavius Galata)
Sicily:
—katane: (3) imp. IG xiv 467 (f. Πριμιγένις)

**Γαλατίας**
Messenia:
—prote*: (1) iii ad SEG xi 1009 (s. Ἀλέξανδρος)

**Γαλάτισσα**
S. Italy (Campania):
—neapolis: (1) iii-iv ad IG xiv 826. 9 (INap 240) (Γαλά[τισσ]α?, Γαλα[τίχ]α?—IG)

**Γάλαυρος**
Illyria:
—taulantioi: (1) iv bc Polyaen. iv 1; cf. Schol. Pers., Sat. i 99 (Lat. Calandrus: king)

**Γαλεός**
Sicily: (1) ii-iii ad Clem. Al., Strom. i 134. 3

**Γαλήνη**
Korinthia:
—korinth: (1) f. ii ad Corinth viii (3) 237, 8 (Lat. –nia Gaiene—ed., Galene—LGPN: m. Π. Αἰφίκιος Ἀτίμητος Λικινιανός)

S. Italy (Apulia):
—venusia: (2) imp. CIL ix 565 (Lat. Satrena Calene); (3) ~ ib. 593 (Lat. Calene)
S. Italy (Calabria):
—brentesion-brundisium: (4) imp. NScav 1887, p. 207 (Eph. Ep. viii 42) (Lat. Pomponia Calene)
Sicily:
—katane: (5) imp. IG xiv 479
—syracuse: (6) iii-v ad Strazzulla 180 (Wessel 1386)
Sicily?: (7) iii ad Epigraphica 3 (1941) p. 267 no. 37 (ILat. Palermo 88) (Lat. Cassia Galene)

**Γαληνός**
Korinthia:
—korinth: (1) f. ii ad Ag. vii p. 96 no. 291; Corinth iv (2) p. 207 no. 718 (lamps) (Γαλ[ηνός]—Ag.)
Lakonia:
—sparta:
——Neopolitai: (2) c. 175 ad IG v (1) 680, 13 (Bradford (-)) (s. Σπένδων)

**Γάλυκος**
Epiros:
—dodona: (1) iii bc Antoniou, Dodone Ba, 36 (Γλαῦκος?)

**Γαμήτη**
S. Italy (Campania):
—pompeii*: (1) ?i ad NScav 1961, p. 200 no. 3 (Lat. Sutoria Gamete: freed.)

**Γαμική**
S. Italy (Calabria):
—brentesion-brundisium: (1) i-ii ad Necropoli via Cappuccini p. 261 no. E3 (Lat. Gamice)
S. Italy (Campania):
—dikaiarchia-puteoli: (2) imp. CIL x 2131 (Lat. Aufidia Gamice)
Sicily:
—katane: (3) imp. IG xiv 496 (Πεσκεννία Γ.)
—katane*: (4) imp. CIL x 7063 (Lat. Decimia Gamice: freed.)
—lipara: (5) imp. Epigraphica 51 (1989) p. 195 no. 90 (Lat. Iulia Gamice: m. Ὑγίεια)

**Γαμίων**
S. Italy (Campania):
—dikaiarchia-puteoli: (1) imp. CIL x 2852 (Lat. L. Domitius Gamio)

**Γάμος**
S. Italy (Apulia):
—canusium*: (1) imp. Epig. Rom. di Canosa 207 (CIL ix 408) (Lat. Gamus: slave?)
S. Italy (Campania):
—pompeii: (2) i bc-i ad ib. iv 1445 (Lat. Gamus); (3) ~ ib. 2310 i (Lat. Gamus); (4) ~ ib. 4513 (Lat. Gamus)
S. Italy (Lucania):
—grumentum: (5) imp. ib. x 237 (Lat. Gamus)
Sicily:
—katane: (6) imp. IG xiv 510, 2; (7) ~ CIL x 7050 (Lat. C. Aulius Gamus)

**Γάνγριος**
Illyria:
—ardiaioi: (1) v bc PAE 1966, p. 76 no. 2 + BE 1967, no. 334

**Γαρέας**
Lakonia:
—sparta*: (1) f. vi bc SEG ii 68; LSAG² p. 198 no. 6 (date); BSA 24 (1919-21) pp. 92-3 no. 5 (name) (Poralla² 180a) (Γαρέας, Γαρέας?: sculptor)

## Γαρτύδας
S. Italy (Bruttium):
—kroton: (1) iv bc Iamb., *VP* 265

## Γάστρος
Akarnania:
—oiniadai: (1) m. ii bc *IG* ix (1)² (2) 209, 17 (s. Ἄνδρων)

## Γάστρων
Aitolia: (1) f. iii bc *Das Heroon von Kalydon* p. 293, 12 (s. Ἀμφώνυμος)
Lakonia:
—sparta: (2) ?c. 350 bc Polyaen. ii 16; Front., *Strat.* ii 3. 13 (Poralla² 181)

## Γάτιμος
Leukas: (1) ?256 bc *SGDI* 2659, 2 (*ZPE* 101 (1994) pp. 223 f.) (f. Τίμων)

## Γαυδεντία
Sicily:
—syracuse: (1) iii–v ad *Rend. Pont.* 22 (1946-7) p. 236 no. 37 (Γαυδεν[τία])

## Γαῦσος
Aitolia: (1) ?273-272 bc *FD* iii (1) 298, 2; 473, 2; iii (3) 185, 2; 203, 2

## Γαψίας
Argolis:
—argos: (1) iii bc *IG* iv (1) 618 II, 7 (f. Ἐπικράτης)

## Γάψων
Argolis:
—argos: (1) 337-328 bc *CID* ii 74 I, 73; 76 II, 23; 120 A, 2; 121 III, 15 (s. Ἀλκίας)

## Γειτιάδας
Lakonia: (1) ?vi bc Paus. iii 17. 2; 18. 8; *REG* 99 (1986) p. 136 (name) (Poralla² s.v. Γιτιάδας 186) (Γιτιάδας—Paus.: sculptor)

## Γείτων
Epiros:
—votonosi (mod.): (1) ?m. iii bc *SEG* xxiv 464 (f. Νικοδίκα)

## Γειτωνίδας
Kynouria:
—tyros*: (1) vi/v bc *IG* v (1) 1521 (vase) (Lazzarini 751) (-τō-)

## Γελάδας
Argolis:
—argos: (1) v bc Schol. Ar., *Ran.* 501 a

## Γελασῖνος
S. Italy (Campania):
—dikaiarchia-puteoli: (1) imp. *CIL* x 2852 (Lat. L. Plutius Gelasinus); (2) ~ ib. 3063 (Lat. Q. Hordeonius Gelasinus: f. Valeria Ianuaria)

## Γελάσις
S. Italy (Campania):
—dikaiarchia-puteoli: (1) ?iii ad *IG* xiv 846, 5 (threptos)

## Γελάστη
S. Italy (Campania):
—pompeii: (1) i bc-i ad *CIL* iv 8381

## Γέλη
Sicily:
—herbessos: (1) vi–v bc *Kokalos* 14-15 (1968-9) p. 200 (vase); cf. Dubois, *IGDS* p. 195 (-λē̄)

## Γελλίας
Sicily:
—akragas: (1) v bc *RE* (-) (Τελλίας—Ath.)

## Γέλλιος
Argolis:
—troizen: (1) 198-211 ad *IG* iv (1) 793, 9 (s. Ἀφροδίσιος)

## Γελώι
Sicily:
—gela-phintias: (1) vi/v bc Dubois, *IGDS* 157 (vase) (Arena, *Iscr. Sic.* ii 59) (Γελṓι (n. pr.?))

## Γελῶιος
Sicily:
—gela-phintias: (1) f. v bc Dubois, *IGDS* 131. 10 (Arena, *Iscr. Sic.* ii 45) (Γελṓιος—ethn.?); (2) f. ii bc *IG* xiv 256, 42 (Dubois, *IGDS* 161); cf. *SEG* xl 804 (s. Γοργύλος)
—herbessos: (3) vi/v bc Dubois, *IGDS* 166 a-b (vase) (Arena, *Iscr. Sic.* ii 120) (-λṓ-)
—kamarina: (4) f. v bc Cordano, *Tessere Pubbliche* 111 (-λṓ-: s. Μέγων); (5) s. v bc Dubois, *IGDS* 121, 19-20 (Arena, *Iscr. Sic.* ii 143; *SEG* xxxviii 940; Cordano, 'Camarina VII' 18) (-λṓ-: f. —δας); (6) ?iv/iii bc *SEG* xxxiv 940, 9 (Dubois, *IGDS* 124; *PdelP* 44 (1989) p. 192 no. 3; Cordano, 'Camarina VII' 85) (Γ[ε]λṓιος: f. Σίμος); (7) iv/iii bc *SEG* xxxiv 942, 5 (Dubois, *IGDS* 123; Cordano, 'Camarina VII' 86)

## Γέλων
Achaia:
—pellene: (1) c. 400 bc *IG* ii² 1386, 6; 1388, 33; 1407, 33 (s. Τλασωνίδας)
Aitolia: (2) ?254 bc *Syll*³ 436, 3; Nachtergael, *Les Galates* 9, 4
Epiros:
—bouthrotos (prasaiboi): (3) a. 163 bc *IBouthrot* 115, 5, 7-8 (s. Φίλιππος)
——Prakeleoi: (4) a. 163 bc ib. 68, 12
—charadroi: (5) iii/ii bc Cabanes, *L'Épire* p. 561 no. 35, 8; Robert, *Hell.* 1 pp. 95 ff. (locn.) (f. —ων)
—dodona: (6) iii bc Antoniou, *Dodone* Ab, 48
—molossoi: (7) ?c. 343-331 bc Cabanes, *L'Épire* p. 577 no. 50, 9; (8) iv/iii bc *RE* (5); (9) ii bc *SGDI* 1357, 3; cf. Cabanes, *L'Épire* p. 583 no. 61
—pharganaioi: (10) f. ii bc ib. p. 589 no. 75, 10 (*SEG* xxxvii 510) (f. Ἀνάξανδρος)
Lakonia:
—sparta: (11) 604 bc Moretti, *Olymp.* 76 (Poralla² 182)
S. Italy (Campania):
—pompeii: (12) i bc-i ad *CIL* x 8058. 52 (seal) (Castrèn 249. 4) (Lat. T. Mescinius Gelo)
Sicily:
—gela-phintias: (13) c. 540-478 bc *RE* (3); Moretti, *Olymp.* 185; ML 28 (and Sicily Syracuse: Γέλōν—ML: s. Δεινομένης: tyrant)
—kamarina: (14) ?iv bc *SEG* xxxii 917 (Cordano, 'Camarina VII' 88) (sculptor); (15) ?iv/iii bc *SEG* xxxiv 940, 10 (Dubois, *IGDS* 124; *PdelP* 44 (1989) p. 192 no. 3; Cordano, 'Camarina VII' 89) (s. Καλλίστρατος)
—leontinoi: (16) 433 bc *IG* i³ 54, 5 (-λōν: s. Ἐξήκεστος)
—syracuse: (17) c. 270-216 bc *RE* (4) (s. Ἱάρων, Φιλιστίς, f. Ἱαρώνυμος, Ἁρμονία)
——(Περηκυαταῖος): (18) iv bc Manganaro, *PdelP* forthcoming no. 3, 10 (f. Σωσίστρατος)

## Γέλως
S. Italy (Bruttium):
—rhegion*: (1) f. i ad *Suppl. It.* 5 p. 64 no. 16 (Lat. C. Iulius Gelos: imp. freed.)
S. Italy (Campania):
—dikaiarchia-puteoli: (2) imp. *CIL* x 2451 (Lat. Gelos)

## Γέμελλα
Akarnania:
—alyzia: (1) imp. *IG* ix (1)² (2) 447
Epiros:
—nikopolis: (2) imp. *Wiss. Mitth. Bosn.* 4 (1896) p. 389 no. 7 (Sarikakis 25) (Γαίμελα)

## Γεμελλῖνα
S. Italy (Campania):
—neapolis: (1) iii–v ad Wessel 777 A (Γαιμαιλῖνα)

## Γέμελλος
S. Italy (Campania):
—dikaiarchia-puteoli: (1) imp. *NScav* 1897, p. 530 fig. 3 (Audollent, *Defix. Tab.* 202 (terracotta))
Sicily:
—syracuse: (2) iii–v ad *IG* xiv 89 (Strazzulla 30; Wessel 834); *ASSicilia* 1938-9, p. 29 (s. Κλωδία)

## Γενεθλία
Korinthia:
—korinth: (1) byz. *Corinth* viii (1) 170 + *SEG* xi 103; (2) ~ Bees 58 A ([Γεν]εθλ[ία])
Sicily:
—syracuse: (3) iii–v ad Strazzulla 370; cf. Ferrua, *NG* 136 (Γενεχλία—lap.)

## Γενεθλίδιος
Korinthia:
—korinth: (1) byz. *Corinth* viii (3) 516; cf. *TMByz* 9 (1985) p. 364 no. 50 (Φλ. Γενεθλίδ(ιος) Ἰοῦστος)

## Γενέθλιος
Elis: (1) 233 ad *IvOl* 116, 9 (s. Μ. Αὐρ. Ἑλληνοκράτης)
Lakonia:
—sparta: (2) ?ii ad *EILakArk* 3 (s. Ἀρίων); (3) m. ii ad *SEG* xi 643, 4 (Bradford (-)) (Γενέθλιος)
S. Italy (Apulia):
—canusium: (4) imp.? *Epig. Rom. di Canosa* 77 (*CIL* ix 355) (Lat. Genetlius)
S. Italy (Calabria):
—taras-tarentum*: (5) imp. *Misc. Gr. Rom.* 3 p. 175 (Lat. Genethlius: slave?)

## Γένεσις
S. Italy (Campania):
—pompeii: (1) i bc-i ad *CIL* iv 4300; 4321 (Lat. Genesis); (2) ~ ib. 8216 (Lat. Genes[is])

## Γενθέας
Illyria:
—epidamnos-dyrrhachion: (1) imp. *IDyrrh* 151 (s. Ζαρρέας)

## Γενθήνα
Illyria:
—epidamnos-dyrrhachion: (1) hell.-imp. ib. 256 (Ἰσνθηνα—apogr., Γενθήνα?—ed.: d. Πλάτωρ)

## Γενθιανή
Illyria:
—dardanioi: (1) s. ii ad *ZA* 24 (1974) p. 255, 1, 6 (m. Ῥήδων, Χάρης)

## Γενθιανός
Illyria:
—apollonia: (1) i/ii ad *IApoll* 189 (Μ. Πεδού. Γ.)
—pogradec (mod.): (2) imp. *Stud. Alb.* 1969 (2), p. 170 (1972 (1), p. 84) (s. Πλάτωρ)

## Γένθιος
Illyria: (1) f. ii bc *RE* (-); Russu (1); *SNG Cop. Thessaly–Illyricum* 529; cf. *Schweizer Münzblätter* 162 (1991) pp. 25-30 (date) (s. Πλευρᾶτος, Εὐρυδίκα, f. Σκερδιλαΐδας, Πλευρᾶτος: king)
—apollonia: (2) hell.-imp. *IApoll* 191 (f. Νικάνωρ); (3) imp. ib. 212 (Κλ. Γ.)

—EPIDAMNOS-DYRRHACHION: (4) c. 250-50 BC
Ceka 123 (coin) (money.); (5) f. ii BC IC 3
p. 112 no. 14; SEG XXXI 1521, 8 (IDyrrh
518-19) (f. Φιλώτας); (6) hell.-imp. ib. 153 (s.
Δαζαῖος); (7) ~ ib. 154 (s. Νικύλος); (8) ~ ib.
337
—KORCA (MOD.): (9) hell. Iliria 1972, p. 18;
SEG XXXIII 487 (pithoi)
—LYCHNIDOS?: (10) ii-i BC ib. I 254 (f. Μαχά-
τας)

**Γενθίς**
ILLYRIA:
—APOLLONIA: (1) i/ii AD IApoll 189 (Φλ. Γ.: d.
Τ. Φλ. Φιλωνίδης)
—EPIDAMNOS-DYRRHACHION: (2) hell.-imp.
IDyrrh 152 (-θείς: d. Τραῦζος)

**Γενική**
S. ITALY (CAMPANIA):
—DIKAIARCHIA-PUTEOLI: (1) imp. CIL x 2645
(Lat. Genice)

**Γέννα**
S. ITALY (CAMPANIA):
—MISENUM*: (1) imp. ib. 3498 (Lat. Arruntia
Genna)

**Γεννάδας**
AITOLIA: (1) ?a. 264 BC SGDI 2508, 3
EPIROS:
—ONOPERNOI?: (2) ?c. 370-344 BC Cabanes,
L'Épire p. 536 no. 2, 8

**Γεννάδιος**
ARGOLIS:
—EPIDAUROS: (1) ii-iii AD IG IV (1)² 516, 7

**Γεννάδις**
SICILY:
—SYRACUSE: (1) iv AD ib. XIV 179 (Strazzulla
117; Agnello 13; Wessel 626); cf. Riv. Arch.
Crist. 18 (1941) p. 166 no. 26 (Ὑγῖνος (ὁ)? καὶ
Γ.)

**Γενναῖος**
LAKONIA:
—SPARTA: (1) m. ii AD IG V (1) 71 II, 15; 154,
12; Artemis Orthia pp. 139-40 no. 85? (Brad-
ford (-)) (Π. Μέμμιος Γ.)
S. ITALY (APULIA):
—LUCERIA: (2) imp. ASP 34 (1981) p. 23 no.
26 (Lat. C. Sallustius Gennaeus: f. Ἑρμιόνη)
S. ITALY (CAMPANIA):
—POMPEII: (3) c. 51-62 AD CIL IV 3340. 74,
10; 130, 1 (Castrèn 205. 11) (Lat. Ti. Iul.
Gennaeus)

**Γενναΐς**
S. ITALY (CAMPANIA):
—DIKAIARCHIA-PUTEOLI: (1) imp. CIL x 3144
(Lat. Volumnia Gennais)

**Γεννικός**
MESSENIA:
—MESSENE: (1) ?202 BC IG VII 292, 3 (IOrop
202) (s. Λεωνίδας)

**Γέννιος**
SICILY:
—ENTELLA: (1) ii-i BC SEG XXXVIII 928 (tile)

**Γεντιανός**
SICILY:
—KATANE: (1) 435 AD Agnello 96 + Ferrua, NG
405 ([Κε]ντιανός—edd., [Γε]ντιανός—Ferrua: f.
Ἄπρα)

**Γένυς**
EPIROS:
—GITANA: (1) f. iii BC AD 18 (1963) Chron. p.
156 (f. Νίκαιος)

**Γένυσος**
ARGOLIS:
—EPIDAUROS*: (1) c. 370-360 BC Peek, IAEpid
52 A, 33, 39; BSA 61 (1966) p. 272 no. 4, 8

**Γεράδας**
LAKONIA:
—SPARTA: (1) arch. Plu., Lyc. 15; Mor. 228
C (Poralla² 183) (Γεραδάτας—228 C); (2) c.
372 BC Plu., Pelop. 25; REG 99 (1986) p.
136 (name) (Poralla² s.v. Γεράνδας 184) (Γεράνδας—Plu.)

**Γεράνωρ**
LAKONIA:
—SPARTA: (1) 369 BC X., HG vii 1. 25 (Poralla²
185)

**Γεράσιμος**
KORINTHIA:
—KORINTH*: (1) byz. IG IV (1) 388 (amph.)
(bp.?)

**Γερμανός**
ARKADIA:
—TEGEA: (1) ii AD ib. v (2) 55, 33 (f. Στόλος)
KORINTHIA:
—KORINTH: (2) byz. Corinth VIII (3) 575
(Γερ[μα]νός)
SICILY:
—AKRILLAI: (3) iii-v AD Epigraphica 12 (1950)
p. 106 no. 2 (biling.); cf. Riv. Arch. Crist. 18
(1941) p. 206 no. 80

**Γερόντιος**
SICILY:
—KATANE: (1) iii-v AD SEG IV 60 (Wessel 878)
—SYRACUSE: (2) iii-v AD Strazzulla 362 (Barreca
91)

**Γέρυλλος**
ARGOLIS:
—HERMIONE: (1) iii/ii BC IG IV (1) 712, 3 (f.
Ἄριστις)

**Γέρων**
EPIROS: (1) s. iv BC ib. IV (1)² 95, 77 (Perlman
E.2); Perlman pp. 46-9 (date) (s. Ἀριστόδαμος)
—BOUTHROTOS (PRASAIBOI): (2) a. 163 BC
IBouthrot 76, 4; cf. L'Illyrie mérid. 2 p. 220
n. 6 (f. Φάλακρος)

**Γέτας**
ILLYRIA:
—DARDANIOI: (1) s. ii AD ZA 24 (1974) p. 255,
1, 5 (f. Ῥήδων, Χάρης)
—EPIDAMNOS-DYRRHACHION: (2) hell.-imp.
IDyrrh 155 (s. Μελάνθιος); (3) ~ ib. 306 (f.
Μελάνθιος); (4) ~ ib. 424 (f. Τρυφέρα)

**Γέτος**
ILLYRIA:
—APOLLONIA: (1) hell.-imp. IApoll 65 (s. Πλά-
τωρ)

**Γεῦμα**
S. ITALY (APULIA):
—CANUSIUM*: (1) imp. Epig. Rom. di Canosa
207 (CIL IX 408) (Lat. Graecidia Geuma:
freed.)

**Γεωργία**
KORINTHIA:
—KORINTH: (1) byz. Corinth VIII (3) 646, 3; cf.
TMByz 9 (1985) p. 363 no. 46 (d. Κλημ—)

**Γεωργίας**
S. ITALY (CALABRIA):
—BRENTESION-BRUNDISIUM: (1) imp. IG XIV
675 (Γεωρ-)

**Γεωργικός**
S. ITALY (CAMPANIA):
—AMALFI (MOD.): (1) iii-iv AD ib. 694 a (p. 689)
(Γεωρ-)

**Γεώργιος**
ARGOLIS:
—EPIDAUROS: (1) iii AD SEG XXII 290, 8; Peek,
NIEpid 52, 2; cf. IG IV (1)² 455 (?s. Βρασίδας)
EPIROS:
—NIKOPOLIS?: (2) v-vi AD PAE 1925-6, p. 127
(mosaic)
KORINTHIA:
—KORINTH: (3) byz. Corinth VIII (1) 200; cf.
TMByz 9 (1985) p. 361 no. 19 (Γεώρ-); (4) ~
Corinth VIII (3) 556, 2; cf. TMByz 9 (1985)
p. 363 no. 40
LAKONIA:
—THALAMAI: (5) byz. IG V (1) 1326 (pithos)
MESSENIA:
—METHONE: (6) byz. PAE 1967, p. 27

**Γεῶργος**
S. ITALY (CAMPANIA):
—MISENUM: (1) f. i AD De Franciscis, Sacello
Augustali p. 38 (Lat. Sex. Gellius Georgus)

**Γηρέας**
AKARNANIA:
—PHOITIAI: (1) iv BC IG IX (1)² (2) 602, 2 (s.
Ἡρακ—)

**Γῆρις**
EPIROS:
—DODONA*: (1) iv BC Ep. Chron. 10 (1935) p.
260 no. 37 + Arch. Pap. 15 (1953) p. 78
(name—Wilhelm)

**Γηρίων**
ARGOLIS:
—HERMIONE: (1) iii BC IG IV (1) 729 II, 18 (s.
Στίχος)

**Γῆρυς**
SICILY:
—KAMARINA: (1) s. v BC Dubois, IGDS 121, 21
(Arena, Iscr. Sic. II 143; SEG XXXVIII 940;
Cordano, 'Camarina VII' 20)

**Γίγας**
SICILY:
—KAMARINA: (1) iv/iii BC SEG XXXIV 942,
4 (Dubois, IGDS 123; Cordano, 'Camarina
VII' 90)

**Γίλλος**
S. ITALY (CALABRIA):
—TARAS-TARENTUM: (1) vi/v BC Hdt. iii 138

**Γιρίων**
KORINTHIA:
—KORINTH: (1) byz. Corinth VIII (3) 551, 3; cf.
TMByz 9 (1985) p. 362 no. 36 (Γερύων—ed.)

**Γλάγος**
S. ITALY (BRUTTIUM):
—KROTON: (1) ?i AD CIL x 109 (Lat. C. Iulius
Glagus: ?s. Πρεπίς)
S. ITALY (CAMPANIA):
—POMPEII: (2) i BC-i AD ib. IV 4886 (Lat.
Glagus)

**Γλαύκα**
AKARNANIA:
—THYRREION: (1) iii BC IG IX (1)² (2) 259
S. ITALY (CALABRIA):
—TARAS-TARENTUM: (2) iii-ii BC SEG XXX
1219 (Landi, DISMG 207)

**Γλαυκατίας**
LAKONIA:
—SPARTA: (1) c. 530-500 BC CEG I 376 (Po-
ralla² 187) ([Γ]λαυκατ[ίας]: s. —οίδας)

## Γλαυκέας

AITOLIA:
—KALLION/KALLIPOLIS: (**1**) 143 BC *IG* IX (1)²
(3) 639. 8, 3 (f. Φιλομήλα)

## Γλαυκέτας

AITOLIA: (**1**) ?209 or 205 BC Flacelière p. 407
no. 38 b, 2; Nachtergael, *Les Galates* 68, 2
EPIROS: (**2**) iv BC *IG* II² 8534 (f. Δέξανδρος)

## Γλαύκη

EPIROS:
—NIKOPOLIS: (**1**) imp. *Wiss. Mitth. Bosn.* 4
(1896) p. 387 no. 3 (Sarikakis 26)
S. ITALY (CAMPANIA):
—DIKAIARCHIA-PUTEOLI: (**2**) ii-iii AD *IG* XIV
839 (Βαία Γλαύκη)
—NEAPOLIS: (**3**) i BC/i AD *INap* 151, 5 (Γ. Πα-
πειρία)

## Γλαυκίας

AIGINA: (**1**) vi/v BC *RE* (11); *Alt-Ägina* II (2)
p. 35 f.; *LSAG²* p. 113 no. 12 (sculptor)
AITOLIA:
—PHISTYON: (**2**) ii BC *IG* IX (1)² (1) 110 a, 7
—THESTIEIS: (**3**) ii BC *SBBerlAk* 1936, p. 380
no. 1 A, 6
AKARNANIA:
—PHOITIAI: (**4**) iv BC *IG* IX (1)² (2) 602, 5 (s.
Εὐαν—)
ARGOLIS:
—ARGOS*: (**5**) ii BC *BCH* 33 (1909) pp. 456-7
no. 23, 11 (slave/freed.?)
—EPIDAUROS: (**6**) i BC Peek, *NIEpid* 109
—EPIDAUROS*: (**7**) c. 290-270 BC *IG* IV (1)² 110
B, 3
—HERMIONE: (**8**) iii BC ib. IV (1) 728, 1 (s. Κάλ-
λων)
—TROIZEN: (**9**) iii BC ib. 774, 10
EPIROS:
—AVARICE (MOD.): (**10**) ii BC *SEG* XXIV 468 (f.
Ἀλκινόα)
—BOUTHROTOS (PRASAIBOI):
——Essyrioi: (**11**) f. ii BC *IBouthrot* 2, 6; 3, 6; 4,
5; 9, 2; 54, 6; 59, 6 (*SEG* XXXVIII 489; 505;
510); *IBouthrot* 69, 16; 70, 12; 71, 10 (*BCH*
118 (1994) p. 129 B 1-3); *IBouthrot* 75, 9; 76,
6; 102, 5; 105, 6; 106, 5; 108, 5 (f. Σωκλῆς,
Ἀρχίας)
——Essyrioi?: (**12**) a. 163 BC ib. 134, 7, 13 (s.
Σωκλῆς)
—DODONA: (**13**) iii BC Antoniou, *Dodone* Ba, 12
—DODONA*: (**14**) iv BC *Ep. Chron.* 10 (1935) p.
254 no. 11
ILLYRIA:
—APOLLONIA: (**15**) iv BC *IApoll* 385; (**16**) hell.
ib. 348 (Γλαυκ[ίας], Γλαῦκ[ος]?); (**17**) ii-i BC ib.
142 (Γλαυ[κίας]?: f. Πατώ)
—DARDANIOI: (**18**) 139 BC *FD* III (3) 27, 4, 5,
8 etc. (slave/freed.)
—EPIDAMNOS-DYRRHACHION: (**19**) imp.
*IDyrrh* 102 (f. Ἀνναία)
—KORCA (MOD.): (**20**) hell.? *Iliria* 1992, p. 207
(sherd)
—TAULANTIOI: (**21**) iv/iii BC *RE* (7); Berve 227
(?f. Τίτος)
ITHAKE: (**22**) hell. *IG* IX (1) 669 (Γ(λ)αυκίας)
KEPHALLENIA:
—PALE: (**23**) iii/ii BC Unp. (*IG* arch.)
KORINTHIA:
—SIKYON: (**24**) iv BC *IG* II² 10296 (s. Δαμά-
τριος)
S. ITALY (BRUTTIUM):
—KROTON: (**25**) 588 BC Moretti, *Olymp.* 87
(Γλύκων—Afric.)
—LOKROI EPIZEPHYRIOI:
——(Θρα.): (**26**) iv/iii BC De Franciscis 12, 7;
27, 2; 30, 6 (s. Σωσίβιος)
S. ITALY (CALABRIA):
—TARAS-TARENTUM: (**27**) f. ii BC *RE* (8);
Deichgräber, *Griech. Empirikerschule* pp. 168
ff. (doctor)

S. ITALY (LUCANIA):
—METAPONTION: (**28**) iv BC *Atti Conv. Taranto*
16 (1976) p. 857, pl. 139.2 (vase) (Γλαυκία
(gen.?): potter?)
SICILY:
—KAMARINA: (**29**) f. v BC Cordano, *Tessere Pub-
bliche* 66 (s. Εὐκλήτας)
—LEONTINOI: (**30**) 433 BC *IG* I³ 54, 5 (f. Σῶσις)
—MORGANTINA: (**31**) iv/iii BC *SEG* XXXIX 1010,
5 (f. —ανδρος); (**32**) ~ ib. 1013, 6
—SELINOUS: (**33**) s. vi BC Dubois, *IGDS* 30
(Arena, *Iscr. Sic.* I 62)

## Γλαυκίδας

ARKADIA:
—MANTINEIA-ANTIGONEIA:
——(Epalea): (**1**) m. iv BC *IG* V (2) 271, 4 (f.
Ἄρχυλλος)
——(Posoidaia): (**2**) c. 425-400 BC *SEG* XXXI
348, 26; Dubois, *RDA* 2 p. 126 (Γλαυσίδας—
lap., Γλαυ(κ)ίδας—Solin and Dubois)

## Γλαυκιδώ

EPIROS:
—MIKHALITSI (MOD.): (**1**) iv BC *SEG* XXVII
231

## Γλαυκίης

S. ITALY (BRUTTIUM):
—RHEGION: (**1**) ?m. v BC Dubois, *IGDGG* I 39
a (Arena, *Iscr. Sic.* III 63); *LSAG²* p. 244
(date) (Γλαυκίν (gen.): f. Κλεόφαντος); (**2**) c.
420-410 BC Paus. v 27. 8; Dubois, *IGDGG* I
36 (Arena, *Iscr. Sic.* III 65; *IvOl* 271; Lazzarini 362; *CEG* I 388); cf. *LSAG²* p. 248 no.
16 ([Γλ]αυκίης—lap.: s. Λυκκίδης)

## Γλαυκῖνος

AKARNANIA:
—ECHINOS?: (**1**) iii BC *IG* IX (1)² (2) 368
—THYRREION: (**2**) 216 BC ib. 583, 19, 64 (s. Διό-
φαντος)
ARGOLIS:
—ARGOS: (**3**) 470-450 BC ib. I³ 858 (f. Ἀριστο-
μάχα, Χαρίκλεια)

## Γλαύκιππος

S. ITALY (BRUTTIUM):
—LOKROI EPIZEPHYRIOI:
——(Κοβ.): (**1**) iv/iii BC De Franciscis 7, 2 (f.
Ἀρίστιππος)
——(Τηλ.): (**2**) iv/iii BC ib. 38, 2 (s. Εὔθυμος)

## Γλαυκίων

KORINTHIA:
—KORINTH: (**1**) iv-iii BC *RE* (-) (painter)

## Γλαῦκον

ARGOLIS:
—ARGOS: (**1**) ii BC *IG* II² 8361 a, 1 (Γλ[α]ῦκον:
d. Ἀγαθοκλῆς)
EPIROS: (**2**) f. iii BC ib. 8533

## Γλαῦκος

AITOLIA: (**1**) s. iv BC Berve 230; (**2**) ?209 or 205
BC Flacelière p. 407 no. 38 b, [2]; Nachtergael, *Les Galates* 68, 3
AKARNANIA: (**3**) iii-ii BC *PAE* 1912, p. 186 no.
21 (s. Κλεομένης); (**4**) c. 170 BC Plb. xxviii 5.
1 + 5
ARGOLIS:
—ARGOS: (**5**) f. v BC *RE* (47) (sculptor); (**6**) c.
80-70 BC *IG* VII 3195, 16; *BSA* 70 (1975) pp.
121-2 (date); cf. Stephanis 572 (f. Δαμαίνετος)
—EPIDAUROS: (**7**) c. 365-335 BC *IG* IV (1)² 103,
63
ELIS: (**8**) m. i BC *IvOl* 407, 2; 409, 1-2
([Γλ]α[ῦ]κος—407, [Γλαῦ]κος—409: s. Θεότιμος)
EPIROS: (**9**) 234-168 BC Franke, *Münz. v. Epirus* p. 175 II ser. 22 (coin)

ILLYRIA:
—EPIDAMNOS-DYRRHACHION: (**10**) c. 250-50
BC Maier 164; 315; 380 (coin) (Ceka 124-6)
(money.)
KERKYRA: (**11**) 500 BC Paus. vi 9. 9; cf. Ebert,
*Gr. Sieg.* 11; cf. Page, *FGE* 802 (f. Φίλων);
(**12**) f. iii BC *IG* IX (1) 691, 11 (*Iscr. Gr. Ve-
rona* p. 22 A); (**13**) ii BC *IG* IX (1) 694, 37
(*RIJG* XXV B); cf. *SEG* XXV 609 (f. Μολώ-
τας); (**14**) i BC-i AD *IG* IX (1) 905
KORINTHIA:
—KORINTH: (**15**) 156 BC *ID* 1417 C, 61 (I f.
Γλαῦκος II); (**16**) c. 156-145 BC ib. l. 60; 1442
A, 61 (II s. Γλαῦκος I); (**17**) s. i BC *Corinth*
VIII (3) 311 (Lat. Glaucus: f. M. Ἀντ. Μιλή-
σιος); (**18**) imp. *IEph* 2243, 3 (Γν. Κορνήλιος
Γ.)
LAKONIA:
—SPARTA: (**19**) ?vii/vi BC Hdt. vi 86 (Poralla²
188) (s. Ἐπικύδης)
MESSENIA:
—THOURIA: (**20**) f. ii BC *SEG* XI 972, 39 (f.
Ἀλεξίων); (**21**) ~ ib. l. 81 (f. Φίλαιος)
S. ITALY (APULIA):
—LUCERIA: (**22**) imp. *IG* XIV 2413. 11 (ring)
S. ITALY (BRUTTIUM):
—LOKROI EPIZEPHYRIOI: (**23**) hell.? *RE* (41)
(Γλαύκων?)
—RHEGION: (**24**) v/iv BC ib. (36)
—RHEGION*: (**25**) m. vi BC Rumpf, *Chalkid.
Vas.* p. 46 no. 4 (vase) (Arena, *Iscr. Sic.* III
p. 102-3 no. 7) (-ρος: her.?)
S. ITALY (CALABRIA):
—TARAS-TARENTUM: (**26**) iv/iii BC *IG* XIV 668
II, 8 (Landi, *DISMG* 194)
S. ITALY (CAMPANIA):
—HERCULANEUM: (**27**) i BC-i AD *CIL* IV 2509,
8 (5449) (Lat. Glaucus)
SICILY:
—GELA-PHINTIAS: (**28**) s. iv BC *IG* IV (1)² (1)
95, 85 (Perlman E.2); Perlman pp. 46-9 (date)
(f. Ἡρακλείδας)
—LILYBAION: (**29**) s. ii AD *CIL* X 7237 (Lat. M.
Marcius Bietis Glaucus)
—MORGANTINA?: (**30**) iv/iii BC *PdelP* 44 (1989)
p. 214 ([Γλ]αῦκος)
—TAUROMENION: (**31**) inc. *IOrop* 675 (f. Ποσεί-
δης)
—(Ἀχαιο.): (**32**) ?ii/i BC *IG* XIV 421 D an. 4;
421 [D] an. 1 (*SGDI* 5219) (s. Ὄλυμπις)
—ZANKLE-MESSANA: (**33**) ?ii BC *IG* XIV 401, 7
(Γηαουκος—apogr., Γ.—Burmann: s. Θευφεί-
δης)

## Γλαύκων

ARKADIA: (**1**) s. i BC *GP* 2200 (fict.)
EPIROS:
—DODONA*: (**2**) iii-ii BC Carapanos, *Dodone* p.
47 no. 18
SICILY?: (**3**) 250 BC *FGrH* 567 F 1 (Λεύκιος Γ.:
fict.?)

## Γλαῦξ

LAKONIA:
—AMYKLAI*: (**1**) c. 510-500 BC *IG* V (1) 832 A;
*LSAG²* p. 200 no. 32 (date) (Γλαῦχς (n. pr.?))

## Γλαφύρα

S. ITALY (APULIA):
—CANUSIUM: (**1**) imp. *Epig. Rom. di Canosa* 9
(Lat. Glaphera)
S. ITALY (CAMPANIA):
—DIKAIARCHIA-PUTEOLI: (**2**) imp. *CIL* X 3067
(Lat. Aviania Glafyra: m. Valeria Pia)
—DIKAIARCHIA-PUTEOLI*: (**3**) imp. ib. 2310
(Lat. Cocceia Glaphyra: freed.)

## Γλάφυρος

LAKONIA:
—HYPERTELEATON*: (**1**) imp. *IG* V (1) 1038
(freed.)

**Γλύκα**
S. ITALY (CAMPANIA):
—DIKAIARCHIA-PUTEOLI*: (2) 56 AD CIL x 1574 (Lat. C. Iulius Glaphyr(us): freed.)
—POMPEII: (3) i BC-i AD ib. IV 8432 (Lat. G(l)afyrus)
SICILY:
—LILYBAION: (4) imp. ib. x 7216 (Lat. C. Cornelius Glaphyr(us))

**Γλύκα**
S. ITALY (CALABRIA):
—HYDROUS-HYDRUNTUM: (1) iii-iv AD JIWE I 134 (CIJ I 632); cf. Puglia Paleocrist. Altomed. 3 p. 108 (d. Σαβῖνος, —μη: Jew)

**Γλυκᾶς**
KEPHALLENIA:
—SAME: (1) hell. IG IX (1) 636 ([Γ]λυκᾶς
MESSENIA:
—MESSENE: (2) byz. DIEEE 6 (1901) p. 388 no. 10

**Γλύκεια**
S. ITALY (BRUTTIUM):
—KROTON: (1) imp. Costabile, Ist. Bruzio p. 176 (Lat. Glucia)

**Γλυκέρα**
AIGINA: (1) hell. IG IV (1) 140
EPIROS:
—NIKOPOLIS: (2) imp. CIG 1811 b (Sarikakis 82) (Κλ. Γ.: d. Μεμμία Κλεοπάτρα)
KORINTHIA:
—KORINTH: (3) iv BC IG II² 9061; (4) iv/iii BC Men., Pk. 472 f. (d. Πάταικος: fict.)
—SIKYON: (5) iv BC RE (-) (Skalet 82) (Lat. Glycera)
LEUKAS: (6) inc. AM 27 (1902) p. 367 no. 29; (7) iv-iii BC SEG XXIX 483
S. ITALY (CAMPANIA):
—DIKAIARCHIA-PUTEOLI: (8) imp. AJA 2 (1898) p. 384 no. 27 (Lat. Larcia Glycera)
—DIKAIARCHIA-PUTEOLI*: (9) imp. CIL x 2867 (Lat. Pompeia Glychera: freed.)
—POMPEII: (10) i BC-i AD ib. IV 5120 (Lat. Glycera)
SICILY:
—KENTORIPA: (11) imp. IG XIV 578

**Γλυκερός**
S. ITALY (CAMPANIA):
—NEAPOLIS: (1) ii-iii AD ib. 717, 3 (INap 4); cf. Leiwo p. 160 no. 133 (Π. Πλώτιος Γ.)

**Γλύκη**
S. ITALY (CALABRIA):
—BRENTESION-BRUNDISIUM: (1) imp. CIL IX 192 (Lat. Statilia [G]lyce)

**Γλύκιννα**
EPIROS:
—BOUTHROTOS (PRASAIBOI): (1) a. 163 BC IBouthrot 27, 4 (SEG XXXVIII 485)
S. ITALY (APULIA):
—TEANUM APULUM*: (2) i BC/i AD Teanum Apulum p. 74 no. 19 (Lat. Porcia Glycinna: freed.)
S. ITALY (CAMPANIA):
—NOLA: (3) imp. CIL x 1267 (Lat. Critonia Glycinna)

**Γλυκῖνος**
S. ITALY (LUCANIA):
—METAPONTION: (1) iv BC Iamb., VP 267 (FVS I p. 446)

**Γλύκος**
AIGINA: (1) ?iii-iv AD Alt-Ägina I (2) p. 49 no. 39 (I f. Αὐρ. Γλύκος II); (2) ~ ib. (Αὐρ. Γ.: II s. Γλύκος I)

**Γλυκύρα**
DALMATIA:
—ISSA: (1) ii BC Brunšmid p. 25 no. 14, 6 + VAHD 84 (1991) p. 248 no. 1 (d. Τιμασίων)

**Γλυκύσπορος**
KORINTHIA:
—KORINTH: (1) iv BC SEG XI 204

**Γλύκων**
ARKADIA:
—TEGEA: (1) ii AD IG v (2) 55, 67 (I f. Γλύκων II); (2) ~ ib. l. 67 (II s. Γλύκων I)
LAKONIA:
—SPARTA: (3) imp. ib. v (1) 796 b (Bradford (3)); (4) c. 90-130 AD IG v (1) 79, 9; 99, [7]; 284, 2; SEG XI 517, 5; 539, 5 (Bradford (5)) (f. Ἑρμογένης); (5) ?ii AD IG v (1) 523 (Bradford (5)) ([Γ]λύκων?); (6) ?m. ii AD IG v (1) 329; Artemis Orthia pp. 317-18 no. 39 (date) (Bradford (2)) (s. Ἑρμογένης); (7) c. 155-170 AD IG v (1) 39, 33; 71 III, 47; 86, 25; 154, 10 (Bradford (4)) (I f. Γλύκων II); (8) ~ IG v (1) 39, 33; 71 III, 47; 86, 25; 154, 10 (Bradford (1)) (II s. Γλύκων I)
MESSENIA:
—MESSENE: (9) 31 BC-14 AD SEG XXIII 207, 16 (Λ. Βέννιος Γ.)
S. ITALY (CALABRIA):
—BRENTESION-BRUNDISIUM: (10) imp. NScav 1881, p. 249 (Lat. M. Anto[nius] Glyco)
S. ITALY (CAMPANIA):
—AEQUANA: (11) imp. CIL x 764 (Lat. Gaius Curatius Gluco: I f. Γλύκων II); (12) ~ ib. (Lat. Gaius Curatius Gluco: II s. Γλύκων I, Ἐλπίς)
—DIKAIARCHIA-PUTEOLI: (13) imp. ib. 2180 (Lat. -tesius Glyco)
—POMPEII: (14) i BC-i AD ib. IV 3999; 4001 (Lat. Glyco); (15) s. i AD ib. 89; Kockel p. 90 (date) (Lat. Glyco)

**Γλυκωνίς**
S. ITALY (APULIA):
—CANUSIUM: (1) i AD Epig. Rom. di Canosa 105 (Lat. Campila [Gl]yconi[s])

**Γλύμμα**
S. ITALY (CALABRIA):
—BRENTESION-BRUNDISIUM: (1) i AD Epigraphica 25 (1963) p. 74 no. 75; cf. Scritti Degrassi 3 p. 70 f. (Lat. Cornificia Glymma: m. C. Caninius Rufus)

**Γλύπτη**
S. ITALY (CAMPANIA):
—DIKAIARCHIA-PUTEOLI: (1) imp. CIL x 2483 (Lat. Glypte)
—POMPEII: (2) i BC-i AD NScav 1916, p. 303 (Lat. Glypte)

**Γλύπτος**
AKARNANIA:
—ANAKTORION (NR.): (1) ii AD SEG XXXVI 533 ([Ἰ]ούλιος [Γ]λύπτος)
S. ITALY (CAMPANIA):
—BAIAI*: (2) s. i AD Puteoli 3 (1979) p. 160 no. 4 (Lat. L. Acilius Glyptus: freed.?)
—PITHEKOUSSAI-AENARIA: (3) imp. CIL x 6803 (Lat. Cominius Glyptus: s. Εἰρήνη)

**Γλώτιος**
S. ITALY (APULIA):
—SALAPIA: (1) 300-225 BC SNG ANS Etruria-Calabria 736-7 (coin) ((Π)λώτιος?)

**Γνάθαινα**
AKARNANIA:
—THYRREION: (1) s. iii BC IG IX (1)² (2) 283

**Γνάθιος**
ARGOLIS:
—ARGOS: (1) f. iii BC GVI 1074
KERKYRA: (2) c. 500 BC SEG XXX 523; (3) ?iii BC IG IX (1) 682, 4; cf. Fraser–Rönne, BWGT p. 181 (s. Σωκράτης); (4) s. ii BC IG IX (2) 5 b, 5 (f. Στράτιος)

**Γνάθις**
ARGOLIS:
—ARGOS: (1) ?c. 480-475 BC JÖAI 14 (1911) Beibl. p. 142 no. 2, 3 (Lazzarini 938); LSAG² p. 169 no. 21 (date); (2) c. 365-335 BC IG IV (1)² 103, 53
S. ITALY (BRUTTIUM): (3) ?ii-i BC ib. XIV 2401. 1-2 (Landi, DISMG 247); Riv. Stor. Calab. NS 6 (1985) p. 213 (tiles); SEG XXXIX 1044
—LOKROI EPIZEPHYRIOI:
——(Ἀγφ.): (4) iv/iii BC De Franciscis 7, 6 (f. Θράσων)
——(Ἀγκ.): (5) iv/iii BC ib. 14, 6
——(Φαω.): (6) iv/iii BC ib. 22, 9 (f. Φίλων)
——(Ψαθ.): (7) iv/iii BC ib. 32, 4 (s. Φρυνίων)

**Γνάθων**
ARKADIA:
—DIPAIA: (1) s. v BC RE (-); Moretti, Olymp. 314
SICILY: (2) iv BC Plu., Mor. 707 E; 1128 B
—KAMARINA: (3) iv/iii BC SEG XXXIX 999, 6 (Dubois, IGDS 125; Cordano, 'Camarina VII' 91) (Γνάθ[ω]ν)

**Γναῖφα**
S. ITALY (APULIA):
—GRAVINA (MOD.): (1) s. v BC Santoro, NSM I p. 169 no. IM 0.322 (vase)

**Γναῖος**
ACHAIA:
—AIGION: (1) imp.? BCH 57 (1933) p. 261
AIGINA: (2) ii BC SEG XI 10, 1; (3) ?f. i BC Alt-Ägina I (2) p. 43 no. 4, 4 (f. Καλλίμαχος)
DALMATIA:
—ISSA: (4) iii/ii BC Brunšmid p. 24 no. 12 (f. Πούλιος)
S. ITALY (CAMPANIA):
—NEAPOLIS: (5) iv/iii BC BMC Italy p. 105 no. 106 (coin) (Sambon 482); (6) i BC-i AD? INap 121; cf. Leiwo p. 68 no. 9 (f. Εὔδρομος)
SICILY:
—ENTELLA: (7) f. iii BC SEG XXX 1121, 3 (Dubois, IGDS 208); SEG XXX 1123, 4 (Dubois, IGDS 211); SEG XXXV 999, 3 (Dubois, IGDS 212) (s. Ὄππιος)

**Γνίκων**
ARGOLIS:
—TROIZEN: (1) ?146 BC IG IV (1) 757 B, 28, 29 (Γνίκων: s. Νικοκλῆς)

**Γνίφων**
S. ITALY (BRUTTIUM):
—LOKROI EPIZEPHYRIOI:
——(Κρα.): (1) iv/iii BC De Franciscis 3, 7 (s. Καλλῖνος)
——(Τυν.): (2) iv/iii BC ib. 25, 1

**Γνωΐλας**
LAKONIA:
—AMYKLAI*: (1) ?iii BC SEG XVII 188 b (Bradford (-))

**Γνώμη**
EPIROS:
—BOUTHROTOS (PRASAIBOI): (1) imp. AEp 1978, no. 772 (Lat. Plaetoria Gnome: m. Μουσικός)
S. ITALY (CALABRIA):
—BRENTESION-BRUNDISIUM: (2) imp. CIL IX 183 (Lat. Sergia Gnome)
S. ITALY (CAMPANIA):
—NEAPOLIS: (3) imp. NScav 1892, p. 317; cf. Leiwo p. 112 no. 83 (Lat. Clodia Gnome)
—POMPEII: (4) i BC-i AD CIL IV 8488 (Lat. Gnome?)

**Γνωμικός**
S. ITALY (CAMPANIA):
—HERCULANEUM: (**1**) m. i AD *PdelP* 8 (1953) p. 461 no. 49, 6 (Lat. M. Rufus Gnomicus)

**Γνώμων**
ARGOLIS:
—EPIDAUROS*: (**1**) c. 335-325 BC *IG* IV (1)² 106 I, 111 ([Γ]νώμων)
SICILY:
—AKRAI (NR.): (**2**) imp. *Epigraphica* 3 (1941) p. 270 no. 44 (Lat. Gnomoni (gen.?))
—KATANE: (**3**) imp. *CIL* X 8059. 183 (seal) (Lat. Gnomon)

**Γνώριμος**
S. ITALY (CAMPANIA):
—HERCULANEUM: (**1**) m. i AD *PdelP* 3 (1948) p. 177 no. 23 (Lat. Sex. Vibidius Gnorimus)
—HERCULANEUM*: (**2**) i BC-i AD *CIL* X 1403 l II, 11; cf. *Cron. Erc.* 7 (1977) p. 116 c, 11 (Lat. A. Vibidius Gnorimus: freed.)

**Γνωσέας**
ARKADIA:
—TEUTHIS: (**1**) 191-146 BC *BMC Pelop.* p. 15 no. 174 (coin)

**Γνώσιππος**
LAKONIA:
—SPARTA: (**1**) s. iii BC *FGrH* 86 F 12 (Bradford (-))

**Γνῶσις**
SICILY:
—SYRACUSE: (**1**) 411 BC X., *HG* i 1. 29 (f. Πόταμις)

**Γνώστας**
LAKONIA:
—OINOUS: (**1**) c. 475 BC *SEG* XIII 239, 2; *BE* 1955, no. 102 (locn.) (Γνόσσ-)

**Γνωστή**
S. ITALY (CALABRIA):
—BRENTESION-BRUNDISIUM*: (**1**) imp. *Epigraphica* 25 (1963) p. 52 no. 42. 1; cf. *Scritti Montevecchi* p. 141 (Lat. Aulia Gnoste: m. Ti. Aulius Felicio: freed.)
SICILY:
—LIPARA: (**2**) ii/iii AD *Epigraphica* 3 (1941) p. 259 no. 15 (Νεαρχία Γ.)

**Γνωστός**
S. ITALY (CAMPANIA):
—DIKAIARCHIA-PUTEOLI*: (**1**) imp. *CIL* X 1917 (Lat. Gnostus: imp. freed.)

**Γόγγος**
SICILY:
—KATANE: (**1**) imp. *IG* XIV 510, 3 (Οὐρβανίων Γόγγε (voc.)—lap., (Λ)όγγε? (voc.)—*IG*)

**Γογγύλος**
KORINTHIA:
—KORINTH: (**1**) 414 BC *RE* (2)

**Γονατία**
SICILY:
—AKRAI: (**1**) imp. *SEG* XLII 829

**Γόνος**
S. ITALY (CAMPANIA):
—POMPEII: (**1**) i BC-i AD *NScav* 1916, p. 303 no. 118 (Lat. Gonus)

**Γόργασος**
AITOLIA:
—KALYDON: (**1**) m. ii BC *IG* IX (1)² (1) 137, 24
ARGOLIS:
—EPIDAUROS: (**2**) s. iii BC Peek, *NIEpid* 45 (s. Πολυκλῆς) ?= (3)

—(Dymanes): (**3**) 146 BC *IG* IV (1)² 28, 4 (Γόργασος: f. Πολυκλῆς) ?= (2)
PELOPONNESE: (**4**) s. iii BC *SEG* XIII 278, 13

**Γοργέας**
ARKADIA:
—MEGALOPOLIS: (**1**) 369-361 BC *IG* V (2) 1, 28; Tod, *GHI* II 132 (date)
ILLYRIA:
—EPIDAMNOS-DYRRHACHION: (**2**) c. 250-50 BC Ceka, *Probleme* p. 151 no. 15 (coin) (pryt.) ?= (3); (**3**) ~ Maier 475 (coin) (Ceka 155; 157) (pryt.) ?= (2)
S. ITALY (LUCANIA):
—HERAKLEIA: (**4**) s. iv BC *BCH* 23 (1899) p. 501 no. 17, 2; cf. 62 (1938) p. 342 n. 1 (date) (s. Αἰσχύλος)
SICILY:
—GELA-PHINTIAS: (**5**) vi BC Dubois, *IGDS* 145 (vase) (Arena, *Iscr. Sic.* II 36); *QUCC* 78 (1995) p. 123 n. 7 (name) (Γόργε—vase, Γοργēς?—Arena)

**Γοργήν**
ILLYRIA:
—EPIDAMNOS-DYRRHACHION: (**1**) c. 250-50 BC Maier 152-4; Münsterberg Nachtr. p. 14 (coin) (Ceka 54; 64; 351; 388) (pryt.); (**2**) hell.-imp. *IDyrrh* 136 = 85 (f. Βάδυλα)

**Γοργιάδας**
ARKADIA:
—MANTINEIA-ANTIGONEIA: (**1**) c. 300-221 BC *IG* V (2) 323. 25 (tessera) (s. Γόργυθος)
—TEGEA: (**2**) m. iv BC ib. 6, 70 (Γοργιάδα[s])
LAKONIA:
—SPARTA: (**3**) s. i BC ib. V (1) 93, 16 (Bradford (1)) (s. Εὐάμερος) ?= (4); (**4**) c. 25-1 BC *IG* V (1) 210, 30 (Bradford (2)) (f. Χαρῖνος) ?= (3)

**Γοργίας**
ARGOLIS:
—EPIDAUROS: (**1**) iv/iii BC *IG* IV (1)² 305
—EPIDAUROS*: (**2**) c. 370 BC ib. 102, 84
—HERMIONE: (**3**) iv BC ib. IV (1) 742, 13
EPIROS:
—AMBRAKIA: (**4**) ?f. iii BC *SEG* XXXIX 522 (s. Δάμιος); (**5**) ii-i BC *CIG* 1797; 1799 (s. Ἀνδρόνικος, f. Ἀνδρόνικος)
—DODONA: (**6**) iii BC Antoniou, *Dodone* Aa, 12
ILLYRIA:
—APOLLONIA: (**7**) imp.? *IApoll* 190; cf. *SEG* XXXVII 533 (s. Ποδᾶς)
—EPIDAMNOS-DYRRHACHION: (**8**) c. 250-50 BC Maier 155 (coin) (Ceka 71) (pryt.)
KORINTHIA:
—KORINTH: (**9**) ?269 BC *CID* II 120 A, 39; 121 II, 16 ([Γορ]γίας: s. Φερεκλῆς)
—SIKYON: (**10**) c. 80-70 BC *IG* IX (2) 534, 23; Kramolisch p. 116 n. 74 (date) (Skalet 83) (f. Κάναχος)
LAKONIA: (**11**) c. 510-500 BC *IG* I³ 637-41; Plin., *NH* xxxiv 49 (Poralla² 190) (sculptor); (**12**) c. 250-230 BC *IG* VII 337, 2 (*IOrop* 113; Bradford (-)) (s. Παντίας)
—LEUKTRA: (**13**) imp. *IG* V (1) 1328
LEUKAS: (**14**) iv BC *AM* 27 (1902) p. 369 no. 40 a
S. ITALY (BRUTTIUM):
—LOKROI EPIZEPHYRIOI:
—(Αγκ.): (**15**) iv/iii BC De Franciscis 7, 8 (s. Ἡράκλητος)
S. ITALY (CAMPANIA):
—DIKAIARCHIA-PUTEOLI: (**16**) imp. *CIL* X 2459 (Lat. Gorgia: f. Primus)
—HERCULANEUM*: (**17**) i BC-i AD ib. 1403 g III, 53 (Lat. C. Opsius Gorgia: freed.)
S. ITALY (LUCANIA):
—HERAKLEIA: (**18**) c. 85 BC *ID* 2002, 1 (s. Δαμόξενος)

SICILY:
—LEONTINOI: (**19**) v BC *RE* (8); *FVS* 82 (s. Χαρμαντίδης)
—MORGANTINA: (**20**) iv/iii BC *SEG* XXXIX 1012, 7 (s. Παρμόνιμος)
—SELINOUS: (**21**) m. v BC Dubois, *IGDS* 34 (Arena, *Iscr. Sic.* I 70) (Γοριγας—apogr.)
—SYRACUSE?:
—(Ὑπα.): (**22**) hell. Manganaro, *PdelP* forthcoming no. 4 II, 4 (s. Ὀλύμπις)
—TAUROMENION: (**23**) c. 198 BC *IG* XIV 421 an. 43 (*SGDI* 5219); (**24**) c. 188-145 BC *IG* XIV 421 an. 53; 421 an. 75; 421 an. 83; 421 an. 96 (*SGDI* 5219) (s. Λύσανδρος, f. Λύσανδρος); (**25**) c. 148 BC *IG* XIV 421 an. 93 (*SGDI* 5219); *IGSI* 4 III (IV), 55 an. 93 (s. Ἀγάθαρχος)

**Γοργίδας**
LAKONIA:
—HIPPOLA: (**1**) ii-i BC *IG* V (1) 1334 a + *AAA* 1 (1968) p. 119 no. 1 (locn.) (date—*LGPN*)
MESSENIA:
—THOURIA: (**2**) f. ii BC *SEG* XI 972, 27 (s. Ἀριστέας)
S. ITALY (BRUTTIUM):
—LOKROI EPIZEPHYRIOI:
—(Ἀστ.): (**3**) iv/iii BC De Franciscis 7, 5 (f. Εὐφρονίσκος); (**4**) 276 BC ib. 23, 2 (f. Μενάλκης)
—(Λακ.): (**5**) iv/iii BC ib. 20, 4 (f. Νέαιθος)

**Γοργίλος**
ARGOLIS:
—ARGOS: (**1**) vi BC Arist., *Ath.* 17. 4 (f. Τιμώνασσα); (**2**) ii AD *SEG* XVI 258 c, 7 (s. Μενεκλῆς)
ARKADIA:
—MANTINEIA-ANTIGONEIA: (**3**) c. 300-221 BC *IG* V (2) 323. 57 (tessera) (f. Βοάθοος)
—TEGEA: (**4**) m. iv BC ib. 6, 86
ELIS: (**5**) ii-i BC *IvOl* 403; 404 (I f. Γοργίλος II); (**6**) ~ ib. 403; [404]? (II s. Γοργίλος I)
ILLYRIA:
—EPIDAMNOS-DYRRHACHION: (**7**) c. 250-50 BC Maier 156 (coin) (Ceka 85) (pryt.)

**Γοργιλώ**
DALMATIA:
—PHAROS: (**1**) hell. Brunšmid p. 14 no. 1 ([Γ]οργιλώ, Ὀργιλώ—*CIG*: d. Δήμαρχος)

**Γοργίππα**
AIGINA: (**1**) m. iv BC *IG* II² 7952 + *AM* 67 (1942) p. 212 no. 5
LAKONIA: iii-ii BC *IG* V (1) 1341, 5 (Bradford (-))

**Γοργιππίδας**
ARKADIA:
—TEGEA: (**1**) f. iii BC *IG* V (2) 36, 63 (f. Ἐπαίνετος)
LAKONIA:
—SPARTA: (**2**) s. i BC ib. V (1) 94, 18 (Bradford (2)) ([Γορ]γιππίδας); (**3**) m. i AD *IG* V (1) 509, 4 (Bradford (1)) (Π. Μέμμιος Γ. Φιλάδελφος: s. Λυσάνικος); (**4**) c. 80-100 AD *SEG* XI 511, 1; 560, 5 (Bradford (3); (5)); (**5**) c. 160-170 AD *IG* V (1) 109, 16 (Bradford (4))

**Γοργιππίς**
LAKONIA:
—PYRRHICHOS: (**1**) imp.? *IG* V (1) 1288 (-ιπίς)

**Γόργιππος**
AIGINA: (**1**) i-ii AD *Alt-Ägina* I (2) p. 46 no. 23 (f. —τος)
ARGOLIS:
—ARGOS: (**2**) a. 324 BC *CID* II 120 A, 9-10 (f. —ντος, —θος)
—EPIDAUROS: (**3**) iv BC *IG* IV (1)² 319; (**4**) iii BC ib. 167, 4
—EPIDAUROS*: (**5**) c. 340-330 BC ib. 112, 29
ARKADIA:
—MANTINEIA-ANTIGONEIA: (**6**) c. 300-221 BC ib. V (2) 323. 95 (tessera); (**7**) ?15 AD ib. 274,

17

—MEGALOPOLIS: (**8**) s. ii BC ib. 436, 11

—PHENEOS: (**9**) m. iii BC ib. IV (1)² 96, 48 (Perlman E.3); Perlman p. 63 f. (date) (s. *Τυχανίδας*)

—TEGEA: (**10**) s. iii BC *IG* v (2) 116, 6 (f. *Γόργων*)

——(Krariotai): (**11**) iv BC ib. 38, 27 (s. *Ἀρχέας*); (**12**) m. iii BC ib. 36, 89 (s. *Γόργις*)

ILLYRIA:

—EPIDAMNOS-DYRRHACHION: (**13**) c. 250-50 BC Maier 158 (coin) (Ceka 55) (pryt.)

LAKONIA:

—SPARTA: (**14**) s. i BC *IG* v (1) 124, 15 (Bradford (5)) (s. *Φιλι*—); (**15**) ~ *IG* v (1) 135, 5 (Bradford (11)) (f. *Πολυκλῆς*); (**16**) c. 30-20 BC *IG* v (1) 141, 27; *SEG* XXXV 329 (date) (Bradford (6)) (*Γόργιπ[πος]*); (**17**) c. 25-1 BC *IG* v (1) 212, 10 (Bradford (1)) (s. *Γοργίων*); (**18**) i BC/i AD *IG* v (1) 48, 14 (Bradford (9)) (f. *Ἵππαρχος*); (**19**) c. 170-210 AD *IG* v (1) 89, 7; 129, 3; 307, 6 (*Artemis Orthia* pp. 328-9 no. 60); *IG* v (1) 308, 4 (*Artemis Orthia* p. 329 no. 61); *SEG* XXXVI 360, 5; *BSA* 81 (1986) pp. 323-4 no. 1 (ident., date) (Bradford (7); (8)) (I f. *Γόργιππος* II); (**20**) ~ *IG* v (1) 89, 7; 129, 3; 307, 6 (*Artemis Orthia* pp. 328-9 no. 60); *IG* v (1) 308, 3 (*Artemis Orthia* p. 329 no. 61); *IG* v (1) 309, 5 (*Artemis Orthia* p. 329 no. 62); *IG* v (1) 557, 2; *SEG* XI 555, 2, 5; XXXVI 360, 5; *BSA* 79 (1984) p. 283 no. 1; 81 (1986) pp. 323-4 no. 1 (ident., date) (Bradford (2); (3)) (II s. *Γόργιππος* I); (**21**) c. 220 AD *IG* v (1) 653 b, 6 (*Artemis Orthia* pp. 356-8 no. 143); *BSA* 79 (1984) pp. 279-82 (ident., stemma) (Bradford (4)) (*Σέξ. Πομπ. Γ.*: s. *Σέξ. Πομπ. Ὀνασικράτης*)

——Pitana: (**22**) c. 105 AD *IG* v (1) 675, 7 (Bradford (10)) (f. *Λαοδαμίδας*)

## Γόργις

ACHAIA:

—DYME: (**1**) s. iii BC *SEG* XIII 278, 28 (s. *Δρακόντιος*)

ARKADIA:

—TEGEA:

——(Krariotai): (**2**) m. iii BC *IG* v (2) 36, 89 (f. *Γόργιππος*)

LAKONIA:

—SPARTA: (**3**) ii BC ib. v (1) 29, 15 (*Syll*³ 669; Bradford (-)) (s. *Ἀλκαμένης*)

MESSENIA:

—MESSENE: (**4**) ii BC *PAE* 1969, p. 106, 16

## Γόργις

S. ITALY (CALABRIA):

—HYDROUS-HYDRUNTUM*: (**1**) ii AD Susini, *Fonti Salento* p. 100 no. 35 (Lat. Iulia Gorgis: freed.)

## Γόργις

ILLYRIA:

—EPIDAMNOS-DYRRHACHION: (**1**) hell.-imp. *IDyrrh* 158 (s./d. *Ἀντίοχος*); (**2**) ~ ib. 159 (s./d. *Ἀριστήν*)

## Γοργίων

ARGOLIS:

—EPIDAUROS:

——(Azantioi): (**1**) 146 BC *IG* IV (1)² 28, 37 (s. *Λεοχάρης*)

LAKONIA:

—SPARTA: (**2**) c. 300-281 BC ib. XI (4) 542, 3, 24 (Bradford (2)) (f. *Δαμάρατος*); (**3**) c. 25-1 BC *IG* v (1) 212, 10 (Bradford (3)) (f. *Γόργιππος*); (**4**) c. 150-160 AD *IG* v (1) 69, 31; 71 III, 23; *SEG* XI 554, [3]; 585, 13; XXX 410, [22] (Bradford (1)) (s. *Κλεόβουλος*)

## Γόργοι

ARGOLIS:

—EPIDAUROS: (**1**) iv/iii BC Peek, *IAEpid* 340, 3 (d. *Κύδιμος*, ?d. *Θεοδότα*)

---

LEUKAS: (**2**) hell. *IG* IX (1) 575

## Γοργολέων

LAKONIA:

—SPARTA: (**1**) 375 BC Plu., *Pelop.* 17 (Poralla² 191)

## Γόργος

ACHAIA?: (**1**) 193 BC *IG* v (2) 293, 11 (s. *Ἑρμογένης*)

AITOLIA: (**2**) 213 or 205 BC Nachtergael, *Les Galates* 66, 3

AKARNANIA:

—ALYZIA: (**3**) s. iv BC *IG* IV (1)² 95, 70 (Perlman E.2); Perlman pp. 46-9 (date) (f. *Ἀργεῖος*)

ARKADIA: (**4**) ?253 BC Nachtergael, *Les Galates* 10, 28; cf. Stephanis 2493 (f. *Φιλινίων*) ?= (7)

—KAPHYAI: (**5**) s. ii BC *BMI* 1154 a, 2; *BE* 1972, no. 37 (date) (I f. *Γόργος* II); (**6**) ~ *BMI* 1154 a, 2; *BE* 1972, no. 37 (date) ([Γ]όργος: II s. *Γόργος* I)

—KLEITOR: (**7**) ?262 or 258 BC Nachtergael, *Les Galates* 5, 43; cf. Stephanis 2774 (f. —s) ?= (4)

—TEGEA:

——(Apolloniatai): (**8**) m. iii BC *IG* v (2) 36, 101 (f. *Μικίων*)

ELIS: (**9**) hell.? Moretti, *Olymp.* 961-966

—OLYMPIA*: (**10**) c. 65-75 AD *IvOl* 83, 10 ([Γ]όργος: slave?)

EPIROS:

—BOUTHROTOS (PRASAIBOI):

——Bouthrotioi: (**11**) a. 163 BC *IBouthrot* 114, 10; 126, 8 (f. *Σωσίπατρος*)

——Eschatioi: (**12**) a. 163 BC ib. 116, 2, 8 (*BCH* 118 (1994) p. 121 A)

ILLYRIA:

—BERAT (MOD.): (**13**) ii/i BC *SEG* XXXVIII 542 (s. *Κέββας*)

—EPIDAMNOS-DYRRHACHION: (**14**) c. 250-50 BC *SNG Lockett* pl. 31 no. 1629

KORINTHIA:

—KORINTH: (**15**) s. vii BC *FGrH* 90 F 59-60 with Comm.; cf. 303 F 1; Arist., *Pol.* 1315b 26; cf. Beloch, *GG* I (2) pp. 274 ff.; Ravel, *Colts of Ambracia* p. 23 no. 122; p. 60 (and Epiros Ambrakia: *Γορδίας*—Arist. *Pol.* mss.: s. *Κύψελος*, ?s. *Κράτεια*, f. *Ψαμμήτιχος*, *Κύψελος*: oikist) (f. *Περίανδρος*); (**16**) vii/vi BC *FGrH* 90 F 59. 1 (s. *Περίανδρος*)

—SIKYON: (**17**) 207 BC *IMM* 41, 18 (s. *Μενεκλῆς*)

LAKONIA:

—SPARTA: (**18**) f. vi BC *SEG* XI 180 a; *LSAG*² p. 199 no. 15 (date) (Poralla² 191a); (**19**) m. ii BC Phld., *Ind. Sto.* 76, 5

MESSENIA: (**20**) vii BC *RE* (8) (s. *Ἀριστομένης*)

—MESSENE: (**21**) f. iii BC *PAE* 1991, p. 100 no. 8, 6; cf. 1989, p. 96; (**22**) s. iii BC Moretti, *Olymp.* 573; *RE* (5); (9) (s. *Εὔκλητος*)

SICILY:

—AKRAGAS: (**23**) c. 488 BC Polyaen. vi 51 (s. *Θήρων*)

—GELA-PHINTIAS: (**24**) ii/i BC *SEG* XXXI 837, 3 (Γ. *Πλώτις*)

—KEPHALOIDION: (**25**) s. iii BC *Thess. Mnem.* 158 (s. *Διόγνητος*); (**26**) ?iii-v AD *SEG* XXXVI 846 (s. *Ζωΐλος*)

—LIPARA: (**27**) imp. *IG* XIV 387 + *SEG* XXXIV 957. 6 (Γ. *Πουβλείλιος Γ.*)

—MORGANTINA: (**28**) c. 133 BC D.S. xxxiv/xxxv 11 (I f. *Γόργος* II); (**29**) ~ ib. (Γ. ἐπικαλ. *Κάμβαλος*: II s. *Γόργος* I)

—SELINOUS: (**30**) ?m. vi BC Dubois, *IGDS* 63 (Arena, *Iscr. Sic.* I 28; *IGLMP* 81)

—SYRACUSE: (**31**) iii-v AD *IG* XIV 90 (Strazzulla 31) (Γό(υ)ργος?)

## Γοργοσθενίδας

LAKONIA:

—SPARTA: (**1**) iii BC *SEG* XL 348 B, 5 (Γοργοσθενίδας)

---

## Γοργυθίων

ARKADIA:

—MANTINEIA-ANTIGONEIA: (**1**) c. 300-221 BC *IG* v (2) 323. 76; 79 (tesserae) (s. *Κλεῖσκος*, f. *Κλεῖσκος*)

## Γόργυθος

ARKADIA:

—MANTINEIA-ANTIGONEIA: (**1**) c. 300-221 BC ib. 323. 25 (tessera) (f. *Γοργιάδας*); (**2**) f. iii BC ib. 278, 5; *EILakArk* 17 (date)

—TEGEA: (**3**) m. iv BC *IG* v (2) 6, 73

## Γοργύλος

SICILY: (**1**) iii BC Vandermersch p. 164 (amph.)

—GELA-PHINTIAS: (**2**) f. ii BC *IG* XIV 256, 42 (Dubois, *IGDS* 161; cf. *SEG* XL 804 (Γ.—apogr. *IG*, Γοργύλος—Dubois: f. *Γελώϊος*)

—SYRACUSE:

——(Κραταιμείος): (**3**) iv BC Manganaro, *PdelP* forthcoming no. 3, 7 (s. *Ῥάδων*)

## Γοργώ

ELIS: (**1**) c. 95-105 AD *IvOl* 438, 5; *ZPE* 99 (1993) p. 232 (stemma) (Φλ. Γ.: m. *Νουμισία Τεισίς*)

EPIROS:

—AMBRAKIA: (**2**) iv/iii BC Unp. (Arta Mus., inscr.) ([Γ]οργώ: d. *Εὐκλείδας*)

—BOUTHROTOS (PRASAIBOI): (**3**) a. 163 BC *IBouthrot* 21, 43 (*SEG* XXXVIII 478); (**4**) ~ *IBouthrot* 26, 15 (*SEG* XXXVIII 484); (**5**) ~ *IBouthrot* 27, 8 (*SEG* XXXVIII 485); (**6**) ~ *IBouthrot* 32, 2 (*SEG* XXXVIII 491)

LAKONIA:

—SPARTA: (**7**) f. v BC *RE* (2) (Poralla² 192) (d. *Κλεομένης*, m. *Πλείσταρχος*); (**8**) hell. *IG* v (1) 811 (Bradford (2))

SICILY:

—SYRACUSE: (**9**) c. 272 BC Theoc., *Id.* xv passim (fict.)

## Γοργώι

LAKONIA:

—SPARTA: (**1**) i BC/i AD *SEG* XI 676, 2 (Bradford (1)) ([Γ]οργώι: d. *Ἀριστόλας*)

MESSENIA:

—MESSENE: (**2**) ii BC *Ergon* 1995, p. 29

## Γόργων

ARKADIA:

—MANTINEIA-ANTIGONEIA:

——(Hoplodmia): (**1**) m. iv BC *IG* v (2) 271, 12 (s. *Διονύσιος*)

—TEGEA: (**2**) s. iii BC ib. 116, 6 (Γόργ[ω]ν: s. *Γόργιππος*)

——(Hippothoitai): (**3**) f. iii BC ib. 36, 17 ([Γόρ]γων?)

## Γοργώπας

LAKONIA: (**1**) hell.? *SEG* XXXII 397

—GYTHEION: (**2**) 195 BC Liv. xxxiv 9-12

—SPARTA: (**3**) 389-388 BC *RE* (-) (Poralla² 193); (**4**) iv/iii BC *CID* II 120 A, 31 (Poralla² 194; Bradford (3)) (I f. *Γοργώπας* II); (**5**) ~ *CID* II 120 A, 31 (Poralla² 195; Bradford (1)) ([Γοργ]ώπας: II s. *Γοργώπας* I); (**6**) c. 25-1 BC *IG* v (1) 212, 43 (Bradford (2)) (s. *Ἀβρίας*); (**7**) c. 80-100 AD *SEG* XI 608, 5 (Bradford (4)) (f. *Πασικλῆς*)

MESSENIA:

—MESSENE: (**8**) f. iii BC *SEG* XLI 342, 14; cf. *PAE* 1991, p. 100 no. 8

## Γόργως

LAKONIA:

—SPARTA: (**1**) c. 25-1 BC *IG* v (1) 212, 42 (Bradford (-)) (s. *Κορείδας*)

## Γράβος

ILLYRIA: (**1**) m. iv BC *RE* Supplbd. 3 (-); *TAPA* 69 (1938) pp. 44 ff. (king)

—APOLLONIA: (2) i BC Maier 140 (coin) (pryt.); (3) i AD *NZ* 41 (1908) p. 16 no. 140 (coin)
ILLYRIA?: (4) 440-415 BC *IG* I³ 162, 5; cf. *SEG* XXXII 5 ([Γ]ράβος) ?= (5); (5) 409 BC *IG* I³ 339, 17 ([Γρ]άβος) ?= (4)

**Γράβων**
ILLYRIA: (1) f. iv BC *IvOl* 695, 1 + *Ol. Ber.* 6 pp. 145 ff. (f. Φερζάν)

**Γραῖα**
S. ITALY (APULIA):
—GNATHIA-EGNATIA: (1) s. iv BC *CVA Genova* 1 IV D r, pl. 10, 5

**Γραῖος**
ILLYRIA:
—EPIDAMNOS-DYRRHACHION: (1) c. 210-172 BC *IDyrrh* 517 (f. Πλάτων)

**Γράμμα**
S. ITALY (BRUTTIUM):
—KROTON: (1) ?i AD *CIL* X 111 (Lat. Iulia Gramma)

**Γράνιος**
LAKONIA:
—SPARTA: (1) c. 105-110 AD *IG* V (1) 97, 7; *SEG* XI 564, 7 (Bradford (2)) (I f. Γράνιος II); (2) ~ *IG* V (1) 97, 7; *SEG* XI 564, 7 (Bradford (1)) (II s. Γράνιος I)

**Γράπτη**
S. ITALY (CALABRIA):
—TARAS-TARENTUM: (1) inc. *NScav* 1894, p. 63 no. 14 (Lat. Crapte)
S. ITALY (CAMPANIA):
—DIKAIARCHIA-PUTEOLI: (2) imp. *CIL* X 3090 (Lat. Verria Grapte); (3) ?i-ii AD ib. 2290 (Lat. Claudia Grapte)
SICILY:
—KATANE: (4) imp. *IG* XIV 468 + *Riv. Arch. Crist.* 18 (1941) p. 179 no. 42

**Γράπτος**
EPIROS:
—NIKOPOLIS: (1) imp. *Wiss. Mitth. Bosn.* 4 (1896) p. 389 no. 7 (Sarikakis 27)
LAKONIA:
—SPARTA: (2) c. 140-160 AD *IG* V (1) 149, 7 (Bradford (-)) (Ἰούλ. Γ.)
S. ITALY (CALABRIA):
—BRENTESION-BRUNDISIUM: (3) imp. *CIL* IX 96 (Lat. Cl. Graptus)
S. ITALY (CAMPANIA):
—DIKAIARCHIA-PUTEOLI: (4) imp. ib. X 2727 (Lat. L. Memmius Graptus)
—MISENUM*: (5) imp. ib. 3419 (Lat. P. Paconius Graptus: freed.)

**Γρατιανός**
S. ITALY (BRUTTIUM):
—RHEGION: (1) imp. *IG* XIV 2400. 1 (tile) (Γρατιαν[ός]); (2) ~ ib. 2400. 2 (tile) (Γρατιαν[ός])

**Γράτος**
KORINTHIA:
—KORINTH: (1) byz. *PAE* 1962, p. 52; cf. *TMByz* 9 (1985) p. 367 no. 84

**Γραφιάδας**
AIGINA*: (1) s. vi BC *AA* 1993, p. 579 no. 12 (vase)

**Γραφική**
S. ITALY (CAMPANIA):
—DIKAIARCHIA-PUTEOLI: (1) imp. *CIL* X 2490 (Lat. Graphice: d. Ἄνθος)

—POMPEII: (2) 70-79 AD ib. IV 7649; 7650 (Lat. Graphice)
—SURRENTUM: (3) imp. ib. X 723 (Lat. Caesennia Graphice)

**Γραφικός**
LAKONIA:
—SPARTA: (1) c. 90-100 AD *SEG* XI 558, 4 (Bradford (-)) (f. Μένανδρος)
S. ITALY (CALABRIA):
—BRENTESION-BRUNDISIUM: (2) imp. *CIL* IX 154 (Lat. O(c)tavius Graphicus)
S. ITALY (CAMPANIA):
—DIKAIARCHIA-PUTEOLI: (3) ?i-ii AD ib. X 2273 (Lat. Ti. Claudius Graphicus: f. Herennia Fortunata)
—SALERNUM*: (4) ?i-ii AD *IItal* I (1) 152 (*CIL* X 574) (Lat. Claudius Graphicus: freed.)

**Γρηγορία**
SICILY: (1) byz. *BZ* 19 (1910) p. 470 (ring)

**Γρηγόριος**
S. ITALY (BRUTTIUM):
—HIPPONION-VIBO VALENTIA: (1) byz. *IG* XIV 2412. 10 (Γρι-)
S. ITALY (CAMPANIA):
—DIKAIARCHIA-PUTEOLI*: (2) c. 170 AD *CIL* X 1729; cf. *Puteoli* 11 (1987) pp. 38-40 (Lat. Gregorius: s. Νικηφόρος, Ulpia Fortunata: slave?)
SICILY:
—CALTAGIRONE (MOD.): (3) byz. *Epigraphica* 5-6 (1943-4) p. 93 (Γρηγόρη[ος])

**Γρόσφος**
SICILY: (1) i BC/i AD Hor., *Ep.* i 12, 22; *Carm.* ii 16, 7 (Lat. Pompeius Grosphus)
—KENTORIPA: (2) i BC *SEG* XLII 838 ?= (3); (3) f. i BC Cic., *In Verr.* II iii 56; cf. Masson, *OGS* 2 p. 381 (name) (Lat. Eubulidas Grosp(h)us) ?= (2)

**Γρόττος**
AKARNANIA:
—STRATOS: (1) c. 425-400 BC *IG* IX (1)² (2) 390, 7

**Γύγας**
SICILY:
—KAMARINA: (1) f. v BC Cordano, *Tessere Pubbliche* 98 (f. Χρόμιος)

**Γυίας**
EPIROS: (1) iv-iii BC Cabanes, *L'Épire* p. 585 no. 68, 10

**Γύλαξ**
KORINTHIA:
—KORINTH: (1) vii BC St. Byz. svv. Ἀπολλωνία and Γυλάκεια (and Illyria Apollonia: oikist)

**Γύλιππος**
LAKONIA:
—SPARTA: (1) ?viii-vii BC *HE* 2719 (Poralla² 197) (s. Ἰφικρατίδας, Ἀλεξίππα: fict.?); (2) s. v BC *RE* (1); *IPr* 316, 7 (Poralla² 196) (s. Κλεανδρίδας, ?f. Κλεανδρίδας); (3) f. iii BC Plu., *Cleom.* 1 (Bradford (1)) (f. Ἀγιᾶτις); (4) c. 140-160 AD *IG* V (1) 149, 6 (Bradford (2))

**Γῦλις**
LAKONIA:
—SPARTA: (1) 648 BC Moretti, *Olymp.* 50 (Poralla² 198); (2) 394 BC X., *HG* iv 3. 21, 23 (Poralla² 199)

**Γυλλίας**
ARKADIA:
—MANTINEIA-ANTIGONEIA:
——(Posoidaia): (1) c. 425-400 BC *SEG* XXXI 348, 28; Dubois, *RDA* 2 p. 126 ([Γ]υλλίας, [Κ]υλλίας—Dubois)
—TEGEA:
——(Krariotai): (2) s. iv BC *IG* V (2) 41, 43 (s. Προ—)

**Γύλων**
S. ITALY (CAMPANIA):
—POMPEII: (1) 70-79 AD *CIL* IV 1015; cf. p. 461; Mouritsen p. 109 (date) (Lat. Gylo)

**Γυμνάς**
SICILY:
—LIPARA: (1) imp. *Epigraphica* 51 (1989) p. 195 f. no. 91 (Lat. Atilia Gymn[as])

**Γυμνάσιον**
ARGOLIS:
—HERMIONE: (1) ii-i BC *IG* IV (1) 732 III, 1 (d. Κλειταγόρας)

**Γυμνικός**
S. ITALY (CAMPANIA):
—DIKAIARCHIA-PUTEOLI: (1) imp. *CIL* X 2132 (Lat. Augurius Gymnicus)

**Γυμνίλος**
S. ITALY (LUCANIA):
—POSEIDONIA-PAESTUM: (1) m. iv BC *RVP* p. 84 no. 125 (vase) (fict.)

**Γύρακος?**
SICILY:
—NAXOS: (1) vii/vi BC Arena, *Iscr. Sic.* III 72 (-ρος (gen.?, n. pr.?))

**Γύρας**
EPIROS:
—ARGOS (AMPHILOCH.): (1) iv BC Cabanes, *L'Épire* p. 586 no. 70, 7

**Γυρίδας**
AIGINA?: (1) ?c. 450 BC *IG* I³ 1341; *LSAG*² p. 439 no. 24 (date)
LAKONIA:
—SPARTA: (2) 220 BC Plb. iv 35. 5 (Bradford (1))

**Γυρτιάς**
LAKONIA:
—SPARTA: (1) iv BC Plu., *Mor.* 240 E (Poralla² 201)

**Γύττιος**
S. ITALY (BRUTTIUM):
—LOKROI EPIZEPHYRIOI: (1) iv BC Iamb., *VP* 267 (*FVS* 1 p. 447)

**Γώνιππος**
MESSENIA:
—ANDANIA: (1) ?viii BC Paus. iv 27. 1-2 (dub.)

**Γῶρος**
ILLYRIA:
—EPIDAMNOS-DYRRHACHION (NR.)?: (1) ii BC *SEG* XXXVIII 572, 4; cf. *L'Illyrie mérid.* 2 p. 206; *CRAI* 1991, p. 197 ff.

**Δαάλκης**
KORINTHIA:
—SIKYON: (1) ?255 BC Nachtergael, *Les Galates* 8, 69; cf. Stephanis 1994 (f. *Πανтакλῆς*) ?= (*Δαϊάλκης* (1))

**Δααλκίδας**
ILLYRIA:
—EPIDAMNOS-DYRRHACHION: (1) c. 250-50 BC Ceka, *Probleme* p. 151 no. 16 (coin) (pryt.) ?= (2); (2) ~ Maier 159-60 (coin) (Ceka 31 a; 319) (pryt.) ?= (1)

**Δαδοῦχος**
S. ITALY (CAMPANIA):
—POMPEII: (1) i BC-i AD *CIL* IV 7090

**Δάδων**
AKARNANIA:
—ALYZIA: (1) ?354 BC Tod, *GHI* II 160, 6 (f. *Χάροψ*)

**Δάζα**
ILLYRIA:
—EPIDAMNOS-DYRRHACHION: (1) imp.? *Iliria* 1984 (2), p. 129 (*Δαζα τα*——lap.)

**Δαζαῖος**
ILLYRIA:
—EPIDAMNOS-DYRRHACHION: (1) hell.-imp. *IDyrrh* 153 (f. *Γένθιος*); (2) ~ ib. 161 (s. *Ἀπολλώνιος*); (3) ~ ib. 246 (*Δαζέου* (gen.): f. *Θερσιάν*); (4) imp. ib. 30

**Δάζας**
S. ITALY (CAMPANIA):
—MISENUM: (1) imp. *AJA* 96 (1992) pp. 82-4 (Lat. Dazas)

**Δαζέτα**
ILLYRIA?: (1) ?10 BC Helly, *Gonnoi* 117, 12 (or S. Italy?: slave/freed.)

**Δαζία**
S. ITALY (APULIA):
—S. SEVERO (MOD.): (1) iv/iii BC Santoro, *NSM* I pp. 193-4 no. IM 0.462 (loomweight)

**Δαζίμα**
ILLYRIA?: (1) 170 BC *SGDI* 1789, 4 (or S. Italy?: slave/freed.)
S. ITALY?: (2) 170 BC ib. l. 4 (or Illyria: slave/freed.)

**Δάζιμος**
AKARNANIA:
—THYRREION: (1) ii BC *IG* IX (1)² (2) 247, 13; 248, 12-13; 250, 9, 18; 251, 2-3 (I f. *Δάζιμος* II, *Εὔξενος*, *Ξενόφαντος*); (2) ~ ib. 248, 13; 250, 9 (II s. *Δάζιμος* I); (3) i BC ib. 342
ILLYRIA?: (4) 185 BC *SGDI* 1952, 2-4 (or S. Italy?: slave/freed.); (5) ii AD *PAmh* 44, 15 (or S. Italy?)
S. ITALY (APULIA): (6) iv BC *Studi Ribezzo* pp. 300-1 (vase)
—AZETIUM: (7) iii-ii BC *Taras* 9 (1989) pp. 105-110 (loomweight); cf. 14 (1994) p. 456
—BUTUNTUM: (8) iii/ii BC ib. p. 455
—GNATHIA-EGNATIA: (9) iii-ii BC Santoro, *NSM* I pp. 183-4 no. IM 0.446 (loomweight)
S. ITALY (CALABRIA):
—TARAS-TARENTUM: (10) 156 BC *ID* 1416 B II, 114 (f. *Παρμενίων*)
—UZENTUM: (11) iv/iii BC Unp. (A.W.J.)
S. ITALY (CAMPANIA):
—PITHEKOUSSAI-AENARIA*: (12) vii/vi BC Dubois, *IGDGG* I 10 (vase) (Arena, *Iscr. Sic.* III 10; *LSAG*² p. 453 no. C)

S. ITALY (LUCANIA):
—HERAKLEIA: (13) iv/iii BC *IGSI* I II, 1 (*DGE* 63; Uguzzoni–Ghinatti II); (14) f. iii BC *Festschr. Neutsch* p. 141
——(*Aἱ. πέλτα*): (15) iv/iii BC *IGSI* I I, 5, 9, 97 (*DGE* 62; Uguzzoni–Ghinatti I); *IGSI* I II, 5, 8 (*DGE* 63; Uguzzoni–Ghinatti II) (s. *Πύρρος*)
—METAPONTION*: (16) iv/iii BC *SEG* XLII 912 (tile) (potter)
S. ITALY?: (17) ?c. 175-150 BC Ag. Inv. 146 (amph.)

**Δάζιος**
ILLYRIA:
—EPIDAMNOS-DYRRHACHION: (1) c. 250-50 BC Maier 172 (coin) (Ceka 127) (money.); (2) hell.-imp. *IDyrrh* 163; (3) ~ ib. 164 (s. *Ἀλεξίων*); (4) ~ ib. 165 (s. *Ἀριστέας*); (5) ~ ib. 203 (f. *Εὐκλέα*); (6) imp. ib. 84 (f. *Ἀδίστα*)
S. ITALY (CAMPANIA):
—POMPEII*: (7) i BC-i AD *NScav* 1893, p. 333 ter (Castrèn 303. 3) (Lat. M. Petacius Dasius: freed.)

**Δαξίς**
ILLYRIA: (1) m. iii BC *Thess. Mnem.* 86
—EPIDAMNOS-DYRRHACHION: (2) hell.-imp. *IDyrrh* 162 (-ζείς)

**Δαζίσκος**
S. ITALY (APULIA):
—AZETIUM: (1) 185 BC *ID* 424, [10]; 439 a, 50; 442 B, 53 (f. *Δάζος*)

**Δαζιώ**
ILLYRIA:
—APOLLONIA: (1) ?iii-ii BC *IApoll* 20

**Δαζίωνος?**
ILLYRIA:
—BESSE-SELCE (MOD.): (1) imp. *Stud. Alb.* 1969 (2), p. 170 (Russu s.v. Dazeion) (*Δαζείωνος* (gen.?): s. *Κλεῖτος*)

**Δάζος**
DALMATIA:
—KERKYRA MELAINA?: (1) iv/iii BC Brunšmid p. 7, 2 (s. *Πύλλος*)
ILLYRIA:
—ALINIOI: (2) c. 215-200 BC *SEG* XV 272, 7 (*IOrop* 134); *SEG* XV 273, 7 (*IOrop* 135); *AE* 1967, Chron. p. 9 no. 4 (locn.); cf. *L'Illyrie mérid.* 2 p. 165 (f. *Πύλλος*, *Πλάτυρ*)
—LYCHNIDOS: (3) ?s. ii AD *ZA* 6 (1956) p. 167 no. 3 (f. *Λεόννατος*)
S. ITALY (APULIA):
—ARGYRIPPA-ARPI: (4) m. iii BC *HN*² p. 45 (coin)
—AZETIUM: (5) 185 BC *ID* 424, [10]; 439 a, 50; 442 B, 53 (s. *Δαζίσκος*)
—CANUSIUM: (6) ii/i BC *IG* IV (1)² 225 (I f. *Δάζος* II); (7) ~ ib. (II s. *Δάζος* I)
—RUBI: (8) iii BC *HN*² p. 48 (coin)
—SALAPIA: (9) iii BC ib. p. 49; *BMC Italy* p. 144 no. 5 (coin)
S. ITALY (CALABRIA):
—BRENTESION-BRUNDISIUM: (10) f. ii BC Cabanes, *L'Épire* p. 554 f. no. 33, 6, 10 (*SEG* XXXVII 511) (f. *Γ. Πολφέννιος*)
—HYRIA?: (11) c. 293-168 BC *Polemon* 4 (1949-50) p. 163 no. 300; cf. *SEG* XXXIII 455; cf. *Synedrio Archaia Thessalia* pl. 79 e (s. *Πλαρίας*)
—TARAS-TARENTUM: (12) s. ii BC *EAD* XXX 381 (f. *Δημήτριος*)

S. ITALY (LUCANIA):
—METAPONTION: (13) b. 158 BC *ID* 2136, 1 (f. *Εὔτυχος*)

**Δαήμων**
ARKADIA:
—ORESTHASION: (1) 472 BC *IvOl* 147; 148; cf. Ebert, *Gr. Sieg.* 14 (f. *Τέλλων*)

**Δαϊάλκης**
KORINTHIA:
—SIKYON: (1) ?269 BC *CID* II 120 A, [48]; 122 I, 13 (s. *Πανтакλείδας*) ?= (*Δαάλκης* (1))

**Δαϊαλκος**
S. ITALY (CALABRIA):
—TARAS-TARENTUM?: (1) 373-347 BC *FD* III (1) p. 232, 1; cf. *REG* 25 (1912) p. 16 (locn.)

**Δαίδαλος**
AKARNANIA:
—THYRREION: (1) c. 101-81 BC *IG* IX (1)² (2) 242, 8; *FD* III (3) 338, 1 (s. *Μένανδρος*, f. *Μένανδρος*)
EPIROS:
—BOUTHROTOS (PRASAIBOI): (2) a. 163 BC *IBouthrot* 14, 13 (*SEG* XXXVIII 471) (s. *Ἀριστείδας*)
ILLYRIA:
—BYLLIONES BYLLIS: (3) ?f. ii BC ib. 538
KORINTHIA:
—SIKYON: (4) v/iv BC *RE* (2); Marcadé I 22 ff.; *FD* III (4) 202 (Skalet 86) (s. *Πατροκλῆς*: sculptor)

**Δαίθος**
LAKONIA:
—SPARTA: (1) 421 BC Th. v 19. 2; 24 (Poralla² 202)

**Δαιθράσης**
ARKADIA:
—ORCHOMENOS: (1) f. iii BC *BCH* 38 (1914) p. 459 no. 4, 9 ([*Δ*]*αιθράσης*)

**Δαϊκλῆς**
ARGOLIS:
—ARGOS: (1) c. 458 BC *IG* I³ 1149, 73 (-κλῆς)
MESSENIA:
—MESSENE: (2) 752 BC Moretti, *Olymp.* 7 (*RE* (-))

**Δαϊκράτεια**
ARGOLIS:
—ARGOS?: (1) v BC *IG* IV (1)² 140 (Lazzarini 281)

**Δαϊκράτης**
ARGOLIS:
—ARGOS: (1) i AD *SEG* XXVI 429, 4 (f. *Θρασέας*); (2) ~ ib. l. 9 (s. *Θρασέας*)
——Paionis?: (3) a. 316 BC ib. XXX 357, 3 (Perlman A.9) (*Δαΐ*[κ]*ρ*[άτης]?, *Δαΐ*[φ]*ρ*[ων]?—ed.: name—*LGPN*)
—EPIDAUROS: (4) ?c. 415-400 BC *IG* IV (1)² 145, 3
SICILY:
—AKRAI: (5) ?iii BC *SGDI* 3240, 2 (*Akrai* p. 156 no. 7) (s. *Ἀριστόξενος*)
—KAMARINA: (6) f. v BC Cordano, *Tessere Pubbliche* 17 (Arena, *Iscr. Sic.* II 130 A) (-τῆς: s. *Λυκίσκος*)

**Δαϊκρατίδας**
ARGOLIS:
—EPIDAUROS: (1) iv BC *IG* IV (1)² 175-7

**Δαϊκρέτης**
ARKADIA:
—MANTINEIA-ANTIGONEIA:
——(Posoidaia): (1) c. 425-400 BC *SEG* XXXI 348, 2

**Δαϊλέων**
ARKADIA:
—MANTINEIA-ANTIGONEIA: (1) c. 300-221 BC
IG v (2) 323. 26 (tessera) (s. Λισσίδας)

**Δαΐλοχος**
AITOLIA:
—KALYDON: (1) 129 BC ib. IX (1)² (1) 137, 96
(f. Δαμόκριτος)
ARKADIA: (2) 312 BC ib. v (2) 549, 39 (Δαΐ-
λ[οχ]ος: f. Πισταγόρας)
S. ITALY (CAMPANIA):
—NEAPOLIS: (3) imp. ib. XIV 775 (INap 105);
cf. Leiwo p. 105 no. 63 (Δαϊλο(χ)ος)
SICILY: (4) f. v BC X., Hier. i 31 ff.

**Δαΐμαχος**
AITOLIA: (1) c. 232-228 BC Syll³ 499, 2;
Nachtergael, Les Galates 62, [3]
ARGOLIS:
—ARGOS: (2) 327-324 BC CID II 97, 33; 99 A,
5; 102 II B, 30; 120 A, 5 (s. Ἄρχιππος)
ARKADIA:
—PALLANTION: (3) a. 316 BC SEG XI 1084, 37
(Perlman A.3) (s. Ἀγαθίας)
ARKADIA?: (4) hell. Syringes 649 (?f. Ἀμφίμαχος)
EPIROS:
—AMBRAKIA: (5) a. 167 BC SEG XXXV 665 A,
1, 5; 665 B, 23 (f. Διοφάνης) ?= (6); (6) ~ ib.
665 A, 6 ?= (5)
LAKONIA:
—SPARTA: (7) m. iii BC IG IV (1)² 96, 30 (Perl-
man E.3); Perlman p. 63 f. (date) (Bradford
(-)) (s. Σωκλείδας)
LEUKAS: (8) c. 315-280 BC FD III (1) 183 (f.
Δαμῖνος)
S. ITALY (CALABRIA):
—TARAS-TARENTUM: (9) c. 235-228 BC Vlasto
938-9 (coins) (Evans, Horsemen p. 194 IX
A.1)
SICILY:
—SYRACUSE: (10) c. 415-413 BC Polyaen. i 43. 1
TRIPHYLIA: (11) 399-369 BC SEG XXXV 389, 8

**Δαϊμένης**
AIGINA?: (1) i AD EAD XXX p. 357 no. 22 (f.
Σιβοίτης)
AITOLIA:
—THERMOS*: (2) s. iii BC IG IX (1)² (1) 60 VI,
10; (3) ~ ib. 60 VII, 8
ARGOLIS:
—EPIDAUROS*: (4) c. 340-320 BC Peek, NIEpid
19 A, 20 (Δαϊμένης)
ARKADIA:
—MANTINEIA-ANTIGONEIA: (5) f. iii BC IG v
(2) 278, 9; EILakArk 17 (date)
LEUKAS: (6) c. 330-315 BC SEG XXIII 189 I,
8; Hesp. 57 (1988) p. 148 B, 10 (SEG XXXVI
331); cf. Hesp. 48 (1979) pp. 78 f. with pl. 22
(s. Πειθωνίδας)
SICILY?: (7) 397 BC D.S. xiv 53. 4
TRIPHYLIA:
—MAKISTOS: (8) 399-369 BC SEG XXXV 389, 13

**Δαϊοδάμας**
LAKONIA:
—SPARTA: (1) iii BC IG v (1) 145, 3 (Bradford
(-))

**Δαΐοχος**
LAKONIA:
—SPARTA: (1) c. 450-434 BC IG v (1) 1228, 6;
LSAG² p. 201 no. 53 (date) (Poralla² 303)

**Δάϊππος**
ARGOLIS:
—EPIDAUROS*: (1) c. 370 BC IG IV (1)² 102,
183, 213, 227, 233, 290, 296, 300 + SEG XXV
383, 190; (2) iv/iii BC Peek, NIEpid 21, 14
(SEG XXV 403, 6) (Δάϊππος)

---

EPIROS: (3) s. iii BC IOrop 136, 1, 5 (s. Νικάνωρ)
KORINTHIA:
—SIKYON: (4) iv/iii BC RE (3); SEG XL 387
(Skalet 87) (s. Λύσιππος: sculptor)
S. ITALY (BRUTTIUM):
—KROTON: (5) 672 BC Moretti, Olymp. 38

**Δαΐπυλος**
KORINTHIA:
—KORINTH: (1) c. 570-550 BC Amyx 107. 1 and
3 (vase) (Lorber 147) (her.?)

**Δαΐστρατος**
ARKADIA:
—MANTINEIA-ANTIGONEIA: (1) 369-361 BC IG
v (2) 1, 38; Tod, GHI II 132 (date)

**Δαΐτας**
AITOLIA:
—LYSIMACHEIA?: (1) hell. SBBerlAk 1936, p.
364 ([Δ]αΐτας)
—POTIDANIA: (2) m. ii BC ib. p. 371 a, 14 (SEG
XLI 528 A); SBBerlAk 1936, p. 371 b, 15
(SEG XLI 528 B) (Δαιπα (gen.)—b per err.: f.
Λυσίας, Καλλίστρατος)

**Δαΐτις**
SICILY:
—HIMERA: (1) c. 475-450 BC Himera 2 p. 681
no. 45 (Dubois, IGDS 11; Arena, Iscr. Sic.
III 51)

**Δαιτίφαντος**
PELOPONNESE: (1) c. 192 BC SEG XIII 327, 17
(Δαιτίφαν[τος]: f. Φειδόλαος)

**Δαιτόφρων**
ACHAIA:
—AIGION: (1) c. 400 BC IG II² 7946 (s. Εὐδαι-
τίδας)

**Δαιτώνδας**
KORINTHIA:
—SIKYON: (1) iv/iii BC Marcadé I 25 (Skalet 88)
(sculptor)

**Δαΐφαντος**
ARKADIA:
—KLEITOR: (1) ?262-253 BC Nachtergael, Les
Galates 5, 18?; 10, 32; cf. Stephanis 132 (f.
Ἀλκίας)

**Δαΐφονος**
KORINTHIA:
—KORINTH: (1) c. 570-550 BC Amyx 70. 10
(vase) (Lorber 126) (her.)

**Δαϊφόντης**
ARGOLIS:
—ARGOS: (1) her. RE (-)

**Δαΐφων**
KORINTHIA:
—KORINTH: (1) c. 600-575 BC Amyx 24. 1
(vase) (Lorber 44) (-φōν: her.)

**Δάκιος**
LAKONIA:
—HIPPOLA?: (1) byz. SEG XXVIII 406 (Δακήου
(gen.))

**Δαμάγης**
ILLYRIA:
—APOLLONIA: (1) hell. IApoll 349 (tile); (2) iii
BC ib. 5 (f. Παρμονίσκος); (3) c. 250-50 BC
Maier 117 + Münsterberg p. 35 (coin) (Ceka
46; 48) ([Δαμ]άγεος?—Münsterberg: pryt.)
—EPIDAMNOS-DYRRHACHION: (4) c. 250-50 BC
Ceka, Probleme p. 151 no. 18; cf. IApoll Ref.
Bibl. n. 43 (coin) (pryt.) ?= (5); (5) ~ Maier
161-8; Münsterberg p. 38 (coin) (Ceka 23; 32;
72; 124; 143; 161; 163; 171; 287; 370; 434)
(pryt.) ?= (4)

---

**Δαμάγητος**
ARGOLIS:
—EPIDAUROS: (1) c. 370-335 BC IG IV (1)² 103,
42, 70, 78; Peek, IAEpid 52 B, 7 (Δαμά-
γη[τος]); (2) ii BC IG IV (1)² 250 (s. Δαμοκλῆς)
——(Azantioi): (3) 146 BC ib. 28, 43
([Δ]αμάγητος: s. Νικόστρατος)
ARKADIA:
—KLEITOR: (4) 369-361 BC ib. v (2) 1, 56; Tod,
GHI II 132 (date)
—MEGALOPOLIS: (5) ?145 BC IG v·(2) 439, 63
(I f. Δαμάγητος II); (6) ~ ib. l. 63 (II s. Δαμά-
γητος I)
—TEGEA: (7) f. iii BC ib. 35, 16 (f. Ἀλκαῖος)
EPIROS:
—ARGOS (AMPHILOCH.): (8) c. 315-280 BC FD
III (1) 86, 1 (SEG XVIII 182) (s. Πυθ—)
LAKONIA:
—SPARTA: (9) f. vi BC D.L. i 68 (Poralla² 205)
(f. Χίλων); (10) 421 BC Th. v 19. 2; 24 (Po-
ralla² 207); (11) c. 30-20 BC IG v (1) 211, 35
(Bradford (-)) (s. Τιμοκράτης)
PELOPONNESE?: (12) s. iii BC RE (4); HE 1375
ff. with Comm.

**Δαμαγίδας**
ARKADIA:
—KYNAITHA: (1) c. 230-200 BC BCH 45 (1921)
p. 12 II, 65 (s. Πελοπίδας)

**Δαμαγόρας**
AIGINA: (1) iii BC SEG XXVI 919, 23 (s. Θεόκο-
σμος, f. Θεόκοσμος, Ἀνδρομήδης)
ARGOLIS:
—EPIDAUROS: (2) inc. IG IV (1)² 29 (f. —κλείτα)
ARKADIA:
—MANTINEIA-ANTIGONEIA:
——(Epalea): (3) m. iv BC ib. v (2) 271, 3 (s.
Ἑξάκης)
EPIROS:
—AMBRAKIA: (4) f. ii BC AD 39 (1984) Chron.
p. 190 + pl. 77 γ (Δαμαγ[όρας]: f. —κριτος)

**Δαμαγορίς**
ARGOLIS:
—KALAURIA: (1) imp. IG IV (1) 852

**Δαμάγων**
LAKONIA:
—SPARTA: (1) 426 BC Th. iii 92. 5 (Poralla² 209)
(and Thessaly Herakleia Trachinia: oikist)

**Δαμαιθίδας**
ARKADIA:
—ORESTHASION: (1) m. iv BC SEG XX 716, 23
(Suppl. Cir. 103); BCH 87 (1963) pp. 388-90
(name) (Δαματρίδας—Suppl. Cir.)
ELIS: (2) i BC/i AD IvOl 209 (Moretti, Olymp.
740) (s. Μένιππος)

**Δάμαινα**
AITOLIA: (1) inc. FD III (1) 575 (IG IX (1)² (1)
200) (her.?)

**Δαμαινέτα**
LAKONIA:
—SPARTA: (1) s. iii BC HE 1667 (Poralla² 229)
(Δημαινέτη: fict.?)
LEUKAS: (2) ?ii BC Unp. (Leukas Mus., inscr.)
inv. 26

**Δαμαίνετος**
ACHAIA: (1) 146 BC IG IV (1)² 28, 158 (f. Πυρ-
βαλίων: synoikos)
ARGOLIS:
—ARGOS: (2) ?ii BC SEG XXXVIII 312, 2 (f. Εὔδι-
κος); (3) c. 80-70 BC IG VII 3195, 16; BSA 70
(1975) pp. 121-2 (date) (Stephanis 572) (-μή-:
s. Γλαῦκος)
—EPIDAUROS: (4) c. 290-270 BC IG IV (1)² 109
II, 146
——(Hysminatai): (5) 146 BC ib. 28, 17 (f. Σθε-
νείδας)
—EPIDAUROS*: (6) c. 290-270 BC ib. 109 IV,
121 ([Δαμαίν]ετος)

—PHLEIOUS: (7) iii BC ib. IV (1) 457
ARKADIA:
—PARRHASIOI: (8) i AD Plin., NH viii 82 (Lat. Demaenetus: fict.)
—TEGEA: (9) ?s. iv BC IG v (2) 39, 5 (f. —ίας); (10) ?ii BC ib. 249 (Δαμαίνε[τος])
——(Apolloniatai): (11) f. iii BC ib. 36, 53 (s. Εὐρύτιμος)
——(Krariotai): (12) f. iii BC ib. l. 64 (s. Ἀγαθίας); (13) s. iii BC ib. l. 119 (s. Δει—)
EPIROS:
—AMBRAKIA: (14) hell.? BCH 79 (1955) p. 267 (f. Ἀγάθυμος); (15) a. 167 BC SEG XXXV 665 A, 6 (f. Ἀριστομήδης)
KEPHALLENIA:
—PALE: (16) c. 475-450 BC IG I³ 1358
KERKYRA: (17) iv/iii BC ib. IX (1) 976, 4 (Δα[μ]αίνετος: s. Φιλανδρίδας)
KORINTHIA:
—KORINTH: (18) s. iv BC Corinth VIII (1) 11, 8; cf. SEG XI 60 (s. Δαμωνίδας); (19) iv/iii BC Corinth VIII (3) 28 + 31 (SEG XXV 336) (s. Ἀγησι—, Δαμώ)
—SIKYON: (20) vi/v BC ib. XI 244, 74 (Δαμαίνε(τ)ος)
LAKONIA:
—SPARTA: (21) ?ii AD IG v (1) 248 (Bradford (4)) (f. Ἀνθοῦσα); (22) m. ii AD IG v (2) 544, 10; SEG XLI 317, 5; BSA 80 (1985) pp. 215; 223-4 (ident., locn., date, stemma); cf. 89 (1994) p. 438 (Πομπ. Δ.: f. Πομπ. Ἀριστοκράτης); (23) ~ SEG XI 623, 6 (Bradford (3)) (Γ. Ἰούλ. Δαμαί[νετος]: s. Ξεναρχίδας); (24) s. ii AD IG v (1) 529, 3; 530, 9; 653 a, 5 (Artemis Orthia p. 356 no. 142); IG v (1) 680, 8; BSA 79 (1984) pp. 266-7 (ident., stemma) (Bradford (1); (5)) (s. Ἀριστοκράτης, f. Μ. Αὐρ. Ἀριστοκράτης); (25) c. 160-180 AD IG v (1) 531, 2; 680, 3; BSA 79 (1984) pp. 266-7 (ident., stemma) (Bradford (6)) (f. Λύσιππος, ?f. Ἀριστοκράτης); (26) f. iii AD IG v (1) 324, 2 (Artemis Orthia p. 336 no. 74); SEG XXXIV 308, 14; BSA 80 (1985) pp. 244-6 (ident., stemma) (Bradford (2)) (Σέξ. Πομπ. Δ.: s. Σέξ. Πομπ. Θεόξενος)
MESSENIA:
—MESSENE: (27) iii BC SEG XXIII 209, 7
S. ITALY (BRUTTIUM):
—LOKROI EPIZEPHYRIOI:
——(Κοβ.): (28) iv/iii BC De Franciscis 39, 7 (s. Πρωτογένης)
S. ITALY (CALABRIA):
—TARAS-TARENTUM: (29) iv/iii BC IG XIV 668 II, 11 (Landi, DISMG 194)
SICILY:
—AKRAI: (30) ?iii BC SGDI 3240, 7 (Akrai p. 156 no. 7) (s. Λύκων)
—ECHETLA: (31) s. v BC PdelP 47 (1992) pp. 455-8; cf. SEG XLII 884 (s. Μνασίας)
—SYRACUSE: (32) c. 340-335 BC Plu., Tim. 37 (Δη-)

**Δάμαινος**
ARKADIA:
—MEGALOPOLIS: (1) 182 BC IvOl 46, 8 (IPArk 31 IIB) (f. Καλλίφιλος)

**Δαμάιππος**
ARGOLIS:
—ARGOS: (1) c. 458 BC IG I³ 1149, 55 (Δαμ[ά]hι[ππος])

**Δαμαισίδας**
LAKONIA:
—SPARTA: (1) ii BC ib. v (1) 29, 16 (Syll³ 669; Bradford (-)) (s. Ἀνδρόβολος)

**Δαμαΐστρατος**
ARGOLIS:
—ARGOS: (1) ?iii BC BCH 28 (1904) p. 420 no. 1 (s. Νικόστρατος)

**Δαμαίων**
ELIS: (1) c. 146-32 BC BMC Pelop. p. 6 no. 69 (coin)

**Δαμακίων**
ARKADIA:
—TEGEA: (1) ii AD IG v (2) 55, 55 (f. Νίκιππος); (2) 165 AD ib. 50, 4 (s. Ἄμυκος)
LAKONIA:
—SPARTA: (3) m. ii AD ib. v (1) 108, 4 (Bradford (2)) (s. Θεο—); (4) c. 140-160 AD IG v (1) 65, 11; 115, 3 (Bradford (3)) (I f. Δαμακίων II); (5) ~ IG v (1) 65, 11; 115, 3 (Bradford (1)) (II s. Δαμακίων I); (6) c. 150 AD IG v (1) 71 II, 12 (Bradford (4)) (f. Φίλητος)

**Δαμαλίς**
ILLYRIA:
—APOLLONIA: (1) imp. IApoll 201
LEUKAS: (2) iv/iii BC AD 26 (1971) Chron. p. 353 no. 6
S. ITALY (CAMPANIA):
—POMPEII: (3) i BC-i AD CIL IV 1507, 10 (Lat. Damalis)
S. ITALY (LUCANIA):
—POTENTIA: (4) imp. ib. x 168 (Lat. Damalis)

**Δαμάλκης**
ARKADIA:
—MEGALOPOLIS: (1) ?130 BC IG v (2) 441, 8 (s. Σωσίστρατος)

**Δάμαλκος**
ITHAKE: (1) hell. SEG XVII 253

**Δάμανδρος**
MESSENIA:
—MESSENE: (1) 208 or 207 BC FD III (4) 21, 2; 22, 9 (f. Δαμοκράτης)

**Δαμάρατος**
ARGOLIS:
—HERMIONE: (1) ?f. ii BC SEG XVII 169, 1
ARKADIA:
—HERAIA: (2) 520-516 BC RE (3); Moretti, Olymp. 132; 138; SEG XXXII 217, 10 ([Δ]ημάρα[τ]ος—SEG, Δαμάρετος—Paus.: f. Θεόπομπος)
DALMATIA:
—ISSA: (3) iii BC Brunšmid p. 9 fr. G, 9 + VAMZ 1970, p. 37 frr. G and M (s. Ἡρακλείδας)
KORINTHIA:
—KORINTH: (4) vii BC RE s.v. Tarquinius (1) (stemma) + Supplbd. 1 (3a) (and Etruria Tarquinii: f. Ἄρρων (Tarquinii), Λυκόμων Λεύκιος Ταρκύνιος (Tarquinii): fict.?); (5) c. 400-328 BC ib. s.v. Demaratos (4); Berve 253 (Δημάρατος—Plu. and Arr., Δημάρετος—D. and Plu. Tim.)
—KORINTH?: (6) ?s. iv BC RE s.v. Demaratos (7)
LAKONIA:
—HYPERTELEATON*: (7) ?c. 500-480 BC SEG II 170 (Lazzarini 285); LSAG² p. 201 no. 43 (date) (Δαμάρ[ατος])
—SPARTA: (8) c. 530-460 BC RE (1); Moretti, Olymp. 157 (Poralla² 210) (and Mysia Teuthrania: s. Ἀρίστων: king); (9) iv/iii BC S.E., M. i 258; D.L. v 53 (Poralla² 211) (Δη-: s. Προκλῆς, Πυθιάς (Stageiros)); (10) c. 300-281 BC IG XI (4) 542, 7, 23 (Bradford (-)) (Δη-: s. Γοργίων); (11) c. 200 BC IG XI (4) 716, 3, 9 (Bradford (-)) (f. Νάβις)
SICILY:
—TYNDARIS: (12) hell.-imp. IG XIV 377 (Δαμυατος—apogr., Δαμ(άρ)ατος—IG)

**Δαμαρέτα**
ACHAIA:
—PHARAI: (1) iii-ii BC Achaean Grave Stelai 59 (d. Σάτυρος)

AIGINA: (2) hell.? IG VII 127
ARGOLIS:
—ARGOS: (3) ii/i BC ib. IV (1) 694 (Δαμαρέτ[α]: d. Ξένων, m. Δαμάρετος)
—EPIDAUROS: (4) iii BC ib. IV (1)² 320; (5) ii BC ib. 211 (d. Λυσικλείδας, m. Δαμοφάνης); (6) i BC-i AD ib. 31
—TROIZEN: (7) iii BC SEG XXXVII 310 (d. Σικυώνιος)
ARKADIA:
—TEGEA: (8) ?iv BC IG v (2) 102 (bronze) (Lazzarini 291)
EPIROS:
—BOUTHROTOS (PRASAIBOI): (9) a. 163 BC IBouthrot 25, 15 (SEG XXXVIII 483)
LAKONIA:
—SPARTA: (10) s. vii BC PMGF I 1, 76 (Poralla² 208) (Δαμαρ[έ]τα)
SICILY:
—AKRAGAS: (11) vi/v BC Schol. Pi., O. ii Inscr.; O. ii 29 b and d (d. Θήρων)
—KAMARINA: (12) ?m. v BC Dubois, IGDS 118 (Arena, Iscr. Sic. II 144; SEG XXXVIII 936)
—SYRACUSE: (13) 215 BC RE s.v. Damarete (2) (d. Ἱάρων)

**Δαμάρετος**
ARGOLIS:
—ARGOS: (1) c. 458 BC IG I³ 1149, 94 ([Δαμ]άρετος); (2) ii/i BC ib. IV (1) 694 (Δαμάρε[τος]: s. Μεγακλῆς, Δαμαρέτα)
—EPIDAUROS:
——Selegeis: (3) c. 365-335 BC ib. IV (1)² 103, 128
—HERMIONE: (4) ii-i BC ib. IV (1) 732 II, 13 (f. Ἀπολλώνιος)
ARKADIA:
—PHIGALEIA: (5) ?384 or 368 BC Paus. vi 6. 1; cf. Ebert, Gr. Sieg. 36 (f. Ναρυκίδας); (6) c. 240 BC IG v (2) 419, 9 (IPArk 28) ([Δ]αμάρετος)
—TEGEA: (7) iv/iii BC IG v (2) 32, 7
ELIS: (8) iv/iii BC Paus. v 5. 1 (s. Ἐτύμων, f. Ἀριστότιμος); (9) ?i AD IvOl 413 (f. Ἀλκίας) ?= (10); (10) ~ ib. 414 (s. Ἀλκίας, Δαμώ) ?= (9)
KERKYRA: (11) hell.-imp. AD 45 (1990) Chron. p. 293 (f. Στρατονίκα)
LAKONIA:
—SPARTA?: (12) ?iii BC HE 1907 (f. Ἀγελόχεια)
MESSENIA:
—MESSENE: (13) ?m. iv BC Moretti, Olymp. 448 (RE (-)); (14) f. iii BC PAE 1991, p. 100 no. 8, 8; cf. 1989, p. 96 (Δεμάρετος—ed., Δ(α)μάρετος—LGPN)
PELOPONNESE: (15) s. iii BC SEG XIII 278, 12 (s. Ἀ—ίμαχος)
SICILY:
—AGYRION: (16) i BC Manganaro, PdelP forthcoming no. 5, 6 ([Δ]αμάρε[τ]ος)
—TAUROMENION: (17) c. 202-186 BC IG XIV 421 an. 39; 421 an. 55 (SGDI 5219) (f. Ὀλυμπις); (18) c. 163 BC IG XIV 421 an. 78 (SGDI 5219) (s. Ὀλυμπις)

**Δαμάρης**
ARKADIA:
—MEGALOPOLIS: (1) ii BC IG v (2) 536 (s. Θεάγγελος, Ἀριστώ)
LAKONIA: (2) ii BC ib. v (1) 1110, 12
—HYPERTELEATON*: (3) imp. ib. 1047 (s. Τύχιππος)
—SPARTA: (4) ii BC ib. 811 (Bradford (10)) ([Δ]αμ<δ>άρης); (5) s. i BC IG v (1) 135, 3 (Bradford (6)); (6) 35-31 BC Münzpr. der Laked. p. 154 Group 17 series 12; pp. 159-60 Group 21 series 1-2 (coin monogram); BSA 80 (1985) pp. 215-16 (ident., stemma) (f. Ἀριστοκράτης); (7) c. 25-1 BC IG v (1) 210, 22 (Bradford (2)) (s. Ἄρχων); (8) i BC/i AD IG IV (1)² 670 I, 2; v (1) 478, 5; BSA 80 (1985) pp. 215-16 (ident., stemma) (Bradford (18)) (Δ[αμά]ρης—670, [Δα]μ[ά]ρη[s]—478: ?s.

Ἀριστοκράτης, f. Λ. Οὐολοσσηνὸς Ἀριστοκράτης, Στατιλία Τιμοσθενίς); **(9)** i BC/i AD? *IG* v (1) 186, 2 (Bradford (9)); **(10)** i/ii AD *IG* v (1) 477, 4; 581; *BSA* 80 (1985) pp. 215; 220-1 (ident., stemma) (Bradford (13)) (Λ. Οὐολοσσηνὸς Δ.: Ι ?s. Λ. Οὐολοσσηνὸς Ἀριστοκράτης, f. Λ. Οὐολοσσηνὸς Ἀριστοκράτης, ?f. Λ. Οὐολοσσηνὸς Δαμάρης ΙΙ, Οὐολοσσηνὴ Ὀλυμπίς, Οὐολοσσηνὴ Ὀλυμπίχα); **(11)** c. 100-115 AD *SEG* XI 559, 5; *BSA* 80 (1985) pp. 215; 221 (ident., stemma) (Bradford (8)) (ΙΙ ?s. Λ. Οὐολοσσηνὸς Δαμάρης Ι, Μεμμία Δαμοκρατία); **(12)** c. 100-160 AD *IG* v (1) 38, 2; 63, 20; 68, 16; 311, [4]; 536, 2; 541, 11; 542, 6; 543, 9; 544, 16; 547, 11; 548, 5; 1314, 32; *SEG* XI 497, 4; 585, 14; XLI 317, 3; *BSA* 80 (1985) pp. 194; 208-9 (ident., stemma) (Bradford (5); (15); (16)) (Π. Μέμμιος Δ., (Δα)μάρης—541: s. Π. Μέμμιος Σιδέκτας, Οὐολοσσηνὴ Ὀλυμπίς, f. Π. Μέμμιος Πρατόλαος ὁ καὶ Ἀριστοκλῆς, Π. Μέμμιος Λογγίνος); **(13)** c. 105-140 AD *SEG* XI 524, 10; 569, 16; *BSA* 75 (1980) p. 219 (stemma) (Bradford (1); (14)) (Γ. Ἰούλ. Δ.: s. Γ. Ἰούλ. Ἀγαθοκλῆς, f. Γ. Ἰούλ. Βροῦτος); **(14)** m. ii AD *IG* v (1) 39, 21; 162, [14]; *BSA* 75 (1980) p. 219 (stemma) (Bradford (3)) (s. Γ. Ἰούλ. Βροῦτος); **(15)** c. 140 AD *IG* v (1) 65, 27 (Bradford (11)) (Σέξ. Πομπ. Δ.); **(16)** f. iii AD *IG* v (1) 312, 4 (*Artemis Orthia* p. 333 no. 68); *IG* v (1) 547, 13; *BSA* 80 (1985) pp. 194; 211 (ident., stemma) (Bradford (4); (17)) (Π. Μέμμιος Δ.: s. Π. Μέμμιος Πρατόλαος ὁ καὶ Ἀριστοκλῆς, Κλ. Λογγῖνα, f. Π. Μέμμιος Σπαρτιατικός)

**Δαμαριλίς**
LAKONIA:
—ASOPOS: **(1)** imp. *IG* v (1) 972

**Δαμάριν**
LAKONIA:
—ASOPOS: **(1)** imp. *SEG* XI 903
—OITYLOS: **(2)** imp. *IG* v (1) 1302

**Δαμάριον**
LAKONIA:
—OITYLOS: **(1)** imp. ib. 1304

**Δαμαρίς**
LAKONIA:
—SPARTA: **(1)** iii BC *SEG* XI 669 a-b (vase); *BSA* 30 (1928-30) p. 243 (date) (Bradford (-)) (Δαμα[ρίς])

**Δαμαρίστα**
KORINTHIA:
—KORINTH: **(1)** iv BC Plu., *Tim.* 3 (Δημαρίστη: m. Τιμολέων, Τιμοφάνης)

**Δαμάριστος**
ARKADIA:
—TEGEA: **(1)** f. iii BC *IG* v (2) 35, 11 (f. Δᾶμις)
ELIS: **(2)** ii/i BC *IvOl* 398, 1 (s. Τιμαίνετος); **(3)** 36-24 BC ib. 61, 6; 62, 8 (s. Ἀντίοχος: Δ.); **(4)** ii-iii AD ib. 125, 4 (Δαμά[ριστος]: f. —ος) ?= (5); **(5)** f. ii AD ib. 92, 7 (Τ. Φλ. Δ.) ?= (4)
LAKONIA:
—SPARTA: **(6)** s. i BC *IG* v (1) 96, 2 (Bradford (4)) (Δαμάρισ[τος]); **(7)** c. 105-115 AD *IG* v (1) 42, 18; *SEG* XI 540, 3 (Bradford (5)) (f. Σπαρτιάτης); **(8)** c. 110 AD *SEG* XI 542, 4 (Bradford (2)) (Δαμάρ[ιστο]s: s. Φιλόστρατος); **(9)** 197 or 198 AD *IG* v (1) 448, 11 (Bradford (1)) (s. Ἀνδρίων); **(10)** c. 217-230 AD *SEG* XI 616 a, 6 (Bradford (3)) (Αὐρ. Δαμάριστος: ?s. Ῥοῦφος)

**Δαμαρμενίδας**
LAKONIA: **(1)** f. i AD *IG* v (1) 1243, 6
—PYRRHICHOS: **(2)** i-ii AD ib. 1524, 5, 43 (s. Εὐάμερος)
—SPARTA: **(3)** c. 240-200 BC *SEG* XI 413, 27 + Peek, *IAEpid* 330 (Perlman E.4; Bradford (-)) ([Δα]μαρμενίδας: s. Βρέμων)

—TAINARON-KAINEPOLIS: **(4)** imp.? *IG* v (1) 1236 (s. Ἀριστοτέλης)

**Δαμάρμενος**
AITOLIA:
—THERMOS: **(1)** 163 BC ib. IX (1)² (1) 102, 3
ARGOLIS:
—ARGOS: **(2)** c. 220-200 BC *SEG* XI 414, 2 (Perlman E.5)
—EPIDAUROS: **(3)** c. 290-270 BC *IG* IV (1)² 109 II, 146
——Dorimachis: **(4)** c. 220-200 BC *SEG* XI 414, 26 (Perlman E.5)
ILLYRIA:
—OLYMPE: **(5)** s. iii BC *SEG* XXXV 697 (f. Ξένυλλος)
LAKONIA: **(6)** 75 BC *IG* v (1) 1146, 11
—SPARTA: **(7)** f. vi BC Hdt. v 41. 3; vi 65. 2 (Poralla² 230) (?s. Χίλων, f. Πρινητάδας, Χίλων)
—TAINARON-KAINEPOLIS: **(8)** imp. *IG* v (1) 1244 (f. Λυσικράτης)
S. ITALY (LUCANIA):
—METAPONTION: **(9)** iv BC Iamb., *VP* 267 (*FVS* I p. 446)

**Δαμαρχίας**
LAKONIA:
—SPARTA: **(1)** 127 AD *IG* v (1) 1314, 29 (Bradford (-)) (s. Σεβῆρος)

**Δαμαρχίδας**
ARKADIA:
—MANTINEIA-ANTIGONEIA: **(1)** ?iii BC *IG* v (2) 318, 23
—MEGALOPOLIS: **(2)** ?145 BC ib. 439, 56 (f. Λεοντομένης, Λάζυγος)
LAKONIA:
—SPARTA: **(3)** s. i BC ib. v (1) 900 (tiles) (Bradford (-))
MESSENIA:
—MESSENE: **(4)** ?i BC *PAE* 1969, p. 100 a, 4; **(5)** i AD *SEG* XXIII 220 a, 1 (f. Τιμαρχίς)
—THOURIA: **(6)** f. ii BC ib. XI 972, 25 (s. Κλεώνυμος)

**Δαμαρχίς**
LAKONIA:
—GYTHEION: **(1)** f. i AD *IG* v (1) 1167, 12 (d. Μήνιος)
—HIPPOLA: **(2)** ?iv AD ib. 1276
—TAINARON-KAINEPOLIS: **(3)** imp.? ib. 1257 (d. Ἐτέαρχος, m. Ἐτεαρχίς)

**Δάμαρχος**
ACHAIA: **(1)** s. iii BC *SGDI* 1338, 6, 10; Hammond, *Epirus* p. 649 (date) (s. Δαμέας)
AITOLIA:
—AGRINION: **(2)** 161 BC *IG* IX (1)² (1) 100, 3
—BOUKATION: **(3)** 190 BC ib. 97, 13
—KALYDON: **(4)** ii-i BC ib. 140 (s. —ων)
—POTIDANIA: **(5)** m. ii BC *SBBerlAk* 1936, p. 371 a, 13 (*SEG* XLI 528 A); *SBBerlAk* 1936, p. 371 b, 3, 11 (*SEG* XLI 528 B) (s. Μίκος)
AKARNANIA: **(6)** iv/iii BC *HG* p. 42 (f. Διοκλῆς)
—THYRREION: **(7)** ii BC *IG* IX (1)² (2) 249, 3 (s. Σωτ—)
ARGOLIS:
—ARGOS: **(8)** f. i BC Unp. (Ch. Kritzas) (s. Ἐπικράτης)
ARKADIA:
—MANTINEIA-ANTIGONEIA: **(9)** c. 300-221 BC *IG* v (2) 323. 31 (tessera) (f. Κλεόνικος)
——(Posoidaia): **(10)** c. 425-400 BC *SEG* XXXI 348, 24; Dubois, *RDA* 2 p. 126 (name) (Δάμαρχος, Δαμάρ[υ]ος—*SEG*)
—PARRHASIOI: **(11)** v/iv BC *RE* (3); Moretti, *Olymp.* 359 (date) (s. Διννύτας)
—TEGEA: **(12)** m. iii BC *IG* v (2) 368, 73 (s. Ἀλέως)

DALMATIA:
—ISSA: **(13)** iv/iii BC *VAHD* NS 8 (1905) p. 97 no. 177 (*VAMZ* 1970, p. 33 f. frr. I-J); **(14)** f. ii BC Brunšmid p. 23 no. 10, 6 (f. Σαβάθυρος)
ILLYRIA:
—APOLLONIA: **(15)** c. 250-50 BC Maier 53; 14; 21; 41 (Ceka 35-39); Maier 80 (Münsterberg p. 37 (coin); Ceka 40) (money.)
—EPIDAMNOS-DYRRHACHION: **(16)** a. 179 BC *Syll*³ 638, 14 (*IDyrrh* 520); Kramolisch p. 54 A, 18 (date) (f. Κλεόστρατος)
KORINTHIA:
—SIKYON?: **(17)** iii-ii BC *IG* IV (1) 429, 8; cf. Stephanis 222 (f. Ἀντιφάνης)
LAKONIA:
—KARDAMYLE: **(18)** imp.? *SEG* XXV 429
—MESSA?: **(19)** imp. *IG* v (1) 1280, 11 (f. Ἐπικράτις)
—SPARTA: **(20)** i BC ib. 125, 2 (Bradford (4)); **(21)** s. i BC *IG* v (1) 93, 14 (Bradford (1)) (s. Ἀλεξίμαχος); **(22)** c. 105-110 AD *SEG* XI 569, 14 (Bradford (5)) (I f. Δάμαρχος II); **(23)** ~ *SEG* XI 569, 14 (Bradford (2)) (II s. Δάμαρχος I); **(24)** c. 175-200 AD *IG* v (1) 150, 4 (Δάμαρχ[ος]?)
——Limnai: **(25)** a. 212 AD ib. 564, 2 (Bradford (3)) (Μ. Αὐρ. Δ.: s. Παρδαλᾶς)
—TEUTHRONE: **(26)** imp. *IG* v (1) 1220 a (f. Κλέων, Ἐπικράτις); **(27)** ii AD *SEG* XXII 308 (s. Φίλιππος)
MESSENIA:
—KORONE: **(28)** ii BC *IG* v (1) 1397, 2
—MESSENE: **(29)** imp. *PAE* 1970, p. 139
PELOPONNESE: **(30)** s. iii BC *SEG* XIII 278, 14 (f. Ἀρίστων)
S. ITALY (LUCANIA):
—HERAKLEIA:
——(ha. ἔμβολος): **(31)** iv/iii BC *IGSI* I I, 182 (*DGE* 62; Uguzzoni–Ghinatti I) (s. Φιλώνυμος)
SICILY: **(32)** iv/iii BC *SEG* XXXIX 1034 (n. pr.?: ?s. Ἄχυρις)
—KAMARINA: **(33)** ?iv/iii BC ib. 1001, 10 (Δάμαρχ[ος]: f. Ἀγήσανδρος); **(34)** iii BC Manganaro, *PdelP* forthcoming no. 1, 4 ([Δ]άμαρχος: f. Ἱέρων)
—MORGANTINA: **(35)** ?iv/iii BC *SEG* XXXIX 1008, 6 (f. Θέστων)
—MT. ERYX*: **(36)** hell.? *IG* XIV 2398. 3 (tile)
—SELINOUS: **(37)** f. v BC Arena, *Iscr. Sic.* I 65; cf. Dubois, *IGDS* p. 39 n. 61
—SYRACUSE: **(38)** 411-406 BC *RE* s.v. Demarchos (4) (Δή-: s. Ἐπικύδης)

**Δαμαρώ**
ARGOLIS:
—EPIDAUROS: **(1)** c. 150-175 AD *IG* IV (1)² 686, 3 (Κλ. Δ.: d. Τιβ. Κλ. Πολυκράτης, m. Τιβ. Κλ. Φαιδρίας, Τιβ. Κλ. Παῦλος)

**Δάμας**
ARGOLIS:
—HERMIONE: **(1)** ii-i BC ib. IV (1) 732 V, 1 (Δαμᾶς—*IG*: s. Ἀμφικλῆς)
EPIROS:
—BOUTHROTOS: **(2)** iii-ii BC *IBouthrot* 172 (Ugolini, *Alb. Ant.* 3 p. 118)
ILLYRIA:
—SKODRAI: **(3)** a. 168 BC *Iliria* 1972, p. 404 (coin)
KORINTHIA:
—KORINTH: **(4)** c. 570-550 BC Amyx 85. 5 (vase) (Lorber 145) (her.?)
LAKONIA:
—SPARTA:
——Mesoa: **(5)** s. vii BC *Suda* A 1289 (Poralla² 212) (?f. Ἀλκμάν: dub.)
MESSENIA:
—MESSENE: **(6)** ii-i BC *SEG* XXXIX 385 + XLI 364
SICILY:
—SYRACUSE: **(7)** iv BC *RE* (3)

## Δαμᾶς
S. Italy (Calabria):
—brentesion-brundisium*: (1) ii ad *Epigraphica* 27 (1965) p. 164 (Lat. Dama: s. Ἀγάθη: imp. freed.?)
—taras-tarentum: (2) imp. *Misc. Gr. Rom.* 3 p. 194 no. T1 (Lat. Dama)
S. Italy (Campania): (3) imp. *IG* xiv 2414. 16 (tessera)
—dikaiarchia-puteoli: (4) ?i-ii ad *CIL* x 2263 (Lat. Ti. Claudius Damas); (5) 38 ad Camodeca, *L'Archivio Puteolano* i pp. 143-4 no. 1 (Lat. C. Suettius Dama)
—herculaneum*: (6) i bc-i ad *REA* 44 (1942) pp. 135-9 (*RAAN* 33 (1958) p. 254 nos. 112-13); cf. *Cron. Erc.* 8 (1978) p. 151 no. 49 (Lat. M. Nonius Dama: freed.); (7) ~ *CIL* x 1403 g II, 24 (Lat. M. Papirius Dama: freed.)
—pompeii: (8) i bc-i ad ib. iv 1866 (Lat. Dama)
—pompeii*: (9) 7 bc ib. x 924, 1 (Lat. Dama: freed.?)
S. Italy (Campania)*: (10) i bc/i ad ib. 8042. 41 (Lat. Dama: imp. freed.)
Sicily:
—halaisa: (11) hell.? *NScav* 1961, p. 303 no. 8 with fig. 30 d (brick)

## Δαμασία
Achaia:
—dyme: (1) iii bc *AJPh* 31 (1910) p. 399 no. 74 c, 14 (-σσ-: m. Διόκλεια)

## Δαμασιάδας
Epiros:
—dodona: (1) ?iv-iii bc *SEG* xix 434 (f. Ἀρχέγονος: date—A.W.J.)

## Δαμασίας
Achaia:
—patrai: (1) ii-i bc *BMC Pelop.* p. 22 no. 4 (coin) ?= (3) (2); (2) ~ ib. p. 22 nos. 2-3 (coin) ?= (1); (3) c. 146-32 bc *SNG Cop. Phliasia-Laconia* 156 (coin) (s. Ἀγησίλαος) ?= (1)
Aitolia: (4) f. iii bc *SEG* xvi 373, 1-2 (s. Πρόξενος)
Argolis:
—hermione: (5) iii bc *IG* iv (1) 728, 13 (s. Δάμων)

## Δαμασικράτης
Lakonia:
—sparta: (1) ?i bc *SEG* 11 60, 2 (Δαμα[σι]κράτης)

## Δαμασίλας
Arkadia:
—mantineia-antigoneia: (1) 46 or 44 bc *IG* v (2) 266, 21 (f. Φαηνά)
Messenia:
—asine: (2) hell.-imp. ib. v (1) 1407 (s. Καλλίστων)

## Δαμάσιππος
Lakonia:
—sparta: (1) c. 145-150 ad ib. 55, 7 (Bradford (-)) (*M. Οὔλπ. Δ.*)
S. Italy (Bruttium):
—lokroi epizephyrioi:
——(Προ.): (2) 279 bc De Franciscis 13, 5; 33, [4] (s. Τίμαιος)

## Δαμασίς
Ithake: (1) iv bc *AM* 27 (1902) p. 377 no. 60 (*REG* 15 (1902) p. 132 no. 2)

## Δαμασίστρατος
Akarnania:
—thyrreion: (1) ii bc *IG* ix (1)² (2) 248, 2 (Δαμασίσ[τρατος])

## Δαμασκηνός
S. Italy (Campania):
—dikaiarchia-puteoli: (1) 61 ad *Puteoli* 9-10 (1985-6) p. 31 no. 5 (Lat. C. Suettius Damascenus)

## Δάμασος
S. Italy (Lucania):
—siris: (1) c. 575 bc Hdt. vi 127. 1 (s. Ἄμυρις)

## Δαμάστας
Argolis:
—epidauros:
——Melkidon: (1) c. 365-335 bc *IG* iv (1)² 103, 153
Lakonia:
—sparta: (2) iii bc *SEG* xl 348 B, 9

## Δαμάστιχος
Argolis:
—epidauros: (1) c. 290-270 bc *BSA* 61 (1966) p. 307 no. 20, 127
—epidauros*: (2) c. 370-365 bc Peek, *IAEpid* 52 A, 38 (Δαμάσ[τιχος]?—Peek)

## Δάμαστος
S. Italy?: (1) ii-i bc *Summa Gall. Auction I* 46 (f. Σῖμος)

## Δαματρία
Argolis:
—hermione: (1) ii-i bc *IG* iv (1) 732 I, 14; (2) ~ ib. 732 III, 28 (d. Θεογένης)
Dalmatia:
—issa?: (3) iii-ii bc Brunšmid p. 34 no. 32
Lakonia:
—sparta: (4) ?iv-iii bc Plu., *Mor.* 240 F (Poralla² 213) (m. Δαμάτριος: fict.?)
Messenia:
—messene: (5) i bc-i ad *SEG* xxiii 218 (d. Ζώπυρος, m. Ἀμμώνιος)
Sicily:
—thermai himeraiai: (6) imp. *CIL* x 7445 (*ILat. Term. Imer.* 157) (Lat. Damatria: m. Βερενίκη)

## Δαμάτριος
Achaia: (1) hell. *IEph* 2287 A, 2 (Δημή-: s. Σύμμαχος); (2) 146 bc *IG* iv (1)² 28, 76 (f. Εὐάμερος: synoikos); (3) ~ ib. l. 145 (s. Ἀνδρόνικος: synoikos); (4) ~ ib. l. 159 (s. Ὀνάσιμος: synoikos)
—dyme*: (5) c. 219 bc *SGDI* 1612, 75 (*Tyche* 5 (1990) p. 124) (s. Ἀπολλοφάνης)
Aigina: (6) m. iv bc *IG* ii² 7953 (Δημή-: s. Δεξίθεος); (7) s. iv bc ib. 7959 (Δημή-: f. Μυρτώ); (8) imp. ib. iv (1) 95 (I f. Δαμάτριος II); (9) ~ ib. (II s. Δαμάτριος I); (10) i-ii ad *Alt-Ägina* 1 (2) p. 47 no. 27, 3 (Δαμάτ[ριος]: f. Εὔνους)
Aitolia: (11) iii bc *IG* v (2) 10, 3 (I f. Δαμάτριος II); (12) ~ ib. l. 3 (II s. Δαμάτριος I)
Argolis:
—argos: (13) m. iii bc ib. iv (1)² 96, 14 (Perlman E.3); Perlman p. 63 f. (date) (s. Μεγακλείδας)
—epidauros: (14) c. 335-325 bc *IG* iv (1)² 108, 108, 117
——(Azantioi): (15) 146 bc ib. 28, 40 ([Δα]μάτριος: s. Δαμόλας)
—hermione: (16) ii-i bc ib. iv (1) 732 IV, 3 (s. Μουσίς); (17) ~ ib. 732 V, 4 (Δα[μ]άτρι[ος]: s. Σωτήρ)
—methana-arsinoe: (18) i bc ib. 853, 6 ([Δ]αμάτρ[ι]ος)
Arkadia:
—kleitor: (19) iii bc *Achaean Grave Stelai* 4
—mantineia-antigoneia: (20) c. 300-221 bc *IG* v (2) 323. 77 (tessera) (Φασοκρέτης); (21) ii bc ib. 297; (22) ~ ib. 328 (f. Ἱεροτίμα); (23) 46 or 44 bc ib. 266, [1], 32, 38 (f. Φαηνά)
—tegea: (24) iv bc ib. 31, 8 (f. Δαμόκριτος); (25) iv/iii bc ib. 192 ([Δα]μάτριος?); (26) hell.

ib. 170. 9 (tile) ([Δ]αμάτριος); (27) f. iii bc ib. 35, 6 ([Δαμάτ]ριος?); (28) iii/ii bc Moretti, *Olymp.* 593; 600; Moretti, *IAG* 44 (s. Ἀρίστιππος); (29) ?i ad *IG* v (2) 209; (30) ii ad ib. 55, 38 (f. Ἀφροδίσιος); (31) ~ ib. l. 72 (s. Ὀρβανός); (32) ~ ib. l. 88 (f. Διονύσιος)
——(Krariotai): (33) f. iii bc ib. 36, 43 (s. Ἀπολλωνίδας: metic)
Dalmatia:
—issa:
——(Dymanes): (34) iv/iii bc Brunšmid p. 7, 20 ([Δα]μάτριος: s. Ἀρίσταρχος); (35) ~ ib. p. 9, 50 (f. —ρ)
——(Pamphyloi): (36) iv/iii bc ib. p. 8, 36 (f. Ζέφυρος)
—issa?: (37) iii-ii bc ib. p. 32 no. 30, 1 (Δαμά[τριος]: f. Τρίτος); (38) ~ ib. l. 2 (s. Τρίτος) ?= (39); (39) ~ ib. l. 4 (f. Δάμων) ?= (38)
Elis: (40) s. iii bc *IvOl* 179; Paus. vi 16. 9 (f. Παιάνιος)
Epiros:
—dodona*: (41) ?iii bc *SEG* xix 432 a
Illyria:
—epidamnos-dyrrhachion: (42) c. 250-50 bc Maier 381 (coin) (Ceka 128) (money.)
Kerkyra: (43) f. iii bc *IG* ix (1) 691, 2 (*Iscr. Gr. Verona* p. 22 A) ([Δαμ]άτριος)
Korinthia:
—korinth: (44) s. iii bc *IG* vii 513, 3, 4; *Horos* 2 (1984) p. 119 f. (date) (s. Φείδιμος, f. Πιστόλαος); (45) ii-i bc *IG* ii² 9067 (Δημή-: f. Ἐπίκτησις)
—sikyon: (46) iv bc ib. 10296 (Δημή-: f. Γλαυκίας); (47) f. iv bc ib. 10297 (Δημή-: f. Διονύσιος)
Lakonia: (48) ii/i bc *RE* (89); De Falco, *L'Epicureo Demetrio Lacone*; Cartledge-Spawforth p. 177 (date) (Bradford (2))
—sparta: (49) ?iv-iii bc *GP* 203; 2270; *HE* 3620; Plu., *Mor.* 240 F (Poralla² 214) (s. Δαματρία); (50) i ad *SEG* xi 729, 1 (Bradford (2)); (51) s. i ad *IG* v (1) 334; *Artemis Orthia* p. 339 no. 84 (date) (Bradford (2)); (52) ii-iii ad *Laconia Survey* 2 p. 219 no. 13
Messenia: (53) ?i bc *IG* v (1) 1502
—asine: (54) hell.-imp. ib. 1407 (s. Ὀνάτιχος)
—messene: (55) ii/i bc *SEG* xxiii 224; *PAE* 1988, p. 59 (date) (f. Ἀρχυλίς)
—thouria: (56) ii-i bc *IG* v (1) 1385, 37; (57) f. ii bc *SEG* xi 972, 119 (s. Τιμοκράτης); (58) ~ ib. l. 123 (I f. Δαμάτριος II); (59) ~ ib. l. 123 (II s. Δαμάτριος I)
Peloponnese: (60) m. iv bc ib. xx 716, 29
Peloponnese?: (61) s. iii bc ib. xxv 449, 50 (*IPArk* 26) (Δαμάτρι[ος])
S. Italy (Bruttium):
—rhegion:
——(Χιω.): (62) s. ii bc *IG* xiv 612, 1 (*Syll*³ 715; Dubois, *IGDGG* i 40) (f. Σωσίπολις)
S. Italy (Lucania):
—metapontion: (63) iii/ii bc *IG* xiv 2404. 4; *SEG* xxx 1176 C. 1-2 (Landi, *DISMG* 257 (tile))
Sicily:
—akrai: (64) ?iii bc *SGDI* 3243, 10 (*Akrai* p. 155 no. 5) (f. Δαμοκλῆς); (65) ii bc ib. p. 156 no. 6, 11 (f. Ἡρακλείδας)
—henna: (66) ?iii bc *Arch. Class.* 17 (1965) p. 188 (Δαμά[τρι]—ed.: ?f. Ἄρχος)
—iaiton*: (67) ?iv/iii bc *AA* 1994, p. 241 no. 10 a (s.p.) ?= (68); (68) ~ *Kokalos* 17 (1971) p. 174 (*AA* 1994, pp. 245 no. PB 1 (bullet)) (?s. Ἄττος) ?= (67)
—kamarina: (69) iv/iii bc Manganaro, *PdelP* forthcoming no. 2, 2 ([Δ]αμάτρ[ιος]); (70) ?ii bc *SEG* xxxix 996, 7 (Dubois, *IGDS* 126; Cordano, 'Camarina VII' 92) (f. Ἀμείνων)
—kentoripa?: (71) hell. *Cron. Arch.* 16 (1977) p. 151 n. 18 (bullet) (?s. Μάμαρκος)
—lilybaion: (72) f. ii bc *SEG* xxxiv 951 (f. Διόγνητος Μήγας)

—MORGANTINA: (73) ?iv/iii BC ib. XXXIX 1010, 7 ([Δα]μάτριος: s. Κρίθων)
—SYRACUSE: (74) ?334 BC Plu., *Tim.* 39 (Δημή-); (75) ?iii BC *Arch. Class.* 17 (1965) p. 192; (76) ~ *IG* II² 10397 (Δημήτριος: f. Φαλέας); (77) c. 247-199 BC *SGDI* 2609, 2 (Δημή-: s. Ἡρακλείδας); (78) 243 BC *PP* 2543 (Δημή-); (79) f. ii BC *IG* IX (2) 526, 7 (Δημή-: I f. Δαμάτριος II); (80) ~ ib. l. 7 (Δημή-: II s. Δαμάτριος I)
—TAUROMENION: (81) c. 239 BC ib. XIV 421 an. 2 (*SGDI* 5219); (82) c. 237 BC *IG* XIV 421 an. 4 (*SGDI* 5219) (s. Νυμφόδωρος); (83) c. 220 BC *IG* XIV 421 an. 21 (*SGDI* 5219); (84) c. 174 BC *IG* XIV 421 an. 67 (*SGDI* 5219); (85) c. 172 BC *IGSI* 4 II (III), 2 an. 69 (s. Νυμφόδωρος); (86) c. 152 BC ib. 4 III (IV), 28 an. 89 (f. Φίλων); (87) c. 151 BC *IG* XIV 421 an. 90 (*SGDI* 5219) (f. Ἀριστόπολις); (88) c. 147 BC *IG* XIV 421 an. 94 (*SGDI* 5219); *IGSI* 4 III (IV), 63 an. 94 (s. Ἀριστόβουλος); (89) ?ii/i BC *IG* XIV 421 D an. 4 (*SGDI* 5219) (s. Φίλων) ?= (90)
——(Πεα.): (90) ?ii/i BC *IG* XIV 421 D an. 7; 421 D an. 13 (*SGDI* 5219); *IGSI* 4 III (IV), 118 D an. 7 (s. Φίλων) ?= (89)

## Δαμάτρις
ARKADIA:
—TEGEA: (1) ii-iii AD *SEG* XXXVI 384 (date—LGPN)
SICILY:
—LILYBAION: (2) s. iii BC ib. XXVI 1075; *Lilibeo* p. 178 no. 193 (Δάματρι (voc.): ?s. Πόπλιος)

## Δαμέας
ACHAIA: (1) s. iii BC *SGDI* 1338, 6, 10; Hammond, *Epirus* p. 649 (date) (f. Δάμαρχος)
—BOURA: (2) 177 BC *Syll*³ 585, 259 (s. Θέαντος)
—PELLENE: (3) 336-334 BC *IG* VII 3055, 10; *JHS* 91 (1971) pp. 15 ff. (date) (f. Ἀρχεμαχίδας)
ACHAIA?: (4) 193 BC *IG* V (2) 293, 2, 4 (s. Δεξικλῆς)
AITOLIA:
—KALYDON: (5) s. ii BC *SEG* XXV 621, 4 (Δαμέ[ας]: I f. Δαμέας II); (6) ~ ib. l. 4 (II s. Δαμέας I); (7) c. 142 BC *IG* IX (1)² (1) 137, 45 (f. Ξένιππος) ?= (8)
—KALYDON?: (8) m. ii BC ib. l. 22 (s.p.) ?= (7)
ARGOLIS:
—ARGOS: (9) iv-iii BC Unp. (Ch. Kritzas); (10) iii BC *IG* IV (1) 527, 4; cf. *BCH* 37 (1913) p. 308 (Δαμέας—apogr.); (11) f. iii BC Moretti, *ISE* 41, 2, 10 (Perlman A.24)
—EPIDAUROS: (12) c. 370 BC *IG* IV (1)² 102, 10 (Δαμ[έας]: f. Νικασίλας); (13) hell.? *PAE* 1992, p. 52 (Δαμ[έ]ω (gen.): ?f. Καλλίστρατος); (14) i AD *IG* IV (1)² 659 (?s. Λαφάντα, f. Κλ. Λαφάντα)
——(Hysminatai): (15) 146 BC ib. 28, 15 (f. Τιμοκλείδας)
—MYKENAI: (16) iii BC ib. IV (1) 499
ARKADIA:
—KLEITOR: (17) c. 400 BC *RE* (5) (sculptor); (18) 168-146 BC *IG* V (2) 367, 13, 34 (*IPArk* 19) (Δαμ[έας]: f. Δωρόθεος)
—MANTINEIA-ANTIGONEIA: (19) c. 300-221 BC *IG* V (2) 323. 71 (tessera) ([Δα]μέας: s. Σωτίας); (20) f. iii BC ib. 278, 10; *EILakArk* 17 (date)
—MEGALOPOLIS: (21) iii BC *IvOl* 299, 2; (22) 182 BC ib. 46, 5 (*IPArk* 31 IIB) (s. Θε—); (23) ?145 BC *IG* V (2) 439, 42 (f. Ἐπαίνετος)
—PHIGALEIA: (24) ii/i BC ib. 426
—TEGEA: (25) s. iii BC ib. 116, 2 (s. Φίντων); (26) ii BC ib. 43, 5 (Δαμέ[ας]: f. Καλλίμαχος)
——(Athaneatai): (27) iv BC ib. 38, 55 (s. Ἀριστόδαμος); (28) s. iv BC ib. 41, 37 (s. Τεῖσις); (29) s. iii BC ib. 36, 108 (s. Φύτιος)
——(Hippothoitai): (30) iv/iii BC ib. 38, 42 (s. Μενεκλῆς)

ELIS: (31) ?320 BC ib. 549, 3 (s. Τίμων); (32) iii BC *IvOl* 299, 2 (f. (ad.) Εὐανορίδαρ); (33) 28-24 BC ib. 64, 16; 65, [21] (f. Μοσχίων: Δ.)
LAKONIA:
—OITYLOS: (34) iii/ii BC *IG* V (1) 1295, 4 (Bradford (3))
—SPARTA: (35) c. 146-32 BC *Münzpr. der Laked.* p. 25 fig. 3 no. 14; pp. 121-2 Group 8 series 14 (coin monogram) (Δαμέ(ας)); (36) c. 30-20 BC *IG* V (1) 211, 32 (Bradford (2)) (s. Νικίας); (37) c. 90-100 AD *IG* V (1) 80, 4; *SEG* XI 558, 1; 559, 7 (Bradford (1)) (s. Ἀρχιάδας)
—TAINARON-KAINEPOLIS: (38) imp.? *IG* V (1) 1257 (f. Ἐτεαρχίς)
MESSENIA:
—MESSENE: (39) i BC ib. II² 9341 (Δη-: s. Θεόδοτος)
—THOURIA: (40) f. ii BC *SEG* XI 972, 26 (f. Νικοτέλης)
S. ITALY (APULIA): (41) c. 425-400 BC *Second Suppl. RVAp* I p. 6 no. 46 a (vase) (f. Κληνίας)
S. ITALY (BRUTTIUM):
—KROTON: (42) m. vi BC *RE* (4) (sculptor)
S. ITALY (CALABRIA):
—TARAS-TARENTUM: (43) 267 BC *SEG* XXVII 1114 A, 8; cf. Stephanis 1124 (Δη-: f. Ἀφαιστίων)
SICILY:
—KAMARINA: (44) f. v BC Cordano, *Tessere Pubbliche* 142 (Δαμέ[ας]: s. Ἐπίστασις); (45) m. v BC Dubois, *IGDS* 120, 1 (Arena, *Iscr. Sic.* II 142 A-B; *SEG* XXXVIII 939; Cordano, 'Camarina VII' 22) (f. Μένων); (46) iii BC Manganaro, *PdelP* forthcoming no. 1, 1 ([Δα]μέας?)

## Δάμεον
ARGOLIS:
—ARGOS: (1) a. 303 BC *CEG* II 816, 13; (2) ii BC *SEG* XLII 279, 6 (d. Λυκόφρων)

## Δαμεύχης
SICILY:
—KAMARINA: (1) f. v BC Cordano, *Tessere Pubbliche* 96 (-χἔς: s. N-β—)

## Δαμήν
ARGOLIS:
—ARGOS?: (1) iv BC *FGrH* 304; *RE* s.v. Demetrios (82)
ILLYRIA:
—APOLLONIA: (2) iii/ii BC *IApoll* 22 bis; cf. *Le Arti* 5 (1943) p. 116 no. 1; Fraser–Rönne, *BWGT* p. 161; p. 174 n. 5 (date) (f. Παρμενίσκος)
—DIMALE: (3) iii/ii BC *Iliria* 1986 (1), p. 102 no. 2
—EPIDAMNOS-DYRRHACHION: (4) c. 250-50 BC Ceka, *Probleme* p. 151 no. 19 (coin) (pryt.) ?= (5); (5) ~ Maier 169-77; 179; 181-3; 185-7; 189 (Ceka 33; 73; 94; 127; 164; 172; 201; 276; 342; 357; 372; 389; 412; 422; 430; 435; 449); Maier 178; 180; 188 (coin) (pryt.) ?= (4); (6) ii-i BC *IDyrrh* 535 (tile)

## Δαμιάδας
LAKONIA:
—SPARTA: (1) 338 BC Plu., *Mor.* 219 F; *REG* 99 (1986) p. 136 (name) (Poralla² s.v. Δαμίνδας 215) (Δαμίνδας—Plu.); (2) c. 70 BC *IG* V (1) 1145, 7, [9], 36, 48, [51] (Bradford (2)) (s. -κλῆς: doctor); (3) c. 100-125 AD *IG* V (1) 137, 4 (Bradford (3))
——Amyklai: (4) ii/i BC *IG* V (1) 26, 5 (Bradford (4)) (I f. Δαμιάδας II); (5) ~ *IG* V (1) 26, 5 (Bradford (1)) (II s. Δαμιάδας I)

## Δαμιάνη
S. ITALY (LUCANIA):
—BLANDA IULIA: (1) imp. *CIL* X 456 (*NScav* 1921, p. 468) (Lat. Cominia Damiane)

SICILY: (2) imp. *CIL* X 8059. 139 (seal) (Lat. Damiane)

## Δαμίας
AKARNANIA:
—PALAIROS: (1) iii BC *IG* IX (1)² (2) 479; Fraser–Rönne, *BWGT* pl. 24

## Δαμίερος
ARKADIA: (1) f. iii BC *SEG* XXXII 246, 5 (Stephanis 573)

## Δαμίνας
ARKADIA:
—TEGEA: (1) m. iv BC *IG* V (2) 6, 112 (f. Λίσων)

## Δαμῖνος
ARGOLIS:
—EPIDAUROS: (1) 191-146 BC *SNG Cop. Phliasia–Laconia* 338; Unp. (Athens, NM) (coin)
——Alamais: (2) c. 365-335 BC *IG* IV (1)² 103, 121
—EPIDAUROS*: (3) c. 370-360 BC *BSA* 61 (1966) p. 272 no. 4 B II, 1, 8; (4) c. 365-335 BC *IG* IV (1)² 103, 65, 80, 83, 92, 97; (5) c. 330-310 BC *SEG* XXV 395, 17 ([Δαμῖ]νος)
LEUKAS: (6) c. 315-280 BC *FD* III (1) 183 (s. Δαΐμαχος)
MESSENIA:
—MESSENE: (7) i BC/i AD *IG* V (1) 1438 a, 10

## Δαμιόι
EPIROS:
—AMBRAKIA: (1) s. iv BC *SEG* XVII 304 (d. Δάμις)

## Δάμιον
ARGOLIS:
—ARGOS: (1) i BC-i AD Unp. (Argos, Kavvadias) (-μη-)

## Δάμιος
EPIROS:
—AMBRAKIA: (1) ?f. iii BC *SEG* XXXIX 522 (Δαμίου (gen.): f. Γοργίας)

## Δαμίππα
AITOLIA:
—KONOPE-ARSINOE: (1) ii-i BC *IG* IX (1)² (1) 132

## Δαμιππίδας
LAKONIA:
—SPARTA: (1) ii AD ib. V (1) 1523, 1, 5 (Bradford (-)) (f. Λαΐδας)
MESSENIA:
—MESSENE: (2) iii BC *SEG* XXIII 209, 15; (3) s. ii BC ib. XLI 341, 4 (f. Χαρμωνίδας)

## Δάμιππος
AKARNANIA:
—PHOITIAI: (1) iv BC *IG* IX (1)² (2) 602, 4 (s. Στ—)
ARGOLIS:
—EPIDAUROS: (2) i-ii AD ib. IV (1)² 545 (f. Τιμοκράτης)
KORINTHIA:
—KORINTH: (3) s. i AD *SEG* XXVII 36. 1 (lamp) (Δά[μ]ιπ[π]ος)
LAKONIA:
—GYTHEION: (4) f. ii AD *IG* V (1) 1170, 7; 1171, 8 (II² 3596) (f. Σωκρατίδας); (5) 211 AD ib. V (1) 1163, 9 (f. Σωκρατίδας)
—HIPPOLA: (6) ?ii-i BC ib. 1277 k ([Δ]άμιππ[ος])
—HYPERTELEATON*: (7) imp. ib. 1084 ([Δ]άμιππ[ος])
—SPARTA: (8) s. iii BC *RE* (1) (Bradford (7)); (9) s. i BC *IG* V (1) 95, 16 (Bradford (10)) (f. Εὐρυβιάδας); (10) ~ *IG* V (1) 135, 7; 260, 1 (*Artemis Orthia* pp. 302-3 no. 11); *IG* V (1) 261, 3 (*Artemis Orthia* p. 303 no. 12); *IG* V (1) 465, 3; 578, 9 (Bradford (1)) (s. Ἀβόλητος, f. Τεισαμενός); (11) ?s. i BC *IG* V (1) 262

(*Artemis Orthia* pp. 303-4 no. 13; Bradford (12)) (f. Σίων); (12) c. 25-1 BC *IG* v (1) 210, 9 (Bradford (5)) (s. Εὐαμερίδας); (13) c. 1-10 AD *IG* v (1) 209, 27; *SEG* xxxv 331 (date) (Bradford (2)) (s. Ἀγαθοκλῆς); (14) c. 80-90 AD *IG* v (1) 674, 12 (Bradford (6)) (s. Τιμοκράτης); (15) c. 105-110 AD *IG* v (1) 97, 23; *SEG* xi 564, 23 (Bradford (11)) (*Δά(μ)ιππος—SEG*: f. Νικοκλῆς); (16) ~ *SEG* xi 569, 18 (Bradford (4)) (s. Διοκλῆς); (17) m. ii AD *IG* v (1) 505; 1174, 9; Cartledge–Spawforth p. 140 (ident.) (Bradford (13)) (f. Ξεναρχίδας); (18) c. 175-200 AD *SEG* xi 503, 9 (Bradford (8))
MESSENIA:
—MESSENE: (19) f. iii BC *SEG* xli 342, 10; cf. *PAE* 1991, p. 100 no. 8
—MESSENE?: (20) ii/i BC *SEG* xi 979, 54

**Δᾶμις**
ARKADIA: (1) 320 BC *IG* v (2) 549, 4 (f. Εὐπόλεμος)
—MANTINEIA-ANTIGONEIA: (2) c. 300-221 BC ib. 323. 105 (tessera) (s. Ἀμάδας)
—MEGALOPOLIS: (3) s. iv BC *RE* (1); Berve 240
—TEGEA: (4) iv BC *IG* v (2) 38, 69 (s. Θυμ—); (5) f. iii BC ib. 35, 11 (*Δᾶμ[ι]ς*: s. Δαμάριστος)
ARKADIA?: (6) iv/iii BC *HE* 696
EPIROS:
—AMBRAKIA: (7) s. iv BC *SEG* xvii 304 (f. Δαμιόι)
ILLYRIA:
—EPIDAMNOS-DYRRHACHION: (8) i BC Mionnet, *Suppl.* 3 p. 352 no. 307 (coin) (*Δάμιος* (gen.))
KERKYRA: (9) imp. *IG* ix (1) 947 ([Δ]ᾶμις)
KORINTHIA:
—KORINTH: (10) ii AD Luc., *DMort.* 27. 7 (fict.)
—OINOE: (11) vi-v BC *IG* iv (1) 418 (Δάμις?)
LAKONIA:
—SPARTA: (12) 324 BC Plu., *Mor.* 219 E (Poralla² 216)
LEUKAS: (13) iv/iii BC *SEG* xxvii 178 = Unp. (*IG* arch.); (14) iii BC *AM* 27 (1902) p. 370 no. 45 a (*Δάμιδος* (gen.))
MESSENIA: (15) viii BC Paus. iv 10. 5-6; 11. 3; 13. 5
—MESSENE: (16) iii BC *SEG* xxiii 209, 9
SICILY:
—GELA-PHINTIAS?: (17) f. v BC Dubois, *IGDS* 134 a, 1 (Arena, *Iscr. Sic.* II 80) (s. Κόβετος, f. Μύσκων)

**Δαμισίας**
AITOLIA:
—KONOPE-ARSINOE: (1) 250-150 BC *SBBerlAk* 1936, p. 363 no. 6 b

**Δαμίσκος**
MESSENIA:
—MESSENE: (1) 368 BC Moretti, *Olymp.* 417 (*RE* (-))
—MESSENE?: (2) ii/i BC *SEG* xi 979, 53
—THOURIA: (3) f. ii BC ib. 972, 31 (f. Σοϊξίνικος)

**Δάμιχος**
EPIROS:
—DODONA*: (1) iv-iii BC *PAE* 1932, p. 51 no. 2

**Δαμίων**
ACHAIA:
—PELLENE: (1) hell.? *SEG* viii 522
AKARNANIA:
—THYRREION: (2) ii BC *IG* ix (1)² (2) 248, 4 (s. Νικαι—)
ARGOLIS:
—EPIDAUROS: (3) c. 350-200 BC *SEG* xxvi 452. 3
EPIROS:
—AMBRAKIA: (4) 238-168 BC *BMC Thessaly* p. 96 nos. 29-30 (coin); (5) f. ii BC *AD* 39 (1984) Chron. p. 190 + pl. 77 γ (f. —θλος); (6) ~ *IG*

v (1) 4, 1, 9 (s. Θεόκριτος); (7) ~ *IC* 2 p. 25 no. 8 C (f. Τίμων); (8) a. 167 BC *SEG* xxxv 665 A, 11 (f. Ἀριστομήδης)
LAKONIA:
—OITYLOS: (9) iii/ii BC *IG* v (1) 1295, 6 (Bradford (4))
—SPARTA: (10) c. 50-25 BC *IG* v (1) 208, 6 (Bradford (2)) (s. Δίων); (11) c. 25-1 BC *IG* v (1) 212, 4 (Bradford (5)) (f. Δαμοκράτης); (12) c. 70-100 AD *IG* v (1) 281, 3 (*Artemis Orthia* pp. 314-15 no. 34; Bradford (3)) (s. Μ. Ἀνθέστιος Φιλοκράτης); (13) ii AD *IG* v (1) 159, 6 (Bradford (5)); (14) c. 175-200 AD *IG* v (1) 89, 11; 129, 2 (Bradford (1)) (s. Βέλλων)
MESSENIA:
—ASINE: (15) ii AD *IG* v (1) 1408 (s. Δαμόκριτος)
—MESSENE: (16) hell. *BMC Pelop.* p. 111 nos. 29-31 (coin); (17) ?35-44 AD *IG* v (1) 1433, 26; *SEG* xxix 396 (date)
—THOURIA: (18) f. ii BC ib. xi 972, 1; (19) ~ ib. l. 67 (s. Καλλικράτης); (20) ~ ib. l. 74 (s. Νικάδας); (21) ~ ib. l. 96 (f. Ὀνασικλῆς); (22) ~ ib. l. 114 (*Δάμων—ed.*: f. Θεοκλείδας); (23) ii/i BC *IG* v (1) 1384, 19 (f. Δαμοκράτης)

**Δάμμυλα**
S. ITALY (APULIA):
—CANUSIUM: (1) i/ii AD *Epig. Rom. di Canosa* 63 (Lat. Dammu[la]: m. Νάρδις)

**Δαμναγόρα**
EPIROS:
—MOLOSSOI: (1) hell. Cabanes, *L'Épire* p. 584 no. 63, 2, 6 (*SEG* xxvi 705) (m. Φορμίσκος, Ἐχενίκα)

**Δαμνασυλλίς**
SICILY:
—SYRACUSE: (1) v BC *Suda* Σ 893 (*CGF* p. 152 T 1) (m. Σώφρων)

**Δαμοδίκα**
ARKADIA:
—PHIGALEIA: (1) i BC *SEG* xxiii 247 (Δαμοδίκα)
—TEGEA: (2) her.? *RE* (5) (*Δημοδίκη*: d. Ῥηξίμαχος)

**Δαμόδικος**
ARKADIA:
—PHENEOS: (1) her.? *FGrH* 42 F 5 (*Δη*-: s. Δαμόστρατος: fict.)

**Δαμόδοκος**
ACHAIA: (1) 217 BC Plb. v 95. 7 (*Δη*-)
ARKADIA:
—MEGALOPOLIS: (2) ?145 BC *IG* v (2) 439, 52 (f. Λάζυγος)
DALMATIA:
—PHAROS: (3) iv BC Brunšmid p. 20 no. 6 ([Δα]μόδοκος: s. Δαμόμαχος, f. Κλεύδαμος)
KERKYRA: (4) her. Wehrli, *Schule Arist.* iv fr. 192

**Δαμοθάλης**
MESSENIA:
—MESSENE: (1) ?f. i AD *PAE* 1992, p. 79, 4 (*Δαμοθάμης—lap. and ed.*: f. (nat.) Ἵππαρχος)
—THOURIA: (2) f. ii BC *SEG* xi 972, 56 (f. Δαμόφαντος); (3) ~ ib. l. 58 (s. Δαμόφαντος); (4) ~ ib. l. 76 (s. Χαρησίδαμος)
S. ITALY: (5) s. iv BC *Misc. Etrusco-Italica* 1 p. 196 no. A6 (bronze)

**Δαμοθάρσης**
AKARNANIA:
—OINIADAI: (1) c. 325-315 BC *Hesp.* 57 (1988) p. 148 A, 36 (*SEG* xxxvi 331); cf. *Hesp.* 48 (1979) pp. 78 f. with pl. 22 c (f. Πορφυρίων, ?f. Φείδων)

**Δαμόθεος**
KORINTHIA:
—SIKYON: (1) c. 230-200 BC *BCH* 45 (1921) p. 11 II, 34-5

**Δαμοθέρρης**
KORINTHIA:
—KORINTH: (1) s. iv BC *Corinth* viii (1) 11, 4 (s. Θράσυλλος)

**Δαμοθέρσης**
MESSENIA:
—THOURIA: (1) ii-i BC *IG* v (1) 1385, 19 (f. —ασις); (2) ii/i BC ib. 1384, 13 (f. Ἀρίστιππος)

**Δαμοθοΐδας**
TRIPHYLIA:
—LEPREON: (1) vii BC Paus. iv 24. 1

**Δαμοίτας**
AITOLIA:
—KALYDON: (1) c. 142 BC *IG* ix (1)² (1) 137, 46 (f. Μυννίων); (2) a. 142 BC ib. l. 78 (*Δαμοί[τας]*)
ARKADIA:
—TEGEA: (3) c. 400 BC *SEG* xxxvi 385 (*Δαμοίτ[ας]*)
EPIROS:
—AMYMNOI: (4) 370-368 BC Cabanes, *L'Épire* p. 534 no. 1, 18
—CHARADROS: (5) a. 167 BC *SEG* xxxv 665 A, 14
—CHERADROI: (6) hell. Cabanes, *L'Épire* p. 581 no. 56, 10

**Δαμοκάδης**
ACHAIA: (1) f. ii BC *IC* 2 p. 23 no. 6 F, 4 (f. Ἀρίσταινος) ?= (Τιμοκάδης (1))
—OLENOS?: (2) ?vii BC Wilhelm, *Beitr.* p. 121; *LSAG²* p. 224 no. 1 (date)
ARGOLIS:
—TROIZEN*: (3) iv BC *IG* iv (1) 823, 58, 59
KEPHALLENIA:
—PALE: (4) iii/ii BC Unp. (*IG* arch.)
S. ITALY (BRUTTIUM):
—KROTON: (5) s. vi BC *RE* (-); *FVS* 19 (*Δημοκήδης—lit. test.*: s. Καλλιφῶν: doctor)

**Δαμόκαμος**
LAKONIA:
—AMYKLAI*: (1) c. 510-500 BC *SEG* i 83 + xxxii 389 (Poralla² 216a) (*Δαμοκρίνιος* (gen.)—83)

**Δαμοκήδης**
S. ITALY (BRUTTIUM):
—KROTON: (1) inc. *MkB* 2 (1876-8) p. 13; cf. Masson, *OGS* 2 p. 494 (s. Βλόσων)

**Δαμοκλέα**
ARGOLIS:
—HERMIONE: (1) ?ii-i BC *IG* iv (1) 731 II, 4 (m. Σωτηρίων); (2) ii-i BC ib. 732 III, 3; (3) i BC-i AD? ib. 730 IV, 2 (m. Ζωπυρῖνα)
DALMATIA:
—ISSA: (4) ii BC *SEG* xxxi 602, 4 (*VAHD* 84 (1991) p. 257 no. 7) (d. Πυθοκράτης)

**Δαμόκλεια**
MESSENIA:
—MESSENE?: (1) imp. *IG* v (1) 1499; 1500

**Δαμοκλείδας**
ARGOLIS:
—EPIDAUROS: (1) c. 221 BC ib. IV (1)² 42, 13
—(Hylleis): (2) 146 BC ib. 28, 51 (s. Νικομένης)
—Hysminaia: (3) c. 335-325 BC ib. 108, 161-2
EPIROS:
—BOUTHROTOS (PRASAIBOI):
—Ambrakioi: (4) a. 163 BC *IBouthrot* 75, 8; 170 (f. Λύκος)
LAKONIA:
—SPARTA: (5) c. 200 BC *SEG* iii 312, 8 (Bradford (2)) (*Δα[μ]οκλείδας*: s. Θεόδωρος); (6) ?s. i

AD *IG* v (1) 282; *Artemis Orthia* pp. 313-14 no. 31 (date) (Bradford (1)) (s. Χαλέας)

MESSENIA:
—THOURIA: (**7**) ii-i BC *IG* v (1) 1385, 31 (s. Χαρῖνος)

## Δαμοκλῆς

ACHAIA: (**1**) 146 BC ib. IV (1)² 28, 65 (s. Φιλο-κράτης: synoikos)
—AIGION: (**2**) 157 BC *FD* III (3) 126, 4, 5 (s. Τι-μοκράτης); (**3**) 153-144 BC ib. III (1) 154, 2-3 with n. (locn.) (f. Θέοξις)
ACHAIA?: (**4**) 193 BC *IG* v (2) 293, 24 (Δαμοκλῆς: s. Ἀριστόμαχος)
AIGINA: (**5**) hell. ib. IV (1) 96
AITOLIA: (**6**) m. iii BC ib. IX (1)² (1) 191, 12 ([Δ]αμοκλ[ῆς])
ARGOLIS:
—ARGOS: (**7**) s. iii BC ib. IV (1) 727 A, 2 (Perl-man H.1) (s. Σ..ο....ς); (**8**) 195 BC Liv. xxxiv 25. 7; (**9**) 105 BC *JÖAI* 14 (1911) Beibl. p. 146 no. 4, 22 (s. Φιλήμων)
—EPIDAUROS: (**10**) iv/iii BC *IG* IV (1)² 200 (f. Δαμοτέλης); (**11**) ~ ib. 203 (s. Ἰσχέμαχος); (**12**) iii BC ib. 304; (**13**) iii/ii BC Peek, *IAEpid* 129, 2 (Δαμοκλ[ῆ]ς); (**14**) ~ ib. 153. 16; (**15**) ii BC *IG* IV (1)² 246, 1 (Δαμο[κλῆς]: I f. Δαμοκλῆς II); (**16**) ~ ib. l. 1 (Δ[αμ]οκλῆς: II s. Δαμοκλῆς I); (**17**) ~ ib. 250 (f. Δαμάγητος); (**18**) ii/i BC ib. 212 (f. Ἐχεκράτεια); (**19**) i BC ib. 223 (I f. Δαμοκλῆς II); (**20**) ~ ib. (II s. Δαμοκλῆς I)
——(Azantioi): (**21**) 146 BC ib. 28, 45 (f. Θιο-κλείδας)
——(Azantioi?): (**22**) ii/i BC ib. 234, 1 (s. Θιο-κλείδας, ?s. Ἀρχώ)
——(Hylleis): (**23**) c. 150-146 BC ib. 28, 56; *SEG* XI 377, 9; 405, [8] (s. Καλλιμένης)
——Mysias: (**24**) m. iii BC *IG* IV (1)² 96, 44 (Perlman E.3); Perlman p. 63 f. (date) (?f. Ἀριστόλας)
—EPIDAUROS*: (**25**) c. 370-365 BC Peek, *IA-Epid* 52 A, 3
ARKADIA:
—MANTINEIA-ANTIGONEIA:
——(Enyalia): (**26**) m. iv BC *IG* v (2) 271, 9 (s. Κάβαισος)
——(Posoidaia): (**27**) c. 425-400 BC *SEG* XXXI 348, 8 ([Δ]αμοκλῆς)
—TEGEA: (**28**) s. v BC *IG* v (2) 175, 3 (-κλēς); (**29**) s. iv BC ib. 41, 59 (Δαμοκλ[ῆς]?)
——(Apolloniatai): (**30**) m. iii BC ib. 36, 103 (s. Ἀπολλωνίδας); (**31**) ~ ib. l. 105 (metic)
——(Hippothoitai): (**32**) iv/iii BC ib. 38, 40 (f. Φιλέας)
——(Krariotai): (**33**) iii BC ib. 40, 15 (f. Εὐάνθης)
—THELPHOUSA: (**34**) i BC/i AD *SEG* XI 1127; *BCH* 88 (1964) p. 179 (date)
EPIROS:
—AMBRAKIA: (**35**) f. ii BC Unp. (Arta Mus., inscr.) (f. Δαμότιμος)
ILLYRIA:
—APOLLONIA: (**36**) i BC-i AD *Iliria* 1975, p. 205 (tile graffito)
—EPIDAMNOS-DYRRHACHION: (**37**) c. 250-50 BC Ceka 396 (coin) (pryt.)
KORINTHIA:
—KORINTH (NR.): (**38**) hell.? *IG* IV (1) 1558 (fals.?)
LAKONIA:
—SPARTA: (**39**) c. 25-1 BC ib. v (1) 212, 16 (Bradford (6)) (s. Σιωνίδας); (**40**) i BC/i AD *IG* v (1) 49, 4; 210, 26; *SEG* XI 676, 1 (Bradford (1)) (s. Ἀριστοκράτης); (**41**) s. i AD *IG* v (1) 51, 32; 52, 7; 103, 10; *SEG* XI 538, 3; 546 b, 2; 609, 3; xxxvi 361, 31 (Bradford (8)) (I s. Φιλοκράτης, f. Δαμοκλῆς II ὁ καὶ Φιλοκράτης) ?= (**45**); (**42**) c. 90-100 AD *SEG* XI 558, 10 (Bradford (5)) (s. Καλλικράτης) ?= (**48**); (**43**) c. 100-105 AD *SEG* XI 537 a, 4 (Bradford (4)) (Γ. Ἰούλ. Δ.: s. Καλλικλείδας); (**44**) c. 100-120

AD *IG* v (1) 32 B, 1; 51, 32; 52, 7; 60, 1-2; 65, [1] + *SEG* XI 549; *IG* v (1) 103, 10; 138, 2; 291, 6?; 492, 2; *SEG* XI 523, 1; 538, 3; 545, [4]; 546 a, 1; 546 b, 1; 548, 18; 549, 2; 582, 2 (Bradford (2)) (Δ. ὁ καὶ Φιλοκράτης: II s. Δαμοκλῆς I, f. Δαμοκλῆς III, Δαμονίκης); (**45**) c. 105-110 AD *IG* v (1) 52, 10 (Bradford (10)) (f. Νικιππίδας) ?= (*41*); (**46**) c. 105-140 AD *IG* v (1) 32 B, 1; 60, 1; 65, [1] + *SEG* XI 549; *IG* v (1) 138, 1; 492, 2; *SEG* XI 481, 4; 523, 1; 545, [4]; 548, 18; 549, 1; 582, [1] (Bradford (3)) (III s. Δαμοκλῆς II ὁ καὶ Φιλο-κράτης, f. Δαμονίκης) ?= (*47*); (**47**) c. 120 AD *IG* v (1) 1315, 23 (Bradford (7)) ?= (*46*); 127 AD *IG* v (1) 1314, 28 (Bradford (9)) (f. Καλλικράτης) ?= (*42*); (**49**) c. 202-205 AD *SEG* XXXVI 360, 6; *BSA* 81 (1986) p. 324 no. 4 (ident.) (I f. Δαμοκλῆς II); (**50**) ~ *SEG* XXXVI 360, 6; *BSA* 81 (1986) p. 324 no. 4 (ident.) (II s. Δαμοκλῆς I)
MESSENIA:
—MESSENE: (**51**) iii BC *RE* (7); Phld., *Ind. Sto.* 76, 4; (**52**) ?i BC *PAE* 1969, p. 100 a, 6; (**53**) i AD *IG* v (1) 1479 (s. Ἀριστομένης)
—THOURIA: (**54**) ii-i BC ib. 1385, 1 (f. Ἐπικρά-της)
S. ITALY (BRUTTIUM):
—KROTON: (**55**) iv BC Iamb., *VP* 267 (*FVS* 1 p. 446)
—LOKROI EPIZEPHYRIOI:
——(Βοω.): (**56**) iv/iii BC De Franciscis 15, 6 (s. Ἀρκείδας)
SICILY:
—AKRAI: (**57**) ?iii BC *SGDI* 3243 (*Akrai* p. 155 no. 5) (s. Ἀρτέμων); (**58**) ~ *SGDI* 3243 (*Akrai* p. 155 no. 5) (s. Δαμάτριος)

## Δαμόκοπος

SICILY:
—SYRACUSE: (**1**) v BC *RE* s.v. Demokopos (-); Sophr. fr. 128 (Δ. ὁ Μύριλλα)

## Δαμοκρᾶς

ARKADIA:
—TEGEA: (**1**) ii-iii AD *Classical Heritage* 121 (terracotta)

## Δαμοκράτεια

AITOLIA:
—KALLION/KALLIPOLIS: (**1**) hell. *IG* IX (1)² (1) 158
—KONOPE-ARSINOE: (**2**) ii-i BC ib. 132 ([Δα]μοκράτεια: d. Εὐρυκλείδας)

## Δαμοκράτη

LAKONIA:
—GYTHEION: (**1**) a. 212 AD ib. v (1) 1177, 11; *BCH* 97 (1973) pp. 248-9 (name) (Αὐρ. Δαμο-κράτης (gen.): d. Μ. Αὐρ. Λυσικράτης)

## Δαμοκράτης

ACHAIA: (**1**) 221 BC *Milet* 1 (3) 42, 3 (Δη-: f. Πολεμοκράτης)
—BOURA: (**2**) c. 210-207 BC *IG* IV (1)² 73, 16; *SEG* XXXV 303 (date) (f. Δίφιλος)
AITOLIA: (**3**) 224 or 221 BC *SGDI* 2524, 4; Nachtergael, *Les Galates* 64, 3
—EITEAIOI: (**4**) ?205-203 BC *FD* III (2) 134 b, 6 (*Syll*³ 564)
AKARNANIA:
—PALAIROS: (**5**) c. 200 BC *IG* IX (1)² (2) 503
—THYRREION: (**6**) imp. ib. 312 b (s. Διονύσιος)
ARGOLIS:
—ARGOS: (**7**) ?ii BC Unp. (Ch. Kritzas)
—ARGOS*: (**8**) ii BC *SEG* XLII 279, 12 (Δαμο-κράτη<η>ς: slave/freed.?)
—EPIDAUROS: (**9**) ?iv-iii BC ib. XXXIX 356 (Δαμοκράτειος—ed., Δαμοκράτε<ι>ος? (gen.): I f. Δαμοκράτης II); (**10**) ~ ib. (Δαμοκράτη (masc./fem. voc.?): II s. Δαμοκράτης I)
—EPIDAUROS*: (**11**) c. 370-360 BC Peek, *IA-Epid* 52 B, 65, 67

—HERMIONE: (**12**) i BC-i AD? *IG* IV (1) 730 V, 6 (f. Νικίας)
ARKADIA:
—MEGALOPOLIS: (**13**) s. ii BC ib. v (2) 461 (?s. Φιλοποίμην, f. Μεγάκλεια)
—MEGALOPOLIS?: (**14**) 42 AD ib. 516, 3 (s. Κλεί-τωρ)
—PHIGALEIA: (**15**) c. 100-90 BC *SEG* XXXIII 290 A, 6; *BSA* 70 (1975) pp. 129-31 (date) (Stephanis 576) ([Δ]αμοκράτης: s. Ἄλυπος)
—TEGEA: (**16**) iv/iii BC *IG* v (2) 32, 8; (**17**) f. ii BC ib. 44, 28 (Δαμοκρά[της])
KERKYRA: (**18**) iii/ii BC ib. IX (1) 683, 13
KORINTHIA:
—SIKYON: (**19**) c. 370-365 BC Peek, *IAEpid* 52 B, 42, 45; (**20**) iii BC *TrGF* 1 p. 284 (Δη-); (**21**) ii BC *SEG* XI 248; cf. Skalet 90 (f. —τος)
LAKONIA:
—GYTHEION*: (**22**) m. ii AD *IG* v (1) 1174, 5 (Λ. Μίνδιος Δ.)
—SPARTA: (**23**) m. iii BC Plu., *Cleom.* 4 (Bradford (17)); (**24**) s. i BC *IG* v (1) 93, 27 (Bradford (38)) (f. —κλῆς); (**25**) c. 30-20 BC *IG* v (1) 141, 2; *SEG* XXXV 329 (date) (Bradford (11)) (s. Ἵππων) ?= (**26**); (**26**) ~ *IG* v (1) 141, 12 (Bradford (28)) (f. Δαμοκρατία) ?= (**25**); (**27**) ~ *IG* v (1) 211, 16 (Bradford (24)) (f. Ἀμείνιππος); (**28**) c. 25-1 BC *IG* v (1) 210, 2 (Bradford (36)) (f. Τιμοκράτης); (**29**) ~ *IG* v (1) 210, 5; 212, 56 (Bradford (25)) (f. Ἀρήξιπ-πος); (**30**) ~ *IG* v (1) 210, 13 (Bradford (1)) (s. Ἀφροδίσιος); (**31**) ~ *IG* v (1) 210, 48 (Bradford (20)); (**32**) ~ *IG* v (1) 210, 51; 212, 56; cf. Stephanis 578 (Bradford (29)) (f. Δαμοκρα-τίδας); (**33**) ~ *IG* v (1) 212, 4 (Bradford (5)) ([Δαμ]οκράτης: s. Δαμίων); (**34**) ~ *SEG* XI 505, 6 (Bradford (4)) (s. Ἀθηνόδωρος); (**35**) c. 1-10 AD *IG* v (1) 209, 12; *SEG* XXXV 331 (date) (Bradford (3)) (s. Ἀριστοκρατίδας); (**36**) ~ *IG* v (1) 209, 17; *SEG* XXXV 331 (date) (Bradford (26)) (I f. Δαμοκράτης II); (**37**) ~ *IG* v (1) 209, 17; *SEG* XXXV 331 (date) (Bradford (7)) (II s. Δαμοκράτης I); (**38**) ~ *IG* v (1) 209, 19; *SEG* XXXV 331 (date) (Bradford (27)) (I f. Δαμοκρά-της II); (**39**) ~ *IG* v (1) 209, 19; *SEG* XXXV 331 (date) (Bradford (8)) (II s. Δαμοκράτης I); (**40**) ~ *IG* v (1) 209, 30; *SEG* XXXV 331 (date) (Bradford (12)) (s. Λύσιππος); (**41**) f. i AD *IG* v (1) 270, 2; *Artemis Orthia* pp. 306-7 no. 20 (date) (Bradford (18)) (Δαμοκράτ (dat.)); (**42**) ~ *IG* v (1) 336; *Artemis Orthia* p. 308 no. 23 (date) (Bradford (37)) (f. —μος); (**43**) c. 90-100 AD *IG* v (1) 79, 2, 5; *SEG* XI 539, 2-3 (Bradford (33); (34)) (f. Νικιππίδας, Φιλάκων); (**44**) c. 100 AD *SEG* XI 513, 8 (Bradford (23)) (f. Ἁγησικλείδας); (**45**) c. 100-110 AD *IG* v (1) 97, 6; *SEG* XI 511, 5; 564, 6 (Bradford (14)) (s. Φιλέρως); (**46**) c. 100-120 AD *IG* v (1) 79, 7; *SEG* XI 517, 4; 539, 4 (Bradford (30)) (f. Γ. Ἰούλ. Δαμόκριτος); (**47**) c. 100-125 AD *IG* v (1) 152, 9 (Bradford (21)) (Γ. Ἰούλ. Δ.); (**48**) ii AD *IG* v (1) 159, 35 (Bradford (19)); (**49**) f. ii AD *SEG* XI 491, 1 (Bradford (16)) (s. Σπένδων, f. Εὐδόκιμος); (**50**) c. 115-125 AD *SEG* XI 543, 2; 575, [13] (Bradford (1)) (Δα[μ]οκράτης—543: s. Φιλάκων); (**51**) c. 140-150 AD *IG* v (1) 64, 8, 15; 289, 3 (*Artemis Orthia* p. 321 no. 46; Bradford (10)) (Δαμοκράτηρ—289: s. Εὐδόκι-μος, f. Εὐδόκιμος ὁ καὶ Ἀριστείδας); (**52**) ~ *IG* v (1) 607, 4; *BSA* 75 (1980) p. 219 (stemma) (Bradford (2)) (Τιβ. Κλ. Δ.: ?s. Τιβ. Κλ. Ἀρι-στοκράτης, Ἰουλ. Ἀπατάριον, f. Κλ. Νίκιον, ?f. Πολύευκτος); (**53**) c. 140-160 AD *IG* v (1) 74, 3 (Bradford (22)) (Μ. Βέττιος Δ.); (**54**) ~ *IG* v (1) 112, 4 (Bradford (31)) (f. Λυσικράτης); (**55**) s. ii AD *IG* v (1) 293, 2; 493, 2-3 (Bradford (9)) (s. Διοκλῆς); (**56**) c. 160-170 AD *IG* v (1) 109, 10 (Bradford (32)) (f. Μᾶρκος); (**57**) c. 175-210 AD *SEG* XI 555, 8 (Bradford (35)) (f. Πυθάγγελος); (**58**) m. iii AD *IG* v (1) 562,

9?; 572, 2 (Bradford (15)) (*M. Aὐρ. Δ.*: s. *Πο-σειδώνιος*, f. *Aὐρ. Δαμοκρατία*, *Aὐρ. Ὀνασιφορίς*)
—THALAMAI: (59) ?211-212 AD *IG* v (1) 1318, 7 (s. *Κράτων*)
LEUKAS: (60) c. 167-50 BC *BMC Thessaly* p. 179 no. 85; p. 181 nos. 108-9; p. 183 nos. 136-9; *SNG Cop. Epirus–Acarnania* 388 (coins)
MESSENIA:
—MESSENE: (61) iii BC *SEG* XXIII 209, 8; (62) iii/ii BC *PAE* 1991, p. 91 (f. *Χαιρήμων*) ?= (65); (63) 208 or 207 BC *FD* III (4) 21, 2; 22, 9 (s. *Δάμανδρος*); (64) 179 BC *ID* 442 B, 116
—THOURIA: (65) f. ii BC *SEG* XI 972, 57 (f. *Χαιρήμων*) ?= (62); (66) ii/i BC *IG* v (1) 1384, 3 (f. *Ξενοκλῆς*); (67) ~ ib. l. 8 (s. *Χαιρήμων*); (68) ~ ib. l. 19 (s. *Δαμίων*)
S. ITALY (CALABRIA):
—BRENTESION-BRUNDISIUM: (69) imp. ib. XIV 676
—TARAS-TARENTUM: (70) 210 BC Liv. xxvi 39. 6; (71) ii BC *SEG* XXIX 1216, 1, [22] (f. *Ἐπί-γονος*)
S. ITALY (LUCANIA):
—METAPONTION?: (72) iii-ii BC Vandermersch p. 165 (amph.) (Desy, *Timbres amphoriques* 11)
SICILY:
—AKRAI: (73) ii BC *Akrai* p. 156 no. 6, 6 (s. *Ἀρι-στοκράτης*); (74) ~ ib. l. 19 (s. *Φίλιος*); (75) ii-i BC *SGDI* 3246, 26 (*Akrai* pp. 152-3 no. 2; Dubois, *IGDS* 109) (*Δαμοκράτ*[ης]: s. *Φίλιος*)
—SYRACUSE?:
——(*Λογ.*): (76) hell. Manganaro, *PdelP* forthcoming no. 4 I, 9 (f. *Ζώπυρος*)

**Δαμοκρατία**
LAKONIA:
—SPARTA: (1) c. 30-20 BC *IG* v (1) 141, 12; *SEG* XXXV 329 (date) (Bradford (1)) (d. *Δα-μοκράτης*); (2) s. i AD *IG* v (1) 581; *BSA* 80 (1985) pp. 215; 220-1 (ident., stemma) (Brad-ford (4)) (*Μεμμία Δ.*: ?d. *Π. Μέμμιος Πρατό-λαος*, *Μεμμία Πασιχάρεια* (Epidauros), ?m. *Λ. Οὐολοσσηνὸς Ἀριστοκράτης*, *Λ. Οὐολοσσηνὸς Δα-μάρης*, *Οὐολοσσηνὴ Ὀλυμπίς*, *Οὐολοσσηνὴ Ὀλυμ-πίχα*); (3) c. 239-244 AD *IG* v (1) 572, 12 (Bradford (2)) (*Aὐρ. Δ.*: d. *M. Aὐρ. Δαμοκρά-της*)

**Δαμοκρατίδας**
ARGOLIS:
—ARGOS: (1) s. vii BC Paus. iv 24. 4 (king)
ARKADIA:
—TEGEA: (2) 369-361 BC *IG* v (2) 1, 15; Tod, *GHI* II 132 (date)
LAKONIA:
—SPARTA: (3) hell.-imp. *IG* v (1) 195, 2 (Brad-ford (11)) ([*Δα*]*μ*[*ο*]*κρατίδας*); (4) c. 25-1 BC *IG* v (1) 210, 50; 212, 56 (Bradford (5); Stephanis 578) (s. *Δαμοκράτης*); (5) i BC/i AD *IG* v (1) 49, 2 (Bradford (1)); (6) i BC/i AD? *IG* v (1) 177, 2 (Bradford (10)) (f. *Ἀγητορί-δας*); (7) c. 1-10 AD *IG* v (1) 209, 6; *SEG* XXXV 331 (date) (Bradford (6)) (s. *Eὐδαμίδας*); (8) i/ii AD *IG* v (1) 31, 1; 79, 10; *SEG* XI 539, 6; 641, 1 (Bradford (2)) (s. *Ἀγιάδας*) ?= (10); (9) c. 90-100 AD *SEG* XI 558, 6 (Bradford (8)) (f. *Ἀριστοκράτης*); (10) c. 105-110 AD *IG* v (1) 97, 11; *SEG* XI 564, 18; 569, 5 (Bradford (7)) (f. *Ἀγιάδας*) ?= (8); (11) c. 110-120 AD *IG* v (1) 298, 1; *Artemis Orthia* pp. 315-16 no. 35 (date) (Bradford (9)) (f. *Χαρίξενος*); (12) c. 170-230 AD *IG* v (1) 144 b-c; 305, 8 (*Artemis Orthia* pp. 333-4 no. 69); *IG* v (1) 553, 2; 554, 2; 555 a-b, 10; 556, 2; 682, 1; *SEG* XI 802, [2]; 803, 3; 831, [1], 10; *IvOl* 238; *BSA* 79 (1984) pp. 279-283 (date); 80 (1985) pp. 246-8 (ident., stemma) (Bradford (3)) (*Π. Aἰλ. Δ.*: s. *Π. Aἰλ. Ἀλκανδρίδας*, *Πομπ. Πόλλα*, ?f. (nat.) *Τιβ. Κλ. Aἰλ. Πρατόλαος ὁ καὶ Δαμοκρατίδας*, f.

*Π. Aἰλ. Ἀλκανδρίδας*); (13) ii/iii AD *IG* v (1) 497, 10; 587, 11; *BSA* 80 (1985) pp. 225; 246-8 (ident., stemma) (Bradford s.v. *Πρατό-λαος* (11)) (*Τιβ. Κλ. Aἰλ. Πρατόλαος ὁ καὶ Δ.*: II ?s. (nat.) *Π. Aἰλ. Δαμοκρατίδας*, ?s. (ad.) *Τιβ. Κλ. Πρατόλαος*); (14) f. iii AD *IG* v (1) 589, 21; *BSA* 80 (1985) pp. 225; 238-9 (ident., stemma) (Bradford s.v. *Πρατόλαος* (10)) (*Τιβ. Κλ. Πρατόλαος ὁ καὶ Δ.*: s. *Τιβ. Κλ. Eὔδαμος*, *Κλ. Δαμοσθένεια*, f. *Κλ. Ἀλκανδρίδας*, *Κλ. Ἐλπὶς ἡ καὶ Καλλιστονίκη*)

**Δαμοκράτις**
ARGOLIS:
—HERMIONE: (1) ii-i BC *IG* IV (1) 732 IV, 18
LAKONIA:
—SPARTA: (2) i BC-i AD ib. v (1) 744 (Bradford (-)) (?d. *Ἀντ*—)

**Δαμοκρίνης**
ARGOLIS:
—ARGOS: (1) i AD *SEG* XXVI 429, 8 (s. *Σαωνίδας*)
—EPIDAUROS:
——Politas: (2) c. 370-335 BC *IG* IV (1)² 102, 14; 103, 38

**Δαμοκρίτα**
ARGOLIS:
—ARGOS: (1) ii BC *SEG* XLII 279, 24 (d. *Σωί-κρατης*)
EPIROS:
—AMBRAKIA: (2) iv/iii BC Unp. (Arta Mus., in-scr.) ([*Δαμ*]*οκρίτα*, [*Τιμ*]*οκρίτα?*)
ITHAKE: (3) ?ii BC *AM* 27 (1902) p. 377 no. 64 (*REG* 15 (1902) p. 132 no. 3) ([*Δα*]*μοκρίτα*, [*Τι*]*μοκρίτα?*)
LAKONIA:
—SPARTA: (4) f. v BC Plu., *Mor.* 775 C-E (Po-ralla² 217)

**Δαμόκριτος**
ACHAIA: (1) 149-146 BC Paus. vii 13. 1-5; Plb. xxxviii 17. 9; (2) 146 BC *IG* IV (1)² 28, 102 (f. *Σωκράτης*: synoikos)
—AIGEIRA: (3) c. 266 BC ib. XII (9) 1187, 34; Robert, *Ét. Num. Gr.* p. 179 ff. (date) (*Δη-*: f. *Ἀγάθαρχος*)
—DYME: (4) iii-ii BC *Syll³* 530, 2; cf. *Achaia und Elis* p. 115
AITOLIA:
—KALYDON: (5) 208-193 BC *IG* IX (1)² (1) p. L, s.a. 200 BC, 193 BC; 30, 21, 26, [31]; 31, 61, 131, 135; *IMM* 28, [5] (*IG* IX (1)² (1) 186); *IG* IX (1)² (3) 617, 1 (s. *Στράταγος*); (6) 129 BC ib. IX (1)² (1) 137, 95 (s. *Δαΐλοχος*)
—KONOPE-ARSINOE?: (7) s. iii BC ib. 24, 2 (or Korinthia Korinth?)
—METAPA: (8) c. 215-200 BC *FD* III (2) 86, 7 (*Syll³* 539 A); cf. Nachtergael, *Les Galates* p. 291 (date)
—PHILOTAIEIS: (9) 190 BC *IG* IX (1)² (1) 97, 14
ARGOLIS:
—ARGOS: (10) iii BC Peek, *NIEpid* 46 = *SEG* XVII 179 (s. *Δαμόχαρτος*); (11) c. 220-200 BC ib. XI 414, 1 (Perlman E.5) ([*Δα*]*μό*[*κ*]*ριτος*: s. [.]*α*[.]*ο*——*ης*); (12) c. 210-207 BC *IG* IV (1)² 73, 7; *SEG* XXXV 303 (date) (f. *Λύσιππος*); (13) 105 BC *JÖAI* 14 (1911) Beibl. p. 146 no. 4, 25 (f. *Κάλλης*)
——(Kerkadai): (14) iv/iii BC Peek, *IAEpid* 24, 2 ([*Δα*]*μόκρι*]*τος*)
—EPIDAUROS: (15) c. 370-360 BC *BSA* 61 (1966) p. 273 no. 4 B III, 10 (*Δαμόκ*[*ριτος*]) ?= (16); (16) c. 365-335 BC *IG* IV (1)² 103, 10, 14, 16-18, [19] ?= (15); (17) ii/i BC ib. 64, 3 + Peek, *IAEpid* 19
—HERMIONE: (18) m. iv BC Unp. (Ch. Kritzas) (f. *Ἀρχεύς*); (19) ~ ib. (s. ——*έδαμος*); (20) iii BC *IG* IV (1) 729 II, 17 (f. *Ἐπικύδης*)
—TROIZEN: (21) hell.-imp. *Certamen* 21 (*Δη-*)

ARKADIA:
—TEGEA: (22) iv BC *IG* v (2) 31, 8 (s. *Δαμά-τριος*); (23) ?s. iv BC ib. 39, 2; (24) s. ii BC *BMI* 1154 a, 3; *BE* 1972, no. 37 (date) (f. *Τελέας*)
EPIROS:
—AMBRAKIA: (25) c. 215-200 BC *FD* III (2) 86, 10 (*Syll³* 539 A); cf. Nachtergael, *Les Galates* p. 291 (date)
—BOUTHROTOS (PRASAIBOI): (26) a. 163 BC *IBouthrot* 26, 9 (*SEG* XXXVIII 484) (f. *Φίλ-ιστος*)
——Kestrinoi Asantoi: (27) a. 163 BC *IBouthrot* 91, 12 (*SEG* XXXII 623) (s. *Τείσαρχος*)
KEPHALLENIA:
—SAME: (28) hell. *IG* IX (1) 635 ([*Δ*]*αμόκριτ*[*ος*])
KORINTHIA:
—SIKYON: (29) f. iv BC *RE* (3) (Skalet 90) (sculptor); (30) 46 BC Cic., *ad Fam.* xiii 78 (Skalet 98)
LAKONIA:
—SPARTA: (31) c. 100-120 AD *IG* v (1) 79, 6; *SEG* XI 517, 4; 539, 4 (Bradford (-)) (*Γ. Ἰούλ. Δ.*: s. *Δαμοκράτης*) ?= (32); (32) c. 105 AD *IG* v (1) 98, 3 ([*Γ.*] [*Ἰούλ.*] *Δ.*) ?= (31)
MESSENIA:
—ASINE: (33) ii AD ib. 1408 (f. *Δαμίων*)
S. ITALY (CALABRIA):
—TARAS-TARENTUM: (34) 281-272 BC Evans, *Horsemen* p. 158 no. 4 (coin) (*Δαμόκρι*(*τος*)); (35) c. 272-235 BC Vlasto 913-26 (coins) (Evans, *Horsemen* p. 181 VIII L.3)
TRIPHYLIA:
—PTELEA: (36) ii BC *SEG* XVI 282, 2

**Δαμοκύδης**
ARGOLIS:
—EPIDAUROS: (1) iii BC *IG* IV (1)² 337; cf. Peek, *IAEpid* 146 (*Δαμο*[*κ*]*ύδης*: f. *Φιλοκλῆς*)

**Δαμόλα**
ARGOLIS:
—EPIDAUROS: (1) iv BC ib. 86

**Δαμόλαος**
EPIROS:
—DODONA*: (1) iv-iii BC *SGDI* 1569 B (f. *Λυ-σίας*)

**Δαμόλας**
ARGOLIS:
—EPIDAUROS:
——(Azantioi): (1) 146 BC *IG* IV (1)² 28, 40 (f. *Δαμάτριος*)
LAKONIA:
—SPARTA: (2) c. 25-1 BC ib. v (1) 212, 32 (Brad-ford (2)) (s. *Φιλόξενος*) ?= (3); (3) i BC/i AD *IG* v (1) 48, 15 (Bradford (4)) (f. *Φιλόξενος*) ?= (2); (4) m. ii AD *IG* v (1) 160, 5 (Bradford (3)) (*Δαμ*[*όλας*]?: f. *Ἀρίστων*)

**Δαμολέων**
ARGOLIS:
—ARGOS: (1) her. D.S. v 54. 4; *RE* (-) (f. *Ἴοκλος*: oikist)
KEPHALLENIA:
—KRANIOI: (2) ?162 BC *FD* III (3) 204, 1 (*Δ*[*αμ*]*ολέων*: f. *Λέων*)

**Δαμόλυτος**
ELIS: (1) ?308 BC *IG* v (2) 550, 9 (s. *Ἀλεξιμένης*)
MESSENIA:
—MESSENE?: (2) ii/i BC *SEG* XI 979, 45

**Δαμόμαχος**
DALMATIA:
—PHAROS: (1) iv BC Brunšmid p. 20 no. 6 (*Δα-μόμα*[*ρχος?*]——ed., *Δ.*—*LGPN*: f. *Δημόδοκος*)

**Δαμονίδας**
ACHAIA:
—DYME*: (1) c. 219 BC *SGDI* 1612, 46 (*Tyche* 5 (1990) p. 124) (s. *Νικόλαος*)

**Δαμονίκα**
ARGOLIS:
—EPIDAUROS: (1) iv/iii BC *IG* IV (1)² 200
KORINTHIA:
—KORINTH: (2) ?iv BC ib. II² 9062 (Δημονίκη)
LAKONIA:
—SPARTA: (3) hell.? ib. v (1) 791 (Bradford (-))

**Δαμονίκης**
LAKONIA:
—SPARTA: (1) f. ii AD *IG* v (1) 20 B, 10; 488, 3 (Bradford (3)) (Τιβ. Κλ. Δαμονείκης: f. Τιβ. Κλ. Ὀνάσιππος); (2) c. 105-110 AD *IG* v (1) 32 B, 4 + *SEG* XI 477 (Bradford (2)) (-νεί-: s. Δαμοκλῆς); (3) c. 120-130 AD *IG* v (1) 60, 1 (Bradford (1)) (s. Δαμοκλῆς ὁ καὶ Φιλοκράτης)

**Δαμονικίδας**
LAKONIA:
—GYTHEION: (1) f. i AD *IG* v (1) 1167, 3 (s. Ῥοῦφος); (2) f. ii AD ib. 1171, 9 = II² 3596 (f. Ἀτίλιος); (3) ~ ib. v (1) 1171, 10 = II² 3596 (s. Ἀγαθοκλῆς)
—MESSA?: (4) imp. ib. v (1) 1279
—SPARTA: (5) i BC ib. 126, 8 (Bradford (8)) ([Δα]μονικίδας); (6) c. 25-1 BC *IG* v (1) 212, 38 (Bradford (11)) (f. Πρατόνικος); (7) c. 100-125 AD *IG* v (1) 137, 20 (Bradford (1)) (s. Βασιλίδας); (8) c. 105-110 AD *SEG* XI 569, 19 (Bradford (7)); (9) c. 110-120 AD *IG* v (1) 40, 12; 326, 3; *SEG* XI 478, 2; 489, 4; 490, 3 (Bradford (6)); (10) c. 120 AD *IG* v (1) 1315, 30 (Bradford (9)); (11) c. 140-160 AD *IG* v (1) 156 a, 4; *SEG* XI 600, 5 (Bradford (3)) (-νει-: II s. Δαμονικίδας I); (12) ~ *IG* v (1) 156 a, [4]; *SEG* XI 600, 6 (Bradford (10)) (-νει-: I f. Δαμονικίδας II)

**Δαμόνικος**
AKARNANIA:
—OINIADAI: (1) s. iii BC *IG* IX (1)² (2) 422; Fraser–Rönne, *BWGT* pl. 25 (f. Σωτίων)
ARGOLIS:
—HERMIONE: (2) ii-i BC *IG* IV (1) 732 IV, 11 (f. Λίβυς)
ARKADIA:
—MEGALOPOLIS: (3) ?262-255 BC Nachtergael, *Les Galates* 5, [16]; 18, 1 (s. Ἰασίδαμος); (4) c. 210 BC *IG* IX (1)² (1) 31, 78 (f. Ἡραιος, Λυσίων)
—TEGEA: (5) i BC/i AD ib. v (2) 83 (Δαμόνικ[ος]: s. Φιλοκράτης); (6) ~ ib. (Δαμόνικ[ος]: f. Φιλοκράτης)
—TORTHYNEION: (7) ?iii BC *FD* III (2) 193, 5 (f. Εὐρύδικος) ?= (9); (8) 263 BC *IG* IX (1)² (1) 17, 37 (s. Εὐρύδικος); (9) c. 230-200 BC *BCH* 45 (1921) p. 14 II, 123 (f. Εὐρύδικος) ?= (7)
ELIS: (10) 12 BC Paus. v 21. 16 (f. Πολύκτωρ)
ILLYRIA:
—BYLLIONES: (11) i BC Cabanes, *L'Épire* p. 562 no. 36 (*SEG* XXXVIII 570) (s. Νικαν—)
KORINTHIA:
—KORINTH: (12) i BC-i AD *ILGR* 98, 3 (Lat. L. Antonius Damonicus: f. Antonia)
LAKONIA: (13) ii-i BC *BCH* 19 (1895) p. 373 no. 23 (s. —ικίδας)
—BOIAI: (14) imp.? *IG* v (1) 952, 16
—SPARTA: (15) s. i BC ib. 94, 12; 95, 4 (Bradford (10)) (Δαμό[νικος]: I f. Δαμόνικος II); (16) ~ *IG* v (1) 94, 12; 95, 4 (Bradford (2)) (II s. Δαμόνικος I); (17) i AD *SEG* XI 828 (Bradford (7)) (II s. Δαμόνικος I); (18) ~ *SEG* XI [828] (I f. Δαμόνικος II); (19) c. 90-100 AD ib. 560, 6 (Bradford (8)) ?= (2); (20) c. 90-110 AD *IG* v (1) 80, 7; *SEG* XI 563, 4 (Bradford (11)) (f. Καλλικράτης); (21) c. 105-110 AD *SEG* XI 564, 20 (Bradford (8)) (Τιβ. Κλ. Δαμόνεικο[ς]); (22) c. 105-122 AD *SEG* XI 569, 21; 574, 3 (Bradford (12)) ([Δαμόν]εικος—574: f. Φίλιππος); (23) c. 125 AD *IG* v (1) 1314, 7 (Bradford (1)) (s.

Ἀρίων); (24) m. ii AD *IG* v (1) 108, 5 (Bradford (3)) (-νει-); (25) ~ *SEG* XI 838, 7; cf. Stephanis 1164 (Bradford (13)) (f. Θεόδωρος); (26) ?134 AD *IG* v (1) 62, 10 (Bradford (6)) (-νει-: s. Ἰεροκλῆς); (27) c. 140-160 AD *IG* v (1) 65, 28; 85, 7; *SEG* XI 528, 3 (Bradford (5)) (I s. Εὔτυχος, f. Δαμόνικος II); (28) ~ *IG* v (1) 65, 28; 85, 6; *SEG* XI 528, 3 (Bradford (3)) (II s. Δαμόνικος I); (29) ~ *IG* v (1) 112, 5 (Bradford (3)) (I f. Δαμόνικος II); (30) ~ *IG* v (1) 112, 5 (Bradford (4)) (II s. Δαμόνικος I); (31) ~ *IG* v (1) 112, 14 (Bradford (3)) (I f. Δαμόνικος II); (32) ~ *IG* v (1) 112, 14 (Bradford (4)) (II s. Δαμόνικος I); (33) c. 230-260 AD *SEG* XI 633, 5 (Bradford (9)) (f. Αὐρ. Ἀρίστων)
MESSENIA:
—MESSENE: (34) f. iii BC *PAE* 1991, p. 99 no. 7, 10; (35) 243 BC *SEG* XII 371, 18 (s. Μαντικράτης); (36) i AD ib. XXIII 220 a, 1; 220 b, 2 (f. Μεγώ); (37) 33 AD ib. XLI 335, 6 (s. Μαντικράτης)

**Δαμονίκων**
ILLYRIA:
—APOLLONIA: (1) hell. *IApoll* 350 (tile) ([Δ]αμονίκων?: s. Θερσέας)

**Δαμονοῖς**
ARGOLIS:
—ARGOS: (1) 105 BC *JÖAI* 14 (1911) Beibl. p. 146 no. 4, 8 (Δαμο[ν]ο[ῖ]s: d. Δάτος)

**Δαμόνομος**
ARKADIA:
—MEGALOPOLIS: (1) iii BC *Coll. Alex.* p. 206 no. 5, 3

**Δαμόνοος**
ACHAIA:
—PELLENE: (1) 336 BC *CID* II 24 II, 19
ARGOLIS:
—EPIDAUROS*: (2) c. 370 BC *IG* IV (1)² 102, 32 (Δαμ[ό]νοος)

**Δαμοξένα**
ARGOLIS:
—EPIDAUROS: (1) iii/ii BC ib. 354 (Peek, *IAEpid* 153. 2)
ARKADIA:
—KLEITOR: (2) imp. *IG* v (2) 378
—MEGALOPOLIS: (3) iii BC ib. 478, 6
ELIS: (4) s. i AD *IvOl* 429, 7 (Κλ. Δ.: d. Ἀντ. Κλεοδίκη)
EPIROS:
—BOUTHROTOS (PRASAIBOI): (5) a. 163 BC *IBouthrot* 25, 25 (*SEG* XXXVIII 483); (6) ~ *IBouthrot* 29, 40 (*SEG* XXXVIII 487); (7) ~ *IBouthrot* 39, 6 (*SEG* XXXVIII 498)
—MOLOSSOI: (8) iii/ii BC *Syll*³ 1206, 3; cf. Cabanes, *L'Épire* p. 583 no. 60 ([Δ]αμοξένα)
KERKYRA: (9) hell.-imp. *IG* IX (1) 587 + Unp. (*IG* arch.) (locn.)

**Δαμοξενίδας**
ARKADIA:
—MAINALIOI: (1) c. 400-370 BC *RE* (-); Moretti, *Olymp.* 393
LAKONIA:
—SPARTA: (2) c. 500 BC *SEG* XI 638, 7; *LSAG*² p. 201 no. 44 (date)

**Δαμόξενος**
ACHAIA: (1) c. 185 BC *Milet* I (3) 148, 18; *Chiron* 19 (1989) pp. 279 ff. (date) (Δα[μόξενος]) ?= (2)
—AIGION: (2) 196 BC Plb. xviii 42. 6 ?= (1)
AITOLIA: (3) ?252-248 BC *Syll*³ 422, 4
AKARNANIA:
—ANAKTORION: (4) hell. *AD* 44 (1989) Chron. p. 145
—ECHINOS?: (5) ii BC *IG* IX (1)² (2) 374

ARKADIA:
—MANTINEIA-ANTIGONEIA: (6) c. 315-280 BC *FD* III (1) 43, 2 (f. Καλλίερος); (7) c. 300-221 BC *IG* v (2) 323. 58 (tessera) (s. Νέαρχος)
—ORCHOMENOS: (8) ?ii BC ib. 345, 5 (s. Ἀ—, Ἄντεια: date—*LGPN*); (9) ~ ib. l. 8 (s. Ἀγίας, f. Ἄντεια: date—*LGPN*)
—TEGEA: (Hippothoitai): (10) iv/iii BC ib. 38, 51 (s. Ὠφελίων)
ELIS: (11) 191-146 BC *ZfN* 9 (1882) p. 270 no. 24; Unp. (Paris, BN) (coins)
ILLYRIA:
—EPIDAMNOS-DYRRHACHION: (12) hell.-imp. *IDyrrh* 78 (f. Ἀγάθων)
PELOPONNESE: (13) 112 BC *FD* III (2) 70 A, 30
S. ITALY (CALABRIA):
—TARAS-TARENTUM: (14) f. iv BC *IG* II² 248, [1], [15], 18 ([Δα]μόξεν[ος]: s. Φιλόδαμος) ?= (15); (15) c. 356-355 BC ib. IV (1)² 95, 44 (Perlman E.2); Perlman pp. 46-9 (date) ?= (14)
S. ITALY (LUCANIA):
—HERAKLEIA: (16) c. 85 BC *ID* 2002, 1 (f. Γοργίας)
SICILY:
—SYRACUSE: (17) ?v-iv BC Paus. viii 40. 3-5

**Δαμοπείθης**
AKARNANIA:
—ASTAKOS: (1) iii/ii BC *IG* IX (1)² (2) 439
ARGOLIS:
—ARGOS: (2) iii/ii BC ib. IV (1)² 205, 4; 208, 4; 243, 4; 244, 9; 318; 696; 697 (f. Λαβρέας)
—EPIDAUROS: (3) iv BC ib. 178; 179; 180; Peek, *NIEpid* 34; (4) c. 365-335 BC *IG* IV (1)² 103, 139, 141 ?= (5)
——(Azantioi): (5) c. 335-325 BC ib. 106 III, 40; 108, 160 ?= (4)
ARKADIA:
—TEGEA:
——(Athaneatai): (6) iv/iii BC ib. v (2) 38, 19 (f. Θῆρις)

**Δᾶμος**
ARGOLIS:
—ARGOS*: (1) ii BC *BCH* 33 (1909) pp. 456-7 no. 23, 12 (slave/freed.?)
—EPIDAUROS: (2) ?ii BC *IG* IV (1)² 335, 2; cf. Peek, *IAEpid* 144 (f. Μίκυλλος)

**Δαμοσθένεια**
ARGOLIS:
—ARGOS: (1) ii BC *SEG* XLII 279, 23 (d. Νικόδαμος)
—ARGOS*: (2) f. iii BC *IG* IV (1) 529, 16 ([Δα]μοσθένεια: slave/freed.?)
—TROIZEN: (3) iii BC ib. 772, 2 (d. Ἀπολλόδωρος, Εὐτυχίς)
LAKONIA:
—OITYLOS: (4) a. 212 AD ib. v (1) 1301 a (Αὐρ. Δ.: d. Φιλάριστος)
—PYRRHICHOS: (5) ?ii-i BC ib. 1282, 18, 19 (-νηα)
—SPARTA: (6) m. i AD ib. 509, 3; *ID* 1629, 2 (Bradford (2)) (and Athens Marathon: Δαμοσθένια—*ID*: d. Λυσίνικος); (7) ?s. ii AD *IG* v (1) 576 (Bradford (1)); (8) ii/iii AD *IG* v (1) 497, 21; 499; 587, 12; 589, 4; 590, 5; *SEG* XXXV 315, [4]; *BSA* 80 (1985) pp. 225; 232-5 (ident., stemma) (Bradford (3)) (Κλ. Δ.: I d. Τιβ. Κλ. Πρατόλαος, m. Τιβ. Κλ. Πρατόλαος ὁ καὶ Δαμοκρατίδας, Κλ. Δαμοσθένεια II, Κλ. Τυραννίς, Κλ. Πόλλα); (9) c. 198-212 AD *IG* v (1) 590, 4; *BSA* 79 (1984) pp. 279-83 (date); 80 (1985) pp. 225; 238-9 (ident., stemma) (Bradford (1)) (Κλ. Δ.: II d. Τιβ. Κλ. Εὔδαμος, Κλ. Δαμοσθένεια I)

**Δαμοσθένης**
AITOLIA: (1) ?209 or 205 BC Nachtergael, *Les Galates* 68, 1 (f. Δε←—της)
—APERANTOI: (2) ii-i BC *SEG* XVII 275, 4 (*L'Illyrie mérid.* I p. 110 fig. 8)

—KALYDON: (**3**) a. 142 BC *IG* IX (1)² (1) 137, 80

ARGOLIS:

—ARGOS: (**4**) c. 365-335 BC ib. IV (1)² 103, 167; (**5**) iii BC ib. II² 8364 ([Δ]αμοσθ[ένης]: s. Τιμοκράτης); (**6**) ~ ib. IV (1) 585 (Δαμοσθέ[νης]: I f. Δαμοσθένης II); (**7**) ~ ib. (Δαμο[σθένης]: II s. Δαμοσθένης I); (**8**) ~ ib. 618 I, 5 ([Δα]μοσθένης: s. Ἄλκις); (**9**) f. iii BC *CID* II 122 I, 14 (s. Ἀρίσταρχος); (**10**) c. 146-32 BC *BMC Pelop.* p. 145 no. 112 (coin) (Δαμοσθέ(νης)); (**11**) i-ii AD *IG* IV (1) 587, 5 (Γ. Δαμοσθέ[νης])

——(Dionysioi): (**12**) f. iii BC ib. 529, 21

——(Paionidai): (**13**) ii/i BC *BCH* 33 (1909) p. 176 no. 2, 5 (s. Νικοκράτης)

—EPIDAUROS: (**14**) iv BC *IG* IV (1)² 252 (s. Ἐπικράτης); (**15**) iv-iii BC ib. 10 ([Δα]μοσθένης, [Τι]μοσθένης?); (**16**) c. 370 BC ib. 102, 93; (**17**) iii BC *SEG* xxx 396 (Δαμοσθέν[ης]: s. Ἀρισ—); (**18**) i-ii AD *IG* IV (1)² 505

—EPIDAUROS*: (**19**) c. 370-365 BC Peek, *IA-Epid* 52 A, 46

—PHLEIOUS: (**20**) c. 220-200 BC *SEG* XI 414, 10 (Perlman E.5) (f. Κλέανδρος)

ARKADIA:

—MANTINEIA-ANTIGONEIA: (**21**) i BC *IG* V (2) 329

—STYMPHALOS: (**22**) iii BC ib. 355, 5 (Δαμοσθ[ένης])

—TEGEA: (**23**) iv-iii BC ib. 103

——(Athaneatai): (**24**) iv/iii BC ib. 38, 14 ([Δ]αμοσθένης)

EPIROS: (**25**) hell. *SGDI* 1360; cf. Cabanes, *L'Épire* p. 584 no. 64 (Δαμοσ[θένης])

ITHAKE: (**26**) ?i BC *IG* IX (1) 679 (Fraser-Rönne, *BWGT* p. 119 no. 6)

KERKYRA: (**27**) 214 BC *IG* IX (1)² (1) 31, 158 (I f. Δαμοσθένης II); (**28**) ~ ib. l. 158 (II s. Δαμοσθένης I)

LAKONIA:

—SPARTA: (**29**) inc. Plu., *Mor.* 801 C (Poralla² 231); (**30**) c. 160-170 AD *IG* V (1) 109, 6 (Bradford (-)) (Γ. Ἰο[ύ]λ. Δαμο[σθέ]νης)

—TEUTHRONE: (**31**) imp. *IG* V (1) 1220 b

MESSENIA:

—THOURIA: (**32**) f. ii BC *SEG* XI 972, 71 (f. Κλέων); (**33**) ii/i BC *IG* V (1) 1384, 11 (f. Δεινίας)

**Δαμοσσός**

AIGINA: (**1**) vi/v BC *SEG* XXIII 169; *LSAG*² p. 439 no. 10 (f. Κλήνα)

**Δαμοστράτα**

ACHAIA:

—PELLENE: (**1**) ?ii-iii AD *SEG* XI 1274, 3; (**2**) ~ ib. l. 5

KORINTHIA:

—SIKYON: (**3**) hell. *IG* VII 2631

LEUKAS: (**4**) iii BC *AM* 27 (1902) p. 370 no. 41 b

**Δαμοστράτη**

AIGINA: (**1**) imp. *IG* IV (1) 97

**Δαμόστρατος**

ARGOLIS:

—ARGOS: (**1**) ii/i BC ib. 608 (Δαμόστ[ρ]ατος: s. Σῶσος)

—EPIDAUROS: (**2**) iv/iii BC ib. IV (1)² 200

—EPIDAUROS*: (**3**) c. 290-270 BC ib. 109 II, 97, 148; IV, 113

ARKADIA:

—PHENEOS: (**4**) her.? *FGrH* 42 F 5 (Δη-: f. Δαμόδικος: fict.)

—TEGEA: (**5**) m. iv BC *IG* V (2) 6, 97, 99; (**6**) f. iii BC ib. 36, 60; (**7**) i BC ib. 164 (Δαμόσ[τρ]ατος); (**8**) i/ii AD ib. 63

——(Hippothoitai): (**9**) m. iii BC ib. 36, 82 (s. Ἀριστόλας)

EPIROS:

—BOUTHROTOS: (**10**) ?i AD *IBouthrot* 201 (Τίτος Πομπώνιος Δ.)

KEPHALLENIA:

—PALE: (**11**) iii/ii BC Unp. (*IG* arch.)

KERKYRA: (**12**) c. 229-48 BC *BMC Thessaly* p. 147 nos. 499-503; *SNG Cop. Epirus-Acarnania* 230 (coins); (**13**) ?ii BC *IG* IX (1) 762-8; *Korkyra* 1 p. 167 no. 7 (tiles); (**14**) i BC ib. p. 167 no. 8

KORINTHIA:

—KORINTH: (**15**) ?vi/v BC *Hesp.* 41 (1972) p. 211 no. 11; (**16**) 343 BC *CID* II 31, 101

KYNOURIA:

—GLYMPEIS?: (**17**) ?i AD *SEG* XXXV 281 (s. Πολυκράτης)

LAKONIA:

—SPARTA: (**18**) hell.? *IG* V (1) 800 (Bradford (3)) (f. Πλειστονίκα); (**19**) s. i BC *IG* V (1) 95, 14 (Bradford (2)) (f. Φιλόστρατος); (**20**) c. 1-10 AD *IG* V (1) 209, 7; *SEG* XXXV 331 (date) (Bradford (4)) (f. Τιμόδαμος) ?= (**21**); (**21**) ~ *IG* V (1) 209, 29; *SEG* XXXV 331 (date) (Bradford (1)) ?= (**20**)

MESSENIA:

—MESSENE: (**22**) iii BC *SEG* XXIII 210, 21

—MESSENE?: (**23**) ii/i BC ib. XI 979, 19, 60

—THOURIA: (**24**) f. ii BC ib. 972, 65 (s. Εὐνικίδας)

**Δαμόσων**

ARGOLIS:

—ARGOS: (**1**) 31 BC-14 AD *IvOl* 420, 3 (f. Κλεογένης)

**Δαμοτάγης**

ARKADIA:

—KLEITOR: (**1**) c. 230-200 BC *BCH* 45 (1921) p. 12 II, 70 + *SEG* XXX 494 (s. Ἀλειός)

S. ITALY (LUCANIA):

—METAPONTION: (**2**) iv BC Iamb., *VP* 267 (*FVS* 1 p. 446)

**Δαμότας**

KORINTHIA:

—SIKYON?: (**1**) 263 BC *IG* IX (1)² (1) 17, 53 (s. Νικάνωρ)

**Δαμοτέλης**

ARGOLIS:

—ARGOS: (**1**) ?m. v BC ib. IV (1) 615, 4 (Δαμοτ[έ]λη[ς]: ?f. —ικράτης)

—EPIDAUROS: (**2**) iv/iii BC ib. IV (1)² 200 (s. Δαμοκλῆς)

—EPIDAUROS*: (**3**) c. 370-365 BC Peek, *IAEpid* 52 B, 6, 54, 71

—TROIZEN: (**4**) iv BC *IG* IV (1) 764, 6 (s. Πατρέας)

—TROIZEN*: (**5**) iv BC ib. 823, 63

ARKADIA:

—ASEA: (**6**) c. 230-200 BC *BCH* 45 (1921) p. 15 III, 9 (s. Δα—)

—MANTINEIA-ANTIGONEIA: (**7**) c. 300-221 BC *IG* V (2) 323. 74 (tessera) (f. Ἀριστόνικος)

—MEGALOPOLIS: (**8**) s. ii BC ib. 439, 79

—METHYDRION: (**9**) a. 420 BC *REG* 62 (1949) p. 6, 6 (Δ[αμ]οτέλης)

KEPHALLENIA:

—SAME: (**10**) f. iii BC *Op. Ath.* 10 (1971) p. 66 no. 12 (*BCH* 83 (1959) p. 658)

KORINTHIA:

—SIKYON: (**11**) 262 or 258 BC Nachtergael, *Les Galates* 5, 32-3; cf. Stephanis 2775-6

LAKONIA:

—SPARTA: (**12**) iv/iii BC J., *AJ* xii 227; xiii 167 (Bradford (-)) (fict.?); (**13**) 222 BC Plu., *Cleom.* 28 (Bradford (1)); (**14**) c. 90-125 AD *IG* V (1) 152, 6; *SEG* XI 570, 2 (Bradford (3)) (I f. Δαμοτέλης II); (**15**) ~ *IG* V (1) 152, 6; *SEG* XI 570, 2 (Bradford (2)) (II s. Δαμοτέλης I)

—SPARTA?: (**16**) 367 BC X., *HG* vii 1. 32 (Poralla² 232) (Δη-)

MESSENIA:

—THOURIA: (**17**) ii/i BC *IG* V (1) 1384, 5 (f. Ἀρασίδαμος)

S. ITALY (BRUTTIUM):

—LOKROI EPIZEPHYRIOI: (**18**) 425 BC Th. iv 25. 11 (Δη-)

S. ITALY (CALABRIA):

—TARAS-TARENTUM: (**19**) iv/iii BC *IG* XIV 668 I, 19 (Landi, *DISMG* 194)

S. ITALY (LUCANIA): (**20**) c. 420-400 BC Trendall, *Early S. It. Vase-painting* 371; cf. *RA* 1993, p. 59 no. 10

**Δαμότιμος**

ACHAIA:

—PATRAI: (**1**) c. 146-32 BC *BMC Pelop.* p. 22 no. 6 (coin) (f. Λύκων)

AITOLIA: (**2**) 244 or 240 BC *SGDI* 2511, 2 (Flacelière p. 402 no. 29); (**3**) ~ *SGDI* 2511, 2 (Flacelière p. 402 no. 29); (**4**) 138-135 BC *IG* IX (1)² (3) 635, 1

—AGRINION: (**5**) 193 BC *Syll*³ 603, 3

—TRICHONION: (**6**) 185 BC *IG* IX (1)² (1) 32, 43

AKARNANIA:

—ANAKTORION: (**7**) c. 325-315 BC *Hesp.* 57 (1988) p. 148 A, 22 (*SEG* XXXVI 331); cf. *Hesp.* 48 (1979) pp. 78 f. with pl. 22 c (s. Ἀνδρόμαχος)

ARGOLIS:

—ARGOS: (**8**) m. v BC Unp. (Ch. Kritzas); (**9**) a. 303 BC *CEG* II 816, 22

—TROIZEN: (**10**) ?c. 550-525 BC ib. I 138 (s. Ἀμφιδάμα)

ARKADIA:

—TEGEA: (**11**) f. iii BC *IG* V (2) 35, 24 (s. Εὔδαμος)

——(Hippothoitai): (**12**) ?s. iv BC ib. 39, 10

EPIROS:

—AMBRAKIA: (**13**) ?253 BC Nachtergael, *Les Galates* 10, 62 (s. Τίμων); (**14**) f. ii BC Unp. (Arta Mus., inscr.) (s. Δαμοκλῆς)

KEPHALLENIA:

—SAME: (**15**) hell.-imp.? *SEG* XL 466

KORINTHIA:

—SIKYON: (**16**) 423 BC Th. iv 119. 2 (Skalet 92) (s. Ναυκράτης)

LAKONIA:

—SPARTA: (**17**) s. vii BC *PMGF* 1 10 b, 12 (Δαμοτιμίδας (patr. adj.): f. Ἀγησίδαμος)

MESSENIA:

—THOURIA: (**18**) ii-i BC *IG* V (1) 1385, 36 (f. Λο...πης)

**Δαμοτίων**

AKARNANIA:

—STRATOS: (**1**) a. 167 BC ib. IX (1)² (1) 36, 4, 9 (f. Μεννέας)

LAKONIA:

—SPARTA: (**2**) c. 25-1 BC ib. V (1) 50, 28 (Bradford (-)) (Δαμοτί[ων]: f. Δεινοκράτης)

PELOPONNESE: (**3**) c. 192 BC *SEG* XIII 327, 14 (s. Ἀριστόδικος)

**Δαμοῦς**

LAKONIA:

—SPARTA: (**1**) ii AD *IG* V (1) 1187 (*GVI* 1548); cf. *SEG* XXXVI 355 (Bradford (-)) (Δαμοῦ (voc.)—*IG*, Δαμού (voc.)—*SEG*)

**Δάμουσα**

LAKONIA:

—SPARTA: (**1**) ii AD *SEG* XXXVI 363; (**2**) ii-iii AD *IG* V (1) 779 (Bradford (-))

—ZARAX: (**3**) ii-iii AD *SEG* XI 894 b III (d. Καλλίστρατος)

**Δαμουχίδας**

KERKYRA: (**1**) ?iii BC *IG* IX (1) 695, 5 (s. Εὐκλείδας)

**Δαμοφάνης**

AITOLIA:

—POTIDANIA: (**1**) 193 BC *Syll*³ 603, 4

ARGOLIS:

—ARGOS: (**2**) c. 458 BC *IG* I³ 1149, 71 (-νε̄ς)

—EPIDAUROS: (3) ii BC ib. IV (1)² 211 (s. Δάμων, Δαμαρέτα) ?= (5); (4) ~ ib. (f. Δάμων); (5) m. i BC ib. 170; 220; 251; 650; 661 (f. Κλεαιχμίδας, Σώδαμος, Λαφάντα) ?= (3)
—EPIDAUROS*: (6) c. 370-360 BC ib. 102, 62, 72-3, 93, 110, 268, 291; 103, 34, 45, 48-51, 66, 74-5, 81, 92, 117; Peek, IAEpid 52 A, 20; BSA 61 (1966) p. 271 no. 4 A, 23-5; (7) ii-i BC Peek, IAEpid 276 ([Δα]μοφάνης)
—TROIZEN*: (8) iv BC IG IV (1) 823, 6, 20, 23, 28

KORINTHIA:
—KORINTH: (9) 357-343 BC CID II 10 A I, 11; 31, 12, 21, 22, 76, 87, 95; 120 A, 33 (s. Μναισίδαμος); (10) iii BC Peek, NIEpid 13, 5 (Δαμοφάνης: s. Ἀκεστορίδας)

## Δαμόφαντος

ARGOLIS:
—ARGOS: (1) ?253 BC Nachtergael, Les Galates 6, [6]; 10, 47; cf. Stephanis 1199 (f. Θέστων)
—TROIZEN: (2) iv BC IG IV (1) 823, 50

ARKADIA:
—TEGEA*: (3) f. iii BC ib. v (2) 36, 9

ELIS: (4) 209 BC Plu., Phil. 7

LAKONIA:
—HYPERTELEATON*: (5) imp. IG v (1) 1078

MESSENIA:
—THOURIA: (6) f. ii BC SEG XI 972, 56 (s. Δαμοθάλης, f. Δαμοθάλης)

SICILY:
—GELA-PHINTIAS?: (7) f. v BC Dubois, IGDS 134 b, 9 (Arena, Iscr. Sic. II 47)

## Δαμοφάων

ARKADIA:
—MANTINEIA-ANTIGONEIA:
——(Posoidaia): (1) c. 425-400 BC SEG XXXI 348, 15
—TEGEA: (2) m. iv BC IG v (2) 6, 91

S. ITALY (BRUTTIUM):
—LOKROI EPIZEPHYRIOI:
——(Ϝαγ.): (3) iv/iii BC De Franciscis 19, 7 (f. Χαιρέλας)

## Δαμοφίλη

ILLYRIA:
—APOLLONIA: (1) hell.-imp. IApoll 66

## Δαμόφιλος

AITOLIA: (1) hell. ZPE 108 (1995) p. 91 no. 5 (s. Ἀλεξίμαχος); (2) iii/ii BC Pantos, Sphragismata p. 150 no. 120; p. 447 f.

ARGOLIS:
—ARGOS: (3) i BC IG IV (1)² 700 (f. Δίων)
——(Pamphyloi-Olisseidai): (4) ii-i BC Mnem. NS 47 (1919) p. 164 no. 9, 10 (f. —λος)
—EPIDAUROS: (5) c. 365-335 BC IG IV (1)² 103, 142; (6) c. 350-250 BC AAA 5 (1972) p. 358 fig. 20; (7) c. 310-300 BC IG IV (1)² 114, 3, 10; SEG XXV 399, 10; (8) iii BC IG IV (1)² 349 (f. Τιμώ, Λέων)
——(Azantioi): (9) 146 BC ib. 28, 46 (f. Λυσέας)
——Agrias: (10) c. 335-325 BC ib. 108, 152, 155-6, 168
—EPIDAUROS*: (11) c. 335-325 BC ib. 106 I, 63, 85, 94, 96, 114
—HERMIONE: (12) ?ii-i BC ib. IV (1) 733, 8 (s. Ἐθ—)

ARKADIA:
—MEGALOPOLIS: (13) c. 272 BC ib. IX (1)² (1) 13, 8 (f. Σάνοννος)
—TEGEA: (14) ?s. iv BC ib. v (2) 39, 6 (f. —νετος)
——(Hippothoitai): (15) iv/iii BC ib. 38, 44 (f. Καλλίας)

EPIROS:
—AMBRAKIA: (16) s. iv BC SEG XVII 304 (f. Λῆνα)

ILLYRIA:
—APOLLONIA: (17) i BC Ceka, Probleme p. 139 no. 8 (coin) (pryt.)

---

—EPIDAMNOS-DYRRHACHION: (18) c. 250-50 BC IApoll Ref. Bibl. n. 32 (coin) (pryt.)

ITHAKE: (19) hell. IG IX (1) 665

KEPHALLENIA:
—KRANIOI: (20) c. 230-200 BC BCH 45 (1921) p. 14 II, 139 (s. Δαμοφῶν)

KERKYRA: (21) ?ii BC IG IX (1) 769; Korkyra I pp. 167-8 nos. 9-11 (tiles)

KORINTHIA:
—KORINTH: (22) vi BC IG IV (1) 307 (pinax)

LAKONIA: (23) i BC ib. II² p. 884 no. 9152 a (f. Πασινίκα)
—LEUKAS: (24) iv/iii BC Carapanos, Dodone p. 40 no. 2 (IGA 339) (f. Φιλοκλείδα); (25) iii BC AM 27 (1902) p. 370 no. 45 b

SICILY:
—HENNA: (26) c. 139 BC RE (6)
—HIMERA: (27) vi/v BC ib. (8); Overbeck 616 (sculptor/painter)
—SYRACUSE?: (28) 312-307 BC RE s.v. Demophilos (7)
—TAUROMENION:
——(Δαμ.): (29) ?ii/i BC IG XIV 421 D an. 8; 421 D an. 12 (SGDI 5219) (s. Ἐπαίνετος, f. Ἐπαίνετος)
—THERMAI HIMERAIAI*: (30) i-ii AD Eph. Ep. VIII 706 (ILat. Term. Imer. 112) (Lat. Damop[hilus]: freed.)

## Δαμοφόων

AIGINA: (1) ?c. 480-470 BC IG IV (1) 7 (Lazzarini 719; CEG I 349); LSAG² p. 113 no. 15 (date) (f. Φιλόστρατος)

## Δαμοφῶν

AKARNANIA:
—THYRREION: (1) iii-ii BC SEG XXVII 159, 7; cf. PAE 1977, pl. 244 a (f. Διονύσιος)

ARGOLIS:
—ARGOS: (2) s. ii BC Unp. (Ch. Kritzas) (f. Κλεήρατος)
—EPIDAUROS: (3) c. 335-325 BC IG IV (1)² 108, 111
—EPIDAUROS*: (4) c. 370 BC ib. 102, 67

ELIS:
—PISA: (5) vii/vi BC Paus. v 16. 5; vi 22. 3 (s. Πανταλέων)

ILLYRIA:
—APOLLONIA: (6) c. 250-50 BC Maier 36 (coin) (Ceka 115) (pryt.)

KEPHALLENIA:
—KRANIOI: (7) c. 230-200 BC BCH 45 (1921) p. 14 II, 139 (f. Ἀρίστων, Σατυρίων, Δαμόφιλος)

LAKONIA:
—SPARTA: (8) c. 450-434 BC IG v (1) 1230, 5; LSAG² p. 201 no. 54 (date) (Poralla² 218) (-φῶν)

MESSENIA:
—MESSENE: (9) ii BC SEG XLI 349 (f. Ξενόφιλος) ?= (11); (10) ~ ib. 352 A (s. Ξενόφιλος, f. Ξενόφιλος, Φίλιππος: sculptor); (11) f. ii BC Kl. Pauly (-); Sculpture from Arcadia and Laconia p. 102, 2, 36 (SEG XLI 333) (I s. Φίλιππος, f. Δαμοφῶν II: sculptor) ?= (9); (12) ii/i BC IG v (2) 539-40; SEG XLI 352 B (II s. Δαμοφῶν I, Νικίππα, f. Ξενόφιλος, Δαμοφῶν III); (13) ~ IG v (2) 539-40 + SEG XLI 352 B (III s. Δαμοφῶν II: sculptor?)
—MESSENE?: (14) ii BC IG v (2) 454

S. ITALY (BRUTTIUM):
—KROTON: (15) s. vi BC Iamb., VP 265 (f. Ἀρισταῖος)

SICILY:
—LIPARA: (16) iii-ii BC SEG XLII 862

## Δαμοχάρης

ACHAIA: (1) 146 BC IG IV (1)² 28, 82 (s. Φοινικίδας: synoikos); (2) ~ ib. l. 138 (f. Βότρυς: synoikos)

ARGOLIS:
—EPIDAUROS: (3) iii BC ib. 160

---

KORINTHIA:
—KORINTH: (4) 324 BC CID II 102 I, 7

LAKONIA:
—SPARTA: (5) 241 BC Plu., Agis 18-19 (Bradford (-))

## Δαμόχαρις

ARKADIA:
—MEGALOPOLIS: (1) hell.? IG v (2) 448, 7 (Δαμόχαρις)

ELIS?: (2) iii BC CIRB 1194 ([Δ]ημόχαρις: s. Νικασίων)

KORINTHIA:
—SIKYON: (3) vi/v BC SEG XI 244, 40

LAKONIA:
—GERONTHRAI: (4) 72 BC IG v (1) 1114, 1
—MESSA?: (5) imp. ib. 1280, 1 (s. Σωτιμίδας)
—SPARTA: (6) i BC/i AD ib. 48, 2 (Bradford (1)) (s. Μελάνιππος); (7) ~ IG v (1) 48, 9; SEG XI 974, 1, 27 (Bradford (2)) (s. Τιμόξενος); (8) ~ IG v (1) 146, 3 (Bradford (3)) ([Δα]μόχαρις); (9) c. 1-10 AD IG v (1) 209, 21; SEG XXXV 331 (date) (Bradford (4)) (f. (ad.) Ἀριστόπολις)
—TEUTHRONE: (10) i BC/i AD IG v (2) 538 (s. Σωτιμίδας, f. Σωτιμίδας)

## Δαμόχαρτος

ARGOLIS:
—ARGOS: (1) iii BC Peek, NIEpid 46 = SEG XVII 179 (f. Δαμόκριτος); (2) iii/ii BC IG IV (1) 498, 2; SEG XI 303 a (locn.)

## Δαμυλίς

SICILY:
—PALAGONIA (MOD.): (1) iii-ii BC ib. XLII 850

## Δάμυλλος

ARKADIA:
—MEGALOPOLIS?: (1) m. i AD IG v (2) 516, 3; 541; 542 (s. Ζευξίας)

## Δάμυλος

ARGOLIS:
—EPIDAUROS: (1) ii/i BC ib. IV (1)² 232, 1 (f. Ἀριστοκράτης); (2) ~ ib. l. 4 (s. Ἀριστοκράτης, Εὐαρέτα)

ARKADIA:
—TEGEA: (3) 165 AD ib. v (2) 50, 49 (freed.)

LAKONIA:
—HYPERTELEATON*: (4) imp. ib. v (1) 1033
—SPARTA: (5) ?ii-i BC ib. 914 (Bradford (2)) (s. Κόσμος); (6) ii-iii AD IG v (1) 802 b (Bradford (1)) (s. Καλλίστρατος)

LEUKAS: (7) c. 167-50 BC BMC Thessaly p. 179 no. 86; p. 181 nos. 104 and 110; p. 183 f. nos. 140-4; p. 186 nos. 173-6; SNG Cop. Epirus–Acarnania 381; 389 (coins); (8) f. i BC IG IX (1) 534, 6 (Iscr. Gr. Verona p. 24) (I f. Δαμύλος II); (9) ~ IG IX (1) 534, 6 (Iscr. Gr. Verona p. 24) (II s. Δαμύλος I)

S. ITALY (CALABRIA):
—TARAS-TARENTUM: (10) c. 280-272 BC Vlasto 750-3 (coins)

## Δᾶμυς

EPIROS:
—DODONA*: (1) v-iv BC SEG XV 391 c

PELOPONNESE: (2) s. iii BC ib. XIII 278, 13

## Δαμώ

AIGINA?: (1) imp. EAD XXX p. 356 no. 20 (d. Διογένης)

ARGOLIS:
—ARGOS: (2) iii BC IG II² 8365
—EPIDAUROS: (3) ii/i BC ib. IV (1)² 232, 5 (d. Ἀριστοκράτης, Εὐαρέτα)
—KLEONAI: (4) c. 230-200 BC BCH 45 (1921) p. 15 II, 148 (d. Εὐρύδαμος)

ARKADIA:
—STYMPHALOS: (5) ii BC SEG XLII 363 ([Δ]αμώ)

DALMATIA:
—ISSA: (6) iii/ii BC ib. XXXI 601 (VAHD 84 (1991) p. 258 no. 8) (d. Πυθήν)

**Δάμων**

ELIS: (**7**) m. i BC *IvOl* 410 (d. Θεότιμος); (**8**) ?i AD ib. 414 (d. Ἀριστόμαχος, m. Δαμάρετος)

EPIROS:
—BOUTHROTOS (PRASAIBOI): (**9**) a. 163 BC *IBouthrot* 33, 3 (*SEG* XXXVIII 492)

ILLYRIA:
—APOLLONIA: (**10**) ii BC *IApoll* 67
—EPIDAMNOS-DYRRHACHION: (**11**) hell.-imp. *IDyrrh* 167 (Δαμώ: d. Μυρτίλος)

ITHAKE: (**12**) hell. *IG* IX (1) 660 (Δαμῶς (gen.?)); (**13**) ?ii BC *AM* 27 (1902) p. 377 no. 63 (*REG* 15 (1902) p. 132 no. 5) (ΔΑΜΩ (gen.)—lap., [Εὔ]δαμος?)

KERKYRA: (**14**) imp. *IG* IX (1) 864 (ring) (Δαμ(ώ))

KORINTHIA:
—KORINTH: (**15**) iv/iii BC *Corinth* VIII (3) 28 + *SEG* XXV 336 (m. Δαμαίνετος); (**16**) s. i BC *IG* II² 9063 (Δη-: d. Ἱππίας)

LAKONIA: (**17**) 192 BC *SGDI* 2129, 3, 5 (slave/freed.)
—KARDAMYLE: (**18**) ii AD *SEG* XI 966, 6 (*GVI* 1931) (m. Πρατεόνικος)

S. ITALY (BRUTTIUM):
—TERINA: (**19**) m. iv BC *IG* II² 10438 ([Δ]ημώ: d. Εὔφρων)

**Δάμων**

ACHAIA: (**1**) 146 BC ib. IV (1)² 28, 149 (f. Ὠφελίων: synoikos); (**2**) ii AD *IvOl* 472, 6 (f. M. Ἀντ. Ἀριστέας); (**3**) 119-138 AD *IG* V (1) 1352, 10 (s. Ἀριστέας)
—DYME: (**4**) 165 BC *ZPE* 101 (1994) p. 128, 7, 11 (s. Νεαγένης)
—PATRAI: (**5**) c. 146-32 BC *BMC Pelop.* p. 22 no. 5; *Coll. Hunter* 2 p. 125 no. 2 (coin) (f. Ἀρίσταρχος); (**6**) 122 BC *SEG* XV 254, 8 (s. Ἀλκισθένης)
—PELLENE: (**7**) m. iii BC *IG* V (2) 368, 93 (f. Κλεόδωρος); (**8**) i BC-i AD *SEG* XI 1270 (s. Σώσανδρος)

ACHAIA?: (**9**) 193 BC *IG* V (2) 293, 9 (I f. Δάμων II); (**10**) ~ ib. l. 9 (II s. Δάμων I)

AIGINA: (**11**) ?205 BC *AE* 1936, Chron. p. 39 no. 212, 6 (f. Εὐκράτης)

AITOLIA: (**12**) ?278-277 BC *FD* III (1) 87, 3; 88, 3; (**13**) ii BC *IG* II² 7988
—KALLION/KALLIPOLIS: (**14**) 175 BC *SGDI* 1987, 5 (f. Ξενίων, Εἰρανίων)
—KONOPE-ARSINOE: (**15**) 154 BC ib. 1908, 12 (f. Λέων, Ξενίας)
—TRICHONION: (**16**) s. iii BC *IG* IX (1)² (1) 117, 5

AKARNANIA:
—PALAIROS: (**17**) iii BC ib. IX (1)² (2) 480

ARGOLIS:
—ARGOS: (**18**) ?i AD Page, *FGE* 1898 (δαίμων—mss.)
—EPIDAUROS: (**19**) ii BC *IG* IV (1)² 211 (s. Δαμοφάνης, f. Δαμοφάνης)
—EPIDAUROS*: (**20**) c. 370-365 BC Peek, *IAEpid* 52 A, 35, 45; (**21**) c. 335-325 BC *IG* IV (1)² 106 I, 39 (*SEG* XXV 389) ([Δ]άμων); (**22**) c. 290-270 BC *IG* IV (1)² 109 II, 147, 155
—HERMIONE: (**23**) iii BC ib. IV (1) 728, 13 (f. Δαμασίας); (**24**) ii-i BC ib. 732 III, 9 (f. Ζωπυρίων)
—PHLEIOUS: (**25**) f. ii BC *FD* III (4) 435 (s. Ὀλυμπιόδωρος)

ARKADIA:
—MANTINEIA-ANTIGONEIA: (**26**) f. iii BC *IG* V (2) 272, 5
—STYMPHALOS: (**27**) hell. *PAE* 1929, p. 92
—TEGEA: (**28**) 165 AD *IG* V (2) 50, 34 (s. Ἐπικτᾶς)
—(Krariotai): (**29**) iv/iii BC ib. 38, 25 (s. Χαρικλῆς)

DALMATIA:
—ISSA: (**30**) iii-ii BC Brunšmid p. 28 no. 20, 1 (s. Ἀγάθων)

—ISSA?: (**31**) iii-ii BC ib. p. 32 no. 30, 3 (s. Τρίτος); (**32**) ~ ib. l. 4 (s. Δαμάτριος)

ELIS:
—OLYMPIA*: (**33**) 185-189 AD *IvOl* 104, 27 (?s. Ἰουλιανός: slave?)

EPIROS:
—AMBRAKIA: (**34**) iii-ii BC *Op. Ath.* 10 (1971) p. 64 no. 11 (s. Ἀλεξίων); (**35**) 238-168 BC *SNG Cop. Epirus-Acarnania* 37 (coin)
—PRASAIBOI: (**36**) a. 163 BC *IBouthrot* 59, 4 (*SEG* XXXVIII 510)

ILLYRIA:
—SKODRAI: (**37**) a. 168 BC *Iliria* 1972, p. 404 (coin)

KERKYRA: (**38**) ?i BC *IG* IX (1) 770; *BM Terracottas* E 192 (tiles)

KORINTHIA:
—KORINTH: (**39**) c. 570-550 BC Amyx 68. 5; 78. 3 (vases) (Lorber 125); Lorber 110 (-μῶν: her.); (**40**) s. vi BC *SEG* XVII 133 (vase) (Lazzarini 840) (-μῶν)
—SIKYON: (**41**) vi-v BC Iamb., *VP* 267 (*FVS* 58 A) (Δη-)

LAKONIA: (**42**) ii BC *IG* II² 9238 (Bradford (1)); (**43**) hell.-imp.? *Bronzes grecs et romains (Madrid)* 563 (?f. Ἀντιγόνη); (**44**) imp. *IG* V (1) 1343 (Bradford (2)) (f. Φιλλώ)
—SPARTA: (**45**) i BC/i AD *IG* V (1) 48, 13 (Bradford (3)) (f. Τιμάριστος)

MESSENIA:
—MESSENE: (**46**) ?35-44 AD *IG* V (1) 1433, 14, 22; 1433 a; *SEG* XXIX 396 (date)
—THOURIA: (**47**) ii-i BC *IG* V (1) 1385, 13 (f. Νικίας); (**48**) ~ ib. l. 25 (s. Οἰνεύς); (**49**) f. ii BC *SEG* XI 972, 18 (f. Λύσων); (**50**) ~ ib. l. 72 (f. Ἀριστόδαμος); (**51**) ~ ib. l. 79 (f. Κλεόνικος); (**52**) ~ ib. l. 86 (s. Φιλόμηλος); (**53**) ii/i BC *IG* V (1) 1384, 16 (f. Νίκων)

S. ITALY (BRUTTIUM):
—LOKROI EPIZEPHYRIOI:
——(Ψαθ.): (**54**) iv/iii BC De Franciscis 17, 4 (s. Σώσανδρος)
—SYBARIS-THOURIOI-COPIAE: (**55**) iv BC *SNG Lloyd* 502; *Samml. Ludwig* 178 (coins); (**56**) 376-372 BC Moretti, *Olymp.* 403; 407; (**57**) s. iv BC *IG* IV (1)² 95, 53 (Perlman E.2); Perlman pp. 46-9 (date)

S. ITALY (CALABRIA):
—TARAS-TARENTUM: (**58**) imp. *Misc. Gr. Rom.* 3 p. 194 no. T1 (Lat. Damo)
—URIA: (**59**) iii/ii BC Santoro, *NSM* 1 p. 163 no. IM 0.317 (vase) (Δαμωναιας—Messap. patr.?: f. Νίκων)

S. ITALY (CAMPANIA):
—NEAPOLIS: (**60**) iv/iii BC *IGSI* 1 I, 187 (*DGE* 62; Uguzzoni-Ghinatti I) (f. Χαιρέας)

S. ITALY (LUCANIA):
—METAPONTION: (**61**) iv-iii BC *SEG* XXX 1176 F. 7 (?f. —φίων)

SICILY:
—GELA-PHINTIAS: (**62**) f. v BC Dubois, *IGDS* 131. 4 (Arena, *Iscr. Sic.* II 45) (-μῶν)
—KAMARINA: (**63**) ?iv/iii BC *SEG* XXXIV 940, 10 (Dubois, *IGDS* 124; *PdelP* 44 (1989) p. 192 no. 3; Cordano, 'Camarina VII' 93) (f. Θεύδωρος); (**64**) ?ii BC *SEG* XXXIX 996, 8 (Dubois, *IGDS* 126; Cordano, 'Camarina VII' 94) (f. Νυμφόδωρος)
—KENTORIPA: (**65**) 396 BC D.S. xiv 78. 7 (tyrant)
—LIPARA: (**66**) c. 315-280 BC *FD* III (4) 401, 3 (s. Διονύσιος)
—MORGANTINA: (**67**) ?iv/iii BC *SEG* XXXIX 1008, 6 (f. Σάτυρος) ?= (68); (**68**) ~ ib. l. 8 (f. Ἐμμενίδας) ?= (67)
—SYRACUSE: (**69**) f. iv BC *RE* (18); *FVS* 55; (**70**) ~ *CGF* p. 9 sect. 16; cf. Str. 671 (or Cilicia Soloi: f. Φιλήμων); (**71**) 208 BC *IMM* 72, 10 (Dubois, *IGDS* 97)

**Δαμῶναξ**

ARKADIA:
—MANTINEIA-ANTIGONEIA: (**1**) m. vi BC *RE* Supplbd. 3 (-); *FGrH* 70 F 54 (Δαμέας—*FGrH*)

**Δαμωνίδας**

KORINTHIA:
—KORINTH: (**1**) s. iv BC *Corinth* VIII (1) 11, 8; *SEG* XI 60 (name) (Δαμωνίδ[ας]: f. Δαμαίνετος)

LAKONIA:
—SPARTA: (**2**) inc. Plu., *Mor.* 219 E (Poralla² 220)

**Δαμώνων**

LAKONIA:
—SPARTA: (**1**) b. 433 BC *IG* V (1) 213, 1, 6, 12 etc. (Moretti, *IAG* 16; Poralla² 219) (-μόνōν: f. Ἐνυμακρατίδας)

**Δανάα**

AITOLIA:
—PHISTYON: (**1**) c. 125-100 BC *SBBerlAk* 1936, p. 367 no. 2, 4, 13 (*SEG* XII 303)

**Δανάη**

EPIROS:
—BOUTHROTOS (PRASAIBOI): (**1**) imp. *AEp* 1978, no. 774 (Lat. Danae)

S. ITALY (APULIA):
—LARINUM: (**2**) imp. *CIL* IX 772 (Lat. Danae: m. Baebia Vinatris)

S. ITALY (CAMPANIA):
—DIKAIARCHIA-PUTEOLI: (**3**) imp. ib. X 2360 (Lat. Danae: m. Τυραννίς)
—DIKAIARCHIA-PUTEOLI*: (**4**) imp. *AJA* 2 (1898) p. 388 no. 39 (Lat. Titinia Danae: freed.)

**Δαναΐς**

ILLYRIA:
—APOLLONIA: (**1**) ii AD *IApoll* 229

S. ITALY (LUCANIA):
—VOLCEI?: (**2**) imp. *IItal* III (1) 11 (*CIL* X 449) (or Italy (Hirpini) Compsa: Lat. Allia Danais)

**Δαναός**

ILLYRIA:
—EPIDAMNOS-DYRRHACHION: (**1**) imp. *IDyrrh* 73 (f. Ἀγαθίων)

S. ITALY (CAMPANIA):
—POMPEII: (**2**) i BC-i AD *CIL* IV 4324 (Lat. Danaus)

**Δάνδις**

ARGOLIS:
—ARGOS: (**1**) f. v BC Ebert, *Gr. Sieg.* 15 (name); Moretti, *Olymp.* 210; 222

**Δάνδων**

ILLYRIA: (**1**) inc. *FGrH* 273 F 17 (Lat. Dandon: dub.)

**Δάολκος**

ARKADIA:
—PHENEOS: (**1**) c. 315-280 BC *FD* III (1) 42, 2 (s. Σάτυρος)

**Δᾶος**

ARGOLIS:
—EPIDAUROS: (**1**) ii-iii AD *IG* IV (1)² 550

S. ITALY (BRUTTIUM):
—SYBARIS-THOURIOI-COPIAE: (**2**) m. iv BC ib. II² 8895 (f. Δορκάς)

**Δάρδανα**

ILLYRIA:
—DARDANIOI: (**1**) 134 or 130 BC *SGDI* 2194, 11, 20 (slave/freed.)

**Δαρδανία**

SICILY:
—SYRACUSE: (**1**) imp. *NScav* 1907, p. 776 no. 41 (Lat. [Dar]dania—Solin)

**Δαρδάνιος**
ARGOLIS:
—EPIDAUROS: (**1**) ii–iii AD *IG* IV (1)² 466
S. ITALY (CAMPANIA):
—DIKAIARCHIA-PUTEOLI: (**2**) f. iii AD *CPh.* 64
(1969) pp. 229-33; 65 (1970) pp. 107-9 (Lat.
L. Valerius Valerianus Dardanius)

**Δαρδανίς**
ILLYRIA:
—DARDANIOI: (**1**) v BC Ar., *V.* 1371 with Schol.
(n. pr.?)

**Δάρδανος**
ILLYRIA:
—EPIDAMNOS-DYRRHACHION: (**1**) hell.-imp.
*IDyrrh* 31 (Δάρδανε (voc.?))
LAKONIA: (**2**) c. 425-400 BC *Eretria* VI 124 (Po-
ralla² 220a) (Δάρδ[ανος], Δαρδ[άνιος]?)
S. ITALY (CAMPANIA):
—DIKAIARCHIA-PUTEOLI*: (**3**) imp. *CIL* X
2752 (Lat. M. Munatius Dardanus: freed.);
(**4**) ~ ib. 2820 b (Lat. M. Laelius Dardanus:
freed.)
—POMPEII: (**5**) i BC-i AD ib. IV 4324 (Lat. Dar-
danus)

**Δαρεῖος**
ACHAIA:
—PELLENE: (**1**) ?c. 315-280 BC *FD* III (4) 403
VI, 1 (f. Τιμοκλῆς)

**Δάρσης**
SICILY:
—SYRACUSE: (**1**) iii-v AD Strazzulla 158 + Fer-
rua, *NG* 3 (Wessel 308) (Δ. πρεσβύτ.)

**Δαρχωνίδας**
SICILY:
—KAMARINA: (**1**) s. v BC Dubois, *IGDS* 121, 15
(Arena, *Iscr. Sic.* II 143; *SEG* XXXVIII 940;
Cordano, 'Camarina VII' 94) (Δαρχōν[ίδας],
Δάρχōν—Dubois)

**Δάρωγος?**
MESSENIA:
—MESSENE: (**1**) c. 80 AD *SEG* XLI 340, 2
(Δάρωγος (n. pr.?))

**Δασίμα**
AKARNANIA:
—PALAIROS: (**1**) iii BC *IG* IX (1)² (2) 481
(Δασίμας (gen.?))

**Δασίμιος**
S. ITALY (APULIA):
—HERDONIA: (**1**) imp. *CIL* IX 689 (Lat. C.
Dasimius: f. Busia Sabula)

**Δάσιμος**
AKARNANIA:
—ANAKTORION: (**1**) iii BC *IG* IX (1)² (2) 213
S. ITALY (LUCANIA):
—PERTOSA (MOD.): (**2**) s. v BC Landi, *DISMG*
256 (Δασιτος—helm., Δάσι(μ)ος—Landi)

**Δάσιος**
S. ITALY (APULIA):
—ARGYRIPPA-ARPI: (**1**) 213 BC *RE* (4) (Lat.
Altinius Dasius)
S. ITALY (APULIA)?: (**2**) i AD Mart. vi 70, 6
(Lat. Dasius: doctor) ?= (3); (**3**) ~ *RE* (3);
Mart. ii 52 (Lat. Dasius) ?= (2)
S. ITALY (CALABRIA):
—BRENTESION-BRUNDISIUM: (**4**) 218 BC *RE* (1)
(Lat. Dasius); (**5**) 210 BC ib. (2) (Lat. Dasius)
S. ITALY (CAMPANIA):
—KYME?: (**6**) ?i BC Audollent, *Defix. Tab.* 197
(Lat. M. Dassius)

**Δάσκων**
SICILY:
—SYRACUSE: (**1**) c. 600 BC Th. vi 5. 3 (Cordano,
'Camarina VII' 2) (and Sicily Kamarina: oi-
kist)

**Δάσμος**
S. ITALY (APULIA):
—CANUSIUM: (**1**) 67 BC *Epig. Rom. di Canosa*
158 (*CIL* IX 390) (Lat. Dasmus: f. Μέδελλα)

**Δάσμων**
KORINTHIA:
—KORINTH: (**1**) 724 BC Moretti, *Olymp.* 14
(Δέσμων—Afric.)

**Δάστα**
S. ITALY (APULIA):
—AZETIUM: (**1**) inc. Parlangèli, *Studi Messapici*
p. 237 O. 31 (vase) (Δάστας (gen.))

**Δαστώ**
DALMATIA:
—EPETION: (**1**) imp. *CIL* III 8551 (Lat. Dasto)

**Δατῖβος**
SICILY:
—SYRACUSE: (**1**) iii-v AD *IG* XIV 91 (Strazzulla
32) (-τεῖ-)

**Δάτος**
ARGOLIS:
—ARGOS: (**1**) 105 BC *JÖAI* 14 (1911) Beibl. p.
146 no. 4, 9 (f. Δαμονοῖς)

**Δαυδᾶτος**
S. ITALY (CALABRIA):
—TARAS-TARENTUM*: (**1**) byz. *JIWE* I 118
(*CIJ* I 627) (s. Ἀζαρία: Jew)

**Δαφίστας**
EPIROS:
—DODONA: (**1**) iii BC Antoniou, *Dodone* Ab, 14;
(**2**) ~ ib. l. 26

**Δαφναῖος**
DALMATIA:
—ISSA: (**1**) iii BC *SEG* XXXV 691, 1 (*VAHD* 84
(1991) p. 256 no. 6) (f. Ξενοκλῆς); (**2**) ~ *SEG*
XXXV 691, 10 (*VAHD* 84 (1991) p. 256 no. 6)
(s. Ξενοκλῆς); (**3**) iii-ii BC Brunšmid p. 28 no.
20, 2 (Δαφν[αῖος]: f. Θευτακώ)
——(Hylleis): (**4**) iv/iii BC ib. p. 9, 57
(Δαφν[αῖος]: f. Ἀγλωτρόφης)
——(Pamphyloi): (**5**) iv/iii BC ib. p. 8, 35 (f.
Δωρικλῆς)
—ISSA?: (**6**) iii/ii BC ib. p. 31 no. 27; *Istros* 2
(1935-6) pp. 18 ff. (or Dalmatia Tragurion)
SICILY:
—SYRACUSE: (**7**) 406 BC *RE* (2)

**Δάφνη**
ARGOLIS:
—HERMIONE: (**1**) imp. *IG* IV (1) 725 (d. Καλλι-
σθένης)
—TROIZEN: (**2**) imp. ib. 820
S. ITALY (APULIA):
—CANUSIUM: (**3**) ii-iii AD *Epig. Rom. di Canosa*
154 (*CIL* IX 389) (Lat. Baebia Dapne: m.
Livius Tertius)
S. ITALY (CALABRIA):
—TARAS-TARENTUM: (**4**) imp. ib. 253 (Lat.
Titinia Daphne); (**5**) ~ ib. 6161 (Lat. Dafne)
S. ITALY (CAMPANIA):
—DIKAIARCHIA-PUTEOLI: (**6**) imp. ib. X 2183
(Lat. Cossinia Daphne); (**7**) ~ ib. 2423 (Lat.
Fisia Daphne); (**8**) ~ *Territorio Flegreo* I p. 92
no. 8 (Lat. Pontia Daphne)
—NOLA*: (**9**) imp. *RAAN* 30 (1955) p. 200
(Lat. Septumuleia Daphne: freed.)
—POMPEII: (**10**) i BC-i AD *CIL* IV 680 (Lat.
Dafne); (**11**) ~ ib. X 1053 (Lat. Daphine)

—POMPEII?: (**12**) i AD ib. IV 2393 (Lat. Dapna
Ionice)
—SURRENTUM: (**13**) imp. ib. X 740 (Lat. Licinia
Daphne)
S. ITALY (LUCANIA):
—VOLCEI: (**14**) imp. *IItal* III (1) 96 (*CIL* X 383)
(Lat. Daphne)
SICILY:
—KATANE: (**15**) imp. *IG* XIV 469
—THERMAI HIMERAIAI: (**16**) i-ii AD *CIL* X 7398
a (*ILat. Term. Imer.* 88) (Lat. Daphne)

**Δάφνης**
KORINTHIA:
—KORINTH: (**1**) hell.-imp.? *FGrH* 156 F 12

**Δαφνική**
ILLYRIA:
—APOLLONIA: (**1**) ii-iii AD *IApoll* 211 (Κλαυδία
Δ.)

**Δαφνικός**
S. ITALY (CAMPANIA):
—NOLA: (**1**) imp. *CIL* X 1332 (Lat. M. Valerius
Daphnicus)
—POMPEII: (**2**) i BC-i AD ib. IV 4066; 4477 (Lat.
Daphnicus)

**Δάφνις**
S. ITALY (CAMPANIA):
—NEAPOLIS: (**1**) ?i AD *GVI* 182 (*INap* 98); cf.
Leiwo p. 121 no. 107

**Δαφνίς**
S. ITALY (CALABRIA):
—RUDIAE: (**1**) imp. *NScav* 1897, p. 404 no.
7 = Bernardini, *Rudiae* p. 87 (Susini, *Fonti
Salento* p. 120 no. 63) (Lat. Tutora Daphnis)

**Δάφνος**
ARKADIA:
—TEGEA: (**1**) ii AD *IG* V (2) 55, 54 (f. Πρῖμος)
LAKONIA:
—SPARTA: (**2**) c. 140-160 AD ib. V (1) 154, 12
(Bradford (2)) (I f. Δάφνος II); (**3**) ~ *IG* V (1)
154, 12 (Bradford (1)) (II s. Δάφνος I)
S. ITALY (APULIA):
—CANUSIUM*: (**4**) i AD *Epig. Rom. di Canosa*
119 (Lat. L. Dasimius Daphnus: freed.); (**5**)
~ ib. Add. 2 (Lat. P. Valeri[us] Daphnus:
freed.?)
—CONVERSANO (MOD.): (**6**) i/ii AD *CIL* IX 274
(Lat. Daphnus: f. Φίλωμα: freed.)
S. ITALY (CAMPANIA):
—ATELLA*: (**7**) imp. ib. X 3750 (Lat. A. Plau-
tius Daphnus: freed.)
—CAPREAE: (**8**) imp. ib. 8059. 430 (seal) (Lat.
T. Vestricius Daphnus)
—DIKAIARCHIA-PUTEOLI: (**9**) imp. ib. 2966
(Lat. Sosius Daf[nus]); (**10**) ?ii AD *NScav*
1888, p. 198 no. 6 (*Eph. Ep.* VIII 398) (Lat.
M. Ulpius Daphnus)
—HERCULANEUM*: (**11**) i BC-i AD *CIL* X 1403 g
III, 28 (Lat. M. Antonius Daphnus: freed.)
—POMPEII: (**12**) i BC-i AD ib. IV 8191 (Lat.
Daphnus); (**13**) ~ ib. 2393-4 (Lat. Dapnus
Asiaticus); (**14**) 23 AD ib. 895 (Lat. Daph-
nus); (**15**) c. 51-62 AD ib. 3340. 88, 9; 98, 8
(Castrèn 232. 1) (Lat. Maetennius Daphnus);
(**16**) ~ *CIL* IV 3340. 92, 1 (Castrèn 238. 1)
(Lat. Mancius Daphnus)
—STABIAE: (**17**) i AD *CIL* X 772 (Lat. –aesius
Daphnus)
S. ITALY (LUCANIA):
—GRUMENTUM: (**18**) imp. ib. 232 (Lat. L.
Turcius Dafnus)
SICILY:
—KATANE: (**19**) imp. ib. 7074 (Lat. L. Lollius
Daphnus)
—SYRACUSE: (**20**) iii-v AD *IG* XIV 92 (Strazzulla
33); cf. Ferrua, *NG* 161 (Δάφρος—lap.)
SICILY*: (**21**) imp. *CIL* X 7154 (Lat. L. Li-
cinius Daphnus: freed.)

**Δαψιλιανός**
SICILY:
—SYRACUSE: (**1**) iii-v AD *IG* XIV 93 (Strazzulla 34) (*Δαψι*[*λ*]*ιανός*)

**Δάων**
ARKADIA:
—TEGEA: (**1**) f. ii BC *IG* V (2) 44, 10 (*Δάων*: s. *Εὐαρείδας*)

**Δεαδότα**
SICILY:
—SYRACUSE: (**1**) iii-v AD Strazzulla 404 (Wessel 379) ([*Δ*]*εαδότα*, [*Δωροθ*]*έα?*—Wessel)

**Δειναγόρας**
LAKONIA: (**1**) iii-ii BC *IG* V (1) 706 (Bradford (-))

**Δεινακῶν**
LAKONIA:
—SPARTA: (**1**) f. ii AD *IG* V (1) 51, 14; 52, 4; 490, 9; *SEG* XI 506, [2]; 606, 3 (Bradford (-)) (f. *Εὐκλείδας*)

**Δείναρχος**
AITOLIA: (**1**) m. ii BC Liv. xliii 22. 4
—THERMOS*: (**2**) s. iii BC *IG* IX (1)² (1) 60 IV, 20
ARGOLIS:
—ARGOS: (**3**) 328-324 BC *CID* II 95, [12]; 97, 22; 102 II B, 27; 121 III, 13 (f. *Φίλλις*)
ARKADIA:
—KLEITOR: (**4**) c. 230-200 BC *BCH* 45 (1921) p. 12 II, 71 (s. *Ἀλεξίλοχος*)
—TEGEA:
——(Hippothoitai): (**5**) iv/iii BC *IG* V (2) 38, 45 (f. *Δεινίας*)
DALMATIA:
—ISSA:
——(Dymanes): (**6**) iv/iii BC Brunšmid p. 7, 21 (f. *Διονύσιος*)
EPIROS:
—KASSOPE: (**7**) f. ii BC *BCH* 45 (1921) p. 23 IV, 51 (*Δείναρ*[*χος*])
—MOLOSSOI: (**8**) f. iii BC *FGrH* 703 F 9 (s. *Νικίας*)
KORINTHIA:
—KORINTH: (**9**) c. 361-290 BC *RE* (1); Berve 247 (s. *Σώστρατος*); (**10**) c. 360-318 BC *RE* (2); Berve 248 (and Athens) *?= (11)*; (**11**) 344 BC Plu., *Tim.* 21; 24 *?= (10)*
LAKONIA:
—SPARTA: (**12**) c. 130 AD *IG* V (1) 60, 2 (Bradford (-)) (s. *Ἀγιάδας*)
S. ITALY (BRUTTIUM):
—LOKROI EPIZEPHYRIOI:
——(*Ἀγφ.*): (**13**) iv/iii BC De Franciscis 39, 9 (*Δείναρ*[*χος*]: s. *Κάλλιππος*)
——(*Ἀγκ.*): (**14**) iv/iii BC ib. 5, 6 (s. *Χάριππος*)
——(*Τιω.*): (**15**) iv/iii BC ib. 7, 8 (f. *Πρώταρχος*)
SICILY:
—KAMARINA: (**16**) ?iv/iii BC *SEG* XXXIV 940, 2 (Dubois, *IGDS* 124; *PdelP* 44 (1989) p. 192 no. 3) (*Δίνα*[*ρχος*]: s. *Κλέανδρος*)

**Δεινῆς**
MESSENIA:
—MESSENE: (**1**) 263 BC *IG* IX (1)² (1) 17, 62 (s. *Σάτυρος*)

**Δεινιάδας**
LAKONIA: (**1**) 412 BC Th. viii 22. 1 (Poralla² 221)

**Δεινίας**
ACHAIA: (**1**) 146 BC *IG* IV (1)² 28, 77 (s. *Ἀλέξαρχος*: synoikos)
—DYME*: (**2**) c. 219 BC *SGDI* 1612, 50 (*Tyche* 5 (1990) p. 124) (s. *Θηρύων*) *?= (3)*; (**3**) ~ *SGDI* 1612, 58 (*Tyche* 5 (1990) p. 124) (f. *Σωσίστρατος*) *?= (2)*

AKARNANIA:
—PALAIROS: (**4**) c. 300 BC *IG* IX (1)² (2) 462 (*CEG* II 661) (s. *Λέαρχος*)
—STRATOS: (**5**) a. 167 BC *IG* IX (1)² (1) 36, 4, 10 (*Δι*-: s. *Εὔδαμος*)
—THYRREION: (**6**) m. iii BC *SEG* XL 464 II side 1, 4; (**7**) ii BC *IG* IX (1)² (2) 252, 9 (f. *Δείνων*)
ARGOLIS:
—ARGOS: (**8**) 326-324 BC *CID* II 32, 35; 97, 35; 99 A, 8; 102 II B, 31; 120 A, 4; 122 III, 3 (s. *Φιλέας*); (**9**) i BC *IG* II² 8369, 4
—ARGOS?: (**10**) iii BC *RE* (8); *FGrH* 306 T 1 (ident.) *?= (11)*; (**11**) s. iii BC *RE* (7); *FGrH* 306; Schol. Pi., *I.* iv, 104 g; *GGM* I p. 112 (*Αἰνείας*—Schol. Pi., *Κλεινίας*—*GGM*) *?= (10)*
ARKADIA: (**12**) 320 BC *IG* V (2) 549, 15 (f. *Δείνων*); (**13**) 316 BC ib. l. 25 (s. *Λάανδρος*)
—KLEITOR: (**14**) ?253 BC Nachtergael, *Les Galates* 10, 36; cf. Stephanis 163 (f. *Ἀμφαρείδας*)
—TEGEA: (**15**) ii BC *IG* V (2) 43, 16; (**16**) ?ii BC ib. 211
——(Hippothoitai): (**17**) iv/iii BC ib. 38, 45 (s. *Δείναρχος*)
—TEGEA*: (**18**) f. iii BC ib. 36, 10 ([*Δ*]*εινίας*?)
KORINTHIA:
—SIKYON: (**19**) vi/v BC *SEG* XI 244, 17
MESSENIA:
—MESSENE: (**20**) s. iv BC ib. XX 716, 26
—THOURIA: (**21**) f. ii BC ib. XI 972, 19 (s. *Κορίνθιος*); (**22**) ~ ib. l. 30 (f. *Λύσιππος*); (**23**) ii/i BC *IG* V (1) 1384, 11 (s. *Δαμοσθένης*)
S. ITALY (LUCANIA):
—HYELE-VELIA: (**24**) imp. *PdelP* 21 (1966) p. 336 no. 7 (s. *Ζώϊλος*)
SICILY:
—GELA-PHINTIAS: (**25**) s. vi BC Dubois, *IGDS* 146 a-b (vases) (Arena, *Iscr. Sic.* II 10-12) (*Ἀδεινίας*—Arena 11-12)
—IAITON: (**26**) iii-ii BC *SEG* XXVII 649 (tile); (**27**) ii-i BC ib. XXVI 1070. 4 (tiles) (f. *Νικίας*)
—KAMARINA: (**28**) f. v BC Cordano, *Tessere Pubbliche* 15 (f. *Ἀριστίων*)
—KAMARINA?: (**29**) v/iv BC Manganaro, *PdelP* forthcoming no. 14
—LIPARA: (**30**) hell. *SEG* XXXIV 958
—SELINOUS: (**31**) vi/v BC Manganaro, *PdelP* forthcoming no. 18 (s. *Σφύρας*)
—SELINOUS?: (**32**) v BC *SEG* XXXIX 1021 I, 3; (**33**) ~ ib. 1021 II, 4
—TAUROMENION: (**34**) c. 172-150 BC *IG* XIV 421 an. 80; 421 an. 91; 421 an. 100 (*SGDI* 5219); *IGSI* 4 II (III), 6 an. 70 (s. *Ἔλωρις*); (**35**) c. 171 BC *IG* XIV 421 an. 70 (*SGDI* 5219)

**Δεινίδας**
LAKONIA:
—SPARTA: (**1**) c. 48-31 BC *Münzpr. der Laked.* p. 37 fig. 6 no. 29; p. 161 Group 22 series 5 (coin) (Bradford (-))

**Δεινιππίδας**
KORINTHIA:
—KORINTH: (**1**) m. iii BC *Corinth* VIII (3) 33 a, 7
LAKONIA:
—OITYLOS: (**2**) ?ii-i BC *IG* V (1) 1297

**Δείνιππος**
ARKADIA:
—MEGALOPOLIS: (**1**) ?145 BC ib. V (2) 439, 32 (s. *Εὔδαμος*)
KORINTHIA:
—KORINTH: (**2**) 3 AD *Corinth* VIII (1) 14, 7; cf. *SEG* XI 61 ([*Δ*]*είνιππος*: f. *Σθενο*—); (**3**) m. i AD *Corinth* VIII (2) 86-90; VIII (3) 158-63 (Lat. Ti. Claudius Dinippus)
—THALAMAI: (**4**) i BC-i AD *IG* V (1) 1321 d
MESSENIA:
—MESSENE: (**5**) 321 BC *FD* III (4) 6, 1 (s. *Δεινύλος*)

—THOURIA: (**6**) ii-i BC *IG* V (1) 1385, 5 (f. *Λεόντιχος*)

**Δεῖνις**
AIGINA: (**1**) m. v BC Pi., *N.* viii, 16; cf. Klee p. 103 no. 121 (*Δεινίας*—Schol.: s. *Μέγας*)
LAKONIA:
—SPARTA: (**2**) ?c. 600 BC *SEG* XXVI 457; *LSAG*² p. 446 no. 3a (date) (Poralla² 221a) (*Δεῖνι*[*ς*])
SICILY:
—SELINOUS?: (**3**) v BC *SEG* XXXIX 1021 III, 3

**Δεινίχα**
LAKONIA:
—SPARTA: (**1**) m. iv BC Paus. iii 10. 3; Cartledge, *Agesilaos* pp. 147-8 (stemma) (Poralla² 222) (?d. *Εὐδαμίδας*, m. *Ἆγις*, *Εὐδαμίδας*, *Ἀγησίλαος*)

**Δεινόβιος**
ARKADIA:
—PHIGALEIA: (**1**) c. 230-200 BC *BCH* 45 (1921) p. 12 II, 83 (s. *Πολύαινος*)

**Δεινοκλῆς**
ILLYRIA:
—APOLLONIA: (**1**) s. iv BC *L'Illyrie mérid.* 2 p. 55 (*IApoll* 340)
—EPIDAMNOS-DYRRHACHION: (**2**) c. 250-50 BC Maier 191-6; Münsterberg Nachtr. p. 15 (Ceka 14; 99; 110; 133; 182; 262; 297; 379); cf. *IApoll Ref. Bibl.* nn. 42 and 46 (coins) (pryt.)
LAKONIA:
—SPARTA: (**3**) c. 25 BC-10 AD *IG* V (1) 209, 10; 210, 32 (Bradford (-)) (*Δι*-: f. *Δεινοκράτης*)

**Δεινοκράτεια**
ILLYRIA:
—APOLLONIA: (**1**) imp. *IApoll* 68 (-τια)

**Δεινοκράτης**
ARGOLIS:
—EPIDAUROS: (**1**) iii/ii BC Peek, *IAEpid* 95 I ([*Δ*]*εινοκράτης*: f. *Δαι*—)
ARKADIA: (**2**) ?254 BC Nachtergael, *Les Galates* 9, 33; cf. Stephanis 2445 (f. *Ὕμνος*)
ILLYRIA:
—APOLLONIA: (**3**) c. 250-50 BC Maier 37 (coin) (Ceka 113) (pryt.); (**4**) i BC Maier 123 (coin) (*Δι*-: s. *Ἐρίμναστος*: money.); (**5**) ~ ib. 141-3; 132 + Münsterberg p. 36 (coin) (pryt.)
KORINTHIA:
—SIKYON: (**6**) s. iii BC *SEG* XXXIX 1334, 1; cf. *Chiron* 19 (1989) p. 499 f. (I f. *Δεινοκράτης* II, *Διονυσόδωρος*); (**7**) 201 BC Plb. xvi 3. 7 f.; *Chiron* 19 (1989) pp. 508-10 (ident., locn.) (II s. *Δεινοκράτης* I)
LAKONIA:
—HYPERTELEATON*: (**8**) imp. *IG* V (1) 1034 (*Δι*-)
—SPARTA: (**9**) c. 25-1 BC ib. 50, 27 (Bradford (1)) (*Δεινοκρά*[*της*]: s. *Δαμοτίων*); (**10**) c. 25 BC-10 AD *IG* V (1) 209, 10; 210, 32 (Bradford (3)) (*Δι*-: s. *Δεινοκλῆς*)
MESSENIA:
—MESSENE: (**11**) iii/ii BC *RE* (4)
S. ITALY (CALABRIA):
—TARAS-TARENTUM: (**12**) iv BC Iamb., *VP* 267 (*FVS* I p. 446); (**13**) c. 302-280 BC Vlasto 692-4 (coin) (Evans, *Horsemen* p. 134 VI D.2); (**14**) s. iii BC *FD* III (1) 444, 2 (f. *Ἀγέμαχος*)
SICILY:
—SYRACUSE: (**15**) iv/iii BC *RE* (3)

**Δεινοκρατίδας**
LAKONIA:
—SPARTA: (**1**) c. 100 AD *SEG* XI 515, 5 (Bradford (-)) (*Δι*-: s. *Ἀρισταγόρας*)

## Δεινόλας

ARKADIA:
—LOUSOI: (1) iv/iii BC *IG* v (2) 389, 14 (Perlman L.1); (2) iii BC *IG* v (2) 395, 4

## Δεινολέων

ARKADIA:
—PSOPHIS: (1) c. 230-200 BC *BCH* 45 (1921) p. 14 II, 124 (s. Σθενόλαος)

## Δεινόλοχος

ELIS: (1) f. iv BC Moretti, *Olymp.* 401 (s. Πύρρος)
SICILY:
—SYRACUSE: (2) v BC *RE* (2); *CGF* i pp. 149-51 (or Sicily Akragas)

## Δεινομάχα

EPIROS:
—BOUTHROTOS (PRASAIBOI): (1) a. 163 BC *IBouthrot* 14, 29 (*SEG* XXXVIII 471) ?= (2); (2) ~ *IBouthrot* 15, 14 (*SEG* XXXVIII 472) ?= (1); (3) ~ *IBouthrot* 151, 8
——Messaneoi: (4) a. 163 BC ib. 14, 9; 17, [3], [5]; 19, 8; 21, 18; 38, 13; 41, 6 (*SEG* XXXVIII 471; 476; 497; 500); *IBouthrot* 48, 12 (II d. Μενοίτας, Δεινομάχα I)
——Messaneoi?: (5) a. 163 BC ib. 17, 3, 5; 19, 8; 21, 17; 26, 5; 27, 6; 29, 45; 38, 12; 41, 6, 10 (*SEG* XXXVIII 471; 474; 476; 478; 484-5; 487; 497; 500); *IBouthrot* 48, 13; 50, 12; 146, [3] (I d. Πολέμων, m. Βοΐσκος, Δεινομάχα II, Βουβάλιον, ?m. Θερσώ)

## Δεινόμαχος

AITOLIA: (1) ii AD Luc., *DMeretr.* 15. 1-2 (fict.)
AKARNANIA:
—MATROPOLIS: (2) m. ii BC *IG* IX (1)² (2) 209, 4 (f. Δείνων)
EPIROS:
—BOUTHROTOS (PRASAIBOI): (3) a. 163 BC *IBouthrot* 29, 49 (*SEG* XXXVIII 487)
LAKONIA: (4) c. 550 BC *Cl. Rh.* 8 p. 86; *LSAG*² p. 199 no. 16 (Δε-)
SICILY:
—KAMARINA: (5) f. v BC Cordano, *Tessere Pubbliche* 19 (f. —λος)

## Δεινομένης

ARGOLIS:
—ARGOS: (1) 343 BC *CID* II 36 I, 26
ARKADIA:
—KYNAITHA: (2) ?253 BC Nachtergael, *Les Galates* 10, 34; cf. Stephanis 124 (f. Ἀλέξιππος)
LAKONIA:
—SPARTA: (3) ?s. i AD *IG* v (1) 678, 2 (Bradford (-)) (Δεινομ[ένης])
S. ITALY (BRUTTIUM):
—LOKROI EPIZEPHYRIOI:
——(Προ.): (4) iv/iii BC De Franciscis 38, 7 (f. Φειδίλας)
SICILY:
—GELA-PHINTIAS: (5) vi BC *RE* (3) (f. Γέλων, Ἱέρων, Πολύζαλος, Θρασύβουλος); (6) f. v BC ib. (4) (and Sicily Syracuse: s. Ἱέρων)
—SYRACUSE: (7) 214 BC ib. (5)

## Δεινόροψ

ILLYRIA:
—EPIDAMNOS-DYRRHACHION: (1) c. 250-50 BC Maier 197 (Ceka 233); *IApoll Ref. Bibl.* n. 47 (coin) (Δεινόρωπος (gen.): pryt.)

## Δεῖνος

SICILY:
—GELA-PHINTIAS: (1) f. v BC Dubois, *IGDS* 131. 9 (Arena, *Iscr. Sic.* II 45)

## Δεινοσθένης

LAKONIA:
—SPARTA: (1) 316 BC *IvOl* 171 (Poralla² 223) (Δε[ι]νοσθέ[ν]η[ς]: I f. Δεινοσθένης II); (2) ~ *RE*

(-); Moretti, *Olymp.* 478 (Poralla² 224; Bradford (-)) (II s. Δεινοσθένης I)

## Δεινύλος

AITOLIA: (1) 224 or 221 BC *SGDI* 2524, 4; Nachtergael, *Les Galates* 64, 3
MESSENIA:
—MESSENE: (2) 321 BC *FD* III (4) 6, 1 (f. Δείνιππος)
S. ITALY (APULIA):
—MONTE SANNACE (MOD.): (3) v BC *Monte Sannace* p. 136 (vase)

## Δεινῦς?

LAKONIA:
—SPARTA: (1) iii BC *SEG* XL 348 B, 2 (Δεινῦς?—ed.)

## Δεινώ

S. ITALY: (1) vi/v BC Iamb., *VP* 132 (Δειωνώ—ms.: name—Scalig.)

## Δείνων

ACHAIA?: (1) 193 BC *IG* v (2) 293, 14 (f. Εὐνομίδας)
AIGINA: (2) f. iii BC Nachtergael, *Les Galates* 7, 28; *IG* II² 3080 (Stephanis 590) (s. Ἡρακλείδας)
AITOLIA:
—KONOPE-ARSINOE: (3) 184 BC *IG* IX (1)² (1) 131, 9 (s. Ἀριστώνυμος)
AKARNANIA:
—MATROPOLIS: (4) m. ii BC ib. IX (1)² (2) 209, 4 (s. Δεινόμαχος)
—PALAIROS: (5) iii BC ib. 482
—THYRREION: (6) ii BC ib. 252, 8 (s. Δεινίας)
ARGOLIS:
—EPIDAUROS*: (7) c. 365-335 BC ib. IV (1)² 103, 130; 113, 3, 10
ARKADIA: (8) 320 BC ib. v (2) 549, 15 (s. Δεινίας)
—TEGEA:
——(Hippothoitai): (9) ?s. iv BC ib. 39, 9 (Δείνω[ν])
EPIROS: (10) c. 250 BC ib. XI (4) 635, 10 (s. Φίλιππος)
—BOUTHROTOS (PRASAIBOI): (11) a. 163 BC *IBouthrot* 43, 19, 23 (*SEG* XXXVIII 502) (f. Λέαινα); (12) ~ *IBouthrot* 101, 4 (f. Μενοίτας)
——Bouthrotioi: (13) a. 163 BC ib. 108 (s. Φίλιππος)
——Eschatioi: (14) a. 163 BC ib. 129, 5; 137, 12; 144, 6; 147, 11 (f. Θύρμαξ)
——Kestrinoi: (15) a. 163 BC ib. 25, 1 (*SEG* XXXVIII 483) (s. Ἀλέξανδρος)
——ETHNESTAI: (16) 370-368 BC Cabanes, *L'Épire* p. 534 no. 1, 15, 31
—EUROPIOI: (17) c. 200 BC *IG* IX (1)² (1) 31, 132 (s. Νέστωρ)
—THESPROTOI: (18) c. 330 BC Cabanes, *L'Épire* p. 580 no. 55, 10 (s. Θοξούχαρος?)
ILLYRIA:
—APOLLONIA: (19) i BC Maier 124; 143; 145 (coin) (money.); (20) ~ ib. 130 (coin) (Δί-: f. Ζώπυρος)
—BYLLIONES (RABIJE (MOD.))*: (21) ?s. ii BC *SEG* XXXII 626, 8 + XXXVIII 520; cf. *CRAI* 1991, p. 197 ff. (Δίνω[ν?], Δινω—?: f. Νικάνωρ)
—EPIDAMNOS-DYRRHACHION: (22) hell.-imp. *IDyrrh* 114 (f. Ἀπολλώνιος)
KORINTHIA:
—KORINTH: (23) ?255 BC Nachtergael, *Les Galates* 8, 34 (Stephanis 588)
LAKONIA:
—SPARTA: (24) 371 BC X., *HG* v 4. 33; vi 4. 14 (Poralla² 225)
MESSENIA:
—MESSENE: (25) ii-i BC *IG* v (1) 1453, 2; (26) ~ ib. l. 7
—THOURIA: (27) f. ii BC *SEG* XI 972, 107 (f. Στράτις); (28) ii/i BC *IG* v (1) 1384, 12 (s. Στράτις)

S. ITALY (CALABRIA):
—TARAS-TARENTUM: (29) ?v-iv BC Thphr. fr. 133
SICILY:
—MORGANTINA: (30) ?iv/iii BC *SEG* XXXIX 1008, 10 (s. Φιντίας)
—SYRACUSE: (31) c. 272 BC Theoc., *Id.* xv 1 (f. Ζωπυρίων: fict.)
—SYRACUSE?:
——(Ὑπα.): (32) hell. Manganaro, *PdelP* forthcoming no. 4 V, 9 (s. Σιμίας)

## Δέκαρθος?

EPIROS:
—DODONA: (1) iii BC Antoniou, *Dodone* Ab, 2 (Δέκαρθος)

## Δεκαρχίς

S. ITALY (CAMPANIA):
—POMPEII: (1) f. i AD *Impegno per Pompeii* 11 OS no. 13 (Castrèn 315. 4) (Lat. Pomponia Decharcis: m. Alleius Maius)

## Δεκένιος

SICILY:
—KATANE: (1) iii-v AD *IG* XIV 527 (Wessel 911)

## Δέκιος

S. ITALY (CAMPANIA): (1) f. iii BC D.H. xx 4. 2
SICILY:
—SEGESTA: (2) iv/iii BC *SEG* XXX 1119, 7 (Dubois, *IGDS* 206) (Δέκ[ι]ος: f. Διονύσιος); (3) 49 BC *IG* XIV 282 (Δέκ<κ>ιος: f. Πασίων Σισυρίων)

## Δέκμος

LAKONIA:
—SPARTA: (1) ?m. ii AD ib. v (1) 161, 1 (Bradford (2)) (I f. Δέκμος II); (2) ~ *IG* v (1) 161, 1 (Bradford (1)) (II s. Δέκμος I)

## Δεκόμανος

SICILY:
—THERMAI HIMERAIAI: (1) ?ii-iii AD *IG* XIV 319

## Δέκομος

ILLYRIA:
—EPIDAMNOS-DYRRHACHION: (1) hell.-imp. *IDyrrh* 168 (I f. Δέκομος II); (2) ~ ib. (II s. Δέκομος I)
SICILY:
—IAITON: (3) i BC-i AD? *SEG* XXXVIII 932 ([Δ]έκομος)
—SYRACUSE: (4) hell. *IG* XIV Add. 9 a

## Δεκριανός

ACHAIA:
—PATRAI: (1) ii AD *RE* s.v. Decrianus (2); Luc., *Asin.* 2

## Δελμάτας

AKARNANIA:
—ASTAKOS: (1) ii BC *IG* IX (1)² (2) 434, 19 (f. Βάβος)

## Δελμάτιος

MESSENIA:
—KORONE: (1) 246 AD ib. v (1) 1398, 32 (Κλ. Δ.)

## Δελφιάς

ARKADIA:
—PHENEOS?: (1) ii BC *SEG* XXI 992 ([Δε]λφιάς)

## Δελφική

S. ITALY (APULIA):
—SIPONTUM: (1) ii AD *Epigraphica* 32 (1970) p. 164 (Serricchio, *Iscrizioni di Siponto* 10) (Lat. Aelia Delphice)

## Δελφικός

S. ITALY (APULIA):
—CANUSIUM: (1) imp. *Epig. Rom. di Canosa* Instr. 3 (tile) (Lat. Delphicus)

**Δέλφινα**
S. ITALY (CAMPANIA):
—POMPEII: (2) i BC-i AD *CIL* IV 1686 (Lat. Delphicus)

**Δέλφινα**
S. ITALY (CAMPANIA):
—DIKAIARCHIA-PUTEOLI: (1) imp. ib. x 2461 (Lat. Delphina: m. Fortunatus)

**Δέλφις**
SICILY:
—GELA-PHINTIAS: (1) m. v BC *Classical Vases* no. 27

**Δελφίων**
ARGOLIS:
—ARGOS:
——Mykenai (Daiphonteis): (1) 195 BC *IG* IV (1) 497, 5 (s. *Τιμόκριτος*)

**Δελφός**
LAKONIA:
—SPARTA: (1) her. *FGrH* 26 F I xxxvi 2; 26 F I xlvii 1; Plu., *Mor.* 247 D; 296 C (Poralla² 226) (and Crete: oikist/dub.)
S. ITALY (CAMPANIA):
—HERCULANEUM*: (2) i BC-i AD *CIL* X 1403 l II, 14; cf. *Cron. Erc.* 7 (1977) p. 116 c, 14 (Lat. L. Aquillius Delphus: freed.)

**Δέμαστος**
EPIROS:
—DODONA: (1) iii BC Antoniou, *Dodone* Ab, 28 (*Δ(ά)-?*)

**Δένδας**
SICILY:
—HERBESSOS: (1) f. v BC Guarducci, *Ep. Gr.* 3 p. 349 (bronze) (Arena, *Iscr. Sic.* II 122) (*Δενδᾶς*—Arena)

**Δενδίλος**
SICILY:
—SELINOUS: (1) m. v BC Dubois, *IGDS* 36, 2 (Arena, *Iscr. Sic.* I 69) (s. *Μνάμων*)

**Δένομος**
LEUKAS: (1) iii BC Unp. (*IG* arch.) (*Δείνομος?*)

**Δεξαγορίδας**
LAKONIA:
—GYTHEION: (1) 195 BC Liv. xxxiv 9

**Δεξαμεναῖος**
EPIROS:
—BOUTHROTOS (PRASAIBOI):
——Phonidatoi: (1) ii-i BC *IBouthrot* 53, 6 (*SEG* XXXVIII 504) (f. *Ἀσ*—)

**Δεξαμένης**
MESSENIA:
—MESSENE: (1) i AD *IG* v (1) 1436, 40 ([*Δ*]*εξαμένη*[*ς*])

**Δέξανδρος**
AKARNANIA:
—MATROPOLIS: (1) m. ii BC ib. IX (1)² (2) 588 (f. *Φιλιστίων*)
ARGOLIS:
—EPIDAUROS: (2) c. 370 BC ib. IV (1)² 102, 23
EPIROS: (3) iv BC ib. II² 8534 (s. *Γλαυκέτας*); (4) ?s. iii BC Cabanes, *L'Épire* p. 553 no. 32, 4 (f. —*νίσκος*); (5) 234-168 BC *BMC Thessaly* p. 89 no. 19; Franke, *Münz. v. Epirus* p. 179 II ser. 39; p. 156 no. 2 (coins) (*Ἀλέξανδρος*—*BMC* per err.)
—BOUTHROTOS (PRASAIBOI): (6) a. 163 BC *IBouthrot* 17, 21; 22, 1; 31, 84 (*SEG* XXXVIII 474; 479; 490) (s. *Θύρμαξ*) ?= (7); (7) ~ *IBouthrot* 25, 13 (*SEG* XXXVIII 483) ?= (6); (8) ~ *IBouthrot* 128, 6; 129, [5] ?= (9); (9) ~ ib. 147, 10 ?= (8)

——Ancheropaioi: (10) a. 163 BC ib. 68, 5; 69, 5; 70, 4; 71, 3 (*BCH* 118 (1994) pp. 129 f. B 1-3) (s. *Νικάδας*)
—KOLPAIOI: (11) f. ii BC Cabanes, *L'Épire* p. 580 no. 54, 7 (s. *Κέφαλος*)
—VOTONOSI (MOD.): (12) ?f. iii BC *SEG* XXIV 459 (f. *Ἀνερείας*)
KORINTHIA:
—KORINTH: (13) viii BC Plu., *Mor.* 772 D-E
—SIKYON: (14) vi/v BC *SEG* XI 244, 54
S. ITALY (BRUTTIUM):
—LOKROI EPIZEPHYRIOI: (15) iv/iii BC *CEG* II 835 (*SEG* XL 836) (*Δέξανδρος*)

**Δεξέας**
ARGOLIS:
—EPIDAUROS: (1) i-ii AD *IG* IV (1)² 520 (*Δεξῆ* (gen.): f. *Ξενοφάνης*)

**Δεξεύς**
ARGOLIS:
—ARGOS: (1) iv-iii BC Unp. (Ch. Kritzas)

**Δεξιάδας**
KORINTHIA:
—SIKYON: (1) vi/v BC *SEG* XI 244, 45
MESSENIA:
—THOURIA: (2) f. ii BC ib. 972, 94 (f. *Σωτέλης*)

**Δεξιάδης**
S. ITALY (CAMPANIA):
—NUCERIA ALFATERNA*: (1) i AD ib. XXXII 1023 (biling.) (Lat. P. Tillius Dexiades: freed.)

**Δεξίας**
AITOLIA:
—KALLION/KALLIPOLIS: (1) ?165 BC *SGDI* 1818, 6
AKARNANIA:
—PALAIROS: (2) iii BC *IG* IX (1)² (2) 483
ARGOLIS:
—ARGOS: (3) ii-i BC *Mnem.* NS 47 (1919) p. 164 no. 9, 7 (s. *Σωσίων*)
—EPIDAUROS: (4) 345 BC *CID* II 31, 77; 120 A, [53?]
ARKADIA:
—TEGEA: (5) m. iv BC *IG* v (2) 6, 60 ([*Δ*]*εξίας?*)
——(Apolloniatai): (6) f. iii BC ib. 36, 69 (s. *Σωτέλης*)
——(Hippothoitai): (7) iv/iii BC ib. 38, 46 (f. *Δεξιφάνης*); (8) m. iii BC ib. 36, 81 (s. *Μνασίστρατος*)
ILLYRIA:
—EPIDAMNOS-DYRRHACHION: (9) c. 76 BC ib. VII 417, 24 + *AE* 1923, p. 50 no. 126 (*IOrop* 525) (s. *Ἐχελαΐδας*)
KORINTHIA:
—SIKYON: (10) iv BC *Eretria* VI 181; (11) c. 210-207 BC *IG* IV (1)² 73, 11; *SEG* XXXV 303 (date) (s. *Δέξις*)
MESSENIA:
—MESSENE: (12) hell. *BMC Pelop.* p. 111 nos. 32-3 (coin) ?= (13); (13) 191-146 BC ib. p. 13 no. 154 (coin) ?= (12); (14) s. ii BC *SEG* XLI 341, 20 (f. —*ης*)
—THOURIA: (15) s. iii BC *IG* v (1) 1386, 9 (f. *Νικεύς*); (16) f. ii BC *SEG* XI 972, 33 (s. *Καλλινόμας*); (17) ~ ib. l. 106 (s. *Ἀντιγένης*)
S. ITALY (BRUTTIUM):
—LOKROI EPIZEPHYRIOI:
——(Ἀνα.): (18) iv/iii BC De Franciscis 22, 14 (f. *Φιλιστίων*)
S. ITALY (CAMPANIA):
—NEAPOLIS: (19) c. 240-225 BC *IG* VII 342, 1 (*IOrop* 111); *IG* VII 505, 4 (f. *Πέλοψ*)

**Δεξίδαμος**
AKARNANIA:
—THYRREION: (1) iii BC ib. IX (1)² (2) 263 (f. *Κλέων*)

EPIROS:
—BOUTHROTOS (PRASAIBOI): (2) a. 163 BC *IBouthrot* 28, 9 (*SEG* XXXVIII 486) (s. *Δόκιμος*)
LAKONIA:
—GERONTHRAI: (3) i BC-i AD ib. II 169
—SPARTA: (4) s. i BC *IG* v (1) 94, 8 (Bradford (3)) (*Δεξίδ*[*αμος*]: f. *Τιμοκλῆς*); (5) c. 30-20 BC *IG* v (1) 141, 24; *SEG* XXXV 329 (date) (Bradford (2))

**Δεξίθεος**
AIGINA: (1) m. iv BC *IG* II² 7953 (f. *Δαμάτριος*)
AKARNANIA:
—ASTAKOS: (2) ii BC ib. IX (1)² (2) 434, 7 (s. *Καλλικράτης*)
DALMATIA:
—ISSA: (3) iii/ii BC Brunšmid p. 24 no. 12 (s. *Ἀλε*—)
KORINTHIA:
—SIKYON: (4) vi/v BC *SEG* XI 244, 56
MESSENIA:
—KYPARISSIA: (5) c. 100-90 BC ib. XXXIII 290 A, 19; *BSA* 70 (1975) pp. 129-31 (date); cf. Stephanis 2444 (f. *Τυχαμένης*)
S. ITALY (CALABRIA): (6) ii/i BC *IG* XII (3) Suppl. 1299, 22 (s. *Χα*—)

**Δεξικλέα**
ARGOLIS:
—ARGOS: (1) 105 BC *JÖAI* 14 (1911) Beibl. p. 146 no. 4, 16 (*Δεξικλ*[*έ*]*α*)

**Δεξικλῆς**
ACHAIA?: (1) 193 BC *IG* v (2) 293, 4 (f. *Δαμέας*)
LAKONIA:
—HIPPOLA: (2) ii-iii AD *SEG* XXVI 456, 5 (-*κλέης*: f. *Δέξιππος*)
MESSENIA:
—MESSENE: (3) ?i BC *PAE* 1969, p. 100 a, 5

**Δεξικράτεια**
AKARNANIA:
—PALAIROS: (1) f. iii BC *IG* IX (1)² (2) 467

**Δεξικράτης**
ACHAIA: (1) 146 BC ib. IV (1)² 28, 126 (s. *Δεξίλας*: synoikos)
ARGOLIS:
—ARGOS:
——(Dymanes-Amphiareteidai): (2) c. 400 BC *SEG* XXIX 361, 36
—EPIDAUROS: (3) ii BC *IG* IV (1)² 247 (f. *Ἱέρων*)
—EPIDAUROS*: (4) c. 335-325 BC ib. 106 III, 96 (*Δεξικ*[*ράτης*])
ARKADIA:
—TEGEA:
——(Athaneatai): (5) s. iii BC ib. v (2) 36, 113 (s. *Δεξι*—: metic)
LAKONIA:
—SPARTA: (6) c. 30-20 BC ib. v (1) 211, 14 (Bradford (-)) (f. *Ἄρατος*)
S. ITALY (BRUTTIUM):
—RHEGION: (7) iv/iii BC D.H. xx 5. 2 (doctor)
S. ITALY (CALABRIA):
—TARAS-TARENTUM: (8) f. ii BC *IG* XI (4) 810; cf. Wilhelm, *Neue Beitr.* 6 p. 58 (name) (*Δεξι*[*κ*]*ράτης*)

**Δεξίλαος**
S. ITALY (BRUTTIUM):
—SYBARIS-THOURIOI-COPIAE: (1) f. vi BC Guarducci, *Ep. Gr.* I p. 110 no. 3 (Lazzarini 859; Landi, *DISMG* 252; Ebert, *Gr. Sieg.* p. 251 f.; *CEG* I 394); *BE* 1973, no. 557 (locn.); cf. *SEG* XXIX 1017; *LSAG²* p. 456 no. 1a (date) (f. *Κλεόμβροτος*)

**Δεξίλαος**
ACHAIA:
—AIGION: (1) hell. *SEG* XLI 401 A
—TRITAIA: (2) iii BC ib. XL 400, 10-12
ARKADIA:
—TEGEA:

## Δεξίλας

——(Krariotai): (3) iii BC *IG* v (2) 40, 19 (s. *Τοξότας*)

EPIROS:
—MOLOSSOI: (4) ?164 BC Cabanes, *L'Épire* p. 586 no. 71, 4 (s. *Εὐρύνους*); (5) ~ ib. l. 5 (f. *Φερένικος*)

ITHAKE: (6) ii BC *SEG* XVII 254; cf. Fraser–Rönne, *BWGT* pl. 23

## Δεξίλας

ACHAIA: (1) 146 BC *IG* IV (1)² 28, 126 (f. *Δεξικράτης*: synoikos)

ARGOLIS:
—EPIDAUROS*: (2) c. 370-360 BC *BSA* 61 (1966) p. 272 no. 4 B II, 16 (*Δεξίλα[ς]*)

LAKONIA?: (3) vii/vi BC *Ol. Ber.* 7 pp. 119; 127; *LSAG*² p. 446 no. 1 a (date—*LGPN*)

## Δεξίλλος

ARGOLIS:
—ARGOS: (1) ?c. 460-450 BC *IG* IV (1) 515 (Lazzarini 401); *LSAG*² p. 170 no. 33 (date) (-ξξι-)

## Δεξίλος

KORINTHIA:
—KORINTH: (1) c. 610-590 BC Amyx 18. 8 (vase) (Lorber 28); *LSAG*² p. 131 no. 9 (date)

## Δεξίλοχος

ARKADIA:
—LOUSOI: (1) iv/iii BC *IG* v (2) 390, 5 (Perlman L.3)

## Δεξιμάχα

AKARNANIA:
—PALAIROS: (1) iii BC *IG* IX (1)² (2) 484

## Δεξίμαχος

EPIROS:
—DODONA*: (1) iv-iii BC *SGDI* 1584 B (*Δεξίμαχος*)

LAKONIA:
—SPARTA: (2) s. i BC *IG* v (1) 141, 19; 142, [2]; 209, 4, 11; 374, 10; 644?; *BSA* 80 (1985) pp. 193-7 (ident., stemma) (Bradford (2)) (*Γ. Ἰούλ. Δ.*: s. *Πρατόλας*, ?s. *Εὐρυβάνασσα*, f. *Πρατόλας*); (3) c. 35 BC-10 AD *PIR*² I 290; *IG* II² 3926, 5; v (1) 141, 18; *BSA* 80 (1985) pp. 193; 195 (ident., date) (Bradford (1)) (*Γ. Ἰούλ. Δ.*: s. *Γ. Ἰούλ. Εὐρυκλῆς*); (4) c. 10-20 AD *IG* v (1) 206, 1; *SEG* XI 847?; XXXV 330 (date); *BSA* 80 (1985) pp. 194; 197 (ident., stemma) (Bradford (6)) (*[Δεξί]μαχος?*—*SEG* XI: s. *Σιδέκτας*); (5) c. 40-100 AD *IG* v (1) 53, 11; 54, [13]; 57, 7; 101, 3; 290, 2 (*Artemis Orthia* pp. 316-17 no. 37); *IG* v (1) 470, 6; *SEG* XI 488, 2; 508, 7; 536, 2; 605, 11; *BSA* 80 (1985) pp. 194; 201-4 (ident., stemma) (Bradford (3); (8); (11); (14)) (*Π. Μέμμιος Δ.*: s. *Π. Μέμμιος Πρατόλας*, *Μεμμία Πασιχάρεια*, f. *Π. Μέμμιος Σιδέκτας*, *Π. Μέμμιος Πρατόλας*, ?f. *Π. Μέμμιος Πρατόλαος Δέξτρος*, *Μεμμία Εὐρυβάνασσα*); (6) c. 95-100 AD *SEG* XI 490, 1 (Bradford (7)) (*Δεξί[μα]χος ὁ καὶ Νικοκράτης*); (7) ii AD *SEG* XI 790, 1 (Bradford (12)); (8) c. 110-170 AD *IG* v (1) 285 (*Artemis Orthia* p. 319 no. 42); *IG* v (1) 537, 2; 584, 4; 585; 586, 3; *SEG* XI 494, 6; XXXV [325]; XXXVI 353, 4; *BSA* 80 (1985) pp. 194; 204-5 (ident., stemma) (Bradford (5); (9); (15)) (*Π. Μέμμιος Δ.*: s. *Π. Μέμμιος Πρατόλαος*, f. *Μέμμιος Μνάσων*, *Μέμμιος Πρατόλαος*, *Μεμμία Ξενοκράτεια*); (9) c. 125-150 AD *IG* v (1) 107, 2 (Bradford (16))

## Δεξιμένης

ARKADIA:
—MEGALOPOLIS: (1) ii BC *IG* v (2) 443, 49 (*IPArk* 32) (*Δεξιμέν[ης]*: s. *Θεαρίδας*)

## Δεξίνικος

KORINTHIA:
—SIKYON: (1) ?255-254 BC Nachtergael, *Les Galates* 8, 42; 9, 15 (Stephanis 600) (s. *Παντοῖος*)

LAKONIA:
—SPARTA: (2) c. 25-1 BC *IG* v (1) 212, 24 (Bradford (-)) (s. *Ὀνασικλείδας*)

## Δεξίνομος

MESSENIA:
—MESSENE: (1) i BC *SEG* XXIII 211, 2

## Δέξιος

AIGINA?: (1) 405 BC *IG* I³ 1032, 429

ARGOLIS:
—EPIDAUROS*: (2) c. 370-360 BC *BSA* 61 (1966) p. 271 no. 4 A, 15; p. 272 no. 4 B II, 10, 18; Peek, *IAEpid* 52 A, 48
—HERMIONE: (3) ?ii-i BC *IG* IV (1) 731 I, 3 (f. *Ἡμερώ*); (4) ~ ib. l. 15 (f. *Κόσμος*); (5) ~ ib. 731 III, 3-4 (f. *Πύρων*, *Κέρδων*)

S. ITALY (CAMPANIA):
—HERCULANEUM: (6) imp. *SB* 11979 (*Λ. Δ.*)

SICILY:
—SYRACUSE: (7) imp. *IG* XIV 35

## Δεξιππίδας

ACHAIA:
—PELLENE: (1) c. 315-280 BC *FD* III (4) 403 X, 1 (s. *—άλης*)

## Δέξιππος

ARGOLIS:
—ARGOS: (1) iv-iii BC Unp. (Ch. Kritzas)

EPIROS:
—BOUTHROTOS (PRASAIBOI): (2) a. 163 BC *IBouthrot* 39, 2; 42, 17 (*SEG* XXXVIII 498; 501) (I ?f. *Φιλόξενος*, *Δέξιππος* II, *Ἀρσινόα*, *Φιλίστα*) ?= (4); (3) ~ *IBouthrot* 39, 2 (*SEG* XXXVIII 498) (II ?s. *Δέξιππος* I, *Ἀρσινόα*); (4) ~ *IBouthrot* 128, 10; 131, 7; 147, 11; 156, 10; 157, 6 (*BCH* 118 (1994) p. 127 nos. 12-13) (s. *Φιλόξενος*) ?= (2)

LAKONIA: (5) 406 BC *RE* (3) (Poralla² 227) ?= (6); (6) 400 BC X., *An.* v 1. 15; vi 1. 32; vi 6. 5 ff.; vi 21 ff. ?= (5)
—HIPPOLA: (7) ii-iii AD *SEG* XXVI 456, 2, 8, 10 (s. *Δεξικλῆς*, f. *Εὐαμερίδας*)
—SPARTA: (8) ?f. vi BC *CEG* I 369 (Lazzarini 131); cf. *SEG* XXX 503 (or Boiotia: -ιπος: f. -δας); (9) ?i AD ib. XI 621, 3 (Bradford (1)) (*[Δ]έξιππο[ς]*); (10) c. 175-200 AD *SEG* XI 503, 18 (Bradford (2)) (f. —*ης*)

MESSENIA: (11) ii/i BC *SEG* XI 981 = *AD* 25 (1970) Chron. p. 174; cf. *SEG* XXXIV 322
—MESSENE: (12) c. 225 BC ib. XI 414, 15 (Perlman E.5) (*Δέξι[ππ]ος*)

## Δέξις

KORINTHIA:
—KORINTH: (1) 353-352 BC *CID* II 31, 53, 60
—SIKYON: (2) c. 210-207 BC *IG* IV (1)² 73, 11; *SEG* XXXV 303 (date) (f. *Δεξίας*)

LAKONIA:
—SPARTA: (3) hell.? *IG* v (1) 808 (Bradford (2)); (4) s. i BC *IG* v (1) 96, 9 (Bradford (1)) (s. *Λυσικράτης*)

## Δεξίστρατος

ARGOLIS:
—ARGOS: (1) iii-ii BC *IG* IV (1) 580 (s. *Ἄρχιππος*)
——(Dymanes?): (2) iv/iii BC *SEG* XI 293, 5
——(Pamphyloi-Aischiadai): (3) c. 400 BC ib. XXIX 361, 13 (*[Δ]εξίστρατος*)

ILLYRIA:
—APOLLONIA: (4) c. 250-50 BC *NZ* 20 (1927) p. 54 (coin) (Ceka 41) (money.)

## Δεξιφάνης

ARKADIA:
—TEGEA:

## Δεξίων

(Hippothoitai): (1) iv/iii BC *IG* v (2) 38, 46 (s. *Δεξίας*)

EPIROS:
—BOUTHROTOS (PRASAIBOI): (2) a. 163 BC *IBouthrot* 29, 18 (*SEG* XXXVIII 487)

## Δεξίων

ACHAIA:
—KARYNEIA: (1) 134 or 130 BC *FD* III (3) 119, 3, 6 (f. *Ἀνδρότιμος*)

MESSENIA:
—KOLONIDES: (2) ii BC *IG* v (1) 1402, 4 (s. *Ἀλκιάδας*)

## Δέξτερ

KERKYRA: (1) imp. Unp. (*IG* arch.)

## Δεξτριανός

SICILY:
—KATANE: (1) iii-v AD Agnello 59 (Wessel 353); cf. Ferrua, *NG* 417 (*Δεξτρανός*—edd., *Δεξτρ(ι)ανός*—Ferrua)

## Δέξτρος

S. ITALY (CAMPANIA):
—POMPEII: (1) i BC-i AD *CIL* IV 1564 (?f. *Κόρινθος*)

## Δεξύλος

S. ITALY (CALABRIA):
—TARAS-TARENTUM (NR.): (1) vi/v BC *SEG* XLI 884

## Δέξων

ARKADIA:
—TEGEA: (1) m. iv BC *IG* v (2) 6, 114

KERKYRA: (2) c. 229-48 BC Postolakas p. 16 no. 154 (coin)

MESSENIA:
—THOURIA: (3) ii-i BC *IG* v (1) 1385, 21 (s. *Ὄρθων*)

SICILY:
—TYNDARIS: (4) f. i BC Cic., *In Verr.* II v 108; 110; 128 (f. *Ἀριστεύς*)

## Δέρδας

EPIROS: (1) 234-168 BC Liv. xxix 12. 11; Franke, *Münz. v. Epirus* p. 178 II ser. 35
—BOUTHROTOS (PRASAIBOI): (2) a. 163 BC *IBouthrot* 26, 7 (*SEG* XXXVIII 484) (f. —*ων*); (3) ~ *IBouthrot* 26, 7 (*SEG* XXXVIII 484) (s. —*ων*)
——Cheirakioi: (4) a. 163 BC *IBouthrot* 56, 4 (*SEG* XXXVIII 507) ?= (6)
—BOUTHROTOS?: (5) a. 163 BC *IBouthrot* 91, 17 (*SEG* XXXII 623) (s. *Μελάνθιος*)
—CHEIRAKIOI: (6) iii/ii BC Cabanes, *L'Épire* p. 558 no. 34, 1 (*SEG* XXVI 701); *ZPE* 63 (1986) p. 145 (locn.) ?= (4)

## Δέρκας

ARGOLIS:
—TROIZEN: (1) iv BC *IG* IV (1) 764, 3 (*Δέρκας*, *Δερίας*—ed.: s. *Στόμας*)

EPIROS:
—DODONA*: (2) iv BC *PAE* 1967, p. 48 no. 1
—MOLOSSOI: (3) c. 317-297 BC Cabanes, *L'Épire* p. 545 no. 12
—TALAONOI/TALAIANES: (4) iii-ii BC *SGDI* 1349, 7; cf. Cabanes, *L'Épire* p. 580 no. 53 (f. *Εὐρύνους*)

KEPHALLENIA:
—PALE: (5) iii/ii BC Unp. (*IG* arch.) (*Δέρ[κας]*, *Δερ[κύλος]?*)

## Δέρκετος

ARGOLIS:
—ARGOS: (1) ?c. 460-450 BC *Mnem.* NS 47 (1919) p. 161 no. 6, 8; *LSAG*² p. 170 no. 31 (date) (*Δέρ[κ]ετ[ος]*); (2) c. 458 BC *IG* I³ 1149, 22 (*[Δ]έρκετος*); (3) ~ ib. l. 75; (4) f. iii BC ib. IV (1) 529, 24; cf. *BCH* 37 (1913) p. 309 (*[Δέρ]κετος*)

**Δερκέτυς**
ARKADIA:
—TEGEA: (1) iii BC *IG* V (2) 248

**Δερκίδας**
LAKONIA:
—SPARTA: (1) m. iii BC Peek, *IAEpid* 42,
13 (Perlman E.3); Perlman p. 63 f. (date)
(*Δερκίδας*: f. *Εὔδωρος*)

**Δερκυλίδας**
LAKONIA:
—SPARTA: (1) v/iv BC *RE* (1) (Poralla² 228) (*Δ.*
*ὁ ἐπικαλ. Σίσυφος*); (2) 272 BC Plu., *Mor.* 219
F (Bradford (-)) ?= (*Μανδροκλείδας* (1))

**Δερκύλος**
ARGOLIS:
—ARGOS: (1) ?s. iv BC *RE* (2); *FGrH* 305; cf.
Fraser, *Ptol. Alex.* 2 p. 1010 nn. 42 and 63
ARKADIA:
—TEGEA: (2) iv BC *SEG* XXXVI 382, 4
(*Δερκύ[λος]*: f. *Διεύχης*)

**Δέρκων**
ARKADIA:
—MANTINEIA-ANTIGONEIA: (1) c. 300-221 BC
*IG* V (2) 323. 97 (tessera) (*Δέρκω[ν]*: f.
*Μελια—*)

**Δερφέας**
ARGOLIS:
—PITYONESOS: (1) v BC ib. IV (1) 192 (Lazza-
rini 266) (*Δερφέας* (n. pr.?))

**Δεσπόσιος**
LAKONIA:
—SPARTA: (1) v BC *IG* V (1) 1590 (s. *Παλάμων*)

**Δέτας**
SICILY:
—SELINOUS: (1) m. v BC Dubois, *IGDS* 34
(Arena, *Iscr. Sic.* I 70)

**Δέτος**
ARGOLIS:
—PHLEIOUS: (1) ?iii BC *IG* IV (1) 458

**Δευκαλίων**
ELIS:
—CHALADRIOI: (1) c. 500-475 BC *IvOl* 11, 1;
*LSAG*² p. 220 no. 8 (date)

**Δευτέρα**
S. ITALY (CAMPANIA):
—DIKAIARCHIA-PUTEOLI: (1) imp. *CIL* X 2353
(Lat. Aviania Deutera)

**Δευτερία**
SICILY:
—KATANE: (1) iii-v AD *IG* XIV 526 (Wessel 241)

**Δευτερικός**
S. ITALY (CAMPANIA):
—POMPEII: (1) c. 51-62 AD *CIL* IV 3340. 132,
3 (Castrèn 324. 2) (Lat. P. Proculeus Deu-
teri[cus]?)

**Δεύτερος**
S. ITALY (CAMPANIA)*: (1) ?i-ii AD *CIL* X
8042. 64; *AJA* 2 (1898) p. 392 no. 46 (tile)
(Lat. C. Iulius Deuterus)
S. ITALY (LUCANIA):
—COSILINUM?: (2) imp. *Apollo* 2 (1962) pp.
117-18 (Lat. T. Helvius Deuterus Prior)
—GRUMENTUM: (3) imp. *CIL* X 250 (Lat. Deu-
terus)

**Δέων**
AITOLIA: (1) ?204 BC *IG* VII 303, 61 (Petra-
kos, *Oropos* pp. 188-91 no. 45; *IOrop* 324)
((*Λ*)*έων*?)

**ARGOLIS:**
—ARGOS: (2) ii AD *SEG* XVI 253, 3 ((*Λ*)*έων*?)

**Δϝεινίας**
KORINTHIA:
—KORINTH: (1) m. vii BC *CEG* I 132 (*GVI*
53; *LSAG*² p. 131 no. 6); cf. *SEG* XXIII 174
(*Δϝε-*)

**Δηϊδάμεια**
EPIROS:
—MOLOSSOI: (1) iv/iii BC *RE* (5) (d. *Αἰακίδης*,
*Φθία* (Thessaly, Pharsalos)); (2) c. 250-232 BC
ib. Supplbd. 1 (6) (d. *Πύρρος*)

**Δηϊκράτης**
SICILY:
—LEONTINOI: (1) s. v BC Paus. vi 17. 7; *IvOl*
293, 2 (*CEG* II 830) (f. *Ἱπποκράτης*)

**Δηΐφονος**
ILLYRIA:
—APOLLONIA: (1) vi/v BC Hdt. ix 92; 95 (s. *Εὐή-*
*νιος*)

**Δήλιος**
S. ITALY (CAMPANIA):
—POMPEII: (1) i BC-i AD *CIL* IV 1290 (Lat. De-
lius); (2) ~ ib. 4215 (Lat. Delius)

**Δηλιώ**
DALMATIA:
—ISSA: (1) iii/ii BC *SEG* XXXV 684 (*VAHD* 84
(1991) p. 254 no. 5) (d. *Εὐχηρίδας*)

**Δημαίνετος**
ARGOLIS:
—ARGOS*: (1) iii BC *SEG* XXX 364, 2, 4
(*Δ[ημ]αίν[ετος]*: I f. *Τίμαρχος*, *Δημαίνετος* II);
(2) ~ ib. l. 4 (*Δημαίνε[το]ς*: II s. *Δημαίνετος* I)

**Δημάρετος**
EPIROS:
—NIKOPOLIS: (1) c. 30 BC ib. XXXVII 526
(Sarikakis 31) (f. *Δικαία*)
LEUKAS: (2) c. 167-50 BC *BMC Thessaly* p. 179
no. 84; p. 182 nos. 123-6; p. 184 nos. 145-9;
*SNG Cop. Epirus–Acarnania* 390-1 (coins)

**Δημαρχία**
LAKONIA:
—SPARTA: (1) ii AD *SEG* XLI 319, 7 (m. *Εὐφρό-*
*συνος*)

**Δημαρχίδης**
MESSENIA:
—MESSENE: (1) i AD *IG* V (1) 1440, 1 (*Τ. Φλ. Δ.*)

**Δήμαρχος**
DALMATIA:
—PHAROS: (1) hell. Brunšmid p. 14 no. 1 (f.
*Γοργιλώ*)
S. ITALY (BRUTTIUM):
—HIPPONION-VIBO VALENTIA: (2) c. 315-280
BC *FD* III (1) 176, 1; cf. *SEG* XL 421 (f. *Φι-*
*λώτας*)

**Δήμασις**
ARGOLIS:
—TROIZEN: (1) imp. *IG* IV (1) 819

**Δημέας**
AIGINA: (1) iv BC ib. 100
ARGOLIS:
—ARGOS: (2) c. 100-90 BC *SEG* XXXIII 290
A, 4; *BSA* 70 (1975) pp. 129-31 (date); cf.
Stephanis 2663 (f. *—as*)
LAKONIA:
—SPARTA: (3) c. 100-125 AD *IG* V (1) 40, 4; 57,
9; *SEG* XI 514, 3 (Bradford (2)) (f. *Ἀμάραν-*
*τος*); (4) c. 130-150 AD *IG* V (1) 65, 16; 112, 1;
*SEG* XI 549, 6 (Bradford (1)) (s. *Ἀμάραντος*)

**Δημητρία**
KORINTHIA:
—KORINTH: (1) ?i AD *Corinth* VIII (3) 282 (Lat.
Demetria)
S. ITALY (CAMPANIA):
—DIKAIARCHIA-PUTEOLI: (2) imp. *CIL* X 2025
(Lat. Aimilia Demetria); (3) ~ ib. 2241; 8368
(Lat. Castricia Demetria)
—MISENUM*: (4) ?ii-iii AD ib. 3349 (Lat. Aure-
lia Demetria)
—NEAPOLIS: (5) i BC *IG* II² 9991 (d. *Λεύκιος*)
S. ITALY (LUCANIA):
—ATINA LUCANA: (6) imp. *IItal* III (1) 162
(*CIL* X 355) (Lat. –lia Demetria)
S. ITALY?: (7) c. 365-340 BC *IG* II² 8942 (d.
*Ἀρίστων*)
SICILY:
—SYRACUSE: (8) iii-v AD *NScav* 1907, p. 756
no. 7; cf. Ferrua, *NG* 80

**Δημητριάς**
ILLYRIA:
—LYCHNIDOS: (1) ii-iii AD Demitsas 340 (d. *Νι-*
*κάνωρ*, *Ἀρτεμιδώρα*)

**Δημήτριος**
ACHAIA: (1) 146 BC *IG* IV (1)² 28, 134 (f. *Ἄν-*
*δρων*: synoikos)
AIGINA: (2) hell.? ib. IV (1) 117 (f. *Θεοδότη*); (3)
ii/i BC *Alt-Ägina* I (2) p. 43 no. 3, 2 (f. *Ξένων*);
(4) ?i BC ib. p. 44 no. 11, 2 (s. *Ἀρίστανδρος*);
(5) ?s. i BC ib. p. 44 no. 6, 1 (*Δημήτριος*); (6)
~ ib. l. 3 (f. *—ης*)
AITOLIA:
—THERMOS*: (7) s. iii BC *IG* IX (1)² (1) 60 II,
5; (8) ~ ib. l. 8; (9) ~ ib. l. 13; (10) ~ ib. 60
IV, 6; (11) ~ ib. 60 V, 2; (12) ~ ib. l. 9; (13)
~ ib. 60 VI, 9
AKARNANIA:
—THYRREION: (14) ii BC ib. IX (1)² (2) 247, 18
(f. *Πρῶτος*); (15) ~ ib. 319
ARGOLIS:
—ARGOS: (16) iii BC *SEG* XI 331; (17) ii BC Le
Rider, *Monnaies crétoises* p. 258 II (f. *Πτολε-*
*μαῖος*); (18) ~ *SEG* XLII 279, 20 (s. *Ἀρίστων*);
(19) ii-i BC *Syringes* 44 (s. *Εὔφρων*); (20) m.
ii BC Siebert, *Ateliers* pp. 30-1; 170 (date)
(*Δημή(τριος)*?: ?s. *Ἰάσων*: potter); (21) 536 AD
Unp. (Oikonomou-Laniado) (f. *Στεφανίς*)
—EPIDAUROS: (22) iii/ii BC Peek, *NIEpid* 15, 13
(f. *Ἀμύντας*); (23) ii BC Peek, *IAEpid* 130 (f.
*Ἀμύντας*)
—EPIDAUROS*: (24) c. 290-270 BC *IG* IV (1)²
109 II, 118, 128, 158; III, 121, 135; *SEG*
XXV 401 B, [120], [129]
—HERMIONE: (25) ?ii-i BC *IG* IV (1) 731 III,
11 (f. *Ζευξαγόρα*); (26) ii-i BC ib. 732 I, 3
([*Δ*]*ημήτριος*: s. *Ἀνδροκλῆς*)
—TROIZEN: (27) imp.? ib. 813, 5; (28) ?i AD *RE*
(106)
ARKADIA:
—TEGEA: (29) iii-ii BC *SEG* XXXIX 391, 3 (f.
*Διόγνητος*: sculptor); (30) ii AD *IG* V (2) 55,
43 (f. *Ἧρος*)
DALMATIA:
—PHAROS: (31) s. iii BC *RE* Supplbd. 1 (44a);
(32) 221 BC *PP* 8134 (s. *Ποιανός*)
ELIS:
—OLYMPIA*: (33) 265 AD *IvOl* 122, 17 (?s. *Εὐ-*
*τύχης*: slave?)
EPIROS:
—NIKOPOLIS?: (34) ?iv AD *BCH* 89 (1965) p.
765
—THESPROTOI?: (35) 200-193 BC *IKourion* 42;
*PP* 15100; *Arch. Class.* 25-6 (1973-4) pp. 316
f. (or Thessaly?: s. *Μαχάτας*)
ILLYRIA:
—APOLLONIA: (36) ?iii BC *IApoll* 313
—EPIDAMNOS-DYRRHACHION: (37) c. 250-50
BC Maier 317; 357 (coin) (Ceka 129-30)
(money.); (38) hell.-imp. *IDyrrh* 220 (f. *Ζή-*
*νων*)

KEPHALLENIA: **(39)** f. vi AD *RE* (68)
KERKYRA: **(40)** ii AD *Ag.* XVII 518 (f. Ξένιον)
KORINTHIA:
—KORINTH: **(41)** i BC *BGU* 1285, 7 (s. Μύστα);
**(42)** i BC-i AD *SEG* XI 440, 2 (f. Ἐρωτίς); **(43)**
i AD *RE* (91); Philostr., *VA* iv 25 etc. (locn.);
Sen., *De Benef.* 7 (locn.); **(44)** byz. *Corinth*
VIII (1) 196
LAKONIA:
—SPARTA: **(45)** c. 140-160 AD *IG* V (1) 154, 8;
*SEG* XI 600, 3 (Bradford (4)) (f. Φιλοκλείδης)
—SPARTA?: **(46)** f. iii AD *IG* V (1) 538, 33; 539,
16; 540, 11 (Loewy 347-9); *BSA* 79 (1984)
pp. 274-7 (date) (Bradford (1)) (II s. Δημή-
τριος I: sculptor); **(47)** ~ *IG* V (1) 538, 34;
539, [16], 540, 11; *BSA* 79 (1984) pp. 274-7
(date) (Bradford (3)) (I f. Δημήτριος II)
MESSENIA:
—ABIA: **(48)** ii/iii AD *IG* V (1) 1253
([Δ]ημήτρι[ος])
—KORONE: **(49)** 246 AD ib. 1398, 65 (Αὐρ. Δ.)
—MESSENE: **(50)** imp.? *Ergon* 1995, p. 31 (f. Διο-
νύσιος)
——(Kleolaidai): **(51)** 11 AD *PAE* 1992, p. 71
A, 28 (f. Φιλέας)
S. ITALY (APULIA):
—CANUSIUM*: **(52)** i AD *Epig. Rom. di Canosa*
126 (*CIL* IX 375) (Lat. -ius Demetrius:
freed.)
S. ITALY (BRUTTIUM):
—CONSENTIA: **(53)** ii AD *Mus. Naz. Reggio* p.
158 no. 27 (f. Ἴα)
—KROTON: **(54)** 206 AD *NScav* 1911, Suppl. p.
122 (Lat. Aur. Demetrius)
S. ITALY (CALABRIA):
—TARAS-TARENTUM: **(55)** s. ii BC *EAD* XXX 381
(s. Δάζος)
S. ITALY (CAMPANIA):
—BAIAI: **(56)** imp. *AJA* 2 (1898) p. 393 no. 50
(Lat. Demetrius)
—DIKAIARCHIA-PUTEOLI: **(57)** imp. *CIL* X
2836 (Lat. A. Perpernius Demetrius); **(58)**
~ ib. 2855 (Lat. Demetrius); **(59)** ~ ib.
2862 (Lat. Sex. Pompeius Demetrius); **(60)** ~
*NScav* 1886, p. 130 (*Eph. Ep.* VIII 401) (Lat.
Demetrius: s. Εὔτυχος, Rufina); **(61)** 211-217
AD *NScav* 1954, pp. 285-7 (Lat. Demetrius)
—DIKAIARCHIA-PUTEOLI*: **(62)** imp. *CIL* X
1746 (Lat. Demetrius: slave?); **(63)** ~ ib. 1923,
1 (Lat. C. Caesonius Demetrius: freed.)
—MISENUM: **(64)** ?i/ii AD De Franciscis, *Sacello
Augustali* p. 29 no. 10 (Lat. Sex. Sextilius
Demetrius)
—MISENUM*: **(65)** imp. *CIL* X 3498 (Lat. De-
metrius: I f. Δημήτριος II); **(66)** ~ ib. (Lat.
L. Domitius Demetrius: II s. Δημήτριος I);
**(67)** ~ ib. 3545 (Lat. Iulius Demetrius); **(68)**
~ *NScav* 1928, p. 198 no. 9 ([Ἰ]ούλιος Δη-
μή[τριος])
—NEAPOLIS: **(69)** i BC *IG* XIV 776 (*INap* 106)
(s. Ἀρχίας)
—POMPEII: **(70)** i BC-i AD *CIL* IV 1276 (Lat.
Demetrius); **(71)** ~ ib. 6719 (Lat. [Pop]idius?
Demetrius); **(72)** ~ ib. 6883; **(73)** 70-79 AD ib.
2993 z; 2993 za; 3359; 3200 h-i; 3200 k; Mou-
ritsen pp. 110-11 (date) (Lat. Demetrius)
—SALERNUM: **(74)** imp. *IItal* I (1) 201 (*CIL* X
596) (Lat. A. Geminius Demetrius)
S. ITALY (LUCANIA):
—HYELE-VELIA: **(75)** iv/iii AD *SEG* XXVIII 818
(Landi, *DISMG* 232) (f. Ζῆνις)
SICILY: **(76)** m. i BC Cic., *ad Fam.* xiii 36. 1
(Lat. P. Cornelius Demetrius Megas)
—SYRACUSE: **(77)** 173 BC *ID* 455 A b, 30-3; 458
41; 460 b, 24; **(78)** s. ii BC *Acragas Graeca* I
p. 34 no. 5, 9, 13, 19, 24 (*IGDS* 185); Dubois,
*IGDS* 185); *IG* XIV 953, 2, 9, 16, 25 (*IGUR*
3) (s. Διόδοτος); **(79)** iii-v AD *Riv. Arch. Crist.*
36 (1960) p. 34 no. 30 (Δημή[τριος]); **(80)** ~
Strazzulla 192 (*Riv. Arch. Crist.* 18 (1941) p.

193 no. 61); cf. *ASSicilia* 1938-9, p. 28 (*Γ.
Βέτουος Δ.*)
—TYNDARIS: **(81)** f. i BC Cic., *In Verr.* II iv 92
(Lat. Demetrius)
—ZANKLE-MESSANA: **(82)** imp. *Mon. Ant.* 24
(1916) p. 165 (Lat. -ius Demetrius)

## Δημήτρις
ARKADIA:
—TEGEA: **(1)** ii AD *IG* V (2) 55, 44 (s. Δημητρ—)
EPIROS:
—NIKOPOLIS: **(2)** imp. *SEG* XXIV 429 (Sarika-
kis 73) (*Κλ. Δ.*)

## Δημόδοκος
S. ITALY (BRUTTIUM):
—RHEGION*: **(1)** m. vi BC Rumpf, *Chalkid.
Vas.* p. 46 no. 4 (vase) (Arena, *Iscr. Sic.* III
p. 102-3 no. 7) (-δοφος: her.?)

## Δημοκήδης
LAKONIA:
—SPARTA: **(1)** hell. *IG* V (1) 237 (Bradford (-))
(s. Δημόστρατος)

## Δημόκλεια
MESSENIA
—KORONE: **(1)** i-ii AD *IG* II² 9082 (d. Δημοκλῆς)

## Δημοκλῆς
AKARNANIA: **(1)** iv BC ib. IX (1)² (2) 586
MESSENIA:
—KORONE: **(2)** i-ii AD ib. II² 9082 (f. Δημόκλεια)
SICILY: **(3)** iv BC *FGrH* 566 F 32

## Δημοκράτης
KORINTHIA:
—SIKYON: **(1)** hell. *IG* IX (1) 935 (s. Δημόστρα-
τος)

## Δημόκριτος
ILLYRIA:
—EPIDAMNOS-DYRRHACHION: **(1)** c. 250-50 BC
Maier 295 (coin) (Ceka 131) (money.)
—LYCHNIDOS: **(2)** ii-iii AD *Sp.* 75 (1933) p. 59
no. 179 (s. Ἀννία Ὀλβίστη)

## Δημόνικος
MESSENIA:
—ASINE: **(1)** hell.-imp. *IG* V (1) 1407 (s. Ἁρμό-
διος)

## Δημοσθένης
ARGOLIS:
—EPIDAUROS: **(1)** 171 AD ib. IV (1)² 392, 4 (f.
Εὔπορος); **(2)** iii AD ib. 553 (I f. Δημοσθένης
II); **(3)** ~ ib. ([Δημοσθ]ένης: II s. Δημοσθένης
I)
ELIS: **(4)** c. 100-90 BC *SEG* XXXIII 290 A, 16;
*BSA* 70 (1975) pp. 129-31 (date) (Stephanis
653) (s. Φυσσίας)
ILLYRIA:
—EPIDAMNOS-DYRRHACHION: **(5)** imp. *IDyrrh*
57 (s. Φίλιππος)
S. ITALY (APULIA):
—VENUSIA: **(6)** imp. *CIL* IX 559 (Lat. Q. Pub-
licius Demosthenes)
S. ITALY (BRUTTIUM):
—RHEGION: **(7)** iv BC Iamb., *VP* 267 (*FVS* I p.
447)
S. ITALY (CAMPANIA):
—HERCULANEUM: **(8)** m. i AD *PdelP* 6 (1951) p.
225 no. 4, 4 (Lat. C. Iulius Demostenes)
—NEAPOLIS: **(9)** ii-iii AD *NScav* 1935, p. 290;
cf. Leiwo p. 101 no. 53 (Lat. T. Fl. Demos-
thenes)
—SALERNUM*: **(10)** imp. *IItal* I (1) 66 (*CIL*
X 597) (Lat. Sex. Helenius Demosthenes:
freed.); **(11)** ?i AD *IItal* I (1) 238 II, 19 (*CIL* X
557) (Lat. L. Appuleius Demosthenes: freed.)

SICILY:
—THERMAI HIMERAIAI: **(12)** imp. *SGDI* 3250
(*Kokalos* 20 (1974) pp. 246-7 no. 17) (s. Ἀρ-
χεβούλα)

## Δημόστρατος
ILLYRIA:
—APOLLONIA: **(1)** imp. *IApoll* 175 (*Γ. Καλπή-
τανος Δ.*)
KORINTHIA:
—SIKYON: **(2)** hell. *IG* IX (1) 935 (f. Δημοκρά-
της)
LAKONIA:
—SPARTA: **(3)** hell. ib. V (1) 237 (Bradford (2))
(f. Δημοκήδης)
SICILY: **(4)** f. iv BC *IG* II² 10288 (Δη-
μό[στρ]ατος: f. Διονύσιος)

## Δημοφάνης
S. ITALY (BRUTTIUM):
—RHEGION: **(1)** c. 425-400 BC Dubois, *IGDGG*
I 39 c (Arena, *Iscr. Sic.* III 63) (Δε̄μ(ο)φάνης:
s. Θράρυς)

## Δημόφαντος
AITOLIA: **(1)** c. 210-200 BC Paus. viii 49. 7 (or
Elis)

## Δημόφιλος
ARGOLIS:
—ARGOS?: **(1)** i BC-i AD Unp. (Argos, Kavva-
dias)
EPIROS:
—AMBRAKIA?: **(2)** inc. Hammond, *Epirus* index
SICILY:
—HIMERA: **(3)** c. 420 BC Plin., *NH* XXXV 61
(painter)

## Δημοφῶν
MESSENIA:
—MESSENE?: **(1)** iii/ii BC *IG* V (2) 539 (f. Νικίπ-
πα)

## Δημόχαρις
S. ITALY (CAMPANIA):
—KYME: **(1)** vi/v BC Dubois, *IGDGG* I 17 b
(Arena, *Iscr. Sic.* III 14); *LSAG*² p. 240 no.
9 (date) (Δε̄-)

## Δημύλος
S. ITALY (LUCANIA):
—HYELE-VELIA: **(1)** f. v BC *FVS* I p. 249 no.
29 A 7 (tyrant)

## Δημώ
ARGOLIS:
—ARGOS: **(1)** i BC *GP* 3199 (het.?)
—HERMIONE: **(2)** ?ii-i BC *IG* IV (1) 731 I, 1 (d.
Ἀπολλωνίδης)
S. ITALY (CAMPANIA):
—KYME: **(3)** arch. *RE* (2) (fict.?)
SICILY:
—ZANKLE-MESSANA: **(4)** i BC-i AD *NS* 604
(or Messenia Messene: d. Λεύκιος, Πλουτίχα
(Lokroi Epizephyrioi))

## Δήμων
S. ITALY (CAMPANIA):
—KYME: **(1)** ?c. 450 BC Dubois, *IGDGG* I 21
a (vase) (Arena, *Iscr. Sic.* III 28); *LSAG*² p.
240 no. 14 (date) (Δέμōν)
S. ITALY (LUCANIA):
—HYELE-VELIA: **(2)** imp.? *IG* XIV 659 a (p. 689)
(f. Ὄνησος)
SICILY:
—HERBITA: **(3)** v/iv BC ib. I³ 228, 21, [23-4]
(date—M.J.O.)

## Δημῶναξ
AIGINA: **(1)** hell.-imp. ib. IV (1) 43 (s. Πύρρος);
**(2)** i BC-i AD *Alt-Ägina* I (2) p. 45 no. 15 (f.
—ριος)
AKARNANIA:
—ASTAKOS: **(3)** ii BC *IG* IX (1)² (2) 435, 17 (s.
Αἰσχύλος)

**Δημώνασσα**
KORINTHIA:
—KORINTH: (**1**) ii AD Luc., *DMeretr.* 5. 2-3 (fict.)

**Δηνίππα**
LAKONIA:
—PYRRHICHOS?: (**1**) iv BC *SEG* XI 1002

**Δῆρις**
KORINTHIA:
—KORINTH: (**1**) vi BC *IG* IV (1) 308 (pinax) (Δἔ-)

**Δῖα**
KORINTHIA:
—KORINTH: (**1**) c. 570-550 BC Amyx 74. 6 (vase) (Lorber 129) (her.)
S. ITALY (BRUTTIUM):
—TERINA: (**2**) c. 325-300 BC *IGSI* 21, 2 (*SEG* IV 73; Landi, *DISMG* 170) (d. Κόνων)
S. ITALY (CAMPANIA):
—DIKAIARCHIA-PUTEOLI: (**3**) imp. *CIL* X 2799 (Lat. Octabia Dia)
—DIKAIARCHIA-PUTEOLI*: (**4**) imp. *Territorio Flegreo* 1 p. 90 no. 4 (Lat. Ostoria Dia: freed.)
—NEAPOLIS: (**5**) 59 AD *CIL* X 1504 (*INap* 132) (Lat. Quintia Dia: m. M. Cominius Verecundus)

**Διαγόρας**
S. ITALY (CAMPANIA)?: (**1**) imp.? *IG* XIV 2414. 17 (tessera)

**Διαδουμενός**
LAKONIA:
—SPARTA: (**1**) c. 132 AD *SEG* XI 579, 6 (Bradford (-))
S. ITALY: (**2**) imp. *CIL* X 8059. 434 (seal) (Lat. C. Vibbius Diadumenus)
S. ITALY (APULIA):
—CANUSIUM: (**3**) ?i-ii AD *Epig. Rom. di Canosa* Instr. 5 (tile) (Lat. Ti. Claudius Diadume(nus))
S. ITALY (CALABRIA):
—BRENTESION-BRUNDISIUM: (**4**) imp. *Epigraphica* 25 (1963) p. 35 no. 5; cf. 42 (1980) p. 154 (Lat. Gerellanus Diadumenus)
S. ITALY (CAMPANIA):
—DIKAIARCHIA-PUTEOLI: (**5**) imp. *CIL* X 1610 (Lat. Diadumenus); (**6**) ~ ib. 2863 (Lat. Iulius Diadumenus); (**7**) ?i-ii AD ib. 2265 (Lat. Ti. Claudius Diadumenus); (**8**) 176 AD ib. 1877 (Lat. Q. Insteius Diadumenus)
—HERCULANEUM: (**9**) m. i AD *PdelP* 6 (1951) p. 228 no. 10, 5 (Lat. Umbrius Diadumenus)
—MISENUM*: (**10**) imp. *CIL* X 3347 (Lat. Diadumenus: freed.?)
—NEAPOLIS*: (**11**) 65 AD *NScav* 1883, p. 51 (*Eph. Ep.* VIII 335-7) (Lat. Diadumenus: imp. freed.)
—PICENTIA: (**12**) imp. *CIL* X 509 (Lat. Diadumenus: s. Felix)
—POMPEII: (**13**) i BC-i AD ib. IV 2356; cf. p. 219 (Lat. Diadumenus); (**14**) ~ ib. 3926 (Lat. Diadum(en)us); (**15**) ~ ib. 7296 (Lat. Diadumenus); (**16**) ~ ib. 7991 (Lat. Diadumenus); (**17**) ~ ib. X 883 (Castrèn 298. 1) (Lat. M. Pacuius Diadumenus); (**18**) 50-79 AD *CIL* IV 2975 (Lat. Diadumenus); (**19**) 55 AD ib. 3340. 14, 17; 28, 14 (Castrèn 161. 6) (Lat. M. Fab. Diadumenus)
—POMPEII*: (**20**) i BC-i AD *CIL* X 8058. 24 (seal) (Castrèn 129. 17) (Lat. C. Corn. Diadumenus: freed.); (**21**) s. i AD *CIL* X 861 (Lat. Diadumenus: freed.)
—SALERNUM: (**22**) imp. *IItal* 1 (1) 121 (Lat. Diadumenus: f. Felix)
SICILY:
—HENNA*: (**23**) ?i/ii AD *CIL* X 7189 (Lat. T. Flavius Diadumenus: f. Flavia Victorina: imp. freed.)

**—ZANKLE-MESSANA:** (**24**) imp. *IG* XIV 408

**Διαίθων**
ARKADIA:
—MANTINEIA-ANTIGONEIA: (**1**) c. 425-385 BC *SEG* XI 1099 (21a) (tessera); cf. *LSAG²* pl. 41 no. 37 (-θõν)

**Διαικλῆς**
LAKONIA:
—SPARTA: (**1**) 345 BC *CID* II 31, 75; 120 A, [18] (Poralla² 233)

**Διαίνετος**
ARKADIA:
—TEGEA: (**1**) iii BC *IG* V (2) 40, 28 (I f. Διαίνετος II); (**2**) ~ ib. l. 28 (II s. Διαίνετος I)

**Δίαιος**
ARKADIA:
—MANTINEIA-ANTIGONEIA: (**1**) c. 300-221 BC ib. 323. 102 (tessera) (s. Ἀγήμων)
—MEGALOPOLIS: (**2**) iii/ii BC Paus. viii 30. 5; 51. 1; *IvOl* 46, [5] (*IPArk* 31 IIB) (f. Διοφάνης); (**3**) m. ii BC *RE* Supplbd. 11 (-) (?s. Διοφάνης); (**4**) s. ii BC *IG* V (2) 460 (and Lakonia Sparta: f. Προάγορος)

**Διαίτης**
S. ITALY (BRUTTIUM):
—KAULONIA?: (**1**) ?c. 475 BC *IGSI* 20, 2 (*SEG* IV 71; Landi, *DISMG* 168); *LSAG²* p. 261 no. 29 (date) (Διαίτēς (n. pr.?))

**Διάκονος**
S. ITALY (CAMPANIA):
—HERCULANEUM: (**1**) m. i AD *PdelP* 8 (1953) p. 461 no. 50, 3 (Lat. L. Mammius Diaconus)

**Διάκριτος**
AITOLIA:
—THESTIEIS: (**1**) 213 BC *IG* IX (1)² (1) 96, 12 (f. Ξενόδοκος)
LAKONIA:
—SPARTA: (**2**) 431 BC Th. ii 12. 1 (Poralla² 234) (f. Μελήσιππος)
LEUKAS: (**3**) c. 167-50 BC *BMC Thessaly* p. 179 no. 87; p. 181 nos. 111-12; p. 186 nos. 177-9; p. 187 nos. 192-3 (coin); (**4**) f. i BC *IG* IX (1) 534, 6 (*Iscr. Gr. Verona* p. 24) (s. Σάθων)

**Διακτορίδας**
LAKONIA:
—SPARTA: (**1**) s. vi BC Hdt. vi 71. 2 (Poralla² 235) (-δης: f. Εὐρυδάμα, Μένιος)

**Διακτόριος**
LAKONIA:
—SPARTA: (**1**) 182 BC Plb. xxiii 18. 5 (Bradford (-))

**Διάκτωρ**
ARGOLIS:
—ARGOS: (**1**) i AD *SEG* XXVI 429, 5 (f. Τεισίας); (**2**) ~ ib. l. 7 (s. Τεισίας)

**Διάλκης**
ARKADIA:
—MANTINEIA-ANTIGONEIA: (**1**) 464 or 460 BC Paus. vi 6. 1; Moretti, *Olymp.* 256 (date) (f. Πρωτόλαος)

**Διάνοια**
KERKYRA: (**1**) i BC-i AD *IG* IX (1) 936

**Διανόμα**
ILLYRIA:
—EPIDAMNOS-DYRRHACHION: (**1**) hell.-imp. *IDyrrh* 169 (Διανέμα—ed.: d. Ἀπολλώνιος)

**Διάπυρος**
S. ITALY (APULIA):
—BUTUNTUM*: (**1**) imp. *Mus. Arch. di Bari* p. 166 no. 15 (Lat. M. Massius Diapyrus)
SICILY:
—LIPARA: (**2**) hell.-imp. *IG* XIV 391 (Libertini, *Isole Eolie* p. 219 no. 9) ([Δ]ιάπυρος)

**Διάρης**
ARKADIA:
—PHENEOS: (**1**) c. 225 BC *SEG* XI 414, 7 (Perlman E.5) (Διάρης)
LAKONIA:
—SPARTA: (**2**) iv/iii BC *IG* V (1) 649 (Poralla² 237; Bradford (-))

**Δίας**
KEPHALLENIA: (**1**) imp. *SEG* XXX 516 (Πόπλιος Βείβιος Δ.)

**Διατάγης**
ARKADIA:
—MANTINEIA-ANTIGONEIA: (**1**) c. 316-222 BC *Mnem.* NS 43 (1915) pp. 376-7 G, 1 (Perlman A.16)

**Διαφάνης**
LAKONIA:
—SPARTA: (**1**) s. i BC *IG* V (1) 95, 15 (Bradford (-)) (f. Νικίας)

**Δίαχος**
LAKONIA:
—SPARTA: (**1**) ii BC *IG* V (1) 475

**Δίδυμα**
AITOLIA:
—APERANTOI: (**1**) ?iv/iii BC ib. IX (1)² (1) 166, 6 + *AbhBerlAk* 1958 (2), p. 9 (*L'Illyrie mérid.* 1 p. 109 fig. 6)

**Διδύμη**
S. ITALY (APULIA):
—LARINUM: (**1**) ?ii AD *CIL* IX 763 (Lat. Flavia Didyma)
S. ITALY (CAMPANIA):
—DIKAIARCHIA-PUTEOLI: (**2**) ?ii AD ib. X 2446 (Lat. Flavia Didyme: I m. Διδύμη II); (**3**) ~ ib. (Lat. Flavia Didyme: II d. Διδύμη I)
—POMPEII: (**4**) i BC-i AD ib. IV 4101 (Lat. Dindyma); (**5**) ~ *Impegno per Pompeii* 8 EN no. 1 (Castrèn 29. 3) (Lat. Aninia Didime)
SICILY:
—SYRACUSE (NR.): (**6**) ?iii AD *NScav* 1951, p. 165 no. 2 (Lat. Didyme)

**Δίδυμος**
AITOLIA:
—KLAUSEION (MOD.): (**1**) vi AD *PAE* 1959, p. 34
ARKADIA:
—TEGEA: (**2**) 165 AD *IG* V (2) 50, 43 (f. Φιλοκράτης)
LAKONIA:
—SPARTA: (**3**) ?m. ii AD ib. V (1) 161, 3 (Bradford (-)) (s. Διοσκουρίδας); (**4**) a. 212 AD *BSA* 89 (1994) p. 435 no. 6, 5 (Αὐρ. Δ.: s. Στράτιος)
S. ITALY (CAMPANIA):
—DIKAIARCHIA-PUTEOLI*: (**5**) ?i-ii AD *CIL* X 1878 (Lat. C. Iulius Didymus: freed.)
—KYME: (**6**) imp. *NScav* 1893, p. 211 (Lat. Didym(us))
—MISENUM*: (**7**) imp. *CIL* X 3587 (Lat. C. Iulius Didymus)
—POMPEII: (**8**) i BC-i AD ib. IV 2319 d (Lat. Didimus); (**9**) ~ ib. 5274 (Lat. Didymus)
SICILY:
—THERMAI HIMERAIAI: (**10**) imp. *IG* XIV 324 (f. Μάξιμος)

**Διεύχης**
AIGINA: (**1**) hell. ib. IV (1) 101 (Διε[ύχ]ης)
ARKADIA: (**2**) 316 BC ib. V (2) 549, 33 (s. Ξενόστρατος)
—MANTINEIA-ANTIGONEIA: (**3**) s. iv BC Peek, *NIEpid* 16, 29 (Perlman E.6) (s. Καλλείδας)

**Διϝαΐδας**
—TEGEA: (4) iv BC SEG XXXVI 382, 4 ([Δ]ιεύχης: s. Δερκύλος)
ELIS: (5) m. i BC IvOl 407 (Δι[ε]ύχ[ης])
SICILY:
—HIMERA: (6) c. 475-450 BC Himera 2 p. 681 no. 45 (Dubois, IGDS 11; Arena, Iscr. Sic. III 51) (-χες̄)

**Διϝαΐδας**
ARGOLIS:
—NEMEA*: (1) ?vi BC SEG XXXI 303 (2) a

**Δίζας**
ILLYRIA:
—LYCHNIDOS: (1) ii AD Šašel, IL 457 (Lat. Dizae (gen.): f. Μουκάκενθος)
S. ITALY (CAMPANIA):
—MISENUM*: (2) ?i-ii AD CIL x 8374 a (Lat. A. Iulius Valens qui et Diza: f. A. Iulius Iulianus, A. Iulius Staleianus)

**Διζομα**
S. ITALY (APULIA):
—CONVERSANO (MOD.): (1) ii BC Taras 10 (1990) p. 355 (ring)

**Διήγυρις**
ITHAKE: (1) hell.-imp. BCH 29 (1905) p. 167 (tile)

**Διηνέκης**
LAKONIA:
—SPARTA: (1) 480 BC Hdt. vii 226 (Poralla² 238)

**Διθύραμβος**
S. ITALY (CAMPANIA):
—DIKAIARCHIA-PUTEOLI: (1) imp. CIL x 1834 (Lat. Dithyramb[us])

**Δίκα**
S. ITALY (CAMPANIA):
—NEAPOLIS: (1) i BC IG XIV 777 (INap 108) (d. Μεγακλῆς); (2) i BC/i AD ib. 107; cf. Leiwo p. 83 no. 30 (d. Βίβιος); (3) ~ INap 109, 2; cf. Leiwo p. 77 no. 21 (d. Τρέβιος); (4) ~ INap 172, 4; cf. Leiwo p. 77 no. 20 (d. Ἐπίλυτος)

**Δικαία**
AITOLIA:
—KALYDON: (1) f. ii BC SEG XVIII 116, 1 (d. Δικαῖος)
AKARNANIA:
—PALAIROS: (2) ?s. iii BC IG IX (1)² (2) 539
EPIROS:
—NIKOPOLIS: (3) c. 30 BC SEG XXXVII 526 (Sarikakis 32) (d. Δημάρετος, ?m. Νικάνωρ)
ITHAKE: (4) hell. SEG XVII 259
LEUKAS: (5) hell.-imp.? IG IX (1) 576
SICILY:
—LIPARA: (6) hell.-imp. NScav 1947, p. 217 no. 2 (Epigraphica 3 (1941) p. 259 no. 14)
—SELINOUS: (7) vii/vi BC Dubois, IGDS 70 (Arena, Iscr. Sic. I 17; IGLMP 77); (8) ?vi BC Manganaro, PdelP forthcoming no. 17

**Δικαιαγόρα**
SICILY:
—KAMARINA: (1) ?iv/iii BC SEG XXXIX 1002, 5 (d. Ἄνταλλος)

**Δικαίαρχος**
ACHAIA:
—PATRAI: (1) c. 146-32 BC BMC Pelop. p. 23 no. 7; Mionnet 2 p. 191 no. 320 (coin) (f. Ἀρχικράτης)
AITOLIA: (2) ?254 BC Syll³ 436, 3; Nachtergael, Les Galates 9, 4; (3) c. 232-228 BC Syll³ 499, 2; Nachtergael, Les Galates 62, [3]; (4) c. 201 BC RE (1) ?= (6); (5) f. ii BC IG IX (1)² (1) 104, 10; (6) 198 BC PP 10072 ?= (4); (7) m. ii BC IG IX (1)² (3) 681, 22
—BOUKATION: (8) c. 164 BC ib. IX (1)² (1) 99, 9
—PHISTYON: (9) ii BC ib. 110 a, 3

—THERMOS: (10) 214 BC ib. 177, 19 (s. Κρινόλαος)
—TRICHONION: (11) c. 198-?187 BC ib. p. LI, s.a. 195 BC, 187 BC; 30, 15; IX (1)² (3) 616, 1; Plb. xviii 10. 9 ff.; 11. 1 ff.; xx 10. 5; xxi 31. 13; Liv. xxv 12. 6 ff.; xxxvi 28. 3; cf. BCH 56 (1932) pp. 314 ff. (s. Ἀλέξανδρος)
AKARNANIA:
—THYRREION: (12) iii-ii BC SEG XXVII 162; (13) ii BC ib. xxv 628, 9 ([Δικ]αίαρχος)
EPIROS:
—BOUTHROTOS (PRASAIBOI): (14) a. 163 BC IBouthrot 121, 9
KEPHALLENIA:
—KRANIOI: (15) iii/ii BC IG IX (1) 276, 2 (s. Εὔιππος)
KERKYRA?: (16) hell. ib. 834 (bullet)
KORINTHIA:
—KORINTH: (17) a. 191 BC SEG XXVI 392, 9 (s. Δαμ—)
—KORINTH?: (18) s. iii BC IG IX (1)² (1) 24, 2 (or Aitolia Konope-Arsinoe: f. Λύσανδρος)
LAKONIA:
—SPARTA: (19) c. 140-150 AD ib. v (1) 64, 13 (Bradford (-)) ([Δικ]αίαρχος: s. Ἀγιάδας)
—SPARTA?: (20) ii BC Suda Δ 1063; RE (4) (dub.?)
SICILY:
—KAMARINA: (21) f. v BC Cordano, Tessere Pubbliche 113 (Δ[ικα]ίαρχος: s. Ἱππίας)
—MENAI: (22) inc. Riv. Stor. Antica 5 (1900-1) p. 57 no. 34 (f. Μενέστρατος)
—ZANKLE-MESSANA: (23) iv/iii BC RE (3) + Supplbd. 11; Wehrli, Schule Arist. i (s. Φειδίας)

**Δικαιογένης**
AIGINA: (1) hell.-imp. IG IV (1) 42 (f. Ἀριστώ)

**Δικαιόπολις**
AITOLIA:
—BOUKATION: (1) 190 BC ib. IX (1)² (1) 97, 6
—KALLION/KALLIPOLIS: (2) iii/ii BC ib. 157
—PHISTYON: (3) imp. ib. 113, 5 (-κεό-: s. Λυκίδας)

**Δικαῖος**
AIGINA: (1) ?i BC Alt-Ägina I (2) p. 44 no. 10 (s. Δωρόθεος)
AITOLIA: (2) c. 315-280 BC FD III (1) 144; cf. BCH 68-9 (1944-5) p. 100 (s. Καλλιτέλης)
—KALYDON: (3) f. ii BC SEG XVIII 116, 2 (f. Δικαία)
—KONOPE-ARSINOE: (4) 250-150 BC Fraser–Rönne, BWGT p. 143 no. 2
AKARNANIA:
—THYRREION: (5) iii BC SEG XXVII 160 (f. Λαμίσκα)
ARGOLIS:
—HERMIONE: (6) i BC-i AD? IG IV (1) 734, 2
EPIROS:
—AMBRAKIA: (7) ?ii BC AD 10 (1926) p. 67 fig. 4 (f. Ἀσκληπίων)
—BOUTHROTOS (PRASAIBOI): (8) a. 163 BC IBouthrot 30, 20 (SEG XXXVIII 488); (9) ~ IBouthrot 32, 14 (SEG XXXVIII 491)
—NIKOPOLIS: (10) imp. AE 1950-1, Chron. p. 39 no. 14 (Sarikakis 33) (f. Περιγένης)
LAKONIA:
—TAINARON-KAINEPOLIS: (11) 213-217 AD IG v (1) 1240, 16 (Αὐρ. Δ.: II s. Δικαῖος I); (12) ~ ib. l. [16] (I f. Αὐρ. Δικαῖος II)
S. ITALY (CALABRIA):
—RUDIAE: (13) i-ii AD Susini, Fonti Salento p. 112 no. 49 (Lat. Ti. Clau[dius] Dicaeus)
S. ITALY (CAMPANIA):
—DIKAIARCHIA-PUTEOLI: (14) imp. CIL x 3156 (Lat. Dicaeus: f. Ζώσιμος)
SICILY:
—LIPARA: (15) iii BC Meligunis-Lipara 5 p. 151 no. 2162; cf. SEG XLI 808

**Δικαιοσύνα**
SICILY:
—SYRACUSE: (1) f. iv BC Plu., Mor. 338 C; cf. Beloch, GG III (2) pp. 102-7 (-νη: d. Διονύσιος, Δωρίς (Lokroi Epizephyrioi))

**Δικαιοσύνη**
ILLYRIA:
—APOLLONIA: (1) ?ii AD IApoll 234 (Βιλλία Δ.)
S. ITALY (CAMPANIA):
—SALERNUM: (2) imp. IItal 1 (1) 234 (CIL x 649) (Lat. Vettiena Dicaeosyne)

**Δικαιοτέλης**
ARGOLIS:
—ARGOS: (1) ?i AD Page, FGE 1899

**Δικάις**
S. ITALY (LUCANIA):
—METAPONTION: (1) m. iii BC SEG XXX 1175, 12 (doctor)

**Δικαιύλις**
SICILY:
—LIPARA: (1) ?iii BC IG XIV 388 (Libertini, Isole Eolie p. 219 no. 5) (Δικαιύλιος (gen.))

**Δικαιώ**
KORINTHIA:
—KORINTH: (1) i BC IG II² 9064 (d. Νικόστρατος)
SICILY:
—GELA-PHINTIAS: (2) m. vi BC Dubois, IGDS 155 (vase) (Arena, Iscr. Sic. II 48; Lazzarini 586) (-καιό)

**Δικαρχία**
S. ITALY (CAMPANIA):
—DIKAIARCHIA-PUTEOLI: (1) imp. CIL x 2390 (Lat. Claudia Dicarchia)

**Δικᾶς**
S. ITALY (CALABRIA):
—TARAS-TARENTUM: (1) iv BC Iamb., VP 267 (FVS 1 p. 446) (δίκας—ms.: name—Diels)

**Δικκώ**
AKARNANIA:
—STRATOS: (1) ?iii BC IG IX (1)² (2) 406 (d. Λάμπων)

**Δίκων**
AITOLIA:
—THERMOS: (1) 214 BC ib. IX (1)² (1) 177, 19 (s. Πολύχαρμος)
ELIS:
—OLYMPIA*: (2) f. v BC CEG 1 387 (Lazzarini 819); LSAG² p. 450 no. C (date) (-κōν)
S. ITALY (BRUTTIUM):
—KAULONIA: (3) iv BC Iamb., VP 267 (FVS 1 p. 447) ?= (4); (4) ~ RE (-); Moretti, Olymp. 379; 388-9 (and Sicily Syracuse: s. Καλλίμβροτος) ?= (3)

**Δίνδυλα**
AKARNANIA:
—PALAIROS: (1) s. iii BC IG IX (1)² (2) 522 (Δινδύλας (fem. gen./masc. nom.?))

**Δινία**
ARGOLIS:
—HERMIONE: (1) ?ii-i BC ib. IV (1) 731 II, 1 (d. Ἀφροδισία)

**Δινύμιος**
KORINTHIA:
—KORINTH: (1) ii-iii AD SEG XI 141 c

**Δινύτας**
ARKADIA:
—PARRHASIOI: (1) v/iv BC Paus. vi 8. 2 (-ννύ-: f. Δάμαρχος)

**Διογένεια**
KORINTHIA:
—SIKYON: (1) m. ii AD *Syll*³ 846, 6 (Τιβ. Κλ. Δ.: m. Τιβ. Κλ. Πολυκράτεια Ναυσικάα)
SICILY:
—SYRACUSE: (2) iii-v AD *IG* XIV 94 (Strazzulla 35; Wessel 1142); cf. Ferrua, *NG* 162 (Διωγένια)

**Διογένης**
AIGINA: (1) imp. *IG* IV (1) 83, 3; (2) ?f. i AD *Alt-Ägina* 1 (2) p. 45 no. 17, 5 (f. Κρίτων)
AIGINA?: (3) imp. *EAD* XXX p. 356 no. 20 (f. Δαμώ)
AITOLIA:
—THERMOS*: (4) s. iii BC *IG* IX (1)² (1) 60 II, 11; (5) ~ ib. l. 16; (6) ~ ib. 60 III, 6; (7) ~ ib. 60 IV, 14; (8) ~ ib. l. 24
AKARNANIA: (9) c. 170 BC Plb. xxviii 5. 3 + 6
ARGOLIS:
—ARGOS: (10) 105 BC *JÖAI* 14 (1911) Beibl. p. 146 no. 4, 10 (s. Ἑρμαῖος)
—EPIDAUROS: (11) imp. *IG* IV (1)² 449 + Peek, *IAEpid* 175; *IG* IV (1)² 450 + Peek, *IAEpid* 176 (s. Ἀρτεμίδωρος); (12) ~ Peek, *NIEpid* 65; (13) ii-iii AD Peek, *IAEpid* 334, 2 (Διογέν[ης]: s. —ρίδας); (14) 298 AD *IG* IV (1)² 417-27
—HERMIONE: (15) i BC-i AD? ib. IV (1) 730 IV, 3 (f. Πρῶτος); (16) ~ ib. 730 V, 4 (f. Ἑρμίας)
ARKADIA:
—HERAIA: (17) c. 230-200 BC *BCH* 45 (1921) p. 12 II, 76 (f. Ἱεροκλῆς)
—MANTINEIA-ANTIGONEIA: (18) i-ii AD *IG* V (2) 287 (Δει-)
—TEGEA: (19) i BC ib. 164; (20) ii AD ib. 55, 32 (I f. Διογένης II); (21) ~ ib. l. 32 (II s. Διογένης I); (22) 165 AD ib. 50, 37 (s. Ἀφροδᾶς)
ELIS: (23) 28-16 BC *IvOl* 64, 13, 17; 65, 14, [22]; 69, [14] (f. Παυσανίας: mantis/Iamidai); (24) c. 177-185 AD ib. 103, 26-7 (?f. Ὀλυμπικός); (25) c. 177-189 AD ib. 138, 6 (?f. —τυς); (26) m. iii AD ib. 119, 6 (Διογέν[ης]: I f. Διογένης II); (27) ~ ib. l. 6 ([Διογ]ένης: II s. Διογένης I)
EPIROS:
—BOUTHROTOS (PRASAIBOI): (28) a. 163 BC *IBouthrot* 17, 17; 41, 21; 43, 26 (*SEG* XXXVIII 474; 500; 502) (s. Ἀπολλώνιος, Νίκα); (29) ~ *IBouthrot* 35, 4 (s.p.) (*SEG* XXXVIII 494); *IBouthrot* 133, 6 (s. Φιλώτας) ?= (33); (30) ~ ib. 43, 25 (*SEG* XXXVIII 502) (f. Ἀπολλώνιος); (31) ~ *IBouthrot* 45, 17 (f. Τάτιον, Πραξίλας); (32) ~ ib. 100, 9
——Bouthrotioi: (33) a. 163 BC ib. 8, 2 (*SEG* XXXVIII 480) (s. Φιλώτας) ?= (29)
—NIKOPOLIS: (34) f. ii AD *FD* III (4) 83, 2 (Sarikakis 34) (f. Ἀριστοκλείδης)
ILLYRIA:
—APOLLONIA: (35) ii-i BC *IApoll* 165 (f. Φιλτέρα)
—EPIDAMNOS-DYRRHACHION: (36) c. 250-50 BC Maier 193; 286; 332; 408; Münsterberg Nachtr. p. 15 (coin) (Ceka 132-42) (money.)
KERKYRA: (37) ii-iii AD Unp. (*IG* arch.) (Διογένηνος (gen.): f. Νίκα)
KORINTHIA:
—KORINTH: (38) imp. *IG* IV (1) 1604, 4 (s. Ἑρμόλαος)
—SIKYON: (39) hell.? *FGrH* 503 (Skalet 99)
LAKONIA:
—SPARTA: (40) c. 90-100 AD *SEG* XI 570, 3 (Bradford (3)) (f. Νικοκράτης); (41) c. 100-120 AD *SEG* XI 572, 5 (Bradford (5)) (Διογέ[νης]: f. —κλῆς); (42) c. 105-110 AD *IG* V (1) 51, 17; 52, 4; *SEG* XI 506, [3] (Bradford (4)) (f. Φιλοκράτης); (43) c. 150-160 AD *SEG* XI 528, 2; 552, 6? Bradford (2)) (f. Εὐβαβερίσκος); (44) c. 170 AD *IG* V (1) 116, 12 (Bradford (1)) (s. Ἀρίστων); (45) ii/iii AD *IG* V (1) 546, 6; 547, 2; 684, [3]; *BSA* 79 (1984) pp. 281-3 (date); 80 (1985) pp. 241-2 (ident., stemma) (Bradford

s.v. Πανθάλης (2)) (Γ. Πομπώνιος Πανθάλης Δ. Ἀριστέας: f. Πομπώνιος Πανθάλης ὁ καὶ Ἀριστοκλῆς, Πομπωνία Καλλιστονίκη ἡ καὶ Ἀρέτη)
LEUKAS: (46) 216 BC *IG* IX (1)² (2) 583, 1, 6, 63 (s. Λέων); (47) ~ ib. l. 3 (f. Ἀθηνογένης)
MESSENIA:
—MESSENE: (48) 31 BC-14 AD *SEG* XXIII 207, 29 (I f. Διογένης II); (49) ~ ib. l. 29 (II s. Διογένης I, f. Φιλωνίδας, Φιλόξενος); (50) f. ii AD *IvOl* 445, 2 (f. Φιλωνίδας)
S. ITALY (APULIA):
—SIPONTUM*: (51) i AD Serricchio, *Iscrizioni di Siponto* 7 (Lat. P. Memmius Diogenes: freed.)
—TEANUM APULUM: (52) imp. *Teanum Apulum* p. 126 no. 55 (tile) (Lat. Diogenes)
S. ITALY (BRUTTIUM):
—LOKROI EPIZEPHYRIOI: (53) iii AD *Suppl. It.* 3 p. 22 no. 3 (Lat. M. Aurelius Diogenes)
——(Γαβ.): (54) iv/iii BC De Franciscis 4, 4 (s. Ἀγαθοκλῆς, f. Ἀγαθοκλῆς)
S. ITALY (CALABRIA):
—RUDIAE: (55) ii AD Bernardini, *Rudiae* p. 108 (Susini, *Fonti Salento* p. 109 no. 46) (Lat. L. Caelius Diogenes)
S. ITALY (CAMPANIA):
—DIKAIARCHIA-PUTEOLI: (56) i AD *Puteoli* 4-5 (1980-1) pp. 262-3 (brick) (Lat. Diogenes); (57) ?ii AD *CIL* X 2429 (Lat. T. Flavius Diogenes: f. Albanus)
—MISENUM*: (58) imp. ib. 3432 (Lat. C. Iulius Diogenes: I f. Διογένης II); (59) ~ ib. (Lat. Diogenes: II s. Διογένης I); (60) ~ ib. 3459 (Lat. Q. Aelius Diogenes); (61) ?i-ii AD ib. 3358 (Lat. Ti. Iulius Diogenes: imp. freed.); (62) ?ii AD ib. 3506 (Lat. Flavius Diogenes)
—NEAPOLIS*: (63) imp. ib. 8042. 42 (tile) (Lat. Diogenes)
—POMPEII: (64) i BC-i AD ib. IV 2046 (Lat. Diogenes); (65) ~ ib. 2462; (66) ~ ib. 4063 (Castrèn 413. 1) (Lat. Titius Diogenes); (67) ~ *CIL* IV 10048; 10050 (Lat. Diogenes); (68) ~ ib. X 805, 4 (Lat. Diogene[s]); (69) ~ ib. 868 (Lat. Diogenes); (70) ~ ib. 8058. 14 (seal) (Castrèn 91. 2) (Lat. L. Calp(urnius) Diog(enes))
—POMPEII*: (71) i BC-i AD *Eph. Ep.* VIII 326 (Castrèn 238. 2) (Lat. P. Mancius Diogenes: freed.)
—SALERNUM: (72) s. i AD *IItal* I (1) 23 (Lat. Diogenes: I f. Διογένης II); (73) ~ ib. (Lat. Ti. Claudius Diogenes: II s. Διογένης I: doctor)
—SALERNUM*: (74) ?i AD ib. 238 II, 5 (*CIL* X 557) (Lat. L. Appuleius Diogenes: freed.)
—SURRENTUM: (75) imp. ib. 751 (Lat. C. Fufius Diogenes)
S. ITALY (LUCANIA):
—HERAKLEIA: (76) 74 BC *ID* 1758, 1 (s. Πρωτογένης)
—POSEIDONIA-PAESTUM: (77) i BC-i AD Mello–Voza 13 (Lat. [Di]ogenes?); (78) imp. ib. 178 (Lat. L. Lollius Diogenes); (79) ?s. i AD ib. 88 (Lat. G. Pomponius Diogenes: s. M. Pomponius Libo); (80) ?ii AD ib. 89 (Lat. M. Pomponius Diogenes: s. M. Pomponius Libo)
SICILY:
—HALAISA: (81) ii BC *IG* XIV 353 (*IGLMP* 127); *IG* XIV 354 (I f. Διογένης II Λαπίρων); (82) ~ ib. 353 (*IGLMP* 127); *IG* XIV 354 (Δ. Λαπίρων: II s. Διογένης I); (83) ~ *IGSI* 2 B II, 14 (Dubois, *IGDS* 196) (Διογέν[ης]: f. Ἡράκλειος)
—LIPARA: (84) i BC *SEG* XLII 854 b (Διω-: s. Παμφίλα); (85) hell.-imp. *NScav* 1929, p. 82 no. 4
—MORGANTINA: (86) ?iv/iii BC *SEG* XXXIX 1009, 1
—SYRACUSE: (87) ii-i BC *IG* XIV 8, 2 (*IGLMP* 105) ([Δι]ογένη[s])

—TAUROMENION: (88) f. i BC *Cron. Arch.* 3 (1964) p. 42 II, 1
——(Σπαρ.): (89) f. i BC ib. p. 45 III, 30 (s. Ἄθανις)

**Διογενιανός**
KORINTHIA:
—KORINTH*: (1) byz. *Corinth* VIII (1) 157 (*TMByz* 9 (1985) pp. 283-4 no. 21) (f. Εἰρηναῖος)

**Διογενίς**
ILLYRIA:
—LYCHNIDOS: (1) ii-iii AD *Sp.* 71 (1931) p. 222 no. 592 (Δει-)

**Διόγνητος**
AKARNANIA:
—THYRREION: (1) ii BC *IG* IX (1)² (2) 251, 1 (Διόγ[νη]τος: f. —χος)
ARGOLIS:
—EPIDAUROS: (2) ii-iii AD ib. IV (1)² 470; cf. Peek, *IAEpid* 186 (f. Κρατῖνος)
—TROIZEN: (3) f. ii AD *IG* IV (1) 758, 18 (s. Ἀπολλωνίδης)
ARKADIA:
—TEGEA: (4) iii-ii BC *SEG* XXXIX 391, 3 (s. Δημήτριος: sculptor)
KORINTHIA:
—KORINTH: (5) iii-ii BC *IG* IV (1) 366 ([Δ]ιόγνη[τος])
S. ITALY: (6) imp. *CIL* X 8059. 421 (seal) (Lat. L. Valerius Diognetus)
S. ITALY (BRUTTIUM):
—KROTON: (7) 548 BC Moretti, *Olymp.* 109
—LOKROI EPIZEPHYRIOI:
——(Πυρ.): (8) iv/iii BC De Franciscis 23, 1, 12
S. ITALY (CAMPANIA):
—DIKAIARCHIA-PUTEOLI*: (9) imp. *CIL* X 1561 (Lat. Diognetus: slave?)
SICILY:
—KEPHALOIDION: (10) s. iii BC *Thess. Mnem.* 158 (f. Γόργος)
—LILYBAION: (11) hell.-imp. *IG* XIV 279 (*Semitica* 26 (1976) pp. 94 ff.; *Lilibeo* p. 124 no. 153) (f. Λύσων); (12) imp. *SEG* XXXIV 951 (Δ. Μήγας: s. Δαμάτριος, f. Μ. Οὐαλέριος Χόρτων)
—SYRACUSE: (13) c. 310 BC *POxy* 2399, 34 (Δ. ὁ Φαλαίνιος ἐπικαλούμενος)

**Διοδότα**
EPIROS:
—NIKOPOLIS: (1) imp. *Hellenika* 22 (1969) p. 69 no. 5 (Sarikakis 35) (d. Τιμέας, Χρυσέα)

**Διοδότη**
S. ITALY (CAMPANIA):
—POMPEII: (1) i BC-i AD *CIL* IV 3905, 4 (Castrèn 195. 3) (Lat. Diodote)

**Διόδοτος**
AIGINA: (1) imp. *IG* IV (1) 106 (I f. Διόδοτος II); (2) ~ ib. (II s. Διόδοτος I)
ARGOLIS:
—ARGOS: (3) i AD ib. 606, 1 (I f. Τιβ. Κλ. Διόδοτος II); (4) ~ ib. l. 2 (Τιβ. Κλ. Δ.: II s. Διόδοτος I); (5) 37 AD ib. VII 2711, 2; (6) ii AD *SEG* XVI 258 a, 4 (Γν. Πομπ. Δ.: s. Γν. Πομπ. Κλεοσθένης, ?s. Κλ. Φιλομάθεια); (7) 135 AD Peek, *IAEpid* 154, 4 (f. Ἀλεξᾶς)
—EPIDAUROS: (8) 232 AD *IG* IV (1)² 410, 8 (s. Ἀφροδίσιος)
ARKADIA?: (9) c. 200 BC *SEG* XVII 829, 9, 14
SICILY:
—SYRACUSE: (10) s. ii BC *Acragas Graeca* 1 p. 34 no. 5, 9, 13, 19, 24 (*IGUR* 2; Dubois, *IGDS* 185); *IG* XIV 953, 3, 10, 17, 25 (*IGUR* 3) (f. Δημήτριος)
—TAUROMENION:
——(Ἀ—): (11) ii/i BC *IGSI* 6 IV, 32 (f. Σέλινις)

**Διοδώρα**
ARGOLIS:
—HERMIONE: (1) ?ii-i BC *IG* IV (1) 731 I, 7 (d. Θεύνοστος)
S. ITALY (BRUTTIUM):
—TORANO CASTELLO (MOD.): (2) iv BC *GRBS* 26 (1985) p. 181 no. 127
S. ITALY (CAMPANIA):
—DIKAIARCHIA-PUTEOLI: (3) ?i-ii AD *CIL* x 2573 (Lat. Iulia Diodora: m. Θεόδωρος)

**Διόδωρος**
ACHAIA: (1) hell. *IDidyma* II 138, 1 (f. Φίλων) ?= (2); (2) ?c. 250 BC *IG* XI (4) 1191, 1 (f. Φίλων) ?= (1)
—AIGION: (3) i BC ib. II² 7947 (s. Λύκος)
AIGINA: (4) ?69 BC ib. IV (1) 2, 1, 3, 25 (s. Ἡρακλείδας)
AITOLIA: (5) ?209 BC ib. IX (1)² (1) 190, 9 (XII Suppl. p. 6 no. 16)
ARGOLIS:
—ARGOS: (6) 337-336 BC *CID* II 74 I, 73; 76 II, 22 (f. Ξενόφαντος)
—ARGOS*: (7) ii-i BC *IG* IV (1) 530, 22; cf. *BCH* 33 (1909) p. 183 n. 2 (Διόδωρ[ος], Διοδώρ[α]?: slave/freed.?)
—EPIDAUROS: (8) iii BC *IG* IV (1)² 168, 1; *SEG* XVII 178, [5]; (9) c. 221 BC *IG* IV (1)² 42, 12; (10) 32 AD Peek, *IAEpid* 45, 44 (s. Κορνήλιος); (11) ii-iii AD *IG* IV (1)² 556 (f. Εὔτυχος); ——(Hylleis): (12) 146 BC ib. 28, 58 (s. Ἵππων); (13) ~ ib. l. 53-4 (f. Ἀρίσταρχος, Λάκριτος)
—EPIDAUROS*: (14) c. 370-365 BC Peek, *IAEpid* 52 B, 20 (Διόδω[ρος])
—HERMIONE: (15) ?ii-i BC *IG* IV (1) 731 II, 18 (s. Ἐτεοκλῆς)
—TROIZEN: (16) c. 240-220 BC *SEG* XXIII 286, 2 (Διόδ[ω]ρ[ος]: f. ——θίδης)
ARKADIA:
—MEGALOPOLIS?: (17) iv/iii BC ib. XXVIII 417 (f. ——ηνίων)
—TEGEA:
——(Athaneatai): (18) iv/iii BC *IG* v (2) 38, 7
ELIS: (19) c. 77 or 81 AD *IvOl* 85, 3, [7] (I ?f. Διόδωρος II); (20) ~ ib. l. 7 (II ?s. Διόδωρος I)
—OLYMPIA*: (21) iii BC *SEG* XXII 356
EPIROS:
—AMBRAKIA: (22) ii-i BC *CIG* 1800, 4 (s. Μένανδρος)
ILLYRIA:
—EPIDAMNOS-DYRRHACHION: (23) c. 250-50 BC Maier 198-200 (coin) (Ceka 194; 366; 450) (pryt.)
KEPHALLENIA?: (24) 230-225 BC *PP* 2277; cf. Launey 1 p. 618 on p. 209
KORINTHIA:
—KORINTH: (25) v BC *IG* IV (1) 355 b (bronze) (f. Καλλίστρατος); (26) 480 BC Plu., *Mor.* 870 F; Page, *FGE* 730; (27) iii BC *IG* IV (1) 361 (bronze) (f. Ξενιάδας)
—SIKYON: (28) 140 BC Moretti, *Olymp.* 642 (Skalet 100)
LAKONIA:
—SPARTA: (29) c. 100 AD *SEG* XI 515, 6 (Bradford (-)) (s. Διονύσιος)
MESSENIA:
—MESSENE: (30) hell. *PAE* 1993, p. 65
—THOURIA: (31) ii-i BC *IG* v (1) 1385, 22 (s. Ἀριστέας); (32) f. ii BC *SEG* XI 972, 120 (f. Εὐάμερος)
S. ITALY (APULIA):
—LUCERIA: (33) imp. *ASP* 34 (1981) p. 26 no. 32 (Lat. Diodorus: I f. Διόδωρος II); (34) ~ ib. (Lat. Diodorus: II s. Διόδωρος I, Εὐτυχίς)
S. ITALY (BRUTTIUM):
—KROTON: (35) vi/v BC Iamb., *VP* 257
S. ITALY (CALABRIA):
—BRENTESION-BRUNDISIUM: (36) imp. *CIL* IX 151 (Lat. [D]iodorus)
—TARAS-TARENTUM?: (37) ii BC *SEG* XXXI 888 (vase)

S. ITALY (CAMPANIA):
—DIKAIARCHIA-PUTEOLI: (38) imp. *CIL* x 2926 (Lat. M. Sallubius Diodorus)
—HERCULANEUM: (39) i BC-i AD ib. 1403 d III, 20 (Lat. M. Calatorius Diodorus)
—NEAPOLIS: (40) imp. ib. 3041; cf. Leiwo p. 185 (locn.) (Lat. Valerius Diodoreus)
—POMPEII: (41) i BC-i AD *CIL* IV 4794 (Lat. Diodorus); (42) ~ ib. 9119 (Lat. Diodor(us))
—SALERNUM*: (43) ?i AD *IItal* I (1) 238 I, 13 (*CIL* x 557) (Lat. L. Appuleius Diodorus: freed.)
S. ITALY (CAMPANIA)*: (44) imp. ib. 8042. 10 (tiles) (Lat. L. Ansius Diodorus)
SICILY:
—AGYRION: (45) i BC *RE* (38); (46) i BC-i AD? *IG* XIV 588 (s. Ἀπολλώνιος)
—AKRAI: (47) ?iii BC *SGDI* 3243 (*Akrai* p. 155 no. 5) (I f. Διόδωρος II, ?f. Ἡρακλείδας); (48) ~ *SGDI* 3243 (*Akrai* p. 155 no. 5) (II s. Διόδωρος I)
—HALAISA: (49) s. ii BC *IG* XIV 355 ([Δι]όδωρος: f. Ἡράκλειος)
—LICODIA EUBEA (MOD.): (50) hell. *RQ* 1904, p. 248 = Pace, *Camarina* p. 164 no. 27 (Διόδω[ρος]?: ?f. Νυμφόδωρος)
—LILYBAION: (51) f. i BC Cic., *In Verr.* II iv 37 (Lat. Q. Lutatius Diodorus); (52) imp. *IGLMP* 22 (Διόδω[ρος]); (53) ~ ib. 24 (*Lilibeo* p. 169 no. 187)
—MELITA: (54) f. i BC Cic., *In Verr.* II iv 38-42 (Lat. Diodorus)
—SEGESTA: (55) iv/iii BC *IG* XIV 290, 4 (Dubois, *IGDS* 215); *SEG* XLI 825 (date) ([Δι]όδωρος: f. Ξέναρχος); (56) ?ii BC *IG* XIV 287 (Dubois, *IGDS* 213) (Δ. Ἀππειραῖος: s. Τίττελος); (57) ?ii-i BC *IG* XIV 288 (Dubois, *IGDS* 214 a; *IGLMP* 46) ([Δ]ιόδωρος: f. Φάλακρος Ἐρύσσιος)
—SYRACUSE: (58) 70 BC Cic., *In Verr.* II iv 138 (Lat. Diodorus: s. Τιμαρχίδας)
—TAUROMENION: (59) c. 221 BC *IG* XIV 421 an. 20 (*SGDI* 5219) (s. Ἄνδρων); (60) c. 40 BC *Cron. Arch.* 3 (1964) p. 54 I, 27 (s. Διονύσιος)

**Διόζοτος**
EPIROS:
—MIKHALITSI (MOD.): (1) s. iv BC *SEG* XXXVII 530 (s. Κλεοπτόλεμος)
—PANDOSIA: (2) 356-354 BC *IG* IV (1)² 95, 24 (Perlman E.2); Perlman p. 40 f. (date) (-σζο-)

**Διοίτας**
KORINTHIA:
—SIKYON: (1) 134 or 130 BC *FD* III (2) 68, 26 = *IG* II² 1132, 67 (s. Νικόστρατος)

**Διοκκῆς**
PELOPONNESE: (1) c. 192 BC *SEG* XIII 327, 14 (f. Ἀντίφιλος)

**Διοκλέα**
ARKADIA:
—KLEITOR: (1) i-ii AD *IG* v (2) 384 ([Δι]οκλέα)

**Διοκλέας**
AITOLIA: (1) ?269-268 BC *CID* II 128, 9; 129 A, [1] ?= (2); (2) ?255 BC Flacelière p. 398 no. 21 c, 2; Nachtergael, *Les Galates* 8, 4; 19, [3] ?= (1)

**Διόκλεια**
ACHAIA:
—DYME: (1) iii BC *AJPh* 31 (1910) p. 399 no. 74 c, 5; (2) ~ ib. l. 15 (d. Θεόδωρος, Δαμασία)
AKARNANIA:
—ANAKTORION: (3) iii BC *IG* IX (1)² (2) 589
ARGOLIS:
—ARGOS*: (4) ii BC *SEG* XLII 279, 20 (slave/freed.?)

LAKONIA:
—SPARTA: (5) i BC-i AD *IG* v (1) 749 (Bradford (-)) (-κλια)
S. ITALY (CAMPANIA):
—SALERNUM: (6) i BC/i AD *IItal* I (1) 206 (*CIL* x 608) (Lat. Iulia Dioclea)

**Διοκλείδας**
ARGOLIS:
—EPIDAUROS*: (1) c. 370-360 BC Peek, *IAEpid* 52 B, 3, 60; *BSA* 61 (1966) p. 271 no. 4 A, 15
LAKONIA:
—KYTHERA: (2) c. 400-375 BC *IG* II² 9110 (-δης)
LEUKAS: (3) iii BC *AD* 26 (1971) Chron. p. 351; (4) ~ *AM* 27 (1902) p. 370 no. 43 ([Δ]ιοκλείδα[ς?])
MESSENIA:
—KORONE: (5) i BC *IG* v (1) 1392, 3 (f. Νικαγόρας)
SICILY:
—SYRACUSE: (6) c. 272 BC Theoc., *Id.* xv 18 (fict.)

**Διοκλῆς**
ACHAIA: (1) 208 BC *IMM* 39, 47; *Philol.* 126 (1982) pp. 198 ff. (date)
—DYME: (2) 218 BC Plb. v 17. 4; (3) ?s. ii BC *Achaean Grave Stelai* 33 (f. Πυθίων)
AITOLIA: (4) 192 BC Liv. XXXV 34. 5 (Lat. Diocles)
—BOUKATION: (5) 164 BC *IG* IX (1)² (1) 99, 10
—KALYDON: (6) 263 BC ib. 17, 73, 88 (f. Λύκος) ?= (8); (7) c. 200 BC ib. 70 (f. Λύκος)
—KALYDON?: (8) c. 250 BC *FD* III (3) 149, 2 (f. Σκύλλα) ?= (6)
AKARNANIA: (9) iv/iii BC *PP* 15144 (s. Δάμαρχος)
—ASTAKOS: (10) ii BC *IG* IX (1)² (2) 434, 13, 17 (s. Νικόδικος, f. Νικόδικος)
—MATROPOLIS: (11) 198 BC ib. IX (2) 61, 4 (Δι<ι>οκλῆς: f. Νικόμαχος)
—PALAIROS: (12) c. 330-315 BC *SEG* XXIII 189 I, 5; *Hesp.* 57 (1988) p. 148 A, 18 (*SEG* XXXVI 331); cf. *Hesp.* 48 (1979) pp. 78 f. with pl. 22 c (s. Θερσίλοχος)
ARGOLIS:
—ARGOS: (13) ii BC *SEG* XLII 279, 18 (f. Ἀριστίππα)
—EPIDAUROS: (14) iv BC Peek, *NIEpid* 35 ([Δι]οκλῆς); (15) iii/ii BC Peek, *IAEpid* 95 I ([Δ]ιο[κλ]ῆς?: s. Δαι——); (16) imp. *IG* IV (1)² 447 (f. Νίκων)
—PHLEIOUS: (17) iv BC *RE* (49)
ARKADIA:
—KYNAITHA: (18) m. iii BC ib. (56) (Stephanis 702)
—MANTINEIA-ANTIGONEIA: (19) c. 185 BC *Milet* I (3) 148, 20; *Chiron* 19 (1989) pp. 279 ff. (date) (s. Ἀγησίλοχος)
—THELPHOUSA: (20) i BC/i AD *SEG* XXII 324 ([Δ]ιοκλῆς)
DALMATIA:
—ISSA: (21) iii BC Brunšmid p. 9 fr. H, 6 ([Δι]οκλῆς: s. Ἀκουσίλας)
ELIS: (22) 36 AD *IvOl* 59, 4 (f. ——ης); (23) 229-232 AD *SEG* XV 258, 3 (Τ[ι]β. Κλ. Δ.)
EPIROS:
—AMBRAKIA: (24) a. 167 BC ib. XXXV 665 A, 12 (s. Ἀλεξιάδας)
—DODONA*: (25) iv-iii BC *PAE* 1932, p. 51 no. 1 (s. Λύκος)
ILLYRIA:
—APOLLONIA: (26) hell. *IApoll* 351 (tile)
—BYLLIONES: (27) imp. *SEG* XXIV 476 (XXXVIII 551)
—EPIDAMNOS-DYRRHACHION: (28) hell.-imp. *IDyrrh* 170 (Διο[κ]λῆς: s. Παρμήν)
KORINTHIA:
—KORINTH: (29) 728 BC Moretti, *Olymp.* 13 (s. Ἀλκυόνη); (30) s. iii BC *IG* IX (1)² (1) 24, 3 (f. Ἀγησίων)

LAKONIA:
—LAS: **(31)** ?iii BC ib. V (1) 1214
—SPARTA: **(32)** s. i BC ib. 92, 10 (Bradford (16)) (f. *Τιμογένης*); **(33)** ~ *IG* V (1) 136, 5 (Bradford (1)) (s. *Δα—*); **(34)** 43-31 BC *Münzpr. der Laked.* p. 148 Group 16 series 19; p. 155 Group 17 series 15; p. 161 Group 22 series 2 (coin) (Bradford (11)); **(35)** imp. *SEG* XI 685 (Bradford (7)); **(36)** c. 90-100 AD *SEG* XI 512, 4 (Bradford (15)) (f. *Ἕλενος*); **(37)** ~ *SEG* XI 558, 5 (Bradford (3)) (s. *Κεχαρισμενός*); **(38)** c. 100 AD *SEG* XI 513, 4 (Bradford (14)) (I f. *Διοκλῆς* II); **(39)** ~ *SEG* XI 513, 4 (Bradford (2)) (II s. *Διοκλῆς* I); **(40)** c. 100-120 AD *SEG* XI 557 a, 4 (Bradford (9)) (*Διοκλ[ῆς]*?); **(41)** ~ *SEG* XI 607, 3 (Bradford (4)) (s. *Νικιάδας*); **(42)** ii AD *IG* V (1) 159, 20 (Bradford (8)); **(43)** c. 105-110 AD *IG* V (1) 97, 2; *SEG* XI 564, 2 (Bradford (5)) (*Διοκλεῖς—SEG*: s. *Νικίας*); **(44)** ~ *SEG* XI 569, 18 (Bradford (12)) (f. *Δάμιππος*); **(45)** c. 140-145 AD *IG* V (1) 1314, 43 (Bradford (10)); **(46)** s. ii AD *IG* V (1) 293, 2; 493, 5 (Bradford (13)) (f. *Δαμοκράτης*)
LEUKAS: **(47)** c. 167-50 BC Unp. (Oxford, AM) A.J. Evans 1934; Postolakas p. 80 nos. 813-15 (*NZ* 10 (1878) p. 135 no. 12 (coin))
S. ITALY (BRUTTIUM):
—SYBARIS-THOURIOI-COPIAE: **(48)** vi/v BC Iamb., *VP* 267 (*FVS* I p. 446)
S. ITALY (CALABRIA):
—TARAS-TARENTUM: **(49)** s. iii BC *IG* VII 1726, 3; cf. Roesch, *Thespies* p. 15 no. 3 (-κλεῖς: s. *Διοφάνης*)
S. ITALY (CAMPANIA):
—MISENUM: **(50)** ?ii AD *CIL* X 3334 (Lat. Patulcius Diocles)
—MISENUM*: **(51)** imp. ib. 3430 (Lat. Cl. Gallicanus Diocles: f. *Πόη*)
—NOLA*: **(52)** imp. *Atti Acc. Pontan.* 21 (1971-2) pp. 392-7 (Lat. —cius Diocles: freed.)
—POMPEII: **(53)** i BC-i AD *CIL* IV 9258 (Lat. M. Diocl[es] Asteropeus); **(54)** ~ ib. 10229 b (Lat. Diocl[es])
SICILY:
—ABAKAINON: **(55)** i BC-i AD? *IGLMP* 125 (*Διόκλε* (voc.), *Διόκλος* (nom.)—ed.)
—AKRAGAS: **(56)** s. ii BC *Acragas Graeca* I p. 34 no. 5, 6 (*IGUR* 2; Dubois, *IGDS* 185) (I f. *Διοκλῆς* II); **(57)** ~ *Acragas Graeca* I p. 34 no. 5, 6 (*IGUR* 2; Dubois, *IGDS* 185) (II s. *Διοκλῆς* I)
—GELA-PHINTIAS: **(58)** c. 321-300 BC Michel 368, 5 (s. *Ἀναξαγόρας*)
—KAMARINA: **(59)** s. v BC Dubois, *IGDS* 121, 5 (Arena, *Iscr. Sic.* II 143; *SEG* XXXVIII 940; Cordano, 'Camarina VII' 24) (*Διοκλ[ἐς*]: ?s. *Τίτας*, ?f. *Πύθων*); **(60)** iii BC Manganaro, *PdelP* forthcoming no. 1, 7 (f. *Ἀριστίων*)
—KATANE: **(61)** m. iv BC *IG* II² 162 a, 1
—KENTORIPA: **(62)** f. i BC Cic., *In Verr.* II iii 129 (Lat. Diocles)
—LILYBAION: **(63)** f. i BC ib. *In Verr.* II iv 35 (Lat. Diocles Popillius)
—PANORMOS: **(64)** f. i BC ib. *In Verr.* II iii 93 (Lat. Diocles Phimes) ?= **(65)**; **(65)** ~ ib. *In Verr.* II v 16 (Lat. Diocles: f. *Ἀπολλώνιος Γεμῖνος*) ?= **(64)**
—SYRACUSE: **(66)** 413-408 BC *RE* (33); **(67)** 317 BC ib. (34)
—SYRACUSE?:
——(*Λαβ.*): **(68)** hell. Manganaro, *PdelP* forthcoming no. 4 V, 3 (s. *Κέφαλος*)

**Διοκλητιανός**
SICILY:
—SYRACUSE: **(1)** iii-v AD *IG* XIV 110 (Strazzulla 48; Wessel 1078) + *ASSicilia* 1938-9, p. 27 (*Εὔπρα—* ὁ καὶ *Δ.*)

**Διοκλῆς**
KORINTHIA:
—KORINTH: **(1)** i AD *IG* II² 9065 (d. *Ξενόδοκος*)

**Διόμαχος**
MESSENIA:
—MESSENE: **(1)** iii BC *SEG* XXIII 210, 13; **(2)** ~ ib. l. 24; **(3)** ~ ib. l. 25
TRIPHYLIA:
—LEPREON: **(4)** iii/ii BC ib. XXII 360, 2; **(5)** ~ ib. l. 6

**Διομέδων**
EPIROS:
—DODONA*: **(1)** ?iv-iii BC Robert, *Coll. Froehner* 39 (f. *Κλέαρχος*)
S. ITALY (LUCANIA):
—HYELE-VELIA: **(2)** v BC *FVS* I p. 247 no. 29 A 1

**Διομήδης**
AIGINA?: **(1)** v BC *IG* IV (1) 1585 (Lazzarini 55) ([*Δ*]*ιομέδε*[*s*])
ARGOLIS:
—ARGOS: **(2)** 237 BC *PPetr²* I *Wills* 6, 17
——Elaion?: **(3)** c. 316-222 BC *Mnem.* NS 43 (1915) pp. 376-7 G, 5 (Perlman A.16) ([*Δ*]*ιομήδης*, [*Θ*]*ιομήδης*?)
—TROIZEN: **(4)** c. 275 BC *SEG* XIII 341, 2 (*IOrop* 389)
ARKADIA:
—MEGALOPOLIS: **(5)** imp. *IG* V (2) 484
—TEGEA: **(6)** ii AD ib. 55, 71 (s. *Ὀρβανός*)
ILLYRIA:
—APOLLONIA: **(7)** iii-ii BC *IApoll* 34 (*Διομήδη* (voc.))
S. ITALY (APULIA):
—VENUSIA: **(8)** imp. *CIL* IX 569 (Lat. M. Turellius Diomedes)
S. ITALY (CALABRIA):
—TARAS-TARENTUM: **(9)** imp. ib. 6162 (Lat. C. Domitius Diomedes)
S. ITALY (CAMPANIA):
—DIKAIARCHIA-PUTEOLI: **(10)** imp. ib. X 2086 (Lat. Marcellus Diomedes: s. Antonia Saturnine); **(11)** ~ ib. 2708 (Lat. Diomedes); **(12)** ~ ib. 8205 + *Puteoli* 11 (1987) p. 63 (Lat. [Di]omedes)
—HERCULANEUM: **(13)** i BC-i AD *RAAN* 33 (1958) p. 277 no. 471 (Lat. Diomedes); **(14)** ~ Maiuri, *Nuovi Scavi* p. 345; cf. *Cron. Erc.* 8 (1978) p. 152 no. 52 (Lat. [Di]omedes)
—PITHEKOUSSAI-AENARIA: **(15)** imp. *CIL* X 6790 (Lat. Diomedes)
—POMPEII: **(16)** i BC-i AD ib. IV 2400; **(17)** ~ ib. 4828 (Lat. Diomedes)
—POMPEII*: **(18)** i BC-i AD ib. X 1042-3 (Castrèn 42. 12) (Lat. M. Arrius Diomedes: freed.)
SICILY:
—SYRACUSE: **(19)** iii-v AD *IG* XIV 95 (Strazzulla 36; Wessel 719)

**Δίομος**
SICILY: **(1)** arch.? *RE* (3); *CGF* I p. 91 fr. 4 (fict.)

**Δῖον**
S. ITALY (APULIA):
—CANUSIUM*: **(1)** imp. *Epig. Rom. di Canosa* 114 (*CIL* IX 370) (Lat. Nonia Dium: freed.)

**Διόνικος**
ELIS: **(1)** imp. *IvOl* 729-731 (tiles) (-νει-) ?= **(2)**; **(2)** f. ii AD ib. 92, 14; 95, 10 (*Διόνεικος*—92: s. *Ὄλυμπος*: mantis/Klytiadai/Φ.) ?= **(1)** **(3)**; **(3)** 197-213 AD ib. 106, 12; 107, [9]; 108, 3; 110, 15; 112, [4] (-νει-: f. *Ὄλυμπος*) ?= **(2)**

**Διονῦς**
SICILY:
—AKRAGAS: **(1)** imp. *IG* XIV 262 (*Νικομήδης* ὁ καὶ *Δ.*)

**Διόνυσα**
KORINTHIA:
—KORINTH: **(1)** byz. Bees 42; cf. *TMByz* 9 (1985) p. 359 no. 2 (-νοί-)

**Διονυσᾶς**
AIGINA: **(1)** imp. *IG* IV (1) 108
AITOLIA:
—THERMOS: **(2)** 163 BC ib. IX (1)² (1) 102, 8

**Διονυσία**
ARGOLIS:
—HERMIONE: **(1)** ii-i BC ib. IV (1) 732 II, 1 ([*Διον*]*υσία*: d. *Κλεομήδης*); **(2)** i BC-i AD? ib. 734, 4 (m. *Πίστα*); **(3)** imp. *SEG* XI 385 e, 5
ARKADIA:
—MEGALOPOLIS: **(4)** ii-iii AD *IG* V (2) 472 (*GVI* 1163)
KERKYRA: **(5)** i BC-i AD *IG* IX (1) 907; **(6)** imp. ib. 906
LAKONIA:
—OITYLOS: **(7)** iii AD ib. V (1) 1301 c (m. *Θέων*)
S. ITALY (BRUTTIUM):
—KROTON: **(8)** imp. *Epigraphica* 26 (1964) p. 78 (Lat. Sextilia Dionysia)
S. ITALY (CALABRIA):
—BRENTESION-BRUNDISIUM: **(9)** imp. *CIL* IX 33 (Lat. Atilia Dionysia); **(10)** ~ *NScav* 1901, p. 505 (Lat. Sextilia Dionysia)
S. ITALY (CAMPANIA):
—DIKAIARCHIA-PUTEOLI: **(11)** imp. *CIL* X 2306 (Lat. Laconis Dionysia: m. *Κορινθία*)
—DIKAIARCHIA-PUTEOLI*: **(12)** imp. ib. 2826, 4 (Lat. —a Dionysia: freed.)
—NEAPOLIS: **(13)** i BC/i AD *INap* 110; cf. Leiwo p. 85 nos. 33-4 (*Δ*(*ιο*)*ν*(*υ*)*σία*: d. *Διονύσιος*)
—POMPEII: **(14)** i BC-i AD *CIL* IV 1425; cf. p. 207 (Lat. [Di]onusia)
S. ITALY (LUCANIA):
—VOLCEI*: **(15)** ii AD *IItal* III (1) 69 (Lat. Poppaedia Dionysia: freed.)
SICILY:
—KATANE: **(16)** iii-v AD *IG* XIV 470; cf. Ferrua, *NG* 431 ([*Διο*]*νυσία*)
—MELITA: **(17)** iv-v AD *JIWE* I 166 (*Δ.* ἡ καὶ *Εἰρήνα*: Jew)
—SYRACUSE: **(18)** iii-v AD *IG* XIV 98 (Strazzulla 39; Wessel 1332); **(19)** ~ *IG* XIV 99 (Strazzulla 40; Wessel 1163) ([*Δι*]*ονυσία*); **(20)** ~ *IG* XIV 100 (Strazzulla 41); **(21)** 403 AD ib. 166 (Wessel 778); Ferrua, *NG* 8 (date) ([*Δι*]*ονυσία*: m. *Πομπήία*)

**Διονυσιάδης**
ELIS: **(1)** 85 AD *EA* 1905, p. 255 no. 1, 5 (*Κάσσανδρος* [*Δι*]*ονυσιά*[*δης*]: s. *Λάχης*)

**Διονυσιανός**
S. ITALY (CAMPANIA):
—DIKAIARCHIA-PUTEOLI: **(1)** ?i AD *CIL* X 3042 (Lat. C. Val. Dionysian(us) Iulianus: s. Valerius Iulianus, *Διονυσιάς*)

**Διονυσίαρχος**
SICILY:
—KATANE: **(1)** f. i BC Cic., *In Verr.* II iv 50 (Lat. Dionysiarchus)

**Διονυσιάς**
S. ITALY (CAMPANIA):
—DIKAIARCHIA-PUTEOLI: **(1)** imp. *CIL* X 3446 (Lat. Cornelia Dionysias); **(2)** ?i AD ib. 3042 (Lat. Varia(ia) Dionysias: m. *Διονυσιανός*)
—MISENUM*: **(3)** imp. ib. 3516 (Lat. Annia Dionysias: freed.); **(4)** ~ ib. 3517 (Lat. Dionysias)

**Διονυσιοδώρα**
SICILY:
—PANORMOS: **(1)** imp. *Atti Acc. Palermo* 1955-6, pp. 144 ff. no. 67 (Lat. Volusia Longina q(uae) et Dionysiodora)

**Διονυσιόδωρος**
SICILY:
—PANORMOS: (1) imp. ib. (Lat. Dionysiodorus Longinus)

**Διονύσιον**
ARGOLIS:
—HERMIONE: (1) ?ii-i BC *IG* IV (1) 731 I, 2 (d. Φαιναγόρας)

**Διονύσιος**
ACHAIA: (1) hell. *IEph* 2287 A, 5 (s. Σύμμαχος); (2) iii BC *IG* XII (9) 827 (f. Πολέμαρχος: date—Knoepfler); (3) 146 BC ib. IV (1)² 28, 69 (f. Πραξίας: synoikos); (4) ~ ib. l. 100 (s. Ἀλέξανδρος: synoikos); (5) ~ ib. l. 108 (s. Ἀρτεμίδωρος: synoikos); (6) ~ ib. l. 112 (s. Ὠφελίων: synoikos); (7) ~ ib. l. 160 (f. Κλείδικος: synoikos)
—AIGEIRA: (8) c. 83-60 BC *FD* III (1) 223, 2 (f. Ἀπολλώνιος)
—DYME*: (9) c. 219 BC *SGDI* 1612, 78 (*Tyche* 5 (1990) p. 124) (f. Νικόστρατος)
—PATRAI?: (10) hell.? Thomopoulos, *Hist. Patr.* p. 202 n. 1 (sculptor)
—PELLENE: (11) iii/iv AD *SEG* XI 1281
—TRITAIA: (12) hell.-imp. Thomopoulos, *Hist. Patr.* p. 237 (*Achaie* II 313) (f. Κλεονίκη); (13) ~ Neratzoulis p. 19 no. 1 (*Achaie* II 315) (f. Φίλα)
AIGINA: (14) ii BC *IG* II² 7954 (s. Φιλιστίδας); (15) ii-i BC ib. IV (1) 132 (f. Μαχαλία); (16) ~ ib. 134 (f. Μενέμαχος); (17) i BC-i AD *Alt-Ägina* I (2) p. 46 no. 22 (I f. Διονύσιος II); (18) ~ ib. (II s. Διονύσιος I); (19) iii AD ib. p. 47 no. 28 (Δ.: I f. Αὐρ. Διονύσιος II); (20) ~ ib. (Αὐρ. Δ.: II s. Διονύσιος I); (21) ?iii-iv AD *IG* IV (1) 28 + *Alt-Ägina* I (2) p. 50 no. 48 (*M. Αὐρ. Δ.*: I f. M. Αὐρ. Διονύσιος II); (22) ~ *IG* IV (1) 28 + *Alt-Ägina* I (2) p. 50 no. 48 (*M. Αὐρ. Δ.*: II s. M. Αὐρ. Διονύσιος I)
AITOLIA:
—KALLION/KALLIPOLIS: (23) byz. *BCH* 98 (1974) p. 635
—KALYDON: (24) m. ii BC *IG* IX (1)² (1) 137, 3, 7 (I f. Διονύσιος II); (25) ~ ib. l. 4 (II s. Διονύσιος I, ?s. Ἀγεμάχα); (26) a. 142 BC ib. l. 75 (Διονύσ[ιος])
—THERMOS*: (27) s. iii BC ib. 60 III, 8
AKARNANIA:
—PALAIROS: (28) iii/ii BC ib. IX (1)² (2) 547
—STRATOS: (29) ii BC ib. 394, 3 (I f. Διονύσιος II); (30) ~ ib. l. 3 (II s. Διονύσιος I)
—THYRREION: (31) iii-ii BC *SEG* XXVII 159, 7; cf. *PAE* 1977, pl. 244 a (s. Δαμοφῶν); (32) ii BC *IG* IX (1)² (2) 320; (33) imp. ib. 312 b (f. Δαμοκράτης)
ARGOLIS:
—ARGOS: (34) f. v BC *RE* (158); Overbeck 401-2 (sculptor); (35) hell. *FGrH* 308; (36) iii BC *IG* IV (1) 570; (37) ?263-261 BC Nachtergael, *Les Galates* 3, 19; cf. Stephanis 959 (f. Εὐκλῆς); (38) ii BC *IPhilae* 13, 7 (f. Μνᾶσις); (39) c. 100-90 BC *SEG* XXXIII 290 A, 8; *BSA* 70 (1975) pp. 129-31 (date); cf. Stephanis 2043 (f. Περιγένης); (40) c. 50 BC *BGU* 1972, 2 (s. Ἡρακλείδης)
—EPIDAUROS: (41) iv-iii BC *IG* IV (1)² 22 ([Διο]νύσιος); (42) c. 350-250 BC *AD* 28 (1973) Chron. pl. 81 γ; (43) c. 350-200 BC *SEG* XXVI 452. 3; (44) c. 335-325 BC *IG* IV (1)² 106 I, 10, 12; *BSA* 61 (1966) p. 319 no. 26 (date); (46) ~ Peek, *NIEpid* 59 (f. Ματερώ); (47) hell.? *SEG* XXIX 380; (48) iii BC Peek, *IAEpid* 43, 34 (Διονύσ[ιος]); (49) ~ ib. l. 35 (s. Τηλέας); (50) ?iii BC *IG* IV (1)² 313; (51) 242-238 BC ib. 71, 2 ([Δι]ονύσιος); (52) ii BC ib. 247 (s. Ἱέρων, Νικαγόρα, f. Ἱέρων); (53) imp. ib. 491 (I f. Διονύσιος II); (54) ~ ib. (II s. Διονύσιος I); (55) i-ii AD Peek, *IAEpid* 237; (56) ~ *IG*

IV (1)² 395 I (I f. Διονύσιος II); (57) ~ ib. ([Διο]νύσιος: II s. Διονύσιος I); (58) ~ ib. 459; 495; Peek, *IAEpid* 237, 2 (f. Πυθοκλῆς); (59) ~ *IG* IV (1)² 460; 506 (I f. Διονύσιος II); (60) ~ ib. 460; 506 (II s. Διονύσιος I); (61) ii AD ib. 480 (Π. Αἴλ. Δ.: s. Ἀντίοχος); (62) iii AD ib. 401, 3; (63) iii-iv AD ib. 587 (s. Ζώσιμος); (64) 207 AD ib. 400, 6 (f. Κερδωνίς); (65) 259 AD ib. 415 (*M. Αὐρ. Δ.*)
——(Azantioi): (66) 146 BC ib. 28, 27 (s. Εὔδαμος)
——Agrias: (67) c. 335-325 BC ib. 108, 156
—EPIDAUROS*: (68) c. 370-365 BC Peek, *IAEpid* 52 A, 23, 30, 32; (69) c. 370-360 BC *BSA* 61 (1966) p. 272 no. 4 B II, 9; (70) c. 335-325 BC *IG* IV (1)² 108, 108, 114
—HERMIONE: (71) iii BC ib. IV (1) 728, 23; (72) ii-i BC ib. 691, 1 (Διον[ύσιος]: I f. Διονύσιος II); (73) ~ ib. l. 3 (Διονύ[σιος]: II s. Διονύσιος I); (74) ~ ib. 732 I, 12 (s. Ἀρχίππα)
—METHANA-ARSINOE: (75) i BC ib. 853, 9 (f. Σώσανδρος); (76) c. 132-212 AD *SEG* XXXVII 316, 1
—TROIZEN: (77) imp. *IG* IV (1) 821 A
—TROIZEN?: (78) s. ii BC *SEG* 11 868; cf. *PP* 5349; Fraser, *Ptol. Alex.* 2 p. 180 n. 31 (locn.)
ARKADIA: (79) hell. *Memnonion* 66
—KLEITOR: (80) m. iii AD *SEG* XXXV 350 I, 1 (Διονύσιος)
—MANTINEIA-ANTIGONEIA:
——(Hoplodmia): (81) m. iv BC *IG* v (2) 271, 12 (f. Γόργων)
——(Posoidaia): (82) c. 425-400 BC *SEG* XXXI 348, 16
—MEGALOPOLIS: (83) ?145 BC *IG* v (2) 439, 33 (f. Πραξίδαμος)
—ORCHOMENOS: (84) ?ii BC ib. 345, 12 (f. Πόλις: date—LGPN)
—ORCHOMENOS*: (85) ?ii BC ib. l. 24 (s. Ἀγα—: date—LGPN)
—TEGEA: (86) f. iii BC ib. 35, 2 ([Δι]ον[ύ]σιος); (87) i-ii AD ib. 561 ([Δι]ονύσιος); (88) ii AD ib. 55, 25 (f. Σωτήριχος); (89) ~ ib. l. 28 (Ἰούλ. Δ.); (90) ~ ib. l. 75 (Ὀφίλλιος Δ.); (91) ~ ib. l. 88 (s. Δαμάτριος); (92) 191 AD ib. 52, 4 (Π. Σύλλιος Δ.)
——(Athaneatai): (93) iv/iii BC ib. 38, 4 (s. Σωκλείδας)
DALMATIA:
—ISSA: (94) iv/iii BC *VAHD* NS 8 (1905) p. 97 no. 177 (*VAMZ* 1970, p. 33 f. frr. I-J); (95) hell.? Brunšmid p. 24 no. 13 (*VAHD* 84 (1991) p. 258 no. 9); (96) hell. Novak, *Vis* fig. 24 (s. Σύμμαχος); (97) iii BC *SEG* XXXI 596 (s. Λυσίμαχος); (98) ~ ib. (s. Θεύδωρος, f. Λυσίμαχος); (99) ~ Brunšmid p. 9 fr. G, 7 + *VAMZ* 1970, p. 37 frr. G and M (f. Ζώπυρος) ?= (100); (100) ~ Brunšmid p. 9 fr. G, 8 + *VAMZ* 1970, p. 37 frr. G and M (Δ[ιο]νύσιος: f. Ὅρθων) ?= (99); (101) ~ Brunšmid p. 9 fr. G, 16 ([Διονύ]σιο[ς]: s. Πρώταρχος); (102) ii BC ib. p. 25 no. 14, 3 (s. Καλλισθένης) ?= (104); (103) ~ ib. l. 4 + *VAHD* 84 (1991) p. 248 no. 1 (f. Πάμφιλος); (104) ~ Brunšmid p. 25 no. 14, 8 + *VAHD* 84 (1991) p. 248 no. 1 (f. Καλλισθένης) ?= (102); (105) ~ Brunšmid p. 25 no. 14, 1-2 + *VAHD* 84 (1991) p. 248 no. 1 (f. Θρασύμαχος, f. Τιμασίων); (106) ~ Brunšmid p. 26 no. 15 (s. Θρασύμαχος); (107) ii-i BC *SEG* XXXI 593 (Διονύ[σιος]: s. Μνα—); (108) i/ii AD Unp. (Split Museum) (Τίτιος Δ.)
——(Dymanes): (109) iv/iii BC Brunšmid p. 7, 21 ([Δ]ιονύσιος: s. Δείναρχος); (110) ~ ib. p. 8, 34 (f. —ανδρος); (111) ~ ib. p. 9, 52 (f. —δας)
——(Hylleis): (112) iv/iii BC ib. p. 7, 26 (Διονύσιος: s. —ν); (113) ~ ib. p. 8, 35 (Διον[ύσι]ος: f. Ἀρχέβιος); (114) ~ ib. l. 44 (f. Νουμήνιος); (115) ~ ib. l. 47 (s. Εὔβατος); (116) ~ ib. p. 9, 62
——(Pamphyloi): (117) iv/iii BC ib. l. 50; (118) ~ ib. l. 52 (Διονύσ[ιος])

—ISSA?: (119) hell. *SEG* XXXI 607; (120) iii-ii BC Brunšmid p. 34 no. 32 (f. Ἀγάθων); (121) iii/ii BC *CIG* 6913; *SEG* XL 512 (locn.) (s. Λεύκιος)
—TRAGURION: (122) 56 BC Sherk 24 A, 9 (f. Φιλόξενος)
ELIS: (123) imp. *IvOl* 732-733 (tiles); (124) ?i AD *EA* 1905, p. 259 no. 2, 9 (I f. Διονύσιος II); (125) ~ ib. l. 9 ([Δ]ιονύσιος: II s. Διονύσιος I); (126) c. 5 AD *IvOl* 69, 18 (s. Ἀ—); (127) 68 AD ib. 287, 3 ([Διο]νύσιος); (128) 113-117 AD ib. 91, 17 (f. Λυκολέων); (129) ii/iii AD ib. 105, 2 ([Δι]ονύσιος); (130) 181-185 AD ib. 102, 4 (I f. Διονύσιος II); (131) ~ ib. l. 4, 8 ([Διον]ύσιος: II s. Διονύσιος I, f. Διονύσιος III: Δ.); (132) ~ ib. l. 8 ([Διον]ύσιος: III s. Διονύσιος II, ?f. Νάρκισσος)
—KYLLENE: (133) v BC *SEG* XXXV 377 ([Δι]ονύσιος)
—OLYMPIA*: (134) 209-213 AD *IvOl* 110, 25 (Δι[ο]νύσιος: ?s. Αὐρ. Ὀνησιφόρος: slave?)
EPIROS:
—AMBRAKIA: (135) 359 BC *CID* II 5 I, 19 (Διονύ[σι]ος); (136) ii-i BC *CIG* 1800 + Leake, *Northern Greece* 4 plate xxxv no. 170, 25 (s. Πλάτωρ)
—BOUTHROTOS (PRASAIBOI): (137) a. 163 BC *IBouthrot* 29, 34 (*SEG* XXXVIII 487); (138) ~ *IBouthrot* 37, 9 (*SEG* XXXVIII 496); (139) ~ *IBouthrot* 43, 32 (*SEG* XXXVIII 502) (s. Φρυνίων); (140) ~ *IBouthrot* 104, 16
—DELVINE (MOD.): (141) iii BC *AE* 1914, p. 237 no. 12 (Διν-: f. Ἄνδρων)
—DODONA*: (142) vi BC *PAE* 1932, p. 52 no. 4
—NIKOPOLIS (NR.): (143) imp. *AD* 36 (1981) Chron. p. 279 no. 4
ILLYRIA:
—APOLLONIA: (144) c. 250-50 BC Maier 92 (coin) (Ceka 42) (money.); (145) ?ii BC *IApoll* 102 (f. Ἱπποσθένης); (146) imp. ib. 31 (Διονύσι[ος])
—EPIDAMNOS-DYRRHACHION: (147) c. 250-50 BC Münsterberg p. 38; Nachtr. p. 16 (coin) (Ceka 143-5) (money.); (148) ~ Maier 201 (coin) (Ceka 320) (pryt.); (149) hell.-imp. *BCH* 19 (1895) pp. 369 ff. no. 19, 5; cf. *IDyrrh* 522 (f. Σωκράτης); (150) ~ ib. 171 (s. Αἴνυτος); (151) ~ ib. 172 (s. Λεωνίδας); (152) imp. *AEp* 1978, no. 756 (Lat. Terentius Dionusius); (153) i BC/i AD *IG* II² 8487 (f. Κασσάνδρα)
—SKAMPIS: (154) imp. *BUST* 1961 (1), p. 122 no. 21 (Lat. Dionysius: s. Sucessus); (155) ~ Hammond, *Epirus* p. 736 no. 17 c (Lat. Dionysius)
KEPHALLENIA: (156) 249 BC *PP* 9206
—SAME: (157) iii AD *IG* IX (1) 643 (T. Φλ. Δ.)
KERKYRA: (158) ?ii-i BC ib. 771; 820; *AAA* 13 (1980) p. 290 (*SEG* XXXVIII 434 (tiles)); (159) i BC-i AD *IG* IX (1) 908; (160) imp.? ib. 931 (Διω-)
KORINTHIA:
—KORINTH: (161) c. 570-550 BC Amyx 86. 1 (vase) (Lorber 146) (her.?); (162) 344 BC Plu., *Tim.* 24; (163) hell.? *RE* (91); (164) m. iii BC *Corinth* VIII (3) 33 d, 5 + *SEG* XXX ([Διον]ύσιος: s. Ζώπυρος); (165) imp.? *Syringes* 765 d (s. Μεγάλος); (166) ii AD *RE* (151) (bp.); (167) ii-iii AD *SEG* XI 132, 4; 133 (f. Φιλωνᾶς); (168) f. iii AD *Ag.* VII p. 96 no. 292; *BM Lamps* 3 p. 405 no. Q3261 (lamps) (Διονύσι[ος]); (169) byz. Bees 42; cf. *TMByz* 9 (1985) p. 359 no. 2
—KORINTH*: (170) 536 AD Schwartz, *ACO* III p. 29, 16; p. 127, 39; p. 163, 13; p. 171, 30
—KROMMYON: (171) imp. *IG* IV (1) 195
—SIKYON: (172) f. iv BC ib. II² 10297 (s. Δαμάτριος); (173) iii BC ib. 10298 (s. Σωκράτης); (174) ?212-210 BC *SEG* XII 223, 1 (f. Σωκλείδας); (175) s. ii BC *AD* 21 (1966) Mel. p. 56, 7, 18

LAKONIA:

—SPARTA: (176) hell.? IG v (1) 793 (Bradford (13)) (I f. Διονύσιος II); (177) ~ IG v (1) 793 (Bradford (1)) (II s. Διονύσιος I); (178) s. i BC IG v (1) 901 a; 901 c (tiles) (Bradford (7)); (179) ?i AD IG v (1) 180, 8 (Bradford (9)) (Διονύσι[ος]); (180) ~ IG v (1) 185, 3 (Διονύσ[ιος]?); (181) c. 100 AD SEG XI 515, 6 (Bradford (12)) (f. Διόδωρος); (182) c. 120 AD IG v (1) 32 B, 12; 82, 1 (Bradford (10)) (Π. Αἴλ. Δ., Διονύσ(ι)ος—82); (183) c. 130-150 AD SEG XI 481, 1 (Bradford (15)) (f. Ἐπάγαθος); (184) c. 140-160 AD IG v (1) 112, 6 (Bradford (17)) (f. Πολύευκτος); (185) ~ IG v (1) 115, 2 (Bradford (3)) ([Διον]ύσιος: s. Ἐπάγαθος); (186) ~ IG v (1) 149, 5 (Bradford (6)) (s. Ζώσιμος); (187) c. 150-160 AD SEG XI 585, 11; XXX 410, 14 (Bradford (11)) (Τιβ. Κλ. Δ.); (188) c. 170 AD IG v (1) 116, 6 (Bradford (16)) (f. Ἐπαφρόδιτος); (189) ii/iii AD IG v (1) 548, 3 (Bradford (5)) (?s. Νικόστρατος, f. Νικόστρατος); (190) iii AD SEG XLII 322; (191) c. 225-250 AD IG v (1) 528, 7; 529, 7 (Bradford (2)); (192) ~ SEG XXXIV 308, 16 (Bradford (14)) (I f. Φλ. Διονύσιος II); (193) ~ SEG XXXIV 308, 16 (Bradford (2)) (Φλ. Δ.: II s. Διονύσιος I); (194) c. 230-260 AD SEG XI 633, 2 (Bradford (4)) (Αὐρ. Δ.: s. Εὐτυχᾶς)

LEUKAS: (195) f. i BC IG IX (1) 534, 8 (Iscr. Gr. Verona p. 24) (f. Εὐκλείδας)

MESSENIA:

—MESSENE: (196) s. iv BC Berve 278; (197) hell. SEG XXXIX 383 (Διονύ[σιος]); (198) c. 140 BC IvOl 52, 4, 32 (f. Μηνόδωρος); (199) 31 BC-14 AD SEG XXIII 207, 10 (f. Τείσαρχος); (200) ~ ib. l. 27 (s. Ἀριστομένης, Πλειστάρχεια); (201) imp.? Ergon 1995, p. 31 (s. Δημήτριος); (202) 54-68 AD IG v (1) 1450, 9 (f. Τι. Κλ. Ἀριστομένης); (203) 174 AD SEG XLI 337, 8 (?s. Λαίστρατος)

PELOPONNESE: (204) 112 BC FD III (2) 70 A, 35

PELOPONNESE?: (205) 11 AD PAE 1992, p. 72 B, 7 (I f. Διονύσιος II); (206) ~ ib. l. 7 (II s. Διονύσιος I)

S. ITALY: (207) imp. CIL x 8059. 35 (seal) (Lat. M. Amul. Diony(sius))

S. ITALY (APULIA):

—AECAE: (208) ii/iii AD Ann. Fac. Lett. Fil. Bari 27-8 (1984-5) p. 30 no. 3 (Lat. –lius Dionysius)

—CANUSIUM: (209) imp. Epig. Rom. di Canosa 157 (Lat. Dionysius); (210) 223 AD ib. 35 III, 38 (CIL IX 338) (Lat. C. Peticius Dionysius)

—GNATHIA-EGNATIA: (211) i AD Suppl. It. 11 p. 40 no. 20 (Lat. –onius [Dio]nysius); (212) ii AD ib. p. 42 no. 23 (Lat. Helvius Dionysius)

—TEANUM APULUM?: (213) ii AD Teanum Apulum pp. 152-3 no. 3a (or S. Italy (Apulia) Luceria: Lat. Dionysius: slave?)

—TURENUM: (214) ii AD Epig. Rom. di Canosa 113 (CIL IX 310) (Lat. Peticius Dionysius: s. Πάνθεια)

S. ITALY (BRUTTIUM):

—HIPPONION-VIBO VALENTIA: (215) imp. ib. x 80 (Lat. Pullius Dionysius: I f. Διονύσιος II); (216) ~ ib. (Lat. T. Scaefius Dionysius: II s. Διονύσιος I)

—RHEGION: (217) ii AD Suppl. It. 5 p. 70 no. 25 (Lat. M. Petronius Dionysius)

—(Ἐργ.): (218) ii BC IG XIV 616, 5 with Add. p. 688 (Mus. Naz. Reggio p. 159 no. 29) (s. Ὄρθων)

S. ITALY (CALABRIA):

—BRENTESION-BRUNDISIUM: (219) i AD Desy, Timbres amphoriques 852; 922 (amph.) (Lat. L. All(ius) Diony(sius))

—BRENTESION-BRUNDISIUM*: (220) ii-i BC Museo Ribezzo 10 (1977) p. 113 no. 1 (vase) (potter)

—TARAS-TARENTUM: (221) m. iv BC SEG XXXI 879. 3 + Getty Mus. Journ. 9 (1981) p. 47 (terracotta); (222) imp. CIL IX 246 (Lat. C. Memmius Dionysius)

—VALETIUM: (223) imp. ib. 6083. 100 (Susini, Fonti Salento p. 178 no. 174 (seal)) (Lat. L. Negilius Dionysius)

S. ITALY (CAMPANIA):

—DIKAIARCHIA-PUTEOLI: (224) iii/ii BC SEG IV 91, 5 (GVI 868) (f. Θευδώρα); (225) hell.-imp. IG XIV 2406. 14; (226) imp. CIL x 2753 (Lat. L. Munatius Dionisius); (227) ~ ib. 2983 (Lat. Dionysius); (228) ~ ib. 3021 (Lat. Dionysius); (229) ~ ib. 3094 (Lat. C. Vettenius Dionysius); (230) i AD AJA 77 (1973) p. 167 no. 18 (Lat. –nuleius Dionysius); (231) ?i-ii AD CIL x 2218 (Lat. C. Iulius Dionysius); (232) ~ ib. 2614 (Lat. C. Iulius Dionysius: f. Ἀφροδίσιος); (233) ?ii-iii AD ib. 2002 (Lat. Aur. Aelius Dionysius)

—DIKAIARCHIA-PUTEOLI*: (234) imp. ib. 1949 (Lat. M(anius) Poplicius Dionysius: freed.?)

—MISENUM*: (235) imp. ib. 3597 (Lat. L. Sossius Dionysius)

—NEAPOLIS: (236) hell. SEG XXXV 1059 (s. Ἀθήναιος); (237) 100 BC IG II² 1028, 157 (Διονύ[σιος]: s. Δίφιλος); (238) imp. CIL x 1517; cf. Leiwo p. 113 no. 94 (Lat. M. Tullius Dionysius); (239) i BC/i AD INap 109, 6; cf. Leiwo p. 77 no. 21 (f. Ἡρακλείδης); (240) ~ INap 110; cf. Leiwo p. 85 no. 34 (f. Διονυσία)

—NEAPOLIS (NR.): (241) imp. Pausilypon p. 214 no. 15

—NOLA: (242) imp. Atti Acc. Pontan. 21 (1971-2) pp. 397-8 (Lat. M. Tulius Dionysius)

—PITHEKOUSSAI-AENARIA: (243) imp. CIL x 6798 (Lat. T. Turranius Dionusius)

—POMPEII: (244) i BC-i AD ib. IV 2021 (Lat. Dionysius Samellius); (245) ~ ib. 3885 (Lat. Dionysius)

—POMPEII*: (246) 70-79 AD ib. 1041; 2966; 2974-5 (Castrèn 318. 14) (Lat. L. Popidius Dionysius: freed.)

—SALERNUM: (247) imp. IItal I (1) 54 (Lat. [Di]onisius)

—SALERNUM*: (248) iii AD ib. 36 (CIL x 563) (Lat. Aur. Dionysius: imp. freed.)

S. ITALY (LUCANIA):

—EBURUM: (249) s. iv BC Arch. Class. 25-6 (1973-4) p. 361 (vase) (fals.?) (s. Μάταλος)

—HYELE-VELIA: (250) inc. SEG XXVIII 820 (s. Εὔνικος); (251) iv BC IG XIV 656 (Landi, DISMG 48) (Δι(ο)νύσιος: f. Αἰσχρίων); (252) hell.? PdelP 21 (1966) p. 336 no. 9 (f. Κληνόμαχος); (253) ~ ib. p. 337 no. 13; (254) 180-178 BC Syll³ 585, 229-30; Nachtergael, Les Galates 35, 2, 6; BCH 45 (1921) p. 23 IV, 68 (s. Ληγέτης); (255) ii/i BC ID 2631, 17 (f. Ἀπολλόδωρος); (256) imp.? IG XIV 660 (Landi, DISMG 47) (f. Τερτία Πακία)

—LEUKANOI: (257) c. 208 BC FD III (4) 135, 14 (s. Σειράνιος)

—VOLCEI: (258) imp. IItal III (1) 31 (CIL x 419) (Lat. Dionysius: I f. Διονύσιος II) ?= (260); (259) ~ IItal III (1) 31 (CIL x 419) (Lat. C. Bruttius Dionysius: II s. Διονύσιος I); (260) ~ IItal III (1) 32 (CIL x 420) (Lat. Dionysius) ?= (258)

SICILY: (261) inc. FGrH 567 (fict.?); (262) f. iv BC IG II² 10288 (s. Δημόστρατος); (263) f. iv AD RE (86); Seeck, Libanius D VII

—AKRAI: (264) ?iii BC SGDI 3243 (Akrai p. 155 no. 5) (s. Ἡρακλείδας); (265) iii-ii BC SGDI 3242, 8 (Akrai p. 157 no. 8) (s. Ἵππων); (266) ii BC ib. p. 154 no. 3, 13 (s. Ἡράκλειος, ?f. Ἄπελλις); (267) ii-i BC SGDI 3246, 28 (Akrai pp. 152-3 no. 2; Dubois, IGDS 109) (f. Αἰσχύλος)

—(Κρα.): (268) ii-i BC SGDI 3246, 42 (Akrai pp. 152-3 no. 2; Dubois, IGDS 109) (f. Ἡράκλειος)

—ERGETION: (269) iii-v AD Röm. Mitt. 17 (1902) p. 117 (Wessel 762)

—HALIKYAI: (270) s. vi AD Sic. Arch. 7 (1975) p. 52 (mosaic) = Felix Ravenna 113-114 (1977) p. 55 (Lat. Dionisius)

—IAITON: (271) ii-i BC SEG XXVI 1070. 3 (tiles); (272) ~ ib. 1070. 10 (tiles) (s. Κόλοβος)

—INESSA-AITNA?: (273) ii BC IG XIV 12*; Sic. Gymn. 16 (1963) p. 57 n. 42

—KAMARINA: (274) f. v BC Cordano, Tessere Pubbliche 103 (Δι(ο)νύσιος); (275) iv/iii BC SEG XXXIV 942, 1 (Dubois, IGDS 123; Cordano, 'Camarina VII' 96) (s. Φίλινος)

—KATANE: (276) hell.-imp. IG XIV 471 (vase); (277) iii-v AD Wessel 732 (Ferrua, NG 414)

—LIPARA: (278) c. 315-280 BC FD III (4) 401, 3 (f. Δάμων)

—MORGANTINA: (279) ?iv/iii BC SEG XXXIX 1009, 7 (s. Φίλινος) ?= (280); (280) ~ ib. 1012, 6 (Διονύ[σιος]: f. Φίλινος) ?= (279)

—PETRA: (281) imp.? BTCGI 13 p. 495 (f. Ἡράκλειος)

—SEGESTA: (282) iv/iii BC SEG XXX 1119, 7 (Dubois, IGDS 206) (s. Δέκιος); (283) 27 BC-14 AD HN² p. 190; RPC I p. 648 (coin)

—SYRACUSE: (284) c. 430-367 BC RE (1); cf. Beloch, GG III (2) pp. 102-7 (I s. Ἑρμοκράτης, f. Διονύσιος II, Ἑρμόκριτος, Ἱππαρῖνος, Νυσαῖος, Σωφροσύνα, Ἀρέτα, Δικαιοσύνα: tyrant); (285) c. 400-330 BC RE (2); cf. Beloch, GG III (2) pp. 102-7 (II s. Διονύσιος I, f. Ἀπολλοκράτης); (286) ?iv BC IApoll 15; (287) s. iv BC Suppl. Cir. 205 + SEG XXVII 1143 (Διονύσ[ιος]); (288) iii BC ib. XVIII 123, 2 ([Διον]ύσ[ιος]); (289) 183 BC FD III (3) 240, 30 (IG IX (1)² (1) 179) (Δ[ιο]νύσιος: f. Πέρσας); (290) 179 BC PP 9619; (291) imp. IG XIV 23 (f. Ἀφροδισιάς); (292) ~ NScav 1912, p. 298 (Lat. L. Arrius Dionusius); (293) iii-v AD IG XIV 96 (Strazzulla 37; Agnello 2; Wessel 864); (294) ~ Strazzulla 296; (295) byz. SEG IV 8 (Wessel 1348; Ferrua, NG 271 b) (Διονύσ[ιος]?); (296) ~ SEG IV 13

—SYRACUSE?:

—(Νητ.): (297) hell. Manganaro, PdelP forthcoming no. 4 III, 5 (s. Θίων)

—TAUROMENION: (298) hell.? IG XIV 2396; (299) c. 233 BC ib. 421 an. 8 (SGDI 5219) (s. Ἀρτεμίδωρος); (300) c. 231 BC IG XIV 421 an. 10 (SGDI 5219) (f. Φρῦνις); (301) c. 200-149 BC IG XIV 421 an. 41; 421 an. 51; 421 an. 62; 421 an. 92 (SGDI 5219) (s. Σωσιφάνης, f. Σωσιφάνης); (302) c. 179 BC IG XIV 421 an. 62 (SGDI 5219); (303) c. 172 BC IG XIV 421 an. 69; 421 an. 79 (SGDI 5219) (f. Ἀγάθαρχος); (304) c. 170-162 BC IG XIV 421 an. 79 (SGDI 5219); IGSI 4 II (III), 14 an. 71 (f. Ἡράκλητος); (305) c. 153 BC IG XIV 421 an. 88 (SGDI 5219) (s. Θεόκριτος); (306) c. 40 BC Cron. Arch. 3 (1964) p. 54 I, 28 (f. Διόδωρος)

—(Ἀρεθ.): (307) ?ii/i BC IG XIV 421 D an. 10 (SGDI 5219) (s. Ἀπολλόδωρος)

—(Χαλκ.): (308) ?ii/i BC IG XIV 421 D an. 12 (SGDI 5219) (f. Ἀγάθαρχος)

—THERMAI HIMERAIAI: (309) imp. Epigraphica 3 (1941) p. 263 no. 25 (ILat. Term. Imer. 89) (Lat. [Di]onysius); (310) ~ CIL x 7441 (ILat. Term. Imer. 150) (Lat. Dionysius); (311) ~ ib. 110 (Lat. M. Iuli(us) Dionysius)

—TYNDARIS: (312) ?iii AD SEG XXXIII 756 (Donderer A 28); Wilson, Sicily p. 315 fig. 268

SICILY?: (313) s. iii BC HE 3526 (s. Πρώταρχος: fict.?)

Διονύσις

KERKYRA: (1) imp. IG IX (1) 948 (s. Εὔβουλος)

SICILY:

—SELINOUS: (2) m. v BC Dubois, IGDS 77 (Arena, Iscr. Sic. I 23; IGLMP 94); cf. SEG XL 808 (s. Σέλινις)

**Διονυσίς**

—SYRACUSE: (3) iii–v AD *IG* XIV 97 (Strazzulla 38); (4) ~ ib. 221 (Wessel 753) (Πετρώνιος Δ.); (5) ~ Ferrua, *NG* 206 (s. Μαρκία)

**Διονυσίς**
KORINTHIA:
—KORINTH: (1) i AD *SEG* XXXIII 269 (Διονυσές—lap.); (2) byz. *Corinth* VIII (3) 544, 3; cf. *TMByz* 9 (1985) p. 365 no. 60 ([Δι]ωννσίς)

**Διονυσογένης**
AIGINA: (1) ?f. i AD *Alt-Ägina* I (2) p. 45 no. 17, 3 (I f. Διονυσογένης II); (2) ~ ib. l. 3 (II s. Διονυσογένης I)

**Διονυσόδοτος**
ILLYRIA:
—APOLLONIA: (1) 190 BC *Syll*³ 585, 95 (*IApoll* 316) (f. Στρόμβιχος)
LAKONIA: (2) ?m. vi BC *FGrH* 595 F 5 (Poralla² 240); cf. *Suda* Δ 486 (date—Wade-Gery)

**Διονυσοδώρα**
S. ITALY (LUCANIA):
—METAPONTION: (1) f. ii BC Landi, *DISMG* 157

**Διονυσόδωρος**
AIGINA: (1) m. ii BC *Alt-Ägina* I (2) p. 43 no. 2
ARGOLIS:
—EPIDAUROS: (2) c. 365–335 BC *IG* IV (1)² 103, 147
——Bounoia (Hylleis): (3) m. iii BC Peek, *IAEpid* 42, 52 (Perlman E.3); Perlman p. 63 f. (date)
—EPIDAUROS*: (4) c. 335–325 BC *IG* IV (1)² 108, 162
—HALIEIS: (5) c. 221 BC ib. 42, 10
—NEMEA*: (6) v–iv BC *SEG* XXXIV 287
—TROIZEN: (7) iii BC *RE* (18); Luc., *Laps.* 10; (8) s. iii BC *IG* IV (1) 727 A, 1 (Perlman H.1) (Διονυσό[δωρος], Διονυσό[δοτος], Διόνυσος—ed.: s. —ιος)
ARKADIA:
—MANTINEIA-ANTIGONEIA: (9) i–ii AD *IG* V (2) 342 a, 7
—TEGEA: (10) i BC ib. 45, 4
EPIROS:
—BOUTHROTOS: (11) f. ii BC *IBouthrot* 2, 5; 3, 5; 4, 6; 76, 7 (f. Νικίας)
—DODONA*: (12) ?iii–ii BC *AE* 1959, p. 175 no 29 ([Διον]νσόδωρος)
ILLYRIA:
—APOLLONIA: (13) i BC Maier 151; cf. *IApoll Ref. Bibl.* n. 50 (coin) (money.)
KORINTHIA:
—KORINTH: (14) m. iii BC *Corinth* VIII (3) 33 a, 10 ([Διον]νσόδωρ[ος]); (15) s. iii BC ib. 38, 4 (f. —ατος)
—SIKYON: (16) iii/ii BC Plb. xvi 3. 7 f.; 8. 4; xviii 1. 3; 2. 2; *SEG* XXXIX 1334, 3; *Chiron* 19 (1989) p. 499 f. (ident.) (s. Δεινοκράτης)
LAKONIA:
—PYRRHICHOS?: (17) iv BC *SEG* XI 1002
—SPARTA: (18) c. 25–1 BC *IG* V (1) 210, 24 (Bradford (2)) (f. Τιμοκράτης); (19) ii AD *IG* V (1) 159, 13 (Bradford (1))
MESSENIA:
—KYPARISSIA: (20) m. iii BC *IG* IV (1)² 96, 67 (Perlman E.3); Perlman p. 63 f. (date) (s. Φιλόδαμος)
S. ITALY (CALABRIA):
—TARAS-TARENTUM: (21) 380 BC Moretti, *Olymp.* 397
SICILY: (22) c. 250 BC *PSI* 626 I, 11 (s. Ἀντίλοχος)
—AKRAI: (23) ?iii BC *SGDI* 3239, 7 (*Akrai* p. 157 no. 9) (s. Φιλιστίων); (24) ~ *SGDI* 3240, 6 (*Akrai* p. 156 no. 7) (f. Ἀριστόμαχος); (25) ii BC ib. p. 156 no. 6, 3 (s. Ζώπυρος)
—SYRACUSE: (26) f. i BC Cic., *In Verr.* II ii 50 (Lat. Dionysodorus)

**Διονυσοκλῆς**
DALMATIA:
—TRAGURION: (1) imp. *CIL* III 2682 (Lat. Statius Dionysocles)

**Διονυσοφάνης**
ARGOLIS:
—EPIDAUROS*: (1) c. 335–325 BC *IG* IV (1)² 106 III, 65, 103
ILLYRIA:
—DALOS: (2) f. ii BC *BCH* 45 (1921) p. 22 IV, 29; *REG* 62 (1949) p. 28, 6 (f. Ἰσίδωρος: reading—Oulhen)

**Διοπείθης**
AKARNANIA:
—MATROPOLIS: (1) m. ii BC *IG* IX (1)² (2) 208, 5, 35 (f. Πρόϊτος)
—PALAIROS: (2) iii/ii BC ib. 548
ARGOLIS:
—ARGOS: (3) c. 210 BC *ILind* 137, 6 (sculptor)
—EPIDAUROS: (4) 149 AD Peek, *IAEpid* 157 (f. Σπόνδος)
—HERMIONE: (5) iii BC *IG* IV (1) 729 I, 7 (f. Κρύτων)
ELIS: (6) vi/v BC *Suda* I 543 (f. Ἱππίας)
EPIROS:
—DODONA*: (7) iv BC Carapanos, *Dodone* p. 41 no. 6 (-πέθ-)
KEPHALLENIA:
—SAME: (8) hell. Fraser–Rönne, *BWGT* p. 118 no. 6, 1
LAKONIA:
—SPARTA: (9) v/iv BC X., *HG* iii 3. 3; Plu., *Ages.* 3; *Lys.* 22 (Poralla² 241)

**Διόπομπος**
ACHAIA:
—DYME: (1) iii BC *AJPh* 31 (1910) p. 399 no. 74 a, 7 (I f. Διόπομπος II); (2) ~ ib. l. 7 (II s. Διόπομπος I)

**Διόπος**
KORINTHIA:
—KORINTH: (1) vii BC Plin., *NH* XXXV 152 (Overbeck 262) (and Etruria: Lat. Diopus: potter)
SICILY:
—KAMARINA: (2) m. vi BC Dubois, *IGDS* 112 (Cordano, 'Camarina VII' 3)

**Δῖος**
ARKADIA:
—TEGEA: (1) ?ii BC *IG* V (2) 210 (Δεῖ-); (2) 165 AD ib. 50, 24 (Δεῖ-: s. Ἡρᾶς)
S. ITALY: (3) imp. *CIL* X 8059. 171 (seal) (Lat. L. Fulvius Dius)
SICILY:
—KATANE: (4) imp. ib. 7090 (Lat. L. Silius Dius: s. Τύχη)

**Διοσκορᾶς**
LAKONIA:
—SPARTA: (1) ?s. ii AD *IG* V (1) 816 (Bradford (-))

**Διόσκορος**
LAKONIA:
—SPARTA: (1) ii AD *IG* V (1) 159, 24 (Bradford (1)); (2) c. 130 AD *IG* V (1) 60, 3 (Bradford s.v. Ἀριστονικίδας (1)) (Ἀριστονικίδας ὁ καὶ Δ.: s. Ἀγαθοκλῆς); (3) s. ii AD *SEG* XI 598, 9 (Bradford (2))
S. ITALY: (4) imp. *CIL* X 8059. 276 (seal) (Lat. A. Nituranius Dioscorus)
S. ITALY (CAMPANIA):
—BAIAI: (5) ii/iii AD *NScav* 1897, p. 12 (Lat. L. Caecilius Dioscorus)

—DIKAIARCHIA-PUTEOLI: (6) imp. *CIL* X 2548 (Lat. Iulius Dios(c)orus)
—HERCULANEUM: (7) m. i AD *PdelP* 16 (1961) p. 70 no. 94 (Lat. Dioscorus)
—POMPEII: (8) i BC–i AD *NScav* 1916, p. 303 no. 66 (Castrèn 158. 13) (Lat. M. Epidius Dioscorus)
SICILY:
—SYRACUSE: (9) iii–v AD *Rend. Pont.* 22 (1946-7) p. 234 no. 32 + *Nuovo Didask.* 6 (1956) p. 54 no. 5 ([Δι]όσκορος); (10) ~ Ferrua, *NG* 259

**Διόσκουθος**
MESSENIA:
—MESSENE: (1) imp. *SEG* XLI 376 G; *PAE* 1988, p. 68 (*Proc. Sympos. Olympic Games* p. 89)

**Διοσκουρίδας**
ACHAIA:
—DYME: (1) ?ii–i BC *SGDI* 1621
LAKONIA:
—SPARTA: (2) ?m. ii AD *IG* V (1) 161, 3 (Bradford (-)) (f. Δίδυμος)
MESSENIA:
—MESSENE: (3) iii/ii BC *SEG* XLI 365 (s. Ἀντικράτης)

**Διοσκουρίδης**
ARKADIA:
—KLEITOR: (1) a. 212 AD *IG* V (2) 369, 15 ([Δι]οσκω[ρίδ]ης)
LEUKAS: (2) ?f. iii BC ib. II² 9205 (f. —ίσκος)
S. ITALY (CAMPANIA):
—NEAPOLIS: (3) 110 BC *ID* 2126; 2265 (f. Ἀπολλώνιος)
—POMPEII*: (4) i BC–i AD *Römische Gräberstrassen* p. 205 a (Lat. L. Caecilius Dioscurides: freed.)

**Διοτίμα**
ARKADIA:
—MANTINEIA-ANTIGONEIA: (1) v BC *RE* (1) (fict.?)

**Διότιμος**
AIGINA?: (1) ?v BC *SEG* XXIX 296 (*CEG* I 130)
LEUKAS: (2) hell.? *IG* IX (1) 560
MESSENIA:
—MESSENE: (3) iv/iii BC ib. V (1) 1435, 15; *SEG* XI 1037 (Θιότιμος—*IG*)
S. ITALY (BRUTTIUM):
—KROTON: (4) vi BC Paus. vi 14. 5 (f. Μίλων)

**Διούνιος**
SICILY:
—LIPARA: (1) imp. *Meligunis-Lipara* 5 p. 182; cf. *SEG* XLI 814 (s. —ων)

**Διοφάνης**
ARKADIA:
—HERAIA: (1) 480 BC Moretti, *Olymp.* 205 ([Διο]φάνης?—Moretti, [Θεο]φάνης?)
—LOUSOI?: (2) iii BC *SEG* XI 1122, 9 (*IPArk* 22)
—MANTINEIA-ANTIGONEIA: (3) c. 300–221 BC *IG* V (2) 323. 96 (tessera) (f. Σῖμος)
—MEGALOPOLIS: (4) 204–169 BC *RE* Supplbd. II (1a); *SEG* XXV 445, 12 (*IPArk* 18); *IvOl* 46, 5 (*IPArk* 31 IIB) (s. Δίαιος, ?f. Δίαιος)
—PHENEOS: (5) c. 210–207 BC *IG* IV (1)² 73, 14; *SEG* XXXV 303 (date) (f. Πανταίνετος)
EPIROS:
—AMBRAKIA: (6) a. 167 BC ib. 665 A, 1, 5; 665 B, 22 (s. Δαΐμαχος)
ILLYRIA:
—EPIDAMNOS-DYRRHACHION: (7) hell.-imp. *IDyrrh* 173 (s. Ἀγάθων)
S. ITALY (CALABRIA):
—TARAS-TARENTUM: (8) s. iii BC *IG* VII 1726, 3; cf. Roesch, *Thespies* p. 15 no. 3 (f. Διοκλῆς)
S. ITALY (CAMPANIA):
—NEAPOLIS: (9) iv/iii BC Sambon 437 ff. (coins) (*SNG Oxford* 91) (Διφάνης—*SNG*)

## Διοφάντης
LAKONIA:
—SPARTA: (1) c. 140-150 AD IG v (1) 64, 1 (Bradford (-)) ([Δι]οφάντης)

## Διόφαντος
ACHAIA: (1) 146 BC IG IV (1)² 28, 133 (f. Ἀγάθων: synoikos)
AIGINA: (2) ?i BC Alt-Ägina I (2) p. 45 no. 13 (Διόφ[αντος]?, Διοφ[άνης]?, Διόφ[ιλος]—ed.)
AITOLIA:
—THERMOS*: (3) s. iii BC IG IX (1)² (1) 60 II, 17
AKARNANIA:
—PALAIROS: (4) c. 325-315 BC Hesp. 57 (1988) p. 148 A, 17 (SEG XXXVI 331); cf. Hesp. 48 (1979) pp. 78 f. with pl. 22 c (s. Λυκοφρονίδας)
—THYRREION: (5) s. iii BC IG IX (1)² (2) 285 (f. Κλεώ); (6) 216 BC ib. 583, 19 (f. Γλαυκῖνος); (7) ii BC ib. 250, 5 (f. Σωτίων); (8) ~ ib. l. 16 (s. Σωτίων); (9) ~ ib. 251, 14 (f. Σωσίβιος); (10) ii/i BC ib. 256, 4
ARGOLIS:
—EPIDAUROS: (11) 191 AD ib. IV (1)² 396 (I f. Διόφαντος II); (12) ~ ib. ([Διό]φαντος: II s. Διόφαντος I); (13) 216 AD ib. 404 (f. M. Αὐρ. Τρύφων)
ARKADIA:
—TEGEA: (14) ?ii BC ib. v (2) 212; (15) ii AD ib. 55, 50 (f. Ὀνήσιμος); (16) 165 AD ib. 50, 42 (I f. Διόφαντος II); (17) ~ ib. l. 42 (II s. Διόφαντος I)
——(Athaneatai): (18) f. iii BC ib. 36, 76 (f. Ἱππαρχος)
DALMATIA:
—ISSA:
——(Pamphyloi): (19) iv/iii BC Brunšmid p. 8, 30 (f. Ὀνασίλας)
—TRAGURION: (20) imp. CIL III 2701 (Lat. Diophantus)
KORINTHIA:
—SIKYON: (21) ii AD Luc., DMort. 10 (fict.)
LAKONIA:
—PYRRHICHOS: (22) imp.? IG v (1) 1287 a
—SPARTA: (23) s. iv BC SEG XI 668 (vase); BSA 30 (1928-30) p. 250 fig. 5, 3 (Poralla² 242a)
MESSENIA:
—MESSENE: (24) f. iii BC SEG XLI 342, 5; cf. PAE 1991, p. 100 no. 8
——(Hylleis): (25) 11 AD ib. 1992, p. 71 A, 16 (s. Κάλλων)
S. ITALY (CAMPANIA):
—POMPEII: (26) iii BC Atti Conv. Taranto 15 (1975) p. 187 (vase); (27) i BC-i AD CIL IV 2462 (Διώ-); (28) ~ ib. 7296 (Lat. [D]iopha[ntus]?); (29) ~ ib. 10249 (Lat. Dioph[antus]?, Dioph[anes]?); (30) f. i AD ib. x 1034 (Castrèn 381. 5); Kockel p. 184 (date) (Lat. P. Sittius Diophantus)
S. ITALY (LUCANIA):
—ATINA LUCANA: (31) i AD IItal III (1) 124 (CIL x 331) (Lat. P. Nanonius Diophantus)
SICILY: (32) imp.? IG XIV 2395. 2 (tile)
ZAKYNTHOS: (33) ?205 BC ib. VII 296, 8 (IOrop 177) (f. Ἀριστόνικος)

## Διοχάρης
ARGOLIS:
—EPIDAUROS*: (1) c. 335-325 BC IG IV (1)² Addenda 106 II, 133-4
S. ITALY (APULIA):
—SIPONTUM*: (2) f. i AD Serricchio, Iscrizioni di Siponto 6; BCH 90 (1966) pp. 144-9 (Lat. D. Iulius Diochares: f. Iulia Tertulla: freed.)

## Δίσκος
ILLYRIA:
—APOLLONIA: (1) hell. IApoll 352 (tile)
S. ITALY (CAMPANIA):
—POMPEII: (2) i BC-i AD CIL IV 4324 (Lat. Discus)
—SALERNUM: (3) ii AD IItal I (1) 149 (CIL x 553) (Lat. C. Ampedius Discus)

## Δίυλλος
ARKADIA: (1) 316 BC IG v (2) 549, 32 (s. Ἐπίγονος)
—THELPHOUSA: (2) a. 228 BC ib. IV (1)² 72 B, 20 (Δίυλλ[ος]: f. Ὀξυτίων)
KORINTHIA:
—KORINTH: (3) vi/v BC Paus. x 13. 7 (sculptor)
S. ITALY (CALABRIA):
—TARAS-TARENTUM: (4) iv BC SEG XXXIX 1077 (loomweight) (Δίυλ(λος)?)

## Διφιλία
S. ITALY (CALABRIA):
—LUPIAE: (1) imp. Susini, Fonti Salento p. 149 no. 99 (Lat. Diphilia)

## Δίφιλος
ACHAIA:
—BOURA: (1) c. 210-207 BC IG IV (1)² 73, 16; SEG XXXV 303 (date) (s. Δαμοκράτης)
ACHAIA?: (2) 193 BC IG v (2) 293, 6 (f. Εὔβουλος)
AKARNANIA:
—THYRREION: (3) iii-ii BC SEG XXVII 159, 5; cf. PAE 1977, pl. 244 a (s. Ἐπιτ—)
ARKADIA: (4) iv BC IG IX (2) 773 (s. Ζατέας)
ILLYRIA:
—EPIDAMNOS-DYRRHACHION: (5) hell.-imp. IDyrrh 174
S. ITALY (CAMPANIA):
—DIKAIARCHIA-PUTEOLI: (6) imp.? NScav 1891, p. 168 (Δεί-)
—NEAPOLIS: (7) 100 BC IG II² 1028, 157 ([Δί]φιλος: f. Διονύσιος)
—POMPEII: (8) 78 BC CIL I² 735 (IV 1842; Castrèn 326. 1) (Lat. C. Pumidius Dipilus)
—POMPEII*: (9) i BC CIL I² 1638 (x 1049; Castrèn 129. 18) (Lat. Q. Cornelius Diphilus: freed.)
S. ITALY (LUCANIA):
—HYELE-VELIA: (10) imp. IG II² 8483 (Δεί-: s. Ἀρτέμων)

## Διφρίδας
LAKONIA:
—SPARTA: (1) v/iv BC RE (-); cf. D.S. xiv 97. 3 (Poralla² 243) (Διφίλας—D.S)

## Διχίνας
SICILY:
—AKRAGAS: (1) vi/v BC Manganaro, QUCC forthcoming no. 1

## Διώ
KORINTHIA:
—KORINTH: (1) c. 570-550 BC Amyx 77. 1; 78. 2 and 5; 119. 2 (vases) (Lorber 111); Lorber 110; 99 (-όι: her.)

## Δίων
ACHAIA: (1) ?257 BC Nachtergael, Les Galates 7, 52 (s. Θεύδωρος); (2) 146 BC IG IV (1)² 28, 73 (s. Νικάτας: synoikos)
—DYME: (3) c. 270 BC ib. IX (1)² (1) 13, 36 (f. Μυννίων); (4) ii BC Achaean Grave Stelai 45 (f. Νικαία); (5) ~ ICos ED 232, 13 (f. Ἀμεινίας)
AITOLIA: (6) m. iii BC IG IX (1)² (1) 22, 6; (7) ?255 BC Nachtergael, Les Galates 8, 5; 19, 3; Flacelière p. 398 no. 21 c, 3; (8) ?247 BC Syll³ 444 A, 3; CID II 139, 3; (9) 244 or 240 BC SGDI 2511, 2 (Flacelière p. 402 no. 29); (10) ?c. 214-210 BC SEG III 343, 3; cf. Hyettos pp. 307-9 (date) (f. Νικάνωρ); (11) 200-150 BC BMC Thessaly p. 196 no. 21 (coin) (Δίω(ν)?)
—KASILIOI: (12) c. 245-236 BC IG IX (1)² (1) 25, 55
AKARNANIA: (13) 213 BC PRain Cent. p. 317 no. 47 A, 2; p. 317 no. 47 B, 1
—ALYZIA: (14) ?353 BC Tod, GHI II 160, 19 (s. Πολυλ—)
ARGOLIS:
—ARGOS: (15) a. 324 BC CID II 120 A, 7 (f. —τος); (16) iii BC IG v (2) 34, 21; (17) ?257-253 BC Nachtergael, Les Galates 7, 39; 10, 51; cf. 1094 (f. Ἡράκλειτος); (18) i BC IG IV (1)² 700 (s. Δαμόφιλος: sculptor); (19) ii/iii AD ib. IV (1) 653
—EPIDAUROS: (20) c. 405 BC Paus. x 9. 10; cf. CEG II 819
—EPIDAUROS*: (21) c. 370-365 BC Peek, IAEpid 52 B, 68 (Δίων)
—TROIZEN*: (22) iv BC IG IV (1) 823, 7, 53
ARKADIA:
—TEGEA:
——(Athaneatai): (23) s. iii BC ib. v (2) 36, 114 (f. Ἀριστείδας: metic)
——(Krariotai): (24) s. iv BC ib. 41, 46 (Δίω[ν]: f. Σακλῆς)
EPIROS:
—DODONA*: (25) iv BC SEG XV 400
ILLYRIA:
—APOLLONIA:
——(Ip.): (26) iii/ii BC IApoll 7; cf. L'Illyrie mérid. 2 p. 207 (f. Ζωῖλος)
KORINTHIA:
—KORINTH: (27) c. 570-550 BC Amyx 59. 2; 78. 1; 84. 1; 102. 1; 104 A. 4 and 7; 104 B. 11; 109. 1-2; 119. 3 and 5 (vases) (Lorber 94); Lorber 90; 91; 93; 99; 110 (her.?); (28) i BC BGU 1285, 7 (s. Μύστα)
—SIKYON: (29) m. v BC IG IV (1) 425, 1 (-ōν)
LAKONIA: (30) ii BC ib. II² 9147 (Bradford (5)) (f. Ἀσία)
—SPARTA: (31) c. 50-25 BC IG v (1) 208, 6 (Bradford (7)) (f. Δαμίων); (32) s. i BC IG v (1) 133, 5 (Bradford (2)) (s. Τιμοφάνης); (33) c. 25-1 BC IG v (1) 210, 3 (Bradford (9)) (f. Νικόστρατος); (34) c. 90-100 AD IG v (1) 31, 6 (Bradford (3)); (35) c. 100 AD SEG XI 536, 6 (Bradford (8)) (I f. Δίων II); (36) ~ SEG XI 536, 6 (Bradford (1)) (II s. Δίων I); (37) c. 140 AD IG v (1) 65, 10 (Bradford (4)) (Π. Αἰλ. Δ.); (38) ii/iii AD IG v (1) 89, 9; 561, 12 (Bradford (6)) (f. M. Αὐρ. Χρυσόγονος); (39) iii AD SEG XLII 321 (Δή-)
LEUKAS: (40) ii BC AM 27 (1902) p. 370 no. 47; (41) c. 167-50 BC BMC Thessaly p. 181 nos. 106-7; p. 183 nos. 127-8; p. 184 nos. 150-1 (coins)
MESSENIA:
—KYPARISSIA: (42) 76 BC Moretti, Olymp. 677
—MESSENE: (43) m. iv BC IG II² 9347, 2 (f. Φιλόξενος); (44) ~ ib. l. 4 (s. Φιλόξενος); (45) hell. BMC Pelop. p. 111 nos. 34-6 (coin); (46) hell.-imp. IG v (1) 1486
S. ITALY (CAMPANIA):
—NEAPOLIS: (47) i BC RE (23) (Lat. Dio)
—POMPEII: (48) i BC-i AD CIL IV 9968 (Lat. Dion)
—SALERNUM: (49) imp. IItal I (1) 199 (CIL x 583) (Lat. Dio)
S. ITALY (LUCANIA):
—HERAKLEIA: (50) iv/iii BC IGSI I I, 14 (DGE 62; Uguzzoni–Ghinatti I) (f. Κωνέας)
SICILY: (51) v/iv BC ZPE 111 (1996) p. 137 no. 1; (52) f. iii BC Vandermersch p. 165; Arch. Subacquea 2 p. 63 (amph.)
—AKRAGAS: (53) iii BC Arch. Class. 17 (1965) p. 192 (?s. Δαι—)
—AKRAI: (54) ii-i BC SGDI 3246, 5, 7 (Akrai pp. 152-3 no. 2; Dubois, IGDS 109) (s. Θεόδωρος, f. Θεόδωρος)
—HALAISA: (55) iii BC NScav 1959, p. 321 no. 25; 1961, p. 293 no. 5 with fig. 30 b (bricks); (56) f. i BC Cic., In Verr. II i 27 ff.; In Verr. II ii 19 ff. (Lat. Q. Caecilius Dio)
—KAMARINA: (57) f. v BC Cordano, Tessere Pubbliche 69 (-ōν: s. Νεμονάιος); (58) s. v BC Dubois, IGDS 121, 11 (Arena, Iscr. Sic. II

143; *SEG* XXXVIII 940; Cordano, 'Camarina VII' 25) (*-ον*: s. *Παρμένων*); (**59**) ?iv/iii BC *SEG* XXXIV 940, 3, 5 (Dubois, *IGDS* 124; *PdelP* 44 (1989) p. 192 no. 3; Cordano, 'Camarina VII' 97) (s. *Ἡρακλείδας*)
—MORGANTINA: (**60**) ii BC *SEG* XXVII 655, 3 (Dubois, *IGDS* 194)
—SELINOUS: (**61**) m. v BC ib. 36, 4 (Arena, *Iscr. Sic.* I 69) (*-ον*: s. *Πίακις*); (**62**) s. v BC Dubois, *IGDS* 61 (*IGLMP* 99) (f. *Σέλινις*) ?= (*63*); (**63**) ~ Dubois, *IGDS* 62 (*IGLMP* 100) (f. *Φιλῖνος*) ?= (*62*)
—SYRACUSE: (**64**) c. 410-354 BC *RE* (2); *IG* IV (1)² 95, 39 (Perlman E.2) (s. *Ἱππαρῖνος*, f. *Ἱππαρῖνος*, *Ἀρεταῖος*)
——(Ἑρμεῖος): (**65**) ?iv BC Manganaro, *PdelP* forthcoming no. 3, 2 (s. *Ἀρίσταρχος*)
—SYRACUSE?:
——(Λαβ.): (**66**) hell. ib. no. 4 II, 10 (*Δίω(ν)*: f. *Ζώπυρος*)
——(Πλη.): (**67**) hell. ib. no. 4 IV, 6 (f. *Ζώπυρος*)
—TAUROMENION: (**68**) 217 BC *IG* XIV 421 an. 24 (*SGDI* 5219)
ZAKYNTHOS: (**69**) c. 350-250 BC *BMC Pelop.* p. 97 no. 33 (coin); Kraay, *Greek Coins and History* pp. 3 f. (ident.)

**Διώνασσα**
LAKONIA:
—SPARTA: (**1**) ?viii-vii BC Plu., *Lyc.* 1 (Poralla² 245) (?m. *Λυκοῦργος*: dub.)

**Διώνδας**
ARGOLIS:
—EPIDAUROS*: (**1**) iv/iii BC Peek, *NIEpid* 20, 27 (*Διών[δ]ας*)

**Διώνη**
S. ITALY (CAMPANIA):
—DIKAIARCHIA-PUTEOLI: (**1**) imp. *CIL* X 2365 (Lat. Dione)

**Διωνίδας**
DALMATIA:
—ISSA:
——(Hylleis): (**1**) iv/iii BC Brunšmid p. 8, 36 (*Διω[νίδ]ας*: f. *Φιλίαρχος*)
LAKONIA:
—SPARTA: (**2**) c. 25-1 BC *IG* V (1) 210, 28 (Bradford (-)) (s. *Λυσίξενος*)

**Διώξιππος**
KORINTHIA:
—KORINTH: (**1**) inc. *FGrH* 454 (Lat. Dioxippus)

**Δοία**
SICILY:
—KATANE: (**1**) iii-v AD *IG* XIV 532 (Wessel 1360) + Ferrua, *NG* 439 (*Δό(μν)α*?—Kaibel and Wessel)

**Δοκήτιος**
EPIROS:
—NIKOPOLIS: (**1**) ii AD *FD* III (1) 544, 3 (Sarikakis 124) (*Μ. Οὔλπιος Δ. Λούκιος*)

**Δόκιμος**
ARKADIA: (**1**) hell. *BMC Pelop.* p. 175 no. 68 (coin) (*Δόκ[ιμος]*)
EPIROS:
—BOUTHROTOS (PRASAIBOI): (**2**) a. 163 BC *IBouthrot* 28, 9 (*SEG* XXXVIII 486) (f. *Δεξίδαμος*); (**3**) ~ *IBouthrot* 32, 4 (*SEG* XXXVIII 491); (**4**) ~ *IBouthrot* 100, 8 (f. *Μεγάρτας*); (**5**) ~ ib. 140, 9; (**6**) ~ ib. 160, [9]; 161, 6 (f. *Στράτων*)
——Tharioi: (**7**) a. 163 BC ib. 91, 13 (*SEG* XXXII 623) (s. *Σαμίας*)
—LARISAIOI: (**8**) c. 330 BC Cabanes, *L'Épire* p. 580 no. 55, 8

—MOLOSSOI: (**9**) c. 343-330 BC ib. p. 588 no. 74, 10 (*SEG* XXVI 700) (s. *Ἔρυξις*); (**10**) iv/iii BC Unp. (Arta Mus., inscr.) (s. *Ἀσανδρος*)
—OMPHALES: (**11**) m. iv BC Cabanes, *L'Épire* p. 539 no. 3, 8
—ORESTOI: (**12**) ?164 BC ib. p. 586 no. 71, 8 (f. *Ἀντίνους*)
—TALAONOI/TALAIANES: (**13**) iii-ii BC *SGDI* 1349, 6; cf. Cabanes, *L'Épire* p. 580 no. 53 (s. *Βοΐσκος*); (**14**) c. 200 BC *IG* IX (1)² (1) 31, 126 (s. *Ἀντίοχος*); (**15**) a. 163 BC *IBouthrot* 99, 7 (*BCH* 118 (1994) p. 121 B)
—TORYDAIOI: (**16**) f. ii BC Cabanes, *L'Épire* p. 554 no. 33, 3 (*SEG* XXXVII 511) (s. *Κεφαλῖνος*)
ILLYRIA:
—APOLLONIA: (**17**) imp. *IApoll* 338 (I f. *Δόκιμος* II); (**18**) ~ ib. (II s. *Δόκιμος* I)
S. ITALY (CALABRIA):
—TARAS-TARENTUM: (**19**) m. iv BC Polyaen. iv 2. 1; (**20**) c. 302-280 BC Vlasto 696 (coin) (*Δ(ό)κιμος*?)
S. ITALY (CAMPANIA):
—SALERNUM*: (**21**) 98-117 AD *IItal* I (1) 92 (*CIL* X 653) (Lat. M. Ulp. Docimus: imp. freed.)
SICILY: (**22**) f. i BC Cic., *In Verr.* II iii 78-9; 83 (Lat. Docimus)

**Δόκων**
MESSENIA:
—THOURIA: (**1**) f. ii BC *SEG* XI 972, 69 (f. *Καλλίμαχος*)

**Δόλιχος**
S. ITALY (CAMPANIA):
—DIKAIARCHIA-PUTEOLI*: (**1**) imp. *CIL* X 2412 (Lat. M. Faltonius Dolicus: freed.?)

**Δόλος**
KORINTHIA:
—KORINTH: (**1**) c. 570-550 BC Amyx 117. 2 (vase) (Lorber 102) (*Δόλō(ν)*—Banti, *Δόλοψ*, *δδλος*—Arena: her.)

**Δομέστιχος**
KORINTHIA:
—KORINTH: (**1**) ii AD *Corinth* IV (2) p. 207 no. 719 (lamp)

**Δομέτιος**
EPIROS:
—NIKOPOLIS?: (**1**) ?iv AD *BCH* 89 (1965) p. 765 (*-μήτ-*)
MESSENIA:
—MESSENE: (**2**) 31 BC-14 AD *SEG* XXIII 207, 33

**Δόμνα**
SICILY:
—HYKKARA: (**1**) imp. *IG* XIV 294 (d. *Βόττος*, *Μελιτίνη*)

**Δομνῖνα**
SICILY:
—SYRACUSE: (**1**) iii-v AD ib. 101 (Strazzulla 42)

**Δόναξ**
ILLYRIA:
—APOLLONIA: (**1**) c. 250-50 BC Maier 71; 88 (coin) (Ceka 43-4) (money.)
—EPIDAMNOS-DYRRHACHION: (**2**) c. 250-50 BC ib. 146 (coin) (money.)
S. ITALY (CAMPANIA):
—DIKAIARCHIA-PUTEOLI: (**3**) imp. *CIL* X 2627 (Lat. D. Iuniu(s) Donax)
—HERCULANEUM*: (**4**) i BC-i AD ib. 1403 g III, 1 (Lat. -nius Donax: freed.)

**Δόντας**
LAKONIA: (**1**) vii/vi BC Paus. vi 19. 14 (Poralla² 246) (*Μεδόντας*?—Wade-Gery) ?= (*Μέδων* (1))

**Δόξα**
AKARNANIA:
—THYRREION: (**1**) ii-i BC *SEG* XL 463
ARKADIA:
—MANTINEIA-ANTIGONEIA: (**2**) m. ii AD *IG* V (2) 312 (m. *Ἰσόχρυσος*)
KEPHALLENIA: (**3**) ii AD *Miscellanea* p. 183 no. 3 (*Δ. Νίκη*)
KERKYRA: (**4**) imp. *IG* IX (1) 939
S. ITALY (CAMPANIA):
—NOLA: (**5**) imp. *Atti Acc. Pontan.* 21 (1971-2) pp. 399-400 (Lat. Publilia Doxa)
SICILY:
—SYRACUSE: (**6**) iii BC *IG* II² 10390 (d. *Μενίσκος*)

**Δοξία**
EPIROS:
—BOUTHROTOS (PRASAIBOI): (**1**) a. 163 BC *IBouthrot* 48, 14 (*Δοξ<ί>α*?)

**Δόξξος**
SICILY:
—KAMARINA: (**1**) f. v BC Cordano, *Tessere Pubbliche* 37 (s. *Αἴσχρων*)

**Δορίσκος**
EPIROS:
—BOUTHROTOS (PRASAIBOI):
——Bouthrotioi: (**1**) a. 163 BC *IBouthrot* 120, 9 (*Δορίσκος*: s. *Ἱππόστρατος*)

**Δορκάς**
ARGOLIS:
—ARGOS: (**1**) m. iii BC *Thess. Mnem.* 107; *BCH* 93 (1969) p. 689 no. 1
KORINTHIA:
—SIKYON: (**2**) m. iii BC *IG* II² 10299
S. ITALY (APULIA):
—CANUSIUM*: (**3**) imp. *Epig. Rom. di Canosa* 90 (*CIL* IX 6188) (Lat. Baebia Dorcas: freed.)
—GIOVINAZZO (MOD.): (**4**) imp. ib. 307 (Lat. Messia Dorcas: m. Petilia Secundina)
—LUCERIA: (**5**) imp. *ASP* 34 (1981) p. 23 no. 25 (Lat. Traebonia Dorcas)
—MELFI (MOD.): (**6**) imp. *CIL* IX 6406 (Lat. Accia Dorcas: m. Q. Sedecianus Rufinus)
—VENUSIA: (**7**) imp. *NScav* 1903, p. 204 (Lat. Carpinia Dorcas: m. *Ἡράκλεια*)
S. ITALY (BRUTTIUM):
—SYBARIS-THOURIOI-COPIAE: (**8**) m. iv BC *IG* II² 8895 (d. *Δᾶος*)
S. ITALY (CAMPANIA):
—DIKAIARCHIA-PUTEOLI: (**9**) imp. *CIL* X 2376 (Lat. Dorcas)
—NOLA: (**10**) imp. ib. 1319 (Lat. Gavia Dorcas: d. *Λυρίς*, m. Q. Ovius Modestus)
—POMPEII: (**11**) i BC-i AD ib. IV 8770-1 (Lat. Dorcas)
S. ITALY (LUCANIA):
—ATINA LUCANA: (**12**) imp. *IItal* III (1) 174 (*CIL* X 381) (Lat. Antonia Dorcas)
—HERAKLEIA: (**13**) iv/iii BC *IG* XIV 646, 4 (Landi, *DISMG* 212)

**Δορκέας**
ARGOLIS:
—ARGOS: (**1**) ii AD *SEG* XLI 285 I, 10

**Δορκεύς**
S. ITALY (BRUTTIUM):
—KAULONIA?:
——(Ξαν.): (**1**) ?c. 475 BC *IGSI* 20, 8 (*SEG* IV 71; Landi, *DISMG* 168); *LSAG*² p. 261 no. 29 (date)

**Δορκίας**
ACHAIA:
—PATRAI: (**1**) 185 BC *IG* IX (1)² (1) 32, 44 (s. *Ἀλέξανδρος*)

**Δορκίνας**
AITOLIA: (**1**) iii BC *AD* 23 (1968) Mel. p. 109 no. 64 (f. *Στράταγος*: locn.—Knoepfler)
—APERANTOI: (**2**) iii/ii BC *SEG* XVII 275, 1 (*L'Illyrie mérid.* I p. 110 fig. 8)

—KALLION/KALLIPOLIS: (3) c. 200 BC *IG* IX
(1)² (2) 405 (*Δορκίνα*[ς])
—KALYDON: (4) c. 243-229 BC *SEG* XXXIII 317
?= (5); (5) iii/ii BC *IG* IX (1)² (1) 136, 10 ?=
(4)
—PHILOTAIEIS: (6) f. ii BC ib. 96, 18
([Δ]*ορ*[*κ*]*ίνας*: f. *Λάμαχος*)
AKARNANIA:
—ECHINOS: (7) c. 266 BC ib. XII (9) 1187, 28;
Robert, *Ét. Num. Gr.* pp. 179 ff. (date) (s.
*Εὔχειρος*)
—STRATOS: (8) a. 167 BC *IG* IX (2) 6 a, 3; cf.
Stählin p. 220 (date) (s. *Μενεκράτης*)

**Δόρκιππος**
S. ITALY (BRUTTIUM):
—LOKROI EPIZEPHYRIOI:
——(Εὐρ.): (1) iv/iii BC De Franciscis 11, 5; 26,
6 (f. *Δορκίων*)
——(Φαω.): (2) iv/iii BC ib. 21, 3

**Δόρκις**
ARGOLIS:
—EPIDAUROS: (1) iv BC *IG* IV (1)² 185
LAKONIA:
—SPARTA: (2) 477 BC Th. i 95. 6 (Poralla² 247)

**Δόρκις**
ILLYRIA:
—APOLLONIA: (1) imp. *IApoll* 87 (Ζορκεις)

**Δορκίων**
ACHAIA:
—DYME: (1) c. 203-201 BC *IG* IX (1)² (1) 30, 13
(f. *Δωρόθεος*)
ARKADIA:
—ALIPHEIRA: (2) iii BC Orlandos, *Alipheira* p.
218 no. 2
KORINTHIA:
—SIKYON: (3) iii BC *IG* II² 10300
S. ITALY (BRUTTIUM):
—LOKROI EPIZEPHYRIOI:
——(Δυσ.): (4) iv/iii BC De Franciscis 4, 5; 22,
5 (s. *Εὐφρονίσκος*)
——(Εὐρ.): (5) iv/iii BC ib. 11, 5; 26, 6 (s. *Δόρ-
κιππος*)
——(Τηλ.): (6) iv/iii BC ib. 16, 3 (s. *Καλλῖνος*)

**Δόρκος**
ARKADIA:
—MEGALOPOLIS: (1) ii BC *IG* V (2) 447, 5
LAKONIA: (2) iii-ii BC ib. V (1) 1341, 3 (Brad-
ford (1))

**Δορκύλος**
AKARNANIA:
—PALAIROS: (1) ii BC *IG* IX (1)² (2) 451, 15 (s.
*Ἀλέξων*)
ARGOLIS:
—ARGOS: (2) c. 458 BC ib. I³ 1149, 57
(Δορρυί[*λος*])
—TROIZEN: (3) f. ii BC ib. IV (1) 756, 4 (s.
*Δαμ....τος*)
EPIROS:
—DODONA*: (4) hell. *SEG* XIX 429 (-κίλ-)
MESSENIA:
—MESSENE: (5) f. iii BC *PAE* 1991, p. 99 no. 7,
15

**Δορκωΐλίδας**
LAKONIA:
—SPARTA?: (1) vii/vi BC *SEG* XI 689 (bronze)
(Lazzarini 355 (name)); *LSAG*² p. 198 no. 5
(date) (Poralla² 247a) (Δορκōϊλίδα(ς), Δορκωνί-
δας—*SEG* and Poralla)

**Δόρκων**
ACHAIA?: (1) 193 BC *IG* V (2) 293, 15 (s. *Στύμ-
φαλος*)


ARGOLIS:
—ARGOS: (2) c. 365-335 BC ib. IV (1)² 103, 12,
44, 53 (?s. *Πολύξενος*); (3) iii BC ib. IV (1) 618
II, 4
—EPIDAUROS*: (4) c. 340-330 BC *SEG* XXV 387
A, 15 ([Δ]*όρ*[*κ*]*ω*[*ν*])
EPIROS:
—DODONA*: (5) iv BC ib. XV 400 (f. *Βοστρύχα*)
KORINTHIA:
—KORINTH: (6) ?c. 500 BC *IG* IV (1) 226 (pinax)
(-κō̄ν); (7) c. 370 BC ib. IV (1)² 102, 30, 51,
179

**Δορκωνίδας**
MESSENIA:
—MESSENE: (1) c. 140 BC *IvOl* 52, 5 (f. *Χαρητί-
δας*); (2) 31 BC-14 AD *SEG* XXIII 207, 15 (f.
*Τυχαμένης*)

**Δόροψος**
EPIROS:
—CHAONES: (1) 356-354 BC *IG* IV (1)² 95, 29
(Perlman E.2); Perlman p. 40 f. (date)

**Δορυκλείδας**
LAKONIA: (1) vii/vi BC Paus. v 17. 1-2 (*RE* (-);
Poralla² 248) (sculptor)

**Δορύμαχος**
LAKONIA:
—KYTHERA: (1) imp. *IG* V (1) 946

**Δορυμένης**
AITOLIA: (1) iii BC *RE* (-); *PP* 15199 ?= (2); (2)
c. 243-229 BC *SEG* XXXIII 317 ?= (1)

**Δορυσσός**
LAKONIA:
—SPARTA: (1) her. *RE* (-) (Poralla² 249) (s. *Λα-
βώτας*, f. *Ἀγησίλαος*: king/dub.)

**Δορυφορίς**
S. ITALY (BRUTTIUM):
—LOKROI EPIZEPHYRIOI: (1) ii-iii AD *Suppl. It.*
3 p. 27 no. 10 (Lat. Duc. Doryphoris)

**Δορυφόρος**
S. ITALY (CALABRIA):
—BRENTESION-BRUNDISIUM: (1) i AD *Epi-
graphica* 25 (1963) p. 70 no. 67 (Lat. L.
Longinus Dorephorus)
S. ITALY (CAMPANIA):
—BAIAI: (2) imp. *IG* XIV 877
—DIKAIARCHIA-PUTEOLI*: (3) imp. *CIL* X 540
(Lat. Cn. Haius Doryphorus: imp. freed.)
—KYME: (4) ?ii AD *NScav* 1886, p. 457 (*Eph.
Ep.* VIII 448) (Lat. Doryphorus: f. T. Flavius
Castrensis)
—POMPEII: (5) ?33-34 AD *CIL* X 909 (Castrèn
109. 7) (Lat. L. Ceius Doryp[horus])
SICILY:
—SYRACUSE: (6) iii-v AD *IG* XIV 25 (Strazzulla
135)

**Δόσσεννος**
S. ITALY (LUCANIA):
—POSEIDONIA-PAESTUM: (1) 410-350 BC *SNG
Cop. Apulia–Lucania* 606; Coll. Santangelo
4386; *Samml. Ludwig* 162 (coins) (Δόσσεν-
νο(ς))

**Δόσσις**
SICILY:
—SEGESTA: (1) m. iii BC *NScav* 1931, p. 398 (Δ.
*Γραδαναῖος*: f. *Ἀρτεμίδωρος*)

**Δότα**
EPIROS:
—NIKOPOLIS: (1) imp. *PAE* 1913, p. 97 no. 10
= p. 111 (Sarikakis 83) (Κλ. Δ.)


**Δουκέτιος**
SICILY:
—MENAI: (1) 461-440 BC *RE* (-) (and Sicily
Kale Akte: oikist)

**Δουλκίτιος**
ARGOLIS:
—ARGOS (NR.): (1) byz. *SEG* XXIX 372, 7

**Δουμέτιος**
EPIROS:
—NIKOPOLIS?: (1) v-vi AD *PAE* 1925-6, p. 129
(mosaic)

**Δράϊππος**
EPIROS:
—DODONA: (1) c. 330 BC Cabanes, *L'Épire* p.
580 no. 55, 6 (-ϊππος)

**Δράκας**
ACHAIA:
—DYME*: (1) c. 219 BC *SGDI* 1612, 59 (*Tyche*
5 (1990) p. 124) (s. *Θεόδοτος*)

**Δρακόντιος**
ACHAIA:
—DYME: (1) s. iii BC *SEG* XIII 278, 28 (f. *Γόρ-
γις*)
LAKONIA:
—SPARTA: (2) 400 BC X., *An.* iv 8. 25 (Poralla²
250)
SICILY:
—KAMARINA: (3) iv/iii BC *SEG* XXXIV 942,
3 (Dubois, *IGDS* 123; Cordano, 'Camarina
VII' 98) (Δρακόντι[ος])

**Δρακοντίς**
AITOLIA:
—KALLION/KALLIPOLIS: (1) 190 BC Sherk 37
B, 7; cf. *SEG* XXVII 123

**Δράκων**
ACHAIA: (1) iii BC ib. XXVI 919, 63 (Δράκω[ν])
—KALLISTAI: (2) c. 230-200 BC *BCH* 45 (1921)
p. 12 II, 61 (s. *Λεπτίνας*: reading—Oulhen)
—PELLENE: (3) 397 BC *RE* (11)
—PHARAI?: (4) ii-i BC *AD* 43 (1988) Chron. p.
172 (f. —ηβούλη)
AITOLIA: (5) c. 285 BC *IG* IX (1)² (1) 51 (f.
*Σκορπίων*)
—THESTIEIS: (6) ii BC *SBBerlAk* 1936, p. 380
no. 1 A, 9
AKARNANIA:
—MEDION: (7) 216 BC *IG* IX (1)² (2) 583, 21 (f.
*Χρέμας*)
—PHOITIAI: (8) 362 BC *CID* II 1 II, 23
ARGOLIS:
—EPIDAUROS: (9) c. 290-270 BC *IG* IV (1)² 109
II, 69, 108, 134-5, 156
ARKADIA:
—KLEITOR: (10) ?i BC *AR* 1994-5, p. 17 (f. *Ἡρα-
κλῆς*)
ILLYRIA:
—APOLLONIA: (11) imp. *IApoll* 237
KEPHALLENIA: (12) c. 215-200 BC *FD* III (2)
86, 12 (*Syll*³ 539 A); Nachtergael, *Les Gala-
tes* 66, 6; cf. p. 291 (date)
KERKYRA: (13) i AD *RE* (16)
LAKONIA:
—SPARTA: (14) c. 115-135 AD *IG* V (1) 114, 8;
*SEG* XI 543, 3 (Bradford (-)) (s. *Κλέαρχος*)
PELOPONNESE: (15) 112 BC *FD* III (2) 70 A, 35
(Sherk 15)
S. ITALY (CALABRIA):
—TARAS-TARENTUM: (16) 279-259 or 255 BC *IG*
XI (2) 108, 18; 161 A, 86; Nachtergael, *Les
Galates* 8, 50 (Stephanis 802) (s. *Λύκων*)
S. ITALY (CAMPANIA):
—DIKAIARCHIA-PUTEOLI*: (17) ii-iii AD *CIL* X
1584 (Lat. Aurelius Draco: imp. freed.)
—MISENUM*: (18) imp. ib. 3386 (Lat. Domitius
Draco); (19) ~ ib. 3621 (Lat. Draco)
SICILY: (20) ii-i BC *Meligunis-Lipara* 2 p. 152
T. 422; cf. *Kokalos* 32 (1986) pp. 223-4 nos.
20-3 (tiles); (21) ?i AD *CIL* X 8053. 105 (Lat.
C. Iunius Draco: potter)
—AKRAGAS: (22) c. 262 BC *IG* IX (1)² (1) 17 A,
93 (Δ[*ράκ*]*ων*: s. *Χαρίλαος*)

—MORGANTINA: (23) iv/iii BC *SEG* XXXIX 1013, 4, 6 (f. Φιλωνίδας, Ἀπολλόδωρος)

**Δραῦκος**
KORINTHIA:
—KORINTH*: (1) iii AD *AE* 1977, p. 76 no. 21

**Δρείγαλος?**
ILLYRIA:
—APOLLONIA: (1) imp. *IApoll* 233 (Δρείπαλος?: f. Χαρίτων)

**Δρίμακος**
ARGOLIS:
—EPIDAUROS*: (1) c. 335-325 BC Peek, *IAEpid* 50, 9, 14-15, 25
ILLYRIA:
—AMANTIA: (2) imp. Cabanes, *L'Épire* p. 562 no. 39 (f. Μένεμος)
S. ITALY (APULIA):
—CANUSIUM*: (3) imp. *Epig. Rom. di Canosa* 206 (*CIL* IX 6191) (Lat. C. Vettius Drimachus: freed.)
—VENUSIA: (4) imp. ib. 501 (Lat. Drimacus)

**Δριμύλος**
MESSENIA:
—MESSENE?: (1) ii/i BC *SEG* XI 979, 61

**Δρίμων**
ILLYRIA:
—BYLLIONES BYLLIS: (1) ?f. ii BC ib. XXXVIII 538

**Δροάτας**
EPIROS:
—KELAITHOI: (1) ?c. 370-344 BC Cabanes, *L'Épire* p. 536 no. 2, 2

**Δρόμας**
ACHAIA:
—DYME: (1) iii-ii BC *Syll*[3] 530, 14; cf. *Achaia und Elis* p. 115 (f. Ἀσκλαπιάδας)

**Δρομέας**
ARKADIA:
—MANTINEIA-ANTIGONEIA: (1) c. 475-450 BC *IG* V (2) 262, 7 (*IPArk* 8); *LSAG*[2] p. 216 no. 29 (date) (Δρομέας)
SICILY:
—NEAITON: (2) f. ii BC *IIasos* 174, 20-1 (s. Θεόδωρος)

**Δρομεύς**
ARKADIA:
—MANTINEIA-ANTIGONEIA: (1) 480 BC Moretti, *Olymp.* 202
—STYMPHALOS: (2) f. v BC *RE* (2); Moretti, *Olymp.* 188; 199; (3) c. 315-280 BC *FD* III (1) 38, 3 (*Syll*[3] 516) (s. Ἀλεξίων)

**Δρόμων**
ACHAIA:
—DYME*: (1) c. 219 BC *SGDI* 1612, 83 (*Tyche* 5 (1990) p. 124) (s. —μων)
ARGOLIS:
—ARGOS*: (2) 105 BC *JÖAI* 14 (1911) Beibl. p. 146 no. 4, 25 (slave/freed.?)
—EPIDAUROS: (3) iv/iii BC Peek, *NIEpid* 97 (Δρ[ό]μων?: f. Μνασικλῆς)
—HERMIONE: (4) i BC-i AD? *IG* IV (1) 730 III, 8 (s. Μεγακλῆς)
EPIROS:
—BOUTHROTOS (PRASAIBOI): (5) a. 163 BC *IBouthrot* 21, 24 (*SEG* XXXVIII 478); (6) ~ *IBouthrot* 30, 18 (*SEG* XXXVIII 488) (f. Ξενις)
ILLYRIA:
—EPIDAMNOS-DYRRHACHION: (7) c. 250-50 BC Maier 233 (coin) (Ceka 147) (money.)


**Δροσίς**
S. ITALY (CAMPANIA):
—DIKAIARCHIA-PUTEOLI: (1) imp. *CIL* X 2277 (Lat. Mindia Drosis: m. Ἡράκλεια)
—NEAPOLIS: (2) imp. *NScav* 1892, p. 317; cf. Leiwo p. 99 no. 50 (Lat. Brinnia Drosis)

**Δρόσος**
S. ITALY (CAMPANIA):
—POMPEII: (1) i BC-i AD *CIL* IV 2506

**Δροσσος**
DALMATIA:
—ISSA: (1) hell. Brunšmid p. 21 no. 7 + *VAHD* 53 (1950-51) p. 35; cf. Robert, *EEP* p. 209 no. 7 (ΔΡΩNON—apogr., Δρ(οσσ)ου—*VAHD*, Δρω(πίω)ν[ος]?—Robert: f. Κίντος); (2) iii/ii BC Brunšmid p. 21 no. 8; *Istros* 2 (1935-6) pp. 18 ff. (date); (3) ii/i BC Brunšmid p. 27 no. 19 (*SEG* XL 515) + *VAHD* 84 (1991) p. 254 no. 4 (Δροσ[σος]: f. Πάτρων)

**Δρύας**
ILLYRIA:
—DASSARETIOI: (1) ii-iii AD *Sp.* 71 (1931) p. 109 no. 262 (s. Καιπίων); (2) ~ ib. 98 (1941-8) p. 122 no. 268 (f. Καιπίων)

**Δρύμος**
ARGOLIS:
—ARGOS: (1) s. iv BC *IG* IV (1)[2] 618 (*CEG* II 815) (s. Θεόδωρος); (2) iv/iii BC *SEG* XXVI 445, 4 (Perlman E.12) (s. Ἐπικράτης)
—NEMEA*: (3) iv/iii BC *SEG* XXXVIII 300

**Δρύμων**
S. ITALY (BRUTTIUM):
—KAULONIA: (1) vi-v BC *RE* (-)

**Δρυπέτης**
ILLYRIA:
—LYCHNIDOS: (1) ?s. ii AD *ZA* 6 (1956) p. 167 no. 3 (f. Ἀνθοῦσα)

**Δρύων**
ACHAIA:
—PELLENE: (1) v/iv BC Paus. vi 8. 6; 27. 5 (f. Πρόμαχος)

**Δρωνίλος**
AKARNANIA:
—ECHINOS: (1) c. 266 BC *IG* XII (9) 1187, 8; Robert, *Ét. Num. Gr.* pp. 179 ff. (date) (f. Ἴδας)

**Δρωξίας**
AKARNANIA:
—LIMNAIA: (1) c. 325-315 BC *Hesp.* 57 (1988) p. 148 A, 33 (*SEG* XXXVI 331); cf. *Hesp.* 48 (1979) pp. 78 f. with pl. 22 c (s. Ἀριστόμαχος)

**Δρώπακος**
AITOLIA: (1) ?263-261 BC *FD* III (3) 184, 1; [190]; *Syll*[3] 498, 2; Nachtergael, *Les Galates* 3, [2]

**Δρωπίνα**
AITOLIA:
—PELEIOI: (1) 190 BC *IG* IX (1)[2] (1) 97, 14 (Δρωπίνα(ς)? (masc. nom.))

**Δρωπίνας**
AITOLIA:
—KALLION/KALLIPOLIS: (1) ?c. 225-200 BC *FD* III (4) 240 (*IG* IX (1)[2] (3) 783); cf. *SEG* XLI 513 (f. Λάδικος); (2) 200 BC *SGDI* 2116, 13, 17 (s.p.); cf. *SEG* XLI 513 (?s. Λάδικος)

**Δρωπίων**
DALMATIA:
—ISSA?: (1) hell.? Brunšmid p. 32 no. 28 (f. Φιλίσκος)


**Δρωπύλος**
ARGOLIS:
—HERMIONE: (1) i BC-i AD? *IG* IV (1) 730 III, 3 (Δ[ρωπ]ύλος—*IG*, Δορκύλος?—*LGPN*: s. Κλειναγόρας)
EPIROS:
—BOUTHROTOS (PRASAIBOI): (2) a. 163 BC *IBouthrot* 27, 9 (*SEG* XXXVIII 485); (3) ~ *IBouthrot* 134, 16; 138, 6 (f. Μενοίτας) ?= (7); (4) ~ ib. l. 6 (Δρωπ[ύλος]: ?s. Μενοίτας)
——Pelmatioi: (5) a. 163 BC ib. 127, 9 (*BCH* 118 (1994) p. 128 A) (f. Ἀριστόμαχος); (6) ~ *IBouthrot* 142, 7; (7) ~ ib. 145, 5 (f. Μενοίτας) ?= (3)
KORINTHIA:
—OINOE: (8) vi BC *IG* IV (1) 414 + *SEG* XXVII 33 (Δροόπυλος—Gallavotti)

**Δρωσίμη**
S. ITALY (CAMPANIA):
—NEAPOLIS: (1) iii-iv AD *IG* XIV 826. 11 (*INap* 238)

**Δυαῖος**
ARKADIA:
—TEGEA: (1) c. 240-229 BC *IG* V (2) 11, 15; 13, 9

**Δυλύπορις**
AIGINA: (1) i BC-i AD? ib. IV (1) 112 (s. Πατᾶς)

**Δύμας**
S. ITALY (BRUTTIUM):
—KROTON: (1) iv BC Iamb., *VP* 267 (*FVS* I p. 446)

**Δυμειάδας**
S. ITALY (CAMPANIA):
—FRATTE DI SALERNO (MOD.): (1) ?c. 500-480 BC Landi, *DISMG* 127 (bronze); *LSAG*[2] p. 252; p. 260 no. 6 (date)

**Δύναμις**
LAKONIA:
—SPARTA: (1) ii-iii AD *IG* V (1) 742 (Bradford (-)) (Ἀντ. Δ.)
S. ITALY (CALABRIA):
—BRENTESION-BRUNDISIUM: (2) imp. *NScav* 1891, p. 172 (Lat. Dynamis)
S. ITALY (CAMPANIA):
—DIKAIARCHIA-PUTEOLI: (3) imp. *CIL* X 2963 (Lat. Siternia Dynamis); (4) ~ *NScav* 1910, p. 192 (Lat. Arrenia Dynamis: d. Arrenius Victor, ?d. Arrenia Mellita)

**Δυνάτη**
S. ITALY (CAMPANIA):
—DIKAIARCHIA-PUTEOLI: (1) imp. *CIL* X 2895; cf. *Puteoli* 11 (1987) p. 55 (Lat. Dynate)

**Δυοκλῆς**
ARKADIA:
—TEGEA:
——(Krariotai): (1) s. iii BC *IG* V (2) 36, 117 (s. Ἐπάλκης)

**Δυοτέλης**
ARKADIA:
—TEGEA:
——(Athaneatai): (1) s. iv BC ib. 174 a, 10

**Δυραχῖνα**
EPIROS:
—NIKOPOLIS: (1) imp. *SEG* XXVII 237
ILLYRIA:
—EPIDAMNOS-DYRRHACHION: (2) imp. *BUST* 1961 (1), p. 110 no. 8 (Lat. Iulia Durachina)

**Δυρώ**
KORINTHIA:
—KORINTH: (1) c. 570-550 BC Amyx 81. 3 (vase) (Lorber 130) (-ρόι: her.?)

**Δυσπσετα**
SICILY:
—SABUCINA (MOD.): (1) f. v BC Dubois, *IGDS* 172 (bronze) (Arena, *Iscr. Sic.* II 107)

**Δυστρίων**
AKARNANIA:
—LEKKA (MOD.): (1) iii BC *IG* IX (1)² (2) 595 ([*Δ*?]*υστρίωνος*—ed.: f. *Σωτίων*)

**Δύσωπος**
ILLYRIA:
—APOLLONIA: (1) c. 213 BC ib. IX (1)² (1) 188, 34

**Δύων**
ARKADIA:
—TEGEA: (1) m. iv BC ib. v (2) 6, 92 (*Δύων*?: f. *Δυσικλῆς*)

**Δωνᾶτος**
SICILY:
—AKRAI: (1) iii-v AD *Akrai* p. 175 no. 68
—SYRACUSE: (2) ?s. i BC *Sic. Gymn.* 16 (1963) p. 61 ([*Δω*]*νᾶτος*: s. *Ἀπολλώνιος*); (3) iii-v AD *Rend. Pont.* 22 (1946-7) p. 233 no. 21 (*Δω*[*νᾶτος*]); (4) ~ ib. p. 237 no. 45; (5) ~ Strazzulla 183 (*Δο-*)

**Δωρᾶς**
ARGOLIS:
—EPIDAUROS: (1) 231 AD *IG* IV (1)² 408 (*Δωρᾶι* (gen.): f. *Ἀπολλώνιος*); (2) 237 AD ib. 412 + Peek, *IAEpid* 167 ([*Δ*]*ωρᾶς*: s. *Ἀπολλώνιος*)
ARKADIA:
—KLEITOR: (3) a. 212 AD *IG* v (2) 369, 7 (*Ἰούλ. Δ.*)
S. ITALY (CALABRIA):
—BRENTESION-BRUNDISIUM: (4) imp. *Necropoli via Cappuccini* p. 283 no. E37 (Lat. Doras)

**Δωρεύς**
AITOLIA: (1) c. 220-150 BC *Coll. Walcher* 1375 (coin) (*Δωρεύ*(*s*), *Δωρ*(*ι*)*εύ*(*s*)?)

**Δωριεύς**
ARGOLIS:
—EPIDAUROS: (1) c. 370 BC *IG* IV (1)² 102, 36 ?= (2); (2) 360 BC *CID* II 4 II, 47; III, 48 ?= (1); (3) iii/ii BC *IG* IV (1)² 243 (f. *Ἀρισταγόρα*)
ILLYRIA:
—EPIDAMNOS-DYRRHACHION: (4) c. 250-50 BC *SNG Cop. Thessaly–Illyricum* 519; cf. *IApoll Ref. Bibl.* n. 51 (coin) (pryt.) ?= (5); (5) ~ *Bakërr Hoard* p. 66 no. 42 (Ceka 271); cf. Ceka 78; *IApoll Ref. Bibl.* n. 51 (coin) (pryt.) ?= (4)
KYNOURIA:
—TYROS*: (6) vi/v BC *IG* v (1) 1521 (vase) (Lazzarini 751) (*Δο-*)
LAKONIA:
—SPARTA: (7) s. vi BC *RE* (3); *IPr* 316, 10 (Poralla² 252) (s. *Ἀναξανδρίδας*, f. *Εὐρυάναξ*)

**Δωρικλῆς**
ARKADIA:
—PHIGALEIA: (1) ii/i BC *IG* v (2) 426
DALMATIA:
—ISSA: (2) hell.? Brunšmid p. 24 no. 13 (*VAHD* 84 (1991) p. 258 no. 9) (f. *Ἀγησίδαμος*)
——(Pamphyloi): (3) iv/iii BC Brunšmid p. 8, 35 (s. *Δαφναῖος*)

**Δωρικός**
SICILY:
—SYRACUSE: (1) 404 BC D.S. xiv 7. 7 (*Δ.*—mss., *Δώριχος*—Dindorf)

**Δωρίλαος**
EPIROS:
—DODONA*: (1) hell. *SEG* XIX 428

**Δωρίμαχος**
AITOLIA: (1) ?279 BC *FD* III (2) 68, 64 = *IG* II² 1132, 5
—KALLION/KALLIPOLIS: (2) 139 BC *SGDI* 2137, 9 ?= (3)

—KALLION/KALLIPOLIS?: (3) a. 166 BC *IG* IX (1)² (3) 676, 19 (f. *Καλλίμαχος*) ?= (2)
—KALYDON: (4) c. 213 BC ib. IX (1)² (1) 188, 2
—KONOPE-ARSINOE: (5) f. ii BC ib. 96, 17 (s. *Στράτων*)
—THESTIEIS: (6) 213 BC ib. l. 11 (s. *Θεόκριτος*)
—TRICHONION: (7) 263-262 BC ib. 3 A, 20; (8) s. iii BC ib. 24, 10; 31, 74 (s. *Σώσανδρος*); (9) c. 219-202 BC *RE* (-); *IG* IX (1)² (1) p. L, s.a. 219 BC, 211 BC, 207 BC, 202 BC; p. XLVIII, 56; 30, 2; *FD* III (1) 352-3; *Ergon* 1990, p. 47 (s. *Νικόστρατος*); (10) 185 BC *IG* IX (1)² (1) 32, 18 (f. *Νίκανδρος*) ?= (11); (11) 184 BC ib. 33, 3 (f. *Κυδρίων*) ?= (10); (12) 153-144 BC p. LII, s.a. 147 BC, 140 BC; (13) c. 141 BC ib. 34, 22 (?s. *Ἀλέξων*)
AITOLIA?: (14) ?iii BC ib. 43, 10
AKARNANIA:
—THYRREION: (15) ii BC ib. IX (1)² (2) 247, 6 (f. *Ἐπικράτης*); (16) ~ ib. 249, 4 (*Δωρίμ*[*αχος*]: f. *Σωτίων*)
KORINTHIA:
—KORINTH: (17) c. 590-570 BC Amyx 33. 3 (vase) (Lorber 52) (*Δō-*: her.?); (18) c. 570-550 BC Amyx 114. 5 (vase) (*Δō-*: her.?)
S. ITALY (BRUTTIUM):
—LOKROI EPIZEPHYRIOI:
——(*Ψαθ.*): (19) 276 BC De Franciscis 23, 1 (s. *Ζωῖλος*)

**Δώριος**
EPIROS:
—DODONA*: (1) iv BC *Ep. Chron.* 10 (1935) p. 257 no. 23

**Δωρίς**
AIGINA: (1) ii-iii AD *AE* 1913, p. 95 no. 6 β (m. *Νίκη*)
AKARNANIA:
—THYRREION: (2) ii BC *IG* IX (1)² (2) 322
ARGOLIS:
—HERMIONE: (3) ii-i BC ib. IV (1) 732 II, 25 (d. *Χαριτώ*)
ARKADIA:
—MANTINEIA-ANTIGONEIA: (4) i AD ib. v (2) 341
S. ITALY (APULIA):
—RUBI: (5) ?ii AD *Suppl. It.* 5 p. 25 no. 7 (Lat. Luxilia Doris: m. *Ναῖs*)
S. ITALY (BRUTTIUM):
—LOKROI EPIZEPHYRIOI: (6) v/iv BC *RE* Supplbd. 3 (4a) (d. *Ξένετος*, m. *Διονύσιος* (Syracuse), *Ἑρμόκριτος* (Syracuse))
S. ITALY (CAMPANIA):
—DIKAIARCHIA-PUTEOLI: (7) imp. *CIL* x 1800 (Lat. Plotia Doris); (8) ~ ib. 3097 (Lat. Vettia Doris); (9) ?ii AD ib. 3133 (Lat. Ulpia Doris)
—DIKAIARCHIA-PUTEOLI*: (10) imp. *Eph. Ep.* VIII 387 (Lat. Modia Doris: freed.)
—MISENUM*: (11) imp. *CIL* x 3643 (Lat. Doris); (12) ii AD *Puteoli* 11 (1987) p. 148 no. 11 (Lat. Doris: freed.)
—POMPEII: (13) i BC-i AD *CIL* IV 1507, 13 (Lat. Doris)
—POMPEII*: (14) i BC-i AD *Eph. Ep.* VIII 326 (Castrèn 238. 3) (Lat. Mancia Doris: freed.)
S. ITALY (LUCANIA):
—VOLCEI: (15) imp. *IItal* III (1) 89 (Lat. Otacilia Doris: d. Otacilius Privatus, *Ἀπολλωνία*)
SICILY:
—KATANE: (16) imp. *CIL* x 7092 (Lat. -atia Doris: d. *Νικηφόρος*)

**Δωρίων**
ARGOLIS:
—EPIDAUROS*: (1) c. 370-365 BC Peek, *IAEpid* 52 B, 46
ILLYRIA:
—APOLLONIA: (2) hell. *IApoll* 353 (tile); (3) i BC Maier 144-7 (coin) (pryt.); (4) imp. *IApoll* 58 (f. *Ἀριστίων*); (5) ~ ib. 69

LEUKAS: (6) f. i BC *IG* IX (1) 534, 12 (*Iscr. Gr. Verona* p. 24) (f. *Ζεῦξις*)

**Δωρόβιος**
EPIROS:
—DODONA*: (1) iv BC Carapanos, *Dodone* p. 41 no. 6

**Δωροθέα**
ILLYRIA:
—EPIDAMNOS-DYRRHACHION: (1) hell.-imp. *IDyrrh* 175 (d. *Ἡρακλείδας*)
SICILY:
—LIPARA: (2) i BC-i AD? Libertini, *Isole Eolie* p. 222 no. 32 + *Kokalos* 13 (1967) p. 199 no. 4 (*Ἀλλιήνα Δ.*)

**Δωρόθεος**
ACHAIA: (1) 146 BC *IG* IV (1)² 28, 95 (f. *Ἀπολλόδωρος*: synoikos)
—DYME: (2) c. 203-201 BC ib. IX (1)² (1) 30, 13 (s. *Δορκίων*)
AIGINA: (3) ?i BC *Alt-Ägina* I (2) p. 44 no. 10 (f. *Δικαῖος*); (4) ~ ib. p. 46 no. 19
AITOLIA:
—KALLION/KALLIPOLIS: (5) 190 BC Sherk 37 B, 61; cf. *SEG* XXVII 123
AKARNANIA: (6) m. iii BC *IG* IX (1)² (2) 578 (s. *Δῶρος*)
—THYRREION: (7) 94 BC ib. 242, 7 (s. *Ἰάσων*)
ARGOLIS:
—ARGOS: (8) ?c. 460-450 BC Marcadé I 30-1; *LSAG*² p. 170 no. 34 (date) (*Δō-*: sculptor)
—EPIDAUROS: (9) iii-ii BC Peek, *IAEpid* 312 (s. *Ἀλέξανδρος*); (10) iii/ii BC *IG* IV (1)² 375; Peek, *IAEpid* 153. 22 (name) (*Δ*[*ωρό*]*θεος*, *Δ*[*ωσί*]*θεος*—IG)
ARKADIA:
—KLEITOR: (11) 168-146 BC *IG* v (2) 367, 13, 34 (*IPArk* 19) (*Δ*[*ω*]*ρόθεος*: s. *Δαμέας*)
—THELPHOUSA: (12) iii BC Phld., *Acad. Ind.* 20, 8
DALMATIA:
—ISSA: (13) ii BC *SEG* XXXI 599, 2 (s. *Κλεψίας*)
EPIROS:
—ANTIGONEIA: (14) v-vi AD *Iliria* 1977-8, p. 234 pl. V c (mosaic)
—BOUTHROTOS (PRASAIBOI): (15) a. 163 BC *IBouthrot* 30, 43, 46; cf. *SEG* XXXVIII 499, 22, 25
ILLYRIA:
—APOLLONIA: (16) c. 250-50 BC *Bakërr Hoard* p. 63 nos. 39-42 (coin) (Ceka 45) (money.)
—EPIDAMNOS-DYRRHACHION: (17) hell.-imp. *IDyrrh* 313 (f. *Μηνογένης*)
KORINTHIA:
—KORINTH: (18) c. 575-550 BC Amyx Gr 19 (vase) (Arena, *Iscr. Cor.* 89) (*Δōρόθ*[*ε*]*os*); (19) hell. *AE* 1915, p. 130 no. 8, 1; (20) c. 225-200 BC *BCH* 23 (1899) p. 93 no. 3, 15 (f. *Ἀγήσανδρος*)
LEUKAS: (21) ?v BC Polyaen. v 36
S. ITALY (CALABRIA):
—TARAS-TARENTUM: (22) c. 100-60 BC *IG* VII 3197, 27; *SEG* XXXIII 290 A, 22; cf. *BSA* 70 (1975) pp. 121-2; p. 130 (date); cf. Stephanis 807 (I f. *Δωρόθεος* II); (23) ~ *IG* VII 3197, 27; *SEG* XXXIII 290 A, 22; cf. *BSA* 70 (1975) pp. 121-2; p. 130 (date) (Stephanis 807) (II s. *Δωρόθεος* I)
S. ITALY (CAMPANIA):
—DIKAIARCHIA-PUTEOLI: (24) iii/iv AD *Puteoli* 4-5 (1980-1) p. 117 no. 3 (Lat. L. Aur. Dorot(heus)
S. ITALY (LUCANIA):
—VOLCEI*: (25) ii AD *IItal* III (1) 69 (Lat. Q. Poppaedius Dorotheus: freed.)
SICILY:
—SOLOUS: (26) ?ii-i BC *IG* XIV 312
—SYRACUSE?:
——(*Νητ.*): (27) hell. Manganaro, *PdelP* forthcoming no. 4 II, 6 (f. *Ἱστιόδωρος*)

**Δῶρον**

—THERMAI HIMERAIAI: (28) ?ii/i BC *SGDI* 3248 (*Kokalos* 20 (1974) p. 219 no. 1) (s. *Λυσ*—) ?= (29); (29) f. i BC Cic., *In Verr.* II ii 89 (Lat. Dorotheus) ?= (28)

**Δῶρον**
KORINTHIA:
—KORINTH*: (1) i BC/i AD *SEG* XI 214 d

**Δῶρος**
AKARNANIA: (1) m. iii BC *IG* IX (1)² (2) 578 (f. *Δωρόθεος*)
ARKADIA:
—MANTINEIA-ANTIGONEIA: (2) i AD ib. V (2) 341 (*Γ. Ἰούλ. Δ.*)
DALMATIA:
—ISSA: (3) iii BC Brunšmid p. 9 fr. G, 10 + *VAMZ* 1970, p. 37 frr. G and M (s. *Λέων*)
——(Dymanes): (4) iv/iii BC Brunšmid p. 8, 37 (f. —*λῆς*); (5) ~ ib. l. 45 ([Ἀρ]χίδωρος?)
——(Hylleis): (6) iv/iii BC ib. p. 9, 60 (s. *Λέων*)
LEUKAS: (7) iv BC *AM* 27 (1902) p. 369 no. 37
MESSENIA:
—MESSENE: (8) ii-iii AD *SEG* XLI 366 B (*Κλ. Δ. Τρυφωνιανός*)

S. ITALY (CAMPANIA):
—POMPEII: (9) i BC-i AD *NScav* 1908, p. 369 no. 9 (Lat. Dorus)

**Δωροφόρος**
S. ITALY (LUCANIA):
—VOLCEI: (1) imp. *IItal* III (1) 37 (*CIL* X 8111) (Lat. M. Isteius Doroporus)

**Δωρώ**
AITOLIA:
—CHRYSOVITSA (MOD.): (1) vi BC *IG* IX (1)² (1) 93 with Add. + Antonetti, *Les Étoliens* p. 217 (*Δōρό̄, Πορώ?*—Antonetti)
KORINTHIA:
—SIKYON?: (2) ?vi BC *IG* IX (1)² (1) 93; *LSAG*² p. 144 no. 19 (*Δōρό̄*)

**Δωρώι**
KORINTHIA:
—KORINTH: (1) c. 570-550 BC Amyx 92 A. 1 (vase) (Lorber 120) (*Δōρό̄ι*: het.?/fict.?)

**Δώρων**
KORINTHIA:
—KORINTH: (1) c. 570-550 BC Amyx 114. 1 (vase) (*Δόρō̄ν*: her.?)

**Δωσιθέα**
ARGOLIS:
—ARGOS*: (1) 105 BC *JÖAI* 14 (1911) Beibl. p. 146 no. 4, 28 (slave/freed.?)

**Δωσίθεος**
ILLYRIA:
—EPIDAMNOS-DYRRHACHION: (1) imp. *IDyrrh* 369 (f. *Ῥοῦφος*)
KORINTHIA:
—SIKYON: (2) i-ii AD *SEG* XVI 240 (*Δωσίθε[ος]*)

**Δωτάδας**
MESSENIA: (1) 740 BC Moretti, *Olymp.* 10 (*RE* (2))

**Δωτώ**
S. ITALY (CAMPANIA):
—DIKAIARCHIA-PUTEOLI: (1) imp. *CIL* X 2377 (Lat. Doto)

# E

**Ἑάρινος**
KORINTHIA:
—KORINTH: (1) ii-iii AD *Corinth* IV (2) p. 207 nos. 715?, 720-3 (lamps)
S. ITALY (CAMPANIA):
—NEAPOLIS: (2) 113 AD *CIL* VI 221, 11 (Lat. C. Ant. Earinus)
—POMPEII: (3) i BC-i AD ib. IV 1092 (Castrèn 207. 11) (Lat. Cn. Iun. Iarinus); (4) ~ *CIL* IV 1228 (Lat. Iarinus); (5) ~ ib. 2111 (Lat. Iarinus); (6) ~ ib. 2181; 2220; 2251 (Lat. Iarinus); (7) ~ ib. 4250 (Lat. Earinus); (8) ~ ib. 7243 (Lat. Iarinus); (9) ~ ib. 3933-4; 3938-9 (Lat. Iarinus); (10) 70-79 AD ib. 124; 223; 821?; Mouritsen p. 109 (date) (Lat. Iarinus); (11) ~ *CIL* IV 7387; Mouritsen p. 109 (date) (Lat. Earinus)

**Ἕβρος**
EPIROS:
—NIKOPOLIS: (1) imp. *Ep. Chron.* 31 (1994) p. 42 no. 8 (*AD* 45 (1990) Chron. p. 257 no. 5)
SICILY:
—LIPARA: (2) i BC/i AD Hor., *C.* iii 12, 6 (Lat. Hebrus)

**Ἐγκαίριος**
S. ITALY (CAMPANIA):
—CUBULTERIA: (1) iii AD *Iscr. Trebula Caiatia Cubulteria* 101 (*CIL* X 4628) (Lat. Encherius)

**Ἐγκάρπιν**
SICILY:
—KATANE: (1) imp. *IG* XIV 473; *Riv. Arch. Crist.* 18 (1941) p. 201 no. 74 (*Ἐνκ*-)
—SYRACUSE: (2) iii-v AD Strazzulla 146 (Wessel 974); cf. *Riv. Arch. Crist.* 18 (1941) p. 181 no. 45 (*Ἐνκά*-, *Ἐνκαρπί[α]*—Strazzulla)

**Ἐγκολπος**
SICILY:
—PANORMOS: (1) imp. *CIL* X 7320 (Lat. Enco[l]pus)

**Ἐγρετίων**
ARKADIA:
—MANTINEIA-ANTIGONEIA: (1) c. 425-385 BC *IG* V (2) 323. 17 (tessera) (-*ōν*: f. *Πραξίνοος*)

**Ἐγχειρίδιον**
S. ITALY (APULIA):
—VENUSIA*: (1) i AD *Rend. Linc.* 29 (1974) p. 629 no. 38 (*Eph. Ep.* VIII 85) (Lat. Titia Enchiridium: freed.)

**Ἐδασηνός**
MESSENIA:
—MESSENE: (1) 192 AD *PAE* 1969, p. 104, 10 (s. *Σύμφορος*)

**Ἐθελήν**
ILLYRIA:
—EPIDAMNOS-DYRRHACHION: (1) hell. *IDyrrh* 176

**Ἐθέλιππος**
SICILY:
—MENAI: (1) inc. *Riv. Stor. Antica* 5 (1900-1) p. 57 no. 34 (*Ἐθέλιπ[π]ος*: f. *Σμᾶς*)

**Εἰδύμμας**
EPIROS:
—ARKTANES: (1) 370-368 BC Cabanes, *L'Épire* p. 534 no. 1, 7, 25 (*Εἰδύμας*—l. 25)

**Εἴελος**
SICILY:
—ENTELLA: (1) f. iii BC *SEG* XXX 1121, 3 (Dubois, *IGDS* 208); *SEG* XXX 1123, 3 (Dubois, *IGDS* 211); *SEG* XXXV 999, 3 (Dubois, *IGDS* 212) (f. *Ἀρτεμίδωρος*)

**Εἰκάδις**
S. ITALY (CALABRIA):
—BRENTESION-BRUNDISIUM*: (1) i BC Desy, *Timbres amphoriques* 474-5; 689; 832 (amph.) (slave/potter?)

**Εἰκονικός**
S. ITALY (CAMPANIA):
—DIKAIARCHIA-PUTEOLI: (1) imp. *CIL* X 2091 (Lat. D. Apul. Iconicus)

**Εἰκόνιον**
EPIROS: (1) iii BC *IG* II² 8537 (*Ἰκ*-)

**Εἰκονίς**
S. ITALY (CAMPANIA):
—MISENUM*: (1) imp. *CIL* X 3539 (Lat. Iconis: freed.)

**Εἰκών**
S. ITALY (BRUTTIUM):
—AGER TEURANUS: (1) imp. ib. 105 (Lat. Claudia Ico)

**Εἰνάλιος**
ARGOLIS:
—TROIZEN: (1) imp. *IG* IV (1) 797, 1 (*Εἰνάλ[ιος]*: s. *Ἡρακλέων*)

**Εἰραμένης**
SICILY:
—SYRACUSE: (1) c. 262 BC ib. IX (1)² (1) 17 A, 68 (f. *Πυρρ*—)

**Εἰράνα**
ILLYRIA:
—EPIDAMNOS-DYRRHACHION: (1) hell.-imp. *IDyrrh* 307 (*Εἰράν[α]*: m. *Μέλισσα*)
KERKYRA: (2) iv-iii BC *IG* IX (1) 887
MESSENIA:
—MESSENE: (3) ii/iii AD *SEG* XXIII 215, 5 (d. *Νυμφόδοτος*)

**Εἰρανίων**
AITOLIA:
—KALLION/KALLIPOLIS: (1) 175 BC *SGDI* 1987, 5 (*Ἰρ*-: s. *Δάμων*)
ARKADIA:
—KLEITOR: (2) m. iii AD *SEG* XXXV 350 I, 7 (*Αὐρ. Ἰρανίων*: s. *Ἰταλός*)
LAKONIA:
—SPARTA: (3) ii AD *IG* V (1) 159, 42 (Bradford (3)); (4) c. 160 AD *IG* V (1) 71 III, 43; 86, 21 (Bradford (2)) (s. *Κλεάνωρ*); (5) c. 212-220 AD *IG* V (1) 653 a, 7 (*Artemis Orthia* p. 356 no. 142; Bradford (1)) (*Τιβ. Κλ. Ε.*: s. *Ὑγῖνος*)

**Εἰρήνα**
ACHAIA:
—DYME: (1) ii BC SEG XIV 371
AKARNANIA:
—THYRREION: (2) iii BC IG IX (1)² (2) 260
ILLYRIA:
—EPIDAMNOS-DYRRHACHION: (3) hell.-imp. IDyrrh 178
SICILY:
—MELITA: (4) iv-v AD JIWE 1 166 (Διονυσία ἡ καὶ Ἐ.: Jew)
—SYRACUSE: (5) ?iii AD ib. 151 (CIJ 1 651) (Jew); (6) iii-v AD IG XIV 116 (Strazzulla 57; Wessel 871) (Ἰ-); (7) iv-v AD Ferrua, NG 339 a (Ἰ-)

**Εἰρηναῖος**
ARGOLIS:
—EPIDAUROS: (1) imp. IG IV (1)² 458 (Εἰρη[ναῖ]ος: I f. Εἰρηναῖος II); (2) ~ ib. (Ε[ἰρηναῖ]ος: II s. Εἰρηναῖος I)
KORINTHIA:
—KORINTH*: (3) byz. Corinth VIII (1) 157 (TMByz 9 (1985) pp. 283-4 no. 21) (Ἰ-: s. Διογενιανός)
MESSENIA:
—PROTE*: (4) i/ii AD IG V (1) 1546 (Sandberg, Euploia 9) (f. Ἱρα—)
S. ITALY (APULIA):
—AZETIUM: (5) c. 100 BC ID 1713, 9 (s. Ζωῖλος)
S. ITALY (CALABRIA):
—LUPIAE: (6) f. ii AD CIL IX 20 (Susini, Fonti Salento p. 142 no. 90) (Lat. C. Iulius Irenaeus)
S. ITALY (CAMPANIA):
—DIKAIARCHIA-PUTEOLI: (7) imp. CIL X 3076 (Lat. L. Istaverus Ireneus: s. Valeria Victoria, ?f. Istaverus Victorinus, Istavera Victorina); (8) ?ii AD ib. 2516 (Lat. Irenaeus: f. Ἑρμιόνη)
—HERCULANEUM: (9) c. 70 AD PdelP 1 (1946) p. 383 no. 7, 2 (Lat. M. Ulpius Irenaeus)
—SALERNUM: (10) 98-117 AD IItal I (1) 92 (CIL X 653) (Lat. T. Claudius Irenaeus)
SICILY:
—KATANE: (11) iii-v AD Wessel 855 (JIWE 1 148; SEG XVII 439); cf. Ferrua, NG 412 (Εἰρήνες); (12) ~ Wessel 866; cf. Ferrua, NG 413 (Εἰρήνμιος—lap.)
—MOTYKA (NR.): (13) iii-v AD IG XIV 248 (Ἱρη[ν]αῖο[ς])
—SYRACUSE: (14) iii-v AD Riv. Arch. Crist. 36 (1960) p. 29 no. 26; cf. Ferrua, NG 107 (Εἰρήνες); (15) ~ NScav 1893, p. 292 no. 58 + Ferrua, NG 24 (Εἰρηνέ(ο)ς); (16) ~ NScav 1947, p. 190 no. 5 + Ferrua, NG 346 (Lat. Hirineus); (17) ~ ib. 215

**Εἰρήνη**
ARGOLIS:
—EPIDAUROS: (1) i BC-i AD? Peek, NIEpid 56 a (Εἰρήνη: d. Σώπολις)
KORINTHIA:
—KORINTH: (2) inc. IG II² 9066
LAKONIA:
—SPARTA: (3) i-ii AD ib. V (1) 774 (Bradford (1)); (4) ii-iii AD IG V (1) 230 (Bradford (2))
S. ITALY (BRUTTIUM):
—TRAPEIA: (5) byz. CIL X 8076 (ICI V 14) (Lat. Hireni); (6) ~ CIL X 8077 (ICI V 20) (Lat. Hireni)
S. ITALY (CALABRIA):
—BRENTESION-BRUNDISIUM: (7) imp. Epigraphica 25 (1963) p. 43 no. 22 (Lat. Irene); (8) ~ ib. p. 68 no. 65 (Lat. Maecia Irene)
—TARAS-TARENTUM: (9) i BC ID 2619 II, 10 (d. Σίμαλος)
S. ITALY (CAMPANIA):
—DIKAIARCHIA-PUTEOLI: (10) imp. CIL X 2422 a (Lat. Irena: m. Firmus); (11) ?i-ii AD ib. 1872 (Lat. Iulia Irene: m. Antonia

Iucunda); (12) ~ ib. 2567 (Lat. Iulia Irene); (13) ?ii AD ib. 2516 (Lat. Flavia Irene)
—NEAPOLIS: (14) v AD JIWE 1 32 (Lat. Erena: Jew)
—PITHEKOUSSAI-AENARIA: (15) imp. CIL X 6803 (Lat. Albia Irene: m. Γλῦπτος, Cominia Marcellina)
—POMPEII: (16) i BC-i AD ib. IV 10079 (Lat. Irene)
SICILY:
—SYRACUSE: (17) iii-v AD IG XIV 103 bis (Strazzulla 52; Wessel 1126); (18) ~ IG XIV 177 (Strazzulla 115; Agnello 12; Wessel 1108) (Ἰρήνα: m. Κρισκωνία); (19) ~ Strazzulla 195; (20) ~ ib. 230 (Barreca 121) (Εἰρήν[η]); (21) ~ Strazzulla 332 (Wessel 1268); cf. Ferrua, NG 115 (Εἰρήνες (gen.), Εἰρηνέ(ο)ς—Ferrua); (22) 383 AD JIWE 1 145 (CIJ 1 650) (Lat. Lasie Erine: Jew)
—TAUROMENION: (23) iii-v AD IG XIV 102 (Strazzulla 51; Wessel 844); cf. Ferrua, NG 475 (locn.)
—ZANKLE-MESSANA: (24) ii-iii AD Epigraphica 3 (1941) p. 256 no. 9; cf. p. 255 no. 7 (Lat. Cartilia Irene: m. Ti. Cl. Claudianus)

**Εἰρηνικός**
S. ITALY (CAMPANIA):
—KYME: (1) 251 AD CIL X 3699 II, 15 (Lat. C. Cartilius Irenicus)

**Εἰρηνοῦς**
SICILY:
—SYRACUSE: (1) ?iii-iv AD NScav 1951, p. 297 (Lat. Lollia Irenus)

**Εἰρίσκος**
S. ITALY (LUCANIA):
—METAPONTION: (1) iv BC Iamb., VP 267 (FVS 1 p. 446)

**Εἰρώνεια**
S. ITALY (CAMPANIA):
—DIKAIARCHIA-PUTEOLI: (1) imp. CIL X 2694 (Lat. Magnia Ironia)

**Ἑκάς**
LAKONIA:
—SPARTA: (1) her. Paus. iv 16. 1 (Poralla² 254) (dub.); (2) m. vii BC Paus. iv 16. 1; 21. 7, 12 (Poralla² 255) (mantis)

**Ἑκαταῖος**
SICILY:
—HIMERA: (1) m. v BC Himera 2 p. 693 no. 203 (sherd) (Dubois, IGDS 14 a; Arena, Iscr. Sic. III 49) (ℎεκαταῖος)

**Ἑκατάων?**
ARKADIA:
—KAPHYAI: (1) c. 230-200 BC BCH 45 (1921) p. 14 II, 120 (Ἑκατάων?—Oulhen: s. Ἱεραῖος)

**Ἑκατόδωρος**
ARGOLIS:
—ARGOS: (1) ?114 BC IG IV (1) 558, 1, 30, 34, [40]; cf. Stephanis 1028 (f. Ζήνων)

**Ἑκάτων**
ARKADIA:
—TEGEA: (1) m. iv BC IG V (2) 6, 111 (Ἑκ[ά]τω[ν]?)

**Ἔκδαμος**
ARKADIA:
—MEGALOPOLIS: (1) m. iii BC RE (-); cf. Walbank 2 pp. 223-4 (-δη-, Ἔκδηλος—Plu. Arat. and Paus.)

**Ἔκδηλος**
AIGINA: (1) m. v BC IG IV (1) 48 (Ἐγδε̄-)
KORINTHIA:
—SIKYON?: (2) m. iii BC Plu., Arat. 7 (Skalet 105)

**Ἔκδικος**
LAKONIA:
—SPARTA: (1) 391 BC X., HG iv 8. 20 ff.; D.S. xiv 97. 3 (Poralla² 256) (Εὐδόκιμος—D.S.)

**Ἐκδόχη**
S. ITALY (CAMPANIA):
—POMPEII: (1) m. i AD Impegno per Pompeii 17b OS no. 4 (Castrèn 318. 16) (Lat. Popidia Ecdoche)

**Ἐκεθαῖος**
ARGOLIS:
—ARGOS: (1) c. 550-525 BC SEG XXVI 423 (Lazzarini 275 b) (Ἐκε[θα]ῖος (n. pr.?): ?f. Ἀρίστεια)

**Ἐκεσθένης**
AIGINA: (1) c. 470 BC SEG III 310 (bronze) (Guarducci, Ep. Gr. 1 pp. 198-9 no. 3; Lazzarini 56); LSAG² p. 113 no. 16 (date) (-νε̄ς: s. Προκλῆς)
ARGOLIS:
—TROIZEN*: (2) iv BC IG IV (1) 823, 9, 22, 26, 36-8, etc.

**Ἐκέφυλος**
ACHAIA:
—PELLENE: (1) 340 BC FD III (1) 398, 2 (s. Χαρμίδας)
LAKONIA:
—SPARTA: (2) c. 450-434 BC IG V (1) 1230, 2; LSAG² p. 201 no. 54 (date) (Poralla² 257)

**Ἐκηβόλος**
S. ITALY (BRUTTIUM):
—RHEGION: (1) f. i AD Suppl. It. 5 p. 68 no. 23 (Lat. Hecebolus)

**Ἐκκελώ**
S. ITALY (LUCANIA):
—LEUKANOI: (1) iv BC Iamb., VP 267 (FVS 1 p. 448)

**Ἔκκριτος**
LAKONIA:
—SPARTA: (1) 413 BC Th. vii 19. 3 (Poralla² 258)

**Ἐκλέκτη**
S. ITALY (CAMPANIA):
—SALERNUM: (1) imp. IItal I (1) 55 (Lat. Eclecte)

**Ἐκλεκτιανός**
S. ITALY (CAMPANIA):
—DIKAIARCHIA-PUTEOLI: (1) ?ii AD CIL X 1583-5 (Lat. T. Flavius Eclectianus)

**Ἔκλεκτος**
S. ITALY (CAMPANIA):
—DIKAIARCHIA-PUTEOLI*: (1) imp. ib. 2618 (Lat. M. Iunius Eglectus: freed.)

**Ἐκλόγη**
ILLYRIA:
—APOLLONIA: (1) imp. IApoll 35 (Ἐγ-)
KEPHALLENIA:
—SAME: (2) imp.? IG IX (1) 621
S. ITALY (APULIA):
—VENUSIA*: (3) imp. CIL IX 509 + NScav 1939, p. 149 no. 2 (Lat. Egnatia Egloge: freed.)
S. ITALY (CAMPANIA):
—MISENUM*: (4) imp. CIL X 3528 (Lat. Antonia Egloge: freed.)
—POMPEII: (5) i BC-i AD ib. IV 2148 (Lat. Egloge); (6) ~ ib. 9934 a (Castrèn 409. 2) (Lat. [T]iburtia Egloge); (7) ~ CIL X 1067 (Lat. Caesia Egloge)
S. ITALY (LUCANIA):
—COSILINUM: (8) imp. IItal III (1) 211 (CIL X 294) (Lat. Ansia Egloge)

**Ἕκοτις**
SICILY:
—SELINOUS: (**1**) f. v BC Dubois, *IGDS* 38, 13, 17 (Arena, *Iscr. Sic.* I 63) (-ϙο-: s. Μάγων)

**Ἐκπρέπης**
LAKONIA:
—SPARTA: (**1**) s. v BC Plu., *Agis* 10; *Mor.* 220 C (Poralla² 259) (Ἐμπρέπης—220 C)

**Ἔκτικος**
ARKADIA:
—KLEITOR: (**1**) i-ii AD *IG* v (2) 375 (Fraser-Rönne, *BWGT* p. 202 no. 1)
S. ITALY (CAMPANIA):
—HERCULANEUM: (**2**) i BC-i AD *Cron. Erc.* 7 (1977) pp. 115-16 B (Lat. N. Vibius Hecticus—Solin)
—POMPEII: (**3**) i BC-i AD *CIL* IV 4485; 10543 (Lat. Hecticus)

**Ἑκτορίδας**
ARGOLIS:
—EPIDAUROS*: (**1**) iv BC *IG* IV (1)² 102, 89, 104, 111; 695 (sculptor)

**Ἕκτωρ**
EPIROS: (**1**) ii BC Cabanes, *L'Épire* p. 590 no. 76, 14 (*SEG* XXVI 704)
—OMPHALES: (**2**) ?c. 370-344 BC Cabanes, *L'Épire* p. 536 no. 2, 9
—OMPHALES CHIMOLIOI: (**3**) c. 330-310 BC ib. p. 578 no. 51, 10 (s. Ἄνδρ—)

**Ἐκφάνης**
LAKONIA:
—SPARTA: (**1**) iv/iii BC Plu., *Agis* 6 (Bradford (-)) (f. Μανδροκλείδας)

**Ἐκφαντίδας**
SICILY:
—KAMARINA: (**1**) f. v BC Cordano, *Tessere Pubbliche* 84 ([Ἐκ]φαντίδας: f. Ἄρατος)

**Ἔκφαντος**
ACHAIA:
—PELLENE: (**1**) ?iii BC *Klio* 15 (1918) p. 58 no. 81 (Ἐχ-: f. Εὔγνωτος)
ILLYRIA:
—APOLLONIA: (**2**) c. 250-50 BC Maier 117; Münsterberg p. 35; Nachtr. p. 13; *NZ* 20 (1927) p. 54 (coin) (Ceka 46-8) (money.); (**3**) i BC Maier 146; 160 (coin) (Ἐκφαντο[ς]: s. Ἀρισ—: money.)
KORINTHIA:
—KORINTH: (**4**) arch. Plin., *NH* XXXV 16 (Lat. Ecphantus: painter); (**5**) vii BC ib. (Lat. Ecphantus)
S. ITALY (BRUTTIUM):
—KROTON: (**6**) iv BC Iamb., *VP* 267 (*FVS* I p. 446)
S. ITALY (CALABRIA):
—TARAS-TARENTUM: (**7**) c. 315-280 BC *FD* III (1) 135 (Ἐκχ-: f. Ἵππις)
SICILY:
—SYRACUSE: (**8**) ?415 BC Polyaen. i 39. 2; (**9**) ?iv BC *RE* (3) (or S. Italy (Bruttium) Kroton)

**Ἐλάϊνος**
S. ITALY (CAMPANIA):
—POMPEII: (**1**) i BC-i AD *CIL* IV 597 (Lat. Elainus)

**Ἔλαιος**
S. ITALY (CAMPANIA):
—NEAPOLIS: (**1**) hell.-imp. *SEG* XXXVII 786 (*INap* 123); cf. Leiwo p. 117 no. 100 (Ἐλ(α)ῖος: f. Ἡρακλείδης)

**Ἔλανδρος**
S. ITALY (CALABRIA):
—TARAS-TARENTUM: (**1**) iv BC Iamb., *VP* 267 (*FVS* I p. 446)

**Ἐλάσιππος**
AIGINA?: (**1**) ?v BC *RE* (3) (Lat. Elasippus: painter)

**Ἐλάτη**
S. ITALY (CAMPANIA):
—DIKAIARCHIA-PUTEOLI: (**1**) imp. *CIL* X 2209 (Lat. Calpurnia Elate)
SICILY:
—KATANE: (**2**) imp. *IG* XIV 504 (Σοσία Ἐ.)

**Ἔλατος**
LAKONIA:
—SPARTA: (**1**) m. viii BC Plu., *Lyc.* 7 (Poralla² 260)

**Ἐλαφεύς**
SICILY:
—HALAISA: (**1**) ii BC *IGSI* 2 A II 46, 51 (Dubois, *IGDS* 196)

**Ἐλάφινα**
TRIPHYLIA:
—PTELEA: (**1**) ii BC *SEG* XVI 282, 1

**Ἐλάφιον**
EPIROS: (**1**) ?iii/ii BC *IG* VII 468 (*IOrop* 586) (d. Πατροκλῆς)
S. ITALY (CAMPANIA):
—DIKAIARCHIA-PUTEOLI*: (**2**) imp. *CIL* X 2912 (Lat. Ravia Elapio: freed.)

**Ἐλαφίς**
ITHAKE: (**1**) i BC-i AD? *IG* IX (1) 677; cf. Fraser-Rönne, *BWGT* p. 161

**Ἐλαφίτη**
S. ITALY (CAMPANIA):
—KYME: (**1**) c. 525 BC Dubois, *IGDGG* I 21 e (vase) (Arena, *Iscr. Sic.* III 17); *LSAG²* p. 453 no. D (date) (-τε, ἀλ(λ)ε Φί(λ)τες—Arena)

**Ἐλεγχία**
S. ITALY (CAMPANIA):
—POMPEII: (**1**) i BC-i AD *CIL* IV 8739 (Lat. Elencia)

**Ἔλεγχος**
LAKONIA:
—SPARTA: (**1**) i-ii AD *IG* V (1) 783 (Bradford s.v. Ἔλενχος (-)) (-λενχ-)

**Ἐλένα**
ARGOLIS:
—HERMIONE: (**1**) ii-i BC *IG* IV (1) 732 I, 5 (d. Θεόδωρος)
S. ITALY (CAMPANIA):
—ATELLA*: (**2**) imp. *CIL* X 3745 (Lat. Curredia Helena: freed.)

**Ἑλένη**
ACHAIA:
—DYME: (**1**) i BC-i AD ib. III 7254 (Lat. Fulvinia Helene)
KORINTHIA:
—KORINTH: (**2**) byz. *Corinth* VIII (3) 564, 4; cf. *TMByz* 9 (1985) p. 366 no. 68
S. ITALY (APULIA):
—LARINUM: (**3**) f. i AD *Forma Italiae* 36 p. 131 no. 2 (Lat. Helena)
S. ITALY (CAMPANIA): (**4**) imp. *CIL* X 8059. 217 (seal) (Lat. Iulia Helene)
—DIKAIARCHIA-PUTEOLI: (**5**) ?ii AD ib. 2013 (Lat. Aelia Elena)
—DIKAIARCHIA-PUTEOLI*: (**6**) f. i AD *AJA* 2 (1898) p. 386 no. 32; cf. *Puteoli* 9-10 (1985-6) p. 43 no. 1 (Lat. Plotia Helena: freed.)
—MISENUM*: (**7**) imp. *CIL* X 3500 (Lat. Varenia Helena)
—POMPEII: (**8**) i BC-i AD ib. IV 1225 (Lat. Helena); (**9**) ~ ib. 1352 b (Lat. Helena); (**10**) ~ ib. 4637 (Castrèn 129. 23) (Lat. Corn.

Hele[na]); (**11**) m. i AD *CIL* IV 9252; cf. *GRBS* 26 (1985) p. 181 no. 128 (Κλ. Ἑλένα)
—SALERNUM: (**12**) imp. *IItal* I (1) 34 (*CIL* X 559) (Lat. Asinia Helene: m. Asinia Venusta); (**13**) ~ *IItal* I (1) 72 (Lat. Helene)
S. ITALY (LUCANIA):
—TEGIANUM: (**14**) imp. ib. III (1) 260 (*CIL* X 316) (Lat. Helena)
SICILY:
—SYRACUSE: (**15**) ?iii-v AD *IG* XIV 104 (Strazzulla 53; Wessel 1102) ([Ἑ]λένη)

**Ἑλενιανός**
ARKADIA:
—TEGEA: (**1**) ii AD *IG* v (2) 55, 47 (f. Σώτηρος)

**Ἑλενίς**
S. ITALY (CAMPANIA):
—DIKAIARCHIA-PUTEOLI: (**1**) ?ii-iii AD *CIL* X 2152 (Lat. Aurelia Helenis)

**Ἑλενίων**
S. ITALY (CAMPANIA):
—NEAPOLIS: (**1**) imp. *IG* XIV 813 (*INap* 175); cf. Leiwo p. 107 no. 72 (f. Τύχη)

**Ἕλενος**
ARKADIA:
—KLEITOR: (**1**) a. 212 AD *IG* v (2) 369, 6 (Κλ. Ἑ.)
—TEGEA: (**2**) ii AD ib. 55, 30 (s. Μιλτιάδης); (**3**) 165 AD ib. 50, 47 (f. Ζώπυρος)
EPIROS:
—MOLOSSOI: (**4**) f. iii BC Plu., *Pyrr.* 9. 2; 33. 1; 34. 8; cf. *SEG* XXXVII 513 (s. Πύρρος, Βίρκεννα)
KERKYRA: (**5**) imp. *IG* IX (1) 855 (loomweight) (Ἕλενο(ς)?—ed., Ἑλεν(ώ)?)
LAKONIA:
—SPARTA: (**6**) c. 90-100 AD *SEG* XI 512, 4 (Bradford (1)) (s. Διοκλῆς); (**7**) c. 105-110 AD *SEG* XI 569, 4 (Bradford (5)) (I f. Ἕλενος II); (**8**) ~ *SEG* XI 569, 4 (Bradford (2)) ([Ἕ]λενος: II s. Ἕλενος I); (**9**) c. 140-160 AD *IG* v (1) 68, 18; *SEG* XI 587, 2 (Bradford (4)) (s. Σωτηρίδας); (**10**) ~ *IG* v (1) 68, 20 (Bradford (7)) (Ἕ[λενος]?: f. Ὀνάσιμος); (**11**) c. 160-170 AD *IG* v (1) 109, 20 (Bradford (4)); (**12**) c. 217-230 AD *SEG* XI 616 a, 2 (Bradford (6)) (I f. Ἕλενος II); (**13**) ~ *SEG* XI 616 a, 2, 4 (Bradford (3)) (M. Αὐρ. Ἑ.: II s. Ἕλενος I)
S. ITALY (APULIA):
—TEANUM APULUM: (**14**) i AD *Teanum Apulum* p. 66 no. 12 (Lat. Helenus)
—VENUSIA: (**15**) i AD *Rend. Linc.* 29 (1974) p. 619 no. 20 (Lat. Helenus)
S. ITALY (CALABRIA):
—BRENTESION-BRUNDISIUM*: (**16**) imp. *NScav* 1900, p. 153 no. 2 (Lat. L. Boionius Helenus: freed.)
S. ITALY (CAMPANIA):
—POMPEII: (**17**) i BC-i AD *CIL* IV 4206 (Lat. Helenus); (**18**) 37 BC ib. 2437 (Castrèn 205. 13) (Lat. C. Iul. Helenus); (**19**) f. i AD *CIL* X 1027-8 (Castrèn 204. 12); Kockel p. 99 (date) (Lat. N. Istacidius Helenus)

**Ἐλευθέρα**
SICILY:
—LIPARA: (**1**) imp. *NScav* 1947, p. 218 no. 6 (*Epigraphica* 11 (1949) p. 55 no. 4) (n. pr.?)
—SYRACUSE: (**2**) iii-v AD Strazzulla 177 (Wessel 879)

**Ἐλευθερᾶς**
SICILY:
—SYRACUSE: (**1**) iii-v AD Strazzulla 363 (Wessel 225); cf. Ferrua, *NG* 133 (Ἐλευθέρας (gen.)—Ferrua)

**Ἐλευθερία**
S. ITALY (CALABRIA):
—TARAS-TARENTUM: (1) imp. *NScav* 1894, p.
68 no. 47 (Lat. Acerronia Eleutheria)

**Ἐλευθέριν**
ILLYRIA:
—EPIDAMNOS-DYRRHACHION: (1) hell.-imp.
*IDyrrh* 180 (d. Φίλων)

**Ἐλευθερίνη**
S. ITALY (CAMPANIA):
—DIKAIARCHIA-PUTEOLI*: (1) imp. *CIL* x
2245 (Lat. Caucia Eleutherine: freed.?)

**Ἐλευθέριος**
AKARNANIA:
—ALYZIA: (1) byz. *IG* IX (1)² (2) 446 a
([Ἐλ]ε[υ]θέριος)
KORINTHIA:
—SIKYON: (2) c. 80-70 BC ib. IX (2) 534, 25;
Kramolisch p. 116 n. 74 (date) (Skalet 106)
(f. —ης)

**Ἐλευθερίς**
ARGOLIS:
—HERMIONE: (1) iii AD *IG* IV (1) 720, 6 (Αὐρ.
[Ἐλευ]θερίς)
KERKYRA: (2) ii-iii AD ib. IX (1) 949 (Νουμερία
Ἐ.)
S. ITALY (CAMPANIA):
—POMPEII*: (3) i BC-i AD *Atti Acc. Pontan.*
39 (1990) p. 289 no. 64 (Lat. Ancarsulena
Eleutheris: freed.)
—SURRENTUM: (4) imp. *CIL* x 717 a (Lat.
Eleutheris: m. Ἀτίμητος)

**Ἐλευθεριώ**
SICILY:
—KATANE: (1) imp. ib. 7082 (Lat. Petillia
Eleutherio)

**Ἐλευθερίων**
SICILY:
—SYRACUSE: (1) iii-v AD *SEG* XVIII 401

**Ἐλεύθερος**
ARKADIA:
—TEGEA: (1) ii AD *IG* V (2) 55, 68 (f. Λέων)
S. ITALY (CAMPANIA):
—MISENUM: (2) imp. De Franciscis, *Sacello
Augustali* p. 21 (Lat. L. Avidius Eleuther(us))
SICILY:
—KENTORIPA: (3) i BC-i AD? *SEG* IV 61
(Ἐλε(ύ)θ[ε]ρος (n. pr.?))
—SYRACUSE: (4) iii-v AD *Riv. Arch. Crist.* 18
(1941) p. 169 no. 30

**Ἐλευσῖνος**
S. ITALY (CAMPANIA):
—NEAPOLIS: (1) imp. *CIL* x 1523 (Lat.
Heleusinus)

**Ἐλέφας**
ARGOLIS:
—EPIDAUROS*: (1) c. 370 BC *IG* IV (1)² 102,
104
LAKONIA:
—SPARTA: (2) vi/v BC ib. V (1) 699 (Poralla²
261)

**Ἑλικάων**
S. ITALY (BRUTTIUM):
—RHEGION: (1) vii-vi BC *RE* (4)

**Ἑλίκη**
S. ITALY (CALABRIA):
—LUPIAE: (1) ii AD *NScav* 1957, p. 193 (Susini,
*Fonti Salento* p. 105 no. 93) (Lat. Vipstania
Helice: m. Sex. Silettius Maximus)
S. ITALY (LUCANIA):
—VOLCEI: (2) imp. *IItal* III (1) 32 (*CIL* x 420)
(Lat. Bruttia Helice)

**Ἑλικίς**
KYNOURIA:
—THYREATIS*: (1) vi/v BC *SEG* XXXV 302
(bronze); cf. XXXIX 368 and *SEG* XLII 290
(or Arkadia Paos: hε-: ?d. Πάρταρος)

**Ἑλικών**
ARGOLIS:
—EPIDAUROS: (1) ii/i BC *IG* IV (1)² 248 (f. Ἔπ-
αινος); (2) ii-iii AD ib. 485 (I f. Ἑλικών II); (3)
~ ib. (II s. Ἑλικών I); (4) iii AD ib. 693 (Αὐρ.
Ἐ.); (5) 307 AD ib. 432; 435
S. ITALY (CAMPANIA):
—DIKAIARCHIA-PUTEOLI?: (6) c. 70-200 AD
*CIL* x 2192 (D'Isanto 68. 2) (Lat. A. Caesel-
lius Helico)
—DIKAIARCHIA-PUTEOLI*: (7) imp. *CIL* x
1748 (Lat. Ti. Iulius Helico: s. Λάλος: imp.
freed.)

**Ἕλιξ**
S. ITALY (CAMPANIA):
—DIKAIARCHIA-PUTEOLI: (1) imp. ib. 2497
(Lat. Helix)
—HERCULANEUM*: (2) i BC-i AD ib. 1403 g III,
27 (Lat. C. Epidius Helix: freed.)

**Ἑλιξώ**
MESSENIA: (1) iii AD *IG* V (1) 1376 (Αὐρ. Ἐ.)

**Ἑλίχρυσος**
ILLYRIA:
—APOLLONIA: (1) ii-iii AD *IApoll* 71

**Ἑλλάδιος**
KERKYRA:
—KASSIOPA: (1) imp. *AD* 26 (1971) Chron. p.
348 (vase)

**Ἕλλαν**
ARKADIA:
—TEGEA: (1) ?253 BC Nachtergael, *Les Galates*
10, 63; cf. Stephanis 2544 (f. Φιλόξενος)

**Ἑλλανίας**
AITOLIA:
—APERANTOI: (1) iii/ii BC *SBBerlAk* 1936, p.
388 no. 2, 9 (*L'Illyrie mérid.* 1 p. 110 fig. 7)

**Ἑλλάνικος**
AITOLIA:
—KALLION/KALLIPOLIS: (1) m. i BC *IG* IX (1)²
(3) 639. 8, 5; *SBBerlAk* 1936, p. 371 a, 2
(*SEG* XLI 528 A) (s. Ἀντισθένης)
—TRICHONION: (2) 217 BC Nachtergael, *Les
Galates* 65, 1 (f. Ξεννίας)
AKARNANIA:
—ANAKTORION: (3) 216 BC *IG* IX (1)² (2) 583,
66 (Ἑ[λ]λάν(ι)κος)
ARGOLIS:
—ARGOS: (4) s. iv BC ib. II² 3078, 5; *Hesp.* 3
(1934) p. 113 no. 178, [3] (Stephanis 832);
(5) ~ *SEG* I 355, 1, 4, 18 (s. Πυθόδωρος)
—EPIDAUROS*: (6) c. 370-365 BC Peek, *IAEpid*
52 B, 60 (Ἑλ(λ)άνικος)
ELIS: (7) 272 BC Plu., *Mor.* 251 F; 252 D, F;
253 A; Paus. v 5. 1; (8) f. i BC *SEG* XVII
199, 2 (f. Θεότιμος ὁ καὶ Σάμιππος); (9) 72 BC
Moretti, *Olymp.* 695-6
LAKONIA:
—TAINARON-KAINEPOLIS: (10) c. 212-225 AD
*IG* V (1) 530, 2; 601, 4; 1240, 13; *BSA*
79 (1984) pp. 265-7 (ident., date); p. 284
(stemma) (Bradford (1); (2)) (f. M. Αὐρ. Παγ-
κρατίδας, Αὐρ. Ἀριστοτέλης)
SICILY:
—SYRACUSE: (11) 356 BC Plu., *Dio* 42
TRIPHYLIA:
—LEPREON: (12) 424 BC Moretti, *Olymp.* 331;
*RE* (1); cf. *IvOl* 155 (Lazzarini 867) (s. Ἀλ-
καίνετος)

**Ἑλλανοκράτης**
ARGOLIS:
—EPIDAUROS: (1) ii AD *IG* IV (1)² 519 (s. Ἡρα-
κλείδης)

**Ἕλλη**
S. ITALY (CAMPANIA):
—POMPEII: (1) m. i AD *Impegno per Pompeii* 19a
OS (Lat. Helle)

**Ἕλλην**
KERKYRA: (1) imp. *IG* IX (1) 956
S. ITALY (CAMPANIA):
—POMPEII: (2) i BC-i AD *CIL* x 8147 (Lat. Hel-
len)

**Ἑλληνοκράτης**
ELIS: (1) 233 AD *IvOl* 116, 6, 9-10 (M. Αὐρ. Ἐ.:
f. Γενέθλιος: Φ.)

**Ἑλλησποντιανός**
S. ITALY (CALABRIA):
—BRENTESION-BRUNDISIUM: (1) ?i-ii AD
*NScav* 1897, p. 326 no. 1 (Lat. Ti. Claudius
Hellespontianus)

**Ἑλλοπίδας**
SICILY:
—SYRACUSE?: (1) 396 BC Ael., *VH* iv 8 (-δης)

**Ἑλλότιος**
ARGOLIS:
—TROIZEN*: (1) iv BC *IG* IV (1) 823, 34

**Ἐλξίππα**
MESSENIA:
—MESSENE: (1) ii BC *Ergon* 1995, p. 29

**Ἕλος**
SICILY:
—COMISO (MOD.): (1) f. v BC *CEG* I 147
(Dubois, *IGDS* 127; Arena, *Iscr. Sic.* II 150;
Cordano, 'Camarina VII' 1); cf. *SEG* XLII
847 (κΑ[π]ελος—Guarducci, κα[ὶ] Ἕλος—*CEG*
and Dubois, κΑ[τ]ελος—Arena)

**Ἐλπίας**
ARGOLIS:
—METHANA-ARSINOE: (1) i BC *IG* IV (1) 853, 5
(Ἐλπ[ίας]: s. Πραξιδάμας)

**Ἐλπιδηφόρος**
ARGOLIS:
—ARGOS: (1) byz. *SEG* XXVI 436, 2; cf. *TMByz*
9 (1985) p. 370 no. 117 (Ἐλπιδηφό(ρος))
LAKONIA:
—SPARTA: (2) c. 212-240 AD *IG* V (1) 501, 2
(Bradford (-)) (Αὐρ. Ἐ.)
MESSENIA:
—KORONE: (3) 246 AD *IG* V (1) 1398, 62 (Αὐρ.
Ἐλπιδοφόρος)
S. ITALY (CAMPANIA):
—DIKAIARCHIA-PUTEOLI: (4) imp. *CIL* x 1790
(Lat. Q. Aemilius Helpidephorus); (5) ~ ib.
2739 (Lat. Mindius Elpidephorus)
SICILY:
—PACHINO (MOD.): (6) ii-iii AD *Arch. Class.* 17
(1965) p. 199, 6 (f. Τρυφέρα)

**Ἐλπιδία**
KERKYRA: (1) imp. *IG* IX (1) 951
S. ITALY (CAMPANIA):
—MISENUM*: (2) imp. *CIL* x 3445 (Lat. Anto-
nia Elpidia)

**Ἐλπιδιανός**
KORINTHIA:
—KORINTH: (1) byz. *Corinth* VIII (3) 664; cf.
*TMByz* 9 (1985) p. 359 no. 1
S. ITALY (BRUTTIUM):
—SKYLLETION?: (2) ?i AD *Atti Centro Studi Do-
cumentazione* 2 (1969-70) p. 120 no. 2 (Lat.
Elpidianus: s. Εὐέλπιστος)

**Ἐλπίδιος**

S. Italy (Campania):
—surrentum: (3) imp. *CIL* x 726 (Lat. Q. Cominius Elpidianus)
Sicily:
—syracuse: (4) iii-v ad *ASSiracusano* 1974, p. 11

**Ἐλπίδιος**

Argolis:
—argos: (1) byz. *SEG* xxvi 435; cf. *TMByz* 9 (1985) p. 370 no. 118
S. Italy (Campania):
—baiai: (2) ?ii-iii ad *IG* xiv 879 (ναύκληρος)
S. Italy (Lucania):
—poseidonia-paestum: (3) 344 ad *CIL* x 478 (Mello–Voza 108) (Lat. Helpidius)

**Ἐλπίδις**

Korinthia:
—korinth: (1) ii ad *Corinth* iv (2) p. 193 no. 598 (lamp)

**Ἐλπιδῦς**

Arkadia:
—mantineia-antigoneia: (1) iii ad *IG* v (2) 295 (Αὐρ. Ἐ.: Jew)

**Ἐλπίνας**

Aitolia:
—prosch(e)ion: (1) 163 bc ib. ix (1)² (1) 101, 3

**Ἐλπινίκη**

Illyria:
—lychnidos: (1) ii-iii ad *Sp.* 98 (1941-8) p. 231 no. 461 (-πεινεί-)

**Ἐλπίνικος**

Argolis:
—argos: (1) f. i bc Unp. (Ch. Kritzas) ([Ἐ]λπίνικος: f. Καλλίστρατος)
Lakonia:
—sparta: (2) c. 220 ad *IG* v (1) 544, 10 (*Artemis Orthia* pp. 358-9 no. 145; Bradford (-)) (f. Μ. Αὐρ. Φιλοκράτης)

**Ἐλπίς**

Achaia:
—patrai: (1) imp. *CIL* iii 499 (Lat. Paconia [Hel]pis)
Argolis:
—argos: (2) ii-iii ad *BCH* 66-7 (1942-3) p. 326
Arkadia:
—kleitor: (3) i-ii ad *IG* v (2) 385
—mantineia-antigoneia*: (4) ii ad ib. 277 (d. Εὐοδία: slave/freed.)
Epiros:
—nikopolis: (5) imp. *IBouthrot* 179 (Ugolini, *Alb. Ant.* 3 p. 123)
Illyria:
—apollonia: (6) imp. *IApoll* 72 (-πείς); (7) ~ ib. 339 (Ἐλπί (voc.))
—epidamnos-dyrrhachion: (8) i bc-i ad *AEp* 1978, no. 755 (Lat. Grania Helpis: m. Grania Secunda)
Kerkyra: (9) imp. *AD* 25 (1970) Chron. p. 322 with Pl. 276 a
Lakonia:
—karyai: (10) imp. *SEG* xi 891
—sparta: (11) ii-iii ad *IG* v (1) 802 a (Bradford (2)); (12) c. 250-260 ad *IG* v (1) 593, 10; *BSA* 80 (1985) pp. 225; 243-4 (ident., stemma) (Bradford (1)) (Κλ. Ἐ. ἡ καὶ Καλλιστονίκη: ?d. Τιβ. Κλ. Πρατόλαος ὁ καὶ Δαμοκρατίδας, d. Ἰουλ. Ἐτεαρχίς)
Messenia:
—abia: (13) ii ad *GVI* 1555 (m. Θεοφάνης, Ἰλαρος)
S. Italy (Apulia):
—canusium: (14) imp. *Epig. Rom. di Canosa* 130 (Lat. Helpis)

—canusium*: (15) imp. ib. 110 (Lat. Herennia Helpis: freed.)
—luceria: (16) imp. *CIL* ix 848 (Lat. Talania Helpis: freed.)
—teanum apulum: (17) i-ii ad ib. 706 (*Teanum Apulum* p. 100 no. 38) (Lat. Claudia Helpis: d. Ἀριάδνη)
S. Italy (Calabria):
—brentesion-brundisium: (18) imp. *CIL* ix 87 (Lat. Caesellia Helspis); (19) ~ ib. 6117 (Lat. Curia Helpis); (20) ~ *NScav* 1901, p. 307 no. 4 (Lat. Vibia Helpis)
—brentesion-brundisium*: (21) imp. *CIL* ix 165 (Lat. Plaetoria Helpis: freed.); (22) ~ ib. 6124 (Lat. Helpis: slave?)
—hydrous-hydruntum: (23) imp. *Ann. Univ. Lecce* 8-9 (1977-80) p. 232 e (Lat. Fla. Elpis)
—taras-tarentum: (24) imp. *NScav* 1896, p. 375 no. 2 (Lat. Hordionia Helpis)
—taras-tarentum*: (25) imp. *Misc. Gr. Rom.* 3 p. 176 (Lat. Pomponia Helpis: freed.)
S. Italy (Campania):
—aequana: (26) imp. *CIL* x 764 (Lat. Curatia Elpis: m. Γλύκων)
—dikaiarchia-puteoli: (27) imp. *AJA* 2 (1898) p. 387 no. 37 (Lat. Septimia Elpis); (28) ~ *CIL* x 2103 (Lat. [Arri]a Elpis); (29) ~ ib. 2758 (Lat. Musidia Elpis); (30) ~ ib. 3047 (Lat. Larcia Helpis); (31) ~ ib. 3092 (Lat. Vestoria Elpis); (32) ~ ib. 3118 (Lat. Vitellia Helpis: m. Vitellia Felicitas); (33) ~ *NScav* 1885, p. 169 (Lat. Geminia Helpis); (34) ?ii ad *CIL* x 2002 (Lat. Iulia Helpis); (35) ~ ib. 3124 a (Lat. Ulpia Elpis)
—dikaiarchia-puteoli*: (36) imp. ib. 2412 (Lat. Faltonia Helpis: freed.?); (37) ?i-ii ad ib. 2550 (Lat. Elpis: freed.)
—misenum: (38) imp. *Eph. Ep.* viii 428 (Lat. Helpis)
—misenum*: (39) imp. *CIL* x 3369 (Lat. Helpis); (40) ~ ib. 3552 (Lat. Calpurnia Elpis: freed.); (41) ~ ib. 3622 (Lat. Curtia Help(d)is); (42) ?i-ii ad ib. 3606 (Lat. Iulia Helpis); (43) ii/iii ad *Forma Italiae* 14 p. 116 (Lat. Barbia Helpis)
—nuceria alfaterna: (44) imp. *NScav* 1922, p. 146 (Lat. Helpis)
—pithekoussai-aenaria: (45) s. ii ad *CIL* x 6801; cf. *Epigraphica* 34 (1972) p. 131 (date) (Lat. Funisulana Helpis)
—pompeii: (46) i bc-i ad *CIL* iv 2189 (Lat. Helpis); (47) ~ ib. 6801 (Lat. Helpis); (48) ~ *NScav* 1916, p. 303 no. 13 (Castrèn 129. 24) (Lat. Cornelia Helpis); (49) m. i ad *Impegno per Pompeii* 9 ES no. 4 (Lat. Helpis); (50) 70-79 ad *CIL* iv 2993 z γ; Mouritsen p. 109 (date) (Lat. Helpis Afra)
—salernum: (51) imp. *CIL* x 533 (Lat. Valeria Helpis)
—salernum*: (52) imp. *IItal* i (1) 202 (*CIL* x 601) (Lat. Herennuleia Helphis: freed.); (53) ?s. i ad *IItal* i (1) 14 (*CIL* x 535) (Lat. Fl. Elpis: m. Θαλλίων)
Sicily:
—akragas: (54) ii-iii ad *IGLMP* 1 + *SEG* xxvi 1059 (Ἀγρ[ία] [Ἐ]λπίς)
—katane: (55) imp. *NScav* 1915, p. 219 (Lat. Elpis)
—kentoripa: (56) imp. *Riv. Stor. Antica* 5 (1900-1) p. 48 no. 14 (Lat. Calpurnia Helpis)
—lipara: (57) imp.? *Meligunis-Lipara* 5 p. 149 no. 2153; cf. *SEG* xli 805 (m. Παιδέρως)
—syracuse: (58) iii-v ad *IG* xiv 96 (Strazzulla 37; Agnello 2; Wessel 864); (59) ~ *IG* xiv 105 (Strazzulla 43; Agnello 3); (60) ~ Strazzulla 271 (Wessel 186 b) (Ἐλ[π]ίς); (61) vi ad *DCB* (3)
—thermai himeraiai*: (62) imp. *ILat. Term. Imer.* 76 (Lat. Elpis: freed.)

**Ἐλπιστος**

Sicily:
—syracuse: (1) iii-v ad *IG* xiv Add. 45 a (Strazzulla 149) (Πομπ. Ἐ.); (2) ~ Barreca 389; cf. *Rend. Pont.* 22 (1946-7) p. 236 no. 40

**Ἐλωρις**

Dalmatia:
—issa:
——(Hylleis): (1) iv/iii bc Brunšmid p. 9, 66; cf. Wilhelm, *Neue Beitr.* 3 p. 17 (Ἐλω[ρις]—ed., Ἐλω[ρος?], Ἐλώ[ριος?]—Wilhelm)
Sicily: (2) hell. Vandermersch p. 166 (amph.) (Ἐλω(ρις)?)
—akrai: (3) iii-ii bc *SGDI* 3242, 10 (*Akrai* p. 157 no. 8) (s. Ἡρακλείδας); (4) ii bc ib. p. 156 no. 6, 9 (s. Ἀπολλώνιος)
—syracuse: (5) ii-i bc *IG* ii² 10391 (s. Ἐπιγένης)
—syracuse?: (6) 404-391 bc *RE* (-)
—tauromenion: (7) c. 172-150 bc *IG* xiv 421 an. 80; 421 an. 91; 421 an. 100 (*SGDI* 5219); *IGSI* 4 II (III), 6 an. 70 (f. Δεινίας)

**Ἐμαύτα**

S. Italy (Apulia): (1) ?iv bc *SEG* xxxvii 773 A (vase)
S. Italy (Lucania):
—poseidonia-paestum: (2) m. iv bc *RVP* pp. 148-9 no. 248 (vase)

**Ἐμαυτίων**

Arkadia: (1) s. iii bc Moretti, *Olymp.* 576 ?= (2)
—thelphousa: (2) s. iii bc *IG* iv (1)² 72 B, 28; cf. *Arch. Class.* 7 (1955) pp. 18 ff. (s. Σταδ—) ?= (1)

**Ἐμαυτός**

Aitolia:
—kalydon: (1) 129 bc *IG* ix (1)² (1) 137, 101 (f. Νικόβουλος, Φιλο—)
S. Italy (Campania):
—neapolis: (2) ii-i bc *IG* xiv 724 (*INap* 12) (s. Ζωΐλος)
—neapolis (nr.): (3) f. iv bc *INap* 190 (vase) (Dubois, *IGDGG* 1 31)

**Ἐμιναύτα**

Akarnania:
—thyrreion: (1) ii bc *IG* ix (1)² (2) 321 + 314, 1 + *AbhBerlAk* 1958 (2), pp. 29 ff. ([Ἐμιν]αύτα)
Epiros:
—kassope: (2) hell. *SEG* xvii 311 (d. Σωτηρίχα)
Kephallenia:
—same: (3) hell. Fraser–Rönne, *BWGT* p. 118 no. 6, 4; cf. Klaffenbach, *Var. Epigr.* pp. 27 ff. no. 12 (name)
Leukas: (4) hell. *Ep. Chron.* 31 (1994) p. 49 no. 1 (*AD* 45 (1990) Chron. p. 254 no. 1)

**Ἐμίναυτος**

Aitolia:
—eidaioi: (1) 213 bc *IG* ix (1)² (1) 96, 3 (*IE-MNAYTOΣ*—lap., Ἐμ(ί)ναυτος, Ἐμ<ν>αυτός?)
Arkadia:
—pheneos: (2) c. 100-90 bc *SEG* xxxiii 290 A, 3; *BSA* 70 (1975) pp. 129-31 (date); *BCH* 109 (1985) p. 382; cf. Stephanis 2825 (Ἐμίνατος, Ἐμίνα(υ)τος?, [Βελ]εμίνατος—SEG)

**Ἐμμενίδας**

Kephallenia:
—kranioi: (1) ?s. v bc *IG* ix (1) 610 (Ἐμ[με]νίδας: f. Μελήσιος)
Korinthia:
—korinth: (2) vi bc *SEG* xi 227 (Lazzarini 274) (Ἐμεν-)
S. Italy (Bruttium):
—lokroi epizephyrioi:
——(Δυσ.): (3) 279 bc De Franciscis 13, 5 (s. Ἀριστεύς)

——(Φαω.): (4) iv/iii BC ib. 18, 3 (f. Μενέστρα-
τος)
SICILY:
—AKRAGAS: (5) vi BC RE s.v. Emmenidai (-); cf.
Schol. Pi., O. iii 68 a; Cordano, Tessere Pubb-
liche 6 (Ἐμμενίδαι (n. gent.), Ἐμμένης—Schol.
Pi.: s. Τηλέμαχος, f. Αἰνησίδαμος)
—KAMARINA: (6) ?iv/iii BC SEG XXXIV 940, 6
(Dubois, IGDS 124; PdelP 44 (1989) p. 192
no. 3; Cordano, 'Camarina VII' 99) (f. Ἀρί-
στων)
—KENTORIPA: (7) c. 60 BC IG VII 420, 46, 56,
62 (IOrop 528) (s. Βεβαῖος)
—MORGANTINA: (8) ?iv/iii BC SEG XXXIX 1008,
8 (s. Δάμων); (9) ~ ib. l. 11 (f. Φίλων) ?= (10);
(10) ~ ib. l. 11 (f. Πολύξενος) ?= (9)
—SYRACUSE?:
——(Ριπ.): (11) hell. NScav 1961, p. 349 with
fig. 15 b (bullet); cf. BE 1965, no. 502 (Ἐμεν-:
f. Ὄρθων)
—TAUROMENION:
——(Δαμ.): (12) ?ii/i BC IG XIV 421 D an. 8
(SGDI 5219) (f. Ἐπαίνετος)

**Ἐμμενίδης**
S. ITALY (BRUTTIUM):
—RHEGION: (1) ?m. v BC Dubois, IGDGG I 39
b (Arena, Iscr. Sic. III 63); LSAG² p. 244
(date) (Ἐμμενίδευ (gen.): f. Κλεομένης)
SICILY:
—LEONTINOI?: (2) m. ii BC IG IX (1)² (2) 208,
38 (Ἐμμε[νίδης])

**Ἐμπεδίας**
LAKONIA:
—SPARTA: (1) 421 BC Th. v 19. 2; 24 (Poralla²
262); (2) f. iii BC CID II 122 I, 6 (Bradford
s.v. Ἐνπεδίας (-)) (Ἐνπε-: f. Ἀριστοκλείδας)

**Ἐμπεδίχων**
AITOLIA?:
—TRAGAS: (1) ?153 BC IG IX (1)² (1) 109, 7
([Ἐμπε?]δίχων—ed.)

**Ἐμπεδίων**
SICILY:
—SELINOUS: (1) 409 BC D.S. xiii 59. 3

**Ἐμπεδοκλῆς**
AKARNANIA:
—PALAIROS: (1) iv/iii BC IG IX (1)² (2) 463
(Ἐνπ-)
ARGOLIS:
—TROIZEN: (2) ?iii BC HE 3206
LAKONIA:
—SPARTA: (3) v BC SEG XI 663 (bronze) (Laz-
zarini 92; Poralla² 262a) (Ἐνπεδοκλέες)
S. ITALY (BRUTTIUM):
—LOKROI EPIZEPHYRIOI:
——(Γαψ.): (4) iv/iii BC De Franciscis 20, 12 (f.
Θεόδοτος)
SICILY:
—AKRAGAS: (5) v BC RE (3); FVS 31; cf. Bidez,
Biographie d'Empédocle pp. 72-3 (?s. Μέτων,
Ἐξαίνετος, Ἀρχίνομος, ?f. Ἐξαίνετος); (6) 496 BC
RE (1); Moretti, Olymp. 170 (?s. Ἐξαίνετος, f.
Μέτων, Ἐξαίνετος)
—GELA-PHINTIAS?: (7) f. v BC Dubois, IGDS
134 A 6 (Arena, Iscr. Sic. II 80) (Ἐνπεδοκλἕς:
s. Μνασίμαχος)

**Ἔμπεδος**
S. ITALY (BRUTTIUM):
—SYBARIS-THOURIOI-COPIAE: (1) vi/v BC
Iamb., VP 267 (FVS I p. 446)

**Ἐμπεδοσθένης**
ARGOLIS:
—ARGOS: (1) ?125 BC FD III (2) 69, 8 = IG II²
1134, 13; FD III (4) 277 B, 10 (s. Ἀγίας)


**Ἐμπεδότιμος**
ARKADIA:
—TEGEA: (1) i BC/i AD SEG XXXVI 384 (date—
LGPN)
S. ITALY (CALABRIA):
—TARAS-TARENTUM: (2) v/iv BC CEG II 833 (f.
Ἱπποτίων)
SICILY:
—SYRACUSE: (3) arch.? Suda E 1007; RE Sup-
plbd. 4 (-); cf. s.v. Herakleides (45) cols. 476-
7 (fict.?)

**Ἐμπέδων**
KORINTHIA:
—SIKYON: (1) vi/v BC SEG XI 244, 14 (Ἐνπέδōν)

**Ἐμπέραμος**
LAKONIA:
—SPARTA: (1) m. vii BC Paus. iv 20. 5, 10; 21.
1, 12 (Poralla² 263)

**Ἔμπορος**
S. ITALY (APULIA):
—CANUSIUM*: (1) imp. Epig. Rom. di Canosa
175 (CIL IX 6190) (Lat. Emporus: freed.)

**Ἐμπύλος**
ARGOLIS:
—HERMIONE: (1) iii BC IG IV (1) 729 II, 6 (s.
Βωλαγόρας)

**Ἔνδιος**
LAKONIA:
—SPARTA: (1) s. v BC RE (-) (Poralla² 264) (s.
Ἀλκιβιάδας)
S. ITALY (BRUTTIUM):
—SYBARIS-THOURIOI-COPIAE: (2) vi/v BC
Iamb., VP 267 (FVS I p. 447)

**Ἔνδοξος**
S. ITALY: (1) imp. CIL X 8059. 387 (seal) (Lat.
M. Suetrius Endoxus)

**Ἐνδυμίων**
S. ITALY (CAMPANIA):
—HERCULANEUM*: (1) c. 72-79 AD ib. 1403 i +
Cron. Erc. 7 (1977) p. 117 C b, 18 (Lat. L.
Mammius Endymio: freed.)

**Ἐννεάτωρ**
ILLYRIA:
—EPIDAMNOS-DYRRHACHION: (1) hell.-imp.
IDyrrh 181 (s. Ἀριστήν); (2) ~ ib. 190 (f. Ἐπί-
κτησις)

**Ἐννέων**
ARKADIA:
—PALLANTION: (1) a. 316 BC SEG XI 1084, 36
(Perlman A.3) (s. Λυσίδικος)

**Ἔννιος**
S. ITALY (CALABRIA):
—RUDIAE: (1) 239-169 BC RE (3) (Lat. Ennius)

**Ἐννόϊος**
SICILY:
—KATANE: (1) iii AD ASSiciliaOrientale 1958-9,
pp. 20 ff.; cf. MEFRA 106 (1994) p. 96 no.
10

**Ἔννυχος**
LAKONIA:
—SPARTA: (1) c. 100-120 AD SEG XI 537 a, 2;
637, 2 (Bradford (-)) (f. Πρατόνικος)
S. ITALY (CAMPANIA):
—HERCULANEUM: (2) m. i AD Cron. Erc. 7
(1977) p. 116 B a, 12 (Lat. L. Venidius Ennychus); (3) 60 AD PdelP I (1946) p. 380 no.
2; p. 382 no. 5; 6 (1951) p. 225 no. 4, 2; 9
(1954) p. 57 no. 62; p. 68 no. 72; 10 (1955)
p. 358 no. 81; 83; 16 (1961) p. 67 no. 89, 3
(Lat. L. Venidius Ennychus)


—HERCULANEUM*: (4) i BC-i AD CIL X 1403 g
II, 39 (Lat. M. Magius Ennychus: freed.)
—STABIAE: (5) imp. RAAN 19 (1938-9) p. 99
(Lat. C. Iylius Ennychus)

**Ἔνοδος**
S. ITALY (CAMPANIA):
—DIKAIARCHIA-PUTEOLI: (1) imp. CIL X 3215;
cf. Puteoli 11 (1987) p. 61 (Lat. [E]nhod[us])

**Ἔνοπλος**
S. ITALY (CAMPANIA):
—HERCULANEUM: (1) m. i AD PdelP 8 (1953) p.
461 no. 50, 1 (Lat. P. Brinnius Enhoplus)

**Ἔνορμος**
SICILY:
—SELINOUS: (1) f. v BC Arena, Iscr. Sic. I 65;
cf. Dubois, IGDS p. 39 n. 61

**Ἐντελλίνιος**
SICILY:
—SYRACUSE: (1) iii-iv AD NScav 1895, p. 488
no. 170 + Ferrua, NG 38; Wessel 1381
([Ἐ]ντελλίνιος)

**Ἔντελλος**
S. ITALY (APULIA):
—VENUSIA: (1) ii-iii AD CIL IX 459 (Museo di
Venosa p. 217 no. 26) (Lat. C. Iulius Entel-
lus)

**Ἔντιμος**
ARGOLIS:
—EPIDAUROS: (1) c. 370 BC IG IV (1)² 102, 93
S. ITALY (APULIA):
—VENUSIA: (2) imp. CIL IX 470 (Lat. C. Eg-
natius Entimus: I f. Ἔντιμος II: doctor); (3) ~
ib. (Lat. C. Egnatius Entimus: II s. Ἔντιμος
I)

**Ἐντρόπη**
SICILY:
—SYRACUSE: (1) iii-v AD Barreca 393 + Rend.
Pont. 22 (1946-7) p. 238 no. 40

**Ἐνυμακρατίδας**
LAKONIA:
—SPARTA: (1) b. 433 BC IG V (1) 213, 35, 39, 45
(Moretti, IAG 16; Poralla² 265) (s. Δαμώνων)

**Ἐνυμαντιάδας**
LAKONIA:
—SPARTA: (1) c. 70-110 AD IG V (1) 97, 20, 21;
280, 2 (Artemis Orthia p. 312 no. 29); SEG XI
564, 21 (Bradford (-)) ((Ἐ)νυμαντιάδας—SEG)

**Ἐνύμαντος**
LAKONIA:
—MARIOS*: (1) vi BC SEG XI 920 (Lazzarini
286) (Ἐ[ν]ύμαντος)

**Ἐνυώ**
KORINTHIA:
—KORINTH (NR.): (1) hell.? IG IV (1) 1560
(fals.?)

**Ἐξαγορίς**
LAKONIA:
—SPARTA: (1) f. iii BC SEG XI 669 f (vase);
BSA 30 (1928-30) p. 245 fig. 2, 15 (Bradford
(-)) ([Ἐ]ξαγορίς)

**Ἐξαίνετος**
ARKADIA:
—MANTINEIA-ANTIGONEIA: (1) c. 300-221 BC
IG V (2) 323. 27-8 (tesserae) ([Ἐ]ξα(ί)νετος—
28: s. Κλεαίνετος); (2) ?253 BC ib. II² 9282;
Nachtergael, Les Galates 10, 54; cf. Stephanis
2033 (f. Πειθίας)
SICILY:
—AKRAGAS: (3) s. vi BC Satyr. ap. D.L. viii 53
(f. Ἐμπεδοκλῆς); (4) 496 BC RE (1); Moretti,
Olymp. 167 (s. Ἐμπεδοκλῆς, ?f. Ἐμπεδοκλῆς,
Καλλικρατίδας); (5) 416-412 BC RE (2); Mo-
retti, Olymp. 341; 346; cf. Bidez, Biographie
d'Empédocle pp. 72-3 (?s. Ἐμπεδοκλῆς)

**Ἐξακέστας**
MESSENIA:
—MESSENE: (1) s. ii BC *SEG* XLI 341, 16 (s.
Νικοκλῆς)

**Ἐξακεστίδας**
SICILY:
—KAMARINA: (1) f. v BC Cordano, *Tessere Pub-
bliche* 133 (['Εξ]ακεστί[δας])
—KAMARINA?: (2) s. v BC *RE* (12);
Westermark–Jenkins pp. 47 ff.; pp. 82 ff.
etc.; *Samml. Ludwig* 313 (Cordano, 'Camar-
ina VII' 27 (coin)) (coin engraver)

**Ἐξάκεστος**
AITOLIA: (1) 224 or 221 BC *SGDI* 2524, 4;
Nachtergael, *Les Galates* 64, 3
ARGOLIS:
—ARGOS: (2) ?c. 575-550 BC *SEG* XI 314, 8;
*LSAG²* p. 168 no. 8 (date)
ILLYRIA:
—EPIDAMNOS-DYRRHACHION: (3) c. 250-50 BC
Ceka, *Probleme* p. 151 no. 21 (pryt.) ?= (4);
(4) ~ Maier 203-8; Münsterberg p. 260 (coin)
(Ceka 111; 134; 189; 195; 209; 335; 348; 380;
461) (pryt.) ?= (3); (5) hell.-imp. *IDyrrh* 182
(s. Μενέλαος); (6) ~ ib. 183 (s. Λέων); (7) ~ ib.
309 (f. Μενέλαος); (8) ~ ib. 492 (f. —ιος)
SICILY:
—GELA-PHINTIAS: (9) m. v BC Dubois, *IGDS*
140 (vase) (Arena, *Iscr. Sic.* II 53) (-κεσσ-)
—HELOROS: (10) vi BC Dubois, *IGDS* 98
—SELINOUS: (11) v BC ib. 35, 2 (Arena, *Iscr.
Sic.* I 64)
—SYRACUSE: (12) 415 BC Th. vi 73. 1 (-ξή-: f.
Σικανός)

**Ἐξάκης**
ARKADIA:
—MANTINEIA-ANTIGONEIA: (1) f. iii BC *IG* v
(2) 272, 3
——(Epalea): (2) m. iv BC ib. 271, 3 ('Εξ(ί)κης:
f. Δαμαγόρας)
—MEGALOPOLIS: (3) iv/iii BC ib. 34, 2
(['Εξ]άκεος (gen.), ['Εξ]άκης?: name—LGPN)

**Ἐξακίδας**
ARKADIA:
—MANTINEIA-ANTIGONEIA: (1) ?iv BC ib. 294
(f. Ἐπικράτης)

**Ἐξάκιος**
ILLYRIA:
—BALAIITAI: (1) ii BC *SEG* XXXVIII 521, 2; cf.
*CRAI* 1991, pp. 197 ff.; *L'Illyrie mérid.* 2 p.
204 f. (f. Ἀριστήν)

**Ἐξακις**
SICILY:
—KAMARINA: (1) f. v BC Cordano, *Tessere Pub-
bliche* 83 (f. Ξένος)

**Ἐξάκων**
EPIROS:
—DODONA*: (1) iv BC *PAE* 1967, p. 49 no. 6
SICILY:
—KAMARINA: (2) s. v BC Dubois, *IGDS* 121, 7
(Arena, *Iscr. Sic.* II 143; *SEG* XXXVIII 940;
Cordano, 'Camarina VII' 32) ('Εξάκō[ν]: II
s. Ἐξάκων I); (3) ~ Dubois, *IGDS* 121, 8
(Arena, *Iscr. Sic.* II 143; *SEG* XXXVIII 940;
Cordano, 'Camarina VII' 32) (-κōν: I f. Ἐξά-
κων II)

**Ἐξαρχος**
LAKONIA:
—SPARTA: (1) 428 BC X., *HG* ii 3. 10 (Poralla²
266)

**Ἐξήκεστος**
SICILY:
—LEONTINOI: (1) 433 BC *IG* I³ 54, 5 ('Εχσέ-: f.
Γέλων)

**Ἐξηκίας**
ARGOLIS:
—ARGOS: (1) v BC *SEG* XXXI 318 ('Εξηκία
(gen.?))

**Ἐξοίδα**
KEPHALLENIA: (1) c. 550-525 BC *BMI* 952
(*CEG* I 391) ('Εχσοίδα (masc. nom.))

**Ἐορταῖος**
ILLYRIA:
—EPIDAMNOS-DYRRHACHION: (1) hell. *IDyrrh*
24 (f. Τιμώ); (2) ~ ib. (s. Φίλιππος); (3) c. 250-
50 BC Schlosser p. 63 no. 324; Unp. (Paris,
BN) 271 (coin) (pryt.) ?= (4); (4) ~ Maier
209-11 (Ceka 56; 112; 299; 305; 390) (pryt.)
?= (3); (5) ii-i BC *IDyrrh* 536 (tiles); (6) hell.-
imp. ib. 281 (f. Λαήν)

**Ἐορτάσιος**
SICILY:
—KATANE: (1) iii-v AD Wessel 732 (Ferrua, *NG*
414)

**Ἐόρτη**
SICILY:
—KATANE: (1) iii-v AD *ASSiciliaOrientale* 1931,
pp. 39-41 no. 11 (Καιλία Ἐ.: m. Βλάστη)
—SYRACUSE: (2) iii-v AD Strazzulla 321 (Wessel
837); cf. Ferrua, *NG* 72 ('Ιώρ-)

**Ἐορτος**
SICILY:
—KENTORIPA: (1) imp. *Epigraphica* 51 (1989) p.
166 no. 30 (Lat. C. Rustius Eortus: f. Rustia
Festa)

**Ἐπάγαθος**
ARKADIA:
—TEGEA: (1) ii AD *IG* v (2) 55, 94 (s. Ὀρβανός)
EPIROS:
—BOUTHROTOS (PRASAIBOI): (2) i AD *AEp*
1978, no. 770 (Lat. Q. Caecilius Epagatus)
KORINTHIA:
—KORINTH: (3) ?ii AD *Hesp.* 33 (1964) p. 141;
(4) ii-iii AD *Ag.* VII p. 96 nos. 293-5; *Corinth*
IV (2) pp. 188 nos. 557-9; 208 nos. 724-9;
*SEG* XXVII 35. 6 (lamps); (5) a. 212 AD *IG* IX
(1) 12, 44
LAKONIA:
—ASOPOS: (6) imp. ib. v (1) 999 (I f. Ἐπάγαθος
II); (7) ~ ib. (II s. Ἐπάγαθος I)
—SPARTA: (8) imp. *SEG* XI 589, 5 (Bradford
(2)) (['Επάγα]θος?: I f. Ἐπάγαθος II); (9) ~
*SEG* XI 589, 5 (Bradford (1)) (['Επάγα]θος?:
II s. Ἐπάγαθος I); (10) i/ii AD *IG* v (1) 188,
3 (Bradford (4)) ('Επάγα[θος]); (11) c. 130-150
AD *SEG* XI 481, 1 (Bradford (1)) (['Επάγα]θος:
s. Διονύσιος) ?= (12); (12) c. 140-160 AD *IG* v
(1) 115, 2 (Bradford (6)) (f. Διονύσιος) ?= (11)
——Limnai: (13) c. 70-100 AD *IG* v (1) 676, 8;
*SEG* XI 488, 1 (Bradford (3)) (s. Σωκράτης)
S. ITALY (CALABRIA):
—BRENTESION-BRUNDISIUM: (14) imp. *NScav*
1884, p. 399 (*Eph. Ep.* VIII 21); cf. *Epi-
graphica* 42 (1980) p. 157 (Lat. Epagathus:
f. Εὐκλῆς)
—BRENTESION-BRUNDISIUM*: (15) imp. *CIL*
IX 141 = *NScav* 1880, p. 501 (Lat. L. Do-
mitius Epagathus: freed.)
—RUDIAE: (16) i-ii AD Bernardini, *Rudiae* p. 108
(Susini, *Fonti Salento* p. 121 no. 64) (Lat. P.
Valerius Epagatus)
S. ITALY (CAMPANIA):
—DIKAIARCHIA-PUTEOLI: (17) imp. *CIL* x
2343 (Lat. L. Cornificius Epagathus); (18)
~ ib. 2384 (Lat. Ennius Epagathus: f. En-
nia Putiolana); (19) m. i AD Camodeca,
*L'Archivio Puteolano* I p. 125 no. 5 (Lat. M.
Amullius Epagathus)

—DIKAIARCHIA-PUTEOLI*: (20) imp. *Röm.
Mitt.* 19 (1904) p. 186 no. 1 (Lat. C. Heius
Epagathus: freed.)
—HERCULANEUM: (21) m. i AD *PdelP* 16
(1961) p. 71 no. 98, 6 (Lat. [P.] Vitellius
Epag[athus]); (22) ~ *Cron. Erc.* 7 (1977) p.
116 B a, 17 (Lat. Epagathus); (23) ~ ib. p.
116 B b, 3 (Lat. M. Claudius Epagathus);
(24) 69 AD *PdelP* 8 (1953) p. 462 no. 53, 6
(*Cron. Erc.* 24 (1994) pp. 137-46) (Lat. Livius
Epagathus)
—KYME: (25) imp. *CIL* x 3701 (Lat. C.
Avianius Epagathus)
—NOLA*: (26) imp. ib. 1335 (Lat. Epagathus:
freed.)
—POMPEII: (27) i BC-i AD ib. IV 2242 (Lat.
Epagathus); (28) ~ ib. 2462; (29) ~ ib. 4897;
(30) ~ ib. 4539-40 (Lat. Epagathus); (31) 70-
79 AD ib. 1015; Mouritsen p. 109 (date) (Lat.
Epagatus)
SICILY:
—DREPANON: (32) ?v AD *NScav* 1919, p. 85
('Επάγαθ[ος])
—SYRACUSE (NR.): (33) ?iii AD ib. 1951, p. 165
no. 2 (Lat. Epacathus)

**Ἐπαγαθώ**
KORINTHIA:
—KORINTH: (1) byz. *Corinth* VIII (3) 532, 3; cf.
*TMByz* 9 (1985) p. 363 no. 41
SICILY:
—KATANE: (2) imp. *GVI* 1936 (*MEFRA* 106
(1994) p. 94 no. 6); cf. *BE* 1980, no. 593 (Ρο-
δογούνη τὸ πρὶν Ἐ.)

**Ἐπαίνετος**
AIGINA: (1) f. v BC *IG* IV (1) 58; *LSAG²* p. 113
no. 10 (date)
ARGOLIS:
—ARGOS: (2) 80 BC Moretti, *Olymp.* 676
—TROIZEN: (3) iv BC *IG* IV (1) 764, 6 (f. Ἀρι-
στόδικος)
ARKADIA: (4) ?255 BC Nachtergael, *Les Galates*
8, 59; cf. Stephanis 1744 (f. Μοσχίων)
—MEGALOPOLIS: (5) ?145 BC *IG* v (2) 439, 42
(s. Δαμέας)
—TEGEA:
——(Krariotai): (6) f. iii BC ib. 36, 63 (s. Γορ-
γιππίδας)
ARKADIA?: (7) c. 200 BC *SEG* XVII 829, 3
EPIROS:
—KELAITHOI: (8) c. 230-200 BC *BCH* 45 (1921)
p. 16 III, 28; cf. Cabanes, *L'Épire* p. 124
(locn.) (f. Ἐπίγονος)
KERKYRA: (9) hell. *Syll*³ 1174, 4
KORINTHIA:
—KORINTH: (10) s. iv BC *Hesp.* 43 (1974) p. 28
no. 37
—SIKYON: (11) c. 545-530 BC *ABV* p. 146 no.
20
LAKONIA:
—SPARTA: (12) inc. Plu., *Mor.* 220 C (Poralla²
267)
S. ITALY (APULIA):
—LARINUM: (13) imp. *CIL* IX 734 (Lat. C.
Iulius Epaenitus)
S. ITALY (BRUTTIUM):
—LOKROI EPIZEPHYRIOI:
——(Ταγ.): (14) iv/iii BC De Franciscis 32, 1
——(Λογ.): (15) iv/iii BC ib. 26, 7 (s. Σιμίας) ?=
(16); (16) ~ ib. 30, 5 (f. Πέλλις) ?= (15)
S. ITALY (CALABRIA):
—TARAS-TARENTUM: (17) iv/iii BC *IG* XIV 668
I, 15 (Landi, *DISMG* 194)
SICILY:
—TAUROMENION: (18) ?ii/i BC *IG* XIV 421 D
an. 12 (*SGDI* 5219) (s. Δαμόφιλος)
——(Δαμ.): (19) ?ii/i BC *IG* XIV 421 D an. 8
(*SGDI* 5219) (s. Ἐμμενίδας); (20) ~ *IG* XIV
421 D an. 8 (*SGDI* 5219) (f. Δαμόφιλος); (21)
~ *IG* XIV 421 III (*SGDI* 5219)

**Ἐπαίνης**
ARKADIA:
—MANTINEIA-ANTIGONEIA:
——(Posoidaia): **(1)** c. 425-400 BC SEG XXXI 348, 23

**Ἐπαινία**
S. ITALY (CAMPANIA):
—POMPEII: **(1)** i BC-i AD CIL IV 1861 (Lat. Epaenia)

**Ἐπαινις**
LAKONIA:
—AIGILIA*: **(1)** ?ii-i BC IG v (1) 951 d-e (bullets)

**Ἐπαινος**
ARGOLIS:
—EPIDAUROS: **(1)** ii/i BC ib. IV (1)² 248 (s. Ἑλικών)

**Ἐπάκας**
S. ITALY (CALABRIA):
—TARAS-TARENTUM: **(1)** hell.? RA 1932 (1), p. 47 no. 106 (loomweight) (Ἐπάκα?)

**Ἐπάλκης**
ARGOLIS:
—ARGOS*: **(1)** 105 BC JÖAI 14 (1911) Beibl. p. 146 no. 4, 17 (Ἐ[π]άλκης, Ε[ὐ]άλκης?: slave/freed.?)
ARKADIA:
—TEGEA:
——(Krariotai): **(2)** s. iii BC IG v (2) 36, 117 (f. Δυοκλῆς)
MESSENIA:
—MESSENE: **(3)** f. iii BC SEG XLI 342, 7; cf. PAE 1991, p. 100 no. 8

**Ἐπαμείνων**
SICILY:
—SELINOUS: **(1)** vii/vi BC Dubois, IGDS 80 (vase) (Arena, Iscr. Sic. I 73) ([Ἐ]παμείνōν)

**Ἐπαμένης**
SICILY:
—NAXOS: **(1)** s. v BC SEG XXXVIII 953. 2 (Arena, Iscr. Sic. III 77); cf. L'Incidenza dell'Antico pp. 418-9 (Ἐπαμένōν—Arena: f. Ὀνομάστατος)

**Ἐπαμίων**
AKARNANIA: **(1)** m. ii BC IG IX (1)² (2) 209, 3

**Ἐπανδρίδας**
LAKONIA:
—GERONTHRAI: **(1)** ?iv/iii BC ib. v (1) 1119 (CEG II 822)

**Ἐπανδρος**
ARKADIA:
—MANTINEIA-ANTIGONEIA: **(1)** c. 300-221 BC IG v (2) 323. 51 (tessera) (s. Ἑρμαῖος)
EPIROS:
—AMBRAKIA: **(2)** iii BC SEG XXIV 413 (f. Ἄρκισα)

**Ἐπανίδας**
LAKONIA:
—SPARTA: **(1)** f. vi BC ib. II 64 (Lazzarini 80); LSAG² p. 198 no. 6 (date) (Poralla² 267a)

**Ἐπάρατος**
SICILY:
—TYNDARIS: **(1)** imp. Manganaro, QUCC forthcoming no. 22 (s. Καλλίας)

**Ἐπαφος**
S. ITALY (CAMPANIA):
—POMPEII: **(1)** c. 51-62 AD CIL IV 3340. 100, 6 (Castrèn 314. 6) (Lat. Sex. Pompeius Epaphus)

**Ἐπαφρᾶς**
ARGOLIS:
—EPIDAUROS: **(1)** 227 AD IG IV (1)² 407, 5 (s. Μᾶρκος)
ARKADIA:
—TEGEA: **(2)** i AD ib. v (2) 47, 11
ELIS: **(3)** ?i AD EA 1905, p. 259 no. 2, 6 (f. Ἐπίγονος)
EPIROS:
—NIKOPOLIS: **(4)** imp. CIG 1820 (Sarikakis 40) (s. Φῆλιξ)
LAKONIA:
—SPARTA: **(5)** c. 150-160 AD SEG XXX 410, 24
MESSENIA:
—MESSENE: **(6)** ?f. i AD PAE 1992, p. 79, 8
PELOPONNESE?: **(7)** 11 AD ib. p. 72 B, 14 (I f. Ἐπαφρᾶς II); **(8)** ~ ib. l. 14 (II s. Ἐπαφρᾶς I)
S. ITALY (APULIA):
—ACERUNTIA: **(9)** imp. CIL IX 419 (Lat. Epaphra)
—GNATHIA-EGNATIA: **(10)** i-ii AD Suppl. It. 11 p. 45 no. 27 (CIL IX 270) (Lat. Sex. Numitorius Epaphra)
—LARINUM: **(11)** imp. NScav 1902, p. 70 no. 3 (Lat. M. Lindius Epaphra)
—VENUSIA: **(12)** i AD Epigraphica 35 (1973) p. 147 no. 9 (Museo di Venosa p. 235 no. 6) (Lat. Q. Herennius Epaphra: s. C. Turranius Crescens, Magia Felicia)
S. ITALY (BRUTTIUM):
—HIPPONION-VIBO VALENTIA*: **(13)** imp. CIL x 8041. 12 (tile) (Lat. Epaphra)
S. ITALY (CALABRIA):
—BRENTESION-BRUNDISIUM: **(14)** imp. Athenaeum 48 (1970) p. 101 no. 6 (Lat. [Ep]afra); **(15)** ~ NScav 1884, p. 140 a (Lat. Epafra); **(16)** ~ Eph. Ep. VIII 19 (Lat. Q. Egnatius Epaphra); **(17)** ~ ib. 20 (Lat. Epafra)
—BRENTESION-BRUNDISIUM*: **(18)** imp. Epigraphica 25 (1963) p. 52 no. 42. 2; cf. Scritti Degrassi 3 p. 67 (Lat. L. Pacilius Epaphra: s. Pacilia Fausta: freed.); **(19)** ?i AD Necropoli via Cappuccini p. 281 no. E32 (Lat. T. Latinius Epaphra: freed.)
S. ITALY (CAMPANIA):
—DIKAIARCHIA-PUTEOLI: **(20)** imp. CIL x 2039 a (Lat. L. Allius Epaphra); **(21)** i AD Puteoli 11 (1987) p. 130 no. 3 (Lat. M. Titius Epaphra)
—DIKAIARCHIA-PUTEOLI*: **(22)** imp. CIL x 2679 (Lat. Epaphra: freed.?); **(23)** f. i AD AJA 77 (1973) p. 162 no. 12 (Lat. Epaphra: freed.)
—HERCULANEUM*: **(24)** i BC-i AD CIL x 1403 g I, 16 (Lat. Ti. Claudius Epaphra: freed.)
—POMPEII: **(25)** i BC-i AD ib. IV 1787; 1816; 1916; 1926; 1936 (Lat. Epaphra); **(26)** ~ ib. 2374 (Lat. Epaphra); **(27)** ~ ib. 4382 (Lat. Epapra); **(28)** ~ ib. 4899 (Lat. Epaphra); **(29)** ~ NScav 1913, p. 32 (terracotta); **(30)** 3 BC CIL IV 2450 (Lat. Epaphra); **(31)** 70-79 AD ib. 7357; Mouritsen p. 111 (date) (Lat. Epaphra)
SICILY:
—LIPARA*: **(32)** imp. IG XIV 389 (Libertini, Isole Eolie p. 219 no. 7) (Ε. Ἱρτιανός: freed.)

**Ἐπαφρίων**
ARKADIA:
—MEGALOPOLIS: **(1)** byz.? IG v (2) 485

**Ἐπαφροδίτα**
KORINTHIA:
—KORINTH: **(1)** byz. Corinth VIII (1) 161; cf. TMByz 9 (1985) p. 359 no. 3

**Ἐπαφροδιτᾶς**
ARGOLIS:
—EPIDAUROS: **(1)** 152 AD IG IV (1)² 389, 4 (f. Πόμπων)

**Ἐπαφροδίτη**
S. ITALY (CAMPANIA):
—DIKAIARCHIA-PUTEOLI: **(1)** imp. CIL x 2902 (Lat. Pullia Epaphrodite)
SICILY:
—SYRACUSE: **(2)** ?iii AD ASSicilia 1938-9, p. 23 (Ἀλφία Ἐπαφροδείτε—apogr.)

**Ἐπαφροδιτιανός**
S. ITALY (CAMPANIA):
—DIKAIARCHIA-PUTEOLI: **(1)** imp. CIL x 2662 (Lat. L. Lollius Epaphroditianus)

**Ἐπαφροδιτίων**
SICILY:
—SYRACUSE: **(1)** iii-v AD IG XIV 26; cf. Riv. Arch. Crist. 18 (1941) p. 192 no. 59 (-δει-)

**Ἐπαφρόδιτον**
ARGOLIS:
—EPIDAUROS?: **(1)** ?i BC SEG I 71
TRIPHYLIA:
—PHRIXA (NR.): **(2)** ii-iii AD ib. XXV 468 (-δει-)

**Ἐπαφρόδιτος**
AIGINA: **(1)** iii AD IG IV (1) 18 (-δει-: f. Νικόστρατος)
AIGINA?: **(2)** imp. EAD XXX p. 357 no. 26 (Ἐ(π)αφρ(ό)διτος: f. Ὀνησᾶς)
ARGOLIS:
—ARGOS: **(3)** ii AD SEG XVI 253, 12 (Τι. Ἰούλ. Ἐπαφρόδιτος)
—EPIDAUROS: **(4)** i BC-i AD IG IV (1)² 35; **(5)** i AD ib. 501 (f. Πόπλιος); **(6)** ii-iii AD Peek, IAEpid 242 (doctor); **(7)** ~ IG IV (1)² 532 ([Ἐπα]φρόδειτος: s. Ἀριστόβουλος); **(8)** 170 AD ib. 391 (-δει-: s. Λεωνίδας); **(9)** ?iii AD ib. 534; 535; 540; **(10)** 260 AD ib. 416 (-δει-: I f. Ἐπαφρόδιτος II); **(11)** ~ ib. (-δει-: II s. Ἐπαφρόδιτος I)
—HERMIONE: **(12)** ii AD ib. IV (1) 719 (M. Αὐρ. Ἐπαφρό[διτος]: s. Εὔτυχος); **(13)** ?iii AD IKyz I 184, 2 (IPrusa II p. 186) (-δει-)
—TROIZEN: **(14)** imp.? IG IV (1) 813 (-δει-)
ARKADIA:
—KLEITOR: **(15)** m. iii AD SEG XXXV 350 I, 2 (Αὐρ. Ἐ.: s. Ἀφροδίσιος); **(16)** ~ ib. l. 6 (Αὐρ. Ἐ.: s. Ἐπαφρῦς)
—TEGEA: **(17)** imp. ib. XXXVI 384; **(18)** ii AD IG v (2) 54, 5 ([Ἐπ]αφρόδ[ει]τ[ος]); **(19)** ~ ib. 55, 26 (-δει-: s. Ἀθηνόδωρος); **(20)** ~ ib. l. 51 (Κορν. Ἐπαφρόδειτος); **(21)** ~ ib. l. 87 (-δει-: I f. Ἐπαφρόδιτος II); **(22)** ~ ib. l. 87 (-δει-: II s. Ἐπαφρόδιτος I); **(23)** ?ii AD ib. 214 (Ἐ[παφ]ρόδειτος)
ELIS: **(24)** i BC/i AD IvOl 74, 12 (Ἐπαφ[ρόδει]τος]); **(25)** f. ii AD ib. 91 a ([Ἐπαφρ]όδειτος)
—OLYMPIA*: **(26)** 113-117 AD ib. 91, 20 (?s. Σόφων: slave?)
EPIROS:
—AMBRAKIA: **(27)** imp. SEG XXXVII 507 (-δει-)
—NIKOPOLIS: **(28)** imp. CIG 1811 (Sarikakis 42) (I f. Ἐπαφρόδιτος II); **(29)** ~ CIG 1811 (Sarikakis 41) (-δει-: II s. Ἐπαφρόδιτος I)
ILLYRIA:
—BYLLIONES BYLLIS: **(30)** imp. AEp 1978, no. 768 (Lat. [Epaphr]odit[us])
—EPIDAMNOS-DYRRHACHION: **(31)** 52 AD CIL x (1) 769 (Lat. T. Pomponius Epaphroditus)
KORINTHIA:
—KORINTH: **(32)** imp. IEph 2243, 1 (Γν. Κορνήλιος Ἐπαφρόδειτος)
LAKONIA: **(33)** 163 AD IG v (1) 1346, 2 (Bradford (5)) (Γ. Ἰούλ. Ἐπαφρόδειτος)
—SPARTA: **(34)** c. 100-105 AD SEG XI 537 a, 6; 537 b, 1 (Bradford (11)) (f. Μελίχρους); **(35)** f. ii AD IG v (1) 162, 8 (Bradford (4)) ([Ἐπα]φρόδειτος: s. T—); **(36)** c. 105-110 AD IG v (1) 20 B, 3; BSA 26 (1923-5) p. 168 C 7, 3 (Bradford (13)) (-δει-: f. Τρύφερος); **(37)** ~ IG v (1) 97, 27 (Bradford (7)) (M. Ἐ.); **(38)** c. 110-150 AD IG v (1) 65, 17; SEG XI 549, 7; 585, 4; 586, [3] (Bradford (12)) (Ἐπαφρόδειτος—SEG XI 585: f. Σωσικράτης); **(39)** c. 140-145 AD SEG XI 583, 2 (Bradford (6)) ([Ἐπαφρό]δειτος); **(40)** c. 140-160 AD IG v (1) 149,

4 (Bradford (10)) (-δει-: I f. Ἐπαφρόδιτος II);
(41) ~ IG v (1) 149, 4 (Bradford (2)) (-δει-:
II s. Ἐπαφρόδιτος I); (42) c. 150-160 AD IG
v (1) 71 II, 18 (Bradford (3)) (s. Φίλιππος);
(43) c. 170 AD IG v (1) 116, 5 (Bradford (1))
(-δει-: s. Διονύσιος); (44) c. 170-190 AD SEG
XI 620, 2 (Bradford (8)) (Κ. Σόσ. Ἐπαφρόδειτος); (45) c. 175 AD IG v (1) 680, 6 (Bradford
(9)) (Πεδουκαῖος Ἐπαφρόδειτος)
—TEUTHRONE: (46) imp. SEG XXXI 337 (-δει-)
MESSENIA:
—MESSENE: (47) i/ii AD IG v (1) 1473 (-δει-);
(48) 192 AD PAE 1969, p. 104, 14 (-δει-)
S. ITALY: (49) imp. CIL x 8059. 66 (seal)
(Lat. M. Aurelius E[pa]phrodi[tus]); (50) ~
ib. 8059. 147 (seal) (Lat. Epaphroditus); (51)
~ ib. 8059. 313 (seal) (Lat. G. Petronius Ep-
aphroditus)
S. ITALY (APULIA):
—CANUSIUM*: (52) i/ii AD Epig. Rom. di Canosa
80 (Lat. Q. Raius Epaproditus: freed.)
—GNATHIA-EGNATIA: (53) imp. CIL IX 267
(Lat. -iedius Epaproditus)
—RUBI: (54) imp. Epigrafia e Territorio 2 p. 72
no. 13 (CIL IX 656) (Lat. Epafroditus: f. Εὔ-
πλους, Felicitas)
—TEANUM APULUM*: (55) i-ii AD Teanum
Apulum p. 72 no. 18 (Lat. [M.] [Plo-
tius] [Epap]hroditus: f. M. Plotius Placidus:
freed.)
—VENUSIA: (56) imp. CIL IX 423 (Lat. C. Avit-
tius Epaphroditus)
S. ITALY (CALABRIA):
—BRENTESION-BRUNDISIUM: (57) imp. Eph.
Ep. VIII 7 (Lat. Cn. Pomponius Epaphrodi-
tus Cissianus)
S. ITALY (CAMPANIA):
—ABELLA: (58) imp. CIL x 1209 (Lat. Q. Cali-
dius Epaphroditus)
—BAIAI: (59) ii-iii AD IG XIV 878, 2 (Σαίνις Ἐπ-
αφρόδειτος: II s. Σαίνις Ἐπαφρόδιτος I, Σαι-
νία Εὐκαρπία); (60) ~ ib. l. 6 (Σαίνις Ἐπα-
φρ(ό)δειτος: I f. Σαίνις Ἐπαφρόδιτος II)
—CUBULTERIA*: (61) i AD Iscr. Trebula Caiatia
Cubulteria 100 (CIL x 4623) (Lat. L. Brittius
Epaproditus: freed.)
—DIKAIARCHIA-PUTEOLI: (62) imp. ib. 1883
(Lat. M. Manlius Epaphroditus); (63) ~ ib.
2187 (Lat. Q. Granius Epaphroditus); (64) ~
ib. 2245 (Lat. A. Caucius Epaphroditus); (65)
~ ib. 2732 (Lat. C. Messius [Epap]hroditus);
(66) ~ ib. 2988 (Lat. C. Clodius Epaphroditus); (67) ~ Eph. Ep. VIII 388 (Lat. M.
Amullius Epaperoditus); (68) ?i-ii AD CIL x
2588 (Lat. Iulius Aepafroditus: f. Κοιτωνίς);
(69) i-ii AD Puteoli 7-8 (1983-4) p. 298 no.
2 (Lat. Epaphroditus); (70) m. i AD Camodeca, L'Archivio Puteolano 1 p. 93 no. 21
(Lat. C[o]cceius Epaphro[ditus]); (71) ~ ib. p.
125 no. 5 (Lat. C. Iulius Epaphroditus); (72)
43 AD ib. p. 211 (Lat. C. Nummius Epaphroditus); (73) 44 AD ib. p. 31 (Lat. L. Patulcius
Epaphroditus); (74) 55-56 AD ib. p. 125 no. 5;
pp. 131-4 (Lat. M. Barbatius Epaphroditus)
—DIKAIARCHIA-PUTEOLI*: (75) imp. AJA 77
(1973) p. 156 no. 5 (Lat. L. Herennius Epaphroditus: freed.); (76) ~ CIL x 2182 (Lat.
M. Caecilius Epaphroditus: freed.); (77) ~
ib. 2818 (Lat. C. Pac. Epaphroditus: freed.);
(78) ~ Eph. Ep. VIII 424 (Lat. Epaphroditus:
freed.)
—HERCULANEUM: (79) i BC-i AD CIL IV 10675
(Lat. Epaphroditus)
—HERCULANEUM*: (80) i BC-i AD ib. x 1403 l
II, 8; cf. Cron. Erc. 7 (1977) p. 116 c, 8 (Lat.
Q. Iunius Epaphroditus: freed.); (81) c. 72-79
AD CIL x 1403 i + Cron. Erc. 7 (1977) p. 117
C b, 22 (Lat. C. Vibius Epaphroditus: freed.)
—NOLA*: (82) imp. Atti Acc. Pontan. 21 (1971-
'2) pp. 392-7 (Lat. C. Gletranus Epaphrodi-
tus)

—POMPEII: (83) i BC-i AD CIL IV 2319 l; cf.
p. 218 (Lat. Apaphroditus); (84) ~ ib. 2443
(Lat. Epaphroditus); (85) ~ ib. 4873; (86) ~
Neue Forsch. in Pompeji p. 264 no. 19 (Lat.
Epaphrodi(tus)); (87) ~ ib. p. 266 nos. 58; 63-
4 (Lat. Epaphroditos); (88) f. i AD CIL x 1013
(Castrèn 439. 2); Kockel p. 67 (date) (Lat. C.
Venerius Epaphroditus)
S. ITALY (LUCANIA):
—EBURUM (NR.): (89) imp. CIL x 8059. 16
(seal) (Lat. Cn. Aemilius Epaphroditus)
SICILY:
—HERBITA: (90) ii-iii AD Arch. Class. 17 (1965)
p. 200 d (Γν. Πομπώνις Ἐ.)
—KATANE: (91) iii-v AD NScav 1937, p. 78
(-δει-)
—PANORMOS: (92) imp. CIL x 7320 (Lat. P.
Servilius Epaphroditus)
—SYRACUSE: (93) iii-v AD IG XIV 27 (Strazzulla
123); cf. Riv. Arch. Crist. 18 (1941) p. 188 no.
55; (94) ~ IG XIV 106 (Strazzulla 44; Wessel
1162); cf. ASSicilia 1938-9, p. 29 (name)
(Ἐπαφρό(δ)ειτος, Ἔπαφρος—IG)
—SYRACUSE*: (95) imp. CIL x 7144 (Lat.
[E]paphroditu[s]: imp. freed.)
—THERMAI HIMERAIAI: (96) i-ii AD ib. 7401
(ILat. Term. Imer. 92) (Lat. C. Ducenius Ep-
aphroditus)
SICILY?: (97) i BC-i AD IGLMP 138 (-δει-)

### Ἔπαφρῦς
ARKADIA:
—KLEITOR: (1) m. iii AD SEG XXXV 350 I, 6
(Ἐπαφρ[ῦ] (gen.): f. Αὐρ. Ἐπαφρόδιτος)
—TEGEA: (2) 165 AD IG v (2) 50, 41 (I f. Ἐπα-
φρῦς II); (3) ~ ib. l. 41 (II s. Ἔπαφρῦς I); (4)
~ ib. l. 68 (s. Ἀμέθυστος); (5) ~ ib. l. 71 (f.
Καλλιστίων)
S. ITALY (CAMPANIA):
—NOLA: (6) imp. CIL x 1296 (Lat. Epaphrys: I
f. Ἔπαφρῦς II); (7) ~ ib. (Lat. Epaphrys: II s.
Ἔπαφρῦς I, Λύκα)

### Ἐπαφρώ
ARKADIA:
—TEGEA: (1) ii-iii AD EILakArk 12, 6 (GVI
2056) (m. Νικάνωρ)
LAKONIA:
—SPARTA: (2) a. 212 AD IG v (1) 594, 2 (Brad-
ford (1)) (Αὐρ. Ἐ.); (3) ~ IG v (1) 594, 9
(Bradford (2)) (Κλ. Ἐπαφρ[ώ])

### Ἐπειός
MESSENIA:
—PYLOS: (1) iv BC IG v (1) 1418

### Ἐπέραστος
ACHAIA:
—PELLENE: (1) ?ii-iii AD SEG XI 1274, 7
ELIS: (2) iv/iii BC Moretti, Olymp. 530 (s. Θεό-
γονος: mantis/Klytiadai); (3) 69-73 AD IvOl
84, 20 (s. Φίλλις)
S. ITALY (CAMPANIA):
—HERCULANEUM: (4) i BC-i AD CIL x 1403 d I,
13 (Lat. M. Nonius Eiperastus)
S. ITALY (LUCANIA):
—GRUMENTUM*: (5) i/ii AD Atti Conv. Taranto
16 (1976) p. 870 (Lat. Eperastus: slave?)

### Ἐπέτινος
ILLYRIA:
—EPIDAMNOS-DYRRHACHION: (1) ?i AD AEp
1978, no. 744 (Lat. Ti. Claudius Epetinus)

### Ἔπευκτος
ACHAIA:
—DYME*: (1) c. 219 BC SGDI 1612, 16 (Tyche
5 (1990) p. 124) (f. Ἀθανάδας)

### Ἐπήβολος
MESSENIA: (1) viii BC Paus. iv 9. 5, 8; 10. 5

### Ἐπηρατίδας
ARKADIA:
—MANTINEIA-ANTIGONEIA: (1) c. 300-221 BC
IG v (2) 323. 94 (tessera) (f. Τίμαρχος)
LAKONIA:
—SPARTA: (2) ii/i BC ib. v (1) 966, 1, 10, 18
(Bradford (-)) (s. Τιμομένης)

### Ἐπήρατος
ACHAIA:
—PHARAI: (1) c. 219 BC Plb. iv 82. 8; v 1 and
passim; Plu., Arat. 48
ARKADIA:
—MANTINEIA-ANTIGONEIA: (2) iii-ii BC IG v
(2) 319, 1, 4, 10
—MEGALOPOLIS: (3) c. 279-248 BC Nachtergael,
Les Galates 3, 7; 8, 22; 17, 1 (Stephanis 851)
(s. Ἀλκῖνος)
—TEGEA: (4) ?vi BC Schol. E., Hipp. 264 (f. Σώ-
δαμος); (5) hell.? IG v (2) 171 (?s. Βάκχιος);
(6) ii AD ib. 55, 36 (s. Λεοντᾶς)
KORINTHIA:
—SIKYON: (7) ?254 BC Nachtergael, Les Galates
9, 47; cf. Stephanis 944 (f. Εὔδοξος)
LAKONIA:
—SPARTA: (8) 414 BC X., HG ii 3. 10 (Poralla²
268); (9) ii BC IG v (1) 29, 17 (Syll³ 669;
Bradford (-)) (f. Λαχάρης)

### Ἐπιάναξ
SICILY:
—ZANKLE-MESSANA: (1) imp. IG XIV 417

### Ἐπιβάτης
S. ITALY (LUCANIA):
—HERAKLEIA: (1) iv BC Unp. (A.W.J.)

### Ἐπιβολίδας
LAKONIA:
—SPARTA: (1) s. i BC IG v (1) 94, 23 (Bradford
(-)) ([Ἐπ]ιβολίδας: s. Εὐ—)

### Ἐπιγένεια
MESSENIA: (1) imp.? IG v (1) 1502
S. ITALY (CAMPANIA):
—DIKAIARCHIA-PUTEOLI*: (2) imp. CIL x
2777 (Lat. Ninia Epigenia: freed.)
SICILY:
—LIPARA: (3) imp.? NScav 1947, p. 217 (-νεα)

### Ἐπιγένης
ARGOLIS:
—ARGOS: (1) ii BC SEG XLII 279, 11 (f. —ος)
—ARGOS?: (2) v BC IG IV (1) 552, 6
ARKADIA:
—ORCHOMENOS: (3) iv-iii BC SEG XI 1104
ILLYRIA:
—EPIDAMNOS-DYRRHACHION: (4) c. 250-50 BC
Bakërr Hoard p. 67 no. 99 (coin) (Ceka 397)
(pryt.); (5) hell.-imp. IDyrrh 288 ([Ἐ]πιγένης:
f. Λαμίσκα); (6) ~ ib. 346 (f. Πιστόξενος); (7) ~
ib. 418 (f. Τραῦζος); (8) ~ ib. 428 (f. Φάφιλος)
—KERKYRA: (9) m. ii BC IG IX (1)² (2) 209, 20 (s.
Πασίων)
KORINTHIA:
—SIKYON: (10) arch. RE (12) (Skalet 109)
(dub.)
LAKONIA:
—GERENIA: (11) m. iv BC IG II² 11335, 4; SEG
XIII 194 (locn.) (s. Ἑρμογένης)
—SPARTA: (12) c. 217-230 AD ib. XI 616 a, 5
(Bradford (-)) (Αὐρ. Ἐ.: s. Ἀπολλωνι—)
—LEUKAS: (13) i BC-i AD? IG IX (1) 595 (f. Βου-
βαλίς)
MESSENIA:
—KORONE: (14) ii BC ib. v (1) 1397, 8
SICILY:
—SYRACUSE: (15) ii-i BC ib. II² 10391 (f. Ἔλω-
ρις)
—TAUROMENION: (16) c. 209 BC ib. XIV 421
an. 32 (SGDI 5219) (s. Ἀριστοκράτης); (17)
c. 209-189 BC IG XIV 421 an. 32; 421 an. 54
(SGDI 5219) (s. Εὐδαμίδας, f. Εὐδαμίδας); (18)

c. 185 BC *IG* XIV 421 an. 56 (*SGDI* 5219) (Ἐ[πιγ]ένης, Ἐ[πισθ?]ένης: f. Θεόχρηστος); (19) c. 156 BC *IG* XIV 421 an. 85 (*SGDI* 5219) (s. Εὐδαμίδας); (20) c. 152 BC *IGSI* 4 III (IV), 27 an. 89 (s. Ἀριστοκράτης)
——(Σπαρ.): (21) ?ii/i BC *IG* XIV 421 [D] an. 1 (*SGDI* 5219) (s. Ἀθανις)

**Ἐπιγήθης**
ACHAIA:
—PELLENE: (1) 241 BC Plu., *Arat.* 32

**Ἐπίγνητος**
AKARNANIA:
—STRATOS: (1) ii BC *IG* IX (1)² (2) 394, 14 (s. Αἰσχρίων); (2) a. 167 BC ib. IX (2) 6 a, 3; cf. Stählin p. 220 (date) (s. Ἀγέλαος)

**Ἐπιγόνη**
AIGINA: (1) imp. *IG* IV (1) 111
ARKADIA:
—MANTINEIA-ANTIGONEIA: (2) 27 BC-15 AD ib. v (2) 268 (d. Ἀρτέμων)
ARKADIA?: (3) ii AD ib. 506 (Κλ. Ἐ.)
EPIROS:
—NIKOPOLIS: (4) imp. *SEG* XXVII 236 (Λουτατία Ἐ.); (5) ~ *Wiss. Mitth. Bosn.* 4 (1896) p. 387 no. 4 (Sarikakis 43) (d. Στράτων)
ILLYRIA:
—APOLLONIA: (6) imp. *IApoll* 74
S. ITALY (CALABRIA):
—BRENTESION-BRUNDISIUM: (7) imp. *CIL* IX 6119 (Lat. Epigone)
S. ITALY (CAMPANIA):
—DIKAIARCHIA-PUTEOLI: (8) ?i-ii AD ib. X 2592 (Lat. Iulia Epigone)
—MISENUM*: (9) ?ii AD ib. 3550 (Lat. Fla. Epigone)

**Ἐπιγονία**
S. ITALY (CAMPANIA):
—DIKAIARCHIA-PUTEOLI: (1) imp. ib. 2176 (Lat. Brinnia Epigonia)

**Ἐπιγόνιος**
S. ITALY (LUCANIA):
—METAPONTION: (1) hell. *IG* XIV 2406. 15 (*RA* 1932 (1), p. 37 no. 11; Landi, *DISMG* 155 (loomweight)) (or S. Italy (Calabria) Taras-Tarentum?)

**Ἐπίγονος**
AIGINA: (1) m. iv BC *Athenian Democratic Accounts* p. 183
AKARNANIA:
—THYRREION: (2) ii BC *IG* IX (1)² (2) 323
ARKADIA: (3) 316 BC ib. v (2) 549, 33 (f. Δίυλλος)
—TEGEA: (4) ii AD ib. 55, 73 (s. Ὀρβανός); (5) ~ ib. l. 93 (s. Ὀρβανός); (6) m. ii AD ib. 48, 23
ELIS: (7) ?i AD *EA* 1905, p. 259 no. 2, 6 (Ἐ[π]ίγονος: s. Ἐπαφρᾶς); (8) 113 AD *IvOl* 90, 9 (I f. Ἐπίγονος II); (9) ~ ib. l. 9 (II s. Ἐπίγονος I)
EPIROS:
—AMBRAKIA: (10) vi BC *RE* (7) (and Korinthia Sikyon)
—KELAITHOI: (11) c. 230-200 BC *BCH* 45 (1921) p. 16 III, 28; cf. Cabanes, *L'Épire* p. 124 (locn.) (s. Ἐπαίνετος)
ILLYRIA:
—BYLLIONES (CAKRAN (MOD.)): (12) iii AD *SEG* XXXVIII 546
LAKONIA:
—SPARTA: (13) i BC-i AD *IG* v (1) 652, 2 (Bradford (1)) (s. Φιλόστρατος); (14) c. 125-160 AD *IG* v (1) 114, 12; *SEG* XI 552, [1] (Bradford (4)) (f. Νικασίων); (15) s. iv AD *PLRE* I (3) (Bradford (3))
——Konosoura: (16) c. 212-230 AD *IG* v (1) 684, 13 (Bradford (2)) (Αὐρ. Ἐ.)


MESSENIA:
—ASINE: (17) ii AD *IG* v (1) 1408 (s. Ἀπολλώνιος)
—KORONE: (18) 246 AD ib. 1398, 31 (Κλ. Ἐ.)
—MESSENE: (19) i AD ib. 1467, 7
PELOPONNESE?: (20) a. 164 BC *IvOl* 47, 3
S. ITALY (BRUTTIUM):
—LOKROI EPIZEPHYRIOI:
——(Κρα.): (21) iv/iii BC De Franciscis 24, 2; 38, 7 (s. Ἀρίστων)
S. ITALY (CALABRIA):
—TARAS-TARENTUM: (22) ii BC *SEG* XXIX 1216, 1, 22 (s. Δαμοκράτης)
S. ITALY (CAMPANIA):
—DIKAIARCHIA-PUTEOLI: (23) imp. *CIL* X 2073 (Lat. M. Antonius Aepigonus)
—DIKAIARCHIA-PUTEOLI*: (24) imp. ib. 2790 (Lat. Q. Occius Epigonus: freed.)
—NEAPOLIS*: (25) imp. *NScav* 1892, p. 55 no. 1; cf. Leiwo p. 112 no. 85 (Lat. Corn. Epigonus: freed.)
SICILY:
—AKRAI: (26) ii BC *Akrai* p. 156 no. 6, 14 (I f. Ἐπίγονος II); (27) ~ ib. l. 14 (II s. Ἐπίγονος I)
—KAMARINA: (28) iv/iii BC Dubois, *IGDS* 122, 6 (Cordano, 'Camarina VII' 100) (f. Ἀρίστων)
—TAUROMENION: (29) c. 178 BC *IG* XIV 421 an. 63 (*SGDI* 5219)

**Ἐπίδαμος**
ARGOLIS:
—EPIDAUROS: (1) 32 AD Peek, *IAEpid* 45, 43 (f. Ἀπολλώνιος)
SICILY:
—GELA-PHINTIAS?: (2) ?v/iv BC Manganaro, *PdelP* forthcoming no. 12 (?s. Φειδίας)

**Ἐπίδικος**
ACHAIA?: (1) 37 AD *IG* VII 2711, 36 (f. —ος)

**Ἐπίδοξον**
ARKADIA:
—HERAIA: (1) ?iii-ii BC *SEG* XXII 326

**Ἐπίδοξος**
ARGOLIS:
—ARGOS: (1) ?271 BC *Syll*³ 419, 6 (f. Εὔδοξος)

**Ἐπίδοον**
ILLYRIA:
—EPIDAMNOS-DYRRHACHION (NR.)?: (1) ii BC *SEG* XXXVIII 572, 2; cf. *CRAI* 1991, p. 197 ff.; *L'Illyrie mérid.* 2 p. 206 (s. Θείρων)

**Ἐπίδρομος**
ARGOLIS:
—EPIDAUROS: (1) iii/ii BC *IG* IV (1)² 696 + Peek, *IAEpid* 304 (Ἐπίδρομ[ο]ς: f. Καλλικράτεια)

**Ἐπίδωρος**
SICILY:
—TAUROMENION:
——(Καλ.): (1) c. 169-147 BC *IG* XIV 421 an. 84; 421 an. 94 (*SGDI* 5219); *IGSI* 4 III (IV) an. 72? + *SEG* XXXIII 755; cf. XXXVIII 975 n. on l. 23: *IGSI* 4 III (IV), 19 an. 88 (Πολύξενος—Manganaro on 4 III an. 72: f. Ξένιος)

**Ἐπιείκης**
SICILY:
—KAMARINA: (1) s. v BC ib. 935, 2 (Arena, *Iscr. Sic.* II 147) (n. pr.?: s. Φάϋλλος)

**Ἐπιθάλης**
MESSENIA:
—MESSENE: (1) s. ii BC *SEG* XLI 341, 5 (f. Χάριππος)

**Ἐπιθυμήτη**
SICILY:
—SYRACUSE: (1) iii-v AD Barreca 385 + *Rend. Pont.* 22 (1946-7) p. 238 no. 40


**Ἐπίκαδος**
ILLYRIA: (1) 168 BC *RE* Supplbd. 3 (1) (Lat. Epicadus); (2) i BC ib. s.v. Asinius (12) (Lat. Asinius Epicadus: freed.); (3) ~ ib. s.v. Cornelius (150) (Lat. Cornelius Epicadus: freed.)
—APOLLONIA: (4) c. 250-50 BC Maier 38 (Ceka 3); Münsterberg Nachtr. p. 13 (coin) (Ceka 26) (pryt.); (5) imp. *IApoll* 204
—APOLLONIA*: (6) imp. ib. 29 (I f. Ἐπίκαδος II, Τευταία); (7) ~ ib. (II s. Ἐπίκαδος I)
—DIMALE: (8) c. 240-230 BC *IG* VII 282, 2 (*IOrop* 51) (f. Πλάτωρ)
—DIMALE*: (9) hell. *Iliria* 1982 (1), p. 120 no. 24 (tile)
—EPIDAMNOS-DYRRHACHION: (10) ii-i BC *IDyrrh* 236 (f. Ἡρακλείδας); (11) hell.-imp. ib. 74 (f. Ἀγαθίων); (12) ~ ib. 103 (f. Ἀνναία); (13) ~ ib. 172 (Ἐπίκ[αδος]: f. Ἀντ—); (14) ~ ib. 184 (s. Βέρσαντος); (15) ~ ib. 185 (Ἐπίκα[δ]ος: I f. Ἐπίκαδος II); (16) ~ ib. (Ἐπί[καδ]ος: II s. Ἐπίκαδος I); (17) ~ ib. 187 (s. Λύκος); (18) ~ ib. 298 (f. Μαλλίκα); (19) ~ ib. 344 (f. Περιγένης); (20) ~ ib. 353 (f. Πλάτωρ); (21) ~ ib. 495; (22) imp. ib. 110 (Ἐπίκ<ι>αδος: f. Ἀντις); (23) ~ ib. 186 (s. Εὐταξία)
—LYCHNIDOS?: (24) ii-i BC *SEG* I 254 (s. Λεύκιος)
—PARTHINI: (25) 168 BC *RE* Supplbd. 3 (2) (Lat. Epicadus)
S. ITALY (APULIA):
—VENUSIA*: (26) imp. *CIL* IX 542 (Lat. C. Murrasius Epicadus: freed.)
S. ITALY (CALABRIA):
—BRENTESION-BRUNDISIUM: (27) imp. ib. 6111 (Lat. C. Caesius Epicadus)

**Ἐπικαρπία**
ARGOLIS:
—ARGOS: (1) iii BC *SEG* XI 371, 6 (*GVI* 1328) (m. Κράτερος)
ILLYRIA:
—APOLLONIA: (2) ii BC *IApoll* 76; (3) imp. ib. 75
—EPIDAMNOS-DYRRHACHION: (4) hell.-imp. *IDyrrh* 188 (d. Ἱέρων); (5) ~ ib. 189 (d. Σωστρίων)
KERKYRA: (6) imp. *IG* IX (1) 909 (Ἐβ(ι)καρπία)
S. ITALY (CALABRIA):
—BRENTESION-BRUNDISIUM: (7) imp. *CIL* IX 67 (Lat. Aemilia Epicarpia)

**Ἐπίκατος**
EPIROS:
—BOUTHROTOS (PRASAIBOI): (1) a. 163 BC *IBouthrot* 44, 6

**Ἐπικλείδας**
LAKONIA:
—SPARTA: (1) c. 25-1 BC *SEG* XI 505, 1 (Bradford (1)) (-κλί-: s. Εὔδαμος)

**Ἐπικλῆς**
AIGINA: (1) ?f. iii AD *Alt-Ägina* I (2) p. 49 no. 43 (f. Αὐρ. Ἀλέξανδρος)
ARGOLIS:
—ARGOS:
——(Dionysioi): (2) f. iii BC *IG* IV (1) 529, 20
—HERMIONE: (3) vi/v BC *RE* (6) (Stephanis 858)
LAKONIA:
—SPARTA: (4) 411 BC Th. viii 107. 2; D.S. xiii 41. 1-2 (Poralla² 269)
MESSENIA:
—MESSENE: (5) ?i/ii AD *SEG* XLI 338, 5 (Τ. Φλ. Ἐπικλῆς)
SICILY:
—SYRACUSE: (6) s. vi BC ib. XII 406 + *LSAG*² p. 265 n. 5 (name); Guarducci, *Ep. Gr.* I p. 343 (-κλἔς)

**Ἐπίκορος**
S. ITALY (BRUTTIUM):
—PETELIA: (1) ?c. 475 BC *IGSI* 19, 7-8 (Landi, *DISMG* 171); *LSAG*² p. 261 no. 28 (date)

## Ἐπικουρίδας

S. Italy (Calabria):
—taras-tarentum: (2) iii-ii BC SEG xxx 1219 (Landi, DISMG 207) (f. Λέων)

## Ἐπικουρίδας

Messenia:
—messene: (1) 99 AD SEG XLI 336, 6, 8 (s. Φιλατάδας, f. Φιλατάδας)

## Ἐπίκουρος

Korinthia:
—sikyon: (1) 344 BC IG II² 3068, 4 (Skalet 111; Stephanis 859) ([Ἐ]πίκουρος)

## Ἐπικράδιος

Arkadia:
—mantineia-antigoneia: (1) f. v BC RE (-); Moretti, Olymp. 193

## Ἐπικράτεια

Aigina: (1) imp. IG IV (1) 76 (-τηα: m. Φίλα)
Argolis:
—argos: (2) ii BC SEG XLII 279, 14

## Ἐπικράτης

Achaia:
—pharai: (1) 134 or 130 BC SGDI 2683, 3, 6 (s. Καμβίας)
Aigina: (2) c. 225 BC SEG XI 414, 36 (Perlman E.5) (f. Σῖμος)
Aitolia:
—thermos*: (3) s. iii BC IG IX (1)² (1) 60 IV, 4
Akarnania:
—palairos: (4) ii BC ib. IX (1)² (2) 451, 23
—thyrreion: (5) c. 200 BC ib. 295; (6) ii BC ib. 247, 6 (s. Δωρίμαχος)
Argolis:
—argos: (7) s. iv BC CEG II 814 (f. Κλεαίνετος); (8) iv/iii BC SEG XXVI 445, 4 (Perlman E.12) (f. Δρύμος); (9) iii BC IG IV (1) 618 II, 7 (s. Γαψίας); (10) f. iii BC ib. 529, 17 (Ἐπικρά[της]); (11) 284 BC ib. XI (2) 105, 26 (Stephanis 862) (Ἐ. Τελληνοκράτης); (12) ?253 BC Nachtergael, Les Galates 10, 22 (Stephanis 866) (s. Νικομήδης); (13) c. 172 BC Syll³ 644 I, 11 (Perlman A.26); (14) c. 146-32 BC BMC Pelop. p. 145 no. 113 (coin); (15) f. i BC Unp. (Ch. Kritzas) (f. Δάμαρχος)
——(A-): (16) ii-i BC Mnem. NS 47 (1919) p. 164 no. 9, 8 (f. —ος)
——(Pamphyloi): (17) ?c. 475 BC SEG XIII 239, 5; LSAG² p. 169 no. 22 (date) (-τε̄ς: s. Ρίνων)
—epidauros: (18) iv BC IG IV (1)² 187; (19) ~ ib. 252 (f. Δαμοσθένης); (20) iv-iii BC ib. 5 (f. —ας); (21) 360 BC CID II 4 II, 46 (f. Παγκρά-της); (22) i BC-i AD IG IV (1)² 32; cf. Peek, IAEpid 5
——Selegeis: (23) c. 335-325 BC IG IV (1)² 108, 142 (Ἐπικ[ρ]άτης); (24) m. iii BC ib. 96, 10 (Perlman E.3); Perlman p. 63 f. (date)
—epidauros*: (25) c. 335-325 BC IG IV (1)² 106 II, 137
—nemea*: (26) hell. SEG XXIX 349 g + Nemea Guide p. 188 (kalos)
—phleious: (27) iii BC IG IV (1) 459
Arkadia:
—mantineia-antigoneia: (28) ?iv BC ib. v (2) 294 (s. Ἐξακίδας, f. Θέμιστος)
—tegea: (29) i AD ib. 46, 8 (Ἐπικράτης)
Epiros:
—ambrakia: (30) iv BC RE (21); CAF 2 p. 282
—bouthrotos (prasaiboi): (31) a. 163 BC IBouthrot 36, 21 (SEG XXXVIII 495) (s. Νικό-μαχος); (32) ~ IBouthrot 101, 2 (f. Ἀντίπατρος)
Kerkyra: (33) iii BC SEG XXXVIII 457 (f. Μέ-λισσος)
Korinthia:
—sikyon: (34) hell. Memnonion 202 ?= (35)
—sikyon?: (35) hell. ib. 209 (s. Νικόλαος) ?= (34)

Lakonia:
—kythera: (36) hell.-imp. IG V (1) 942, 2 (s. Ἀβρίας)
—sparta: (37) c. 80-90 AD ib. 674, 6 (Bradford (-)) (f. —ιππίδας)
Messenia:
—messene: (38) ?i BC PAE 1969, p. 100 a, 10
—thouria: (39) ii-i BC IG V (1) 1385, 1 (s. Δα-μοκλῆς); (40) f. ii BC SEG XI 972, 34 (s. Σάων)
S. Italy (Bruttium):
—rhegion: (41) iv-iii BC IG XIV 2400. 3 (tile)
Sicily:
—agyrion: (42) f. i BC Cic., In Verr. II ii 25 (Lat. Epicrates)
—bidis: (43) f. i BC ib. 53 ff.; 140 (Lat. Epicrates)
—naxos: (44) f. v BC SEG XXXVIII 953. 1 (Arena, Iscr. Sic. III 76); cf. L'Incidenza dell'Antico pp. 418-9 (f. Πρώταρχος)
—neaiton: (45) iii/ii BC SGDI 5260 (Sic. Gymn. 16 (1963) p. 55); cf. Rupes loquentes p. 454 (f. Φιλιστίων)
—syracuse: (46) hell.? IG XIV 10 (SGDI 3235) (s. Ἀγέας)

## Ἐπικρατίδας

Messenia:
—thouria: (1) f. ii BC SEG XI 972, 82 (f. Τρί-τιος)
S. Italy (Calabria):
—taras-tarentum: (2) 472 BC Moretti, Olymp. 230; cf. FGrH 415 F 1, 28 (name) ([Ἐπι]κρατίδας—Jacoby)

## Ἐπικρατῖνος

Argolis:
—argos: (1) ?254 BC Nachtergael, Les Galates 9, 24 (Stephanis 867) (s. Νικομήδης)

## Ἐπικράτις

Lakonia:
—messa?: (1) imp. IG V (1) 1280, 11 (Ἐ. πρεσ-βυτ.: d. Δάμαρχος)
—teuthrone: (2) imp. ib. 1220 a (d. Δάμαρχος)
Triphylia:
—lepreon: (3) iii/ii BC SEG XXII 360, 4

## Ἐπικρέτης

Arkadia:
—tegea: (1) f. iii BC IG V (2) 35, 12 (f. —σίας)

## Ἐπικτᾶς

Arkadia:
—tegea: (1) ii AD ib. 55, 27 (f. Σπένδων); (2) ~ ib. l. 64-5 (-πει-: f. Ζωσιμᾶς, Λουκᾶς); (3) ii-iii AD ib. 215 b; (4) 165 AD ib. 50, 10 (s. Ρούφος); (5) ~ ib. l. 34 (f. Δάμων)
Lakonia:
—oitylos: (6) imp. ib. V (1) 1300
—sparta: (7) ii AD ib. 159, 34 (Bradford (1)); (8) c. 175-210 AD IG V (1) 479, 2; SEG XXXVI 360, 6; BSA 81 (1986) pp. 324 no. 3; 329-30 (ident., date) (Bradford (2)) (Σέξ. Πομπ. Ἐ.)

## Ἐπικτέας

Argolis:
—argos?: (1) v BC IG IV (1) 552, 12 ([Ἐ]πικτέας)

## Ἐπίκτησις

Achaia:
—tritaia: (1) imp. Achaean Grave Stelai 9 (d. Ἐ—ων); (2) ~ ib. 10
Aigina: (3) imp. IG IV (1) 78 (m. Ἀπάτη)
Argolis:
—argos: (4) i AD BCH 33 (1909) p. 460 no. 24
—epidauros: (5) ?ii AD IG IV (1)² 33 ([Ἐπί]κτησις)
—hermione: (6) ?ii-i BC ib. IV (1) 731 III, 8 (d. Σωσίδαμος)
Arkadia:
—tegea: (7) ?i AD ib. V (2) 213

Dalmatia:
—rizon (nr.): (8) imp. IGR I 553 (Μουκ. Ἐ.)
Epiros:
—nikopolis: (9) imp. AEMÖ 15 (1892) p. 127 no. 1 (Sarikakis 44) (d. Ἵππαρχος)
Illyria:
—epidamnos-dyrrhachion: (10) hell.-imp. IDyrrh 32; (11) ~ ib. 138 (m. Βάτουνα); (12) ~ ib. 190 (Ἐπικρησις—ed. pr.: d. Ἐννεάτωρ); (13) ~ ib. 191; (14) ~ ib. 192 (d. Τρίτος); (15) ~ ib. 193 (d. Φίλιππος); (16) ~ ib. 227 (m. Ζώπυρος)
Kerkyra: (17) imp. IG IX (1) 910 (-κτε-)
Korinthia:
—korinth: (18) ii-i BC ib. II² 9067 (d. Δαμά-τριος)
Lakonia:
—kythera: (19) ?f. iv BC ib. 9111 (d. Ὄνασος)
S. Italy (Calabria):
—brentesion-brundisium: (20) imp. NScav 1900, p. 245 no. 2; cf. Rend. Linc. 24 (1969) p. 172 no. 4
S. Italy (Campania):
—dikaiarchia-puteoli: (21) imp. CIL X 2385 (Lat. Epictesis); (22) ~ ib. 2775 (Lat. Nicinia Epictesis); (23) ~ ib. 2784 (Lat. Numeria Epictesis); (24) ~ ib. 2964 (Lat. Sittia Epictesis); (25) ~ ib. 3031 (Lat. Turronia Epictesis: m. L. Turronius Adiutor)
—pompeii: (26) i BC-i AD ib. IV 1286 (Lat. Epictesis)
S. Italy (Lucania):
—volcei: (27) imp. IItal III (1) 53 (CIL X 426) (Lat. Epictesis: d. Ἐπίκτητος, Νέμεσις)
Sicily:
—katane: (28) imp. ib. 7086 (Lat. Pompeia Epictesis)
—syracuse: (29) iii-v AD Führer p. 817 n.

## Ἐπίκτητος

Argolis:
—epidauros*: (1) ii AD IG IV (1)² 683
—hermione: (2) ii AD SEG XI 385, 2 (s. Μυρ-τίλος); (3) ~ ib. XVII 163, 1 (s. Λούκιος, Θεο-δώρα); (4) ~ ib. l. 2 (f. Λούκιος); (5) iii AD IG IV (1) 726, 4 (s. Λούκιος)
Arkadia:
—tegea: (6) 165 AD ib. V (2) 50, 79 (s. Ἀλέ-ξανδρος); (7) ?182 AD ib. 84 ([Ἐ]πίκτητος: f. Ἡδύμη)
Elis:
—olympia*: (8) 28-24 BC IvOl 64, 29 (?s. Ἡρα-κλείδης: Δου.); (9) ~ ib. l. 30 (?s. Ἀφροδίσιος: Δου.)
Korinthia:
—korinth: (10) ii-iii AD Corinth IV (2) p. 208 no. 730; SEG XXVII 35. 7 (lamps); (11) m. ii AD IG VII 1773, 15 (Stephanis 868) (Αἰμίλιος Ἐ.)
—tenea: (12) c. 150-175 AD Corinth VIII (3) 228 a, 2 (f. Θαύμαστος)
Lakonia:
—gytheion: (13) imp. IG V (1) 1192 (Κλ. Ἐ.); (14) f. ii AD ib. 1170, 4 (Ἐπίκτ[ητος]: s. Ἀγα-θόπους)
—sparta: (15) i BC-i AD ib. 652, 5 (Bradford (1)) (s. Φιλόστρατος); (16) i/ii AD IG V (1) 97, 4; 674, 5 + SEG XI 842; 524, 4?; 564, 4; 597, 7? (Bradford (3)) (f. Ἀριστομένης); (17) f. ii AD IG V (1) 763 (Papaefthimiou p. 131 no. 2; Bradford (2))
S. Italy (Apulia):
—luceria: (18) imp. CIL IX 812 (Lat. A. Pilius Epictetus: f. Pilia Valeria); (19) ~ ib. 842 (Lat. Epictetus)
S. Italy (Bruttium):
—kroton: (20) imp. NScav 1921, p. 495 (Lat. Epictet[us])
S. Italy (Calabria):
—leuka*: (21) imp. SEG XXVIII 784
—rudiae: (22) ii-iii AD Susini, Fonti Salento p. 135 no. 81 (Lat. Epictetus)

S. Italy (Campania):
—dikaiarchia-puteoli: (23) imp. CIL x 2120 (Lat. Attius Aepictetus)
—neapolis: (24) i AD IG xiv 720 (INap 8); cf. Leiwo p. 161 no. 134 (M. Μάριος Ἐ.); (25) ii AD IG xiv 790 (INap 128); cf. Leiwo p. 106 no. 67 (Λάρκιος Ἐπίκτητο[s])
—pompeii: (26) i BC-i AD CIL IV 9188 (Castrèn 121. 5) (Lat. C[oe]lius Epictetus)
—salernum: (27) i AD IItal I (1) 217 (CIL x 624) (Lat. D. Petronius Epictetus: f. D. Petronius Mercurius); (28) 121 AD IItal I (1) 4 (CIL x 514) (Lat. Q. –nius Epictetus)
S. Italy (Lucania):
—volcei: (29) imp. IItal III (1) 53 (CIL x 426) (Lat. Epictetus: f. Ἐπίκτησις)

**Ἐπικτώ**
Arkadia:
—tegea: (1) imp. IG v (2) 218

**Ἐπικύδης**
Argolis:
—argos*: (1) ii/i BC BCH 33 (1909) p. 176 no. 2, 3 (f. Ἱέρων)
—hermione: (2) iii BC IG IV (1) 729 II, 17 (s. Δαμόκριτος)
Lakonia:
—sparta: (3) ?vii/vi BC Hdt. vi 86; Paus. ii 18. 2 (Poralla² 270) (f. Γλαῦκος); (4) 427 BC IG v (1) 1231, 10 (Poralla² 271)
Sicily:
—syracuse: (5) 410 BC X., HG i 1. 29 (f. Δά-μαρχος); (6) b. 212 BC Liv. xxv 28. 5 (Lat. Epicydes Sindon); (7) 214-210 BC RE (4); (8) 208 BC IMM 72, 2 (Dubois, IGDS 97) (s. Ξεν—)

**Ἐπικυδίδας**
Lakonia:
—sparta: (1) 422 BC Th. v 12. 1 (Poralla² 272); (2) c. 405 BC Paus. x 9. 10; cf. ML 95; CEG II 819 (Poralla² 274) (Ἐπικυρίδας—mss.) ?= (3); (3) 394-378 BC X., HG iv 2. 2; v 4. 39; Plu., Ages. 15 (Poralla² 273) (Ἐπιλυτίδας—HG v) ?= (2)

**Ἐπιλάνθανος**
Sicily:
—zankle-messana: (1) imp. CIL x 6983 (Lat. Epilantanus)

**Ἐπίλαος**
Akarnania:
—derion: (1) 263-262 BC IG IX (1)² (1) 3 A, 22-3

**Ἐπιλήναιος**
Korinthia:
—korinth: (1) ?iii AD Hesp. 63 (1994) pp. 116 ff. no. 5 col. IV, 2 (lead) (Ἐπιλήναι[ος])

**Ἐπίλυτος**
S. Italy (Campania):
—neapolis: (1) i BC/i AD SEG IV 96 (INap 152, 2); cf. Leiwo pp. 62 ff. (f. Πακέα); (2) ~ SEG IV 96 (INap 152, 4); cf. Leiwo p. 62 ff. (f. Λάρχιος); (3) ~ SEG IV 96 (INap 152, 5); cf. Leiwo pp. 62 ff. (f. Ἀριστόλη); (4) ~ SEG IV 96 (INap 152, 7); cf. Leiwo pp. 62 ff. (f. Τρέβιος); (5) ~ SEG IV 96 (INap 152, 3); cf. Leiwo pp. 62 ff. (I f. Ἐπίλυτος II); (6) ~ SEG IV 96 (INap 152, 6); cf. Leiwo pp. 62 ff. (I f. Ἐπίλυτος II); (7) ~ SEG IV 96 (INap 152, 3); cf. Leiwo pp. 62 ff. (II s. Ἐπίλυτος I); (8) ~ SEG IV 96 (INap 152, 6); cf. Leiwo pp. 62 ff. (II s. Ἐπίλυτος I); (9) ~ SEG IV 97 (INap 102); cf. Leiwo p. 62 no. 3 (f. Βίβιος); (10) ~ SEG IV 98 (INap 116); cf. Leiwo pp. 62 ff. (s. Τρέβιος); (11) ~ SEG IV 99 (INap 115, 4); cf. Leiwo pp. 62 ff. (f. Βίβιος); (12) ~ SEG IV 99 (INap 115, 5); cf. Leiwo pp. 62


ff. (f. Μονίς); (13) ~ SEG IV 99 (INap 115, 1); cf. Leiwo pp. 62 ff. (I f. Ἐπίλυτος II); (14) ~ SEG IV 99 (INap 115, 1); cf. Leiwo pp. 62 ff. (II s. Ἐπίλυτος I); (15) ~ SEG IV 100 (INap 114); cf. Leiwo pp. 62 ff. (s. Βίβιος); (16) ~ INap 81, 1; cf. Leiwo p. 141 (Ἐπίλ[υτος]: I f. Ἐπίλυτος II); (17) ~ INap 81, 1; cf. Leiwo p. 141 (II s. Ἐπίλυτος I); (18) ~ INap 172, 4; cf. Leiwo p. 77 no. 20 (f. Δίκα)
—neapolis?: (19) f. iv BC X., Oec. xi 4; cf. Leiwo p. 63 (name)

**Ἐπιλώϊον?**
Sicily:
—apollonia: (1) hell.-imp. IG xiv 360 (Εὐλω-ίων, —πλωιον (apogr.): d. Εὔξενος)

**Ἐπιμαχίς**
S. Italy (Campania):
—dikaiarchia-puteoli: (1) ?ii-iii AD CIL x 1731 (Lat. Aurelia Epimachis)

**Ἐπίμαχος**
Korinthia:
—korinth: (1) imp. JÖAI 15 (1912) p. 55 no. 27, 10 (Νούμμιος Ἐ.)
Peloponnese: (2) c. 192 BC SEG XIII 327, 19 (Ἐπίμ[αχος]?: f. Μνασικλῆς)
S. Italy (Campania):
—dikaiarchia-puteoli: (3) imp. CIL x 8181 (Lat. Epimachus: I f. Ἐπίμαχος II); (4) ~ ib. (Lat. Epimachus: II s. Ἐπίμαχος I)

**Ἐπιμέλεια**
Lakonia: (1) ii BC IG II² 9148 (Bradford (-))

**Ἐπιμέλης**
Elis:
—olympia*: (1) s. i BC IvOl 66, 7 (?s. Πρέπων)

**Ἐπιμένης**
Argolis:
—argos: (1) c. 458 BC IG I³ 1149, 93 (['Ἐπ]ιμένης)
Arkadia:
—orchomenos*: (2) ?ii BC ib. v (2) 345, 23 (s. Ἀρχ—: date—LGPN)

**Ἐπιμενίδας**
Sicily:
—syracuse:
——(Μνε.): (1) 208 BC IMM 72, 43 (Dubois, IGDS 97)

**Ἐπινίκη**
Sicily:
—syracuse: (1) imp. CIL x 7148 (Lat. [Co]rnelia Epinice)

**Ἐπινικίδας**
Lakonia: (1) 96-98 AD IG v (1) 1161, 7 (-νει-: s. Φιλοχαρῖνος)
—sparta: (2) i BC/i AD? ib. 264 (Artemis Orthia p. 298 no. 4; Bradford (-)) (f. Τιμοκράτης)

**Ἐπινίκιος**
S. Italy (Campania):
—dikaiarchia-puteoli: (1) imp. CIL x 2046 (Lat. M. Amulius Epinicius: s. Σῶσος, Amulia Maximilla)
—nola: (2) imp. ib. 1325 (Lat. Epinicius)

**Ἐπίνικος**
Achaia:
—patrai: (1) i AD ib. III 500; cf. 7256 (Lat. M. Lollius Epinicus)
Aigina: (2) ?iii-iv AD Alt-Ägina I (2) p. 48 no. 34 (Ἐπίνεικ[ος])
Aitolia:
—boukation?: (3) imp. IG IX (1)² (1) 114
—daianes: (4) 161 BC ib. 100, 8
—kalydon: (5) 263 BC ib. 17, 115


—kasilioi: (6) s. ii BC SEG XXV 621, 7 (f. Ἀρ-κίσων)
—pholantioi: (7) s. iii BC IG IX (1)² (1) 24, 11, 13 (f. Ἀγέμαχος)
—potana: (8) 139 BC SGDI 2137, 15 (s. Καλ-λίμαχος)
Akarnania:
—stratos: (9) 208 BC IG IX (1)² (1) 31, 66 (f. Φιλλέας)
Argolis:
—argos*: (10) ii BC SEG XLII 279, 22 (slave/freed.?)
—hermione: (11) iii BC IG IV (1) 729 I, 22 (s. Λαχάρης)
Elis: (12) c. 146-32 BC BM coin 1920 5-15-92; Coll. McClean 6583 (coins); (13) 20-16 BC IvOl 65, 10 (I f. Ἐπίνικος II); (14) ~ ib. l. 10 (II s. Ἐπίνικος I); (15) 68 AD ib. 287, 2 (Δ(έκμος) Ἰούνιος Ἐ.)
Epiros:
—zmaratha: (16) s. iv BC IG IV (1)² 95, 74 (Perlman E.2); Perlman pp. 46-9 (date) (Ἐπίν(ι)κος: s. Νίκανδρος)
Messenia:
—messene: (17) hell. SEG XXXI 346 (Ἐπί-νικ[ος]); (18) 31 BC-14 AD ib. XXIII 207, 4, 39-40, 42; (19) 84 AD ib. XLI 334, 2 (f. Σῶι-σις)
—thouria: (20) ii-i BC IG v (1) 1385, 2 (s. Φί-λαιθος)
S. Italy (Campania):
—pompeii: (21) i BC-i AD CIL IV 8299 (Lat. [Ep]inicus?)

**Ἐπίνοια**
S. Italy (Campania):
—neapolis: (1) i BC/i AD INap 161

**Ἐπίνομος**
Argolis:
—epidauros*: (1) c. 290-270 BC SEG XXV 402, 56
Korinthia:
—sikyon?: (2) c. 325-300 BC IG XI (4) 511; cf. Stephanis 1411 (f. Κλεαγόρας)

**Ἐπίξενος**
Sicily:
—akrai: (1) ii-i BC SGDI 3246, 44 (Akrai pp. 152-3 no. 2; Dubois, IGDS 109) (f. Ζώπυρος)
—tauromenion: (2) c. 189 BC IG xiv 421 an. 52 (SGDI 5219) (f. Σῖμος)

**Ἐπίπολις**
S. Italy (Campania):
—neapolis: (1) iii-iv AD IG xiv 826. 12 (INap 224-5)

**Ἐπισθένης**
Argolis:
—epidauros: (1) c. 370-335 BC IG IV (1)² 103, [23], 98; Peek, IAEpid 52 A, 11, 15, 21; BSA 61 (1966) p. 271 no. 4 A, 6, 20, 21
Arkadia:
—tegea: (2) s. iii BC IG v (2) 116, 4 (s. Λυσί-δαμος)
——(Apolloniatai): (3) iv/iii BC ib. 38, 36 (f. Παντισθένης)
Sicily:
—kamarina: (4) f. v BC Cordano, Tessere Pubbliche 77 (-νēς: f. Γελ—)
—tauromenion: (5) c. 175 BC IG xiv 421 an. 66 (SGDI 5219) (f. Θεόχρηστος)

**Ἐπισκοπιανός**
Korinthia:
—korinth: (1) vi-vii AD SEG XXIX 311, 8 (?f. Θεόδωρος)

**Ἐπίσκοπος**
S. Italy (Bruttium):
—kroton*: (1) 200 AD NScav 1921, p. 495 (Lat. Episcopus (n. pr.?): imp. freed.)

**Ἐπίστασις**
SICILY:
—KAMARINA: (1) f. v BC Cordano, *Tessere Pubbliche* 142 (Ἐπίσστα[σις]—ed., Ἐπίσστρ[ατος]?: f. Δαμέας)

**Ἐπίστατος**
LAKONIA:
—LAS: (1) vi/v BC Giannakopoulou, *Gytheion* pp. 51-3
—SPARTA: (2) iv BC *SEG* 11 158 (Bradford (-))

**Ἐπιστήμη**
S. ITALY (CAMPANIA):
—POMPEII: (1) i BC-i AD *CIL* IV 4300 (Lat. Episte(me?): name—Solin)

**Ἐπιστόλη**
S. ITALY (APULIA):
—CANUSIUM: (1) imp. *Epig. Rom. di Canosa* 176 (Lat. Epist[ole])

**Ἐπίστρατος**
AKARNANIA: (1) 220 BC Plb. iv 11. 6
ARGOLIS:
—EPIDAUROS: (2) iv BC *IG* IV (1)² 175; 176; 177 ?= (4); (3) ~ ib. 317 (f. Ἀρχέλοχος); (4) c. 370 BC ib. 102, 28, 40 ?= (5) (2); (5) c. 370-365 BC Peek, *IAEpid* 52 A, 82-3 ([Ἐπ]ίστρατος) ?= (4)
ARKADIA:
—MANTINEIA-ANTIGONEIA:
——(Posoidaia): (6) m. iv BC *IG* v (2) 271, 16 (f. Σακλῆς)
—MEGALOPOLIS: (7) ?145 BC ib. 439, 50 (Ἐπίστρατος: s. Θρασύμαχος)
—TEGEA: (8) i AD ib. 46, 9
LAKONIA:
—OITYLOS: (9) iii/ii BC ib. v (1) 1295, 2 (Bradford (2)) (Ἐπίσ[τρ]ατ[ος])
—SPARTA: (10) i BC/i AD *IG* v (1) 48, 4; 212, 48 (Bradford (3)) (f. Πρατόνικος)
LEUKAS: (11) 216 BC *IG* IX (1)² (2) 583, 19, 63 (s. Φίλιστος)

**Ἐπίστροφος**
ILLYRIA:
—EPIDAMNOS-DYRRHACHION: (1) vi BC Hdt. vi 127. 2 (f. Ἀμφίμναστος)

**Ἐπίσυλος**
S. ITALY (BRUTTIUM):
—KROTON: (1) iv BC Iamb., *VP* 267 (*FVS* 1 p. 446)

**Ἐπιτάδας**
AKARNANIA:
—STRATOS: (1) ?153 BC *IG* IX (1)² (1) 109, 6 (Ἐπιτά[δας])
LAKONIA:
—SPARTA: (2) 425 BC Th. iv 8. 9; 31. 2; 33. 1; 38. 1 (Poralla² 275) (s. Μόλοβρος)

**Ἐπιτάδευς**
LAKONIA:
—SPARTA: (1) ?f. iv BC Plu., *Agis* 5 (Poralla² 276)

**Ἐπιτέλης**
ACHAIA:
—DYME*: (1) c. 219 BC *SGDI* 1612, 17-18 (s. Κόνων, f. Κλέων)
AKARNANIA:
—OINIADAI: (2) iii BC *IG* IX (1)² (2) 421 (f. Ξενίας)
—THYRREION: (3) ii BC ib. 247, 10 (f. Σωτέλης)
ARGOLIS:
—ARGOS: (4) f. iv BC Paus. iv 26. 7-8 (s. Αἰσχίνας)
ARKADIA:
—MANTINEIA-ANTIGONEIA: (5) ?iii BC *IG* v (2) 319, 41

—TEGEA: (6) s. v BC ib. 175, 4 (-λ̄ες); (7) m. iv BC ib. 6, 60; (8) ?218 BC ib. 16, 14; (9) ii BC *SEG* XXIII 233; (10) ~ *EILakArk* 14 (?f. Καλλίας)
——(Athaneatai): (11) s. iv BC *IG* v (2) 41, 33 (f. Καλλίας); (12) m. iii BC ib. 36, 85 (f. Ἀγαθοκλῆς)
MESSENIA:
—KORONE: (13) ii BC ib. v (1) 1397, 4
—THOURIA: (14) s. iii BC ib. 1386, 10 (f. Ξένων); (15) ii-i BC ib. 1385, 8, 9 (f. Σωσικλῆς, Ὀνάτας)

**Ἐπιτελίδας**
LAKONIA:
—SPARTA: (1) 580 BC Moretti, *Olymp.* 91 (Poralla² 277)

**Ἐπίτεξος**
AIGINA: (1) s. vi BC *AA* 1993, p. 579 no. 13 (vase) (-χσος)

**Ἐπιτευκτᾶς**
LAKONIA:
—SPARTA: (1) ii AD *IG* v (1) 159, 40 (Bradford (2)) (Ἐπ[ιτ]ευκτᾶς: I f. Ἐπιτευκτᾶς II); (2) ~ *IG* v (1) 159, 40 (Bradford (1)) (Ἐπ[ιτ]ευκτᾶς: II s. Ἐπιτευκτᾶς I)

**Ἐπιτευκτικός**
LAKONIA:
—SPARTA: (1) c. 125 AD *SEG* XI 575, 6 (Bradford (1)) (s. Δημ—); (2) c. 175-210 AD *SEG* XI 555, 11 (Bradford (4)) ([Ἐπιτευ]κτικός?: s. Σω—); (3) c. 225-250 AD *SEG* XI 806 a, 9 (Bradford (3)) (I s. Κλησᾶς, f. Μ. Αὐρ. Ἐπιτευκτικός II); (4) ~ *SEG* XI 806 a, 9 (Bradford (2)) (Μ. Αὐρ. Ἐ.: II s. Ἐπιτευκτικός I)

**Ἐπίτευξις**
LAKONIA:
—PYRRHICHOS: (1) imp. *IG* v (1) 1287 c
S. ITALY (CALABRIA):
—BRENTESION-BRUNDISIUM: (2) imp. *CIL* IX 107 (Lat. Epiteuxis)
S. ITALY (CAMPANIA):
—DIKAIARCHIA-PUTEOLI: (3) ?ii AD ib. X 2129 (Lat. Aufidia Epiteuxis)
—MISENUM*: (4) ?i-ii AD ib. 3584 (Lat. Iulia Epiteuxis)
—SURRENTUM: (5) imp. *NScav* 1928, p. 213 (Lat. Valeria Epiteusis)
SICILY:
—SYRACUSE: (6) iii-v AD ib. 1915, p. 206 (Lat. Epiteyxis)

**Ἐπιτιμάδας**
ARGOLIS:
—ARGOS?: (1) 468 BC Moretti, *Olymp.* 241; *FGrH* 415. 1, 39 ([Ἐ]πιτιμάδας)

**Ἐπιτιμίδας**
KORINTHIA:
—KORINTH: (1) ii/i BC *Corinth* VIII (3) 47 a

**Ἐπίτιμος**
ARGOLIS:
—ARGOS: (1) c. 458 BC *IG* I³ 1149, 16
ARKADIA:
—TEGEA: (2) ?i AD ib. v (2) 216
EPIROS:
—AMBRAKIA: (3) ?257 BC Nachtergael, *Les Galates* 7, 63

**Ἐπιτρέπων**
S. ITALY (CAMPANIA):
—HERCULANEUM: (1) i BC-i AD *CIL* X 1403 d II, 11 (Lat. C. Vibius Epitrepon)

**Ἐπιτύγχανος**
ARGOLIS:
—PITYOUSSA: (1) byz. *SEG* XVII 170, 4; cf. *TMByz* 9 (1985) p. 371 no. 128 (s. Ἰωάννης)

ARKADIA:
—MANTINEIA-ANTIGONEIA: (2) m. ii AD *IG* v (2) 312 (-τύν-: f. Ἰσόχρυσος)
KORINTHIA:
—KORINTH: (3) f. ii AD *Ag.* VII p. 97 no. 296; *Corinth* IV (2) p. 204 no. 691; *SEG* XXVII 35. 8; 36. 5 (lamps) (Ἐπειτύγχανος—Corinth)
S. ITALY (APULIA):
—CANUSIUM: (4) ii-iii AD *Epig. Rom. di Canosa* 179 (*CIL* IX 2106) (Lat. Q. Saccidius Epitincanus: f. Q. Saccidius Primus, C. Saccidius Primus)
S. ITALY (BRUTTIUM):
—RHEGION*: (5) imp. *IG* XIV 618, 6 (-τύνχα-: slave?)
S. ITALY (CALABRIA):
—BRENTESION-BRUNDISIUM*: (6) imp. *NScav* 1897, p. 327 no. 10 = *Epigraphica* 25 (1963) p. 42 no. 17; cf. 42 (1980) p. 154 (Lat. Epitynchanus: freed.); (7) 108 AD *CIL* IX 36 (Lat. C. Fulvius Epitynchanus: freed.)
—LUPIAE: (8) ii AD *NScav* 1957, p. 193 (Susini, *Fonti Salento* p. 145 no. 93) (Lat. Sex. Silettius Epitynchanus: f. Sex. Silettius Maximus)
S. ITALY (CAMPANIA):
—DIKAIARCHIA-PUTEOLI: (9) ?ii AD *CIL* X 3126 (Lat. M. Ulpius Epitynchanus)
—POMPEII: (10) i BC-i AD ib. IV 5088 (-τύνχα-); (11) ~ *NScav* 1896, p. 229 (seal) (Castrèn 394. 1) (Lat. C. Stlaccius Epitynchanus)
SICILY:
—SYRACUSE: (12) iii-v AD Strazzulla 356 (Wessel 1192); (13) ~ Ferrua, *NG* 260

**Ἐπιτυγχάνων**
ARGOLIS:
—EPIDAUROS: (1) 151 AD *IG* IV (1)² 388, 2 (-τυν-: s. Ἀρίστων)
ARKADIA:
—MANTINEIA-ANTIGONEIA: (2) ii AD ib. v (2) 277 (Κορν. Ἐπιτυγχάν<ι>ων)
LAKONIA:
—SPARTA: (3) c. 80-120 AD ib. v (1) 20 B, 1; 147, 7; *SEG* XI 574, [10] (Bradford (2)) (-τυν-: s. Κλεώνυμος); (4) c. 120 AD *SEG* XI 518, 4 (Bradford (4)) (Ἐ[πι]τυνχάν[ων]: s. —κρ]άτης); (5) c. 125-150 AD *IG* v (1) 64, 2; *SEG* XI 575, 5 (Bradford (3)) (Ἐπιτυνχάνων—SEG: s. Ὀνησιφόρος); (6) c. 140-145 AD *SEG* XI 524, 20 (Bradford (1)) ([Ἐπιτυγχά]ν(ω)ν?: II s. Ἐπιτυγχάνων I); (7) ~ *SEG* XI 524, [20]? (Bradford (5)) (I f. Ἐπιτυγχάνων II)

**Ἐπιτυχία**
S. ITALY (CAMPANIA):
—DIKAIARCHIA-PUTEOLI*: (1) imp. *Eph. Ep.* VIII 400 (Lat. Decia Epitychia: freed.)
SICILY:
—THERMAI HIMERAIAI: (2) ii AD *Epigraphica* 3 (1941) p. 262 no. 21 (*ILat. Term. Imer.* 60) (Lat. Caninia Epitychia)

**Ἐπιτυχίων**
ELIS:
—OLYMPIA*: (1) f. ii AD *IvOl* 92, 21 (?s. Ἀπολλοφάνης: slave?)

**Ἐπίτυχος**
KERKYRA: (1) f. iii BC *IG* IX (1) 691, 15 (*Iscr. Gr. Verona* p. 22 A)

**Ἐπιφανέας**
ACHAIA:
—KARYNEIA: (1) i BC-i AD *Achaean Grave Stelai* 25

**Ἐπιφάνεια**
ARGOLIS:
—HERMIONE: (1) iii AD *SEG* XXIV 1081, 8 (-νια)
KORINTHIA:
—KORINTH: (2) ii-iii AD ib. XI 141 b, 4 (-νηα)
S. ITALY (CAMPANIA):
—DIKAIARCHIA-PUTEOLI*: (3) imp. *CIL* X 1980 (Lat. Valeria Epiphania: freed.)

**Ἐπιφάνης**

SICILY:
—SYRACUSE: (**4**) iii-v AD Strazzulla 339 (Wessel 226) (-νια); (**5**) ~ Strazzulla 405 (Barreca 129) (-νια)

**Ἐπιφάνης**

ILLYRIA:
—EPIDAMNOS-DYRRHACHION: (**1**) hell.-imp. IDyrrh 194 (Ἐπιφάνε (voc.))
KEPHALLENIA:
—SAME?: (**2**) ?ii AD Clem. Al., Strom. iii 5. 2 (s. Ἀλεξάνδρεια: dub.)

**Ἐπιφάνιος**

ARGOLIS:
—HERMIONE*: (**1**) vi AD PAE 1955, p. 236; cf. TMByz 9 (1985) pp. 297-8 no. 39 (bp.)
KORINTHIA:
—KORINTH: (**2**) byz. Corinth VIII (3) 568, 7; cf. TMByz 9 (1985) p. 362 no. 28
SICILY:
—SYRACUSE: (**3**) iii-v AD IG XIV 86 (Strazzulla 27; Wessel 1104) (Ἐπει-: ?f. Βικτωρῖνος)

**Ἐπίφρων**

ACHAIA:
—PELLENE: (**1**) v/iv BC Milet I (1) 13, 10 f. (s. Φιλόδωρος)
AKARNANIA:
—PALAIROS: (**2**) c. 325-315 BC Hesp. 57 (1988) p. 148 A, 19 (SEG XXXVI 331); cf. Hesp. 48 (1979) pp. 78 f. with pl. 22 c (f. Εὔφρων)
S. ITALY (LUCANIA):
—METAPONTION: (**3**) iv BC Iamb., VP 267 (FVS I p. 446)

**Ἐπιχάρεια**

LAKONIA:
—SPARTA: (**1**) c. 30-20 BC IG V (1) 142, 15 (Bradford (-)) (-ρια: d. Φιλόστρατος)

**Ἐπιχάρης**

AKARNANIA:
—THYRREION: (**1**) ii BC IG IX (1)² (2) 252, 7 (s. Ἀριστοφῶν)
ARGOLIS:
—KALAURIA: (**2**) iii BC ib. IV (1) 845 (Ἐ[πι]χάρης: f. Εὐάνωρ)
ILLYRIA:
—EPIDAMNOS-DYRRHACHION: (**3**) c. 250-50 BC Ceka, Probleme p. 151 no. 23 (coin) (pryt.) ?= (**4**); (**4**) ~ Maier 212-3; Münsterberg Nachtr. p. 15 (coin) (Ceka 113; 210; 367) (pryt.) ?= (3); (**5**) hell.-imp. IDyrrh 195 (s. Καλλίστρατος)
KEPHALLENIA:
—PRONNOI: (**6**) c. 230-200 BC BCH 45 (1921) p. 14 II, 142 (f. Εὔανδρος)
KORINTHIA:
—SIKYON: (**7**) m. iv BC D. xviii 295 (Skalet 112) ?= (8); (**8**) 336 BC CID II 60, 7 (Skalet 113) ?= (9) (7)
—SIKYON?: (**9**) c. 320 BC CID II 113, 4 ?= (8)
LAKONIA:
—MESSA?: (**10**) imp. IG V (1) 1280, 4 ([Ἐπι]χάρεως (gen.): f. Σωτιμίδας)
MESSENIA:
—KORONE: (**11**) ?ii BC ib. 1395, 2 (f. Πολυκλῆς)
—MESSENE: (**12**) iii BC SEG XXIII 210, 26 ([.]μιχάρης—ed., [Ἐ]πιχάρης—LGPN); (**13**) 208 or 207 BC FD III (4) 23, 4; 24, 4 (s. Φιλίας)
S. ITALY (CAMPANIA):
—NEAPOLIS: (**14**) s. iv BC INap 117 (Dubois, IGDGG I 26); cf. Leiwo p. 65 no. 7

**Ἐπιχαρίς**

MESSENIA:
—MESSENE: (**1**) ii BC SEG XLI 345 (Ἐπιχαρίν (acc.): d. Πολυκλῆς)

S. ITALY (CAMPANIA):
—DIKAIARCHIA-PUTEOLI: (**2**) imp. CIL X 3151 (Lat. Epicharis: d. Ζευξίδαμος, Gailla)
SICILY:
—AKRAI*: (**3**) ii AD ib. 7188 (Akrai p. 164 no. 25) (Lat. Aelia Aepicharis: freed.)

**Ἐπίχαρμος**

ARKADIA: (**1**) 361 BC CID II 4 I, 48
KORINTHIA:
—KORINTH: (**2**) iv BC Hesp. 43 (1974) p. 26 no. 36 (s. Μενοίτιος)
SICILY: (**3**) ?f. iv BC Iamb., VP 241 (f. Ματρόδωρος, Θύρσος)
—SELINOUS: (**4**) f. v BC Arena, Iscr. Sic. I 21 (Dubois, IGDS 76; IGLMP 90) (s. Μνασανδρίδας)

**Ἐπίχαρτος**

MESSENIA:
—MESSENE?: (**1**) ii/i BC SEG XI 979, 14 ([Ἐ]πίχαρτος)

**Ἔποχος**

SICILY:
—GELA-PHINTIAS: (**1**) vi BC Dubois, IGDS 129 (Arena, Iscr. Sic. II 5) (f. Κύναιθος)

**Ἔρανος**

S. ITALY (CAMPANIA):
—POMPEII: (**1**) i BC-i AD CIL IV 1450 (Lat. Eranus)

**Ἐρασίδαμος**

ARKADIA:
—MEGALOPOLIS: (**1**) 134 or 130 BC FD III (3) 120, 9, 15 (f. Πειθίας)

**Ἐρασινίδας**

KORINTHIA:
—KORINTH: (**1**) 414 BC Th. vii 7. 1 (Ἐρασινίδης—vulg., Θρασωνίδης—ms. B)

**Ἐρασίνιος**

ARGOLIS:
—ARGOS: (**1**) ?ii AD Unp. (Argos, Kavvadias) (-σεί-)

**Ἐρασῖνος**

S. ITALY (CAMPANIA):
—SALERNUM: (**1**) imp. IItal I (1) 67 (Lat. L. Irius Erasinus)

**Ἐρασίππα**

ARKADIA:
—KAPHYAI: (**1**) s. iv BC IG IV (1)² 122, 122

**Ἐράσιππος**

ACHAIA: (**1**) s. iv BC IMM 258 (f. Ἀγησίλαος)
—AIGION: (**2**) m. iii BC Peek, IAEpid 42, 18, 22 (Perlman E.3); Perlman p. 63 f. (date) (f. Ἀγήσιππος)
AITOLIA:
—TRICHONION: (**3**) s. iv BC SBBerlAk 1936, p. 386 no. 1
ARKADIA:
—LYKOSOURA*: (**4**) i BC IG V (2) 521 (f. Αἰνησώ)
KORINTHIA:
—SIKYON: (**5**) m. v BC ib. IV (1) 425, 5
S. ITALY (BRUTTIUM):
—LOKROI EPIZEPHYRIOI: (**6**) ?viii/vii BC RE (2)
S. ITALY (CALABRIA):
—UZENTUM: (**7**) iv/iii BC Unp. (A.W.J.)

**Ἔρασις**

LAKONIA:
—SPARTA: (**1**) 345 BC CID II 31, 75; 120 A, [17] (Poralla² 278)

**Ἐρασίστρατος**

LAKONIA:
—SPARTA: (**1**) ?134 AD IG V (1) 62, 14 (Bradford (-))
S. ITALY (CAMPANIA):
—POMPEII: (**2**) i BC-i AD CIL X 930 (Castrèn 298. 2) (Lat. Pacuvius Erasistratus)

**Ἐράσμιος**

LAKONIA:
—SPARTA: (**1**) ?ii AD IG V (1) 677, 8 (Bradford (-)) ([Ἐ]ράσμιος)

**Ἔραστος**

ACHAIA?: (**1**) m. i AD Act. Ap. 19, 22; Ep. Rom. 16, 23; 2 Ep. Tim. 4, 20
KORINTHIA:
—KORINTH: (**2**) m. i AD Corinth VIII (3) 232 (Lat. Erastus); (**3**) ii AD SEG XXIX 301 (Βιτέλλιος [Ἔ]ραστος)
LAKONIA:
—SPARTA: (**4**) c. 150-160 AD IG V (1) 69, 29; 70, 6; 71 III, 20; SEG XI 622, 1 (Bradford (-)) (f. Ἀπολλώνιος)
S. ITALY (CAMPANIA):
—DIKAIARCHIA-PUTEOLI: (**5**) imp. CIL X 2519 (Lat. Erastus); (**6**) ?i-ii AD ib. 1878 (Lat. C. Iulius Erastus); (**7**) ?ii AD ib. 2002 (Lat. P. Aelius Erastus)
—POMPEII: (**8**) i BC-i AD ib. IV 4614; 4641 (Lat. Era[s]tus); (**9**) ~ NScav 1906, p. 154 no. 8 (Lat. Erastus); (**10**) c. 51-62 AD CIL IV 3340. 57, 11 (Castrèn 129. 20) (Lat. P. Corn. Erastus); (**11**) 70-79 AD CIL IV 179; Mouritsen p. 109 (date) (Lat. Erastus)
—SALERNUM*: (**12**) m. i AD IItal I (1) 172 (CIL X 527) (Lat. Ti. Claudius Erastus: imp. freed.)

**Ἐράσων**

KERKYRA: (**1**) ?ii-i BC IG IX (1) 772 (tile)

**Ἐράτα**

KORINTHIA:
—KORINTH: (**1**) c. 570-550 BC Amyx 65 (vase) (Lorber 81) (het.?/fict.?)

**Ἐράτεια**

ARGOLIS:
—ARGOS: (**1**) hell. IG IV (1) 638

**Ἐρατέων**

S. ITALY (LUCANIA):
—HYELE-VELIA: (**1**) hell.? PdelP 25 (1970) p. 264 no. 6 (f. Εὐβάτης)

**Ἐρατίας**

ARKADIA:
—MANTINEIA-ANTIGONEIA: (**1**) c. 425-385 BC IG V (2) 323. 20 (tessera) (Ἐρατίδας—IG: f. Γρυψίδας)
MESSENIA:
—MESSENE?: (**2**) ii/i BC SEG XI 979, 42

**Ἐρατογένης**

AIGINA: (**1**) ?i BC Alt-Ägina I (2) p. 45 no. 13 (Ἐρατογ[ένης])

**Ἐρατοκλέα**

ARGOLIS:
—HERMIONE: (**1**) ii-i BC IG IV (1) 732 II, 22 (m. Καλλικλῆς)

**Ἐρατοκλείδας**

KORINTHIA:
—KORINTH: (**1**) vii BC Th. i 24. 2 (f. Φάλιος)

**Ἐρατοκλῆς**

AIGINA: (**1**) ?f. i BC Alt-Ägina I (2) p. 43 no. 4, 2 (f. Ἀγαθοκλῆς)
ARGOLIS:
—HERMIONE: (**2**) m. iv BC Unp. (Ch. Kritzas) (Ἐρατοκλῆς, Πρατοκλῆς): s. Ἀντιλαΐδας)
—TROIZEN: (**3**) iv BC SEG XXII 280, 29
ARKADIA:
—STYMPHALOS: (**4**) c. 225 BC ib. XI 414, 16 (Perlman E.5)

KORINTHIA:
—SIKYON: (5) iii BC *IG* IV (1) 426, 6 (Skalet 115)

**Ἔρατος**
ARGOLIS:
—ARGOS: (1) s. viii BC Paus. ii 36. 4 (king)
S. ITALY (BRUTTIUM):
—KROTON: (2) iv BC Iamb., *VP* 267 (*FVS* 1 p. 446)
S. ITALY (CAMPANIA):
—POMPEII: (3) i BC-i AD *CIL* IV 1571 (Lat. Eratus)
SICILY:
—CAPITIUM: (4) imp. ib. x 7462 (Lat. M. Volumnius Eratus)

**Ἐρατοσθένης**
ARKADIA:
—STYMPHALOS: (1) 191-146 BC Unp. (Paris, BN) 170-1 (coins) (Ἐρατοσθ[έ]ν[η]s)
MESSENIA:
—PROTE*: (2) imp. *SEG* XI 1021 (s. Βαθυκλῆς); (3) ii AD *IG* V (1) 1547, 7 + Sandberg, *Euploia* 10 comm.
S. ITALY (BRUTTIUM):
—KROTON: (4) 576 BC Moretti, *Olymp.* 92

**Ἐρατυϊϊος?**
ARGOLIS:
—ARGOS: (1) ?c. 575-550 BC *SEG* XI 314, 6; *LSAG*² p. 168 no. 8 (date)

**Ἐρατώ**
AIGINA: (1) hell. *IG* IV (1) 114 (?d. Λακρείδας)
ARGOLIS:
—ARGOS*: (2) ii BC *BCH* 33 (1909) pp. 456-7 no. 23, 9 (slave/freed.?)
ARKADIA?: (3) iv/iii BC *HE* 689
LAKONIA:
—MESSA?: (4) imp. *IG* V (1) 1528 = *SEG* XXX 401
S. ITALY (APULIA):
—LARINUM: (5) imp. *CIL* IX 747 (Lat. Fulvia Erato)
SICILY:
—MEGARA HYBLAIA: (6) vii/vi BC *SEG* XXVI 1085 (-τό, —εράτō? (gen.))

**Ἐρατώι**
KORINTHIA:
—KORINTH: (1) c. 570-550 BC Amyx 92 A. 6 (vase) (Lorber 120) (-τόι: het.?/fict.?); (2) ~ Amyx 110. 2 (vase) (-τόι: fict.?)

**Ἐράτων**
ARKADIA: (1) 277 BC *IG* II² 3081, 4; 3082, 4 (Stephanis 882)
LAKONIA:
—KARDAMYLE: (2) i AD *SEG* XI 948, 19 (s. Σώσικλῆς)
—SPARTA: (3) ?viii-vii BC *HE* 2717 (Poralla² 279) (s. Ἰφικρατίδας, Ἀλεξίππα: fict.?)
LEUKAS: (4) 190 BC *Syll*³ 585, 99 (s. Ἀμφίτιμος)
SICILY:
—KAMARINA: (5) f. v BC Cordano, *Tessere Pubbliche* 72 (-τōν: s. Στράτων)
—TAUROMENION: (6) c. 235-184 BC *IG* XIV 421 an. 6; 421 an. 57 (*SGDI* 5219) (s. Ἀπολλόδωρος, f. Ἀπολλόδωρος); (7) 152-150 BC *IG* XIV 421 an. 89 (*SGDI* 5219); *IGSI* 4 III (IV), 43 an. 91 (s. Ἀπολλόδωρος)

**Ἐρατώνομος**
ARKADIA:
—MANTINEIA-ANTIGONEIA: (1) iii-ii BC *IG* V (2) 319, 18

**Ἐργαῖος**
ARKADIA:
—PHIGALEIA: (1) f. iii BC *SEG* XXIII 238 (Ἐργαῖο[s]?)

**Ἐργάσιμος**
S. ITALY (APULIA):
—VENUSIA*: (1) imp. *CIL* IX 479 (Lat. C. Antistius Ergasimus: freed.)

**Ἐργασίων**
ACHAIA: (1) 146 BC *IG* IV (1)² 28, 107 (s. Ἀριστογένης: synoikos)
AIGINA: (2) i BC-i AD *Alt-Ägina* 1 (2) p. 46 no. 22 (f. Ἀρχέδαμος)
ILLYRIA:
—EPIDAMNOS-DYRRHACHION: (3) imp. *IDyrrh* 196 (s. Πτολεμαῖος)

**Ἐργίας**
SICILY: (1) ?iv BC Manganaro, *QUCC* forthcoming no. 68

**Ἐργίλος**
ARGOLIS:
—EPIDAUROS: (1) iv/iii BC Peek, *IAEpid* 142. 5; 142. 7 (s. Ἀρίσταρχος, f. Ἀρχίδαμος); (2) ~ ib. 142. 6 (s. Ἀρχίδαμος); (3) ~ *IG* IV (1)² 235; 254; 254 a; 289; Peek, *IAEpid* 142. 4 (f. Ἀρίσταρχος); (4) iii BC *IG* IV (1)² 163

**Ἐργῖνος**
MESSENIA:
—ABIA: (1) i BC/i AD ib. V (1) 1353 (f. Τρίτιος)

**Ἐργιππος**
ARKADIA:
—STYMPHALOS: (1) c. 315-280 BC *FD* III (1) 38, 3 with Add. (*Syll*³ 516); Daux sub F11 (ident.) (s. Ἀλεξίων); (2) iii BC *SEG* XI 1109, 3 (s. Ἀλεξίμαχος); (3) c. 230-200 BC *BCH* 45 (1921) p. 13 II, 117 (s. Ἀλεξίων)

**Ἐργίων**
MESSENIA:
—MESSENE?: (1) ii/i BC *SEG* XI 979, 3

**Ἐργοίτας**
ARKADIA:
—MANTINEIA-ANTIGONEIA: (1) ?253 BC *FD* III (1) 20, 1 (s. Ἀνδροκλῆς)

**Ἐργόνικος**
ARKADIA:
—TEGEA:
——(Krariotai): (1) m. iii BC *IG* V (2) 36, 92 (f. Ὀδαῖος)

**Ἐργοτέλεια**
S. ITALY (CALABRIA):
—TARAS-TARENTUM: (1) iv-iii BC Troisi, *Epigrafi mobili* 98 (*SEG* XL 909 (terracotta))

**Ἐργοτέλης**
EPIROS:
—BOUTHROTOS (PRASAIBOI): (1) a. 163 BC *IBouthrot* 18, 19; 33, 16 (*SEG* XXXVIII 475; 492) (f. Ἀγαθοκλῆς) ?= (2)
—PRASAIBOI: (2) a. 163 BC *IBouthrot* 78, 11; 79, 10; 80, 9; 81, 9; 82, 9; 83, 9; 84, 9; 85, 9; 86, 11; 87, 10; 88, 8 (*BCH* 118 (1994) pp. 122 f. nos. 1-11) (f. Ἀγαθοκλῆς) ?= (1)
SICILY:
—KAMARINA: (3) iv/iii BC *SEG* XXXIV 942, 2-3 (Dubois, *IGDS* 123; Cordano, 'Camarina VII' 101) (f. Νεομήνιος, Φ—)

**Ἐργόφιλος**
ELIS: (1) m. ii BC *BGU* 1939 A, 9 (f. Πυριλάμπης)

**Ἐρέδαμος**
ACHAIA:
—AIGEIRA: (1) c. 100-90 BC *SEG* XIX 335, 3; *BSA* 70 (1975) pp. 127 ff. (date) (f. Ἀντανδρος)

**Ἐρεμένα**
ARKADIA:
—TEGEA: (1) iv-iii BC *IG* V (2) 71

**Ἐρεννιανός**
ELIS: (1) 113 AD *IvOl* 90, 8 (f. Θράσων); (2) ?iv AD *SEG* XXII 331, [2], 4; cf. *TMByz* 9 (1985) p. 373 no. 152 (Ἐρεν(ν)ιανός)

**Ἐρετριάδας**
ARGOLIS:
—EPIDAUROS*: (1) c. 370-365 BC Peek, *IAEpid* 52 B, 58 (Ἐρετριά[δας])
ARKADIA:
—MANTINEIA-ANTIGONEIA: (2) c. 425-385 BC *IG* V (2) 323. 7 (tessera) (f. Παντίνας)

**Ἐρίανθος**
ARGOLIS:
—ARGOS: (1) ii BC *SEG* XI 348

**Ἐριασπίδας**
ARKADIA:
—TEGEA: (1) ?iv/iii BC *HE* 668 (f. Κλεύβοτος)

**Ἐριήις**
S. ITALY (BRUTTIUM):
—KRIMISA: (1) ?iii BC *AMSMG* 1932, p. 130 (n. pr.?)

**Ἐρίμανθος**
MESSENIA:
—KYPARISSIA: (1) ?iv/iii BC *IG* V (2) 390 (Perlman L.3)

**Ἐρίμναστος**
ILLYRIA:
—APOLLONIA: (1) i BC Maier 123 (coin) (f. Δεινοκράτης)
KERKYRA: (2) ?ii-i BC *IG* IX (1) 773-4 (tiles)

**Ἐριοκόμας**
ARGOLIS:
—EPIDAUROS*: (1) c. 370-365 BC Peek, *IAEpid* 52 B, 58 ([Ἐ]ριοκόμας)

**Ἐρισθένεια**
ARKADIA:
—ORCHOMENOS?: (1) s. vii BC Wehrli, *Schule Arist.* vii fr. 144; *IG* V (2) p. xii, 116 ff. (stemma) (and Argolis Epidauros: d. Ἀριστοκράτης, m. Λυσιδίκα (Epidauros))

**Ἔριστος**
S. ITALY (CAMPANIA):
—DIKAIARCHIA-PUTEOLI: (1) imp. *Eph. Ep.* VIII 399 (Lat. Curius Eristus)

**Ἐρίτιμος**
AIGINA: (1) ii BC *IG* IV (1) 13 (f. Φοίνισσα)
ARGOLIS:
—PHLEIOUS: (2) iv/iii BC ib. IV (1)² 620 + Peek, *IAEpid* 145 (Ἐρίτ[ιμος]: f. Πραξιώ)
KORINTHIA:
—KORINTH: (3) vi/v BC Schol. Pi., *O.* xiii, 58 b-c; *SLG* 339 a, 6-7; *Dionysiaca* pp. 1-16 (ident.) (?s. Τερψίας); (4) m. v BC Schol. Pi., *O.* xiii, 58 b-c; *SLG* 339 a, 6-7; *Dionysiaca* pp. 1-16 (ident.) (?s. Ναμερτίδας)

**Ἔριφος**
KYNOURIA:
—THYREATIS: (1) v BC *SEG* XXXV 290 (vase) ([Ἔ]ριφος)

**Ἐρίφυλος**
ELIS:
—THRAISTOS: (1) f. iv BC *IG* IX (1)² (1) 138, 2, 14

**Ἐριχύων?**
ILLYRIA:
—EPIDAMNOS-DYRRHACHION: (1) c. 250-50 BC *SNG Cop. Thessaly–Illyricum* 504; cf. *IApoll Ref. Bibl.* n. 53 (coin) (pryt.)

**Ἑρμαγόρας**
KORINTHIA:
—KORINTH: (1) c. 570-550 BC Amyx 92 A. 3 (vase) (Lorber 120) ([hε]ρμαγόρας: fict.?)

**Ἑρμάγορος**
DALMATIA:
—PHAROS: (1) iv/iii BC Brunšmid p. 15 no. 2 (f. Κλευνίκη)

**Ἑρμαδίων**
ARGOLIS:
—TROIZEN*: (1) iv BC IG IV (1) 823, 54 (Ἑρμαδ[ίων])
DALMATIA:
—EPETION: (2) imp. CIL III 14649 (Lat. C. Iul. Hermadio)
EPIROS:
—NIKOPOLIS: (3) imp. Unp. (Nikopolis Mus.) (Κορν. Ἑ.)
ILLYRIA:
—EPIDAMNOS-DYRRHACHION: (4) ?i AD AEp 1978, no. 740 (Lat. P. Clodius Hermadion)
S. ITALY (APULIA):
—LUCERIA: (5) imp. CIL IX 859 (Lat. Hermadio)
—VENUSIA: (6) imp. ib. 549 (Lat. M. Pacuvius Hermadio)
S. ITALY (CAMPANIA):
—DIKAIARCHIA-PUTEOLI: (7) imp. ib. X 1567 (Lat. Q. Aurelius Hermadion)
SICILY:
—PANORMOS: (8) s. ii AD ib. 7292 (ILat. Palermo 29) (Lat. [Sex.] Clod. Hermadion: f. Clodia Granilla)
—SYRACUSE: (9) iii-v AD IG XIV 107 (Strazzulla 45) (Ἑρμάδι(ο)ν?—IG)

**Ἑρμαῖος**
ACHAIA?: (1) hell.? AM 27 (1902) p. 378 no. 68 (Ἑ. Ἀχαιοῦ Δ)
AIGINA: (2) ?c. 475-450 BC CEG I 129; LSAG² p. 113 no. 18 (date) (s. Κυδόνικος); (3) hell. IG II² 7966, 3 (f. Σίμων)
AIGINA*: (4) iv BC D. xxxvi 29
AKARNANIA:
—STRATOS: (5) i BC IG IX (1)² (1) 110, 10 (s. Στράτων)
ARGOLIS:
—ARGOS: (6) 105 BC JÖAI 14 (1911) Beibl. p. 146 no. 4, 10 (f. Διογένης); (7) i-ii AD IG IV (1) 587, 9 (s. Καλλι—)
—EPIDAUROS: (8) c. 50-40 BC SEG XXXIV 153, 63 (Ἑρμαῖος: I f. Ἑρμαῖος II); (9) ~ ib. l. 63 (Ἑρμαῖος: II s. Ἑρμαῖος I)
—HERMIONE: (10) iii BC IG IV (1) 728, 7 (f. Ἑρμων); (11) ~ ib. l. 9 (s. Ἑρμων); (12) ?ii-i BC ib. 731 III, 5 (f. Ὠφελίων); (13) ii-i BC ib. 732 I, 8 (f. Κέρδων)
—TROIZEN*: (14) iv BC ib. 823, 48, 52
ARKADIA:
—MANTINEIA-ANTIGONEIA: (15) c. 300-221 BC ib. v (2) 323. 51 (tessera) (f. Ἔπανδρος)
—TEGEA:
——(Athaneatai): (16) iv/iii BC ib. 38, 11
——(Hippothoitai): (17) iii BC ib. 40, 42
KORINTHIA:
—KORINTH: (18) c. 570-550 BC Amyx 92 A. 5 (vase) (Lorber 120) (h(ε)ρμαῖος: fict.!)
—SIKYON: (19) iii BC SEG XI 261
SICILY:
—KAMARINA: (20) f. v BC Cordano, Tessere Pubbliche 64 (hερ-: f. Εὐκλῆς)

**Ἑρμαΐς**
S. ITALY (CALABRIA):
—BRENTESION-BRUNDISIUM: (1) imp. CIL IX 184 (Lat. Sergia Secunda et Hermais); (2) ii AD Studi Ribezzo p. 59 no. 3 (Lat. Hermais)
S. ITALY (CAMPANIA):
—CAPREAE: (3) imp. ZPE 71 (1988) p. 196 no. 7, 4 (Lat. Antistia Hermais)

SICILY:
—KATANE: (4) imp. CIL X 7094 (Lat. Statilia Hermais)
—THERMAI HIMERAIAI: (5) imp. IG XIV 326 (Μαρκία Ἑ.)

**Ἑρμαΐσκος**
ARGOLIS:
—EPIDAUROS: (1) f. iii AD ib. IV (1)² 410, 2; 411 + Peek, IAEpid 166 (s. Μᾶρκος); (2) 226-231 AD IG IV (1)² 407, 3; 410, 6 (f. Μᾶρκος)
S. ITALY (CAMPANIA):
—NOLA: (3) imp. CIL X 1335 (Lat. L. Vibius Hermaiscus)

**Ἑρμαίων**
KERKYRA: (1) imp. IG IX (1) 911

**Ἑρμάξοος**
ARKADIA:
—PHENEOS: (1) 146-31 BC BMC Pelop. p. 196 no. 25 (coin)

**Ἕρμαρχος**
ARGOLIS:
—HERMIONE: (1) imp. IG IV (1) 715 (Ἑρμα[ρ]χος: s. Λούκιος)

**Ἑρμᾶς**
ARGOLIS:
—TROIZEN: (1) i AD ib. 799
S. ITALY (APULIA):
—LUCERIA: (2) imp. CIL IX 805 (Lat. Lucerinus Hermas)
S. ITALY (BRUTTIUM):
—RHEGION: (3) hell. NScav 1892, p. 490
S. ITALY (CALABRIA):
—BRENTESION-BRUNDISIUM: (4) imp. CIL IX 143 (Lat. L. Messius Herma); (5) ~ NScav 1900, p. 153 no. 3 (Lat. C. Iulius Herma); (6) 108 AD CIL IX 36 (Lat. Herma)
—BRENTESION-BRUNDISIUM*: (7) imp. NScav 1892, p. 101 (freed.)
—LUPIAE: (8) imp. Susini, Fonti Salento p. 150 no. 100 (Lat. Claudius Herma)
—RUDIAE: (9) ii AD ib. p. 108 no. 43 (Lat. Herma)
S. ITALY (CAMPANIA):
—DIKAIARCHIA-PUTEOLI: (10) imp. IG XIV 2414. 24 (tessera)
—DIKAIARCHIA-PUTEOLI*: (11) imp. CIL X 1732 (Lat. Ti. Claud. Hermas: imp. freed.)
—HERCULANEUM: (12) m. i AD PdelP 10 (1955) p. 453 no. 79 (Lat. L. Opsius Hermas)
—HERCULANEUM*: (13) i BC-i AD CIL X 1403 g II, 5 (Lat. —us Herma: freed.)
—KYME: (14) imp. ib. 3700, 4 (Lat. Nulanius Herma)
—KYME*: (15) ?i-ii AD Eph. Ep. VIII 446 (Lat. C. Iulius Hermas: freed.)
—MISENUM*: (16) imp. CIL X 3646 (Lat. Herma)
—NUCERIA ALFATERNA: (17) imp. ib. 1094 (Lat. Herma)
—POMPEII: (18) i BC-i AD ib. IV 1466; (19) ~ ib. 2508, 24 (Lat. Herma); (20) ~ ib. 3101 (Ἑρμᾶ(s)); (21) ~ ib. 4512 (Lat. Hermas); (22) c. 51-62 AD ib. 3340. 87, 8; 95, 9; 5140; 5141; 5143 (Castrèn 361. 3) (Lat. Cn. Seius Herma); (23) ?55 AD CIL IV 3340. 18, 8; 51, 6; 69, 13 (Castrèn 81. 14) (Lat. L. Caecilius Hermas)
SICILY:
—KATANE: (24) imp. Epigraphica 51 (1989) p. 171 no. 39 (Lat. L. Arrius Hermas)
—KATANE*: (25) ii-iii AD CIL X 7097 (ILat. Palermo 3) + Epigraphica 51 (1989) p. 171 (Lat. Herma: slave?)
—KENTORIPA: (26) imp. IG XIV 579
—THERMAI HIMERAIAI: (27) i-ii AD CIL X 7440 (ILat. Term. Imer. 149) (Lat. L. Tennius Herma)

**Ἑρμάφιλος**
ILLYRIA:
—EPIDAMNOS-DYRRHACHION: (1) hell.-imp. IDyrrh 80 (f. Ἄγησις)

**Ἑρμαφρόδιτος**
S. ITALY (APULIA):
—LUCERIA: (1) imp. CIL IX 826 (Lat. C. Pontius Ermaprodi[tus])
S. ITALY (CAMPANIA):
—SALERNUM: (2) imp. IItal I (1) 143 (CIL X 8345) (Lat. Hermaphroditus)

**Ἑρμείας**
ARKADIA:
—MANTINEIA-ANTIGONEIA: (1) ii-iii AD IG v (2) 275, 10 (s. Ἰούνιος)
—TEGEA: (2) 165 AD ib. 50, 51 (I f. Ἑρμείας II); (3) ~ ib. l. 51 (II s. Ἑρμείας I)
KORINTHIA:
—KORINTH: (4) c. 100-110 AD FD III (4) 99 (Λ. Ἀρρούντιος Ἑ.)
MESSENIA:
—KORONE: (5) 246 AD IG v (1) 1398, 67 (Αὐρ. Ἑ.)
SICILY:
—SYRACUSE: (6) iii-v AD NScav 1907, p. 755 no. 4 + Ferrua, NG 78 (Ἑρμεί[ας])

**Ἑρμέρως**
ARKADIA:
—TEGEA: (1) ii AD IG v (2) 55, 58 (f. Ἑρμογένης)
EPIROS:
—NIKOPOLIS: (2) imp. SEG XXXV 677
S. ITALY (APULIA):
—LUCERIA: (3) imp. CIL IX 872 (Lat. Hermeros)
—VIBINUM*: (4) imp. ib. 6252 (Lat. C. Octavius Hermeros: freed.)
S. ITALY (BRUTTIUM):
—RHEGION*: (5) i BC/i AD SEG XXXIX 1062 B (slave?/potter)
S. ITALY (CALABRIA):
—BRENTESION-BRUNDISIUM: (6) imp. CIL IX 85 (Lat. Hermeros)
S. ITALY (CAMPANIA):
—DIKAIARCHIA-PUTEOLI: (7) imp. ib. X 1565 (Lat. P. Acilius Hermeros); (8) ~ ib. 1599 (Lat. C. Novius [Her]meros); (9) ~ ib. 2652 (Lat. C. Licinius Hermeros); (10) ~ ib. 2707 (Lat. C. Iulius Hermeros); (11) 47 AD Camodeca, L'Archivio Puteolano I p. 58 no. 1 (Lat. L. Marius Hermeros); (12) 53 AD ib. p. 229 no. 3 (Lat. P. Vedius Hermeros)
—HERCULANEUM: (13) m. i AD PdelP 9 (1954) p. 57 no. 62 (Lat. M. Nonius Hermer[os]); (14) ~ Cron. Erc. 7 (1977) p. 116 B a, 8 (Lat. M. Nonius Hermeros)
—HERCULANEUM*: (15) i BC-i AD CIL IV 10676 (Lat. Hermeros: slave?)
—NEAPOLIS: (16) iii-iv AD IG XIV 826. 14 (INap 227) (Ἑ[ρ]μέρως)
—POMPEII: (17) i BC-i AD CIL IV 1109; cf. p. 696 (Castrèn 454. 16) (Lat. Q. Vettius Her(r)meros); (18) ~ CIL IV 1254; 1256 (Lat. Hermeros); (19) ~ ib. 1466; (20) ~ ib. 2191; 2195 (Lat. Hermeros); (21) ~ ib. 2192; 2195 (Lat. Hermeros); (22) ~ ib. 3969 (Lat. Hermeros); (23) ~ ib. 5082 (Lat. Hermeros)
SICILY:
—PANORMOS*: (24) ii-iii AD ib. X 7303 (Lat. M. Aurelius Hermeros: freed.)

**Ἑρμερωτίς**
S. ITALY (CAMPANIA):
—DIKAIARCHIA-PUTEOLI: (1) imp. ib. 2156 (Lat. Babullia Hermerotis)

## Ἑρμῆς

ACHAIA:
—PATRAI: **(1)** imp. *NScav* 1895, p. 267 a (Lat. Hermes)

ARGOLIS:
—TROIZEN: **(2)** imp. *IG* IV (1) 781 (f. Εὔτυχος)

ARKADIA:
—TEGEA: **(3)** ii AD ib. v (2) 217; **(4)** 165 AD ib. 50, 46 (s. Ἔφηβος)

DALMATIA:
—TRAGURION: **(5)** imp. *CIL* III 2682 (Lat. Iul. Hermes)

ELIS:
—OLYMPIA*: **(6)** 245-265 AD *IvOl* 121, 29; 122, 24

EPIROS:
—BOUTHROTOS (PRASAIBOI): **(7)** f. ii AD *RAAN* 21 (1941) p. 289 (Sestieri, *ILat. Albania* 12) (Lat. C. Papirius Hermes)

ILLYRIA:
—EPIDAMNOS-DYRRHACHION*: **(8)** ?ii AD *JÖAI* 23 (1926) Beibl. p. 239 no. 1 (Lat. P. Clodius Hermes: f. P. Clodius Valerianus: freed.)

KORINTHIA:
—KORINTH: **(9)** f. ii AD *Corinth* VIII (3) 286, 2 (Lat. Marcius Ermes: ?f. Marcia Fervida, Μάρκιος Εὐέλπιστος)

LAKONIA:
—SPARTA: **(10)** ii AD *IG* v (1) 159, 4 (Bradford (3)) (I f. Ἑρμῆς II); **(11)** ~ *IG* v (1) 159, 4 (Bradford (1)) (II s. Ἑρμῆς I); **(12)** ii-iii AD *IG* v (1) 778 (Bradford (2))

S. ITALY: **(13)** imp. *CIL* x 8059. 62 (seal) (Lat. Cn. Lucretius Hermes)

S. ITALY (APULIA):
—BARION: **(14)** f. ii AD *Suppl. It.* 8 p. 39 no. 7 (Lat. L. Plutius Hermes)

—LUCERIA: **(15)** imp. *CIL* IX 854 (Lat. Erucius Hermes)

—SIPONTUM*: **(16)** ii AD *Epigraphica* 34 (1972) p. 135 (Serricchio, *Iscrizioni di Siponto* 11) (Lat. Hermes: freed.)

—TEANUM APULUM: **(17)** imp. *Teanum Apulum* p. 114 no. 46 (*CIL* IX 710; 723) (Lat. Hermes: s. Urbanus)

—VENUSIA: **(18)** imp. *CIL* IX 507 (Lat. Q. Publicius Hermes); **(19)** i/ii AD *Epigraphica* 35 (1973) p. 148 no. 10 (*Museo di Venosa* p. 237 no. 10) (Lat. Iulius Hermes: f. Iulius Musteolus, Ἑρμιόνη)

—VENUSIA (NR.): **(20)** imp. *Eph. Ep.* VIII 87 (Lat. Hermes: f. –licius Maximus)

S. ITALY (BRUTTIUM):
—RHEGION: **(21)** f. i AD *SEG* XXIX 987, 11 (*Suppl. It.* 5 p. 60 no. 12)

S. ITALY (CALABRIA):
—BRENTESION-BRUNDISIUM: **(22)** imp. *NScav* 1894, p. 17 no. 4 = *Epigraphica* 25 (1963) p. 43 no. 21 (Lat. M. Aeficius Hermes); **(23)** ~ *Eph. Ep.* VIII 22 (Lat. M. Fabiu[s] Herme[s]); **(24)** i-ii AD *CIL* IX 129 (Susini, *Fonti Salento* p. 182 no. 1 a) (Lat. L. Iulius Hermes)

—BRENTESION-BRUNDISIUM*: **(25)** imp. *NScav* 1892, p. 242 (Lat. A. Gabinius Hermes: freed.)

S. ITALY (CAMPANIA):
—AEQUANA: **(26)** imp. ib. 1897, p. 200 (Lat. Hermes)

—DIKAIARCHIA-PUTEOLI: **(27)** imp. *IG* XIV 2414. 23 (tessera); **(28)** ~ *CIL* x 2065 (Lat. T. Iunius Hermes); **(29)** ~ ib. 2115 (Lat. D. Aterius Hermes); **(30)** ~ ib. 2285 (Lat. L. Munatius Hermes); **(31)** ~ ib. 2512 (Lat. Hermes); **(32)** ~ ib. 2513 (Lat. Hermes); **(33)** ~ ib. 2634 (Lat. Sex. Patulcius Hermes); **(34)** ~ ib. 2705 (Lat. L. Laecanius Hermes); **(35)** ~ ib. 2754 (Lat. M(anius) Paccius Hermes); **(36)** ~ ib. 2940 (Lat. L. Laelius Hermes); **(37)** ~ ib. 3009 (Lat. Q. Volusius Hermes); **(38)** ~ ib. 3047 (Lat. M. Valerius Hermes); **(39)** ~ ib. 3097 (Lat. C. Valerius Hermes); **(40)** ~ ib. 8202 (Lat. A. Vesonius Hermes) ?= (*80*); **(41)** ~ *NScav* 1891, p. 321 (Lat. Hermes); **(42)** ?i-ii AD *CIL* x 2556 (Lat. C. Iulius Hermes); **(43)** ~ ib. 2606 (Lat. Hermes: f. Iulia Primigenia); **(44)** ~ ib. 2614 (Lat. P. Apuleius Hermes); **(45)** 47 AD *Puteoli* 6 (1982) p. 51 (Lat. Hermes); **(46)** ?ii AD *CIL* x 2129 (Lat. T. Flavius Hermes); **(47)** ~ ib. 3140 (Lat. Ulpius Hermes)

—DIKAIARCHIA-PUTEOLI*: **(48)** imp. ib. 1906 (Lat. C. Poppaeus Hermes: imp. freed.); **(49)** ?i-ii AD ib. 2129 (Lat. Ti. Claudius Hermes: freed.?); **(50)** i/ii AD *Puteoli* 7-8 (1983-4) p. 299 no. 3 (*CIL* x 2109) (Lat. L. Asellius Hermes: f. L. Asellius Mamilianus: freed.)

—HERCULANEUM*: **(51)** i BC-i AD ib. 1403 g II, 12 (Lat. M. Volusius Hermes: freed.); **(52)** ~ ib. 1403 g III, 64 (Lat. C. Castricius Hermes: freed.); **(53)** ~ ib. l. 65 (Lat. C. Calvisius Hermes: freed.); **(54)** ~ ib. 1403 k, 7 (Lat. Hermes: freed.); **(55)** c. 50-75 AD ib. 1403 a I, 10 (Lat. P. Petronius Hermes: freed.)

—MISENUM: **(56)** 112-113 AD De Franciscis, *Sacello Augustali* p. 25 no. 6; p. 27 (Lat. L. Laninius Hermes: I s. Φίλιππος, f. Ἑρμῆς II); **(57)** ~ ib. p. 25 no. 6; p. 27 (Lat. L. Laninius Hermes: II s. Ἑρμῆς I)

—MISENUM*: **(58)** imp. *CIL* x 3401 (Lat. Hermes); **(59)** ~ ib. 3460 (Lat. Hermes: freed.); **(60)** ~ ib. 3547 (Lat. C. Bebius Hermes); **(61)** ~ ib. 3622 (Lat. M. Seius Hermes)

—NEAPOLIS: **(62)** ?i AD *NScav* 1892, p. 99; cf. Leiwo p. 112 no. 87 (Lat. Hermes: f. Ῥοδόπη); **(63)** ii AD *IG* XIV 802 (*INap* 147); cf. Leiwo p. 105 no. 66 (f. Νοονία Ἑρμιόνη)

—POMPEII: **(64)** i BC-i AD *CIL* IV 544; 545 (Lat. Hermes); **(65)** ~ ib. 1365 (Lat. Hermes); **(66)** ~ ib. 1511 (Lat. Ermes); **(67)** ~ ib. 1723 (Lat. Hermes); **(68)** ~ ib. 2164; **(69)** ~ ib. 2261; **(70)** ~ ib. 2341 (Lat. Hermes); **(71)** ~ ib. 2367; cf. p. 220 (Lat. Hermes); **(72)** ~ ib. 3145 a (Lat. Ermes); **(73)** ~ ib. 3355 (Lat. Hermes); **(74)** ~ ib. 3961 (Lat. Ermes); **(75)** ~ ib. 4893; **(76)** ~ ib. 5083 (Lat. Hermes); **(77)** ~ ib. 5281 (Lat. Hermes); **(78)** ~ *NScav* 1910, p. 477 no. 71 (amph.) (Lat. Hermes); **(79)** ~ ib. 1946, p. 129 no. 411 (Castrèn 42. 13) (Lat. Arri(us) H(er)mes); **(80)** m. i AD *CIL* IV 3340. 66 (Castrèn 450. 3) (Lat. Vesonius Hermes) ?= (*40*); **(81)** 54 AD *CIL* IV 3340. 7, 18 (Castrèn 68. 1) (Lat. M. Badius Hermes); **(82)** 57 AD *CIL* IV 3340. 28, [20] (Castrèn 443. 2) (Lat. M. Veratius Hermes); **(83)** c. 70 AD *CIL* x 1025, 6 (Castrèn 288. 2); Kockel p. 84 (date) (Lat. C. Olius Hermes); **(84)** 70-79 AD *CIL* IV 85; Mouritsen p. 109 (date) (Lat. Hirmis); **(85)** ~ *CIL* IV 241; Mouritsen p. 110 (date) (Lat. Hermes); **(86)** ~ *CIL* IV 7489; 7722; Mouritsen pp. 110-11 (date) (Lat. Hermes)

—SALERNUM: **(87)** ?i AD *IItal* I (1) 128 (*CIL* x 602) (Lat. Hermes)

—SALERNUM*: **(88)** imp. *IItal* I (1) 219 (*CIL* x 628) (Lat. M. Quirinius Hermes: freed.)

S. ITALY (LUCANIA):
—POSEIDONIA-PAESTUM*: **(89)** i BC-i AD Mello–Voza 10 (Lat. [L.] Fundanius Hermes: freed.)

—POTENTIA: **(90)** imp. *CIL* x 158 (Lat. Hermes)

SICILY:
—AKRILLAI (NR.): **(91)** iii-v AD *NScav* 1912, p. 363 (Pace, *Camarina* p. 164 no. 25)

—HALAISA*: **(92)** ii AD *Kokalos* 17 (1971) p. 19 no. 9 (Lat. Iulius Acilius Hermes)

—KATANE: **(93)** imp. *CIL* x 7056 (Lat. L. Cassius Hermes)

—PANORMOS: **(94)** imp. ib. 7319 (Lat. Hermes)

—SYRACUSE: **(95)** imp. ib. 7148 (Lat. [Co]rnelius Herm[es]?); **(96)** iii-v AD *ASSiracusano* 1956, p. 63

—SYRACUSE*: **(97)** imp. *CIL* x 8314 (Lat. Q. Cornificius Hermes: freed.)

—TAUROMENION: **(98)** imp. *Arch. Class.* 15 (1963) p. 30 (Λ. Μάλιος Ἑ.)

## Ἑρμήσανδρος

ARKADIA: **(1)** 228-1 BC *PTeb* III 815 fr. 11

## Ἑρμητιανός

S. ITALY (CALABRIA):
—VALETIUM: **(1)** ii-iii AD *CIL* IX 24 and Add. p. 652 (Susini, *Fonti Salento* p. 164 no. 129) (Lat. P. Tutorius Hermetianus: s. Ἰλαριανός)

## Ἑρμία

EPIROS:
—NIKOPOLIS: **(1)** imp. *SEG* XXXIX 534 (m. Ἰλαρος, Ἰλαρος (sic), Πλόκαμος)

## Ἑρμιανός

S. ITALY (CAMPANIA):
—DIKAIARCHIA-PUTEOLI: **(1)** imp. *Eph. Ep.* VIII 359 (Lat. Hermianus)

## Ἑρμίας

ARGOLIS:
—ARGOS*: **(1)** 105 BC *JÖAI* 14 (1911) Beibl. p. 146 no. 4, 24 (slave/freed.?)

—EPIDAUROS*: **(2)** c. 335-325 BC Peek, *IAEpid* 50, 26

—HERMIONE: **(3)** ii BC *IG* IV (1) 689 (I f. Ἑρμίας II, Σώδαμος); **(4)** ~ ib. (II s. Ἑρμίας I); **(5)** ii-i BC ib. 732 III, 25 (s. Καλλισθένης); **(6)** i BC-i AD? ib. 730 V, 3 (s. Διογένης); **(7)** v-vi AD *SEG* XI 385 c, 1; cf. *TMByz* 9 (1985) p. 298 no. 40 (bp.?)

ARKADIA:
—MANTINEIA-ANTIGONEIA: **(8)** iv/iii BC *IG* v (2) 279 ([Ἑρ]μίας: s. Ἀνδροκλῆς)

ELIS: **(9)** ii-iii AD *IvOl* 139, 6

EPIROS:
—AMBRAKIA: **(10)** ii-i BC *BCH* 79 (1955) p. 267

ILLYRIA:
—APOLLONIA: **(11)** imp. *IApoll* 77 (Ἑρμία (voc.))

—EPIDAMNOS-DYRRHACHION: **(12)** hell.-imp. *IDyrrh* 197 ([Ἑ]ρμίας)

ILLYRIA?:
—APOLLONIA: **(13)** f. ii BC *SEG* XXII 130, 13 (*IApoll* 318) (resid. Athens Rhamnous)

KERKYRA: **(14)** hell. *IG* IX (1) 835 (bullet) (Ἑρ[μί?]ας)

KORINTHIA:
—KORINTH: **(15)** ii-iii AD *SEG* XI 134, 6

LAKONIA:
—SPARTA: **(16)** c. 100-120 AD ib. 610, 9 (Bradford (-)) (s. Παα—)

PELOPONNESE?: **(17)** ii AD *PAE* 1992, p. 71 A, 32 (f. Ἡρακλείδας)

S. ITALY (APULIA):
—VENUSIA: **(18)** imp. *CIL* IX 599 (Lat. Q. Veturius Hermias)

S. ITALY (CAMPANIA): **(19)** imp. *IG* XIV 2414. 124

—BAIAI: **(20)** ii/iii AD *NScav* 1897, p. 12 (Lat. L. Caecilius Hermias)

—DIKAIARCHIA-PUTEOLI: **(21)** imp. *CIL* x 2591 (Lat. Hermias); **(22)** ~ ib. 2826, 3 (Lat. [L.] [Patu]lcius Hermia)

—HERCULANEUM: **(23)** i BC-i AD ib. IV 10594

—POMPEII: **(24)** i BC-i AD ib. 4775 (Lat. Hermias); **(25)** ~ ib. 8697 b (Castrèn 378. 2) (Lat. P. Siculius Hermias)

## Ἑρμιόνα

ACHAIA:
—PELLENE: **(1)** ii-i BC *SEG* XI 1278

ARGOLIS:
—HERMIONE: **(2)** i BC-i AD? *IG* IV (1) 730 II, 1 (d. Μ—)

EPIROS: **(3)** hell. *SGDI* 1360; cf. Cabanes, *L'Épire* p. 584 no. 64 ([Ἑρμ]ιόνα: ?m. Ἑρμων)

## Ἑρμιόνη

ACHAIA: (1) i BC-i AD *Achaean Grave Stelai* 7
ARGOLIS:
—ARGOS: (2) iii/ii BC *PP* 17209; *BE* 1949, no. 202 (family) (d. Πολυκράτης, Ζευξώ (Cyrene))
ILLYRIA:
—EPIDAMNOS-DYRRHACHION: (3) imp. *AEp* 1978, no. 751 (Lat. Hermione: m. Ianuaria: slave?)
S. ITALY (APULIA):
—LUCERIA: (4) imp. *ASP* 34 (1981) p. 23 no. 26 (Lat. Sallustia Hermione: d. Γενναῖος)
—VENUSIA: (5) i/ii AD *Epigraphica* 35 (1973) p. 148 no. 10 (*Museo di Venosa* p. 237 no. 10) (Lat. Iulia Hermione: d. Ἑρμῆς, Εὐτυχία)
S. ITALY (CALABRIA):
—KALLIPOLIS: (6) i-ii AD *Athenaeum* 48 (1970) p. 94 no. 1 (*CIL* IX 8; Susini, *Fonti Salento* p. 86 no. 19) (Lat. Pomponia Hermione: m. D. Vibuleius Fuscus)
S. ITALY (CAMPANIA):
—DIKAIARCHIA-PUTEOLI: (7) imp. *AJA* 2 (1898) p. 379 no. 15 (Lat. Cornelia Hermione: m. Cornelius Aquilinus, Ἑρμογένης); (8) ~ *CIL* X 2646 (Lat. Hermione); (9) ?ii AD ib. 2516 (Lat. Hermione: d. Εἰρηναῖος, Καρπιάς)
—DIKAIARCHIA-PUTEOLI*: (10) imp. ib. 1917 (Lat. Hermione: freed.?)
—MISENUM*: (11) ?i-ii AD ib. 3497 (Lat. Iulia Hermione)
—NEAPOLIS: (12) ii AD *IG* XIV 802 (*INap* 147); cf. Leiwo p. 105 no. 66 (Νοουία Ἑ.: d. Ἑρμῆς, Περπέτουα)
—POMPEII*: (13) i BC-i AD *Römische Gräberstrassen* p. 214 a (Lat. Lollia Hermiona: freed.)
S. ITALY (LUCANIA):
—GRUMENTUM: (14) ?ii-iii AD *CIL* X 248 (Lat. Aurelia Hermione)
SICILY:
—SYRACUSE: (15) iii-v AD Strazzulla 249 b (Wessel 1063); cf. *Riv. Arch. Crist.* 18 (1941) p. 168 no. 29 (-νι: d. Μάξιμος); (16) ~ Strazzulla 305 (Agnello 24; Wessel 860) (d. Καισάριος)
—ZANKLE-MESSANA: (17) imp. *IG* XIV 414 (Ρωσκία Ἑ.)

## Ἑρμιος

SICILY:
—SELINOUS: (1) vi/v BC Dubois, *IGDS* 47 (Arena, *Iscr. Sic.* I 51; Lazzarini 880 e); cf. *SEG* XL 807 (h(ε)ρμιος—Dubois, h(ε)ρμίας—Arena, h(ε)ρμ(α)ῖος?)

## Ἑρμιππος

S. ITALY (CAMPANIA):
—DIKAIARCHIA-PUTEOLI*: (1) imp. *CIL* X 1952 (Lat. L. Pl. Hermippus: freed.)

## Ἑρμίς

ILLYRIA:
—EPIDAMNOS-DYRRHACHION: (1) i AD *Stud. Alb.* 1965, p. 70 no. 45 (Lat. Claudiae Hermi[di?] (dat.))

## Ἑρμίσκος

S. ITALY (BRUTTIUM):
—HIPPONION-VIBO VALENTIA*: (1) imp. *CIL* X 8041. 16 (tile) (Lat. Hermeiscus)

## Ἑρμίων

S. ITALY (CAMPANIA):
—POMPEII: (1) i BC-i AD ib. IV 1466

## Ἑρμογένεια

S. ITALY (CAMPANIA):
—MISENUM*: (1) ?ii-iii AD ib. X 3438 (Lat. Aurelia Ermogenia)

## Ἑρμογένης

ACHAIA?: (1) 193 BC *IG* V (2) 293, 11 (Ἑρμογ[ένης]: f. Γόργος)
AIGINA: (2) hell.-imp. ib. IV (1) 104; (3) ?f. i AD *Alt-Ägina* I (2) p. 45 no. 17, 4 (s. Νηρεύς)
ARGOLIS:
—ARGOS*: (4) ii-i BC *IG* IV (1) 530, 5; cf. *BCH* 33 (1909) p. 183 n. 2 (slave/freed.?)
—HERMIONE: (5) ii-iii AD *SEG* XI 383, 4 (*GVI* 1867) (Ἑρμογέν[ης])
—METHANA-ARSINOE: (6) i BC *IG* IV (1) 853, 8 (Ἑρμογ[έ]νης: f. Πρωτίων); (7) c. 132-212 AD ib. 858, 3; cf. *SEG* XXXVII 316
—PHLEIOUS: (8) c. 400-375 BC *IG* II² 10479 (f. Ἀντίοχος)
—TROIZEN: (9) c. 295-288 BC ib. VII 7, 1; Urban, *Wachstum* pp. 66-70 (date) (f. Ἑρμῶναξ)
ARKADIA:
—TEGEA: (10) ii AD *IG* V (2) 55, 58 (s. Ἑρμέρως)
EPIROS:
—BOUTHROTOS (PRASAIBOI): (11) imp. Ugolini, *Alb. Ant.* 3 p. 219 (Lat. Hermogenes)
KORINTHIA:
—KORINTH: (12) 185 BC *IG* IX (1)² (1) 32, 19 (Ἑρμογένης: s. —ίδας)
—KORINTH*: (13) 353-358 AD *Corinth* VIII (3) 503, 1 (Φλ. Ἑ.)
LAKONIA:
—GERENIA: (14) m. iv BC *IG* II² 11335, 1; *SEG* XIII 194 (locn.) (II s. Ἑρμογένης I, f. Ἐπιγένης); (15) ~ *IG* II² 11335, 3; *SEG* XIII 194 (locn.) (I f. Ἑρμογένης II)
—KYTHERA: (16) imp.? Paus. iii 2. 8; *RE* (25) (sculptor)
—SPARTA: (17) s. i BC *SEG* XI 874 (brick) (Bradford (4)); (18) c. 90-130 AD *IG* V (1) 65, 23; 79, 8; 99, 7; 284, 1; *SEG* XI 493, 2; 517, 5; 539, 5 (Bradford (2)) (s. Γλύκων) ?= (20); (19) c. 105-122 AD *SEG* XI 569, 23; 574, [4] (Bradford (1)) (s. Ἀσκλαπος); (20) ?m. ii AD *IG* V (1) 329; *Artemis Orthia* pp. 317-18 no. 39 (date) (Bradford (5)) (f. Γλύκων) ?= (18); (21) f. iii AD *IG* V (1) 330; *Artemis Orthia* p. 331 no. 65 (Bradford (3)) ([Ἑ]ρμογένης: s. Μ. Αὐρ. [—])
S. ITALY (APULIA):
—RUBI: (22) ii AD *Epigrafia e Territorio* 2 pp. 77 ff. no. 16 (*CIL* IX 6185) (Lat. M. Licinius Hermogenes: f. M. Licinius M–ilus)
S. ITALY (CAMPANIA):
—DIKAIARCHIA-PUTEOLI: (23) imp. *AJA* 2 (1898) p. 379 no. 15 (Lat. Cornelius Hermogenes: s. Ἑρμιόνη); (24) ~ *CIL* X 3067 (Lat. Valerius Hermogenes: f. Valeria Pia); (25) ?i-ii AD ib. 2580 (Lat. Hermogenes: s. Ἀγάθη)
—DIKAIARCHIA-PUTEOLI*: (26) imp. ib. 3021 (Lat. L. Triarius Hermoge[nes]: freed.)
—MISENUM*: (27) imp. ib. 3652 (Lat. Iulius Hermogenes)
S. ITALY (LUCANIA):
—GRUMENTUM?: (28) imp. ib. 8092 (or S. Italy (Lucania) Potentia: Lat. Iulius Hermo[ge]nes)
SICILY: (29) c. 250 BC *PSI* 626 I, 9-10 (s. Ἀντίλοχος) ?= (31)
—KATANE: (30) c. 80 BC *IG* VII 416, 40 (*IOrop* 523) (f. Ζώπυρος)
—SYRACUSE: (31) c. 227 BC *PPetr* III 21 (d), 5, 13-14 (f. Πτολεμαῖος) ?= (29)

## Ἑρμόδωρος

ACHAIA:
—PATRAI?: (1) ii-i BC *GVI* 530 (Ἑρμόδωρος: f. Ἀρτέμων)
ILLYRIA:
—BYLLIONES BYLLIS: (2) imp. *SEG* II 365
MESSENIA:
—PROTE*: (3) imp. *IG* V (1) 1543 (Sandberg, *Euploia* 6)

## S. ITALY (CAMPANIA):

—POMPEII: (4) i BC-i AD *CIL* IV 5194 (Lat. H(e)rmodorus)
SICILY: (5) ?v BC *ASSiciliaOrientale* 1919-20, p. 197 (hερμόδō[ρος])
—ECHETLA: (6) vi/v BC Manganaro, *PdelP* forthcoming 5 (hερμόδō[ρ]ος)
—SYRACUSE: (7) iv BC *RE* (5)
—ZANKLE-MESSANA: (8) imp. *IG* XIV 416 (f. Φηλικίτα)

## Ἑρμοκλῆς

AIGINA: (1) s. iii BC ib. IV (1) 727 A, 8 (Perlman H.1) (f. Ἀριστίων)
KERKYRA: (2) imp. *IG* IX (1) 952 (Ἑρμολεες (voc.)—lap., Ἑρμό(κ)λεες—ed.)

## Ἑρμοκράτης

AITOLIA:
—THERMOS*: (1) s. iii BC ib. IX (1)² (1) 60 II, 23; (2) ~ ib. 60 IV, 8
ARGOLIS:
—ARGOS: (3) ii AD *SEG* XVI 253, 14 (f. Καλλίστρατος)
KORINTHIA:
—KORINTH: (4) c. 315-280 BC *FD* III (1) 179, 2 (s. Ἀνδροσθένης); (5) f. iii BC *IG* II² 1957, 13; (6) 191-146 BC *BMC Pelop.* p. 12 no. 139 (coin); (7) ii/i BC *Corinth* VIII (3) 47 a
LAKONIA:
—GYTHEION: (8) f. ii AD *IG* V (1) 1170, 4 ([Ἑρ]μοκράτης: f. Νεόπολις); (9) ~ ib. 1171, 11 (II² 3596, 11) (s. Νεόπολις)
MESSENIA:
—MESSENE: (10) f. iii BC *PAE* 1991, p. 99 no. 7, 23
SICILY:
—SYRACUSE: (11) v BC *RE* s.v. Dionysios (1) col. 882; Tod, *GHI* II 108; Plu., *Dio* 21; cf. Beloch, *GG* III (2) pp. 102-7 (Ἑρμόκριτος—Beloch: f. Διονύσιος, Λεπτίνας, Θεαρίδας, Θέστα); (12) 424-407 BC *RE* (1) (s. Ἑρμων)

## Ἑρμόκριτος

SICILY:
—SYRACUSE: (1) 368 BC ib. (-) + Supplbd. 3 (2); Tod, *GHI* II 133; cf. Beloch, *GG* III (2) pp. 102-7 (s. Διονύσιος, Δωρίς (Lokroi Epizephyrioi))

## Ἑρμόλαος

KORINTHIA:
—KORINTH: (1) imp. *IG* IV (1) 1604, 3 (f. Διογένης)
S. ITALY (CALABRIA):
—BRENTESION-BRUNDISIUM: (2) imp. *NScav* 1892, p. 101

## Ἑρμόνικος

S. ITALY (CAMPANIA):
—DIKAIARCHIA-PUTEOLI: (1) 79 AD *FD* III (4) 34, 2 + Guarducci, *Ep. Gr.* 2 p. 57 no. 7 (Stephanis 906) (Μ. Τουρράνιος Ἑρμόνεικος)

## Ἑρμόξενα

ARGOLIS:
—ARGOS:
——(Amphisseis): (1) s. iv BC *SEG* XXIX 363, 4 (or Lokris (Western) Amphissa: hερ-)

## Ἑρμότιμος

ARKADIA: (1) f. v BC Richter, *Engraved Gems* no. 216
—TEUTHIS?: (2) vi BC Boardman, *Archaic Greek Gems* p. 147 no. 516 (gem)

## Ἑρμόφαντος

AITOLIA: (1) s. iii BC *FD* III (4) 232 (Ἑρμόφα[ντος], Ἑρμοφά[νης]?: ?s. Ἀριστοφ—)

## Ἑρμύλος

S. ITALY (CAMPANIA):
—POMPEII: (1) i BC-i AD *CIL* IV 8690 (Lat. Hermulus)

## Ἕρμων

ACHAIA: (**1**) 146 BC *IG* IV (1)² 28, 72 (f. Ἀθηνα-γόρας: synoikos)

AKARNANIA:
—THYRREION: (**2**) hell.? *SEG* XXIX 481 (Ἔρμων)

ARGOLIS:
—HERMIONE: (**3**) iii BC *IG* IV (1) 728, 7 (s. Ἑρ-μαῖος); (**4**) ~ ib. l. 9 (f. Ἑρμαῖος)
—TROIZEN: (**5**) arch.? *RE* (11) (sculptor)

DALMATIA:
—ISSA: (**6**) i BC-i AD Brunšmid p. 29 no. 23 (f. Μνασικράτης)

EPIROS: (**7**) hell. *SGDI* 1360; cf. Cabanes, *L'Épire* p. 584 no. 64 (?s. Ὑμένιος, Ἑρμιόνα)
—AMBRAKIA: (**8**) iii BC *SEG* XXIV 413 (s. Ξάν-θιππος, f. Ἡρόδωρος)
—DODONA: (**9**) iii BC Antoniou, *Dodone* Ba, 2
—DODONA*: (**10**) vi/v BC *PAE* 1931, p. 88 no. 1

ILLYRIA:
—EPIDAMNOS-DYRRHACHION?: (**11**) vi BC Paus. vi 19. 8 (s. Πύρρος)

S. ITALY (LUCANIA):
—HYELE-VELIA: (**12**) s. ii BC *ID* 1713, 5-6; 1965 a, 2; 2368, 3; 2595, 32; 2602, [8-9]; *Athenaeum* 63 (1985) p. 496 (stemma) (s. Θρασυ-δήιος, f. Θέων, Ζήνων) ?= (*14*); (**13**) ~ *ID* 1965 b, 2; 2004, [2]; 2595, 8; *Athenaeum* 63 (1985) p. 496 (stemma) (s. Ἀγαθοκλῆς, ?f. Ἀγαθοκλῆς); (**14**) ~ *ID* 2619 b II, 12 ?= (*12*); (**15**) c. 140 BC ib. 1965 a, 1; 1965 b, 1; *Athenaeum* 63 (1985) p. 496 (stemma) (f. Ἀγαθοκλῆς, Θρασυδήιος); (**16**) ii/i BC *SEG* XIX 400, 3 (s. Πολύστρατος)

SICILY:
—AKRAGAS: (**17**) iv/iii BC *Acragas Graeca* 1 p. 41 no. 11, 5 (Cabanes, *L'Épire* p. 543 no. 8; Dubois, *IGDS* 184)
—NAXOS: (**18**) s. v BC *SEG* XXXVIII 953. 2 (Arena, *Iscr. Sic.* III 77); cf. *L'Incidenza dell'Antico* pp. 418-9 (date) (Ἑρμωνίδαι—n. gent.)
—SEGESTA: (**19**) f. v BC *SEG* XXX 1127 bis a (vase); cf. Dubois, *IGDS* p. 271 (ἑρμῶν)
—SYRACUSE: (**20**) v BC *RE* (4); X., *HG* i 3. 13 (f. Ἑρμοκράτης, Πρόξενος)
—SYRACUSE?:
——(Μακ.): (**21**) hell. Manganaro, *PdelP* forthcoming no. 4 II, 7 (f. Αἰσχρίων)
——(Πλη.): (**22**) hell. ib. no. 4 III, 8 (f. Σῶσις)
—TAUROMENION: (**23**) c. 229-212 BC *IG* XIV 421 an. 12; 421 an. 29 (*SGDI* 5219) (s. Φι-λέας)
—TYNDARIS: (**24**) imp. *IG* II² 10293 (s. Ἀθάνιπ-πος)

## Ἑρμῶναξ

ARGOLIS:
—ARGOS: (**1**) ?253 BC Nachtergael, *Les Galates* 10, 61; cf. Stephanis 1892 (f. Νουμήνιος)
—EPIDAUROS*: (**2**) c. 335-325 BC *SEG* XXV 389, 58 ([Ἑρ]μῶναξ)
—TROIZEN: (**3**) c. 295-288 BC *IG* VII 7, 1; Urban, *Wachstum* pp. 66-70 (date) (s. Ἑρμο-γένης)

SICILY:
—SYRACUSE?: (**4**) hell. Manganaro, *PdelP* forthcoming no. 4 V, 11 (s. Ἀλκίας)

## Ἐροῦσα

S. ITALY (CAMPANIA):
—DIKAIARCHIA-PUTEOLI: (**1**) imp. *CIL* X 2688 (Lat. Maecenatia Erusa)

## Ἑρπέας

ARGOLIS:
—ARGOS:
——Zarax (Aischiadai): (**1**) c. 316-222 BC *SEG* XVII 143, 3 (Perlman A.15); *SEG* XVIII 146 (name)

## Ἑρπίς

ARGOLIS:
—ARGOS: (**1**) ?i AD Unp. (Ch. Kritzas) (vase)

LAKONIA:
—SPARTA: (**2**) byz. *IG* V (1) 820 (Bradford (-))

## Ἑρπυλίδας

LAKONIA:
—SPARTA: (**1**) ?viii-vii BC *HE* 2717 (Poralla² 311) (Εὐπυλίδας—ms. P: s. Ἰφικρατίδας, Ἀλεξ-ίππα: fict.?)

## Ἑρπυλλίς

ARGOLIS:
—ARGOS: (**1**) iv-iii BC *BCH* 27 (1903) p. 265 no. 14

## Ἑρύκοιρος?

ARGOLIS:
—ARGOS: (**1**) ?c. 575-550 BC *SEG* XI 314, 10; *LSAG*² p. 168 no. 8 (date) (Ἐρύϙο[ιρος]?)

## Ἑρύμανθος

ARGOLIS:
—ARGOS: (**1**) ?308 BC *IG* V (2) 550, 11 (f. Ὀνό-μαντος)

## Ἑρυμνίδας

LAKONIA:
—LAS: (**1**) vi/v BC Giannakopoulou, *Gytheion* pp. 51-3

## Ἑρυμνίων

AITOLIA?: (**1**) s. iv BC *Klio* 15 (1918) p. 56 no. 79, 2 (f. Θεότιμος)

## Ἑρύμνων

AITOLIA: (**1**) 310 BC D.S. xx 16. 1; cf. *Klio* 15 (1918) p. 56 sub no. 79 (Ἐρυμν(ί)ων—*Klio*)

## Ἔρυξ

S. ITALY (BRUTTIUM):
—PETELIA: (**1**) i-ii AD *Klearchos* 22 (1980) p. 25 (Lat. M(anius) Megonius Eryx)

## Ἐρυξιλαΐδας

LAKONIA:
—SPARTA: (**1**) 423 BC Th. iv 119. 2 (Poralla² 281) (Ἐρυξιδαΐδας—mss. and Poralla: f. Φιλο-χαρίδας)

## Ἔρυξις

EPIROS:
—MOLOSSOI: (**1**) c. 343-330 BC Cabanes, *L'Épire* p. 588 no. 74, 9-10 (*SEG* XXVI 700) (f. Ἀμύνανδρος, Δόκιμος)

## Ἐρύσσιος

SICILY:
—SEGESTA: (**1**) ?ii-i BC *IG* XIV 288 (Dubois, *IGDS* 214 a; *IGLMP* 46) (Φάλακρος Ἐ.: s. Διόδωρος, f. Σώπολις)

## Ἐρχέλαος

EPIROS:
—DODONA: (**1**) iv BC Cabanes, *L'Épire* p. 586 no. 70, 6

## Ἔρως

ACHAIA:
—PATRAI: (**1**) i BC-i AD *CIL* III 512 (Lat. L. Durcatius Eros)

ARGOLIS:
—ARGOS: (**2**) i BC *SEG* I 70 (*GVI* 618) (f. Εὐα-μερώ)

ARKADIA:
—TEGEA: (**3**) ii AD *IG* V (2) 55, 35 (f. Ἄνθος); (**4**) 165 AD ib. 50, 82 (f. Καλλίβιος)

ITHAKE*: (**5**) imp. *BSA* 39 (1938-9) p. 38 no. 2 (Lat. Eros)

KEPHALLENIA:
—KRANIOI: (**6**) imp. *IG* IX (1) 613 (s. Ὀνασιφό-ρον)

KORINTHIA:
—KORINTH: (**7**) iii AD *Ag.* VII p. 97 no. 297 (lamp) ([Ἔρ]ωτος (gen.))

LAKONIA:
—HYPERTELEATON*: (**8**) imp. *IG* V (1) 1038
—SPARTA: (**9**) imp. ib. 1014 (Bradford (1)) (s. Ἀτ—); (**10**) c. 100-125 AD *IG* V (1) 152, 7 (Bradford (2)) (f. Ἀργεῖος)

S. ITALY: (**11**) imp. *CIL* X 8059. 228 (seal) (Lat. L. Latuelius Eros); (**12**) ~ ib. 8059. 335 (seal) (Lat. Eros); (**13**) ?ii-iii AD ib. 8059. 65 (seal) (Lat. M. Aur. Eros)

S. ITALY (APULIA):
—CANUSIUM: (**14**) imp. *Epig. Rom. di Canosa* 46 (Lat. Eros); (**15**) ~ ib. 182 (*CIL* IX 398) (Lat. L. Seius Eros)
—CANUSIUM*: (**16**) imp. *Epig. Rom. di Canosa* 125 (*CIL* IX 6189) (Lat. P. Decimius Eros: freed.); (**17**) ~ *Epig. Rom. di Canosa* 171 (*CIL* IX 396) (Lat. C. Poblicius Eros: freed.); (**18**) ~ *Epig. Rom. di Canosa* 187 (Lat. C. Tampius Eros: freed.); (**19**) ~ ib. Add. 11 (Lat. C. Casellius Eros: freed.?); (**20**) i AD ib. 91 (Lat. Q. Baebius Eros: freed.); (**21**) ~ ib. 127 (Lat. A. Ditonius Eros: freed.); (**22**) ii/iii AD ib. 65 (Lat. P. Fabricius Eros: freed.)
—LUCERIA: (**23**) imp. *CIL* IX 899 (Lat. P. Tamullius Eros)
—LUCERIA*: (**24**) imp. ib. 876 (Lat. T. Boa-tius Eros: freed.); (**25**) ~ *Lucera Romana* p. 27 (Lat. Eros: freed.)
—TEANUM APULUM: (**26**) ii/iii AD *Teanum Apu-lum* p. 63 no. 10 (Lat. Eros)
—VENUSIA*: (**27**) imp. *CIL* IX 673 (Lat. C. Cosconius Eros: freed.)

S. ITALY (CALABRIA):
—BRENTESION-BRUNDISIUM: (**28**) imp. ib. 147 (Lat. Eros: f. Εὐτυχία ἡ καὶ Βύττιν); (**29**) ~ *NScav* 1892, p. 353 u (Lat. D. Paprius Eros)
—BRENTESION-BRUNDISIUM*: (**30**) imp. *Epigraphica* 25 (1963) p. 58 no. 46 (Lat. M. Publius Eros: freed.); (**31**) i AD *Athenaeum* 45 (1967) pp. 155-7 (Lat. C. Iulius Eros: freed.)

S. ITALY (CAMPANIA):
—ATELLA*: (**32**) imp. *CIL* X 3748 (Lat. Q. Hos-tius Eros: freed.)
—DIKAIARCHIA-PUTEOLI: (**33**) imp. *AJA* 2 (1898) p. 382 no. 22 (Lat. L. Genucius Aeros?); (**34**) ~ *CIL* x 2367 (Lat. Cn. Do-mitius Eros Baianus); (**35**) ~ ib. 2675 (Lat. M. Lucilius Eros: f. Lucilia Primigenia); (**36**) ~ ib. 2939 (Lat. C. Scribonius Eros); (**37**) ~ ib. 3095 (Lat. Vettenius Aeros: f. Τιμόθεος); (**38**) ~ *NScav* 1913, p. 25 no. 4 (Lat. M. Crit-tius Eros: s. Ὀλυμπιάς); (**39**) 35 AD Camodeca, *L'Archivio Puteolano* 1 p. 116 no. 3 (Lat. A. Castricius Eros Hordionianus); (**40**) 43 AD ib. p. 211 (Lat. C. Iulius Eros) ?= (*43*); (**41**) 47 AD *Puteoli* 6 (1982) p. 51 (Lat. Ero[s]); (**42**) ~ Camodeca, *L'Archivio Puteolano* 1 p. 65 no. 5 (Lat. Q. Baebius Ero[s])
—DIKAIARCHIA-PUTEOLI*: (**43**) imp. *CIL* X 1915 (Lat. C. Iulius Eros: freed.?) ?= (*40*); (**44**) ~ ib. 2389 (Lat. P. Annius Eros: freed.) = *ZPE* 71 (1988) p. 195 no. 3 (Lat. P. Annius Eros: freed.); (**45**) ~ *CIL* X 2752 (Lat. M. Hostius Eros: freed.)
—HERCULANEUM: (**46**) i BC-i AD *RAAN* 33 (1958) p. 295 no. 732; cf. *Cron. Erc.* 8 (1978) p. 155 no. 63 (Lat. M. Helvius Eros)
—HERCULANEUM*: (**47**) i BC-i AD *CIL* X 1403 g II, 6 (Lat. M. Gallicius Eros: freed.)
—MISENUM: (**48**) imp. *ZPE* 73 (1988) p. 93 no. 4 (Lat. Iulius Eros)
—NEAPOLIS: (**49**) i AD *CIL* X 1499; cf. Leiwo p. 89 (Lat. M. Caecilius Eros)
—NUCERIA ALFATERNA: (**50**) i AD *Boll. Arch.* 1-2 (1990) p. 243 (Lat. L. Lollius Eros)
—PITHEKOUSSAI-AENARIA: (**51**) ?ii AD Monti, *Ischia* p. 614 (Lat. T. Flavius Eros)
—POMPEII: (**52**) i BC-i AD *CIL* IV 1419 (Lat. Eros); (**53**) ~ ib. 1562 (Lat. Eros); (**54**) ~ ib.

2446; 3201 a; **(55)** ~ ib. 2474; 2476 (Lat. Eros); **(56)** ~ ib. 3186 (Lat. Eros); **(57)** ~ ib. 3200 b (Lat. Eros); **(58)** ~ ib. 4081 (Lat. Eros); **(59)** ~ ib. 4220; **(60)** ~ ib. 4323 (Castrèn 229. 1) (Lat. Q. Luscius Eros); **(61)** ~ CIL IV 4602; 4679 (Lat. Eros); **(62)** ~ ib. 5234 (Lat. Eros); **(63)** ~ ib. 5320 (Lat. Eros); **(64)** ~ NScav 1929, p. 436 no. 53 (Castrèn 389. 2) (Lat. Stallius Eros); **(65)** ~ NScav 1933, p. 295 (Castrèn 320. 4) (Lat. Q. Poppaeus Eros); **(66)** c. 51-62 AD CIL IV 3340. 71, 4; 90, 2 (Castrèn 99. 5) (Lat. D. Caprisius Eros); **(67)** ~ CIL IV 3340. 96, 6; NScav 1895, p. 210 (seal) (Castrèn 76. 2) (Lat. L. Brittius Eros); **(68)** ?55 AD CIL IV 3340. 18, 10; 85, 7 (Castrèn 402. 6) (Lat. P. Terentius Eros); **(69)** 57 AD CIL IV 3340. 32, 6, 9, [20] (Castrèn 207. 10) (Lat. D. Iunius Eros)
—POMPEII*: **(70)** i BC-i AD NScav 1893, p. 334 no. 7 (Lat. Q. Caecilius Eros: freed.); **(71)** i AD CIL X 8042. 48 (tiles) (Lat. L. Eumachius Eros); **(72)** f. i AD Impegno per Pompeii 11 OS no. 10 (Castrèn 23. 9) (Lat. Cn. Alleius Eros: freed.)
—SALERNUM: **(73)** ii-iii AD IItal 1 (1) 137 (CIL X 564) (Lat. M. Aurelius Eros)
—SALERNUM*: **(74)** ?i AD IItal 1 (1) 238 I, 20 (CIL X 557) (Lat. L. Appuleius Eros: freed.); **(75)** ~ IItal 1 (1) 238 III, 19 (CIL X 557) (Lat. L. Appuleius Eros: freed.)
—STABIAE*: **(76)** i BC ib. I² 1681 (X 8133) (Lat. Sex. Attius Eros: freed.)
—SURRENTUM: **(77)** imp. ib. 753 (Lat. Valerius Eros)
SICILY: **(78)** imp. ib. 8059. 150 (seal) (Lat. Eros)
—AKRAGAS*: **(79)** ii/iii AD Kokalos 9 (1963) p. 167 f. = 28-9 (1982-3) p. 321 (tiles) (Lat. A. Annius Eros: freed.)
—AKRAI: **(80)** imp. SEG XLII 829 (slave?)
—LILYBAION: **(81)** imp. Mon. Ant. 33 (1929) p. 58 (Lat. Eros)
—SYRACUSE: **(82)** iii-v AD SEG XVIII 399 (-ος)
—THERMAI HIMERAIAI*: **(83)** i-ii AD CIL X 7390 (ILat. Term. Imer. 70) (Lat. T. Cispius Eros: freed.)
—TYNDARIS*: **(84)** imp. ib. 7483 (Lat. Eros: s. Ἀντέρως: freed.)

**Ἐρῶσα**
KORINTHIA:
—KORINTH: **(1)** ?s. vi BC Amyx 126. 1 (vase) (Corinth XV (3) p. 360 no. 15) (Ἐρόσας (gen., n. pr.?))

**Ἐρωτάριν**
S. ITALY (CAMPANIA):
—POMPEII: **(1)** i BC-i AD CIL IV 9945 (Gnomon 45 (1973) p. 268) (Lat. Erotarin)

**Ἐρωταρίων**
SICILY:
—SYRACUSE: **(1)** iii-v AD NScav 1913, p. 263 (Ἐρο-); **(2)** ~ Strazzulla 368 (Agnello 27; Wessel 1387; cf. Ferrua, NG 135 (-ρεί-)

**Ἐρωτιανός**
ACHAIA:
—AIGION: **(1)** imp. SEG XXXIX 403

**Ἐρωτική**
SICILY:
—MORGANTINA*: **(1)** i BC-i AD? ib. XXIX 929 (slave?)

**Ἐρωτικός**
S. ITALY (CAMPANIA):
—DIKAIARCHIA-PUTEOLI: **(1)** imp. CIL X 1937 (Lat. L. Numis. Eroticus)
—POMPEII: **(2)** i BC-i AD Atti Acc. Pontan. 39 (1990) p. 318 no. 196 (Lat. Eroticus)

**Ἐρωτίς**
ACHAIA:
—PATRAI: **(1)** i BC-i AD CIL III 516 (Lat. Aemilia Erotis: m. P. Aemilius Urbanus, Aemilia Secunda)
ARGOLIS:
—ARGOS: **(2)** i AD IG II² 8366 (d. Πιτύλος)
—HERMIONE: **(3)** iii BC ib. IV (1) 728, 33
EPIROS:
—NIKOPOLIS: **(4)** imp. AD 43 (1988) Chron. p. 308 no. 3 (d. Κόϊντος)
ILLYRIA:
—APOLLONIA: **(5)** hell.-imp. IApoll 79 (d. Φιλοκλῆς); **(6)** imp. ib. 78 (-τείς)
—EPIDAMNOS-DYRRHACHION: **(7)** hell.-imp. IDyrrh 198; **(8)** ii-iii AD AEp 1978, no. 759 (Lat. Aeliae Erotidi (dat.))
KORINTHIA:
—KORINTH: **(9)** i BC-i AD SEG XI 440, 1 (d. Δημήτριος)
S. ITALY (APULIA):
—BUTUNTUM: **(10)** imp. Mus. Arch. di Bari p. 166 no. 15 (Lat. Domitia Erotis)
—CANUSIUM*: **(11)** imp. Epig. Rom. di Canosa 160 (CIL IX 392) (Lat. Minucia Erotis: freed.)
—LUCERIA: **(12)** inc. Lucera Romana p. 27 (Lat. Erotis: freed.?)
—TEANUM APULUM*: **(13)** ii/iii AD Teanum Apulum p. 64 no. 10 (Lat. Avieddia Erotis: freed.)
S. ITALY (CAMPANIA):
—BAIAI: **(14)** ?i AD NScav 1894, p. 287 (Lat. Iulia Erotis)
—DIKAIARCHIA-PUTEOLI*: **(15)** imp. CIL X 2245 (Lat. Caucia Erotis: freed.); **(16)** ~ ib. 2831 (Lat. Pavillia Erotis: freed.); **(17)** 44 AD Camodeca, L'Archivio Puteolano 1 p. 31 (Lat. Patulcia Erotis: freed.)
—NEAPOLIS: **(18)** ii-iii AD IG XIV 782 (INap 120); cf. Leiwo p. 108 no. 74

**Ἐρωτίων**
KORINTHIA:
—SIKYON: **(1)** 341 BC CID II 12 I, 61 (s. Κλεότιμος)
MESSENIA:
—KORONE: **(2)** 246 AD IG V (1) 1398, 42 (Αὐρ. Ἐ.)

**Ἐσθήρ**
S. ITALY (APULIA):
—VENUSIA: **(1)** v AD JIWE I 47 (CIJ I 579) (Ἀσ-: d. Συριανός: Jew)

**Ἐσθλαγόρας**
DALMATIA:
—ISSA:
——(Dymanes): **(1)** iv/iii BC Brunšmid p. 8, 49

**Ἐσπερᾶτος**
S. ITALY (APULIA):
—VENUSIA: **(1)** v AD JIWE I 99 (Ἡσπε-: Jew)

**Ἐσπεριανός**
SICILY:
—SYRACUSE: **(1)** iii-v AD IG XIV 156 (Strazzulla 97; Wessel 1064) (f. Οὔρβικα)

**Ἐσπερίς**
S. ITALY (APULIA):
—LUCERIA: **(1)** ?i-ii AD CIL IX 862 (Lat. Iulia Esperis)
—MELFI (MOD.): **(2)** ii-iii AD Epigrafia del Villaggio p. 449 no. 3 (Lat. Seppia Esperis)
S. ITALY (CALABRIA):
—BRENTESION-BRUNDISIUM: **(3)** imp. CIL IX 81 (Lat. Avidia Hesperis)
S. ITALY (CAMPANIA):
—NEAPOLIS: **(4)** imp. NScav 1894, p. 173 no. 1; cf. Leiwo p. 112 no. 91 (Lat. Sentia Hesperis)

S. ITALY (LUCANIA):
—MURO LUCANO (MOD.): **(5)** imp. Atti Conv. Taranto 17 (1977) p. 440 (CIL X 441) (Lat. Tattia Esperis: d. Tattia Marcella)
—VOLCEI: **(6)** s. ii AD Suppl. It. 3 p. 77 no. 6 (Lat. Pont. Esperis)
SICILY:
—KATANE: **(7)** imp. CIL X 7073 (Lat. Iulia Hesperis)
—SYRACUSE: **(8)** iii-v AD Ferrua, NG 59

**Ἐσπερίων**
AKARNANIA:
—ASTAKOS: **(1)** ii BC IG IX (1)² (2) 434, 11 (f. Σωτίων); **(2)** 167 BC Klio 75 (1993) p. 132, 7 (s. Ἀντικράτης)

**Ἔσπερος**
AKARNANIA:
—ANAKTORION: **(1)** iii BC IG IX (1)² (2) 590
ARKADIA:
—TEGEA: **(2)** m. ii AD ib. V (2) 48, 10 (Ἐσπε[ρος])
ILLYRIA:
—APOLLONIA: **(3)** imp. IApoll 73 (Ἑ(σ)περος: s. Αἰσχίνας)
S. ITALY (APULIA): **(4)** imp. Epigraphica 34 (1972) pp. 134-5 (Κλ. Ἑ.)
S. ITALY (CALABRIA):
—BRENTESION-BRUNDISIUM: **(5)** imp. CIL IX 127 (Lat. Hesper)
—TARAS-TARENTUM: **(6)** imp. Eph. Ep. VIII 61 (Lat. A. Hordionius Essper)
S. ITALY (CAMPANIA):
—BAIAI: **(7)** imp. NScav 1887, p. 154 (Eph. Ep. VIII 408) (Lat. Insteius Hesper)
—HERCULANEUM*: **(8)** m. i AD Cron. Erc. 7 (1977) p. 118 D, 3 (Lat. C. Lusius Hesper: freed.)
—LITERNUM: **(9)** imp. CIL X 3720 (Lat. Cossinius Hesperus)
S. ITALY (LUCANIA):
—COSILINUM: **(10)** imp. IItal III (1) 229 (Lat. T. Helvius Hesperus)

**Ἑστάτας**
ARKADIA: **(1)** 308 BC IG V (2) 550, 6

**Ἑστιαῖος**
PELOPONNESE?: **(1)** ii AD PAE 1992, p. 72 B, 2 (s. Θεόδωρος)
S. ITALY (CALABRIA):
—TARAS-TARENTUM: **(2)** f. iv BC FVS 1 pp. 421-2 no. 47 A 1-2 (?f. Ἀρχύτας)

**Ἑστίας**
SICILY:
—KAMARINA: **(1)** iii BC Manganaro, PdelP forthcoming no. 1, 2

**Ἑστιόδωρος**
SICILY:
—KENTORIPA: **(1)** i BC-i AD? IG XIV 576; cf. Sic. Gymn. 16 (1963) pp. 53-4 ((Ἑ)στιόδωρος: f. Ἀρχύτας Σάντρα)

**Ἑσφαντίδας**
ARKADIA:
—MEGALOPOLIS: **(1)** 320 BC IG V (2) 549, 1 (f. Εὐκαμπίδας)

**Ἔσφαντος**
ARKADIA:
—TEGEA: **(1)** m. iv BC ib. 6, 107; **(2)** f. iii BC ib. 35, 33 (s. Ἀριστοκλῆς)

**Ἑταιρεία**
ILLYRIA:
—BYLLIONES BYLLIS: **(1)** imp. BUST 1961 (1), p. 107 (Lat. Heterea Saturnina)

**Ἐταίριχος**
ARKADIA:
—THISOA?: **(1)** f. iv BC SEG XIV 455, 2 (?s. Πέτηλος)

TRIPHYLIA:
—MAKISTOS: (2) 399-369 BC ib. XXXV 389, 12

**Ἑταῖρος**
S. ITALY (CAMPANIA):
—DIKAIARCHIA-PUTEOLI: (1) ?ii-iii AD CIL X 2005 (Lat. L. Aelius Hetaerus)

**Ἕταρις**
DALMATIA:
—ISSA: (1) iii/ii BC SEG XXXV 687 (s./d. Θρασυκλῆς)

**Ἑτεαρχίς**
LAKONIA:
—BOIAI: (1) ii AD IG V (1) 955 (Μινδία Ἑ.)
—SPARTA: (2) c. 250-260 AD ib. 593, 2; BSA 80 (1985) p. 225; p. 243 (ident., stemma) (Bradford (-)) (Ἰουλ. Ἑ.: m. Κλ. Ἀλκανδρίδας, Κλ. Ἐλπὶς ἡ καὶ Καλλιστονίκη) ?= (4)
—TAINARON-KAINEPOLIS: (3) imp.? IG V (1) 1257 (d. Δαμέας, Δαμαρχίς); (4) imp. ib. 1258 (Ἰουλ. Ἑ.) ?= (2)

**Ἑτέαρχος**
ARKADIA:
—TEGEA: (1) f. ii BC ib. V (2) 44, 3 (Ἐτέ<λ>αρχος: s. Ἀ—)
——(Hippothoitai): (2) iv/iii BC ib. 38, 50 (s. Νικασίας)
ELIS: (3) s. i BC IvOl 425 (Ἐτέαρχ[ος]: I f. Ἐτέαρχος II); (4) ~ ib. (Ἐτέαρχο[ς]: II s. Ἐτέαρχος I)
LAKONIA:
—SPARTA: (5) ?s. i AD IG V (1) 661 (Bradford (3)) (Ἐτ]έαρχος: I f. Ἐτέαρχος II); (6) ~ IG V (1) 661 (Bradford (1)) (Ἐτ]έαρχος: II s. Ἐτέαρχος I)
—TAINARON-KAINEPOLIS: (7) imp.? IG V (1) 1257 (f. Δαμαρχίς); (8) imp. ib. 1258 (Bradford (2)); (9) ~ IG V (1) 1259 (s. Νικανδρίδας)

**Ἑτεοίτας**
LAKONIA:
—SPARTA: (1) ?c. 510-500 BC SEG XI 653 (Lazzarini 89); LSAG² p. 200 no. 30 (date) (Poralla² 281a) (Ἐτεοί[τας]?)

**Ἑτεοκλῆς**
ARGOLIS:
—HERMIONE: (1) ?ii-i BC IG IV (1) 731 II, 18 (f. Διόδωρος)
ARKADIA:
—TEGEA:
——(Hippothoitai): (2) iii BC ib. V (2) 40, 36 (f. Θηρίνας)
LAKONIA:
—SPARTA: (3) iv BC Plu., Lys. 19 ?= (4); (4) 331 or 330 BC RE (3) (Poralla² 282) ?= (3)

**Ἑτέοκλος**
ARGOLIS:
—HERMIONE: (1) iii BC IG IV (1) 729 I, 11 (s. Ὑπεράνωρ)

**Ἑτεόνικος**
LAKONIA:
—SPARTA: (1) v/iv BC RE (-) (Poralla² 283)

**Ἕτευτα**
ILLYRIA:
—DARDANIOI: (1) 168 BC RE Supplbd. 3 (-) (Lat. Etuta: d. Μονούνιος) ?= (Ἕτλευα (1))

**Ἕτλευα**
ILLYRIA: (1) 168 BC ib. (Lat. Etleva: m. Σκερδιλαΐδας, Πλευρᾶτος) ?= (Ἕτευτα (1))

**Ἑτοιμαρίδας**
LAKONIA:
—SPARTA: (1) c. 475 BC D.S. xi 50. 6-7 (Poralla² 284)

**Ἑτοιμοκλῆς**
LAKONIA:
—SPARTA: (1) vii/vi BC RE (-); Moretti, Olymp. 82-6 (Poralla² 285) (s. Ἱπποσθένης)

**Ἑτροῦσκος**
SICILY:
—ZANKLE-MESSANA: (1) s. i BC GP 2290 ff.

**Ἐτυμοκλείδας**
EPIROS:
—DODONA: (1) ?c. 500 BC LSAG² p. 230 no. 14 (Lazzarini 141) (-κλέδας)

**Ἐτυμοκλήδεια**
LAKONIA:
—SPARTA: (1) ii-i BC SEG XI 677 c, 1 (Bradford (2)) (Ἐτυμοκ(λ)ήιδεια: d. Ἀνδροτέλεια); (2) c. 125-150 AD IG V (1) 488, 4 (Bradford (3)) (d. Σοϊξιτέλης, m. Ὀνάσιππος); (3) ii/iii AD IG V (1) 534, 13; 591, 5; SEG XI 817, 4; XXXVI 353, 14; BSA 80 (1985) pp. 194; 206-8 (ident., stemma) (Bradford (1); (4)) (Ἰουλ. Ἑ.: d. Γ. Ἰούλ. Ἀγαθοκλῆς, Μεμμία Ξενοκράτεια, m. Κλ. Φιλοκράτεια)

**Ἐτυμοκλῆς**
LAKONIA:
—SPARTA: (1) c. 550 BC HE 1365 (Poralla² 286) (Ἐτυμοκλεῖος—patr. adj.: f. Κλεύας: dub.); (2) f. iv BC X., HG v 4. 22; vi 5. 33; Plu., Ages. 25 (Poralla² 287)

**Ἕτυμος**
S. ITALY (CAMPANIA):
—HERCULANEUM*: (1) m. i AD Cron. Erc. 7 (1977) p. 118 D, 4 (Lat. Sex. Arellius Etymus: freed.)

**Ἐτύμων**
ELIS: (1) iv BC Paus. v 5. 1 (f. Δαμάρετος)

**Εὐάγαθος**
ARKADIA:
—PHIGALEIA: (1) c. 272 BC IG IX (1)² (1) 13, 19 (s. Φιλόξενος)

**Εὐαγγελίς**
SICILY:
—KATANE: (1) iii-v AD Agnello 57 (Wessel 823) (Μακαρία Εὐαγγελίς: Jew?)

**Εὐάγγελος**
KORINTHIA:
—SIKYON: (1) iv-iii BC SEG XIX 357 s ([Ε]ὐάγγ[ε]λος)
LAKONIA:
—SPARTA: (2) s. i BC IG V (1) 94, 22; 210, 29 (Bradford (1); (2)) (-άνγε-: s. Ἀρήξιππος, f. Ἀρήξιππος)
S. ITALY: (3) imp. CIL X 8059. 391 (seal) (Lat. P. T. Euangelus)
S. ITALY (APULIA):
—CANUSIUM: (4) imp. Epig. Rom. di Canosa 54 (CIL IX 345) (Lat. M. Apronius Euangelus)
S. ITALY (CALABRIA):
—TARAS-TARENTUM: (5) v BC Luc., Ind. 8 f. (Stephanis 916)
S. ITALY (CAMPANIA):
—DIKAIARCHIA-PUTEOLI: (6) ?i-ii AD CIL X 3036 (Lat. C. Iulius Euangelus); (7) ?ii AD ib. 2886 (Lat. M. Ulpius Euangelus); (8) iii-iv AD Puteoli 7-8 (1983-4) p. 178 (Lat. Euangelus)
SICILY:
—KAMARINA: (9) f. v BC Cordano, Tessere Pubbliche 25 (Arena, Iscr. Sic. II 133 A) (-άνγε-: s. Σῖμος)
—SYRACUSE: (10) imp. CIL X 7150 (Lat. Euange[lus]: s. Τύχη)

**Εὐάγης**
ARGOLIS:
—HYDREA: (1) ?iv BC PCG 5 p. 183
ARKADIA:
—MANTINEIA-ANTIGONEIA: (2) c. 300-221 BC IG V (2) 323. 69 (tessera) (f. Χαιρίων)

**Εὐάγητος**
KORINTHIA:
—KORINTH: (1) viii BC FGrH 239 A 31 (f. Ἀρχίας)

**Εὐαγόρας**
ACHAIA:
—AIGION: (1) m. ii BC IG IX (1)² (3) 667, 4 (f. Ἀριστόβουλος); (2) 147 BC Plb. xxxviii 13. 4; cf. Walbank 3 p. 707 (s. Ἀριστόβουλος)
ARGOLIS:
—EPIDAUROS*: (3) c. 370-365 BC Peek, IAEpid 52 A, 50
—METHANA-ARSINOE: (4) iii-ii BC IG IV (1) 863
—TROIZEN: (5) 146 BC ib. 757 A, 27 (Εὐαγόρα[ς])
ARKADIA:
—PHIGALEIA: (6) f. iii BC SEG XXIII 238 (Εὐαγόρ[ας])
ELIS: (7) 408 BC Moretti, Olymp. 350; SEG XXXII 217, [13]
ILLYRIA:
—EPIDAMNOS-DYRRHACHION: (8) c. 250-50 BC BMC Thessaly p. 77 no. 170 (coin) (pryt.) ?= (9); (9) ~ Bakërr Hoard p. 66 no. 43 (coin) (Ceka 272) (pryt.) ?= (8)
KORINTHIA:
—KORINTH: (10) vii/vi BC FGrH 90 F 59. 1 (and Macedonia Potidaia-Kassandreia: s. Περίανδρος, ?s. Λυσιδίκα (Epidauros): oikist); (11) 326 BC Berve 307 (s. Εὐκλέων)
LAKONIA:
—SPARTA: (12) m. vi BC RE (6); Moretti, Olymp. 110; 113; 117 (Poralla² 288)
PELOPONNESE: (13) s. iii BC SEG XIII 278, 10 (f. Λίχας)
SICILY:
—ZANKLE-MESSANA: (14) s. vi BC Paus. v 25. 11

**Εὐαγόρης**
S. ITALY (BRUTTIUM):
—RHEGION: (1) m. v BC L'Incidenza dell'Antico 1 p. 416 (-ρἐς: s. Λυκίσκος)

**Εὐάγορος**
ARKADIA:
—MEGALOPOLIS: (1) hell.? IG V (2) 448, 10 ([Ε]ὐάγορος)
DALMATIA:
—ISSA: (2) iii BC Brunšmid p. 9 fr. H, 7 ([Εὐ]άγορος, [Ἑρμ]άγορος?: s. Ἀρχιτέλης)
EPIROS:
—MOLOSSOI: (3) f. iii BC FGrH 703 F 9 (s. Θεόδωρος)
S. ITALY (LUCANIA):
—HYELE-VELIA: (4) hell.? PdelP 21 (1966) p. 336 no. 5 (s. Ὄνησος)

**Εὐάγριος**
SICILY:
—KATANE: (1) iii-v AD IG XIV 542 (Agnello 53; Wessel 852; cf. Riv. Arch. Crist. 18 (1941) p. 241 no. 138

**Εὔαγρος**
AIGINA: (1) vi/v BC SEG XXXVIII 289; cf. XXXIX 331; (2) ii-iii AD ib. XI 21

**Εὔαθλος**
LEUKAS: (1) vi BC PMG fr. 277 (dub.)

**Εὐαίνετος**
ARGOLIS:
—ARGOS: (1) iii BC Mnem. NS 47 (1919) p. 162 no. 8 a (s. Εὐφάνης)
—EPIDAUROS: (2) iii BC Peek, IAEpid 93 (s. Εὐα—)

## Εὔαινος

ARKADIA: (3) 320 BC *IG* v (2) 549, 6 (f. Χιονίδας)
—MANTINEIA-ANTIGONEIA: (4) iv/iii BC ib. 279 (Εὐαίνε[τος]: f. Ἀνδροκλῆς); (5) iii-ii BC ib. 319, 17 (Ἐὐαίνετ[ος])
—TEGEA: (6) hell.? ib. 170. 14 (tile); (7) c. 240-229 BC ib. 11, 20
KORINTHIA:
—SIKYON: (8) vi/v BC *SEG* XI 244, 63
LAKONIA:
—SPARTA: (9) 480 BC Hdt. vii 173. 2; D.S. xi 2. 5 (Poralla² 289) (s. Κάρανος)
MESSENIA:
—MESSENE: (10) s. iii BC *IG* IV (1) 727 B, 3 (Perlman H.2) (f. Χαιρήμων)
SICILY: (11) f. iv BC *IG* II² 10287 (f. Ἀπολλωνίδης)
—SYRACUSE?: (12) v BC *RE* (5); Liegle, *Euainetos*; Gallatin, *Euainetos*; Westermark–Jenkins pp. 47 ff.; *Samml. Ludwig* 455 (Cordano, 'Camarina VII' 28 (coin)) (coin engraver)

## Εὔαινος

ARGOLIS:
—EPIDAUROS: (1) c. 370 BC *IG* IV (1)² 102, 288; (2) iii BC Peek, *IAEpid* 147 (s. —αρχίδας); (3) ii BC ib. 153. 20 (f. Ἄκρων)
——Rhopitais: (4) c. 365-335 BC *IG* IV (1)² 103, 137
—EPIDAUROS*: (5) c. 370-360 BC *BSA* 61 (1966) p. 271 no. 4 A, 14
ILLYRIA:
—EPIDAMNOS-DYRRHACHION: (6) c. 250-50 BC *IApoll Ref. Bibl.* Addenda n. 7; (7) ii-i BC *IDyrrh* 537 (tiles)

## Εὔαιφνος

LAKONIA:
—SPARTA: (1) m. viii BC Paus. iv 4. 5-8; 5. 2; D.S. viii 7. 1 (Poralla² 290) (dub.)

## Εὐάκης

KERKYRA: (1) c. 315-280 BC *FD* III (4) 406, 3 (Εὐά(λ)κης?: f. Λυσήν)

## Εὔακρος

S. ITALY (CALABRIA):
—LUPIAE: (1) imp. *Ann. Univ. Lecce* 8-9 (1977-80) p. 216 b (Lat. Euacrus)

## Εὐάλας

LAKONIA:
—SPARTA: (1) 412 BC Th. viii 22. 1 (Poralla² 291)

## Εὐάλκης

ACHAIA: (1) 146 BC *IG* IV (1)² 28, 113 (f. Ἀπελλῆς: synoikos)
ARGOLIS:
—ARGOS: (2) c. 458 BC ib. I³ 1149, 66 (Ε[ὐά]λ[κε]ς)
ARKADIA:
—MANTINEIA-ANTIGONEIA: (3) c. 300-221 BC ib. v (2) 323. 59 (tessera) (s. Εὐαλκίδας)
LAKONIA:
—GERONTHRAI: (4) ?418 BC ib. v (1) 1124; *LSAG²* p. 202 no. 60 (date) (Poralla² 298) (-κēς)
LEUKAS: (5) iii BC Unp. (*IG* arch.)

## Εὐαλκίδας

AKARNANIA:
—THYRREION: (1) ii BC *SEG* XXV 628, 2; *IG* IX (1)² (2) 251, 7 (I f. Εὐαλκίδας II); (2) ~ *SEG* XXV 628, 2; *IG* IX (1)² (2) 251, 7 (II s. Εὐαλκίδας I); (3) f. i BC *AE* 1917, p. 167, 17 (Stephanis 2756)
ARKADIA:
—MANTINEIA-ANTIGONEIA: (4) c. 300-221 BC *IG* v (2) 323. 59 (tessera) (f. Εὐάλκης)
—MEGALOPOLIS: (5) s. iii BC ib. 479, 7

---

ELIS: (6) inc. Moretti, *Olymp.* 958
EPIROS:
—BOUTHROTOS (PRASAIBOI): (7) a. 163 BC *IBouthrot* 36, 14 (*SEG* XXXVIII 495) (f. Ἀγώνιππος)

## Εὔαλκος

AKARNANIA:
—EURIPOS: (1) c. 325-315 BC *Hesp.* 57 (1988) p. 148 A, 30 (*SEG* XXXVI 331); cf. *Hesp.* 48 (1979) pp. 78 f. with pl. 22 c (s. Χαιρμένης)
—THYRREION: (2) 216 BC *IG* IX (1)² (2) 583, 64; (3) ii BC ib. 248, 9, 18 (s. Κλεομένης, f. Κλεομένης, Ἀθανάδας)
EPIROS:
—AMBRAKIA: (4) c. 200 BC ib. IX (1)² (1) 31, 127 (f. Ἄεροπος)
—MOLOSSOI:
——Arianteis: (5) f. ii BC *IBouthrot* 1, 2; Cabanes, *L'Épire* p. 589 no. 75, 2 (*SEG* XXXVII 510); *L'Illyrie mérid.* 1 p. 134
KORINTHIA:
—SIKYON: (6) vi/v BC *SEG* XI 244, 39
LAKONIA:
—SPARTA: (7) 272 BC Plu., *Pyrrh.* 30 (Bradford (-))
SICILY:
—TAUROMENION: (8) c. 226 BC *IG* XIV 421 an. 15 (*SGDI* 5219) ?= (9); (9) c. 220-176 BC *IG* XIV 421 an. 21; 421 an. 35; 421 an. 65; 421 an. 77 (*SGDI* 5219) (s. Νυμφόδωρος, f. Νυμφόδωρος) ?= (8)

## Εὐαμᾶς

LAKONIA: (1) imp. *SEG* XXXII 394 (Εὐαμᾶ (gen.))

## Εὐαμερίδας

LAKONIA:
—HIPPOLA: (1) ii-iii AD ib. XXVI 456, 17, 19 (s. Δέξιππος, Κλεοπάτρα); (2) ~ ib. l. 17-18 (f. Κλεοπάτρα)
—SPARTA: (3) c. 25-1 BC *IG* v (1) 210, 9 (Bradford (-)) (f. Δάμιππος)

## Εὐαμέριος

LAKONIA:
—SPARTA: (1) ii-i BC *IG* IX (2) 518 (Bradford (-)) (f. Ἀριστόνικος)

## Εὐαμερίς

ARGOLIS:
—EPIDAUROS: (1) iii-ii BC *SEG* XI 452; (2) ?i AD ib. XXXIX 356 bis (date—*LGPN*)

## Εὐαμερίων

LAKONIA:
—SPARTA: (1) 101-60 BC *Klio* 15 (1918) p. 33 no. 54, [2], 7; (2) c. 25-1 BC *IG* v (1) 210, 4 (Bradford (-)) (f. Φιλόξενος)

## Εὐάμερος

ACHAIA: (1) 146 BC *IG* IV (1)² 28, 76 (s. Δαμάτριος: synoikos)
AIGINA: (2) i BC-i AD ib. IV (1) 44 + *AD* 31 (1976) Chron. p. 7 (s. Ἀγνόθεμις)
ARGOLIS:
—TROIZEN: (3) ?ii/i BC *IG* IV (1) 811
LAKONIA:
—PYRRHICHOS: (4) i-ii AD ib. v (1) 1524, 6, 26, 44 (f. Δαμαρμενίδας)
—SPARTA: (5) s. i BC ib. 93, 16 (Bradford (7)) (Εὐάμ[ερ]ος: f. Γοργιάδας); (6) ~ *IG* v (1) 143 a (Bradford (6)) (f. Εὐδαιμοτέλης); (7) ~ *IG* v (1) 902; *SEG* XI 873 a (tiles) (Bradford (3)); (8) c. 30-20 BC *IG* v (1) 211, 52 (Bradford (2)); (9) c. 25-1 BC *IG* v (1) 210, 49; 212, 49 (Bradford (2)) (II s. Εὐάμερος I); (10) ~ *IG* v (1) 212, 49 (Bradford (5)) (I f. Εὐάμερος II); (11) c. 105-110 AD *IG* v (1) 20 B, 1 (Bradford (1)) (s. Ἀρίων); (12) f. iii AD *FD* III (1) 215;

---

Cartledge–Spawforth p. 197 (date) (Bradford (4)) (M. Αὐρ. Ἐ.)
MESSENIA:
—MESSENE: (13) ii-i BC *SEG* XLI 343, 6 ([Εὐ]άμερος); (14) 31 BC-14 AD ib. XXIII 207, 22 (s. Φιλοκράτης)
—MESSENE?: (15) iv/iii BC *RE* s.v. Euemeros (3); *Evemero di Messene*; Fraser, *Ptol. Alex.* 2 p. 447 n. 800 (locn.)
—THOURIA: (16) f. ii BC *SEG* XI 972, 120 (s. Διόδωρος)
PELOPONNESE?: (17) 11 AD *PAE* 1992, p. 72 B, 16 (f. Λαέρτιος)
SICILY:
—KAMARINA: (18) ?ii BC *SEG* XXXIX 997, 8 (Cordano, 'Camarina VII' 102) ([Ε]ὐάμερ[ος])

## Εὐαμερώ

ARGOLIS:
—ARGOS: (1) i BC *SEG* I 70 (*GVI* 618) (d. Ἔρως, Μόσχιον)

## Εὐάνδρα

AITOLIA:
—KALLION/KALLIPOLIS: (1) hell.? *IG* IX (1)² (1) 156

## Εὐανδρίδας

ELIS: (1) ii AD Luc., *Herm* 39 (fict.)
KORINTHIA:
—SIKYON: (2) iv/iii BC *CID* II 120 A, 47; 122 I, 2 (f. —ος)

## Εὐάνδριος

ARGOLIS:
—EPIDAUROS*: (1) c. 360-350 BC *IG* IV (1)² 113, 11 (Εὐάνδριος) ?= (2); (2) c. 335-325 BC Peek, *IAEpid* 50, 17 (Εὐάν[δριος]) ?= (1)

## Εὐανδρίς

ACHAIA:
—TRITAIA: (1) hell.-imp. Neratzoulis p. 20 no. 3 with fig. 13 (*Achaie* II 312) ([Εὐ]ανδρίς: d. Λυκίσκος)

## Εὔανδρος

ACHAIA:
—ASCHEION: (1) c. 230-200 BC *BCH* 45 (1921) p. 12 II, 63 (s. Ἀπολλωνίδας)
—DYME*: (2) c. 219 BC *SGDI* 1612, 38 (*Tyche* 5 (1990) p. 124) (f. Τίμων)
AITOLIA: (3) ?225 BC Nachtergael, *Les Galates* 63, 9; cf. Stephanis 972 (f. Εὔνικος)
ARGOLIS:
—ARGOS: (4) c. 100-90 BC *SEG* XXXIII 290 A, 13; *BSA* 70 (1975) pp. 129-31 (date); cf. Stephanis 1519 (f. Κυδίας)
—EPIDAUROS: (5) iii/ii BC *IG* IV (1)² 306 A, 3
—HERMIONE: (6) iii BC ib. IV (1) 697 (f. Καλλιστώ)
—NEMEA*: (7) v BC *SEG* XXXIII 273
ARKADIA:
—TEGEA: (8) iii BC *IG* v (2) 30, 19 ([Ε]ὔανδρος)
EPIROS:
—DODONA*: (9) iv-iii BC *SGDI* 1582 (Εὔβ(ϝ)ανδρος)
ILLYRIA:
—EPIDAMNOS-DYRRHACHION: (10) c. 250-50 BC Maier 214; *Jubice Hoard* p. 96 no. 4 (coin) (Ceka 6; 86 (coin)) (pryt.); (11) ~ Maier 358; 475; *Bakërr Hoard* p. 67 nos. 108-9; Münsterberg Nachtr. p. 17 (coin) (Ceka 155-60) (money.); (12) hell.-imp. *IDyrrh* 101 (Εὐάποδρο[s]—ed., Εὐαν<ο>δρο[s]?: f. Ἀνθρωπίων); (13) ~ ib. 199 (Εὐανδ[ρος]: s. Νέων)
KEPHALLENIA:
—PRONNOI: (14) c. 230-200 BC *BCH* 45 (1921) p. 14 II, 142 (s. Ἐπιχάρης)
KORINTHIA:
—SIKYON: (15) ii BC *IG* II² 10304 (f. Ἴλαρον)
LEUKAS: (16) iv/iii BC Peek, *IAEpid* 14, 7 (s. Νικόμαχος)

MESSENIA:
—MESSENE: (17) s. ii BC *SEG* XLI 341, 8 (s. Εὐνοστίδας); (18) i AD *IG* V (1) 1436, 22 (Εὐανθ[ρος])
S. ITALY (BRUTTIUM):
—KROTON: (19) iv BC Iamb., *VP* 267 (*FVS* I p. 446) (Ἔνανδρος—ms., *E.*—edd.)
—RHEGION: (20) i BC/i AD *Suppl. It.* 5 p. 65 no. 17 (Lat. C. Iulius Evander: s. Νεοπτόλεμος)
S. ITALY (CALABRIA):
—TARAS-TARENTUM: (21) imp. *CIL* IX 6166 (Lat. Ti. Iulius Euander)
S. ITALY (CAMPANIA):
—POMPEII: (22) 54 AD ib. IV 3340. 9, 5, 9; 10, 19 (Castrèn 55. 2) (Lat. C. Atullius Evander)
S. ITALY (LUCANIA):
—METAPONTION: (23) iv BC Iamb., *VP* 267 (*FVS* I p. 446)
SICILY:
—SYRACUSE: (24) iii-v AD Strazzulla 391 (Wessel 1335)
—TAUROMENION: (25) c. 239-216 BC *IG* XIV 421 an. 2; 421 an. 3; 421 an. 9; 421 an. 25 (*SGDI* 5219) (f. Ἀγάθαρχος, Εὐπόλεμος) ?= (26); (26) c. 224 BC *IG* XIV 421 an. 17 (*SGDI* 5219) (f. Ἄρχιππος) ?= (25)
——(Σακ.): (27) ?ii/i BC *IG* XIV 421 D an. 11 (*SGDI* 5219) (s. Φιλίαρχος)

### Εὐάνθα
ARKADIA:
—MEGALOPOLIS: (1) hell. *IG* V (2) 479, 9

### Εὐάνθη
ARKADIA:
—THELPHOUSA: (1) ii/i BC *SEG* XI 1125; *BCH* 88 (1964) p. 174 (date)
SICILY:
—SYRACUSE: (2) iii-v AD *IG* XIV 108 (Strazzulla 46; Wessel 845)

### Εὐάνθης
ARGOLIS:
—ARGOS: (1) ii AD *SEG* XVI 253, 17 (f. Νίκανδρος)
—EPIDAUROS: (2) c. 370 BC *IG* IV (1)² 102, 41; (3) iii BC Peek, *IAEpid* 43, 34; (4) s. iii BC *IG* IV (1)² 221 (f. Ἀρχέδαμος); (5) f. ii BC ib.; 222; 649, [2] (s. Ἀρχέδαμος, Ἱερόκλεια, f. Εὔνομος); (6) ii/i BC ib. 216; 224; 649, [1]; 656 (s. Εὔνομος, f. Λαφάντα); (7) i BC ib. 647; 648; 654; 657; 658, 3-4 (s. Εὔνομος, f. Πολυκράτης); (8) f. i BC ib. 66, 1, 20, 25, 44, 48, 55, 60, 66, 70, 72; 67 a, 2; 216, 3; 224, 1; 648; 649, 2; 656, 2; Peek, *IAEpid* 22, 4, 9, [13]; Peek, *NIEpid* 84 (s. Εὔνομος, f. Εὔνομος, Λαφάντα)
ARKADIA:
—TEGEA:
——(Krariotai): (9) iii BC *IG* V (2) 40, 15 ([Εὐά]νθης: s. Δαμοκλῆς)
ILLYRIA:
—EPIDAMNOS-DYRRHACHION: (10) hell.-imp. *IDyrrh* 200
S. ITALY (BRUTTIUM):
—LOKROI EPIZEPHYRIOI:
——(Ὀμβ.): (11) 279 BC De Franciscis 13, 4 (s. Εὐκλείσκος)
S. ITALY (CALABRIA):
—TARAS-TARENTUM?: (12) f. iii BC *HE* 2178 (f. Ἄγνων)
S. ITALY (CAMPANIA):
—NEAPOLIS: (13) 170 AD *IG* XIV 748 A, 2 (*INap* 52) (Τ. Φλ. Ἐ.: s. Τ. Φλ. Ζώσιμος, Φλ. Φορτουνάτα)
—SALERNUM*: (14) imp. *IItal* I (1) 60 (*CIL* X 586) (Lat. Euanthes: I f. Εὐάνθης II: freed.); (15) ~ *IItal* I (1) 60 (*CIL* X 586) (Lat. L. Faenius Euanthes: II s. Εὐάνθης I: freed.)

### Εὐανθίδας
ARKADIA:
—TEGEA: (1) iii BC *IG* V (2) 30, 23 ([Εὐ]ανθίδας?, —ανθίδας—ed.)

### Εὐανθίδης
EPIROS:
—BOUTHROTOS (PRASAIBOI): (1) a. 163 BC *IBouthrot* 14, 43 (*SEG* XXXVIII 471) (II s. Εὐανθίδης I); (2) ~ *IBouthrot* 14, 42-3 (*SEG* XXXVIII 471) (I s. Εὔπορος, f. Εὐανθίδης II)

### Εὐάνθιος
AITOLIA:
—TITRAI: (1) c. 265-260 BC *FD* III (3) 199 (Κυάνθιος—lap. and *FD*, (Ε)ὐάνθιος—Pomtow: f. Βουθήρας)

### Εὐανθίς
S. ITALY (CAMPANIA):
—DIKAIARCHIA-PUTEOLI: (1) imp. *CIL* X 3085 (Lat. Veratia Euanthis)

### Εὔανθος
S. ITALY (APULIA):
—ARGYRIPPA-ARPI*: (1) imp. ib. IX 934 (Lat. [E]uanthus: ?f. Ἄρχη: freed.)
S. ITALY (CAMPANIA):
—HERCULANEUM*: (2) m. i AD *Cron. Erc.* 7 (1977) p. 118 D, 7 (Lat. Q. Iunius Euanthus: freed.)
—POMPEII: (3) i BC-i AD *CIL* IV 8518 (Lat. Evanthus); (4) 56 AD ib. 3340. 19, 17 (Lat. C. Atillius Euanthus)
—POMPEII*: (5) i BC-i AD ib. 10126 (*Gnomon* 45 (1973) p. 270) (Lat. Evantus: freed.?)

### Εὐάνιος
KORINTHIA:
—SIKYON: (1) vi/v BC *SEG* XI 244, 32

### Εὐανορίδαρ
ELIS: (1) iii BC *IvOl* 299 ([Εὐανο]ρίδαρ: s. (ad.) Δαμέας) ?= (Εὐανορίδας (1))

### Εὐανορίδας
ELIS: (1) ?iii BC *RE* (-); Moretti, *Olymp.* 570; cf. *FGrH* 416 T 2 ?= (2) Εὐανορίδαρ (1); (2) 217 BC Plb. v 94. 6 ?= (1)

### Εὐάντας
KORINTHIA:
—KORINTH: (1) vii/vi BC Amyx Gr 5 a. 2 (vase) (Lorber 2 a) (Εὐάντας, [M]ελάντας?)

### Εὐαντίδας
EPIROS:
—AMBRAKIA: (1) c. 405 BC Paus. x 9. 10; cf. *CEG* II 819

### Εὔαντος
ARKADIA:
—PHENEOS: (1) c. 315-280 BC *FD* III (1) 40, 2 (s. Ξενόδικος)

### Εὐάνωρ
ACHAIA?: (1) 193 BC *IG* V (2) 293, 17 (Εὐάν[ωρ]: s. Ἀλεξι—)
ARGOLIS:
—EPIDAUROS: (2) iii/ii BC ib. IV (1)² 358 (Peek, *IAEpid* 153. 6)
—KALAURIA: (3) iii BC *IG* IV (1) 845 (s. Ἐπιχάρης)
ARKADIA: (4) 316 BC ib. V (2) 549, 34 (s. Εὔαρχος)
EPIROS:
—DODONA: (5) iii BC Antoniou, *Dodone* Ab, 17
MESSENIA:
—MESSENE: (6) f. iii BC *PAE* 1991, p. 99 no. 7, 24
S. ITALY (BRUTTIUM):
—SYBARIS-THOURIOI-COPIAE: (7) iv BC Iamb., *VP* 267 (*FVS* I p. 446)

### Εὔαπτος
ACHAIA:
—DYME*: (1) c. 219 BC *SGDI* 1612, 23 (*Tyche* 5 (1990) p. 124) (s. Μεγακλῆς)

### Εὐαρείδας
ARKADIA:
—TEGEA: (1) f. ii BC *IG* V (2) 44, 10 (Εὐαρείδας: f. Δάων); (2) c. 146-32 BC *BMC Pelop.* p. 11 no. 132 (coin) (Εὐαρεί[δας]?)

### Εὐάρεστος
AIGINA: (1) imp. *Alt-Ägina* I (2) p. 46 no. 25 (I f. Εὐάρεστος II); (2) ~ ib. (II s. Εὐάρεστος I)
EPIROS:
—IGOUMENITSA (MOD.): (3) iii AD *SEG* XXXIII 478 (Ἀντώνιος Εὐά[ρεσ]τος)
—NIKOPOLIS: (4) imp. *PAE* 1913, p. 97 no. 6 (Sarikakis 47) (s. Κλεόμαχος); (5) ii AD *Hellenika* 22 (1969) p. 70 no. 7 (Sarikakis 46) (s. Ἀγρίππας)
LAKONIA:
—SPARTA: (6) c. 212-220 AD *IG* V (1) 653 a, 3 (*Artemis Orthia* p. 356 no. 142; Bradford (-)) (M. Αὐρ. Ἐ.: s. Ζωῖλος)
S. ITALY (CAMPANIA):
—DIKAIARCHIA-PUTEOLI: (7) imp. *CIL* X 2328 (Lat. C. Cornelius Euarestus)

### Εὐαρέτα
ARGOLIS:
—EPIDAUROS: (1) s. iii BC *IG* IV (1)² 209 (m. Τι—); (2) ii/i BC ib. 232, 2 (d. Ξενόδοκος, m. Δαμύλος, Δαμώ); (3) i AD ib. 34
EPIROS:
—AMBRAKIA: (4) hell.? *SEG* XXXIX 523 (d. Τιμωνίδας); (5) hell. ib. ([Ε]ὐαρέτα)

### Εὐάρετος
ARKADIA:
—TEGEA: (1) s. iii BC *IG* V (2) 116, 7 (s. Σακλῆς)

### Εὐάρης
DALMATIA:
—ISSA: (1) hell. *SEG* XXXI 594 (s. Κλεέμπορος); (2) iii BC ib. 597 (f. Ἀγησίδαμος)
——(Dymanes): (3) iv/iii BC Brunšmid p. 8, 43 ([Εὐ]άρης—*LGPN*: s. Ἀντίμαχος)
—ISSA?: (4) iii/ii BC ib. p. 31 no. 27; *Istros* 2 (1935-6) pp. 18 ff. (or Dalmatia Tragurion: s. Τιμασίων)
S. ITALY (BRUTTIUM):
—LOKROI EPIZEPHYRIOI:
——(Θρα.): (5) iv/iii BC De Franciscis 21, 2

### Εὐαρίδας
S. ITALY (LUCANIA):
—METAPONTION: (1) vii/vi BC *SEG* XXX 1176 A. 3 (Landi, *DISMG* 135)

### Εὐάριστος
DALMATIA:
—EPETION: (1) imp. *CIL* III 8520 (Lat. Evvaristus)
S. ITALY (APULIA):
—CANUSIUM*: (2) ii AD *Epig. Rom. di Canosa* 86 (Lat. L. Marius Euaristus: freed.); (3) ii-iii AD ib. 53 (Lat. Euaristus: freed.)
—LUCERIA: (4) imp. *CIL* IX 867 (Lat. Minatius Euaristus)
S. ITALY (CAMPANIA):
—DIKAIARCHIA-PUTEOLI: (5) imp. ib. X 3020 (Lat. M. Tribonius Euaristus: f. Trebonia Marsilla)
—DIKAIARCHIA-PUTEOLI*: (6) imp. ib. 1560 (Lat. Euaristus: slave?)
—HERCULANEUM: (7) i BC-i AD ib. 1403 d III, 16 (Lat. L. Minicius Euaristus)
—POMPEII: (8) i BC-i AD ib. IV 1804 (Lat. Evaristus); (9) ~ ib. 9981; cf. *Gnomon* 45 (1973) p. 268 (Lat. Euaritmus?—*CIL*, Evaristus—*Gnomon*)

**Εὐαρμίδας**
AITOLIA:
—KALLION/KALLIPOLIS: (1) ?160 BC *SGDI* 2280, 1 (f. Σωκράτεια)

**Εὐάρμοστος**
KORINTHIA:
—SIKYON: (1) 337-336 BC *CID* II 74 I, 75; 75 II, 49; 76 II, 24 (s. Στίλπας)

**Εὐαρχίδαμος**
ARGOLIS:
—EPIDAUROS*: (1) c. 370-360 BC Peek, *IAEpid* 52 A, 41; *BSA* 61 (1966) p. 272 no. 4 A, 20

**Εὐαρχίδας**
ACHAIA:
—PELLENE: (1) m. iv BC *CID* II 19, 2 (f. —ιος)
AIGINA: (2) ?s. i BC *Alt-Ägina* I (2) p. 44 no. 6, 2 (f. —ος)
AITOLIA: (3) ?228-215 BC *FD* III (4) 364, 4
ARGOLIS:
—ARGOS: (4) c. 458 BC *IG* I³ 1149, 80 ([Εὐ]αρχί[δ]ας)
—EPIDAUROS: (5) iv BC ib. IV (1)² 174; (6) ~ ib. XII (5) 542, 15 (Εὐαρχ[ίδας], Εὐαρχ[ος]—*IG*: f. Ξενόδοκος: name—*LGPN*); (7) s. iii BC *SEG* XI 440 a-b (s. Εὔαρχος); (8) ~ ib. (f. Εὔαρχος); (9) iii/ii BC *IG* IV (1)² 378 (Peek, *IAEpid* 153. 25); (10) ii BC ib. 143. 24
ARKADIA:
—TEGEA: (11) c. 369-362 BC *IG* v (2) 173, 5; cf. *CEG* II 657 (Εὐαρχ[ί]δας)
LAKONIA?: (12) ?v-iv BC *CGFP* 236, 12, 14 (fict.?)
S. ITALY (CALABRIA):
—TARAS-TARENTUM: (13) c. 302-280 BC Vlasto 709 (coin) (Evans, *Horsemen* p. 135 VI H)
SICILY:
—KAMARINA: (14) f. v BC Cordano, *Tessere Pubbliche* 75 (Arena, *Iscr. Sic.* II 140 A) (s. Καλλισθένης)
—SYRACUSE: (15) v/iv BC *HN²* p. 177; *Samml. Ludwig* 461-2 (coin) (coin engraver)

**Εὐάρχιππος**
LAKONIA:
—SPARTA: (1) 408 BC X., *HG* ii 3. 10 (Poralla² 292)

**Εὔαρχος**
ACHAIA:
—DYME*: (1) c. 219 BC *SGDI* 1612, 63 (*Tyche* 5 (1990) p. 124) (f. Σαμίας)
AITOLIA: (2) iv BC *IG* IX (1)² (1) 116; (3) ?c. 230 BC *FD* III (3) 219 bis, 3; (4) 217 BC Nachtergael, *Les Galates* 65, 9; cf. Stephanis 1203 (f. Θεύφραστος)
—APEIRIKOI?: (5) m. ii BC *SBBerlAk* 1936, p. 371 b, 14 (*SEG* XLI 528 B) (Εὔα(ρ)χος: s. Βιαῖος)
—BOUKATION: (6) 190 BC *IG* IX (1)² (1) 97, 5 ?= (8); (7) 163 BC ib. 101, 7 (s. Ἄνταγρος); (8) ~ ib. l. 13 (s. Νικιάδας) ?= (6); (9) 161 BC ib. 100, 5
—EGGORAIOI: (10) 223 BC ib. 31, 51
—POTIDANIA: (11) m. ii BC *SBBerlAk* 1936, p. 371 a, 10 (*SEG* XLI 528 A); *SBBerlAk* 1936, p. 371 b, 2, 10, 13 (*SEG* XLI 528 B) (s. Νεοπτόλεμος, f. Νεοπτόλεμος)
AKARNANIA: (12) 375 BC Tod, *GHI* II 126, 26; (13) iii/ii BC *AM* 7 (1882) p. 21; cf. Fraser, *Ptol. Alex.* 2 p. 116 n. 23 (vase)
—ASTAKOS: (14) 431 BC Th. ii 30. 1; 33. 1 (tyrant)
—PHOKREAI: (15) 216 BC *IG* IX (1)² (2) 583, 4 (f. Σίμων)
ARGOLIS:
—ARGOS:
——Pedion: (16) iii BC *SEG* XVII 141, 3
—EPIDAUROS: (17) s. iii BC ib. XI 440 a-b (s. Εὐαρχίδας, f. Εὐαρχίδας); (18) iii/ii BC Peek,

*NIEpid* 15, 12 (Εὔαρ[χος]: s. Σκύμνος); (19) i BC *IG* IV (1)² 64, 4 + Peek, *IAEpid* 19 (f. Κίτος)
——Lasieis: (20) c. 365-335 BC *IG* IV (1)² 103, 151
ARKADIA: (21) 316 BC ib. v (2) 549, 34 (f. Εὐάνωρ)
—TEGEA: (22) iii BC ib. 40, 4; (23) s. iii BC ib. 116, 2 (s. Κλέων)
DALMATIA:
—ISSA:
——(Hylleis): (24) iv/iii BC Brunšmid p. 8, 40-1 (f. Κόκκαλος, Θρασύμαχος)
ELIS: (25) c. 400 BC *IG* II² 8528

**Εὐατέας**
ARKADIA:
—KYNAITHA: (1) c. 230-200 BC *BCH* 45 (1921) p. 12 II, 66 (s. Πελοπίδας)

**Εὐβαβερίσκος**
LAKONIA:
—SPARTA: (1) c. 150-160 AD *SEG* XI 528, 2; 552, 6?; *REG* 99 (1986) p. 139 (name) (Bradford (-)) (Εὐβ(ϝ)αβ(ϝ)ερίσκος, Εὐβ(ϝ)αβ(ϝ)ε[ρίσκος]—552: s. Διογένης)

**Εὐβάβερος**
LAKONIA:
—SPARTA: (1) c. 140-160 AD *IG* v (1) 154, 13 (Bradford (2)) (Εὐβ(ϝ)άβ(ϝ)ερος: I f. Εὐβάβερος II); (2) ~ *IG* v (1) 154, 13; *REG* 99 (1986) p. 139 (name) (Bradford (1)) (Εὐβ(ϝ)άβ(ϝ)ερος: II s. Εὐβάβερος I)

**Εὐβάλκης**
LAKONIA:
—SPARTA: (1) iv/iii BC *IG* v (1) 649; Moretti, *Olymp.* 510; cf. *Artemis Orthia* p. 289 (Poralla² 299; Bradford (1)) (Εὐβ(ϝ)άλκης (n. pr.?)); (2) c. 25-1 BC *IG* v (1) 210, 17 (Bradford (2)) (Εὐβ(ϝ)άλκης: f. Λίβυς)

**Εὐβάμερος**
LAKONIA:
—SPARTA: (1) ii BC *Mél. Daux* p. 233, 4 (Εὐβ(ϝ)άμερος: s. Εὐτυχᾶς)

**Εὐβάνωρ**
LAKONIA:
—GYTHEION*: (1) ii BC *IG* v (1) p. 210 (vase) (Εὐβ(ϝ)άνωρ)

**Εὐβάτης**
S. ITALY (LUCANIA):
—HYELE-VELIA: (1) hell.? *PdelP* 25 (1970) p. 264 no. 6 (s. Ἐρατέων)

**Εὐβατίδας**
KORINTHIA:
—KORINTH: (1) ii AD Luc., *Philops.* 30-1 (fict.)

**Εὔβατος**
DALMATIA:
—ISSA:
——(Hylleis): (1) iv/iii BC Brunšmid p. 8, 47 (f. Διονύσιος)

**Εὐβήσυχος**
LAKONIA:
—PYRRHICHOS: (1) imp. *IG* v (1) 1285 (Εὐβ(ϝ)ήσυχος)

**Εὔβιος**
MESSENIA:
—MESSENE: (1) m. iii BC *IC* I p. 247 no. 4 A, 28; cf. Stephanis 927 (I f. Εὔβιος II, Ζώβιος); (2) ~ *IC* I p. 247 no. 4 A, 28; Stephanis 927 (II s. Εὔβιος I)
S. ITALY (CAMPANIA): (3) 226 BC *PPetr²* I *Wills* 26, 4 (Καμπανὸς τῶν Ἀ—)

SICILY:
—SYRACUSE: (4) c. 350-320 BC *SEG* XVIII 772 (s. Εὐβίοτος)
—ZANKLE-MESSANA: (5) ?ii BC *IG* XIV 401, 3, 6 (f. Ἀριστόδαμος, Θεύγνις)

**Εὐβιότα**
S. ITALY (BRUTTIUM):
—LOKROI EPIZEPHYRIOI: (1) imp. *Suppl. It.* 3 p. 28 no. 11 (Lat. —ia Eubiot[a])

**Εὐβίοτος**
ILLYRIA:
—APOLLONIA: (1) c. 250-50 BC Maier 57; Münsterberg Nachtr. p. 13 (coin) (Ceka 49) (money.)
—EPIDAMNOS-DYRRHACHION: (2) c. 250-50 BC Maier 165 (coin) (Ceka 161) (money.)
KEPHALLENIA:
—SAME: (3) hell. *IG* IX (1) 636 ([E]ὐβίοτος)
PELOPONNESE: (4) s. iii BC *SEG* XIII 278, 13 (f. Εὐχύλος)
SICILY:
—SYRACUSE: (5) c. 350-320 BC ib. XVIII 772 (f. Εὔβιος)

**Εὐβοΐδας**
LAKONIA:
—SPARTA: (1) inc. Plu., *Mor.* 220 D (Poralla² 293)

**Εὐβολλεύς**
ACHAIA:
—DYME?: (1) iv BC *SEG* XXIV 340, 1 (f. Ἀγησώ)

**Εὐβούλα**
ARGOLIS:
—NEMEA*: (1) s. iv BC ib. XXX 353, 1, 10 (d. Αἰνέας)
EPIROS:
—AMBRAKIA: (2) iv BC *Op. Ath.* 10 (1971) p. 64 no. 7 (d. Ἀγέλοχος)
ILLYRIA:
—BYLLIONES BYLLIS: (3) iii AD *SEG* XXXVIII 553 (Εὐβούλ[α?])
KORINTHIA:
—SIKYON: (4) imp. *IG* II² 10301

**Εὐβουλία**
SICILY:
—SYRACUSE: (1) hell.? ib. XII (2) 310 (d. Ἀρίστων)

**Εὐβουλίδας**
AITOLIA:
—POTIDANIA: (1) m. ii BC *SBBerlAk* 1936, p. 371 a, 13 (*SEG* XLI 528 A) (f. Τίμαρχος, Ἀρίστων) ?= (2); (2) ~ *SBBerlAk* 1936, p. 371 b, 16 (*SEG* XLI 528 B) (f. Φίλλακος) ?= (1)
ARGOLIS:
—ARGOS:
——(Amphisseis): (3) s. iv BC ib. XXIX 363, 2 (or Lokris (Western) Amphissa)
—EPIDAUROS*: (4) c. 370-365 BC Peek, *IAEpid* 52 B, 17 (Εὐβ[ο]υ[λίδ]ας)
DALMATIA:
—ISSA:
——(Hylleis): (5) iv/iii BC Brunšmid p. 9, 52 (f. Εὐκλῆς)
ILLYRIA:
—APOLLONIA: (6) imp. *IApoll* 80
KORINTHIA:
—SIKYON: (7) s. iv BC *IG* II² 10302 (-δης)
SICILY:
—HERBITA: (8) f. i BC Cic., *In Verr.* II v 110; 128 (Lat. Eubulidas)
—INESSA-AITNA: (9) ?ii-i BC *Riv. Stor. Antica* 5 (1900-1) p. 55 no. 28 + *Sic. Gymn.* 16 (1963) p. 57 (s. Ἡράκλειος)
—KENTORIPA: (10) ?s. iii BC ib. 2 (1949) p. 91 no. 1, 2 + 16 (1963) p. 54; *BE* 1953, no. 279 ([Εὐ]βουλίδας, Βουλίδας?—*BE*: ?s. Ἡ—); (11) i BC-i AD *IGLMP* 29 (s. Ἀγάθαρχος); (12) f. i BC Cic., *In Verr.* II iii 56 (Lat. Eubulidas Grospus)

—MENAI: (13) i BC-i AD *NScav* 1903, p. 436 ([Εὐ]βουλί[δας])
—MORGANTINA: (14) ?iv/iii BC *SEG* XXXIX 1012, 7 ([Εὐβου]λίδας)
—TAUROMENION:
——(Ἀσσιτ.): (15) ii/i BC *IGSI* 12 I, 23; II, 21; III, 17 (f. Ζωτικός)

**Εὐβουλίων**
S. ITALY (CAMPANIA):
—POMPEII: (1) i BC-i AD *CIL* IV 4773; 4727; 5221 (Lat. Euboulio)

**Εὔβουλος**
ACHAIA?: (1) 193 BC *IG* V (2) 293, 6 (s. Δίφιλος); (2) ~ ib. l. 7 (f. Ἀλκαίνετος)
AITOLIA:
—KALLION/KALLIPOLIS: (3) 175 BC *SGDI* 1843, 13 (f. Νικόλαος)
—PLEURON: (4) ?iii BC *IG* IX (2) 202 (*RÉnip* 124) (f. Σώσανδρος)
—THERMOS*: (5) s. iii BC *IG* IX (1)² (1) 60 III, 25
ARGOLIS:
—EPIDAUROS:
——Sinias: (6) c. 370-335 BC ib. IV (1)² 102, 106; 103, 135-6 (Εὔβο(υ)λ[ος]—102)
—EPIDAUROS*: (7) c. 370-360 BC *BSA* 61 (1966) p. 272 no. 4 B II, 14, 16-17
—TROIZEN: (8) ?146 BC *IG* IV (1) 757 B, 39; (9) imp. ib. 812
DALMATIA:
—ISSA: (10) iv/iii BC *VAHD* NS 8 (1905) p. 97 no. 177 (*VAMZ* 1970, p. 33 f. frr. I-J); (11) hell. Brunšmid p. 26 no. 16 (s. Σώδαμος)
——(Hylleis): (12) iv/iii BC ib. p. 9, 50 ([Ε]ὔβολος: s. Φιλώτας)
EPIROS: (13) v/iv BC Unp. (Ioannina Mus.) (Εὔβ(ο)υλος)
KERKYRA: (14) imp. *IG* IX (1) 948 (f. Διονύσις)
KORINTHIA:
—KORINTH: (15) iii AD *IGUR* 1210 (*IG* XIV 1595; *GVI* 1994)
MESSENIA:
—AMPHEIA: (16) ii AD *IG* V (1) 1531
PELOPONNESE?: (17) ii AD *PAE* 1992, p. 72 B, 9 (f. Σοϊξίας)
S. ITALY (CAMPANIA):
—DIKAIARCHIA-PUTEOLI*: (18) imp. *CIL* X 1882 (Lat. Eubulus: freed.)
SICILY:
—AKRAGAS: (19) f. vi BC *FGrH* 577 F 3 (fict.?)
—SYRACUSE: (20) i BC-i AD? Manganaro, *QUCC* forthcoming no. 52 (Εὔβουλ[ος])
—TAUROMENION: (21) c. 180 BC *IG* XIV 421 an. 61 (*SGDI* 5219) (f. Ἀ...ρος); (22) ii/i BC *IGSI* 9 II, 1 (Εὔβουλ[ος], Εὐβουλ[ίδας]?: f. Εὐκλείδας)
—ZANKLE-MESSANA: (23) f. iv BC Iamb., *VP* 127 (*FVS* 1 p. 473)

**Εὐβωλίδας**
ARGOLIS:
—MYKENAI*: (1) iv-iii BC *IG* IV (1) 500 (f. Πρόνομος)

**Εὔβωλος**
LAKONIA:
—OITYLOS: (1) iii/ii BC ib. V (1) 1295, 3 (Bradford (-))

**Εὔγαμος**
LAKONIA:
—HYPERTELEATON*: (1) imp. *IG* V (1) 1080
S. ITALY (CAMPANIA):
—POMPEII: (2) c. 70-79 AD *CIL* IV 9877 (Castrèn 177. 1) (Lat. Fundilius Eugamus)

**Εὐγειτονίδας**
ARKADIA:
—MAINALIOI: (1) 369-361 BC *IG* V (2) 1, 18; Tod, *GHI* II 132 (date)

**Εὐγείτων**
ACHAIA:
—DYME: (1) iii BC *AJPh* 31 (1910) p. 399 no. 74 c, 8 (f. Φιλόξενος)
ARKADIA:
—ORCHOMENOS: (2) 369-361 BC *IG* V (2) 1, 47; Tod, *GHI* II 132 (date)
SICILY:
—SYRACUSE: (3) imp. *Riv. Arch. Crist.* 36 (1960) p. 36 no. 32 (-γή-)

**Εὐγένεια**
KORINTHIA:
—KORINTH: (1) byz. *Corinth* VIII (3) 561, 3; cf. *TMByz* 9 (1985) p. 363 no. 38 (-νια: m. Ἀναστασία); (2) ~ *Corinth* VIII (3) 686 (-νια)
S. ITALY (CAMPANIA):
—MISENUM*: (3) imp. *CIL* X 3406 (Lat. Suillia Eugenia: freed.)

**Εὐγενιανός**
KORINTHIA:
—KORINTH: (1) iii-iv AD *Corinth* VIII (3) 512 ([Εὐ]γενιανός)

**Εὐγενίδας**
S. ITALY (BRUTTIUM):
—LOKROI EPIZEPHYRIOI:
——(Ὀμβ.): (1) iv/iii BC De Franciscis 5, 4 (s. Φιλοκράτης)

**Εὐγένιος**
ILLYRIA:
—EPIDAMNOS-DYRRHACHION: (1) iii-iv AD *IDyrrh* 60 (f. Στέφανος)
KORINTHIA:
—KORINTH: (2) byz. *PAE* 1962, p. 54; cf. *TMByz* 9 (1985) p. 367 no. 87
S. ITALY (APULIA):
—CANUSIUM: (3) s. iii AD *Epig. Rom. di Canosa* 50 (Lat. P. Libuscidius Victorinus Eugenius)

**Εὔγνωτος**
ACHAIA:
—PELLENE: (1) ?iii BC *Klio* 15 (1918) p. 58 no. 81 (s. Ἔκφαντος)

**Εὔγραμμος**
KORINTHIA:
—KORINTH: (1) vii BC Plin., *NH* XXXV 152 (and Etruria: Lat. Eugrammus: potter)

**Εὐδαιμάκων**
LAKONIA:
—SPARTA: (1) c. 130-160 AD *IG* V (1) 68, 24; 112, 8; *SEG* XI 585, 8; XXX 410, 10 (Bradford (-)) (Εὐδαιμάκ(ω)ν—68: s. Εὐκτήμων)

**Εὐδαιμίων**
LAKONIA:
—SPARTA: (1) c. 30-20 BC *IG* V (1) 211, 51 (Bradford (-))

**Εὐδαιμόκλεια**
LAKONIA:
—SPARTA: (1) i-ii AD *IG* V (1) 740 (Bradford (-))

**Εὐδαιμοκλῆς**
LAKONIA:
—SPARTA: (1) i BC-i AD *IG* V (1) 745 (Bradford (5)) (f. Νικοκράτης); (2) s. i BC *IG* V (1) 94, 15 (Bradford (3)) (s. Κα—); (3) c. 1-10 AD *IG* V (1) 209, 16; *SEG* XXXV 331 (date) (Bradford (8)) (I f. Εὐδαιμοκλῆς II); (4) ~ *IG* V (1) 209, 16; *SEG* XXXV 331 (date) (Bradford (1)) (II s. Εὐδαιμοκλῆς I); (5) c. 80-90 AD *IG* V (1) 674, 14 (Bradford (2)) (s. Εὔδαμος); (6) c. 100-125 AD *IG* V (1) 137, 9 (Bradford (6)); (7) ii AD *IG* V (1) 159, 16 (Bradford (5)); (8) c. 140-160 AD *IG* V (1) 154, 10 (Bradford (4)) (s. Φιλόστρατος); (9) c. 160-170 AD *IG* V (1) 109, 12 (Bradford (7)) (f. Ἀριστότιμος)

MESSENIA:
—MESSENE: (10) 263 BC *IG* IX (1)² (1) 17, 7 (s. Εὐδαίμων); (11) ii AD *PAE* 1992, p. 71 A, 5 (s. Ἀρίστων)

**Εὐδαιμονίδας**
LAKONIA:
—SPARTA: (1) iii BC *SEG* XL 348 B, 2; (2) ?i-ii AD *IG* V (1) 672 (Bradford (3)) (Εὐδα(ι)μονίδας: f. Μένιππος); (3) c. 80-100 AD *SEG* XI 608, 2 (Bradford (2)) (f. Ἀγαθοκλῆς); (4) ii AD *IG* V (1) 176, 2 (Bradford (1)) (s. Νικοκλῆς); (5) c. 140 AD *IG* V (1) 128, 8 (f. —λης)
MESSENIA:
—THOURIA: (6) f. ii BC *SEG* XI 972, 98 (f. Χαίρων)

**Εὐδαιμοτέλης**
LAKONIA:
—SPARTA: (1) s. i BC *IG* V (1) 143 a-c (Bradford (1); (3); (5)) (Εὐ(δ)αιμοτέλης—143 a: I s. Εὐάμερος, f. Εὐδαιμοτέλης II, —λα) ?= (3); (2) ~ *IG* V (1) 143 c (Bradford (2)) (II s. Εὐδαιμοτέλης I); (3) c. 30-20 BC *IG* V (1) 211, 9 (Bradford (4)) (f. Καλλιάδας) ?= (1)

**Εὐδαίμων**
AITOLIA: (1) s. iii BC *IG* IX (1)² (1) 204, 1 ([Εὐ]δαίμ[ων]?)
ARKADIA:
—TEGEA: (2) 165 AD ib. V (2) 50, 4 (Γ. Ἰούλ. Ἐ.); (3) ~ ib. l. 18 (I f. Εὐδαίμων II); (4) ~ ib. l. 18 (II s. Εὐδαίμων I)
—ELIS: (5) i/ii AD *IvOl* 83, 7; 86, 12; 92, 19 (Εὐδάμων—92: I f. Εὐδαίμων II); (6) ~ ib. 83, 7; 86, 12; 92, 19 (Εὐδάμων—92, Εὐδα(ί)μων—ed.: II s. Εὐδαίμων I: X.)
LAKONIA:
—KARYSTOS?: (7) iii BC *IG* V (1) 918 (Bradford (3))
—SPARTA: (8) iii BC *SEG* XL 348 B, 7; (9) ~ ib. l. 8 (νεώτ.); (10) ii BC *Mél. Daux* p. 233, 3 ([Ε]ὐδαίμων: s. Εὐθύμιος); (11) c. 100-125 AD *IG* V (1) 137, 7 (Bradford (2)); (12) c. 175-200 AD *IG* V (1) 89, 3 (Bradford (4)) (I f. Εὐδαίμων II); (13) ~ *IG* V (1) 89, 3 (Bradford (1)) (II s. Εὐδαίμων I)
MESSENIA:
—MESSENE: (14) iii BC *SEG* XXIII 209, 8; (15) 263 BC *IG* IX (1)² (1) 17, 7 (f. Εὐδαιμοκλῆς); (16) ?ii BC *PAE* 1991, p. 119 no. 3, 7
—MESSENE?: (17) ii/i BC *SEG* XI 979, 15 ([Εὐ]δαίμων)
—PHARAI: (18) ii BC *IG* V (1) 1366
S. ITALY (CAMPANIA):
—DIKAIARCHIA-PUTEOLI: (19) 196 AD *CIL* X 1786 (Lat. P. Aelius Eudaemon)
—MISENUM*: (20) imp. ib. 3515 (Lat. Iulius Eudemon)
SICILY:
—AKRILLAI: (21) iii-v AD Agnello 68; cf. Ferrua, *NG* 504 (-δέ-: doctor)
—SYRACUSE: (22) iii-v AD Strazzulla 382 (Wessel 750); cf. Ferrua, *NG* 141 a (-δέ-)

**Εὐδαιτίδας**
ACHAIA:
—AIGION: (1) c. 400 BC *IG* II² 7946 (-δης: f. Δαιτόφρων)

**Εὐδάμας**
SICILY: (1) m. vi BC *Argive Heraeum* 2 p. 338 no. 2252 (*LSAG*² p. 168 no. 13)

**Εὐδαμία**
LAKONIA:
—GYTHEION: (1) i-ii AD *IG* V (1) 1176, 3 (d. Εὔτυχος, Σωτηρίς)
—SPARTA: (2) a. 212 AD ib. 596, 3 (Bradford (-)) (Ἀντ. Ἐ.: d. Ἀρτεμᾶς)
MESSENIA:
—MESSENE: (3) i/ii AD *IG* V (1) 1473

## Εὐδαμίδας

ARGOLIS:
—EPIDAUROS: (1) iv/iii BC Peek, *IAEpid* 51, 11; *BSA* 61 (1966) p. 319 no. 26 (date)

ARKADIA:
—MANTINEIA-ANTIGONEIA: (2) 369-361 BC *IG* V (2) 1, 37; Tod, *GHI* II 132 (date)

KORINTHIA:
—KORINTH: (3) ii AD Luc., *Tox.* 22-3
—SIKYON: (4) vi/v BC *SEG* XI 244, 67

LAKONIA: (5) m. ii BC ib. XIII 259, 31-2
—LAS: (6) ?iii BC *IG* V (1) 1214
—SPARTA: (7) c. 400-375 BC ib. 1232, 8 (Poralla² 294); (8) 382 BC *RE* (3); Cartledge, *Agesilaos* pp. 147-8 (stemma) (Poralla² 295) (?f. Δεινίχα); (9) c. 370-300 BC *RE* (4) (Bradford (1)) (s. Ἀρχίδαμος, Δεινίχα, f. Ἀρχίδαμος: king); (10) iv/iii BC Plb. iv 35. 13 (f. Ἀγησίλαος, Ἀγησιστράτα); (11) c. 300-244 BC Plu., *Agis* 3 (Bradford (2)) (s. Ἀρχίδαμος, f. Ἆγις, Ἀρχίδαμος: king); (12) m. ii BC *IG* V (1) 889; 890; 892; 893 (tiles) (Bradford (11)); (13) c. 140 BC *IvOl* 62, 61 (Bradford (4)) (s. Εὐθυκλῆς); (14) hell.-imp. *IG* V (1) 195, 6 (Bradford (14)); (15) 80-70 BC *IG* IX (2) 534, 21; Kramolisch p. 116 n. 74 (date) (Bradford (19)) (f. Ἁρμόνικος); (16) s. i BC *IG* V (1) 92, 6 (Bradford (5)) (s. Ἁρμόνικος); (17) c. 25-1 BC *IG* V (1) 210, 54 (Bradford (13)); (18) i BC/i AD *IG* V (1) 48, 12; 95, 5 (Bradford (6)) (s. Κλεώνυμος); (19) c. 1-10 AD *IG* V (1) 209, 6; *SEG* XXXV 331 (date) (Bradford (18)) (f. Δαμοκρατίδας); (20) c. 100-120 AD *IG* V (1) 99, 5; *SEG* XI 569, 11 (Bradford (23)) (f. Σωκρατίδας); (21) ~ *SEG* XI 610, 5 (Bradford (3)) (Ε. ὁ καὶ Πο—τομ—: s. Ἀγαθοκλῆς); (22) c. 100-125 AD *IG* V (1) 137, 18 (Bradford (15)); (23) c. 105-115 AD *IG* V (1) 103, 11 (Bradford (21)) (Εὐ[δ]αμίδας: f. Ὀνησιφόρος); (24) c. 110 AD *SEG* XI 516, 13 (Bradford (9)) (s. Σωσικράτης); (25) m. ii AD *IG* V (1) 160, 2 (Bradford (16)); (26) c. 140 AD *SEG* XI 582, 9 (Bradford (24)) ([Εὐδ]αμίδας); (27) ~ *SEG* XI 597, 1 (Bradford (8)) ([Εὐδα]μίδας: s. Σωκρατίδας); (28) c. 140-160 AD *IG* V (1) 74, 6; 85, 14; 128, 10; *SEG* XI 528, 6 (Bradford (20)) (f. Καλλικράτης Μωλόχιος); (29) ~ *IG* V (1) 154, 7 (Bradford (10)) (s. Θαλίαρχος); (30) c. 150 AD *IG* V (1) 71 III, 2, 15; *SEG* XI 497, 5 (Bradford (12)); (31) c. 150-160 AD *IG* V (1) 53, 26 (Bradford (7)) (s. Νικίας); (32) c. 221 AD *IG* V (1) 541, 4; *BSA* 79 (1984) pp. 270-3 (date) (Bradford (22)) (f. Μ. Αὐρ. Φιλοκρατίδας)
—SPARTA?: (33) 316 BC *IG* V (2) 549, 28 (Bradford (17)) (f. Ἀνδρόβιος)

MESSENIA:
—MESSENE: (34) c. 250 BC *SEG* XI 413, 26 (f. Εὔδαμος); (35) 87 AD ib. XLI 335, 7; (36) 192 AD *PAE* 1969, p. 103, 4 (s. Μουσικός)
—THOURIA: (37) f. ii BC *SEG* XI 972, 63 (Εὐδαιμονίδας—ed.: f. Ἀγαθίας)

SICILY:
—TAUROMENION: (38) c. 209 BC *IG* XIV 421 an. 32 (*SGDI* 5219) (f. Ἐπιγένης); (39) c. 187-156 BC *IG* XIV 421 an. 54; 421 an. 85 (*SGDI* 5219) (s. Ἐπιγένης, f. Ἐπιγένης)

## Εὔδαμος

AIGINA: (1) ?i BC *Alt-Ägina* I (2) p. 44 no. 10 (f. Φιλόξενος)

AITOLIA:
—KONOPE-ARSINOE: (2) c. 200 BC *FD* III (4) 163, 6; (3) 173 BC *SGDI* 1853, 2 (s. Τίμαιος)
—TRICHONION: (4) 187 BC *Syll*³ 585, 158 (f. Φίλων) ?= (5); (5) 185 BC *IG* IX (1)² (1) 32, 19 ?= (4)

AKARNANIA: (6) iii BC *SEG* XXV 539, 2, 12 (-δη-: I f. Εὔδημος II); (7) ~ ib. l. 2, 12 (-δη-: II s. Εὔδαμος I)
—ANAKTORION: (8) 216 BC *IG* IX (1)² (2) 583, 65

—STRATOS: (9) a. 167 BC ib. IX (1)² (1) 36, 5, 10 (f. Δεινίας)

ARGOLIS:
—ARGOS: (10) iii BC ib. IV (1) 618 I, 7 (f. —ικράτης); (11) ?255 BC Nachtergael, *Les Galates* 8, 56; cf. Stephanis 1794 (Εὔ[δ]ημος: f. Νεοκλῆς); (12) imp. *SEG* XI 321, 3 (Εὔ[δ]αμος: f. —νιος)
—EPIDAUROS: (13) ii BC *IG* IV (1)² 213 (s. Τελέας, f. Τελέας)
——(Azantioi): (14) 146 BC ib. 28, 27 (f. Διονύσιος)
——Hysidrias: (15) c. 365-335 BC ib. 103, 123
——Stratitis: (16) c. 335-325 BC ib. 106 III, 45
—EPIDAUROS*: (17) c. 370-360 BC ib. 102, 49, 259; *BSA* 61 (1966) p. 272 no. 4 B I, 3

ARKADIA: (18) 55 BC *BGU* 1002, 3 (-δη-: f. Μήδοκος)
—MANTINEIA-ANTIGONEIA: (19) c. 300-221 BC *IG* V (2) 323. 60 (tessera)
—MEGALOPOLIS: (20) m. iii BC ib. IV (1)² 96, 39 (Perlman E.3); Perlman p. 63 f. (date) (f. Νικάσιππος); (21) s. ii BC *IG* V (2) 439, 36, 77 (s. Λησίας) ?= (22); (22) ?145 BC ib. l. 31, 32 (f. Δείνιππος, Λησίας) ?= (21)
—MEGALOPOLIS?: (23) ii BC ib. 534 (f. Λυδιάδας)
—TEGEA: (24) m. iv BC ib. 6, 98 (s. Τιμοκρέτης); (25) iv/iii BC ib. 38, 66; (26) f. iii BC ib. 35, 24 ([Εὔδ]αμος: f. Δαμότιμος)

ELIS: (27) 28-24 BC *IvOl* 64, 4 (s. Εὐθυμένης: K.); (28) i/ii AD ib. 470, 6 (Γ. Μέμμιος Ἐ.: f. Π. Μέμμιος Φιλόδαμος)

EPIROS:
—MOLOSSOI: (29) ii BC *SGDI* 1357, 9; cf. Cabanes, *L'Épire* p. 583 no. 61
—NIKOPOLIS: (30) f. i AD *Syll*³ 791 B, 8 (*FD* III (1) 530, 8); *Syll*³ 791 C, 2; 791 D, 2 (*FD* III (1) 312, 2); *BCH* 75 (1951) p. 307 no. 1, 2 (Sarikakis 48) (f. Θεοκλῆς Φιλόκαισαρ (Nikopolis and Delphi))
—PRASAIBOI: (31) a. 163 BC *IBouthrot* 58, 9 (*SEG* XXXVIII 509); *IBouthrot* 105, 5 (f. Σατύρα)

ILLYRIA:
—APOLLONIA:
——(Litai): (32) iii/ii BC *IApoll* 7; *L'Illyrie mérid.* 2 p. 207 (locn.) (f. Σωτακλῆς)

KORINTHIA:
—KORINTH: (33) her. D.S. vii fr. 9 (king)

LAKONIA: (34) c. 100-90 BC *SEG* XXXIII 290 A, 11; *BSA* 70 (1975) pp. 129-31 (date) (Stephanis 938) (s. Λυκίσκος)
—GYTHEION: (35) 211 AD *IG* V (1) 1163, 15 (s. Καλλινικίδας)
—OITYLOS: (36) iii/ii BC ib. 1295, 3 (Bradford (20))
—SPARTA: (37) ii-i BC *IG* V (1) 1112, 2, 10 (Bradford (8)) (s. Εὐκράτης); (38) i BC-i AD? *IG* V (1) 754 (Bradford (24)); (39) s. i BC *IG* V (1) 92, 1 (Bradford (10)) ([Εὔ]δαμος: s. Κρατήσιππος); (40) ~ *IG* V (1) 124, 9 (Bradford (31)) (I f. Εὔδαμος II); (41) ~ *IG* V (1) 124, 9 (Bradford (2)) (II s. Εὔδαμος I); (42) ~ *IG* V (1) 124, 13 (Bradford (45)) (Εὔδ[α]μος: f. —άδης); (43) ~ *IG* V (1) 134, 7 (Bradford (39)) (f. Σίτιμος); (44) c. 25-1 BC *IG* V (1) 212, 40 (Bradford (33)) (f. Καλλικράτης); (45) ~ *SEG* XI 505, 1 (Bradford (25)) (f. Ἐπικλείδας); (46) ~ *SEG* XI 505, 8 (Bradford (28)) (Εὔδαμ[ο]ς: I f. Εὔδαμος II); (47) ~ *SEG* XI 505, 8 (Bradford (3)) (II s. Εὔδαμος I); (48) c. 50-80 AD *IG* V (1) 277, 5 (*Artemis Orthia* pp. 308-9 no. 25 (date); Bradford (23)); (49) c. 80-90 AD *IG* V (1) 674, 10 (Bradford (9)) (s. Ἵππαρχος); (50) ~ *IG* V (1) 674, 14 (Bradford (26)) (f. Εὐδαμοκλῆς); (51) c. 90-100 AD *IG* V (1) 80, 3 (Bradford (30)) (I f. Γ. Ἰούλ. Εὔδαμος II); (52) ~ *IG* V (1) 80, 3 (Bradford (6)) (Γ. Ἰούλ. Ἐ.: II s. Εὔδαμος I); (53) ~ *SEG* XI 570, 7 (Bradford (1)) (s. Ἄρχιππος); (54) c. 100 AD *SEG* XI 536, 3 (Bradford (34)) (f. Κλέαρχος); (55)

c. 100-125 AD *IG* V (1) 137, 14, 17 (Bradford (40)) (f. Σοϊξιτέλης); (56) ~ *IG* V (1) 152, 4 (Bradford (16)) (s. Πάμφιλος); (57) ~ *IG* V (1) 152, 5; 153, 26 (Bradford (42)) (f. Σωκλείδας) ?= (65); (58) ?ii AD *IG* V (1) 119, 3 (Bradford (44)); (59) ii AD *IG* V (1) 159, 10 (Bradford (21)); (60) ~ *IG* V (1) 159, 41 (Bradford (22)); (61) ~ *SEG* XI 782, 3 (Bradford (35)) (f. Μενεκλείδας); (62) ?f. ii AD *IG* V (1) 296, 2; *Artemis Orthia* pp. 318-19 no. 41 (date) (Bradford (6)); (63) c. 105 AD *SEG* XI 517, 3 (Bradford (14)) (s. Νικοκράτης); (64) c. 105-110 AD *IG* V (1) 20 B, 10; 75 B, 8 (Bradford (17)) (s. Σωκλείδας); (65) ~ *IG* V (1) 20 B, 11 (Bradford (37)) (f. Πρατόνικος) ?= (57); (66) c. 120 AD *IG* V (1) 1315, 27 (Bradford (13)) (I f. Εὔδαμος II); (67) ~ *IG* V (1) 1315, 27 (Bradford (5)) (II s. Εὔδαμος I); (68) ~ *SEG* XI 544, 6 (Bradford (29)) (I f. Εὔδαμος II); (69) ~ *SEG* XI 544, 6 (Bradford (4)) (II s. Εὔδαμος I); (70) c. 133 AD *SEG* XI 580, 3 (Bradford (41)) (f. Σωσίπολις); (71) c. 140-145 AD *IG* V (1) 63, 17; *SEG* XI 490, 7; 550, [2] (Bradford (6)) (Γ. Ἰούλ. Ἐ.); (72) c. 150-160 AD *SEG* XI 528, 5 (Bradford (43)) (s. Μενίσκος); (73) s. ii AD *IG* V (1) 554, 13; *SEG* XXXV 327; *BSA* 80 (1985) pp. 194; 212-13 (ident., stemma) (Bradford (43)) (Π. Μέμμιος Ἐ.: ?s. Π. Μέμμιος Σπαρτιατικός, f. Σπαρτιατικός); (74) c. 170 AD *SEG* XI 530, 4 (Bradford (38)) ([Εὔ]δαμος: f. Ῥοῦφος); (75) c. 170-190 AD *SEG* XI 627, 9 (Bradford (27)) (I f. Εὔδαμος II); (76) ~ *SEG* XI 627, 9 (Bradford (7)) (II s. Εὔδαμος I); (77) c. 175-210 AD *SEG* XI 555, 10 (f. —δας); (78) ii/iii AD *IG* V (1) 589, 21; 590, 5, 10; 602, 19; *BSA* 79 (1984) pp. 279-83 (date); 80 (1985) p. 225; pp. 238-41 (ident., stemma) (Bradford (18); (36)) (Τιβ. Κλ. Ἐ.: s. Τιβ. Κλ. Σπαρτιατικός, f. Τιβ. Κλ. Πρατόλαος ὁ καὶ Δαμοκρατίδας, Κλ. Δαμοσθένεια, Κλ. Τυραννίς, Κλ. Πῶλλα); (79) a. 217 AD *IG* V (1) 559, 4 (Bradford (15)) (Σέξ. Ἐ.: s. Σέξ. Πομπ. Ὀνασικράτης); (80) c. 220 AD *IG* V (1) 653 b, 11 (*Artemis Orthia* pp. 356-8 no. 143); *BSA* 79 (1984) pp. 279-82 (ident., stemma) (Bradford (32)) (f. Αὐρ. Ἄγιον)

MESSENIA:
—MESSENE: (81) c. 250 BC *SEG* XI 413, 26 (s. Εὐδαμίδας); (82) ii/i BC *IG* V (1) 1428, 2 ([Εὔδ]αμος)
—THOURIA: (83) ii-i BC ib. 1385, 4 (f. Κλεανδρίδας)

S. ITALY (BRUTTIUM):
—LOKROI EPIZEPHYRIOI:
——(Κρα.): (84) iv/iii BC De Franciscis 22, 8 (s. Τίμων)
—RHEGION: (85) hell.-imp. *IG* XIV 2406. 18

SICILY:
—ADRANON: (86) iii-ii BC *PdelP* 16 (1961) p. 127 (f. Ἀγάθων)
—SELINOUS: (87) ?v BC Manganaro, *PdelP* forthcoming no. 16 (Εὐδαμ[ος])
—SYRACUSE: (88) 361 BC *CID* II 4 I, 40; (89) c. 200 BC *IG* XI (4) 723 (-δη-: f. Ἡρακλείδας)
—SYRACUSE?:
——(Μακ.): (90) hell. Manganaro, *PdelP* forthcoming no. 4 III, 4 (s. Σωσίπατρος)
—TAUROMENION: (91) c. 163 BC *IG* XIV 421 an. 78 (*SGDI* 5219)

## Εὐδάμων

KORINTHIA:
—KORINTH: (1) her. *FGrH* 244 F 331 (s. Ἀγέλας, f. Ἀριστόδαμος: king)

## Εὔδημος

AIGINA: (1) ?iii AD *Alt-Ägina* I (2) p. 50 no. 46 (Αὐρ. Ἐ.: s. Ἀντέρως)

ARGOLIS:
—ARGOS: (2) imp.? *RE* (15) (dub.)

ELIS: (3) c. 177-185 AD *IvOl* 103, 7 (Μ. Ἀν[τ.] [Εὔ]δημος)

**Εὐδία**
ARKADIA:
—MANTINEIA-ANTIGONEIA: (1) i AD IG v (2) 269; 270 (Ἰουλ. Ἐ.: d. Εὐτελῖνος)
S. ITALY (CAMPANIA):
—DIKAIARCHIA-PUTEOLI: (2) imp. AJA 2 (1898) p. 375 no. 4 (Lat. Lutatia Eudia: m. Q. Lutatius Domitus)
SICILY:
—LIPARA: (3) imp. Libertini, Isole Eolie p. 225 no. 45 (Μελπομένη Ἐ.)

**Εὐδίαιτος**
LAKONIA:
—SPARTA: (1) c. 140-150 AD IG v (1) 85, 12 (Bradford (3)) (f. Σωτηρίδας) ?= (2); (2) c. 160-170 AD IG v (1) 109, 6 (Bradford (2)) ([Εὐ]δία(ι)τος: I f. Εὐδίαιτος II) ?= (1); (3) ~ IG v (1) 109, 6 (Bradford (1)) ([Εὐ]δία(ι)τος: II s. Εὐδίαιτος I)

**Εὐδιάκονος**
S. ITALY (CAMPANIA):
—DIKAIARCHIA-PUTEOLI: (1) imp. CIL x 1874 (Lat. C. Caesonius Eudiaconus)

**Εὐδίκας**
KORINTHIA:
—OINOE: (1) vi-v BC IG IV (1) 416 (masc. nom./fem. gen.?)

**Εὔδικος**
ACHAIA:
—DYME*: (1) c. 219 BC SGDI 1612, 28 (Tyche 5 (1990) p. 124) (f. Φιλόμηλος)
AITOLIA: (2) c. 315-280 BC FD III (1) 142, 1 + SEG XXVII 129 (Λυδικός—edd., Εὔδικος— Daux: s. Βάθυς)
ARGOLIS:
—ARGOS: (3) m. v BC IG IV (1) 566 (Εὔδ[ιφο]ς); (4) ?ii BC SEG XXXVIII 312, 2 (s. Δαμαίνετος); (5) i AD ib. XXVI 429, 6 (s. Σαωνίδας)
—TROIZEN: (6) iv BC IG IV (1) 764, 5 (s. Θεσσαλός)
EPIROS:
—AMBRAKIA: (7) iii BC Op. Ath. 10 (1971) p. 64 no. 10 (f. Ξενόι); (8) 263 BC IG IX (1)² (1) 17, 95 (f. Καλλικράτης)
KORINTHIA:
—KORINTH: (9) c. 610-590 BC Amyx 18. 5 (vase) (Lorber 28); LSAG² p. 131 no. 9 (date) (-διρος)
LAKONIA: (10) 378 BC X., HG v 4. 39 (Poralla² 296)
S. ITALY (BRUTTIUM):
—LOKROI EPIZEPHYRIOI: (11) iv BC Iamb., VP 267 (FVS I p. 447)
SICILY:
—PANTALICA (MOD.): (12) arch. Manganaro, QUCC forthcoming no. 67 (Εὐδικō (gen.))

**Εὔδιος**
LAKONIA:
—SPARTA: (1) 404 BC X., HG ii 3. 1; ii 3. 10 (Poralla² 297)

**Εὐδόκιμος**
LAKONIA:
—SPARTA: (1) c. 100-110 AD SEG XI 563, 6 (Bradford (5)) (E[ὐ]δόκιμος: s. Πρατομηλίδας); (2) f. ii AD IG v (1) 64, 8; SEG XI 491, 1 (Bradford (1)); (7)) (I s. Δαμοκράτης, f. Δαμοκράτης, Εὐδόκιμος II); (3) c. 140 AD IG v (1) 289, 1 (Artemis Orthia p. 321 no. 46; Bradford (3)) (II ?s. Εὐδόκιμος I, f. Εὐδόκιμος III); (4) ~ IG v (1) 289, 1 (Artemis Orthia p. 321 no. 46; Bradford (4)) (-μορ: III s. Εὐδόκιμος II); (5) c. 140-150 AD IG v (1) 64, 15; 289, 2 (Artemis Orthia p. 321 no. 46; Bradford (2)) (Ἐ. ὁ καὶ Ἀριστείδας, Εὐδόκιμορ—289: s. Δαμοκράτης)

**Εὐδοξία**
KORINTHIA:
—KORINTH: (1) m. v AD Cyr. S., V. Cyriac. 1 (m. Κυριακός)

**Εὐδοξίδας**
ARKADIA:
—TEGEA: (1) c. 240-229 BC IG v (2) 11, 16

**Εὐδόξιος**
MESSENIA:
—KYPARISSIA: (1) vi AD Peloponnesiaka Suppl. 18 (1991) pp. 407 ff.; cf. BZ 89 (1996) p. 325 (Ἐ. πρεσβύτ.)

**Εὔδοξος**
ACHAIA:
—DYME*: (1) c. 219 BC SGDI 1612, 32 (Tyche 5 (1990) p. 124) (s. Θεόξενος)
ARGOLIS:
—ARGOS: (2) ?iv BC SEG XVII 154; (3) ?271 BC Syll³ 419, 6 etc. (s. Ἐπίδοξος)
ARKADIA:
—MANTINEIA-ANTIGONEIA:
——(Epalea): (4) m. iv BC IG v (2) 271, 2 (s. Ἱμπεδέας)
—ORCHOMENOS: (5) ?c. 369-361 BC BCH 102 (1978) p. 348, 32 (IPArk 14)
—TEGEA:
——(Hippothoitai): (6) f. iii BC IG v (2) 36, 72 (s. Κλεαίνετος)
KORINTHIA:
—SIKYON: (7) ?254 BC Nachtergael, Les Galates 9, 47 (Stephanis 944) (s. Ἐπήρατος)
PELOPONNESE?: (8) 11 AD PAE 1992, p. 71 A, 35 (s. Πασικράτης)
S. ITALY (CAMPANIA):
—POMPEII: (9) i BC-i AD CIL IV 3091 (Lat. Eudoxus); (10) ~ ib. 4456 (Castrèn 402. 7) (Lat. M. Terentius Eudoxsus)
S. ITALY (LUCANIA):
—HYELE-VELIA: (11) 188 BC Syll³ 585, 132 (s. Αἰσχρίων)
SICILY: (12) iv-iii BC RE (5) (s. Ἀγαθοκλῆς)
—GELA-PHINTIAS: (13) ?277 BC FD III (1) 125, 3 (s. Ζώιλος)
—KAMARINA: (14) iv/iii BC SEG XXXIX 999, 2 (Dubois, IGDS 125; Cordano, 'Camarina VII' 103) (f. Εὐθυκλῆς)
—TAUROMENION: (15) ?ii/i BC IG XIV 421 D an. 8 (SGDI 5219); IGSI 4 III (IV), 136 D an. 8 (s. Σῶσις)

**Εὔδοτος**
ACHAIA: (1) iii BC IG II² 8402 (s. Λύκων)
AKARNANIA:
—THYRREION: (2) s. iii BC ib. IX (1)² (2) 289 = 345? (Εὔδοξος—no. 345)

**Εὐδραῖος**
ARGOLIS:
—ARGOS: (1) c. 245-236 BC ib. IX (1)² (1) 25, 9 (f. Μνασίας)

**Εὐδράμων**
SICILY:
—NAXOS: (1) v/iv BC Arena, Iscr. Sic. III 74 (vase) (-μōν)

**Εὔδρομος**
S. ITALY (CAMPANIA):
—NEAPOLIS: (1) i BC-i AD? INap 121; cf. Leiwo p. 68 no. 9 (s. Γναῖος)
SICILY:
—SYRACUSE: (2) ?iv BC Unp. (Attica) (s. Εὔδωρος: date—M.J.O.)

**Εὐδωρίδας**
ARKADIA:
—MEGALOPOLIS: (1) 359 BC CID II 5 I, 46 ([Εὐ]δωρ[ίδ]ας)

**Εὐδωρίχας?**
ITHAKE: (1) hell. IG IX (1) 661 (Εὐδ(ο)ρίχας— IG, Εὐδ(ω)ρί(δ)ας?)

**Εὔδωρος**
AIGINA: (1) iv BC SEG XXV 970
AKARNANIA?: (2) iii/ii BC IG IX (1)² (2) 574; Fraser–Rönne, BWGT pl. 28
ARKADIA:
—MANTINEIA-ANTIGONEIA: (3) iii-ii BC IG v (2) 319, 16 (Εὔδωρ[ος])
——(Posoidaia): (4) c. 425-400 BC SEG XXXI 348, 6
ITHAKE: (5) hell. Rev. Épig. 1 (1913) p. 47 no. 11
KORINTHIA:
—KORINTH: (6) c. 570-550 BC Amyx 104 A. 4 (vase) (Lorber 92) (-δō-: her.?)
LAKONIA:
—SPARTA: (7) m. iii BC Peek, IAEpid 42, 13 (Perlman E.3); Perlman p. 63 f. (date) (Bradford (-)) (s. Δερκίδας)
SICILY:
—SYRACUSE: (8) ?iv BC Unp. (Attica) (f. Εὔδρομος: date—M.J.O.)

**Εὐέλθων**
ARGOLIS:
—ARGOS: (1) v-iv BC Iamb., VP 267 (FVS I p. 447)

**Εὐελπίας**
ARGOLIS:
—ARGOS:
——(Pholygadai): (1) m. iv BC Unp. (Ch. Kritzas) (Εὐελπίας)

**Εὐελπίστιος**
LAKONIA: (1) m. iv AD Seeck, Libanius p. 132 (Bradford (-))

**Εὐέλπιστος**
ARKADIA:
—MANTINEIA-ANTIGONEIA: (1) imp.? IG v (2) 298 (Εὐέλπιστος)
—TEGEA: (2) ii AD ib. 54, 25
KEPHALLENIA:
—SAME: (3) imp. ib. IX (1) 640
KORINTHIA:
—KORINTH: (4) f. ii AD Corinth VIII (3) 286, 3 (Lat. Marcius Euelpistus: s. Μάρκιος Ἑρμῆς); (5) ii/iii AD ib. 206 (Γ. Οὐίβι[ος] Εὐέλπισ[τος]: s. Μέγης: doctor)
LAKONIA:
—SPARTA: (6) ii AD IG v (1) 176, 1 (Bradford (4)); (7) c. 220 AD SEG XXXIV 311, 7 (Bradford (3)) (Αὐρ. [Εὐέλπι]στος?)
——Limnai: (8) a. 212 AD IG v (1) 564, 8 (Bradford (2)) (Λ. Ἀπρώνιος Ἐ.); (9) c. 225 AD IG v (1) 547, 17; 682, 9; 683, 7 (Bradford (5)) (f. Μ. Αὐρ. Ἀλκισθένης)
S. ITALY (APULIA):
—CANUSIUM: (10) imp. Epig. Rom. di Canosa 164 (CIL IX 394) (Lat. M. Numisius Euhelpistus)
S. ITALY (BRUTTIUM):
—SKYLLETION?: (11) ?i AD Atti Centro Studi Documentazione 2 (1969-70) p. 120 no. 2 (Lat. Euelpistus: f. Ἐλπιδιανός)
S. ITALY (CALABRIA):
—MANDURIA*: (12) i AD Atti Conv. Taranto 12 (1972) p. 369 (Ann. Univ. Lecce 6 (1971-3) p. 69 no. 1) (Lat. Annius Euhelpistus: freed.)
S. ITALY (CAMPANIA):
—DIKAIARCHIA-PUTEOLI: (13) imp. CIL x 2392 (Lat. Euhelpistus); (14) ~ ib. 2778 (Lat. M. Ninnius Euhelpistus)
—KYME: (15) ii-iii AD Audollent, Defix. Tab. 198, 27, 33 (Βετρούβιος Ἐ.: f. Βετρούβιος Φῆλιξ)

## Εὐέμπολος

—SALERNUM: (16) imp. IItal 1 (1) 224 (CIL x 652) (Lat. M. Claudius Euhelpistus)
SICILY:
—PACHINO (MOD.): (17) imp. ASSiracusano 1961, pp. 24-5 no. 3 (Lat. L. Offonius Euhelpistus: f. L. Offonius Fructuosus)

## Εὐέμπολος
LAKONIA?: (1) ?v-iv BC CGFP 236, 15 (fict.?)

## Εὐεργέτας
MESSENIA:
—THOURIA: (1) f. ii BC SEG XI 972, 29 (s. Ἀρισταῖος)

## Εὐεργετίδας
MESSENIA: (1) vii BC Paus. iv 21. 2; 23. 2

## Εὐεργίδας
ARGOLIS:
—EPIDAUROS: (1) s. iv BC SEG XI 438 (f. Ἀρχέλοχος)

## Εὐέστιος
KORINTHIA:
—SIKYON: (1) vi/v BC ib. 244, 37

## Εὐετήριος
ELIS: (1) iii-ii BC PAE 1983, p. 165 with pl. 143 β (vase) (Εὐετήρ[ιος]?, Εὐέτηρ?)

## Εὐετηρίς
ILLYRIA:
—EPIDAMNOS-DYRRHACHION: (1) iv BC IDyrrh 39 (Εὐετηρίδι (dat.))

## Εὐέτης
ARGOLIS:
—ARGOS: (1) c. 220-200 BC SEG XI 414, 30 (Perlman E.5) (f. Αἰσχίνας); (2) i BC SEG XI 313 a, 3 ([Ε]ὐέτης)
—EPIDAUROS: (3) iv/iii BC ib. XIV 327
LAKONIA:
—SPARTA: (4) f. i AD IG v (1) 269, 2; Artemis Orthia p. 306 no. 19 (date) (Bradford (-))
S. ITALY (APULIA):
—CANNAE: (5) ii AD Epig. Rom. di Canosa 150 (CIL IX 385) (Lat. L. Lepidius Euetes: s. Λύρα)
S. ITALY (BRUTTIUM):
—LOKROI EPIZEPHYRIOI: (6) iv BC Iamb., VP 267 (FVS I p. 447)
SICILY:
—HIMERA?: (7) vii/vi BC Suda Σ 1095 (?f. Τεισίας Στησίχορος, Ἡλιάναξ, Μαμερτῖνος)

## Εὐϝαίνετος
S. ITALY (LUCANIA):
—PADULA (MOD.): (1) vi/v BC Apollo 9 (1993) pp. 5-6 (Arena, Iscr. Sic. IV 32) (Πα. Ε.)

## Εὔϝαινος
ARKADIA:
—MANTINEIA-ANTIGONEIA: (1) c. 425-385 BC IG v (2) 323. 2 (tessera) (Εὔϝαιν[ος]: f. Εὔνο-ος)

## Εὐϝάνιος
LAKONIA:
—SPARTA: (1) ?c. 500-450 BC SEG XXVI 476; LSAG² p. 450 no. D (date) (Poralla² 299a) (Εὐϝανίου (gen.))

## Εὐϝάνωρ
ARKADIA:
—MANTINEIA-ANTIGONEIA: (1) c. 425-385 BC IG v (2) 323. 15 (tessera) (-νōρ: f. Ζευξίας)

## Εὔϝαρχος
KORINTHIA:
—KORINTH: (1) c. 560 BC Amyx 101 B. 5 (vase) (Lorber 88) (fict.?)

SICILY:
—GELA-PHINTIAS: (2) s. vi BC Arena, Iscr. Sic. II 14 (vase)

## Εὔϝετος
ARKADIA:
—MANTINEIA-ANTIGONEIA: (1) c. 425-385 BC IG v (2) 323. 5 (tessera) (Εὔϝετος: f. Ϝιωνίδας)

## Εὐήθης
S. ITALY (CALABRIA):
—TARAS-TARENTUM: (1) imp. CIL IX 240 (Lat. M. Kaninius Euhethes)

## Εὐηθίδας
AIGINA: (1) ii/i BC IG IV (1) 40 (f. Ἀριστοπείθης)
KEPHALLENIA:
—SAME: (2) 208 BC IMM 35, 2 ([Εὐ]ηθίδας)

## Εὐημερίς
S. ITALY (BRUTTIUM):
—TAURIANA: (1) iii AD Eph. Ep. VIII 251 (Rend. Linc. 19 (1964) p. 133 no. 6) (Lat. [Eu]hemeris: m. Vitalio, Emo)
S. ITALY (CAMPANIA):
—DIKAIARCHIA-PUTEOLI: (2) imp. CIL x 2881 (Lat. Pontia Euhemeris)

## Εὐήμερος
ARKADIA:
—TEGEA: (1) ii AD IG v (2) 55, 86 (s. Ὀνησίφορος)
ILLYRIA:
—APOLLONIA: (2) ii AD IApoll 209 (Κ. Ἰούλι. Ε.)
—EPIDAMNOS-DYRRHACHION: (3) hell.-imp. IDyrrh 201 (s. Νικηφόρος)
LAKONIA:
—HYPERTELEATON*: (4) imp. IG v (1) 1079
—SPARTA: (5) c. 125-145 AD ib. 67, 5; SEG XI 524, 17; 548, 12 (Bradford (2)) (f. Νικάσιππος); (6) c. 125-150 AD IG v (1) 114, 7 (Bradford (1)) (s. Ἀφροδίσιος)
S. ITALY (CAMPANIA):
—NOLA: (7) imp. CIL x 1307 (Lat. L. Apusius Euhemer(us): f. Ἀτίμητος)
SICILY: (8) imp. ib. 8059. 343 (seal) (Lat. C. Rubellius Euemerus)
—HIMERA: (9) ?iii BC Himera 2 p. 701 no. 302 (tile)
—KATANE: (10) imp. NScav 1918, p. 62 no. 2 (Lat. [E]uhemerus)

## Εὐήνα
SICILY:
—GELA-PHINTIAS: (1) vi/v BC Dubois, IGDS 144 g (vase) (Arena, Iscr. Sic. II 77) (-ϝα: kala)

## Εὐήνιος
ILLYRIA:
—APOLLONIA: (1) s. vi BC Hdt. ix 92-95 (f. Δηίφονος)

## Εὐηνίων
MESSENIA:
—ANDANIA*: (1) s. v AD SEG XXIX 394; cf. RE Supplbd. 3 (-) (fict.?)

## Εὔηνος
S. ITALY (CAMPANIA):
—DIKAIARCHIA-PUTEOLI*: (1) 37 AD Camodeca, L'Archivio Puteolano 1 pp. 182-3; pp. 184-5; Bove, Documenti finanziarie pp. 24-5 T.P. 7 (Lat. Euenus Primianus: imp. freed.)
—HERCULANEUM: (2) i BC-i AD CIL IV 10549 (Lat. Euenus); (3) m. i AD ib. x 8058. 20 (seal) (Lat. Ti. Claud. Euenus)
SICILY: (4) i BC-i AD? RE (8); GP 2296 ff. with Comm. p. 289
—TAUROMENION:
——(Ταυ.): (5) ii/i BC IGSI 5 III, 9

## Εὐήνωρ
ARGOLIS:
—EPIDAUROS: (1) hell. Peek, NIEpid 111 (Εὐήνωρ: s. Κρατῖνος)
ARKADIA: (2) 232 BC CPR XVIII 12, 238, 239 (f. Ἄριστις, Σιμάλη)
EPIROS:
—ARGOS (AMPHILOCH.): (3) c. 337-318 BC RE (1); IG II² 242 + 373, 1-15, 16 ff.; 374; SEG XL 74 (link, date); cf. XLI 44 (ethn.); cf. Osborne, Naturalization D 50; IG IX (1)² (2) p. XVIII, s.a. 321 BC (and Athens: s. Εὐήπιος: doctor)
LAKONIA:
—BOIAI: (4) ii AD ib. v (1) 956 (f. Γ. Ἰούλ. Πανθάλης)

## Εὐήπιος
EPIROS:
—ARGOS (AMPHILOCH.): (1) 322 BC ib. II² 374; cf. IX (1)² (2) p. XVIII, s.a. 321 BC (f. Εὐήνωρ)

## Εὐήπολις
AIGINA: (1) ii-iii AD SEG XI 22 (Εὐήπολις—apogr., Εὔ<η>πολις?)

## Εὐήρης
ARKADIA:
—MANTINEIA-ANTIGONEIA: (1) ii-i BC IG II² 9279 (Ag. XVII 538) (f. Ἀγώ)
S. ITALY (CAMPANIA):
—NEAPOLIS: (2) her. IG XIV 730 (INap 29); cf. Leiwo p. 147 no. 121 (Εὐηρείδαι (n. gent.))

## Εὐθέας
KORINTHIA:
—KORINTH?: (1) iv/iii BC SEG XXX 990, 2 (or Argolis Phleious)

## Εὐθηνία
S. ITALY (CAMPANIA):
—DIKAIARCHIA-PUTEOLI: (1) imp. NScav 1924, p. 84 (Lat. Egnatia Euthenia)

## Εὔθηρος
ELIS:
—OLYMPIA*: (1) 265 AD IvOl 122, 19 (?s. Π. Ἐγνάτιος Βενυστεῖνος: slave?)

## Εὐθίας
ARGOLIS:
—ARGOS: (1) s. iv BC SEG XXXV 799 (s. Λυσίας)

## Εὔθιος
ILLYRIA:
—BYLLIONES BYLLIS: (1) imp. AEp 1978, no. 766 (Lat. Euthius)
S. ITALY (CAMPANIA):
—NEAPOLIS: (2) 184 BC IG IX (1)² (1) 33, 2 (Εὔθιος: II s. Εὔθιος I); (3) ~ ib. l. 3 ([Εὔθ]ιος: I f. Εὔθιος II)

## Εὔθιππος
LAKONIA:
—SPARTA: (1) 326 BC CID II 32, 43; 99 B, 15 (Poralla² 300) (Εὔθ[ιππος]—99 B, Εὔθρεπτος—Poralla)

## Εὖθις
ARKADIA: (1) 362 BC CID II 1 II, 39

## Εὔθοινος
AIGINA: (1) v BC SEG XXXVII 262 (?f. Ἀρίσταρχος)

## Εὐθοσίων
S. ITALY (BRUTTIUM):
—RHEGION: (1) iv BC Iamb., VP 267 (FVS I p. 447); Rh. Mus. 78 (1929) p. 25 (name)

## Εὐθράσης
ARKADIA:
—TEGEA: (1) f. ii BC IG v (2) 19 (f. Καλλικράτης)

**Εὐθύβιος**
KORINTHIA:
—KORINTH: (2) iii-ii BC *Hesp.* 41 (1972) p. 204 no. 6 ([*E*]ὐθράσης)

**Εὐθύβιος**
KORINTHIA:
—SIKYON: (1) m. iv BC *IG* II² 10302 a

**Εὐθύβουλος**
SICILY:
—SYRACUSE?:
——(Ὑπα.): (1) hell. Manganaro, *PdelP* forth-coming no. 4 IV, 9 (Εὐ<ε>θύβουλος: s. Εὐθυμίδας)

**Εὐθύδαμος**
ACHAIA: (1) 146 BC *IG* IV (1)² 28, 83 (f. Τίμων: synoikos)
—KALLISTAI: (2) c. 230-200 BC *BCH* 45 (1921) p. 12 II, 62 (f. Νέων: reading—Oulhen)
AITOLIA:
—KONOPE-ARSINOE: (3) i BC/i AD *IG* IX (1)² (1) 134
ARGOLIS:
—ARGOS: (4) ii BC *SEG* XLII 279, 7 (f. Μναῖς)
ARKADIA:
—ALIPHEIRA: (5) c. 230-200 BC *BCH* 45 (1921) p. 12 II, 80 (s. Ξενοκράτης)
—KAPHYAI: (6) hell.? *IEph* 1459 (s. Εὐμήδης)
—MANTINEIA-ANTIGONEIA: (7) c. 300-221 BC *IG* V (2) 323. 86 (tessera) (f. Φίλιππος)
—TEGEA:
——(Athaneatai): (8) s. iv BC ib. 41, 34 (Εὐθύδ[α]μος: s. Ἁγησίας)
ITHAKE: (9) iii-ii BC *GVI* 102 (*Gr. Gr.* 224) (f. Τιμέας)
KORINTHIA:
—SIKYON: (10) vi/v BC *SEG* XI 244, 55; (11) f. iii BC Paus. ii 8. 2 (Skalet 123) (-δη-); (12) ?272 BC *FD* III (1) 298, 4; III (3) 185, 4
LAKONIA:
—SPARTA: (13) s. i BC *IG* V (1) 93, 36 (Bradford (-))
MESSENIA:
—MESSENE: (14) c. 170-130 BC *SEG* XXIII 201, 10; (15) ?ii AD ib. XLI 335, 14 (s. Νίκαρχος); (16) ~ ib. l. 16 (Εὐθύδα(μος): f. Θαλλίεπος)
S. ITALY (BRUTTIUM):
—LOKROI EPIZEPHYRIOI:
——(Δυσ.): (17) iv/iii BC De Franciscis 21, 4, 9
SICILY:
—SELINOUS: (18) f. vi BC *Lex Sacra from Selinous* p. 14 A, 17 (her.?)
—SYRACUSE: (19) s. v BC Pl., *R.* 328 B; Plu., *Mor.* 835 D; cf. *APF* C 9 (-δη-: s. Κέφαλος)

**Εὐθυδίκα**
KORINTHIA:
—KORINTH?: (1) c. 540-525 BC *SEG* XXIII 264 a (pinax); cf. Guarducci, *Ep. Gr.* 3 p. 29

**Εὐθύδικος**
ARKADIA:
—MEGALOPOLIS?: (1) ?iii BC *Coll. Alex.* p. 210 fr. 8, 5
S. ITALY (CAMPANIA):
—KYME: (2) v BC Arena, *Iscr. Sic.* III 24 (vase) (Εὐθύδι(ϙ)ος?)

**Εὐθυκλῆς**
ARGOLIS:
—ARGOS: (1) c. 146-32 BC *Coll. Hunter* 2 p. 153 no. 13; BM coin 1920 5-15-132 (coins)
—EPIDAUROS*: (2) c. 290-270 BC *IG* IV (1)² 109 II, 109, 150
ELIS: (3) ?i AD *EA* 1905, p. 259 no. 2, 11 ([Εὐ]θυκλῆς: s. Σωτήριχος)
ILLYRIA:
—APOLLONIA: (4) 14-29 AD *IApoll* 173
—EPIDAMNOS-DYRRHACHION: (5) hell. *IDyrrh* 282 (f. Λαήν)

KORINTHIA:
—KORINTH: (6) 433-426 BC Th. i 46. 2; iii 114. 4 (f. Ξενοκλείδας)
—KORINTH?: (7) 288 BC *IG* IX (1)² (1) 5, 9 (f. -δωρος)
LAKONIA:
—SPARTA: (8) 367 BC X., *HG* vii 1. 33 (Poralla² 301); (9) 333 BC Arr., *An.* ii 15 (Berve 312; Poralla² 302); (10) c. 140 BC *IvOl* 62, 61 (Bradford (3)) (f. Εὐδαμίδας); (11) s. i BC *IG* V (1) 92, 4 (Bradford (1)) (s. Λίχας); (12) c. 1-10 AD *IG* V (1) 209, 33; *SEG* XXXV 331 (date) (Bradford (2))
MESSENIA: (13) ?i AD *IG* V (1) 1374 (f. Χάρτος, Θεοξενίδας)
S. ITALY (BRUTTIUM):
—LOKROI EPIZEPHYRIOI: (14) vi/v BC *RE* Supplbd. 3 (3a); Moretti, *Olymp.* 180
—RHEGION: (15) iv BC Iamb., *VP* 267 (*FVS* 1 p. 447)
SICILY:
—KAMARINA: (16) iv/iii BC *SEG* XXXIX 999, 2 (Dubois, *IGDS* 125) ([Εὐ]θυκλῆς—*SEG*, [Βα]θυκλῆς—Dubois: s. Εὔδοξος); (17) hell. *SEG* XXXIX 1001, 2 (f. Ἡρακλείδας)

**Εὐθυκράτης**
ACHAIA:
—PATRAI: (1) ii-i BC *Achaean Grave Stelai* 19 (f. Σοφία)
KERKYRA: (2) iv/iii BC Unp. (*IG* arch.) (s. Μίρων)
KORINTHIA:
—KORINTH: (3) s. iv BC D.L. vi 90
—SIKYON: (4) iv/iii BC *RE* (6) (Skalet 124) (Lat. Euthycrates: s. Λύσιππος: sculptor)
LEUKAS: (5) iii BC *AD* 26 (1971) Chron. p. 353 (Εὐθυκράτ[ης])

**Εὐθυκρέτεια**
ARKADIA:
—TEGEA: (1) ?iv-iii BC *IG* V (2) 563 ([Ε]ὐθυκρέτει[α])

**Εὐθυκρίνης**
LAKONIA:
—SPARTA: (1) v BC *SEG* XXVI 459 (Poralla² 302a) (-νēς: name, date—*LGPN*)

**Εὐθύλαος**
ARKADIA:
—TEGEA: (1) f. iii BC *IG* V (2) 35, 26 (Εὐθύ[λ]αος: s. Εὐρυμένης)

**Εὐθύμας**
SICILY:
—LIPARA: (1) v BC *SEG* XLII 868 (vase)

**Εὐθύμαχος**
AKARNANIA:
—PALAIROS: (1) iii/ii BC *IG* IX (1)² (2) 538 (Εὐθύμαχ[ος])
ARGOLIS:
—EPIDAUROS: (2) iv/iii BC ib. IV (1)² 272
ARKADIA:
—TEGEA:
——(Athaneatai): (3) s. iv BC ib. V (2) 41, 29 (f. -χος)
LAKONIA:
—SPARTA: (4) v BC ib. V (1) 1589

**Εὐθυμένης**
AIGINA: (1) f. v BC Pi., *N.* v, 41; *I.* vi, 58; cf. Klee pp. 89-90 nos. 28 and 30
ARGOLIS:
—ARGOS: (2) 228-146 BC *BMC Pelop.* p. 146 no. 131 (coin) (Εὐθυμέ(νης))
ARKADIA:
—MAINALIOI: (3) v/iv BC *RE* (2); Moretti, *Olymp.* 362; 377
—THELPHOUSA: (4) a. 228 BC *IG* IV (1)² 72 B, 30 (s. Λάκων)

ELIS: (5) 28-24 BC *IvOl* 64, 4 (f. Εὔδαμος)
EPIROS:
—AMBRAKIA: (6) s. iv BC *SEG* XVII 307 b (f. Κλιόι)
LAKONIA: (7) 173 BC *SGDI* 1853, 3, 4, 6, 7 (slave/freed.)
SICILY:
—KAMARINA: (8) ?iv/iii BC *SEG* XXXIV 940, 9 (Dubois, *IGDS* 124; *PdelP* 44 (1989) p. 192 no. 3; Cordano, 'Camarina VII' 104) (f. Νίκων)

**Εὐθυμήδης**
ARGOLIS:
—HERMIONE: (1) iii BC *IG* IV (1) 729 II, 2 (f. Σχῦρος)

**Εὐθυμία**
S. ITALY (CAMPANIA):
—DIKAIARCHIA-PUTEOLI: (1) imp. *CIL* X 2710 (Lat. Maria Euthymia: d. Εὐτύχης)

**Εὐθυμίδας**
ARGOLIS:
—HERMIONE: (1) iii BC *IG* IV (1) 729 I, 14 (f. Ἀπταραῖος)
—TROIZEN: (2) ?c. 450-425 BC ib. 760, 1 (Lazzarini 279); *LSAG*² p. 181 no. 6 (date)
EPIROS:
—CHAONES: (3) c. 300 BC *FD* III (4) 409, 8 ([Ε]ὐθυμίδας: f. Ἀντάνωρ)
S. ITALY (APULIA):
—TURI (MOD.): (4) ?v BC *SEG* XXXI 852 (bronze)
S. ITALY (BRUTTIUM):
—LOKROI EPIZEPHYRIOI:
——(Τηλ.): (5) iv/iii BC De Franciscis 4, 9; 33, [1]
SICILY:
—SELINOUS: (6) m. v BC Dubois, *IGDS* 59 (Arena, *Iscr. Sic.* I 22; *IGLMP* 93) (f. Σιλανός)
—SYRACUSE?:
——(Ὑπα.): (7) hell. Manganaro, *PdelP* forth-coming no. 4 IV, 9 (f. Εὐθύβουλος)

**Εὐθύμιος**
LAKONIA:
—SPARTA: (1) ii BC *Mél. Daux* p. 233, 3 (f. Εὐδαίμων)

**Εὐθυμίσκος**
S. ITALY (BRUTTIUM):
—LOKROI EPIZEPHYRIOI:
——(Φαω.): (1) iv/iii BC De Franciscis 15, 7 (f. Ἀρχέλας)
——(Ταγ.): (2) iv/iii BC ib. 7, 1 ?= (3); (3) 276 BC ib. 23, 5 (f. Εὔθυμος) ?= (2)
S. ITALY (LUCANIA):
—HYELE-VELIA: (4) iv/iii BC *SEG* XXXII 921; cf. *Chiron* 22 (1992) p. 386 and pl. 2, 2

**Εὐθυμοκλῆς**
LAKONIA:
—SPARTA: (1) c. 120-125 AD *IG* V (1) 1314, 14; 1315, 28; *SEG* XI 596, 3; *BSA* 43 (1948) p. 218 (stemma) (Bradford (-)) (s. Ἀμάραντος)

**Εὔθυμος**
AKARNANIA:
—THYRREION: (1) m. iii BC *SEG* XL 464 II side 1, 5 (?f. Σωτίων)
ARGOLIS:
—ARGOS: (2) m. v BC Unp. (Ch. Kritzas)
—EPIDAUROS*: (3) c. 370 BC *IG* IV (1)² 102, 164
—HERMIONE: (4) iii BC ib. IV (1) 729 I, 17 (s. Βωλαγόρας); (5) f. ii BC *IC* 2 p. 24 no. 7 B, 1 (s. Ἀλεξίβιος)
ELIS: (6) 28-24 BC *IvOl* 64, 32 (s. Σωτίων: Με.)
KORINTHIA:
—SIKYON: (7) hell.? *IG* IX (1) 593 ([Εὔ]θυμος: f. Πυθιάδας)

## Εὐθύνας

LAKONIA:
—SPARTA: (8) c. 100 AD SEG XI 515, 4 (Bradford (1)) (s. Ἀριστόδαμος)
——Amyklai: (9) ii/i BC IG v (1) 26, 5 (Bradford (2)) (s. Λυσικράτης)
LEUKAS: (10) s. iv BC RE (2)
S. ITALY (BRUTTIUM):
—LOKROI EPIZEPHYRIOI: (11) 484-472 BC Moretti, Olymp. 191; 214; 227; Call. frr. 98-9; IvOl 144 (Lazzarini 853; Landi, DISMG 235; Ebert, Gr. Sieg. 16; CEG I 399); cf. SEG XXXVII 779 (s. Ἀστυκλῆς); (12) v/iv BC Landi, DISMG 239 (Εὔθυμ[ο]ς); (13) c. 350-250 BC SEG XXX 1172; (14) i AD NScav 1890, p. 265 (tile); cf. Costabile, Municipium Locrensium pp. 73-4 (date)
——(Ἀνξ.): (15) iv/iii BC De Franciscis 24, 5 (s. Ὀναῖος)
——(Δυσ.): (16) iv/iii BC ib. 4, 2; 5, 3; 22, 3; 39, 5 (s. Φίλιστος)
——(Γαυ.): (17) 276 BC ib. 23, 5 (s. Εὐθυμίσκος)
——(Κρα.): (18) iv/iii BC ib. 26, 7 (s. Ἀρίστιππος)
——(Τηλ.): (19) iv/iii BC ib. 38, 3 (f. Γλαύκιππος)
——(Ψαθ.): (20) iv/iii BC ib. 39, 4 (s. Ζωῖλος)
S. ITALY (CAMPANIA):
—HERCULANEUM: (21) i BC-i AD RAAN 33 (1958) p. 274 no. 431; cf. Cron. Erc. 8 (1978) p. 154 no. 59 (Lat. L. Antonius Ethymus)
SICILY:
—GELA-PHINTIAS: (22) f. ii BC IG XIV 256, 38 (Dubois, IGDS 161); cf. SEG XL 804 (f. Ἀρτέμων)
—KAMARINA: (23) s. v BC Dubois, IGDS 121, 17 (Arena, Iscr. Sic. II 143; SEG XXXVIII 940; Cordano, 'Camarina VII' 29) (s. Εὐφραῖος)
—LEONTINOI?: (24) 339 BC Plu., Tim. 32 (or Sicily Syracuse)
—SYRACUSE: (25) v BC HN² p. 175 (coin) (Εὐθ[υμος]?: coin engraver)
—TAUROMENION: (26) c. 219-218 BC IG XIV 421 an. 22; 421 an. 23 (SGDI 5219) (f. Ἀρίσταρχος, Ζωπυρίσκος)

## Εὐθύνας

S. ITALY (BRUTTIUM):
—LOKROI EPIZEPHYRIOI: (1) vi/v BC Landi, DISMG 66 (vase)

## Εὐθυνίων

ACHAIA:
—DYME: (1) ii BC Achaean Grave Stelai 43 (f. Ἀριστίων)

## Εὐθύνοος

S. ITALY (BRUTTIUM):
—TERINA: (1) ?vi-v BC Plu., Mor. 109 B-D (s. Ἡλύσιος)

## Εὔθυνος

S. ITALY (CALABRIA):
—TARAS-TARENTUM: (1) iv BC Iamb., VP 267 (FVS I p. 446)

## Εὐθύνους

S. ITALY (BRUTTIUM):
—LOKROI EPIZEPHYRIOI: (1) iv BC Iamb., VP 267 (FVS I p. 447)

## Εὔθυς

LAKONIA:
—SPARTA: (1) ?s. viii BC Paus. iii 2. 7 (Poralla² 303) (f. Χαρμίδας: fict.?)

## Εὐθύφρων

ARKADIA:
—MAINALIOI: (1) c. 400-370 BC Moretti, IAG 20; Paus. vi 9. 2; cf. Ebert, Gr. Sieg. 32 (f. Ξενοκλῆς)
—MT. KYLLENE*: (2) iv-iii BC IG v (2) 362

## Εὐθωλίς

EPIROS:
—BOUTHROTOS (PRASAIBOI): (1) a. 163 BC IBouthrot 17, 19 (SEG XXXVIII 474) ?= (4); (2) ~ IBouthrot 18, 16; 32, 17 (SEG XXXVIII 475; 491); (3) ~ IBouthrot 32, 12 (SEG XXXVIII 491); (4) ~ IBouthrot 43, 45 (SEG XXXVIII 502) (d. Σώσιππος) ?= (1)

## Εὖιδος

ARKADIA:
—TEGEA: (1) f. ii BC IG v (2) 44, 11 (s. Φλέγων)

## Εὖιος

KORINTHIA:
—KORINTH: (1) ?205 BC ib. VII 1721, 6 (f. Νικάνωρ)

## Εὐίππα

ARKADIA:
—MANTINEIA-ANTIGONEIA: (1) ?i BC ib. v (2) 335

## Εὐίππη

ARGOLIS:
—ARGOS?: (1) 135 AD Peek, IAEpid 154, 6 (or Argolis Epidauros: Εὐίπ[π]η)

## Εὔιππος

KEPHALLENIA:
—KRANIOI: (1) iii/ii BC IG IX (1) 276, 2 (f. Δικαίαρχος)
LAKONIA:
—SPARTA: (2) b. 433 BC ib. v (1) 213, 74 (Moretti, IAG 16; Poralla² 304)
S. ITALY: (3) f. iii BC SNG Cop. Apulia-Lucania 1109; van Keuren, Coinage of Heraclea p. 83 nos. 106-7 (coin) (-hιππος)

## Εὐκάδης

AKARNANIA:
—THYRREION: (1) m. iii BC SEG XL 464 II side 1, 3

## Εὔκαιρος

KORINTHIA:
—SIKYON: (1) hell.? IG IV (1) 436, 2 (f. Ζωτικός)
S. ITALY (CALABRIA):
—BRENTESION-BRUNDISIUM: (2) ?i-ii AD CIL IX 96 (Lat. Tib. Cl. Eucaerus)

## Εὐκαλίς

S. ITALY (CAMPANIA):
—DIKAIARCHIA-PUTEOLI: (1) imp. ib. X 3107 (Lat. Eucalis)

## Εὐκαμίδας

S. ITALY (BRUTTIUM):
—LOKROI EPIZEPHYRIOI:
——(Πυρ.): (1) iv/iii BC De Franciscis 3, 8 (Εὐ(δ)αμίδας?, Εὐκα(δ)μίδας?—ed.: s. Φιλωνίδας)

## Εὐκαμπίδας

ARKADIA:
—MAINALIOI: (1) m. iv BC D. xviii 295; Paus. viii 27. 2; Plb. xviii 14. 2, 12 (and Arkadia Megalopolis: oikist)
—MEGALOPOLIS: (2) 320 BC IG v (2) 549, 1 (s. Ἐσφαντίδας)

## Εὐκαρίμων

SICILY:
—SYRACUSE: (1) byz. SEG IV 22 (Εὐκαρ(π)ίμων?)

## Εὐκάρπη

S. ITALY (CAMPANIA):
—NEAPOLIS: (1) iii-iv AD IG XIV 826. 15 (INap 222)

## Εὐκαρπία

DALMATIA:
—KERKYRA MELAINA: (1) imp. CIL III 10089 (Lat. Eucarpia)
S. ITALY (CALABRIA):
—TARAS-TARENTUM: (2) imp. NScav 1897, p. 224 (Lat. Eucarpia)
S. ITALY (CAMPANIA):
—BAIAI: (3) ii-iii AD IG XIV 878, 8 (Σαινία Ἐ.: m. Σαίνις Ἐπαφρόδιτος)
—SALERNUM: (4) imp. IItal I (1) 41 (Lat. Caesia Eucarpia)
SICILY:
—KATANE: (5) iii-v AD IG XIV 540 (Agnello 51; Wessel 592); cf. Ferrua, NG 442 ([E]ὐκαρπία)
—KENTORIPA: (6) i-ii AD Epigraphica 51 (1989) pp. 166-7 no. 30 (Lat. Publicia Eucarpia); (7) iii-v AD NScav 1907, p. 494
—SYRACUSE: (8) iii-v AD Strazzulla 85 (Wessel 401) ([E]ὐκαρπία); (9) ~ Strazzulla 414 (Barreca 139); cf. Riv. Arch. Crist. 18 (1941) p. 197 no. 67
—TYNDARIS: (10) imp. Epigraphica 51 (1989) p. 165 no. 19 (Lat. [Euc]arpia)

## Εὐκαρπίων

SICILY:
—SYRACUSE: (1) m. iv AD Riv. Arch. Crist. 36 (1960) p. 30 no. 27

## Εὔκαρπος

ARGOLIS:
—ARGOS: (1) ii/iii AD IG VII 4151, 4, 6 (Stephanis 956) (Κορ(ν). Ἐ.)
ARKADIA:
—KLEITOR: (2) a. 212 AD IG v (2) 369, 25; SEG XXXI 347, 18 (f. Αὐρ. Θάλλος)
—TEGEA: (3) ii AD IG v (2) 55, 46 (Εὔκαρπ[ος]: f. —ης)
—THELPHOUSA?: (4) ?iii AD SEG XVI 280
DALMATIA:
—RIZON*: (5) ii AD Šašel, IL 1855 A (Λούκιος Λοῦσκος Ἐ.: doctor)
KORINTHIA:
—KORINTH: (6) ?ii-iii AD Corinth VIII (1) 132
LAKONIA:
—SPARTA: (7) c. 120 AD IG v (1) 1315, 24 (Bradford (1)) (s. Χιδ—); (8) c. 221 AD IG v (1) 541, 2; BSA 79 (1984) pp. 270-3 (date) (Bradford (3)) (I f. M. Αὐρ. Εὔκαρπος II); (9) ~ IG v (1) 541, 2; BSA 79 (1984) pp. 270-3 (date) (Bradford (2)) (M. Αὐρ. Ἐ.: II s. Εὔκαρπος I)
MESSENIA:
—KORONE: (10) 246 AD IG v (1) 1398, 52 (Αὐρ. Ἐ.)
S. ITALY (BRUTTIUM):
—LOKROI EPIZEPHYRIOI:
——(Πυρ.): (11) iv/iii BC De Franciscis 10, 6 (Εὔκ(α)ρπος)
S. ITALY (CAMPANIA):
—POMPEII: (12) i BC-i AD CIL IV 4709 (Lat. Eucarpus); (13) ~ Atti Acc. Pontan. 39 (1990) p. 296 no. 92 (Lat. Eucarpus)
SICILY:
—KATANE: (14) imp. IG XIV 474 b, 1
—SYRACUSE: (15) iii-v AD Ferrua, NG 193 ([Πο]λύκ]αρπος—ed., [Εὔκ]αρπος—LGPN)

## Εὐκατάλλακτος

LAKONIA:
—SPARTA: (1) c. 225-250 AD SEG XXXIV 308, 11 (Bradford (-)) (f. Ἀφροδίσιος)

## Εὐκέλαδος

S. ITALY (BRUTTIUM):
—LOKROI EPIZEPHYRIOI: (1) ?c. 475-450 BC Guarducci, Ep. Gr. I p. 303 no. 6 (Lazzarini 197; Landi, DISMG 61); LSAG² p. 286 no. 6 (date)
——(Στρ.): (2) iv/iii BC De Franciscis 3, 6 (f. Ἀρχιππος)

**Εὐκλέα**

DALMATIA:

—ISSA: **(1)** iii/ii BC *SEG* XXXV 684 (*VAHD* 84 (1991) p. 254 no. 5) (d. *Κλέων*); **(2)** ?ii BC *SEG* XXXV 692 (d. *Καλλίστρατος*)

ILLYRIA:

—EPIDAMNOS-DYRRHACHION: **(3)** hell.-imp. *IDyrrh* 63 (d. *Λύκος*); **(4)** ~ ib. 202 (d. *Ἀσκλαπος*); **(5)** ~ ib. 203 (d. *Δάζιος*)

**Εὐκλέας**

SICILY:

—SELINOUS: **(1)** vi/v BC Dubois, *IGDS* 47 (Arena, *Iscr. Sic.* I 51; Lazzarini 880 e)

**Εὔκλεια**

AKARNANIA:

—PALAIROS: **(1)** iii BC *IG* IX (1)$^2$ (2) 485

ARGOLIS:

—ARGOS: **(2)** ii BC *SEG* XLII 279, 13

—HERMIONE: **(3)** iii BC *IG* IV (1) 728, 30 (d. *Νίκων*)

—KALAURIA: **(4)** iii BC ib. 841, 4

EPIROS:

—KEPHALOS: **(5)** s. iii BC *Op. Ath.* 10 (1971) p. 65 no. 2

ILLYRIA:

—APOLLONIA: **(6)** imp. *IApoll* 252

**Εὐκλείδας**

AIGINA: **(1)** c. 650 BC *Alt-Ägina* II (2) p. 48 no. 1; *LSAG*$^2$ p. 439 no. Aa (date); **(2)** f. vi BC *Alt-Ägina* II (2) p. 12; Overbeck 340 ff. (f. *Σμῖλις*)

AITOLIA:

—TRICHONION: **(3)** iii-ii BC *IG* IX (1)$^2$ (1) 120

AKARNANIA:

—THYRREION: **(4)** f. iii BC *SEG* XXVII 161

ARGOLIS:

—ARGOS: **(5)** v BC *Mnem.* NS 57 (1929) p. 206; **(6)** hell. *IG* IV (1) 636; **(7)** ii BC *BCH* 33 (1909) pp. 456-7 no. 23, 9

—ARGOS*: **(8)** iii BC *SEG* XVII 152, 2 (sculptor)

—HERMIONE: **(9)** ?ii-i BC *IG* IV (1) 731 I, 12 (-κλί-: f. *Ζωπυρίων*); **(10)** imp. ib. II$^2$ 8499 (-κλί-: I f. *Εὐκλείδας* II); **(11)** ~ ib. (-κλί-: II s. *Εὐκλείδας* I)

—METHANA-ARSINOE: **(12)** hell.? *SEG* XXXIX 363 (s. *Πραξιμίας*)

—PHLEIOUS: **(13)** 401 BC X., *An.* vii 8. 1 (-δης: s. *Κλεαγόρας*: mantis)

EPIROS:

—AMBRAKIA: **(14)** iv/iii BC Unp. (Arta Mus., inscr.) (f. *Γοργώ*)

—MOLOSSOI: **(15)** iii/ii BC *Syll*$^3$ 1206, 6; cf. Cabanes, *L'Épire* p. 583 no. 60

ILLYRIA:

—APOLLONIA: **(16)** ii BC *IApoll* 39; **(17)** ~ Cabanes, *L'Épire* p. 562 no. 37 (*IApoll* 6) (f. *Πάτρων*)

—EPIDAMNOS-DYRRHACHION: **(18)** hell. *IDyrrh* 204 (-κλίδ-: s. *Τρίτος*); **(19)** hell.-imp. ib. 444 (f. *Φιλώ*)

KERKYRA: **(20)** ?iii BC *IG* IX (1) 695, 5 (f. *Δαμουχίδας*)

KORINTHIA:

—KORINTH: **(21)** 344 BC Plu., *Tim.* 13 (-δης); **(22)** iii BC *IG* IV (1) 201 (*Εὐκλί<α>δας*); **(23)** ~ ib. XII (9) 806 (f. *Θεοκλῆς*)

—KORINTH*: **(24)** s. iv BC *Hesp.* 43 (1974) p. 29 no. 37 (sculptor)

—SIKYON: **(25)** 263 BC *IG* IX (1)$^2$ (1) 17, 80 (f. *Ἀρχωνίδας*)

LAKONIA: **(26)** v/iv BC Plu., *Art.* 5 (Poralla$^2$ 305)

—MESSA?: **(27)** imp. *IG* V (1) 1280, 10 (f. *Κρατησικλέα*)

—SPARTA: **(28)** c. 260-222 BC *RE* (19); Paus. ii 9. 1-3 (Bradford (1)) (*Ἐπικλείδας*—Paus.: s. *Λεωνίδας*, *Κρατησίκλεια*: king); **(29)** i BC-i AD *IG* V (1) 750 (Bradford (7)) (f. *Πρατόνικος*); **(30)** c. 30-20 BC *IG* V (1) 142, 11 (Bradford (6)) (f. *Πασικλῆς*); **(31)** c. 25-1 BC *IG* V (1) 212, 7 (Bradford (5)) (f. *Νικανδρίδας*); **(32)** c. 50-75 AD *IG* V (1) 278, 2; *Artemis Orthia* pp. 310-11 no. 27 (date) (Bradford (4)); **(33)** f. ii AD *IG* V (1) 51, 13; 52, [3]; 490, 2, 8; *SEG* XI 506, 2; 606, [3] (Bradford (2)) (s. *Δεινακῶν*, f. *Βέλλων*)

LEUKAS: **(34)** iii BC Unp. (*IG* arch.); **(35)** f. i BC *IG* IX (1) 534, 8 (*Iscr. Gr. Verona* p. 24) (*Εὐκλε[ίδ]ας*: s. *Διονύσιος*)

MESSENIA:

—MESSENE: **(36)** 323 BC *FD* III (4) 8, 1 (-δης: f. *Εὔκλητος*)

S. ITALY (BRUTTIUM):

—LOKROI EPIZEPHYRIOI:

——(*Γαγ.*): **(37)** iv/iii BC De Franciscis 28, 3 (f. *Ἀλκίδας*)

——(*Γαψ.*): **(38)** 277 BC ib. 8, 2; 31, 2 (f. *Εὔφραστος*)

——(*Δυσ.*): **(39)** iv/iii BC ib. 20, 5 (f. *Φίλων*)

——(*Θρα.*): **(40)** iv/iii BC ib. 2, 1; 16, 3; 28, 2 (s. *Θράσων*, f. *Θράσων*)

——(*Κρα.*): **(41)** iv/iii BC ib. 20, 13 (s. *Σιλανός*)

SICILY:

—GELA-PHINTIAS: **(42)** vi/v BC Hdt. vii 155. 1 (-δης: s. *Ἱπποκράτης*)

—KAMARINA: **(43)** f. v BC Cordano, *Tessere Pubbliche* 81 (f. *—υς*); **(44)** s. v BC Dubois, *IGDS* 119, 2 (Arena, *Iscr. Sic.* II 145; Cordano, 'Camarina VII' 30) (?f. *Ναιρογένης*)

—MORGANTINA: **(45)** iv/iii BC *SEG* XXXIX 1013, 3; **(46)** ~ ib. l. 5 (f. *Φρῦνος*); **(47)** ~ Dubois, *IGDS* 191 (f. *Ἀρχέλας*)

—SYRACUSE?: **(48)** c. 415-405 BC *RE* (20) (coin engraver)

—TAUROMENION: **(49)** c. 218 BC *IG* XIV 421 an. 23 (*SGDI* 5219); **(50)** c. 188 BC *IG* XIV 421 an. 53 (*SGDI* 5219) (s. *Ἀριστομέδων*); **(51)** 173-144 BC *IG* XIV 421 an. 68; 421 an. 82; 421 an. 97 (*SGDI* 5219); *IGSI* 4 II (III), 7 an. 70 (*Εὐκλε(ί)δας*—68: f. *Νυμφόδωρος*); **(52)** ?ii/i BC *IG* XIV 421 D an. 13 (*SGDI* 5219) (s. *Ἱέρων*); **(53)** ~ *IG* XIV 421 III (*SGDI* 5219) ([*Εὐκλε*]*ίδας*: s. *Μεγιστέας*); **(54)** ii/i BC *IGSI* 5 II, 8; 5 III, 6, 20, 31; 5 IV, 10; 6 I, 5; 6 III, 8, [26]; 6 IV, 7, 27; 7 I, 2, 18, 32; 7 II, 13, 28; 8 I, 18; 8 II, 8, 20; 9 I, 10; 9 II, 16; 10 I, 8, 15, 24, 33; 10 II, 24; 11 I, 15; 11 II, 21; 12 I, 42; 12 II, 37; 12 III, 33; *Cron. Arch.* 3 (1964) pp. 43-4 II, 15; III, 11, 26; IV, 1 etc.; **(55)** ~ *IGSI* 9 II, 1 ([*Εὐκλ*]*είδας*: s. *Εὔβουλος*)

——(*Ἀρεθ.*): **(56)** s. ii BC *SEG* XXXII 937 (f. *Νυμφόδωρος*)

——(*Ἀσ.*): **(57)** c. 147 BC *IGSI* 4 III (IV), 65 an. 94 (s. *Νυμφόδωρος*)

——(*Ἰδομ.*): **(58)** ?ii/i BC *IG* XIV 421 D an. 10; 421 D an. 13 (*SGDI* 5219) (s. *Ἀγάθων*, f. *Ἀγάθων*)

——(*Οἰν.*): **(59)** ?ii/i BC *IG* XIV 421 D an. 5 (*SGDI* 5219); *IGSI* 4 III (IV), 119 D an. 7 (s. *Νυμφόδωρος*)

**Εὐκλείδης**

MESSENIA:

—MESSENE: **(1)** i BC *SEG* XIII 248, 11; cf. Stephanis 389 (f. *Ἀρίστων*)

SICILY:

—HIMERA: **(2)** m. v BC Dubois, *IGDS* 12 (Arena, *Iscr. Sic.* III 44; *IGLMP* 17) (*Εὐκλεί[δης]*)

—HIMERA?: **(3)** vii/vi BC *Suda* Σ 1095; *IG* XIV 1213 (?f. *Τεισίας Στησίχορος*, *Ἡλιάναξ*, *Μαμερτῖνος*)

—ZANKLE-MESSANA: **(4)** c. 650 BC Th. vi 5. 1 (and Sicily Himera: oikist)

**Εὔκλεινος**

ARGOLIS:

—EPIDAUROS: **(1)** c. 370 BC *IG* IV (1)$^2$ 102, 101, 272, 286 + Peek, *IAEpid* 297, 46 (name) (*Εὔκλιν[ος]*, *Εὐκλῆς*—*IG*)

**Εὐκλεΐσκος**

S. ITALY (BRUTTIUM):

—LOKROI EPIZEPHYRIOI:

——(*Ὀμβ.*): **(1)** 279 BC De Franciscis 13, 4 (f. *Εὐάνθης*)

**Εὔκλειτος**

MESSENIA:

—THOURIA: **(1)** ?iv BC *CEG* II 709

**Εὐκλείων**

ARKADIA:

—STYMPHALOS: **(1)** iv BC *PAE* 1929, p. 92

**Εὐκλέων**

ARGOLIS:

—EPIDAUROS*: **(1)** c. 370 BC *IG* IV (1)$^2$ 102, 48

ARKADIA: **(2)** hell. *IEph* 1412 (f. *Φανόστρατος*)

KORINTHIA:

—KORINTH: **(3)** iv BC Arr., *Ind.* xviii 9 (f. *Εὐαγόρας*)

**Εὐκληΐδας**

LAKONIA:

—SPARTA: **(1)** iii BC *SEG* XL 348 B, 10

**Εὐκλῆς**

AIGINA?: **(1)** i BC-i AD *EAD* XXX p. 356 no. 21 (I f. *Εὐκλῆς* II, *Θεόφιλος*, ?f. *Ἀπολλωνίς*); **(2)** ~ ib. (II s. *Εὐκλῆς* I)

AKARNANIA:

—PALAIROS: **(3)** iii BC *IG* IX (1)$^2$ (2) 486

ARGOLIS:

—ARGOS: **(4)** c. 475-450 BC *SEG* XXVI 449, 2; *LSAG*$^2$ p. 444 no. F (date) (f. *Κάλλιππος*); **(5)** ?263-261 BC Nachtergael, *Les Galates* 3, 19; *IG* XI (2) 110, 31 (Stephanis 959) (s. *Διονύσιος*)

—EPIDAUROS: **(6)** c. 370 BC *IG* IV (1)$^2$ 102, 71 ?= (*9*); **(7)** c. 365-335 BC ib. 103, 90, 93, 95, 100, 102-3, 106 ?= (*9*); **(8)** iii AD ib. 401, 3 + Peek, *IAEpid* 160 (*Εὐκ[λῆς]*: s. *Κύπρις*)

——Mesogais: **(9)** c. 365-335 BC *IG* IV (1)$^2$ 103, 150 ?= (*7*) (*6*)

—EPIDAUROS (TRACHEIA (MOD.)): **(10)** 400-375 BC *SEG* XXIX 382 (?s. *Σωσθένης*)

—EPIDAUROS*: **(11)** c. 370-360 BC *BSA* 61 (1966) p. 271 no. 4 A, 19

DALMATIA:

—ISSA:

——(Dymanes): **(12)** iv/iii BC Brunšmid p. 8, 27 (s. *Σῶσις*); **(13)** ~ ib. p. 9, 53 ([*Εὐ*]*κλῆ[ς]*: s. *—ίσκος*)

——(Hylleis): **(14)** iv/iii BC ib. l. 52 ([*Ε*]*ὐκλῆς*?: s. *Εὐβουλίδας*)

KORINTHIA:

—KORINTH: **(15)** ?411 BC *IG* XII (8) 402 (f. *Λυσίστρατος*); **(16)** iii BC *Mnem.* NS 43 (1915) p. 372 D, 1

S. ITALY (CALABRIA):

—BRENTESION-BRUNDISIUM: **(17)** imp. *NScav* 1885, p. 113 h (*Eph. Ep.* VIII 21); cf. *Epigraphica* 42 (1980) p. 157 (Lat. Eucliis: s. *Ἐπάγαθος*)

—TARAS-TARENTUM: **(18)** 156 BC *ID* 1417 B II, 97 (s. *Ἡρακλείδας*)

SICILY:

—AKRAI: **(19)** iii-ii BC *SGDI* 3242, 12 (*Akrai* p. 157 no. 8) (s. *Φίλαρχος*)

——(*Νητ.*): **(20)** ii-i BC *SGDI* 3246, 19 (*Akrai* pp. 152-3 no. 2; Dubois, *IGDS* 109) (f. *Σιμύλος*)

—HYBLA: **(21)** m. iv BC Page, *FGE* 1552; cf. Stephanis 440 (f. *Ἀρχίας*)

—KAMARINA?: **(22)** f. vi BC *SEG* XXXIV 939

—LIPARA: **(23)** hell.? Libertini, *Isole Eolie* p. 226 no. 50; **(24)** imp. ib. p. 226 no. 51 (*ΚΕΥΛΕΙΣ*—lap.: ?f. *Νεμέριον*)

—SELINOUS: **(25)** s. vi BC Dubois, *IGDS* 31, 1, 6 (Arena, *Iscr. Sic.* I 60); cf. *SEG* XXXVIII 962; **(26)** vi/v BC Arena, *Iscr. Sic.* I 58 (*Εὐκ(λ)ῆς*: f. *Ἀρχέτιος*)

## Εὐκλήσιον

—SELINOUS?: (27) vi/v BC SEG XXXIX 1020 A, 1 (s. Ἀδείμαντος)
—SYRACUSE: (28) 414-410 BC RE (15) (s. Ἱππων); (29) 341 BC CID II 12 II, 22
—TAUROMENION: (30) c. 160 BC IG XIV 421 an. 81 (SGDI 5219)

## Εὐκλήσιον
S. ITALY (APULIA):
—CANUSIUM*: (1) imp. Epig. Rom. di Canosa 160 (CIL IX 392) (Lat. Minucia Euclesium: freed.)

## Εὐκλήσιος
ARGOLIS:
—EPIDAUROS*: (1) c. 370-365 BC Peek, IAEpid 52 B, 72 ([Εὐ]κλήσιος)

## Εὐκλήτας
SICILY:
—KAMARINA: (1) f. v BC Cordano, Tessere Pubbliche 26 (-κλέ-: s. Ἄσαρος); (2) ~ ib. 66 (-κλέ—ed., Εὐκλείδας—LGPN: f. Γλαυκίας)

## Εὔκλητος
LAKONIA:
—SPARTA: (1) c. 100 AD SEG XI 593, 3 (Bradford (3)); (2) c. 105-110 AD IG V (1) 20 B, 8 (Bradford (1)) (s. Μελήσιππος); (3) ~ SEG XI 569, 2 (Bradford (4)) (f. Μελήσιππος); (4) c. 120-137 AD IG V (1) 59, 5; SEG XI 521 b, 4; 574, 2 (Bradford (2)) (s. Νυμφόδοτος)
MESSENIA:
—MESSENE: (5) 323 BC FD III (4) 8, 1 (s. Εὐκλείδας); (6) iii BC Paus. vi 14. 11 (f. Γόργος)

## Εὔκλιππος
ARGOLIS:
—EPIDAUROS: (1) iii BC IG IV (1)² 167, 5; (2) ii BC ib. 214; 216; 217; 219; Peek, IAEpid 96 (f. Σώδαμος); (3) ii/i BC IG IV (1)² 340 (Εὔκλιππ[ος]); (4) f. i BC ib. 219 (s. Σώδαμος, Λαφάντα)

## Εὐκολίς
KORINTHIA:
—KORINTH?: (1) c. 540-525 BC SEG XXIII 264 a (pinax); cf. Guarducci, Ep. Gr. 3 p. 29 (-ϙο-)

## Εὐκόλυμβος
SICILY:
—SYRACUSE: (1) iii-v AD NScav 1907, p. 758 no. 12 (Wessel 193); cf. Ferrua, NG 82 ([Ε]ὐκόλυν[βος])

## Εὔκοσμος
ELIS:
—OLYMPIA*: (1) iv BC IvOl 845 ([Ε]ὔκοσμος)
LAKONIA:
—SPARTA: (2) her. Paus. iii 16. 6 (Poralla² 306) (s. Λυκοῦργος: dub.)

## Εὐκρατέα
ARGOLIS:
—EPIDAUROS: (1) ii-iii AD IG IV (1)² 39 (m. Σωτηρίων)
—HERMIONE: (2) i BC-i AD? ib. IV (1) 730 V, 8

## Εὐκράτεια
ARGOLIS:
—ARGOS: (1) a. 303 BC CEG II 816, 16; (2) ~ ib. l. 17; (3) iii BC IG IV (1)² 321; (4) iii/ii BC PP 17210; BE 1949, no. 202 (family) (d. Πολυκράτης, Ζευξώ (Cyrene)); (5) ii-i BC IG IV (1) 575 ([Ε]ὐκράτεια)
—ARGOS*: (6) ii BC SEG XLII 279, 15 (slave/freed.?)
KORINTHIA:
—SIKYON: (7) m. iv BC IG II² 10303 (d. Ἀρίστων)

## Εὐκράτης
ACHAIA: (1) 146 BC ib. IV (1)² 28, 98 (I f. Εὐκράτης II: synoikos); (2) ~ ib. l. 98 (II s. Εὐκράτης I: synoikos); (3) ~ ib. l. 130 (s. Σωσικράτης: synoikos)
—DYME*: (4) c. 219 BC SGDI 1612, 31 (Tyche 5 (1990) p. 124) (s. Στρομβιχίδας)
AIGINA: (5) ?205 BC AE 1936, Chron. p. 39 no. 212, 6 (-τεις: s. Δάμων)
AKARNANIA:
—THYRREION: (6) iii BC IG IX (1)² (2) 245, 14
ARGOLIS:
—ARGOS: (7) iii BC Mnem. NS 47 (1919) p. 163 no. 8 b (s. Εὐφάνης); (8) imp. IG IV (1) 589, 2 (f. Ἀρχένους); (9) ~ ib. 613 (f. Φιλοῦσα); (10) ii AD SEG XVI 253, 8 (I f. Εὐκράτης II); (11) ~ ib. l. 8 (II s. Εὐκράτης I)
——(-eis): (12) iii BC ib. XXXI 306, 5 (Perlman A.25) (s. Εὐ—)
—EPIDAUROS: (13) iii BC Peek, IAEpid 342; (14) i-ii AD IG IV (1)² 503 (I f. Εὐκράτης II); (15) ~ ib. (II s. Εὐκράτης I)
——Isarnia: (16) c. 365-335 BC ib. 103, 77
——Kolonaia: (17) c. 335-325 BC ib. 108, 151
—EPIDAUROS*: (18) c. 370 BC ib. 102, 78, 294
ARKADIA:
—MANTINEIA-ANTIGONEIA: (19) iv/iii BC ib. v (2) 330
—TEGEA: (20) iv BC ib. 31, 4 (s. Ἀμφίας)
ELIS:
—KYLLENE: (21) iii BC SEG XI 1171 ([Εὐ]κράτης)
LAKONIA:
—GYTHEION: (22) imp. Giannakopoulou, Gytheion p. 177
—SPARTA: (23) ii-i BC IG V (1) 1112, 2, 10 (Bradford (3)) (f. Εὔδαμος); (24) c. 1-10 AD IG V (1) 209, 13; SEG XXXV 331 (date) (Bradford (1)) (s. Εὐρυκράτης: mantis)
LEUKAS: (25) iv BC D. lix 29-32; 36; (26) c. 167-50 BC BMC Thessaly p. 184 no. 152; p. 186 nos. 180-1 (coins)
MESSENIA:
—MESSENE: (27) iii BC SEG XXIII 209, 7; (28) c. 250 BC FD III (4) 14, 4 (f. Εὐκρατίδας)
S. ITALY (CAMPANIA):
—HERCULANEUM: (29) m. i AD PdelP 1 (1946) p. 383 no. 8 (Lat. Eucrates)

## Εὐκρατιανός
S. ITALY (CAMPANIA):
—KYME: (1) imp. CIL X 3700, 20 (Lat. Mammius Eucratianus)

## Εὐκρατίδας
LAKONIA:
—KOTYRTA: (1) ii BC IG V (1) 962, 33
MESSENIA:
—MESSENE: (2) c. 250 BC FD III (4) 14, 4 (s. Εὐκράτης)
—THOURIA: (3) f. ii BC SEG XI 972, 112 (s. Καλλικλῆς)

## Εὐκράτις
ARGOLIS:
—ARGOS: (1) ii/i BC IG IV (1) 640 (d. Εὔστρατος)

## Εὔκρατος
S. ITALY (CAMPANIA):
—KYME: (1) imp. CIL X 3700, 19 (Lat. Mammius Eucratus)

## Εὐκράτων
ARGOLIS:
—EPIDAUROS:
——(Hysminatai): (1) 146 BC IG IV (1)² 28, 20 (f. Φιλιστίδας)

## Εὐκρίνας
KORINTHIA:
—KORINTH: (1) f. vi BC Corinth XV (3) p. 359 no. 8 (pinax) (Εὐκρίνας)

## Εὐκρίνης
ARGOLIS:
—EPIDAUROS: (1) i BC IG IV (1)² 64, 4 + Peek, IAEpid 19 (f. —ος)
LAKONIA:
—SPARTA: (2) f. ii AD IG V (1) 32 B, 16 (Bradford (2)) (f. Νικίας); (3) c. 150-160 AD SEG XI 585, 4; 586, [2]; 600, 4; XXX 410, 5 (Bradford (1); (3)) (s. Φιλωνίδας, f. Φιλωνίδας)

## Εὐκρίτα
ARKADIA:
—TEGEA: (1) hell.? IG V (2) 174 b
ITHAKE: (2) ?ii BC AM 27 (1902) p. 377 no. 64; cf. REG 15 (1902) p. 132 no. 5 (Εὐκρίπα—REG)

## Εὔκριτος
ARGOLIS:
—ARGOS: (1) iii BC IG IV (1) 618 II, 2 (s. Κυλλίας)
ARKADIA:
—ORCHOMENOS*: (2) ?ii BC ib. V (2) 345, 11 (f. —ομενείδας: date—LGPN)
SICILY:
—MEGARA HYBLAIA: (3) f. v BC Dubois, IGDS 25 (Arena, Iscr. Sic. I 12) (-γρι-: f. Φυτύλος)
—SELINOUS: (4) s. vii BC Dubois, IGDS 72 (Arena, Iscr. Sic. I 79; IGLMP 74) (s. —ανδρος)

## Εὐκταῖος
AITOLIA: (1) ?257 BC Nachtergael, Les Galates 7, 5

## Εὔκτη
SICILY:
—SYRACUSE: (1) iii-v AD Strazzulla 182 (Wessel 1205)

## Εὐκτήμων
ILLYRIA:
—EPIDAMNOS-DYRRHACHION: (1) c. 250-50 BC Maier 105; 173; 296; 365; Münsterberg p. 39; Nachtr. p. 15 (Ceka 162-7); cf. IApoll Ref. Bibl. n. 56 (coin) (money.)
LAKONIA:
—SPARTA: (2) c. 130-150 AD IG V (1) 68, [24]; 112, 8; SEG XI 585, 8; XXX 410, 10 (Bradford (-)) (f. Εὐδαιμάκων)
SICILY:
—FILICUDI (MOD.): (3) hell. Libertini, Isole Eolie p. 227 no. 61
—LIPARA: (4) f. v BC SEG XLII 865 (vase); cf. BTCGI 9 p. 87 (-κκτέμον)
—SYRACUSE: (5) hell. IG XIV Add. 9 a

## Εὔκτος
ARGOLIS:
—ARGOS: (1) 219 BC PEnt 66, 1 verso (f. Μάρων); (2) ~ ib. l. 2 verso (s. Μάρων)

## Εὔκτωρ
S. ITALY (CAMPANIA):
—NEAPOLIS: (1) ?iv AD INap 247 (Οὐ(ί)κτωρ—INap)

## Εὐκώμιος
ARGOLIS:
—PHLEIOUS: (1) vi BC Suda Π 2230 (?f. Πρατίνας)

## Εὐλαΐδας
KORINTHIA:
—SIKYON: (1) ?221 or 220 BC IG VII 213, 6, [9] (f. Θεόφαντος)

## Εὐλαλία
SICILY:
—PANORMOS: (1) 488 AD CIL X 7329 (ILat. Palermo 36) (Lat. Munatia Eul[alia])
—SYRACUSE: (2) iii-v AD Strazzulla 333 + Ferrua, NG 116 (Wessel 944) (Νεραλλία—Strazzulla, Ἑρ(μα)ία—Wessel)

**Εὐλάλιος**
SICILY:
—SYRACUSE: (1) iii-v AD Ferrua, *NG* 240
([Εὐλ]άλιος)

**Εὔλαλος**
S. ITALY (CAMPANIA):
—POMPEII: (1) i BC-i AD *CIL* IV 1573-4 (Lat.
Eulalus)

**Εὔλιβα?**
SICILY:
—SYRACUSE: (1) iii-v AD *IG* XIV 537 (Strazzulla
147; Agnello 49; Wessel 505; *SEG* XXVI
1121); cf. Ferrua, *NG* 26 (Εὐλιβα—apogr.,
Εὐσεβία?—*IG*)

**Εὐλιμένης**
S. ITALY (CAMPANIA):
—HERCULANEUM*: (1) i BC-i AD *CIL* X 1403 g
III, 33 (Lat. C. Vibius Eulimines: freed.)

**Εὐλίμενος**
ILLYRIA:
—EPIDAMNOS-DYRRHACHION: (1) imp. *IDyrrh*
205 (s. Ἀλκίων)
S. ITALY (CALABRIA):
—BRENTESION-BRUNDISIUM: (2) s. i AD *Necro-
poli via Cappuccini* p. 286 no. E42 (Lat. T.
Paphrius Eul[i]menus)
S. ITALY (CAMPANIA):
—DIKAIARCHIA-PUTEOLI*: (3) imp. *CIL* X
3071 (Lat. A. Valerius Eulimenus: freed.)
—HERCULANEUM*: (4) m. i AD *Cron. Erc.* 7
(1977) p. 117 C b, 10 (Lat. [M.] Saluvius
Eulimenus: freed.)
—POMPEII: (5) i BC-i AD *CIL* IV 4900; 4903
(Lat. Eulymenus)

**Εὐλογία**
SICILY:
—MELITA: (1) iv-v AD *SEG* XXXV 995 (*JIWE* I
163) (Jew)

**Εὐλυτίδας**
LAKONIA:
—KYTHERA: (1) v/iv BC *Suda* Φ 393 (f. Φιλόξε-
νος)

**Εὔλυτος**
ARKADIA:
—ORCHOMENOS: (1) f. iii BC *SEG* XXXIII 319,
1

**Εὐμάθης**
ARKADIA:
—TEGEA: (1) iii BC *IG* V (2) 30, 21 (Ἐυμάθης)

**Εὐμαθίδας**
LAKONIA: (1) ?254 BC Nachtergael, *Les Gala-
tes* 9, 59; cf. Stephanis 1881 (Bradford (-)) (f.
Νίκων)

**Εὐμαΐδας**
SICILY:
—SELINOUS: (1) m. vi BC Dubois, *IGDS* 42
(Arena, *Iscr. Sic.* I 40; *IGLMP* 57)

**Εὔμαιος**
ACHAIA: (1) 146 BC *IG* IV (1)² 28, 154 (s. Φίλων:
synoikos)
MESSENIA:
—MESSENE: (2) imp.? ib. V (1) 1496 (Εὔμ(αι)ος)

**Εὔμαος**
MESSENIA:
—KYPARISSIA?: (1) c. 200 BC *AD* 25 (1970)
Chron. p. 174 (Εὔμα(ι)ος?)

**Εὐμάρας**
S. ITALY (BRUTTIUM):
—SYBARIS-THOURIOI-COPIAE: (1) iii BC
Theoc., *Id.* v 10, 73 (fict.)

**Εὐμάρης**
AIGINA: (1) f. iv BC *IG* II² 7963 (?f. Νικασώ)
ARGOLIS:
—EPIDAUROS*: (2) c. 370-365 BC Peek, *IAEpid*
52 B, 67 ([*E*]ὐμάρης)
—METHANA-ARSINOE: (3) ?c. 600 BC *CEG* I
137; cf. Guarducci, *Ep. Gr.* I p. 362 f. (-ρε̄ς:
f. Ἀνδροκλῆς)
—PHLEIOUS: (4) ?iv BC *Suda* Σ 829
MESSENIA:
—MESSENE?: (5) ii/i BC *SEG* XI 979, 58
S. ITALY (BRUTTIUM):
—SYBARIS-THOURIOI-COPIAE:
——(Βοι.): (6) iv/iii BC Landi, *DISMG* 118

**Εὐμαρίδας**
ARKADIA:
—MEGALOPOLIS: (1) s. ii BC *IG* V (2) 438, 16;
443, 6; 444, 5; 453 (*IPArk* 32) (s. Ἵππων, f.
Ἵππων)
MESSENIA:
—MESSENE?: (2) ii/i BC *SEG* XI 979, 37
—THOURIA: (3) f. ii BC ib. 972, 109 (s. Ὀλκιάδας)

**Εὐμάριχος**
ARGOLIS:
—HERMIONE: (1) iii BC *IG* IV (1) 685

**Εὐμᾶς**
S. ITALY (CALABRIA):
—TARAS-TARENTUM: (1) m. iv BC *Phlyax Vases*
p. 87 no. 199 (fict.)

**Εὐμαχία**
S. ITALY (CAMPANIA):
—POMPEII: (1) f. i AD *CIL* X 810; 811; 812; 813;
*Impegno per Pompeii* 11 OS (Lat. Eumachia)

**Εὐμαχίδας**
AIGINA: (1) ii BC *IG* II² 7957 (f. Κριτόλα)
ARKADIA:
—TEGEA: (2) iv/iii BC ib. V (2) 32, 8

**Εὔμαχος**
ARGOLIS:
—EPIDAUROS*: (1) c. 335-325 BC ib. IV (1)²
108, 148-9
KERKYRA: (2) ?i AD *RE* (5)
KORINTHIA:
—KORINTH: (3) c. 570-550 BC Amyx 85. 2
(vase) (Lorber 145) (her.?); (4) 431 BC Th.
ii 33. 1 (s. Χρύσις)
MESSENIA:
—MESSENE: (5) hell. *SEG* XXXVIII 346 b + XLI
370 (Εὔμαχος)
S. ITALY (CAMPANIA):
—NEAPOLIS: (6) iii/ii BC *RE* (4); *FGrH* 178
SICILY: (7) 307 BC D.S. xx 57. 4; 58. 6; 60. 4-7
—AKRAI: (8) i BC-i AD? *IG* XIV 222 (Akrai p.
164 no. 27) (s. Ζώπυρος)
—HALOUNTION: (9) i BC-i AD *IG* XIV 371 (Φίν-
των Ἐ.)
—HERBESSOS: (10) vi/v BC Dubois, *IGDS* 166 c
(vase) (Arena, *Iscr. Sic.* II 120)

**Εὐμέλης**
LAKONIA:
—HYPERTELEATON*: (1) imp. *IG* V (1) 1048

**Εὐμένεια**
S. ITALY (BRUTTIUM):
—KAULONIA: (1) ii AD *NScav* 1957, p. 188
(brick) (Lat. Eumenia)
S. ITALY (CAMPANIA):
—DIKAIARCHIA-PUTEOLI: (2) imp. *RAAN* 42
(1967) pp. 4-6 (Lat. Eumenia Primitiva)

**Εὐμένης**
ARGOLIS:
—EPIDAUROS: (1) i BC-i AD *SEG* XI 450
—EPIDAUROS*: (2) iv/iii BC Peek, *IAEpid* 51, 6,
8; *BSA* 61 (1966) p. 319 no. 26 (date)

—HERMIONE: (3) ?ii-i BC *IG* IV (1) 731 III, 6
(s. Κλεοπάτρα)
ELIS: (4) c. 177-185 AD *IvOl* 103, 10 (*M.
Εὐμ(έν)ης*)
EPIROS:
—PHOINIKE: (5) ?iii BC *SEG* XXXII 628 (f. Πευ-
κόλαος)
LAKONIA:
—GYTHEION: (6) imp. Giannakopoulou, *Gy-
theion* p. 177 (I f. Κλ. Εὐμένης II); (7) ~ ib.
(Κλ. Ἐ.: II s. Εὐμένης I); (8) ~ ib. p. 178 (f.
Κλεοκρατίδας)
—SPARTA: (9) c. 125 AD *IG* V (1) 1314, 6 (Brad-
ford (-)) (f. Ἰούλ. Σωκράτης)
MESSENIA:
—ASINE: (10) hell.-imp. *IG* V (1) 1407 (f. Κρά-
των)
—KOLONIDES: (11) ii BC ib. 1402, 1
S. ITALY (APULIA):
—TEANUM APULUM: (12) i AD *Teanum Apulum*
p. 72 no. 17 (Lat. A. Muttienus Eumenes: s.
Muttiena Tertulla)
S. ITALY (CAMPANIA):
—DIKAIARCHIA-PUTEOLI: (13) 48 AD Camo-
deca, *L'Archivio Puteolano* I p. 59 no. 2; p.
61 no. 3; p. 106 no. 2 (Lat. L. Faenius Eu-
menes)
SICILY:
—LILYBAION: (14) iii-iv AD *Kokalos* 9 (1963)
pp. 232 ff. (Lat. Eumeni, Eumenius—ed.)

**Εὐμενίδας**
SICILY:
—HALIKYAI: (1) f. i BC Cic., *In Verr.* II v 15
(Lat. Eumenides)

**Εὐμενίδοτος**
SICILY:
—SELINOUS: (1) vi/v BC Dubois, *IGDS* 50
(Arena, *Iscr. Sic.* I 50; Lazzarini 880 a); cf.
*SEG* XL 806 (Εὐμενιδότō (gen.)—Dubois, Εὐ-
μενίδō τō̄—Arena)

**Εὐμένιος**
S. ITALY (LUCANIA):
—HERAKLEIA: (1) iii BC *NC* 1917, p. 174 no. 5
n (coin)

**Εὐμένων**
ARGOLIS:
—EPIDAUROS:
——Nymphais: (1) c. 365-335 BC *IG* IV (1)²
103, 93

**Εὐμήδης**
ACHAIA:
—PELLENE: (1) f. iv BC *CEG* II 888, 18 (f. Σύμ-
μαχος)
ARKADIA:
—KAPHYAI: (2) hell.? *IEph* 1459 (f. Εὐθύδαμος)
EPIROS:
—AMBRAKIA: (3) hell.? *SEG* XXIV 421 (s.
Πολυαν—)
S. ITALY (BRUTTIUM):
—SYBARIS-THOURIOI-COPIAE: (4) iii BC
Theoc., *Id.* v 132 (fict.)

**Εὐμηλίδας**
AITOLIA: (1) ?255 BC Nachtergael, *Les Galates*
8, 5; 19, 3; Flacelière p. 398 no. 21 e, 3
ARKADIA: (2) iii BC *IG* V (2) 415, 3 (*IPArk* 23)
([Εὐ]μηλίδας)
—TEGEA:
——(Apolloniatai): (3) m. iii BC *IG* V (2) 36, 99
(f. Ξενότιμος)
——(Athaneatai): (4) s. iv BC ib. 41, 39 (s. Ξε-
νότιμος)
—TEUTHIS?: (5) ii BC *SEG* XXXV 347 C
(Εὐμηλίδας)
KEPHALLENIA:
—PALE: (6) iii/ii BC Unp. (*IG* arch.)
(Εὐμηλ(ί)[δας]?)

**Εὔμηλος**

LAKONIA:
—SPARTA: (7) iv BC *IG* V (1) 1233, 7 (Poralla²
307)

**Εὔμηλος**

ACHAIA:
—DYME*: (1) c. 219 BC *SGDI* 1612, 68 (*Tyche*
5 (1990) p. 124) ([Εὔ]μηλος: s. Ἀσκλαπιόδωρος)

ARGOLIS:
—ARGOS: (2) c. 330-300 BC *SEG* XXXIV 282, 18

ARKADIA:
—ALIPHEIRA: (3) ?273 BC ib. XXV 447, 19
(*IPArk* 24); *Chiron* 3 (1973) pp. 85-93 (date)
—MANTINEIA-ANTIGONEIA: (4) f. iii BC *IG* V
(2) 278, 12; *EILakArk* 17 (date)
—MEGALOPOLIS?: (5) ii/iii AD *IG* V (2) 518; 519
(f. Ἡράκλεια)

ELIS: (6) ?v BC *RE* s.v. Thespis (2); Luc., *Ind.*
10 (Stephanis 966)

KORINTHIA:
—KORINTH: (7) 8 or iv BC *RE* (12); *FGrH*
451 (s. Ἀμφίλυτος); (8) ?iii BC *IG* VII 135
([Εὔ]μηλος)

S. ITALY (CAMPANIA):
—NEAPOLIS: (9) her. ib. XIV 715 (*INap* 2);
*IG* XIV 748 A, 13 (*INap* 52) (Εὐμηλεῖδαι (n.
gent.))

**Εὔμηνος**

SICILY:
—SYRACUSE?: (1) v BC *RE* (-); *Samml. Ludwig*
456; 459; 460; 480 + *Chiron* 2 (1972) pp. 52-3
(coin) (coin engraver)

**Εὐμναστίδας**

KORINTHIA:
—SIKYON: (1) vi/v BC *SEG* XI 244, 70

**Εὔμναστος**

AITOLIA:
—TRICHONION: (1) f. ii BC *BCH* 45 (1921) p. 22
IV, 47 ?= (2); (2) 183 BC *SGDI* 2133, 9, 11
(f. Κλευπάτρα, Κρίνων (Trichonion and Amphissa)) ?= (1)

LAKONIA:
—SPARTA: (3) c. 550 BC *AM* 87 (1972) pp. 140-
4; *LSAG*² p. 446 no. 16a (date)

MESSENIA:
—THOURIA: (4) f. ii BC *SEG* XI 972, 42 (f. —
ητος); (5) ~ ib. l. 66 (f. Ἀριστόδαμος)

**Εὐμόλπη**

MESSENIA:
—MESSENE: (1) ii/iii AD *IG* V (1) 1483

**Εὔμολπος**

ARKADIA:
—TEGEA: (1) ii AD ib. V (2) 54, 15 (I f. Εὔμολπος
II); (2) ~ ib. l. 15 (Ε[ὔ]μολπος: II s. Εὔμολπος
I)

KORINTHIA:
—KORINTH: (3) 3 AD *Corinth* VIII (1) 14, 88
(Stephanis 969) (Γ. Ἀντ. Εὐμο[λ]πο[ς])

MESSENIA:
—MESSENE: (4) ii-iii AD *SEG* XLI 366 F

SICILY:
—LEONTINOI: (5) iv BC Paus. vi 17. 7; *IvOl* 293,
4 (*CEG* II 830) (s. Ἱπποκράτης)

**Εὐμορφία**

KORINTHIA:
—KORINTH: (1) byz. *Corinth* VIII (1) 200; cf.
*TMByz* 9 (1985) p. 361 no. 19

**Εὐμορφιανός**

S. ITALY (CAMPANIA):
—DIKAIARCHIA-PUTEOLI: (1) imp. *CIL* X 3043
(Lat. C. Valerius Eumorphianus: s. Valerius,
Sempronia)


**Εὔμορφος**

S. ITALY (CAMPANIA):
—NEAPOLIS: (1) i BC/i AD *IG* XIV 788 (*INap*
182; Dubois, *IGDGG* I 27); cf. Leiwo p.
66 (Ε(ὔ)μορφος—C. Keil, Ἔσμορφου—apogr.:
f. Μόσχος)

**Εὔμυθις**

LAKONIA:
—SELLASIA*: (1) vi BC *IG* V (1) 920 (Lazzarini
288; Poralla² 308) (Εὔμυθις: sculptor?)

**Εὐμωλίων**

LAKONIA:
—SPARTA: (1) c. 30-20 BC *IG* V (1) 94, 5 (Bradford (1)) (s. Βωρθίας) ?= (2); (2) ~ *IG* V (1)
211, 12 (Bradford (2)) (f. Καλλικράτης) ?= (1)

**Εὐνέτη**

S. ITALY (CALABRIA):
—LUPIAE?: (1) i-ii AD Susini, *Fonti Salento* p.
159 no. 120 (Lat. Anton(ia) Eunete)

**Εὐνικίδας**

MESSENIA:
—THOURIA: (1) f. ii BC *SEG* XI 972, 65
(Εὐνικίδας: f. Δαμόστρατος)

**Εὔνικος**

AITOLIA: (1) ?f. iii BC Pantos, *Sphragismata* p.
149 no. 119; p. 447 f.; (2) ?262 BC *FD* III (4)
358, 4; (3) ?257 BC Nachtergael, *Les Galates*
7, 5; (4) ?225 BC ib. 63, 9 (Stephanis 972) (s.
Εὔανδρος)

AKARNANIA:
—PALAIROS: (5) ii BC *IG* IX (1)² (2) 451, 19 (s.
Ἀρκολέων)

ARGOLIS:
—EPIDAUROS*: (6) c. 370-335 BC ib. IV (1)²
103, 19; *BSA* 61 (1966) p. 272 no. 4 B II,
7; Peek, *IAEpid* 52 B, 15

EPIROS?:
—AMPRA: (7) f. ii BC *BCH* 45 (1921) p. 23 IV,
59

LAKONIA:
—SPARTA: (8) c. 80-90 AD *IG* V (1) 674, 8 (Bradford (-)) ([E]ὔνικος)

S. ITALY (BRUTTIUM):
—RHEGION: (9) s. iv BC *IG* II² 10133 (f. Ἀριστοφῶν)

S. ITALY (CAMPANIA):
—CAPREAE: (10) i BC-i AD? ib. XIV 899
(Ὀηγικου—apogr., (Εὔ)νικος, Θείνικος?—*IG*: f.
Θεανώ)

S. ITALY (LUCANIA):
—HYELE-VELIA: (11) inc. *SEG* XXVIII 820
(-νει-: f. Διονύσιος)

SICILY:
—GELA-PHINTIAS?: (12) f. v BC Dubois, *IGDS*
134 b, 1, 3, 11, 13-14 (Arena, *Iscr. Sic.* II 47)
(-ϙος)
—SYRACUSE: (13) iv/iii BC *SEG* XVII 406 (Εὔ-)

**Εὖνις**

ILLYRIA:
—EPIDAMNOS-DYRRHACHION: (1) hell.-imp.
*IDyrrh* 206

**Εὐνίσκος**

KERKYRA: (1) c. 200 BC *IBouthrot* 10; cf. *SEG*
XXXVIII 464 (f. Μοσχίδας)

**Εὐνόα**

ARGOLIS:
—ARGOS: (1) a. 303 BC *CEG* II 816, 9

**Εὔνοια**

ILLYRIA:
—EPIDAMNOS-DYRRHACHION: (1) hell.-imp.
*IDyrrh* 207 (d. Βένετος)


LEUKAS: (2) iii/ii BC Unp. (*IG* arch.)

S. ITALY (CAMPANIA):
—DIKAIARCHIA-PUTEOLI: (3) imp. *CIL* X 1747
(Lat. Eunea); (4) ~ ib. 2817 (Lat. Pa. Eunia:
freed.)
—KYME: (5) ii-iii AD *IG* XIV 872, 14, 23, etc.
(Audollent, *Defix. Tab.* 198) (Οὐαλερία Ἐ.: m.
Οὐαλερία Κοδράτιλλα)

**Εὐνοΐδας**

ARKADIA:
—KLEITOR: (1) a. 212 AD *IG* V (2) 369, 11; *SEG*
XXXI 347, 3

**Εὐνοῖς**

ILLYRIA:
—APOLLONIA: (1) imp. *IApoll* 251 (-εῖς: d. Εὐφράντα, Μάριος)

**Εὐνομία**

ILLYRIA:
—EPIDAMNOS-DYRRHACHION: (1) i BC-i AD
*CIL* III 617 (Sestieri, *ILat. Albania* 34) (Lat.
[F]r[e]gania [Eu]nom[ia]: m. Ἀλεξάνδρεια)

MESSENIA:
—PHARAI: (2) ii/i BC *IG* V (1) 1363 + *SEG*
XXXIX 387 ([Εὔ]νομία)

SICILY:
—SYRACUSE: (3) iii-v AD *NScav* 1907, p. 766
no. 31 (Barreca 143)

**Εὐνομίδας**

ACHAIA?: (1) 193 BC *IG* V (2) 293, 14 (s. Δείνων)

**Εὐνόμιος**

KORINTHIA:
—KORINTH: (1) ii AD Luc., *DMort.* 11. 2 (fict.)

**Εὔνομος**

ACHAIA:
—DYME: (1) 191-146 BC BM coins 1920 5-15-
108/9 (coin)

ARGOLIS:
—EPIDAUROS: (2) iii/ii BC *IG* IV (1)² 222 (f. Ἱερόκλεια); (3) ii BC ib. 246, 2 (Εὔ[νο]μος: s. Ἀρχέλαος); (4) ~ ib. l. 5; 289, 4 (f. Εὔνους); (5) ii/i
BC ib. 649, 2 (s. Εὐάνθης, f. Εὐάνθης); (6) i BC
ib. 648; 657; 658, 4 (s. Εὐάνθης, ?s. Χαρικώ, f.
Εὐάνθης); (7) f. i BC ib. 66, [1], 48, 55, 60, 70,
72; 648; Peek, *IAEpid* 22, 5; Peek, *NIEpid* 84
(f. Εὐάνθης); (8) 32 AD *IG* IV (1)² 101, 46 +
Peek, *IAEpid* 45 (s. Τιβ. Κλ. Νικοτέλης); (9)
49-54 AD *IG* IV (1)² 602, 4; Peek, *NIEpid* 76,
4 (s. Νικοτέλης, f. Τιβ. Κλ. Νικοτέλης)

EPIROS:
—BOUTHROTOS (PRASAIBOI):
—Metoreis: (10) a. 163 BC *IBouthrot* 91, 6
(*SEG* XXXII 623) (f. Νικάνωρ)
—PHOINIKE: (11) iii BC ib. 629

LAKONIA:
—SPARTA: (12) her. *RE* (7); Hdt. viii 131.
2; Plu., *Lyc.* 1 (Poralla² 309) (s. Πρύτανις, ?s. Πολυδέκτας, ?f. Λυκοῦργος, Χάριλλος:
king/dub.)

MESSENIA:
—MESSENE: (13) i AD *IG* V (1) 1436, 27
(Εὔνομ[ος])

S. ITALY (BRUTTIUM):
—LOKROI EPIZEPHYRIOI: (14) ?vi-v BC *RE* (10)
(Stephanis 973)

S. ITALY (CAMPANIA):
—HERCULANEUM: (15) i BC-i AD *Cron. Erc.*
18 (1988) p. 199 (Lat. C. Messenius
Euno(m)us); (16) i AD *CIL* X 8058. 51 (seal)
(Lat. C. Mes. Eunom(us))

SICILY:
—KALE AKTE?: (17) 156 BC *IG* II² 1937, 13

**Εὔνοος**

ARGOLIS:
—ARGOS: (1) iv BC Peek, *IAEpid* 52 B, 51
—EPIDAUROS: (2) c. 370 BC *SEG* XXV 383, 117
(Εὔ[ν]ο[ος])
—EPIDAUROS*: (3) c. 290-270 BC *BSA* 61
(1966) p. 306 no. 20, 119

## Εὐνοστίδας

ARKADIA:
—MANTINEIA-ANTIGONEIA: (4) c. 425-385 BC *IG* v (2) 323. 2 (tessera) ([Ε]ὔνοος: s. Εὔφαινος)
LAKONIA:
—SPARTA: (5) c. 90-100 AD *SEG* XI 605, 4 (Bradford (-)) (f. Νικανδρίδας)

## Εὐνοστίδας

EPIROS:
—THESPROTOI: (1) c. 223 BC *IG* IX (1)² (1) 31, 46
LAKONIA:
—SPARTA?: (2) ii BC ib. XII (9) 900 Ac, 3, 6 (Bradford (-)) (f. Κλέων)
MESSENIA:
—MESSENE: (3) s. ii BC *SEG* XLI 341, 8 (f. Εὔανδρος)

## Εὔνοστος

ARKADIA:
—TEGEA:
——(Hippothoitai): (1) iv/iii BC *IG* v (2) 38, 53 (f. Φαυΐδας)

## Εὐνούδας

MESSENIA*:
—ANDANIA*: (1) s. v AD *RE* Supplbd. 3 (-); cf. *SEG* XXIX 394 (fict.?)

## Εὔνους

ACHAIA: (1) 146 BC *IG* IV (1)² 28, 139 (I f. Εὔνους II: synoikos); (2) ~ ib. l. 139 (II s. Εὔνους I: synoikos)
AIGINA: (3) ?i BC *Alt-Ägina* I (2) p. 45 no. 13 (Εὔνο[υς]?); (4) i-ii AD ib. p. 47 no. 27, 3 (s. Δαμάτριος)
AKARNANIA:
—THYRREION: (5) ii BC *IG* IX (1)² (2) 250, 11
ARGOLIS:
—EPIDAUROS: (6) ii BC ib. IV (1)² 246, 5; 247, 3; 653, 9 + Peek, *IAEpid* 284; 289, 4 (s. Εὔνομος: sculptor)
EPIROS: (7) i AD *CIL* III 12300, 4 (Lat. T. Flavius Eunus: f. Τύχη)
—AMBRAKIA: (8) ii-i BC *CIG* 1800, 6 (s. Ἀπολλοφάνης)
—PHOTIKE: (9) imp. *AE* 1914, p. 241 no. I (Lat. Eunous)
ILLYRIA:
—EPIDAMNOS-DYRRHACHION: (10) c. 250-50 BC Maier 106; 126; 151; 161; 174; 225; 260; 297; 324; 366; 400; 482; Münsterberg Nachtr. p. 17 (coins) (Ceka 154; 168-80) (money.); (11) ii BC *IDyrrh* 33; (12) hell.-imp. ib. 208 (s. Ἀνδρίων)
KORINTHIA:
—KORINTH: (13) c. 590-570 BC Amyx 40. I (vase) (Lorber 42) (-νῦς: fict.?)
—SIKYON: (14) ii AD *SEG* XXX 372 (tile)
S. ITALY (CAMPANIA):
—DIKAIARCHIA-PUTEOLI: (15) imp. *CIL* X 1886 (Lat. Sex. Patul. Eunus); (16) ~ ib. 3089 (Lat. Eunus); (17) 37-39 AD Camodeca, *L'Archivio Puteolano* I pp. 182-3; pp. 183-4; Bove, *Documenti finanziarie* pp. 24-5 T.P. 7; p. 44 T.P. 17; pp. 45-7 T.P. 18 (Lat. C. Novius Eunus)
—HERCULANEUM: (18) i BC-i AD *CIL* IV 10598 (-νυς)
—POMPEII: (19) i BC-i AD ib. 7309 f (Castrèn 205. 8) (Lat. [C.] Iul. Eunus)
SICILY:
—THERMAI HIMERAIAI: (20) i-ii AD *CIL* X 7402 (*ILat. Term. Imer.* 93) (Lat. Eunus)

## Εὐνοῦσα

ARKADIA:
—TEGEA: (1) imp. *IG* v (2) 218

## Εὐνσιβίυος?

LAKONIA: (1) m. vi BC *AA* 1964, p. 571 no. 52 a (sherd)

## Εὔξεινος

S. ITALY (CAMPANIA):
—POMPEII: (1) 70-79 AD *CIL* IV 9851; *Archaeology* 20 (1967) pp. 36-44; Mouritsen p. 109 (date) (Lat. Euxinus)
S. ITALY (LUCANIA):
—HYELE-VELIA: (2) i AD *SEG* XXXVIII 1020. 1; *PdelP* 25 (1970) p. 262 (οὖλις Εὐξίνου: doctor)

## Εὐξένα

EPIROS:
—BOUTHROTOS (PRASAIBOI): (1) a. 163 BC *IBouthrot* 36, 8; 43, 44 (*SEG* XXXVIII 495; 502)

## Εὐξένη

ELIS: (1) f. iii BC ib. XXXI 354

## Εὐξενίδας

ARGOLIS:
—EPIDAUROS*: (1) c. 290-270 BC *IG* IV (1)² 109 III, 102 (Εὐξε(ν)ίδας)
—KLEONAI: (2) ?i BC *SEG* XI 297 c
ARKADIA:
—TEGEA: (3) iii-ii BC *IG* v (2) 219; (4) f. ii BC ib. 44, 17 (Εὐξενίδ[ας]: f. Ἀλκισθένης)

## Εὔξενος

ACHAIA:
—DYME*: (1) c. 219 BC *SGDI* 1612, 34 (*Tyche* 5 (1990) p. 124) (f. Πυθίων)
AIGINA: (2) her. Pi., *N.* vii, 70 (Εὐξενίδαι (n. gent.))
AKARNANIA:
—THYRREION: (3) ii BC *IG* IX (1)² (2) 247, 13; 248, 12; 250, 17; 251, 2 (s. Δάζιμος: mantis)
ARGOLIS:
—HERMIONE: (4) ii-i BC ib. IV (1) 732 II, 24 (f. Ζήνων)
—TROIZEN: (5) ?146 BC ib. 757 A, 12; (6) ~ ib. 757 B, 32
—TROIZEN*: (7) iv BC ib. 823, 43 (Εὔξεν[ος])
DALMATIA:
—ISSA:
——(Dymanes): (8) iv/iii BC Brunšmid p. 8, 36 ([Εὔξ]ενος: s. Φίλων); (9) ~ ib. p. 9, 57 (s. Ἄνθιππος)
EPIROS:
—AMBRAKIA: (10) vi BC *SEG* XLI 540; cf. *BE* 1994, no. 38
ITHAKE?: (11) inc. *AM* 27 (1902) p. 375 (Λυκνοιος Ἐ.—apogr.)
LAKONIA:
—SPARTA: (12) 394 BC X., *HG* iv 2. 5 (Poralla² 310); (13) 242 BC *SEG* XII 371, 2 (Bradford (1)); (14) c. 30-20 BC *IG* v (1) 211, 23 (Bradford (2)) (f. Σήριππος)
MESSENIA:
—THOURIA: (15) f. ii BC *SEG* XI 972, 117 (s. Θάλινος)
S. ITALY (LUCANIA):
—METAPONTION: (16) f. iv BC *IG* XIV 648 (Landi, *DISMG* 152) (s. Φιλιστίδας)
SICILY: (17) f. iii BC Vandermersch p. 166; *Arch. Subacquea* 2 p. 63 (amph.)
—APOLLONIA: (18) hell.-imp. *IG* XIV 360 (f. Ἐπιλάϊων)
—GELA-PHINTIAS: (19) f. v BC Dubois, *IGDS* 130 (Arena, *Iscr. Sic.* II 37) (f. Φιλιστίδας)
—SYRACUSE: (20) 266 BC *IG* XII (9) 1187, 15; Robert, *Ét. Num. Gr.* pp. 179 ff. (date) (f. Ἄρχιππος)
—TAUROMENION: (21) c. 172 BC *IGSI* 4 II (III), 2 an. 69

## Εὐξίδαμος

ARGOLIS:
—HERMIONE: (1) ?ii-i BC *IG* IV (1) 733, I ([Ζ]ευξίδαμος—Boeckh)

## Εὐξίθεος

AITOLIA:
—ATTALEIA: (1) 204 BC ib. IX (1)² (1) 95, 2
ARGOLIS:
—MYKENAI: (2) s. iv BC *SEG* XV 197
ELIS: (3) c. 343 BC D. xviii 295; xix 294
KORINTHIA:
—KORINTH: (4) c. 360-330 BC *CID* II 120 A, 34 (f. Λαβώτας)

## Εὐξίθιος

ARGOLIS:
—ARGOS: (1) c. 315 BC *SEG* XXXII 370, 17 ([Εὐ]ξίθιος)

## Εὖξις

SICILY:
—HALOUNTION: (1) iii/ii BC *Arch. Class.* 17 (1965) p. 202; cf. *SEG* XXVI 1060

## Εὐοδία

ARKADIA:
—MANTINEIA-ANTIGONEIA*: (1) ii AD *IG* v (2) 277 (d. Σύμμαχος, m. Ἐλπίς: freed.)
S. ITALY (CAMPANIA):
—DIKAIARCHIA-PUTEOLI: (2) imp. ib. XIV 855 (Τρεβωνία Ἐ.); (3) ~ *CIL* X 2030 (Lat. Aeuodia); (4) ~ ib. 2336 (Lat. Cornelia Euhodia); (5) ~ ib. 2782 (Lat. Novia Euhodia: m. C. Novius Sabinianus, Novia Iusta)
—MISENUM*: (6) imp. ib. 3426 (Lat. Marcia Euhodia); (7) ~ ib. 3525 (Lat. Euvodia); (8) ~ ib. 3570 (Lat. -lia Euhodia: freed.); (9) ~ ib. 3648 (Lat. Mestria Euhodia)
—POMPEII: (10) i BC-i AD ib. IV 8154 (Lat. Euhodia); (11) ~ *NScav* 1916, p. 303 no. 109 (Castrèn 158. 14) (Lat. Epidia Euhodia); (12) 70-79 AD *CIL* IV 3595; Mouritsen p. 110 (date) (Lat. Euhodia)
SICILY:
—SYRACUSE: (13) iii-v AD *Riv. Arch. Crist.* 36 (1960) p. 40 no. 39 + Ferrua, *NG* 243 ([Εὐ]οδία)
—THERMAI HIMERAIAI: (14) ?iv AD *Epigraphica* 3 (1941) p. 264 no. 27 (*ILat. Term. Imer.* 94) (Lat. Euodia: d. Salutaris)

## Εὐοδιανός

S. ITALY (CAMPANIA):
—DIKAIARCHIA-PUTEOLI: (1) imp. *CIL* X 2808 (Lat. C. Olius Euhodianus: s. Εὔοδος)

## Εὐόδιος

S. ITALY (CAMPANIA):
—NEAPOLIS?: (1) iv-v AD *IG* XIV 822 (*INap* 2 p. 10); *IG* XIV 2410. 7 (glass) (Εὐόδι (voc./n. pr.?))

## Εὐοδίς

S. ITALY (BRUTTIUM):
—HIPPONION-VIBO VALENTIA: (1) imp. *Rend. Pont.* 60 (1987-8) p. 273 no. 19 (Lat. [Eu]hodis)
—PETELIA: (2) imp. *CIL* X 8086 (Lat. Megonia Euhodis)

## Εὐοδίων

MESSENIA:
—KORONE: (1) 246 AD *IG* v (1) 1398, 38 (Αὐρ. Ἐ.)
SICILY?: (2) imp. *IGUR* 794

## Εὔοδος

ARGOLIS:
—HERMIONE: (1) ii-i BC *IG* IV (1) 732 II, 28 (s. Ἡρακλείδας)
ARKADIA:
—KLEITOR: (2) a. 212 AD ib. v (2) 369, 28 (Αὐρ. Ἐ.: s. Ἱέρων)
ELIS:
—OLYMPIA*: (3) c. 65-75 AD *IvOl* 83, 9 (?s. Ἰσιγένης: slave?)

**Εὔορμος**

ILLYRIA:
—EPIDAMNOS-DYRRHACHION: (**4**) imp. *AEp* 1978, no. 743 (Lat. Bennius [Euh]odos)
KERKYRA: (**5**) ii-iii AD *GVI* 1978, 14, 17
KORINTHIA:
—KORINTH: (**6**) iii AD *SEG* XXVII 36. 3 (lamp) (Εὔγοδος—lamp, Εὔπο(ρ)ος?)
S. ITALY (APULIA):
—HERDONIA: (**7**) imp. *Ordona* 2 p. 139 no. 14 (Lat. Lucilius Euhodus)
—LARINUM: (**8**) imp. *CIL* IX 749 (Lat. Q. Calavius Euodus)
S. ITALY (BRUTTIUM):
—HIPPONION-VIBO VALENTIA: (**9**) imp. ib. x 66 (Lat. Atilius Euhodus)
—PETELIA: (**10**) imp.? *IG* XIV 639
S. ITALY (CALABRIA):
—BRENTESION-BRUNDISIUM*: (**11**) imp. *Epigraphica* 25 (1963) p. 60. no. 49 (Lat. L. Audius Euhodus: f. Ἄργος: freed.)
S. ITALY (CAMPANIA):
—ATELLA: (**12**) imp. *CIL* x 3750 (Lat. A. Plautius Euhodus)
—CAPREAE*: (**13**) imp. *ZPE* 71 (1988) p. 197 no. 8, 6 (Lat. Euhodus)
—DIKAIARCHIA-PUTEOLI: (**14**) i BC-i AD *CIL* IV 10528 (Lat. Euhodus); (**15**) imp. ib. x 1834 (Lat. Euhodu[s]); (**16**) ~ ib. 2808 (Lat. C. Olius Euhodus: f. Εὐοδιανός); (**17**) ~ ib. 2905 (Lat. M. Octavius Euhodus); (**18**) ~ *NScav* 1927, p. 332 no. 6 (Lat. Euhodus); (**19**) f. ii AD *Rend. Linc.* 30 (1975) p. 370 (Lat. [Clo]dius Euhodus: f. Clodius Sabinus)
—HERCULANEUM: (**20**) i BC-i AD *CIL* IV 2509, 2 (5449) (Lat. Euodus); (**21**) ~ ib. 10679 (Lat. Euhodus)
—HERCULANEUM*: (**22**) c. 50-75 AD ib. x 1403 a I, 17 (Lat. L. Mammius Euhodus: freed.)
—KYME: (**23**) imp. ib. 3700, 7 (Lat. Seius Euhodus)
—POMPEII: (**24**) i BC-i AD ib. IV 4803 (Lat. Euhodu[s]); (**25**) ~ ib. 7984 (Lat. Euhodus); (**26**) ~ ib. 8876 (Lat. Euodus); (**27**) ~ ib. 8894 (Lat. Euodus); (**28**) ~ ib. 10116 (Lat. Euo[d]us); (**29**) ~ ib. 10159 (Lat. Heuodos); (**30**) 70-79 AD ib. 515; Mouritsen p. 110 (date) (Lat. Euhodus); (**31**) ~ *CIL* IV 840; Mouritsen p. 109 (date) (Lat. Euhodus)
—SARNUM: (**32**) imp. *CIL* x 1112 (Lat. Crispinus Euodus)
—STABIAE: (**33**) i BC ib. I² 3146 (Lat. Euhodus); (**34**) imp. *RAAN* 19 (1938-9) p. 90 (Lat. P. Granius Euhodus)
SICILY:
—ZANKLE-MESSANA*: (**35**) imp. *CIL* x 6985 (Lat. A. Magullius Euhodus: freed.)

**Εὔορμος**
SICILY:
—KAMARINA: (**1**) f. v BC Cordano, *Tessere Pubbliche* 63 (-hορ-: f. Ἡρακλείδας)

**Εὔοχος**
ACHAIA:
—ASCHEION: (**1**) c. 230-200 BC *BCH* 45 (1921) p. 12 II, 63 (f. Ἀγέας)

**Εὐπαίδευτος**
KORINTHIA:
—KORINTH: (**1**) ii AD *FD* III (4) 96 (Γ. Ἥιος Ἐ.)

**Εὐπαΐδας**
ARGOLIS:
—EPIDAUROS: (**1**) 423 BC Th. iv 119. 2 (f. Ἀμφίας)

**Εὐπάμων**
ARGOLIS:
—HERMIONE: (**1**) i BC-i AD? *IG* IV (1) 734, 11 (Εὐπά(μ)ων—C. Keil, Εὐπαντονος (gen.)—apogr.: f. Ῥόδα)

**Εὔπαστος**
ARGOLIS:
—ARGOS: (**1**) iv BC ib. 629

**Εὐπάτας**
ARKADIA:
—ALIPHEIRA: (**1**) iv/iii BC Orlandos, *Alipheira* p. 237
—MEGALOPOLIS: (**2**) s. ii BC *IG* V (2) 439, 72

**Εὐπατινός?**
KORINTHIA:
—KORINTH: (**1**) hell.? ib. IV (1) 208 (Εὐπα(λ)ῖνος—CIG, Εὔπ[ρ]α[ξ]ῖνος—IG: s. Καλλίστρατος)

**Εὐπειθίδας**
KORINTHIA:
—KORINTH: (**1**) 337 BC *CID* II 74 I, 75 (s. Τιμόλας)

**Εὐπίδας**
S. ITALY (CALABRIA):
—TARAS-TARENTUM: (**1**) ?c. 500-490 BC Landi, *DISMG* 178 (Lazzarini 343); *LSAG²* p. 284 no. 4 (date) (sculptor)

**Εὔπλοια**
MESSENIA:
—KOLONIDES: (**1**) i AD *IG* V (1) 1404
SICILY:
—THERMAI HIMERAIAI: (**2**) imp. *NScav* 1902, p. 130 (*ILat. Term. Imer.* 136) (Lat. Publicia Euplea); (**3**) iii AD *Eph. Ep.* VIII 704 (*Epigraphica* 3 (1941) p. 262 no. 24); *ILat. Term. Imer.* 95 (Lat. Euplia)

**Εὔπλοιος**
S. ITALY (CAMPANIA):
—POMPEII: (**1**) i BC-i AD *CIL* IV 6631 (Lat. Euplius)

**Εὔπλους**
ARGOLIS:
—HERMIONE: (**1**) ii-i BC *IG* IV (1) 732 III, 6 (s. Ὀνάσιμος)
KORINTHIA:
—KORINTH: (**2**) s. iv AD *Corinth* VIII (3) 530, 2, 4; cf. *TMByz* 9 (1985) p. 362 no. 34
S. ITALY (APULIA):
—RUBI: (**3**) imp. *Epigrafia e Territorio* 2 p. 72 no. 13 (*CIL* IX 656) (Lat. Eyplus: s. Ἐπαφρόδιτος, Secunda)
S. ITALY (BRUTTIUM):
—PETELIA: (**4**) i-ii AD *Klearchos* 14 (1972) p. 124 (Lat. Q. Blattius Euplus)
S. ITALY (CALABRIA):
—BRENTESION-BRUNDISIUM: (**5**) f. i AD *Studi di Antichità* 5 p. 219 no. 4 (Lat. Euplus)
S. ITALY (CAMPANIA):
—HERCULANEUM: (**6**) i BC-i AD *CIL* IV 10478 (Lat. Campanus Secundus Euplus)
—KYME: (**7**) imp. *Eph. Ep.* VIII 446 (Lat. Euplus)
—POMPEII: (**8**) i BC-i AD *CIL* IV 1294; (**9**) ~ ib. 4904 (Lat. Euplus); (**10**) ~ *Riv. Stud. Pomp.* 6 (1993-4) p. 219 (Lat. C. Iulius Euplus)
—SALERNUM: (**11**) imp. *IItal* I (1) 72 (Lat. Euplus)
SICILY:
—KATANE: (**12**) imp. *IG* XIV 452 + Ferrua, *NG* 428 (Εὔπλ[ους]: s. Ἀρτέμων); (**13**) iii-v AD *IG* XIV 533 (Wessel 1357) + *Riv. Arch. Crist.* 18 (1941) p. 222 no. 108 (name—Ferrua)
—SYRACUSE: (**14**) iii-v AD *SEG* XV 588 ([Εὔ]πλο[υς]); (**15**) ~ *Nuovo Didask.* 6 (1956) p. 61 no. 23 (Εὔπλ[ους]); (**16**) byz. *CIL* x 7172 (Strazzulla 424) (Lat. Euplus)

**Εὔπλουτος**
S. ITALY (CAMPANIA):
—CAPREAE: (**1**) f. i AD *NScav* 1895, p. 235 (Lat. Euplutus)

**Εὐπόλεμος**
ACHAIA: (**1**) 146 BC *IG* IV (1)² 28, 151 (f. Λαφυράδας: synoikos)
AITOLIA: (**2**) ?255 BC Nachtergael, *Les Galates* 8, 3; 19, 2; cf. Flacelière p. 398 no. 21 c, 2
—KALLION/KALLIPOLIS: (**3**) 273 BC *IG* IX (1)² (1) 11, 39
AKARNANIA:
—OINIADAI: (**4**) v/iv BC Hp., *Epid.* v 7; *Abh-MainzAk* 1982 (9) p. 35 (locn.) (or Thessaly?)
—THYRREION: (**5**) ii BC *IG* IX (1)² (2) 248, 7 (Εὐπόλ[εμος]: f. Πολύδωρος)
ARGOLIS:
—ARGOS: (**6**) v/iv BC *RE* (13); (**7**) b. 364 BC *ID* 104, 29; 104-12, [21]
ARKADIA: (**8**) 320 BC *IG* V (2) 549, 4 (s. Δᾶμις)
DALMATIA:
—ISSA: (**9**) s. iii BC *SEG* XXXV 682; cf. *BCH* 114 (1990) p. 507-8; (**10**) ii BC *SEG* XXXI 599, 1 ([Εὐ]πόλε[μ]ος: s. Κλεψίας); (**11**) ~ ib. l. 3 (Ε[ὐ]πόλε[μ][ος])
ELIS: (**12**) c. 400-390 BC Moretti, *Olymp.* 367 ?= (Εὔπολις (1))
ILLYRIA:
—APOLLONIA: (**13**) i BC *BMC Thessaly* p. 62 nos. 81-2 (coin); (**14**) imp. *IApoll* 82
KERKYRA: (**15**) ?ii-i BC *IG* IX (1) 754 (tile) (f. Ἀριστοκλῆς)
KORINTHIA:
—SIKYON: (**16**) 283-246 BC *PPetr* II 35 (III 54 b) d, 8
SICILY:
—ADRANON: (**17**) iii-ii BC *PdelP* 16 (1961) p. 127 (f. Νικασίων)
—KALE AKTE: (**18**) f. i BC Cic., *In Verr.* II iv 49 (Lat. Eupolemus)
—MORGANTINA: (**19**) ?iv/iii BC *SEG* XXXIX 1008, 8 (f. Θεύδωρος)
—SYRACUSE: (**20**) 339 BC Plu., *Tim.* 32 (and Sicily Leontinoi: s. Ἱκέτας); (**21**) f. iii BC *NScav* 1907, p. 751 (f. Μοσ—)
—SYRACUSE?:
——(Ἀλτρι.): (**22**) hell. *Mem. Linc.* 8 (1938) p. 127 no. 35. 2 (bullet); cf. *L'Incidenza dell'Antico* pp. 420 ff. (f. Φιλωνίδας)
—TAUROMENION: (**23**) c. 238-232 BC *IG* XIV 421 an. 3; 421 an. 9 (*SGDI* 5219) (s. Εὔανδρος)

**Εὔπολις**
ELIS: (**1**) v/iv BC D.S. xiv 54. 1 ?= (Εὐπόλεμος (12))
S. ITALY (APULIA): (**2**) f. iv BC *CVA London* 7 IV Eb pl. 4, 2 (kalos)
S. ITALY (BRUTTIUM):
—LOKROI EPIZEPHYRIOI:
——(Ἀλχ.): (**3**) iv/iii BC De Franciscis 6, 4; 12, 9 (s. Φαικίων, f. Φαικίων)
S. ITALY (CAMPANIA):
—DIKAIARCHIA-PUTEOLI*: (**4**) imp. *CIL* x 2738 a (Lat. Minatia Eupolis: freed.)

**Εὔπομπος**
KORINTHIA:
—SIKYON: (**1**) v/iv BC *RE* (2) (Skalet 127) (Lat. Eupompus: painter)

**Εὐπόρα**
LAKONIA:
—TAINARON-KAINEPOLIS: (**1**) imp. *IG* V (1) 1269

**Εὐπορᾶς**
LAKONIA:
—SPARTA: (**1**) c. 170 AD ib. 116, 1 (Bradford (-)) (Γ. Σίλβιος Ἐ.)
S. ITALY (CAMPANIA):
—DIKAIARCHIA-PUTEOLI: (**2**) imp. *CIL* x 8368 (Lat. Euporas)

**Εὐπορία**
ILLYRIA:
—EPIDAMNOS-DYRRHACHION: (1) hell.-imp. *IDyrrh* 209
KORINTHIA:
—KORINTH: (2) iii-iv AD *Corinth* VIII (1) 133 (Ἐουπω-)
—SIKYON: (3) iii BC *Eretria* VI 182
LAKONIA:
—SPARTA: (4) imp. *SEG* XI 686 (Bradford (-)) (d. Σωσθένα)
S. ITALY (CAMPANIA):
—NEAPOLIS: (5) f. iii AD *ILS* 6453 (*Napoli Antica* p. 389 no. 115. 3); cf. Leiwo p. 157 no. 127 (Lat. Iulia Euporia)
SICILY:
—KATANE: (6) imp. *CIL* X 7052 (Lat. Cabaria Euporia)
—SYRACUSE: (7) iii-v AD Strazzulla 344 (Barreca 145)

**Εὐποριανός**
S. ITALY (LUCANIA):
—VOLCEI: (1) 323 AD *CIL* X 407 (Lat. F. Euporianus)

**Εὐπόριος**
SICILY:
—KATANE: (1) imp. *IG* XIV 475

**Εὐπόριστος**
LAKONIA:
—SPARTA: (1) c. 150-160 AD ib. V (1) 53, 14; 54, 5 (Bradford (-)) (f. Ἀνέγκλητος)
MESSENIA:
—KORONE: (2) 246 AD *IG* V (1) 1398, 84 (Αὐρ. Ἐ.)
SICILY:
—THERMAI HIMERAIAI: (3) i-ii AD *CIL* X 7368 (*ILat. Term. Imer.* 37) (Lat. P. Acellius Eyporistus)

**Εὐπορίων**
ILLYRIA:
—EPIDAMNOS-DYRRHACHION: (1) i BC-i AD *CIL* III 623 (Sestieri, *ILat. Albania* 39) (Lat. Memmius Euporion)

**Εὔπορος**
ACHAIA: (1) 146 BC *IG* IV (1)² 28, 115 (s. Ἀπολλόδωρος: synoikos)
AIGINA: (2) ?f. i AD *Alt-Ägina* I (2) p. 46 no. 20, 1 (s. Λυ—)
ARGOLIS:
—ARGOS: (3) ii/i BC *IG* IV (1) 539 (s. Ἀντέρως)
—EPIDAUROS: (4) ii-iii AD ib. IV (1)² 526 (s. Μενεκλῆς); (5) ?135 AD Peek, *IAEpid* 240; (6) 167 AD *IG* IV (1)² 390 (I f. Εὔπορος II); (7) ~ ib. (II s. Εὔπορος I); (8) 171 AD ib. 392, 4 (s. Δημοσθένης); (9) 194 AD ib. 555, 6 + Peek, *IAEpid* 231 ([Εὔ]πορος: f. Καλλιτέλης)
ELIS: (10) 28-24 BC *IvOl* 64, 6 (f. Ἀφροδίσιος); (11) c. 201-265 AD ib. 107, [14]; 110, 22; 117, 18; 122, 22
EPIROS:
—BOUTHROTOS: (12) iii AD *IBouthrot* 192 (Γά(λ)λιος Ἐ.)
—BOUTHROTOS (PRASAIBOI): (13) a. 163 BC ib. 14, 42 (*SEG* XXXVIII 471) (f. Εὐανθίδης)
—NIKOPOLIS: (14) c. 75-100 AD *FD* III (4) 114, 4 (Sarikakis 92) (Πο. Κορνήλιος Ἐ.); (15) ~ *FD* III (4) 114, 5-6 (Sarikakis 91) (Πο. Κορνήλιος Ἐ. [Λού]πος)
ILLYRIA:
—EPIDAMNOS-DYRRHACHION: (16) c. 250-50 BC Maier 124; 194; 223; 234; 311; 316 (coin) (Ceka 181-6) (money.); (17) hell.-imp. *IDyrrh* 213 (f. Εὐτυχίς); (18) ~ ib. 389 (?f. Σωτηρίς); (19) ?ii AD *Stud. Alb.* 1965, p. 72 no. 46 (Lat. Euporus: f. Ἄννυλα)
—SKODRAI: (20) a. 168 BC *Iliria* 1972, p. 400 (coin)

KORINTHIA:
—KORINTH: (21) ii-iii AD *SEG* XI 132, 2; 134, 3; (22) ~ *IAquil* 711 (Τ. Φλ. Ἐ.); (23) iii AD *Corinth* IV (2) p. 208 nos. 731-734; *SEG* XXVII 36. 2 (lamps)
—SIKYON*: (24) ii AD *ILGR* 82 (Lat. M. Pacuvius Euporus: freed.?)
LAKONIA:
—SPARTA: (25) c. 125-150 AD *IG* V (1) 73, 4; 113, 4; *SEG* XI 575, 7 (Bradford (6)) (f. Κλέανδρος); (26) m. ii AD *IG* V (1) 71 II, 13; 154, 6 (Bradford (2)) (II s. Εὔπορος I); (27) ~ *IG* V (1) 71 II, 14; 154, 6 (Bradford (5)) (I f. Εὔπορος II); (28) c. 150-160 AD *IG* V (1) 53, 32 (Bradford (1)) (Κανίνιος Ἐ.: s. Κανίνιος Ἀριστόνικος); (29) c. 220 AD *IG* V (1) 544, 6 (Artemis Orthia pp. 358-9 no. 145; Bradford (3)) (Μ. Αὐρ. Ἐ.: s. Ἅρμοστος); (30) c. 230-250 AD *IG* V (1) 314, 10 (Artemis Orthia p. 335 no. 71); *BSA* 79 (1984) p. 285 no. 17 (date) (Bradford (4)) (Μ. Αὐρ. Ἐ.: s. Κλέανδρος ὁ καὶ Μήνιος)
S. ITALY (CAMPANIA):
—DIKAIARCHIA-PUTEOLI: (31) ?i-ii AD *CIL* X 2592 (Lat. Ti. Iulius Eupor(us))
—POMPEII: (32) i BC-i AD ib. IV 8491 (Lat. Eupor(us))
—POMPEII*: (33) 57 AD ib. 117; 120; 3340. 37, 15; 71, 9; 92, 3; 97, 5 (Castrèn 161. 7) (Lat. M. Fabius Eupor(us): freed.)
ZAKYNTHOS: (34) i BC-i AD *IG* IX (1) 606

**Εὐποσία**
ILLYRIA:
—EPIDAMNOS-DYRRHACHION: (1) imp. *AEp* 1928, no. 93 (Lat. Aelia Euposia)
S. ITALY (APULIA):
—CANUSIUM*: (2) ii-iii AD *Epig. Rom. di Canosa* 53 (Lat. Coelia Euposia: freed.)
S. ITALY (CALABRIA):
—TARAS-TARENTUM: (3) i-ii AD *Misc. Gr. Rom.* 3 p. 197 no. T7 (Lat. Euposia)
SICILY:
—KAMARINA: (4) imp. Pace, *Camarina* p. 159 nos. 1-2 (Cordano, 'Camarina VII' 106)

**Εὐποσιώ**
S. ITALY (CAMPANIA):
—DIKAIARCHIA-PUTEOLI*: (1) imp. *CIL* X 2820 a-b (Lat. Paccia Euposio: freed.)

**Εὐπράγιος**
MESSENIA:
—KORONE: (1) iii AD *SEG* XI 988

**Εὐπραισία**
S. ITALY (CAMPANIA):
—DIKAIARCHIA-PUTEOLI*: (1) imp. *CIL* X 2185 (Lat. Caecilia Eupraesia: freed.?)

**Εὐπράκτας**
ARKADIA:
—TEGEA:
——(Apolloniatai): (1) f. iii BC *IG* V (2) 36, 55 (f. Ἀριστόβιος: metic)

**Εὔπρακτος**
ARGOLIS:
—ARGOS: (1) iv-v AD *SEG* XI 325, 4; cf. *TMByz* 9 (1985) p. 289 no. 29
SICILY:
—MOTYKA (NR.): (2) iv-v AD *IG* XIV 244 + *ASSiciliaOrientale* 1938-9, p. 27; cf. *SEG* XXXIX 994 note (Ἀντ. Ἐ.)
—SYRACUSE: (3) byz. *IG* XIV 110 (Wessel 1078) + *ASSicilia* 1938-9, p. 27 (name) (Εὔπρα— ὁ καὶ Διοκλητιανός?—*IG* and Strazzulla, Εὔπτα[—]—Wessel)

**Εὐπραξία**
ARKADIA:
—STYMPHALOS: (1) iv AD *IG* V (2) 359

LAKONIA:
—SPARTA?: (2) ii-iii AD *SEG* XXXI 342 (Κλ. Ἐ.)
S. ITALY (CAMPANIA):
—DIKAIARCHIA-PUTEOLI*: (3) imp. *CIL* X 3062 (Lat. Valeria Eupraxia: m. Ἀπόλαυστος, Νέστωρ: freed.)
SICILY:
—KENTORIPA: (4) imp. Manganaro, *QUCC* forthcoming no. 16 ([E]ὐπραξ[ία]); (5) i-ii AD *CIL* X 7006 (*ILat. Palermo* 5) (Lat. Maria Eupraxia: m. Εὐτυχιανός)

**Εὔπραξις**
ARGOLIS:
—ARGOS: (1) ii/i BC *IG* IV (1) 539
ILLYRIA:
—APOLLONIA: (2) iii-ii BC *IApoll* 34 (s./d. Νίκων); (3) imp. ib. 83 (Εὔπραξ[ις]?)
KERKYRA: (4) imp. *IG* IX (1) 912

**Εὐπρέπεια**
S. ITALY (CAMPANIA):
—DIKAIARCHIA-PUTEOLI: (1) ?ii AD *CIL* X 3134 (Lat. Ulpia Euprepia)

**Εὐπρέπης**
ACHAIA:
—PATRAI: (1) ii-iii AD *ILGR* 57, 2 (Lat. Q. Cassius Euprepes)
S. ITALY: (2) imp. *CIL* X 8059. 175 (seal) (Lat. Euprepes)
S. ITALY (CAMPANIA):
—DIKAIARCHIA-PUTEOLI: (3) imp. ib. 2393 (Lat. Eyprepes)

**Εὐπυρίδης**
ARGOLIS:
—PHLEIOUS: (1) iii-iv AD *IG* IV (1) 449, 2 (Κλ. Κλαυδιανὸς Εὐπυρίδης: s. Κλ. Μινουκιανός)

**Εὐπυρίων**
KERKYRA: (1) c. 240-220 BC ib. VII 369, 2 (*IOrop* 155) (s. Νίκων: reading—Petrakos)

**Εὐπωλία**
LAKONIA:
—SPARTA: (1) c. 460-390 BC Plu., *Ages.* 1 (Poralla² 312) (d. Μελησιππίδας, m. Ἀγησίλαος, Κυνίσκα, Τελευτίας); (2) f. iv BC Plu., *Ages.* 19 (Poralla² 313) (d. Ἀγησίλαος, Κλεόρα)

**Εὐρέας**
ACHAIA: (1) 165 BC Plb. XXX 30. 1; 32. 3

**Εὕρημα**
S. ITALY (APULIA):
—CANUSIUM: (1) i-ii AD *Epig. Rom. di Canosa* 58, 1 (*CIL* IX 348) (Lat. Maria Heurema: d. Villanus)
S. ITALY (CAMPANIA):
—SURRENTUM: (2) i AD *NScav* 1956, p. 79 (Lat. Passiena Heurema)

**Εὐρήμων**
ARGOLIS:
—EPIDAUROS*: (1) c. 365-335 BC *IG* IV (1)² 103, 131
ARKADIA:
—STYMPHALOS: (2) 189 BC *SEG* XXV 445, 21 (*IPArk* 18) (s. Ἰσαγόρας)
S. ITALY (CAMPANIA):
—KYME: (3) ii/iii AD *Puteoli* 3 (1979) p. 162 no. 5 (Lat. P. Aelius Aeuremo: I f. Εὐρήμων II); (4) ~ ib. (Lat. P. Aelius Aeuremo: II s. Εὐρήμων I)

**Εὐρήσιος**
S. ITALY (CAMPANIA):
—DIKAIARCHIA-PUTEOLI: (1) imp. *CIL* X 2444 (Lat. Euresius)

**Εὕρησις**
S. ITALY (CAMPANIA):
—ACERRAE: (1) imp. ib. 3759 (Lat. Heuresis)

**Εὑρησίς**
SICILY:
—SYRACUSE: (2) iii-iv AD ib. 7130. 10 + *Epigraphica* 51 (1989) p. 185 ([Εὑ]ρησις?)

**Εὑρησίς**
S. ITALY (BRUTTIUM):
—PETELIA: (1) imp. *CIL* x 116 (Lat. Aufidia Heuresis)
S. ITALY (CALABRIA):
—BRENTESION-BRUNDISIUM: (2) imp. *Eph. Ep.* VIII 43 (Lat. Pompon[ia] Heuresis)
S. ITALY (CAMPANIA):
—DIKAIARCHIA-PUTEOLI: (3) imp. *CIL* x 1870 (Lat. Betubia Euresis); (4) s. iii AD *Puteoli* 6 (1982) p. 150 no. 5 (Lat. Heuresis)

**Εὔρητος**
S. ITALY (CAMPANIA):
—HERCULANEUM*: (1) m. i AD *Cron. Erc.* 7 (1977) p. 118 D, 1 (Lat. C. Lusius Euretus: freed.)

**Εὐρίας?**
EPIROS:
—BOUTHROTOS (PRASAIBOI): (1) a. 163 BC *IBouthrot* 96, 4

**Εὐρίοπος?**
EPIROS:
—BOUTHROTOS (PRASAIBOI):
——Cherrioi: (1) a. 163 BC ib. 98, 8 (f. Ἀπολλώνιος)

**Εὐριπίδας**
AITOLIA: (1) 219 BC Plb. iv 19. 5; 59. 1 + 4; 60. 3; 68-72 etc.; Pantos, *Sphragismata* p. 129 no. 104
—KALLION/KALLIPOLIS: (2) 139 BC *SGDI* 2137, 3 (name—Mulliez)

**Εὖρις**
SICILY:
—SELINOUS: (1) f. v BC Dubois, *IGDS* 41 (Arena, *Iscr. Sic.* 1 48; Lazzarini 880 f) (he[ὑ]ρις)

**Εὖρος**
S. ITALY (CAMPANIA):
—POMPEII: (1) i BC-i AD *CIL* IV 4679 (Lat. Eurus)

**Εὐρυάδης**
LAKONIA:
—SPARTA: (1) iii BC *IG* v (1) 708; Moretti, *Olymp.* 565 (Bradford (-))

**Εὐρύαλος**
LAKONIA:
—SPARTA: (1) m. vii BC Paus. iv 20. 8 (Poralla² 314)
S. ITALY (APULIA):
—CANUSIUM: (2) 223 AD *Epig. Rom. di Canosa* 35 III, 12 (*CIL* IX 338) (Lat. L. Abuccius Euryalus)

**Εὐρυάναξ**
LAKONIA:
—SPARTA: (1) 479 BC Hdt. ix 10, 53, 55 (Poralla² 315) (s. Δωριεύς)

**Εὐρύας**
ACHAIA:
—AIGION: (1) c. 230-200 BC *BCH* 45 (1921) p. 12 II, 60 (f. Εὐρυφάων, Ἀρίστανδρος, Θευπροπίδας)
AITOLIA: (2) ?265-264 BC *FD* III (3) 202, 2; (4) 359, 34; *SEG* XVIII 242, 2; *CID* II 130, [2]; *IG* XII (9) 1187, 21; cf. Robert, *Ét. Num. Gr.* p. 179 ff. (date) (s. Στρατόνικος)
ARKADIA:
—MANTINEIA-ANTIGONEIA: (3) iv/iii BC *SEG* XXXVI 378, 2 (f. —άρδιος)

**Εὐρυβάνασσα**
LAKONIA:
—SPARTA: (1) c. 50 BC-20 AD *IG* v (1) 209, 2; 212, 58; *BSA* 80 (1985) pp. 194-7 (ident., stemma) (Bradford (1)) (Εὐρυβ(ϝ)άνασσα: d. Σιδέκτας, ?m. Γ. Ἰούλ. Δεξίμαχος, Σιδέκτας); (2) i/ii AD *IG* v (1) 507, 9; 573-4; *BSA* 75 (1980) p. 219 (stemma); 80 (1985) pp. 194; 203 (ident., stemma) (Bradford (2)) (Μεμμία Εὐρυβ(ϝ)άνασσα: ?d. Π. Μέμμιος Δεξίμαχος)

**Εὐρυβάτας**
ARGOLIS:
—ARGOS: (1) c. 525-488 BC *RE* (4)
KORINTHIA:
—KORINTH: (2) c. 570-550 BC Amyx 71. 1 (vase) (Lorber 127) (her.?)

**Εὐρύβατος**
ARGOLIS:
—HERMIONE: (1) ii BC *IG* IV (1) 733, 3 (s. Ἀρι—)
KERKYRA: (2) 433 BC Th. i 47. 1
LAKONIA:
—SPARTA: (3) 708 BC Moretti, *Olymp.* 22 (Poralla² 316) (or Arkadia Lousoi)

**Εὐρυβιάδας**
ARKADIA:
—TEGEA: (1) m. iv BC *IG* v (2) 6, 71
LAKONIA:
—SPARTA: (2) vi/v BC *RE* (-) (Poralla² 317) (s. Εὐρυκλείδας); (3) 384 BC Moretti, *Olymp.* 396; *SEG* XXXII 217, 15 (Poralla² 318) (Εὐρυβιά[δας]); (4) s. i BC *IG* v (1) 95, 16 (Bradford (-)) (s. Δάμιππος)

**Εὐρύβιος**
ARKADIA:
—MEGALOPOLIS: (1) ?225-221 BC Nachtergael, *Les Galates* 63, 6; 64, 6 (Stephanis 982) (s. Λυκίσκος)
SICILY:
—SYRACUSE?: (2) f. iv BC [Pl.], *Ep.* 348 E

**Εὐρυβίοτος**
AIGINA?: (1) iv-iii BC *IG* IV (1) 115 (s. Τεῖσις)

**Εὐρυδάμα**
LAKONIA:
—SPARTA: (1) f. v BC Hdt. vi 71. 2 (Poralla² 319) (d. Διακτορίδας, m. Λαμπιτώ)

**Εὐρυδάμας**
AKARNANIA:
—OINIADAI: (1) v/iv BC Hp., *Epid.* v 5; *Abh. MainzAk* 1982 (9) p. 35 (locn.) (or Thessaly?)

**Εὐρυδαμίδας**
LAKONIA:
—SPARTA: (1) c. 241-227 BC Paus. ii 9. 1; iii 10. 5; Cartledge—Spawforth p. 242 n. 22 (name) (Bradford (-)) (Εὐδαμίδας?: s. Ἄγις, Ἀγιᾶτις: king)

**Εὐρύδαμος**
AITOLIA: (1) f. iii BC *BCH* 64-5 (1940-1) p. 65 no. 4, 1; *IG* IX (1)² (1) p. XVII; p. XLIX, s.a. 279 BC; cf. Flacelière p. 109 (f. Πλείσταινος); (2) c. 280-275 BC ib. p. 414 no. 47; *SEG* XV 338; (3) ?255 BC Nachtergael, *Les Galates* 8, 4; 19, 2
—CHALKIS: (4) ?iii BC *SEG* XXV 623 b = XXIX 470
—DARDEOI: (5) f. ii BC *IG* IX (1)² (1) 96, 21 (f. Σύμμαχος)
—KALLION/KALLIPOLIS: (6) a. 170 BC ib. IX (1) 226, 14
ARGOLIS:
—KLEONAI: (7) c. 230-200 BC *BCH* 45 (1921) p. 15 II, 148 (f. Δαμώ)

**Εὐρυδάμων**
AITOLIA:
—TRICHONION: (1) 263 BC *IG* IX (1)² (1) 17, 83

**Εὐρυδίκα**
AITOLIA:
—KALYDON: (1) ii BC ib. 145 (m. Ἀρισταρχίς)
ARGOLIS:
—ARGOS: (2) 105 BC *JÖAI* 14 (1911) Beibl. p. 146 no. 4, 26 (d. Κλέανδρος)
—EPIDAUROS: (3) iii/ii BC *IG* IV (1)² 336 (d. Κλεώνυμος)
EPIROS:
—BOUTHROTOS (PRASAIBOI): (4) a. 163 BC *IBouthrot* 92, 5
ILLYRIA: (5) 168 BC *RE* Supplbd. 3 (20) (m. Γένθιος, Πλάτωρ, Καραβάντιος)
—APOLLONIA: (6) ?ii BC *IApoll* 375
—EPIDAMNOS-DYRRHACHION: (7) i BC-i AD *CIL* III 615 (Sestieri, *ILat. Albania* 32) (Lat. Cassia Eurudica)

**Εὐρυδίκη**
S. ITALY (APULIA):
—VENUSIA: (1) imp. *CIL* IX 511 (Lat. Eurycis—lap.?)

**Εὐρύδικος**
ARKADIA:
—TORTHYNEION: (1) ?iii BC *FD* III (2) 193, 4 (Εὐρύ[δικος]: s. Δαμόνικος) ?= (3); (2) 263 BC *IG* IX (1)² (1) 17, 37 (f. Δαμόνικος); (3) c. 230-200 BC *BCH* 45 (1921) p. 14 II, 123 (s. Δαμόνικος) ?= (1)

**Εὐρύκλεια**
ARGOLIS:
—EPIDAUROS: (1) iii BC *IG* IV (1)² 337 (d. Σωτέλης)
LEUKAS: (2) iv/iii BC Unp. (Leukas Mus., inscr.) inv. 8

**Εὐρυκλείδας**
AITOLIA:
—KONOPE-ARSINOE: (1) ii-i BC *IG* IX (1)² (1) 132 ([Εὐ]ρυκλείδας: f. Δαμοκράτεια)
LAKONIA:
—SPARTA: (2) 632 BC Moretti, *Olymp.* 59 (Poralla² 320); (3) vi/v BC Hdt. viii 2. 2; 42. 2 (Poralla² 321) (f. Εὐρυβιάδας); (4) 227 BC Plu., *Cleom.* 8 (Bradford (-))

**Εὐρυκλῆς**
LAKONIA:
—SPARTA: (1) 592 BC Moretti, *Olymp.* 80 (Poralla² 322); (2) c. 60-2 BC *RE* (5); s.v. Iulius (220); *PIR*² I 301; *IG* v (1) 141, 17-18; *SEG* XI 883 a (tile); XXII 310, 2; XXIX 383, 2; *Münzpr. der Laked.* pp. 162-70 Groups 25-30; *RPC* I p. 247 nos. 1102-7 (coins) (Bradford (1); (4); (5)) (Γ. Ἰούλ. Ἐ.: s. Λαχάρης, f. Ῥαδάμανθυς, Γ. Ἰούλ. Δεξίμαχος, Γ. Ἰούλ. Λάκων); (3) c. 73-136 AD *RE* s.v. Iulius (221); *PIR*² I 302; *SEG* XXVIII 412, [2]; Cartledge-Spawforth pp. 110-12; *BSA* 73 (1978) pp. 249-60 (date, stemma) (Bradford (2)) (Γ. Ἰούλ. Ἐ. Ἡρκλανός Λ. Βιβούλιος Πῖος: s. Γ. Ἰούλ. Λάκων); (4) c. 134 AD *IG* v (1) 287, 4 (*Artemis Orthia* p. 320 no. 44); *Artemis Orthia* pp. 320-1 no. 45, [1] (Bradford (3)) (Ἰούλ. Ἐ.)
SICILY:
—SYRACUSE: (5) 413 BC Plu., *Nic.* 28

**Εὐρυκράτης**
LAKONIA: (1) vi BC Iamb., *VP* 267 (*FVS* 1 p. 447; Poralla² 324)
—SPARTA: (2) f. vii BC Hdt. vii 204; Paus. iii 3. 4; iv 15. 3 (Poralla² 323) (s. Πολύδωρος, f. Ἀνάξανδρος: king); (3) c. 1-10 AD *IG* v (1) 209, 13; *SEG* XXXV 331 (date) (Bradford (2)) (f. Εὐκράτης)

**Εὐρυκρατίδας**
LAKONIA:
—SPARTA: (1) vii/vi BC RE (-) (Poralla² 325); cf. Paus. iii 3. 5 (Εὐρυκράτης—Paus.: s. Ἀνάξανδρος, Λεανδρίς, f. Λέων: king)

**Εὐρυκρέτης**
ARKADIA:
—TEGEA:
——(Hippothoitai): (1) f. iii BC IG v (2) 36, 59 (s. Πολέας)

**Εὐρυλέων**
ACHAIA: (1) 211 BC Plb. x 21. 1 ?= (2)
—AIGION: (2) c. 210-195 BC IG ix (1)² (1) 29, 27; Syll³ 585, 29 (f. Ξενοφῶν) ?= (1)
LAKONIA:
—SPARTA: (3) ?s. viii BC Paus. iv 7. 8; 8. 11 (Poralla² 326) (dub.?)

**Εὐρυλεωνίς**
LAKONIA:
—SPARTA: (1) iv BC Moretti, Olymp. 418 (Poralla² 328)

**Εὔρυλλος**
KERKYRA:
——(Amphineis): (1) c. 500 BC SEG xxx 521 + L'Illyrie mérid. 2 p. 205
KORINTHIA:
—SIKYON: (2) iv BC BCH 52 (1928) p. 217 no. 21, 3 (f. Καλλιφάων)

**Εὐρύλοχος**
AITOLIA:
—KALYDON: (1) a. 142 BC IG ix (1)² (1) 137, 60
AKARNANIA:
—ASTAKOS: (2) m. ii BC ib. ix (1)² (2) 209, 2 (s. Ἀγήσαρχος)
ARKADIA: (3) 308 BC ib. v (2) 550, 1 ([Εὐ]ρύλοχος)
—LOUSOI: (4) 401 BC RE Supplbd. 4 (10)
EPIROS:
—VOTONOSI (MOD.): (5) f. iii BC SEG xxiv 456 (Εὐρύλο[χος]: I f. Εὐρύλοχος II); (6) ~ ib. (Εὐρύλο[χος]: II s. Εὐρύλοχος I)
KORINTHIA:
—KORINTH: (7) c. 570-550 BC Amyx 68. 11 (vase) (Lorber 125) (her.)
LAKONIA:
—SPARTA: (8) 426 BC Th. iii 100-2; 105-9 (Poralla² 329)
S. ITALY (CAMPANIA):
—POMPEII: (9) i BC-i AD IG xiv 2414. 26 (tessera) (-ρό-)

**Εὐρυμαχίδας**
ARKADIA:
—TORTHYNEION: (1) c. 230-200 BC BCH 45 (1921) p. 14 II, 122 (Εὐρυμα[χί]δας: s. Κρατύιος)

**Εὐρύμαχος**
AIGINA: (1) f. v BC IG iv (1) 56; LSAG² p. 113 no. 10 (date) (or Phoenicia: ?s. Φοῖνιξ)
KORINTHIA:
—KORINTH: (2) c. 570-550 BC Amyx 53. 2; 74. 10 (vases) (Lorber 138); Lorber 129 (her.)

**Εὐρυμέδων**
ARKADIA:
—MEGALOPOLIS: (1) hell. IG v (2) 486
KORINTHIA:
—KORINTH: (2) c. 570-550 BC Amyx 68. 2 (vase) (Lorber 125) ([Εὐ]ρυμέδōν: her.)
S. ITALY (CALABRIA):
—TARAS-TARENTUM: (3) iv BC Iamb., VP 267 (FVS 1 p. 446)

**Εὐρυμένης**
ARKADIA:
—TEGEA: (1) f. iii BC IG v (2) 35, 26 (f. Εὐθύλαος)
SICILY:
—SYRACUSE: (2) f. iv BC FGrH 84 F 31 b (Iamb., VP 189); Iamb., VP 191 (s. Ἱππαρῖνος)

**Εὐρυμήδης**
ARGOLIS:
—EPIDAUROS:
——Pierias (Hysminatai): (1) c. 365-335 BC IG iv (1)² 103, 64 ([Ε]ὐρυμήδης)
KORINTHIA:
—KORINTH: (2) c. 600-575 BC ib. iv (1) 227 (pinax) (Lazzarini 267); LSAG² p. 131 no. 15 (date) (-μέδēς)

**Εὐρύμμας**
EPIROS:
—BOUTHROTOS (PRASAIBOI): (1) a. 163 BC IBouthrot 17, 31; 25, 29; 29, 62 (SEG xxxviii 474; 483; 487) ?= (7); (2) ~ IBouthrot 29, 27 ?= (8); (3) ~ ib. 30, 14 (SEG xxxviii 488); (4) ~ IBouthrot 43, 10; cf. SEG xxxviii 502 (f. Φιλόξενος) ?= (8); (5) ~ IBouthrot 126, 5 (Ε[ὐρύμ]μας: f. Κέφαλος); (6) ~ ib. 143, 6 (-ρύμας)
——Cheilioi: (7) a. 163 BC ib. 116, 3, 8 (BCH 118 (1994) p. 121 A) (Εὐρύμας—l. 3: f. Ταυρίσκος) ?= (1)
——Phorrioi: (8) a. 163 BC IBouthrot 48, 2 (f. Φιλόξενος) ?= (2) (4); (9) ~ ib. 129, 1 ([Εὐρ]ύμμας)
—ORESTOI: (10) ?164 BC Cabanes, L'Épire p. 586 no. 71, 8 (f. Φιλόνικος)
—PRASAIBOI: (11) a. 163 BC IBouthrot 66, 4 (s. Λυκῖνος)
KORINTHIA:
—KORINTH: (12) c. 570-550 BC Amyx 68. 1 (vase) (Lorber 125) (Ἐ<υ>ρύμας?—Amyx: her.)

**Εὐρύνδας**
SICILY:
—KENTORIPA: (1) i BC-i AD? IG xiv 241 (s. Ἀγαθ—)

**Εὐρυνόα**
EPIROS:
—BOUTHROTOS (PRASAIBOI): (1) a. 163 BC IBouthrot 19, 6 (SEG xxxviii 476)

**Εὐρυνόμη**
AITOLIA:
—APERANTOI: (1) iii-ii BC IG ix (1)² (1) 162 (d. Τιμάγορος)

**Εὐρύνομος**
AITOLIA:
—APERANTOI: (1) hell. ib. 163 (Εὐ(ρ)ύνομ[ος]: s. Αἴνιχος)

**Εὐρύνους**
EPIROS:
—DODONA*: (1) iv-iii BC PAE 1932, p. 52 no. 6
—MOLOSSOI: (2) ?164 BC Cabanes, L'Épire p. 586 no. 71, 4 (f. Δεξίλαος)
—TALAONOI/TALAIANES: (3) iii-ii BC SGDI 1349, 7; cf. Cabanes, L'Épire p. 580 no. 53 (s. Δέρκας)

**Εὐρυσθένεια**
LAKONIA:
—SPARTA: (1) iv/iii BC SEG xi 669 c (vase); BSA 30 (1928-30) pp. 243-4 (date) (Bradford (-))

**Εὐρυσθένης**
LAKONIA:
—SPARTA: (1) her. RE (3); cf. D.S. xii 45. 1 (Poralla² 331) (Εὐρυσθεύς—D.S.: s. Ἀριστόδαμος, Ἀργεία, f. Ἆγις: king/dub.); (2) 399 BC X., HG iii 1. 6 (Poralla² 332) (and Mysia Teuthrania)

**Εὐρυστρατίδας**
LAKONIA: (1) ?c. 550-525 BC Lazzarini 791 (CEG 1 371); LSAG² p. 199 no. 19 (date) (Poralla² 332b)

**Εὐρυτίδας**
ARGOLIS:
—TROIZEN: (1) iii BC IG iv (1) 774, 4 (Εὐρυτί[δας]: f. Ἀριστόδαμος); (2) ?146 BC ib. 757 B, 8

**Εὐρύτιμος**
ARKADIA:
—TEGEA: (1) f. iii BC ib. v (2) 35, 32 (s. Πρατόλαος)
——(Apolloniatai): (2) f. iii BC ib. 36, 53 (f. Δαμαίνετος)
KORINTHIA:
—KORINTH: (3) 435 BC Th. i 29. 2 (f. Ἀρχέτιμος)

**Εὐρυτίων**
KORINTHIA:
—KORINTH: (1) c. 570-550 BC Amyx 107. 5 (vase) (Lorber 147) (her.?)

**Εὔρυτος**
LAKONIA:
—SPARTA: (1) inc. Lyd., Mens. 154; (2) 480 BC Hdt. vii 229. 1 (Poralla² 333)
S. ITALY (BRUTTIUM):
—KROTON: (3) s. v BC RE (10); FVS 45 (or S. Italy (Lucania) Metapontion or S. Italy (Calabria) Taras-Tarentum)
S. ITALY (CALABRIA):
—TARAS-TARENTUM: (4) iv/iii BC IG xiv 668 I, 9 (Landi, DISMG 194)
S. ITALY (CAMPANIA):
—DIKAIARCHIA-PUTEOLI: (5) m. i AD Puteoli 12-13 (1988-9) p. 24 (Lat. C. Vibius Eurytus)
—HERCULANEUM: (6) 59 AD Ostraka 2 (1993) pp. 201-3 (Lat. C. Vibius Eurytus)

**Εὐρύφαμος**
SICILY:
—SYRACUSE: (1) vi BC RE (-)

**Εὐρυφάων**
ACHAIA:
—AIGION: (1) c. 230-200 BC BCH 45 (1921) p. 11 II, 59 (s. Εὐρύας)

**Εὐρυφῶν**
ARGOLIS:
—EPIDAUROS: (1) c. 350-200 BC SEG xxvi 452. 3
LAKONIA:
—SPARTA: (2) her. Hdt. viii 131; Bechtel, KOS pp. 169-170 (name); RE s.v. Eurypon (Poralla² 330); FGrH 70 F 118; cf. Plu., Lys. 19 (Εὐρυπῶν—FGrH, Εὐρυπωντίδας—Plu.: ?s. Προκλῆς, Σόος, f. Πρύτανις: king/dub.)
SICILY:
—SELINOUS: (3) m. v BC Dubois, IGDS 68 (Arena, Iscr. Sic. 1 32; IGLMP 95) (-φōν: s. Ἀρχινίδας)

**Εὐρυώδας**
SICILY: (1) ?v-iv BC RE (-) (-δης: doctor)

**Εὐρώπα**
AKARNANIA:
—THYRREION: (1) ii BC IG ix (1)² (2) 320

**Εὐρώπας**
LAKONIA:
—SPARTA: (1) her. Paus. iii 15. 8 (RE (-)) (s. Ὑραῖος: dub.)

## Εὐρώπη
S. Italy (Calabria):
—brentesion-brundisium*: (1) imp. *CIL* ix 6396 c (Lat. Valeria Aeuropa: freed.)

## Εὐρώτας
Kynouria:
—prasiai?: (1) imp. *IG* v (1) 1516, 3 (Bradford (-)) (*Τιβ. Κλ. Ἐ.*)
Lakonia:
—sparta: (2) c. 160-170 AD *IG* v (1) 109, 15 (Bradford (-))

## Εὐσαμβάτις
Korinthia:
—korinth: (1) iii-iv AD *SEG* xxxv 260

## Εὔσαμος
Akarnania:
—oiniadai: (1) f. ii BC *BCH* 45 (1921) p. 23 IV, 62 (*Εὔσα[μος]*)

## Εὐσέβεια
Kephallenia:
—panormos: (1) byz. *IG* xiv 895; cf. *SEG* xxxvii 790 (n. pr.?)
Sicily:
—syracuse: (2) iii-v AD *IG* xiv 59 a (Wessel 1083) (*Εὐσεβ[ής]—IG, Εὐσέβ[ια] [ἡ] καὶ Ἀγάθη—*Wessel)

## Εὐσέβης
Illyria:
—epidamnos-dyrrhachion: (1) imp. *BUST* 1961 (1), p. 115 no. 13 (Lat. Vibius (Eus)ebes: I f. *Εὐσέβης* II); (2) ~ ib. (Lat. [Vale]rio Eusebenti (dat.): II s. *Εὐσέβης* I, Popilia Ianuaria)
Messenia:
—messene: (3) imp. *SEG* xli 339 (*Εὐσέβ[ιο]s*— ed., *Εὐσέβ[η]s?*—LGPN)
S. Italy (Campania):
—dikaiarchia-puteoli: (4) imp. *CIL* x 2394 (Lat. Eusebes: f. Albanus); (5) ?i-ii AD ib. 2202 (Lat. N. Calavius Eusebes)
—salernum: (6) s. i AD *IItal* i (1) 162 (*CIL* x 651) (Lat. Vibius Eusebes: s. *Καλλιτύχη*)
Sicily:
—adranon: (7) ?ii-iii AD *PdelP* 16 (1961) p. 132 (Ferrua, *NG* 472); cf. *Rupes loquentes* p. 497 no. 8
—katane: (8) imp. *IG* xiv 472 (*CIL* x 7064 (biling.)) (*Κ. Δομίτιος Ἐ.*, Lat. Q. Domitius Pius)

## Εὐσέβιος
Argolis:
—argos: (1) byz. *BCH* 27 (1903) p. 261 no. 3, 4; cf. *TMByz* 9 (1985) p. 369 no. 107
Korinthia:
—korinth: (2) s. iv AD *Corinth* viii (3) 522, 2; cf. *TMByz* 9 (1985) p. 362 no. 35 (?s. *Ἀνατολικός*)
S. Italy (Apulia):
—canusium: (3) c. 509-549 AD *Epig. Rom. di Canosa* 166 b (*CIL* ix 412) (Lat. Eusevius)
S. Italy (Campania):
—dikaiarchia-puteoli: (4) imp. ib. x 2665 (Lat. L. Lol. Severus Eusebius: s. L. Lol. Severus, *Ἀπολλωνία*)
Sicily:
—katane: (5) iii-v AD *IG* xiv 534 (Wessel 310) (*[Εὐ]σέβιος*)
—syracuse: (6) iii-v AD *IG* xiv 88 (Strazzulla 29; Wessel 160) (f. *Βονιφάτιος*); (7) ~ *IG* xiv 111 (Strazzulla 49; Agnello 4; Wessel 949); (8) ~ *ASSiracusano* 1956, p. 62; (9) ~ *Rend. Pont.* 22 (1946-7) p. 235 no. 36 (*[Εὐ]σέβιος*); (10) ~ Wessel 848 (Barreca 18)

## Εὐσέβις
Sicily:
—syracuse: (1) iii-v AD *SEG* iv 26; (2) ~ Strazzulla 323 (Barreca 147) (*Εὐσεβις* (gen.))

## Εὔσεινος
Lakonia:
—sparta: (1) iii BC *SEG* xl 348 B, 3; *PdelP* 45 (1990) pp. 284-8 (name)

## Εὐσθένης
Aigina: (1) ?275 BC *FD* iii (1) 195, 3 (f. *Τιμόμαχος*)
Argolis:
—epidauros: (2) c. 365-335 BC *IG* iv (1)² 103, 35
Arkadia:
—mantineia-antigoneia: (3) iv/iii BC *SEG* xxxvi 378, 3 (I f. *Εὐσθένης* II); (4) ~ ib. l. 3 (*[E]ὐσθένης* II s. *Εὐσθένης* I)
Korinthia:
—korinth: (5) s. iv BC *Corinth* viii (1) 32 (sculptor?); (6) iii BC *IG* xi (4) 1173, 4 (f. *Ἀριστόφιλος*)

## Εὔσκανος
Kerkyra?: (1) hell. ib. ix (1) 836 (bullet)

## Εὐσκία
Sicily:
—syracuse: (1) iv-v AD Strazzulla 165 (Agnello 20; Wessel 456-8; Guarducci, *Ep. Gr.* 4 p. 526 no. 4); cf. *Riv. Arch. Crist.* 18 (1941) p. 183 no. 47; Ferrua, *NG* 109 (*Εὐσ(εβ)ία*—Wessel)

## Εὔσκιος
Sicily:
—motyka (nr.): (1) 398 AD *IG* xiv 246 + Agnello 92; cf. *ASSicilia* 1938-9, p. 30; *SEG* xxxix 992

## Εὔσκις
Sicily:
—zankle-messana: (1) f. iv AD *Epigraphica* 3 (1941) p. 253 no. 2

## Εὐσοΐδας
Arkadia:
—mantineia-antigoneia: (1) f. iii BC *IG* v (2) 278, 7; *EILakArk* 17 (date)

## Εὐσταθία
S. Italy (Campania):
—misenum*: (1) m. ii AD *Puteoli* 11 (1987) p. 137 no. 5 (Lat. Iulia Eustathia)

## Εὐστάθιος
Korinthia:
—korinth: (1) byz. *Corinth* viii (1) 189 (*Εὐστάθ[ιος]*)
—korinth*: (2) ?v AD *PAE* 1961, p. 133 (bp.)
Sicily:
—syracuse: (3) iii-v AD Wessel 1368 (Barreca 153)

## Εὐστάθις
Elis: (1) m. iii AD *IvOl* 120, 14 (*[Εὐ]στάθις*)

## Εὔστατος
S. Italy (Campania):
—herculaneum*: (1) i BC-i AD *CIL* x 1403 g III, 11 (Lat. Eustatus: freed.)

## Εὐσταχίς
Sicily:
—syracuse: (1) iii-v AD *SEG* iv 12 (Wessel 977); cf. Ferrua, *NG* 273 (name) (*Εὐσταχὶς ἡ κὲ Βῶκυς*)

## Εὐστόλων
S. Italy (Campania):
—pompeii: (1) i BC-i AD *CIL* iv 8816 (Lat. Eustolo)

## Εὐστόχιος
Sicily:
—syracuse: (1) imp.? Ferrua, *NG* 394

## Εὔστρατος
Achaia:
—dyme?: (1) ?f. iii BC *HE* 2875 (s. *Ἔχελλος*)
Aitolia: (2) ?253 BC Nachtergael, *Les Galates* 10, 5
Argolis:
—argos: (3) c. 316-222 BC *Mnem.* NS 43 (1915) p. 377 G, 3 (Perlman A.16); (4) ii/i BC *IG* iv (1) 640 (*[E]ὔστρα[τος]*: f. *Εὐκράτις*)
Arkadia:
—mantineia-antigoneia: (5) f. iii BC ib. v (2) 278, 11; *EILakArk* 17 (date)
—megalopolis: (6) m. iii BC *IG* iv (1)² 96, 34 (Perlman E.3); Perlman p. 63 f. (date) (f. *Ἀναξίδαμος*)
Epiros:
—ambrakia: (7) s. iv BC Unp. (Arta Mus., inscr.) (f. *Φρύνεος*)
—kelaithoi: (8) 370-368 BC Cabanes, *L'Épire* p. 534 no. 1, 13, 29
Illyria:
—epidamnos-dyrrhachion: (9) hell.-imp. *IDyrrh* 211 (s. *Τρίτος*)
Korinthia:
—korinth: (10) vi BC *IG* iv (1) 228 (pinax) (Lazzarini 268)
—sikyon: (11) 326 BC *CID* ii 32, 36; 120 A, 44 (s. *Ξενότιμος*)

## Εὔστροφος
Argolis:
—argos: (1) 420 BC Th. v 40. 3

## Εὔσχημος
Illyria:
—epidamnos-dyrrhachion: (1) i BC-i AD *AEp* 1978, no. 755 (Lat. D. Granius Euschemus)
S. Italy (Apulia):
—canusium: (2) ?ii AD *Epig. Rom. di Canosa* 129 (*CIL* ix 377) (Lat. Euschemus: I f. *Εὔσχημος* II); (3) ~ *Epig. Rom. di Canosa* 129 (*CIL* ix 377) (Lat. Euschemus: II s. *Εὔσχημος* I)
S. Italy (Calabria):
—hydrous-hydruntum: (4) ii AD Susini, *Fonti Salento* p. 101 no. 36 (Lat. Ulp. Euschemus)
S. Italy (Campania):
—dikaiarchia-puteoli: (5) imp. *CIL* x 2793 (Lat. M. Oct. Euscem(us))
—herculaneum: (6) i BC-i AD ib. 1408 (Lat. Q. Pont. Euschemus)

## Εὐσχήμων
Achaia:
—pellene: (1) ?ii-iii AD *SEG* xi 1274, 6

## Εὔτακτος
Lakonia:
—sparta: (1) imp. *IG* v (1) 795 (Bradford (-))
S. Italy (Apulia):
—luceria: (2) imp. *ASP* 34 (1981) p. 5 no. 2 (Lat. Eutactus)
—venusia: (3) imp. *CIL* ix 481 (Lat. M. Antonius Eutactus)
S. Italy (Campania):
—dikaiarchia-puteoli: (4) imp. *Eph. Ep.* viii 375 (Lat. L. Balabius Eutactus)
—herculaneum: (5) i BC-i AD *Riv. Stud. Pomp.* 3 (1989) p. 291 (tile) (Lat. Eutaktos)
—nola: (6) imp. *CIL* x 1331 (Lat. Q. Sulpicius Eutactus)

—POMPEII: (7) i BC-i AD *NScav* 1923, p. 274 (pithos) (Lat. A. Plautius Eutactus); (8) c. 51-62 AD *CIL* IV 3340. 61, 13 (Castrèn 205. 9) (Lat. C. Iul. Eutactus); (9) 54 AD *CIL* IV 3340. 5, [19]; 37, 22; 38, 18 (Castrèn 220. 2) (Lat. L. Livineus Eutactus)
—POMPEII*: (10) i BC-i AD *CIL* IV 4572

**Εὐταξία**
ILLYRIA:
—APOLLONIA: (1) imp. *IApoll* 30; (2) ~ ib. 84
—EPIDAMNOS-DYRRHACHION: (3) imp. *IDyrrh* 186 (m. Ἐπίκαδος)
S. ITALY (APULIA):
—RUBI: (4) ii/iii AD *Suppl. It.* 5 p. 24 no. 6 (*CIL* IX 6184) (Lat. Iulia Eutaxia)

**Εὐτέλης**
AITOLIA: (1) ?228-215 BC *SGDI* 2525, 3
ARKADIA:
—MANTINEIA-ANTIGONEIA:
——(Posoidaia): (2) m. iv BC *IG* V (2) 271, 15 (s. Ὀριπίων)
—TEGEA: (3) hell.? ib. 170. 13 (tile)
KEPHALLENIA?: (4) c. 330 BC *SEG* XXIII 189 I, 22 (f. —ων)
KORINTHIA:
—KORINTH: (5) s. iii BC *Corinth* VIII (1) 59
—SIKYON: (6) ?255 BC Nachtergael, *Les Galates* 8, 13; cf. Stephanis 334 (f. Ἀριστόδαμος)
MESSENIA:
—MESSENE: (7) s. ii BC *SEG* XLI 341, 18 (f. —λης)
—THOURIA: (8) s. iii BC *IG* V (1) 1386, 4 (f. —θυμος)

**Εὐτελίδας**
ARGOLIS:
—ARGOS: (1) vi/v BC *RE* (2) (sculptor)
—PHLEIOUS: (2) c. 210-207 BC *IG* IV (1)² 73, 13; *SEG* XXXV 303 (date) (-λει-: f. Ἀρχέας)
ARKADIA: (3) ?iii BC Ael. fr. 60
LAKONIA:
—SPARTA: (4) 628 BC Moretti, *Olymp.* 63-4; *SEG* XXXII 217, 4 (Poralla² 334); (5) i BC/i AD *IG* V (1) 48, 11 (Bradford (1)) (f. Ἀριστοκράτης)

**Εὐτελῖνος**
ARKADIA:
—MANTINEIA-ANTIGONEIA: (1) i AD *IG* V (2) 269; 270 (-λεῖ-: f. Ἰουλ. Εὐδία); (2) i-ii AD ib. 342 a, 6

**Εὐτελίων**
ARGOLIS:
—PHLEIOUS: (1) c. 366-338 BC Petrakos, *Oropos* pp. 196-7 no. 47, 21 (*IOrop* 520)
ARKADIA:
—MANTINEIA-ANTIGONEIA:
——(Posoidaia): (2) c. 425-400 BC *SEG* XXXI 348, 18

**Εὐτέρπη**
EPIROS:
—BOUTHROTOS (PRASAIBOI): (1) ii AD Ugolini, *Alb. Ant.* 3 p. 223 c (Sestieri, *ILat. Albania* 4) (Lat. Julia Euterpe: m. Ποθεύνη)
SICILY:
—SYRACUSE: (2) 360 AD *IG* XIV 112 (Strazzulla 50; Agnello 91; Wessel 1017/18; Guarducci, *Ep. Gr.* 4 pp. 524-5 no. 3)

**Εὐτερπίδας**
KORINTHIA:
—KORINTH: (1) c. 370 BC *IG* IV (1)² 102, 14, 27, 230-1, 234

**Εὐτιμίδας**
LAKONIA:
—GERONTHRAI: (1) 72 BC ib. V (1) 1114, 1

**Εὐτραπελίων**
SICILY:
—KATANE: (1) iii-v AD Ferrua, *NG* 455

**Εὐτράπελος**
LAKONIA:
—SPARTA: (1) ii-iii AD *IG* V (1) 742 (Bradford (-)) (*M. Ἀντ. Ε.*)
S. ITALY (APULIA):
—LUCERIA*: (2) imp. *NScav* 1899, p. 276 (*Lucera Romana* p. 26) (Lat. Allius Eutraphilus: freed.)
—VENUSIA: (3) imp. *CIL* IX 595 (Lat. Eutrapelus)
S. ITALY (CAMPANIA):
—DIKAIARCHIA-PUTEOLI: (4) imp. *NScav* 1902, p. 630 (Lat. Eutrapelus: f. Plutia Pia)
—POMPEII: (5) m. i AD *Impegno per Pompeii* 9 ES no. 2 (Castrèn 265. 1) (Lat. L. Naevoleius Eutrapel(us))

**Εὐτρήσιος**
MESSENIA:
—VASILIKO (MOD.): (1) c. 500-475 BC *SEG* XXXVII 332 (vase); *LSAG*² p. 206 no. 4 (date) (ethn.?)

**Εὔτροπος**
S. ITALY (BRUTTIUM):
—PATERNUM?: (1) imp. *CIL* X 120 (Lat. Eutropus: f. Valentina)

**Εὐτρόφιμος**
MESSENIA:
—MESSENE: (1) ?272 BC *SEG* XII 220 (Εὐτρόφ[ιμος]—LGPN: f. Φαρσάλιος)

**Εὔτυχα**
ARGOLIS:
—HERMIONE: (1) ii-i BC *IG* IV (1) 732 III, 10 (d. Τεισικράτης)

**Εὐτυχαία**
KORINTHIA:
—KORINTH: (1) byz. *Corinth* VIII (3) 543, 4 (Εὐτυ[χαί]α)

**Εὐτυχᾶς**
ARKADIA:
—TEGEA: (1) ii AD *IG* V (2) 55, 95 (I f. Εὔτυχᾶς II); (2) ~ ib. l. 95 (II s. Εὔτυχᾶς I); (3) 165 AD ib. 50, 56 (f. Ἄρχιππος)
LAKONIA:
—HYPERTELEATON*: (4) imp. ib. V (1) 1024 (s. Ἀρσινέα)
—SPARTA: (5) ii BC *Mél. Daux* p. 233, 4 (Εὐ[τυχ]ᾶς?: f. Εὐβάμερος); (6) ii AD *IG* V (1) 159, 8 (Bradford (1)); (7) c. 225-250 AD *IG* V (1) 529, 15 (Bradford (4)) (f. Ἀβίδιος Σάτυρος); (8) c. 230-260 AD *SEG* XI 633, 3 (Bradford (3)) (f. Διονύσιος); (9) ~ *SEG* XI 633, 7 (Bradford (2)) (Αὐρ. Εὐ[τυχ]ᾶς)
MESSENIA:
—KORONE: (10) 246 AD *IG* V (1) 1398, 40 (Αὐρ. Ε.)
S. ITALY (CAMPANIA):
—DIKAIARCHIA-PUTEOLI: (11) ?i-ii AD *CIL* X 2550 (Lat. C. Iulius Eutuchas)

**Εὐτύχη**
ARGOLIS:
—HERMIONE: (1) ?ii-i BC *IG* IV (1) 731 I, 4
KORINTHIA:
—KORINTH: (2) byz. *Corinth* VIII (1) 160 (d. Χρυσέρως)
S. ITALY (CAMPANIA):
—MISENUM: (3) imp. *AJA* 2 (1898) p. 394 no. 53 (Lat. Fl. Eutyce: d. Ζωτικός)
SICILY:
—SYRACUSE: (4) imp. *Sic. Gymn.* 16 (1963) p. 62 (Ἰουλ. Εὐ[μά]χη—ed., Εὐ[τύ]χη—LGPN); (5) iii-v AD Strazzulla 415; (6) ~ *Sic. Gymn.* 3

(1950) p. 123; cf. Ferrua, *NG* 112 ([E]ὐτύχη, [E]ὐτύχητος—Ferrua)

**Εὐτύχημος**
LAKONIA:
—KYTHERA: (1) c. 230-200 BC *BCH* 45 (1921) p. 19 III, 101

**Εὐτύχης**
ARKADIA:
—KLEITOR: (1) a. 212 AD *IG* V (2) 369, 16; *SEG* XXXI 347, 8 (f. Σύμφορος); (2) ~ ib. l. 2; (3) m. iii AD ib. XXXV 350 I, 3 (Εὐτύχης: f. Αὐρ. Σωσικράτης)
—TEGEA: (4) ii AD *IG* V (2) 55, 63 (s. Φαυσίων); (5) ~ ib. l. 80 (s. Παράμονος); (6) 165 AD ib. 50, 29 (s. Ζώσιμος); (7) ~ ib. l. 33 (f. Εὔτυχος)
ELIS: (8) 265 AD *IvOl* 122, 3, 7, 17 (Αὐρ. Ε.: f. Ἀφροδᾶς, ?f. Δημήτριος)
EPIROS:
—NIKOPOLIS: (9) imp. *CIG* 1815
ILLYRIA:
—APOLLONIA: (10) imp. *IApoll* 277
ITHAKE: (11) imp. *BCH* 54 (1930) p. 489
KERKYRA: (12) imp. *IG* IX (1) 953 (s. Ἡρᾶς)
KORINTHIA:
—KORINTH: (13) ?ii AD *SEG* XVII 132 (Γ. Ἰούλ. Ε.); (14) ii-iii AD *Corinth* I (1) 183 (Εὐτύχηδος (gen.)); (15) ~ *Lampes antiques BN* I 32; *SEG* XXVII 35. 9 (lamps) (Εὐτυχᾶ (gen.)—*Lampes*, Εὐτύχηδος (gen.)—*SEG*)
LAKONIA:
—GYTHEION: (16) imp. *IG* V (1) 1201
—SPARTA:
——Konosoura: (17) c. 212-230 AD ib. 684, 14 (Bradford (-)) (Αὐρ. Ε.)
MESSENIA:
—KORONE: (18) 246 AD *IG* V (1) 1398, 48 (Ἰγν. Εὐτύχης)
S. ITALY: (19) imp. *CIL* X 8059. 152 (seal) (Lat. Eutiches)
S. ITALY (APULIA):
—CANUSIUM: (20) ii-iii AD *Epig. Rom. di Canosa* 82 (*CIL* IX 357) (Lat. L. Attius Eutyches); (21) ~ *Epig. Rom. di Canosa* 154 (*CIL* IX 389) (Lat. T. Livius Eutyches: f. Livius Tertius)
—GNATHIA-EGNATIA*: (22) imp. ib. 265 and Add. p. 657 (Lat. Clodius Eytyches: freed.)
—TEANUM APULUM: (23) imp. ib. 719 (Lat. Eutiches)
—TEANUM APULUM?: (24) imp. *Teanum Apulum* p. 151 no. 2 a (or S. Italy (Apulia) Luceria: Lat. Eutiches)
S. ITALY (BRUTTIUM):
—RHEGION: (25) f. i AD *SEG* XXIX 987, 8 (*Suppl. It.* 5 p. 60 no. 12)
—RHEGION*: (26) imp. *IG* XIV 620, 6 (Γ. Ἰο[ύλ.] [Εὐ]τύχης: freed.)
S. ITALY (CALABRIA):
—BRENTESION-BRUNDISIUM: (27) imp. *CIL* IX 183 (Lat. Sergius Eutuches)
S. ITALY (CAMPANIA):
—DIKAIARCHIA-PUTEOLI: (28) imp. *AJA* 2 (1898) p. 381 no. 20 (Lat. Eutyches: f. Fortunatus); (29) ~ *CIL* X 2182 (Lat. M. Caelilius Eutyches); (30) ~ ib. 2636 (Lat. Laecanius Eutyches: f. Laecanius Venerianus); (31) ~ ib. 2710 (Lat. L. Marius Eutyches: f. Εὐθυμία); (32) ~ ib. 2868 (Lat. Q. Pompeius Eutyche(s)); (33) ~ ib. 8196 (Lat. Eutyces); (34) ~ ib. 8059. 151 (seal) (Lat. Eutiches); (35) ~ *Eph. Ep.* VIII 414 (Lat. C. Oppius Eutiches Magonianus); (36) ?i-ii AD *CIL* X 2266 (Lat. Ti. Claudius Eutyches); (37) ~ ib. 2267 (Lat. Ti. Claudius Eutyches); (38) 168 AD ib. 1563 (Lat. Nemonius Eutyches: f. Καλλίστη, Εὐτυχιανός, M. Nemonius Gemellianus)
—DIKAIARCHIA-PUTEOLI*: (39) imp. ib. 1723 (Lat. Eutyches: freed.); (40) ~ ib. 3091 (Lat. Eutyches: freed.)
—HERCULANEUM: (41) iii AD ib. 8189 = *NScav* 1880, p. 184 (Lat. Eutyces: I f. Εὐτύχης II);

(42) ~ *CIL* x 8189 = *NScav* 1880, p. 184 (Lat. Eutyces: II s. *Εὐτύχης* I)
—KYME: (43) 251 AD *CIL* x 3699 II, 24 (Lat. M. Valerius Eutyches)
—NEAPOLIS: (44) imp. *Gnomon* 45 (1973) pp. 270-1 (*Εὐτυχῖ* (dat.)); (45) ~ *NScav* 1892, p. 273; cf. Leiwo p. 112 no. 84 (Lat. C. Comin[ie]nus Eutyches); (46) iii-iv AD *IG* XIV 826. 16 (*INap* 229); (47) ~ ib. 241
—NOLA: (48) imp. *Atti Caserta* 27 (1896) p. 29 no. 1 (Lat. C. Varius Eutyches)
—NUCERIA ALFATERNA: (49) imp. *CIL* x 1085 (Lat. Eutuches)
—SALERNUM: (50) ii AD *IItal* 1 (1) 93 (Lat. Ulpius Eutyches)
—SALERNUM*: (51) i BC/i AD ib. 190 (*CIL* x 1753) (Lat. L. Atilius Eutyches: freed.); (52) m. ii AD *IItal* 1 (1) 171 (*CIL* x 526) (Lat. Eutyches: s. T. Aelius Celsus: imp. freed.)
SICILY: (53) imp. ib. 8045. 21 (tile) (Lat. C. Sextius Eutyches); (54) ~ ib. 8059. 211 (seal) (Lat. M. Iulius Eutyches)
—AKRAI: (55) ii AD ib. 7188 (Akrai p. 164 no. 25) (Lat. P. Ael. Eutyces); (56) iii-v AD *IG* XIV 236 (Führer–Schultze p. 136 no. 4; Agnello 64; Wessel 795; Akrai p. 166 no. 38)
—KATANE: (57) imp. *CIL* x 7094 (Lat. Eutyches); (58) ~ ib. 7099 (Lat. Valerius Eutyches: f. Valeria Thermitana); (59) iv-v AD Libertini, *Museo Biscari* p. 318 no. 6 (*Στά-τειος Ἐ.*)
—KENTORIPA: (60) ?ii AD *CIL* x 7005 (Lat. [E]u[t]ych[e]s: f. T. Aelius Pius)
—LILYBAION: (61) ?ii AD ib. 7242 (Lat. P. Aelius Eutyches: f. *Ἰλάρα*)
—SYRACUSE (NR.): (62) imp. *Helikon* 2 (1962) p. 499
—SYRACUSE: (63) iii-v AD *IG* XIV 114 (Strazzulla 55; Wessel 259); cf. *ASSicilia* 1938-9, p. 31; (64) ~ Strazzulla 361 (Barreca 160); (65) ~ Strazzulla 390 (Agnello 29; Wessel 859); cf. Ferrua, *NG* 144 (s. *Ἀρτεμισία*); (66) ~ ib. 261; (67) ~ ib. 367/8 (*Εὐτύχεις*—lap., *Εὐτύχι(ο)ς*—Ferrua); (68) ~ *Nuovo Didask.* 6 (1956) p. 67 no. 42 (*Εὐτύ[χης]?*)
—TAUROMENION: (69) imp. *IG* XIV 439 (*Στά-τειος Ἐ.*)
—ZANKLE-MESSANA*: (70) ?ii AD *Mon. Ant.* 24 (1916) p. 147 (Lat. M. Ulpius Eutyc[he]s: freed.)

**Εὐτυχία**
ILLYRIA:
—EPIDAMNOS-DYRRHACHION: (1) i BC *IG* II² 8485 (d. *Εὔτυχος*)
—LYCHNIDOS: (2) ii-iii AD *BSA* 18 (1911-12) p. 176 no. 18
KORINTHIA:
—KORINTH: (3) imp. *SEG* XIII 234
S. ITALY (APULIA):
—BARION: (4) imp. *CIL* IX 287 (Lat. Anton[ia] Euthycia: m. Barinus)
—CANUSIUM: (5) i-ii AD *Epig. Rom. di Canosa* 111 (*CIL* IX 368 with Add.) (Lat. Baebia Eutychia: m. *Σελήνη*)
—LUCERIA: (6) imp. ib. 817 (Lat. Sulpicia Euticia)
—TEANUM APULUM: (7) imp. *Taras* 2 (1982) p. 182 (Lat. Eutychia)
—VENUSIA: (8) i/ii AD *Epigraphica* 35 (1973) p. 148 no. 10 (*Museo di Venosa* p. 237 no. 10) (Lat. Valeria Euthycia: m. Iulius Musteolus, *Ἑρμιόνη*)
S. ITALY (BRUTTIUM):
—HIPPONION-VIBO VALENTIA: (9) imp. *CIL* x 77 (Lat. Minicia Eutychia)
—RHEGION: (10) 79 AD ib. 7, 6; cf. *Suppl. It.* 5 p. 41 (Lat. Eutychia)


S. ITALY (CALABRIA):
—BRENTESION-BRUNDISIUM: (11) imp. *CIL* IX 109 (Lat. Eutychia); (12) ~ ib. 147 (Lat. Eutychia quae et Buttin: d. *Ἔρως*, *Μυρρίνη*)
—BRENTESION-BRUNDISIUM*: (13) imp. *NScav* 1900, p. 153 no. 4 (Lat. —arcia Eutychia: freed.)
—TARAS-TARENTUM: (14) imp. ib. 1896, p. 375 no. 1 (Lat. Eutychia); (15) ~ *Misc. Gr. Rom.* 3 p. 176 (Lat. Publicia Eytycia)
S. ITALY (CAMPANIA):
—DIKAIARCHIA-PUTEOLI: (16) imp. *CIL* x 1918 (Lat. Pompeia Eutychia); (17) ~ ib. 2048 (Lat. Amullia Eutychia); (18) ~ ib. 2064, 2 (Lat. Annia Eutychia); (19) ~ ib. 2074 (Lat. Pontia Eutychia); (20) ~ ib. 2155 (Lat. Rupilia Eutychia: m. *Ῥοδίνη*); (21) ~ ib. 2332 (Lat. Sabinia Euthycia); (22) ~ ib. 2523 (Lat. Horatia Eutychia); (23) ~ ib. 2866 (Lat. Pompeia Eutychia); (24) ~ *NScav* 1885, p. 499 (*Eph. Ep.* VIII 383) (Lat. Maria Eutychia); (25) ~ *NScav* 1891, p. 340 no. 1 (Lat. Annia Eutychia); (26) ?ii AD *CIL* x 2014 (Lat. Aelia Eutychia); (27) ~ ib. 2447 (Lat. Flavia Eutychia)
—DIKAIARCHIA-PUTEOLI*: (28) imp. ib. 2965 (Lat. Sittia Euthycia: freed.)
—MISENUM: (29) ?iii AD *AJPh* 30 (1909) p. 167 no. 18 (Lat. Cincia Eutychia)
—MISENUM*: (30) imp. *CIL* x 3361 (Lat. Silia Eutychia); (31) ~ ib. 3463 (Lat. Naevia Eutychia); (32) ~ ib. 3519 (Lat. Pomponia Eutychia); (33) ?i-ii AD ib. 3358 (Lat. Nigidia Eutychia: freed.)
—NEAPOLIS: (34) iii-iv AD *IG* XIV 826. 17 (*INap* 237)
—POMPEII: (35) i BC-i AD *CIL* IV 8321 a (Lat. Eutychia)
—SALERNUM: (36) imp. *IItal* 1 (1) 50 (Lat. [Cl]audia Eu[t]ych[i]a: d. *Ζωσίμη*); (37) ~ ib. 197 (*CIL* x 577) (Lat. Claudia Eutychia); (38) ~ *Rass. Stor. Salern.* 10 (1988) p. 44 no. 7 (Lat. Eutychia); (39) ?s. i AD *IItal* 1 (1) 179 (*CIL* x 558) (Lat. Flavia Eutychia)
S. ITALY (LUCANIA):
—POSEIDONIA-PAESTUM: (40) imp. ib. 491 (Mello–Voza 202) (Lat. Eutychia)
SICILY:
—AKRAGAS?: (41) imp. *Epigraphica* 3 (1941) p. 269 no. 43 (seal) (-*χεία*)
—MOTYKA (NR.): (42) iii-v AD *IG* XIV 247 (-*κεία*); (43) iv-v AD *ASSiciliaOrientale* 1938-9, pp. 27-8; cf. *SEG* XXXIX 993 (*Ἀντωνεία Εὐ-τυχεία*)
—MOTYKA (HORTENSIANA): (44) iii-v AD ib. XXVII 662 (d. *Τρύγητος*)
—SYRACUSE: (45) iii-v AD *ASSiracusano* 1956, p. 62 (-*χεία*); (46) ~ *NScav* 1920, p. 318 (*Μάρκελλ[α] Εὐτυχ[ία]*); (47) ~ Strazzulla 288; cf. Ferrua, *NG* 55 (*Εὐτιχία*—Strazzulla, *Εὐπλία?*—Ferrua); (48) ~ Strazzulla 291 + *Nuovo Didask.* 6 (1956) p. 58 no. 14; cf. Ferrua, *NG* 58 ([*Εὐ*]*τυχία*—Agnello, [*Εὐ*]*τυχια*[*νός*]—Ferrua); (49) ~ Strazzulla 328 (Wessel 1111); cf. Ferrua, *NG* 111; (50) ~ Strazzulla 367 (Wessel 691); (51) ~ Strazzulla 379 (Wessel 1005); cf. Ferrua, *NG* 141 ([*E*]*ὐτυχία*, *Εὐ-τυχια*[*νή*]?—Ferrua); (52) ~ Strazzulla 386 (Wessel 1000); (53) iii/iv AD *Act. Sanct.* 11 (2) p. 647 (m. *Λουκία*)

**Εὐτυχιανή**
DALMATIA:
—BOUTHOE: (1) imp. Šašel, *IL* 594 (Lat. Baleria Eytychiana)
ILLYRIA:
—APOLLONIA: (2) ii AD *IApoll* 205
KORINTHIA:
—KORINTH: (3) byz. *Corinth* VIII (3) 556, 3; cf. *TMByz* 9 (1985) p. 363 no. 40; (4) ~ *Corinth* VIII (3) 650 (*Εὐτυχ[ιανή]*)


S. ITALY (CAMPANIA):
—NEAPOLIS: (5) ii-iii AD *BdA* 9 (1929-30) pp. 351-4 (Lat. Aurelia Euticiane)
SICILY:
—SYRACUSE: (6) iii-v AD *IG* XIV 113 (Strazzulla 54; Wessel 194) (*Εὐτυχ(ι)ανή*); (7) ~ *ASSiracusano* 1956, p. 63 (-*χει-*); (8) ~ Strazzulla 260 (Wessel 829); cf. Ferrua, *NG* 33; (9) ~ ib. 205

**Εὐτυχιανός**
AITOLIA:
—KLAUSEION (MOD.): (1) byz. *PAE* 1958, p. 61 with pl. 49 *a*; cf. *BCH* 83 (1959) p. 664
ARGOLIS:
—ARGOS: (2) v-vi AD Unp. (Oikonomou-Laniado) (*Εὐτυχιαν(ός)*)
ARKADIA:
—TEGEA: (3) ii AD *IG* V (2) 55, 62 (s. *Βουδᾶς*)
KORINTHIA:
—KORINTH: (4) ii-iii AD *Corinth* VIII (3) 502 (*TMByz* 9 (1985) pp. 291-2 no. 31) (*Αὐρ. Ἐ.*); (5) m. ii AD *IG* VII 1773, 18 (Stephanis 993)
—KORINTH?: (6) ii-iii AD *Corinth* VIII (1) 89, 5; cf. *PIR²* E 130 ?= (7); (7) c. 350 AD *Corinth* VIII (3) 502, 6 (*Αὐρ. Ἐ.*) ?= (6)
LAKONIA:
—SPARTA: (8) f. iii AD *SEG* XLII 320, 6 (*Αὐρ. Ἐ.*: s. *Ὀνασίων*); (9) m. iii AD *IG* V (1) 598, 13; 599, 14 (Bradford (1)) (*M. Αὐρ. Εὐτυχια-νὸς ὁ καὶ Αὐρηλιανός*: II s. *Εὐτυχιανός*); (10) ~ *IG* V (1) 598, 14; 599, 15 (Bradford (2)) (*Εὐτυχ[ιανός]*: I f. *M. Αὐρ. Εὐτυχιανὸς* II *ὁ καὶ Αὐρηλιανός*)
MESSENIA:
—KORONE: (11) 246 AD *IG* V (1) 1398, 30 (*Ποσ. Ἐ.*)
S. ITALY (APULIA):
—CANUSIUM: (12) 223 AD *Epig. Rom. di Canosa* 35 III, 16 (*CIL* IX 338) (Lat. Ti. Claudius Euthychianus)
—HERDONIA*: (13) imp. *Ordona* 2 p. 152 no. 42 (Lat. Eutychian[us]: freed.)
S. ITALY (CAMPANIA):
—ATELLA: (14) ?i-ii AD *RAAN* 38 (1963) p. 19 (Lat. Ti. Cl. Eutychianus: f. Ti. Cl. Menodotus)
—DIKAIARCHIA-PUTEOLI: (15) imp. *CIL* x 2678 (Lat. M. Valerius Eutychianus: f. *Τύχιος*); (16) ~ ib. 2713 (Lat. L. Marius Eutychianus: s. *Σύντροφος*); (17) ?ii-iii AD ib. 1947 (Lat. Aurel. Eutychianus); (18) m. ii AD ib. 1576 (Lat. M. Nemonius Eutychianus); (19) 168 AD ib. 1563 (Lat. M. Nemonius Eutychianus: s. *Εὐτύχης*)
—MISENUM*: (20) ?ii AD ib. 3594 (Lat. Aelius Eutychianus)
—SALERNUM: (21) ?s. i AD *IItal* 1 (1) 179 (*CIL* x 558) (Lat. Aprius Eutychianus)
—SURRENTUM: (22) imp. *Rend. Torn. Acc. Arch. Napoli* 1 (1887) p. 9 no. 3 (Lat. Eutychianus)
S. ITALY (LUCANIA):
—ATINA LUCANA: (23) imp. *IItal* III (1) 195 (*CIL* x 300) (Lat. Eutichianus)
SICILY:
—KATANE: (24) 408 AD *IG* XIV 535 (*IGLMP* 9; Agnello 94; Wessel 777)
—KENTORIPA: (25) i-ii AD *CIL* x 7006 (*ILat. Palermo* 5) (Lat. Marius Eutychianus: s. *Πι-στιανός*, *Εὐπραξία*)

**Εὐτυχίδας**
ACHAIA: (1) 146 BC *IG* IV (1)² 28, 143 (s. *Πά-πας*: synoikos)
ARGOLIS:
—EPIDAUROS: (2) iii/ii BC ib. 353 (Peek, *IAEpid* 153. 1)
—EPIDAUROS*: (3) c. 335-325 BC ib. 50, 18 (*Εὐ-τυχίδ[ας]*)
—HERMIONE: (4) iv BC *SEG* XI 382, 14 (*Εὐ-τυ[χί]δας*: s. *Θεώνιχος*)

ARKADIA:
—TEGEA: (5) iii BC *IG* v (2) 30, 3 (f. Ἡράκλειτος); (6) imp. ib. 221
——(Krariotai): (7) iv/iii BC ib. 38, 22 (s. Θεοτέλης)
ILLYRIA:
—EPIDAMNOS-DYRRHACHION: (8) iii BC *IDyrrh* 19 (f. Σώστρατος); (9) hell.-imp. ib. 212 (s. Εὔτυχος); (10) ~ ib. 439 (Εὐτ(υ)χίδας: f. Φιλουμένα)
KORINTHIA:
—SIKYON: (11) iv/iii BC *RE* (2) (Skalet 131) (sculptor/painter)
LAKONIA: (12) c. 100-105 AD *SEG* XI 537 b, 5 (Bradford (4); Stephanis 995)
—SPARTA: (13) ii BC *Mél. Daux* p. 233, 5 (f. Εὔτυχος); (14) ~ *PAE* 1964, p. 115 (f. —κίδων); (15) s. i BC *IG* v (1) 127, 6; 210, 11 (Bradford (6)) (Εὐ[τυχίδας]—127: f. Νηκλῆς); (16) c. 30-20 BC *IG* v (1) 141, 7; *SEG* XXXV 329 (date) (Bradford (1)); (17) c. 90-110 AD *IG* v (1) 97, 5; *SEG* XI 561, 5; 564, 5; 605, 3 (Bradford (5)) (f. Ἀριστονικίδας); (18) c. 100-105 AD *SEG* XI 537 b, 8 (Bradford (7)) (f. Σίτμος); (19) c. 110 AD *SEG* XI 516, 5 (Bradford (3)) (Τιβ. Κλ. Ἐ.)
MESSENIA:
—THOURIA: (20) ii/i BC *IG* v (1) 1384, 21 (s. Νικάρετος)

## Εὐτυχίδης

LAKONIA:
—TAINARON-KAINEPOLIS: (1) hell.-imp. ib. 1261; (2) imp. ib. 1248 (I f. Τιβ. Κλ. Εὐτυχίδης II); (3) ~ ib. l. 3 (Τιβ. Κλ. Ἐ.: II s. Εὐτυχίδης I)
SICILY:
—SYRACUSE: (4) iii-v AD Strazzulla 309 + Ferrua, *NG* 65 (Wessel 843) (Εὐτύχη—Strazzulla and Wessel)

## Εὐτύχιμος

SICILY:
—KATANE: (1) iii-v AD *IG* XIV 551 (Wessel 853) + Ferrua, *NG* 445 (-χη-, Εὐ(θ)ύ(δ)ημος?—Ferrua, Τύχημος—*IG* and Wessel)

## Εὐτύχιος

ACHAIA:
—AIGEIRA?: (1) byz. *EA* 1872, p. 404 no. 4
ILLYRIA:
—EPIDAMNOS-DYRRHACHION: (2) imp. *AEp* 1984, nos. 812-13 (Lat. Eutychius)
LAKONIA:
—SPARTA: (3) i AD *SEG* XXVI 462, 5 ([E]ὐτύ[χι]ος)
S. ITALY (LUCANIA):
—POTENTIA: (4) i BC-i AD *ZPE* 106 (1995) p. 281 no. 2, 6 (Lat. Eutychius)
SICILY:
—KATANE: (5) iii-v AD *IG* XIV 536 (Agnello 48; Wessel 799); cf. Ferrua, *NG* 441 (Εὐτύχι[ος])
—SYRACUSE: (6) iii-v AD Strazzulla 250 (Wessel 157) ([Εὐτ]ύχειος)
—TAUROMENION: (7) iii-v AD *IG* XIV 115 (Strazzulla 56; Wessel 1329); Ferrua, *NG* 476 (locn.)

## Εὐτύχις

SICILY:
—KATANE: (1) iii-v AD *NScav* 1915, p. 223 (Wessel 1362)

## Εὐτυχίς

ARGOLIS:
—HERMIONE: (1) ii-i BC *IG* IV (1) 732 IV, 1 (d. Μελανειός)
—TROIZEN: (2) iii BC ib. 772, 1 (d. Ἀπολλόδωρος)
EPIROS: (3) f. ii BC ib. II² 8535 (d. Νεοπτόλεμος)
—NIKOPOLIS: (4) imp. *CIG* 1817; cf. Hammond, *Epirus* p. 712 n. 1 (Sarikakis 134) (Πομπηία Ἐ.: d. Μ. Πομπήιος Λύκος)

ILLYRIA:
—APOLLONIA: (5) imp. *IApoll* 85 (Εὐτ(υ)χεί (voc.)); (6) ~ ib. 86; (7) ~ ib. 328 (Εὐτυχεί (voc.))
—EPIDAMNOS-DYRRHACHION: (8) hell.-imp. *IDyrrh* 213 (d. Εὔπορος); (9) ~ ib. 214 (Ἐ. Καρνήα: d. Οὐρβᾶνος)
KORINTHIA:
—KORINTH: (10) hell. Demitsas 901
—SIKYON*: (11) ii AD *ILGR* 82 (Lat. Fulvia Eutychis: m. Calpetanus Ianuarius, Calpetana Magna)
LEUKAS: (12) inc. *Alt-Ithaka* p. 329 γ
S. ITALY (APULIA):
—LUCERIA: (13) imp. *ASP* 34 (1981) p. 26 no. 32 (Lat. Eutychis: m. Διόδωρος)
S. ITALY (CAMPANIA):
—DIKAIARCHIA-PUTEOLI: (14) imp. *CIL* X 1758 (Lat. Claudia Eutychis); (15) ~ ib. 2878 (Lat. Castricia Eutychis); (16) ~ ib. 3089 (Lat. Verria Eutychis); (17) ?ii AD ib. 2448 (Lat. Flavia Eutychis)
—DIKAIARCHIA-PUTEOLI*: (18) imp. ib. 2396 (Lat. Eutychis: freed.); (19) ?ii AD ib. 2593 (Lat. Iulia Eutychis: freed.)
—POMPEII?: (20) i AD ib. IV 4592 (Lat. Eutychis)
—SALERNUM: (21) imp. *IItal* I (1) 218 (*CIL* X 626) (Lat. Popilia Eutychis)
SICILY:
—KATANE: (22) imp. ib. 7072 (Lat. Iulia Eutychis); (23) iii-v AD Ferrua, *NG* 456 ([Εὐ]τυχίς, [Εὐ]τύχις—Ferrua)
TRIPHYLIA:
—LEPREON: (24) iii/ii BC *SEG* XXII 361

## Εὐτυχίων

ARKADIA:
—TEGEA: (1) ii AD *IG* v (2) 55, 49 (f. Ξένων)
LAKONIA:
—HYPERTELEATON*: (2) imp. ib. v (1) 1039
—SPARTA: (3) c. 230-260 AD ib. 556, 10 (Bradford (1)) (Αὐρ. Ἐ.: s. Φιλοκράτης); (4) ~ *SEG* XI 633, 5 (Bradford (2)) (Α[ὐρ.] Ἐ.: s. Ῥωμανός)
S. ITALY (CALABRIA):
—PORTO CESAREO (MOD.): (5) imp. *CIL* IX 13 (Susini, *Fonti Salento* p. 93 no. 26) (Lat. Pomponius Euticio)
S. ITALY (CAMPANIA):
—DIKAIARCHIA-PUTEOLI: (6) imp. *CIL* X 1888 (Lat. L. Plutius Eutychio)
SICILY:
—DREPANON?: (7) f. iii AD *IG* XIV 284 (*IGR* I 502)
—SYRACUSE: (8) ?ii AD *CIL* X 7141 (Lat. Aelius Eutychio: I f. Εὐτυχίων II); (9) ~ ib. (Lat. Aelius Eutychio: II s. Εὐτυχίων I, Aelia Gemella); (10) iii-v AD *IG* XIV 116 (Strazzulla 57; Wessel 871); (11) ~ Strazzulla 248 (Wessel 746) (Εὐχίων—lap., Εὐ(τυ)χίων—edd.); (12) ~ *Nuovo Didask.* 4 (1950) p. 63 no. 22 (Ἀλφιος Ἐ.)

## Εὔτυχος

ACHAIA:
—PHARAI: (1) iii-ii BC *Achaean Grave Stelai* 30 (f. Λυκίσκα)
AIGINA: (2) f. v BC *IG* IV (1) 70; *LSAG²* p. 113 no. 10 (date); (3) c. 480-470 BC *SEG* XI 14
AKARNANIA: (4) 139 BC *PP* 2787 (I f. Εὔτυχος II); (5) ~ *PTeb* 806, 2 (Εὐτύ[χος]: II s. Εὔτυχος I)
—AKTION: (6) s. i BC *RE* (1)
ARGOLIS:
—ARGOS: (7) imp. *IG* IV (1) 651 ([E]ὔτυχος); (8) 252-253 AD ib. X (2) (1) 38 B, 6 (Αὐρ. Ἐ.)
—EPIDAUROS: (9) ii-iii AD ib. IV (1)² 556 (s. Διόδωρος); (10) ~ ib. 569 (Π. Αἰλ. Ἐ.: f. Αἰλ. Ἀκυλεΐνη); (11) 133 AD ib. 383, 7 (f. Ἱεροκλῆς); (12) 134 AD ib. 384, 6 (I f. Εὔτυχος II); (13) ~

ib. l. 6 (II s. Εὔτυχος I, f. Εὔτυχος III); (14) ~ ib. l. 6 (III s. Εὔτυχος II) ?= (15); (15) ~ ib. l. 8 (f. Στέφανος) ?= (14); (16) iii-iv AD ib. 541 (I f. Εὔτυχος II); (17) ~ ib. (II s. Εὔτυχος I); (18) 207 AD ib. 400, 8 (f. Ἴλαρος); (19) 212 AD ib. 403 (I f. Εὔτυχος II); (20) ~ ib. (II s. Εὔτυχος I)
—EPIDAUROS*: (21) c. 370-335 BC ib. 102, 294; 103, 108, 112, 114, 125, 131, 133, 136, 138; (22) c. 335-325 BC ib. 106 I, 105 ?= (23); (23) ~ ib. 108, 127 ?= (22)
—HERMIONE: (24) iii AD ib. IV (1) 719, 2 (f. Μ. Αὐρ. Ἐπαφρόδιτος)
—TROIZEN: (25) i BC ib. II² 10462 (f. Ἀφροδίσιος); (26) imp. ib. IV (1) 781 (s. Ἑρμῆς, f. Ἰσίων)
ARKADIA:
—KLEITOR: (27) i-ii AD ib. v (2) 385 (doctor)
—MEGALOPOLIS: (28) ii/i BC ib. 442, 21 (I f. Εὔτυχος II); (29) ~ ib. l. 21 (II s. Εὔτυχος I)
—TEGEA: (30) ii-iii AD ib. 180 (*GVI* 1036) (Εὐτύχου (gen.)); (31) 165 AD *IG* v (2) 50, 12 (s. Τυχικός); (32) ~ ib. l. 33 (s. Εὐτύχης); (33) ~ ib. l. 65 (s. Λεοντομένης); (34) iii-iv AD ib. 156 (s. Ἀριστομένης)
ELIS: (35) imp. *IvOl* 754 (tile) ([E]ὔτυχος); (36) f. ii AD ib. 93, 5 (Εὔτυ[χος]: ?f. —ος); (37) c. 177-189 AD ib. 103, 11; 104, 6, [10] (II s. Εὔτυχος I, f. Εὔτυχος III: M.); (38) ~ ib. 103, 11, 28-9; 104, 10, 25 (III s. Εὔτυχος II, ?f. Πρῖμος); (39) 185-189 AD ib. l. 6 (I f. Εὔτυχος II)
—PYLOS: (40) iii/ii BC *SEG* XXV 458
EPIROS:
—BOUTHROTOS (PRASAIBOI): (41) a. 163 BC *IBouthrot* 21, 37 (*SEG* XXXVIII 478)
—PHOTIKE: (42) imp. *BCH* 79 (1955) p. 267 (Lat. Euthycos)
ILLYRIA:
—EPIDAMNOS-DYRRHACHION: (43) c. 250-50 BC Maier 121; 203; 231; 302; Münsterberg Nachtr. p. 15 (coin) (Ceka 187-91) (money.); (44) i BC *IG* II² 8485-6 (s. Σωσιμένης, f. Εὐτυχία); (45) hell.-imp. *IDyrrh* 212 (f. Εὐτυχίδας); (46) ~ ib. 215 (s. Θεόδωρος); (47) ~ ib. 224 (f. Ζωΐλος); (48) imp. *AEp* 1928, no. 93 (Lat. C. Vin(i)cius Eutychus); (49) ~ ib. 1978, no. 756 (Lat. P. Cetetranius/C(aet)r(o)nius? [Eu]tychus)
ITHAKE: (50) imp. *IG* IX (1) 681 (f. Θεόδωρος)
KORINTHIA:
—KORINTH: (51) iii BC ib. IV (1) 201; (52) ?f. i AD *Hesp.* 42 (1973) p. 464 no. 209; (53) s. i AD *IG* X (2) (1) 69, 38 (f. Θάλλος)
LAKONIA:
—GYTHEION: (54) i-ii AD ib. v (1) 1176, 1 (s. Ἀγίας, f. Εὐδαμία: doctor)
—HYPERTELEATON*: (55) imp. ib. 1049 (s. Γλο—)
—SPARTA: (56) ii BC *Mél. Daux* p. 233, 5 (Εὐτ(υ)χος: s. Εὐτυχίδας); (57) ii-i BC *IG* v (1) 886 (Bradford (6)) ([E]ὔτυχος); (58) c. 50-25 BC *IG* v (1) 208, 7 (Bradford (7)); (59) c. 30-20 BC *IG* v (1) 142, 12 (Bradford (15)) (f. Ἀριστοφάνης); (60) i/ii AD *IG* v (1) 39, 20 (Bradford (2)) (II s. Εὔτυχος I) ?= (77); (61) ~ *IG* v (1) 39, [20] (Bradford (18)) (I f. Εὔτυχος II) ?= (76); (62) c. 130 AD *IG* v (1) 60, 4 (Bradford (10)); (63) ?134 AD *IG* v (1) 62, 15 + *SEG* XI 520 (Bradford (23)) (Ε[ὔ]τυχ[ος]); (64) c. 140-145 AD *IG* v (1) 1314, 44 (Bradford (9)); (65) c. 140-160 AD *IG* v (1) 65, 28; 85, 7; *SEG* XI 528, 3 (Bradford (16)) (f. Δαμόνικος); (66) ~ *IG* v (1) 112, 9 (Bradford (14)) (f. Ἀρίων); (67) ~ *IG* v (1) 154, 15 (Bradford (21)) (f. Κλεώνυμος); (68) c. 150-160 AD *IG* v (1) 53, 18; 54, 10 (Bradford (5)) (s. Νυμφᾶς); (69) f. iii AD *IG* v (1) 535, 19 (Bradford (22)) (f. Αὐρ. Ξενώ); (70) ~ *IG* v (1) 538, 29; *BSA* 79 (1984) pp. 274-7 (date) (Bradford (20)) (I f. Μέμμιος Αὐρ. Εὔτυχος II); (71)

~ *IG* v (1) 538, 29; *BSA* 79 (1984) pp. 274-7 (date) (Bradford (4)) (*Μέμμιος* [*Αὐρ.*] *'Ε.*: II s. *Εὔτυχος* I); **(72)** c. 225-250 AD *IG* v (1) 529, 13 (I f. *Μέμμιος Εὔτυχος* II); **(73)** ~ ib. l. 13 (Bradford (11)) (*Μέμμιος 'Ε.*: II s. *Εὔτυχος* I); **(74)** 359 AD *SEG* XI 464, 7 (Bradford (13))
——Konosoura: **(75)** c. 212-230 AD *IG* v (1) 684, 9 (Bradford (12)) (*Αὐρ. 'Ε.*)
——Limnai: **(76)** c. 70-100 AD *IG* v (1) 676, 17 (Bradford (17)) (I f. *Εὔτυχος* II) ?= **(61)**; **(77)** ~ *IG* v (1) 676, 17 (Bradford (1)) (II s. *Εὔτυχος* I) ?= **(60)**
——SPARTA?: **(78)** i BC-i AD *FD* III (1) 464 (Bradford (19)); **(79)** ii AD *IG* v (1) 1317 a, 12
PELOPONNESE?: **(80)** II AD *PAE* 1992, p. 72 B, 11 (f. *Λεύκιος*)
S. ITALY (APULIA):
——CANUSIUM: **(81)** imp. *Epig. Rom. di Canosa* 130 (Lat. [P.] [Libuscidius] Eutychus)
——LARINUM: **(82)** imp. *CIL* IX 725 (Lat. C. Salvius Eutychus)
——VENUSIA*: **(83)** imp. *Epigraphica* 35 (1973) p. 151 no. 16 (Lat. C. Torius Eutychus: freed.)
S. ITALY (BRUTTIUM):
——LOKROI EPIZEPHYRIOI: **(84)** hell.? Landi, *DISMG* 248
S. ITALY (CALABRIA):
——BASTA: **(85)** ii AD *NScav* 1957, p. 192 (Susini, *Fonti Salento* p. 83 no. 16) (Lat. L. Aemilius Eutychus)
——BRENTESION-BRUNDISIUM*: **(86)** imp. *NScav* 1880, p. 189 (Lat. Clodius Eutychus: freed.?)
——TARAS-TARENTUM: **(87)** imp. *CIL* IX 6165 a (Lat. Lucretius Eutychus)
S. ITALY (CAMPANIA):
——ATELLA: **(88)** imp. ib. x 3746 (Lat. Eutychus)
——CAPREAE: **(89)** imp. *ZPE* 71 (1988) p. 197 no. 8 (Lat. A. Cossinius Eutychus)
——DIKAIARCHIA-PUTEOLI: **(90)** imp. *IG* XIV 859, 9 (Audollent, *Defix. Tab.* 208); **(91)** ~ *CIL* x 2003 (Lat. M. Aelius Eutychus); **(92)** ~ ib. 2126 (Lat. C. Aufid. Eutychus); **(93)** ~ ib. 2365 (Lat. Eutychus); **(94)** ~ ib. 2397 (Lat. Eutychus: s. *Ποντικός*); **(95)** ~ ib. 2445 (Lat. C. Aufidius Eutychus); **(96)** ~ ib. 2474 (Lat. L. Gavidius Eutychus); **(97)** ~ ib. 2681 (Lat. L. Sutorius Eutychus); **(98)** ~ ib. 2772 (Lat. C. Netaninus Eutychus); **(99)** ~ ib. 2837 (Lat. M. Perpernius Eutychus); **(100)** ~ ib. 3044 (Lat. Q. Valerius Eutychus); **(101)** ~ *NScav* 1886, p. 130 (*Eph. Ep.* VIII 401) (Lat. Eutychus: f. *Δημήτριος*); **(102)** ?i-ii AD *CIL* x 2540 (Lat. C. Iulius Eutychus: f. C. Iulius Agrippa); **(103)** ~ ib. 3036, 7 (Lat. T. Oculatius Eutychus); **(104)** 51 AD Bove, *Documenti finanziarie* pp. 126-7 T.P. 39 pag. 2, 5 (Lat. C. Sulpicius Eutychus); **(105)** 61 AD *Puteoli* 9-10 (1985-6) p. 31 no. 5 (Lat. C. Mateius Eutychus); **(106)** ?ii AD *CIL* x 2449 (Lat. T. F[l]. Eutychus)
——DIKAIARCHIA-PUTEOLI*: **(107)** imp. ib. 2225 (Lat. M. Kanius Eutychus: freed.)
——HERCULANEUM*: **(108)** i BC-i AD ib. 1403 g I, 15 (Lat. Ti. Iulius Eutychus: freed.); **(109)** ~ ib. 1403 g II, 4 (Lat. Eutychus: freed.); **(110)** ~ ib. 1471-2; cf. *Cron. Erc.* 8 (1978) pp. 145-6 no. 19 (Lat. [M.] [Nonius] Eutychus [Marcianus]: freed.)
——MISENUM: **(111)** 102 AD De Franciscis, *Sacello Augustali* p. 22, 5, 10 (Lat. Tullius Eutychus); **(112)** 113 AD ib. p. 27 (Lat. L. Iulius Eutychus)
——MISENUM*: **(113)** imp. *CIL* x 3413 (Lat. C. Atinius Eutyc[hus])
——NEAPOLIS: **(114)** imp. ib. 1480; cf. Leiwo p. 158 no. 129 (Lat. P. Mevius Eutychus); **(115)** ~ *NScav* 1893, p. 522 no. 4; cf. Leiwo p. 112 no. 86 (Lat. M. Hortensius Eutychus)
——POMPEII: **(116)** i BC-i AD *CIL* IV 676; cf. p. 196 (Lat. Eutychus); **(117)** ~ ib. 1369 (Lat.

Eutychus); **(118)** ~ ib. 9197 (Lat. Eutychus); **(119)** ~ ib. x 8058. 13 (seal) (Castrèn 87. 1) (Lat. Cn. Caetronius Eutychus); **(120)** ~ *CIL* x 8058. 33 (seal) (Lat. Eutychus); **(121)** ~ *NScav* 1916, p. 303 no. 104 bis a (Castrèn 158. 11) (Lat. M. Epidius Eutychus: name-Solin); **(122)** c. 51-62 AD *CIL* IV 3340. 75, 9 (Castrèn 204. 11) (Lat. L. Istacidius Eutychus); **(123)** 54 AD *CIL* IV 3340. 5, [10]; 13, 16; 14, 16; 17, 17; 49, 17; 61, 9; 69, 8; 73, 5; 85, 5; 90, 4; 91, 3; 101, 6; 106, 4; 110, 6; 113, 6; 116, 3 (Castrèn 382. 3) (Lat. T. Sornius Eutychus)
——POMPEII*: **(124)** m. i AD *NScav* 1922, p. 460 (seal) (Castrèn 118. 9) (Lat. Tib. Cl. Eutychus: imp. freed.)
——SALERNUM: **(125)** imp. *IItal* I (1) 199 (*CIL* x 583) (Lat. Eutychus); **(126)** ~ *IItal* I (1) 236 (*CIL* x 622) (Lat. M. Perperna Eytychus)
——SURRENTUM: **(127)** imp. ib. 756 (Lat. Eutychus); **(128)** ~ *Rend. Torn. Acc. Arch. Napoli* I (1887) p. 9 no. 2 (Lat. Eutychus)
S. ITALY (LUCANIA):
——METAPONTION: **(129)** b. 158 BC *ID* 2136, 1 (s. *Δάζος*)
SICILY:
——HERBESSOS*: **(130)** imp. *Epigraphica* 51 (1989) p. 186 no. 71 (Lat. Eutychus: freed.)
——KATANE: **(131)** imp. *CIL* x 7046 (Lat. Eutychus); **(132)** ii-iii AD *Epigraphica* 51 (1989) p. 170 no. 37 (Lat. C. Iulius Eutychus)
——PANORMOS*: **(133)** ?ii AD *CIL* x 7267 (Lat. M. Ulpius Eutychus: freed.)
——SYRACUSE: **(134)** iii-v AD Ferrua, *NG* 203

**Εὐτυχῶ**
ARGOLIS:
——ARGOS: **(1)** v-vi AD Unp. (Oikonomou-Laniado)

**Εὐτύχης**
S. ITALY (CAMPANIA):
——NOLA: **(1)** imp. *NScav* 1900, p. 101 no. 1 (Lat. C. Varius Euthyces)

**Εὐφάης**
ARKADIA:
——TEGEA: **(1)** m. iv BC *IG* v (2) 6, 82
MESSENIA: **(2)** vii BC Paus. iv 5. 8 ff. (s. *Ἀντίοχος*: king)

**Εὐφαμίδας**
ARGOLIS:
——EPIDAUROS*: **(1)** c. 370-365 BC Peek, *IAEpid* 52 A, 14
KORINTHIA:
——KORINTH: **(2)** 431-419 BC *RE* (-) (s. *Ἀριστώνυμος*)

**Εὐφαμίδης**
AIGINA: **(1)** ?v BC *IG* IV (1) 184

**Εὔφαμος**
ACHAIA:
——DYME*: **(1)** c. 219 BC *SGDI* 1612, 27 (*Tyche* 5 (1990) p. 124) (s. *Φιλόδαμος*)
KORINTHIA:
——KORINTH: **(2)** c. 570-550 BC Amyx 100. 2 (vase) (Lorber 90) (her.); **(3)** ~ Amyx 114. 4 (vase) (her.?); **(4)** iii AD *Corinth* VIII (3) 366 (Lat. Euphami (gen.?))

**Εὐφάνης**
ACHAIA:
——DYME: **(1)** iii-ii BC *Syll*³ 530, 13; cf. *Achaia und Elis* p. 115 ([*Εὐ*]φάνης)
——PATRAI: **(2)** m. iii BC *Achaean Grave Stelai* 17 (s. *Αἰσχρίων*)
AIGINA: **(3)** ?473 BC Pi., *N.* iv, 89
ARGOLIS:
——ARGOS: **(4)** iii BC *Mnem.* NS 47 (1919) p. 163 no. 8 a-b (f. *Εὐαίνετος, Εὐκράτης*)

Eutychus); **(118)** ~ ib. 9197 (Lat. Eutychus);
——EPIDAUROS: **(5)** s. iv BC *IG* IV (1)² 121, 68
——HERMIONE: **(6)** iv BC *SEG* XI 382, 22 (f. *Τέλεσις*)
——TROIZEN: **(7)** 327-324 BC *CID* II 32, 37, 40; 97, 31; 99 A, 2; 102 II B, 37 (s. *Σωφάνης*)
ARKADIA:
——PHENEOS: **(8)** c. 230-200 BC *BCH* 45 (1921) p. 13 II, 119 (reading—Oulhen)
——STYMPHALOS?: **(9)** iii BC *IG* v (2) 352, 7, 12-13
EPIROS:
——NIKOPOLIS: **(10)** imp. *Ep. Chron.* 31 (1994) p. 42 no. 9 (*AD* 45 (1990) Chron. p. 257 no. 6) (-βεί- *'Ε.*)
S. ITALY (BRUTTIUM):
——LOKROI EPIZEPHYRIOI:
——(*Ἀνα.*): **(11)** 275 BC De Franciscis 25, 5 (f. *Κοπρίων*)
——(*Θρα.*): **(12)** iv/iii BC ib. 7, 7; 26, 4 (s. *Μενέδαμος*)

**Εὔφαντος**
ARGOLIS:
——EPIDAUROS*: **(1)** c. 370 BC *IG* IV (1)² 102, 227

**Εὐφάτας**
ACHAIA?: **(1)** c. 300 BC *SEG* XIV 375, 5

**Εὐφημία**
ARGOLIS:
——ARGOS: **(1)** v-vi AD Unp. (Oikonomou-Laniado)
S. ITALY (CAMPANIA):
——DIKAIARCHIA-PUTEOLI: **(2)** ?i-ii AD *CIL* x 1872 (Lat. Iulia Euphemia)
——MISENUM*: **(3)** imp. ib. 3505 (Lat. Euphemia)
——POMPEII: **(4)** i BC-i AD ib. IV 4125 (Lat. Euphemia)

**Εὐφήμιος**
S. ITALY (LUCANIA):
——MARSICI NOVI: **(1)** imp. ib. x 184 (Lat. T. Helvius Heufemius)

**Εὐφημίων**
MESSENIA:
——MESSENE: **(1)** ii AD *IG* v (1) 1460 (*PAE* 1987, p. 98) (*Κόϊντος Πλώτιος 'Ε.*)

**Εὔφημος**
ARGOLIS:
——PITYOUSSA: **(1)** i AD *A. Barn.* 11 (dub.)
DALMATIA:
——EPETION: **(2)** imp. Cambi, *Stobreč* p. 13 no. 3 (Lat. Iul. Euphemus)
ELIS: **(3)** iii AD *IvOl* 119, 9; *SEG* XV 259, 11 (*Εὔφ*[ημος]—*IvOl*, [*Εὔφ*]ημος—*SEG*: mantis/Klytiadai)
KORINTHIA:
——KORINTH: **(4)** f. iii AD *Corinth* VIII (3) 302, 5 (Lat. Clodius Euphemus: s. *Γρανία Ὁμόνοια*)
S. ITALY (APULIA):
——BARION*: **(5)** i-ii AD *Suppl. It.* 8 p. 40 no. 8 (Lat. T. Flavius Euphemus: freed.)
S. ITALY (CAMPANIA):
——DIKAIARCHIA-PUTEOLI: **(6)** imp. *CIL* x 2198 (Lat. Sacconius Eufemus); **(7)** m. i AD Camodeca, *L'Archivio Puteolano* I p. 196 (Lat. M. Valerius Euphemus)
——HERCULANEUM: **(8)** i BC-i AD *CIL* x 1403 l I, 2 + *Cron. Erc.* 7 (1977) p. 116 b, 8 (Lat. A. Tetteius Euphemus); **(9)** m. i AD *PdelP* 8 (1953) p. 463 no. 56, 3 (Lat. M. Burrius Euphemus)
——POMPEII: **(10)** i BC-i AD *CIL* IV 1415 (Lat. -s Eupemus); **(11)** ~ ib. 1754 (Lat. Euphemus)
S. ITALY (LUCANIA):
——METAPONTION: **(12)** iv BC Iamb., *VP* 267 (*FVS* I p. 446)

**Εὐφία**

SICILY:
—HIMERA?: **(13)** vii/vi BC *RE* (9) + s.v. Stesichoros (1) col. 2460 (?f. Ἡλιάναξ, Μαμερτῖνος, Τεισίας Στησίχορος)

**Εὐφία**

S. ITALY (CAMPANIA):
—POMPEII: **(1)** i BC-i AD *CIL* IV 2310 b; 5048; 10004 (Lat. Euphia)

**Εὐφίλητος**

S. ITALY (CAMPANIA):
—POMPEII: **(1)** i BC-i AD ib. 4165 (Castrèn 146. 4) (Lat. C. Cuspius Cresces Euphiletus)

**Εὐφίλιστος**

S. ITALY (BRUTTIUM):
—LOKROI EPIZEPHYRIOI:
——(Λακ.): **(1)** iv/iii BC De Franciscis 17, 7 (Εὐφίλετος—ed., Εὐφίλ(ι)στος—*LGPN*: f. Χαρίξενος)

**Εὔφορβος**

MESSENIA:
—MESSENE: **(1)** ii/i BC *SEG* XXIII 224; *PAE* 1988, p. 59 (date) (s. Νίκων, Ἀρχυλίς)
S. ITALY (CAMPANIA):
—SALERNUM*: **(2)** f. ii AD *IItal* I (1) 163 (*CIL* X 654; Sinn, *Stadtröm. Marmorurnen* 526) (Lat. M. Ulpius Euphorvus: imp. freed.)
SICILY:
—HIMERA?: **(3)** vii/vi BC *Suda* Σ 1095 (?f. Τεισίας Στησίχορος, Ἡλιάναξ, Μαμερτῖνος)

**Εὐφοριανός**

S. ITALY (CAMPANIA):
—DIKAIARCHIA-PUTEOLI: **(1)** imp. *CIL* X 2501 (Lat. C. Helvius Euphorianus: s. C. Helvius Marcianus)

**Εὐφορίων**

ARKADIA:
—PAOS: **(1)** c. 575 BC Hdt. vi 127. 3 (f. Λαφάνης)
KORINTHIA:
—SIKYON: **(2)** 263 BC *IG* IX (1)² (1) 17, 14 (f. Πυθοκλῆς)

**Εὔφορος**

ARGOLIS:
—HERMIONE: **(1)** f. iv BC *SEG* XI 379 a (s. Λύων)
SICILY:
—TAUROMENION: **(2)** c. 225-215 BC *IG* XIV 421 an. 16; 421 an. 26 (*SGDI* 5219) (s. Πυθόδωρος); **(3)** c. 140 BC *IG* XIV 421 an. 101 (*SGDI* 5219) ([Εὔ?]φ[ο]ρος: f. Ἀρτεμίδωρος)

**Εὐφραγόρας**

ARGOLIS:
—TROIZEN: **(1)** ?255 BC Nachtergael, *Les Galates* 8, 52; cf. Stephanis 1730 (f. Μνασιφῶν)

**Εὐφραίνετος**

S. ITALY (BRUTTIUM):
—LOKROI EPIZEPHYRIOI:
——(Ἀγκ.): **(1)** iv/iii BC De Franciscis 4, 1; 5, 1; 22, 1
——(Ἀλχ.): **(2)** iv/iii BC ib. 32, 6 (f. Μένων)
——(Ἀνα.): **(3)** iv/iii BC ib. 19, 4 (s. Πλάτιος)

**Εὐφραίνουσα**

SICILY:
—SYRACUSE: **(1)** iii-v AD Ferrua, *NG* 369 (-φρέ-)

**Εὐφραίνων**

SICILY:
—KENTORIPA: **(1)** imp. *IG* XIV 580

**Εὐφραῖος**

ARGOLIS:
—EPIDAUROS*: **(1)** c. 370 BC ib. IV (1)² 102, 87
LEUKAS: **(2)** vi BC Lazzarini 145; cf. *LSAG*² p. 229 no. 1 (Εὐφαῖος—*LSAG*² per err.)

S. ITALY (BRUTTIUM):
—LOKROI EPIZEPHYRIOI:
——(Κυλ.): **(3)** iv/iii BC De Franciscis 11, 8; 18, 4 (s. Νικόδαμος)
——(Πυρ.): **(4)** iv/iii BC ib. 28, 4 (s. Χαρίλας)
SICILY:
—AKRAI: **(5)** iii-ii BC *SGDI* 3242, 11 (*Akrai* p. 157 no. 8) (f. Θεόδωρος); **(6)** ~ *SGDI* 3242, 11 (*Akrai* p. 157 no. 8) (I f. Εὐφραῖος II); **(7)** ~ *SGDI* 3242, 11 (*Akrai* p. 157 no. 8) (II s. Εὐφραῖος I); **(8)** ii BC ib. p. 156 no. 6, 4 (s. Καλλικράτης)
—KAMARINA: **(9)** s. v BC Dubois, *IGDS* 121, 18 (Arena, *Iscr. Sic.* II 143; *SEG* XXXVIII 940; Cordano, 'Camarina VII' 31) ([E]ὐφραῖος: f. Εὔθυμος)
—TAUROMENION: **(10)** c. 205 BC *IG* XIV 421 an. 36 (*SGDI* 5219) (s. Καλλίας)

**Εὐφραῖς**

ILLYRIA:
—EPIDAMNOS-DYRRHACHION: **(1)** hell.-imp. *IDyrrh* 216 (d. Περιγένης)

**Εὐφράντα**

ARGOLIS:
—PHLEIOUS: **(1)** iv-iii BC *SEG* XLII 354
ILLYRIA:
—APOLLONIA: **(2)** imp. *IApoll* 251 (m. Εὐνοΐς)
—SHKOZE (MOD.): **(3)** imp. Ugolini, *Alb. Ant.* I p. 192 no. 12 (d. Πολυνίκης)

**Εὐφραντίς**

S. ITALY (CAMPANIA):
—MISENUM*: **(1)** ?ii AD *CIL* X 3398 (Lat. Ulpia Euphrantis)

**Εὔφραντος**

PELOPONNESE: **(1)** s. iii BC *SEG* XIII 278, 7 (f. Εὐχέας)

**Εὐφράνωρ**

ACHAIA:
—DYME?: **(1)** i BC ib. XIV 370
ARGOLIS:
—TROIZEN: **(2)** ii BC *IG* II² 10463 (s. Πύρρος)
ARKADIA:
—TEGEA:
——(Krariotai): **(3)** s. iii BC ib. v (2) 36, 125 (Εὐφρά[νωρ]: f. Φιλιστίδας: metic)
EPIROS:
—BOUTHROTOS (PRASAIBOI):
——Prochtheioi: **(4)** a. 163 BC *IBouthrot* 168, 12 (*SEG* XXXVIII 469) (Εὐφρά[νωρ]: f. Ξένων) ?= (5); **(5)** ~ *IBouthrot* 168, 13 (*SEG* XXXVIII 469) (Εὐφρά<σ>νωρ: f. Οὔλατος) ?= (4)
—MESOPOTAMON (MOD.): **(6)** i BC Ugolini, *Alb. Ant.* I p. 193 no. 13
—PHOINIKE: **(7)** imp. *AE* 1914, p. 235 no. 6 (f. Ναΐς); **(8)** ~ ib. p. 237 no. 11
KORINTHIA:
—KORINTH: **(9)** m. iv BC *RE* (8) (sculptor/painter)
—SIKYON: **(10)** ?253 BC Nachtergael, *Les Galates* 10, 25; cf. Stephanis 325 (f. Ἀριστογένης); **(11)** 251 BC Plu., *Arat.* 6 (Skalet 132)
LAKONIA:
—SPARTA: **(12)** s. i BC *IG* v (1) 870 (tiles) (Bradford (-))
LEUKAS: **(13)** f. i BC *IG* IX (1) 534, 8 (*Iscr. Gr. Verona* p. 24) (s. Ἀρχέλαος)
S. ITALY (BRUTTIUM):
—SYBARIS-THOURIOI-COPIAE: **(14)** s. iv BC Men. fr. 286 (fict.?)

**Εὐφρᾶς**

MESSENIA:
—KORONE: **(1)** 246 AD *IG* V (1) 1398, 88 (Αὐρ. Ἐ.)

**Εὐφρασία**

KORINTHIA:
—KORINTH: **(1)** byz. *Corinth* VIII (3) 589; cf. *TMByz* 9 (1985) p. 366 no. 70
SICILY:
—SYRACUSE: **(2)** iii-v AD *NScav* 1895, p. 485 no. 164 + *BZ* 8 (1899) p. 108; cf. Ferrua, *NG* 35 ([Εὐφ]ρασία?)

**Εὐφραστίων**

S. ITALY (BRUTTIUM):
—LOKROI EPIZEPHYRIOI:
——(Γαψ.): **(1)** iv/iii BC De Franciscis 18, 1

**Εὔφραστος**

KORINTHIA:
—SIKYON: **(1)** vi/v BC *SEG* XI 244, 72
S. ITALY (BRUTTIUM):
—LOKROI EPIZEPHYRIOI:
——(Γαψ.): **(2)** 277 BC De Franciscis 8, 2; 31, [2] (s. Εὐκλείδας)
——(Θρα.): **(3)** iv/iii BC ib. 29, 7 ?= (4); **(4)** 279 BC ib. 13, 7 (s. Εὐφρονίσκος) ?= (3)
——(Λακ.): **(5)** iv/iii BC ib. 16, 1; 24, 4 (Εὔφρασ τ(ος): s. Σωσίπολις)
——(Μνα.): **(6)** 277 BC ib. 8, 2; 31, 2 (s. Ξένων); **(7)** ~ ib. 14, 1
——(Σκα.): **(8)** iv/iii BC ib. 10, 1
——(Φαω.): **(9)** iv/iii BC ib. 32, 8 (s. Χαρμίδας)

**Εὐφράτας**

LAKONIA:
—SPARTA: **(1)** ?v/iv BC Aen. Tact. xxvii 7 (-της)

**Εὐφράτης**

S. ITALY (CAMPANIA):
—DIKAIARCHIA-PUTEOLI: **(1)** imp. *CIL* X 2719 (Lat. L. Marius Euphrates); **(2)** ~ ib. 2872 (Lat. Euphrates: f. Pomponius Crescens, Pomponius Rhenus, Pomponius Damivius)
—POMPEII*: **(3)** 15 AD ib. IV 3340. 1, 6 (Castrèn 111. 8) (Lat. M. Cerrinius Euphrates: freed.)
SICILY:
—LIPARA: **(4)** hell.? Libertini, *Isole Eolie* p. 222 no. 30
—SYRACUSE: **(5)** iv BC Call. T 1; *Suda* K 227

**Εὐφρατύας**

S. ITALY (BRUTTIUM):
—SYBARIS-THOURIOI-COPIAE: **(1)** c. 600 BC *NScav* 1970, Suppl. 3 p. 171 no. 335 with fig. 178 (vase); cf. *LSAG*² p. 456 no. A (date) (Εὐφρατύας)

**Εὐφρόνειος**

SICILY:
—SELINOUS?: **(1)** ?m. vi BC Arena, *Iscr. Sic.* I 81; cf. *BE* 1988, no. 1042 (Εὐφρονεῖο (gen.), Εὐφρόν<ε>ιος?—*BE*)

**Εὐφρονίδας**

KORINTHIA:
—SIKYON?: **(1)** iii BC *Suda* A 3933 (Skalet 134) (or Korinthia Korinth)
S. ITALY (BRUTTIUM):
—TERINA:
——(Τι.): **(2)** c. 325-300 BC *IGSI* 21, 15 (*SEG* IV 73; Landi, *DISMG* 170)

**Εὐφρονῖνος**

MESSENIA:
—MESSENE: **(1)** s. ii BC *SEG* XLI 341, 7 (Εὐφρονίδας—ed. per err.: f. Χαρμῖνος)

**Εὐφρόνιος**

AKARNANIA: **(1)** c. 300 BC *IEph* 1449, 3 (s. Ἀγήμων)
LAKONIA:
—SPARTA: **(2)** 359 AD *SEG* XI 464, 7 (Bradford (-)) (Ε[ὐ]φρόνιος)
S. ITALY?: **(3)** v/iv BC van Keuren, *Coinage of Heraclea* p. 58 no. 17

**Εὐφρονίς**
LEUKAS: (**1**) f. iii BC Unp. (*IG* arch.)

**Εὐφρονίσκα**
SICILY:
—LIPARA: (**1**) hell.-imp. *IG* XIV 390 (Libertini, *Isole Eolie* p. 219 no. 8)

**Εὐφρονίσκος**
AIGINA: (**1**) v BC *IG* XII (9) 300
S. ITALY (BRUTTIUM):
—LOKROI EPIZEPHYRIOI:
——(Ἀστ.): (**2**) iv/iii BC De Franciscis 7, 5 (s. Γοργίδας)
——(Δυσ.): (**3**) iv/iii BC ib. 4, 5; 22, 6 (f. Δορκίων); (**4**) ~ ib. 24, 6 (s. Σώσιππος)
——(Θρα.): (**5**) 279 BC ib. 13, 7 (f. Εὔφραστος)
——(Κρα.): (**6**) iv/iii BC ib. 22, 22 (f. Σωτήριχος)
——(Μνα.): (**7**) iv/iii BC ib. 28, 2 (s. Ἀμύνανδρος)
——(Τιω.): (**8**) iv/iii BC ib. 3, 9; 25, 2 (s. Λύσων)

**Εὐφροσύνα**
ARGOLIS:
—HERMIONE: (**1**) ii-i BC *IG* IV (1) 732 III, 17 (d. Θεοκλείδας); (**2**) i BC-i AD? ib. 730 III, 5 (Εὐφροσύν[α]: d. Κλειναγόρας)
EPIROS:
—NIKOPOLIS: (**3**) imp. *CIG* 1813 (Sarikakis 9) (Ἀλ. Ἐ.: d. Κο. Ἀλβίδιος Ἵππαρχος)
SICILY:
—SYRACUSE: (**4**) ii-i BC *IG* XII (1) 471

**Εὐφροσύνη**
KORINTHIA:
—KORINTH: (**1**) imp. *Corinth* VIII (3) 361 (n. pr.?)
MESSENIA:
—MESSENE: (**2**) hell.-imp. *IG* V (1) 1489
S. ITALY (APULIA):
—CANUSIUM: (**3**) i AD *Taras* 14 (1994) p. 465 no. 1 (Lat. Vettia Euphrosine)
S. ITALY (BRUTTIUM):
—RHEGION: (**4**) imp. *IG* XIV 627 (Φαβρ[ικία] Εὐφρο[σύνη])
S. ITALY (CALABRIA):
—BRENTESION-BRUNDISIUM: (**5**) imp. *NScav* 1892, p. 353 z (Lat. Seia Euphrosyne)
S. ITALY (CAMPANIA):
—DIKAIARCHIA-PUTEOLI: (**6**) imp. *IG* XIV 850 (Δομιτ(ία) Εὐφρ(οσύνη)?); (**7**) ~ *CIL* X 2355 (Lat. Culcia Euphrosyne)
—DIKAIARCHIA-PUTEOLI*: (**8**) imp. ib. 2130 (Lat. Aufidia Euphrosyne: m. T. Aufidius Templitanus: freed.)
—STABIAE: (**9**) imp. *PBSR* 40 (1972) p. 128 no. 6 (Lat. Gerulana Euphrosyne)
SICILY: (**10**) imp. *Epigraphica* 5-6 (1943-4) p. 94 (seal)
—ACATE (MOD.): (**11**) iii-v AD *Rend. Pont.* 45 (1972-3) p. 189 no. 1
—KATANE: (**12**) imp. *IG* XIV 477 (m. Θρεπτύλος); (**13**) ~ ib. 485
—LIPARA: (**14**) imp. Libertini, *Isole Eolie* p. 229 no. 6 (*ILat. Palermo* 8) (Lat. Vibia Euphrosyne: d. Θεοφάνης, Ποθείνη)
—MOTYKA (NR.): (**15**) iv-v AD *IG* XIV 250 + *SEG* XXXIX 994 (Ἀντ. Εὐφροσ[ύ]νη)
—SYRACUSE: (**16**) iii-v AD *IG* XIV 29 (Strazzulla 138); cf. *Riv. Arch. Crist.* 18 (1941) p. 188; (**17**) ~ *SEG* XV 584 (Εὐφροσ[ύνη], Εὐφρόσ[υνος]); (**18**) ~ Strazzulla 232 (Εὐφρο[σύνη]?); (**19**) ~ ib. 303 + *Nuovo Didask.* 6 (1956) pp. 58-9 no. 16 (-οσύ-); (**20**) ~ *IG-LMP* 154; cf. Ferrua, *NG* 357
—TAUROMENION: (**21**) i-ii AD *CIL* X 6998 (*ILat. Palermo* 51) (Lat. Nasennia Euphrosyne)
—ZANKLE-MESSANA: (**22**) inc. *Epigraphica* 51 (1989) p. 162 no. 1 (Lat. Cottia Euphrosyne: m. Cerrinia Cottia)

**Εὐφρόσυνον**
AKARNANIA:
—THYRREION: (**1**) ii BC *IG* IX (1)² (2) 316
EPIROS:
—BOUTHROTOS (PRASAIBOI): (**2**) a. 163 BC *IBouthrot* 29, 6 (*SEG* XXXVIII 487)
KERKYRA: (**3**) i BC-i AD *IG* IX (1) 936; (**4**) ~ ib. 937

**Εὐφρόσυνος**
AIGINA: (**1**) ?iii AD *Alt-Ägina* I (2) p. 50 no. 47 (Αὐρ. Ἐ.: s. Πάμφιλος)
ARKADIA:
—MANTINEIA-ANTIGONEIA: (**2**) 27 BC-15 AD *IG* V (2) 268, 7; 307 (s. Τίτος); (**3**) ii-iii AD ib. 275, 7 (Ἡος Ἐ.); (**4**) ii/iii AD ib. VII 4151, 11 (Stephanis 1003) (Λ. Οὐεν[τίδιος] [Εὐφρ]όσυνος)
—TEGEA: (**5**) imp. *IG* V (2) 253, 3 4; (**6**) ii AD ib. 55, 34 (s. Σωσικράτης); (**7**) ~ ib. l. 61 (f. Ἀφροδᾶς); (**8**) 165 AD ib. 50, 11 (s. Τυχικός)
ELIS: (**9**) ?i AD *EA* 1905, p. 259 no. 2, 4 ([Ε]ὐφρόσυνος: s. Ἀθανάδας)
EPIROS:
—NIKOPOLIS?: (**10**) ?iv AD *BCH* 89 (1965) p. 765
KEPHALLENIA: (**11**) i BC-i AD *SEG* XXX 516
LAKONIA:
—SPARTA: (**12**) ii AD ib. XLI 319, 2, 3 (s. Δημαρχία)
MESSENIA:
—KORONE: (**13**) 246 AD *IG* V (1) 1398, 34 (Αὐρ. Εὐφρόσυν[ος]); (**14**) ~ ib. l. 51 (Ἀντ. Ἐ.); (**15**) ~ ib. l. 76 (Ἰγν. Ἐ.); (**16**) ~ ib. l. 89 (Αὐρ. Ἐ.)
S. ITALY (CAMPANIA):
—DIKAIARCHIA-PUTEOLI: (**17**) imp. *CIL* X 2549 (Lat. Iulius Euphrosynus); (**18**) ~ ib. 2861; cf. *NScav* 1923, p. 270 (Lat. Cn. Pompeius Euphrosynus)
—HERCULANEUM: (**19**) 66 AD *PdelP* 8 (1953) p. 459 no. 42 + *Cron. Erc.* 23 (1993) pp. 110-5 (name, date) (Lat. D. Laelius Euphrosynus); (**20**) 67 AD ib. p. 111 no. 1 (Lat. D. Laelius Euphrosynus)
S. ITALY (LUCANIA):
—POSEIDONIA-PAESTUM: (**21**) ii-iii AD *CIL* X 489 (Mello–Voza 200) (Lat. Iulius Eufrosynus)
SICILY:
—SYRACUSE: (**22**) iii-v AD *IG* XIV 79 (Strazzulla 20; Wessel 205)

**Εὐφρώ**
EPIROS:
—NIKOPOLIS: (**1**) imp. *Ep. Chron.* 31 (1994) p. 41 no. 4 (*AD* 45 (1990) Chron. p. 257 no. 1) (d. Τρίτος)

**Εὐφρώι**
ARGOLIS:
—ARGOS: (**1**) iii BC *IG* IV (1)² 321

**Εὔφρων**
AKARNANIA:
—PALAIROS: (**1**) c. 325-315 BC *Hesp.* 57 (1988) p. 148 A, 19 (*SEG* XXXVI 331); cf. *Hesp.* 48 (1979) pp. 78 f. with pl. 22 c (s. Ἐπίφρων); (**2**) hell.? *IG* IX (1)² (2) 563
ARGOLIS:
—ARGOS: (**3**) ii-i BC *Syringes* 44 (f. Δημήτριος); (**4**) 102 BC *FD* III (1) 227, 3, 7 (f. Ἀρίσταρχος)
—HERMIONE: (**5**) iii BC *IG* IV (1) 729 I, 13 (s. Ἀγαθόλας)
DALMATIA:
—ISSA: (**6**) f. ii BC Brunšmid p. 22 no. 9, 8 (Εὔ(φ)ρων?)
KORINTHIA:
—SIKYON: (**7**) c. 410-366 BC *RE* (1) (Skalet 135) (f. Ἀδέας: tyrant); (**8**) c. 350-318 BC *RE* (2); Osborne, *Naturalization* D 38 (Skalet 136) (s. Ἀδέας)

S. ITALY (BRUTTIUM):
—LOKROI EPIZEPHYRIOI:
——(Ἀνξ.): (**9**) iv/iii BC De Franciscis 15, 4 (s. Ζώϊππος)
——(Δυσ.): (**10**) iv/iii BC ib. 18, 6 (f. Μεγακλῆς)
——(Θρα.): (**11**) iv/iii BC ib. 4, 4; 22, 4 (s. Σαύρων)
——(Μνα.): (**12**) iv/iii BC ib. 19, 5 (f. Χαρίξενος)
——(Πετ.): (**13**) iv/iii BC ib. 4, 6; 22, 6 (f. Ἡράκλητος)
——(Ψαθ.): (**14**) iv/iii BC ib. 15, 6 (s. Πλάτων)
—TERINA: (**15**) m. iv BC *IG* II² 10438 (f. Δαμώ)
S. ITALY (CAMPANIA):
—NEAPOLIS: (**16**) i BC/i AD ib. XIV 783, 1 (*INap* 137); cf. Leiwo p. 121 no. 106 (f. Λευκία); (**17**) ~ *IG* XIV 783, 3, 5 (*INap* 137); cf. Leiwo p. 121 no. 106 (s. Ἡρακλείδης)
TRIPHYLIA:
—LEPREON: (**18**) m. iv BC Paus. vi 3. 4 (f. Λάβαξ)

**Εὐχάνωρ**
ARKADIA:
—PHENEOS: (**1**) c. 315-280 BC *FD* III (1) 41, 1 (f. Μνασέας)

**Εὐχάρης**
ARGOLIS:
—EPIDAUROS:
——Teichias: (**1**) c. 365-335 BC *IG* IV (1)² 103, 112
KORINTHIA:
—KORINTH: (**2**) byz. *Corinth* VIII (3) 684 (-κά-)
MESSENIA:
—THOURIA: (**3**) f. ii BC *SEG* XI 972, 102 (s. Φίλων)

**Εὐχαρίδας**
ARKADIA:
—MANTINEIA-ANTIGONEIA:
——(Vanakisia): (**1**) m. iv BC *IG* V (2) 271, 20 (s. Πιστόξενος)
LEUKAS: (**2**) iii BC Unp. (*IG* arch.) (Εὐχαρίδ[ας])
SICILY:
—GELA-PHINTIAS: (**3**) f. v BC Dubois, *IGDS* 144 c (vase) (Arena, *Iscr. Sic.* II 55) (Εὐχ(α)ρίδας, Εὐαρίδας?)

**Εὐχάριον**
S. ITALY (CAMPANIA):
—SALERNUM: (**1**) imp. *IItal* I (1) 58 (*CIL* X 584) (Lat. Euchario (dat.))

**Εὐχαρίστα**
LEUKAS: (**1**) hell.? *IG* IX (1) 547 ([Εὐ]χαρίστα)

**Εὐχάριστος**
KORINTHIA:
—KORINTH: (**1**) s. ii AD *Corinth* VIII (1) 15, 39 (Λικίνιος Ἐ.)
MESSENIA:
—MESSENE: (**2**) 174 AD *SEG* XLI 337, 4 (f. Τρυφωνιανός)

**Εὐχάριτος**
SICILY:
—SYRACUSE: (**1**) iii-v AD *NScav* 1903, p. 534 (-ρει-)

**Εὔχαρμος**
ARGOLIS:
—EPIDAUROS*: (**1**) c. 290-270 BC *IG* IV (1)² 109 III, [52], 74; *SEG* XXV 401 B, [130]
SICILY:
—KAMARINA: (**2**) f. v BC Cordano, *Tessere Pubbliche* 68 (s. Θ—)

**Εὐχάρων**
EPIROS:
—THESPROTOI: (**1**) c. 223 BC *IG* IX (1)² (1) 31, 46 (Εὐχάρων)

**Εὐχέας**
PELOPONNESE: (**1**) s. iii BC *SEG* XIII 278, 7 (s. Εὔφραντος)

Εὔχειρος
AKARNANIA:
—ECHINOS: (1) c. 266 BC IG XII (9) 1187, 28;
Robert, Ét. Num. Gr. pp. 179 ff. (date) (f.
Δορκίνας)
EPIROS:
—VOTONOSI (MOD.): (2) f. iii BC SEG XXIV 456
(I f. Εὔχειρος II); (3) ~ ib. (II s. Εὔχειρος I)
KORINTHIA:
—KORINTH: (4) vii BC RE s.v. Eucheir (1) (and
Etruria: Lat. Eucheirus: potter)
MESSENIA:
—PROTE*: (5) imp. IG V (1) 1557 (-χι-)

Εὐχέλας
S. ITALY (BRUTTIUM):
—LOKROI EPIZEPHYRIOI:
——(Κοβ.): (1) iv/iii BC De Franciscis 3, 4; 38,
4 (s. Ἀριστεύς) ?= (2); (2) ~ ib. 28, 1 ?= (1)

Εὔχη
S. ITALY (CALABRIA):
—BRENTESION-BRUNDISIUM: (1) imp. CIL IX
84 = Epigraphica 25 (1963) p. 81 no. 89 (Lat.
Ba[e]bia Eu[c]he)
S. ITALY (CAMPANIA):
—POMPEII: (2) i BC-i AD CIL IV 4126 (Lat.
Eyce); (3) ~ ib. 1590-2 (Lat. Euche); (4) ~
ib. 5345-6 (Lat. Euche); (5) m. i AD Impegno
per Pompeii 9 ES no. 3 (Castrèn 259. 3) (Lat.
Munatia Euche)

Εὐχηρίδας
ARGOLIS:
—PHLEIOUS: (1) iii/ii BC IG IV (1) 460
DALMATIA:
—ISSA: (2) iii BC VAMZ 1970, p. 36 fr. K (Εὐ-
χη[ρίδας]); (3) iii/ii BC SEG XXXV 684 (VAHD
84 (1991) p. 254 no. 5) (f. Πρώταρχος); (4) ~
SEG XXXV 684 (VAHD 84 (1991) p. 254 no.
5) (I s. Πρώταρχος, f. Εὐχηρίδας II, Πρώταρχος, Δηλιώ); (5) ~ SEG XXXV 684 (VAHD 84
(1991) p. 254 no. 5) (II s. Εὐχηρίδας I)

Εὐχόρα
ARGOLIS:
—EPIDAUROS: (1) iv/iii BC Peek, NIEpid 75

Εὔχορος
S. ITALY (CAMPANIA):
—POMPEII: (1) i BC-i AD CIL IV 10026; Gnomon
45 (1973) p. 268 (name) (Lat. Eucorus)

Εὖχος
ILLYRIA:
—EPIDAMNOS-DYRRHACHION: (1) hell.-imp.
IDyrrh 322 (Εὖχος: f. Ναυσήν)

Εὐχρηστος
S. ITALY (CAMPANIA):
—SURRENTUM: (1) imp. CIL X 749 (Lat. Eu-
chrestus)

Εὔχρους
S. ITALY (CAMPANIA):
—POMPEII: (1) i BC-i AD ib. IV 8359 (Lat. Eu-
crus)

Εὐχύλος
PELOPONNESE: (1) s. iii BC SEG XIII 278, 13 (s.
Εὐβίοτος)

Εὔψηφος
ARKADIA:
—LYKOSOURA*: (1) ii-iii AD IG V (2) 526
(Εὔψηφος)

Εὐωνίας
ARKADIA:
—PALLANTION: (1) a. 316 BC SEG XI 1084, 36
(Perlman A.3) (f. —πος)

Εὐωνύμα
LAKONIA:
—SPARTA: (1) ?vi/v BC SEG XI 662 (bronze)
(Lazzarini 91; Poralla² 334a) (-ōνύ-: date—
LGPN)

Εὐώνυμος
ELIS: (1) iii-ii BC IG IV (1) 429, 9; cf. Stephanis
194 ([E]ὐ[ώνυ]μος: f. Ἀντανδρος)
LAKONIA:
—HYPERTELEATON*: (2) vi/v BC IG V (1) 983
(bronze) (Lazzarini 95; Poralla² 335) (-ōνυ-)

Εὐωπίδας
SICILY:
—HIMERA: (1) c. 475-450 BC Himera 2 p. 681
no. 45 (Dubois, IGDS 11; Arena, Iscr. Sic.
III 51) (Εὐōπίδας (n. gent.?))
—KAMARINA: (2) f. v BC Cordano, Tessere Pub-
bliche 50 (Εὐō-: f. Ζευξίας)

Εὐῶπις
ARGOLIS:
—PHLEIOUS: (1) iv BC SEG XXVI 416, 2

Ἐφεσία
S. ITALY (APULIA):
—VENUSIA*: (1) f. i AD Rend. Linc. 29 (1974)
p. 614 no. 12 (Museo di Venosa p. 235 no. 5)
(Lat. Camuria Fausta et Ephe[sia]: freed.)
S. ITALY (CAMPANIA):
—DIKAIARCHIA-PUTEOLI: (2) ?i AD CIL X 2500
(Lat. Iulia Ephesia); (3) ii AD Puteoli 11
(1987) p. 129 no. 2 (Lat. Clodia Ephesia)
—DIKAIARCHIA-PUTEOLI*: (4) imp. CIL X
3078 (Lat. Varia Ephesia: freed.)
—KYME: (5) imp. NScav 1898, p. 192 (Lat.
Aemilia Ephesia)
—SALERNUM: (6) s. i AD IItal I (1) 211 (CIL X
617) (Lat. Iuventia Ephesia: m. Πάρθενος)
S. ITALY (LUCANIA):
—POSEIDONIA-PAESTUM: (7) imp. ib. 486
(Mello–Voza 198) (Lat. Bennia Ephesia)

Ἐφέσιος
AKARNANIA:
—STRATOS: (1) c. 325-315 BC Hesp. 57 (1988)
p. 148 A, 40 (SEG XXXVI 331); cf. Hesp. 48
(1979) pp. 78 f. with pl. 22 c (s. Ἐχεκράτης)

Ἔφεσος
S. ITALY (CAMPANIA):
—POMPEII: (1) i BC-i AD CIL IV 1503 (Lat.
Ephesus)

Ἐφηβικός
S. ITALY (CAMPANIA):
—DIKAIARCHIA-PUTEOLI: (1) imp. ib. x 2355
(Lat. M. Culcius Ephoebicus)

Ἔφηβος
ACHAIA:
—PATRAI: (1) imp. ILGR 70, 5 (Lat. L.?
Aemilius Ephebus)
ARKADIA:
—TEGEA: (2) 165 AD IG V (2) 50, 46 (f. Ἑρμῆς)
ELIS: (3) 141-145 AD IvOl 95, 5 (Λ. Καικίλιος
Φοῖβος [ὁ] καὶ Ε.: T.)
LAKONIA:
—CHEN?: (4) imp. IG VII 2936 (Bradford (-))
(n. pr.?)
S. ITALY (CAMPANIA):
—DIKAIARCHIA-PUTEOLI: (5) imp. CIL X 2164
(Lat. Aephebus: I f. Ἔφηβος II); (6) ~ ib. (Lat.
Q. Bellicius Aephebus: II s. Ἔφηβος I)
—POMPEII: (7) i BC-i AD ib. IV 1478 (Lat. Ephe-
bus); (8) ~ ib. 3963 (Lat. Ephebus); (9) ~
ib. 4753; 4765 (Lat. Aephebus: f. Successus);
(10) ~ ib. 9127 (Lat. Ephebus); (11) c. 51-62
AD ib. 3340. 82, 5 (Castrèn 320. 3) (Lat. C.
Poppaeus Ephebus)

Ἐφύρα
S. ITALY (CAMPANIA):
—KYME: (1) imp. AJA 2 (1898) p. 398 no. 66
(Lat. Pontia Hepyre)

Ἐφωτίων
ARKADIA:
—MAINALIOI: (1) 466-464 BC Moretti, Olymp.
253; Klee pp. 80 no. 48; 93 no. 114; 102 no.
109; FGrH 241 F 15 a (name) (Ἐφουδίων—
Ar., Ἐφωδίων—Polem. and Hsch.)

Ἐχεδαμίδας
ARGOLIS:
—ARGOS: (1) ?c. 575-550 BC SEG XI 336, 4;
LSAG² p. 168 no. 7 (date) (f. Σθενέλας)

Ἐχέδαμος
AKARNANIA: (1) 197 BC RE Supplbd. 11 (2)
(Lat. Echedamus) ?= (3)
KEPHALLENIA: (2) iii-ii BC Op. Ath. 10 (1971)
p. 65 no. 10
LEUKAS: (3) 216 BC IG IX (1)² (2) 583, 2, 63 (s.
Μνασίλοχος) ?= (1)
MESSENIA:
—MESSENE: (4) 87 AD SEG XLI 335, 10 (s. Χάρ-
τις)
—THOURIA: (5) f. ii BC ib. XI 972, 32 (f. Σόφιος)
S. ITALY (BRUTTIUM):
—LOKROI EPIZEPHYRIOI:
——(Προ.): (6) iv/iii BC De Franciscis 17, 3 (s.
Ζωίλος)
SICILY:
—APOLLONIA: (7) hell.? IG XIV 363 (Ὀχέδα-
μου (gen)—apogr., (Ε)χεδάμου—Wilamowitz,
(Αρ)χέδαμος—CIG and IG)

Ἐχεκλείδας
EPIROS:
—AMBRAKIA: (1) iii-ii BC Op. Ath. 10 (1971) p.
64 no. 12, 2, 5; cf. VAHD 84 (1991) p. 262
(s. Χαιρήν, f. Πολυστράτα)

Ἐχεκλῆς
KORINTHIA:
—KORINTH: (1) v BC Amyx Gr 21 (vase) (Co-
rinth XV (3) p. 360 no. 16) (-κλ̄ς: potter)

Ἐχεκράτεια
ARGOLIS:
—EPIDAUROS: (1) v/iv BC AD 25 (1970) Mel.
pp. 31-2 no. 5; (2) ii/i BC IG IV (1)² 212 (d.
Δαμοκλῆς, m. Ἀρχώ)
—PHLEIOUS: (3) iv BC Iamb., VP 267 (FVS I
p. 447)
ITHAKE: (4) hell. SEG XVII 257; cf. Fraser-
Rönne, BWGT pl. 23 (d. Κλεοφῶν)

Ἐχεκράτης
ACHAIA:
—AIGION: (1) c. 210-207 BC IG IV (1)² 73, 18;
SEG XXXV 303 (date) (f. Τεισίας)
AKARNANIA:
—STRATOS: (2) c. 325-315 BC Hesp. 57 (1988)
p. 148 A, 40 (SEG XXXVI 331); cf. Hesp. 48
(1979) pp. 78 f. with pl. 22 c (f. Ἐφέσιος)
ARGOLIS:
—ARGOS: (3) 337-324 BC CID II 74 I, 46; 77 I,
[7]; 97, 34; 99 A, [6], 102 II B, 31; 120 A, 3;
122 III, [1] (f. Ὁρμασίλας); (4) ?165 BC Syll³
585, 308 (Stephanis 1009) (II s. Ἐχεκράτης I);
(5) ~ Syll³ 585, 309; cf. Stephanis 1009 (I f.
Ἐχεκράτης II)
—EPIDAUROS: (6) c. 350-250 BC AD 28 (1973)
Chron. pl. 84 a
—PHLEIOUS: (7) v-iv BC Iamb., VP 251; 267
(FVS I p. 443); D.L. viii 43 ?= (8); (8) f. iv
BC Pl., Ph. 57A; Ep. ix 358b ?= (s. Φρυνίων) ?=
(9) (7)
—PHLEIOUS?: (9) iv BC Plb. xii 10. 7; Walbank
2 p. 346 ?= (8)
EPIROS:
—EMBESOS (MOD.): (10) ii BC AD 22 (1967)
Chron. p. 321 (s. Φράσων, f. Ἐχέμμας)

Ἐχελαΐδας

KORINTHIA:
—KORINTH: (11) viii/vii BC Hdt. v 92 (f. Ἀε-τίων); (12) m. iii BC *Corinth* VIII (3) 33 b, 4 + *SEG* XXV 330 (['E]χεκρ[άτης])
S. ITALY (BRUTTIUM):
—LOKROI EPIZEPHYRIOI: (13) iv/iii BC Plb. xii 10. 7; (14) ~ De Franciscis 3, 14 (f. Μενέδαμος) —(Ἀγφ.): (15) iv/iii BC ib. 21, 4, 19
S. ITALY (CALABRIA):
—TARAS-TARENTUM: (16) iv BC Iamb., *VP* 267 (*FVS* I p. 446)

Ἐχελαΐδας

ILLYRIA:
—EPIDAMNOS-DYRRHACHION: (1) c. 76 BC *IG* VII 417, 24 + *AE* 1923, p. 50 no. 126 (*IOrop* 525) (f. Δεξίας)

Ἐχέλαος

AITOLIA:
—PHISTYON: (1) f. ii BC *IG* IX (1)² (1) 111, 5 (s. Τίμαιος) ?= (2); (2) c. 170-150 BC ib. 98, 9; 99, 11; 101, 9 ?= (1)
—PHISTYON?: (3) f. ii BC ib. 104, 5 (Ἐχέ[λαος])
EPIROS:
—PAROROI: (4) f. ii BC Cabanes, *L'Épire* p. 580 no. 54, 3

Ἔχελλος

ACHAIA:
—DYME?: (1) ?f. iii BC *HE* 2875 (f. Μαντιάδας, Εὔστρατος)

Ἐχέμβροτος

ARGOLIS:
—ARGOS: (1) iii BC *SEG* XXXIII 283 (Ἐχέμ[βροτος], Ἐχεμ[ένης]?)
—KLEONAI: (2) v/iv BC *IG* II² 632, 2, 8; *SEG* XXX 66, 47 (Ἐχέν[βροτος]—SEG: s. Λάπυρις, ?f. Καλλίας)
ARKADIA: (3) f. vi BC *RE* (-) (Stephanis 1011)

Ἐχεμένης

AKARNANIA?:
—THERMINEA: (1) 356-354 BC *IG* IV (1)² 95, 36 (Perlman E.2); Perlman p. 40 f. (date)
ARGOLIS:
—ARGOS: (2) c. 458 BC *IG* I³ 1149, 23 (['Ἐχ]εμένες)
ARKADIA:
—TEGEA: (3) iv BC ib. v (2) 31, 9 (f. Ἀριστίων)
KORINTHIA:
—KORINTH: (4) s. iv BC *Corinth* VIII (1) 11, 10 (s. Ἐχε—)
LAKONIA:
—SPARTA: (5) b. 433 BC *IG* v (1) 213, 66, 90 (Moretti, *IAG* 16; Poralla² 336)
LEUKAS: (6) 216 BC *IG* IX (1)² (2) 583, 5 (f. Φαίαξ)

Ἐχεμήδης

LAKONIA:
—SELLASIA*: (1) iii BC *SEG* XXXII 397

Ἐχέμμας

EPIROS:
—EMBESOS (MOD.): (1) ii BC *AD* 22 (1967) Chron. p. 321 (s. Ἐχεκράτης)

Ἐχενίκα

EPIROS:
—BOUTHROTOS (PRASAIBOI): (1) a. 163 BC *IBouthrot* 28, 19 (*SEG* XXXVIII 486); *IBouthrot* 144, 5; (2) ~ ib. 29, 62 (*SEG* XXXVIII 487); (3) ~ *IBouthrot* 36, 24 (*SEG* XXXVIII 495)


—KASSOPE: (4) ii BC *GVI* 1078, 2 (*IG* IX (1)² (2) 312 a) (d. Μενέδαμος, Ἀριστοκράτεια)
—MOLOSSOI: (5) hell. Cabanes, *L'Épire* p. 584 no. 63, 2 (*SEG* XXVI 705) (d. Βοῖσκος, Δαμνα-γόρα)

Ἐχενίκη

ARGOLIS:
—PHLEIOUS: (1) 361 BC *CID* II 4 I, 51

Ἐχένικος

AITOLIA:
—KONOPE-ARSINOE: (1) ii BC *SBBerlAk* 1936, p. 360 no. I, 10

Ἐχεσθένης

ACHAIA:
—DYME: (1) ?145 BC Sherk 43, 21; *SEG* XXXVIII 372 (date) (f. Φορμίσκος)
—PATRAI: (2) ii BC *Achaean Grave Stelai* 57 (Ἐχεσθ[ένης])
ARGOLIS:
—EPIDAUROS*: (3) iv/iii BC Peek, *IAEpid* 51, 6; *BSA* 61 (1966) p. 319 no. 26 (date) (Ἐχεσ[θ]έν[η]ς)
ARKADIA:
—PHENEOS: (4) ?265 BC *BCH* 82 (1958) p. 87 C (s. —άνης)
S. ITALY (BRUTTIUM):
—KROTON: (5) ?c. 500-475 BC *SEG* XXXIII 768 (bronze); cf. *LSAG*² p. 457 no. R (date) (f. Αἰσχύλος)

Ἐχέστρατος

ARKADIA:
—MEGALOPOLIS: (1) ii/i BC *IG* v (2) 443, 2 (*IPArk* 32)
LAKONIA:
—SPARTA: (2) her. *RE* (-) (Poralla² 338) (s. Ἆγις, f. Λαβώτας: king/dub.)

Ἐχέταρμος

AITOLIA: (1) ?228-215 BC *FD* III (4) 364, 4; *SGDI* 2525, 4

Ἐχετέλης

LAKONIA:
—SPARTA: (1) 362-360 BC *CID* II I I, 35; 4 II, 53 (Poralla² 339)

Ἐχετέρμων

AKARNANIA:
—THYRREION: (1) ii BC *IG* IX (1)² (2) 250, 14 (f. Ἀπολλώνιος)

Ἐχετιμίδας

LAKONIA:
—SPARTA: (1) 423 BC Th. iv 119. 2; Schol. Ar., *Eq.* 79b (Poralla² 340) (f. Ταῦρος)

Ἐχέτιμος

ARGOLIS:
—EPIDAUROS:
——(Azantioi): (1) 146 BC *IG* IV (1)² 28, 39 (f. Θεύδωρος)
——Dexelis: (2) c. 365-335 BC ib. 103, 78
—EPIDAUROS*: (3) c. 370 BC ib. 102, 52
KORINTHIA:
—SIKYON: (4) ?v BC Paus. ii 10. 3 (Skalet 137)

Ἐχέφρων

ILLYRIA:
—EPIDAMNOS-DYRRHACHION: (1) c. 250-50 BC Maier 112; 145; 198; 204; 215; 281; 401 (coin) (Ceka 192-8) (money.)


Ἐχεφυλίδας

ELIS?: (1) iv/iii BC *FGrH* 409
PELOPONNESE?: (2) s. iii BC *IG* v (1) 1426, 24 (s. Πανταλέων)

Ἐχέφυλος

ARKADIA: (1) ?iii BC Breccia, *Iscriz.* 294 (s. Κλεόδωρος)
LAKONIA: (2) iii-ii BC *IG* v (1) 1341, 2 (Bradford (-))
ZAKYNTHOS: (3) iv BC Carapanos, *Dodone* p. 39 no. I, 5 (f. Ἀγάθων)

Ἔχθρων

EPIROS:
—DODONA: (1) iii BC Antoniou, *Dodone* Ba, 39 (Ἐχθρων)

Ἐχιάδας

KORINTHIA:
—KORINTH: (1) s. vii BC *FGrH* 90 F 57. 7 (and Akarnania Anaktorion: s. Κύψελος: oikist)

Ἐχίας

ARKADIA:
—THELPHOUSA: (1) 369-361 BC *IG* v (2) 1, 67; Tod, *GHI* II 132 (date)

Ἐχῖνος

S. ITALY (CAMPANIA):
—POMPEII: (1) i BC-i AD *CIL* IV 4513 (Lat. Echinus)
S. ITALY (LUCANIA):
—METAPONTION: (2) iii BC *SEG* XXX 1176 F. 17 (potter)

Ἔχιππος

ARKADIA: (1) c. 230-200 BC *BCH* 45 (1921) p. 13 II, 110 (f. Ἱπποκράτης)
S. ITALY (BRUTTIUM):
—RHEGION*: (2) m. vi BC Rumpf, *Chalkid. Vas.* pp. 46-7 no. 5 (vase) (Arena, *Iscr. Sic.* III pp. 103-4 no. 8) (her.?)
SICILY:
—AKRAGAS: (3) inc. Manganaro, *QUCC* forthcoming no. 7 (Ἐχιπ[πος]: f. -ων)

Ἐχίων

S. ITALY (CAMPANIA):
—DIKAIARCHIA-PUTEOLI: (1) imp. *CIL* X 3023 (Lat. L. Trisenius Echio)
—HERCULANEUM: (2) i BC-i AD ib. IV 10596 (Lat. Echio)
—POMPEII: (3) i BC-i AD ib. 1110; 1303; 2377 (Lat. Echio); (4) ~ ib. 5414 (Lat. Echio)

Ἔχυλλος

ILLYRIA:
—EPIDAMNOS-DYRRHACHION: (1) hell.? *IDyrrh* 217 (s. Θερσήν)

Ἐχύντας

EPIROS:
—DODONA: (1) iii BC Antoniou, *Dodone* Ba, 10; (2) ~ ib. l. 11

# F

**Ϝαγέας**
KORINTHIA:
—KORINTH: (1) ?vi BC *Corinth* XV (3) p. 361 no. 20 (Ϝαγέας)

**Ϝαγιάδας**
SICILY:
—MONTE SARACENO (MOD.): (1) vi/v BC Arena, *Iscr. Sic.* II 104 (*IGLMP* 36)

**Ϝάδήσιος**
KORINTHIA:
—KORINTH: (1) c. 590-570 BC Amyx 19 B. 6 (vase) (Lorber 37) (Ϝhαδέ-: fict.?)

**Ϝάδων**
ARKADIA:
—MANTINEIA-ANTIGONEIA:
——(Posoidaia): (1) c. 425-400 BC *SEG* XXXI 348, 13

**Ϝαιράντιος**
MESSENIA: (1) ?f. v BC *AD* 2 (1916) p. 114 no. 78; *LSAG²* p. 206 no. 7 (date)

**Ϝαναξίβιος**
LAKONIA:
—SPARTA: (1) ?c. 525-500 BC *IG* v (1) 215 (Lazzarini 405); *LSAG²* p. 200 no. 27 (date) (Poralla² 85)

**Ϝαναξίλας**
ARGOLIS:
—ARGOS: (1) c. 458 BC *IG* I³ 1149, 21 (Ϝαναξίλας)
ELIS: (2) v BC *Boston Bronzes* 622

**Ϝάρις**
KORINTHIA:
—KORINTH: (1) c. 570-550 BC Amyx 105 A. 5 (vase) (Lorber 93) (fict.?)

**Ϝάριχος**
S. ITALY (CALABRIA):
—TARAS-TARENTUM: (1) iv/iii BC *IG* XIV 668 I, 17 (Landi, *DISMG* 194)

**Ϝασίας**
S. ITALY (LUCANIA):
—METAPONTION: (1) vii/vi BC *SEG* XXIX 954; cf. *LSAG²* p. 457 no. J (date)

**Ϝαστύοχος**
ARKADIA:
—TEGEA: (1) v BC *IG* v (2) 77, 1a (Ϝαστύ-)

**Ϝαττίδας**
EPIROS:
—MOLOSSOI: (1) iii/ii BC *Syll³* 1206, 5; cf. Cabanes, *L'Épire* p. 583 no. 60

**Ϝάχας**
KORINTHIA:
—KORINTH: (1) c. 570-550 BC Amyx 103. 3 (vase) (Ϝάχας: her.?)

**Ϝᾶχος**
ARKADIA:
—MANTINEIA-ANTIGONEIA: (1) 369-361 BC *IG* v (2) 1, 36; Tod, *GHI* II 132 (date)

**Ϝᾶχυς**
KORINTHIA:
—KORINTH: (1) c. 570-550 BC Amyx 63; 67. 1; 105 B. 10; 119. 1 (vases) (Lorber 87); Lorber 123; 93; 99; cf. Masson, *OGS* 2 p. 391 (name) (her.?)

---

S. ITALY (BRUTTIUM):
—RHEGION*: (2) m. vi BC Rumpf, *Chalkid. Vas.* p. 47 no. 8 (vase) (Arena, *Iscr. Sic.* III p. 105 no. 12) (her.?)

**Ϝαχώι**
KORINTHIA:
—KORINTH: (1) c. 570-550 BC Amyx 81. 9 (vase) (Lorber 130) (-χ̣όι̣: her.?)

**Ϝεΐδυς**
EPIROS:
—AMYMNOI: (1) ?c. 343-331 BC Cabanes, *L'Épire* p. 577 no. 50, 5

**Ϝειλάτα?**
AITOLIA:
—KALLION/KALLIPOLIS: (1) arch. *Rev. Épig.* I (1913) p. 200; cf. *IG* IX (1)² (1) 156 note

**Ϝειράνα**
LAKONIA:
—SPARTA: (1) iv BC ib. v (1) 1509; Masson, *OGS* 2 p. 515 (name) (Bradford (-))

**Ϝέπις**
KORINTHIA:
—SIKYON: (1) vi/v BC *SEG* XI 244, 26; Masson, *OGS* I p. 338 (name)

**Ϝερζάν**
ILLYRIA: (1) f. iv BC *IvOl* 695, 1, 2 + *Ol. Ber.* 6 pp. 145 ff. (s. Γράβων)

**Ϝέσκλαρος**
ARKADIA:
—MANTINEIA-ANTIGONEIA: (1) c. 475-450 BC *IG* v (2) 262, 12 (*IPArk* 8); *LSAG²* p. 216 no. 29 (date)

**Ϝιανθεμίς**
LAKONIA:
—SPARTA: (1) s. vii BC *PMGF* I 1, 76 (Poralla² 382)

**Ϝιανθίς**
SICILY:
—SYRACUSE: (1) vi/v BC Dubois, *IGDS* 87 (vase) (*SEG* XXXVI 885; XXXVIII 971) (Ϝιαθίς—*SEG* XXXVI, Ϝια(ν)θίς—Dubois)

**Ϝικαδέων**
ARGOLIS:
—ARGOS:
——(Ophellokleidai): (1) ?iv-iii BC ib. XXXIII 286 (Ϝικαδέω[ν])

**Ϝικάδιος**
ARKADIA:
—MANTINEIA-ANTIGONEIA:
——(Enyalia): (1) m. iv BC *IG* v (2) 271, 8 (f. Τρίτιος)

**Ϝίκελος**
SICILY:
—SELINOUS?: (1) vi/v BC *SEG* XXXIX 1020 B, 1, 4 + *BE* 1990, no. 863 (f. Μήστωρ)

**Ϝινναδεύς**
S. ITALY (APULIA):
—RUBI: (1) hell.? *RA* 1932 (1), p. 38 no. 14 (loomweight); cf. *SEG* XXX 1222 (name) (Ϝ. Πλάτυρ)

**Ϝιόπα**
KORINTHIA:
—KORINTH: (1) c. 550 BC Amyx Gr 15. 1 (vase) (Lorber 153) (het.?/fict.?)

---

**Ϝίος**
KORINTHIA:
—KORINTH: (1) c. 570-550 BC Amyx 67. 3 (vase) (Lorber 123; Arena, *Iscr. Cor.* 74) (Ϝίος, Ϝίον̣?: her.?)

**Ϝίσϝαρχος**
KORINTHIA:
—SIKYON: (1) vi/v BC *SEG* XI 244, 59

**Ϝισϝόδαμος**
ARKADIA:
—MANTINEIA-ANTIGONEIA: (1) c. 425-385 BC *IG* v (2) 323. 21 (tessera) (s. Πάνθις)

**Ϝίσιππος**
KORINTHIA:
—KORINTH: (1) c. 570-550 BC Amyx 64. 2 (vase) (Lorber 97) (Ϝίσιππος?—Amyx, Κίσιππος—Lorber: her.?)

**Ϝισόδαμος**
ARKADIA:
—MANTINEIA-ANTIGONEIA: (1) c. 300-221 BC *IG* v (2) 323. 91 (tessera) (f. Κλέας)

**Ϝισοκρέτης**
ARKADIA:
—MANTINEIA-ANTIGONEIA: (1) c. 300-221 BC ib. 323. 77 (tessera) (f. Δαμάτριος)

**Ϝιστίας**
ARKADIA:
—MANTINEIA-ANTIGONEIA:
——(Posoidaia): (1) m. iv BC ib. 271, 18 (f. Ἀλύγας)
——PHIGALEIA: (2) s. v BC ib. 429, 8 (*IPArk* 27) ([Ϝ]ιστίας (n. pr.?))

**Ϝισύλος**
S. ITALY (CAMPANIA):
—FRATTE DI SALERNO (MOD.): (1) vi BC Arena, *Iscr. Sic.* IV 29 (vase)

**Ϝίσων**
ARGOLIS:
—TROIZEN: (1) ?c. 500 BC *CEG* I 139; cf. Guarducci, *Ep. Gr.* I p. 364 (sculptor)

**Ϝîφις**
KORINTHIA:
—KORINTH: (1) c. 570-550 BC Amyx 81. 5 (vase) (Lorber 130) (her.?)

**Ϝίφιτος**
KORINTHIA:
—KORINTH: (1) c. 570-550 BC Amyx 107. 6 (vase) (Lorber 147) (Ϝίφιτος: her.?)
S. ITALY (BRUTTIUM):
—KROTON: (2) vii/vi BC Arena, *Iscr. Sic.* IV 38 (loomweight)

**Ϝιώι**
KORINTHIA:
—KORINTH: (1) c. 570-550 BC Amyx 71. 3; 77; 78; 81. 2; 119. 4 (vases) (Lorber 127); Lorber 111; 81; 110; 99 (-όι̣: her.?)

**Ϝίων**
KORINTHIA:
—KORINTH: (1) c. 570-550 BC Amyx 59. 3; 99 A. 1; 99 B. 6; 102. 2-4; 108. 1 (vases) (Lorber 91); Lorber 94 (-όν: her.?)
LAKONIA:
—GERONTHRAI: (2) c. 500 BC *IG* v (1) 1134, 5; *LSAG²* p. 201 no. 45 (date) (Poralla² 777)
S. ITALY (BRUTTIUM):
—RHEGION*: (3) m. vi BC Rumpf, *Chalkid. Vas.* p. 47 no. 8 (vase) (Arena, *Iscr. Sic.* III p. 105 no. 11) (-όν: her.?)

## Ϝιωνίδας
ARKADIA:
—MANTINEIA-ANTIGONEIA: (1) c. 425-385 BC *IG* v (2) 323. 5 (tessera) (Ϝιωνίδα[ς]: s. Εὔϝετος)

## Ϝοινάνθα
SICILY:
—SELINOUS: (1) c. 600 BC Dubois, *IGDS* 79 (vase) (Arena, *Iscr. Sic.* I 80; Amyx Gr 8); cf. *SEG* XXXV 1018

## Ϝοινεύς
KORINTHIA:
—KORINTH: (1) c. 590-570 BC Amyx 41. 1 (vase) (Lorber 64) (her.?)
S. ITALY (CAMPANIA):
—NEAPOLIS: (2) m. vi BC Landi, *DISMG* 24

## Ϝοινίδας
AKARNANIA:
—PHOITIAI: (1) iv BC *IG* IX (1)² (2) 602, 10 (Ϝοινίδας, Ϝοινι(ά)δας?—ed.: s. Βιάνωρ)

## Ϝοινίων
S. ITALY (CAMPANIA):
—NEAPOLIS (NR.): (1) f. iv BC *INap* 190 (vase) (Dubois, *IGDGG* I 31) (-ōν)

## Ϝόλτεσκος
SICILY:
—ECHETLA: (1) c. 500 BC *Kokalos* 14-15 (1968-9) pp. 201-2 (vase) (-ϙος)

## Ϝόλχας
S. ITALY (CAMPANIA):
—FRATTE DI SALERNO (MOD.): (1) f. v BC *SEG* XXXVII 817 A (vase) (Arena, *Iscr. Sic.* IV 33)

## Ϝορθαγόρας
ARGOLIS:
—ARGOS: (1) ?c. 575-550 BC *SEG* XI 336, 8; *LSAG*² p. 168 no. 7 (date)

## Ϝουλιάδας
SICILY:
—GELA-PHINTIAS: (1) s. vi BC Arena, *Iscr. Sic.* II 15 (vase) (Ϝουλιάδας)

## Ϝράδων
ARKADIA:
—MANTINEIA-ANTIGONEIA: (1) c. 425-385 BC *IG* v (2) 323. 1 (tessera) (-δōν: s. Περίανδρος)

## Ϝρίθισα
LAKONIA:
—SPARTA: (1) c. 600 BC ib. v (1) 1587 (vase); *LSAG*² p. 198 no. 2 a (date) (Poralla² 343)

## Ϝρικνίδας
ARGOLIS:
—ARGOS: (1) m. vi BC *CEG* II 813

## Ϝριψίδας
ARKADIA:
—MANTINEIA-ANTIGONEIA: (1) c. 425-385 BC *IG* v (2) 323. 20 (tessera) (s. Ἐρατίας)

## Ϝρωσις?
AKARNANIA:
—THYRREION: (1) ?ii BC ib. IX (1)² (2) 337 with note

# Z

## Ζαίμινα
ILLYRIA:
—EPIDAMNOS-DYRRHACHION: (1) hell.-imp. *IDyrrh* 218

## Ζακύνθιος
ARKADIA:
—MANTINEIA-ANTIGONEIA: (1) c. 425-385 BC *IG* v (2) 323. 3 (tessera) (s. Ξανθίας)

## Ζάκυνθος
S. ITALY (CAMPANIA):
—DIKAIARCHIA-PUTEOLI: (1) imp. *CIL* x 2243 (Lat. C. Ca– Zacynthu[s])

## Ζάλευκος
S. ITALY (BRUTTIUM):
—LOKROI EPIZEPHYRIOI: (1) vii BC *RE* (-)

## Ζᾶλος
S. ITALY (CALABRIA):
—TARAS-TARENTUM: (1) c. 280-272 BC Vlasto 803-8 (coins) (Evans, *Horsemen* p. 161 VIII G) (Ζᾶλο(ς))

## Ζανούβιος
SICILY:
—AKRILLAI: (1) iii-v AD *Epigraphica* 12 (1950) p. 105 no. 1; cf. Ferrua, *NG* 505 (Ζ(η)νό<υ>βιος?—Ferrua)

## Ζαοτύχα
S. ITALY (BRUTTIUM):
—KRIMISA: (1) ?c. 475 BC *IGSI* 18, 6 (*SEG* IV 75; Landi, *DISMG* 173); *LSAG*² p. 261 no. 30 (date) (Ζαο[τ]ύχ[α])

## Ζαρρέας
ILLYRIA:
—EPIDAMNOS-DYRRHACHION: (1) imp. *IDyrrh* 151 (f. Γενθέας)

## Ζατέας
ARKADIA: (1) iv BC *IG* IX (2) 773 (f. Δίφιλος)

## Ζευξαγόρα
ARGOLIS:
—HERMIONE: (1) ?ii-i BC ib. IV (1) 731 III, 11 (d. Δημήτριος)

## Ζεύξαυλος
ARGOLIS:
—EPIDAUROS:
——Agrias: (1) c. 335-325 BC ib. IV (1)² 108, 156

## Ζευξίας
ARGOLIS:
—EPIDAUROS:
——Pagasina (Azantioi): (1) m. iii BC ib. 96, 47 (Perlman E.3); Perlman p. 63 f. (date)
—HERMIONE: (2) ?ii-i BC *IG* IV (1) 733, 7 (s. Ξενόστρατος)
ARKADIA:
—MANTINEIA-ANTIGONEIA: (3) c. 425-385 BC ib. v (2) 323. 15 (tessera) (s. Εὐϝάνωρ); (4) c. 300-221 BC ib. 323. 48-9 (tesserae) (f. Σάτυρος)
—MEGALOPOLIS: (5) ?130 BC ib. 441, 8 (s. Σωσίστρατος)
—MEGALOPOLIS?: (6) 42 AD ib. 516, 3 (f. Δάμυλλος)
ELIS?: (7) ?c. 450-425 BC *IvOl* 15, 1, 3; *LSAG*² p. 221 no. 18 (date)
SICILY:
—KAMARINA: (8) f. v BC Cordano, *Tessere Pubbliche* 50 (s. Εὐωπίδας)

## Ζευξίδαμος
LAKONIA:
—SPARTA: (1) f. vii BC Paus. iii 7. 6 (Poralla² 344) (s. Ἀρχίδαμος, f. Ἀναξίδαμος: king/dub.); (2) vi/v BC *RE* (2); *IPr* 316, 12 (Poralla² 345) (Ζ. ὁ ἐπικαλ. Κυνίσκος: s. Λατυχίδας, f. Ἀρχίδαμος)
MESSENIA:
—MESSENE: (3) i AD *IG* v (1) 1467, 1
S. ITALY (CAMPANIA):
—DIKAIARCHIA-PUTEOLI: (4) imp. *CIL* x 3151 (Lat. Zeyxidamus: f. Ἐπιχαρίς)

## Ζευξίδας
LAKONIA:
—SPARTA: (1) 421 BC Th. v 19. 2; 24 (Poralla² 346)

## Ζεύξιλα
ARGOLIS:
—HERMIONE: (1) ?ii-i BC *IG* IV (1) 731 II, 8, 10 (m. Σίνδης, Ἀφροδίσιος)

## Ζευξίμαχος
ARGOLIS:
—EPIDAUROS:
——Aphylonia (Azantioi): (1) c. 365-335 BC ib. IV (1)² 103, 39

## Ζεύξιππος
ARGOLIS:
—HERMIONE*: (1) i BC/i AD ib. IV (1) 745 (s. Φιλέας: sculptor)
ARKADIA:
—MEGALOPOLIS: (2) ii BC ib. v (2) 143 (I f. Φιλέας, Ζεύξιππος II); (3) ~ ib. [143]? (II s. Ζεύξιππος I: sculptor)
—MEGALOPOLIS?: (4) ?i AD ib. IV (1) 745 (Loewy 141) (s. Φιλέας: sculptor)
KORINTHIA:
—KORINTH*: (5) iii BC *Corinth* VIII (3) 34 (her.?)
LAKONIA:
—SPARTA: (6) 424 BC X., *HG* ii 3. 10 (Poralla² 347); (7) i/ii AD Plu., *Mor.* 122 B ff.; 749 B; 762 B; 767 C; 1086 D ff.; Cartledge-Spawforth pp. 178-9 (ident.) (Bradford (5)) (?f. Τυνδάρης); (8) c. 90-100 AD *SEG* XI 570, 6 (Bradford (1)) (s. Καλλικράτης); (9) ii AD *IG* v (1) 194, 5 (Bradford (2)) ([Ζε]ύξιππος: s. Φ—); (10) c. 105-110 AD ib. v (1) 97, 14 (Bradford (6)); (11) c. 140-160 AD *IG* v (1) 74, 4; 87, 5; 446, 6; *SEG* XI 585, 10; XXX 410, 13; cf. Cartledge-Spawforth pp. 178-9 (Bradford (4)) (s. Τυνδάρης); (12) c. 212-235 AD *IG* v (1) 305, 3 (*Artemis Orthia* pp. 333-4 no. 69); *BSA* 79 (1984) p. 283 no. 5 (date) (Bradford s.v. Ζεύξιππος (3)) (Μ. Αὐρ. Ζεύξιππορ ὁ καὶ Κλεάνδρορ: s. Φιλόμουσος)
—TAINARON-KAINEPOLIS: (13) imp. *IG* v (1) 1245 (s. Φιλόδαμος: doctor)

**Ζεῦξις**
AKARNANIA: (1) 197 BC Liv. xxxiii 16. 5 (Lat.
Zeuxis)
LAKONIA:
—SPARTA: (2) i-ii AD *IG* v (1) 741 (Bradford (-))
(Δεκ. Λείβιος (Ζ)εῦξις)
LEUKAS: (3) f. i BC *IG* IX (1) 534, 11 (*Iscr. Gr.
Verona* p. 24) (s. Δωρίων)
S. ITALY (LUCANIA):
—HERAKLEIA: (4) v BC *RE* Supplbd. 15 (1)
(painter)

**Ζευξώ**
ARGOLIS:
—ARGOS: (1) iii/ii BC *PP* 17212 (*PPC* Z 2); *BE*
1949, no. 202 (family) (II d. Πολυκράτης, Ζευ-
ξώ I (Cyrene))
ARKADIA:
—MEGALOPOLIS: (2) ?145 BC *IG* v (2) 439, 45
(d. Σάϋλλος, m. Ἱέρων, Κλεοννώ)

**Ζέφυρος**
ACHAIA:
—DYME: (1) 170-164 BC *OGIS* 252 (*SEG* XIV
368); *SEG* XIV 369, 2; *Historia* 7 (1958) pp.
376-78 (date) (f. Ἀγημονίδας)
DALMATIA:
—ISSA:
——(Pamphyloi): (2) iv/iii BC Brunšmid p. 8, 36
(s. Δαμάτριος)
S. ITALY (CAMPANIA): (3) i AD *NScav* 1889, p.
404; *Cron. Erc.* 20 (1990) p. 166 no. 10 (tiles)
(Lat. L. Ansius Zephyrus)
S. ITALY (LUCANIA):
—HYELE-VELIA: (4) ii/i BC *CIG* 6986 (Noll, *Ins-
chr. Wien.* p. 44 no. 97) (f. Σαραπίων)

**Ζῆθος**
ELIS: (1) 225-241 AD *IvOl* 113, [4]; 114, 9;
116, 13; 117, 14; *SEG* XV 258, 9 (M. Ἀντ.
Ζ.: mantis/Klytiadai); (2) 265 AD *IvOl* 122,
21 (Αὐρ. Ζ.)
ILLYRIA:
—EPIDAMNOS-DYRRHACHION: (3) hell.-imp.
*IDyrrh* 271 (f. Κοΐα)
LAKONIA:
—SPARTA: (4) imp. *SEG* XI 645, 1 (Bradford
(-)) (Ζήθος); (5) i-ii AD *IG* v (1) 746 (Bradford
s.v. Ἀριστοκλῆς (17)) (Ἀριστοκλῆς ὁ καὶ Ζ.)
S. ITALY (CALABRIA):
—BRENTESION-BRUNDISIUM: (6) imp. *CIL* IX
6112 (Lat. Calavius Zethus)
—BRENTESION-BRUNDISIUM*: (7) imp. *NScav*
1892, p. 352 p = *Epigraphica* 25 (1963) p. 82
no. 91; cf. *Scritti Degrassi* 3 p. 74 (Lat. L.
Negilius Zeth[us]: freed.)
S. ITALY (CAMPANIA):
—DIKAIARCHIA-PUTEOLI: (8) imp. *AJA* 2
(1898) p. 384 no. 27 (Lat. M. Minucius
Zethus); (9) ~ *CIL* x 1767 (Lat. Munatius
Zethus: f. M. Munatius Priminus); (10) ~ ib.
3150 (Lat. Zethus)
—DIKAIARCHIA-PUTEOLI*: (11) imp. ib. 2637
(Lat. C. Laecanius Zethus: freed.)
—POMPEII: (12) i BC-i AD ib. 8058. 90 (seal)
(Castrèn 429. 1) (Lat. P. Vale. Zetus)
—SALERNUM*: (13) ?i AD *IItal* 1 (1) 238 II,
12 (*CIL* x 557) (Lat. L. Appuleius Zethus:
freed.)
SICILY:
—HALAISA: (14) imp. *Epigraphica* 51 (1989) p.
190 no. 80 (Lat. A. Mevius Zethus)
—HENNA: (15) imp. *CIL* x 7190 (*ILat. Palermo*
1) (Lat. Zethus)

**Ζηλίας**
DALMATIA:
—PHAROS: (1) iii/ii BC *SEG* XXIII 489, 1; cf.
XLI 545 ([Ζ]ηλίας?)

**Ζῆλος**
LAKONIA:
—SPARTA: (1) c. 124-145 AD *IG* v (1) 59, 6;
*SEG* XI 494, 1; 521 b, 5; 583, [4] (Bradford
(2)) (f. Νικάρων)
——Limnai: (2) c. 70-100 AD *IG* v (1) 676, 16
(Bradford (1)) (s. Ἀγαθόνικος)

**Ζηλουμενός**
ARGOLIS:
—ARGOS: (1) iii BC *BCH* 27 (1903) p. 265 no.
13 (Ζηλουμ[ενός], Ζηλουμ[ένη]?: s. Στρατόλας)

**Ζηλωτός**
S. ITALY (CAMPANIA):
—DIKAIARCHIA-PUTEOLI: (1) imp. *CIL* x 1557
(Lat. T. Vestorius Zelotus)

**Ζηναΐς**
S. ITALY (LUCANIA):
—MARSICI NOVI: (1) imp. ib. 198 (Lat.
Zenai(s)?)

**Ζηνάριον**
SICILY:
—LILYBAION: (1) i BC/i AD *SEG* XV 512 (d.
Λεύκιος)

**Ζηνᾶς**
KORINTHIA:
—KORINTH: (1) imp. ib. XI 50, 4 (Γν. Πομπ. Ζ.)
S. ITALY (CAMPANIA):
—LITERNUM: (2) ?i-ii AD *CIL* x 3717 (Lat. Ti.
Cl. Zenas)

**Ζηνίας**
ARKADIA?: (1) c. 200 BC *SEG* XVII 829, 8, 13

**Ζῆνις**
S. ITALY (LUCANIA):
—HYELE-VELIA: (1) iv/iii BC ib. XXVIII 818
(Landi, *DISMG* 232) (s. Δημήτριος); (2) hell.?
*IG* XII (5) 1018 (s. Καλλικράτης)

**Ζηνίς**
S. ITALY (CAMPANIA):
—MISENUM: (1) imp. *Eph. Ep.* VIII 441 (Lat.
Popilia Zenis)

**Ζηνοβία**
S. ITALY (CAMPANIA):
—ABELLA: (1) 490 AD *CIL* x 1231 (Lat. Zaeno-
bia)

**Ζηνόδοτος**
ARGOLIS:
—TROIZEN: (1) m. ii BC *RE* (9); *FGrH* 821

**Ζηνοδώρα**
S. ITALY (CAMPANIA):
—DIKAIARCHIA-PUTEOLI: (1) imp. *CIL* x 2373
(Lat. Domitia Zenodora)

**Ζηνοφάνης**
S. ITALY (BRUTTIUM):
—SYBARIS-THOURIOI-COPIAE: (1) i-ii AD
Charito i 7. 2 (fict.)

**Ζηνόφιλος**
ELIS: (1) iii AD *IvOl* 479 (Κλ. Ζ.)
SICILY:
—LILYBAION: (2) imp. *CIL* x 7234 (Lat. Do-
mitius Zenofilus)

**Ζηνωΐς**
ILLYRIA:
—LYCHNIDOS: (1) ii-iii AD *GVI* 1943, 11 (m.
Ἀπτυρίς)

**Ζήνων**
ACHAIA:
—AIGEIRA: (1) s. i BC Frazer, *Paus. Descr. of
Greece* 4 p. 177 (Π. Κανείνιος Ζ.)

ARGOLIS:
—ARGOS: (2) ?114 BC *IG* IV (1) 558, 1, 30, [33],
[40] (Stephanis 1028) (s. Ἑκατόδωρος); (3) 105
BC *JÖAI* 14 (1911) Beibl. p. 146 no 4, 2
([Ζ]ήνων)
—EPIDAUROS: (4) i-ii AD *IG* IV (1)² 544 (f. Ζώ-
σιμος); (5) ii AD ib. 729
—HERMIONE: (6) ii-i BC ib. IV (1) 732 II, 23 (s.
Εὔξενος)
ARKADIA:
—TEGEA: (7) ?i BC ib. v (2) 163; (8) ~ ib. 220;
(9) i AD ib. 46, 3 (f. Στρατόνικος); (10) ~ ib. l.
11 (Ζήνων); (11) ~ ib. 47, 6 (Ζήνων)
DALMATIA:
—ISSA:
——(Hylleis): (12) iv/iii BC Brunšmid p. 9, 58
(Ζήνων: s. Ζώπυρος)
EPIROS:
—AMBRAKIA: (13) ii-i BC *CIG* 1797 (s. Νίκαν-
δρος)
ILLYRIA:
—EPIDAMNOS-DYRRHACHION: (14) hell.-imp.
*IDyrrh* 219; (15) ~ ib. 220 (s. Δημήτριος)
KORINTHIA:
—KORINTH: (16) byz. *Corinth* VIII (1) 192; cf.
*TMByz* 9 (1985) p. 360 no. 17
LAKONIA:
—EPIDAUROS LIMERA: (17) m. ii BC *SEG* XIII
259, 1, 25 (f. Ἀγγελῆς, Θεόδωρος)
—GYTHEION: (18) imp. *IG* v (1) 1198 (Ζήν[ων]?:
?f. Σωτη—); (19) f. ii AD ib. 1170, 10 (f. Λύ-
κος)
—SPARTA: (20) s. i BC *SEG* XI 873 b (brick)
(Bradford (-))
S. ITALY (APULIA):
—CANUSIUM*: (21) i AD *Epig. Rom. di Canosa*
121 (*CIL* IX 373) (Lat. P. Dasimius Zeno:
freed.)
S. ITALY (CALABRIA):
—BRENTESION-BRUNDISIUM: (22) imp. *NScav*
1900, p. 153 no. 1 (Lat. L. Boionius Zeno)
—IAPYGES: (23) c. 221 BC *PP* 3936
S. ITALY (CAMPANIA):
—DIKAIARCHIA-PUTEOLI: (24) imp. *CIL* x
2057 (Lat. L. Marius Zeno: f. M. Annius
Fortunatus); (25) ~ ib. 2169 (Lat. Martius
Zenon); (26) ~ *NScav* 1891, p. 340 no. 2 (Lat.
Zeno)
—HERCULANEUM: (27) m. i AD *PdelP* 10 (1955)
p. 467 no. 85 (Lat. C. Caecilius Zenon)
S. ITALY (LUCANIA):
—HERAKLEIA: (28) c. 125-100 BC *ID* 1689;
1854, 3; 2234, 10; 2253, 1; 2254, 1; 2288, 1
(f. Μίδας)
—HYELE-VELIA: (29) v BC *RE* (1); *FVS* 29 (s.
(nat.) Τελευταγόρας, ?s. (ad.) Παρμενίδης); (30)
hell.? *PdelP* 25 (1970) p. 264 no. 7 (s. Ἀπο-
λλωνίδης); (31) c. 100 BC *ID* 1713, 4 (s. Ἕρμων,
?s. Θεοδότη) (Other)
—MARSICI NOVI: (32) imp. *CIL* x 198 (Lat.
Zeno)
SICILY:
—PANORMOS: (33) imp. ib. 7288 (Lat. Zeno)

**Ζηνωνίς**
S. ITALY (CAMPANIA):
—SALERNUM: (1) imp. *IItal* 1 (1) 47 (*CIL* x 572)
(Lat. Cicereia Zenonis: m. Aur. Victor); (2) ~
*IItal* 1 (1) 90 (*CIL* x 644) (Lat. Attia Zenonis:
m. M. Val. Punicus Aemilianus)

**Ζῆραξ**
S. ITALY (CAMPANIA):
—KYME: (1) 251 AD ib. 3699 I, 16 (Lat. M.
Herennius Zerax)

**Ζητουμενός**
S. ITALY (CAMPANIA):
—HERCULANEUM*: (1) i BC-i AD ib. 1403 g II,
22 (Lat. C. Lusius Zetemenus: freed.)

**Ζιλιαν?**
SICILY:
—SELINOUS: (1) s. v BC Dubois, *IGDS* 40, 2
(Ζιλιαν?)

## Ζύβιος

SICILY: (1) iv-iii BC Vandermersch p. 167 (amph.) (or S. Italy: Z(ώ)βιος?)

## Ζύγης

S. ITALY (CAMPANIA):
—DIKAIARCHIA-PUTEOLI*: (1) imp. NScav 1886, p. 457 (Lat. A. Titinius Zyges maior: freed.)

## Ζώαρχος

S. ITALY (CALABRIA): (1) ii/i BC IG XII (3) Suppl. 1299, 23 (Zό-)
SICILY:
—KENTORIPA: (2) f. ii BC Dubois, IGDS 189, [2], 10 (s. Μενίσκος)

## Ζώβιος

KORINTHIA:
—KORINTH: (1) 195 BC Syll³ 585, 26 (f. Λάτροπος)
MESSENIA:
—MESSENE: (2) m. iii BC IC I p. 247 no. 4 A, 29 (s. Εὔβιος)
S. ITALY (LUCANIA):
—HYELE-VELIA: (3) imp. PdelP 21 (1966) p. 341 no. 28

## Ζώγριος

AKARNANIA:
—THYRREION: (1) iii-ii BC SEG XXVII 159, 4; cf. PAE 1977, pl. 244 a (f. Ἀλκίστρατος)

## Ζώη

KORINTHIA:
—KORINTH: (1) byz. Corinth VIII (3) 660 (Zό-); (2) vi-vii AD SEG XXIX 311, 3 (Zό-)
S. ITALY (BRUTTIUM):
—HIPPONION-VIBO VALENTIA: (3) ?i AD CIL X 3485 (Lat. Iulia Zoe: d. Ζωΐλος)
S. ITALY (CAMPANIA):
—POMPEII: (4) c. 51-62 AD ib. IV 3340. 80, 1 (Castrèn 99. 12) (Lat. Caprasi Zoeni (dat.))
S. ITALY (LUCANIA):
—POSEIDONIA-PAESTUM: (5) imp. Mello–Voza 177 (Lat. Nonia Zoe)
—TRICARICO (MOD.): (6) imp. CIL X 128 (Lat. Ven[t]ulania Zoe)
SICILY:
—ACATE (MOD.): (7) iii-v AD Kokalos 7 (1961) pp. 199 ff. (Ferrua, NG 510) (Lat. Zoe)
—SYRACUSE: (8) imp. IG XIV 30; cf. Riv. Arch. Crist. 18 (1941) p. 188; (9) iii-v AD IG XIV 164 (Strazzulla 105; Wessel 873); cf. Ferrua, NG 173 (Zό-)

## Ζωΐλα

EPIROS:
—NIKOPOLIS: (1) imp. Wiss. Mitth. Bosn. 4 (1896) p. 388 no. 6 (Sarikakis 52) (Zo-)
ILLYRIA:
—APOLLONIA: (2) m. i BC IApoll 319 (d. Ζωΐλος); (3) imp. ib. 88; (4) ~ ib. 89; (5) ~ ib. 90 (d. Φίλων); (6) ~ ib. 137 (Ὀππία Z.: d. Φίλων)
—EPIDAMNOS-DYRRHACHION: (7) hell.-imp. IDyrrh 221 (Zo-: d. Ἡρίμναστος); (8) ~ ib. 222 (d. Λεύκιος)
S. ITALY (LUCANIA):
—METAPONTION: (9) hell. IG XIV 2406. 22 (RA 1932 (1), p. 38 no. 15; Landi, DISMG 155 (loomweight)) (or S. Italy (Calabria) Taras-Tarentum)

## Ζωΐλος

AIGINA: (1) i BC IG II² 7955 (f. Θεόφιλος)
AITOLIA:
—KONOPE-ARSINOE: (2) iii BC SEG XXV 625; AD 22 (1967) Chron. p. 320 (tiles)
AKARNANIA:
—OINIADAI: (3) ?iv-iii BC IG IX (1)² (2) 426. 6 (tile)

ARGOLIS:
—ARGOS?: (4) ii/i BC ib. XII (5) 925 (sculptor)
—EPIDAUROS: (5) i-ii AD ib. IV (1)² 552 (s. Μενεκράτης)
——(Hysminatai): (6) 146 BC ib. 28, 23 (f. Μηνόφιλος)
—HERMIONE: (7) iii BC HE 1910
DALMATIA:
—ISSA: (8) hell. Brunšmid p. 30 no. 25 (f. Παρμονίσκος); (9) ~ ib. (s. Ἡροδ—); (10) iii BC SEG XXXV 691, 7 (VAHD 84 (1991) p. 256 no. 6) (f. Ξενώ); (11) ~ VAMZ 1970, p. 36 fr. K; (12) ii BC SEG XXXI 600 (Zo-: s. Ζώπυρος); (13) f. ii BC Brunšmid p. 23 no. 10, 3 (s. Κλεύδικος)
——(Dymanes): (14) iv/iii BC ib. p. 7, 22 (f. Φαναῖος); (15) ~ ib. l. 22 (s. Φαναῖος); (16) ~ ib. p. 8, 29 ([Ζω]ΐλος: s. Φαναῖος); (17) ~ ib. p. 9, 56 (s. Σώπατρος)
——(Hylleis): (18) iv/iii BC ib. p. 8, 45 ([Z]ωΐλος: s. Πρωτέας); (19) ~ ib. l. 46 (f. Φιλικός); (20) ~ ib. p. 9, 61 (s. Διων—)
ELIS: (21) 36-24 BC IvOl 62, 9 (I f. Ζωΐλος II); (22) ~ ib. l. 9 (II s. Ζωΐλος I: Γ.); (23) 67 AD ib. 82, 15; (24) 85 AD EA 1905, p. 255 no. 1, 9 (s. Λέων); (25) 245-249 AD IvOl 121, 9 (f. Αὐρ. Ἀβάσκαντος)
EPIROS:
—AKRALESTOI: (26) iii/ii BC Cabanes, L'Épire p. 561 no. 35, 7
—AMBRAKIA: (27) ii-i BC BCH 79 (1955) p. 267; (28) a. 167 BC SEG XXXV 665 A, 11 (f. Λυσίων)
—BOUTHROTOS (PRASAIBOI): (29) a. 163 BC IBouthrot 33, 9 (SEG XXXVIII 492) ?= (32); (30) ~ IBouthrot 48, 14
——Bouthrotioi: (31) ii-ii BC ib. 57 (SEG XXXVIII 508); (32) a. 163 BC IBouthrot 92, 6; 100, 8; 133, 3 (s. Ἀγήσανδρος) ?= (29)
ILLYRIA:
—APOLLONIA: (33) c. 250-50 BC NZ 20 (1927) p. 54; Bakërr Hoard p. 64 nos. 54-8 (coin) (Ceka 53-5) (money.); (34) ~ Maier 41 (coin) (Ceka 38) (pryt.); (35) i BC Maier 138 (coin) (money.); (36) ~ ib. 148 (coin) (pryt.); (37) m. i BC IApoll 319 (f. Ζωΐλα); (38) imp. ib. 91; (39) ~ ib. 253 (Zo-)
——(Ip.): (40) iii/ii BC ib. 7; cf. L'Illyrie mérid. 2 p. 207 (s. Δίων)
—BYLLIONES NIKAIA (KLJOS (MOD.)): (41) hell. Iliria 1982 (1), p. 112 no. 54 = p. 120 no. 26 (tile)
—EPIDAMNOS-DYRRHACHION: (42) c. 250-50 BC Maier 217; Münsterberg p. 260; Nachtr. p. 15 (coin) (Ceka 199-200) (money.); (43) hell.-imp. IDyrrh 223; (44) ~ ib. 224 (s. Εὔτυχος)
—OLYMPE: (45) s. iii BC SEG XXXV 697 (s. Ἀντάνωρ)
ITHAKE: (46) hell.? IG IX (1) 680 (Σω-)
KEPHALLENIA:
—KRANIOI?: (47) c. 230 BC ib. X (2) (1) *1, 4; cf. Robert, OMS 5 pp. 281 f. (locn.)
KERKYRA: (48) i BC IG IX (1) 709
KORINTHIA:
—KORINTH: (49) iii-ii BC ib. IV (1) 366 (?s. Φιλ—)
—SIKYON: (50) c. 146-32 BC NC 1984, p. 15 Group 10 no. 6 (coin)
LAKONIA:
—SPARTA: (51) f. iii AD SEG XLII 323 (Ζωΐ[λ]ος); (52) c. 212-220 AD IG V (1) 653 a, 3 (Artemis Orthia p. 356 no. 142; Bradford (-)) (f. Μ. Αὐρ. Εὐάρεστος)
MESSENIA:
—MESSENE: (53) iii BC SEG XXIII 209, 12
S. ITALY (APULIA):
—AZETIUM: (54) c. 100 BC ID 1713, 9-10 (f. Εἰρηναῖος)

S. ITALY (APULIA)*: (55) i BC Desy, Timbres amphoriques 1065; 1092; 1128 (amph.) (Ζωΐλο(ς): slave/potter?) ?= (85)
S. ITALY (BRUTTIUM):
—HIPPONION-VIBO VALENTIA: (56) ?i AD CIL X 3485 (Lat. C. Iulius Zoilus: f. Iulius Silius, Ζώη)
—LOKROI EPIZEPHYRIOI:
——(Ἀγκ.): (57) iv/iii BC De Franciscis 3, 4 (f. Ὀναῖος); (58) ~ ib. 27, 3 (f. Φίλυκος)
——(Δυσ.): (59) iv/iii BC ib. 6, 5; 11, 3 (s. Σώσιππος)
——(Κυλ.): (60) iv/iii BC ib. 12, 3 (f. Ξενάρης)
——(Λακ.): (61) iv/iii BC ib. 15, 2 (s. Θέων)
——(Προ.): (62) iv/iii BC ib. 17, 3 (f. Ἐχέδαμος)
——(Τυν.): (63) iv/iii BC ib. 10, 5; (64) ~ ib. 19, 2 (f. Ὀναῖος)
——(Ψαθ.): (65) iv/iii BC ib. 11, 6; 18, 4 (s. Ὀνάσιμος) ?= (67); (66) ~ ib. 39, 4 (f. Εὔθυμος) ?= (67); (67) 276 BC ib. 23, 1 (f. Δωρίμαχος) ?= (66) (65)
S. ITALY (CAMPANIA):
—DIKAIARCHIA-PUTEOLI: (68) imp. CIL X 2651 (Lat. Granius Zoilus: s. Ἀτίμητος, Μένουσα); (69) iii AD Culte des divinités orientales en Campanie pp. 180-1 (Lat. Plutius Zoillus)
—KYME: (70) hell.? IG XIV 860 (Zo-?: s. Ἀγάθων)
—NEAPOLIS: (71) hell. ib. 725 (INap 13) (I f. Ζωΐλος II) ?= (73); (72) ~ IG XIV 725 (INap 13) (II s. Ζωΐλος I) ?= (74); (73) ii-i BC IG XIV 724 (INap 12) (I f. Ζωΐλος II, Ἐμαυτός) ?= (71); (74) ~ IG XIV 724 (INap 12) (II s. Ζωΐλος I) ?= (72); (75) i BC-i AD IG XIV 762 (INap 90); cf. Leiwo p. 117 no. 98 (f. Αἴγλη); (76) i BC/i AD INap 173, 3; cf. Leiwo p. 60 no. 1 ([Z]ωΐλος: f. Τρέβιος); (77) ~ INap 173, 5; cf. Leiwo p. 60 no. 1
—POMPEII: (78) i BC-i AD CIL IV 4469 (Castrèn 129. 43) (Lat. P. Cornelius Zoilus)
S. ITALY (LUCANIA):
—HYELE-VELIA: (79) iv/iii BC IG XIV 659; cf. SEG XXIX 1024 (date) (Ζωΐλ[ος]?: f. Νίκα); (80) c. 50 BC IG VII 1765, 9; cf. BSA 70 (1975) pp. 132-3 (date) (s. Ἀλέξανδρος); (81) imp.? IG XIV 2403. 12 (tile); (82) imp. PdelP 21 (1966) p. 336 no. 7 (f. Δεινίας); (83) ~ ib. p. 336 no. 11 (s. Πόσις)
—METAPONTION: (84) m. iii BC SEG XXX 1175, 17 (doctor)
S. ITALY?: (85) i BC Desy, Timbres amphoriques 1251; 1254; 1267 (amph.) (Ζωΐλο(ς): slave/potter?) ?= (55)
SICILY:
—GELA-PHINTIAS: (86) ?277 BC FD III (1) 125, 3 (f. Τιμαγόρας, Εὔδοξος)
—HALOUNTION: (87) iii/ii BC Arch. Class. 17 (1965) p. 202 a; cf. SEG XXVI 1060 (s. Θέστων); (88) ~ Arch. Class. 17 (1965) p. 202 b; cf. SEG XXVI 1060
—HELOROS: (89) ii-i BC Dubois, IGDS 100, 3 (s. Νύμφων)
—KAMARINA: (90) f. v BC Cordano, Tessere Pubbliche 65 (Arena, Iscr. Sic. II 139 A) (Ζō-: s. Πολέμαρχος); (91) hell. SEG XXXIX 1001, 6 (f. Ἀρίστων); (92) ~ ib. l. 9 (f. —ων)
—KATANE: (93) imp. IG XIV 501 (Σαβούκις Z.)
—KEPHALOIDION: (94) ?iii-v AD SEG XXXVI 846 (Ζωΐλος]: f. Γόργος)
—LIPARA*: (95) i-ii AD Kokalos 32 (1986) p. 225 nos. 28-31 (tiles) (Ζωΐ(λος))
—SYRACUSE: (96) c. 60 BC IG VII 420, 28 (IOrop 528); cf. Stephanis 1035 (I f. Ζωΐλος II); (97) ~ IG VII 420, 28 (IOrop 528; Stephanis 1035) (II s. Ζωΐλος I); (98) iii AD CIL X 7120 (Lat. C. Marcius Zoilus); (99) iii-v AD IG XIV 108 (Strazzulla 46; Wessel 845) (Ζωΐλος)
—TAUROMENION: (100) c. 227 BC IG XIV 421 an. 14 (SGDI 5219) (s. Μένανδρος); (101) c. 170-146 BC IG XIV 421 an. 71; 421 an. 85; 421 an. 95 (SGDI 5219); IGSI 4 II (III),

[48] an. 75 (s. Θάρριππος); (102) c. 167 BC IG XIV 421 an. 74 (SGDI 5219); (103) c. 154 BC IG XIV 421 an. 87 (SGDI 5219); IGSI 4 III (IV), 10 an. 87 (s. Ἰστίαρχος); (104) c. 40 BC Cron. Arch. 3 (1964) p. 54 I, 23; (105) ~ ib. l. 27 (f. Ζώπυρος)
——(Καλ.): (106) ?ii/i BC IG XIV 421 D an. 2; 421 D an. 14 (SGDI 5219) (s. Θάρριππος)

**Ζώιππος**
LAKONIA:
—TAINARON-KAINEPOLIS: (1) ii-iii AD IG V (1) 1249, 1 (GVI 2028) ([Z]ώϊπος: ?f. Κλεῖνος)
S. ITALY (BRUTTIUM):
—LOKROI EPIZEPHYRIOI:
——(Ἀνξ.): (2) iv/iii BC De Franciscis 15, 4 (f. Εὔφρων)
——(Μνα.): (3) iv/iii BC ib. l. 4 (f. Ὀναῖος)
——(Σκι.): (4) iv/iii BC ib. 33, 3 (f. Σωσῖνος); (5) 280 BC ib. 35, 2 (s. Ἀριστώνυμος)
——(Σωτ.): (6) iv/iii BC ib. 2, 5 (f. Φορμίων)
SICILY:
—LIPARA: (7) ?m. iv BC SEG XLI 813
—SYRACUSE: (8) 215 BC RE (-) (PP 14823)

**Ζωῖτα**
SICILY:
—SELINOUS: (1) m. v BC Dubois, IGDS 36, 5 (Arena, Iscr. Sic. I 69) (Ζōῖτα—Arena, Ζοξ̄τα—Dubois)

**Ζωναρίων**
S. ITALY (CAMPANIA):
—POMPEII: (1) i BC-i AD CIL IV 8343 (Zonasíων—lap.)

**Ζωπύρα**
ARGOLIS:
—HERMIONE: (1) ii-i BC IG IV (1) 732 II, 26 ([Z]ωπύρα: d. Καλλιστράτα); (2) ~ ib. 732 III, 19 (d. Νικαρέτα)
ILLYRIA: (3) 171 BC SGDI 1810, 5, 8 (slave/freed.)
KORINTHIA:
—KORINTH: (4) ii BC IG II² 9068 (d. Ἀλκίμαχος)
LAKONIA: (5) s. i BC ib. 9149 (d. Νικοκλῆς)
S. ITALY (CALABRIA):
—TARAS-TARENTUM: (6) m. iv BC SEG XXXI 879. 5-6; (7) iv/iii BC IG XIV 668 I, 13 (Landi, DISMG 194) + SEG XXX 1223 (Z. Μαχαν[.]ο)
S. ITALY (CAMPANIA):
—NEAPOLIS*: (8) i BC/i AD NScav 1926, p. 235; cf. Leiwo p. 97 no. 46 (Lat. Fuficia Zopyra: freed.)

**Ζωπυρῖνα**
ARGOLIS:
—HERMIONE: (1) i BC-i AD? IG IV (1) 730 IV, 2 (Ζωπυρῖνα: d. Δαμοκλέα)

**Ζωπυρίς**
ARGOLIS:
—ARGOS*: (1) 105 BC JÖAI 14 (1911) Beibl. p. 146 no. 4, 27 (slave/freed.?)
KORINTHIA:
—TENEA: (2) i AD IG II² 10437 (d. Σωσίβιος)

**Ζωπυρίσκα**
SICILY:
—SYRACUSE: (1) hell. SEG XXXII 923 + XLII 858 (d. Ἡρακλείδας)

**Ζωπυρίσκος**
S. ITALY (LUCANIA):
—HERAKLEIA: (1) iv/iii BC ib. XXX 1153-6
——(Fε. τρίπους): (2) iv/iii BC IGSI 1 I, 3, 9, 96 (DGE 62; Uguzzoni–Ghinatti I); IGSI 1 II, 3, 7 (DGE 63; Uguzzoni–Ghinatti II) (f. Φιλώνυμος)

SICILY:
—TAUROMENION: (3) c. 219 BC IG XIV 421 an. 22 (SGDI 5219) (s. Εὔθυμος); (4) c. 201 BC IG XIV 421 an. 40 (SGDI 5219) (s. Νίκων)

**Ζωπυρίων**
AITOLIA:
—APERANTOI: (1) i BC-i AD SEG XVII 275, 5 (L'Illyrie mérid. 1 p. 110 fig. 8)
ARGOLIS:
—HERMIONE: (2) ?ii-i BC IG IV (1) 731 I, 12 (s. Εὔκλείδας); (3) ii-i BC ib. 732 I, 9 (s. Κλεοπάτρα); (4) ~ ib. 732 III, 8 (s. Δάμων)
—TROIZEN: (5) iii BC ib. 774, 3 (s. Παντακλῆς)
ARKADIA:
—TEGEA: (6) i BC ib. V (2) 45, 9; (7) i AD ib. 47, 2
EPIROS?: (8) 226-225 BC PPetr² 1 Wills 26, 6 (f. Νικάνωρ)
LAKONIA: (9) iv/iii BC IG V (1) 1348; (10) 194 BC SGDI 2075, 3 (slave/freed.)
S. ITALY: (11) iii BC Epig. Rom. di Canosa Instr. 55-7 (vases) (potter)
S. ITALY (CALABRIA):
—TARAS-TARENTUM: (12) c. 235-228 BC Vlasto 940-1 (coins) (Evans, Horsemen p. 194 IX B.1)
SICILY:
—SYRACUSE: (13) c. 272 BC Theoc., Id. xv 13 (s. Δείνων, Πραξινόα: fict.)

**Ζώπυρος**
ACHAIA: (1) 146 BC IG IV (1)² 28, 85 (s. Φίλιππος: synoikos); (2) ~ ib. l. 104 (s. Νούϊος: synoikos); (3) ~ ib. l. 123 (s. Σωτηρίων: synoikos)
AIGINA?: (4) imp. EAD XXX p. 357 no. 26 (f. Ἀφροδώ)
AKARNANIA:
—THYRREION: (5) iii BC IG IX (1)² (2) 596, 8 ([Z]ώπυ[ρος]); (6) ii/i BC ib. 341
ARGOLIS:
—ARGOS: (7) 105 BC JÖAI 14 (1911) Beibl. p. 146 no. 4, 24 (s. Οἰώνιχος); (8) ii/iii AD IG IV (1) 594 (f. Σπένδων)
—EPIDAUROS*: (9) c. 335-325 BC ib. IV (1)² 108, 120, 144 ?= (10); (10) ~ SEG XXV 390, [117] ?= (9); (11) c. 290-270 BC IG IV (1)² 109 III, 153
—HERMIONE: (12) ii-i BC IG IV (1) 732 II, 5; (13) ~ ib. 732 III, 14, 16 (s. Ἀγαπάτις)
—PHLEIOUS: (14) ii-i BC ib. 461 (s. Ἀριστόβουλος)
—TROIZEN: (15) iii BC ib. 774, 9
ARKADIA:
—STYMPHALOS: (16) ?262 or 258 BC Nachtergael, Les Galates 5, 44; cf. Stephanis 2697 (f. —ιμος)
—TEGEA: (17) 165 AD IG V (2) 50, 47 (s. Ἕλενος); (18) ~ ib. l. 62 (f. Θάλλος)
DALMATIA:
—ISSA: (19) iv/iii BC SEG XXXV 685 (s. Ὀλτίων); (20) iii BC Brunšmid p. 9 fr. G, 7 + VAMZ 1970, p. 37 frr. G and M (s. Διονύσιος); (21) ii BC SEG XXXI 600 (f. Ζωῖλος); (22) 56 BC Sherk 24 A, 5
——(Hylleis): (23) iv/iii BC Brunšmid p. 9, 58 (f. Ζήνων)
—ISSA?: (24) iii/ii BC CIG 6913; SEG XL 512 (locn.) (f. Ματερίσκα)
ELIS: (25) 28-24 BC IvOl 64, 23 (s. Ὀλύμπιχος); (26) 245-249 AD ib. 121, 10 (I f. Αὐρ. Ζώπυρος II); (27) ~ ib. l. 10 (Αὐρ. Ζ.: II s. Ζώπυρος I)
EPIROS:
—AMBRAKIA: (28) hell. SEG XXXIX 524 (tile)
—BOUTHROTOS (PRASAIBOI): (29) a. 163 BC IBouthrot 13, 15; cf. Ugolini, Alb. Ant. 3 p. 120 (Ζώπυ[ρος]: I f. Ζώπυρος II); (30) ~ IBouthrot 13, 15; cf. Ugolini, Alb. Ant. 3 p. 120 ([Z]ώπυρος: II s. Ζώπυρος I); (31) ~ IBouthrot 50, 3; (32) ~ ib. 89, 9 ?= (33); (33)

~ ib. l. 9 ?= (32); (34) ~ ib. 128, 8 (f. Παυσανίας)
—PRASAIBOI: (35) a. 163 BC ib. 78, [12]; 79, [11]; 80, 10; 81, 10; 82, 9; 83, 9; 84, 10; 85, 10; 86, [11]; 87, 10; 88, 8 (BCH 118 (1994) pp. 122 f. nos. 1-11); IBouthrot 92, 7; 103, 8; 153, 7 (f. Θεμίσων)
ILLYRIA:
—APOLLONIA: (36) hell.? IApoll 354 (tile); (37) iii-ii BC ib. 33; (38) c. 250-50 BC Münsterberg Nachtr. p. 13; Maier 42 (coin) (Ceka 117; 82) (pryt.); (39) ~ Münsterberg Nachtr. p. 13 (coin) (Ceka 56) (money.); (40) ii-i BC IApoll 98 (f. Ἱέρων); (41) i BC Maier 130 (coin) (s. Δείνων: money.); (42) ~ ib. 161 (coin) (f. Φίλων: pryt.); (43) imp. IApoll 25 ([Ζώπ]υρος: f. Ἀνθρωπία); (44) ~ ib. 92; (45) ~ ib. 93 (f. —ος); (46) ~ ib. 329
—EPIDAMNOS-DYRRHACHION: (47) c. 250-50 BC Ceka, Probleme p. 151 no. 25 (coin) (pryt.); (48) ~ Maier 175; 261; 350 (coin) (Ceka 201-3) (money.); (49) ~ Maier 215; 217-9; 221 (coin) (Ceka 196; 199; 300; 306; 451) (pryt.); (50) ii-i BC IDyrrh 538 (tile); (51) hell.-imp. ib. 225 (s. Ἱέρων); (52) ~ ib. 227 (s. Ἐπίκτησις); (53) ~ ib. 228 (s. Κέρδων); (54) ~ ib. 330 (f. Νικηφόρος); (55) imp. ib. 226; (56) ~ ib. 229 (Ζώπυρ[ος]: s. Πλάτωρ); (57) ~ ib. 230 (Z. Φαινίας—lap.: ?s. Φαινίας)
KORINTHIA:
—KORINTH: (58) m. iii BC Corinth VIII (3) 33 d, 5 (Ζώπυ[ρος]: f. Διονύσιος)
LAKONIA:
—SPARTA: (59) s. iv BC SEG XI 668 (vase); BSA 30 (1928-30) p. 249 fig. 4, 8 (Poralla² 251a) (Δώπυρ[ος])
MESSENIA:
—KORONE: (60) 246 AD IG V (1) 1398, 45 (Κλ. Z.); (61) ~ ib. l. 74 (Ὀπ(πιος) Z.)
—MESSENE: (62) i BC-i AD SEG XXIII 218 (f. Δαματρία); (63) 31 BC-14 AD ib. 207, 33 (f. Μηνᾶς, Λεύκιος Σάλβιος)
S. ITALY (BRUTTIUM):
—RHEGION: (64) 190 BC Syll³ 585, 82 (f. Ὀρθων); (65) m. ii BC Nachtergael, Les Galates 70, 4, 8; cf. Stephanis 55 (f. Ἀθανάδας)
S. ITALY (CALABRIA):
—TARAS-TARENTUM: (66) iv BC Iamb., VP 267 (FVS 1 p. 446); (67) ~ BCH 70 (1946) p. 38 a; (68) iv/iii BC IG XIV 668 II, 14 (Landi, DISMG 194); (69) c. 315-280 BC FD III (1) 109, 2 (s. Λυκίσκος); (70) c. 280-272 BC Vlasto 769-72; 809-13 (coins) (Evans, Horsemen p. 159 VII C.8; p. 161 VII H-K) (Ζώπυ(ρος)); (71) c. 272-235 BC Vlasto 855-6 (coins) (Evans, Horsemen p. 176 VIII A.2-3; p. 178 VIII B.2)
S. ITALY (LUCANIA):
—HERAKLEIA:
——(Με. ἐπιστύλιον): (72) iv/iii BC IGSI 1 I, 7, 10, 98 (DGE 62; Uguzzoni–Ghinatti I) (f. Ἡρακλείδας)
SICILY: (73) hell. SEG XXXIII 455 (s. Ἄνταλλος)
—AKRAI: (74) hell. Akrai p. 75 no. 1 = p. 162 no. 22. 14; (75) i BC ib. p. 156 no. 6, 3 (f. Διονυσόδωρος); (76) ~ ib. l. 21 (f. Ἀριστομένης); (77) ii-i BC SGDI 3246, 11 (Akrai pp. 152-3 no. 2; Dubois, IGDS 109) (s. Ἀρτεμίδωρος); (78) ~ SGDI 3246, 44 (Akrai pp. 152-3 no. 2; Dubois, IGDS 109) (s. Ἐπίξενος); (79) ?i BC IG XIV 222 (Akrai p. 164 no. 27) (s. Εὔμαχος); (80) hell.-imp. Manganaro, QUCC forthcoming no. 15 (f. Μέλισσα)
—GELA-PHINTIAS: (81) f. ii BC IG XIV 256, 10, 20, 32 (Dubois, IGDS 161); cf. SEG XL 804 (f. Ἡρακλείδας)
——(Χαρ.): (82) f. ii BC IG XIV 256, 47 (Dubois, IGDS 161); cf. SEG XL 804 (s. Ἡρακλείδας)
—IAITON: (83) iii-ii BC ib. XXVI 1070. 8 (tiles)
—KAMARINA: (84) ?iv/iii BC ib. XXXIV 940, 8 (Dubois, IGDS 124; PdelP 44 (1989) p. 192

no. 3; Cordano, 'Camarina VII' 107) (f. Σάν-
νων)
—KATANE: (85) c. 80 BC IG VII 416, 40 (IOrop
523) (s. Ἑρμογένης)
—LIPARA: (86) iv-iii BC NScav 1947, p. 220 fig.
1
—SYRACUSE: (87) 476 BC Moretti, Olymp. 219
([Ζώπ]υρος); (88) 244 BC SEG XXXII 118 I,
59; (89) 220 BC Moretti, Olymp. 579
—(Ἑρμεῖος): (90) iv BC Manganaro, PdelP
forthcoming no. 3, 6 (f. Λυκῖνος)
—SYRACUSE?:
——(Ὑπα.): (91) hell. ib. no. 4 IV, 7 (s. Κλείδα-
μος)
——(Λαβ.): (92) hell. ib. no. 4 II, 10 (s. Δίων)
——(Λογ.): (93) hell. ib. no. 4 I, 9 (s. Δαμοκρά-
της)
——(Πλη.): (94) hell. ib. no. 4 IV, 6 (s. Δίων)
—TAUROMENION: (95) c. 222 BC IG XIV 421 an.
19 (SGDI 5219) (s. Ὄλυμπις); (96) c. 181 BC
IG XIV 421 an. 60 (SGDI 5219) ?= (97); (97)
c. 180 BC IG XIV 421 an. 61 (SGDI 5219) ?=
(96); (98) c. 174 BC IG XIV 421 an. 67 (SGDI
5219) (s. Φιλιστίων); (99) c. 165 BC IG XIV 421
an. 76 (SGDI 5219) (s. Στροῦθος); (100) c. 151
BC IG XIV 421 an. 90 (SGDI 5219); IGSI 4
III (IV), 33 an. 90 (s. Χαιρέδαμος); (101) c.
146 BC ib. l. 71 an. 95 (f. Ἀριστοκράτης); (102)
c. 40 BC Cron. Arch. 3 (1964) p. 54 I, 27 (s.
Ζωΐλος)
——(Δεξ.): (103) ?ii/i BC IG XIV 421 D an. 14
(SGDI 5219) (f. Ἀρίσταρχος)
——(Καλ.): (104) ?ii/i BC IG XIV 421 D an. 3;
421 D an. 9 (SGDI 5219) (s. Ἀρτεμίδωρος)
—THERMAI HIMERAIAI: (105) ?i BC IG XIV 340
(Ζ. Ὠκιδίας: s. Ἀρτέμων, ?f. Φαινώ)
—ZANKLE-MESSANA: (106) ?ii BC ib. 401, 12
(Ξούπυρος (apogr.): s. Ναυκράτης)

## Ζωπυρώ
SICILY:
—CALTANISSETA (MOD.): (1) s. iv BC Guarducci, Ep. Gr. 3 p. 482 (vase) (Dubois, IGDS
170) (Ζωπυροῖ (dat.))

## Ζωσάρα?
S. ITALY (CALABRIA):
—BRENTESION-BRUNDISIUM*: (1) imp. CIL IX
149 (Lat. Valeria Zosara: freed.)

## Ζωσᾶς
LAKONIA:
—SPARTA: (1) c. 140 AD IG V (1) 65, 29 (Brad-
ford (-)) (s. Ἀρίων)

## Ζωσίμα
ILLYRIA:
—EPIDAMNOS-DYRRHACHION: (1) hell.-imp.
IDyrrh 231 (d. Νίκων); (2) ~ ib. 232 (d. Κλευ-
μήδης)
SICILY:
—KATANE: (3) iii-v AD Oikoumene p. 606 no. 5
—LIPARA: (4) imp.? Libertini, Isole Eolie p. 223
no. 34
—ZANKLE-MESSANA: (5) imp. IG XIV 407

## Ζωσιμᾶς
ARKADIA:
—TEGEA: (1) ii AD ib. v (2) 55, 64 (s. Ἐπικτᾶς)
ELIS: (2) b. 165 AD IvOl 99, 18 ?= (Ζώσιμος
(22))
KORINTHIA:
—KORINTH: (3) ii AD Corinth IV (2) pp. 190 no.
577; 204 no. 694; Lampes antiques BN 1 25;
SEG XLII 268 A (lamps)
LAKONIA:
—SPARTA: (4) c. 230-260 AD ib. XI 633, 7 (Brad-
ford (-)) (f. Πασικλῆς)
MESSENIA:
—KORONE: (5) 246 AD IG V (1) 1398, 69 (Αὐρ.
Ζ.)

SICILY:
—SYRACUSE: (6) iii-v AD Rend. Pont. 22 (1946-
7) p. 236 sub 41 (Wessel 659); cf. Ferrua, NG
87 (Αὐφίδιος Z.)

## Ζωσίμη
AIGINA: (1) imp. IG IV (1) 135 (Ζωσι Μνη—IG,
Ζωσίμ<ν>η—LGPN)
ARGOLIS:
—ARGOS: (2) imp. SEG XI 349 ([Ζ]ωσίμη)
ARKADIA:
—TEGEA: (3) imp. IG V (2) 221
ELIS:
—KEPIDES: (4) iii AD CIG 9294 b, 1 (A(ὐ)ρ. Z.:
d. Ἄβρος)
ILLYRIA:
—APOLLONIA: (5) ii-iii AD IApoll 228
([Z]ωσίμη)
—BYLLIONES: (6) imp. SEG XXIV 477 (XXXVIII
552)
KERKYRA: (7) ii-iii AD IG IX (1) 950
KORINTHIA:
—KORINTH: (8) ii-iii AD SEG XI 138 e, 2
S. ITALY (APULIA):
—BARION: (9) i-ii AD Suppl. It. 8 p. 36 no. 4
(CIL IX 283; Mus. Arch. di Bari p. 160 no.
11) (Lat. Petronia Zosima)
—CANUSIUM: (10) imp. Epig. Rom. di Canosa 93
(CIL IX 362) (Lat. Verronia Zosim[a]); (11) ~
Epig. Rom. di Canosa Add. 38 (Lat. Zosima)
—CANUSIUM*: (12) imp. ib. 125 (CIL IX 6189)
(Lat. Decimia Zosima: freed.); (13) ~ Epig.
Rom. di Canosa 153 (CIL IX 388) (Lat. Li-
cinia Sosima: freed.); (14) ii AD Epig. Rom. di
Canosa Add. 21 (Lat. Etria Zosima: freed.)
—VENUSIA*: (15) imp. CIL IX 527 (Lat. Her-
minia Zosima: freed.)
S. ITALY (BRUTTIUM):
—INTERAMNIUM*: (16) inc. NScav 1926, p.
332 + Puteoli 11 (1987) p. 139 no. 6 (Lat.
Zosima: freed.)
—LOKROI EPIZEPHYRIOI*: (17) i AD Suppl. It.
3 p. 31 no. 16 (Lat. Tullia Zosima: freed.)
—SYBARIS-THOURIOI-COPIAE*: (18) imp.
NScav 1925, p. 323 (Lat. Zosima: freed.)
S. ITALY (CALABRIA):
—BRENTESION-BRUNDISIUM: (19) imp. CIL IX
140 (Lat. Mamia Zozima); (20) ~ ib. 6137
(Lat. Tituria Zosima); (21) ~ NScav 1891,
p. 173 = Epigraphica 25 (1963) p. 65 no. 59;
cf. Scritti Degrassi 3 p. 70 (Lat. Zosima); (22)
i AD NScav 1892, p. 243 = Epigraphica 25
(1963) p. 72 no. 71; cf. Scritti Degrassi 3 p. 70
(Lat. Seia Zosima); (23) ?i-ii AD Epigraphica
25 (1963) p. 73 no. 72; cf. Scritti Degrassi 3
p. 70 (Lat. Iulia Zosima: d. L. Iulius Bales,
Θρέπτη); (24) s. i AD Necropoli via Cappuccini
p. 258 no. E1; Atti Conv. Taranto 23 (1983)
p. 438 (Lat. Iulia Zosima); (25) ?ii AD CIL IX
6121 = Epigraphica 25 (1963) p. 47 no. 30 +
p. 84 no. 95 (Lat. Flavia Zosime)
—TARAS-TARENTUM: (26) inc. NScav 1883, p.
298 (Lat. Sosime); (27) imp. CIL IX 6398 a
(Lat. Zosime)
—VALETIUM: (28) f. i AD Studi di Antichità 5
pp. 222-3 (Lat. [M]agia Zosi[m]a)
S. ITALY (CAMPANIA):
—DIKAIARCHIA-PUTEOLI: (29) imp. CIL X
1912; cf. Puteoli 11 (1987) p. 45 (name) (Lat.
Haia Zosime); (30) ~ CIL X 2400 (Lat. –teia
Zosime); (31) ~ ib. 2480 (Lat. Iunia Zosime); (32) ~
ib. 2630 (Lat. Iunia Zosime); (33) ~ ib. 2683
(Lat. Lysia Zosime. d. Lysius Crescens, Cu-
tia Incenua); (34) ~ ib. 3152 (Lat. Zosi[me]);
(35) ~ ib. 3153 (Lat. Zosime); (36) ~ ib. 3154
(Lat. Zosime); (37) ?i-ii AD ib. 2295 (Lat.
Claudia Zosima: m. Ὀνησίμη)
—DIKAIARCHIA-PUTEOLI*: (38) imp. ib. 2234
(Lat. Zosima: freed.); (39) ~ ib. 2925 (Lat.
Sallie[na] [Z]osima: freed.); (40) ?i-ii AD ib.
2616 (Lat. Iulia Zosima: freed.)

SICILY:
—MISENUM: (41) imp. ib. 8209 (Lat. Cl.
Zosime)
—MISENUM*: (42) imp. ib. 3396 (Lat. Arria
Zosime: freed.); (43) ~ NScav 1928, p. 198
no. 12 (Lat. Zosime)
—NEAPOLIS: (44) imp. IG XIV 814 (INap 176);
cf. Leiwo p. 108 no. 75 (Φαβία Z.)
—POMPEII: (45) i BC-i AD CIL IV 10072 b;
Gnomon 45 (1973) p. 262 (Lat. Iosime)
—SALERNUM: (46) imp. IItal I (1) 50 (Lat.
Claudia Zosime: m. Εὐτυχία); (47) ~ ib. 80
(Lat. Pom(peia) Zosime: m. Iucundus); (48)
?i-ii AD ib. 152 (CIL X 574) (Lat. Memmia
Zosime)
—SUESSULA: (49) imp. ib. 3770 (Lat. Severia
Zosime)
S. ITALY (LUCANIA):
—ATINA LUCANA: (50) imp. IItal III (1) 185
(CIL X 350) (Lat. Fabia Zosime)
SICILY:
—KATANE: (51) imp. ib. 7016 (Lat. Annia
Zosima); (52) iii-v AD IG XIV 529 (Wessel
856); (53) 345 AD Agnello 88 (Lat. Zosime)
—SYRACUSE: (54) iii-v AD ASSiracusano 1956,
p. 63; (55) ~ Riv. Arch. Crist. 36 (1960) p. 29
no. 25; (56) ~ Rend. Pont. 22 (1946-7) p. 236
no. 38; cf. Nuovo Didask. 6 (1956) p. 53 no.
2; (57) ~ Strazzulla 257 (Wessel 153); (58) ~
Strazzulla 381 + Nuovo Didask. 6 (1956) p.
63 no. 29 (Wessel 994)
—THERMAI HIMERAIAI*: (59) imp. CIL X
7426 (ILat. Term. Imer. 124) (Lat. Munatia
Zosime: m. Νικάριον: freed.)
—ZANKLE-MESSANA: (60) imp. CIL X 6979
(Lat. Nonia Zosima)

## Ζωσιμιανίδης
SICILY:
—KATANE: (1) imp. IG XIV 502 (ASSicilia-
Orientale 1958-9, pp. 15 ff.); cf. MEFRA 106
(1994) p. 97 no. 11 (Ζωσυμιανείδης Σεβῆρος)

## Ζωσιμιανός
KORINTHIA:
—KORINTH: (1) ii-iii AD Corinth VIII (3) 369, 2
(Ζωσιμια[νός])
SICILY:
—KATANE?: (2) iv-v AD CIJ I 654 (IGLMP 10)
(Jew)

## Ζωσιμίων
S. ITALY (CAMPANIA):
—POMPEII: (1) 70-79 AD CIL IV 229; cf. p. 696;
Mouritsen p. 109 (date) (Lat. Zosimio)
SICILY:
—MELITA: (2) imp. IG XIV 603 (Wessel 868)
(Ζωσιμήτινος?—IG, Ζωσιμή(ω)νος (gen.)—
Wessel)
—SYRACUSE: (3) iii-v AD Ferrua, NG 334

## Ζώσιμος
AIGINA: (1) ii-iii AD AE 1913, p. 95 no. 6 β (f.
Ὠρότυχος)
AITOLIA:
—KALLION/KALLIPOLIS: (2) byz. BCH 98
(1974) p. 635 ([Ζ]ώσιμος)
ARGOLIS:
—ARGOS: (3) c. 160 AD SEG III 334, 27
(Stephanis 1046) ([Ζώ]σιμος: s. Τρύφων)
—EPIDAUROS: (4) i-ii AD IG IV (1)² 544 (s. Ζή-
νων); (5) iii-iv AD ib. 587 (f. Διονύσιος)
ARKADIA:
—KLEITOR: (6) a. 212 AD ib. v (2) 369, 12; SEG
XXXI 347, 4 (s. Κόρινθος)
—TEGEA: (7) ii AD IG V (2) 55, 29 (s. Ἀλέξαν-
δρος); (8) ~ ib. l. 39 (s. Τατιανός); (9) ~ ib. l.
52 (f. Ἀκμάζων); (10) ~ ib. l. 79 (s. Λιβυρνός);
(11) 165 AD ib. 50, 26 (I f. Ζώσιμος II); (12)
~ ib. l. 26 (II s. Ζώσιμος I); (13) ~ ib. l. 28
(s. Στρατέας); (14) ~ ib. l. 29 (f. Εὐτύχης); (15)
~ ib. l. 50 (Παχώνιος Z.); (16) ~ ib. l. 55 (I
f. Ζώσιμος II); (17) ~ ib. l. 55 (II s. Ζώσιμος
I); (18) ~ ib. l. 57 (I f. Ζώσιμος II); (19) ~

ib. l. 57 (II s. Ζώσιμος I); (20) ~ ib. l. 80 (s. Μυστικός)

——(Krariotai): (21) s. iv BC ib. 41, 45 (f. Πόλλιχος)

ELIS: (22) 181-185 AD IvOl 102, 25 (s. Ἀντίπατρος) ?= (Ζωσιμᾶς (2))

—OLYMPIA*: (23) 245-249 AD ib. 121, 20 (?s. Αὐρ. Βασιλείδης: slave?)

EPIROS:

—BOUTHROTOS (PRASAIBOI): (24) ii AD Ugolini, Alb. Ant. 3 p. 223 c (Sestieri, ILat. Albania 4) (Lat. C. Clodius Zosimus: f. Ποθείνη)

—KASTANIA (MOD.): (25) imp. Hammond, Epirus p. 734 no. 2 (Lat. P. Patunius Zosimus Pinerus)

—NIKOPOLIS: (26) imp. AE 1950-1, Chron. p. 36 (Sarikakis 53); (27) ~ SEG XXXIX 535 (Μέμιος Z.); (28) ~ ib. 538 ([Z]ώσιμος)

ILLYRIA:

—APOLLONIA: (29) imp. IApoll 94 (s. Νικόμαχος); (30) ~ ib. 202 (Ζώσι[μος]: f. Ἰσίδωρος); (31) ~ ib. 248

—EPIDAMNOS-DYRRHACHION: (32) hell.-imp. IDyrrh 233

—LYCHNIDOS: (33) ii-iii AD Sp. 98 (1941-8) p. 231 no. 461 (-σει-)

KORINTHIA:

—KORINTH: (34) imp. Corinth VIII (2) 173 (Lat. -us Zosi[mus]); (35) ~ ib. VIII (3) 362 (Lat. Zosim[us]); (36) ~ ib. 364 d (Lat. Zosimu[s]); (37) ~ ib. 365 (Lat. Zosim[us]); (38) ii AD Ag. VII p. 97 no. 298; SEG XXVII 35. 10 (lamps); (39) ii-iii AD ib. XI 136 a; (40) ~ Corinth VIII (3) 369, 5; (41) m. ii AD IG VII 1773, 8; SEG III 334, 13 (Stephanis 1041) (and Boiotia Thespiai: Γν. Πομπ. Z.); (42) ~ Corinth VIII (3) 296 (Λ. Γέ[λλιος] Ζώσ[ιμος])

LAKONIA:

—GYTHEION: (43) m. ii AD IG V (1) 1174, 11 (I f. Ζώσιμος II); (44) ~ ib. l. 11 (II s. Ζώσιμος I)

—HYPERTELEATON*: (45) imp. ib. 1022; (46) ~ ib. 1023

—SPARTA: (47) c. 140-160 AD ib. 149, 5 (Bradford (4)) (f. Διονύσιος); (48) ~ IG V (1) 154, 3 (Bradford (1)) (s. Μᾶρκος); (49) c. 170-190 AD SEG XI 627, 6 (Bradford (2)) (f. Ἀπολλώνιος) ?= (50); (50) f. iii AD IG V (1) 170, 18; BSA 80 (1985) p. 245 (date) (Bradford (3)) (f. Αὐρ. Ἀπολλώνιος) ?= (49)

MESSENIA:

—KORONE: (51) 246 AD IG V (1) 1398, 55 (Αὐρ. Z.); (52) ~ ib. l. 75 (Ἰγν. Z.)

S. ITALY (APULIA):

—CANUSIUM: (53) i AD Epig. Rom. di Canosa 161 (Lat. P. Min– Zosim[us])

—CANUSIUM*: (54) i AD ib. 84 (CIL IX 358) (Lat. P. Avillius Zosim(us): freed.); (55) i-ii AD Epig. Rom. di Canosa 64 (Lat. Zosimus: freed.)

—LARINUM: (56) imp. CIL IX 753 (Lat. C. Gabbius Zosimus)

—LARINUM*: (57) i AD Athenaeum 51 (1973) p. 348; cf. Forma Italiae 36 p. 112 (Lat. Zosimus: freed.)

—VENUSIA: (58) imp. CIL IX 492 (Lat. Calvius [Z]osimus)

—VENUSIA*: (59) i AD Rend. Linc. 31 (1976) p. 283 no. 1 (Museo di Venosa p. 236 no. 7) (Lat. C. Salvius Zosimus: freed.)

S. ITALY (BRUTTIUM):

—RHEGION*: (60) imp. IG XIV 617, 9 (slave?); (61) ~ ib. 620, 7 (slave?)

—TAURIANA: (62) imp. Rend. Linc. 19 (1964) pp. 135-6 no. 7 (Lat. -ius Zosimus)

S. ITALY (CALABRIA):

—BRENTESION-BRUNDISIUM: (63) imp. NScav 1885, p. 112 c (Eph. Ep. VIII 51) (Lat. Zosimus); (64) ~ NScav 1896, p. 239 no. 1 (Lat. P. Sextilius Zosimus)

—HYDROUS-HYDRUNTUM: (65) imp. Ann. Univ. Lecce 8-9 (1977-80) p. 229 b (Lat. P. Vinidius Zosimus)

—TARAS-TARENTUM: (66) imp. Eph. Ep. VIII 241 (Lat. A. Fulvius Zosimus)

—TARAS-TARENTUM*: (67) imp. Misc. Gr. Rom. 3 p. 175 (Lat. P. Lelius Zosimus: freed.?)

—VALETIUM: (68) imp. BABesch 62 (1987) p. 98 (Lat. Zosi[mus]: f. Dacia)

S. ITALY (CAMPANIA):

—DIKAIARCHIA-PUTEOLI: (69) imp. CIL X 2106 (Lat. L. Arulenus Zosimus); (70) ~ ib. 2238 (Lat. Cn. Cassius Zosimus); (71) ~ ib. 2309 (Lat. M. Cocceius Zosimus); (72) ~ ib. 2879 (Lat. Cn. Pontius Zosimus); (73) ~ ib. 3155 (Lat. Zosimus: s. Arcanius); (74) ~ ib. 3156 (Lat. Zosimus: s. Δικαῖος, Apisia Fortunata); (75) ~ Eph. Ep. VIII 389 (Lat. Annius Zosimus); (76) ?50 AD Camodeca, L'Archivio Puteolano I pp. 194-5 (Lat. P. Urvinus Zosimus); (77) ?ii AD CIL X 1933 (Lat. M. Ulpius Zosimus); (78) ~ ib. 3131 (Lat. M. Ulpius Zosimus); (79) ~ Puteoli 12-13 (1988-9) p. 213 no. 2 (Lat. Q. Castricius Caulius Zosimus: f. Ἀνδραγαθιανός)

—DIKAIARCHIA-PUTEOLI*: (80) i AD AJA 77 (1973) p. 167 no. 18 (Lat. Zosimus: freed.)

—MISENUM: (81) imp. ib. 2 (1898) p. 394 no. 52 (Lat. Zosimus)

—NEAPOLIS: (82) imp. IG XIV 792 (INap 131); cf. Leiwo p. 105 no. 65 (M. Κλώδιος Z.); (83) 170 AD IG XIV 748 A, 9 (INap 52) (T. Φλ. Z.: II s. T. Φλ. Ζώσιμος I, Φλ. Φορτουνᾶτα); (84) ~ IG XIV 748 B, 3 (INap 52) (T. Φλ. Z.: I f. T. Φλ. Ζώσιμος II, T. Φλ. Εὐάνθης); (85) s. iv AD DCB (2) (bp.)

—POMPEII: (86) i BC-i AD CIL IV 1684 (Lat. Zosimus); (87) ~ ib. 2310 h; cf. p. 216 (Lat. Zosim(us)); (88) ~ ib. 4242 (Lat. Zosimus); (89) ~ ib. 4599 (Lat. Iosimus); (90) ~ ib. 5007; 5051; 5052 (Lat. Zosimus); (91) ~ ib. 6814 (Lat. Zosimus); (92) ~ ib. 8317 b (Lat. Zosimus); (93) ~ ib. 8866 (Lat. Zosimus); (94) ~ ib. 8936; (95) ~ ib. 10170 (Lat. Zosimus); (96) ~ NScav 1887, p. 380 (seal) (Castrèn 129. 44) (Lat. Cornelius Zosimus); (97) ?i AD Mem. Accad. Arch. Napoli 6 (1940) p. 274 no. 138 (Castrèn 204. 19) (Lat. L. Istacidius Zosimus); (98) c. 55-60 AD CIL IV 3340. 43, 16 (Castrèn 381. 13) (Lat. P. Sittius Zosimus)

—SALERNUM*: (99) imp. IItal I (1) 89 (CIL X 641) (Lat. L. Taietius Zosimus)

—SURRENTUM: (100) imp. ib. 742 (Lat. M. Livius Zosimus)

S. ITALY (LUCANIA):

—HERAKLEIA: (101) iii BC NC 1917, p. 174 no. 5 u (coin) ([Z]ώσιμος)

SICILY:

—HALIKYAI: (102) s. vi AD SEG XXXVI 830 (Wessel 508 (mosaic))

—KATANE: (103) imp. IG XIV 494 (M. Βιβάνιος Z.); (104) iii AD CIL X 7075 (ILat. Palermo 2) (Lat. Lurius Zosimus: s. Μελάνθιν)

—MOTYKA: (105) 402 AD Ferrua, NG 499 (Z[ώσι]μος)

—NEAITON: (106) iv-v AD Rend. Linc. 18 (1963) p. 57 f. (Ζό-)

—SYRACUSE: (107) imp. IG XIV 5 a; (108) ~ NScav 1912, p. 293 (I f. Ζώσιμος II); (109) ~ ib. (II s. Ζώσιμος I); (110) iii-v AD IG XIV 31 (Strazzulla 132; Wessel 232); cf. Riv. Arch. Crist. 18 (1941) p. 185 no. 51; (111) ~ ASSiracusano 1956, p. 63 = Ferrua, NG 339 b; (112) ~ SEG IV 11 (Agnello 40); (113) ~ SEG XV 584 (Ζώσιμ[ος], Ζωσίμ[η]?); (114) ~ Strazzulla 365 (Wessel 1314)

—TAUROMENION: (115) imp. Rend. Linc. 19 (1964) p. 135-6 no. 7 (Lat. [Ca]ius Zosimus)

—ZANKLE-MESSANA: (116) imp. IG XIV 414; (117) ~ Mon. Ant. 24 (1916) p. 175 (Lat. P. Avillius Zosimus)

## Ζώτη

S. ITALY (BRUTTIUM):

—HIPPONION-VIBO VALENTIA: (1) imp. CIL X 82 (Lat. Mallia Zote)

## Ζωτικά

SICILY:

—AKRAI: (1) ?i BC IG XIV 224 (Akrai p. 164 no. 28) (Ζωτικὰ Γενυκία)

## Ζωτική

S. ITALY (CAMPANIA): (1) imp. CIL X 8059. 205 (seal) (Lat. Zotice)

SICILY:

—SYRACUSE: (2) iii-v AD Strazzulla 346 (Wessel 1320)

—THERMAI HIMERAIAI*: (3) ?i AD CIL X 7398 (ILat. Term. Imer. 90) (Lat. Alfia Zotice: freed.)

—TYNDARIS: (4) imp. Epigraphica 51 (1989) pp. 163-4 no. 12 (Lat. Caecilia Zotice)

## Ζωτικός

DALMATIA:

—EPETION: (1) imp. CIL III 14650 (Lat. Zoticus)

KORINTHIA:

—SIKYON: (2) hell.? IG IV (1) 436, 1 ([Z]ωτικός: s. Εὔκαιρος)

S. ITALY (CAMPANIA):

—DIKAIARCHIA-PUTEOLI: (3) ?i-ii AD CIL X 2576 (Lat. Ti. Iulius Zoticus)

—DIKAIARCHIA-PUTEOLI?: (4) imp. ib. 1833; cf. Puteoli 11 (1987) p. 42 (Lat. -lius Zoticus)

—DIKAIARCHIA-PUTEOLI*: (5) imp. CIL X 3091 (Lat. Zoticus: freed.)

—KYME: (6) imp. ib. 3684 (Lat. C. Pomponius Zoticus)

—MISENUM: (7) ?ii AD AJA 2 (1898) p. 394 no. 52 (Lat. Fl. Zoticus: f. Εὐτύχη, Fl. Vitalis)

—SURRENTUM: (8) imp. NScav 1928, p. 213 (Lat. Zoticus)

SICILY:

—ACATE (MOD.): (9) iii-v AD Rend. Pont. 45 (1972-3) p. 192 no. 3 (Ζωτ[ικός]?)

—KATANE: (10) imp. IG XIV 476; (11) ~ ib. 495 (Βειβάνιος Z.)

—MENAI: (12) imp. Riv. Stor. Antica 5 (1900-1) p. 57 no. 33

—SYRACUSE: (13) hell. IG XIV Add. 9 a

—TAUROMENION: (14) c. 152 BC IGSI 4 III (IV), 25 an. 89 (f. Ἱέρων)

——(Ἀσσιτ.): (15) ii/i BC ib. 12 I, 23; 12 II, 20; 12 III, 17 (s. Εὐβουλίδας)

## Ζώτιχος

ARGOLIS:

—HERMIONE: (1) ?ii-i BC IG IV (1) 731 II, 2 (s. Ἀφροδισία)

## Ζωτίων

AKARNANIA: (1) ?iv BC Unp. (Brauron Mus., sherd)

S. ITALY (CAMPANIA):

—DIKAIARCHIA-PUTEOLI: (2) imp. CIL X 1882 (Lat. L. Lollius Zotio)

Ἡγέας
S. Italy (Campania):
—neapolis: (1) 216 BC Liv. xxiii 1. 9 (Lat. Hegeas)

Ἡγέμαχος
Aitolia:
—thermos*: (1) s. iii BC IG ix (1)² (1) 60 III, 5

Ἡγεμονίς
S. Italy (Campania):
—dikaiarchia-puteoli*: (1) imp. Eph. Ep. viii 400 (Lat. Decia Hegemonis: freed.)

Ἡγέμων
S. Italy (Campania):
—dikaiarchia-puteoli*: (1) imp. CIL x 2741 (Lat. Mindius Hegemo: freed.?)
—herculaneum*: (2) c. 50-75 AD ib. 1403 a III, 8 (Lat. A. Tetteius Hegemon: freed.)
—misenum: (3) ?i-ii AD ib. 3679 (Lat. Hegemon: I f. Ἡγέμων II); (4) ~ ib. (Lat. C. Iulius Hegemon: II s. Ἡγέμων I, Cassia Urbana)

Ἡγήμων
Akarnania: (1) c. 300 BC IEph 1449, 3 (f. Εὐφρόνιος); (2) ii BC IG ix (1)² (2) 581 (s. Μόσχος)

Ἡγήσανδρος
Sicily:
—akragas (nr.)?: (1) ?iv BC Manganaro, QUCC forthcoming no. 39 A, 3

Ἡγησίας
Illyria:
—epidamnos-dyrrhachion: (1) hell.-imp. IDyrrh 234 (s. Σωστρίων)

Ἡγησίστρατος
Sicily:
—katane: (1) imp. CIL x 7059 (Lat. T. Clatius He(g)esistratus)

Ἡγίας
Argolis:
—troizen: (1) hell.? RE Supplbd. 7 (-); cf. s.v. Hagias (1); FGrH 606

Ἡγίων
Aitolia: (1) hell. Plaut., Capt. passim (Lat. Hegio: fict.)

Ἡδεῖα
S. Italy (Campania):
—dikaiarchia-puteoli: (1) imp. CIL x 2647 (Lat. Larcia Hedia)
—pompeii: (2) i BC-i AD ib. IV 1983 (Lat. Hedia)

Ἡδίστα
S. Italy (Bruttium):
—brettioi: (1) 197 BC SGDI 2045, 2-3 (slave/freed.)

Ἡδίστη
S. Italy (Bruttium):
—lokroi epizephyrioi*: (1) imp. Costabile, Municipium Locrensium 32 (CIL x 30) (Lat. Ediste: freed.?)
—tauriana: (2) ii-iii AD Rend. Linc. 19 (1964) p. 133 no. 2 (Lat. Hediste: d. Βίθυς, Successa)
S. Italy (Campania):
—capreae: (3) imp. Eph. Ep. viii 673/4 (Lat. Hediste)
—dikaiarchia-puteoli: (4) ?ii AD CIL x 1737 (Lat. Aelia Hediste)

—dikaiarchia-puteoli*: (5) imp. ib. 3006 (Lat. -caea [H]ediste: freed.)

Ἡδιστος
Illyria:
—epidamnos-dyrrhachion: (1) imp. AEp 1978, no. 752 (Lat. Tadius Hedistus)
Lakonia:
—sparta: (2) c. 221 AD IG v (1) 541, 8; BSA 79 (1984) pp. 270-3 (date) (Ἡδί[στος]?: f. M. Αὐρ. Παράμονος: name—LGPN)
S. Italy (Campania):
—pompeii: (3) i BC-i AD CIL IV 1837; 1936 (Lat. Hedystus)

Ἡδόνη
S. Italy (Apulia):
—rubi: (1) m. ii AD Epigrafia e Territorio 2 p. 73 no. 14 (CIL ix 6183) (Lat. Flavia Hedone)
—venusia: (2) imp. ib. 577 (Lat. Ceciena Edone)
S. Italy (Calabria):
—brentesion-brundisium*: (3) imp. ib. 122 (Lat. Gerellana Hedone: m. Ἰσίδωρος: freed.)
S. Italy (Campania):
—dikaiarchia-puteoli: (4) imp. ib. x 2112 (Lat. Falconia Hedone); (5) ~ ib. 2840 (Lat. Peticia Hedone); (6) ~ ib. 2842 (Lat. Petronia Hedone: m. Φιλήμων); (7) ~ ib. 2849 (Lat. Hedone)
—dikaiarchia-puteoli*: (8) imp. ib. 3024 (Lat. Trolia Hedone: freed.)
—neapolis: (9) imp. ib. 1522 (Lat. Edone)
—pompeii: (10) i BC-i AD ib. IV 10233 (Lat. Edone)
Sicily:
—syracuse: (11) imp.? NScav 1913, p. 267 (vase)

Ἡδύλιον
S. Italy (Apulia):
—canusium*: (1) imp. Epig. Rom. di Canosa 206 (CIL ix 6191) (Lat. Ossidia Hedylium: freed.)

Ἡδυλίων
S. Italy (Lucania):
—hyele-velia: (1) imp. PdelP 21 (1966) p. 337 no. 19 (Lat. Hedylio); (2) ~ CIL x 464 (Lat. Hedilio)

Ἡδύλος
Illyria:
—apollonia: (1) imp. IApoll 206
S. Italy (Campania):
—dikaiarchia-puteoli: (2) s. iii AD CIL x 1687 (Lat. L. Caesonius Hedylus)
—herculaneum: (3) b. 79 AD IG xiv 2414. 27 (tessera)
S. Italy (Lucania):
—hyele-velia: (4) imp. PdelP 21 (1966) p. 337 no. 13 (Lat. Hedyl(us))
—poseidonia-paestum?: (5) s. i AD IItal i (1) 24* (CIL x 470) (or S. Italy (Lucania) Hyele-Velia: Lat. M. Allienius Hedylus)

Ἡδύμη
Arkadia:
—tegea: (1) ?182 AD IG v (2) 84 (Ἡδύμ[η]: d. Ἐπίκτητος)

Ἡδύς
S. Italy (Campania):
—kyme: (1) imp. CIL x 3693 (Lat. P. Avius Hedus)

Ἡδυχρώ
Sicily:
—lipara: (1) hell.-imp. Epigraphica 11 (1949) p. 52 no. 2 (Ἡδυχρό?: d. Ἀρχυλις)

Ἡδωνός
S. Italy (Lucania):
—atina lucana: (1) imp. IItal iii (1) 156 (CIL x 8100) (Lat. Helvius Edonus)

Ἡϊονεύς
Epiros:
—molossoi: (1) iv BC D.S. xix 89. 3 (Ἡσιονεύς—ms. ed.: s. Ἀλκέτας: name—Dindorf)

Ἡλας?
S. Italy (Calabria):
—taras-tarentum: (1) hell.? RA 1932 (1), p. 38 no. 16 (loomweight) (nom./gen.?)

Ἡλείας?
S. Italy (Calabria):
—taras-tarentum: (1) hell.? IG xiv 2406. 23 (RA 1932 (1), p. 38 no. 17; Wessel 429 (loomweight)) (nom./gen.?)

Ἡλεῖος
Argolis:
—epidauros: (1) i BC-i AD? Peek, NIEpid 56 b (Ἡλεῖ<ει>ος: f. Μονᾶς)

Ἡλία
S. Italy (Apulia):
—canusium: (1) i BC-i AD Epig. Rom. di Canosa Instr. 157 (vase) (Lat. Helia)

Ἡλιάναξ
Sicily:
—himera?: (1) vii/vi BC Suda Σ 1095 (?s. Εὔφορβος, Εὔφημος, Εὐκλείδης, Εὐέτης)

Ἡλιάς
S. Italy (Apulia):
—canusium: (1) ii AD Epig. Rom. di Canosa 99 (Lat. Balonia Helias)
S. Italy (Campania):
—dikaiarchia-puteoli: (2) ?i-ii AD CIL x 2559 (Lat. Iulia Aelias)
—herculaneum: (3) m. i AD PdelP 6 (1951) p. 229 no. 15, 3 (Lat. Laelia Helias)
—neapolis: (4) imp. CIL x 2247; cf. Leiwo p. 103 no. 56 (Lat. Ceionia Helias: m. L. Ceionius Fructuosus); (5) ~ NScav 1892, p. 317; cf. Leiwo p. 99 no. 50 (Lat. Brinnia Helias: d. Μένανδρος, Παρθενόπη)
—pompeii: (6) i BC-i AD CIL IV 6716 (Lat. Helias)
Sicily:
—thermai himeraiai*: (7) imp. ib. x 7369 (ILat. Term. Imer. 38) (Lat. Helias: slave?)

Ἡλίας
Korinthia:
—korinth: (1) vi AD Hesp. 36 (1967) p. 423, 3; cf. TMByz 9 (1985) p. 367 no. 88
S. Italy (Calabria):
—taras-tarentum*: (2) byz. JIWE I 119 (CIJ I 628) (s. Ἰαακώβ: Jew)
Sicily:
—syracuse: (3) iii-v AD Strazzulla 388 (Wessel 1330) (Jew?)

Ἡλιόδωρος
Argolis:
—argos*: (1) ii BC SEG xlii 279, 17 (slave/freed.?)
—epidauros: (2) ii/iii AD Peek, IAEpid 243, 4 (?f. Ζω—, —κα, —πο—)
Elis: (3) 237-241 AD IvOl 117, 10, 21 (?f. Πολυκράτης)
Illyria:
—epidamnos-dyrrhachion: (4) c. 250-50 BC Maier 222; Münsterberg Nachtr. p. 15 (coin)

(Ceka 249; 252) ((Ἡλι)όδω(ρος)—Ceka 249: pryt.)

KORINTHIA:
—KORINTH: (5) inc. *SEG* XXXI 297 (vase); (6) ii-iii AD *Corinth* VIII (1) 102

LAKONIA:
—HYPERTELEATON*: (7) imp. *IG* V (1) 1040 (*Τιβ. Κλ. Ἥ.*)

S. ITALY (BRUTTIUM):
—RHEGION (NR.): (8) hell.? Landi, *DISMG* 33. 3 (brick)

S. ITALY (CAMPANIA):
—DIKAIARCHIA-PUTEOLI: (9) imp. *CIL* X 1598 (Lat. Heliodorus); (10) ~ ib. 2107 (Lat. Heliodorus: ?f. Σιδωνίη); (11) ~ ib. 2305 (Lat. M(anius) Cluvius Heliodorus); (12) ~ *NScav* 1901, p. 19 (Lat. C. Cornelius Heliodorus)
—NEAPOLIS*: (13) imp. *Mon. Ant.* 41 (1951) p. 592; cf. Leiwo p. 158 no. 130 (Lat. Q. Granius Heliodor(us): freed.); (14) ~ *Storia di Napoli* 1 pp. 430-2 (Lat. L. Granius Heliodor(us): freed.)
—POMPEII: (15) i BC-i AD *CIL* IV 8372 (Lat. Heliodorus)
—POMPEII*: (16) i BC-i AD ib. 2462

Ἥλιος
S. ITALY: (1) imp. ib. X 8059. 209 (seal) (Lat. Sex. Iulius Helius)

S. ITALY (APULIA):
—CANUSIUM: (2) imp. *Epig. Rom. di Canosa* 137 (Lat. Fufius Helius) ?= (3); (3) ii AD ib. 88 (Lat. Q. Fufius Helius) ?= (2); (4) 223 AD ib. 35 III, 7 (*CIL* IX 338) (Lat. M. Servilius Helius)

S. ITALY (BRUTTIUM):
—TRAPEIA: (5) ii AD *ICI* V 30 (Lat. Cl. Helius)

S. ITALY (CALABRIA):
—BRENTESION-BRUNDISIUM: (6) i AD *NScav* 1894, p. 17 no. 1; cf. *Epigraphica* 32 (1970) p. 166 (Lat. Iulius Helius)

S. ITALY (CAMPANIA):
—DIKAIARCHIA-PUTEOLI: (7) imp. *CIL* X 2016 (Lat. Helius); (8) ~ *Eph. Ep.* VIII 406 (Lat. C. Hostius Helius)
—NUCERIA ALFATERNA: (9) imp. *NScav* 1922, p. 146 (Lat. A. Gabinius Helius)
—POMPEII*: (10) i BC-i AD *CIL* IV 5036-7; 5039 (slave/freed.?)

S. ITALY (LUCANIA):
—ATINA LUCANA: (11) imp. *IItal* III (1) 144 (Lat. M. Tihonius Helius: I f. Ἥλιος II); (12) ~ ib. (Lat. M. Tihonius Helius: II s. Ἥλιος I)
—CALLE (MOD.): (13) imp. *BdA* 52 (1967) p. 44 (Lat. Cor(nelius) Helius: s. Τύχη)
—METAPONTION: (14) imp. *Atti Conv. Taranto* 19 (1979) p. 405 (Lat. Helius)

Ἡλιοφῶν
S. ITALY (APULIA):
—BARION: (1) imp. *CIL* IX 288 (Lat. M. Appalenus Aeliofon)

Ἡλίων
S. ITALY (LUCANIA):
—GRUMENTUM: (1) imp. ib. X 8094 (Lat. Helion: I f. Ἡλίων II); (2) ~ ib. (Lat. Helion: II s. Ἡλίων I, Ἰλάρα)
—POSEIDONIA-PAESTUM: (3) i BC/i AD Mello-Voza 72 (Lat. [H]elio)

Ἡλύσιος
S. ITALY (BRUTTIUM):
—TERINA: (1) ?vi-v BC Plu., *Mor.* 109 B (f. Εὐθύνοος)

Ἡμερώ
ARGOLIS:
—HERMIONE: (1) ?ii-i BC *IG* IV (1) 731 I, 3 (d. Δέξιος)

Ἡμετέρη
SICILY:
—ZANKLE-MESSANA (NR.): (1) f. v BC Dubois, *IGDS* 16 (vase) (Arena, *Iscr. Sic.* III 43) (hἐμετέρē)

Ἡμέτερος
S. ITALY (CAMPANIA):
—DIKAIARCHIA-PUTEOLI: (1) imp. *NScav* 1888, p. 198 no. 5 (*Eph. Ep.* VIII 391) (Lat. Aurelius Tertullus Hemeterus)

Ἡμιθέων
S. ITALY (BRUTTIUM):
—SYBARIS-THOURIOI-COPIAE: (1) arch. Luc., *Ind.* 23; *Pseudol.* 3 (fict.?)

Ἡνίοχος
ACHAIA:
—AIGEIRA: (1) ii-i BC *BMC Pelop.* p. 2 no. 17 (coin) (Ἡνί[οχος])

LAKONIA:
—GYTHEION: (2) c. 120-140 AD *IG* V (1) 1147, 5

S. ITALY (CAMPANIA):
—DIKAIARCHIA-PUTEOLI: (3) imp. *CIL* X 2389 = *ZPE* 71 (1988) p. 195 no. 3 (Lat. C. Erucius Heniochus)

Ἤπειρος
S. ITALY (CAMPANIA):
—DIKAIARCHIA-PUTEOLI: (1) m. i AD *Puteoli* 6 (1982) p. 151 no. 6 (Lat. Cn. Pompeius Epirus) ?= (2); (2) 41 AD Camodeca, *L'Archivio Puteolano* 1 p. 238 (Lat. Epirus) ?= (1)

Ἠπειρωτικός
KERKYRA: (1) imp. *IG* IX (1) 710 (Κορν. Ἥ.)

Ἠπία
S. ITALY (CAMPANIA):
—POMPEII*: (1) i BC-i AD *NScav* 1905, p. 213 (Castrèn 109. 9) (Lat. Ceia Hepia: freed.)

Ἠπιόνη
SICILY:
—KENTORIPA: (1) iii-v AD *Nuovo Didask.* 4 (1950) p. 65 no. 26

Ἡραγόρης
S. ITALY (LUCANIA):
—HYELE-VELIA: (1) f. v BC *Atti Conv. Taranto* 20 (1980) p. 295 (gem) (Ἡραγ(όρης)?)

Ἡραιος
ARKADIA:
—MEGALOPOLIS: (1) c. 210 BC *IG* IX (1)² (1) 31, 78 (s. Δαμόνικος); (2) ?145 BC ib. V (2) 439, 35 (s. Θρασύμαχος)
—ORCHOMENOS: (3) ?c. 369-361 BC *BCH* 102 (1978) p. 347, 30 (*IPArk* 14)

ILLYRIA:
—APOLLONIA?: (4) hell.? *IApoll* 355 (amph.)

S. ITALY (CALABRIA):
—BRENTESION-BRUNDISIUM*: (5) i BC Desy, *Timbres amphoriques* 487-9; 724; 811; 833; 880 1083; 1107 (amph.) (slave/potter?)

Ἡραῖς
ACHAIA: (1) ?c. 250 BC *IG* XI (4) 1191, 2 (d. Φίλων)

DALMATIA:
—ISSA: (2) hell. Brunšmid p. 27 no. 18, 2 (*SEG* XL 514; *VAHD* 84 (1991) p. 253 no. 3) (-εῖς: d. Ἀγάθων)

S. ITALY (CAMPANIA):
—DIKAIARCHIA-PUTEOLI: (3) ?ii-iii AD *CIL* X 2150 (Lat. Aurelia Aerais)
—POMPEII*: (4) i BC ib. I² 1638 (X 1049; Castrèn 129. 25) (Lat. Corn. Heraes: freed.)

S. ITALY (LUCANIA):
—VOLCEI: (5) ii AD *Suppl. It.* 3 p. 84 no. 16 (Lat. Ulpia [H]erais)

SICILY:
—THERMAI HIMERAIAI: (6) i-ii AD *Kokalos* 20 (1974) p. 236 no. 9 (d. Ἡρύλος)

Ἡραίων
ILLYRIA:
—APOLLONIA: (1) hell. *IApoll* 356 (tile)

Ἡρακᾶς
S. ITALY (LUCANIA):
—METAPONTION: (1) iv BC *NScav* 1977, Suppl. p. 454 no. 21 (Landi, *DISMG* 153 (tile)) (hηρα-)

Ἡρακλανός
KORINTHIA:
—KORINTH: (1) i/ii AD Amandry pp. 51-2; 148-50; *RPC* I p. 252 no. 1138 (coin) (Lat. C. Iulius Herac(lanus))

Ἡρακλᾶς
AIGINA: (1) ?f. iii AD *Alt-Ägina* I (2) p. 48 no. 38 ([Αὐρ.] Ἥ.: s. Βάσσος)

ARKADIA:
—TEGEA: (2) ii AD *IG* V (2) 55, 78 (f. Ἀντώνις)

LAKONIA:
—SPARTA: (3) imp. ib. V (1) 915 (Bradford (1)); (4) c. 230-260 AD *IG* V (1) 556, 9 (Bradford (2)) (f. Αὐρ. Ἀριστοκράτης)

S. ITALY (APULIA):
—CANNAE*: (5) i-ii AD *Epig. Rom. di Canosa* 57 (*CIL* IX 319) (Lat. C. Iulius Heracula: freed.)

S. ITALY (CAMPANIA):
—CAPREAE*: (6) imp. *ZPE* 71 (1988) p. 197 no. 8, 7 (Lat. Heracla: freed.)
—DIKAIARCHIA-PUTEOLI: (7) imp. *CIL* X 2319-20 (Lat. L. Cominius Heracla); (8) ?i-ii AD *Eph. Ep.* VIII 396 (Lat. Iulius Heracla)
—HERCULANEUM*: (9) i BC-i AD *CIL* X 1403 g I, 6 (Lat. M. Nonius Heracla: freed.); (10) ~ ib. 1403 g III, 60 (Lat. Ti. Iulius Heracla: freed.)
—KYME: (11) imp. *AJPh* 30 (1909) p. 70 no. 6 (Lat. [L.] Vinulli[us] Heracla)
—POMPEII: (12) i BC-i AD *CIL* IV 726 (Lat. Heracla); (13) ~ ib. 1235; 4829 (Lat. Heracla); (14) ~ ib. 3542 (Lat. Heracla); (15) ~ ib. 4914 (Lat. Heracla); (16) ~ ib. 5110 (Lat. Eracla); (17) ~ ib. X 927 (Lat. Heracla)

Ἡρακλέα
ARGOLIS:
—PHLEIOUS: (1) iii-ii BC *IG* IV (1) 474

LAKONIA:
—BOIAI: (2) ii AD ib. V (1) 958, 4; 959, 4 (d. Ἡρωίδης, m. Πρόνοια, Μελίχρως); (3) ~ ib. l. 1 (d. Λεωνίδας)

SICILY:
—SYRACUSE: (4) iii BC ib. II² 10392 (d. Νυμφόδωρος)

Ἡράκλεια
AKARNANIA:
—ANAKTORION: (1) iii BC ib. IX (1)² (2) 220
—THYRREION: (2) s. iii BC ib. 290

ARKADIA:
—MEGALOPOLIS?: (3) ii/iii AD ib. V (2) 518; 519 (d. Εὔμηλος)

KERKYRA: (4) hell. ib. IX (1) 589, 3 (d. Ἀριστομέδων); (5) ?i-ii AD Unp. (*IG* arch.)

LAKONIA: (6) 196 BC *SGDI* 2050, 3, 4 (slave/freed.)
—SPARTA: (7) m. iii AD *IG* V (1) 599, 4, 23 (Bradford (-)) (d. Τεισαμενός)

S. ITALY (APULIA):
—VENUSIA: (8) imp. *NScav* 1903, p. 204 (Lat. Pomponia Heraclia: d. Δορκάς)

S. ITALY (CAMPANIA):
—DIKAIARCHIA-PUTEOLI: (9) imp. *CIL* X 2186 (Lat. Caecilia Heraclia); (10) ?i-ii AD ib. 2277 (Lat. Cl. Heraclia: d. Στέφανος, Δροσίς)
—DIKAIARCHIA-PUTEOLI*: (11) imp. *NScav* 1886, p. 457 (Lat. Titinia Heraclea: freed.)

—POMPEII: (12) i BC-i AD *CIL* IV 1507, 5 (Lat. Heracla (fem.))

SICILY:

—KATANE: (13) imp. *IG* XIV 495 (Ἡράκλ[εια])

—SELINOUS: (14) inc. *ASSiciliano* 1955, p. 248 n. 20

—SYRACUSE: (15) iii-v AD Ferrua, *NG* 332 (-κλια)

—ZANKLE-MESSANA: (16) imp. *CIL* X 6984 (Lat. Coponia Heraclia)

## Ἡρακλειανός

ARGOLIS:

—EPIDAUROS: (1) ii-iii AD *IG* IV (1)² 476; 477 (-κλι-)

S. ITALY (CAMPANIA):

—DIKAIARCHIA-PUTEOLI: (2) imp. *CIL* X 2369 (Lat. Heraclianus: I f. Ἡρακλειανός II); (3) ~ ib. (Lat. Domitius Heraclianus: II s. Ἡρακλειανός I)

## Ἡρακλείδας

ACHAIA: (1) 146 BC *IG* IV (1)² 28, 88 (s. Ἀλέξανδρος: synoikos)

—DYME*: (2) c. 219 BC *SGDI* 1612, 65 (*Tyche* 5 (1990) p. 124) ([Ἡρ]ακλείδας: f. Σώσιππος); (3) ~ *SGDI* 1612, 74 (*Tyche* 5 (1990) p. 124) (f. Φίλιστος)

AIGINA: (4) f. iii BC Nachtergael, *Les Galates* 7, 28; cf. Stephanis 590 (f. Δείνων); (5) ?69 BC *IG* IV (1) 2, 1, 3, 25 (f. Διόδωρος)

AKARNANIA:

—ASTAKOS: (6) c. 325-315 BC *Hesp.* 57 (1988) p. 148 A, 53 (*SEG* XXXVI 331); cf. *Hesp.* 48 (1979) pp. 78 f. with pl. 22 c (s. Ὀφρυάδας); (7) ii BC *IG* IX (1)² (2) 434, 2-3 (s. Λύκων, f. Λύκων)

—ECHINOS?: (8) hell.-imp. ib. 379

—KORONTA: (9) iii-ii BC ib. 432, 1 (s. Θεωνίδας)

—THYRREION: (10) iii-ii BC *SEG* XXVII 159, 10; cf. *PAE* 1977, pl. 244 a (s. Ἀρχέδαμος); (11) ii BC *IG* IX (1)² (2) 249, 12

ARGOLIS:

—EPIDAUROS: (12) iv BC ib. IV (1)² 154; (13) ?i-ii AD Peek, *IAEpid* 225 a (-κλί-)

—EPIDAUROS*: (14) c. 370-365 BC ib. 52 A, 12; 52 B, 61; (15) c. 335-325 BC *IG* IV (1)² 106 I, 23; (16) c. 290-270 BC ib. 109 II, 43; *BSA* 61 (1966) p. 307 no. 20, 127

—HERMIONE: (17) iv BC *IG* IV (1) 741, 5 (s. Σωσα—); (18) ?ii-i BC ib. 731 III, 8 (f. Θαΐς); (19) ii-i BC ib. 732 II, 27-31 (f. Εὔοδος, Ὑλαῖος, Κέρδων, Θεσσαλός, —νάσιον); (20) i BC-i AD? ib. 734, 5 (Ἡρ[α]κλείδας)

ARKADIA:

—TEGEA: (21) s. iv BC ib. v (2) 41, 63 (Ἡρακλείδ[ας]); (22) iii BC ib. 30, 8 (s. Κερκίδας); (23) f. iii BC ib. 35, 7 ([Ἡ]ρακλείδας); (24) i-ii AD ib. 561 (Ἡρακλείδας); (25) i/ii AD ib. 81; (26) ii AD ib. 55, 89 (s. Λύκος); (27) 165 AD ib. 50, 49 (-κλί-); (28) ~ ib. l. 76 (Φλάβιος Ἡ.)

DALMATIA:

—ISSA: (29) iv/iii BC *VAHD* NS 8 (1905) p. 97 no. 177 (*VAMZ* 1970, p. 33 f. frr. I-J); (30) iii BC Brunšmid p. 9 fr. G, 9 + *VAMZ* 1970, p. 37 frr. G and M (f. Δαμάρατος)

——(Dymanes): (31) iv/iii BC Brunšmid p. 9, 60 (f. Θεόδοτος)

——(Hylleis): (32) iv/iii BC ib. p. 7, 19 (Ἡρα[κλείδας]?: s. —ιμος); (33) ~ ib. p. 8, 49 (f. Κλεαίνετος)

——(Pamphyloi): (34) iv/iii BC ib. p. 7, 23 (f. Πανθέας); (35) ~ ib. p. 8, 47

ELIS: (36) ?257 BC Nachtergael, *Les Galates* 7, 50; cf. Stephanis 1095 ([Ἡρ]ακλείδης: f. Ἡράκλειτος); (37) m. i AD *IvOl* 78, 4 (s. Ξεν—); (38) iii AD *SEG* XV 259, 8, 19 ([Ἡ]ρακλείδας)

EPIROS:

—AMBRAKIA: (39) ?254-253 BC Nachtergael, *Les Galates* 9, 79; 10, 75 (-δης: s. Λύκος)

—BOUTHROTOS (PRASAIBOI): (40) a. 163 BC *IBouthrot* 21, 32 (*SEG* XXXVIII 478); (41) ~ *IBouthrot* 28, 2 (*SEG* XXXVIII 486) ?= (46); (42) ~ *IBouthrot* 28, 2 (*SEG* XXXVIII 486) ?= (47); (43) ~ *IBouthrot* 30, 10; 36, 12 (s. Νικίας); (44) ~ ib. 43, 34-5 (*SEG* XXXVIII 502) (s. Λυκίσκος, f. Λυκίσκος) ?= (45); (45) ~ *IBouthrot* 103, 9 (f. Λυκίσκος) ?= (44); (46) ~ ib. 117, 6, 9 (-κλι-) ?= (41); (47) ~ ib. l. 7 (-κλι-) ?= (42)

—DODONA*: (48) iv-iii BC *SGDI* 1561 (*Syll*³ 1160)

—MOLOSSOI: (49) hell. Cabanes, *L'Épire* p. 581 no. 56, 3

ILLYRIA:

—APOLLONIA: (50) c. 250-50 BC *Bakërr Hoard* p. 65 no. 131 (coin) (Ceka 135) (pryt.); (51) i BC Unp. (Paris, BN) 72 (coin) (pryt.); (52) imp. *IApoll* 31 (-κλί-); (53) ~ ib. 95; (54) ii AD ib. 207 (s. Ξένων); (55) ~ ib.

—EPIDAMNOS-DYRRHACHION: (56) c. 250-50 BC Maier 115 (coin) (Ceka 204) (money.); (57) ii-i BC *IDyrrh* 236 (s. Ἐπίκαδος); (58) hell.-imp. ib. 86 (f. Ἀθηναΐς); (59) ~ ib. 175 (-κλί-: f. Δωροθέα); (60) ~ ib. 247 (-κλί-: f. Θερσίας); (61) ~ ib. 264 (f. Κλέα); (62) ~ ib. 361 (f. Πορτία)

KORINTHIA:

—KORINTH: (63) 172 BC *PMich* III 190, 15 (-δης: f. Ἀριστοκλῆς); (64) ~ ib. l. 38 (-δης: s. Ἀριστοκλῆς: t.e.)

LAKONIA:

—HYPERTELEATON*: (65) imp. *IG* V (1) 1019 (-κλί-)

—SPARTA: (66) i BC-i AD *Laconia Survey* 2 p. 217 no. 9 (Ἡρακλε[ίδας]: f. —ης) ?= (67); (67) s. i BC *SEG* XXVIII 410 (f. Λαχάρης) ?= (66); (68) f. i AD *IG* V (1) 270, 1; *Artemis Orthia* pp. 306-7 no. 20 (date) (Bradford (1)) (-κλί-: s. Πακώνιος); (69) c. 220 AD *SEG* XXXIV 311, 7; *BSA* 79 (1984) pp. 267-9 (date) (Bradford (3)) (Αὐρ. Ἡρακλείδ[ας])

PELOPONNESE?: (70) 11 AD *PAE* 1992, p. 71 A, 32 (s. Ἑρμίας)

S. ITALY (APULIA):

—VENUSIA: (71) imp. *CIL* IX 524 (Lat. Heraclida)

S. ITALY (BRUTTIUM):

—HIPPONION-VIBO VALENTIA*: (72) imp. ib. X 68 (Lat. M. Caerellius Heraclida: freed.)

—LOKROI EPIZEPHYRIOI:

——(Τυν.): (73) iv/iii BC De Franciscis 19, 6 (s. Θεώνδας)

—TERINA: (74) inc. *EM* p. 752 s.v. Τέρινα

S. ITALY (CALABRIA):

—BRENTESION-BRUNDISIUM: (75) imp. *IG* XIV 679 (-κλί-: f. Κυρίων)

—TARAS-TARENTUM: (76) iii/ii BC *RE* (63); (77) c. 160 BC *ID* 1716, 1 (I s. Ἀριστίων, f. Ἀριστίων, Αἰσχρίων, Ἡρακλείδας II, Μενεκράτης, Ἀρίστακος, Νικασώ, Κλεανώ); (78) ~ ib. l. 5 (II s. Ἡρακλείδας I, Μυραλλίς (Syracuse)); (79) 156 BC ib. 1417 B II, 97 (f. Εὐκλῆς); (80) ii/i BC *RE* (54); cf. Deichgräber, *Griech. Empirikerschule* pp. 172 ff. (doctor); (81) c. 70-60 BC *BCH* 44 (1920) p. 251 no. 10, 24; cf. *BSA* 70 (1975) pp. 122-3; cf. Stephanis 1082 (Ἡ[ρακλ]είδης: I f. Ἡρακλείδας II); (82) ~ *BCH* 44 (1920) p. 251 no. 10, 24; cf. *BSA* 70 (1975) pp. 122-3 (Stephanis 1082) (-δης: II s. Ἡρακλείδας I)

S. ITALY (CAMPANIA):

—DIKAIARCHIA-PUTEOLI: (83) imp. *CIL* X 3064 (Lat. Val. Heraclida)

—KYME: (84) imp. ib. 3700, 5 (Lat. Mevius Heraclida); (85) ~ *Eph. Ep.* VIII 451 (Lat. C. Sulpicius Heraclida: I f. Ὑγῖνος, Ὄνειρος, Ἡρακλείδας II, Faustus); (86) ~ ib. (Lat. Heraclida: II s. Ἡρακλείδας I, Ἁρμονία)

—KYME*: (87) f. i AD *Puteoli* 3 (1979) p. 169 no. 9 (Lat. M. Messius Heraclida: freed.)

—MISENUM*: (88) ?i-ii AD *CIL* X 3359 (Lat. C. Iulius Heraclida); (89) ~ ib. (Lat. Heraclida)

S. ITALY (LUCANIA):

—HERAKLEIA: (90) iv/iii BC *IGSI* 1 I, 1, 165 (*DGE* 62; Uguzzoni–Ghinatti I) (ηρα-: f. Ἀρίσταρχος)

——(ἡα. ἔμβολος): (91) iv/iii BC *IGSI* 1 I, 166 (*DGE* 62; Uguzzoni–Ghinatti I) (ηηρα-: s. Τιμοκράτης)

——(Με. ἐπιστύλιον): (92) iv/iii BC *IGSI* 1 I, 7, 10, 98 (*DGE* 62; Uguzzoni–Ghinatti I) (ηηρα-: s. Ζώπυρος)

SICILY:

—ADRANON: (93) iii-ii BC *PdelP* 16 (1961) p. 127 (f. Νεμήνιος)

—AKRAI: (94) ?iii BC *SGDI* 3240, 3 (*Akrai* p. 156 no. 7) (s. Ἀπολλόδωρος); (95) ~ *SGDI* 3243 (*Akrai* p. 155 no. 5) (Ἡερα-: ?s. Διόδωρος); (96) ~ *SGDI* 3243 (*Akrai* p. 155 no. 5) (f. Διονύσιος); (97) ~ *SGDI* 3243 (*Akrai* p. 155 no. 5) (I f. Ἡρακλείδας II, Ἀρχάγαθος); (98) ~ *SGDI* 3243 (*Akrai* p. 155 no. 5) (II s. Ἡρακλείδας I); (99) iii-ii BC *SGDI* 3242, 10 (*Akrai* p. 157 no. 8) (f. Ἔλωρις); (100) ii BC ib. p. 156 no. 6, 11 (s. Δαμάτριος); (101) ~ *IGLMP* 30, 4 (*Akrai* p. 155 no. 4 a) ([Ἡ]ρακλείδας)

——(Πε.): (102) ii-i BC *SGDI* 3246, 23 (*Akrai* pp. 152-3 no. 2; Dubois, *IGDS* 109) (I f. Ἡρακλείδας II); (103) ~ *SGDI* 3246, 23 (*Akrai* pp. 152-3 no. 2; Dubois, *IGDS* 109) (II s. Ἡρακλείδας I)

—GELA-PHINTIAS: (104) f. iv BC *Ag.* XVII 455 (*IG* II² 8460) (f. Τεισίας); (105) s. iv BC ib. IV (1)² 95, 84 (Perlman E.2); Perlman pp. 46-9 (date) (s. Γλαῦκος); (106) f. ii BC *IG* XIV 256, 10, 20, 32 (Dubois, *IGDS* 161); cf. *SEG* XL 804 (s. Ζώπυρος) ?= (107)

——(Χαρ.): (107) f. ii BC *IG* XIV 256, 47 (Dubois, *IGDS* 161); cf. *SEG* XL 804 (f. Ζώπυρος) ?= (106)

—HALAISA: (108) ii BC *IGSI* 2 A II, 73 (Dubois, *IGDS* 196) (s. Ἀπολλώνιος)

—HIMERA: (109) v/iv BC *Himera* 2 p. 688 no. 147 (sherd) (Dubois, *IGDS* 14 b)

—KAMARINA: (110) f. v BC Cordano, *Tessere Pubbliche* 5 (Arena, *Iscr. Sic.* II 127 A) (hēρα-: s. Ἀρχωνίδας); (111) ~ Cordano, *Tessere Pubbliche* 9 a (Arena, *Iscr. Sic.* II 128 A) ([h]ερακλείδας: s. Κρατίνος); (112) ~ Cordano, *Tessere Pubbliche* 63 (hερακλείδ[ας]: s. Εὔορμος); (113) m. v BC Dubois, *IGDS* 120, 3 (Arena, *Iscr. Sic.* II 142 A; *SEG* XXXVII 939; Cordano, 'Camarina VII' 35) (hερακλι-: f. Ἀρ—ας); (114) s. v BC Dubois, *IGDS* 119, 6 (Arena, *Iscr. Sic.* II 145) ([Ἡ]ρακλείδας: s. Νικίας); (115) ?iv/iii BC *SEG* XXXIV 940, 5 (Dubois, *IGDS* 124; *PdelP* 44 (1989) p. 192 no. 3; Cordano, 'Camarina VII' 108) (f. Δίων); (116) ~ *SEG* XXXIV 940, 7 (Dubois, *IGDS* 124; *PdelP* 44 (1989) p. 192 no. 3; Cordano, 'Camarina VII' 108) (f. Ἀρταμίδωρος); (117) iv/iii BC *SEG* XXXIX 999, 5 (Dubois, *IGDS* 125; Cordano, 'Camarina VII' 109); (118) hell. *SEG* XXXIX 1001, 2 (s. Εὐθυκλῆς)

—KATANE: (119) 413-404 BC *HN*² p. 133; *Samml. Ludwig* 338 (coin) (coin engraver)

—KENTORIPA: (120) ?s. iii BC *Sic. Gymn.* 2 (1949) p. 91 no. 1, 8 + 16 (1963) p. 54 (s. Φάλακρος); (121) imp. Manganaro, *QUCC* forthcoming no. 16 (I f. Ἡρακλείδας II); (122) ~ ib. (II s. Ἡρακλείδας I)

—LIPARA: (123) imp.? *NScav* 1929, p. 82 no. 5 (Ἡρακλείδ[ας])

—LIPARA*: (124) i BC-i AD *Kokalos* 32 (1986) p. 226 nos. 32-3 (tiles)

—MORGANTINA: (125) iv/iii BC *SEG* XXXIX 1008, 9; 1010, 6 (f. Φιλωνίδας); (126) ~ ib. 1012, 7 (s. Θευ-); (127) ~ ib. 1013, 3 (Ἡρακλείδ[ας]); (128) ~ ib. l. 4 ([Ἡρ]ακλεί[δ]ας: f. Φιλωνίδας); (129) ~ ib. l. 8 ([Ἡρ]ακλείδ[ας]: f. Ἄνταλλος)

—MORGANTINA (NR.): (130) ?iii BC Manganaro, *PdelP* forthcoming no. 7, 4 (f. Ξενότιμος)
—PETRA: (131) f. iii BC *SEG* XXX 1121, 26 (Dubois, *IGDS* 208) (f. Ἡράκλειος)
—SYRACUSE: (132) 415 BC *RE* s.v. Herakleides (21) (-δης: s. Λυσίμαχος); (133) 414-409 BC ib. s.v. Herakleides (22) (-δης: s. Ἀριστογένης); (134) 413 BC Plu., *Nic.* 24 (-δης); (135) iv BC *RE* s.v. Herakleides (-δης); (136) ?iv BC ib. s.v. Herakleides (58) (-δης); (137) f. iv BC ib. s.v. Herakleides (24); *IG* IV (1)² 95, 40 (Perlman E.2); Perlman p. 40 (date) (-δης: s. Λυσίμαχος); (138) c. 330-307 BC *RE* s.v. Herakleides (26) (s. Ἀγαθοκλῆς); (139) hell.? ib. s.v. Herakleides (59); (140) hell. *SEG* XXXII 923; cf. XLII 858 (f. Ζωπυρίσκα); (141) ~ *NScav* 1892, p. 361; (142) c. 247-199 BC *SGDI* 2609, 2 (-δης: I s. Λύκων, f. Δαμάτριος, Ἡρακλείδα II); (143) ~ ib. l. 3 (-δης: II s. Ἡρακλείδας I); (144) c. 220 BC *PPetr* III 112 (c), 18-19 (f. Στράτιππος); (145) c. 200 BC *IG* XI (4) 723 (-δης: s. Εὔδαμος)
—SYRACUSE?:
——(Δυν.): (146) hell. *Mem. Linc.* 8 (1938) p. 128 no. 35. 9 (bullet) (f. Ἄνδρων)
——(Μακ.): (147) hell. Manganaro, *PdelP* forthcoming no. 4 III, 2 (s. Φίλων)
——(Ὑπα.): (148) hell. ib. no. 4 IV, 8 (f. Θράσων)
—TAUROMENION: (149) c. 236 BC *IG* XIV 421 an. 5 (*SGDI* 5219); (150) c. 177 BC *IG* XIV 421 an. 64 (*SGDI* 5219); (151) c. 170 BC *IGSI* 4 II (III), 17 an. 71 (s. Ὀλυμπίς); (152) c. 152 BC *IG* XIV 421 an. 89 (*SGDI* 5219) (s. Φίλιστος)
——(Μαυ.): (153) ii/i BC *IGSI* 9 II, 21 (s. Σῖμος)
—TYRAKION: (154) f. ii BC *BCH* 45 (1921) p. 25 IV, 101 + *SEG* XXII 455; cf. *Sic. Gymn.* 17 (1964) pp. 47 f. (Ἡρακλε[ίδας]?, Ἡράκλε[ιος]?)
SICILY?: (155) m. v BC *Essays M. Thompson* p. 285 (terracotta) (date—A.W.J.)

## Ἡρακλείδης

AIGINA: (1) ?i BC *Alt-Ägina* I (2) p. 44 no. 11, 3 (s. Σαραπίων)
AITOLIA?: (2) iii BC *IG* IX (1)² (1) 64 (sculptor)
ARGOLIS:
—ARGOS: (3) c. 50 BC *BGU* 1972, 3 (f. Διονύσιος)
—EPIDAUROS: (4) ii AD *IG* IV (1)² 519 (f. Ἑλλανοκράτης)
ARKADIA: (5) 285 BC *PEleph* 2, 17 (*MChr* 311) (f. Πολυκράτης)
ELIS: (6) 36-24 BC *IvOl* 62, 4; 64, 9 (I f. Ἡρακλείδης II); (7) ~ ib. 62, 4, 21; 64, 9, 29 (Ἡρακλίδης—62 l. 21: II s. Ἡρακλείδης I, ?f. Ἐπίκτητος, Σωσίνικος: N.); (8) 28-24 BC ib. l. 25 (I f. Ἡρακλείδης II); (9) ~ ib. l. 25 (II s. Ἡρακλείδης I: Π.); (10) 113-117 AD ib. 91, 16 (-κλί-: f. Ἡρᾶς)
—OLYMPIA*: (11) s. v BC *Ol. Forsch.* 5 p. 150 no. 5 (ℎερακλέδε); (12) s. i BC *IvOl* 66, 9 (?s. Πρέπων)
ILLYRIA:
—EPIDAMNOS-DYRRHACHION: (13) hell.-imp. *IDyrrh* 235 (s. Βάντιος)
KORINTHIA:
—KORINTH: (14) s. i AD *Ag.* VII p. 90 no. 215 (lamp) (-κλί-)
S. ITALY (CAMPANIA):
—NEAPOLIS: (15) i BC *SEG* XXXVII 786 (*INap* 123); cf. Leiwo p. 117 no. 100 (s. Ἐλαῖος); (16) i BC/i AD *IG* XIV 783, 4 (*INap* 137); cf. Leiwo p. 121 no. 106 (f. Εὔφρων); (17) ~ *INap* 109, 5; cf. Leiwo p. 77 no. 21 (s. Διονύσιος); (18) ~ *INap* 113, 1; (19) ~ ib. l. 5 (f. Ἄστος); (20) ~ ib. 134; cf. Leiwo p. 78 no. 24 (Ἡρα[κλεί]δης: f. Κρευμένων); (21) ~ *INap* 170, 4; (22) i BC/i AD? ib. 186 (Ἡ[ρα]κλῆδης); (23) 194 AD ib. 44 col. II, 6 (Κανείνιος Ἡ.)

SICILY:
—LEONTINOI: (24) 278 BC D.S. xxii 8. 5 (tyrant)
—THERMAI HIMERAIAI: (25) c. 361-354 BC ib. xix 2. 5-6; cf. *RE* (25) (s. Ἀγαθοκλῆς)

## Ἡρακλειόδωρος

EPIROS?: (1) iii BC Robert, *Hell.* 10 p. 283 ff. (*CRAI* 1991, p. 197 ff. 10)

## Ἡράκλειος

ACHAIA:
—AIGION: (1) 191-146 BC Unp. (Athens, NM) (coin) (Ἡράκλει[ος], Ἡρακλεί[δας]?, Ἡράκλει[τος]?)
AKARNANIA:
—STRATOS: (2) iii BC *IG* IX (1)² (2) 401
SICILY:
—AKRAI: (3) ?iii BC *SGDI* 3239, 1 (*Akrai* p. 157 no. 9) (s. Νυμφόδωρος); (4) ~ *SGDI* 3240, 1 (*Akrai* p. 156 no. 7) (s. Πόσειδις); (5) ~ *SGDI* 3240, 4 (*Akrai* p. 156 no. 7) (s. Ἀγάθων); (6) ii BC ib. p. 154 no. 3, 14 (f. Διονύσιος); (7) ii-i BC *SGDI* 3246, 9 (*Akrai* p. 152-3 no. 2; Dubois, *IGDS* 109) (f. Ἀρτεμίδωρος)
——(Κρα.): (8) ii-i BC *SGDI* 3246, 42 (*Akrai* pp. 152-3 no. 2; Dubois, *IGDS* 109) (s. Διονύσιος)
——(Σαλ.): (9) iii-ii BC *SGDI* 3242, 4 (*Akrai* p. 157 no. 8) (I f. Ἡράκλειος II); (10) ~ *SGDI* 3242, 4 (*Akrai* p. 157 no. 8) (II s. Ἡράκλειος I)
—AMESTRATOS: (11) f. i BC Cic., *In Verr.* II iii 88 (Lat. Heraclius)
—HALAISA: (12) ii BC *IGSI* 2 B II, 14 (Dubois, *IGDS* 196) (s. Διογένης)
—HALAISA?: (13) s. ii BC *IG* XIV 355 (Ἡ. Κα—: s. Διόδωρος)
—HALOUNTION: (14) i BC-i AD? ib. 369 (f. Ἀγάθαρχος)
—INESSA-AITNA: (15) ii-i BC *Riv. Stor. Antica* 5 (1900-1) p. 55 no. 28 + *Sic. Gymn.* 16 (1963) p. 57 (f. Εὐβουλίδας)
—KAMARINA: (16) f. v BC Cordano, *Tessere Pubbliche* 42 (Arena, *Iscr. Sic.* II 135 A) (ℎεράκλει[ος]: s. Θέστων); (17) ?iv/iii BC *SEG* XXXIV 940, 8 (Dubois, *IGDS* 124; *PdelP* 44 (1989) p. 192 no. 3; Cordano, 'Camarina VII' 110) (s. Νίκων)
—KENTORIPA: (18) hell. *IG* XIV 574, 1 (Dubois, *IGDS* 188) (Ἡ. Ἀριστόνικος: s. Ἀ—); (19) ?i BC *IG* XIV 575 (s. Ἀριστόφυλος); (20) f. i BC *RE* (6) (Lat. Heraclius)
—LIPARA*: (21) ii/i BC *Meligunis-Lipara* 2 p. 60 T. 180; cf. *Kokalos* 32 (1986) pp. 226-7 nos. 34-9 (tiles)
—MORGANTINA: (22) iv/iii BC *SEG* XXXIX 1012, 5 (Ἡρ[άκλει]ος?: s. Φιλωνίδας); (23) ~ ib. l. 5 (f. —ικλῆς)
—PETRA: (24) f. iii BC ib. XXX 1121, 25 (Dubois, *IGDS* 208) (s. Ἡρακλείδας); (25) imp.? *BTCGI* 13 p. 495 (s. Διονύσιος)
—SEGESTA: (26) 72 BC *RE* (7) (Lat. Heraclius)
—SYRACUSE: (27) 73-70 BC ib. (4) (Lat. Heraclius: s. Ἱέρων); (28) 70 BC ib. (5) (Lat. Heraclius)
SICILY?: (29) hell. *IG* XIV 2406. 1 (vase); *Sic. Gymn.* 2 (1949) p. 105; *AJA* 64 (1960) pp. 80 ff. nos. 2 A-B (or S. Italy?)

## Ἡράκλειτος

ACHAIA: (1) ?ii BC *Memnonion* 188 (s. Πολέμαρχος); (2) f. ii BC *Aegyptus* 49 (1969) pp. 5-8; cf. *Achaia und Elis* p. 64
—PATRAI: (3) ii BC *Achaean Grave Stelai* 35 (Ἡρά]κλειτος)
ACHAIA?: (4) 193 BC *IG* V (2) 293, 9 (f. Ἀριστείδας)
AITOLIA:
—PROSCH(E)ION: (5) 192 BC ib. IX (1)² (1) 31, 26 (f. Λύκος, Σιμίας)

AKARNANIA: (6) iii BC Robert, *EEP* p. 114, 6; (7) 213 BC *PRain Cent.* p. 317 no. 47 A, [14]; p. 317 no. 47 B, 9
—ANAKTORION: (8) 208 BC *IMM* 31, 5 (*IG* IX (1)² (2) 582) (f. Ἀν—)
—ASTAKOS: (9) m. iii BC *SEG* XXVII 153, 4; cf. *PAE* 1977, pl. 244 b (f. Κνέφιος); (10) ii BC *IG* IX (1)² (2) 435, 12 (s. Λεοντίσκος)
—PHOITIAI: (11) m. ii BC ib. 208, 4, 33 (f. Φιλόξενος)
—THYRREION: (12) c. 315-280 BC *SGDI* 2658 (Ἡράκ]λειτος)
ARGOLIS:
—ARGOS: (13) ?257-253 BC Nachtergael, *Les Galates* 7, 39; 10, 51; cf. Osborne, *Naturalization* T96 (Stephanis 1089) + Stephanis 1094 (and Athens: s. Δίων); (14) ii-i BC *NZ* 9 (1877) pp. 54-6; *BMC Pelop.* p. 147 no. 147 (coins); (15) 105 BC *JÖAI* 14 (1911) Beibl. 146 no. 4, 19 (Ἡ]ράκλειτος); (16) i BC-i AD Unp. (Argos, Kavvadias)
ARKADIA:
—MANTINEIA-ANTIGONEIA: (17) ?iii BC *IG* V (2) 318, 7
—TEGEA: (18) iii BC ib. 30, 3 (Ἡρ]άκλειτ[ο]ς: s. Εὐτυχίδας)
ELIS: (19) ?257 BC Nachtergael, *Les Galates* 7, 50 (Stephanis 1095) (Ἡράκλει]τος: s. Ἡρακλείδας); (20) i BC/i AD *IvOl* 61, 7 (Ἡ]ρά[κλ]ειτ[ος]: f. Κλεόδαμος)
EPIROS: (21) ?255-254 BC Nachtergael, *Les Galates* 8, 80; 9, 65 (f. Νίκων)
—AMBRAKIA: (22) ii-i BC *CIG* 1800, 7 (f. Κράτης); (23) ~ ib. l. 8 (s. Κράτης)
—BOUTHROTOS (PRASAIBOI): (24) a. 163 BC *IBouthrot* 13, 17; cf. Ugolini, *Alb. Ant.* 3 p. 120 (Ἡ]ράκλειτος: s. Κλευκράτης); (25) ~ *IBouthrot* 17, 29 (*SEG* XXXVIII 474) (s. Φιλιστίων); (26) ~ *IBouthrot* 30, 40 (Ἡρά[κλει]τος)
ILLYRIA:
—EPIDAMNOS-DYRRHACHION: (27) ii-i BC *IDyrrh* 237 (s. Θεοτέλης)
—KERKYRA: (28) c. 85 BC *IOrop* 521, 29, 33, 37, 61 (f. Μικίνας)
KORINTHIA:
—SIKYON: (29) hell. Ps.-Plu., *Fluv.* 13. 4 (Skalet 138)
S. ITALY (APULIA):
—VENUSIA*: (30) imp. *Epigraphica* 35 (1973) p. 150 no. 12 (Lat. Q. Ovius Heraclitus: freed.)
S. ITALY (CALABRIA):
—TARAS-TARENTUM: (31) f. iv BC *IG* XII (9) 187 (*Syll*³ 106); (32) 324 BC *RE* Supplbd. 4 (6a) (Berve 351; Stephanis 1093); (33) ?253 BC Nachtergael, *Les Galates* 10, 46 (Stephanis 1103) (s. Νικόδαμος)
SICILY:
—LIPARA: (34) hell. *IG* II² 9214 (f. Καλλίας)

## Ἡρακλείων

S. ITALY (CAMPANIA):
—NOLA*: (1) imp. *Atti Acc. Pontan.* 21 (1971-2) pp. 392-7 (Lat. [C.] [Au]relius Heraclio: freed.)
SICILY:
—KATANE: (2) iii-v AD *Oikoumene* p. 604 no. 1 (-κλίων)
—SYRACUSE: (3) iii-v AD Ferrua, *NG* 207 (-κλίων)
—ZANKLE-MESSANA: (4) imp. *Epigraphica* 3 (1941) p. 256 no. 10 (-κλίων)

## Ἡρακλεόδωρος

AKARNANIA:
—STRATOS: (1) iv/iii BC *IG* IX (1)² (2) 395, 9 (Ἡρακλεό[δωρος]: f. Θυϊωνίδας)

## Ἡρακλέων

ARGOLIS:
—TROIZEN: (1) imp. ib. IV (1) 797, 3 (Ἡρα[κ]λέων: f. Εἰνάλιος)
EPIROS:
—NIKOPOLIS: (2) imp. *Hellenika* 22 (1969) p. 68 no. 4 (Sarikakis 54)

ILLYRIA:
—AMANTIA: (3) hell.? Ugolini, *Alb. Ant.* 1 p. 197 no. 19 (f. *M. Λυκόφρων*)
—EPIDAMNOS-DYRRHACHION: (4) c. 250-50 BC Maier 133; Münsterberg p. 39 (coin) (Ceka 205-6) (money.)
KEPHALLENIA:
—KRANIOI: (5) imp.? *IG* IX (1) 612 (I f. *Ἡρακλέων* II); (6) ~ ib. (II s. *Ἡρακλέων* I)
S. ITALY (CAMPANIA):
—DIKAIARCHIA-PUTEOLI: (7) imp. *CIL* X 2503 (Lat. Heracleon)
—DIKAIARCHIA-PUTEOLI*: (8) imp. ib. 2829 (Lat. C. Pavillius Heracleo: freed.)
—NEAPOLIS: (9) i AD *SEG* XXXVII 783 B (*INap* 153); cf. Leiwo p. 118 no. 105 (*Πάκκ(ιος) Ἡ.*)

**Ἡρακληΐδας**
S. ITALY (CALABRIA):
—TARAS-TARENTUM: (1) c. 280-272 BC Vlasto 814-17 (Evans, *Horsemen* pp. 161 VII L.1; p. 162 VII M.1); cf. *SNG ANS Etruria–Calabria* 1155 (coins) (*ηηρακληΐ(δας)*)
—TARAS-TARENTUM?: (2) ?iv BC *IG* XIV 2405. 13 (lamp) (*ηηρα*-: s. *Νευμήνιος*)

**Ἡρακλῆς**
S. ITALY (CALABRIA):
—TARAS-TARENTUM: (1) inc. Ael., *NA* viii 22 (fict.?); (2) iv-iii BC *SEG* XXXVI 896 (Troisi, *Epigrafi mobili* 73 (loomweight)) (*ηηρα*-)

**Ἡρακλῆς**
ARKADIA:
—KLEITOR: (1) ?i BC *AR* 1994-5, p. 17 (s. *Δράκων*)
KORINTHIA:
—KORINTH: (2) imp. *SEG* XXVII 59

**Ἡράκλητος**
S. ITALY (APULIA):
—AUSCULUM: (1) c. 340-320 BC *RVAp* p. 720 no. 880 (vase)
S. ITALY (BRUTTIUM):
—LOKROI EPIZEPHYRIOI:
——(*Ἀγκ*.): (2) iv/iii BC De Franciscis 7, 8 (f. *Γοργίας*)
——(*Θρα*.): (3) iv/iii BC ib. 3, 7 (f. *Φίντων*) ?= (4); (4) 281 BC ib. 1, 3; 34, 3, 14 ?= (3)
——(*Πετ*.): (5) iv/iii BC ib. 4, 5; 22, 6 (s. *Εὔφρων*)
——(*Προ*.): (6) iv/iii BC ib. 19, 5 (f. *Φιλίαρχος*)
—RHEGION: (7) hell. *IG* XIV 2400. 4 (tile); (8) s. ii BC ib. 615, 3; *Klearchos* 21 (1979) pp. 83-96 (date) (f. *Σύμμαχος*)
S. ITALY (CALABRIA):
—TARAS-TARENTUM: (9) hell.? *IG* XIV 2406. 25 (*RA* 1932 (1), p. 39 no. 20) (*ηηρά*-); (10) c. 272-235 BC Vlasto 890-3; 1089-90 (coins) (Evans, *Horsemen* p. 179 VIII G.1-2; p. 182 no. 2) (*ηηρά*-)
S. ITALY (LUCANIA):
—HERAKLEIA:
——(*Πε. καρυκεῖον*): (11) iv/iii BC *IGSI* 1 I, 4, 9, 97, 186 (*DGE* 62; Uguzzoni–Ghinatti I); *IGSI* 1 II, 4, 8 (*DGE* 63; Uguzzoni–Ghinatti II) (*ηηρά*-: f. *Ἀπολλώνιος*)
SICILY:
—TAUROMENION: (12) c. 238 BC *IG* XIV 421 an. 3 (*SGDI* 5219) (s. *Ἀγώνιππος*); (13) c. 213-159 BC *IG* XIV 421 an. 28; 421 an. 40; 421 an. 82 (*SGDI* 5219) (s. *Κλείνιππος*, f. *Κλείνιππος*); (14) c. 170-162 BC *IG* XIV 421 an. 71; 421 an. 79 (*SGDI* 5219); *IGSI* 4 II (III), 15 an. 71 (s. *Διονύσιος*); (15) c. 155 BC *IG* XIV 421 an. 86 (*SGDI* 5219) (f. *Ἀρίσταρχος*); (16) c. 149 BC *IG* XIV 421 an. 92 (*SGDI* 5219); *IGSI* 4 III (IV), 50 an. 92 (s. *Ἀπολλόδωρος*)
——(*Ἀχαιο*.): (17) ?ii/i BC *IG* XIV 421 D an. 7 (*SGDI* 5219)
——(*Οἰτ*.): (18) ii/i BC *IGSI* 5 III, 18; 7 II, 18 (f. *Ὀλυμπις*)

——(*Πιπρε*.): (19) ii/i BC ib. 12 II, 1 (s. *Ἀπολλόδωρος*)

**Ἡράκλις**
SICILY:
—SYRACUSE: (1) iii-v AD Strazzulla 198 (Wessel 1331)

**Ἡρακώ**
AIGINA?: (1) imp. *EAD* XXX p. 356 no. 16 with n. 1 (d. *Νικηφᾶς*)

**Ἡρᾶς**
ARKADIA:
—KLEITOR: (1) imp. *IG* V (2) 378
—TEGEA: (2) i-ii AD ib. 53 (?s. *K—*); (3) 165 AD ib. 50, 24 (f. *Δῖος*)
ELIS: (4) 113-117 AD *IvOl* 91, 16 (s. *Ἡρακλείδης*)
KERKYRA: (5) imp. *IG* IX (1) 953 (f. *Εὐτύχης*)
KORINTHIA:
—SIKYON: (6) ii-iii AD *SEG* XI 256, 12 (?s. *Σωσικράτης*)
LAKONIA:
—SPARTA: (7) c. 90-105 AD ib. 512, 2; 562, 2 (Bradford (-)) (f. *Ἀριστοκράτης*)
MESSENIA:
—KORONE: (8) 246 AD *IG* V (1) 1398, 82 (*Αὐρ. Ἡ.*)
S. ITALY (CAMPANIA):
—DIKAIARCHIA-PUTEOLI: (9) imp. *CIL* X 2330 (Lat. L. Cornelius Hera)
—MISENUM*: (10) imp. ib. 3421 (Lat. M. Sabinius Hera)

**Ἡρέας**
LAKONIA:
—SPARTA: (1) c. 125 AD *IG* V (1) 1314, 11 (Bradford (-)) (*Ἡρ[έ]ας*: f. *Φιλόμηλος*)
SICILY:
—MELITA: (2) s. ii BC *IGUR* 3, 7 (*IG* XIV 953)
—TAUROMENION: (3) c. 186 BC ib. 421 an. 55 (*SGDI* 5219); (4) c. 170 BC *IG* XIV 421 an. 71 (*SGDI* 5219) (s. *Ὀνόμαστος*)

**Ἡρέννη**
S. ITALY (CAMPANIA):
—NEAPOLIS: (1) i BC-i AD *INap* 124; cf. Leiwo p. 84 no. 32 (d. *Νύμφιος*)

**Ἡρίγονος**
KORINTHIA:
—SIKYON: (1) m. iii BC Overbeck 2105 (Skalet 139) (Lat. Erigonus: painter)

**Ἡριδανός**
LAKONIA:
—GYTHEION: (1) imp. *IG* V (1) 1191

**Ἡρίδας**
LAKONIA:
—SPARTA: (1) s. i BC ib. 94, 14 (Bradford (-)) (*Ἡρίδ[ας]*?—ed., *Ἰφιδ[άμας]*?—Fraenkel: f. *Πασιτέλης*)

**Ἡρίμναστος**
ILLYRIA:
—EPIDAMNOS-DYRRHACHION: (1) hell.-imp. *IDyrrh* 221 (f. *Ζωΐλα*)

**Ἡριππίδας**
LAKONIA:
—SPARTA: (1) c. 430-379 BC *RE* (-) (Poralla² 349)

**Ἡρίφιλος**
SICILY:
—SELINOUS: (1) vi/v BC Manganaro, *PdelP* forthcoming no. 18, 3 (*Ἐρί*-: s. *Τερπέφιλος*)

**Ἡρόδικος**
SICILY:
—LEONTINOI: (1) v BC *RE* (4) (s. *Χαρμαντίδης*: doctor)

**Ἡρόδοτος**
AITOLIA:
—THERMOS*: (1) s. iii BC *IG* IX (1)² (1) 60 III, 23
ARKADIA:
—TEGEA: (2) 78 AD ib. V (2) 49, 9 (*[Ἡ]ρόδοτος*)
ILLYRIA:
—EPIDAMNOS-DYRRHACHION: (3) c. 250-50 BC Maier 116; 205; 213; 312; 333; 340; 383; 391; 486 (Ceka 207-16); *SNG Fitz. Macedonia–Acarnania* pl. 46 no. 2544 (coin) (*Ἡρό(δοτος)*—Ceka 207: money.)
S. ITALY (CAMPANIA):
—POMPEII?: (4) i BC-i AD *CIL* IV 8406 (Lat. Herodotus)
S. ITALY (LUCANIA):
—HYELE-VELIA: (5) hell. *Op. Ath.* 10 (1971) p. 65 no. 8 (f. *Φιλίσκος*)
SICILY:
—KEPHALOIDION: (6) f. i BC Cic., *In Verr.* II ii 128; 130 (Lat. Herodotus)

**Ἡρόδωρος**
ARGOLIS:
—EPIDAUROS: (1) m. iv BC *IG* II² 8489 (*Ἡρό[δ]ωρος*: f. *Λυσίς*)
EPIROS:
—AMBRAKIA: (2) iii BC *SEG* XXIV 413 (*Πρόδωρος*—Peranthes *Ambrakia* ad loc.: s. *Ἕρμων*)

**Ἡρος**
ARKADIA:
—TEGEA: (1) ii AD *IG* V (2) 55, 43 (*Ἡρος*: s. *Δημήτριος*)

**Ἡροφάνης**
ARGOLIS:
—TROIZEN: (1) imp.? *FGrH* 605

**Ἡροφίλα**
S. ITALY (CAMPANIA):
—DIKAIARCHIA-PUTEOLI*: (1) imp. *CIL* X 2669 (Lat. Lucceia Herophila: freed.)

**Ἡρόφιλος**
ACHAIA:
—PATRAI: (1) i AD *ILGR* 60, 2 (Lat. M. Fulvius Herophilus: doctor)
ARGOLIS:
—ARGOS: (2) i BC-i AD Unp. (Argos, Kavvadias)

**Ἡρύλος**
SICILY:
—THERMAI HIMERAIAI: (1) i-ii AD *Kokalos* 20 (1974) p. 236 no. 9 (f. *Ἡραΐς*)

**Ἡρυτος**
SICILY:
—KENTORIPA: (1) ?s. iii BC *Sic. Gymn.* 2 (1949) p. 91 no. 1, 15 + 16 (1963) p. 54 (*Ἡρυτ[ος]*)

**Ἡρώ**
ARGOLIS:
—ARGOS: (1) iv BC *SEG* XIV 321 (*Ἡρ[ώ]*)

**Ἡρωΐδας**
ARKADIA:
—MANTINEIA-ANTIGONEIA: (1) c. 300-221 BC *IG* V (2) 323. 56 (tessera) (f. *Ἀρχίας*)
—PHENEOS: (2) ?ii BC *SEG* XIX 328 (f. *Θηρίλαος*); (3) 191-146 BC *BMC Pelop.* p. 14 no. 158 (coin)
DALMATIA:
—ISSA:
——(Pamphyloi): (4) iv/iii BC Brunšmid p. 8, 49 (s. *Βουλαγόρας*)
S. ITALY (LUCANIA):
—HERAKLEIA: (5) iv/iii BC *IGSI* 1 I, 15, 42, 55, 87, etc. (*DGE* 62; Uguzzoni–Ghinatti I) (*ηηρωΐδεια* (estate))
SICILY:
—SYRACUSE: (6) 397 BC X., *HG* iii 4. 1 (-*ρώ*-)

**Ἡρωΐδης**
ARGOLIS:
—KLEONAI: (1) i BC-i AD SEG XXV 277, 2 (f. Σωσικράτεια)
ARKADIA:
—TEGEA: (2) 191 AD IG V (2) 52, 7 (Ἰούλ. Ἡρώδης)
ELIS: (3) imp. IvOl [734]; 735 (tiles)
KERKYRA: (4) c. 229-48 BC BMC Thessaly p. 147 nos. 504-9; SNG Cop. Epirus–Acarnania 231 (coins) (-ρώδ-)
LAKONIA:
—BOIAI: (5) ii AD IG V (1) 958, 4; 959, 4 (f. Ἡρακλέα)
PELOPONNESE: (6) 112 BC FD III (2) 70 A, 31 (-ώδης: f. Φίλιππος)
S. ITALY (CAMPANIA):
—MISENUM*: (7) imp. CIL X 3449 (Lat. Herodes)

**Ἡρωΐς**
ILLYRIA:
—APOLLONIA: (1) imp. IApoll 238 (?d. Φιλιππίδης)
S. ITALY (APULIA):
—LUCERIA: (2) imp. CIL IX 871 (Lat. Allia Herois: m. Naevia Allia)
—LUCERIA*: (3) imp. ASP 34 (1981) p. 7 no. 5 (Lat. Herois: freed.)

**Ἡρων**
AIGINA: (1) hell.? IG IV (1) 1589; (2) ii BC ib. 10
ARGOLIS:
—ARGOS: (3) imp. ib. 648 (f. Ἀτίμητος)
DALMATIA:
—EPETION: (4) imp. CIL III 8524 (Lat. Sex. Gellius Ero)
S. ITALY (CAMPANIA):
—PITHEKOUSSAI-AENARIA: (5) ?iii AD Epigraphica 34 (1972) p. 133 (Lat. Haero)

**Ἡρῶναξ**
S. ITALY (CALABRIA):
—TARAS-TARENTUM: (1) ?iii BC HE 2542 (fict.?)

**Ἡρώνδας**
LAKONIA:
—SPARTA: (1) inc. Plu., Mor. 221 C (Poralla² 350)

**Ἡσίδωρος**
PELOPONNESE?: (1) ii AD PAE 1992, p. 72 B, 19 (s. Κλεόνικος)

**Ἡσίοδος**
ARKADIA:
—MEGALOPOLIS: (1) c. 225 BC SEG XI 414, 27 (Perlman E.5) (f. Ἀλεξιμένης)

**Ἡσιόνη**
SICILY:
—THERMAI HIMERAIAI: (1) imp. Eph. Ep. VIII 707 (ILat. Term. Imer. 150) (Lat. Modia Hesione: m. Trebonia Modia)

**Ἧσις?**
ILLYRIA:
—EPIDAMNOS-DYRRHACHION: (1) iv BC IDyrrh 34 (s./d. Ἀριστείδας)

**Ἡσυχία**
ARGOLIS:
—ARGOS: (1) imp. IG II² 8367
EPIROS: (2) iii BC ib. 8536
S. ITALY (LUCANIA):
—HERAKLEIA*: (3) f. iv BC SEG XXX 1162; cf. XXXVI 914 (ἡσυ-: slave?)
ZAKYNTHOS: (4) ?iv BC ib. XL 507

**Ἡσύχιον**
ACHAIA:
—KARYNEIA?: (1) ii BC Achaean Grave Stelai 24
S. ITALY (CALABRIA):
—MESSAPIOI: (2) ii BC IG XII (1) 517

**Ἡσύχιος**
KORINTHIA:
—KORINTH: (1) iii-iv AD Corinth VIII (1) 92; cf. SEG XI 79; cf. TMByz 9 (1985) p. 360 no. 8
S. ITALY (CALABRIA):
—BRENTESION-BRUNDISIUM: (2) imp. CIL IX 6128 (Lat. L. Negilius Esych(ius))
S. ITALY (CAMPANIA):
—DIKAIARCHIA-PUTEOLI: (3) imp. ib. X 2518 (Lat. Esychius)
—HERCULANEUM*: (4) i BC-i AD ib. 1403 e, 9 (Lat. A. Tetteius Hesych[ius]: freed.)
SICILY:
—SYRACUSE: (5) iii-v AD Strazzulla 256 + Nuovo Didask. 6 (1956) pp. 55-6 no. 10

**Ἡσύχις**
SICILY:
—SYRACUSE: (1) iii-v AD Barreca 395; (2) ~ Nuovo Didask. 4 (1950) p. 60 no. 11

**Ἡσυχος**
LAKONIA:
—SPARTA: (1) c. 100-120 AD SEG XI 610, 10 (Bradford (-)) (s. No—)
S. ITALY: (2) imp. CIL X 8059. 17 (seal) (Lat. L. Aemilius Hesycus)
S. ITALY (CAMPANIA):
—DIKAIARCHIA-PUTEOLI: (3) imp. ib. 3284 (Lat. Esichus)
—POMPEII: (4) i BC-i AD ib. IV 8557

**Ἡφαιστίων**
S. ITALY (CAMPANIA):
—POMPEII*: (1) 3 BC ib. X 796 (I f. Γ. Ἰούλ. Ἡφαιστίων II); (2) ~ ib. (Γ. Ἰούλ. Ἡ.: II s. Ἡφαιστίων I)

**Ἦχος**
SICILY:
—SYRACUSE: (1) ii-i BC SEG XVI 538 i; cf. Rend. Linc. 28 (1973) pp. 541-2

# Θ

**Θαηΐς**
ARGOLIS:
—ARGOS: (1) iii BC Mnem. NS 47 (1919) p. 166 no. 14

**Θαΐς**
ARGOLIS:
—HERMIONE: (1) ?ii-i BC IG IV (1) 731 III, 8 (d. Ἡρακλείδας)
S. ITALY (CALABRIA):
—BRENTESION-BRUNDISIUM: (2) imp. CIL IX 188 (Lat. Sextia Thais)
—TARAS-TARENTUM: (3) 281 BC RE s.v. Philocharis (-) (Φιλόχαρις ὁ ἐπικαλ. Θ.)
S. ITALY (CAMPANIA):
—DIKAIARCHIA-PUTEOLI: (4) imp. CIL X 2220 (Lat. Iunia Thais)
—DIKAIARCHIA-PUTEOLI*: (5) imp. ib. 2162 (Lat. Fabia Thais: freed.)
—POMPEII: (6) i BC-i AD ib. IV 8137 (Lat. Taine)
S. ITALY (LUCANIA):
—VOLCEI: (7) imp. IItal III (1) 88 (CIL X 382) (Lat. Arria Thais)
SICILY:
—SYRACUSE?: (8) iii-v AD Riv. Arch. Crist. 18 (1941) p. 235 no. 129 (Θ[αΐ]δος (gen.))

**Θαλάμη**
S. ITALY (CALABRIA):
—TARAS-TARENTUM*: (1) imp. NScav 1897, p. 68 (Lat. Thalame: d. Quinta: imp. slave?)
S. ITALY (CAMPANIA):
—DIKAIARCHIA-PUTEOLI: (2) 144 AD CIL X 1597 (Lat. Thalame)

**Θάλαμος**
ILLYRIA:
—APOLLONIA: (1) i BC IApoll 219 (f. Μᾶρκος)
S. ITALY (APULIA):
—CANUSIUM: (2) 223 AD Epig. Rom. di Canosa 35 III, 15 (CIL IX 338) (Lat. Q. Fabius Thalamus)
S. ITALY (CAMPANIA):
—POMPEII: (3) i BC-i AD Atti Acc. Pontan. 39 (1990) p. 301 no. 133 (Lat. Thalamus); (4) 70-79 AD CIL IV 933; Mouritsen p. 111 (date) (Lat. Thalamus); (5) ~ CIL IV 1083; Mouritsen p. 109 (date) (Lat. Thalamus)

**Θαλάσσιος**
S. ITALY (CALABRIA):
—TARAS-TARENTUM: (1) iii AD Arch. Class. 31 (1979) p. 133 no. 1 (Lat. Tala[ssi]us)

**Θάλεια**
ARGOLIS:
—ARGOS: (1) ii AD SEG XI 304, 1
MESSENIA:
—MESSENE?: (2) ii/i BC ib. 979, 38 (-λια)
S. ITALY (APULIA):
—GNATHIA-EGNATIA: (3) i AD Suppl. It. 11 p. 46 no. 30 (Lat. Thalia)
S. ITALY (CAMPANIA):
—POMPEII: (4) i BC-i AD CIL IV 1309 a-b (Lat. Thalia); (5) ~ Neue Forsch. in Pompeji p. 266 no. 58 (Lat. Thaleia)
SICILY:
—THERMAI HIMERAIAI*: (6) i-ii AD CIL X 7392 (ILat. Term. Imer. 74) (Lat. Clodia Thalia: freed.?)

**Θαλῆς**
AIGINA: (1) ?c. 550-525 BC SEG XI 1 (Lazzarini 53); LSAG² p. 112 no. 5 (date); (2) s. v BC Favorin. fr. 64 (f. Φειδιάδας)
KORINTHIA:
—SIKYON: (3) iv BC RE (6) (Skalet 140) (painter)
S. ITALY (CAMPANIA):
—HERCULANEUM*: (4) i BC-i AD CIL X 1403 g III, 36 (Lat. C. Volasenna Thales: freed.)

**Θαλησικλῆς**
Messenia:
—Messene: **(1)** c. 240-220 bc *IG* vii 359, 3 (*IOrop* 166) (f. *Πανίτας*)

**Θαλιαρχίδας**
Messenia?: **(1)** ii/i bc *SEG* xi 979, 8

**Θαλιαρχίς**
Argolis:
—Argos: **(1)** f. iii bc Tat., *Orat.* 33 (het.?)

**Θαλίαρχος**
Argolis:
—Argos: **(1)** iii bc *SEG* xiii 370; Marcadé i 105 (s. *Θευγένης*: sculptor)
Elis: **(2)** c. 146-32 bc Clerk, *Coins Ach. League* p. 17 no. 271 (coin); **(3)** s. i bc Moretti, *Olymp.* 718; 722 (s. *Σωτήριχος*); **(4)** 69-73 ad *IvOl* 84, 23 (?f. —ανός)
Lakonia:
—sparta: **(5)** f. ii bc *IC* 2 p. 23 no. 6 D (Bradford (4)) (f. *Πεισίδαμος*); **(6)** c. 90-100 ad *SEG* xi 558, 8 (Bradford (1)) (s. *Φιλόξενος*); **(7)** c. 140-160 ad *IG* v (1) 109, 14 + *SEG* xi 588 (Bradford (3)) (*Θύ(ν)αρχος*—*IG*, *Θ(α)λίαρχος*—*SEG*: f. *Καλλικράτης*) ?= (*8*); **(8)** ~ *IG* v (1) 154, 7 (Bradford (2)) (f. *Εὐδαμίδας*) ?= (7)
—tainaron-kainepolis: **(9)** 238-244 ad *IG* v (1) 1241, 7 (I f. *M. Αὐρ. Θαλίαρχος* II); **(10)** ~ ib. l. 7 (*M. Αὐρ. Θ.*: II s. *Θαλίαρχος* I)
Messenia:
—kyparissia: **(11)** iii bc ib. 1424 (f. *Ἀριστέας*)
—messene: **(12)** i ad ib. 1436, 5 (*Σέκστος Πομπ. Θ.*)

**Θαλίδαμος**
Messenia:
—messene: **(1)** ii/iii ad ib. 1472

**Θάλινος**
Messenia:
—thouria: **(1)** f. ii bc *SEG* xi 972, 117 (f. *Εὔξενος*)

**Θάλιος**
Lakonia:
—karyai?: **(1)** ii/i bc *IG* v (1) 923
—sparta: **(2)** c. 25-1 bc ib. 210, 8 (Bradford (-)) (s. *Λυίξενίδας*)
Messenia:
—thouria: **(3)** f. ii bc *SEG* xi 972, 110 (f. *Κλεάρετος*)

**Θάλιππος**
Messenia:
—messene: **(1)** ?f. i ad *PAE* 1992, p. 79, 6 (s. *Ἀρίστων*) ?= (2)
——(Kleolaidai): **(2)** ii ad ib. p. 71 A, 24 (s. *Ἀρίστων*) ?= (1)

**Θαλλέας**
Messenia:
—messene: **(1)** i bc *AM* 67 (1942) p. 220 no. 16 (s. *Θήριππος*)

**Θαλλία**
S. Italy (Campania):
—salernum: **(1)** imp. *IItal* i (1) 223 (Lat. Thallia)

**Θαλλίεπος**
Messenia:
—messene: **(1)** ?ii ad *SEG* xli 335, 16 (s. *Εὐθύδαμος*)

**Θάλλινος**
Argolis:
—argos: **(1)** 105 bc *JÖAI* 14 (1911) Beibl. p. 146 no. 4, 23 (f. *Ξηναγόρα*)

**Θαλλίσκος**
Sicily:
—katane: **(1)** imp. *Helikon* 2 (1962) p. 489 (*Θαλλί(σ)κος*)

**Θαλλίων**
S. Italy (Apulia):
—barion: **(1)** imp. *Mus. Arch. di Bari* p. 153 no. 7 (Lat. Thallion)
S. Italy (Campania):
—salernum*: **(2)** ?s. i ad *IItal* i (1) 14 (*CIL* x 535) (Lat. T. Fla. Tallio: s. *Ἐλπίς*)

**Θάλλος**
Arkadia:
—kleitor: **(1)** a. 212 ad *SEG* xxxi 347, 18 (*Αὐρ. Θ.*: s. *Εὔκαρπος*)
—tegea: **(2)** s. iv bc ib. xxxvi 383, 8 (*Θάλος*: f. *Κόλχος*); **(3)** 165 ad *IG* v (2) 50, 62 (s. *Ζώπυρος*)
——(Apolloniatai): **(4)** s. iv bc ib. 41, 10 (f. —ος)
Korinthia:
—korinth: **(5)** s. i ad ib. x (2) (1) 69, 38 (s. *Εὔτυχος*)
S. Italy (Apulia):
—vibinum: **(6)** ii ad *Taras* 12 (1992) p. 156 no. 3 (Lat. Thallus: ?f. *Ἀφροδισία*)
S. Italy (Bruttium):
—rhegion: **(7)** imp. *CIL* x 8339 d (Lat. Publicius Tallus)
—skylletion: **(8)** imp. *Atti Centro Studi Documentazione* 2 (1969-70) p. 122 no. 4 (Lat. –ius Thallus)
S. Italy (Calabria):
—brentesion-brundisium: **(9)** imp. *NScav* 1892, p. 353 v = *Epigraphica* 25 (1963) p. 68 no. 64 (Lat. C. Publicius Thallus)
S. Italy (Campania):
—capreae*: **(10)** imp. *ZPE* 71 (1988) p. 197 no. 9 (Lat. Thallus: freed.)
—dikaiarchia-puteoli: **(11)** imp. *CIL* x 2231 (Lat. M. Carvilius Thallus); **(12)** ~ ib. 2775 (Lat. C. Aulius Thallus); **(13)** ~ ib. 2782 (Lat. C. Novius Thallus: f. C. Novius Sabinianus, Novia Iusta); **(14)** ~ ib. 3004 (Lat. Thallus: f. Flora); **(15)** m. i ad Camodeca, *L'Archivio Puteolano* i p. 125 no. 5 (Lat. A. Mevius Thallus); **(16)** 48 ad ib. p. 106 no. 2 (Lat. L. Faenius Thallus)
—herculaneum: **(17)** 62 ad *Ostraka* 2 (1993) pp. 203-7 (Lat. C. Vibius Thallus)
—herculaneum*: **(18)** i bc-i ad *CIL* x 1403 f III, 4 (Lat. Thallus: freed.); **(19)** ~ ib. 1403 g III, 48 (Lat. L. Sestius Thallus: freed.)
—pompeii: **(20)** i bc-i ad ib. iv 10085 b; *Gnomon* 45 (1973) p. 269 (Lat. Thallus); **(21)** ?i ad *NScav* 1921, p. 428 (seal) (Castrèn 46. 3) (Lat. Thallus); **(22)** 56 ad *CIL* iv 3340. 25, 23, 26; 40, 18 (Castrèn 474. 2) (Lat. D. Volcius Thallus)
Sicily:
—aigates islands: **(23)** imp. *CIL* x 7493 (Lat. Thallus: f. *Νάρκισσος*)
—kephaloidion: **(24)** ?iii-v ad *IGLMP* 11

**Θάλλουσα**
Argolis:
—argos: **(1)** i bc-i ad Unp. (Argos, Kavvadias)
Korinthia:
—korinth: **(2)** imp. *CIL* iii 7277, 5 (Lat. Atilia Thallusa: d. T. Atilius)
Messenia:
—messene: **(3)** ?i ad *IG* v (1) 1482; cf. p. 311 (*Θάλουσα(α)*, *Θαλοῦς*?—Wilhelm)
S. Italy (Apulia):
—canusium*: **(4)** ii ad *Epig. Rom. di Canosa* 86 (Lat. Maria Thallusa: freed.)
S. Italy (Bruttium):
—tauriana: **(5)** imp. *Eph. Ep.* viii 252 (Lat. [La]ridia [Th]allusa)

**Θαλλώ**
Arkadia:
—tegea: **(1)** imp. *IG* v (2) 86 (*Θαλλ[ώ]*)

**Θάλπις**
Lakonia:
—sparta: **(1)** 680 bc Moretti, *Olymp.* 32 (Poralla² 353)

**Θάλπων**
Sicily:
—akrai: **(1)** iii-v ad *Riv. Arch. Crist.* 18 (1941) p. 218 no. 99

**Θάλων**
Leukas: **(1)** 216 bc *IG* ix (1)² (2) 583, 20 (f. *Βίανωρ*)
Messenia:
—messene: **(2)** ?35-44 ad ib. v (1) 1433, 24; *SEG* xxix 396 (date) (f. *Ἱππίσκα*, *Καλλίστα*)

**Θαμόφιλος**
Argolis:
—argos: **(1)** ?c. 550-525 bc *Argive Heraeum* 2 p. 366 no. 1877 (Lazzarini 841 bis); *LSAG*² p. 168 no. 12 (date)

**Θάμυρις**
Korinthia:
—korinth: **(1)** imp. *CIL* iii 7273, 3 (Lat. P. Caesennius Thamyris)

**Θάμυρος**
S. Italy (Campania):
—surrentum*: **(1)** imp. ib. x 722 (Lat. A. Caesennius Thamyrus: freed.)

**Θάρνα?**
Illyria:
—epidamnos-dyrrhachion: **(1)** hell.-imp.? *IDyrrh* 239 (d. *Ἀριστήν*)

**Θαρραγόρας**
S. Italy (Lucania):
—metapontion: **(1)** s. iv bc *HN*² p. 78 (coin) (her.?)

**Θαρρέδαμος**
Sicily:
—lipara*: **(1)** ii/i bc *Meligunis-Lipara* 5 p. 183 T. 2181; cf. *Kokalos* 32 (1986) p. 228 nos. 40-4 (tiles)

**Θαρρίας**
Sicily:
—tauromenion: **(1)** c. 240-226 bc *IG* xiv 421 an. 1; 421 an. 15 (*SGDI* 5219) (f. *Φιλιστίων*)

**Θάρριππος**
Sicily:
—tauromenion: **(1)** c. 195-181 bc *IG* xiv 421 an. 46; 421 an. 60 (*SGDI* 5219) (s. *Ἀγέστρατος*); **(2)** c. 170-146 bc *IG* xiv 421 an. 71; 421

an. 85; 421 an. 95; *IGSI* 4 II (III), 46 an. 75 (f. *Ζωΐλος*); (3) ?f. i BC ib. 4 I, 4 + *SEG* XXXIII 755 + XXXVIII 975 (*Θ[άρρι]π[πος?]*)
——(*Καλ.*): (4) ?ii/i BC *IG* XIV 421 D an. 2; 421 D an. 14 (*SGDI* 5219) (f. *Ζωΐλος*)

**Θαρρύδαμος**
SICILY:
—AKRAGAS: (1) c. 262 BC *IG* IX (1)² (1) 17 A, 93 (f. *Ἱκέτας*)
—KAMARINA: (2) iii BC Manganaro, *PdelP* forthcoming no. 1, 8 (f. *Σώσανδρος*)

**Θαρρύμαχος**
S. ITALY (BRUTTIUM):
—LOKROI EPIZEPHYRIOI:
——(*Ἀγφ.*): (1) iv/iii BC De Franciscis 9, 5

**Θαρρύνων**
KORINTHIA:
—SIKYON: (1) c. 225-200 BC *SEG* XIX 80, 15 (s. *Ἀπολλᾶς*); (2) ~ ib. l. 22 (*Θαρ[ρύνων]*: f. *Ἀπολλᾶς*)

**Θάρρων**
SICILY:
—SEGESTA: (1) f. v BC ib. XXX 1127 bis a + *Cron. Arch.* 16 (1977) p. 149 (vase); cf. Dubois, *IGDS* p. 271 n. 31 (*Θάρōν*)

**Θαρσαγόρας**
SICILY:
—SYRACUSE?:
——(*Ὑπα.*): (1) hell. Manganaro, *PdelP* forthcoming no. 4 IV, 4 (f. *Λεάναξ*)

**Θαρσίας**
ARGOLIS:
—HERMIONE: (1) iii BC *IG* IV (1) 729 I, 10 (s. *Ἄστωχος*)

**Θάρσος**
S. ITALY (CAMPANIA):
—SALERNUM*: (1) ?i AD *IItal* 1 (1) 238 III, 16 (*CIL* X 557) (Lat. L. Appuleius Tharsus: freed.)
—SURRENTUM: (2) imp. ib. 705 (Lat. Tharsus)

**Θαρσύας**
ARKADIA:
—ORCHOMENOS: (1) m. iii BC *IG* IV (1)² 96, 42 (Perlman E.3); Perlman p. 63 f. (date) (s. *Λαγορίδας*)

**Θαρσύννων**
DALMATIA:
—ISSA?: (1) iii/ii BC Brunšmid p. 31 no. 27; *Istros* 2 (1935-6) pp. 18 ff. (or Dalmatia Tragurion)

**Θαρσύνων**
S. ITALY (CAMPANIA):
—DIKAIARCHIA-PUTEOLI: (1) imp. *CIL* X 3005 (Lat. Tharsynon)
SICILY:
—MORGANTINA: (2) ?iv/iii BC *SEG* XXXIX 1009, 5 (f. *Λίσσος*)

**Θαρσύτας**
ARGOLIS:
—HERMIONE: (1) iii BC *IG* IV (1) 729 I, 6 (s. *Φιλητάδας*)

**Θαρτέας**
ILLYRIA:
—EPIDAMNOS-DYRRHACHION: (1) hell.-imp. *IDyrrh* 240

**Θαρυκίδας**
ARKADIA:
—PHIGALEIA: (1) c. 240 BC *IG* V (2) 419, 7 (*IPArk* 28)

**Θάρυξ**
ARKADIA:
—PHIGALEIA: (1) f. vii BC Paus. iv 24. 1

**Θάρυψ**
EPIROS:
—MOLOSSOI: (1) v/iv BC *RE* (-); Th. ii 80. 6 (name); cf. Osborne, *Naturalization* T6 (and Athens: *Θαρύπας*—Plut. & Paus.: f. *Ἀλκέτας*: king); (2) 356-354 BC *IG* IV (1)² 95, 31 (Perlman E.2); Perlman p. 40 f. (date)

**Θασίς**
KORINTHIA:
—KORINTH: (1) iv BC *SEG* XVIII 138 (Lazzarini 352) (m. *Κλεώ*)

**Θαύμανδρος**
AITOLIA:
—APERANTOI: (1) ?iii BC *L'Illyrie mérid.* 1 p. 108 no. 4; cf. p. 98 (locn.) (*SEG* XXXVII 434) (s. *Ἀριστόβουλος*)

**Θαυμαρέτα**
S. ITALY (BRUTTIUM):
—LOKROI EPIZEPHYRIOI: (1) iv/iii BC *HE* 2815

**Θαυμασία**
SICILY:
—KATANE: (1) imp. *CIL* X 7099 (Lat. Lysidia Thaumasie: m. Valeria Thermitana)

**Θαύμαστος**
KORINTHIA:
—TENEA: (1) c. 150-175 AD *Corinth* VIII (3) 228 a, 2 (s. *Ἐπίκτητος*)
S. ITALY (CAMPANIA):
—POMPEII: (2) i BC-i AD *CIL* IV 383 (Lat. Thaumastus); (3) ~ ib. 10085 b; *Gnomon* 45 (1973) p. 269 (Lat. Thaumastus)

**Θαυμέας**
ARGOLIS:
—ARGOS:
——(Pholygadai): (1) iii BC *SEG* XXXI 306, 2 (Perlman A.25) (f. *—στρατος*)

**Θαῦμις**
ARKADIA:
—PALLANTION*: (1) ?c. 500-475 BC *SEG* XXX 416 (bronze); *LSAG*² p. 449 no. 11a (date)
LAKONIA: (2) ?s. vi BC *CEG* 1 370 (Lazzarini 133); *SEG* XXX 501 (date)

**Θεάγγελος**
ARKADIA:
—MANTINEIA-ANTIGONEIA: (1) c. 300-221 BC *IG* V (2) 323. 61 (tessera) (s. *Θεομήδης*)
—MEGALOPOLIS: (2) ii BC ib. 536 (f. *Δαμάρης*)

**Θεαγένης**
ACHAIA:
—PATRAI: (1) ii AD *RE* (11)
ARKADIA:
—MEGALOPOLIS: (2) ii-iii AD *IG* V (2) 474 (*Θεαγέν[ης]*)
DALMATIA:
—ISSA: (3) f. ii BC Brunšmid p. 23 no. 10, 5 (*Θεάγ[ης]*: f. *Σωσύλος*)
EPIROS:
—NIKOPOLIS: (4) imp. *SEG* XXXVII 527 (Sarikakis 60) (*Ἰούλιος Θ.*: locn.—Cabanes)
LAKONIA:
—SPARTA: (5) 359 AD *SEG* XI 464, 5 (Bradford (-))
MESSENIA:
—KORONE: (6) f. iii AD *IvOl* 451, 5; *IG* V (1) 1398, 5, 13 (*Γ. Ἰούλ. Θ.*: II s. *Γ. Ἰούλ. Θεαγένης* I, f. *Γ. Κλώδιος Ἰούλ. Κλεόβουλος*); (7) ~ *IvOl* 452, 8; *IG* V (1) 1398, 11 (*Γ. Φούφ(ιος) Ἰούλ. Θ.*: s. *Γ. Κλώδιος Ἰούλ. Κλεόβουλος*); (8) a. 212 AD *IvOl* 451, 6 (*Γ. Ἰούλ. Θ.*: I f. *Γ. Ἰούλ. Θεαγένης* II)

—MESSENE: (9) 174 AD *SEG* XLI 337, 11
S. ITALY: (10) imp. *CIL* X 8059. 401 (seal) (Lat. Theagenes)
S. ITALY (BRUTTIUM):
—RHEGION: (11) s. vi BC *RE* (9); *FVS* 8
S. ITALY (CAMPANIA):
—MISENUM*: (12) ?ii-iii AD *AJA* 2 (1898) p. 393 no. 51 (Lat. P. Aelius Theagenes)

**Θεαγενίς**
SICILY:
—KATANE: (1) imp. *IG* XIV 505 (*Στατειλία Θ.*)

**Θεάγης**
ILLYRIA:
—AMANTIA: (1) f. ii BC *BCH* 45 (1921) p. 23 IV, 56 (*Θεάγ[ης?]*, *Θεαγ[ένης?]*: reading—Oulhen)
—EPIDAMNOS-DYRRHACHION: (2) c. 250-50 BC Maier 223 (coin) (Ceka 183) (pryt.); (3) ii-i BC *IDyrrh* 539 (tile) (*Θεάγ[ης?]*)
S. ITALY (BRUTTIUM):
—KROTON: (4) vi/v BC *RE* (1)
S. ITALY (LUCANIA):
—METAPONTION: (5) ?c. 550-525 BC Lazzarini 883 (Landi, *DISMG* 134); cf. *LSAG*² p. 260 no. 14 (date) (?s. *Βύρος*)

**Θεάδουσα**
LAKONIA: (1) ?v/iv BC Iamb., *VP* 267 (*FVS* 1 p. 448; Poralla² 552) (*Νισθεάδουσα*—ms. F & Diels: name—Deubner)

**Θεαίνετος**
ARKADIA:
—MANTINEIA-ANTIGONEIA: (1) c. 316-222 BC *SEG* XVII 143, 3, 9 (Perlman A.15) (s. *Περίανδρος*)

**Θεαῖος**
ARGOLIS:
—ARGOS: (1) ?444 BC Pi., *N.* x, 24, 37 (s. *Οὐλίας*)

**Θεαίσιος**
KORINTHIA:
—KORINTH: (1) f. iii BC Peek, *NIEpid* 39, 2 (*Θεαίσιος*: s. *Σαμοκλῆς*)

**Θεαίτητος**
KERKYRA: (1) imp. *IG* IX (1) 954
S. ITALY (BRUTTIUM):
—RHEGION: (2) vii-vi BC *RE* (3)

**Θέανδρος**
AIGINA: (1) her. Pi., *N.* iv, 73 (*Θεανδρίδαι* (n. gent.))

**Θεάντας**
S. ITALY (CALABRIA):
—TARAS-TARENTUM: (1) hell.? *Syringes* 329

**Θέαντος**
ACHAIA:
—BOURA: (1) 177 BC *Syll*³ 585, 259 (f. *Δαμέας*)
S. ITALY (LUCANIA):
—METAPONTION:
——(*Πωγ.*): (2) iv/iii BC *SEG* XXXVIII 997 (f. *—α*)
TRIPHYLIA:
—LEPREON: (3) f. v BC Paus. vi 7. 8 (f. *Ἀλκαίνετος*); (4) c. 420 BC Moretti, *Olymp.* 338 (s. *Ἀλκαίνετος*)

**Θεανώ**
AKARNANIA:
—ANAKTORION: (1) iii BC *IG* IX (1)² (2) 591
ARGOLIS:
—ARGOS: (2) s. vii BC *Suda* K 2499
—ARGOS*: (3) ii BC *SEG* XLII 279, 17 (*[Θ]εανώ*: d. *Ἀπολλόδωρος*: katoikos)
EPIROS:
—BOUTHROTOS (PRASAIBOI): (4) a. 163 BC *IBouthrot* 17, 17; 43, 27 (*SEG* XXXVIII 474;

502) (d. Ἀπολλώνιος, Νίκα); (5) ~ IBouthrot 43, 45 (SEG XXXVIII 502)

ILLYRIA:

—EPIDAMNOS-DYRRHACHION: (6) iii BC IDyrrh 19 (Θεανώι?: d. Ἀριστοκλῆς)

LAKONIA:

—SPARTA: (7) vi/v BC Polyaen. viii 34 (Poralla² p. 62) (?m. Παυσανίας, Νικομήδης)

S. ITALY (BRUTTIUM):

—LOKROI EPIZEPHYRIOI: (8) ?vi BC RE (6)

S. ITALY (CAMPANIA):

—CAPREAE: (9) i BC-i AD? IG XIV 899 (d. Εὔνικος)

S. ITALY?: (10) vi/v BC RE (5); cf. Delatte, VP pp. 138 f.; pp. 246 ff.; cf. LGPN I (2) (?d. Λεώφρων (Sybaris-Thourioi-Copiae): fict.?)

SICILY:

—AKRAGAS: (11) imp. IG XIV 264 (d. Σαβῖνα)

**Θεάνωρ**

S. ITALY (BRUTTIUM):

—KROTON: (1) f. iv BC RE (-)

**Θεάρης**

ARGOLIS:

—HERMIONE: (1) c. 405 BC Paus. x 9. 10; cf. CEG II 819; (2) iii BC IG IV (1) 728, 4; cf. SEG XXIII 190 (s. Θεαρίδας); (3) ?ii-i BC IG IV (1) 733, 6 (s. Ἀγησίας)

LAKONIA:

—SPARTA: (4) c. 450-434 BC ib. v (1) 1228, 3; LSAG² p. 201 no. 53 (date) (Poralla² 354)

**Θεαρία**

MESSENIA:

—MESSENE: (1) i BC IG v (1) 1476

**Θεαρίδας**

AITOLIA:

—KALYDON: (1) c. 143 BC ib. IX (1)² (1) 137, 38 (s. Νικόδαμος)

AKARNANIA:

—HYPOREIAI: (2) iv BC ib. II² 7998 (IX (1)² (2) 587) (-δης)

ARGOLIS:

—HERMIONE: (3) iii BC ib. IV (1) 697; (4) ~ ib. 728, 4; cf. SEG XXIII 190 (f. Θεάρης)

ARKADIA: (5) 304 BC IG v (2) 550, 28

—MEGALOPOLIS: (6) iii BC ib. 478, 2; (7) ~ ib. l. 4; (8) s. iii BC RE (1); IG v (1)² 624 (f. Λυκόρτας); (9) ii BC ib. v (2) 443, 49 (IPArk 32) (f. Δεξιμένης); (10) f. ii BC RE (2); IG IV (1)² 623; v (2) 535 (s. Λυκόρτας, f. Φιλοποίμην); (11) m. ii BC RE (3); IG v (2) 442, 8; 535 (s. Φιλοποίμην, f. —εια)

—STYMPHALOS: (12) 189 BC SEG XXV 445, 21 (IPArk 18) (s. Ἰσαγόρας)

ELIS:

—LASION: (13) ?iii/ii BC HE 478 (or Arkadia Megalopolis: f. Λυκόρτας)

EPIROS:

—DODONA*: (14) c. 425-400 BC Ep. Chron. 10 (1935) p. 256 no. 17; LSAG² p. 230 no. 17 (date)

LAKONIA:

—SPARTA: (15) inc. Plu., Mor. 221 C (Poralla² 355)

MESSENIA:

—MESSENE: (16) ii BC PAE 1969, p. 106, 8 (I f. Θεαρίδας II); (17) ~ ib. l. 9 (II s. Θεαρίδας I)

S. ITALY (LUCANIA):

—METAPONTION: (18) iv BC Clem. Al., Strom. v 133. 1; Iamb., VP 36; cf. Zeller III (2) p. 102 no. 38

SICILY:

—KAMARINA: (19) f. v BC Cordano, Tessere Pubbliche 24 (Arena, Iscr. Sic. II 132 A) (s. Βράχυλλος); (20) ~ Cordano, Tessere Pubbliche 61 (s. Ποδ—)

—SYRACUSE: (21) v/iv BC RE Supplbd. 8 (4); cf. Beloch, GG III (2) pp. 102-7 (s. Ἑρμοκράτης)

**Θεαρίς**

ARGOLIS:

—TROIZEN: (1) iv BC IG IV (1) 805

ARKADIA:

—MANTINEIA-ANTIGONEIA: (2) hell. ib. II² 9280 (d. Ἀρισταγόρας)

S. ITALY (BRUTTIUM):

—TORANO CASTELLO (MOD.): (3) iv BC GRBS 26 (1985) p. 181 no. 127 (d. Στ—)

**Θεαρις**

ARGOLIS:

—EPIDAUROS: (1) iv BC IG IV (1)² 322 ([Θ]εαρις: s./d. Ἀλεξικλῆς)

—HERMIONE: (2) iii BC ib. IV (1) 697

ARKADIA:

—KLEITOR: (3) i AD ib. v (2) 379

**Θεάριχος**

ARGOLIS:

—KALAURIA: (1) iii BC ib. IV (1) 841, 10

**Θεαρίων**

AIGINA: (1) ?485 BC Pi., N. vii, 7, 58 (f. Σωγένης)

ARGOLIS:

—EPIDAUROS*: (2) c. 370-365 BC Peek, IAEpid 52 B, 57; (3) c. 320-300 BC IG IV (1)² 110 A, 41, 43; 111, 6

—HERMIONE: (4) iii BC ib. IV (1) 729 II, 12 (s. Πεισίνοος)

—TROIZEN: (5) 153-144 BC SGDI 2295, 16 (s. Ἀριστοτέλης)

MESSENIA:

—MESSENE:

——(Aristomachidai): (6) 11 AD PAE 1992, p. 71 A, 9 (f. Καλλιτέλης)

S. ITALY (CALABRIA):

—BRENTESION-BRUNDISIUM*: (7) i BC Desy, Timbres amphoriques 752 (amph.) (slave/potter?)

**Θεάρκης**

ACHAIA:

—PELLENE: (1) 341 BC CID II 12 I, 63 (f. Τιμοξένα)

ARKADIA:

—KLEITOR: (2) 228-222 BC Plb. ii 55. 9 (or Arkadia Orchomenos)

**Θέαρος**

ARKADIA: (1) iii BC IG v (2) 415, 2 (IPArk 23) ([Θέ]αρος?: s. Φιλίσκος)

**Θεασίδας**

LAKONIA:

—SPARTA: (1) vi/v BC Hdt. vi 85. 2 (Poralla² 356) (Θεαρίδας?—Wade-Gery: s. Λαπρέπης)

**Θεάσων**

ARGOLIS:

—KLEONAI: (1) ?c. 229 BC SEG XXIII 178, 26 (or Argolis Argos: s. Πολέμαρχος)

**Θεατρικός**

S. ITALY (CAMPANIA):

—SALERNUM: (1) imp. IItal I (1) 203 (CIL x 606) (Lat. T. Iulius Theatricus)

**Θεδώρα**

EPIROS:

—AMBRAKIA: (1) f. iii BC Unp. (Arta Mus., inscr.) (d. Πυθόδωρος)

**Θέδωρος**

AKARNANIA:

—THYRREION: (1) iii BC IG IX (1)² (2) 261

KERKYRA: (2) c. 500 BC SEG XXX 523; cf. L'Illyrie mérid. 2 p. 202 (Θέδō-)

**Θειναμάξης?**

S. ITALY (CAMPANIA):

—KYME: (1) ii-iii AD IG XIV 868 (GVI 367)

**Θειογήτων**

SICILY:

—KAMARINA: (1) vi BC SEG XXXII 918 B (vase) (-γέτōν)

**Θείρων**

ILLYRIA:

—EPIDAMNOS-DYRRHACHION (NR.)?: (1) ii BC ib. XXXVIII 572, 2; cf. CRAI 1991, p. 197 ff.; L'Illyrie mérid. 2 p. 206 (Θείρων[ος] (gen.): f. Ἐπίδοον)

**Θέκλεια**

ILLYRIA:

—APOLLONIA: (1) hell.? IApoll 40 (Θέκλει[α])

**Θεκλῆς**

KERKYRA: (1) hell. Unp. (IG arch.) (f. Τίμων)

**Θεκταμένης?**

LAKONIA:

—SPARTA: (1) inc. Plu., Mor. 221 F; REG 99 (1986) p. 137 (name) (Poralla² 357) (Θηκταμένης?—Wade-Gery, Τεκταμένης?—Masson)

**Θέλγων**

LAKONIA:

—SPARTA: (1) c. 90-100 AD SEG XI 558, 16 (Bradford (1)) (II s. Θέλγων I); (2) ~ SEG XI 558, 17 (Bradford (2)) (I f. Θέλγων II)

**Θελξαγόρας**

KORINTHIA:

—SIKYON: (1) c. 500-480 BC SEG XIV 309, 2

**Θελξινόα**

LAKONIA:

—SPARTA: (1) ii-iii AD X. Eph. v 1. 5 ff. (-νόη: fict.)

**Θελξίνοος**

LAKONIA:

—SPARTA: (1) s. i BC IG v (1) 124, 3 (Bradford (-)) (Θε[λ]ξίνοος: s. Ἀρίστων)

**Θέλπουσα**

LAKONIA:

—GYTHEION: (1) iii-iv AD SEG II 179

**Θέλυτος**

EPIROS:

—DODONA*: (1) ?v/iv BC ib. XV 388

**Θέλων**

S. ITALY (CAMPANIA):

—POMPEII: (1) i BC-i AD CIL IV 8784; cf. Epigraphica 30 (1968) p. 120 (name) (Lat. Thelon)

**Θέμανδρος**

ARKADIA:

—MANTINEIA-ANTIGONEIA: (1) c. 475-450 BC IG v (2) 262, 13, 30 (IPArk 8); LSAG² p. 216 no. 29 (date)

**Θεμίας**

ARGOLIS:

—EPIDAUROS*: (1) c. 335-325 BC Peek, IAEpid 50, 22 (Θεμί[α]s)

**Θέμις**

EPIROS:

—DODONA*: (1) iv-iii BC SGDI 1581

S. ITALY (APULIA):

—CANUSIUM*: (2) imp. Epig. Rom. di Canosa 201 (CIL IX 405) (Lat. Cluatia Them(i)s: freed.)

S. ITALY (CAMPANIA):

—HERCULANEUM: (3) m. i AD PdelP 3 (1948) p. 168 no. 13; p. 169 no. 14; p. 173 no. 17; p. 175 no. 20; p. 177 no. 23 (Lat. Calatoria Themis)

—NEAPOLIS*: **(4)** i AD *CIL* x 1499; cf. Leiwo p. 89 (Lat. Flavia Themis: freed.)

**Θεμιστέας**
ARGOLIS:
—ARGOS?: **(1)** s. v BC *SEG* XI 317, 2 ([Θε]μιστέας)

**Θεμιστίας**
ARKADIA:
—MANTINEIA-ANTIGONEIA: **(1)** ?iii BC *IG* v (2) 318, 27

**Θεμίστιος**
AIGINA: **(1)** ?483-480 BC Pi., *N.* v, 50; *I.* vi, 65
AKARNANIA:
—STRATOS: **(2)** vi BC *IG* IX (1)² (2) 398, 4
ARGOLIS:
—TROIZEN: **(3)** iii BC ib. IV (1) 774, 5 (f. Κλειτέας)
DALMATIA:
—ISSA:
——(Dymanes): **(4)** iv/iii BC Brunšmid p. 8, 30 (f. —άσιος?) ?= (5); **(5)** ~ ib. l. 47 (f. —τρος) ?= (6) (4); **(6)** ~ ib. p. 9, 54 (Θ[ε]μίστιος: f. Ἀγησιάναξ) ?= (5)

**Θεμιστογένης**
SICILY:
—SYRACUSE: **(1)** v/iv BC *RE* (-); *FGrH* 108 with comm. (fict.?)

**Θεμιστοκλῆς**
EPIROS:
—BOUTHROTOS (PRASAIBOI):
——Bouthrotioi: **(1)** a. 163 BC *IBouthrot* 59, 7-8 (*SEG* XXXVIII 510) (s. Θεόδοτος, f. Σοφοκλῆς)
ILLYRIA:
—APOLLONIA: **(2)** c. 250-50 BC Maier 43 (Ceka 10); Maier 44 (118; 477; Ceka 12-13; 63D); *IApoll Ref. Bibl.* n. 15 (locn.) (coin) (pryt.); **(3)** ii BC ib. 26 ([Θ]εμισστοκλῆς); **(4)** i BC Maier 149 (coin) (pryt.)

**Θεμιστόλα**
DALMATIA:
—ISSA: **(1)** ii BC *SEG* XXXI 602, 8 (*VAHD* 84 (1991) p. 257 no. 7) (d. Φίλιος)

**Θέμιστος**
ARKADIA:
—MANTINEIA-ANTIGONEIA: **(1)** ?iv BC *IG* v (2) 294 (s. Ἐπικράτης)
SICILY:
—SYRACUSE: **(2)** 214 BC *RE* (-) (Lat. Themistus)

**Θεμιστώ**
ARGOLIS:
—ARGOS: **(1)** her. *IMM* 17, 14 (*FGrH* 482. 3); cf. *SEG* XXXV 1128
S. ITALY (LUCANIA):
—HYELE-VELIA: **(2)** hell.? *PdelP* 21 (1966) p. 336 no. 10

**Θεμίσων**
AIGINA: **(1)** imp. *GVI* 605 (s. Παμμένης, Πόσιλλα)
EPIROS:
—BOUTHROTOS (PRASAIBOI): **(2)** a. 163 BC *IBouthrot* 159
—PRASAIBOI: **(3)** a. 163 BC ib. 78, [12]; 79, [10]; 80, 9; 81, 10; 82, 9; 83, 9; 84, 10; 85, 10; 86, 11; 87, 10; 88, 8 (*BCH* 118 (1994) pp. 122 f. nos. 1-11); *IBouthrot* 92, 6; 103, 7; 153, 7 (s. Ζώπυρος) ?= (4); **(4)** ~ ib. 92, 6 (f. Σοφοκλῆς) ?= (3)
KERKYRA: **(5)** hell. *IG* IX (1) 913
S. ITALY (LUCANIA):
—HERAKLEIA: **(6)** c. 125-100 BC *EAD* XXX 297 (f. Ἀπελλῆς)


**Θενιανα**
S. ITALY (CALABRIA):
—TARAS-TARENTUM: **(1)** iv-iii BC *RA* 1932 (1), p. 39 no. 21; p. 41 no. 56 (Troisi, *Epigrafi mobili* 74 (loomweight)) (nom./gen.?)

**Θεογείτων**
AKARNANIA:
—ANAKTORION: **(1)** ?iv/iii BC *IG* IX (1)² (2) 219 (Θε[ογε]ίτων)
ARKADIA: **(2)** 304 BC ib. v (2) 550, 22
—TEGEA: **(3)** 165 AD ib. 50, 15 (-γί-: f. Ἀλέξανδρος)

**Θεογένης**
AIGINA: **(1)** i-ii AD *Alt-Ägina* I (2) p. 47 no. 27, 1 (I f. Θεογένης II); **(2)** ~ ib. l. 1 (II s. Θεογένης I)
AIGINA?: **(3)** hell.? *RE* (9); *FGrH* 300
AKARNANIA:
—ASTAKOS: **(4)** ii BC *IG* IX (1)² (2) 435, 2-3 (s. Πεισίθεος, f. Καλλιφῶν)
ARGOLIS:
—HERMIONE: **(5)** ii-i BC ib. IV (1) 732 III, 28 (f. Δαματρία)
DALMATIA:
—ISSA: **(6)** hell. Brunšmid p. 27 no. 18, 3 (*SEG* XL 514; *VAHD* 84 (1991) p. 253 no. 3) (s. Ἀγάθων)
ELIS: **(7)** 53 AD *IvOl* 435, 3; *ZPE* 99 (1993) p. 232 (stemma) (Κλ. Θ.: f. Κλ. Ἀλκινόα); **(8)** 113-117 AD *IvOl* 91, 5 (Δ(έκμος) Ἀνθέστιος Θ.: Γ.)
ILLYRIA:
—APOLLONIA: **(9)** i BC/i AD *GP* 307 (s.e.) (Θειογένης—metr. c.) ?= (10); **(10)** ~ *RE* (10) (Lat. Theogenes) ?= (9)
—EPIDAMNOS-DYRRHACHION: **(11)** c. 250-50 BC Maier 224-8 (coin) (Ceka 66; 173; 221; 253; 425; 436) (pryt.)
LAKONIA:
—SPARTA: **(12)** i AD *IG* v (1) 297, 2-3; *Artemis Orthia* pp. 310-11 (date) (Bradford (3)) (f. Θεοδότη, Νικοκράτης); **(13)** c. 90-120 AD *SEG* XI 545, [3]?; 559, 5; 605, 7 (Bradford (2)) (I f. Θεογένης II); **(14)** ~ *SEG* XI 545, [3]?; 559, 5; 605, 7 (Bradford (1)) ([Θεογ]ένης—605: II s. Θεογένης I)
MESSENIA:
—PROTE*: **(15)** imp. *IG* v (1) 1540 (Sandberg, *Euploia* 3) ([Θ]εο[γέν]ε[ι] (dat.))
S. ITALY (BRUTTIUM):
—KROTON: **(16)** ?ii AD Costabile, *Ist. Bruzio* p. 176 (Lat. Flavius Theogenes)

**Θεογενίς**
AIGINA: **(1)** imp.? *IG* IV (1) 157

**Θεόγνητος**
AIGINA: **(1)** f. v BC *RE* (1); Moretti, *Olymp.* 217; Ebert, *Gr. Sieg.* 12; cf. Page, *FGE* 804
ARGOLIS:
—TROIZEN: **(2)** iv BC *IG* IV (1) 823, 38; **(3)** ?287 BC ib. 750, 15, 41 (s. Θεόξενος)
ILLYRIA:
—APOLLONIA: **(4)** c. 250-50 BC Maier 45 (coin) (Ceka 34) (pryt.); **(5)** ii-i BC *IApoll* 381 ([Θ]εόγνητος)
SICILY:
—KAMARINA: **(6)** f. v BC Cordano, *Tessere Pubbliche* 16 (-γνē-: f. —νυτος)

**Θέογνις**
S. ITALY (BRUTTIUM):
—KROTON: **(1)** ?c. 475 BC *SEG* XXXIII 767 (bronze); cf. *LSAG*² p. 456 no. 23a (date) (f. Ἀκάνθωπος)
SICILY:
—SELINOUS: **(2)** ?vii/vi BC Dubois, *IGDS* 57 (Arena, *Iscr. Sic.* I 15; *IGLMP* 75)


**Θεογνίς**
S. ITALY (CALABRIA):
—BRENTESION-BRUNDISIUM: **(1)** imp. *NScav* 1894, p. 17 no. 3 (Lat. Iunia [T]heogn[is])

**Θεογνωτίδας**
ITHAKE: **(1)** hell. *Rev. Épig.* 1 (1913) p. 47 no. 3 (Θεογνωτί(δα)[ς]?, Θεογνωτιλο—apogr.)

**Θεόγονος**
ELIS: **(1)** iv/iii BC Paus. vi 17. 5 (f. Ἐπέραστος: mantis/Klytiadai)
ILLYRIA:
—LYCHNIDOS: **(2)** ii-iii AD Demitsas 348 (Ἰούλ. Θηΐγονος)

**Θεοδέκτης**
ACHAIA: **(1)** 146 BC *RE* (3)

**Θεοδοσία**
ARGOLIS:
—ARGOS: **(1)** ii-i BC *IG* IV (1) 530, 14; cf. *BCH* 33 (1909) p. 183 n. 2
—ARGOS*: **(2)** ii BC *SEG* XLII 279, 19 (d. Θεόδοτος: katoikos)
KORINTHIA:
—KORINTH: **(3)** byz. *Corinth* VIII (3) 562; cf. *TMByz* 9 (1985) p. 366 no. 66 (Θεω-)
S. ITALY (CAMPANIA):
—BAIAI: **(4)** iii-iv AD *Puteoli* 6 (1982) p. 160 no. 11 (Lat. Theodosia)
SICILY:
—SYRACUSE: **(5)** iii-v AD *IG* XIV 118 (Strazzulla 59; Wessel 1349) (Θεοδοσ[ία])

**Θεοδόσιος**
ELIS: **(1)** 20-16 BC *IvOl* 65, 5 (s. Ποσειδώνιος: M.); **(2)** 185-189 AD ib. 104, 20 (s. Ἀντίοχος: K.)
KORINTHIA:
—KORINTH?: **(3)** v-vi AD *SEG* XXII 222, 4 (*TMByz* 9 (1985) pp. 293-4 no. 33) (Θεοδόσ[ιος])
LAKONIA:
—SPARTA: **(4)** 384-394 AD *SEG* XXXII 400 (Φλ. Θεοδόσ[ιος])
MESSENIA:
—KORONE: **(5)** 246 AD *IG* v (1) 1398, 58 (Αὐρ. Θ.)
S. ITALY (CALABRIA):
—HYRIA: **(6)** imp. *CIL* IX 233 (Lat. Theodosius)
S. ITALY (CAMPANIA):
—NEAPOLIS: **(7)** c. 80 BC *IG* VII 416, 14 (*IOrop* 523); cf. Stephanis 26 (f. Ἀγαθοκλῆς)
—NOLA: **(8)** 490 AD *CIL* x 1345 (Lat. Theodosios)
SICILY:
—KAMARINA: **(9)** ?ii BC *SEG* XXXIX 996, 9 (Dubois, *IGDS* 126; Cordano, 'Camarina VII' 112) (f. Ἀρταμίδωρος)

**Θεοδότα**
ARGOLIS:
—EPIDAUROS: **(1)** iv/iii BC Peek, *IAEpid* 340, 6 (?m. Κλεινοξένα, Κορινθία, Γοργόι)
ELIS: **(2)** f. iii BC D.L. iv 40 (-τη: het.); **(3)** f. i BC *IvOl* 203; Moretti, *Olymp.* 675 (d. Ἀντιφάνης); **(4)** ~ *IvOl* 204, 3 (m. Στρογιήν, Τιμαρέτα)
EPIROS:
—BOUTHROTOS (PRASAIBOI): **(5)** a. 163 BC *IBouthrot* 14, 24, 27 (*SEG* XXXVIII 471) (?m. Βοΐσκος)
SICILY?: **(6)** i BC-i AD *IGLMP* 138 (Θ. Κέλτα)

**Θεοδότας**
SICILY:
—SYRACUSE: **(1)** f. iv BC [Pl.], *Ep.* 318 C; 320 E; 348 B ff.; Plu., *Dio* 12; D.L. iii 21

**Θεοδότη**
AIGINA: **(1)** hell.? *IG* IV (1) 117 (d. Δημήτριος)
ARGOLIS:
—ARGOS: **(2)** byz. *BCH* 28 (1904) p. 420 no. 4; cf. *TMByz* 9 (1985) p. 370 no. 112

ILLYRIA:
—APOLLONIA: (3) ii-iii AD *IApoll* 276
LAKONIA:
—SPARTA: (4) i AD *IG* V (1) 297, 1; *Artemis Orthia* pp. 310-11 (date) (Bradford (-)) (d. Θεογένης)
S. ITALY (APULIA):
—CANUSIUM: (5) s. ii AD *Epig. Rom. di Canosa* 131 (*CIL* IX 378) (Lat. Galbia [Theo]dote: m. Μερόπη)
S. ITALY (CALABRIA):
—PORTO CESAREO (MOD.): (6) ii AD *NScav* 1957, p. 198 (Lat. Theodo(t)e?: d. Honoratus)
S. ITALY (CAMPANIA):
—DIKAIARCHIA-PUTEOLI: (7) imp. *CIL* X 2629 (Lat. Iunia Theodote); (8) ?ii AD ib. 2598 (Lat. Aelia Theodote)
—MISENUM*: (9) imp. ib. 3403 (Lat. Valeria Theodote)
—NEAPOLIS: (10) i BC-i AD *IG* XIV 786 (*INap* 125) (d. Ἰατροκλῆς); (11) iii-iv AD ib. 228
SICILY:
—SYRACUSE: (12) iii-v AD *NScav* 1893, p. 312 no. 138 b + Ferrua, *NG* 296 ([Θεο]δότη)

### Θεοδοτιανός

S. ITALY (APULIA):
—LUCERIA: (1) imp. *CIL* IX 891 (Lat. M. Terentius Theodotianus)

### Θεόδοτος

ACHAIA:
—DYME*: (1) c. 219 BC *SGDI* 1612, 60 (*Tyche* 5 (1990) p. 124) (f. Δράκας)
—PATRAI: (2) m. i BC *IPhilae* 55, 7 (s. Ἁγησιφῶν)
AIGINA: (3) ?i BC *Alt-Ägina* I (2) p. 46 no. 19
AITOLIA: (4) s. iii BC *RE* (11); *PP* 15045 ?= (8)
—APERANTOI: (5) ?iv/iii BC *IG* IX (1)² (1) 166, 2 (*L'Illyrie mérid.* 1 p. 109 fig. 6); (6) c. 215-200 BC *FD* III (2) 86, 8 (*Syll*³ 539 A); cf. Nachtergael, *Les Galates* p. 291 (date) ?= (7)
—APERANTOI?: (7) 214 BC *IG* IX (1)² (1) 177, 8 (f. —ς) ?= (6)
—KALYDON: (8) s. iii BC *FD* III (1) 519, 2 (s. Ἀντίβολος) ?= (4)
AKARNANIA:
—THYRREION: (9) ii BC *IG* IX (1)² (2) 247, 2 (f. Πολύευκτος)
ARGOLIS:
—ARGOS: (10) byz. *BCH* 99 (1975) p. 699 (glass)
—ARGOS*: (11) ii AD *SEG* XLII 279, 19 (Θ[ε]όδοτος: f. Θεοδοσία: katoikos)
—EPIDAUROS*: (12) c. 370 BC *IG* IV (1)² 102, 9, 31, 54 etc.
—TROIZEN: (13) f. ii BC ib. IV (1) 752, 9-10 + IV (1)² 77, 15
ARKADIA:
—TEGEA: (14) ii AD ib. V (2) 55, 40 (s. Ἐπικτο—)
DALMATIA:
—ISSA:
——(Dymanes): (15) iv/iii BC Brunšmid p. 9, 60 (s. Ἡρακλείδας)
ELIS: (16) 113 AD *IvOl* 90, 10 (I f. Θεόδοτος II); (17) ~ ib. l. 10 (II s. Θεόδοτος I)
EPIROS: (18) c. 330 BC Cabanes, *L'Épire* p. 580 no. 55, 2
—AMBRAKIA: (19) iii/ii BC Unp. (Arta Mus., inscr.) (f. Σώστρατος)
—ANTIGONEIA: (20) hell. *AE* 1914, p. 234 no. 2 (*SEG* XXXVII 508); Cabanes, *L'Épire* p. 234 n. 96 (locn.) (f. Λυκόφρων)
—BOUTHROTOS (PRASAIBOI): (21) a. 163 BC *IBouthrot* 19, 6 (*SEG* XXXVIII 476); (22) ~ *IBouthrot* 47, 17 (f. Στρατώ); (23) ~ ib. l. 18 (?s. Στρατώ)
——Bouthrotioi: (24) a. 163 BC ib. 59, 7 (*SEG* XXXVIII 510) (f. Θεμιστοκλῆς)
—MOLOSSOI: (25) f. ii BC *RE* (12)

—MOLOSSOI?: (26) iv/iii BC Plu., *Pyrr.* 6. 7 (mantis)
—NIKOPOLIS: (27) a. 30 BC *SEG* XXIV 434 (Sarikakis 55) (s. Ὑπερβάλλων)
—PHOINIKE: (28) ii-iii AD Ugolini, *Alb. Ant.* 2 p. 155 no. 9
ILLYRIA:
—APOLLONIA: (29) c. 250-50 BC Maier 26; cf. Ceka 61 (coin) (Θεόδωτος—Ceka per err.)
—EPIDAMNOS-DYRRHACHION: (30) c. 250-50 BC Maier 117; 226; 241; 313; 334; 363; 392; 487; Münsterberg p. 260 = Nachtr. p. 15 (coin) (Ceka 218-30) (money.)
KORINTHIA:
—KORINTH: (31) ii-i BC *IG* II² 9078 (f. Σωτήριχος); (32) hell.-imp. *Corinth* VIII (3) 41
LAKONIA:
—GYTHEION: (33) 211 AD *IG* V (1) 1163, 8 (Κλ. Θ.)
MESSENIA:
—MESSENE: (34) i BC ib. II² 9341 (f. Δαμέας)
—THOURIA: (35) f. ii BC *SEG* XI 972, 99 (f. Ξένων); (36) ~ ib. l. 121 (I f. Θεόδοτος II); (37) ~ ib. l. 121 (II s. Θεόδοτος I)
S. ITALY (APULIA):
—CANUSIUM: (38) s. ii AD *Epig. Rom. di Canosa* 131 (*CIL* IX 378) (Lat. Artorius [Theo]dotus: ?s. Μερόπη)
S. ITALY (BRUTTIUM):
—HERA LAKINIA*: (39) iv BC *PdelP* 45 (1990) pp. 302-4 (Θεόδοτ[ος])
—LOKROI EPIZEPHYRIOI:
——(Γαψ.): (40) iv/iii BC De Franciscis 20, 12 (s. Ἐμπεδοκλῆς)
S. ITALY (CAMPANIA):
—DIKAIARCHIA-PUTEOLI: (41) imp. *CIL* X 2768 (Lat. M. Nemonius Theodotus)
—DIKAIARCHIA-PUTEOLI*: (42) imp. ib. 2220 (Lat. C. Iunius Theodotus: freed.)
—SALERNUM: (43) byz. *IItal* I (1) 107 (*CIL* X 663) (Lat. Theodotus)
S. ITALY (LUCANIA):
—HYELE-VELIA*: (44) ii/i BC *ID* 2602, 10
SICILY: (45) byz. *BZ* 19 (1910) p. 472 (-δω-)
—LIPARA: (46) ?vi-v BC Call. fr. 93 dieg.
—SYRACUSE: (47) 238 BC *PPetr*² I *Wills* 3, 87 (*PP* 3957); (48) 215-214 BC *RE* (13) (Lat. Theodotus); (49) iii-v AD *IG* XIV 119 (Strazzulla 60; Wessel 771)

### Θεοδούλα

SICILY:
—SYRACUSE: (1) iii-v AD Strazzulla 412; cf. Ferrua, *NG* 321 (Θε-)

### Θεοδούλη

SICILY:
—KATANE: (1) iii-v AD *Oikoumene* p. 605 no. 4; cf. Ferrua, *NG* 425; (2) 419 AD ib. 415 a ([Θεο]δούλη)
—SYRACUSE: (3) iii-v AD *Riv. Arch. Crist.* 36 (1960) p. 42 no. 44; (4) ~ *NScav* 1907, p. 756 no. 7; cf. Ferrua, *NG* 80; (5) ~ Strazzulla 191 (*Riv. Arch. Crist.* 18 (1941) p. 205 no. 78; Wessel 325); (6) ~ Ferrua, *NG* 327; (7) byz. *SEG* XV 583

### Θεόδουλος

KORINTHIA:
—KORINTH: (1) byz. *Corinth* VIII (3) 661; cf. *TMByz* 9 (1985) p. 367 no. 81
LAKONIA:
—ASOPOS: (2) byz. *IG* V (1) 974 (s. Σισίνιος, Φλωρεντία)
SICILY:
—KATANE: (3) iii-v AD ib. XIV 538 (Agnello 50; Wessel 862); cf. *Riv. Arch. Crist.* 18 (1941) p. 240 no. 137 (Θέ-); (4) ~ *IG* XIV 542 (Agnello 53; Wessel 852); cf. *Riv. Arch. Crist.* 18 (1941) p. 241 no. 138; (5) ~ *SEG* XVIII 397

—SYRACUSE: (6) iii-v AD *IG* XIV 120 (Strazzulla 127); (7) ~ *IG* XIV 121 (Strazzulla 128) (Θέ-); (8) ~ *IG* XIV 122 (Strazzulla 129) (Θέ-); (9) ~ ib. 223 (Θέ-); (10) ~ ib. 255 + *Nuovo Didask.* 6 (1956) p. 55 no. 9 (Wessel 1086) (Θεόδου[λ]ος); (11) ~ Strazzulla 441 (Agnello 75); cf. Ferrua, *NG* 40 (Lat. Patricius Teodulus, Marina Teodule—Ferrua); (12) ~ ib. 349 ([Θεόδ]ουλος); (13) ~ Wessel 327; (14) ~ ib. 720 + Ferrua, *NG* 90; (15) ~ *Nuovo Didask.* 6 (1956) p. 67 no. 41 ([Θεό]δουλος?)
—SYRACUSE?: (16) iii-v AD *Riv. Arch. Crist.* 18 (1941) p. 223 no. 109 ([Θέ(ο)δο]υλος)
—TAUROMENION: (17) iii-v AD *IG* XIV 102 (Strazzulla 51; Wessel 844); Ferrua, *NG* 475 (locn.); (18) ~ *IGLMP* 117 + Ferrua, *NG* 487 ([Θεό]δουλος)

### Θεοδώρα

ACHAIA:
—AIGEIRA?: (1) byz. *EA* 1872, p. 404 no. 4
ARGOLIS:
—ARGOS*: (2) 105 BC *JÖAI* 14 (1911) Beibl. p. 146 no. 4, 20 (slave/freed.?)
—EPIDAUROS: (3) ii BC Peek, *IAEpid* 153. 13 (Θεοδώ[ρ]α)
—HERMIONE: (4) ii AD *SEG* XVII 163, 3 (d. Χαρίξενος, m. Ἐπίκτητος)
ARKADIA:
—MANTINEIA-ANTIGONEIA: (5) 46 or 44 BC *IG* V (2) 266, 20 (d. Φαηνά, m. Φαηνά)
ILLYRIA:
—EPIDAMNOS-DYRRHACHION: (6) hell.-imp. *IDyrrh* 241 (d. Ἀπολλώνιος)
ITHAKE: (7) imp. *BCH* 82 (1958) p. 732 + Unp. (*IG* arch.) (Θεοδώρ[α])
KERKYRA: (8) ?s. ii AD *IG* IX (1) 734 (Ἰουλ. Θ.)
KORINTHIA:
—KORINTH: (9) a. 43 AD *SEG* XVIII 143, 1 etc.; cf. XXXVI 307 (Ἰουνία Θ.: d. Λεύκιος: katoikos); (10) ii-iii AD ib. XXIX 321 (Τερεντία Θ.); (11) byz. *Corinth* VIII (3) 705 ([Θ]εοδώρα)
LEUKAS: (12) iv/iii BC Unp. (*IG* arch.)
S. ITALY (CAMPANIA):
—DIKAIARCHIA-PUTEOLI: (13) imp. *CIL* X 2659 (Lat. Limbricia Theodora)
S. ITALY (LUCANIA):
—HERAKLEIA: (14) ii/i BC *EAD* XXX 502; cf. *ID* 1713 (stemma) (d. Τίτος)
SICILY:
—LIPARA: (15) imp.? Libertini, *Isole Eolie* p. 224 no. 41
—SYRACUSE: (16) iii-v AD *SEG* IV 2 (Wessel 185); (17) ~ *SEG* IV 5 (Wessel 1372) (-ώιρα)

### Θεοδώρητος

ILLYRIA:
—LYCHNIDOS: (1) byz. Demitsas 354 (ὁ Φιλοκτίστης (n. pr.?))

### Θεοδωρίδας

ILLYRIA:
—EPIDAMNOS-DYRRHACHION: (1) hell.-imp. *IDyrrh* 242 (s. Ἀγαθίων); (2) ~ ib. 243 (Θε[οδ]ωρίδας: s. Φρουνίλος?)
KORINTHIA:
—SIKYON: (3) 187-169 BC Plb. xxii 3. 6; xxix 23. 6
SICILY:
—SYRACUSE: (4) s. iii BC *RE* (-); *HE* 3506 ff.; *Suppl. Hell.* 739-48

### Θεόδωρος

ACHAIA: (1) c. 235 BC *IG* II² 1299, 117; (2) 146 BC ib. IV (1)² 28, 87 (s. Ἀρσενάδας: synoikos); (3) ~ ib. l. 150 (Θευώ-: f. Ὀνάσιμος: synoikos)
—DYME: (4) iii BC *AJPh* 31 (1910) p. 399 no. 74 c, 13 (s. Νικοκράτης, f. Διόκλεια)
—PATRAI: (5) 246 BC *IG* IX (1)² (1) 17, 132 (s. Τιμανορίδας); (6) ii-iii AD *Rh. Mus.* 21 (1866) p. 398 no. 265 (s. Κριτόλαος)
AIGINA: (7) ii/i BC *Alt-Ägina* I (2) p. 43 no. 3, 4 (f. Κλεῖτος); (8) byz. *IG* IV (1) 190 (*CIJ* I 722) (Jew); (9) ~ *IG* IV (1) 190 (*CIJ* I 723) (Θ. νεώτ.: Jew)

AITOLIA:
—KOTTAEIS: (10) c. 200 BC FD III (4) 163, 5
—POTIDANIA: (11) 153 BC IG IX (1)² (3) 632, 7
(f. Μενέστρατος)
ARGOLIS:
—ARGOS: (12) s. iv BC ib. IV (1)² 618 (CEG II
815) (f. Δρύμος); (13) iii-ii BC IG IV (1) 687;
Peek, IAEpid 306 (s. Πόρος: sculptor); (14)
?iv-v AD IG IV (1) 628, 7
—EPIDAUROS: (15) ?iv-iii BC SEG XXXIX 357 c
—EPIDAUROS*: (16) c. 370-360 BC Peek, IA-
Epid 52 B, 9; (17) c. 320-300 BC IG IV (1)²
110 A, 37, 39
—HERMIONE: (18) ii-i BC ib. IV (1) 732 I, 5 (f.
Ἑλένα)
—TROIZEN: (19) iv BC ib. 823, 33, 53, 64, 66;
(20) iii BC ib. 824, 5 (s. Κλείτανδρος); (21) iv
AD ib. 787; cf. TMByz 9 (1985) p. 371 no.
127
ARKADIA: (22) iii BC SB 7204, 5 (f. Ἀσκλαπιά-
δας)
—MEGALOPOLIS: (23) ?131 BC IG V (2) 440, 13
(s. Φίλαρχος, f. Φίλαρχος)
—PHIGALEIA: (24) iii BC ib. 428
—TEGEA: (25) c. 315-280 BC FD III (1) 37, 2
(s. Ἀνδρόβιος); (26) f. iii BC IG V (2) 35, 17 (f.
Ἀρίσταρχος); (27) c. 225 BC SEG XI 414, 23
(Perlman E.5) (Θ[ε]όδωρος: s. Τελέστας); (28)
ii-i BC IG V (2) 222
——(Krariotai): (29) m. iii BC ib. 36, 94 (s. Πρα-
ξιδάμος: metic)
—TEUTHIS?: (30) ii BC SEG XXXV 347 C (Θεό-
δωρ[ος], Θεοδώρ[α]?)
DALMATIA:
—ISSA: (31) iii BC Brunšmid p. 9 fr. H, 3 (Θεό-
δω[ρος])
——(Dymanes): (32) iv/iii BC ib. p. 9, 62 (s.
Κλέαρχος)
——(Hylleis): (33) iv/iii BC ib. p. 8, 27
(Θεόδωρ[ος]: s. —ις)
——(Pamphyloi): (34) iv/iii BC ib. p. 8, 34 (f.
Ἀγέλοχος)
—ISSA?: (35) iii/ii BC CIG 6913; SEG XL 512
(locn.) (f. Ματερίσκα)
ELIS: (36) hell.? IG II² 8527 (f. Ἀσκλαπιάς); (37)
hell.? Moretti, Olymp. 978; (38) m. iii BC IG
V (2) 368, 58 (s. Πίθων); (39) i BC/i AD ib.
XII (8) 176, 4 (f. Ἄντανδρος)
EPIROS:
—ARGETHIA: (40) iv/iii BC Cabanes, L'Épire p.
544 no. 9, 2 (s. Στόμιος)
—ARGOS (AMPHILOCH.): (41) c. 200 BC FD III
(4) 163, 4
—ATHAMANES: (42) iii/ii BC RE (11); BCH 45
(1921) p. 16 III, 34; Welles, RC 35 (SEG
XXXVIII 1227); ID 338 Bb, 29; 385 a, 24 (f.
Φίλα: king)
—BOUTHROTOS: (43) ii-i BC IBouthrot 174
(Ugolini, Alb. Ant. 3 p. 118) (Θ. Μαάλλιος (n.
pr.?))
—KASSOPE: (44) f. ii BC Cabanes, L'Épire p. 564
no. 41, 5 (f. Σάτυρος)
—MOLOSSOI: (45) f. iii BC FGrH 703 F 9 (f.
Εὐάγορος)
ILLYRIA:
—APOLLONIA: (46) c. 250-50 BC Maier 100
(coin) (Ceka 60) (money.); (47) ~ Maier 119;
46 (coin) (Ceka 100; 160) (pryt.); (48) iii/ii BC
IApoll 176; cf. SEG XXXIX 550 (f. Μύσκαλ-
λος); (49) i BC SNG Cop. Thessaly-Illyricum
395 (coin); (50) ~ Maier 150 (coin) (pryt.)
—EPIDAMNOS-DYRRHACHION: (51) hell.-imp.
IDyrrh 215 (f. Εὔτυχος); (52) ~ ib. 244
ITHAKE: (53) hell. IG IX (1) 670 (Fraser-Rönne,
BWGT p. 119 no. 4); (54) imp. IG IX (1) 681
(s. Εὔτυχος)
KEPHALLENIA:
—PALE: (55) c. 210 BC ib. IX (1)² (1) 31, 80 (f.
Καλλικράτης)

KERKYRA: (56) imp. ib. IX (1) 961 (f. Νεοκλῆς)
—KASSIOPA: (57) byz. SEG XXVII 182
(Θεόδ[ω]ρος)
KORINTHIA:
—KORINTH: (58) inc. AJA 33 (1929) p. 499;
(59) c. 370-365 BC Peek, IAEpid 52 B, 9, 40,
43, [52]; (60) byz. Bees 3; cf. TMByz 9 (1985)
p. 362 no. 27 ([Θεό]δωρος); (61) vi-vii AD SEG
XXIX 311, 8 (?s. Ἐπισκοπιανός)
—KORINTH*: (62) i BC/i AD ib. XI 214 b (-δο-);
(63) ?m. iv AD Corinth VIII (3) 517; cf.
TMByz 9 (1985) pp. 364-5 no. 51
—SIKYON: (64) iv AD IG IV (1) 437, 11
LAKONIA:
—ASINE: (65) iv AD RE (35); PLRE I (4)
—EPIDAUROS LIMERA: (66) m. ii BC SEG XIII
259, 1, [17], [25] ([Θε]όδωρος: s. Ζήνων)
—PSAMATHOUS: (67) ?v BC IG V (1) 1225 (Po-
ralla² 359) (Θ(ε)όδōρος)
—SPARTA: (68) m. v BC ib. 360 (f. Τελευτίας;
(69) c. 200 BC SEG III 312, 9 (Bradford (4))
(Θεόδω[ρο]ς: f. Δαμοκλείδας); (70) c. 30-20 BC
IG V (1) 141, 6; SEG XXXV 329 (date) (Bradford (5)) (f. Νικοκλείδας); (71) i BC/i AD? IG V
(1) 177, 5; SEG XI 634 (ident.) (Bradford (3))
([Θ]εόδωρος: freed.?); (72) c. 80-90 AD IG V
(1) 674, 15 (Bradford (8)) (f. Σώστρατος); (73)
c. 80-120 AD IG V (1) 147, 10; 481, 9; SEG
XI 512, 5; 565, 6 (Bradford (2)) (s. Θεοκλῆς);
(74) c. 100-105 AD SEG XI 561, 2 (Bradford
(7)) (Θεόδω[ρος]: f. Σωσικράτης); (75) c. 100-
110 AD IG V (1) 97, 18; SEG XI 534, 3; 564,
12 (Bradford (9)) (Θεόδοτος—SEG XI 564 per
err. lap.: f. Τιμοκλῆς); (76) c. 105-115 AD IG
V (1) 103, 14 (Bradford (6)) (f. Φιλοκράτης);
(77) m. ii AD SEG XI 838, 7 (Bradford (1);
Stephanis 1164) (s. Δαμόνικος)
LEUKAS: (78) c. 325-315 BC Hesp. 57 (1988)
p. 148 B, 13 (SEG XXXVI 331); cf. Hesp. 48
(1979) pp. 78 f. with pl. 22 (s. Καλλίας); (79)
c. 167-50 BC BMC Thessaly p. 179 nos. 88-9
(coins)
MESSENIA:
—MESSENE: (80) i BC Moretti, Olymp. 713; 716;
(81) 2 AD SEG XXIII 206, 1
—THOURIA: (82) ?iv BC CEG II 709
PELOPONNESE: (83) vi/v BC BMI 948 a (bronze)
(-δō-)
PELOPONNESE?: (84) 11 AD PAE 1992, p. 72 B,
1-2 (f. Ἀριστίων, Ἑστιαῖος)
S. ITALY: (85) c. 200-175 BC IG XI (4) 808 (f.
Σωτίων); (86) imp. ib. XIV 2412. 16
S. ITALY (APULIA):
—VENUSIA*: (87) i BC/i AD Museo di Venosa p.
209 no. 7 (Lat. Theodorus: freed.)
S. ITALY (BRUTTIUM):
—LOKROI EPIZEPHYRIOI:
——(Αστ.): (88) iv/iii BC De Franciscis 20, 19
(s. Πύραμος)
——(Γαγ.): (89) iv/iii BC ib. 21, 3
S. ITALY (CALABRIA):
—TARAS-TARENTUM: (90) vi-v BC RE (29); (91)
s. iv BC Berve 363 (Stephanis 1163)
S. ITALY (CAMPANIA): (92) i AD Cron. Erc. 20
(1990) p. 166 no. 12 (tile) (Lat. Tfeodorus)
—DIKAIARCHIA-PUTEOLI: (93) ?i-ii AD CIL X
2573 (Lat. L. Iulius Theodorus: s. Διοδώρα);
(94) ?iii AD ib. 1578; cf. Puteoli 11 (1987) p.
37 (Lat. Aur. Theodorus)
—NEAPOLIS: (95) 98 BC ID 1761, 5 (f. Σωσιγέ-
νης)
S. ITALY (LUCANIA):
—HERAKLEIA: (96) iv/iii BC IGSI 1 I, 182 (DGE
62; Uguzzoni-Ghinatti I) (I f. Θεόδωρος II);
(97) ~ IGSI 1 I, 182 (DGE 62; Uguzzoni-
Ghinatti I) (II s. Θεόδωρος I)
—LEUKANOI: (98) c. 208 BC FD III (4) 135, 11
(s. Ἀρτεμίδωρος)
—METAPONTION: (99) c. 262 BC IG IX (1)² (1)
17 A, 74 (s. Πασικλῆς)

SICILY: (100) f. i BC Cic., In Verr. II ii 102
(Lat. Cn. Pompeius Theodorus)
—AKRAGAS: (101) s. ii BC Acragas Graeca 1 p.
34 no. 5, 12 (IGUR 2; Dubois, IGDS 185) (I
s. Ξηνιάδας, f. Θεόδωρος II); (102) ~ Acragas
Graeca 1 p. 34 no. 5, 12 (IGUR 2; Dubois,
IGDS 185) (II s. Θεόδωρος I)
—AKRAI: (103) iii-ii BC SGDI 3242, 11 (Akrai
p. 157 no. 8) (s. Ἀρτέμων); (104) ii BC ib. p.
154 no. 3, 3 (s. Ἀρτέμων); (105) ii-i BC SGDI
3246, 1 (Akrai pp. 152-3 no. 2; Dubois,
IGDS 109) (s. Σα—); (106) ~ SGDI 3246, 5
(Akrai pp. 152-3 no. 2; Dubois, IGDS 109)
(f. Δίων); (107) ~ SGDI 3246, 7 (Akrai pp.
152-3 no. 2; Dubois, IGDS 109) (s. Δίων)
—ENTELLA: (108) iv/iii BC SEG XXX 1120, 2
(Dubois, IGDS 207) (s. Μᾶμος)
—HENNA: (109) f. i BC Cic., In Verr. II iv 113
(Lat. Theodorus)
—KAMARINA: (110) f. v BC Cordano, Tessere
Pubbliche 40 (Θεόδ[ō]ρος: f. Ταυ—ς); (111) ?ii
BC SEG XXXIX 996, 8 (Dubois, IGDS 126;
Cordano, 'Camarina VII' 114) (s. Ἀριστογέ-
νης)
—LIPARA: (112) imp. Epigraphica 3 (1941) p.
270 no. 47 b
—MENAI: (113) hell. Riv. Stor. Antica 5 (1900-
1) p. 57 no. 35, 5 (s. Ἀπολλόδωρος)
—NEAITON: (114) f. ii BC IIasos 174, 21 (f. Δρο-
μέας)
—PETRA:
——(Σάννειος): (115) f. iii BC SEG XXX 1121, 24
(Dubois, IGDS 208) (s. Πράτων)
—SYRACUSE: (116) 396 BC D.S. xiv 64. 5; 70. 1;
(117) hell.? D.L. ii 104; (118) c. 210 BC IG
IX (1)² (1) 29, 19 (s. —όστρ[ατος]); (119) iii-v
AD ib. XIV 104 (Strazzulla 53; Wessel 1102);
(120) ~ IG XIV 123 (Strazzulla 61; Wessel
328); cf. ASSicilia 1938-9, p. 31; (121) ~
Strazzulla 358 (Wessel 1227); (122) ~ ib. 886
+ Ferrua, NG 27 ([Θε]όδορος: I f. Θεόδωρος
II); (123) ~ Wessel 886 + Ferrua, NG 27
(Θεόδο[ρος]: II s. Θεόδωρος I)
—SYRACUSE (NR.): (124) ii-i BC IG XIV 4
(SGDI 3233); cf. Rupes loquentes p. 451 no. 2
(f. Ἀριστοβούλα)
—SYRACUSE?:
——(Μακ.): (125) hell. Manganaro, PdelP forth-
coming no. 4 III, 1 (s. Πάμμαχος)
—TAUROMENION: (126) c. 230 BC IG XIV 421
an. 11 (SGDI 5219) (s. Ἀντίπατρος); (127) c.
224 BC IG XIV 421 an. 17 (SGDI 5219); (128)
c. 222-205 BC IG XIV 421 an. 19; 421 an. 36
(SGDI 5219) (s. Φιλίσκος); (129) c. 216-170
BC IG XIV 421 an. 25; 421 an. 47; 421 an. 62
(SGDI 5219) (s. Σωσίπατρος, f. Σωσίπατρος);
(130) c. 208-183 BC IG XIV 421 an. 33; 421
an. 44; 421 an. 58 (SGDI 5219) (f. Λέων) ?=
(131); (131) f. ii BC BCH 45 (1921) p. 25 IV,
95 + SEG XXII 455; Sic. Gymn. 17 (1964) p.
49 ([Θεό]δωρος: f. Λέων) ?= (130); (132) c. 170
BC IGSI 4 II (III), 8 an. 70 (s. Λέων); (133) c.
145-143 BC IG XIV 421 an. 98 (SGDI 5219);
IGSI 4 III (IV), 81 an. 96 (f. Ὄλυμπις); (134)
ii/i BC ib. 11 I, 3; 12 III, 32 (s. Ὄλυμπις)
——(Δαμ.): (135) c. 153 BC ib. 4 III (IV), 20 an.
88 (f. Ἀρίσταρχος)
—TYNDARIS: (136) f. i BC ASAA NS 1-2 (1939-
40) p. 168 no. 21 B I, 10 (Θεύ-)

## Θεοίτας

AIGINA: (1) m. vi BC SEG XXXII 356; LSAG²
p. 112 no. 4 (date); p. 439 no. 4 (name)
([Θ]εοίτας, [Κλ]εοίτας?)
ARKADIA:
—TEGEA: (2) c. 400-375 BC IG II² 10435 (GVI
1653) (-της: s. Τελέσων, Νικαρέτα)
—THELPHOUSA: (3) a. 228 BC IG IV (1)² 72 B,
22 (s. Κλεισ—)

**Θεοκλέα**
LAKONIA:
—SPARTA: (**1**) c. 30-20 BC ib. v (1) 141, 23; *SEG* XXXV 329 (date) (Bradford (-)) (d. Σωσ—)

**Θεοκλείδας**
ARGOLIS:
—HERMIONE: (**1**) ii-i BC *IG* IV (1) 732 III, 18 (f. Εὐφροσύνα); (**2**) c. 135-130 BC *FD* III (4) 169, 3, 9 (II s. Θεοκλείδας I); (**3**) ~ ib. l. [3], 9 (I f. Θεοκλείδας II)
ARKADIA:
—TEGEA:
——(Hippothoitai): (**4**) f. iii BC *IG* v (2) 36, 57 (s. Θεοκλῆς)
KORINTHIA:
—SIKYON: (**5**) vi/v BC *SEG* XI 244, 75
MESSENIA:
—THOURIA: (**6**) f. ii BC ib. 972, 114 (s. Δαμίων)

**Θεοκλῆς**
ACHAIA:
—DYME*: (**1**) c. 219 BC *SGDI* 1612, 39 (*Tyche* 5 (1990) p. 124) (s. Σίμων)
AKARNANIA:
—STRATOS: (**2**) iv/iii BC *IG* IX (1)² (2) 395, 7 (s. Θέων)
ARGOLIS:
—HERMIONE: (**3**) iii BC ib. IV (1) 728, 3 (f. Θεύπομπος)
ARKADIA:
—TEGEA:
——(Apolloniatai): (**4**) iv/iii BC ib. v (2) 38, 32 (s. Φιλοκράτης)
——(Hippothoitai): (**5**) iii BC ib. 40, 23 (s. Σωκλῆς) ?= (6); (**6**) f. iii BC ib. 36, 57 (f. Θεοκλείδας) ?= (5)
EPIROS:
—NIKOPOLIS: (**7**) f. i AD *Syll*³ 791 B, 8 (*FD* III (1) 530, 8); *Syll*³ 791 C, 2; 791 D, 2 (*FD* III (1) 312); *FD* III (4) 503, 21; III (6) 22, 16; 43, 13; 107, 2; 108, 2-3; 116, 18-19; *BCH* 75 (1951) p. 307 no. 1, 2 (Sarikakis 57) (and Phokis Delphi: Θ. Φιλόκαισαρ: I s. Εὔδαμος, f. Πόπλιος Μέμμιος Θεοκλῆς II (Delphi))
ILLYRIA:
—EPIDAMNOS-DYRRHACHION: (**8**) c. 250-50 BC Maier 229 (coin) (Ceka 426) (pryt.)
KORINTHIA:
—KORINTH: (**9**) inc. Ael., *VH* xiv 24; (**10**) iii BC *IG* XII (9) 806 (s. Εὐκλείδας); (**11**) 215 BC *BGU* 1278, 5, 6, 11, etc.; *PFrankf* 4, 3; *SB* 6303, 6; *PP* 3960 (f. Στάχυς)
LAKONIA: (**12**) m. vi BC *RE* Supplbd. 8 (5) (Poralla² 361) (s. Ἄγυλος: sculptor)
—SPARTA: (**13**) vi/v BC *IG* v (1) 457 (Poralla² 362) (Θιοκλέ̄—lap.); (**14**) c. 75-100 AD *IG* v (1) 31, 8, 15; 57, 12; 273, 6 (Bradford (2)) (Π. Μέμμιος Θ.); (**15**) c. 80-120 AD *IG* v (1) 147, 11; 481, 9; *SEG* XI 512, 5; 565, 6 (Bradford (5)) (f. Θεόδωρος); (**16**) c. 105-110 AD *IG* v (1) 20 B, 2; *BSA* 26 (1923-5) p. 168 C 7, 6 (Bradford (4)) (f. Παρδαλᾶς); (**17**) f. iii AD *IG* v (1) 748 (*Artemis Orthia* pp. 364-5 no. 159; Papaefthimiou p. 146 no. 19; Bradford (6)) (I f. Θεοκλῆς II); (**18**) ~ *IG* v (1) 748 (*Artemis Orthia* pp. 364-5 no. 159; Papaefthimiou p. 146 no. 19; Bradford (1)) (II s. Θεοκλῆς I)
MESSENIA:
—THOURIA: (**19**) s. iii BC *IG* v (1) 1386, 14 (s. Χαρμῖνος); (**20**) ii-i BC ib. 1385, 27 (s. Λυσικλῆς); (**21**) f. ii BC *SEG* XI 972, 124 (f. Νικάνωρ)
S. ITALY (BRUTTIUM):
—RHEGION: (**22**) arch. Iamb., *VP* 130

**Θεόκλος**
MESSENIA: (**1**) m. vii BC *RE* (1) (f. Μάντικλος: mantis)

**Θεοκλύμενος**
LAKONIA:
—SPARTA: (**1**) c. 100-150 AD *SEG* XI 492, 1; 510, 2 (Bradford (-)) (s. Κλύμενος, f. Θεόφραστος)

**Θεόκοσμος**
AIGINA: (**1**) iii BC *SEG* XXVI 919, 23 (f. Δαμαγόρας); (**2**) ~ ib. l. 24 (s. Δαμαγόρας)
ARKADIA:
—MANTINEIA-ANTIGONEIA: (**3**) c. 475-450 BC *IG* v (2) 262, 5 (*IPArk* 8); *LSAG*² p. 216 no. 29 (date) (Θεό[κ]οσσμος)

**Θεόκριτος**
ACHAIA:
—DYME: (**1**) iii BC *AJPh* 31 (1910) p. 399 no. 74 a, 1; p. 399 no. 74 c, 11 (s. Κλεόξενος, Ξενοκράτεια); (**2**) 128 BC *FD* III (3) 123, 2 (s. Λέων)
AITOLIA:
—THESTIEIS: (**3**) 213 BC *IG* IX (1)² (1) 96, 12 (f. Δωρίμαχος)
ARKADIA: (**4**) c. 265-260 BC *FD* III (1) 18, 2 (s. Θεότιμος)
—MANTINEIA-ANTIGONEIA: (**5**) c. 300-221 BC *IG* v (2) 323. 107 (tessera) (f. Κάμων)
—MEGALOPOLIS: (**6**) 263 BC ib. IX (1)² (1) 17, 12 (s. Κλεόδαμος)
—TEGEA: (**7**) c. 240-229 BC ib. v (2) 11, 13; (**8**) ?218 BC ib. 16, 1; (**9**) ~ ib. l. 13
EPIROS:
—AMBRAKIA: (**10**) f. ii BC ib. v (1) 4, 2, 9 (f. Δαμίων)
ILLYRIA:
—EPIDAMNOS-DYRRHACHION: (**11**) hell.-imp. *IDyrrh* 245 (s. Καλλήν)
S. ITALY (LUCANIA):
—METAPONTION (NR.): (**12**) c. 450-425 BC *SEG* XXXVII 781 (vase) (Landi, *DISMG* 146)
SICILY:
—BUTERA (MOD.): (**13**) ?v AD *SEG* XVI 569 (Θεό(κ)ριτος)
—SYRACUSE: (**14**) f. iii BC *RE* (1); Gow, *Theocritus* I pp. xv ff. (s. Πραξαγόρας, Φίλιννα)
—TAUROMENION: (**15**) c. 214 BC *IG* XIV 421 an. 27 (*SGDI* 5219); (**16**) 211 BC *IG* XIV 421 an. 30 (*SGDI* 5219) (f. Ὄρθων); (**17**) c. 176 BC *IG* XIV 421 an. 65 (*SGDI* 5219) (s. Ὄρθων); (**18**) c. 158-145 BC *IG* XIV 421 an. 83; 421 an. 93; 421 an. 96 (*SGDI* 5219) (f. Ἀρίσταρχος); (**19**) c. 153 BC *IG* XIV 421 an. 88 (*SGDI* 5219) (f. Διονύσιος); (**20**) ?ii/i BC *IG* XIV 421 [D] an. 2 (*SGDI* 5219) (s. Ὄλυμπις); (**21**) c. 40 BC *Cron. Arch.* 3 (1964) p. 54 I, 7, 13, 30, 39 (s. Ὄλυμπις)

**Θεοκτᾶς**
ARKADIA:
—HERAIA: (**1**) m. iii BC *IG* IV (1)² 96, 35 (Perlman E.3); Perlman p. 63 f. (date) (s. Ἀρίσταινος)

**Θεοκτίστη**
SICILY:
—SYRACUSE: (**1**) iii-v AD *IG* XIV 124 (*GVI* 1203; Strazzulla 62; Agnello 101; Wessel 258) (d. Οὐλπία)

**Θεόκτιστος**
ELIS: (**1**) iv-v AD *SEG* XXII 332, 1; cf. *TMByz* 9 (1985) p. 373 no. 152 (πρεσβύτ.)
SICILY:
—SYRACUSE: (**2**) iii-v AD Wessel 885; cf. Ferrua, *NG* 90 a (Θεώ-)

**Θεόλλος**
SICILY:
—SYRACUSE: (**1**) iv BC Manganaro, *PdelP* forthcoming no. 3, 2 (f. Παιάνιος)

**Θεόλυτος**
AIGINA: (**1**) 183 BC *FD* III (3) 240, 9, [31] (*IG* IX (1)² (1) 179) (s. Ἀρίστων)
AKARNANIA:
—KORONTA: (**2**) 429 BC Th. ii 102. 1 (f. Κύνης)
ARGOLIS:
—EPIDAUROS*: (**3**) c. 370-365 BC Peek, *IAEpid* 52 B, 53 (Θεόλυ[τ]ο[s])

**Θεόμαντις**
ARKADIA:
—MANTINEIA-ANTIGONEIA:
——(Hoplodmia): (**1**) m. iv BC *IG* v (2) 271, 11 (I f. Θεόμαντις II); (**2**) ~ ib. l. 11 (II s. Θεόμαντις I)

**Θεομένης**
ILLYRIA:
—APOLLONIA: (**1**) imp. *IApoll* 376 (Θεομέν[ης]: f. Κλεοπάτρα)

**Θεομήδης**
ARKADIA:
—MANTINEIA-ANTIGONEIA: (**1**) c. 300-221 BC *IG* v (2) 323. 61 (tessera) (f. Θεάγγελος)
ILLYRIA:
—EPIDAMNOS-DYRRHACHION: (**2**) hell.-imp. *IDyrrh* 210 (Θεομήδ[ης]: f. Εὐρύγ—); (**3**) ~ ib. 450 (f. Φιλώτας)
KERKYRA: (**4**) hell. *IG* IX (1) 890 (s. Ἀριστολαΐδας)

**Θεομηλίδας**
LAKONIA:
—SPARTA: (**1**) her. Paus. iii 14. 2

**Θεόμναστος**
AITOLIA:
—PHISTYON: (**1**) 161 BC *IG* IX (1)² (1) 100, 3; 101, 9
ARGOLIS:
—ARGOS: (**2**) 334 BC *CID* II 79 A I, 36 (-μνη-); (**3**) iii BC *BCH* 27 (1903) p. 278 no. 30 (s. Μνασέας)
KORINTHIA:
—SIKYON: (**4**) 333 BC *CID* II 81 A, 5 (Skalet 141) (-μνη-)
SICILY:
—SYRACUSE: (**5**) 73-70 BC *RE* (-) (Lat. Theomnastus)
—TAUROMENION: (**6**) c. 223 BC *IG* XIV 421 an. 18 (*SGDI* 5219) (s. Κάλλιππος)

**Θεόμνηστος**
ARGOLIS:
—METHANA-ARSINOE: (**1**) imp. *IG* IV (1) 870 (Θεόμν[η]στος)
ILLYRIA:
—APOLLONIA: (**2**) i AD *IApoll* 180 (Κλαύδιος Θ.: f. Κλαυδία Προβᾶτα)
KORINTHIA:
—KORINTH: (**3**) iv-v AD *IG* XII (5) 565, 5 (-νισθος: f. Θεοσέβεια)
S. ITALY (APULIA):
—VENUSIA: (**4**) imp. *Epigraphica* 35 (1973) p. 147 no. 7 (Lat. M. Creperius Theomnestus)
S. ITALY (CAMPANIA):
—DIKAIARCHIA-PUTEOLI: (**5**) imp. *CIL* X 2372 (Lat. M. Sittius Theomnestus)
—POMPEII: (**6**) i BC-i AD ib. IV 4772 (Lat. Theomnestus)

**Θεονίκα**
EPIROS:
—PHOTIKE: (**1**) imp. *AE* 1914, p. 241 no. II (Lat. [T]heonica)

**Θεονόη**
S. ITALY (CAMPANIA):
—DIKAIARCHIA-PUTEOLI: (**1**) imp. *CIL* X 3037 (Lat. Val. Theonoe)

**Θεόνομος**
S. ITALY (CAMPANIA):
—HERCULANEUM*: (**1**) i BC-i AD ib. 1403 g III, 31 (Lat. M. Laronius Theonomus: freed.)

## Θεόνοστος

ARGOLIS:
—HERMIONE: (1) ?ii-i BC *IG* IV (1) 731 III, 1
(f. Νικάσιον)

## Θεοξένα

AIGINA: (1) ii BC *SEG* XI 9, 2
ARGOLIS:
—HERMIONE: (2) i BC-i AD? *IG* IV (1) 730 IV, 5
(d. Σωκράτεια)
ELIS: (3) ?i AD *IvOl* 413 (d. Τελέστας, m. Ἀλκίας)
SICILY:
—SYRACUSE: (4) f. iii BC *POxy* 2821 (II d.
Ἀγαθοκλῆς, Θεοξένα I (Egypt), m. Ἀγαθοκλῆς
(Egypt))

## Θεοξενίδας

ARGOLIS:
—EPIDAUROS: (1) c. 370 BC *IG* IV (1)² 102, 98,
99
ARKADIA:
—MANTINEIA-ANTIGONEIA: (2) ?iii BC ib. V (2)
318, 29
—PHENEOS: (3) 139-122 BC *Syll*³ 703; cf.
Stephanis 1228; 1439 (f. Κλεόδωρος, Θρασύ-
βουλος)
—STYMPHALOS: (4) iii BC *IG* V (2) 356, 7
MESSENIA: (5) ?i AD ib. V (1) 1374 (s. Εὔθυκλῆς)

## Θεόξενος

ACHAIA: (1) f. ii BC *RE* (3); *ID* 396 B, [51]; 425,
11; 439a, [63]; 442 B, 68; 1417 A I, 21 ?= (3)
—DYME*: (2) c. 219 BC *SGDI* 1612, 32 (*Tyche*
5 (1990) p. 124) (f. Εὔδοξος)
—LEONTION: (3) 179 BC *Syll*³ 634 (f. Καλλικρά-
της) ?= (1)
—PATRAI: (4) ii-iii AD *IG* II² 10046 a (s. Ἀχιλ-
λεύς)
—PELLENE: (5) m. iii BC ib. V (2) 368, 104 (f.
Ξενότιμος)
AIGINA: (6) hell.-imp. ib. IV (1) 42 (f. Μόμμιος)
AIGINA?: (7) imp. *EAD* xxx p. 356 no. 18
ARGOLIS:
—TROIZEN: (8) ?287 BC *IG* IV (1) 750, [15], 41
(f. Θεόγνητος)
ARKADIA:
—HERAIA: (9) 191-146 BC *BMC Pelop.* p. 14 no
164 (coin)
—KLEITOR: (10) ?ii BC *IG* V (2) 376
—PARRHASIOI: (11) c. 369 BC Paus. viii 27. 2
(and Arkadia Megalopolis: oikist)
ELIS: (12) c. 100-90 BC *SEG* XXXIII 290 A,
26; *BSA* 70 (1975) pp. 129-31 (date); cf.
Stephanis 1179 (I f. Θεόξενος II); (13) ~ *SEG*
XXXIII 290 A, 26; *BSA* 70 (1975) pp. 129-31
(date) (Stephanis 1179) (II s. Θεόξενος I)
EPIROS: (14) iii-ii BC Cabanes, *L'Épire* p. 587
no. 72 (Θεόξ[ενος])
ILLYRIA:
—EPIDAMNOS-DYRRHACHION: (15) c. 250-50
BC Ceka, *Probleme* p. 151 no. 27 (coin) (pryt.)
?= (16); (16) ~ Maier 230-1; Münsterberg
Nachtr. p. 15 (coin) (Ceka 19; 57; 190) (pryt.)
?= (15)
LAKONIA:
—GYTHEION: (17) c. 100-75 BC *IG* V (1) 1144,
22; 1181 (s. Φιλήμων); (18) ~ ib. 1144, 22;
1181 (f. Φιλήμων)
—SPARTA: (19) s. i BC ib. 124, 2 (Bradford (3));
(20) c. 70-100 AD *IG* V (1) 676, 5 (Bradford
(6)) (f. Φιλέρως) ?= (23); (21) f. ii AD *IG* V
(1) 587, 2; *BSA* 80 (1985) p. 244 (ident.,
stemma) (Bradford (8)) (Θ.: f. Πομπ. Πῶλλα);
(22) c. 140-160 AD *IG* V (1) 112, 15 (Bradford (1)) (s. Γ. Ἰούλ. Φιλέρως); (23) c. 150-160
AD *IG* V (1) 68, 15 (Bradford (7)) (f. Γ. Ἰούλ.
Φιλέρως) ?= (20); (24) f. iii AD *IG* V (1) 170, 7;
464, 2; *SEG* XLI 384, 3; *BSA* 80 (1985) pp.
244-6 (ident., stemma) (Bradford (4)) (Σέξ.
Πομπ. Θ.: I f. Σέξ. Πομπ. Θεόξενος II, Σέξ.
Πομπ. Μηνοφάνης, Πομπ. Πῶλλα); (25) ~ *IG*

v (1) 324, [3]; 464, 13; *SEG* XXXIV 308, 14;
*BSA* 79 (1984) pp. 285-6 (Bradford (5)) (Σέξ.
Πομπ. Θ.: II s. Σέξ. Πομπ. Θεόξενος I, f. Σέξ.
Πομπ. Δαμαίνετος)
SICILY:
—SELINOUS: (26) s. vi BC Arena, *Iscr. Sic.* I 20
(Dubois, *IGDS* 74; *IGLMP* 85) (s. Νικόλα)

## Θέοξις

ACHAIA:
—AIGION: (1) ii BC *IG* IV (1)² 628 (f. Ἀβροσύνα); (2) 153-144 BC *FD* III (1) 154, 1, 3 with
n. (locn.) (s. Δαμοκλῆς); (3) c. 32-31 BC *BMC
Pelop.* pp. 18-19 nos. 4-9 (coin); *Ag.* XXVI p.
233 (date) (f. Κληταῖος)
ARKADIA:
—LOUSOI: (4) m. iii BC *BCH* 38 (1914) p. 457
no. 3, 2 ([Θ]έοξις: s. Ἀλέως); (5) iii/ii BC *IG* V
(2) 394, 3 (Perlman L.5)

## Θεοπείθης

ARKADIA:
—BASSAI*: (1) m. iv BC *SEG* XXVIII 416 (Θεο-
πεί[θης])
—TEGEA: (2) iv/iii BC *IG* V (2) 32, 9

## Θεοπομπίδας

MESSENIA:
—MESSENE?: (1) ii/i BC *SEG* XI 979, 43

## Θεόπομπος

ACHAIA:
—DYME*: (1) c. 219 BC *SGDI* 1612, 45 (*Tyche*
5 (1990) p. 124) (f. Μενέστρατος)
ACHAIA?: (2) 37 AD *IG* VII 2711, 35 (s. Ἀ—
δαμος)
ARGOLIS:
—HERMIONE: (3) i BC-i AD? ib. IV (1) 734, 1 (f.
Σθένιος)
—TROIZEN: (4) iii BC ib. 774, 12; (5) ?146 BC ib.
757 B, 19 (f. Νικοτέλης)
ARKADIA:
—HERAIA: (6) f. vii BC Paus. iv 24. 1; (7) vi/v
BC Moretti, *Olymp.* 189; 200 (I s. Δαμάρα-
τος, f. Θεόπομπος II); (8) ?440-436 BC ib. 313;
317 (II s. Θεόπομπος I); (9) a. 420 BC *REG* 62
(1949) p. 6, 12 (Θεόπομ[πο]ς); (10) 369-361 BC
*IG* V (2) 1, 61; Tod, *GHI* II 132 (date)
—MEGALOPOLIS: (11) m. iii BC *SEG* XI 412, 67
(Perlman E.3); Perlman p. 63 f. (date) ([Θεό-
πο]μπος: s. Ἱστιαῖος); (12) c. 200 BC *FD* III
(4) 145, 2 (Stephanis 1182) (Θε[όπ]ονπος: s.
Ἱστιαῖος)
EPIROS:
—AMBRAKIA: (13) 263 BC *IG* IX (1)² (1) 17, 42
(f. Ἄνταρχος)
KORINTHIA:
—KORINTH: (14) ii-i BC *Corinth* XIII p. 319 no.
X-115
—SIKYON: (15) ?165 BC *Syll*³ 585, 311 (Skalet
142) (s. Νίκων); (16) c. 146-95 BC Roesch, *Ét.
Béot.* p. 190 no. 35 (Skalet 143; Stephanis
1184) (s. Σωκράτης)
LAKONIA:
—SPARTA: (17) s. viii BC *RE* (3) (Poralla²
363) (s. Νίκανδρος, f. Ἀναξανδρίδας, Ἀρχίδαμος:
king); (18) 375 BC Plu., *Pelop.* 17 (Poralla²
364)
MESSENIA:
—MESSENE: (19) f. iii BC *PAE* 1991, p. 99 no.
7, 21; (20) m. iii BC *IC* 2 p. 29 no. 13
(s. —άτων); (21) ii BC *PAE* 1969, p. 106,
10 ([Θεό]πομπος); (22) c. 146-32 BC Imhoof-
Blümer, *MGr* p.170 no. 74; BM coin 1899
4-6-1 (coin)

## Θεοπρέπεια

AKARNANIA:
—ANAKTORION (NR.): (1) byz. *AAA* 4 (1971)
p. 188 (-πια)

## Θεοπρόκα

KEPHALLENIA:
—PRONNOI: (1) s. v BC *SEG* XXV 607

## Θεοπροκίδας

S. ITALY (LUCANIA):
—PADULA (MOD.): (1) vi/v BC *Apollo* 9 (1993)
pp. 5-6 (Arena, *Iscr. Sic.* IV 32) (Δυ. Θ.)

## Θεοπροπίδας

AKARNANIA:
—KORONTA: (1) c. 325-315 BC *Hesp.* 57 (1988)
p. 148 A, 50 (*SEG* XXXVI 331); cf. *Hesp.* 48
(1979) pp. 78 f. with pl. 22 c (Θ(ε)οπροπίδας?:
f. Παυσανίας)
—STRATOS: (2) 356-354 BC *IG* IV (1)² 95, 10
(Perlman E.2); Perlman p. 40 f. (date)
ARGOLIS:
—EPIDAUROS*: (3) c. 335-325 BC Peek, *IAEpid*
50, 23-4

## Θεοπρόπιος

LAKONIA:
—SPARTA: (1) ?i/ii AD *IG* V (1) 513 (Bradford
(-))

## Θεόπροπος

AIGINA: (1) f. v BC Marcadé I 106 (Lazzarini 895); *Alt-Ägina* II (2) pp. 44-5; cf. *SEG*
XXXVIII 417 (sculptor)

## Θεόσαμος

SICILY:
—KEPHALOIDION: (1) hell.-imp. *IG* XIV 2395.
3 (tile)

## Θεοσέβεια

KORINTHIA:
—KORINTH: (1) iv-v AD ib. XII (5) 565, 3 (-βια:
d. Θεόμνηστος)

## Θεοσχώτης

S. ITALY (CAMPANIA):
—NEAPOLIS: (1) i BC/i AD *INap* 126 ter, 3
(Θεοσχώτ[ης]—ed., Θεοσχώ?: s. Καλλίνικος)

## Θεότεκνα

ARGOLIS:
—ARGOS: (1) byz. *BCH* 28 (1904) p. 420 no. 4;
cf. *TMByz* 9 (1985) p. 370 no. 112

## Θεότεκνος

S. ITALY (CAMPANIA):
—NEAPOLIS: (1) imp. *CIL* X 1525 (Lat.
Theotecnus)

## Θεοτέλης

ACHAIA:
—PELLENE?: (1) ?263-261 BC *FD* III (3) 190, 4
(f. —τέλης)
ARKADIA: (2) 320 BC *IG* V (2) 549, 8 (Θεοτή-
λες—lap.: s. Νικάσιππος); (3) 304 BC ib. 550,
21
—MANTINEIA-ANTIGONEIA: (4) c. 300-221 BC
ib. 323. 63 (tessera) (s. Ἀριστο—)
—TEGEA
——(Krariotai): (5) iv/iii BC ib. 38, 22 (f. Εὐτυ-
χίδας)
ELIS:
—THRAISTOS: (6) f. iv BC ib. IX (1)² (1) 138, 2
ILLYRIA:
—EPIDAMNOS-DYRRHACHION: (7) c. 250-50 BC
Maier 232-5; Münsterberg Nachtr. p. 15
(coin) (Ceka 114; 147; 184; 212?; 222; 258)
(pryt.); (8) ii-i BC *IDyrrh* 237 (f. Ἡράκλειτος)
MESSENIA:
—MESSENE: (9) iii BC *SEG* XXIII 210, 12

## Θεοτιμίδας

LAKONIA:
—SPARTA: (1) c. 225 BC ib. XI 414, 29 (Perlman
E.5; Bradford (9)) (f. Θεότιμος)

**Θεότιμος**
AITOLIA?: (**1**) s. iv BC *Klio* 15 (1918) p. 56 no. 79, 1 (s. Ἐρυμνίων)
ARGOLIS:
—ARGOS*: (**2**) 105 BC *JÖAI* 14 (1911) Beibl. p. 146 no. 4, 11 (Θεότιμ[ος]: slave/freed.?)
—EPIDAUROS*: (**3**) c. 370 BC *IG* IV (1)² 102, 196; *SEG* XXV 383, 42, 167
ARKADIA: (**4**) iii BC *IG* V (2) 415, 4 (*IPArk* 23) (Θεότιμ[ος]); (**5**) c. 265-260 BC *FD* III (1) 18, 2 (Θεότιμ[ος]: f. Θεόκριτος)
—MANTINEIA-ANTIGONEIA: (**6**) iv BC *IG* V (2) 331
—MEGALOPOLIS: (**7**) ?145 BC ib. 439, 37 (s. Ἀλεξάνωρ); (**8**) ii/i BC ib. 443, 3 (*IPArk* 32) (f. —νος)
—PHENEOS: (**9**) i BC *SEG* XXXIII 291, 3; cf. Stephanis 2765 (f. .αγλ..ρης)
—TEGEA:
——(Apolloniatai): (**10**) iv/iii BC *IG* V (2) 38, 35 (I f. Θεότιμος II); (**11**) ~ ib. l. 35 (II s. Θεότιμος I) ?= (*12*); (**12**) f. iii BC ib. 36, 51 (f. Ἰμπεδοκλῆς) ?= (*11*)
DALMATIA:
—ISSA: (**13**) iv/iii BC *VAHD* NS 8 (1905) p. 97 no. 177 (*VAMZ* 1970, p. 33 f. frr. I-J)
——(Dymanes): (**14**) iv/iii BC Brunšmid p. 7, 25 (f. -ολθων)
ELIS: (**15**) c. 325-300 BC Moretti, *Olymp.* 489 (s. Μοσχίων); (**16**) f. i BC *SEG* XVII 199, 2 (Θ. ὁ καὶ Σάμιππος: s. Ἑλλάνικος); (**17**) m. i BC *IvOl* 407, 2; 409, 2; 410 (f. Γλαῦκος, Δαμώ); (**18**) i BC/i AD ib. 75, 11 ([Θ]εότιμος); (**19**) f. i AD ib. 80, 3; cf. 76, 2; 77, [7] (Φιλίκων ὁ καὶ Θεότιμος: s. Ὀλυμπιόδωρος: mantis/Iamidai)
EPIROS:
—BOUTHROTOS (PRASAIBOI): (**20**) a. 163 BC *IBouthrot* 32, 31; 34, 2 (*SEG* XXXVIII 491; 493); (**21**) ~ *IBouthrot* 134, 17 (s. Σώσανδρος) ?= (*23*)
——Kleonaioi: (**22**) a. 163 BC ib. 120, 10 (s. Κλέων)
——Tharioi: (**23**) a. 163 BC ib. 126, 7 (f. Σώσανδρος) ?= (*21*)
ILLYRIA:
—EPIDAMNOS-DYRRHACHION: (**24**) hell.-imp. *IDyrrh* 88 (f. Αἰσχύλος)
KORINTHIA:
—SIKYON: (**25**) iv/iii BC *CID* II 120 A, 45 (Skalet 144) (f. —τος)
LAKONIA:
—SPARTA: (**26**) vi BC *IEG* 1 p. 215 l. 881 (Poralla² 365); (**27**) c. 225 BC *SEG* XI 414, 29 (Perlman E.5; Bradford (-)) (s. Θεοτιμίδας)
MESSENIA:
—MESSENE: (**28**) f. iii BC *PAE* 1991, p. 99 no. 7, 20; (**29**) ii/i BC *IG* V (1) 1446 (s. Παυλῖνος)
S. ITALY (CAMPANIA):
—STABIAE: (**30**) b. 79 AD ib. XIV 700 (s. Μύρινος, Ὑγίεια)
SICILY:
—GELA-PHINTIAS: (**31**) v BC Dubois, *IGDS* 156 (loomweight) (Arena, *Iscr. Sic.* II 60)
—KAMARINA: (**32**) iv/iii BC *SEG* XXXIX 999, 7 (Dubois, *IGDS* 125; Cordano, 'Camarina VII' 116) (Θεότ[ι]μος: s. Λαμίσκος); (**33**) ?ii BC *SEG* XXXIX 996, 7 (Dubois, *IGDS* 126; Cordano, 'Camarina VII' 115) (s. Λαμίσκος)
—LEONTINOI: (**34**) 433 BC *IG* I³ 54, 7 (s. Ταυρίσκος)

**Θεοφάνεια**
MESSENIA:
—MESSENE?: (**1**) ii BC *SEG* XXIII 219 (d. Φιλωνίδας, m. Φίλιππος, Ξενόφιλος)

**Θεοφάνης**
AIGINA: (**1**) i-ii AD *Alt-Ägina* I (2) p. 47 no. 27, 5 (s. Ἀφροδίσιος)

ARGOLIS:
—ARGOS: (**2**) hell.? *BCH* 78 (1954) p. 167 (terracotta)
—EPIDAUROS*: (**3**) c. 365-335 BC *IG* IV (1)² 103, 50
LAKONIA:
—SPARTA: (**4**) s. i BC ib. V (1) 124, 18 (Bradford (-)) ([Θ]εοφάνης: s. T—)
MESSENIA:
—ABIA: (**5**) ii AD *GVI* 1555 (Θειο-: s. Ἀρχιτέλης, Ἐλπίς)
—MESSENE: (**6**) ii BC *SEG* XLI 348 (f. Κράτων); (**7**) ii/i BC ib. 346; 348; cf. *PAE* 1991, p. 115 (s. Κράτων)
SICILY:
—LIPARA: (**8**) imp. Libertini, *Isole Eolie* p. 229 no. 6 (*ILat. Palermo* 8) (Lat. Theophanes: f. Εὐφροσύνη)

**Θεοφανίσκος**
AKARNANIA:
—PALAIROS: (**1**) iii BC *IG* IX (1)² (2) 487 (-σχος)

**Θεόφαντος**
KORINTHIA:
—SIKYON: (**1**) ?221 or 220 BC ib. VII 213, 5-6, 8 (Skalet 145) (s. Εὐλαΐδας)

**Θεοφείδης**
ARGOLIS:
—EPIDAUROS: (**1**) c. 370 BC *IG* IV (1)² 102, 48
—KALAURIA: (**2**) iv BC ib. IV (1) 839, 3

**Θεοφίλα**
S. ITALY (CAMPANIA):
—CAPREAE*: (**1**) ?iii AD *Epigraphica* 34 (1972) p. 142 (Lat. Aurelia Theophila: freed.)
SICILY:
—LIPARA: (**2**) hell. *NScav* 1947, p. 218 no. 4 (*Epigraphica* 11 (1949) p. 50 no. 2)

**Θεοφίλης**
ARGOLIS:
—EPIDAUROS: (**1**) m. iv BC *IvOl* 165; Paus. vi 13. 6 (f. Ἀριστίων)

**Θεοφιλίδας**
ARKADIA:
—MANTINEIA-ANTIGONEIA: (**1**) c. 300-221 BC *IG* V (2) 323. 29 (tessera) (s. Αὐτίας)

**Θεόφιλος**
AIGINA: (**1**) hell.? ib. IV (1) 117 (s. Μηνόδωρος); (**2**) i BC ib. II² 7955 (s. Ζωῖλος); (**3**) iii AD *SEG* XI 15 ([Θε]όφιλος)
AIGINA?: (**4**) i BC-i AD *EAD* XXX p. 356 no. 21 (s. Εὐκλῆς)
ARGOLIS:
—EPIDAUROS: (**5**) i-ii AD *IG* IV (1)² 460 (sculptor)
——(Hysminatai): (**6**) 146 BC ib. 28, 18 (f. Ἀριστοκράτης)
—EPIDAUROS*: (**7**) c. 370-365 BC Peek, *IAEpid* 52 B, 8, 12
—KLEONAI: (**8**) imp. *IG* IV (1) 490, 2 (Κορν. Βετούριος Θ.)
—MYKENAI*: (**9**) ?ii-i BC *SEG* III 315 e (tile) ([Θ]εόφιλο[ς])
ARKADIA:
—TEGEA: (**10**) i BC-i AD *IG* V (2) 224; (**11**) i AD ib. 46, 15 ([Θε]όφιλο[ς]); (**12**) 165 AD ib. 50, 73 (I f. Θεόφιλος II); (**13**) ~ ib. l. 73 (II s. Θεόφιλος I)
ILLYRIA:
—APOLLONIA: (**14**) c. 250-50 BC Maier 47 (coin) (Ceka 14) (pryt.); (**15**) i BC Ceka, *Probleme* p. 139 no. 13 (coin) (pryt.); (**16**) ~ Maier 134 (coin) (money.)
—EPIDAMNOS-DYRRHACHION: (**17**) imp. *IDyrrh* 145 (Γάει Σέργει Θεόφιλε (voc.))
KERKYRA: (**18**) 126 BC *ID* 1923, 11 (I f. Θεόφιλος II); (**19**) ~ ib. l. 11 (II s. Θεόφιλος I)

KORINTHIA:
—KORINTH: (**20**) i BC *IG* II² 9146, 5; (**21**) 30 BC Amandry pp. 138-40; *RPC* 1 p. 251 nos. 1129-31 (coin) (Lat. M. Ant. Theophil(us)) ?= (*22*)
—KORINTH*: (**22**) 31 BC Plu., *Ant.* 67 (f. M. Ἀντ. Ἵππαρχος: freed.) ?= (*21*); (**23**) i AD *Corinth* VIII (2) 107 (Lat. Q. Cispuleius Theophilus)
LAKONIA:
—SPARTA: (**24**) s. i BC *IG* V (1) 93, 17 (Bradford (4)) (I f. Θεόφιλος II); (**25**) ~ *IG* V (1) 93, 17 (Bradford (2)) (II s. Θεόφιλος I); (**26**) c. 105-115 AD *IG* V (1) 103, 9 (Bradford (1)) ([Θε]όφιλος: s. Καλλικρατίδας); (**27**) c. 110-150 AD *IG* V (1) 114, 9; *SEG* XI 540, 6 (Bradford (3)) (s. Ξενοκράτης)
LEUKAS: (**28**) c. 167-50 BC *BMC Thessaly* p. 181 no. 113 (coin) (Θεόφιλ[ος])
MESSENIA:
—PHARAI?: (**29**) imp. *IG* V (1) 1365; cf. PM 1684 (s. Ἀλέξανδρος)
—THOURIA: (**30**) ii/i BC *IG* V (1) 1384, 14 (f. Ἀριστόμαχος)
S. ITALY (APULIA):
—CANUSIUM*: (**31**) imp. *Epig. Rom. di Canosa* 94 (*CIL* IX 363) (Lat. L. Maecius Theopilus: freed.)
—LUCERIA: (**32**) imp. ib. 817 (Lat. Q. Sulpicius Theophilus)
S. ITALY (CALABRIA):
—TARAS-TARENTUM: (**33**) imp. *Misc. Gr. Rom.* 3 p. 177 no. N2 (Lat. Theophi[lus])
S. ITALY (CAMPANIA):
—DIKAIARCHIA-PUTEOLI: (**34**) imp. *CIL* X 2189 (Lat. M. Valerius Theophilus); (**35**) m. i AD *RAAN* 47 (1972) p. 312 no. 2 (Lat. Theophilus)
—HERCULANEUM: (**36**) 60 AD *PdelP* 1 (1946) p. 381 no. 4; *Ostraka* 2 (1993) pp. 201-3 (Lat. Q. Iunius Theophilus)
—HERCULANEUM*: (**37**) m. i AD *Cron. Erc.* 7 (1977) p. 118 D, 6 (Lat. M. Antonius Theophilus: freed.)
—NEAPOLIS: (**38**) c. 95-92 BC *ID* 1934, 1 ([Θε]όφιλος: s. Φιλόστρατος (Palestine, Askalon))
—POMPEII: (**39**) i BC-i AD *CIL* IV 4189; (**40**) ~ ib. 8898; *Epigraphica* 30 (1968) pp. 115-8 (Lat. Tiopilus)
S. ITALY (LUCANIA):
—HERAKLEIA: (**41**) c. 125-100 BC *EAD* XXX 295 (s. Ἀρίστων)
—HYELE-VELIA: (**42**) ?i AD *PdelP* 33 (1978) p. 65 no. 10 (Lat. Gabinius Theophilus: f. Λαΐς)
SICILY:
—AKRAI: (**43**) ?iii BC *SGDI* 3240, 4 (*Akrai* p. 156 no. 7) (f. Εὐ—ος)
—SYRACUSE: (**44**) iii-v AD Strazzulla 202 (Wessel 842) (Θεόφιλ[ος], Θεοφίλ[η]?)
—TAUROMENION: (**45**) c. 184-179 BC *IG* XIV 421 an. 57; 421 an. 58; 421 an. 69 (*SGDI* 5219) (f. Θεόχρηστος, Μένων); (**46**) 168 BC *IG* XIV 421 an. 73 (f. Φίλιστος); (**47**) ii/i BC *IGSI* 6 II, 2 (Θε[ό]φ[ιλος]: s. Θεόχρηστος); (**48**) c. 40 BC *Cron. Arch.* 3 (1964) p. 56 I, 9, 34 (f. Ὀλυμπις)
——(K.): (**49**) c. 146 BC *IGSI* 4 III (IV), 78 an. 96 (f. Ἀρτεμίδωρος)
——(Ταυ.): (**50**) ?ii/i BC *IG* XIV 421 D an. 7 (*SGDI* 5219) (f. Φιλόδαμος)

**Θεόφραστος**
AIGINA: (**1**) c. 100-90 BC *IG* VII 2448, 2; cf. Stephanis 454 (f. Ἀσκληπιάδης); (**2**) c. 75-60 BC *IG* VII 419, 8 (*IOrop* 526); *IG* VII 3196, 3; *BSA* 70 (1975) p. 121 (date) (Stephanis 1190) (s. Ἀσκληπιάδης)
ARGOLIS:
—EPIDAUROS: (**3**) c. 350-200 BC *SEG* XXVI 452. 3

Θεόφρις
ELIS: (4) i/ii AD *IvOl* 87, 4-5 (?f. Σύντροφορ)
LAKONIA:
—SPARTA: (5) c. 100-150 AD *IG* v (1) 506; *SEG*
11 62, 2; XI 492, 1; 494, 5; 496, 4; 522, 5; 623,
4 (Bradford (-)) (Γ. Ἰούλ. Θ.: s. Θεοκλύμενος)

Θεόφρις
S. ITALY (BRUTTIUM):
—KROTON: (1) iv BC Iamb., *VP.* 267 (*FVS* 1 p.
448) (f. Φιλτύς, Βύνδακος)

Θεοφύλακτος
S. ITALY (BRUTTIUM):
—HIPPONION-VIBO VALENTIA: (1) byz. *IG* XIV
2412. 17 (-φίλ-)
S. ITALY (CAMPANIA):
—NEAPOLIS: (2) byz. *Bull. Arch. Crist.* 5 (1867)
pp. 72-4 (Lat. Theophilactus)

Θεοχάρης
ARKADIA:
—MANTINEIA-ANTIGONEIA: (1) c. 300-221 BC
*IG* v (2) 323. 78 (tessera) (s. Ἀγησίδαμος)
—TEGEA:
——(Krariotai): (2) s. iii BC ib. 36, 120 (Θεο-
χάρ[ης]: f. Νεοκλῆς)
EPIROS: (3) imp. *Syringes* 1516

Θεόχαρις
ARKADIA: (1) ?255 BC Nachtergael, *Les Gala-*
*tes* 8, 25 (Stephanis 1192) (Θεόχ[α]ρις: s. Ἱεροκλῆς)

Θεοχαρμίδας
AIGINA: (1) ii BC *IG* II² 7956 (-δης: f. Καλλινώ)

Θεόχρηστος
SICILY:
—TAUROMENION: (1) c. 185-175 BC ib. XIV 421
an. 56 (*SGDI* 5219) (s. Ἐπιγένης); (2) c. 184-
172 BC *IG* XIV 421 an. 57; 421 an. 69 (*SGDI*
5219) (s. Θεόφιλος); (3) c. 175 BC *IG* XIV 421
an. 66 (*SGDI* 5219) (s. Ἐπισθένης); (4) ii/i
BC *IGSI* 6 II, 2 (f. Θεόφιλος); (5) ?f. i BC
ib. 4 I, 4 + *SEG* XXXIII 755 + XXXVIII 975
(Θε[όχρ]ησ[τος])

Θεράπων
KERKYRA: (1) imp. *IG* IX (1) 955

Θερειός
AITOLIA:
—KALYDON: (1) f. iv BC ib. IX (1)² (1) 138, 3

Θερινή
ILLYRIA:
—APOLLONIA: (1) imp. *IApoll* 241 (Κλαυδία Θ.)

Θερμοξένα
AIGINA: (1) imp. *AE* 1913, p. 95 no. 6 γ

Θέρμων
LAKONIA:
—SPARTA: (1) 412 BC Th. viii 11. 2 (Poralla²
366)

Θέρπις
ARKADIA:
—MANTINEIA-ANTIGONEIA: (1) c. 300-221 BC
*IG* v (2) 323. 52 (tessera) (f. Καλλίερος)

Θερρίλας
ARKADIA:
—ORCHOMENOS: (1) s. iv BC *SEG* XI 1051 =
*EILakArk* 19 (f. Νικέας)

Θερσαγόρας
ARGOLIS:
—ARGOS: (1) ?c. 460-450 BC *Mnem.* NS 47
(1919) p. 161 no. 6, 7; *LSAG²* p. 170 no.
31 (date) (Θερσαγό[ρας])
——(Dmaihippidai): (2) ii/i BC *BCH* 33 (1909)
p. 176 no. 2, 10 (s. Νικοφάης)

EPIROS:
—ARGOS (AMPHILOCH.): (3) c. 315-280 BC *FD*
III (4) 407, 2 (s. Κριτολαΐδας)

Θέρσανδρος
ARGOLIS:
—ARGOS: (1) c. 550 BC *FGrH* 287 F 2a
—EPIDAUROS: (2) iv BC *IG* IV (1)² 173
—HALIEIS: (3) s. iv BC ib. 122, 69, 73-4
—TROIZEN: (4) iv BC ib. IV (1) 823, 32, 38
KERKYRA: (5) ?s. v BC *CEG* II 469
KORINTHIA:
—KORINTH: (6) c. 590-570 BC Amyx 33. 8
(vase) (Lorber 52) (her.?); (7) hell.? *SEG*
XXVIII 292 (f. Ἀριστοκράτης)
—SIKYON: (8) vi/v BC ib. XI 244, 50; (9) ~ ib. l.
62

Θερσάνωρ
KORINTHIA:
—SIKYON: (1) f. iii BC *CID* II 120 A, 42; 122
II, 1 (Skalet 146) (s. Θερσικλῆς)

Θέρσας
ARGOLIS:
—ARGOS:
——Selligon (Vanidai): (1) iii BC *Mnem.* NS 43
(1915) p. 375 E, 10 (Θέρ[σ]ας)

Θερσέας
ILLYRIA:
—APOLLONIA: (1) hell. *IApoll* 350 (tile) (f. Δα-
μονίκων)

Θερσήν
ILLYRIA:
—APOLLONIA: (1) imp. ib. 281 (f. —α)
—EPIDAMNOS-DYRRHACHION: (2) hell.? *IDyrrh*
217 (f. Ἔχυλλος)

Θερσιάν?
ILLYRIA:
—EPIDAMNOS-DYRRHACHION: (1) hell.-imp. ib.
246 (s. Δαζαῖος)

Θερσίας
ARKADIA:
—TEGEA: (1) ?iii BC *IG* v (2) 104
——(Krariotai): (2) f. iii BC ib. 36, 40 (f. Ἰσόδα-
μος)
ILLYRIA:
—APOLLONIA: (3) c. 250-50 BC Münsterberg
Nachtr. p. 13 (Ceka 17); Maier 48 (Ceka 99);
cf. *IApoll Ref. Bibl.* n. 23 (coin) (pryt.); (4) i
BC Maier 149 (coin) (money.)
—EPIDAMNOS-DYRRHACHION: (5) c. 250-50 BC
Ceka, *Probleme* p. 151 no. 28 (coin) (pryt.)
?= (6); (6) ~ Maier 236 (coin) (Ceka 68; 407)
(pryt.) ?= (5); (7) ii-i BC *IDyrrh* 401 (f. Τι-
μᾶς); (8) ~ ib. 540 (tile); (9) hell.-imp. ib. 247
(s. Ἡρακλείδας)
KERKYRA: (10) ?ii-i BC *IG* IX (1) 775 + *BM*
*Terracottas* E 133 (tile)

Θερσίδαμος
ARGOLIS:
—ARGOS: (1) c. 315 BC *SEG* XXXII 370, 11, 14

Θερσικλῆς
KORINTHIA:
—SIKYON: (1) f. iii BC *CID* II 120 A, 42; 122
II, 1 (Skalet 147) (f. Θερσάνωρ)

Θερσίλας
KORINTHIA:
—KORINTH: (1) f. ii BC *Corinth* VIII (1) 2, 1; cf.
*SEG* XI 54 ([Θ]ερσίλας)

Θερσίλοχος
AKARNANIA:
—PALAIROS: (1) c. 325-315 BC *Hesp.* 57 (1988)
p. 148 A, 18 (*SEG* XXXVI 331); cf. *Hesp.* 48
(1979) pp. 78 f. with pl. 22 c (f. Διοκλῆς)

EPIROS:
—BOUTHROTOS (PRASAIBOI): (2) a. 163 BC
*IBouthrot* 14, 24 (*SEG* XXXVIII 471) (f. Βοΐ-
σκος)
KERKYRA: (3) 372 BC Moretti, *Olymp.* 409

Θερσιμένης
ARGOLIS:
—ARGOS: (1) iv BC *SEG* XVIII 145; *BCH* 33
(1909) p. 448 no. 13

Θερσίνους
KORINTHIA:
—SIKYON: (1) ?257-255 BC Nachtergael, *Les*
*Galates* 7, 70; 8, 73 (Skalet 148; Stephanis
1195) (s. Νικωνίδας)

Θερσίππα
AKARNANIA:
—PALAIROS: (1) s. iii BC *IG* IX (1)² (2) 524

Θέρσις
AIGINA: (1) vi/v BC *SEG* XL 301; *LSAG²* p.
113 no. 7; p. 439 no. 10b (gem)

Θερσίς
ARKADIA?: (1) iv/iii BC *HE* 695

Θερσίων
ARGOLIS:
—ARGOS:
——(Daiphonteis): (1) f. iii BC *IG* IV (1) 529, 18
KERKYRA: (2) iv/iii BC ib. IX (1) 976, 3
(Θε[ρσ]ίων: s. Ἀμφισθένης)

Θερσόπολις
EPIROS:
—BOUTHROTOS (PRASAIBOI): (1) a. 163 BC
*IBouthrot* 16 (*SEG* XXXVIII 473)

Θερσώ
EPIROS:
—BOUTHROTOS (PRASAIBOI):
——Messaneoi?: (1) a. 163 BC *IBouthrot* 14, 10;
41, 7, 10 (*SEG* XXXVIII 471; 500); *IBouthrot*
146, 4 (?d. Μενοίτας, Δεινομάχα)

Θέσμος
S. ITALY (APULIA):
—CANNAE: (1) i-ii AD *Epig. Rom. di Canosa* 57
(*CIL* IX 319) (Lat. Thesmus: slave?)
S. ITALY (CALABRIA):
—RUDIAE: (2) ii AD Bernardini, *Rudiae* p. 87
(Susini, *Fonti Salento* p. 164 no. 129) (Lat.
Claudius Thesmus)
S. ITALY (CAMPANIA):
—HERCULANEUM*: (3) i BC-i AD *CIL* X 1403 g
I, 18 (Lat. C. Novius Thesmus: freed.)
—POMPEII: (4) i BC-i AD ib. IV 2160 (Lat. Thes-
mus); (5) c. 50-61 AD ib. 2983; 3340. 71, 10
(Castrèn 22. 2) (Lat. L. Albucius Thesmus:
freed.)

Θέσπις
S. ITALY (CAMPANIA):
—HERCULANEUM: (1) ?i AD *RAAN* 45 (1970)
pp. 139-58 (Lat. T[he]spis)

Θεσπρωτός
S. ITALY (CAMPANIA):
—DIKAIARCHIA-PUTEOLI*: (1) s. i BC *Puteoli*
4-5 (1980-1) p. 267 no. 3 (Lat. Thesprotus:
freed.)

Θεσσαλίων
ARGOLIS:
—TROIZEN*: (1) iv BC *IG* IV (1) 823, 36, [58],
59

Θεσσαλός
ARGOLIS:
—EPIDAUROS: (1) iii BC Peek, *IAEpid* 43, 35
([Θ]εσσαλός)

—HERMIONE: (2) ii-i BC *IG* IV (1) 732 II, 31 (Θεσ[σ]αλός: s. Ἡρακλείδας)
—TROIZEN: (3) iv BC ib. 764, 5 (f. Εὔδικος); (4) 360 BC *CID* II 4 II, 41 (s. Τιμοκλῆς)
KORINTHIA:
—KORINTH: (5) 504 BC Moretti, *Olymp.* 154; Pi., *O.* xiii, 35; cf. *Dionysiaca* pp. 1-16 (s. Πτωΐόδωρος, f. Ξενοφῶν)
LAKONIA:
—SPARTA: (6) s. vi BC Hdt. v 46. 1 (Poralla² 367)
SICILY:
—MEGARA HYBLAIA: (7) f. v BC Dubois, *IGDS* 26 (Arena, *Iscr. Sic.* I 9) (Θεσα-)

**Θέστα**
SICILY:
—SYRACUSE: (1) c. 425-355 BC Plu., *Dio* 21; cf. Beloch, *GG* III (2) pp. 102-7 (-τη: d. Ἑρμο-κράτης)

**Θεστίας**
SICILY:
—AKRAGAS: (1) s. iv BC *IG* IV (1)² 95, 91 (Perlman E.2); Perlman pp. 46-9 (date) (s. Φιλο-κλῆς)

**Θέστιος**
ARGOLIS:
—ARGOS: (1) her. *FGrH* 115 F 393 (s. Κίσσιος, f. Μέροψ: king)

**Θεστορίδας**
S. ITALY (BRUTTIUM):
—LOKROI EPIZEPHYRIOI:
——(Mνα.): (1) iv/iii BC De Franciscis 2, 4 (s. Ἀμύνανδρος)

**Θεστυλίς**
SICILY:
—SYRACUSE?: (1) v BC *CGF* p. 155 fr. 5; Theoc., *Beren.* ii 1 f. (fict.?)

**Θέστων**
ARGOLIS:
—ARGOS: (1) ?253 BC Nachtergael, *Les Galates* 6, [6]; 10, 47 (Stephanis 1199) (s. Δαμόφαντος)
SICILY:
—HALAISA: (2) ii BC *IGSI* 2 A II, 80 (Dubois, *IGDS* 196) (f. Ἱστιειός)
—HALOUNTION: (3) iii/ii BC *Arch. Class.* 17 (1965) p. 202 a (Θέστ[ων]: f. Ζωῖλος); (4) i BC-i AD *IG* XIV 373 (*IGLMP* 45)
—KAMARINA: (5) f. v BC Cordano, *Tessere Pubbliche* 42 (Arena, *Iscr. Sic.* II 135 A) (-τōν: f. Ἡράκλειος)
—MORGANTINA: (6) ?iv/iii BC *SEG* XXXIX 1008, 5 (s. Δάμαρχος)

**Θέστωρ**
S. ITALY (LUCANIA):
—POSEIDONIA-PAESTUM: (1) vi BC Iamb., *VP* 239

**Θέτις**
S. ITALY (APULIA):
—VENUSIA: (1) imp. *CIL* IX 584 (Lat. Thetis)
S. ITALY (CALABRIA):
—VALETIUM: (2) ii-iii AD ib. 24 (Susini, *Fonti Salento* p. 164 no. 129) (Lat. Aelia Thetis)
S. ITALY (CAMPANIA):
—DIKAIARCHIA-PUTEOLI: (3) imp. *CIL* X 1743 (Lat. Octavia Thetis)
—KYME: (4) imp. ib. 3689 (Lat. Lucce[ia] [Th]etis)
—SALERNUM*: (5) imp. *IItal* I (1) 76 (Lat. Thetis: freed.)
S. ITALY (LUCANIA):
—MURO LUCANO (MOD.): (6) imp. *Atti Conv. Taranto* 17 (1977) p. 441 (Lat. Thetis)

**Θευγένης**
ACHAIA:
—DYME: (1) iii BC *AJPh* 31 (1910) p. 399 no. 74 c, 10 (s. Φιλόξενος, Φίλα)
ARGOLIS:
—ARGOS: (2) iii BC *SEG* XIII 370; cf. Marcadé I 105 (Θευγ[έ]νης: f. Θαλίαρχος)
KERKYRA: (3) ii AD *IG* IX (1) 881 (doctor)

**Θεῦγνις**
SICILY:
—ZANKLE-MESSANA: (1) ?ii BC ib. XIV 401, 3 (s. Εὔβιος)

**Θεύδαμος**
EPIROS:
—AMBRAKIA: (1) f. v BC Unp. (Arta Mus.) (Θεύ-δαμ[ος])

**Θευδᾶς**
ILLYRIA:
—EPIDAMNOS-DYRRHACHION: (1) imp. *IDyrrh* 135
S. ITALY (CAMPANIA):
—HERCULANEUM: (2) i AD *CIL* X 8058. 48 (seal) (Lat. Q. Maecius Theuda)
SICILY:
—KATANE: (3) imp. *SGDI* 5237 (*IGLMP* 7) ([Θε]υδᾶς)

**Θεύδετος**
DALMATIA:
—ISSA: (1) hell. Brunšmid p. 26 no. 17 (*SEG* XL 513) + *VAHD* 84 (1991) p. 252 no. 2 (name) (s. Ἀριστήν)

**Θευδίων**
ACHAIA:
—DYME: (1) iii BC *AJPh* 31 (1910) p. 399 no. 74 a, 19 (f. Σιμίας)

**Θευδοσία**
ILLYRIA:
—EPIDAMNOS-DYRRHACHION: (1) imp. *IDyrrh* 11

**Θευδόσιος**
SICILY:
—KAMARINA: (1) ?iv/iii BC *PdelP* 44 (1989) p. 203; cf. *SEG* XXXIX 1002 note (Θευδόσιος: s. Ἱππίας); (2) ?ii BC ib. 996, 6 (Dubois, *IGDS* 126; Cordano, 'Camarina VII' 117) (s. Θεύ-δωρος)

**Θευδότα**
AKARNANIA:
—OINIADAI: (1) iii/ii BC *IG* IX (1)² (2) 419. 9
SICILY:
—SYRACUSE: (2) ?ii BC ib. XII (5) 440 (-τη)

**Θεύδοτος**
AITOLIA: (1) 244 or 240 BC *SGDI* 2511, 3 (Flacelière p. 402 no. 29)
AKARNANIA:
—ANAKTORION: (2) m. ii BC *Syll*³ 669, 2 (s. Σώτων)
ARGOLIS:
—ARGOS (MAGOULA (MOD.)): (3) iii BC *SEG* XI 367
ARKADIA?: (4) ?iv/iii BC *HE* 673
DALMATIA:
—ISSA: (5) hell. Brunšmid p. 26 no. 17 (*SEG* XL 513) + *VAHD* 84 (1991) p. 252 no. 2 (s. Ἄνταλλος); (6) iii/ii BC *SEG* XXXV 689 (f. Ἀν-ναῖος); (7) ~ ib. 690 (s. Ἀνναῖος)
EPIROS: (8) iii BC *Thess. Mnem.* 28 (f. Ἀφροδι-σία)
—AMBRAKIA: (9) iii/ii BC Unp. (Arta Mus., inscr.) (f. Ἀνίκατος)
—ATHAMANES: (10) 217-207 BC *FD* III (3) 221, 9
—BOUTHROTOS (PRASAIBOI):

—Opatai: (11) a. 163 BC *IBouthrot* 69, 18; 70, 13; 71, 11 (*BCH* 118 (1994) pp. 129 f. B 1-3) (s. Ἀνεροίτας) ?= (12); (12) ~ *IBouthrot* 99, 6 (*BCH* 118 (1994) p. 121 B) ?= (11)
—CHERADROI: (13) hell. Cabanes, *L'Épire* p. 581 no. 56, 11
—KORONEIATAI: (14) c. 343-330 BC ib. p. 588 no. 74, 3 (*SEG* XXVI 700)
—VOTONOSI (MOD.): (15) ?m. iii BC ib. XXIV 464 (s. Ἀλέξανδρος)
ILLYRIA:
—EPIDAMNOS-DYRRHACHION: (16) hell.-imp. *IDyrrh* 248 (s. Ἀγαθοκλῆς)
S. ITALY (BRUTTIUM):
—LOKROI EPIZEPHYRIOI:
——(Tνν.): (17) 278 BC De Franciscis 30, 4 (f. Θεώνδας)
——(Φαω.): (18) iv/iii BC ib. 11, 6; 17, 8 (f. Θέων)
SICILY:
—LIPARA: (19) c. 315-280 BC *FD* III (4) 401, 1 (s. Μνασικλῆς)

**Θευδώρα**
S. ITALY (CAMPANIA):
—DIKAIARCHIA-PUTEOLI: (1) iii/ii BC *SEG* IV 91, 2 (*GVI* 868) (d. Κλειορόδη, Διονύσιος)
SICILY:
—LILYBAION: (2) iii-iv AD *IGLMP* 26
—SYRACUSE: (3) iii-v AD *NScav* 1895, p. 497 no. 197 (Barreca 454) (Lat. Teudora)

**Θευδωρίδας**
S. ITALY (LUCANIA):
—METAPONTION: (1) m. iii BC *SEG* XXX 1175, 14 (Θευδωρίδ[ας]: doctor)

**Θεύδωρος**
ACHAIA: (1) ?257 BC Nachtergael, *Les Galates* 7, 52 (f. Δίων)
ARGOLIS:
—ARGOS: (2) f. iii BC *CID* II 122 I, 3 (f. —μος)
—EPIDAUROS: (3) iii BC *IG* IV (1)² 341 (s. Μενε-κλῆς)
——(Azantioi): (4) 146 BC ib. 28, 39 (s. Ἐχέτι-μος)
—TROIZEN: (5) ii/i BC ib. IV (1) 790 (s. Κάλλιπ-πος, f. Βίτος)
DALMATIA:
—ISSA: (6) iii BC *SEG* XXXI 596 (f. Διονύσιος); (7) ~ ib. 598 (s. Φιλικός)
ELIS: (8) m. iii BC *IG* IV (1)² 96, 46 (Perlman E.3); Perlman p. 63 f. (date) (f. Λυσίβιος)
KERKYRA: (9) hell. ib. IX (1) 694, 38 (*RIJG* XXV B); cf. *SEG* XXV 609 (Θεύδ[ω]ρος: f. Σώ-σανδρος)
S. ITALY (BRUTTIUM):
—LOKROI EPIZEPHYRIOI: (10) iii BC *IG* IX (1) 685, 5, 21 (Landi, *DISMG* 242) (f. Φιλιστίων)
S. ITALY (LUCANIA):
—METAPONTION: (11) m. iii BC *SEG* XXX 1175, 12 (Θεύδ[ωρος])
SICILY:
—ADRANON: (12) iii-ii BC *PdelP* 16 (1961) p. 127
—AKRAGAS: (13) iv/iii BC *Acragas Graeca* 1 p. 32 no. 3 (Dubois, *IGDS* 183) (f. Φάλακρος)
—KAMARINA: (14) ?iv/iii BC *SEG* XXXIV 940, 10 (Dubois, *IGDS* 124; *PdelP* 44 (1989) p. 192 no. 3; Cordano, 'Camarina VII' 118) (Θεύδω[ρ]ος: s. Δάμων); (15) ?ii BC *SEG* XXXIX 996, 6 (Dubois, *IGDS* 126; Cordano, 'Camarina VII' 119) (Θευδόσιος)
—MORGANTINA: (16) ?iv/iii BC *SEG* XXXIX 1008, 8 (s. Εὐπόλεμος); (17) iv/iii BC ib. 1012, 8 (s. Λέοντις)

**Θεύκλεια**
LEUKAS: (1) hell.? *IG* IX (1) 548 ([Θ]εύκλεια)

**Θευκλῆς**
ACHAIA:
—AIGION: (1) ?228-215 BC *SGDI* 2525, 6 (s. Τιμόλοχος)

**Θευκύδης**
PELOPONNESE: (1) c. 230-200 BC *BCH* 45 (1921) p. 11 II, 43

**Θέϋλλος**
SICILY:
—SELINOUS: (1) f. v BC Dubois, *IGDS* 54 (Arena, *Iscr. Sic.* 1 39; Lazzarini 744); *IGLMP* 56 (name) (Θέϋλλος: s. Πυρρίας)

**Θεύμναστος**
KORINTHIA:
—KORINTH: (1) s. iv BC *Corinth* VIII (1) 11, 11

**Θεύνοστος**
ARGOLIS:
—HERMIONE: (1) ?ii-i BC *IG* IV (1) 731 I, 7 (f. Διοδώρα)

**Θευξένα**
ACHAIA:
—DYME: (1) hell.? *SGDI* 1616 (d. Ξενόφιλος)

**Θεύξενος**
ACHAIA:
—DYME: (1) c. 210-207 BC *IG* IV (1)² 73, 21; *SEG* XXXV 303 (date) (f. Σαμοφάνης)
ARKADIA:
—KYNAITHA: (2) c. 230-200 BC *BCH* 45 (1921) p. 12 II, 67 (f. Σάτυρος)

**Θευόδοτος**
ILLYRIA:
—APOLLONIA: (1) ?ii-i BC *IApoll* 96; cf. *BE* 1974, no. 706 (s. Σωτίων)

**Θεύπομπος**
ARGOLIS:
—HERMIONE: (1) iii BC *IG* IV (1) 728, 3 (s. Θεοκλῆς)
EPIROS:
—AMBRAKIA: (2) s. iii BC *HE* 1393 (f. Ἀρισταγόρας)
SICILY:
—SYRACUSE:
——(Ἑρμείος): (3) iv BC Manganaro, *PdelP* forthcoming no. 3, 8 (f. Φράστωρ)

**Θευπροπίας**
PELOPONNESE: (1) c. 230-200 BC *BCH* 45 (1921) p. 11 II, 55 ([Θευ]προπίας)

**Θευπροπίδας**
ACHAIA:
—AIGION: (1) c. 230-200 BC ib. p. 12 II, 60 (s. Εὐρύας)

**Θευτακώ**
DALMATIA:
—ISSA: (1) iii-ii BC Brunšmid p. 28 no. 20, 2 (d. Δαφναῖος)

**Θευτᾶς**
PELOPONNESE?: (1) s. iii BC *SEG* XXV 449, 49 (*IPArk* 26)

**Θεύτιμος**
KORINTHIA:
—SIKYON: (1) c. 275-265 BC *IG* XI (4) 704, 4, [10]; Vial p. 98 (date) (Skalet 149) (f. Τιμοκλείδας)

**Θευφάνης**
EPIROS:
—AMBRAKIA: (1) ?v BC *SEG* XXIV 414 (Θευφάν[ης])
LAKONIA: (2) iii BC *IG* V (1) 1340, 2 (Bradford (-)) ([Θ]ευφάνης)

**Θευφείδης**
SICILY:
—ZANKLE-MESSANA: (1) ?ii BC *IG* XIV 401, 7 (Θευφε[ίδ]ης, Εὐφε[ίδ]ης—*IG*: f. Γλαῦκος)

**Θευφιλίς**
S. ITALY (BRUTTIUM):
—LOKROI EPIZEPHYRIOI: (1) iv/iii BC *HE* 2802 (d. Κλεόχα, m. Νοσσίς)

**Θεύφιλος**
ARKADIA:
—MANTINEIA-ANTIGONEIA: (1) ?iii BC *IG* V (2) 318, 1
S. ITALY (CAMPANIA):
—NEAPOLIS: (2) ?vii AD *INap* 266

**Θεύφραστος**
AITOLIA: (1) 217 BC Nachtergael, *Les Galates* 65, 9 (s. Εὔαρχος)

**Θεώ**
AIGINA: (1) v/iv BC *IG* IV (1) 66 (-ṓ)

**Θέων**
ACHAIA: (1) s. iii BC *PTeb* 815 fr. 3 recto, 2 (f. Ἄρειος)
—DYME: (2) hell. *BCH* 4 (1880) p. 521 no. 3 (f. Ἀσπασία)
—PATRAI?: (3) iii BC *Achaean Grave Stelai* 5 (s. Τίμανδρος)
AITOLIA:
—KALYDON: (4) s. iv BC *IG* IV (1)² 95, 7 (Perlman E.2); Perlman p. 40 f. (date) (s. Πολέμαρχος)
AKARNANIA:
—ANAKTORION: (5) 263-262 BC *IG* IX (1)² (1) 3 A, 23
—STRATOS: (6) iv/iii BC ib. IX (1)² (2) 395, 7 (f. Θεοκλῆς)
—THYRREION: (7) iii-ii BC *SEG* XXVII 159, 2; cf. *PAE* 1977, pl. 244 a (s. Κλε—)
ARGOLIS:
—PHLEIOUS: (8) ii-i BC *IG* IV (1) 475
ARKADIA:
—ALIPHEIRA: (9) iii BC *EILakArk* 11, 3 (*GVI* 1505; *Gr. Gr.* 196) (s. Τιμείας, Κλεαρίστη)
—ORCHOMENOS: (10) 191-146 BC BM Hawkins p. 463 no. 3 (coin)
—STYMPHALOS: (11) ?303-301 BC *IG* V (2) 351, 11; *SEG* XXXI 351 (date)
—TEGEA: (12) m. iii BC Peek, *IAEpid* 42, 22 (Perlman E.3); Perlman p. 63 f. (date) (s. Πολίας); (13) ii BC *IG* IV (1)² 226 (f. Πολίας); (14) ~ ib. V (2) 143 (f. Πολίας) ?= (16); (15) ~ ib. 144 ([Θ]έω[ν]?: s. Πολίας); (16) f. ii BC ib. 44, 5 (f. Πολίας) ?= (14)
——(Hippothoitai): (17) iii BC ib. 40, 37 (s. Κλεόδωρος)
KEPHALLENIA:
—KRANIOI: (18) c. 230-200 BC *BCH* 45 (1921) p. 14 II, 135
LAKONIA:
—OITYLOS: (19) iii AD *IG* V (1) 1301 c (s. Διονυσία); (20) a. 212 AD ib. 1301 b (Θ[έ]ων: f. Αὐρ. [—])
—SPARTA: (21) c. 30-20 BC ib. 211, 31 (Bradford (1)) (s. Μνασικράτης); (22) c. 100 AD *IG* V (1) 80, 6 (Bradford (2)) (s. Ὀνησιφόρος); (23) ii-iii AD *IG* V (1) 739, 1 (Bradford (5)); (24) c. 105-110 AD *SEG* XI 569, 20 (Bradford (4)) (f. Ὀνησιφόρος); (25) c. 220 AD *IG* V (1) 817 (Papaefthimiou p. 142 no. 16); *BSA* 79 (1984) pp. 268-9 (date) (Bradford (3)) (f. M. Αὐρ. Ἀλεξύς)
MESSENIA:
—MESSENE: (26) i BC/i AD *IG* V (1) 1374; *SEG* XXIII 207, 17, 19 (f. Τίμαρχος, Νικήρατος)
——(Kresphontidai): (27) 11 AD *PAE* 1992, p. 71 A, 18 (s. Ὀνάσων)
S. ITALY (BRUTTIUM):
—LOKROI EPIZEPHYRIOI:
——(Ἀγκ.): (28) iv/iii BC De Franciscis 18, 4 (f. Ἀριστοκλῆς)
——(Λακ.): (29) iv/iii BC ib. 15, 2 (f. Ζωΐλος); (30) ~ ib. 28, 3 (s. Κάλλιππος)
——(Τηλ.): (31) iv/iii BC ib. 14, 7

——(Φαω.): (32) iv/iii BC ib. 11, 6; 17, 8 (s. Θεύδοτος)
S. ITALY (CAMPANIA):
—DIKAIARCHIA-PUTEOLI: (33) imp. *CIL* X 1997 (Lat. Cassius Theo: f. Βασιλεύς)
S. ITALY (LUCANIA):
—HYELE-VELIA: (34) c. 100 BC *ID* 1713, 5 (s. Ἕρμων, ?s. Θεοδότη (Other))
S. ITALY?: (35) iii-ii BC Vandermersch p. 167 (amph.)
SICILY:
—KAMARINA: (36) f. v BC Cordano, *Tessere Pubbliche* 45 (-ōν: s. Νικίας); (37) ?iv/iii BC *SEG* XXXIV 940, 2 (Dubois, *IGDS* 124; *PdelP* 44 (1989) p. 192 no. 3; Cordano, 'Camarina VII' 120) (f. Σωσίστρατος) ?= (38); (38) iv/iii BC Manganaro, *PdelP* forthcoming no. 2, 7 (f. Σωσίστρατος) ?= (37)
—MORGANTINA: (39) iv/iii BC *SEG* XXXIX 1012, 6 (f. Αἴνησις)
—SYRACUSE: (40) c. 100 BC *IG* XII (3) Suppl. 1299, 18 (f. Ἰσίδωρος)
—SYRACUSE?:
——(Πλη.): (41) hell. Manganaro, *PdelP* forthcoming no. 4 I, 5 (f. Ἀνδρέας)

**Θεώνδας**
S. ITALY (BRUTTIUM):
—LOKROI EPIZEPHYRIOI:
——(Τυν.): (1) iv/iii BC De Franciscis 19, 6 (f. Ἡρακλείδας); (2) 278 BC ib. 30, 4 (s. Θεύδοτος)

**Θεωνίδας**
AKARNANIA:
—KORONTA: (1) iii-ii BC *IG* IX (1)² (2) 432, 2 (Θεο-: f. Ἡρακλείδας)

**Θεωνίς**
EPIROS:
—NIKOPOLIS: (1) imp. *CIG* 1816 (Sarikakis 94; *SEG* XXXIV 593); cf. *BE* 1990, no. 177 (Κορν. Θ.)

**Θεώνιχος**
ARGOLIS:
—HERMIONE: (1) iv BC *SEG* XI 382, 15 (Θε[ώνι]χος, Θε[άρι]χος?: s. Σωσίστρατος, f. Εὐτυχίδας)

**Θεώνυμος**
EPIROS:
—AMBRAKIA: (1) f. ii BC *AD* 39 (1984) Chron. p. 190 + pl. 77 γ

**Θέωρις**
ARGOLIS:
—TROIZEN: (1) iii BC *IG* IV (1) 773 (Θεώριδος (gen.): f. Σωσίας)

**Θεωρίς**
KORINTHIA:
—SIKYON: (1) s. v BC Hsch. s.v.; *Suda* I 451 (Skalet 150) (Θεοδωρίς—*Suda*: m. Ἀρίστων (Athens, Kolonos?): fict.?)
S. ITALY (CALABRIA):
—BRENTESION-BRUNDISIUM: (2) imp. *CIL* IX 198 (Lat. Theoris)

**Θέωρος**
S. ITALY (CAMPANIA):
—NOLA: (1) byz. ib. X 1383 (Lat. Teorus)

**Θεώτας**
S. ITALY (CAMPANIA):
—NEAPOLIS: (1) her. *IG* XIV 723 (*INap* 11) (Θεωτάδαι (nom. gent.))

**Θήβα**
MESSENIA:
—MESSENE: (1) ii BC *Ergon* 1995, p. 29

**Θηβαΐς**
ARGOLIS:
—HERMIONE: (**1**) iv BC *SEG* XI 382, 24 (d. Ἀγασικλῆς)
ARKADIA: (**2**) hell. *Memnonion* 78
EPIROS:
—BOUTHROTOS (PRASAIBOI): (**3**) a. 163 BC *IBouthrot* 21, 28 (*SEG* XXXVIII 478)

**Θηβασίμαχος**
AIGINA: (**1**) ?c. 550-525 BC ib. XI 1 (Lazzarini 53) (Θεβ-: her.?)

**Θήβη**
S. ITALY (CAMPANIA):
—DIKAIARCHIA-PUTEOLI: (**1**) imp. Audollent, *Defix. Tab.* 208, 14

**Θηλύμορφος**
S. ITALY: (**1**) imp. *CIL* X 8059. 320 (seal) (Lat. Q. Planius Thelymor(phus))

**Θῆλυς**
S. ITALY (CAMPANIA):
—HERCULANEUM*: (**1**) i BC-i AD ib. 1403 f I, 5 (Lat. M. Volusius Thelys: freed.)
—POMPEII: (**2**) 57 AD ib. IV 3340. 34, 7; 77, 7; 97, 4 (Castrèn 161. 21) (Lat. M. Fabius Thelus)

**Θῆμος**
S. ITALY (CALABRIA):
—BRENTESION-BRUNDISIUM*: (**1**) f. i AD *Studi di Antichità* 6 pp. 311-18 (Lat. Themus: f. Τρίτων)

**Θηραία**
LEUKAS: (**1**) iv BC *AM* 27 (1902) p. 369 no. 34

**Θηραμένης**
ILLYRIA:
—APOLLONIA: (**1**) imp. *IApoll* 97 (s. Φιλέρως)
MESSENIA:
—MESSENE: (**2**) hell. Peek, *NIEpid* 43 (f. Θηρόμαχος)

**Θηρήας**
ARKADIA:
—PHENEOS: (**1**) ?274 BC *FD* III (1) 83, 14

**Θηρικλῆς**
KORINTHIA:
—KORINTH: (**1**) v/iv BC *RE* (2) (potter); (**2**) 225-218 BC *Kafizin* 40, 2; 41, 2; 42, 2 (θηρικλεῖον (noun): potter)

**Θηρικύων**
LAKONIA:
—SPARTA: (**1**) inc. *IPr* 316, 5 ?= (2); (**2**) iv/iii BC *CID* II 120 A, 30; Plu., *Mor.* 221 F (Poralla² 368) (Θωρυκίων—Plu.: f. —ππος) ?= (*1*); (**3**) 227-222 BC Plu., *Cleom.* 8; 31; Masson, *OGS* 2 p. 512 (name) (Bradford (-)) (Θηρυκίων—Plu.)

**Θηρίλαος**
ARKADIA:
—PHENEOS: (**1**) ?ii BC *SEG* XIX 328 (s. Ἡρωΐδας)

**Θηρίμαχος**
LAKONIA:
—SPARTA: (**1**) 389 BC X., *HG* iv 8. 29; D.S. xiv 94. 4 (Poralla² 370)

**Θηριμένης**
LAKONIA:
—SPARTA: (**1**) 412 BC *RE* (-) (Poralla² 371)

**Θηρίνας**
ARKADIA:
—TEGEA:
——(Hippothoitai): (**1**) iii BC *IG* V (2) 40, 36 (s. Ἐτεοκλῆς)

**Θηριππίδας**
LAKONIA:
—SPARTA: (**1**) 377 BC D.S. xv 30. 3 (Poralla² 372) (Θηριπίδης—D.S.)

**Θήριππος**
MESSENIA:
—MESSENE: (**1**) i BC *AM* 67 (1942) p. 220 no. 16 (f. Θαλλέας); (**2**) ii-iii AD *SEG* XLI 366 D (Φ. M. Θ.)

**Θῆρις**
ARKADIA:
—MEGALOPOLIS: (**1**) ii AD *IG* V (2) 465 (s. —ος)
—TEGEA: (**2**) hell.? ib. 149 (s. Ἵππων); (**3**) ii BC ib. 141 (f. Ἀριστοκράτης); (**4**) f. ii BC ib. 44, 16 (f. Ἵππων); (**5**) ii AD ib. 54, 22
——(Athaneatai): (**6**) iv/iii BC ib. 38, 19 ([Θῆ]ρις?: s. Δαμοπείθης)
LAKONIA:
—TAINARON-KAINEPOLIS: (**7**) imp.? ib. v (1) 1260 (I f. Θῆρις II); (**8**) ~ ib. (II s. Θῆρις I)
S. ITALY (CAMPANIA):
—DIKAIARCHIA-PUTEOLI: (**9**) imp. *CIL* X 2986 (Lat. C. Sulpicius Teris: s. C. Sulpicius Saturninus)

**Θηριώτης**
KORINTHIA:
—KORINTH: (**1**) ?iii AD *Hesp.* 63 (1994) pp. 116 ff. no. 5 col. V, 6-8 (lead) (Μαρκίων ὁ καὶ Θ.)

**Θηρόμαχος**
MESSENIA:
—MESSENE: (**1**) hell. Peek, *NIEpid* 43 (s. Θηραμένης)
—MESSENE?: (**2**) ii/i BC *SEG* XI 979, 41

**Θηρύλος**
MESSENIA:
—MESSENE: (**1**) ii/iii AD ib. XL 367 (XLI 376 E) (θηρυλοσενικαιθιδας—lap.)

**Θηρύων**
ACHAIA:
—DYME*: (**1**) c. 219 BC *SGDI* 1612, 51 (*Tyche* 5 (1990) p. 124) (f. Δεινίας)

**Θήρων**
AIGINA: (**1**) v BC *IG* IV (1) 69 (Θέρōν); (**2**) f. v BC ib. 64; *LSAG²* p. 113 no. 10 (date) (Θέρōν)
ARKADIA:
—MANTINEIA-ANTIGONEIA: (**3**) i-ii AD *IG* V (2) 321. 4 (amph.)
—TEGEA: (**4**) ii AD ib. 54, 17 (Θή[ρω]ν)
ELIS:
—PISATIS: (**5**) ?c. 425 BC *IvOl* 18, 1; *LSAG²* p. 221 no. 20 (date)
KORINTHIA:
—KORINTH: (**6**) c. 610-590 BC Amyx 18. 3 (vase) (Lorber 28); *LSAG²* p. 131 no. 9 (date) (Θέρōν)
S. ITALY (BRUTTIUM):
—LOKROI EPIZEPHYRIOI:
——(Θρα.): (**7**) 279 BC De Franciscis 13, 2 (f. Κράτων)
——(Ὀμβ.): (**8**) iv/iii BC ib. 2, 3 (s. Ἀρκεσίλας); (**9**) ~ ib. 6, 3 (s. Σωσικράτης)
SICILY:
—AKRAGAS: (**10**) c. 530-472 BC *RE* (1); Moretti, *Olymp.* 220 (s. Αἰνησίδαμος, f. Γόργος, Θρασυδαῖος, Φιλοκράτης, Δαμαρέτα: tyrant)
—SELINOUS: (**11**) ?vi BC Polyaen. i 28. 2; cf. *RE* Supplbd. 11 (4) (s. Μιλτιάδας: tyrant)

**Θησεύς**
LAKONIA:
—GYTHEION: (**1**) i-ii AD *IG* V (1) 1178, 3 (f. Σμηλίδας)
S. ITALY (CAMPANIA):
—DIKAIARCHIA-PUTEOLI: (**2**) imp. *CIL* X 1588 (Lat. Theseus); (**3**) ~ ib. 2739; cf. *Puteoli* 11

(1987) pp. 53-4 (name) (Lat. Cl. Theseus); (**4**) ?ii-iii AD *CIL* X 3058 (Lat. Aurelius Theseus)
SICILY:
—ZANKLE-MESSANA: (**5**) ii-iii AD *Epigraphica* 3 (1941) p. 255 no. 7; p. 256 no. 9 (Lat. T. Cl. Theseus: f. T. Cl. Claudianus); (**6**) ?v AD *NScav* 1942, pp. 83-4 nos. 4-5 (Κλ. Θ.: f. Κλ. Ῥωμανός, Κλ. Ῥωμάντιλλα)

**Θιαῖος**
ARGOLIS:
—ARGOS: (**1**) ?c. 460-450 BC *IG* IV (1)² 139 (Lazzarini 76); *LSAG²* p. 170 no. 38 (date) ([Θ]ιαῖος: s. Ἀρχιτέλης)
—EPIDAUROS: (**2**) c. 365-335 BC *IG* IV (1)² 103, 107, 109, 112

**Θιάρης**
ARGOLIS:
—EPIDAUROS: (**1**) iv BC ib. 191 + Peek, *NIEpid* 6; *IG* IV (1)² 192; *SEG* XXXVIII 319 ?= (*2*); (**2**) c. 370 BC *IG* IV (1)² 102, 49 ?= (*1*); (**3**) iv/iii BC ib. 197 (s. Ἀναξίδωρος)

**Θίασος**
ARGOLIS:
—EPIDAUROS: (**1**) ii-iii AD ib. 688 (s. Ἀριστόδαμος)
KORINTHIA:
—KORINTH: (**2**) ii AD Apul., *Met.* x 18 (Lat. Thiasus)
S. ITALY (BRUTTIUM):
—RHEGION*: (**3**) f. i AD *Suppl. It.* 5 p. 64 no. 16 (Lat. C. Iulius Thiasus: imp. freed.)
S. ITALY (CAMPANIA):
—DIKAIARCHIA-PUTEOLI: (**4**) imp. *CIL* X 1585 (Lat. Thiasus)
—HERCULANEUM*: (**5**) c. 50-75 AD ib. 1403 a III, 4 (Lat. L. Mammius Thiasus: freed.)
S. ITALY (LUCANIA):
—POTENTIA: (**6**) ?ii AD *Misc. Gr. Rom.* 8 p. 436 no. 2 (Lat. P. Petronius Tiasus)
SICILY:
—GELA-PHINTIAS: (**7**) f. v BC Dubois, *IGDS* 136 (vase) (Arena, *Iscr. Sic.* II 43)

**Θίβραχος**
LAKONIA:
—SPARTA: (**1**) 403 BC X., *HG* ii 4. 33 (Poralla² 373)

**Θίβρων**
ARKADIA:
—TEGEA: (**1**) m. iv BC *IG* V (2) 6, 93 (s. Βράχυλλος)
——(Apolloniatai): (**2**) f. iii BC ib. 36, 50 (Θίβρων: f. Σμίδας)
LAKONIA:
—SPARTA: (**3**) c. 430-391 BC *RE* (1); cf. *FGrH* 70 F 71; Isoc. iv 144 (Poralla² 374) (Θίμβρων—*FGrH* and Isoc.) ?= (*4*); (**4**) v/iv BC Arist., *Pol.* 1333b 18 (Poralla² 375) (Θίμβρων—mss., Θί<μ>βρων—edd.) ?= (*3*); (**5**) m. iv BC *RE* (2); Berve 372; *CGFP* p. 196 F 19 (Poralla² 376) (?s. Τάνταλος)

**Θιγγωνίδας**
ARKADIA:
—MANTINEIA-ANTIGONEIA: (**1**) iv-iii BC *SEG* XI 347 (Θιγγωνίδας: s. Ἀστίδας)

**Θιοδέκτας**
ARGOLIS:
—ARGOS: (**1**) f. iii BC Moretti, *ISE* 41, 2 (Perlman A.24); (**2**) 228-146 BC BM coin 1887 6-6-15 (coin); cf. *NC* 1888, p. 10 (Θιοδέ(κτας))
—ARGOS?: (**3**) f. i BC *SEG* XXIII 180, 3 (f. Φαηνός: date—Kritzas)

**Θιόδοτος**
ARGOLIS:
—EPIDAUROS*: (**1**) c. 370 BC *IG* IV (1)² 102, 92

KORINTHIA:
—KORINTH?: (2) s. iii BC *Corinth* VIII (1) 8 + *HSCP* 53 (1942) p. 111 (Θιόδο[τος])
S. ITALY (CAMPANIA):
—SALERNUM: (3) imp. *IItal* I (1) 136 (Lat. [Th]iodotu[s])

**Θιοκλείδας**
ARGOLIS:
—EPIDAUROS:
——(Azantioi): (1) 146 BC *IG* IV (1)² 28, 45; 234, 2 (s. Δαμοκλῆς, f. Δαμοκλῆς, Ἀστυλαΐδας)

**Θιοκλῆς**
ARGOLIS:
—ARGOS:
——Laparea (Moklai): (1) s. iii BC *Mnem.* NS 43 (1915) p. 366 A, 3 (Perlman A.17); *Mnem.* NS 43 (1915) pp. 366-7 B, 2 (Perlman A.18); *SEG* XVI 247, 4 (Perlman A.19); *SEG* XXXIII 279 (locn.) (f. Θιότιμος)

**Θιοκορμίδας**
LAKONIA:
—SPARTA: (1) f. vi BC Lazzarini 79; *LSAG*² p. 198 no. 6 (date); Masson, *OGS* 2 p. 512 (name) (Poralla² 376b)

**Θιόκριτος**
ARGOLIS:
—ARGOS: (1) ?c. 460-450 BC *Mnem.* NS 47 (1919) p. 161 no. 6, 6; *LSAG*² p. 170 no. 31 (date) (Θιόκρι[τος]); (2) f. iii BC *CID* II 120 A, 12 (f. —τος) ?= (3); (3) ~ ib. 121 II, 15 ([Θι]όκριτος?: s. Ἄρχιππος) ?= (2)
——Kolouris: (4) a. 316 BC *SEG* XI 1084, 26, 40 (Perlman A.3); *SEG* XXXIII 276, 5, 18

**Θιοκύδης**
ARGOLIS:
—EPIDAUROS: (1) iii BC *IG* IV (1)² 98, 1

**Θιόνοος**
ARKADIA:
—MANTINEIA-ANTIGONEIA:
——(Posoidaia): (1) c. 425-400 BC *SEG* XXXI 348, 3 + Dubois, *RDA* 2 pp. 123-4; cf. Pritchett, *Topography* 2 p. 51 (Οἰόνθος?— Pritchett, Οἰόνοος?)

**Θιοπαλίδας**
MESSENIA:
—THOURIA: (1) ?m. vi BC *LSAG*² p. 448 no. 1a (pithos)

**Θιοτέλης**
ARGOLIS:
—EPIDAUROS: (1) c. 290-270 BC *IG* IV (1)² 109 II, 147
——Isarnia: (2) m. iii BC ib. 96, 36, 38 (Perlman E.3); Perlman p. 63 f. (date)

**Θιότιμος**
ARGOLIS:
—ARGOS:
——Laparea (Moklai): (1) s. iii BC *Mnem.* NS 43 (1915) p. 366 A, 3 (Perlman A.17); *Mnem.* NS 43 (1915) pp. 366-7 B, 3 (Perlman A.18); *SEG* XVI 247, [3] (Perlman A.19); *SEG* XXXIII 279 (locn.) (s. Θιοκλῆς)
—EPIDAUROS: (2) iv/iii BC *IG* IV (1)² 169, 2 (Θιότι[μος])

**Θιόφαμος**
ARGOLIS:
—ARGOS: (1) a. 316 BC *SEG* XXX 360, 18 (Perlman A.8) (f. Νίθων)

**Θιοφάνης**
ARGOLIS:
—ARGOS: (1) ii-i BC *IG* IV (1) 530, 18; cf. *BCH* 33 (1909) p. 183 n. 2 (Θιοφάν[ης])
—EPIDAUROS:

——Nymphais: (2) m. iii BC *IG* IV (1)² 96, 33 (Perlman E.3); Perlman p. 63 f. (date)

**Θιοχάρης**
ARGOLIS:
—EPIDAUROS:
——Lower Teichias: (1) c. 220-200 BC *SEG* XI 414, 28 (Perlman E.5)

**Θίοψ**
ARGOLIS:
—ARGOS: (1) ?c. 500-480 BC *IG* IV (1) 561; cf. *SEG* XI 328; *LSAG*² p. 169 no. 17 (date) (f. Αἰσχύλος)

**Θίσβη**
S. ITALY (APULIA):
—AUSCULUM: (1) imp. *CIL* IX 672 (Lat. Betitia Thisbe)

**Θίων**
ARGOLIS:
—ARGOS:
——Poimonis: (1) iv/iii BC Moretti, *ISE* 40, 32
—EPIDAUROS:
——Politas: (2) c. 370-365 BC Peek, *IAEpid* 52 B, 35
MESSENIA:
—MESSENE: (3) iii BC *SEG* XXIII 210, 19
SICILY:
—SYRACUSE?:
——(Νητ.): (4) hell. Manganaro, *PdelP* forthcoming no. 4 III, 5 (f. Διονύσιος)

**Θιωνίς**
ARGOLIS:
—ARGOS: (1) iii/ii BC *IG* IV (1)² 208, 1

**Θιώτας**
MESSENIA:
—MESSENE: (1) i/ii AD *SEG* XXIII 221 (f. Τιμαρέτα)

**Θόας**
ACHAIA:
—PELLENE: (1) ?274 BC *FD* III (4) 403 I, 1 (s. Φηρῆς)
AITOLIA:
—TRICHONION: (2) 205-173 BC *RE* (8); cf. Liv. xxxv 12. 6; *IG* IX (1)² (1) pp. L f., s.a. 203 BC, 194 BC, 181 BC, 173 BC; 31, 108 (s. Ἀλέξανδρος, f. Ἀλέξανδρος)
ITHAKE: (3) ?iv BC *RE* Supplbd. 14 (11)
KORINTHIA:
—KORINTH: (4) m. vii BC Amyx 1. 3 (vase) (Lorber 1) (Θόας: her.?)
LAKONIA:
—SPARTA: (5) c. 105-110 AD *IG* V (1) 20 B, 4; *BSA* 26 (1923-5) p. 168 C 7, 6 (Bradford (2)) (I f. Θόας II); (6) ~ *IG* V (1) 20 B, 4; *BSA* 26 (1923-5) p. 168 C 7, 6 (Bradford (1)) (II s. Θόας I)
SICILY:
—ECHETLA: (7) vi/v BC Manganaro, *PdelP* forthcoming 2
—RAGUSA (MOD.) (NR.): (8) ii-i BC *SEG* XLII 873. 1

**Θοινίας**
KORINTHIA:
—SIKYON: (1) iv/iii BC *IG* VII 267 (*IOrop* 385); *AD* 25 (1970) Mel. p. 139 no. 2 (Skalet 151) (f. Τεισικράτης); (2) iii BC *RE* (-); Marcadé II 128-30; *SEG* XXXIX 1334, 5; cf. *Chiron* 19 (1989) pp. 499-521 (Skalet 152) (s. Τεισικράτης: sculptor)

**Θοῖνος**
EPIROS:
—BOUTHROTOS (PRASAIBOI): (1) a. 163 BC *IBouthrot* 30, 22, 25; 40, 9 (*SEG* XXXVIII 488; 499)

—OMPHALES: (2) 370-368 BC Cabanes, *L'Épire* p. 534 no. 1, 17

**Θοίνων**
SICILY:
—SYRACUSE: (1) 279-278 BC D.S. xxii 7. 2-3, 6; 8. 4; Plu., *Pyrrh.* 23; cf. *RE* s.v. Sosistratos (5) (Θυνίων—D.S. mss.: s. Μαμεύς)

**Θοξούχαρος?**
EPIROS:
—THESPROTOI: (1) c. 330 BC Cabanes, *L'Épire* p. 580 no. 55, 10 (Ὀξούχαρος—Fick: f. Δείνων)

**Θορίων**
AITOLIA: (1) ?228-215 BC *SGDI* 2525, 4

**Θορσύλοχος**
ACHAIA:
—PELLENE: (1) iii BC *BCH* 38 (1914) p. 464 no. 8, 3 (f. Νεοκλῆς)

**Θραικίδας**
EPIROS:
—KHOSEPSI (MOD.): (1) imp. *SEG* XXIV 415; cf. XXIX 559 (Ὀραικίδας—Hammond, Αἰκίλας— *SEG* XXIX: s. Ἀρχίας: name—*LGPN*)

**Θραικίων**
ACHAIA:
—DYME: (1) iii-ii BC *Syll*³ 530, 7; cf. *Achaia und Elis* p. 115 (εἴτε Ἀντι[—])

**Θραικώ**
AITOLIA?: (1) m. ii BC *SBBerlAk* 1936, p. 371 b, 7 (*SEG* XLI 528 B) (slave/freed.)

**Θρᾶιξ**
SICILY:
—THERMAI HIMERAIAI: (1) imp. *CIL* X 7364 (Lat. [T]raeci (dat.))

**Θράπυς**
S. ITALY (BRUTTIUM):
—RHEGION: (1) c. 425-400 BC Dubois, *IGDGG* I 39 c (Arena, *Iscr. Sic.* III 63) (f. Δημοφάνης)

**Θρασέας**
ARGOLIS:
—ARGOS: (1) 105 BC *JÖAI* 14 (1911) Beibl. p. 146 no. 4, 28 (s. Πολ—); (2) i AD *SEG* XXVI 429, 4, 9, 10 (s. Δαϊκράτης, f. Δαϊκράτης, Ἀγαῖος)
ARKADIA:
—KLEITOR: (3) i AD *IG* V (2) 379
—LYKOSOURA*: (4) ii/i BC ib. 522 (f. Κλέων)
—MANTINEIA-ANTIGONEIA: (5) c. 300-221 BC ib. 323. 30 (tessera) (s. Θρασύλας)
—TEGEA: (6) 191-146 BC *BMC Pelop.* p. 15 no. 171 (coin)
——(Apolloniatai): (7) m. iii BC *IG* V (2) 36, 97 (s. Φίλων)
——(Krariotai): (8) s. iii BC ib. l. 116 (f. Κλέας)
—THELPHOUSA: (9) c. 210 BC ib. IX (1)² (1) 31, 89 (f. Σθένιππος)
KORINTHIA:
—KORINTH: (10) s. ii AD *Corinth* VIII (1) 15, 10
LAKONIA:
—BOIAI: (11) ii AD *IG* V (1) 956; 957 a-b (Γ. Ἰούλ. Θ.: f. Ἰουλ. Φιλοκράτις)
S. ITALY (LUCANIA):
—METAPONTION: (12) iv BC Iamb., *VP* 267 (*FVS* 1 p. 446) (Θράσεος—ms., Θράσιος— Rohde: name—Schweigh.)

**Θράσεια**
SICILY:
—SYRACUSE: (1) imp. *IG* XIV 32 (Θράσεια?—*IG*)

**Θρασίας**
S. ITALY (BRUTTIUM):
—RHEGION: (1) ii-i BC ib. 613 (f. Ἄνδρων)

—SYBARIS-THOURIOI-COPIAE: (2) s. ii AD
*NScav* 1972, Suppl. 4 p. 228 (Lat. Trasias:
f. Flavia Turina)
S. ITALY (CAMPANIA):
—POMPEII: (3) i BC-i AD ib. 1910, p. 262 (Lat.
Trasia)
SICILY:
—APOLLONIA: (4) ii BC *IG* XIV 359; cf. *Kokalos*
17 (1971) p. 179 (f. Ἄνδρων)

**Θράσιος**
ACHAIA:
—DYME: (1) s. iii BC *SEG* XIII 278, 27 (f. Θρά-
σων)

**Θράσιππος**
AKARNANIA:
—THYRREION: (1) iii-ii BC ib. XXVII 159, 4; cf.
*PAE* 1977, pl. 244 a (s. Ἁ—)
ARKADIA:
—TEGEA: (2) iv/iii BC *IG* v (2) 32, 10; (3) iii BC
ib. 30, 9
KORINTHIA:
—KORINTH: (4) m. iv BC *Corinth* VIII (1) 41; (5)
imp. ib. VIII (3) 300, 7 (*GVI* 2020) (doctor)

**Θρασύας**
ARKADIA:
—MANTINEIA-ANTIGONEIA: (1) v-iv BC
Thphr., *HP* ix 16. 8; 17. 1

**Θρασυβουλίδας**
AKARNANIA:
—STRATOS: (1) 225-205 BC *FD* III (3) 220, 5

**Θρασύβουλος**
ACHAIA:
—DYME*: (1) c. 219 BC *SGDI* 1612, 24 (*Tyche*
5 (1990) p. 124) (s. Ἀδείμαντος)
—TRITAIA: (2) iii-ii BC *Achaean Grave Stelai* 6
(f. Σόφων)
AITOLIA:
—KALYDON: (3) 410 BC *RE* (8); *IG* I³ 102, 6 f.;
cf. Osborne, *Naturalization* D2 (and Athens)
ARKADIA:
—PHENEOS: (4) 139-122 BC *Syll*³ 703
(Stephanis 1228) (s. Θεοξενίδας)
—PYLAI?: (5) vi-v BC *SEG* XVIII 157 (f. Σαέας)
—THELPHOUSA: (6) c. 230-200 BC *BCH* 45
(1921) p. 12 II, 74 (s. Λάττυπος)
—TORTHYNEION: (7) a. 420 BC *REG* 62 (1949)
p. 6, 9 (Θρασύβο[υλ]ος)
ELIS: (8) c. 250 BC *RE* (9) (s. Αἰνέας, f. Ἀγαθῖνος:
mantis/Iamidai)
EPIROS:
—DODONA*: (9) f. v BC *PAE* 1932, p. 52 no. 3
(-βολος)
LAKONIA:
—SPARTA: (10) c. 70-90 AD *IG* v (1) 280, 1
(*Artemis Orthia* p. 312 no. 29; Bradford (1))
(s. Καλλικράτης); (11) ?ii AD *IG* v (1) 677, 4
(Bradford (2))
——Pitana: (12) ?vi BC *HE* 1651; Plu., *Mor.* 234
F (Poralla² 377) (s. Τύννιχος)
PELOPONNESE?: (13) s. iii BC *IG* v (1) 1426, 12
(s. Αἰγύπτιος)
SICILY:
—AKRAGAS: (14) f. v BC Pi., *P.* vi 15; *I.* ii 1, 31;
Pi. fr. 124, 1 (s. Ξενοκράτης)
—GELA-PHINTIAS: (15) f. v BC *RE* (2) (and Si-
cily Syracuse: s. Δεινομένης: tyrant)

**Θρασυδαῖος**
ELIS: (1) v/iv BC ib. (1); (2) 374 BC *FGrH* 115
F 103, 12
SICILY:
—AKRAGAS: (3) f. v BC D.S. xi 48. 6-7; 53. 1;
Schol. Pi., *O.* ii 15; *O.* iii 38 (s. Θήρων: tyrant)

**Θρασύδαμος**
ARGOLIS:
—ARGOS: (1) v-iv BC Iamb., *VP* 267 (*FVS* I p.
447)

KEPHALLENIA:
—SAME: (2) hell. *IG* IX (1) 635 ([Θρ]ασύδα[μος],
[Θρ]ασυδα[ῖος?])
KORINTHIA:
—KORINTH: (3) 354 BC *CID* II 31, 35 ?= (4);
(4) ?269 BC ib. 120 A, 40; 121 II, 17 ([Θρα-
σύ]δαμος: I f. Θρασύδαμος II) ?= (3); (5) ~ ib.
120 A 40; 121 II, 17 (II s. Θρασύδαμος I)
S. ITALY (BRUTTIUM):
—LOKROI EPIZEPHYRIOI:
——(Θρα.): (6) 279 BC De Franciscis 14, 5

**Θρασυδήϊος**
S. ITALY (LUCANIA):
—HYELE-VELIA: (1) c. 140 BC *ID* 1965 a, 1-2;
1965 b, [1]; 2368, 3; 2595, 32; 2602, 9 (s. Ἕρμων, f. Ἕρμων, —ανα)

**Θρασυκλείης**
AIGINA: (1) ?s. v BC Unp. (Aigina Mus. Inv. I
1)

**Θρασυκλῆς**
ARGOLIS:
—ARGOS: (1) ?274 BC *CID* II 120 A, 14; 122 II,
11 (f. Ὀλυμπιάδας); (2) 196 BC *IG* IX (1)² (1)
30, 29 (s. Ἄνδρ—)
ARKADIA:
—TEGEA: (3) m. iv BC ib. v (2) 6, 60
DALMATIA:
—ISSA: (4) iii/ii BC *SEG* XXXV 687 (f. Ἕταρις)
KORINTHIA:
—KORINTH: (5) ii AD Luc., *DMort.* 11. 2 (fict.)
—SIKYON: (6) c. 146-32 BC *BMC Pelop.* p. 51
no. 194 (coin)
LEUKAS: (7) iv/iii BC PH 291

**Θράσυκλος**
ARGOLIS:
—ARGOS: (1) ?444 BC Pi., *N.* x, 39

**Θρασύκριτος**
AKARNANIA:
—ALYZIA: (1) ?f. iv BC *SEG* XLII 1041 (f. Πόλ-
λυς)

**Θρασύλαος**
AITOLIA:
—APERANTOI: (1) iii BC *SBBerlAk* 1936, p. 388
no. 2, 3 (*L'Illyrie mérid.* 1 p. 110 fig. 7) (s.
Κρατίνος)

**Θρασύλας**
ARKADIA:
—MANTINEIA-ANTIGONEIA: (1) c. 300-221 BC
*IG* v (2) 323. 30 (tessera) (Θρασύλαυ (gen.): f.
Θρασέας)

**Θρασυλέων**
ELIS: (1) c. 146-32 BC *BMC Pelop.* p. 6 no. 70
(coin)
LAKONIA:
—ASOPOS: (2) imp. *IG* v (1) 1003 (f. —των)

**Θράσυλλος**
ARGOLIS:
—PHLEIOUS: (1) v/iv BC *RE* (8)
ARKADIA:
—STYMPHALOS: (2) iii BC *IG* v (2) 356, 7
EPIROS:
—AMBRAKIA: (3) hell.-imp. *BCH* 17 (1893) p.
632 no. 3
KERKYRA: (4) c. 500 BC *SEG* XXX 520; cf.
*L'Illyrie mérid.* 2 p. 202
KORINTHIA:
—KORINTH: (5) s. iv BC *Corinth* VIII (1) 11, 4
(f. Δαμοθέρρης)
S. ITALY (BRUTTIUM):
—LOKROI EPIZEPHYRIOI:
——(Γαυ.): (6) 279 BC De Franciscis 13, 3 (s.
Φιλοχάρης)

SICILY:
—KAMARINA: (7) ?iv/iii BC *SEG* XXXIV 940, 4
(Dubois, *IGDS* 124; *PdelP* 44 (1989) p. 192
no. 3; Cordano, 'Camarina VII' 122) (Θρά-
συλλ(ο)ς)

**Θρασύλος**
ARGOLIS:
—ARGOS: (1) 418 BC Th. v 59. 5; 60. 6
ARKADIA:
—TEGEA: (2) i BC *IG* v (2) 225

**Θρασύλοχος**
LEUKAS: (1) c. 325-315 BC *Hesp.* 57 (1988) p.
148 B, 12 (*SEG* XXXVI 331); cf. *Hesp.* 48
(1979) pp. 78 f. with pl. 22 (f. Θράσων)
MESSENIA:
—MESSENE: (2) m. iv BC Berve 379 (*RE* (2)) (s.
Φιλιάδας); (3) ii BC *Ergon* 1995, p. 29

**Θρασύμαχος**
ACHAIA:
—BOURA: (1) ?s. iv BC *Achaean Grave Stelai* 2
(f. Ψαμώνιος)
AKARNANIA:
—STRATOS: (2) iv/iii BC *IG* IX (1)² (2) 395, 14
(s. Φιλόξενος)
—THYRREION: (3) ii BC ib. 324
ARGOLIS:
—ARGOS: (4) f. iii BC ib. XI (4) 546, 2, 5, [7]
ARKADIA:
—MEGALOPOLIS: (5) ?145 BC ib. v (2) 439, 35
(f. Ἥραιος); (6) ~ ib. l. 50 (f. Ἐπίστρατος)
DALMATIA:
—ISSA: (7) ii BC Brunšmid p. 25 no. 14, 1 +
*VAHD* 84 (1991) p. 248 no. 1 (f. Διονύσιος);
(8) ~ Brunšmid p. 26 no. 15 (f. Διονύσιος)
——(Hylleis): (9) iv/iii BC ib. p. 8, 40 (s. Εὔαρ-
χος)
EPIROS:
—BOUTHROTOS (PRASAIBOI): (10) a. 163 BC
*IBouthrot* 22, 19 (*SEG* XXXVIII 479); (11) ~
*IBouthrot* 38, 7 (*SEG* XXXVIII 497) (f. Λέων)
—CHIMERA: (12) f. ii BC *BCH* 45 (1921) p. 23
IV, 55; cf. p. 63 n. 1
ILLYRIA:
—APOLLONIA: (13) hell. *IApoll* 357 (tile)
KORINTHIA:
—KORINTH: (14) vi BC *IG* IV (1) 229 (pinax)
(Lazzarini 64) (Θρασύμα[χος]); (15) v/iv BC *RE*
(2)
S. ITALY (BRUTTIUM):
—LOKROI EPIZEPHYRIOI:
——(Τηλ.): (16) iv/iii BC De Franciscis 15, 2;
33, 3 (s. Νικίας); (17) 276 BC ib. 23, 4 (f. Καλ-
λίστρατος)
SICILY:
—TAUROMENION: (18) c. 234 BC *IG* XIV 421 an.
7 (*SGDI* 5219) (f. Ἀντίμαχος); (19) c. 221 BC
*IG* XIV 421 an. 20 (*SGDI* 5219); (20) c. 172
BC *IG* XIV 421 an. 69 (*SGDI* 5219); *IGSI* 4
II (III), [1] an. 69
TRIPHYLIA:
—HYPANA: (21) 191-146 BC *ZfN* 2 (1875) p. 164
no. 3; *BMC Pelop.* p. 13 no. 151 (coin)

**Θρασυμένης**
AITOLIA:
—KONOPE-ARSINOE?: (1) 184 BC *IG* IX (1)² (1)
131, 18 (Θρασυμ[έ]νης)
ARKADIA:
—ORCHOMENOS: (2) c. 230-200 BC *BCH* 45
(1921) p. 13 II, 115 (Θρασυμ[έ]νης: s. Πανάν-
δριος)
ZAKYNTHOS: (3) c. 293-168 BC *Polemon* 5
(1952-3) p. 11 no. 328, 2 (f. Λυκίδας)

**Θρασυμήδης**
ACHAIA:
—PELLENE: (1) ?278 BC *FD* III (4) 403 IX, 1 (s.
—σθένης)
AITOLIA: (2) iii/ii BC *IG* IX (1) 272, 3 (f. Ἀντί-
φιλος)

—THERMOS*: (3) s. iii BC ib. IX (1)² (1) 60 III, 2

ARGOLIS:
—EPIDAUROS*: (4) iv BC ib. IV (1)² 198 (sculptor); (5) c. 370-365 BC Peek, *IAEpid* 52 B, 57, 70, 75

ARKADIA:
—HERAIA: (6) ?f. i AD Plu., *Mor.* 437 F
—TEGEA*: (7) f. iii BC *IG* v (2) 36, 7 ([Θρ]ασυμήδης)

ELIS: (8) 20-16 BC *IvOl* 65, 7, 11 (s. Κλεινίας, f. Ἀγαθοκλῆς)

S. ITALY (LUCANIA):
—METAPONTION: (9) iv BC Iamb., *VP* 267 (*FVS* I p. 446)

**Θρασυμηλίδας**
LAKONIA:
—SPARTA: (1) 425 BC Th. iv 11. 2; D.S. xii 61. 3 (Poralla² 378) (Θρασυμήδης—D.S.: s. Κρατησικλῆς)

**Θρασύξενος**
ACHAIA:
—DYME: (1) s. iii BC *SEG* XIII 278, 24
ZAKYNTHOS: (2) ?257 BC Nachtergael, *Les Galates* 7, 49; cf. Stephanis 1559 (Θρασ[ύξ]ενος: f. Λυκίδας)

**Θράσυς**
ELIS: (1) v/iv BC Paus. vi 3. 4; Page, *FGE* 899; cf. Ebert, *Gr. Sieg.* 34 (Θράσις—Paus., Θ.—edd.: f. Ἀριστόδαμος)

S. ITALY (LUCANIA):
—HYELE-VELIA: (2) inc. *SEG* XXVIII 819 (f. Φιλιστώ)

SICILY:
—AKRAI: (3) iv BC *Helikon* 2 (1962) pp. 494-5
—KAMARINA: (4) f. v BC Cordano, *Tessere Pubbliche* 2 (f. -οσις); (5) ~ ib. 6; cf. *Riv. Fil.* 122 (1994) pp. 5 ff. (Θ. Ἐμμενίδας)

—SYRACUSE?:
——(Μακ.): (6) hell. Manganaro, *PdelP* forthcoming no. 4 V, 8 (f. Πολύξενος)

**Θράσων**
ACHAIA:
—AIGEIRA: (1) ?161 BC *FD* III (1) 49, 2, 7 (s. Πάτρων)
—DYME: (2) iii BC *AJPh* 31 (1910) p. 399 no. 74 a, 21 (f. Σώστρατος); (3) s. iii BC *SEG* XIII 278, 27 (s. Θράσιος); (4) i BC-i AD? *Achaean Grave Stelai* 36 (s. Ἡρακλε—)
—DYME*: (5) c. 219 BC *SGDI* 1612, 12 (*Tyche* 5 (1990) p. 124) (f. Φίλων)
—PELLENE: (6) ii AD Loewy 406, 7 (Ugolini, *Alb. Ant.* 3 p. 223 a) (sculptor)
—PHARAI: (7) ii/i BC *AE* 1973, p. 167 (s. Ξενοφῶν)

AITOLIA:
—KALYDON: (8) 129 BC *IG* IX (1)² (1) 137, 96 (s. Σώτακος)

AKARNANIA:
—ALYZIA: (9) m. ii BC ib. IX (1)² (2) 209, 18 (f. Φιλήσιος)

ARGOLIS:
—EPIDAUROS: (10) c. 370 BC ib. IV (1)² 102, 293, 295

ARKADIA:
—TEGEA: (11) ii BC ib. v (2) 43, 14 (s. Δαμο—)

ELIS: (12) iii BC *BCH* 45 (1921) p. 15 II, 145; *IG* v (2) 368, 55 (s. Τηρεύς, f. Τηρεύς); (13) imp. *IvOl* 755-756 (tiles); (14) 113 AD ib. 90, 8 (s. Ἑρεννιανός)

EPIROS:
—AMBRAKIA: (15) s. ii BC Cabanes, *L'Épire* p. 548 no. 19 (*SEG* XXVI 694) (s. Κλεομήδης)
—KELAITHOI: (16) iv-iii BC Cabanes, *L'Épire* p. 585 no. 68, 8; p. 592 no. 77, 12
KERKYRA: (17) imp. *IG* IX (1) 865; (18) ii AD ib. 881 (doctor)

KORINTHIA:
—KORINTH: (19) ii AD *Lampes antiques BN* I 27; *SEG* XXXVII 287 (lamps) ([Τ]άσων—*SEG*)
—SIKYON: (20) ii/i BC ib. XI 251, 2 (Skalet 154) (s. Κρίτων)
LEUKAS: (21) c. 325-315 BC *Hesp.* 57 (1988) p. 148 B, 12 (*SEG* XXXVI 331); cf. *Hesp.* 48 (1979) pp. 78 f. with pl. 22 ((Θ)ράσων: s. Θρασύλοχος)

S. ITALY (APULIA):
—CANUSIUM: (22) ?i-ii AD *Epig. Rom. di Canosa* 112 (*CIL* IX 369) (Lat. Ti. Claudius Thraso)

S. ITALY (BRUTTIUM):
—KROTON: (23) i BC ib. I² 2542 (Lat. T. Annaeus Trhaso)
—LOKROI EPIZEPHYRIOI:
——(Ἀγφ.): (24) 280 BC De Franciscis 7, 6; 35, 1 (s. Γνάθις)
——(Ἀστ.): (25) iv/iii BC ib. 29, 7
——(Θρα.): (26) iv/iii BC ib. 2, 2 (f. Εὐκλείδας); (27) ~ ib. 14, 2; (28) ~ ib. 16, 3; 28, 2 (s. Εὐκλείδας)

S. ITALY (CAMPANIA):
—POMPEII: (29) i BC-i AD *CIL* IV 5036; 5037; 5039; 5040 (Lat. Thraso)

SICILY:
—SYRACUSE: (30) 215 BC *FGrH* 268 F 4 (Θ. ὁ Κάρχαρος ἐπικαλούμενος) ?= (31); (31) ~ *RE* (2) ?= (30)
—SYRACUSE?:
——(Ὑπα.): (32) hell. Manganaro, *PdelP* forthcoming no. 4 IV, 8 (s. Ἡρακλείδας)
—TYNDARIS: (33) f. i BC Cic., *In Verr.* II iv 48 (Lat. Thraso)

**Θρασωνίδας**
ARKADIA:
—ORCHOMENOS: (1) f. iii BC *BCH* 38 (1914) p. 461 no. 5, 6
ELIS: (2) c. 365 BC X., *HG* vii 4. 15
KORINTHIA:
—KORINTH: (3) inc. Ael., *VH* xiv 24 (-δης)

**Θρασωνίδης**
ELIS: (1) s. iii BC Moretti, *Olymp.* 585 (s. Παιανόδωρος)

**Θράϋλλος**
ARGOLIS:
—ARGOS: (1) iii BC *IG* IV (1) 618 II, 5

**Θρέπτη**
S. ITALY (CALABRIA):
—BRENTESION-BRUNDISIUM: (1) ?i-ii AD *Epigraphica* 25 (1963) p. 73 no. 72; cf. *Mem. Linc.* 11 (1962-3) p. 262 (Lat. Iulia Threpte: m. Iulius Bales, Ζωσίμη)

S. ITALY (CAMPANIA):
—DIKAIARCHIA-PUTEOLI: (2) imp. *AJA* 2 (1898) p. 382 no. 24 (Lat. Trhepte)
—NEAPOLIS: (3) imp. *CIL* X 1530 (Lat. Trepte)

**Θρέπτος**
ARKADIA:
—TEGEA: (1) imp. *IG* v (2) 253, 5 (Στέπτος—*IG*, Θ.?); (2) 165 AD ib. 50, 54 (I f. Θρέπτος II); (3) ~ ib. l. 54 (II s. Θρέπτος I)
LAKONIA:
—SPARTA: (4) ii-iii AD ib. v (1) 734, 1 (*GVI* 1828; Bradford (-))

S. ITALY (CALABRIA):
—BRENTESION-BRUNDISIUM: (5) imp. *NScav* 1892, p. 351 b (Lat. L. Argentarius Treptus); (6) ~ ib. p. 353 cc (Lat. L. Valerius T[re]hptus)

S. ITALY (CAMPANIA):
—DIKAIARCHIA-PUTEOLI: (7) imp. *CIL* X 3086 b (Lat. M. Verrius Threptus); (8) m. i AD Camodeca, *L'Archivio Puteolano* I p. 125 no. 5 (Lat. L. Iulius Threptus)
—DIKAIARCHIA-PUTEOLI*: (9) imp. *CIL* X 3007 (Lat. Threptus: freed.)

—HERCULANEUM*: (10) c. 50-75 AD ib. 1403 a I, 22 (Lat. L. Mammius Threptus: freed.)
—NUCERIA ALFATERNA*: (11) imp. ib. 1092 (Lat. Q. Constantius Threptus: freed.)
—POMPEII: (12) i BC-i AD ib. IV 5028 (Lat. Threptus); (13) ~ ib. 7082 (Lat. Threptus)
SICILY:
—LILYBAION: (14) imp. ib. x 7243 (Lat. C. Curtius Threptus: I f. Θρέπτος II); (15) ~ ib. (Lat. C. Curtius Threptus: II s. Θρέπτος I)

**Θρεπτύλος**
SICILY:
—KATANE: (1) imp. *IG* XIV 477 (s. Εὐφροσύνη)

**Θρίπαινος**
SICILY:
—KAMARINA: (1) f. v BC Cordano, *Tessere Pubbliche* 85 (s. Ἀντίγονος)

**Θριπύλος**
SICILY:
—HIMERA: (1) vi/v BC *CEG* I 392 (vase) (Dubois, *IGDS* 8; Arena, *Iscr. Sic.* III 45)

**Θύας**
S. ITALY (CAMPANIA):
—POMPEII: (1) i BC-i AD *CIL* IV 4498 (Lat. Thyas)

**Θυέστας**
LAKONIA:
—SPARTA: (1) 220 BC Plb. iv 22. 11 (Bradford (-))

**Θυῆλος**
S. ITALY (CALABRIA):
—TARAS-TARENTUM: (1) imp. *CIL* IX 6164 (Lat. Thyielus)

**Θυϊνός**
EPIROS: (1) ?iv BC *IG* II² 8540 (Θ(υ)ϊνός: s. Λυκίσκος)

**Θυῖων**
ACHAIA:
—DYME: (1) c. 210-207 BC ib. IV (1)² 73, 20; *SEG* XXXV 303 (date) (s. Λύκων)
AKARNANIA:
—OINIADAI: (2) ?iii BC *IG* IX (1)² (2) 423 (f. Φορμίων)

**Θυϊωνίδας**
AKARNANIA:
—STRATOS: (1) iv/iii BC ib. 395, 9 (s. Ἡρακλεόδωρος)
LAKONIA:
—SPARTA: (2) 403-399 BC *ID* 87 b, 10 (Poralla² 379)

**Θυμάρης**
ARGOLIS:
—ARGOS: (1) c. 458 BC *IG* I³ 1149, 72 (-ρε̄ς)

**Θυμαρίδας**
ARGOLIS:
—ARGOS:
——(Hyrnathioi-Temenidai): (1) c. 400 BC *SEG* XXIX 361, 22
S. ITALY (CALABRIA):
—TARAS-TARENTUM: (2) iv BC Iamb., *VP* 145

**Θυμέλη**
S. ITALY (CAMPANIA):
—DIKAIARCHIA-PUTEOLI: (1) ?ii AD *CIL* X 2215 (Lat. Flavia Thimele: d. Βρέμουσα)
—POMPEII: (2) i BC-i AD ib. IV 1378; 1387-8; 1388 1; 1390; 4442-3 (Lat. Timele); (3) ~ ib. 8653 (Lat. Thymeli)
—RUFRAE: (4) imp. ib. x 4832 (Lat. Sattia Tymele: m. M. Sattius Ianuarius)
S. ITALY (LUCANIA):
—POTENTIA: (5) imp. ib. 168 (Lat. Tymale)

**Θυμοτέλης**
S. Italy (Campania):
—kyme: (1) vi/v bc Plu., *Mor.* 262 C

**Θύμων**
Arkadia:
—thelphousa: (1) iii/ii bc *IG* v (2) 511 (s.
Παυσίων)

**Θυρίων**
Arkadia: (1) vi bc D.L. i 29 (s. Βαθυκλῆς)

**Θύρμαξ**
Epiros:
—bouthrotos (prasaiboi): (1) a. 163 bc
*IBouthrot* 17, 13; 31, 67 (*SEG* xxxviii 474;
490) (I s. Φάλακρος, f. Φάλακρος, Θύρμαξ II,
?f. Φιλίστα) ?= (5); (2) ~ *IBouthrot* 17, 13; 31,
67 (*SEG* xxxviii 474; 490) (II s. Θύρμαξ I);
(3) ~ *IBouthrot* 22, 1; 31, 84 (*SEG* xxxviii
479; 490) (f. Δέξανδρος) ?= (4); (4) ~ *IBouthrot* 25, 13 (*SEG* xxxviii 483) ?= (3); (5) ~
*IBouthrot* 43, 7 (*SEG* xxxviii 502) ?= (1);
(6) ~ *IBouthrot* 107; (7) ~ ib. 116, 11 (*BCH*
118 (1994) p. 121 A); (8) ~ *IBouthrot* 153, 6
([Θύ]ρμα[ξ])
——Bouthrotioi: (9) a. 163 bc ib. 139, 10 (s.
Ἀρχίδαμος)
——Eschatioi: (10) a. 163 bc ib. 93, 1; 94, [1];
99, 2 (*BCH* 118 (1994) p. 121 B) ?= (11);
(11) ~ *IBouthrot* 128, 6; 129, 4; 137, 12; 144,
6; 147, 11 (s. Δείνων) ?= (10)

**Θυρρειάδας**
Argolis:
—troizen: (1) 337-336 bc *CID* ii 74 I, 76; 76
II, 25 (Θυ[ρ]ρ[ει]άδας: f. Φάντος)

**Θυρσιάδας**
Achaia:
—pellene: (1) m. iv bc ib. 19, 5 (f. Ἀλεξίων)

**Θύρσις**
Sicily?: (1) f. iii bc Theoc., *Id.* i 65 and
passim; cf. *SP* III 123, 9 (Heitsch 17) (fict.)

**Θύρσος**
Arkadia:
—heraia: (1) iv bc Peek, *AG* 2 p. 24 no. 60
(Θύρ[σ]ος)
—tegea*: (2) s. iv ad *SEG* xxxiv 327 (bp.)
Epiros:
—nikopolis: (3) imp. ib. xxxv 678 (Ἰούλ. Θ.)

**Kerkyra:** (4) imp. *IG* ix (1) 957 (Π. Αἴλ. Θ.)
Messenia:
—messene: (5) iii bc *SEG* xxiii 209, 21
S. Italy (Campania):
—dikaiarchia-puteoli: (6) imp. *CIL* x 2641
(*Epigraphica* 57 (1995) p. 167 no. 1) (Lat.
Thyrsus)
—pompeii: (7) i bc-i ad *CIL* iv 829 (Lat.
Thirsus); (8) ~ ib. 7190 (Lat. Tyrsus); (9) 70-
79 ad ib. 3640; Mouritsen p. 110 (date) (Lat.
Thyrsus)
S. Italy (Lucania):
—potentia: (10) imp. *Misc. Gr. Rom.* 8 pp.
436-8 (Lat. P. Petronius Tirsus)
Sicily: (11) ?v bc Iamb., *VP* 241 (s. Ἐπίχαρ-
μος)
—syracuse: (12) imp. *IG* xiv 34 + *Riv. Arch.
Crist.* 18 (1941) p. 196 no. 64 (Κλ. Θύ[ρσος]?)

**Θύτας**
Epiros: (1) c. 200 bc Cabanes, *L'Épire* p. 558
no. 34, 5 (*SEG* xxvi 701) (n. pr.?: f. Μένανδρος)

**Θύτης**
S. Italy (Bruttium):
—rhegion: (1) i ad *IG* xiv 617, 6 (*Suppl. It.*
5 p. 45); cf. *SEG* xl 855 (Γ. Ἀντώνιος Θ. (n.
pr.?))

**Θύων**
Akarnania: (1) c. 250-167 bc *NZ* 10 (1878) p.
31 no. 36 (coin) (*BMC Thessaly* p. 169 no.
14)

**Θυωνίδας**
Arkadia:
—mantineia-antigoneia: (1) 64 or 62 bc *IG*
v (2) 265, 47 (I f. Θυωνίδας II); (2) ~ ib. l. 47
(II s. Θυωνίδας I)
Illyria:
—apollonia: (3) c. 250-50 bc Münsterberg
Nachtr. p. 13 (coin) (Ceka 107) (Οὐωνίδας—
Münsterberg per err?: pryt.)

**Θωμαδία**
Korinthia:
—korinth: (1) byz. *Corinth* VIII (3) 664; cf.
*TMByz* 9 (1985) p. 359 no. 1

**Θωμάντα**
Argolis:
—phleious: (1) iii bc *IG* iv (1) 462 (d. Ἀρχι-
κλείδας)

**Θώπας**
Akarnania:
—thyrreion: (1) iii bc ib. ix (1)² (2) 262

**Θωπίας**
Aitolia:
—kallion/kallipolis: (1) 190 bc Sherk 37
B, 45; cf. *SEG* xxvii 123 ?= (2); (2) 177 bc
*SGDI* 1869, 3 ?= (1)

**Θωπίνας**
Akarnania:
—limnaia: (1) s. iv bc *IG* iv (1)² 95, 56 (Perlman E.2); Perlman pp. 46-9 (date) (s. Ἀριστόλαος)

**Θωπίων**
Epiros:
—dodona*: (1) iv-iii bc *Ep. Chron.* 10 (1935)
p. 259 no. 32

**Θωπύλος**
Sicily:
—selinous: (1) vi/v bc Manganaro, *PdelP*
forthcoming no. 18, 6 (-Θό-: s. Ξένων)

**Θωρακίδας**
Arkadia:
—mantineia-antigoneia:
——(Posoidaia): (1) m. iv bc *IG* v (2) 271, 17
([Θ]ωρακίδας: s. Ἀγησίνοος)
Korinthia:
—korinth: (2) i-ii ad ib. ii² 9070 (f. Μενέστρα-
τος)

**Θωρακίς**
Epiros:
—dodona*: (1) c. 425-400 bc *Ep. Chron.* 10
(1935) p. 256 no. 17; *LSAG*² p. 230 no. 17
(date) (Θό-)

**Θώραξ**
Epiros:
—chimera: (1) f. ii bc *BCH* 45 (1921) p. 23
IV, 54; cf. p. 63 n. 1
Lakonia:
—sparta: (2) s. v bc *RE* (6) (Poralla² 380)

**Θωροπίδας**
Argolis:
—argos: (1) s. iv bc *SEG* xx 716, 27 + xxvii
1194 ?= (2); (2) c. 343-336 bc *CID* ii 58 I,
[2]; 59 II, 22, 25; cf. p. 90 ?= (1)

Ἴα
S. Italy (Bruttium):
—Consentia: (1) ii AD *Mus. Naz. Reggio* p. 158 no. 27 (d. Δημήτριος)
S. Italy (Campania):
—Dikaiarchia-Puteoli: (2) imp. *CIL* X 2531 (Lat. Ia: m. Νεβρίς)

Ἴακχος
Kerkyra: (1) ?ii BC *IG* IX (1) 708 (f. Φιλώτας)
S. Italy (Lucania):
—Hyele-Velia: (2) imp. Dito, *Velia* p. 94 no. 20 (Lat. C. Aquillius Iacchus)

Ἰακώβ
S. Italy (Apulia):
—Venusia: (1) v AD *JIWE* I 48 (*CIJ* I 594) (f. Σεβῆρα: Jew)
S. Italy (Calabria):
—Taras-Tarentum*: (2) byz. *JIWE* I 119 (*CIJ* I 628) (Ἰαα[κώβ]: f. Ἠλίας: Jew)

Ἰαλλίς
Korinthia:
—Korinth: (1) v BC *SEG* XXV 339 (bronze) (Lazzarini 350); cf. *SEG* XXVIII 379

Ἴαμβος
S. Italy (Campania):
—Dikaiarchia-Puteoli: (1) imp. *IG* XIV 855 (Λ. Τρεβώνιος Ἰ.)

Ἴαμος
Elis: (1) her. *RE* (1); (2) c. 57-93 AD *IvOl* 80, 4; 81, [12]; 84, [13]; 85, [10]; 86, 8; *EA* 1905, p. 255 no. 1, 8 (Ἴαμορ—86: s. Φιλίκων: mantis/Iamidai)
Lakonia:
—Sparta: (3) c. 110-120 AD *IG* V (1) 258, [1]?; 298, 4; *Artemis Orthia* pp. 315-16 no. 35 (date) (Bradford (2)) (f. Τεισαμενός); (4) m. ii AD *IG* V (1) 466, 9 (f. Μοῦσα)

Ἰανουαρία
S. Italy (Campania):
—Neapolis: (1) iii-iv AD ib. XIV 826. 19 (*INap* 229)
Sicily:
—Syracuse: (2) iii-v AD *Riv. Arch. Crist.* 18 (1941) p. 213 no. 88 ([Ἰε]ν-); (3) ~ *Rend. Pont.* 22 (1946-7) p. 233 no. 19 (Ἰανα-); (4) ~ *SEG* XVIII 396 (Ἰενα-); (5) ~ Strazzulla 176 (Wessel 1043) (Ἰενα-); (6) ~ Strazzulla 226 (Ἰενα-)

Ἰανουαριανός
Sicily:
—Syracuse: (1) iii-v AD ib. 299 + Ferrua, *NG* 61 (Wessel 192) (Ἰενα-)

Ἰανουάριος
Korinthia:
—Korinth?: (1) v-vi AD *CIG* 8824 (*TMByz* 9 (1985) p. 294 no. 34 A)
S. Italy (Apulia):
—Venusia: (2) v AD *JIWE* I 101 (*CIJ* I 582) (Ἰεν-: Jew)
Sicily:
—Akrai: (3) iii-v AD Agnello 66 (Wessel 7; *Akrai* p. 167 no. 39); cf. *Riv. Arch. Crist.* 18 (1941) p. 204 no. 77
—Katane: (4) iii-v AD Agnello 61; cf. Ferrua, *NG* 407 (Ἰενα-: s. Πρῖμος)
—Syracuse: (5) iii-v AD *NScav* 1893, p. 282 no. 18 + Ferrua, *NG* 7 ([Ἰε]νάρις); (6) ~ *NScav* 1907, p. 758 no. 13 (Ἰεν-); (7) ~ ib. 1915, p. 203 (Wessel 643) (-άρις); (8) ~ Strazzulla 224; cf. Ferrua, *NG* 287 ([Ἰε]νά-); (9) ~ Strazzulla 380 (Wessel 721) (Ἰανά-)

Ἰαπετός
S. Italy (Campania):
—Pompeii: (1) i BC-i AD *CIL* IV 1686 (Lat. Iapetus)

Ἴᾱπυξ
S. Italy (Calabria):
—Iapyges: (1) iv BC *PCG* 2 p. 386 fr. 137 (slave)

Ἰαροκλῆς
Argolis:
—Epidauros:
——(Azantioi): (1) 146 BC *IG* IV (1)² 28, 32 (f. Λυσικράτης)
——Nymphais: (2) m. iii BC ib. 96, 33 (Perlman E.3); Perlman p. 63 f. (date)
——Selegeis: (3) c. 335-325 BC *IG* IV (1)² 108, 153
—Epidauros*: (4) c. 370-335 BC ib. 103, 106; Peek, *IAEpid* 52 A, 16; (5) iii/ii BC *IG* IV (1)² 306 B (f. Νίκων)
Arkadia:
—Tegea: (6) c. 225 BC *SEG* XI 414, 22 (Perlman E.5) (f. Ἀνδρόμαχος)
Sicily:
—Syracuse: (7) ?327 BC *BCH* 64-5 (1940-1) p. 144 B, 2 (f. Μάγνης); (8) iv/iii BC Paus. vi 12. 2; *FD* III (3) 157 (Ἰερο-: s. Ἰάρων, f. Ἰάρων)

Ἴαρυς
Sicily:
—Lipara: (1) ?iii BC *Meligunis-Lipara* 5 p. 150 no. 2160; cf. *SEG* XLI 806 (ἱάρυος (gen.)—ed., Κάρυς?—*LGPN*)

Ἰάρων
Argolis:
—Epidauros: (1) c. 320-300 BC *IG* IV (1)² 110 A, 13
——(Azantioi): (2) 146 BC ib. 28, 44 (s. Ἰαρώνυμος)
——(Hysminatai): (3) 146 BC ib. l. 21 (f. Νικασίλας); (4) ~ ib. l. 22 (s. Καλλήν)
—Epidauros*: (5) c. 335-325 BC ib. 106 I, 72
—Methana-Arsinoe: (6) i BC ib. IV (1) 853, 8 (Ἰά[ρω]ν: s. Σώδαμος)
Epiros:
—Ambrakia: (7) iv BC *Op. Ath.* 10 (1971) p. 64 no. 7 with fig. 20 (s. Κλεύμαχος)
Lakonia:
—Sparta?: (8) v/iv BC *IvOl* 274 (Poralla² p. 66) (hιά- (n. pr.?))?= (Ἰέρων (40))
S. Italy (Bruttium):
—Nicotera: (9) inc. *Studi Merid.* 2 (1969) p. 383
Sicily:
—Echetla: (10) vi/v BC Manganaro, *PdelP* forthcoming 4 (hιάρōν, ΙΙΑΡΟΝ?—ed.)
—Gela-Phintias: (11) c. 530-467 BC *RE* (11); Moretti, *Olymp.* 221; 234; 246; ML 29 (and Sicily Syracuse: hιάρōν—ML, Ἰέρων—lit. test.: s. Δεινομένης, f. Δεινομένης: tyrant)
—Morgantina: (12) ?iv/iii BC *SEG* XXXIX 1008, 9 (s. Φιλίαρχος); (13) ~ ib. 1009, 6 (s. Ἀγάθαρχος); (14) iv/iii BC ib. 1013, 6 (s. Κλέων)
—Syracuse: (15) c. 306-215 BC *RE* (13) (Ἰέρων—lit. test.: s. Ἰαροκλῆς, f. Γέλων: tyrant); (16) 290-280 BC *FD* III (3) 157 (Ἰε-: f. Ἰαροκλῆς); (17) c. 264 BC *IG* XII (5) 1061, 2 (*PP* 15148); cf. *RE* (14) (Ἰέ-: s. Τιμοκράτης)
—Syracuse?:
——(Λαβ.): (18) hell. Manganaro, *PdelP* forthcoming no. 4 IV, 5 (s. Σῖμος)

Ἰαρώνυμος
Argolis:
—Epidauros: (1) iii/ii BC *IG* IV (1)² 243 (s. Ἀκρυπτίδας, f. Ἀκρυπτίδας, Ἀδεισιτίδας)
——(Azantioi): (2) 146 BC ib. 28, 44 (f. Ἰάρων)
——Pagasina (Azantioi): (3) c. 365-335 BC ib. 103, 120
—Epidauros*: (4) c. 370-365 BC Peek, *IAEpid* 52 B, 14 (Ἰαρώνυμ[ος])
Sicily:
—Syracuse: (5) c. 230-214 BC *RE* (8) (Ἰερώνυμος—lit. test.: s. Γέλων, Νηρηΐς (Molossoi): tyrant)

Ἴας
S. Italy (Campania):
—Dikaiarchia-Puteoli: (1) imp. *CIL* X 2118 (Lat. Atilia Ias); (2) ~ ib. 2476 (Lat. Gellia Ias); (3) ~ ib. 2564 (Lat. Iade (dat.))
—Kyme: (4) imp. ib. 2930 (Lat. Ia)
—Pompeii: (5) i BC-i AD ib. IV 1379; 1384 (Lat. Ias); (6) ~ ib. 2174; 2231 (Lat. Ias)

Ἰασίδαμος
Arkadia:
—Megalopolis: (1) ?262-255 BC Nachtergael, *Les Galates* 5, 16?; 18, 1 (f. Δαμόνικος); (2) ?145 BC *IG* V (2) 439, 1

Ἴασις
Lakonia:
—Amyklai*: (1) c. 510-500 BC *SEG* I 84; *LSAG*² p. 200 no. 32 (date); Masson, *OGS* 2 p. 512 (name) (Poralla² 381b)

Ἴασος
S. Italy (Apulia):
—Venusia: (1) imp. *CIL* IX 572 (Lat. C. Stat. Iasus)

Ἴασπις
S. Italy (Campania):
—Dikaiarchia-Puteoli*: (1) i/ii AD ib. X 2433 (Lat. T. F. Iaspis: imp. freed.)

Ἰάσων
Achaia: (1) 226 BC *PPetr*² I *Wills* 24, 2; (2) f. ii BC *IC* 2 p. 23 no. 6 F, 1 (s. Σάμος)
Akarnania:
—Thyrreion: (3) 94 BC *IG* IX (1)² (2) 242, 7 (f. Δωρόθεος)
Argolis:
—Argos: (4) m. ii BC Siebert, *Ateliers* pp. 30-1; 170 (date) (Ἰάσο(νος)? (gen.): ?f. Δημήτριος); (5) ii AD *RE* (12); *FGrH* 446
—Argos*: (6) ii BC *SEG* XLII 279, 14 (slave/freed.?)
—Epidauros: (7) i BC *IG* IV (1)² 227 (f. —λος)
Elis: (8) ii/i BC *IvOl* 197, 1 (f. Ἀντιγένης)
Epiros:
—Antigoneia?: (9) ?f. iii BC *Iliria* 1972, p. 375; cf. p. 341 (tile)
Illyria:
—Epidamnos-Dyrrhachion: (10) c. 200-172 BC *RA* 1948, p. 826 no. 2, 5 (*IDyrrh* 523) (Ἰά[σ]ων: s. Λύσων)
Korinthia:
—Korinth: (11) ii-iii AD *IG* IV (1) 395, 2 (*GVI* 317) (Ἰή-)
S. Italy (Bruttium):
—Varapodio (mod.): (12) f. iii BC *Klearchos* 8 (1966) p. 64 (tile)
S. Italy (Calabria):
—Brentesion-Brundisium: (13) imp. *IG* XII (5) 86 (f. Τερτία)
S. Italy (Campania):
—Herculaneum: (14) i BC-i AD *CIL* X 1403 d III, 1 (Lat. Iaso)
—Misenum*: (15) imp. ib. 3527 (Lat. Ammo. Iaso)

—POMPEII: (16) c. 51-62 AD ib. IV 3340. 80, 7 (Castrèn 281. 4) (Lat. C. Numitorius Iason)
SICILY:
—AKRILLAI: (17) ?iv AD *JIWE* I 155 (Jew)
—KATANE: (18) iv-v AD ib. 149 (*SEG* XVII 440; Libertini, *Museo Biscari* p. 317 no. 5) (*I.*)
—LILYBAION: (19) iii-iv AD *IGLMP* 26 (s. Ἀρτάφαν)
—TAUROMENION (NR.): (20) imp. *Epigraphica* 3 (1941) p. 270 no. 44 (seal) (Lat. Sex. Iul. Iason)
—THERMAI HIMERAIAI: (21) imp. *IG* XIV 325 (f. Μάξιμος)

**Ἰατρόκλεια**
LAKONIA: (1) ii-i BC ib. II² 9150 (d. Βίων)

**Ἰατροκλείδας**
ARGOLIS:
—EPIDAUROS: (1) iii/ii BC ib. IV (1)² 374 (Peek, *IAEpid* 153. 21)

**Ἰατροκλῆς**
ILLYRIA:
—APOLLONIA: (1) c. 250-50 BC Maier 65 (coin) (Ceka 62) (money.)
S. ITALY (CAMPANIA):
—NEAPOLIS: (2) i BC-i AD *IG* XIV 786 (*INap* 125) (f. Θεοδότη)
SICILY:
—SYRACUSE?: (3) f. iv BC [Pl.], *Ep.* 363 E

**Ἰάχη**
S. ITALY (CAMPANIA):
—DIKAIARCHIA-PUTEOLI*: (1) imp. *CIL* X 1943 (Lat. Calpurnia Iache: freed.?)

**Ἴβυκος**
S. ITALY (BRUTTIUM):
—RHEGION: (1) vi BC *RE* (1); *PMGF* I pp. 236 ff.; cf. *Arch. Class.* 25-6 (1973-4) pp. 464 ff. (?s. Φύτιος, Πολύζηλος, Κέρδας)

**Ἰγέρτας**
ITHAKE: (1) 208 BC *IMM* 36, 23 (s. Πραΰλος)

**Ἰγνατία**
ILLYRIA:
—BYLLIONES: (1) imp. *SEG* XXIV 476 (XXXVIII 551)

**Ἰγνᾶτις**
SICILY:
—KATANE: (1) imp. *IG* XIV 484 (*I.* Καρικός)

**Ἴγρων**
KORINTHIA:
—KORINTH: (1) vi BC ib. IV (1) 230; 231 (pinax) (Lazzarini 269) (-ρōν)

**Ἰδαία**
S. ITALY (CAMPANIA):
—POMPEII: (1) i BC-i AD *CIL* IV 3131 (Lat. Idaia)

**Ἰδαῖος**
AITOLIA:
—THERMOS*: (1) s. iii BC *IG* IX (1)² (1) 60 II, 12
ARGOLIS:
—ARGOS:
——(Pholygadai): (2) a. 316 BC *Mnem.* NS 43 (1915) pp. 375-6 F, 5 (Perlman A.7) (s. Ἀ—)
LAKONIA:
—SPARTA?: (3) v/iv BC X., *HG* iv 1. 39; Plu., *Ages.* 13 (Poralla² 382) (Ἀδαῖος—Plu.)
S. ITALY (CAMPANIA):
—DIKAIARCHIA-PUTEOLI: (4) imp. *CIL* X 2308 (Lat. Cocceius Idaeus); (5) ~ ib. 2358 (Lat. M. Valer. Idaeus)
—SALERNUM: (6) i BC/i AD *IItal* I (1) 178 (*CIL* X 530) (Lat. Q. Maecius Idaeus)

S. ITALY (LUCANIA):
—TEGIANUM*: (7) 177 AD *IItal* III (1) 259 (*CIL* X 285) (Lat. Idaeus)
SICILY:
—HIMERA: (8) ?v BC *FVS* 63

**Ἰδάλιος**
S. ITALY (CAMPANIA):
—POMPEII: (1) i BC-i AD *CIL* IV 4787 (Lat. Idalius)

**Ἴδας**
AKARNANIA:
—ECHINOS: (1) c. 266 BC *IG* XII (9) 1187, 8; Robert, *Ét. Num. Gr.* pp. 179 ff. (date) (s. Δρωνίλος)

**Ἴδη**
S. ITALY (CAMPANIA):
—DIKAIARCHIA-PUTEOLI: (1) imp. *CIL* X 2367 (Lat. Domitia Ide)

**Ἰδρόμας**
AKARNANIA:
—ECHINOS: (1) c. 266 BC *IG* XII (9) 1187, 10; Robert, *Ét. Num. Gr.* pp. 179 ff. (date) (f. Ὑβρίλας)

**Ἰέρα**
S. ITALY (APULIA):
—VENUSIA: (1) imp. *CIL* IX 504 (Lat. Creperia Hiera: d. M. Creperius Iustus, Salvia Veneria)

**Ἱεραῖος**
ARKADIA:
—KAPHYAI: (1) c. 230-200 BC *BCH* 45 (1921) p. 14 II, 121 (Ἱεραῖος—Oulhen: f. Κάλλιστος, Ἑκατάων)

**Ἱέραξ**
LAKONIA:
—SPARTA: (1) 389 BC X., *HG* v 1. 3 ff. (Poralla² 383)
S. ITALY (APULIA):
—TEANUM APULUM*: (2) imp. *Teanum Apulum* p. 126 no. 56; *CIL* IX 6078. 94 (tiles) (Lat. Hierax)
S. ITALY (BRUTTIUM):
—RHEGION: (3) imp. ib. X 8422. 5 (tile) (Lat. Ierax)
S. ITALY (CAMPANIA):
—DIKAIARCHIA-PUTEOLI: (4) imp. ib. 2076 (Lat. [An]tonius Hierax); (5) ~ *NScav* 1897, p. 532 (Audollent, *Defix. Tab.* 206 (terracotta))
—MISENUM*: (6) imp. *CIL* X 3446 (Lat. H(i)erax)
SICILY:
—KENTORIPA: (7) hell.? *IG* XIV 2397. 3 (tile)
—SYRACUSE: (8) iii-v AD *NScav* 1913, p. 268 (Εἰ-); (9) ~ Strazzulla 243

**Ἱέραρχος**
ARKADIA:
—MANTINEIA-ANTIGONEIA: (1) ?iii BC *IG* v (2) 318, 26 (Ἱέραρχος)
LAKONIA:
—SPARTA: (2) s. i BC ib. v (1) 135, 13 (Bradford (2)) (Ἱέρα(ρ)χος: f. Φιλόμουσος); (3) c. 30-20 BC *IG* v (1) 211, 36 (Bradford (1)) (s. Ἄρχιππος)

**Ἱερατικός**
S. ITALY (CAMPANIA):
—DIKAIARCHIA-PUTEOLI*: (1) i/ii AD *CIL* X 2433 (Lat. T. F. Hieraticus: imp. freed.)

**Ἱέρεια**
S. ITALY (CAMPANIA):
—DIKAIARCHIA-PUTEOLI: (1) imp. ib. 2868 (Lat. Pompeia Hieria)

**Ἱερήν**
ILLYRIA:
—EPIDAMNOS-DYRRHACHION: (1) ?iii BC *IDyrrh* 35 (s. Ταυρίσκος); (2) ~ ib. 250 (s. Ἀμφικλῆς); (3) hell.-imp. ib. 251

**Ἱερίς**
ELIS:
—LASION: (1) c. 230-200 BC *BCH* 45 (1921) p. 14 II, 126 (s. Ἀγέλοχος)

**Ἱεροδώρα**
ACHAIA:
—AIGION: (1) i AD *IG* II² 7948; cf. Peek, *AG* I p. 19 no. 58 (Ἱε[ροδ]ώρα—ed., Ἰσ[ιδ]ώρα?)

**Ἱεροκλέα**
ARGOLIS:
—HERMIONE: (1) ii-i BC *IG* IV (1) 732 III, 12 (d. Τισικράτης)

**Ἱερόκλεια**
ARGOLIS:
—EPIDAUROS: (1) s. iii BC ib. IV (1)² 222 (d. Εὔνομος, m. Εὐάνθης)
ARKADIA:
—MEGALOPOLIS?: (2) hell.? *Platon* 26 (1974) p. 13 no. 152

**Ἱεροκλείδης**
SICILY:
—ZANKLE-MESSANA: (1) s. i BC *GP* 2291 (fict.)

**Ἱεροκλῆς**
ARGOLIS:
—ARGOS: (1) 105 BC *JÖAI* 14 (1911) Beibl. p. 146 no. 4, 22 (f. Οἰνοκλῆς)
—ARGOS*: (2) 105 BC ib. l. 22 (slave/freed.?)
—EPIDAUROS: (3) i-ii AD *IG* IV (1)² 484, 3 (s. Χαρικλῆς); (4) ~ ib. 513; (5) ~ ib. 549 (s. Ἀφροδίσιος); (6) 133 AD ib. 383, 6 (s. Εὔτυχος)
—HERMIONE: (7) i BC-i AD? ib. IV (1) 730 I, 7 (s. Ὀλυμπιόδωρος)
—TROIZEN: (8) ?200 BC *Memnonion* 31-32 bis (f. Φιλοκλῆς)
ARKADIA: (9) iii BC *IG* v (2) 415, 12 (*IPArk* 23) (Ἱερ[ο]κλῆς); (10) ?255 BC Nachtergael, *Les Galates* 8, 25; cf. Stephanis 1192 (Ἱε[ροκλῆς: f. Θεόχαρις) ?= (15)
—HERAIA: (11) c. 230-200 BC *BCH* 45 (1921) p. 12 II, 76 (s. Διογένης)
—MANTINEIA-ANTIGONEIA: (12) c. 300-221 BC *IG* v (2) 323. 90 (tessera) (s. Ἱερότιμος); (13) ~ ib. 323. 98 (tessera) (s. Κλεόμαχος)
—TEGEA: (14) m. iv BC ib. 6, 63 (Ἱεροκλῆς); (15) ?265-253 BC Nachtergael, *Les Galates* 2, 35; 10, 60; cf. Stephanis 1261 (f. Ἱερότιμος) ?= (10)
EPIROS:
—AMBRAKIA: (16) iii/ii BC Unp. (Arta Mus., inscr.) (f. Καλλιόι); (17) c. 200 BC *IG* II² 4931 (f. —ώ)
LAKONIA:
—HYPERTELEATON*: (18) imp. *SEG* XI 907 b (bronze) ([Ἱ]εροκλ[ῆς])
—SPARTA: (19) i BC-i AD ib. II 156 (Bradford (4)); (20) s. i BC *IG* v (1) 136, 6 (Bradford (7)) (I f. Ἱεροκλῆς II); (21) ~ *IG* v (1) 136, 6 (Bradford (2)) (II s. Ἱεροκλῆς I); (22) c. 25-1 BC *IG* v (1) 210, 37 (Bradford (6)) (I f. Ἱεροκλῆς II); (23) ~ *IG* v (1) 210, 37 (Bradford (1)) (II s. Ἱεροκλῆς I); (24) c. 105-110 AD *IG* v (1) 20 B, 3; 97, 21; *SEG* XI 564, 21; *BSA* 26 (1923-5) p. 168 C 7, 2 (Bradford (8)) (I f. Ἱεροκλῆς II); (25) ~ *IG* v (1) 20 B, 3; 97, 21; *SEG* XI 564, 21; *BSA* 26 (1923-5) p. 168 C 7, 2 (Bradford (3)) (II s. Ἱεροκλῆς I); (26) ?134 AD *IG* v (1) 62, 10 (Bradford (5)) (f. Δαμόνικος)
MESSENIA:
—MESSENE:
——(Kleolaidai): (27) 11 AD *PAE* 1992, p. 71 A, 26 (s. Καλλίστρατος)

**Ἱερονίκη**

S. Italy (Campania):
—Dikaiarchia-Puteoli: (28) imp. *CIL* x 1909 (Lat. Hierocles)

Sicily:
—Akragas: (29) 191 BC Liv. xxxvi 31. 12 (Lat. Hierocles)

**Ἱερονίκη**

S. Italy (Campania):
—Dikaiarchia-Puteoli: (1) imp. *Eph. Ep.* VIII 373 (Lat. Hieronice)

**Ἱερόνικος**

Argolis:
—Epidauros: (1) imp.? Peek, *IAEpid* 229 ([Ἱ]ερόνει[κος])

**Ἱερόνομος**

Arkadia:
—Mantineia-Antigoneia:
——(Posoidaia): (1) c. 425-400 BC *SEG* xxxi 348, 22

**Ἱερός**

Epiros:
—Dodona: (1) ?164 BC Cabanes, *L'Épire* p. 586 no. 71, 9 (f. Φίλιππος)

S. Italy (Campania):
—Dikaiarchia-Puteoli: (2) imp. *CIL* x 2761 (Lat. L. Aufillius Hierus)

**Ἱεροτίμα**

Arkadia:
—Mantineia-Antigoneia: (1) ii BC *IG* v (2) 328 (d. Δαμάτριος)

**Ἱερότιμος**

Arkadia:
—Mantineia-Antigoneia: (1) c. 300-221 BC ib. 323. 90 (tessera) (f. Ἱεροκλῆς)
—Tegea: (2) ?265-253 BC Nachtergael, *Les Galates* 2, 35; 10, 60 (Stephanis 1261) (s. Ἱεροκλῆς)

**Ἱερώ**

Argolis:
—Argos: (1) byz. *SEG* xxvi 435; cf. *TMByz* 9 (1985) p. 370 no. 118 (Εἱ-)

**Ἱέρων**

Achaia:
—Aigeira: (1) 156 BC *IG* vii 411, 1, 14, 31 (Petrakos, *Oropos* pp. 187-8 no. 44; *IOrop* 307) (s. Τηλεκλῆς)

Akarnania:
—Astakos: (2) s. iii BC *IG* ix (1)² (2) 438 ([Ἱ]έρων)
—Palairos: (3) iii/ii BC ib. 549

Argolis:
—Argos: (4) c. 366-338 BC Petrakos, *Oropos* pp. 196-7 no. 47, 15 (*IOrop* 520); (5) c. 146-32 BC *BMC Pelop.* p. 145 nos. 114-15 (coins)
—Argos*: (6) ii/i BC *BCH* 33 (1909) p. 176 no. 2, 2 (s. Ἐπικύδης)
—Epidauros: (7) iii/ii BC Peek, *IAEpid* 153. 11; (8) ii BC *IG* iv (1)² 247 (s. Δεξικράτης, f. Διονύσιος); (9) ~ ib. (s. Διονύσιος)

Arkadia:
—Kleitor: (10) a. 212 AD ib. v (2) 369, 28 (f. Αὐρ. Εὔοδος)
—Megalopolis: (11) ii BC ib. 447, 10 ([Ἱ]έρων); (12) ?145 BC ib. 439, 43 (f. Πασικράτης); (13) ~ ib. l. 48 (s. Πασικράτης, Ζευξώ); (14) ii/i BC ib. 443, 8; 444, 6 (*IPArk* 32) (s. Ἀντικράτης)
—Tegea: (15) iv BC *IG* v (2) 31, 7 (s. Σίκων); (16) s. iv BC *SEG* xxxvi 383, 3; (17) f. iii BC *IG* v (2) 42, 3 (s. Ἱερ—); (18) f. ii BC ib. 44, 14 (s. Ἵππων); (19) ii AD ib. 55, 83 (s. Ὀνησιφόρος)
——(Apolloniatai): (20) iv/iii BC ib. 38, 34 (f. Καλλικράτης)
——(Krariotai): (21) m. iii BC ib. 36, 90 (s. Ἵππων)

Elis: (22) 191-146 BC *SNG Cop. Phliasia-Laconia* 350 (coin)

Epiros:
—Kassope: (23) ?c. 215-195 BC *BMC Thessaly* p. 99 no. 14; Franke, *Münz. v. Epirus* p. 80 IX ser. 3 (coin) (Ἱέρω(ν))

Illyria:
—Apollonia: (24) hell. *IApoll* 358 (tile); (25) ~ ib. 359 (tile) (s. Ἀριστήν); (26) ~ ib. 389 (f. —ν); (27) c. 250-50 BC Bakërr Hoard p. 64 no. 68; *Jubice Hoard* p. 98 no. 38-9 (coin) (Ceka 63-4) (money.); (28) ~ Maier 49-50 (coin) (Ceka 129; 134) (pryt.); (29) ii BC *IApoll* 178 (s. Νικήν); (30) ii-i BC ib. 98 (s. Ζώπυρος)
—Bylliones: (31) ii BC *SEG* xxxviii 534 (f. Τράσος)
—Bylliones (Margellic (mod.)): (32) hell. ib. 549
—Epidamnos-Dyrrhachion: (33) hell.-imp. *IDyrrh* 100 (f. Ἀνθίνα); (34) ~ ib. 188 (f. Ἐπικαρπία); (35) ~ ib. 225 (f. Ζώπυρος); (36) ~ ib. 252 (s. Ἀνδρόνικος); (37) ~ ib. 253 (Ἱ. Κρασσίων: s. Λυκίσκος)

Korinthia:
—Korinth: (38) ?254 BC Nachtergael, *Les Galates* 9, 56; cf. Stephanis 400 (f. Ἀρκεσίλαος); (39) imp. *CIL* iii 7276, 1 (Lat. Hiero)

Lakonia:
—Sparta: (40) f. iv BC X., *HG* vi 4. 9; Plu., *Mor.* 397 E (Poralla² 384) ?= (Ἱάρων (8))

S. Italy (Bruttium):
—Lokroi Epizephyrioi:
——(Γαγ.): (41) iv/iii BC De Franciscis 3, 10; 33, 2 (f. Σαμίων)

S. Italy (Campania):
—Pompeii: (42) i BC-i AD *CIL* iv 3937 (Lat. Hiero); (43) i AD ib. x 891 (Castrèn 42. 14) (Lat. Q. Arrius Hiero)

Sicily: (44) iii/ii BC Vandermersch p. 167 (amph.) (or S. Italy: Ἱέρω(ν), Ἱερώ(νυμος)?); (45) i BC-i AD *NScav* 1959, p. 334 no. 22; *Kokalos* 32 (1986) p. 229 no. 45 (tiles) (n. pr.?)
—Akrai: (46) hell.? *SGDI* 3244 (*Akrai* p. 158 no. 12) (f. Νυμφόι); (47) ii-i BC *SGDI* 3246, 38 (*Akrai* pp. 152-3 no. 2; Dubois, *IGDS* 109) (s. Φίλων)
—Kamarina: (48) iii BC Manganaro, *PdelP* forthcoming no. 1, 3, 6 (s. Δάμαρχος)
—Leontinoi: (49) m. v BC *JNG* 33 (1983) p. 14 (coin graffito) (s. Πόλυς)
—Lipara: (50) inc. *NScav* 1929, p. 83 no. 14 ?= (53); (51) hell. *Meligunis-Lipara* 5 p. 69 T. 1944; cf. *SEG* xli 798 ([Ἱ]έρων); (52) ii-i BC *Meligunis-Lipara* 5 p. 149 no. 2145; cf. *SEG* xli 803 ?= (51)
—Syracuse: (53) inc. *JNG* 33 (1983) p. 14 (coin graffito) (-ōν); (54) ii/i BC Cic., *In Verr.* II ii 35 (Lat. Hiero: f. Ἡράκλειος)
—Tauromenion: (55) c. 152 BC *IG* xiv 421 an. 89 (*SGDI* 5219); *IGSI* 4 III (IV), 25 an. 89 (s. Ζωτικός); (56) c. 141 BC *IG* xiv 421 an. 100 (*SGDI* 5219) (Φίλων?—*LGPN*: s. —ρος); (57) ?ii/i BC *IG* xiv 421 D an. 13 (*SGDI* 5219) (f. Εὐκλείδας)

**Ἱερωνᾶς**

Argolis:
—Epidauros: (1) i BC-i AD *IG* iv (1)² 658, 2 (f. Λαδάμα)

Messenia:
—Andania*: (2) s. v AD *SEG* xxix 394; cf. *RE* Supplbd. 3 (-) (fict.?)

**Ἱερωνίς**

S. Italy (Campania):
—Misenum*: (1) imp. *CIL* x 3493 (Lat. Valeria Hieronis)

**Ἱερώνυμος**

Aigina: (1) ?i BC *Alt-Ägina* I (2) p. 44 no. 11, 1 (f. Μηνόδοτος); (2) i BC-i AD ib. p. 45 no. 12, 4 (Ἱερώνυ[μος]); (3) ~ ib. p. 46 no. 21

Argolis:
—Argos: (4) ii/i BC *IG* iv (1) 598, 3 (f. Κλεαινέτα); (5) ii AD *SEG* xvi 253, 15 (s. Αὖλος)
—Epidauros: (6) ii-i BC *IG* ii² 8488 (s. Ἀντισθένης); (7) i-ii AD ib. iv (1)² 523 (f. Φιλωνίδας)

Arkadia:
—Mainalioi: (8) m. iv BC *RE* (3) (and Arkadia Megalopolis: oikist)
—Mantineia-Antigoneia: (9) i/ii AD *IG* v (2) 287 (s. Πίος)
—Megalopolis: (10) c. 210-207 BC ib. iv (1)² 73, 25; *SEG* xxxv 303 (date) (f. Πύρρανθος)
—Phigaleia: (11) imp. ib. xxiii 249

Elis: (12) 401-400 BC *RE* (1)

Peloponnese?: (13) s. iii BC *IG* v (1) 1426, 23 (-ρό-: f. Σιργεύς)

S. Italy (Lucania):
—Hyele-Velia: (14) i AD *SEG* xxxviii 1020. 3; *PdelP* 25 (1970) p. 262 (οὖλις Ἱερωνύμου: doctor)

Sicily:
—Echetla: (15) vi/v BC Manganaro, *PdelP* forthcoming 6 (ἱερό-)
—Solous?: (16) byz.? *IG* xiv 2415. 8 (lead) (Ἱερώνυ(μος))

**Ἱερωσύνα**

Arkadia:
—Paos: (1) s. iv BC *SEG* xxiv 290 (Ἱερωσύνα)

**Ἰεσωρῖνος**

Sicily:
—Syracuse?: (1) iii-v AD *Riv. Arch. Crist.* 18 (1941) p. 236 no. 130 (Ἰεναρῖνος?—Ferrua)

**Ἰηρίας**

S. Italy (Bruttium):
—Lokroi Epizephyrioi:
——(Εὐρ.): (1) iv/iii BC De Franciscis 12, 2 (f. Ἀγησίδαμος)

**Ἰθαιγένης**

Sicily:
—Kamarina: (1) f. v BC Cordano, *Tessere Pubbliche* 10 (Arena, *Iscr. Sic.* II 129 A) (-νēς: f. Σιλανός)

**Ἰθάκη**

S. Italy (Apulia):
—Luceria: (1) imp. *CIL* ix 845 (Lat. Itace)
—Venusia: (2) imp. ib. 530 (Lat. Iunia Ithace)

**Ἴθακος**

S. Italy (Campania):
—Pompeii: (1) i BC-i AD ib. iv 1421 (Lat. Itacus: f. Faustus Neronianus)

**Ἰθμονίκα**

Achaia:
—Pellene: (1) s. iv BC *IG* iv (1)² 121, 10

**Ἰθμονικώ**

Akarnania:
—Lykoniko (mod.): (1) iii BC ib. ix (1)² (2) 381

**Ἰκαδεύς**

Messenia:
—Messene: (1) iv/iii BC ib. v (1) 1425, 1 (f. Τείσων)

**Ἰκάδιος**

Aitolia:
—Thermos*: (1) s. iii BC ib. ix (1)² (1) 60 III, 4 (Εἰ-)

Sicily?: (2) ii-i BC *IGLMP* 33 (Εἰ-: f. Κισσός, Τρύφων)

**Ἰκαδίων**

Argolis:
—Argos: (1) 105 BC *JÖAI* 14 (1911) Beibl. p. 146 no. 4, 12 (f. —όρας)

**Ἴκαρος**
—EPIDAUROS*: (2) c. 370 BC *IG* IV (1)² 102, 80

**Ἴκαρος**
ACHAIA:
—AIGEIRA (HYPERESIA): (1) 688 BC *RE* (6);
Moretti, *Olymp.* 28
S. ITALY (CAMPANIA):
—DIKAIARCHIA-PUTEOLI: (2) 53 AD Camodeca,
*L'Archivio Puteolano* 1 p. 125 no. 5; pp. 229-
30 (Lat. Q. Attius Icarus)
—POMPEII: (3) i BC-i AD *CIL* IV 1093 (Lat.
Ikarus) ?= (7); (4) ~ ib. 2177 (Lat. Ikarus); (5)
~ ib. 2350 (Lat. Icarus); (6) ~ ib. 2369; 2375
(Lat. Ikarus); (7) ~ ib. 3056 (Lat. Ikarus) ?=
(3); (8) ~ ib. 8600 (Lat. Icarus); (9) ~ ib. 8636
(Lat. Icar(us))

**Ἴκελος**
KORINTHIA:
—KORINTH: (1) imp. *JÖAI* 15 (1912) p. 55 no.
27, 11 (*T. Σάλιος Ἴ.*)

**Ἰκεσίη**
S. ITALY (LUCANIA):
—HYELE-VELIA: (1) imp. *PdelP* 21 (1966) p.
336 no. 8 (d. Σώσανδρος)

**Ἰκέσιος**
KORINTHIA:
—KORINTH: (1) f. i AD *Corinth* VIII (3) 231 (Lat.
Hicesius); (2) 127 AD *Hesp.* 39 (1970) p. 80,
10; *Corinth* VIII (3) 223 (—ήιος Ἴ.)
SICILY:
—LIPARA: (3) hell. *BTCGI* 4 p. 15

**Ἰκέτα**
S. ITALY (BRUTTIUM):
—SYBARIS-THOURIOI-COPIAE: (1) vi BC
*AMSMG* NS 13-14 (1973-4) p. 45 (loom-
weight) (Ἱρέ-)

**Ἰκεταΐδας**
KERKYRA: (1) hell. *IG* IX (1) 707

**Ἰκέτας**
ARKADIA:
—ORCHOMENOS: (1) viii/vii BC Paus. iv 17. 2;
viii 5. 13 (or Arkadia Trapezous: s. Ἀριστο-
κράτης, f. Ἀριστοκράτης)
SICILY:
—AKRAGAS: (2) c. 262 BC *IG* IX (1)² (1) 17 A,
93 (s. Θαρρύδαμος)
—HERAKLEIA MINOA?: (3) iii BC *SEG* IX 821 (f.
Ἀπολλόδωρος)
—MELITA: (4) s. ii BC *IGUR* 3, 6 (*IG* XIV 953)
(I f. Ἰκέτας II); (5) ~ *IGUR* 3, 6 (*IG* XIV 953)
(II s. Ἰκέτας I)
—MORGANTINA (NR.): (6) ?iii BC Manganaro,
*PdelP* forthcoming no. 7, 1 (f. Μολοσσός)
—SYRACUSE: (7) iv BC *RE* (4); *FVS* 50; (8) c.
390-339 BC *RE* (2); *IG* IV (1)² 95, 67 (Perl-
man E.2); Perlman p. 46 (date) and Sicily
Leontinoi: s. Νικάνωρ, f. Εὐπόλεμος: tyrant);
(9) 289-278 BC *RE* (3); *Samml. Ludwig* 516
(coin)

**Ἰκέτης**
S. ITALY (CAMPANIA):
—DIKAIARCHIA-PUTEOLI: (1) imp. *CIL* X 2795
(Lat. C. Octavius Hicetes)
—POMPEII: (2) i BC-i AD ib. IV 4244 (Lat. Hiceti
(dat.))

**Ἰκετῖνος**
ARGOLIS:
—ARGOS?: (1) f. i BC *SEG* XXIII 180, 4
(Ἰκε[τῖνος]?: I f. Ἰκετῖνος II: date—Kritzas); (2)
~ ib. l. 4 (II s. Ἰκετῖνος I: date—Kritzas)
—MYKENAI*: (3) hell. ib. XIII 238 b (tiles)

**Ἰκέτις**
MESSENIA:
—MESSENE?: (1) imp. *IG* V (1) 1499 (Ἰκέτι—
lap.)

**Ἴκκος**
ARGOLIS:
—EPIDAUROS: (1) 492 BC Paus. vi 9. 6; cf. Mo-
retti, *Olymp.* 174
S. ITALY (APULIA):
—RUBI: (2) iv BC *SEG* XXXVII 816 a-b (Troisi,
*Epigrafi mobili* 52-3) (Ἴκκω, Ἴκω (gen.)) ?= (3)
S. ITALY (CALABRIA):
—TARAS-TARENTUM: (3) m. v BC *RE* (-); *FVS*
25; Moretti, *Olymp.* 307 (s. Νικολαΐδας: doc-
tor) ?= (2)

**Ἰκμάς**
S. ITALY (CAMPANIA):
—POMPEII: (1) 56 AD *CIL* IV 3340. 22, 1, 6, 10,
[26] (Castrèn 196. 1) (Lat. Histria Ichmas)

**Ἰλαϊκός**
ARGOLIS:
—EPIDAUROS: (1) c. 350-200 BC *SEG* XXVI 452.
3

**Ἰλάρα**
DALMATIA:
—EPETION: (1) imp. *CIL* III 8535 (Lat. Ilara)
EPIROS:
—NIKOPOLIS: (2) imp.? *SEG* XXXIX 540
ILLYRIA:
—APOLLONIA: (3) ii AD *IApoll* 235 (Ἰλάρ[α]?)
KORINTHIA:
—KORINTH: (4) m. ii AD *Corinth* VIII (3) 287, 3
(Lat. Calliana Hilara: m. *M. Αἴνιος Ὀνησιφό-
ρος*)
LAKONIA:
—SPARTA: (5) m. ii AD *IG* V (1) 490, 10 (Brad-
ford (-)) (Ἰλά[ρ]α: d. Βέλλων, m. Βέλλων)
S. ITALY (APULIA):
—CANUSIUM: (6) i AD *Epig. Rom. di Canosa* 32
(*CIL* IX 336) (Lat. –dia Hilara: freed.)
—CANUSIUM*: (7) imp. *Epig. Rom. di Canosa*
187 (Lat. Tampia Hilara: freed.)
—LARINUM: (8) imp. *CIL* IX 6250 (Lat. Pedia
Hilara)
—TEANUM APULUM*: (9) imp. *Teanum Apulum*
p. 84 no. 27 (*CIL* IX 718) (Lat. Pilia Hilara:
freed.)
—VENUSIA*: (10) imp. ib. 589 (Lat. Tullia Hi-
lara: freed.)
S. ITALY (CALABRIA):
—BRENTESION-BRUNDISIUM*: (11) i BC ib. I²
1699 (IX 171) (Lat. Pomponia Hilara: freed.)
S. ITALY (CAMPANIA):
—DIKAIARCHIA-PUTEOLI: (12) imp. ib. X 2158
(Lat. Hilara); (13) ~ ib. 2725 (Lat. Medullina
Hilara: m. Medullina Flora); (14) ~ *NScav*
1888, p. 197 no. 1 (Lat. Hilara); (15) ~ ib.
1924, p. 85 (Lat. Aulia Hilara)
—DIKAIARCHIA-PUTEOLI*: (16) imp. *CIL* X
2457; *Puteoli* 11 (1987) p. 50 (name) (Lat. Fo-
lia Hila(ra): freed.); (17) ~ *CIL* X 2733 (Lat.
Messia Hilara: d. C. Messius Primigenius:
freed.); (18) ~ ib. 2831 (Lat. Pavillia Hilara:
freed.)
—MISENUM*: (19) ?i-ii AD ib. 3351 (Lat. Iulia
Hilara)
—POMPEII*: (20) m. i AD *Impegno per Pom-
peii* 22 EN (Castrèn 8. 3) (Lat. Aebia Hilara:
freed.)
S. ITALY (LUCANIA):
—GRUMENTUM: (21) imp. *CIL* X 8094 (Lat. Hi-
lara: m. Ἡλίων)
SICILY:
—LILYBAION: (22) ?ii AD ib. 7242 (Lat. Aelia
Hilara: d. Εὐτύχης)
—LIPARA: (23) imp. *IG* XIV 387 (Libertini, *Isole
Eolie* p. 219 no. 6) (Κλωδία Ἴ.)

**Ἰλαρία**
AITOLIA:
—KALLION/KALLIPOLIS: (1) byz. *BCH* 98
(1974) p. 635 (m. Ἀλέξανδρος)
EPIROS:
—BOUTHROTOS (PRASAIBOI): (2) a. 163 BC
*IBouthrot* 28, 13 (*SEG* XXXVIII 486) (?d. Νι-
κάνωρ); (3) ~ *IBouthrot* 32, 9 (*SEG* XXXVIII
491)
ILLYRIA:
—EPIDAMNOS-DYRRHACHION: (4) hell.-imp.
*IDyrrh* 254
S. ITALY (APULIA):
—LUCERIA: (5) imp. *CIL* IX 892 (Lat. Hilaria)

**Ἰλαριανός**
LAKONIA:
—SPARTA: (1) ii AD *IG* IV (1)² 511 (Bradford
(-)) (Σέξ. Πομπ. Ἴ.: s. Ἄλκαστος)
S. ITALY (APULIA):
—CANUSIUM: (2) v-vi AD *Puglia Paleocrist.
Altomed.* 4 p. 135 (Lat. Ilaria[nus]: Jew)
S. ITALY (CALABRIA):
—VALETIUM: (3) ii-iii AD *CIL* IX 24 with Add.
p. 652 (Susini, *Fonti Salento* p. 164 no. 129)
(Lat. P. Tutorius Hilarianus: f. Ἑρμητιανός)
S. ITALY (CAMPANIA):
—ATELLA: (4) imp. *Mem. Accad. Arch. Napoli*
2 (1913) pp. 151-75 (Lat. L. Munatius Hila-
rianus)
—DIKAIARCHIA-PUTEOLI: (5) imp. *NScav*
1901, p. 19 (Lat. C. Cornelius Hilarianus)
—DIKAIARCHIA-PUTEOLI*: (6) ?i-ii AD *CIL* X
2557, 4 (Lat. Iulius Hilarianus: ?s. Iulia
Primigenia: freed.)
—NEAPOLIS: (7) imp. *Eph. Ep.* VIII 344; cf.
Leiwo p. 156 no. 126 (Lat. Munatius Hila-
rianus) ?= (8); (8) 194 AD *INap* 44 col. I, 7,
21; col. II, 4, 7 (Λ. Μουνάτιος Ἴ.: f. Μάριος
Οὖῆρος) ?= (7)
S. ITALY (LUCANIA):
—MARSICI VETERES: (9) imp. *CIL* X 197 (Lat.
Hilarianus)

**Ἰλαρῖνος**
SICILY:
—SYRACUSE: (1) iii-v AD *IG* XIV 109 (Strazzulla
227; Wessel 1155); cf. Ferrua, *NG* 290 (Εἰ-,
Εὔνομος—*IG*)

**Ἰλαρίων**
DALMATIA:
—PHAROS: (1) imp. *CIL* III 3107 (Lat. Hilario)
ILLYRIA:
—APOLLONIA: (2) imp. *IApoll* 99
S. ITALY (APULIA):
—CANUSIUM: (3) imp. *Epig. Rom. di Canosa* 200
(*CIL* IX 403) (Lat. Q. Martius Hilario)
S. ITALY (BRUTTIUM):
—SYBARIS-THOURIOI-COPIAE*: (4) imp.
*NScav* 1925, p. 323 (Lat. L. Marcius Hilario:
freed.)
S. ITALY (CAMPANIA): (5) imp. *Misc. Gr. Rom.*
8 p. 521 no. 12 (vase) (Lat. Hilario); (6) m.
i AD *CIL* X 8047. 3; *Atti Conv. Taranto* 32
(1992) p. 738 = *Boll. Arch.* 19-21 (1993) p.
127 (pithoi) (Lat. A. Appuleius Hilario)
—DIKAIARCHIA-PUTEOLI: (7) imp. *CIL* X 1963
(Lat. Hilario); (8) ~ *NScav* 1889, p. 228 (Lat.
Hilarion Pammusus)
—DIKAIARCHIA-PUTEOLI*: (9) ?ii/iii AD *Eph.
Ep.* VIII 358 (Lat. M. Aurelius Hilario: imp.
freed.)
—POMPEII: (10) c. 51-62 AD *CIL* IV 3340. 93, 5;
97, 5; 98, 5 (Castrèn 150. 1) (Lat. L. Deccius
Hilarion); (11) 70-79 AD *CIL* IV 913; Mou-
ritsen p. 112 (date) (Lat. Hilario)
SICILY:
—SYRACUSE: (12) imp. *CIL* X 7130. 22 (Lat.
Hilario); (13) iii-v AD *SEG* XV 580; (14) ~
*IGLMP* 148; cf. Ferrua, *NG* 311 (Εἰ-); (15)
~ *Nuovo Didask.* 4 (1950) p. 56 no. 3 + Fer-
rua, *NG* 99 ([Εἰλ]αρίων—Ferrua)

**Ἰλαροκλῆς**
LAKONIA:
—SPARTA: (**1**) ii AD *IG* v (1) 159, 9 (Bradford (-))

**Ἴλαρον**
KORINTHIA:
—SIKYON: (**1**) ii BC *IG* II² 10304 (Skalet 155) (d. Εὔανδρος)

**Ἴλαρος**
ACHAIA:
—DYME*: (**1**) ii-iii AD *GVI* 1091, 5 (Raffeiner, *Sklaven* 19) (imp. slave)
AIGINA: (**2**) ?f. iii AD *Alt-Ägina* 1 (2) p. 49 no. 44 (I s. Ἀγαπᾶς, f. Αὐρ. Ἴλαρος II); (**3**) ~ ib. (Αὐρ. Ἴ.: II s. Ἴλαρος I)
ARGOLIS:
—ARGOS: (**4**) imp. *Mnem.* NS 47 (1919) p. 166 no. 13 (Π. Πάκκιος Ἴ.)
—EPIDAUROS: (**5**) ?iv-iii BC Peek, *NIEpid* 13, 12 (Perlman E.15) (Ἴλαρος); (**6**) 184 AD *IG* IV (1)² 393, 3 (f. Ἀρχιμήδης); (**7**) 184-207 AD ib. l. 6; 400, 3 (s. Ἀρχιμήδης); (**8**) 207 AD ib. l. 7 (s. Εὔτυχος)
ARKADIA:
—TEGEA: (**9**) 165 AD ib. v (2) 50, 53 (f. Στράτυλλος); (**10**) ~ ib. l. 61 (Μέμμιος Ἴ.)
ELIS:
—OLYMPIA*: (**11**) 28-24 BC *IvOl* 64, 29 (?s. Ἀντίοχος: Δου.)
EPIROS:
—NIKOPOLIS: (**12**) imp. *SEG* XXXIX 534 (s. Ἑρμεία); (**13**) ~ ib. (s. Ἑρμεία)
ILLYRIA:
—APOLLONIA: (**14**) imp. *IApoll* 100
KORINTHIA:
—KORINTH: (**15**) iv/v AD *Lampes d'Argos* 438-441; *Ag.* VII p. 98 no. 321 (lamps) (Ναρος—*Ag.*)
LAKONIA:
—SPARTA: (**16**) ii AD *IG* v (1) 189, 3 (Bradford (2)) (f. —ων); (**17**) a. 212 AD *IG* v (1) 597, 3 (Bradford (1)) (f. Αὐρ. Σωκλήδεια)
MESSENIA:
—ABIA: (**18**) ii AD *GVI* 1555 (s. Ἀρχιτέλης, Ἐλπίς)
S. ITALY (APULIA):
—CANUSIUM*: (**19**) i AD *Epig. Rom. di Canosa* 89 (Lat. A. Baebius Hilarus: freed.); (**20**) ~ ib. 121 (*CIL* IX 373) (Lat. P. Dasimius Hilarus: freed.)
—TEANUM APULUM*: (**21**) i BC *Teanum Apulum* p. 65 no. 11 (Lat. Q. Avillius Hilarus: freed.)
—VENUSIA*: (**22**) imp. *Epigraphica* 35 (1973) p. 145 no. 6 (Lat. M. Cuperius Hilarus: freed.); (**23**) i AD *Museo di Venosa* p. 209 no. 8 (Lat. M. Creperius Hilarus: freed.)
S. ITALY (APULIA)?: (**24**) imp. *Epig. Rom. di Canosa* Instr. 28 (amph.) (Lat. Hilarus)
S. ITALY (BRUTTIUM):
—RHEGION: (**25**) inc. *NScav* 1888, p. 593 no. 8 (tile) (Lat. Hilarus)
S. ITALY (CALABRIA):
—BRENTESION-BRUNDISIUM*: (**26**) iii AD *Museo Ribezzo* 7 (1974) p. 127 (Lat. [Pu]blic[ius] Hil[arus]: freed.?)
—TARAS-TARENTUM: (**27**) imp. *NScav* 1894, p. 67 no. 43 (Lat. C. Scaevius Hilarus)
S. ITALY (CAMPANIA): (**28**) i AD *CIL* X 8047. 13 (pithos) (Lat. M. Paccius Hilarus)
—DIKAIARCHIA-PUTEOLI: (**29**) imp. ib. 2521 (Lat. Hilarus: I f. Ἴλαρος II); (**30**) ~ ib. (Lat. Hilarus: II s. Ἴλαρος I, Ποιμενία); (**31**) ~ ib. 2617 (Lat. M. Iunius Hilarus: s. Ἀττικός, Πρέπουσα); (**32**) ~ *RAAN* 42 (1967) pp. 4-6 (Lat. Q. Aemilius Hilarus)
—DIKAIARCHIA-PUTEOLI*: (**33**) imp. *CIL* X 2669 (Lat. P. Carpinarius Hilarus: freed.); (**34**) ~ ib. 2777 (Lat. L. Maecius Hilarus: freed.); (**35**) i AD ib. 1582 (Lat. L. Safinius

Hilarus: freed.); (**36**) ?i-ii AD ib. 2557, 1 (Lat. C. Iulius Hilarus: f. Iulia Primigenia: freed.)
—HERCULANEUM: (**37**) i BC-i AD ib. IV 10609 (Lat. [H]ila(r)u[s])
—HERCULANEUM*: (**38**) i BC-i AD ib. X 1403 g I, 32 (Lat. A. Vibidius Hilarus: freed.)
—KYME: (**39**) f. i AD *Arch. Class.* 34 (1982) pp. 190-5 (Lat. N. Naevius Hilarus); (**40**) 251 AD *CIL* X 3699 I, 20 (Lat. L. Modestius Hilarus); (**41**) ~ ib. 3699 II, 37 (Lat. M. Plautius Hilarus)
—NEAPOLIS: (**42**) iii-iv AD *IG* XIV 826. 20 (*INap* 230); (**43**) ~ *IG* XIV 826. 21 (*INap* 231)
—POMPEII: (**44**) i BC-i AD *CIL* IV 5392 (Lat. Hilarus); (**45**) ~ ib. 10237-8 (Lat. Hilarus); (**46**) 48 BC ib. I² 937 (X 8069. 1) (Lat. Hilarus); (**47**) 37 BC ib. IV 2437 (Castrèn 205. 14) (Lat. C. Iulius Hilarus); (**48**) 70-79 AD *CIL* IV 3521; Mouritsen p. 111 (date) (Lat. Hilarus)
—POMPEII*: (**49**) i BC-i AD *CIL* IV 3864 (Lat. Q. Decius Hilarus: freed.); (**50**) ~ *NScav* 1961, p. 200 no. 5 (Lat. N. Mettius Hilarus: freed.); (**51**) i AD *CIL* X 8042. 74 (tiles) (Lat. M. Minicius Hilarus)
—SALERNUM*: (**52**) ?i AD *IItal* I (1) 238 I, 5 (*CIL* X 557) (Lat. L. Appuleius Hilarus: freed.); (**53**) ~ *IItal* I (1) 238 II, 11 (*CIL* X 557) (Lat. L. Appuleius Hilarus: freed.); (**54**) ~ *IItal* I (1) 238 III, 4 (*CIL* X 557) (Lat. L. Appuleius Hilarus: freed.); (**55**) ~ *IItal* I (1) 238 III, 7 (*CIL* X 557) (Lat. L. Appuleius Hilarus: freed.); (**56**) ~ *IItal* I (1) 238 III, 8 (*CIL* X 557) (Lat. L. Appuleius Hilarus: freed.)
—STABIAE: (**57**) imp. ib. 8059. 196 (seal) (Lat. Hilarus); (**58**) ~ *RAAN* 19 (1938-9) p. 85 (Lat. -us Hilarus)
—SURRENTUM: (**59**) imp. *St. Rom.* 2 (1914) p. 346 no. 9 = *NScav* 1928, p. 211 no. 19 (Lat. Hilarus: s. Πλόκαμος)
S. ITALY (LUCANIA):
—ATINA LUCANA: (**60**) imp. *IItal* III (1) 170 (*CIL* X 369) (Lat. Hilarus: I f. Ἴλαρος II); (**61**) ~ *IItal* III (1) 170 (*CIL* X 369) (Lat. M. Valerius Hilarus: II s. Ἴλαρος I)
—GRUMENTUM*: (**62**) imp. ib. 245 (Lat. M. Artorius Hilarus: freed.)
—POSEIDONIA-PAESTUM: (**63**) imp. Mello-Voza 115 (Lat. Hilarus); (**64**) ~ ib. 167 (Lat. Hilarus)
—TRICARICO (MOD.): (**65**) imp. *CIL* X 126 (Lat. M. Annius Hilarus)
SICILY: (**66**) imp. ib. 8059. 195 (seal) (Lat. Hilarus)
—KAMARINA (NR.): (**67**) iii-v AD *Riv. Arch. Crist.* 21 (1944-5) p. 71
—THERMAI HIMERAIAI: (**68**) imp. *ILat. Term. Imer.* 147 (Lat. P. Stat. Hil(arus))

**Ἴλαρχος**
LAKONIA:
—SPARTA: (**1**) 420 BC X., *HG* ii 3. 10 (Poralla² 385)

**Ἰλαρώ**
DALMATIA:
—EPETION: (**1**) imp. *CIL* III 8534 (Lat. Hilaro: m. Φυσκίων)

**Ἴλας**
S. ITALY (BRUTTIUM):
—LOKROI EPIZEPHYRIOI: (**1**) 476 BC Pi., *O.* x, 17

**Ἰλάσιος**
SICILY:
—SYRACUSE: (**1**) iii-v AD Strazzulla 345 (Wessel 591); cf. Ferrua, *NG* 127 (Ἰλά(ρ)ιος?—Strazzulla)

**Ἰλιάδη**
ILLYRIA:
—EPIDAMNOS-DYRRHACHION: (**1**) hell.-imp. *IDyrrh* 177 (Εἰ-: d. Κέρδων)

**Ἰλιακός**
S. ITALY (CAMPANIA):
—POMPEII: (**1**) c. 51-62 AD *CIL* IV 3340. 65, 15; 78, 7 (Castrèn 454. 17) (Lat. A. Vettius Iliacus)

**Ἱμέρα**
SICILY: (**1**) ?v/iv BC Manganaro, *QUCC* forthcoming no. 72 (ring) (n. pr.?)

**Ἱμεραῖος**
SICILY:
—HALAISA*: (**1**) i/ii AD *Kokalos* 17 (1971) p. 16 no. 6 (Lat. Q. Caecilius Hime[raeus]?: freed.)
—KAMARINA: (**2**) f. v BC Cordano, *Tessere Pubbliche* 132 (ῑμ-: f. Σωσίας)
—MORGANTINA (NR.): (**3**) ?iii BC Manganaro, *PdelP* forthcoming no. 7, 2
—THERMAI HIMERAIAI: (**4**) ?i AD *CIL* X 7398 (*ILat. Term. Imer.* 90) (Lat. Domitius Himeraeus)

**Ἵμερος**
S. ITALY (CAMPANIA):
—DIKAIARCHIA-PUTEOLI: (**1**) ?i-ii AD *CIL* X 3036, 4; cf. *Puteoli* 11 (1987) p. 57 (Lat. T. Claudius Hime[r])
—HERCULANEUM: (**2**) i BC-i AD *CIL* IV 10639 (Lat. Himme(r))
—HERCULANEUM*: (**3**) i BC-i AD ib. X 1403 g III, 49 (Lat. Q. Novius Himer: freed.)
—POMPEII: (**4**) i BC-i AD ib. IV 1682 (Lat. Himer); (**5**) ~ ib. 3820 (Lat. Himer)

**Ἱμερώ**
KORINTHIA:
—KORINTH: (**1**) c. 550 BC Amyx Gr 15. 2 (vase) (Lorber 153) (ῑμερόῑ: het.?/fict.?)

**Ἰμίλχων**
SICILY:
—LILYBAION: (**1**) ii BC *IG* XIV 279; *Semitica* 26 (1976) pp. 93 ff. (name) (f. Ἰμύλχ Ἰνίβαλος Χλῶρος)

**Ἰμίων**
S. ITALY (CALABRIA):
—BRENTESION-BRUNDISIUM: (**1**) imp. *CIL* IX 79 (Lat. M. Arruntius Imio)

**Ἰμπεδέας**
ARKADIA:
—MANTINEIA-ANTIGONEIA: (**1**) c. 425-385 BC *IG* v (2) 323. 6 (tessera) ([Ἰ]μπεδέας: s. —εσίας)
——(Epalea): (**2**) m. iv BC ib. 271, 2 (f. Εὔδοξος)

**Ἰμπεδις**
ARKADIA:
—TEGEA: (**1**) s. iii BC ib. 116, 3 (s. Ἀντάγορος)

**Ἰμπεδοκλῆς**
ARKADIA:
—TEGEA:
——(Apolloniatai): (**1**) f. iii BC ib. 36, 51 (s. Θεότιμος)

**Ἰμπεδόκριτος**
ARKADIA:
—TEGEA:
——(Hippothoitai): (**1**) iii BC ib. 40, 21 (Ἰμπε[δό]κριτος: s. Πεδάριτος)

**Ἰμύλχ**
SICILY:
—LILYBAION: (**1**) ii BC ib. XIV 279; *Semitica* 26 (1976) pp. 93 ff. (name) (Ἰ. Ἰνίβαλος Χλῶρος: s. Ἰμίλχων)

## Ἰναίσιμος
ARKADIA:
—TEGEA: (1) v BC *IG* v (2) 105 (Lazzarini 293) ([Ἰ]ναίσιμος); (2) f. ii BC *IG* v (2) 44, 9 (Ἰναίσιμ[ος]: f. Σῖμος)
——(Apolloniatai): (3) iv/iii BC ib. 38, 37 (f. Ξενόκριτος)

## Ἰναχίδας
ARGOLIS:
—ARGOS: (1) ii/i BC *SEG* XXVIII 1246, 31 (s. Σώανδρος)

## Ἰνίβαλος
SICILY:
—LILYBAION: (1) ii BC *IG* XIV 279; *Semitica* 26 (1976) pp. 93 ff. (name) (Ἰμύλχ Ἰ. Χλῶρος: s. Ἰμίλχων)

## Ἰνυκος
SICILY:
—SELINOUS: (1) vi/v BC Manganaro, *PdelP* forthcoming no. 18, 11 (ἵνυγος: f. Ξένων)

## Ἰνων
EPIROS:
—MOLOSSOI: (1) c. 343-330 BC Cabanes, *L'Épire* p. 588 no. 74, 5, 9?, 11 (*SEG* XXVI 700) (Σίνων—l. 9: f. Ἀμύνανδρος, Μέγας, Φειδέτα)

## Ἰνωπός
S. ITALY (CAMPANIA):
—SALERNUM*: (1) s. i AD *IItal* I (1) 133 (*CIL* X 582; Sinn, *Stadtröm. Marmorurnen* 194) (Lat. Ti. Claudius Inopus: imp. freed.)

## Ἰξίων
KORINTHIA:
—KORINTH: (1) her. *RE* (3) (s. Ἀλήτης, f. Ἀγέλας: king)

## Ἰόβακχος
SICILY:
—SYRACUSE: (1) imp. *CIL* X 7152 (Lat. Iobacchus)

## Ἰοκάδης
ARKADIA:
—MEGALOPOLIS: (1) 359 BC *CID* II 5 I, 44 (Ἰοκάδη[s])

## Ἰοκράτης
LAKONIA:
—SPARTA: (1) iii BC *SEG* XL 348 B, 4

## Ἰολαΐδας
ARGOLIS:
—ARGOS: (1) 224 BC Moretti, *Olymp.* 578

## Ἰόλαος
AITOLIA:
—KALYDON: (1) 129 BC *IG* IX (1)² (1) 137, 91 (f. Λάμιος)
MESSENIA:
—ASINE: (2) i BC-i AD *SEG* XI 986 (Γεγάνιος Ἰόλα[ος])

## Ἰόλη
ARKADIA:
—MANTINEIA-ANTIGONEIA: (1) ?ii AD *IG* v (2) 327, 5 (*GVI* 1066) (d. Πρῖμος)
S. ITALY (CAMPANIA):
—POMPEII: (2) i BC-i AD *CIL* IV 8685 (Lat. Iole—Solin); (3) ~ ib. 9969 (Lat. Iole)

## Ἰόλλη
S. ITALY (CALABRIA):
—BRENTESION-BRUNDISIUM: (1) imp. *NScav* 1892, p. 352 i = *Epigraphica* 25 (1963) p. 38 no. 12 (Lat. Iolle); (2) ~ *NScav* 1893, p. 443 no. 3 (Lat. –ia Iolle)

## Ἰόνιος
DALMATIA:
—ISSA: (1) s. iv BC Brunšmid p. 61 nos. 5-6 (coins)
SICILY:
—KATANE: (2) imp. *CIL* X 7068; *Sic. Gymn.* 14 (1961) p. 195 (Lat. T. Flavius Ionius)
—ZANKLE-MESSANA*: (3) imp. *CIL* X 8053. 98 (lamp) (Lat. Ionius)

## Ἰουβεντιανός
KORINTHIA:
—KORINTH: (1) imp. *Corinth* VIII (3) 201; (2) ii AD *SEG* XVII 131

## Ἰουβῖνος
SICILY:
—SYRACUSE: (1) iii-v AD *IG* XIV 125 (Strazzulla 63; Wessel 1382); (2) ~ Strazzulla 122 (*ASSicilia* 1938-9, p. 31; Ferrua, *NG* 362)

## Ἰούδας
SICILY:
—GELA-PHINTIAS (NR.): (1) ?iv AD *JIWE* I 158 ([Ἰ]ούδας Σαββατίας: Jew)
—PHILOSOPHIANA: (2) byz. *Riv. Arch. Crist.* 40 (1964) p. 177 (Ἰ. Σαβάνας)

## Ἰουκοῦνδα
ILLYRIA:
—APOLLONIA*: (1) imp. *IApoll* 29 (Ἰοκόν-: d. Τευταία)

## Ἰουλία
EPIROS:
—NIKOPOLIS: (1) imp. *SEG* XLII 545
MESSENIA:
—KORONE: (2) i AD *IG* v (1) 1400
S. ITALY (CAMPANIA):
—NEAPOLIS: (3) iii-iv AD ib. XIV 826. 22 (*INap* 232)

## Ἰουλιανή
SICILY:
—SYRACUSE: (1) iii-v AD *IG* XIV 127 (Strazzulla 64); cf. *ASSicilia* 1938-9, p. 32

## Ἰουλιανός
ARKADIA:
—TEGEA: (1) ii-iii AD *IG* v (2) 179, 4 (Εἰ-)
ELIS: (2) 185-189 AD *IvOl* 104, 12, 27 (?f. Δάμων); (3) 241 AD ib. 118, 9 (Ἰουλιαν[ός])
KORINTHIA:
—KORINTH: (4) byz. *Corinth* VIII (3) 534; cf. *TMByz* 9 (1985) p. 365 no. 55; (5) ~ *Corinth* VIII (3) 587; cf. *TMByz* 9 (1985) p. 366 no. 69
S. ITALY (BRUTTIUM):
—RHEGION: (6) imp. *IG* XIV 618, 6
S. ITALY (CAMPANIA):
—DIKAIARCHIA-PUTEOLI: (7) imp. *SEG* XXXII 1031 ([Ἰ]ουλιανός)
SICILY: (8) iv AD *IGUR* 60 (*IG* XIV 1078 a) (Ἰουλι(α)νός)
—KATANE: (9) iii-v AD ib. 539 (Wessel 1209)
—SYRACUSE: (10) iii-v AD *IG* XIV 126 (Strazzulla 65); cf. Ferrua, *NG* 316 (Ἰουλι(α)νός, Ἰουλῖνος—Ferrua); (11) ~ *Riv. Arch. Crist.* 36 (1960) p. 27 no. 19; (12) ~ Ferrua, *NG* 202 (-λει-)

## Ἰούλιος
ARKADIA:
—TEGEA: (1) ii-iii AD *EILakArk* 9, 4 (?s. Ἀργεία)
LAKONIA:
—SPARTA: (2) f. ii AD *IG* v (1) 162, 5 (Bradford (2)) (f. Ἰσόδαμος); (3) c. 150-160 AD *SEG* XXX 410, 12 (Bradford (5)) (I f. Ἰούλιος II); (4) ~ *SEG* XXX 410, 12 (Bradford (4)) (II s. Ἰούλιος I)
S. ITALY (CAMPANIA):
—MISENUM: (5) imp. *IG* XIV 876

## Ἰούλις
SICILY:
—SYRACUSE: (6) iii-v AD ib. 128 (Strazzulla 66)

## Ἰούλις
ARKADIA:
—TEGEA: (1) ii AD *IG* v (2) 55, 31 (I f. Ἰούλις II); (2) ~ ib. l. 31 (II s. Ἰούλις I)
SICILY:
—SYRACUSE: (3) iii-v AD *Rend. Pont.* 22 (1946-7) p. 232 (Ἰού[λις])

## Ἰούλιττα
ARGOLIS:
—ARGOS: (1) ii AD *SEG* XLI 285 I, 4; *BCH* 115 (1991) p. 322 (name)
ARKADIA:
—MEGALOPOLIS: (2) ii AD *IG* v (2) 463; 464 (Κλ. Ἰ.: m. Τάδιος Σωτήριχος, Τάδιος Τιμοκράτης)

## Ἰουλίων
SICILY:
—SYRACUSE: (1) iii-v AD *NScav* 1893, p. 282 no. 17 (Wessel 760)

## Ἰούνιος
ARKADIA:
—MANTINEIA-ANTIGONEIA: (1) ii-iii AD *IG* v (2) 275, 10 (f. Ἑρμείας)
LAKONIA:
—SPARTA: (2) ii AD ib. v (1) 1369, 2 (Bradford (1)) (s. Χαριτέλης, Τιμάς); (3) ~ *IG* v (1) 1369, 9 (Bradford (2)) (f. Τιμάς)

## Ἰοῦστα
S. ITALY (APULIA):
—VENUSIA: (1) v AD *JIWE* I 69 (*CIJ* I 583) (Jew)
S. ITALY (CAMPANIA):
—NEAPOLIS: (2) iii-iv AD *IG* XIV 826. 23 (*INap* 233)
SICILY:
—SYRACUSE: (3) iii-v AD Barreca 399

## Ἰουστῖνος
SICILY:
—AKRAI: (1) iii-v AD *Akrai* p. 167 no. 40 (*SEG* XIV 587) (Ἰωάννης Ἰοστῖνος)

## Ἰοῦστος
SICILY:
—KATANE: (1) iii-v AD *IG* XIV 555 + Ferrua, *NG* 447 ([Ἰο]ῦστος); (2) ?iii-v AD *SEG* XXVI 1173 (s. Ἀμάχιος)
—SYRACUSE: (3) iii-v AD *IG* XIV 33 (Strazzulla 139); cf. *Riv. Arch. Crist.* 18 (1941) p. 230 no. 123
—THERMAI HIMERAIAI: (4) imp. *IGLMP* 121 (s. Νίγρος)

## Ἱππαγόρας
SICILY:
—LEONTINOI: (1) ?f. v BC Paus. v 22. 7
SICILY?: (2) ?iii BC *RE* (2); *FGrH* 743

## Ἱππαγρέτας
LAKONIA:
—SPARTA: (1) 425 BC Th. iv 38. 1 (Poralla² 386)

## Ἵππαινος
KEPHALLENIA:
—PALE: (1) ?iv BC *IG* I² 1070. 2

## Ἱππαῖος
ARKADIA:
—MANTINEIA-ANTIGONEIA: (1) c. 300-221 BC ib. v (2) 323. 23 (tessera) (f. Ἀλκίμαχος)
ELIS: (2) ?f. iii BC *HE* 1226 (f. Κίμων)

## Ἵππακος
ARKADIA:
—KYNAITHA: (1) ?253 BC Nachtergael, *Les Galates* 10, 31; cf. Stephanis 1707 (f. Μικύλος)

## Ἱππάλκιμος

KORINTHIA:
—KORINTH: (1) c. 570-550 BC Amyx 66. 20 (vase) (Lorber 122) (ἱππάλρμος, ἱππάλρ(ι)μος: her.)

## Ἵππανθος

ILLYRIA:
—APOLLONIA: (1) c. 250-50 BC *Bakërr Hoard* p. 64 no. 68; *Jubice Hoard* p. 98 nos. 38-9 (coin) (Ceka 63-4) (pryt.); (2) 208 BC *IMM* 45, 48 (*IApoll* 315) (Ἰ.: ?s. Φ—)

## Ἱππαρῖνος

S. ITALY (LUCANIA):
—HERAKLEIA: (1) v-iv BC Wehrli, *Schule Arist.* ix Phainias fr. 16; cf. Plu., *Mor.* 770 C (or S. Italy (Lucania) Metapontion)
SICILY:
—KAMARINA: (2) f. v BC Cordano, *Tessere Pubbliche* 62 (ἱ[ππ]αρῖνος: s. —σαῖος)
—SYRACUSE: (3) v/iv BC *RE* (1); *IG* IV (1)² 95, 39 (Perlman E.2); *FGrH* 84 F 31 (f. Δίων, Μεγακλῆς, Εὐρυμένης, Ἀριστομάχα); (4) c. 385-351 BC *RE* (2); cf. Beloch, *GG* III (2) pp. 102-7 (s. Διονύσιος, Ἀριστομάχα); (5) m. iv BC *RE* (3) (Ἱππορῖνος—Plu. mss., Ἵππαρις—Schol. Aristeid. iii p. 629, Ἱππαρίων—Polyaen.: s. Δίων, Ἀρέτα)

## Ἵππαρμος

ARGOLIS:
—PHLEIOUS: (1) 336-334 BC *CID* II 26, 3; 75 II, 50; 76 II, 25; 79 A I, 16

## Ἱππαρχία

LAKONIA:
—SPARTA: (1) i BC *SEG* II 157 (Bradford (2))

## Ἱππαρχίδας

MESSENIA:
—MESSENE: (1) iii BC *SEG* XXIII 209, 14

## Ἱππαρχίδης

S. ITALY (BRUTTIUM):
—RHEGION: (1) iv BC Iamb., *VP* 267 (*FVS* I p. 447)

## Ἵππαρχος

ACHAIA:
—PELLENE: (1) m. iii BC *IG* IV (1)² 96, 49 (Perlman E.3); Perlman p. 63 f. (date) (Ἵπ[π]αρχος)
AITOLIA: (2) c. 225-200 BC *FD* III (4) 366, 2
AITOLIA?: (3) iii BC *SEG* XXV 622 (bullet)
AKARNANIA:
—ASTAKOS: (4) ii BC *IG* IX (1)² (2) 435, 13 (f. Νίκων)
AKARNANIA?: (5) ii BC Unp. (Agrinion Mus.) (f. Τιμόξενος)
ARGOLIS:
—TROIZEN: (6) ?287 BC *IG* IV (1) 750, 14 (Ἵππα[ρχος])
ARKADIA: (7) 308 BC ib. V (2) 550, 2
—PALLANTION: (8) 191-146 BC *BMC Pelop.* p. 14 no. 167 (coin)
—TEGEA: (9) c. 240-229 BC *IG* V (2) 11, 18
——(Athaneatai): (10) f. iii BC ib. 36, 76 (Ἵπ[π]αρχος: s. Διόφαντος)
ELIS: (11) ii BC *SEG* XXXIII 329; XXXVII 361 (date) (f. Ἀσάμων)
EPIROS:
—KASSOPE: (12) iv/iii BC ib. XXXIV 589 (s. Νικίας, f. Αἰσχρίας); (13) c. 130 BC Dakaris, *Kassope* p. 25 (*SEG* XXXVI 555); cf. *SEG* XLI 541 (s. Φιλόξενος)
—NIKOPOLIS: (14) imp. *CIG* 1812-13 (Sarikakis 8) (Κο. Ἀλβίδιος Ἰ.: f. Ἀλ. Εὐφροσύνα); (15) ~ *AEMÖ* 15 (1892) p. 127 no. 1 (Sarikakis 56) (f. Ἐπίκτησις); (16) s. i AD *SEG* XVIII 198, 3; *FD* III (1) 537, 5 (Sarikakis 75) (Τιβ. Κλ. Ἰ.)

ILLYRIA:
—AMANTIA: (17) hell.? *BUST* 1958 (2), p. 107 (*BE* 1967, no. 338)
—APOLLONIA: (18) imp.? *IApoll* 190; cf. *SEG* XXXVII 533 (s. Ποδᾶς)
KERKYRA: (19) s. iii BC Unp. (*IG* arch.)
KORINTHIA:
—KORINTH: (20) c. 225-200 BC *IG* VII 309, 1, 4 (*IOrop* 85) (s. Μέμνων); (21) m. i BC *RE* (9) (Lat. M. Antonius Hipparchus: s. Θεόφιλος: freed.) ?= (22); (22) 10-1 BC Amandry pp. 142-8; *RPC* 1 pp. 251-2 nos. 1134-7 (coin) (Lat. M. Ant. Hipparchus) ?= (21)
LAKONIA:
—SPARTA: (23) s. i BC *IG* V (1) 95, 13 (Bradford (8)) (f. Σωκράτης); (24) ?s. i BC *IG* V (1) 894 (tile) (Bradford (4)) (Ἵππαρ[χος]); (25) c. 30-20 BC *IG* V (1) 142, 4 (Bradford (9)) (Ἵ]ππαρχος); (26) i BC/i AD *IG* V (1) 48, 14 (Bradford (1)): s. Γόργιππος); (27) ~ Plu., *Lyc.* 4; 31; Cartledge–Spawforth p. 177 (date) (Bradford (6)) (f. Ἀριστοκράτης); (28) ~ *SEG* XI 677, 2 (Bradford (5)) (f. Ἀγηιππία); (29) f. i AD *IG* V (1) 269, 6; *Artemis Orthia* p. 306 no. 19 (date) (Bradford (2)); (30) c. 80-90 AD *IG* V (1) 674, 10 (Bradford (7)) (f. Εὔδαμος)
MESSENIA:
—MESSENE: (31) hell.? *SEG* XXIII 213 (f. Φιλοκράτεια); (32) c. 146-32 BC *Boston Coins* p. 155 no. 1185 (coin); (33) ?f. i AD *PAE* 1992, p. 79, 3 (s. nat.) Δαμοθάλης, s. (ad.) Λύσιππος)
S. ITALY (CAMPANIA):
—DIKAIARCHIA-PUTEOLI: (34) imp. *CIL* x 2830 (Lat. Hipparchus)
—NOLA: (35) imp. ib. 1267 (Lat. M. Critonius Hipparcus)
SICILY: (36) vi/v BC Dubois, *IGDS* 219, 5 (Arena, *Iscr. Sic.* I 76); cf. *SEG* XLII 885 (ἱπάρχος (n. pr.?))
—KAMARINA: (37) f. v BC Cordano, *Tessere Pubbliche* 53 ([ἱπ]παρχος: s. Ἀθανις)
—MORGANTINA: (38) iv/iii BC *SEG* XXXIX 1013, 8 (f. Ξένων)

## Ἵππασος

EPIROS:
—AMBRAKIA: (1) iv AD *RE* Supplbd. 10 (17) (fict.?)
KORINTHIA:
—KORINTH: (2) c. 570-550 BC Amyx 116. 1 (vase) (ἱί-: her.?); (3) ~ ib. 66. 18 (vase) (Lorber 122) (ἱπασος: her.)
LAKONIA:
—SPARTA: (4) ?iii-ii BC *FGrH* 589 (Poralla² 387; Bradford (-))
S. ITALY (BRUTTIUM):
—SYBARIS-THOURIOI-COPIAE: (5) vi/v BC *RE* (15); *FVS* 18 (or S. Italy (Lucania) Metapontion or S. Italy (Bruttium) Kroton)

## Ἱππέας

ARKADIA:
—KLEITOR: (1) c. 140-120 BC *BCH* 60 (1936) p. 12 no. 1, 8, 16 (s. Χίλιος)

## Ἵππεια

ELIS:
—LASION: (1) vi BC *SEG* XI 1173 a, 4

## Ἱππήν

S. ITALY (CALABRIA):
—TARAS-TARENTUM: (1) v-iv BC *IG* XIV 2405. 15 (lamp) (ἱππήνο[ς]? (gen.)—*LGPN*, ἱππίνο[υ] (gen.)—ed.)

## Ἱππιάδας

LAKONIA:
—SPARTA: (1) c. 500 BC *SEG* XI 638, 4; *LSAG²* p. 201 no. 44 (date) (ἱππιάδα[ς]?)

## Ἱππίας

AIGINA: (1) ?i BC *Alt-Ägina* I (2) p. 46 no. 19 ([Ἱ]ππίας)
AKARNANIA:
—ASTAKOS: (2) m. iii BC *IG* VII 12, 7 (s. Περικλῆς)
—MEDION: (3) 216 BC ib. IX (1)² (2) 583, 21 (f. Μνασίθεος)
ARGOLIS:
—EPIDAUROS: (4) iv BC *ZPE* 103 (1994) p. 106 no. 1 (f. Τιμοκράτης); (5) iii BC *IG* IV (1)² 324; 328?; (6) ii BC *SEG* XV 211 (f. Τιμοκράτις)
ARKADIA: (7) 427 BC Th. iii 34. 3
—KYNAITHA: (8) i BC *Achaean Grave Stelai* 21 (f. Λοχίτας)
—STYMPHALOS: (9) ?263-255 BC Nachtergael, *Les Galates* 3, 8; 5, 31; 8, 43; cf. Stephanis 1800 (f. Νέων)
—TEGEA: (10) c. 240-229 BC *IG* V (2) 11, 17
ELIS: (11) v BC *RE* (13) (*FGrH* 6; *FVS* 86) (s. Διοπείθης); (12) c. 365 BC X., *HG* vii 4. 15; (13) 36-24 BC *IvOl* 62, 10; 64, 16; 65, 20 (s. Χάροψ: Φ.)
EPIROS:
—AMBRAKIA: (14) imp. *SEG* XXIV 420 (Ἡππίας—apogr.: f. Νεοπτόλεμος)
—MOLOSSOI: (15) s. iv BC Plu., *Pyrr.* 2. 2; (16) f. iii BC *BCH* 64-5 (1940-1) p. 83, 1
ILLYRIA:
—EPIDAMNOS-DYRRHACHION: (17) hell.-imp. *IDyrrh* 121 (f. Ἀριστομένεια)
KERKYRA: (18) ?ii BC *Korkyra* I p. 168 no. 12 ([Ἱ]ππίας)
KORINTHIA:
—KORINTH: (19) s. i BC *IG* II² 9063 (f. Δαμώ)
LAKONIA:
—SPARTA: (20) iii BC *SEG* XL 348 B, 2 (ἱππ-)
—SPARTA?: (21) 333 BC Arr., *An.* ii 13. 6 (Poralla² 388)
PELOPONNESE: (22) c. 230-200 BC *BCH* 45 (1921) p. 13 II, 108
SICILY: (23) ?vi BC Manganaro, *PdelP* forthcoming no. 10 (ἱππί-)
—AKRAGAS: (24) f. v BC Dubois, *IGDS* 180 b, 3 (Arena, *Iscr. Sic.* II 90) (ἱππί-)
—AKRAGAS (NR.)?: (25) ?iv BC Manganaro, *QUCC* forthcoming no. 39 B, 4
—GELA-PHINTIAS: (26) iii BC *SEG* VIII 611 (f. Ἀπολλωνίδας)
—KALE AKTE: (27) m. i BC Cic., *ad Fam.* xiii 37 (Lat. Hippias: s. Φιλόξενος)
—KAMARINA: (28) f. v BC Cordano, *Tessere Pubbliche* 113 (ἱ[π]πίας: f. Δικαίαρχος); (29) ?iv/iii BC *PdelP* 44 (1989) p. 203; cf. *SEG* XXXIX 1002 note (f. Θευδόσιος)
—MORGANTINA: (30) ?iv/iii BC ib. 1008, 5 (f. Λύσων)

## Ἵππις

S. ITALY (CALABRIA):
—TARAS-TARENTUM: (1) c. 315-280 BC *FD* III (1) 135, 1 (s. Ἔκφαντος)

## Ἱππίσκα

MESSENIA:
—MESSENE: (1) ?35-44 AD *IG* V (1) 1433, 24; *SEG* XXIX 396 (date) (d. Θάλων)

## Ἱππίτας

LAKONIA:
—SPARTA: (1) 219 BC Plb. v 37. 8; Plu., *Cleom.* 37 (Bradford (-))

## Ἱππίχα

LAKONIA:
—SPARTA: (1) c. 30-20 BC *IG* V (1) 141, 15; *SEG* XXXV 329 (date) (Bradford (-)) (d. Ἵππων)

## Ἵππιχος

ARGOLIS:
—ARGOS:
——(Hyrnathioi-Temenidai): (1) c. 400 BC *SEG* XXIX 361, 20 (ἱίπ-)
ARKADIA:
—TEGEA:

——(Apolloniatai): (2) f. iii BC *IG* v (2) 36, 52 (s. Ἀλεξιάδας)

KORINTHIA:
—KORINTH: (3) c. 590-570 BC Amyx 44. 2 (vase) (Lorber 63) (hίπι-: her.)

**Ἱππίων**
S. ITALY (BRUTTIUM):
—RHEGION: (1) s. iv BC *IG* IV (1)² 95, 47 + Peek, *IAEpid* 41 (Perlman E.2); Perlman pp. 46-9 (date) (Ἱππίων—*IG*, Ζήγων—Fraenkel, Ἱππων?: f. Ἀρχέδαμος)
SICILY:
—KENTORIPA: (2) hell.-imp. Gal. xiv 442 (doctor)

**Ἱπποβάτας**
KORINTHIA:
—KORINTH: (1) c. 610-590 BC Amyx 7. 1 (vase) (Lorber 18); cf. Arena, *Iscr. Cor.* 46 (hιπ-: her.?)

**Ἱπποδάμεια**
S. ITALY (CAMPANIA):
—DIKAIARCHIA-PUTEOLI: (1) imp. *CIL* X 2759 (Lat. Ippodamia: m. Ὀλόκαλος)

**Ἱππόδαμος**
DALMATIA:
—ISSA:
——(Hylleis): (1) iv/iii BC Brunšmid p. 9, 59 ([Ἱ]ππόδαμος: s. Μενητίδας)
ILLYRIA:
—APOLLONIA: (2) c. 250-50 BC *Bakёrr Hoard* p. 64 nos. 55-8; Maier 51; Münsterberg Nachtr. p. 13 (coin) (Ceka 55; 114) (pryt.)
—EPIDAMNOS-DYRRHACHION: (3) hell.-imp. *IDyrrh* 324 (?f. Νεσσίκα)
KORINTHIA:
—SIKYON: (4) 367 BC X., *HG* vii 1. 45 (Skalet 157)
LAKONIA:
—SPARTA: (5) vi/v BC *SEG* XI 658 (Lazzarini 406; Poralla² 389a) ([h]ιππόδαμ[ος], [h]ιποδάμ[ας]?); (6) c. 435-352 BC *FGrH* 124 F 13; Plu., *Mor.* 222 A; Polyaen. ii 15 (Poralla² 389) (Ἱπποδάμας—Polyaen.); (7) hell.? *IG* v (1) 650; (8) c. 30-20 BC ib. 211, 38 (Bradford (1)) (f. Ἀλκισοΐδας); (9) c. 170 AD *IG* v (1) 116, 15 (Bradford (2)) ([Ἱπ]πόδαμος: f. Ἰούλ. Φιληρατίδας)
S. ITALY (CALABRIA):
—TARAS-TARENTUM: (10) c. 272-235 BC Vlasto 904-7 (coins) (Evans, *Horsemen* p. 180 VIII K.1) (hιππόδα(μος))
S. ITALY (CAMPANIA):
—CAPREAE: (11) imp. *ZPE* 71 (1988) p. 196 no. 6 (Lat. Hippod[amus])

**Ἱππόδικος**
KORINTHIA:
—KORINTH: (1) c. 590-570 BC Amyx 26. 3 (vase) (Lorber 101) ([h]ιππόδιρος: fict.?)

**Ἱπποδρόμη**
SICILY: (1) vi/v BC Dubois, *IGDS* 17 a (vase) (Arena, *Iscr. Sic.* II 78; Lazzarini 752 a); Callipolitis-Feytmans, *Plats* p. 250 no. 17 (hιπο-)

**Ἱπποθράής**
LAKONIA:
—SPARTA: (1) ii BC *IG* v (1) 8, 7 (Bradford (3)) (Ἱπποθρά[ής]: I f. Ἱπποθράής II); (2) ~ *IG* v (1) 8, 7 (Bradford (1)) (II s. Ἱπποθράής I); (3) s. ii AD *IG* v (1) 534, 4; *BSA* 75 (1980) p. 219 (stemma) (Bradford (2)) (?s. Γ. Ἰούλ. Ἀγαθοκλῆς, f. Γ. Ἰούλ. Ἀγαθοκλῆς)

**Ἱπποθράσης**
MESSENIA:
—MESSENE: (1) f. iii BC *PAE* 1991, p. 99 no. 7, 29

**Ἱπποκλείδας**
KORINTHIA:
—KORINTH: (1) m. vii BC *RE* Supplbd. 11 s.v. Patrokleides (1) (-δης, Πατροκλείδης—*FGrH* 90 F 57. 6)

**Ἱπποκλῆς**
DALMATIA:
—PHAROS: (1) iii BC *SEG* XXXI 606 (Šašel, *IL* 2928) (f. Σελινώ)
KORINTHIA:
—KORINTH: (2) c. 590-570 BC Amyx 30. 4 (vase) (Lorber 34) (hιποκλές: her.)
LAKONIA:
—SPARTA?: (3) ?378-371 BC *IG* VII 1904; *LSAG*² p. 447 no. 62a (Poralla² 390) (hιποκλέές)
SICILY:
—GELA-PHINTIAS: (4) f. ii BC *IG* XIV 256, 6 (Dubois, *IGDS* 161); cf. *SEG* XL 804 (I f. Ἱπποκλῆς II); (5) ~ *IG* XIV 256, 6 (Dubois, *IGDS* 161); cf. *SEG* XL 804 (II s. Ἱπποκλῆς I)

**Ἱπποκράτης**
AKARNANIA:
—ALYZIA: (1) c. 330 BC ib. XXIII 189 I, 6
ARGOLIS:
—PHLEIOUS: (2) vi BC ib. XI 275, 1 (hιπποκράτ[ης])
ARKADIA: (3) hell. *Syringes* 29 (s. Φαίδιμος); (4) c. 230-200 BC *BCH* 45 (1921) p. 13 II, 110 (s. Ἔχιππος)
EPIROS: (5) 234-168 BC Franke, *Münz. v. Epirus* p. 173 II ser. 16-17 (coin)
LAKONIA:
—SPARTA: (6) c. 450-409 BC Th. viii 35. 1; 99; 107. 2; X., *HG* i 1. 23; i 3. 5-6; D.S. xiii 66. 2 (Poralla² 391)
MESSENIA:
—MESSENE: (7) iii BC *SEG* XXIII 209, 16
—THOURIA: (8) ii/i BC *IG* v (1) 1384, 7 (s. Ἱππων)
S. ITALY (BRUTTIUM):
—SYBARIS-THOURIOI-COPIAE: (9) vii/vi BC Hdt. vi 127 (f. Σμινδυρίδας)
S. ITALY (CALABRIA):
—TARAS-TARENTUM (NR.): (10) f. v BC *SEG* XLI 885. 1 ([hι]ποκρά(τēς))
S. ITALY (CAMPANIA):
—NEAPOLIS: (11) ii-iii AD *IG* XIV 815 (*INap* 178); cf. Leiwo p. 126 no. 113
SICILY:
—AKRAGAS: (12) vi/v BC *RE* (8) (s. Ξενόδικος); (13) f. v BC Dubois, *IGDS* 180 a, 1 (Arena, *Iscr. Sic.* II 90) (hιποκράτēς)
—GELA-PHINTIAS: (14) c. 530-491 BC *RE* (7) (s. Παντάρης, f. Εὔκλειδας, Κλέανδρος)
—KAMARINA: (15) f. v BC Cordano, *Tessere Pubbliche* 14 ((h)ιπποκρ[άτēς]: s. Παρβόλας)
—KATANE?: (16) hell.-imp. *IG* XIV 2412. 20 (seal)
—LEONTINOI: (17) vi/v BC Schol. Aeschin. iii 189; (18) m. iv BC *IvOl* 293 (*CEG* II 830) (s. Δήϊκράτης, f. Εὔμολπος)
—NEAITON: (19) hell. *NScav* 1900, p. 210
—SYRACUSE: (20) 214-212 BC *RE* (10) (and N. Africa Carthage)
—TAUROMENION: (21) c. 145 BC *IGSI* 4 III (IV), 85 an. 97 (f. Ἀρτέμων)

**Ἱπποκρατίδας**
LAKONIA:
—SPARTA: (1) vii/vi BC Hdt. viii 131 (Poralla² 392) (s. Λατυχίδας, f. Ἀγησίλαος, ?f. Ἀγησικλῆς: king); (2) ?v/iv BC Plu., *Mor.* 222 A (Poralla² 393)

**Ἱππόλαος**
AKARNANIA:
—OINIADAI: (1) 263-262 BC *IG* IX (1)² (1) 3 A, 24

**Ἱππολέων**
MESSENIA:
—THOURIA: (1) f. ii BC *SEG* XI 972, 127 (f. Ξενόδαμος) —

**Ἱππόλοχος**
AITOLIA: (1) m. ii BC Plb. xxvii 15. 14
ARKADIA:
—KLEITOR: (2) f. iii BC *IG* XI (4) 532 (Ἱππό[λ]ο[χ]ος: s. Κλεοκράτης)

**Ἱππολύτα**
KORINTHIA:
—KORINTH: (1) c. 590-570 BC Amyx 42 (vase) ([h]ιππολύτα: her.?)

**Ἱππολύτη**
ARGOLIS:
—EPIDAUROS: (1) ?iv-iii BC Peek, *IAEpid* 127
S. ITALY (BRUTTIUM):
—RHEGION*: (2) m. vi BC Rumpf, *Chalkid. Vas.* p. 46 no. 4 (vase) (Arena, *Iscr. Sic.* III p. 102-3 no. 7) (hιππολύτē: her.?)
S. ITALY (CAMPANIA):
—SALERNUM: (3) ?ii-iii AD *CIL* X 8123 (Lat. Aurelia Hippolyte)

**Ἱππόλυτος**
KORINTHIA:
—KORINTH: (1) c. 615-550 BC Amyx 24. 9; 61; 68. 12 (vases) (Lorber 44); Lorber 85; 125 (hιπ-: her.)
S. ITALY (CAMPANIA):
—HERCULANEUM: (2) m. i AD *Cron. Erc.* 7 (1977) p. 116 B b, 4 (Lat. M. Nonius Hippolytus)
S. ITALY (LUCANIA):
—VOLCEI: (3) imp. *IItal* III (1) 109 (*CIL* X 301 and p. 1004) (Lat. Hippolitus)

**Ἱππόμαχος**
AKARNANIA?: (1) hell. Unp. (Agrinion Mus.)
ELIS: (2) iv/iii BC Moretti, *Olymp.* 506 (s. Μοσχίων)
KORINTHIA:
—KORINTH: (3) c. 570-550 BC Amyx 70. 7 (vase) (Lorber 126) (hιπ-: her.)
LEUKAS: (4) f. v BC *RE* Supplbd. 4 (-)

**Ἱππομέδων**
ARGOLIS:
—ARGOS: (1) ?c. 575-550 BC *SEG* XI 336, 5; *LSAG*² p. 168 no. 7 (date) (Ἱπομέδōν); (2) v-iv BC *RE* (10)
KORINTHIA:
—KORINTH: (3) c. 570-550 BC Amyx 81. 8 (vase) (Lorber 130) (hιπομέδōν: her.?)
LAKONIA:
—SPARTA: (4) c. 270-215 BC *RE* (14); *PP* 14605 + *Historia* 28 (1979) pp. 76 ff. (Bradford (1)) (s. Ἀγησίλαος); (5) c. 1-10 AD *IG* v (1) 209, 23; *SEG* XXXV 331 (date) (Bradford (2)) (s. Νίκανδρος)
S. ITALY (CAMPANIA):
—KYME: (6) vi/v BC *RE* (11)

**Ἱππονίκα**
AKARNANIA:
—ALYZIA: (1) c. 200 BC *IG* IX (1)² (2) 445
ARGOLIS:
—ARGOS: (2) 105 BC *JÖAI* 14 (1911) Beibl. p. 146 no. 4, 21 (Ἱππο[νί]κα: d. —εοδ—)
KORINTHIA:
—KORINTH: (3) c. 570-550 BC Amyx 91. 2 (vase) (Lorber 84) ([h]ιπονίκα: her.)

**Ἱππονίκη**
AIGINA: (1) hell. *IG* IV (1) 102

**Ἱππόνικος**
AITOLIA:
—THERMOS*: (1) s. iii BC ib. IX (1)² (1) 60 VII, 16
ARGOLIS:
—PHLEIOUS: (2) v/iv BC X., *HG* v 3. 13 (f. Προκλῆς)
ARKADIA: (3) 219 BC *PP* 2738
ELIS:
—LASION: (4) vi BC *SEG* XI 1173 a, 1 (s. Κλεώνυμος)
ILLYRIA:
—APOLLONIA: (5) hell.-imp. *IApoll* 210 (-νει-: I f. Ἱππόνικος II); (6) ~ ib. (-νει-: II s. Ἱππόνικος I)
KERKYRA: (7) i AD *IG* II² 9013 (f. Λυκώτας)
LAKONIA: (8) ii BC ib. v (1) 709 (Bradford (-)) ([Ἱπ]πόνικος)

**Ἱππονοΐδας**
LAKONIA:
—SPARTA: (1) 418 BC Th. v 71. 3; 72. 1 (Poralla² 394)

**Ἵππος**
ARGOLIS:
—EPIDAUROS: (1) iii BC Peek, *IAEpid* 73, 2 ([Ἵ]ππος); (2) ii BC ib. 153. 27 (Ἵ[π]πος)
ELIS: (3) f. iv BC Moretti, *Olymp.* 402

**Ἱπποσθένης**
ARGOLIS:
—ARGOS: (1) c. 458 BC *IG* I³ 1149, 9 ([ἱ]πποσθ[ένēς]); (2) c. 100-90 BC *SEG* XXXIII 290 A, 8; *BSA* 70 (1975) pp. 129-31 (date); cf. Stephanis 1823 (f. Νικίας)
ARKADIA:
—HERAIA: (3) 369-361 BC *IG* v (2) 1, 63; Tod, *GHI* II 132 (date)
—TEGEA*: (4) f. iii BC *IG* v (2) 36, 24 ([Ἱ]πποσθένης)
ILLYRIA:
—APOLLONIA: (5) ?ii BC *IApoll* 102 (s. Διονύσιος)
LAKONIA:
—SPARTA: (6) 632-608 BC *RE* (2); Moretti, *Olymp.* 61; 66; 68; 70; 73; 75 (Poralla² 395) (f. Ἑτοιμοκλῆς)
SICILY:
—AKRAGAS: (7) iv/iii BC *Acragas Graeca* 1 p. 41 no. 11, 4 (Cabanes, *L'Épire* p. 543 no. 8; Dubois, *IGDS* 184)
—MORGANTINA: (8) ?iv/iii BC *SEG* XXXIX 1009, 8 (Ἱπποσθ(θ)ένης: s. Πράτων)
—SYRACUSE: (9) 214 BC Plb. vii 4. 1

**Ἱππόστρατος**
EPIROS:
—BOUTHROTOS (PRASAIBOI):
——Bouthrotioi: (1) a. 163 BC *IBouthrot* 120, 9 (Ἱπό-: f. Δορίσκος)
—DODONA*: (2) iv-iii BC *SGDI* 1583
ILLYRIA:
—APOLLONIA: (3) c. 250-50 BC Münsterberg p. 36 (coin) (Ceka 78) (pryt.)
KEPHALLENIA:
—PRONNOI: (4) s. v BC *SEG* XXV 607 (ἱπό-)
S. ITALY (BRUTTIUM):
—KROTON: (5) 564-560 BC Moretti, *Olymp.* 100; 104
—SYBARIS-THOURIOI-COPIAE: (6) iii BC *Coll. Santangelo* 5161-2 (coin) (Ἱππόστρα(τος))
SICILY?: (7) ?iii BC *RE* (7); *FGrH* 568

**Ἱππόστροφος**
KORINTHIA:
—KORINTH: (1) c. 610-590 BC Amyx 7. 2 (vase) (Lorber 18) (ἱπό-: her.?)

**Ἱππότας**
LAKONIA:
—SPARTA: (1) c. 225 BC *SEG* XI 414, 39 (Perlman E.5; Bradford (-)) (s. Ἀριστόλας)

**Ἱπποτίων**
KORINTHIA:
—KORINTH: (1) c. 570-550 BC Amyx 92 B. 10; 66. 8 (vases) (Lorber 120); Lorber 122 (ἱπιοτίōν: her.?)
S. ITALY (CALABRIA):
—TARAS-TARENTUM: (2) v/iv BC Paus. v 25. 7 ?= (3); (3) ~ *CEG* II 833 ([Ἱππ]οτίω[ν]: s. Ἐμπεδότιμος) ?= (2)

**Ἱππότυρος**
S. ITALY (BRUTTIUM):
—HIPPONION-VIBO VALENTIA*: (1) imp. *CIL* X 88 (Lat. L. Pullius Hippotyrus: freed.)

**Ἵππυς**
S. ITALY (BRUTTIUM):
—RHEGION: (1) ?iv BC *RE* (-); *FGrH* 554 with Komm. (date)

**Ἱππώ**
SICILY:
—KAMARINA: (1) iv/iii BC *SEG* XLII 848; cf. *BE* 1993, no. 714 ([Ἱ]ππώ)

**Ἱππώι**
KORINTHIA:
—KORINTH: (1) c. 570-550 BC Amyx 71. 4 (vase) (Lorber 127) (ἱπόι (n. pr.?): her.?)

**Ἵππων**
AKARNANIA:
—ANAKTORION: (1) 216 BC *IG* IX (1)² (2) 583, 65
ARGOLIS:
—EPIDAUROS:
——(Hylleis): (2) 146 BC ib. IV (1)² 28, 58 (f. Διόδωρος)
ARKADIA:
—MEGALOPOLIS: (3) s. ii BC ib. v (2) 438, 16; 443, 7; 444, 5; 453 (*IPArk* 32) (f. Εὐμαρίδας); (4) ~ *IG* v (2) 438, 17 (s. Εὐμαρίδας)
—TEGEA: (5) hell.? ib. 149 (f. Θῆρις) ?= (8); (6) ii BC *SEG* XI 1058, 3; (7) f. ii BC *IG* v (2) 44, 14 (f. Ἱέρων); (8) ~ ib. l. 16 (s. Θῆρις) ?= (5); (9) 191-146 BC *Coll. McClean* 6528 (coin); (10) ?i AD *IG* v (2) 226; (11) ii AD ib. 54, 6 ([Ἵ]ππων: s. Θεο—); (12) 165 AD ib. 50, 48 (s. Φιλόμουσος)
——(Krariotai): (13) m. iii BC ib. 36, 90 (Ἱέρων)
ILLYRIA:
—EPIDAMNOS-DYRRHACHION: (14) hell.-imp. *IDyrrh* 255 (s. Ἀρχιτέλης)
KORINTHIA:
—SIKYON: (15) ?253 BC Nachtergael, *Les Galates* 10, 38 (Skalet 158; Stephanis 1288) (s. Ἀριστοκράτης)
LAKONIA:
—SPARTA: (16) c. 30-20 BC *IG* v (1) 141, 2, 15; *SEG* XXXV 329 (date) (Bradford (-)) (f. Δαμοκράτης, Ἱππίχα)
MESSENIA:
—MESSENE: (17) s. ii BC *BCH* 95 (1971) p. 544, [3], 12, 18 + *SEG* XXXVII 447 (name) (f. Φιλοκράτης)
—THOURIA: (18) ii/i BC *IG* v (1) 1384, 7 (f. Ἱπποκράτης)
S. ITALY (BRUTTIUM):
—LOKROI EPIZEPHYRIOI:
——(Ἀλχ.): (19) 279 BC De Franciscis 13, 1 (Ἵπων-)
S. ITALY (CALABRIA):
—TARAS-TARENTUM: (20) c. 356-355 BC *IG* IV (1)² 95, 44 (Perlman E.2); Perlman pp. 46-9 (date)

SICILY:
—AKRAI: (21) iii-ii BC *SGDI* 3242, 8 (*Akrai* p. 157 no. 8) (f. Διονύσιος)
—SYRACUSE: (22) 410 BC X., *HG* i 2. 8 (f. Εὐκλῆς); (23) 357 BC Plu., *Dio* 37
—TAUROMENION: (24) ?ii/i BC *IG* XIV 421 D an. 7 (*SGDI* 5219); *IGSI* 4 III (IV), 117 D an. 7 (f. Φίλιστος)
—ZANKLE-MESSANA: (25) 339 BC Plu., *Tim.* 34 (tyrant)

**Ἵρα**
S. ITALY (LUCANIA):
—HYELE-VELIA: (1) inc. *SEG* XXVIII 819

**Ἱράνα**
ARGOLIS:
—ARGOS: (1) iv BC ib. XVII 151

**Ἴρβος?**
LAKONIA:
—SPARTA: (1) her. Paus. iii 16. 9; Masson, *OGS* 2 p. 512 (name) (Poralla² 396) (s. Ἀμφισθένης, f. Ἀστράβακος, Ἀλώπεκος: dub.)

**Ἴρις**
ARGOLIS:
—ARGOS: (1) iii BC *IG* IV (1) 527, 7; cf. *BCH* 37 (1913) p. 308 (Δαιρίς—*IG*)
ILLYRIA:
—LYCHNIDOS: (2) ii AD Šašel, *IL* 457 (Lat. Iris)
S. ITALY (BRUTTIUM):
—PETELIA: (3) imp. *Eph. Ep.* VIII 261 (Lat. Caedicia Iris)
S. ITALY (CAMPANIA):
—POMPEII: (4) i BC-i AD *CIL* IV 8258; 8259 (Lat. Hiris)

**Ἱρόμαχος**
EPIROS:
—BOUTHROTOS (PRASAIBOI): (1) a. 163 BC *IBouthrot* 30, 37 (*SEG* XXXVIII 488) (Ἱ(ε)ρόμαχος?)
——Prakeleoi: (2) ii-i BC *IBouthrot* 94, 11 (Εἱρό-: f. Μενοίτας)

**Ἰσαγόρας**
ARKADIA:
—STYMPHALOS: (1) 189 BC *SEG* XXV 445, 21 (*IPArk* 18) (Ἱ[σ]αγόρας: f. Εὐρήμων, Θεαρίδας)
LAKONIA:
—SPARTA: (2) iii AD *IG* v (1) 727, 8 (*GVI* 1374; Bradford (-)) (Ἰσαγό[ρας]: f. Καλλιστονίκη)

**Ἰσάδας**
LAKONIA:
—SPARTA: (1) c. 380-362 BC Plu., *Ages.* 34; Ael., *VH* vi 3 (Poralla² 397); cf. Polyaen. ii 9 (Ἰσίδας—Polyaen.: s. Φοιβίδας)

**Ἰσάνωρ**
LAKONIA:
—SPARTA: (1) 430 BC X., *HG* ii 3. 10 (Poralla² 398)

**Ἰσάργυρος**
S. ITALY (APULIA):
—CANUSIUM*: (1) i AD *Epig. Rom. di Canosa* 146 (Lat. Isargyrus: freed.)
—VENUSIA: (2) ii AD *ZPE* 103 (1994) p. 166 no. 5 (Lat. Satrius Isargyrus)

**Ἰσαρχίδας**
KORINTHIA:
—KORINTH: (1) 435 BC Th. i 29. 2 (s. Ἴσαρχος)

**Ἴσαρχος**
AITOLIA:
—THESTIEIS: (1) hell. *SBBerlAk* 1936, p. 386 no. 4 (tile) (Εἴσ-)
ELIS:
—OLYMPIA*: (2) s. v BC *Ol. Forsch.* 5 p. 150 no. 6
KORINTHIA:
—KORINTH: (3) 435 BC Th. i 29. 2 (f. Ἰσαρχίδας)

## Ἰσᾶς
ARKADIA:
—TEGEA: (1) ii AD *IG* V (2) 55, 92 (*Eἰ*-: s. Φρο-νιμᾶς)
—TEGEA?: (2) a. 116 AD ib. 151 (*M. Πομπ. Εἰσᾶς Αἰλιανός*)
MESSENIA:
—KORONE: (3) 246 AD ib. V (1) 1398, 90 (*Aὐρ. Εἰσᾶς*)
S. ITALY (APULIA):
—TEANUM APULUM: (4) 521 AD *Studi Storici* pp. 87-95 (Lat. Isas: ?s. Symonas, f. Augusta: Jew)
—VENUSIA: (5) v AD *JIWE* I 76 (*CIJ* I 600) (*Ἰσα(ά)κ*—*CIJ*: f. Φαυστῖνος: Jew)

## Ἰσέας
ACHAIA:
—KARYNEIA: (1) f. iii BC *RE* (-)

## Ἰσθμός
AIGINA: (1) ?f. iii AD *Alt-Ägina* I (2) p. 49 no. 41 (I f. *Aὐρ. Ἰσθμός* II); (2) ~ ib. (*Aὐρ. Ἰ.*: II s. Ἰσθμός I)
EPIROS:
—ARGETHIA: (3) 157 BC *SGDI* 1689, 1, 4 etc. (s. Νικαία: slave/freed.)
KORINTHIA:
—KORINTH: (4) i-ii AD *SEG* XX 30, 4 (Stephanis 1290)
S. ITALY (CAMPANIA):
—POMPEII: (5) i BC-i AD *CIL* IV 2015 (Lat. Isthmus); (6) ~ ib. 2994 (Lat. Istmus); (7) c. 51-62 AD ib. 3340. 77, 6 (Castrèn 118. 11) (Lat. Claudius Isthmus)

## Ἰσίας
ARGOLIS:
—PHLEIOUS?: (1) s. iv BC Peek, *NIEpid* 16, 22 (Perlman E.6) (f. —σις)
KORINTHIA:
—KORINTH: (2) 344 BC Plu., *Tim.* 21
LAKONIA:
—SPARTA: (3) 410 BC X., *HG* ii 3. 10 (Poralla² 399)

## Ἰσιάς
ARGOLIS:
—EPIDAUROS: (1) ?iv-iii BC *SEG* XXXIX 356 (d. Σαραπίων)
—HERMIONE: (2) ii-i BC *IG* IV (1) 732 III, 17 (-σει-: d. Πεισιδίκα)
S. ITALY (APULIA):
—VENUSIA: (3) imp. *CIL* IX 587 (Lat. Titiolaeia Isias: d. Πλιάς)
S. ITALY (CAMPANIA):
—DIKAIARCHIA-PUTEOLI: (4) imp. ib. X 2451 (Lat. Ela Isias); (5) ~ ib. 2682 (Lat. Valeria Isias); (6) ~ ib. 2910 (Lat. Rasidia Isias); (7) ~ ib. 2920 (Lat. Rutilia Isias); (8) ~ ib. 8194 (Lat. Lucceia Isias: d. Ὑγίεια); (9) ~ *NScav* 1927, p. 333 no. 8 B (Lat. Otacilia Isias)
—DIKAIARCHIA-PUTEOLI*: (10) imp. *CIL* X 2180 (Lat. -ellia Isia: freed.)
—NEAPOLIS: (11) i BC/i AD *INap* 113, 3 (*Eἴσει*-: d. Ἄστος)
—POMPEII: (12) i BC-i AD *Cron. Pomp.* 5 (1979) p. 190 (Lat. Isias)
SICILY:
—LIPARA: (13) imp.? *SEG* XLI 819 (*Eἰ*-); (14) imp. *NScav* 1929, p. 78 with fig. 30 (*Eἰουλ. Eἰσιάς*)

## Ἰσιας
KYNOURIA:
—THYREATIS: (1) ii AD *SEG* XXXV 280 (*Eἰ*-)

## Ἰσιγένεια
S. ITALY (CAMPANIA):
—LITERNUM: (1) ?i-ii AD *CIL* X 3717 (Lat. Aelia Isicenia)

## Ἰσιγένης
ELIS: (1) c. 65-75 AD *IvOl* 83, 9 (*Eἰ[σιγέ]νης*: ?f. Eὔοδος: slave?)
LAKONIA:
—SPARTA: (2) c. 150-160 AD *SEG* XI 585, 12; XXX 410, [21] (Bradford (-)) (*Eἰ*-: s. Στρατόνι-κος)

## Ἰσιδώρα
S. ITALY (CAMPANIA):
—DIKAIARCHIA-PUTEOLI: (1) imp. *CIL* X 2326 (Lat. Valeria Isidora: m. Ἀσκλᾶς)
—MISENUM: (2) imp. ib. 3444 (Lat. Valeria Isidora)
SICILY:
—KATANE: (3) iii-v AD Libertini, *Museo Biscari* p. 318 no. 10
—LIPARA: (4) imp. *BTCGI* 9 p. 97 (Κλωδία Eἰσιδώρα)

## Ἰσίδωρος
ARGOLIS:
—HERMIONE: (1) ii-i BC *IG* IV (1) 732 II, 14 (*Eἰ*-: s. Σωσθένης)
ARKADIA:
—TEGEA: (2) 165 AD ib. V (2) 50, 70 (*Eἰ*-: s. Ὧρος)
—THELPHOUSA: (3) ii-iii AD *SEG* XI 1131 (*Eἰσίδω[ρος]?, Eἰσιδώ[ρα]?*)
ELIS: (4) 36-24 BC *IvOl* 62, 22 (s. Μολοσσός); (5) 233 AD ib. 116, 5 (*T. Φλ. Eἰσίδωρος*: Γ.); (6) ~ ib. l. 8 (*Eἰ*-: s. Πυθίων)
EPIROS:
—AMBRAKIA: (7) iii/ii BC Unp. (Arta Mus., inscr.) (*Eἰ*-: f. Φιλίστα)
ILLYRIA:
—APOLLONIA: (8) imp. *IApoll* 202 (*Eἰσίδωρ[ος]*: s. Ζώσιμος)
—DALOS: (9) f. ii BC *BCH* 45 (1921) p. 22 IV, 29; *REG* 62 (1949) p. 28, 6 (s. Διονύσιος: reading—Oulhen)
KORINTHIA:
—KORINTH: (10) v AD *SEG* XI 142 (Ἡσήδο-)
LAKONIA:
—SPARTA: (11) s. ii AD ib. 598, 6 (Bradford s.v. Eἰσίδωρος (-)) (*Eἰ*-)
S. ITALY (APULIA): (12) imp. *CIL* X 8059. 272 (seal) (Lat. Isidorus)
S. ITALY (APULIA):
—VENUSIA: (13) imp. ib. IX 552 (Lat. Cn. Petronius Isidorus: I f. Ἰσίδωρος II); (14) ~ ib. (Lat. Cn. Petronius Isidorus: II s. Ἰσίδωρος I)
S. ITALY (CALABRIA):
—BRENTESION-BRUNDISIUM: (15) imp. *NScav* 1892, p. 352 m (Lat. Isido[rus])
—BRENTESION-BRUNDISIUM*: (16) imp. *CIL* IX 122 (Lat. Isidorus: s. Ἡδόνη: freed.)
S. ITALY (CAMPANIA):
—DIKAIARCHIA-PUTEOLI: (17) imp. ib. X 2077 (Lat. [An]tonius Isidorus); (18) ~ *NScav* 1885, p. 499 (*Eph. Ep.* VIII 383) (Lat. M. Antonius Isidorus)
—MISENUM*: (19) imp. *CIL* X 3352 (Lat. Saturninus Isidorus: f. Memorius); (20) f. i AD *Epigraphica* 34 (1972) p. 141 (Lat. Isidorus: imp. freed./doctor)
—NEAPOLIS: (21) ii/i BC *IG* IX (2) 528, 15; cf. Stephanis 2687 (f. —ης); (22) 106 BC *IG* II² 1011, 113 (I f. Ἰσίδωρος II); (23) ~ ib. l. 113 (II s. Ἰσίδωρος I)
—POMPEII: (24) i BC-i AD *CIL* IV 1383; 4699; 4700 (Lat. Isidorus) ?= (25); (25) ~ ib. 3117 (Lat. Isidorus) ?= (24); (26) ~ ib. 4441 (Lat. Isidorus)
S. ITALY (LUCANIA):
—POSEIDONIA-PAESTUM?: (27) imp. ib. X 469 (Lat. Arrius Isidorus Missicius: f. Silvanus)
SICILY:
—GELA-PHINTIAS: (28) f. ii BC *IG* XIV 256, 44 (Dubois, *IGDS* 161); cf. *SEG* XL 804 (f. Σω-σίπολις)

—SYRACUSE: (29) c. 100 BC *IG* XII (3) Suppl. 1299, 17 (s. Θέων)

## Ἰσιτύχη
S. ITALY (CAMPANIA):
—DIKAIARCHIA-PUTEOLI: (1) imp. *CIL* X 2197 (Lat. Caesia Isityche)

## Ἰσίων
ARGOLIS:
—ARGOS: (1) hell.? *SEG* XL 329 (terracotta)
—EPIDAUROS: (2) i AD *IG* IV (1)² 642, 3; 643 (s. Ἀπολλώνιος)
—HERMIONE: (3) ?ii-i BC ib. IV (1) 731 I, 17 (*Eἰ*-: s. Κλειναγόρας)
—TROIZEN: (4) imp. ib. 781 (*Eἰ*-: s. Eὔτυχος); (5) f. ii AD ib. 758, 2, 29 (*Eἰ*-: s. Τιμόθεος)
LAKONIA:
—SPARTA: (6) c. 125 AD *SEG* XI 575, 9 (Bradford (1)) ([Οὐ]άριος Eἰσίων)
S. ITALY (CAMPANIA):
—DIKAIARCHIA-PUTEOLI: (7) imp. *CIL* X 2015 (Lat. Isio)
—DIKAIARCHIA-PUTEOLI*: (8) i AD *Puteoli* 11 (1987) p. 130 no. 3 (Lat. L. Furius Isio: freed.)
SICILY:
—THERMAI HIMERAIAI*: (9) imp. *CIL* X 7403 (*ILat. Term. Imer.* 96) (Lat. Q. Fabius Isio: freed.)

## Ἰσμαριανός
S. ITALY (APULIA):
—LUCERIA: (1) imp. *ASP* 34 (1981) p. 16 no. 17 (Lat. C. Sallustius Ismarianus: I f. Ἰσμαριανός II); (2) ~ ib. (Lat. C. Sallustius Ismarianus: II s. Ἰσμαριανός I)

## Ἴσμαρος
S. ITALY (CAMPANIA):
—POMPEII: (1) i BC-i AD *CIL* IV 5297-8; 5300 (Lat. Ismarus)

## Ἰσμηνίας
SICILY:
—TYNDARIS: (1) f. i BC Cic., *In Verr.* II iv 92 (Lat. Hismenias)

## Ἰσμήνιχος
S. ITALY (CAMPANIA):
—NEAPOLIS: (1) iii-iv AD *INap* 234 (Ἰσμήν(ι)χος)

## Ἰσμηνός
S. ITALY (CAMPANIA):
—POMPEII: (1) i BC-i AD *CIL* IV 2169-70 (Lat. Ismenus)

## Ἰσοδαμίς
MESSENIA:
—MESSENE: (1) ii-i BC *SEG* XXXIX 385; *PAE* 1988, p. 68 (*Proc. Sympos. Olympic Games* p. 89)

## Ἰσόδαμος
ARGOLIS:
—EPIDAUROS*: (1) c. 370 BC *IG* IV (1)² 102, 252, 258, 271, 285
—TROIZEN: (2) ii AD Luc., *Dem. Enc.* 27 (fict.?)
ARKADIA:
—TEGEA: (3) ii BC *IG* V (2) 43, 10 (f. Πεισίας)
—(Krariotai): (4) f. iii BC ib. 36, 40 (s. Θερσίας)
KEPHALLENIA:
—PRONNOI: (5) c. 210 BC ib. IX (1)² (1) 31, 95 (s. Τιμοκράτης)
KORINTHIA:
—SIKYON: (6) vii/vi BC *FGrH* 90 F 61 (Skalet 159) (?s. Ἀριστώνυμος: tyrant)
LAKONIA:
—SPARTA: (7) f. ii AD *IG* V (1) 162, 5 (Bradford (-)) (s. Ἰούλιος)

LEUKAS: (**8**) 368 BC Tod, *GHI* II 134, 4 (-δη-)
MESSENIA:
—MESSENE: (**9**) iii BC *SEG* XXIII 209, 10; (**10**) i BC/i AD *IG* v (1) 1438 a, 12
—MESSENE?: (**11**) ii/i BC *SEG* XI 979, 50

**Ἰσοδίκη**
S. ITALY (LUCANIA):
—SIRIS: (**1**) ?c. 575-550 BC Guarducci, *Ep. Gr.* 3 p. 350 (loomweight) (Dubois, *IGDGG* 1 46); *LSAG*² p. 288 no. 1 (date)

**Ἰσόδικος**
SICILY:
—TAUROMENION: (**1**) c. 230-202 BC *IG* XIV 421 an. 11; 421 an. 21; 421 an. 27; 421 an. 39 (*SGDI* 5219) (f. Λύσανδρος)

**Ἰσοκράτης**
ARGOLIS:
—ARGOS: (**1**) hell.-imp. *AD* 32 (1977) Chron. p. 343; cf. *AR* 1985-6, p. 100 (or Rhodes)
KORINTHIA:
—KORINTH: (**2**) 429 BC Th. ii 83. 4
MESSENIA:
—KORONE: (**3**) ii/iii AD *SEG* XI 989 (Εἰσοκράτη (fem./masc. voc.?))
—MESSENE: (**4**) ?i BC *PAE* 1969, p. 100 a, 11

**Ἰσομέλης**
MESSENIA:
—MESSENE: (**1**) iii BC *SEG* XXIII 209, 16

**Ἰσομέντωρ**
ARGOLIS:
—ARGOS: (**1**) ?272 BC *FD* III (1) 82 (s. Φίλιππος)

**Ἰσοχρύση**
S. ITALY (CAMPANIA):
—POMPEII: (**1**) i BC-i AD *CIL* IV 1655 (Lat. Hysocryse)
—STABIAE: (**2**) i AD ib. X 779 (Lat. Isochryse)

**Ἰσόχρυσος**
ARGOLIS:
—HERMIONE: (**1**) imp. *IG* IV (1) 723, 3 (f. Ἀ—ρα)
ARKADIA:
—MANTINEIA-ANTIGONEIA: (**2**) m. ii AD ib. v (2) 312 (s. Ἐπιτύγχανος, Δόξα)
LAKONIA:
—SPARTA: (**3**) f. ii AD ib. v (1) 62, 3; 107, 3; *SEG* XI 606, 5 (Bradford (3)) (f. Πωλλίων); (**4**) c. 125-155 AD *SEG* XI 493, 1 (Bradford (2)) (I f. Ἰσόχρυσος II); (**5**) ~ *SEG* XI 493, 1 (Bradford (1)) ([Ἰσόχρ]υσος: II s. Ἰσόχρυσος I)
S. ITALY (CAMPANIA):
—DIKAIARCHIA-PUTEOLI: (**6**) 35 AD Camodeca, *L'Archivio Puteolano* 1 p. 116 no. 3; Bove, *Documenti processuali* pp. 79-80 T.P. 14 (Lat. A. Castricius Isochrysus); (**7**) 61 AD *Puteoli* 9-10 (1985-6) p. 31 no. 5 (Lat. M. Amullius Isochrysus); (**8**) ii AD *AJA* 77 (1973) p. 164 no. 15 (Lat. Hisochrysus)
—DIKAIARCHIA-PUTEOLI*: (**9**) imp. *CIL* X 2179 (Lat. M. Bubbius Isochrysus: freed.)
—HERCULANEUM: (**10**) 41-79 AD *Cron. Erc.* 7 (1977) p. 115 A c, 4 (Lat. C. Novius Isochrysus)
—POMPEII: (**11**) i BC-i AD *CIL* IV 1289 (Ἰσώ-)

**Ἰσπῆς**
SICILY:
—SYRACUSE: (**1**) iii-v AD *IG* XIV 48; cf. *Riv. Arch. Crist.* 18 (1941) p. 229 no. 122

**Ἴσσα**
S. ITALY (CAMPANIA):
—DIKAIARCHIA-PUTEOLI: (**1**) imp. *CIL* X 1568 (Lat. Issa: d. Κυπρογένεια)

**Ἴσσος**
S. ITALY (APULIA):
—CANUSIUM: (**1**) ii AD *Epig. Rom. di Canosa* 78 (Lat. M. Arruntius Issus: f. Ἀσιατικός)

**Ἰστιαία**
S. ITALY (CALABRIA):
—TARAS-TARENTUM: (**1**) iv/iii BC *IG* XIV 668 I, 14 (Landi, *DISMG* 194) (ʰιστ-)

**Ἰστιαῖος**
ARGOLIS:
—ARGOS: (**1**) ii-i BC *IG* IV (1) 530, 3; cf. *BCH* 33 (1909) p. 183 n. 2 (Ἱστια[ῖος])
ARKADIA:
—MEGALOPOLIS: (**2**) m. iii BC *SEG* XI 412, 67 (Perlman E.3); Perlman p. 63 f. (date) (Ἱστι[αῖ]ος: f. Θεόπομπος); (**3**) c. 200 BC *FD* III (4) 145, 2; cf. Stephanis 1182 (Ἱστ[ιαῖος]: f. Θεόπομπος)
EPIROS:
—BOUTHROTOS (PRASAIBOI):
——Bouthrotioi: (**4**) a. 163 BC *IBouthrot* 91, 16 (*SEG* XXXII 623); *IBouthrot* 153, 7 (f. Λυκῖνος)
ILLYRIA:
—EPIDAMNOS-DYRRHACHION: (**5**) arch. *IDyrrh* 1 (ʰιστ-)
KORINTHIA:
—KORINTH: (**6**) f. iv BC *Corinth* VIII (3) 20
LAKONIA:
—SPARTA: (**7**) s. i BC *SEG* XI 877 (brick) (Bradford (-))
S. ITALY (BRUTTIUM):
—TERINA: (**8**) c. 325-300 BC *IGSI* 21, 4-6 (*SEG* IV 73; Landi, *DISMG* 170); cf. *Gnomon* 3 (1927) pp. 372 ff. (f. Νίκυλις, Ἀριστοκρέτης, Φιλότας)
S. ITALY (CALABRIA):
—TARAS-TARENTUM: (**9**) v BC *IG* XIV 2405. 16 (lamp) (ʰιστιαῖ[ος]); (**10**) iv/iii BC ib. 668 II, 4 (Landi, *DISMG* 194) (ʰιστ[ι]αῖος Ὀλ.); (**11**) ~ *IG* XIV 668 II, 17 (Landi, *DISMG* 194) (ʰιστιαῖος Λι.)

**Ἰστίαρχος**
S. ITALY (CALABRIA):
—TARAS-TARENTUM: (**1**) c. 272-235 BC Vlasto 842-5; 1091-3 (coins) (Evans, *Horsemen* p. 177 VIII A.10; p. 182 no. 3) (ʰιστ-)
SICILY:
—SELINOUS: (**2**) v BC Dubois, *IGDS* 35, 5 (Arena, *Iscr. Sic.* I 64) (ʰιστ-); (**3**) f. v BC Dubois, *IGDS* 39, 5 (Arena, *Iscr. Sic.* I 71) (ʰιστία(ρχος)?); (**4**) ~ Dubois, *IGDS* 39, 12 (Arena, *Iscr. Sic.* I 71) (ʰιστί(αρχος)?)
—SELINOUS?: (**5**) v BC *SEG* XXXIX 1021 II, 7 (ʰιστίαρχ(ο)ς)
—TAUROMENION: (**6**) c. 154 BC *IGSI* 4 III (IV), 9 an. 87 (f. Ζωῖλος)

**Ἰστιειός**
S. ITALY (CALABRIA):
—TARAS-TARENTUM: (**1**) s. iv BC Guarducci, *Ep. Gr.* 1 p. 290 no. 10 (Landi, *DISMG* 189) (ʰιστιη-: s. Ἴστων)
S. ITALY (LUCANIA):
—HERAKLEIA: (**2**) iii BC ib. 214 ([Ἰσ]τιει[ός]: s. Ἀρίστυλος)
——(Κυ. θρῖναξ): (**3**) iv/iii BC *IGSI* 1 I, 6, 9, 98 (*DGE* 62; Uguzzoni–Ghinatti I) (ʰιστ-: f. Φιλώτας)
SICILY:
—GELA-PHINTIAS: (**4**) f. ii BC *IG* XIV 256, 2 (Dubois, *IGDS* 161); cf. *SEG* XL 804 (Ἱστ[ια]ῖος—Dubois: f. Ἀριστίων)
—HALAISA: (**5**) ii BC *IGSI* 2 A II, 80 (Dubois, *IGDS* 196) (s. Θέστων)
—KAMARINA: (**6**) ?iv/iii BC *SEG* XXXIX 1001, 11 ([Ἱ]στιειός: f. —ων)

—TAUROMENION: (**7**) c. 240 BC *IG* XIV 421 an. 1 (*SGDI* 5219); (**8**) c. 171 BC *IG* XIV 421 an. 70 (*SGDI* 5219) (s. Στράτων)

**Ἰστίη**
S. ITALY (LUCANIA):
—HYELE-VELIA: (**1**) imp.? *IG* XIV 658

**Ἰστιόδωρος**
SICILY:
—SYRACUSE?:
——(Νητ.): (**1**) hell. Manganaro, *PdelP* forthcoming no. 4 II, 6 (s. Δωρόθεος)

**Ἰστληῖα**
KORINTHIA:
—KORINTH: (**1**) iv-v AD *Corinth* VIII (3) 689, 2

**Ἴστρος**
AITOLIA:
—THERMOS*: (**1**) s. iii BC *IG* IX (1)² (1) 60 II, 26

**Ἴστων**
S. ITALY (CALABRIA):
—TARAS-TARENTUM: (**1**) s. iv BC Guarducci, *Ep. Gr.* 1 p. 290 no. 10 (Landi, *DISMG* 189) (ʰίστ-: f. Ἰστιειός)

**Ἴστωρ**
S. ITALY (BRUTTIUM):
—SYBARIS-THOURIOI-COPIAE: (**1**) c. 410-400 BC *Coll. de Luynes* 581; *NC* 1896, pp. 138 ff. (coins)

**Ἴσυλλος**
ARGOLIS:
—EPIDAUROS: (**1**) c. 280 BC *RE* (-); *Coll. Alex.* pp. 132 ff. (s. Σωκράτης)

**Ἰσχαγόρας**
LAKONIA:
—SPARTA: (**1**) 422-421 BC *RE* (-) (Poralla² 400)

**Ἴσχανδρος**
ARKADIA: (**1**) 348 BC D. xix 303
MESSENIA:
—MESSENE: (**2**) ii-i BC *SEG* XLI 343, 10 ([Ἴσ]χανδρος, [Ἄρ]χανδρος?, [Τύ]χανδρος—*LGPN*)

**Ἰσχέμαχος**
ARGOLIS:
—EPIDAUROS: (**1**) iv/iii BC *IG* IV (1)² 203 (f. Δαμοκλῆς)
ARKADIA:
—TEGEA: (**2**) c. 225 BC *SEG* XI 414, 22 (Perlman E.5) (f. Αὐτόνοος)

**Ἰσχένοος**
AIGINA: (**1**) vi/v BC Hdt. vii 181; viii 92 (f. Πυθέας)

**Ἰσχόλαος**
LAKONIA:
—SPARTA: (**1**) v/iv BC *RE* (-) (Poralla² 401); cf. D.S. xv 64. 3 (Ἰσχόλας—D.S.)

**Ἰσχόμαχος**
AITOLIA:
—MESATA: (**1**) f. iii BC *IG* XII (8) 151, 12 (f. Σείρακος)
ARKADIA:
—MEGALOPOLIS: (**2**) iv/iii BC ib. v (2) 479, 3
—TEGEA: (**3**) s. iii BC ib. 116, 4 (f. Ἀριστίων); (**4**) c. 240-229 BC ib. 12 (Ἰσχόμ[αχος])
PELOPONNESE: (**5**) c. 230-200 BC *BCH* 45 (1921) p. 11 II, 38 (Ἰσκό-: f. —μαχος: name—Oulhen)
S. ITALY (BRUTTIUM):
—KROTON: (**6**) 508-504 BC Moretti, *Olymp.* 148; 153

**Ἰσχόπολις**
AKARNANIA:
—STRATOS: (**1**) iv/iii BC Unp. (Lazaros Kolonos–E.L. Schwandner) (s./d. Νίκων)

**Ἰσχυρός**
SICILY:
—HIMERA: (1) 516 BC Moretti, *Olymp.* 137

**Ἰταλία**
EPIROS:
—NIKOPOLIS?: (1) imp. Unp. (Nikopolis Mus.)
ILLYRIA:
—EPIDAMNOS-DYRRHACHION: (2) hell.-imp. *IDyrrh* 179 (Εἰτ-: d. Πατούλκιος)
S. ITALY (CALABRIA):
—BRENTESION-BRUNDISIUM: (3) imp. *CIL* IX 172 (Lat. Pomponia Hitalia)
S. ITALY (CAMPANIA):
—DIKAIARCHIA-PUTEOLI*: (4) imp. *Eph. Ep.* VIII 400 (Lat. Decia Italia: freed.)
—NEAPOLIS*: (5) i BC/i AD *NScav* 1926, pp. 235-6; cf. Leiwo p. 97 no. 47 (Lat. Fuficia Italia: freed.)

**Ἰταλικός**
SICILY:
—PANORMOS: (1) ?ii AD *CIL* X 7267 (Lat. Italicus)

**Ἰταλός**
ARKADIA:
—KLEITOR: (1) m. iii AD *SEG* XXXV 350 I, 7 (f. Αὐρ. Εἰρανίων)
SICILY:
—HERBESSOS: (2) ?s. vi BC *Kokalos* 14-15 (1968-9) p. 200 (vase)

**Ἰταναῖος**
S. ITALY (BRUTTIUM):
—KROTON: (1) iv BC Iamb., *VP* 267 (*FVS* 1 p. 446)

**Ἰφιάνασσα**
SICILY:
—NEAITON: (1) ii-iii AD *Helikon* 2 (1962) p. 497 (Εἰφιόνισα?)

**Ἰφιγένεια**
S. ITALY (CAMPANIA):
—POMPEII: (1) i BC-i AD *CIL* IV 457 (Lat. Iphigenia)

**Ἰφικλῆς**
EPIROS?: (1) 375 AD *PLRE* I (-)

**Ἰφικρατίδας**
LAKONIA:
—SPARTA: (1) ?viii-vii BC *HE* 2718 (Poralla² 402) (f. Ἑρπυλίδας, Ἐράτων, Χαῖρις, Λύκος, Ἆγις, Ἀλέξων, Γύλιππος: fict.?)

**Ἰφίς**
S. ITALY (LUCANIA):
—VILLA POTENZA (MOD.): (1) f. i AD *BdA* 69 (1984) pp. 40-3 (Lat. Petrusidia Iphis)
SICILY:
—KATANE: (2) imp. *CIL* X 7087 (Lat. Publicia Ifis)

**Ἰφιστείδας**
MESSENIA:
—MESSENE: (1) f. iii BC *SEG* XLI 342, 2; cf. *PAE* 1991, p. 100 no. 8 (Ἰφιστείδας, —σιξίδας—ed. pr.)

**Ἰφιτος**
ELIS: (1) ?viii BC *RE* (2) (II ?s. Αἵμων, Πραξωνίδης, Ἰφιτος I: fict.?)

**Ἰφίων**
AIGINA: (1) f. v BC Pi., *O.* viii, 81 with Schol. ad loc. (f. Ἀλκιμέδων, Τιμοσθένης)
KORINTHIA:
—KORINTH: (2) vi/v BC *RE* (-); Page, *FGE* 810, 812 (painter)

**Ἰχαίων**
SICILY:
—SELINOUS: (1) m. v BC Dubois, *IGDS* 36, 5 (Arena, *Iscr. Sic.* I 69) (Ἰχαίōν—Dubois, Χαίōν—Arena: s. Μαμμάρειος)

**Ἰχωνίδας**
ARGOLIS:
—ARGOS: (1) ?c. 575-550 BC *SEG* XI 336, 11; *LSAG*² p. 168 no. 7 (date) (-χō-)

**Ἰώ**
ARGOLIS:
—ARGOS: (1) ii AD *SEG* XXVIII 223, 3 (Βηδία Εἰώ: d. Βήδιος Πρόφαντος, Κλ. Ἀρτεμώ)

**Ἰώαννα**
KORINTHIA:
—KORINTH: (1) v-vi AD ib. XXIX 315 (d. Ἰωάννης, Μαρία)
SICILY:
—SYRACUSE: (2) iii-v AD Strazzulla 448 + Ferrua, *NG* 67 (Lat. Ioanetis (gen.))

**Ἰωάννης**
AITOLIA:
—KLAUSEION (MOD.): (1) byz. *PAE* 1958, p. 61 δ; cf. *BCH* 83 (1959) p. 664
ARGOLIS:
—ARGOS: (2) ?iv-v AD *IG* IV (1) 628, 4; cf. *TMByz* 9 (1985) p. 369 no. 109
—PITYOUSSA: (3) byz. *SEG* XVII 170, 2; cf. *TMByz* 9 (1985) p. 371 no. 128 (f. Ἐπιτύγχανος)
—TROIZEN: (4) byz. *IG* IV (1) 784; cf. *TMByz* 9 (1985) p. 370 no. 126
EPIROS:
—VOTONOSI (MOD.): (5) byz. *SEG* XXIV 457 b (Ἰοάνις)
ILLYRIA:
—EPIDAMNOS-DYRRHACHION: (6) c. 440-482 AD *PLRE* II (29); (7) f. vi AD Procop., *Vand.* iii 11. 7
KORINTHIA:
—KORINTH: (8) byz. *Corinth* VIII (1) 207; cf. *TMByz* 9 (1985) p. 361 no. 22 (-νις); (9) ~ *Corinth* VIII (3) 563; cf. *TMByz* 9 (1985) p. 366 no. 67; (10) ~ *Corinth* VIII (3) 605 (Ἰω[άννης]?); (11) ~ ib. 721; (12) ~ Bees 42; cf. *TMByz* 9 (1985) p. 359 no. 2 (Ἰωάν[νης]); (13) v-vi AD *SEG* XXIX 315 (f. Ἰώαννα); (14) ~ *Corinth* VIII (3) 531, 3, 8; cf. *TMByz* 9 (1985) p. 365 no. 54 (Ἰωάν(ν)ης: s. Ἀφοβία); (15) m. v AD Cyr. S., *V. Cyriac.* 1 (f. Κυριακός)
MESSENIA:
—MESSENE*: (16) 431-458 AD *ABME* 11 (1969) p. 89 (bp.)
SICILY: (17) byz. *Epigraphica* 5-6 (1943-4) p. 93
—AKRAI: (18) iii-v AD *Akrai* p. 167 no. 40 (*SEG* XIV 587) (Ἰοάνις Ἰουστῖνος)
—KATANE: (19) imp. *CIL* X 7116; cf. Ferrua, *NG* 452 (Lat. Ioannes)
—SYRACUSE: (20) iii-v AD *SEG* IV 7; cf. Ferrua, *NG* 271 a (Ἰ. (gen.?)—Ferrua)

**Ἰωάννιος**
SICILY:
—SYRACUSE: (1) iii-v AD Agnello 31; cf. Ferrua, *NG* 84 a; (2) ~ Wessel 329 (*SEG* XXXIX 1030); (3) 439 AD *IG* XIV 130 (Strazzulla 68; Wessel 950)

**Ἰώαννος**
SICILY:
—SYRACUSE: (1) iii-v AD Strazzulla 311 (Ἰό-)

**Ἰωβινιανός**
SICILY:
—SYRACUSE: (1) iii-v AD *IG* XIV 129 (Strazzulla 67)

**Ἰων**
AKARNANIA: (1) iii BC *IG* IX (1)² (2) 575; Fraser–Rönne, *BWGT* pl. 27 (f. Ξενίας)
—ASTAKOS: (2) ?iii-ii BC *AD* 26 (1971) Chron. p. 321 (f. Σῶσις)
ARGOLIS:
—ARGOS: (3) c. 220-200 BC *SEG* XI 414, 31 + Peek, *IAEpid* 331 (Perlman E.5) (Ἰάρων— *SEG*: s. Καλλίστρατος)
KORINTHIA:
—KORINTH: (4) m. i AD *Corinth* VIII (1) 19, 4, 8 (Stephanis 1306) (and Argolis Argos: Γ. Ἰούλ. Ἰ.)
LAKONIA:
—SPARTA: (5) iii BC *SEG* XL 348 B, 3

**Ἰωναθᾶς**
MESSENIA:
—KYPARISSIA: (1) iii AD *PAE* 1958, p. 215; cf. *BE* 1966, no. 197 (Jew?)
SICILY:
—SYRACUSE: (2) iii-v AD *Riv. Arch. Crist.* 31 (1955) p. 47; cf. Ferrua, *NG* 353

**Ἰωνᾶς**
S. ITALY (CAMPANIA):
—POMPEII: (1) i BC-i AD *CIL* IV 2402-3; 2406 (Lat. Ionas/Ionis)

**Ἰωνία**
S. ITALY (CAMPANIA):
—DIKAIARCHIA-PUTEOLI: (1) imp. *Röm. Mitt.* 19 (1904) p. 187 (Lat. Ionia: d. Φιλαινίς)

**Ἰωνική**
S. ITALY (CAMPANIA):
—DIKAIARCHIA-PUTEOLI: (1) imp. *CIL* X 2817 (Lat. Pa. Ionice); (2) ?i-ii AD ib. 2609 (Lat. Lollia Ionice: m. Iulia Secunda)
—POMPEII: (3) i BC-i AD ib. IV 2049 (Lat. Ionice)
—POMPEII?: (4) i AD ib. 2393 (Lat. Dapna Ionice)

**Ἰωνικός**
S. ITALY (APULIA):
—VENUSIA: (1) imp. *NScav* 1939, p. 149 no. I (Lat. Ionicus: s. Pompeia Faceta)
S. ITALY (CAMPANIA):
—POMPEII: (2) i BC-i AD *CIL* IV 1588 (Lat. Ionicus); (3) ~ ib. 1879 (Lat. Ionicus); (4) ~ ib. 3048 (Lat. Ionicus); (5) ~ ib. 10092 (Lat. Ionicus)
—SURRENTUM: (6) imp. ib. X 746 (Lat. Q. Otincius Ionicus)

**Ἰωσῆς**
ARGOLIS:
—ARGOS: (1) iii AD *BCH* 27 (1903) p. 262 no. 4, 1 (Αὐρ. Ἰ.: Jew)
MESSENIA:
—KORONE: (2) 246 AD *IG* V (1) 1398, 91; Robert, *Hell.* 3 p. 100 (Αὐρ. Ἰ.: Jew); (3) ~ *IG* V (1) 1398, 92; Robert, *Hell.* 3 p. 100 (Αὐρ. Ἰ.: Jew)
S. ITALY (APULIA):
—VENUSIA: (4) iv-v AD *JIWE* I 94 (*CIJ* I 585) (Εἰω-: Jew); (5) v AD *JIWE* I 43 (Εἰοσ[ῆς]: Jew); (6) ~ ib. 59 (*CIJ* I 581) (f. Βερονίκη: Jew)

**Ἰωσήφ**
S. ITALY (APULIA):
—VENUSIA: (1) v AD *JIWE* I 70 (*CIJ* I 584) (I f. Ἰωσήφ II: Jew); (2) ~ *JIWE* I 70 (*CIJ* I 584) (Ἰο-: II s. Ἰωσήφ I: Jew); (3) ~ *JIWE* I 79 (*CIJ* I 586) ([Ἰ]ωσήφ: s. —άριος: Jew)

**Ἰωτάπη**
ARGOLIS:
—HERMIONE: (1) iii AD *IG* IV (1) 699, 3 (Ἰουλ. Ἰ.: I m. Ἰωτάπη II); (2) ~ ib. l. 5 (II d. Αὐρ. Ἀμάραντος, Ἰουλ. Ἰωτάπη I)

# K

Κάβαισος
ARKADIA:
—MANTINEIA-ANTIGONEIA:
——(Enyalia): (1) m. iv BC IG v (2) 271, 9 (f. Δαμοκλῆς)

Κάβαλλος
SICILY:
—KENTORIPA: (1) hell. ib. XIV 574, 5 (Dubois, IGDS 188) (Ἀρτεμίσκος Κάβαλλος, Κάβαμος—apogr.: s. Νύμφων)

Κάβας
ARGOLIS:
—ARGOS:
——Kerkas: (1) v BC Suda A 942; FGrH 2 T. 1 (Σκάβρας?: f. Ἀκουσίλαος)

Καβιρίας
TRIPHYLIA:
—TYPANEAI: (1) c. 230-200 BC BCH 45 (1921) p. 12 II, 79 (f. Καλλίστρατος)

Καβωνίδας
LAKONIA:
—SPARTA: (1) i BC/i AD IG v (1) 48, 1 (Bradford (-)) (s. Ἀνδρόνικος)

Καγψίας
AITOLIA:
—POTIDANIA: (1) m. ii BC SBBerlAk 1936, p. 371 a, 8 (SEG XLI 528 A) (s. Λαδάμης)

Κάδμεια
EPIROS:
—MOLOSSOI: (1) iv/iii BC Plu., Pyrr. 5. 10 (d. Ἀλέξανδρος, Κλεοπάτρα)

Κάδμος
S. ITALY (APULIA):
—LARINUM: (1) imp. CIL IX 6243 (Lat. Cadmus)
S. ITALY (CAMPANIA):
—DIKAIARCHIA-PUTEOLI: (2) m. i AD Camodeca, L'Archivio Puteolano I p. 87 no. 18 (Lat. Ti. C[lau]dius Cadmus)

Κάδοσις
SICILY:
—SELINOUS: (1) f. v BC Dubois, IGDS 38, 13 (Arena, Iscr. Sic. I 63) (s. Ματυλαῖος)

Καθήκων
LAKONIA:
—SPARTA: (1) c. 160 AD IG v (1) 71 III, 49; 86, 27 (Bradford (1)) (f. Νικηφόρος)
——Limnai: (2) c. 70-100 AD IG v (1) 676, 19 (Bradford (2)) (Καθήκων: f. Σωτήριχος)

Καθήχουσα
S. ITALY (CALABRIA):
—BRENTESION-BRUNDISIUM: (1) imp. CIL IX 154 (Lat. Catecusa)

Καιίλαος
ILLYRIA:
—SKAMPIS*: (1) v-iv BC Stud. Alb. 1969 (2), p. 176

Καίκαλος
ARGOLIS:
—ARGOS: (1) ?iv BC RE (-) (dub.)

Καικιλία
SICILY:
—AKRAI: (1) imp. SEG XLII 832, 5; (2) iii-v AD IG XIV 235 (Agnello 63); cf. Ferrua, NG 490 (-κει-: m. Ἀλφ. Κλώδις)

—KATANE: (3) iii-v AD IG XIV 542 (Agnello 53; Wessel 852); cf. Riv. Arch. Crist. 18 (1941) p. 241 no. 138 (Κε-)
—MELITA: (4) imp.? IG XIV 2406. 27 (vase) (-κελ-: d. Κάσσιος)
—SYRACUSE: (5) iii-v AD Strazzulla 358 (Wessel 1227)

Καικιλιανός
SICILY:
—KATANE: (1) iii-v AD IG XIV 541 (Agnello 52; Wessel 590) (Κεκι-)

Καικινιάδας
S. ITALY (BRUTTIUM):
—LOKROI EPIZEPHYRIOI:
——(Γαγ.): (1) iv/iii BC De Franciscis 19, 3 (f. Χαρίδαμος)

Κάϊκος
SICILY:
—KAMARINA: (1) f. v BC Cordano, Tessere Pubbliche 105 (-ρος: f. Κλεάριστος)

Καιλεσῖνα
SICILY:
—SYRACUSE: (1) iii-v AD Strazzulla 287 (Barreca 228); cf. Ferrua, NG 54 (Καιλε(ρ)ῖνα?, Καιλεσ(τ)ῖνα?)

Καίλιος
SICILY:
—SELINOUS: (1) f. v BC Dubois, IGDS 38, 6, 17 (Arena, Iscr. Sic. I 63) (f. Ῥῶμις); (2) ~ Dubois, IGDS 38, 15 (Arena, Iscr. Sic. I 63) (f. Φοῖνιξ)

Καινίας
S. ITALY (CALABRIA):
—TARAS-TARENTUM: (1) iv BC Iamb., VP 267 (FVS I p. 446)

Καινίς
S. ITALY (APULIA):
—VENUSIA: (1) ?ii AD CIL IX 517 (Lat. Flavia Caenis: m. Flaminia Lucilla)
S. ITALY (CAMPANIA):
—DIKAIARCHIA-PUTEOLI: (2) ?i-ii AD ib. X 2286 (Lat. Cl. Caenis)

Καιπίων
ILLYRIA:
—DASSARETIOI: (1) ii-iii AD Sp. 71 (1931) p. 109 no. 262; 98 (1941-8) p. 122 no. 268 (s. Δρύας, f. Δρύας)

Καισάρεια
ILLYRIA:
—EPIDAMNOS-DYRRHACHION: (1) s. v AD PLRE II (1) (m. Ὑπάτιος (Other))

Καισάριος
SICILY:
—SYRACUSE: (1) iii-v AD Strazzulla 305 (Agnello 24; Wessel 860) (Κε-: f. Ἑρμιόνη)

Καίσιος
S. ITALY (CALABRIA):
—UZENTUM: (1) f. iii BC Coll. Hunter I p. 152 no. 9 with pl. 11. 7 (coin)
SICILY:
—ENTELLA: (2) iv/iii BC SEG XXX 1119, 1 (Dubois, IGDS 206) (f. Λεύκιος)

Κάλα
ILLYRIA:
—EPIDAMNOS-DYRRHACHION: (1) hell.-imp. IDyrrh 257 (Κάλα: d. Σωστρίων)

TRIPHYLIA:
—SAMIKON: (2) iii BC SEG XXV 471

Κάλαικος
SICILY:
—KAMARINA: (1) f. v BC Cordano, Tessere Pubbliche 41 (f. —ων)

Κάλαϊς
S. ITALY (BRUTTIUM):
—RHEGION: (1) iv BC Iamb., VP 267 (FVS I p. 447)
—SYBARIS-THOURIOI-COPIAE: (2) s. i BC Hor., Carm. iii 9. 14 (Lat. Calais: s. Ὄρνυτος)
S. ITALY (CAMPANIA):
—POMPEII: (3) i BC-i AD CIL IV 2495 (Lat. Calaes)

Κάλαισος
LAKONIA:
—SPARTA: (1) s. vii BC PMGF I 5 fr. 2, 9, 12

Κάλαμος
S. ITALY (CAMPANIA):
—POMPEII: (1) i BC-i AD CIL IV 9127 (Lat. Calamus)

Καλανδίων
KORINTHIA:
—SIKYON (NR.): (1) ii AD SEG XI 273
SICILY:
—KATANE: (2) iii-v AD Ferrua, NG 419 (Καλαν[δίων])
—SYRACUSE: (3) iii-v AD Agnello 33 (Guarducci, Ep. Gr. 4 p. 524 no. 2) (Καλα(ν)δίων)

Κάλανδρος
ARKADIA:
—KLEITOR: (1) i-ii AD IG v (2) 377

Καλανεύς
ARGOLIS:
—EPIDAUROS*: (1) c. 370-365 BC Peek, IAEpid 52 A, 26

Κάλαρχος
LAKONIA:
—HIPPOLA: (1) byz. SEG XLII 304

Κάλας
ELIS: (1) 72 BC Moretti, Olymp. 692

Καλάτυχος
SICILY:
—KATANE: (1) imp. IG XIV 496 (Πεσκέννις Καλάτιχος)

Καλβασία
SICILY:
—SYRACUSE: (1) iii-v AD Ferrua, NG 333

Καλεδίας
SICILY:
—GELA-PHINTIAS?: (1) f. v BC Dubois, IGDS 134 b, 6 (Arena, Iscr. Sic. II 47)

Κάλεια
KEPHALLENIA:
—SAME: (1) f. iii BC Op. Ath. 10 (1971) p. 66 no. 12 (BCH 83 (1959) p. 658)

Καλεῖς
AKARNANIA:
—PALAIROS: (1) hell.-imp. SEG XXVII 158 (?d. Ἀρτεμιδώρα)

Καλένδιος
SICILY:
—AKRAI: (1) iii-v AD Akrai p. 167 no. 41 (Καλήδις)

## Καλεύς
SICILY:
—SELINOUS: (1) vi/v BC Manganaro, *PdelP* forthcoming no. 18, 4 (f. *Μυτάλας*)

## Κάλη
S. ITALY (APULIA):
—CANNAE*: (1) m. i AD *Epig. Rom. di Canosa* 195 a (Lat. Minucia Cale: freed.)
—LUCERIA*: (2) imp. *ASP* 34 (1981) p. 32 no. 39 (Lat. –ia Cale: freed.)
S. ITALY (CAMPANIA):
—DIKAIARCHIA-PUTEOLI: (3) m. i AD *Rend. Linc.* 30 (1975) pp. 361-2 (Lat. Cassia Cale: m. L. Cassius Cerialis)
—POMPEII: (4) i BC-i AD *CIL* IV 2139 (Lat. Caleni (dat.))
SICILY:
—KATANE: (5) imp. ib. X 7081 (Lat. Cale)
—SYRACUSE: (6) iii-v AD Strazzulla 353 (Barreca 206)

## Καλημέρα
S. ITALY (CAMPANIA):
—SALERNUM: (1) ?ii AD *IItal* 1 (1) 63 (*CIL* X 589) (Lat. Flavia Calemera)
SICILY:
—KENTORIPA: (2) iii-v AD *IGLMP* 13 (Wessel 651); cf. Ferrua, *NG* 473 (*Καλὴ πρε(σ)β.—IGLMP*)
—SYRACUSE: (3) iii-v AD Strazzulla 359; cf. Ferrua, *NG* 131 a (*Καλη[μ]έρα*)
—THERMAI HIMERAIAI: (4) i-ii AD *CIL* X 7381 (*ILat. Term. Imer.* 58) (Lat. Calemera)

## Καλήμερος
LAKONIA:
—SPARTA: (1) f. iii AD *IG* V (1) 170, 1; *BSA* 80 (1985) p. 245 (date) (Bradford (-)) (*Αὐρ. Κ.*: s. *Ἀγαθοκλῆς*)

## Καλήν
AKARNANIA: (1) iii BC Cook, *Hadra Vases* 16 (*Κα.ηνο.* (gen.), *Κα[λ]ήν*: f. *Κλῆμις*)

## Καλία
ITHAKE*: (1) inc. *BSA* 39 (1938-9) p. 28 no. 3

## Καλίας
S. ITALY (LUCANIA):
—METAPONTION: (1) s. v BC *SEG* XXIX 963 (*Καλ(λ)ίας*—ed.)

## Καλικλέας
ITHAKE: (1) ?m. vii BC *LSAG*² pp. 230-1; p. 234 no. 2 (potter)

## Καλικράτεια
LAKONIA:
—SPARTA: (1) v BC *SEG* XI 664 (bronze) (Lazzarini 93; Poralla² 407a) (-τια)

## Καλικράτης
SICILY: (1) s. vi BC Dubois, *IGDS* 217 (vase) (Arena, *Iscr. Sic.* I 74) (-τēς: f. *Μενναρώ*)
—KASMENAI: (2) vi BC *Arch. Class.* 17 (1965) p. 193 + *ZPE* 99 (1993) pp. 123-4 (-τēς: s. —ιπος, *Αἶσα*: kalos)

## Καλικρατώ
ARKADIA:
—TEGEA: (1) imp. *IG* V (2) 218

## Καλινόμας
MESSENIA:
—THOURIA: (1) f. ii BC *SEG* XI 972, 33 (f. *Δεξίας*)

## Καλιόπα
KORINTHIA:
—KORINTH: (1) c. 590-570 BC Amyx 26. 1 (vase) (Lorber 101) (*Καλιόπ[α]*: fict.?)

## Καλίοψις
SICILY:
—MEGARA HYBLAIA: (1) vi/v BC Dubois, *IGDS* 24 (Arena, *Iscr. Sic.* I 6); cf. *SEG* XXXVIII 946 (*Καλίοψ[ις], Καλιόψ[ιος]?*)

## Κάλιππος
EPIROS:
—AMBRAKIA: (1) ?iii BC *BCH* 79 (1955) p. 267 (f. *Καλλίας*)

## Καλιστεύς
SICILY:
—MEGARA HYBLAIA: (1) vi/v BC Dubois, *IGDS* 23 (Arena, *Iscr. Sic.* I 5)

## Καλιστίων
ARGOLIS:
—EPIDAUROS: (1) c. 360-350 BC *IG* IV (1)² 113, 6 (*Καλιστίων*)

## Καλιστόλας
MESSENIA:
—THOURIA: (1) ii-i BC ib. V (1) 1385, 15 (s. *Ξενόδαμος*)

## Καλίστρατος
KORINTHIA:
—KORINTH: (1) v BC ib. IV (1) 355 b (bronze) (s. *Διόδωρος*)

## Κάλλαισχρος
AKARNANIA:
—PALAIROS: (1) ?iii BC ib. IX (1)² (2) 540

## Καλλᾶς
ARKADIA:
—TEGEA: (1) ii AD ib. V (2) 55, 42 (s. *Σωσικράτης*)

## Καλλέας
AITOLIA: (1) c. 315-280 BC *FD* III (1) 143, 1 (f. *Τηλεφάνης*)
AKARNANIA:
—ASTAKOS: (2) s. iv BC *IG* IV (1)² 95, 63 + IX (1)² (2) p. XVII n. 1 (Perlman E.2); Perlman pp. 46-9 (date) (*Καλλίας*—ed.: s. *Νίκων*)
ARGOLIS:
—ARGOS: (3) iii BC *SEG* XI 371, 5 (*GVI* 1328) (f. *Κράτερος*); (4) ?i AD *RE* s.v. Kallias (21); *AP* xi 232; (5) ii AD *SEG* XVI 258 c, 4 (*Γν. Πομπ. Κ.*: s. *Γν. Πομπ. Κλεοσθένης*, ?s. *Κλ. Φιλομάθεια*)
ARKADIA: (6) iii BC ib. I 360
LAKONIA:
—SPARTA: (7) 140-160 AD *IG* V (1) 64, 12; 74, 7; 358, [1] (Bradford (2)) (s. *Καλλικράτης*); (8) c. 140-160 AD *IG* V (1) 154, 10 (Bradford (3)) (I f. *Καλλέας* II); (9) ~ *IG* V (1) 154, 10 (Bradford (1)) (II s. *Καλλέας* I)

## Καλλείδας
ARKADIA:
—MANTINEIA-ANTIGONEIA: (1) s. iv BC Peek, *NIEpid* 16, 29 (Perlman E.6) (f. *Διεύχης*)
—ORCHOMENOS: (2) ?c. 369-361 BC *BCH* 102 (1978) p. 347, 2 (*IPArk* 14)
ARKADIA?: (3) 369 BC *BCH* 39 (1915) p. 55 no. III, 2 ([*Κ*]*αλλείδας*)

## Καλλενίκα
S. ITALY (CAMPANIA):
—NEAPOLIS (NR.): (1) f. iv BC *INap* 190 (vase) (Dubois, *IGDGG* I 31)

## Κάλλεον
ARGOLIS:
—ARGOS: (1) ii BC *Mnem.* NS 47 (1919) p. 170 no. 24, 14 (*Κάλλε[ον]*)
—TIRYNS: (2) iii/ii BC *IG* IV (1) 668

## Καλλήν
ARGOLIS:
—EPIDAUROS:
——(Hysminatai): (1) 146 BC ib. IV (1)² 28, 12 (s. *Μνασίας*); (2) ~ ib. l. 22 (f. *Ἱάρων*)
DALMATIA:
—ISSA: (3) ii BC *SEG* XXXI 600 (s. *Σωτέλης*)
——(Hylleis): (4) iv/iii BC Brunšmid p. 8, 42 (f. *Σιμίας*)
ILLYRIA:
—APOLLONIA: (5) hell. *IApoll* 342 (tile) (s. *Παυσήν*); (6) ~ ib. 360 (tile); (7) iii-ii BC ib. 33; (8) c. 250-50 BC *NZ* 20 (1927) p. 53; Maier 11; 84 (coin) (Ceka 65-6) (money.); (9) ~ *Bakërr Hoard* p. 64 no. 62 (coin) (Ceka 58) (pryt.); (10) i BC Unp. (Paris, BN) 71; *IApoll Ref. Bibl.* n. 37 (coin); (11) imp. ib. 36 (*Καλλήν*)
—EPIDAMNOS-DYRRHACHION: (12) iii BC *IDyrrh* 12 (s. *Καλλιππίδας*); (13) c. 250-50 BC Ceka, *Probleme* p. 151 no. 29 (coin) (pryt.) ?= (14); (14) ~ Maier 238-50; 478; Münsterberg p. 39; Nachtr. p. 15; *Jubice Hoard* p. 97 nos. 44-5 (Ceka 24; 58; 115; 144; 206; 223; 254; 259; 277) + *IApoll Ref. Bibl.* n. 68 (307; 321; 336; 349; 352) + *IApoll Ref. Bibl.* n. 94 (368; 384; 391; 408; 452) (pryt.) ?= (13); (15) ii-i BC *IDyrrh* 541 (tiles); (16) hell.-imp. ib. 245 (f. *Θεόκριτος*); (17) ~ ib. 258 (I f. *Καλλήν* II); (18) ~ ib. (II s. *Καλλήν* I); (19) ~ ib. 259 (s. *Φίλων*)
—SKODRAI: (20) a. 168 BC *Iliria* 1972, p. 404; *God. Balk. Isp.* 13. 11 (1976) pp. 226 f. nos. 7-10 (coin)

## Κάλλης
AITOLIA:
—THERMOS*: (1) s. iii BC *IG* IX (1)² (1) 60 III, 1 ([*Κ*]*άλλης*)
ARGOLIS:
—ARGOS: (2) 105 BC *JÖAI* 14 (1911) Beibl. p. 146 no. 4, 25 (s. *Δαμόκριτος*)
S. ITALY (LUCANIA):
—METAPONTION: (3) m. iii BC *SEG* XXX 1175, 15; cf. XXXIV 1006 (*Κάλλε̄ς*—ed., [*Βα*]*κάλλε̄ς*—Guarducci: doctor)

## Καλλιάδας
LAKONIA:
—SPARTA: (1) iii BC ib. XL 348 B, 7 (*Καλλιάδ[ας]* νεώτ.); (2) c. 30-20 BC *IG* V (1) 211, 9 (Bradford (1)) (s. *Εὐδαιμοτέλης*); (3) ~ *IG* V (1) 211, 11 (Bradford (2)) (s. *Καλλικράτης*)

## Καλλίαρ
ELIS: (1) 101-109 AD *IvOl* 89, 1 (I f. *Καλλίαρ* II); (2) ~ ib. l. 1, 5 ([*Καλλί*]*αρ*: II s. *Καλλίαρ* I, f. *Καλλίαρ* III: *Α*.); (3) ~ ib. l. 5 (III s. *Καλλίαρ* II)

## Καλλίας
ACHAIA:
—DYME: (1) s. iii BC *SEG* XIII 278, 16
—PELLENE: (2) m. iii BC *IG* V (2) 368, 97 (s. *Λ—*); (3) ?257-253 BC Nachtergael, *Les Galates* 7, 13; 10, 11 (s. *Πολύξενος*)
AIGINA: (4) f. v BC Pi., *N.* vi, 36; cf. Klee p. 79 no. 43; p. 91 no. 62; p. 101 no. 56; (5) m. ii BC *Alt-Ägina* 1 (2) p. 43 no. 2
AITOLIA: (6) ?271 BC *Syll*³ 419, 2; (7) ?265-259 BC Nachtergael, *Les Galates* 4, 3; (8) ?228-215 BC *FD* III (4) 364, 3
—KALLION/KALLIPOLIS: (9) 263-262 BC *IG* IX (1)² (1) 3 A, 19; (10) 139 BC *SGDI* 2137, 1
—KALYDON: (11) f. iv BC *IG* IX (1)² (1) 138, 7
AKARNANIA: (12) iv/iii BC *Thess. Mnem.* 160 (*IG* IX (1)² (2) 584) (f. *Ἄνδρων*)
ARGOLIS:
—ARGOS: (13) s. iv BC ib. II² 8370 (f. *Μένης*)
—ARGOS?: (14) c. 400-375 BC ib. 78, 4 (f. *Μελάνθιος*)
—EPIDAUROS: (15) c. 370 BC ib. IV (1)² 102, 53 ?= (17); (16) c. 365-335 BC ib. 103, 77-8, 80, 82, 84, 87-9 ?= (17)
——Naupheis: (17) c. 365-335 BC ib. l. 113 ?= (16) (15)

—EPIDAUROS*: **(18)** c. 340-320 BC Peek, *NIEpid* 19 B, 22
—HERMIONE: **(19)** ii-i BC *IG* IV (1) 732 II, 6 (s. Ἀριστοκλῆς); **(20)** c. 135-130 BC *FD* III (4) 169, 2, 9 (f. Κυλοίας)
—KLEONAI: **(21)** 323 BC *SEG* xxx 66, 42 (Καλλί[ας]: ?s. Ἐχέμβροτος, f. Λάπυρις)
—TROIZEN: **(22)** ?146 BC *IG* IV (1) 757 A, 25 (f. —νιος); **(23)** ~ ib. 757 B, 8
ARKADIA:
—KLEITOR: **(24)** ?253 BC Nachtergael, *Les Galates* 10, 30; cf. Stephanis 1428 (f. Κλειτίας)
—TEGEA: **(25)** m. iv BC *IG* v (2) 6, 88; **(26)** s. iv BC *SEG* xxxvi 383, 4 ([Κα]λλίας: s. Σάστρατος); **(27)** iv/iii BC *IG* v (2) 38, 62; **(28)** iii BC ib. 30, 12; **(29)** ~ ib. 356, 1 ([Κ]αλλίας: s. Καλλισθένης); **(30)** f. iii BC ib. 35, 22 (s. Ἀρχαγόρας) ?= **(32)**; **(31)** ~ ib. l. 27 (f. Λακράτης); **(32)** ~ ib. ix (2) 430 (*GVI* 1460) (Κα(λ)(λ)ίας: s. Ἀρχαγόρας) ?= **(30)**; **(33)** ?254 BC Nachtergael, *Les Galates* 9, 44 ([Καλ]λίας?: I f. Καλλίας II); **(34)** ~ ib. l. 44 (Κ[αλλίας]?: II s. Καλλίας I); **(35)** ii BC *SEG* xxiii 233; **(36)** ~ *EILakArk* 14 (?s. Ἐπιτέλης)
——(Athaneatai): **(37)** s. iv BC *IG* v (2) 41, 19 ([Κα]λλίας); **(38)** ~ ib. l. 33 (s. Ἐπιτέλης); **(39)** iv/iii BC ib. 38, 18 ([Καλ]λίας: s. Στίλπυρος); **(40)** iii BC ib. 40, 31 (s. Εὐα—)
——(Hippothoitai): **(41)** iv/iii BC ib. 38, 44 (s. Δαμόφιλος)
——(Krariotai): **(42)** f. iii BC ib. 36, 41 (s. Ἀρίστων); **(43)** ~ ib. l. 46 (f. Ὀνάσιμος: metic); **(44)** s. iii BC ib. l. 126 (f. Σωσικράτης: metic)
DALMATIA:
—ISSA:
——(Hylleis): **(45)** iv/iii BC Brunšmid p. 8, 43 (s. Πρώταρχος)
—PHAROS: **(46)** iv/iii BC *GVI* 1532 (*CEG* II 662) (f. Χάρμος)
ELIS: **(47)** s. vi BC Hdt. v 44-5 (-ης: mantis/Iamidai); **(48)** 28-16 BC *IvOl* 64, 15; 65, 18 (s. Παυσανίας: X.)
—OLYMPIA*: **(49)** imp. ib. 469, 3
EPIROS: **(50)** ii/i BC *IG* II² 8546 (f. Χλίδανον)
—AMBRAKIA: **(51)** ?iii BC *BCH* 79 (1955) p. 267 (s. Κάλιππος)
—ELATREIA: **(52)** ?iv-iii BC *SEG* xxiv 418; Hammond, *Epirus* p. 427 (locn.) (f. Μνάσιππος)
—KERKYRA: **(53)** iv/iii BC *IG* ix (1) 976, 6 (s. Ἀριστοκράτης)
KORINTHIA:
—KORINTH: **(54)** 435 BC Th. i 29. 2 (f. Καλλικράτης)
—SIKYON: **(55)** c. 365-340 BC *IG* II² 10305 (Skalet 160) (f. Πάμφιλος); **(56)** ?254 BC Nachtergael, *Les Galates* 9, 35 (Skalet 161; Stephanis 1327) (s. Ὀλυμπιόδωρος); **(57)** 116 BC *Syll*³ 704 K (Skalet 162) ([Κ]αλλίας)
LAKONIA:
—KOTYRTA: **(58)** hell.? *SEG* II 173
—SPARTA: **(59)** v/iv BC X., *HG* iv 1. 15; Plu., *Ages.* 8; *Mor.* 213 D (Poralla² 404); **(60)** iii BC *SEG* xl 348 B, 5 (Καλλίας)
LEUKAS: **(61)** c. 325-315 BC *Hesp.* 57 (1988) p. 148 B, 13 (*SEG* xxxvi 331); cf. *Hesp.* 48 (1979) pp. 78 f. with pl. 22 (f. Καλλικλῆς, Θεόδωρος)
MESSENIA:
—MESSENE: **(62)** 31 BC-14 AD *SEG* xxiii 207, 20 (s. Ἀπολλώνιος)
S. ITALY (BRUTTIUM):
—LOKROI EPIZEPHYRIOI:
——(Στρ.): **(63)** iv/iii BC De Franciscis 24, 5 (f. Κάλλιππος)
——(Τω.): **(64)** iv/iii BC ib. 32, 5 (f. Κάλλιππος); **(65)** 278 BC ib. 30, 6 (s. Κάλλιππος)
SICILY?: **(66)** ?iv-iii BC Manganaro, *QUCC* forthcoming no. 55 (bronze)
SICILY:
—KATANE: **(67)** f. v BC Ael. fr. 2 (dub.)

—LIPARA: **(68)** hell. *IG* II² 9214 (s. Ἡράκλειτος)
—SYRACUSE: **(69)** iv/iii BC *RE* (22); *FGrH* 564; Plu., *Mor.* 844 C; **(70)** ?265-259 BC Nachtergael, *Les Galates* 4, 13 (Stephanis 1326) (s. Ἀρχέτιμος)
—SYRACUSE?:
——(Τηλ.): **(71)** hell. Manganaro, *PdelP* forthcoming no. 4 V, 6 (s. Ἀριστοκλῆς)
—TAUROMENION: **(72)** c. 205 BC *IG* XIV 421 an. 36 (*SGDI* 5219) (f. Εὔφραῖος)
—TYNDARIS: **(73)** imp. Manganaro, *QUCC* forthcoming no. 22 (f. Ἐπάρατος)

## Καλλίβιος
ARGOLIS:
—ARGOS: **(1)** iii BC *SEG* XVI 249, 3 ([Κ]αλλίβιος)
ARKADIA:
—MEGALOPOLIS: **(2)** s. ii BC *IG* v (2) 439, 70 (f. Πολυήρατος); **(3)** ii/i BC ib. 442, 20 (Κ[α]λλίβιος: f. Ἀγαθάμερος)
—TEGEA: **(4)** 371 BC X., *HG* vi 5. 6-8; **(5)** 165 AD *IG* v (2) 50, 82 (s. Ἔρως)
KORINTHIA:
—SIKYON: **(6)** vi/v BC *SEG* XI 244, 41; **(7)** ?254 BC Nachtergael, *Les Galates* 9, 32 (Skalet 163; Stephanis 1329) (s. Βίων)
LAKONIA:
—SPARTA: **(8)** 404 BC X., *HG* ii 3. 14; Arist., *Ath.* 37. 2; 38. 2; Plu., *Lys.* 15 (Poralla² 405); **(9)** iii BC *SEG* xl 348 B, 4
SICILY:
—SYRACUSE: **(10)** ?ii-i BC *NScav* 1920, pp. 318-19 ([Καλ]λίβιος)

## Καλλιβούλα
SICILY:
—TYNDARIS: **(1)** iv-iii BC *IGLMP* 122

## Καλλίγειτος
AIGINA: **(1)** ?iii BC *IG* IV (1) 150 + *SEG* XI 39 (or Boiotia?: -γι-: f. Πρόξενος)

## Καλλιγένης
AKARNANIA:
—ASTAKOS: **(1)** ii BC *IG* IX (1)² (2) 434, 8 (s. Λεσφίνας)
ARKADIA:
—MEGALOPOLIS: **(2)** ii/i BC ib. v (2) 442, 10 (Καλ[λιγένης]: f. Ξένων); **(3)** ~ ib. l. 11 (s. Ξένων)
LAKONIA:
—SPARTA: **(4)** s. i BC ib. v (1) 903 a; 903 b (Bradford (-))
MESSENIA:
—MESSENE: **(5)** f. ii AD *IvOl* 458, 2 (Τιβ. Κλ. Κ.); **(6)** s. ii AD *SEG* xxxi 372 (Τιβ. Κλ. Κ.)
S. ITALY (CAMPANIA):
—DIKAIARCHIA-PUTEOLI: **(7)** ?i-ii AD *CIL* x 2274 (Lat. Calligenes: f. Σκύμνος)

## Καλλίγνωτος
ARKADIA:
—MEGALOPOLIS: **(1)** ?iv-iii BC Paus. viii 31. 7

## Καλλιδάμα
SICILY:
—THERMAI HIMERAIAI: **(1)** f. i BC Cic., *In Verr.* II ii 89 (Lat. Callidama: d. Ἀγαθῖνος)

## Καλλιδαμίδας
LAKONIA:
—TAINARON-KAINEPOLIS: **(1)** 198-211 AD *SEG* xxiii 199, 16 (f. Λύσιππος)

## Καλλίδαμος
ACHAIA:
—BOURA: **(1)** c. 271 BC *IG* IX (1)² (1) 12, 27 (f. Ἀρχέδαμος)
AITOLIA:
—TRICHONION: **(2)** 185 BC ib. 32, 16 (f. Π—ος)

ARGOLIS:
—ARGOS: **(3)** 362 BC *CID* II 1 II, 37; **(4)** iii BC *IG* IV (1) 618 II, 1 (Καλλίδ[α]μος: s. Τιμάγητος)
—EPIDAUROS: **(5)** ii BC ib. IV (1)² 247 (f. Νικαγόρα)
——Bounoia (Hylleis): **(6)** m. iii BC ib. 96, 52 (Perlman E.3); Perlman p. 63 f. (date)
ARKADIA: **(7)** 360 BC *CID* II 4 III, 43
—MANTINEIA-ANTIGONEIA: **(8)** c. 300-221 BC *IG* v (2) 323. 44 (tessera) (s. Καλλίφαμος)
—MEGALOPOLIS: **(9)** c. 210-207 BC ib. IV (1)² 73, 27; *SEG* xxxv 303 (date) (s. Καλλίμαχος)
—TEGEA: **(10)** i BC *IG* v (2) 45, 7
LAKONIA:
—SPARTA: **(11)** c. 50-25 BC ib. v (1) 208, 1 (Bradford (-)) (s. Καλλι—)
S. ITALY (BRUTTIUM):
—LOKROI EPIZEPHYRIOI:
——(Σκι.): **(12)** iv/iii BC De Franciscis 11, 3; 18, 5 (f. Σωφρονίσκος)
SICILY:
—SYRACUSE?: **(13)** hell. *IG* XIV 2407. 16; cf. *L'Incidenza dell'Antico* pp. 420 ff. (bullet) (Κα(λλ)ίδα(μο)ς: f. Τυνδαρίων)

## Καλλιδίκα
LEUKAS: **(1)** iii BC Unp. (*IG* arch.)

## Καλλίδικος
ARGOLIS:
—EPIDAUROS*: **(1)** c. 370 BC *IG* IV (1)² 102, 21, 299

## Καλλίδρομος
ITHAKE: **(1)** iii BC ib. IX (1) 1075
S. ITALY (CAMPANIA):
—POMPEII: **(2)** i BC-i AD *CIL* IV 2206 (Lat. Callidromus)
—SALERNUM: **(3)** imp. *IItal* I (1) 225 (*CIL* x 655) (Lat. [Cal]lidromus)

## Καλλιέρα
ARKADIA:
—ALIPHEIRA: **(1)** iii BC *EILakArk* 11 = Orlandos, *Alipheira* pp. 218-9 no. 3
—STYMPHALOS: **(2)** iii BC *SEG* XLII 360

## Καλλίερος
ARKADIA:
—MANTINEIA-ANTIGONEIA: **(1)** c. 315-280 BC *FD* III (1) 43, 1 (Κ[α]λλίερ[ος]: s. Δαμόξενος); **(2)** c. 300-221 BC *IG* v (2) 323. 52 (tessera) (s. Θέρπις)

## Καλλιέτης
LAKONIA:
—SPARTA: **(1)** ii AD ib. v (1) 159, 38 (Bradford (-))

## Καλλίθυια
ARGOLIS:
—ARGOS: **(1)** arch. Plu. fr. 158 (d. Πείρας: dub.)

## Καλλίκλεια
MESSENIA:
—MESSENE?: **(1)** ii/i BC *SEG* XI 979, 59

## Καλλικλείδας
LAKONIA:
—SPARTA: **(1)** ?i AD *IG* v (1) 514, 2 (Bradford (1)) (II s. Καλλικλείδας I); **(2)** ~ *IG* v (1) 514, 3-4 (Bradford (3)) (I f. Καλλικλείδας II, Φιλοκράτεια); **(3)** c. 100-105 AD *SEG* XI 537 a, 4 (Bradford (2)) (Καλλικλεί[δας]: f. Γ. Ἰούλ. Δαμοκλῆς)

## Καλλικλῆς
AIGINA: **(1)** vi/v BC Pi., *N.* iv, 80; cf. Klee p. 89 no. 25
AIGINA?: **(2)** 405 BC *IG* I³ 1032, 167
ARGOLIS:
—ARGOS*: **(3)** ii BC *SEG* XLII 279, 9 ([Κα]λλικλῆς: slave/freed.?)
—EPIDAUROS: **(4)** c. 335-325 BC *IG* IV (1)² 108, 141, 144; **(5)** iv/iii BC ib. 204 (s. Καλλιφάνης);

(6) ii-i BC Peek, *IAEpid* 33, 1 (f. Ἀριστείδας);
(7) ii/i BC ib. 151 (s. Τιμοκράτης, ?f. Πασικλῆς);
(8) i BC-i AD *IG* IV (1)² 645 (s. Ἀριστείδας) ?=
(*10*); (9) i AD Peek, *IAEpid* 274 (f. Πολυκράτης); (10) ~ *IG* IV (1)² 644 (f. Ἀριστείδας) ?=
(*8*); (11) ~ *SEG* XI 398, 1 (Καλλι[κλῆς]: f. Ἀρι-
στίδας); (12) i-ii AD ib. XXX 394 (Καλλικλῆ(ς))
—HERMIONE: (13) ii-i BC *IG* IV (1) 732 II, 21
(s. Ἐρατοκλέα)

ARKADIA:
—KYNOURIOI: (14) 369-361 BC ib. V (2) 1, 42;
Tod, *GHI* II 132 (date)
—MEGALOPOLIS: (15) s. ii BC *IG* V (2) 438, 14
([Κ]αλλικλῆς)
—TEGEA:
——(Krariotai): (16) s. iv BC ib. 41, 55 (Καλλι-
κλ[ῆς])

EPIROS:
—AMBRAKIA: (17) f. ii BC *AD* 39 (1984) Chron.
p. 190 + pl. 77 γ ([Κα]λλικλῆς: s. Τιμοκράτης)
—BOUTHROTOS: (18) ii-i BC *IBouthrot* 178
(Ugolini, *Alb. Ant.* 3 p. 125)

KORINTHIA:
—SIKYON: (19) vi/v BC *SEG* XI 244, 44 (-κλές)

LAKONIA:
—SPARTA:
——Amyklai: (20) ii/i BC *IG* V (1) 26, 18 (Bradford (-))
LEUKAS: (21) c. 325-315 BC *Hesp.* 57 (1988)
p. 148 B, 13 (*SEG* XXXVI 331); cf. *Hesp.* 48
(1979) pp. 78 f. with pl. 22 (s. Καλλίας)

MESSENIA:
—MESSENE: (22) iii BC *SEG* XIII 243, 4 (f.
Καφισοκλῆς); (23) ii/i BC *IG* V (1) 1437, 13
(Κα(λλ)ικλῆς—*IG*, Ἀ[μ]φικλ[ῆς]?—Hiller)
——(Kleolaidai): (24) 11 AD *PAE* 1992, p. 71
A, 25 (f. Νικόδαμος)
—THOURIA: (25) f. ii BC *SEG* XI 972, 112 (f.
Εὐκρατίδας)

SICILY:
—EUONYMOS: (26) ?iv BC *BTCGI* 13 p. 322

## Καλλικράτεια

ARGOLIS:
—EPIDAUROS: (1) iii BC Peek, *IAEpid* 141 (d.
Μνασικλῆς); (2) iii/ii BC *IG* IV (1)² 696 + Peek,
*IAEpid* 304 (d. Ἐπίδρομος); (3) ?i BC *IG* IV
(1)² 730 (-τηα); (4) c. 30 AD Peek, *IAEpid* 293;
*BSA* 80 (1985) pp. 249-50 (ident., stemma)
(d. Τ. Στατίλιος Λαμπρίας)
—PHLEIOUS: (5) iii BC *IG* IV (1) 463 (d. Χαιρέ-
μαχος)

ARKADIA:
—GORTYS: (6) ii BC *SEG* XXXV 349 (m. Κράτεια)

KORINTHIA:
—KORINTH: (7) f. i AD *Corinth* VIII (2) 110
(*ILGR* 116) (Lat. Callicratea: d. Φιλήσιος)

LAKONIA:
—SPARTA: (8) c. 30-20 BC *IG* V (1) 141, 13;
*SEG* XXXV 329 (date) (Bradford (1)) (-τια: d.
Καλλικράτης); (9) c. 100-125 AD *IG* V (1) 481,
1 (Bradford (2)) (-τια: d. Φιλοκρατίδας, ?m. Φι-
λοκράτης)

## Καλλικράτης

ACHAIA: (1) 231 BC *CPR* XVIII 25, 47 (f. Φι-
λοναύτης); (2) 146 BC *IG* IV (1)² 28, 155 (s.
Λυσίμαχος: synoikos)
—LEONTION: (3) 181-150 BC *RE* Supplbd. 4
(7g) (s. Θεόξενος)
ACHAIA?: (4) 193 BC *IG* V (2) 293, 19 (f. Σιμίας)
AIGINA: (5) i BC-i AD *Alt-Ägina* I (2) p. 45 no.
12, 3 (Καλλικρ[άτης])

AKARNANIA:
—ASTAKOS: (6) ii BC *IG* IX (1)² (2) 434, 7 (f.
Δεξίθεος)
—PALAIROS: (7) iii BC ib. 488
—THYRREION: (8) ii BC ib. 247, 21 (s. Τιμοκρά-
της); (9) ~ ib. 251, 5 (Καλ[λικρά]της: f. Αὐτό-
λυκος)

ARGOLIS:
—ARGOS: (10) m. iv BC ib. II² 8368 (s. Ἄνοχις);
(11) iii BC ib. IV (1)² 238; 239; 240; *Mnem.*
NS 47 (1919) p. 163 no. 8 a (s. Ἀριστεύς:
sculptor); (12) ii/i BC *IG* IV (1) 612; (13) f.
i BC Unp. (Ch. Kritzas) (s. Καλλίστρατος)
—EPIDAUROS: (14) c. 365-335 BC *IG* IV (1)²
103, 143, 146, 156, 161; (15) iv/iii BC ib. 204;
(16) iii BC ib. 242; 242a (f. Καλλισθένης); (17)
~ Peek, *NIEpid* 67 (K(α)λλικράτης); (18) ii BC
Peek, *IAEpid* 95 II (Καλλ[ικράτης]?)
——(Hylleis): (19) 146 BC *IG* IV (1)² 28, 55 (s.
Ἀρίστανδρος)
——Naupheis: (20) c. 290-270 BC ib. 109 II,
146; III, 134
—EPIDAUROS*: (21) c. 370-365 BC Peek, *IA-
Epid* 52 A, 2, 6; (22) c. 290-270 BC *IG* IV (1)²
109 II, 153; *SEG* XXV 401 B, [94]
—TROIZEN*: (23) iv BC *IG* IV (1) 823, 3
ARKADIA: (24) ?255 BC Nachtergael, *Les Galates*
8, 27 (Stephanis 1337) (s. Ἀριστόξενος)
—KLEITOR: (25) c. 340-323 BC *CID* II 51, 6; 55,
[4]?; 58 I, 24; 62 I B I, 66; 79 B, [3]?; 107,
15?
—MEGALOPOLIS: (26) m. iii BC *IG* VII 11, 6 (f.
Μένανδρος); (27) ii BC *SEG* XXXIII 291, 7; cf.
Stephanis 98 (Καλλ[ικρ]άτης: f. Ἀλ—); (28) i
BC-i AD *IG* IV (1)² 656, 7; *SEG* XI 382 a (f.
Φιλοκλῆς)
—PHIGALEIA: (29) i BC ib. XXXIII 291, 16; cf.
Stephanis 2833 ([Καλ]λικράτης)
—TEGEA: (30) c. 225 BC *SEG* XI 414, 8 (Perl-
man E.5) (s. Κρατῖνος); (31) f. ii BC *IG* V (2)
19 (s. Εὐθράσης); (32) ii AD ib. 123
ELIS: (33) 141-145 AD *IvOl* 95, 4 (Καλλι[κράτ]ης:
f. Λούκιος)

EPIROS:
—AMBRAKIA: (34) iv/iii BC Unp. (Arta Mus.,
inscr.) (f. Ἀρισταγόρα); (35) 263 BC *IG* IX (1)²
(1) 17, 95 (s. Εὔδικος); (36) ii-i BC *CIG* 1800,
9 (f. Ἀγαθίδας)
—BOUTHROTOS (PRASAIBOI): (37) a. 163 BC
*IBouthrot* 18, 14 (*SEG* XXXVIII 475) (f. Φιλώτας) ?= (*39*) (*38*); (38) ~ *IBouthrot* 35, 5
(s.p.) (*SEG* XXXVIII 494); *IBouthrot* 133, 6
(s. Φιλώτας) ?= (*37*)
——Bouthrotioi: (39) a. 163 BC ib. 67, 6; 95, 4
(s. Φιλώτας, f. Φιλώτας) ?= (*37*)
—DODONA*: (40) hell. *SEG* XIX 426 a

ILLYRIA:
—EPIDAMNOS-DYRRHACHION: (41) hell. *IDyrrh*
36 (Καλλικράτ[της]); (42) c. 250-50 BC Ceka,
*Probleme* p. 151 no. 30 (coin) (pryt.) ?= (*44*);
(43) ~ Maier 146; 341; 383 (coin) (Ceka 245-
7) (money.); (44) ~ Maier 251 (coin) (Ceka
150) (pryt.) ?= (*42*); (45) hell.-imp. *IDyrrh*
27 (f. Ἀριστομένης); (46) ~ ib. 260 (s. Ἀντίοχος)

KEPHALLENIA:
—PALE: (47) c. 210 BC *IG* IX (1)² (1) 31, 80 (s.
Θεόδωρος)

KORINTHIA:
—KORINTH: (48) 435 BC Th. i 29. 2 (s. Καλλίας)
—SIKYON: (49) 176 BC *Syll*³ 585, 272 (Skalet
164) (s. Νέων)

LAKONIA: (50) arch. *RE* (12) (Poralla² 406)
—AMYKLAI*: (51) ?iii BC *SEG* XVII 188 a
(Bradford (32)) (Καλλικράτης: s. Σακίντας)
—EPIDAUROS LIMERA: (52) imp. *IG* V (1) 1008
(Καλλ[ι]κράτης)
—HYPERTELEATON*: (53) imp. ib. 1050; (54) ~
ib. 1051
—SPARTA: (55) c. 505-479 BC Hdt. ix 72; 85.
1; Plu., *Arist.* 17 (Poralla² 407); (56) ?ii-i BC
*IG* V (1) 232, 1 (Bradford (37)); (57) ?i BC
*SEG* XI 881 c (tile) (Bradford (35)); (58) i
BC-i AD *IG* V (1) 749 (Bradford (43)); (59)
s. i BC *IG* V (1) 93, 24 (Bradford (69)) (f.
—αρχίδας); (60) ~ *IG* V (1) 94, 7 (Bradford
(7)) (s. Εὐ—); (61) ~ *IG* V (1) 127, 5 (Bradford (36)); (62) ~ *IG* V (1) 135, 11 (Bradford
(19)) (s. Λυκῖνος); (63) imp. *IG* V (1) 510; (64)

c. 30-20 BC ib. 141, 3, 13-14; *SEG* XXXV 329
(date) (Bradford (3); (44); (58)) (s. Ἀριστοκλῆς,
f. Ἀριστοκλῆς, Καλλικράτεια); (65) ~ *IG* V (1)
142, 5 (Bradford (70)) ([Καλ]λικράτης); (66) ~
*IG* V (1) 211, 11 (Bradford (52)) (f. Καλλιάδας); (67) ~ *IG* V (1) 211, 12 (Bradford (10))
(s. Εὐμωλίων); (68) ~ *IG* V (1) 211, 26 (Bradford (65)) (f. Πρατόνικος); (69) c. 25-1 BC *IG*
V (1) 50, 1; 210, 1; 254, 5 (*Artemis Orthia*
p. 355 no. 141); *IG* V (1) 872, 2; *SEG* XI
505, 5; 873-879 (tiles) (Bradford (33)); (70) ~
*IG* V (1) 210, 20 (Bradford (60)) (f. Κλέων);
(71) ~ *IG* V (1) 212, 40 (Bradford (9)) (s. Εὔδαμος); (72) i-ii AD *IG* V (1) 836 (Bradford
(48)) ([Καλ]λικράτης: ?f. Ἀριστοτέλης); (73) c.
1-10 AD *IG* V (1) 209, 14; *SEG* XXXV 331
(date) (Bradford (22); Stephanis 1341) (s. Νίκων); (74) s. i AD Plu., *Ages.* 35; (75) c. 70-90
AD *IG* V (1) 280, 1 (*Artemis Orthia* p. 312
no. 29; Bradford (67)) (f. Θρασύβουλος); (76)
c. 80-90 AD *IG* V (1) 674, 11 (Bradford (24))
(s. Φιλόστρατος); (77) c. 80-100 AD *SEG* XI
608, 4 (Bradford (28)) (s. Σώστρατος); (78) c.
90-100 AD *SEG* XI 558, 10 (Bradford (50))
(f. Δαμοκλῆς); (79) ~ *SEG* XI 570, 5 (Bradford (56)) (I f. Καλλικράτης II); (80) ~ *SEG*
XI 570, 6 (Bradford (68)) (f. Ζεύξιππος); (81)
c. 90-110 AD *IG* V (1) 80, 7; *SEG* XI 563, 4
(Bradford (6)) (s. Δαμόνικος); (82) c. 100 AD
*SEG* XI 510, 3 (Bradford (25)) (s. Πολυκλῆς);
(83) c. 100-120 AD *IG* V (1) 192 (Bradford
(31)) (I f. Καλλικράτης II); (84) ~ *IG* V (1) 192
(Bradford (16)) ([Κ]αλλικρά[τ]ης: II s. Καλλικράτης I); (85) ~ *SEG* XI 610, 6 (Bradford
(2)) (s. Ἄρχιππος); (86) c. 100-125 AD *IG* V (1)
137, 21 (Bradford (30)) (s. Τιμόστρατος); (87)
~ *IG* V (1) 481, 3 (Bradford (64)) (f. Φιλοκρατίδας); (88) ?ii AD *SEG* II 62 (Bradford (42));
(89) ii AD *SEG* XI 791, 13 (Bradford s.v. Δαΐ-
κράτης (-)) ((Κα)λλικράτ[ης]); (90) ~ *SEG* XI
882 (Bradford (34)) ?= (Καλλικρατίδας (17));
(91) f. ii AD *IG* V (1) 162, 2; 163, 1, 5; 189,
1; *SEG* XI 570, 5 (Bradford (17)) (Κλούβιος
Κ. ὁ καὶ Σαπφίων νέος—162-3: II s. Καλλικράτης I); (92) ~ *IG* V (1) 163, 4 (Bradford
(18)); (93) ?f. ii AD *IG* V (1) 319 (*Artemis Orthia* p. 326 no. 54) (Καλλικράτ[ης]?: ?f. Μνάσων); (94) c. 105-110 AD *IG* V (1) 97, 12;
*SEG* XI 564, 19 (Bradford (45)) (f. Ἀριστοκλῆς); (95) ~ *IG* V (1) 97, 24; *SEG* XI 564, 24
(Bradford (45)) (f. Ἀριστοκλῆς); (96) ~ *SEG*
XI 565, 4 (Bradford (20)) ([Κ]αλλικ[ρ]άτη[ς:
s. Νίκαρχος); (97) c. 120 AD *SEG* XI 518, 6
(Bradford (47)) (Καλ[λικρά]της: f. Ἀριστοκράτης); (98) c. 125-134 AD *IG* V (1) 62, 7; *SEG*
XI 575, 3 (Bradford (39)) (Μ. Οὔλπ. Κ.); (99)
m. ii AD *IG* V (1) 37, 12 (Bradford (1)) (s.
Ἀπελλάκων); (100) 127 AD *IG* V (1) 1314, 27
(Bradford (49)) (f. Χαρίτων); (101) ~ *IG* V (1)
1314, 28 (Bradford (5)) (s. Δαμοκλῆς); (102) c.
130-140 AD *IG* V (1) 66, 11 (Bradford (23))
([Καλλ]ικράτης: s. Πασικλῆς); (103) c. 130-160
AD *IG* V (1) 64, 10; 69, 24, [32]; 70, 2; 71
II, 2; 71 [III]; 71 III, 32; *SEG* XI 554, 5;
579, 2 (Bradford (4)) (I s. Ἀριστοκλῆς, f. Καλλικράτης II, Πασικλῆς); (104) c. 134 AD *IG* V
(1) 287, 2 (Bradford (46)) (f. Μ. Οὔλπ. Ἀριστοκράτης); (105) c. 140-150 AD *IG* V (1) 64,
4 (Bradford (54)) (f. Κλεόδαμος); (106) ~ *IG*
V (1) 64, 14 (Bradford (14)) ([Κα]λλικράτης:
I f. Καλλικράτης II); (107) ~ *IG* V (1) 64, 14
(Bradford (14)) ([Καλ]λικράτης: II s. Καλλικράτης I); (108) ~ *IG* V (1) 68, 23 (Bradford (40));
(109) c. 140-160 AD *IG* V (1) 64, 10; 69, 24;
70, 2; 71 II, 2; 71 [III]; 71 III, 32 (II
s. Καλλικράτης I); (110) 140-160 AD *IG* V (1)
64, 12; 74, 7; 358, 1 (Bradford (51)) (f. Καλλέας); (111) c. 140-160 AD *IG* V (1) 74, 6; 85,
13; 128, 10; *SEG* XI 528, 6 (Bradford (8)) (Κ.
Μώλοχος: s. Εὐδαμίδας); (112) ~ *SEG* XI 600,
1 (Bradford (41)) (Κλούβιος Κ.); (113) c. 150-

160 AD *IG* v (1) 53, 2; 54, [2]; 64, 11; 276, 1; *SEG* XI 480, 11; 495, 2 (Bradford (26)) (s. *Ῥοῦφος*); (**114**) ~ *SEG* XI 585, 7; XXX 410, 8; *BSA* 43 (1948) p. 236 (ident.) (Bradford (27)) (s. *Σωσικράτης*); (**115**) ~ *SEG* XI 585, 11; XXX 410, [16] (Bradford (55)) (I f. *Καλλικράτης* II); (**116**) ~ *SEG* XI 585, 11; XXX 410, 16 (Bradford (15)) (II s. *Καλλικράτης* I); (**117**) ?s. ii AD *IG* v (1) 259, 3; *Artemis Orthia* p. 299 no. 6 (date) (Bradford (11)) (s. *Πούλχρα*); (**118**) c. 160-170 AD *IG* v (1) 109, 14 (Bradford (29)) (s. *Θαλίαρχος*); (**119**) c. 175-200 AD *IG* v (1) 129, 2 (Bradford (21)) (s. *Νικηφόρος*) ?= (*124*); (**120**) ii/iii AD *IG* v (1) 548, 13 (Bradford (62)) (f. *Νικόστρατος*); (**121**) f. iii AD *IG* v (1) 503; 504, 10 (Bradford (66)) (f. *Π. Οὔλπιος Πύρρος*); (**122**) a. 212 AD *BSA* 89 (1994) p. 439 no. 12, 2, 7 (*Μ. Αὐρ. Κ.*: I f. *Καλλικράτης* II, *Νικιππία*); (**123**) ~ ib. l. 8 (II s. *Μ. Αὐρ. Καλλικράτης*); (**124**) ~ *IG* v (1) 568; 692 (Bradford (61)) ([*Καλ*]λικράτης: f. *Μ. Αὐρ. Νικηφόρος*) ?= (*119*)

—TAINARON-KAINEPOLIS: (**125**) 198-211 AD *SEG* XXIII 199, 17 (*Κλ. Κ.*); (**126**) ~ ib. l. 18 (s. *Νικάδας*)

—TAINARON-KAINEPOLIS?: (**127**) ?ii-i BC *IG* v (1) 1250 (f. *Λυσικράτης*)

—ZARAX: (**128**) ii-iii AD *SEG* XI 894 b I (s. *Μενεκλείδας*)

MESSENIA:

—MESSENE: (**129**) iii BC ib. XXIII 209, 17; (**130**) c. 223 BC *IG* IX (1)² (1) 31, 34 (s. *Αἰσχρίων*); (**131**) ii BC *PAE* 1969, p. 106, 14; (**132**) ?35-44 AD *IG* v (1) 1432, 19, 42 (f. *Ἀριστοκλῆς*)

——(Hylleis): (**133**) II AD *PAE* 1992, p. 71 A, 13 (f. *Λυκίσκος*)

—MESSENE?: (**134**) ii/i BC *SEG* XI 979, 22 ([*Καλ*]ικράτης)

—THOURIA: (**135**) f. ii BC ib. 972, 67 (f. *Δαμίων*); (**136**) ~ ib. l. 85 (f. *Τεισικλῆς*); (**137**) ~ ib. l. 100 (f. *Πλειστίας*); (**138**) ~ ib. l. 111 (s. *Σώστρατος*)

S. ITALY (BRUTTIUM):

—LOKROI EPIZEPHYRIOI:

——(*Μνα.*): (**139**) iv/iii BC De Franciscis 12, 8 (f. *Κάλλιππος*)

——(*Τω.*): (**140**) iv/iii BC ib. 6, 1; 19, 3; 26, 5; 39, 8 (s. *Πρωτογένης*, f. *Πρωτογένης*); (**141**) ~ ib. 20, 16 (f. *Τίμων*)

—RHEGION: (**142**) hell. *IG* XIV 2400. 5 (tile) ([*Καλ*]λικράτης)

S. ITALY (CALABRIA):

—TARAS-TARENTUM: (**143**) iv/iii BC ib. 668 II, 7 (Landi, *DISMG* 194); (**144**) c. 235-228 BC Vlasto 963-70 (coins) (Evans, *Horsemen* p. 196 IX H.1-2)

S. ITALY (CAMPANIA):

—DIKAIARCHIA-PUTEOLI: (**145**) 174 AD *OGIS* 595, 21 (*Γ. Οὐαλ. Κ.*)

S. ITALY (LUCANIA):

—HYELE-VELIA: (**146**) hell.? *IG* XII (5) 1018 (f. *Ζῆνις*)

SICILY?: (**147**) hell.? Manganaro, *QUCC* forthcoming no. 57 (bronze)

SICILY:

—AKRAI: (**148**) ii BC *Akrai* p. 156 no. 6, 4 (f. *Εὔφραιος*)

—LEONTINOI: (**149**) ?iv-iii BC *QUCC* 78 (1995) p. 126 ([*Καλ*]λικράτης)

—SYRACUSE: (**150**) 414 BC Plu., *Nic.* 18

**Καλλικρατίδας**

ARKADIA:

—TEGEA: (**1**) ?ii BC *IG* v (2) 194

LAKONIA: (**2**) inc. *RE* (2) (Poralla² 410)

—HIPPOLA: (**3**) ii-i BC *IG* v (1) 1334 a + *AAA* I (1968) p. 119 no. 1 (locn.) (date—*LGPN*)

—PYRRHICHOS: (**4**) ?ii-i BC *IG* v (1) 1282, 6

—SPARTA: (**5**) 407-406 BC *RE* (1) (Poralla² 408); (**6**) 330 BC Berve 402 (Poralla² 409); (**7**) c. 50-25 BC *IG* v (1) 208, 5 (Bradford (7)) (f. *Καλλίστρατος*); (**8**) c. 25-1 BC *IG* v (1) 210,

15 (Bradford (6)) (I f. *Καλλικρατίδας* II); (**9**) ~ *IG* v (1) 210, 15 (Bradford (2)) (II s. *Καλλικρατίδας* I); (**10**) ~ *IG* v (1) 212, 33 (Bradford (8)) (f. *Νεόλας*); (**11**) ~ *SEG* XI 505, 3 (Bradford (9)) (*K<ι>αλλικρατίδας*: f. *Νικίας*); (**12**) i BC/i AD *IG* v (1) 48, 6 (Bradford (5)) (s. *Τιμόξενος*); (**13**) ~ *IG* v (1) 146, 5 (Bradford (12)) ([*Καλ*]λικρατίδας); (**14**) i BC/i AD? *IG* v (1) 263; *Artemis Orthia* p. 305 no. 17 (date) (Bradford (10)) (f. *Νίκιππος*); (**15**) c. 95-105 AD *SEG* XI 562, 3 (Bradford (3)) (*Καλλικ*[*ρατίδ*]*ας*: s. *Φιλοκράτης*); (**16**) c. 100-120 AD *SEG* XI 637, 3 (Bradford (14)) ([*Καλλ*]ικρατίδας); (**17**) ii AD *IG* v (1) 871-4 (tiles) (Bradford (34)) ?= (*Καλλικράτης* (*90*)); (**18**) c. 105-110 AD *SEG* XI 569, 9 (Bradford (1)) ([*K*]αλλικρατίδας: s. *Ἁγησίνικος*); (**19**) c. 105-115 AD *IG* v (1) 103, 9 (Bradford (11)) (f. *Θεόφιλος*); (**20**) c. 125-150 AD *IG* v (1) 107, 4 (Bradford (13)) ([*Κα*]λλικρατίδας)

—TAINARON-KAINEPOLIS: (**21**) 213-217 AD *IG* v (1) 1240, 14 (*Αὐρ. Κ.*: II s. *Καλλικρατίδας* I); (**22**) ~ ib. l. 15 (I f. *Αὐρ. Καλλικρατίδας* II)

MESSENIA:

—MESSENE: (**23**) 33 AD *SEG* XLI 335, 1

SICILY:

—AKRAGAS: (**24**) v BC D.L. viii 53; *Suda E* 1002 (-δης: ?s. *Μέτων*, *Ἀρχίνομος*, *Ἐξαίνετος*)

**Καλλικράτις**

ARGOLIS:

—HERMIONE: (**1**) ?iii-ii BC *IG* IV (1) 735, 1 (d. *Οἶκις*)

LAKONIA:

—PYRRHICHOS: (**2**) ?ii-i BC ib. v (1) 1282, 11 (d. *Νίκανδρος*)

MESSENIA:

—MESSENE: (**3**) ii/i BC *SEG* XXXVIII 341, 2 (*Καλλι*[*κράτις*]: d. *Φιλοκράτης*)

**Καλλικρέτεια**

ARKADIA:

—TRIPOLIS (MOD.): (**1**) ii/i BC Unp. (Tripolis Mus.)

**Καλλικρέτης**

ARKADIA:

—TEGEA: (**1**) iii BC *IG* v (2) 30, 11

——(Apolloniatai): (**2**) iv/iii BC ib. 38, 34 (s. *Τέρων*)

——(Krariotai): (**3**) iv/iii BC ib. l. 24 (f. *Τιμίων*)

**Καλλίκριτος**

ARGOLIS:

—ARGOS?: (**1**) m. iv BC Unp. (Ch. Kritzas)

ARKADIA:

—TEGEA: (**2**) ii-i BC *IG* v (2) 165, 6

**Καλλικώ**

ARGOLIS:

—EPIDAUROS: (**1**) imp. Peek, *IAEpid* 98 (d. *Λακλῆς*)

ARKADIA:

—TEGEA: (**2**) imp. *IG* v (2) 227

**Καλλικῶν**

ARGOLIS:

—EPIDAUROS: (**1**) iv BC ib. IV (1)² 178; 179; 180; Peek, *NIEpid* 34; (**2**) iii/ii BC *IG* IV (1)² 357 (Peek, *IAEpid* 153. 5); (**3**) f. ii BC *REG* 62 (1949) p. 28 face B, 19 (s. *Τιμαίνετος*) ?= (*4*); (**4**) c. 150 BC *SEG* XI 377, 10; Peek, *IAEpid* 30, [8] (f. *Τιμαίνετος*) ?= (*3*)

**Καλλιλαΐδας**

LEUKAS: (**1**) iii BC *IG* IV (1)² 350 (f. *Πυστακίων*)

**Καλλίλας**

KEPHALLENIA:

—SAME: (**1**) c. 230-200 BC *BCH* 45 (1921) p. 14 II, 136 (s. *Ἀρχέμβροτος*)

**Καλλιμάχα**

AITOLIA:

—PHISTYON: (**1**) 204 BC *IG* IX (1)² (1) 95, 9 ([*Κα*]λλιμάχα)

**Καλλιμαχίδας**

ARGOLIS:

—TROIZEN: (**1**) ?146 BC ib. IV (1) 757 B, 22 (or Arkadia: *Καλλιμαχίδα*<ς> (gen.): f. *Πάντις*)

DALMATIA:

—ISSA:

——(Pamphyloi): (**2**) iv/iii BC Brunšmid p. 7, 24 (s. *Ὀνάσιμος*)

**Καλλίμαχος**

AIGINA: (**1**) 460 BC Pi., *O.* viii, 82; (**2**) ii BC *IG* IV (1) 13 (I f. *Καλλίμαχος* II); (**3**) ~ ib. (II s. *Καλλίμαχος* I); (**4**) ?f. i BC *Alt-Ägina* I (2) p. 43 no. 4, 4 (s. *Γναῖος*)

AIGINA?: (**5**) 210-197 BC *AE* 1913, p. 91 no. 3

AITOLIA:

—KALLION/KALLIPOLIS?: (**6**) a. 166 BC *IG* IX (1)² (3) 676, 19 (s. *Δωρίμαχος*)

—POTANA: (**7**) 139 BC *SGDI* 2137, 15 (f. *Ἐπίνικος*)

ARGOLIS:

—EPIDAUROS: (**8**) iii BC *IG* IV (1)² 205 (s. *Κλεισθένης*, ?s. *Κλειταρώ*); (**9**) imp. ib. 509; (**10**) ii-iii AD ib. 467; 574, [3] (f. *Νικέρως*); (**11**) 163 AD ib. 88, 24 + Peek, *IAEpid* 37, 24 (s. *Νικέρως*)

—HERMIONE: (**12**) iii BC *IG* IV (1) 688 (s. *Καλλῖνος*)

—METHANA-ARSINOE: (**13**) ii BC ib. 855, 1 (s. *Ἀριστόδαμος*, f. *Ἀριστόδαμος*)

—TROIZEN: (**14**) iii BC ib. 825, 2

ARKADIA:

—KAPHYAI: (**15**) 191-146 BC *Coll. McClean* 6458 (coin)

—MANTINEIA-ANTIGONEIA: (**16**) c. 300-221 BC *IG* v (2) 323. 33 (tessera) (f. *Σαμωνίδας*)

—MEGALOPOLIS: (**17**) s. iii BC *FD* III (1) 22, 1 (s. *Κάλλων*); (**18**) c. 210-207 BC *IG* IV (1)² 73, 27; *SEG* XXXV 303 (date) (*Καλλίμα*[*χος*]: f. *Καλλίδαμος*); (**19**) ?145 BC *IG* v (2) 439, 5 (*Καλλίμα*[*χος*])

—PARRHASIOI: (**20**) 401 BC *RE* Supplbd. 4 (3b)

—STYMPHALOS: (**21**) ?271 BC *FD* III (1) 14, 2 (s. *Λαμέδων*)

—TEGEA: (**22**) ii BC *IG* v (2) 43, 5 (s. *Δαμέας*); (**23**) f. ii BC ib. 44, 18 (s. *Ἀγαθίας*)

EPIROS:

—DODONA: (**24**) iii BC Antoniou, *Dodone* Aa, 37

—KASSOPE: (**25**) ii BC Dakaris, *Kassope* p. 23 (s. *Λυκίσκος*)

ILLYRIA:

—APOLLONIA: (**26**) iii/ii BC *IApoll* 176; cf. *SEG* XXXIX 550 (s. *Ναυκράτης*)

ITHAKE: (**27**) hell. *Rev. Épig.* I (1913) p. 47 no. 14

KORINTHIA:

—SIKYON: (**28**) c. 100-90 BC *SEG* XXXIII 290 A, 14; *BSA* 70 (1975) pp. 129-31 (date) (Skalet 165; Stephanis 1342) (s. *Μηνόφιλος*)

LAKONIA:

—SPARTA: (**29**) s. i BC *IG* v (1) 133, 7 (Bradford (3)) (I f. *Καλλίμαχος* II); (**30**) ~ *IG* v (1) 133, 7 (Bradford (1)) (II s. *Καλλίμαχος* I); (**31**) c. 140 AD *IG* v (1) 138, 4 (Bradford (2)) (*Καλλίμαχο*[*ς*]: s. *—κλῆς*)

MESSENIA:

—MESSENE: (**32**) i BC *IG* v (1) 1463, 1 (s. *Νικόξενος*) ?= (*34*); (**33**) hell.-imp. ib. 1484; (**34**) ~ *PAE* 1991, p. 106 no. 8, 6 (s. *Νικόξενος*) ?= (*32*)

—THOURIA: (**35**) f. ii BC *SEG* XI 972, 69 (s. *Δόκων*)

S. ITALY (APULIA):

—VENUSIA: (**36**) imp. *Epigraphica* 35 (1973) p. 147 no. 8 (Lat. Callimachus)

S. ITALY (CAMPANIA):

—NUCERIA ALFATERNA: (**37**) imp. *NScav* 1922, p. 486 no. 1 (Lat. M. Asellinus Callimachus)

Καλλίμβροτος

S. ITALY (LUCANIA):
—POSEIDONIA-PAESTUM: (38) imp. CIL x 479 (Mello-Voza 196) (Lat. Q. Ceppius Callimachus)
SICILY:
—TAUROMENION: (39) c. 211-199 BC IG XIV 421 an. 30; 421 an. 42 (SGDI 5219) (f. Φιλωνίδας)
——(Πεα.): (40) c. 154-149 BC IG XIV 421 an. 92 (SGDI 5219); IGSI 4 III (IV), 13 an. 87 (s. Φίλων)

Καλλίμβροτος
ARKADIA:
—TEGEA:
——(Hippothoitai): (1) f. iii BC IG v (2) 36, 23 (-ινβρο-)
S. ITALY (BRUTTIUM):
—KAULONIA: (2) v/iv BC Paus. vi 3. 11; AP xiii 15 (Καλλίβροτος—Paus.: f. Δίκων) ?= (3); (3) iv BC Iamb., VP 267 (FVS I p. 447) (Καλλίβροτος—ms. F) ?= (2)

Καλλιμέδων
KORINTHIA:
—SIKYON: (1) ?254 BC Nachtergael, Les Galates 9, 78 (Skalet 167); cf. Stephanis 1344 (I f. Καλλιμέδων II); (2) ~ Nachtergael, Les Galates 9, 78 (Skalet 166; Stephanis 1344) (II s. Καλλιμέδων I)

Καλλιμένης
ARGOLIS:
—EPIDAUROS: (1) iv BC IG IV (1)² 199
——(Hylleis): (2) c. 150-146 BC ib. 28, 56; SEG XI 377, 9; 405, [8] (f. Δαμοκλῆς)
——Pagasina (Azantioi): (3) c. 365-335 BC IG IV (1)² 103, 145 (Καλλ<λ>ιμένης)
—TROIZEN: (4) c. 365-335 BC ib. l. 55
SICILY:
—SYRACUSE: (5) 343 BC D.S. xvi 70. 6 (s. Ἀλκάδας)

Καλλιμήδης
ARGOLIS:
—NEMEA*: (1) hell.? SEG XXIII 185, 2
KORINTHIA:
—KORINTH: (2) 354 BC CID II 31, 35

Καλλίμορφος
S. ITALY (LUCANIA):
—HYELE-VELIA: (1) imp. CIL x 463 (Lat. Galimorphus); (2) ~ Dito, Velia p. 95 no. 22 (Lat. Callimorphus)
SICILY:
—KATANE: (3) imp. IG XIV 501 (Σαβούκις Κ.)

Καλλιμορφώ
ACHAIA:
—PATRAI: (1) ii-iii AD SEG XXXIV 348 (Μαρκία Κ.)

Καλλινίκη
LAKONIA:
—TAINARON-KAINEPOLIS: (1) ii-iii AD IG v (1) 1249, 15 (GVI 2028) (-νεί-: m. Καλλίνικος)
S. ITALY (CAMPANIA):
—NEAPOLIS: (2) ii/i BC EAD XXX 49 (IG II² 9992) (Καλλινίκη: d. Πολέμαρχος); (3) i BC/i AD INap 126 ter, 1 ([Κ]α[λ]λινίκη: d. Αἰσχύλος); (4) i-ii AD ib. 126 bis (Καλλινείκ[η]?, Καλλίνεικ[ος]?)
—POMPEII: (5) i BC-i AD NScav 1928, pp. 374-5 (Lat. [C]allinice)

Καλλινίκης
LAKONIA:
—SPARTA: (1) c. 30-20 BC IG v (1) 211, 15 (Bradford (-)) (f. Χαιρήμων)

Καλλινικίδας
LAKONIA:
—GYTHEION: (1) 211 AD IG v (1) 1163, 15 (f. Εὔδαμος)

Καλλίνικος
ARGOLIS:
—EPIDAUROS*: (1) c. 340-330 BC SEG XXV 387 A, 20
EPIROS:
—VOTONOSI (MOD.): (2) byz. ib. XXIV 457 b (Καλλίνικ[ος])
KORINTHIA:
—KORINTH*: (3) 536 AD Schwartz, ACO III p. 29, 16; p. 127, 39; p. 163, 13; p. 171, 30 (bp.)
—SIKYON: (4) f. vi BC Paus. vi 14. 10 (Skalet 168) (f. Πυθόκριτος)
LAKONIA:
—TAINARON-KAINEPOLIS: (5) ii-iii AD IG v (1) 1249, 17 (GVI 2028) (Καλίνει-: s. Ξύστος, Καλλινίκη)
S. ITALY (CAMPANIA):
—DIKAIARCHIA-PUTEOLI: (6) imp. CIL x 2205 (Lat. Callinicus I f. Καλλίνικος II); (7) ~ ib. (Lat. Callinicus: II s. Καλλίνικος I, Νικομήδεια)
—KYME: (8) 251 AD ib. 3699 I, 13 (Lat. Ti. Iulius Callinicus)
—NEAPOLIS: (9) i BC/i AD INap 126 ter, 4 (Καλ[λί]νικ[ος]: f. Θεοσχώτης)
—NUCERIA ALFATERNA: (10) imp. CIL x 1098 (Lat. L. Pontius Callinicus: s. L. Pontius Fortunatus, Coelia Secundilla)
SICILY:
—PANORMOS: (11) ?ii/iii AD ib. 7303 (Lat. M. A(ur). Callinicus)

Καλλῖνος
ARGOLIS:
—ARGOS: (1) iv-iii BC Unp. (Ch. Kritzas)
—EPIDAUROS: (2) c. 365-335 BC SEG XXV 386, 5 (Καλλί[νος]) ?= (3); (3) c. 335-325 BC IG IV (1)² 106 I, 31 ([Κ]αλλί[νος]) ?= (2)
—EPIDAUROS*: (4) c. 370-365 BC SEG XXV 383, 201; Peek, IAEpid 52 A, 24, 28, 31, 35, 46 (Καλ(λ)ῖνος—35)
—HERMIONE: (5) iii BC IG IV (1) 688 ([Κ]αλλῖνος: f. Καλλίμαχος); (6) ~ ib. 693 ([Κα]λλῖνος); (7) m. iii BC Wehrli, Schule Arist. vi fr. 15
ARKADIA:
—TEGEA: (8) ?s. iii BC IG v (2) 94
EPIROS:
—DODONA: (9) iii BC Antoniou, Dodone Ab, 36
MESSENIA:
—MESSENE: (10) s. ii BC SEG XLI 341, 9 (f. Χάρυλλος)
S. ITALY (BRUTTIUM):
—LOKROI EPIZEPHYRIOI:
——(Κρα.): (11) iv/iii BC De Franciscis 3, 7 (Καλ(λ)ῖνος: f. Γνίφων)
——(Τηλ.): (12) iv/iii BC ib. 16, 3 (f. Δορκίων)

Καλλινώ
AIGINA: (1) ii BC IG II² 7956 (d. Θεοχαρμίδας)

Καλλίξενος
AITOLIA: (1) c. 249-239 BC FD III (3) 167, 3 ([Κ]αλλίξενος)
ARGOLIS:
—ARGOS: (2) f. i BC ASAA NS 1-2 (1939-40) p. 168 no. 21 B I, 12 (-ξει-)

Καλλιόι
EPIROS:
—AMBRAKIA: (1) iii/ii BC Unp. (Arta Mus., inscr.) (d. Ἱεροκλῆς)
LEUKAS: (2) iii BC SEG XXXV 484

Κάλλιον
SICILY:
—LIPARA: (1) hell.-imp. Libertini, Isole Eolie p. 220 no. 21

Καλλιόπα
KERKYRA: (1) b. 227 BC GVI 922, 2 (Gr. Gr. 140) (m. Ἀλέξανδρος)

Καλλιόπη
ILLYRIA:
—BYLLIONES BYLLIS: (1) iii AD SEG XXXVIII 555 (Καλιώ-: m. Κρωταμήνη)
LAKONIA:
—GYTHEION: (2) imp. IG v (1) 1191
S. ITALY (CAMPANIA): (3) i BC-i AD NScav 1916, p. 302 no. 7 b (Castrèn 219. 3) (Lat. Livia Calliope)
S. ITALY (CAMPANIA):
—DIKAIARCHIA-PUTEOLI*: (4) imp. CIL x 2402 (Lat. Aemilia Calliopa: freed.); (5) ~ ib. 2741 (Lat. Mindia Calliope: freed.?)
SICILY:
—KATANE: (6) imp. ib. 7055 (Lat. Calliope); (7) iii-v AD IG XIV 543; cf. Wilson, Sicily pp. 310-11 with fig. 264 b (Jew)
—SYRACUSE: (8) iii-v AD NScav 1909, p. 353 no. 16; cf. Ferrua, NG 96 (Καλλιό[π]η); (9) ~ Strazzulla 259 (Wessel 1321); cf. Ferrua, NG 32; (10) ~ Strazzulla 343 (Wessel 948)

Καλλίοπος
S. ITALY (CALABRIA):
—TARAS-TARENTUM (NR.): (1) hell. SEG XLI 885. 2 (lamp)

Καλλιπάρθενος
S. ITALY (CAMPANIA):
—DIKAIARCHIA-PUTEOLI: (1) imp. CIL x 2520 (Lat. A. Plautius Calliparthnus (sic))

Καλλιπάτας
ARKADIA:
—MEGALOPOLIS: (1) m. iii BC IG IV (1)² 96, 67 (Perlman E.3); Perlman p. 63 f. (date) (s. Ἀριστολαΐδας)
—TEGEA:
——(Krariotai): (2) s. iii BC IG v (2) 36, 122 (f. Ἱερο—)

Καλλιπείθης
MESSENIA:
—MESSENE: (1) f. iii BC SEG XLI 342, 4; cf. PAE 1991, p. 100 no. 8

Καλλίπολις
ILLYRIA:
—APOLLONIA: (1) hell. IApoll 28 (d. Ὀνασικλῆς)
LAKONIA:
—SPARTA: (2) s. i BC IG v (1) 94, 16 (Bradford (-)) (s. Εὐρυ—)
S. ITALY (CALABRIA):
—BRENTESION-BRUNDISIUM: (3) imp. CIL IX 89 (Lat. Caesia Callipolis)
S. ITALY (CAMPANIA):
—DIKAIARCHIA-PUTEOLI: (4) imp. ib. X 3059 (Lat. Valeria Callipolis)
—NEAPOLIS: (5) 41-54 AD INap 17 (Καλλίπο[λις])

Καλλίππα
S. ITALY (LUCANIA):
—METAPONTION: (1) ?iii BC NScav 1966, p. 153 no. 21 (terracotta) (Καλ(λ)ίπ(π)α)

Καλλιππίδας
ARGOLIS:
—HERMIONE: (1) ii-i BC IG IV (1) 732 IV, 19 (f. Νικώ)
ARKADIA:
—HELISSON: (2) c. 221 BC ib. IV (1)² 42, 3
ILLYRIA:
—EPIDAMNOS-DYRRHACHION: (3) iii BC IDyrrh 12 (f. Καλλήν, Παρμένων)
MESSENIA:
—THOURIA: (4) ii-i BC IG v (1) 1385, 32 (s. Χαῖρις)
SICILY:
—HALOUNTION: (5) hell.? Manganaro, QUCC forthcoming no. 23 (f. Σιμύλος)

## Καλλιππῖνος

ARGOLIS:
—ARGOS: **(1)** iii AD *SEG* XI 325, 2

## Κάλλιππος

ACHAIA: **(1)** 146 BC *IG* IV (1)² 28, 161 (f. Νί-καιος: synoikos)
AIGINA: **(2)** c. 225 BC *SEG* XI 414, 36 (Perlman E.5) (s. Τιμέας)
AKARNANIA:
—THYRREION: **(3)** ii BC *IG* IX (1)² (2) 247, 19 (s. Πολύευκτος)
ARGOLIS:
—ARGOS: **(4)** c. 475-450 BC *SEG* XXVI 449, 1; cf. XXX 393; *LSAG*² p. 444 no. F (date) (-ιπος: s. Εὐκλῆς)
—EPIDAUROS*: **(5)** c. 290-270 BC *IG* IV (1)² 109 I, 128; III, 109
—HERMIONE: **(6)** i BC-i AD? ib. IV (1) 730 III, 9 (Κάλλιππ[ος]: f. Νικώνυμος)
—TROIZEN: **(7)** iv BC ib. 823, 55; **(8)** iii BC ib. 774, 4; **(9)** ii/i BC ib. 790 (f. Θεύδωρος)
ARKADIA:
—MEGALOPOLIS: **(10)** c. 250-175 BC *IC* 4 p. 282 no. 206 E (f. Ἀγέπολις); **(11)** ?145 BC *IG* V (2) 439, 39 (s. Τριτέας)
—ORCHOMENOS: **(12)** iii/ii BC *BCH* 38 (1914) p. 465 no. 8, 11 (Κάλλι[ππος]?, Καλλί[βιος]?)
—TEGEA:
——(Hippothoitai): **(13)** iii BC *IG* V (2) 40, 41 (f. Κλεόστρατος)
ELIS: **(14)** c. 146-32 BC *BMC Pelop.* pp. 6-7 nos. 71-74 (coin); **(15)** 72 BC Moretti, *Olymp.* 698; **(16)** 36 BC *IvOl* 59, 8 (f. —ων ὁ καὶ Τη-λέμαχος); **(17)** ~ ib. l. 14 (Κάλλιπ[πος]); **(18)** i BC/i AD ib. 242, 2 (Κάλλιπ[πος] [Τηλέμα]χος: s. Τηλέμαχος); **(19)** m. i AD Moretti, *Olymp.* 782 (Κ. Πεισανός: s. Κλ. Κλεοδίκη); **(20)** 213-214 AD *IvOl* 111, 5 ([Φ]λ. Κ.: Χ.)
ILLYRIA:
—EPIDAMNOS-DYRRHACHION: **(21)** c. 250-50 BC Ceka, *Probleme* p. 151 no. 31 (coin) (pryt.) ?= **(22)**; **(22)** ~ Maier 252; Münsterberg p. 261; Nachtr. p. 15 (coin) (Ceka 34; 100) (pryt.) ?= **(21)**
KEPHALLENIA:
—PRONNOI: **(23)** f. iii BC *IG* IX (1)² (1) 8, 2
KORINTHIA:
—KORINTH: **(24)** iii BC *D.L.* vii 38; **(25)** i-ii AD *RE* (19); *FGrH* 385
LAKONIA:
—SPARTA: **(26)** s. i BC *IG* V (1) 904 (tiles) (Bradford (-)) (Κάλλ(ι)ππος)
MESSENIA:
—THOURIA: **(27)** ii/i BC *IG* V (1) 1384, 18 (s. Ἀριστόνικος)
PELOPONNESE?: **(28)** s. iii BC ib. 1426, 27 (f. Ὀλυμπιόδωρος)
S. ITALY (BRUTTIUM):
—LOKROI EPIZEPHYRIOI:
——(Ἀγφ.): **(29)** iv/iii BC De Franciscis 39, 10 (f. Δείναρχος)
——(Ἀστ.): **(30)** iv/iii BC ib. 34, 2
——(Γαψ.): **(31)** iv/iii BC ib. 7, 4 (s. Ποιγένης)
——(Κοβ.): **(32)** iv/iii BC ib. 21, 5
——(Λακ.): **(33)** iv/iii BC ib. 28, 3 (f. Θέων)
——(Μνα.): **(34)** iv/iii BC ib. 12, 8 (s. Καλλικρά-της); **(35)** ~ ib. 24, 1
——(Στρ.): **(36)** iv/iii BC ib. l. 5 (s. Καλλίας)
——(Τω.): **(37)** iv/iii BC ib. 32, 5 (s. Καλλίας); **(38)** 278 BC ib. 30, 6 (f. Καλλίας)
——(Φαω.): **(39)** iv/iii BC ib. 2, 3 (s. Ἀρίστιππος)
S. ITALY (CAMPANIA):
—HERCULANEUM*: **(40)** i BC-i AD *CIL* X 1403 g I, 33 (Lat. P. Brinnius Callippus: freed.)
S. ITALY (LUCANIA):
—VOLCEI: **(41)** iii-iv AD *IItal* III (1) 86 (Lat. Callippus)
SICILY:
—TAUROMENION: **(42)** c. 223 BC *IG* XIV 421 an. 18 (*SGDI* 5219) (f. Θεόμναστος)

## Καλλιρρόη

DALMATIA:
—EPETION: **(1)** imp. *CIL* III 12818 (Lat. Caetennia Calliroe)
—TRAGURION: **(2)** imp. ib. 9707 (Lat. Stallia Callirhoe)
EPIROS:
—NIKOPOLIS: **(3)** imp. *Ep. Chron.* 31 (1994) p. 42 no. 8 (*AD* 45 (1990) Chron. p. 257 no. 5) (-ιρό-)
SICILY:
—SYRACUSE: **(4)** i-ii AD Charito i 1. 1 (d. Ἑρμο-κράτης: fict.); **(5)** iii-v AD *SEG* IV 2 (Wessel 185); cf. Ferrua, *NG* 340 b (-λε-)

## Κάλλις

ARGOLIS:
—EPIDAUROS*: **(1)** c. 370 BC *IG* IV (1)² 102, 70
ARKADIA: **(2)** ?263-261 BC Nachtergael, *Les Galates* 3, 9; cf. Stephanis 2705 (f. —κλῆς)
—TEGEA:
——(Krariotai): **(3)** s. iv BC *IG* V (2) 41, 50 (f. Ἀγαλλίας)
SICILY:
—LIPARA: **(4)** iii BC *Meligunis-Lipara* 5 p. 151 no. 2166; cf. *SEG* XLI 810

## Καλλίς

AKARNANIA:
—PALAIROS: **(1)** iii BC *IG* IX (1)². (2) 455
KEPHALLENIA:
—KRANIOI?: **(2)** iv BC Unp. (Argostoli Mus.)
MESSENIA:
—MESSENE: **(3)** ii/iii AD *SEG* XXIII 216 (d. Ἀρι-στοκλῆς)

## Καλλις

ARGOLIS:
—HERMIONE: **(1)** ii BC *IG* IV (1) 738 (Καλλις: s./d. Ἀθανίων)
LEUKAS: **(2)** hell.-imp. ib. IX (1) 538; cf. *AM* 27 (1902) p. 355

## Καλλισθένεια

ELIS?: **(1)** v-iv BC *NY Bronzes* pp. 454-5 nos. 1778-9 (bronze)
LAKONIA:
—SPARTA: **(2)** c. 1-10 AD *IG* V (1) 209, 34; *SEG* XXXV 331 (date) (Bradford (-)) (-νια)

## Καλλισθένης

ARGOLIS:
—ARGOS: **(1)** ii BC *IG* IV (1)² 99, 18 (f. Φίλιστος)
—EPIDAUROS: **(2)** iii BC ib. 242; 242a (s. Καλλι-κράτης)
——(Hysminatai): **(3)** 146 BC ib. 28, 13 (f. Φάϋλ-λος)
—EPIDAUROS*: **(4)** c. 290-270 BC *SEG* XXV 402, 57 ([Καλ]λισθένης)
—HERMIONE: **(5)** ii-i BC *IG* IV (1) 732 III, 25 (-σσθέ-: s. Ξένων, f. Ἑρμίας); **(6)** imp. ib. 725 (f. Δάφνη)
ARKADIA:
—MANTINEIA-ANTIGONEIA: **(7)** c. 300-221 BC ib. V (2) 323. 55 (tessera) (f. Ἀριστοξενίδας)
—MEGALOPOLIS: **(8)** c. 315-280 BC Nachtergael, *Les Galates* 6, [4]; 12, 2 ([Καλ]λισθένης: f. Σί-μος); **(9)** ?262-255 BC ib. 5, [19]; 6, [2]; 8, 23 (Stephanis 1355) (s. Ἄρχων)
—TEGEA: **(10)** iii BC *IG* V (2) 356, 1 (f. Καλλίας)
DALMATIA:
—ISSA: **(11)** hell. Brunšmid p. 27 no. 18, 5 (*SEG* XL 514; *VAHD* 84 (1991) p. 253 no. 3) (f. Κυννίς); **(12)** iii BC Brunšmid p. 9 fr. G, 11 + *VAMZ* 1970, p. 37 frr. G and M ([Κ]αλλισθ[ένης: s. Ὀλύμπιος); **(13)** ii BC Brunšmid p. 25 no. 14, 3 + *VAHD* 84 (1991) p. 248 no. 1 (f. Διονύσιος); **(14)** ~ Brunšmid p. 25 no. 14, 8 + *VAHD* 84 (1991) p. 248 no. 1 (s. Διονύσιος)
——(Dymanes): **(15)** iv/iii BC Brunšmid p. 9, 58 (s. Νίκανδρος)

## Καλλιστιανός

ELIS: **(16)** ii BC *GVI* 453 (s. Ξεινόφαντος); **(17)** f. i BC *SEG* XVII 199, 1
EPIROS:
—DODONA*: **(18)** iv BC ib. XV 399 (Καλ[λισ]θένης)
ILLYRIA:
—APOLLONIA: **(19)** c. 250-50 BC Maier 52 (Ceka 72); Ceka 79 (coin) (pryt.)
—EPIDAMNOS-DYRRHACHION: **(20)** c. 250-50 BC *BMC Thessaly* p. 77 no. 178 (coin) (pryt.) ?= **(21)**; **(21)** ~ Münsterberg p. 39 = Nachtr. p. 15 (coin) (Ceka 15) (pryt.) ?= **(20)**
KORINTHIA:
—KORINTH: **(22)** s. iv BC *Corinth* VIII (1) 32 (?s. Ἀ—); **(23)** 336-324 BC *CID* II 23, 4; 76 II, [31]; 79 A I, 17; 95, 13; 97, 24; 102 II B, [32]; 120 A, 36 (s. Σαίγαλος)
LAKONIA:
—GERONTHRAI: **(24)** iii-ii BC *IG* V (1) 1127, 4 ([Καλλι]σθένης?)
—SPARTA: **(25)** 676 BC Moretti, *Olymp.* 34 (Po-ralla² 411); **(26)** ii AD *IG* V (1) 159, 5 (Bradford (-))
—LEUKAS: **(27)** iv BC *AM* 27 (1902) p. 369 no. 40 b; **(28)** iii/ii BC *SEG* XXVII 175
MESSENIA:
—MESSENE: **(29)** ?i BC *PAE* 1969, p. 100 a, 9
——(Kleolaidai): **(30)** 11 AD ib. 1992, p. 71 A, 27 (f. Ὀνασικράτης)
—THOURIA: **(31)** f. ii BC *SEG* XI 972, 16 (s. Σωτάδας); **(32)** ii/i BC *IG* V (1) 1384, 10 (f. Ἀρίστων)
S. ITALY (BRUTTIUM):
—SYBARIS-THOURIOI-COPIAE: **(33)** inc. *RE* (3); *FGrH* 291
SICILY:
—GELA-PHINTIAS: **(34)** f. v BC Dubois, *IGDS* 144 f (vase) (Arena, *Iscr. Sic.* II 27) (-νε̃ς)
—KAMARINA: **(35)** f. v BC Cordano, *Tessere Pubbliche* 75 (Arena, *Iscr. Sic.* II 140 A) (Καλλ[ι]σ[θ]ένε̃ς: f. Εὐαρχίδας)

## Καλλίστα

MESSENIA:
—MESSENE: **(1)** ?35-44 AD *IG* V (1) 1433, 24; *SEG* XXIX 396 (date) (d. Θάλων)

## Καλλίστη

ARGOLIS:
—EPIDAUROS: **(1)** hell.-imp. ib. XXV 420
KORINTHIA:
—KORINTH: **(2)** byz. *Corinth* VIII (3) 557, 2; cf. *TMByz* 9 (1985) p. 365 no. 63
S. ITALY (APULIA):
—LUCERIA: **(3)** imp. *CIL* IX 898 (Lat. Vesonia [Cal]lista)
S. ITALY (BRUTTIUM):
—LOKROI EPIZEPHYRIOI*: **(4)** s. i BC *Suppl. It.* 3 p. 25 no. 8 (Lat. —nucia Calliste: freed.)
—RHEGION: **(5)** imp. *NScav* 1888, p. 67 (*Eph. Ep.* VIII 248) (Lat. Caliste)
S. ITALY (CAMPANIA):
—DIKAIARCHIA-PUTEOLI: **(6)** imp. *CIL* X 1734 (Lat. Calliste); **(7)** ?i-ii AD ib. 2149 (Lat. Aquilia Calliste); **(8)** 168 AD ib. 1563 (Lat. Nemonia Calliste: d. Εὐτύχης, m. Nemonia Ianuaris)
—DIKAIARCHIA-PUTEOLI*: **(9)** imp. ib. 2180 (Lat. —ellia Callista: freed.)
—NEAPOLIS: **(10)** i BC/i AD *SEG* XXXVII 783 (*INap* 112) (Δομιτία Κ.)
—POMPEII: **(11)** i BC-i AD *CIL* IV 1854; cf. p. 213 (Lat. Cal[l]iste); **(12)** ?i AD *NScav* 1896, p. 230; 1928, p. 377; *Riv. Stud. Pomp.* 1 (1987) pp. 161-2 (tiles) (Lat. Attia Calliste)

## Καλλιστιανός

S. ITALY (CAMPANIA):
—DIKAIARCHIA-PUTEOLI: **(1)** ii AD *Puteoli* 12-13 (1988-9) p. 211 no. 1 (Lat. M. Annius Cal-listianus: s. Κάλλιστος)

## Καλλίστιν
KERKYRA: (1) imp. *IG* IX (1) 914

## Καλλιστῖνος
S. ITALY (CAMPANIA):
—DIKAIARCHIA-PUTEOLI: (1) imp. *CIL* X 2312
(Lat. M. Coelius Callistinus: s. *Κάλλιστος*)

## Καλλίστιον
ARGOLIS:
—ARGOS: (1) imp. *IG* IV (1) 589, 12 (m. Ἀρχέ-
νους)
—EPIDAUROS: (2) ?iii BC Peek, *NIEpid* 119

## Καλλιστίων
ARGOLIS:
—EPIDAUROS: (1) iii AD *SEG* XXX 397 (Καλλι-
στίω[ν])
ARKADIA:
—TEGEA: (2) 165 AD *IG* V (2) 50, 71 (s. Ἐπαφρῦς)
S. ITALY (LUCANIA):
—HYELE-VELIA: (3) imp. *PdelP* 33 (1978) p. 64
no. 9 (Lat. L. Cominius C[al]listio)

## Καλλιστοκλῆς
LAKONIA:
—SPARTA: (1) c. 217-230 AD *SEG* XI 616 a, 5
(Bradford (-)) (Αὐρ. Καλλισ[τ]οκ[λῆ]s)

## Καλλιστονίκα
LAKONIA:
—SPARTA: (1) 54-68 AD *SEG* XLI 315 (Κλ. Κ.)

## Καλλιστονίκη
LAKONIA:
—SPARTA: (1) ii AD *IG* V (1) 518 and Add.
(Bradford (1)) (-νεί-: d. Κλ. Ἀπο—); (2)
?ii-iii AD *IG* V (1) 694 (Bradford (5))
([Κα]λλιστονείκη); (3) s. ii AD *SEG* XI 817,
3; XXXVI 353, 13; *BSA* 80 (1985) pp. 194;
206-8 (stemma) (Καλλίστο[κλῆς]?—ed., Καλ-
λιστο[νίκη]?—Spawforth: d. Μεμμία Ξενοκράτεια); (4) ii/iii AD *IG* V (1) 547, 7 (Bradford
(4)) (Πομπωνία Κ. ἡ καὶ Ἀρέτη: d. Πομπώνιος
Πανθάλης Διογένης Ἀριστέας, Μεμμία Λογγῖνα);
(5) iii AD *IG* V (1) 727, 2 (*GVI* 1374; Bradford
(3)) (d. Ἰσαγόρας); (6) m. iii AD *IG* V (1) 602,
1; *BSA* 80 (1985) p. 242 (stemma) (Bradford
(2)) (Πομπωνία Καλλιστονείκη: d. Γ. Πομπώνιος Ἀριστέας ὁ καὶ Περικλῆς, Κλ. Πῶλλα); (7) c.
250-260 AD *IG* V (1) 593, 11; *BSA* 80 (1985)
pp. 225; 239 (ident., stemma) (Bradford s.v.
Ἐλπίς (1)) (Κλ. Ἐλπὶς ἡ καὶ Κ.: ?d. Τιβ. Κλ.
Πρατόλαος ὁ καὶ Δαμοκρατίδας, d. Ἰουλ. Ἐτεαρχίς)

## Κάλλιστος
ACHAIA:
—PATRAI*: (1) c. 200 AD *SEG* XXXII 422; 423
ARGOLIS:
—ARGOS: (2) imp. *BCH* 98 (1974) p. 770 (tile);
(3) ii AD *ILGR* 85-8 (Lat. L. Naevius Callis-
tus)
ARKADIA:
—KAPHYAI: (4) c. 230-200 BC *BCH* 45 (1921) p.
14 II, 120 (Κ[ά]λλισ[τος]—Oulhen: s. Ἱεραῖος)
—TEGEA: (5) ii AD *IG* V (2) 55, 37 (s. Φίλνυς);
(6) ~ ib. l. 85 (f. Σωτήριχος)
ELIS: (7) 113-117 AD *IvOl* 91, 21 (Γ. Μελφέννιος
Κ.)
—OLYMPIA*: (8) i AD ib. 80, 12 (slave?)
EPIROS:
—PHOINIKE: (9) ii-iii AD Ugolini, *Alb. Ant.* 2
p. 155 no. 8
ILLYRIA:
—LYCHNIDOS: (10) ii-iii AD *BSA* 18 (1911-12)
p. 176 no. 18 (f. Βαυκιδίων)
KORINTHIA:
—KORINTH: (11) iii-iv AD *SEG* XXVI 413, 6;
(12) f. iii AD *Ag.* VII pp. 94 no. 272; 97 nos.
299-300; *Corinth* IV (2) pp. 189 nos. 570-1;

193 no. 600; 209 nos. 737-741; *SEG* XXVII
35. 11; XXX 348 (lamps)
LAKONIA:
—SPARTA: (13) c. 80-100 AD ib. XI 632, 3 (Brad-
ford (3)) (I f. *Κάλλιστος* II); (14) ~ *SEG* XI
632, 3 (Bradford (1)) (II s. *Κάλλιστος* I); (15)
c. 140-160 AD *IG* V (1) 154, 14 (Bradford (2))
(s. Σῶσος)
MESSENIA:
—MESSENE: (16) ii/i BC *IG* V (1) 1437, 10
([Κάλ]λιστος)
S. ITALY (APULIA):
—VENUSIA: (17) v AD *JIWE* I 53 (*CIJ* I 587)
(Jew)
S. ITALY (CALABRIA):
—BRENTESION-BRUNDISIUM: (18) ii AD *Epi-
graphica* 27 (1965) pp. 163-4 (Lat. T. Duxius
Callistus)
S. ITALY (CAMPANIA):
—DIKAIARCHIA-PUTEOLI: (19) imp. *CIL* X
2206 (Lat. Callistus: I f. *Κάλλιστος* II); (20)
~ ib. (Lat. Callistus: II s. *Κάλλιστος* I); (21)
~ ib. 2312 (Lat. Callistus: f. *Καλλιστῖνος*); (22)
?ii AD ib. 1546 (Lat. Callistus: doctor); (23)
~ ib. 3124 (Lat. M. Ulpius Callistus); (24)
~ ib. 3139 (Lat. Ulpius Callistus: f. Ulpia
Valentina); (25) ii AD *Puteoli* 12-13 (1988-
9) p. 211 no. 1 (Lat. M. Annius Callistus: f.
*Καλλιστιανός*); (26) m. ii AD *CIL* X 1576 (Lat.
M. Nemonius Callistus)
—DIKAIARCHIA-PUTEOLI?: (27) imp. ib. 1547
(Lat. Callistus); (28) ii AD *IG* XIV 842 (*GVI*
405); cf. *Puteoli* 3 (1979) pp. 158-60 no. 3
—MISENUM: (29) 97 AD De Franciscis, *Sacello
Augustali* p. 28 no. 9 (Lat. P. Herennius Cal-
listus)
—POMPEII: (30) i BC-i AD *CIL* IV 2413 i (Lat.
Callistus); (31) ~ ib. 4462 (Lat. Callistus);
(32) ~ ib. 8546 (Lat. Calistus)
—POMPEII*: (33) 57 AD ib. 3340. 28, 13; 61, 11;
68, 10; 71, 8; 74, 9; 75, 6; 87, 6; 102, 10; 114,
4; X 1033 (Castrèn 458. 1) (Lat. Cn. Vibrius
Callistus: freed.)
—SALERNUM*: (34) 117-137 AD *IItal* I (1) 191
(*CIL* X 549) (Lat. Callistus: freed.)
S. ITALY (LUCANIA):
—HYELE-VELIA: (35) imp. *PdelP* 25 (1970) p.
265 no. 11 (Lat. [Iul]ius Callistus: s. Iulius
Acianus)
—VOLCEI: (36) imp. *IItal* III (1) 61 (*CIL* X 390)
(Lat. M. Insteius Callistus: f. M. Insteius
Firminus)
SICILY: (37) iii-v AD *Sic. Gymn.* 2 (1949) p. 97
—KATANE: (38) imp. ib. 14 (1961) p. 184 (Lat.
M. Antonius Cal[l]istus); (39) iii-v AD *IG* XIV
540 (Agnello 51; Wessel 592)

## Καλλιστράτα
ARGOLIS:
—ARGOS: (1) a. 303 BC *CEG* II 816, 15
—HERMIONE: (2) ?ii-i BC *IG* IV (1) 731 II, 3 (m.
Νικηφόρος); (3) ii-i BC ib. 732 II, 26 (-σστρά-:
m. Ζωπύρα)
ARKADIA:
—TEGEA: (4) hell. ib. V (2) 562
LEUKAS: (5) iii BC *AM* 27 (1902) p. 370 no. 44
S. ITALY (CALABRIA):
—TARAS-TARENTUM: (6) hell. *ASAA* 2 (1916)
p. 129 no. 14 (Καλλισ[τράτα])
S. ITALY (LUCANIA):
—METAPONTION: (7) ?s. iv BC *SEG* XXX 1176
D. 2 (loomweight)

## Καλλίστρατος
ACHAIA: (1) 281 BC *Hesp.* 65 (1996) p. 252 (s.
Τερμόνιος)
—PATRAI: (2) c. 146-32 BC *BMC Pelop.* p. 23
nos. 12-13 (coin) (f. Νικόστρατος)
AITOLIA: (3) c. 260 BC *FD* III (4) 178, 3 (Καλ-
λίσ[τρατος?])

—PHISTYON: (4) imp. *IG* IX (1)² (1) 113, 1 (s.
Αἰσχρίων, f. Στρατώ)
—PLEURON: (5) i BC-i AD ib. IX (2) 401 (*RÉnip*
100) (f. Φρίκων)
—POTIDANIA: (6) m. ii BC *SBBerlAk* 1936, p.
371 a, 14 (*SEG* XLI 528 A) (Καλί-: s. *Δαίτας*)
AKARNANIA:
—OINIADAI: (7) iii/ii BC *IG* IX (1)² (2) 419. 7
ARGOLIS:
—ARGOS: (8) c. 220-200 BC *SEG* XI 414, 31
(Perlman E.5); cf. Peek, *IAEpid* 331, 31 (f.
Ἴων); (9) f. i BC Unp. (Ch. Kritzas) (s. Ἐλ-
πίνικος); (10) ~ ib. (f. Καλλικράτης); (11) ii AD
*SEG* XVI 253, 14 (s. Ἑρμοκράτης)
——Mansetos (Vanidai): (12) iv/iii BC Moretti,
*ISE* 40, 3
—ARGOS?: (13) v BC *IG* IV (1) 552, 10
—EPIDAUROS: (14) ?c. 450 BC ib. IV (1)² 144
(Lazzarini 78); *LSAG*² p. 182 no. 16 (date);
(15) hell.? *PAE* 1992, p. 52 (Καλλίστρατ[ος]:
?s. *Δαμέας*); (16) imp. *IG* IV (1)² 441; (17) ii
AD ib. 488 (f. Πάντις)
—HERMIONE: (18) c. 245-236 BC ib. IX (1)² (1)
25, 65 (s. Νικοκράτης); (19) m. ii BC *SEG* XI
377, 8; XXXI 328, 7; Peek, *IAEpid* 30, 7 (f.
Φίλων)
—NEMEA*: (20) ?iv BC *SEG* XXVIII 392
([Κα]λλίστρατος)
ARKADIA: (21) ii/i BC ib. XLI 1635, 6 (s. Ἀσκλη-
πιάδης)
—ALIPHEIRA: (22) s. iii BC ib. XXV 448, 1, 8
(*IPArk* 25)
—TEGEA: (23) c. 365-335 BC *IG* IV (1)² 103, 54,
61; (24) 349 BC *SEG* XXVII 19, 4 (Stephanis
1359); (25) f. iii BC *IG* V (2) 35, 19 (s. Σαιθίων)
——(Athaneatai): (26) s. iv BC ib. 41, 27 (f. —
ος); (27) ~ ib. l. 32 with index (s. Τελέσας);
(28) s. iii BC ib. 36, 110 (f. Ἱπα—)
DALMATIA:
—ISSA: (29) ?ii BC *SEG* XXXV 692 (f. Εὐκλέα)
ELIS: (30) 191 BC Plb. XX 3. 1; (31) 185-189 AD
*IvOl* 104, 11, 26 (Καλλίστρ[ατος]: s. —της, ?f.
Παράμονος)
EPIROS:
—AMBRAKIA: (32) ii-i BC *CIG* 1800, 3 (f. Σώ-
των)
—BOUTHROTOS (PRASAIBOI): (33) a. 163 BC
*IBouthrot* 17, 23 (*SEG* XXXVIII 474)
——Bouthrotioi: (34) a. 163 BC *IBouthrot* 139,
10 (f. Λέων)
ILLYRIA:
—APOLLONIA: (35) c. 250-50 BC Maier 76 (coin)
(Ceka 67) (money.)
—EPIDAMNOS-DYRRHACHION: (36) c. 250-50
BC Maier 254 (coin) (Ceka 418) (pryt.);
(37) hell.-imp. *IDyrrh* 89 (Καλλίσ[τρα]τος: f.
Ἀλεξ—); (38) ~ ib. 195 (f. Ἐπιχάρης)
KERKYRA?: (39) hell. *IG* IX (1) 837; cf. *SEG*
XXXIX 1744 (bullet); (40) ii-iii AD ib. XXX 518
KORINTHIA:
—KORINTH: (41) v BC *IG* IV (1) 355 b
(bronze) (Καλί-: s. Διόδωρος); (42) hell.? ib.
208 (Καλλ[ίστρ]ατ[ος]?: f. Εὐπατινός)
—SIKYON: (43) s. iii BC ib. 428, 1 (Skalet 169)
(s. Φιλοθάλης)
LAKONIA:
—GYTHEION: (44) m. ii AD *IG* V (1) 1174, 10
(Ἥϊος Κ.)
—SPARTA: (45) c. 50-25 BC ib. 208, 5 (Bradford
(1)) (s. Καλλικρατίδας); (46) s. i BC *IG* V (1)
96, 7 (Bradford (2)) (s. Σω—); (47) c. 25-1
BC *IG* V (1) 210, 14 (Bradford (7)) (f. Φίλιπ-
πος); (48) c. 100-137 AD *IG* V (1) 59, 7; *SEG*
XI 521 b, 6; 611, 5 (Bradford (3); (8)) (s. Τιμοκράτης, f. Τιμοκράτης); (49) ii-iii AD *IG* V
(1) 802 b (Bradford (5)) (Κα[λλί]στρατ[ος]: f.
Δαμύλος); (50) c. 160-170 AD *IG* V (1) 109,
17 (Καλλίστρα[τος]); (51) ii/iii AD ib. 307, 3
(*Artemis Orthia* pp. 328-9 no. 60); *IG* V (1)
601, 9; *BSA* 79 (1984) p. 283 no. 1 (date)
(Bradford (6)) (f. Αὐρ. Κλέανδρος ὁ καὶ Μήνιος)

—ZARAX: (52) ii-iii AD *SEG* XI 894 b III; 894 b IV (Καλλίστρ[ατ]ος—b IV: s. Μενεκλείδας, f. Δάμουσα)

LEUKAS: (53) iii BC Unp. (*IG* arch.)

MESSENIA:

—MESSENE: (54) i BC/i AD *IG* V (1) 1438 a, 11

——(Kleolaidai): (55) 11 AD *PAE* 1992, p. 71 A, 26 (f. Ἱεροκλῆς)

—THOURIA: (56) f. ii BC *SEG* XI 972, 61 (s. Νόμας)

PELOPONNESE?: (57) 11 AD *PAE* 1992, p. 72 B, 18 (s. Ἀφροδίσιος)

S. ITALY (BRUTTIUM):

—LOKROI EPIZEPHYRIOI:

——(Τηλ.): (58) 276 BC De Franciscis 23, 3 (s. Θρασύμαχος)

S. ITALY (CALABRIA):

—TARAS-TARENTUM: (59) hell. *ASAA* 2 (1916) p. 158 no. 66

S. ITALY (LUCANIA):

—POSEIDONIA-PAESTUM: (60) imp. Mello–Voza 80 (Lat. N. Numestius Callistratus)

SICILY:

—ADRANON: (61) i BC-i AD? *IG* XIV 570 (Κα(λλ)ίστρατος: s. Ῥάτωρ)

—KAMARINA: (62) ?iv/iii BC *SEG* XXXIV 940, 10 (Dubois, *IGDS* 124; *PdelP* 44 (1989) p. 192 no. 3; Cordano, 'Camarina VII' 124) (f. Γέλων)

—SYRACUSE?:

——(Μακ.): (63) hell. Manganaro, *PdelP* forthcoming no. 4 III, 9 (s. Χαιρήμων)

TRIPHYLIA:

—TYPANEAI: (64) c. 230-200 BC *BCH* 45 (1921) p. 12 II, 79 (s. Καβιρίας)

## Καλλιστώ

ARGOLIS:

—ARGOS: (1) i BC *IG* II² 8369, 1 (d. Φαιδιμίδας)

—HERMIONE: (2) iii BC ib. IV (1) 693 (d. Κ—, m. Ἀριστωνύμα); (3) ~ ib. 697 (d. Εὔανδρος)

ARKADIA:

—ALEA: (4) f. iii BC ib. IX (1)² (1) 9, 3 (d. Ἀρίσταιχμος)

ILLYRIA:

—APOLLONIA: (5) imp. *IApoll* 278 ([Κ]αλλιστ[ώ])

## Καλλίστων

MESSENIA:

—ASINE: (1) hell.-imp. *IG* V (1) 1407 (f. Δαμασίλας)

## Καλλίτας

EPIROS:

—AMBRAKIA: (1) vi BC *SEG* XLI 540; cf. *BE* 1994, no. 38

## Καλλιτέλης

AIGINA: (1) f. v BC Paus. v 27. 8; x 13. 10; Overbeck 426; cf. *Alt-Ägina* II (2) p. 23; p. 26 n. 67 (Κάλυνθος—Paus. x: ?s. Ὀνάτας: sculptor)

AITOLIA: (2) c. 315-280 BC *FD* III (1) 144 + *BCH* 68-9 (1944-5) p. 100 (Καλλιτ[έλε]ος (gen.), Καλλικ[ράτε]ος (gen.)—ed.: f. Δικαῖος)

ARGOLIS:

—ARGOS: (3) ii-i BC *IG* II² 8376 (f. Ὑμνίς)

—EPIDAUROS: (4) c. 340-320 BC Peek, *NIEpid* 19 C, 12 (Καλλ[ιτέ]λης); (5) 194 AD *IG* IV (1)² 555, 4 + Peek, *IAEpid* 231 (Καλ[λι]τέλης: s. Εὔπορος)

EPIROS:

—AMBRAKIA: (6) ?iv BC *SEG* XXXIX 269

LAKONIA:

—SPARTA: (7) vi/v BC Moretti, *Olymp.* 149 (Poralla² 412) (f. Πολυπείθης); (8) s. i BC *IG* V (1) 96, 6 (Bradford (-)); (9) c. 25-1 BC *IG* V (1) 212, 9 (Bradford (-))

LEUKAS: (10) iii/ii BC *SEG* XXVII 175

MESSENIA:

—MESSENE: (11) iv/iii BC *IG* V (1) 1435, 17

——(Aristomachidai): (12) 11 AD *PAE* 1992, p. 71 A, 9 (s. Θεαρίων)

TRIPHYLIA:

—LEPREON: (13) ?a. 369 BC Paus. vi 15. 1 (f. Ξένων)

## Καλλιτελίδας

LAKONIA:

—GERONTHRAI: (1) v BC *IG* V (1) 1116 (Lazzarini 101) ([Καλ]λιτελίδα[ς])

—SPARTA: (2) c. 240-200 BC Peek, *IAEpid* 330, 18 (Perlman E.4) ([Καλ]λιτελίδας: s. Κλεανδρίδας)

## Καλλιτίβερις

MESSENIA:

—KORONE: (1) 246 AD *IG* V (1) 1398, 27 (Αὐρ. Κ.)

## Καλλιτίμα

ARGOLIS:

—EPIDAUROS: (1) iii BC Peek, *IAEpid* 102 ([Κ]αλλιτίμα)

## Καλλίτιμος

ARGOLIS:

—EPIDAUROS: (1) iii BC ib. (s. Ξενόδοκος)

KORINTHIA:

—KORINTH: (2) c. 445-430 BC *IG* I³ 1348

## Καλλιτίων

ARGOLIS:

—EPIDAUROS: (1) iv BC Peek, *NIEpid* 32, 5 ([Καλλ]ιτίων?)

## Κάλλιτος

ELIS: (1) c. 28 BC-5 AD *IvOl* 64, 12; 65, 13; 69, 13 (s. Ἀντίας: mantis/Klytiadai/Π.)

## Καλλιτύχη

ARKADIA:

—TEGEA: (1) imp. *IG* V (2) 228 (Καλι-)

ITHAKE: (2) ?i BC *SEG* XVII 260

S. ITALY (APULIA):

—CANUSIUM*: (3) i AD *Epig. Rom. di Canosa* 89 (Lat. Antonia Calityche: freed.)

—LUCERIA: (4) imp. *CIL* IX 884 (Lat. Caletyche)

S. ITALY (BRUTTIUM):

—HIPPONION-VIBO VALENTIA: (5) imp. *Klearchos* 26 (1984) p. 59 no. 3 (Lat. Iunia Caletyce)

S. ITALY (CALABRIA):

—BRENTESION-BRUNDISIUM: (6) imp. *CIL* IX 6111 (Lat. Caesia Callityche)

—BRENTESION-BRUNDISIUM*: (7) imp. *Eph. Ep.* VIII 28 (Lat. Iuleia [Ca]llityche: freed.?)

S. ITALY (CAMPANIA):

—DIKAIARCHIA-PUTEOLI: (8) imp. *CIL* X 2863 (Lat. Duronia Callityche); (9) ~ ib. 2911 (Lat. Vibbia Callituche); (10) ?iii AD *IG* XIV 846, 2 (threpte)

—DIKAIARCHIA-PUTEOLI*: (11) imp. *AJA* 2 (1898) p. 384 no. 28 (Lat. Marcia Callityche: freed.); (12) ~ *CIL* X 1942 (Lat. Valeria Callityche: freed.) ?= (14); (13) ~ ib. 2912 (Lat. Ravia Callityche: freed.); (14) f. i AD *AJA* 77 (1973) p. 162 no. 12 (Lat. Valeria Callityche: freed.) ?= (12)

—KYME: (15) ii-iii AD *Puteoli* 3 (1979) p. 165 no. 7 (*CIL* X 2221) (Lat. Calvia Callityche)

—MISENUM*: (16) imp. ib. 3425 (Lat. Antonia Callityche: m. Ποντικός); (17) ~ ib. 3568 (Lat. Callitic(e))

—POMPEII: (18) i BC-i AD ib. IV 2997 (Lat. Callityche)

—SALERNUM: (19) s. i AD *IItal* I (1) 162 (*CIL* X 651) (Lat. Vibia Callityche: m. Εὐσέβης)

—SURRENTUM: (20) ?i-ii AD ib. 739 (Lat. Iulia Callityche)

S. ITALY (LUCANIA):

—POSEIDONIA-PAESTUM: (21) i-ii AD Mello–Voza 176 (Lat. Amatia Callityche)

SICILY:

—NEAITON: (22) ?iv AD *IGLMP* 111; cf. *SEG* XXVI 1120; Ferrua, *NG* 497 (locn.)

## Καλλίτυχος

LAKONIA:

—SPARTA: (1) a. 212 AD *IG* V (1) 562, 10 (Bradford (-)) (Καλίτυ[χος])

S. ITALY (LUCANIA):

—VOLCEI: (2) imp. *IItal* III (1) 97 (Lat. M. Insteius Callitychus: f. M. Insteius Pulcher)

SICILY:

—KAMARINA (NR.): (3) iii-v AD Führer–Schultze p. 196; Pace, *Camarina* p. 165 no. 32 (Wessel 494) (-του-)

## Καλλιφάης

ARGOLIS:

—EPIDAUROS: (1) iv/iii BC *IG* IV (1)² 204 + Peek, *IAEpid* 92 (Καλλικλῆς—*IG*); (2) ii-i BC ib. 318, 1; (3) ~ ib. l. 5 (Καλλιφάη[ς]: s. Τιμόστρατος)

## Καλλίφαμος

ARKADIA:

—MANTINEIA-ANTIGONEIA: (1) c. 300-221 BC *IG* V (2) 323. 44 (tessera) (f. Καλλίδαμος)

## Καλλιφάνη

S. ITALY (LUCANIA):

—HYELE-VELIA: (1) f. i BC *RE* (-) (Lat. Calliphana)

## Καλλιφάνης

ARGOLIS:

—EPIDAUROS: (1) iv/iii BC *IG* IV (1)² 204 (f. Καλλικλῆς)

——Bounoia (Hylleis): (2) c. 365-335 BC ib. 103, 108 ?= (4)

—EPIDAUROS*: (3) c. 440-425 BC ib. 46, 4; *LSAG²* p. 182 no. 17 (date); (4) c. 370-365 BC Peek, *IAEpid* 52 A, 10 ?= (2)

ARKADIA:

—TEGEA:

——(Athaneatai): (5) iii BC *IG* V (2) 40, 30 (s. Ξεν—)

EPIROS:

—BOUTHROTOS (PRASAIBOI): (6) a. 163 BC *IBouthrot* 47, 21 ([Καλ]λιφάνης)

## Καλλιφάων

KORINTHIA:

—SIKYON: (1) iv BC *BCH* 52 (1928) p. 217 no. 21, 2 (s. Εὔρυλλος)

S. ITALY (BRUTTIUM):

—KRIMISA: (2) ?c. 475 BC *IGSI* 18, 1 (*SEG* IV 75; Landi, *DISMG* 173); *LSAG²* p. 261 no. 30 (date)

## Καλλίφιλος

ARKADIA:

—MEGALOPOLIS: (1) 182 BC *IvOl* 46, 7 + *IPArk* 31 IIB (Κ[αλ]λίφιλος: s. Δάμαινος)

## Καλλίφρων

KERKYRA: (1) hell.? *IG* IX (1)² (2) 233

## Καλλίφυτος

SICILY:

—AKRAI?: (1) imp. *CIL* X 8059. 90 (seal) (Lat. D. Caecilius Calliphytus)

## Καλλιφῶν

AKARNANIA:

—ASTAKOS: (1) ii BC *IG* IX (1)² (2) 435, 3 (s. Θεογένης)

ARGOLIS:

—TROIZEN: (2) c. 405 BC *FD* III (1) 64; cf. *CEG* II 819 (Καλλιφῶνος (gen.): f. Ἀπολλόδωρος)

EPIROS:

—AMBRAKIA: (3) s. iv BC Unp. (Arta Mus.)

S. Italy (Bruttium):
—kroton: (**4**) vi bc Hdt. iii 125. 1; cf. *FVS* 19
(f. Δαμοκάδης)
Sicily: (**5**) iv/iii bc D.S. xxii 5. 2

**Καλλιχάρης**
Aitolia: (**1**) iii/ii bc *Ag.* XVII 398 (s. Νίκων)

**Κάλλιχον**
Lakonia:
—kotyrta: (**1**) hell.? *SEG* 11 173

**Καλλιώ**
Akarnania:
—anaktorion: (**1**) iii bc *IG* IX (1)² (2) 221

**Καλλίων**
Argolis:
—epidauros: (**1**) iv/iii bc Peek, *IAEpid* 51,
7; *BSA* 61 (1966) p. 319 no. 26 (date)
(Καλλ[ίω]ν) ?= (*2*); (**2**) ~ Peek, *NIEpid* 21, 9
(*SEG* XXV 403, 1) ?= (*1*)
Illyria:
—apollonia: (**3**) c. 250-50 bc Ceka 9; *IApoll
Ref. Bibl.* n. 7 (coin) (pryt.); (**4**) ~ Maier 70
(coin) (Ceka 68) (money.)
Sicily:
—lipara: (**5**) hell.? *IG* XIV 392 (Libertini, *Isole
Eolie* p. 219 no. 10)

**Καλλόνη**
Illyria:
—dimale: (**1**) iii bc *Iliria* 1986 (1), p. 102 no.
1 ([K]αλλόνη)

**Κάλλος**
Arkadia:
—tegea: (**1**) s. iv bc *SEG* XXXVI 383, 6 (f. Κώκαλος)

**Κάλλουσα**
Arkadia:
—mantineia-antigoneia: (**1**) ?i ad *IG* v (2)
338 (Ἰουλ. Κ.)
Lakonia:
—sparta: (**2**) iii ad ib. v (1) 251 (Bradford (-))
(Αὐρ. Κ.: d. Σάτυρος)

**Καλλώ**
Achaia:
—dyme: (**1**) ii-i bc *SGDI* 1617 a (d. Τερμόνιος)
Akarnania:
—thyrreion: (**2**) ?iii/ii bc *IG* IX (1)² (2) 353;
cf. Fraser–Rönne, *BWGT* pp. 169 f. (Καλλοῖ
(voc.))
Argolis:
—epidauros: (**3**) iv/iii bc *IG* IV (1)² 200; (**4**) c.
115 bc D.S. xxxii 11 (Κ. ἡ ὕστερον Κάλλων)
Illyria:
—epidamnos-dyrrhachion: (**5**) hell.-imp.
*IDyrrh* 261
Messenia:
—messene: (**6**) c. 30-50 ad *IvOl* 428, 4 (Ἀντωνία
Κ.)
S. Italy (Bruttium):
—lokroi epizephyrioi: (**7**) iv/iii bc *HE* 2811

**Κάλλων**
Aitolia: (**1**) ?254-237 bc Nachtergael, *Les Galates* 9, 17; 60, 6; cf. Stephanis 323 (f. Ἀρίστιππος)
Argolis:
—epidauros: (**2**) c. 115 bc D.S. xxxii 11 (Κ. ὁ
πρότερον Καλλώ)
—hermione: (**3**) iii bc *IG* IV (1) 728, 1 (f. Γλαυκίας); (**4**) ii-i bc ib. 732 IV, 12
Arkadia:
—megalopolis: (**5**) s. iii bc *FD* III (1) 22, 1
(f. Καλλίμαχος); (**6**) ?ii ad *IG* v (2) 122 (f.
Ὀλυμπιόδωρος)
Elis: (**7**) iv/iii bc Moretti, *Olymp.* 497 (s. Ἁρμόδιος)

—olympia*: (**8**) 36-24 bc *IvOl* 62, 20 (?s. Κλέιππος: Δου.)
Epiros:
—ambrakia: (**9**) 238-168 bc *BMC Thessaly*
p. 95 no. 24 (coin) (Κάλλων); (**10**) s. ii bc
Cabanes, *L'Épire* p. 548 no. 19 (*SEG* XXVI
694) (s. Νικοσθένης)
—charadros: (**11**) a. 167 bc ib. xxxv 665 A,
15
Illyria:
—epidamnos-dyrrhachion: (**12**) c. 250-50
bc Maier 255-6; Münsterberg Nachtr. p. 15
(coin) (Ceka 224; 322) (pryt.)
Lakonia:
—sparta: (**13**) ?ii ad *IG* v (1) 179, 7 (Bradford
s.v. Κάλπων (-)) (Κάλπων—apogr.)
Messenia:
—messene: (**14**) s. ii bc *SEG* XLI 341, 11 (s.
Ἀπολλόδωρος)
——(Hylleis): (**15**) 11 ad *PAE* 1992, p. 71 A, 14
(f. Χρύσιππος); (**16**) ~ ib. l. 16 (f. Διόφαντος)
—thouria: (**17**) ii-i bc *IG* v (1) 1385, 16 (f.
Κράτων)
Sicily:
—syracuse: (**18**) ?s. v bc *SGDI* 5246 (*SEG*
XLI 837) (Κάλλ[ων]); (**19**) 215 bc Liv. xxiv 5.
9 (Lat. Callo)

**Καλογένητος**
Korinthia:
—korinth: (**1**) byz. *Corinth* VIII (3) 560, 4; cf.
*TMByz* 9 (1985) p. 366 no. 65 (-λω-: f. Λαυρέντιος)

**Καλόδρυς**
Elis:
—olympia*: (**1**) 181-185 ad *IvOl* 102, 23
([Κα]λόδρυς: ?s. Μ. Ἀντ. Ἀντικός: slave?)

**Καλοῖς**
Messenia:
—messene: (**1**) s. ii bc *IG* v (1) 1445 (Κ. (n.
pr.?)—*LGPN*, Καλοῖς (dat.)—*IG*)

**Καλόκαιρος**
Illyria:
—epidamnos-dyrrhachion: (**1**) i bc-i ad
*CIL* III 615 (Sestieri, *ILat. Albania* 32) (Lat.
Calocaerus)
S. Italy (Campania):
—salernum*: (**2**) imp. *IItal* I (1) 205 (*CIL* x
607) (Lat. Calocaerus: imp. freed.)

**Καλοκλείνας**
Lakonia:
—oitylos: (**1**) v bc *IG* v (1) 1293 (Poralla²
413) (-κλέ-: s. Κλεόμαχος)

**Καλοκλῆς**
Lakonia:
—gytheion: (**1**) a. 212 ad *IG* v (1) 1179, 3 (Μ.
Αὐρ. Κ.: s. Νίκανδρος)
—sparta: (**2**) c. 145-155 ad *SEG* XI 529, 3
(Bradford (-)) (s. Φιλο—)

**Καλονίκα**
Aitolia:
—kallion/kallipolis: (**1**) hell. *IG* IX (1)² (1)
158 bis

**Καλόνιος**
S. Italy (Bruttium):
—catanzaro (mod.): (**1**) hell. *SEG* IV 76 (terracotta) (Πάκιος Κ.)

**Κάλος**
S. Italy (Campania):
—pompeii: (**1**) i bc-i ad *CIL* IV 3952 (Castrèn
315. 3) (Lat. C. Pomponius Calus)

**Καλότυχος**
S. Italy (Campania):
—neapolis: (**1**) ii ad *IG* XIV 789 (*INap* 127);
cf. Leiwo p. 105 no. 64

**Κάλσος**
Illyria:
—epidamnos-dyrrhachion: (**1**) hell.-imp.
*IDyrrh* 104 (f. Ἀνναία)

**Καλύβη**
S. Italy (Campania):
—dikaiarchia-puteoli: (**1**) imp. *CIL* X 2223
(Lat. Calybe: m. Fuscina, Faustinus)
S. Italy (Lucania):
—atina lucana: (**2**) imp. *IItal* III (1) 179; cf.
Solin, *Lukan. Inschr.* pp. 43-4 (Lat. Allidia
Calibe: d. Σοφωνιανός, Κλαδίσκη)

**Καλύκα**
Argolis:
—epidauros: (**1**) ?iv bc Peek, *NIEpid* 92

**Καλύκη**
Leukas: (**1**) vi bc *PMG* fr. 277 (dub.)
S. Italy (Campania):
—salernum*: (**2**) imp. *IItal* I (1) 81 (*CIL* x
627) (Lat. Proculeia Calyce: m. Proculeius
Magnus: freed.)

**Καλυκία**
Korinthia:
—korinth: (**1**) ?v-iv bc UP (Corinth Mus. C-
39-170) (vase) (n. pr.?)

**Καλχηδόνιος**
S. Italy (Campania):
—salernum: (**1**) imp. *IItal* I (1) 79 (*CIL* x 625)
(Lat. C. Plutius Calchedonius)

**Κάλων**
Aigina: (**1**) vi/v bc *RE* (1); *IG* I³ [752]; 753;
cf. *Alt-Ägina* II (2) p. 13 f. (sculptor)
Elis: (**2**) ?c. 450-425 bc *RE* (2); *CEG* I 388
(Arena, *Iscr. Sic.* III 65; Dubois, *IGDGG* I
36); *LSAG*² p. 221 no. 19 (date) (Κάλλων—
Paus.: sculptor)

**Καλωνᾶς**
Sicily:
—syracuse: (**1**) iii-v ad Strazzulla 408 (Wessel
1121); cf. Ferrua, *NG* 355

**Κάμανδρος**
Epiros:
—votonosi (mod.): (**1**) ?s. iii bc *SEG* XXIV
458 (s. Τίμαιος: slave/freed.)

**Κάμβαλος**
Sicily:
—morgantina: (**1**) c. 133 bc D.S. xxxiv/xxxv
11 (Γόργος ἐπικαλ. Κ.)

**Καμένη**
Lakonia:
—thalamai: (**1**) byz. *IG* v (1) 1324

**Κάμιλλος**
Lakonia:
—sparta: (**1**) c. 100-125 ad ib. 103, 7; 483, 2;
*SEG* XI 537 a, 5; 569, 25 (Bradford (-)) (f.
Ἀριστοκράτης)

**Καμινᾶς**
Lakonia:
—sparta: (**1**) c. 230-260 ad *SEG* XI 633, 4
(Bradford (-)) (-μει-: f. Αὐρ. Ἀπολλώνιος)

**Καμοφίας**
Korinthia:
—korinth: (**1**) arch. *Corinth* XVIII (1) p. 152
no. 374 (vase) (f. —ρετα (n. pr.?))

**Κάμπα**
S. Italy (Lucania):
—metapontion: (**1**) ?iii bc Guarducci, *Ep. Gr.*
3 p. 351 (Landi, *DISMG* 151 (loomweight))

**Καμπάνη**
ILLYRIA:
—APOLLONIA: (1) imp. *IApoll* 262 (*Καν*-)

**Κάμπας**
ARKADIA:
—TEGEA: (1) c. 240-229 BC *IG* v (2) 11, 15

**Κάμπος**
ARKADIA:
—ORCHOMENOS: (1) ?c. 369-361 BC *BCH* 102 (1978) p. 348, 32 (*IPArk* 14)

**Καμύδων**
AITOLIA:
—KALYDON: (1) f. iv BC *IG* IX (1)² (1) 138, 3

**Καμψίας**
ACHAIA:
—PHARAI: (1) 134 or 130 BC *SGDI* 2683, 3, 6 (f. Ἐπικράτης)

**Καμώ**
ARKADIA:
—MELPEIA*: (1) ?c. 500-480 BC *IG* v (2) 554 (bronze) (Lazzarini 111); *LSAG²* p. 215 no. 12 (date)

**Κάμων**
ARKADIA:
—MANTINEIA-ANTIGONEIA: (1) c. 300-221 BC *IG* v (2) 323. 107 (tessera) (*Κάμων*: s. Θεόκριτος)

**Κάνακις**
SICILY:
—AKRAI: (1) imp. *SEG* XLII 832, 10 (*K. Ὄππις K.*)

**Κάναχος**
ACHAIA:
—LEONTION?: (1) c. 200 BC *IG* VII 2835; *Hyettos* pp. 157 ff. (locn.) (sculptor)
KORINTHIA:
—SIKYON: (2) s. vi BC *RE* (1) (Skalet 171) (sculptor); (3) v/iv BC *RE* (2) (Skalet 172) (sculptor); (4) c. 80-70 BC *IG* IX (2) 534, 23; Kramolisch p. 116 n. 74 (date) (Skalet 173) ([K]άναχος: s. Γοργίας)

**Κάνδιδα**
SICILY:
—SYRACUSE: (1) iii-v AD Barreca 400

**Κανθαρίων**
ARKADIA: (1) ?364 BC Plu., *Mor.* 300 C

**Κάνθαρος**
KORINTHIA:
—SIKYON: (1) m. iv BC *RE* (4) (Skalet 175) (s. Ἄλεξις: sculptor)
SICILY:
—SYRACUSE?:
——(Πλε.): (2) hell. *NScav* 1961, p. 349 (bullet); cf. *BE* 1965, no. 502; *L'Incidenza dell'Antico* pp. 420 ff. (s. Ἀγέλοχος)

**Κανθίας**
ARGOLIS:
—ARGOS?: (1) v BC *IG* IV (1) 552, 11

**Κάνθος**
S. ITALY (CAMPANIA):
—POMPEII: (1) i BC-i AD *CIL* IV 1140; 1149 (Lat. Canthus)

**Κανών**
S. ITALY (CAMPANIA):
—HERCULANEUM*: (1) i BC-i AD ib. X 1403 f I, 10 (Lat. P. Brennius Cano: freed.)

**Κάνωπος**
ACHAIA:
—DYME: (1) ii BC *Achaean Grave Stelai* 32 (f. Φιλοστράτα)
LAKONIA:
—HYPERTELEATON*: (2) imp. *IG* v (1) 1052 (I f. Κάνωπος II); (3) ~ ib. ([K]άνωπος: II s. Κάνωπος I)

**Καπάρων**
S. ITALY (BRUTTIUM):
—LOKROI EPIZEPHYRIOI: (1) ?c. 450-425 BC Th. iii 103. 3; Lazzarini 342 (Landi, *DISMG* 62); *SEG* XXIX 952 (name); *LSAG²* p. 286 no. 7 (-ρὸν, Καπάτων—Th. mss.: f. Πρόξενος)

**Καπιτωλία**
SICILY:
—SYRACUSE: (1) iii-v AD Strazzulla 410 (Agnello 35; Wessel 238) ([Κα]πιτωλία)

**Καπιτωλῖνα**
SICILY:
—SYRACUSE: (1) iii-v AD *Rend. Pont.* 22 (1946-7) p. 236 no. 39 ([Κ]απιτω[λῖ]να)

**Καπίτων**
SICILY:
—GELA-PHINTIAS: (1) ii-i BC *SEG* XXXI 837, 8
—SYRACUSE: (2) iii-v AD *IG* XIV 131 (Strazzulla 69); cf. Ferrua, *NG* 288 (Καπίτω(ν)); (3) ~ ib. 210

**Κάποσος**
SICILY:
—GELA-PHINTIAS: (1) f. v BC Dubois, *IGDS* 131. 3 (Arena, *Iscr. Sic.* II 45)
—SELINOUS: (2) m. v BC Dubois, *IGDS* 36, 2 (Arena, *Iscr. Sic.* I 69) (f. Νίκυλλος)

**Καπρόγονον**
SICILY:
—MEGARA HYBLAIA: (1) vi/v BC Guarducci, *Ep. Gr.* 1 pp. 315-6 no. 6 (Dubois, *IGDS* 27; Arena, *Iscr. Sic.* I 7) (d. Ἀγίας)

**Κάπρος**
AKARNANIA:
—KORONTA: (1) ii/i BC *GVI* 308 (*IG* IX (1)² (2) 431) (Κάπ[ρος])
—PALAIROS: (2) ?iii BC ib. 541 (Κάπρου? (gen.))
ELIS: (3) 212 BC Moretti, *Olymp.* 587-8 (s. Πυθαγόρας)
S. ITALY (APULIA):
—CANUSIUM: (4) ii-iii AD *Epig. Rom. di Canosa* 152 (*CIL* IX 387) (Lat. Caprus: f. P. Libuscidius Faustinus)

**Κάπυς**
SICILY:
—AKRAGAS: (1) vi/v BC *FGrH* 568 F 2 (s. Ξενόδικος)

**Καραβάντιος**
ILLYRIA: (1) f. ii BC Liv. xliv 30. 9 (Lat. Caravantius: s. Εὐρυδίκα)

**Καράϊκος**
SICILY:
—MORGANTINA: (1) iv/iii BC *SEG* XXXIX 1008, 12 (f. Πυρρίας)
—SYRACUSE?:
——(Ῥιπε.): (2) hell. *NScav* 1961, p. 349 (bullet); cf. *BE* 1965, no. 502 (f. Σῶσις)

**Καραῖος**
ARGOLIS:
—HERMIONE: (1) iii BC *IG* IV (1) 729 II, 16 (s. Ἀλκιμένης)

**Καράνιος**
ARKADIA:
—TEGEA:

——(Krariotai): (1) s. iii BC ib. v (2) 36, 123 (s. Αἴσχρων)

**Κάρανος**
ARGOLIS:
—ARGOS: (1) her. *RE* (-) (and Macedonia: s. Φείδων: king)
ELIS: (2) iv BC *SEG* XV 241, 5, 8
LAKONIA:
—SPARTA: (3) vi/v BC Hdt. vii 173. 2 (Poralla² 414) (-ρη-: f. Εὐαίνετος)

**Καρᾶς**
SICILY:
—AKRAGAS (NR.): (1) ?iv BC Manganaro, *QUCC* forthcoming no. 39, 5 ?= (*2*); (2) ~ Manganaro, *QUCC* forthcoming no. 39, 7 ?= (*1*)

**Καρδαμίων**
AKARNANIA:
—LIMNAIA: (1) m. ii BC *Syll³* 669, 9 (*IG* v (1) 29, 9) (f. Ἀλεξίμαχος)
ARGOLIS:
—EPIDAUROS: (2) c. 240-200 BC Peek, *IAEpid* 330, 8 (Perlman E.4) (Καρδ[α]μ[ίων])

**Καρίας**
SICILY:
—SELINOUS: (1) s. vi BC Dubois, *IGDS* 75 (Arena, *Iscr. Sic.* I 29; *IGLMP* 84) (f. Ἀγασίας)

**Καρική**
S. ITALY (CALABRIA):
—HYRIA: (1) ii/iii AD *Studi Ribezzo* p. 64 no. 8 (Lat. Carice)

**Καρικός**
S. ITALY (CAMPANIA):
—NEAPOLIS*: (1) imp. *IG* XIV 792 (*INap* 131); cf. Leiwo p. 105 no. 65 (M. Κλώδιος K.: threptos)
SICILY:
—KATANE: (2) imp. *IG* XIV 484 (Ἰγνάτις K.)

**Καρίων**
AIGINA?: (1) 405 BC ib. I³ 1032, 422
AITOLIA: (2) f. iii BC *SGDI* 2590, 2; cf. *IG* IX (1)² (1) p. XIX, 85 (Κα[ρ]ίων: f. Τελέσων)
S. ITALY (LUCANIA):
—POSEIDONIA-PAESTUM: (3) m. iv BC *RVP* p. 84 no. 125 (vase) (fict.)

**Καρκίνος**
S. ITALY (BRUTTIUM):
—RHEGION: (1) 317 BC D.S. xix 2 (and Sicily Syracuse: f. Ἀγαθοκλῆς, Ἀντανδρος (Syracuse))
SICILY:
—AKRAGAS: (2) ?v-iv BC *Suda* K 394 (dub.)

**Καρμόννη**
EPIROS:
—AMBRAKIA: (1) ii BC *SEG* XVII 308 (d. Παυσανίας)

**Κάρμων**
LEUKAS: (1) f. i BC *IG* IX (1) 534, 11 (*Iscr. Gr. Verona* p. 24) (s. Ἀρχανδρος)

**Καρνεάδας**
ARGOLIS:
—PHLEIOUS: (1) s. iv BC Peek, *NIEpid* 16, 25 (Perlman E.6) (s. Χάροψ)
ARKADIA:
—MEGALOPOLIS: (2) ii-iii AD *GVI* 1091, 2 (Raffeiner, *Sklaven* 19) (f. Συμφορίς)

**Κάρνεια**
ILLYRIA:
—EPIDAMNOS-DYRRHACHION: (1) hell.-imp. *IDyrrh* 214 (Εὐτυχὶς Κάρνηα: d. Οὐρβάνος)

**Κᾶρος**
S. Italy (Campania):
—dikaiarchia-puteoli?: (1) imp. *Bull. Mus. Imp. Rom.* 61 (1933) pp. 43-5 no. 9; cf. *Storia di Napoli* 1 p. 621 (sculptor)
Sicily:
—syracuse: (2) iii-v AD *NScav* 1918, p. 277 (Barreca 212)

**Καροφαντίδας**
S. Italy (Calabria):
—taras-tarentum: (1) iv BC Iamb., *VP* 267 (*FVS* 1 p. 446) (Καρνεοφαντίδας—Schweigh., Κλεοφαντίδας—Nauck)

**Καρπία**
Sicily:
—syracuse: (1) iii-v AD Strazzulla 52 bis

**Καρπιάς**
S. Italy (Campania):
—dikaiarchia-puteoli: (1) ?ii AD *CIL* x 2516 (Lat. Carpias: m. Ἑρμιόνη)

**Καρπίμη**
Epiros:
—nikopolis: (1) imp. *Hellenika* 22 (1969) p. 72 no. 12 (Sarikakis 164) (Τιτία Κ., Καπίμη—ed.)
S. Italy (Campania):
—misenum*: (2) imp. *CIL* x 3611 (Lat. Carpime: m. Ἀμμιάς)

**Κάρπιμος**
Sicily:
—mt. eryx*: (1) imp. *IG* xiv 281 ([Κάρ]πιμος: s. Ἀρίστων)

**Κάρπιον**
S. Italy (Calabria):
—taras-tarentum: (1) ii/i BC ib. ii² 10412 a, 1

**Καρπίων**
Arkadia:
—tegea: (1) ii AD ib. v (2) 55, 24 (f. Κλέανδρος)
Kephallenia:
—same: (2) imp. ib. ix (1) 642 ([Κ]αρπίων)
Sicily:
—zankle-messana: (3) iii AD *Epigraphica* 3 (1941) p. 254 no. 4 (Lat. Carpio: I f. Καρπίων II); (4) ~ ib. (Lat. Carpio: II s. Καρπίων I)

**Καρπόδωρος**
Achaia: (1) imp.? *IG* ii² 8401 (Καρπ(ό)δωρος: f. Ἀριστοκλέας)
Ithake: (2) iv BC *AM* 27 (1902) p. 377 no. 62 (*REG* 15 (1902) p. 132 no. 1) ([Π]ονπόδωρος?—*AM*, [Κ]αρπόδωρος—*REG*)

**Καρποκρᾶς**
Sicily:
—syracuse: (1) iii-v AD *NScav* 1893, p. 290 no. 46 + Ferrua, *NG* 16 (Χαρ[ποκ]ρᾶς: f. Αἴσωπος)

**Κάρπος**
Arkadia:
—tegea: (1) hell.-imp.? *IG* v (2) 257
Illyria:
—epidamnos-dyrrhachion: (2) imp. *IDyrrh* 37
Kerkyra: (3) imp. *IG* ix (1) 915
Korinthia:
—korinth: (4) f. ii AD *Ag.* vii p. 97 no. 301; *Corinth* iv (2) pp. 187 no. 553; 209 no. 743; *SEG* xxvii 35. 12 (lamps)
Lakonia:
—gytheion: (5) f. ii AD *IG* v (1) 1156; 1171, 9 = ii² 3596 (II s. Κάρπος I); (6) ~ ib. v (1) [1156]; 1171, 10 = ii² 3596 (I f. Κάρπος II)

—sparta: (7) c. 25-1 BC ib. v (1) 210, 25 (Bradford (2)) (f. Φιλοκλείδας); (8) c. 75-100 AD *IG* v (1) 31, 12 (Bradford (1)) (s. Ὀνήσιμος)
S. Italy (Apulia):
—luceria: (9) imp. *CIL* ix 827 (Lat. P. Vedius Carpus: freed./doctor)
S. Italy (Calabria):
—brentesion-brundisium*: (10) imp. ib. 6126 (Lat. C. Marcius Carpus: freed.)
—taras-tarentum: (11) imp. *NScav* 1896, p. 375 no. 1 (Lat. Carpus)
S. Italy (Campania):
—dikaiarchia-puteoli: (12) imp. *CIL* x 2102 (Lat. [Ar]rius Carpus); (13) ~ ib. 2134 (Lat. Carpus); (14) ~ ib. 2230 (Lat. Carpus); (15) ~ ib. 2379 (Lat. A. Ducennius Carpus); (16) ~ ib. 2462 (Lat. A. Fraucius Carpus); (17) m. i AD Camodeca, *L'Archivio Puteolano* 1 p. 68 no. 7 (Lat. Carpus)
—herculaneum: (18) m. i AD *PdelP* 3 (1948) p. 182 no. 30; 8 (1953) p. 463 no. 56, 4 (Lat. Sex. Caecilius Carpus)
—herculaneum*: (19) i BC-i AD *CIL* x 1403 g II, 31 (Lat. P. Valerius Carpus: freed.)
—misenum*: (20) ii AD ib. vi 8684; cf. *Puteoli* 12-13 (1988-9) p. 65 no. 1 (locn.) (Lat. Claudius Carpus: f. Αὔξιμος)
—pompeii: (21) 27 AD *CIL* iv 3340. 2, 4, 6; 21, 5, 18; 74, 12 (Castrèn 23. 6) (Lat. M. Alleius Carpus)
—salernum: (22) imp. *IItal* 1 (1) 132 (*CIL* x 571) (Lat. Carpus)
Sicily:
—syracuse: (23) iii-v AD Ferrua, *NG* 370

**Καρποφοριανός**
S. Italy (Campania):
—stabiae: (1) imp. *CIL* x 8135 (Lat. Cornelius Carpophorian(us): s. Cornelia Ferocia)

**Καρποφόρος**
Korinthia:
—korinth: (1) ii-iii AD *SEG* xxvii 35. 5 (lamp) ((Κ)α(ρ)ποφόρος?)
S. Italy (Apulia):
—canusium: (2) 223 AD *Epig. Rom. di Canosa* 35 III, 13 (*CIL* ix 338) (Lat. P. Marcius Carpophorus)
S. Italy (Calabria):
—brentesion-brundisium: (3) ?ii AD ib. 205 (Lat. Assius Carpophorus: f. Ulpia Prima)
S. Italy (Campania):
—salernum: (4) imp. *IItal* 1 (1) 222 (*CIL* x 642) (Lat. C. Terentius Carpoforus: f. C. Terentius Rarus)

**Καρπῦς**
Korinthia:
—korinth: (1) iii-iv AD *Corinth* viii (3) 68

**Κάρπων**
S. Italy (Campania):
—pompeii: (1) i BC-i AD *CIL* iv 8422 (Lat. Carpo)

**Κάρτομος**
Epiros:
—onopernoi: (1) 370-368 BC Cabanes, *L'Épire* p. 534 no. 1, 17

**Καρφίνας**
Akarnania: (1) 338 BC Osborne, *Naturalization* D 16, 8, 15 ?= (2)
—stratos: (2) c. 325-315 BC *Hesp.* 57 (1988) p. 148 B, 40 (*SEG* xxxvi 331); cf. *Hesp.* 48 (1979) pp. 78 f. with pl. 22 c; cf. Tod, *GHI* II 178 (f. Μεννέας) ?= (1)

**Κάρχαξ**
Epiros:
—phoinike?: (1) c. 330 BC *SEG* xxiii 189 I, 12 (Κάρχαξ (n. pr.?))

**Κάρχαρος**
Sicily:
—syracuse: (1) 215 BC *FGrH* 268 F 4 (Θράσων ὁ Κ. ἐπικαλούμενος)

**Καρχηδών**
Lakonia:
—leuktra: (1) hell.-imp. *IG* v (1) 1330 a

**Κάρων**
S. Italy?: (1) ?vi BC *CIG* 8338; cf. Arndt, *Vasenkunde* p. 112 (vase) (Κάρōν—vase, (Χ)άρōν—*CIG* and Arndt)

**Κάσαμβος**
Aigina: (1) vi/v BC Hdt. vi 73 (s. Ἀριστοκράτης)

**Κασία**
Argolis:
—troizen: (1) imp. *IG* iv (1) 821 B
Elis: (2) 21 AD *IvOl* 233 + *ZPE* 99 (1993) p. 227 f. (date, stemma); Moretti, *Olymp.* 866 (d. Μ. Βετληνὸς Λαῖτος)

**Κασίλης**
Argolis:
—hermione: (1) imp. *IG* iv (1) 700

**Κασίννιος**
Sicily:
—paterno (mod.): (1) iv-iii BC *Silver for the Gods* pp. 58-61 nos. 25-7 (Πάμπελος Κ.)

**Κάσιος**
Lakonia:
—sparta: (1) ii AD *IG* v (1) 491, 2 (Bradford (-)) (Κλ. Κ.: s. Τυχικός)

**Κασσάνδρα**
Illyria:
—epidamnos-dyrrhachion: (1) i BC/i AD *IG* ii² 8487 (d. Διονύσιος)
—lychnidos: (2) ii-iii AD *Sp.* 77 (1934) p. 50 no. 44 (Κασά-)

**Κάσσανδρος**
Aigina: (1) 185 BC *RE* (5); (2) i BC-i AD *Alt-Ägina* 1 (2) p. 45 no. 12, 1 (Κάσσαν[δρος])
Aitolia:
—kalydon: (3) a. 142 BC *IG* ix (1)² (1) 137, 79 (Κάσσα[νδρος])
Akarnania:
—thyrreion: (4) iii BC ib. ix (1)² (2) 271 = *SEG* xxvii 166? (Κάσα-: f. Νικάσιος)
Elis: (5) 85 AD *EA* 1905, p. 255 no. 1, 5 (Κ. Διονυσιάδης: s. Λάχης)
Epiros:
—kassope: (6) hell. *Ep. Chron.* 29 (1988-9) pp. 89 ff.; cf. *BE* 1991, no. 360
Korinthia:
—korinth: (7) 217 BC Plb. v 95. 3
Lakonia:
—sparta: (8) s. i AD *IG* v (1) 516, 5; *BSA* 75 (1980) pp. 205-6 (date) (Bradford (-)) (f. Τ. Ὀκτ. Λογγῖνος, Τιβ. Κλ. .ατ...ς)
S. Italy (Campania):
—dikaiarchia-puteoli*: (9) i AD *CIL* x 3146; cf. *Puteoli* 11 (1987) p. 59 (date) (Lat. C. Volusius Cassander: freed.)

**Κασσιανός**
Epiros:
—bouthrotos*: (1) imp. *IBouthrot* 182-3 (*SEG* xxxviii 518-19) (Κασι-)

**Κάσσιος**
Sicily:
—melita: (1) imp.? *IG* xiv 2406. 27 (vase) (-σει-: f. Καικελία)

**Κασσίς**
Kephallenia:
—same: (1) hell. *Op. Ath.* 10 (1971) p. 66 no. 11

**Κάστα**
S. ITALY (APULIA):
—VENUSIA: (1) v AD *JIWE* I 46 (*CIJ* I 588)
(Jew)

**Κασταλία**
ITHAKE: (1) hell.? *Rev. Épig.* I (1913) p. 47 no.
12 (Κασσαλιας—apogr., Κασ(τ)αλίας? (gen.))

**Κάσταλος**
S. ITALY (CAMPANIA):
—POMPEII: (1) i BC-i AD *CIL* IV 8554 (Lat.
Castalus)

**Καστάνις**
SICILY:
—SYRACUSE: (1) iii-v AD Ferrua, *NG* 371

**Καστίνα**
SICILY:
—SYRACUSE?: (1) byz. *SEG* XIV 582 (Καστεῖνα
Ῥωμαία)

**Καστορίδης**
S. ITALY (CAMPANIA):
—NEAPOLIS: (1) i BC/i AD *INap* 151, 4 (Π. Οὐι-
κίριος [Κ]αστορίδης?)

**Κάστωρ**
S. ITALY (APULIA):
—VENUSIA: (1) imp. *CIL* IX 486 (Lat. Castor)
S. ITALY (CALABRIA):
—TARAS-TARENTUM: (2) iv BC *SEG* XXXIII 812
([Κ]άστωρ)
S. ITALY (CAMPANIA):
—DIKAIARCHIA-PUTEOLI*: (3) ?i-ii AD *CIL* X
2545 (Lat. C. Iulius Castor: freed.)
—POMPEII*: (4) i BC-i AD *NScav* 1894, p. 384
(Castrèn 246. 11) (Lat. L. Melissaeus Castor:
freed.)
S. ITALY (LUCANIA):
—VOLCEI: (5) imp. *IItal* III (1) 116 (*CIL* X 372)
(Lat. Bruttius Castor)
SICILY:
—THERMAI HIMERAIAI: (6) i-ii AD *ILat. Term.
Imer.* 83 (Lat. Cornelius Castor)

**Κασώπας**
EPIROS: (1) s. iv BC *IG* IV (1)² 95, 73 (Perlman
E.2); Perlman pp. 46-9 (date)

**Κατάγραφος**
S. ITALY (CAMPANIA):
—DIKAIARCHIA-PUTEOLI: (1) imp. *CIL* X 3084
(Lat. Catagraphus)

**Κατάκοος**
ELIS: (1) m. iv BC *IvOl* 44, 10 (Κατά[κ]οος)

**Κατάνικος**
EPIROS:
—VOTONOSI (MOD.): (1) f. iii BC *SEG* XXIV 456
(Κατόνικος—ed.)

**Κατάπλους**
S. ITALY (CAMPANIA):
—DIKAIARCHIA-PUTEOLI: (1) imp. *AJA* 2
(1898) p. 384 no. 27 (Lat. C. Larcius Cata-
plus)

**Κάτελλα**
SICILY:
—SYRACUSE: (1) iii-v AD Strazzulla 338 (Wessel
1354); cf. Ferrua, *NG* 122

**Κατιάνιλλα**
SICILY:
—SYRACUSE: (1) iii-v AD ib. 308 (Κατιάνιλ<α>λα)

**Κάτιλλος**
S. ITALY (BRUTTIUM):
—KROTON: (1) arch. Paus. vi 19. 6 (f. Πατρο-
κλῆς)

**Κατυλλῖνος**
SICILY:
—SYRACUSE: (1) iii-v AD Wessel 846 (Barreca
237)

**Καῦλος**
S. ITALY (CALABRIA):
—LEPORANO (MOD.): (1) ?v-iv BC Santoro,
*NSM* I p. 108 (vase) (potter)

**Κάφις**
ACHAIA:
—ASCHEION?: (1) c. 315-280 BC *FD* III (1) 413,
3 (f. Φανοκλῆς, —χος)

**Καφισίας**
AITOLIA: (1) c. 232-228 BC *Syll*³ 499, 3;
Nachtergael, *Les Galates* 62, [3]
ARGOLIS:
—EPIDAUROS*: (2) c. 370 BC *IG* IV (1)² 102, 68
KORINTHIA:
—SIKYON?: (3) 251 BC Plu., *Arat.* 6; 7 (Skalet
176)

**Καφίσιος**
LAKONIA:
—GERONTHRAI: (1) 72 BC *IG* V (1) 1114, 2

**Καφισόδωρος**
ARKADIA:
—MANTINEIA-ANTIGONEIA: (1) ii-i BC ib. V (2)
319, 7 ([Κα]φισόδωρος)
KORINTHIA:
—KORINTH: (2) s. iv BC *Corinth* VIII (1) 11, 2
(s. Ἄριστ—); (3) 336 BC *CID* II 60, 16, 23
—KORINTH?: (4) c. 450-425 BC *IG* IV (1) 356
(bronze) (XIV 2282; Lazzarini 347); *LSAG*²
p. 132 no. 40 (date) (-δō-)
—SIKYON: (5) iii BC *IG* II² 10306 (Skalet 177)
(Κη-)

**Καφισοκλῆς**
MESSENIA:
—MESSENE: (1) iii BC *SEG* XIII 243, 4 (s. Καλ-
λικλῆς)

**Καφισός**
S. ITALY (CAMPANIA):
—POMPEII: (1) i BC-i AD *CIL* IV 2192 (Lat.
Caphisus)

**Καφισοτέλης**
KORINTHIA:
—KORINTH: (1) m. iii BC *Corinth* VIII (1) 60 (s.
Τιμοσθένης)

**Καφισοφῶν**
LAKONIA:
—SPARTA?: (1) ?v-iv BC Plu., *Mor.* 239 C (Κη-)

**Κέββας**
ILLYRIA:
—BERAT (MOD.): (1) ii/i BC *SEG* XXXVIII 542
(I f. Κέββας II, Γόργος); (2) ~ ib. (II s. Κέββας
I)

**Κέδρος**
S. ITALY (CAMPANIA):
—POMPEII: (1) i BC-i AD *CIL* IV 3376 (Castrèn
4. 2) (Lat. Acilius Cedrus)

**Κείαλος**
EPIROS:
—DODONA: (1) iii BC Antoniou, *Dodone* Ab, 3

**Κελαδιανός**
SICILY:
—ADRANON: (1) ?ii-iii AD *PdelP* 16 (1961) p.
132 (Ferrua, *NG* 472); cf. *Rupes loquentes* p.
497 no. 8

**Κελαδῖνος**
S. ITALY (CAMPANIA):
—CAPREAE: (1) imp. *CIL* X 6810 (Lat. Ge-
ladinus)

**Κέλαδος**
ARGOLIS:
—ARGOS: (1) iii BC *IG* IV (1) 618 I, 6 ([Κέ]λαδος:
s. Ξενοκλῆς)
—EPIDAUROS: (2) imp. ib. IV (1)² 446 (I f. Κέ-
λαδος II); (3) ~ ib. (II s. Κέλαδος I)
—HERMIONE: (4) iii AD ib. IV (1) 716, 2-3
(Κέλ[αδ]ος: f. Χαρίξενος)
ELIS: (5) 69-73 AD *IvOl* 84, 21 (?s. Νικ—)
S. ITALY: (6) imp. *CIL* X 8059. 278 (seal) (Lat.
A. Non. Celad(us))
S. ITALY (APULIA):
—LARINUM: (7) s. i BC ib. IX 755; cf. *Forma
Italiae* 36 p. 62 no. 2 (Lat. Q. Itius Celadus)
—VENUSIA: (8) i AD *Rend. Linc.* 29 (1974) p.
616 no. 15 (Lat. Celad[us])
S. ITALY (CAMPANIA):
—DIKAIARCHIA-PUTEOLI: (9) 52 AD Bove, *Do-
cumenti processuali* p. 106 T.P. 34 (Lat. C.
Blossius Celadus); (10) 55 AD ib. p. 87 T.P.
25 (Lat. D. Marcius Celadus); (11) 61 AD
*Puteoli* 9-10 (1985-6) p. 31 no. 5 (Lat. Sex.
Afranius Celadus)
—DIKAIARCHIA-PUTEOLI*: (12) imp. *CIL* X
2726 (Lat. A. Memmius Celadus: freed.)
—HERCULANEUM*: (13) i BC-i AD ib. 1403 f I,
14 (Lat. L. Numisius Celadus: freed.)
S. ITALY (LUCANIA):
—POSEIDONIA-PAESTUM*: (14) 245 AD Mello-
Voza 102 (Lat. L. Digitius Celadus: freed.)
—VOLCEI: (15) imp. *Suppl. It.* 3 p. 83 no. 14
(Lat. [Ce]ladus); (16) ~ *IItal* III (1) 106 +
Solin, *Lukan. Inschr.* p. 35 (Lat. M. Atulius
Celadus)

**Κελέας**
LAKONIA:
—SPARTA: (1) s. vi BC Hdt. v 46. 1 (Poralla²
415) (-ης)

**Κέλερ**
S. ITALY (CAMPANIA):
—DIKAIARCHIA-PUTEOLI: (1) imp. *IG* XIV 859,
10 (Audollent, *Defix. Tab.* 208)

**Κελεστῖνα**
S. ITALY (CAMPANIA):
—NEAPOLIS: (1) iii-iv AD *INap* 234 (-στεῖ-); (2)
~ ib. 235 (-στεῖ-)

**Κέλσος**
ARGOLIS:
—EPIDAUROS: (1) ii AD *IG* IV (1)² 387
SICILY:
—KAMARINA: (2) ii/i BC *SEG* XXXI 837, 1

**Κέλτα**
SICILY?: (1) i BC-i AD *IGLMP* 138 (Θεοδότα
Κ.—ethn.?)

**Κέλων**
ACHAIA:
—HELIKE: (1) f. v BC *SEG* XXXVI 718 (f. Φιλό-
ξενος)

**Κενδίων**
S. ITALY (CAMPANIA):
—KYME: (1) ii-iii AD *IG* XIV 868 (*GVI* 367)

**Κέντος**
SICILY:
—AKRAGAS (NR.)?: (1) ?iv BC Manganaro,
*QUCC* forthcoming no. 39 B, 7 (Κέντ[ος])
—CASTEL DI IUDICA (MOD.): (2) ?iii BC Man-
ganaro, *PdelP* forthcoming no. 6, 3 (Κέν[τ]ος:
f. Μόθων)
—SYRACUSE?:
——(Κατηλ.): (3) hell. *Mem. Linc.* 8 (1938)
p. 127 no. 35. 3 (bullet); cf. *L'Incidenza
dell'Antico* pp. 420 ff. (s. Στράτων)

## Κέος

ARKADIA?: (1) f. v BC *Musée de Mariemont* p. 87 no. G.57

## Κέπιον

SICILY:
—LIPARA: (1) iv/v AD Bernabò Brea, *Isole Eolie* p. 97 with fig. 55

## Κέραμβος

S. ITALY (LUCANIA):
—LEUKANOI: (1) iv BC Iamb., *VP* 267 (*FVS* 1 p. 447)

## Κέραμος

LAKONIA:
—SPARTA: (1) iv/iii BC *SEG* XI 668 (vase); *BSA* 30 (1928-30) p. 245 fig. 2, 17 (Poralla² 415b) (Κέραμο[s])

## Κέρας

ARGOLIS:
—ARGOS: (1) 300 BC Moretti, *Olymp.* 502; *RE* (5)

## Κέραυνος

S. ITALY (BRUTTIUM):
—RHEGION: (1) hell. *NScav* 1892, p. 488 (vase)
S. ITALY (CAMPANIA):
—STABIAE: (2) m. i AD *CIL* X 1081 (*PBSR* 40 (1972) p. 130 no. 10) (Lat. M. Virtius Ceraunus)

## Κέρδας

S. ITALY (BRUTTIUM):
—RHEGION: (1) vi BC *Suda* I 80 (?f. Ἴβυκος)

## Κέρδιππος

S. ITALY (CALABRIA):
—HYRIA: (1) imp. *CIL* IX 218 (Lat. Cerdippus)

## Κέρδος

S. ITALY (CALABRIA):
—BRENTESION-BRUNDISIUM*: (1) i BC Desy, *Timbres amphoriques* 510 (amph.) (slave/potter?)

## Κερδοφόρος

S. ITALY (CAMPANIA):
—DIKAIARCHIA-PUTEOLI*: (1) imp. *CIL* X 2741; cf. *Puteoli* 11 (1987) p. 54 (Lat. T. Mindius Cerdophorus: freed.)

## Κέρδων

ACHAIA: (1) 146 BC *IG* IV (1)² 28, 81 (s. Νικομήδης: synoikos)
AIGINA: (2) ii BC ib. II² 7960 (f. Μῦς)
AIGINA?: (3) hell.? *EAD* XXX p. 357 no. 23 (s. Ἀλέξανδρος); (4) i-ii AD ib. 357 no. 25 (s. Ῥόδων, f. Παρθένιν)
ARGOLIS:
—HERMIONE: (5) ?ii-i BC *IG* IV (1) 731 III, 4 (s. Δέξιος); (6) ii-i BC ib. 732 I, 6 (s. Ἑρμαῖος); (7) ~ ib. 732 II, 30 (s. Ἡρακλείδας); (8) ~ ib. 732 IV, 25 (s. Σώδαμος)
ARKADIA:
—TEGEA: (9) i AD ib. V (2) 46, 10 (Κέρδων)
DALMATIA:
—ISSA: (10) imp. *CIL* III 3081 (Lat. C. Fadius Cerdo)
—TRAGURION: (11) imp. ib. 2695 (Lat. C. Pomp. Cerdo)
ELIS:
—KYLLENE: (12) iv BC *SEG* XI 1170
—OLYMPIA*: (13) imp. *IvOl* 659
EPIROS:
—NIKOPOLIS: (14) c. 75-100 AD *FD* III (4) 114, 6 (Sarikakis 93) (Πο. Κορνήλιος [Κέ]ρδων)
ILLYRIA:
—APOLLONIA: (15) ?i BC *IApoll* 17; cf. *SGDI* 3222; *ZPE* 63 (1986) p. 154; Robert, *Hell.* 9 p. 70 (locn.) ([Κ]έρδων)

—EPIDAMNOS-DYRRHACHION: (16) iii-ii BC *IDyrrh* 262; (17) c. 250-50 BC Maier 141; 127; 222; 227; 242; 335; 410 + 420; Münsterberg p. 38; Nachtr. p. 15 (Ceka 248?; 249-56) (money.); (18) ii-i BC *IDyrrh* 381 (f. Σύρα); (19) hell.-imp. ib. 177 (f. Ἰλιάδη); (20) ~ ib. 228 (f. Ζώπυρος); (21) ~ ib. 354 (f. Πλάτωρ); (22) ~ ib. 372 (f. Σαπφώ)
KORINTHIA:
—KORINTH: (23) i AD *Hesp.* 42 (1973) p. 462 no. 196 (vase); (24) byz. *Corinth* VIII (1) 136, 4; cf. *TMByz* 9 (1985) p. 360 no. 10
LAKONIA:
—HYPERTELEATON*: (25) imp. *IG* V (1) 1053 ([Κ]έρδων)
—SPARTA: (26) s. i BC *SEG* XI 873 c (brick); (27) i BC/i AD *IG* V (1) 146, 7 (Bradford (2)); (28) 116 or 117 AD *IG* V (1) 380, 7 (Bradford (1))
S. ITALY (APULIA):
—LUCERIA*: (29) imp. *CIL* IX 885 (Lat. L. Saenius Cerdo: freed.)
—TEANUM APULUM: (30) i BC/i AD *Taras* 7 (1987) p. 44 no. 1, 1 (Lat. Cerdo: f. Optatus)
S. ITALY (CALABRIA):
—BRENTESION-BRUNDISIUM: (31) imp. *Epigraphica* 25 (1963) p. 76 no. 79 (Lat. Granius Cerdo)
—BRENTESION-BRUNDISIUM*: (32) imp. *CIL* IX 195 (Lat. N. Terraeus Cerdo: freed.); (33) ~ *NScav* 1889, p. 167 c (*Eph. Ep.* VIII 13) (Lat. Cerdo: freed.); (34) ~ *Necropoli via Cappuccini* p. 283 no. E37 (Lat. [C]er[d]o?: freed.)
S. ITALY (CAMPANIA):
—CAPREAE: (35) imp. *ZPE* 71 (1988) p. 197 no. 8, 1, 5 (Lat. L. Antonius Cerdo)
—DIKAIARCHIA-PUTEOLI: (36) imp. *CIL* X 2488 (Lat. Cerdo); (37) ~ ib. 2826, 2 (Lat. [L.] Patu]lcius Cerdo); (38) m. i AD Bove, *Documenti processuali* p. 115 T.P. 24 pag. 2, 5 (Lat. Q. Laber[ius] Cerdo maior); (39) ?ii AD *CIL* X 2516 (Lat. Q. Cissonius Cerdo)
—HERCULANEUM*: (40) i BC-i AD ib. 1403 g II, 14 (Lat. Q. Iunius Cerdo: freed.)
—KYME: (41) i BC ib. I² 3128 (X 8214; Audollent, *Defix. Tab.* 199 (lead)) (Lat. M. Allius Cerdo)
—POMPEII: (42) i BC-i AD *CIL* IV 2109; cf. p. 215 (Lat. Cerdo); (43) ~ ib. 2413 f (Lat. Cerdo); (44) ~ ib. 7079 (Lat. Cerdo); (45) ~ ib. 8283 (Lat. Cerdo); (46) ~ ib. 6867-9; 6971 (Lat. Cerdo)
—SALERNUM*: (47) ?i AD *IItal* I (1) 238 I, 8 (*CIL* X 557) (Lat. L. Appuleius Cerdo: freed.); (48) ~ *IItal* I (1) 238 III, 9 (*CIL* X 557) (Lat. L. Appuleius Cerdo: freed.)
—SURRENTUM*: (49) imp. ib. 695 (Lat. Cerdo: imp. freed.)
S. ITALY (LUCANIA):
—HYELE-VELIA: (50) imp. *PdelP* 21 (1966) p. 337 no. 19 (Lat. Cerdo)
SICILY:
—KAMARINA: (51) s. v BC Dubois, *IGDS* 121, 3 (Arena, *Iscr. Sic.* II 143; *SEG* XXXVIII 940; Cordano, 'Camarina VII' 37) (-δōν: s. Ἐλαχ—)

## Κερδωνίς

ARGOLIS:
—EPIDAUROS: (1) 207 AD *IG* IV (1)² 400, 5 (d. Διονύσιος)

## Κέρκα

KERKYRA: (1) i BC-i AD ib. IX (1) 916 (masc./fem. voc.?)

## Κερκίδας

ARKADIA: (1) c. 338 BC *RE* (1); (2) 308 BC *IG* V (2) 550, 3

—MEGALOPOLIS: (3) c. 290-220 BC *RE* (2); *Coll. Alex.* pp. 201 ff.; (4) ?145 BC *IG* V (2) 439, 40 (s. Ἀγησίστρατος)
—METHYDRION?: (5) ?iv BC *IEG* 2 p. 25 no. 49
—TEGEA: (6) iii BC *IG* V (2) 30, 8 (Κερκ[ίδας]: f. Ἡρακλείδας: name—*LGPN*)

## Κερκίνος

ILLYRIA:
—APOLLONIA: (1) iii BC *IApoll* 369 (s. Νικοσ—); (2) c. 250-50 BC Maier 53 (Ceka 35); Ceka 39 (coin) (pryt.); (3) ~ Maier 54 (coin) (Ceka 125) (pryt.)
—EPIDAMNOS-DYRRHACHION: (4) ii-i BC *IDyrrh* 542 (tile)
LEUKAS: (5) iv/iii BC *Alt-Ithaka* p. 329 a

## Κερκίων

EPIROS:
—KASSOPE: (1) iii BC *SEG* XXXII 616 (tile)

## Κέρκων

DALMATIA:
—ISSA:
——(Hylleis)?: (1) iii BC Brunšmid p. 9 fr. G, 12

## Κερρίων

SICILY:
—LICODIA EUBEA (MOD.): (1) v BC *NScav* 1905, p. 444 (tile)

## Κεφαλίδας

ARGOLIS:
—ARGOS:
——(Moklai): (1) iii BC *SEG* XXXI 306, 7 (Perlman A.25) (f. —δωρος)

## Κεφαλῖνος

EPIROS:
—BOUTHROTOS (PRASAIBOI): (1) a. 163 BC *IBouthrot* 41, 4 (*SEG* XXXVIII 500) (f. Σατυρῖνος) ?= (4); (2) ~ *IBouthrot* 41, 4 (*SEG* XXXVIII 500) (s. Σατυρῖνος) ?= (6); (3) ~ *IBouthrot* 46, 6 (f. Νέστωρ); (4) ~ ib. 47, 5 (f. Παμφίλα) ?= (1); (5) ~ ib. 152, 6 (s. Λέων)
——Kolonoi: (6) a. 163 BC ib. 119; 158, 3 ?= (2) (7); (7) ~ ib. 141, 11 (?s. Σατυρῖνος) ?= (6)
—PHOINIKE: (8) iii-ii BC *AE* 1914, p. 236 no. 8 (-λεῖ-: f. Ἄντανδρος)
—TORYDAIOI: (9) f. ii BC Cabanes, *L'Épire* p. 554 no. 33, 4 (*SEG* XXXVII 511) (f. Δόκιμος)

## Κεφαλίς

EPIROS:
—BOUTHROTOS (PRASAIBOI): (1) a. 163 BC *IBouthrot* 159

## Κεφαλίων

ACHAIA: (1) 146 BC *IG* IV (1)² 28, 111 (s. Πραξίας: synoikos)

## Κεφαλλήν

ELIS: (1) 252 BC *PP* 3982

## Κέφαλος

AITOLIA:
—KALYDON: (1) f. iv BC *IG* IX (1)² (1) 138, 12
AKARNANIA:
—STRATOS: (2) hell.? ib. IX (1)² (2) 414 a (s. Πράϋχος)
ARGOLIS:
—EPIDAUROS:
——Selegeis: (3) c. 365-335 BC ib. IV (1)² 103, 69 (Κέ[φα]λος)
DALMATIA:
—ISSA:
——(Pamphyloi): (4) iv/iii BC Brunšmid p. 7, 19 (f. Ὀνάσιμος)
EPIROS:
—BOUTHROTOS (PRASAIBOI): (5) a. 163 BC *IBouthrot* 18, 8 (*SEG* XXXVIII 475) (f. Λυσανίας); (6) ~ *IBouthrot* 29, 16 (*SEG* XXXVIII 487) (f. Φίλιππος); (7) ~ *IBouthrot* 29, 61 (*SEG* XXXVIII 487); (8) ~ *IBouthrot* 31, 70 (*SEG* XXXVIII 490) (s. Νίκανδρος); (9) ~

*IBouthrot* 42, 10-11 (*SEG* XXXVIII 501); **(10)** ~ *IBouthrot* 126, 5 (s. Εὐρύμμας, f. Φιλίς)
——Kammeoi: **(11)** a. 163 BC ib. 90, 8 (f. Ἀνάξανδρος)
——Opatai: **(12)** a. 163 BC ib. 104, 13; 160, [9]; 161, 5 (f. Τιμάνωρ)
——Sakaronoi: **(13)** a. 163 BC ib. 114, 9; 120, 8 (f. Ἀνδρίσκος)
—CHAONES: **(14)** f. ii BC ib. 6, 15-16 (*SEG* XXXVIII 468) (f. Ἀνάξανδρος)
—HOPLAINOI: **(15)** hell. Cabanes, *L'Épire* p. 584 no. 63, 9 (*SEG* XXVI 705)
—KASSOPE: **(16)** iii-ii BC ib. XVII 309 (f. Ἀνίκατος)
—KOLPAIOI: **(17)** f. ii BC Cabanes, *L'Épire* p. 580 no. 54, 7 (f. Δέξανδρος)
—PEIALES: **(18)** hell. *RE* Supplbd. 4 (3a); Cabanes, *L'Épire* p. 581 no. 56, 1
KORINTHIA:
—KORINTH: **(19)** m. iv BC D.S. xiii 35. 3; xvi 82. 7; Plu., *Tim.* 24
S. ITALY (CALABRIA):
—TARAS-TARENTUM: **(20)** hell.? *IG* XIV 2406. 48 (*RA* 1932 (1), p. 37 no. 10 (loomweight))
SICILY:
—KAMARINA: **(21)** f. v BC Cordano, *Tessere Pubbliche* 131 (s. Λεπτίνας)
—SYRACUSE: **(22)** vi BC Pl., *R.* 330 B; Plu., *Mor.* 835 C; cf. *APF* C 9 (f. Λυσανίας); **(23)** v BC *RE* (2); cf. *APF* C 9 (s. Λυσανίας, f. Λυσίας, Πολέμαρχος, Εὐθύδαμος)
—SYRACUSE?:
——(Λαβ.): **(24)** hell. Manganaro, *PdelP* forthcoming no. 4 V, 3 (f. Διοκλῆς)

**Κεφάλων**
S. ITALY (APULIA):
—HERDONIA: **(1)** ?ii/i BC *Taras* 9 (1989) p. 224 (Lat. Pilipus Cepalo Faber Alexsander)
S. ITALY (CALABRIA):
—BRENTESION-BRUNDISIUM*: **(2)** i BC Desy, *Timbres amphoriques* 511-14; 888-90; 894; 1046 (amph.) (slave/potter?)

**Κεχαρισμενός**
LAKONIA:
—SPARTA: **(1)** c. 90-100 AD *SEG* XI 558, 5 (Bradford (-)) (f. Διοκλῆς)

**Κήρινθος**
S. ITALY (BRUTTIUM):
—RHEGION: **(1)** ii AD *Suppl. It.* 5 p. 67 no. 21 (Lat. Cerinthus)
S. ITALY (CAMPANIA):
—CUBULTERIA*: **(2)** i BC/i AD *Iscr. Trebula Caiatia Cubulteria* 99 (*CIL* X 533*) (Lat. L. Aulius Cerintus: freed.)
—DIKAIARCHIA-PUTEOLI: **(3)** imp. ib. 1920 (Lat. Sexstius Cerinthus)
—POMPEII: **(4)** i BC-i AD ib. IV 4371 (Lat. Cerinth[u]s); **(5)** 54 AD ib. 3340. 7, 19; 18, 5 (Castrèn 297. 3) (Lat. P. Paccius Cerinthus)

**Κήτων**
S. ITALY (BRUTTIUM):
—LOKROI EPIZEPHYRIOI: **(1)** 448 BC Moretti, *Olymp.* 297

**Κηφισόδοτος**
ARGOLIS:
—LERNA: **(1)** iv/iii BC *IG* IV (1) 667

**Κηφισόδωρος**
ACHAIA: **(1)** hell. ib. II² 8403 (IV (1) 125) (s. Πολύαρχος)
KORINTHIA:
—KORINTH: **(2)** iv BC *Corinth* VIII (3) 24 ([Κ]ηφισόδω[ρος]); **(3)** m. iii BC ib. 33 f, 7 ([Κη]φισόδωρος: I f. Κηφισόδωρος II); **(4)** ~ ib. l. 7 (II s. Κηφισόδωρος I)


**Κιθαιρών**
LAKONIA:
—SPARTA: **(1)** s. i BC *IG* V (1) 133, 6 (Bradford (-)) (s. Ἀνδρόνικος)

**Κίθιος**
ARGOLIS:
—MYKENAI: **(1)** ?c. 500-480 BC *IG* IV (1) 492, 7; *LSAG²* p. 174 no. 2 (date)

**Κικκώ**
ILLYRIA:
—EPIDAMNOS-DYRRHACHION: **(1)** iv BC *IDyrrh* 8

**Κικνίας**
ILLYRIA:
—BYLLIONES: **(1)** m. iii BC *SEG* XXXV 695 (XXXVIII 567)

**Κῖκος**
ARGOLIS:
—ARGOS: **(1)** v BC ib. XI 339, 6 (s. Ἀρίσταρχος); **(2)** m. v BC Unp. (Ch. Kritzas)

**Κίκων**
SICILY:
—SELINOUS?: **(1)** v BC *SEG* XXXIX 1021 I, 4 + *BE* 1990, no. 863 (-ϙõν)

**Κιλικᾶς**
LEUKAS: **(1)** hell. *Ep. Chron.* 31 (1994) p. 49 no. 3 (*AD* 45 (1990) Chron. p. 254 no. 3)

**Κίλιξ**
S. ITALY (CALABRIA):
—LUPIAE: **(1)** i BC-i AD? Praschniker–Schober p. 2 no. 3 (Lat. [C.] Marcius Cilix)
S. ITALY (CAMPANIA):
—HERCULANEUM*: **(2)** i BC-i AD *CIL* IV 10681 (Lat. Cilix: slave?)
—POMPEII: **(3)** ?f. i AD ib. X 857 a (Castrèn 204. 10) (Lat. N. Istacidius Cilix)

**Κίλισσα**
S. ITALY (CAMPANIA):
—POMPEII: **(1)** i BC-i AD *CIL* IV 8953 (Lat. Cilissa)

**Κιλλανός**
DALMATIA:
—RIZON: **(1)** imp. ib. III 1723 (Lat. Hordionius Cillanus, Cyranus—ed.)

**Κίλλος**
ARKADIA:
—HELISSON: **(1)** c. 221 BC *IG* IV (1)² 42, 4 + Peek, *IAEpid* 8 (Κίλ[λ]ος)

**Κίλλων**
ARKADIA:
—TEGEA:
——(Krariotai): **(1)** iii BC *IG* V (2) 40, 26 (f. Μελαγκόμας)

**Κίμος**
SICILY:
—LIPARA: **(1)** ?iv BC *BTCGI* 9 p. 99

**Κίμων**
ARGOLIS:
—KLEONAI: **(1)** ?vi/v BC *RE* (10); Page, *FGE* 815; 817 (painter)
ELIS: **(2)** ?f. iii BC *HE* 1225 (s. Ἱππαῖος)
SICILY:
—SYRACUSE?: **(3)** v/iv BC *RE* (12); *Samml. Ludwig* 457; 463-5; 473 (coin) (coin engraver)


**Κινάδων**
LAKONIA:
—SPARTA: **(1)** c. 425-399 BC *RE* (-) (Poralla² 416)

**Κίναιδος**
S. ITALY (CAMPANIA):
—SALERNUM: **(1)** imp. *IItal* I (1) 221 (*CIL* X 637) (Lat. Cinadus)

**Κιναίθων**
LAKONIA: **(1)** arch. *RE* (-); *PEG* p. 115 (Poralla² 417)

**Κίναρος**
S. ITALY (BRUTTIUM):
—RHEGION: **(1)** iii AD *Suppl. It.* 5 p. 66 no. 18 (Lat. Cinarus)

**Κινέας**
LAKONIA:
—SPARTA: **(1)** hell.? *IG* V (1) 808 (Bradford (-)) (Κι[ν]έας)

**Κινναμίς**
S. ITALY (CAMPANIA):
—DIKAIARCHIA-PUTEOLI: **(1)** 62 AD *CIL* X 1549 (Lat. Vellia Cinnamis)

**Κίνναμος**
S. ITALY (CAMPANIA):
—DIKAIARCHIA-PUTEOLI: **(1)** imp. ib. 2380 (Lat. C. Egnatius Cinnamus: f. Ἄμωμος, Νάρδος); **(2)** 43-52 AD *Puteoli* 6 (1982) pp. 13-21; pp. 22-7 nos. 1-2; p. 34 no. 1; 7-8 (1983-4) p. 39 no. 1; p. 45 no. 6; p. 47 no. 8; p. 56 no. 13; p. 57 no. 14; p. 60 no. 16; p. 61 no. 17; p. 66 no. 20; 9-10 (1985-6) p. 18 no. 2; p. 28 no. 4; 12-13 (1988-9) pp. 4-24 no. 1; p. 38 (Lat. C. Sulpicius Cinnamus); **(3)** 45 AD Camodeca, *L'Archivio Puteolano* 1 p. 189 (Lat. C. Av[i]lius Cinnamus)
—HERCULANEUM*: **(4)** i BC-i AD *CIL* X 1403 g III, 3 (Lat. –ius Cinnamus: freed.); **(5)** c. 50-75 AD ib. 1403 a I, 6 (Lat. L. Caninius C(i)nnamus: freed.)
—POMPEII: **(6)** i BC-i AD ib. IV 6829; 6834 (Lat. Cinnamus); **(7)** ~ ib. 8532 (Lat. Cinn[amus])
S. ITALY (LUCANIA):
—VOLCEI: **(8)** imp. *IItal* III (1) 28 (*CIL* X 8113) (Lat. C. Allius Cinnamus); **(9)** ~ *IItal* III (1) 43 (Lat. [Cin]namus)

**Κίντος**
DALMATIA:
—ISSA: **(1)** hell. Robert, *EEP* p. 209 no. 7 (s. Δροσσος)

**Κινύρα**
S. ITALY (CALABRIA):
—BRENTESION-BRUNDISIUM: **(1)** ?i AD *Necropoli via Cappuccini* p. 275 no. E22 (Lat. Cinura)

**Κινύρας**
KORINTHIA:
—KORINTH: **(1)** ii-iii AD *SEG* XI 141 b, 2
S. ITALY (APULIA):
—TEANUM APULUM*: **(2)** i AD *Teanum Apulum* p. 56 no. 5 (Lat. Cn. Aemilius Cinyra: freed.?)

**Κίνυψ**
S. ITALY (CALABRIA):
—LUPIAE: **(1)** imp. *CIL* IX 17 (Susini, *Fonti Salento* p. 138 no. 87) (Lat. T. Memmius Cinyps Tiberinus)

**Κῖπος**
LAKONIA:
—SPARTA: **(1)** c. 146-32 BC *Münzpr. der Laked.* p. 120 Group 8 series 10 (coin) (Κῖπ[ος]?)
SICILY:
—ENTELLA: **(2)** iv/iii BC *SEG* XXX 1120, 1 (Dubois, *IGDS* 207) (s. Σώϊος)

—HALAISA: (3) ?f. i BC *SEG* XXXVII 761; cf. *Chiron* 22 (1992) p. 390 (f. *M. Aἰμίλιος Ῥο—*)
—KATANE: (4) c. 340-338 BC *IG* IV (1)² 95, 71-2 + *Chiron* 22 (1992) p. 390 n. 38 (Perlman E.2 (date)); Perlman p. 46 (s. *Μᾶρκος*)

**Κίρων**
ILLYRIA:
—APOLLONIA: (1) ?ii BC *IApoll* 16; cf. *SEG* XXXVI 558 (f. *Μυρτώ*)

**Κισκιβᾶς**
SICILY:
—LIPARA: (1) inc. *Chiron* 22 (1992) p. 386; (2) iv-iii BC *SEG* XLII 856

**Κίσσα**
S. ITALY (CAMPANIA):
—POMPEII: (1) i BC-i AD *NScav* 1946, p. 88 no. 26 b (Lat. Cissa)

**Κισσῆς**
S. ITALY (BRUTTIUM):
—LOKROI EPIZEPHYRIOI:
——(*Mva.*): (1) 280 BC De Franciscis 35, 2 (*Κισσῆ[s]*)

**Κισσίδας**
SICILY:
—SYRACUSE: (1) 373-368 BC X., *HG* vii 1. 28; D.S. xv 47. 7 (*Κισσίδης*—D.S.)

**Κισσός**
S. ITALY (CAMPANIA):
—POMPEII: (1) i BC-i AD *CIL* IV 3178 (Lat. Cissus); (2) ~ ib. 4146 (Lat. Cissus); (3) ~ ib. 8334 (Lat. Cissus); (4) ~ ib. 2388-9 (Lat. Cissus)
SICILY: (5) ii-i BC *Kokalos* 32 (1986) p. 229 no. 46 (tiles)
—AKRAI: (6) imp. *Akrai* p. 175 no. 63 (Lat. Al. Cissus)
SICILY?: (7) ii-i BC *IGLMP* 33 (s. *Ἰκάδιος*)

**Κισσώ**
S. ITALY (CALABRIA):
—TARAS-TARENTUM: (1) iv-iii BC Wuilleumier, *Tarente* p. 413 (terracotta) ?= (2)
S. ITALY (LUCANIA):
—HERAKLEIA: (2) iv-iii BC Unp. (A.W.J.) ?= (1)

**Κιτιάς**
S. ITALY (CAMPANIA):
—DIKAIARCHIA-PUTEOLI: (1) imp. *CIL* X 3098, 2 (Lat. Veturia Citias: I d. *Ἀνίκητος*); (2) ~ ib. l. 3 (Lat. Veturia Citias: II d. *Ἀνίκητος*)

**Κίτος**
ARGOLIS:
—EPIDAUROS: (1) i BC *IG* IV (1)² 64, 4 + Peek, *IAEpid* 19 (name) (s. *Εὔαρχος*)
—HERMIONE: (2) iii BC *IG* IV (1) 729 II, 14 (s. *Ἀσπάσιος*)

**Κίων**
LAKONIA:
—SPARTA: (1) iii BC *SEG* XL 348 B, 3

**Κλάδη**
S. ITALY (CAMPANIA):
—DIKAIARCHIA-PUTEOLI: (1) imp. *AJA* 77 (1973) p. 156 no. 5 (Lat. Herennia Clade)

**Κλαδίσκη**
S. ITALY (LUCANIA):
—ATINA LUCANA: (1) imp. *IItal* III (1) 179 (Lat. Allidia Cladisce: m. *Σόφων*, Allidius Epulianus, *Καλύβη*)

**Κλάδος**
S. ITALY (APULIA):
—CANUSIUM: (1) ii/iii AD *Epig. Rom. di Canosa* 65 (Lat. P. Fabricius Cladus: freed.?)

S. ITALY (CAMPANIA):
—DIKAIARCHIA-PUTEOLI*: (2) imp. *CIL* X 2255 (Lat. Cladus: slave?)
—POMPEII: (3) i BC-i AD ib. IV 3093 a (Lat. Cladus)
—SALERNUM: (4) imp. *IItal* I (1) 135 (*CIL* X 635) (Lat. A. Sergius Cladus); (5) f. i AD *IItal* I (1) 19, 11 (Lat. Cn. Maius Cladus)
—SARNUM*: (6) imp. *CIL* X 8363 (Lat. Cladus: freed.)
SICILY:
—AKRAI: (7) 35 AD *SEG* XLII 833, 6 (*Λ. Βηβήϊος Κ.*)

**Κλάρα**
KORINTHIA:
—KORINTH: (1) byz. *Corinth* VIII (3) 548, 5 (*Κλᾶ[ρ]α*)

**Κλᾶρος**
ARGOLIS:
—KLEONAI: (1) imp. *IG* IV (1) 490, 11

**Κλάσις**
ARGOLIS:
—ARGOS: (1) 327-324 BC *CID* II 97, 28; 102 II B, 30 (f. *Μικίων*)

**Κλαυδιανός**
ARGOLIS:
—EPIDAUROS: (1) imp. *IG* IV (1)² 453
—TROIZEN: (2) f. ii AD ib. IV (1) 758, 17 ([*Κλ*]*αυδιανός*)
LAKONIA:
—SPARTA: (3) ii AD ib. V (1) 176, 3 (Bradford (-)) (s. *Μακεδών*)

**Κλαύδιος**
ARGOLIS:
—EPIDAUROS: (1) 152 AD *IG* IV (1)² 389, 5
EPIROS:
—AMBRAKIA: (2) imp. *BCH* 17 (1893) p. 632 no. 1
—NIKOPOLIS: (3) i-ii AD *SEG* XIV 410, 5 (*Κλαύ[διος]*)
ILLYRIA:
—APOLLONIA*: (4) imp. *IApoll* 277 (threptos)
MESSENIA:
—MESSENE: (5) ii-iii AD *SEG* XLI 366 G (*Κλαύδ[ιος]*)

**Κλέα**
ARGOLIS:
—EPIDAUROS: (1) ii-iii AD *IG* IV (1)² 711 + *Horos* 6 (1988) pp. 65-7
ILLYRIA:
—APOLLONIA: (2) hell.-imp. *IApoll* 103 (d. *Πολυμήδης*)
—EPIDAMNOS-DYRRHACHION: (3) hell.-imp. *IDyrrh* 263 (d. *Βάντιος*); (4) ~ ib. 264 (d. *Ἡρακλείδας*); (5) ~ ib. 265 (d. *Κλειτόριος*)

**Κλεαγένης**
KORINTHIA:
—KORINTH: (1) 166 BC *IG* II² 2316, 12, 14 (s. *Λυκῖνος*)

**Κλεαγόρα**
ARGOLIS:
—TROIZEN: (1) hell.-imp. ib. IV (1) 815

**Κλεαγόρας**
AKARNANIA:
—THYRREION: (1) ii BC ib. IX (1)² (2) 325 (nom./gen.?)
ARGOLIS:
—ARGOS: (2) ii BC Siebert, *Ateliers* pp. 41; 171 (date) (potter)
—PHLEIOUS: (3) v/iv BC X., *An.* vii 8. 1 (f. *Εὐκλείδας*: painter)
ARKADIA:
—MEGALOPOLIS: (4) ?145 BC *IG* V (2) 439, 15

KEPHALLENIA:
—SAME: (5) iv/iii BC Fraser–Rönne, *BWGT* p. 117 no. 2. 2
KORINTHIA:
—SIKYON?: (6) c. 325-300 BC *IG* XI (4) 511 (Stephanis 1411) (*Κ[λεα]γόρας*: s. *Ἐπίνομος*)

**Κλεάδας**
ARGOLIS:
—ARGOS: (1) ?ii/iii AD *AP* ix 688
LAKONIA:
—SPARTA: (2) viii BC Polyaen. viii 34 (Poralla² 418) (f. *Χιλωνίς*)

**Κλεαιθίδας**
MESSENIA:
—THOURIA: (1) f. ii BC *SEG* XI 972, 113 (s. *Φιλόδαμος*)

**Κλεαινέτα**
ARGOLIS:
—ARGOS: (1) ii/i BC *IG* IV (1) 598, 2 (*Κλαινέτα*—lap., *Κ.*—*IG* index: d. *Ἱερώνυμος*)
ARKADIA:
—TEGEA: (2) hell.? ib. V (2) 255 (d. *Βράχυλλος*)
LAKONIA:
—BOIAI: (3) ii AD ib. V (1) 957 b (*Ἰουλ. Κ.*: d. *Γ. Ἰούλ. Πανθάλης*, m. *Ἰουλ. Φιλοκράτις*)

**Κλεαίνετος**
ARGOLIS:
—ARGOS: (1) s. iv BC *CEG* II 814 (s. *Ἐπικράτης*); (2) f. i BC Unp. (Ch. Kritzas) (s. *Ἀριστοκράτης*)
—EPIDAUROS: (3) c. 370-360 BC Peek, *IAEpid* 52 B, 28-30, 33-4, 36-7; *BSA* 61 (1966) p. 273 no. 4 III, 7; (4) iii BC Peek, *IAEpid* 43, 35
ARKADIA:
—MANTINEIA-ANTIGONEIA: (5) c. 300-221 BC *IG* V (2) 323. 27-8 (tesserae) (*Κλεα(ί)νετος*—28: f. *Ἐξαίνετος*)
—TEGEA: (6) m. iv BC ib. 6, 84; (7) c. 240-229 BC ib. 11, 15
——(Hippothoitai): (8) f. iii BC ib. 36, 72 (f. *Εὔδοξος*)
DALMATIA:
—ISSA:
——(Hylleis): (9) iv/iii BC Brunšmid p. 8, 49 ([*Κ*]*λεαίνετος*: s. *Ἡρακλείδας*)
MESSENIA:
—MESSENE: (10) iii BC *SEG* XXIII 209, 5
S. ITALY (BRUTTIUM):
—RHEGION (NR.): (11) f. iv BC Dubois, *IGDGG* I 42 (s. *Νικόμαχος*)

**Κλεαῖος**
ARKADIA:
—PHENEOS: (1) iii BC *IG* IV (1)² 96, 70 (Perlman E.3); Perlman p. 63 f. (date) (*Κλεα[ῖ]ος*: s. *Ἀριστομήδης*)

**Κλεαίχμα**
LAKONIA:
—SPARTA: (1) m. vi BC Iamb., *VP* 267 (*FVS* 1 p. 448; Poralla² 419)

**Κλεαιχμίδας**
ARGOLIS:
—EPIDAUROS: (1) iii BC *Mnem.* NS 43 (1915) pp. 375-6 F, 9 (Perlman A.7) (f. *Κλέανδρος*); (2) ii BC *IG* IV (1)² 99, 14 (s. *Ἀριστοκλῆς*); (3) i BC ib. 170; 251 (s. *Δαμοφάνης*); (4) ~ ib. 220; 224 (s. *Κλέανδρος*, f. *Χαρικώ*)

**Κλέαιχμος**
AITOLIA:
—KALYDON: (1) f. iv BC ib. IX (1)² (1) 138, 5

**Κλεᾶναξ**
ARGOLIS:
—ARGOS: (1) viii BC Ps.-Hdt., *Vit. Hom.* 1-2 (fict.)

**Κλεανδρίδας**

KORINTHIA:
—KORINTH: (1) c. 370 BC *IG* IV (1)² 102, 29 (Κλεανδρίδ[ας]); (2) ?274 BC *CID* II 120 A, 33 (f. Πάσαρχος)

LAKONIA:
—SPARTA: (3) m. v BC *RE* (1) (Poralla² 420) (and S. Italy (Bruttium) Sybaris-Thourioi-Copiae: f. Γύλιππος); (4) 371 BC D.S. xv 54. 1 (Poralla² 421) (Λεανδρίας—mss., K.— Müller, Λεανδρίδας—Dindorf: ?s. Γύλιππος); (5) c. 240-200 BC Peek, *IAEpid* 330, 18 (Perlman E.4) (Κλε[ανδ]ρίδας: f. Καλλιτελίδας)

MESSENIA:
—THOURIA: (6) ii-i BC *IG* v (1) 1385, 4 (s. Εὔδαμος)

S. ITALY (BRUTTIUM):
—SYBARIS-THOURIOI-COPIAE: (7) f. i AD *NScav* 1970, Suppl. 3 p. 60 nos. 197-8; p. 496 nos. 697; 702; 704 (tiles); cf. *Atti Conv. Taranto* 32 (1992) pp. 413 ff. (date) (Lat. Cleandridas)

**Κλέανδρος**

AIGINA: (1) s. vii BC Plu., *Mor.* 403 C; (2) 478 BC Pi., *I.* viii, 1, 66; cf. Klee p. 91 no. 51; p. 100 no. 44 (s. Τελέσαρχος)

AITOLIA: (3) f. iii BC *Das Heroon von Kalydon* p. 293, 12 (s. Ἀνδρόβουλος); (4) ?240-228 BC *FD* III (3) 218 A, 3; (5) c. 152 BC *IG* IX (1)² (3) 627, 1 (Κλεανς—apogr., Κλεάν(ορο)ς (gen.)—Fick, Κλεάνδ(ρου) (gen.)—*IG*)

AKARNANIA:
—ANAKTORION: (6) m. ii BC *Syll*³ 669, 4 (s. Λυκίσκος)

ARGOLIS:
—ARGOS: (7) 105 BC *JÖAI* 14 (1911) Beibl. p. 146 no. 4, 26 (f. Εὐρυδίκα)
—EPIDAUROS: (8) iii BC *Mnem.* NS 43 (1915) p. 375 F, 1, 8 (Perlman A.7) (s. Κλεαιχμίδας); (9) ii/i BC *IG* IV (1)² 224 (f. Κλεαιχμίδας)
—MYKENAI?: (10) ?c. 525 BC *SEG* XXVI 419, 2 (Lazzarini 721); *LSAG*² p. 174 no. 7 (date) (or Argolis Argos: [Κλ]έανδρος)
—PHLEIOUS: (11) c. 220-200 BC *SEG* XI 414, 10 (Perlman E.5) (s. Δαμοσθένης)

ARKADIA:
—MANTINEIA-ANTIGONEIA: (12) m. iii BC *RE* Supplbd. 4 (8) (and Arkadia Megalopolis)
—MEGALOPOLIS: (13) iv BC *IG* v (2) 470 (bullet)
—PHIGALEIA: (14) c. 479-468 BC Hdt. vi 83
—TEGEA: (15) s. iv BC *SEG* XXXVI 383, 5 (s. Ἀρύβας); (16) ?iii-ii BC *IG* v (2) 229; (17) f. ii BC ib. 44, 7 (s. Νικίας); (18) ?ii/i BC ib. 119 (f. Νικίας); (19) ii AD ib. 55, 24 (s. Καρπίων)

EPIROS:
—AMBRAKIA: (20) 238-168 BC *Coll. Hunter* 2 p. 10 no. 6; Unp. (Oxford, AM) 19. 10. 1911 (coins)
—DODONA: (21) iii BC Antoniou, *Dodone* Aa, 6; (22) ~ ib. Ba, 15; (23) ~ ib. l. 32 (Κλέανδρος); (24) ~ ib. l. 35

KERKYRA: (25) i AD *IG* IX (1) 712

KORINTHIA:
—KORINTH: (26) 66-67 AD Amandry pp. 215-21; *RPC* I pp. 255-6 nos. 1203-6 (coins); *Corinth* VIII (3) 81, 8 (Lat. P. Mem. Cleander); (27) ii-iii AD *Kenchreai* v App. I (lamp)
—SIKYON: (28) 367-364 BC X., *HG* vii 1. 45; *Syll*³ 171 (Skalet 179); (29) c. 146-32 BC *BMC Pelop.* p. 52 nos. 195-6 (coins) ?= (30); (30) i BC *NC* 1984, p. 19 Group 12 no. 5 (coin) ?= (29)

LAKONIA:
—HYPERTELEATON*: (31) imp. *IG* v (1) 1045 ([Κλ]έανδρος?)
—SPARTA: (32) 406-400 BC *RE* (2) (Poralla² 422); (33) i BC/i AD *IG* v (1) 49, 3; 95, 18; 212, 17 (Bradford (1)) (s. Ἀλκαμένης); (34) c. 70-100 AD *IG* v (1) 281, 6 (*Artemis Orthia* pp.

314-15 no. 34; Bradford (6)) (f. Ἄγις); (35) c. 75-100 AD *IG* v (1) 31, 4; *SEG* XI 512, 1; 539, 1; 609, 1 (Bradford (5)) (Γ. Ἰούλ. Κ.); (36) c. 125-150 AD *IG* v (1) 73, 4; 113, 4; *SEG* XI 575, 7 (Bradford (2)) (s. Εὔπορος); (37) ~ *IG* v (1) 73, 6; 87, 6; 446, 7 (Bradford (7)) (f. Φιλοκράτης); (38) m. ii AD *SEG* XI 643, 3 (Bradford (4)) (s. Τιμ—); (39) ii/iii AD *IG* v (1) 307, 1 (*Artemis Orthia* pp. 328-9 no. 60); *IG* v (1) 313, 4 (*Artemis Orthia* pp. 334-5 no. 70); *IG* v (1) 314, 11 (*Artemis Orthia* p. 335 no. 71); *IG* v (1) 601, 8, 14; *BSA* 79 (1984) p. 284 no. 13 (date, stemma) (Bradford (3)) (Αὐρ. Κ. ὁ καὶ Μήνιος, Κλέανδρορ—307: s. Καλλίστρατος, f. Μ. Αὐρ. Εὔπορος); (40) c. 212-235 AD *IG* v (1) 305, 4 (*Artemis Orthia* pp. 333-4 no. 69); *BSA* 79 (1984) p. 283 no. 5 (date) (Bradford s.v. Ζεύξιππος (3)) (Μ. Αὐρ. Ζεύξιππορ ὁ καὶ Κλέανδρορ: s. Φιλόμουσος)

MESSENIA:
—MESSENE: (41) hell.-imp. *IG* v (1) 1486
—THOURIA: (42) f. ii BC *SEG* XI 972, 95 (I f. Κλέανδρος II); (43) ~ ib. l. 95 (II s. Κλέανδρος I)

S. ITALY (BRUTTIUM):
—LOKROI EPIZEPHYRIOI:
——(Αστ.): (44) iv/iii BC De Franciscis 33, 5 (f. Ἀρχέλας)
—RHEGION: (45) c. 433 BC *IG* I³ 53, 2 (s. Ξεν—)

S. ITALY (CALABRIA):
—TARAS-TARENTUM?: (46) c. 315-280 BC *FD* III (1) 132 + *SEG* XXIII 306 (f. Ἀρχίμυθος)

SICILY:
—GELA-PHINTIAS: (47) s. vi BC Arist., *Pol.* 1316 a 37; Hdt. vii 154-5 (s. Πανταρης: tyrant); (48) vi/v BC ib. 155. 1 (s. Ἱπποκράτης)
—HALOUNTION: (49) iii/ii BC *Arch. Class.* 17 (1965) p. 202 no. a (s. Ἀρπ—)
—KAMARINA: (50) ?iv/iii BC *SEG* XXXIV 940, 2 (Dubois, *IGDS* 124; *PdelP* 44 (1989) p. 192 no. 3; Cordano, 'Camarina VII' 125) (f. Δείναρχος)
—LIPARA: (51) hell.? *Meligunis-Lipara* 5 p. 152; cf. 2 p. 167 and pl. F and pl. 37
—SYRACUSE: (52) hell.? *Schol. Il.* E 6, ver. B; cf. *Ar. Byz.* (Nauck) p. 16 n. 6

**Κλεάνθης**

KORINTHIA:
—KORINTH: (1) arch. *RE* (4) (painter)
—SIKYON: (2) 362-360 BC *SEG* XXVII 13, 4; 15, 5

S. ITALY (CALABRIA):
—TARAS-TARENTUM: (3) iv BC *RE* (3); Wehrli, *Schule Arist.* iii fr. 89

**Κλέανθος?**

S. ITALY (LUCANIA):
—POTENTIA: (1) imp. *CIL* x 8059. 283 (seal) (Lat. C. Numisius Cleantus)

**Κλεαντίδας**

LAKONIA:
—TEUTHRONE: (1) imp. *SEG* XXII 307

**Κλεανώ**

S. ITALY (CALABRIA):
—TARAS-TARENTUM: (1) c. 160 BC *ID* 1716, 7 (d. Ἡρακλείδας, Μυραλλίς (Syracuse))

SICILY:
—LIPARA: (2) ?i BC *Meligunis-Lipara* 5 p. 181 T. 2173; cf. *SEG* XLI 812

**Κλεάνωρ**

ARGOLIS:
—EPIDAUROS: (1) c. 370 BC *IG* IV (1)² 102, 5, 31
—PHLEIOUS?: (2) c. 220-200 BC *SEG* XI 414, 10 (Perlman E.5) (f. Φαῖδρος)

ARKADIA:
—ORCHOMENOS: (3) 401 BC *RE* Supplbd. 4 (-)

EPIROS:
—DODONA*: (4) v/iv BC *Ep. Chron.* 10 (1935) p. 255 no. 15

ILLYRIA:
—AMANTIA (NR.): (5) ii BC *SEG* XXXIX 553 (f. Ἀρίσταρχος)
—EPIDAMNOS-DYRRHACHION: (6) c. 250-50 BC Schlosser p. 63 no. 325; p. 64 no. 345 (coin) (pryt.) ?= (7); (7) ~ Maier 257-8; 410 + 420; Münsterberg p. 261; Nachtr. p. 15 (coin) (Ceka 25; 200; 225; 255; 392; 427; 453) (pryt.) ?= (6); (8) ii-i BC *IDyrrh* 543 (tiles); (9) hell.-imp. ib. 38

LAKONIA:
—(10) m. vi BC Iamb., *VP* 267 (*FVS* 1 p. 447; Poralla² 423); (11) c. 100-75 BC *IG* v (1) 1144, 33
—SPARTA: (12) hell. ib. 811 (Bradford (2)); (13) i BC/i AD *IG* v (1) 48, 16 (Bradford (4)) (f. Πασιτέλης); (14) c. 160 AD *IG* v (1) 71 III, 43; 86, 21 (Bradford (3)) (f. Εἰρανίων); (15) f. iii AD *IG* v (1) 563, 8; *SEG* XXXIV 308, 12; 314; *BSA* 79 (1984) pp. 275; 287 (Bradford (1)) (Μ. Αὐρ. Κ.: I s. Ῥοῦφος, f. Μ. Αὐρ. Κλεάνωρ II); (16) m. iii AD *SEG* XXXIV 308, 12; 314; *BSA* 79 (1984) pp. 275; 287 (date) (Μ. Αὐρ. Κ.: II s. Μ. Αὐρ. Κλεάνωρ I)

**Κλεάρατος**

S. ITALY (CALABRIA):
—TARAS-TARENTUM: (1) iv BC Iamb., *VP* 267 (*FVS* 1 p. 446)

**Κλεαρέτα**

AITOLIA: (1) 139-122 BC *FD* III (6) 83, 3, 12, 14 (m. Ἀλέξανδρος)

ARGOLIS:
—EPIDAUROS: (2) iv/iii BC Peek, *IAEpid* 142. 2

**Κλεαρέτας**

LAKONIA:
—OITYLOS: (1) iii/ii BC *IG* v (1) 1295, 7 (Bradford (2)) (Κλεαρέτας)

**Κλεάρετος**

ELIS: (1) hell.? Moretti, *Olymp.* 967

LAKONIA:
—AKRIAI: (2) ii/i BC *IG* v (1) 1189 (f. Ὀνάσανδρος); (3) ~ ib. (s. Ὀνάσανδρος)
—BOIAI: (4) ii AD ib. 958, 2; 959, 1 (Π. Μέμμιος Κ.: s. Χαίρων)
—SPARTA: (5) c. 220 AD *SEG* XXXIV 311, 1; *BSA* 79 (1984) pp. 267-9 (date); 284 no. 12 (ident.) (Bradford (1)) (Μ. Αὐρ. Κλεάρε[τος]: s. Τιμοκλῆς)

MESSENIA:
—THOURIA: (6) f. ii BC *SEG* XI 972, 110 (s. Θάλιος)

**Κλεάρης**

ARGOLIS:
—EPIDAUROS: (1) c. 365-335 BC *IG* IV (1)² 103, 152, 155, [174], 178

**Κλεαρίδας**

LAKONIA:
—SPARTA: (1) 423-421 BC *RE* (-) (Poralla² 424) (s. Κλεώνυμος)

**Κλέαρις**

KEPHALLENIA:
—KRANIOI: (1) ?v BC *IG* IX (1) 610 (fals.?); cf. *LSAG*² p. 231 n. 5 (f. Μνασίας)

**Κλεαρίστα**

ARGOLIS:
—EPIDAUROS: (1) iii BC Peek, *IAEpid* 142. 3 (d. Ἀρίσταρχος) ?= (2); (2) ~ *IG* IV (1)² 239 (d. Ἀρίσταρχος, m. Ὀξυμένης) ?= (1)

LAKONIA:
—KYTHERA: (3) ?c. 525-500 BC *LSAG*² p. 447 no. 21 c (bronze)

**Κλεαρίστη**
ARKADIA:
—ALIPHEIRA: (**1**) iii BC *EILakArk* 11, 5 (*GVI* 1505; *Gr. Gr.* 196) (m. Θέων)

**Κλεάριστος**
ARGOLIS:
—PHLEIOUS: (**1**) s. iii BC *IG* IV (1) 727 A, 4 (Perlman H.1) (f. —ασίλας)
SICILY:
—KAMARINA: (**2**) f. v BC Cordano, *Tessere Pubbliche* 105 (Κλεάριστ[ος]: s. Κάϊκος)

**Κλεάριτος**
ARKADIA: (**1**) 279 BC *IG* II² 3080, 5 (Stephanis 1417)

**Κλεαρχίς**
AITOLIA:
—KONOPE-ARSINOE?: (**1**) 213 BC *IG* IX (1)² (1) 96, 3 (or Aitolia Thestieis?: m. Φιλόξενος, Σκορπίων)
LEUKAS: (**2**) iv/iii BC *AD* 26 (1971) Chron. p. 353 no. 8

**Κλέαρχος**
AITOLIA: (**1**) c. 315-280 BC *FD* III (1) 145, 1 (s. Κριτόδαμος)
—THERMOS*: (**2**) s. iii BC *IG* IX (1)² (1) 60 VI, 20
AKARNANIA:
—TYRBEION/TORYBEIA: (**3**) c. 334 BC *CID* II 26, 19 ([Κ]λέαρχος)
ARKADIA:
—MANTINEIA-ANTIGONEIA: (**4**) c. 225 BC *SEG* XI 414, 24 (Perlman E.5)
—METHYDRION: (**5**) iv BC *FGrH* 115 F 344 (fict.?)
DALMATIA:
—ISSA:
——(Dymanes): (**6**) iv/iii BC Brunšmid p. 8, 35 (f. —λων); (**7**) ~ ib. p. 9, 62 (f. Θεόδωρος)
ELIS: (**8**) 217 BC Plb. v 94. 6
EPIROS: (**9**) c. 200 BC *IG* IX (1)² (1) 31, 129 (s. Ἀντάνωρ)
—AMBRAKIA: (**10**) 238-168 BC *BMC Thessaly* p. 96 no. 32 (coin)
—DODONA*: (**11**) ?iv BC *AEMÖ* 4 (1880) p. 64; (**12**) ?iv-iii BC Robert, *Coll. Froehner* 39 (s. Διομέδων); (**13**) iv-iii BC *SGDI* 1576 (Κλέαρχος)
—KHALIKI (MOD.): (**14**) hell.? Heuzey, *Excursion* p. 111
—THESPROTOI: (**15**) iv AD *RE* (7); *PLRE* I (1)
KERKYRA: (**16**) hell. *IG* IX (1) 707 (Κ[λ]έαρχος: s. Λέων); (**17**) iii/ii BC *Korkyra* 1 p. 165 no. 4
KORINTHIA:
—TENEA: (**18**) 191-146 BC BM coin 1920 5-15-114; 1920 5-15-123 (coins)
LAKONIA:
—LAS: (**19**) ?iii BC *IG* V (1) 1214
—SPARTA: (**20**) c. 450-401 BC *RE* (3) (Poralla² 425) (s. Ῥαμφίας); (**21**) c. 100 AD *SEG* XI 536, 3 (Bradford (1)) (s. Εὔδαμος); (**22**) c. 115-135 AD *IG* V (1) 114, 8; *SEG* XI 543, 3 (Bradford (3)) (f. Δράκων); (**23**) c. 175-200 AD *IG* V (1) 129, 1 (Bradford (2)) (II s. Κλέαρχος I); (**24**) ~ *IG* V (1) 129, [1] (Bradford (4)) (I f. Κλέαρχος II)
MESSENIA:
—KORONE: (**25**) 191-146 BC *ZfN* 9 (1882) p. 267 no. 2 (coin) (Κλέαρχ[ος])
—THOURIA: (**26**) f. ii BC *SEG* XI 972, 23 (f. Ἀριστόταξενος)
S. ITALY (BRUTTIUM):
—RHEGION: (**27**) vi BC *RE* (13); Overbeck 332 ff. (sculptor)
SICILY:
—SYRACUSE: (**28**) s. iv BC *IG* IV (1)² 95, 65 (Perlman E.2); Perlman pp. 46-9 (date)

**Κλεαρώ**
ARKADIA:
—TEGEA: (**1**) ii-iii AD *IG* V (2) 182 (*GVI* 1857)

**Κλέας**
ARGOLIS:
—TROIZEN: (**1**) s. iv BC *IG* IV (1) 766 (f. —νδρος)
ARKADIA:
—MANTINEIA-ANTIGONEIA: (**2**) c. 300-221 BC ib. v (2) 323. 91 (tessera) (s. Ϝισόδαμος)
—TEGEA:
——(Hippothoitai): (**3**) iii BC ib. 40, 42 ([Κ]λέας: s. Φίλων)
——(Krariotai): (**4**) s. iii BC ib. 36, 116 (s. Θρασέας)
EPIROS:
—BOUTHROTOS (PRASAIBOI): (**5**) a. 163 BC *IBouthrot* 151, 7
——Drymioi: (**6**) a. 163 BC ib. 14, 1 (*SEG* XXXVIII 471); *IBouthrot* 139, 1 ?= (7); (7) ~ ib. 21, 48 (*SEG* XXXVIII 478); *IBouthrot* 130, 4; 131, 6; 156, 4; 157, 3 (*BCH* 118 (1994) p. 127 nos. 12-13) (s. Μυρτίλος) ?= (6)
—DODONA: (**8**) iii BC Antoniou, *Dodone* Ab, 9
LAKONIA:
—SPARTA: (**9**) 378 BC X., *HG* v 4. 39 (Poralla² 426)
LEUKAS: (**10**) c. 325-315 BC *Hesp.* 57 (1988) p. 148 B, 11 (*SEG* XXXVI 331); cf. *Hesp.* 48 (1979) pp. 78 f. with pl. 22

**Κλεαφάνης**
ACHAIA:
—DYME*: (**1**) c. 219 BC *SGDI* 1612, 14 (*Tyche* 5 (1990) p. 124) (s. Τιμοφάνης)

**Κλεβέριος**
ILLYRIA:
—EPIDAMNOS-DYRRHACHION: (**1**) hell.-imp. *IDyrrh* 266 (s. Λοβαῖος)

**Κλεβέτα**
ILLYRIA:
—EPIDAMNOS-DYRRHACHION: (**1**) hell.-imp. ib. 267 (Κλεβ(ϝ)έτα); (**2**) ~ ib. 268 (Κλεβ(ϝ)έτα: d. Φιλόνικος)

**Κλέβετος**
ILLYRIA:
—EPIDAMNOS-DYRRHACHION: (**1**) hell.-imp. ib. 355 (Κλέβ(ϝ)ετος: f. Πλάτωρ)

**Κλέδωρος**
EPIROS:
—AMBRAKIA: (**1**) f. ii BC *AD* 39 (1984) Chron. p. 190 + pl. 77 γ

**Κλεέμπορος**
DALMATIA:
—ISSA: (**1**) hell. *SEG* XXXI 594 (f. Εὐάρης); (**2**) iii BC ib. 596 (s. Λυσίμαχος, f. Μνασίς); (**3**) s. iii BC App., *Ill.* 7; (**4**) ii BC *SEG* XXXI 602, 1, 5, 6, 9 (*VAHD* 84 (1991) p. 257 no. 7) (s. Φιλήσιος, f. Νικασώ, Φιλήσιος, Μνασιφῶν)
—TRAGURION: (**5**) 56 BC Sherk 24 A, 8 (Κλεέμ[πορ]ος: s. Τιμασίων)

**Κλέη**
ARGOLIS:
—ARGOS: (**1**) ?ii/iii AD *AP* ix 688

**Κλεήρατος**
ARGOLIS:
—ARGOS: (**1**) s. ii BC Unp. (Ch. Kritzas) (s. Δαμοφῶν)
LAKONIA:
—LAS: (**2**) ?iii BC *IG* V (1) 1214

**Κλεήσιππος**
LAKONIA:
—SPARTA: (**1**) arch. *PMGF* 1 174

**Κλεησισήρα**
LAKONIA:
—SPARTA: (**1**) s. vii BC ib. 1, 72; Masson, *OGS* 2 p. 512 (name) (Poralla² 427)

**Κλειγένης**
ILLYRIA:
—BALAIITAI: (**1**) ii BC *SEG* XXXVIII 521, 1; cf. *CRAI* 1991, pp. 197 ff.; *L'Illyrie mérid.* 2 p. 204 f. (f. Βίων)

**Κλείδαμος**
ARGOLIS:
—EPIDAUROS:
——Koleis: (**1**) c. 335-325 BC *IG* IV (1)² 108, 143 (Κλείδα[μος])
EPIROS:
—AMBRAKIA: (**2**) f. iii BC Unp. (Arta Mus., inscr.) (f. Πειθόι)
SICILY:
—SYRACUSE?:
——(Ὑπα.): (**3**) hell. Manganaro, *PdelP* forthcoming no. 4 IV, 7 (Κλε<α>ίδ(α)μος—ed.: f. Ζώπυρος)

**Κλείδης**
EPIROS:
—AMBRAKIA?: (**1**) her. *FGrH* 69 F 1

**Κλειδίκα**
ARGOLIS:
—HERMIONE: (**1**) i BC-i AD? *IG* IV (1) 730 I, 8 (Κ[λε]ιδίκα: m. Πατ—)

**Κλείδικος**
ACHAIA: (**1**) 146 BC ib. IV (1)² 28, 160 (Κλί-: s. Διονύσιος: synoikos)
ARGOLIS:
—EPIDAUROS: (**2**) c. 370 BC ib. 102, 30 ?= (5)
——(Hysminatai?): (**3**) c. 340-320 BC Peek, *NIEpid* 19 C, 11
——Erilais: (**4**) m. iii BC Peek, *IAEpid* 42, 28 (Perlman E.3); Perlman p. 63 f. (date)
——Upper Oiseia: (**5**) c. 365-320 BC *IG* IV (1)² 103, 144; 106 III, 41; *SEG* XXV 394 B, 12 ?= (2)
—EPIDAUROS*: (**6**) c. 370-365 BC Peek, *IAEpid* 52 A, 36
KERKYRA: (**7**) 208 BC *IMM* 44, 40 (s. Ἀλεξικλῆς)

**Κλείμαχος**
ARGOLIS:
—EPIDAUROS*: (**1**) c. 370-365 BC Peek, *IAEpid* 52 B, 62

**Κλειμένης**
ARGOLIS:
—ARGOS: (**1**) s. iv BC *IG* IV (1)² 122, 102
KORINTHIA:
—KORINTH: (**2**) ?274 BC *CID* II 120 A, 32 (s. Κλεινοφάνης)

**Κλείνα**
ARKADIA?: (**1**) iv/iii BC *HE* 680 (Κ.—*AP*, Κλεινώ?—Reiske: m. Φιλαινίς)
KERKYRA: (**2**) iii BC *SEG* XXV 612

**Κλειναγόρας**
ARGOLIS:
—HERMIONE: (**1**) ?ii-i BC *IG* IV (1) 731 I, 17, 18 (f. Ἰσίων, Φαενίκης); (**2**) i BC-i AD? ib. 730 I, 6 (Κλι-: f. Χ—λος); (**3**) ~ ib. 730 III, 3-5 (Κλι-: f. Δρωπύλος, Ἀγάθων, Εὐφροσύνα)
S. ITALY (CALABRIA):
—TARAS-TARENTUM: (**4**) iv BC Iamb., *VP* 267 (*FVS* 1 p. 446)

**Κλεινίας**
ARGOLIS:
—EPIDAUROS*: (**1**) c. 370 BC *IG* IV (1)² 102, 57, 82, 304
ARKADIA:
—KLEITOR: (**2**) i BC *SEG* XXXIII 291, 4; cf. Stephanis 128 (f. Ἄλεξις)

**Κλείνιππος**
ELIS: **(3)** 265 BC *IG* II² 686, 12 (f. Ἀργεῖος); **(4)** 20-16 BC *IvOl* 65, 7 (f. Θρασυμήδης)
KORINTHIA:
—SIKYON: **(5)** c. 300-264 BC *IG* IV (1) 788; Paus. ii 7. 5; 8. 2; 10. 7; Plu., *Arat.* 2; 8 (Skalet 180) (f. Ἄρατος)
S. ITALY (BRUTTIUM):
—KROTON: **(6)** v BC D.H. xx 7. 1
S. ITALY (CALABRIA):
—TARAS-TARENTUM: **(7)** f. iv BC *RE* (6); *FVS* 54

**Κλείνιππος**
SICILY:
—TAUROMENION: **(1)** c. 213-201 BC *IG* XIV 421 an. 28; 421 an. 40 (*SGDI* 5219) (f. Ἡράκλητος); **(2)** c. 159 BC *IG* XIV 421 an. 82 (*SGDI* 5219) (s. Ἡράκλητος)

**Κλεῖνις**
KORINTHIA:
—KORINTH: **(1)** c. 570-550 BC Amyx 48 (vase) (Lorber 78; Arena, *Iscr. Cor.* 38) (Κενις—vase, Κεῖνις—*IG* and Payne, Κ(λ)εῖνις—Bechtel and Arena, Κένις—Amyx: fict.?)

**Κλεινόμαχος**
ARKADIA:
—PHIGALEIA: **(1)** c. 230-200 BC *BCH* 45 (1921) p. 12 II, 82 (f. Κλείξενος)
ELIS: **(2)** ?iv-iii BC Moretti, *Olymp.* 968
KERKYRA: **(3)** iii BC *SEG* XXXIII 444 ([Κ]λεινόμαχος)
LAKONIA:
—SPARTA: **(4)** 421 BC X., *HG* ii 3. 10 (Poralla² 428)

**Κλεινοξένα**
ARGOLIS:
—EPIDAUROS: **(1)** iv/iii BC Peek, *IAEpid* 340, 1 (?d. Κύδιμος, Θεοδότα)

**Κλεινόξενος**
PELOPONNESE: **(1)** s. iii BC *SEG* XIII 278, 13

**Κλεῖνος**
LAKONIA:
—TAINARON-KAINEPOLIS: **(1)** ii-iii AD *IG* V (1) 1249, 1 (*GVI* 2028) (n. pr.?: ?s. Ζώιππος)

**Κλεινοφάνης**
KORINTHIA:
—KORINTH: **(1)** ?274 BC *CID* II 120 A, 32 (f. Κλειμένης)

**Κλεινώ**
ARGOLIS:
—PHLEIOUS: **(1)** 361 BC ib. 4 I, 49
ILLYRIA:
—APOLLONIA: **(2)** hell. *IApoll* 107 (Κλι-); **(3)** ii-i BC ib. 105 (d. Φίλων); **(4)** imp. ib. 104
SICILY:
—KAMARINA: **(5)** s. vi BC Dubois, *IGDS* 113 (Arena, *Iscr. Sic.* II 113; Cordano, 'Camarina VII' 5)

**Κλείξενος**
ARKADIA:
—PHIGALEIA: **(1)** c. 230-200 BC *BCH* 45 (1921) p. 12 II, 82 (s. Κλεινόμαχος)

**Κλειορόδη**
S. ITALY (CAMPANIA):
—DIKAIARCHIA-PUTEOLI: **(1)** iii/ii BC *SEG* IV 91, 2 (*GVI* 868) (m. Θευδώρα)

**Κλέιππος**
ELIS: **(1)** 36-24 BC *IvOl* 62, 3, 20 (s. Ἀριστόδημος, ?f. Κάλλων: Κ.)
LAKONIA:
—OITYLOS: **(2)** iii/ii BC *IG* V (1) 1295, 8 (Bradford (-))

**Κλέϊς**
ARKADIA:
—LOUSOI: **(1)** c. 210-207 BC *IG* IV (1)² 73, 24; *SEG* XXXV 303 (date) (f. Ἀκράγας)

**Κλεισθένης**
AIGINA: **(1)** ?c. 525-500 BC ib. XXXVI 305, 6; *LSAG*² p. 439 no. D (date) (-νες)
ARGOLIS:
—ARGOS: **(2)** imp. *IG* IV (1) 550 (tiles) (Κλοισσθέ-)
—EPIDAUROS: **(3)** iv BC ib. IV (1)² 189; 190 (f. Λαχάρης); **(4)** iii BC ib. 205 (f. Νικοτέλης, Καλλίμαχος)
——(Azantioi): **(5)** 146 BC ib. 28, 34 (f. Ἀντικράτης) ?= (6); **(6)** ~ ib. l. 41 (f. Ἀρίστων) ?= (5)
——Pagasina (Azantioi): **(7)** m. iii BC ib. 96, 49 (Perlman E.3); Perlman p. 63 f. (date)
—TROIZEN: **(8)** ?146 BC *IG* IV (1) 757 B, 42 (f. Κλεωνίδας)
KORINTHIA:
—SIKYON: **(9)** vii/vi BC *RE* (1); Moretti, *Olymp.* 96 (Skalet 181) (s. Ἀριστώνυμος, f. Ἀγαρίστα)

**Κλεισίας**
AITOLIA:
—PLEURON: **(1)** m. iii BC *IG* IX (1)² (1) 53 (Κλεισίας: s. Λύκος)

**Κλεΐσκος**
ARKADIA:
—MANTINEIA-ANTIGONEIA: **(1)** c. 300-221 BC ib. V (2) 323. 76 (tessera) (f. Γοργυθίων); **(2)** ~ ib. 323. 79 (tessera) (s. Γοργυθίων); **(3)** ~ ib. 323. 87 (tessera) (Κ[λ]εῖσκο[s])

**Κλεισταινέτη**
AIGINA: **(1)** ?i BC ib. IV (1) 126 (d. Ἀγαθάμερος)

**Κλείτα**
S. ITALY (CAMPANIA):
—HERCULANEUM*: **(1)** m. i AD *PdelP* 10 (1955) p. 470 no. 87 (Lat. Iunia Cleta: freed.)

**Κλειταγόρα**
LAKONIA:
—SPARTA?: **(1)** ?v BC *RE* (-) (Poralla² 429); Hsch. s.v. Κλειταγόρα (locn.) (or Lesbos)

**Κλειταγόρας**
ARGOLIS:
—EPIDAUROS*: **(1)** c. 370-360 BC Peek, *IAEpid* 52 A, 51; *BSA* 61 (1966) p. 272 no. 4 B II, 17
—HERMIONE: **(2)** ii-i BC *IG* IV (1) 732 III, 2 (f. Γυμνάσιον)

**Κλειτάνδρα**
SICILY: **(1)** inc. Manganaro, *PdelP* forthcoming no. 11 (Κλι-)

**Κλείτανδρος**
ARGOLIS:
—TROIZEN: **(1)** iii BC *IG* IV (1) 824, 5 (f. Θεόδωρος)

**Κλείταρχος**
AIGINA: **(1)** ii-i BC *RE* (4)

**Κλειταρώ**
ARGOLIS:
—EPIDAUROS: **(1)** iii BC *IG* IV (1)² 205 (?m. Νικοτέλης, Καλλίμαχος)

**Κλειτέας**
ARGOLIS:
—TROIZEN: **(1)** iii BC ib. IV (1) 774, 5 (s. Θεμίστιος)

**Κλειτέλης**
ARGOLIS:
—EPIDAUROS*: **(1)** c. 320-300 BC ib. IV (1)² 110 A, 44
KORINTHIA:
—KORINTH: **(2)** 371 BC X., *HG* vi 5. 37

**Κλείτη**
SICILY:
—ZANKLE-MESSANA: **(1)** ?ii-iii AD *NScav* 1942, p. 82 no. 1 (Λικινία Κ.)

**Κλειτία**
ILLYRIA:
—EPIDAMNOS-DYRRHACHION: **(1)** hell.-imp. *IDyrrh* 64 with index (d. Λύσανδρος); **(2)** ~ ib. 269 with index (d. Φίλων)

**Κλειτίας**
ARKADIA:
—KLEITOR: **(1)** ?253 BC Nachtergael, *Les Galates* 10, 30 (Stephanis 1428) (s. Καλλίας)
KORINTHIA:
—SIKYON: **(2)** vi/v BC *SEG* XI 244, 31
S. ITALY?: **(3)** v/iv BC ib. XXXIII 820 (Κλε-)

**Κλειτόλας**
KORINTHIA:
—OINOE: **(1)** v BC *IG* IV (1) 415 (Κλετ-)

**Κλειτομάχα**
EPIROS:
—BOUTHROTOS (PRASAIBOI): **(1)** a. 163 BC *IBouthrot* 19, 5 (*SEG* XXXVIII 476); **(2)** ~ *IBouthrot* 42, 18 (*SEG* XXXVIII 501)

**Κλειτόμαχος**
AIGINA: **(1)** f. v BC Pi., *P.* viii, 37; cf. Klee p. 91 no. 55

**Κλειτόριος**
ARKADIA: **(1)** ?265-253 BC Nachtergael, *Les Galates* 4, 12; 7, 11; 8, 10; 10, 8 (Stephanis 1429) (s. Ἀριστείδας)
ILLYRIA:
—EPIDAMNOS-DYRRHACHION: **(2)** c. 250-50 BC *BMC Thessaly* p. 77 no. 171 (coin) (Κλε[ιτό]ρι[ος]: pryt.) ?= (3); **(3)** ~ Maier 259-69; Münsterberg p. 39; Nachtr. p. 15 (coin) (Ceka 95; 165; 174; 202; 278) + *IApoll Ref. Bibl.* n. 71 (293; 301; 323; 358; 373; 413; 431; 454) (pryt.) ?= (2); **(4)** hell.-imp. *IDyrrh* 265 (f. Κλέα)

**Κλεῖτος**
AIGINA: **(1)** ii/i BC *Alt-Ägina* I (2) p. 43 no. 3, 4 (s. Θεόδωρος)
ARKADIA:
—TEGEA: **(2)** m. ii AD *IG* V (2) 48, 24
ILLYRIA: **(3)** iv BC *RE* (11); Berve 426 (s. Βάρδυλλις, ?f. Βάρδυλλις)
—BESSE-SELCE (MOD.): **(4)** imp. *Stud. Alb.* 1969 (2), p. 170 (f. Δαζίωνος)
S. ITALY: **(5)** imp. *Epig. Rom. di Canosa* Instr. 24 (amph.) (Lat. Clitus)
S. ITALY (CALABRIA):
—BRENTESION-BRUNDISIUM: **(6)** 31 AD *Athenaeum* 42 (1964) pp. 299-306 (Lat. Clitus)
S. ITALY (CAMPANIA):
—HERCULANEUM: **(7)** i BC-i AD *CIL* X 1403 d III, 19 (Lat. L. Mammius Clitus); **(8)** m. i AD *PdelP* 1 (1946) p. 383 no. 8; 3 (1948) p. 181 no. 26 (Lat. C. Petronius Clitus)

**Κλειτοφῶν**
LEUKAS: **(1)** ?iii BC Unp. (*IG* arch.)

**Κλειτώ**
ARGOLIS:
—EPIDAUROS: **(1)** v/iv BC *SEG* XXXI 330

**Κλείτων**
MESSENIA:
—PROTE*: **(1)** ii BC *IG* V (1) 1534 (Κλέτ-)

**Κλείτωρ**
ARKADIA:
—MEGALOPOLIS?: (1) 42 AD ib. v (2) 516, 4 (f. Δαμοκράτης)

**Κλειφάνης**
ARGOLIS:
—EPIDAUROS:
——Erilais: (1) m. iii BC Peek, IAEpid 42, 28 (Perlman E.3); Perlman p. 63 f. (date)

**Κλειφαντίς**
ARGOLIS:
—EPIDAUROS: (1) hell.-imp. IG IV (1)² 731, 4 (d. Ἀγιάδας)

**Κλειώ**
AKARNANIA:
—THYRREION: (1) hell.? ib. IX (1)² (2) 354; Fraser–Rönne, BWGT pp. 169 f. ([Κ]λειοῖ (voc.))

**Κλεμήδης**
EPIROS:
—DODONA*: (1) ?iii BC SEG XIX 431 (f. Ὀλυμπιάς)

**Κλενάγορος**
ARGOLIS:
—HERMIONE: (1) c. 370 BC ib. XI 379 b, 1 (s. Λύων)

**Κλέοβις**
ARGOLIS:
—ARGOS: (1) s. vii BC RE s.v. Biton (1) (s. Κυδίππα)

**Κλεόβουλος**
ARGOLIS:
—ARGOS:
——(Amphisseis): (1) s. iv BC SEG XXIX 363, 1 (or Lokris (Western) Amphissa)
DALMATIA:
—ISSA: (2) iii BC Brunšmid p. 9 fr. H, 5 ([Κλε]όβουλος: s. Κλεόμηλος)
EPIROS:
—VOTONOSI (MOD.): (3) f. iii BC SEG XXIV 456
LAKONIA:
—SPARTA: (4) 421 BC Th. v 36-8 (Poralla² 430); (5) ii AD IG v (1) 159, 7 (Bradford (2)) (Κ[λε]όβουλος); (6) ?ii AD IG v (1) 179, 9 (Bradford (1)) (Κλεόβο[υλος]); (7) c. 150-160 AD IG v (1) 69, 31; 71 III, 23; SEG XI 554, 3; 585, 13; XXX 410, [22] (Bradford (3)) (f. Γοργίων)
MESSENIA:
—KORONE: (8) f. iii AD IvOl 451, 8-9; 452, 7; IG v (1) 1398, 3, 12 (Γ. Κλώδιος Ἰούλ. Κ.: s. Γ. Ἰούλ. Θεαγένης, f. Γ. Φούφιος Ἰούλ. Θεαγένης); (9) 246 AD ib. l. 37 (Αὐρ. Κ.)

**Κλεογένα**
EPIROS:
—DODONA*: (1) v BC PAE 1968, p. 56

**Κλεογένεια**
MESSENIA:
—KYPARISSIA: (1) ii BC SEG XXV 436 = AD 25 (1970) Chron. p. 174

**Κλεογένης**
ACHAIA:
—AIGION: (1) m. ii BC IG IX (1)² (3) 721 B, 4 (s. Ἀλκίθοος)
ARGOLIS:
—ARGOS: (2) 31 BC-14 AD IvOl 420, 1 (s. (nat.) Δαμόσων, s. (ad.) Σωτέλης); (3) i-ii AD IG IV (1) 587, 1 (s. —ένης)
ELIS: (4) f. iv BC Moretti, Olymp. 387 (s. Σιληνός); (5) s. ii BC IG IX (1)² (3) 721 C, 2 (s. Ἀνδρόνικος)

LAKONIA:
—SPARTA: (6) ?ii BC SEG XI 459 (Bradford (-)) (Κλεογένη[ς])

**Κλεοδάμας**
MESSENIA: (1) iii BC SEG XI 980 a (Κ[λεοδ]άμα[ς]: name—LGPN)

**Κλεόδαμος**
ARGOLIS:
—ARGOS: (1) v BC ib. 339, 7 ([Κ]λεόδαμος); (2) a. 303 BC CEG II 816, 10
——(Dorieis): (3) c. 330-300 BC SEG XXX 355, 5
——Kolonos: (4) a. 316 BC ib. 360, 6 (Perlman A.8)
ARKADIA:
—LYKOSOURA*: (5) ii/i BC IG v (2) 522 (s. Πολυδεύκης)
—MEGALOPOLIS: (6) 263 BC ib. IX (1)² (1) 17, 12 (f. Θεόκριτος, Ἀγιάδας)
—TEGEA: (7) ii-i BC ib. v (2) 165, 3 (s. Κρατέας); (8) ?i BC ib. 230 (Κλεόδα[μος])
——(Athaneatai): (9) s. iv BC ib. 41, 36 (s. Πάχων)
ELIS: (10) i BC/i AD IvOl 61, 7 (s. Ἡράκλειτος)
KEPHALLENIA:
—SAME: (11) iv/iii BC Fraser–Rönne, BWGT p. 117 no. 2. 1 ([Κλ]εόδαμος); (12) ~ ib. p. 117 no. 2. 3
LAKONIA:
—SPARTA: (13) c. 30-20 BC IG v (1) 211, 13 (Bradford (5)) (f. Ἀριστείδας); (14) c. 90-100 AD SEG XI 609, 6 (Bradford (6)) (I f. Κλεόδαμος II); (15) ~ SEG XI 609, 6 (Bradford (2)) (II s. Κλεόδαμος I); (16) c. 100 AD SEG XI 515, 2; 637, 1? (Bradford (7)) (f. Μενεκλῆς); (17) ~ SEG XI 534, 1 (Bradford (3)); (18) c. 100-125 AD IG v (1) 483, 10 (Bradford (9)) (Κλεώ-: f. Σωσικράτεια); (19) c. 131-133 AD IG v (1) 61, 2; SEG XI 579, 4 (Bradford (4)); (20) c. 140 AD SEG XI 522, 8 (Bradford (8)) (f. Γ. Ἰούλ. Σωσίβιος); (21) c. 140-150 AD IG v (1) 64, 4 (Bradford (1)) ([Κ]λεόδαμος: s. Καλλικράτης)
MESSENIA:
—MESSENE: (22) f. iii BC PAE 1991, p. 99 no. 7, 30; (23) m. iii BC IC 2 p. 29 no. 13 B, 2 ([Κλε]όδαμος—IC, [Φιλ]όδαμος?—ed.: f. Φιλιππίδας)
S. ITALY (BRUTTIUM):
—RHEGION:
——(Nav.): (24) ii BC IG XIV 616, 7 with Add. p. 688 (Mus. Naz. Reggio p. 159 no. 29) (s. Μυΐσκος)
S. ITALY (CALABRIA):
—TARAS-TARENTUM: (25) iv BC IG XIV 2406. 49 (RA 1932 (1), p. 39 no. 23; SEG XXX 1222. 6; Troisi, Epigrafi mobili 75 (loomweight))
S. ITALY (CAMPANIA):
—POMPEII: (26) i BC-i AD CIL IV 5158 (Lat. Cle(o)damus)

**Κλεοδίκα**
ACHAIA: (1) iv/iii BC IG XII (9) 810 (d. Λυσίας: date—Knoepfler)

**Κλεοδίκη**
ELIS: (1) m. i AD IvOl 223, 1; 428, 1; 429, 5 (Κλ. Κ.: I m. Κάλλιππος Πεισανός, Ἀντ. Κλεοδίκη II); (2) s. i AD ib. l. 3; 430, 3 (Ἀντ. Κ.: II d. Μ. Ἀντ. Ἀλεξίων, Κλ. Κλεοδίκη I, m. Τιβ. Κλ. Πέλοψ, Κλ. Δαμοξένα, Τιβ. Κλ. Ἀριστομένης)

**Κλεόδικος**
AIGINA: (1) iv BC IG IV (1) 41 (s. Ἀγέμαχος)
ARKADIA:
—ORCHOMENOS: (2) ?c. 369-361 BC BCH 102 (1978) p. 347, 30 (IPArk 14)
—PHIGALEIA: (3) 191-146 BC BMC Pelop. p. 15 no. 169 (coin)

DALMATIA:
—ISSA:
——(Hylleis): (4) iv/iii BC Brunšmid p. 8, 34 (s. Μνάστηρ)
—ISSA?: (5) hell.? ib. p. 32 no. 29 (f. Ἀρχέβιος)

**Κλεοδόξα**
ARKADIA?: (1) s. v BC SEG XLI 386 a

**Κλεόδωρος**
ACHAIA:
—PELLENE: (1) m. iii BC IG v (2) 368, 93 (s. Δάμων)
ARGOLIS:
—ARGOS: (2) 356 BC CID II 31, 11
ARKADIA: (3) ?iii BC Breccia, Iscriz. 294 (f. Ἐχέφυλος)
—PHENEOS: (4) 139-122 BC Syll³ 703 (Stephanis 1439) (s. Θεοξενίδας)
—TEGEA:
——(Hippothoitai): (5) iii BC IG v (2) 40, 37 (f. Θέων)
——(Krariotai): (6) iii BC ib. l. 18 (f. Φιλοκλῆς)
KEPHALLENIA:
—SAME (NR.): (7) ?v BC Op. Ath. 10 (1971) p. 65 no. 7 + Unp. (IG arch.) (Κλεόδωρ[—]—IG arch., Κλέοδος—Fraser–Rönne)
SICILY:
—TAUROMENION: (8) c. 100-95 BC IG XIV 421 an. 35; 421 an. 45; 421 an. 46 (SGDI 5219) (f. Ἀγάθαρχος, Στράτων)

**Κλεόθοινος**
ARKADIA:
—MANTINEIA-ANTIGONEIA: (1) c. 300-221 BC IG v (2) 323. 75 (tessera) (f. Ἀρίστιππος)

**Κλεοίτας**
ARKADIA:
—TEGEA: (1) s. iii BC ib. 60 (Κλεοίτας)
LAKONIA:
—SPARTA: (2) c. 217-230 AD SEG XI 616 a, 3; BSA 79 (1984) p. 284 no. 11 (ident., date) (Bradford s.v. Τιμοκλῆς (5)) (Μ. Αὐρ. Τιμοκλῆς ὁ καὶ Κλεο[ίτ]ας: s. Τιμοκλῆς)

**Κλεοκράτεια**
LEUKAS: (1) iii BC Unp. (IG arch.)

**Κλεοκράτης**
ARKADIA:
—KLEITOR: (1) f. iii BC IG XI (4) 532 (f. Ἱππόλοχος)

**Κλεοκρατίδας**
LAKONIA:
—GYTHEION: (1) imp. Giannakopoulou, Gytheion p. 178 (s. Εὐμένης)

**Κλεοκρατῖνος**
ARGOLIS:
—HERMIONE: (1) ii-i BC IG IV (1) 732 IV, 17 (Κλεοκρατῖν[ος]); (2) i BC-i AD? ib. 730 IV, 4 (f. —ερμος)

**Κλεόκριτος**
ARGOLIS:
—ARGOS: (1) ?205 BC AE 1936, Chron. p. 39 no. 213, 7 (s. Κλεόνικος)
ARKADIA:
—MANTINEIA-ANTIGONEIA:
——(Posoidaia): (2) c. 425-400 BC SEG XXXI 348, 20
—TEGEA: (3) c. 240-229 BC IG v (2) 11, 17
KORINTHIA:
—KORINTH: (4) 480 BC Plu., Arist. 8
SICILY:
—NAXOS: (5) vi BC Paus. vi 13. 8 (f. Τείσανδρος)

**Κλεόλα**
LAKONIA:
—SPARTA: (1) v/iv BC Plu., Ages. 19; cf. Keil, Analecta Epigr. p. 160 (Poralla² 440) (Κλεόρα—Plu., Κ.—Dindorf, Keil and Masson: ?d. Ἀριστομενίδας, m. Ἀρχίδαμος, Εὐπωλία, Προαύγα)

**Κλεολαεύς**
EPIROS:
—DODONA*: (**1**) iv BC *PAE* 1973, p. 94 no. 1
with n. 1

**Κλεολαΐς**
AKARNANIA:
—THYRREION: (**1**) ii BC *IG* IX (1)² (2) 332
EPIROS:
—DODONA*: (**2**) ?iv BC *Ep. Chron.* 10 (1935) p.
256 no. 18 B

**Κλεόλαος**
AITOLIA:
—BOUKATION: (**1**) c. 162 BC *IG* IX (1)² (1) 106,
9 (Κλε(ό)λαος)
ARKADIA:
—KLEITOR: (**2**) c. 369 BC Paus. viii 27. 2 (and
Arkadia Megalopolis: oikist)

**Κλεόλας**
ARGOLIS:
—PHLEIOUS: (**1**) hell.? ib. v 22. 1
ARKADIA:
—STYMPHALOS: (**2**) 373-347 BC *SEG* XXIV 379,
3 ([Κ]λε[ό]λας?)
KEPHALLENIA:
—KRANIOI: (**3**) hell. ib. XVII 250; cf. *Op. Ath.*
10 (1971) p. 71 fig. 29

**Κλεόμαντις**
ARKADIA:
—KAPHYAI: (**1**) 341 BC *CID* II 12 II, 2
—KLEITOR: (**2**) 336 BC *RE* (1); Moretti, *Olymp.*
456
—ORCHOMENOS: (**3**) c. 230-200 BC *BCH* 45
(1921) p. 13 II, 114 (s. Τιμόδαμος)
—TEGEA:
——(Athaneatai): (**4**) s. iv BC *IG* V (2) 41,
20 (Κλεόμαντ[ις], Κλεόμαν[δρος]—ed.: name—
*LGPN*)
LAKONIA: (**5**) s. iv BC Plu., *Alex.* 50 (Berve
430; Poralla² 431) (Κλεομένης—Wyttenbach:
mantis: name—mss.)

**Κλεόμαχος**
ACHAIA:
—AIGION: (**1**) ?228-215 BC *SGDI* 2525, 7 (s.
Ἀρχέλαος)
—DYME: (**2**) iii BC *AJPh* 31 (1910) p. 399 no.
74 c, 1
—PELLENE?: (**3**) ?263-261 BC *FD* III (3) 190, 5
AITOLIA:
—KALLION/KALLIPOLIS: (**4**) 223-192 BC *IG* IX
(1)² (1) 31, 24, 39
—KALYDON: (**5**) 129 BC ib. 137, 98 (s. Πολέμων)
ARGOLIS:
—ARGOS: (**6**) v BC ib. IV (1) 511 (Lazzarini 400)
—EPIDAUROS: (**7**) iii-ii BC Le Rider, *Monnaies
crétoises* p. 258 I, 7 (s. Ἀφθόνητος)
ARKADIA:
—MANTINEIA-ANTIGONEIA: (**8**) iv/iii BC *SEG*
XXVI 330 (f. Νόστων); (**9**) c. 300-221 BC *IG* V
(2) 323. 98 (tessera) (f. Ἱεροκλῆς)
—MEGALOPOLIS: (**10**) hell.? ib. 448, 11
([Κλε]όμαχο[ς]?)
—TEGEA: (**11**) c. 240-229 BC ib. 12
ELIS: (**12**) i BC/i AD *IvOl* 61, 10 (Κλ[εόμ]αχος:
f. —ος); (**13**) ii/iii AD ib. 100, 13; 102, [12];
103, 13, 16; 104, 14; 106, 13; 107, [10];
110, 16; 112, [3] (I s. Πολύβιος, f. Κλεόμα-
χος II: mantis/Klytiadai/*A.*) ?= (*15*); (**14**) c.
177-213 AD ib. 103, 16; 106, 13; 107, [10];
110, 16; 112, 3 (Αὐρ. Κ.—110: II s Κλεόμαχος
I: mantis/Klytiadai); (**15**) 209-213 AD ib. 110,
10 (f. Αὐρ. Ὀνησιφόρος) ?= (*13*)
—PISA: (**16**) 365-363 BC ib. 36, 7 (Perlman O.1)
([Κλ]εόμαχος: f. Βάθυλλος)
EPIROS:
—AMBRAKIA: (**17**) 238-168 BC *JIAN* 12 (1909-
10) p. 45 no. 15; *BMC Thessaly* p. 96 no. 33
(coins) (Κλεόμαχ(ος)—*BMC*)

—BOUTHROTOS (PRASAIBOI): (**18**) a. 163 BC
*IBouthrot* 14, 36; 22, 4; 28, 12 (*SEG* XXXVIII
471; 479; 486) (s. Νικάνωρ); (**19**) ~ *IBouth-
rot* 14, 36; 28, 11 (*SEG* XXXVIII 471; 486)
(f. Νικάνωρ); (**20**) ~ *IBouthrot* 31, 29 (*SEG*
XXXVIII 490) (f. Μάχανδρος); (**21**) ~ *IBouthrot*
31, 44 (*SEG* XXXVIII 490); (**22**) ~ *IBouthrot*
53, 7 (*SEG* XXXVIII 504) (f. Βοΐσκος); (**23**) ~
*IBouthrot* 145, 11 (f. Σαώτας)
——Polleioi: (**24**) a. 163 BC ib. 98, 6 (f. Νικάνωρ)
—DODONA: (**25**) iii BC Antoniou, *Dodone* Ab, 10
—NIKOPOLIS: (**26**) imp. *PAE* 1913, p. 97 no.
6 (Sarikakis 88) (f. Εὐάρεστος); (**27**) a. 30 BC
*SEG* XXIV 435 (Sarikakis 89) (s. Λυκίσκος);
(**28**) s. i AD *Syll*³ 813 B, 4 (*FD* III (3) 181, 4;
Sarikakis 77) (Τιβ. Κλ. Κ.)
—TEPELENE (MOD.): (**29**) i BC-i AD? *SEG* XXIV
474, 1; cf. Hammond, *Epirus* p. 738 (locn.)
(s. Νικανός)
ILLYRIA:
—APOLLONIA: (**30**) c. 250-50 BC Maier 55 (coin)
(Ceka 108) (pryt.)
LAKONIA:
—OITYLOS: (**31**) v BC *IG* V (1) 1293 (Poralla²
432) ([Κ]λεόμαχος: f. Καλοκλείνας)
—SPARTA: (**32**) c. 30-20 BC *IG* V (1) 211, 2
(Bradford (3)) (s. Σηρανδρίδας); (**33**) c. 80-90
AD *IG* V (1) 674, 13 (Bradford (5)) (I f. Κλεό-
μαχος II); (**34**) ~ *IG* V (1) 674, 13 (Bradford
(1)) (II s. Κλεόμαχος I); (**35**) c. 120-130 AD
*SEG* XI 518, 5; 544, 7; 579, [6] (Bradford
(4)) (f. Ἀριστομενίδας); (**36**) c. 175-200 AD *IG*
V (1) 89, 16 (Bradford (6)) (I f. Κλεόμαχος
II); (**37**) ~ *IG* V (1) 89, 16 (Bradford (2)) (II
s. Κλεόμαχος I)
MESSENIA:
—MESSENE: (**38**) ii-i BC *SEG* XLI 343, 5
([Κλ]εόμαχος)
SICILY:
—LIPARA: (**39**) vi/v BC *Meligunis-Lipara* 2 p.
140 T. 395 (vase); cf. *SEG* XLII 864

**Κλεόμβροτος**
ACHAIA?: (**1**) c. 300 BC ib. XIV 375, 6
ARGOLIS:
—EPIDAUROS: (**2**) c. 350-250 BC *AAA* 5 (1972)
p. 358 fig. 20
ARKADIA: (**3**) iii BC *IG* V (2) 415, 3 (*IPArk* 23)
([Κλεό]μβροτος: f. Φιλέας)
—MEGALOPOLIS: (**4**) 359 BC *CID* II 5 I, 29
(Κλε[ό]μβροτος)
EPIROS:
—AMBRAKIA: (**5**) v/iv BC *HE* 1273
LAKONIA:
—SPARTA: (**6**) c. 535-479 BC *RE* (1); cf. *FGrH*
287 F 4 (Poralla² 433) (s. Ἀναξανδρίδας, f.
Παυσανίας, Νικομήδης: regent); (**7**) c. 410-371
BC *RE* (2) (Poralla² 434) (s. Παυσανίας, f. Ἀγη-
σίπολις, Κλεομένης: king); (**8**) m. iii BC *RE*
(3) (Bradford (1)) (f. Ἀγησίπολις, Κλεομένης:
king); (**9**) s. i AD *RE* (4); Plu., *Mor.* 409 E
ff.; Cartledge-Spawforth pp. 178-80 (ident.)
(Bradford (2)) ?= (*10*); (**10**) c. 100 AD *SEG* XI
513, 7 (Bradford (3)) ?= (*9*)
S. ITALY (BRUTTIUM):
—SYBARIS-THOURIOI-COPIAE:
——(Δο.): (**11**) f. vi BC *Klio* 52 (1970) pp. 295-
6; Guarducci, *Ep. Gr.* 1 p. 110 no. 3 (Lazzarini 859; Landi, *DISMG* 252; Ebert, *Gr.
Sieg.* p. 251 f.; *CEG* 1 394); cf. *BE* 1973, no.
557; *SEG* XXIX 1017; *LSAG*² p. 456 no. 1a
(Κλεόμρ-: s. Δεξίλαϝος)

**Κλεομένης**
ACHAIA:
—PATRAI: (**1**) m. iii BC *IG* V (2) 368, 61 (f. Ἀ-
γυλλος)
AITOLIA:
—TRICHONION: (**2**) s. iii BC ib. IX (1)² (1) 117,
5

AKARNANIA: (**3**) iii-ii BC *PAE* 1912, p. 186 no.
21 (f. Γλαῦκος)
—THYRREION: (**4**) ii BC *IG* IX (1)² (2) 248, 18
(s. Εὔαλκος); (**5**) ~ ib. l. 19 (s. Ἀλκιφῶν); (**6**) ~
ib. l. 8-9 (f. Ἀλκιφῶν, Εὔαλκος)
LAKONIA:
—SPARTA: (**7**) c. 600 BC Plu., *Sol.* 10 (Poralla²
435); (**8**) c. 540-487 BC *RE* (3); *IPr* 316,
2 (Poralla² 436) (s. Ἀναξανδρίδας, f. Γοργώ:
king); (**9**) 427 BC Th. iii 26. 2 (Poralla² 438)
(s. Παυσανίας: regent?); (**10**) c. 390-309 BC *RE*
(5) (Poralla² 437) (s. Κλεόμβροτος, f. Κλεώνυμος, Ἀκρότατος: king); (**11**) c. 260-219 BC *RE*
(6); *IvOl* 309 (Bradford (1)) (s. Λεωνίδας, Κρατησίκλεια: king); (**12**) s. iii BC Plb. iv 35. 10,
12 (Bradford (2)) (s. Κλεόμβροτος, Χιλωνίς: regent); (**13**) f. iii AD *IG* V (1) 550, 1 (Bradford
(3)) (Μ. Αὐρ. Κ.: s. Νικηφόρος)
MESSENIA:
—MESSENE: (**14**) ii-i BC *SEG* XLI 343, 10
([Κλ]εομένης)
S. ITALY (BRUTTIUM):
—LOKROI EPIZEPHYRIOI:
——(Ἀνα.): (**15**) iv/iii BC De Franciscis 21, 6
—RHEGION: (**16**) ?vi BC *PMG* 838; *PCG* 5 p.
156 fr. 4; (**17**) ?m. v BC Dubois, *IGDGG* 1
39 b (Arena, *Iscr. Sic.* III 63); *LSAG*² p. 248
(date) (s. Ἐμμενίδης)
S. ITALY (CAMPANIA):
—DIKAIARCHIA-PUTEOLI: (**18**) imp. *CIL* X
1916 (Lat. Cleomenes)
SICILY:
—HERAKLEIA MINOA: (**19**) ?iii-ii BC *SEG* XIX
613 (vase-stamp)
—SYRACUSE: (**20**) s. vi BC ib. XXXI 841 (Dubois,
*IGDS* 86; Lazzarini 821); cf. *LSAG*² p. 265
no. 3 (Κλεομ[έν]ες, Κλεομ[έδ]ες?: ?s. Κνιδιείδας);
(**21**) 72 BC *RE* (10) (Lat. Cleomenes)

**Κλεομήδης**
ARGOLIS:
—HERMIONE: (**1**) ?ii-i BC *IG* IV (1) 731 I, 5 (f.
Ἄρχων); (**2**) ~ ib. 731 II, 16 (s. Μνασικλῆς, f.
Σύμφορον); (**3**) ii-i BC ib. 732 II, 2 (f. Διονυσία)
ARKADIA:
—TEGEA:
——(Krariotai): (**4**) iii BC ib. V (2) 40, 17
(Κλεο[μ]ήδης: f. Νικάρατος)
EPIROS:
—AMBRAKIA: (**5**) s. ii BC Cabanes, *L'Épire* p.
548 no. 19 (*SEG* XXVI 694) (Κλεομίδης: f.
Θράσων)
—BOUTHROTOS (PRASAIBOI): (**6**) a. 163 BC
*IBouthrot* 93, 5
ITHAKE: (**7**) 208 BC *IMM* 36, 2 (f. Ἀναξίλαος);
(**8**) hell.-imp. *AM* 27 (1902) p. 376 no. 59 (s.
Φρύνων)
KORINTHIA:
—SIKYON: (**9**) vi/v BC *SEG* XI 244, 73 (-μέδες)
SICILY:
—MEGARA HYBLAIA: (**10**) f. vi BC Arena, *Iscr.
Sic.* 1 8 (-μέδες)

**Κλεόμηλος**
ARGOLIS:
—EPIDAUROS*: (**1**) c. 365-335 BC *IG* IV (1)²
103, 164-5, 170-2, 176
DALMATIA:
—ISSA:
——(Dymanes): (**2**) iv/iii BC Brunšmid p. 9, 61
(f. Ἀθηναγόρας)
——(Dymanes)?: (**3**) iii BC ib. p. 9 fr. H, 5
(Κλεόμ[ηλος]: f. Κλεόβουλος)
——(Pamphyloi): (**4**) iv/iii BC ib. p. 8, 31 (f.
Κλεύστρατος)

**Κλεόμητις**
EPIROS:
—BOUTHROTOS (PRASAIBOI): (**1**) a. 163 BC
*IBouthrot* 18, 11; 33, 14 (*SEG* XXXVIII 475;
492); (**2**) ~ *IBouthrot* 21, 45 (*SEG* XXXVIII
478); (**3**) ~ *IBouthrot* 22, 10; 41, 18 (*SEG*
XXXVIII 479; 500) (s. Σωσίπατρος) ?= (*8*); (**4**)
~ *IBouthrot* 22, 23; 41, 8 (*SEG* XXXVIII 479;

## Κλεόμητος (continued)

500) (s. Νικόστρατος); (5) ~ *IBouthrot* 30, 8
(*SEG* XXXVIII 488); (6) ~ *IBouthrot* 31, 45
(*SEG* XXXVIII 490); (7) ~ *IBouthrot* 42, 15
(*SEG* XXXVIII 501); (8) ~ *IBouthrot* 122, 6 ?=
(3)

## Κλεόμητος
LAKONIA:
—SPARTA: (1) imp.? *Syringes* 339 (Bradford (-))

## Κλεόμμας
EPIROS:
—BOUTHROTOS (PRASAIBOI): (1) a. 163 BC
*IBouthrot* 31, 77 (*SEG* XXXVIII 490); *SEG*
XXXVIII 134, 15 (f. Κρίσων); (2) ~ *IBouthrot*
31, 79 (*SEG* XXXVIII 490) (s. Κρίσων); (3) ~
*IBouthrot* 42, 7 (*SEG* XXXVIII 501)

## Κλεόμναστος
ILLYRIA:
—APOLLONIA: (1) imp. *IApoll* 70

## Κλεονίκα
AKARNANIA:
—PALAIROS: (1) iii BC *IG* IX (1)² (2) 489
ARGOLIS:
—EPIDAUROS: (2) iii/ii BC ib. IV (1)² 336 (d.
Κλεώνυμος)
—PHLEIOUS: (3) 361 BC *CID* II 4 I, 53
S. ITALY (CAMPANIA):
—SURRENTUM: (4) ?ii AD *CIL* X 733 (Lat. Flavia
Cleonica)

## Κλεονίκη
ACHAIA:
—TRITAIA: (1) hell.-imp. Thomopoulos, *Hist.
Patr.* p. 237 (*Achaïe* II 313) (d. Διονύσιος)

## Κλεονίκης
MESSENIA:
—PHARAI: (1) ii BC *IG* V (1) 1366

## Κλεονικίδας
LAKONIA:
—SPARTA: (1) imp. ib. 609, 4 (Bradford (-))
([Κ]λεονικίδας); (2) c. 150-160 AD *IG* V (1) 53,
29 (Bradford s.v. Νικίας (3)) (Νικίας ὁ καὶ Κ.:
s. Νικίας)

## Κλεόνικος
AIGINA: (1) ?480-478 BC Pi., *I.* V, 55; VI, 16
AITOLIA:
—ATTALEIA: (2) 204 BC *IG* IX (1)² (1) 95, 5
—KALYDON: (3) c. 142 BC ib. 137, 47 (f. Λυσί-
ξενος)
AKARNANIA:
—PALAIROS: (4) iii BC ib. IX (1)² (2) 490
ARGOLIS:
—ARGOS: (5) ?205 BC *AE* 1936, Chron. p. 39
no. 213, 7 (Κλεόν[ι]κος: f. Κλεόκριτος)
—EPIDAUROS: (6) c. 365-335 BC *IG* IV (1)² 103,
46; (7) iii BC Peek, *NIEpid* 38 (Κλεόνικ[ος])
ARKADIA: (8) 284 BC *PEleph* 4, 8
—KAPHYAI: (9) f. iii BC *BCH* 38 (1914) p. 459
no. 4, 2 (f. Κλεοφάης)
—MANTINEIA-ANTIGONEIA: (10) c. 300-221 BC
*IG* V (2) 323. 31 (tessera) (s. Δάμαρχος); (11)
~ ib. 323. 81 (tessera) (f. Μνασίλας)
LAKONIA:
—SPARTA: (12) i BC/i AD *SEG* XI 677, 1 (Brad-
ford (1)) (f. Νικιππία); (13) c. 100-120 AD
*SEG* XI 545, 2?; 561, [1]; 562, 1; 637, 4
(Bradford (2)) ([Κλ]εόνικος—637: f. Σίπομπος)
MESSENIA:
—THOURIA: (14) ii-i BC *IG* V (1) 1385, 7 (s.
Κλεοσθένης); (15) f. ii BC *SEG* XI 972, 79 (s.
Δάμων)
PELOPONNESE?: (16) 11 AD *PAE* 1992, p. 72 B,
19 (f. Ἡσίδωρος)

## Κλέοννις
AKARNANIA:
—STRATOS: (1) ii BC *IG* IX (1)² (2) 410
([Κ]λέονν[ις?], [Κ]λεονν[ώ?])
MESSENIA: (2) viii BC Paus. iv 7. 4; 8; 8. 11; 10.
5-6; 11. 2; 13. 5; D.S. viii 12

## Κλεοννώ
ARKADIA:
—MEGALOPOLIS: (1) ?145 BC *IG* V (2) 439, 46
(Κλεον[νώ]: d. Πασικράτης, Ζευξώ)

## Κλεοξένα
KERKYRA: (1) imp. ib. IX (1) 856 (loomweight)

## Κλεόξενος
ACHAIA:
—DYME: (1) iii BC *AJPh* 31 (1910) p. 399 no.
74 a, 1; p. 399 no. 74 c, 11 (f. Θεόκριτος)
AITOLIA:
—PSOLOUNTIOI: (2) s. ii BC *SEG* XXV 621, 10
(f. Ἄγριος)
—TRICHONION: (3) iii/ii BC *SBBerlAk* 1936, p.
387 no. 2
AKARNANIA:
—THYRREION: (4) ?iii BC *IG* IX (1)² (2) 300 a
([Κ]λεόξ[ενος], [Κ]λεοξ[ένα?])
ARKADIA:
—MEGALOPOLIS: (5) ii BC ib. V (2) 443, 46
(*IPArk* 32)
—THELPHOUSA: (6) 175 BC *SGDI* 1865, 1 (f.
Μένανδρος)
LAKONIA:
—SPARTA: (7) ?s. ii BC *SEG* XI 470, 2, [12]
(Bradford (1)) (s. Νικόλας); (8) i BC/i AD *SEG*
XI 707 (Κλεόξ[ενος]?); (9) ?i AD *IG* V (1) 911
(tiles) (Bradford (2))

## Κλεοπάμων
SICILY:
—GELA-PHINTIAS: (1) iv BC *IG* II² 8459 (s. Ἀρ-
χέτιμος)

## Κλεοπάτρα
ARGOLIS:
—HERMIONE: (1) ?ii-i BC ib. IV (1) 731 III, 6
(m. Εὐμένης); (2) ~ ib. l. 12 (m. Φιλόδαμος);
(3) ii-i BC ib. 732 I, 10 (m. Ζωπυρίων); (4) i
BC-i AD? ib. 730 I, 2, 3, 4 (m. Ὀνασικράτις,
Λεοντίς, Βελτίς)
ARKADIA:
—TEGEA: (5) imp. ib. V (2) 196; (6) i/ii AD ib.
81 (d. Σεκοῦνδος)
EPIROS:
—BOUTHROTOS (PRASAIBOI): (7) a. 163 BC
*IBouthrot* 21, 9, 11 (*SEG* XXXVIII 478);
*IBouthrot* 184 (d. Ἀφροδίσιος, Λαοδίκα); (8) ~
ib. 21, 40 (*SEG* XXXVIII 478); (9) ~ *IBouthrot*
25, 19 (*SEG* XXXVIII 483); *IBouthrot* 47, 12,
15; (10) ~ ib. 27, 9 (*SEG* XXXVIII 485); (11)
~ *IBouthrot* 28, 24 (*SEG* XXXVIII 486); (12) ~
*IBouthrot* 29, 41 (*SEG* XXXVIII 487); (13) ~
*IBouthrot* 31, 52, 64 (*SEG* XXXVIII 490); (14)
~ *IBouthrot* 31, 92 (*SEG* XXXVIII 490); (15) ~
*IBouthrot* 32, 15 (*SEG* XXXVIII 491); (16) ~
*IBouthrot* 40, 11 (*SEG* XXXVIII 499)
—NIKOPOLIS: (17) imp. *CIG* 1811 b (Sarikakis
108) (Μεμμία Κ.: m. Κλ. Γλυκέρα)
ILLYRIA:
—APOLLONIA: (18) hell. *IApoll* 106; (19) imp.
ib. 376 (d. Θεομένης)
KORINTHIA:
—KORINTH: (20) c. 570-550 BC Amyx 77. 2
(vase) (Lorber 111) (Κλεοπά[τ]ρα: her.)
—SIKYON: (21) i BC-i AD *IG* II² 10307 (Skalet
182) (d. Ἀρτέμων)
—HIPPOLA: (22) ii-iii AD *SEG* XXVI 456, 9 (d.
Εὐαμερίδας, m. Εὐαμερίδας)
S. ITALY (APULIA):
—CANUSIUM*: (23) ?s. i BC *Epig. Rom. di
Canosa* 132 (Lat. Firmilia Cleopatra: freed.)

—LARINUM*: (24) imp. *CIL* IX 6253 (Lat. Me-
dia Cleopatra: m. Νικηφόρος: freed.)
S. ITALY (CALABRIA):
—BRENTESION-BRUNDISIUM*: (25) imp.
*NScav* 1893, p. 443 no. 5 (Lat. Servaea
Cleopatra: freed.)
S. ITALY (CAMPANIA):
—ATELLA: (26) imp. *CIL* X 3746 (Lat. Cleo-
patra)
—DIKAIARCHIA-PUTEOLI: (27) imp. ib. 1945
(Lat. Tuccia Cleopatra); (28) ~ ib. 2303 (Lat.
Clodia Cleopatra: d. Σωτηρίς)
—NEAPOLIS: (29) imp. *IG* XIV 793, 1, 9 (*INap*
130)
—POMPEII: (30) i BC-i AD *CIL* IV 8324 (Lat.
Cleopatra)
SICILY:
—SYRACUSE: (31) ii-i BC *IG* II² 10393
—THERMAI HIMERAIAI: (32) imp. ib. XIV 329;
*Kokalos* 20 (1974) p. 242 no. 14 (date) (d. Νε-
μηνίδας); (33) ?ii AD *CIL* X 7352 (*ILat. Term.
Imer.* 18) (Lat. Antia Cleopatra)

## Κλεόπατρος
ACHAIA: (1) c. 220 BC Plu., *Arat.* 40
AITOLIA: (2) m. iii BC *IG* V (2) 419, 2 (*IPArk*
28) ?= (Κλεύπατρος (1))
ILLYRIA:
—LYCHNIDOS: (3) ii-iii AD Demitsas 331
KERKYRA: (4) imp. *IG* IX (1) 958

## Κλεοπείθης
AKARNANIA:
—THYRREION: (1) 167 BC *Klio* 75 (1993) p. 132,
5-6 (s. Κλεοσθένης)

## Κλεόπολις
ACHAIA:
—PATRAI: (1) ii BC *Achaean Grave Stelai* 64
(s./d. Τρύφων)
ARGOLIS:
—ARGOS: (2) f. iii BC *IG* IV (1) 529, 24
(Κλε[όπ]ολις)

## Κλεοπτόλεμος
EPIROS:
—BOUTHROTOS (PRASAIBOI): (1) a. 163 BC
*IBouthrot* 22, 28 (*SEG* XXXVIII 479); (2) ~
*IBouthrot* 28, 38 (*SEG* XXXVIII 478) (s. Νι-
κόλαος); (3) ~ *IBouthrot* 42, 14 (*SEG* XXXVIII
501); (4) ~ *IBouthrot* 43, 38 (*SEG* XXXVIII
502); *IBouthrot* 48, 4 (s. Μύρτων)
—MIKHALITSI (MOD.): (5) s. iv BC *SEG* XXXVII
530 (f. Διόζοτος)
LAKONIA:
—SPARTA: (6) 684 BC Moretti, *Olymp.* 30 (Po-
ralla² 439)

## Κλέος
EPIROS:
—DODONA: (1) iii BC Antoniou, *Dodone* Aa, 26
([Κλ]έος?)

## Κλεοσθένης
ACHAIA:
—AIGION: (1) c. 271 BC *IG* IX (1)² (1) 12, 15 (f.
Ἀγίας)
AKARNANIA:
—THYRREION: (2) 167 BC *Klio* 75 (1993) p. 132,
6 (f. Κλεοπείθης)
ARGOLIS:
—ARGOS: (3) imp. *IG* IV (1) 609, 3 (Πομπ. Κ.);
(4) ii AD *SEG* XVI 258 a, 3; 258 b, 3; 258 c, 3;
259, 5 (Γν. Πομπ. Κ.: I f. Γν. Πομπ. Διόδοτος,
Γν. Πομπ. Κλεοσθένης II, Γν. Πομπ. Καλλέας);
(5) ~ ib. 258 b, 4 (Γν. Πομπ. Κ.: II s. Γν.
Πομπ. Κλεοσθένης I, ?s. Κλ. Φιλομάθεια); (6) ~
*Corinth* VIII (1) 15, 48
—(Pamphyloi): (7) iv/iii BC *SEG* XI 293, 3
ARKADIA:
—KLEITOR: (8) c. 140-120 BC *BCH* 60 (1936)
p. 12 no. 1, 8, 16 (f. Νικέας)
—PHIGALEIA: (9) imp. *SEG* XXIII 249 (Κλεο-
σθέν[ης], Κλεοσθέν[εια]?)
—TEGEA: (10) ?i BC *IG* V (2) 167

**Illyria:**
—EPIDAMNOS-DYRRHACHION: (11) 516 BC Moretti, *Olymp.* 141; cf. Ebert, *Gr. Sieg.* 4 (s. Πόντις)
**Lakonia:**
—SPARTA: (12) 416 BC X., *HG* ii 3. 10 (Poralla² 441)
**Leukas:** (13) hell. *IG* IX (1) 561
**Messenia:**
—MESSENE: (14) f. iii BC *PAE* 1991, p. 99 no. 7, 5
—THOURIA: (15) ii-i BC *IG* v (1) 1385, 7 (f. Κλεόνικος)
**Peloponnese?:** (16) s. iii BC ib. 1426, 28 (s. Ἀλέξιππος)
**S. Italy (Bruttium):**
—KROTON: (17) iv BC Iamb., *VP* 267 (*FVS* 1 p. 446)
—LOKROI EPIZEPHYRIOI:
——(Προ.): (18) iv/iii BC De Franciscis 6, 5; 8, 5; 31, 5 (s. Τιμασίπολις, f. Τιμασίπολις)
**Sicily:**
—GELA-PHINTIAS: (19) c. 525-500 BC Dubois, *IGDS* 142 b (vase) (Arena, *Iscr. Sic.* II 13) (Κλεο[σ]θένἒς)

**Κλεοσθένιος**
**Argolis:**
—MYKENAI: (1) iii BC *IG* IV (1) 501

**Κλεοσιμένης**
**Lakonia:**
—SPARTA: (1) 345-340 BC *CID* II 31, 76; 32, 9; 120 A, 20 (Poralla² 442; Bradford (-))

**Κλεόστρατος**
**Akarnania:**
—THYRREION: (1) ii/i BC *IG* IX (1)² (2) 256, 6
**Argolis:**
—ARGOS: (2) 408 BC X., *HG* i 3. 13; (3) c. 340-335 BC *CID* II 46 B II, [4]?; 54, 8; 59 I, 25; 62 III B, 79 (Κλεύστρατος—59)
—ARGOS?: (4) v BC *IG* IV (1) 552, 7
**Arkadia:**
—TEGEA: (5) m. iv BC ib. v (2) 6, 74
——(Hippothoitai): (6) iii BC ib. 40, 41 (s. Κάλλιππος)
**Dalmatia:**
—ISSA:
——(Hylleis): (7) iv/iii BC Brunšmid p. 9, 65 (Κλεόστ[ρατος])
**Illyria:**
—EPIDAMNOS-DYRRHACHION: (8) a. 179 BC *Syll³* 638, 13 (*IDyrrh* 520); Kramolisch p. 54 A, 18 (date) (s. Δάμαρχος)
**Lakonia:**
—KYTHERA: (9) ?255-254 BC Nachtergael, *Les Galates* 8, 33; 9, 45; cf. Stephanis 2308 (f. Στρατοκλῆς)
**Leukas:** (10) hell.-imp. *AD* 44 (1989) Chron. p. 266 (*Ep. Chron.* 31 (1994) p. 43)
**Messenia:**
—MESSENE: (11) iii BC *SEG* XXIII 210, 28 ([Κλ]ε[ό]στρατος: name—*LGPN*); (12) c. 223 BC *IG* IX (1)² (1) 31, 36 (f. Στέφανος)

**Κλεότας**
**Aitolia:**
—APERANTOI: (1) ?ii BC ib. 163 (s. Τέλεμμος)

**Κλεότιμος**
**Aitolia:**
—KALLION/KALLIPOLIS: (1) a. 170 BC ib. IX (1) 226, 11
**Argolis:**
—EPIDAUROS: (2) s. vii BC Plu., *Mor.* 403 D
**Elis:** (3) c. 343 BC D. xviii 295
**Epiros:**
—BOUTHROTOS (PRASAIBOI): (4) a. 163 BC *IBouthrot* 14, 15 (*SEG* XXXVIII 471) (f. Ἀνδρόνικος)

**Korinthia:**
—SIKYON: (5) 341 BC *CID* II 12 I, 61 (f. Ἐρωτίων)

**Κλεούτας**
**Epiros:**
—DODONA*: (1) iv-iii BC *SGDI* 1559 (*Syll³* 1165)

**Κλεοφάης**
**Arkadia:**
—KAPHYAI: (1) f. iii BC *BCH* 38 (1914) p. 459 no. 4, 1 (Κλε[ο]φάης: s. Κλεόνικος)

**Κλεοφάνης**
**Achaia:**
—DYME*: (1) c. 219 BC *SGDI* 1612, 54 (*Tyche* 5 (1990) p. 124) (f. Νίκαρχος)
**Arkadia:**
—TEGEA: (2) f. iii BC *IG* v (2) 35, 25 (f. Σῖμος)
**Epiros:**
—PEUKESTOI: (3) iii BC ib. IX (1)² (2) 243, 2 (s. Ἀλύπητος)
**Leukas:** (4) iv BC *AM* 27 (1902) p. 369 no. 38

**Κλεοφάντα**
**Argolis:**
—HERMIONE: (1) ii-i BC *IG* IV (1) 732 I, 2 ([Κ]λεοφάντα: m. Σωσίστρατος); (2) ii/i BC ib. 721 (d. Ὀλυμπιόδωρος)

**Κλεοφαντίς**
**Arkadia:**
—MANTINEIA-ANTIGONEIA: (1) f. iv BC ib. II² 9281 + *ZPE* 29 (1978) p. 68, 1 (d. Σαώτας, m. Λαμιεύς)

**Κλεόφαντος**
**Lakonia:**
—SPARTA: (1) c. 70-100 AD *IG* v (1) 676, 2 (Bradford (2)) (f. Ἀγαθοκλῆς); (2) c. 140-160 AD *IG* v (1) 156 a, 2 (Bradford (1)) (Γ. Ἰούλ. Κ.)
**S. Italy (Bruttium):**
—RHEGION: (3) ?m. v BC Dubois, *IGDGG* I 39 a (Arena, *Iscr. Sic.* III 63); *LSAG²* p. 244 (date) (s. Γλαυκίης)

**Κλεόφατος**
**Messenia:**
—MESSENE: (1) i AD *IG* v (1) 1436, 9 (Κλεόφα(ν)τος?); (2) 54-68 AD ib. 1449, 6 (Κλεόφα(ν)τος?: s. Ἀριστεύς)

**Κλεόφρων**
**Arkadia:**
—ORCHOMENOS: (1) imp. ib. v (2) 349 b ([Κ]λεόφρων)
**S. Italy (Bruttium):**
—KROTON: (2) iv BC Iamb., *VP* 267 (*FVS* 1 p. 446)
—RHEGION: (3) vi/v BC Schol. Pi., *P.* ii 20 (s. Ἀναξίλας: tyrant)

**Κλεοφῶν**
**Dalmatia:**
—ISSA: (1) iii BC Brunšmid p. 9 fr. G, 4 ([Κλ]εοφῶντο[ς] (gen.), [Θ]εοφῶντο[ς]?, [Λ]εοφῶντο[ς]?)
**Ithake:** (2) hell. *SEG* XVII 257; cf. Fraser-Rönne, *BWGT* pl. 23 (f. Ἐχεκράτεια)
**Korinthia:**
—KORINTH: (3) inc. Clem. Al., *Strom.* i 132. 3

**Κλεόχα**
**S. Italy (Bruttium):**
—LOKROI EPIZEPHYRIOI: (1) iv/iii BC *HE* 2802 (m. Θευφιλίς)

**Κλεοχάρης**
**Lakonia:**
—SPARTA: (1) ?c. 550-525 BC *IG* v (1) 216 (Lazzarini 831); *LSAG²* p. 199 no. 21 (date) (Poralla² 443) (Κλεοχά[ρης])

**Κλεόχαρμος**
**Epiros:**
—BOUTHROTOS (PRASAIBOI): (1) a. 163 BC *IBouthrot* 36, 6 (*SEG* XXXVIII 495) (f. Μενέχαρμος)

**Κλεπάτρα**
**Lakonia:**
—PYRRHICHOS: (1) ii-i BC *IG* v (1) 1286

**Κλέπτιος**
**S. Italy (Lucania):**
—LEUKANOI: (1) 103 BC D.S. xxxvi 8

**Κλέπωρ**
**Illyria:**
—EPIDAMNOS-DYRRHACHION: (1) hell. *IDyrrh* 304 (f. Ματιώ)

**Κλεσθένης**
**Illyria:**
—EPIDAMNOS-DYRRHACHION: (1) iv BC ib. 39

**Κλέστρατος**
**Illyria:**
—EPIDAMNOS-DYRRHACHION: (1) c. 250-50 BC Maier 271 (coin) (Ceka 234; 324) (pryt.)

**Κλευάνδρα**
**Argolis:**
—ARGOS: (1) a. 303 BC *CEG* II 816, 10; (2) ~ ib. l. 20 ([Κ]λευάνδρα)

**Κλεύας**
**Lakonia:**
—SPARTA: (1) c. 550 BC *HE* 1365 (Poralla² 444) (s. Ἐτυμοκλῆς: dub.)

**Κλεύβοτος**
**Arkadia:**
—TEGEA: (1) ?iv/iii BC *HE* 669 (s. Ἐριασπίδας)

**Κλεύβουλος**
**Illyria?:**
—DAULIA: (1) f. ii BC *BCH* 45 (1921) p. 22 IV, 32; p. 65 n. 3 (locn.) (s. Νικόστρατος)

**Κλευγένης**
**Arkadia:** (1) s. iv BC *Thess. Mnem.* 176 (s. Περίανδρος)

**Κλευγενίδας**
**Lakonia:**
—AMYKLAI*: (1) vi BC *IG* v (1) 827 (Poralla² 445) (Κ[λ]ευγενίδας—*IG*, Εὐγενίδας?)

**Κλευδάμας**
**Kynouria:**
—THYREA?: (1) iv BC *SEG* XXXV 284 (or Kynouria Eua?: date—*LGPN*)

**Κλεύδαμος**
**Aitolia:** (1) ?209 or 205 BC Flacelière p. 407 no. 38 b, [2]; Nachtergael, *Les Galates* 68, 3
**Argolis:**
—ARGOS: (2) iii BC *IG* IV (1)² 321 (s. Σώδαμος)
**Dalmatia:**
—PHAROS: (3) iv BC Brunšmid p. 20 no. 6 (μικρός: s. Δημόδοκος)

**Κλεύδικος**
**Dalmatia:**
—ISSA: (1) f. ii BC ib. p. 23 no. 10, 3 (f. Ζώϊλος)

**Κλεύδωρος**
**S. Italy (Lucania):**
—HYELE-VELIA: (1) s. iv BC *Silver Coinage of Velia* pp. 73-92

**Κλεύθηρος**
**S. Italy (Bruttium):**
—LOKROI EPIZEPHYRIOI:
——(Λακ.): (1) 276 BC De Franciscis 23, 4 (f. Ξεναίνετος)

## Κλευκράτης

ARGOLIS:
—ARGOS: (**1**) ii-i BC *IG* IV (1) 530, 12; cf. *BCH* 33 (1909) p. 183 n. 2
EPIROS:
—BOUTHROTOS (PRASAIBOI): (**2**) a. 163 BC *IBouthrot* 13, 17; cf. Ugolini, *Alb. Ant.* 3 p. 120 (Κλευκ[ράτης]?, Κλεύκ[ριτος]?: f. Ἡράκλειτος)

## Κλεύκριτος

ARKADIA:
—MANTINEIA-ANTIGONEIA: (**1**) ?272 BC *FD* III (1) 33, 1 (s. Περικλῆς)

## Κλεϋλλίς

SICILY:
—KAMARINA: (**1**) s. iv BC Dubois, *IGDS* 115 (vase) (Cordano, 'Camarina VII' 126)

## Κλεῦλος

SICILY:
—SELINOUS: (**1**) ?m. vi BC Dubois, *IGDS* 45 (Arena, *Iscr. Sic.* I 41; Lazzarini 880 d; *IG-LMP* 58) (Κλεϋλίδαι (n. gent.))

## Κλευμάχη

KEPHALLENIA:
—KRANIOI: (**1**) hell.-imp. *IG* IX (1) 615

## Κλεύμαχος

EPIROS:
—AMBRAKIA: (**1**) iv BC *Op. Ath.* 10 (1971) p. 64 no. 7 (f. Ἰάρων)

## Κλευμένης

AITOLIA:
—CHALKIS: (**1**) hell. *SEG* XXV 623 a
—KOTTAEIS: (**2**) ?268 BC *SGDI* 2598 (s. Κρεύθων)
AKARNANIA:
—PALAIROS: (**3**) ?iii BC *IG* IX (1)² (2) 542 (?s. Στίλπων)

## Κλευμήδης

ILLYRIA:
—EPIDAMNOS-DYRRHACHION: (**1**) hell.-imp. *IDyrrh* 232 ([Κ]λ(ε)υμήδης: f. Ζωσίμα)

## Κλεύμναστος

ITHAKE: (**1**) hell.? *BCH* 29 (1905) p. 164 no. 3

## Κλευνίκα

ILLYRIA:
—EPIDAMNOS-DYRRHACHION: (**1**) i BC/i AD *GP* 215 (-κη)

## Κλευνίκη

DALMATIA:
—PHAROS: (**1**) iv/iii BC Brunšmid p. 15 no. 2 (d. Ἑρμάγορος)

## Κλευπάτρα

ACHAIA:
—DYME: (**1**) ii BC *SEG* XXXI 379, 2
AITOLIA:
—TRICHONION: (**2**) 183 BC *SGDI* 2133, 10 (d. Εὔμναστος)
EPIROS:
—BOUTHROTOS (PRASAIBOI): (**3**) a. 163 BC *IBouthrot* 104, 8
—PRASAIBOI: (**4**) a. 163 BC ib. 99, 4 (*BCH* 118 (1994) p. 121 B)

## Κλεύπατρος

AITOLIA: (**1**) c. 249-239 BC *FD* III (3) 167, 2 ?= (Κλεόπατρος (2))

## Κλευσθένης

ARGOLIS:
—EPIDAUROS: (**1**) c. 365-335 BC *IG* IV (1)² 103, 137

## Κλεύστρατος

DALMATIA:
—ISSA:
——(Pamphyloi): (**1**) iv/iii BC Brunšmid p. 8, 31 (s. Κλεόμηλος)

## Κλευφάνης

KEPHALLENIA:
—SAME: (**1**) 208 BC *IMM* 35, 34 (s. Σίμακος)

## Κλεψίας

DALMATIA:
—ISSA: (**1**) ii BC *SEG* XXXI 599, 1-2 (f. Δωρόθεος, Εὐπόλεμος)

## Κλεώ

AKARNANIA:
—THYRREION: (**1**) s. iii BC *IG* IX (1)² (2) 285 (d. Διόφαντος); (**2**) f. ii BC ib. 297
ARGOLIS:
—HERMIONE: (**3**) ii/i BC *SEG* XVII 162 (d. Ἀριστίων)
ARKADIA:
—KLEITOR: (**4**) i AD *IG* V (2) 379 (Κ(λ)εώ)
—MEGALOPOLIS: (**5**) iv/iii BC ib. 479, 4
ARKADIA?: (**6**) s. v BC *SEG* XLI 386 a
EPIROS:
—AMBRAKIA: (**7**) hell.? ib. XXIV 416 (d. Ἀρχίας)
ILLYRIA: (**8**) 186 BC *SGDI* 2046, 2 etc. (slave/freed.)
KEPHALLENIA:
—PRONNOI: (**9**) hell. Unp. (*IG* arch.)
KORINTHIA:
—KORINTH: (**10**) iv BC *SEG* XVIII 138 (Lazzarini 352) (d. Θασίς)
MESSENIA: (**11**) vii BC Paus. iii 14. 4
S. ITALY (CALABRIA):
—BRENTESION-BRUNDISIUM: (**12**) inc. *NScav* 1901, p. 307 no. 5 (Lat. Clio)
S. ITALY (LUCANIA):
—METAPONTION: (**13**) v BC *SEG* XXIX 961 (Κλεό)

## Κλέων

ACHAIA: (**1**) 146 BC *IG* IV (1)² 28, 94 (s. Νίκανδρος: synoikos)
—AIGION: (**2**) 214 BC ib. IX (1)² (1) 31, 175 (s. Αἰσχρίας)
—DYME: (**3**) iii BC *AJPh* 31 (1910) p. 399 no. 74 b, 2 (f. Ἀσκλαπιάδας); (**4**) iii-ii BC *Syll*³ 530, 3; cf. *Achaia und Elis* p. 115
—DYME*: (**5**) c. 219 BC *SGDI* 1612, 18 (*Tyche* 5 (1990) p. 124) (s. Ἐπιτέλης); (**6**) ~ *SGDI* 1612, 33 (*Tyche* 5 (1990) p. 124) (s. Ἀλεξίων)
—PELLENE: (**7**) m. iii BC *IG* V (2) 368, 110 (s. Πομπίας)
—PHARAI: (**8**) iv/iii BC ib. XII (8) 637
AIGINA: (**9**) ?i BC *Alt-Ägina* I (2) p. 45 no. 14 (Κλέω[ν]); (**10**) ?f. i BC ib. p. 43 no. 4, 3 (s. Ἀσκληπιάδης); (**11**) ?s. i BC ib. p. 44 no. 6, 4 ([Κ]λέων, Λέων?)
AITOLIA: (**12**) c. 249-239 BC *FD* III (3) 167, 4
—KALYDON: (**13**) m. ii BC *IG* IX (1)² (1) 137, 24
—POTIDANIA: (**14**) m. ii BC *SBBerlAk* 1936, p. 371 b, 3, 10 (*SEG* XLI 528 B) (s. Φιλάνβροτος)
AKARNANIA:
—ALYZIA: (**15**) iv BC *IG* IX (1)² (2) 444 (s. Μένετος)
—ASTAKOS: (**16**) ii BC ib. 435, 14 (f. Σωτίων)
—PALAIROS: (**17**) iii BC ib. 525; (**18**) ii BC ib. 451, 2 ([Κλ]έων: f. Φιλόξενος)
—THYRREION: (**19**) iii BC ib. 263 (s. Δεξίδαμος)
ARGOLIS:
—ARGOS: (**20**) c. 458 BC ib. I³ 1149, 77 (-ōν)
—ARGOS?: (**21**) v BC ib. IV (1) 552, 11 (-ōν); (**22**) s. iv BC *AR* 1990-1, p. 17 (sculptor)
—ARGOS*: (**23**) ii BC *SEG* XLII 279, 19 (slave/freed.?)
—EPIDAUROS: (**24**) 608 BC Moretti, *Olymp.* 74
—HERMIONE: (**25**) iii BC *IG* IV (1) 729 II, 4 (f. Πεισίνοος)
—PHLEIOUS: (**26**) iii-ii BC ib. 476

ARKADIA:
—LYKOSOURA*: (**27**) ii/i BC ib. V (2) 522 (s. Θρασέας)
—MEGALOPOLIS: (**28**) ii BC ib. 447, 3 ([Κ]λέων: s. Κλ—); (**29**) ?145 BC ib. 439, 59 (f. Νικανδρία); (**30**) ii AD *SEG* XIV 347, 5, 7 (f. —ππος)
—PHENEOS: (**31**) i-ii AD *IG* II² 10478 (Κλέω[ν]: s. Ἀνδρόνικος)
—TEGEA: (**32**) s. v BC ib. V (2) 175, 1 (-ōν); (**33**) m. iv BC ib. 6, 67; (**34**) f. iii BC ib. 35, 21 (f. Νικόλας); (**35**) s. iii BC ib. 116, 2 (f. Εὔαρχος); (**36**) f. ii BC ib. 44, 8 (f. Χαρέας)
DALMATIA:
—ISSA: (**37**) iii/ii BC *SEG* XXXV 684 (*VAHD* 84 (1991) p. 254 no. 5) (f. Εὐκλέα)
EPIROS:
—AMBRAKIA: (**38**) hell.? *CIG* 1805 (f. Φιλία); (**39**) f. iii BC Unp. (Arta Mus., inscr.) (f. Λέων)
—BOUTHROTOS (PRASAIBOI):
——Kleonaioi: (**40**) a. 163 BC *IBouthrot* 120, 10 (f. Θεότιμος)
ILLYRIA:
—EPIDAMNOS-DYRRHACHION: (**41**) c. 250-50 BC Maier 235; 364; Münsterberg p. 40; Nachtr. p. 14 (coin) (Ceka 257-61) (money.); (**42**) hell.-imp. *IDyrrh* 90 (f. Ἀλεξήν); (**43**) ~ ib. 364 (f. Πρεύρατος)
ITHAKE: (**44**) hell. *IG* IX (1) 662
KORINTHIA:
—SIKYON: (**45**) vi/v BC *SEG* XI 244, 9 (-ōν); (**46**) f. iv BC Marcadé I 60-1 (Skalet 183) (sculptor); (**47**) 279 BC *IG* XI (2) 108, 23 (Skalet 185; Stephanis 1460); (**48**) c. 270 BC *RE* (2) (Skalet 186) (tyrant); (**49**) ?255 BC Nachtergael, *Les Galates* 8, 29 (Skalet 184; Stephanis 1466) (s. Σωσικράτης)
LAKONIA:
—GYTHEION: (**50**) hell. *IG* V (1) 1203
—KARDAMYLE: (**51**) ?ii-i BC *SEG* XXVIII 405 (Κλεοφ[ῶ]ν?—*LGPN*
—SPARTA: (**52**) c. 146-32 BC *Münzpr. der Laked.* p. 124 Group 8 series 21 (coin) (Bradford (34)); (**53**) i BC-i AD? *IG* V (1) 690 (Bradford (10)) (s. Πεικλείδας); (**54**) s. i BC *IG* V (1) 94, 13 (Bradford (23)) (I f. Κλέων II); (**55**) ~ *IG* V (1) 94, 13 (Bradford (8)) (II s. Κλέων I); (**56**) ~ *SEG* XI 873 d (brick) (Bradford (16)); (**57**) c. 30-20 BC *IG* V (1) 211, 28 (Bradford (32)) (f. Τιμοκλῆς); (**58**) c. 25-1 BC *IG* V (1) 210, 20 (Bradford (2)) (s. Καλλικράτης); (**59**) ~ *IG* V (1) 212, 46 (Bradford (15)) (freed.); (**60**) ?i-ii AD *IG* V (1) 668 (Bradford (14)) (s. Τίμαρχος); (**61**) c. 100-125 AD *IG* V (1) 137, 8 (Bradford (19)); (**62**) f. ii AD *IG* V (1) 20 B, 3; 99, 6; 502, 9; *BSA* 26 (1923-5) p. 168 C 7, [1] (Bradford (24); (28)) (I f. Κλέων II); (**63**) ~ *IG* V (1) 20 B, 3; 99, 6; 138, 5; 502, 2, 9; *BSA* 26 (1923-5) p. 168 C 7, [1] (Bradford (8); (24)) (II s. Κλέων I, Ἀγησιππία, f. Κλέων III); (**64**) ~ *IG* V (1) 20 B, 7; 51, 35; 52, 7; 660, 2; *SEG* XI 537 a, 7; 537 b, 3; 538, [4]; 594, 3 (Bradford (13)) (s. Σωσικράτης); (**65**) c. 105 AD *SEG* XI 546 a, 3; 546 b, 3 (Bradford (29)) (f. Λυκοῦργος); (**66**) c. 110-125 AD *IG* V (1) 32 B, 27; *SEG* XI 542, 6; 575, [1]; 613, [2] (Bradford (31)) (f. Σίπομπος); (**67**) m. ii AD *IG* V (1) 138, 5; 502, 2 (Bradford (5); (9)) (III s. Κλέων II); (**68**) 127 AD *IG* V (1) 1314, 29 (Bradford (6)) (II s. Κλέων I); (**69**) ~ *IG* V (1) 1314, [29] (Bradford (26)) (I f. Κλέων II); (**70**) c. 130 AD *IG* V (1) 60, 4 (Bradford (27)) (I f. Κλέων II); (**71**) ~ *IG* V (1) 60, [4] (Bradford (7)) (II s. Κλέων I); (**72**) c. 132 AD *SEG* XI 579, 5 (Bradford (17)); (**73**) ?134 AD *IG* V (1) 62, 13 (Bradford (12)) (s. Σίπομπος); (**74**) c. 140-145 AD *IG* V (1) 1314, 39 (Bradford (20)); (**75**) c. 140-160 AD *IG* V (1) 112, 10 (Bradford (30)) (f. Νικοκλῆς); (**76**) 147 AD *SEG* XI 493, 1; 498, 2; 551, 2 (Bradford (18)); (**77**) c. 150-160 AD *IG* V (1) 53, 16 (Bradford (11)) (s. Φιλόθεος); (**78**)

c. 170 AD *IG* v (1) 116, 1 (Bradford (21)) ([Γ.]
Ἰούλ. Κ.)
—SPARTA?: (**79**) ii BC *IG* XII (9) 900 A c, 2, 6
(Bradford (1)) (s. Εὐνοστίδας)
—TEUTHRONE: (**80**) imp. *IG* v (1) 1220 a (s.
Δάμαρχος, f. Φίλιππος)
MESSENIA:
—KORONE: (**81**) ii BC ib. 1397, 9
—MESSENE: (**82**) iii BC *SEG* XXIII 209, 5
—THOURIA: (**83**) f. ii BC ib. XI 972, 71 (s. Δαμο-
σθένης); (**84**) ~ ib. l. 88 (f. Τιμοσθένης)
S. ITALY: (**85**) iv BC *RE* (10) (Stephanis 1457)
?= (*96*)
S. ITALY (APULIA):
—SPINAZZOLA (MOD.): (**86**) ?i BC *SEG* XXXIII
759 (biling.) (Lat. [C.] [Ma]rcius Cleon: doc-
tor/freed.)
S. ITALY (BRUTTIUM):
—SYBARIS-THOURIOI-COPIAE: (**87**) f. iii BC
*SNG ANS Etruria–Calabria* 1196 (coin)
S. ITALY (CALABRIA):
—TARAS-TARENTUM: (**88**) iv BC Iamb., *VP* 267
(*FVS* 1 p. 446)
SICILY: (**89**) s. iv BC Berve 437 (Lat. Cleo) ?=
(*95*)
—AKRAI: (**90**) ?iii BC *SGDI* 3239, 10 (*Akrai* p.
157 no. 9) (s. Νυμφόδωρος)
—GELA-PHINTIAS: (**91**) 311 BC *PEleph* 1, 17
—MEGARA HYBLAIA: (**92**) vi/v BC *Arch. Sicilia
sud-orient.* p. 168 no. 478 (terracotta) (-ōν)
—MORGANTINA: (**93**) iv/iii BC *SEG* XXXIX 1013,
6 ([Κ]λέων?: f. Ἰάρων); (**94**) ~ ib. l. 7
—SYRACUSE: (**95**) ?s. iv BC *RE* (8) ?= (*89*); (**96**)
s. iv BC Curt. viii 5.8 (Berve 437) (Lat. Cleon)
?= (*85*)
—TAUROMENION: (**97**) c. 193 BC *IG* XIV 421 an.
48 (*SGDI* 5219) (s. Σώσανδρος)
ZAKYNTHOS: (**98**) iii-ii BC *AA* 1932, p. 155 no.
4 (f. Ἀριστονίκη)

**Κλεωναῖος**
S. ITALY (CAMPANIA):
—DIKAIARCHIA-PUTEOLI: (**1**) c. 165-172 AD
*Puteoli* 7-8 (1983-4) p. 81 (Lat. L. Flavius
Cleonaeus: f. Πολυμνία)

**Κλεωνίδας**
ARGOLIS:
—TROIZEN: (**1**) ?146 BC *IG* IV (1) 757 B, 42 (s.
Κλεισθένης)

**Κλεωνίκα**
LAKONIA:
—SPARTA: (**1**) imp. ib. v (1) 522 (Bradford (-))

**Κλεωνίς**
ARGOLIS:
—ARGOS: (**1**) iii-ii BC *IG* IV (1) 630 b
ARKADIA:
—MANTINEIA-ANTIGONEIA: (**2**) ?iv BC ib. v (2)
291
—TEGEA: (**3**) ?i AD ib. 231

**Κλεώνομος**
ARKADIA:
—MANTINEIA-ANTIGONEIA: (**1**) c. 300-221 BC
ib. 323. 80 (tessera) (s. Τιμαίνετος)
—TEGEA:
——(Hippothoitai): (**2**) iii BC ib. 40, 38 (f. Ἀγέ-
μαχος)
——(Krariotai): (**3**) c. 369-362 BC ib. 173, 32;
cf. *CEG* II 657 ([Κλεώ]νομος?: name—*LGPN*)

**Κλεώνυμος**
ACHAIA: (**1**) ?253 BC Nachtergael, *Les Galates*
10, 57
ACHAIA?: (**2**) c. 300 BC *SEG* XIV 375, 5
AITOLIA: (**3**) 290-280 BC *FD* III (1) 149, 1 (f.
Ἀνδρομένης)
AKARNANIA: (**4**) 208 BC *IMM* 31, 2 (*IG* IX (1)²
(2) 582) (s. Λαμίσκος)

—THYRREION: (**5**) 216 BC ib. 583, 18
(Κλεώνυμ[ος]: f. Αἰσχρίων); (**6**) 167 BC *Klio* 75
(1993) p. 132, 4 (f. Αἰσχρίων)
ARGOLIS:
—ARGOS?: (**7**) m. iv BC Thphr. fr. 83 (Stephanis
1467)
—EPIDAUROS: (**8**) iii/ii BC *IG* IV (1)² 336 (f.
Κλεονίκα, Εὐρυδίκα)
—MYKENAI*: (**9**) hell. *SEG* XIII 238 b (tiles)
—PHLEIOUS: (**10**) s. iii BC Plb. ii 44. 6; *RE* (4)
(tyrant)
ARKADIA:
—ALIPHEIRA*: (**11**) ?273 BC *SEG* XXV 447, 3,
7, 16 (*IPArk* 24); *Chiron* 3 (1973) pp. 85-93
(ident., date) ?= (*20*)
ELIS:
—LASION: (**12**) vi BC *SEG* XI 1173 a, 2 (f. Ἱπ-
πόνικος)
ILLYRIA:
—APOLLONIA: (**13**) c. 250-50 BC Maier 17; 107
(Münsterberg Nachtr. p. 12-13 (coin); Ceka
70-1) (money.)
—BYLLIONES NIKAIA (KLJOS (MOD.)): (**14**) iii
BC *SEG* XXXVIII 568 (Κλεό-)
—EPIDAMNOS-DYRRHACHION: (**15**) c. 250-50
BC Maier 270; cf. *IApoll Ref. Bibl.* n. 72
(coin) (Κλειώ-: pryt.)
KORINTHIA:
—KORINTH: (**16**) s. v BC *SEG* XXII 251 e (Κλεό-)
LAKONIA:
—GERONTHRAI: (**17**) ii BC ib. II 163, 5
([Κλεώ]νυμος?: s. Ἐτ—)
—SPARTA: (**18**) 423 BC Th. iv 132. 3 (Poralla²
446) (f. Κλεαρίδας); (**19**) c. 393-371 BC X., *HG*
v 4. 25 ff.; vi 4. 14; Plu., *Ages.* 25; 28 (Poralla² 447) (s. Σφοδρίας); (**20**) c. 340-270 BC
*RE* (3) (Bradford (1)) (s. Κλεομένης, f. Λεωνίδας) ?= (*11*); (**21**) hell. *SEG* XI 858 (Bradford (7)) (Κλεώνυ[μος]); (**22**) c. 30-20 BC *IG*
v (1) 211, 46 (Bradford (6)) (s. Κλήτωρ); (**23**)
i BC/i AD *IG* v (1) 48, 12; 95, [5] (Bradford
(11)) (f. Εὐδαμίδας); (**24**) c. 80-120 AD *IG* v
(1) 20 B, 1; 147, 8; *SEG* XI 574, 10? (Bradford (10)) (f. Ἐπιτυγχάνων); (**25**) c. 105-110 AD
*SEG* XI 569, 12 (Bradford (12)) (I f. Κλεώνυμος II); (**26**) ~ *SEG* XI 569, 12 (Bradford (4))
([Κ]λεώνυμος: II s. Κλεώνυμος I); (**27**) c. 105-
122 AD *IG* v (1) 20 B, 1; 97, 19; *SEG* XI 564,
13; 574, 9 (Bradford (14)) (f. Σωκλείδας); (**28**)
c. 140-160 AD *IG* v (1) 154, 15 (Bradford (2))
(s. Εὔτυχος); (**29**) c. 170-190 AD *SEG* XI 627,
3 (Bradford (13)) (I f. Κλεώνυμος II); (**30**) ~
*SEG* XI 627, 3 (Bradford (5)) (II s. Κλεώνυμος
I); (**31**) c. 220 AD *IG* v (1) 653, 5; 653 b, 2
(*Artemis Orthia* pp. 356-8 no. 143; Bradford
(3)) (Μ. Αὐρ. Κ. ὁ καὶ Ὑμνος: s. Ὑμνος); (**32**)
c. 225-250 AD *SEG* XXXIV 308, 10 (Bradford
(13)) (I f. Κλεώνυμος II); (**33**) ~ *SEG* XXXIV
308, 10 (Bradford (5)) (II s. Κλεώνυμος I)
MESSENIA:
—THOURIA: (**34**) f. ii BC *SEG* XI 972, 25 (f. Δαμαρχίδας)

**Κληγόρα**
ARGOLIS:
—ARGOS: (**1**) iv-iii BC *BCH* 27 (1903) p. 265 no.
14; (**2**) iii BC *IG* IV (1) 527, 16; cf. *BCH* 37
(1913) p. 309
KORINTHIA:
—KORINTH?: (**3**) iv BC *IG* II² 9069 (Κληγόρας
(gen.))

**Κληγόρας**
ARGOLIS:
—ARGOS: (**1**) 105 BC *JÖAI* 14 (1911) Beibl. p.
146 no. 4, 25 ([Κ]ληγόρας)

**Κληίνίκα**
LAKONIA:
—SPARTA: (**1**) ?ii BC *IG* v (1) 229 (Bradford (-))

**Κληΐνικος**
LAKONIA:
—SPARTA: (**1**) iii BC *SEG* XL 348 B, 1

**Κλημεντῖνα**
SICILY:
—SYRACUSE: (**1**) iii-v AD *IG* XIV 132 (Strazzulla
71; Wessel 1145) (Κλημε(ν)τεῖνα)

**Κλήμης**
SICILY:
—KATANE: (**1**) imp. *Sic. Gymn.* 14 (1961) p. 190
(f. Ἀρτεμίδωρος)

**Κλῆμις**
AKARNANIA: (**1**) iii BC *PP* 15011 (s. Καλήν)

**Κλήνα**
AIGINA: (**1**) vi/v BC *SEG* XXIII 169; *LSAG*² p.
439 no. 10 (Κλέ-: d. Δαμοσσός)

**Κληναγόρα**
S. ITALY (BRUTTIUM):
—TORANO CASTELLO (MOD.): (**1**) iv BC *GRBS*
26 (1985) p. 181 no. 127

**Κληναγόρας**
KEPHALLENIA:
—PRONNOI: (**1**) s. v BC *SEG* XXV 607 (Κλ̄ε-)
LEUKAS: (**2**) hell.? *IG* IX (1) 577 (Fraser-Rönne,
*BWGT* p. 116 no. 3) = *IG* IX (1) 671? (Κλη-
ναγόρα (masc./fem. voc.?))
SICILY:
—MORGANTINA: (**3**) ?iv/iii BC *SEG* XXXIX 1009,
3 (Κληναγό[ρας]: s. Ἀρίστων)

**Κλήνετος**
DALMATIA:
—ISSA: (**1**) ii/i BC Brunšmid p. 27 no. 19 (*SEG*
XL 515) + *VAHD* 84 (1991) p. 254 no. 4 (f.
Ἀγησίδαμος)

**Κληνίας**
ARKADIA:
—TEGEA: (**1**) iii BC *IG* v (2) 61 b
S. ITALY (APULIA): (**2**) c. 425-400 BC *Second
Suppl. RVAp* 1 p. 6 no. 46a (vase) (s. Δαμέας)
S. ITALY (BRUTTIUM):
—LOKROI EPIZEPHYRIOI:
——(Γαγ.): (**3**) iv/iii BC De Franciscis 39, 6 (f.
Σωσικράτης)

**Κληνίδας**
ARKADIA:
—PHIGALEIA: (**1**) f. iii BC *SEG* XXIII 238 (Κλη-
νίδ[ας])

**Κληνίκης**
LAKONIA:
—SPARTA: (**1**) i BC *IG* v (1) 126, 3 (Bradford
(-)) (Κληνίκεος (gen.): f. Κληνικίδας)

**Κληνικίδας**
LAKONIA:
—SPARTA: (**1**) i BC *IG* v (1) 126, 3 (Bradford
(2)) (s. Κληνίκης); (**2**) c. 25-1 BC *IG* v (1) 210,
31 (Bradford (1)) (s. Ἆγις)

**Κλήνικος**
LAKONIA:
—SPARTA: (**1**) c. 30-20 BC *IG* v (1) 211, 50
(Bradford (2)) (I f. Κλήνικος II); (**2**) ~ *IG* v
(1) 211, 50 (Bradford (1)) (II s. Κλήνικος I)

**Κληνίππα**
ARKADIA:
—PHIGALEIA: (**1**) ii/i BC *IG* v (2) 426
KEPHALLENIA:
—PRONNOI: (**2**) hell. Unp. (*IG* arch.)
ZAKYNTHOS: (**3**) hell. *IG* IX (1) 600 (d. Ἀρχι-
κλῆς, Ἀλκιδάμα)

**Κλήνιππος**
KEPHALLENIA:
—PALE: (**1**) iii/ii BC Unp. (*IG* arch.)
([Κ]λήνιππος)

**Κλῆνις**
ARKADIA:
—PHIGALEIA: (1) s. v BC *IG* v (2) 429, 2 (*IPArk* 27)
SICILY:
—LIPARA: (2) hell.? Libertini, *Isole Eolie* p. 221 no. 23

**Κληνίς**
ACHAIA:
—DYME: (1) ?iii-ii BC *SGDI* 1619 (d. Ἀγίας, m. Φερέμβροτος)

**Κληνιώ**
SICILY:
—LIPARA: (1) ii-i BC *Meligunis-Lipara* 5 p. 148 T. 2143; cf. *SEG* XLI 801 (Ληνιώ—ed., [Κ]ληνιώ—*SEG*)

**Κληνόμαχος**
S. ITALY (LUCANIA):
—HYELE-VELIA: (1) hell.? *PdelP* 21 (1966) p. 336 no. 9 (s. Διονύσιος)

**Κλῆνος**
S. ITALY (CALABRIA):
—TARAS-TARENTUM: (1) iv-iii BC *Boston Mus. Rep.* 38 (1913) p. 98; Wuilleumier, *Tarente* p. 364 (Κληνός? (gen.): date—A.W.J.)

**Κληρέτα**
ARGOLIS:
—EPIDAUROS: (1) iv/iii BC *IG* IV (1)² 203

**Κλήρικος**
S. ITALY (CAMPANIA):
—POMPEII: (1) c. 51-62 AD *CIL* IV 3340. 54, 18 (Castrèn 319. 1) (Lat. Popillius Clericus)

**Κληρισσία**
EPIROS:
—AMBRAKIA: (1) imp.? *Arch. Miss. scient.* III 3 (1876) p. 331 no. 199

**Κλῆρος**
S. ITALY (CAMPANIA):
—HERCULANEUM: (1) 41-79 AD *Cron. Erc.* 7 (1977) p. 115 A c, 9 (Lat. Cn. Octavius Clerus)

**Κλήσαρχος**
S. ITALY (BRUTTIUM):
—LOKROI EPIZEPHYRIOI:
——(Πυρ.): (1) iv/iii BC De Franciscis 16, 5 (s. Ἀριστείδας)
S. ITALY (LUCANIA):
—PADULA (MOD.): (2) vi/v BC *Apollo* 9 (1993) pp. 5-6 (Arena, *Iscr. Sic.* IV 32) (Βυ. Κλέσαρχος)

**Κλησᾶς**
LAKONIA:
—SPARTA: (1) c. 225-250 AD *SEG* XI 806 a, 10 (Bradford (-)) (f. Ἐπιτευκτικός)

**Κλησιμβρότα**
LAKONIA:
—SPARTA: (1) s. vii BC *PMGF* 1 4 fr. 1, 9 (Κλησιμβ[ρότα])

**Κλήσιππος**
ARGOLIS:
—HERMIONE: (1) iii BC *IG* IV (1) 729 II, 13 (f. Φωκύλος)

**Κλησις**
LEUKAS: (1) iv/iii BC *AD* 25 (1970) Chron. p. 332

**Κλήτα?**
ILLYRIA:
—BYLLIONES BYLLIS: (1) ?f. ii BC *SEG* XXXVIII 538

**Κληταγόρα**
AITOLIA:
—APERANTOI: (1) iii/ii BC *SBBerlAk* 1936, p. 388 no. 2, 10 (*L'Illyrie mérid.* 1 p. 110 fig. 7)

**Κληταῖος**
ACHAIA:
—AIGION: (1) c. 32-31 BC *BMC Pelop.* pp. 18-19 nos. 4-9; *Coll. Weber* 3951 (s.p.) (coin); *Ag.* XXVI p. 233 (date) (s. Θέοξις)

**Κλητέας**
ARKADIA:
—TEGEA: (1) s. v BC *IG* v (2) 175, 6 (Κλε̄-)

**Κλητίας**
ELIS: (1) 72 BC Moretti, *Olymp.* 697

**Κλῆτις**
LAKONIA:
—SPARTA: (1) 182 BC Plb. xxiii 18. 5 (Bradford (-))

**Κλητις**
AKARNANIA:
—ANAKTORION: (1) iv/iii BC *IG* IX (1)² (2) 237 (Κλήτιος (gen.), Κλῆτις (nom.)—*IG* index)
EPIROS:
—PRASAIBOI: (2) a. 163 BC *IBouthrot* 58, 8 (*SEG* XXXVIII 509); *IBouthrot* 105, 4? ([Κ]λητώ—105: s./d. Ἀντιφῶν)

**Κλητίων**
ARGOLIS:
—ARGOS:
——(Achaioi): (1) iv/iii BC *SEG* XXX 356, 3

**Κλήτων**
MESSENIA:
—THOURIA: (1) f. ii BC ib. XI 972, 105 (f. Πολυκράτης)

**Κλήτωρ**
LAKONIA:
—SPARTA: (1) c. 30-20 BC *IG* V (1) 211, 46 (Bradford (-)) (f. Κλεώνυμος)

**Κλιμάτιος**
SICILY:
—KATANE: (1) imp. *IG* XIV 2412. 23 (or Sicily Panormos?)

**Κλιμαχίας**
SICILY:
—KEPHALOIDION: (1) f. i BC Cic., *In Verr.* II ii 128-9 (Lat. Artemo Climachias)

**Κλινοσώ?**
ARGOLIS:
—HERMIONE: (1) ?ii-i BC *IG* IV (1) 731 I, 11 (n. pr.?)

**Κλιόι**
EPIROS:
—AMBRAKIA: (1) s. iv BC *SEG* XVII 307 b (d. Εὐθυμένης)

**Κλόγατος?**
S. ITALY (CAMPANIA)?: (1) iv-iii BC *CIG* 8493 (vase)

**Κλύκα?**
KORINTHIA:
—KORINTH: (1) c. 590-570 BC Amyx 25. 2 (vase) (Lorber 35) ((Γ)λύκα?, Κ(α)λύκα—Amyx: het.?/fict.?)

**Κλυμένη**
S. ITALY (BRUTTIUM):
—RHEGION: (1) imp. *CIL* X 8337. 3 (seal) (Lat. Clymene)

S. ITALY (CALABRIA):
—PORTO CESAREO (MOD.): (2) imp. Susini, *Fonti Salento* p. 192 no. 182 (Lat. [Cl]ymaene)
S. ITALY (CAMPANIA):
—DIKAIARCHIA-PUTEOLI: (3) imp. *CIL* X 1941 (Lat. Clymene)
—POMPEII: (4) i BC-i AD ib. IV 1281 (Lat. Clymene); (5) ~ ib. 4756 (Lat. Clymene)
SICILY:
—THERMAI HIMERAIAI: (6) i-ii AD ib. X 7347 (*ILat. Term. Imer.* 11) (Lat. Clymene)

**Κλυμένης**
S. ITALY (CAMPANIA):
—DIKAIARCHIA-PUTEOLI*: (1) imp. *AJA* 2 (1898) p. 378 no. 10 (Lat. M. Caecilius Clymenes: freed.)

**Κλύμενος**
ELIS:
—KOILE (GASTOUNI (MOD.)): (1) imp.? *SEG* XXXIX 397 (tile)
KORINTHIA:
—KORINTH: (2) imp. *CIL* III 6100, 4 (Lat. L. Rutilius Clymenus)
LAKONIA:
—SPARTA: (3) c. 100 AD *SEG* XI 510, 2 (Bradford (-)) (f. Θεοκλύμενος)
S. ITALY (CAMPANIA):
—DIKAIARCHIA-PUTEOLI: (4) imp. *AJA* 2 (1898) p. 378 no. 11 (Lat. M. Caecilius Clymenus)
—POMPEII: (5) i BC-i AD *CIL* IV 1583 (Lat. Clumenus)
S. ITALY (LUCANIA):
—BLANDA IULIA: (6) s. ii AD *Epigraphica* 38 (1976) pp. 138-41 no. 8 (Lat. M. Arrius Clymenus)
—POTENTIA: (7) ?ii-iii AD *CIL* X 8091 (Lat. M. Aurelius Clyminus: I f. Κλύμενος II); (8) ~ ib. (Lat. Aur. Clyminus: II s. Κλύμενος I)

**Κλύτη**
S. ITALY (CAMPANIA):
—DIKAIARCHIA-PUTEOLI*: (1) imp. ib. 2415 (Lat. Clyte: freed.)

**Κλύτιος**
ELIS: (1) her. *RE* (9); (2) 57-61 AD *IvOl* 79, 7 ([Κλ]ύτιος)

**Κλύτος**
AKARNANIA: (1) 191 BC *RE* Supplbd. 11 (9) (Lat. Clytus)
EPIROS:
—NIKOPOLIS: (2) imp. *SEG* XLII 545
KORINTHIA:
—KORINTH: (3) c. 570-550 BC Amyx 113. 1 (vase) (Lorber 100) (ϙλύ-: her.)
S. ITALY (CAMPANIA):
—DIKAIARCHIA-PUTEOLI: (4) imp. *AJA* 2 (1898) p. 379 no. 14 (Lat. Clytus)

**Κλυτώ**
S. ITALY (BRUTTIUM):
—RHEGION*: (1) m. vi BC Rumpf, *Chalkid. Vas.* p. 46 no. 4 (Arena, *Iscr. Sic.* III p. 102-3 no. 7) (ϙλυτό̄: her.?)

**Κλωδία**
SICILY:
—SYRACUSE: (1) iii-v AD *IG* XIV 89 (Strazzulla 30; Wessel 834); *ASSicilia* 1938-9, p. 29 (m. Γέμελλος)

**Κλωδιανός**
SICILY:
—AKRAI: (1) iii-v AD *IG* XIV 237 (Wessel 206; *Akrai* p. 167 no. 42); *IGLMP* 157; cf. Ferrua, *NG* 491
—SYRACUSE: (2) iii-v AD *IG* XIV 133 (Strazzulla 73); (3) ~ ib. 213
—TAUROMENION: (4) iii-v AD *IG* XIV 446 (Wessel 411)

**Κλώδιος**
ILLYRIA:
—APOLLONIA: (**1**) imp. *IApoll* 108 (I f. *Κλώδιος*
II); (**2**) ~ ib. (*Κλώδι* (voc.): II s. *Κλώδιος* I)
PELOPONNESE?: (**3**) II AD *PAE* 1992, p. 72 B,
12 (I f. *Κλώδιος* II); (**4**) ~ ib. l. 12 (II s. *Κλώ-
διος* I)
S. ITALY (CAMPANIA):
—NEAPOLIS: (**5**) inc. Porph., *Abst.* i 3. 3, with
Budé ed. I pp. 25-30
SICILY:
—MOTYKA: (**6**) iii-v AD *NScav* 1907, p. 485

**Κλώδις**
SICILY:
—LIPARA: (**1**) iii-iv AD ib. 1947, p. 218 no. 5 (*K.
Σύντροφος*)

**Κνέφιος**
AKARNANIA:
—ASTAKOS: (**1**) m. iii BC *SEG* XXVII 153, 4; cf.
*PAE* 1977, pl. 244 b (s. *Ἡράκλειτος*)

**Κνῆμος**
LAKONIA:
—SPARTA: (**1**) s. v BC *RE* (-) (Poralla² 448)

**Κνιδιείδας**
SICILY:
—SYRACUSE: (**1**) s. vi BC *SEG* XXXI 841
(Dubois, *IGDS* 86; Lazzarini 821); cf.
*LSAG²* p. 265 no. 3 (*Κνιδιείδᾳ* (gen., n. pr.?):
?f. *Κλεομένης*)

**Κνίδις**
LAKONIA:
—SPARTA: (**1**) s. v BC Th. v 51. 2 (Poralla² 449)
(f. *Ξενάρης*)

**Κνίδος**
S. ITALY (CAMPANIA):
—HERCULANEUM*: (**1**) i BC-i AD *CIL* x 1403 g
I, 34 (Lat. M. Antonius Cnidus: freed.)

**Κνοῖθος**
AIGINA: (**1**) vi/v BC Hdt. vi 88 (f. *Νικόδρομος*)

**Κνύμων**
LAKONIA:
—SPARTA: (**1**) v BC *SEG* XI 859 (Poralla² 449a)
(-μῶν)

**Κόβετος**
SICILY:
—GELA-PHINTIAS?: (**1**) f. v BC Dubois, *IGDS*
134 a, 1 (Arena, *Iscr. Sic.* II 80) (f. *Δᾶμις*)

**Κόγχων**
SICILY:
—SYRACUSE?: (**1**) hell. Manganaro, *PdelP* forth-
coming no. 4 II, 1 (f. *Φίλων*)

**Κοδράτης**
KORINTHIA:
—KORINTH*: (**1**) a. 250 AD *SEG* XXXIV 273

**Κοδράτιλλα**
SICILY:
—AKRAGAS: (**1**) ii-iii AD *IGLMP* 1
([*Κο*]δράτιλλα)

**Κοδρᾶτος**
ILLYRIA:
—APOLLONIA: (**1**) ii AD *IApoll* 109

**Κοθόδιος?**
SICILY:
—LIPARA: (**1**) hell.? *NScav* 1929, p. 65

**Κόθων**
DALMATIA:
—ISSA:
——(Hylleis): (**1**) iv/iii BC Brunšmid p. 7, 21
(*Κόθων*: f. *Ἀπολλ*—)

**Κοΐα**
ILLYRIA:
—EPIDAMNOS-DYRRHACHION: (**1**) hell.-imp.
*IDyrrh* 271 (d. *Ζῆθος*)

**Κοιάτωρ**
SICILY:
—MORGANTINA (NR.): (**1**) ?iii BC Manganaro,
*PdelP* forthcoming no. 8 (*Κοιά*[*τωρ*]: f. *Ὄλτος*)

**Κοικόα**
SICILY:
—SYRACUSE: (**1**) v/iv BC *CGF* pp. 156-7 frr. 16-
18

**Κοίνα**
SICILY:
—GELA-PHINTIAS: (**1**) c. 525-500 BC Dubois,
*IGDS* 142 d (vase) (n. pr.?)

**Κοῖνος**
S. ITALY (CAMPANIA):
—DIKAIARCHIA-PUTEOLI: (**1**) imp. *CIL* x 2026
(Lat. P. Firmus Coenus)

**Κόϊντος**
ARGOLIS:
—ARGOS: (**1**) byz.? *IG* IV (1) 653; cf. *TMByz* 9
(1985) p. 369 no. 108
ELIS: (**2**) ii-iii AD *IvOl* 125, 5 (f. —ος)
EPIROS:
—NIKOPOLIS: (**3**) imp. *AD* 43 (1988) Chron. p.
308 no. 3 (f. *Ἐρωτίς*)
KORINTHIA:
—KORINTH: (**4**) ii-iii AD *SEG* XXVII 35. 13
(lamp)
LAKONIA:
—SPARTA: (**5**) c. 80-100 AD ib. XI 511, 4; 559, 3
(Bradford (2)) (I f. *Κόϊντος* II); (**6**) ~ *SEG* XI
511, 4; 559, 3 (Bradford (1)) (II s. *Κόϊντος* I)
S. ITALY: (**7**) 192 BC *ID* 399 B, 141 ?= (**8**); (**8**)
179 BC ib. 442 B, 34 ?= (**7**)

**Κοῖος**
ELIS:
—OLYMPIA*: (**1**) ?c. 550-525 BC *IvOl* 629;
*LSAG²* p. 220 no. 1 (date) (ϙοῖ-, ϙοῖος?)

**Κοίρανος**
AIGINA?: (**1**) ?c. 450 BC *IG* I³ 1341; *LSAG²* p.
439 no. 24 (date)
KORINTHIA:
—KORINTH*: (**2**) i BC/i AD *SEG* XI 214 c
S. ITALY (CAMPANIA):
—DIKAIARCHIA-PUTEOLI: (**3**) imp. *CIL* x 1931
(Lat. P. Gaulius Coeranus); (**4**) ~ ib. 2311
(Lat. Cocceius Coeranus)
—POMPEII: (**5**) c. 51-62 AD ib. IV 3340. 103, 8
(Lat. L. Melissaeus Coeranus)

**Κοῖρις**
LAKONIA?: (**1**) vi BC *IvOl* 720 (Lazzarini 833);
*LSAG²* p. 202 no. 63 (locn., date)

**Κοιρόμαχος**
AKARNANIA:
—EURIPOS: (**1**) 356-354 BC *IG* IV (1)² 95, 15
(Perlman E.2); Perlman p. 40 f. (date); cf.
*SEG* XXXV 306

**Κοισέας**
AITOLIA:
—KALYDON: (**1**) iii/ii BC *IG* IX (1)² (1) 136, 10

**Κοῖσος**
ARKADIA:
—PALLANTION: (**1**) a. 316 BC *SEG* XI 1084, 36
(Perlman A.3) ([*K*]οῖσος: f. *Ξένιππος*)

**Κοιτωνίς**
S. ITALY (CAMPANIA):
—DIKAIARCHIA-PUTEOLI: (**1**) imp. *CIL* x 3009
(Lat. Titia Coetonis); (**2**) ?i-ii AD ib. 2588
(Lat. Iulia Coetonis: d. *Ἐπαφρόδιτος*)
SICILY:
—KENTORIPA: (**3**) ?ii AD ib. 7005 (Lat.
Coe[t]onis: m. Aelius Pius)

**Κοκκαίειος**
ARKADIA:
—TEGEA: (**1**) ii AD *IG* v (2) 55, 77

**Κόκκαλος**
DALMATIA:
—ISSA:
——(Hylleis): (**1**) iv/iii BC Brunšmid p. 8, 41 (s.
*Εὔαρχος*)

**Κοκκήϊος**
S. ITALY (CAMPANIA):
—NEAPOLIS: (**1**) i BC/i AD *INap* 151, 2 (?s.
*Ἄστος*)

**Κόκκος**
KORINTHIA:
—KORINTH: (**1**) iii-iv AD *SEG* XIII 228, 1; cf.
XXII 223 (*Κόκ*(*κ*)*ος*)

**Κοκκύς**
S. ITALY (LUCANIA):
—HYELE-VELIA: (**1**) hell.? *PdelP* 25 (1970) p.
264 no. 8 (d. *Προκλῆς*)

**Κόλαξ**
LAKONIA:
—SPARTA: (**1**) c. 125 AD *IG* v (1) 1314, 13
(Bradford (-)) (f. *Πίστος*)
SICILY:
—THERMAI HIMERAIAI*: (**2**) imp. *ILat. Term.
Imer.* 76 a (Lat. Colax: freed.)

**Κόλαφος**
SICILY:
—SYRACUSE?: (**1**) inc. *CGF* p. 91 fr. 1 (dub.)

**Κολήβας**
S. ITALY (BRUTTIUM):
—LOKROI EPIZEPHYRIOI: (**1**) hell.? *IG* XIV
2401. 4 (Landi, *DISMG* 249 (tile)) (*Κολή-
βα*[*s*])

**Κολλίων**
ILLYRIA:
—BYLLIONES NIKAIA (KLJOS (MOD.)): (**1**)
hell. *Iliria* 1982 (1), p. 120 no. 32 (tile)
(*Κ*(*α*)*λλίων*?)

**Κολλύρα**
S. ITALY (BRUTTIUM): (**1**) hell.? Landi,
*DISMG* 114, 1, 9

**Κόλοβος**
SICILY:
—IAITON: (**1**) ii-i BC *SEG* XXVI 1070. 10 (tile)
(f. *Διονύσιος*)

**Κολοῖος**
ILLYRIA:
—APOLLONIA: (**1**) c. 250-50 BC Maier 56 (coin)
(Ceka 119; 120) (pryt.)

**Κολοιφῶν**
ARKADIA:
—PHIGALEIA: (**1**) v BC *IG* v (2) 425, 3 (-φῶν)

**Κολοκύνθη**
SICILY:
—KATANE: (**1**) ii-iii AD *CIL* x 7097 (*ILat.
Palermo* 2; *Epigraphica* 51 (1989) p. 171)
(Lat. Culucui(n)tas)

**Κολομβίων**
LEUKAS: (1) ?iii BC *SBBerlAk* 1935, p. 709

**Κόλχος**
ARKADIA:
—TEGEA: (1) s. iv BC *SEG* XXXVI 383, 8
([Κ]όλχος: s. Θάλλος)

**Κόλων**
S. ITALY (CAMPANIA):
—MISENUM*: (1) imp. *CIL* X 3395 (Lat. Antonius Colo: I f. Κόλων II); (2) ~ ib. (Lat. Camurius Colo: II s. Κόλων I)

**Κομάδας**
ARKADIA: (1) ?c. 550-525 BC *SEG* XI 1044 (bronze) (Lazzarini 289); *LSAG*² p. 214 no. 1 (name, date) (ϙομάδας, ϙομάρας—SEG)

**Κόμαιθος**
AITOLIA: (1) ?228-215 BC *SGDI* 2525, 2

**Κομαῖος**
ARKADIA:
—TEGEA: (1) ii AD *IG* V (2) 54, 11 ([Κ]ομαῖος)

**Κομᾶς**
ARGOLIS:
—TROIZEN: (1) ?146 BC ib. IV (1) 757 B, 37 (f. Ἀρίστων)

**Κομάτας**
S. ITALY (BRUTTIUM):
—SYBARIS-THOURIOI-COPIAE*: (1) iii BC Theoc., *Id.* v passim; cf. vii 83 (slave/fict.)

**Κόμιος**
KORINTHIA:
—KORINTH: (1) c. 590-570 BC Amyx 19 B. 8 (vase) (Lorber 37) (ϙό-, ϙōμιος?: fict.?)

**Κομμαγηνή**
S. ITALY (CAMPANIA): (1) imp. *IG* XIV 885 (Ἰουλ. Μαρκέλλα Κ.: d. Ἰούλ. Βάσσος)

**Κομμοῦνος**
EPIROS:
—NIKOPOLIS: (1) imp. *SEG* XLII 545 (f. Ὑγῖνος)

**Κομνιάδας**
KORINTHIA:
—KORINTH: (1) vi BC ib. XLI 540 B (ϙομν[ι]άδ[ας])

**Κόμψη**
S. ITALY (CAMPANIA):
—POMPEII: (1) i BC-i AD *CIL* IV 4587 (Lat. Compse); (2) ~ ib. 10171 (Castrèn 368. 1) (Lat. Comse); (3) ~ *CIL* IV 4544-5 (Castrèn 20. 1) (Lat. Alficia Compse)
S. ITALY (LUCANIA):
—HYELE-VELIA: (4) imp. *PdelP* 25 (1970) p. 266 no. 12 (Lat. Terentia Compse)

**Κόμψις**
AITOLIA:
—APERANTOI: (1) iv/iii BC *SEG* XVII 274, 2 (*L'Illyrie mérid.* I p. 111 fig. 9)

**Κόμων**
ARGOLIS:
—ARGOS: (1) ?253 BC Nachtergael, *Les Galates* 10, 72; cf. Stephanis 2305 (f. Στράτιος)
DALMATIA:
—PHAROS: (2) iv/iii BC *SEG* XXXI 605 (s. Φιλοξενίδης)
ILLYRIA:
—EPIDAMNOS-DYRRHACHION: (3) c. 250-50 BC Maier 195 (Ceka 262); cf. *IApoll Ref. Bibl.* n. 46 (coin) (money.)
MESSENIA: (4) s. v BC Paus. iv 26. 2-3 (and Lokris (Western) Naupaktos)

**Κόνα**
ILLYRIA:
—EPIDAMNOS-DYRRHACHION: (1) hell.-imp. *IDyrrh* 273

**Κόνδων**
KERKYRA: (1) c. 500 BC *SEG* XXX 520

**Κονκορδία**
SICILY:
—SYRACUSE: (1) iii-v AD *IG* XIV 135 (Strazzulla 75; Wessel 1326); cf. Ferrua, *NG* 167 ([Κο]νκορδία)

**Κοννακίς**
S. ITALY (CALABRIA):
—TARAS-TARENTUM: (1) m. iv BC *CVA* Taranto 3 IV D pl. 22, 2 (vase) (het./fict.?)

**Κοννίδας**
SICILY:
—SELINOUS*: (1) v-iv BC Call. fr. 201 dieg.; *FGrH* 566 F 148 (Κύνναρος—FGrH: metic)

**Κόνοσος**
S. ITALY (CALABRIA):
—TARAS-TARENTUM: (1) f. v BC *ASP* 22 (1969) pp. 88-9 no. 1 (terracotta)

**Κοντεύς**
SICILY:
—TYRAKION: (1) f. ii BC *BCH* 45 (1921) p. 25 IV, 102 (*SEG* XXII 455); cf. *Sic. Gymn.* 17 (1964) pp. 47 f.

**Κονώ**
ILLYRIA:
—EPIDAMNOS-DYRRHACHION: (1) hell.-imp. *IDyrrh* 40 (Κονοῦς (gen.): d. Λαήν); (2) ~ ib. 274

**Κόνων**
ACHAIA:
—DYME*: (1) c. 219 BC *SGDI* 1612, 17 (*Tyche* 5 (1990) p. 124) (f. Ἐπιτέλης)
AITOLIA: (2) ?269 BC *FD* III (4) 415, 8
ILLYRIA:
—EPIDAMNOS-DYRRHACHION: (3) c. 250-50 BC Maier 374 (coin) (Ceka 263) (money.); (4) hell.-imp. *IDyrrh* 275 (s. Περιγένης)
KERKYRA: (5) iv/iii AD Unp. (*IG* arch.) (Κόνω[ν])
S. ITALY (BRUTTIUM):
—TERINA: (6) c. 325-300 BC *IGSI* 21, 2 (*SEG* IV 73; Landi, *DISMG* 170) (Κόνōν[ος] (gen.): f. Δία)
S. ITALY (CAMPANIA):
—DIKAIARCHIA-PUTEOLI: (7) imp. *CIL* X 1870 (Lat. P. Aemilius Cono)

**Κονωνεύς**
S. ITALY (CALABRIA):
—TARAS-TARENTUM: (1) s. iii BC App., *Hann.* 32; Front., *Str.* iii 3. 6

**Κοπαίνα**
ILLYRIA: (1) inc. Aratus ap. Eustath. *Odyss.* iii 68 (K. (masc.)—Eustath., Κοπαίνης?)

**Κοπρία**
SICILY:
—KATANE: (1) imp. *IG* XIV 497 b; cf. *Riv. Arch. Crist.* 18 (1941) p. 231 no. 124 (m. Κούϊντα)

**Κοπριανός**
SICILY:
—AKRAI: (1) imp. *Akrai* p. 164 no. 26 + *Arch. Class.* 17 (1965) p. 205 (name) (Ἄππιος Κ.)
—SYRACUSE: (2) iii-iv AD *NScav* 1951, p. 297 (Lat. L. Helvius Coprianus); (3) iii-v AD *IG* XIV 137 (Strazzulla 77; Agnello 5; Wessel 1363) (Κ(υ)πριανός?—Strazzulla); (4) ~ Strazzulla 211; cf. Ferrua, *NG* 279 (Κροπι-)

**(5)** ~ Strazzulla 241 (Wessel 695); Ferrua, *NG* 294 (name) ([Κο]πριανός, Πριανός—Strazzulla, [Ἀσ]πριανός—Wessel); (6) ~ ib. 372

**Κόπριλλα**
SICILY:
—LIPARA: (1) iii-v AD Libertini, *Isole Eolie* p. 229 no. 7 (*NScav* 1929, p. 85); cf. *Riv. Arch. Crist.* 18 (1941) p. 186 f. no. 53 (Lat. Coprilla)
—SYRACUSE: (2) iii-v AD ib. p. 187 no. 53
—SYRACUSE?: (3) ?iii-v AD *ASSicilia* 1938-9, p. 33 (Lat. C. Coprilla)
—THERMAI HIMERAIAI*: (4) imp. *CIL* X 7403 (*ILat. Term. Imer.* 96) (Lat. Laelia Coprilla: freed.)

**Κόπρις**
AIGINA: (1) ii/i BC *Alt-Ägina* I (2) p. 43 no. 3, 3 (f. Χαρμύλος)
KORINTHIA:
—KORINTH: (2) ?vi BC *IG* IV (1) 233 + Amyx p. 607 no. 33 (pinax) (ϙό[π]ρις, ϙό[ρ]ρις—IG)
LAKONIA:
—SPARTA: (3) f. vi BC *SEG* II 73 (Lazzarini 403a); *LSAG*² p. 198 no. 6 (date) (Poralla² 449b; Bradford (-))

**Κοπρίων**
S. ITALY (BRUTTIUM):
—LOKROI EPIZEPHYRIOI:
——(Ἀνα.): (1) 275 BC De Franciscis 25, 5 (s. Εὐφάνης)

**Κόπρολλα**
SICILY:
—SYRACUSE: (1) iii-v AD Strazzulla 234 (Κρόπολλα)

**Κοραγίων**
S. ITALY (LUCANIA):
—METAPONTION: (1) iv BC *Coll. McClean* 924; cf. *JNG* 33 (1983) p. 14 (coin graffito)

**Κόραξ**
SICILY:
—SYRACUSE: (1) v BC *RE* (3)

**Κορβουλίων**
ILLYRIA:
—APOLLONIA: (1) imp. *IApoll* 239; cf. *SEG* XXIII 486 ([Κ]ορβουλίων)

**Κόργισις**
PELOPONNESE?: (1) s. iii BC ib. XXV 449, 48 (*IPArk* 26)

**Κόρδαφος**
TRIPHYLIA:
—LEPREON: (1) ?c. 475-450 BC *SEG* XV 253 (Lazzarini 866); Moretti, *Olymp.* 267; *LSAG*² p. 220 no. 14 (date) (s. Ἀλκάνωρ)

**Κορδίρας?**
AKARNANIA:
—STRATOS: (1) vi BC *IG* IX (1)² (2) 399 (Κορδίρας?—IG)

**Κορείδας**
LAKONIA:
—SPARTA: (1) c. 25-1 BC ib. V (1) 212, 42 (Bradford (-)) (f. Γόργως)

**Κόρειος**
SICILY:
—KAMARINA: (1) f. v BC Cordano, *Tessere Pubbliche* 129 (s. Ἀπολλωνίδας)

**Κορέτα**
ILLYRIA:
—EPIDAMNOS-DYRRHACHION: (1) ii-i BC *IDyrrh* 276 (d. Πλάτωρ)

**Κορίνθα**
S. Italy (Apulia):
—canusium: **(1)** imp. *Epig. Rom. di Canosa* 200
(*CIL* ix 403) (Lat. Vavidia Corintha)

**Κορινθᾶς**
Argolis:
—argos: **(1)** iii ad *SEG* xxii 268 (*Αὐρ. Κ.*)
Korinthia:
—korinth: **(2)** byz. ib. xxxv 256
Lakonia:
—sparta: **(3)** c. 150-190 ad *IG* v (1) 45, 7;
*BSA* 80 (1985) p. 226 (date) (Bradford (-))
(s. *Νικηφόρος*)

**Κορινθία**
Argolis:
—epidauros: **(1)** iv/iii bc Peek, *IAEpid* 340, 2
(n. pr.?: ?d. *Κύδιμος, Θεοδότα*)
S. Italy (Campania):
—dikaiarchia-puteoli: **(2)** imp. *CIL* x 2306
(Lat. Cluvia Corinthia: d. *Διονυσία*)
—pompeii: **(3)** i bc-i ad ib. iv 2077 (Lat. Corinthia); **(4)** ~ ib. 4628 (Lat. Corintia)

**Κορινθιάς**
S. Italy (Campania):
—dikaiarchia-puteoli: **(1)** ?ii ad *NScav*
1888, p. 198 no. 6 (*Eph. Ep.* viii 398) (Lat.
Corinthias)
—salernum: **(2)** 98-117 ad *IItal* i (1) 92 (*CIL*
x 653) (Lat. Venuleia Corinthias)
S. Italy (Lucania):
—potentia: **(3)** ?i-ii ad ib. 138 (Lat. Iulia Corinthias)

**Κορίνθιος**
Aitolia: **(1)** ?273 bc *FD* iii (2) 205
Kerkyra: **(2)** m. iv bc Fraser–Rönne, *BWGT*
p. 113 no. 5 (*Miscellanea* p. 186 n. 5) (n. pr.?:
?f. *Πάγκιος*)
Korinthia:
—korinth: **(3)** i bc/i ad *AE* 1977, p. 78 no. 24,
1 (Lat. C. Heius Corinthius: f. *Ἥϊος Ἀγάθων*)
Messenia:
—thouria: **(4)** f. ii bc *SEG* xi 972, 19 (f. *Δεινίας*)

**Κορινθίς**
S. Italy (Campania):
—surrentum: **(1)** imp. *CIL* x 692 (Lat. Corin-
this)

**Κόρινθος**
Argolis:
—argos: **(1)** ?m. v bc *IG* iv (1) 516
Arkadia:
—kleitor: **(2)** a. 212 ad ib. v (2) 369, 12; *SEG*
xxxi 347, 4 (f. *Ζώσιμος*)
Korinthia:
—korinth: **(3)** imp. *Corinth* viii (3) 345, 2
(Lat. Corint[hu]s); **(4)** ii-iii ad *SEG* xxix
340, 3 (Stephanis 1480) (*Λ. Κορνήλιος Κ.*: I
f. *Λ. Κορνήλιος Σαβῖνος, Λ. Κορνήλιος Κόρινθος*
II); **(5)** ~ *SEG* xxix 340, 7 (Stephanis 1481)
(*Λ. Κορνήλιος Κ.*: II s. *Λ. Κορνήλιος Κόρινθος*
I)
—sikyon*: **(6)** ii ad *ILGR* 82 (Lat. M. Calpetanus Corinthus: f. Calpetanus Ianuarius,
Calpetana Magna)
S. Italy (Apulia):
—luceria: **(7)** imp. *CIL* ix 814 (*ASP* 34
(1981) p. 27 no. 33) (Lat. L. Ocratius Corinthus: s. Ocratia Silvana)
S. Italy (Bruttium):
—lokroi epizephyrioi*: **(8)** i/ii ad Costabile,
*Municipium Locrensium* 47 (brick) (Lat. C.
Flavius Corinthus)
S. Italy (Calabria):
—brentesion-brundisium: **(9)** imp. *CIL* ix
125 (Lat. L. Granius Corinthus); **(10)** ~ ib.
6121 (Lat. L. Afranius Corin[thus])

S. Italy (Campania):
—capreae: **(11)** imp. *IG* xiv 896 ([*Κό*]*ρινθος
Τροπιανός?—IG*)
—dikaiarchia-puteoli: **(12)** imp. *CIL* x
1747 (Lat. Corinthus); **(13)** ~ ib. 2064, 4 (Lat.
L. Annius Corinthus); **(14)** ~ ib. 2539 (Lat.
Iulius Corintus)
—dikaiarchia-puteoli*: **(15)** ?i-ii ad ib.
8042. 63 (tile) (Lat. C. Iulius Corinthus)
—kyme: **(16)** 251 ad ib. 3699 I, 41 (Lat. Q.
Granius Chorintus)
—nola: **(17)** i ad ib. iv 7025 (Lat. Corinthus)
—pompeii: **(18)** i bc-i ad ib. 1564 (?s. *Δέξτρος*); **(19)** ~ ib. 2024 (Lat. Corinthus); **(20)**
~ ib. 4620 (Lat. Corinthus); **(21)** ~ ib. 5161
(Lat. Corinthus); **(22)** ~ ib. 6803 (Lat. Corintus); **(23)** ~ ib. 8069 (Lat. Corinthus); **(24)** ~ ib.
8448 (Lat. Corinthus); **(25)** ~ ib. 8977 (Lat.
C[o]rintus); **(26)** ~ ib. 9040 (Lat. Corinthus);
**(27)** ~ ib. 9154 (Castrèn 225. 3) (Lat. P. Luc-
cus Corinthus); **(28)** ~ *NScav* 1910, p. 450 no.
27 (Lat. Corinthus); **(29)** 55 ad *CIL* iv 3340.
12, 18; 13, 19; 87, 7; 89, 11 (Castrèn 207. 9)
(Lat. L. Iun. Corinthus)

**Κόριννα**
S. Italy (Campania):
—pompeii: **(1)** i bc-i ad *NScav* 1894, p. 384
(Castrèn 320. 2) (Lat. Poppaea Corinna)

**Κορινvίς**
Sicily:
—syracuse?: **(1)** iii-v ad *IG* xiv 28 + *SEG*
xxxviii 696; cf. *Riv. Arch. Crist.* 18 (1941)
p. 221 no. 105 (locn.) (*Κωρηννίς*)

**Κορίσκος**
S. Italy (Campania):
—herculaneum*: **(1)** i bc-i ad *CIL* x 1403 g
III, 51 (Lat. A. Ofillius Coriscus: freed.)

**Κορίων**
Sicily:
—eryx: **(1)** imp. ib. 8045, 3 (Lat. M. Aemilius
Corion)

**Κορκυραῖος**
Sicily:
—kamarina: **(1)** f. v bc Cordano, *Tessere Pubbliche* 79 (f. *Ξένων*)

**Κορμίνας**
Korinthia:
—sikyon: **(1)** f. v bc *SEG* xxiv 271 + *Hesp.*
41 (1972) p. 205 no. 7; *LSAG*² p. 442 no 14b
(date) (*ηηρμίνας—SEG*: f. *Πασέδας*)

**Κορνηλία**
Sicily:
—kentoripa: **(1)** imp. *IG* xiv 581 (-*νε*-)
—motyka (nr.): **(2)** iii-v ad ib. 249 (Wessel
1048)
—syracuse: **(3)** iii-v ad *IG* xiv 136 (Strazzulla
76) (*Κορνη*[*λία*])
—syracuse?: **(4)** imp.? ib. 137

**Κορνήλιος**
Argolis:
—epidauros: **(1)** 32 ad Peek, *IAEpid* 45, 44 (f.
*Διόδωρος*)
S. Italy (Bruttium):
—rhegion: **(2)** inc. *IG* xiv 623; cf. *Rend. Pont.*
60 (1987-8) p. 274 no. 25

**Κόροιβος**
Elis: **(1)** 776 bc *RE* (2); Moretti, *Olymp.* 1
Lakonia:
—sparta: **(2)** 368 bc *IG* ii² 106, 11 (Poralla²
450) (*Κ*[*όρ*]*ο*[*ιβ*]*ος?*)
S. Italy (Lucania):
—grumentum: **(3)** imp. Ramagli, *Cuore del
Sud* pp. 92-3 (Lat. C. Alidius Choroibus)

**Κόρραγος**
Epiros:
—votonosi (mod.): **(1)** f. iii bc *SEG* xxiv 462
(f. *Ἄρροπος*)
Sicily:
—kamarina: **(2)** iv/iii bc ib. xxxiv 941 with
note (Dubois, *IGDS* 125, 2 a; Cordano, 'Camarina VII' 127) (*Κόρα*-)

**Κόρριθος**
Epiros:
—bouthrotos (prasaiboi): **(1)** a. 163 bc
*IBouthrot* 28, 41; cf. *SEG* xxxviii 478 (s. *Πο-
λέμων*); **(2)** ~ *IBouthrot* 31, 74 (*SEG* xxxviii
490)
—Aphobioi: **(3)** a. 163 bc *IBouthrot* 29, 1
(*SEG* xxxviii 487)
—Kestrinoi: **(4)** ?164 bc Cabanes, *L'Épire* p.
586 no. 71, 1 (*Κόρι*-: s. *Μενέλαος*)

**Κοροαῖος**
Lakonia:
—sparta: **(1)** c. 175-200 ad *IG* v (1) 129, 1
(Bradford (-)) (*Γ. Ἰούλ. Κ.*)

**Κορύδων**
Arkadia: **(1)** s. i bc *GP* 2200 (fict.)

**Κορύμβιος**
Aitolia: **(1)** ?262-253 bc Nachtergael, *Les Galates* 5, 29; 10, 35; cf. Stephanis 1974 (f. *Παγ-
κλῆς*)

**Κόρυμβος**
Elis: **(1)** 36 bc *IvOl* 59, 5 (f. *Λεωνίδας*)
Peloponnese?: **(2)** s. iii bc *IG* v (1) 1426, 20
(s. *Σιλανός*)
S. Italy (Campania):
—dikaiarchia-puteoli: **(3)** imp. *CIL* x 2969
(Lat. Corym[bus])
—surrentum*: **(4)** imp. ib. 697 (Lat. Chorin-
bus: imp. freed.)

**Κόρυνθις**
Sicily:
—megara hyblaia: **(1)** s. vii bc Dubois,
*IGDS* 18 (vase) (Arena, *Iscr. Sic.* I 14) (*ϙορύν-
θιος* (gen.?, ethn.?))

**Κορύς**
Sicily:
—kamarina: **(1)** ?iv bc *SEG* xxxii 917 (Cordano, 'Camarina VII' 128)

**Κόρων**
Argolis:
—argos: **(1)** v bc *Argive Heraeum* 2 p. 186 no.
9 and pl. 69 (sherd) (*ϙόρōν*)

**Κοσίνα**
Argolis:
—argos: **(1)** c. 500 bc *SEG* xi 305, 1 (*ϙο*-)

**Κοσμᾶς**
Argolis:
—argos: **(1)** v-vi ad Unp. (Oikonomou-
Laniado) (f. *Πέτρος*)
Korinthia:
—korinth: **(2)** iv/v ad *Corinth* viii (3) 525;
cf. *TMByz* 9 (1985) p. 365 no. 53; **(3)** v-vi
ad *SEG* xi 173, 3; cf. *Corinth* viii (3) 595
(*Κο*[*σμᾶς*], *Κο*[*σμόδωρος*]—*Corinth*)

**Κοσμία**
Leukas: **(1)** hell.? *IG* ix (1) 562 ([*Κ*]*οσμία*)
S. Italy (Calabria):
—brentesion-brundisium: **(2)** ?i ad *CIL* ix
131 (Lat. Iulia Cosmia)
Sicily:
—syracuse: **(3)** iii-v ad Ferrua, *NG* 204
—thermai himeraiai: **(4)** imp. *CIL* x 7397
(*ILat. Term. Imer.* 87) (Lat. Cosmia)

**Κοσμιανός**
S. Italy (Calabria):
—taras-tarentum*: (1) i-ii ad *SEG* xxxiv
1020; cf. *Mus. Arch. Taranto* iv (1) p. 208
(*Κοσσμιανό*[*s*])

**Κοσμίερος**
Arkadia:
—mantineia-antigoneia: (1) c. 425-385 bc
*IG* v (2) 323. 8 (tessera) (s. *Αὐτάριστος*)

**Κόσμιλλα**
Epiros:
—tepelene (mod.): (1) hell.-imp. *Iliria* 1976,
p. 320 with pl. 7 (d. *Ἀλέξανδρος*)

**Κοσμόπολις**
Elis: (1) c. 67-105 ad *IvOl* 431, 2; 432, 2-3;
433, 4 (*Τιβ. Κλ. Λύσων Κ.*: s. *Τιβ. Κλ. Ἀγίας,
Γιγανία Πῶλλα*)

**Κόσμος**
Achaia: (1) 146 bc *IG* iv (1)² 28, 89 (I f.
*Κόσμος* II: synoikos); (2) ~ ib. l. 89 (II s. *Κόσ-
μος* I: synoikos)
Argolis:
—hermione: (3) ?ii-i bc ib. iv (1) 731 I, 15
([*Κ*]*όσμος*: s. *Δέξιος*)
—methana-arsinoe: (4) imp.? *SEG* xxxviii
326
Illyria:
—apollonia: (5) c. 250-50 bc Maier 52 (coin)
(Ceka 72) (money.)
Lakonia:
—sparta: (6) ?ii-i bc *IG* v (1) 914 (Bradford
(-)) (*Κόσσ-*: f. *Δαμύλος*); (7) s. ii ad *SEG* xi
598, 2 (Bradford (-)) (f. *Νικίας*)
S. Italy (Apulia):
—barion: (8) i-ii ad *Suppl. It.* 8 p. 37 no. 5
(Lat. M. Caesius Cosmus)
—canusium: (9) imp. *Epig. Rom. di Canosa*
Add. 1 (Lat. [Co]smus)
—canusium*: (10) imp. ib. 90 (*CIL* ix 6188)
(Lat. L. Baebius Cosmus: freed.); (11) ~
*Epig. Rom. di Canosa* 123 (*CIL* ix 374) (Lat.
Cosmus: freed.?); (12) i-ii ad *Epig. Rom. di
Canosa* 58, 7 (*CIL* ix 348) (Lat. Cosmus:
freed.)
S. Italy (Calabria):
—brentesion-brundisium: (13) imp. ib. 169
(Lat. Cosmu[s])
—rudiae: (14) ii ad Bernardini, *Rudiae* p. 100
(Susini, *Fonti Salento* p. 104 no. 39) (Lat. L.
Marcius Cosmus)
S. Italy (Campania):
—dikaiarchia-puteoli: (15) imp. *CIL* x
2632 (Lat. Cosmus)
—herculaneum: (16) i bc-i ad ib. iv 10597
(Lat. Cosmus)
—neapolis: (17) i ad *IG* xiv 795, 1, 9 (*INap*
133); cf. Leiwo p. 124 no. 111 (*Ναούιος Κ.*)
—nuceria alfaterna: (18) ii-iii ad *CIL* x
1086 (Lat. Aelius Cosmus)
—pompeii: (19) i bc-i ad ib. iv 1825 (Lat. Cosmus); (20) ~ ib. 6863 (Lat. Cosmus); (21) ~
ib. 8221 (Lat. Cosmus); (22) ~ ib. 8479 (Lat.
Cosmu(s)); (23) ~ ib. 10181 d (Castrèn 34.
4) (Lat. P. Antistius Cosmus); (24) 70-79 ad
*CIL* iv 737; 2626 (Castrèn 26. 1) (Lat. An-
nullius Cosmus)
Sicily:
—syracuse: (25) iii-v ad Strazzulla 360
(Wessel 941)
Sicily?: (26) imp.? *IG* xiv 2393. 341 (vase)

**Κοσπίννιος**
Lakonia:
—hyperteleaton*: (1) imp. ib. v (1) 1054
([*Κ*]*οσπίννιος*)

**Κόσσα**
Korinthia:
—korinth: (1) viii bc Schol. Call., *Aet.* ii fr.
43, 28-30 (d. *Ἀρχίας*)

**Κοσσαῖος**
Lakonia:
—sparta: (1) c. 160-165 ad *IG* v (1) 45, 12;
*BSA* 80 (1985) p. 226 (date) (Bradford (-))

**Κόσσας**
Achaia:
—pellene: (1) arch. Suda K 2134; cf. T 834
(*Κόσας*—834: fict.?)

**Κοσσύφα**
Epiros:
—argos (amphiloch.): (1) iv/iii bc *SEG*
xxxii 563 (d. *Αἰσχύλος*)
Kerkyra: (2) iv/iii bc *IG* ix (1) 888

**Κόσσυφος**
Illyria:
—epidamnos-dyrrhachion: (1) c. 250-50 bc
Münsterberg p. 39 (coin) (Ceka 7) (pryt.)

**Κόσων**
Akarnania:
—echinos: (1) 356-354 bc *IG* iv (1)² 95, 17
(Perlman E.2); Perlman p. 40 f. (date)

**Κότας**
Sicily:
—kamarina: (1) ?ii bc *SEG* xxvii 651; *PdelP*
44 (1989) p. 191 no. II (Cordano, 'Camarina
VII' 129); cf. Cordano, 'Camarina VII' 105
(*-κοτα-*)

**Κότης**
Sicily:
—akragas: (1) s. ii bc *Acragas Graeca* 1 p. 34
no. 5, 12 (*IGUR* 2; Dubois, *IGDS* 185) (f.
*Πασίων*)
—melita: (2) s. ii bc *IGUR* 3, 7 (*IG* xiv 953)
(*Κ*[*ό*]*της*)

**Κοτίων**
Argolis:
—mykenai: (1) hell. *SEG* xv 198

**Κόtταβος**
Arkadia: (1) 361 bc *CID* ii 4 I, 43

**Κοττείης**
S. Italy (Bruttium):
—hipponion-vibo valentia: (1) hell.
*Klearchos* 16 (1974) p. 82 (tile) (*Κοττε*[*ί*]*ης*)

**Κόττινα**
Lakonia:
—sparta: (1) ?iv/iii bc Polem. fr. 18 (Poralla²
452) (het.)

**Κότυς**
Aigina: (1) imp. *IG* iv (1) 127 (*REG* 15 (1902)
p. 138 no. 1) (*Κοξιος*—apogr.: s. *Αἴπολος*)

**Κουαδρᾶτος**
S. Italy (Campania):
—kyme: (1) ii-iii ad *Puteoli* 6 (1982) pp. 159-60
no. 10 ([*Κου*]*αδρᾶτος*)

**Κούαρτα**
Illyria:
—apollonia: (1) ii-iii ad *IApoll* 214

**Κουίδας**
Argolis:
—epidauros: (1) iv/iii bc *IG* iv (1)² 162

**Κούϊντα**
S. Italy (Bruttium):
—rhegion?: (1) ii ad *IGUR* 1165 (*GVI* 1025)
(m. *Ἀτίμητος*)

**Sicily:**
—katane: (2) imp. *IG* xiv 497 b (*Κού*[*ε*]*ιντα*: d.
*Κοπρία*)
—syracuse: (3) iii-v ad Ferrua, *NG* 262

**Κουϊντιανή**
Kephallenia:
—kranioi?: (1) imp. *SEG* iii 448 (*Κυϊ-*)

**Κούϊντος**
Sicily: (1) iii-v ad *IG* xiv 599 (Wessel 641)
(*Κούειν-*)
—akrai: (2) imp. *Akrai* p. 165 no. 30 + *Riv.
Arch. Crist.* 18 (1941) p. 198 no. 70 (*-ειν-*)
—syracuse: (3) iii-v ad *Rend. Pont.* 22 (1946-
7) p. 234 no. 26 (*Κούειν-*); (4) ~ *Nuovo Didask.*
6 (1956) p. 64 no. 34 (*Κύ-*)

**Κραῖνυς**
Epiros:
—dodona: (1) iii bc Antoniou, *Dodone* Aa, 13;
(2) ~ ib. Ba, 25; (3) ~ ib. l. 31 ([*Κρ*]*α*[*ῖν*]*υς*)
—phoinatoi: (4) c. 330 bc Cabanes, *L'Épire*
p. 580 no. 55, 7

**Κραινώ**
Epiros:
—bouthrotos (prasaiboi):
——Kammeoi: (1) a. 163 bc *IBouthrot* 118, 4;
119 (d. *Φίλιππος*)

**Κρανaός**
Korinthia:
—sikyon: (1) 145 ad Moretti, *Olymp.* 858
S. Italy (Lucania):
—poseidonia-paestum: (2) vi bc Iamb., *VP*
267 (*FVS* 1 p. 448) (*Κρανοος*—ms.: name—
C. Keil)

**Κρασσίων**
Illyria:
—epidamnos-dyrrhachion: (1) hell.-imp.
*IDyrrh* 253 (*Ἱέρων Κ.* (n. pr.?))

**Κραταΐδας**
Lakonia:
—sparta: (1) her. Plu., *Mor.* 247 D (Poralla²
453) (*Κραταιμένης*?—Wade-Gery: oikist/dub.)

**Κραταιμένης**
Arkadia:
—phigaleia: (1) c. 240 bc *IG* v (2) 419, 8
(*IPArk* 28)
Lakonia:
—sparta: (2) s. i bc *IG* v (1) 127, 4; 211, 34
(Bradford (1); (2)) (s. *Ἀνδρομένης*)
S. Italy (Bruttium-Lucania): (3) c. 625-
600 bc *Arch. Coll. Johns Hopkins Univ.* pp.
38-9 no. 24 (bronze) (Arena, *Iscr. Sic.* iv 89);
cf. *LSAG*² p. 456 no. 30a

**Κρατέα**
Argolis:
—hermione: (1) i bc-i ad? *IG* iv (1) 730 IV, 6
(d. *Φιλο—*)

**Κρατέας**
Arkadia:
—tegea: (1) ?255-253 bc Nachtergael, *Les Galates* 8, 38; 10, 70; cf. Stephanis 2136 (f. *Πραξίας*); (2) ii-i bc *IG* v (2) 165, 3 (f. *Κλεόδαμος*)
Epiros:
—bouthrotos (prasaiboi):
——Cheilioi: (3) a. 163 bc *IBouthrot* 98, 7 (s.
*Σώσανδρος*)
Kerkyra: (4) c. 500 bc *SEG* xxx 520; cf.
*L'Illyrie mérid.* 2 p. 202
Korinthia:
—korinth: (5) c. 225 bc *SEG* xi 414, 15 (Perlman E.5); Peek, *IAEpid* 331, 15 (ethn.)
Lakonia:
—sparta: (6) c. 25-1 bc *IG* v (1) 212, 25 (Bradford (-)) (s. *Τιμάγορος*)

MESSENIA:
—MESSENE: (7) f. iii BC *PAE* 1991, p. 99 no. 7, 8
SICILY:
—KASMENAI: (8) vi BC Dubois, *IGDS* 103

## Κράτεια

AITOLIA:
—KALYDON: (1) imp. *IG* IX (1)² (1) 141 (Κρά-τει[α])
ARKADIA:
—GORTYS: (2) ii BC *SEG* XXXV 349 (d. Φιλοποί-μην, Καλλικράτεια)
EPIROS:
—KELAITHOI: (3) 170 BC *SGDI* 1756, 3-4 (slave/freed.)
KORINTHIA:
—KORINTH: (4) vii BC D.L. i 96 (m. Περίανδρος, ?m. Γόργος)
LEUKAS: (5) hell.? *IG* II² 9206
S. ITALY (CAMPANIA):
—DIKAIARCHIA-PUTEOLI: (6) imp. *CIL* X 2561 a (Lat. Apuleia Cratia)
SICILY:
—SYRACUSE: (7) hell. *NScav* 1892, p. 359

## Κρατεραῖος

EPIROS:
—MOLOSSOI: (1) c. 237-232 BC *SGDI* 1348, 5; Hammond, *Epirus* p. 593 (date) (?f. Κανθάρα (Other))

## Κράτερος

ARGOLIS:
—ARGOS: (1) iii BC *SEG* XI 371, 6 (*GVI* 1328) (s. Καλλέας, Ἐπικαρπία)
ELIS: (2) 210-220 AD *IvOl* 477, 1 (Λ. Πομπ. Κ. Κασσιανός: s. Ἀπρία Κασσία, f. Π. Ἐγνάτιος Μά-ξιμος Βεννστεῖνος)
EPIROS:
—BOUTHROTOS (PRASAIBOI): (3) a. 163 BC *IBouthrot* 31, 61 (*SEG* XXXVIII 490) (f. Μυρ-τίχα)
KEPHALLENIA:
—PRONNOI: (4) iii AD ib. XIX 408-9; cf. XXIII 388 (mosaic) (Donderer C5)
S. ITALY (CAMPANIA):
—PITHEKOUSSAI-AENARIA: (5) imp. *CIL* X 6788 (Lat. M. Verrius Craterus)

## Κρατηιδάμεια

LAKONIA:
—HYPERTELEATON*: (1) iii BC *IG* V (1) 977, 13 (Bradford (-)) (d. Πεικράτης)

## Κρατηίππίδας

LAKONIA:
—SPARTA: (1) ii BC *SEG* XI 856, 3 (Bradford (-)) (Κρατηίπ[πίδας]: s. Νικοκλῆς)

## Κρατήιππος

LAKONIA:
—OITYLOS: (1) iii/ii BC *IG* V (1) 1295, 8 (Bradford (-))

## Κράτης

ARGOLIS:
—ARGOS: (1) m. iii BC Peek, *IAEpid* 42, 30 (Perlman E.3); Perlman p. 63 f. (date) (s. —σ—ιος); (2) 105 BC *JÖAI* 14 (1911) Beibl. p. 146 no. 4, 17 (f. —οτος)
—EPIDAUROS*: (3) iv/iii BC Peek, *IAEpid* 51, 8; *BSA* 61 (1966) p. 319 no. 26 (date)
—HERMIONE: (4) iii BC *IG* IV (1) 728, 15 (s. Μενεκλῆς)
ELIS: (5) 396 BC Moretti, *Olymp.* 375 (Stephanis 1491)
EPIROS:
—AMBRAKIA: (6) ii-i BC *CIG* 1800, 7-8 (s. Ἡρά-κλειτος, f. Ἡράκλειτος)

ILLYRIA:
—DASSARETIOI: (7) iii AD *ZA* 20 (1970) p. 160 (Αὐρ. Κ.: s. Πτολεμαῖος)
KORINTHIA:
—SIKYON: (8) 327-326 BC *CID* II 32, 35; 97, 30; 99 A, [1]; 120 A, [43]; p. 262 n. on l. 41 (Skalet 187) (s. Τιμοκράτης); (9) ?221 BC *PUG* III 101-2 (f. Τίμαρχος, Μενέλαος)
S. ITALY (CAMPANIA):
—CELLOLE (MOD.): (10) imp. *Romans in N. Campania* p. 105 no. 15 (Lat. C. Caius Crates)
SICILY:
—GELA-PHINTIAS: (11) s. vi BC Guarducci, *Ep. Gr.* 1 p. 252 no. 2 (Dubois, *IGDS* 128; Arena, *Iscr. Sic.* II 3; *IGLMP* 15) (-τε̄ς)

## Κρατησικλέα

LAKONIA:
—MESSA?: (1) imp. *IG* V (1) 1280, 10 (d. Εὐκλεί-δας)

## Κρατησίκλεια

LAKONIA:
—SPARTA: (1) ?m. vi BC Iamb., *VP* 267 (*FVS* 1 p. 448; Poralla² 454); (2) c. 280-219 BC Plu., *Cleom.* 6; 22; 38 (Bradford (-)) (m. Κλεομένης, Εὐκλείδας, Χιλωνίς)

## Κρατησικλῆς

LAKONIA:
—SPARTA: (1) 425 BC Th. iv 11. 2 (Poralla² 455) (f. Θρασυμηλίδας); (2) c. 100 AD *IG* V (1) 273 (Bradford (-)) (Κ. ὁ καὶ Στράτων: s. Στράτων)
MESSENIA:
—MESSENE?: (3) f. iii BC *IG* XII (9) 217, 2, 9 (s. Χαρτίων: name, locn.—Knoepfler)

## Κρατησίλοχος

ACHAIA:
—PATRAI: (1) 160-150 BC ib. v (2) 367, 10, 34 (*IPArk* 19) (s. Παυσίμαχος)

## Κρατησίνικος

ACHAIA: (1) 146 BC *IG* IV (1)² 28, 152 (f. Κρα-τῖνος: synoikos)
LAKONIA:
—ASOPOS: (2) ii BC ib. v (1) 962, 1, 15 (f. Πεῖ-τας)

## Κρατησιππίδας

LAKONIA:
—SPARTA: (1) 409 BC X., *HG* i 1. 32; i 5. 1; D.S. xiii 15. 3 (Poralla² 456)

## Κρατήσιππος

LAKONIA:
—SPARTA: (1) s. i BC *IG* V (1) 92, 1 (Bradford (3)) (f. Εὔδαμος); (2) ~ *IG* V (1) 134, 2 (Brad-ford (1)); (3) ?i AD *IG* V (1) 520 (Bradford (4)) (Γ. Ἰούλ. Κ.)
MESSENIA:
—MESSENE: (4) ?ii-i BC *SEG* XLI 343, 4 ([Κρα]τήσιππος, [Κ]τήσιππος—ed. pr.)
S. ITALY (BRUTTIUM):
—RHEGION: (5) c. 420-410 BC Herzfelder, *Mon-naies de Rhégion* pp. 102-3 nos. 62-4 (coins)

## Κρατησώ

ARKADIA:
—PHIGALEIA: (1) ii BC *IG* V (2) 428

## Κρατιάδας

AITOLIA:
—BOUKATION: (1) 163 BC ib. IX (1)² (1) 103, 8
ARGOLIS:
—ARGOS: (2) c. 458 BC ib. I³ 1149, 78

## Κρατίας

LAKONIA:
—SPARTA: (1) i-ii AD ib. v (1) 774 (Bradford (-)) (Κ(ρ)ατίας)

SICILY:
—MORGANTINA: (2) ?iv/iii BC *SEG* XXXIX 1008, 7 (f. Νικίας)

## Κρατίδας

AITOLIA: (1) 217 BC Nachtergael, *Les Galates* 65, 2
ARKADIA: (2) iii BC Breccia, *Iscriz.* 307 (s. Πρα-ξίας)
S. ITALY (BRUTTIUM):
—SYBARIS-THOURIOI-COPIAE: (3) iii BC Theoc., *Id.* v 90, 99

## Κράτιλλος

ILLYRIA:
—BYLLIONES: (1) i BC Cabanes, *L'Épire* p. 562 no. 36 (*SEG* XXXVIII 570) (s. Μαχάτας)
—BYLLIONES BYLLIS: (2) hell. *Iliria* 1982 (1), p. 107 no. 19 = p. 120 no. 33 (tile) (Κράτι̣[λ]λος)

## Κρατῖνος

ACHAIA: (1) 146 BC *IG* IV (1)² 28, 152 (s. Κρα-τησίνικος: synoikos)
—AIGEIRA: (2) ?272 BC *RE* (1); Moretti, *Olymp.* 541
AITOLIA: (3) ?262 BC *FD* III (4) 357, 4 ([Κρ]ατῖνος)
—APERANTOI: (4) iii BC *SBBerlAk* 1936, p. 388 no. 2, 4 (*L'Illyrie mérid.* 1 p. 110 fig. 7) (f. Θρασύλαος); (5) ~ *SBBerlAk* 1936, p. 388 no. 2, 5 (*L'Illyrie mérid.* 1 p. 110 fig. 7) (s. Τιμό-λαος)
ARGOLIS:
—EPIDAUROS: (6) hell. Peek, *NIEpid* 111 (Κρα[τῖ]νος: f. Εὐήνωρ, Λαφιλ—); (7) imp. Peek, *IAEpid* 186 (Κ̣[ρ]α̣[τ]ῖνος: s. Διόγνητος)
ARKADIA:
—MEGALOPOLIS: (8) i BC *SEG* XLII 746 B, 11
—TEGEA: (9) c. 225 BC ib. XI 414, 8 (Perlman E.5) (f. Καλλικράτης)
KORINTHIA:
—KORINTH: (10) 191-146 BC *BMC Pelop.* p. 12 no. 140 (coin)
LAKONIA:
—SPARTA: (11) arch.? Paus. vi 9. 4; *RE* (5); cf. Moretti, *Olymp.* 975 (sculptor); (12) f. i AD *RE* s.v. Iulius (200) (Bradford (-)) (Γ. Ἰούλ. Κ.: s. Γ. Ἰούλ. Λάκων)
MESSENIA:
—MESSENE: (13) ii-i BC *SEG* XLI 343, 8 ([Κρ]ατῖνος)
S. ITALY (CALABRIA):
—TARAS-TARENTUM: (14) c. 302-280 BC Vlasto 677-8 (coin) (Evans, *Horsemen* p. 133 VI A.4)
S. ITALY (CAMPANIA):
—NEAPOLIS: (15) i BC/i AD *INap* 161 ([Κρ]ατῖνος?, [Πρ]ατῖνος?)
S. ITALY (LUCANIA):
—HERAKLEIA: (16) iv/iii BC *IGSI* 1 I, 168 (*DGE* 62; Uguzzoni–Ghinatti I) (f. Φιντίας)
SICILY:
—KAMARINA: (17) f. v BC Cordano, *Tessere Pubbliche* 9 a (Arena, *Iscr. Sic.* II 128 A) ([Κ]ρατῖνος: f. Ἡρακλείδας)

## Κράτιος

MESSENIA:
—MESSENE: (1) c. 140 BC *IvOl* 52, 32 (f. Φίλοι-τος)

## Κρατιππίδας

MESSENIA:
—THOURIA: (1) ii/i BC *IG* V (1) 1384, 22 (f. Ἀρι-στείδας)

## Κράτιππος

AITOLIA:
—THERMOS*: (1) s. iii BC ib. IX (1)² (1) 60 VI, 25 ([Κρ]άτιππος); (2) ~ ib. 60 VII, 17
AKARNANIA:
—ANAKTORION: (3) iii BC ib. IX (1)² (2) 222 ([Κρ]άτιππος, [Πρ]άτιππος?—*IG*)
—ASTAKOS: (4) ii BC ib. 434, 4 (s. Ἀθάναιος)
ARKADIA:
—TEGEA: (5) ii AD ib. v (2) 54, 19

Κράτις (continued)

MESSENIA:
—MESSENE: (6) f. iii BC *PAE* 1991, p. 99 no. 7, 9
—THOURIA: (7) f. ii BC *SEG* XI 972, 90 (f. —ης)
S. ITALY (BRUTTIUM):
—LOKROI EPIZEPHYRIOI: (8) ?c. 500-480 BC Robert, *Coll. Froehner* 82 (Landi, *DISMG* 58); cf. *LSAG*² p. 286 no. 3 (date) (Κρά-τιπ[πος])
——(Πετ.): (9) iv/iii BC De Franciscis 19, 1
—RHEGION: (10) s. ii BC *IG* XIV 615, 5; *Klearchos* 21 (1979) pp. 83-96 (date) (I f. Κρά-τιππος II); (11) ~ *IG* XIV 615, 5; *Klearchos* 21 (1979) pp. 83-96 (date) (II s. Κράτιππος I)
S. ITALY (CAMPANIA):
—NEAPOLIS: (12) i BC/i AD *INap* 170, 1 ?= (13); (13) ~ ib. l. 2 (f. Σῶσις) ?= (14) (12); (14) ~ ib. l. 3 ?= (13)
SICILY:
—TYNDARIS: (15) f. i BC Cic., *In Verr.* II iv 29 (Lat. Cratippus)

Κράτις
S. ITALY (CALABRIA):
—TARAS-TARENTUM: (1) iii/ii BC *ASP* 22 (1969) p. 92 no. 4 (loomweight)

Κρᾶτις
SICILY:
—SELINOUS: (1) s. vi BC Dubois, *IGDS* 58 (Arena, *Iscr. Sic.* I 19; *IGLMP* 82) (Κρᾶτις—Dubois and Arena, Κρᾶτις—*IGLMP*, Κρα-τίς?—*LGPN*)

Κρατισθένης
ARGOLIS:
—PHLEIOUS: (1) ?iv BC Ath. 19e (Stephanis 1496)

Κρατίσκος
S. ITALY (CALABRIA):
—TARAS-TARENTUM: (1) iv/iii BC *IG* XIV 668 II, 5 (Landi, *DISMG* 194)

Κρατίστη
S. ITALY (CALABRIA):
—TARAS-TARENTUM: (1) imp. *CIL* IX 238 (Lat. Calpurnia Cratista)

Κρατιστόλας
LAKONIA:
—SPARTA: (1) c. 30-20 BC *IG* V (1) 211, 18 (Bradford (-)) (s. Ἀριστόλας)
MESSENIA:
—MESSENE: (2) f. iii BC *SEG* XLI 342, 15; cf. *PAE* 1991, p. 100 no. 8 (Ματιοτος—ed. pr., K.—*SEG*)

Κρατίστολος
SICILY:
—SYRACUSE: (1) f. iv BC [Pl.], *Ep.* 310 C (Κρα-τιστόλαος?)

Κράτιστος
S. ITALY (CALABRIA):
—TARAS-TARENTUM: (1) imp. *CIL* IX 237 (Lat. T. Calpurnius Cratistus)

Κρατύϊος
ARKADIA:
—TORTHYNEION: (1) c. 230-200 BC *BCH* 45 (1921) p. 14 II, 122 (f. Εὐρυμαχίδας)

Κρατύλος
AIGINA: (1) v BC *BMI* 947 (*SEG* XLI 1708 (fals.?))
S. ITALY (CAMPANIA):
—POMPEII: (2) i BC-i AD *CIL* IV 1439 (Lat. C. Kratilus)


Κράτων
AITOLIA:
—KONOPE-ARSINOE: (1) hell.-imp. *SEG* XXXIV 468
ARGOLIS:
—EPIDAUROS: (2) imp. *IG* IV (1)² 464; 465
—HERMIONE: (3) i BC *SEG* XII 190 a (f. Μό-σχιον)
EPIROS:
—AMBRAKIA: (4) a. 167 BC ib. XXXV 665 A, 12 (f. Μένανδρος)
KORINTHIA:
—SIKYON: (5) arch. *RE* (3) (Skalet 188) (painter); (6) c. 208 BC *FD* III (4) 135, 12 (s. Μενέμαχος)
LAKONIA:
—THALAMAI: (7) ?211-212 AD *IG* V (1) 1318, 8 (f. Δαμοκράτης)
MESSENIA:
—ASINE: (8) hell.-imp. ib. 1407 (s. Εὐμένης)
—MESSENE: (9) ii/i BC *SEG* XLI 346; 348 (s. Θεοφάνης, f. Θεοφάνης); (10) 31 BC-14 AD ib. XXIII 207, 12; *PAE* 1992, p. 71 A, 1 (s. Ἀρ-χέδαμος)
—THOURIA: (11) ii-i BC *IG* V (1) 1385, 16 (s. Κάλλων); (12) f. ii BC *SEG* XI 972, 108 (s. Φιλοκλῆς)
S. ITALY (BRUTTIUM):
—HIPPONION-VIBO VALENTIA: (13) imp. *CIL* X 71 (Lat. Crato)
—LOKROI EPIZEPHYRIOI:
——(Ἀγκ.): (14) 278 BC De Franciscis 15, 5; 30, 7 (f. Ἀντίδωρος)
——(Θρα.): (15) 279 BC ib. 13, 2; 25, 3 (s. Θή-ρων)
S. ITALY (CAMPANIA):
—DIKAIARCHIA-PUTEOLI: (16) imp. *CIL* X 2709 (Lat. Marius Crato)
SICILY:
—LIPARA*: (17) imp.? *Meligunis-Lipara* 2 p. 331; cf. *Kokalos* 32 (1986) p. 253 no. 128 (tile) (Lat. Crato)

Κραύγατος
KORINTHIA:
—KORINTH: (1) f. iv AD *Ag.* VII p. 153 no. 1818; *Corinth* IV (2) p. 205 no. 700 (lamps)

Κραῦγις
ARKADIA:
—MEGALOPOLIS: (1) hell. *AR* 1994-5, p. 13 (f. Ξεναίρετος); (2) iii BC *RE* Supplbd. 4 (-); *FD* III (1) 47, 2 (f. Φιλοποίμην)
—ORCHOMENOS: (3) i BC/i AD? *GP* 372 (s. Νεο-λαΐδας: fict.?)

Κράφαγος
SICILY:
—KEPHALOIDION: (1) i BC-i AD *IG* XIV 351 + *SEG* XXXVII 763 (Σῶσις K.: ?s. Νύμφων)

Κρέκων
S. ITALY (CAMPANIA):
—HERCULANEUM*: (1) i BC-i AD *CIL* X 1403 g II, 9 (Lat. Q. Harius Crecon: freed.)

Κρεομάχα
AKARNANIA:
—PALAIROS: (1) hell.? *IG* IX (1)² (2) 564

Κρεοντίδας
AIGINA: (1) ?f. v BC ib. IV (1) 1595 (gem); *LSAG*² p. 439 no. 10a (date); (2) ?465 BC Pi., *N.* vi, 40

Κρέπα
S. ITALY (LUCANIA):
—POSEIDONIA-PAESTUM: (1) m. iv BC *RVP* p. 225 no. 863 (vase)


Κρεσφόντης
MESSENIA:
—MESSENE: (1) 126 AD *IG* V (1) 1469, 1; cf. *SEG* XL 366

Κρεταία
EPIROS:
—DODONA*: (1) vi/v BC *PAE* 1931, p. 88 no. 1

Κρέτεια
ARKADIA:
—MANTINEIA-ANTIGONEIA: (1) v/iv BC *IG* IV (1)² 149 (Peek, *IAEpid* 67; Lazzarini 284)

Κρεύγας
ILLYRIA:
—EPIDAMNOS-DYRRHACHION: (1) ?v/iv BC *RE* (-)

Κρεύθων
AITOLIA:
—KOTTAEIS: (1) ?268 BC *SGDI* 2598 (f. Κλευ-μένης)

Κρευμένων
S. ITALY (CAMPANIA):
—NEAPOLIS: (1) i BC/i AD *INap* 134; cf. Leiwo p. 78 no. 24 (s. Ἡρακλείδης)

Κρηθεύς
ARGOLIS:
—ARGOS: (1) iii BC *IG* IV (1) 618 II, 3 (f. Αἰσχί-νας)
—EPIDAUROS: (2) iv/iii BC ib. IV (1)² 305

Κρηΐλα
ARGOLIS:
—ARGOS?: (1) f. v BC ib. 138 + *AE* 1975, p. 24 no. 16 (name) (Lazzarini 280) (Κρηΐ-)

Κρήνη
ILLYRIA:
—APOLLONIA: (1) ii AD *IApoll* 254 (Ἰουν. Κρήνν[η])

Κρής
ARGOLIS:
—EPIDAUROS*: (1) c. 370-335 BC *IG* IV (1)² 103, 132; Peek, *IAEpid* 52 A, 14, 16

Κρήσκενς
KORINTHIA:
—KORINTH: (1) iii AD *Ag.* VII pp. 90 no. 222; 97 nos. 302-3; *Corinth* IV (2) pp. 185 no. 538; 203 no. 679; *BM Lamps* 3 p. 404 nos. Q3246-7; *Lampes antiques BN* I 28; II 325; *SEG* XXVII 35. 14; 36. 9; XXX 348 (lamps)

Κρησκεντίων
EPIROS:
—BOUTHROTOS: (1) iii AD *IBouthrot* 194 (Ugolini, *Alb. Ant.* 3 p. 210 no. 6)

Κρήσκης
SICILY:
—SYRACUSE: (1) iii-v AD *SEG* XV 585 (Κρήσ[κης])

Κρησκώνις
SICILY:
—SYRACUSE: (1) iii-v AD Ferrua, *NG* 196 (-νεις)

Κρῆσσα
AIGINA: (1) iv BC *SEG* XXXIV 270 (Κρῆσα)

Κρητικός
S. ITALY (CAMPANIA):
—HERCULANEUM*: (1) m. i AD *CIL* X 1403 g III, 61 (Lat. L. Velleius Creticus: freed.)

Κρητίνης
S. ITALY (BRUTTIUM):
—RHEGION: (1) vi BC Hdt. vii 165 (f. Ἀναξίλας)

Κρήτων
S. ITALY (CAMPANIA):
—NEAPOLIS: (1) her. *IG* XIV 743 (*INap* 31) (Κρήτονδαι (n. gent.))

**Κριάννιος**

SICILY:
—KAMARINA: (2) hell. *SEG* XXXIX 1001, 7 (s. Ὄλυμπις)

**Κριάννιος**

ELIS: (1) hell.? Moretti, *Olymp.* 969

**Κριθέας**

ARGOLIS:
—ARGOS: (1) iii BC *IG* IV (1) 618 II, 6 (f. Ἀγηΐδαμος)

**Κριθύλος**

ARGOLIS:
—ARGOS: (1) ?c. 480-475 BC *JÖAI* 14 (1911) Beibl. p. 142 no. 2, 2 (Lazzarini 938); *LSAG*² p. 169 no. 21 (date)

**Κρίθων**

ACHAIA:
—AIGION: (1) 191-146 BC *SNG Cop. Phliasia-Laconia* 326 (coin)
ARKADIA: (2) iv BC *IG* V (2) p. xxii l. 9 (s. Ἀρχέπολις)
—THELPHOUSA: (3) a. 228 BC ib. IV (1)² 72 B, 31 (f. Φέρις)
SICILY:
—AKRAI: (4) ?iii BC *SGDI* 3239, 8 (*Akrai* p. 157 no. 9) (s. Φιλιστίων)
—MORGANTINA: (5) ?iv/iii BC *SEG* XXXIX 1010, 7-8 (f. Δαμάτριος, Φιλόδωρος)
—SYRACUSE?: (6) hell. *IG* XIV 2407. 17; cf. *L'Incidenza dell'Antico* pp. 420 ff. (bullet) (s. Ἀριστόβουλος)
—TAUROMENION: (7) 178 BC *IG* XIV 421 an. 63 (s. Ἀρτεμίδωρος)
——(Ἀσαι.): (8) c. 146-142 BC ib. 421 an. 99 (*SGDI* 5219); *IGSI* 4 III (IV), 73 an. 95 + *Comptes et Inventaires* p. 178 (*SEG* XXXVIII 975 n. on l. 72) (f. Φιλωνίδας)

**Κριθώνιος**

S. ITALY (LUCANIA):
—GRUMENTUM: (1) ?iv BC *IG* XIV 654; cf. *Epigraphica* 35 (1973) pp. 7 ff. (Κρει-)

**Κρίνιον**

AITOLIA:
—TRICHONION: (1) 183 BC *SGDI* 2133, 9 (and Lokris (Western) Amphissa: d. Εὔμναστος)

**Κρίνιππος**

SICILY:
—HIMERA: (1) s. vi BC Hdt. vii 165 (f. Τήριλλος)
—SYRACUSE: (2) 373 BC X., *HG* vi 2. 36; D.S. xv 47. 7; Polyaen. iii 9. 55

**Κρίνις**

ARKADIA:
—MANTINEIA-ANTIGONEIA: (1) c. 480-460 BC *CEG* I 380 i (f. Πραξιτέλης)

**Κρινόλαος**

AITOLIA: (1) ?252-248 BC *Syll*³ 422, 4
—OPHIONEIS: (2) iii BC *IG* IX (1)² (1) 160
—THERMOS: (3) 214 BC ib. 177, 19 (Κρινό[λαος]: f. Δικαίαρχος)
AKARNANIA:
—STRATOS: (4) 223 BC ib. 31, 49

**Κρινοτέλης**

ARKADIA:
—MT. KYLLENE*: (1) iv-iii BC ib. V (2) 364 ([Κ]ρινοτέλης)

**Κρίνουσα**

S. ITALY (CAMPANIA):
—MISENUM*: (1) imp. *CIL* X 3544 (Lat. Pettia Crinusa)

**Κρινώ**

AIGINA: (1) vi/v BC *SEG* XXXIX 332 (-νό)
AKARNANIA?: (2) iii BC Unp. (Agrinion Mus.)

**Κριός**

AIGINA: (1) vi/v BC Hdt. vi 50; 73; viii 92; *PMG* 507; *RE* Supplbd. 4 (9) (s. Πολύκριτος, f. Πολύκριτος)
ARGOLIS:
—EPIDAUROS: (2) iii BC Peek, *IAEpid* 73, 3 ([Κ]ριός)

**Κρισκωνία**

SICILY:
—SYRACUSE: (1) iii-v AD *IG* XIV 177 (Strazzulla 115; Agnello 12; Wessel 1108); cf. Ferrua, *NG* 176 (d. Τιμόθεος, Εἰρήνη)

**Κρῖσος**

ARKADIA:
—TEGEA: (1) arch.? Paus. viii 48. 1 (Κροῖσος—mss.)

**Κρισπῖνα**

SICILY:
—SYRACUSE: (1) iii-v AD *IG* XIV 39 (Strazzulla 140); cf. *Riv. Arch. Crist.* 18 (1941) p. 194 no. 62; (2) ~ *IG* XIV 138 (Strazzulla 78); (3) ~ *Rend. Pont.* 22 (1946-7) p. 234 no. 31 (Χρη-); (4) ~ Führer p. 817 n. + Ferrua, *NG* 310 (Κρισπῖ[να]?)

**Κρισπῖνος**

ACHAIA:
—PATRAI: (1) i BC/i AD *SEG* XXVI 485, 1 (brick) (-πεῖ-)
SICILY:
—SYRACUSE: (2) iii-v AD *NScav* 1905, p. 398 no. 4 (Wessel 1189)

**Κρίσπος**

KORINTHIA:
—KORINTH: (1) m. i AD *Act. Ap.* 18. 8; *1 Ep. Cor.* 1. 15 (Jew)

**Κρίσων**

EPIROS: (1) 208 BC *IMM* 32, 37
—BOUTHROTOS (PRASAIBOI): (2) a. 163 BC *IBouthrot* 31, 77 (*SEG* XXXVIII 490); *SEG* XXXVIII 134, 1 (s. Κλεόμμας, f. Κλεόμμας, Σωκράτης); (3) ~ *IBouthrot* 143, 10 (Κρί[σων]: f. Σατυρῖνος)
—MOLOSSOI:
——Kyestoi: (4) c. 230-219 BC Cabanes, *L'Épire* p. 546 nos. 14-15 (s. Σαβύρτιος, f. Μενέλαος)
ILLYRIA:
—APOLLONIA: (5) ii-i BC *IApoll* 119 (f. Μενέδαμος)
SICILY:
—HIMERA: (6) 448-440 BC *RE* (-); Moretti, *Olymp.* 294; 306; 312 (Κρίσσων—D.S., Κρίτων—*FGrH* 415, Γρίσων—Hesych., Βρίσων—Plu. *Mor.* 471 E); (7) s. iv BC Berve 451

**Κριτίας**

ARGOLIS:
—KLEONAI: (1) iv AD Alciphr. iii 12 (Stephanis 1506) (fict.?)

**Κριτοβούλα**

AKARNANIA:
—PALAIROS: (1) hell.? *IG* IX (1)² (2) 565

**Κριτοβούλη**

S. ITALY (CAMPANIA):
—KYME: (1) ?f. vi BC Dubois, *IGDGG* I 17 a (Arena, *Iscr. Sic.* III 13); *LSAG*² p. 240 no. 4 (date) (Κριτοβόλε̄—Dubois, Κριτοβόλε̄—Arena)

**Κριτόβουλος**

ACHAIA:
—AIGION: (1) c. 230-200 BC *BCH* 45 (1921) p. 11 II, 59 (f. Αἰγιαλεύς)
MESSENIA:
—MESSENE: (2) iv/iii BC *IG* V (1) 1435, 12

**Κριτοβώλα**

AIGINA: (1) ?v BC Unp. (Aigina Mus.); cf. *PdelP* 31 (1976) p. 209 no. 10

**Κριτόδαμος**

AITOLIA: (1) c. 315-280 BC *FD* III (1) 145, 1 (f. Κλέαρχος)
—POTIDANIA: (2) m. ii BC *SBBerlAk* 1936, p. 371 b, 11 (*SEG* XLI 528 B) (Κριτόδ[αμος]: s. Φιλάνβροτος)
ARKADIA:
—KLEITOR: (3) iv BC Moretti, *Olymp.* 406 (s. Λίχας)
ILLYRIA:
—EPIDAMNOS-DYRRHACHION: (4) iv BC *IDyrrh* 9 ?= (5); (5) ~ ib. 41 ?= (4)
KORINTHIA:
—SIKYON: (6) ?254 BC Nachtergael, *Les Galates* 9, 9 (Skalet 189); cf. Stephanis 18 (-δη-: f. Ἀγαθῖνος)
LAKONIA:
—SPARTA: (7) c. 30-20 BC *IG* V (1) 141, 22; *SEG* XXXV 329 (date) (Bradford (2)); (8) c. 110-120 AD *IG* V (1) 298, 3; *Artemis Orthia* pp. 315-16 no. 35 (date) (Bradford (1)) (s. Τεισαμενός)
MESSENIA:
—MESSENE: (9) ?202 BC *IG* VII 292, 3 (*IOrop* 202) (-δη-: s. Λεωνίδας)

**Κριτόλα**

AIGINA: (1) ii BC *IG* II² 7957 (d. Εὐμαχίδας)

**Κριτολαΐδας**

EPIROS:
—ARGOS (AMPHILOCH.): (1) c. 315-280 BC *FD* III (4) 407, 2 (f. Θερσαγόρας)

**Κριτόλαος**

ACHAIA: (1) ii BC *RE* (1)
—PATRAI: (2) imp. *Rh. Mus.* 21 (1866) p. 398 no. 265 (f. Θεόδωρος)
AITOLIA: (3) c. 261 BC *IG* IX (1)² (1) 18, 19
—APERANTOI: (4) ?iv/iii BC ib. 166, 4 (*L'Illyrie mérid.* 1 p. 109 fig. 6)
—ATTALEIA: (5) ii BC *SBBerlAk* 1936, p. 380 no. 1 A, 2
—PHISTYON: (6) ii BC *IG* IX (1)² (1) 110 a, 3 ?= (7); (7) c. 164 BC ib. 99, 3 ?= (6)
—TRICHONION: (8) f. ii BC Fraser–Rönne, *BWGT* p. 144 no. 1 ?= (9) (10); (9) 165 BC *ZPE* 101 (1994) p. 128, 5?, 18 ?= (8); (10) c. 157 BC *IG* IX (1)² (1) p. LII, s.a. 157 BC ?= (8)
AKARNANIA:
—PALAIROS: (11) ii BC ib. IX (1)² (2) 451, 14 (f. Νικίας)
ARKADIA:
—TEGEA: (12) her.? *FGrH* 42 F 5 (s. Ῥηξίμαχος: fict.)
ITHAKE: (13) hell. *IG* IX (1) 672 (Fraser–Rönne, *BWGT* p. 118 no. 1)
SICILY:
—INESSA-AITNA: (14) f. i BC Cic., *In Verr.* II iv 59 (Lat. Critolaus)
ZAKYNTHOS: (15) hell.? *IG* IX (1) 607

**Κριτόλας**

ARGOLIS:
—PHLEIOUS: (1) 331 BC *CID* II 86, 10 ([Κρι]τόλας)
S. ITALY (BRUTTIUM):
—LOKROI EPIZEPHYRIOI:
——(Φαω.): (2) iv/iii BC De Franciscis 21, 6
S. ITALY (CALABRIA):
—TARAS-TARENTUM: (3) iv BC *SEG* XXX 1218 (Landi, *DISMG* 191) (f. Ἀρτεμίδωρος)

**Κριτόνικος**
LAKONIA:
—SPARTA: (**1**) c. 160-170 AD *IG* v (1) 109,
18 (Bradford (2)) ([Κρ]ιτόνικος: I f. Κριτόνι-
κος II); (**2**) ~ *IG* v (1) 109, 18 (Bradford (2))
([Κρ]ιτόνικος: II s. Κριτόνικος I)

**Κριτόνιλλα**
S. ITALY (LUCANIA):
—MURO LUCANO (MOD.): (**1**) imp. *NScav* 1883,
p. 564 (*Eph. Ep.* VIII 278) (Lat. Allia Cri-
tonilla)

**Κρῖτος**
S. ITALY (CALABRIA):
—TARAS-TARENTUM: (**1**) c. 212-209 BC Vlasto
978-80 (coins) (Evans, *Horsemen* p. 210 X
C.1)

**Κρίτυλλα**
ARGOLIS:
—ARGOS:
——(Lykophronidai): (**1**) ii-i BC *IG* IV (1) 530,
19; cf. *BCH* 33 (1909) p. 183 n. 2

**Κρίτων**
AIGINA: (**1**) ?f. i AD *Alt-Ägina* I (2) p. 45 no.
17, 5 (f. Διογένης)
ARGOLIS:
—ARGOS: (**2**) v-iv BC Iamb., *VP* 267 (*FVS* 1 p.
447); (**3**) ii BC *IG* IV (1) 557, 8
KORINTHIA:
—KORINTH: (**4**) f. ii BC *Corinth* VIII (1) 73, 1 (s.
Λυκῖνος, f. Τιμασίων)
—SIKYON: (**5**) ii/i BC *SEG* XI 251, 2 (f. Θράσων)
S. ITALY: (**6**) hell. *Memnonion* 55 (s. Ἀγαθοκλῆς)
SICILY:
—AKRAI: (**7**) ii BC *Akrai* p. 156 no. 6, 13 (I f.
Κρίτων II); (**8**) ~ ib. l. 13 (II s. Κρίτων I)
—SYRACUSE: (**9**) c. 146-140 BC *ID* 1443 B I,
133; 1444 Aa 16; 1449 B a I c, 19

**Κροίας**
ARKADIA:
—MANTINEIA-ANTIGONEIA:
——(Posoidaia): (**1**) c. 425-400 BC *SEG* XXXI
348, 17; cf. Dubois, *RDA* 2 p. 125 (K.—lap.,
Κρ(ι)θίας—Dubois)

**Κροκίνη**
ILLYRIA:
—EPIDAMNOS-DYRRHACHION: (**1**) imp. *CIL* III
12308 (Lat. Iulia Crocine)
S. ITALY (CAMPANIA):
—POMPEII: (**2**) i BC-i AD ib. IV 5297-8 (Lat.
Crocine); (**3**) ~ *NScav* 1916, p. 303 no. 104
bis c (Castrèn 457. 9) (Lat. Vivia Crocine)

**Κρόκος**
S. ITALY (CAMPANIA):
—DIKAIARCHIA-PUTEOLI: (**1**) ?i-ii AD *CIL* x
2547 (Lat. C. Iulius Crocus)
—POMPEII: (**2**) 56 AD ib. 826; 10036 a (Castrèn
348. 2) (Lat. M. Salarius Crocus) ?= (*3*); (**3**)
70-79 AD *CIL* IV 3491; 6645; 6647; 6667 (Lat.
Crocus) ?= (2)

**Κροκύλος**
S. ITALY (BRUTTIUM):
—SYBARIS-THOURIOI-COPIAE: (**1**) iii BC
Theoc., *Id.* v 11 (fict.)

**Κρονίων**
KORINTHIA:
—KORINTH: (**1**) ?iii AD *Hesp.* 63 (1994) pp. 116
ff. no. 5 col. I, 6 (lead) (K. ὁ καὶ Λαῖτος)

**Κροτίς**
S. ITALY (APULIA):
—BARION: (**1**) imp. *CIL* IX 291 (Lat. Atilia
Crotis)

**Κρότος**
ILLYRIA:
—EPIDAMNOS-DYRRHACHION: (**1**) imp. *AEp*
1978, no. 749 (Lat. Crotus: freed./doctor)

**Κρότων**
MESSENIA:
—KORONE: (**1**) 246 AD *IG* v (1) 1398, 43 (Ἀττ.
K.)

**Κροτωνίς**
S. ITALY (BRUTTIUM):
—PETELIA: (**1**) i AD *Misc. Gr. Rom.* 10 pp. 153-
4 (Lat. Octavia Crotonis)

**Κρύπτη**
SICILY:
—SYRACUSE: (**1**) iii-v AD *NScav* 1893, p. 295
no. 60 + Ferrua, *NG* 25 (Γρύ(π)τη)

**Κρύτων**
ARGOLIS:
—HERMIONE: (**1**) iii BC *IG* IV (1) 729 I, 7 (s.
Διοπείθης)

**Κρωβύλος**
AITOLIA: (**1**) ?254 BC *Syll*³ 436, 3; Nachtergael,
*Les Galates* 9, 4
KORINTHIA:
—KORINTH: (**2**) s. iv BC Berve 454

**Κρωμύθα**
EPIROS:
—AMBRAKIA: (**1**) ?iii/ii BC Unp. (Arta Mus., in-
scr.)

**Κρωταμήνη**
ILLYRIA:
—BYLLIONES BYLLIS: (**1**) iii AD *SEG* XXXVIII
555 (Κρωταμήνι (dat.): d. Καλλιόπη)

**Κτησίας**
ARGOLIS:
—EPIDAUROS: (**1**) ii-iii AD *IG* IV (1)² 478
DALMATIA:
—ISSA: (**2**) ?i AD *VAHD* 53 (1950-51) p. 211 no.
1 (Šašel, *IL* 927)

**Κτησίβις**
SICILY:
—SYRACUSE: (**1**) iii-v AD *IG* XIV 98 (Strazzulla
39; Wessel 1332)

**Κτησικλῆς**
ACHAIA: (**1**) 146 BC *IG* IV (1)² 28, 103 (s. Νι-
κίας: synoikos)
MESSENIA:
—THOURIA: (**2**) s. iii BC ib. v (1) 1386, 5 (s.
Φαινοκλείδας)

**Κτήσιππος**
KORINTHIA:
—SIKYON: (**1**) iii BC ib. IV (1) 426, 7
TRIPHYLIA:
—PYRGOI: (**2**) 205 BC ib. IX (1)² (1) 31, 111 (f.
Μύρτιλος, Σωτέας)

**Κτησιφῶν**
S. ITALY (CAMPANIA)?: (**1**) imp. ib. XIV 2414.
37 (tessera)

**Κτήσων**
ACHAIA: (**1**) 146 BC ib. IV (1)² 28, 93 (I f. Κτή-
σων II: synoikos); (**2**) ~ ib. l. 93 (II s. Κτήσων
I: synoikos)
ARGOLIS:
—EPIDAUROS*: (**3**) c. 290-270 BC ib. 109 II, 98,
106, 122
EPIROS:
—MOLOSSOI?: (**4**) ?342-326 BC Cabanes,
*L'Épire* p. 541 no. 5, 6

ILLYRIA:
—APOLLONIA: (**5**) hell. *IApoll* 110; (**6**) ~ ib. 111
(s. Ἀριστήν)
—EPIDAMNOS-DYRRHACHION: (**7**) c. 250-50 BC
Ceka 264; 265 + Maier 273 (*BMC Thes-
saly* p. 71 no. 91); Maier 128; Münsterberg
Nachtr. pp. 16-17; *Bakërr Hoard* p. 66 nos.
40-3 (coin) (Ceka 267-74) (Κτή(σων)—264:
money.)
ITHAKE: (**8**) i AD *FGrH* 616 F 36
SICILY:
—AKRAGAS*: (**9**) iv BC *SEG* XXX 1116 (amph.)

**Κτῆτος**
ARGOLIS:
—ARGOS: (**1**) ?c. 575-550 BC ib. XI 336, 9;
*LSAG*² p. 168 no. 7 (date) (Κτε̄-: s. Μίντων)
ELIS: (**2**) ii-iii AD *IvOl* 125, 7
ILLYRIA:
—EPIDAMNOS-DYRRHACHION: (**3**) c. 250-50 BC
Maier 107; 176; 243; 262; 298; 304; 367; 384;
467; Münsterberg Nachtr. p. 16-17 (Ceka
266; 275-85); cf. *IApoll Ref. Bibl.* n. 71 (coin)
(Κτή(τος)—266: money.)
S. ITALY (BRUTTIUM):
—RHEGION*: (**4**) imp. *IG* XIV 618, 5 (slave?)

**Κυάνη**
SICILY:
—DREPANON: (**1**) imp. *CIL* X 7261 (Lat. Petro-
nia Cyane)
—SYRACUSE: (**2**) hell.? *FGrH* 290 F 7 (d. Κυά-
νιππος: fict.)

**Κυάνιππος**
SICILY:
—SYRACUSE: (**1**) hell.? ib. (f. Κυάνη: fict.)

**Κύδας**
ARKADIA:
—TEGEA: (**1**) iii BC *IG* v (2) 30, 22 (Κύδας)

**Κυδίας**
ARGOLIS:
—ARGOS: (**1**) c. 100-90 BC *SEG* XXXIII 290
A, 13; *BSA* 70 (1975) pp. 129-31 (date)
(Stephanis 1519) (s. Εὔανδρος)
—HERMIONE: (**2**) v BC *PMG* 948 (Stephanis
1520); Schol. Ar., *Nub.* 967; *RE* s.v.
Kedeides (Κυδίδου—ms. Schol. Ar.)
ARKADIA:
—MANTINEIA-ANTIGONEIA: (**3**) ii AD Luc.,
*Nav.* 38 (fict.)

**Κυδίμαχος**
ARGOLIS:
—TROIZEN: (**1**) s. ii BC *BMI* 1154 a, 4; *BE* 1972,
no. 37 (date) (f. Φιλίσκος)

**Κυδιμένης**
AIGINA: (**1**) ?f. i BC *Alt-Ägina* I (2) p. 43 no. 4,
1 (s. Πεισιτέλης)

**Κύδιμος**
ARGOLIS:
—ARGOS: (**1**) iii/ii BC *IG* v (2) 263, 1, 15 (f.
Ἀφροδίσιος)
—EPIDAUROS: (**2**) iv/iii BC Peek, *IAEpid* 340, 3
(?f. Κλεινοξένα, Κορινθία, f. Γοργόι)
S. ITALY (CAMPANIA):
—POMPEII: (**3**) i BC-i AD *CIL* IV 3376 (Castrèn
11. 4) (Lat. L. Ael. Cydimus)

**Κυδίππα**
ARGOLIS:
—ARGOS: (**1**) s. vii BC *RE* s.v. Biton (1); *AP* iii
18, 2 (m. Βίτων, Κλέοβις)

**Κυδίππη**
SICILY:
—HIMERA: (**1**) f. v BC Hdt. vii 165 (d. Τήριλλος)

**Κύδιππος**
AKARNANIA:
—KORONTA: (**1**) iii BC *IG* IX (1)² (2) 427

ARGOLIS:
—EPIDAUROS*: (2) c. 370-360 BC BSA 61 (1966) p. 271 no. 4 A, 14
ARKADIA:
—MANTINEIA-ANTIGONEIA: (3) ?iv-iii BC RE (-)
ILLYRIA:
—APOLLONIA: (4) c. 250-50 BC Maier 57; Münsterberg Nachtr. p. 13 (coin) (Ceka 49) (pryt.)
—EPIDAMNOS-DYRRHACHION: (5) c. 250-50 BC Maier 108; 167; 299 (coin) (Ceka 286-8) (money.); (6) ~ Maier 272 (coin) (Ceka 8) (pryt.)

**Κυδοιμοκλῆς**
LAKONIA:
—SPARTA: (1) iii BC SEG XL 348 B, 6

**Κυδόνικος**
AIGINA: (1) ?c. 475-450 BC CEG I 129; IC 2 p. 113 (name); LSAG² p. 113 no. 18 (date) (-δό-: ?s. Ἀγρίτας, f. Ἑρμαῖος)

**Κυδρίων**
AITOLIA: (1) ?269 BC FD III (4) 415, 7; (2) c. 240 BC Syll³ 515 A, 1 (IG IX (1)² (1) 181); Syll³ 515 B, 1 (f. Χαρίξενος)
—BOUKATION: (3) 164-161 BC IG IX (1)² (1) 99, 10; 100, 6
—LYSIMACHEIA: (4) 263-262 BC ib. 3 A, 20; 13, 7
—TRICHONION: (5) 184 BC ib. 33, 3 (s. Δωρίμαχος)

**Κύδων**
ARGOLIS:
—HERMIONE: (1) i BC-i AD? ib. IV (1) 730 IV, 1 (s. Ὀνάσιμος)
KORINTHIA:
—KORINTH: (2) inc. Apostol. xvi 59 (Arsen. xlix 57; Diogenian. viii 42; Zen. ii 42; Ps.-Plu., Prov. ii 29; Suda A 642) (fict.)
S. ITALY (CAMPANIA):
—POMPEII: (3) i BC-i AD CIL IV 1106 (Lat. Cydo)

**Κυδωνίας**
ITHAKE: (1) ?ii BC Unp. (IG arch.) (f. Ἀλεξίλαος)

**Κύδωρος**
AITOLIA?: (1) ?c. 230 BC FD III (3) 219 bis, 4

**Κύζικος**
S. ITALY (CAMPANIA):
—HERCULANEUM: (1) i BC-i AD Cron. Erc. 20 (1990) p. 161 no. 7 (tile) (Lat. Q. Mu. Cizicus)

**Κύθηρα**
S. ITALY (CAMPANIA):
—POMPEII: (1) i BC-i AD CIL IV 8792 (Lat. Cithera)

**Κυθηρία**
S. ITALY (CAMPANIA):
—DIKAIARCHIA-PUTEOLI: (1) ?ii AD ib. x 2280 (Lat. Flavia Cyteria)

**Κυθηρίς**
S. ITALY (CAMPANIA):
—DIKAIARCHIA-PUTEOLI: (1) imp. ib. 2037 (Lat. -vidia Cytheris); (2) ~ ib. 2049 (Lat. Pompeia Cytheris)

**Κύθηρος**
S. ITALY (CAMPANIA):
—POMPEII: (1) i BC-i AD Römische Gräberstrassen p. 216 e (Lat. L. Calventius Cytherus)

**Κυκλάς**
S. ITALY (CALABRIA):
—BRENTESION-BRUNDISIUM: (1) imp. CIL IX 6118 = Epigraphica 25 (1963) p. 92 no. 121 (Lat. Cyclas)
S. ITALY (CAMPANIA):
—ATELLA: (2) imp. CIL X 3734 (Lat. Plinia Cyclas)

**Κυκλιάδας**
ACHAIA: (1) iii/ii BC RE (-)

**Κυκλίας**
ARGOLIS:
—NEMEA*: (1) iv BC SEG XXVI 421. 2

**Κύκνος**
S. ITALY (CAMPANIA):
—POMPEII: (1) i BC-i AD CIL IV 2508, 21 (Lat. Cycnus); (2) ~ ib. 10057 (Lat. Cicnus)

**Κυκυίης**
SICILY:
—TERRAVECCHIA DI CUTI (MOD.): (1) vi/v BC Arena, Iscr. Sic. II 117 A (Dubois, IGDS 176) (-ίες)

**Κυκυώι**
SICILY:
—TERRAVECCHIA DI CUTI (MOD.): (1) vi/v BC ib. 175 a (loomweight) (Arena, Iscr. Sic. II 114) (Κυκυῶς (gen.))

**Κύλαμος**
KORINTHIA:
—KORINTH: (1) ?vi BC IG IV (1) 328 (pinax); cf. LSAG² p. 116 ([ϙ]ύλαμος—IG, [Ο]ύλαμος—LSAG)

**Κύλαός**
ARGOLIS:
—ARGOS:
——(Hyadai): (1) v BC IG IV (1) 553, 2; BCH 37 (1913) p. 308 (locn.)

**Κύλινδρος**
S. ITALY (CALABRIA):
—TARAS-TARENTUM: (1) c. 344-334 BC Evans, Horsemen p. 66 n. 84 (coin); cf. pl. V no. 2 (Κυλικ——Evans, Κύλιν(δρος)—LGPN)

**Κύλισος**
EPIROS:
—KASSOPE: (1) c. 130 BC Dakaris, Kassope p. 25 (SEG XXXVI 555); cf. SEG XLI 541 (s. Πολύξενος)

**Κυλίχα**
SICILY:
—SELINOUS: (1) s. vi BC Dubois, IGDS 30 (Arena, Iscr. Sic. I 62) (ϙυ-)

**Κύλλα**
KERKYRA: (1) iii BC SEG XXV 614

**Κυλλάνιος**
ACHAIA:
—DYME: (1) iii-ii BC Syll³ 530, 10; cf. Achaia und Elis p. 115 ([Κυλλ]άνιος ἢ εἰ Πανταλέων); (2) ?145 BC Sherk 43, 5; SEG XXXVIII 372 (date)

**Κυλλίας**
ARGOLIS:
—ARGOS: (1) iii BC IG IV (1) 618 II, 2, 9 (f. Εὔκριτος)
KORINTHIA:
—KORINTH: (2) c. 570-550 BC Amyx 50 (vase) (Lorber 79; IG IV (1) 349) (ϙυλί-: fict.?)

**Κύλλις**
ACHAIA:
—DYME: (1) c. 219 BC SGDI 1612, 3 (Tyche 5 (1990) p. 124) (Κύλ[λ]ις)

**Κύλλος**
ARKADIA?: (1) i-ii AD IG V (2) 508 (?f. Λυσικράτης)

**Κύλλων**
ELIS: (1) ?252-248 BC FD III (3) 191, 2 (I f. Κύλλων II); (2) ~ ib. l. 2 (II s. Κύλλων I) ?= (Κύλων (2))

**Κυλοίας**
ARGOLIS:
—HERMIONE: (1) c. 135-130 BC ib. III (4) 169, 2, 9 (s. Καλλίας)

**Κυλωϊάδας**
LAKONIA:
—SPARTA: (1) 334-324 BC CID II 32, 37; 79 A I, 22; 95, [15]; 97, 26; 102 II B, [34]; 113, 31?; 120 A, 23 (Poralla² 458; Bradford (-)) (Κυλωϊ(ά)δας—79 A)

**Κυλωΐδας**
KORINTHIA:
—KORINTH: (1) ?vi BC IG IV (1) 210 (pinax) (Lazzarini 59) (ϙυλō-)
SICILY:
—KAMARINA: (2) f. v BC Cordano, Tessere Pubbliche 29 (Κυλō[ίδα]s: s. Ἀντίοχος)

**Κύλων**
ARGOLIS:
—ARGOS: (1) 395 BC X., HG iii 5. 1; Paus. iii 9. 8
ELIS: (2) 272 BC ib. v 5. 1; vi 14. 11; Plu., Mor. 252 D; 253 A-B ?= (Κύλλων (2))
LAKONIA:
—HYPERTELEATON*: (3) imp. IG v (1) 1055 (Κύλōνος (gen.), Κυνίσκος?—Fraenkel, Tod)
S. ITALY (BRUTTIUM):
—KROTON: (4) v BC RE (2) (Γύλων—D.L.)
S. ITALY (CAMPANIA):
—POMPEII: (5) i BC-i AD CIL IV 8894 (Lat. Cylo)

**Κυμαῖος**
S. ITALY (CAMPANIA):
—HERCULANEUM: (1) m. i AD PdelP 10 (1955) p. 453 no. 79 (Lat. M. Offellius Cymaeus)

**Κυματοθέα**
KORINTHIA:
—KORINTH: (1) c. 570-550 BC Amyx 77. 5 (vase) (Lorber 111) (ϙυματοθ(έ)α—Amyx: her.)

**Κυμβάδεια**
LAKONIA:
—SPARTA: (1) iii BC SEG XI 677 b with add. (Bradford (-))

**Κύμβαλος**
ARKADIA:
—TEGEA: (1) s. iv BC SEG XI 1070
——(Hippothoitai): (2) iv/iii BC IG V (2) 38, 52 (s. Ἀρίστων)

**Κύμβας**
ARKADIA: (1) ?i AD Ant. Diog. 4; 5; 7; 10-12 (fict.)

**Κύναγος**
LAKONIA: (1) vi/v BC IG V (1) 829 (Bradford (-))

**Κύναιθος**
SICILY:
—GELA-PHINTIAS: (1) vi BC Dubois, IGDS 129 (Arena, Iscr. Sic. II 5) ([Κ]ύναιθος: s. Ἔποχος)

**Κυνήγιος**
S. ITALY (CAMPANIA):
—NOLA: (1) byz. CIL X 1370 (Lat. Cinegius)

**Κυνηγίς**
S. Italy (Campania):
—dikaiarchia-puteoli: (1) imp. ib. 2358
(Lat. Cynegis)

**Κύνης**
Akarnania:
—koronta: (1) 429 BC Th. ii 102. 1 (s. Θεόλυτος)

**Κύνθιος**
S. Italy (Campania):
—pompeii: (1) i BC-i AD *CIL* IV 9203; cf.
*Gnomon* 45 (1973) p. 268 (Lat. Cyntius (n.
pr.?))

**Κυνίσκα**
Lakonia:
—sparta: (1) v/iv BC *RE* (-); Moretti, *Olymp.*
373; 381; *CEG* II 820; cf. Ebert, *Gr. Sieg.* 33
(Poralla² 459) (d. Ἀρχίδαμος, Εὐπωλία) ?= (2);
(2) ?c. 400 BC *IG* V (1) 235, 1 ?= (1)

**Κυνίσκος**
Arkadia:
—mantineia-antigoneia: (1) m. v BC *IvOl*
149 (Lazzarini 852); Paus. vi 4. 11; cf. Ebert,
*Gr. Sieg.* 21 (I f. Κυνίσκος II); (2) ~ *RE*
(2); Moretti, *Olymp.* 265; Lazzarini 852; cf.
Ebert, *Gr. Sieg.* 21 (II s. Κυνίσκος I)
Epiros:
—bouthrotos (prasaiboi): (3) a. 163 BC
*IBouthrot* 13, 13; cf. Ugolini, *Alb. Ant.* 3 p.
120 (f. —ας)
Illyria:
—apollonia: (4) c. 250-50 BC Maier 58 (coin)
(Ceka 30) (pryt.)
—epidamnos-dyrrhachion:· (5) hell.-imp.
*IDyrrh* 458 ([Κ]υνίσκος, [Ε]ὐνίσκος?: f. Ἄνα—)
Kerkyra: (6) ?525-500 BC *Korkyra* I p. 171 no.
8; *LSAG*² p. 234 no. 14 (date) (ϙυνίσϙ(ο)ς)
Lakonia:
—sparta: (7) vi/v BC Hdt. vi 71 (Poralla² 345)
(Ζευξίδαμος ὁ ἐπικαλ. Κ.: s. Λατυχίδας, f. Ἀρχίδαμος); (8) 400 BC X., *An.* vii 1. 13 (Poralla²
460)
S. Italy (Bruttium):
—s. sosti (mod.): (9) m. vi BC Guarducci, *Ep.
Gr.* 3 p. 43 (Landi, *DISMG* 119) (ϙυνίσϙος)

**Κυνίσκυλος**
S. Italy (Campania):
—pompeii: (1) i BC-i AD *CIL* IV 3784 (Lat.
Cynisculus)

**Κυννίς**
Dalmatia:
—issa: (1) hell. Brunšmid p. 27 no. 18, 5 (*SEG*
XL 514; *VAHD* 84 (1991) p. 253 no. 3) (d.
Καλλισθένης)

**Κύνορτος**
S. Italy (Apulia):
—rubi?: (1) ?iv BC Kretschmer p. 4 n. 4 (vase)

**Κύνων**
S. Italy (Calabria):
—taras-tarentum: (1) c. 272-235 BC Vlasto
859-62 (coins) (Evans, *Horsemen* p. 178 VIII
B.4)

**Κυπάρη**
S. Italy (Apulia):
—canusium: (1) ii AD *Epig. Rom. di Canosa* 88
(Lat. Babullia Cypare: m. Babullia Severa)
—gnathia-egnatia*: (2) i/ii AD *Suppl. It.* 11
p. 28 no. 1 (Lat. Flavi[a] Cypa[re]: freed.)
—luceria*: (3) imp. *Lucera Romana* p. 26
(Lat. [All]ia Cypare: freed.)
—teanum apulum: (4) imp. *Teanum Apulum*
p. 123-4 no. 53 (Lat. Cypare)

S. Italy (Campania):
—dikaiarchia-puteoli: (5) imp. *CIL* x 2273
(Lat. Herennia Cypare: m. Herennia Fortunata)
—nuceria alfaterna: (6) imp. *NScav* 1922,
p. 487 no. 3 (Lat. Claudia Cypare)
—pompeii: (7) i BC-i AD *CIL* IV 99; cf. p. 460
(Lat. Chypare); (8) ~ ib. 4713; [4724] (Lat.
Cypare); (9) ~ ib. 8219 (Lat. [C]ypare)
S. Italy (Lucania):
—cosilinum: (10) imp. *IItal* III (1) 211 (*CIL*
x 294) (Lat. Cypare: d. Ansia Urbana)

**Κυπαρίνη**
S. Italy (Campania):
—pompeii: (1) i BC-i AD ib. IV 4141-2

**Κύπαρος**
S. Italy (Campania):
—pompeii: (1) i BC-i AD ib. 8411 b (Lat.
Ciparus)

**Κύπειρος**
S. Italy (Apulia):
—canusium*: (1) imp. *Epig. Rom. di Canosa*
156 (Lat. L. Marcius Cypaerus: freed.)
S. Italy (Campania):
—dikaiarchia-puteoli: (2) 37 AD Camodeca,
*L'Archivio Puteolano* 1 pp. 184-5; Bove, *Documenti finanziarie* pp. 24-5 T.P. 7 (Lat. C.
Novius Cypaerus)
—herculaneum: (3) 62 AD *Ostraka* 2 (1993)
pp. 203-7 (Lat. M. Nonius C[yp]aerus)

**Κυπίας**
Sicily:
—akragas (nr.)?: (1) ?iv BC Manganaro,
*QUCC* forthcoming no. 39 A, 4

**Κυπριανός**
Argolis:
—argos: (1) v-vi AD Unp. (Oikonomou-
Laniado) (Κυπρ[ιανός])

**Κύπρις**
Argolis:
—epidauros: (1) iii AD *IG* IV (1)² 401, 4; cf.
Peek, *IAEpid* 160 (f. Εὐκλῆς)

**Κυπρίς**
S. Italy (Apulia):
—canusium*: (1) imp. *Epig. Rom. di Canosa*
156 (Lat. Marcia Cypris: freed.)
S. Italy (Calabria):
—lupiae: (2) i AD *CIL* IX 19 (Susini, *Fonti
Salento* p. 140 no. 89) (Lat. Acilia Cypris:
m. Curtia Secunda)
S. Italy (Campania):
—dikaiarchia-puteoli: (3) imp. *CIL* x 2989;
cf. *Puteoli* 11 (1987) p. 57 (Lat. Sulpicia Cypris)

**Κυπρογένεια**
S. Italy (Campania):
—dikaiarchia-puteoli: (1) imp. *CIL* x 1568
(Lat. Galeria Cyprogenia: m. Πτολεμαΐς, Ἴσσα); (2) ~ ib. 2356, 3 (Lat. Minucia Cyprigenia: m. Χρῆστος)

**Κυπύρα**
Sicily:
—terravecchia di cuti (mod.): (1) v BC
Dubois, *IGDS* 175 b (loomweight) (Arena,
*Iscr. Sic.* II 112-13); cf. *Di Terra in Terra*
pp. 55-6 nos. 70-72 (Κύπρα—Arena 112); (2)
f. v BC *SEG* XXVII 657, 9 (Dubois, *IGDS*
177; Arena, *Iscr. Sic.* II 118) (?d. Ἄρχων)

**Κύρα**
Sicily:
—lipara: (1) iv/v AD Bernabò Brea, *Isole Eolie*
p. 97 and fig. 55

**Κυράνα**
Korinthia:
—korinth: (1) v BC *RE* (4); Schol. Ar., *Pl.* 149
(-ρήνη)

**Κυραναῖος**
Lakonia:
—hyperteleaton*: (1) ?c. 500-480 BC *SEG* II
170 (Lazzarini 285); *LSAG*² p. 201 no. 43 (n.
pr.?: sculptor)

**Κύρβασος**
Illyria:
—epidamnos-dyrrhachion: (1) c. 250-50 BC
Ceka, *Probleme* p. 151 no. 35 (coin) (pryt.)
?= (2); (2) ~ Maier 273 (coin); *Bakërr Hoard*
p. 67 no. 111 (Ceka 265; 416) (pryt.) ?= (1);
(3) hell.-imp. *IDyrrh* 572 (tile) ([Κυρβ?]άσου
(gen.))

**Κυριακή**
Argolis:
—argos: (1) byz. *SEG* XXVI 434, 1; cf. *TMByz*
9 (1985) p. 370 no. 119 (d. Ῥόδη)
S. Italy (Campania):
—dikaiarchia-puteoli: (2) imp. *CIL* x 1689
(Lat. Aria Cyriace)
Sicily:
—katane: (3) iii-v AD *NScav* 1931, p. 370 no.
4 (Ferrua, *NG* 420)
—syracuse: (4) iii-v AD *IG* XIV 139, 10
(Strazzulla 79; Agnello 44; Wessel 557)
(d. Κυριακός, Σαλβία); (5) ~ *IG* XIV 140
(Strazzulla 80; Wessel 1037); (6) ~ *IG* XIV 141
(Strazzulla 81; Wessel 876); (7) ~ *Riv. Arch.
Crist.* 18 (1941) p. 227 no. 119 ([Κυ]ριακή);
(8) ~ Strazzulla 266 (Wessel 934); cf. Ferrua, *NG* 37 (Κυρια[κή]?); (9) ~ Strazzulla 277
(Wessel 1355); cf. Ferrua, *NG* 45 ([Κυρι]ακή);
(10) ~ Strazzulla 279 ([Κυ]ριακή); (11) ~ ib.
286 (Wessel 1084); cf. Ferrua, *NG* 53 ?= (12);
(12) ~ Strazzulla 286 (Wessel 1084); cf. Ferrua, *NG* 53 ?= (11); (13) ~ Strazzulla 339
(Wessel 226); (14) ~ Strazzulla 366 (Agnello
26); (15) ~ Strazzulla 398 (Agnello 30; Wessel
725; Ferrua, *NG* 148) (Κυρα-); (16) ~ *ASSiciliaOrientale* 1954, p. 112 no. 1 (Κυρ[ιακή]);
(17) ~ Ferrua, *NG* 396

**Κυριακός**
Argolis:
—argos: (1) v-vi AD Unp. (Oikonomou-
Laniado)
Elis:
—olympia*: (2) f. v AD *IvOl* 656, 1
Korinthia:
—korinth: (3) byz. *Corinth* VIII (3) 561, 7; cf.
*TMByz* 9 (1985) p. 363 no. 38; (4) 449-56
AD Cyr. S., *V. Cyriac.* 1 f.; *V. Euthym.* 19;
22; 28 (s. Ἰωάννης, Εὐδοξία); (5) vi AD *SEG*
XXIX 316
Sicily:
—katane: (6) iii-v AD Agnello 62
—syracuse: (7) iii-v AD *IG* XIV 139, 1
(Strazzulla 79; Agnello 44; Wessel 557) (I
f. Κυριακός II, Κυριακή); (8) ~ *IG* XIV 139,
4 (Strazzulla 79; Agnello 44; Wessel 557)
(II s. Κυριακός I, Σαλβία); (9) ~ *IG* XIV 163
(Strazzulla 104; Wessel 1316); cf. Ferrua, *NG*
318; (10) ~ *Riv. Arch. Crist.* 36 (1960) p. 26
no. 16 (Κυρ(ι)α[κός]?); (11) ~ *SEG* XVIII 396;
(12) ~ Strazzulla 264 (Wessel 717); (13) ~
Strazzulla 286 (Wessel 1084); cf. Ferrua, *NG*
53; (14) ~ Strazzulla 314 (Wessel 1350); (15)
~ Strazzulla 411 (Barreca 227); (16) ~ Führer
p. 816 n.

**Κυριάρχης**
Illyria:
—lychnidos: (1) ii-iii AD Demitsas 341

**Κύριλλα**
S. Italy (Apulia):
—venusia: (1) imp. *CIL* IX 498 (Lat. Claudia Cyrilla)
S. Italy (Campania):
—dikaiarchia-puteoli: (2) imp. ib. x 2462 (Lat. Fraucia Cyrilla)
—misenum*: (3) imp. ib. 3439 (Lat. -a Cyrilla); (4) ?i-ii AD ib. 3643 a (Lat. Iulia Cyrila)
Sicily:
—lipara: (5) iv/v AD Bernabò Brea, *Isole Eolie* p. 97 and fig. 55

**Κυρῖνος**
S. Italy (Campania):
—neapolis: (1) iii-iv AD *IG* XIV 826. 25 (*INap* 237) (-ρεῖ-)

**Κύριος**
Lakonia:
—sparta?: (1) arch.? *IPr* 316, 3

**Κυρίων**
S. Italy (Calabria):
—brentesion-brundisium: (1) iii-v AD *IG* XIV 679 (s. Ἡρακλείδας)

**Κύρνος**
S. Italy (Campania):
—pompeii: (1) i BC-i AD *CIL* IV 1424 (Lat. Cyrnu)

**Κῦρος**
Argolis:
—epidauros*: (1) ii-iii AD Peek, *IAEpid* 311
Elis: (2) 36-24 BC *IvOl* 59, [19]; 62, 6 (f. Ἀρίσταρχος: mantis/Iamidai)
S. Italy (Campania):
—dikaiarchia-puteoli: (3) imp. *CIL* X 2252 (Lat. L. Charisius Cyrus)
—pompeii*: (4) m. i AD *Impegno per Pompeii* 17 ES (Castrèn 146. 5) (Lat. C. Cuspius Cyrus: freed.)

**Κύρτος**
Lakonia:
—sparta: (1) iv/iii BC *CID* II 120 A, 27 (Bradford (-)) (Κύρτος: f. —ίλας)

**Κύτισος**
S. Italy: (1) imp. *CIL* X 8059. 134 (seal) (Lat. Cytisus)
S. Italy (Campania):
—pompeii: (2) 55 AD ib. IV 3340. 13, 21 (Castrèn 372. 2) (Lat. L. Sest. Cytissus)
Sicily:
—zankle-messana: (3) imp. *Mon. Ant.* 24 (1916) p. 173 (Lat. Cytisus: s. Ἀμάρανθος)

**Κύτων**
Korinthia:
—korinth?: (1) ?ii BC Page, *FGE* 936 (Κύλων—Bergk, Κύδων?—*LGPN*: fict.?)

**Κύψελος**
Aitolia: (1) c. 232-228 BC *Syll³* 499, 3; Nachtergael, *Les Galates* 62, [3]

Korinthia:
—korinth: (2) vii BC *RE* (2) (s. Ἀετίων, Λάβδα, f. Περίανδρος, Γόργος, Ἐχιάδας, Πυλάδας); (3) vii/vi BC Wehrli, *Schule Arist.* vii fr. 144 (s. Περίανδρος, Λυσιδίκα (Epidauros)); (4) ~ *FGrH* 90 F 60. 1 (s. Γόργος)

**Κώβιος**
Leukas: (1) hell.? *IG* IX (1) 563

**Κωθίων**
Kerkyra: (1) ?ii-i BC ib. 776 (tile) (reading—Strauch)

**Κώκαλος**
Arkadia:
—tegea: (1) s. iv BC *SEG* XXXVI 383, 6 (Κώκαλος: s. Κάλλος)

**Κώμαρχος**
Elis?: (1) ?iii BC *FGrH* 410

**Κωμάσιος**
Argolis:
—epidauros: (1) iii AD *IG* IV (1)² 451
—epidauros*: (2) c. 370-365 BC Peek, *IAEpid* 52 A, 40 ([Κ]ωμά[σιος])

**Κωμάστας**
Argolis:
—epidauros: (1) i BC ib. 19, 5 (s. Παράμονος)

**Κώμη**
S. Italy (Lucania):
—tegianum: (1) imp. *IItal* III (1) 271 (*CIL* X 328) (Lat. Anicia Coma: m. Cominus)

**Κωμική**
S. Italy (Apulia):
—luceria: (1) imp. ib. IX 872 (Lat. Nummia Comice)
S. Italy (Calabria):
—brentesion-brundisium: (2) imp. *Epigraphica* 25 (1963) p. 33 no. 1 (Lat. Ania Comice)

**Κωμικός**
S. Italy (Campania):
—dikaiarchia-puteoli: (1) imp. *CIL* X 2401 (Lat. A. Fabius Comicus)
—herculaneum: (2) i BC-i AD ib. 1403 d III, 8 (Lat. Sex. Atellius Comicus)
—pompeii: (3) i BC-i AD ib. IV 4745 (Lat. Comicus)

**Κῶμος**
S. Italy (Apulia):
—canusium: (1) i-ii AD *Epig. Rom. di Canosa* 58, 3 (*CIL* IX 348) (Lat. P. Libuscidius Comus)
—teanum apulum*: (2) imp. *Teanum Apulum* p. 84 no. 27 (*CIL* IX 718) (Lat. C. Titius Comus: freed.)
S. Italy (Campania):
—pompeii: (3) i BC-i AD ib. IV 9110 (Lat. M. Comus); (4) ~ ib. 9947 (Lat. Comus)
S. Italy (Lucania):
—tegianum: (5) imp. *IItal* III (1) 269 (*CIL* X 297) (Lat. L. Cincius Comus)

**Κωμύλος**
Sicily:
—katane: (1) imp. *IG* XIV 487 (Κωμύ[λος])

**Κωμωιδίων**
Argolis:
—epidauros*: (1) c. 365-335 BC ib. IV (1)² 103, 90, 94, 104

**Κωνέας**
S. Italy (Lucania):
—herakleia: (1) iv/iii BC *IGSI* I I, 14 (*DGE* 62; Uguzzoni–Ghinatti I) (s. Δίων)

**Κωνσταντία**
Sicily:
—syracuse: (1) iii-v AD *IG* XIV 142 (Strazzulla 82; Wessel 858; *IGLMP* 112) (Κωσστα-); (2) ~ *IG* XIV 190 (Strazzulla 133; Wessel 1317) (Κω(ν)σταντία); (3) ~ *NScav* 1907, p. 766 no. 32

**Κωνσταντῖνα**
Argolis:
—argos: (1) v-vi AD Unp. (Oikonomou-Laniado)

**Κωνσταντινιανός**
Illyria: (1) vi AD Procop., *Pers.* ii 24. 3; 28. 2

**Κωνσταντῖνος**
Korinthia:
—korinth: (1) byz. *Corinth* VIII (3) 589; cf. *TMByz* 9 (1985) p. 366 no. 70 (Κωνστα[ντῖν]ος)
Sicily:
—lilybaion?: (2) iv-v AD *SEG* XLII 869

**Κωνστάντις**
Sicily:
—katane: (1) iii-v AD *IG* XIV 542 (Agnello 53; Wessel 852); cf. *Riv. Arch. Crist.* 18 (1941) p. 241 no. 138
—tauromenion: (2) iii-v AD *IG* XIV 143 (Strazzulla 83; Wessel 1315; *ASSicilia* 1938-9, p. 52); Ferrua, *NG* 477 (ident., locn.) (Κοστάν-: s. Βονιφᾶς)

**Κωνώπα**
Epiros:
—ambrakia: (1) v/iv BC *BCH* 79 (1955) p. 267 (d. Σώτων)

**Κώνωψ**
S. Italy (Campania):
—pompeii: (1) i BC-i AD *CIL* IV 3905, 1 (Lat. C. Hostilius Conops)
Sicily:
—lipara: (2) vi/v BC *SEG* XLII 866 (vase) (Κόνōπος (gen.))

**Κωσίλος**
S. Italy (Lucania):
—poseidonia-paestum: (1) m. iv BC *RVP* p. 84 no. 125 (vase) (Κωσί[λ]ος: fict.)

**Λάαλκος**
ARKADIA:
—PHENEOS: (1) m. iii BC *IG* IX (1)² (1) 22, 2 (s. Ἀγίας)

**Λαάνασσα**
AKARNANIA:
—ALYZIA: (1) ii-i BC ib. IX (1)² (2) 446 a ([Λα]άνασσα?, [Εὐ]άνασσα?—Klaffenbach: d. Λεοντεύς)

**Λαανδρίας**
SICILY:
—KAMARINA: (1) f. v BC Cordano, *Tessere Pubbliche* 95 (Λ[α]ανδρίας)

**Λάανδρος**
ARKADIA: (1) 316 BC *IG* v (2) 549, 25 (f. Δεινίας)

**Λααρχίδας**
ARGOLIS:
—EPIDAUROS*: (1) c. 365-335 BC ib. IV (1)² 103, 124, 126, 132-3 (Λααρχίδας—132-3)

**Λάαρχος**
AITOLIA: (1) ?209 or 205 BC Flacelière p. 407 no. 38 b, 3; Nachtergael, *Les Galates* 68, [3]
—PHOLANTIOI: (2) 263 BC *IG* IX (1)² (1) 17, 27
ARGOLIS:
—NEMEA*: (3) hell.? *SEG* XXIII 185, 1
ARKADIA:
—MEGALOPOLIS: (4) 369-361 BC *IG* v (2) 1, 32; Tod, *GHI* II 132 (date)
—TEGEA:
——(Apolloniatai): (5) iv/iii BC *IG* v (2) 38, 30 (s. Φαιδιμίδας)

**Λάβαξ**
TRIPHYLIA:
—LEPREON: (1) ?m. iv BC Moretti, *Olymp.* 405 (s. Εὔφρων)

**Λάβδα**
KORINTHIA:
—KORINTH: (1) vii BC *RE* (-) (d. Ἀμφίων, m. Κύψελος)

**Λάβδακος**
SICILY: (1) iv/iii BC *CAF* 3 p. 296 fr. 1, 3

**Λαβία**
ILLYRIA:
—EPIDAMNOS-DYRRHACHION: (1) hell.-imp. *IDyrrh* 277; (2) ~ ib. 278 (d. Γάϊος)

**Λαβιάδας**
ARKADIA:
—STYMPHALOS: (1) hell.? *PAE* 1929, p. 92

**Λαβίππα**
LAKONIA:
—HIPPOLA: (1) ?ii-i BC *IG* v (1) 1277 e (Λαβ(ϝ)ίπα)
—MESSA?: (2) imp. ib. 1280, 5 (Λαβ(ϝ)ίππα: d. Φιλοκλῆς)

**Λαβίων**
LAKONIA:
—SPARTA: (1) iii AD *Sculpture from Arcadia and Laconia* pp. 242-3 (*SEG* XLII 324) (-βεί-)

**Λαβρέας**
ARGOLIS:
—ARGOS: (1) iii/ii BC *IG* IV (1)² 205, 4; 208, 4; 243, 4; 244, 9; 318; 696; 697 (s. Δαμοπείθης: sculptor)

**Λαβώτας**
KORINTHIA:
—KORINTH: (1) 360-330 BC *CID* II 4 II, 62; 31, 21, 22, 76, 85, 87; 120 A, 34 (s. Εὐξίθεος)
LAKONIA:
—SPARTA: (2) her. Hdt. i 65. 4; vii 204; Paus. iii 2. 3-4 (Poralla² 461) (Λεωβώτης—Hdt.: s. Ἐχέστρατος, f. Δορυσσός: king/dub.); (3) 409 BC X., *HG* i 2. 18 (Poralla² 462)

**Λαγένης**
ACHAIA?: (1) 193 BC *IG* v (2) 293, 16 (s. Φιλαρχίδας)

**Λάγιος**
ACHAIA: (1) 146 BC Plb. xxxviii 18. 2 ff.

**Λαγίσκος**
AKARNANIA:
—ANAKTORION: (1) iv/iii BC *IG* IX (1)² (2) 212, 3 (Ἀλγισκος—apogr.: f. Ἀγάνωρ)
ILLYRIA:
—GUREZEZE (MOD.): (2) hell. *Iliria* 1982 (1), p. 112 no. 56 = p. 120 no. 34 (tile); cf. *IApoll* 361
S. ITALY (BRUTTIUM):
—LOKROI EPIZEPHYRIOI:
——(Φαω.): (3) iv/iii BC De Franciscis 6, 8; 17, 6; 28, 6 (f. Μενέδαμος)

**Λαγόρας**
ARGOLIS:
—EPIDAUROS: (1) 336 BC *CID* II 76 II, 29 (f. Τιμύλος)
SICILY:
—AKRAGAS: (2) vi BC Luc., *Phal.* 1 9 (Λεω-: fict.)

**Λαγορίδας**
ARKADIA:
—ORCHOMENOS: (1) m. iii BC *IG* IV (1)² 96, 42 (Perlman E.3); Perlman p. 63 f. (date) (f. Θαρσύας)

**Λάγορος**
EPIROS:
—BATELONOI: (1) hell. Cabanes, *L'Épire* p. 584 no. 63, 9 (*SEG* XXVI 705)

**Λαδάμα**
ARGOLIS:
—EPIDAUROS: (1) i BC-i AD *IG* IV (1)² 658, 2 (d. Ἱερωνᾶς)

**Λαδάμαρος**
KORINTHIA:
—KORINTH: (1) c. 570-550 BC Amyx 92 B. 8 (vase) (Lorber 120) (her.?)

**Λαδάμας**
AIGINA: (1) iii BC *IG* IV (1)² 256 (f. Ἀρισαμίδας)
KORINTHIA:
—KORINTH: (2) c. 570-550 BC Amyx 92 B. 9 (vase) (Lorber 120) (her.?)

**Λαδάμεια**
ARKADIA:
—PHIGALEIA: (1) m. iii BC *SEG* XXIII 239, 3

**Λαδάμης**
AITOLIA: (1) 244 or 240 BC *SGDI* 2512, 2 (Flacelière p. 402 no. 28 a); Nachtergael, *Les Galates* 59, [2]
—KALYDON: (2) s. ii BC *IG* IX (1)² (1) 36, 11; 137, 22 (s. Νικίας, f. Νικίας); (3) c. 84 BC ib. 139 (s. Νικίας)
—POTIDANIA: (4) m. ii BC *SBBerlAk* 1936, p. 371 a, 8 (*SEG* XLI 528 A) (f. Τηλέμαχος, Καγψίας)

**Λαδαμίδας**
ARGOLIS:
—EPIDAUROS: (1) iv-iii BC *IG* IV (1)² 5 (f. —υς)
——(Hylleis): (2) 146 BC ib. 28, 48 (s. Ἀριστόφαντος)

**Λάδας**
ACHAIA:
—AIGION: (1) 280 BC Moretti, *Olymp.* 535
ARGOLIS:
—ARGOS?: (2) m. v BC *RE* (1); (2); (3); Moretti, *Olymp.* 260 (or Lakonia Sparta)
LAKONIA:
—GYTHEION*: (3) imp. *IG* v (1) p. 210 (tile)

**Λαδέκτας**
KERKYRA: (1) f. ii BC *BCH* 45 (1921) p. 24 IV, 82 (*SEG* XXII 455); cf. *Sic. Gymn.* 17 (1964) pp. 47 f. (?s. Λεω—)

**Λάδη**
S. ITALY (CAMPANIA):
—DIKAIARCHIA-PUTEOLI: (1) imp. *CIL* X 2026 (Lat. Aimilia Lade)

**Λάδης**
ARGOLIS:
—EPIDAUROS: (1) ?vi-v BC *BCH* 73 (1949) p. 377

**Λαδίκα**
ARKADIA:
—TEGEA: (1) ?ii-i BC *IG* v (2) 232 (Λαδίκα)
EPIROS:
—AMBRAKIA: (2) her. *FGrH* 69 F 1, 7
—BOUTHROTOS (PRASAIBOI): (3) a. 163 BC *IBouthrot* 32, 6; cf. *SEG* XXXVIII 491

**Λάδικος**
AITOLIA: (1) 213 or 205 BC Nachtergael, *Les Galates* 66, 3; *SEG* XLI 513 (ident.) ?= (2)
—KALLION/KALLIPOLIS: (2) ?c. 225-200 BC *FD* III (4) 240 (*IG* IX (1)² (3) 783); cf. *SEG* XLI 513 (s. Δρωπίνας, ?f. Δρωπίνας) ?= (1); (3) 153-144 BC *SGDI* 2279, 1 (s. Πλείσταινος) ?= (4); (4) ~ ib. l. 11, 13 (f. Ἀριστόφυλος) ?= (3)
—KONOPE-ARSINOE: (5) 213 BC *IG* IX (1)² (1) 59, 6; (6) c. 158-151 BC ib. IX (1)² (3) 638. 11, 1
AKARNANIA: (7) 219 BC Plb. iv 80. 15
EPIROS:
—ARGOS (AMPHILOCH.): (8) c. 330 BC *SEG* XXIII 189 I, 9
LAKONIA:
—SPARTA: (9) ii AD *IG* v (1) 1369, 8 (Bradford (-)) (f. Χαριτέλης)

**Λάδοκος**
ARGOLIS:
—ARGOS: (1) iv-iii BC Unp. (Ch. Kritzas)
ELIS: (2) s. i BC *IvOl* 61, 12 (Λάδο[κος]: f. —οντις) ?= (3); (3) ~ ib. [289]; 290, 1, 2; [291] (f. Ἀπολλώνιος) ?= (2)

**Λάδρομος**
ELIS: (1) a. 191 BC *SEG* XXVI 392, 14
LAKONIA:
—SPARTA: (2) 552 BC Moretti, *Olymp.* 108 (Poralla² 464)

**Λαέας**
ARKADIA:
—ORCHOMENOS: (1) ?c. 378 BC *BCH* 102 (1978) p. 335, 98 (*IPArk* 15)

**Λαέρτιος**
PELOPONNESE?: (1) ii AD *PAE* 1992, p. 72 B, 16 (Λαέ[ρτι]ος: s. Εὐάμερος)

**Λαέτιος**
ILLYRIA:
—EPIDAMNOS-DYRRHACHION: (1) hell.-imp. *IDyrrh* 333 (f. Νικώ)

**Λαϝάναξ**
LAKONIA:
—GERONTHRAI: (1) c. 500 BC *IG* V (1) 1133, 2; *LSAG*² p. 201 no. 46 (date) (Poralla² 465) ([Λ]αϝάναξ)

**Λαϝοδάμας**
KORINTHIA:
—KORINTH: (1) c. 570-550 BC Amyx 79. 3 (vase) (Λαϝοδά[μας]: her.?)

**Λαϝοπτόλεμος**
KORINTHIA:
—KORINTH: (1) c. 570-550 BC ib. 89. 1 (vase) (Lorber 108) (her.?)

**Λάζιος**
ILLYRIA:
—EPIDAMNOS-DYRRHACHION: (1) imp. *IDyrrh* 146 (Γάεις Ἑπτάνις Λάζιε (voc./ethn.?), Δά-ζιε?—ed.)

**Λάζυγος**
ARKADIA:
—MEGALOPOLIS: (1) ?145 BC *IG* V (2) 439, 52 (s. Δαμόδοκος); (2) ~ ib. l. 56 (s. Δαμαρχίδας)

**Λαήν**
ILLYRIA:
—EPIDAMNOS-DYRRHACHION: (1) hell. *IDyrrh* 282 (s. Εὐθυκλῆς); (2) c. 250-50 BC *BMC Thessaly* p. 77 no. 180 (coin) (pryt.) ?= (3); (3) ~ Maier 274; *Jubice Hoard* p. 97 no. 35 (coin) (Ceka 35; 337) (pryt.) ?= (2); (4) hell.-imp. *IDyrrh* 40 (f. Κονώ); (5) ~ ib. 280 (s. Ἀρίανθος); (6) ~ ib. 281 (s. Ἑορταῖος); (7) ~ ib. 283 (s. Ὀλύμπιχος)

**Λαθέμεια**
ARGOLIS:
—EPIDAUROS: (1) iv BC Peek, *NIEpid* 72 = *AD* 25 (1970) Mel. pp. 32-3 no. 6

**Λαϊάδας**
ARKADIA:
—MEGALOPOLIS: (1) 359 BC *CID* II 5 I, 37

**Λαίανδρος**
ITHAKE: (1) hell. *IG* IX (1) 665 ((Μ)αίανδρος?)

**Λαίαρχος**
AITOLIA:
—PHISTYON*: (1) f. ii BC ib. IX (1)² (1) 104, 6
ARGOLIS:
—EPIDAUROS*: (2) c. 370-365 BC Peek, *IAEpid* 52 A, 29

**Λαίας**
LAKONIA:
—SPARTA: (1) her. *RE* (1) (s. Ὑραῖος: dub.)

**Λαιδάν**
ILLYRIA:
—EPIDAMNOS-DYRRHACHION: (1) hell.-imp. *IDyrrh* 284 (s. Ὀλόμμνιος)

**Λαΐδας**
ARGOLIS:
—HERMIONE: (1) iii-ii BC *IG* IV (1) 679, 26 (Perlman H.3)
KORINTHIA:
—KORINTH: (2) c. 570-550 BC Amyx 64. 3; 67. 2; 105 B. 9; 111. 1; 115. 1 (vases) (Lorber 97); Lorber 123; 93; 140; 103 (her.?)
LAKONIA:
—SPARTA: (3) ii AD *IG* V (1) 1523, 1, 5 (Bradford (-)) (s. Δαμιππίδας)

**Λαιδίας**
ILLYRIA:
—EPIDAMNOS-DYRRHACHION: (1) hell.-imp. *IDyrrh* 451 (f. Φιλώτας); (2) imp. ib. 49 (f. Τάτα)

**Λαίδων**
ILLYRIA:
—EPIDAMNOS-DYRRHACHION: (1) ii-i BC ib. 440 (f. Φιλουμένα)

**Λαιετίων**
ARGOLIS:
—ARGOS?: (1) iii BC *BCH* 96 (1972) p. 138; cf. *BE* 1973, no. 181 (sculptor)

**Λάιος**
ELIS: (1) 229-232 AD *SEG* XV 258, 4 (Φλ. Λ., Λαῖος?)

**Λάϊππος**
AKARNANIA:
—OINIADAI: (1) 356-354 BC *IG* IV (1)² 95, 9 (Perlman E.2); Perlman p. 40 f. (date)

**Λαΐς**
ARGOLIS:
—ARGOS: (1) iii BC *IG* IV (1) 571
ILLYRIA:
—EPIDAMNOS-DYRRHACHION: (2) hell. *IDyrrh* 279 (-εἴς); (3) hell.-imp. ib. 285; (4) ~ ib. 286 (d. Ἀρχάγαθος)
KORINTHIA:
—KORINTH: (5) f. iv BC *RE* (1) (?d. Μεγακλῆς, d. Τιμάνδρα (Hykkara, Sicily): het.); (6) imp. *CIL* III 7273, 2 (Lat. V. Caesennia Lais); (7) i-ii AD *IG* XII (9) 66 (?d. Σόφος (Paphlagonia, Amastris))
S. ITALY (APULIA):
—LUCERIA: (8) imp. *CIL* IX 839 (Lat. Babbia Lais: freed.)
—VENUSIA: (9) imp. ib. 461 (Lat. Livia Lais)
S. ITALY (CALABRIA):
—BRENTESION-BRUNDISIUM: (10) imp. *NScav* 1900, p. 245 no. 1 (Lat. Aufidia Lais)
—BRENTESION-BRUNDISIUM*: (11) imp. *Epigraphica* 25 (1963) p. 64 no. 58; cf. 42 (1980) p. 155 (Lat. Annia Laeis: freed.)
S. ITALY (CAMPANIA):
—DIKAIARCHIA-PUTEOLI: (12) imp. *CIL* X 2083 (Lat. Antonia Lais); (13) ~ ib. 2379 (Lat. Ducenia Lais); (14) ?ii-iii AD ib. 3049 (Lat. Aurelia Lais: m. Λᾶος ὁ καὶ Ἀφρικανός)
—DIKAIARCHIA-PUTEOLI*: (15) imp. ib. 2645 (Lat. Lais: freed.)
—PITHEKOUSSAI-AENARIA*: (16) imp. ib. 6804 (Lat. Antonia Lais: imp. freed.)
—POMPEII: (17) i BC-i AD ib. IV 1578 (Lat. Lais) ?= (18); (18) ~ ib. 1969 (Lat. Lahis) ?= (17); (19) ~ *NScav* 1916, p. 303 no. 108 (Castrèn 158. 18) (Lat. Epidia Lais)
—SALERNUM: (20) imp. *IItal* I (1) 135 (*CIL* X 635) (Lat. Sergia Lais)
S. ITALY (LUCANIA):
—HYELE-VELIA: (21) ?i AD *PdelP* 33 (1978) p. 65 no. 10 (Lat. Iulia Lais: d. Θεόφιλος, m. Μένανδρος)
SICILY:
—HYKKARA: (22) v/iv BC *RE* (2) (d. Τιμάνδρα: het.)
—KATANE: (23) imp. *NScav* 1915, p. 216 (Lat. -cia Lais)
—TAUROMENION: (24) imp. *NS* 1920, pp. 340-1 (Lat. Servilia Lais)
—THERMAI HIMERAIAI: (25) i-ii AD *ILat. Term. Imer.* 145 (Lat. Seppiena Lais)

**Λαΐστας**
AITOLIA:
—HYPOSIRIA: (1) c. 215-200 BC *FD* III (2) 86, 6 (*Syll*³ 539 A); cf. Nachtergael, *Les Galates*

p. 291 (date); *BCH* 54 (1930) p. 395 no. 3, 4, 10 (s. Λι—)
—PHISTYON: (2) s. ii BC *SBBerlAk* 1936, p. 364 no. 1, 8

**Λαΐστρατος**
LAKONIA:
—SPARTA: (1) s. i BC *IG* V (1) 94, 17 (Bradford (2)) (Λαΐσ[τρατος], Λ.?: I f. Λαΐστρατος II); (2) ~ *IG* V (1) 94, 17 (Bradford (1)) (Λ.?: II s. Λαΐστρατος I)
MESSENIA:
—MESSENE: (3) 174 AD *SEG* XLI 337, 9 (ἀπὸ [Λ]αϊστράτου—ed.: ?f. Διονύσιος)

**Λάϊτος**
AKARNANIA:
—STRATOS: (1) ?277 BC Plu., *Mor.* 911 F; 913 D; *FD* III (1) 106, 2

**Λαῖτος**
ARKADIA:
—MANTINEIA-ANTIGONEIA: (1) i AD *IG* V (2) 339
KORINTHIA:
—KORINTH: (2) ?iii AD *Hesp.* 63 (1994) pp. 116 ff. no. 5 col. I, 6-7 (lead) (Κρονίων ὁ καὶ Λ.)

**Λακάδης**
ARGOLIS:
—ARGOS: (1) f. vi BC *RE* (-); Plu., *Mor.* 89 E (Λεωκήδης—Hdt., Λακύδης—Plu.: s. Φείδων, f. Μέλτας: king)

**Λάκαινα**
S. ITALY (APULIA):
—BARION*: (1) imp. *CIL* IX 288 (Lat. Lacaena: freed.)
S. ITALY (CALABRIA):
—BRENTESION-BRUNDISIUM: (2) imp. ib. 108; *Epigraphica* 42 (1980) p. 156 (name) (Lat. Ulpia Lacena)
S. ITALY (CAMPANIA):
—DIKAIARCHIA-PUTEOLI: (3) imp. *CIL* X 2217 (Lat. Calpurnia Lacaena); (4) ~ ib. 2275 (Lat. Antonia Lacena); (5) ~ ib. 2339 (Lat. Cornelia Lacaena); (6) ~ ib. 2635 (Lat. Lacaena); (7) ~ ib. 2723 (Lat. Matutina Lacaena)
—POMPEII: (8) i BC-i AD ib. IV 8535 (Lat. Lacene (dat.))
SICILY:
—KAMARINA: (9) ?m. v BC Dubois, *IGDS* 118 (Arena, *Iscr. Sic.* II 144; *SEG* XXXVIII 936) (n. pr.?)

**Λακιππίδας**
LAKONIA:
—SPARTA: (1) f. ii BC ib. XI 471, 9 (Bradford (4)) (date—*LGPN*); (2) c. 25-1 BC *IG* V (1) 212, 29 (Bradford (3)) (f. Σιδέκτας); (3) m. iii AD *IG* V (1) 595, 8 (Bradford (1)) (Λακιπ[πίδας]: II s. Λακιππίδας I); (4) ~ *IG* V (1) 595, 9 (Bradford (2)) (Λακιπ[πίδας]?: I f. Λακιππίδας II)

**Λακισθένης**
LAKONIA: (1) 395 BC D.S. xiv 82. 8 (Poralla² 467) (Λ.—mss., Ἀλκισθένης—Keil)

**Λακλείδας**
ACHAIA:
—AIGEIRA?: (1) ii BC *SEG* XXIV 337, 1 (f. Πολύκαστος)
—AIGINA: (2) iv BC *Ag.* XVII 519, 8 (f. Πλαγγών)

**Λακλῆς**
ARGOLIS:
—EPIDAUROS: (1) imp. Peek, *IAEpid* 98 (s. ..όδωρος); (2) ~ ib. (Λακλ[ῆς]: f. Καλλικώ)
——(Hylleis): (3) 146 BC *IG* IV (1)² 28, 50 (s. Σωσιφάνης)

**Λάκος**
ARGOLIS:
—ARGOS?: (1) vi BC *BMI* 948

**Λακρατεύς**
ARGOLIS:
—HERMIONE: (1) iii BC *IG* IV (1) 728, 6 (f. Τι-
μόστρατος)

**Λακράτης**
AITOLIA: (1) 288 BC ib. IX (1)² (1) 5, 2 ?= (2);
(2) 279 BC Paus. x 20. 4 ?= (1)
AKARNANIA:
—ECHINOS?: (3) ii BC *IG* IX (1)² (2) 375
ARGOLIS:
—ARGOS: (4) 228-146 BC *BMC Pelop.* p. 146
no. 133; BM coin 1925 1-15-11 (coins) (Λα-
κρά(της))
—TROIZEN: (5) iii BC *IG* IV (1) 825, 8
ARKADIA:
—TEGEA: (6) f. iii BC ib. v (2) 35, 27 (s. Καλλίας)
ILLYRIA:
—EPIDAMNOS-DYRRHACHION: (7) c. 250-50 BC
Ceka p. 64 (Δακράτης—Ceka)
—EPIDAMNOS-DYRRHACHION?: (8) vi BC Paus.
vi 19. 8 (s. Πύρρος)
KEPHALLENIA:
—PALE: (9) iii/ii BC *IG* VII 377, 3, 8 (*IOrop* 80)
(f. Ἄλκων)
LAKONIA:
—SPARTA: (10) 479 BC Plu., *Mor.* 868 F (Po-
ralla² 469); (11) s. v BC Moretti, *Olymp.* 342
(Poralla² 468)
LEUKAS: (12) c. 167-50 BC *BMC Thessaly* p.
187 nos. 194-6; *SNG Cop. Epirus–Acarnania*
396 (coins)
S. ITALY (LUCANIA):
—METAPONTION: (13) iv BC Iamb., *VP* 267
(*FVS* 1 p. 446)

**Λακρατίδας**
ARGOLIS:
—METHANA-ARSINOE: (1) iii BC *SEG* XXXVII
320 (-τεί-)
LAKONIA:
—SPARTA: (2) c. 390 BC *FGrH* 70 F 207; Plu.,
*Mor.* 229 F (Poralla² 470) (Κρατίδας—Plu.)

**Λακρίδας**
AIGINA: (1) hell. *IG* IV (1) 114 (-εί-: ?f. Ἐρατώ)

**Λακρίνης**
ARGOLIS:
—EPIDAUROS: (1) c. 370 BC ib. IV (1)² 102, 35,
41, [95], 243; (2) iii BC *SB* 2130
LAKONIA:
—SPARTA: (3) m. vi BC Hdt. i 152. 3 (Poralla²
471)

**Λᾶκρις**
ARGOLIS:
—EPIDAUROS: (1) iv BC *IG* IV (1)² 155; 189; 190
(s. Λαφείδης)
——(Dymanes): (2) 146 BC ib. 28, 6 (f. Ὀρσίας)
——Selegeis: (3) m. iii BC Peek, *IAEpid* 42,
9, 15 (Perlman E.3); Perlman p. 63 f. (date)
([Λᾶ]κρις)

**Λάκριτος**
ARGOLIS:
—EPIDAUROS: (1) c. 365-335 BC *IG* IV (1)² 103,
148, 152, 162, 174; (2) iii BC ib. 168, 3; *SEG*
XVII 178, 3; (3) iii/ii BC Peek, *IAEpid* 129, 2
(f. Ἀριστοκράτης)
——(Hylleis): (4) 146 BC *IG* IV (1)² 28, 54 (s.
Διόδωρος)
ARKADIA:
—MANTINEIA-ANTIGONEIA: (5) iii BC ib. v (2)
319, 9
—TEGEA:
——(Krariotai): (6) s. iii BC ib. 36, 118
(Λάκριτ[ος]: f. Νικασίας)
KERKYRA: (7) hell. ib. IX (1) 838 (bullet); (8)
imp. ib. 728 (f. Νίκαρχος); (9) s. ii AD ib. 730
(Λάκ[ριτ]ος: f. Παρμενίσκος)

S. ITALY (LUCANIA):
—METAPONTION: (10) iv BC Iamb., *VP* 267
(*FVS* 1 p. 446)

**Λακύδας**
S. ITALY (LUCANIA):
—METAPONTION: (1) iv BC Iamb., *VP* 267
(*FVS* 1 p. 446) (Δακίδας—ms.: name—C.
Keil)

**Λακώ**
ARGOLIS:
—ARGOS: (1) iii BC *IG* IV (1) 527, 6 + *Hesp.* 16
(1947) p. 86 no. 9; cf. *BCH* 37 (1913) p. 308
(d. Αὐγείας)

**Λάκων**
ACHAIA:
—PATRAI: (1) m. iii BC *IG* v (2) 368, 60 (s. Σκύ-
λων)
ARKADIA:
—TEGEA:
——(Athaneatai): (2) s. iv BC ib. 41, 38
(Λάκω[ν]: f. Αὐτόπας)
——THELPHOUSA: (3) a. 228 BC ib. IV (1)² 72 B,
30 (Λάκ[ων]: f. Εὐθυμένης)
ELIS:
—OLYMPIA*: (4) f. iv BC *SEG* XI 1254 (vase)
(*Ol. Forsch.* 23 p. 78 no. T 87)
KORINTHIA:
—KORINTH: (5) c. 590-570 BC Amyx 33. 6
(vase) (Lorber 52) (-ϙōν: her.?)
LAKONIA:
—SPARTA: (6) c. 20 BC-50 AD *RE* s.v. Iulius
(309); *PIR²* I 372; *Münzpr. der Laked.* p. 73;
pp. 171-4 Groups 32-4; pp. 79-80; pp. 174-
8 Groups 35-6; *RPC* I p. 248 nos. 1109-15
(coins) (Bradford (1)) (Γ. Ἰούλ. Λ.: s. Γ. Ἰούλ.
Εὐρυκλῆς, f. Γ. Ἰούλ. Σπαρτιατικός, Γ. Ἰούλ.
Κρατῖνος, Ἀργολικός, Ἰούλ. Παντιμία); (7) s. i
AD *IG* v (1) 280, 3 (*Artemis Orthia* p. 312 no.
29); *IG* v (1) 281, 2 (*Artemis Orthia* pp. 314-
15 no. 34); *IG* v (1) 480, 14; *BSA* 73 (1978)
p. 260 (stemma) (Bradford (2)) (Γ. Ἰούλ. Λ.: f
?s. Γ. Ἰούλ. Σπαρτιατικός, f. Γ. Ἰούλ. Λάκων II,
Γ. Ἰούλ. Εὐρυκλῆς Ἡρκλανὸς Λ. Βιβούλιος Πῖος);
(8) c. 70-100 AD *IG* v (1) 280, 5 (*Artemis Orthia* p. 312 no. 29); *IG* v (1) 281, 1 (*Artemis
Orthia* pp. 314-15 no. 34); *BSA* 73 (1978)
p. 260 (stemma) (Bradford (3)) (Γ. Ἰούλ. Λ.:
II s. Γ. Ἰούλ. Λάκων I); (9) ?ii AD *IG* v (1)
119, 6 (Bradford (5)) ([Λ]άκων); (10) c. 133
AD *IG* v (1) 286, 1; *Artemis Orthia* p. 319 no.
43 (name) (Bradford s.v. Λακρίνης (-)) (Φλ.
Λάκω[ν]: s. Ἀριστοτέλης); (11) ~ *SEG* XI 547
a, [8]; 547 b, 4; 547 c, [1]; *BSA* 80 (1985)
pp. 194; 212 (ident., stemma) (Bradford (4))
(Π. Μέμμιος Λ.: ?s. Π. Μέμμιος Σπαρτιατικός);
(12) c. 140-145 AD *IG* v (1) 1314, 47 (n. pr.?)
MESSENIA:
—MESSENE: (13) iii BC *SEG* XXIII 210, 8
S. ITALY (BRUTTIUM):
—LOKROI EPIZEPHYRIOI: (14) ii AD Costabile,
*Municipium Locrensium* 11 (*CIL* x 35) (Lat.
P. Vagellius Lacon)
—SYBARIS-THOURIOI-COPIAE*: (15) iii BC
Theoc., *Id.* v passim (s. Καλαιθίς: slave/fict.)
S. ITALY (CAMPANIA):
—DIKAIARCHIA-PUTEOLI: (16) imp. *CIL* x
2784 (Lat. L. Licinius Laco); (17) ~ ib. 2916
(Lat. Lacon: f. Ῥόδη)
S. ITALY (LUCANIA):
—METAPONTION: (18) c. 500 BC *SEG* XXX 1176
F. 5 (Landi, *DISMG* 136); cf. *LSAG²* p. 457
no. P (date); *SEG* XL 844 (vase) (-κōν)
SICILY: (19) ii-i BC ib. XXVI 1070. 5; XL 789;
*Entella* I pp. 173-4 nos. 12-15 (tiles) (Λάκōν—
*SEG* XL)

**Λακωνικός**
LAKONIA:
—SPARTA: (1) 192 BC Liv. XXXV 36. 8 (Bradford
(-)) (Lat. Laconicus) ?= (Λεωνίδας (28))

**Λακωνίς**
S. ITALY (CAMPANIA):
—DIKAIARCHIA-PUTEOLI: (1) imp. *CIL* x 2306
(Lat. Laconis Dionysia: m. Κορινθία)

**Λάλα**
S. ITALY (LUCANIA):
—METAPONTION: (1) iv-iii BC *JNG* 33 (1983)
p. 16 (coin graffito)

**Λαλάγη**
S. ITALY (APULIA):
—CANUSIUM*: (1) imp. *Epig. Rom. di Canosa*
202 (*CIL* IX 406) (Lat. Vellaea Lalage: freed.)
S. ITALY (CAMPANIA):
—POMPEII: (2) i BC-i AD ib. IV 1507, 7 (Lat.
Lalage); (3) ~ ib. 4391 (Lat. Lalage); (4) ~ ib.
3041-2 (Lat. Lalage)

**Λάλος**
S. ITALY (CALABRIA):
—BRENTESION-BRUNDISIUM: (1) imp. ib. IX
6127 (Lat. C. Laelius Lalus)
S. ITALY (CAMPANIA):
—DIKAIARCHIA-PUTEOLI*: (2) imp. ib. x 1748
(Lat. Lalus: f. Ἑλικών: imp. freed.)
—HERCULANEUM*: (3) i BC-i AD ib. 1403 g III,
50 (Lat. C. Novius Lalus: freed.)
—POMPEII: (4) i BC-i AD ib. IV 1888 (Lat.
Lalus); (5) ~ ib. 9836 (Lat. L. Saetilius
Lalus); (6) ~ ib. x 8058. 35 (seal) (Castrèn
161. 10) (Lat. M. Fabius Lalus)
SICILY:
—ADRANON: (7) ?ii-iii AD *PdelP* 16 (1961) p.
132 (Ferrua, *NG* 472); cf. *Rupes loquentes* p.
497

**Λαμάγα**
ARGOLIS:
—HERMIONE: (1) ?ii-i BC *IG* IV (1) 731 II, 21

**Λάμαχος**
AITOLIA:
—KASILIOI: (1) s. ii BC *SEG* XXV 621, 12 (s.
Νικολέων)
—PHILOTAIEIS: (2) f. ii BC *IG* IX (1)² (1) 96, 18
(s. Δορκίνας)
—TRICHONION: (3) s. iii BC ib. 117, 3
ARGOLIS:
—EPIDAUROS: (4) iv BC ib. IV (1)² 184
—EPIDAUROS*: (5) c. 370-365 BC Peek, *IAEpid*
52 A, 18 (Λάμαχ[ος])
ARKADIA:
—MEGALOPOLIS: (6) hell.? *IG* v (2) 448, 6
([Λ]άμαχος)
MESSENIA:
—MESSENE: (7) hell.-imp. *PAE* 1991, p. 106 no.
8, 11
SICILY:
—TAUROMENION: (8) 56 BC Moretti, *Olymp.*
706

**Λαμέδων**
AITOLIA:
—KALYDON: (1) 263-262 BC *IG* IX (1)² (1) 3 A,
18; 17, 16
ARGOLIS:
—EPIDAUROS: (2) iv BC Peek, *NIEpid* 31 ?= (3);
(3) c. 370 BC *IG* IV (1)² 102, 108 ?= (2); (4)
hell.-imp. ib. 731, 1 (s. Ἀγιάδας)
ARKADIA:
—STYMPHALOS: (5) ?271 BC *FD* III (1) 14, 2 (f.
Καλλίμαχος)
ELIS: (6) 36 BC *IvOl* 59, 12
LAKONIA:
—SPARTA: (7) s. i BC *IG* v (1) 94, 6 (Bradford
(-)) (Λαμέ[δων]: f. Παυσανίας); (8) c. 25-1 BC
*IG* v (1) 210, 40 (Λαμ[έδων]?: f. —ίδας)

**Λαμηριώ**
Leukas: (1) ?iv-iii bc *SEG* xxxv 483

**Λαμία**
Achaia:
—pellene: (1) ?ii-iii ad ib. xi 1274, 2
Aitolia: (2) 213 bc *IG* ix (1)² (1) 96, 19 (slave/freed.)
Akarnania:
—palairos: (3) s. iii bc ib. ix (1)² (2) 526; (4) f. ii bc ib. 556
Epiros:
—bouthrotos (prasaiboi): (5) a. 163 bc *IBouthrot* 25, 7 (*SEG* xxxviii 483); (6) ~ *IBouthrot* 29, 18 (*SEG* xxxviii 487); (7) ~ *IBouthrot* 30, 4 (*SEG* xxxviii 488); *IBouthrot* 48, 12; (8) ~ ib. 30, 37 (*SEG* xxxviii 488) ?= (10); (9) ~ *IBouthrot* 31, 74 (*SEG* xxxviii 490); (10) ~ *IBouthrot* 33, 18 (*SEG* xxxviii 492) (d. Ἄδματος) ?= (8); (11) ~ *IBouthrot* 38, 10 (*SEG* xxxviii 497); (12) ~ *IBouthrot* 55, 8 (*SEG* xxxviii 506); (13) ~ *IBouthrot* 135, 11 (d. Λυσανίας)
—Cherrioi: (14) a. 163 bc ib. 49, 3; 111, 6; 112, 7 (d. Μένανδρος)
—passaron: (15) ii bc *AE* 1914, p. 239 no. 19 (d. Ἄδματος)
Kerkyra: (16) hell. *IG* ix (1) 895 (d. Σόφιος)
Sicily:
—segesta: (17) f. i bc Cic., *In Verr.* II iv 59 (Lat. Lamia)

**Λαμιάδας**
Akarnania:
—thyrreion: (1) s. iii bc *IG* ix (1)² (2) 291

**Λαμίας**
Elis: (1) ii-iii ad ib. v (1) 1150, 1 = II² 4526; *AAA* 7 (1974) pp. 250-60 (date) (Λ. Αἴλ. Λ.)

**Λαμιάς**
Akarnania:
—palairos: (1) ?s. iii bc *IG* ix (1)² (2) 545

**Λαμιεύς**
Arkadia:
—mantineia-antigoneia: (1) f. iv bc ib. II² 9281 + *ZPE* 29 (1978) p. 68, 1, 2 (s. Κλεοφαντίς)

**Λάμιος**
Aitolia:
—daianes: (1) 161 bc *IG* ix (1)² (1) 100, 7
—kalydon: (2) 129 bc ib. 137, 91 (s. Ἰόλαος)
—lysimacheia: (3) 225-205 bc *FD* iii (3) 220, 5 ([Λ]άμιος)
—pamphia: (4) c. 162 bc *IG* ix (1)² (1) 105, 10
—phistyon: (5) 163 bc ib. 103, 10
—prosch(e)ion: (6) m. ii bc *SBBerlAk* 1936, p. 371 a, 1 (*SEG* xli 528 A) (s. Ἀγήσανδρος)
—thermos (nr.): (7) hell. *IG* ix (1)² (1) 94
—thermos: (8) 214 bc ib. 177, 20
—thestieis: (9) 213 bc ib. 96, 13
—titrai: (10) c. 245 bc ib. 11, 48
Aitolia?: (11) s. ii bc *FD* iii (4) 233
Akarnania:
—astakos: (12) ii bc *IG* ix (1)² (2) 435, 8 (s. Σωτύλος)
—stratos: (13) ii bc ib. 394, 15 ([Λάμ]ιος: s. Ξένων) ?= (14); (14) a. 167 bc ib. ix (2) 6 a, 3; cf. Stählin p. 220 (date) (f. Ξένων) ?= (13)
Epiros:
—ambrakia: (15) 238-168 bc *SNG Evelpidis* ii 1784; Unp. (Oxford, AM) July 1971 (coins); (16) iii/ii bc Plb. xviii 10. 9; (17) f. ii bc *IC* 2 p. 25 no. 8 C (f. Λέων)
—bouthrotos (prasaiboi): (18) a. 163 bc *IBouthrot* 18, 9 (*SEG* xxxviii 475) ?= (21); (19) ~ *IBouthrot* 36, 8; 43, 43 (*SEG* xxxviii 495; 502) (f. Σώσιππος); (20) ~ *IBouthrot* 56, 9 (*SEG* xxxviii 507) (s. Φιλιππίδας) ?= (22); (21) ~ *IBouthrot* 134, 17 (s. Λαμίσκος) ?= (18)

—Aigorrioi: (22) a. 163 bc ib. 90, 7 (s. Φιλιππίδας) ?= (20)
—Euryoi: (23) a. 163 bc ib. 97, 18 (s. Φιλιππίδας)
Illyria:
—apollonia: (24) c. 200 bc *FD* iii (4) 163, 6
Lakonia:
—sparta: (25) c. 350 bc D.S. xvi 48. 2 (Poralla² 472)

**Λάμις**
Korinthia:
—korinth: (1) s. vi bc *SEG* xi 239; *IG* iv (1) 418 (Δᾶμις?, Λάμις?—*IG*)

**Λαμίσκα**
Akarnania:
—thyrreion: (1) iii bc *SEG* xxvii 160 (d. Δικαῖος)
Arkadia:
—alipheira: (2) i bc-i ad *IG* II² 8046 (d. Σωτάδης)
Epiros:
—kassope: (3) hell. *SEG* xvii 310 (Λαμίσκ[α])
—tatarna (mod.): (4) hell.? Hammond, *Epirus* p. 738 no. 22
Illyria:
—epidamnos-dyrrhachion: (5) hell.-imp. *IDyrrh* 287; (6) ~ ib. 288 ([Λ]αμίσκα: d. Ἐπιγένης)
Leukas: (7) ?f. ii bc *AD* 26 (1971) Chron. p. 352
S. Italy (Calabria):
—s. pancrazio salentino (mod.): (8) iii ad *NScav* 1884, p. 378 (*Eph. Ep.* viii 18); cf. *Epigraphica* 25 (1963) p. 70 no. 69 (Lat. Lamisca: m. Φίλλα)

**Λαμίσκος**
Akarnania: (1) 208 bc *IMM* 31, 2 (*IG* ix (1)² (2) 582) (f. Κλεώνυμος)
—thyrreion: (2) iii bc ib. 246, 12; (3) ii bc ib. 247, 11 (s. Λέων)
Epiros:
—ambrakia: (4) iii bc *BCH* 17 (1893) p. 633 (s. Σώτων); (5) a. 167 bc *SEG* xxxv 665 A, 10 (s. Ἀρίσταρχος); (6) ~ ib. l. 11 (Λα[μίσκος]: f. Σώτων)
—argos (amphiloch.): (7) ?205-203 bc *FD* iii (2) 134 b, 7 (*Syll*³ 564)
—bouthrotos (prasaiboi): (8) iii-ii bc *IBouthrot* 167 (Cabanes, *L'Épire* p. 568 no. 46: s. Σώστρατος); (9) a. 163 bc *IBouthrot* 18, 9 (*SEG* xxxviii 475) ?= (10); (10) ~ *IBouthrot* 134, 17 (f. Λάμιος) ?= (9)
—Bouthrotioi: (11) f. ii bc ib. 1, 9; 97, 7 (f. Ἀγήσανδρος); (12) ~ ib. 1, 9; 76, 7; 97, 7 (s. Ἀγήσανδρος)
—charadros: (13) a. 167 bc *SEG* xxxv 665 A, 14 (f. Νίκανδρος)
—kassope: (14) ii bc Dakaris, *Kassope* p. 23 (s. Λυκίσκος)
—molossoi: (15) ?iv/iii bc *SGDI* 1353, 5; cf. Cabanes, *L'Épire* p. 582 no. 57
Illyria:
—apollonia: (16) f. ii bc *BCH* 45 (1921) p. 22 IV, 35 (s. Ἀρίστιππος)
Ithake: (17) i bc-i ad? *IG* ix (1) 677
Kephallenia:
—same: (18) 293-168 bc *PAE* 1912, p. 188 no. 148 (Λαμ[ίσ]κος: f. Ἀλεξάνωρ)
Leukas: (19) f. i bc *IG* ix (1) 534, 6, 10, 12 (*Iscr. Gr. Verona* p. 24) (f. Σώστρατος)
S. Italy (Calabria):
—taras-tarentum: (20) iv bc *RE* (-)
S. Italy (Campania):
—neapolis: (21) i bc *IG* xiv 796 (*INap* 135); cf. Leiwo p. 117 no. 101 (I f. Λαμίσκος II); (22) ~ *IG* xiv 796 (*INap* 135); cf. Leiwo p. 117 no. 101 (II s. Λαμίσκος I)

S. Italy (Lucania):
—leukanoi: (23) arch.? Arist. fr. 611. 48 (Heraclid. Lemb. 48) (king)
Sicily:
—kamarina: (24) iv/iii bc *SEG* xxxix 999, 7 (Dubois, *IGDS* 125; Cordano, 'Camarina VII' 130) (f. Θεότιμος); (25) ?ii bc *SEG* xxxix 996, 7 (Dubois, *IGDS* 126; Cordano, 'Camarina VII' 131) (f. Θεότιμος)
—tauromenion: (26) c. 40 bc *Cron. Arch.* 3 (1964) p. 54 I, 21 (s. Νίκανδρος)

**Λαμίχα?**
Aitolia:
—konope-arsinoe: (1) 250-150 bc *SBBerlAk* 1936, p. 363 no. 6 a + Fraser–Rönne, *BWGT* p. 166 no. 15 (Λαμί[.]ας (gen.))

**Λάμιχος**
Arkadia:
—tegea: (1) m. iii bc *IG* v (2) 36, 95 (s. Ὑπεράνθης: metic)

**Λαμπαδίας**
Kerkyra: (1) imp. ib. ix (1) 860

**Λαμπάδιος**
S. Italy (Campania):
—dikaiarchia-puteoli: (1) imp. *CIL* x 1704 (Lat. Postumius Lampadius)

**Λαμπάδις**
S. Italy (Campania):
—neapolis: (1) iii-iv ad *IG* xiv 826. 26 (*INap* 226)

**Λαμπάς**
Illyria:
—apollonia: (1) imp. *IApoll* 101 (Ἰουλία Λ.)
S. Italy (Campania):
—dikaiarchia-puteoli*: (2) imp. *CIL* x 8201 (Lat. Turrania Lampas: freed.)

**Λαμπετίδας**
Arkadia:
—tegea: (1) s. v bc *IG* v (2) 175 (Λανπετί[δας]?, Λαμπετίων?—*CIG*)

**Λάμπις**
Aigina: (1) iv bc *RE* (2); Vélissaropoulos, *Nauclères* pp. 50-1 (ident.)
Akarnania: (2) ii ad Luc., *DMort.* 27. 7 (fict.)
Elis: (3) inc. Paus. vi 15. 7 (f. Τιμόπτολις); (4) iv/iii bc ib. 16. 8 (f. Πύτταλος); (5) 272 bc ib. v 5. 1; Plu., *Mor.* 253 B
Lakonia:
—sparta: (6) 708 bc Moretti, *Olymp.* 21 (Poralla² 473); (7) c. 80-100 ad *SEG* xi 511, 6 (Bradford (1)) (s. Ἀρίστανδρος) ?= (8); (8) c. 115-120 ad *IG* v (1) 137, 16; *SEG* xi 478, 4 (Bradford (3)) (Γ. Ἰούλ. Λ.) ?= (7); (9) c. 170-190 ad *SEG* xi 499, 11; 620 (Bradford (2)) (II s. Λάμπις I); (10) ~ *SEG* xi 499, 12; 620 (Bradford (4)) (I f. Λάμπις II)

**Λαμπιτώ**
Lakonia:
—sparta: (1) v bc Hdt. vi 71. 2; Pl., *Alc.* I 123 E; Plu., *Ages.* 1 (Poralla² 474) (Λαμπιδώ—Pl. and Plu.: d. Λατυχίδας, Εὐρυδάμα, m. Ἆγις); (2) 411 bc Ar., *Lys.* 77 ff. (Poralla² 475) (fict.)

**Λάμπιχος**
Sicily:
—gela-phintias: (1) arch.? Luc., *DMort.* 10. 4 (dub.)

**Λάμπος**
Arkadia:
—thelphousa: (1) c. 230-200 bc *BCH* 45 (1921) p. 12 II, 75 (f. Τιμογένης)
Elis: (2) inc. Paus. v 2. 4 (s. Πρόλαος, Λυσίππα: fict.); (3) ~ ib. vi 16. 7 (s. Ἀρνίσκος)

**Λάμπρα**
ACHAIA: (1) iii BC *Eretria* VI 167

**Λαμπρέας**
KORINTHIA:
—KORINTH: (1) s. iv BC *Corinth* VIII (1) 11, 6 (s. Νικόξενος)

**Λαμπρῆς**
ARKADIA:
—KLEITOR: (1) ?262 or 258 BC Nachtergael, *Les Galates* 5, 40; cf. Stephanis 2764 (f. —ρατος)

**Λαμπρίας**
ARGOLIS:
—ARGOS: (1) m. iv AD Jul., *Ep.* 35
—EPIDAUROS: (2) s. i BC *IG* IV (1)² 674; Peek, *IAEpid* 289, 5; *BSA* 80 (1985) pp. 249-51 (ident., stemma) (I f. Τ. Στατίλιος Λαμπρίας II); (3) c. 25 BC-50 AD *IG* IV (1)² 84, 41; 674, 2; Peek, *IAEpid* 36, 19; 289, 5; 293, 2; *BSA* 80 (1985) pp. 249-53 (ident., stemma) (Τ. Στατίλιος Λ.: II s. Λαμπρίας I, f. Τ. Στατίλιος Τιμοκράτης, Καλλικράτεια); (4) c. 25-50 AD *IG* IV (1)² 82, 5; 83, 17; 84, 26, 38; 85, 2; 86, 8, 30 + Peek, *IAEpid* 36; *IG* IV (1)² 671, 1; 676, 3; 677, 3; 679, 5; 681, 3; *BSA* 80 (1985) pp. 249-54 (ident., date, stemma) (Τ. Στατίλιος Λ.: s. Τ. Στατίλιος Τιμοκράτης, Στατιλία Τιμοσθενίς (Sparta)); (5) m. ii AD *IG* IV (1) 590, 2; *BSA* 80 (1985) pp. 249; 258 (ident., stemma) (?s. Τ. Στατίλιος Τιμοκράτης, f. Τ. Στατίλιος Τιμοκράτης Μεμμιανός)
—TROIZEN: (6) iii BC *IG* IV (1) 774, 12 (Λα[μ]πρίας)
ARKADIA:
—STYMPHALOS?: (7) iii BC ib. V (2) 354, 4 (Λαμπρί[ας]?: ?f. —ιπυλος)
LAKONIA:
—SPARTA?: (8) m. i AD ib. IV (1)² 675, 3 (Peek, *IAEpid* 294); *BSA* 80 (1985) pp. 249; 254-5 (ident., stemma) (and Argolis Epidauros: Τ. Στατίλιος Λ. Μεμμιανός: ?s. (nat.) Π. Μέμμιος Πρατόλαος, Μεμμία Πασιχάρεια (Epidauros), ?s. (ad.) Τ. Στατίλιος Τιμοκράτης (Epidauros), ?f. Τ. Στατίλιος Τιμοκράτης)

**Λαμπρίων**
AITOLIA: (1) ?264 BC *FD* III (3) 202, 3

**Λάμπρον**
ARKADIA:
—STYMPHALOS: (1) s. ii BC *EAD* XXX 270

**Λαμπροτύχη**
ARGOLIS:
—EPIDAUROS: (1) 184 AD *IG* IV (1)² 393, 7 (Λαν-)

**Λαμπυρίδας**
ILLYRIA:
—APOLLONIA: (1) i BC Münsterberg p. 36; Nachtr. p. 12 + *IApoll Ref. Bibl.* n. 76 (coin) ?= (2); (2) ~ Ceka, *Probleme* p. 139 no. 16; cf. *IApoll Ref. Bibl.* n. 76 (coin) ?= (1)

**Λαμπυρίς**
S. ITALY (CAMPANIA):
—POMPEII: (1) 57 AD *CIL* IV 3340. 40, 5, 8, 26 (Castrèn 420. 8) (Lat. Tallia Lampyris)

**Λαμπυρίων**
ELIS:
—OLYMPIA*: (1) v/iv BC Moretti, *Olymp.* 371 (?s. Ἀ—)

**Λάμπων**
AIGINA: (1) f. v BC Hdt. ix 78; Paus. iii 4. 10; Pi., *N.* v, 4; *I.*, 21; vi, 3, 66 (s. Πυθέας, f. Πυθέας, Φυλακίδας)
AKARNANIA:
—STRATOS: (2) ?iii BC *IG* IX (1)² (2) 406 (f. Δικκώ)

EPIROS:
—AMBRAKIA: (3) a. 167 BC *SEG* XXXV 665 A, 9 (s. Λέων)
SICILY: (4) iii BC Vandermersch p. 167 (amph.) (or S. Italy)
—KENTORIPA: (5) ii-i BC Dubois, *IGDS* 189, 2 (*SEG* XLII 837) (Λάμπ[ων])

**Λαμύρα**
S. ITALY (APULIA):
—LUCERIA: (1) ?i-ii AD *CIL* IX 861 (Lat. Iulia Lamyra: d. Ἀπάτη)
S. ITALY (CAMPANIA):
—DIKAIARCHIA-PUTEOLI: (2) imp. ib. X 2347 (Lat. Lamyra: m. A. Cossinius Primigenius)

**Λάμυρος**
AIGINA: (1) ?f. i AD *Alt-Ägina* I (2) p. 46 no. 20, 3 (s. Ἀριστο—)
ILLYRIA:
—BYLLIONES BYLLIS: (2) imp. *Iliria* 1987 (2), p. 107 no. 67 (Lat. Lamyrus)
S. ITALY (CAMPANIA):
—DIKAIARCHIA-PUTEOLI: (3) imp. *AJA* 77 (1973) p. 156 no. 5 (Lat. Volussius Lamyrus)

**Λάνασσα**
AITOLIA: (1) inc. *FD* III (1) 575 (*IG* IX (1)² (1) 200) (her.?)
SICILY: (2) iv/iii BC *RE* (2); cf. Beloch, *GG* IV (2) pp. 255-6 (d. Ἀγαθοκλῆς, ?d. Ἀλκία, m. Ἀλέξανδρος (Molossoi))

**Λανδρίδας**
LAKONIA:
—SPARTA: (1) f. iv BC *FD* III (4) 196

**Λάνδρος**
ARKADIA:
—HELISSON: (1) c. 221 BC *IG* IV (1)² 42, 5

**Λανθάνουσα**
S. ITALY (CALABRIA):
—BRENTESION-BRUNDISIUM: (1) imp. *Eph. Ep.* VIII 15 (Lat. Clitia Lan[t]hanusa)
S. ITALY (CAMPANIA):
—DIKAIARCHIA-PUTEOLI: (2) ?i-ii AD ib. 396 (Lat. Cloatia Lanthanusa)
S. ITALY (LUCANIA):
—VOLCEI: (3) imp. *IItal* III (1) 117 (Lat. Insteia Lantenusa)
SICILY:
—LICODIA EUBEA (MOD.): (4) ?vi AD *IG* XIV 254 (*IGLMP* 18; Wessel 614); cf. *Riv. Arch. Crist.* 18 (1941) p. 209 no. 82 (Λ. (ἡ) καὶ Ἀγάθη)

**Λανίκα**
EPIROS:
—BOUTHROTOS (PRASAIBOI): (1) a. 163 BC *IBouthrot* 25, 13 (*SEG* XXXVIII 483)

**Λανικία**
LAKONIA:
—THALAMAI*: (1) f. iv BC *IG* V (1) 1313 (Lazzarini 104; Poralla² 476) (Λανίκ(ι)α?)

**Λάνικος**
AITOLIA: (1) ?265-264 BC *FD* III (4) 359, 37; *SEG* XVIII 242, [6]; *CID* II 130, 4; (2) ?240-228 BC *FD* III (3) 218 A, 3

**Λάνομος**
ARKADIA:
—HERAIA: (1) m. iii BC *SEG* XI 413, 28 (Perlman E.4) (f. Ἀπελλίας)
—TEGEA:
——(Athaneatai): (2) s. iv BC *IG* V (2) 174 a, 7

**Λαοδάμας**
AIGINA: (1) vi BC Hdt. iv 152 (f. Σώστρατος)
EPIROS:
—AMBRAKIA: (2) c. 320 BC *SEG* XXXI 535 (Λαοδά[μαν]τι (dat.): s. Στράτιος)
LAKONIA:
—SPARTA: (3) ii-i BC *IG* V (1) 1113, 2 (Bradford (-)) (f. Πέλοψ)

**Λαοδάμεια**
S. ITALY (BRUTTIUM):
—PETELIA: (1) imp. *CIL* X 118 (Lat. Laudamia: m. Secundus)

**Λαοδαμίδας**
LAKONIA:
—SPARTA:
——Pitana: (1) c. 105 AD *IG* V (1) 675, 7 (Bradford (-)) ([Λα]οδαμίδας: s. Γόργιππος)

**Λαοδίκα**
AITOLIA:
—KONOPE-ARSINOE: (1) ?ii BC *SEG* XXXIV 467
AKARNANIA:
—PALAIROS: (2) f. iii BC *IG* IX (1)² (2) 468
ARGOLIS:
—ARGOS: (3) 105 BC *JÖAI* 14 (1911) Beibl. p. 146 no. 4, 21 (d. Τ—ο—)
EPIROS:
—BOUTHROTOS (PRASAIBOI): (4) a. 163 BC *IBouthrot* 21, 10, 12 (*SEG* XXXVIII 478); *IBouthrot* 184 (m. Ἀφροδίσιος, Κλεοπάτρα)

**Λαοδίκη**
ARGOLIS:
—HERMIONE: (1) imp. *SEG* XVII 173
EPIROS:
—ORIKOS PYLLE: (2) imp. Patsch, *Sandschak Berat* p. 80
S. ITALY (CAMPANIA):
—DIKAIARCHIA-PUTEOLI: (3) imp. *CIL* X 2084 (Lat. Antonia Laodice)

**Λαομέδων**
SICILY:
—ZANKLE-MESSANA: (1) 399 BC D.S. xiv 40. 4

**Λαόμμας**
EPIROS:
—DODONA: (1) iii BC Antoniou, *Dodone* Ab, 4

**Λαόνικος**
LAKONIA:
—SPARTA: (1) 336-324 BC *CID* II 76 II, 31; 79 A I, 20; 95, [15]; 97, 26; 102 II B, 34; 120 A, 21 (Poralla² 477; Bradford (-))

**Λᾶος**
AITOLIA:
—TRICHONION: (1) s. iii BC *IG* IX (1)² (1) 117, 2
S. ITALY (CAMPANIA):
—DIKAIARCHIA-PUTEOLI: (2) ?ii-iii AD *CIL* X 3049 (Lat. M. Val. Laos qui et Africanus: s. Λαΐς)

**Λαοφῶν**
AIGINA: (1) ?270 BC *FD* III (4) 149, 1 (f. Χαρικλῆς)

**Λαπίρων**
S. ITALY (BRUTTIUM):
—LOKROI EPIZEPHYRIOI: (1) ii/i BC *SEG* XXXII 1018
SICILY:
—HALAISA: (2) ii BC *IG* XIV 353 (*IGLMP* 127); *IG* XIV 354 (Διογένης Λ.: s. Διογένης); (3) f. i BC Cic., *In Verr.* II ii 19 (Lat. Apollodorus Laphiro)
——(Σαλ.): (4) ii-i BC *SEG* XXXVII 759 (s. Ἀπολλόδωρος)

**Λαπομπίδας**
ACHAIA:
—AIGEIRA: (1) c. 225-200 BC *BCH* 23 (1899) p. 93 no. 3, 11; cf. *SEG* III 362 (s. Ἀριστόδαμος)

**Λαπρέπης**
ARGOLIS:
—ARGOS: (2) iii BC *IG* IV (1) 618 I, 1 (*Λα-πομπί*[δας]: I f. *Λαπομπίδας* II); (3) ~ ib. l. 1 ([*Λαπ*]ομπίδας: II s. *Λαπομπίδας* I)

**Λαπρέπης**
LAKONIA:
—SPARTA: (1) vi/v BC Hdt. vi 85. 2 (Poralla² 486) (*Λεω*-: f. *Θεασίδας*)

**Λάπυρις**
ARGOLIS:
—KLEONAI: (1) v/iv BC *SEG* XXX 66, 48 (f. *Ἐχέμβροτος*); (2) 323 BC ib. l. 8, 37, 42 (s. *Καλλίας*)

**Λαρέτα**
ELIS:
—OLYMPIA*: (1) imp. *IvOl* 285

**Λάριξ**
S. ITALY (CAMPANIA):
—DIKAIARCHIA-PUTEOLI: (1) ?ii AD *CIL* X 2019 (Lat. M. Caesius Larix)

**Λᾶρις**
SICILY:
—ZANKLE-MESSANA: (1) f. ii BC *BCH* 45 (1921) p. 24 IV, 90 (*SEG* XXII 455); cf. *Sic. Gymn.* 17 (1964) pp. 47 f. (*Λᾶρις*: name—Nikitsky)

**Λάρισα**
LAKONIA: (1) ii-i BC *SEG* XVIII 117

**Λαρχίδας**
ARGOLIS:
—EPIDAUROS: (1) iv/iii BC Peek, *NIEpid* 95 (f. *Ἀλκιβία*)

**Λάρχιππος**
ARKADIA:
—TEGEA: (1) f. iii BC *SEG* XXXIII 319, 6 (s. *Στίπακος*)

**Λάρων**
S. ITALY (CAMPANIA):
—NEAPOLIS: (1) i BC/i AD *INap* 136 (s. *Νύμφιος*) ?= (2); (2) ~ ib. (f. *Νύμφιος*) ?= (1)

**Λασθένεια**
ARKADIA: (1) iv BC *RE* (1) ?= (2)
—MANTINEIA-ANTIGONEIA: (2) iv BC ib. (2) ?= (1)

**Λασθένης**
AKARNANIA:
—LEKKA (MOD.): (1) hell.? *IG* IX (1)² (2) 238-9 (f. *Λαφάνης*)
ARKADIA:
—MT. KYLLENE*: (2) iv-iii BC ib. V (2) 362 (*Λασθέν*[η]ς)
ELIS: (3) i BC Moretti, *Olymp.* 68; *SEG* XV 255 (s. *Σόφων*)
LAKONIA:
—KYTHERA?: (4) ii BC ib. XLI 326, 4 (*Λασθέ*[νης]: f. *Παγκρατίδας*)
PELOPONNESE: (5) c. 192 BC ib. XIII 327, 19 (f. *Ἐπι*—)

**Λασίας**
ARKADIA:
—DIPAIA: (1) 191-146 BC *ZfN* 9 (1882) p. 257 (coin)

**Λάσιος**
ARKADIA:
—TEGEA: (1) m. iv BC *IG* V (2) 6, 117

**Λασκίβος**
ILLYRIA:
—APOLLONIA: (1) ii AD *IApoll* 215 (-σκεί-)

**Λασοΐδας**
SICILY:
—SELINOUS: (1) vi/v BC Dubois, *IGDS* 69 (Arena, *Iscr. Sic.* I 30; *IGLMP* 87) (Λ.—Guarducci and Dubois, *Λασόρας*—*IGLMP* and Arena: f. *Σέλινις*)

**Λάσος**
ARGOLIS:
—HERMIONE: (1) vi BC *RE* (2) (?s. *Χαρμῖνος*, *Χαβρῖνος*, *Χαρμαντίδας*, *Σισύμβρινος*, *Ἰκέλαος*)

**Λαστρατίδας**
ELIS: (1) m. iii BC Moretti, *Olymp.* 562 (s. *Παραβάλλων*)
LAKONIA:
—SPARTA: (2) c. 25-1 BC *IG* V (1) 212, 21 (Bradford (-)) (f. *Τιμάγορος*)

**Λάστρατος**
ARGOLIS:
—PHLEIOUS: (1) vi BC *SEG* XI 275, 7 (*Λάστρατος*)

**Λασύρτας**
ELIS:
—LASION: (1) iii BC Meineke, *Anal. Alex.* fr. 121 (fict.?)

**Λάτροπος**
ARGOLIS:
—ARGOS: (1) iii BC *SEG* XVII 152 (s. *Ἀγέστρατος*)
ARKADIA:
—THISOA?: (2) iii BC ib. XXXVI 388
KORINTHIA:
—KORINTH: (3) 195 BC *Syll*³ 585, 25 (s. *Ζώβιος*)

**Λάτταβος**
AITOLIA: (1) c. 334 BC *FD* III (1) 148, 1 (*Λάττ*[α]βος: f. *Στρόμβιχος*); (2) c. 220 BC *RE* (-)

**Λάτταμος**
AITOLIA:
—BOUKATION: (1) iii/ii BC *IG* IX (1)² (1) p. L, s.a. 216 BC; *FD* III (4) 163, 6

**Λάττυπος**
AITOLIA: (1) ?228-215 BC *SGDI* 2525, 4
ARKADIA:
—THELPHOUSA: (2) c. 230-200 BC *BCH* 45 (1921) p. 12 II, 74 (f. *Θρασύβουλος*)

**Λατυχίδας**
LAKONIA:
—SPARTA: (1) m. vii BC *RE* s.v. Leotychidas (1); *PMGF* I 5 fr. 2, 14, 19; *ZPE* 91 (1992) pp. 1 ff. (ident., stemma) (Poralla² 487) (*Λεωτυχίδας*—lit. test., *Λεωτυχίδης*—Hdt.: s. *Ἀναξίλας*, f. *Ἱπποκρατίδας*, *Εὔκρατ*—: king); (2) c. 530-469 BC *RE* s.v. Leotychidas (2); *IPr* 316, 14 (Poralla² 488) (*Λεωτυχίδας*—lit. test., *Λεωτρεφίδας*—*IPr*: s. *Μενάρης*, f. *Ζευξίδαμος ὁ ἐπικαλ. Κυνίσκος*, *Λαμπιτώ*: king); (3) v/iv BC Plu., *Ages.* 3; *Lys.* 22; *Alc.* 23; Paus. iii 8. 7-10 (Poralla² 489) (*Λεωτυχίδης*—Paus. and Plu.: s. *Ἆγις*, *Τιμαία*: king); (4) iv/iii BC Plu., *Pyrrh.* 26 (Bradford (-)) (*Λεω*-: f. *Χιλωνίς*)

**Λαυδίκα**
ARGOLIS:
—EPIDAUROS: (1) ?i BC *IG* IV (1)² 36
S. ITALY (CAMPANIA):
—DIKAIARCHIA-PUTEOLI*: (2) imp. *CIL* X 2829 (Lat. Marcia Laudica: freed.)
—POMPEII*: (3) i BC-i AD *Eph. Ep.* VIII 319 (Castrèn 118. 12) (Lat. Claudia Laudica: imp. freed.)

**Λαυδίκη**
KEPHALLENIA:
—SAME: (1) i/ii AD *IGUR* 1239 (Λ., Lat. Iulia Laudice: m. Flavia Titiane)
SICILY:
—KATANE: (2) imp. *CIL* X 7049 (Lat. Arruntia Laudice)

**Λαῦδος**
ILLYRIA:
—EPIDAMNOS-DYRRHACHION: (1) hell.-imp. *IDyrrh* 393 (f. *Τάτα*)

**Λαυρέντιος**
KORINTHIA:
—KORINTH: (1) byz. *Corinth* VIII (3) 560, 3; cf. *TMByz* 9 (1985) p. 366 no. 65 (*Λαυρέ*(ν)*τηος*: s. *Καλογένητος*, f. *Παῦλα*)

**Λαφάης**
ARGOLIS:
—ARGOS: (1) iii BC *IG* IV (1) 527, 11; cf. *BCH* 37 (1913) p. 309 ([Λ]αφάης); (2) ?iii BC Paus. ii 21. 8 (tyrant)
—PHLEIOUS: (3) arch. *RE* (2) (sculptor)
KORINTHIA:
—KORINTH*: (4) 325-300 BC *Corinth* XIII p. 287 no. 479-1 (*Λαφά*[ης]?)

**Λαφάνης**
AKARNANIA:
—LEKKA (MOD.): (1) hell.? *IG* IX (1)² (2) 238-9 (s. *Λασθένης*)
ARGOLIS:
—TROIZEN: (2) ?146 BC ib. IV (1) 757 B, 20 (s. *Νίκαρχος*)
ARKADIA:
—KYNOURIOI: (3) 369-361 BC ib. V (2) 1, 43; Tod, *GHI* II 132 (date)
—PAOS: (4) c. 575 BC Hdt. vi 127. 3 (s. *Εὐφορίων*)

**Λαφάντα**
ARGOLIS:
—EPIDAUROS: (1) ii/i BC *IG* IV (1)² 214; 216; 217; 218 + Peek, *IAEpid* 96; *IG* IV (1)² 219; 223; Peek, *IAEpid* 96 (d. *Τηλέμαχος*, *Χαρικώ*, m. *Εὔκλιππος*, *Χαρικώ*); (2) f. i BC *IG* IV (1)² 216; 224; 656 (d. *Εὐάνθης*, ?d. *Χαρικώ*, ?m. *Χαρικώ*); (3) i BC/i AD ib. 220; 661 (d. *Δαμοφάνης*, *Χαρικώ*, ?m. *Δαμέας*); (4) i AD ib. 659 (Κλ. Λ.: d. *Δαμέας*, m. *Τιβ. Κλ. Κλαυδιανός*)

**Λαφάων**
S. ITALY (LUCANIA):
—METAPONTION: (1) iv BC Iamb., *VP* 267 (*FVS* I p. 446)

**Λαφείδης**
ARGOLIS:
—EPIDAUROS: (1) iv BC *IG* IV (1)² 189; 190 (f. *Λᾶκρις*)

**Λάφιλος**
ARGOLIS:
—EPIDAUROS: (1) ?271 BC *Syll*³ 419, 6
——Pierias (Hysminatai): (2) c. 335-325 BC *IG* IV (1)² 108, 143
LAKONIA:
—SPARTA: (3) 421 BC Th. v 19. 2; 24 (Poralla² 478)

**Λάφριος**
AKARNANIA:
—STRATOS: (1) ii BC *IG* IX (1)² (2) 394, 16 (f. *Πρωτόμαχος*)

**Λαφυράδας**
ACHAIA: (1) 146 BC ib. IV (1)² 28, 151 (s. *Εὐπόλεμος*: synoikos)

**Λαφύργας**
EPIROS:
—BOUTHROTOS (PRASAIBOI):
——Chrausinoi: (1) a. 163 BC *IBouthrot* 139, 9 (s. *Στράτων*)
—TRIPOLITAI: (2) 370-368 BC Cabanes, *L'Épire* p. 534 no. 1, 12, 28

**Λαφύστιος**
SICILY:
—SYRACUSE: (**1**) c. 340-335 BC Plu., *Tim.* 37

**Λαχανᾶς**
S. ITALY (BRUTTIUM):
—TERINA: (**1**) v-iv BC *JNG* 33 (1983) p. 13 (coin graffito) (*Λαχ(α)νᾶς* (n. pr.?))
S. ITALY (CAMPANIA):
—KYME: (**2**) imp. *AJA* 77 (1973) p. 153 no. 2 (Lat. Ti. Pontius Lachan(as)?)

**Λαχάρης**
ARGOLIS:
—ARGOS:
——Upper Hysea (Melanippidai): (**1**) iii BC *Mnem.* NS 43 (1915) pp. 372-3 D, 10 (Perlman A.23) (s. *Μίθων*)
—EPIDAUROS: (**2**) iv BC *IG* IV (1)² 181; 182; Peek, *NIEpid* 36; 37 ?= (*3*); (**3**) ~ *IG* IV (1)² 189; 190 (s. *Κλεισθένης*) ?= (*2*); (**4**) iii BC Peek, *NIEpid* 38 ([*Λ*]αχ[ά]ρης); (**5**) ii BC Peek, *IAEpid* 95 II (*Λαχά[ρης]*)
——(Dymanes): (**6**) 146 BC *IG* IV (1)² 28, 5 (f. *Πυθόδωρος*)
——Tenias: (**7**) c. 290-270 BC ib. 109 III, 51
—EPIDAUROS*: (**8**) c. 370 BC ib. 102, 245
—HERMIONE: (**9**) iii BC ib. IV (1) 729 I, 9 (f. *Παρμενίτας*); (**10**) ~ ib. l. 22 (f. *Ἐπίνικος*)
—HERMIONE?: (**11**) iv BC ib. 747 A, 9 (*Λαχάρ[ης]*)
ARKADIA:
—ORCHOMENOS: (**12**) f. iii BC *BCH* 38 (1914) p. 467 no. 10, 8
LAKONIA: (**13**) 77 BC *IG* V (1) 1146, 7
—SPARTA: (**14**) ii BC ib. 29, 17 (*Syll*³ 669; Bradford (1)) (s. *Ἐπήρατος*); (**15**) ?i BC *IG* V (1) 610 (Bradford (6)) (f. *Λεωνίς*); (**16**) m. i BC *IG* II² 3885; 3926 a; *SEG* XI 924 (*ILGR* 40); *SEG* XXIX 383; Plu., *Ant.* 67 (Bradford (2); (3)?) (s. *Εὐρυκλῆς*, f. *Εὐρυκλῆς*); (**17**) ~ *IG* V (1) 94, 11; 265; 267, 1; 1146, 7; 1332 (Bradford (3)) (I ?s. *Ἡρακλείδας*, f. *Λαχάρης* II); (**18**) s. i BC *SEG* XXVIII 410 (s. *Ἡρακλείδας*); (**19**) c. 25-1 BC *IG* V (1) 210, 16 (Bradford (5)) (f. *Ἀγησίνικος*); (**20**) i BC/i AD *IG* V (1) 267 (II s. *Λαχάρης* I)
—SPARTA?: (**21**) i BC-i AD ib. ʹ332
MESSENIA: (**22**) 736 BC Moretti, *Olymp.* 11 (*Λεω-*)
PELOPONNESE: (**23**) s. iii BC *SEG* XIII 278, 8

**Λάχαρτος**
KORINTHIA:
—KORINTH: (**1**) c. 464 BC Plu., *Cim.* 17

**Λάχης**
ELIS: (**1**) i BC *IvOl* 68, 3 (*Λάχη[s]*); (**2**) 85 AD *EA* 1905, p. 255 no. 1, 5 (*Λάχ[ης]*: f. *Κάσσανδρος Διονυσιάδης*)
S. ITALY (CAMPANIA):
—POMPEII: (**3**) i BC-i AD *CIL* IV 1572 c (Lat. Laches)

**Λαχίας**
ARGOLIS:
—ARGOS:
——(Lykophronidai): (**1**) 105 BC *JÖAI* 14 (1911) Beibl. p. 144 no. 4, 3; *Mnem.* NS 44 (1916) p. 58 (locn.) (*Λαχίας*: s. *Παμφάης*)

**Λαώ**
AITOLIA:
—APERANTOI: (**1**) iii BC *SBBerlAk* 1936, p. 388 no. 2, 1 (*L'Illyrie mérid.* 1 p. 110 fig. 7) (d. *Ἀγέλαος*)
S. ITALY (CALABRIA):
—TARAS-TARENTUM: (**2**) hell.? *IG* XIV 2405. 20; cf. 23 (lamp)
S. ITALY (LUCANIA):
—HERAKLEIA: (**3**) iii BC Landi, *DISMG* 216. 2 (loomweight)

**Λέαιθος**
ARGOLIS:
—KLEONAI: (**1**) c. 330-300 BC *SEG* XXX 355, 3

**Λέαινα**
ACHAIA:
—DYME: (**1**) hell.? ib. XIV 373 a (d. *Τρωίλος*)
AITOLIA:
—KALYDON?: (**2**) c. 250 BC *FD* III (3) 149, 1 (d. *Λύκος*)
—PLEURON: (**3**) ?iii BC *SEG* XXXIV 471
AKARNANIA:
—THYRREION: (**4**) iii BC *IG* IX (1)² (2) 265 (d. *Λέων*)
EPIROS:
—BOUTHROTOS (PRASAIBOI): (**5**) a. 163 BC *IBouthrot* 14, 38 (*SEG* XXXVIII 471) ?= (*11*); (**6**) ~ *IBouthrot* 14, 40; 31, 57 (*SEG* XXXVIII 471; 492); (**7**) ~ *IBouthrot* 17, 27 (*SEG* XXXVIII 474); (**8**) ~ *IBouthrot* 27, 9 (*SEG* XXXVIII 485); (**9**) ~ *IBouthrot* 29, 27 (*SEG* XXXVIII 487); (**10**) ~ *IBouthrot* 30, 48; cf. *SEG* XXXVIII 499, 27; (**11**) ~ *IBouthrot* 31, 53, 65 (*SEG* XXXVIII 490) ?= (*5*); (**12**) ~ *IBouthrot* 31, 98 (*SEG* XXXVIII 490) (d. *Λέων*) ?= (*13*); (**13**) ~ *IBouthrot* 37, 10 (*SEG* XXXVIII 496) (d. *Λέων*) ?= (*12*); (**14**) ~ *IBouthrot* 43, 19, 23 (*SEG* XXXVIII 502) (d. *Δείνων*); (**15**) ~ *IBouthrot* 47, 24 ([*Λέ*]αινα); (**16**) ~ ib. 50, 4, 10 ?= (*19*); (**17**) ~ ib. 58, 9 (*SEG* XXXVIII 509); *IBouthrot* 105, 5 (d. *Ἀντιφῶν*); (**18**) ~ ib. 152, 4
——Porronoi: (**19**) a. 163 BC ib. 69, 8; 70, 7; 71, 5 (*BCH* 118 (1994) pp. 129 f. B 1-3) (d. *Σίμακος*) ?= (*16*)
KEPHALLENIA:
—SAME: (**20**) hell.-imp. *IG* IX (1) 622 (*Λέαινα<s>*)
KORINTHIA:
—KORINTH: (**21**) iv/iii BC *RE* (4) (het.)
LEUKAS: (**22**) hell. *Ep. Chron.* 31 (1994) p. 49 no. 2 (*AD* 45 (1990) Chron. p. 254 no. 2)
MESSENIA:
—KYPARISSIA: (**23**) iii BC *SEG* XV 225

**Λεάναξ**
S. ITALY (BRUTTIUM):
—SYBARIS-THOURIOI-COPIAE: (**1**) iv BC Iamb., *VP* 267 (*FVS* 1 p. 446) (*Δεάναξ*—ms.: name—C. Keil)
SICILY:
—SYRACUSE?:
——(Ὑπα.): (**2**) hell. Manganaro, *PdelP* forthcoming no. 4 IV, 4 (s. *Θαρσαγόρας*)

**Λεανδρίς**
LAKONIA:
—SPARTA: (**1**) m. vii BC Paus. iii 14. 4 (Poralla² 479) (m. *Εὐρυκρατίδας*)

**Λέανδρος**
S. ITALY (CALABRIA):
—BRENTESION-BRUNDISIUM: (**1**) imp. *CIL* IX 130 (Lat. L. Iulius Laeander)

**Λεαρέτα**
SICILY:
—APOLLONIA: (**1**) hell. *SEG* XXXIV 933 (loomweight)

**Λέαρχος**
AKARNANIA:
—PALAIROS: (**1**) c. 300 BC *IG* IX (1)² (2) 462 (*CEG* II 661) (f. *Δεινίας*)

**Λέβινθος**
S. ITALY (CAMPANIA):
—POMPEII: (**1**) i BC-i AD *CIL* IV 1123 (Lat. Lebinthus)

**Λεϝκάνα**
SICILY:
—SELINOUS (NR.): (**1**) c. 600 BC *SEG* XLII 875; cf. *BE* 1993, no. 714

**Λειτός**
ARGOLIS:
—EPIDAUROS: (**1**) c. 290-270 BC *IG* IV (1)² 109 II, 155

**Λέκαδος?**
S. ITALY (BRUTTIUM):
—RHEGION: (**1**) hell. ib. XIV 2400. 6 (tile) (*Λεκάδου* (gen.), (*Κ*)ε(*λ*)άδου?)

**Λελία**
SICILY:
—PANORMOS?: (**1**) imp. ib. 2412. 28 (seal) (d. *Πρώπινκος*)

**Λένεον**
ARGOLIS:
—MYKENAI: (**1**) hell.? *SEG* III 315 a (loomweight)

**Λεντῖνος**
ARGOLIS:
—EPIDAUROS: (**1**) c. 365-335 BC *IG* IV (1)² 103, 73

**Λεξειάτας**
KERKYRA: (**1**) f. v BC *LSAG*² p. 233; p. 234 no. 16

**Λέξις**
S. ITALY (CAMPANIA):
—DIKAIARCHIA-PUTEOLI: (**1**) imp. *CIL* X 2627 (Lat. Poblicia Lexis)

**Λεοκράτεια**
S. ITALY (CALABRIA):
—TARAS-TARENTUM (NR.): (**1**) c. 530 BC *SEG* XL 898 (vase)

**Λεοκράτης**
EPIROS:
—AMBRAKIA: (**1**) 238-168 BC *BMC Thessaly* p. 96 no. 31 (coin) ([*Λ*]εοκράτης)

**Λεομένης**
ARKADIA:
—TEGEA: (**1**) iv BC *SEG* XXXVI 382, 2 (f. —ος)

**Λεονᾶς**
AKARNANIA:
—THYRREION (NR.): (**1**) ?ii-iii AD ib. 538

**Λεόνικος**
AITOLIA:
—PHOLAI: (**1**) 217-207 BC *FD* III (3) 221, 2 + *BCH* 73 (1949) p. 268 no. 19 (*Λεονί[κ?]ος*)
S. ITALY (APULIA):
—VENUSIA: (**2**) imp. *CIL* IX 426 (Lat. Leonicus: s. Sentia Rufina)

**Λεόννατος**
ILLYRIA:
—LYCHNIDOS: (**1**) ?s. ii AD *ZA* 6 (1956) p. 167 no. 3 + *BE* 1958, no. 301 (*Λέννα-*: s. *Δάζος*)

**Λεοντᾶς**
ARKADIA:
—TEGEA: (**1**) ii AD *IG* V (2) 55, 36 (f. *Ἐπήρατος*)
ELIS:
—OLYMPIA*: (**2**) 209-213 AD *IvOl* 110, 24 (?s. *Αὐρ. Νικηφόρος*: slave?)
LAKONIA:
—GYTHEION: (**3**) f. ii AD *IG* V (1) 1170, 6; 1174, 10 (s. *Λυσικράτης*)
—SPARTA: (**4**) ?ii-i BC ib. 780 (Bradford (5)); (**5**) ii AD *IG* V (1) 118, 3 (Bradford (1)) ([*Λε*]οντᾶς: s. *N*—); (**6**) ~ *IG* V (1) 159, 29 (Bradford (6)); (**7**) c. 140-160 AD *IG* V (1) 154, 13 (Bradford (2)) (s. *Φιλουμενός*); (**8**) f. iii AD *IG* V (1) 541, 6; 552, 7; 555, 2; *BSA* 79 (1984) p. 270 (name) (Bradford (3)) (*Μάμιος Λ.*)

**S. Italy (Campania):**
—DIKAIARCHIA-PUTEOLI: (9) imp. *CIL* x 2647 (Lat. Larcius Leontas)

**Λεοντεύς**
AKARNANIA:
—ALYZIA: (1) ii-i BC *IG* IX (1)² (2) 446 a ([Λε]οντεύς: f. Λάνασσα)
—STRATOS: (2) s. iii BC ib. IX (1)² (1) 24, 5
ARGOLIS:
—ARGOS: (3) s. i BC *RE* (4) (Stephanis 1534)
EPIROS:
—ARGOS (AMPHILOCH.): (4) 356-354 BC *IG* IV (1)² 95, 33 (Perlman E.2); Perlman p. 40 f. (date); (5) f. ii BC *BCH* 45 (1921) p. 23 IV, 49
—BOUTHROTOS (PRASAIBOI):
——Lykourgoi: (6) a. 163 BC *IBouthrot* 137, 13 (s. Λέων)
LAKONIA:
—SPARTA: (7) c. 262 BC *IG* IX (1)² (1) 17, 79 (Bradford (2)) (f. Ἀπ—ο—); (8) ?s. ii AD *IG* v (1) 257; *Artemis Orthia* pp. 299-300 no. 7 (date) (Bradford (1))
LEUKAS: (9) 240 BC *ID* 298 A, 116; 1409 B a II, 62
MESSENIA:
—THOURIA: (10) ii-i BC *IG* v (1) 1385, 12 (s. Τίμων)
S. ITALY (CALABRIA):
—TARAS-TARENTUM: (11) iv BC Iamb., *VP* 267 (*FVS* 1 p. 446)

**Λεοντία**
S. ITALY (APULIA):
—VENUSIA: (1) c. 448-503 AD *Vetera Christianorum* 13 (1976) pp. 157-9 (*Puglia Paleocrist. Altomed.* 3 p. 123) (Lat. Leontia: Jew?)
S. ITALY (CAMPANIA):
—DIKAIARCHIA-PUTEOLI: (2) imp. *CIL* x 2383 (Lat. Gerontia Leontia)
—POMPEII: (3) i BC-i AD ib. IV 1617 (Lat. Leontia)
SICILY:
—KATANE: (4) iii-v AD *JIWE* 1 146 (*CIJ* 1² 650 a; *IG* XIV 543; Wessel 1342); cf. Wilson, *Sicily* pp. 310-11 with fig. 264 b (Jew)
—SYRACUSE: (5) imp. *NScav* 1947, p. 189 no. 4 + *Riv. Arch. Crist.* 22 (1946) p. 259 (Lat. Leontia); (6) iii-v AD *SEG* IV 2 (Wessel 185)

**Λεοντίας**
ARKADIA:
—TEGEA: (1) m. iv BC *IG* v (2) 6, 64

**Λεοντίδας**
ARGOLIS:
—HERMIONE: (1) imp. ib. IV (1) 723, 1 (f. Σμυρναία: doctor)

**Λεοντῖνος**
S. ITALY (CAMPANIA):
—POMPEII: (1) i BC-i AD *CIL* IV 2471 (Lat. Leontinus)

**Λεόντιον**
KERKYRA: (1) hell.-imp. *IG* IX (1) 587 + Unp. (*IG* arch.) (locn.)

**Λεόντιος**
AKARNANIA:
—PALAIROS: (1) 356-354 BC *IG* IV (1)² 95, 21 (Perlman E.2); Perlman p. 40 f. (date)
ARKADIA: (2) iii BC *SEG* II 863 (Λεόν[τι]ος)
—MANTINEIA-ANTIGONEIA: (3) c. 300-221 BC *IG* v (2) 323. 45 (tessera) (s. Πολυήρατος); (4) ~ ib. 323. 83 (tessera) (f. Πολυχάρης)
EPIROS:
—DODONA*: (5) iv/iii BC *PAE* 1931, p. 90 no. 2 (f. Λέων)

**S. ITALY (APULIA):**
—VENUSIA: (6) v AD *JIWE* 1 104 (Λεό[ντιος]?: Jew)
S. ITALY (CAMPANIA):
—NOLA: (7) imp. *CIL* x 1252 (Lat. Leontius)
—SALERNUM: (8) imp. *IItal* 1 (1) 21 (*CIL* x 539) (Lat. Acerius Firmius Leontius)
SICILY: (9) byz. *BZ* 19 (1910) p. 472 (ring) (Λεόντ(ι)ος)

**Λεοντίς**
ARKADIA: (1) 320 BC *IG* v (2) 549, 22 (f. Πάντιχος)
S. ITALY (LUCANIA):
—MONTESCAGLIOSO (MOD.): (2) iii BC *St. Etr.* 52 (1984) p. 479 (tiles)
SICILY:
—AKRAGAS: (3) 190 BC *Syll*³ 585, 91 (s. Σωσικράτης)
—KAMARINA: (4) iv/iii BC *SEG* XXXIX 999, 5 (Dubois, *IGDS* 125; Cordano, 'Camarina VII' 132)
—MORGANTINA: (5) iv/iii BC *PdelP* 44 (1989) p. 214 ([Λέ]οντι[ς]); (6) ~ *SEG* XXXIX 1012, 8 (f. Θεύδωρος)

**Λεοντίς**
ARGOLIS:
—ARGOS: (1) i BC-i AD Unp. (Argos, Kavvadias) (Λη-)
—HERMIONE: (2) i BC-i AD? *IG* IV (1) 730 I, 3 (d. Κλεοπάτρα); (3) ~ ib. 730 V, 7
—PHLEIOUS: (4) iii-ii BC ib. 477
EPIROS: (5) iv/iii BC ib. II² 8539 (d. Νικάδας)
—AMBRAKIA: (6) v/iv BC *BCH* 79 (1955) p. 267 (d. Λέων)
—NIKOPOLIS: (7) imp. *PAE* 1913, p. 98 no. 13 (Sarikakis 98) (d. Πύριχος)
ILLYRIA:
—APOLLONIA: (8) ii-i BC *IApoll* 112 (-τείς)
ITHAKE: (9) hell. *SEG* XVII 255
KORINTHIA:
—KORINTH: (10) c. 570-550 BC Amyx 66. 7 (vase) (Lorber 122) (Λho-: her.)
LEUKAS: (11) hell.-imp. *IG* IX (1) 578
MESSENIA:
—KYPARISSIA: (12) iii BC *SEG* XV 225
—MESSENE: (13) ?iv-ii BC *IG* v (1) 1488
S. ITALY (BRUTTIUM):
—LOKROI EPIZEPHYRIOI: (14) s. iv AD ib. XIV 625, 3 (*ICI* v 6); cf. Costabile, *Municipium Locrensium* p. 74 (locn., date) (Λεω-: d. Σεκουνδίων, Φήλικλα)
S. ITALY (CALABRIA):
—TARAS-TARENTUM (NR.): (15) iii BC *Atti Conv. Taranto* 22 (1982) p. 457 (Λεοντὶς Βιωτώ)

**Λεοντίς**
EPIROS:
—BOUTHROTOS (PRASAIBOI): (1) a. 163 BC *IBouthrot* 48, 9; (2) ~ ib. 102, 3
—NIKOPOLIS: (3) imp. *SEG* XLII 545, 2

**Λεοντίσκος**
AKARNANIA:
—ASTAKOS: (1) ii BC *IG* IX (1)² (2) 435, 12 (-σχος: f. Ἡράκλειτος)
—THYRREION: (2) ii BC ib. 247, 15 (f. Λέων)
EPIROS: (3) iii BC Brown, *Ptolemaic Paintings* 22 (f. —ος)
—AMBRAKIA: (4) s. ii BC Cabanes, *L'Épire* p. 548 no. 19 (*SEG* XXVI 694) (f. Νίκαρχος)
—NIKOPOLIS: (5) imp. *Hellenika* 22 (1969) p. 72 no. 11 (Sarikakis 99) (s. Ἀθήναιος)
—TEPELENE (MOD.): (6) ii-iii AD *Iliria* 1976, p. 320 with pl. 7 = 1989 (2), p. 222; cf. *SEG* XXXIX 552 note
ILLYRIA:
—EPIDAMNOS-DYRRHACHION: (7) c. 250-50 BC Münsterberg Nachtr. p. 16 (coin) (pryt.) ?= (8); (8) ~ Maier 275 (Ceka 96); *IApoll Ref.*

**Bibl.** n. 88 (coin) (pryt.) ?= (7); (9) ii-i BC *IDyrrh* 544 (tiles)
KORINTHIA:
—SIKYON: (10) s. iii BC *RE* (3) (Skalet 191) (painter)
S. ITALY (LUCANIA):
—HERAKLEIA:
——(Fε. γυῖον): (11) iv/iii BC *IGSI* 1 I, 183 (*DGE* 62; Uguzzoni–Ghinatti I) (f. Πεισίας)
SICILY:
—ZANKLE-MESSANA: (12) 456-452 BC *RE* (2); Moretti, *Olymp.* 271; 285

**Λεόντιχος**
ACHAIA:
—ASCHEION: (1) c. 210-207 BC *IG* IV (1)² 73, 28; *SEG* XXXV 303 (date) ([Λεόντ]ιχος: f. Ἀριστόβουλος); (2) 188 BC *Syll*³ 585, 150 (s. Ἀριστόβουλος)
ARKADIA:
—TEGEA: (3) m. iv BC *IG* v (2) 6, 65
ELIS: (4) c. 50 BC *SEG* XXXVII 388, 7 ([Λε]όντιχος: s. Φόσυρος)
MESSENIA:
—THOURIA: (5) ii-i BC *IG* v (1) 1385, 5 (s. Δείνιππος)

**Λεοντίων**
EPIROS:
—AMBRAKIA: (1) a. 167 BC *SEG* XXXV 665 A, 6 (s. Λέων)
ILLYRIA:
—APOLLONIA: (2) imp. *IApoll* 207 ([Λ]εοντίων: s. Ἀρχήν)

**Λεοντομένης**
ACHAIA:
—DYME: (1) s. iii BC *SEG* XIII 278, 23
AITOLIA: (2) c. 334 BC *FD* III (1) 147, 1 (Λεοντομ[ένης]: s. Στρογγυλίων); (3) ?263-261 BC ib. III (3) 184, 1; [190]; *Syll*³ 498, 2; Nachtergael, *Les Galates* 3, 1
—KALLION/KALLIPOLIS: (4) a. 170 BC *IG* IX (1) 226, 14
—PHYTAION: (5) ?205-203 BC *FD* III (2) 134 b, 4 (*Syll*³ 564)
ARKADIA:
—MEGALOPOLIS: (6) ?145 BC *IG* v (2) 439, 55 (s. Δαμαρχίδας)
—TEGEA: (7) 165 AD ib. 50, 65 (f. Εὔτυχος)
ELIS: (8) ii BC *SEG* XLI 387 (f. Φίλα)

**Λεότιμος**
ARKADIA:
—MANTINEIA-ANTIGONEIA: (1) c. 225 BC ib. XI 414, 37 (Perlman E.5) (Λ[ε]ότιμος: s. Τιμούχος)

**Λεόφρων**
S. ITALY (BRUTTIUM):
—KROTON: (1) iv BC Iamb., *VP* 267 (*FVS* 1 p. 446)
S. ITALY (LUCANIA):
—METAPONTION: (2) iii BC *IG* IV (1)² 263

**Λεοχάρης**
ARGOLIS:
—EPIDAUROS:
——(Azantioi): (1) 146 BC ib. 28, 37 (f. Γοργίων)
—EPIDAUROS*: (2) c. 370-365 BC Peek, *IAEpid* 52 B, 10 (Λεοχ[άρης])

**Λέπιδα**
LAKONIA:
—OITYLOS: (1) imp. *IG* v (1) 1306

**Λεπούσκλα**
LAKONIA:
—ASOPOS: (1) i/ii AD *SEG* XXXIX 372, 3

**Λεπτίνας**
ACHAIA:
—DYME*: (1) c. 219 BC *SGDI* 1612, 35 (*Tyche* 5 (1990) p. 124) (I f. Λεπτίνας II); (2) ~ *SGDI*

## Λέπτος (cont.)

1612, 35 (*Tyche* 5 (1990) p. 124) (II s. Λεπτίνας I)

—KALLISTAI: (3) c. 230-200 BC *BCH* 45 (1921) p. 12 II, 61 (f. Δράκων: reading—Oulhen)

AITOLIA: (4) m. iii BC *IG* IX (1)² (1) 22, 6; 23, 2

—KALYDON: (5) ?iii BC ib. IX (2) 458, 4 (Λεπτιναία (patr. adj.): f. Ἀρχαρέτα)

ARKADIA:

—ORCHOMENOS*: (6) ?ii BC ib. v (2) 345, 10 (f. Σωτέλης)

KORINTHIA:

—SIKYON: (7) ?257-255 BC Nachtergael, *Les Galates* 7, 73; 8, 75; cf. Stephanis 2350 (f. Σωσικράτης)

SICILY: (8) ?iv BC Vandermersch p. 168 (amph.) (or S. Italy) ?= (9); (9) hell. ib. (amph.) (or S. Italy) ?= (8)

—KAMARINA: (10) f. v BC Cordano, *Tessere Pubbliche* 131 ([Λ]επ(π)[τ]ίνας: f. Κέφαλος)

—KATANE: (11) f. ii BC *BCH* 45 (1921) p. 25 col. IV, 98 (*SEG* XXII 455); cf. *Sic. Gymn.* 17 (1964) pp. 47 f. (Λεπτίν[ας])

—SYRACUSE: (12) iv BC *RE* (3) (II ?s. Λεπτίνας I, ?f. Λεπτίνας III); (13) f. iv BC Iamb., *VP* 267 (*FVS* 1 p. 447) (-νης); (14) 397-383 BC *RE* (2); cf. Beloch, *GG* III (2) pp. 102-7 (I s. Ἑρμοκράτης, f. Ἀλκέτας, ?f. Λεπτίνας II); (15) iv/iii BC *RE* (4) (III ?s. Λεπτίνας II, f. Φιλιστίς)

—TERRAVECCHIA DI CUTI (MOD.): (16) vi/v BC Arena, *Iscr. Sic.* II 117 A (Dubois, *IGDS* 176)

## Λέπτος

SICILY:

—GELA-PHINTIAS: (1) vi/v BC ib. 143 b (vase) (Arena, *Iscr. Sic.* II 20) ([Λ]έπτος: ?s. Σκυ—)

## Λέπτων

ARGOLIS:

—ARGOS:

——(Dymanes-Doriadai): (1) c. 400 BC *SEG* XXIX 361, 33 (-πτōν)

## Λεσβία

S. ITALY (CAMPANIA):

—NEAPOLIS: (1) imp. *CIL* X 1516; cf. Leiwo p. 113 no. 93 (Lat. Valeria Lesvia)

## Λεσβιανός

S. ITALY (CAMPANIA):

—POMPEII: (1) 70-79 AD *CIL* IV 9870; 10070; Mouritsen p. 111 (date) (Lat. Lesbianus)

## Λέσβιος

MESSENIA:

—ASINE: (1) ii AD *IG* V (1) 1408 (f. Μηνᾶς)

S. ITALY (CAMPANIA):

—POMPEII: (2) 56 AD *CIL* IV 3340. 25, 21 (Castrèn 187. 6) (Lat. Q. Granius Lesbius)

SICILY:

—THERMAI HIMERAIAI*: (3) i-ii AD *Eph. Ep.* VIII 706 (*ILat. Term. Imer.* 112) (Lat. Lesbius: freed.)

## Λεσφίνας

AKARNANIA:

—ASTAKOS: (1) ii BC *IG* IX (1)² (2) 434, 8; cf. *SEG* XXIX 473 (f. Καλλιγένης)

## Λεύκα

S. ITALY (APULIA):

—LUCERIA: (1) imp. *ASP* 34 (1981) p. 29 no. 35 (Lat. Obsitia Leuca: m. Felicitas)

S. ITALY (CALABRIA):

—TARAS-TARENTUM: (2) iv/iii BC *IG* XIV 668 II, 13 (Landi, *DISMG* 194) (<Δ>ευκα—apogr.)

## Λευκάδιος

ARGOLIS:

—ARGOS: (1) iv AD *SEG* XVI 261, 3; cf. *TMByz* 9 (1985) p. 289 no. 28

LEUKAS?: (2) v/iv BC *Suda* O 1091 (n. pr.?: ?f. Φιλόξενος)

## Λεύκαρος

AKARNANIA: (1) ?f. iv BC Arist., *Fr.* 475; cf. Moretti, *Olymp.* 1013

ARKADIA:

—MANTINEIA-ANTIGONEIA:

——(Posoidaia): (2) c. 425-400 BC *SEG* XXXI 348, 25

EPIROS:

—DODONA: (3) iii BC Antoniou, *Dodone* Ab, 25

—MOLOSSOI: (4) iv/iii BC Cabanes, *L'Épire* p. 543 no. 8, 2 (Dubois, *IGDS* 184) (Λεύκαρος)

## Λεύκαρχος

EPIROS:

—ARGOS (AMPHILOCH.): (1) ?270 BC *FD* III (2) 179, 1 (f. Πάλλιχος)

## Λευκάς

S. ITALY (CAMPANIA):

—POMPEII: (1) i BC-i AD *CIL* IV 1417 (Lat. Leucas)

## Λεύκασπις

ELIS:

—OLYMPIA*: (1) v BC *IvOl* 658 (s. Προῖτος)

## Λευκία

S. ITALY (CAMPANIA):

—NEAPOLIS: (1) i BC-i AD *IG* XIV 783, 1 (*INap* 137); cf. Leiwo p. 121 no. 106 (d. Εὔφρων)

## Λευκίας

AITOLIA: (1) 244 or 240 BC *SGDI* 2511, 2 (Flacelière p. 402 no. 29)

EPIROS:

—DODONA: (2) iii BC Antoniou, *Dodone* Aa, 7; (3) ~ ib. Ba, 1; (4) ~ ib. l. 20 (Λε[υκ]ίας)

## Λευκίδας

AITOLIA:

—THESTIEIS: (1) 213 BC *IG* IX (1)² (1) 96, 14, 16 ?= (2); (2) ii BC *SBBerlAk* 1936, p. 381 no. 1 B, 1 ?= (1)

## Λεύκιος

AITOLIA:

—THERMOS*: (1) s. iii BC *IG* IX (1)² (1) 60 II, 7; (2) ~ ib. 60 VI, 17

AKARNANIA:

—ASTAKOS: (3) ii BC ib. IX (1)² (2) 435, 18 (f. Σωτίων)

ARGOLIS:

—ARGOS: (4) c. 146-32 BC BM coin 1887 6-6-14 (coin)

—EPIDAUROS: (5) i-ii AD Peek, *IAEpid* 214 (f. Φιλόνικος)

DALMATIA:

—ISSA?: (6) iii/ii BC *CIG* 6913; *SEG* XL 512 (locn.) (f. Διονύσιος)

EPIROS:

—BOUTHROTOS: (7) ?i BC *IBouthrot* 197 (Ugolini, *Alb. Ant.* 3 p. 209 no. 4) (f. Οὐεργιλία)

—BOUTHROTOS (PRASAIBOI): (8) a. 163 BC *IBouthrot* 22, 13 (*SEG* XXXVIII 479)

ILLYRIA:

—EPIDAMNOS-DYRRHACHION: (9) c. 250-50 BC Maier 118; 308; 488 (coin) (Ceka 290-2) (money.); (10) i BC *IDyrrh* 290; (11) hell.-imp. ib. 222 (f. Ζωΐλα); (12) ~ ib. 291 (I f. Λεύκιος II); (13) ~ ib. (II s. Λεύκιος I)

—LYCHNIDOS?: (14) ii-i BC *SEG* I 254 (f. Ἐπίκαδος)

KERKYRA: (15) i BC *IG* IX (1) 709 (f. Πόπλιος)

KORINTHIA:

—KORINTH: (16) a. 43 AD *SEG* XVIII 143, 16 (f. Θεοδώρα: katoikos)

PELOPONNESE?: (17) ii AD *PAE* 1992, p. 72 B, 11 (s. Εὔτυχος); (18) ~ ib. l. 13 (s. Φῆσος)

S. ITALY: (19) 179 BC *ID* 442 B, 85

S. ITALY (BRUTTIUM):

—LOKROI EPIZEPHYRIOI: (20) iii-ii BC Landi, *DISMG* 244, 10

—PETELIA:

——(Ὀρ.): (21) i BC *SEG* XXXIV 1009 (brick)

—RHEGION: (22) s. ii BC *IG* XIV 615, 2; *Klearchos* 21 (1979) pp. 83-96 (date) (f. Νίκανδρος)

—ROSSANO (MOD.): (23) iii BC *Atti Conv. Taranto* 12 (1972) p. 336 no. 2

S. ITALY (CAMPANIA):

—NEAPOLIS: (24) i BC *IG* II² 9991 (f. Δημητρία)

SICILY:

—ENTELLA: (25) iv/iii BC *SEG* XXX 1117, 2 (Dubois, *IGDS* 204); *SEG* XXX 1118, 2 (Dubois, *IGDS* 205) (s. Πάκκιος); (26) ~ *SEG* XXX 1119, 1 (Dubois, *IGDS* 206) (s. Καίσιος)

—LILYBAION: (27) i BC/i AD *SEG* XV 512 (f. Ζηνάριον)

—SYRACUSE: (28) ii-i BC *NScav* 1913, p. 279 (?s. Πολλίας); (29) i BC-i AD? *IG* XIV 13 (*Sic. Gymn.* 16 (1963) p. 59) (f. Ἀπολλόδοτος)

—ZANKLE-MESSANA: (30) i BC-i AD *NS* 604 (or Messenia Messene: f. Δημώ)

SICILY?: (31) 250 BC *FGrH* 567 F 1 (Λ. Γλαύκων: fict.?)

## Λεύκιππος

ARGOLIS:

—ARGOS?: (1) v BC *IG* IV (1) 552, 9 (Λεύκιπ[πος])

ARKADIA:

—MANTINEIA-ANTIGONEIA: (2) c. 300-221 BC ib. v (2) 323. 46 (tessera) (s. Τιμοτέλης)

LAKONIA:

—SPARTA: (3) arch. D.H. xvii 4 (Poralla² 480) (and S. Italy (Calabria) Kallipolis: oikist)

## Λευκόϊον

ILLYRIA:

—APOLLONIA: (1) hell. *IApoll* 113; (2) ~ ib. 114

## Λεῦκος

ILLYRIA:

—EPIDAMNOS-DYRRHACHION: (1) hell. *IDyrrh* 293 (s. Φαλίος)

## Λευκόσιν

ILLYRIA:

—APOLLONIA: (1) imp. *IApoll* 332 (Λευκόσιν, Λευκοσία—ed.)

## Λευκόσιος

S. ITALY (BRUTTIUM):

—TAURIANA: (1) m. iv AD *ICI* V 8 (Lat. Leucosius: bp.)

## Λευκτριάδας

LAKONIA:

—SPARTA: (1) ?ii-i BC *IG* V (1) 755 (Bradford (-)) (f. Ὀλυμπίχα); (2) c. 25-1 BC *IG* V (1) 210, 41 (Λευκτρι[άδας]: f. Ἀ—ς); (3) i BC/i AD? ib. 577 (Bradford (-)) (f. —α)

## Λεύκων

AKARNANIA:

—PALAIROS: (1) iii BC *IG* IX (1)² (2) 491

S. ITALY (LUCANIA):

—LEUKANOI: (2) c. 316-309 BC ib. II² 1956, 50; *Ancient Macedonia* 5 p. 445 with n. 10 (date)

SICILY:

—GELA-PHINTIAS: (3) m. v BC Arena, *Iscr. Sic.* II 63 (Lazzarini 393) (-κōν, Τεύκōν?)

—ZANKLE-MESSANA*: (4) f. ii BC *BCH* 45 (1921) p. 24 IV, 91 (*SEG* XXII 455); cf. *Sic. Gymn.* 17 (1964) pp. 47 f. (freed.?)

## Λεχώι

SICILY: (1) v/iv BC *ZPE* 111 (1996) p. 136 no. 4 (-χōι)

## Λεωκύδης

ARKADIA:
—MEGALOPOLIS: (1) 331 BC Paus. viii 10. 6, 10
S. ITALY (LUCANIA):
—METAPONTION: (2) iv BC Iamb., VP 267 (FVS 1 p. 446)

## Λεώμαχος

ILLYRIA:
—ATINTANES: (1) c. 313-297 BC Cabanes, L'Épire p. 545 no. 12 ([Κ]λεώμαχος—edd.)

## Λεωμήδης

ILLYRIA:
—EPIDAMNOS-DYRRHACHION: (1) c. 250-50 BC Mionnet 2 p. 39 no. 111; cf. Ceka 289 (coin) (Λεαμήδης—Mionnet)

## Λέων

ACHAIA: (1) c. 235-225 BC SEG XV 276, 2 (IOrop 65) (Λέο[ν]τ[α] (acc.)—IOrop: s. Φιλόστρατος); (2) ii BC IG XII (9) 1127 (f. Ἀπολλόδωρος)
—DYME: (3) ii-i BC SEG XIV 373 c (f. Φίλα); (4) ?145 BC Sherk 43, 1; SEG XXXVIII 372 (date); (5) 128 BC FD III (3) 123, 2 (f. Θεόκριτος)
—DYME*: (6) c. 219 BC SGDI 1612, 52 (Tyche 5 (1990) p. 124) (s. Βουθύων)
—TRITAIA?: (7) m. iii BC IG V (2) 368, 81 with index (f. Παντίας)
AITOLIA: (8) ?316 BC FD III (4) 387, 1 (s. Φυρταῖος); (9) ?253 BC Nachtergael, Les Galates 10, 5; (10) ?252-248 BC Syll³ 422, 3; (11) ?a. 246 BC SGDI 2508, 2; (12) 244 or 240 BC ib. 2512, 2 + Flacelière p. 402 no. 28 a; Nachtergael, Les Galates 59, 3
—APEIRIKOI: (13) 143-141 BC IG IX (1)² (1) 34, 16; IX (1)² (3) 634, 10 (f. Νικιάδας)
—APERANTOI: (14) iv/iii BC SEG XVII 274, 4 (L'Illyrie mérid. 1 p. 111 fig. 9)
—KALLION/KALLIPOLIS: (15) c. 20-45 AD FD III (6) 13, 53 (Λέ[ων]: s. Πιστέας: reading—Mulliez)
—KALYDON: (16) s. ii BC SEG XXV 621, 3 (s. Λύσων); (17) c. 143 BC IG IX (1)² (1) 137, 37 (f. Ἀγάθυμος); (18) a. 142 BC ib. l. 79
—KONOPE-ARSINOE: (19) c. 200 BC BCH 50 (1926) p. 125 no. 2 b, 4, 10 ([Λ]έων, [Κ]έων?—ed.: f. Πανταλέων); (20) 154 BC SGDI 1908, 12 (s. Δάμων)
—PELEIOI: (21) c. 162 BC IG IX (1)² (1) 105, 9
—PHILOTAIEIS: (22) f. ii BC ib. 96, 22 (s. Μικκίας)
—PHISTYON: (23) c. 125-100 BC SBBerlAk 1936, p. 367 no. 2, 3, 14 (SEG XII 303) (s. Ἀντιλέων)
—THESTIEIS: (24) ?212-210 BC FD III (4) 363, 5
AKARNANIA: (25) c. 250-167 BC NZ 10 (1878) p. 29 no. 30; BMC Thessaly p. 169 no. 12 (coins); cf. Stud. D. M. Robinson 2 p. 218 ff. (s. Ὀρσικράτης)
—ASTAKOS: (26) ii BC IG IX (1)² (2) 434, 12 (f. Σωτίων); (27) ~ ib. l. 16 (s. Σωτίων)
—PALAIROS: (28) ii BC ib. 451, 11 ([Λ]έων: s. Ἀγέλαος); (29) ~ ib. l. 18 (f. Μνασίλοχος); (30) ~ ib. l. 21
—STRATOS: (31) iv/iii BC ib. 395, 10 (s. Περικλῆς)
—THYRREION: (32) iii BC ib. 265 (f. Λέαινα); (33) ~ ib. 266 (f. —ος); (34) ~ ib. 598 (f. Ἀνδροτέλης) ?= (37); (35) ~ ib. 599 (Λέ[ων]: f. Λέων II); (36) ~ ib. (II s. Λέων I); (37) ~ ib. 600 (f. Λεωνίδας) ?= (34); (38) iii-ii BC SEG XXVII 159, 3; cf. PAE 1977, pl. 244 a (s. Τιμοκλῆς); (39) ii BC IG IX (1)² (2) 247, 11 (f. Λαμίσκος); (40) ~ ib. 248 (s. Λεοντίσκος); (41) ~ ib. 248, 17 (f. Λυσίξενος); (42) ~ ib. l. 20 (f. Ἀλέξων); (43) ~ ib. 314, 1, 4 (?f. Σώπολις); (44) hell.-imp. ib. 355; (45) ?94 BC Phegos pp. 267 f. (coins) (s. Φατνιάδας)

ARGOLIS:
—ARGOS:
—Posidaon: (46) a. 338 BC IG XII (3) 1259, 14; cf. Mnem. NS 44 (1916) pp. 61-4
—EPIDAUROS: (47) iii BC IG IV (1)² 349 (s. Δαμόφιλος)
—EPIDAUROS*: (48) c. 335-325 BC Peek, IAEpid 50, 23
—HERMIONE: (49) iii BC IG IV (1) 728, 2 (s. Σωκράτης)
—KLEONAI: (50) c. 315 BC SEG XXXII 370, 5 ([Λ]έων)
—TROIZEN: (51) 480 BC Hdt. vii 180
ARKADIA: (52) iii BC BSAAlex 15 (1914) p. 89 (f. Ἀπολλόδωρος) ?= (53); (53) ~ ib. ?= (52)
—GORTYS: (54) ii-i BC SEG XXXV 348 (s. Ὀλυμπιάδας, f. Ὀλυμπιάδας)
—MEGALOPOLIS: (55) 359 BC CID II 5 I, 39; (56) ?145 BC IG V (2) 439, 49 (f. Πολυκράτης)
—TEGEA: (57) ii AD ib. 55, 68 (s. Ἐλεύθερος)
DALMATIA:
—ISSA:
—(Hylleis): (58) iv/iii BC Brunšmid p. 9, 60 (f. Δῶρος)
—(Hylleis)?: (59) iii BC ib. p. 9 fr. G, 10 + VAMZ 1970, p. 37 frr. G and M (f. Δῶρος)
ELIS: (60) f. i BC IvOl 199; 406, 3 (Λέοντος (gen.)—199, Λέωνος (gen.)—406: f. Τηλέμαχος); (61) ~ ib. 200 ([Λέ]ων: f. Πραξαγόρας); (62) 67 AD ib. 82, 6 (Γ. [Ἀν]τ. Λ.: Π.); (63) ~ ib. l. 16 (s. Λύσων); (64) 85 AD EA 1905, p. 255 no. 1, 9 (f. Ζωΐλος)
—OLYMPIA*: (65) m. i BC IvOl 400 (?s. Ἀπ—); (66) 237-249 AD ib. 117, 18; 121, 25
EPIROS: (67) 234-168 BC BMC Thessaly p. 89 no. 17; Franke, Münz. v. Epirus p. 182 II ser. 51; p. 156 no. 4 (coin); (68) 241 AD Cabanes, L'Épire p. 552 no. 30 (SEG XXXVII 512) (Πόπλιος Μέμμιος Λ.)
—AMBRAKIA: (69) v/iv BC BCH 79 (1955) p. 267 (f. Λεοντίς); (70) ~ Paus. vi 3. 7; (71) f. iii BC Unp. (Arta Mus., inscr.) (s. Κλέων); (72) m. iii BC IG V (2) 368, 20 (s. Μενεκράτης); (73) f. ii BC IC 2 p. 25 no. 8 C (s. Λάμιος); (74) a. 167 BC SEG XXXV 665 A, 6 (f. Λεοντίων); (75) ~ ib. l. 9 (f. Λάμπων)
—BOUTHROTOS (PRASAIBOI): (76) a. 163 BC IBouthrot 14, 38; 31, 51, 63 (SEG XXXVIII 471; 490) (s. Νικάνωρ, f. Νικάνωρ) ?= (79); (77) ~ IBouthrot 14, 40; 31, 56; 33, 23 (SEG XXXVIII 471; 490; 492) (s. Σωσίπατρος); (78) ~ IBouthrot 18, 9 (SEG XXXVIII 475) (f. Αἴσχρα); (79) ~ IBouthrot 18, 17 (SEG XXXVIII 475) ?= (97) (76); (80) ~ IBouthrot 21, 13; 42, 4, 13 (SEG XXXVIII 478; 501) (s. Νίκανδρος) ?= (92); (81) ~ IBouthrot 22, 12 (SEG XXXVIII 479); (82) ~ IBouthrot 28, 15 (SEG XXXVIII 486) (f. Νικόλαος); (83) ~ IBouthrot 29, 14; 40, 8 (SEG XXXVIII 487; 499); (84) ~ IBouthrot 29, 36 (SEG XXXVIII 487); (85) ~ IBouthrot 29, 65 (SEG XXXVIII 487); (86) ~ IBouthrot 31, 97 (SEG XXXVIII 490) (s. Ἀλεξίμαχος, f. Λέαινα) ?= (88); (87) ~ IBouthrot 32, 11; cf. SEG XXXVIII 491; (88) ~ IBouthrot 37, 10 (SEG XXXVIII 496) (f. Λέαινα) ?= (105) (86); (89) ~ IBouthrot 38, 7 (SEG XXXVIII 497) (I s. Θρασύμαχος, f. Λέων II); (90) ~ IBouthrot 38, 7 (SEG XXXVIII 497) (II s. Λέων I); (91) ~ IBouthrot 43, 30 (SEG XXXVIII 502) (f. Ἀνδρόνικος); (92) ~ IBouthrot 100, 4 (s. Νίκανδρος) ?= (80); (93) ~ ib. 110, 10 (s. Λε—); (94) ~ ib. 121, 13 (f. Φίλιππος) ?= (101); (95) ~ ib. 128, 8 (s. Ἀνδροσθένης); (96) ~ ib. l. 10; 131, 7 (s. Φιλόξενος); (97) ~ ib. 130, 8 (s. Νικάνωρ) ?= (79); (98) ~ ib. 133, 5 (s. Λύκος); (99) ~ ib. 152, 6 (s. Κεφαλῖνος)
—Bouthrotioi: (100) a. 163 BC ib. 139, 11 (s. Καλλίστρατος)
—Euryoi: (101) a. 163 BC ib. 97, 4 (s. Φιλιππίδας, f. Φίλιππος) ?= (94)

—Lykourgoi: (102) a. 163 BC ib. 137, 13 (f. Λεοντεύς)
—Opatai: (103) a. 163 BC ib. 99, 7 (BCH 118 (1994) p. 121 B) ?= (104); (104) ~ IBouthrot 111, 3, 8; 112, 3, 10, 113, 4 (s. Σώσιππος) ?= (103); (105) ~ ib. 139, 9 (s. Ἀλεξίμαχος) ?= (88)
—Thymaioi: (106) a. 163 BC ib. 23, 1; 24, 1 (SEG XXXVIII 481-2) ?= (108); (107) ~ IBouthrot 66, 8; 93, 6 (s. Νίκανωρ) ?= (108); (108) ~ ib. 68, 12 ?= (107) (106)
—DODONA*: (109) iv/iii BC PAE 1931, p. 90 no. 2 (s. Λεόντιος)
ILLYRIA:
—EPIDAMNOS-DYRRHACHION: (110) hell.-imp. IDyrrh 183 (f. Ἐξάκεστος); (111) ~ ib. 294 (s. Μενέλαος)
KEPHALLENIA:
—KRANIOI: (112) ?162 BC FD III (3) 204, 1 (s. Δαμολέων)
—PRONNOI: (113) ii BC Op. Ath. 10 (1971) p. 66 no. 15
—SAME: (114) f. iii BC ib. p. 66 no. 12 (BCH 83 (1959) p. 658)
KERKYRA: (115) hell. IG IX (1) 707 (f. Κλέαρχος); (116) ii BC Korkyra 1 p. 168 nos. 13-17; (117) f. ii BC BCH 45 (1921) p. 24 IV, 82 + SEG XXII 455; (118) i BC-i AD IG IX (1) 917
KORINTHIA:
—KORINTH: (119) a. 324 BC CID II 120 A, 38; 122 I, 12 (f. Φυλακίδας); (120) hell. SEG XIII 232 (tile) (Corinth II 35) (Λέο(ν)τος (gen.)); (121) iii BC ITrall I 33 B, 9 (s. Ἀπολλώνιος)
LAKONIA:
—SPARTA: (122) f. vi BC RE (10) (Poralla² 481) (s. Εὐρυκρατίδας, f. Ἀναξανδρίδας: king); (123) 440 or 424 BC RE (9); Moretti, Olymp. 332; cf. Ebert, Gr. Sieg. 28 (Poralla² 482) (s. Ἀντικλείδας) ?= (124); (124) 426 BC Th. iii 92. 5 (and Thessaly Herakleia Trachinia: oikist) ?= (125) (123); (125) 420 BC ib. v 44. 3 ?= (126) (124); (126) 419 BC X., HG ii 3. 10 ?= (127) (125); (127) 411 BC Th. viii 28. 5 (f. Πεδάριτος) ?= (126); (128) ~ ib. 61. 2 (Poralla² 482); (129) f. iv BC Plu., Art. 21 (Poralla² 482) (f. Ἀνταλκίδας); (130) ~ ib. IG V (1) 8, 5 (Bradford (3)); (131) i-ii AD IG V (1) 766 (Bradford (2)); (132) c. 230 AD IG V (1) 551, 3; BSA 79 (1984) pp. 281-2 (date) (Bradford (4)) (f. Γ. Ἀσίννιος Λεωνίδης); (133) ~ IG V (1) 551, 4; BSA 79 (1984) pp. 281-2 (date) (Bradford (1)) (Αὐρ. Ἀσίννιος Λ.: s. Γ. Ἀσίννιος Λεωνίδης)
LEUKAS: (134) hell. SEG XXVII 177 (Λέ[ων]); (135) 216 BC IG IX (1)² (2) 583, 2 (f. Διογένης); (136) c. 167-50 BC BMC Thessaly p. 180 nos. 91-2; SNG Cop. Epirus-Acarnania 382 (coins); (137) f. i BC IG IX (1) 534, 11 (Iscr. Gr. Verona p. 24) (f. Ἀριστομένης)
MESSENIA:
—MESSENE: (138) hell. Unp. (Paris, BN) 1724A (coin); (139) c. 220 BC SEG XXXVIII 339; cf. PAE 1971, p. 166 no. 7 (f. Τιμαρχίς); (140) c. 191 BC Ebert, Gr. Sieg. 71 (s. Λεωνίδας); (141) s. ii BC SEG XLI 341, 15 (I f. Λέων II); (142) ~ ib. l. 15 (II s. Λέων I); (143) hell.-imp. PAE 1991, p. 106 no. 8, 1 (s. —αρχος)
—THOURIA: (144) f. ii BC SEG XI 972, 60 (s. Ἀλκέτας)
S. ITALY (APULIA):
—LUCERIA: (145) byz. Lucera Romana p. 34 (Lat. Leo)
S. ITALY (BRUTTIUM):
—LOKROI EPIZEPHYRIOI:
—(Σκα.): (146) iv/iii BC De Franciscis 28, 4 (f. Σιμίας)
—PETELIA: (147) imp. CIL X 117 (Lat. C. Marius Leo); (148) ~ ib. 113-14 (NScav 1894, p. 20); Eph. Ep. VIII 260-1 (Lat. M(anius) Meconius Leo)
—RHEGION*: (149) m. vi BC Rumpf, Chalkid. Vas. p. 47 no. 8 (vase) (Arena, Iscr. Sic. III p. 105 no. 11) (Λ[έ]ōν: her.?)

—SYBARIS-THOURIOI-COPIAE: **(150)** 400 BC X., *An.* v 1. 2; **(151)** 196 BC *IG* IX (1)² (1) 31, 18 (s. Ἄνταλλος)

S. ITALY (CALABRIA):

—TARAS-TARENTUM: **(152)** m. iv BC *SEG* XXXI 879. 7-8; *Taras* 9 (1989) pl. 92, 2 (terracotta); **(153)** iii-ii BC *SEG* XXX 1219 (Landi, *DISMG* 207) (s. Ἐπίκορος); **(154)** c. 272-235 BC Vlasto 857-8; 1093; 1416 (coins) (Evans, *Horsemen* p. 178 VIII B.3; p. 182 no. 5); **(155)** c. 266 BC *IG* XII (9) 1187, 19; Robert, *Ét. Num. Gr.* pp. 179 ff. (date) (s. Πανταλέων); **(156)** imp.? *IG* XII (3) 1233, 7 (f. Νευμήνιος)

S. ITALY (CAMPANIA):

—DIKAIARCHIA-PUTEOLI*: **(157)** imp. *CIL* X 8179 with Add. p. 1009 (Lat. Leo: f. C. Rafidius Sabinus: freed.)

—MISENUM*: **(158)** imp. ib. 3511 (Lat. L. Acutius Leo)

—NOLA: **(159)** byz. ib. 1376 (Lat. Leo); **(160)** ~ ib. 1377 (Lat. Leo)

—POMPEII: **(161)** i BC-i AD ib. IV 8669; 8671 (Lat. Leo)

—SALERNUM: **(162)** imp. *IItal* I (1) 110 (*CIL* X 666) (Lat. Leo)

S. ITALY (LUCANIA):

—HERAKLEIA: **(163)** f. iii BC *NC* 1918, p. 141 nos. 71-2; *Coll. McClean* 853 (coins); **(164)** i BC *SEG* XXIV 552 (biling.) (f. Ἀθηνόδωρος)

—LEUKANOI: **(165)** c. 316-309 BC *IG* II² 1956, 49; *Ancient Macedonia* 5 p. 445 with n. 10 (date)

—METAPONTION: **(166)** iv BC Iamb., *VP* 267 (*FVS* I p. 446); D.L. viii 83; **(167)** m. iii BC *SEG* XXX 1175, 14 (doctor); **(168)** c. 262 BC *IG* IX (1)² (1) 17 A, 75 (s. Ἀντιλέων)

SICILY: **(169)** f. iii BC Vandermersch p. 168 (amph.) (or S. Italy: Λέω[ν])

—IMACHARA: **(170)** f. i BC Cic., *In Verr.* II v 15 (Lat. Leo)

—SYRACUSE: **(171)** ?205-203 BC *FD* III (4) 427 A, 1 (f. Νέων); **(172)** iv-v AD Ferrua, *NG* 307 ([Λέ]ω, Lat. Leo)

—SYRACUSE?:

——(Ἀρχ.): **(173)** hell. Manganaro, *PdelP* forthcoming no. 4 I, 10 (f. Ἀρίστων)

—TAUROMENION: **(174)** c. 208-170 BC *IG* XIV 421 an. 33; 421 an. 44; 421 an. 58 (*SGDI* 5219); *IGSI* 4 II (III), 9 an. 70 (s. Θεόδωρος, f. Θεόδωρος) ?= (*175*); **(175)** f. ii BC *BCH* 45 (1921) p. 25 IV, [94-5] + *SEG* XXII 455; *Sic. Gymn.* 17 (1964) p. 49 (s. Θεόδωρος) ?= (*174*)

—ZANKLE-MESSANA: **(176)** s. iii BC *SEG* XVIII 196 (s. Λεωνίδας)

**Λεωνᾶς**

ARGOLIS:

—ARGOS: **(1)** ii/iii AD *IG* IV (1) 650

ARKADIA:

—TEGEA: **(2)** ii AD ib. v (2) 55, 23 (Βήδιος Λ.); **(3)** 165 AD ib. 50, 67 (s. Πανθήρας)

ILLYRIA:

—EPIDAMNOS-DYRRHACHION?: **(4)** i BC-i AD *CIL* III 621 (Sestieri, *ILat. Albania* 38) (Lat. Leonas)

KORINTHIA:

—KORINTH: **(5)** byz. *Corinth* VIII (1) 200; cf. *TMByz* 9 (1985) p. 361 no. 19 (Λεων[έ]ας—Meritt, Λεων(τι)ανό(ς)—Feissel: name—*LGPN*)

S. ITALY (CAMPANIA):

—DIKAIARCHIA-PUTEOLI: **(6)** imp. *CIL* X 2527 (Lat. C. Hosidius Leona)

—POMPEII: **(7)** i BC-i AD ib. IV 3151 a ?= (*8*); **(8)** ~ ib. 5116 ?= (*7*)

**Λεώνη**

DALMATIA:

—EPETION: **(1)** imp. ib. III 12816 (Lat. Vibia Lione)

**Λεωνίδας**

ACHAIA:

—DYME: **(1)** iii BC *AJPh* 31 (1910) p. 399 no. 74 a, 9 (s. Πιστίας)

—PATRAI: **(2)** ?i-ii AD *AD* 16 (1960) Chron. p. 140 no. 2; p. 142 no. 9 (Λεονεί-)

AKARNANIA:

—THYRREION: **(3)** iii BC *IG* IX (1)² (2) 600 (s. Λέων); **(4)** ii BC ib. 247, 7 (I f. Λεωνίδας II); **(5)** ~ ib. l. 7 (II s. Λεωνίδας I)

ARGOLIS:

—ARGOS: **(6)** ii AD *SEG* XVI 253, 7 (I f. Λεωνίδας II); **(7)** ~ ib. l. 7 (II s. Λεωνίδας I)

——Paionis: **(8)** iii BC ib. XVII 141, 4

—EPIDAUROS: **(9)** 133-134 AD *IG* IV (1)² 383, 5; 384, 6 (s. Περιγένης); **(10)** 170 AD ib. 391 (f. Ἐπαφρόδιτος)

ARKADIA:

—THELPHOUSA: **(11)** a. 228 BC ib. 72 B, 32 ([Λε]ωνίδας?: s. Πειθ—)

ELIS: **(12)** s. i BC *IvOl* 59, 21; 66, 1; **(13)** 36 BC ib. 59, 5 (s. Κόρυμβος); **(14)** i BC/i AD ib. 61, 11 (f. —ος); **(15)** ii/iii AD ib. 111, 4; 467, 7 (Φλ. Λ.: N.)

EPIROS:

—ARGOS (AMPHILOCH.): **(16)** ?272 BC *FD* III (1) 123, 2 (f. Σιμίας)

—MOLOSSOI: **(17)** m. iv BC *RE* (4); Berve 469

ILLYRIA:

—BYLLIONES NIKAIA (KLJOS (MOD.)): **(18)** hell. *Iliria* 1982 (1), p. 120 no. 35 (tile); cf. p. 124

—EPIDAMNOS-DYRRHACHION: **(19)** iii BC *IGB* I² 37; cf. *IDyrrh* 516 (f. Φιλοκράτης); **(20)** c. 250-50 BC Maier 263; 290; 368; 404 (coin) (Ceka 293-6) (money.); **(21)** hell.-imp. *IDyrrh* 172 (f. Διονύσιος)

KEPHALLENIA:

—PRONNOI: **(22)** ii BC *Op. Ath.* 10 (1971) p. 66 no. 15

LAKONIA:

—BOIAI: **(23)** ii AD *IG* V (1) 959, 1 (f. Ἡρακλέα)

—LEUKTRA*: **(24)** imp. ib. 1327 (Τιβ. Κλ. Λ.)

—SPARTA: **(25)** her. Plu., *Lyc.* 3 (Poralla² 483) (dub.); **(26)** c. 530-480 BC *RE* (2); *IPr* 316, 15 (Poralla² 484) (s. Ἀναξανδρίδας, f. Πλείσταρχος: king); **(27)** c. 316-235 BC *RE* (3) (Bradford (1)) (s. Κλεώνυμος, ?s. Χιλωνίς, f. Κλεομένης, Εὐκλείδας, Χιλωνίς: king); **(28)** 171 BC Liv. xlii 51. 8 (Bradford (2)) (Lat. Leonides) ?= (Λακωνικός (*1*))

MESSENIA:

—MESSENE: **(29)** ?202 BC *IG* VII 292, 3 (*IOrop* 202) (Λεων(ί)δας—Petrakos: f. Γεννικός, Κριτόδαμος); **(30)** c. 191 BC Ebert, *Gr. Sieg.* 71; *IG* II² 2314, 27, 59; *SEG* XXII 484 (Λεωνίδης—*IG*: f. Λέων, Νικόμαχος)

—THOURIA: **(31)** s. iii BC *IG* V (1) 1386, 7 (s. Πτολεμαῖος)

S. ITALY (BRUTTIUM):

—LOKROI EPIZEPHYRIOI:

——(Ἀγκ.): **(32)** iv/iii BC De Franciscis 27, 6 (s. Ἄπτος)

S. ITALY (CALABRIA):

—TARAS-TARENTUM: **(33)** f. iii BC *RE* (14); *HE* 1955 ff.

SICILY:

—TRIOCALA: **(34)** f. i BC Cic., *In Verr.* II v 10 (Lat. Leonidas)

—ZANKLE-MESSANA: **(35)** s. iii BC *SEG* XVIII 196 (f. Λέων)

**Λεωνίδης**

AITOLIA:

—KLAUSEION (MOD.): **(1)** byz. *PAE* 1958, p. 61 δ; cf. *BCH* 83 (1959) p. 664

ARKADIA:

—TEGEA: **(2)** iii AD *IG* V (2) 152 (Π. Αἴλ. Λεωνείδης: s. Πλόκαμος)

LAKONIA:

—SPARTA: **(3)** c. 230 AD ib. v (1) 551, 2; *BSA* 79 (1984) pp. 282-3 (date) (Bradford (-)) (Γ. Ἀσίννιος Λ.: s. Λέων, f. Αὐρ. Ἀσίννιος Λέων)

MESSENIA:

—KORONE: **(4)** 246 AD *IG* V (1) 1398, 54 (Αὐρ. Λ.)

S. ITALY (CAMPANIA):

—DIKAIARCHIA-PUTEOLI: **(5)** m. i AD Camodeca, *L'Archivio Puteolano* 1 p. 66 no. 6 (Lat. Q. Acilius Leon[ides])

—KYME: **(6)** ii-iii AD *SEG* XXIX 948 (s. Ἀλέξανδρος)

S. ITALY (LUCANIA):

—POTENTIA: **(7)** imp. *CIL* X 160 (Lat. Iulius Claudius Leonides)

**Λεωνίδιος**

KORINTHIA:

—KORINTH: **(1)** s. iv AD *Corinth* VIII (3) 522, 2; cf. *TMByz* 9 (1985) p. 362 no. 35

**Λεωνίς**

AKARNANIA:

—THYRREION: **(1)** hell. *IG* IX (1)² (2) 346

LAKONIA:

—SPARTA: **(2)** hell. ib. v (1) 811 (Bradford (2)); **(3)** ?i BC *IG* V (1) 610 (Bradford (1)) (d. Λαχάρης)

**Λεώνυμος**

LAKONIA: **(1)** 401 BC X., *An.* iv 1. 18 (Poralla² 485)

**Λεωσθένης**

SICILY:

—SYRACUSE: **(1)** imp. *IG* XIV 40 + *Wien. Stud.* 46 (1928) p. 227; cf. *Riv. Arch. Crist.* 18 (1941) p. 174 no. 37; cf. *BE* 1952, no. 197 (Λεο(σ)θένης)

**Λεώφρων**

S. ITALY (BRUTTIUM):

—SYBARIS-THOURIOI-COPIAE: **(1)** vi/v BC *Suda* Θ 83; cf. Delatte, *VP* pp. 246 ff. (or S. Italy (Lucania) Metapontion: ?f. Θεανώ: fict.?)

**Ληγέτης**

S. ITALY (LUCANIA):

—HYELE-VELIA: **(1)** 180-178 BC Nachtergael, *Les Galates* 35, 2, 6; *Syll*³ 585, 229; *BCH* 45 (1921) p. 23 IV, [68] (f. Διονύσιος)

**Λήδα**

S. ITALY (CALABRIA):

—BRENTESION-BRUNDISIUM: **(1)** imp. *NScav* 1893, p. 275 no. 4 (Lat. Sergia Leda)

S. ITALY (CAMPANIA):

—NOLA: **(2)** imp. *CIL* X 1326 (Lat. Sabidia Leda)

—POMPEII: **(3)** i BC-i AD ib. IV 9202 (Lat. Leda)

S. ITALY (LUCANIA):

—COSILINUM: **(4)** imp. *Suppl. It.* 3 p. 49 no. 4 (Lat. Leda)

**Λῆδος**

S. ITALY (CALABRIA):

—BRENTESION-BRUNDISIUM*: **(1)** imp. *NScav* 1893, p. 121 (Lat. Q. Camurius Ledus: freed.)

**Ληΐλοχος**

LAKONIA:

—SPARTA: **(1)** ii/i BC *IG* V (1) 256; *Artemis Orthia* p. 297 no. 2 (name, date) (Bradford (-))

**Λήμνιος**

S. ITALY (CAMPANIA):

—POMPEII: **(1)** i BC-i AD *CIL* IV 1253 (Lat. Lemnius); **(2)** ~ ib. 4546 (Lat. Lemnius)

**Λῆμνος**

ARKADIA:

—MT. KYLLENE*: **(1)** imp.? *IG* V (2) 366 ([Λ]ῆμνος)

**Λῆνα**

—TEGEA: (2) ?i AD ib. 215 a; (3) ii-iii AD ib. 215 b; (4) 165 AD ib. 50, 8 (I f. Λῆμνος II); (5) ~ ib. l. 8 (II s. Λῆμνος I)
S. ITALY (APULIA):
—LAVELLO (MOD.): (6) imp. CIL IX 659 (Lat. Savonius Lemnus)
S. ITALY (CAMPANIA):
—HERCULANEUM*: (7) m. i AD Cron. Erc. 7 (1977) p. 117 C b, 24 (Lat. –ulius Lemnus: freed.)

**Λῆνα**

AITOLIA: (1) ?ii BC Fraser–Rönne, BWGT p. 145 no. 2 (Lat. Allia Lena: freed.)
EPIROS:
—AMBRAKIA: (2) s. iv BC SEG XVII 304 (d. Δαμόφιλος); (3) s. iii BC ib. 307 a (d. Ἀπολλόδωρος)
—NIKOPOLIS (NR.): (4) imp. AD 36 (1981) Chron. p. 279 no. 4 (Λê-, (Ἐ)λένα?)
KEPHALLENIA:
—PRONNOI: (5) ii BC Op. Ath. 10 (1971) p. 66 no. 15

**Ληναῖς**

S. ITALY (CAMPANIA)?: (1) imp. IG XIV 2414. 39 (tessera) (Ληναί(ο)ς?—IG)

**Ληνᾶς**

S. ITALY (CAMPANIA):
—POMPEII: (1) i BC-i AD CIL IV 5263 (Lat. Lenas)

**Λῆνος**

S. ITALY (CAMPANIA):
—POMPEII: (1) i BC-i AD ib. 9127 (Lat. Lenus)

**Λησίας**

ARKADIA:
—MEGALOPOLIS: (1) s. ii BC IG V (2) 439, 36, 77 (f. Εὔδαμος); (2) ?145 BC ib. l. 31 (s. Εὔδαμος)

**Λητώ**

SICILY:
—THERMAI HIMERAIAI: (1) ?ii-iii AD ib. XIV 332 (Πετρηΐα Λητώι)

**Λιβανίς**

S. ITALY (CAMPANIA):
—POMPEII: (1) i BC-i AD CIL IV 2028 (Lat. Libanis)

**Λίβανος**

S. ITALY (CAMPANIA):
—HERCULANEUM*: (1) imp. ib. X 1403 g III, 58 (Lat. C. Pompeius Libanus: freed.)
—POMPEII: (2) i BC-i AD ib. IV 9241 (n. pr.?); (3) ~ ib. X 8058. 27 (seal) (Castrèn 133. 1) (Lat. A. Cors. Libanus)
—SALERNUM*: (4) ?i AD IItal I (1) 238 II, 9 (CIL X 557) (Lat. L. Appuleius Libanus: freed.)
—STABIAE: (5) imp. ib. 777 (Lat. T. Cornelius Libanus)

**Λιβάς**

S. ITALY (APULIA):
—VIBINUM: (1) i AD Bovino p. 240 no. 303 (Ann. Fac. Lett. Fil. Bari 19-20 (1976-7) p. 15 no. 3) (Lat. Libas)

**Λίβερα**

SICILY:
—SYRACUSE: (1) iii-v AD Strazzulla 210 (Wessel 1224)

**Λίβερτος**

SICILY:
—KENTORIPA: (1) ii-iii AD MEFRA 106 (1994) p. 85 no. 3 (Λεί-)

**Λίβιος**

SICILY:
—KATANE: (1) imp. IG XIV 488

**Λιβύρνας**

S. ITALY (CAMPANIA):
—DIKAIARCHIA-PUTEOLI: (1) imp. CIL X 2092 (Lat. Liburnas); (2) ~ ib. 2374 (Lat. Liburnas)

**Λιβυρνός**

ARKADIA:
—TEGEA: (1) ii AD IG V (2) 55, 79 (f. Ζώσιμος)

**Λίβυς**

ARGOLIS:
—HERMIONE: (1) iii BC ib. IV (1) 729 I, 15 (s. Σήραμβος); (2) ii-i BC ib. 732 IV, 11 (s. Δαμόνικος)
LAKONIA:
—SPARTA: (3) 404 BC X., HG ii 4. 28; D.S. xiv 3. 6 (Poralla² 490) (s. Ἀριστόκριτος); (4) m. iii BC Plu., Agis 6 (Bradford (2)) (f. Λύσανδρος); (5) c. 25-1 BC IG V (1) 210, 17 (Bradford (1)) (s. Εὐβάλκης)
S. ITALY (BRUTTIUM):
—SYBARIS-THOURIOI-COPIAE: (6) f. iv BC SNG Oxford 948 (coin graffito); cf. JNG 33 (1983) p. 14
SICILY:
—GELA-PHINTIAS: (7) f. v BC Dubois, IGDS 149 f (vase) (Arena, Iscr. Sic. II 33)

**Λίβυσσα**

S. ITALY (APULIA): (1) s. iv BC RVAp p. 510 no. 131 (vase) (SEG XL 908 b) (n. pr.?)

**Λίβων**

ELIS: (1) c. 475-456 BC RE (2)

**Λίδοκος**

S. ITALY (CALABRIA):
—LUPIAE: (1) hell. Susini, Fonti Salento p. 179 no. 178 (ring) (n. pr.?)

**Λιμένη**

S. ITALY (BRUTTIUM):
—HIPPONION-VIBO VALENTIA: (1) imp. CIL X 78 (Lat. Munatia Limene)

**Λιμένιος**

SICILY:
—SYRACUSE: (1) iii-v AD Wessel 846 (Barreca 237)

**Λιμήν**

EPIROS:
—NIKOPOLIS: (1) ?s. i AD SEG XXXIX 541 (Τιβ. Κλαύ. Λ.)
S. ITALY (CAMPANIA):
—HERCULANEUM*: (2) imp. CIL X 1403 g III, 39 (Lat. A. Fuficius Limen: freed.)

**Λιμναῖος**

ARGOLIS:
—TROIZEN*: (1) iv BC IG IV (1) 823, 24
ELIS: (2) m. ii BC BGU 1939 A, 8 (s. Πυριλάμπης)
KERKYRA: (3) iii-ii BC SEG XXXVI 568 (f. Νικόλαος: locn.—Strauch)
TRIPHYLIA:
—LEPREON: (4) c. 230-200 BC BCH 45 (1921) p. 12 II, 81 (s. Ἀνδρίας)

**Λιπαρίων**

KORINTHIA:
—SIKYON: (1) vi/v BC SEG XI 244, 42 (-ōν)

**Λίπαρος**

SICILY:
—TYNDARIS (NR.): (1) ?iii AD Epigraphica 11 (1949) p. 60

**Λίπων**

LAKONIA:
—KYTHERA*: (1) c. 425-400 BC Kythera p. 203 ω 321 (sherd) (n. pr.?: ?s. Φιλομ—)

**Λίσας**

ARKADIA:
—TEGEA: (1) c. 400 BC IG II² 10436

**Λισσίας**

SICILY:
—HELOROS (NR.): (1) s. v BC Dubois, IGDS 99 (s. Νεμήνιος)

**Λισσίδας**

ARKADIA:
—MANTINEIA-ANTIGONEIA: (1) c. 300-221 BC IG V (2) 323. 26 (tessera) (f. Δαιλέων)

**Λίσσος**

SICILY:
—MORGANTINA: (1) ?iv/iii BC SEG XXXIX 1009, 5 (s. Θαρσύνων)

**Λισφίνας**

AKARNANIA:
—KORONTA: (1) f. iii BC ib. XXIX 473

**Λίσων**

ARKADIA:
—TEGEA: (1) m. iv BC IG V (2) 6, 61; (2) ~ ib. l. 112 (s. Δαμίνας)
—(Apolloniatai): (3) s. iv BC ib. 174 a, 5
—(Athaneatai): (4) iv BC ib. l. 9
—(Krariotai): (5) m. iii BC ib. 36, 87 (s. Μικίων)

**Λιτάγης**

S. ITALY (BRUTTIUM):
—KROTON: (1) iv BC Iamb., VP 263 (Λιτάτης—mss., Θεάγης?—Kiessling)

**Λίτη**

S. ITALY (CAMPANIA):
—POMPEII: (1) i BC-i AD CIL IV 10119 (Lat. Lite)
—SURRENTUM: (2) imp. ib. X 747 (Lat. Lite)

**Λίχας**

AKARNANIA: (1) 221-204 BC RE (4); PP 4422 (s. Πύρρος) ?= (2)
AKARNANIA?: (2) iii BC ib. 1938 ?= (1)
ARKADIA:
—KLEITOR: (3) f. iv BC IvOl 167 (f. Κριτόδαμος)
—MEGALOPOLIS: (4) 182 BC ib. 46, 5 (IPArk 31 IIB) ([Λί]χας?)
LAKONIA:
—SPARTA: (5) f. vi BC Hdt. i 67-8 (Poralla² 491) (-χης); (6) 421-411 BC RE (3); Moretti, Olymp. 339 (Poralla² 492) (s. Ἀρκεσίλαος); (7) s. i BC IG V (1) 92, 4 (Bradford (3)) (f. Εὐθυκλῆς); (8) 43-31 BC Münzpr. der Laked. p. 148 Group 16 series 18; p. 160 Group 22 series 1 (coin) (Bradford (2)); (9) i AD IG V (1) 297, 6; Artemis Orthia pp. 310-11 no. 27 (date) (Bradford (1))
PELOPONNESE: (10) s. iii BC SEG XIII 278, 10 (s. Εὐαγόρας)
S. ITALY (CAMPANIA):
—POMPEII: (11) i BC-i AD CIL IV 8900 (Lat. Licas)
SICILY:
—AKRAGAS: (12) vi BC JNG 33 (1983) p. 13 (coin graffito)

**Λιχμέας**

ARKADIA: (1) ?255 BC Nachtergael, Les Galates 8, 28; cf. Stephanis 1805 ([Λ]ιχμέας?, [Ἀ]ἰχμέας?: f. Νικαγόρας)

**Λοβαῖος**

ILLYRIA:
—EPIDAMNOS-DYRRHACHION: (1) hell.-imp. IDyrrh 266 (f. Κλεβέριος)

**Λοβίας**
ARKADIA:
—MANTINEIA-ANTIGONEIA: (1) c. 425-385 BC
IG v (2) 323. 18 (tessera) (f. Ἀριστοκλῆς)

**Λόβων**
ARGOLIS:
—ARGOS: (1) hell. RE (-)

**Λογάριος**
SICILY:
—AKRAI: (1) iii-v AD Agnello 66 (Wessel 7;
Akrai p. 167 no. 39); cf. Riv. Arch. Crist.
18 (1941) p. 204 no. 77 (Λογαριανά (estate))

**Λογάς**
S. ITALY (APULIA):
—TEANUM APULUM: (1) imp. Teanum Apulum
p. 123-4 no. 53 (Lat. Logas: d. L. Sestius
Primus)
S. ITALY (CAMPANIA):
—POMPEII: (2) i BC-i AD CIL IV 2325 (Lat. Lo-
gas); (3) ~ ib. 4276 (Lat. Logas); (4) ~ ib. 5203
(Lat. Logas); (5) ~ ib. 8467 (Lat. Logas—
Solin)

**Λόγγαρος**
ILLYRIA:
—DARDANIOI: (1) 200 BC Liv. xxxi 28. 1-2 (Lat.
Longarus: f. Βάτων: king)

**Λογγῖνος**
LAKONIA:
—SPARTA: (1) c. 160-170 AD IG v (1) 45, 15;
BSA 80 (1985) p. 226 (date) (Bradford (1))
(-γεί-)
S. ITALY (APULIA):
—VENUSIA: (2) v AD JIWE I 44 (CIJ I 589)
(Λογγῖνος]: Jew); (3) ~ JIWE I 62 (CIJ I 590)
(Λογγίνι (gen.): s. Φαυστῖνος, f. Μαννίνα: Jew)

**Λόγγος**
ARGOLIS:
—ARGOS: (1) imp. SEG XVI 262, 5-6 (Λόν-)

**Λόγισμος**
ARGOLIS:
—PHLEIOUS: (1) imp. IG IV (1) 448
S. ITALY (CAMPANIA):
—HERCULANEUM: (2) m. i AD Cron. Erc. 7
(1977) p. 116 B b, 6 (Lat. M. Helvius Lo-
gismus)
S. ITALY (LUCANIA):
—ATINA LUCANA: (3) imp. IItal III (1) 136
(Lat. [L]ogismus)
SICILY:
—KATANE: (4) imp. CIL x 7047 (Lat. L. Arr.
Logismus)

**Λογίστας**
AITOLIA:
—BOUKATION?: (1) c. 162 BC IG IX (1)² (1) 106,
10 (Λογίστα(s))

**Λόγος**
S. ITALY (APULIA):
—VENUSIA: (1) imp. CIL IX 424 (Lat. Cn. Tre-
batius Logus)
S. ITALY (CAMPANIA):
—DIKAIARCHIA-PUTEOLI: (2) ii AD Puteoli 11
(1987) p. 127 no. 1 (Lat. Ti. Claudius Logus)
—HERCULANEUM*: (3) i BC-i AD CIL x 1403 f
I, 12 (Lat. Q. Iunius Logus: freed.)
—POMPEII: (4) i BC-i AD ib. IV 1287 a; 1310
(Lat. Logus); (5) f. i AD ib. 3340. 16; 83; Im-
pegno per Pompeii 11 OS no. 12 (Castrèn 23.
11) (Lat. Cn. Alleius Logus)
—POMPEII*: (6) i BC-i AD Eph. Ep. VIII 321
(Castrèn 85. 8) (Lat. L. Caesius Logus:
freed.)

**Λοκρικός**
ARGOLIS:
—EPIDAUROS*: (1) c. 370-365 BC Peek, IAEpid
52 A, 15

**Λόκρις**
KORINTHIA:
—KORINTH: (1) c. 550-525 BC IG IV (1) 313
(pinax); LSAG² p. 132 no. 24 (date) (fict.?)

**Λοκρίων**
KORINTHIA:
—KORINTH: (1) ?411 BC IG XII (8) 402

**Λολλιάνα**
SICILY:
—SYRACUSE: (1) iii-v AD Strazzulla 413 (Barreca
238)

**Λόλλος**
SICILY:
—PATERNO (MOD.): (1) iv-iii BC Silver for the
Gods pp. 58-61 nos. 25; 27-8

**Λόξιος**
KORINTHIA:
—KORINTH: (1) c. 590-570 BC Amyx 19 B. 9
(vase) (Lorber 37) (fict.?)

**Λόρδιος**
KORINTHIA:
—KORINTH: (1) c. 590-570 BC Amyx 19 B. 5
(vase) (Lorber 37) (fict.?)

**Λουϊάδας**
LAKONIA:
—SPARTA: (1) s. i AD SEG XI 776, 1 (Bradford
(2)) (Λου[ϊ]άδας: f. Λυσανδρία); (2) c. 100-120
AD IG v (1) 103, 5 + SEG XI 568; 537 a, 3
(Bradford (1)) (s. Ἀριστοκράτης)

**Λουκάνιος**
KORINTHIA:
—KORINTH: (1) i/ii AD Plu., Mor. 675 D-E; 676
E

**Λουκᾶς**
ARKADIA:
—TEGEA: (1) ii AD IG v (2) 55, 57 (f. Ἀφροδᾶς);
(2) ~ ib. l. 65 (s. Ἐπικτᾶς)
KORINTHIA:
—KORINTH: (3) byz. Corinth VIII (3) 558 a, 1;
558 b, 6; cf. TMByz 9 (1985) p. 363 no. 39

**Λουκία**
ARGOLIS:
—HERMIONE: (1) imp. IG IV (1) 715, 4 (d. Τρό-
πος); (2) ii AD SEG XI 385, 1 (d. Λούκιος); (3)
iii AD IG IV (1) 726, 1 (II d. Αὐρ. Σώστρατος,
Αὐρ. Λουκία I); (4) ~ ib. l. 13 (Αὐρ. Λ.: I m.
Λουκία II, Αὐρ. Ἀντίγονος, Αὐρ. Νίκη)
S. ITALY (CAMPANIA):
—NEAPOLIS: (5) i BC/i AD INap 139; cf. Leiwo
p. 84 no. 31 (d. Νύμφιος)
SICILY:
—SYRACUSE: (6) iii/iv AD DCB s.v. Lucia (1);
Act. Sanct. 11 (2) p. 647; cf. Guarducci, Ep.
Gr. 4 p. 526 no. 4 (d. Εὐτυχία)

**Λουκιανός**
S. ITALY (CAMPANIA):
—HERCULANEUM: (1) i BC/i AD IG XIV 2412. 29
A
SICILY:
—SYRACUSE: (2) iii-v AD ib. 145 (Strazzulla 86);
(3) ~ Nuovo Didask. 6 (1956) p. 55 no. 7

**Λούκιος**
ARGOLIS:
—HERMIONE: (1) imp. IG IV (1) 715, 1 (f. Ἕρ-
μαρχος); (2) ii AD SEG XI 385, 1 (f. Λουκία);

(3) ~ ib. XVII 163, 1-2 (s. Ἐπίκτητος, f. Ἐπί-
κτητος); (4) ii-iii AD ib. XI 384, 5 (GVI 1773);
(5) iii AD IG IV (1) 726, 5 (f. Ἐπίκτητος)
ARKADIA:
—TEGEA: (6) m. ii AD ib. v (2) 48, 8
ELIS: (7) 141-145 AD IvOl 95, 4 (s. Καλλικράτης:
N.) ?= (8)
—OLYMPIA*: (8) imp. ib. 736-738 (tiles) ?= (7)
KERKYRA: (9) i AD IG IX (1) 918
KORINTHIA:
—KORINTH: (10) ii/iii AD Ag. VII pp. 92-7 nos.
238, 253, 264, 276, 305-7; Corinth IV (2) pp.
191 no. 582; 194 nos. 603 and 606; 209 nos.
745-9; BM Lamps 3 pp. 404-5 nos. Q3245,
Q3251, Q3258; SEG XXVII 35. 15; XXX 348
(lamps)
LAKONIA:
—SPARTA: (11) c. 175-200 AD ib. XI 503, 22
(Bradford (4)) (f. Τίτος); (12) c. 220 AD IG
v (1) 544, 8 (Artemis Orthia pp. 358-9 no.
145); BSA 79 (1984) pp. 270-3 (date) (Brad-
ford (3)) (f. M. Αὐρ. Λούκιος)
S. ITALY (CAMPANIA):
—PITHEKOUSSAI-AENARIA: (13) ?ii BC SEG XIV
603 (f. Μεγακλῆς)
SICILY:
—AKRAI: (14) iii-v AD IG XIV 235 (Agnello 63);
cf. Ferrua, NG 490 (f. Ἀλφ. Κλώδις)
—SYRACUSE: (15) iii-v AD Strazzulla 318
(Wessel 1356)

**Λουκιφέρα**
SICILY:
—KATANE: (1) iii-v AD IG XIV 489; cf. Riv.
Arch. Crist. 18 (1941) p. 242 no. 140
—USTICA: (2) iii-v AD IG XIV 592; cf. Riv. Arch.
Crist. 18 (1941) p. 237 no. 133

**Λουπαρίων**
ILLYRIA:
—BYLLIONES: (1) imp. SEG XXIV 477 +
XXXVIII 551

**Λούπερκος**
SICILY:
—SYRACUSE: (1) iii-v AD NScav 1947, p. 211
no. 3 (Λό-)

**Λοῦπος**
EPIROS:
—NIKOPOLIS: (1) imp. SEG XXVII 238 (?f. Τίθ-
θη)
ILLYRIA:
—SHKOZE (MOD.): (2) imp. Ugolini, Alb. Ant.
1 p. 192 no. 12 (s. Πολυνίκης)

**Λόφιος**
KERKYRA: (1) ?f. vi BC IG IX (1) 705; LSAG²
p. 234 no. 10 (date)

**Λόφος**
S. ITALY (CAMPANIA):
—HERCULANEUM*: (1) i BC-i AD CIL x 1403 g
III, 5 (Lat. —us Lophus: freed.)

**Λόχαγος**
AITOLIA: (1) 214 BC IG IX (1)² (1) 177, 21
—APERANTOI: (2) iii BC AD 22 (1967) Chron.
p. 322 (s. Πολεμαῖος)
—KALLION/KALLIPOLIS: (3) 218 BC IG IX (1)²
(1) 59, 3 (f. Ἀγήτας); (4) 179-C140 BC RE
Supplbd. 11 (2); IG IX (1)² (1) p. LI, s.a. 179
BC; Pantos, Sphragismata p. 148 no. 118; p.
448; cf. SGDI 1765, 1 (s. Ἀγήτας, ?f. Ἀγήτας)
?= (5); (5) 153-144 BC ib. 2279, 2 (s. Ἀγήτας)
?= (4)
—THERMOS*: (6) hell. IG IX (1)² (1) 85. 6 =
SEG XXVII 152? (tile)
AKARNANIA:
—STRATOS: (7) ii BC IG IX (1)² (2) 394, 15 (f.
Πολύξεινος)
LAKONIA:
—SPARTA: (8) f. iv BC Plu., Mor. 225 E (Poralla²
493) (f. Πολυαινίδας, Σείρων)

**Λοχαῖος**
SICILY:
—HIMERA: (9) c. 475-450 BC *Himera* 2 p. 681 no. 45 (Dubois, *IGDS* 11; Arena, *Iscr. Sic.* III 51) (n. pr.?)

**Λοχαῖος**
ARKADIA:
—MAINALIOI: (1) 420 BC Paus. vi 6. 1 (f. Ἀνδρο-σθένης)

**Λοχιάς**
S. ITALY (APULIA):
—LARINUM: (1) imp. *CIL* IX 762 (Lat. Ortoria Lochias)
S. ITALY (CAMPANIA):
—NEAPOLIS: (2) i AD ib. X 1505; cf. Leiwo p. 89 (Lat. Cornelia [L]ochias)

**Λοχίσκος**
EPIROS:
—DODONA*: (1) s. iv BC *SEG* XV 398

**Λοχίτας**
ARKADIA:
—KYNAITHA: (1) i BC *Achaean Grave Stelai* 21 (s. Ἱππίας)

**Λύαιος**
S. ITALY (CAMPANIA):
—POMPEII: (1) i BC-i AD *Neue Forsch. in Pompeji* p. 263 no. 5 (Lat. Lyaeus)

**Λύανδρος**
AIGINA: (1) ?268 BC *FD* III (3) 200; III (4) 415, 10 (s.p.) (s. Ἀναξίλας)

**Λύγδαμις**
SICILY:
—SYRACUSE: (1) m. vii BC *RE* (5); Moretti, *Olymp.* 51

**Λύγδαμος**
S. ITALY: (1) imp. *CIL* X 8059. 240 (seal) (Lat. Lygdamus)
S. ITALY (APULIA):
—LUCERIA: (2) imp. ib. IX 816 (Lat. M. Staius Lygdamus: freed.)
S. ITALY (CAMPANIA):
—HERCULANEUM*: (3) i BC-i AD ib. X 1403 g I, 5 (Lat. –nius Lygdamus: freed.)
S. ITALY (LUCANIA):
—VOLCEI: (4) imp. *IItal* III (1) 286 (Lat. S. Teius Ligdamus: f. S. Teius Arelonius)

**Λυγκεύς**
ARKADIA:
—TEGEA: (1) ii AD *IG* V (2) 131 (M. Ἀντ. Λυγκε[ύς])

**Λύγων**
KORINTHIA:
—KORINTH: (1) ?c. 675 BC *LSAG²* p. 131 no. 5; cf. *SEG* XI 229 ([Πο]λύγονος—*SEG*)

**Λύδη**
S. ITALY (APULIA):
—CANUSIUM*: (1) i-ii AD *Epig. Rom. di Canosa* 58, 6 (*CIL* IX 348) (Lat. Lyde: freed.)

**Λυδία**
SICILY:
—TAUROMENION: (1) iii-v AD Ferrua, *NG* 488

**Λυδιάδας**
ARGOLIS:
—ARGOS: (1) c. 146-32 BC *BMC Pelop.* p. 145 no. 116 (coin)
ARKADIA:
—MEGALOPOLIS: (2) c. 230-200 BC *SEG* XXXVI 379 (Λυδιάδας: f. Ἀριστοπάμων); (3) 180 BC Plb. xxiv 8. 8; (4) s. ii BC *IG* V (2) 439, 80 (s. —φάνης)

—MEGALOPOLIS?: (5) ii BC ib. 534 ([Λ]υδιάδας: s. Εὔδαμος)

**Λυδίας**
ARGOLIS:
—ARGOS: (1) ii-i BC *Mnem.* NS 47 (1919) p. 164 no. 9, 2 (s. Ἀρισ-)

**Λυδίων**
SICILY:
—KAMARINA?: (1) vi BC *QUCC* 78 (1995) pp. 121-2 (vase) (-ōν: potter)

**Λυδός**
SICILY:
—SYRACUSE: (1) iii-v AD *NScav* 1913, p. 263

**Λύδρα**
ILLYRIA:
—EPIDAMNOS-DYRRHACHION: (1) hell.-imp. *IDyrrh* 42

**Λυιγένης**
LAKONIA:
—OITYLOS: (1) iii/ii BC *IG* V (1) 1295, 10 (Bradford (-))

**Λυιξενίδας**
LAKONIA:
—SPARTA: (1) c. 25-1 BC *IG* V (1) 210, 8 (Bradford (-)) (f. Θάλιος)

**Λυῖξηνος**
LAKONIA:
—SPARTA: (1) iii BC *SEG* XL 348 B, 5 (Λυhί-)

**Λυῖων**
LAKONIA:
—SPARTA: (1) i-ii AD *IG* V (1) 740 (Bradford (-))

**Λύκα**
ARGOLIS:
—TROIZEN: (1) imp. *IG* IV (1) 798 (m. Φαῦστος)
EPIROS:
—ONCHESMOS: (2) imp. Ugolini, *Alb. Ant.* I p. 192 no. 10
ILLYRIA:
—APOLLONIA: (3) hell. *IApoll* 115; (4) imp. ib. 199 (m. Ἀφροδίσις)
S. ITALY (CAMPANIA):
—NOLA: (5) imp. *CIL* X 1296 (Lat. Lyca: m. Ἐπαφρῦς)
SICILY:
—HIMERA: (6) ?s. v BC *IG* XIV 597 (n. pr.?)

**Λυκάδας**
DALMATIA:
—ISSA: (1) iv/iii BC *VAHD* NS 8 (1905) p. 97 no. 177 (*VAMZ* 1970, p. 33 f. frr. I-J)

**Λύκαιθος**
ARGOLIS:
—EPIDAUROS: (1) iv BC *IG* IV (1)² 188

**Λυκαῖος**
AIGINA?: (1) ?f. v BC Page, *FGE* 510 (f. Πραξα-γόρας)

**Λυκάριος**
LAKONIA:
—SPARTA: (1) 415 BC X., *HG* ii 3. 10 (Poralla² 494)

**Λυκαρίων**
ELIS:
—OLYMPIA*: (1) 237-241 AD *IvOl* 117, 19 (slave?)
EPIROS:
—NIKOPOLIS: (2) imp. *PAE* 1913, p. 97 no. 8 (Sarikakis 101) (Λυκαρί[ων], Λυκάρι[ος]: Sarikakis)

**Λυκίδας**

ILLYRIA:
—EPIDAMNOS-DYRRHACHION: (3) ?i AD *AEp* 1978, no. 739 (Lat. Sergius Cornelius Castricius Lycario: s. Νίκη)

**Λύκαρος**
ILLYRIA:
—APOLLONIA: (1) i-ii AD *IApoll* 220 (M. Τυρράνιος Λ.)

**Λυκάων**
ELIS: (1) 113-117 AD *IvOl* 91, 6 (I f. Λυκάων II); (2) ~ ib. l. 6, 10 (II s. Λυκάων I, f. Σόφων: N.)

**Λυκέας**
AITOLIA: (1) ?279 BC *FD* III (2) 68, 64 = *IG* II² 1132, 5; (2) ?252-248 BC *Syll³* 422, 3; (3) 224 or 221 BC *SGDI* 2524, 5; Nachtergael, *Les Galates* 64, 4
—RHADANIOI: (4) c. 215-205 BC *FD* III (4) 362, 8
—THESTIEIS: (5) s. iii BC *SBBerlAk* 1936, p. 386 no. 2 a (s. Πολύστρατος)
ARGOLIS:
—ARGOS: (6) imp.? *RE* (2); *FGrH* 312; (7) ii AD *SEG* XVI 253, 4 ([Κορ]ιν. Λ.)
—EPIDAUROS: (8) iv/iii BC *IG* IV (1)² 156
—TROIZEN: (9) iv BC ib. IV (1) 764, 8 (f. Φιλωνίδας)

**Λυκειός**
LAKONIA:
—SPARTA: (1) v BC *SEG* XI 671 (iron) (Lazzarini 354; Poralla² 495b)

**Λυκήν**
ILLYRIA:
—EPIDAMNOS-DYRRHACHION: (1) c. 250-50 BC Maier 276 (coin) (Ceka 398) (pryt.)

**Λυκία**
AKARNANIA:
—THYRREION: (1) ii BC *IG* IX (1)² (2) 332
MESSENIA:
—MESSENE: (2) s. ii BC ib. V (1) 1445

**Λυκιανός**
S. ITALY (CALABRIA):
—TARAS-TARENTUM: (1) c. 302-280 BC Evans, *Horsemen* p. 133 VI B.1 (coin)

**Λυκίας**
ARGOLIS:
—EPIDAUROS*: (1) c. 370-365 BC Peek, *IAEpid* 52 A, 16; 52 B, 73

**Λυκίδας**
AITOLIA: (1) s. iv BC Berve 475
—KALLION/KALLIPOLIS: (2) f. ii BC *BCH* 45 (1921) p. 23 IV, 61
—KONOPE-ARSINOE: (3) m. ii BC *IG* IX (1)² (3) 624 b, 4
—PHISTYON: (4) imp. ib. IX (1)² (1) 113, 6 (f. Δικαιόπολις)
AKARNANIA:
—STRATOS: (5) a. 170 BC ib. 100, 9
ELIS: (6) imp. *IvOl* 739 (tile); (7) 28-24 BC ib. 64, 10 (I f. Λυκίδας II); (8) ~ ib. l. 10 (II s. Λυκίδας I)
EPIROS:
—CHAONES:
——Elinnoi: (9) f. ii BC *IBouthrot* 1, 3; cf. *L'Illyrie mérid.* I p. 134
——DODONA*: (10) ?iv BC *Ep. Chron.* 10 (1935) p. 260 no. 36 (Λυκκ-)
S. ITALY (BRUTTIUM):
—LOKROI EPIZEPHYRIOI:
——(Τυν.): (11) 275 BC De Franciscis 25, 1 (f. Λύκων)
SICILY:
—SYRACUSE?:
——(Νητ.): (12) hell. Manganaro, *PdelP* forthcoming no. 4 II, 5 (s. Νικόστρατος)
ZAKYNTHOS: (13) c. 293-168 BC *Polemon* 5 (1952-3) p. 11 no. 328, 1 (s. Θρασυμένης);

(**14**) ?257 BC Nachtergael, *Les Galates* 7, 49 (Stephanis 1559) (s. Θρασύξενος)

**Λυκίνα**
LAKONIA:
—HIPPOLA: (**1**) ?ii-i BC *IG* v (1) 1277 h

**Λυκίνος**
ACHAIA:
—PATRAI: (**1**) ii/i BC *SEG* XIX 400, 1 (s. Ἀριστόδαμος); (**2**) 121-108 BC *FD* III (4) 52, 2, 9 (f. Ἀριστόδαμος)
AITOLIA:
—KALYDON: (**3**) a. 142 BC *IG* IX (1)² (1) 137, 62
AKARNANIA:
—STRATOS: (**4**) iii BC *SEG* XXV 634 (s. Ἀρίστιππος)
ARGOLIS:
—ARGOS: (**5**) ?m. v BC *IG* IV (1) 516; (**6**) c. 458 BC ib. I³ 1149, 20 ([Λ]υκῖνος)
—EPIDAUROS: (**7**) c. 370 BC ib. IV (1)² 102, 24
—HERMIONE: (**8**) ?ii-i BC ib. IV (1) 731 I, 14 (s. Ἀπολλωνία)
ARKADIA:
—HERAIA: (**9**) c. 400-375 BC Moretti, *Olymp.* 394
—MEGALOPOLIS: (**10**) 208 BC *IMM* 38, 45 (Λυκῖν[ος]); (**11**) ii/i BC *IG* v (2) 443, 7 (*IPArk* 32) (f. Ἄλκιμος)
ELIS: (**12**) s. v BC Moretti, *Olymp.* 323
EPIROS:
—AMBRAKIA: (**13**) f. ii BC *AD* 39 (1984) Chron. p. 190 + pl. 77 γ
—BOUTHROTOS (PRASAIBOI): (**14**) a. 163 BC *IBouthrot* 28, 4 (*SEG* XXXVIII 486); (**15**) ~ *IBouthrot* 66, 4 (f. Εὐρύμμας); (**16**) ~ ib. l. 7; 75, 6 (Λυκεῖνος—66)
——Bouthrotioi: (**17**) a. 163 BC ib. 91, 16 (*SEG* XXXII 623); *IBouthrot* 153, 7 (s. Ἱστιαῖος)
ILLYRIA:
—EPIDAMNOS-DYRRHACHION: (**18**) hell.-imp. *IDyrrh* 404 (-κεῖ-: f. Τεισίας)
KEPHALLENIA:
—SAME: (**19**) 208 BC *IMM* 35, 1 (s. Λύκος)
KORINTHIA:
—KORINTH: (**20**) f. ii BC *Corinth* VIII (1) 73, 1 (f. Κρίτων); (**21**) 166 BC *IG* II² 2316, 12, 14 (f. Κλεαγένης)
—SIKYON: (**22**) f. iv BC ib. 10308 (Skalet 194) (s. Λυκῖνος)
LAKONIA:
—SPARTA: (**23**) iv/iii BC *CID* II 120 A, 28 (Poralla² 497) (f. —άρης); (**24**) s. i BC *IG* v (1) 135, 11 (Bradford (2)) (-κεῖ-: f. Καλλικράτης); (**25**) s. ii AD *SEG* XI 486, 1 (Bradford (3)) (I f. Λυκῖνος II); (**26**) ~ *SEG* XI 486, 1 (Bradford (1)) (-κεῖ-: II s. Λυκῖνος I)
—SPARTA?: (**27**) ?448-432 BC Moretti, *Olymp.* 304; 327 (Poralla² 496); (**28**) i BC/i AD *GP* 1391 (f. Χάρμος)
S. ITALY (BRUTTIUM):
—KROTON: (**29**) 584 BC Moretti, *Olymp.* 90
S. ITALY (CALABRIA):
—TARAS-TARENTUM: (**30**) c. 272-235 BC Vlasto 834-41 (coins) (Evans, *Horsemen* p. 177 VIII A.8-9)
SICILY:
—KAMARINA: (**31**) f. v BC Cordano, *Tessere Pubbliche* 11 ([Γλ]υκῖνος—ed., [Λ]υκῖνος—LGPN: s. Σιμίας)
—SELINOUS: (**32**) f. v BC Dubois, *IGDS* 38, 1, 16 (Arena, *Iscr. Sic.* I 63) (f. Ἄπελος); (**33**) ~ Dubois, *IGDS* 38, 2 (Arena, *Iscr. Sic.* I 63) (s. Ἅλος); (**34**) ~ Dubois, *IGDS* 38, 16 (Arena, *Iscr. Sic.* I 63) (s. Πῦρος)
—SYRACUSE:
——(Ἑρμεῖος): (**35**) iv BC Manganaro, *PdelP* forthcoming no. 3, 6 (s. Ζώπυρος)
—TAUROMENION: (**36**) c. 225 BC *IG* XIV 421 an. 16 (*SGDI* 5219) (f. Ἄνδρων)

**Λύκιος**
ACHAIA:
—DYME*: (**1**) c. 219 BC ib. 1612, 25 (*Tyche* 5 (1990) p. 124) (s. Νίκων)
AKARNANIA:
—ASTAKOS: (**2**) ii BC *IG* IX (1)² (2) 434, 10 (s. Πολύμναστος)
ARGOLIS:
—EPIDAUROS*: (**3**) c. 370-360 BC *BSA* 61 (1966) p. 271 no. 4 A, 13
ARKADIA:
—TEGEA: (**4**) c. 240-229 BC *IG* v (2) 11, 13
—THELPHOUSA: (**5**) 369-361 BC ib. 1, 69; Tod, *GHI* II 132 (date)
KORINTHIA:
—KORINTH: (**6**) c. 370 BC *IG* IV (1)² 102, 5, 18, 24 + *SEG* XXV 383, 119, 147
—SIKYON: (**7**) f. iv BC *IG* II² 10308 (Skalet 195) (f. Λυκῖνος)
SICILY:
—SYRACUSE: (**8**) 401 BC X., *An.* i 10. 14-15

**Λυκίς**
AKARNANIA:
—ANAKTORION: (**1**) ?v BC *AA* 1905, p. 167

**Λυκίσκα**
ACHAIA:
—PHARAI: (**1**) iii-ii BC *Achaean Grave Stelai* 30 (d. Εὔτυχος)
AKARNANIA:
—PALAIROS: (**2**) hell.? *AD* 26 (1971) Chron. p. 324
—THYRREION: (**3**) ii BC *IG* IX (1)² (2) 319; (**4**) ~ ib. 326; Fraser–Rönne, *BWGT* pl. 24 (-σχα)
EPIROS:
—BOUTHROTOS (PRASAIBOI): (**5**) a. 163 BC *IBouthrot* 15, 15 (*SEG* XXXVIII 472); (**6**) ~ *IBouthrot* 15, 19 (*SEG* XXXVIII 472); (**7**) ~ *IBouthrot* 15, 21 (*SEG* XXXVIII 472); (**8**) ~ *IBouthrot* 17, 23 (*SEG* XXXVIII 474); (**9**) ~ *IBouthrot* 29, 29 (*SEG* XXXVIII 487) (d. Φορμίων); (**10**) ~ *IBouthrot* 30, 15 (*SEG* XXXVIII 488) ?= (13); (**11**) ~ *IBouthrot* 32, 9 (*SEG* XXXVIII 491); (**12**) ~ *IBouthrot* 36, 21 (*SEG* XXXVIII 495); (**13**) ~ *IBouthrot* 43, 12 (*SEG* XXXVIII 502) (Λ[υκίσ]κα: d. Φιλόξενος) ?= (10); (**14**) ~ *IBouthrot* 44, 6; (**15**) ~ ib. 113, 13; (**16**) ~ ib. 117, 7
——Pelmatioi: (**17**) a. 163 BC ib. 69, 9; 70, 7; 71, 6 (*BCH* 118 (1994) pp. 129 f. B 1-3) (d. Μενέξιος)
——PRASAIBOI: (**18**) a. 163 BC *IBouthrot* 60, 5 (*SEG* XXXVIII 511)
ILLYRIA:
—APOLLONIA: (**19**) imp. *IApoll* 217 (d. Λύκος)
KEPHALLENIA:
—SAME: (**20**) hell. *IG* IX (1) 633
KERKYRA: (**21**) i BC ib. II² 9012 (d. Λύκος)
SICILY:
—LIPARA: (**22**) hell.-imp. *NScav* 1929, p. 83 no. 7

**Λυκίσκος**
ACHAIA:
—PHARAI: (**1**) ii BC *Achaean Grave Stelai* 71 (f. Ἀσκλάπων)
—TRITAIA: (**2**) hell.-imp. Neratzoulis p. 20 no. 3 with fig. 13 (*Achaie* II 312) (Λυκ[ίσκος]: f. Εὐανδρίς)
ACHAIA?: (**3**) 193 BC *IG* v (2) 293, 22 (s. Λυκομήδης)
AITOLIA: (**4**) ii BC *RE* (3)
—EIDAIOI: (**5**) 214 BC *IG* IX (1)² (1) 177, 21 (Λ[υ]κίσκος); (**6**) c. 162 BC ib. 105, 8
—KALYDON: (**7**) c. 210 BC ib. 31, 96 (s. Αἰσχρίων)
—KONOPE-ARSINOE: (**8**) 163 BC ib. 103, 4 (f. Λύκος)
—RHADEOI: (**9**) f. ii BC ib. 96, 21 (f. Ἀνδρόλαος) ?= (10); (**10**) ~ ib. l. 23 (f. Ἀλκίας) ?= (9)

—THERMOS: (**11**) 214 BC ib. 177, 17 (Λυκίσ[κος]); (**12**) ~ ib. l. 18 (s. Σκορπίων)
AKARNANIA: (**13**) 211 BC Plb. ix 32
—ANAKTORION: (**14**) m. ii BC *Syll*³ 669, 4 (f. Κλέανδρος)
—MEDION: (**15**) hell.? *IG* IX (1)² (2) 387 (Λυκίσκ[ος], Λυκίσκ[α?])
—STRATOS: (**16**) 178-172 BC *RE* (3); *IG* IX (1)² (1) p. LI, s.a. 178 BC, 172 BC
—THYRREION: (**17**) iii BC ib. IX (1)² (2) 245, 14; (**18**) ~ ib. l. 16; (**19**) ~ ib. l. 16; (**20**) ~ ib. 267; (**21**) ii BC ib. 251, 9 (f. Μένανδρος); (**22**) hell.-imp. ib. 356 (s. Φαλακρίων)
ARGOLIS:
—NEMEA*: (**23**) iii BC ib. IV (1) 482 (Λυκίσ[κος])
ARKADIA:
—MEGALOPOLIS: (**24**) ?225-221 BC Nachtergael, *Les Galates* 63, 6; 64, 6; cf. Stephanis 982 (f. Εὐρύβιος)
ARKADIA?: (**25**) f. iii BC *BCH* 38 (1914) p. 461 no. 5, 1 (s. —ατίας)
DALMATIA:
—ISSA: (**26**) ii BC *SEG* XXXI 600 (f. Μνασέας)
ELIS: (**27**) c. 295-288 BC *BSA* 19 (1912-13) p. 85 no. 3, 9 (s. Φύσαλος); (**28**) 57-61 AD *IvOl* 79, 3 ([Σόφω]ν ὁ καὶ Λ.: s. Σόφων) ?= (29); (**29**) 85 AD *EA* 1905, p. 255 no. 1, 11 (Λυκίσ[κος]: f. Σόφων) ?= (28)
EPIROS: (**30**) ?iv BC *IG* II² 8540 (Λυκίσκος: f. Θυϊνός); (**31**) 234-168 BC *BMC Thessaly* p. 90 nos. 37-8; Franke, *Münz. v. Epirus* p. 184 II ser. 54; p. 156 no. 5 (coin); (**32**) ii BC Cabanes, *L'Épire* p. 590 no. 76, 4 (*SEG* XXVI 704) (Λυκίσκος])
—AMBRAKIA: (**33**) hell.? *CIG* 1802 (f. Ἀρίσταρχος); (**34**) 182 BC *Syll*³ 585, 208 (f. Νικάνωρ); (**35**) a. 167 BC *SEG* XXXV 665 A, 9
—AVARICE (MOD.): (**36**) ii BC ib. XXIV 468 (f. Λυκώτας)
—BOUTHROTOS: (**37**) f. ii BC *IBouthrot* 2, 5; 3, 6; 4, 5 (s. Νικάνωρ) ?= (38)
—BOUTHROTOS (PRASAIBOI): (**38**) a. 163 BC ib. 14, 3, 7; 21, 20, 26 (*SEG* XXXVIII 471; 478) (f. Νικάνωρ) ?= (37); (**39**) ~ *IBouthrot* 14, 7 (*SEG* XXXVIII 471) (s. Νικάνωρ, Ἀττέα); (**40**) ~ *IBouthrot* 18, 15 (*SEG* XXXVIII 475) (s. Βοΐσκος) ?= (51); (**41**) ~ *IBouthrot* 18, 16; 32, 17 (*SEG* XXXVIII 475; 491); (**42**) ~ *IBouthrot* 21, 3 (*SEG* XXXVIII 478); (**43**) ~ *IBouthrot* 22, 34 (*SEG* XXXVIII 479); (**44**) ~ *IBouthrot* 27, 10; 31, 23 (*SEG* XXXVIII 485; 490) (s. Λύκος); (**45**) ~ *IBouthrot* 28, 2 (*SEG* XXXVIII 486) ?= (54); (**46**) ~ *IBouthrot* 29, 21 (*SEG* XXXVIII 487); (**47**) ~ *IBouthrot* 43, 14 (*SEG* XXXVIII 502) (s. Λυκώτας) ?= (57); (**48**) ~ *IBouthrot* 43, 34 (*SEG* XXXVIII 502) (s. Ἡρακλείδας); (**49**) ~ *IBouthrot* 43, 35 (*SEG* XXXVIII 502) (s. Ἡρακλείδας) ?= (53); (**50**) ~ *IBouthrot* 51, 27 (f. Σίμακος); (**51**) ~ ib. 52, 10 (*SEG* XXXVIII 517) (s. Βοΐσκος) ?= (40); (**52**) ~ *IBouthrot* 66, 7; 75, 6; (**53**) ~ ib. 103, 8 (s. Ἡρακλείδας) ?= (49); (**54**) ~ ib. 117, 7 ?= (45); (**55**) ~ ib. 122, 7 ([Λυκ]ίσκος: f. Φαλακρίων); (**56**) ~ ib. 128, 9; 130, 7 (s. Λύκος); (**57**) ~ ib. 134, 17 (s. Λυκώτας) ?= (47)
——Bouthrotioi: (**58**) a. 163 BC ib. 180 (*SEG* XXXVI 567) (s. Λύκος, f. Λύκος)
——Erythronioi: (**59**) a. 163 BC *IBouthrot* 91, 4 (*SEG* XXXII 623); *IBouthrot* 92, 3; 153, 2
——Oporronioi: (**60**) a. 163 BC ib. 10, 9 (*SEG* XXXVIII 464) (s. Λύκος)
——Phonidatoi: (**61**) a. 163 BC *IBouthrot* 153, 4
—BOUTHROTOS?: (**62**) hell.? ib. 208 (*RAAN* 21 (1941) p. 278) ([Λ]υκίσκος: s. Λυκώτας)
—HYPORRONIOI: (**63**) a. 163 BC *IBouthrot* 132, 2
—KASSOPE: (**64**) ii BC Dakaris, *Kassope* p. 23 (s. Νικόμαχος, f. Καλλίμαχος, Λαμίσκος)
—MOLOSSOI: (**65**) c. 210 BC *IG* IX (1)² (1) 29, 23 (s. Ἀνεροίτας)

—NIKOPOLIS: (66) imp. *SEG* XXVII 233 (f. *Πει-θόλας*); (67) a. 30 BC ib. XXIV 435 (Sarikakis 102) (f. *Κλεόμαχος*)

—OPHYLLIOI: (68) a. 163 BC *IBouthrot* 115, 13 (s. *Λύκος*)

—TEPELENE (MOD.): (69) i BC-i AD? *SEG* XXIV 474, 2; cf. Hammond, *Epirus* p. 738 (locn.) (-*κίσσ*-: f. *Ξένων*)

ILLYRIA:

—APOLLONIA: (70) hell. *IApoll* 362 (tile); (71) iii-ii BC ib. 42 (f. *Σιμίας*)

—BYLLIONES: (72) c. 200 BC *SEG* XXXV 679 (XXXVIII 524) (f. *Βότιχος*)

—EPIDAMNOS-DYRRHACHION: (73) c. 250-50 BC Unp. (Paris, BN) 276 (coin) (pryt.) ?= (74); (74) ~ Maier 278-9 (coin) (Ceka 325; 364) (pryt.) ?= (73); (75) ii-i BC *IDyrrh* 545 (tile); (76) hell.-imp. ib. 253 (f. *Ἱέρων Κρασσίων*); (77) ~ ib. 331 (-*ίσσκ*-: f. *Νικόστρατος*)

ITHAKE: (78) hell. *BCH* 29 (1905) p. 168 no. 17 (tile)

KEPHALLENIA: (79) ?255-253 BC Nachtergael, *Les Galates* 8, 61; 10, 68 (Stephanis 1561) (s. *Λύκος*)

—PALE: (80) iii/ii BC Unp. (*IG* arch.) (*Λυκ[ί]σκο[ς]*)

KERKYRA: (81) hell. *IG* IX (1) 919; cf. Fraser-Rönne, *BWGT* p. 161; (82) i BC-i AD *IG* IX (1) 937

KORINTHIA:

—KORINTH: (83) i BC-i AD ib. II² 9069 a (*Ag.* XVII 523) (*Λυκί[σκο]ς*)

LAKONIA: (84) c. 100-90 BC *SEG* XXXIII 290 A, 11; *BSA* 70 (1975) pp. 129-31 (date); cf. Stephanis 938 (f. *Εὔδαμος*)

LEUKAS: (85) c. 167-50 BC *BMC Thessaly* p. 180 no. 93; p. 184 no. 153 (coins)

MESSENIA: (86) viii BC Paus. iv 9. 5-6; 10. 1; 12. 5-6

—MESSENE:

——(Hylleis): (87) 11 AD *PAE* 1992, p. 71 A, 13 (s. *Καλλικράτης*)

PELOPONNESE: (88) c. 192 BC *SEG* XIII 327, 21

S. ITALY (BRUTTIUM):

—RHEGION: (89) m. v BC *L'Incidenza dell'Antico* I p. 416 (*Λυκίσκυ* (gen.): f. *Εὐαγόρης*)

S. ITALY (CALABRIA):

—TARAS-TARENTUM: (90) c. 315-280 BC *FD* III (1) 109, 2 (f. *Ζώπυρος*); (91) c. 302-280 BC Vlasto 679 (coins) (*Coll. Hunter* I p. 73 no. 68)

S. ITALY (CAMPANIA):

—SALERNUM: (92) imp. *IItal* I (1) 219 (*CIL* X 628) (Lat. Sex. Vestilius Lycys(c)us)

SICILY: (93) 309 BC D.S. XX 33. 3-5

—KAMARINA: (94) f. v BC Cordano, *Tessere Pubbliche* 17 (Arena, *Iscr. Sic.* II 130 A) (f. *Δαϊκράτης*); (95) ?iv/iii BC *SEG* XXXIX 1001, 8 (f. *Πρόδοξος*)

—LIPARA: (96) hell.? ib. XXXIV 958

—MORGANTINA: (97) ?iv/iii BC ib. XXXIX 1011, 4-5 (f. *Παντίας*, *Φίντων*)

—SELINOUS: (98) m. vi BC Arena, *Iscr. Sic.* I 26 (Dubois, *IGDS* 64; *IGLMP* 78); (99) s. vi BC Dubois, *IGDS* 46 (Arena, *Iscr. Sic.* I 43; Lazzarini 880 c; *IGLMP* 61) (-*σρος*)

—SYRACUSE: (100) hell. *NScav* 1892, p. 358

—TAUROMENION: (101) c. 213 BC *IG* XIV 421 an. 28 (*SGDI* 5219)

——(Ἀσιν.): (102) ii/i BC *IGSI* 12 I, 2 (I f. *Λυκίσκος* II); (103) ~ ib. l. 2 (II s. *Λυκίσκος* I)

TRIPHYLIA:

—LEPREON: (104) iv/iii BC *SEG* XXII 359

**Λύκκας**

EPIROS:

—HORRAION: (1) m. iv BC Cabanes, *L'Épire* p. 539 no. 3, 12 + *BCH* 109 (1985) p. 522; cf. *REG* 95 (1982) p. 192

**Λυκκίδης**

S. ITALY (BRUTTIUM):

—RHEGION: (1) c. 420-410 BC Dubois, *IGDGG* I 36 (Arena, *Iscr. Sic.* III 65; *IvOl* 271; Lazzarini 362; *CEG* I 388; *LSAG*² p. 248 no. 16 (date) (f. *Γλαυκίης*)

**Λυκοδόρκας**

ARGOLIS:

—ARGOS: (1) c. 458 BC *IG* I³ 1149, 76 (-*ϙο*-)

**Λυκόλαος**

AKARNANIA:

—THYRREION: (1) iii BC ib. IX (1)² (2) 245, 6

**Λυκόλας**

AITOLIA:

—TRICHONION: (1) iv BC *FGrH* 115 F 248 (f. *Φυσκίδας*)

**Λυκολέων**

AKARNANIA:

—ANAKTORION: (1) hell. *AD* 44 (1989) Chron. p. 145

ELIS: (2) 113-117 AD *IvOl* 91, 16 (s. *Διονύσιος*)

EPIROS:

—BOUTHROTOS: (3) imp. *AEp* 1978, no. 772 (Lat. Lycoleo: f. *Μουσικός*)

KORINTHIA:

—KORINTH: (4) f. iii BC *Corinth* VIII (3) 32 (f. —*ας*)

**Λυκομήδης**

ACHAIA?: (1) 193 BC *IG* V (2) 293, 22 (f. *Λυκίσκος*)

AKARNANIA:

—PHOITIAI: (2) iv BC ib. IX (1)² (2) 602, 6

ARKADIA:

—MANTINEIA-ANTIGONEIA: (3) 370-366 BC *RE* (6) (and Arkadia Megalopolis: oikist)

ELIS: (4) s. i BC *IvOl* 216, 1 (f. *Ἀριστόδημος*); (5) ~ Moretti, *Olymp.* 720; *IvOl* 216, 2 (s. *Ἀριστόδημος*)

—PISA: (6) 365-363 BC ib. 36, 6 (Perlman O.1) (*Λυκομή[δ]ης*: f. *Φίλων*)

KORINTHIA:

—KORINTH: (7) c. 356-354 BC *IG* IV (1)² 95, 2 (Perlman E.2); Perlman p. 40 f. (date)

LAKONIA:

—SPARTA: (8) s. i BC *IG* V (1) 94, 2 (Bradford (-)) (s. *Ἄρατος*)

**Λυκόρτας**

AITOLIA:

—KALLION/KALLIPOLIS: (1) c. 225 BC *SEG* XI 414, 38 (Perlman E.5) (f. *Φιλόξενος*)

ARKADIA:

—MANTINEIA-ANTIGONEIA: (2) ii BC *IG* V (2) 304 (*Λυκόρτ[ας]*)

—MEGALOPOLIS: (3) f. ii BC *RE* (-); *IG* IV (1)² 623; 624; V (2) 535 (s. *Θεαρίδας*, f. *Θεαρίδας*, *Πολύβιος*); (4) iii AD ib. 473 ([*Λυ*]κόρτας)

ELIS:

—LASION: (5) ?iii/ii BC *HE* 478 (or Arkadia Megalopolis: *Λ.*—Gow, *Λυκόρμας*—*AP*: s. *Θεαρίδας*)

MESSENIA:

—MESSENE: (6) ii AD *IvOl* 449, 1; 450, 10 (f. *Τ. Φλ. Πολύβιος*); (7) s. ii AD *AR* 1983-84, p. 30 with fig. 42 (*M. Τάδιος Λ.*: s. *M. Τάδιος Τιμοκράτης*)

SICILY:

—SYRACUSE: (8) f. v BC Paus. v 27. 7

**Λύκος**

ACHAIA:

—AIGION: (1) i BC *IG* II² 7947 (f. *Διόδωρος*)

—DYME: (2) ?ii BC *SGDI* 1618 (I f. *Λύκος* II); (3) ~ ib. (II s. *Λύκος* I)

—PHARAI: (4) 217 BC Plb. v 94-5

AITOLIA: (5) c. 262 BC *IG* IX (1)² (1) 18, 11; (6) ?257 BC Nachtergael, *Les Galates* 7, 5; (7)

iii/ii BC Pantos, *Sphragismata* p. 133 no. 107; (8) 224 or 221 BC *SGDI* 2524, 3; Nachtergael, *Les Galates* 64, 2; (9) 213 or 205 BC ib. 66, 4; (10) c. 209 BC *IG* IX (1)² (1) 190, 10; cf. 188, 33-4 (XII Suppl. p. 6 no. 16); (11) ?209 or 205 BC Nachtergael, *Les Galates* 68, 4; Flacelière p. 407 no. 38 b, [4]; (12) 208 BC *IG* IX (1)² (1) 31, 62; (13) hell.-imp. ib. 82 (f. *Πολύφρων*)

—HERMATTIOI: (14) 175 BC *SGDI* 1843, 3, 14, 21 (s. *Ἀρίστων*)

—KALLION/KALLIPOLIS: (15) 194 BC ib. 2075, 6

—KALYDON: (16) 263 BC *IG* IX (1)² (1) 17, 73, 88 (s. *Διοκλῆς*) ?= (21); (17) c. 200 BC ib. 70 (s. *Διοκλῆς*); (18) m. ii BC ib. 137, 23; (19) a. 142 BC ib. l. 61 ?= (20); (20) ~ ib. l. 77 ?= (19)

—KALYDON?: (21) c. 250 BC *FD* III (3) 149, 2 (f. —*τομάχα*, *Λέαινα*) ?= (16)

—KONOPE-ARSINOE: (22) 163 BC *IG* IX (1)² (1) 103, 4 (s. *Λυκίσκος*)

—PHISTYON: (23) 163 BC ib. 101, 8

—PLEURON: (24) m. iii BC ib. 53 (f. *Κλεισίας*)

—PROSCH(E)ION: (25) 192 BC ib. 31, 27 (s. *Ἡράκλειτος*)

AKARNANIA:

—ECHINOS?: (26) ?iii BC ib. IX (1)² (2) 370

—PALAIROS: (27) ii BC ib. 451, 7 (s. *Μένιππος*)

—STRATOS: (28) ?153 BC ib. IX (1)² (1) 109, 5?, 7, 10

—THYRREION: (29) iii-ii BC *SEG* XXVII 159, 2; cf. *PAE* 1977, pl. 244 a (s. *Παύσων*); (30) 208 BC *IMM* 31, 6 (*IG* IX (1)² (2) 582) (f. *Νίκανδρος*); (31) ii BC ib. 248, 15; (32) ~ ib. 251, 11 (s. *Ἀριστέας*)

ARKADIA:

—TEGEA: (33) ii AD ib. V (2) 55, 89 (f. *Ἡρακλείδας*)

ELIS: (34) 28-24 BC *IvOl* 64, 5 (f. *Σόφων*) ?= (35); (35) ~ ib. l. 34 (?f. *Ἀλεξᾶς*) ?= (34)

EPIROS: (36) 234-168 BC Franke, *Münz. v. Epirus* p. 173 II ser. 18; p. 156 no. 6 (coin)

—AMBRAKIA: (37) ?254-253 BC Nachtergael, *Les Galates* 9, 79; 10, 75 (f. *Ἡρακλείδης*); (38) s. ii BC Cabanes, *L'Épire* p. 548 no. 19 (*SEG* XXVI 694) (mantis)

—BOUTHROTOS (PRASAIBOI): (39) a. 163 BC *IBouthrot* 14, 34; 31, 40 (*SEG* XXXVIII 471; 490) (f. *Τιμάνωρ*) ?= (60); (40) ~ *IBouthrot* 21, 3 (*SEG* XXXVIII 478); (41) ~ *IBouthrot* 21, 34; 28, 22; 29, 32; 36, 4 (*SEG* XXXVIII 478; 486-7; 495) (s. *Σωσίπατρος*, *Ἀρίστα*); (42) ~ *IBouthrot* 27, 2 (*SEG* XXXVIII 485) (s. *Λυκώτας*); (43) ~ *IBouthrot* 27, 8 (*SEG* XXXVIII 485) (f. *Λυκίσκος*); (44) ~ *IBouthrot* 27, 10; 31, 23 (*SEG* XXXVIII 485; 490) (f. *Λυκίσκος*); (45) ~ *IBouthrot* 30, 23; 40, 9 (*SEG* XXXVIII 488; 499); (46) ~ *IBouthrot* 38, 14 (*SEG* XXXVIII 497) (f. *Νικάδας*); (47) ~ *IBouthrot* 38, 14 (*SEG* XXXVIII 497) (s. *Νικάδας*); (48) ~ *IBouthrot* 42, 1 (*SEG* XXXVIII 501); (49) ~ *IBouthrot* 48, 11; (50) ~ ib. 52, 6-7 (*SEG* XXXVIII 517) (f. *Λυκόφρων*, *Βόϊλλα*, ?f. *Φείδυλλα*); (51) ~ *IBouthrot* 68, 9; (52) ~ ib. 76, 4-5; cf. *L'Illyrie mérid.* 2 p. 220 n. 6 (s. *Φάλακρος*, f. *Φάλακρος*) ?= (70); (53) ~ *IBouthrot* 78, 11; 79, 10; 80, 9; 81, 9; 82, 8; 83, 9; 84, 9; 85, 9; 86, 10; 87, 9; 88, 8 (*BCH* 118 (1994) pp. 122 f. nos. 1-11) (f. *Νικάνωρ*); (54) ~ *IBouthrot* 104, 7, 11 (s. *Λυκώτας*, f. *Λυκώτας*); (55) ~ ib. 117, 10; (56) ~ ib. 128, 9; 130, 8 (f. *Λυκίσκος*); (57) ~ ib. 133, 5 (f. *Λέων*); (58) ~ ib. 143, 9; (59) ~ ib. 150, 10 (s. *Σειμ*—); (60) ~ ib. 152, 3 (f. *Τιμάνωρ*) ?= (39); (61) ~ ib. 159

——Ambrakioi: (62) a. 163 BC ib. 75, 8; 170 (s.e.) (or Epiros Ambrakia?: s. *Δαμοκλείδας*)

——Bouthrotioi: (63) a. 163 BC ib. 180 (*SEG* XXXVI 567) (f. *Λυκίσκος*); (64) ~ *IBouthrot* 180 (*SEG* XXXVI 567) (s. *Λυκίσκος*)

——Opatai: (65) a. 163 BC *IBouthrot* 104, 14

——Oporronioi: (**66**) a. 163 BC ib. 10, 9 (*SEG* XXXVIII 464) (f. Λυκίσκος)

——Sarpingioi: (**67**) a. 163 BC *IBouthrot* 36, 19 (*SEG* XXXVIII 495) (s. Μαχάτας)

——Thymaioi: (**68**) a. 163 BC *IBouthrot* 144, 5 (s. Τιμάνωρ)

—DODONA*: (**69**) iv-iii BC *PAE* 1932, p. 51 no. 1 (f. Διοκλῆς)

—KAMMANOI BOUTHROTIOI: (**70**) a. 163 BC *IBouthrot* 60, 6 (*SEG* XXXVIII 511) (s. Φάλακρος) ?= (*52*)

—KASSOPE: (**71**) ?c. 215-195 BC Franke, *Münz. v. Epirus* p. 77 V ser. 3 (coin); (**72**) f. ii BC Cabanes, *L'Épire* p. 564 no. 41, 4 (f. Λυκώτας)

—NIKOPOLIS: (**73**) imp. *CIG* 1817; cf. Hammond, *Epirus* p. 712 n. 1 (Sarikakis 133) (*M.* Πομπήϊος *Λ.*: f. Πομπηΐα Εὐτυχίς)

—OPHYLLIOI: (**74**) a. 163 BC *IBouthrot* 115, 14 (f. Λυκίσκος)

ILLYRIA:

—APOLLONIA: (**75**) imp. *IApoll* 217 (f. Λυκίσκα); (**76**) ii AD ib. 216

—EPIDAMNOS-DYRRHACHION: (**77**) c. 250-50 BC Ceka, *Probleme* p. 151 no. 39 (coin) (pryt.) ?= (*78*); (**78**) ~ Maier 280-2; Münsterberg Nachtr. p. 16 (coin) (Ceka 65; 74; 197; 369) (pryt.) ?= (*77*); (**79**) ii-i BC *IDyrrh* 295 (s. Φιλιστίδας); (**80**) hell.-imp. ib. 63 (f. Εὐκλέα); (**81**) ~ ib. 115 (f. Ἀπολλωνίς); (**82**) ~ ib. 187 (f. Ἐπίκαδος); (**83**) ~ ib. 270; (**84**) ~ ib. 296

KEPHALLENIA: (**85**) ?255-253 BC Nachtergael, *Les Galates* 8, 61; 10, 68; cf. Stephanis 1561 (f. Λυκίσκος)

—SAME: (**86**) 208 BC *IMM* 35, 1 (f. Λυκῖνος)

KERKYRA: (**87**) hell. *IG* IX (1) 932 (s. Φιλοχάρης); (**88**) i BC ib. II² 9012 (f. Λυκίσκα)

LAKONIA:

—GYTHEION: (**89**) f. ii AD ib. V (1) 1170, 9 (s. Ζήνων: threptos)

—SPARTA: (**90**) ?viii-vii BC *HE* 2717 (Poralla² 498) (s. Ἰφικρατίδας, Ἀλεξίππα: fict.?); (**91**) ii-iii AD *Laconia Survey* 2 p. 219 no. 12; (**92**) c. 150-160 AD *SEG* XI 585, 6; 586, [6] (Bradford (1)) (Ἰούλ. *Λ.*); (**93**) s. ii AD *SEG* XI 598, 8 (Bradford (2)) (freed.); (**94**) c. 230-260 AD *IG* V (1) 556, 12 (Bradford (3)) (f. Αὐρ. Ἀρτεμίδωρος)

MESSENIA: (**95**) hell.? *RE* (43); Moretti, *Olymp.* 1014

—KORONE: (**96**) 246 AD *IG* V (1) 1398, 50 (Ἀντ. *Λ.*)

S. ITALY (BRUTTIUM):

—RHEGION?: (**97**) iv/iii BC *RE* (50); *PP* 16931; *FGrH* 570 (*Λ.* ὁ καὶ Βουθήρας: ?f. (ad.) Λυκόφρων (Chalkis))

S. ITALY (CALABRIA):

—TARAS-TARENTUM: (**98**) 189 BC *Syll*³ 585, 125 (s. Φιλέας)

S. ITALY (CAMPANIA):

—NEAPOLIS: (**99**) ii/i BC *RE* (51) (doctor)

S. ITALY (LUCANIA):

—METAPONTION: (**100**) v BC Landi, *DISMG* 147

SICILY:

—HIMERA: (**101**) c. 500-475 BC *Himera* 2 p. 678 no. 15 (vase) (Dubois, *IGDS* 9; Arena, *Iscr. Sic.* III 46)

—KAMARINA: (**102**) s. v BC Dubois, *IGDS* 119, 8 (Arena, *Iscr. Sic.* II 145); *BE* 1990, no. 860 (Λύκ[ο]ς, [Γ]λύκ[υ]ς—Arena)

## Λυκοῦργος

AKARNANIA: (**1**) c. 250-167 BC *NZ* 10 (1878) pp. 27 f. nos. 20-3; cf. *IG* IX (1)² (2) 249, 9; *BMC Thessaly* p. 168 nos. 2-7; p. 169 nos. 9-10 (coins)

—THYRREION: (**2**) ii BC *IG* IX (1)² (2) 249, 9 ([Λ]υκοῦ[ργος])

ARKADIA:

—TRAPEZOUS: (**3**) c. 575 BC Hdt. vi 127. 3 (f. Ἀμίαντος)

LAKONIA:

—SPARTA: (**4**) her. *RE* s.v. Lykurgos (7) (Poralla² 499; Bradford (3)) (?s. Εὔνομος, Ἄγις, s. Διώνασσα, f. Εὔκοσμος, Ἀντίωρος); (**5**) s. iii BC *RE* (8) (Bradford (1)) (f. Πέλοψ: king); (**6**) f. i BC *Anthemonte–Kalindoia* p. 53 no. A8 (*SEG* XLII 557) (s. Βρασίδας); (**7**) c. 105 AD ib. XI 546 a, 3; 546 b, 3 (Bradford (2)) (Γ. Ἰούλ. *Λ.*: s. Κλέων)

## Λυκοφρονίδας

AKARNANIA:

—PALAIROS: (**1**) c. 325-315 BC *Hesp.* 57 (1988) p. 148 A, 17 (*SEG* XXXVI 331); cf. *Hesp.* 48 (1979) p. 78-9 + pl. 22 c (f. Διόφαντος)

SICILY:

—SELINOUS: (**2**) s. vi BC Dubois, *IGDS* 49 (Arena, *Iscr. Sic.* I 46; *IGLMP* 64) (-φο-)

## Λυκόφρων

AITOLIA:

—BOUKATION: (**1**) 163 BC *IG* IX (1)² (1) 103, 7 (s. Ἀγήτας)

—KALLION/KALLIPOLIS: (**2**) 190 BC *SEG* XXVII 123, 33; cf. Sherk 37 B; (**3**) 153-144 BC *SGDI* 2279, 11

—KALYDON: (**4**) iii BC *IG* IX (1)² (1) 144 (s. Φίλων)

AKARNANIA:

—OINIADAI: (**5**) s. iv BC ib. IV (1)² 95, 58 (Perlman E.2); Perlman pp. 46-9 (date)

ARGOLIS:

—ARGOS: (**6**) ii BC *SEG* XLII 279, 6 (f. Δάμεον)

—ARGOS?: (**7**) v BC *IG* IV (1) 552, 5 (-φρόν)

EPIROS:

—ANTIGONEIA: (**8**) hell. *AE* 1914, p. 234 no. 2 (*SEG* XXXVII 508); Cabanes, *L'Épire* p. 234 n. 96 (locn.) (s. Θεόδοτος)

—BOUTHROTOS (PRASAIBOI): (**9**) a. 163 BC *IBouthrot* 13, 8; cf. Ugolini, *Alb. Ant.* 3 p. 120; (**10**) ~ *IBouthrot* 27, 4 (*SEG* XXXVIII 485) (s. Λύκος) ?= (*11*); (**11**) ~ *IBouthrot* 52, 6 (*SEG* XXXVIII 517) (s. Λύκος) ?= (*10*); (**12**) ~ *IBouthrot* 61 (*SEG* XXXVIII 512); (**13**) ~ *IBouthrot* 127, 5 (f. Ἀντίγονος); (**14**) ~ ib. l. 5 (s. Ἀντίγονος) ?= (*18*)

——Hermiatoi: (**15**) a. 163 BC ib. 77, 7; 94, 9 (f. Φίλιππος)

——Kydestoi: (**16**) a. 163 BC ib. 69, 10; 70, 8; 71, 6 (*BCH* 118 (1994) pp. 129 f. B 1-3) (s. Ἀντίγονος); (**17**) ~ *IBouthrot* 69, 11; 70, 9; 71, 7 (*BCH* 118 (1994) pp. 129 f. B 1-3); *IBouthrot* 77, 7 (f. Ἀντίγονος)

——Opatai: (**18**) a. 163 BC ib. 117, 2; 118, 1, 5; 119?; 168, 2 (*SEG* XXXVIII 469) (s. Ἀντίγονος) ?= (*14*)

—DODONA: (**19**) hell. *IG* IX (1) 688, 3, 18 (f. Βοΐσκος)

—DODONA*: (**20**) iv BC *SEG* XV 406

—KOLPAIOI: (**21**) f. ii BC Cabanes, *L'Épire* p. 580 no. 54, 6 (s. Ἀντίοχος)

—PHOINIKE: (**22**) c. 232-168 BC ib. p. 574 no. 48, 5 (*SEG* XXVI 721) ([Λυ]κόφρων)

ILLYRIA:

—AMANTIA: (**23**) hell.? Ugolini, *Alb. Ant.* 1 p. 197 no. 19 (*M.* Λυκ[ό]φ[ρων]: s. Ἡρακλέων)

—APOLLONIA: (**24**) i BC-i AD *IApoll* 170 (Λυκόφρωνος (gen.): f. Πριμίων)

KORINTHIA:

—KORINTH: (**25**) vii/vi BC *RE* (2) (and Kerkyra: s. Περίανδρος, Λυσιδίκα (Epidauros)); (**26**) 425 BC ib. (7)

—KORINTH*: (**27**) ?v-iv BC *AR* 1974-5, p. 40 nos. 3-4 (bullet)

LAKONIA:

—SPARTA: (**28**) 429 BC Th. ii 85. 1 (Poralla² 500)

MESSENIA:

—MESSENE?: (**29**) ii-i BC *SEG* XI 979, 17 ([Λ]υκόφρων); (**30**) ii/i BC ib. l. 29

SICILY:

—GELA-PHINTIAS: (**31**) s. iv BC Peek, *IAEpid* 41, 5 (Perlman E. 2); Perlman pp. 46-9 (date) (Λυκό[φρω]ν)

—KENTORIPA: (**32**) imp. *CIL* X 7007 (Lat. M. Mestrius Luciffrio)

—SYRACUSE?: (**33**) v/iv BC *RE* Supplbd. 14 (10); *FVS* 83

## Λυκυμνίς

ARGOLIS:

—ARGOS: (**1**) s. iv BC *SEG* XXIX 363, 5 (-μμνίς)

## Λύκων

ACHAIA: (**1**) c. 425-410 BC *IG* I³ 174, 5; (**2**) iii BC ib. II² 8402 (f. Εὔδοτος); (**3**) f. ii BC *RE* (10)

—DYME: (**4**) c. 210-207 BC *IG* IV (1)² 73, 20; *SEG* XXXV 303 (date) (f. Θυίων)

—DYME*: (**5**) c. 219 BC *SGDI* 1612, 13 (*Tyche* 5 (1990) p. 124) (s. Ἀρισταίνετος)

—PATRAI: (**6**) ii BC *Achaean Grave Stelai* 34 (I f. Λύκων II); (**7**) ~ ib. (II s. Λύκων I); (**8**) c. 146-32 BC *BMC Pelop.* p. 22 no. 6 (coin) (s. Δαμότιμος)

AITOLIA:

—EIDAIOI: (**9**) ?153 BC *IG* IX (1)² (1) 109, 8

—PHISTYON: (**10**) f. ii BC ib. 111, 2 (s. Μύννος) ?= (*11*); (**11**) 163 BC ib. 103, 10 ?= (*10*); (**12**) c. 125-100 BC *SBBerlAk* 1936, p. 367 no. 2, 2 (*SEG* XII 303)

AITOLIA?: (**13**) s. iv BC *Ét. Thas.* 3 p. 136 no. 17 (s. Σκύτας)

AKARNANIA:

—ASTAKOS: (**14**) ii BC *IG* IX (1)² (2) 434, 2 (f. Ἡρακλείδας); (**15**) ~ ib. l. 3 (s. Ἡρακλείδας)

—OINIADAI: (**16**) v/iv BC Hp., *Epid.* v 8; *Abh. MainzAk* 1982 (9) p. 35 (locn.) (or Thessaly?)

ARGOLIS:

—TROIZEN*: (**17**) iv BC *IG* IV (1) 823, 2

EPIROS:

—AMBRAKIA: (**18**) f. ii BC *AD* 39 (1984) Chron. p. 190 + pl. 77 γ (f. —οσθένης)

—BOUTHROTOS: (**19**) f. ii BC *IBouthrot* 2, 5; 3, 5; 4, 4 (s. Φιλωνίδας) ?= (*20*)

—BOUTHROTOS (PRASAIBOI): (**20**) a. 163 BC ib. 101, 4 (s. Φιλωνίδας) ?= (*19*)

——Tharioi: (**21**) a. 163 BC ib. 91, 14 (*SEG* XXXII 623) (f. Σίμακος) ?= (*22*)

——PRASAIBOI: (**22**) a. 163 BC *IBouthrot* 60, 5; 62 (*SEG* XXXVIII 511; 513) (f. Σίμακος) ?= (*21*)

KEPHALLENIA:

—SAME: (**23**) ?iv-iii BC ib. XXXIX 486 (I? f. Φιλοπείθης, ?f. Πεισις, Λύκων II?); (**24**) ~ ib. (II? ?s. Λύκων I?)

MESSENIA:

—MESSENE: (**25**) hell. *IG* II² 9343 (f. Σωσίχα); (**26**) iii BC *SEG* XXIII 209, 12

S. ITALY (BRUTTIUM):

—KROTON: (**27**) ?s. iv BC *BMC Italy* p. 356 no. 113 (coin)

—LOKROI EPIZEPHYRIOI:

——(Τυν.): (**28**) 275 BC De Franciscis 25, 1 (s. Λυκίδας)

—RHEGION: (**29**) iv/iii BC Landi, *DISMG* 34

—SYBARIS-THOURIOI-COPIAE: (**30**) iii BC Theoc., *Id.* v 8 (fict.)

S. ITALY (CALABRIA):

—TARAS-TARENTUM: (**31**) iv/iii BC Landi, *DISMG* 200 (vases); (**32**) c. 302-280 BC Vlasto 695 (coin) (Evans, *Horsemen* p. 134 VI D.3); (**33**) c. 280-272 BC Vlasto 727 (coin) (Evans, *Horsemen* p. 157 VII A.6); (**34**) ?255 BC Nachtergael, *Les Galates* 8, 50; cf. Stephanis 802 (f. Δράκων); (**35**) c. 210 BC *IG* IX (1)² (1) 31, 82 (f. Ἀριστόφαμος); (**36**) m. ii BC *ZPE* 1 (1967) p. 230, 6; Stephanis 1570

(II s. Λύκων I); (37) ~ ZPE 1 (1967) p. 260, 6; cf. Stephanis 1570 (I f. Λύκων II)
—TARAS-TARENTUM?: (38) iv/iii BC RE (15); FVS 57 (or Caria Iasos)
SICILY:
—AKRAI: (39) ?iii BC SGDI 3240, 7 (Akrai p. 156 no. 7) (f. Δαμαίνετος)
—AVOLA (MOD.): (40) i BC SEG XXXIV 981, 6 (s. Νύμφων)
—SYRACUSE: (41) 354 BC Plu., Dio 57; (42) c. 247-199 BC SGDI 2609, 2 (f. Ἡρακλείδας)
—TAUROMENION: (43) c. 199 BC IG XIV 421 an. 42 (SGDI 5219)

## Λυκώπας
LAKONIA:
—SPARTA: (1) c. 525 BC Hdt. iii 55. 1 (Poralla² 501) (-πης)
S. ITALY (BRUTTIUM):
—SYBARIS-THOURIOI-COPIAE: (2) iii BC Theoc., Id. v 62 (fict.)

## Λύκωπος
AITOLIA: (1) iv/iii BC Polyaen. viii 70; (2) 190 BC Plb. xxi 25. 11
—KALYDON: (3) c. 263-237 BC IG IX (1)² (1) p. XLIX ff., s.a. 259 BC, 252 BC, 244 BC, 237 BC; cf. 31, 182 n.; FD III (3) 218 B, 5; Syll³ 444 A, 2; CID II 139, 2; (4) m. ii BC IG IX (1)² (1) 137, 24; (5) s. ii BC ib. 72 (s. Πολέμαρχος); (6) 129 BC ib. 137, 93 (s. Ἀγήσων)
—THERMOS*: (7) hell. ib. 85. 8 (tile)
ARKADIA:
—MANTINEIA-ANTIGONEIA: (8) iii/ii BC ib. v (2) 319, 22; (9) ii-i BC ib. l. 25
EPIROS:
—KASSOPE: (10) f. ii BC Cabanes, L'Épire p. 564 no. 41, 8 (f. Σωτίων)

## Λυκωρίς
ARKADIA:
—TEGEA: (1) imp. IG v (2) 233
S. ITALY (CALABRIA):
—BRENTESION-BRUNDISIUM*: (2) imp. NScav 1904, p. 300 (Lat. Terraea Lycoris: freed.)

## Λυκωτάδας
ARGOLIS:
—ARGOS:
——(Hylleis): (1) c. 450 BC ML 42 B, 44 (-κō-)

## Λυκώτας
EPIROS:
—AVARICE (MOD.): (1) ii BC SEG XXIV 468 (s. Λυκίσκος, f. Παμφίλα)
—BOUTHROTOS (PRASAIBOI): (2) a. 163 BC IBouthrot 17, 33 (SEG XXXVIII 474) ?= (10); (3) ~ IBouthrot 23, 3 (SEG XXXVIII 481); (4) ~ IBouthrot 25, 27 (SEG XXXVIII 483); (5) ~ IBouthrot 27, 2 (SEG XXXVIII 485) (f. Λύκος); (6) ~ IBouthrot 28, 26; 143, 5 (SEG XXXVIII 486) ?= (16); (7) ~ IBouthrot 29, 23 (SEG XXXVIII 487) (f. Λυσανίας); (8) ~ IBouthrot 31, 36 (SEG XXXVIII 490) (f. Φίλιππος); (9) ~ IBouthrot 31, 37 (SEG XXXVIII 490) (s. Φίλιππος, Παμφίλα); (10) ~ IBouthrot 33, 11 (SEG XXXVIII 492); IBouthrot 134, 12 ?= (2); (11) ~ ib. 43, 1 (SEG XXXVIII 502) (s. Λυσανίας); (12) ~ IBouthrot 43, 14 (SEG XXXVIII 502) (f. Λυκίσκος) ?= (15); (13) ~ IBouthrot 104, 7 (f. Λύκος); (14) ~ ib. l. 8 (s. Λύκος); (15) ~ ib. 134, 17 (f. Λυκίσκος) ?= (12); (16) ~ ib. 160, 10; 161, 5 (s. Στράτων) ?= (6)
——Dranoi: (17) a. 163 BC ib. 132, 6-8 (s. Φιλιππίδας, ?f. Φίλιππος)
——Sarpingioi: (18) a. 163 BC ib. 139, 8 (f. Φίλιππος)
——Thoiatoi: (19) a. 163 BC ib. 137, 2; 141, 4
—BOUTHROTOS?: (20) hell.? ib. 208 (RAAN 21 (1941) p. 278) ([Λυ]κώτας: f. Λυκίσκος)
—EPHYRA*: (21) iii-ii BC PAE 1964, p. 51

—KASSOPE: (22) hell. Ep. Chron. 29 (1988-9) pp. 89 ff.; cf. BE 1991, no. 360; (23) f. ii BC Cabanes, L'Épire p. 564 no. 41, 3 (s. Λύκος)
—ORESTOI: (24) ?164 BC ib. p. 586 no. 71, 7 (f. Σιμίας)
—TEPELENE (MOD.): (25) i BC-i AD? SEG XXIV 474, 3; cf. Hammond, Epirus p. 738 (locn.) (f. Φίλιστος)
ILLYRIA:
—BYLLIONES BYLLIS: (26) imp. Iliria 1987 (2), p. 104 no. 63 (Lat. Lycotas)
KERKYRA: (27) i AD IG II² 9013 (s. Ἱππόνικος)
LAKONIA:
—SPARTA: (28) 612 BC Moretti, Olymp. 72 (Poralla² 502)

## Λύλης
ILLYRIA:
—EPIDAMNOS-DYRRHACHION: (1) c. 250-50 BC Jubice Hoard p. 97 no. 43 (coin) (Ceka 399); cf. IApoll Ref. Bibl. n. 80 (coin) (pryt.)

## Λῦος
EPIROS:
—KELAITHOI: (1) ?iv/iii BC SGDI 1354, 9; cf. Cabanes, L'Épire p. 582 no. 58
—PHOINATOI: (2) iii/ii BC Syll³ 1206, 9; cf. Cabanes, L'Épire p. 583 no. 60

## Λύρα
S. ITALY (APULIA):
—CANNAE: (1) ii AD Epig. Rom. di Canosa 150 (CIL IX 385) (Lat. Titinia Lyre: m. Εὐέτης)

## Λύρακος?
SICILY:
—NAXOS?: (1) vii/vi BC SEG XXXV 1014; cf. BE 1988, no. 1035 (Λύραφος ἡύρος)

## Λυρικός
S. ITALY (CAMPANIA):
—POMPEII: (1) i BC-i AD CIL IV 2172 (Lat. Lyricus)

## Λυρίς
S. ITALY (CAMPANIA):
—DIKAIARCHIA-PUTEOLI*: (1) i/ii AD Puteoli 7-8 (1983-4) p. 299 no. 3 (CIL X 2109) (Lat. Mamilia Lyris: m. L. Asellius Mamilianus: freed.)
—NOLA: (2) imp. ib. 1319 (Lat. Gavia Lyris: m. Δορκάς)

## Λυσαγόρας
DALMATIA:
—BOUTHOE: (1) hell.? BE 1941, no. 82

## Λυσαιθίδας
MESSENIA:
—MESSENE: (1) s. ii BC SEG XLI 341, 13 (f. Λυσίμαχος)

## Λυσανδρία
LAKONIA:
—SPARTA: (1) s. i AD ib. XI 776, 1 (Bradford (-)) (d. Λουϊάδας, m. Ἰουλ. Νίκιον)

## Λυσανδρίδας
ARKADIA:
—MEGALOPOLIS: (1) 222 BC RE (2)
KORINTHIA:
—KORINTH: (2) c. 610-590 BC Amyx 18. 6 (vase) (Lorber 28); LSAG² p. 131 no. 9 (date)
LAKONIA:
—SPARTA: (3) f. iv BC FGrH 115 F 240 (Poralla² 503) (s. Ξενοπείθεια) ?= (Λυσανορίδας (2)); (4) imp. IG v (1) 797 (Bradford (-))
LAKONIA?: (5) ?v-iv BC CGFP 236, 23 (fict.)

## Λύσανδρος
ARGOLIS:
—EPIDAUROS: (1) iii BC IG IV (1)² 159

—EPIDAUROS*: (2) c. 370-365 BC Peek, IAEpid 52 B, 67
ARKADIA:
—PHIGALEIA: (3) imp. SEG XXIII 250
ILLYRIA:
—EPIDAMNOS-DYRRHACHION: (4) hell.-imp. IDyrrh 64 (f. Κλειτία)
KORINTHIA:
—KORINTH?: (5) s. iii BC IG IX (1)² (1) 24, 2 (or Aitolia Konope-Arsinoe: s. Δικαίαρχος)
—SIKYON: (6) ?vi BC FGrH 328 F 23 (Skalet 198); (7) 367 BC X., HG vii 1. 45 (Skalet 196); (8) ?255 BC Nachtergael, Les Galates 8, 24; cf. Stephanis 1921 (Λύσ[αν]δρος: f. Ξένων)
LAKONIA:
—SPARTA: (9) c. 440-395 BC RE (1); ML 95; IPr 316, 6 (Poralla² 504) (s. Ἀριστόκριτος); (10) m. iii BC Bradford (1) (s. Λίβυς); (11) s. i BC IG v (1) 905 (Λύσα[νδρος]?)
MESSENIA:
—MESSENE: (12) f. iii BC PAE 1991, p. 99 no. 7, 11; (13) m. iii BC IG v (2) 368, 83 (f. Ξενοκλῆς)
—THOURIA: (14) f. ii BC SEG XI 972, 75 (s. Φιλοκράτης)
SICILY:
—TAUROMENION: (15) 230-214 BC IG XIV 421 an. 11; 421 an. 21; 421 an. 27; 421 an. 39 (SGDI 5219) (s. Ἰσόδικος) ?= (16); (16) c. 228 BC IG XIV 421 an. 13 (SGDI 5219) ?= (15); (17) c. 188-166 BC IG XIV 421 an. 53; 421 an. 75 (SGDI 5219) (f. Γοργίας); (18) c. 158-145 BC IG XIV 421 an. 83; 421 an. 96 (SGDI 5219) (s. Γοργίας)

## Λυσανίας
AITOLIA:
—KONOPE-ARSINOE: (1) iii-ii BC IG IX (1)² (1) 133 c; SBBerlAk 1936, p. 364 no. 7 a (tile)
DALMATIA:
—ISSA:
——(Pamphyloi): (2) iv/iii BC Brunšmid p. 8, 27 (s. Ξενότιμος)
EPIROS: (3) 234-168 BC Franke, Münz. v. Epirus p. 177 II ser. 32; p. 156 no. 7 (coin)
—BOUTHROTOS: (4) iii-ii BC IBouthrot 195 (f. Λυσώ)
—BOUTHROTOS (PRASAIBOI): (5) a. 163 BC ib. 13, 14; cf. Ugolini, Alb. Ant. 3 p. 120 (Λυσ[ανίας]: I f. Λυσανίας II); (6) ~ IBouthrot 13, 14; cf. Ugolini, Alb. Ant. 3 p. 120 ([Λυ]σανίας: II s. Λυσανίας I); (7) ~ IBouthrot 13, 18; cf. Ugolini, Alb. Ant. 3 p. 120 (Λυσα[νίας?]: f. Σαώτας); (8) ~ IBouthrot 14, 32 (SEG XXXVIII 471) ?= (13); (9) ~ IBouthrot 17, 25 (SEG XXXVIII 474); (10) ~ IBouthrot 18, 9 (SEG XXXVIII 475) (s. Κέφαλος); (11) ~ IBouthrot 18, 17 (SEG XXXVIII 475) ?= (12); (12) ~ IBouthrot 22, 31 (SEG XXXVIII 479) ?= (11); (13) ~ IBouthrot 24, 4; 25, 4 (SEG XXXVIII 482-3) ?= (8); (14) ~ IBouthrot 25, 6; 28, 7 (SEG XXXVIII 483; 486); (15) ~ IBouthrot 26, 16; 29, 11; 32, 19, 23 (SEG XXXVIII 484; 487; 491) (s. Νίκανδρος); (16) ~ IBouthrot 26, 18 (SEG XXXVIII 484); IBouthrot 137, 9? (f. Φυσκίνος); (17) ~ ib. 29, 2 (SEG XXXVIII 487); (18) ~ IBouthrot 29, 11; 32, 19, 23 (SEG XXXVIII 487; 491); (19) ~ IBouthrot 29, 23 (SEG XXXVIII 487) (s. Λυκώτας); (20) ~ IBouthrot 31, 73 (SEG XXXVIII 490) (s. Ἀριστόμαχος) ?= (31); (21) ~ IBouthrot 31, 101, 109 (SEG XXXVIII 490) (f. Ἄλκιμος); (22) ~ IBouthrot 33, 11 (SEG XXXVIII 492); IBouthrot 134, 11; (23) ~ ib. 42, 5-6 (SEG XXXVIII 501); (24) ~ IBouthrot 43, 2 (SEG XXXVIII 502); (25) ~ IBouthrot 46, 2 (f. Μύρτων); (26) ~ ib. 50, 1; 152, 5 (s. Τελεσίδας); (27) ~ ib. 50, 4, 10; (28) ~ ib. 56, 5 (SEG XXXVIII 507) (Λυσα[νίας]); (29) ~ IBouthrot 66, 4 (f. Νίκανδρος); (30) ~ ib. 78, 10; 79, 9; 80, 8; 81, 8; 82, 8; 83, 8; 84, 8; 85, 8; 86, 9;

87, 9; 88, 7 (*BCH* 118 (1994) pp. 122 f. nos. 1-11) (f. *Μυρτίλος*) ?= (*41*); (**31**) ~ *IBouthrot* 110, 7 (s. *Ἀριστόμαχος*) ?= (*36*) (*20*) (*36*); (**32**) ~ ib. 132, 4 (f. *Βοῖσκος*); (**33**) ~ ib. 135, 11 (f. *Λαμία*); (**34**) ~ ib. l. 14 (f. —*ακλῆς*); (**35**) ~ ib. 147, 13 (f. —*κης*)
——Aixonioi: (**36**) a. 163 BC ib. 111, 11; 112, 12; 122, 7 (s. *Ἀριστόμαχος*) ?= (*31*) (*31*); (**37**) ~ ib. 126, 3; 127, 3, 7 (*BCH* 118 (1994) p. 128 A); *IBouthrot* 134, 4 (?s. *Φυσκίων*)
——Belyoi: (**38**) a. 163 BC ib. 72, 7
——Bouthrotioi: (**39**) a. 163 BC ib. 91, 15 (*SEG* XXXII 623) (s. *Λυσίμαχος*)
——Drymioi: (**40**) a. 163 BC *IBouthrot* 15, 4; 21, 48; 38, 2 (*SEG* XXXVIII 472; 478; 497); *IBouthrot* 130, 4; 131, 5; 140, 7; 144, 6; 156, 4; 157, 3 (*BCH* 118 (1994) p. 127 no. 12-13) (s. *Μυρτίλος*); (**41**) ~ *IBouthrot* 21, 47 (*SEG* XXXVIII 478) (f. *Μυρτίλος*) ?= (*30*)
——Kotylaioi: (**42**) a. 163 BC *IBouthrot* 168, 8 (*SEG* XXXVIII 469) (f. *Λυσώ*)
——Parthaioi: (**43**) a. 163 BC *IBouthrot* 149, 9 (f. *Φυσκίων*)
——Pelmatioi: (**44**) a. 163 BC ib. 53, 4 (*SEG* XXXVIII 504); *IBouthrot* 146, 7 (s. *Μενέξιος*) ?= (*45*); (**45**) ~ ib. 69, 9; 70, 7; 71, 6 (*BCH* 118 (1994) p. 129 B 1-3) (s. *Μενέξιος*) ?= (*47*) (*44*); (**46**) ~ *IBouthrot* 69, 12; 70, 10; 71, 8 (*BCH* 118 (1994) pp. 129 f. B 1-3) (f. *Μενέξιος*); (**47**) ~ *IBouthrot* 72, 1; 73; 74; 98, 2; 140, 1 ?= (*45*)
—DODONA: (**48**) iii BC Antoniou, *Dodone* Aa, 31; (**49**) ~ ib. Ab, 27
—DODONA*: (**50**) iv-iii BC Carapanos, *Dodone* p. 111 no. 6 (tile); (**51**) iii/ii BC *Syll*3 1163; (**52**) ?i BC Cabanes, *L'Épire* p. 551 no. 27
—KAR(I)OPOI: (**53**) f. ii BC ib. p. 554 no. 33, 5 (*SEG* XXXVII 511) (s. *Νικόλαος*); (**54**) ~ Cabanes, *L'Épire* p. 580 no. 54, 2
—OMPHALES: (**55**) m. iv BC ib. p. 539 no. 3, 7
—PASSARON: (**56**) ii BC *AE* 1914, p. 239 no. 19
ILLYRIA:
—AMANTIA: (**57**) ?i BC *Iliria* 1972, p. 91 no. 2, 5, 6, 9, 16
—APOLLONIA: (**58**) c. 250-50 BC Maier 77 (Ceka 73); cf. Ceka 298 + *IApoll Ref. Bibl.* n. 81 (locn.); Maier 104 (coin) (Ceka 74) (money.); (**59**) ~ Maier 59-60 (coin) (Ceka 75; 101) (pryt.)
—EPIDAMNOS-DYRRHACHION: (**60**) c. 250-50 BC Münsterberg p. 261 (Ceka 298?; 299); cf. *IApoll Ref. Bibl.* n. 81 (coin) (money.); (**61**) hell.-imp. *IDyrrh* 68 ([*Λ*]*υσανίας*, [*Πα*]*υσανίας*?: f. *Ἀβαία*)
KERKYRA: (**62**) s. ii AD *IG* IX (1) 730-1 (f. *Ἀρίοστα*)
PELOPONNESE: (**63**) m. iii BC *RE* (9) (Lat. Lysanias: f. *Ἀρχάγαθος*: doctor?)
S. ITALY (CALABRIA):
—TARAS-TARENTUM: (**64**) 248 BC *PP* 8679
SICILY: (**65**) ?v BC *ASSiciliaOrientale* 1919-20, p. 197
—ECHETLA: (**66**) vi/v BC Manganaro, *PdelP* forthcoming 9
—GELA-PHINTIAS: (**67**) s. iv BC Peek, *IAEpid* 41, 5 (Perlman E. 2); Perlman pp. 46-9 (date) (*Λυ*[*σ*]*ανίας*)
—SYRACUSE: (**68**) f. v BC Pl., *R.* 330 B; Plu., *Mor.* 835 C; cf. *APF* C 9 (s. *Κέφαλος*, f. *Κέφαλος*)

**Λυσανορίδας**
LAKONIA:
—SPARTA: (**1**) ?f. iv BC Plu., *Mor.* 233 E; cf. 576 A (*Λύσανδρος*—mss., *Λ.*—Wyttenbach); (**2**) f. iv BC Poralla2 505 ?= (*Λυσανδρίδας* (*3*))

**Λυσάνωρ**
AKARNANIA:
—PALAIROS: (**1**) ii BC *AD* 22 (1967) Chron. p. 324 (s. *Τιμασικράτης*)

ILLYRIA:
—APOLLONIA: (**2**) c. 250-50 BC Maier 62 (coin) (Ceka 109) (pryt.); (**3**) a. 179 BC *Syll*3 638 (*IDyrrh* 520); Kramolisch p. 54 (date) (*Λυσάνο*[*ρος*] (gen.)—*IG* and *Syll*2, *Λυσάνδ*[*ρου*] (gen.)—*Syll*3: s. *Φιντύλος*)
—GUREZEZE (MOD.): (**4**) hell. *Iliria* 1982 (1), p. 104 no. 5 = p. 120 no. 36 (tile)

**Λυσαρχίδας**
MESSENIA:
—MESSENE: (**1**) iii BC *SEG* XXIII 210, 30 (*Λυσαρχί*[*δ*]*ας*)

**Λυσαρχίς**
MESSENIA:
—ABIA: (**1**) i BC/i AD *IG* V (1) 1353 (d. *Σοίξιππος*)

**Λυσαρώ**
ARGOLIS:
—ARGOS: (**1**) ?i AD Unp. (Argos, Kavvadias)

**Λύσας**
MESSENIA:
—MESSENE: (**1**) 317 BC *PAE* 1991, p. 96 no. 1 (*Λίσας*—ed., *Λ.*—LGPN)

**Λυσέας**
ARGOLIS:
—EPIDAUROS:
——(Azantioi): (**1**) 146 BC *IG* IV (1)2 28, 46 (s. *Δαμόφιλος*)
——Pleiatios (Hylleis): (**2**) m. iii BC ib. 96, 69 (Perlman E.3); Perlman p. 63 f. (date)
KORINTHIA:
—KORINTH: (**3**) v BC *SEG* XI 202 (*Λυσέ*[*ας*])

**Λυσέρως**
S. ITALY (CALABRIA):
—BRENTESION-BRUNDISIUM: (**1**) imp. *NScav* 1895, p. 267 b = *Epigraphica* 25 (1963) p. 86 no. 100 (Lat. Lyseros)

**Λυσήν**
ARGOLIS:
—EPIDAUROS*: (**1**) c. 370-365 BC Peek, *IAEpid* 52 A, 36
EPIROS: (**2**) 234-168 BC *BMC Thessaly* p. 90 no. 41; Franke, *Münz. v. Epirus* p. 173-5 II ser. 19-22; p. 156 no. 8 (coin)
—ANTIGONEIA: (**3**) imp. *AE* 1914, p. 238 no. 15; Cabanes, *L'Épire* p. 234 n. 96 (locn.) (f. *Ἄνδρων*)
—BOUTHROTOS: (**4**) hell.? *IBouthrot* 214 (Ugolini, *Alb. Ant.* 3 p. 210 no. 8) (*Λυσ*[*ήν*]*ος* (gen.), *Λύσ*[*ων*]*ος*?)
ILLYRIA:
—APOLLONIA: (**5**) c. 250-50 BC Maier 63 (Ceka 27); Maier 65 (coin) (Ceka 62) (pryt.); (**6**) ii BC Cabanes, *L'Épire* p. 562 no. 37 (*IApoll* 6) (s. *Σωστρίων*); (**7**) i BC Maier 133 (coin) (f. *Ἄριστων*)
—EPIDAMNOS-DYRRHACHION: (**8**) c. 250-50 BC ib. 218 (coin) (Ceka 300) (money.); (**9**) ~ Maier 277 + 483; Münsterberg Nachtr. p. 16 (Ceka 106; 235; 243); cf. *IApoll Ref. Bibl.* n. 67 (coin) (pryt.)
KERKYRA: (**10**) c. 315-280 BC *FD* III (4) 406, 3 (s. *Χλεμύτας*); (**11**) ~ ib. l. 3 (s. *Εὐάκης*)

**Λυσιάδας**
ARGOLIS:
—ARGOS: (**1**) c. 365-335 BC *IG* IV (1)2 103, 14, 53, 73, 85, 87, 115 (s. *Πολύξενος*)
KORINTHIA:
—KORINTH: (**2**) c. 575-550 BC ib. IV (1) 232 (pinax)
LAKONIA:
—SPARTA: (**3**) c. 130 AD ib. V (1) 60, 3 (Bradford (-)) (f. *Πρατόνικος*)

TRIPHYLIA:
—MAKISTOS: (**4**) 399-369 BC *SEG* XXXV 389, 10

**Λυσιάδης**
SICILY:
—KATANE: (**1**) ?f. iv BC Iamb., *VP* 267 (*FVS* 1 p. 448)

**Λυσιάναξ**
ELIS: (**1**) m. iv BC Paus. vi 4. 5 (f. *Σάτυρος*: mantis/Iamidai) ?= (*2*); (**2**) ?320 BC *IG* V (2) 549, 18 (f. *Ἀνδρόμαχος*) ?= (*1*)

**Λυσίας**
ACHAIA: (**1**) iv/iii BC ib. XII (9) 810 (f. *Κλεοδίκα*: date—Knoepfler)
—DYME: (**2**) iii BC *AJPh* 31 (1910) p. 399 no. 74 a, 11 (s. *Ξενοκλῆς*, f. *Ἀριστονίκα*)
—PATRAI: (**3**) c. 146-32 BC BM coin 1887 6-6-11 (coin) (f. *Αἰσχρίων*)
AITOLIA:
—POTIDANIA: (**4**) m. ii BC *SBBerlAk* 1936, p. 371 b, 15 (*SEG* XLI 528 B) (s. *Δαίτας*)
AKARNANIA:
—ANAKTORION: (**5**) iii BC *IG* IX (1)2 (2) 592
—THYRREION: (**6**) ii BC ib. 247, 4; 251, 4 (s. *Μενοίτιος*)
ARGOLIS:
—ARGOS: (**7**) s. iv BC *SEG* XXXV 799 ([*Λ*]*υσία*[*s*]: f. *Εὐθίας*); (**8**) ii-i BC *Mnem.* NS 47 (1919) p. 164 no. 9, 5 (s. *Ἀντισθένης*)
—EPIDAUROS: (**9**) iii BC *IG* IV (1)2 325 ([*Λυ*]*σίας*)
—HERMIONE: (**10**) iii BC ib. IV (1) 728, 14
DALMATIA:
—ISSA?: (**11**) iii/ii BC Brunšmid p. 31 no. 27; *Istros* 2 (1935-6) pp. 18 ff. (or Dalmatia Tragurion)
EPIROS: (**12**) iv/iii BC *IG* XII Suppl. 631 (s. *Λύσων*: date—Knoepfler)
—AMBRAKIA: (**13**) hell. *SEG* XXIV 421 (*Λυσί*[*as*]: f. *Φιλόμηλος*)
—CHAONES: (**14**) ?198 BC *IG* II2 2313, 34; *SEG* XLI 113; Habicht, *Athen hell. Zeit* p. 134 (date) (f. —*τος*)
—DODONA*: (**15**) iv-iii BC *SGDI* 1569 B (s. *Δαμόλαος*); (**16**) ?iv/iii BC *SEG* XXIII 475 a
ILLYRIA:
—LYCHNIDOS: (**17**) ii-iii AD *Sp.* 71 (1931) p. 223 no. 592
KEPHALLENIA:
—PALE: (**18**) iii/ii BC Unp. (*IG* arch.) (*Λυσιαν*-apogr.)
LEUKAS: (**19**) hell.? *IG* IX (1) 580; cf. *AM* 27 (1902) p. 360
MESSENIA:
—MESSENE: (**20**) f. iii BC *PAE* 1991, p. 100 no. 8, 5; cf. 1989, p. 96
—THOURIA: (**21**) f. ii BC *SEG* XI 972, 20 (s. *Παγκράτης*)
S. ITALY (CAMPANIA):
—AEQUANA: (**22**) imp. *CIL* X 768 (Lat. L. Sergius Lysias)
—DIKAIARCHIA-PUTEOLI*: (**23**) imp. ib. 2687 (Lat. Lysia: freed.)
S. ITALY (LUCANIA):
—LEUKANOI: (**24**) imp. *IG* II2 9207 (f. *Νικήτης*)
SICILY:
—AKRAI: (**25**) iii-ii BC *SGDI* 3242, 7 (*Akrai* p. 157 no. 8) (f. *Νύμφων*)
—SYRACUSE: (**26**) c. 450-370 BC *RE* (13); *APF* C 9 (s. *Κέφαλος*); (**27**) v/iv BC Wehrli, *Schule Arist.* iii fr. 8
—TAUROMENION:
——(*Παμ.*): (**28**) ii/i BC *IGSI* 7 I, 8; 10 I, 17 (f. *Νικίας*)

**Λυσίβιος**
ELIS: (**1**) m. iii BC *IG* IV (1)2 96, 46 (Perlman E.3); Perlman p. 63 f. (date) (s. *Θεύδωρος*)
S. ITALY (CALABRIA):
—TARAS-TARENTUM: (**2**) iv BC Iamb., *VP* 267 (*FVS* 1 p. 446)

## Λυσίδαμος
AITOLIA:
—LITHOVOUNI (MOD.) (AKRAI?): (1) v/iv BC
SEG XXXIV 466 (vase)
AKARNANIA:
—THYRREION: (2) ii BC ib. XXV 628, 6
ARGOLIS:
—LYRKEIA (MOD.): (3) iv BC AAA 3 (1970) p.
118
ARKADIA:
—TEGEA: (4) s. iii BC IG V (2) 116, 4
(Λυσί[δ]αμος: f. Ἐπισθένης); (5) i BC SEG XI
1079
KORINTHIA:
—SIKYON: (6) vi/v BC ib. 244, 57
MESSENIA:
—KORONE: (7) ii BC IG V (1) 1397, 10
—MESSENE: (8) i BC-i AD SEG XXIII 212 (f. Λυ-
σικράτης) ?= (9); (9) 11 AD PAE 1992, p. 71
A, 4 (s. Λυσικράτης) ?= (8)
SICILY:
—AKRAGAS: (10) f. v BC Dubois, IGDS 180 a,
2 (Arena, Iscr. Sic. II 90)

## Λυσίδας
KORINTHIA:
—KORINTH: (1) ?i BC Corinth VIII (1) 67

## Λυσίδη?
ARGOLIS:
—EPIDAUROS: (1) c. 500-450 BC AA 1957, p. 22

## Λυσίδημος
ARGOLIS:
—TROIZEN: (1) imp. IG IV (1) 779 ([Λ]υσίδημος:
I f. Λυσίδημος II); (2) ~ ib. (Λυσί[δημος]: II s.
Λυσίδημος I)

## Λυσιδίκα
ARGOLIS:
—EPIDAUROS: (1) vii/vi BC Wehrli, Schule Arist.
vii fr. 144 (and Korinthia Korinth: Λ. ἡ καὶ
Μέλισσα, Λυσίδη—mss., Λυσιδίκη—Reiske: d.
Προκλῆς, Ἐρισθένεια (Orchomenos), m. Κύψε-
λος (Korinth), Λυκόφρων (Korinth)); (2) iv/iii
BC IG IV (1)² 732 + Peek, IAEpid 316
EPIROS:
—BOUTHROTOS (PRASAIBOI): (3) a. 163 BC
IBouthrot 48, 8; (4) ~ ib. 75, 7; (5) ~ ib. 93, 5
—PHOINIKE: (6) iii BC Ugolini, Alb. Ant. 2 p.
153 no. 5
ITHAKE: (7) hell. IG IX (1) 663

## Λυσιδίκη
ARKADIA:
—MT. KYLLENE*: (1) ?iv-iii BC ib. V (2) 365
(Λυσι<ο>δίκη?)

## Λυσίδικος
ARKADIA:
—PALLANTION: (1) a. 316 BC SEG XI 1084, 37
(Perlman A.3) (f. Ἐννέων)

## Λυσιδώι
KYNOURIA:
—THYREA?: (1) iv/iii BC SEG XXX 378 (or Ky-
nouria Eua?: date—LGPN)

## Λυσίθεος
ARGOLIS:
—HERMIONE: (1) iv BC IG IV (1) 742, 6

## Λυσικλείδας
ARGOLIS:
—EPIDAUROS: (1) ii BC ib. IV (1)² 211 (f. Δαμα-
ρέτα)

## Λυσικλείδης
SICILY: (1) f. iv BC [Pl.], Ep. 315 A

## Λυσικλῆς
AITOLIA:
—KALYDON: (1) s. ii BC SEG XXV 621, 4
(Λ[υσι]κλῆς: s. Τίμων)

AKARNANIA:
—THYRREION: (2) iii BC IG IX (1)² (2) 268; (3)
ii BC ib. 252, 9 (s. Σώστρατος)
ARKADIA:
—MEGALOPOLIS: (4) ?268 BC FD III (1) 27, 1
(s. Πολύμναστος)
—TEGEA: (5) m. iv BC IG V (2) 6, 92 (s. Δύων)
LEUKAS: (6) hell.? ib. IX (1) 564
MESSENIA:
—THOURIA: (7) ii-i BC ib. V (1) 1385, 27 (f. Θεο-
κλῆς)

## Λυσικράτεια
ARGOLIS:
—ARGOS: (1) iv/iii BC ib. IV (1) 569

## Λυσικράτης
ARGOLIS:
—ARGOS: (1) f. i BC Unp. (Ch. Kritzas) (f. Πο-
λέας)
—EPIDAUROS: (2) c. 365-335 BC IG IV (1)² 103,
6; cf. SEG XXV 386
——(Azantioi): (3) 146 BC IG IV (1)² 28, 32 (s.
Ἱαροκλῆς)
—EPIDAUROS*: (4) c. 370 BC ib. 102, 33
ARKADIA?: (5) i-ii AD ib. V (2) 508 (Λυσι-
κράτ[ης]: ?s. Κύλλος)
DALMATIA:
—ISSA: (6) iv/iii BC VAHD NS 8 (1905) p. 97
no. 177 (VAMZ 1970, p. 33 f. frr. I-J)
——(Dymanes): (7) iv/iii BC Brunšmid p. 8, 44
(f. —ιος)
ELIS: (8) c. 146-32 BC BM coin 1926 1-16-845
(coin)
LAKONIA:
—GYTHEION: (9) f. ii AD IG V (1) 1170, 6; 1174,
11 (f. Λεοντᾶς); (10) a. 212 AD ib. 1177, 3 (M.
Αὐρ. Λυσικρά[της]: II s. Λυσικράτης I, f. Αὐρ.
Δαμοκράτης, Αὐρ. Λυσικράτης III); (11) ~ ib. l.
4 (I f. M. Αὐρ. Λυσικράτης II); (12) ~ ib. l. 12
(Αὐρ. Λυσικράτης: III s. M. Αὐρ. Λυσικράτης
II)
—SPARTA: (13) s. i BC ib. 96, 9 (Bradford (6))
(f. Δέξις); (14) imp. IG V (1) 1015 (Bradford
(4)); (15) i AD IG V (1) 274 (Artemis Orthia
pp. 309-10 no. 26) (s. Χαρίξενος) ?= (16); (16)
i/ii AD IG V (1) 275, 4 (Artemis Orthia pp.
312-13 no. 30); SEG XI 534, 5; 594 (Bradford (1)) (Γ. Ἰούλ. Λ.: f. Γ. Ἰούλ. Χαρίξενος) ?=
(15); (17) m. ii AD IG V (1) 53, 7; 55, 2; 283,
4; SEG XI 498, 4; 629, 3; BSA 75 (1980) p.
219 n. 3 (date) (Bradford (1)) (Γ. Ἰούλ. Λ.:
s. Χαρίξενος) ?= (20); (18) ~ SEG XI 623, 8
(Bradford (3)) ([Γ.] [Ἰού]λ. Λ. νεώτ.); (19) c.
140-160 AD IG V (1) 112, 4 (Bradford (2)) (s.
Δαμοκράτης); (20) c. 175-200 AD IG V (1) 663,
7; SEG XI 503, 3 (Bradford (5)) (f. Γ. Ἰούλ.
Ἀντίπατρος) ?= (17)
——Amyklai: (21) ii/i BC IG V (1) 26, 5 (Bradford (7)) (f. Εὔθυμος)
—TAINARON-KAINEPOLIS: (22) imp. IG V (1)
1244 (s. Δαμάρμενος); (23) 238-244 AD ib.
1241, 10 (f. M. Αὐρ. Λυσίξενος)
—TAINARON-KAINEPOLIS?: (24) ?ii-i BC ib.
1250 (s. Καλλικράτης)
LEUKAS: (25) iv/iii BC AD 26 (1971) Chron. p.
353 no. 5
MESSENIA:
—MESSENE: (26) i BC-i AD SEG XXIII 212 (s.
Λυσίδαμος); (27) 11 AD PAE 1992, p. 71 A, 4
(f. Λυσίδαμος)
—MESSENE?: (28) ii/i BC SEG XI 979, 55
—THOURIA: (29) f. ii BC ib. 972, 37 (s. Ξενάρης);
(30) ~ ib. l. 40 ([Λ]υσικράτης: s. Νικίας); (31) ~
ib. l. 64 (f. Λυσίστρατος)

## Λυσικράτις
ARGOLIS:
—HERMIONE: (1) iii BC IG IV (1) 728, 37

## Λυσικύδης
ARGOLIS:
—HERMIONE*: (1) iv BC ib. 742, 18

## Λυσίλαος
KEPHALLENIA: (1) iii BC SEG XLI 323, 16

## Λυσίλοχος
ARGOLIS:
—ARGOS: (1) ?320 BC IG V (2) 549, 13 (s. Περί-
λας)

## Λυσιμάχα
AKARNANIA:
—PALAIROS: (1) iii BC ib. IX (1)² (2) 492
ARGOLIS:
—ARGOS: (2) ii-i BC ib. IV (1) 611 (Nachtergael,
Les Galates 79) ([Λυ]σιμάχα: d. Πολ—)
DALMATIA:
—ISSA: (3) ii BC SEG XXXI 602, 2 (VAHD 84
(1991) p. 257 no. 7) (d. Μνασιφῶν, ?m. Μνασι-
φῶν)
EPIROS:
—BOUTHROTOS (PRASAIBOI): (4) a. 163 BC
IBouthrot 43, 15 (SEG XXXVIII 502) (d. Σαώ-
τας); (5) ~ IBouthrot 50, 8
MESSENIA:
—MESSENE: (6) ii BC PAE 1969, p. 116 no. 3
(d. Περίτας)

## Λυσιμαχίδας
ILLYRIA:
—EPIDAMNOS-DYRRHACHION: (1) 328 BC IG
II² 3052 (Stephanis 1581) (-δης)

## Λυσίμαχος
ACHAIA: (1) 146 BC IG IV (1)² 28, 155 (f. Καλ-
λικράτης: synoikos)
AKARNANIA: (2) iv BC RE (14); Berve 481
ARGOLIS:
—ARGOS: (3) 330-329 BC CID II 69, 21; 89, 9;
(4) 196 BC IG IX (1)² (1) 30, 24 (Λυσίμα[χος]:
s. Φάυλλος)
—ARGOS?: (5) v BC ib. IV (1) 552, 5
—EPIDAUROS: (6) ii-iii AD ib. IV (1)² 570
——(Azantioi): (7) 146 BC ib. 28, 29
(Λυσ(ί)μαχος: f. Ἀριστομήδης)
—TROIZEN: (8) ?146 BC ib. IV (1) 757 B, 26
([Λ]υσίμαχος)
ARKADIA:
—MEGALOPOLIS: (9) c. 210-207 BC ib. IV (1)²
73, 26; SEG XXXV 303 (date) (s. Λύσιππος)
DALMATIA:
—ISSA: (10) iii BC ib. XXXI 596 (s. Διονύ-
σιος, f. Κλεέμπορος, Διονύσιος); (11) ~ ib. 598
(Λυσίμα[χος])
EPIROS:
—ANTIGONEIA: (12) imp. AE 1914, p. 238 no.
15; Cabanes, L'Épire p. 234 n. 96 (locn.) (s.
Φίλιππος)
—BOUTHROTOS (PRASAIBOI): (13) a. 163 BC
IBouthrot 14, 31 (SEG XXXVIII 471); (14)
~ IBouthrot 25, 23 (SEG XXXVIII 483) (Λυ-
σίμα[χος], Λυσιμά[χα]?); (15) ~ IBouthrot 29,
43 (SEG XXXVIII 487) ([Λυ]σίμαχος); (16) ~
IBouthrot 38, 5-6 (SEG XXXVIII 497); (17)
~ IBouthrot 42, 12 (SEG XXXVIII 501) (I? f.
Λυσίμαχος II?); (18) ~ IBouthrot 42, 12 (SEG
XXXVIII 501) (II? s. Λυσίμαχος I?); (19) ~
IBouthrot 100, 7 (f. Φιλόξενος)
——Bouthrotioi: (20) a. 163 BC ib. 91, 15 (SEG
XXXII 623) (f. Λυσανίας)
——Cherrioi: (21) a. 163 BC IBouthrot 90, 4 (s.
Ἀνδρόνικος)
ILLYRIA:
—APOLLONIA: (22) hell. IApoll 24; cf. Le Arti
5 (1943) p. 117 no. 2; cf. Fraser–Rönne,
BWGT p. 174 n. 5 (date) ([Λ]υσίμαχος: f.
Φαλάκρα); (23) c. 250-50 BC Maier 67 (coin)
(Ceka 90) (pryt.); (24) imp. IApoll 41
—BYLLIONES NIKAIA (KLJOS (MOD.)): (25) iii
BC SEG XXXVIII 571 (Λυσ[ίμ]αχος)

—LYCHNIDOS: (**26**) ii-iii AD *Sp.* 71 (1931) p. 109 no. 265 (f. *Π. Κουϊντιανός*)

KEPHALLENIA:

—PRONNOI: (**27**) ii BC *Op. Ath.* 10 (1971) p. 66 no. 15 (*Λυσίμαχος*)

KERKYRA: (**28**) ii BC *IG* IX (1) 934 (f. *Φιλοξένα*)

LAKONIA: (**29**) m. ii BC *SB* 7169, 10; *PP* 13413 (f. *Σ—χος*)

—SPARTA: (**30**) c. 206 BC *IG* IX (1)² (1) 28, 3 (Bradford (3)) (*Λυσίμα[χος]*: f. *Ἀριστόμαχος*); (**31**) s. i BC *IG* v (1) 93, 22; 212, 52 (Bradford (5)) (f. *Πρατόνικος*); (**32**) c. 25-1 BC *IG* v (1) 210, 27 (Bradford (6)) (f. *Ξενοκλῆς*); (**33**) c. 100-110 AD *SEG* XI 611, 1 (Bradford (1)) (*Λυσίμαχος*); (**34**) ?ii AD *IG* v (1) 731, 4 (*GVI* 1341; Bradford (4)) (f. *Πασικλῆς*); (**35**) c. 110 AD *IG* v (1) 99, 1 (Bradford (1)) (s. *Μνάσων*); (**36**) m. ii AD *INap* 59, 5 (Bradford (2)); (**37**) c. 140-160 AD *IG* v (1) 68, 27; 69, 25; 70, 3; *SEG* XI 533 a, [2] (Bradford (1)) (*Λυσίμ(αχος)*—69, *Λυσίμα(χος)*—70)

LEUKAS: (**38**) c. 167-50 BC *BMC Thessaly* p. 180 no. 94 (coin)

MESSENIA:

—ASINE: (**39**) hell.-imp. *IG* v (1) 1407 (s. *Νικάνωρ*)

—MESSENE: (**40**) s. ii BC *SEG* XLI 341, 3 (s. *Τιμασικράτης*); (**41**) ~ ib. l. 13 (s. *Λυσαιθίδας*)

PELOPONNESE?: (**42**) ii AD *PAE* 1992, p. 72 B, 21 (I f. *Λυσίμαχος* II); (**43**) ~ ib. l. 21 (II s. *Λυσίμαχος* I)

S. ITALY (CAMPANIA):

—SALERNUM: (**44**) i AD *CIL* x 8343 (Lat. Q. Fabius Lysimachus)

—SALERNUM*: (**45**) ?i AD *IItal* I (1) 238 II, 15 (*CIL* x 557) (Lat. L. Appuleius Lysimachus: freed.)

—SURRENTUM: (**46**) imp. ib. 720 (Lat. P. Aurelius Lysimachus)

SICILY:

—AKRAI: (**47**) imp. *SGDI* 5258 (*PdelP* 6 (1951) p. 70 no. 3); cf. *Rupes loquentes* p. 459 no. 5

—SYRACUSE: (**48**) 415 BC Th. vi 73. 1 (f. *Ἡρακλείδας*); (**49**) 356-354 BC *SEG* XLII 829 (f. *Ἡρακλείδας*)

**Λύσιμβος**

AITOLIA: (**1**) 217 BC Nachtergael, *Les Galates* 65, 5

**Λυσιμένης**

KEPHALLENIA?: (**1**) c. 330 BC *SEG* XXIII 189 I, 23 (*Λυσ[ι]μέν[ης]*: f. —ας)

KORINTHIA:

—SIKYON: (**2**) 367 BC X., *HG* vii 1. 45 (Skalet 200)

**Λυσινίκη**

S. ITALY (CAMPANIA):

—SURRENTUM: (**1**) imp. *CIL* x 717 (Lat. Atilia Lycinice)

**Λυσίνικος**

ARKADIA:

—TEGEA: (**1**) iv BC *IG* v (2) 31, 5 (s. *Ξενοκράτης*)

LAKONIA:

—SPARTA: (**2**) c. 30-20 BC ib. v (1) 141, 26; *SEG* XXXV 329 (date) (Bradford (3)); (**3**) i BC/i AD *SEG* XI 679, 4, 6 (Bradford (2)) (*Λυσίνικ[ος]*: s. *Σωτηρίδας*); (**4**) m. i AD *IG* v (1) 509, 1 (Bradford s.v. *Λυσίνεικος* (1)) (*Π. Μέμμιος Λυσινείκ[ος] Φιλάδελφος*: II s. *Λυσίνικος* I); (**5**) ~ *IG* v (1) 509, 6; *ID* 1629, 2 (Bradford s.v. *Λυσίνεικος* (4)) (*Λυσινείκης*—*IG*: I f. *Π. Μέμμιος Γοργιππίδας Φιλάδελφος, Π. Μέμμιος Λυσίνικος* II *Φιλάδελφος, Δαμοσθένεια*)

——Amyklai: (**6**) ii/i BC *IG* v (1) 26, 1 (Bradford (2)) (s. *Σωτηρίδας*)

MESSENIA:

—MESSENE: (**7**) m. iii BC *IG* v (2) 368, 84 (s. *Παυσέας*)

**Λυσῖνος**

MESSENIA:

—MESSENE: (**1**) i AD ib. v (1) 1436, 3

**Λυσιξενίδας**

LAKONIA:

—SPARTA: (**1**) 31-7 BC *Münzpr. der Laked.* pp. 71-2; pp. 169-70 Group 30; *RPC* 1 p. 248 no. 1107 (coin)

**Λυσίξενος**

ACHAIA: (**1**) iii BC Breccia, *Iscriz.* 283 (Pagenstecher, *Nekrop.* p. 59 no. 73)

—PATRAI: (**2**) c. 146-32 BC *Coll. Hunter* 2 p. 126 no. 3 (coin) (f. *Ἄνδρων*)

AITOLIA:

—KALYDON: (**3**) a. 143 BC *IG* IX (1)² (1) 137, 47 (s. *Κλεόνικος*); (**4**) 129 BC ib. l. 97 (s. *Νικόβουλος*)

AKARNANIA:

—THYRREION: (**5**) ii BC *GVI* 1078, 5 (*IG* IX (1)² (2) 312 a); (**6**) ~ ib. 248, 17 (s. *Λέων*)

ARGOLIS:

—HERMIONE: (**7**) iii-ii BC *SEG* XVII 172 (*Λ[υ]σίξενος*: s. *Ἀρχέπολις*)

ARKADIA:

—TEGEA: (**8**) iii/ii BC *IG* IV (1)² 318 (s. *Ἀρχέπολις*)

LAKONIA:

—SPARTA: (**9**) c. 25-1 BC ib. v (1) 210, 28 (Bradford (-)) (f. *Διωνίδας*)

—TAINARON-KAINEPOLIS: (**10**) 238-244 AD *IG* v (1) 1241, 9 (*M. Αὐρ. Λ.*: s. *Λυσικράτης*)

MESSENIA:

—MESSENE: (**11**) 361 BC *CID* II 4 I, 28

**Λυσίπονος**

EPIROS:

—BOUTHROTOS (PRASAIBOI): (**1**) a. 163 BC *IBouthrot* 32, 21; 42, 9 (*SEG* XXXVIII 491; 501)

**Λυσίππα**

ARGOLIS:

—ARGOS: (**1**) hell. *BCH* 27 (1903) p. 278 no. 29 (d. *Λυσι—*)

ELIS: (**2**) inc. Paus. v 2. 4 (-πη: m. *Φίλανθος, Λάμπος*)

**Λύσιππος**

ACHAIA: (**1**) m. iii BC *TCal* 32, 5, 16 (s. *Ἀγίας*)

ACHAIA?: (**2**) 201 BC Plu., *Phil.* 12

AKARNANIA:

—STRATOS: (**3**) a. 167 BC *IG* IX (2) 6 a, 2; cf. Stählin p. 220 (date) (I f. *Λύσιππος* II); (**4**) ~ *IG* IX (2) 6 a, 2; cf. Stählin p. 220 (date) (II s. *Λύσιππος* I)

ARGOLIS:

—ARGOS: (**5**) c. 365-335 BC *IG* IV (1)² 103, 53; (**6**) iii BC ib. IV (1) 618 I, 9 (f. —ος); (**7**) c. 220-200 BC *SEG* XI 414, 11 (Perlman E.5) (s. *Φείδιππος*); (**8**) 213 or 205 BC Nachtergael, *Les Galates* 66, 7; cf. Stephanis 2530 (f. *Φιλοκράτης*); (**9**) c. 210-207 BC *IG* IV (1)² 73, 7; *SEG* XXXV 303 (date) (s. *Δαμόκριτος*)

ARKADIA: (**10**) ?253 BC *IG* II² 3083, 10; Nachtergael, *Les Galates* 10, 17 (Stephanis 1587) (s. *Ξενότιμος*)

—MEGALOPOLIS: (**11**) c. 210-207 BC *IG* IV (1)² 73, 26; *SEG* XXXV 303 (date) (*Λύσιππ[ος]*: f. *Λυσίμαχος*)

—TEGEA: (**12**) iii BC *IG* v (2) 30, 6 (f. *Ἀριστοκλῆς*)

ELIS: (**13**) f. ii BC Moretti, *Olymp.* 621

—OLYMPIA*: (**14**) v BC *SEG* XI 1237 (-ιπος)

EPIROS: (**15**) inc. Schol. A.R. iv 1093-5 a (dub.)

ILLYRIA:

—EPIDAMNOS-DYRRHACHION: (**16**) c. 250-50 BC Ceka, *Probleme* p. 151 no. 41 (coin) (pryt.) ?= (*17*); (**17**) ~ Maier 284-7; 481 (coin) (Ceka 20; 36; 101; 135; 289) (pryt.) ?= (*16*); (**18**) hell.-imp. *IDyrrh* 442 (f. *Φιλυλλίς*)

KORINTHIA:

—KORINTH: (**19**) ?c. 550 BC *IG* IV (1) 314 (pinax) (-ιπος)

—SIKYON: (**20**) iv BC *RE* (6); Marcadé 1 66 ff.; *SEG* XXII 460, 7 (Skalet 201) (s. *Λυσ—*, f. *Βοΐδας, Δάιππος, Εὐθυκράτης*: sculptor); (**21**) ?184 BC Klee p. 8 II B, 9 (Stephanis 2835)

LAKONIA:

—SPARTA: (**22**) c. 401 BC X., *HG* iii 2. 29-30; Paus. iii 8. 5 (Poralla² 506) (*Λυσίστρατος*—Paus.); (**23**) c. 60-20 BC *IG* v (1) 211, 48; VII 420, 42, 54 (*IOrop* 528; Bradford (9)) (f. *Ἀρέτιππος*: mantis); (**24**) s. i BC *IG* v (1) 95, 20 (Bradford (5)) (s. *Πολλίων*); (**25**) c. 30-20 BC *IG* v (1) 142, 25 (Bradford (6)); (**26**) c. 1-10 AD *IG* v (1) 209, 30; *SEG* XXXV 331 (date) (Bradford (11)) (f. *Δαμοκράτης*); (**27**) ?i/ii AD *IG* v (1) 187 (*Λύσιππο[ς]*: f. —ης); (**28**) c. 90-100 AD *SEG* XI 558, 11; 613, [3]? (Bradford (-)) (-ιπος: f. *Ξενοκλῆς*); (**29**) c. 100-120 AD *IG* v (1) 80, 5; *SEG* XI 571 (Bradford (2)) (s. *Γάιος*); (**30**) c. 100-125 AD *IG* v (1) 51, 30; 103, 3 + *BSA* 27 (1925-6) p. 219; *SEG* XI 538, 2 (Bradford (3)) (f. (nat.) *Ἀλεξικράτης*); (**31**) c. 105-115 AD *IG* v (1) 20 B, 8; 51, 38; 52, 8; *SEG* XI 538, 6 (Bradford (10)) (f. *Ἀριστοκλῆς*); (**32**) c. 105-160 AD *IG* v (1) 32 B, 19; 65, 19; 85, 15; 114, 3; 128, 11; 292, 4; *SEG* XI 546 a, 5; 546 b, 5; XXXVI 361, 13 (Bradford (4); (13)) (s. *Φιλοχαρῖνος*, f. *Φιλοχαρῖνος*); (**33**) c. 115-130 AD *IG* v (1) 32 B, 15; 60, 2; 65, 24; *SEG* XI 544, 5; XXXVI 361, 23 (Bradford (3)) (s. *Μνάσων*) ?= (*36*); (**34**) c. 128-133 AD *IG* v (1) 486, 4; *SEG* XI 547 a, [8]; 547 b, 3; 547 c, 1; 579, 4 (*Γ. Ἰούλ. Λ.*: II ?s. *Λύσιππος* II); (**35**) c. 133 AD ib. 547 a, 8? ([*Λύσ*]ιπ[πος]?: I ?f. *Λύσιππος* II); (**36**) c. 147-170 AD *IG* v (1) 87, 7; 446, 8; *SEG* XI 486, [3]; 552, [4]; 585, 11; XXX 410, [17] (Bradford (1)) (f. *Μνάσων*) ?= (*33*); (**37**) c. 160-180 AD *IG* v (1) 531, 2; 680, 2; *BSA* 79 (1984) pp. 266-7 (ident., stemma) (Bradford (1)) (s. *Δαμαίνετος*)

—TAINARON-KAINEPOLIS: (**38**) 198-211 AD *SEG* XXIII 199, 16 (s. *Καλλιδαμίδας*)

MESSENIA:

—MESSENE: (**39**) f. iii BC ib. XLI 342, 13; cf. *PAE* 1991, p. 100 no. 8; (**40**) ?f. i AD ib. 1992, p. 79, 3 (f. (ad.) *Ἵππαρχος*)

—THOURIA: (**41**) f. ii BC *SEG* XI 972, 30 (s. *Δεινίας*)

S. ITALY (LUCANIA):

—HERAKLEIA: (**42**) ii/i BC Marcadé II 64-6 (I f. *Λύσιππος* II); (**43**) ~ *RE* (8); Marcadé II 64-6 (II s. *Λύσιππος* I: sculptor)

SICILY:

—KAMARINA?: (**44**) ?v/iv BC Manganaro, *PdelP* forthcoming no. 14

**Λῦσις**

AKARNANIA:

—THYRREION: (**1**) iii BC *IG* IX (1)² (2) 246, 9-10

ARGOLIS:

—ARGOS: (**2**) iii BC ib. IV (1) 527, 14; cf. *BCH* 37 (1913) p. 309

—TROIZEN: (**3**) ?146 BC *IG* IV (1) 757 B, 15 (s. *Ἀριστοκλῆς*)

LAKONIA:

—SPARTA: (**4**) 184 BC Plb. xxiii 4. 2 (Bradford (-))

S. ITALY (CALABRIA):

—TARAS-TARENTUM: (**5**) v/iv BC *RE* (2); *FVS* 46

SICILY:

—AKRAI: (**6**) s. vi BC *Akrai* p. 161 no. 20 (Dubois, *IGDS* 107) ([*Λ*]ῦσις: s. *Χίμαρος*)

**Λυσίς**

ARGOLIS:

—EPIDAUROS: (**1**) m. iv BC *IG* II² 8489 (d. *Ἡρόδωρος*)

SICILY:
—SYRACUSE: (2) iv/iii BC *Ag.* XVII 669 (*SEG* XIV 227) ([Λ]υσίς: d. Φιλικός)

**Λυσίστρατος**
ARGOLIS:
—ARGOS: (1) s. viii BC Paus. ii 36. 5
—EPIDAUROS: (2) c. 335-325 BC *IG* IV (1)² 106 I, 31 ([Λυ]σίστρατος?)
——(Hylleis): (3) 146 BC ib. 28, 49 (s. Σωκλῆς)
——Aphylonia (Azantioi): (4) m. iii BC ib. 96, 66 (Perlman E.3); Perlman p. 63 f. (date)
ARKADIA:
—TEGEA:
——(Krariotai): (5) f. iii BC *IG* v (2) 36, 62 (f. Ἀλκισθένης)
KERKYRA: (6) hell.? ib. IX (1) 891 (?f. Πειθίας)
KORINTHIA:
—KORINTH: (7) vii BC Paus. iv 19. 2; (8) ?411 BC *IG* XII (8) 402 (s. Εὐκλῆς)
—SIKYON: (9) f. iv BC *RE* (12) (Skalet 202) (sculptor)
LEUKAS: (10) iv BC Unp. (*IG* arch.) (f. Νίκαρχος)
MESSENIA:
—THOURIA: (11) f. ii BC *SEG* XI 972, 64 (s. Λυσικράτης)

**Λυσιφάνης**
ARGOLIS:
—EPIDAUROS:
——Miltias (Azantioi): (1) m. iii BC ib. 412, 72 (Perlman E.3); Perlman p. 63 f. (date)

**Λυσιώ**
EPIROS:
—BOUTHROTOS (PRASAIBOI): (1) a. 163 BC *IBouthrot* 66, 7; 75, 7

**Λυσίων**
ARGOLIS:
—ARGOS:
——(Aithaleis): (1) ii/i BC *BCH* 33 (1909) p. 176 no. 2, 16 (f. Φιλοκράτεια)
—EPIDAUROS: (2) c. 370 BC *IG* IV (1)² 102, 69, 102, 103, 264, 280, 287, 291
ARKADIA:
—MEGALOPOLIS: (3) c. 210 BC ib. IX (1)² (1) 31, 78 (s. Δαμόνικος)
EPIROS:
—AMBRAKIA: (4) a. 167 BC *SEG* XXXV 665 A, 11 (s. Ζωῖλος)
ILLYRIA:
—EPIDAMNOS-DYRRHACHION: (5) c. 250-50 BC Ceka, *Probleme* p. 151 no. 42 (coin) (pryt.) ?= (6); (6) ~ Maier 289-90; Münsterberg Nachtr. p. 16; *SNG Cop. Thessaly–Illyricum* 449 (coin) (Ceka 21; 26; 37; 294; 393) (pryt.) ?= (5); (7) ?ii-i BC *IG* XII (8) 196, 4; cf. *IDyrrh* 515 (s. Ἐ—)
KORINTHIA:
—SIKYON: (8) vi/v BC *SEG* XI 244, 13 (-ōν)
PELOPONNESE?: (9) s. iii BC *IG* v (1) 1426, 17 (f. Ἀλεξάνωρ)

**Λῦσος**
AKARNANIA:
—STRATOS: (1) f. iii BC ib. IX (1)² (2) 391, 9

**Λυσώ**
DALMATIA:
—TRAGURION: (1) hell.? *SEG* XXXI 613 (d. Σωσίας)
EPIROS:
—BOUTHROTOS: (2) iii-ii BC *IBouthrot* 195 (d. Λυσανίας)
—BOUTHROTOS (PRASAIBOI): (3) a. 163 BC ib. 53, 5 (*SEG* XXXVIII 504)
——Kotylaioi: (4) a. 163 BC *IBouthrot* 168, 8, 12 (*SEG* XXXVIII 469) (d. Λυσανίας)
—PHOINIKE: (5) c. 232-168 BC Cabanes, *L'Épire* p. 574 no. 48, 15 (*SEG* XXVI 721) (Λύσων?—Cabanes)
ILLYRIA:
—APOLLONIA: (6) iii-ii BC *IApoll* 33
KERKYRA?: (7) c. 200 BC *IBouthrot* 10; cf. *SEG* XXXVIII 464 (m. Ἀρίστων)
MESSENIA:
—MESSENE: (8) i BC *IG* v (1) 1480 (Λυσοι—lap.)
S. ITALY (BRUTTIUM):
—SYBARIS-THOURIOI-COPIAE: (9) c. 550 BC *SEG* XLI 853 (loomweight) (-σό)

**Λυσώι**
MESSENIA:
—MESSENE: (1) ii BC *Ergon* 1995, p. 29

**Λύσων**
ACHAIA:
—PATRAI: (1) m. i BC *RE* (2) (Lat. Lyso); (2) 32-31 BC *BMC Pelop.* p. 23 nos. 14-15; *RPC* I p. 259 no. 1245 (coin) (f. Ἀγίας)
AITOLIA:
—KALYDON: (3) s. ii BC *SEG* XXV 621, 3 (f. Λέων)
—PHILOTAIEIS?: (4) c. 157 BC *IG* IX (1)² (1) 108, 10
AKARNANIA:
—STRATOS: (5) 148 BC ib. IX (1)² (3) 640 e, 1; Pantos, *Sphragismata* p. 155 no. 127; p. 447 (Λύσων—*IG*)
ARGOLIS:
—HERMIONE: (6) s. iv BC *IG* IV (1)² 121, 125; (7) ?ii-i BC ib. IV (1) 733, 5 (s. Ἀγλωφάνης)
—TROIZEN: (8) ?146 BC ib. 757 B, 27, 28 (s. Ἀλφειόδωρος)
ELIS: (9) m. i AD *IvOl* 77, [6]; 82, 4 (f. Ἀγίας); (10) 67 AD ib. l. 13 (?f. —ρος) ?= (11); (11) ~ ib. l. 16 (f. Λέων) ?= (10); (12) c. 67-105 AD ib. l. [8]; 86, 4; 431-434 (Τιβ. Κλ. Λ. Κοσμόπολις: s. Τιβ. Κλ. Ἀγίας, Γιγανία Πῶλλα)
EPIROS: (13) iv/iii BC *IG* XII Suppl. 631 (f. Λυσίας: date—Knoepfler); (14) 234-168 BC Franke, *Münz. v. Epirus* p. 182 II ser. 50 (coin)
—EUROPIOI: (15) f. ii BC Cabanes, *L'Épire* p. 554 no. 33, 5 (*SEG* XXXVII 511)
ILLYRIA:
—APOLLONIA: (16) iii BC *IApoll* 5 (s. Ἀγέστρατος); (17) c. 250-50 BC Maier 108; Münsterberg Nachtr. p. 13 (Ceka 7; 97); Münsterberg p. 36 (Ceka 69; 93?; 96); Maier 69 (coin) (Ceka 126) (pryt.); (18) i BC *BMC Thessaly* p. 61 no. 75 (coin) ?= (19); (19) ~ Maier 151 (coin) (pryt.) ?= (18); (20) imp. *IApoll* 55 (s. Ἀντίμαχος)

—EPIDAMNOS-DYRRHACHION: (21) c. 200-172 BC *RA* 1948, p. 826 no. 2, 5 (*IDyrrh* 523) (Λού-: f. Ἰάσων)
MESSENIA:
—MESSENE: (22) ii/i BC *IG* v (1) 1437, 14; (23) 31 BC-14 AD *SEG* XXIII 207, 35 (s. Νίκιππος)
—THOURIA: (24) f. ii BC ib. XI 972, 18 (s. Δάμων)
S. ITALY (BRUTTIUM):
—LOKROI EPIZEPHYRIOI:
——(Τιω.): (25) 275 BC De Franciscis 10, 3; 25, 2 (f. Εὐφρονίσκος)
SICILY:
—GELA-PHINTIAS: (26) s. iv BC *IG* IV (1)² (1) 95, 86 (Perlman E.2); Perlman pp. 46-9 (date)
—LILYBAION: (27) ?i BC *IG* XIV 279 (*Semitica* 26 (1978) pp. 93 ff.; *Lilibeo* p. 124 no. 153) (s. Διόγνητος) ?= (28); (28) f. i BC Cic., *In Verr.* II iv 37 (Lat. Lyso) ?= (27) (29); (29) 46 or 45 BC ib. *ad Fam.* xiii 34 (Lat. Lyso: I f. Λύσων II) ?= (28); (30) ~ ib. (Lat. Lyso: II s. Λύσων I)
—MORGANTINA: (31) ?iv/iii BC *SEG* XXXIX 1008, 5 (s. Ἱππίας)

**Λυταίδα**
LEUKAS: (1) iv BC *AD* 26 (1971) Chron. p. 353 no. 3; cf. *SEG* XXVII 169 (nom., gen.?)

**Λυχνίς**
S. ITALY (CAMPANIA):
—DIKAIARCHIA-PUTEOLI: (1) imp. *CIL* X 2498 (Lat. Helvia Lychn[is]); (2) ~ ib. 2807; cf. *Puteoli* 11 (1987) p. 55 (Lat. [L]uchnis)

**Λύων**
ARGOLIS:
—HERMIONE: (1) ?c. 460-450 BC *IG* IV (1) 683 (Lazzarini 74); cf. *SEG* XI 378; *LSAG*² p. 181 no. 8 (date) (f. Ἀλεξίας); (2) ~ ib. *SEG* XI 379 a (f. Εὔφορος); (3) m. iv BC Unp. (Ch. Kritzas); (4) c. 370 BC *SEG* XI 379 b, 1 (f. Κλενάγορος)
ARKADIA:
—TEGEA: (5) m. iv BC *IG* v (2) 6, 90
LAKONIA:
—SPARTA: (6) c. 450-434 BC ib. v (1) 1228, 7; *LSAG*² p. 201 no. 53 (date) (Poralla² 507) (-ōν)

**Λώϊνος**
MESSENIA:
—MESSENE: (1) iii BC *SEG* XXIII 210, 3

**Λωρχίδας**
ELIS:
—PISA: (1) 365 BC ib. XXIX 405 b, 3 (Λωρχί[δας]?)

**Λωτός**
S. ITALY (BRUTTIUM):
—SYBARIS-THOURIOI-COPIAE: (1) f. i AD *NScav* 1970, Suppl. 3 p. 551 (Lat. T. Annius Lotus)
S. ITALY (CAMPANIA):
—POMPEII: (2) i BC-i AD *CIL* X 1050 (Castrèn 129. 27) (Lat. C. Cornelius Lotus)

# M

**Μάα**
SICILY:
—ACATE (MOD.): **(1)** iii-v AD *Rend. Pont.* 45 (1972-3) p. 191 no. 2 + Ferrua, *NG* 512 (*Μι-νία*—ed.)

**Μάαρκος**
EPIROS:
—BOUTHROTOS (PRASAIBOI): **(1)** a. 163 BC *IBouthrot* 29, 48 (*SEG* XXXVIII 487) (f. *Στρα-ταγίς*)
ILLYRIA:
—APOLLONIA: **(2)** c. 250-50 BC Maier 59 (coin) (Ceka 75) (money.)
—EPIDAMNOS-DYRRHACHION: **(3)** c. 250-50 BC Maier 264 (coin) (Ceka 301) (money.); **(4)** hell.-imp. *IDyrrh* 359 (f. *Πολλία*)

**Μαγγάνης**
SICILY:
—SYRACUSE: **(1)** iii-v AD Strazzulla 247 (Wessel 1206) (*Μανγά-*)

**Μάγης**
SICILY:
—GELA-PHINTIAS: **(1)** m. v BC Arena, *Iscr. Sic.* II 83 (vase) (*Μάγεδ* (gen.))

**Μαγίων**
KORINTHIA:
—KORINTH: **(1)** 105 AD *IG* V (1) 659, 1; *SEG* XI 835 (name) (*Γ. Ἥιος Μ.*)

**Μάγνης**
SICILY:
—SYRACUSE: **(1)** ?327 BC *BCH* 64-5 (1940-1) p. 144 B, 2 ([*Μ*]*άγ*[*νη*]*ς*: s. *Ἰαροκλῆς*)

**Μαγνησία**
S. ITALY (LUCANIA):
—HYELE-VELIA: **(1)** imp. *PdelP* 33 (1978) p. 64 no. 9 (Lat. Magnesia)
—VOLCEI: **(2)** imp. *IItal* III (1) 79 (*CIL* x 8115) (Lat. Magnisia)

**Μαγνήσιος**
S. ITALY (LUCANIA):
—POTENTIA: **(1)** ii-iii AD *ZPE* 106 (1995) p. 289 no. 9 (Lat. Magnesius: s. Prisca)

**Μάγνος**
SICILY:
—SYRACUSE: **(1)** iii-v AD *NScav* 1947, p. 211 no. 3; **(2)** ~ Strazzulla 173 (Wessel 153 A); cf. Ferrua, *NG* 14; **(3)** ~ ib. 397 (*Μά*[*γ*]*νος*)

**Μάγων**
SICILY:
—SELINOUS: **(1)** f. v BC Dubois, *IGDS* 38, 13, 17 (Arena, *Iscr. Sic.* I 63) (-*γōν*: f. *Ἔκοτις*)

**Μαδήνα**
ILLYRIA:
—EPIDAMNOS-DYRRHACHION: **(1)** hell.-imp. *IDyrrh* 43; **(2)** ~ ib. 111 (*Ἀντωνία Μ.*)

**Μαζάν**
SICILY:
—KAMARINA: **(1)** f. v BC Cordano, *Tessere Pubbliche* 18 (s. *Σωσίας*)

**Μαθαῖος**
SICILY:
—MORGANTINA (NR.): **(1)** hell. Manganaro, *PdelP* forthcoming no. 9

**Μαθθέας**
KORINTHIA:
—KORINTH: **(1)** byz. *Corinth* VIII (3) 564, 1; cf. *TMByz* 9 (1985) p. 366 no. 68

**Μαθις**
DALMATIA:
—PHAROS: **(1)** iv BC Brunšmid p. 20 no. 5 (s./d. *Πύθεος*)

**Μαία**
AKARNANIA:
—PALAIROS: **(1)** hell.-imp. *IG* IX (1)² (2) 379
SICILY:
—HERBESSOS: **(2)** ?s. vi BC *Kokalos* 14-15 (1968-9) p. 200 (vase); cf. Dubois, *IGDS* 168 d

**Μαίεις**
S. ITALY (BRUTTIUM):
—HIPPONION-VIBO VALENTIA: **(1)** hell. *Klearchos* 16 (1974) p. 82 (tile)

**Μαίκιος**
KORINTHIA:
—KORINTH: **(1)** f. iii AD *Corinth* IV (2) p. 209 no. 750 (lamp)

**Μάιος**
S. ITALY (CAMPANIA):
—PITHEKOUSSAI-AENARIA: **(1)** ?s. iii BC *IG* XIV 894; *BE* 1951, no. 252 (date) (s. *Πάκυλλος*)

**Μαῖσις**
LAKONIA:
—SPARTA: **(1)** her. Paus. iii 15. 8 (*RE* (-)) (s. *Ὑραῖος*: dub.)

**Μαίσων**
ILLYRIA:
—APOLLONIA:
——(Amphineis): **(1)** iii BC Robert, *Hell.* 10 p. 283 ff.; cf. *CRAI* 1991, p. 197 ff.; *L'Illyrie mérid.* 2 p. 204 f. (s. *Φιλωνίδας*)

**Μαίων**
ARKADIA:
—TEGEA: **(1)** m. ii AD *IG* V (2) 48, 5
SICILY: **(2)** hell. Vandermersch p. 169 (amph.) (or S. Italy: *Μαίω*[*ν*], *Μάιος*?)

**Μαίωρ**
ARGOLIS:
—EPIDAUROS: **(1)** 307 AD *IG* IV (1)² 433

**Μακαρία**
S. ITALY (CALABRIA):
—BRENTESION-BRUNDISIUM: **(1)** imp. *CIL* IX 119 (Lat. Gabinia Magaria)
S. ITALY (CAMPANIA):
—MISENUM*: **(2)** imp. ib. x 3628 (Lat. Silia Macaria: freed.)
SICILY:
—HALAISA: **(3)** iii-v AD Ferrua, *NG* 526
—KATANE: **(4)** iii-v AD Agnello 57 (Wessel 823) (*Μ. Εὐαγγελίς* (n. pr.?))

**Μακάριος**
LAKONIA:
—SPARTA: **(1)** 426 BC Th. iii 100. 2; 109. 1 (Poralla² 508)
S. ITALY (APULIA):
—LARINUM: **(2)** imp. *CIL* IX 757 (Lat. Macarius: s. Fructosa)
SICILY:
—SYRACUSE: **(3)** iii-v AD *IG* XIV 146 (Strazzulla 87; Agnello 45; Wessel 539) (*Μακάρι*[*ος*], *Μα-καρί*[*α*]?)

**Μακεδονία**
KORINTHIA:
—KORINTH: **(1)** byz. *Corinth* VIII (3) 644, 2; cf. *TMByz* 9 (1985) p. 362 no. 29
SICILY:
—SYRACUSE: **(2)** iii-v AD Wessel 1056 (*SEG* XXXIX 1025)

**Μακεδονικός**
SICILY:
—THERMAI HIMERAIAI*: **(1)** 27-22 BC *CIL* x 7351 (*ILat. Term. Imer.* 16) (Lat. M. Livius Macedonicus: freed.?)

**Μακεδόνιος**
KORINTHIA:
—KORINTH: **(1)** byz. *Corinth* VIII (3) 602; cf. *TMByz* 9 (1985) p. 366 no. 71

**Μακεδών**
ILLYRIA:
—APOLLONIA: **(1)** ii AD *IApoll* 116; **(2)** ~ ib. 117 (*Μακεδ*[*ών*]: ?s. *Θεαγ*—)
KERKYRA: **(3)** hell.? *IG* IX (1) 885 (n. pr.?: s. *Μεγάθυρσος*)
LAKONIA:
—SPARTA: **(4)** i BC/i AD? ib. v (1) 616 (Bradford (1)); **(5)** ii AD *IG* v (1) 176, 3 (Bradford (2)) (f. *Κλαυδιανός*)
—TAINARON-KAINEPOLIS*: **(6)** imp. *IG* v (1) 1268 (*Αὐφίδιος Μ.*)
S. ITALY (BRUTTIUM):
—TRAPEIA: **(7)** byz. *ICI* v 11 (Lat. Macedo)
S. ITALY (CAMPANIA):
—DIKAIARCHIA-PUTEOLI: **(8)** ?ii AD *CIL* x 2436 (Lat. Flavius Macedo); **(9)** ii AD *Puteoli* 11 (1987) p. 129 no. 2 (Lat. Macedo: f. P. Clodius Celsianus)
—MISENUM*: **(10)** ?ii-iii AD *CIL* x 3366 (Lat. Aurelius Macedo: f. Aurelia Iulia)
SICILY:
—SYRACUSE: **(11)** iii-v AD ib. 7149 (Strazzulla 427; Agnello 72); cf. Ferrua, *NG* 185 (Lat. Dominicus Macedo)
SICILY?: **(12)** iii AD *Epigraphica* 3 (1941) p. 267 no. 37 (*ILat. Palermo* 88) (Lat. C. Iulius Macedo)

**Μακέτα**
ILLYRIA:
—BYLLIONES BYLLIS: **(1)** iii AD *SEG* XXXVIII 554 (*Μακάτα*—ed.: d. *Σωσιπάτρα*)

**Μακίας**
ARGOLIS:
—ARGOS: **(1)** imp. *IG* IV (1) 546 (tiles) (*Κορ*(*ν*). *Μ.*)

**Μακρίνα**
SICILY:
—SYRACUSE: **(1)** iii-v AD *SEG* IV 4 (Wessel 938); cf. Ferrua, *NG* 270 (*Μαρκῖνα*—lap., *Μαρκι*(*α*)*νά*—Ferrua)

**Μακρῖνος**
ELIS:
—OLYMPIA*: **(1)** byz. *IvOl* 811 (-*κρεῖ*-)

**Μάκρων**
S. ITALY (CALABRIA):
—TARAS-TARENTUM: **(1)** inc. *Mon. Piot* 30 (1929) p. 53 no. 5; cf. Wuilleumier, *Tarente* p. 420 n. 1 ([*Μ*]*άκρω*[*ν*]?, *Ἄκρω*[*ν*]?)
SICILY:
—SOLOUS: **(2)** f. i BC Cic., *In Verr.* II ii 102 (Lat. Posides Macro)

**Μαλακός**
S. ITALY (CAMPANIA):
—KYME: **(1)** vi/v BC *RE* s.v. Aristodemos (8) (*Ἀριστόδημος ὁ ἐπικαλ. Μ.*: s. *Ἀριστοκράτης*: tyrant)

**Μαλάκων**
ELIS:
—PYLOS: (1) s. iii BC *SEG* XXV 459

**Μαλαυῖδας**
LAKONIA:
—GERENIA: (1) v BC *IG* v (1) 1337; Masson, *OGS* 2 p. 512 (name) (Poralla² 509) (Μαλαυή{δ]ας: s. Νικόλοχος)

**Μάληκος**
ARKADIA:
—PHIGALEIA: (1) v BC *IG* v (2) 425, 5 (-λε̄-)
KORINTHIA:
—KORINTH: (2) vii/vi BC Amyx Gr 5 a. 6 (vase) (Lorber 2 a) (-λε̄ρος)

**Μάληξ**
ELIS?: (1) v BC *IvOl* 13, 1 (f. Τιμοκράτης)

**Μάλης**
AITOLIA: (1) f. vi BC Hdt. vi 127

**Μαλία**
SICILY:
—SYRACUSE: (1) iii-v AD Strazzulla 236 (Barreca 249)

**Μαλιάδας**
ELIS: (1) f. i BC *IvOl* 399 (s. Χαιρόλας)

**Μαλίκα**
EPIROS:
—BOUTHROTOS (PRASAIBOI): (1) a. 163 BC *IBouthrot* 141, 9

**Μάλιος**
SICILY:
—SYRACUSE: (1) iii-v AD Strazzulla 283; cf. Ferrua, *NG* 51 ([Μ]άλιος, [Εὐλ]άλιος?—Ferrua)

**Μαλίχα**
LAKONIA:
—KYTHERA: (1) f. iv BC *IG* II² 9112 (*GVI* 493)

**Μαλλίκα**
ILLYRIA:
—EPIDAMNOS-DYRRHACHION: (1) hell.-imp. *IDyrrh* 298 (d. Ἐπίκαδος)

**Μάλλιος**
ELIS: (1) ?i AD *EA* 1905, p. 259 no. 2, 12 (f. Μᾶρκος)

**Μάλλος**
ARKADIA:
—ORESTHASION?: (1) v BC *IG* IX (2) 1098 (Lazzarini 740) (f. Πατροκλέας)
S. ITALY (CALABRIA):
—TARAS-TARENTUM: (2) imp. *NScav* 1894, p. 68 no. 48 (Lat. M. A[nto]nius Mallus)
S. ITALY (CAMPANIA):
—DIKAIARCHIA-PUTEOLI: (3) imp. *CIL* X 1912 (Lat. Mallus)

**Μᾶλος**
ARKADIA:
—MEGALOPOLIS: (1) ii/i BC *IG* v (2) 442, 17 (s. Μαντίας)
LAKONIA:
—KYTHERA: (2) v BC *SEG* XXII 300; *LSAG*² p. 447 no. 51c (her.?)

**Μαλούσιος**
AITOLIA:
—THERMOS*: (1) s. iii BC *IG* IX (1)² (1) 60 II, 14

**Μαλχίς**
S. ITALY (CALABRIA):
—BRENTESION-BRUNDISIUM*: (1) i-ii AD *Epigraphica* 25 (1963) p. 57 no. 44 (Lat. Sentia Malchis: freed.)

**Μαλχίων**
KORINTHIA:
—KORINTH: (1) imp. *IG* IV (1) 401 (f. Νικηφόρος: Jew?)
S. ITALY (CAMPANIA):
—DIKAIARCHIA-PUTEOLI: (2) imp. *CIL* X 2644 (Lat. Egnatius Malchio)
—DIKAIARCHIA-PUTEOLI*: (3) i-ii AD *NScav* 1913, p. 24 no. 1 (Lat. Malchio: imp. freed.)
—HERCULANEUM: (4) m. i AD *PdelP* 3 (1948) p. 177 no. 23 (Lat. T. Hordionius Malchio)
—POMPEII: (5) i BC-i AD *NScav* 1898, p. 499 (Castrèn 260. 1) (Lat. M. Mundicius Malchio)
—POMPEII*: (6) i BC-i AD *Römische Gräberstrassen* p. 212 a (Lat. Malchio: freed.); (7) ~ ib. p. 212 b (Lat. M. Blaesius Malchio: freed.)

**Μάλχος**
S. ITALY (CAMPANIA):
—MISENUM: (1) imp. *Eph. Ep.* VIII 431 (Lat. Malchus)

**Μαλώι**
KORINTHIA:
—KORINTH: (1) c. 570-550 BC Amyx 74. 7 (vase) (Lorber 129) (-λόι: her.)

**Μάμαρκος**
S. ITALY (CAMPANIA):
—NEAPOLIS: (1) iii/ii BC *IG* XIV 718 (*INap* 5) (f. —ανός); (2) i BC ib. 146; cf. Leiwo p. 83 no. 28 (f. Μονίς); (3) ~ *INap* 165; cf. Leiwo p. 83 no. 26 (f. Στατία); (4) s. i BC *INap* 141; cf. Leiwo p. 83 no. 27 (s. Τίνθωρ)
SICILY: (5) iv/iii BC Vandermersch p. 170 (amph.) (or S. Italy: Μάμαρ(κος)?, Μαμαρ(τίνων) (ethn.?))
—KENTORIPA*: (6) hell. *Cron. Arch.* 16 (1977) p. 151 n. 18 (bullet) (n. pr.?: ?f. Δαμάτριος)

**Μάμαρχος**
DALMATIA:
—ISSA: (1) iii BC Brunšmid p. 9 fr. G, 5 (f. Ἀριστίων)

**Μάμερκος**
SICILY:
—HIMERA: (1) vii/vi BC *RE* (1); cf. s.v. Stesichoros (1) (or Sicily Matauros)
—KATANE: (2) m. iv BC ib. (2) ?= (Μᾶρκος (34))

**Μαμερτίνας**
EPIROS:
—DODONA: (1) iii BC Antoniou, *Dodone* Ba, 19 ([Μαμ]ε[ρτ]ίνας)

**Μαμερτῖνος**
SICILY:
—HIMERA?: (1) vii/vi BC *Suda* Σ 1095 (?s. Εὔφημος, Εὔφορβος, Εὐκλείδης, Εὐέτης)
—ZANKLE-MESSANA: (2) iv-iii BC *SEG* XXX 1121, 27 (Μνᾶτος Κορούϊος Μ. (n. pr.?))

**Μαμεύς**
SICILY:
—SYRACUSE: (1) iv/iii BC D.S. xxii 7. 2 (f. Θοίνων)

**Μαμμάρειος**
SICILY:
—SELINOUS: (1) m. v BC Dubois, *IGDS* 36, 5 (Arena, *Iscr. Sic.* 1 69) (f. Ἰχαίων)

**Μαμμία**
ARKADIA:
—MEGALOPOLIS: (1) ii-iii AD *IG* v (2) 492 (Ἀσιννία Μ.)

**Μᾶμος**
S. ITALY (CAMPANIA):
—NEAPOLIS: (1) i BC/i AD *INap* 93; cf. Leiwo p. 74 no. 17 (f. Ἀπολλόδωρος); (2) ~ *INap* 142; cf. Leiwo p. 74 no. 19 and p. 123 no. 110 (I f. Μᾶμος II, Νύμφιος); (3) ~ *INap* 142; cf. Leiwo p. 74 no. 19 and p. 123 no. 110 (II s. Μᾶμος I)
SICILY:
—ENTELLA: (4) iv/iii BC *SEG* XXX 1120, 2 (Dubois, *IGDS* 207) (f. Θεόδωρος)

**Μανδρηκίδας**
ARKADIA:
—MANTINEIA-ANTIGONEIA: (1) 64 or 62 BC *IG* v (2) 265, 49 (f. Ἀλκαμένης)

**Μανδροκλείδας**
LAKONIA:
—SPARTA: (1) c. 310-241 BC *RE* (1); (2) (Bradford (-)) (s. Ἐκφάνης) ?= (Δερκυλίδας (2))

**Μανδροκλῆς**
SICILY:
—MEGARA HYBLAIA: (1) m. vi BC Guarducci, *Ep. Gr.* 1 p. 314 no. 5 (Dubois, *IGDS* 22; Arena, *Iscr. Sic.* 1 3) (f. Σωμροτίδας)

**Μάνης**
S. ITALY (APULIA):
—CANUSIUM*: (1) imp. *Epig. Rom. di Canosa* 160 (*CIL* IX 392) (Lat. P. Minucius Manes: freed.)

**Μανία**
ARGOLIS:
—HERMIONE: (1) imp. *SEG* XVII 176

**Μανίδας**
ACHAIA:
—AIGEIRA: (1) s. iv BC *BCH* 62 (1938) p. 341 (s. Ἀψέφης)

**Μαννήϊα**
KERKYRA: (1) ?i AD *IG* IX (1) 942

**Μάννικος**
ILLYRIA:
—EPIDAMNOS-DYRRHACHION: (1) hell.-imp. *IDyrrh* 69 (f. Ἀβαία)

**Μαννίνα**
S. ITALY (APULIA):
—VENUSIA: (1) v AD *JIWE* 1 62 (*CIJ* 1 590) (Μαννίνες (gen.): d. Λογγῖνος: Jew)

**Μαντιάδας**
ACHAIA:
—DYME?: (1) ?f. iii BC *HE* 2875 (s. Ἔχελλος)
ILLYRIA:
—EPIDAMNOS-DYRRHACHION: (2) c. 250-50 BC Maier 291; Münsterberg Nachtr. p. 16 (coin) (Ceka 343; 417) (pryt.)

**Μαντίας**
ARKADIA: (1) c. 247-199 BC *SGDI* 2609, 3 (s. Πρωτογένης)
—MANTINEIA-ANTIGONEIA: (2) c. 300-221 BC *IG* v (2) 323. 65 (tessera) (s. Σάστρατος)
—MEGALOPOLIS: (3) ii/i BC ib. 442, 17 (Μαν[τίας]?: f. Μᾶλος)
—STYMPHALOS: (4) iii BC ib. 356, 5
—TEGEA: (5) m. iv BC ib. 6, 80

**Μαντικλῆς**
LAKONIA:
—SPARTA: (1) c. 1-10 AD ib. v (1) 209, 18; *SEG* XXXV 331 (date) (Bradford (-)) (s. Σωσικράτης)

**Μάντικλος**
MESSENIA: (1) vii BC *RE* (2) (s. Θέοκλος)

**Μαντικράτης**
MESSENIA:
—MESSENE: (1) 243 BC *SEG* XII 371, 18 (f. Δαμόνικος); (2) 208 or 207 BC *FD* III (4) 21, 2; 22, 8 (f. Μνασάγορος); (3) ii-i BC *SEG* XLI

343, 9 ([M]αντικράτης); (4) 33 AD ib. 335, 6 (f. Δαμόνικος)

**Μαντικρέτης**
ARKADIA:
—MANTINEIA-ANTIGONEIA:
——(Posoidaia): (1) c. 425-400 BC ib. XXXI 348, 14 (Μαντικρέ[τ]η[s])

**Μάντις**
S. ITALY (LUCANIA):
—ATINA LUCANA: (1) iv-iii BC NScav 1901, p. 503 (loomweight) (n. pr.?)

**Μάξιμα**
ILLYRIA:
—EPIDAMNOS-DYRRHACHION: (1) hell.-imp. IDyrrh 299 (d. Βάργος)
SICILY:
—HALIKYAI: (2) s. vi AD Agnello 67 (mosaic) (SEG XXXVI 828) (Μά[ξ]ιμα)

**Μαξιμῖνος**
ILLYRIA:
—APOLLONIA: (1) imp. IApoll 218 (Μα(ξ)ιμῖνος)

**Μάξιμος**
ELIS: (1) c. 177-189 AD IvOl 138, 3 (M[ά]ξιμος)
EPIROS:
—NIKOPOLIS: (2) iii-iv AD SEG XXXIV 596
KORINTHIA:
—KORINTH: (3) ?ii AD IG IV (1) 442 (I f. Λ. Σερβίλιος Μάξιμος II); (4) byz. Corinth VIII (3) 540, 5; cf. TMByz 9 (1985) p. 365 no. 57
SICILY:
—SYRACUSE: (5) iii-v AD Strazzulla 249 b (Wessel 1063); cf. Riv. Arch. Crist. 18 (1941) p. 168 no. 29 (f. Ἑρμιόνη)
—THERMAI HIMERAIAI: (6) imp. IG XIV 324 (s. Δίδυμος); (7) ~ ib. 325 (s. Ἰάσων)

**Μαξιμοῦλα**
SICILY:
—KATANE: (1) ?v AD Sic. Gymn. 14 (1961) p. 196

**Μάπιλλα**
ITHAKE: (1) iv BC AM 27 (1902) p. 377 no. 61; cf. REG 15 (1902) p. 132 no. 4 (reading—Strauch)

**Μάρα**
S. ITALY (BRUTTIUM):
—BRETTIOI: (1) hell.-imp. AD 22 (1967) Chron. p. 539 no. [17] (Μαραβρετία—ed.)

**Μαραῖος**
LEUKAS: (1) c. 167-50 BC BMC Thessaly p. 184 nos. 154-5; SNG Cop. Epirus-Acarnania 392; SNG Lockett 1679 (coins)
S. ITALY (CAMPANIA):
—MAMERTINOI: (2) hell. SB 417 f (s. Βακχεῖος)
—NEAPOLIS: (3) i BC/i AD INap 109, 8; cf. Leiwo p. 77 no. 21 (Μαραῖος: f. Χαιρέας); (4) ~ INap 110; cf. Leiwo p. 85 no. 34 (s. Νύμφιος)

**Μαρακός**
SICILY:
—SYRACUSE: (1) ?v-iv BC Arist., Pr. 954 a 38

**Μαργαρίς**
S. ITALY (BRUTTIUM):
—LOKROI EPIZEPHYRIOI: (1) iii-iv AD Costabile, Municipium Locrensium 36 (Lat. Margaris: m. Χαρίτη)
S. ITALY (CAMPANIA):
—DIKAIARCHIA-PUTEOLI: (2) imp. CIL X 2261 (Lat. Rutilia Margaris); (3) ~ ib. 2707 (Lat. Margaris)
—DIKAIARCHIA-PUTEOLI*: (4) imp. ib. 2708 (Lat. Margaris: freed.)
—POMPEII: (5) 61 AD ib. IV 3340. 155, 7, 31 (Castrèn 149. 3) (Lat. Dicidia Margaris)

SICILY:
—THERMAI HIMERAIAI: (6) imp. CIL X 7420 (ILat. Term. Imer. 118) (Lat. Margar[is])

**Μαργαρίτα**
S. ITALY (CAMPANIA):
—MISENUM*: (1) ?i-ii AD CIL X 3358 (Lat. Staberia Margarita: freed.)

**Μάργος**
ACHAIA:
—KARYNEIA: (1) iii BC RE (1)
ARGOLIS:
—HERMIONE: (2) iii BC IG IV (1) 729 II, 3 (f. Βάρις); (3) ~ ib. l. 5 (s. Ἀκέστωρ)

**Μαρδόνιος**
LAKONIA:
—SPARTA: (1) ii BC SEG XI 856, 1 (Bradford (-)) (Μαρδόν[ιος])

**Μάρθα**
LAKONIA: (1) ii-iii AD SEG XIV 637 (IGUR 771) (Jew)
S. ITALY (CAMPANIA):
—DIKAIARCHIA-PUTEOLI: (2) i AD Puteoli 7-8 (1983-4) p. 306 no. 6 (Lat. Iulia Martha)

**Μαρία**
AIGINA: (1) v-vi AD IG IV (1) 54 (M. ἡ καὶ Πατρικία)
KORINTHIA:
—KORINTH: (2) byz. Corinth VIII (3) 564, 3; cf. TMByz 9 (1985) p. 366 no. 68; (3) s. iv AD Corinth VIII (3) 530, 1; cf. TMByz 9 (1985) p. 362 no. 34; (4) v-vi AD SEG XXIX 315 (m. Ἰώαννα)
S. ITALY (BRUTTIUM):
—RHEGION: (5) 530 AD Wessel 692 (SEG XL 861)
S. ITALY (CALABRIA):
—TARAS-TARENTUM: (6) ?i-ii AD CIL IX 246 (Lat. Iulia Maria)
S. ITALY (CAMPANIA):
—DIKAIARCHIA-PUTEOLI: (7) ?i-ii AD ib. X 2292 (Lat. Claudia Maria)
—NEAPOLIS: (8) iii-iv AD INap 259; (9) vi-vii AD ib. 266
—POMPEII: (10) i BC-i AD CIL IV 1507, 6 (Lat. Maria); (11) ~ ib. 8224 (Lat. Maria); (12) 70-79 AD ib. 7866; Mouritsen p. 110 (date) (Lat. Maria)
SICILY:
—LILYBAION: (13) imp. IGLMP 20 (Lilibeo p. 166 no. 186)

**Μαριανός**
SICILY:
—SYRACUSE: (1) iii-v AD Strazzulla 282 (Barreca 252)

**Μαρῖνος**
KORINTHIA:
—KORINTH: (1) byz. Corinth VIII (1) 215, 6; (2) ~ ib. VIII (3) 722

**Μάριος**
ILLYRIA:
—APOLLONIA: (1) imp. IApoll 251 (-ρει-: f. Εὐνοῦς)

**Μάρις**
S. ITALY (CAMPANIA):
—NOLA: (1) iv-v AD JIWE I 22 (SEG XXIX 968) (Ἀββᾶ M.: Jew)
SICILY: (2) iii-v AD Wessel 2
—SYRACUSE: (3) iii-v AD Strazzulla 443 (-ρης); (4) ~ Ferrua, NG 263; (5) iv-v AD Führer-Schultze p. 294 (Wessel 712)

**Μαρίων**
S. ITALY (CAMPANIA):
—HERCULANEUM: (1) i BC-i AD Ann. S. Chiara 13 (1963) pp. 304-9 (Lat. Mario)
—NEAPOLIS*: (2) imp. Mon. Ant. 8 (1898) p. 223 (Lat. L. Licinius Mario: s. Νίκη: freed.)

**Μαρκαρίων**
SICILY:
—LEONTINOI: (1) ?iii-iv AD MEFRA 106 (1994) p. 89 no. 7 (M. Βαλέρις Μαρκαρίων)

**Μάρκελλα**
SICILY:
—SYRACUSE: (1) iii-v AD IG XIV 147 (Strazzulla 88); (2) ~ IG XIV 152 (Strazzulla 93; Agnello 8; Wessel 492); cf. ASSicilia 1938-9, p. 35 (name) (Μάσκελλα—lap., Μά(ρ)κελλα—Wessel)

**Μαρκελλῖνα**
SICILY:
—SYRACUSE: (1) iii-v AD IG XIV 148 (Strazzulla 89; Wessel 1369)

**Μαρκελλῖνος**
KORINTHIA:
—KORINTH: (1) vii-viii AD SEG XXIX 307
MESSENIA:
—PROTE*: (2) imp. ib. XI 1021 (-λεῖ-)

**Μάρκελλος**
ILLYRIA:
—BYLLIONES (GRESHICE (MOD.)): (1) iii AD ib. XXXVIII 543 (-κελος)
S. ITALY (APULIA):
—VENUSIA: (2) iv-v AD JIWE I 114 (Jew)
S. ITALY (CAMPANIA):
—NEAPOLIS?: (3) ii AD IG XIV 807 (INap 158)

**Μαρκία**
ARGOLIS:
—ARGOS: (1) imp. SEG XVI 262, 5
SICILY:
—SYRACUSE: (2) iii-v AD Strazzulla 148 (Führer-Schultze p. 305; Wessel 496); cf. Ferrua, NG 330 c; (3) ~ ib. 206 (m. Διονύσις)

**Μαρκιανή**
KYNOURIA:
—EUA?: (1) imp. IG IV (1) 678
S. ITALY (LUCANIA):
—POTENTIA (NR.): (2) imp. CIL X 8090 = NScav 1881, p. 123 (Lat. Sabia Marciane)
SICILY:
—AKRAI: (3) iii-v AD IG XIV 238 (Agnello 65; Wessel 615; Akrai p. 168 no. 44); cf. Ferrua, NG 492 (Μάριννα—Wessel)

**Μαρκιανός**
ILLYRIA:
—APOLLONIA: (1) ii AD IApoll 205
KORINTHIA:
—KORINTH: (2) ii-iii AD Corinth IV (2) p. 191 no. 583; SEG XXVII 35. 16 (lamps)
S. ITALY (CAMPANIA):
—NEAPOLIS: (3) iii-iv AD IG XIV 826. 27 (INap 238) (-κει-)
SICILY:
—SYRACUSE: (4) ?ii AD NScav 1947, p. 202; (5) iii-v AD IG XIV 149 (Strazzulla 90); (6) ~ IG XIV 150 (Strazzulla 91; Agnello 6; Wessel 839); (7) ~ SEG XIV 592; (8) ~ Strazzulla 262 (Agnello 21; Wessel 857); (9) 423 AD Strazzulla 384 (Barreca 246)

**Μαρκίων**
KORINTHIA:
—KORINTH: (1) ?iii AD Hesp. 63 (1994) pp. 116 ff. no. 5 col. V, 6-8 (lead) (M. ὁ καὶ Θηριώτης)
S. ITALY (CAMPANIA):
—KYME: (2) ?i-ii AD CIL X 3692 (Lat. Ti. Claudius Marcion)

SICILY:
—THERMAI HIMERAIAI: (3) imp. *IG* XIV 327 (I
f. *Μαρκίων* II); (4) ~ ib. (II s. *Μαρκίων* I)

**Μᾶρκος**
AIGINA: (1) imp. ib. IV (1) 131 ([*M*]ᾶρκος: ?s.
*Πάρος*); (2) ?f. i AD *Alt-Ägina* 1 (2) p. 45 no.
17, 2 (f. *Σωτηρίων*)
ARGOLIS:
—ARGOS: (3) imp. *SEG* XVI 263
—EPIDAUROS: (4) f. iii AD *IG* IV (1)² 407, 2, 6;
410, 3, 5; 411 + Peek, *IAEpid* 166 (s. *Ἑρμαΐ-
σκος*, f. *Ἐπαφρᾶς*, *Ἑρμαΐσκος*)
ARKADIA:
—MANTINEIA-ANTIGONEIA: (5) ?16 AD *IG* V (2)
274, 4 (s. *Τίτος*)
—TEGEA: (6) imp. *SEG* XXXVI 384; (7) 165 AD
*IG* V (2) 50, 2 (f. *Σωτηρᾶς*); (8) ~ ib. l. 19 (s.
*Σωσικράτης*)
ELIS: (9) i AD *IvOl* 444 (I f. *Μᾶρκος* II); (10) ~
ib. (II s. *Μᾶρκος* I, f. *Μᾶρκος* III); (11) ~ ib.
(III s. *Μᾶρκος* II); (12) ?i AD *EA* 1905, p. 259
no. 2, 12 ([*M*]ᾶρκος: s. *Μάλλιος*); (13) 113 AD
*IvOl* 90, 4; 94, 4 (s. *Φαῦστος: Γ.*); (14) 197-
201 AD ib. 106, 5; (15) iii AD *SEG* XV 259, 3
(f. —*ρος*)
EPIROS:
—BOUTHROTOS (PRASAIBOI): (16) a. 163 BC
*IBouthrot* 21, 9, 11 (*SEG* XXXVIII 478) (f.
*Ἀφροδίσιος*)
—NIKOPOLIS: (17) imp. *JHS* 74 (1954) p. 159
(Sarikakis 104) (I f. *Μᾶρκος* II); (18) ~ *JHS*
74 (1954) p. 159 (Sarikakis 103) (II s. *Μᾶρκος*
I); (19) ~ *SEG* XXVII 234
ILLYRIA:
—APOLLONIA: (20) i BC *IApoll* 219 (s. *Θάλαμος*)
—EPIDAMNOS-DYRRHACHION: (21) hell.-imp.
*IDyrrh* 303
—EPIDAMNOS-DYRRHACHION (NR.)?: (22) ii BC
*SEG* XXXVIII 572, 3; cf. *CRAI* 1991, p. 197
ff.; *L'Illyrie mérid.* 2 p. 206
KORINTHIA:
—KORINTH: (23) ii-iii AD *SEG* XXVII 35. 17
(lamp)
LAKONIA:
—GYTHEION: (24) imp. *IG* V (1) 1201
—SPARTA: (25) c. 120-140 AD ib. 1315, 22; *SEG*
XI 522, 6; 548, 16; 575, 10 (Bradford (4)) (f.
*Νικηφόρος*); (26) c. 140-160 AD *IG* V (1) 154,
3 (Bradford (5)) (f. *Ζώσιμος*); (27) c. 150-160
AD *SEG* XI 585, 11; XXX 410, 15 (Bradford
(2)) (s. *Νικηφόρος*); (28) c. 160-170 AD *IG* V
(1) 109, 10 (Bradford (1)) (s. *Δαμοκράτης*)
—SPARTA?: (29) i AD *SEG* XI 948, 20 (sculptor)
MESSENIA:
—KORONE: (30) i AD *IG* V (1) 1400
—MESSENE: (31) imp. ib. 1485
—THOURIA: (32) 102-114 AD ib. 1381, 8 (s. *Σώ-
των*)
SICILY:
—ERYX: (33) inc. *ASSiciliano* 1887, p. 298 no.
811 (vase)
—KATANE: (34) c. 390-340 BC *RE* (1); *IG* IV
(1)² 95, 72 (Perlman E.2); D.S. XVI 69. 4; cf.
*Chiron* 22 (1992) p. 390 n. 88 (f. *Κῖπος*: ty-
rant) ?= (*Μάμερκος* (2))

**Μαρμορίς**
S. ITALY (APULIA):
—LUCERIA*: (1) imp. *CIL* IX 887 (Lat. Servia
Marmoris: freed.)

**Μάρπησσα**
ARKADIA:
—TEGEA: (1) her. Paus. VIII 47. 2; 48. 5 (*M. ἡ
Χοίρα ἐπονομαζομένη*)

**Μαρσύας**
AITOLIA: (1) 207-205 BC *SEG* XII 217, 8
(XXXVIII 412) (*Μαρσ*[*ύας*])
—THERMOS*: (2) iii BC *IG* IX (1)² (1) 60 III, 14

ARGOLIS:
—EPIDAUROS*: (3) c. 370 BC ib. IV (1)² 102, 66
KORINTHIA:
—SIKYON: (4) ?255 BC Nachtergael, *Les Galates*
8, 41 (Skalet 203; Stephanis 1616) (s. *Χαρίτι-
μος*)
SICILY:
—SYRACUSE?: (5) c. 405-367 BC Plu., *Dio* 9
TRIPHYLIA: (6) s. iv BC *IG* II² 10461, 1 (s. *Ἀν-
δροκλῆς*)

**Μαρτίαλις**
ARGOLIS:
—NEMEA*: (1) imp. *SEG* XXIX 349 j + *Nemea
Guide* p. 191

**Μαρτίνη**
S. ITALY (APULIA):
—LUCERIA: (1) imp. *ASP* 34 (1981) p. 28 no.
34 (Lat. Martine: d. Martialis)

**Μαρτύριος**
ARKADIA:
—MEGALOPOLIS*: (1) 344 AD *IG* V (2) p.
XXXIII, 28 (bp.)
SICILY:
—KATANE: (2) iii-v AD ib. XIV 543 a (Wessel
582) (-*τί*-)
—SYRACUSE: (3) iii-v AD *IG* XIV 151 (Strazzulla
92; Agnello 7; Wessel 784); (4) ~ *ASSiracu-
sano* 1956, p. 54 (*Μαρτ*[*ύριος*])

**Μάρτυς**
S. ITALY (CAMPANIA):
—DIKAIARCHIA-PUTEOLI: (1) imp. *CIL* X 2509
(Lat. Herennia Martus)

**Μάρυλλα**
SICILY:
—KATANE: (1) imp. *IG* XIV 491 (*CIL* X 7078
(biling.)) (*M. Μάρυ*[*λλα*]?, Lat. Marylia); (2) ~
*SGDI* 5237 (*IGLMP* 7)

**Μαρύλος**
SICILY:
—MEGARA HYBLAIA: (1) m. vi BC Dubois,
*IGDS* 21 (Arena, *Iscr. Sic.* I 4)

**Μάρων**
ACHAIA:
—PATRAI: (1) ?iii-iv AD *AD* 16 (1960) Chron.
p. 144 β
ARGOLIS:
—ARGOS: (2) 219 BC *PEnt* 66, 1 Verso 2 (s. *Εὔ-
κτος*, f. *Εὔκτος*: t.e.)
ARKADIA:
—TEGEA: (3) ii AD *IG* V (2) 55, 96 (f. *Σῶσος*)
LAKONIA:
—SPARTA: (4) 480 BC Hdt. VII 227; Paus. III 12.
9 (Poralla² 510) (s. *Ὀρσίφαντος*)
S. ITALY (CAMPANIA):
—DIKAIARCHIA-PUTEOLI: (5) imp. *CIL* X 2668
(Lat. Cn. Lucceius Maron); (6) 43 AD Camo-
deca, *L'Archivio Puteolano* I p. 211 (Lat. C.
Hostius Maro)
—MISENUM*: (7) ii/iii AD *Ostraka* 4 (1995) p.
301 (Lat. C. Iulius Maro)
—NEAPOLIS: (8) i BC *IG* XIV 797 (*INap* 143);
cf. Leiwo p. 118 no. 103
—NEAPOLIS*: (9) imp. *INap* 136; cf. Leiwo p.
104 no. 59 (s. *Νύμφιος*)
SICILY:
—SYRACUSE: (10) 46 BC *Sic. Gymn.* 16 (1963) p.
60 no. 2, 3

**Μαρώνιος**
LAKONIA: (1) imp. *IG* V (1) 1349 (Bradford (-))
(f. *Παντώ*: Jew)

**Μαστακίς**
AKARNANIA:
—ANAKTORION: (1) hell.? *IG* IX (1)² (2) 235

**Μασχαλία**
AIGINA: (1) ii-i BC ib. IV (1) 132 (*Μαχαλία*—
apogr., *Μα*(*σ*)*χαλία*—*CIG*: d. *Διονύσιος*)

**Μάταλος**
S. ITALY (LUCANIA):
—EBURUM: (1) s. iv BC *Arch. Class.* 25-6 (1973-
4) p. 361 (vase) (fals.?) (f. *Διονύσιος*)

**Ματερῖνα**
EPIROS:
—BOUTHROTOS (PRASAIBOI): (1) a. 163 BC
*IBouthrot* 78, 7, 9; 79, 7-8; 80, 6, 8; 81, 6,
8; 82, 6-7; 83, 5-6; 84, 6, 8; 85, 6, 8; 86, 7, 9;
87, 7-8; 88, 5-6 (*BCH* 118 (1994) pp. 122 f.
nos. 1-11) ?= (*Μάτρα* (1))

**Μάτερις**
SICILY:
—LIPARA: (1) v BC *SEG* XLII 861 (s. *Πείσαν-
δρος*)

**Ματερίσκα**
DALMATIA:
—ISSA: (1) s. iii BC ib. XXXV 682; cf. *BCH* 114
(1990) p. 507-8
—ISSA?: (2) iii/ii BC *CIG* 6913; *SEG* XL 512
(locn.) (d. *Θεόδωρος*); (3) ~ *CIG* 6913; *SEG*
XL 512 (locn.) (d. *Ζώπυρος*)

**Ματερώ**
ARGOLIS:
—EPIDAUROS: (1) iv/iii BC Peek, *NIEpid* 59
(*Ματερώ*: d. *Διονύσιος*)
EPIROS:
—BOUTHROTOS (PRASAIBOI): (2) a. 163 BC
*IBouthrot* 22, 32 (*SEG* XXXVIII 479); (3) ~
*IBouthrot* 22, 34 (*SEG* XXXVIII 479); (4) ~
*IBouthrot* 26, 3; 28, 4; 29, 25 (*SEG* XXXVIII
484; 486-7); (5) ~ *IBouthrot* 30, 6 (*SEG*
XXXVIII 488); (6) ~ *IBouthrot* 95, 3; 96, 3

**Ματιώ**
ILLYRIA:
—EPIDAMNOS-DYRRHACHION: (1) hell. *IDyrrh*
304 (d. *Κλέπωρ*)

**Ματοῦρος**
S. ITALY (APULIA):
—CANUSIUM: (1) 195 BC *Syll*³ 585, 14 (f. *Βλάτ-
τος*)

**Μάτρα**
EPIROS:
—BOUTHROTOS (PRASAIBOI): (1) f. ii BC
*IBouthrot* 5, 5 ?= (*Ματερῖνα* (1))

**Ματροβία**
AIGINA?: (1) vi/v BC *NC* 1987, pp. 1 ff.; cf.
*ASNP* 20 (1990) p. 421 f.; *SEG* XLI 264 (coin
graffito) (*Στροβίας*?, *Στρο*(*μ*)*βίας*, *Βίαστος*? (n.
pr.?))

**Ματρόδωρος**
ARGOLIS:
—ARGOS: (1) 316-309 BC *IG* II² 1956, 107; *An-
cient Macedonia* 5 p. 445 with n. 10 (date)
(*Μη*-)
KERKYRA: (2) f. iii BC *IG* IX (1) 691, 3 (*Iscr.
Gr. Verona* p. 22 A)
SICILY: (3) f. iv BC Iamb., *VP* 241 (s. *Ἐπίχαρ-
μος*)
—KAMARINA: (4) f. v BC Cordano, *Tessere Pub-
bliche* 70 (-δō-)
—SYRACUSE: (5) ?135 BC *Milet* I (3) 103, 4 (*Μη*-:
f. *Μηνόδοτος*)

**Ματροφάνης**
SICILY:
—SYRACUSE: (1) ?ii BC ib. 79, 9 (*Μη*-: f. *Φιλίστα*); (2) ~ ib. l. 10 (and Caria Miletos: *Μη*-:
s. *Ἀρίβαζος*, *Φιλίστα*)

**Ματροχάρης**
ACHAIA: (1) 146 BC IG IV (1)² 28, 74 (s. Πυθό-κριτος: synoikos)
ARGOLIS:
—EPIDAUROS*: (2) c. 290-270 BC ib. 109 II, 141 (Μ[α]τροχάρης)

**Μάτρων**
AITOLIA:
—THERMOS*: (1) s. iii BC ib. IX (1)² (1) 60 II, 15; (2) ~ ib. 60 IV, 12

**Ματρώνα**
SICILY:
—SYRACUSE: (1) iii-v AD Wessel 1313 (Barreca 82) (n. pr.?)

**Ματτυξίδας**
AITOLIA: (1) ?269 BC FD III (4) 415, 7 (Ματ-τυξ[ί]δας)

**Ματυδίκα**
EPIROS:
—MOLOSSOI: (1) iii/ii BC Syll³ 1206, 1; cf. Cabanes, L'Épire p. 583 no. 60

**Ματυλαῖος**
SICILY:
—SELINOUS: (1) f. v BC Dubois, IGDS 38, 13 (Arena, Iscr. Sic. I 63) (f. Κάδοσις)

**Μαυρίκιος**
KORINTHIA:
—KORINTH: (1) byz. Corinth VIII (3) 148; cf. TMByz 9 (1985) p. 360 no. 12

**Μαῦρος**
S. ITALY (BRUTTIUM):
—HIPPONION-VIBO VALENTIA · (NR.): (1) inc. IG XIV 2412. 31 (s. Μήζωτρος)
S. ITALY (CAMPANIA):
—DIKAIARCHIA-PUTEOLI?: (2) m. i AD Camodeca, L'Archivio Puteolano I p. 69 no. 9 (Lat. C. Vitrasius Maurus)
SICILY:
—SYRACUSE: (3) imp. Epigraphica 5-6 (1943-4) p. 97 (amph.) (Lat. Maurus)

**Μάχα**
EPIROS:
—BOUTHROTOS (PRASAIBOI): (1) a. 163 BC IBouthrot 36, 16 (SEG XXXVIII 495) (d. Ὑβρίμμας)

**Μαχαίρα**
S. ITALY (APULIA):
—LARINUM: (1) imp. CIL IX 767 (Lat. C. Annidius Machaira)

**Μαχαιρίων**
LAKONIA:
—SPARTA: (1) 362 BC Paus. viii 11. 5; RE (-) (or Arkadia Mantineia-Antigoneia: Ἀντικράτης ὁ ἐπικαλ. Μ.? (n. pr.?)—RE)

**Μάχανδρος**
EPIROS:
—BOUTHROTOS (PRASAIBOI): (1) a. 163 BC IBouthrot 31, 29; 32, 27 (SEG XXXVIII 490-1) (s. Κλεόμαχος)

**Μαχανίδας**
LAKONIA:
—SPARTA: (1) iii BC IG V (1) 236; (2) c. 250-207 BC RE (-) (Bradford (-))
—SPARTA?: (3) imp.? SEG XI 970

**Μάχανος**
SICILY:
—KAMARINA: (1) ?ii BC ib. XXXIX 997, 7 (Cordano, 'Camarina VII' 133) (Μάχαν[ος]: f. Φιν-τέας)

**Μάχαος**
EPIROS:
—ATHAMANES?: (1) s. iii BC IG IX (2) 208 + Moretti, ISE 2 94 (Μαχάειος (patr. adj.): f. Ἀμύνανδρος)

**Μαχάτας**
ACHAIA: (1) iii BC HE 1395
AITOLIA: (2) 220-219 BC Plb. iv 34; 36
—POTIDANIA: (3) m. ii BC SBBerlAk :936, p. 371 b, 16 (SEG XLI 528 B) (s. Νικόβουλος)
AKARNANIA: (4) hell.? IG IX (1)² (2) 238-9 (sculptor)
EPIROS:
—AMBRAKIA: (5) ii-i BC CIG 1799 (s. Σωκράτης)
—BOUTHROTOS (PRASAIBOI): (6) a. 163 BC IBouthrot 14, 28; 19, 4 (SEG XXXVIII 471; 476) (s. Φωτεύς, f. Ἀριστοφάνης) ?= (14); (7) ~ IBouthrot 21, 19 (SEG XXXVIII 478) ([Μαχ]άτας); (8) ~ IBouthrot 28, 17 (SEG XXXVIII 486); IBouthrot 144, 4 (I s. Ἀριστοφά-νης, f. Φωτεύς, Μαχάτας II, Φίλιππος) ?= (18); (9) ~ ib. 28, 18 (SEG XXXVIII 486); IBouthrot 144, 5 (II s. Μαχάτας I) ?= (11); (10) ~ ib. 28, 35; cf. SEG XXXVIII 478; IBouthrot 29, 37; 36, 17 (SEG XXXVIII 487; 495) ?= (12); (11) ~ IBouthrot 40, 4 (SEG XXXVIII 499); IBouth-rot 149, 7 ?= (9); (12) ~ ib. 114, 6; 116, 5-6 (BCH 118 (1994) p. 123 A) ?= (10); (13) ~ IBouthrot 114, 7; 116, 6 (BCH 118 (1994) p. 121 A); (14) ~ IBouthrot 137, 5 (s. Φωτεύς) ?= (6)
——Delioi: (15) a. 163 BC ib. l. 3
——Parthaioi: (16) hell. Cabanes, L'Épire p. 552 no. 31; (17) a. 163 BC IBouthrot 93, 3; 94, 3; 136, 4; (18) ~ ib. 111, 11; 112, 11 (f. Φωτεύς) ?= (8)
——Sarpingioi: (19) a. 163 BC ib. 36, 19 (SEG XXXVIII 495) (f. Λύκος)
—OPATOI: (20) iii BC Cabanes, L'Épire p. 548 no. 18; cf. pp. 258 f. (f. Χάροψ) ?= (22); (21) iii/ii BC RE (3); Cabanes, L'Épire index s.v. (s. Χάροψ, f. Χάροψ)
—THESPROTOI: (22) 200-193 BC IKourion 42; Arch. Class. 25-6 (1973-4) pp. 316 f. (ident.) (f. Δημήτριος) ?= (20)
ILLYRIA:
—BYLLIONES: (23) i BC Cabanes, L'Épire p. 562 no. 36 (SEG XXXVIII 570) (f. Κράτιλλος)
—EPIDAMNOS-DYRRHACHION: (24) c. 250-50 BC Maier 119; 122; 134; 210; 219; 244; 303; 305; 309; 326; 342; Münsterberg Nachtr. p. 16-17 (Ceka 302-14); IApoll Ref. Bibl. n. 84 (coin) (money.)
—LYCHNIDOS?: (25) ii-i BC SEG I 254 (s. Γέν-θιος)

**Μαχάων**
KORINTHIA:
—KORINTH: (1) 429 BC Th. ii 83. 4

**Μάχων**
AITOLIA: (1) ?262 BC FD III (4) 357, 3; 358, 3; SGDI 2514, 2
—THERMOS: (2) 214 BC IG IX (1)² (1) 177, 20 (f. Νικόμαχος)
EPIROS:
—NIKOPOLIS: (3) imp. AD 42 (1987) Chron. p. 322 (Lat. Macho)
KORINTHIA:
—SIKYON: (4) iii BC RE (-); PCG 5 pp. 623-5 (Skalet 204) (or Korinthia Korinth)

**Μεγάθυρσος**
KERKYRA: (1) hell.? IG IX (1) 885 (Με(γ)άθυρσος: f. Μακεδών)

**Μεγάκλεια**
ARGOLIS:
—KLEONAI: (1) i BC SEG XI 297 b

ARKADIA:
—MEGALOPOLIS: (2) s. ii BC IG V (2) 461 (d. Δαμοκράτης)

**Μεγακλείδας**
ARGOLIS:
—ARGOS: (1) m. iii BC ib. IV (1)² 96, 14 (Perlman E.3); Perlman p. 63 f. (date) (f. Δαμά-τριος)
—EPIDAUROS: (2) c. 365-335 BC IG IV (1)² 103, 66, 98; (3) ?s. iv BC Peek, NIEpid 94 (f. Με-γακλῆς)

**Μεγακλῆς**
ACHAIA: (1) 316-309 BC IG II² 1956, 195, 197; Ancient Macedonia 5 p. 445 with n. 10 (date) (?f. Ξένων)
—DYME*: (2) c. 219 BC SGDI 1612, 22-3 (Tyche 5 (1990) p. 124) (f. Ἀριστόδαμος, Εὔα-πτος)
ARGOLIS:
—ARGOS: (3) ii/i BC IG IV (1) 694 (f. Δαμάρετος)
—EPIDAUROS: (4) ?s. iv BC Peek, NIEpid 94 (s. Μεγακλείδας)
—EPIDAUROS*: (5) c. 370-365 BC Peek, IAEpid 52 B, 53
—HERMIONE: (6) m. iv BC Unp. (Ch. Kritzas) (f. Ἀριστόκριτος); (7) i BC-i AD? IG IV (1) 730 III, 8 (f. Δρόμων)
ARKADIA:
—TEGEA: (8) m. iv BC ib. V (2) 6, 73
EPIROS:
—MOLOSSOI: (9) f. iii BC Plu., Pyrr. 16
KORINTHIA:
—KORINTH?: (10) v BC CAF I p. 718 fr. 26, 3; cf. PCG 7 p. 636 (or Megarid Megara: μέγα κλέος—PCG: ?f. Λαΐς)
—SIKYON: (11) 423 BC Th. iv 119. 2 (Skalet 205) (f. Ὀνάσιμος)
S. ITALY (BRUTTIUM):
—LOKROI EPIZEPHYRIOI:
——(Δυσ.): (12) iv/iii BC De Franciscis 18, 5 (s. Εὔφρων) ?= (13); (13) ~ ib. 29, 5 ?= (12)
S. ITALY (CAMPANIA):
—NEAPOLIS: (14) ?275 BC FD III (2) 177, 1 (s. Σωσίπατρος); (15) i BC IG XIV 777 (INap 108) (f. Δίκα)
—PITHEKOUSSAI-AENARIA: (16) ?ii BC SEG XIV 603 (Μεγακλ[ῆς] ὁ Ῥωμαῖος: s. Λούκιος)
S. ITALY (LUCANIA):
—POMARICO VECCHIO (MOD.): (17) arch. NScav 1992-3, p. 217 (tile) (Μεγακλ[ῆς])
SICILY:
—AKRAI: (18) ?iii BC Akrai p. 162 no. 22. 16
—SYRACUSE: (19) 358-357 BC RE (8) (s. Ἱππαρί-νος)
—SYRACUSE?: (20) ?s. vi BC ib. (10)
—ZANKLE-MESSANA: (21) c. 315-312 BC Poly-aen. v 15

**Μέγαλα**
SICILY:
—KEPHALOIDION: (1) i BC SEG XLII 849 (Πομπ. Μ.: d. Ῥοῦφος Μέγας)

**Μεγάλη**
S. ITALY (CAMPANIA):
—DIKAIARCHIA-PUTEOLI: (1) s. ii AD AJA 77 (1973) p. 164 no. 14 (Lat. Tantilia Megale)

**Μεγαλίας**
ARKADIA:
—TEGEA: (Hippothoitai): (1) c. 369-362 BC IG V (2) 173, 36 ([Μεγα]λίας?); (2) f. iii BC ib. 36, 58 (I f. Μεγαλίας II); (3) ~ ib. l. 58 (II s. Μεγαλίας I)
LAKONIA:
—GERENIA: (4) v BC ib. V (1) 1337 (Poralla² 511)

**Μέγαλλα**
ARGOLIS:
—HERMIONE: (1) ii-i BC IG IV (1) 732 III, 21 (m. Σώστρατος)

**Μεγαλλῆς**
ZAKYNTHOS: (1) iii/ii BC ib. IX (1)² (2) 229
([Μεγ]αλλῆς)

**Μεγαλλίς**
EPIROS:
—BOUTHROTOS (PRASAIBOI): (1) a. 163 BC
IBouthrot 25, 11; 31, 89 (SEG XXXVIII 483;
490)
SICILY:
—HENNA: (2) c. 135 BC D.S. xxxiv/xxxv 2. 10
ff.
—SYRACUSE: (3) hell. NScav 1892, p. 357 (d.
Σωσίστρατος); (4) ~ ib. p. 360

**Μέγαλλος**
SICILY: (1) arch.? RE (-) (or Athens)

**Μεγαλοκλῆς**
ARGOLIS:
—EPIDAUROS: (1) iv BC IG IV (1)² 184
([Μ]εγαλοκλῆς)

**Μέγαλος**
KORINTHIA:
—KORINTH: (1) imp.? Syringes 765 d (f. Διονύ-
σιος)

**Μεγαλοστράτα**
LAKONIA:
—SPARTA: (1) s. vii BC PMGF I 59 (Poralla²
512)

**Μεγαλοφάνης**
ARKADIA:
—MEGALOPOLIS: (1) m. iii BC RE (-); cf. Wal-
bank 2 pp. 223-4 (Δημοφάνης—Plb.)

**Μεγανίκα**
EPIROS:
—BOUTHROTOS (PRASAIBOI): (1) a. 163 BC
IBouthrot 14, 23; 18, 3; 21, 42; 31, 27; 39,
6 (SEG XXXVIII 471; 475; 478; 490; 498); cf.
Cabanes, L'Épire p. 406 (?d. Ἀνδρόνικος, Φι-
λωτέρα); (2) ~ IBouthrot 159
——Netidioi?: (3) a. 163 BC ib. 91, 9 (SEG
XXXII 623)

**Μεγάρα**
ARGOLIS:
—ARGOS: (1) s. v BC ib. XVI 243, 4

**Μεγαρίστα**
AITOLIA:
—PHISTYON: (1) f. ii BC IG IX (1)² (1) 98, 8

**Μεγάρτας**
EPIROS:
—BOUTHROTOS (PRASAIBOI): (1) a. 163 BC
IBouthrot 100, 8 (s. Δόκιμος)

**Μέγας**
AIGINA: (1) f. v BC Pi., N. viii, 16, 44; cf. Klee
p. 103 no. 120 (f. Δεῖνις)
EPIROS:
—DODONA: (2) iii BC Antoniou, Dodone Ab, 18
(Μέγας)
—MOLOSSOI: (3) c. 343-330 BC Cabanes,
L'Épire p. 588 no. 74, 8 (SEG XXVI 700) (s.
Ἴνων)
SICILY: (4) m. i BC Cic., ad Fam. xiii 36. 1 (Lat.
P. Cornelius Demetrius Megas)
—GELA-PHINTIAS: (5) f. v BC Dubois, IGDS
149 c (vase) (Arena, Iscr. Sic. II 39) (μέλα—
Arena)
—KEPHALOIDION: (6) ?i BC SEG XXXVI 847
(Δέκομος Λαίλιος M.); (7) i BC ib. XLII 849
(Ῥοῦφος M.: f. Πομπ. Μεγάλα)

**Μέγης**
KORINTHIA:
—KORINTH: (1) ii/iii AD Corinth VIII (3) 206 (f.
Γ. Οὐίβιος Εὐέλπιστος)

**Μεγίας**
ARKADIA:
—HERAIA: (1) m. iii BC IG v (2) 368, 144

**Μέγιλα**
S. ITALY (CALABRIA):
—TARAS-TARENTUM: (1) v/iv BC Scritti Sciarra
Bardaro p. 251 no. 1 (loomweight)

**Μέγιλλος**
KORINTHIA:
—KORINTH: (1) ii AD Luc., DMort. 1. 3; Cat.
22 (fict.)
LAKONIA:
—SPARTA: (2) 408 BC FGrH 324 F 44 with note;
RE (1) (Μέτελλος—codd., M.—Usener) ?= (4);
(3) iv BC Pl., Lg. 624 ff.; Epin. 973 ff. (Po-
ralla² 514) (fict.?); (4) 396 BC X., HG iii 4. 6
(Poralla² 513) ?= (2)
S. ITALY (LUCANIA):
—HYELE-VELIA: (5) c. 340 BC Plu., Tim. 35
(and Sicily Akragas)
SICILY:
—AKRAGAS: (6) v/iv BC Wehrli, Schule Arist. ii
fr. 82 + Usener, Kl. Schr. pp. 208-9 (Μέτελ-
λος—codd. Loeb, Μέγυλλος—Wehrli)
TRIPHYLIA:
—PYRGOI: (7) c. 230-200 BC BCH 45 (1921) p.
12 II, 84 (locn.—Oulhen)

**Μέγιππος**
LAKONIA:
—SPARTA: (1) s. i BC IG v (1) 96, 10 (Bradford
(-)) (s. Νικόστρατος)

**Μεγιστέας**
S. ITALY (BRUTTIUM):
—RHEGION: (1) imp.? IG XIV 2400. 8 (tile)
SICILY:
—TAUROMENION: (2) ?ii/i BC ib. 421 III (SGDI
5219) (f. Εὐκλείδας)

**Μεγίστη**
S. ITALY (CALABRIA):
—UZENTUM: (1) iii AD Susini, Fonti Salento p.
77 no. 10 (Lat. Mecista)
S. ITALY (CAMPANIA):
—DIKAIARCHIA-PUTEOLI: (2) imp. CIL x 1774
(Lat. –tia Megiste)
—DIKAIARCHIA-PUTEOLI*: (3) imp. ib. 8203
(Lat. Megiste: freed.)
—POMPEII: (4) i BC-i AD ib. IV 4300 (Lat.
Megiste)

**Μεγιστίας**
AKARNANIA: (1) 480 BC RE (-); IG IX (1)² (2)
p. X, s.a. 480 BC; Page, FGE pp. 702 ff.; cf.
Plu., Mor 221 C (or Lakonia Sparta?: Θεμι-
στέας—Plu.)
S. ITALY (LUCANIA):
—METAPONTION: (2) iv BC Iamb., VP 267
(FVS 1 p. 446)

**Μεγιστίων**
S. ITALY (CALABRIA):
—BRENTESION-BRUNDISIUM*: (1) imp. Epigraphica 25 (1963) p. 73 no. 74 (Lat. C. Ha-
bidius Megistio: freed.)
—RUDIAE: (2) i-ii AD Susini, Fonti Salento p.
128 no. 72 (Lat. Megistio)

**Μεγιστόδαμος**
LAKONIA:
—SPARTA?: (1) i-ii AD SEG XI 131 a (Bradford
(-)) (f. —όδαμος)

**Μεγιστόνους**
LAKONIA:
—SPARTA: (1) m. iii BC Plu., Cleom. 7; 11; 19;
21; Arat. 38; 41 (Bradford (-))

**Μεγιστώ**
ARGOLIS:
—ARGOS: (1) i BC-i AD Mnem. NS 47 (1919) p.
167 no. 16
ARKADIA:
—TEGEA: (2) ii BC IG v (2) 68
ELIS: (3) 272 BC RE (-)
SICILY:
—HALOUNTION: (4) imp. CIL x 7468 (Lat. Li-
cinia Mecisto)

**Μεγυλλίας**
LAKONIA:
—SPARTA: (1) 359 BC CID II 5 I, 16 (Poralla²
515)

**Μέγυλλος**
S. ITALY (LUCANIA):
—POSEIDONIA-PAESTUM: (1) c. 470-460 BC
Arena, Iscr. Sic. IV 36 (coin) (Μέγυλ(λος))

**Μεγώ**
MESSENIA:
—MESSENE: (1) i AD SEG XXIII 220 a, 2; 220 b,
3 (d. Δαμόνικος, Τιμαρχίς)

**Μέγων**
AITOLIA: (1) hell. IEph 2511 (f. Τιμόδαμος)
ARGOLIS:
—EPIDAUROS: (2) iii BC Peek, IAEpid 73, 2
(Μέ[γων])
——Bryantina: (3) c. 370-335 BC IG IV (1)² 103,
43; Peek, IAEpid 52 A, 23
ILLYRIA:
—EPIDAMNOS-DYRRHACHION: (4) hell.-imp.
IDyrrh 44; (5) ~ ib. 305 (f. —ια)
S. ITALY (BRUTTIUM):
—TERINA: (6) c. 356-355 BC IG IV (1)² 95, 45
(Perlman E.2); Perlman p. 40 f. (date) (s.
Ἁγησίδαμος)
SICILY:
—KAMARINA: (7) f. v BC Cordano, Tessere Pub-
bliche 111 (-γōν: f. Γελώιος)

**Μεδέα**
EPIROS:
—PHOTIKE?: (1) imp. ILGR 166 (Lat. Medea)

**Μέδεστις**
ILLYRIA:
—EPIDAMNOS-DYRRHACHION (NR.)?: (1) ii BC
SEG XXXVIII 572, 7; cf. CRAI 1991, p.
197 ff.; L'Illyrie mérid. 2 p. 206; (2) ~ SEG
XXXVIII 572, 8; cf. CRAI 1991, p. 197 ff.;
L'Illyrie mérid. 2 p. 206 (s. Πλατούριος)

**Μέδουσα**
S. ITALY (APULIA):
—VENUSIA: (1) imp. CIL IX 580 (Lat. Badia
Medusa)
S. ITALY (CAMPANIA):
—POMPEII: (2) i BC-i AD ib. IV 4196 (Lat. Mi-
duse)

**Μέδων**
LAKONIA: (1) vii/vi BC Paus. v 17. 2 (Po-
ralla² 516) (Μεδόντας?—Wade-Gery: sculptor)
?= (Δόντας (1))
S. ITALY (BRUTTIUM):
—RHEGION*: (2) m. vi BC Rumpf, Chalkid.
Vas. p. 47 no. 8 (vase) (Arena, Iscr. Sic. III
p. 105 no. 12) (-δōν: her.?)

**Μεδώνη?**
S. ITALY (APULIA):
—BARION*: (1) i BC-i AD Mus. Arch. di Bari
p. 151 no. 5 (CIL IX 301) (Lat. Tarutia
Medona: freed.)

**Μέθη**
EPIROS:
—NIKOPOLIS: (1) imp. PAE 1913, p. 97 no. 3
(Sarikakis 105) (m. Σωτηρίχα)

**Korinthia:**
—korinth*: (2) ii AD *Corinth* VIII (2) 105, 8 (Lat. Papia Methe)
**S. Italy (Apulia):**
—larinum: (3) ii-iii AD *Contr. Ist. Fil. Class.* I (1963) p. 249 no. 7 (Lat. Pacidia Methe)
—venusia*: (4) i AD *Epigraphica* 35 (1973) p. 150 no. 12 (Lat. Ovia Methe: freed.)
**S. Italy (Bruttium):**
—lokroi epizephyrioi: (5) iii AD *Suppl. It.* 3 p. 29 no. 14 (Lat. -ilia Methe)
**S. Italy (Campania):**
—dikaiarchia-puteoli*: (6) imp. *CIL* x 2826, 6 (Lat. -a Methe: freed.)
—pompeii: (7) i BC-i AD ib. IV 2457 (Lat. Methe); (8) ~ ib. 4434 (Lat. Methe); (9) f. i AD *Impegno per Pompeii* 42 EN (Castrèn 153. 1) (Lat. Derecia Methe: d. Spurius); (10) m. i AD *CIL* x 928 (Castrèn 34. 7) (Lat. Antistia Methe: d. Antistius Primigenius)

**Μεθίκων**
**Achaia:**
—dyme: (1) s. iii BC *SEG* XIII 278, 19 (f. Ἀθανάδας)
**Argolis:**
—kleonai: (2) ?c. 229 BC ib. XXIII 178, 24 (or Argolis Argos)
**Peloponnese:** (3) s. iii BC ib. XIII 278, 10 (Μεθίκωνος (gen.): f. Φίλυς)

**Μέθιον**
**Sicily:**
—syracuse: (1) iii-v AD Strazzulla 262 (Agnello 21; Wessel 857) (Μεθίου (gen.), Μέθιος?)

**Μεθοδικός**
**Korinthia:**
—korinth: (1) f. ii AD *SEG* III 335, 31 (*AE* 1936, Chron. p. 44 no. 221) (Π. Ἀλκείνιος M.—*SEG*, Π. Ἀλβείνιος M.—*AE*)

**Μειδίας**
**Aigina:** (1) f. v BC Pi. fr. 4 (Μ(ε)ιδ(ί)ας); (2) ?i BC *Alt-Ägina* I (2) p. 44 no. 11, 4 (s. Ἀμύντας)
**Aitolia:**
—thermos*: (3) s. iii BC *IG* IX (1)² (1) 60 VI, 7; (4) ~ ib. 60 VII, 14 (Μι-); (5) ~ ib. l. 19
**Messenia:**
—messene: (6) inc. Plin., *NH* vii 200 (Lat. Midias: fict.?)

**Μειδύλος**
**Aigina:** (1) her. Pi., *P.* viii, 38; Pi. fr. 190 (Μειδυλίδαι (n. gent.))

**Μειλίχων**
**Arkadia:**
—tegea: (1) iv/iii BC *IG* v (2) 38, 61 (Μειλίχω[ν])

**Μείνων**
**Sicily:**
—leontinoi (nr.): (1) vi BC *QUCC* 78 (1995) pp. 122-4 (vase) (-νōν)

**Μείξις**
**Kerkyra:** (1) c. 575-550 BC *CEG* I 146 (Μhεῖ-: f. Ξενάρης)

**Μειχύλος**
**Sicily:**
—selinous: (1) v BC Dubois, *IGDS* 35, 5 (Arena, *Iscr. Sic.* I 64)

**Μελαγκόμας**
**Aitolia:** (1) f. ii BC *RE* Supplbd. 7 (2); *PP* 5194 + 15120; Ijsewijn 121; *PTeb* 811, 3 + *BPW* 1934, col. 1317 (I s. Φιλόδαμος, f. Μελαγκόμας II); (2) 146-116 BC *PP* 15119 (II s. Μελαγκόμας I)
**Aitolia?:** (3) c. 214 BC Plb. viii 15. 9-10; *PP* 14851

**Arkadia:**
—megalopolis: (4) 208 or 207 BC *FD* III (4) 25 (-λαν-: doctor)
—tegea:
—(Krariotai): (5) iii BC *IG* v (2) 40, 26 (Μ[ε]λαγκόμας: s. Κίλλων)
—thelphousa: (6) a. 228 BC ib. IV (1)² 72 B, 25 (-λαν-: s. Φι—)

**Μέλαγκος**
**Illyria:**
—apollonia: (1) imp. *IApoll* 29 (-νκ-)

**Μελαγχρίδας**
**Lakonia:**
—sparta: (1) 413 BC Th. viii 6. 5 (Poralla² 517)

**Μελαινίς**
**Aigina:** (1) iv BC *IG* IV (1) 41
**Epiros:**
—ambrakia: (2) iv/iii BC Unp. (Arta Mus., inscr.)
**S. Italy (Calabria):**
—brentesion-brundisium*: (3) imp. *CIL* IX 197 = *Epigraphica* 25 (1963) p. 45 no. 26; cf. 42 (1980) p. 158 (Lat. Terraea Melaenis: freed.)

**Μελάμπους**
**Kephallenia:** (1) vi BC Paus. x 7. 4 (Stephanis 1626)

**Μελάνας**
**Korinthia:**
—korinth: (1) c. 570-550 BC Amyx 114. 6 (vase) (her.?)

**Μελάνδρυς**
**Argolis:**
—hermione: (1) iii BC *IG* IV (1) 729 I, 5 (f. Ὀρύας)

**Μελανειός**
**Argolis:**
—hermione: (1) ii-i BC ib. 732 IV, 2 (f. Εὐτυχίς)

**Μελάνθιν**
**Sicily:**
—katane: (1) iii AD *CIL* x 7075 (*ILat. Palermo* 2) (Lat. Luria Melant[hi]n: m. Ζώσιμος)

**Μελάνθιος**
**Aitolia:** (1) ?263-261 BC *FD* III (3) 184, 3; 190, 3; *Syll*³ 498, 4; Nachtergael, *Les Galates* 3, [3]
**Argolis:**
—argos?: (2) c. 400-375 BC *IG* II² 78, [4], 9 (s. Καλλίας)
—epidauros*: (3) c. 340-325 BC *SEG* XXV 387 A, 13; Peek, *IAEpid* 50, 26
—hermione*: (4) iv BC *IG* IV (1) 742, 4
—troizen*: (5) iv BC ib. 823, 45, 47, 48, 51
**Epiros:**
—bouthrotos?: (6) a. 163 BC *IBouthrot* 91, 17 (*SEG* XXXII 623) (f. Δέρδας)
**Illyria:**
—apollonia: (7) ii-i BC *IApoll* 129 (f. Νίκων)
—bylliones: (8) f. ii BC *SEG* XXXVIII 534 (s. Ἀνθρωπίσκος)
—byrliones nikaia (kljos (mod.)): (9) hell. *Iliria* 1982 (1), p. 120 no. 38 (tile) + *BE* 1983, no. 25
—epidamnos-dyrrhachion: (10) hell.-imp. *IDyrrh* 155 (f. Γέτας); (11) ~ ib. 306 (s. Γέτας)
**Kerkyra:** (12) f. iii BC *IG* IX (1) 691, 7, 13 (*Iscr. Gr. Verona* p. 22 A)
**Korinthia:**
—sikyon: (13) m. iv BC *RE* (14) (Skalet 206) (painter)

**Lakonia:** (14) iv/iii BC *IG* v (1) 1348
**Sicily:**
—gela-phintias?: (15) f. v BC Dubois, *IGDS* 134 b, 9 (Arena, *Iscr. Sic.* II 47) ([Μελ]άνθιος)
—kamarina: (16) s. v BC Dubois, *IGDS* 121, 9 (Arena, *Iscr. Sic.* II 143; *SEG* XXXVIII 940; Cordano, 'Camarina VII' 39) (Μελάνθιο[ς]: s. -άτιμος)

**Μέλανθος**
**Lakonia:**
—sparta: (1) 413 BC Th. viii 5. 1 (Poralla² 518)
**S. Italy (Campania):**
—baiai: (2) imp. *NScav* 1897, p. 14 (Lat. Melanthus)

**Μελάνιππος**
**Illyria:**
—apollonia: (1) iii AD *IApoll* 290 ([Με]λάνιπ[πος])
**Lakonia:**
—sparta: (2) i BC/i AD *IG* v (1) 48, 3 (Bradford (-)) (f. Δαμόχαρις)
**Sicily:**
—akragas: (3) f. vi BC Wehrli, *Schule Arist.* vii fr. 65
—syracuse: (4) vii/vi BC *BdA* 67 (1982) p. 53 with fig. 8 (bronze); cf. *SEG* XXXVIII 965; XL 810 (-ιπος)

**Μέλανις**
**Aitolia:**
—philotaieis?: (1) c. 162 BC *IG* IX (1)² (1) 105, 6
—prosch(e)ion: (2) c. 157 BC ib. 108, 3 ?= (3)
—prosch(e)ion?: (3) ii BC ib. 73 ?= (2)

**Μελανίων**
**Sicily:**
—kentoripa: (1) imp. *CIL* x 7010 (tile) (Lat. L. Roscius Melanio)

**Μελάντας**
**Aitolia:** (1) 276 BC Polyaen. iv 6. 18; cf. *IG* IX (1)² (1) p. XVII, 106 (Μελάτας—codd., Μελά(ν)τας—edd.)
**Argolis:**
—argos: (2) c. 450 BC ML 42 B, 43
**Epiros:**
—dodona: (3) iii BC Antoniou, *Dodone* Aa, 29
—leukas: (4) iii BC Unp. (Leukas Mus., inscr.) inv. 31

**Μελάνωπος**
**Argolis:**
—epidauros: (1) iii-iv AD *IG* IV (1)² 537; 538
**Illyria:**
—apollonia: (2) c. 250-50 BC *Jubice Hoard* p. 99 no. 83 (coin) (Ceka 130) (pryt.)

**Μέλας**
**Lakonia:**
—kosmas (mod.): (1) ?f. vi BC *SEG* XI 890 (bronze) (Lazzarini 835); *LSAG*² p. 199 no. 14 (date) (Poralla² 518a)
**Messenia:**
—messene: (2) ii/i BC *IG* v (1) 1437, 3
**S. Italy (Campania):**
—kyme: (3) imp. *Mon. Ant.* 22 (1913) p. 764 (Lat. L. Pontius Mela)
—pompeii: (4) i BC *CIL* I² 1634 (x 8148; Castrèn 231. 4) (Lat. P. Maccius Melas)
**Sicily:**
—syracuse: (5) iv BC *CIRB* 203 (s. Σῖμος)

**Μελέαγρος**
**Illyria:** (1) 238-237 BC *PP* 2312; *PPetr²* I Wills 6, 33
**S. Italy (Campania):**
—pompeii: (2) i BC-i AD *NScav* 1899, p. 496 no. 2 (Castrèn 190. 3) (Lat. Meleager)
—salernum*: (3) ?i AD *IItal* I (1) 238 I, 10 (*CIL* x 557) (Lat. L. Appuleius Meleager: freed.)

**Μελέας**
S. ITALY (LUCANIA):
—POTENTIA: (4) imp. ib. 159 (Lat. M. Insteius Meleager: f. M. Insteius Firmus)

**Μελέας**
LAKONIA: (1) 428 BC Th. iii 5. 2 (Poralla² 519)

**Μέλεος**
S. ITALY (APULIA): (1) s. iv BC RVAp p. 510 no. 131 (vase) (n. pr.?)

**Μελέτη**
S. ITALY (APULIA):
—CANUSIUM: (1) ii-iii AD Epig. Rom. di Canosa 53 (Lat. Melete)
S. ITALY (CALABRIA):
—BRENTESION-BRUNDISIUM*: (2) imp. NScav 1885, p. 501 a (Eph. Ep. VIII 35) (Lat. Melete: slave?)

**Μεληϊππίδας**
LAKONIA:
—SPARTA: (1) ii/i BC IG v (1) 966, 2, 9, 12, [19] (Bradford (-)) ([M]ελnϊππίδας: s. Τάρας)

**Μεληΐων**
LAKONIA: (1) iii BC IG v (1) 1340, 3 (Bradford (-)) ([M]ελnηΐων)

**Μελησίας**
S. ITALY (LUCANIA):
—METAPONTION: (1) iv BC Iamb., VP 267 (FVS I p. 446) (Μελισίας—ms.: name—Keil)

**Μελησίης**
LAKONIA:
—TAINARON*: (1) iv BC IG v (1) 1342 (Poralla² 520) ([M]ελησίης)

**Μελήσιος**
KEPHALLENIA:
—KRANIOI: (1) ?s. v BC IG IX (1) 610 (-λέ-: s. Ἐμμενίδας)

**Μελησιππίδας**
LAKONIA:
—SPARTA: (1) f. v BC Plu., Ages. 1 (Poralla² 521) (f. Εὐπωλία)

**Μελήσιππος**
LAKONIA:
—SPARTA: (1) 431 BC Th. i 139. 3; ii 12. 1 (Poralla² 522) (s. Διάκριτος); (2) c. 105-110 AD IG v (1) 20 B, 8 (Bradford (2)) (f. Εὔκλητος) ?= (3); (3) ~ SEG XI 569, 2 (Bradford (1)) (s. Εὔκλητος) ?= (2)
MESSENIA:
—MESSENE?: (4) ii/i BC SEG XI 979, 7

**Μελητεύς**
ARGOLIS:
—ARGOS: (Leukyridai): (1) a. 316 BC BCH 98 (1974) p. 775, 4 (Perlman A.5) ([Mε]λητεύς)

**Μέλητος**
MESSENIA:
—MESSENE: (1) iii BC SEG XXX 1363

**Μελίανθος**
S. ITALY: (1) imp. CIL X 8059. 321 (seal) (Lat. Q. Plautius Melianthus)

**Μελίβοια**
AKARNANIA:
—PALAIROS: (1) iii BC IG IX (1)² (2) 493

**Μελίβοιος**
S. ITALY (CAMPANIA):
—POMPEII: (1) i BC-i AD CIL IV 4908; 4955

**Μελίζουσα**
KEPHALLENIA:
—SAME: (1) imp. SEG XXXIV 475

**Μελίη**
S. ITALY (CAMPANIA):
—AEQUANA*: (1) imp. NScav 1896, p. 332 (Lat. Livia Melie: freed.)

**Μελιθήριος**
ARGOLIS:
—PHLEIOUS: (1) iv BC IG IV (1) 452 (s. Φιλαρχίδας, Ἀγαθόκλεια)

**Μελικέρτης**
S. ITALY (CAMPANIA):
—POMPEII: (1) i BC-i AD CIL IV 2993 n; 8023 (Lat. Melicertes); (2) ~ ib. 7186 (Lat. Certimeles)

**Μελικράτης**
SICILY:
—SYRACUSE: (1) iii-v AD Ferrua, NG 373

**Μέλιννα**
S. ITALY (BRUTTIUM):
—LOKROI EPIZEPHYRIOI: (1) iv/iii BC HE 2819 (Αὐτομέλιννα)

**Μέλις**
ARGOLIS:
—EPIDAUROS: (1) c. 370 BC IG IV (1)² 102, 290
ELIS?: (2) a. 420 BC REG 62 (1949) p. 6, 11; pp. 8 f. (locn.)

**Μελίς**
KORINTHIA:
—KORINTH: (1) iv-iii BC SEG XXII 237 a (loomweight)

**Μέλισσα**
AKARNANIA:
—THYRREION: (1) f. ii BC IG IX (1)² (2) 297
ARGOLIS:
—ARGOS: (2) iv BC Peek, IAEpid 225; (3) ~ ib. 225 b, 2
—EPIDAUROS: (4) vii/vi BC RE (3) no. 8 (and Korinthia Korinth: Λυσιδίκα ἥ καὶ M.: d. Προκλῆς, Ἐρισθένεια (Orchomenos), m. Κύψελος (Korinth), Λυκόφρων (Korinth))
—HERMIONE: (5) ii BC IG IV (1)² 259 (d. Ἀριστώ)
—NAUPLIA: (6) ?iii BC SEG XXIX 374 ([M]έλισσα)
EPIROS:
—AMBRAKIA: (7) ?f. iii BC ib. XXXIX 522
—BOUTHROTOS (PRASAIBOI): (8) a. 163 BC IBouthrot 33, 3 (SEG XXXVIII 492); (9) ~ IBouthrot 43, 40 (SEG XXXVIII 502); IBouthrot 48, 4; (10) ~ ib. l. 10
—Drymioi?: (11) a. 163 BC ib. 21, 49 (SEG XXXVIII 478); IBouthrot 156, 5; 157, 5 (BCH 118 (1994) p. 127 nos. 12-13) (?d. Μυρτίλος)
ILLYRIA:
—EPIDAMNOS-DYRRHACHION: (12) hell.-imp. IDyrrh 307 (-ισα: d. Εἰράνα)
S. ITALY (CALABRIA):
—BRENTESION-BRUNDISIUM*: (13) imp. CIL IX 6129 = Epigraphica 25 (1963) p. 90 no. 113 + p. 91 no. 119 (Lat. Numisia Melissa: freed.)
—TARAS-TARENTUM: (14) ?s. i AD Petr., Sat. 61. 6 (Lat. Melissa: fict.)
S. ITALY (CAMPANIA):
—NEAPOLIS: (15) ii-iii AD CIL X 1495; cf. Leiwo p. 111 (Lat. Marcia Melissa: m. Marcius Felix)
SICILY:
—AKRAI: (16) hell.-imp. Manganaro, QUCC forthcoming no. 15 (-ισα: d. Ζώπυρος); (17) imp. SEG XLII 829
—GELA-PHINTIAS?: (18) m. v BC Dubois, IGDS 149 a (vase) (Arena, Iscr. Sic. II 54)
—HERBESSOS: (19) hell. Dubois, IGDS 168 c (vase) (-λισα)

**Μελισσίας**
LEUKAS: (1) iv/iii BC SEG XXVII 170

**Μελισσίς**
ARGOLIS:
—ARGOS: (1) iv BC IG IV (1) 629
EPIROS:
—BOUTHROTOS (PRASAIBOI): (2) a. 163 BC IBouthrot 17, 11 (SEG XXXVIII 474) (?d. Νικάνωρ, Ἀδυλώ); (3) ~ IBouthrot 21, 35 (SEG XXXVIII 478) (d. Σωσίπατρος, Ἀρίστα I)
KERKYRA: (4) i BC-i AD IG IX (1) 920

**Μελισσίων**
ARKADIA:
—TEGEA: (1) f. iii BC ib. v (2) 35, 15 (s. Πύθων)

**Μέλισσος**
AITOLIA:
—KLAUSEION (MOD.): (1) byz. PAE 1958, p. 61 α; p. 61 ε; cf. BCH 83 (1959) p. 664 (Μέ[λ]ισσος)
ARKADIA:
—ORCHOMENOS: (2) iv BC IOlbia 4 (f. Ἀρίστανδρος)
KERKYRA: (3) iii BC SEG XXXVIII 457 (s. Ἐπικράτης: sculptor)
KORINTHIA:
—KORINTH: (4) s. viii BC D.S. viii 10; Plu., Mor. 772 E f. (s. Ἄβρων (Argos), f. Ἀκταίων: fict.?)
—SIKYON?: (5) f. v BC Dubois, IGDS 144 a (vase) (Arena, Iscr. Sic. II 81) (and Sicily Gela-Phintias?)
S. ITALY (APULIA):
—CANUSIUM*: (6) imp. Epig. Rom. di Canosa 94 (CIL IX 363) (Lat. Melissus: slave?)
S. ITALY (CAMPANIA):
—POMPEII: (7) i BC-i AD ib. IV 7306 (Lat. Melissus); (8) ~ ib. 8508; 9168 (Lat. Melissus); (9) ~ NScav 1910, p. 407 (Lat. Melissus)
SICILY:
—MENAI: (10) i BC-i AD ib. 1903, p. 436
—THERMAI HIMERAIAI: (11) ?ii-iii AD IG XIV 333 + Epigraphica 3 (1941) pp. 263-4 no. 26 (name) (Κλ. M.)

**Μελίτα**
ARGOLIS:
—ARGOS: (1) a. 303 BC CEG II 816, 11
S. ITALY (BRUTTIUM): (2) hell.? Landi, DISMG 114, 10

**Μελιτέα**
EPIROS:
—BOUTHROTOS: (1) hell. IBouthrot 206 (Ugolini, Alb. Ant. 3 p. 210 no. 7)
—BOUTHROTOS (PRASAIBOI): (2) a. 163 BC IBouthrot 29, 34 (SEG XXXVIII 487); (3) ~ IBouthrot 31, 37 (SEG XXXVIII 490) (d. Φίλιππος, Παμφίλα); (4) ~ IBouthrot 43, 30 (SEG XXXVIII 502); (5) ~ IBouthrot 66, 8; 75, 7; (6) ~ ib. 145, 9
—Pelmatioi: (7) a. 163 BC ib. 142, 8

**Μελίτη**
SICILY:
—SYRACUSE: (1) ii-i BC IG XII (1) 152 (GVI 1393)

**Μελιτίνη**
SICILY:
—HYKKARA: (1) imp. IG XIV 294 (m. Δόμνα)

**Μελίτις**
MESSENIA:
—KORONE: (1) 246 AD ib. v (1) 1398, 44 (Κλ. M.)

**Μέλιττα**
AKARNANIA:
—THYRREION: (1) hell. ib. IX (1)² (2) 347 (-λιτα)

**Μελίτων**

ILLYRIA:
—APOLLONIA: (2) ii BC *IApoll* 118 (-λιτα)
LEUKAS: (3) hell.? *IG* IX (1) 565 (-ιτα)

**Μελίτων**

S. ITALY (CAMPANIA):
—NEAPOLIS: (1) ii-iii AD ib. XIV 798 (*INap* 144); cf. Leiwo p. 106 no. 68 (Μελίθων—*IG* per err.)

**Μελίφθογγος**

S. ITALY (BRUTTIUM):
—RHEGION*: (1) imp. *IG* XIV 617, 8 (-φθονγος: slave?)

**Μελίχρους**

LAKONIA:
—SPARTA: (1) c. 100-105 AD *SEG* XI 537 a, 6; 537 b, 1 (Bradford (-)) (Π. Μέμμιος M.: s. Ἐπαφρόδιτος)
SICILY:
—SYRACUSE: (2) iii-v AD *Rend. Pont.* 22 (1946-7) p. 236 no. 41 (Στάτι Μελίχρου)

**Μελίχρως**

LAKONIA:
—BOIAI: (1) ii AD *IG* V (1) 958, 3, 5, 6; 959, 2, 5, 6 (I s. Μουσαῖος, f. Μελίχρως II, Πρόνοια); (2) ~ ib. 958, 6; 959, 6 (II s. Μελίχρως I, Ἡρακλέα)

**Μέλλαξ**

S. ITALY (CAMPANIA):
—POMPEII: (1) i BC-i AD *CIL* IV 9111 (Lat. Mellax—Solin)

**Μέλλις**

ARGOLIS:
—ARGOS:
——(Hyrnathioi-Temenidai): (1) c. 400 BC *SEG* XXIX 361, 24

**Μέλλουσα**

S. ITALY (APULIA):
—CANUSIUM*: (1) imp. *Epig. Rom. di Canosa* 94 (*CIL* IX 363) (Lat. Baebia Mellusa: freed.)
SICILY:
—THERMAI HIMERAIAI: (2) imp. *IG* XIV 337 (Σειλικία M.)

**Μέλλωσος**

SICILY:
—LILYBAION?: (1) iv-v AD *SEG* XLII 869

**Μέλουσα**

S. ITALY (CALABRIA):
—TARAS-TARENTUM: (1) c. 540-530 BC Landi, *DISMG* 175; *SEG* XL 900 (vase) (Μελόσας (gen.))

**Μελπομένη**

S. ITALY (LUCANIA):
—MURO LUCANO (MOD.): (1) imp. *CIL* X 437 (Lat. Equitia Melpomene)
SICILY:
—LIPARA: (2) imp. Libertini, *Isole Eolie* p. 225 no. 45 (M. Εὐδίας)
—TAUROMENION: (3) i AD *CIL* X 6997 (*ILat. Palermo* 50) (Lat. Coelia Melpomene)

**Μελπομενός**

LAKONIA:
—HYPERTELEATON*: (1) imp. *IG* V (1) 1082

**Μέλτας**

ARGOLIS:
—ARGOS: (1) f. vi BC *RE* (-) (s. Λακάδης: king)

**Μέλων**

MESSENIA:
—MESSENE: (1) iii BC *SEG* XXIII 209, 14

**Μέμμιος**

ACHAIA:
—PATRAI?: (1) 118 AD Vatin, *Delph. à l'ép. imp.* p. 66, 7, 13

**Μέμνων**

ACHAIA:
—PELLENE: (1) s. iii BC *IG* IV (1) 727 A, 7 (Perlman H.1) (f. Πεισίας); (2) 198 BC Liv. xxxii 22. 5 (Lat. Memnon: s. Πεισίας)
KORINTHIA:
—KORINTH: (3) c. 225-200 BC *IG* VII 309, 4 (*IOrop* 85) (f. Ἵππαρχος)
S. ITALY (APULIA):
—LUCERIA: (4) imp. *CIL* IX 834 (Lat. –ius Memno)
S. ITALY (BRUTTIUM):
—RHEGION: (5) iii-ii BC *IG* XIV 2400. 9 (Guarducci, *Ep. Gr.* 2 p. 496; Landi, *DISMG* 33 (tile))
S. ITALY (CALABRIA):
—TARAS-TARENTUM: (6) ii/i BC *IG* II² 10413 (s. Ἀρίστων)
SICILY:
—LIPARA: (7) hell.? Libertini, *Isole Eolie* p. 222 no. 29

**Μέμφις**

KERKYRA: (1) imp. *IG* IX (1) 959, 2 (Μέμ(μιος) M.)
SICILY:
—KATANE: (2) iii-v AD ib. XIV 527 (Wessel 911)

**Μένα**

EPIROS:
—BOUTHROTOS (PRASAIBOI): (1) a. 163 BC *IBouthrot* 76, 5; cf. *L'Illyrie mérid.* 2 p. 220 n. 6

**Μέναιος**

ARGOLIS:
—ARGOS:
——(Kleodaidai): (1) a. 316 BC *SEG* XXX 360, 5 (Perlman A.8)

**Μέναιχμος**

AKARNANIA:
—THYRREION: (1) iii BC *IG* IX (1)² (2) 255 (Μένα(ι)χμος)
KORINTHIA:
—SIKYON: (2) s. iv BC *RE* (1); *FGrH* 131 (Skalet 207) (?s. Ἀλκίβιος, Ἀλκιβιάδας)
SICILY:
—SYRACUSE: (3) hell. Plaut., *Men.* passim (Lat. Menaechmus: fict.)

**Μενάλκης**

ARKADIA:
—MANTINEIA-ANTIGONEIA: (1) c. 300-221 BC *IG* V (2) 323. 73 (tessera) (f. Ἀλεξίας)
—TEGEA: (2) f. iii BC ib. 42, 13 ([Με]νάλκη[ς])
ELIS: (3) inc. Moretti, *Olymp.* 970
—OLYMPIA*: (4) imp. *IvOl* 285 (Μενάλκ[ης])
S. ITALY (BRUTTIUM):
—LOKROI EPIZEPHYRIOI:
——(Ἀστ.): (5) 281 BC De Franciscis 1, 1, 4 ?= (6); (6) 276 BC ib. 23, 2 (s. Γοργίδας) ?= (5)
TRIPHYLIA:
—MAKISTOS: (7) 399-369 BC *SEG* XXXV 389, 11

**Μεναλκίδας**

ARGOLIS:
—ARGOS: (1) c. 315 BC ib. XXXII 370, 18 (Μεναλκ[ίδας])
LAKONIA:
—SPARTA: (2) c. 200-147 BC *RE* (-) (Bradford (1)); (3) s. i BC *IG* V (1) 92, 3 (Bradford (4)) (Μενα(λ)κίδας: f. Τιμοκλῆς); (4) ~ *IG* V (1) 95, 2; 266? (Bradford (3)) ([Μενα]λκίδ[ας]); (5) ~ *IG* V (1) 95, 6 (Bradford (2)) (s. Βρασίδας)
MESSENIA:
—MESSENE: (6) iv/iii BC *IG* V (1) 1435, 6

**Μέναλκος**

ZAKYNTHOS: (1) iv/iii BC ib. 1425, 5 (s. Ἀριστομένης)

**Μενανδρίδας**

ACHAIA: (1) iii BC *SEG* XL 394, 4, 7

**Μένανδρος**

ACHAIA: (1) 146 BC *IG* IV (1)² 28, 84 (f. Ἀνδρικός: synoikos)
—DYME: (2) c. 219 BC *SGDI* 1612, 5 (*Tyche* 5 (1990) p. 124)
AIGINA: (3) ?i BC *Alt-Ägina* I (2) p. 44 no. 8 (Μέναν[δρος]); (4) i BC-i AD ib. p. 45 no. 12, 5 (Μέναν[δρος]); (5) ~ ib. p. 45 no. 15 ([Μέ]νανδρος: s. Μηνόδοτος); (6) ?s. i BC ib. p. 43 no. 5; (7) i-ii AD ib. p. 47 no. 27, 4 (I f. Μένανδρος II); (8) ~ ib. l. 4 (II s. Μένανδρος I)
AITOLIA:
—KALYDON: (9) a. 142 BC *IG* IX (1)² (1) 137, 53 ([Μέ]νανδρος)
—THERMOS*: (10) s. iii BC ib. 60 V, 8; (11) ~ ib. l. 11; (12) ~ ib. 60 VI, 3; (13) ~ ib. l. 8; (14) ~ ib. l. 21; (15) ~ ib. l. 24; (16) ~ ib. 60 VII, 20
AITOLIA?:
—AIKLYMIOI: (17) a. 167 BC ib. 36, 8 (f. Νικόβουλος)
AKARNANIA:
—THYRREION: (18) ii BC ib. IX (1)² (2) 247, 9 (I f. Μένανδρος II); (19) ~ ib. l. 9 (II s. Μένανδρος I); (20) ~ ib. 251, 8 (s. Λυκίσκος); (21) a. 167 BC *NZ* 10 (1878) p. 175 nos. 21-3; *BMC Thessaly* p. 193 no. 12; *SNG Fitz. Macedonia–Acarnania* 2787 (coins); (22) c. 101-81 BC *FD* III (3) 338, 1 (and Epiros Kassope: s. Δαίδαλος); (23) 94 BC *IG* IX (1)² (2) 242, 8 (f. Δαίδαλος)
ARGOLIS:
—ARGOS: (24) iv BC Peek, *IAEpid* 225; (25) ~ ib. 225 b, 1; (26) ii-i BC *Mnem.* NS 47 (1919) p. 165 no. 10, 1 (f. Σοίκράτης); (27) 191-182 BC *IG* II² 2314, 17 (Μέν[ανδ]ρος: s. Μένιππος)
—EPIDAUROS: (28) i BC ib. IV (1)² 227 (s. Ἀσκλαπιάς, —λος); (29) i-ii AD ib. 484, 7 (f. Χαρικλῆς)
—EPIDAUROS*: (30) c. 370-365 BC Peek, *IAEpid* 52 B, 5; (31) c. 335-325 BC *IG* IV (1)² 108, 108, 145 (Μένα[νδρος])
—HERMIONE: (32) ?ii-i BC ib. IV (1) 731 I, 8 (s. Σωτηρίων)
—KALAURIA: (33) m. iii BC ib. IV (1)² 96, 43 (Perlman E.3); Perlman p. 63 f. (date) (s. Φιλοκλῆς)
—METHANA-ARSINOE: (34) i BC *IG* IV (1) 853, 10 (f. Ἀφθόνητος)
—TROIZEN: (35) imp. ib. 778
ARKADIA:
—MEGALOPOLIS: (36) c. 315-280 BC *FD* III (1) 44, 1 ([Μ]έ[ν]ανδ[ρος]: s. Μενέστρατος); (37) m. iii BC *IG* VII 11, 6 (s. Καλλικράτης); (38) ii BC ib. V (2) 447, 11 ([Μ]έναν[δρος])
—TEGEA: (39) f. iii BC ib. 35, 20 (s. Πραξίας)
—THELPHOUSA: (40) 175 BC *SGDI* 1865, 2, 4 (s. Κλεόξενος)
ELIS: (41) ?c. 475 BC *SEG* XXXI 358, 3; *LSAG*² p. 450 no. E (date)
EPIROS: (42) c. 200 BC Cabanes, *L'Épire* p. 558 no. 34, 5 (*SEG* XXVI 701) (s. Θύτας)
—AMBRAKIA: (43) ii-i BC *CIG* 1800, 4 (f. Διόδωρος); (44) a. 167 BC *SEG* XXXV 665 A, 12 (s. Κράτων); (45) s. ii BC Unp. (Arta Mus., inscr.) ([Μ]ένανδρος: f. Σώτων)
—ARGOS (AMPHILOCH.): (46) iv BC *NZ* 10 (1878) p. 95 no. 54 (coin) (Μένα(ν)δρος)
—BOUTHROTOS (PRASAIBOI): (47) a. 163 BC *IBouthrot* 31, 49 (*SEG* XXXVIII 490)
——Cheilioi: (48) a. 163 BC *IBouthrot* 98, 8 (s. Νικάνωρ)
——Cherrioi: (49) a. 163 BC ib. 111, 6; 112, 7 (f. Λαμία)
——Prakeleoi: (50) a. 163 BC ib. 36, 23 (*SEG* XXXVIII 495) (s. Νικάσιος)

——Somitai: (51) a. 163 BC IBouthrot 28, 1 (SEG XXXVIII 486)
——Thyioi: (52) a. 163 BC IBouthrot 102, 1
—CHARADROS: (53) a. 167 BC SEG XXXV 665 A, 1, 13; 665 B, 5 (s. Μητροφάνης)
—PHOINIKE: (54) iii/ii BC Cabanes, L'Épire pp. 569 ff. no. 47, 3 (SEG XXVI 720)
—TIAIOI: (55) c. 330 BC Cabanes, L'Épire p. 580 no. 55, 9
ILLYRIA:
—APOLLONIA: (56) c. 210 BC IG IX (1)² (1) 31, 79 (f. Τίμαιος); (57) 189 BC SGDI 2026, 8 (s. Τίμαιος)
KERKYRA: (58) c. 229-48 BC BMC Thessaly p. 148 nos. 510-13; SNG Cop. Epirus-Acarnania 232 (coins)
KORINTHIA:
—KORINTH: (59) ii AD Hesp. 39 (1970) p. 79, 5; SEG XXXI 285, 6; CIL III 7269, 6; ILGR 94, 10; PIR² G132 (Λ. Γέλλιος Μ.: f. Λ. Γέλλιος Ἰοῦστος, Λ. Γέλλιος Μυστικός); (60) ~ SEG XLI 273 B, 3 (s. Φλαβιανός, f. Ἀριστομένης); (61) iv AD Lib., Or. xiv 5; 9; 20; 46 (f. Ἀριστοφάνης)
—SIKYON: (62) iii/ii BC IG VII 2223, 4 (Skalet 208) (f. Μενέξενος)
LAKONIA:
—KYTHERA: (63) iv BC IG V (1) 937 (Poralla² 523)
—SPARTA: (64) c. 25-1 BC IG V (1) 212, 22 (Bradford (3)); (65) c. 70-110 AD IG V (1) 20 B, 5; 676, [17]; BSA 26 (1923-5) p. 168 no. C 7, 7 (Bradford (4)) (I f. Γ. Ἰούλ. Μένανδρος II); (66) ~ IG V (1) 20 B, 5; 676, 17; BSA 26 (1923-5) p. 168 C 7, 7 (Bradford (2)) (Γ. Ἰούλ. Μ.: II s. Μένανδρος I); (67) c. 90-100 AD SEG XI 558, 4 (Bradford (1)) (s. Γραφικός)
LEUKAS: (68) c. 167-50 BC BMC Thessaly pp. 181-2 nos. 114-15; p. 185 nos. 156-8; p. 186 nos. 182-3 (coins)
MESSENIA:
—KORONE: (69) 246 AD IG V (1) 1398, 26 (Ἰούλ. Μ.)
—MESSENE: (70) c. 146-32 BC Imhoof-Blümer, MGr p. 170 no. 77 (coin); (71) hell.-imp. PAE 1991, p. 106 no. 8, 11
S. ITALY (APULIA):
—HERDONIA: (72) ii/iii AD Ordona 2 pp. 129-32 nos. 1-3 (Lat. L. Arrenius Menander: f. Arrenia Felicissima)
S. ITALY (CAMPANIA):
—DIKAIARCHIA-PUTEOLI: (73) imp. CIL x 2911 (Lat. C. Ravius Menander)
—NEAPOLIS: (74) imp. NScav 1892, p. 317; cf. Leiwo p. 99 no. 50 (Lat. C. Brinnius Menander: f. Ἡλιάς)
—POMPEII: (75) i BC-i AD CIL IV 4024 (Lat. Menander)
S. ITALY (LUCANIA):
—HYELE-VELIA: (76) ?i AD PdelP 33 (1978) p. 65 no. 10 (Lat. A. Gabinius Menander: s. Λαΐς)
SICILY:
—KAMARINA: (77) f. v BC Cordano, Tessere Pubbliche 76 (Μέ[ν]αν[δρος]: f. Ἀρχέας)
—LIPARA: (78) inc. Chiron 22 (1992) p. 386
—PANORMOS: (79) c. 100 BC EAD XXX 429 (Μέναν[δρος]: f. Ἀρισ—)
—SYRACUSE: (80) ?iv/iii BC Plin., NH viii 14 (Lat. Menander)
—TAUROMENION: (81) c. 227 BC IG XIV 421 an. 14 (SGDI 5219) (f. Ζώϊλος) ?= (82); (82) c. 221 BC IG XIV 421 an. 20 (SGDI 5219) (f. Αἴνησις) ?= (81)

## Μενάρης
LAKONIA:
—SPARTA: (1) s. vi BC Hdt. vi 65. 1; 71. 1; viii 131 (Poralla² 524) (s. Ἀγησίλαος, f. Λατυχίδας)

## Μέναρχος
ACHAIA: (1) 316-309 BC IG II² 1956, 192; Ancient Macedonia 5 p. 445 with n. 10 (date)

AITOLIA: (2) ?228-215 BC FD III (4) 364, 2; SGDI 2525, 4; (3) 199 BC IG IX (1)² (3) 615, 2 (Μέναρχος, Ξέναρχος?)
ELIS: (4) hell. Plaut., Capt. 26; cf. Hermes 37 (1902) p. 196 (Lat. Menarchus: doctor/fict.)

## Μένασκος
LAKONIA:
—SPARTA: (1) 394 BC X., HG iv 2. 8; REG 99 (1986) p. 138 (name) (Poralla² 525) (Μενίσκος?—Masson)

## Μενέα
EPIROS:
—BOUTHROTOS (PRASAIBOI): (1) a. 163 BC IBouthrot 29, 46 (SEG XXXVIII 487)

## Μενέας
ARKADIA:
—TEGEA: (1) f. iii BC IG V (2) 35, 30 (s. Ἀριστομένης)
ILLYRIA:
—EPIDAMNOS-DYRRHACHION: (2) hell.-imp. IDyrrh 402 (f. Τιμᾶς)
KORINTHIA:
—KORINTH: (3) c. 610-590 BC Amyx 18. 2 (vase) (Lorber 28); LSAG² p. 131 no. 9 (date) (Με(ν)έας)

## Μενεδάϊος
LAKONIA:
—SPARTA: (1) 426 BC Th. iii 100. 2; 109 (Poralla² 526)

## Μενέδαμος
ACHAIA?: (1) 193 BC IG V (2) 293, 20 (f. Ἀριστέας)
AKARNANIA:
—STRATOS: (2) c. 175 BC ib. IX (1)² (1) 31, 142 (Μενέδ[αμ]ος)
ARGOLIS:
—ARGOS:
——Asine: (3) iv/iii BC Moretti, ISE 40, 32
—EPIDAUROS*: (4) c. 370-360 BC BSA 61 (1966) p. 272 no. 4 B II, 13-14 ([Με]νέδαμος)
—HERMIONE: (5) iii BC IG IV (1) 728, 17
EPIROS:
—BOUTHROTOS (PRASAIBOI):
——Kestrinoi: (6) a. 163 BC IBouthrot 31, 5 (SEG XXXVIII 490) (s. Βοΐσκος)
—DODONA: (7) iii BC Antoniou, Dodone Aa, 33 (Μενέδαμος); (8) ~ ib. Ab, 7
—KASSOPE: (9) ii BC GVI 1078, 1 (IG IX (1)² (2) 312 a) (f. Ἐχενίκα)
—LARRUOI: (10) c. 343-330 BC Cabanes, L'Épire p. 588 no. 74, 4 ?= (11)
—LARRUOI?: (11) m. iv BC ib. p. 541 no. 6, 7 (SEG XXVI 699) ([Με]νέδα[μος]) ?= (10)
—OMPHALES: (12) ?342-326 BC Cabanes, L'Épire p. 540 no. 4, 7 (IApoll 308); Cabanes, L'Épire p. 540 no. 5, 4
—PEIALES: (13) m. iv BC ib. p. 539 no. 3, 13
—PHOTIKE (NR.): (14) hell. SEG XXVII 228 (f. Ἄεροπος)
ILLYRIA:
—APOLLONIA: (15) ii-i BC IApoll 119 (s. Κρίσων)
KORINTHIA:
—KORINTH: (16) 181 BC Syll³ 585, 215 (f. Ἀντίπατρος)
LAKONIA:
—KYTHERA: (17) f. ii BC IC 2 p. 28 no. 12 A (Μενέδ[αμος])
S. ITALY (BRUTTIUM):
—KROTON: (18) 317-295 BC RE (4)
—LOKROI EPIZEPHYRIOI: (19) iv/iii BC De Franciscis 3, 14 (s. Ἐχεκράτης)
——(Φαω.): (20) iv/iii BC ib. 6, 7; 17, 6; 28, 6 (s. Λαγίσκος); (21) ~ ib. 10, 4
——(Θρα.): (22) iv/iii BC ib. 7, 7; 26, 4 (f. Εὐφάνης)
——(Σωτ.): (23) iv/iii BC ib. 9, 2

S. ITALY (LUCANIA):
—LEUKANOI: (24) c. 208 BC FD III (4) 135, 10 (-δη-: s. Φανίδης)

## Μενεδημερούμενος
S. ITALY (CAMPANIA):
—POMPEII: (1) i BC-i AD CIL IV 1211; 1212; 1616; 1637; 1870; 4555; 5189; 5417; 8564; 8581 etc. (Lat. Menedemerumenus)

## Μενέδημος
AIGINA: (1) ?i BC Alt-Ägina I (2) p. 44 no. 10 (s. Ποσειδώνιος)
ELIS: (2) f. i BC IvOl 214, 1; 215, 2 (II s. Μενέδημος I); (3) b. 36 BC ib. l. 1 (Moretti, Olymp. 705) (I s. Πρῶτος, f. Μενέδημος II)
EPIROS:
—DODONA: (4) 168-148 BC BMC Thessaly p. 93 nos. 68-71; Franke, Münz. v. Epirus pp. 37-9; pp. 308 ff. (coin) (M. Ἀργεάδης)
ILLYRIA:
—LYCHNIDOS: (5) iii-iv AD IG IV (1) 449 (Αὐρ. Μ.)

## Μένεια
ARGOLIS:
—HERMIONE: (1) iii BC ib. 728, 38

## Μενεκκᾶς
ILLYRIA:
—EPIDAMNOS-DYRRHACHION: (1) c. 250-50 BC Maier 293-300 (coin) (Ceka 27; 75; 131; 166; 175; 279; 288; 437; 455) (pryt.)

## Μενεκλείδας
ARGOLIS:
—EPIDAUROS:
——Lower Oiseia: (1) c. 365-335 BC IG IV (1)² 103, 57
LAKONIA:
—SPARTA: (2) ii AD SEG XI 782, 2 (Bradford (-)) (Τιβ. Κλ. Μενεκλίδας: s. Εὔδαμος)
—ZARAX: (3) ii-iii AD SEG XI 894 b I; 894 b II; 894 b IV (Τιβ. Κλ. Μ.: f. Καλλικράτης, Καλλίστρατος)
SICILY:
—SYRACUSE?:
——(Λαβ.): (4) hell. Manganaro, PdelP forthcoming no. 4 III, 7 (s. Μέττις)

## Μενεκλῆς
ACHAIA:
—PATRAI: (1) c. 146-32 BC BMC Pelop. p. 23 nos. 8-11 (coin) (f. Μητρόδωρος)
AITOLIA:
—KALYDON: (2) s. ii BC SEG XXV 621, 3 (f. Ἀντίοχος)
—THERMOS*: (3) s. iii BC IG IX (1)² (1) 60 II, 24
ARGOLIS:
—ARGOS: (4) ?277 BC FD III (1) 88, 5 (s. Μενέστρατος); (5) c. 235 BC IG II² 1299, 106; (6) imp. SEG XXVIII 396, 5 (Τιβ. Κλ. Μενεκλῆς); (7) ii AD ib. XVI 258 c, 8 (f. Γοργίλος)
—EPIDAUROS: (8) iii BC IG IV (1)² 341 (f. Θεύδωρος); (9) ii-iii AD ib. 526 ([Μ]ενεκλῆς: f. Εὔπορος)
——(Azantioi): (10) 146 BC ib. 28, 31 (I f. Μενεκλῆς II); (11) ~ ib. l. 31 (II s. Μενεκλῆς I)
—EPIDAUROS*: (12) iv/iii BC Peek, IAEpid 51, 3, 6; BSA 61 (1966) p. 319 no. 26 (date)
—HERMIONE: (13) iii BC IG IV (1) 728, 15 (f. Κράτης)
—PHLEIOUS: (14) iv/iii BC Peek, IAEpid 24, 1, 4 (II s. Μενεκλῆς I); (15) ~ ib. l. 4 (Με[νεκλῆς]: I f. Μενεκλῆς II)
—TROIZEN: (16) ?146 BC IG IV (1) 757 A, 40 ([Με]νεκλῆς: s. Αἰσχ—)
ARKADIA:
—TEGEA: (17) m. iii BC ib. V (2) 368, 74 (s. Νικο—)

——(Hippothoitai): (**18**) iv/iii BC ib. 38, 42 (f. *Δαμέας*)

ELIS: (**19**) 8-4 BC *SEG* XV 257, 4 ([*Με*]*νεκλῆς*); (**20**) ?i AD *EA* 1905, p. 259 no. 2, 3 ([*M*]*ενεκλῆς*)

KEPHALLENIA:

—PALE: (**21**) iii/ii BC Unp. (*IG* arch.) (*Μενεκλῆς*)

KORINTHIA:

—SIKYON: (**22**) ?iii/ii BC *IOrop* 521, 43 (f. —*ας*); (**23**) 207 BC *IMM* 41, 18 (f. *Γόργος*)

LAKONIA:

—SPARTA: (**24**) c. 50-100 AD *IG* V (1) 277, 2, 7 (*Artemis Orthia* pp. 308-9 no. 25 (date)); *SEG* XI 511, 4; 559, 3 (Bradford (5)); (**25**) c. 80-100 AD *SEG* XI 511, 3; 608, 6 (Bradford (1)) (*T. Τρεβελληνὸς M.*: s. *Ἀρεύς*); (**26**) 97 AD *IG* V (1) 667, 7-9 (Bradford (4)) (*Γ. Ἰούλ. M.*); (**27**) c. 100 AD *SEG* XI 515, 2; 637, [1]? (Bradford (2)) (s. *Κλεόδαμος*)

LEUKAS: (**28**) c. 167-50 BC Postolakas p. 67 no. 684; *NZ* 10 (1878) p. 132 no. 49 (coins)

S. ITALY (CAMPANIA):

—MISENUM: (**29**) a. 79 AD De Franciscis, *Sacello Augustali* p. 39 (Lat. C. Volusius Menecles)

SICILY:

—SYRACUSE?:

——(*Νητ*.): (**30**) hell. Manganaro, *PdelP* forthcoming no. 4 I, 6 (*Μενεκλείου* (gen.): f. *Μενέστρατος*)

## Μενεκράτεια

AKARNANIA:

—THYRREION: (**1**) iii BC *IG* IX (1)² (2) 269

## Μενεκράτης

AIGINA: (**1**) f. v BC ib. IV (1) 55; *LSAG*² p. 113 no. 10 (date) (or Phoenicia: ?s. *Φοῖνιξ*); (**2**) hell. *IG* IV (1) 1591 (f. *Μηνοφίλα*)

AITOLIA:

—BOUKATION: (**3**) 161 BC ib. IX (1)² (1) 100, 6

—LEPADA: (**4**) c. 215-205 BC *FD* III (4) 362, 6; Feyel, *Polybe* pp. 174 f. (locn.) (*M*[*ενεκρ*]*άτης*)

—THERMOS*: (**5**) s. iii BC *IG* IX (1)² (1) 60 VII, 21

AKARNANIA:

—STRATOS: (**6**) iv/iii BC ib. IX (1)² (2) 395, 8 (*Μενεκρ*[*άτης*]: f. *Τείσανδρος*); (**7**) a. 167 BC ib. IX (2) 6 a, 3; cf. Stählin p. 220 (date) (f. *Δορκίνας*)

ARGOLIS:

—ARGOS: (**8**) hell. *IG* IV (1) 637; (**9**) ?255-254 BC Nachtergael, *Les Galates* 8, 68; 9, 70; cf. Stephanis 2272 (f. *Σίμακος*)

—EPIDAUROS: (**10**) i-ii AD *IG* IV (1)² 552 (f. *Ζωῖλος*)

—HERMIONE: (**11**) iii BC ib. IV (1) 728, 10 (s. *Ξένων*); (**12**) m. ii BC *SEG* XI 377, 8; XXXI 328, 7 (I f. *Μενεκράτης* II); (**13**) ~ ib. XI 377, 8; XXXI 328, 7 (II s. *Μενεκράτης* I)

—METHANA-ARSINOE: (**14**) iv-iii BC *IG* IV (1) 862 ([*M*]*ενεκράτης*)

—TROIZEN: (**15**) iii BC ib. 810; (**16**) ~ ib. 824, 3 (s. *Φρασισθένης*)

—TROIZEN*: (**17**) iv BC ib. 823, 49 (*Μενεκρά*[*της*])

ARKADIA:

—MANTINEIA-ANTIGONEIA: (**18**) c. 300-221 BC ib. V (2) 323. 41 (tessera) (f. *Ἀριστόδαμος*)

—TEGEA: (**19**) f. iii BC ib. 35, 34 (f. *Μένιππος*)

DALMATIA:

—ISSA:

——(Hylleis): (**20**) iv/iii BC Brunšmid p. 8, 37 (*Μενεκ*[*ρ*]*άτης*: f. *Ἀνταλλος*)

EPIROS:

—AMBRAKIA: (**21**) m. iii BC *IG* V (2) 368, 20 (f. *Λέων*)

—KASSOPE: (**22**) iii BC Helly, *Gonnoi* 10, 2 (f. *Παυσανίας*)

ILLYRIA:

—APOLLONIA: (**23**) c. 250-50 BC Maier 70 (coin) (Ceka 68) (pryt.)

—EPIDAMNOS-DYRRHACHION: (**24**) c. 250-50 BC Maier 301-3 (Ceka 59; 191; 217) + *IApoll Ref. Bibl.* n. 63 (Ceka 308); *IApoll Ref. Bibl.* n. 12 (coin) (pryt.); (**25**) ii-i BC *IDyrrh* 567 (tile) ([*Με*]*νεκράτης*); (**26**) hell.-imp. ib. 308

KERKYRA: (**27**) hell.? *IG* IX (1) 861 (tile)

LAKONIA:

—SPARTA: (**28**) ?v-iv BC Plu., *Mor.* 797 C (Bradford (1)); (**29**) c. 25-1 BC *IG* V (1) 212, 31 (Bradford (2)) (f. *Νικάσιππος*)

S. ITALY: (**30**) 173 BC *Syll*³ 585, 279 (f. *Νίκανδρος*)

S. ITALY (CALABRIA):

—TARAS-TARENTUM: (**31**) c. 160 BC *ID* 1417 B II, 128; 1716, 5 (s. *Ἡρακλείδας, Μυραλλίς* (Syracuse))

S. ITALY (CAMPANIA):

—NEAPOLIS: (**32**) i AD *RE* (10); s.v. Iulius (358); *PIR*² I 430 (Lat. Iulius Menecrates)

—NUCERIA ALFATERNA: (**33**) imp. *CIL* X 1084 (Lat. M. Genicius Menecrates)

—POMPEII: (**34**) i BC-i AD ib. IV 3390 (Lat. Menecrates); (**35**) 70-79 AD ib. 636; Mouritsen p. 109 (date) (Lat. Menecrates); (**36**) ~ *CIL* IV 822; Mouritsen p. 110 (date) (Lat. Menecrates)

SICILY:

—AKRAI: (**37**) ii BC *Akrai* p. 156 no. 6, 22 (s. *Σῶσις*)

—GELA-PHINTIAS: (**38**) c. 530-520 BC *CEG* I 398 (Dubois, *IGDS* 132; Arena, *Iscr. Sic.* II 4; Lazzarini 854; Ebert, *Gr. Sieg.* 5); cf. *Ol. Forsch.* 1 pp. 83 ff. (f. *Παντάρης*)

—NOAI: (**39**) f. ii BC *BCH* 45 (1921) p. 25 col. IV, 109 (*SEG* XXII 455); cf. *Sic. Gymn.* 17 (1964) pp. 47 f. (*Μενεκρ*[*άτης*]? f. *Σῶσις*)

—SYRACUSE: (**40**) 410 BC X., *HG* i 1. 29 (f. *Μύσκων*); (**41**) iv BC *RE* (29); cf. Weinreich, *Menekrates Zeus u. Salmoneus* (doctor); (**42**) c. 160 BC *ID* 1716 (f. *Μυραλλίς*)

—TAUROMENION: (**43**) c. 162 BC *IG* XIV 421 an. 79 (*SGDI* 5219)

——(Ἀλκ.): (**44**) ?ii/i BC *IG* XIV 421 D an. 13 (*SGDI* 5219) (f. *Ἀπολλόδωρος*)

## Μενεκρέτης

ARKADIA:

—TEGEA: (**1**) iv/iii BC *IG* V (2) 38, 64 (*Μενεκρ*[*έτης*])

## Μενέκωλος

SICILY:

—SYRACUSE: (**1**) c. 600 BC Th. vi 5. 3 (and Sicily Kamarina: oikist)

## Μενελαΐδας

ARGOLIS:

—ARGOS: (**1**) a. 303 BC *CEG* II 816, 11 ([*M*]*ενελαΐδας*—*CEG*, [*Σθ*]*ενελαΐδας*?)

## Μενέλαος

AITOLIA:

—KONOPE-ARSINOE: (**1**) c. 143 BC *IG* IX (1)² (1) 34, [7]; 137, 27 (s. *Ἀνδρόνικος*)

AKARNANIA:

—STRATOS: (**2**) 185 BC ib. 32, 37

EPIROS: (**3**) 156 BC *ID* 1417 A I, 24

—AMBRAKIA: (**4**) hell.? *Ep. Chron.* 28 (1986-7) pp. 9 f. (tile); (**5**) ii BC *SEG* XLII 542 (s. *Χαιρέας*)

—BOUTHROTOS (PRASAIBOI):

——Kestrinoi: (**6**) ?164 BC Cabanes, *L'Épire* p. 586 no. 71, 1 (f. *Κόριθος*)

—CHARADROS: (**7**) a. 167 BC *SEG* XXXV 665 A, 15 (s. *Ἀλεξίμαχος*)

—DODONA: (**8**) iii BC Antoniou, *Dodone* Ab, 8; (**9**) ~ ib. l. 38

—MOLOSSOI: (**10**) ?iv/iii BC *SGDI* 1354, 1; cf. Cabanes, *L'Épire* p. 582 no. 58

——Kyestoi: (**11**) s. iii BC ib. p. 546 no. 15 ([*M*]*ενέλαος*: s. *Κρίσων*)

—OMPHALES CHIMOLIOI: (**12**) c. 330-310 BC ib. p. 578 no. 51, 13

ILLYRIA:

—EPIDAMNOS-DYRRHACHION: (**13**) hell.-imp. *IDyrrh* 182 (f. *Ἐξάκεστος*); (**14**) ~ ib. 294 (f. *Λέων*); (**15**) ~ ib. 309 (s. *Ἐξάκεστος*)

KORINTHIA:

—SIKYON: (**16**) ?221 BC *PUG* III 102 (s. *Κράτης*)

S. ITALY (CAMPANIA):

—POMPEII: (**17**) 38 AD *RAAN* 43 (1968) p. 195 ff.

## Μενέμαχος

AIGINA: (**1**) ii-i BC *IG* IV (1) 134 (s. *Διονύσιος*)

AITOLIA:

—PAMPHIA: (**2**) c. 162 BC ib. IX (1)² (1) 105, 11

—THERMOS*: (**3**) s. iii BC ib. 60 II, 10; (**4**) ~ ib. l. 27; (**5**) ~ ib. 60 III, 19; (**6**) ~ ib. l. 26

AKARNANIA: (**7**) iii BC Breccia, *Iscriz.* 293 (s. *Ἀπολλόδωρος*)

ARGOLIS:

—ARGOS: (**8**) 324 BC *CID* II 102 II A, 27

KEPHALLENIA:

—PRONNOI: (**9**) f. iii BC *Op. Ath.* 10 (1971) p. 67 no. 16

KORINTHIA:

—SIKYON: (**10**) c. 208 BC *FD* III (4) 135, 12 (f. *Κράτων*)

LAKONIA:

—SPARTA: (**11**) c. 115-140 AD *SEG* XI 543, 2; 582, [5] (Bradford (2)) (I f. *Μενέμαχος* II); (**12**) ~ *SEG* XI 543, 2; 582, 5 (Bradford (3)) (II s. *Μενέμαχος* I); (**13**) c. 133-160 AD *SEG* XI 547 a, [10]; 547 b, 7; 547 c, 3; 585, 6; 586, [5] (Bradford (3)) (f. *Νικιππίδας*)

## Μένεμος

ILLYRIA:

—AMANTIA: (**1**) imp. Cabanes, *L'Épire* p. 562 no. 39 (s. *Δρίμακος*)

## Μενέξενος

KORINTHIA:

—SIKYON: (**1**) iii/ii BC *IG* VII 2223, 3 (Skalet 209) (s. *Μένανδρος*)

## Μενέξιος

EPIROS:

—BOUTHROTOS (PRASAIBOI): (**1**) a. 163 BC *IBouthrot* 14, 33 (*SEG* XXXVIII 471)

——Pelmatioi: (**2**) a. 163 BC *IBouthrot* 53, 4 (*SEG* XXXVIII 504); *IBouthrot* 146, 7 (f. *Λυσανίας*) ?= (**3**); (**3**) ~ ib. 68, 2; 69, 3, 10; 70, 2, 8-9; 71, 2, 6, 8 (*BCH* 118 (1994) pp. 129 f. B 1-3); *IBouthrot* 162? (s. *Λυσανίας*, f. *Λυσανίας*, *Σώσανδρος*, *Λυκίσκα*) ?= (**2**)

## Μενέπολις

AKARNANIA:

—THYRREION: (**1**) iii BC *IG* IX (1)² (2) 270 (s./d. *Πολύξενος*)

## Μενεπτόλεμος

ILLYRIA:

—APOLLONIA: (**1**) ?vi/v BC Moretti, *Olymp.* 162

SICILY:

—SELINOUS: (**2**) vii/vi BC Guarducci, *Ep. Gr.* I p. 317 no. 9 (Dubois, *IGDS* 71; Arena, *Iscr. Sic.* I 16; *IGLMP* 76) (*Μενεπτό*[*λεμος*]: f. *Μύσκος*)

## Μενέσανδρος

AITOLIA: (**1**) ?228-215 BC *FD* III (4) 364, 2; *SGDI* 2525, 3

## Μενεσθεύς

AKARNANIA:

—PHOITIAI: (**1**) c. 325-315 BC *Hesp.* 57 (1988) p. 148 A, 48 (*SEG* XXXVI 331); cf. *Hesp.* 48 (1979) pp. 78 f. with pl. 22 c (s. *Μιλτιάδας*)

S. ITALY (CAMPANIA)?: (**2**) imp. *IG* XIV 2417. 2 b

**Μενεσθίδας**
KORINTHIA:
—KORINTH: (**1**) ?iv BC ib. II² 9062 (-δης)

**Μενέστας**
AITOLIA: (**1**) ?262 BC *FD* III (4) 357, 3
EPIROS: (**2**) iii/ii BC *RE* s.v. Menestratos (6); cf.
Walbank s.v. Plb. xx 10. 5 (Μενέστρατος—Plb.
xx 10. 5)

**Μενεστικλῆς**
LAKONIA:
—HYPERTELEATON*: (**1**) v BC *IG* v (1) 981
(Lazzarini 97; Poralla² 528) (-κλέˉς)

**Μενεστράτα**
EPIROS:
—BOUTHROTOS (PRASAIBOI): (**1**) a. 163 BC
*IBouthrot* 54, 4-5 (*SEG* XXXVIII 505) (d. Μη-
νόφιλος, m. Σωσίπατρος)
MESSENIA:
—MESSENE: (**2**) i AD *IG* v (1) 1479 (d. Ἀριστομέ-
νης)

**Μενέστρατος**
ACHAIA:
—DYME*: (**1**) c. 219 BC *SGDI* 1612, 44 (*Tyche*
5 (1990) p. 124) (s. Θεόπομπος)
AITOLIA: (**2**) iii BC *SEG* XVIII 244, 3
([Μ]ενέστρατος)
—KALYDON: (**3**) c. 142 BC *IG* IX (1)² (1) 137,
47 (f. Τιμόλοχος)
—POTIDANIA: (**4**) 153 BC ib. IX (1)² (3) 632, 7
(s. Θεόδωρος)
—THERMOS*: (**5**) s. iii BC ib. IX (1)² (1) 60 V,
18
ARGOLIS:
—ARGOS: (**6**) ?278-277 BC *FD* III (1) 87, 6; 88,
5; cf. 83, 6 with *Syll*³ 406 n. 7 (f. Νέων, Βρύας,
Μενεκλῆς, Ἀσκλαπιάδας); (**7**) ii BC *SEG* XLI 282
ARKADIA:
—MEGALOPOLIS: (**8**) c. 315-280 BC *FD* III (1)
44, 2 (f. Μέναν δρος)
ILLYRIA:
—EPIDAMNOS-DYRRHACHION: (**9**) hell.-imp.
*IDyrrh* 105 (f. Ἀνναία)
KERKYRA: (**10**) ?s. i BC *IG* IX (1) 778; *Korkyra*
1 p. 168 no. 18 (tiles)
KORINTHIA:
—KORINTH: (**11**) i-ii AD *IG* II² 9070 (-σστρα-: s.
Θωρακίδας)
LAKONIA:
—SPARTA: (**12**) hell.? ib. v (1) 650 (Bradford (-))
MESSENIA:
—THOURIA: (**13**) s. i BC *SEG* XI 974, 24, 35
(-σστρα-)
S. ITALY (BRUTTIUM):
—LOKROI EPIZEPHYRIOI:
——(Φαω.): (**14**) iv/iii BC De Franciscis 18, 3 (s.
Ἐμμενίδας)
S. ITALY (CAMPANIA):
—POMPEII: (**15**) i BC-i AD *CIL* IV 4804
SICILY:
—MENAI: (**16**) inc. *Riv. Stor. Antica* 5 (1900-1)
p. 57 no. 34 (s. Δικαίαρχος)
—SYRACUSE?:
——(Νητ.): (**17**) hell. Manganaro, *PdelP* forth-
coming no. 4 I, 6 (s. Μενεκλῆς)

**Μενέστωρ**
S. ITALY (BRUTTIUM):
—SYBARIS-THOURIOI-COPIAE: (**1**) vi BC *RE* (-);
*FVS* 32

**Μενέτιμος**
ARKADIA:
—MANTINEIA-ANTIGONEIA: (**1**) m. iii BC *IG* v
(2) 368, 119 (s. Νεοκρέτης)
KORINTHIA:
—SIKYON: (**2**) vi/v BC *SEG* XI 244, 48

**Μένετος**
AKARNANIA:
—ALYZIA: (**1**) iv BC *IG* IX (1)² (2) 444 (Μενέτω
(gen.): f. Κλέων)
ARKADIA:
—TEGEA:
——(Krariotai): (**2**) s. iv BC ib. v (2) 41, 51
(Μέ[ν]ετος: s. Π—)

**Μενέφυλος**
ACHAIA:
—AIGION: (**1**) 380 BC Paus. vi 3. 13 (f. Ξενοφῶν)
EPIROS:
—BOUTHROTOS (PRASAIBOI): (**2**) a. 163 BC
*IBouthrot* 30, 8 (*SEG* XXXVIII 488) ?= (4)
——Aphobioi: (**3**) a. 163 BC *IBouthrot* 27, 1
(*SEG* XXXVIII 485)
——Prakeleoi: (**4**) a. 163 BC *IBouthrot* 94, 7 (s.
Νικάσιος, Πολύκλεια) ?= (2)
—DODONA: (**5**) iii BC Antoniou, Dodone Aa, 11
—IOANNINA (MOD.): (**6**) iii-ii BC *Op. Ath.* 10
(1971) p. 65 no. 3 (*SEG* XXXVII 516) (f. Ἀν-
τίοχος) ?= (8)
—MOLOSSOI: (**7**) ?c. 370-344 BC Cabanes,
*L'Épire* p. 536 no. 2, 6
—TALAONOI/TALAIANES: (**8**) iii-ii BC *SGDI*
1349, 8; cf. Cabanes, *L'Épire* p. 580 no. 53
(f. Ἀντίοχος) ?= (6)

**Μενεχαρίδας**
LAKONIA:
—SPARTA: (**1**) c. 400-375 BC *IG* v (1) 1232, 8
(Poralla² 529)

**Μενέχαρμος**
EPIROS:
—BOUTHROTOS (PRASAIBOI): (**1**) a. 163 BC
*IBouthrot* 36, 6 (*SEG* XXXVIII 495) (s. Κλεό-
χαρμος)
—MOLOSSOI: (**2**) iii/ii BC *Syll*³ 1206, 7; cf.
Cabanes, *L'Épire* p. 583 no. 60

**Μενήν**
ILLYRIA:
—APOLLONIA: (**1**) ii-i BC *IApoll* 120 (s. Ἀνταν-
δρος)

**Μένης**
ARGOLIS:
—ARGOS: (**1**) s. iv BC *IG* II² 8370 (s. Καλλίας)
SICILY:
—KAMARINA: (**2**) 406 BC D.S. xiii 87. 5 (Cor-
dano, 'Camarina VII' 40)

**Μενητίδας**
DALMATIA:
—ISSA: (**1**) hell. Brunšmid p. 27 no. 18, 1 (*SEG*
XL 514; *VAHD* 84 (1991) p. 253 no. 3) (f.
Ἀγάθων)
——(Hylleis): (**2**) iv/iii BC Brunšmid p. 9, 59
(Μενη[τίδας]: f. Ἱππόδαμος)

**Μενήτιος**
ARGOLIS:
—HERMIONE: (**1**) iii BC *IG* IV (1) 729 I, 2 (f.
Σῶσος)

**Μένιος**
EPIROS:
—DODONA: (**1**) iii BC Antoniou, Dodone Ba, 28
(Μένιος)
KORINTHIA:
—KORINTH: (**2**) 334 BC *CID* II 79 A I, 28
(Μέ[ν]ιος)
LAKONIA:
—SPARTA: (**3**) vi/v BC Hdt. vi 71. 2 (Poralla²
530) (s. Διακτορίδας)

**Μενίππα**
AKARNANIA:
—THYRREION: (**1**) iii BC *IG* IX (1)² (2) 601

**Μενίππη**
SICILY:
—TYNDARIS: (**1**) ?ii BC ib. XIV 375

**Μένιππος**
AIGINA: (**1**) hell.-imp. ib. IV (1) 45; (**2**) i BC-i
AD *Alt-Ägina* I (2) p. 45 no. 12, 2 (Μένιπ[πος])
AITOLIA:
—LITHOVOUNI (MOD.) (AKRAI?): (**3**) a. 170 BC
*IG* IX (1) 228, 8
—PHISTYON: (**4**) ii BC ib. IX (1)² (1) 110 a, 6
—THERMOS*: (**5**) s. iii BC ib. 60 III, 13; (**6**) ~
ib. l. 15; (**7**) ~ ib. 60 IV, 22; (**8**) ~ ib. 60 VI,
23
AKARNANIA:
—PALAIROS: (**9**) ii BC ib. IX (1)² (2) 451, 8 (f.
Λύκος)
ARGOLIS:
—ARGOS: (**10**) 191-182 BC ib. II² 2314, 17
(f. Μέανδρος); (**11**) 105 BC *JÖAI* 14 (1911)
Beibl. p. 146 no. 4, 18 ([Μέ]νιππος: s. Μνάσιπ-
πος)
ARKADIA:
—MANTINEIA-ANTIGONEIA: (**12**) 64 or 62 BC
*IG* v (2) 265, 48 (f. Ἀρίσταρχος)
—TEGEA: (**13**) c. 369-362 BC ib. 173, 25; cf.
*CEG* II 657 (Μένι[ππος]?); (**14**) f. iii BC *IG*
v (2) 35, 34 (s. Μενεκράτης)
ELIS: (**15**) i BC/i AD *IvOl* 209, 1 (Μένι[ππ]ος: f.
Δαμαιθίδας)
ILLYRIA: (**16**) ii BC *PP* 15692 (*GVI* 751)
LAKONIA:
—SPARTA: (**17**) ?i-ii AD *IG* v (1) 672 (Bradford
(1)) (s. Εὐδαιμονίδας); (**18**) ?s. i AD *IG* v (1)
661 (Bradford (2)) (s. Πολυκλῆς); (**19**) c. 80-
100 AD *SEG* XI 608, 7; 632, 1 (Bradford (4);
(5)) (Γ. Ἰούλ. Μ.); (**20**) c. 175-200 AD *SEG* XI
503, 21 (Bradford (2)) (Μένι[ππ]ος: s. Πασι-
κράτης)
S. ITALY (BRUTTIUM):
—LOKROI EPIZEPHYRIOI:
——(Πυρ.): (**21**) iv/iii BC De Franciscis 26, 3
(Μένιπ(π)ος: s. Σίλων)
S. ITALY (CAMPANIA):
—DIKAIARCHIA-PUTEOLI: (**22**) imp. *IG* XIV 849
—PITHEKOUSSAI-AENARIA: (**23**) i BC-i AD ib.
892 (doctor); (**24**) imp. Monti, *Ischia* p. 224
n. 43 (Lat. (M)enippus)
—POMPEII: (**25**) i BC-i AD *CIL* IV 1471 (Lat.
Menipus)
S. ITALY (LUCANIA):
—HERAKLEIA: (**26**) c. 250-175 BC *SEG* XXXII
810 (s. Ἀρτεμίδωρος)

**Μενίσκα**
ILLYRIA:
—EPIDAMNOS-DYRRHACHION: (**1**) iv BC *IDyrrh*
16; (**2**) hell.-imp. ib. 310; (**3**) ~ ib. 311 (d.
Αἰσχρίων); (**4**) ~ ib. 312 (d. Ἀρίσταρχος)

**Μενίσκη**
SICILY:
—TYRAKION: (**1**) iv BC *IG* II² 10467

**Μενίσκος**
AITOLIA:
—THERMOS*: (**1**) s. iii BC ib. IX (1)² (1) 60 VII,
5
ILLYRIA:
—EPIDAMNOS-DYRRHACHION: (**2**) c. 250-50 BC
Ceka, *Probleme* p. 151 no. 43 (coin) (pryt.)
?= (4); (**3**) ~ Maier 91; 101; 144; 157; 159;
201; 256; 265; 278; 354; 386; 393; 396; 490;
Münsterberg p. 41 (Ceka 315-32); *IApoll Ref.
Bibl.* n. 88 (coin) (money.); (**4**) ~ Maier 304-6
(coin) (Ceka 280; 309) + *IApoll Ref. Bibl.* n.
84 (438) (pryt.) ?= (2)
KORINTHIA:
—SIKYON: (**5**) vi/v BC *SEG* XI 244, 46; (**6**)
c. 100-90 BC ib. XXXIII 290 A, 18; *BSA*
70 (1975) pp. 129-31 (date) (Skalet 210); cf.
Stephanis 2057 (f. Πετραῖος); (**7**) i BC *SEG*
XIII 248, 9 (Stephanis 1664) (s. Ἁρμόδιος)

Μενναρώ 298 Μερόη

LAKONIA:
—SPARTA: (8) c. 110-135 AD *IG* v (1) 32 B, 18; *SEG* XI 575, 10 (Bradford (3)) (I f. Μενίσκος II); (9) ~ *IG* v (1) 32 B, 18; *SEG* XI 575, 10 (Bradford (1)) (II s. Μενίσκος I); (10) 137 AD *SEG* XI 494, 4; 496, 3; 521 a, [1]; 521 b, 1 (Bradford (1)) (Γ. Ἰούλ. Μ.); (11) c. 150-160 AD *SEG* XI 528, 5 (f. Εὔδαμος); (12) c. 170 AD ib. 530, 3 (Μενίσκ[ος]: f. Πολύβιος)

SICILY:
—ENTELLA: (13) f. i BC Cic., *In Verr.* II iii 200 (Lat. Meniscus)
—HALAISA: (14) ii BC *IGSI* 2 A II, 74 (Dubois, *IGDS* 196) (f. Φιλόξενος)
—KAMARINA: (15) iv/iii BC Manganaro, *PdelP* forthcoming no. 2, 1 ([Με]νίσκος)
—KENTORIPA: (16) ii-i BC Dubois, *IGDS* 189, [2], 10 (*SEG* XLII 837) (f. Ζώαρχος)
—SYRACUSE: (17) c. 321-306 BC *AM* 72 (1957) p. 197 no. 30, 2, 10 (s. Ἐ—); (18) iii BC *IG* II² 10390 (f. Δόξα)

**Μενναρώ**
SICILY: (1) s. vi BC Dubois, *IGDS* 217 (vase) (Arena, *Iscr. Sic.* I 74) (Μενναρῶς (gen.)— Dubois, Μεννάδος (gen.)—Arena: d. Καλικράτης)

**Μέννας**
S. ITALY (BRUTTIUM):
—RHEGION*: (1) inc. *NScav* 1890, p. 196 (terracotta)

**Μεννέας**
AKARNANIA:
—ALYZIA: (1) i BC *IG* IX (1)² (2) 446 b (f. Ἀριστομένης)
—STRATOS: (2) c. 325-315 BC *Hesp.* 57 (1988) p. 148 B, 39 (*SEG* XXXVI 331); cf. *Hesp.* 48 (1979) pp. 78 f. with pl. 22 c; cf. Tod, *GHI* II 78 (s. Καρφίνας); (3) a. 167 BC *IG* IX (1)² (1) 36, 4, 9 (s. Δαμοτίων)

**Μεννείας**
AKARNANIA: (1) c. 250-167 BC *NZ* 10 (1878) pp. 29-30 nos. 31-2; *BMC Thessaly* p. 169 no. 13 (coins)
—ALYZIA: (2) iii/ii BC *IG* IX (1)² (2) 583, 22; Ijsewijn 83; *Hermes* 85 (1957) pp. 501 ff. (ident.) (f. Ἀριστομένης); (3) c. 200 BC *IG* IX (1)² (2) 445

**Μεννώ**
ARKADIA:
—PHIGALEIA: (1) m. iii BC *SEG* XXIII 239, 2

**Μένοικος**
S. ITALY (CAMPANIA):
—POMPEII: (1) f. i AD *CIL* X 1007 (Castrèn 204. 14); Kockel p. 67 (date) (Lat. Istacidius Menoecus)

**Μενοίτας**
AIGINA: (1) ii-i BC *IG* IV (1) 138 b (f. Μηνοδότη)
AITOLIA:
—KALYDON: (2) iii/ii BC ib. IX (1)² (1) 136, 9
EPIROS: (3) ii BC Cabanes, *L'Épire* p. 590 no. 76, 14 (*SEG* XXVI 704) ([Με]νοίτας)
—BOUTHROTOS (PRASAIBOI): (4) a. 163 BC *IBouthrot* 15, 13; (5) ~ ib. 38, 17 (*SEG* XXXVIII 497) (f. Αἴσχρα); (6) ~ *IBouthrot* 68, 8; (7) ~ ib. 101, 4 (s. Δείνων); (8) ~ ib. 134, 15; 138, 5-6 (s. Δρωπύλος, ?f. Δρωπύλος) ?= (12); (9) ~ ib. 135, 12; 152, 5 (s. Βοΐσκος) ?= (11)
——Messaneoi: (10) a. 163 BC ib. 14, 9; 17, 3, 5; 18, 1; 19, 8; 21, 17; 26, 5; 27, 6; 29, 45; 38, 12; 41, 6, 10; cf. *SEG* XXXVIII 471-2; 474-6; 478; 484-5; 487; *IBouthrot* 48, 12; 50, 12; 146, 3 (s. Βοΐσκος, f. Βοΐσκος, Δεινομάχα, Βουβάλιον, ?f. Θερσώ) ?= (11); (11) ~ ib. 72, 2; 73; 74 ?= (9) (10)

——Pelmatioi: (12) a. 163 BC ib. 116, 2, 7 (s.p.) (*BCH* 118 (1994) p. 121 A); *IBouthrot* 145, 5 (s. Δρωπύλος) ?= (8); (13) ~ ib. 144, 2 (f. Σ—ος)
——Prakeleoi: (14) a. 163 BC ib. 52, 7 (*SEG* XXXVIII 517) (f. Παν—); (15) ~ *IBouthrot* 94, 11 (s. Ἰρόμαχος)
——Tharioi: (16) a. 163 BC ib. 68, 8 (s. Νικόμαχος)
ILLYRIA:
—EPIDAMNOS-DYRRHACHION: (17) hell.-imp. *IDyrrh* 433 (f. Φίλιππος)
KORINTHIA:
—SIKYON?: (18) c. 45 AD *FD* III (1) 534, 7

**Μενοίτιος**
AKARNANIA:
—THYRREION: (1) ii BC *IG* IX (1)² (2) 247, 4; 251, 4 (f. Ἀλκαῖος, Λυσίας); (2) ~ ib. 250, 4; (3) ~ ib. 251, 12 (f. Σώστρατος)
EPIROS:
—AMBRAKIA: (4) iii BC *BCH* 17 (1893) p. 633 (f. Πιθάνα)
—BOUTHROTOS (PRASAIBOI):
——Loigyphioi: (5) a. 163 BC *IBouthrot* 137, 14 (Μενοιτίου (gen.): f. Νίκαιος)
KORINTHIA:
—KORINTH: (6) iv BC *Hesp.* 43 (1974) p. 26 no. 36 (f. Ἐπίχαρμος)
KYNOURIA:
—PRASIAI?: (7) ?s. vi BC *IG* v (1) 928 (Lazzarini 85); *LSAG*² p. 194 n. 2 (date) (Poralla² 531) (Μεν[οί]τι[ο]ς)
S. ITALY (BRUTTIUM):
—LOKROI EPIZEPHYRIOI:
——(Φαω.): (8) 279 BC De Franciscis 13, 8 (f. Σιμύλος)

**Μενοκράτης**
S. ITALY (CAMPANIA):
—SALERNUM*: (1) ?i AD *IItal* I (1) 238 II, 4 (*CIL* X 557) (Lat. L. Appuleius Menocrates: freed.)
TRIPHYLIA:
—MAKISTOS (NR.): (2) iii BC *SEG* XVI 283; *BE* 1958, no. 246 (date)

**Μενόμαχος**
S. ITALY (CAMPANIA):
—POMPEII*: (1) f. i AD *CIL* X 1037 (Castrèn 109. 12); Kockel p. 179 (date) (Lat. L. Ceius Menomachus: freed.)

**Μενόστρατος**
ARGOLIS:
—TROIZEN: (1) ?146 BC *IG* IV (1) 757 B, 36 ([Μ]ενό[σ]τρατος: s. Καλ—)

**Μένουσα**
S. ITALY (CAMPANIA):
—DIKAIARCHIA-PUTEOLI: (1) imp. *CIL* X 2651 (Lat. Grania Menusa: m. Ζωῖλος, Ὡραία)

**Μέντας**
ARKADIA:
—MEGALOPOLIS: (1) ?iv-iii BC Paus. viii 31. 7

**Μέντιος**
S. ITALY?: (1) c. 185 BC *ID* 427, 11; 442 B, 89 (Τίτος Μ.)

**Μέντωρ**
ARGOLIS:
—KLEONAI: (1) c. 230-200 BC *BCH* 45 (1921) p. 15 II, 147 (s. Ἄρχιππος)
—PHLEIOUS: (2) 345 BC *CID* II 31, 78, 82
S. ITALY (LUCANIA):
—HERAKLEIA: (3) c. 360-340 BC ib. 6 B, 9 (doctor)
SICILY:
—SYRACUSE: (4) inc. Plin., *NH* viii 56 (Lat. Mentor)

**Μένυλλος**
ARGOLIS:
—ARGOS: (1) hell.? *IG* II² 8375 (f. Σωστράτα); (2) ii BC ib. 8371 ([Μέ]νυλλος)
DALMATIA:
—ISSA:
——(Pamphyloi): (3) iv/iii BC Brunšmid p. 8, 38 (f. Σωνύλος)
SICILY:
—SELINOUS?: (4) v BC *SEG* XXXIX 1021 II, 2

**Μένων**
ACHAIA:
—AIGION: (1) ?f. iv BC *SGDI* 1606 (Μ. (Ἀ)σπευς)
AITOLIA:
—THERMOS*: (2) s. iii BC *IG* IX (1)² (1) 60 VI, 11
ARGOLIS:
—ARGOS: (3) iv BC *SEG* XXXI 313 ([Μ]ένων); (4) hell.? ib. XXXIX 352 (tile)
—HERMIONE: (5) iv BC *IG* IV (1) 742, 12
ARKADIA:
—TEGEA: (6) f. iii BC ib. v (2) 35, 28 (s. Μικίων)
EPIROS:
—ORIKOS: (7) f. ii BC *BCH* 45 (1921) p. 22 IV, 43 (s. Μεν—)
LAKONIA:
—SPARTA: (8) c. 530-500 BC *CEG* I 375, 2 (μενον—lap., μὲν ὀν—ed. pr.); (9) 336 BC *CID* II 24 II, 5 (Poralla² 532)
S. ITALY (BRUTTIUM):
—KROTON: (10) iv BC Iamb., *VP* 170; 267 (*FVS* 1 p. 446)
—LOKROI EPIZEPHYRIOI: (11) hell.? De Franciscis p. 102 (f. Ἀρίσταρχος)
——(Ἀλχ.): (12) iv/iii BC ib. 32, 6 (s. Εὐφραίνετος)
——(Λακ.): (13) iv/iii BC ib. 31, 2 (f. Φορμίων)
——(Προ.): (14) iv/iii BC ib. 11, 4 (f. Ἀριστοκράτης)
S. ITALY (CAMPANIA):
—POMPEII: (15) i BC-i AD *CIL* IV 4253 (Lat. Meno)
SICILY: (16) iv/iii BC Vandermersch pp. 170-1 (amph.) (or S. Italy: Μένω[ν])
—KAMARINA: (17) m. v BC Dubois, *IGDS* 120, 1 (Arena, *Iscr. Sic.* II 142 A-B; *SEG* XXXVIII 939; Cordano, 'Camarina VII' 41) (-νõν: s. Δαμέας)
—SEGESTA: (18) 307-289 BC D.S. xxi 16. 2 ff.; 18. 1 (slave)
—TAUROMENION: (19) c. 219-198 BC *IG* XIV 421 an. 22; 421 an. 31; 421 an. 43 (*SGDI* 5219) (f. Ἀγέας); (20) c. 183 BC *IG* XIV 421 an. 58 (*SGDI* 5219) (s. Θεόφιλος); (21) c. 168-155 BC *IGSI* 4 III (IV), 4 an. 86; *SGDI* 2610, 3 (f. Ἀγάθαρχος)
—ZANKLE-MESSANA: (22) i-ii AD Charito i 7. 2 (fict.)

**Μέριμνος**
S. ITALY (LUCANIA):
—POTENTIA: (1) imp. *CIL* X 8059. 444 (seal) (Lat. M. Vipsanius Merimnus)

**Μερίς**
LEUKAS: (1) iv BC *AM* 27 (1902) p. 369 no. 35

**Μέριτα**
SICILY:
—SYRACUSE: (1) iii-v AD Strazzulla 193 (Wessel 1328)

**Μερόη**
S. ITALY (CAMPANIA):
—DIKAIARCHIA-PUTEOLI: (1) imp. *CIL* X 2731 (Lat. Meroe)
—POMPEII: (2) i BC-i AD ib. IV 2172 (Lat. Mero[e]); (3) ~ ib. 9062 (Lat. Meroe)
S. ITALY (LUCANIA):
—EBURUM: (4) i AD *IItal* III (1) 6 (*CIL* X 452) (Lat. Marcia Meroe)

**Μερόπη**

SICILY:
—SYRACUSE: (5) iii-v AD Strazzulla 347 (Wessel 999)

**Μερόπη**

EPIROS:
—NIKOPOLIS: (1) imp. SEG XXXIX 537
S. ITALY (APULIA):
—CANUSIUM: (2) s. ii AD Epig. Rom. di Canosa 131 (CIL IX 378) (Lat. Faenia [Me]rope: d. Μέροψ, Θεοδότη, ?m. Θεόδοτος)
S. ITALY (CALABRIA):
—HYRIA: (3) imp. Museo Ribezzo 10 (1977) p. 152 no. a (CIL IX 700) (Lat. Rufin(i)a Merope: m. Vinius Etruscus)
SICILY:
—ZANKLE-MESSANA: (4) imp. Mon. Ant. 24 (1916) p. 175 (Lat. Mevia Merope)

**Μερόπιος**

S. ITALY (CAMPANIA):
—DIKAIARCHIA-PUTEOLI: (1) imp. CIL X 2338 (Lat. Antonius Meropius)

**Μέροψ**

ARGOS:
—ARGOS: (1) her. FGrH 115 F 393 (s. Θέστιος, f. Ἀριστοδαμίδας: king)
S. ITALY (APULIA):
—CANUSIUM: (2) s. ii AD Epig. Rom. di Canosa 131 (CIL IX 378) (Lat. Faenius [Mer]ops: f. Μερόπη); (3) 223 AD Epig. Rom. di Canosa 35 II, 16 (CIL IX 338) (Lat. L. Faenius Merops); (4) ~ Epig. Rom. di Canosa 35 III, 19 (CIL IX 338) (Lat. L. Faenius Merops iun(ior))
—VENUSIA*: (5) imp. ib. 518 (Lat. M. Creperius Merops: freed.)

**Μεσόδαμος**

DALMATIA:
—ISSA:
——(Dymanes): (1) iv/iii BC Brunšmid p. 7, 19 (f. Ἀρχέλαος)

**Μέσσαλος**

ILLYRIA:
—EPIDAMNOS-DYRRHACHION: (1) c. 250-50 BC Ceka, Probleme p. 151 no. 44 (coin) (pryt.)

**Μέστης**

S. ITALY (APULIA):
—VENUSIA: (1) imp. NScav 1939, p. 149 no. 1 (Lat. Mestes)

**Μεταγένης**

LAKONIA:
—SPARTA: (1) 421 BC Th. v 19. 1; 24 (Poralla² 533)

**Μέττις**

SICILY:
—SYRACUSE?:
——(Λαβ.): (1) hell. Manganaro, PdelP forthcoming no. 4 III, 7 (f. Μενεκλείδας)

**Μέτων**

S. ITALY (CALABRIA):
—TARAS-TARENTUM: (1) f. iii BC RE (3)
SICILY:
—AKRAGAS: (2) f. v BC ib. (1); D.L. viii 51-2 (s. Ἐμπεδοκλῆς, ?f. Ἐμπεδοκλῆς, Καλλικρατίδας)

**Μετώπα**

KERKYRA: (1) m. iv BC Ag. XVII 517

**Μέτωπος**

S. ITALY (BRUTTIUM):
—SYBARIS-THOURIOI-COPIAE: (1) vi BC RE (-) (or S. Italy (Lucania) Metapontion)

**Μήδειος**

AITOLIA:
—THERMOS*: (1) s. iii BC IG IX (1)² (1) 60 VI, 22

**Μήδοκος**

ARKADIA: (1) 55 BC BGU 1002, 3 (s. Εὔδαμος)

**Μηδόκριτος**

KORINTHIA:
—KORINTH: (1) c. 500-475 BC IG IV (1) 353 (vase); LSAG² p. 132 no. 31 (date) (Μē-)

**Μήζωτρος**

S. ITALY (BRUTTIUM):
—HIPPONION-VIBO VALENTIA (NR.): (1) inc. IG XIV 2412. 31 (f. Μαῦρος)

**Μηλοφῶν**

EPIROS:
—BOUTHROTOS (PRASAIBOI): (1) a. 163 BC IBouthrot 76, 7 (f. Φίλων)

**Μήνας**

LAKONIA:
—SPARTA: (1) 421 BC Th. v 19. 1; 21. 1; 24; Masson, OGS 2 p. 513 (name) (Poralla² 534) (Μηνᾶς—Poralla)

**Μηνᾶς**

ARGOLIS:
—ARGOS: (1) v-vi AD Unp. (Oikonomou-Laniado)
ARKADIA:
—MANTINEIA-ANTIGONEIA: (2) 64 or 62 BC IG V (2) 265, 50 (I f. Μηνᾶς II); (3) ~ ib. l. 50 (II s. Μηνᾶς I)
MESSENIA:
—ASINE: (4) ii AD ib. V (1) 1408 (s. Λέσβιος)
—MESSENE: (5) 31 BC-14 AD SEG XXIII 207, 33 (s. Ζώπυρος)
S. ITALY (CAMPANIA):
—DIKAIARCHIA-PUTEOLI?: (6) imp. IG XIV 799
—POMPEII: (7) i BC-i AD CIL IV 1396 (Lat. Mena—Solin)

**Μηνιάς**

S. ITALY (CAMPANIA):
—DIKAIARCHIA-PUTEOLI: (1) imp. AJA 77 (1973) p. 156 no. 5 (Lat. Herennia Menias)

**Μήνιος**

LAKONIA:
—GYTHEION: (1) f. i AD IG V (1) 1167, 13 (f. Δαμαρχίς)
—SPARTA: (2) ii/iii AD ib. 307, 2 (Artemis Orthia pp. 328-9 no. 60); IG V (1) 313, 4 (Artemis Orthia pp. 334-5 no. 70); IG V (1) 314, 12 (Artemis Orthia p. 335 no. 71); IG V (1) 601, 8, 14; BSA 79 (1984) p. 284 no. 13 (date, stemma) (Bradford s.v. Κλέανδρος (3)) (Κλέανδρος ὁ καὶ Μ., Μήνιρ—307: s. Καλλίστρατος, f. Μ. Αὐρ. Εὔπορος)
S. ITALY (LUCANIA):
—LEUKANOI: (3) 197 BC SGDI 2042, 2-3 (slave/freed.)

**Μῆνις**

AIGINA: (1) iii BC IG II² 7958 (f. Μηνόδωρος); (2) i BC-i AD ib. 7961 (f. Μύστα)

**Μηνογένης**

AITOLIA:
—THERMOS*: (1) s. iii BC ib. IX (1)² (1) 60 II, 4; (2) ~ ib. 60 IV, 16
ARGOLIS:
—EPIDAUROS: (3) 129 AD ib. IV (1)² 381, 6 (II s. Μηνογένης I); (4) ~ ib. l. 7 (I f. Μηνογένης II); (5) ?iv AD ib. 517 + Peek, IAEpid 211 (Μη[ν]ογένης: f. Ἄγλαος)
ILLYRIA:
—EPIDAMNOS-DYRRHACHION: (6) hell.-imp. IDyrrh 313 (Μηνογένη—lap.: s. Δωρόθεος)

**Μηνοδότη**

AIGINA: (1) ii-i BC IG IV (1) 138 b (d. Μενοίτας)

**Μηνόδοτος**

AIGINA: (1) ?i BC ib. II² 7964 (f. Πανική); (2) ~ Alt-Ägina I (2) p. 44 no. 11, 1 (s. Ἱερώνυμος); (3) i BC-i AD ib. p. 45 no. 15 (f. Μένανδρος)
ARGOLIS:
—ARGOS*: (4) 105 BC JÖAI 14 (1911) Beibl. p. 146 no. 4, 18 (slave/freed.?)
EPIROS:
—TREN (MOD.): (5) hell.? Iliria 1971, p. 44 (loomweight) (?f. Γᾶ)
ILLYRIA:
—APOLLONIA: (6) c. 250-50 BC Maier 27 (coin) (Ceka 76) (money.)
KORINTHIA:
—SIKYON: (7) ?39 AD SEG XIV 312 (I f. Μηνόδοτος II); (8) ~ ib. (II s. Μηνόδοτος I)
S. ITALY (CAMPANIA):
—ATELLA: (9) ?i-ii AD RAAN 38 (1963) p. 19 (Lat. Ti. Cl. Menodotus: s. Ti. Cl. Eutychianus)
—DIKAIARCHIA-PUTEOLI: (10) ?i-ii AD CIL X 2149 (Lat. Aurelius Quirinius Me(n)odotus)
—DIKAIARCHIA-PUTEOLI*: (11) imp. ib. 2402 (Lat. P. Fabius Menodotus: freed.)
—POMPEII: (12) i BC-i AD ib. IV 1315
SICILY:
—SYRACUSE: (13) ?135 BC Milet I (3) 103, 4 (s. Ματρόδωρος)

**Μηνοδώρα**

AITOLIA:
—TRICHONION?: (1) c. 200 BC SBBerlAk 1936, p. 387 no. 1 ([Μ]ηνοδώρα)

**Μηνόδωρος**

ACHAIA:
—DYME*: (1) c. 219 BC SGDI 1612, 70 (Tyche 5 (1990) p. 124) ([Μη]νόδωρος: s. Ἀσκλαπιόδωρος)
AIGINA: (2) hell.? IG IV (1) 117 (f. Θεόφιλος); (3) iii BC ib. II² 7958 (s. Μῆνις)
AITOLIA:
—THERMOS*: (4) s. iii BC ib. IX (1)² (1) 60 II, 3; (5) ~ ib. 60 VI, 14; (6) ~ ib. l. 16; (7) ~ ib. l. 18
ARGOLIS:
—EPIDAUROS: (8) i-ii AD ib. IV (1)² 508 (s. Ἄγα—)
ARKADIA: (9) ii/i BC SEG XLI 1635, 5 (s. Ἀσκληπιάδης)
MESSENIA:
—MESSENE: (10) c. 140 BC IvOl 52, 4, 32 (s. Διονύσιος)

**Μηνόθεμις**

S. ITALY (CAMPANIA):
—DIKAIARCHIA-PUTEOLI: (1) imp. CIL X 2955 (Lat. L. Sextilius Menothemis: f. Ταῦρος)

**Μηνοκλῆς**

S. ITALY (APULIA):
—CANUSIUM: (1) imp. Epig. Rom. di Canosa Add. 9 (Lat. Menocle)

**Μῆνος?**

S. ITALY (CAMPANIA):
—POMPEII: (1) i BC-i AD CIL IV 4947

**Μηνοφάνης**

ACHAIA?: (1) 37 AD IG VII 2711, 38
AITOLIA:
—THERMOS*: (2) s. iii BC ib. IX (1)² (1) 60 V, 15 ([Μη]νοφάνης)
LAKONIA:
—SPARTA: (3) f. iii AD ib. V (1) 303, 5 (Artemis Orthia pp. 327-8 no. 57); IG V (1) 325, 2 (Artemis Orthia p. 336 no. 73); IG V (1) 464, 13; SEG XLI 384, 3; BSA 79 (1984) p. 283; 80 (1985) pp. 244; 246 (ident., stemma) (Bradford (-)) (and Arkadia Tegea?: Σέξ.

*Πομπ. Μ.*: s. *Σέξ. Πομπ. Θεόξενος*, f. *Πομπ. Ἀριστοτέλης*)

**Μηνοφάντα**
S. Italy (Campania):
—dikaiarchia-puteoli: (1) imp. *CIL* x 2090 (Lat. Appuleia Menophant[a])

**Μηνόφαντος**
S. Italy (Campania):
—neapolis: (1) i bc *IG* xiv 779 (*INap* 100) (*Αὐφίδιος Μ.*)

**Μηνοφίλα**
Aigina: (1) hell. *IG* iv (1) 1591 (d. *Μενεκράτης*)

**Μηνοφιλίς**
Kerkyra: (1) imp. ib. ix (1) 960 (d. *Μηνόφιλος*)

**Μηνόφιλος**
Aitolia:
—thermos*: (1) s. iii bc ib. ix (1)² (1) 60 II, 28; (2) ~ ib. 60 V, 6; (3) ~ ib. 60 VII, 23
Argolis: (4) imp. *SEG* i 73
—epidauros: (5) i ad *IG* iv (1)² 26, 4; (6) 187 ad ib. 395 II (I f. *Μηνόφιλος* II); (7) ~ ib. (II s. *Μηνόφιλος* I)
——(Hysminatai): (8) 146 bc ib. 28, 11 (s. *Αἰνησίδαμος*); (9) ~ ib. l. 23 (s. *Ζωῖλος*)
—hermione: (10) ?ii-i bc ib. iv (1) 731 III, 2 (f. *Νικίας*)
Epiros:
—bouthrotos (prasaiboi): (11) a. 163 bc *IBouthrot* 54, 5; cf. *SEG* xxxviii 505 (f. *Μενεστράτα*)
Kerkyra: (12) imp. *IG* ix (1) 960 (f. *Μηνοφιλίς*)
Korinthia:
—korinth: (13) imp. ib. ii² 9075 (*Μηνόφι[λος]*: f. *Σωσι—*); (14) ~ ib. iv (1) 400
—sikyon: (15) c. 100-90 bc *SEG* xxxiii 290 A, 14; *BSA* 70 (1975) pp. 129-31 (date); cf. Stephanis 1342 (f. *Καλλίμαχος*)
Lakonia:
—sparta: (16) ?i ad *IG* v (1) 916 (Bradford (-))
S. Italy (Apulia):
—canusium*: (17) imp. *Epig. Rom. di Canosa* 199 (Lat. C. Vavidius Menophilus: freed.)
—venusia: (18) imp. *CIL* ix 479 (Lat. Menophilus)
S. Italy (Calabria):
—brentesion-brundisium: (19) imp. *Epigraphica* 25 (1963) p. 41 no. 15 (Lat. M. Mae[nius] [Me]noph[ilus])
S. Italy (Campania):
—dikaiarchia-puteoli: (20) imp. *CIL* x 1966 (Lat. Decius Menofilus); (21) ?i-ii ad ib. 2569 (Lat. C. Iulius Menophilus: s. *Μουσογένης*, f. C. Iulius Rufus, Iulius Bassus)
—dikaiarchia-puteoli*: (22) i ad *Puteoli* 11 (1987) p. 130 no. 3 (Lat. Q. Granius Menophilus: freed.)
—herculaneum*: (23) i bc-i ad *CIL* x 1403 f III, 9 (Lat. M. Calatorius Menophilus: freed.)
—neapolis: (24) i bc-i ad? *IG* xiv 800 (*INap* 145) (s. *Φιλήμων*)
—pompeii*: (25) i bc-i ad *CIL* x 906 (Castrèn 27. 1) (Lat. Menophil(us))

**Μηστρία**
Messenia:
—messene: (1) ii/iii ad *IG* v (1) 1472

**Μήστωρ**
Sicily:
—selinous?: (1) vi/v bc *SEG* xxxix 1020 A, 3, 5, etc.; 1020 B, 1, etc. (*Μέστōρ*: s. *Γίκελος*)

**Μητίοχος**
S. Italy (Campania):
—pompeii: (1) i bc-i ad *CIL* iv 5054 (Lat. Mettiocus)

**Μητρᾶς**
S. Italy (Campania):
—neapolis*: (1) i bc/i ad *NScav* 1926, p. 235; cf. Leiwo p. 97 no. 46 (Lat. A. Fuficius Metra: freed.)

**Μητρικῶν**
Dalmatia:
—issa:
——(Dymanes): (1) iv/iii bc Brunšmid p. 8, 28 ([*Μ*]*ητρικῶν*: s. *Ἀριστήν*); (2) ~ ib. l. 46

**Μήτριος**
Argolis:
—argos: (1) c. 458 bc *IG* i³ 1149, 17 ([*Μ*]*έτριος*)

**Μητρόβιος**
Elis: (1) 209-213 ad *IvOl* 110, 11, 26 (*Αὐ(ρ). Μ.*: s. *Σωτήριχος*, ?f. *Συγχαίρων*)
S. Italy (Campania):
—pandateria*: (2) i ad *CIL* x 6785 (Lat. Metrobius: imp. freed.)

**Μητρόδωρος**
Achaia:
—patrai: (1) c. 146-32 bc *BMC Pelop.* p. 23 nos. 8-11 (coin) (s. *Μενεκλῆς*)
Aigina: (2) ?f. i ad *Alt-Ägina* I (2) p. 45 no. 17, 1 (f. *Ξενοκλείδας*)
Aitolia:
—thermos*: (3) s. iii bc *IG* ix (1)² (1) 60 IV, 1; (4) ~ ib. 60 VII, 24
Argolis:
—epidauros: (5) iii bc Peek, *IAEpid* 43, 34
Epiros:
—nikopolis: (6) s. ii ad *AEp* 1901, no. 126, 52 (Lat. M. Aur. Metrodorus)
Lakonia:
—sparta: (7) c. 140-160 ad *IG* v (1) 37, 9; 64, 5; *SEG* xi 587, 3 (Bradford (-)) (s. *Ἀπολλώνιος*)
S. Italy (Campania):
—dikaiarchia-puteoli: (8) imp. *CIL* x 3289; cf. *Puteoli* 12-13 (1988-9) p. 74 no. 2 (Lat. Methrod[orus])
—pompeii?: (9) i bc-i ad *CIL* iv 8396 (Lat. Metrodorus)

**Μητροφάνης**
Aitolia:
—thermos*: (1) s. iii bc *IG* ix (1)² (1) 60 VII, 2
Epiros:
—charadros: (2) a. 167 bc *SEG* xxxv 665 A, 2, 13 (f. *Μένανδρος*)
Lakonia:
—sparta?: (3) a. 212 ad *IG* v (1) 563, 2; cf. Cartledge–Spawforth p. 181 (Bradford (-)) (*Αἰλ. Μ.*)
S. Italy (Campania):
—dikaiarchia-puteoli: (4) imp. *CIL* x 1923, 4, 6 (Lat. C. Caesonius Metrophanes: freed.)

**Μητρῶναξ**
S. Italy (Campania):
—neapolis: (1) i ad *RE* (-); cf. Leiwo p. 40

**Μίγκων**
S. Italy (Bruttium):
—petelia: (1) ?c. 475 bc *IGSI* 19, 5 (Landi, *DISMG* 171); *LSAG*² p. 261 no. 28 (date) (*Μίνκōν*)

**Μίδας**
S. Italy (Lucania):
—herakleia: (1) c. 125-100 bc *ID* 1689; 1854, 3; 2234, 9-10; 2253, [1]; 2254, 1; 2288, 1 (s. *Ζήνων*)
Sicily:
—akragas: (2) vi/v bc *RE* (6) (Stephanis 1702)

**Μίθαικος**
Sicily: (1) ?v bc *RE* s.v. Kochbücher col. 934; *CAF* 3 p. 478 fr. 374

**Μίθρης**
S. Italy (Campania):
—pompeii: (1) i bc-i ad *CIL* iv 9197; *Gnomon* 45 (1973) p. 268 (Lat. Mithres)

**Μιθυλῖνος**
Arkadia:
—heraia: (1) iii bc *IG* v (2) 415, 8 (*IPArk* 23) (f. *Τιμέας*)

**Μίθων**
Argolis:
—argos:
——Upper Hysea (Melanippidai): (1) iii bc *Mnem.* NS 43 (1915) pp. 372-3 D, 10 (Perlman A.23) (f. *Λαχάρης*)

**Μίκαρος?**
S. Italy (Campania):
—salernum*: (1) ?i ad *IItal* i (1) 238 II, 17 (*CIL* x 557) (Lat. L. Appuleius Micarus: freed.)

**Μικιάδας**
Kerkyra: (1) 433 bc Th. i 47. 1 (-δης)

**Μίκιλλος**
Achaia:
—aiga: (1) iv bc *IG* ii² 8404; p. 884 (date)

**Μικίνας**
Kerkyra: (1) c. 85 bc *IOrop* 521, 29, 33, 37, 61 (s. *Ἡράκλειτος*)

**Μικίων**
Argolis:
—argos: (1) 345-324 bc *CID* ii 31, 77; 75 II, 44; 97, 28; 102 II B, [30] (s. *Κλάσις*)
—epidauros: (2) iv/iii bc *IG* iv (1)² 285 (*Μικί[ων]*)
Arkadia:
—tegea: (3) f. iii bc ib. v (2) 35, 28 (f. *Μένων*)
——(Apolloniatai): (4) m. iii bc ib. 36, 101 (s. *Γόργος*)
——(Krariotai): (5) m. iii bc ib. l. 87 (f. *Λίσων*)
Korinthia:
—korinth: (6) iv bc ib. ii² 9071; (7) f. iii bc *Das Heroon von Kalydon* p. 294, 2 (s. *Φιλόξενος*)
Messenia:
—messene?: (8) ii/i bc *SEG* xi 979, 40
Sicily:
—akragas: (9) ?c. 400 bc *BMC Sicily* p. 18 no. 121 (coin graffito) (-ōν)
—syracuse: (10) m. iii bc *RE* s.v. Mikon (4); *SEG* xvii 196 (name) (s. *Νικήρατος*: sculptor)

**Μίκκα**
Elis: (1) 272 bc Plu., *Mor.* 251 A-B (d. *Φιλόδαμος*)

**Μικκέας**
Aitolia: (1) ?iii bc *RPh* 1899, p. 282 no. 3
—agrinion (nr.): (2) iii/ii bc *SBBerlAk* 1936, p. 388 no. 2, 8 (*L'Illyrie mérid.* 1 p. 110 fig. 7)
—kallion/kallipolis: (3) 272 bc *IG* ix (1)² (1) 13, 42
—kalydon: (4) 185 bc ib. 71, 2 (ix (1)² (3) 784) (f. *Νικόστρατος*)

**Μικκία**
S. Italy (Apulia):
—cannae: (1) ii-iii ad *Epig. Rom. di Canosa* 33 (Lat. Gaia Miccia: m. *Μικκίων*, Aemilius Fronto)

**Μικκίας**
AITOLIA:
—PHILOTAIEIS: (**1**) f. ii BC *IG* IX (1)² (1) 96, 23 (f. *Λέων*)
ELIS: (**2**) 36-24 BC *IvOl* 59, 18; 62, 5; 69, 20 (s. *Τίμων*, f. *Ἀλεξίων*: mantis/Klytiadai); (**3**) f. i AD ib. 76, 3; 77, 8 (s. *Ἀλεξίων*: mantis/Klytiadai)

**Μικκίνας**
KERKYRA: (**1**) c. 166 BC *IG* II² 2316, 15-16 (s. —*κλείδης*)

**Μικκίων**
S. ITALY (APULIA):
—CANNAE: (**1**) ii-iii AD *Epig. Rom. di Canosa* 33 (Lat. Aemilius Miccio: s. *Τράχαλος*, *Μικκία*)
S. ITALY (CAMPANIA):
—HERCULANEUM: (**2**) m. i AD *PdelP* 8 (1953) p. 461 no. 50, 2 (Lat. M. Ruffellius Miccio)
—POMPEII: (**3**) i BC-i AD *CIL* IV 2416 (Lat. Miccio)

**Μίκκος**
ACHAIA:
—DYME: (**1**) 219 BC Plb. iv 59. 2
—PELLENE: (**2**) s. ii BC *HE* 3600 (or Euboia Histiaia-Oreos Pallene: fict.?)
AITOLIA: (**3**) ?274 BC *FD* III (1) 83, 2 (Flacelière p. 387 no. 5 a); *CID* II 124, [1]
S. ITALY (CAMPANIA):
—KYME: (**4**) f. i AD *Puteoli* 3 (1979) p. 164 no. 6 (Lat. Miccus)

**Μικκύλος**
AITOLIA: (**1**) ?252-248 BC *Syll*³ 422, 3

**Μίκος**
AITOLIA:
—POTIDANIA: (**1**) m. ii BC *SBBerlAk* 1936, p. 371 a, 13 (*SEG* XLI 528 A); *SBBerlAk* 1936, p. 371 b, 3, 11 (*SEG* XLI 528 B) (f. *Δάμαρχος*, *Φιλόχορος*)
ARGOLIS:
—ARGOS: (**2**) v BC *Argive Heraeum* 2 p. 186 no. 8 and pl. 69 (vase)

**Μικύθα**
LEUKAS: (**1**) f. v BC *IG* IX (1) 544; *LSAG*² p. 229 no. 5 (date)

**Μικυθίων**
ARKADIA:
—TEGEA: (**1**) s. iv BC *SEG* XXXVI 383, 7 (f. *Σύρος*)
KORINTHIA:
—KORINTH: (**2**) c. 570-550 BC Amyx 114. 2 (vase) (*Philia Epi* 2 p. 166 no. 2) (*Μιροθίον*: her.?)

**Μίκυθος**
ARGOLIS:
—EPIDAUROS*: (**1**) c. 370 BC *IG* IV (1)² 102, 249
KORINTHIA:
—KORINTH: (**2**) vii/vi BC *SEG* XIII 229 (*Μί<ρι>ρυθος*)
S. ITALY (BRUTTIUM):
—RHEGION: (**3**) f. v BC *RE* (1); *IvOl* 267-9 (Dubois, *IGDGG* 1 35; Arena, *Iscr. Sic.* III 64); Paus. v 26. 2 ff. (and Arkadia Tegea and Sicily Zankle-Messana: s. *Χοῖρος*)
SICILY:
—SELINOUS?: (**4**) vi/v BC *SEG* XXXIX 1020 A, 4 (-ρυ-: f. *Σιμίας*)

**Μικύλα**
LAKONIA:
—ASINE: (**1**) iv BC *IG* II² 8387a (-λη)

**Μικυλίων**
ARGOLIS:
—ARGOS*: (**1**) f. iii BC ib. IV (1) 529, 11 (slave/freed.?)
ARKADIA:
—MEGALOPOLIS: (**2**) ii/i BC ib. v (2) 444, 7 (*IPArk* 32) (*Μ[ικυ]λίων*: s. *Νικολαΐδας*)

**Μίκυλλος**
ARGOLIS:
—EPIDAUROS: (**1**) ?ii BC *IG* IV (1)² 335, 2 + Peek, *IAEpid* 144 (s. *Δᾶμος*)

**Μικύλος**
ACHAIA:
—PELLENE: (**1**) iv BC *SEG* XI 1271 (*Μικύλ[ος]*)
ARGOLIS:
—EPIDAUROS: (**2**) ?c. 500-475 BC *IG* IV (1)² 136 (Lazzarini 77); *LSAG*² p. 182 no. 10 (date)
ARKADIA:
—KYNAITHA: (**3**) ?253 BC Nachtergael, *Les Galates* 10, 31 (Stephanis 1707) (s. *Ἵππακος*)
—TEGEA: (**4**) ?iii/ii BC *IG* v (2) 90
DALMATIA:
—ISSA:
——(Pamphyloi): (**5**) iv/iii BC Brunšmid p. 8, 28 (f. *Σώσανδρος*)
KORINTHIA:
—SIKYON: (**6**) vi/v BC *SEG* XI 244, 15

**Μίκων**
AIGINA: (**1**) vi/v BC Paus. v 25. 10, 13; viii 42. 7, 10; *IPerg* 48; cf. *RE* s.v. Onatas (1) (*Σμίκων*—*IPerg*.: f. *Ὀνάτας*)
DALMATIA:
—ISSA:
——(Hylleis): (**2**) iv/iii BC Brunšmid p. 9, 64 (s. *Ἀθα*—)
LEUKAS: (**3**) iii BC *BCH* 79 (1955) p. 262
S. ITALY (BRUTTIUM):
—SYBARIS-THOURIOI-COPIAE: (**4**) iii BC Theoc., *Id.* v 112 (fict.)

**Μίλατος**
ARGOLIS:
—EPIDAUROS: (**1**) c. 370 BC *IG* IV (1)² 102, 18 ([*M*]*ίλατος*)

**Μιλήσιος**
EPIROS:
—BOUTHROTOS (PRASAIBOI): (**1**) 31 BC-14 AD Imhoof-Blümer, *MGr* p. 140 no. 36; *RAAN* 21 (1941) p. 282 (Sestieri, *ILat. Albania* 7) (Lat. F. Graecinus Milesius)
KORINTHIA:
—KORINTH: (**2**) s. i BC *Corinth* VIII (3) 311 (Lat. M. Antonius Milesius: s. *Γλαῦκος*)

**Μιλήτα**
AKARNANIA:
—PALAIROS: (**1**) iv BC *IG* IX (1)² (2) 452

**Μιλτεύς**
ARGOLIS:
—EPIDAUROS: (**1**) ?c. 475-450 BC ib. IV (1)² 143 (Lazzarini 353); *LSAG*² p. 182 no. 15 (date) (f. *Φιλόμηλος*)

**Μιλτιάδας**
AKARNANIA:
—PHOITIAI: (**1**) c. 325-315 BC *Hesp.* 57 (1988) p. 148 A, 48 (*SEG* XXXVI 331); cf. *Hesp.* 48 (1979) pp. 78 f. with pl. 22 c (f. *Μενεσθεύς*)
ARGOLIS:
—PHLEIOUS: (**2**) 327-324 BC *CID* II 97, 27; 102 II B, 36; 120 A, 50 (f. *Ἀνδρέας*)
ARKADIA:
—TEGEA:
——(Athaneatai): (**3**) iv/iii BC *IG* v (2) 38, 17 (f. *Ἀριστόμαχος*)

SICILY:
—SELINOUS: (**4**) ?vi BC Polyaen. i 28. 2 (f. *Θήρων*)

**Μιλτιάδης**
ARKADIA:
—TEGEA: (**1**) ii AD *IG* v (2) 55, 30 (f. *Ἔλενος*)

**Μίλων**
ARKADIA:
—ALIPHEIRA: (**1**) ?273 BC *SEG* XXV 447, 8 (*IPArk* 24); *Chiron* 3 (1973) pp. 85-93 (date)
—PALLANTION: (**2**) a. 316 BC *SEG* XI 1084, 34 (Perlman A.3) (s. *Τίμων*)
EPIROS: (**3**) m. iii BC Polyaen. viii 52 (s. *Φιλωτέρα*) ?= (**4**)
—MOLOSSOI?: (**4**) m. iii BC *RE* (5) ?= (**3**)
—THESPROTOI: (**5**) s. iii BC Cabanes, *L'Épire* p. 547 no. 17 (s. *Σώσανδρος*)
LAKONIA:
—SPARTA?: (**6**) 395 BC *Hell. Oxy.* vi 3; viii 1; Aeschin. ii 78 (Poralla² 535) (*Χίλων*—Aeschin.)
S. ITALY (BRUTTIUM):
—KROTON: (**7**) m. vi BC *RE* (2); Moretti, *Olymp.* 115; cf. Ebert, *Gr. Sieg.* 61 (s. *Διότιμος*); (**8**) iv BC Iamb., *VP* 104; 249; 267 (*FVS* 1 pp. 446 ff.)
S. ITALY (CAMPANIA):
—NEAPOLIS: (**9**) imp. *CIL* X 8169; cf. Leiwo p. 92 (Lat. Octavius Milo)
—POMPEII: (**10**) i BC-i AD *NScav* 1916, p. 303 no. 107 (Castrèn 12. 9) (Lat. M. Aemilius Milo)

**Μιλωνίδας**
KORINTHIA:
—KORINTH: (**1**) c. 570-550 BC Amyx 120. 1 (pinax) (*IG* IV (1) 244; Lorber 114; *LSAG*² p. 131 no. 20) (-λō-: potter/painter)

**Μιμαλλίς**
S. ITALY (CAMPANIA):
—DIKAIARCHIA-PUTEOLI: (**1**) ?i-ii AD *CIL* X 2602 (2578); cf. *Misc. Gr. Rom.* 8 p. 44? (Lat. Iulia Mimallis)

**Μιμάρα**
S. ITALY (LUCANIA):
—GRUMENTUM: (**1**) imp. *CIL* X 187 (Lat. Mimara)

**Μιμνέας**
AITOLIA: (**1**) ?257 BC Nachtergael, *Les Galates* 7, 5
ARKADIA:
—MANTINEIA-ANTIGONEIA: (**2**) iii-ii BC *IG* v (2) 319, 31

**Μιμνόμαχος**
S. ITALY (CALABRIA):
—TARAS-TARENTUM: (**1**) iv BC Iamb., *VP* 267 (*FVS* 1 p. 446)

**Μίμων**
KORINTHIA:
—KORINTH: (**1**) c. 570-550 BC Amyx 114. 3 (vase) (-μōν: her.?)

**Μίναιχμος**
ARKADIA:
—ORCHOMENOS: (**1**) f. iii BC *BCH* 38 (1914) p. 461 no. 5, 7

**Μίνασσα**
ILLYRIA:
—SKAMPIS: (**1**) imp. *Stud. Alb.* 1969 (2), p. 176 (d. *Μίρος*)

**Μινάτιος**
S. ITALY: (**1**) c. 150 BC *ID* 1520, 6, 21, 29, 39, 41, 45, 52 etc (*Μάαρκος Μ.*: s. *Σέξτος*)

**Μίνατος**
DALMATIA:
—ISSA: (**1**) f. ii BC Brunšmid p. 23 no. 10, 10 (*Μεί*-: s. *Ἀριστίων*)

S. ITALY (BRUTTIUM):
—PETELIA: (2) iii-ii BC *SEG* XXXIV 1008 (I f. *Μίνατος* II Κρίττιος, Μᾶρκος Κρίττιος); (3) ~ ib. (*M. Κρίττιος* —δας: II s. *Μίνατος* I)
S. ITALY (CAMPANIA):
—KYME: (4) 220 BC *ID* 351, 6; 442 B, 147 (I f. *Μίνατος* II Τήϊος); (5) ~ ib. 351, 6; 442 B, 147 (*M. Τήϊος*: II s. *Μίνατος* I)
—MAMERTINOI: (6) ?f. iii BC *SEG* XXX 1121, 27 (Dubois, *IGDS* 208) (*M. Κοροΰϊος*)

**Μίνδαρος**
LAKONIA:
—SPARTA: (1) 411-410 BC *RE* (-); *IPr* 316, 13 (Poralla² 536) (*Ζμίνδαρος—IPr*)

**Μινικιανός**
KORINTHIA:
—KORINTH: (1) ii AD *Corinth* IV (2) p. 188 no. 560 (lamp)

**Μινίκιος**
KORINTHIA:
—KORINTH: (1) ii/iii AD *BM Lamps* 3 p. 405 no. Q3254; *SEG* XXVII 35. 18 (lamps)

**Μινουκία**
SICILY: (1) iii-iv AD *IGUR* 795

**Μίντων**
ARGOLIS:
—ARGOS: (1) ?c. 575-550 BC *SEG* XI 336, 9; *LSAG²* p. 168 no. 7 (date) (-τōν: f. *Κτῆτος*)

**Μινύρα**
SICILY:
—SEGESTA: (1) ?ii BC *IG* XIV 287 (Dubois, *IGDS* 213) (d. *Ἀρτέμων*)
—SYRACUSE: (2) iii BC *NScav* 1905, p. 387 (d. *Χαιρύλος*)

**Μιραλλύς**
S. ITALY (BRUTTIUM):
—PATERNUM?: (1) imp. *CIL* x 120 (Lat. Mirallys: m. Valentina)

**Μιρᾶς**
KERKYRA?: (1) imp. *IG* IX (1) 974 (Μει-: s. *Σάββος*)

**Μιρίκυθος**
ACHAIA?: (1) ?vii BC *LSAG²* p. 224 no. 5 (-ρυθος)

**Μίρκα**
AITOLIA:
—LITHOVOUNI (MOD.) (AKRAI?): (1) v/iv BC *SEG* XXXIV 466; cf. *BCH* 101 (1977) p. 579 (vase) (*Μικρά*?)

**Μίρος**
ILLYRIA:
—SKAMPIS: (1) imp. *Stud. Alb.* 1969 (2), p. 176 (f. *Μίνασσα*)

**Μίρων**
KERKYRA: (1) iv/iii BC Unp. (*IG* arch.) (f. *Εὐθυκράτης*)

**Μισγολαΐδας**
LAKONIA:
—SPARTA: (1) 411 BC X., *HG* ii 3. 10 (Poralla² 537)

**Μιτάλων**
SICILY:
—SYRACUSE: (1) vi/v BC Dubois, *IGDS* 87 (vase) (*SEG* XXXVI 885; XXXVIII 971) (-λōν)

**Μιτιάδας**
SICILY:
—SELINOUS?: (1) v BC ib. XXXIX 1021 II, 3; cf. *BE* 1990, no. 863

**Μιτύλος**
S. ITALY (CAMPANIA):
—DIKAIARCHIA-PUTEOLI: (1) ?i-ii AD *CIL* x 2300 (Lat. M. Iulius Mitulus)

**Μίτυς**
ARGOLIS:
—ARGOS: (1) arch.? Arist., *Po.* 1452 a 8-9; Ps.-Arist., *Mir.* 846 a 22; Plu., *Mor.* 553 D (*Βίτυς*—Ps.-Arist.); (2) v/iv BC D. lix 33

**Μίτων**
AITOLIA:
—LITHOVOUNI (MOD.) (AKRAI?): (1) v/iv BC *SEG* XXXIV 466 (vase) (*Μίτονος* (gen.?))

**Μίων**
ILLYRIA:
—EPIDAMNOS-DYRRHACHION: (1) c. 250-50 BC Münsterberg p. 260 = Nachtr. p. 16 (Ceka 359); cf. *IApoll Ref. Bibl.* s.v. (coin) (*Μύωνος?*—Münsterberg: pryt.)

**Μναΐμαχος**
ARGOLIS:
—ARGOS:
——Prosymna: (1) c. 330-300 BC *SEG* XXX 355, 4 (-hί-)

**Μναῖος**
EPIROS:
—TOSKESI (MOD.): (1) iv BC *AD* 23 (1968) Chron. p. 292 (s. *Οἰνάτας*)

**Μναΐς**
ARGOLIS:
—ARGOS: (1) ii BC *SEG* XLII 279, 7 (d. *Εὐθύδαμος*)

**Μναΐστρατος**
ACHAIA?: (1) 193 BC *IG* v (2) 293, 10 (f. *Αἰσχίνας*)

**Μναιστρία**
AKARNANIA:
—ECHINOS?: (1) ii BC ib. IX (1)² (2) 375

**Μναΐτιμος**
ARGOLIS:
—ARGOS:
——Pallas (Heraieis): (1) s. iii BC *SEG* XVII 144, 4 (Perlman A.20) (f. *Ἀριστεύς*)

**Μνάμαχος**
ARGOLIS:
—ARGOS: (1) iv-iii BC Unp. (Argos, Kavvadias)

**Μναμονίδας**
ILLYRIA:
—DIVJAKA (MOD.): (1) hell. *Iliria* 1982 (1), p. 120 no. 39 (tile); cf. p. 123

**Μναμόσυνον**
ILLYRIA:
—APOLLONIA: (1) ii-i BC *IApoll* 121

**Μνάμων**
ARGOLIS:
—HERMIONE: (1) c. 210-207 BC *IG* IV (1)² 73, 6; *SEG* XXXV 303 (date) (f. *Ἀμφαίνετος*); (2) i BC-i AD? *IG* IV (1) 730 IV, 7 (f. *Νουμήνιος*)
—KLEONAI: (3) c. 315 BC *SEG* XXXII 370, 10
SICILY:
—SELINOUS: (4) m. v BC Dubois, *IGDS* 36, 2 (Arena, *Iscr. Sic.* I 69) (*M(ν)άμōν*: f. *Δενδίλος*)
—SYRACUSE?:
——(Ἐριμ.): (5) hell. Manganaro, *PdelP* forthcoming no. 4 I, 7 (*Μνά[μ]ων*: f. *Ὀνάτωρ*)

**Μνασαγόρας**
AKARNANIA:
—ANAKTORION: (1) iii BC *IG* IX (1)² (2) 223; Fraser-Rönne, *BWGT* pl. 24

S. ITALY (CALABRIA):
—TARAS-TARENTUM: (2) f. iv BC D.L. viii 79; *Suda A* 4121 (*FVS* 47 A 1-2) (?f. *Ἀρχύτας*)

**Μνασάγορος**
MESSENIA:
—MESSENE: (1) 208 or 207 BC *FD* III (4) 21, 2; 22, 8 (s. *Μαντικράτης*)

**Μνασάλκης**
ARGOLIS:
—PHLEIOUS: (1) iii BC *IG* IV (1) 464 (*Μνασάλκ[ης]*, *Μνασαλκ[ίδας]?*)
KORINTHIA:
—SIKYON:
——Plataiai: (2) m. iii BC *RE* (2); *HE* 2599 ff.; *IG* VII 395, 2, 5 (*IOrop* 17; Skalet 212) (s. *Μνάσιππος*)

**Μνασαλκίδας**
KERKYRA: (1) 356-354 BC *IG* IV (1)² 95, 28 (Perlman E.2); Perlman p. 40 f. (date); *SEG* XXIII 189 I, [13] + *REG* 82 (1969) p. 551; Perlman pp. 178 f. (ident.)

**Μνασανδρίδας**
SICILY:
—SELINOUS: (1) f. v BC Arena, *Iscr. Sic.* I 21 (Dubois, *IGDS* 76; *IGLMP* 90) (f. *Ἐπίχαρμος*)

**Μνασαρέτα**
EPIROS:
—PHOINIKE: (1) iii/ii BC Cabanes, *L'Épire* pp. 569 ff. no. 47, 6 (*SEG* XXVI 720)
MESSENIA:
—MESSENE: (2) iii-ii BC ib. XXXVIII 346 a + XLI 370; cf. *PAE* 1987, pl. 80 a

**Μνάσαρχος**
MESSENIA:
—MESSENE?: (1) ii/i BC *SEG* XI 979, 10

**Μνασέας**
ARGOLIS:
—ARGOS: (1) m. iv BC D. xviii 295; Plb. xviii 14. 3; *FGrH* 115 F 231 (Παϲέας—*FGrH* 115) ?= (*Μνασίας* (3)); (2) iii BC *BCH* 27 (1903) p. 278 no. 30 (*Μνασέ[ας]*: f. *Θεόμναστος*)
—HERMIONE: (3) 355 AD *IG* IV (1)² 438, 5 (I f. *Μνασέας* II); (4) ~ ib. l. 5 (II s. *Μνασέας* I)
ARKADIA:
—PHENEOS: (5) c. 315-280 BC *FD* III (1) 41, 1 (s. *Εὐχάνωρ*)
DALMATIA:
—ISSA: (6) ii BC *SEG* XXXI 600 (s. *Λυκίσκος*)
ELIS: (7) 156 BC *ID* 1417 B II, 17
ILLYRIA:
—EPIDAMNOS-DYRRHACHION: (8) hell. *IDyrrh* 93 (f. *Ἄλκιμος*)
KERKYRA*: (9) ?i BC *GVI* 1288, 4; cf. *RE* (8); *SEG* XXXVIII 433 (s. *Ἀθηνίων*)
KORINTHIA:
—KORINTH: (10) a. 191 BC ib. XXVI 392, 8; (11) byz. *Corinth* VIII (1) 191, 1; (12) ~ ib. VIII (3) 673; cf. *TMByz* 9 (1985) p. 367 no. 82
—SIKYON: (13) 116 BC *IG* II² 1009 col. IV, 106 + *SEG* XXXVIII 116 (*Μνασ[έας]*: s. *Πυθοκλῆς*)
LAKONIA:
—SPARTA: (14) c. 105-110 AD *IG* v (1) 20 B, 2; *BSA* 26 (1923-5) p. 168 C 7, 7 (Bradford (2)) (I f. *Μνασέας* II); (15) ~ *IG* v (1) 20 B, 2; *BSA* 26 (1923-5) p. 168 C 7, 7 (Bradford (1)) (II s. *Μνασέας* I)

**Μνασείας**
AKARNANIA:
—STRATOS: (1) iv/iii BC *IG* IX (1)² (2) 395, 5 (s. *Δαμοκ*—)

**Μνασήν**
EPIROS:
—AMBRAKIA: (1) f. ii BC *IC* 2 p. 25 no. 8 C (*Μνασην* (acc.)—lap.: s. *Ὀνασάδας*)

## Μνασιάδας

ILLYRIA:
—APOLLONIA: (2) c. 250-50 BC Münsterberg p. 36 (Ceka 78) (money.); (3) ii-i BC *IApoll* 122 (s. Ἀριστήν); (4) i BC Maier 139 (coin) (pryt.)
—DIMALE: (5) hell. *Iliria* 1982 (1), p. 120 no. 40; cf. p. 124 (tile)
—EPIDAMNOS-DYRRHACHION: (6) c. 250-50 BC Maier 102; 245; 492; *Jubice Hoard* p. 97 nos. 35-7 + 39-40; *Bakërr Hoard* p. 67 no. 93 (coin) (Ceka 333-41) (money.); (7) hell.-imp. *IDyrrh* 314

## Μνασιάδας

ARGOLIS:
—ARGOS: (1) iii BC Moretti, *Olymp.* 1016; *SEG* XXXI 1359 (f. Πολυκράτης)
ARKADIA:
—TEGEA: (2) iii BC ib. XXXIII 283 ([Μν]ασιάδας, [Ἀγ]ασιάδας?: s. Πυρραλίων)

## Μνασίας

AITOLIA: (1) 244 or 240 BC *SGDI* 2511, 3 (Flacelière p. 402 no. 29)
—KALYDON: (2) a. 142 BC *IG* IX (1)² (1) 137, 55
ARGOLIS:
—ARGOS: (3) m. iv BC Hyp., *Ath.* 31 (Μνη-) ?= (Μνασέας (1)); (4) c. 245-236 BC *IG* IX (1)² (1) 25, 9 (s. Εὐδραῖος)
—EPIDAUROS:
——(Hysminatai): (5) 146 BC ib. IV (1)² 28, 12 (f. Καλλήν)
—TROIZEN: (6) iv BC ib. IV (1) 764, 7 (f. Ἀγησικράτης)
ARKADIA: (7) 320 BC ib. V (2) 549, 11 (f. Νικίας)
—MANTINEIA-ANTIGONEIA:
——(Posoidaia): (8) c. 425-400 BC *SEG* XXXI 348, 27
—ORCHOMENOS: (9) ?c. 369-361 BC *BCH* 102 (1978) p. 347, 30 (*IPArk* 14)
EPIROS:
—KATAPHYLLI (MOD.): (10) hell.? *SEG* XXXIII 480
—SELIPIANA (MOD.): (11) inc. *AE* 1915, p. 77 no. 9, 2; Stählin p. 150 n. 5 (locn.) (f. Νικόμαχος)
ILLYRIA:
—APOLLONIA: (12) c. 250-50 BC Maier 73 (coin) (Ceka 21) (pryt.)
KEPHALLENIA:
—KRANIOI: (13) ?v BC *IG* IX (1) 610 (fals.?); cf. *LSAG*² p. 231 n. 5 (s. Κλέαρις)
KERKYRA: (14) ?ii-i BC *IG* IX (1) 779 (tile)
MESSENIA:
—KYPARISSIA: (15) i BC *SEG* XI 1027
S. ITALY (APULIA):
—BARION: (16) i-ii AD *Suppl. It.* 8 p. 36 no. 4 (*CIL* IX 283) (Lat. Petronius Mnasias)
S. ITALY (CALABRIA):
—TARAS-TARENTUM: (17) v/iv BC *Suda* A 3927 (Μνησίας ὁ καὶ Σπίνθαρος: f. Ἀριστόξενος)
SICILY:
—ECHETLA: (18) m. v BC *PdelP* 47 (1992) pp. 455-8; cf. *SEG* XLII 884 (f. Δαμαίνετος)

## Μνασίδαμος

ARKADIA:
—HELISSON: (1) c. 221 BC *IG* IV (1)² 42, 5 (Μνασιδ[α]μος)
KORINTHIA:
—KORINTH: (2) 357-343 BC *CID* II 120 A, 33 (f. Δαμοφάνης); (3) 184 BC *Syll*³ 613, 2 ?= (4)
—KORINTH?: (4) c. 186 BC *FD* III (4) 160, 4; Daux, *Delphes* pp. 675 ff. (ident.) (or Phokis Delphi) ?= (3)

## Μνασιθάλης

SICILY:
—GELA-PHINTIAS: (1) vi/v BC Guarducci, *Ep. Gr.* 1 p. 254 no. 4 (vase) (Dubois, *IGDS* 135; Arena, *Iscr. Sic.* II 29; Lazzarini 198) (-λēς)

## Μνασιθέα

ELIS: (1) f. ii AD *IvOl* 440, 4; *ZPE* 99 (1993) p. 232 (stemma) (Λουκηνὴ Κλ. Μ.: d. Κλ. Λουκηνὸς Σαίκλαρος, Βετληνὴ Κασσία Χρυσαρέτα)

## Μνασίθεος

AIGINA: (1) vi/v BC *IG* XII (9) 285, 7 (*CEG* 1 108) (Μνē-: s. Τιμαρέτα)
AKARNANIA:
—MEDION: (2) 216 BC *IG* IX (1)² (2) 583, 20 (s. Ἱππίας)
KORINTHIA:
—KORINTH: (3) s. iv BC *Corinth* XIV p. 89
—SIKYON: (4) ?iv-iii BC *RE* (2) (Skalet 214; Overbeck 2108) (Lat. Mnasitheus); (5) 251 BC Plu., *Arat.* 7 (Skalet 214)

## Μνασικλείδας

ARGOLIS:
—EPIDAUROS*: (1) c. 370 BC *IG* IV (1)² 102, 54, 123; (2) c. 290-270 BC *SEG* XXV 402, 65 (Μνασικλε[ίδ]ας, Μνασικλ[ῆς]?)
KORINTHIA:
—KORINTH: (3) 207 BC *IMM* 42, 17 (f. Πανταίνετος)

## Μνασικλῆς

ACHAIA:
—DYME: (1) ii-i BC *SEG* XIV 373 e (Μνα[σικ]λῆς)
ARGOLIS:
—EPIDAUROS: (2) c. 370 BC *IG* IV (1)² 102, 3; (3) iv/iii BC Peek, *NIEpid* 97 (Μνασικ[λῆ]ς: s. Δρόμων); (4) iii BC Peek, *IAEpid* 141 (f. Καλλικράτεια); (5) c. 290-270 BC *IG* IV (1)² 109 II, 146
—HERMIONE: (6) ?ii-i BC ib. IV (1) 731 II, 17 (f. Κλεομήδης)
—PHLEIOUS: (7) 352 BC *CID* II 31, 65
ARKADIA: (8) c. 208 BC *FD* III (4) 135, 10 (s. Τελέσαρχος)
KERKYRA: (9) inc. *SEG* XXV 354 (f. —κλείδας)
KORINTHIA:
—KORINTH: (10) ?204 BC *IG* VII 303, 65 (Petrakos, *Oropos* pp. 188-91 no. 45; *IOrop* 324)
PELOPONNESE: (11) c. 192 BC *SEG* XIII 327, 19 (s. Ἐπίμαχος)
SICILY:
—LIPARA: (12) c. 315-280 BC *FD* III (4) 401, 1 (f. Θεύδοτος)

## Μνασικράτης

AKARNANIA:
—PALAIROS: (1) f. iii BC *IG* IX (1)² (2) 469
—THYRREION: (2) iii BC ib. 245, 17; (3) iii/ii BC ib. 307
DALMATIA:
—ISSA: (4) i BC-i AD Brunšmid p. 29 no. 23 (s. Ἕρμων)
LAKONIA:
—SPARTA: (5) c. 30-20 BC *IG* V (1) 211, 30-1 (Bradford (-)) (f. Μνάσων, Θέων)
LEUKAS: (6) iii BC Unp. (*IG* arch.)

## Μνασιλαΐδας

EPIROS:
—AMBRAKIA: (1) s. iii BC *SEG* XIX 379, 3; (2) a. 167 BC ib. XXXV 665 A, 9 (s. Ἀρατθίων)

## Μνασίλαος

AITOLIA: (1) ?265-259 BC Nachtergael, *Les Galates* 4, 6
ARKADIA:
—PHENEOS: (2) 191-146 BC *Coll. McClean* 6516 (coin)

## Μνασίλας

ARKADIA:
—MANTINEIA-ANTIGONEIA: (1) c. 300-221 BC *IG* V (2) 323. 81 (tessera) (s. Κλεόνικος)
KERKYRA: (2) f. ii BC *BCH* 45 (1921) p. 24 IV, 81 (*SEG* XXII 455); cf. *Sic. Gymn.* 17 (1964) pp. 47 f. (Μνασιλ[ας]: ?s. Λεω—); (3) i BC-i AD?

## Μνασίλλος

ARGOLIS:
—EPIDAUROS*: (1) c. 370-365 BC *IG* IV (1)² 102, 40; Peek, *IAEpid* 52 A, 1, 5, 9; 52 B, 62

## Μνασίλοχος

AKARNANIA: (1) iii/ii BC *RE* (2)
—PALAIROS: (2) ii BC *IG* IX (1)² (2) 451, 17 (s. Λέων)
LEUKAS: (3) 216 BC ib. 583, 2 (f. Ἐχέδαμος)

## Μνασιμαχίδας

MESSENIA:
—THOURIA: (1) ii/i BC ib. V (1) 1384, 15 (f. Νεόδαμος)

## Μνασίμαχος

EPIROS: (1) m. iii BC *JHS* 57 (1937) p. 35, 9 (f. Πράϋλα)
S. ITALY?: (2) vi/v BC *Mél. Vatin* p. 183 (bronze)
SICILY:
—GELA-PHINTIAS?: (3) f. v BC Dubois, *IGDS* 134 a, 6 (Arena, *Iscr. Sic.* II 80) (Μνασ[ίμ[αχο]ς: f. Ἐμπεδοκλῆς)

## Μνασιππίδας

ACHAIA:
—DYME*: (1) c. 219 BC *SGDI* 1612, 56 (*Tyche* 5 (1990) p. 124) (f. Πολυξενίδας)

## Μνάσιππος

AITOLIA:
—KALYDON: (1) 129 BC *IG* IX (1)² (1) 137, 94 (s. Τιμοκράτης)
ARGOLIS:
—ARGOS: (2) ii BC ib. II² 8372 (s. Ἀριστοκλῆς); (3) 105 BC *JÖAI* 14 (1911) Beibl. p. 146 no. 4, 18 (f. Μένιππος)
EPIROS:
—ELATREIA: (4) ?iv-iii BC *SEG* XXIV 418; Hammond, *Epirus* p. 427 (locn.) (I? s. Καλλίας, f. Μνάσιππος II?); (5) ~ *SEG* XXIV 418; Hammond, *Epirus* p. 427 (locn.) (II? s. Μνάσιππος I?)
KORINTHIA:
—SIKYON: (6) m. iii BC *IG* VII 395, 2, 5 (*IOrop* 17) (f. Μνασάλκης)
LAKONIA:
—SPARTA: (7) 373-372 BC *RE* (-) (Poralla² 538)

## Μνᾶσις

ARGOLIS:
—ARGOS: (1) ii BC *PP* 2062; *IPhilae* 13, 7 (s. Διονύσιος)
SICILY:
—TAUROMENION: (2) c. 223-207 BC *IG* XIV 421 an. 18; 421 an. 34 (*SGDI* 5219) (f. Νικόμαχος); (3) c. 164-142 BC *IG* XIV 421 an. 86; 421 an. 99 (*SGDI* 5219); *IGSI* 4 II (III), 60 an. 77 (f. Νικόμαχος)

## Μνᾶσις

DALMATIA:
—ISSA: (1) iii BC *SEG* XXXI 596 (s./d. Κλεέμπορος)
EPIROS:
—AMBRAKIA: (2) hell.? ib. XXVII 227

## Μνασισθένης

MESSENIA:
—MESSENE: (1) c. 208 BC *FD* III (4) 135, 9 (or Sicily Zankle-Messana?: f. Ὀνάτας)

## Μνασιστράτα
LEUKAS: (1) ?iii BC Unp. (*IG* arch.)

## Μνασίστρατος
AKARNANIA:
—THYRREION: (1) ii BC *IG* IX (1)² (2) 247, 8 (f. Ἀγησίστρατος)
ARGOLIS:
—ARGOS: (2) c. 220-200 BC Peek, *IAEpid* 331, 1 (Perlman E.5) (Μν[α]σί[στ]ρατος: s. Νομεύς)
ARKADIA:
—TEGEA:
——(Hippothoitai): (3) m. iii BC *IG* V (2) 36, 81 (f. Δεξίας)
LAKONIA:
—SPARTA: (4) f. i AD ib. V (1) 270, 5; *Artemis Orthia* pp. 306-7 no. 20 (date); *SEG* XI 881 e (Bradford (1)); (5) c. 105-110 AD *SEG* XI 569, 13 (Bradford (2)) (f. Στύραξ)
MESSENIA:
—MESSENE: (6) ii/i BC *IG* V (1) 1390, 13, 28 etc. (Sokolowski III 65; *Syll*³ 736); *BCH* 33 (1909) pp. 175-6 no. 2, 21 (*Syll*³ 735) ?= (9); (7) 42 AD *SEG* XXIII 208, 2 etc.; *Ergon* 1995, p. 31 (s. Φιλοξενίδας)
—MESSENE (NR.): (8) f. ii AD *SEG* XI 982 (f. Ἀσκληπιάδης)
—MESSENE?: (9) ii/i BC ib. 979, 11 ?= (6)
SICILY:
—LEONTINOI: (10) f. i BC Cic., *In Verr.* II iii 109 (Lat. Mnasistratus)

## Μνασιτέλης
AIGINA: (1) ii/i BC *IG* IV (1) 40
ARKADIA:
—ORCHOMENOS: (2) ?c. 378 BC *BCH* 102 (1978) p. 334, 42 (*IPArk* 15)

## Μνασίτιμος
AIGINA: (1) ?i BC *Alt-Ägina* I (2) p. 44 no. 11, 6 (s. Στ—)

## Μνασιφάνης
ARGOLIS:
—TROIZEN: (1) iii BC *IG* IV (1) 774, 9

## Μνασιφίλα
ARGOLIS:
—ARGOS: (1) i BC-i AD Unp. (Argos, Kavvadias)

## Μνασίφιλος
ARGOLIS:
—ARGOS: (1) 337 BC *CID* II 74 I, 77 (f. Μνάσων)

## Μνασιφῶν
ARGOLIS:
—TROIZEN: (1) ?255 BC Nachtergael, *Les Galates* 8, 52 (Stephanis 1730) (Μνη-: s. Εὐφραγόρας)
DALMATIA:
—ISSA: (2) ii BC *SEG* XXXI 602, 2 (*VAHD* 84 (1991) p. 257 no. 7) (f. Λυσιμάχα); (3) ~ *SEG* XXXI 602, 6 (*VAHD* 84 (1991) p. 257 no. 7) (s. Κλεέμπορος, ?s. Λυσιμάχα)

## Μνασίων
ARGOLIS:
—ARGOS: (1) ii BC *SEG* XLII 279, 10 (Μνασίω[ν])
ARKADIA:
—MANTINEIA-ANTIGONEIA: (2) c. 300-221 BC *IG* V (2) 323. 66 (tessera) (s. Χαιρήμων)
KORINTHIA:
—SIKYON: (3) vi/v BC *SEG* XI 244, 19 (-ōν); (4) ?253 BC Nachtergael, *Les Galates* 10, 67 (Skalet 216); cf. Stephanis 2351 (f. Σωσικράτης)
MESSENIA:
—KORONE: (5) ?ii-i BC *SEG* XI 991 ([Μ]νασίων, [Ὀ]νασίων?)

## Μνάστηρ
DALMATIA:
—ISSA:
——(Hylleis): (1) iv/iii BC Brunšmid p. 8, 34 (Μν[άστ]ηρ: f. Κλεόδικος); (2) ~ ib. l. 48 (f. Ἀγλωτρόφης)

## Μναστορίδας
LAKONIA:
—SPARTA: (1) c. 478 BC [Themist.], *Ep.* 14 with Doenges edn. p. 101

## Μνάστωρ
S. ITALY (LUCANIA):
—POSEIDONIA-PAESTUM: (1) s. vi BC Arena, *Iscr. Sic.* IV 27 (vase) (-στōρ)

## Μνασώ
AITOLIA:
—TRICHONION: (1) i BC-i AD? *IG* IX (1)² (1) 120
ILLYRIA:
—APOLLONIA: (2) ii-i BC *IApoll* 123 (d. Παρμήν)

## Μνάσων
ACHAIA:
—PELLENE: (1) m. iii BC *IG* V (2) 368, 112 (s. Ἀνδρομένης)
AKARNANIA: (2) c. 250-167 BC *Corolla Num.* p. 297 no. 3 (coin)
ARGOLIS:
—ARGOS: (3) 337 BC *CID* II 74 I, 77 (s. Μνασίφιλος)
—EPIDAUROS*: (4) c. 440-425 BC *IG* IV (1)² 46, 6; *LSAG*² p. 182 no. 17 (date)
EPIROS:
—KELAITHOI: (5) ?iv-iii BC *SGDI* 1365 ([Μν]άσων)
KERKYRA: (6) 208 BC *IMM* 44, 3 (s. Στράτων)
LAKONIA:
—SPARTA: (7) c. 30-20 BC *IG* V (1) 211, 30 (Bradford (4)) (s. Μνασικράτης); (8) c. 90-100 AD *SEG* XI 488, 4 (Bradford (7)); (9) c. 90-110 AD *IG* V (1) 667, 10; *SEG* XI 534, 4; 569, 17; 570, 4 (Bradford (6); (11)) (s. Πασικλῆς, f. Πασικλῆς); (10) c. 100 AD *SEG* XI 534, 6 (Bradford (10)) (I f. Μνάσων II); (11) ~ *SEG* XI 534, 6 (Bradford (5)) (II s. Μνάσων I); (12) ?f. ii AD *IG* V (1) 319 (*Artemis Orthia* p. 326 no. 54) (Μνάσ[ων]?: ?s. Καλλικράτης); (13) ~ *IG* V (1) 322 (*Artemis Orthia* pp. 325-6 no. 53; Bradford (2)) (s. Εὐ—); (14) c. 105 AD *IG* V (1) 98, 1; 675, 2 (Bradford (7)); (15) c. 110 AD *IG* V (1) 99, 1 (Bradford (8)) (f. Λυσίμαχος); (16) c. 115-130 AD *IG* V (1) 60, [2]; 65, 24; *SEG* XI 544, 5; XXXVI 361, 24 (Bradford (9)) (f. Λύσιππος); (17) c. 140-160 AD *IG* V (1) 69, 25; 70, 3; *SEG* XI 525; 533 a, 2 (Bradford (7)) (Μνά(σων)—69 and 70); (18) c. 147-170 AD *IG* V (1) 87, 7; 446, 8; *SEG* XI 486, 3; 552, 4; 585, 11; XXX 410, 17 (Bradford (3)) (s. Λύσιππος); (19) s. ii AD *IG* V (1) 537, 14; *SEG* XXXV 325; *BSA* 80 (1985) pp. 194; 205-6 (ident., stemma) (Bradford (1)) (Μέμμιος Μ., [Μνά]σων—*SEG*: s. Π. Μέμμιος Δεξίμαχος)
S. ITALY (BRUTTIUM):
—LOKROI EPIZEPHYRIOI:
——(Ἀλχ.): (20) iv/iii BC De Franciscis 32, 4 (f. Ἀρίστων)

## Μνήμων
S. ITALY (CAMPANIA):
—DIKAIARCHIA-PUTEOLI: (1) imp. *CIL* X 2507 (Lat. M. Herennius Mnemon)

## Μνησίβουλος
S. ITALY (BRUTTIUM):
—RHEGION: (1) iv BC Iamb., *VP* 267 (*FVS* I p. 447)

## Μνησίθεος
S. ITALY (LUCANIA):
—POTENTIA: (1) imp. *CIL* X 162 (Lat. [M]nesithe[us])

## Μνησίπολις
DALMATIA:
—ISSA:
——(Hylleis): (1) iv/iii BC Brunšmid p. 9, 54 (s. Ἀκουσίλας)

## Μνῆσις
ARGOLIS:
—HERMIONE: (1) 191-146 BC BM coin 1920 5-15-116 (coin)

## Μνησίστρατος
S. ITALY (BRUTTIUM):
—RHEGION: (1) imp. *IG* II² 10134 ([Μ]νησίστρατος)

## Μνησιφίλη
S. ITALY (BRUTTIUM):
—SYBARIS-THOURIOI-COPIAE: (1) iv BC *NScav* 1988-9, Suppl. 3 p. 419 no. 210 and fig. 375 (vase) ([Μνη]σιφίλη—*LGPN*)

## Μνήστηρ
ILLYRIA:
—EPIDAMNOS-DYRRHACHION: (1) ii-i BC *IDyrrh* 568 (tile) ([Μν]ήστηρ[ος]? (gen.))
S. ITALY (CAMPANIA):
—HERCULANEUM*: (2) c. 50-75 AD *CIL* X 1403 a I, 15 (Lat. A. Tetteius Mnester: freed.)
—NEAPOLIS: (3) 71 AD *INap* 84 col. I, 3 (Ἑρέννιος Μ.)
—POMPEII: (4) i BC-i AD *CIL* IV 1373; 1828; 1862 (Lat. Mnester); (5) ~ ib. 7090

## Μόθων
SICILY:
—AKRAGAS: (1) imp. ib. X 7193 (Lat. Calbentius Motho)
—CASTEL DI IUDICA (MOD.): (2) ?iii BC Manganaro, *PdelP* forthcoming no. 6, 3 (s. Κέντος)

## Μοιρᾶς
ARGOLIS:
—EPIDAUROS: (1) iii BC Peek, *IAEpid* 153. 10

## Μοῖρις
SICILY:
—KAMARINA: (1) f. v BC Cordano, *Tessere Pubbliche* 21 (Μο[ῖ]ρις: f. —ν)

## Μοίριχος
KORINTHIA:
—KORINTH: (1) ii AD Luc., *DMort.* 11. 1 (fict.)

## Μοισέας
ARKADIA:
—THELPHOUSA: (1) c. 230-200 BC *BCH* 45 (1921) p. 12 II, 73 + *SEG* XXX 494 (f. Φίλων)

## Μοισύας
PELOPONNESE: (1) c. 230-200 BC *BCH* 45 (1921) p. 13 II, 107

## Μόκων
AKARNANIA:
—PALAIROS: (1) iii BC *IG* IX (1)² (2) 571

## Μόλις
AITOLIA:
—THERMOS*: (1) s. iii BC ib. IX (1)² (1) 60 VII, 4

## Μόλοβρος
LAKONIA:
—SPARTA: (1) 425 BC Th. iv 8. 9 (Poralla² 539) (f. Ἐπιτάδας) ?= (2)
—SPARTA?: (2) s. v BC *IG* V (1) 1 B, 8 (*SEG* XXXIX 370) (Μόλοκρος—lap., Μό[λων] Λοκρός?—Wilamowitz) ?= (1)

**Μολοσσός**
AITOLIA: (**1**) 206 BC *REG* 101 (1988) p. 15, 80
(*SEG* XXXVIII 1476)
ELIS: (**2**) m. iv BC *IG* II² 3827, 2 (f. Σάμιππος);
(**3**) i BC *IvOl* 415 (I f. Μολοσσός II); (**4**) i BC/i
AD ib. 62, 19, 23; 415, 2 (II s. Μολοσσός I, f.
Ἰσίδωρος, ?f. Ἄρεστος)
EPIROS:
—MOLOSSOI: (**5**) iii/ii BC *Syll³* 1206, 9; cf.
Cabanes, *L'Épire* p. 583 no. 60 (Μολ[οσσ]ός
(n. pr.?, ethn.?), Μολ[οσσ]ῶ?—*Syll*: ?s. Ἀγέας)
EPIROS?: (**6**) ii BC *PP* 1953 ?= (7); (**7**) ~ ib. 1954
?= (6)
S. ITALY (BRUTTIUM):
—SYBARIS-THOURIOI-COPIAE: (**8**) f. iv BC *NC*
1896, pp. 138 ff. (coins) (*SNG Oxford* 942;
*Samml. Ludwig* 177)
SICILY:
—MORGANTINA (NR.): (**9**) ?iii BC Manganaro,
*PdelP* forthcoming no. 7, 1 (s. Ἱκέτας)

**Μόλπις**
LAKONIA: (**1**) ii/i BC *FGrH* 590 (Bradford (-))

**Μόλπος**
S. ITALY (CAMPANIA):
—HERCULANEUM: (**1**) m. i AD *PdelP* 10 (1955)
p. 470 no. 87 (Lat. [Q.] Iunius Molpus)

**Μολύσχριος**
AITOLIA:
—KALLION/KALLIPOLIS: (**1**) iii/ii BC *IG* IX (1)²
(1) 157

**Μόλων**
LAKONIA:
—SPARTA: (**1**) 336-335 BC *CID* II 75 II, 45; 76
II, 33
S. ITALY (LUCANIA):
—METAPONTION: (**2**) ?272 BC *FD* III (2) 178, 1
(f. Σωκράτης)

**Μολώτας**
ITHAKE: (**1**) hell. *IG* IX (1) 676 (Fraser–Rönne,
*BWGT* p. 121 no. 13)
KERKYRA: (**2**) hell. *IG* IX (1) 707 (f. Φιλόξενος);
(**3**) ii BC ib. 694, 37 (*RIJG* XXV B); cf. *SEG*
XXV 609 (s. Γλαῦκος); (**4**) i BC *IG* IX (1) 709
([Μολ?]ώτας)

**Μολωτίς**
KERKYRA: (**1**) i BC-i AD ib. 921

**Μόμμιος**
AIGINA: (**1**) hell.-imp. ib. IV (1) 42 (s. Θεόξενος)

**Μομψίδας**
DALMATIA:
—ISSA: (**1**) ii BC *SEG* XXXI 600 (s. Σωτέλης)

**Μονᾶς**
ARGOLIS:
—EPIDAUROS: (**1**) i BC-i AD? Peek, *NIEpid* 56 b
(Μονᾶς: s. Ἠλείος)

**Μονέρις**
SICILY:
—SYRACUSE (NESOS): (**1**) iii-v AD *SEG* IV 18
(Wessel 3); cf. Ferrua, *NG* 274

**Μονίκα**
SICILY:
—SYRACUSE: (**1**) iii-v AD *IG* XIV 167 (Strazzulla
108; Wessel 1150) (?d. Σατορνῖλος)

**Μονίμη**
S. ITALY (CAMPANIA):
—NEAPOLIS: (**1**) i BC/i AD *INap* 96; cf. Leiwo
p. 70 no. 12 (Ἀρτωρία Μ.)

**Μόνιμος**
ARGOLIS:
—ARGOS: (**1**) ii AD *SEG* XLI 285 II, 27

LAKONIA:
—SPARTA: (**2**) 330 BC Berve 538 (Poralla² 540)
S. ITALY (CAMPANIA):
—DIKAIARCHIA-PUTEOLI: (**3**) imp. *CIL* X 2208
(Lat. L. Calpurnius Monimus)
—HERCULANEUM: (**4**) m. i AD *PdelP* 6 (1951) p.
230 no. 18, 3 (Lat. Q. Livius Monimus)
—POMPEII: (**5**) i BC-i AD *CIL* IV 1215; 1218
(Lat. Monimus); (**6**) ~ *NScav* 1916, p. 302
no. 4 (Castrèn 158. 19) (Lat. M. Epidius
Monimus)
SICILY:
—SYRACUSE: (**7**) s. iv BC *RE* (10)

**Μονίς**
S. ITALY (CAMPANIA):
—NEAPOLIS: (**1**) i BC *INap* 146; cf. Leiwo p. 83
no. 28 (d. Μάμαρκος); (**2**) i BC/i AD *SEG* IV 99
(*INap* 115); cf. Leiwo p. 64 n. 28 (name) (d.
Ἐπίλυτος)

**Μονούνιος**
ILLYRIA: (**1**) c. 300 BC *RE* s.v. Monunios (1);
*ZA* 21 (1971) pp. 177 ff.; Morkholm, *EHC*
pp. 83-4; *BMC Thessaly* p. 80 nos. 1-3 (coin)
(king)
—APOLLONIA: (**2**) i BC-i AD? *IApoll* 124
—DARDANIOI: (**3**) f. ii BC *RE* s.v. Monunios (2)
(f. Ἔτευτα: king)
—EPIDAMNOS-DYRRHACHION: (**4**) c. 250-50 BC
Maier 177 (coin) (Ceka 342) (money.)

**Μοντανός**
ELIS: (**1**) 197-201 AD *IvOl* 106, 9 (s. Ἀχαϊκός)
SICILY:
—ACATE (MOD.): (**2**) ii AD *MEFRA* 106 (1994)
p. 105 no. 19, 1 (II s. Μοντανός I: doctor); (**3**)
~ ib. l. 17 (I f. Μοντανός II)

**Μόρκος**
ILLYRIA: (**1**) 168 BC *RE* (-)
S. ITALY (APULIA):
—GRAVINA (MOD.): (**2**) s. v BC Santoro, *NSM*
1 p. 169 no. IM 0.322 (vase)

**Μόρσων**
S. ITALY (BRUTTIUM):
—SYBARIS-THOURIOI-COPIAE: (**1**) iii BC
Theoc., *Id.* v 68, 70 (fict.)

**Μορφίων**
TRIPHYLIA:
—PHRIXA: (**1**) c. 230-200 BC *BCH* 45 (1921) p.
13 II, 87 (s. Ἀγυλλος)

**Μόσχα?**
S. ITALY (LUCANIA):
—POSEIDONIA-PAESTUM: (**1**) imp. Mello–Voza
194 (Lat. –a Mosca)

**Μοσχᾶς**
S. ITALY (CAMPANIA):
—DIKAIARCHIA-PUTEOLI: (**1**) imp. *CIL* X 2346
(Lat. A. Cossinius Moscha)
—POMPEII: (**2**) i BC-i AD ib. IV 10223; *Gnomon*
45 (1973) p. 271

**Μοσχίδας**
KERKYRA?: (**1**) c. 200 BC *IBouthrot* 10; cf. *SEG*
XXXVIII 464 (s. Εὐνίσκος, f. Ἀρίστων)
S. ITALY (CALABRIA):
—TARAS-TARENTUM: (**2**) iv BC ib. XIX 619 a;
Troisi, *Epigrafi mobili* 90-1 (terracotta)

**Μοσχίλος**
ILLYRIA:
—APOLLONIA: (**1**) c. 250-50 BC Ceka 79; cf. p.
64; Maier 82 (coin) (Ceka 80) (money.)
—EPIDAMNOS-DYRRHACHION: (**2**) c. 250-50 BC
*SNG Cop. Thessaly–Illyricum* 505; 514; Unp.
(Paris, BN) 278 (coin) (pryt.); (**3**) ii-i BC
*IDyrrh* 569 (tile) ([Μο]σχίλος)

**Μόσχιν**
EPIROS:
—NIKOPOLIS: (**1**) imp. *Wiss. Mitth. Bosn.* 4
(1896) p. 386 no. 2 (Sarikakis 23) (Βιλλήνη
Μόσχειν: ?m. Γ. Βιλληνὸς Νικίας)
S. ITALY (CALABRIA):
—BRENTESION-BRUNDISIUM*: (**2**) imp. *CIL* IX
87 (Lat. Caeselia Moschin: freed.)

**Μόσχινα**
ILLYRIA:
—EPIDAMNOS-DYRRHACHION: (**1**) iii-ii BC
*IDyrrh* 316

**Μόσχιον**
ACHAIA:
—DYME: (**1**) iii BC *AJPh* 31 (1910) p. 399 no.
74 a, 17 (m. Σωστράτα)
AKARNANIA:
—THYRREION: (**2**) ii BC *IG* IX (1)² (2) 327 (d.
Ἀντικράτης); (**3**) hell.-imp. ib. 357
ARGOLIS:
—ARGOS: (**4**) i BC *SEG* I 70 (*GVI* 618) (m. Εὐα-
μερώ)
—HERMIONE: (**5**) i BC *SEG* XII 190 a (d. Κρά-
των)

**Μοσχίς**
S. ITALY (APULIA):
—VENUSIA: (**1**) imp. *CIL* IX 536 (Lat. Marcia
Moschis)
S. ITALY (CAMPANIA):
—MISENUM*: (**2**) imp. ib. X 3661 (Lat. –a
Moschis)
—NEAPOLIS: (**3**) i AD ib. 1508; cf. Leiwo p. 89
(Lat. Hordionia Moschis)
—POMPEII: (**4**) i BC-i AD *CIL* IV 5339 (Lat.
Moschis)

**Μοσχίων**
ACHAIA:
—DYME: (**1**) iii-ii BC *Achaean Grave Stelai* 74
(f. Ἀσπασία)
AIGINA: (**2**) ?i AD *Alt-Ägina* I (2) p. 45 no. 14
AITOLIA:
—THERMOS*: (**3**) s. iii BC *IG* IX (1)² (1) 60 II,
19 (-κίων)
AKARNANIA:
—KORONTA: (**4**) hell.? *SEG* XL 463
ARGOLIS:
—ARGOS*: (**5**) f. iii BC *IG* IV (1) 529, 13
(slave/freed.?); (**6**) imp. *BCH* 27 (1903) p. 269
no. 22 (amph.) (f. Πυθόνικος)
ARKADIA: (**7**) ?255 BC Nachtergael, *Les Galates*
8, 59 (Stephanis 1744) (s. Ἐπαίνετος)
—MEGALOPOLIS: (**8**) ?131 BC *IG* V (2) 440, 16
ELIS: (**9**) s. iv BC *RE* (1) (Berve 539); cf. Mo-
retti, *Olymp.* 489 (f. Θεότιμος, Ἱππόμαχος);
(**10**) 28-24 BC *IvOl* 64, 18; 65, [21] (s. Δα-
μέας)
EPIROS:
—AMBRAKIA: (**11**) iv/iii BC *SEG* XXXIX 523 (s.
Φιλόξενος)
—BOUTHROTOS (PRASAIBOI): (**12**) a. 163 BC
*IBouthrot* 22, 13 (*SEG* XXXVIII 479)
ILLYRIA: (**13**) ii-i BC ib. XXXIV 820 (s. Αἰσχρίων)
—APOLLONIA: (**14**) c. 250-50 BC Maier 72 (Ceka
52); Münsterberg Nachtr. p. 13 (coin) (Ceka
56) (pryt.)
—EPIDAMNOS-DYRRHACHION: (**15**) hell. *IDyrrh*
126 (-σσχί-: f. Ἀρίστων)
KORINTHIA:
—KORINTH: (**16**) iv/iii BC Men., *Pk.* 267 f. (s.
Πάταικος: fict.)
S. ITALY (BRUTTIUM):
—RHEGION: (**17**) inc. *IG* XIV 622 (terracotta)
(Μασχίων?—apogr.: f. Τίμανδρος)
S. ITALY (CAMPANIA):
—DIKAIARCHIA-PUTEOLI: (**18**) ?i-ii AD *CIL* X
2580 (Lat. Moschio: s. Ἀγάθη)
—HERCULANEUM: (**19**) 69 AD *Cron. Erc.* 23
(1993) p. 116 no. 2 II 4 (Lat. M. Ulpius
Moschio); (**20**) c. 70 AD *PdelP* 1 (1946) p.

383 no. 7, 3; 8; 8 (1953) p. 459 no. 43; 48;
52, 5 (*Cron. Erc.* 23 (1993) pp. 115-9) (Lat.
M. Ulpius Moschio)
SICILY:
—SYRACUSE: (**21**) 350-320 BC *SEG* XVIII 772 (f.
Ἀγέστρατος)
ZAKYNTHOS: (**22**) ?278 BC *FD* III (2) 185 (s.
Φιλόνικος)

## Μοσχόλαος
ACHAIA:
—DYME: (**1**) iii-ii BC *Syll*³ 530, 12; cf. *Achaia
und Elis* p. 115 (I f. Μοσχόλαος II); (**2**) ~ *Syll*³
530, 12; cf. *Achaia und Elis* p. 115 (II s. Μοσχόλαος I)

## Μόσχος
ACHAIA:
—PATRAI: (**1**) imp. *CIL* III 527 (Lat. Moschus)
AIGINA: (**2**) imp.? *REG* 15 (1902) p. 138 no. 3
(I f. Μόσχος II); (**3**) ~ ib. (II s. Μόσχος I)
AKARNANIA: (**4**) ii BC *IG* IX (1)² (2) 581 (f.
Ἡγήμων)
ARGOLIS:
—NEMEA*: (**5**) inc. *SEG* XXIX 349 e (-σκος)
ARKADIA:
—TEGEA: (**6**) 165 AD *IG* V (2) 50, 23 (f. Φοῖβος)
——(Krariotai): (**7**) f. iii BC ib. 36, 45 (f. Σωσι-
κλῆς: metic)
ELIS: (**8**) iv BC *RE* (3)
ILLYRIA:
—APOLLONIA: (**9**) c. 250-50 BC Maier 71 (coin)
(Ceka 43) (pryt.); (**10**) i BC *BMC Thessaly* p.
62 no. 80 (coin) (pryt.)
KORINTHIA:
—KORINTH: (**11**) 27 BC-14 AD *Corinth* VIII (3)
69 (Lat. Cn. Mosch[us]); (**12**) ii AD ib. 214
(Lat. Arruntius Moschus)
—SIKYON: (**13**) ?257-254 BC Nachtergael, *Les
Galates* 7, 74; 8, 72; 9, 77 (Skalet 217-18;
Stephanis 1750) (s. Σωσικλείδας)
MESSENIA:
—ABIA: (**14**) ?i AD *IG* V (1) 1374 (-σσχος: s.
Μεν—)
S. ITALY (CAMPANIA):
—DIKAIARCHIA-PUTEOLI: (**15**) imp. *CIL* X
1807 (Lat. N. Naevius Moschus: f. N.
Naevius Vitulus)
—HERCULANEUM: (**16**) i BC-i AD ib. IV 10604 c
(Lat. Moschus)
—NEAPOLIS: (**17**) i BC/i AD *IG* XIV 788 (*INap*
182; Dubois, *IGDGG* I 27); cf. Leiwo p. 66
(*M.*—C. Keil, ΘΥΟΣΧΩ—apogr.: s. Εὔμορφος)
—POMPEII: (**18**) i BC-i AD *Römische
Gräberstrassen* p. 216 b (Lat. A. Sta-
tius Moschus); (**19**) 2 BC *CIL* X 890, 2;
908 (Castrèn 318. 19) (Lat. N. Popidius
Moschus)
SICILY:
—AKRAGAS: (**20**) s. v BC *RE* (4) (Stephanis
1748)
—SYRACUSE: (**21**) m. ii BC *RE* (2) (*PP* 16873);
Gow, *Bucolici Graeci* pp. 132 ff.; *HE* 2683 ff.
—TAUROMENION: (**22**) c. 236 BC *IG* XIV 421 an.
5 (*SGDI* 5219) (s. Ἀμμωνόδοτος); (**23**) c. 165
BC *IG* XIV 421 an. 76 (*SGDI* 5219); *IG* XIV
422 [an. 76]; (**24**) c. 146 BC ib. 421 an. 95
(*SGDI* 5219) (s. Ἀριστέας)

## Μουδύων
AITOLIA:
—KALYDON: (**1**) f. iv BC *IG* IX (1)² (1) 138, 6

## Μουκάκενθος
ILLYRIA:
—LYCHNIDOS: (**1**) ii AD Šašel, *IL* 457 (Lat. Mu-
cacenthus: s. Δίζας)

## Μουντανός
ILLYRIA:
—LYCHNIDOS?: (**1**) ii-i BC *SEG* I 254 (f. Φίλιπ-
πος)

## Μοῦσα
ACHAIA:
—PATRAI: (**1**) ?i/ii AD *CIL* III 510 (Lat.
Aequana Musa: d. Sex. Aequanus); (**2**) ii-iii
AD *ILGR* 63, 2 (Lat. Apuleia Musa)
ARGOLIS:
—PHLEIOUS: (**3**) i AD *SEG* XI 282
ARKADIA:
—TEGEA: (**4**) ii/iii AD *IG* V (2) 28
DALMATIA:
—TRAGURION: (**5**) imp. *CIL* III 2701 (Lat. Val.
Musa)
LAKONIA:
—SPARTA: (**6**) m. ii AD *IG* V (1) 466, 9 (d.
Ἴαμος, m. Νυμφόδοτος); (**7**) iii AD ib. 773
(Papaefthimiou p. 152 no. 26; Bradford (-))
S. ITALY (CALABRIA):
—BRENTESION-BRUNDISIUM: (**8**) imp. *NScav*
1892, p. 101 (Lat. Musa)
S. ITALY (CAMPANIA):
—DIKAIARCHIA-PUTEOLI: (**9**) imp. *CIL* X 2717
(Lat. Maria Musa: m. Maria Procula, Maria
Procilla); (**10**) ~ ib. 2757 (Lat. Musa); (**11**)
~ *Röm. Mitt.* 19 (1904) p. 187 no. 3 (Lat.
Musa); (**12**) ?i-ii AD *CIL* X 2603 (Lat. Iulia
Musa: d. Titianus)
—DIKAIARCHIA-PUTEOLI*: (**13**) imp. ib. 2225
(Lat. Kania Musa: freed.); (**14**) ~ ib. 2343
(Lat. Cornificia Musa: freed.); (**15**) ~ ib. 3021
(Lat. Clodia Musa: freed.); (**16**) ~ *Eph. Ep.*
VIII 424 (Lat. Arellia Musa: freed.)
—HERCULANEUM: (**17**) m. i AD *PdelP* 6 (1951)
p. 225 no. 2, 5-6, 9-10; 9 (1954) p. 55 no. 59,
5 (Lat. Claudia Musa)
—NEAPOLIS: (**18**) i BC/i AD *IG* XIV 759, 2, 20
(*INap* 43; Dubois, *IGDGG* I 29) (Οὐαλερία
M.); (**19**) ~ Leiwo p. 85 no. 36 ([Μο]ῦσα)
—NEAPOLIS*: (**20**) ?i AD *Mon. Ant.* 8 (1898)
p. 223; cf. Leiwo p. 69 no. 10 (Lat. Licinia
Musa: d. Νίκη: freed.)
—POMPEII: (**21**) i BC-i AD *CIL* IV 4268 (Lat.
Musa); (**22**) ~ ib. 8136 (Lat. Musa (n.pr.?));
(**23**) ~ ib. 8638 (Lat. Musa); (**24**) ~ ib. 9210;
9239; 9244 (Lat. Musa); (**25**) ~ *NScav* 1891,
pp. 133-4 (seal) (Lat. Musa); (**26**) 23 AD *CIL*
X 895, 4 (Castrèn 85. 9) (Lat. Caesia Musa)
—STABIAE?: (**27**) imp. *RAAN* 19 (1938-9) p.
124 (Lat. Terentia Musa)
SICILY:
—INESSA-AITNA: (**28**) imp. *CIL* X 7000 (Lat.
Valeria Musa)
—SYRACUSE: (**29**) iii-v AD Strazzulla 235 (Bar-
reca 244)
—TAUROMENION: (**30**) iii-v AD *IG* XIV 446
(Wessel 411)

## Μουσαῖος
ARKADIA:
—MEGALOPOLIS: (**1**) ?iv-iii BC *IG* V (2) 489
—TEGEA: (**2**) 165 AD ib. 50, 75 (f. Πλόκαμος)
ELIS: (**3**) 85 AD *EA* 1905, p. 255 no. 1, 12
(Μουσ[αῖος]); (**4**) 113-117 AD *IvOl* 91, 4 (f.
Γάϊος); (**5**) ~ ib. l. 8 (s. Γάϊος) ?= (**6**); (**6**) ~ ib.
l. 18 (?f. Ἀπολλώνιος) ?= (**5**)
EPIROS:
—NIKOPOLIS: (**7**) imp. *PAE* 1913, p. 97 no. 5
(Sarikakis 114) (Lat. Musaeus: s. Σίμακος)
ILLYRIA:
—APOLLONIA: (**8**) hell.-imp. *IApoll* 335-6 (f.
Τρίτος)
LAKONIA:
—BOIAI: (**9**) ii AD *IG* V (1) 958, 3; 959, 3 (f.
Μελίχρως)
—SPARTA: (**10**) c. 30-20 BC ib. 141, 4; *SEG*
XXXV 329 (date) (Bradford (1)) (s. Ἀγαθοκλῆς);
(**11**) i BC/i AD? *IG* V (1) 177, 1; *SEG* XI 634
(name) (Bradford (2)) ([Μου]σαῖος: s. Ἀγίων);
(**12**) c. 100-125 AD *IG* V (1) 20 B, 4; *SEG* XI
517, 6; 540, 2; 611, 4; XXXVI 361, 29; *BSA* 26

(1923-5) p. 168 C 7, 4 (Bradford (5)) (f. Ἀρι-
στονικίδας); (**13**) c. 175-200 AD *SEG* XI 503,
10 (Bradford (3))
MESSENIA:
—METHONE: (**14**) ?ii AD *IG* V (1) 1417, 9 (Ἰου-
βέντιος Καικίλιος M.: f. Ἰουβέντιος Καικίλιος Πο-
λύχαρμος)
S. ITALY (CAMPANIA):
—DIKAIARCHIA-PUTEOLI: (**15**) imp. *CIL* X
2724 (Lat. Musaeus); (**16**) ~ ib. 2738 (Lat.
Cn. Minatius Musaes)
—POMPEII: (**17**) i BC-i AD ib. IV 2216; 3101;
(**18**) i AD ib. X 8058. 55 (seal) (Lat. Musaeus)
SICILY:
—ABAKAINON: (**19**) imp. Manganaro, *QUCC*
forthcoming no. 14
—SYRACUSE: (**20**) c. 400-375 BC *IG* II² 10394
—SYRACUSE?:
——(Μακ.): (**21**) hell. Manganaro, *PdelP* forth-
coming no. 4 V, 10 (s. Ἀρέθων)
—THERMAI HIMERAIAI: (**22**) ?ii-iii AD *IG* XIV
332; cf. *Kokalos* 20 (1974) p. 240 no. 13

## Μουσιάς
S. ITALY (CAMPANIA):
—SALERNUM: (**1**) ?ii AD *IItal* I (1) 29 (*CIL* X
547) (Lat. Flavia Musias)

## Μουσική
S. ITALY (BRUTTIUM):
—HIPPONION-VIBO VALENTIA: (**1**) i BC-i AD ib.
7365 (*ILat. Term. Imer.* 34) (Lat. Musice)

## Μουσικία
SICILY:
—SYRACUSE: (**1**) iii-v AD Strazzulla 316 (Wessel
1336) (Μουση[κία])

## Μουσικός
EPIROS:
—BOUTHROTOS: (**1**) imp. *AEp* 1978, no. 772
(Lat. Musicus: s. Λυκολέων, Πλαιτωρία Γνώ-
μη)
MESSENIA:
—MESSENE: (**2**) 192 AD *PAE* 1969, p. 104, 5 (f.
Εὐδαμίδας)
S. ITALY (CAMPANIA):
—HERCULANEUM: (**3**) i BC-i AD *CIL* IV 2509, 4
(5449) (Lat. Musicus)
—POMPEII: (**4**) i BC-i AD ib. 1120; 3013 (Lat.
Musicus); (**5**) ~ ib. 3869 (Lat. Musicus); (**6**) ~
ib. 4062 (Lat. Musicus); (**7**) ~ ib. 4161 (Lat.
Mussicus); (**8**) ~ ib. 4166 (Castrèn 146. 6)
(Lat. Cuspius Musicus); (**9**) ~ *CIL* IV 4478
(Lat. Musicus); (**10**) ~ ib. 4824 (Lat. Mu-
sicus); (**11**) ~ ib. 4874 (Lat. Musicus); (**12**)
~ ib. 9182 (Lat. Musicus)

## Μούσιον
KORINTHIA:
—SIKYON: (**1**) ii BC *IG* II² 10309 (Μού[σι]ον: d.
Σωκράτης)

## Μουσίς
AITOLIA:
—APERANTOI: (**1**) iv/iii BC *SEG* XVII 274, 3
(*L'Illyrie mérid.* I p. 111 fig. 9)
ARGOLIS:
—HERMIONE: (**2**) ii-i BC *IG* IV (1) 732 IV, 4
(M[ο]υσίς: m. Δαμάτριος)

## Μουσογένης
S. ITALY (APULIA):
—CANUSIUM: (**1**) 223 AD *Epig. Rom. di Canosa*
35 IV, 11 (*CIL* IX 338) (Lat. Q. Iunius
Musogenes)
S. ITALY (CAMPANIA):
—DIKAIARCHIA-PUTEOLI: (**2**) ?i-ii AD ib. X 2569
(Lat. Musogenes: f. Μηνόφιλος)

## Μοῦσος
KORINTHIA:
—SIKYON: (**1**) m. v BC *IG* IV (1) 425, 3 (Skalet
219)

**Μούτατος**
ARGOLIS:
—ARGOS: (1) ?119 AD FD III (4) 82, 2 (s. Φιλέρως)

**Μούτιος**
ACHAIA:
—PATRAI: (1) ii BC Achaean Grave Stelai 31 (f. Στράτιος)

**Μόψος**
S. ITALY (CAMPANIA):
—DIKAIARCHIA-PUTEOLI*: (1) imp. CIL x 2225 (Lat. M. Kanius Mopsus: freed.)
—POMPEII: (2) i BC-i AD ib. IV 1979 (Lat. Mopsus); (3) ~ ib. 4226 (Lat. Mopsus); (4) ~ ib. 8680; 8780 (Lat. Mopsus)

**Μρόγος?**
ILLYRIA:
—EPIDAMNOS-DYRRHACHION: (1) hell.-imp. IDyrrh 317

**Μύγδων**
LAKONIA:
—SPARTA: (1) 395 BC X., HG iii 4. 20 (Poralla² 541)

**Μύδρα**
EPIROS:
—DODONA*: (1) v-iv BC Ep. Chron. 10 (1935) p. 259 no. 34

**Μύης**
S. ITALY (LUCANIA):
—POSEIDONIA-PAESTUM: (1) v-iv BC RE (2) ?= (2)
S. ITALY?: (2) ?iv BC ib. (1); cf. FGrH 554 ?= (1)

**Μύθος**
S. ITALY (CAMPANIA):
—POMPEII*: (1) i BC-i AD NScav 1916, p. 303 no. 65 (Lat. Mythus: freed.)

**Μυῖα**
LAKONIA:
—SPARTA: (1) arch.? Suda M 1362 (Poralla² 542) (dub.)

**Μυΐλλος**
ILLYRIA:
—APOLLONIA: (1) c. 250-50 BC Münsterberg Nachtr. p. 13 (coin) (Ceka 81) (money.)

**Μυΐσκος**
S. ITALY (BRUTTIUM):
—RHEGION: (1) f. ii BC BCH 45 (1921) p. 24 col. IV, 89 (SEG XXII 455); cf. Sic. Gymn. 17 (1964) pp. 46 f.; (2) 84-80 BC SEG I 418, 5 (Suppl. It. 5 p. 59 no. 11) (II s. Μυΐσκος I); (3) ~ SEG I 418, 6 (Suppl. It. 5 p. 59 no. 11) (I f. Μυΐσκος II)
——(Nav.): (4) ii BC IG XIV 616, 7 with Add. p. 688 (Mus. Naz. Reggio p. 159 no. 29) (f. Κλεόδαμος)

**Μυκηνᾶς**
SICILY:
—SYRACUSE: (1) imp. IG XIV 43 (fals.?)

**Μυλασώ?**
LAKONIA:
—SPARTA: (1) ?i BC ib. v (1) 229 + SEG XI 675 (Μιλα(σ)ως (gen.))

**Μυλλίας**
S. ITALY (BRUTTIUM):
—KROTON: (1) ?vi/v BC Iamb., VP 267 (FVS I p. 446); RE (-) (fict.?)

**Μύλλος**
ARGOLIS:
—HERMIONE: (1) iii BC IG IV (1) 729 II, 7 (Μ[ύ]λλος)

**Μύλλων**
ARKADIA:
—TEGEA:
——(Athaneatai): (1) s. iv BC ib. v (2) 41, 35 (f. Πρόξενος)

**Μύλος**
SICILY:
—MONTE SARACENO (MOD.): (1) vi/v BC Dubois, IGDS 165 (Arena, Iscr. Sic. II 103) (s. Σάκων, f. Σάκων)

**Μυννίων**
ACHAIA:
—DYME: (1) c. 270 BC IG IX (1)² (1) 13, 36 (s. Δίων)
AITOLIA: (2) f. iii BC CID II p. 255 Inv. 671 (Μυνν[ίων]) ?= (3); (3) 272 BC IG IX (1)² (1) 11, 8 ?= (2)
—KALYDON: (4) c. 142 BC ib. 137, 46 (s. Δαμοίτας)

**Μύννος**
AITOLIA:
—PHISTYON: (1) f. ii BC ib. 98, 5 ?= (2); (2) ~ ib. 111, 2 (f. Λύκων) ?= (1)
AKARNANIA:
—KORONTA: (3) iii/ii BC ib. IX (1)² (2) 603 (s. Πολέμαρχος)

**Μύοχος**
S. ITALY (CAMPANIA):
—DIKAIARCHIA-PUTEOLI: (1) imp. RAAN 42 (1967) pp. 4-6 (Lat. Myocus)

**Μυραλλίς**
SICILY:
—SYRACUSE: (1) c. 160 BC ID 1716 (d. Μενεκράτης, m. Ἀριστίων, Αἰσχρίων, Ἡρακλείδας, Μενεκράτης, Ἀρίστακος, Νικασώ, Κλεανώ (all Taras-Tarentum))

**Μυρθώ**
S. ITALY (APULIA):
—VALENZANO (MOD.): (1) m. v BC Troisi, Epigrafi mobili 112 (LSAG² p. 284 no. 11) (-θό)

**Μύριλλα**
AKARNANIA:
—PALAIROS: (1) iii/ii BC IG IX (1)² (2) 530
SICILY:
—SYRACUSE: (2) v BC RE s.v. Demokopos (-); Sophr. fr. 128 (Δαμόκοπος ὁ M.)

**Μυρίνα**
S. ITALY (CAMPANIA):
—S. CLEMENTE (MOD.): (1) imp. Atti Conv. Taranto 28 (1988) pp. 518-19 (M. πρεσβυτ.: Jew)

**Μύρινος**
S. ITALY (CAMPANIA):
—HERCULANEUM*: (1) i BC-i AD CIL x 1403 g I, 30 (Lat. L. Vitellius Myrinus: freed.)
—POMPEII: (2) i BC-i AD ib. IV 10099 a (Lat. Myrinus)
—STABIAE: (3) b. 79 AD IG XIV 700 (f. Θεότιμος)

**Μύριος**
KORINTHIA:
—KORINTH: (1) c. 570-550 BC Amyx 115. 2 (vase) (Lorber 103) (her.?)

**Μύρις**
KORINTHIA:
—KORINTH: (1) c. 570-550 BC Amyx 105 A. 6 and 8 (vase) (Lorber 93) (fict.?)

**Μύρισμος**
S. ITALY (CAMPANIA):
—DIKAIARCHIA-PUTEOLI*: (1) imp. CIL x 2623 (Lat. Myrismus: imp. freed.)

**Μυρκεύς**
ARKADIA:
—KLEITOR?: (1) 296 BC Moretti, Olymp. 520

**Μύρμαξ**
ARGOLIS:
—EPIDAUROS*: (1) c. 365-335 BC IG IV (1)² 103, 17, 48

**Μυρμίδας**
KORINTHIA:
—KORINTH: (1) c. 610-590 BC Amyx 18. 4 (vase) (Lorber 28); LSAG² p. 131 no. 9 (date)

**Μυρμιδών**
AKARNANIA:
—PALAIROS: (1) hell.? IG IX (1)² (2) 566

**Μύρον**
ACHAIA:
—PATRAI: (1) imp. ib. II² 10047 (Μύρ(ω)ν—IG)

**Μύρος**
ELIS:
—OLYMPIA*: (1) vii/vi BC Ol. Ber. 7 p. 82 no. 31
KORINTHIA:
—KORINTH: (2) c. 570-550 BC Amyx 105 A. 2 (vase) (Lorber 93) (Μύρος: fict.?)

**Μυρρίδας**
ELIS: (1) iv BC SEG XV 241, 7

**Μυρρίνη**
ACHAIA:
—PATRAI: (1) imp. CIL III 7263 (Lat. T(a)dia Myrine)
KORINTHIA:
—KORINTH: (2) iv/iii BC Men., Pk. 402 (fict.)
S. ITALY (BRUTTIUM):
—HIPPONION-VIBO VALENTIA: (3) ?i-ii AD Rend. Pont. 60 (1987-8) p. 273 no. 11 (CIL x 75) (Lat. [Iu]lia Myrine: d. Χάρις)
S. ITALY (CALABRIA):
—BRENTESION-BRUNDISIUM: (4) imp. ib. IX 147 (Lat. Myrine: m. Εὐτυχία ἡ καὶ Βύττιν)
S. ITALY (CAMPANIA):
—HERCULANEUM: (5) i BC-i AD ib. IV 10521 (Lat. Myrine)
—POMPEII: (6) i BC-i AD ib. 1402; 4179; 10033 (Lat. Myrine); (7) ~ ib. 4179 (Lat. Myrine)
S. ITALY (LUCANIA):
—HYELE-VELIA: (8) inc. SEG XXVIII 821 (Μυρί-: d. Ἡ—ει—)
—VOLCEI: (9) imp. IItal III (1) 36 (CIL x 8110) (Lat. Curtia Myrine)

**Μυρσίνη**
DALMATIA:
—TRAGURION: (1) imp. ib. III 2677 (Lat. Titia Myrsine)
S. ITALY (CAMPANIA):
—POMPEII: (2) i BC-i AD ib. IV 2151 (Lat. Myrsine)
—SALERNUM: (3) imp. IItal I (1) 44 (Lat. Calpurnia Myrsine)
—SURRENTUM: (4) inc. NScav 1928, p. 212 no. 4 (Lat. Iunia Myrsine)

**Μύρτα**
AKARNANIA:
—OINIADAI: (1) iii/ii BC IG IX (1)² (2) 419. 8
ARGOLIS:
—ARGOS: (2) s. iv BC SEG XXIX 363, 6
—HERMIONE: (3) i BC-i AD? IG IV (1) 730 I, 9 (m. Πύχνων)

**Μυρτάλη**
EPIROS:
—MOLOSSOI: (1) c. 380-316 BC Plu., Mor. 401 A-B; cf. Chiron 11 (1981) pp. 79 ff. (name)

**Μυρταλίς**

S. Italy (Apulia):
—LARINUM: (**2**) imp. *Contr. Ist. Fil. Class.* 1 (1963) p. 247 no. 5 (Lat. –moedia Myrtale)
S. Italy (Campania):
—POMPEII: (**3**) i BC-i AD *CIL* IV 1363 c (Lat. Myrtale); (**4**) ~ ib. 2268; 2271 (Castrèn 105. 4) (Lat. Myrtale); (**5**) ~ *CIL* IV 3494 a (Lat. Myrtale)
—SURRENTUM: (**6**) imp. ib. X 735 (Lat. Gellia Myrtale)
SICILY:
—KATANE: (**7**) imp. *IG* XIV 492

**Μυρταλίς**

S. Italy (Campania):
—SALERNUM*: (**1**) imp. *IItal* I (1) 158 (Lat. Pomponia Myrtalis: freed.)

**Μύρτης**

S. Italy (Apulia)?: (**1**) ii BC *IG* II² 8943 (f. —ασζος: Ital.)

**Μυρτία**

MESSENIA:
—MESSENE: (**1**) m. iv BC *AM* 67 (1942) p. 111 no. 216

**Μυρτιλλίς**

S. Italy (Bruttium):
—LOKROI EPIZEPHYRIOI: (**1**) hell.? *NScav* 1902, p. 41; cf. Costabile, *Municipium Locrensium* p. 74 (loomweight) (*Μυρτιλλί*[ς]— *LGPN*, *Μύρτιλλος*—Costabile)

**Μυρτίλος**

ARGOLIS:
—ARGOS: (**1**) ii BC *SEG* XXVI 431; (**2**) a. 146 BC ib. II 161, 4-5
—HERMIONE: (**3**) ii AD ib. XI 385, 3 (f. Ἐπίκτητος)
—KLEONAI: (**4**) i BC-i AD ib. XXV 277, 5
EPIROS: (**5**) 234-168 BC *BMC Thessaly* p. 89 no. 18; Franke, *Münz. v. Epirus* p. 183 II ser. 52 (coin) (*Μυγγιλος*—*BMC*)
—BOUTHROTOS (PRASAIBOI): (**6**) a. 163 BC *IBouthrot* 17, 7, 9; 29, 7; 32, 29 (*SEG* XXXVIII 474; 487; 491) (s. Σαώτας, f. Σαώτας) ?= (*10*); (**7**) ~ *IBouthrot* 22, 7 (*SEG* XXXVIII 479); (**8**) ~ *IBouthrot* 30, 32 (*SEG* XXXVIII 488) (M[υ]ρτίλος: f. Ἀδυλω); (**9**) ~ *IBouthrot* 78, 10; 79, 9; 80, 8; 81, 8; 82, 8; 83, 8; 84, 8; 85, 8; 86, 9; 87, 9; 88, 7 (*BCH* 118 (1994) pp. 122 f. nos. 1-11) (s. Λυσανίας) ?= (*14*); (**10**) ~ *IBouthrot* 103, 7 (s. Σαώτας) ?= (*6*); (**11**) ~ ib. 159
——Anemotioi: (**12**) a. 163 BC ib. 114, 4, 8; 115, 4, 13; 133, 2 (s.p.) (s. Σαώτας)
——Drymioi: (**13**) a. 163 BC ib. 15, 4; 21, 48 (*SEG* XXXVIII 472; 478); *IBouthrot* 140, 8; 156, 4; 157, 3 (*BCH* 118 (1994) p. 127 nos. 12-13) (II s. Μύρτιλος I); (**14**) ~ *IBouthrot* 21, 47; 38, 2 (*SEG* XXXVIII 478; 497); *IBouthrot* 131, 5?; 144, 6; 156, 3; 157, 2 (*BCH* 118 (1994) p. 127 nos. 12-13) (I s. Λυσανίας f. Λυσανίας, Κλέας, Μύρτιλος II, Φερενίκα, ?f. Μέλισσα) ?= (*9*)
——Phornaioi: (**15**) a. 163 BC *IBouthrot* 141, 2
—CHAONES: (**16**) s. iii BC Cabanes, *L'Épire* p. 547 no. 16
—MOLOSSOI:
——Kyestoi: (**17**) a. 163 BC *IBouthrot* 69, 15; 70, 11; 71, 9 (*BCH* 118 (1994) pp. 129 f. B 1-3) (f. Πολύνικος)
—MOLOSSOI?: (**18**) iv/iii BC *RE* (4)
ILLYRIA:
—EPIDAMNOS-DYRRHACHION: (**19**) hell.-imp. *IDyrrh* 167 (f. Δαμώ)
KERKYRA: (**20**) ii BC *IG* IX (1) 694, 38 (*RIJG* XXV B); cf. *SEG* XXV 609 (M[υ]ρτίλος: f. Προμαχίδας); (**21**) imp. *IG* IX (1) 945 (Κλ. Μ.)

**Μύρτις**

AIGINA: (**1**) v BC *IG* XII (9) 300 (masc./fem.); (**2**) hell.? ib. IV (1) 149 (masc./fem.)
AKARNANIA:
—ECHINOS?: (**3**) s. ii BC ib. IX (1)² (2) 376
EPIROS:
—AMBRAKIA: (**4**) iv/iii BC Unp. (Arta Mus., inscr.)
LEUKAS: (**5**) s. iii BC Unp. (*IG* arch.)

**Μυρτιφώ**

S. Italy (Apulia): (**1**) iv BC *SEG* XXXVII 773 (Μυρτι(χ)ώ?)

**Μυρτίχα**

EPIROS:
—BOUTHROTOS (PRASAIBOI): (**1**) a. 163 BC *IBouthrot* 29, 14; 40, 8 (*SEG* XXXVIII 487; 499); *IBouthrot* 136, 8 ?= (*3*); (**2**) ~ ib. 31, 60 (*SEG* XXXVIII 490); *IBouthrot* 51, 21 (s.p.) (d. Κρατερός); (**3**) ~ ib. 47, 9 ?= (*1*)
SICILY:
—SELINOUS: (**4**) c. 600 BC Dubois, *IGDS* 79 (vase) (Arena, *Iscr. Sic.* I 80; Amyx Gr 8); cf. *SEG* XXXV 1018 (M[υρ]τίχα?)

LEUKAS: (**22**) iii-ii BC ib. 571 (s. Φιλόνικος)
MESSENIA:
—PROTE*: (**23**) imp. *SEG* XI 1021
S. Italy: (**24**) imp. *CIL* X 8059. 410 (seal) (Lat. L. Trebius Myrtilus)
S. Italy (Campania):
—POMPEII: (**25**) i BC-i AD ib. IV 2083 (Lat. Myrtilus); (**26**) ~ ib. 3804 (Lat. Murtilus); (**27**) ~ ib. 9196 (Lat. Murtulus)
S. Italy (Lucania):
—GRUMENTUM: (**28**) imp. ib. X 230 (Lat. L. Magius Myrtilus) ?= (*29*); (**29**) ~ ib. 261 (Mello–Voza 198) (Lat. L. Magius Myrtilus) ?= (*28*)
S. Italy?: (**30**) ?ii-i BC Desy, *Timbres amphoriques* 1224 (amph.) (Lat. L. Vinius Myrtilus)
SICILY:
—SYRACUSE: (**31**) ?iii-iv AD *IGLMP* 110 ([M]υρτίλος)
—THERMAI HIMERAIAI: (**32**) imp. *CIL* X 7417 (*ILat. Term. Imer.* 115) (Lat. M. Lollius Myrtilus)
TRIPHYLIA:
—PYRGOI: (**33**) 205 BC *IG* IX (1)² (1) 31, 110 (s. Κτήσιππος)

**Μυρτινίς**

S. Italy (Campania):
—DIKAIARCHIA-PUTEOLI*: (**1**) imp. *AJA* 2 (1898) p. 385 no. 29 (Lat. Myrtinis: freed.)

**Μύρτις**

ARGOLIS:
—ARGOS: (**1**) m. iv BC *RE* (2); D. xviii 295; cf. Thphr. fr. 83

**Μύρτις**

MESSENIA:
—ASINE (NR.): (**1**) ii/i BC *IG* V (1) 1403 = *AD* 25 (1970) Chron. p. 174
S. Italy (Campania):
—DIKAIARCHIA-PUTEOLI*: (**2**) imp. *NScav* 1886, p. 457 (Lat. Titinia Myrtis: freed.)
—HERCULANEUM: (**3**) i BC-i AD *Riv. Stud. Pomp.* 3 (1989) p. 271 no. 3 (Lat. Iunia Myrtis)
—LITERNUM: (**4**) ii-iii AD *Puteoli* 4-5 (1980-1) p. 279 no. 12 (Lat. Naevia Myrtis)
—POMPEII: (**5**) i BC-i AD *CIL* IV 2273; 2292-3 (Lat. Myrtis)
SICILY:
—KATANE: (**6**) imp. ib. X 7093 (Lat. Statia Myrtis)

**Μύρτιχος**

ARKADIA:
—MANTINEIA-ANTIGONEIA: (**1**) c. 425-385 BC *IG* V (2) 323. 10 (tessera) (Μύρτιχος)

**Μυρτιώ**

ILLYRIA:
—EPIDAMNOS-DYRRHACHION: (**1**) hell.-imp. *IDyrrh* 318 (Μυρτίω(ν)?: d. Φίλων)
SICILY:
—LIPARA: (**2**) hell.? Libertini, *Isole Eolie* p. 224 no. 43 (Μυρτιῶς (gen.))

**Μυρτίων**

ILLYRIA:
—EPIDAMNOS-DYRRHACHION: (**1**) hell.-imp. *IDyrrh* 319 (s. Παρμενίσκος)

**Μυρτώ**

AIGINA: (**1**) s. iv BC *IG* II² 7959 (d. Δαμάτριος)
ARGOLIS:
—MYKENAI: (**2**) hell.? *SEG* III 315 b (loomweight)
ILLYRIA:
—APOLLONIA: (**3**) hell.? *IApoll* 32; (**4**) ?ii BC ib. 16; cf. *SEG* XXXVI 558 (d. Κίρων); (**5**) ?ii-i BC *IApoll* 125
S. Italy (Lucania):
—METAPONTION: (**6**) hell.? *IG* XIV 2406. 57 (*RA* 1932 (1), p. 39 no. 28; Landi, *DISMG* 155 (loomweight)) (or S. Italy (Calabria) Taras-Tarentum)
SICILY:
—SYRACUSE: (**7**) iii-v AD Wessel 630 + Ferrua, *NG* 84

**Μύρτων**

EPIROS: (**1**) c. 167 BC Plb. xxxii 5. 9 (f. Νικάνωρ) ?= (*2*)
—BOUTHROTOS (PRASAIBOI): (**2**) a. 163 BC *IBouthrot* 36, 10; 43, 37-8 (*SEG* XXXVIII 495; 502); *IBouthrot* 48, 4 (s. Νικάνωρ, f. Κλεοπτόλεμος) ?= (*1*); (**3**) ~ ib. 46, 1 (s. Λυσανίας)
——Kestrinoi: (**4**) a. 163 BC ib. 16 (*SEG* XXXVIII 473) (f. Ἀέροπος)

**Μυρώ**

ARKADIA?: (**1**) iv/iii BC *HE* 743
ELIS: (**2**) 272 BC Plu., *Mor.* 253 D (d. Ἀριστότιμος)
ILLYRIA:
—EPIDAMNOS-DYRRHACHION: (**3**) hell.-imp. *IDyrrh* 320 (d. Φιλώτας); (**4**) imp. ib. 45 (d. Τέφιλος)
SICILY:
—LIPARA: (**5**) inc. *Chiron* 22 (1992) p. 386

**Μύρων**

ILLYRIA:
—APOLLONIA: (**1**) imp. *IApoll* 240 (I f. Μύρων II); (**2**) ~ ib. (II s. Μύρων I)
KORINTHIA:
—SIKYON: (**3**) m. vii BC *RE* (2); Moretti, *Olymp.* 52 (Skalet 220) (s. Ἀνδρέας, f. Ἀριστώνυμος: tyrant?); (**4**) vii/vi BC *FGrH* 90 F 61; cf. *RE* (1) (?s. Ἀριστώνυμος: tyrant)
LAKONIA:
—SPARTA: (**5**) i-ii AD *IG* V (1) 753 (Bradford (1)); (**6**) c. 225-250 AD *SEG* XXXIV 308, 13 (Bradford (2)) (f. Γ. Ἰούλ. Σεκοῦνδος)
MESSENIA:
—ASINE: (**7**) hell.-imp. *IG* V (1) 1407 (s. Ἀσκλάπων)
S. Italy: (**8**) imp. *CIL* X 8059. 289 (seal) (Lat. P. Ofillienius Myro)
S. Italy (Campania):
—CAPREAE*: (**9**) imp. *ZPE* 71 (1988) p. 196 no. 7, 1 (Lat. L. Antistius Myro: freed.)
—DIKAIARCHIA-PUTEOLI: (**10**) imp. *CIL* X 2475 (Lat. Myron: f. Severinus)
—HERCULANEUM: (**11**) m. i AD *PdelP* 6 (1951) p. 227 no. 9, 2 (9 (1954) p. 55 no. 60) (Lat. Myro)
—NUCERIA ALFATERNA: (**12**) imp. *CIL* X 1085 (Lat. Myro)

**Μυρωνιανός**

SICILY:
—AKRAI: (**13**) hell. *Akrai* p. 173 no. 61
TRIPHYLIA:
—EPITALION: (**14**) hell. *AD* 23 (1968) Chron.
pl. 127 a (Μύριννος—per err. *SEG* XXXII 409)

**Μυρωνιανός**

S. ITALY (APULIA):
—VENUSIA: (**1**) iii AD *Museo di Venosa* p. 241
no. 18 (Lat. Myronianus)

**Μυρωνίδας**

ARGOLIS:
—EPIDAUROS:
——Naupheis: (**1**) c. 365-335 BC *IG* IV (1)² 103,
149
SICILY:
—SYRACUSE?: (**2**) f. iv BC [Pl.], *Ep.* 363 E

**Μυρωνίδης**

S. ITALY (CAMPANIA):
—DIKAIARCHIA-PUTEOLI: (**1**) imp. *CIL* X 2759
(Lat. Myronides: f. Ὁλόκαλος)

**Μυρωνίς**

ARGOLIS:
—ARGOS: (**1**) 536 AD Unp. (Oikonomou-
Laniado) (m. Στεφανίς)

**Μυρώτας**

SICILY:
—LIPARA: (**1**) iv-iii BC Libertini, *Isole Eolie* p.
224 no. 39 + *SEG* XLII 860

**Μῦς**

AIGINA: (**1**) ii BC *IG* II² 7960 (s. Κέρδων)
KERKYRA: (**2**) vii-vi BC ib. IX (1) 704; *LSAG²*
p. 234 no. 12 (date)
KORINTHIA:
—KORINTH: (**3**) ?iv BC *IG* IV (1) 367 (lamp)
LEUKAS: (**4**) iii BC Unp. (Leukas Mus., inscr.)
inv. 18
S. ITALY (BRUTTIUM):
—SYBARIS-THOURIOI-COPIAE: (**5**) ?iv BC *JNG*
33 (1983) p. 14 (coin graffito) (Μισανγα—
graff.)
S. ITALY (CALABRIA):
—TARAS-TARENTUM: (**6**) 336 BC *RE* (3); Mo-
retti, *Olymp.* 457
S. ITALY (CAMPANIA):
—HERCULANEUM: (**7**) i BC-i AD *CIL* IV 10678
(Lat. Mus)
—POMPEII: (**8**) i BC-i AD ib. 2056; cf. p. 465
(Lat. D. Mus)

**Μυσίς**

S. ITALY (CAMPANIA):
—POMPEII: (**1**) i BC-i AD ib. 2250 (Lat. Mysine
(abl.))

**Μύσκαλλος**

ILLYRIA:
—APOLLONIA: (**1**) iii/ii BC *IApoll* 176; cf. *SEG*
XXXIX 550 (s. Θεόδωρος)

**Μύσκελλος**

ACHAIA:
—RHYPES: (**1**) s. viii BC *RE* (-) (and S. Italy
(Bruttium) Kroton: s. Ἀλήμων (Argos): oikist)

**Μύσκελος**

SICILY:
—GELA-PHINTIAS?: (**1**) f. v BC Dubois, *IGDS*
134 b, 9 (Arena, *Iscr. Sic.* II 47) (-σσκε-)
—HERBESSOS: (**2**) vi/v BC Dubois, *IGDS* 168 b
(vase) (Arena, *Iscr. Sic.* II 121) (-σχε-, Μύσχε-
λυς—Arena)
—KATANE?: (**3**) c. 410 BC *JNG* 33 (1983) p. 11
(coin graffito)

**Μύσκος**

SICILY:
—SELINOUS: (**1**) vii/vi BC Guarducci, *Ep. Gr.* 1
p. 317 no. 9 (Dubois, *IGDS* 71; Arena, *Iscr.
Sic.* 1 16; *IGLMP* 76) (-ϙος: s. Μενεπτόλεμος)
?= (**2**); (**2**) f. vi BC *Lex Sacra from Selinous* p.
14 A, 9 (-ϙος: her.?) ?= (**1**)

**Μύσκων**

SICILY:
—GELA-PHINTIAS?: (**1**) f. v BC Dubois, *IGDS*
134 a, 1, 4 (Arena, *Iscr. Sic.* II 80) ([M]ύσκῶν:
s. Δᾶμις)
—KAMARINA: (**2**) ?ii BC *SEG* XXXIX 996, 10
(Dubois, *IGDS* 126; Cordano, 'Camarina
VII' 134) (s. Ἄνδρων)
—SYRACUSE: (**3**) 411-410 BC *RE* (-) (s. Μενεκρά-
της)

**Μυσός**

SICILY?: (**1**) c. 480 BC *AJA* 78 (1974) p. 430
(vase)

**Μύσσιος**

KORINTHIA:
—KORINTH: (**1**) ii-iii AD *SEG* XI 138 d (Lat.
Mussius)

**Μυσσκλίας**

AITOLIA:
—KONOPE-ARSINOE: (**1**) ?s. vi BC *AD* 22 (1967)
Chron. p. 320

**Μύστα**

AIGINA: (**1**) i BC-i AD *IG* II² 7961 (d. Μῆνις)
KORINTHIA:
—KORINTH: (**2**) i BC *BGU* 1285, 6, 7 (d. Ἔξ[..ο]υ
(gen.), m. Δημήτριος, Δίων)

**Μύστης**

ARKADIA:
—HERAIA: (**1**) ii-iii AD *IG* V (2) 417
S. ITALY (CAMPANIA):
—HERCULANEUM: (**2**) m. i AD *PdelP* 3 (1948) p.
182 no. 30 (Lat. A. Tetteius Mystis)
—POMPEII: (**3**) i BC-i AD *CIL* IV 1237 (Lat.
Mystes); (**4**) ~ ib. 1639; cf. p. 210 (Lat.
Mystes); (**5**) ~ ib. 2142; cf. p. 215 (Lat.
Mystes)

**Μυστική**

S. ITALY (CAMPANIA):
—POMPEII: (**1**) i BC-i AD ib. 5198 (Lat. Mys-
tiche) ?= (**2**); (**2**) ~ ib. 5241 (Lat. Mystice) ?=
(**1**); (**3**) ~ ib. 8618 (Lat. Mystice)

**Μυστικός**

ARKADIA:
—TEGEA: (**1**) 165 AD *IG* V (2) 50, 80 (f. Ζώσιμος)

**Μύστικος**

KORINTHIA:
—KORINTH: (**2**) m. ii AD *Corinth* VIII (3) 223
a, 3 (Λ. Γέλλιος Μύστικος: s. Λ. Γέλλιος Μέναν-
δρος)
S. ITALY (CALABRIA):
—BRENTESION-BRUNDISIUM: (**3**) imp. *NScav*
1904, p. 300 (Lat. Mysticus)
S. ITALY (CAMPANIA):
—KYME: (**4**) ii-iii AD *IG* XIV 872, 14, 24, etc.
(Audollent, *Defix. Tab.* 198) (Οὐαλέριος M.: f.
Οὐαλερία Κοδράτιλλα)
—POMPEII: (**5**) i BC-i AD *Atti Acc. Pontan.* 39
(1990) p. 293 nos. 68-69 (Lat. Mysticus)
S. ITALY (LUCANIA):
—VOLCEI: (**6**) i AD *IItal* III (1) 112 (Lat. L.
Rufius Mysticus)

**Μύστρων**

EPIROS?:
—AKRIPOS: (**1**) 356-354 BC *IG* IV (1)² 95, 34
(Perlman E.2); Perlman p. 40 f. (date); cf.
Cabanes, *L'Épire* p. 144 n. 59

**Μυτάλας**

SICILY:
—SELINOUS: (**1**) vi/v BC Manganaro, *PdelP*
forthcoming no. 18, 4 (s. Καλεύς)

**Μυτιλήνη**

KORINTHIA:
—KORINTH: (**1**) ii-iii AD *SEG* XI 136 a (-τη-)

**Μυτίλος**

ILLYRIA: (**1**) c. 275-250 BC Cabanes, *L'Épire*
pp. 81 f.; Ceka pp. 66 ff.; cf. *Congr. Int. Num.*
p. 92 (Μυτίλιος—var.: king)

**Μύχα**

SICILY:
—SELINOUS: (**1**) v BC Dubois, *IGDS* 35, 4
(Arena, *Iscr. Sic.* 1 64)

**Μύχων**

ELIS: (**1**) m. i BC *IvOl* 401, 2 (s. Τιμοκ—)

**Μῶκος**

S. ITALY (CAMPANIA):
—NEAPOLIS: (**1**) iii-iv AD *IG* XIV 826. 28 (*INap*
242); cf. Wessel 1112

**Μωλόχιος**

LAKONIA:
—SPARTA: (**1**) c. 140-160 AD *IG* V (1) 74,
6; 85, 13; 128, 10; *SEG* XI 528, 6 (Bradford s.v. Καλλικράτης (8)) (Καλλικράτης M.
(nom./gen.?): s. Εὐδαμίδας)

**Μωσίς**

ARKADIA:
—STYMPHALOS: (**1**) iv-iii BC *SEG* XLII 357

**Μωτέας**

AKARNANIA:
—PALAIROS: (**1**) iii BC *IG* IX (1)² (2) 495

**Μώχας**

SICILY:
—SYRACUSE: (**1**) iii-v AD ib. XIV 193 (Wessel
413 A (name))

# N

**Νααρχίδας**
ILLYRIA:
—EPIDAMNOS-DYRRHACHION: (1) c. 250-50 BC
Maier 307 (coin) (Ceka 38; 123) (pryt.)

**Νάβις**
LAKONIA:
—SPARTA: (1) c. 240-192 BC *RE* (1); *IG* IV (1)
497; V (1) 885; XI (4) 716, 3, 9; *IPerg* 60; 61;
62 a; 63; *Münzpr. der Laked.* p. 126 Group 9
series 4-5 nos. 16-17 (coin) (Bradford (-)) (s.
Δαμάρατος, f. Ἁρμένας: king)

**Ναιρογένης**
SICILY:
—KAMARINA: (1) s. v BC Dubois, *IGDS* 119, 1
(Arena, *Iscr. Sic.* II 145) (-νēς: ?s. Εὐκλείδας)

**Ναῖς**
EPIROS:
—PHOINIKE: (1) imp. *AE* 1914, p. 235 no. 6 (d.
Εὐφράνωρ)
S. ITALY (APULIA):
—RUBI: (2) ?ii AD *Suppl. It.* 5 p. 23 no. 5 (Lat.
Dasumia Nais) ?= (3); (3) ~ ib. p. 25 no. 7
(Lat. Dasumia Nais: d. Δωρίς) ?= (2)
—VENUSIA*: (4) imp. *CIL* IX 512 (Lat. Fadia
Nais: freed.)
S. ITALY (CAMPANIA):
—DIKAIARCHIA-PUTEOLI: (5) imp. ib. X 2541
(Lat. Lucilia Nais); (6) ~ ib. 2740 (Lat. Bae-
bia Nais); (7) ~ ib. 2990 (Lat. Sulpicia Nais);
(8) ~ ib. (Lat. Valeria Nais); (9) ~ ib. 8199
(Lat. Pomponia Nais)
—KYME*: (10) imp. *Eph. Ep.* VIII 446 (Lat.
Nais: freed.)
—NOLA: (11) imp. *CIL* X 1298 (Lat. Firmia
Nais)
—POMPEII: (12) i BC-i AD ib. IV 2230 (Lat.
Nais); (13) ~ ib. 8307 (Lat. Nais)

**Ναϊσσός**
ILLYRIA:
—BYLLIONES BYLLIS: (1) imp. *AEp* 1923, no.
39 (Lat. Lartidius Naissus)

**Νακώ**
SICILY:
—SELINOUS: (1) vi/v BC Manganaro, *PdelP*
forthcoming no. 18 (-ϙδι: d. Φίλων)

**Ναμέρτας**
LAKONIA:
—SPARTA: (1) inc. Plu., *Mor.* 230 A (Poralla²
544) (-της)

**Ναμερτίδας**
KORINTHIA:
—KORINTH: (1) vi/v BC Schol. Pi., *O.* xiii 58 b-
c; *SLG* 340, 8-9; *Dionysiaca* pp. 1-16 (ident.)
(?s. Τερψίας, ?f. Αὐτόλυκος, Ἐρίτιμος)

**Νᾶνα**
ILLYRIA:
—EPIDAMNOS-DYRRHACHION: (1) hell.-imp.
*IDyrrh* 321 (N. Ἀνεκεία)
S. ITALY (CAMPANIA):
—DIKAIARCHIA-PUTEOLI*: (2) imp. *CIL* X
1954 (Lat. Nana: m. Rustius, Numerius:
freed.?)

**Νανελαῖος**
SICILY:
—SELINOUS: (1) f. v BC Dubois, *IGDS* 38, 10
(Arena, *Iscr. Sic.* I 63) (Ναννε-: f. Πλακίτας)
?= (3) (2); (2) ~ Dubois, *IGDS* 38, 17 (Arena,
*Iscr. Sic.* I 63) ?= (1); (3) ~ Dubois, *IGDS* 38,
19 (Arena, *Iscr. Sic.* I 63) (f. Τίτελος) ?= (1)

**Νάνιος**
LAKONIA:
—SPARTA: (1) c. 140-145 AD *IG* V (1) 1314, 45
(Νά[νι]ος)

**Ναννώ**
LAKONIA:
—SPARTA: (1) s. vii BC *PMGF* I 1, 70 (Poralla²
546)
S. ITALY (LUCANIA):
—TEGIANUM: (2) imp. *CIL* X 318 (Lat. Trae-
cidia Nano)

**Νάπη**
S. ITALY (APULIA):
—CANUSIUM*: (1) ii AD *Epig. Rom. di Canosa*
Add. 21 (Lat. Dastidia Nape: freed.)

**Ναραωνίδας**
SICILY:
—KAMARINA: (1) s. v BC Dubois, *IGDS* 121, 26
(Arena, *Iscr. Sic.* II 143; *SEG* XXXVIII 940;
Cordano, 'Camarina VII' 5) (-ραō-: ?f. —ιος)

**Νάργος**
LAKONIA:
—SPARTA: (1) iii AD *SEG* XI 871 (Bradford (-))
(Ναργώ?)

**Ναρδίς**
S. ITALY (APULIA):
—ARGYRIPPA-ARPI: (1) imp. *CIL* IX 934 (Lat.
[Cal]purnia Nardis)
—CANUSIUM: (2) i/ii AD *Epig. Rom. di Canosa*
63 (Lat. Nardis: d. Οἴβαλος, Δαμμύλα)
—LUCERIA: (3) imp. *CIL* IX 867 (Lat. Minatia
Nardis: m. Minatia Victrix)
—SPINAZZOLA (MOD.): (4) m. i AD *Epigrafia
e Territorio* 1 p. 22 no. 2 (Lat. Nardis: d.
Primio, Claudia Hilaritas)
S. ITALY (CAMPANIA):
—DIKAIARCHIA-PUTEOLI: (5) imp. *CIL* X 2349
(Lat. Nardis)

**Νάρδος**
LAKONIA:
—SPARTA: (1) c. 225-250 AD *SEG* XXXIV 308, 6
(Bradford (-)) (M. Αὐρ. N.)
S. ITALY (CAMPANIA):
—DIKAIARCHIA-PUTEOLI: (2) imp. *CIL* X 2380
(Lat. Egnatius Nardus: s. Κίνναμος)
—NOLA: (3) imp. ib. 1284 (Lat. Nardu(s))
—POMPEII: (4) i BC-i AD *NScav* 1896, p. 298
(Castrèn 191. 13) (Lat. M. Heren. Nardus)
—POMPEII*: (5) i BC-i AD *CIL* X 1076 (Lat.
Nardus: freed.)

**Νάρκισσος**
ARGOLIS:
—ARGOS: (1) ii AD *SEG* XLI 285 II, 27
ARKADIA:
—TEGEA: (2) ii AD *IG* V (2) 54, 12 (s. Ὀνησᾶς)
ELIS: (3) f. ii AD *IvOl* 92, 17 (T. Φλ. N.)
—OLYMPIA*: (4) 181-185 AD ib. 102, 24 (?s.
Διονύσιος: slave?)
LAKONIA:
—SPARTA: (5) ii-iv AD Robert, *Gladiateurs* p. 79
no. 12, 3, 5 (Bradford s.v. Νεικηφόρος (13))
(Νικηφόρος ὁ καὶ N.: s. Σύνετος)
S. ITALY (CAMPANIA):
—CAPREAE*: (6) imp. *ZPE* 71 (1988) p. 196 no.
7, 1 (Lat. L. Antistius Narcissus: freed.)
—DIKAIARCHIA-PUTEOLI: (7) imp. *CIL* X 2790
(Lat. Q. Occius Narcissus); (8) ~ *Eph. Ep.*
VIII 394 (*NScav* 1885, p. 72 l) (Lat. Cattius
Narcissus: f. M. Cattius Puteolanus); (9) 45
AD Bove, *Documenti finanziarie* p. 129 T.P.

27 (Lat. P. Servilius Narcissus); (10) ii AD
*AJA* 77 (1973) p. 164 no. 15 (Lat. Narcissus)
—DIKAIARCHIA-PUTEOLI*: (11) i-ii AD *CIL* X
2558; 2561 (Lat. C. Iulius Narcissus: freed.)
—HERCULANEUM*: (12) i BC/i AD ib. 8042. 82
(tiles) (Lat. Narcissus: imp. freed.)
—MISENUM: (13) imp. De Franciscis, *Sacello
Augustali* p. 23 (Lat. M. Calpurnius Narcissus)
—POMPEII: (14) i BC-i AD *CIL* IV 1115 (Castrèn
210. 2) (Lat. Laelius Narcissus); (15) ~ *CIL*
IV 1130 (Lat. Narcissus); (16) ~ ib. 1489 (Lat.
Narces[sus]); (17) ~ ib. 1657 (Lat. Narcissus);
(18) ~ ib. 1825 a b; 1841; 1889 (Lat. Narcissus); (19) ~ ib. 2130; cf. p. 215 (Lat. Narcissus); (20) ~ ib. 3527 (Lat. Narcissus); (21) ~
ib. 4105 (Lat. Narcissus); (22) ~ ib. 4514, 13
(Lat. Narcissus); (23) ~ ib. 5078 (Lat. Nar-
cissus); (24) ~ ib. 8012 (Lat. Narcissus); (25)
~ ib. 8785 (Lat. Narcissus); (26) ~ ib. 10124
(Lat. Nacrissus (sic)); (27) ~ ib. x 908 (Lat.
Narcissus); (28) c. 51-62 AD ib. IV 3340. 69,
11 (Castrèn 320. 8) (Lat. P. Poppaeus Narcissus); (29) 57 AD *CIL* IV 3340. 34, 8; 37,
14; 70, 9; 110, 5 (Castrèn 318. 22) (Lat. N.
Popid[ius] [Nar]cissus)
—SALERNUM: (30) ?i AD *IItal* I (1) 49 (Lat. Ti.
Claudius Narcissus: s. Claudia Prima)
SICILY:
—AIGATES ISLANDS: (31) imp. *CIL* X 7493 (Lat.
Narcissus: s. Θάλλος, Παννυχίς)

**Νάρος**
KORINTHIA:
—KORINTH: (1) f. vi AD *Hesp.* 44 (1975) p. 206
no. 46

**Ναρυκίδας**
ARKADIA:
—PHIGALEIA: (1) f. iv BC Moretti, *Olymp.* 392;
cf. Ebert, *Gr. Sieg.* 36 (Θαρυκίδας?: s. Δαμάρετος)

**Νάρων**
SICILY:
—KAMARINA: (1) iv/iii BC Dubois, *IGDS* 122,
3 (Cordano, 'Camarina VII' 136); cf. Ferrua,
*NG* 64 (s. Αἰσχύλος)

**Νασσιανή**
SICILY:
—SYRACUSE: (1) iii-v AD Agnello 102 (Wessel
1016); cf. Ferrua, *NG* 64 (Μασσιανή—Wessel)

**Νάστας**
S. ITALY (BRUTTIUM):
—KAULONIA: (1) iv BC Iamb., *VP* 267 (*FVS* I
p. 447)
S. ITALY (CAMPANIA):
—POMPEII: (2) i BC-i AD *CIL* X 926 (Castrèn
89. 4) (Lat. M. Calidius Nasta)

**Νατᾶλις**
S. ITALY (BRUTTIUM):
—RHEGION*: (1) imp. *IG* XIV 617, 9 (slave?)

**Ναύαρχος**
ARGOLIS:
—ARGOS: (1) f. iii BC ib. IV (1) 529, 15

**Ναυβάτας**
LAKONIA:
—SPARTA: (1) 398 BC X., *HG* iii 2. 6 (Poralla²
547) (-της); (2) c. 125-150 AD *IG* V (1) 114, 4
(Bradford (-)) (s. Νικανδρίδας)

**Ναυεριάδας**
SICILY:
—SELINOUS: (1) f. v BC Dubois, *IGDS* 38, 18
(Arena, *Iscr. Sic.* I 63) (f. Ἆτος)

## Ναύερος

SICILY:
—SELINOUS: (1) f. v BC Dubois, *IGDS* 38, 4 (Arena, *Iscr. Sic.* I 63) (*N.*—Arena, Ναυέρο-τος—Dubois: s. Ἇλος)

## Ναυκλείδας

LAKONIA:
—SPARTA: (1) 404 BC X., *HG* ii 4. 36; *FGrH* 86 F 11; Ael. *VH* xiv 7 (Poralla² 548) (s. Πολυ-βιάδας, f. Πολυβιάδας)
MESSENIA:
—MESSENE: (2) iii BC *SEG* XXIII 209, 4

## Ναυκλῆς

LAKONIA: (1) ?iii BC *IG* II² 9153 (Bradford (-)) (Ναυκλέϊος (gen.): f. Παυσανίας)
—SPARTA: (2) 367 BC X., *HG* vii 1. 41 (Poralla² 549)

## Ναυκράτης

ARGOLIS:
—EPIDAUROS: (1) c. 315-280 BC *FD* III (1) 95, 2 (s. Ἀρχέστρατος)
ILLYRIA:
—APOLLONIA: (2) iii/ii BC *IApoll* 176; cf. *SEG* XXXIX 550 (f. Καλλίμαχος)
KORINTHIA:
—SIKYON: (3) 423 BC Th. iv 119. 2 (Skalet 221) (f. Δαμότιμος)
SICILY:
—ZANKLE-MESSANA: (4) ?ii BC *IG* XIV 401, 12 (f. Ζώπυρος)

## Ναυκύδης

ARGOLIS:
—ARGOS: (1) s. v BC *RE* (2); cf. Loewy 86 (ident.) (s. Μόθων: sculptor) ?= (2); (2) v/iv BC *RE* (2) (s. Πατροκλῆς: sculptor) ?= (1)

## Ναυμάχιος

EPIROS: (1) m. iv AD *Suda* Φ 295 ?= (2)
EPIROS?: (2) m. iv AD *RE* (1) ?= (1)

## Ναύμαχος

KORINTHIA:
—SIKYON: (1) c. 525-500 BC *SEG* XI 226; *LSAG²* p. 143 no. 7 (date)

## Ναύπηγος

S. ITALY (CAMPANIA):
—POMPEII: (1) i BC-i AD *CIL* IV 4516 (Lat. Naupegus)

## Ναύπλιος

S. ITALY (CAMPANIA):
—POMPEII: (1) i BC-i AD ib. 2093; 2319 k; 3917; 5175; 8639 (Lat. Nauplius); (2) ~ ib. 8633; 8639 (Lat. Nauplius)

## Ναυσήν

ILLYRIA:
—EPIDAMNOS-DYRRHACHION: (1) hell.-imp. *IDyrrh* 322 (s. Εὔχος)

## Ναυσιάδας

LAKONIA:
—SPARTA: (1) 362 BC *CID* II 1 II, 13

## Ναυσιγένης

LEUKAS: (1) iv/iii BC Peek, *IAEpid* 14, 6 (Ναυσιγ[έ]ν[ης]: s. Νικόμαχος)

## Ναυσικάα

KORINTHIA:
—SIKYON: (1) m. ii AD *Syll³* 846, 2 (Τιβ. Κλ. Πολυκράτεια *N.*: d. Τιβ. Κλ. Πολυκράτης, Τιβ. Κλ. Διογένεια)

## Ναυσικλείδας

LAKONIA:
—SPARTA?: (1) 400-399 BC X., *An.* vii 8. 6 (Po-ralla² 550)

## Ναυσικλῆς

ARGOLIS:
—EPIDAUROS*: (1) c. 240-200 BC Peek, *IAEpid* 330, 20 (Perlman E.4) (s. Να—)

## Ναυσικράτης

ARGOLIS:
—ARGOS: (1) iii BC *IG* v (2) 34, 30 ([Ν]αυσικράτης)
KERKYRA: (2) ?ii-i BC ib. IX (1) 782-3 (tiles)

## Ναυσίλοχος

ILLYRIA:
—APOLLONIA: (1) c. 250-50 BC Maier 74 (coin) (Ceka 102) (pryt.)

## Ναυσίμαχος

AKARNANIA: (1) c. 250-167 BC *NZ* 10 (1878) p. 30 no. 34 (coin)
—ASTAKOS: (2) m. ii BC *IG* IX (1)² (2) 208, 3, 33 (s. Ἀριστοκλῆς)

## Ναυσινίκα

KORINTHIA:
—KORINTH: (1) a. 480 BC Plu., *Mor.* 871 A (-κη: d. Ἀδείμαντος)

## Ναυσίνικος

MESSENIA:
—MESSENE: (1) i AD *IG* v (1) 1436, 41 ([Να]υσίνικος, [Λ]υσίνικος?: s. Νικιππίδας)

## Ναυσίστρατος

EPIROS:
—AMBRAKIA: (1) vi BC *SEG* XLI 540; cf. *BE* 1994, no. 38

## Ναύτης

ILLYRIA:
—LYCHNIDOS: (1) ii-iii AD Demitsas 341 (f. Ἀν-τίγονος)

## Ναύτωρ

DALMATIA:
—ISSA:
——(Pamphyloi): (1) iv/iii BC Brunšmid p. 8, 37 (s. Σίβαλις)

## Νεαγένης

ACHAIA:
—DYME: (1) 165 BC *ZPE* 101 (1994) p. 128, 7, 11 (f. Δάμων)
AKARNANIA:
—THYRREION: (2) iii-ii BC *SEG* XXVII 159, 7; cf. *PAE* 1977, pl. 244 a (s. Ἀσκλαπιάδας)
ILLYRIA:
—APOLLONIA: (3) hell. *IApoll* 24; cf. *Le Arti* 5 (1943) p. 117 no. 2; Fraser-Rönne, *BWGT* p. 174 n. 5 (date) (s. Τεισίδαμος)

## Νεάδας

ARKADIA:
—MANTINEIA-ANTIGONEIA: (1) c. 300-221 BC *IG* v (2) 323. 32 (tessera) (f. Ξενοτέλης)

## Νέαιθος

AKARNANIA:
—STRATOS: (1) iv/iii BC ib. IX (1)² (2) 395, 15 (s. Φιλόξενος)
S. ITALY (BRUTTIUM):
—LOKROI EPIZEPHYRIOI:
——(Εὐρ.): (2) 277 BC De Franciscis 8, 1; 31, 1 (s. Χαρίξενος)
——(Λακ.): (3) iv/iii BC ib. 20, 4 (s. Γοργίδας)
——(Τιω.): (4) iv/iii BC ib. 27, 3 (s. Χαρίλας)

## Νεαίθων

S. ITALY (BRUTTIUM):
—LOKROI EPIZEPHYRIOI:
——(Εὐρ.): (1) iv/iii BC ib. 3, 1

## Νέαιρα

EPIROS:
—BOUTHROTOS (PRASAIBOI): (1) a. 163 BC *IBouthrot* 31, 93 (*SEG* XXXVIII 490)

## Νεάλκης

KORINTHIA:
—SIKYON: (1) m. iii BC *RE* (-) (Skalet 32) (f. Ἀναξάνδρα: painter)

## Νέανδρος

AITOLIA:
—PHISTYON: (1) 190 BC *IG* IX (1)² (1) 97, 4, 13
EPIROS:
—DODONA: (2) iii BC Antoniou, *Dodone* Aa, 36 (Μέανδρος—ed., Νέανδρος); (3) ~ ib. Ba, 6
—MOLOSSOI: (4) s. iv BC Plu., *Pyrr.* 2. 2
KORINTHIA:
—KORINTH: (5) v BC *SEG* XI 203 (potter)

## Νεανθίς

ARGOLIS:
—PHLEIOUS: (1) iv BC ib. XXVI 416, 1 (Νεανθίδος (gen.), Νέανθις?)

## Νεανίας

LAKONIA:
—KARYAI?: (1) hell. ib. XL 344

## Νεάπολις

S. ITALY (LUCANIA):
—POTENTIA: (1) imp. *CIL* x 163 (Lat. Neapolis)

## Νεαρέτα

ARGOLIS:
—ARGOS: (1) iv BC *SEG* XXXII 374 (Νεαρ[έ]τα)

## Νεάρετος

MESSENIA:
—MESSENE: (1) iii BC ib. XXIII 210, 4

## Νεαρχία

SICILY:
—LIPARA: (1) imp. *Epigraphica* 3 (1941) p. 259 no. 15 (*N.* Γνωστή); (2) ~ ib. (*N.* Λίβερα); (3) iii-v AD Libertini, *Isole Eolie* p. 230 no. 9 (Lat. Nearchia)

## Νεαρχίς

LAKONIA:
—KYTHERA: (1) hell.-imp. *IG* v (1) 942, 6
—TAINARON-KAINEPOLIS: (2) ?ii-i BC ib. 1262 (?d. Τη—)

## Νέαρχος

AITOLIA:
—POTANA: (1) c. 200 BC *SGDI* 2072, 15
AKARNANIA:
—ASTAKOS: (2) ii BC *IG* IX (1)² (2) 434, 6 (s. Σιμίας)
ARGOLIS:
—ARGOS: (3) iv-iii BC Unp. (Ch. Kritzas)
ARKADIA:
—MANTINEIA-ANTIGONEIA: (4) c. 300-221 BC *IG* v (2) 323. 42 (tessera) (f. Ἀμφίστρατος); (5) ~ ib. 323. 58 (tessera) (f. Δαμόξενος); (6) ~ ib. 323. 82 (tessera) (f. Ξενίας)
—ORCHOMENOS: (7) c. 234 BC ib. 344, 14-15 (tyrant?)
S. ITALY (BRUTTIUM):
—LOKROI EPIZEPHYRIOI:
——(Στρ.): (8) iv/iii BC De Franciscis 20, 1 (f. Ὀνάσιμος)
S. ITALY (CALABRIA):
—TARAS-TARENTUM: (9) 209 BC *RE* (4); (10) imp. *CIL* IX 239 (Lat. Cn. Nearchus Nepos Fabianus)
S. ITALY (LUCANIA):
—HYELE-VELIA: (11) v BC *FGrH* 169
—METAPONTION: (12) m. iii BC *SEG* XXX 1175, 12 (doctor)

**Νέας**
LAKONIA:
—SPARTA: (1) c. 150-160 AD *IG* v (1) 68, 17; *SEG* XI 585, 5; XXX 410, 7 (Bradford (-)) (Γ. Ἰούλ. Ν., Ἰούλ. Νεασμός—no. 585 lap., N.—ed.: s. Σωσικράτης)

**Νεβρίδας**
LAKONIA:
—SPARTA: (1) ii AD *IG* v (1) 159, 32 (Bradford (-)) (doctor)

**Νεβρίς**
KORINTHIA:
—KORINTH: (1) c. 590-570 BC Amyx 25. 1 (vase) (Lorber 35) (het.?/fict.?)
S. ITALY (CAMPANIA):
—DIKAIARCHIA-PUTEOLI: (2) imp. *CIL* X 2123 (Lat. Attia Nebris); (3) ~ ib. 2531 (Lat. Nebris: d. 7a)
—POMPEII: (4) i BC-i AD ib. IV 5118; 5146 (Lat. Nebris)
S. ITALY (LUCANIA):
—GRUMENTUM*: (5) imp. ib. X 227 (Lat. Allidia Nebris: freed.)

**Νεβρίσκος**
ILLYRIA:
—EPIDAMNOS-DYRRHACHION: (1) c. 250-50 BC Ceka, *Probleme* p. 151 no. 46 (coin) (pryt.) ?= (2); (2) ~ Maier 330 (Ceka 39); cf. *IApoll Ref. Bibl.* n. 92; Maier 308-9; 488 (coin) (Ceka 290; 292; 310) (pryt.) ?= (1); (3) ii-i BC *IDyrrh* 546 (tile)

**Νέβρος**
S. ITALY (LUCANIA):
—GRUMENTUM: (1) imp. *CIL* X 227 (Lat. C. Turcius Nebrus)

**Νέζος**
DALMATIA:
—ISSA: (1) iii-ii BC Brunšmid p. 28 no. 21 (f. Φαντώ)

**Νεθαρίς**
SICILY:
—SYRACUSE: (1) imp. *IG* XIV 44; cf. *Riv. Arch. Crist.* 18 (1941) p. 224 no. 112 (Νεθαρί (voc.))

**Νειάδας**
SICILY:
—GELA-PHINTIAS: (1) f. v BC Dubois, *IGDS* 131. 6 (Arena, *Iscr. Sic.* II 45)

**Νειλᾶς**
S. ITALY (CAMPANIA):
—DIKAIARCHIA-PUTEOLI: (1) imp. *CIL* X 2094 with Add. p. 972 (Lat. Nilas)
—SALERNUM: (2) s. i AD *IItal* I (1) 124 (Lat. Q. Lucretius Nilas)

**Νειλεύς**
KORINTHIA:
—KORINTH: (1) ii BC *ZPE* I (1967) p. 230 (Stephanis 1786) (s. Ἀμμώνιος)

**Νειλόδωρος**
ARGOLIS:
—TROIZEN: (1) ?146 BC *IG* IV (1) 757 B, 24 (Νε[ιλό]δωρος: f. Φειδωνίδας)

**Νεῖλος**
KERKYRA: (1) ii-iii AD Unp. (*IG* arch.)
S. ITALY (CALABRIA):
—BRENTESION-BRUNDISIUM: (2) imp. *CIL* IX 97 (Lat. Cl. Nilus)
S. ITALY (CAMPANIA):
—NEAPOLIS: (3) iii-iv AD *IG* XIV 826. 30 (*INap* 240)

**Νεῖσκος**
S. ITALY (CALABRIA):
—TARAS-TARENTUM: (1) imp.? *SEG* XVI 580 (vase)

**Νεκταρεύς**
S. ITALY (APULIA):
—CANUSIUM: (1) 223 AD *Epig. Rom. di Canosa* 35 IV, 21 (*CIL* IX 338) (Lat. T. Aelius Nectareus)

**Νεμέρατος**
SICILY:
—KAMARINA: (1) iv/iii BC Dubois, *IGDS* 122, 4 (Cordano, 'Camarina VII' 137) (s. Ἀριστόμαχος)

**Νεμέριον**
SICILY:
—LIPARA: (1) imp. Libertini, *Isole Eolie* p. 226 no. 51 (?d. Εὐκλῆς)

**Νεμέριος**
MESSENIA:
—KORONE: (1) ii AD *SEG* XI 990 (f. Ῥόδα)
—MESSENE: (2) ?35-44 AD *IG* v (1) 1433, 26; *SEG* XXIX 396 (date) (f. Αὐτόμεια)
SICILY:
—LIPARA*: (3) ii-i BC *Kokalos* 32 (1986) p. 233 nos. 53-4 (tiles)

**Νέμεσις**
LAKONIA:
—LEUKTRA: (1) i AD *IG* v (1) 1330
S. ITALY (CAMPANIA):
—DIKAIARCHIA-PUTEOLI: (2) i BC *CIL* I² 1622 (x 1846) (Lat. Nemesis); (3) imp. ib. 2752 (Lat. Nemesis)
—POMPEII: (4) i BC-i AD ib. IV 1547 e
S. ITALY (LUCANIA):
—HYELE-VELIA: (5) imp. *PdelP* 33 (1978) p. 64 no. 8 (Lat. Furia Nemesis)
—VOLCEI: (6) imp. *IItal* III (1) 53 (*CIL* X 426) (Lat. Nemesis: m. Ἐπίκτησις)

**Νέμη**
S. ITALY (CAMPANIA):
—DIKAIARCHIA-PUTEOLI: (1) imp. ib. 2696 (Lat. Manlia Neme)

**Νεμηνίδας**
SICILY:
—THERMAI HIMERAIAI: (1) ?ii-i BC *IG* XIV 316, 1 (Dubois, *IGDS* 203) (f. Ἀριστόδημος Πέρσιος); (2) imp.? *IG* XIV 329 (s. Ἀριστόδαμος, f. Κλεοπάτρα)

**Νεμήνιος**
SICILY: (1) hell.-imp. ib. 456
—ADRANON: (2) iii-ii BC *PdelP* 16 (1961) p. 127 (s. Ἡρακλείδας)
—HELOROS (NR.): (3) s. v BC Dubois, *IGDS* 99 (f. Λισσίας)
—LIPARA*: (4) ?i AD *Kokalos* 32 (1986) p. 234 nos. 55-6 (tiles)
—NEAITON: (5) i AD *IG* II² 10292 (f. Ξένων)
—SYRACUSE:
——(Περηκυαταῖος): (6) iv BC Manganaro, *PdelP* forthcoming no. 3, 3 (f. Φιλωνίδας)
—SYRACUSE?:
——(Φελ.): (7) hell. ib. no. 4 V, 7 (f. Ἀπολλόδωρος)
—TAUROMENION: (8) c. 232 BC *IG* XIV 421 an. 9 (*SGDI* 5219) (s. Ἀμμωνόδοτος); (9) c. 173 BC *IG* XIV 421 an. 68 (*SGDI* 5219) (s. Ἀρτεμίδωρος) ?= (10); (10) c. 168 BC *IG* XIV 421 an. 73 (*SGDI* 5219) ?= (9); (11) ?ii/i BC *IG* XIV 421 D an. 1 (*SGDI* 5219) (f. Ἀπολλόδωρος); (12) c. 40 BC *Cron. Arch.* 3 (1964) p. 54 I, 2 (s. Φιλιστίων)

**Νεμονάϊος**
SICILY:
—KAMARINA: (1) f. v BC Cordano, *Tessere Pubbliche* 69 (f. Δίων)

**Νεμψίς**
S. ITALY (CAMPANIA):
—SURRENTUM: (1) imp. *CIL* X 742 (Lat. Pullia Nempsis)

**Νένδας**
SICILY:
—KAMARINA (NR.): (1) m. vi BC *SEG* XXXIV 939 (vases)

**Νεόδαμος**
ARKADIA:
—ORCHOMENOS: (1) f. iii BC *BCH* 38 (1914) p. 459 no. 4, 11
LAKONIA:
—SPARTA: (2) c. 208 BC *FD* III (4) 135, 8 (Bradford (-)) (f. Φιλόμαχος)
MESSENIA:
—MESSENE: (3) iv/iii BC *IG* v (1) 1435, 18
—THOURIA: (4) ii/i BC ib. 1384, 15 (s. Μνασιμαχίδας)
S. ITALY (BRUTTIUM):
—LOKROI EPIZEPHYRIOI:
——(Φαω.): (5) iv/iii BC De Franciscis 4, 12

**Νεοικίδας**
AKARNANIA:
—STRATOS: (1) iii BC *SEG* XXIX 475

**Νεοκλῆς**
ACHAIA:
—PELLENE: (1) iii BC *BCH* 38 (1914) p. 464 no. 8, 3 (s. Θορσύλοχος)
ARGOLIS:
—ARGOS: (2) ?255 BC Nachtergael, *Les Galates* 8, 56 (Stephanis 1794) (s. Εὔδαμος); (3) imp. *IG* II² 8373 (Νεοκ[λῆς]: s. Εὔρυμ—)
—PHLEIOUS: (4) s. iv BC Peek, *NIEpid* 16, 24 (Perlman E.6) (s. Ἀριστοκλῆς)
ARKADIA:
—TEGEA: (5) hell. *IG* v (2) 106 (Νεοκλῆ[s]); (6) iii BC ib. 33
——(Krariotai): (7) iv/iii BC ib. 38, 23 (f. Νέων); (8) s. iii BC ib. 36, 120 (s. Θεοχάρης)
—TEGEA?: (9) m. iii BC ib. 368, 3 (s. Νέων)
ELIS: (10) 245-249 AD *IvOl* 121, 8 (Αὐρ. Ν.: s. Αὐρ. Βασιλείδης)
KERKYRA: (11) imp. *IG* IX (1) 961 (s. Θεόδωρος)
LAKONIA:
—SPARTA: (12) s. i BC ib. v (1) 875 (Bradford (-))
LEUKAS: (13) c. 167-50 BC *BMC Thessaly* p. 180 no. 90 (coin) (Νεωκλῆς: reading—J.W.)
MESSENIA:
—ASINE: (14) ?316 BC *SEG* XII 219 (f. Ἀριστεύς, Φιλίδας)
—MESSENE: (15) m. ii BC *IG* II² 986, 12 (s. Ἀθανάδας)
—MESSENE?: (16) ii/i BC *SEG* XI 979, 12
S. ITALY (BRUTTIUM):
—KROTON: (17) hell.? Ath. 57 f

**Νεοκράτεια**
ARKADIA:
—STYMPHALOS: (1) iii BC *SEG* XLII 359

**Νεοκράτης**
ACHAIA:
—KALLISTAI: (1) c. 230-200 BC *BCH* 45 (1921) p. 12 II, 62 (f. Ἀγησίλαος)
ARKADIA:
—TEGEA: (2) iv/iii BC *IG* v (2) 38, 67

**Νεοκρέτης**
ARKADIA:
—MANTINEIA-ANTIGONEIA: (1) m. iii BC ib. 368, 119 (f. Μενέτιμος)

**Νεολαΐδας**
ACHAIA:
—AIGION: (1) c. 210-207 BC ib. IV (1)² 73, 18; *SEG* XXXV 303 (date)

**Νεόλαος**
ARKADIA:
—ORCHOMENOS: (2) i BC/i AD? *GP* 371 (f. Κραύ-
γις: fict.?)
—PHENEOS: (3) f. iv BC Moretti, *Olymp.* 380 (s.
Πρόξενος)
ELIS: (4) hell.? ib. 971-972
LAKONIA:
—SPARTA: (5) iv BC *IG* v (1) 1233, 5 (Poralla²
551)

**Νεόλαος**
LAKONIA:
—SPARTA: (1) c. 105-110 AD *IG* v (1) 20 B, 5;
*BSA* 26 (1923-5) p. 168 C 7, 8 (Bradford (4))
(*Τιβ. Κλ. Ν.*: s. Πρατομηλίδας)

**Νεόλας**
KORINTHIA:
—SIKYON: (1) vi/v BC *SEG* XI 244, 35
LAKONIA:
—SPARTA: (2) s. i BC *IG* v (1) 95, 11 (Bradford
(5)); (3) c. 25-1 BC *IG* v (1) 212, 33 (Bradford
(2)) (s. Καλλικρατίδας); (4) c. 50-75 AD *IG* v
(1) 278, 4 (Bradford (6)) (f. Ἀγησίλαος); (5) c.
90-100 AD *SEG* XI 558, 7 (Bradford (7)) (f.
Ἀγησίνικος); (6) ~ *SEG* XI 609, 6 (Bradford
(3)) (Νεόλ[ας]); (7) f. ii AD *IG* v (1) 473, 4 +
*SEG* XI 785 (name); 540, 4; *BSA* 81 (1986)
p. 324 no. 2 (ident.) (Bradford (1); (8)) (s. Ἀρχιάδας, f. Ἀρχιάδας); (8) m. ii AD *IG* v (1) 73,
2 (Bradford (9))

**Νεολλίς**
ACHAIA:
—PATRAI?: (1) iii-ii BC *Achaean Grave Stelai* 5

**Νεομήνιος**
SICILY:
—KAMARINA: (1) iv/iii BC *SEG* XXXIV 942,
2 (Dubois, *IGDS* 123; Cordano, 'Camarina
VII' 138) (s. Ἐργοτέλης)

**Νεοπάτρα**
AITOLIA:
—POTANA: (1) 186-?161 BC *FD* III (3) 2, 2, 11;
*SGDI* 1725, 1; 2034, 1 etc.; cf. Daux, *Del-
phes* pp. 468 f. (locn.) (and Phokis Delphi: d.
Ὀρθαῖος)
EPIROS:
—OMPHALES CHIMOLIOI: (2) c. 330-310
BC Cabanes, *L'Épire* p. 578 no. 51, 5
((Κλ)εοπάτρα?)

**Νεόπατρος**
ACHAIA:
—DYME: (1) s. iii BC *SEG* XIII 278, 22 (s. Σω—)

**Νεόπολις**
LAKONIA:
—GYTHEION: (1) f. ii AD *IG* v (1) 1170, 3
([Νε]όπολις: II s. Νεόπολις I); (2) ~ ib. l. [3];
1171, 12 = II² 3596 (I s. Ἑρμοκράτης, f. Νεό-
πολις II, Ἑρμοκράτης)
MESSENIA:
—THOURIA: (3) f. ii BC *SEG* XI 972, 92 (s. Ξε-
νόστρατος)
SICILY: (4) inc. Manganaro, *QUCC* forthcom-
ing nos. 64-6

**Νεοπολιτανός**
MESSENIA:
—MESSENE: (1) ii AD *IvOl* 465, 3 (Ἰούλ. Νεοπο-
λειτανός: f. Ἰούλ. Ἀθήναιος)

**Νεοπτόλεμος**
AITOLIA: (1) ?c. 275-254 BC *Syll³* 411; 412, 3,
9, 12 (*IEK* 35); *Syll³* 436, [2] (s.p.); Nachter-
gael, *Les Galates* 9, 3 (s.p.) (s. Φύσκος)
—ATTALEIA: (2) 204 BC *IG* IX (1)² (1) 95, 8
([Νεο]πτόλεμος)
—POTIDANIA: (3) m. ii BC *SBBerlAk* 1936, p.
371 a, 10 (*SEG* XLI 528 A); *SBBerlAk* 1936,

p. 371 b, 2, 10 (*SEG* XLI 528 B) (f. Εὔαρχος);
(4) ~ *SBBerlAk* 1936, p. 371 b, 13 (*SEG* XLI
528 B) (s. Εὔαρχος)
AKARNANIA:
—ASTAKOS: (5) ii BC *IG* IX (1)² (2) 435, 20 (s.
Παυσανίας)
EPIROS: (6) 234-168 BC Franke, *Münz. v. Epi-
rus* pp. 179-80 II ser. 40-1; p. 82 (coin); (7) f.
ii BC *IG* II² 8535 ([Ν]εοπτόλεμος: f. Εὐτυχίς)
—AMBRAKIA: (8) imp. *SEG* XXIV 420 (Νεουπτό-
λημος—apogr.: s. Ἱππίας)
—ARGETHIA: (9) c. 230-200 BC *BCH* 45 (1921)
p. 20 III, 132; *CID* II sub no. 8
—KASSOPE: (10) 168-148 BC *BMC Thessaly* p.
99 no. 16; Franke, *Münz. v. Epirus* p. 82; p.
84 I ser. 2 (coin) (Νεοπτ(όλεμος))
—MOLOSSOI: (11) f. iv BC *RE* (3); Cabanes,
*L'Épire* index s.v. (s. Ἀλκέτας, f. Ἀλέξανδρος,
Τρωϊάς, Ὀλυμπιάς: king); (12) s. iv BC *RE* (4);
Berve 548; (13) iv/iii BC *HE* 1971 (king?) ?=
(14); (14) ~ *RE* (4) (s. Ἀλέξανδρος, Κλεοπάτρα)
?= (13); (15) ii/i BC *GVI* 1063 (*SEG* XII 340)
(f. Ἀλκίμαχος)
S. ITALY (BRUTTIUM):
—RHEGION: (16) i BC/i AD *Suppl. It.* 5 p. 65 no.
17 (Lat. Neoptol(emus): f. Εὔανδρος)
S. ITALY (CAMPANIA):
—SURRENTUM: (17) imp. *NScav* 1928, p. 213
no. 5 (Lat. Neoptolem(us))

**Νέος**
ARKADIA:
—TEGEA: (1) m. iv BC *IG* v (2) 6, 113 (Ν̣έος?)

**Νεοσσός**
S. ITALY (LUCANIA):
—HYELE-VELIA: (1) f. v BC *Palinuro* 2 pp. 167-
170

**Νεόστρατος**
SICILY: (1) ?ii-i BC *Kokalos* 32 (1986) p. 234
no. 57 (tile) (Νεόσ[σ]τρατ[ος])

**Νεοφάνης**
ARKADIA: (1) iii BC *SEG* XXXVII 351

**Νεόφρων**
AKARNANIA:
—PALAIROS: (1) iii BC *IG* IX (1)² (2) 496
KORINTHIA:
—SIKYON: (2) v-iv BC *RE* (-); *TrGF* I pp. 92-4;
Berve 549 (Skalet 223)

**Νεόφυτος**
ARGOLIS:
—NEMEA: (1) v-vi AD *SEG* XXXIII 274

**Νεπτούνιος**
SICILY:
—SYRACUSE: (1) iii-v AD *Riv. Arch. Crist.* 36
(1960) p. 23 no. 8 (-νειος)

**Νεπώτιλλα**
S. ITALY (CAMPANIA):
—DIKAIARCHIA-PUTEOLI: (1) imp. *IG* XIV 851

**Νεσίων**
ILLYRIA:
—EPIDAMNOS-DYRRHACHION: (1) hell.-imp.
*IDyrrh* 76 (f. Ἀγαθοκλέα)

**Νεσσίκα**
ILLYRIA:
—EPIDAMNOS-DYRRHACHION: (1) hell.-imp. ib.
324 (?d. Ἱππόδαμος)

**Νεσσύλος**
ILLYRIA:
—EPIDAMNOS-DYRRHACHION: (1) c. 250-50 BC
*Congr. Int. Num.* p. 92 pl. I. 6; cf. *IApoll
Ref. Bibl.* n. 93 (coin); (2) ii-i BC *IDyrrh* 548
(tiles)

**Νεστίων**
ILLYRIA:
—EPIDAMNOS-DYRRHACHION: (1) hell.-imp. ib.
139 (f. Βάτων)

**Νεστόριος**
S. ITALY (LUCANIA):
—POSEIDONIA-PAESTUM: (1) 347 AD *Misc. Gr.
Rom.* 15 p. 235 f. (Lat. Aquillius Nestorius)

**Νέστωρ**
ARGOLIS:
—EPIDAUROS: (1) c. 340-320 BC Peek, *NIEpid*
19 C, 12 (Νέστ[ωρ])
—HERMIONE: (2) i BC *SGDI* 4108, 76
EPIROS: (3) iii BC *RE* (2)
—BOUTHROTOS (PRASAIBOI): (4) a. 163 BC
*IBouthrot* 14, 19; 22, 25 (*SEG* XXXVIII 471;
479) (s. Νικάνωρ, f. Νικάνωρ) ?= (7); (5)
~ *IBouthrot* 16 (*SEG* XXXVIII 473); (6) ~
*IBouthrot* 18, 10 (*SEG* XXXVIII 475) (f. Νι-
κάνωρ); (7) ~ *IBouthrot* 18, 11; 33, 13 (*SEG*
XXXVIII 475; 492) (s. Νικάνωρ) ?= (4); (8) ~
*IBouthrot* 46, 6 (s. Κεφαλῖνος); (9) ~ ib. 145,
12 (s. Νίκανδρος)
——Loigyphioi: (10) a. 163 BC ib. 29, 9 (*SEG*
XXXVIII 487)
——Moneoi: (11) a. 163 BC *IBouthrot* 103, 3
——Naritioi: (12) a. 163 BC ib. 94, 10 (f. Σίμα-
κος)
——Opatai: (13) a. 163 BC ib. 99, 6 (*BCH* 118
(1994) p. 121 B)
——Temouoi: (14) a. 163 BC *IBouthrot* 53, 3?;
54, 1; 58, 2; 59, 2 (*SEG* XXXVIII 504-5; 509;
510)
—EUROPIOI: (15) c. 200 BC *IG* IX (1)² (1) 31,
132 (Νέσσ-: f. Δείνων)
—KROPIOI: (16) f. ii BC *RE* (3); cf. Walbank on
Plb. xxvii 16. 4 (ὁ Κρώπιος (ethn.?))
ILLYRIA:
—DIMALE: (17) hell. *Iliria* 1982 (1), p. 120 no.
41 (tile); cf. p. 122
—EPIDAMNOS-DYRRHACHION: (18) c. 250-50
BC *SNG Cop. Thessaly–Illyricum* 515 (coin)
(pryt.); (19) ii-i BC *IDyrrh* 549 (tile)
KORINTHIA:
—KORINTH*: (20) ii-iii AD *Corinth* VIII (2) 10
(Lat. Aurelius Nestor)
S. ITALY (APULIA):
—CANUSIUM: (21) imp. *Epig. Rom. di Canosa*
101 (*CIL* IX 365) (Lat. Nestor)
S. ITALY (CAMPANIA):
—DIKAIARCHIA-PUTEOLI: (22) imp. ib. X 3100
(Lat. [V]ibellius Nestor); (23) ~ ib. 3103 (Lat.
M. Vibius Nestor); (24) ?ii-iii AD ib. 2806
(Lat. Aurelius Nestor)
—DIKAIARCHIA-PUTEOLI*: (25) imp. ib. 3062
(Lat. L. Plotius Nestor: s. Εὐπραξία: freed.)
—PITHEKOUSSAI-AENARIA: (26) s. viii BC *CEG*
I 454 (vase) (Dubois, *IGDGG* I 2; Arena,
*Iscr. Sic.* III 2; *LSAG²* p. 239 no. 1) (her.?)

**Νεστωριανός**
S. ITALY (CAMPANIA):
—DIKAIARCHIA-PUTEOLI: (1) imp. *CIL* X 3103
(Lat. M. Vibius Liberalis Nestorianus)
—NEAPOLIS: (2) iii-iv AD *IG* XIV 826. 31 (*INap*
243)

**Νευκλῆς**
ARGOLIS:
—EPIDAUROS*: (1) c. 370-360 BC Peek, *IAEpid*
52 A, 9, 13; *BSA* 61 (1966) p. 271 no. 4 A,
19 + Peek, *IAEpid* 48 (name)

**Νευμήνιος**
ACHAIA:
—DYME*: (1) c. 219 BC *SGDI* 1612, 36 (*Tyche*
5 (1990) p. 124) (f. Ξενόδοκος)
AITOLIA: (2) c. 220-150 BC *Coll. Walcher* 1376
(coin) (Νευ(μήνιος))

**S. Italy (Calabria):**

—taras-tarentum: (**3**) c. 280-272 bc Vlasto 739-47; 1059-63 (coin) (Evans, *Horsemen* p. 158 VII C.1-3; p. 162 nos. 1-2) (*Νευμή(νιος)*— Vlasto 739-47); (**4**) imp.? *IG* xii (3) 1233, 6 (*Νευμ[ή]νιος*: s. *Λέων*)

—taras-tarentum?: (**5**) ?iv bc ib. xiv 2405. 13 (lamp) (f. *Ἡρακλήδας*)

**Νεῦνα**

Illyria:

—epidamnos-dyrrhachion: (**1**) hell.-imp. *IDyrrh* 325 (*Νεῦνα*)

**Νεφέλη**

**S. Italy (Campania):**

—stabiae: (**1**) i ad *CIL* x 781 (Lat. Nepele)

**Νεώ**

**S. Italy (Calabria):**

—taras-tarentum: (**1**) ?v-iv bc *SEG* xxxvi 897 (Troisi, *Epigrafi mobili* 76 (loomweight)) (*Νεως* (gen.?, n. pr.?))

**Νέων**

Achaia:

—kallistai: (**1**) c. 230-200 bc *BCH* 45 (1921) p. 12 II, 62 (s. *Εὐθύδαμος*: reading—Oulhen)

Aitolia:

—thermos*: (**2**) s. iii bc *IG* ix (1)² (1) 60 VI, 13

Argolis:

—argos: (**3**) ?278-277 bc *Syll*³ 405 (*FD* iii (1) 87, [5]); *FD* iii (1) 88, [7]; cf. 83, 6 with *Syll*³ 406 n. 7 (*Λέων—Syll* 405: s. *Μενέστρατος*)

—epidauros: (**4**) iii bc *IG* iv (1)² 343

—halieis: (**5**) 424 bc ib. i³ 75, 34

Arkadia:

—kleitor: (**6**) ?262-255 bc Nachtergael, *Les Galates* 5, [39]; 8, 32 (Stephanis 1799) (s. *Ἀπολλώνιος*)

—pheneos: (**7**) ?265 bc *BCH* 82 (1958) p. 87 C (s. *—άνης*)

—stymphalos: (**8**) ?263-255 bc Nachtergael, *Les Galates* 3, 8; 5, [31]; 8, 43 (Stephanis 1800) (s. *Ἱππίας*)

—tegea: (**9**) hell. *IG* v (2) 106

——(Krariotai): (**10**) iv/iii bc ib. 38, 23 (s. *Νεοκλῆς*) ?= (*11*)

—tegea?: (**11**) m. iii bc ib. 368, 3 (f. *Νεοκλῆς*) ?= (*10*)

Illyria:

—apollonia: (**12**) c. 250-50 bc Maier 75 + Münsterberg Nachtr. p. 13 (coin) (Ceka 131) (pryt.)

—epidamnos-dyrrhachion: (**13**) hell.-imp. *IDyrrh* 199 (f. *Εὔανδρος*)

Korinthia:

—korinth: (**14**) 344 bc Plu., *Tim.* 18; (**15**) 263 bc *IG* ix (1)² (1) 17, 84 (f. *Χαιρίων*); (**16**) 247 bc *SB* 6759, 18 (*PCZ* 59340, 18)

—sikyon: (**17**) f. iii bc *IG* ii² 744, 5 (Skalet 225) (*Νέω[ν]*); (**18**) 176 bc *Syll*³ 585, 273 (Skalet 224) (f. *Καλλικράτης*)

Lakonia:

—asine: (**19**) 401-399 bc *RE* (2) (Poralla² 553)

—sparta: (**20**) c. 100-160 ad *IG* v (1) 38, 1, 7; 68, 16; 1506, 2; *SEG* xi 499, 1; *BSA* 80 (1985) p. 247 (date) (Bradford (1)) (II s. *Νέων* I, f. *Νέων* III); (**21**) m. ii ad *IG* v (1) 38, 1; 68, 16; 1506, 2 (Bradford (3)) (I f. *Νέων* II); (**22**) c. 125-180 ad *IG* v (1) 38, 7; *SEG* xi 499, 1; *BSA* 80 (1985) p. 247 (date) (Bradford (2)) (III s. *Νέων* II)

Messenia:

—messene: (**23**) m. iv bc Berve 550 (*RE* (3)) (s. *Φιλιάδας*) ?= (*24*); (**24**) s. iv bc *SEG* xli 362 (f. *Φιλλιάδας*) ?= (*23*); (**25**) ii bc *Ergon* 1995, p. 29

—thouria: (**26**) ii-i bc *IG* v (1) 1385, 14 (s. *Σωσίδαμος*)

**S. Italy (Calabria):**

—taras-tarentum: (**27**) f. ii bc *BCH* 45 (1921) p. 26 col. IV, 83 + *SEG* xxii 455; cf. *Sic. Gymn.* 17 (1964) pp. 46 f. (*Νέω[ν]*)

**S. Italy (Campania):**

—dikaiarchia-puteoli: (**28**) imp. *CIL* x 2770 (Lat. Neon Nepos)

—pompeii: (**29**) 70-79 ad ib. iv 871 (Castrèn 402. 11); Mouritsen p. 109 (date) (Lat. Terentius Neo)

—stabiae: (**30**) imp. *Arctos* 15 (1981) p. 105 (Lat. Cn. Helvius Neo)

**S. Italy (Lucania):**

—atina lucana: (**31**) imp. *IItal* III (1) 196 (Lat. Luxilius Neo: f. Luxilius Pedo)

—herakleia: (**32**) iii bc *NC* 1917, p. 174 no. 5 q-r; *Coll. McClean* 860 (coins) (van Keuren, *Coinage of Heraclea* p. 80 no. 97); van Keuren, *Coinage of Heraclea* p. 87 no. 122

Sicily:

—syracuse: (**33**) ?205-203 bc *FD* iii (4) 427 A, 1 (s. *Λέων*)

**Νεωνίδας**

Kephallenia:

—pale: (**1**) iii/ii bc Unp. (*IG* arch.)

**Νεωτίς**

Leukas: (**1**) iii bc *AM* 27 (1902) p. 370 no. 41 a

**Νήδυμος**

Illyria:

—epidamnos-dyrrhachion: (**1**) imp. *AEp* 1978, no. 753 (Lat. L. Cluvius Nedymus: s. Primigenia, L. Cluvius Aper); (**2**) 52 ad *CIL* x (1) 769 (Lat. C. Sabinius Nedymus)

Lakonia:

—sparta: (**3**) c. 100-125 ad *IG* v (1) 153, 27; *SEG* xi 569, 22 (Bradford (1)) (s. *Φιλόκαλος*); (**4**) c. 160 ad *IG* v (1) 39, 32, 38; 71 II, 7 (Bradford (2))

**S. Italy (Apulia):**

—canusium*: (**5**) imp. *Epig. Rom. di Canosa* 156 (Lat. L. Marcius Nedimus: freed.)

—venusia: (**6**) imp. *CIL* ix 543 (Lat. Nedymus)

**S. Italy (Campania):**

—capreae: (**7**) imp. *Eph. Ep.* viii 673/4 (Lat. Nedimus)

—herculaneum*: (**8**) i bc-i ad *CIL* x 1403 f III, 15 (Lat. P. Marius Nedymus: freed.); (**9**) ~ ib. 1403 g II, 18 (Lat. M. Nonius Nedymus: freed.)

—pompeii: (**10**) i bc-i ad ib. iv 1561 (Lat. Nedymus); (**11**) ~ ib. 3376 (Castrèn 203. 1) (Lat. P. Instuleius Nedymus); (**12**) ~ *CIL* iv 4822 (Lat. Nedimus); (**13**) c. 51-62 ad ib. 3340. 99, 3 (Castrèn 118. 14) (Lat. Ti. Claudius Nedymus)

**S. Italy (Lucania):**

—poseidonia-paestum: (**14**) f. iii ad Mello–Voza 100 (Lat. Tullius Nedymus)

**Νηκλῆς**

Lakonia:

—sparta: (**1**) s. i bc *IG* v (1) 127, 6; 210, 11 (Bradford (2)) (s. *Εὐτυχίδας*)

——Amyklai: (**2**) ii/i bc *IG* v (1) 26, 1 (Bradford (1)) (s. *Ἀριστοκράτης*)

**Νήνη**

Aigina: (**1**) ii-i bc *IG* iv (1) 138 a (d. *Ἀπολλώνιος*)

**Νηρεῖς**

**S. Italy (Apulia):**

—herdonia: (**1**) ii/iii ad *Ordona* 2 p. 130 no. 2 (Lat. Bruttia Nereis: ?m. Arrenia Felicissima)

**S. Italy (Campania):**

—dikaiarchia-puteoli: (**2**) ?i-ii ad *CIL* x 1878 (Lat. Lollia Nereis)

—misenum*: (**3**) imp. ib. 3572 (Lat. Antonia Nereis)

—pompeii: (**4**) i bc-i ad ib. iv 1353 e; cf. p. 207 (Lat. Niaereis)

—stabiae: (**5**) imp. ib. x 3472 (Lat. Memmia Nereis)

**S. Italy (Lucania):**

—calle (mod.): (**6**) imp. *BdA* 52 (1967) p. 44 (Lat. Caedia Nerais)

**Νηρεύς**

Aigina: (**1**) ?f. i ad *Alt-Ägina* 1 (2) p. 45 no. 17, 4 (f. *Ἑρμογένης*)

Illyria:

—lissos?: (**2**) imp. *SEG* xxiv 469

Korinthia:

—korinth: (**3**) ii ad *FD* iii (4) 92 (*Γ. Ἥϊος Ν.*)

Lakonia:

—sparta: (**4**) c. 50-80 ad *IG* v (1) 277, 2, 6-7; *Artemis Orthia* pp. 308-9 no. 25 (date) (Bradford (-)) (f. *Πρῖμος*)

**S. Italy (Campania):**

—pompeii: (**5**) i bc-i ad *CIL* iv 4514, 14 (Lat. Nereus)

**Νηρηΐς**

Epiros:

—molossoi: (**1**) iii bc *RE* (23); Walbank ad Plb. vii 4, 5 (ident.) (d. *Πύρρος*, m. *Ἱερώνυμος* (Syracuse))

**Νηρως?**

**S. Italy (Calabria):**

—brentesion-brundisium*: (**1**) imp. *CIL* ix 197 = *Epigraphica* 25 (1963) p. 45 no. 26; cf. 42 (1980) p. 158 (Lat. Nerotis (gen.): freed.)

**Νησιας**

Aigina: (**1**) imp.? *IG* iv (1) 139

**Νήσων**

**S. Italy (Calabria):**

—taras-tarentum: (**1**) ?iv-iii bc Unp. (A.W.J.) (terracotta)

**Νήφων**

Elis: (**1**) 233 ad *IvOl* 116, 10 (s. *Λ. Βετληνὸς Στάχυς*)

Lakonia:

—sparta: (**2**) c. 140-145 ad *IG* v (1) 1314, 35 (Bradford (-))

**S. Italy (Calabria):**

—brentesion-brundisium: (**3**) ?i/ii ad *NScav* 1892, p. 242 (Lat. T. Flavius Nepho)

**Νῆψις**

Korinthia:

—korinth: (**1**) ii-iii ad *SEG* xi 132, 3; 135 (f. *Ἀπελλᾶς*)

**Νίγερ**

Elis: (**1**) f. ii ad *IvOl* 92, 6 (I f. *Νίγερ* II); (**2**) ~ ib. l. 6, 10, 11 (II s. *Νίγερ* I, f. *Σόφων*, *Ποσείδιππος*)

**Νιγρῖνος**

**S. Italy (Campania):**

—dikaiarchia-puteoli: (**1**) ii-iii ad *IG* xiv 834 (-γρεῖ-: s. *Τρύφων*)

**Νίγρος**

Sicily:

—thermai himeraiai: (**1**) imp. *IGLMP* 121 (f. *Ἰοῦστος*)

**Νίθων**

Argolis:

—argos: (**1**) a. 316 bc *SEG* xxx 360, 18 (Perlman A.8); *SEG* xxxiii 285 (name) (*Ἴθων—SEG* xxx: s. *Θιόφαμος*)

## Νίκα
ACHAIA:
—DYME: (1) iii BC *AJPh* 31 (1910) p. 399 no. 74 a, 8
ARKADIA:
—ALIPHEIRA: (2) hell.? Orlandos, *Alipheira* p. 218 no. 2
EPIROS:
—BOUTHROTOS (PRASAIBOI): (3) a. 163 BC *IBouthrot* 17, 17; 41, 22; 43, 26 (*SEG* XXXVIII 474; 500; 502) (m. Διογένης, Θεανώ)
KERKYRA: (4) ii-iii AD Unp. (*IG* arch.) (Νεί-: d. Διογένης)
S. ITALY (LUCANIA):
—HYELE-VELIA: (5) iv/iii BC *IG* XIV 659; cf. *SEG* XXIX 1024 (date) (d. Ζωίλος)

## Νικααρίστα
ARGOLIS:
—ARGOS?: (1) v BC *IG* IV (1)² 140 (Lazzarini 281) (-καηαρί-)

## Νικάγαθος
ILLYRIA:
—APOLLONIA: (1) hell. *IApoll* 342 (tile); (2) c. 250-50 BC Münsterberg Nachtr. p. 13 (coin) (Ceka 136) (pryt.)

## Νικαγένης
ARGOLIS:
—EPIDAUROS:
——Tantalis: (1) c. 365-335 BC *IG* IV (1)² 103, 7; cf. *SEG* XXV 386

## Νικαγίδας
AIGINA: (1) iv BC Peek, *IAEpid* 149

## Νικαγόρα
ACHAIA:
—PATRAI?: (1) imp.? Moretti, *IAG* p. 168 (Νικηγόρα—ed.)
AIGINA: (2) iv BC *Ag.* XVII 393 ([Νι]καγόρα: d. Πύθων); (3) hell. *IG* IV (1) 140
ARGOLIS:
—EPIDAUROS: (4) ii BC ib. IV (1)² 247 (d. Καλλίδαμος, m. Διονύσιος)
—KALAURIA: (5) iii BC ib. IV (1) 840, 4 (d. Σωφάνης, Ἁγασιγράτις); (6) ~ ib. 841, 5, 9, 14; (7) ~ ib. 844
—PHLEIOUS: (8) ?iv BC ib. 465
KORINTHIA:
—SIKYON: (9) ?v BC Paus. ii 10. 3 (Skalet 226) (m. Ἁγασικλῆς)
LEUKAS: (10) iv/iii BC *AD* 25 (1970) Chron. p. 332; (11) ~ ib. 26 (1971) Chron. p. 354

## Νικαγόρας
AKARNANIA:
—PALAIROS: (1) iii BC *IG* IX (1)² (2) 497 (Νικαγόρα (masc. nom., fem. gen.?))
ARGOLIS:
—ARGOS:
——Eryneion (Naupliadai): (2) s. iii BC *SEG* XVII 144, 3 (Perlman A.20)
—TROIZEN: (3) 480 BC Plu., *Them.* 10
ARKADIA: (4) ?c. 369-361 BC *BCH* 102 (1978) p. 347, 28 (*IPArk* 14) (Νικαγορες (gen.)—lap., Νικαγόρα? (fem.)); (5) ?255 BC Nachtergael, *Les Galates* 8, 28 (Stephanis 1805) (s. Λιχμέας)
ILLYRIA:
—EPIDAMNOS-DYRRHACHION: (6) hell.-imp. *IDyrrh* 327; (7) ~ ib. 397 (f. —ία)
KEPHALLENIA:
—SAME: (8) hell. *IG* IX (1) 635 ([Ν]ικαγόρ[ας])
LAKONIA:
—SPARTA: (9) c. 105-115 AD ib. v (1) 103, 1 (Bradford s.v. Νικάγορος (2)) (Ν̣ε̣ικαγό[ρας]: f. —ης); (10) byz.? *AP* vi 84 (Poralla² 554)
MESSENIA:
—KORONE: (11) i BC *IG* v (1) 1392, 2 (s. Διοκλείδας)

---

—MESSENE: (12) iii BC ib. 1444 (f. Ἀρισταγόρα); (13) s. iii BC *RE* (2)

## Νικάγορος
LAKONIA:
—SPARTA: (1) ?f. ii AD *IG* v (1) 296, 1; *Artemis Orthia* pp. 318-19 no. 41 (date) (Bradford (1)) (Νει-: s. Σωσίδαμος)

## Νικάδας
ACHAIA:
—AIGION: (1) f. ii BC *Corinth* VIII (1) 2, 2, 7 (s. Ἀλεξάνωρ)
—DYME*: (2) c. 219 BC *SGDI* 1612, 42 (*Tyche* 5 (1990) p. 124) (s. Νικάνωρ)
AITOLIA:
—TRICHONION: (3) f. ii BC *IG* IX (1)² (3) 630, 3
ARKADIA: (4) ?255 BC Nachtergael, *Les Galates* 8, 15; cf. Stephanis 1807 (f. Νικαίας)
EPIROS: (5) iv/iii BC *IG* II² 8539 (f. Λεοντίς)
—BOUTHROTOS (PRASAIBOI): (6) a. 163 BC *IBouthrot* 18, 11; 33, 13 (*SEG* XXXVIII 475; 492) (s. Νικάνωρ) ?= (20); (7) ~ *IBouthrot* 28, 31 (*SEG* XXXVIII 486) (?s. Βόϊλλα); (8) ~ *IBouthrot* 32, 2 (*SEG* XXXVIII 491) ?= (9); (9) ~ *IBouthrot* 37, 1 (*SEG* XXXVIII 496) (f. Φίλιππος) ?= (8); (10) ~ *IBouthrot* 38, 14 (*SEG* XXXVIII 497) (I? s. Λύκος, f. Λύκος, Νικάδας II?); (11) ~ *IBouthrot* 38, 14 (*SEG* XXXVIII 497) (II? s. Νικάδας I?); (12) ~ *IBouthrot* 56, 9 (*SEG* XXXVIII 507) ([Νικ]άδας); (13) ~ *IBouthrot* 129, 8 (s. Φίλιππος)
——Ancheropaioi: (14) a. 163 BC ib. 68, 5 (Νει-: f. Δέξανδρος)
——Bouthrotioi: (15) a. 163 BC ib. 95, 5 (Νει-: f. Νίκαιος)
——Kartonoi: (16) f. ii BC ib. 6, 5 (*SEG* XXXVIII 468); (17) a. 163 BC *IBouthrot* 78, 4; 79, 4; 80, 3; 81, 4; 82, 3; 83, [3]; 84, [4]; 85, 3; 86, 4; 87, 3; 88, [3] (*BCH* 118 (1994) pp. 122 f. nos. 1-11) ?= (18); (18) ~ *IBouthrot* 144, 8 (s. Φίλιππος) ?= (17)
——Loigyphioi: (19) a. 163 BC ib. 78, 2; 79, 2; 80, 2; 81, 2; 82, 1; 83, 2; 84, [2]; 85, 1; 86, 2; 87, 2; 88, 1 (*BCH* 118 (1994) pp. 122 f. nos. 1-11); *IBouthrot* 110, [2]; 126, 2; 127, 2 (*BCH* 118 (1994) p. 128 A); *IBouthrot* 138, 2
——Temouoi: (20) a. 163 BC ib. 15, 1 (*SEG* XXXVIII 472) (s. Νικάνωρ) ?= (21) (6)
——Temouoi?: (21) a. 163 BC *IBouthrot* 52, 3 (*SEG* XXXVIII 517) (Νικ[άδας]) ?= (20)
—BOUTHROTOS*: (22) f. iii BC Ugolini, *Alb. Ant.* 3 p. 131 with Plate XVII (s. Νίκαιος)
—CHAONES: (23) f. ii BC *IBouthrot* 6, 16 (*SEG* XXXVIII 468) (f. Φιλόξενος)
ILLYRIA:
—APOLLONIA: (24) c. 250-50 BC Münsterberg Nachtr. p. 13 (coin) (Ceka 82) (money.)
—EPIDAMNOS-DYRRHACHION: (25) c. 250-50 BC Maier 135; 206; 246; Münsterberg p. 260 = Nachtr. p. 14 (coin) (Ceka 346-9) + *IApoll Ref. Bibl.* n. 94 (money.); (26) hell.-imp. *IDyrrh* 323 (Νει-: I f. Νικάδας II); (27) ~ ib. (Νει-: II s. Νικάδας I)
LAKONIA:
—TAINARON-KAINEPOLIS: (28) 198-211 AD *SEG* XXIII 199, 18 (Νει-: f. Καλλικράτης)
MESSENIA:
—THOURIA: (29) f. ii BC ib. XI 972, 74 (f. Δαμίων); (30) ~ ib. l. 77 (f. Νικάνωρ)

## Νικαία
ACHAIA:
—DYME: (1) ii BC *Achaean Grave Stelai* 45 (d. Δίων)
AIGINA: (2) ii BC *SEG* XI 10, 2
ARGOLIS:
—ARGOS*: (3) ii BC ib. XLII 279, 13 (slave/freed.?)

---

—EPIDAUROS: (4) iii BC Peek, *IAEpid* 342 (Ν[ικ]αία)
DALMATIA:
—ISSA: (5) iii-ii BC Brunšmid p. 29 no. 24 (Νει-: d. Βαιστίρων)
EPIROS:
—ARGETHIA: (6) 157 BC *SGDI* 1689, 1, 4 etc. (m. Ἰσθμός: slave/freed.)
—BOUTHROTOS (PRASAIBOI): (7) a. 163 BC *IBouthrot* 18, 10; 33, 14 (*SEG* XXXVIII 475; 492)
ILLYRIA:
—APOLLONIA: (8) ?ii BC *IApoll* 126 (Νει-: d. Ἁγρων)
LAKONIA: (9) 194 BC *SGDI* 2068, 3, 5 (m. Νικέας, Νικόστρατος: slave/freed.)
S. ITALY?: (10) 200 BC ib. 2116, 5 (slave/freed.)

## Νικαίας
ARKADIA: (1) ?255 BC Nachtergael, *Les Galates* 8, 15 (Stephanis 1807) (s. Νικάδας)

## Νίκαιθος
ARGOLIS:
—PHLEIOUS: (1) m. iii BC *IG* VII 10, 7 (f. Πειθανορίδας)

## Νικαικλῆς
LAKONIA: (1) iv/iii BC ib. v (1) 704 (Bradford (-)) (-καhι-)

## Νικαΐλας
ARGOLIS:
—ARGOS: (1) c. 315 BC *SEG* XXXII 370, 3, 5

## Νίκαιος
ACHAIA: (1) 257 BC *PKöln* 314 (s. Χαρίξενος: t.e.); (2) 146 BC *IG* IV (1)² 28, 161 (s. Κάλλιππος: synoikos)
AITOLIA:
—BOUKATION?: (3) c. 162 BC ib. IX (1)² (1) 106, 11
AKARNANIA:
—KORONTA: (4) 208 BC *IMM* 31, 1 (*IG* IX (1)² (2) 582) (s. Ἐχε—)
ARGOLIS:
—EPIDAUROS: (5) c. 370 BC ib. IV (1)² 102, 70, 293; (6) ii BC Peek, *IAEpid* 130 (Νίκα[ιος]: f. Στρατονίκη)
——Politas: (7) c. 350-275 BC *SEG* XXVI 445, 19 (Perlman E.12)
—HERMIONE: (8) ?ii-i BC *IG* IV (1) 731 III, 14 (s. Ἀριστόδαμος)
ARKADIA:
—PHENEOS: (9) 191-146 BC *BMC Pelop.* p. 15 no. 168 (coin)
EPIROS:
—BOUTHROTOS (PRASAIBOI): (10) a. 163 BC *IBouthrot* 15, 17 (*SEG* XXXVIII 472); (11) ~ *IBouthrot* 48, 11; (12) ~ ib. 57 (*SEG* XXXVIII 508)
——Altharioi: (13) a. 163 BC *IBouthrot* 53, 5 (*SEG* XXXVIII 504) (s. Νικᾶς)
——Bouthrotioi: (14) a. 163 BC *IBouthrot* 95, 5 (Νει-: s. Νικάδας)
——Elaioi: (15) a. 163 BC ib. 66, 9 (f. Νίκανδρος)
——Loigyphioi: (16) a. 163 BC ib. 137, 14 (s. Μενοίτιος)
——Lyktennoi: (17) a. 163 BC ib. 115, 10 (f. Ἄδματος)
——Tharioi: (18) a. 163 BC ib. 114, 10 (f. Νικόλαος)
——Tykonioi: (19) a. 163 BC ib. 102, 2
—BOUTHROTOS*: (20) f. iii BC Ugolini, *Alb. Ant.* 3 p. 131 with Plate XVII (f. Νικάδας)
—GITANA: (21) f. iii AD *AD* 18 (1963) Chron. p. 156 (s. Γένυς)
ILLYRIA:
—AMANTIA: (22) ?i BC *Iliria* 1972, p. 91 no. 2, 1, 12 (Νεί-)
MESSENIA:
—MESSENE: (23) hell. *SEG* XXIII 207, 28
——(Aristomachidai): (24) 11 AD *PAE* 1992, p. 71 A, 8 (f. Φιλοκράτης)

S. Italy (Bruttium):
—Terina:
——(Ὠλ.): (25) c. 325-300 BC IGSI 21, 13 (SEG IV 73; Landi, DISMG 170)
S. Italy (Lucania):
—Metapontion: (26) vi BC Lazzarini 884 a (Landi, DISMG 140) (n. pr.?)
Sicily:
—Adranon: (27) hell.? IG XIV 571
—Syracuse?:
——(Ὑπα.): (28) hell. Manganaro, PdelP forthcoming no. 4 III, 6 (s. Πόλυλλος)

**Νικάιππος**
Lakonia:
—Amyklai*: (1) iii BC IG V (1) 1574 a (Bradford (-)) (Νικάhιππ[ος])

**Νικάνδρα**
Epiros:
—Dodona: (1) m. v BC Hdt. ii 55 (fict.?)

**Νικανδρία**
Arkadia:
—Megalopolis: (1) ?145 BC IG V (2) 439, 59 (d. Κλέων, m. Ξένων)
Lakonia:
—Hippola: (2) s. ii BC SEG XLII 304

**Νικανδρίδας**
Achaia: (1) c. 222 BC Syll³ 519, 14
Korinthia:
—Korinth: (2) c. 240-220 BC IG VII 366, [1] (IOrop 162) (-δης: s. Νικόδαμος: reading—Petrakos)
Lakonia:
—Sparta: (3) c. 25-1 BC IG V (1) 212, 7 (Bradford (1)) (s. Εὐκλείδας); (4) c. 1-10 AD IG V (1) 209, 15; SEG XXXV 331 (date) (Bradford (3); Stephanis 1808) (s. Νικόμαχος); (5) c. 90-100 AD SEG XI 605, 4 (Bradford (2)) (s. Εὔνοος); (6) c. 100-125 AD SEG XI 514, 4 (Bradford (6)) (Νικ[α]νδρί[δας]); (7) c. 125-150 AD IG V (1) 114, 4 (Bradford (5)) (f. Ναυβάτας); (8) m. ii AD IG V (1) 69, 27; 70, 5; 71 III, 14; BSA 80 (1985) pp. 246-7 (ident., stemma) (Bradford (4)) (Π. Αἰλ. Ν.: ?s. Ἀλκανδρίδας, ?f. Π. Αἰλ. Ἀλκανδρίδας); (9) c. 175-210 AD SEG XI 503, 8; 555, 6 (II s. Νικανδρίδας I); (10) ~ ib. 503, [8]; 555, 6 (I f. Νικανδρίδας II)
—Tainaron-Kainepolis: (11) imp. IG V (1) 1259 (Νει-: f. Ἐτέαρχος)
Leukas: (12) hell.? ib. IX (1) 549; (13) ~ ib. 550

**Νικάνδριππος**
Lakonia:
—Hippola: (1) iii/ii BC ib. V (1) 1336, 2, 11 (s. Νικαν—)

**Νίκανδρος**
Achaia: (1) 146 BC ib. IV (1)² 28, 94 (f. Κλέων: synoikos); (2) iii AD SEG XIII 480; cf. BE 1955, no. 95 (f. Ἀμάραντος)
—Dyme: (3) s. iii BC SEG XIII 278, 29 (f. Ξένων)
Aitolia: (4) c. 262-254 BC Flacelière p. 398 no. 21 c, 3; Nachtergael, Les Galates 8, 6; 19, 4 (Νικόδωρος—Flacelière per err.) ?= (8)
—Daianes: (5) 161 BC IG IX (1)² (1) 100, 8
—Philotaieis: (6) m. ii BC ib. 107, 1; 108, 8
—Phytaion: (7) ii/i BC SEG XVII 273, 4 (Νείκ[α]ν[δρος], Νεικ[ά]ν[ωρ]?—ed.: f. Τεῖσις)
—Trichonion: (8) 263 BC IG IX (1)² (1) 17, 8 ?= (4); (9) 194-170 BC RE (4); IG IX (1)² (1) p. LI, s.a. 190 BC, 184 BC, 177 BC; 187, 3; Syll³ 636, 16 (s. Βίττος); (10) 185 BC IG IX (1)² (1) 32, 18 (s. Δωρίμαχος); (11) c. 141 BC ib. 34, 22 (?s. Ἀλέξων)
Akarnania:
—Thyrreion: (12) iii BC ib. IX (1)² (2) 597 (f. Ἀγίας); (13) 216 BC ib. 583, 19 (f. Χαροπίδας); (14) 208 BC IMM 31, 6 (IG IX (1)² (2) 582) (s. Λύκος); (15) ii BC ib. 247, 17; 251, 13 (s.

Σωκράτης); (16) ~ ib. 250, 10; (17) ~ ib. 251, 10 (II s. Νίκανδρος I); (18) ~ ib. l. 11 (I f. Νίκανδρος II)
Argolis:
—Argos: (19) a. 303 BC CEG II 816, 13; (20) ?170 BC IG II² 2315, 18; Habicht, Athen hell. Zeit pp. 118-19 (date); 133 (ethn.) (s. Τίμων); (21) ii/i BC SEG XXVIII 1246, 19 (I f. Νίκανδρος II); (22) ~ ib. l. 19 (II s. Νίκανδρος I); (23) ii AD ib. XVI 253, 17 (s. Εὐάνθης)
—Epidauros: (24) ?c. 270-260 BC ib. XIV 398 b, 11, 14 (s. Νικήρατος)
——(Dymanes): (25) c. 335-325 BC IG IV (1)² 106 III, 39; 108, 159 ?= (27)
——(Hylleis): (26) 146 BC ib. 28, 57 (f. Σωκράτης)
——Nauplias: (27) c. 335-325 BC ib. 106 I, [3], [13], 22 ?= (25)
——Tantalis: (28) c. 290-270 BC ib. 109 II, 153
—Epidauros*: (29) c. 320-300 BC ib. 110 A, 10, 14
—Troizen: (30) iii BC ib. IV (1) 774, 11; (31) 153-144 BC SGDI 2295, 15 (f. Ἀριστοτέλης); (32) ?146 BC IG IV (1) 757 B, 22 (or Arkadia: Νίκανδ[ρ]ος: s. Πεισικράτης); (33) imp. ib. 817
Arkadia:
—Megalopolis: (34) ii BC IvOl 396 (f. Ἀριστέας)
—Tegea: (35) i BC IG V (2) 45, 5
——(Apolloniatai): (36) s. iv BC ib. 174 a, 2
Dalmatia:
—Issa:
——(Dymanes): (37) iv/iii BC Brunšmid p. 9, 58 (f. Καλλισθένης)
Elis: (38) iv/iii BC Moretti, Olymp. 494; 501
Epiros:
—Ambrakia: (39) ?iii/ii BC SEG XXV 700 (s. Φιλιστίων); (40) ii-i BC CIG 1797 (f. Ζήνων); (41) ~ AE 1910, p. 397; cf. AAA 4 (1971) pp. 337 f.; cf. SEG XLII 543 (s. Σόλων)
—Bouthrotos (Prasaiboi): (42) a. 163 BC IBouthrot 10, 1 (SEG XXXVIII 464); (43) ~ IBouthrot 18, 20 (SEG XXXVIII 475); (44) ~ IBouthrot 21, 13; 42, 4, 13 (SEG XXXVIII 478; 501) (f. Λέων) ?= (59); (45) ~ IBouthrot 22, 19 (SEG XXXVIII 479); (46) ~ IBouthrot 22, 19 (SEG XXXVIII 479); (47) ~ IBouthrot 26, 16 (SEG XXXVIII 484) (f. Λυσανίας); (48) ~ IBouthrot 29, 19 (SEG XXXVIII 487); (49) ~ IBouthrot 31, 59 (SEG XXXVIII 490); IBouthrot 51, 20 (f. Σώπατρος) ?= (64); (50) ~ ib. 31, 70 (SEG XXXVIII 490) (f. Κέφαλος); (51) ~ IBouthrot 32, 7; (52) ~ ib. 33, 5 (SEG XXXVIII 492); IBouthrot 50, 7; (53) ~ ib. 38, 1 (SEG XXXVIII 497) (f. Νίκαρχος) ?= (67); (54) ~ IBouthrot 38, 1 (SEG XXXVIII 497) (f. Σωτίων); (55) ~ IBouthrot 38, 11 (SEG XXXVIII 497) (s. Σωτίων); (56) ~ IBouthrot 39, 4 (SEG XXXVIII 498); (57) ~ IBouthrot 41, 12 (SEG XXXVIII 500); (58) ~ IBouthrot 66, 4 (s. Λυσανίας) ?= (72); (59) ~ ib. 100, 4 (f. Λέων) ?= (44); (60) ~ ib. 103, 5; (61) ~ ib. 107; (62) ~ ib. 110, 8 (f. Ἀριστόμαχος); (63) ~ ib. 113, 15; (64) ~ ib. 122, 8 (f. Σώπατρος) ?= (49); (65) ~ ib. 140, 10; (66) ~ ib. 145, 12 (f. Νέστωρ); (67) ~ ib. 151, 5 ?= (53); (68) ~ ib. l. 6
——Elaioi: (69) a. 163 BC ib. 66, 9 (s. Νίκαιος)
——Oporronioi: (70) a. 163 BC ib. 89, 2; 100, 1; 114, 2; 115, 2
——Prakeleoi: (71) a. 163 BC ib. 94, 6 (f. Νικάσιος)
——Somitai: (72) a. 163 BC ib. 67, 2 ?= (58)
—Chaones: (73) f. ii BC ib. 6, 17 (SEG XXXVIII 468) (f. Σαώτας)
—Charadros: (74) a. 167 BC ib. XXXV 665 A, 14 (s. Λαμίσκος)
—Dodona: (75) iii BC Antoniou, Dodone Aa, 19; (76) ~ ib. l. 23; (77) ~ ib. Ab, 44; (78) ~ ib. Ba, 18; (79) ~ ib. l. 33
—Hyporronioi: (80) a. 163 BC IBouthrot 116, 10 (BCH 118 (1994) p. 121 A)

—Kassope: (81) iii-ii BC SEG XXXV 670 (s. Ἀρίστων)
—Molossoi: (82) f. iii BC FGrH 703 F 9 (f. Βάλακρος)
—Nikopolis: (83) imp. PAE 1913, p. 111 (Sarikakis 78) (Τιβ. Κλ. Ν.); (84) ~ Wiss. Mitth. Bosn. 4 (1896) p. 389 no. 8 (Sarikakis 115) (Νεί-)
—Opouoi: (85) iii-ii BC SGDI 1349, 11; cf. Cabanes, L'Épire p. 580 no. 53 (Νεί-: f. Βοΐσκος)
—Pergamoi: (86) iii/ii BC ib. p. 561 no. 35, 5; Robert, Hell. 1 pp. 95 ff. (locn.) (s. Θευ—)
—Talaonoi/Talaianes: (87) iii-ii BC SGDI 1349, 4; cf. Cabanes, L'Épire p. 580 no. 53 (Νεί-: s. Ἀνεροίτας)
—Thesprotoi: (88) s. iii BC FD III (2) 83, 1 (f. Ἄλκιμος)
—Votonosi (mod.): (89) ?iii BC SEG XXIV 465 (Νεί-: f. Ἀδαμάτας)
—Zmaratha: (90) s. iv BC IG IV (1)² 95, 74-5 (Perlman E.2); Perlman pp. 46-9 (date) (f. Ἐπίνικος)
Illyria:
—Apollonia: (91) c. 250-50 BC Maier 13; 24 (coin) (Ceka 83-4) (money.)
—Epidamnos-Dyrrhachion: (92) c. 250-50 BC SNG Cop. Thessaly–Illyricum 516; 520; 522; Unp. (Paris, BN) 268 (coin) (pry.); (93) ~ Maier 153; 247; Münsterberg Nachtr. p. 14 (coin) (Ceka 350-2) (money.); (94) hell.-imp. IDyrrh 326
—Olympe: (95) s. iii BC SEG XXXV 697 (s. Ἀδύλος)
Kerkyra: (96) ?ii-i BC IG IX (1) 784 (tile); (97) imp.? ib. 711
Korinthia:
—Korinth: (98) s. iii BC ib. IV (1) 727 A, 6 (Perlman H.1) (f. Νικόστρατος); (99) iii/ii BC Milet I (3) 78, 1 (and Caria Miletos: Ἀσκλαπιάδας); (100) a. 191 BC SEG XXVI 392, 7 (Νίκανδ[ρος], Νικανδ[ρίδας]?: f. Πολύξενος); (101) f. ii AD Lampes antiques BN 1 29 (lamp) (Νεί-)
Lakonia: (102) a. 400 BC X., An. v 1. 15 (Poralla² 556); (103) iii BC PSI 626 recto I, 3-4 (Bradford (7)) (f. Ἀριστοκλῆς); (104) 196 BC SGDI 1990, 6, 7 (slave/freed.)
—Geronthrai: (105) 72 BC IG V (1) 1114, 3 (s. Νικοκλῆς); (106) ~ ib. l. 4, 20 (f. Ξενοκλῆς)
—Gytheion: (107) a. 212 AD ib. 1179, 4 (f. Μ. Αὐρ. Καλοκλῆς)
—Oitylos: (108) iii/ii BC ib. 1295, 7 (Bradford (5))
—Pyrrhichos: (109) ?ii-i BC IG V (1) 1282, 11 (Νείκανδ[ρος]: f. Καλλικράτις)
—Sparta: (110) viii BC RE (2) (Poralla² 555) (s. Χάριλλος: king); (111) s. i BC IG V (1) 134, 16 (Bradford (8)) (f. Ἀριστομενίδας); (112) c. 30-20 BC IG V (1) 211, 20 (Bradford (4)) (s. Παντοκλῆς); (113) c. 25-1 BC IG V (1) 210, 21 (Bradford (9)) (f. Βίολας); (114) c. 1-10 AD IG V (1) 209, 23; SEG XXXV 331 (date) (Bradford (10)) (f. Ἱππομέδων); (115) c. 140-145 AD SEG XI 550, 14; BSA 29 (1927-8) pp. 23-4 (name) (Bradford (1)) (Νεί[καν]δρ[ος]?: ?s. Φῆλιξ); (116) c. 150-160 AD IG V (1) 71 II, 6 (Bradford (11)) (Νεί-: I f. Νίκανδρος II); (117) ~ IG V (1) 71 II, 6 (Bradford (2)) (II s. Νίκανδρος I); (118) ~ IG V (1) 71 II, 22 (Bradford (2)) (f. Σύντροφος); (119) c. 170-200 AD IG V (1) 89, 13; 116, 9 (Bradford (3)) ([Γ.] Ἰούλ. Ν.: s. Νικοκράτης)
Messenia:
—Messene: (120) iii BC SEG XXIII 210, 17; (121) c. 140 BC IvOl 52, 5 (f. Ἀπολλωνίδας)
—Messene?: (122) ii/i BC SEG XI 979, 24 ([Ν]ίκανδρος)
—Peloponnese: (123) c. 192 BC ib. XIII 327, 13 (f. —όστρατος)

S. Italy: (**124**) 173 BC *Syll*³ 585, 278 (s. Μενεκράτης); (**125**) imp. *CIL* x 8059. 365 (seal) (Lat. M. Septimius Nikander)

S. Italy (Apulia)

—canusium: (**126**) i AD *Taras* 14 (1994) p. 465 no. 1 (Lat. Sex. Pompeius Nikander)

—venusia*: (**127**) i AD *Rend. Linc.* 29 (1974) p. 629 no. 37 (Lat. L. Statius Nicander: freed.)

S. Italy (Bruttium)

—rhegion: (**128**) s. ii BC *IG* xiv 612, 1 (*Syll*³ 715; Dubois, *IGDGG* i 40) (s. Νικόδαμος); (**129**) ~ *IG* xiv 615, 2; *Klearchos* 21 (1979) pp. 83-96 (date) (s. Λεύκιος)

——(Τεισ.): (**130**) ii-i BC *IG* xiv 614 (s. Νίκων)

—sybaris-thourioi-copiae: (**131**) f. iv BC *NC* 1896, pp. 138 ff.; Noe, *Thurian Di-Staters* p. 14 with pl. XI. 7 (coins)

S. Italy (Calabria)

—taras-tarentum: (**132**) hell.? *RA* 1932 (1), p. 39 no. 30 (loomweight) (Νικάναρος—ed.)

S. Italy (Campania)

—dikaiarchia-puteoli: (**133**) imp. *CIL* x 2336 (Lat. L. Calpurnius Nicander)

Sicily

—akragas: (**134**) imp. Manganaro, *QUCC* forthcoming no. 13; (**135**) ?iii AD *IGLMP* 3 + *SEG* xxvi 1059 ([*N*]είκανδρος)

—akrai: (**136**) ?iii BC *SGDI* 3242, 6 (*Akrai* p. 156 no. 7) (f. Φιλιστίων)

—lipara: (**137**) inc. *Chiron* 22 (1992) p. 386

—syracuse: (**138**) 182 BC *PP* 2806 + 8241; (**139**) imp. *NScav* 1913, p. 265 (vase)

—syracuse?: (**140**) hell. *IG* xiv 2407. 23 (bullet)

—tauromenion: (**141**) c. 40 BC *Cron. Arch.* 3 (1964) p. 54 I, 21 (f. Λαμίσκος); (**142**) ~ ib. l. 35 (s. *N*—)

## Νικανός

Epiros

—tepelene (mod.): (**1**) i BC-i AD? *SEG* xxiv 474, 1; cf. Hammond, *Epirus* 738 (locn.) (f. Κλεόμαχος); (**2**) ~ *SEG* xxiv 474, 4; cf. Hammond, *Epirus* p. 738 (locn.) (s. Φίλιστος)

## Νικάνωρ

Achaia: (**1**) ii BC *BGU* 1939 fr. C, 3 (s. Ἀντίοχος); (**2**) 146 BC *IG* iv (1)² 28, 75 (f. Νικόστρατος: synoikos)

—ascheion: (**3**) 339 BC *CID* ii 51, 7 (*N*[ικά]*νωρ*)

—dyme*: (**4**) c. 219 BC *SGDI* 1612, 43 (*Tyche* 5 (1990) p. 124) (f. Νικάδας)

Aitolia: (**5**) ?265-264 BC *FD* iii (3) 202, 2; iii (4) 359, 34; *SEG* xviii 242, 2; *CID* ii 130, [1] ?= (7); (**6**) ?262 BC *FD* iii (4) 357, 3; (7) ?247 BC *Syll*³ 444 A, 3; *CID* ii 139, 2 ?= (5); (**8**) ?c. 214-210 BC *SEG* iii 343, 2; cf. *Hyettos* pp. 307-9 (date) (s. Δίων)

—kalydon: (**9**) 192 BC *IG* ix (1)² (1) 31, 26 (f. Ἀγαθίας)

—ophioneis: (**10**) imp.? ib. 161 (-νορ)

Argolis:

—epidauros*: (**11**) i-ii AD Peek, *IAEpid* 279 (f. Νικοφάνης)

Arkadia: (**12**) ?225 BC *PPetr*² 1 *Wills* 28, 4

—tegea: (**13**) i BC *IG* v (2) 45, 11; (**14**) i AD ib. 46, 5 (Νικάνω[ρ]: s. Ἀπολλώνιος); (**15**) ii-iii AD *EILakArk* 12, 5 (*GVI* 2056) (or Lakonia Sparta: Νει-: s. Ἐπαφρώ)

Dalmatia:

——issa:

——(Pamphyloi): (**16**) iv/iii BC Brunšmid p. 8, 32 (s. Νίκων)

Epiros: (**17**) iii BC *AD* 11 (1927-8) Parart. p. 33 no. 10 (f. Πολεμαῖος); (**18**) s. iii BC *IOrop* 136, 5 (f. Δάϊππος); (**19**) c. 240-220 BC *JHS* 57 (1937) p. 35 no. 9; *IKourion* 60 (f. Ἀντίοχος) ?= (91); (**20**) c. 200 BC *IG* ix (1)² (1) 31, 129 (s. Ἀντάνωρ); (**21**) c. 167 BC Plb. xxxii 5. 9; 6. 3 (s. Μύρτων)

—ambrakia: (**22**) 182 BC *Syll*³ 585, 208 (s. Λυκίσκος)

—bouthrotos: (**23**) f. ii BC *IBouthrot* 2, 5; 3, 6; 4, 5 (f. Λυκίσκος)

—bouthrotos (prasaiboi): (**24**) a. 163 BC ib. 13, 1; cf. Ugolini, *Alb. Ant.* 3 p. 120; (**25**) ~ *IBouthrot* 14, 3, 7; 21, 20, 26 (*SEG* xxxviii 471; 478) (s. Λυκίσκος, f. Λυκίσκος, Πρωτόμαχος); (**26**) ~ *IBouthrot* 14, 19 (*SEG* xxxviii 471) (f. Νέστωρ) ?= (34); (**27**) ~ *IBouthrot* 14, 19; 22, 25 (*SEG* xxxviii 471; 479) (s. Νέστωρ); (**28**) ~ *IBouthrot* 14, 36; 22, 4; 28, 11 (*SEG* xxxviii 471; 479; 486) (I s. Κλεόμαχος, f. Κλεόμαχος, Σαώτας, Νικάνωρ II, ?f. Φιλωτέρα, Ἱλαρία); (**29**) ~ *IBouthrot* 14, 38; 31, 53, 65 (*SEG* xxxviii 471; 490) (s. Λέων) ?= (35); (**30**) ~ *IBouthrot* 15, 6 (*SEG* xxxviii 472); (**31**) ~ *IBouthrot* 15, 22 (*SEG* xxxviii 472); (**32**) ~ *IBouthrot* 17, 1 (*SEG* xxxviii 474); (**33**) ~ *IBouthrot* 17, 11; 21, 30 (*SEG* xxxviii 474; 478) (II s. Νικάνωρ I, ?f. Μελισσίς); (**34**) ~ *IBouthrot* 18, 10; 33, 13 (*SEG* xxxviii 475; 492) (s. Νέστωρ, f. Νέστωρ, Νικάδας) ?= (71) (26); (**35**) ~ *IBouthrot* 18, 17 (*SEG* xxxviii 475) ?= (29); (**36**) ~ *IBouthrot* 20, 2 (*SEG* xxxviii 477); *IBouthrot* 47, 2 (f. Νικόστρατος); (**37**) ~ ib. 21, 30 (*SEG* xxxviii 478) (I f. Νικάνωρ II); (**38**) ~ *IBouthrot* 22, 22; 41, 8 (*SEG* xxxviii 479; 500) (s. Νικόστρατος); (**39**) ~ *IBouthrot* 25, 22 (*SEG* xxxviii 483); (**40**) ~ *IBouthrot* 28, 12 (*SEG* xxxviii 486) (II s. Νικάνωρ I); (**41**) ~ *IBouthrot* 30, 35 (*SEG* xxxviii 488) (s. Συμμαχίδας); (**42**) ~ *IBouthrot* 31, 51, 63 (*SEG* xxxviii 490) (f. Λέων); (**43**) ~ *IBouthrot* 31, 71 (*SEG* xxxviii 490) ?= (54); (**44**) ~ *IBouthrot* 36, 10; 43, 37 (*SEG* xxxviii 495; 502) (f. Μύρτων); (**45**) ~ *IBouthrot* 41, 8 (*SEG* xxxviii 500) (f. Νικόστρατος); (**46**) ~ *IBouthrot* 42, 8 (*SEG* xxxviii 501); (**47**) ~ *IBouthrot* 45, 4 (f. Νικόστρατος); (**48**) ~ ib. l. 5; 49, 6 (s. Νικόστρατος); (**49**) ~ ib. 50, 8; (**50**) ~ ib. l. [5], 11; (**51**) ~ ib. 51, 3; (**52**) ~ ib. 57 (*SEG* xxxviii 508); (**53**) ~ *IBouthrot* 78, 11; 79, 10; 80, 9; 81, 9; 82, 8; 83, 9; 84, 9; 85, 9; 86, 10; 87, [9]; 88, 8 (*BCH* 118 (1994) pp. 122 f. nos. 1-11) (s. Λύκος); (**54**) ~ *IBouthrot* 130, 8 (f. Λέων) ?= (43); (**55**) ~ ib. 131, 8; (**56**) ~ ib. l. 8-9?; 156, 9 (*BCH* 118 (1994) p. 127 no. 12) (f. Ὕβριμος); (**57**) ~ *IBouthrot* 158

——Asteatoi: (**58**) a. 163 BC ib. 144, 7 (f. Σωκράτης)

——Cheilioi: (**59**) a. 163 BC ib. 98, 8 (f. Μένανδρος)

——Cherrioi: (**60**) a. 163 BC ib. 58, 4; 59, 1, 6 (*SEG* xxxviii 509-10) (s. Ἀνδρόνικος)

——Cherrioi?: (**61**) a. 163 BC *IBouthrot* 49, 3; 111, 7; 112, 8

——Datonioi: (**62**) a. 163 BC ib. 66, 9 (s. Βοΐσκος); (**63**) ~ ib. 75, 8 (f. Βοΐσκος)

——Eschatioi?: (**64**) a. 163 BC ib. 128, 6; 129, 5

——Metoreis: (**65**) a. 163 BC ib. 90, 3; 91, 2, 5 (*SEG* xxxviii 623); *IBouthrot* 92, 2 (s. Εὔνομος)

——Pelmatioi: (**66**) a. 163 BC ib. 142, 7 (*N*ικά[*νω*]ρ)

——Phonidatoi: (**67**) a. 163 BC ib. 120, 6 (s. Σίμακος)

——Polleioi: (**68**) a. 163 BC ib. 98, 6 (s. Κλεόμαχος)

——Porronoi: (**69**) a. 163 BC ib. 36, 1 (*SEG* xxxviii 495) (s. Νικόστρατος) ?= (70); (**70**) ~ *IBouthrot* 111, 2; 112, 2; 113, 2; 133, 2 ?= (69)

——Temouoi: (**71**) a. 163 BC ib. 15, 2 (*SEG* xxxviii 472) (f. Νικάδας) ?= (34)

——Tharioi: (**72**) a. 163 BC *IBouthrot* 113, 15

——Thymaioi: (**73**) a. 163 BC ib. 66, 893, 6 (f. Λέων); (**74**) ~ ib. 111, 4, 10; 112, 5, 11; 113, 6 (f. Σάτυρος)

——Tykonioi: (**75**) a. 163 BC ib. 72, 7

—chaones: (**76**) c. 430 BC Th. ii 80. 5

—charadros: (**77**) a. 167 BC *SEG* xxxv 665 A, 15 (s. Χύτρων)

—dodona: (**78**) iii BC Antoniou, *Dodone* Aa, 3; (**79**) ~ ib. l. 22; (**80**) ~ ib. Ab, 32

—doiesstoi: (**81**) f. ii BC Cabanes, *L'Épire* p. 580 no. 54, 4 (f. Ἀντίβολος)

—ikadotoi: (**82**) m. iv BC ib. p. 576 no. 49, 5 (*SEG* xxvi 717, 10) (f. Ξένυς, Ἄνδρων)

—kammanoi bouthrotioi: (**83**) a. 163 BC *IBouthrot* 60, 6 (*SEG* xxxviii 511) (s. Φίλιππος)

—molossoi: (**84**) c. 343-330 BC Cabanes, *L'Épire* p. 588 no. 74, 11 (*SEG* xxvi 700) (s. Ἀλίπων)

—molossoi?: (**85**) f. ii BC Cabanes, *L'Épire* p. 546 no. 13

—nikopolis: (**86**) i BC/i AD *SEG* xxxvii 526 (Νει-: ?s. Δικαία, f. Ἀσκληπιάδης); (**87**) ?i AD *Ep. Chron.* 31 (1994) p. 42 no. 12 (*AD* 45 (1990) Chron. p. 257 no. 8) (Νει-: s. Τίτος)

—omphales chimolioi: (**88**) c. 330-310 BC Cabanes, *L'Épire* p. 578 no. 51, 12 (-ναρ)

—ossonioi: (**89**) a. 163 BC *IBouthrot* 104, 5

—prasaiboi: (**90**) a. 163 BC ib. 92, 8 (s. Πρωτόμαχος)

Epiros?: (**91**) m. iii BC *PP* 1961; cf. *IKourion* 60 comm. (ident.) ?= (19); (**92**) 226-225 BC *PPetr*² 1 *Wills* 26, 6 (s. Ζωπυρίων: t.e.)

Illyria:

—apollonia: (**93**) ?ii BC *IApoll* 146 (f. Σαμίδας); (**94**) i BC Ceka, *Probleme* p. 139 no. 21 (coin) (Νικάν(ωρ)); (**95**) ~ Maier 135 (coin) (pryt.); (**96**) hell.-imp. *IApoll* 191 (Νει-: s. Γένθιος)

—bylliones: (**97**) iii/ii BC *SEG* xxxv 696; cf. xxxviii 569 (s. Νικάσιος)

—bylliones (rabije (mod.)): (**98**) ?s. ii BC ib. xxxii 626, 8 + xxxviii 520; cf. *CRAI* 1991, p. 197 ff. ([Νικά]νορ: s. Δείνων)

—bylliones byllis: (**99**) ?ii BC *SEG* xxxviii 522 ([Νι]κάνωρ)

—epidamnos-dyrrhachion: (**100**) ii-i BC *IDyrrh* 550 (tiles)

—lychnidos: (**101**) ii-iii AD Demitsas 340 (Νει-: f. Δημητριάς)

Kerkyra: (**102**) c. 229-48 BC *BMC Thessaly* p. 148 f. nos. 514-24; *SNG Cop. Epirus-Acarnania* 233 (coin); (**103**) ?ii BC *IG* ix (1) 708 (s. Νικόστρατος)

Korinthia:

—korinth: (**104**) ?205 BC ib. vii 1721, 6 (s. Εὔιος); (**105**) ii BC *BGU* 1939 F, 3

—sikyon?: (**106**) 263 BC *IG* ix (1)² (1) 17, 53 (f. Δαμότας)

Lakonia:

—gytheion: (**107**) 15 AD *SEG* xi 922, 15 (Δέκμος Τυρράνιος Νεικάνωρ)

Leukas: (**108**) c. 167-50 BC Postolakas p. 83 nos. 844-8 (*NZ* 10 (1878) p. 136 no. 24 (coins))

Messenia:

—asine: (**109**) hell.-imp. *IG* v (1) 1407 (f. Λυσίμαχος)

—thouria: (**110**) f. ii BC *SEG* xi 972, 77 (s. Νικάδας); (**111**) ~ ib. l. 124 (s. Θεοκλῆς)

S. Italy (Calabria):

—taras-tarentum: (**112**) hell. *IG* xiv 2405. 25 (lamp)

S. Italy (Campania):

—herculaneum: (**113**) i BC-i AD *CIL* iv 10603 (Lat. Nicanor)

—herculaneum*: (**114**) c. 50-75 AD ib. x 1403 a I, 14 (Lat. M. Remmius Nikanor: freed.)

—pompeii: (**115**) i BC-i AD ib. iv 1097 (c. ?); (**116**) ~ ib. 3950 (Lat. Nicanor); (**117**) ~ ib. 7570 (Lat. Nicanor); (**118**) ~ ib. 8414 (Lat. Nicanor)

Sicily:

—syracuse: (**119**) c. 343-339 BC *IG* iv (1)² 95, 68 (Perlman E.2); Perlman p. 46 (date) (f.

Ἱκέτας); (**120**) ?i BC *CIL* x 7121 (Lat. Cn. Octavius Nicanor)

**Νικάρατος**
ARKADIA:
—TEGEA:
——(Krariotai): (**1**) iii BC *IG* v (2) 40, 17 (s. Κλεομήδης)

**Νικαρέτα**
ARGOLIS:
—ARGOS: (**1**) s. iv BC Unp. (Argos, Kavvadias)
—EPIDAUROS: (**2**) iii BC Peek, *IAEpid* 131 ([Νι]καρέτα); (**3**) ~ Peek, *NIEpid* 67 (Νικαρέτα, Νικαρέτη—Peek); (**4**) iii/ii BC *IG* IV (1)² 228, 6 (d. Ἄρκεσα)
—HERMIONE: (**5**) iii BC ib. IV (1) 728, 31; (**6**) ii-i BC ib. 732 III, 19 (m. Ζωπύρα)
ARKADIA: (**7**) ?ii-iii AD *SEG* XLII 368
—TEGEA: (**8**) c. 400-375 BC *IG* II² 10435 (*GVI* 1653) (-τη: m. Θεοίτας); (**9**) m. iv BC *IG* v (2) 6, 101
EPIROS:
—BOUTHROTOS (PRASAIBOI): (**10**) a. 163 BC *IBouthrot* 31, 102 (*SEG* XXXVIII 490)
—THESPROTOI: (**11**) m. iv BC *IG* II² 8840
ILLYRIA:
—APOLLONIA: (**12**) ii-i BC *IApoll* 131 (d. Φίλων)
LEUKAS: (**13**) hell.? *IG* IX (1) 566

**Νικαρετίδας**
LAKONIA: (**1**) 71 BC ib. v (1) 1146, 37, 52
—SPARTA: (**2**) c. 120 AD ib. 1315, 26 (Bradford (-)) (Νεικαρα-: f. Γ. Σώσιμος)

**Νικαρετίς**
ARGOLIS:
—EPIDAUROS: (**1**) iv/iii BC *IG* IV (1)² 204

**Νικάρετος**
ARGOLIS:
—EPIDAUROS: (**1**) f. ii BC ib. 218 (f. Χαρικώ)
ARKADIA:
—HERAIA: (**2**) iii BC ib. v (2) 415, 7 (*IPArk* 23) ([Νικά]ρετος: I f. Νικάρετος II); (**3**) ~ *IG* v (2) 415, 7 (*IPArk* 23) (II s. Νικάρετος I)
MESSENIA:
—MESSENE: (**4**) f. iii BC *PAE* 1991, p. 99 no. 7, 22
—THOURIA: (**5**) ii/i BC *IG* v (1) 1384, 21 (f. Εὐτυχίδας)

**Νικάριν**
SICILY:
—THERMAI HIMERAIAI: (**1**) imp. *CIL* x 7426 (*ILat. Term. Imer.* 124) (Lat. Nicarin: d. Ζωσίμη); (**2**) i-ii AD ib. 86 (Lat. Cornificia Nicarin)

**Νικαρίστα**
ARGOLIS:
—EPIDAUROS: (**1**) iv/iii BC *IG* IV (1)² 204
—HERMIONE: (**2**) iv BC ib. IV (1) 741, 6; (**3**) ii-i BC ib. 739
EPIROS:
—BOUTHROTOS (PRASAIBOI): (**4**) a. 163 BC *IBouthrot* 42, 7 (*SEG* XXXVIII 501)

**Νικάριστος**
MESSENIA:
—THOURIA: (**1**) f. ii BC ib. XI 972, 122 (s. Φιλοκράτης)

**Νίκαρος**
SICILY:
—GELA-PHINTIAS: (**1**) f. ii BC *IG* XIV 256, 45 (Dubois, *IGDS* 161); cf. *SEG* XL 804 (Νίκαρ(χ)ος—*IG*: s. Πύρρος)

**Νικαροῦς**
ILLYRIA:
—EPIDAMNOS-DYRRHACHION: (**1**) i BC-i AD *CIL* III 615 (Sestieri, *ILat. Albania* 32) (Lat. Nicarus)

**Νικαρχίδας**
ELIS: (**1**) ?c. 450-425 BC *IvOl* 16, 1, 10, 15, [22]; *LSAG*² p. 220 no. 17 (date)
MESSENIA:
—MESSENE: (**2**) 323 BC *FD* III (4) 7, 1 (-δης: f. Νικόδαμος)

**Νίκαρχος**
ACHAIA:
—DYME*: (**1**) c. 219 BC *SGDI* 1612, 19 (*Tyche* 5 (1990) p. 124) (I f. Νίκαρχος II); (**2**) ~ *SGDI* 1612, 19 (*Tyche* 5 (1990) p. 124) (II s. Νίκαρχος I); (**3**) ~ *SGDI* 1612, 53 (*Tyche* 5 (1990) p. 124) (s. Κλεοφάνης)
AITOLIA:
—DAIANES: (**4**) 161 BC *IG* IX (1)² (1) 100, 7
—PHILOTAIEIS?: (**5**) c. 157 BC ib. 108, 10
—PLEURON: (**6**) 196 BC ib. 30, 12 (s. Σῖμος)
AKARNANIA:
—THYRREION: (**7**) ii BC *GVI* 1822, 6 (*IG* IX (1)² (2) 313) (s. Ξένων)
ARGOLIS:
—EPIDAUROS*: (**8**) c. 370-360 BC *BSA* 61 (1966) p. 272 no. 4 B II, 20; Peek, *IAEpid* 52 A, 52
—TROIZEN: (**9**) ?146 BC *IG* IV (1) 757 B, 20 (f. Λαφάνης)
ARKADIA: (**10**) 401 BC X., *An.* ii 5. 33 ?= (*11*); (**11**) ~ ib. iii 3. 5 ?= (*10*)
—TEGEA: (**12**) 369-361 BC *IG* v (2) 1, 13; Tod, *GHI* II 132 (date); (**13**) ii BC *IG* v (2) 43, 4 (I f. Νίκαρχος II); (**14**) ~ ib. l. 4 (II s. Νίκαρχος I)
DALMATIA:
—ISSA: (**15**) f. ii BC Brunšmid p. 23 no. 10, 4 (f. Σώσανδρος)
——(Hylleis): (**16**) iv/iii BC ib. p. 8, 28
——(Pamphyloi): (**17**) iv/iii BC ib. p. 8, 46 (s. Δ—)
ELIS: (**18**) f. iii BC *IvOl* 175 (Moretti, *Olymp.* 540) ([N]ίκαρχος: s. Φυσσίας)
EPIROS:
—AMBRAKIA: (**19**) iv-iii BC *CIG* 1803 (f. Ἀριστόι); (**20**) ii BC *SEG* XLII 543 (s. Σάμος); (**21**) ii-i BC *CIG* 1799 (f. Σάτυρος); (**22**) f. ii AD 39 (1984) Chron. p. 190 + pl. 77 γ (s. —δικος); (**23**) s. ii BC Cabanes, *L'Épire* p. 548 no. 19 (*SEG* XXVI 694) (s. Λεοντίσκος)
—ARBAIOI: (**24**) iii/ii BC Cabanes, *L'Épire* pp. 569 ff. no. 47, 4 (*SEG* XXVI 720) (s. Νικόμαχος)
—BOUTHROTOS (PRASAIBOI): (**25**) a. 163 BC *IBouthrot* 30, 30 (*SEG* XXXVIII 488); (**26**) ~ *IBouthrot* 38, 1 (*SEG* XXXVIII 497) (s. Νίκανδρος) ?= (*27*); (**27**) ~ *IBouthrot* 151, 6 ?= (*26*)
——nioi: (**28**) a. 163 BC ib. 146, 6 (s. Ἐ—)
—DODONA*: (**29**) ?iii BC *SEG* XIX 431
—HYPORRONIOI: (**30**) a. 163 BC *IBouthrot* 121, 2; 122, 2
KERKYRA: (**31**) ?iii-ii BC *BM Terracottas* E 134; *PAE* 1965, p. 76; (**32**) 242 BC *SEG* XII 377 (s. Τιμο—); (**33**) imp. *IG* IX (1) 728 (s. Λάκριτος)
LAKONIA:
—SPARTA: (**34**) c. 100-120 AD ib. v (1) 103, 13; *SEG* XI 610, [8] (Bradford (2)) (Νεί-: f. Νικοκράτης); (**35**) c. 105-110 AD *SEG* XI 565, 4 (Bradford (3)) (Νεί-: f. Καλλικράτης)
——Limnai: (**36**) c. 70-100 AD *IG* v (1) 676, 13 (Bradford (1)) (s. Ἀγαθόνικος)
LEUKAS: (**37**) iv BC Unp. (*IG* arch.) (s. Λυσίστρατος); (**38**) c. 167-50 BC *BMC Thessaly* p. 186 no. 184 (coin)

**Νικασίλας**
MESSENIA:
—MESSENE: (**39**) hell. *BMC Pelop.* p. 112 nos. 37-8; *Coll. McClean* 6725-6 (coin); (**40**) ii AD *SEG* XLI 335, 14 (f. Εὐθύδαμος)
——(Aristomachidai): (**41**) 11 AD *PAE* 1992, p. 71 A, 11 (s. Ἀνδρομένης)
S. ITALY (CALABRIA):
—TARAS-TARENTUM: (**42**) c. 280-272 BC Vlasto 23; 28; 32 etc. (coins) (Evans, *Horsemen* pp. 140-1 nos. 3-4; *Samml. Ludwig* 97) (Νίκαρ(χος))

**Νικαρώ**
ARGOLIS:
—EPIDAUROS: (**1**) ii-i BC Peek, *IAEpid* 318, 4 (d. Λα—)

**Νικάρων**
LAKONIA:
—SPARTA: (**1**) c. 124-145 AD *IG* v (1) 59, 6; *SEG* XI 494, 1; 521 b, 5; 583, 3 (Bradford (2)) (Νει-: s. Ζῆλος); (**2**) c. 140-160 AD *IG* v (1) 112, 13 (Bradford (1)) (s. Ἀρίων); (**3**) f. iii AD *IG* v (1) 301, 8 (*Artemis Orthia* pp. 326-7 no. 55); *BSA* 79 (1984) p. 285 no. 18 (date) (Bradford (3)) (Νει-: f. Μ. Αὐρ. Σωσίνικος)

**Νικᾶς**
DALMATIA:
—PHAROS: (**1**) iii/ii BC *SEG* XXIII 489, 21, [33]; cf. XLI 545 (f. Ἀντίπατρος)
EPIROS:
—BOUTHROTOS (PRASAIBOI):
——Altharioi: (**2**) a. 163 BC *IBouthrot* 53, 5 (*SEG* XXXVIII 504) (f. Νίκαιος)
ILLYRIA:
—EPIDAMNOS-DYRRHACHION: (**3**) hell.-imp. *IDyrrh* 289

**Νικασίας**
ARGOLIS:
—ARGOS: (**1**) m. vi BC *Argive Heraeum* 2 p. 337 no. 1878 (Lazzarini 72) (Ν[ι]κασίας)
ARKADIA:
—MEGALOPOLIS: (**2**) i BC *SEG* XXXIII 291, 5 (Νικασί[ας]?)
—TEGEA: (**3**) m. iv BC *IG* v (2) 6, 110; (**4**) ~ ib. l. 115; (**5**) ii BC ib. 43, 8 (s. Πειθίας); (**6**) f. ii BC ib. 44, 20 (Νικασία[ς])
——(Hippothoitai): (**7**) iv/iii BC ib. 38, 50 (f. Ἐτέαρχος)
——(Krariotai): (**8**) s. iii BC ib. 36, 118 (s. Λάκριτος)

**Νικασίβιος**
KERKYRA: (**1**) c. 500 BC *BSA* 66 (1971) p. 81 no. 8 b with n.

**Νικασιβούλα**
MESSENIA:
—MESSENE: (**1**) s. iv BC *IG* IV (1)² 122, 129

**Νικασίκλεια**
LAKONIA:
—GERONTHRAI: (**1**) ii-i BC *Mél. Daux* p. 226 no. 6 (Νικαβίκλεια—lap., Νικα(h)ίκλεια?: ?d. Λυσι—)

**Νικασικράτης**
S. ITALY (BRUTTIUM):
—LOKROI EPIZEPHYRIOI:
——(Ἀλχ.): (**1**) iv/iii BC De Franciscis 12, 6 (s. Φρυνίσκος)

**Νικασίλαος**
ARKADIA:
—ORCHOMENOS: (**1**) 265 BC *SEG* XXV 443, 10

**Νικασίλας**
ARGOLIS:
—ARGOS*: (**1**) 105 BC *JÖAI* 14 (1911) Beibl. p. 146 no. 4, 21 ([N]ικασίλας: slave/freed.?)
—EPIDAUROS: (**2**) c. 370 BC *IG* IV (1)² 102, 10 (s. Δαμέας)
——(Hysminatai): (**3**) 146 BC ib. 28, 21 (s. Ἰάρων)
EPIROS:
—AMBRAKIA: (**4**) ?ii BC *AD* 10 (1926) p. 66 (f. Πρῶτος)

## Νικασιμάχα

MESSENIA:
—MESSENE: (5) ii/i BC IG v (1) 1437, 11 (Νικασι-χᾶς—apogr., Wilhelm, Νικάσιχ(ο)ς—Foucart, Νικασί(λ)ας—Hiller)

## Νικασιμάχα

ARKADIA:
—LOUSOI?: (1) iii-ii BC Master Bronzes from the Classical World 152

## Νικασίμαχος

SICILY:
—LIPARA: (1) imp. Epigraphica 3 (1941) p. 270 no. 47 a

## Νικάσιον

ARGOLIS:
—HERMIONE: (1) ?ii-i BC IG IV (1) 731 III, 1 (d. Θεόνοστος)

## Νικάσιος

AKARNANIA:
—THYRREION: (1) iii BC ib. IX (1)² (2) 271 = SEG XXVII 166? (s. Κάσσανδρος)
EPIROS:
—BOUTHROTOS (PRASAIBOI): (2) a. 163 BC IBouthrot 22, 29 (SEG XXXVIII 479); (3) ~ IBouthrot 30, 8 (SEG XXXVIII 488) ?= (7); (4) ~ IBouthrot 152, 5 (f. Σίμακος); (5) ~ ib. 158
——Prakeleoi: (6) a. 163 BC ib. 36, 23 (SEG XXXVIII 495) (f. Μένανδρος); (7) ~ IBouthrot 94, 6-7 (s. Νίκανδρος, f. Μενέφυλος) ?= (3)
ILLYRIA:
—BYLLIONES: (8) iii/ii BC SEG XXXV 696; cf. XXXVIII 569 (Ν[ι]κάσιος: f. Νικάνωρ); (9) c. 200 BC ib. XXXV 680, 7; cf. XXXVIII 541 ([Νι]κάσιος: s. Ἀρχέλαος); (10) ~ ib. XXXV 680, 11; cf. XXXVIII 541 ([Νικ]άσιος: s. Νικολαΐδας)

## Νικάσιππος

ARGOLIS:
—EPIDAUROS:
——(Hylleis): (1) 146 BC IG IV (1)² 28, 52 (I f. Νικάσιππος II); (2) ~ ib. l. 52 (II s. Νικάσιππος I)
ARKADIA: (3) 320 BC ib. v (2) 549, 8 (f. Θεοτέ-λης)
—MANTINEIA-ANTIGONEIA: (4) ?ii BC ib. 319, 40
—MEGALOPOLIS: (5) m. iii BC ib. IV (1)² 96, 39 (Perlman E.3); Perlman p. 63 f. (date) (s. Εὔδαμος)
—MEGALOPOLIS?: (6) 42 AD IG v (2) 516, 2 etc. (s. Φίλιππος)
—TEGEA:
——(Hippothoitai): (7) f. iii BC ib. 36, 74 (s. Ἀσφάλιος: metic)
ELIS: (8) 217 BC Plb. v 94. 6
LAKONIA:
—SPARTA: (9) s. i BC IG v (1) 124, 10 (Bradford (4)) (s. Τημένης); (10) c. 25-1 BC IG v (1) 212, 6 (Bradford (1)) (s. Ἀντιάλκης); (11) ~ IG v (1) 212, 31 (Bradford (3)) (s. Μενεκράτης); (12) c. 125-145 AD IG v (1) 67, 5; SEG XI 524, 17; 548, 12 (Bradford (2)) (Νει-: s. Εὐήμερος)
MESSENIA:
—MESSENE: (13) c. 261 BC IG IX (1)² (1) 18, 16 (f. Νικύλος)

## Νικασίς

KORINTHIA:
—KORINTH: (1) 97 BC ib. II² 1337, 5; SEG XVI 111 (date) (d. Φιλίσκος)
LEUKAS: (2) iii BC Unp. (Leukas Mus., inscr.) inv. 16

## Νικασίων

DALMATIA:
—ISSA:
——(Dymanes): (1) iv/iii BC Brunšmid p. 8, 39 (f. —ην)

ELIS?: (2) iii BC CIRB 1194 ([Ν]ικασίων: f. Δα-μόχαρις)
ILLYRIA:
—APOLLONIA: (3) c. 250-50 BC Maier 15; 97 + Münsterberg Nachtr. p. 13; Bakёrr Hoard p. 68. nos. 88-90 (coins) (Ceka 85-7) (money.)
LAKONIA:
—SPARTA: (4) s. i BC SEG XI 878 (brick) (Bradford (2)); (5) c. 125-160 AD IG v (1) 114, 12; SEG XI 552, 1 (Bradford (1)) ([Νικ]ασίων—IG, [Ν]ικασ[ίων]—SEG: s. Ἐπίγονος)
SICILY:
—ADRANON: (6) iii-ii BC PdelP 16 (1961) p. 127 (s. Εὐπόλεμος)
—AKRAI: (7) ?iii BC SGDI 3240, 3 (Akrai p. 156 no. 7) (s. Ἀρτέμων); (8) ~ SGDI 3240, 9 (Akrai p. 156 no. 7) (s. Φίλιστος)
—HENNA: (9) f. i BC Cic., In Verr. II iv 113 (Lat. Nicasio)
—LIPARA: (10) hell.? Libertini, Isole Eolie p. 224 no. 44
—LIPARA*: (11) i BC-i AD? Kokalos 32 (1986) p. 235 no. 59 (tile)
—TAUROMENION: (12) c. 40 BC Cron. Arch. 3 (1964) p. 54 I, 24 (s. Ἀρτεμίδωρος)

## Νικασύλις

SICILY:
—LIPARA: (1) inc. Chiron 22 (1992) p. 385; (2) ~ ib.; (3) ~ ib.; (4) ~ ib. pp. 385-6

## Νικασώ

AIGINA: (1) f. iv BC IG II² 7963 (?d. Εὐμάρης)
AITOLIA:
—PHILOTAIEIS: (2) c. 162 BC ib. IX (1)² (1) 105, 2
ARGOLIS:
—EPIDAUROS: (3) ii-i BC ib. IV (1)² 737
DALMATIA:
—ISSA: (4) hell. Brunšmid p. 30 no. 25 (d. Ἀρι-στόξενος); (5) ii BC SEG XXXI 602, 7 (VAHD 84 (1991) p. 257 no. 7) (d. Πάμφιλος); (6) ~ SEG XXXI 602, 9 (VAHD 84 (1991) p. 257 no. 7) (d. Κλεέμπορος)
EPIROS:
—BOUTHROTOS (PRASAIBOI): (7) a. 163 BC IBouthrot 21, 32 (SEG XXXVIII 478); (8) ~ IBouthrot 41, 12 (SEG XXXVIII 500)
S. ITALY (CALABRIA):
—TARAS-TARENTUM: (9) c. 160 BC ID 1716, 6 (d. Ἡρακλείδας, Μυραλλίς (Syracuse)); (10) imp.? IG XIV 2406. 59 (RA 1932 (1), p. 39 no. 31 (loomweight))
SICILY:
—LIPARA: (11) inc. Chiron 22 (1992) p. 386

## Νικάτας

ACHAIA: (1) 146 BC IG IV (1)² 28, 73 (f. Δίων: synoikos)
AITOLIA:
—KALLION/KALLIPOLIS: (2) c. 263 BC ib. IX (1)² (1) 18, 4; (3) iii/ii BC ib. 157; (4) 195 BC SGDI 2119, 2
ARGOLIS:
—EPIDAUROS: (5) iv BC Peek, NIEpid 110 = AD 25 (1970) Mel. pp. 33-4 no. 7 (s. Νικόστρα-τος); (6) f. iii BC Peek, IAEpid 87 ([Νικ]άτας); (7) m. iii BC IG VII 13, 7 (s. Ἀρχέδαμος); (8) i BC/i AD ib. IV (1)² 651; 652, 2-3 (Γν. Κορν. Ν.: s. Σώδαμος, f. Γν. Κορν. Πούλχερ)
——Erilais: (9) c. 370-335 BC ib. 102, 12; 103, 107
—HERMIONE: (10) ii/i BC ib. 229, 3 (I f. Νικάτας II); (11) ~ ib. l. 3 (II s. Νικάτας I, f. Ὀλυμπιάς, Ὀλυμπιόδωρος, Νῖκις)
KORINTHIA:
—KORINTH: (12) a. 191 BC SEG XXVI 392, 7 (s. Χιωνίδας)
LAKONIA:
—AKRIAI: (13) c. 80-70 BC IG VII 417, 16, 20, 50 (IOrop 525); IG IX (2) 529, 15; RPh 1911,

p. 125 no. 27, 5; BSA 70 (1975) p. 133 (date) (Bradford (-)) (f. Νικοκλῆς)
SICILY:
—MORGANTINA: (14) ?s. iv BC Riv. Stor. Antica 5 (1900-1) p. 54 no. 25

## Νικαφορίς

LAKONIA:
—SPARTA: (1) a. 212 AD IG v (1) 597, 10 (Bradford (-)) (Αὐρ. Νεικαφορίς: d. Ἀρίστων, Αὐρ. Σωκλήδεια)

## Νικέας

ACHAIA:
—PELLENE: (1) m. iii BC IG v (2) 368, 94 (s. Ἀστ—)
AITOLIA:
—THERMOS: (2) 163 BC ib. IX (1)² (1) 102, 8, 11 (Νεικέας—l. 11)
ARGOLIS:
—ARGOS: (3) c. 458 BC ib. I³ 1149, 10 ([Ν]ικέας)
—EPIDAUROS: (4) iii BC Peek, IAEpid 43, 30 (f. Ἀμύντωρ)
—EPIDAUROS (KARATZIA (MOD.)): (5) ?iii BC Peek, NIEpid 121
ARKADIA:
—KLEITOR: (6) c. 140-120 BC BCH 60 (1936) p. 12 no. 1, 8, 16 (s. Κλεοσθένης)
—LOUSOI: (7) c. 230-200 BC ib. 45 (1921) p. 12 II, 69 (f. Πεισίας)
—ORCHOMENOS: (8) ?c. 369-361 BC ib. 102 (1978) p. 348, 32 (IPArk 14); (9) s. iv BC SEG XI 1051 = EILakArk 19 (s. Θερρίλας)
ELIS: (10) c. 146-32 BC BM coin 1920 5-15-94 (coin) (Νικέου (gen.)); (11) i BC IvOl 191; cf. Moretti, Olymp. 711 (f. Ἀγίλοχος) ?= (12); (12) m. i BC IvOl 412 (s. Ἀγίλοχος) ?= (11)
EPIROS:
—DODONA*: (13) iv BC PAE 1932, p. 52 no. 5
ILLYRIA:
—APOLLONIA: (14) ii-iii AD IApoll 230 (Νει-)
KEPHALLENIA:
—PALE: (15) c. 230-200 BC BCH 45 (1921) p. 14 II, 137 (s. Ὀρθαγόρας)
KORINTHIA:
—KORINTH: (16) byz. Corinth VIII (3) 550, 3; cf. TMByz 9 (1985) p. 365 no. 62
—SIKYON: (17) c. 230-200 BC BCH 45 (1921) p. 11 II, 34 ([Νι]κέας, [Λυ]κέας?)
LAKONIA: (18) 194 BC SGDI 2068, 3, 5 (s. Νι-καία: slave/freed.)
—SPARTA: (19) ii/i BC IG v (1) 26, 4 (Bradford (-))
MESSENIA:
—MESSENE: (20) m. iii BC IG v (2) 368, 87

## Νίκεον

ARGOLIS:
—ARGOS: (1) iv/iii BC SEG XXIX 358

## Νικέρως

ARGOLIS:
—EPIDAUROS: (1) ii-iii AD IG IV (1)² 467; 574 (Νει-: s. Καλλίμαχος) ?= (2); (2) 163 AD ib. 88, 24 + Peek, IAEpid 37 (Νει-: f. Καλλίμαχος) ?= (1); (3) iii AD IG IV (1)² 483 (Αὐρ. Ν.)
ELIS: (4) iii AD SEG XV 259, 4 (Νει-)
LAKONIA:
—EPIDAUROS LIMERA: (5) imp. IG v (1) 1012 (f. Σωσάρων)
—SPARTA: (6) imp. SEG XI 684 (Bradford (3)) (Νει-); (7) ii AD IG v (1) 159, 21 (Bradford (1)); (8) ~ IG v (1) 159, 43 (Bradford (2)) (Νει-)
MESSENIA:
—KORONE: (9) 246 AD IG v (1) 1398, 72 (Αὐρ. Νεικέρως)
S. ITALY (CAMPANIA):
—DIKAIARCHIA-PUTEOLI: (10) imp. CIL x 1949 (Lat. M(anius) Poplicius Niceros)
—POMPEII: (11) i BC-i AD ib. IV 4536 (Lat. Niceros); (12) ~ ib. 6746 (Lat. Niceros)

**Σικελύ:**

SICILY:
—KATANE: **(13)** imp. *Epigraphica* 51 (1989) p. 171 no. 38 (Lat. L. Vib. Niceros: f. Σωτήρ)

**Νικεύς**

ARGOLIS:
—ARGOS: **(1)** iii BC *IG* IV (1) 618 II, 5
—ARGOS*: **(2)** ii BC *BCH* 33 (1909) pp. 456-7 no. 23, 12 (slave/freed.?)
MESSENIA:
—THOURIA: **(3)** s. iii BC *IG* v (1) 1386, 6 (s. Νικόδαμος); **(4)** ~ ib. l. 9 ([Νι]κεύς: s. Δεξίας)

**Νίκη**

ACHAIA:
—PATRAI: **(1)** imp. *CIL* III 519 (Lat. Apicia Nice)
AIGINA: **(2)** ii-iii AD *AE* 1913, p. 95 no. 6 β (Νεί-: d. Δῶρις)
ARGOLIS:
—ARGOS: **(3)** ii-iii AD *IG* XIV 1873 (Νεί-)
—ARGOS*: **(4)** ii BC *SEG* XLII 279, 18 (Νίκ<κ>η: slave/freed.?)
—HERMIONE: **(5)** iii AD *IG* IV (1) 726, 9 (Αὐρ. Νείκη: d. Αὐρ. Σώστρατος, Αὐρ. Λουκία)
EPIROS:
—ANTIGONEIA: **(6)** v-vi AD *Iliria* 1977-8, p. 234 pl. V c (mosaic)
—DODONA*: **(7)** hell. *SEG* XIX 426 a
ILLYRIA:
—EPIDAMNOS-DYRRHACHION: **(8)** ?i AD *BUST* 1961 (1), p. 114 no. 12 (Lat. Pomponia Nice); **(9)** ~ *AEp* 1978, no. 739 (Lat. Castricia Nice: m. Λυκαρίων, Cornelius Castricius Saturninus)
KEPHALLENIA: **(10)** ii AD *Miscellanea* p. 183 no. 3 (Δόξα N.)
KERKYRA: **(11)** imp. *IG* IX (1) 962 (Μεμμία Νείκ(η))
S. ITALY (APULIA):
—AECAE: **(12)** imp. *AEp* 1972, no. 141 (Lat. Splatia Nice: m. Turrania Marcella)
—CANUSIUM: **(13)** imp. *Epig. Rom. di Canosa* 48 (*CIL* IX 341) (Lat. Nice: m. Baebia Arbuscula)
—LARINUM*: **(14)** s. i BC Frenz p. 153 no. 139 (Lat. Gavia Nice: freed.)
—LUCERIA: **(15)** imp. *ASP* 34 (1981) p. 16 no. 16 (Lat. Spedia Nice)
—VENUSIA: **(16)** imp. *CIL* IX 426 (Lat. Nice); **(17)** ~ ib. 524 (Lat. Nica); **(18)** ~ ib. 544 (Lat. Nice)
S. ITALY (CALABRIA):
—BRENTESION-BRUNDISIUM: **(19)** imp. *Epigraphica* 25 (1963) p. 42 no. 19 (Lat. Camuria Nice); **(20)** ~ *NScav* 1885, p. 262 (*Eph. Ep.* VIII 11) = *Epigraphica* 25 (1963) p. 36 no. 6 (Lat. Caledia Nice)
—BRENTESION-BRUNDISIUM*: **(21)** i/ii AD *Museo Ribezzo* 12 (1980-87) p. 177 (*CIL* IX 6099); cf. *Epigraphica* 51 (1989) p. 77 (Lat. Publilia Nice: m. Ταῦρος: freed.)
—TARAS-TARENTUM*: **(22)** i/ii AD *Misc. Gr. Rom.* 3 p. 176 (Lat. Cocceia Nice: imp. freed.?)
S. ITALY (CAMPANIA):
—DIKAIARCHIA-PUTEOLI: **(23)** inc. *NScav* 1902, p. 382 no. 3 (Lat. Nice); **(24)** imp. *CIL* x 2022 (Lat. Aemilia Nice); **(25)** ~ ib. 2053 (Lat. Annaea Nice); **(26)** ~ ib. 2188 (Lat. Caecilia Nice: m. M. Oc(t)abius); **(27)** ~ ib. 2654 (Lat. Licinia Nice: m. Licinius Puteolanus); **(28)** ~ ib. 2773 (Lat. Nice); **(29)** ?i-ii AD ib. 2293 (Lat. Claudia Nice); **(30)** ?ii AD ib. 1546 (Lat. Aelia Nice)
—DIKAIARCHIA-PUTEOLI*: **(31)** imp. ib. 2677 (Lat. Nice: freed.); **(32)** ?i-ii AD ib. 2604; cf. *Puteoli* 11 (1987) pp. 40-1 (Lat. Iulia Nice: freed.)
—MISENUM: **(33)** imp. *AJA* 2 (1898) p. 395 no. 56 (Lat. Valeria Nice); **(34)** ~ *Eph. Ep.* VIII 441 (Lat. Popilia Nice)

—MISENUM*: **(35)** imp. *CIL* x 3627 (Lat. Titia Nice); **(36)** ~ ib. 3660 (Lat. Valeria Nice)
—NEAPOLIS: **(37)** i BC/i AD *INap* 168, 6; cf. Leiwo p. 78 no. 23 (Νεί- Ἰουνία); **(38)** iii-iv AD *IG* XIV 826. 29 (*INap* 239) (Νεί-)
—NEAPOLIS*: **(39)** ?i AD *Mon. Ant.* 8 (1898) p. 223; cf. Leiwo p. 69 no. 10 (Lat. Licinia Nice: m. Μαρίων, Μοῦσα: freed.)
—POMPEII: **(40)** i BC-i AD *CIL* IV 4459 (Lat. Nice); **(41)** ~ ib. 4590 (Lat. Nice)
—POMPEII*: **(42)** i BC-i AD *Römische Gräberstrassen* p. 212 a (Lat. Blaisia Nice)
—STABIAE*: **(43)** imp. *RAAN* 19 (1938-9) p. 103 (Lat. Mevia Nica: freed.)
—SURRENTUM: **(44)** imp. *CIL* x 731 (Lat. Faenia Nice)
SICILY:
—LILYBAION: **(45)** imp. *Mon. Ant.* 33 (1929) p. 59 (Lat. Nice)
—LIPARA: **(46)** ?i AD *Meligunis-Lipara* 5 p. 183 T. 2179; cf. *SEG* XLI 817 (Πομπ. Νείκη)
—PACHINO (MOD.): **(47)** ii-iii AD *Arch. Class.* 17 (1965) p. 199, 7 (m. Τρυφέρα)
—SYRACUSE: **(48)** f. i BC Cic., *In Verr.* II v 82 (Lat. Nice); **(49)** iii-v AD Strazzulla 200 (Wessel 1160); **(50)** ~ Strazzulla 259 (Wessel 1321); cf. Ferrua, *NG* 32 (Νεί-); **(51)** ~ Strazzulla 351 (Wessel 637)
—SYRACUSE (NESOS): **(52)** iii-v AD *SEG* IV 18 (Wessel 3)

**Νικήν**

ILLYRIA:
—APOLLONIA: **(1)** c. 250-50 BC Maier 31 (coin) (Ceka 88) (money.); **(2)** ii BC *IApoll* 178 (f. Ἱέρων)
—DIVJAKA (MOD.): **(3)** hell. *Iliria* 1982 (1), p. 111 no. 52 = p. 120 no. 7 (tile)
—EPIDAMNOS-DYRRHACHION: **(4)** hell. *IDyrrh* 24 (f. Ἄγησις); **(5)** ~ ib. 328 (s. Ἀριστήν); **(6)** c. 250-50 BC *SNG Cop. Thessaly–Illyricum* 507 (coin) (pryt.) ?= **(7)**; **(7)** ~ Maier 310-3; Münsterberg Nachtr. p. 16 (coin) (Ceka 116; 185; 211; 226; 456) (pryt.) ?= **(6)**; **(8)** ii-i BC *IDyrrh* 551 (tiles); **(9)** hell.-imp. ib. 329 (s. Φίλιππος); **(10)** ~ ib. 447 (f. Φίλων)

**Νικηράτη**

S. ITALY (CAMPANIA):
—POMPEII: **(1)** i BC-i AD *CIL* IV 2013 (Lat. Nicherate)

**Νικήρατος**

ACHAIA: **(1)** 146 BC *IG* IV (1)² 28, 119 (f. Σῖμος: synoikos)
AIGINA: **(2)** 337-324 BC *CID* II 32, 36; 74 I, 77; 75 II, 51; 76 II, 29; 79 A I, 15; 97, 32; 99 A, [3]; 102 II B, 36 (s. Τιμῶναξ)
AKARNANIA:
—MEDION: **(3)** c. 325-315 BC *Hesp.* 57 (1988) p. 148 A, 45 (*SEG* XXXVI 331); cf. *Hesp.* 48 (1979) pp. 78 f. with pl. 22 c (f. Φρικίνας)
ARGOLIS:
—EPIDAUROS: **(4)** c. 365-335 BC *IG* IV (1)² 103, 142, 157; **(5)** ?c. 270-260 BC *SEG* XIV 398 b, 11 (f. Νίκανδρος)
ARKADIA:
—KLEITOR: **(6)** iii BC *IG* XII (9) 821 (I ?f. Νικήρατος II: date—Knoepfler); **(7)** ~ ib. (II ?s. Νικήρατος I: date—Knoepfler)
—MEGALOPOLIS: **(8)** 208 BC *IMM* 38, 54 (s. Ἀρκεσίλας); **(9)** ?131-130 BC *IG* v (2) 440, 1; 441, 1
ELIS: **(10)** iii AD *IvOl* 478, 3 (Τ. Κλ. N.)
ILLYRIA:
—EPIDAMNOS-DYRRHACHION: **(11)** hell.-imp. *IDyrrh* 129 (f. Ἀρχήν)
MESSENIA:
—MESSENE: **(12)** f. i AD *IG* v (1) 1374; *SEG* XXIII 207, 19 (s. Θέων) ?= (13); **(13)** 42 AD ib. 208, 4 ?= (12); **(14)** s. ii AD *PIR²* C 873 (Τιβ.

Κλ. Φροντῖνος N.: s. Τιβ. Κλ. Φροντῖνος, f. Τιβ. Κλ. Σαιθίδας Φροντῖνος)
SICILY:
—SYRACUSE: **(15)** m. iii BC Paus. vi 12. 4; *SEG* XVII 196 (f. Μικίων)

**Νικῆς**

ARKADIA:
—MANTINEIA-ANTIGONEIA: **(1)** c. 400-370 BC ib. XXXVII 340, 20, 23; cf. XL 371 (Νικῆι (dat.)); **(2)** i-ii AD *IG* v (2) 342 a, 4 (Νικεί (dat.))
—TEGEA: **(3)** f. iii BC ib. 36, 35 (Νικέος (gen.): f. —ης)

**Νικησας**

MESSENIA:
—KYPARISSIA: **(1)** hell.? ib. v (1) 1560 (n. pr.?)

**Νίκησις**

KEPHALLENIA:
—SAME: **(1)** iv/iii BC *Op. Ath.* 10 (1971) p. 66 no. 14

**Νικησώ**

ILLYRIA:
—LYCHNIDOS: **(1)** ii-iii AD Demitsas 331 (Νει-)

**Νικήτας**

S. ITALY (APULIA):
—RUBI: **(1)** iii AD *Suppl. It.* 5 p. 22 no. 3 (Lat. Cornelius [N]icetas)
SICILY:
—LILYBAION?: **(2)** iv-v AD *SEG* XLII 869

**Νικήτης**

AIGINA: **(1)** iii BC *IG* IV (1) 11
S. ITALY (CAMPANIA):
—HERCULANEUM?: **(2)** hell.-imp. ib. XIV 2411. 3
S. ITALY (LUCANIA):
—LEUKANOI: **(3)** imp. ib. II² 9207 (s. Λυσίας)

**Νικητιανός**

S. ITALY (CAMPANIA):
—KYME: **(1)** 251 AD *CIL* x 3699 I, 37 (Lat. Q. Servius Nicetianus)

**Νικηφᾶς**

AIGINA?: **(1)** imp. *EAD* XXX p. 356 no. 16 with n. 1 (Νει-: f. Ἡρακώ, Ἀσιατικός)

**Νικηφορίς**

EPIROS:
—NIKOPOLIS: **(1)** imp. *SEG* XXXVII 527 (Sarikakis 84) (Κλαυδία Νεικηφορίς: locn.— Cabanes)

**Νικηφόρος**

ACHAIA:
—TRITAIA: **(1)** i BC-i AD *Achaean Grave Stelai* 8
AITOLIA:
—PHANA?: **(2)** ?ii BC *SEG* XXIX 474 a
ARGOLIS:
—ARGOS: **(3)** i-ii AD *IG* IV (1) 587, 10 (f. Σῶσος); **(4)** ?ii AD Unp. (Argos, Kavvadias)
—EPIDAUROS: **(5)** ii AD *SEG* XVII 185; Peek, *IAEpid* 343 (date)
—HERMIONE: **(6)** ?ii-i BC *IG* IV (1) 731 II, 3 (s. Καλλιστράτα)
ARKADIA:
—TEGEA: **(7)** ?ii-i BC ib. v (2) 197; **(8)** imp. *SEG* XXXVI 384
ELIS: **(9)** c. 5 AD *IvOl* 69, 16; **(10)** f. ii AD ib. 121, 93, 3 (Νικη[φόρος]); **(11)** 185-189 AD ib. 104, 8 (Νει-: I f. Νικηφόρος II); **(12)** ~ ib. l. 8 ([Νεικη]φόρος: II s. Νικηφόρος I: T.); **(13)** 209-213 AD ib. 110, 9 (Νει-: I f. Αὐρ. Νικηφόρος II); **(14)** ~ ib. l. 9, 24 (Αὐρ. Νεικηφόρος: II s. Νικηφόρος I, ?f. Λεοντᾶς)
EPIROS:
—AMBRAKIA?: **(15)** ?s. ii BC *SEG* XXIX 474

ILLYRIA:
—AMANTIA: (16) imp. Patsch, *Sandschak Berat* p. 44 (*ΝΙΚΗΦΟΙΣ*, Νικηφορίς—ed., Νικηφόρε (voc.)—*LGPN*)
—APOLLONIA: (17) ?ii BC *IApoll* 127 (Νει-); (18) imp. ib. 261 ([*N*]ικηφόρος)
—EPIDAMNOS-DYRRHACHION: (19) hell.-imp. *IDyrrh* 201 (f. Εὐήμερος); (20) ~ ib. 330 (s. Ζώπυρος)

KORINTHIA:
—KORINTH: (21) 43 or 42 BC Amandry pp. 123-4; *RPC* 1 p. 250 no. 1117 (coin) (Lat. C. Iuli(us) Nicep(horus)); (22) imp. *IG* IV (1) 401 (Νει-: s. Μαλχίων)

LAKONIA:
—OITYLOS: (23) 238-240 AD ib. V (1) 1294, 8 (*M. Αὐρ. Νεικηφόρος*: s. Πρόσδεκτος)
—SPARTA: (24) c. 100-110 AD *SEG* XI 563, 5; 595, 2 (Bradford (7)) (s. Νικόστρατος); (25) ii-iv AD Robert, *Gladiateurs* p. 79 no. 12, 2 (Bradford (13)) (Νει- ὁ καὶ Νάρκισσος: s. Σύνετος); (26) c. 120-140 AD *IG* V (1) 1315, 22; *SEG* XI 522, 6; 548, 16; 575, 10 (Bradford (4)) (s. Μᾶρκος) ?= (32); (27) c. 125 AD *IG* V (1) 1314, 3 (Bradford (18)); (28) c. 130-140 AD *IG* V (1) 66, 6; 67, 1 (Bradford (8)) ([*Γ*]. Ἰούλ. Νεικηφ[όρος]: s. Φιλωνίδας); (29) 136 AD *IG* V (1) 65, 25; *SEG* XI 494, 3 (Bradford (17)) (Νει-); (30) c. 137-170 AD *IG* V (1) 116, 7; *SEG* XI 548, [21] (Bradford (20)) (f. Ἀριστονικίδας); (31) c. 150-160 AD *IG* V (1) 69, 32; 71 III, 28; *SEG* XI 554, [4] (Bradford (1)) (s. Ἀριστόβουλος); (32) ~ *SEG* XI 585, 11; XXX 410, 15 (Bradford (24)) (Νει-: f. Μᾶρκος) ?= (26); (33) c. 150-190 AD *IG* V (1) 45, 7; *BSA* 80 (1985) p. 226 (date) (Bradford (23)) (f. Κορινθᾶς); (34) c. 160 AD *IG* V (1) 71 III, 48; 86, 26 (Bradford (3)) (Νεικηφόρος—71: s. Καθήκων); (35) c. 175-200 AD *IG* V (1) 129, 2 (Bradford (21)) (f. Καλλικράτης); (36) iii AD *IG* V (1) 798 (Papaefthimiou p. 166 no. 41; Bradford (16)) (Νει-); (37) f. iii AD *IG* V (1) 301, 1 (*Artemis Orthia* pp. 326-7 no. 55); *BSA* 79 (1984) p. 285 no. 18 (date) (Bradford (6)) (II s. Νικηφόρος I); (38) ~ *IG* V (1) 301, 2 (*Artemis Orthia* pp. 326-7 no. 55); *BSA* 79 (1984) p. 285 no. 18 (date) (Bradford (25)) (I f. Νικηφόρος II, —ος); (39) ~ *IG* V (1) 303, 2 (*Artemis Orthia* pp. 327-8 no. 57); *BSA* 79 (1984) p. 283 no. 3 (Bradford (12)) (Νεικηφόρορ: s. Στέφανος); (40) ~ *IG* V (1) 310, 4 (*Artemis Orthia* pp. 332-3 no. 67); *IG* V (1) 544, 3 (*Artemis Orthia* pp. 358-9 no. 145); *IG* V (1) 547, 15; 549, 2; *SEG* XI 799, [2]; *BSA* 29 (1927-8) pp. 34-5 no. 57; 79 (1984) p. 284 no. 11 (date) (Bradford (9)) (*M. Αὐρ. N.*, Νεικηφόρος—310, 547 and 549: s. Φιλωνίδας); (41) ~ *IG* V (1) 550, 2 (Bradford (22)) (f. *M. Αὐρ. Κλεομένης*); (42) a. 212 AD *IG* V (1) 567, 3 (Bradford (26)) (I f. Αὐρ. Νικηφόρος II); (43) ~ *IG* V (1) 567, 3 (Bradford (5)) (Αὐρ Νεικηφόρος: II s. Νικηφόρος I: sculptor); (44) ~ *IG* V (1) 568; [692] (Bradford (2)) (*M. Αὐρ. N.*: s. Καλλικράτης); (45) ~ *IG* V (1) 600, 4 (Bradford (11)) (Αὐρ. *N.*: s. Σωτηρίδας)
——Konosoura: (46) c. 212-230 AD *IG* V (1) 684, 10 (Αὐρ. Νεικηφόρος)

MESSENIA:
—MESSENE: (47) 31 BC-14 AD *SEG* XXIII 207, 32 (s. Σωτηρίδας, f. Σωτηρίδας)

S. ITALY (APULIA):
—CANUSIUM: (48) imp. *Epig. Rom. di Canosa* 172 (*CIL* IX 397 with Add.) (Lat. L. Postumulenus Nicephorus: f. Sotidia Maxima)
—LARINUM*: (49) imp. ib. 6253 (Lat. N. Maedius Nicephor: s. Κλεοπάτρα: freed.)
—VENUSIA*: (50) imp. ib. 693 (Lat. L. Artorius Nicephor: freed.)
—VIBINUM: (51) i AD *Bovino* p. 240 no. 303 (*Ann. Fac. Lett. Fil. Bari* 19-20 (1976-7) p. 152 no. 3) (Lat. -rius Nicephor: freed.)

S. ITALY (CALABRIA):
—BRENTESION-BRUNDISIUM*: (52) imp. *CIL* IX 6113 (Lat. P. Calavius Nicephorus: freed.); (53) ?ii AD *NScav* 1892, p. 352 i = *Epigraphica* 25 (1963) p. 38 no. 12 (Lat. C. Flavi[us] Niceph[orus]: freed.)

S. ITALY (CAMPANIA):
—ATELLA*: (54) imp. *CIL* X 3737 (Lat. P. Terentius Nicephor(us): freed.)
—BAIAI*: (55) s. i AD *Puteoli* 3 (1979) p. 160 no. 4 (Lat. L. Acilius Nicephorus: freed.)
—DIKAIARCHIA-PUTEOLI: (56) imp. *CIL* X 2774 (Lat. Nicephor); (57) c. 170 AD ib. 3127; cf. *Puteoli* 11 (1987) pp. 38-40 (Lat. M. Ulpius Niceforus)
—DIKAIARCHIA-PUTEOLI*: (58) imp. *CIL* X 2035 (Lat. T. Cornelius Nicephor: freed.); (59) ~ ib. 2174 (Lat. C. Brinnius Nicephorus: freed.); (60) c. 170 AD ib. 1729; cf. *Puteoli* 11 (1987) pp. 38-40 (Lat. M. Ulpius Nicephorus: imp. freed.); (61) ~ *CIL* X 1729; cf. *Puteoli* 11 (1987) pp. 38-40 (Lat. Nicephorus: f. Γρηγόριος)
—HERCULANEUM*: (62) i BC-i AD *CIL* X 1403 f II, 6 (Lat. A. Furius Nicephor: freed.); (63) ~ ib. 1403 g III, 32 (Lat. C. Vibius Nicephor: freed.)
—POMPEII: (64) i BC-i AD ib. IV 1922 (Lat. Nicephor); (65) ~ ib. 3964 (Lat. Nicepor); (66) ~ ib. 4795 (Lat. Nicephorus); (67) ~ ib. 8718 (Lat. Nicephor)
—POMPEII*: (68) i BC-i AD *Atti Acc. Pontan.* 39 (1990) p. 288 no. 62 (Lat. C. Herennius Neicephorus: freed.)
—SALERNUM*: (69) ?i AD *IItal* 1 (1) 238 II, 10 (*CIL* X 557) (Lat. L. Appuleius Nicephor: freed.)
—SURRENTUM*: (70) imp. *NScav* 1928, p. 208 no. 8 (Lat. Nicephor: slave)

S. ITALY (LUCANIA):
—GRUMENTUM*: (71) imp. ib. 1901, p. 26 (Lat. Titius Nicephorus: s. Φιλημάτιον: freed.)
—POSEIDONIA-PAESTUM*: (72) imp. *CIL* X 487 (Mello—Voza 199) (Lat. M. Caedius Nicephor: freed.)

SICILY:
—KATANE: (73) imp. *CIL* X 7092 (Lat. Nice[por]: f. Δωρίς)
—SYRACUSE: (74) imp. *MEFRA* 106 (1994) p. 84 no. 2 (*M. Κοκκηῖς N.*); (75) iii-v AD Strazzulla 265 (vase) (Barreca 262) (Νικηφό[ρος])
—TAUROMENION: (76) byz. *Epigraphica* 5-6 (1943-4) p. 93 (-κι-)

## Νικιάδας

AITOLIA: (1) iii BC *SEG* XVIII 244, 4; (2) ?252-248 BC *Syll³* 422, 3; (3) ?a. 246 BC *SGDI* 2508, 3
—APEIRIKOI: (4) 141 BC *IG* IX (1)² (1) p. LII, s.a. 141 BC; IX (1)² (3) 634, 10; Pantos, *Sphragismata* p. 151 no. 122; p. 447 (s. Λέων)
—ATTALEIA: (5) 204 BC *IG* IX (1)² (1) 95, 2, 5-7
—BOUKATION: (6) f. ii BC ib. 98, 9 ?= (7); (7) 190-163 BC ib. 97, 5; 101, 13 (f. Εὔαρχος) ?= (6)
—KALLION/KALLIPOLIS: (8) hell. ib. 158
—PHISTYON: (9) ii BC ib. 110 a, 2 ?= (10); (10) 163 BC ib. 101, 11; 102, 2; 103, 3 ?= (9)

AKARNANIA:
—ASTAKOS: (11) m. iii BC *SEG* XXVII 153, 5; cf. *PAE* 1977, pl. 244 b (s. Ἄριστων)

ARGOLIS:
—EPIDAUROS: (12) c. 365-335 BC *IG* IV (1)² 103, 115

EPIROS:
—NIKOPOLIS: (13) c. 200 AD *FD* III (6) 96, 3 (Sarikakis 20) (*M. Αὐρ. N.*: s. Σάτυρος)

LAKONIA:
—SPARTA: (14) c. 100-120 AD *SEG* XI 607, 3 (Bradford (-)) (Νικιάδ[ας]: f. Διοκλῆς)
LEUKAS: (15) imp. *IG* IX (1) 599 (Πομπ. Νεικιάδας)

MESSENIA:
—THOURIA: (16) f. ii BC *SEG* XI 972, 128 (f. Φίλιππος)

## Νικιάδης

AKARNANIA: (1) ii BC *BGU* 1939 F, 4

## Νικίαρ

ELIS: (1) 101-109 AD *IvOl* 89, 4, 6 (Νικίαι (gen.): I f. Νικίαρ II, Νικοκλῆρ); (2) ~ ib. l. 4 (II s. Νικίαρ I)

## Νικίας

ACHAIA: (1) 207 BC Liv. xxviii 8. 10 (Lat. Nicias); (2) 146 BC *IG* IV (1)² 28, 64 (s. Νικόστρατος: synoikos); (3) ~ ib. l. 103 (f. Κτησικλῆς: synoikos); (4) ~ ib. l. 106 (I f. Νικίας II: synoikos); (5) ~ ib. l. 106 (II s. Νικίας I: synoikos)
—DYME: (6) iii BC *AJPh* 31 (1910) p. 399 no. 74 a, 6 (s. Σώσιππος); (7) ii BC *SEG* XXXI 379, 1 (doctor); (8) ?145 BC Sherk 43, 23; *SEG* XXXVIII 372 (date) (f. Τιμόθεος)
—PATRAI: (9) c. 80 BC *IG* VII 416, 62 (*IOrop* 523) (I f. Νικίας II); (10) ~ *IG* VII 416, 62 (*IOrop* 523) (II s. Νικίας I)
—PELLENE: (11) m. iii BC *IG* V (2) 368, 107 (s. Ὄνομα—); (12) imp. *SEG* XI 1280
AITOLIA: (13) iii BC Robert, *EEP* p. 114, 4; (14) ?247 BC *Syll³* 444 A, 4; *CID* II 139, 2; (15) ii AD *IG* IX (1)² (1) 92, 4 (s. Βίων)
—KALYDON: (16) c. 210-196 BC ib. 29, 22; 30, 14 (f. Ἀλέξανδρος); (17) 178 BC *Syll³* 636, 12 (s. Ἀλέξανδρος); (18) m. ii BC *IG* IX (1)² (1) 137, 22 (f. Λαδάμης); (19) 154 BC ib. IX (1)² (3) 638 9, 2 (f. Ἀλέξανδρος); (20) s. ii BC ib. IX (1)² (1) 36, 11; [139]; *SBBerlAk* 1936, p. 367. no. 2, 1, 12 (s.p.) (*SEG* XII 303) (s. Λαδάμης, f. Λαδάμης)
—PHISTYON?: (21) i BC *IG* IX (1)² (1) 110 b, 12 (s. Ταλούρας) ?= (22); (22) ~ ib. l. 13 (f. Ἀνδρόνικος) ?= (21)
—PHYTAION: (23) s. iii BC ib. 24, 7 (f. Νίκων)
—POTIDANIA: (24) m. ii BC *SBBerlAk* 1936, p. 371 b, 15 (*SEG* XLI 528 B) (f. Πολέμαρχος)
AKARNANIA: (25) c. 250-167 BC *NZ* 10 (1878) p. 28 no. 25 (coin) (Νικ[ίας]: f. Βάθυος) ?= (28)
—ALYZIA: (26) m. ii BC *IG* IX (1)² (2) 208, 2, [32] (f. Ἀγήτας)
—ANAKTORION?: (27) 305-295 BC *JIAN* 11 (1908) p. 260 no. 25 (coin); *SNR* 56 (1977) pp. 97-8; p. 111 (date) (?s. Ἕλλα—)
—KORONTA: (28) m. ii BC *IG* IX (1)² (2) 209, 18-19 (s. Βάθυος) ?= (25)
—PALAIROS: (29) ii BC ib. 451, 13 (s. Κριτόλαος)
—STRATOS: (30) iv/iii BC *SEG* XXIX 476 (-χί-)
—THYRREION: (31) ii BC *IG* IX (1)² (2) 249, 2 (Νικία[s], Νικιά[δας]?: f. Ἄντοχος)
ARGOLIS:
—ARGOS: (32) m. v BC Unp. (Ch. Kritzas) (Νικί[ας], Νικί[ων]?); (33) ?277 BC *FD* III (1) 80 with Add. p. 384 (f. Νικομήδης); (34) 105 BC *JÖAI* 14 (1911) Beibl. p. 146 no. 4, 15 (f. —μων); (35) c. 100-90 BC *SEG* XXXIII 290 A, 8; *BSA* 70 (1975) pp. 129-31 (date) (Stephanis 1823) (s. Ἱπποθένης); (36) ~ *SEG* XXXIII 290 A, 10; *BSA* 70 (1975) pp. 129-31 (date); cf. Stephanis 1907 (f. Ξενοκράτης); (37) f. i BC Unp. (Ch. Kritzas) (Νι[κί]ας: f. Ἀριστοκλῆς); (38) i-ii AD *IG* IV (1) 587, 8 ([*N*]ικίας: s. Σεραπίων)
—EPIDAUROS: (39) iii BC Peek, *IAEpid* 73, 3 (Νικ[ίας]); (40) 237 AD *IG* IV (1)² 412, 7 (Νει-: II s. Νικίας I); (41) ~ ib. l. 8 (Νει-: I f. Νικίας II)
—HERMIONE: (42) f. iii BC ib. XII (7) 16, 3 (s. Φίλαγρος); (43) ?ii-i BC ib. IV (1) 731 III, 2 (s. Μηνόφιλος); (44) i BC-i AD? ib. 730 V, 5 (s. Δαμοκράτης)

—KLEONAI: **(45)** c. 210-207 BC ib. IV (1)² 73, 10; *SEG* XXXV 303 (date) (s. Ξενοκλῆς)

—TROIZEN: **(46)** iii BC *IG* IV (1) 774, 8; **(47)** ~ ib. 830

ARKADIA: **(48)** 320 BC ib. V (2) 549, 11 (s. Μνασίας)

—KLEITOR: **(49)** 191-146 BC *ZfN* 9 (1882) p. 260 no. 3; Unp. (Athens, NM) Empedocles Coll. 7430 (coin)

—MANTINEIA-ANTIGONEIA: **(50)** c. 425-385 BC *IG* V (2) 323. 14 (tessera)

—MEGALOPOLIS: **(51)** ?165 BC *FD* III (1) 48, 3, 5; *Syll*³ 585, 308; cf. Stephanis 1886 (f. Νίκων)

—TEGEA: **(52)** ?218 BC *IG* V (2) 16, 13; **(53)** f. ii BC ib. 44, 7 (f. Κλέανδρος); **(54)** ?ii/i BC ib. 119 (s. Κλέανδρος); **(55)** i AD ib. 46, 12 (Νικίας)

——(Krariotai): **(56)** iii BC ib. 40, 24 (f. —μόλας); **(57)** f. iii BC ib. 36, 39 (s. Νικόδαμος); **(58)** s. iii BC ib. l. 121 (s. Ἀλκισθένης)

ARKADIA?: **(59)** ?v-iv BC *RE* (25); *FGrH* 318

ELIS: **(60)** c. 146-32 BC BM coins 1926 1-16-839/40 (coins) (*NKIA*—coin, Νικία[ς], Νικιά[δας]?)

—OLYMPIA*: **(61)** c. 177-189 AD *IvOl* 138, 5 (Νει-: ?s. Ἀ—)

EPIROS: **(62)** iii BC *Hist. Rom. Rel.* I² p. 218 fr. 40 (Lat. Nicias, Timochares—alii); **(63)** 167 BC Plb. xxx 13. 4

—AMBRAKIA: **(64)** ii BC *SEG* XLII 542 (f. Ἀγαθίων)

—BOUTHROTOS: **(65)** f. ii BC *IBouthrot* 2, 5; 3, 5; 4, 5; 76, 7 (s. Διονυσόδωρος)

—BOUTHROTOS (PRASAIBOI): **(66)** a. 163 BC ib. 15, 8; 22, 11; 41, 19 (*SEG* XXXVIII 472; 479; 500); *IBouthrot* 45, 10; 47, 7 (s. Σωσίπατρος); **(67)** ~ ib. 30, 10; 36, 12 (*SEG* XXXVIII 488; 495) (f. Ἡρακλείδας)

——Eschatioi: **(68)** a. 163 BC *IBouthrot* 98, 7 (Ν<ισ>ικιου? (gen.): f. Βοΐσκος)

—KASSOPE: **(69)** iv/iii BC *SEG* XXXIV 589 (Νικ[ίας]: f. Ἱππαρχος)

—MOLOSSOI: **(70)** f. iii BC *FGrH* 703 F 9 (f. Δείναρχος)

—NIKOPOLIS: **(71)** imp. *RE* (31); s.v. Plutarchos col. 679; Sarikakis 118 (doctor); **(72)** ~ *Wiss. Mitth. Bosn.* 4 (1896) p. 386 no. 2 (Sarikakis 22) (Γ. Βιλληνὸς Νεικίας: ?s. Βιλλήνη Μόσχιν)

ILLYRIA:

—APOLLONIA: **(73)** c. 250-50 BC Maier 76 (coin) (Ceka 59; 67) (pryt.)

—DASSARETIOI?: **(74)** ii-i BC *SEG* I 254

KORINTHIA:

—KORINTH: **(75)** hell. *IG* II² 9072 (s. Νίκων); **(76)** iii AD *SEG* XVIII 137 a, 6; 137 b, 9 (Νεικίας—137 a); **(77)** iii/iv AD *Corinth* VIII (3) 305, 5 (*GVI* 592); cf. Robert, *OMS* 6 p. 572 (Νεικίης: s. Ἀλέξανδρος)

LAKONIA:

—EPIDAUROS LIMERA: **(78)** ii AD *SEG* XI 894 a, 1 = XLI 311 (Νει-: I f. Νικίας II); **(79)** ~ ib. XI 894 a, 1 = XLI 311 (Νεικ[ία]s: II s. Νικίας I)

—GYTHEION: **(80)** i-ii AD *IG* V (1) 1178, 10 (Νει-: s. Σιμηλίδας)

—SPARTA: **(81)** iv BC Plu., *Ages.* 13; *Mor.* 191 B; 209 F; 808 A (Poralla² 557); **(82)** ii BC *IG* V (1) 961, 1, 9 (Bradford (16)) (f. Ἀρατος); **(83)** s. i BC *IG* V (1) 95, 12; 96, 8; 133, 1 (Bradford (23)) (f. Τίμαρχος); **(84)** ~ *IG* V (1) 95, 15 (Bradford (2)) (I s. Διαφάνης, f. Νικίας II); **(85)** ~ *IG* V (1) 95, 15 (Bradford (7)) (II s. Νικίας I); **(86)** ~ *IG* V (1) 134, 1 (Bradford (22)) (f. Νικόστρατος); **(87)** imp.? *IG* V (1) 247 (Bradford (9)) (s. Φιλέας); **(88)** c. 30-20 BC *IG* V (1) 211, 21 (Bradford (20)) (f. Νικόδαμος); **(89)** ~ *IG* V (1) 211, 32 (Bradford (17)) (f. Δαμέας); **(90)** ~ *IG* V (1) 211, 40 (Bradford (21)) (f. Νικομήδης); **(91)** c. 25-1 BC *SEG* XI 505, 3 (Bradford (5)) (s. Καλλικρατίδας); **(92)** i/ii AD *IG* V (1) 184, 6 (Bradford (12)) (Νικίας); **(93)**

c. 80-100 AD *SEG* XI 511, 2 (Bradford (1)) (Νει-: s. Ἀριστοκρατίδας); **(94)** ?ii AD *IG* V (1) 625, 7 (Bradford (4)) (Νει-); **(95)** f. ii AD *IG* V (1) 32 B, 16 (Bradford (3)) (Νει-: s. Εὐκρίνης); **(96)** c. 105-110 AD *IG* V (1) 97, 2; *SEG* XI 564, 2 (Bradford (18)) (Νει-: f. Διοκλῆς); **(97)** c. 105-135 AD *IG* V (1) 97, 22; 99, 3; *SEG* XI 564, 22; 580, 5 (Bradford (10)) (Νεικίας—*SEG*: s. Τεταρτίων); **(98)** m. ii AD *IG* V (1) 72, 4 (Bradford (24)); **(99)** c. 140-150 AD *IG* V (1) 37, 13; 38, 6; *SEG* XI 497, 3 (Bradford (14)) (Νεικίας—37 and *SEG*); **(100)** c. 150-160 AD *IG* V (1) 53, 27 (Bradford (19)) (I f. Εὐδαμίδας, Νικίας II ὁ καὶ Κλεονικίδας); **(101)** ~ *IG* V (1) 53, 28 (Bradford (8)) (N. ὁ καὶ Κλεονικίδας: II s. Νικίας I); **(102)** s. ii AD *SEG* XI 598, 2 (Bradford (6)) (Νει-: s. Κόσμος); **(103)** c. 160-175 AD *IG* V (1) 45, 1; *BSA* 80 (1985) p. 226 (date) (Bradford (15)) (Τιβ. Κλ. Νεικίας)

—TEUTHRONE: **(104)** i BC/i AD *IG* V (2) 538 (f. Ἀριστήδεια)

MESSENIA:

—MESSENE?: **(105)** ii/i BC *SEG* XI 979, 9; **(106)** ~ ib. l. 52

—THOURIA: **(107)** ii-i BC *IG* V (1) 1385, 13 (s. Δάμων); **(108)** ~ ib. l. 24 (s. Ἀριστόδαμος); **(109)** ~ ib. l. 35 (f. Ὀνασικλῆς); **(110)** f. ii BC *SEG* XI 972, 40 (f. Λυσικράτης); **(111)** ~ ib. l. 89 (f. Παγκράτης)

PELOPONNESE: **(112)** c. 175-150 BC ib. XXXII 435, 5

S. ITALY (BRUTTIUM):

—LOKROI EPIZEPHYRIOI:

——(Προ.): **(113)** iv/iii BC De Franciscis 32, 5 (s. Πύρρων)

——(Τηλ.): **(114)** iv/iii BC ib. 15, 2; 33, 3 (f. Θρασύμαχος)

—RHEGION: **(115)** hell. *IG* XIV 2400. 10 (tile); **(116)** byz. ib. 2405. 46 (lamp)

—SYBARIS-THOURIOI-COPIAE: **(117)** v BC D.H., *Lys.* i

S. ITALY (CAMPANIA):

—DIKAIARCHIA-PUTEOLI*: **(118)** imp. *CIL* x 2305; 2307 (Lat. A. Cluvius Nicia: freed.); **(119)** ~ ib. 2831 (Lat. C. Pavillius Nicia: freed.)

—HERCULANEUM: **(120)** m. i AD *PdelP* 6 (1951) p. 230 no. 18, 6 (Lat. Q. Caninius Nicias); **(121)** 60 AD ib. 1 (1946) p. 381 no. 4 (Lat. L. Caninius N[icias])

—HERCULANEUM*: **(122)** c. 50-75 AD *CIL* x 1403 a I, 7 (Lat. L. Caninius Nicia: freed.)

—POMPEII: **(123)** i BC/i AD ib. IV 1252 (Lat. Nicias); **(124)** ~ ib. 10223; *Gnomon* 45 (1973) p. 271 (Νι[κί]ας)

—POMPEII*: **(125)** i BC-i AD *Römische Gräberstrassen* p. 214 a (Lat. M. Lollius Nicias: freed.); **(126)** c. 51-62 AD *CIL* IV 3340. 45, 11 (Lat. M. Eprius Nicias)

SICILY:

—AKRAGAS (NR.)?: **(127)** ?iv BC Manganaro, *QUCC* forthcoming no. 39 B, 6

—ENGUION: **(128)** c. 214-211 BC Plu., *Marc.* 20

—GELA-PHINTIAS: **(129)** s. iv BC Dubois, *IGDS* 154 (potter)

—IAITON: **(130)** ii-i BC *SEG* XXVI 1070. 4 (tiles) (s. Δεινίας)

—KAMARINA: **(131)** f. v BC Cordano, *Tessere Pubbliche* 45 (f. Θέων); **(132)** ~ ib. 57; **(133)** s. v BC Dubois, *IGDS* 119, 6 (Arena, *Iscr. Sic.* II 145); Cordano, 'Camarina VII' 44 (f. Ἡρακλείδας)

—KENTORIPA: **(134)** ?s. iii BC *Sic. Gymn.* 2 (1949) p. 91 no. 1, 9 (s. Φάλακρος)

—MORGANTINA: **(135)** ?iv/iii BC *SEG* XXXIX 1008, 7 (s. Κρατίας)

—SYRACUSE: **(136)** m. v BC Plu., *Mor.* 835 D

—SYRACUSE?:

——(Ἐκυ.): **(137)** hell. *Mem. Linc.* 8 (1938) p. 127 no. 35. 1 (bullet) (*NScav* 1961, p.

349); cf. *BE* 1965, no. 502; cf. *L'Incidenza dell'Antico* pp. 420 ff. (s. Πολίτας)

—TAUROMENION:

——(Παμ.): **(138)** ii/i BC *IGSI* 7 I, 8; 10 I, 17 (s. Λυσίας)

—TYNDARIS: **(139)** imp. Manganaro, *QUCC* forthcoming no. 21 (Νει-: f. Ἀρτεμίδωρος)

## Νικίδας

LAKONIA: **(1)** ?ii-i BC *IG* V (1) 1282, 14, 17 (Νει-)

## Νικιδώ

ARKADIA:

—ALIPHEIRA: **(1)** iv/iii BC Orlandos, *Alipheira* p. 237

## Νίκιν

LAKONIA:

—SPARTA: **(1)** ii-i BC *SEG* XLII 325

## Νίκιον

ARGOLIS:

—EPIDAUROS: **(1)** i-ii AD ib. XXX 394 (-ηον)

KEPHALLENIA:

—PRONNOI: **(2)** f. iii BC *Op. Ath.* 10 (1971) p. 67 no. 16

—SAME: **(3)** hell. *IG* IX (1) 629

LAKONIA:

—SPARTA: **(4)** s. i AD *SEG* XI 776, 5 (Bradford (2)) (Ἰουλ. Ν.: d. Λυσανδρία, m. Γ. Ἰουλ. Χαρίξενος); **(5)** c. 110-130 AD *BSA* 89 (1994) pp. 437-8 no. 10, 5 (Ἰουλ. Νείκιον: m. Ὀκτ. Ἀγίς); **(6)** c. 140-150 AD *IG* V (1) 607, 2; *BSA* 75 (1980) p. 219 (stemma) (Bradford (1)) (Κλ. Νείκιον: d. Τιβ. Κλ. Δαμοκράτης)

## Νικίππα

AKARNANIA: **(1)** iv/iii BC *Thess. Mnem.* 216 (*IG* IX (1)² 2 585) (-ππη: d. Νίκων)

—THYRREION: **(2)** ii BC ib. 328

ARGOLIS:

—ARGOS: **(3)** hell. *SEG* XXIX 357; **(4)** a. 303 BC *CEG* II 816, 21

ARKADIA:

—MANTINEIA-ANTIGONEIA: **(5)** 64 or 62 BC *IG* V (2) 265, 2 etc. (d. Πασίας) ?= (6); **(6)** ?s. i BC Paus. viii 9. 6 (d. Πασέας) ?= (5)

—MEGALOPOLIS: **(7)** i BC/i AD *IG* V (2) 515 A, 23, 25; C, 10

KEPHALLENIA?: **(8)** i BC-i AD *SEG* XXX 516; cf. *BE* 1981, no. 68 (locn.) (or Messenia?)

LAKONIA?: **(9)** i BC-i AD *SEG* XXX 516; *BE* 1981, no. 68 (locn.)

LEUKAS: **(10)** hell.? *IG* IX (1) 551

MESSENIA:

—MESSENE?: **(11)** f. ii BC ib. V (2) 539 (d. Δαμοφῶν, m. Δημοφῶν)

## Νικιππία

LAKONIA:

—SPARTA: **(1)** i BC/i AD *SEG* XI 677, 1 (Bradford (2)) ([Νι]κιππία: d. Κλεόνικος); **(2)** i/ii AD *IG* V (1) 607, 22; *BSA* 75 (1980) pp. 213-19 (ident., stemma) (Bradford (1)) (Κλ. Νεικιππία: ?m. Γ. Ἰουλ. Σιμήδης, Γ. Ἰουλ. Ἀγαθοκλῆς); **(3)** a. 212 AD *BSA* 89 (1994) p. 439 no. 12, 8 (Νει-: d. Μ. Αὐρ. Καλλικράτης)

## Νικιππίδας

LAKONIA:

—SPARTA: **(1)** c. 90-100 AD *IG* V (1) 79, 4; *SEG* XI 539, 3 (Bradford (4)) (Νει-: s. Δαμοκράτης); **(2)** f. ii AD *IG* V (1) 162, 16 (Bradford (6)) (Νει-: s. —μος); **(3)** ~ *SEG* XXXI 340, 3 (Νει-); **(4)** c. 105-110 AD *IG* V (1) 52, 9 (Bradford (1)) (Νει-: s. Δαμοκλῆς); **(5)** c. 110-120 AD *SEG* XI 483, 2 (Bradford (5)) (Νει-); **(6)** c. 133-160 AD *SEG* XI 547 a, 10?; 547 b, 7?; 547 c, 3?; 585, 6; 586, 2 (Bradford (2)) (Νει-: s. Μενέμαχος); **(7)** c. 150-160 AD *IG* V (1) 71 II, 11 (Bradford (5))

**Νικιππίδης**
MESSENIA:
—MESSENE: (8) i AD *IG* v (1) 1436, 42
([*Νι*]*κιππίδας*: f. *Ναυσίνικος*)

**Νικιππίδης**
ILLYRIA:
—EPIDAMNOS-DYRRHACHION: (1) ii-iii AD *AEp*
1978, no. 759 (Lat. M. Aelius Nicippides)

**Νίκιππος**
ARGOLIS:
—ARGOS: (1) m. iii BC *IG* IV (1)² 96, 24 (Perl-
man E.3); Perlman p. 63 f. (date) (s. *Ἀριστώ-
νυμος*)
ARKADIA:
—MEGALOPOLIS: (2) ii BC *IG* v (2) 453 (s. *Σω-
τίων*: sculptor)
—MT. LYKAION*: (3) hell.? ib. p. 146 no. 553
(13) (tile)
—TEGEA: (4) ii AD ib. 55, 55 (*Νεί-*: s. *Δαμακίων*)
KORINTHIA:
—KORINTH: (5) c. 590-570 BC Amyx 14. 6
(vase) (Lorber 48) (-*ιπος*: her.)
LAKONIA:
—GYTHEION: (6) imp. *IG* v (1) 1184 (*Νεί-*)
—HYPERTELEATON*: (7) imp. ib. 1025 (*Νί-
κιπ*[*πος*])
—SPARTA: (8) s. i BC *SEG* XI 881 f (tile) (Brad-
ford (4)) (*Νίκ*[*ι*]*ππ*[*ος*]); (9) i BC/i AD? *IG* v
(1) 263; *Artemis Orthia* p. 305 no. 17 (date)
(Bradford (2)) (s. *Καλλικρατίδας*); (10) f. ii AD
*Sculpture from Arcadia and Laconia* p. 239
(*SEG* XLII 326); (11) c. 105-110 AD *IG* v (1)
20 B, 3; *BSA* 26 (1923-5) p. 168 C 6/7, 9
(Bradford (6)) (*Νει-*: I f. *Νίκιππος* II); (12) ~
*IG* v (1) 20 B, 3; *BSA* 26 (1923-5) p. 168 C
6/7, 9 (Bradford (3)) (*Νει-*: II s. *Νίκιππος* I);
(13) c. 125-150 AD *IG* v (1) 114, 11 (Brad-
ford (1)) (s. *Ἀγήσιππος*); (14) a. 212 AD *IG* v
(1) 562, 8 (Bradford (5)) (*Αὐρ. Νείκιππος*)
MESSENIA:
—MESSENE: (15) 219 BC Plb. iv 31. 2; (16) 31
BC-14 AD *SEG* XXIII 207, 35 (f. *Λύσων*)
——(Hylleis): (17) 11 AD *PAE* 1992, p. 71 A,
15 (s. *Ὀνασικλῆς*)
—THOURIA: (18) ii-i BC *IG* v (1) 1385, 10 (s.
*Χαιρήμων*); (19) ~ ib. l. 11 (s. *Τίμων*)
S. ITALY (BRUTTIUM):
—LOKROI EPIZEPHYRIOI:
——(Λογ.): (20) 275 BC De Franciscis 25, 6 (s.
*Φιλιστίων*)
S. ITALY (LUCANIA): (21) f. iv BC *SEG* XXX
1173 (vase)

**Νῖκις**
ARGOLIS:
—EPIDAUROS:
——Selegeis: (1) c. 221 BC *IG* IV (1)² 42, 15
—HERMIONE: (2) iii-ii BC ib. IV (1) 687 (s. *Ἀν-
δρωνίδας*); (3) ?iii-ii BC ib. 735, 2 (f. *Ἀνδρο-
κλῆς*); (4) ?265-259 BC Nachtergael, *Les Ga-
lates* 4, 17; cf. Stephanis 2177 (f. *Πυθόνικος*);
(5) ii/i BC *IG* IV (1) 721 (f. *Ὀλυμπιάς*); (6) ~
ib. IV (1)² 229, 2 (s. *Νικάτας*)
—TROIZEN: (7) iv BC ib. IV (1) 764, 2 (f. *Ἀνδρό-
βιος*)
ARKADIA:
—MANTINEIA-ANTIGONEIA: (8) c. 300-221 BC
ib. v (2) 323. 99 (tessera) (f. *Αὐτέας*)
—MEGALOPOLIS: (9) 369-361 BC ib. 1, 31; Tod,
*GHI* II 132 (date)
—TEGEA: (10) f. ii BC *IG* v (2) 44, 15 (f. *Ἀρί-
στων*)
SICILY:
—KAMARINA: (11) iv/iii BC *SEG* XXXIX 999, 3
(Dubois, *IGDS* 125); cf. *BE* 1990, no. 861
(*Ν.—SEG, Ἴνικις—*Dubois: s. *Στράτων*)

**Νικίων**
ARGOLIS:
—ARGOS: (1) a. 303 BC *CEG* II 816, 20

LAKONIA:
—OITYLOS: (2) iii/ii BC *IG* v (1) 1295, 9 (Bradford (1))
—SPARTA: (3) m. ii BC *IG* v (1) 889; 890; 891
a; 891 b; *SEG* XI 881 d (tiles) (Bradford (2));
(4) imp. *IG* v (1) 807 (Bradford (3))
S. ITALY (CAMPANIA):
—POMPEII*: (5) 46 BC *CIL* IV 60, 17 (Castrèn
395. 8) (Lat. M. Stronnius Nicio: freed.)

**Νικοβούλα**
ARGOLIS:
—ARGOS*: (1) ii BC *SEG* XLII 279, 10
(slave/freed.?)
—HERMIONE: (2) ?ii-i BC *IG* IV (1) 731 III, 9
(d. *Ἀγώ*)
SICILY:
—LIPARA: (3) hell.? Libertini, *Isole Eolie* p. 226
no. 55; (4) ~ ib. p. 227 no. 60 (*Νικο(β)ούλα*)

**Νικόβουλος**
AITOLIA: (1) ?a. 246 BC *SGDI* 2508, 3; (2) iii/ii
BC *IG* II² 7990 + 7991 (f. *Στράτιος*); (3) 185
BC ib. IX (1)² (1) 32, 26
—KALYDON: (4) c. 142 BC ib. 137, 48; (5) 129
BC ib. l. 98 (f. *Λυσίξενος*, *Ἄνδρων*, *Φιλόξενος*);
(6) ~ ib. l. 100 (s. *Ἐμαυτός*)
—KONOPE-ARSINOE: (7) 184 BC ib. 131, 8 (s.
*Πολέμων*); (8) a. 167 BC ib. 36, 1 (f. *Στράτων*)
—POTIDANIA: (9) m. ii BC *SBBerlAk* 1936, p.
371 b, 17 (*SEG* XLI 528 B) (f. *Μαχάτας*, *Νι-
κωνίδας*)
AITOLIA?:
—AIKLYMIOI: (10) a. 167 BC *IG* IX (1)² (1) 36,
8 (s. *Μένανδρος*)
LAKONIA:
—SPARTA: (11) c. 105-110 AD ib. v (1) 97, 9;
*SEG* XI 564, 16 (Bradford (-)) (*Νεικόβουλος—
SEG*: f. *Νικοκράτης*)
LEUKAS: (12) c. 167-50 BC *BMC Thessaly* p.
183 no. 129; p. 185 nos. 159-60 (coins)

**Νικοδάμανς**
ARGOLIS:
—ARGOS: (1) iv-iii BC Unp. (Ch. Kritzas)

**Νικοδαμία**
LAKONIA:
—GERONTHRAI: (1) iii-ii BC *IG* v (1) 1127, 3

**Νικόδαμος**
ACHAIA:
—PELLENE?: (1) ?263-261 BC *FD* III (3) 190, 5
AITOLIA: (2) 189 BC *RE* (1) (Lat. Nicodamus)
—BOUKATION: (3) c. 164 BC *IG* IX (1)² (1) 99,
11 (*Νει-*)
—KALYDON: (4) c. 143 BC ib. 137, 39 (f. *Θεαρί-
δας*)
ARGOLIS:
—ARGOS: (5) c. 343-323 BC *CID* II 31, 97, 100,
106; 47 A II, 13?, 16; 49 B II, 9; (6) ii BC
*SEG* XLII 279, 23 (f. *Δαμοσθένεια*)
——(Achaioi): (7) c. 316-222 BC ib. XVII 142, 3
(Perlman A.14)
——(Dymanes-Arkoidai): (8) v BC *SEG* XXIX
351 b
——Skleris: (9) c. 318-316 BC ib. XI 1084, 26,
41 (Perlman A.3); *SEG* XXXIII 276, 5, 18
ARKADIA:
—HERAIA: (10) m. iii BC *IG* v (2) 368, 143
—LOUSOI: (11) iv/iii BC ib. 388, 9 ([*Ν*]*ικόδαμο*[*ς*])
—MAINALIOI: (12) v/iv BC *RE* (2); Marcadé 1
84 (sculptor)
—TEGEA: (13) iii BC *IG* v (2) 30, 13
——(Krariotai): (14) f. iii BC ib. 36, 39 (f. *Νι-
κίας*)
DALMATIA:
—ISSA?: (15) hell. Brunšmid p. 5 (*Νικόδαμ*[*ος*])
ELIS: (16) 187-185 BC Plb. xxii 3. 4; 10. 5 (-*δη*-)
EPIROS:
—TEPELENE (MOD.): (17) imp. *SEG* XXIV 475
(*Νεικόδαμ*[*ος*])

ILLYRIA:
—LISSOS: (18) imp. *Op. Ath.* 10 (1971) p. 81 n.
19 (f. *Πραυγισσός*)
KORINTHIA:
—KORINTH: (19) c. 240-220 BC *IG* VII 366, 2
(*IOrop* 162) (f. *Νικανδρίδας*)
LAKONIA:
—OITYLOS: (20) iii/ii BC *IG* v (1) 1295, 8 (Brad-
ford (4)) (*Νικόδα*[*μος*])
—SPARTA: (21) 104 BC Moretti, *Olymp.* 653
(Bradford s.v. *Νικόδημος* (-)) ?= (22); (22) c.
80 BC *IG* VII 416, 56 (*IOrop* 523; Bradford
(3)) (s. *Νίκων*) ?= (21); (23) c. 30-20 BC *IG*
v (1) 211, 21 (Bradford (1)) (s. *Νικίας*); (24)
c. 140-160 AD *IG* v (1) 154, 6 (Bradford (5))
(I f. *Νικόδαμος* II); (25) ~ *IG* v (1) 154, 6
(Bradford (2)) (II s. *Νικόδαμος* I)
MESSENIA:
—MESSENE: (26) 323 BC *FD* III (4) 7, 1 (-*δη*-: s.
*Νικαρχίδας*) ?= (27); (27) c. 307-297 BC Plu.,
*Dem.* 13. 3 (-*δη*-) ?= (26); (28) i BC/i AD *IG* v
(1) 1438 a, 1 (*Νικόδα*[*μος*])
——(Kleolaidai): (29) 11 AD *PAE* 1992, p. 71
A, 25 (s. *Καλλικλῆς*)
—THOURIA: (30) s. iii BC *IG* v (1) 1386, 6 (f.
*Νικεύς*)
S. ITALY (BRUTTIUM):
—LOKROI EPIZEPHYRIOI:
——(Κυλ.): (31) inc. De Franciscis 27, 1 ?= (32);
(32) iv/iii BC ib. 11, 8; 18, 4 (f. *Εὐφραῖος*) ?=
(31)
——(Στρ.): (33) iv/iii BC ib. 10, 8
——(Σωτ.): (34) 275 BC ib. 12, 5; 25, 3 (s. *Τί-
μων*)
—RHEGION: (35) s. ii BC *IG* XIV 612, 1 (*Syll*³
715; Dubois, *IGDGG* 1 40) (f. *Νίκανδρος*)
S. ITALY (CALABRIA):
—TARAS-TARENTUM: (36) c. 302-280 BC Vlasto
704; 707 (coin) (Evans, *Horsemen* p. 135 VI
F.1; p. 135 VI G); (37) ?253 BC Nachtergael,
*Les Galates* 10, 46; cf. Stephanis 1101 (-*δη*-:
f. *Ἡράκλειτος*)
SICILY:
—KAMARINA: (38) f. v BC Cordano, *Tessere Pub-
bliche* 82a (s. *Παρμενείδας*)
—SYRACUSE: (39) ?iv-iii BC *Riv. Stor. Antica* 5
(1900-1) p. 61 no. 40
—TAUROMENION: (40) c. 227 BC *IG* XIV 421 an.
14 (*SGDI* 5219) ?= (41); (41) iii/ii BC *IG* XIV
421 an. 7; 421 an. 47 (*SGDI* 5219) (s. *Παιά-
νιος*, f. *Παιάνιος*) ?= (40); (42) c. 187 BC *IG*
XIV 421 an. 54 (*SGDI* 5219); (43) c. 185 BC
*IG* XIV 421 an. 56 (*SGDI* 5219)

**Νικόδημος**
ARGOLIS:
—HERMIONE: (1) imp. *IG* IV (1) 714, 3 (*Νει-
κόδ*[*ημος*])
SICILY:
—KENTORIPA: (2) 339 BC D.S. xvi 82. 4 (tyrant)

**Νικοδίκα**
EPIROS:
—BOUTHROTOS (PRASAIBOI): (1) a. 163 BC
*IBouthrot* 14, 15 (*SEG* XXXVIII 471)
—VOTONOSI (MOD.): (2) ?m. iii BC ib. XXIV 464
(*Νει-*: d. *Γείτων*)

**Νικόδικος**
AKARNANIA:
—ASTAKOS: (1) ii BC *IG* IX (1)² (2) 434, 13 (f.
*Διοκλῆς*); (2) ~ ib. l. 17 (s. *Διοκλῆς*)
KORINTHIA:
—KORINTH: (3) s. iii BC *Corinth* VIII (3) 38, 6

**Νικοδρόμας**
ARKADIA:
—TEGEA: (1) ii-i BC *IG* v (2) 163

**Νικόδρομορ**
Elis: (1) iii/ii BC *IvOl* 39, 37 (Perlman O.2)

**Νικόδρομος**
Achaia: (1) 146 BC *IG* IV (1)² 28, 141 (f. Νίκων: synoikos)
Aigina: (2) vi/v BC Hdt. vi 88; 90-1 (s. Κνοῖθος)
Argolis:
—argos: (3) iv-iii BC Unp. (Ch. Kritzas)
Elis: (4) m. iii BC *IG* v (2) 368, 57 (f. Φιλιστέας)
Elis?: (5) i BC *IvOl* 194; cf. Moretti, *Olymp.* 714 (Νικόδρομο[s]: f. —χος)

**Νικόδωρος**
Argolis:
—epidauros:
——Sinias: (1) c. 365-335 BC *IG* IV (1)² 103, 128, 134
Arkadia:
—mantineia-antigoneia: (2) b. 425 BC Ael., *VH* ii 23; *PMG* 738; Eust., *Comm.* 1860, 53

**Νικόθεος**
Argolis:
—troizen: (1) c. 130 BC *FD* iii (3) 124; cf. Stephanis 337 (f. Ἀριστόθεος)

**Νικόι**
Lakonia:
—hippola: (1) ii-i BC *IG* v (1) 1334 a + *AAA* 1 (1968) p. 119 no. 1 (locn.) (date—*LGPN*)

**Νικοκλέα**
Argolis:
—hermione: (1) i BC-i AD? *IG* IV (1) 730 V, 1 (d. Σωτηρίων)

**Νικοκλείδας**
Lakonia:
—sparta: (1) c. 30-20 BC ib. v (1) 141, 6; *SEG* XXXV 329 (date) (Bradford (2)) (s. Θεόδωρος); (2) c. 100-110 AD *IG* v (1) 97, 3; *SEG* XI 561, 4; 564, 3 (Bradford (3)) (I f. Τιβ. Κλ. Νικοκλείδας II); (3) ~ *IG* v (1) 97, 3; *SEG* XI 561, 4; 564, 3 (Bradford (1)) (Τιβ. Κλ. Ν.: II s. Νικοκλείδας I)

**Νικοκλῆρ**
Elis: (1) 101-109 AD *IvOl* 89, 6 (s. Νικίαρ); (2) 101-113 AD ib. l. 2; 90, 5 (Νεικοκλέους (gen.)—90: I f. Νικοκλῆρ II); (3) ~ ib. 89, 2; 90, 5 (Νεικοκλῆς—90: II s. Νικοκλῆρ I: X.)

**Νικοκλῆς**
Achaia: (1) 146 BC *IG* IV (1)² 28, 109 (s. Ὀνασικλῆς: synoikos)
Aigina: (2) vi/v BC Pi., *I.* viii, 61; cf. Klee p. 89 no. 26; (3) ii/i BC *Alt-Ägina* I (2) p. 43 no. 3, 5 (f. Τιμησίων); (4) ?i BC ib. p. 44 no. 11, 5 (s. Τιμησίων)
Akarnania:
—thyrreion: (5) iii-ii BC *SEG* XXVII 159, 6; cf. *PAE* 1977, pl. 244 a (s. M—); (6) ii BC *IG* IX (1)² (2) 329
Argolis:
—epidauros:
——(Dymanes): (7) 146 BC ib. IV (1)² 28, 9 (I f. Νικοκλῆς II); (8) ~ ib. l. 9 (II s. Νικοκλῆς I)
—hermione?: (9) iv BC ib. IV (1) 747 A, 7 (Νι[κ]οκλῆς: s. Αἰσχίνας)
—troizen: (10) ?146 BC ib. 757 B, 29 (f. Γνίκων)
Arkadia:
—kleitor: (11) f. ii BC *RPh* 1911, p. 125 no. 27, 3 (I f. Νικοκλῆς II); (12) ~ ib. l. 3 (II s. Νικοκλῆς I)
—megalopolis: (13) ii/i BC *IG* v (2) 443, 4, 22 (*IPArk* 32) (s. Νικόμαχος)
Arkadia?: (14) ?ii AD *IG* v (2) 505 (Νει-)
Epiros:
—ambrakia: (15) 271 BC ib. II² 3083, 9

Korinthia:
—korinth: (16) a. 191 BC *SEG* XXVI 392, 6 (s. Δια—)
—sikyon: (17) m. iii BC *RE* Supplbd. 7 (5) (Skalet 227) (tyrant); (18) 217 BC Nachtergael, *Les Galates* 65, 11 (Stephanis 1840) (Νικ[οκλῆς], Νικ[ίας]—Flacelière: s. Τιμόδαμος)
—sikyon?: (19) ?265-259 BC Nachtergael, *Les Galates* 4, 20 ([Νικοκ]λῆς: s. Τιμόδαμος)
Lakonia: (20) hell. *FGrH* 587 (Poralla² 559; Bradford (5)); (21) s. i BC *IG* II² 9149 (f. Ζωπύρα)
—akriai: (22) c. 80-70 BC Moretti, *Olymp.* 655-7; 660-1; *IG* VII 417, 16, 20, 50 (*IOrop* 525); *IG* IX (2) 529, 15; *RPh* 1911, p. 125 no. 27, 5; *BSA* 70 (1975) p. 133 (date) (Bradford (3)) (s. Νικάτας)
—geronthrai: (23) 72 BC *IG* v (1) 1114, 3 (f. Νίκανδρος)
—hyperteleaton*: (24) imp. ib. 1057
—kythera: (25) f. ii BC *IC* 2 p. 28 no. 12 A (s. [.]ικο—)
—sparta: (26) ii BC *SEG* XI 856, 4 (Bradford (15)) (f. Κρατηΐππίδας); (27) c. 25-1 BC *IG* v (1) 212, 19 (Bradford (13)) (f. Ἀριστόδαμος); (28) i BC/i AD *BSA* 89 (1994) pp. 433-4 no. 2, 2 (f. —ορ—ος); (29) c. 1-10 AD *IG* v (1) 209, 1; *SEG* XXXV 331 (date) (Bradford (7)); (30) ~ *IG* v (1) 209, 25; *SEG* XXXV 331 (date) (Bradford (12)) (f. Ἀνδρόνικος); (31) ii AD *IG* v (1) 176, 2 (Bradford (14)) (f. Εὐδαιμονίδας); (32) c. 105-110 AD *IG* v (1) 97, 23; *SEG* XI 564, 23 (Bradford (1)) (Νεικοκλῆς—*SEG*: s. Δάμιππος); (33) c. 140-160 AD *IG* v (1) 112, 10 (Bradford (2)) (s. Κλέων); (34) c. 160-170 AD *IG* v (1) 109, 7 (Bradford (16)) (Νικοκλ[ῆς]: I f. Νικοκλῆς II); (35) ~ *IG* v (1) 109, 7 (Bradford (4)) (Νικοκλ[ῆς]: II s. Νικοκλῆς I); (36) f. iv AD *RE* (10) (*PLRE* I (-)); (37) m. iv AD *RE* (9); *PLRE* I (-); Seeck, *Libanius* pp. 221-2 (Bradford (11))
Messenia:
—messene: (38) f. iii BC *SEG* XLI 342, 12; cf. *PAE* 1991, p. 100 no. 8; (39) s. ii BC *SEG* XLI 341, 16 (f. Ἑξακέστας)
—thouria: (40) ii-i BC *IG* v (1) 1385, 30 (s. Ξενόδαμος)
S. Italy (Calabria):
—taras-tarentum: (41) m. iii BC Paus. i 37. 2; *IG* II² 3779, 1; *PP* 17027 (Stephanis 1839) (s. Ἀριστοκλῆς, f. Ἀριστοκλῆς)
Sicily:
—syracuse: (42) vi/v BC *FGrH* 556 F 50
—tauromenion: (43) ?ii/i BC *IG* XIV 421 D an. 14 (*SGDI* 5219) (I f. Νικοκλῆς II); (44) ~ *IG* XIV 421 D an. 14 (*SGDI* 5219) (II s. Νικοκλῆς I)

**Νικοκρατέα**
Argolis:
—phleious: (1) iii BC *IG* IV (1) 466

**Νικοκράτεια**
Aigina: (1) imp. ib. 135
Epiros:
—dodona*: (2) iv-iii BC *SGDI* 1561 B (*Syll*³ 1161) (Νικοκράτ[ει]α)

**Νικοκράτης**
Achaia: (1) 146 BC *IG* IV (1)² 28, 92 (f. Ἀνδρέας: synoikos); (2) ~ ib. l. 162 (f. Ἀριστοκράτης: synoikos)
—dyme: (3) iii BC *AJPh* 31 (1910) p. 399 no. 74 c, 2, 4 ?= (4); (4) ~ ib. l. 13 (f. Θεόδωρος) ?= (3)
Akarnania: (5) iii BC Pagenstecher, *Nekrop.* p. 51 no. 44 (*PP* 4027) (s. Τεισίμαχος)
Argolis:
—argos:

——(Paionidai): (6) ii/i BC *BCH* 33 (1909) p. 176 no. 2, 5 (f. Δαμοσθένης)
—epidauros: (7) c. 365-335 BC *IG* IV (1)² 103, 127, 130
—epidauros*: (8) c. 200-175 BC Peek, *NIEpid* 80 (f. Ἀριστόδαμος)
—hermione: (9) c. 245-236 BC *IG* IX (1)² (1) 25, 65 (f. Καλλίστρατος)
Elis: (10) m. iii BC ib. v (2) 368, 56 (Νι(κο)κράτης: f. Ἀλκέτας)
Epiros:
—bouthrotos: (11) ?ii BC *IBouthrot* 173 (Ugolini, *Alb. Ant.* 3 p. 121) (f. Φιλίαρχος)
—bouthrotos (prasaiboi): (12) a. 163 BC *IBouthrot* 25, 6; 28, 7 (*SEG* XXXVIII 483; 486); (13) ~ *IBouthrot* 28, 6 (*SEG* XXXVIII 486)
Lakonia:
—epidauros limera: (14) imp. *IG* v (1) 1009
—kythera: (15) imp. ib. 941 (I f. Νικοκράτης II); (16) ~ ib. (II s. Νικοκράτης I)
—sparta: (17) i BC-i AD ib. 745 (Bradford (2)) (s. Εὐδαιμοκλῆς); (18) s. i BC *IG* v (1) 92, 12 (Bradford (7)) (s. Πείσιππος); (19) imp. *SEG* XI 645, 2 (Bradford (21)) ([Ν]εικοκράτ[ης]); (20) c. 30-20 BC *IG* v (1) 141, 16; *SEG* XXXV 329 (date) (Bradford (14)) (f. Ἀριστονίκα); (21) c. 25-1 BC *IG* v (1) 210, 7 (Bradford (8)) (s. Σίπομπος); (22) i BC/i AD *BSA* 89 (1994) pp. 433-4 no. 2, 3 (s. Στέφανος); (23) ~ ib. l. 7 (s. Πτολεμαῖος); (24) ~ *RE* (2) (Poralla² 560; Bradford (11)); Cartledge–Spawforth pp. 177-8 (date) (Lat. Nicocrates); (25) i AD *IG* v (1) 297, 3; *Artemis Orthia* pp. 310-11 (date) (Bradford (9)) (s. Θεογένης); (26) i/ii AD *BSA* 89 (1994) p. 434 no. 3 (f. Τιμόλας); (27) c. 80-100 AD *IG* v (1) 147, 5 (Bradford (18)) (Νει-: f. Φιλονικίδας); (28) c. 80-120 AD *IG* v (1) 101, 4; 674, 3; *SEG* XI 610, 7 (Bradford (6)) (I f. Νικοκράτης II); (29) ~ *IG* v (1) 674, 3 (Bradford (6)) (II s. Νικοκράτης I); (30) c. 90-100 AD *SEG* XI 570, 3 (Bradford (1)) (Νει-: s. Διογένης); (31) c. 95-100 AD *SEG* XI 490, 2 (Bradford s.v. Δεξίμαχος (7)) (Δεξίμαχος ὁ καὶ Νεικοκράτης); (32) c. 100 AD *SEG* XI 515, 1; 536, 1; 626, 2 (Bradford (12)); (33) ~ *SEG* XI 536, 5 (Bradford (5)) (s. Νικομήδης) ?= (39); (34) c. 100-120 AD *IG* v (1) 103, 13; *SEG* XI 610, 8 (Bradford (3)) (Νει-: s. Νίκαρχος); (35) ~ *SEG* XI 606, 6 (Bradford (20)) ([Νι]κοκράτης); (36) c. 105 AD *SEG* XI 517, 3 (Bradford (15)) (Νει-: f. Εὔδαμος); (37) c. 105-110 AD *IG* v (1) 97, 9; *SEG* XI 564, 16 (Bradford (4)) (Νεικοκράτης—*SEG*: s. Νικόβουλος); (38) c. 120-130 AD *SEG* XI 544, 8; 579, 8? (Bradford (10)) (Κ. Σόσ. Νεικοκράτης); (39) c. 125 AD *SEG* XI 575, 2 (Νει-) ?= (33); (40) c. 150-160 AD *IG* v (1) 71 II, 11; 674, 3 (Bradford (17)) (Νεικοκράτης: I f. Νικοκράτης II); (41) ~ *IG* v (1) 71 II, 11; 101, 4; 674, 3; *SEG* XI 610, 7 (Bradford (6)) (Νεικοκράτης—71 and 101: II s. Νικοκράτης I); (42) c. 175-200 AD *IG* v (1) 89, 13 (Bradford (16)) (Νει-: f. Ἰούλ. Νίκανδρος); (43) ?359 AD *SEG* XI 465, 2 (Bradford (13)) (Νει-)
Leukas: (44) ii-i BC *Ep. Chron.* 31 (1994) p. 50 no. 6 (*AD* 45 (1990) Chron. p. 254 no. 6); (45) c. 167-50 BC *BMC Thessaly* p. 180 nos. 95-6 (coins)
S. Italy (Calabria):
—taras-tarentum: (46) iv/iii BC *IG* XIV 668 I, 4 (Landi, *DISMG* 194); (47) c. 272-235 BC Vlasto 863 (coin); (48) ~ ib. 883; 934; 1096-1100 (coin) (Evans, *Horsemen* p. 179 VIII D.2; p. 181 VIII N.1; p. 182 no. 6)
S. Italy (Lucania):
—herakleia: (49) ?iii-ii BC Landi, *DISMG* 220 (brick) ([Νι]κοκράτης)

**Νικοκράτις**
Argolis:
—epidauros: (1) iv/iii BC *IG* IV (1)² 200

ARKADIA:
—PHIGALEIA: (2) m. iii BC SEG XXIII 243

**Νικόλα**

SICILY:
—SELINOUS: (1) s. vi BC Arena, *Iscr. Sic.* I 20
(Dubois, *IGDS* 74; *IGLMP* 85); cf. *Scritti
Zambelli* p. 222 n. 7 (Ν[ι]ϙόλα, Ν[α]ϙόλα—
Manganaro, Μ[ι]κόλα—Gallavotti: m. Θεόξε-
νος)

**Νικολαΐδας**

ARGOLIS:
—TROIZEN: (1) iii BC *IG* IV (1) 753, 1 with
Add. (f. —νίας); (2) ?146 BC ib. 757 B, 8 (Νι-
κολ[α]ΐ[δ]ας)
ARKADIA:
—MEGALOPOLIS: (3) s. ii BC ib. v (2) 439, 71 (f.
Ἀρίστανδρος); (4) 104 BC ib. 444, 7 (*IPArk* 32)
(f. Μικυλίων)
ILLYRIA:
—BYLLIONES: (5) c. 200 BC *SEG* XXXV 680, 11;
cf. XXXVIII 541 (f. Νικάσιος)
KORINTHIA:
—KORINTH: (6) ?v BC Page, *FGE* 858; cf. Ebert,
*Gr. Sieg.* 26
LEUKAS: (7) hell. *IG* IX (1) 572 + *AM* 27 (1902)
p. 360
S. ITALY (CALABRIA):
—TARAS-TARENTUM: (8) v BC Paus. vi 10. 5 (f.
Ἴκκος)

**Νικολαΐς**

S. ITALY (CAMPANIA):
—MISENUM*: (1) ?ii AD *CIL* x 3456 (Lat. Aelia
Nicolais)

**Νικόλαος**

ACHAIA:
—DYME*: (1) c. 219 BC *SGDI* 1612, 47 (*Tyche*
5 (1990) p. 124) (Νει-: f. Δαμονίδας)
AIGINA: (2) imp. *IG* IV (1) 82 (s. Φίλαιος)
AITOLIA: (3) ?262 BC *FD* III (4) 357, 2
([Νικ]όλαος); (4) c. 220-200 BC *RE* (2)
—KALLION/KALLIPOLIS: (5) 175 BC *SGDI*
1843, 12 (s. Εὔβουλος)
—PHISTYON: (6) ii BC *IG* IX (1)² (1) 110 a, 4 (s.
Φανέας)
—POTIDANIA: (7) f. iii BC ib. 9, 12
—PROSCH(E)ION: (8) 250 BC ib. XI (2) 287 B,
127; XI (4) 1075 (s. Ἀγίας)
—THERMOS*: (9) s. iii BC ib. IX (1)² (1) 60 II,
18
AKARNANIA:
—MEDION: (10) c. 325-315 BC *Hesp.* 57 (1988)
p. 148 A, 46 (*SEG* XXXVI 331); cf. *Hesp.* 48
(1979) pp. 78 f. with pl. 22 c (s. Σώσανδρος)
—PALAIROS: (11) hell.? *IG* IX (1)² (2) 569, 2
—THYRREION: (12) hell.-imp. ib. 358
ARKADIA:
—PHENEOS: (13) c. 315-280 BC *FD* III (1) 39, 1
(Νικ[ό]λαος: s. Χορέας)
EPIROS: (14) 279 BC *IG* XI (2) 108, 18
(Stephanis 1846)
—BOUTHROTOS: (15) ii-i BC *IBouthrot* 196 (s.
Ὀλώϊχος)
—BOUTHROTOS (PRASAIBOI): (16) a. 163 BC ib.
17, 23 (*SEG* XXXVIII 474) (I f. Νικόλαος II);
(17) ~ *IBouthrot* 17, 23 (*SEG* XXXVIII 474)
(II s. Νικόλαος I); (18) ~ *IBouthrot* 28, 15
(*SEG* XXXVIII 486) (s. Λέων); (19) ~ *IBouthrot*
28, 30 (*SEG* XXXVIII 486) (f. Βόϊλλα); (20) ~
*IBouthrot* 28, 31 (*SEG* XXXVIII 486) (?s. Βόϊλ-
λα); (21) ~ *IBouthrot* 28, 38; cf. *SEG* XXXVIII
478 (f. Κλεοπτόλεμος); (22) ~ *IBouthrot* 29, 41;
(23) ~ ib. 39, 6 (*SEG* XXXVIII 498); (24) ~
*IBouthrot* 66, 7; 75, 6 (-λαιος—66); (25) ~ ib.
108 (s. Σωκράτης); (26) ~ ib. 128, 10 (s. Ἀνδρόνικος)
—Kestrinoi Barrioi: (27) a. 163 BC ib. 41, 1
(*SEG* XXXVIII 500) (f. Ἀριστόμαχος)

——Tharioi: (28) a. 163 BC *IBouthrot* 114, 10
(s. Νίκαιος) ?= (29); (29) ~ ib. 126, 7 ?= (28)
—DODONA*: (30) iv BC *PAE* 1967, p. 48 no. 1
—KAR(I)OPOI: (31) f. ii BC Cabanes, *L'Épire* p.
554 no. 33, 6 (*SEG* XXXVII 511) (f. Λυσανίας)
—KELAITHOI: (32) c. 230-200 BC *BCH* 45
(1921) p. 16 III, 28 (s. Ἀρχῖνος: reading—
Oulhen)
—OPHYLLEIS: (33) f. ii BC *IBouthrot* 6, 7-8
(*SEG* XXXVIII 468) (f. Τιμαγόρα)
—VOTONOSI (MOD.): (34) f. iii BC ib. XXIV 457
a (f. Ἄγέλαος)
ILLYRIA:
—BYLLIONES: (35) c. 200 BC ib. XXXV 680, 9;
cf. XXXVIII 541 ([Νι]κόλαος: s. Πευκόλαος)
—BYLLIONES BYLLIS: (36) iii BC ib. 529 (f. Φι-
λιστίων)
KERKYRA: (37) iii-ii BC ib. XXXVI 568 (s. Λιμ-
ναῖος: locn.—Knoepfler)
KORINTHIA:
—KORINTH: (38) vii/vi BC *FGrH* 90 F 59. 1-2
(s. Περίανδρος); (39) b. 238 BC *IG* IX (1)² (1)
31, 190 (s. Νίκων)
—SIKYON?: (40) hell. *Memnonion* 209 (f. Ἐπι-
κράτης)
LAKONIA:
—SPARTA: (41) vi/v BC Hdt. vii 134. 2 (Poralla²
561) (f. Βοῦλις); (42) m. v BC Hdt. vii 137. 2;
Th. ii 67. 1 (Poralla² 562) (s. Βοῦλις)
S. ITALY (CAMPANIA):
—DIKAIARCHIA-PUTEOLI: (43) ?ii-iii AD *CIL* x
2148 (Lat. M. Aurelius Nicolaus)
—DIKAIARCHIA-PUTEOLI*: (44) imp. ib. 3073
(Lat. Nicolaus: freed.)
S. ITALY (LUCANIA):
—HERAKLEIA: (45) imp. *SEG* XXVI 1132 (f.
Ἀπολλώς)
SICILY:
—AKRAI: (46) hell.? Manganaro, *QUCC* forth-
coming nos. 30-1
—CORLEONE (MOD.): (47) byz. Ferrua, *NG* 525
—LILYBAION: (48) imp. *CIL* x 7213 (Lat. Ni-
colaus)
—SYRACUSE: (49) 413 BC D.S. xiii 19. 6; 28. 1-
3; (50) ii-i BC *NScav* 1913, p. 279 (Νεικόλεος:
s. Σεκονδία)

**Νικόλας**

ARKADIA:
—TEGEA: (1) f. iii BC *IG* v (2) 35, 21 (s. Κλέων);
(2) f. ii BC ib. 44, 19 (Νικόλᾳ[ς]: f. Βάκχιος);
——(Hippothoitai): (3) f. iii BC ib. 36, 19
([Νι]κόλας?)
LAKONIA:
—SPARTA: (4) ?s. ii BC *SEG* XI 470, 2, [12]
(Bradford (-)) (f. Κλεόξενος)

**Νικολέων**

AITOLIA:
—KASILIOI: (1) s. ii BC *SEG* XXV 621, 12 (f.
Λάμαχος)
—PAMPHIA: (2) c. 162 BC *IG* IX (1)² (1) 105, 9
—PHISTYON: (3) 163 BC ib. 101, 11; 102, 2; 103,
3 ?= (4)
—PHISTYON?: (4) c. 162 BC ib. 106, 6, 9 ?= (3)

**Νικόλεως**

ILLYRIA:
—LYCHNIDOS: (1) ii-iii AD *GVI* 1943, 7 (f.
Ἀπτυρίς)

**Νικόλος**

AITOLIA:
—KALYDON: (1) iii BC *IG* IX (1)² (1) 148, 2
([Ν]εικόλου (gen.))

**Νικόλοχος**

ARGOLIS:
—EPIDAUROS:
——(Hysminatai): (1) 146 BC ib. IV (1)² 28, 164
(f. Σώσανδρος)

——(Hysminatai?): (2) iii/ii BC ib. 335, 1 (s. Πα-
τροκλείδας) ?= (3); (3) ~ ib. l. 3 (f. Πατροκλεί-
δας) ?= (2)
ARKADIA: (4) 263 BC ib. XI (2) 113, 25
(Stephanis 1849)
—MEGALOPOLIS: (5) 360 BC *CID* II 4 III, 53,
55 (s. Πρόξενος)
LAKONIA:
—GERENIA: (6) v BC *IG* v (1) 1337 (Poralla²
563) (Νικόλοχος: f. Μαλανίδας)
—SPARTA: (7) v/iv BC X., *HG* v 1. 6-7; v 1. 25;
v 4. 65; Polyaen. iii 10. 4, 12 (Poralla² 564)
SICILY:
—SYRACUSE?:
——(Περ.): (8) hell. Manganaro, *PdelP* forth-
coming no. 4 I, 3 (f. Ἀγέλοχος)

**Νικομᾶς**

EPIROS:
—BOUTHROTOS (PRASAIBOI): (1) a. 163 BC
*IBouthrot* 32, 21; 42, 9 (*SEG* XXXVIII 491;
501) (Νικόμαχος—42)

**Νικομάχα**

EPIROS:
—BOUTHROTOS (PRASAIBOI): (1) a. 163 BC
*IBouthrot* 15, 16 (*SEG* XXXVIII 472); (2) ~
*IBouthrot* 29, 21 (*SEG* XXXVIII 487); (3) ~
*IBouthrot* 38, 7 (*SEG* XXXVIII 497)

**Νικομάχη**

ARKADIA:
—MEGALOPOLIS?: (1) ii AD *IG* v (2) 495 (d. Ἀριστόθεμις)

**Νικόμαχος**

ACHAIA:
—KARYNEIA: (1) 215 BC *SEG* XV 113, 33
(*IRhamnous* 41) (s. Σώστρατος)
AIGINA: (2) ?i BC *Alt-Ägina* I (2) p. 44 no. 7
(Νικόμα[χος])
AITOLIA: (3) ?274 BC *FD* III (1) 83, 2
(Flacelière p. 387 no. 5 a); *CID* II 124, [1]; (4)
c. 249-239 BC *FD* III (3) 167, 2 (Νικόμα[χος]);
(5) 212 BC *SEG* XL 141, 2 ([Νι]κόμαχος: s.
Νίκων)
—KALYDON: (6) m. ii BC *IG* IX (1)² (1) 137, 23
—THERMOS: (7) 214 BC ib. 177, 20 (s. Μάχων)
—THESTIEIS: (8) 213 BC ib. 96, 13
—TRICHONION: (9) s. iii BC ib. 117, 7
AKARNANIA:
—ASTAKOS: (10) ii BC ib. IX (1)² (2) 435, 19 (s.
Ἄνδρων)
—MATROPOLIS: (11) 198 BC ib. IX (2) 61, 4 (s.
Διοκλῆς)
—THYRREION: (12) ii BC ib. IX (1)² (2) 248, 5
(s. Λε—); (13) ~ ib. 250, [3], 15 (s. Πίμφων, f.
Πίμφων); (14) 197 BC Plb. xviii 10. 10; cf. *IG*
IX (1)² (2) p. XXIV, s.a. 210-207 BC
—TYRBEION/TORYBEIA: (15) ?273 BC *FD* III (3)
203, 5; cf. *BCH* 90 (1966) pp. 174 f. (locn.)
(f. Σάτυρος)
ARGOLIS:
—EPIDAUROS: (16) iii BC *IG* IV (1)² 352 (Νι-
κόμ[αχ]ος: f. —χις); (17) ii-i BC *SEG* XXX 398
——(Azantioi): (18) 146 BC *IG* IV (1)² 28, 28 (s.
Σωκρατίδας)
—EPIDAUROS*: (19) ?c. 415-400 BC Peek, *IA-
Epid* 64, 7; *LSAG²* p. 182 no. 19 (date) (Νι-
κόμα[χος])
ARKADIA:
—HERAIA: (20) c. 230-200 BC *BCH* 45 (1921) p.
12 II, 76
—MEGALOPOLIS: (21) hell. *IG* v (2) 469 (20)
(tile); (22) ii/i BC ib. 443, 4, 22 (*IPArk* 32)
(II s. Νικόμαχος I, f. Νικοκλῆς); (23) ~ *IG* v
(2) 443, 5, 22 (*IPArk* 32) (I f. Νικόμαχος II)
—STYMPHALOS?: (24) iii BC *IG* v (2) 354, 5
(Νι[κό]μαχος: s. Νι—)
—TEGEA:
——(Apolloniatai): (25) s. iv BC ib. 41, 9
ARKADIA?: (26) i-ii AD ib. 508 (Νεικόμα[χος])
EPIROS: (27) 263 BC ib. IX (1)² (1) 17, 63 (f.
Σώσανδρος)

—ARBAIOI: (28) iii/ii BC Cabanes, *L'Épire* pp. 569 ff. no. 47, 4 (*SEG* XXVI 720) (f. *Νίκανδρος*)
—ATHAMANES: (29) 175 BC *SGDI* 1987, 7, 9 (slave/freed.)
—BOUTHROTOS (PRASAIBOI): (30) a. 163 BC *IBouthrot* 13, 16; cf. Ugolini, *Alb. Ant.* 3 p. 120; (31) ~ *IBouthrot* 14, 32 (*SEG* XXXVIII 471) (f. *Στρατονίκα*); (32) ~ *IBouthrot* 24, 1 (*SEG* XXXVIII 482) (s. *Φιλίσκος*); (33) ~ *IBouthrot* 29, 55 (*SEG* XXXVIII 487); (34) ~ *IBouthrot* 32, 21; 42, 9 (*SEG* XXXVIII 491; 501) (*Νικομᾶς*—no. 32); (35) ~ *IBouthrot* 36, 21 (*SEG* XXXVIII 495) (f. *Ἐπικράτης*); (36) ~ *IBouthrot* 106; (37) ~ ib. 135, 13 (f. —*ος*)
——Ancheropaioi: (38) a. 163 BC ib. 90, 7; 96, 5 (f. *Ἀπολλώνιος*)
——Dionioi: (39) a. 163 BC ib. 68, 13 (f. *Ἀριστόμαχος*)
——Tharioi: (40) a. 163 BC ib. l. 8 (f. *Μενοίτας*); (41) ~ ib. 100, 7 (s. *Πολέμων*) ?= (42); (42) ~ ib. 117, 4, 10; 168, 6 (*SEG* XXXVIII 469) ?= (41)
——Thymaioi: (43) a. 163 BC *IBouthrot* 141, 12 (s. —*κος*)
—DODONA: (44) iii BC Antoniou, *Dodone* Aa, 16; (45) ~ ib. l. 21; (46) ~ ib. Ab, 12
—DODONA*: (47) c. 300 BC *SEG* XXXV 668 (tile)
—KASSOPE: (48) ii BC Dakaris, *Kassope* p. 23 (f. *Λυκίσκος*)
—MOLOSSOI: (49) f. ii BC Cabanes, *L'Épire* p. 589 no. 75, 14 (*SEG* XXXVII 510) ([*Νι*]*κόμαχος*: f. *Ἀντίνους*)
—PHOINIKE: (50) iii/ii BC Cabanes, *L'Épire* pp. 569 ff. no. 47, 5 (*SEG* XXVI 720)
—SELIPIANA (MOD.): (51) inc. *AE* 1915, p. 77 no. 9, 1; Stählin p. 150 n. 5 (locn.) (s. *Μνασίας*)
—TALAONOI/TALAIANES: (52) iii-ii BC *SGDI* 1349, 9; cf. Cabanes, *L'Épire* p. 580 no. 53 (f. *Ἀνδροκος*)

ILLYRIA:
—APOLLONIA: (53) ii-i BC *IApoll* 132; (54) imp. ib. 94 (f. *Ζώσιμος*)
—BYLLIONES: (55) c. 200 BC *SEG* XXXV 680, 12; cf. XXXVIII 541 (*Νικ*[*όμ*]*αχος*: f. *Φιλιστίων*)
—DIVJAKA (MOD.): (56) hell. *Iliria* 1982 (1), p. 120 no. 44 (tile); cf. p. 123
—EPIDAMNOS-DYRRHACHION: (57) c. 250-50 BC *BMC Thessaly* p. 77 no. 181 (coin) (pryt.) ?= (58); (58) ~ Maier 314 (coin) (Ceka 40) (pryt.) ?= (57); (59) hell.-imp. *IDyrrh* 409 (f. *Τευταία*)
—KERKYRA: (60) hell. *IG* IX (1) 785-8; *AAA* 13 (1980) p. 291 (*SEG* XXXVIII 434 (tiles)) (*Νικόμαχ*[*ος*]—phot., *Νικοκλῆς*—*AAA*)

KORINTHIA:
—SIKYON: (61) iv BC *TCal* 1 C, 20 (s. *Ἀλκαῖος*); (62) 336 BC *CID* II 60, 9 (Skalet 228)

LAKONIA:
—SPARTA: (63) c. 1-10 AD *IG* V (1) 209, 15; *SEG* XXXV 331 (date); cf. Stephanis 1808 (Bradford (3)) (f. *Νικανδρίδας*); (64) c. 125-133 AD *SEG* XI 547 a, [9]; 547 b, 6; 547 c, 2; 575, 1 (Bradford (1)) (*Νει*-: s. *Ἁρμόνικος*); (65) c. 140-145 AD *SEG* XI 550, 5 (Bradford (4)) (I f. *Νικόμαχος* II); (66) ~ *SEG* XI 550, 5 (Bradford (2)) ([*Ν*]*εικόμ*[*α*]*χος*: II s. *Νικόμαχος* I)
—LEUKAS: (67) iv/iii BC Peek, *IAEpid* 14, 7 (f. *Ναυσιγένης*, *Εὔανδρος*); (68) hell.? *IG* IX (1) 573; (69) c. 167-50 BC BM coin 1896 7-3-225 (*Coll. Bunbury* 1 p. 110 no. 910); Naville sale 5 (18. 6. 1923) 1840 (coins)

MESSENIA:
—MESSENE: (70) c. 191 BC *IG* II² 2314, 27, 59; *SEG* XXII 484 (s. *Λεωνίδας*); (71) ii AD *IG* V (1) 1481
—PELOPONNESE: (72) m. iii BC ib. V (2) 368, 91 (s. *Ἀρι*—); (73) c. 230-200 BC *BCH* 45 (1921) p. 11 II, 32 (*Νικόμαχ*[*ος*])

S. ITALY (BRUTTIUM):
—RHEGION (NR.): (74) f. iv BC Dubois, *IGDGG* 1 42 (f. *Κλεαίνετος*)

S. ITALY (CAMPANIA):
—POMPEII: (75) i BC-i AD *CIL* IV 5014 (Lat. Nicom(achus))
—SALERNUM: (76) imp. *IItal* 1 (1) 91 (*CIL* X 646) (Lat. L. Veratius Nicomachus)

S. ITALY (LUCANIA):
—METAPONTION (NR.): (77) ?c. 525-500 BC Lazzarini 804 (Landi, *DISMG* 137; *CEG* I 396; *SEG* XXXIV 1004; XL 843); *LSAG*² p. 261 no. 16 (date) (potter)

SICILY:
—AKRAGAS: (78) ?470 BC Pi., *I.* ii 22
—KAMARINA: (79) f. v BC Cordano, *Tessere Pubbliche* 27 (Arena, *Iscr. Sic.* II 134 A) (s. *Σῖμος*)
—TAUROMENION: (80) c. 223-207 BC *IG* XIV 421 an. 18; 421 an. 34 (*SGDI* 5219) (s. *Μνᾶσις*); (81) c. 164-142 BC *IG* XIV 421 an. 77; 421 an. 86; 421 an. 99 (*SGDI* 5219); *IGSI* 4 II (III), 60 an. 77 (s. *Μνᾶσις*)

TRIPHYLIA:
—MAKISTOS: (82) iv/iii BC *SEG* XXXIX 628 (s. *Τεισαμενός*)

## Νικομένης

ACHAIA:
—DYME*: (1) c. 219 BC *SGDI* 1612, 15 (*Tyche* 5 (1990) p. 124) (s. *Τιμοφάνης*)
ARGOLIS:
—EPIDAUROS: (2) ?iii BC Peek, *IAEpid* 233; (3) iii BC *IG* IV (1)² 168, 2; *SEG* XVII 178, 4
——(Hylleis): (4) 146 BC *IG* IV (1)² 28, 51 (f. *Δαμοκλείδας*)
S. ITALY (LUCANIA):
—HYELE-VELIA: (5) 157 BC *ID* 1416 A I, 76; 1417 B I, 81; 1452 A, 52

## Νικομενίδας

LAKONIA:
—TEUTHRONE: (1) iii/ii BC *SEG* XXII 304, 4 (f. *Νικοτέλης*: date—*LGPN*)

## Νικομήδεια

S. ITALY (CAMPANIA):
—DIKAIARCHIA-PUTEOLI: (1) imp. *CIL* X 2205 (Lat. Cassia Nicomedia: m. *Καλλίνικος*)

## Νικομήδης

ACHAIA: (1) 146 BC *IG* IV (1)² 28, 81 (f. *Κέρδων*: synoikos)
AIGINA: (2) imp. ib. IV (1) 137 (*Νει*- νεώτ.)
AITOLIA:
—KALYDON: (3) a. 142 BC ib. IX (1)² (1) 137, 59
AITOLIA?: (4) iii BC *SEG* XVIII 244, 5 (*Νικομή*[*δη*]*ς*)
ARGOLIS:
—ARGOS: (5) ?277 BC *FD* III (1) 80 with Add. p. 384 (*Νικομή*[*δ*]*ης*: s. *Νικίας*) ?= (6); (6) ?254-253 BC Nachtergael, *Les Galates* 9, 24; 10, 22; cf. Stephanis 866-7 (f. *Ἐπικράτης*, *Ἐπικρατῖνος*) ?= (5)
—EPIDAUROS: (7) c. 290-270 BC *IG* IV (1)² 109 II, 146
ARKADIA?: (8) c. 200 BC *SEG* XVII 829, 2
EPIROS:
—KASSOPE: (9) ii BC ib. XXXIV 590; cf. XXXV 672 (s. *Παυσανίας*, f. *Παυσανίας*)
—NIKOPOLIS: (10) 13-12 BC *Ep. Chron.* 31 (1994) p. 42 no. 11 (*AD* 45 (1990) Chron. p. 257 no. 7) (-*μεί*-: I f. *Νικομήδης* II); (11) ~ *Ep. Chron.* 31 (1994) p. 42 no. 11 (*AD* 45 (1990) Chron. p. 257 no. 7) (-*μεί*-: II s. *Νικομήδης* I)
KERKYRA: (12) ?s. i BC *IG* IX (1) 789-91 (tiles)
KORINTHIA:
—SIKYON?: (13) 336 BC *CID* II 60, 22 (Skalet 229)
LAKONIA:
—SPARTA: (14) f. v BC Th. i 107. 2; D.S. xi 79. 5 (Poralla² 565) (s. *Κλεόμβροτος*, ?s. *Ἀγχιθέα*, *Ἀλκαθόα*, *Θεανώ*: regent); (15) c. 30-20 BC *IG*

v (1) 211, 40 (Bradford (1)) (s. *Νικίας*); (16) c. 100 AD *SEG* XI 536, 5 (Bradford (2)) (f. *Νικοκράτης*)
LEUKAS: (17) c. 167-50 BC *BMC Thessaly* p. 180 nos. 97-8; *SNG Cop. Epirus–Acarnania* 383 (coins)
MESSENIA: (18) viii/vii BC Paus. iv 14. 8 (?f. *Ἀριστομένης*, *Ἀγναγόρα*)
—MESSENE: (19) s. ii BC *BCH* 95 (1971) p. 544, 3, 11, 17 (s. *Τρίτων*)
—THOURIA: (20) ii-i BC *IG* V (1) 1385, 17 (s. *Ἀριστείδας*)
S. ITALY (CAMPANIA):
—HERCULANEUM*: (21) i BC-i AD *CIL* X 1403 g II, 7 (Lat. Ti. Iulius Nicomedes: freed.)
—SARNUM: (22) imp. ib. 1111 (Lat. Nicomedes: freed.?)
SICILY:
—AKRAGAS: (23) imp. *IG* XIV 262 (*Acragas Graeca* i p. 33 no. 4); cf. *SEG* XXXV 996 (*N. ὁ καὶ Διονῦς*—*IG*, *N. ὁ καὶ Ὄνυς*—de Waele)
—LEONTINOI: (24) ?v BC *QUCC* 78 (1995) 124 (vase) (*Νικομέ*[*δὲς*]—ed., *Νικομέ*[*νης*]?: s. -*μενις*)
ZAKYNTHOS: (25) ii/i BC *SBBerlAk* 1935, p. 713 n. 1 (*Νεικομήδ*[*ης*])

## Νικόνομος

LAKONIA:
—SPARTA: (1) s. i BC *IG* V (1) 870; 895 (tiles) (Bradford (-))

## Νικόξενος

ARGOLIS:
—ARGOS: (1) i BC/i AD *IG* IV (1) 633
KORINTHIA:
—KORINTH: (2) s. iv BC *Corinth* VIII (1) 11, 6 (f. *Λαμπρέας*)
MESSENIA:
—MESSENE: (3) s. ii BC *SEG* XLI 341, 6 (f. *Σώστρατος*); (4) i BC *IG* V (1) 1463, 1 (f. *Καλλίμαχος*) ?= (5); (5) ~ ib. l. 2 ?= (6) (4); (6) hell.-imp. *PAE* 1991, p. 106 no. 8, 6 (f. *Καλλίμαχος*) ?= (5)

## Νικοπόλη

SICILY:
—SYRACUSE: (1) iii-v AD *IG* XIV 145 (Strazzulla 86) (*N.*?—edd.)

## Νικόπολις

AKARNANIA:
—KOMBOTI (MOD.): (1) ii BC *IG* IX (1)² (2) 386
—THYRREION: (2) iii BC ib. 272
ARGOLIS:
—ARGOS: (3) iii BC ib. IV (1) 630 a
—EPIDAUROS: (4) iii AD Peek, *NIEpid* 88, 1 ([*Γ.*] *Α*[*ἴλ.*] *Ν*[*ικόπο*]*λις*)
ARKADIA:
—MANTINEIA-ANTIGONEIA: (5) ii BC *IG* V (2) 297 (*Νικόπολι*[*ς*])
—TEGEA: (6) ii AD ib. 181 (*Νει*-)
DALMATIA:
—ISSA: (7) iii BC *SEG* XXXV 691, 6 (*VAHD* 84 (1991) p. 256 no. 6) (s./d. *Ξενοκλῆς*)
EPIROS:
—AMBRAKIA: (8) ?ii BC *AD* 10 (1926) p. 67 fig. 4
—BOUTHROTOS (PRASAIBOI): (9) a. 163 BC *IBouthrot* 38, 11 (*SEG* XXXVIII 497); (10) ~ *IBouthrot* 43, 39 (*SEG* XXXVIII 502); *IBouthrot* 48, 4
ILLYRIA:
—EPIDAMNOS-DYRRHACHION: (11) hell.-imp. *IDyrrh* 72 (f. *Ἀγαθήμερος*)
—LYCHNIDOS: (12) iii-iii AD *Sp.* 71 (1931) p. 110 no. 266 (*SEG* XXXIX 603) (*Νει*-: s. *Ἀρίστων*, *Ἀννία*)
KORINTHIA:
—KORINTH: (13) ii-iii AD ib. XI 138 e, 3 (*Νικόπ*(*ο*)*λις*)

S. ITALY (APULIA):
—GNATHIA-EGNATIA: (14) i AD *Suppl. It.* 11 p. 44 no. 26 (Lat. Nicopo[lis])
S. ITALY (CALABRIA):
—BRENTESION-BRUNDISIUM: (15) imp. *NScav* 1894, p. 17 no. 1 (Lat. Nicopolis)
S. ITALY (CAMPANIA):
—MISENUM*: (16) ?ii AD *CIL* x 3433 (Lat. Flavia Nicopolis)
—POMPEII: (17) i BC-i AD ib. IV 8171; 8218 (Lat. Nicopolis)

**Νικοσάλης**

LAKONIA:
—TEUTHRONE: (1) iii/ii BC *SEG* XXII 304, 7 (date—*LGPN*)

**Νικοσθένης**

ARGOLIS:
—ARGOS: (1) iv-iii BC Unp. (Ch. Kritzas)
EPIROS:
—AMBRAKIA: (2) iv BC *BMC Corinth* p. 105 no. 16; Unp. (Oxford, AM) 21. 7. 1955 (Ravel, *Colts of Ambracia* p. 79 no. 181); Ravel, *Colts of Ambracia* p. 148 (coins) (Νικοσθέ(νης)—Ravel, Νικοσ(θένης)—*BMC*: her.?); (3) 360-338 BC ib. p. 79 no. 181; cf. pp. 147 f. (coin) (Νικοσθ[ένης]); (4) s. ii BC Cabanes, *L'Épire* p. 548 no. 19 (*SEG* XXVI 694) (f. Κάλλων)
ILLYRIA:
—BYLLIONES BYLLIS: (5) f. ii BC *BCH* 45 (1921) p. 22 IV, 37 (s. Κ—ων)
KORINTHIA:
—KORINTH: (6) c. 334 BC *FD* III (2) 191, 1 (*Syll*³ 449 B) (f. Ἀριστόνοος)
LAKONIA:
—HIPPOLA: (7) iii/ii BC *IG* v (1) 1336, 3 ([Νι]κοσθέ[νης]: f. Ξενοκλείδας)

**Νικοσθενίδας**

LAKONIA:
—SPARTA: (1) iii BC ib. 1317, 1 (Bradford (1)); (2) ~ *IG* v (1) 1317, 4, 7 (Bradford (2))

**Νικοστράτα**

ACHAIA:
—DYME: (1) ii-i BC *SEG* XI 1262 (d. Ἀλεξικλῆς)
AKARNANIA:
—THYRREION: (2) s. iii BC *IG* IX (1)² (2) 292
ARKADIA:
—ORCHOMENOS: (3) iii BC ib. v (2) 347
—TEGEA: (4) hell. ib. 562
ELIS:
—KYLLENE: (5) ?f. ii BC *BCH* 85 (1961) pp. 141-2
MESSENIA:
—KYPARISSIA?: (6) c. 200 BC *AD* 25 (1970) Chron. p. 174

**Νικοστράτη**

ARGOLIS:
—EPIDAUROS: (1) i-ii AD *IG* IV (1)² 727 + Peek, *IAEpid* 313 (Νει-: d. Ἀγαθοκλῆς)
—EPIDAUROS*: (2) i-ii AD ib. 272 (Νει-)
SICILY:
—SYRACUSE: (3) iii-v AD Agnello 19

**Νικόστρατος**

ACHAIA: (1) 198 BC *RE* (13) (Lat. Nicostratus); (2) 146 BC *IG* IV (1)² 28, 62 (s. Σωσίας: synoikos); (3) ~ ib. l. 64 (f. Νικίας: synoikos); (4) ~ ib. l. 75 (s. Νικάνωρ: synoikos)
—DYME*: (5) c. 219 BC *SGDI* 1612, 77 (*Tyche* 5 (1990) p. 124) (s. Διονύσιος)
—PATRAI: (6) c. 146-32 BC *BMC Pelop.* p. 23 nos. 12-13 (coin) (s. Καλλίστρατος)
—PELLENE: (7) ?ii-iii AD *SEG* XI 1274, 4 (Νει-)
AIGINA: (8) iii AD *IG* IV (1) 18 (Νει-: s. Ἐπαφρόδιτος)
AITOLIA: (9) 356 BC *FD* III (1) 146, 1 (f. Ξένιππος); (10) ?316 BC ib. III (4) 387, 2 (s. Φυρταῖος); (11) ?273 BC ib. III (2) 205, 2; (12)

?228-215 BC *SGDI* 2525, 4; (13) 214 BC *IG* IX (1)² (1) 31, 170 (f. Ἀπολλώνιος)
—KALYDON: (14) 185 BC ib. 71 (IX (1)² (3) 784) (s. Μικκέας)
—PHILOTAIEIS: (15) m. ii BC ib. IX (1)² (1) 107, 1
—POTANA: (16) 177 BC *SGDI* 2058, 6 (s. Ἀλέξων)
—RHADEOI: (17) f. ii BC *IG* IX (1)² (1) 96, 23 (s. Ἀρίστων) ?= (18); (18) c. 157 BC ib. 108, 8 ?= (17)
—TRICHONION: (19) c. 220-200 BC *RE* (12) (f. Δωρίμαχος)
AKARNANIA:
—THYRREION: (20) s. iii BC *IG* IX (1)² (2) 286; (21) ii/i BC ib. 341
ARGOLIS:
—ARGOS: (22) arch.? Paus. ii 22. 3; (23) m. iv BC *RE* (2); (24) ?iii BC *BCH* 28 (1904) p. 420 no. 1 (f. Δαμαίστρατος); (25) m. iii BC *IG* IV (1)² 96, 54 (Perlman E.3); Perlman p. 63 f. (date) (f. Σμύλος); (26) s. iii BC Plu., *Mor.* 760 A-B
——(Sphyreis): (27) c. 365-334 BC *IG* IV (1)² 103, 12, 44, 53; *CID* II 59 I, 25; 79 A I, 35; *BCH* 107 (1983) p. 272 n. 23 (ident., locn.)
—ARGOS*: (28) s. i AD *SEG* XLII 273 bis, 1 (f. Νικόστρατος II); (29) ~ ib. l. 1 (II s. Νικόστρατος I: katoikos)
—EPIDAUROS: (30) iv BC Peek, *NIEpid* 110 = *AD* 25 (1970) Mel. pp. 33-4 no. 7 (f. Νικάτας); (31) i BC-i AD? Peek, *NIEpid* 60 ([Νι]κόστρα[τος]: f. Τιμοκλῆς)
——(Azantioi): (32) 146 BC *IG* IV (1)² 28, 42 (f. Δαμάγητος)
——Pierias (Hysminatai): (33) c. 365-335 BC ib. 103, 95
——Stratitis: (34) c. 365-335 BC ib. l. 103
—EPIDAUROS*: (35) c. 370-360 BC Peek, *IAEpid* 52 B, 52, 69, 72-3; *BSA* 61 (1966) p. 272 no. 4 B II, 3
—TROIZEN: (36) iii BC *IG* IV (1) 824, 7, 8 (f. Ξενολαΐδας, Σωγένης)
ARKADIA:
—GORTYS: (37) 191-146 BC *ZfN* 9 (1882) p. 258 no. 1 (coin)
—HERAIA: (38) s. v BC Moretti, *Olymp.* 344 (s. Ξενοκλείδας)
—KLEITOR: (39) a. 212 AD *SEG* XXXI 347, 15 (Κλ. Ν.)
—MANTINEIA-ANTIGONEIA: (40) c. 230-200 BC *BCH* 45 (1921) p. 13 II, 113
—MEGALOPOLIS: (41) a. 369 BC *IG* v (2) 548 (Νικόστ[ρατος])
—TEGEA: (42) iv BC ib. 31, 12 (s. Ὀνάσιμος); (43) ii BC ib. 43, 11 (s. Πολ—)
——(Apolloniatai): (44) iv/iii BC ib. 38, 38 (f. Ἀλκιθοΐδας)
EPIROS:
—BOUTHROTOS: (45) imp. *AEp* 1978, no. 776 (Lat. Q. Caecilius Nicostratus)
—BOUTHROTOS (PRASAIBOI): (46) a. 163 BC *IBouthrot* 15, 6 (*SEG* XXXVIII 472); (47) ~ *IBouthrot* 15, 6 (*SEG* XXXVIII 472); (48) ~ *IBouthrot* 20, 2 (*SEG* XXXVIII 477); *IBouthrot* 47, 1 (s. Νικάνωρ); (49) ~ ib. 22, 22; 41, 8 (*SEG* XXXVIII 477; 479; 500) (s. Νικάνωρ, f. Νικάνωρ, Κλεόμητις); (50) ~ *IBouthrot* 45, 4-5; 49, 6 (s. Νικάνωρ, f. Νικάνωρ); (51) ~ ib. 123-5; 155 (*BCH* 118 (1994) p. 120 nos. 2-5)
——Porronoi: (52) a. 163 BC *IBouthrot* 36, 1 (*SEG* XXXVIII 495) (f. Νικάνωρ); (53) ~ *IBouthrot* 54, 3; 56, 3 (*SEG* XXXVIII 505; 507); *IBouthrot* 121, 3; 122, 3; 142, 3
—ORIKOS PYLLE: (54) imp. Patsch, *Sandschak Berat* p. 80 (Νεικόσστ(ρ)ατος)
ILLYRIA:
—EPIDAMNOS-DYRRHACHION: (55) c. 250-50 BC Maier 315-9; 330; Münsterberg p. 40; Nachtr. p. 16 (coin) (Ceka 41?; 117; 125; 129; 136; 186; 381) (pryt.); (56) ii-i BC *IDyrrh* 547 (tile) (Νει-); (57) hell.-imp. ib.

331 (Νικ[όστ]ρατος: s. Λυκίσκος); (58) imp. ib. 29 (Νει-)
ILLYRIA?:
—DAULIA: (59) f. ii BC *BCH* 45 (1921) p. 22 IV, 32; p. 65 n. 3 (locn.) (Νικόστ[ρατος]: f. Κλεύβουλος)
KERKYRA: (60) ?ii BC *IG* IX (1) 708 (f. Νικάνωρ); (61) ?ii-i BC ib. 792 (tile); (62) imp. ib. 963, 2-3 ([Ἀ]πολέ(ι)ος Νικόστ<τ>ρατος)
KORINTHIA:
—KORINTH: (63) s. iii BC ib. IV (1) 727 A, 6 (Perlman H.1) (s. Νίκανδρος); (64) i BC *IG* II² 9064 (f. Δικαιώ)
—SIKYON: (65) s. iii BC *FD* III (1) 107 + *SEG* XXIII 312 (s. Νίκων); (66) 134 or 130 BC *FD* III (2) 68, 27 = *IG* II² 1132, 67 (Skalet 230) (f. Διοίτας); (67) iv AD *IG* IV (1) 437, 2 (Skalet 231)
LAKONIA: (68) 194 BC *SGDI* 2068, 4, 6 (s. Νικαία: slave/freed.)
—OITYLOS: (69) iii/ii BC *IG* v (1) 1295, 5 (Bradford (5))
—SPARTA: (70) s. i BC *IG* v (1) 96, 10 (Bradford (8)) (Νικόστρα[τος]: f. Μέγιππος); (71) ~ *IG* v (1) 134, 1 (Bradford (4)) (s. Νικίας); (72) c. 25-1 BC *IG* v (1) 210, 3 (Bradford (1)) (s. Δίων); (73) c. 100-110 AD *SEG* XI 563, 5; 595, 2 (Bradford (9)) (f. Νικηφόρος); (74) c. 100-125 AD *IG* v (1) 659, 9 (Bradford (6)) (Ὠ(λος) Γαβίνιος Νεικόστρατος); (75) c. 125 AD *IG* v (1) 1314, 9 (Bradford (7)) (f. Ἀνδρίων); (76) ii/iii AD *IG* v (1) 548, 2 (Bradford (2)) (s. Διονύσιος); (77) ~ *IG* v (1) 548, 12 (Bradford (3)) (Νει-: s. Καλλικράτης, ?f. Διονύσιος)
MESSENIA:
—THOURIA: (78) s. iii BC *IG* v (1) 1386, 17; (79) ii/i BC ib. 1384, 1 (f. Νίκων)
S. ITALY (BRUTTIUM):
—RHEGION: (80) hell. ib. XIV 2400. 11 (tile)
S. ITALY (CALABRIA):
—LUPIAE: (81) i-ii AD Susini, *Fonti Salento* p. 150 no. 101 (Lat. C. Geminius Nicostratus)
S. ITALY (CAMPANIA):
—POMPEII: (82) i BC-i AD *CIL* IV 4804; (83) m. i AD *Impegno per Pompeii* 17b OS no. 4 (Castrèn 318. 24) (Lat. Popidius Nicostratus)
SICILY:
—SYRACUSE: (84) 410 AD Strazzulla 4 (Agnello 100; *GVI* 448; Wessel 1036); cf. *Riv. Arch. Crist.* 18 (1941) p. 219 no. 101
—SYRACUSE?:
——(Νητ.): (85) hell. Manganaro, *PdelP* forthcoming no. 4 II, 5 (f. Λυκίδας)
—TAUROMENION: (86) c. 193-167 BC *IG* XIV 421 an. 49; 421 an. 59; 421 an. 74 (*SGDI* 5219) (II s. Νικόστρατος I); (87) c. 192-167 BC *IG* XIV 421 an. 49; 421 an. 59; 421 an. 74 (*SGDI* 5219) (I f. Νικόστρατος II); (88) c. 185 BC *IG* XIV 421 an. 56 (*SGDI* 5219) (f. Ἀντίμαχος); (89) c. 147-144 BC *IG* XIV 421 an. 97 (*SGDI* 5219); *IGSI* 4 III (IV), 66 an. 94 (s. Ἀγάθων); (90) ?ii/i BC *IG* XIV [421 D an. 6] (*SGDI* 5219); *IGSI* 4 III (IV), 99 D an. 6 (s. Φίλων) ?= (93)
——(Ἴδομ.): (91) ii/i BC ib. 6 IV, 12 (I f. Νικόστρατος II); (92) ~ ib. l. 12 (II s. Νικόστρατος I)
——(Πεα.): (93) ?ii/i BC *IG* XIV 421 III (*SGDI* 5219) (s. Φίλων) ?= (90)

**Νικοτέλεια**

MESSENIA: (1) viii/vii BC Paus. iv 14. 7 (m. Ἀριστομένης, Ἁγναγόρα)

**Νικοτέλης**

ARGOLIS:
—ARGOS: (1) 356 BC *CID* II 31, 11; (2) imp. *SEG* XXIV 273; (3) c. 150-175 AD *AJA* 83 (1979) p. 295
—EPIDAUROS: (4) iii BC *IG* IV (1)² 205 (s. Κλεισθένης, ?s. Κλειταρώ); (5) 32-54 AD ib. 101, 46 + Peek, *IAEpid* 45; *IG* IV (1)² 602, 4; Peek,

*NIEpid* 76, 5 (*Τιβ. Κλ. Ν.*: s. *Εὔνομος*, f. *Εὔνομος*) ?= (*6*)

—EPIDAUROS?: (**6**) c. 45 AD *FD* III (1) 534, 6 (*Νει-*) ?= (*5*)

—EPIDAUROS*: (**7**) c. 370-365 BC Peek, *IAEpid* 52 A, 11

—TROIZEN: (**8**) ?146 BC *IG* IV (1) 757 B, 18 (*Ν[ικο]τέλης*: s. *Θεόπομπος*)

ILLYRIA:

—APOLLONIA: (**9**) c. 250-50 BC Maier 77 (Ceka 73); Münsterberg Nachtr. p. 13; *IApoll Ref. Bibl.* n. 81 (coin) (pryt.); (**10**) i BC Maier 152; cf. 126 (coin) (*Νικοτ[έ]λ[ε]ος* (gen.)—152, *Ἀκοτελος*—126 err.: pryt.)

—EPIDAMNOS-DYRRHACHION: (**11**) c. 250-50 BC Ceka, *Probleme* p. 151 no. 51 (coin) (pryt.) ?= (*12*); (**12**) ~ Maier 320-1; Münsterberg Nachtr. p. 16 (coin) (Ceka 42; 102; 212?) (pryt.) ?= (*11*); (**13**) hell.-imp. *IDyrrh* 430 (f. *Φιλαινίς*)

KERKYRA: (**14**) c. 500 BC *SEG* XXX 523

KORINTHIA:

—KORINTH: (**15**) 404 BC *FGrH* 558 F 1; Ael., *VH* ii 41; D.S. xiv 10. 3

LAKONIA:

—SPARTA: (**16**) s. i BC *IG* v (1) 93, 28 (Bradford (-)) (f. —*κράτης*)

—TEUTHRONE: (**17**) iii/ii BC *SEG* XXII 304, 3 (s. *Νικομενίδας*: date—LGPN)

MESSENIA:

—ASINE: (**18**) ii AD *IG* v (1) 1408 (s. *Ξέναρχος*)

—THOURIA: (**19**) f. ii BC *SEG* XI 972, 26 (s. *Δαμέας*)

## Νικοφάης

ARGOLIS:

—ARGOS:

——(Dmaihippidai): (**1**) ii/i BC *BCH* 33 (1909) p. 176 no. 2, 11 (f. *Θερσαγόρας*)

## Νικοφάνης

AKARNANIA:

—KORONTA: (**1**) hell. *AD* 25 (1970) Chron. p. 297 no. γ (f. *Ἀριστοφάνης*)

ARGOLIS:

—EPIDAUROS: (**2**) iv BC *IG* IV (1)² 249 = *SEG* XXXII 386; Peek, *IAEpid* 85; 324; cf. *PdelP* 48 (1993) pp. 394-5 ?= (*3*)

——Miltias (Azantioi): (**3**) c. 365-335 BC *IG* IV (1)² 103, 68 ?= (*2*)

—EPIDAUROS*: (**4**) i-ii AD Peek, *IAEpid* 279 ([*Νικο*]*φάνης*: s. *Νικάνωρ*)

ARKADIA:

—MEGALOPOLIS: (**5**) 223 BC Plb. ii 48. 4; 50. 3, 5

KORINTHIA:

—SIKYON: (**6**) vi/v BC *SEG* XI 244, 60 (-*νēς*); (**7**) s. iv BC *RE* (-) (Skalet 232) (painter)

SICILY:

—KAMARINA: (**8**) f. v BC Cordano, *Tessere Pubbliche* 43 (Arena, *Iscr. Sic.* II 136 A) (*Νικοφάν[ēς*]: f. *Πύρριχος*)

## Νικόφιλος

ACHAIA:

—PATRAI?: (**1**) imp.? Moretti, *IAG* p. 168

## Νικοφῶν

AITOLIA:

—THESTIEIS: (**1**) 213 BC *IG* IX (1)² (1) 96, 13

SICILY:

—SYRACUSE?: (**2**) ?v BC *NScav* 1956, pp. 154-6 (-*φῶν*)

## Νίκυλις

S. ITALY (BRUTTIUM):

—TERINA:

——(Ξα.): (**1**) c. 325-300 BC *IGSI* 21, 6 (*SEG* IV 73; Landi, *DISMG* 170) (s. *Ἱστιαῖος*)

## Νίκυλλα

ACHAIA: (**1**) iii BC *IG* XII (9) 822 (date—Knoepfler)

## Νίκυλλος

ILLYRIA:

—EPIDAMNOS-DYRRHACHION: (**1**) c. 250-50 BC Ceka, *Probleme* p. 151 no. 52 (coin); *Iliria* 1992, p. 159 no. 24 (tile) (pryt.) ?= (*2*); (**2**) ~ Maier 322-9; Münsterberg p. 260; Nachtr. p. 16; p. 40 (coin) (Ceka 60; 67; 76; 87; 176; 256; 311; 428; 439; 457) ([*Νίκ*]*υλλος*—60: pryt.) ?= (*1*)

SICILY:

—SELINOUS: (**3**) m. v BC Dubois, *IGDS* 36, 1 (Arena, *Iscr. Sic.* I 69) (s. *Κάποσος*)

## Νικύλος

ILLYRIA:

—EPIDAMNOS-DYRRHACHION: (**1**) hell.-imp. *IDyrrh* 154 (*Νει-*: f. *Γένθιος*)

MESSENIA:

—MESSENE: (**2**) c. 261 BC *IG* IX (1)² (1) 18, 16 (s. *Νικάσιππος*)

S. ITALY (CALABRIA):

—TARAS-TARENTUM: (**3**) c. 272-235 BC Vlasto 935-7 (coins) (Evans, *Horsemen* p. 182 VIII O.1; *Samml. Ludwig* 102)

## Νικῦς

S. ITALY (BRUTTIUM):

—KROTON: (**1**) s. vi BC *JNG* 33 (1983) p. 12 (coin graffito) (*Νικῦ* (gen.))

## Νικώ

AKARNANIA:

—PALAIROS: (**1**) iii BC *IG* IX (1)² (2) 499

—THYRREION: (**2**) iii BC ib. 273; Fraser–Rönne, *BWGT* pl. 24

ARGOLIS:

—HERMIONE: (**3**) iii BC *IG* IV (1) 728, 36; (**4**) ii-i BC ib. 732 IV, 19 (d. *Καλλιππίδας*)

ARKADIA:

—ALEA: (**5**) hell. ib. VII 2112

—KLEITOR: (**6**) imp. ib. v (2) 378

—ORCHOMENOS: (**7**) iii BC ib. 347

DALMATIA:

—ISSA: (**8**) iii BC *SEG* XXXV 686 (d. *Τιμασίων*)

EPIROS:

—BOUTHROTOS (PRASAIBOI): (**9**) a. 163 BC *IBouthrot* 32, 16 (*SEG* XXXVIII 491); (**10**) ~ *IBouthrot* 159

ILLYRIA:

—APOLLONIA: (**11**) ii-i BC *IApoll* 128 (*Νει-*); (**12**) ~ ib. 133; (**13**) ~ ib. 134 (d. *Βίων*); (**14**) imp. ib. 37

—EPIDAMNOS-DYRRHACHION: (**15**) hell.-imp. *IDyrrh* 332; (**16**) ~ ib. 333 (d. *Λαέτιος*)

KEPHALLENIA:

—PALE: (**17**) hell. *IG* IX (1) 646 (*Νικοι* (apogr.))

KERKYRA: (**18**) imp. *SEG* XXVII 182 bis (*Νει-*)

S. ITALY (CALABRIA):

—TARAS-TARENTUM: (**19**) hell.? *IG* XIV 2406. 60 (*RA* 1932 (1), p. 48 no. 109; Troisi, *Epigrafi mobili* 77 (loomweight)) (*Νίκως* (gen.))

S. ITALY (LUCANIA):

—LEUKANOI: (**20**) s. iv BC *IG* II² 9208

## Νικώι

LAKONIA:

—SPARTA: (**1**) hell.? ib. v (1) 250 (Bradford (-))

## Νίκων

ACHAIA: (**1**) 146 BC *IG* IV (1)² 28, 140 (I f. *Νίκων* II: synoikos); (**2**) ~ ib. l. 140 (II s. *Νίκων* I: synoikos); (**3**) ~ ib. l. 141 (s. *Νικόδρομος*: synoikos)

—DYME*: (**4**) c. 219 BC *SGDI* 1612, 25 (*Tyche* 5 (1990) p. 124) (f. *Λύκιος*)

AIGINA: (**5**) hell. *IG* IV (1) 142; (**6**) iii AD *FD* III (1) 469 + Robert, *OMS* I p. 22 (Stephanis 1785) ([*Αὐ*]*ρ. Νείκων*: I s. *Παράδοξος*, f. *Αὐρ.*

*Νίκων* II, *Αὐρ. Σεβῆρος*); (**7**) ~ *FD* III (1) 469 (*Αὐρ. Νείκων*: II s. *Αὐρ. Νίκων* I)

AITOLIA: (**8**) iii BC *ITrall* 33 B, 1 (s. *Ἀρχίας*); (**9**) iii/ii BC *Ag.* XVII 398 (f. *Καλλιχάρης*); (**10**) 212 BC *SEG* XL 141, 2 (f. *Νικόμαχος*)

—APERANTOI: (**11**) iv/iii BC ib. XVII 274, 1 (*L'Illyrie mérid.* 1 p. 111 fig. 9)

—DAIANES: (**12**) 161 BC *IG* IX (1)² (1) 100, 8

—PHOLAI: (**13**) s. ii BC *SBBerlAk* 1936, p. 364 no. 1, 1 (f. *Σῖμος*)

—PHYTAION: (**14**) s. iii BC *IG* IX (1)² (1) 24, 6 (s. *Νικίας*); (**15**) f. ii BC *BCH* 45 (1921) p. 22 IV, 46

AKARNANIA: (**16**) iv/iii BC *Thess. Mnem.* 216 (*IG* IX (1)² (2) *Νίκιππα*)

—ASTAKOS: (**17**) s. iv BC ib. IV (1)² 95, 63 (Perlman E.2); Perlman pp. 46-9 (date) ([*Ν*]*ίκων*: f. *Καλλέας*); (**18**) a. 229 BC *PAE* 1991, p. 92 no. 3, 21 (*IRhamnous* 24); *IRhamnous* 132; (**19**) ii BC *IG* IX (1)² (2) 435, 13 (s. *Ἵππαρχος*)

—PALAIROS: (**20**) iii/ii BC ib. 534 (f. *Τεισίππα*)

—STRATOS: (**21**) iv/iii BC Unp. (Lazaros Kolonos—E.L. Schwandner) (f. *Ἰσχόπολις*); (**22**) s. ii BC *IG* IX (1)² (1) 36, 14

ARGOLIS:

—ARGOS:

——(Dionysioi): (**23**) a. 316 BC *SEG* XIII 240, 2 (Perlman A.4) (s. *Ἀ—στις*)

—EPIDAUROS: (**24**) ?iv-iii BC *SEG* XXXIX 357 b; (**25**) imp. *IG* IV (1)² 447 (s. *Διοκλῆς*); (**26**) 364 AD Peek, *NIEpid* 55 (*Νεί-*: s. *Αἰσχύλος*)

—EPIDAUROS*: (**27**) c. 370 BC *IG* IV (1)² 102, 222; (**28**) c. 365-335 BC ib. 103, 109; (**29**) c. 340-320 BC Peek, *NIEpid* 19 A, 21 (*Νί[κ]ων*); (**30**) iii/ii BC *IG* IV (1)² 306 B (s. *Ἱαροκλῆς*: sculptor)

—HERMIONE: (**31**) iii BC ib. IV (1) 728, 25; (**32**) ~ ib. l. 30 (f. *Εὔκλεια*)

—TROIZEN: (**33**) c. 163-146 BC ib. IV (1)² 76, 1

ARKADIA:

—MEGALOPOLIS: (**34**) ?165 BC *FD* III (1) 48, 3, 5; *Syll*³ 585, 308 (Stephanis 1886) (s. *Νικίας*); (**35**) 143 BC *ID* 2593, 29

—TEGEA: (**36**) ii AD *IG* v (2) 55, 59 (*Νεί-*: s. *Ἀρίστων*); (**37**) ~ ib. l. 66 (*Νεί-*: s. *Τίμανδρος*); (**38**) 165 AD ib. 50, 27 (s. *Σωτήριχος*)

DALMATIA:

—ISSA: (**39**) f. ii BC Brunšmid p. 23 no. 10, 7 (f. *Ἀνδρέας*)

——(Pamphyloi): (**40**) iv/iii BC ib. p. 8, 32 (f. *Νικάνωρ*) ?= (*41*); (**41**) ~ ib. l. 33 (f. *Ὀρθων*) ?= (*40*)

ELIS: (**42**) i BC *IvOl* 68, 7 (?s. *Ἀ—*)

EPIROS: (**43**) ?255-254 BC Nachtergael, *Les Galates* 8, 80; 9, 65 (s. *Ἡράκλειτος*)

—AMBRAKIA: (**44**) iii-ii BC *Op. Ath.* 10 (1971) p. 64 no. 12, 3; cf. *VAHD* 84 (1991) p. 262 (f. *Ξενώ*); (**45**) ii BC Unp. (Arta Mus., inscr.)

—BOUTHROTOS (PRASAIBOI): (**46**) a. 163 BC *IBouthrot* 106 (f. *Ἀριστοκλῆς*); (**47**) ~ ib. 132, 9

——Opatai: (**48**) a. 163 BC ib. 97, 9 (f. *Φαλακρίων*)

ILLYRIA:

—APOLLONIA: (**49**) iii-ii BC *IApoll* 34 ([*Νί*]*κων*: f. *Εὔπραξις*); (**50**) c. 250-50 BC Maier 19 (coin) (Ceka 89) (money.); (**51**) ~ Maier 78 (coin) (Ceka 104) (pryt.); (**52**) ii-i BC *IApoll* 129 (*Νεί-*: s. *Μελάνθιος*); (**53**) ~ ib. 135

—EPIDAMNOS-DYRRHACHION: (**54**) iv/iii BC *IDyrrh* 10 (f. *Ἔννις*); (**55**) hell.-imp. ib. 231 (f. *Ζωσίμα*); (**56**) ~ ib. 425 (f. *Τρυφέρα*)

—GUREZEZE (MOD.): (**57**) hell. *Iliria* 1982 (1), p. 105 no. 8 = p. 120 no. 43 (tile)

KERKYRA: (**58**) c. 240-220 BC *IG* VII 369, 2 (*IOrop* 155) (f. *Εὐπυρίων*)

KORINTHIA:

—KORINTH: (**59**) c. 570-550 BC Amyx 58. 1 (vase) (-*ϙōν*: her.?); (**60**) hell. *IG* II² 9072 (f. *Νικίας*); (**61**) iii BC ib. IV (1)² 98, 12; (**62**) b. 238 BC ib. IX (1)² (1) 31, 190 (f. *Νικόλαος*);

**(63)** i AD *Corinth* IV (2) p. 167 no. 383; *Ag.* VII p. 73 no. 16 (lamp)
—SIKYON: **(64)** iv/iii BC *SEG* XII 218 (s. Ἄνδρων); **(65)** s. iii BC *FD* III (1) 107 + *SEG* XXIII 312 (f. Νικόστρατος); **(66)** ?165 BC *Syll*³ 585, 311 (Skalet 233) (f. Θεόπομπος)
LAKONIA: **(67)** ?254 BC Nachtergael, *Les Galates* 9, 59 (Bradford (1); Stephanis 1881) (s. Εὐμαθίδας)
—SPARTA: **(68)** c. 400-375 BC *IG* V (1) 1232, 3 (Poralla² 566); **(69)** iv/iii BC *SEG* XI 668 (vase); *BSA* 30 (1928-30) p. 247 fig. 4, 3 (Poralla² 566a) (Ν[ί]κων); **(70)** c. 80 BC *IG* VII 416, 56 (*IOrop* 523; Bradford (5)) (f. Νικόδαμος); **(71)** imp. *IG* V (1) 1593, 3 (Bradford (2)); **(72)** c. 1-10 AD *IG* V (1) 209, 14; *SEG* XXXV 331 (date); cf. Stephanis 1341 (Bradford (4)) (f. Καλλικράτης); **(73)** 359 AD *SEG* XI 464, 6 (Bradford (3)) (Νεί-)
MESSENIA:
—KORONE: **(74)** ii BC *IG* V (1) 1397, 3; **(75)** 246 AD ib. 1398, 39 (Αὐρ. Νείκων); **(76)** ~ ib. l. 46 (Κλ. Νείκων); **(77)** ~ ib. l. 49 (Αὐρ. Νείκων)
—MESSENE: **(78)** c. 140 BC *IvOl* 52, 61 (II s. Νίκων I); **(79)** ~ ib. l. 62 (I f. Νίκων II); **(80)** ii/i BC *SEG* XXIII 224; *PAE* 1988, p. 59 (date) (f. Εὔφορβος); **(81)** ?i BC ib. 1969, p. 100 a, 3; **(82)** ?i/ii AD *SEG* XLI 338, 2-3 (Νεί[κ]ων); **(83)** 174 AD ib. 337, 7 (Κάταρος Ἰούλ. Νείκων)
—PHARAI: **(84)** b. 78 BC *RE* (12)
—THOURIA: **(85)** f. ii BC *SEG* XI 972, 62 (f. Ἀρίστων); **(86)** ii/i BC *IG* V (1) 1384, 1 (s. Νικόστρατος); **(87)** ~ ib. l. 16 (s. Δάμων); **(88)** i BC *SEG* XI 974, 29
S. ITALY (BRUTTIUM):
—RHEGION: **(89)** imp. *IG* XIV 2400. 12 (tile)
—(Τεισ.): **(90)** ii-i BC ib. 614 (f. Νίκανδρος); **(91)** s. ii BC ib. 615, 8; *Klearchos* 21 (1979) pp. 83-96 (date) (f. Αἰνησώ)
S. ITALY (CALABRIA):
—TARAS-TARENTUM: **(92)** iv/iii BC *RE* (20); **(93)** c. 302-280 BC Vlasto 701-3 (Evans, *Horsemen* p. 135 VI E.2 (coin)); **(94)** 213-209 BC *RE* (10) (N. ὁ ἐπικαλ. Πέρκων); **(95)** imp.? *IG* XIV 2406. 61
—URIA: **(96)** iii/ii BC Santoro, *NSM* I p. 163 no. IM 0.317 (vase) (s. Δάμων)
S. ITALY (CAMPANIA):
—DIKAIARCHIA-PUTEOLI*: **(97)** imp. *CIL* X 2175 (Lat. C. Brinnius Nicon: freed.)
—KYME: **(98)** 251 AD ib. 3699 II, 27 (Lat. L. Gentius Nico)
—POMPEII*: **(99)** 15 AD ib. IV 3340. 1, 2 (Castrèn 315. 9) (Lat. [M.] Pomponius Nicon: freed.)
—SALERNUM: **(100)** iii AD *IItal* I (1) 36 (*CIL* X 563) (Lat. Aur. Nico)
S. ITALY (LUCANIA):
—HERAKLEIA: **(101)** iii-ii BC *SEG* XXXIII 765 (f. Φιλημένα)
—(Ἀσ. βότρυς): **(102)** iv/iii BC *IGSI* 1 I, 96 (*DGE* 62; Uguzzoni–Ghinatti I) (f. Τίμαρχος)
—VOLCEI*: **(103)** s. i BC *IItal* III (1) 68 (*CIL* X 398); cf. Frenz p. 109 no. 54 (date) (Lat. M. Plotius Nico: freed.)
SICILY: **(104)** ii/i BC *NScav* 1959, p. 316 no. 4; *Meligunis-Lipara* 2 p. 160 T. 443; cf. *Kokalos* 32 (1986) p. 235 no. 60 (tiles)
—AKRAGAS: **(105)** ?i BC *RE* (17) (doctor)
—AKRAI: **(106)** iii-ii BC *SGDI* 3242, 3 (*Akrai* p. 157 no. 8) (s. Νυμφόδωρος); **(107)** ~ *SGDI* 3242, 9 (*Akrai* p. 157 no. 8) (I f. Νίκων II); **(108)** ~ *SGDI* 3242, 9 (*Akrai* p. 157 no. 8) (II s. Νίκων I)
—DREPANON: **(109)** f. i BC Cic., *In Verr.* II iv 37 (Lat. Nico: f. Αὖλος Κλώδιος Ἀπολλώνιος)
—KAMARINA: **(110)** ?iv/iii BC *SEG* XXXIV 940, 8 (Dubois, *IGDS* 124; *PdelP* 44 (1989) p. 192 no. 3; Cordano, 'Camarina VII' 139) (f. Ἡράκλειος); **(111)** ~ *SEG* XXXIV 940, 9 (Dubois, *IGDS* 124; *PdelP* 44 (1989) p. 192 no. 3;

Cordano, 'Camarina VII' 135) ([Ν]ίκων— Manganaro, Μύων—Cordano and Dubois: s. Εὐθυμένης)
—KATANE: **(112)** imp. *CIL* X 7086 (Lat. Publicius Nicon); **(113)** iii AD *IG* XIV 2412. 6 (seal) (Αὐρ. N.)
—SYRACUSE: **(114)** hell.? *Syringes* 936; **(115)** iii-v AD *IG* XIV 96 (Strazzulla 37; Agnello 2; Wessel 864); **(116)** ~ *IG* XIV 172 (Strazzulla 72; Agnello 11; Wessel 872); cf. Ferrua, *NG* 174; **(117)** ~ *NScav* 1918, p. 275 (Wessel 636); **(118)** ~ Strazzulla 209
—SYRACUSE?:
——(Πλη.): **(119)** hell. Manganaro, *PdelP* forthcoming no. 4 I, 8 (f. Ἀριστέας)
—TAUROMENION: **(120)** c. 216 BC *IG* XIV 421 an. 25 (*SGDI* 5219); **(121)** c. 201 BC *IG* XIV 421 an. 40 (*SGDI* 5219) (f. Ζωπυρίσκος)

**Νικώνδας**
EPIROS:
—DODONA*: **(1)** hell. *SEG* XIX 426 b

**Νικωνίδας**
AITOLIA:
—POTIDANIA: **(1)** m. ii BC *SBBerlAk* 1936, p. 371 b, 16 (*SEG* XLI 528 B) (s. Νικόβουλος)
KORINTHIA:
—SIKYON: **(2)** ?257-255 BC Nachtergael, *Les Galates* 7, 70; 8, 73 (Skalet 234); cf. Stephanis 1195 (-δης: f. Θερσαίνους)
LEUKAS: **(3)** ii-i BC *Ep. Chron.* 31 (1994) p. 50 no. 6 (*AD* 45 (1990) Chron. p. 254 no. 6)
S. ITALY (CALABRIA):
—TARAS-TARENTUM: **(4)** iv-iii BC Wuilleumier, *Tarente* p. 394 (terracotta)

**Νικώνυμος**
ARGOLIS:
—HERMIONE: **(1)** i BC-i AD? *IG* IV (1) 730 III, 9 (Νικώνυμο[ς]: s. Κάλλιππος)
MESSENIA:
—THOURIA: **(2)** hell. *BMC Pelop.* p. 119 nos. 2-3 (coin); **(3)** ii/i BC *IG* V (1) 1384, 9 (f. Σόλων)

**Νικώττας**
S. ITALY (CALABRIA):
—TARAS-TARENTUM: **(1)** c. 302-280 BC Vlasto 699 (coin) (Evans, *Horsemen* p. 134 VI E.1)

**Νίνιος**
SICILY:
—GELA-PHINTIAS: **(1)** ii/i BC *SEG* XXXI 837, 6

**Νίννιον?**
SICILY: **(1)** ?f. iii BC *ZPE* 111 (1996) p. 136 no. 4 (Νίνν[ιον])

**Νῖνος**
S. ITALY (CAMPANIA):
—POMPEII: **(1)** i BC-i AD *CIL* IV 2336 (Lat. Ninus)

**Νίνων**
S. ITALY (BRUTTIUM):
—KROTON: **(1)** v BC *RE* Supplbd. 9 (-)

**Νίξα**
S. ITALY (CALABRIA):
—TARAS-TARENTUM: **(1)** hell.? *RA* 1932 (1), p. 39 no. 32 (loomweight)

**Νιξώ**
S. ITALY (CAMPANIA):
—FRATTE DI SALERNO (MOD.): **(1)** f. v BC *SEG* XXXVII 817 B (vase) (Arena, *Iscr. Sic.* IV 33) (-ξό)

**Νιοβίς**
S. ITALY (CAMPANIA):
—POMPEII: **(1)** i BC-i AD *CIL* IV 1800 (Lat. Niobis)

**Νιράχας**
ARGOLIS:
—ARGOS: **(1)** ?c. 590-570 BC *IG* IV (1) 564; *LSAG*² p. 168 no. 6 (date)

**Νισαία**
MESSENIA:
—KORONE: **(1)** ?i BC *IG* V (1) 1396, 1

**Νίσις**
SICILY:
—MEGARA HYBLAIA: **(1)** f. vi BC Dubois, *IGDS* 19 (Arena, *Iscr. Sic.* I 2) (f. Ἀριστίων)

**Νίσος**
EPIROS: **(1)** iv BC *RE* (4) (s. Ἀλκέτας)
MESSENIA:
—KORONE: **(2)** 246 AD *IG* V (1) 1398, 85 (Αὐρ. Νεῖσος)
S. ITALY (CAMPANIA):
—POMPEII: **(3)** i BC-i AD *CIL* IV 4514, 13 (Lat. Nisus)

**Νιφάς**
S. ITALY (APULIA):
—CANUSIUM*: **(1)** imp. *Epig. Rom. di Canosa* 128 (*CIL* IX 376) (Lat. Niphas: freed.)

**Νοημία**
S. ITALY (LUCANIA):
—EBURUM: **(1)** imp. *Rass. Stor. Salern.* 24-5 (1963-4) pp. 94-5 (Lat. Noemia)

**Νοήμων**
LAKONIA:
—SPARTA: **(1)** f. iii AD *IG* V (1) 549, 12 (Bradford (-)) (f. Αὐρ. Ἀφροδισία)

**Νοήτη**
S. ITALY (CAMPANIA):
—POMPEII: **(1)** i BC-i AD *CIL* IV 168; 1970-1; 8040 (Lat. Noete)

**Νόητος**
LAKONIA:
—SPARTA: **(1)** c. 140-160 AD *IG* V (1) 69, 26; 70, 4; 71 III, 11; *SEG* XXX 410, [25] (Bradford (-)) (Γ. Νερβίνιος N.)
S. ITALY (CAMPANIA):
—HERCULANEUM: **(2)** i BC-i AD *CIL* IV 10604 c (Lat. Noetus); **(3)** ~ *Cron. Erc.* 7 (1977) pp. 114-15 A (Lat. Noetus)
—POMPEII: **(4)** i BC-i AD *CIL* IV 8854 d (Lat. Noetus)

**Νοήτυλος**
S. ITALY (CAMPANIA):
—HERCULANEUM: **(1)** i BC-i AD *RAAN* 33 (1958) p. 244 no. 18; cf. *Cron. Erc.* 8 (1978) p. 152 no. 51 (Lat. No[e]tul[us])

**Νόθη**
S. ITALY (CAMPANIA):
—POMPEII: **(1)** i BC-i AD *CIL* IV 3711 (Lat. Nothe (sinistr.))
—POMPEII*: **(2)** 61 AD ib. 154; 155 (Castrèn 320. 9) (Lat. Poppaea Note: freed.)

**Νοθίς**
S. ITALY (APULIA):
—VENUSIA: **(1)** i AD *Epigraphica* 35 (1973) p. 150 no. 12 (*Museo di Venosa* p. 146 no. 1) (Lat. Nothis)

**Νόθος**
S. ITALY (CALABRIA):
—BRENTESION-BRUNDISIUM: **(1)** imp. *Epigraphica* 25 (1963) p. 41 no. 15; cf. 42 (1980) p. 154 (Lat. Nothu[s])
S. ITALY (CAMPANIA):
—DIKAIARCHIA-PUTEOLI: **(2)** imp. *CIL* X 2415 (Lat. Nothus)

**Νόϊλλα**
S. Italy (Campania): (**1**) iii/ii BC *IG* II² 8953

**Νοῖος**
Argolis:
—ARGOS: (**1**) 328-324 BC *CID* II 95, 13; 97, 23; 102 II B, 28 (s. Νοίων)

**Νοίων**
Argolis:
—ARGOS: (**1**) 345-324 BC ib. 31, 77; 32, 34; 75 II, 44; 97, 23; 102 II B, [28] (f. Νοῖος)

**Νοκερία**
Sicily:
—SYRACUSE (NESOS): (**1**) iii-v AD *IG* XIV 153 (Strazzulla 94; Agnello 9; Wessel 874)

**Νόμας**
Messenia:
—THOURIA: (**1**) f. ii BC *SEG* XI 972, 59 (s. Ἀρίσταρχος) ?= (*2*); (**2**) c. 182 BC ib. l. 61 (f. Καλλίστρατος) ?= (*1*)

**Νομάς**
S. Italy (Apulia):
—CANUSIUM: (**1**) imp. *Epig. Rom. di Canosa* 164 (*CIL* IX 394) (Lat. Claudia Nomas)
S. Italy (Campania):
—POMPEII: (**2**) i BC-i AD ib. IV 5308 (Lat. Nomas)
S. Italy (Lucania):
—VOLCEI: (**3**) imp. *IItal* III (1) 64 (*CIL* X 394) (Lat. Otacilia Nomas)

**Νομεύς**
Argolis:
—ARGOS: (**1**) c. 220-200 BC Peek, *IAEpid* 331, 1 (Perlman E.5) ([Νο]μεύς: f. Μνασίστρατος)

**Νόμη**
S. Italy (Campania):
—NEAPOLIS: (**1**) 71 AD *ILS* 6460 (*INap* 84) (Lat. Plotia Nome)
—POMPEII: (**2**) i BC-i AD *CIL* IV 1462 (Lat. Nome); (**3**) ~ ib. 4695 (Lat. Nome)
Sicily:
—THERMAI HIMERAIAI: (**4**) imp. ib. X 7425 (*ILat. Term. Imer.* 123) (Lat. Modia Nom[e]?)

**Νομία**
S. Italy (Apulia):
—BARION: (**1**) imp. *CIL* IX 293 (Lat. Caelidia Nomia)

**Νόμιος**
Arkadia:
—TEGEA: (**1**) i BC *SEG* XI 1079
S. Italy (Calabria):
—BRENTESION-BRUNDISIUM: (**2**) imp. *NScav* 1889, p. 167 g (*Eph. Ep.* VIII 37) = *Epigraphica* 25 (1963) p. 78 no. 80; cf. 42 (1980) p. 157 (Lat. Nomius)

**Νόμιππος**
Arkadia:
—KLEITOR: (**1**) c. 362-300 BC BM coin 1920 8-5-1392; *SNG Cop. Argolis–Aegean Islands* 223 (coin) (Νόμιπ[πος])

**Νομοκλῆς**
Illyria:
—EPIDAMNOS-DYRRHACHION: (**1**) hell. *IDyrrh* 334 (s. Νουμήνιος)

**Νομωνία**
Argolis:
—KLEONAI: (**1**) ?i AD *SEG* XI 297, 1
Arkadia:
—MEGALOPOLIS: (**2**) ii-i BC *IG* IV (1) 491 (*GVI* 1735)

**Νόννος**
Korinthia:
—KORINTH: (**1**) hell. *SEG* XI 213 (vase)

**Νόσος**
S. Italy (Lucania):
—VOLCEI: (**1**) ii-i BC *Arch. Class.* 24 (1972) p. 270 (terracotta) (Νοσ(σ)ός?)

**Νοσσίς**
S. Italy (Bruttium):
—LOKROI EPIZEPHYRIOI: (**1**) iv/iii BC *RE* (-); *HE* 2791 ff. (d. Θευφιλίς)

**Νοστία**
Achaia:
—PATRAI: (**1**) ?ii BC *Achaean Grave Stelai* 20 (d. Ἀριστόδαμος)

**Νόστων**
Arkadia:
—MANTINEIA-ANTIGONEIA: (**1**) iv/iii BC *SEG* XXVI 330 (s. Κλεόμαχος)

**Νουΐα**
S. Italy (Bruttium):
—LOKROI EPIZEPHYRIOI: (**1**) iii-ii BC Landi, *DISMG* 244, 6 (Νουΐ<λ>α?); (**2**) ~ ib. l. 8
S. Italy?: (**3**) 187 BC *SGDI* 2227, 4, 5, 9 etc. (slave/freed.)

**Νούϊος**
Achaia: (**1**) 146 BC *IG* IV (1)² 28, 104 (f. Ζώπυρος: synoikos)
S. Italy: (**2**) s. iv BC *SEG* XXIX 1026 (N. Βαύνιος)
S. Italy (Bruttium):
—PETELIA:
——(Ἑλε.): (**3**) i BC ib. XXXIV 1009 (brick)
S. Italy (Lucania):
—LEUKANOI: (**4**) 185 BC ib. XXXIX 737 B, 17
S. Italy?: (**5**) 250 BC *IG* XI (2) 287 A, 58; (**6**) c. 200-180 BC ib. IX (1)² (3) 619, 1 (slave/freed.)

**Νουμέριος**
S. Italy (Apulia):
—VENUSIA: (**1**) iv-v AD *JIWE* I 95 (Νω-: Jew)

**Νουμήνιος**
Argolis:
—ARGOS: (**1**) ?253 BC Nachtergael, *Les Galates* 10, 61 (Stephanis 1892) (s. Ἑρμῶναξ)
—EPIDAUROS: (**2**) i BC-i AD *IG* IV (1)² 583 (Νουμή[νιος])
—HERMIONE: (**3**) ii-i BC ib. IV (1) 732 IV, 22 (f. Ἀγάθων); (**4**) i BC-i AD? ib. 730 IV, 7 (Νουμή[ν]ιος: s. Μνάμων)
Dalmatia:
—ISSA:
——(Hylleis): (**5**) iv/iii BC Brunšmid p. 8, 44 ([Ν]ουμήνιος: s. Διονύσιος)
Illyria:
—APOLLONIA: (**6**) c. 250-50 BC Maier 67 (coin) (Ceka 90) (money.)
——(Ar.): (**7**) iii/ii BC *IApoll* 7; cf. *L'Illyrie mérid.* 2 p. 207 (s. Σωσικράτης)
—EPIDAMNOS-DYRRHACHION: (**8**) hell. *IDyrrh* 334 (Νο-: f. Νομοκλῆς); (**9**) imp. ib. 335 (Νομ-)
Korinthia:
—KORINTH: (**10**) c. 300 BC *RE* s.v. Numenios (8)
S. Italy (Calabria):
—BRENTESION-BRUNDISIUM*: (**11**) i BC Desy, *Timbres amphoriques* 571-7; 835-7; 1053 (amph.) (slave/potter?)
S. Italy (Lucania):
—HYELE-VELIA: (**12**) ii/i BC *CIG* 6986 (Noll, *Inschr. Wien.* p. 44 no. 97) (s. Σαραπίων)
Sicily:
—HENNA: (**13**) f. i BC Cic., *In Verr.* II iv 113 (Lat. Numenius)

—KENTORIPA: (**14**) f. i BC ib. *In Verr.* II iii 57 (Lat. Numenius)
—SYRACUSE?: (**15**) 213 or 205 BC Nachtergael, *Les Galates* 66, 8, 10; cf. Stephanis 2339 (f. Σώπολις)

**Νουμήνις**
Argolis:
—EPIDAUROS*: (**1**) c. 370-365 BC Peek, *IAEpid* 52 B, 72
Korinthia:
—KORINTH: (**2**) s. iv AD *Corinth* VIII (3) 522, 11; cf. *TMByz* 9 (1985) p. 362 no. 35 (-μέ-)

**Νουμηνίς**
Sicily: (**1**) i AD *IG* II² 10289

**Νουνφίων**
Sicily:
—KASMENAI: (**1**) vi BC *Arch. Class.* 17 (1965) p. 193 + *ZPE* 99 (1993) pp. 123-4 (f. Αἶσα)

**Νύμμελος**
S. Italy (Lucania):
—SERRA DI VAGLIO (MOD.): (**1**) iv BC Landi, *DISMG* 160

**Νυμφαῖς**
Lakonia:
—TAINARON-KAINEPOLIS: (**1**) hell.-imp. *IG* V (1) 1265

**Νυμφᾶς**
Lakonia:
—SPARTA: (**1**) c. 150-160 AD ib. 53, 19; 54, 10 (Bradford (-)) (f. Εὔτυχος)

**Νυμφέρως**
S. Italy (Campania):
—HERCULANEUM*: (**1**) i BC-i AD *CIL* X 1403 g III, 24 (Lat. Nympheros: freed.)
—POMPEII: (**2**) i BC-i AD ib. IV 1093 (Lat. Nympheros); (**3**) c. 51-62 AD ib. 3340. 81, 7 (Castrèn 266. 2) (Lat. N. Nassenius Nympheros)
—SURRENTUM*: (**4**) imp. *St. Rom.* 2 (1914) p. 346 no. 16 = *NScav* 1928, p. 209 no. 9 (Lat. Nympheros: slave?)
S. Italy (Lucania):
—VOLCEI: (**5**) imp. *IItal* III (1) 98 (*CIL* X 389) (Lat. Nympheros: I f. Νυμφέρως II); (**6**) ~ *IItal* III (1) 98 (*CIL* X 389) (Lat. M. Insteius Nympheros: II s. Νυμφέρως I, Natalis)

**Νύμφη**
S. Italy (Apulia):
—TEANUM APULUM: (**1**) imp. *Teanum Apulum* p. 67 no. 13 (*CIL* IX 711) (Lat. Numpe)
—VENUSIA: (**2**) imp. ib. 545 (Lat. Numpe)
—VENUSIA*: (**3**) imp. ib. 481 (Lat. Antonia Numphe: freed.)
S. Italy (Calabria):
—BRENTESION-BRUNDISIUM: (**4**) imp. *NScav* 1904, p. 300 (Lat. -tiena Nym[p]he)
S. Italy (Campania):
—DIKAIARCHIA-PUTEOLI: (**5**) imp. *CIL* X 2367 (Lat. Domitia Nym[phe])
—DIKAIARCHIA-PUTEOLI*: (**6**) imp. ib. 1923 (Lat. Nymphe: freed.); (**7**) ?i-ii AD *Eph. Ep.* VIII 396 (Lat. Nymphe: freed.?)
—POMPEII: (**8**) i BC-i AD *CIL* IV 1389 (Lat. Nympe); (**9**) ~ ib. 2495 (Castrèn 23. 17) (Lat. Al. Nype); (**10**) ~ *CIL* IV 3580 (Lat. Nupe); (**11**) ~ ib. 4833 (Lat. Nype); (**12**) ~ ib. 8897 (Lat. Nuphe); (**13**) imp. ib. X 8349 (Lat. Alleia Calaes Nuphe)
Sicily:
—SYRACUSE: (**14**) iii-v AD Strazzulla 196 (Wessel 1351); (**15**) iv-v AD *JIWE* I 152 (*CIJ* I 652) (Νύ(μ)φη)

**Νυμφία**
S. Italy (Campania):
—SUESSULA: (**1**) imp. *CIL* X 3767 (Lat. Claudia Nymphia)

**Νυμφιανός**
S. ITALY (CAMPANIA):
—SURRENTUM*: (1) imp. ib. 717 b (Lat. Nymphianus: s. Νύμφος: freed.)

**Νυμφιδία**
S. ITALY (CAMPANIA):
—DIKAIARCHIA-PUTEOLI: (1) imp. ib. 2357 (Lat. Curtia Nymphidia)

**Νυμφιδιανός**
SICILY:
—KATANE: (1) imp. ib. 7057 (Lat. Ceparius Nymphidianus)

**Νυμφιδίων**
S. ITALY (CAMPANIA):
—HERCULANEUM: (1) 41-79 AD Cron. Erc. 7 (1977) p. 115 A b, 13 (Lat. Nymphidio)

**Νυμφικός**
KORINTHIA:
—KORINTH: (1) imp. JÖAI 15 (1912) p. 55 no. 27, 11 (Γ. Παπίριος Ν.)
S. ITALY (CAMPANIA):
—HERCULANEUM: (2) i AD CIL x 8058. 73 (seal) (Lat. M. Publicius Nymphicus); (3) ~ ib. 8058. 92 (seal) (Lat. C. Vibius Nymphicus) ?= (4); (4) m. i AD PdelP 3 (1948) p. 177 no. 23; 16 (1961) p. 72 no. 101, 4 (Lat. C. Vibius Nymphic[us]) ?= (3); (5) ~ Cron. Erc. 7 (1977) p. 116 B a, 16 (Lat. [C.] [Messien]us Numphicus); (6) 62 AD PdelP 6 (1951) p. 226 no. 5; 9 (1954) p. 64 no. 66, 4; Ostraka 2 (1993) pp. 201-3 (Lat. C. Messienius Nymphicus)
—HERCULANEUM*: (7) i BC-i AD CIL x 1403 l II, 7 + Cron. Erc. 7 (1977) p. 116 c, 7 (Lat. C. Vibius Nymphicus: freed.)
—POMPEII: (8) i BC-i AD CIL IV 4492 (Lat. Nymphicus)
S. ITALY (LUCANIA):
—VOLCEI: (9) imp. IItal III (1) 20 (CIL x 410) (Lat. Nymphicus)

**Νύμφιος**
KERKYRA: (1) ii AD IG IX (1) 732 (I f. Νύμφιος II); (2) ~ ib. (II s. Νύμφιος I)
S. ITALY (APULIA):
—VENUSIA: (3) imp. CIL IX 508 (Lat. C. Geminius Nymphius)
S. ITALY (CALABRIA):
—HYRIA: (4) ii AD Athenaeum 48 (1970) p. 99 no. 4 (Rend. Linc. 24 (1969) p. 99) (Lat. Nymphius)
S. ITALY (CAMPANIA):
—NEAPOLIS: (5) 326 BC Liv. viii 25. 9 (Lat. Nymphius); (6) i BC-i AD INap 124; cf. Leiwo p. 84 no. 32 (f. Ἡρέννη) ?= (7); (7) ~ INap 139; cf. Leiwo p. 84 no. 31 (f. Λουκία) ?= (6); (8) i BC/i AD INap 110; cf. Leiwo p. 85 no. 34 (f. Μαραῖος)
—POMPEII: (9) i BC-i AD CIL IV 171 (Lat. Nymphius); (10) ~ ib. 1106 (Lat. Nymphius); (11) ~ ib. 1614 (seal) (Lat. P. G. Nymphius); (12) m. i AD ib. 3340. 81; 103; Impegno per Pompeii 11 ES no. 2 (Castrèn 434. 14) (Lat. A. Veius Nymphius); (13) c. 51-62 AD CIL IV 3340. 57, 9 (Castrèn 318. 25) (Lat. N. Popidius Nymphius); (14) ~ CIL IV 3340. 103, 10 (Castrèn 265. 3) (Lat. L. Naevolius Nymphius)

**Νυμφοδότη**
S. ITALY (CAMPANIA):
—POMPEII: (1) i BC-i AD CIL IV 4760 (Lat. Nunpdote)

**Νυμφόδοτος**
ELIS: (1) ?i AD EA 1905, p. 259 no. 2, 7 ([N]υμφόδοτος: s. Φίλλυς)

**Illyria:**
—EPIDAMNOS-DYRRHACHION: (2) imp. AEp 1978, no. 747 (Lat. L. Scantius Nymphodotus: freed.)
LAKONIA:
—SPARTA: (3) f. ii AD IG V (1) 20 B, 4; 466, 8; 1314, 30; BSA 26 (1923-5) p. 168 C 7, 5 (Bradford (1); (4)) (Νυνφόδοτος—1314: s. Ξενοφῶν, f. Ξενοφῶν); (4) c. 120-137 AD IG v (1) 59, 5; SEG XI 521 b, 4; 574, 2 (Bradford (3)) (f. Εὔκλητος); (5) m. ii AD IG V (1) 466, 2 (Νυμφόδ[οτος]: s. Ξενοφῶν, Μοῦσα); (6) iii AD ib. 781 = SEG XXIV 282 (Bradford (2))
MESSENIA:
—MESSENE: (7) ii/iii AD SEG XXIII 215, 5 (f. Εἰράνα); (8) 192 AD PAE 1969, p. 104, 8 (f. Σπάταλος)
S. ITALY (APULIA):
—CANUSIUM: (9) i AD Epig. Rom. di Canosa 71 (Lat. A. Marcius Nymphodotus)
S. ITALY (CAMPANIA):
—HERCULANEUM*: (10) m. i AD Ann. S. Chiara 13 (1963) pp. 251-4; Cron. Erc. 7 (1977) p. 117 C b, 14 (Lat. M. Caelius Nymphodot(us): freed.)
—NEAPOLIS: (11) i BC/i AD INap 110; cf. Leiwo p. 85 no. 33
—POMPEII: (12) i BC-i AD CIL IV 207 (Lat. Nymph[odot]us); (13) ~ ib. 1235 (Lat. Nymphodotus); (14) ~ ib. 9179 (Lat. Nymphodotus); (15) i BC/i AD ib. x 908 (Castrèn 99. 8) (Lat. Nymphodotus); (16) 23-32 AD CIL x 895, 3; 899, 8 (Castrèn 190. 4 and 15) (Lat. Helvius Nymphodotus); (17) c. 51-62 AD CIL IV 3340. 94, 6; 114, 2 (Castrèn 393. 3) (Lat. M. Stlaborius Nymphodotus); (18) 57 AD CIL IV 3340. 34, 10; 73, 9 (Castrèn 161. 12) (Lat. M. Fabius Nympodotus); (19) 63-79 AD CIL IV 901 (Castrèn 119. 14) (Lat. Clodius Nymphodotus)

**Νυμφοδώρα**
SICILY:
—SYRACUSE: (1) iii-v AD NScav 1892, p. 361 (-φι-)

**Νυμφόδωρος**
SICILY: (1) iv BC FGrH 76 F 57; Wehrli, Schule Arist. iii fr. 93; (2) iii/ii BC Vandermersch p. 172 (amph.)
—ABAKAINON: (3) ii-iii AD IGLMP 126 (Νεμέρις Γρανώνις Ν.)
—AKRAGAS: (4) s. ii BC Acragas Graeca 1 p. 34 no. 5, 2 (IGUR 2; Dubois, IGDS 185) (s. Φίλων); (5) f. i BC Cic., In Verr. II iv 48 (Lat. Nymphodorus)
—AKRAI: (6) ?iii BC SGDI 3239, 2 (Akrai p. 157 no. 9) (f. Ἡράκλειος) ?= (7); (7) ~ SGDI 3239, 10 (Akrai p. 157 no. 9) (f. Κλέων) ?= (6); (8) ~ SGDI 3245, 2 (Akrai p. 158 no. 10; IGLMP 31) (Νυμφόδ[ωρος]: ?f. Ἀρχέδαμος); (9) iii-ii BC SGDI 3242, 3 (Akrai p. 157 no. 8) (f. Νίκων); (10) ~ SGDI 3242, 3 (Akrai p. 157 no. 8) (f. Ἀπολλόδωρος)
—GELA-PHINTIAS: (11) f. ii BC IG XIV 256, 3 (Dubois, IGDS 161); cf. SEG XL 804 (f. Σῶσις); (12) ~ IG XIV 256, 43 (Dubois, IGDS 161); cf. SEG XL 804 (f. Ἀριστίων)
—HALAISA: (13) ii BC IGSI 2 B I, 16 (Dubois, IGDS 196) (Νυμφόδω[ρος])
—INESSA-AITNA: (14) f. ii BC BCH 45 (1921) p. 25 IV, 96 (SEG XXII 455); cf. Sic. Gymn. 17 (1964) pp. 47 f. (Νυμφόδ[ωρος])
—KAMARINA: (15) hell. SEG XXXIX 1001, 3; (16) ?ii BC ib. 996, 8 (Dubois, IGDS 126; Cordano, 'Camarina VII' 140) (s. Δάμων)
—KENTORIPA: (17) ?s. iii BC Sic. Gymn. 2 (1949) p. 91 no. 1, 13 + 16 (1963) p. 54 (Νυμφόδω[ρος]); (18) ~ ib. 2 (1949) p. 91 no. 1, 14 + 16 (1963) p. 54 (Νυμφόδ[ωρος]); (19) f. i BC Cic., In Verr. II iii 57 (Lat. Nymphodorus)

—LICODIA EUBEA (MOD.): (20) hell. RQ 1904, p. 248 = Pace, Camarina p. 164 no. 27 (?s. Διόδωρος)
—LIPARA*: (21) s. iii BC Meligunis-Lipara 2 p. 174 T. 475; cf. Kokalos 32 (1986) p. 235 nos. 61-2 (tiles)
—MENAI: (22) hell.? Riv. Stor. Antica 5 (1900-1) p. 56 no. 30-1 (s. Βομβυλῖνος)
—PALAGONIA (MOD.): (23) iii-ii BC SEG XLII 850
—SYRACUSE: (24) 312 BC D.S. xix 103. 2-3; (25) iii BC IG II² 10392 (f. Ἡρακλέα); (26) s. iii BC RE (6); FGrH 572; (27) iii/ii BC ID 442 B, 74; IG XI (4) 759; XII (5) 816-18 (f. Τίμων); (28) ii-i BC ib. xIV 8, 10 (IGLMP 105) (Νυμφό[δωρος]: ?f. —τος); (29) f. ii BC ID 404, [3]; 405, 30 etc. (s. Τίμων)
—TAUROMENION: (30) c. 240 BC IG XIV 421 an. 1 (SGDI 5219) (s. Σιμίσκος); (31) c. 237 BC IG XIV 421 an. 4 (SGDI 5219) (f. Δαμάτριος); (32) c. 235 BC IG XIV 421 an. 6 (SGDI 5219); (33) c. 231 BC IG XIV 421 an. 10 (SGDI 5219) (f. Σαύλαος); (34) c. 226 BC IG XIV 421 an. 15 (SGDI 5219) (f. Ἀνδρίσκος); (35) c. 223 BC IG XIV 421 an. 18 (SGDI 5219); (36) c. 220-207 BC IG XIV 421 an. 21; 421 an. 35 (SGDI 5219) (f. Εὔαλκος); (37) c. 204 BC IG XIV 421 an. 37 (SGDI 5219) (s. Φιλωνίδας); (38) c. 197 BC IG XIV 421 an. 44 (SGDI 5219) (f. Ἀπολλόδωρος); (39) c. 188 BC IG XIV 421 an. 53 (SGDI 5219); (40) c. 178 BC IG XIV 421 an. 63 (SGDI 5219) (s. Ἀνδρίσκος); (41) c. 176-164 BC IG XIV 421 an. 65; 421 an. 77 (SGDI 5219) (s. Εὔαλκος); (42) c. 173-144 BC IG XIV 421 an. 68; 421 an. 82; 421 an. 97 (SGDI 5219); IGSI 4 II (III), 7 an. 70 (s. Εὐκλείδας); (43) c. 172 BC ib. l. 2 an. 69 (f. Δαμάτριος); (44) c. 146 BC ib. 4 III (IV), 81 an. 96 (f. Ὑπέρβολος); (45) c. 40 BC Cron. Arch. 3 (1964) p. 54, I, 36 (s. N—)
——(Ἀρεθ.): (46) ?s. ii BC SEG XXXII 937 (s. Εὐκλείδας)
——(Ἀσ.): (47) c. 147 BC IGSI 4 III (IV), 65 an. 94 (f. Εὐκλείδας)
——(Οἰν.): (48) ?ii/i BC IG XIV 421 D an. 5 (SGDI 5219); IGSI 4 III (IV), 119 D an. 7 (f. Εὐκλείδας)
——(Ὀμ.): (49) c. 153-150 BC IG XIV 421 an. 91 (SGDI 5219); IGSI 4 III (IV), 12 an. 87 (f. Σῶσις)
——(Σπαρ.): (50) s. ii BC SEG XXXII 936 (s. Φιλιστίων)

**Νύμφος**
S. ITALY (CAMPANIA):
—SURRENTUM*: (1) imp. CIL x 717b (Lat. M. Avillius Nymphus: f. Νυμφιανός: freed.)

**Νύμφων**
S. ITALY (CAMPANIA):
—PANDATERIA: (1) imp. Storia di Napoli 1 p. 252 (Lat. Nymphon)
SICILY: (2) hell. Vandermersch p. 172 (amph.) (or S. Italy) ?= (3); (3) iii-ii BC ib. (amph.) (or S. Italy) ?= (2)
—AKRAI: (4) hell.? SGDI 3244 (Akrai p. 158 no. 12) (Νύμφ(οι)—lap.: s. Ἱέρων); (5) iii-ii BC SGDI 3242, 7 (Akrai p. 157 no. 8) (s. Λυσίας)
—AVOLA (MOD.): (6) i BC SEG XXXIV 981, 6 (f. Λύκων)
—HELOROS: (7) ii-i BC Dubois, IGDS 100, 3 (f. Ζωΐλος)
—KATANE: (8) imp. CIL x 7081 (Lat. Nymphon)
—KENTORIPA: (9) hell. IG XIV 574, 4 (Dubois, IGDS 188) (Νύμ[φ]ων: f. Ἀρτεμίσκος Κάβαλος); (10) f. i BC Cic., In Verr. II iii 53-4 (Lat. Nympho)
—KEPHALOIDION: (11) i BC-i AD IG XIV 351 + SEG XXXVII 763 (?f. Σῶσις Κράφαγος)

## Νυμψία

—SEGESTA: (12) iv/iii BC *IG* XIV 290, 2 (Dubois, *IGDS* 215); *SEG* XLI 825 (date) ([Νύμ]φων: f. Φάων Σωπολιανός); (13) ~ ib. 827 (f. Ἀρτεμιδώρα)
—SYRACUSE: (14) ii-i BC ib. XXXIV 974, 5 (*IG-LMP* 106; Stephanis 1895); (15) f. ii BC *Iasos* 177, 14 (Ἀμφων—*LBW* I 266: s. Ἀρχάγαθος)
—THERMAI HIMERAIAI: (16) ii/i BC *SGDI* 3248; *Kokalos* 20 (1974) p. 219 no. 1 (Νύμφ[ων]—*IG*: f. Ἄνταλλος)

## Νυμψία

S. ITALY (CAMPANIA):
—NEAPOLIS: (1) i BC/i AD *INap* 174 bis (d. Τρέβιος)

## Νύμψιος

S. ITALY (BRUTTIUM):
—PETELIA: (1) c. 200-175 BC *IG* XI (4) 1244-6 (f. Ἀγάθων)

S. ITALY (CAMPANIA):
—NEAPOLIS: (2) 356 BC D.S. xvi 18-19. 1; Plu., *Dio* 41 (Νύψιος—mss.); (3) i BC/i AD *INap* 136 (f. Λάρων); (4) ~ ib. (s. Λάρων); (5) ~ ib. 142; cf. Leiwo p. 74 no. 19 and p. 123 no. 110 (Νύμφιος—Leiwo per err.: s. Μᾶμος); (6) ~ *INap* 148 ([Νύ]μψιο[ς]?); (7) ~ ib. 177, 3 (Ν(ύ)μψιος: f. Φιλλίνων) ?= (8); (8) ~ ib. l. 4 (f. Φαιναρέτη) ?= (7); (9) i AD *IG* XIV 726 (*INap* 14); cf. Leiwo p. 163 no. 139
—PITHEKOUSSAI-AENARIA: (10) ?s. iii BC *IG* XIV 894; *BE* 1951, no. 252 (date) (f. Πάκιος)

## Νῦσα

ARGOLIS:
—HERMIONE: (1) ?ii-i BC *IG* IV (1) 731 I, 6 (d. Σωκράτης)

S. ITALY (APULIA):
—CANUSIUM*: (2) imp. *Epig. Rom. di Canosa* 151 (*CIL* IX 386) (Lat. Marcia Nysa: freed.)

S. ITALY (CALABRIA):
—LUPIAE*: (3) imp. Susini, *Fonti Salento* p. 153 no. 106 (Lat. –ia Nysa: freed.)

## Νυσαῖος

SICILY:
—SYRACUSE: (1) c. 385-347 BC *RE* (2); cf. Beloch, *GG* III (2) pp. 102-7 (s. Διονύσιος, Ἀριστομάχα)

## Νύσιος

EPIROS:
—AMBRAKIA: (1) ii BC *NS* 547 (f. Φιλοκράτης)

# Ξ

## Ξανθίας

AITOLIA:
—ATTALEIA: (1) 204 BC *IG* IX (1)² (1) 95, 5
ARKADIA:
—MANTINEIA-ANTIGONEIA: (2) c. 425-385 BC ib. V (2) 323. 3 (tessera) (f. Ζακύνθιος)
—TEGEA: (3) iv/iii BC ib. 32, 5 ([Ξ]ανθίας)
—TEGEA?: (4) m. iii BC ib. 368, 5 ([Ξ]ανθίας)
EPIROS:
—DODONA: (5) iii BC Antoniou, *Dodone* Ba, 4
KORINTHIA:
—KORINTH (NR.): (6) hell.? *IG* IV (1) 1560 (fals.?)
—SIKYON: (7) vi/v BC *SEG* XI 244, 7
S. ITALY (APULIA): (8) f. iv BC *NScav* 1883, p. 566 (vase) (fict.)

## Ξανθικλῆς

ACHAIA: (1) 401-400 BC *RE* (-)

## Ξανθίππα

ARGOLIS:
—TROIZEN: (1) iii BC *IG* IV (1) 809
KORINTHIA:
—KORINTH: (2) vi/v BC Page, *FGE* 829 (-πη)

## Ξάνθιππος

DALMATIA:
—ISSA: (1) hell. Brunšmid p. 28 no. 22 (f. Πόσθων)
EPIROS:
—AMBRAKIA: (2) iii BC *SEG* XXIV 413 (f. Ἕρμων)
LAKONIA:
—SPARTA: (3) m. iii BC *RE* (9) (Bradford (-))
SICILY:
—TAUROMENION: (4) c. 140 BC *IG* XIV 421 an. 101 (*SGDI* 5219)
——(Ἱππ.): (5) ?ii/i BC *IG* XIV 421 D an. 5 (*SGDI* 5219) (f. Ἀλέξανδρος); (6) ~ *IG* XIV 421 D an. 9 (*SGDI* 5219) (s. Ἀλέξανδρος)
——(Σιπποκ.): (7) f. i BC *Cron. Arch.* 3 (1964) p. 45 IV, 7 (f. Ἀλέξανδρος)

## Ξάνθος

ARGOLIS:
—ARGOS: (1) i-ii AD *IG* IV (1) 587, 7 (Λ. Δεκούμιος Ξ.)
EPIROS:
—NIKOPOLIS: (2) imp. *PAE* 1913, p. 111 (Sarikakis 120)

S. ITALY (CAMPANIA):
—NOLA: (3) imp. *CIL* X 1298 (Lat. Sex. Firmius Xanthus)
—POMPEII: (4) i BC-i AD ib. IV 1361 (Lat. Xantus); (5) ~ ib. 1505 (Lat. Xanthus); (6) ~ ib. 4598; 4635 (Lat. Xanthus); (7) ~ ib. 4825 (Lat. Xanthus)
S. ITALY?: (8) ?vii BC *RE* (26); *PMG* 699-700

## Ξειναγόρης

ELIS:
—OLYMPIA*: (1) iii/ii BC *SEG* XXVIII 435, 2 (Ξειναγόρης)
KORINTHIA:
—KORINTH: (2) ii AD ib. XLI 273 B, 2-3 (s. Φλαβιανός, Σαλβία (Thessaly), f. Φλαβιανή)

## Ξεινόφαντος

ELIS: (1) ii BC *GVI* 453 (f. Καλλισθένης)

## Ξένα

EPIROS:
—BOUTHROTOS (PRASAIBOI): (1) a. 163 BC *IBouthrot* 89, 8-9 ?= (Ξενώ (5))

## Ξενάγατος

S. ITALY (BRUTTIUM):
—LOKROI EPIZEPHYRIOI?: (1) ?c. 500-480 BC *Rend. Linc.* 18 (1963) pp. 16-17 (Landi, *DISMG* 60 (bronze)); cf. *LSAG²* p. 286 no. 5 (date); p. 464 (name) (Ξενάγατ[ος])

## Ξεναγίς

ARKADIA:
—TEGEA: (1) iv/iii BC *IG* V (2) 74

## Ξεναγόρας

LAKONIA:
—SPARTA: (1) m. ii AD *SEG* XI 622, 7 (Bradford (-)) ([Ξ]εναγόρ[ας])

## Ξέναγος

AITOLIA: (1) ?209 or 205 BC Flacelière p. 407 no. 38 b, [3]; Nachtergael, *Les Galates* 68, 4

## Ξέναιθος

S. ITALY (CALABRIA):
—TARAS-TARENTUM: (1) ?232 or 228 BC *FD* III (1) 443, 2 (f. Ξενέας)

## Ξεναίνετος

ARKADIA?: (1) hell.? *IG* V (2) 509 (1) (tile)
ELIS: (2) 191-146 BC *ZfN* 9 (1882) p. 270 no. 23; Unp. (Oxford, AM) (coins)

S. ITALY (BRUTTIUM):
—LOKROI EPIZEPHYRIOI:
——(Εὐρ.): (3) iv/iii BC De Franciscis 10, 7
——(Λακ.): (4) 276 BC ib. 23, 4 (s. Κλεύθηρος)

## Ξέναιος

ACHAIA:
—PHARAI: (1) iii-ii BC *Achaean Grave Stelai* 61 (f. Προξενίδας)
LAKONIA:
—SPARTA: (2) ?i AD *IG* V (1) 180, 6 (Bradford (-))

## Ξεναίρετος

ARKADIA:
—MEGALOPOLIS: (1) hell. *AR* 1994-5, p. 13 (s. Κραῦγις)

## Ξενάκων

LAKONIA:
—SPARTA: (1) hell. *SEG* XI 884 a (tile) (Bradford (2)) ([Ξε]νάκων); (2) c. 80-90 AD *IG* V (1) 674, 16 (Bradford (1)) (s. Ἀντίβιος); (3) f. ii AD *SEG* XXXI 340, 7 (f. —ας); (4) c. 170 AD *IG* V (1) 116, 2 (Bradford (3)) (Κορν. Ξ.)

## Ξένανδρος

ARKADIA:
—MEGALOPOLIS: (1) ?131 BC *IG* V (2) 440, 10 (Ξέναν[δρος]: f. Ἀρχενίκα)

## Ξεναρέτα

EPIROS:
—AMBRAKIA: (1) iii-ii BC *Op. Ath.* 10 (1971) p. 64 no. 12, 4; cf. *VAHD* 84 (1991) p. 262; *BCH* 92 (1968) p. 847 (Ξενν-: d. Τίμανδρος)

## Ξενάρετος

MESSENIA:
—MESSENE: (1) 208 or 207 BC *FD* III (4) 23, 4; 24, 3 (s. Τελέσαρχος)

## Ξενάρης

ACHAIA:
—DYME*: (1) c. 219 BC *SGDI* 1612, 64 (*Tyche* 5 (1990) p. 124) ([Ξ]ενάρης: f. Ξενοχάρης)
LAKONIA:
—SPARTA: (2) 421-420 BC Th. v 36-8; 46. 4; 51. 2 (Poralla² 567) (s. Κνίδις); (3) s. iii BC Plu., *Cleom.* 3 (Bradford (1)); (4) s. i BC *IG* V (1) 94, 9 (Bradford (2)) (s. Δαμοκ—)
MESSENIA:
—THOURIA: (5) f. ii BC *SEG* XI 972, 37 (f. Λυσικράτης)

S. ITALY (BRUTTIUM):
—LOKROI EPIZEPHYRIOI:
——(Κυλ.): (6) iv/iii BC De Franciscis 12, 3 (s. Ζωΐλος)

### Ξεναρία
LAKONIA:
—MESSA?: (1) imp. IG v (1) 1280, 12 (d. Σωσίπατρος)
—SPARTA: (2) ii AD ib. 583, 3 (Bradford (-))

### Ξέναρις
AKARNANIA:
—MEDION: (1) hell.? SEG XL 463 (Ξενάριος (gen.?))

### Ξεναρίστα
ILLYRIA:
—APOLLONIA: (1) s. vi BC IApoll 3

### Ξενάρκης
AIGINA: (1) 446 BC Pi., P. viii, 19, 72 (f. Ἀριστομένης)
EPIROS:
—BOUTHROTOS (PRASAIBOI): (2) a. 163 BC IBouthrot 158 (Ξενά[ρ]κ[ης]?)

### Ξενάρχης
LAKONIA:
—SPARTA: (1) ?iv BC Moretti, Olymp. 386; Paus. vi 2. 1-2 (Poralla² 568)

### Ξεναρχίδας
LAKONIA:
—SPARTA: (1) m. ii AD IG v (1) 39, 30; 505, 2; 1174, 9; Cartledge–Spawforth p. 140 (ident.) (Bradford (1)) (s. Δάμιππος); (2) ~ SEG XI 623, 7 (Bradford (3)) ([Ξ]εναρχίδας: f. Γ. Ἰούλ. Δαμαίνετος); (3) a. 212 AD SEG XI 806, 3 (Bradford (2)) (Μ. Αὐρ. Ξεναρχίδας: s. Πύρρος)

### Ξεναρχίς
AKARNANIA:
—PALAIROS: (1) hell.? IG IX (1)² (2) 567

### Ξέναρχος
ACHAIA:
—AIGEIRA: (1) iii/ii BC RE (1)
—DYME*: (2) c. 219 BC SGDI 1612, 21 (Tyche 5 (1990) p. 124) (s. Τιμέας)
—PELLENE: (3) ?a. 247 BC FD III (4) 403 III, 2 (f. Ἀχαιός); (4) ~ ib. l. 3 (s. Ἀχαιός)
AITOLIA:
—PHISTYON: (5) ii BC IG IX (1)² (1) 110 a, 2
AKARNANIA:
—STRATOS: (6) c. 200 BC ib. 31, 128 (s. Πυθοκλῆς)
ARGOLIS:
—ARGOS: (7) s. iv BC ib. IV (1) 617, 6
—EPIDAUROS*: (8) iv/iii BC Peek, IAEpid 51, 5, 7, 9-10; BSA 61 (1966) p. 319 no. 26 (date)
ARKADIA:
—HELISSON: (9) c. 221 BC IG IV (1)² 42, 6
—MEGALOPOLIS: (10) i BC/i AD ib. v (2) 515 A, 21, 25, 31; C, 9 (s. Ὀνασικράτης)
—MEGALOPOLIS?: (11) imp. ib. 523 (s. Ὀνασικράτης)
EPIROS:
—KASSOPE: (12) iv/iii BC Thess. Mnem. 72 (s. Ξένων)
LAKONIA:
—SPARTA: (13) hell.? IG v (1) 792 (Bradford (2)) ([Ξ]έναρχος: f. Ξενότιμος); (14) m. ii BC IG v (1) 889; 890; 892 (tiles) (Bradford (1))
MESSENIA:
—ASINE: (15) ii AD IG v (1) 1408 (f. Νικοτέλης)
—MESSENE: (16) f. iii BC PAE 1991, p. 99 no. 7, 7
SICILY:
—SEGESTA: (17) iv/iii BC IG XIV 290, 3 (Dubois, IGDS 215); SEG XLI 825 (date) (s. Διόδωρος)


—SYRACUSE: (18) v/iv BC RE (3); CGF I p. 182 (s. Σώφρων)

### Ξενέας
KORINTHIA:
—SIKYON: (1) vi/v BC SEG XI 244, 21
S. ITALY (BRUTTIUM):
—KAULONIA: (2) iv BC Iamb., VP 267 (FVS I p. 447) (Ξέντας—ms.: name—Schweigh.)
S. ITALY (CALABRIA):
—TARAS-TARENTUM: (3) c. 272-235 BC Vlasto 864-6 (coins) (Evans, Horsemen p. 178 VIII C.1); (4) ?232 or 228 BC FD III (1) 443, 2 (Ξ[ε]νέας: s. Ξέναιθος)

### Ξένεια
ARGOLIS:
—PHLEIOUS: (1) ?iv BC IG IV (1) 467 (—ξένεια?)

### Ξενείων
LAKONIA:
—HYPERTELEATON*: (1) vi BC ib. v (1) 980 (Lazzarini 94) (-ōν)

### Ξένετος
S. ITALY (BRUTTIUM):
—LOKROI EPIZEPHYRIOI: (1) v/iv BC RE (-) (f. Δωρίς)
SICILY:
—TAUROMENION: (2) ?ii/i BC IG XIV 421 D an. 11 (SGDI 5219) (s. Ἀγάθων)

### Ξενϝάρηρ
ELIS:
—PISATIS (KOSKINA (MOD.)): (1) ?c. 475-450 BC IvOl 718, 3; LSAG² p. 220 no. 16 (date) (Ξενϝάρ[ηρ]: f. Ῥίπιρ)

### Ξενϝάρης
KERKYRA: (1) c. 575-550 BC CEG I 146 (s. Μείξις)

### Ξενϝοκλῆς
KORINTHIA:
—KORINTH: (1) ?vi BC IG IV (1) 315 (pinax) (-κλễς)

### Ξενϝων
KORINTHIA:
—KORINTH: (1) c. 610-590 BC Amyx 18. 9 (vase) (Lorber 28); LSAG² p. 131 no. 9 (date) (-νϝōν)

### Ξενήν
ILLYRIA:
—EPIDAMNOS-DYRRHACHION: (1) c. 250-50 BC Münsterberg Nachtr. p. 16 (coin) (Ceka 400) (pryt.); (2) hell.-imp. IDyrrh 119 (f. Ἀριστόλαος)

### Ξενία
ARKADIA:
—TEGEA: (1) i BC-i AD? IG v (2) 234 (fem. nom./masc. voc.?)

### Ξενιάδας
KORINTHIA:
—KORINTH: (1) c. 500-475 BC ib. IV (1) 352 (vase) (CVA Robinson 3 p. 46 no. 6); LSAG² p. 132 no. 32 (date); (2) f. v BC RE (1) (-δης); (3) iv BC ib. (2) (-δης); (4) iii BC IG IV (1) 361 (bronze) (s. Διόδωρος)
MESSENIA:
—KOLONIDES: (5) ii BC ib. v (1) 1402, 3 (f. Φιλοκράτης)

### Ξενίας
ACHAIA?: (1) 193 BC ib. v (2) 293, 21 (f. Φίλλυρος)
AITOLIA:
—KONOPE-ARSINOE: (2) 154 BC SGDI 1908, 12 (s. Δάμων)


—MAKYNEIS: (3) s. ii BC SEG XXV 621, 11 (s. Ἀλέξων)
AKARNANIA: (4) iii BC IG IX (1)² (2) 575 (s. Ἴων)
—OINIADAI: (5) iii BC ib. 421 (s. Ἐπιτέλης)
ARKADIA:
—ASEA: (6) 191-146 BC BMC Pelop. p. 14 no. 161 (coin)
—MANTINEIA-ANTIGONEIA: (7) c. 300-221 BC IG v (2) 323. 53 (tessera); (8) ~ ib. 323. 70 (tessera) (f. —θέας); (9) ~ ib. 323. 82 (tessera) (s. Νέαρχος)
—MEGALOPOLIS: (10) ?268 BC FD III (1) 17, 1 (s. Πράγορος)
—PARRHASIOI: (11) 405 BC RE (1)
—TEGEA: (12) s. iv BC SEG XXXVI 383, 9 (Ξενίας: f. Ἀπολλώνιος); (13) f. ii BC IG v (2) 44, 6 (f. Ξενότιμος)
—TEUTHIS?: (14) ii BC SEG XXXV 347 C (Ξενία?)
ELIS: (15) v/iv BC RE (2) ?= (16); (16) ~ Paus. vi 1. 3 (f. Ἀρχέδαμος) ?= (15)
EPIROS:
—KASSOPE: (17) iii BC IG IX (1)² (2) 243, 3 (f. Σωτιμίδας)
KORINTHIA:
—SIKYON: (18) 336 BC CID II 76 III, 13 ?= (19)
—SIKYON?: (19) c. 340-330 BC ib. 58 I, 33 (Skalet 235) ?= (18)
PELOPONNESE?: (20) s. iii BC SEG XXV 449, 41 (IPArk 26) (s. Ἀν—)

### Ξενικόν
SICILY:
—SYRACUSE: (1) hell.? AA 1937, col. 147

### Ξενικός
SICILY: (1) ?f. iv BC IG I³ 1369 bis

### Ξενικράτης
SICILY:
—KAMARINA: (1) iv/iii BC Manganaro, PdelP forthcoming no. 2, 3 (Ξενικρ[άτης]: s. Ἀρχωνίδας)

### Ξένιον
KERKYRA: (1) ii AD Ag. XVII 518 (d. Δημήτριος)

### Ξένιος
ARKADIA:
—MANTINEIA-ANTIGONEIA: (1) ?iii BC IG v (2) 318, 25
SICILY:
—LIPARA: (2) ?iii BC Meligunis-Lipara 5 p. 151 no. 2152; cf. SEG XLI 811
—SELINOUS:
——(Ἡρακλείδας): (3) m. v BC Dubois, IGDS 36, 3 (Arena, Iscr. Sic. I 69) (s. Ἀπόντις)
—TAUROMENION:
——(Καλ.): (4) c. 169-147 BC IG XIV 421 an. 72; 421 an. 84; 421 an. 94 (SGDI 5219); IGSI 4 II (III), 21 an. 72 + SEG XXXIII 755; cf. XXXVIII 975 n. on l. 23; IGSI 4 II (III), 19 an. 88 (s. Ἐπίδωρος)

### Ξένιππος
AITOLIA: (1) 356 BC FD III (1) 146, 1 (s. Νικόστρατος)
—KALYDON: (2) c. 142 BC IG IX (1)² (1) 137, 45 (s. Δαμέας)
ARKADIA:
—PALLANTION: (3) a. 316 BC SEG XI 1084, 36 (Perlman A.3) (s. Κοῖσος)
—TEGEA: (4) ?218 BC IG v (2) 16, 13
LAKONIA:
—OITYLOS: (5) iii/ii BC ib. v (1) 1295, 9 (Bradford (2))
—SPARTA: (6) c. 200 BC IG XI (4) 718, 3 (Bradford (1)) (s. Τράχαλος)
MESSENIA:
—MESSENE: (7) f. iii BC PAE 1991, p. 99 no. 7, 26; (8) ~ SEG XLI 342, 8; cf. PAE 1991, p. 100 no. 8

—THOURIA: (**9**) s. iii BC *IG* V (1) 1386, 15 (f.
Ξένων)

**Ξένις**
SICILY:
—SELINOUS:
——(Ἡρακλείδας): (**1**) m. v BC Dubois, *IGDS*
36, 6 (Arena, *Iscr. Sic.* I 69) (f. Ἀγάθυλλος)

**Ξενις**
ACHAIA:
—PATRAI: (**1**) hell.? *SGDI* 1628 (s./d. Αἰσχρίων)
EPIROS:
—BOUTHROTOS (PRASAIBOI): (**2**) a. 163 BC
*IBouthrot* 30, 18 (*SEG* XXXVIII 488) (s./d.
Δρόμων)

**Ξενίσκα**
ARKADIA:
—MEGALOPOLIS: (**1**) ii/i BC *IG* V (2) 487

**Ξενίσκος**
ILLYRIA:
—EPIDAMNOS-DYRRHACHION: (**1**) c. 250-50 BC
*BMC Thessaly* p. 77 nos. 172-3 (coin) (pryt.)
?= (*2*); (**2**) ~ Maier 273; *Jubice Hoard* p. 97
no. 23; Münsterberg Nachtr. p. 16 (coin)
(Ceka 9; 244) (pryt.) ?= (*1*)

**Ξενίων**
AITOLIA:
—KALLION/KALLIPOLIS: (**1**) 175 BC *SGDI*
1987, 5 (s. Δάμων)

**Ξεννέας**
EPIROS:
—ATHAMANES: (**1**) iii-ii BC *SEG* VIII 518

**Ξεννιάδας**
KORINTHIA:
—KORINTH: (**1**) 217 BC Nachtergael, *Les Gala-
tes* 65, 8; cf. Stephanis 2545 (f. Φιλόξενος)

**Ξεννίας**
AITOLIA: (**1**) ?262 BC *FD* III (4) 358, 3; *SGDI*
2514, 2
—EIDAIOI: (**2**) 214 BC *IG* IX (1)² (1) 177, 21
—TNIMAIOI: (**3**) c. 162 BC ib. 105, 11
—TRICHONION: (**4**) 217 BC Nachtergael, *Les
Galates* 65, 1 (s. Ἑλλάνικος)
ARKADIA: (**5**) ?253 BC ib. 10, 26 (Stephanis
1900) (s. Ἀρχέτιμος)

**Ξεννις**
ILLYRIA:
—EPIDAMNOS-DYRRHACHION: (**1**) iv/iii BC
*IDyrrh* 10 (Ξενμις—lap.: s./d. Νίκων)

**Ξεννος**
S. ITALY (CAMPANIA):
—NEAPOLIS: (**1**) iii-iv AD *INap* 241 (Ξένος—
*INap*)

**Ξεννυς**
AKARNANIA:
—PHOITIAI: (**1**) iv BC *IG* IX (1)² (2) 602, 12
—STRATOS: (**2**) iv/iii BC ib. 395, 13 (s. Σίρων)

**Ξεννώ**
KEPHALLENIA:
—SAME: (**1**) hell. ib. IX (1) 629

**Ξενόδαμος**
ARKADIA:
—PHIGALEIA: (**1**) ii/i BC ib. V (2) 426
(Ξενόδαμ[ος]?)
LAKONIA:
—KYTHERA: (**2**) ?vii BC *RE* (2) (Poralla² 568a)
—OITYLOS: (**3**) iii/ii BC *IG* V (1) 1295, 3 (Brad-
ford (-)) ([Ξ]ενόδαμος)
MESSENIA:
—MESSENE: (**4**) ii/i BC *IG* V (1) 1437, 4
—MESSENE?: (**5**) ii/i BC *SEG* XI 979, 31

—THOURIA: (**6**) ii-i BC *IG* V (1) 1385, 15, 30
(f. Νικοκλῆς, Καλλιστόλας); (**7**) f. ii BC *SEG* XI
972, 70 (s. Σῖμος); (**8**) ~ ib. l. 127 (s. Ἱππολέων)

**Ξενοδίκα**
KORINTHIA:
—SIKYON: (**1**) ?iv BC Paus. ii 7. 3 (Skalet 236)
(-κη)

**Ξενόδικος**
ARKADIA:
—PHENEOS: (**1**) c. 315-280 BC *FD* III (1) 40, 2
(f. Εὔαντος)
SICILY:
—AKRAGAS: (**2**) vi BC *RE* (1) (s. Τηλέμαχος, f.
Ἱπποκράτης, Κάπυς); (**3**) s. iv BC ib. (2) (Ξενό-
δοκος—D.S. xx 56; 62)
—SELINOUS: (**4**) ?vi BC Manganaro, *PdelP*
forthcoming no. 17 ([Ξε]νόδιφος)

**Ξενοδόκα**
S. ITALY (BRUTTIUM):
—LOKROI EPIZEPHYRIOI?: (**1**) ?c. 500 BC Guarducci, *Ep. Gr.* I p. 302 no. 5 (Landi, *DISMG*
63; Lazzarini 194); *LSAG*² p. 286 no. 8 (date)

**Ξενόδοκος**
ACHAIA:
—DYME*: (**1**) c. 219 BC *SGDI* 1612, 36 (*Tyche*
5 (1990) p. 124) (s. Νευμήνιος)
AITOLIA:
—THESTIEIS: (**2**) 213 BC *IG* IX (1)² (1) 96, 12
(s. Διάκριτος)
ARGOLIS:
—EPIDAUROS: (**3**) iv BC ib. XII (5) 542, 15 ([Ξε-
νόδ]οκος: s. Εὐαρχίδας: name—*LGPN*); (**4**) ~
Peek, *NIEpid* 32, 2 ([Ξ]ενόδοκος); (**5**) iii BC
Peek, *IAEpid* 102 (f. Καλλίτιμος, Χοροκλῆς);
(**6**) ii/i BC *IG* IV (1)² 65, 15, 19, [23]; 630, 2-3
(f. Ἀριστόβουλος); (**7**) ~ ib. 232, 2 (f. Εὐαρέτα)
——Pagasina (Azantioi): (**8**) m. iii BC ib. 96, 47
(Perlman E.3); Perlman p. 63 f. (date)
—HERMIONE: (**9**) iii BC *IG* IV (1) 729 I, 19 (s.
Σωσίων)
KORINTHIA:
—KORINTH: (**10**) i AD ib. II² 9065 (f. Διοκλῆς)
MESSENIA: (**11**) 744 BC Moretti, *Olymp.* 9 (Ξ.—
Paus., Ξενοκλῆς—Afric.)
TRIPHYLIA:
—PHRIXA: (**12**) c. 230-200 BC *BCH* 45 (1921)
p. 13 II, 86 (s. Ἀγυλλος)

**Ξενοδώρα**
SICILY:
—MORGANTINA: (**1**) imp. *Epigrafia del Villaggio*
p. 548 (Lat. Iulia Xenodora)

**Ξενόι**
EPIROS:
—AMBRAKIA: (**1**) iii BC *Op. Ath.* 10 (1971) p. 64
no. 10 (d. Εὔδικος)

**Ξένοια**
KEPHALLENIA:
—SAME: (**1**) iv/iii BC ib. p. 66 no. 14

**Ξενοίτας**
ACHAIA: (**1**) m. iii BC *RE* (-)

**Ξενοκάδης**
S. ITALY (CALABRIA):
—TARAS-TARENTUM: (**1**) iv/iii BC *IG* XIV 668 I,
5 (Landi, *DISMG* 194)
S. ITALY (LUCANIA):
—METAPONTION: (**2**) iv BC Iamb., *VP* 267
(*FVS* I p. 446)

**Ξενοκλέα**
ACHAIA:
—PATRAI: (**1**) iii-ii BC *Achaean Grave Stelai* 65
(Ξενοκλέας—index: d. Ἀγεσίλαος)
ARKADIA:
—THELPHOUSA: (**2**) i BC/i AD *SEG* XI 1129

**Ξενοκλέας**
EPIROS:
—AMBRAKIA: (**1**) hell.-imp. *BCH* 17 (1893) p.
632 no. 2 (s. Ξενόλαος)

**Ξενοκλείδας**
AIGINA: (**1**) ?f. i AD *Alt-Ägina* I (2) p. 45 no.
17, 1 (s. Μητρόδωρος)
ARKADIA:
—HERAIA: (**2**) s. v BC Paus. vi 3. 11 (-δης: f.
Νικόστρατος)
KORINTHIA:
—KORINTH: (**3**) 433-426 BC Th. i 46. 2; iii 114.
4 (Ξενοκλείδης—Th. i 46: s. Εὐθυκλῆς)
—SIKYON: (**4**) 356-345 BC *CID* II 120 A, 42
(Skalet 237) (f. Ξενότιμος)
LAKONIA:
—HIPPOLA: (**5**) iii/ii BC *IG* V (1) 1336, 3, 12 (s.
Νικοσθένης)
—KOTYRTA: (**6**) imp. ib. 1013
—SPARTA: (**7**) s. i BC ib. 124, 14 (Bradford (1))
(s. Εὔκ—)

**Ξενοκλῆς**
ACHAIA:
—DYME: (**1**) iii BC *AJPh* 31 (1910) p. 399 no.
74 a, 11 (f. Λυσίας)
ARGOLIS:
—ARGOS: (**2**) iii BC *IG* IV (1) 618 I, 6 (f. Κέλα-
δος)
—EPIDAUROS: (**3**) c. 370 BC ib. IV (1)² 102, 264;
(**4**) f. ii AD ib. 678, 6; 686, 8; *BSA* 80 (1985)
p. 256 (ident., date) (Τιβ. Κλ. Ξ.: s. Φαιδρίας,
f. Τιβ. Κλ. Φαιδρίας, Τιβ. Κλ. Παῦλος) ?= (*5*);
(**5**) ~ Peek, *NIEpid* 90, 4 ((Ξ)ενοκλῆς) ?= (*4*);
(**6**) 225 AD *IG* IV (1)² 406 (Τι(β). Κλ. Ξ.)
——Alamais: (**7**) c. 310-300 BC ib. 114, 13
(Ξενοκλῆ[s])
——Upper Oiseia: (**8**) m. iii BC ib. 96, 41 (Perl-
man E.3); Perlman p. 63 f. (date)
—KLEONAI: (**9**) c. 210-207 BC *IG* IV (1)² 73, 10;
*SEG* XXXV 303 (date) (f. Νικίας)
ARKADIA:
—MAINALIOI: (**10**) c. 400-370 BC Moretti,
*Olymp.* 408; cf. Ebert, *Gr. Sieg.* 32 (s. Εὐ-
θύφρων)
—MEGALOPOLIS: (**11**) ?145 BC *IG* V (2) 439, 57
(s. Ξένων, f. Ξένων)
—TEGEA: (**12**) iv BC ib. 31, 3 (f. Ἀριστοπάμων);
(**13**) c. 240-229 BC ib. 11, 16
——(Apolloniatai): (**14**) s. iv BC ib. 41, 8 (Ξε-
νοκλῆ[s]: f. —ος); (**15**) iv/iii BC ib. 38, 33 (f.
Τιμόστρατος)
DALMATIA:
—ISSA: (**16**) iii BC *SEG* XXXV 691, 1, 10 (*VAHD*
84 (1991) p. 256 no. 6) (s. Δαφναῖος, f. Δαφναῖος); (**17**) ~ *SEG* XXXV 691, 2, 4 (*VAHD*
84 (1991) p. 256 no. 6) (s. Πάμφιλος, f. Πάμφιλος); (**18**) ~ *SEG* XXXV 691, 3 (*VAHD* 84
(1991) p. 256 no. 6) (f. Φιλίστα); (**19**) ~ *SEG*
XXXV 691, 5 (*VAHD* 84 (1991) p. 256 no.
6) (f. Ἀριστόνικος); (**20**) ~ *SEG* XXXV 691, 6
(*VAHD* 84 (1991) p. 256 no. 6) (f. Νικόπολις);
(**21**) ~ *SEG* XXXV 691, 8 (*VAHD* 84 (1991) p.
256 no. 6) (f. Ἀριστόνικος); (**22**) ~ *SEG* XXXV
691, 9 (*VAHD* 84 (1991) p. 256 no. 6) (f.
Ὀνάσιμος); (**23**) f. ii BC Brunšmid p. 22 no. 9,
9 (f. —ιτος)
ILLYRIA:
—APOLLONIA: (**24**) c. 250-50 BC Maier 99 (coin)
(Ceka 91) (money.)
KERKYRA: (**25**) hell. *IG* IX (1) 839 (bullet); (**26**)
?ii BC ib. 793-4; *Korkyra* I p. 169 no. 20
(tiles)
KORINTHIA:
—KORINTH: (**27**) c. 500-475 BC *IG* IV (1) 353
(vase); *LSAG*² p. 132 no. 31 (date) (-κλῆς)
—SIKYON: (**28**) vi/v BC *SEG* XI 244, 22 (-κλῆς);
(**29**) 251 BC Plu., *Arat.* 5 (Skalet 238)
LAKONIA: (**30**) 192 BC *SGDI* 2129, 3, 5
(slave/freed.)

—GERONTHRAI: (31) 72 BC *IG* V (1) 1114, 3, [10], 20 (s. *Νίκανδρος*)
—SPARTA: (32) 395-394 BC *RE* (4) (Poralla² 569); (33) ii/i BC *IG* V (1) 256 (Bradford (2)) (s. *Ἀριστόκριτος*); (34) s. i BC *IG* V (1) 95, 9 (Bradford (3)) (s. *Χαρίξενος*); (35) ~ *IG* V (1) 876 (Bradford (9)); (36) c. 30-20 BC *IG* V (1) 142, 22 (Bradford (1)) (s. *Ἁ*—); (37) c. 25-1 BC *IG* V (1) 210, 27 (Bradford (4)) (s. *Λυσίμαχος*); (38) f. i AD *IG* V (1) 269, 1; *Artemis Orthia* p. 306 no. 19 (date) (Bradford (12)) (I f. *Ξενοκλῆς* II); (39) ~ *IG* V (1) 269, 1; *Artemis Orthia* p. 306 no. 19 (date) (Bradford (8)) (II s. *Ξενοκλῆς* I); (40) c. 90-100 AD *SEG* XI 558, 11; 613, 3? (Bradford (5)) (s. *Λύσιππος*); (41) ii AD *IG* V (1) 159, 26 (Bradford (10)); (42) c. 140-150 AD *IG* V (1) 64, 3 (Bradford (7)) (*Ξ. Σκορδίας*: s. *Φιλοξενίδας*); (43) f. iii AD *IG* V (1) 541, 5; 545, [3] (Bradford (11)) (f. *M. Αὐρ. Τιμάκων*)
MESSENIA:
—MESSENE: (44) m. iii BC *IG* V (2) 368, 83 (s. *Λύσανδρος*)
—THOURIA: (45) ii/i BC ib. V (1) 1384, 3 (s. *Δαμοκράτης*)
PELOPONNESE: (46) s. iii BC *SEG* XIII 278, 15 (s. *Τιμόθεος*)
SICILY:
—KAMARINA: (47) f. v BC Cordano, *Tessere Pubbliche* 101 (-κλἔς: s. *Σῶσις*)
—MORGANTINA: (48) iv/iii BC *SEG* XXXIX 1013, 5 (*Ξεν[οκ]λῆς*: f. *Σωσίας*)
—SELINOUS: (49) s. vi BC Dubois, *IGDS* 30 (Arena, *Iscr. Sic.* 1 62) (-κλἔς)
ZAKYNTHOS: (50) s. iv BC *Iasos* 27

**Ξενοκρατέας**
ARKADIA:
—TEGEA?: (1) ii BC *IG* IV (1)² 226

**Ξενοκράτεια**
ACHAIA:
—DYME: (1) iii BC *AJPh* 31 (1910) p. 399 no. 74 a, 2; p. 399 no. 74 c, 12 (m. *Θεόκριτος*)
KEPHALLENIA:
—SAME: (2) hell. *IG* IX (1) 623
LAKONIA:
—SPARTA: (3) s. ii AD ib. V (1) 584, 3; [585]; 586, 2; *SEG* XXXVI 353, 3; *BSA* 80 (1985) pp. 194; 206-8 (ident., stemma) (Bradford (-)) (*Μεμμία Ξ.*: d. *Π. Μέμμιος Δεξίμαχος*, m. *Καλλιστονίκη, Ἄλκαστος, Ἰουλ. Ἐτυμοκλήδεια*)

**Ξενοκράτης**
AITOLIA: (1) ?254 BC *Syll³* 436, 3; Nachtergael, *Les Galates* 9, 5
AKARNANIA:
—STRATOS: (2) ?205-203 BC *FD* III (2) 134 b, 4 (*Syll³* 564); (3) ii BC *IG* IX (1)² (2) 409; (4) 154 BC *SGDI* 1908, 14 (I f. *Ξενοκράτης* II); (5) ~ ib. l. 14 (II s. *Ξενοκράτης* I)
ARGOLIS:
—ARGOS: (6) c. 100-90 BC *SEG* XXXIII 290 A, 10; *BSA* 70 (1975) pp. 129-31 (date) (Stephanis 1907) (s. *Νικίας*)
ARKADIA:
—ALIPHEIRA: (7) ?273 BC *SEG* XXV 447, 12 (*IPArk* 24); *Chiron* 3 (1973) pp. 85-93 (date); (8) c. 230-200 BC *BCH* 45 (1921) p. 12 II, 80 (f. *Εὐθύδαμος*)
—MEGALOPOLIS: (9) s. ii BC *IG* V (2) 439, 73 (s. *Ἀλκιμέδων*)
—TEGEA: (10) iv BC ib. 31, 5 (f. *Λυσίνικος*)
DALMATIA:
—ISSA:
——(Hylleis): (11) iv/iii BC Brunšmid p. 8, 30 (s. *Λ...ων*)
EPIROS:
—AMBRAKIA: (12) 284 BC *IG* XI (2) 105, 24
LAKONIA:
—OITYLOS: (13) ii BC ib. V (1) 1595 (*Ξενοκράτ[ης]*)

—SPARTA: (14) c. 70-90 AD ib. 480, 12 (Bradford (2)) (s. *Φιλωνίδας*); (15) c. 110 AD *SEG* XI 542, 4 (Bradford (3)) (f. *Ἀγαθοκλῆς*); (16) c. 110-150 AD *IG* V (1) 114, 9; *SEG* XI 540, 6 (Bradford (5)) (f. *Θεόφιλος*); (17) c. 115-120 AD *SEG* XI 543, 3 (Bradford (1)) (s. *Φιλόμουσος*); (18) c. 140-145 AD *IG* V (1) 63, 18 (Bradford (4)) (f. *Ἀνδρόνικος*)
LEUKAS: (19) c. 450-425 BC *AM* 27 (1902) p. 368 no. 31; *LSAG²* p. 229 no. 9 (date) ([*Ξ*]*ενοκράτἔς*)
MESSENIA:
—MESSENE: (20) iii BC *SEG* XXIII 210, 29; (21) f. iii BC *PAE* 1991, p. 99 no. 7, 14; (22) s. ii BC *SEG* XLI 341, 14 (f. *Πολυκράτης*); (23) 139 BC *FD* III (1) 455, 1 (*Ξενοκρά[της]*); (24) 31 BC-14 AD *SEG* XXIII 207, 31 (s. *Τιμοκράτης*)
—MESSENE?: (25) ii/i BC ib. XI 979, 49
S. ITALY (CALABRIA):
—TARAS-TARENTUM: (26) c. 235-228 BC Vlasto 955-61 (coins) (Evans, *Horsemen* p. 195 IX G.1)
SICILY:
—AKRAGAS: (27) vi/v BC *RE* (1) (s. *Αἰνησίδαμος*, f. *Θρασύβουλος*)
—KAMARINA: (28) f. v BC Cordano, *Tessere Pubbliche* 74 (-τἔς: s. *Ἁ*—)
—LIPARA: (29) hell.? Libertini, *Isole Eolie* p. 220 no. 20 (—*εν*—*οκρατεος*—apogr., [*Ξ*]*ενοκράτης, Δεινοκράτης*—ed.)

**Ξενοκρίτη**
S. ITALY (CAMPANIA):
—KYME: (1) vi/v BC *RE* (9)

**Ξενόκριτος**
AITOLIA:
—TRICHONION: (1) 154 BC *SGDI* 1908, 17 (s. *Ποτάμων*)
ARKADIA:
—TEGEA:
——(Apolloniatai): (2) iv/iii BC *IG* V (2) 38, 37 (s. *Ὑναίσιμος*)
KORINTHIA:
—SIKYON: (3) iv BC *SEG* XI 260; (4) i BC *NC* 1984, p. 19 Group 12 no. 6 (coin) (*Ξενόκρι(τος)*)
S. ITALY (BRUTTIUM):
—LOKROI EPIZEPHYRIOI: (5) vii BC *RE* (2)

**Ξενολαΐδας**
ARGOLIS:
—TROIZEN: (1) iii BC *IG* IV (1) 824, 7 (s. *Νικόστρατος*)

**Ξενόλαος**
EPIROS:
—AMBRAKIA: (1) hell.-imp. *BCH* 17 (1893) p. 632 no. 2 (f. *Ξενοκλέας*)
—ARGOS (AMPHILOCH.): (2) i BC-i AD *IG* IX (1) 533
KEPHALLENIA:
—SAME: (3) c. 230-200 BC *BCH* 45 (1921) p. 14 II, 140 (s. *Τιμόμαχος*)

**Ξενόλας**
KORINTHIA:
—KORINTH: (1) hell. *SEG* XI 220 a (*Corinth* II p. 35)

**Ξενόλυτος**
SICILY:
—KAMARINA: (1) f. v BC Cordano, *Tessere Pubbliche* 123 (*Ξενόλυτ[ος]*)

**Ξενομένης**
ACHAIA:
—AIGION: (1) c. 230-200 BC *BCH* 45 (1921) p. 11 II, 57 (f. *Ἀρίστανδρος*: name—Oulhen)
AITOLIA:
—PHILOTAIEIS?: (2) c. 157 BC *IG* IX (1)² (1) 108, 10

AKARNANIA:
—THYRREION: (3) ii BC ib. IX (1)² (2) 251, 6 (I f. *Ξενομένης* II); (4) ~ ib. l. 6 (II s. *Ξενομένης* I); (5) a. 167 BC *NZ* 10 (1878) p. 176 nos. 26-8; *NC* 1900, p. 284; *BMC Thessaly* p. 193 no. 13; *SNG Lockett* 2787 (coins); (6) m. i BC *RE* (-) (Lat. Xenomenes)
ARKADIA:
—KLEITOR: (7) imp. *IG* V (2) 378; (8) a. 212 AD ib. 369, 14; *SEG* XXXI 347, 6
LAKONIA:
—SPARTA: (9) c. 132 AD ib. XI 579, 5 (Bradford (-)) (f. *Στράτων*)

**Ξενοπείθεια**
LAKONIA:
—SPARTA: (1) v/iv BC *FGrH* 115 F 240 (Poralla² 570) (m. *Λυσανδρίδας*)

**Ξενοπείθηρ**
ELIS:
—KOILE (DAPHNIOTISSA (MOD.)): (1) imp. *SEG* XXII 335

**Ξενοπείθης**
ACHAIA:
—TRITAIA: (1) c. 230-200 BC *BCH* 45 (1921) p. 14 II, 129 ([*Ξ*]*ενοπείθη[ς]*)
ARKADIA:
—PALLANTION: (2) c. 230-200 BC ib. p. 15 III, 8 (?s. *Ξενο*—: name—Oulhen)
—TEGEA: (3) 369-361 BC *IG* V (2) 1, 14; Tod, *GHI* II 132 (date)
KORINTHIA:
—SIKYON: (4) vi/v BC *SEG* XI 244, 53 (-θἔς)

**Ξένος**
ARGOLIS:
—EPIDAUROS: (1) f. iv BC Peek, *IAEpid* 1
EPIROS:
—BOUTHROTOS (PRASAIBOI): (2) a. 163 BC *IBouthrot* 19, 9 (*SEG* XXXVIII 476) (n. pr.?)
S. ITALY (CAMPANIA):
—NEAPOLIS: (3) iii-iv AD *INap* 242
SICILY:
—KAMARINA: (4) f. v BC Cordano, *Tessere Pubbliche* 83 (s. *Ἔξακις*)
—SYRACUSE: (5) iii-v AD Strazzulla 227 (Wessel 1155); cf. Ferrua, *NG* 290 ([*Φιλό*]*ξενος?*—Ferrua)

**Ξενοστράτα**
ARKADIA:
—THISOA?: (1) iii-ii BC *IG* V (2) 501

**Ξενόστρατος**
ARGOLIS:
—HERMIONE: (1) ?ii-i BC ib. IV (1) 733, 7 (*Ξενός[τρατος]*: f. *Ζευξίας*)
ARKADIA: (2) 316 BC ib. V (2) 549, 33 (f. *Διεύχης*)
—MEGALOPOLIS: (3) 312 BC ib. l. 37
LAKONIA:
—KARDAMYLE: (4) i BC-i AD ib. V (1) 1334 (*Ξενόσστ[ρατος]*: s. *Ἀγάσιππος*)
—SPARTA: (5) c. 25-1 BC ib. 212, 15 (Bradford (1)) (f. *Ἀριστόκριτος*); (6) c. 70-100 AD *IG* V (1) 676, 3 (Bradford (2)) (f. *Ξένων*)
MESSENIA:
—MESSENE: (7) iii BC *SEG* XXIII 210, 27
—THOURIA: (8) ii-i BC *IG* V (1) 1385, 20 (f. *Αὐτολαΐδας*); (9) f. ii BC *SEG* XI 972, 92 (f. *Νεόπολις*)

**Ξενοτέλης**
ARGOLIS:
—EPIDAUROS*: (1) c. 320-300 BC *IG* IV (1)² 110 A, 25, 27, 29, 31, 33, 36
ARKADIA:
—MANTINEIA-ANTIGONEIA: (2) c. 300-221 BC ib. V (2) 323. 32 (tessera) (s. *Νεάδας*)
—PALLANTION: (3) a. 420 BC *REG* 62 (1949) p. 6, 2 (*Ξενοτέλ[ης]*)

**Ξενοτίμα**
ELIS:
—LASION: (1) vi BC *SEG* XI 1173 c
EPIROS:
—PHOINIKE: (2) iii/ii BC Cabanes, *L'Épire* pp. 569 ff. no. 47, 7 (*SEG* XXVI 720)

**Ξενότιμος**
ACHAIA: (1) 146 BC *IG* IV (1)² 28, 80 (f. Ἀφρο-δίσιος: synoikos)
—DYME: (2) s. iii BC *SEG* XIII 278, 26 (f. Ἀντι-γένης)
—PELLENE: (3) m. iii BC *IG* v (2) 368, 104 (s. Θεόξενος)
AKARNANIA:
—PALAIROS: (4) hell.? ib. IX (1)² (2) 568
ARGOLIS:
—HERMIONE: (5) ii-i BC ib. IV (1) 692 (s. Πολυ-κλῆς)
ARKADIA: (6) ?253 BC ib. II² 3083, 10; Nachter-gael, *Les Galates* 10, 17; cf. Stephanis 1587 (f. Λύσιππος)
—TEGEA: (7) f. ii BC *IG* v (2) 44, 6 (s. Ξενίας); (8) imp. ib. 234
——(Apolloniatai): (9) m. iii BC ib. 36, 99 (s. Εὐμηλίδας)
——(Athaneatai): (10) s. iv BC ib. 41, 39 (f. Εὐ-μηλίδας)
——(Hippothoitai): (11) iii BC ib. 40, 39 (s. Φά-λαρος)
DALMATIA:
—ISSA: (12) f. ii BC Brunšmid p. 22 no. 9, 7 ([Ξ]ενότιμος: s. Σάλλας)
——(Pamphyloi): (13) iv/iii BC ib. p. 8, 27 (f. Λυσανίας)
ELIS: (14) ?180 BC Klee p. 12 II B, 74
KORINTHIA:
—SIKYON: (15) b. 356 BC *CID* II 8 II, 12 ?= (16); (16) 356-345 BC ib. 31, 12, 22, 44, 76, 82; 120 A, 42, 44 (Skalet 240) ([Ξενότι]μος—no. 120: s. Ξενοκλείδας, f. Εὔστρατος) ?= (15); (17) c. 146-32 BC BM coin 1920 5-15-136; *NC* 1984, p. 15 Group 10 no. 3 (coin)
LAKONIA:
—SPARTA: (18) hell.? *IG* v (1) 792 ([Ξ]ενότιμ[ος]?: s. Ξέναρχος)
SICILY:
—MORGANTINA (NR.): (19) ?iii BC Manganaro, *PdelP* forthcoming no. 7, 4 (s. Ἡρακλείδας)

**Ξενοφάης**
KORINTHIA:
—SIKYON: (1) vi/v BC *SEG* XI 244, 29 (-ῆς)

**Ξενοφάνης**
ARGOLIS:
—EPIDAUROS: (1) i-ii AD *IG* IV (1)² 520 (s. Δε-ξέας)
ARKADIA:
—MEGALOPOLIS: (2) i BC/i AD ib. v (2) 515 A, 33 ([Ξε]νοφάνης)
—TEGEA:
——(Apolloniatai): (3) m. iii BC ib. 36, 98 (f. Πατροκλείδας)
LAKONIA: (4) ii BC ib. v (1) 1111, 36
—SPARTA: (5) s. i BC ib. 95, 7 (Bradford (2)) (s. Μεν—); (6) c. 25-1 BC *IG* v (1) 212, 30 (Bradford (4)) (I f. Ξενοφάνης II); (7) ~ *IG* v (1) 212, 30 (Bradford (3)) (II s. Ξενοφάνης I); (8) c. 100-105 AD *IG* v (1) 79, 14; *SEG* XI 546 a, 7; 546 b, 7 (Bradford (1)) (Τιβ. Κλ. Ξ.: s. Τιβ. Κλ. Ἁρμόνικος)
MESSENIA:
—MESSENE: (9) i AD *IG* v (1) 1436, 1
SICILY:
—SYRACUSE: (10) v BC *FGrH* 555 T 1 (f. Ἀντί-οχος)

**Ξενοφάντα**
ARGOLIS:
—METHANA-ARSINOE: (1) ii BC *IG* IV (1) 855, 2 (d. Τιμασικράτης, m. Ἀριστόδαμος)

**Ξενοφάντης**
S. ITALY (LUCANIA):
—METAPONTION: (1) iv BC Iamb., *VP* 267 (*FVS* 1 p. 446)

**Ξενοφαντίδας**
LAKONIA: (1) 412 BC Th. viii 55. 2 (Poralla² 571)

**Ξενόφαντος**
ACHAIA: (1) 220 BC *PPetr* III 112 g, 11 (f. Σω-σίβιος)
—PATRAI: (2) c. 146-32 BC Mionnet 2 p. 191 no. 319 (coin) (s. Σωσίστρατος)
AIGINA: (3) s. v BC *SEG* XXXVII 254 (vase)
AKARNANIA:
—PALAIROS: (4) f. iv BC *IG* IX (1)² (2) 460 (Ξε-νοφάντō (gen.))
—THYRREION: (5) ii BC ib. 250, 17; 251, 3 (s. Δάζιμος); (6) ~ ib. l. 10 (I f. Ξενόφαντος II); (7) ~ ib. l. 10 (II s. Ξενόφαντος I)
ARGOLIS:
—ARGOS: (8) 337-336 BC *CID* II 74 I, 73; 76 II, 22 (s. Διόδωρος) ?= (Ξενοφάων (1))
——(Dmaihippidai): (9) ii/i BC *BCH* 33 (1909) p. 176 no. 2, 12 (f. Φιλοκλῆς)
——(Hyrnathioi-Temenidai): (10) c. 400 BC *SEG* XXIX 361, 25
—EPIDAUROS*: (11) c. 370-365 BC Peek, *IA-Epid* 52 A, 8 (Ξ[ενό]φαντος)
ARKADIA:
—PHIGALEIA: (12) m. iii BC *SEG* XXIII 239, 3
—TEGEA:
——(Krariotai): (13) f. iii BC *IG* v (2) 36, 38 (s. Ἀριστίων)
ILLYRIA:
—APOLLONIA: (14) c. 250-50 BC Maier 79 (coin) (Ceka 111) (pryt.); (15) i BC *BMC Thessaly* p. 62 no. 80 (coin) (Ξενόφ(αντος))
ITHAKE: (16) hell. *BCH* 29 (1905) p. 164 no. 2
KERKYRA: (17) a. 179 BC *Syll*³ 638, 12 (*IDyrrh* 520); Kramolisch p. 54 A 18 (date) (s. —μέας)
S. ITALY (CAMPANIA):
—KYME: (18) f. v BC Dubois, *IGDGG* I 21 d (vase) (Arena, *Iscr. Sic.* III 20); *LSAG*² p. 240 no. 11 (date)

**Ξενοφάων**
ARGOLIS:
—ARGOS: (1) 336-334 BC *CID* II 75 II, 43; 79 A I, 18 ?= (Ξενόφαντος (8))

**Ξενόφιλος**
ACHAIA:
—DYME: (1) hell.? *SGDI* 1616 (f. Θευξένα); (2) ii BC *Achaean Grave Stelai* 32 (f. Ἀριστώ)
ARGOLIS:
—ARGOS: (3) 251 BC Plu., *Arat.* 6; (4) c. 146-32 BC *BMC Pelop.* p. 145 nos. 117-18 (coins); (5) ii/i BC Marcadé 1 109-11 + *SEG* XIX 400; cf. *Corinth* VIII (3) 47; p. 20 with n. 10; *SEG* XVII 153 (s. Στράτων, f. Στράτων: sculptor) ?= (6); (6) 105 BC *JÖAI* 14 (1911) Beibl. p. 146 no. 4, 15 ([Ξε]νόφιλος: s. Στράτων) ?= (5)
ARKADIA:
—GORTYS: (7) ii-i BC *SEG* XXXV 348 (f. Πασι-ξένα)
MESSENIA:
—MESSENE: (8) ii BC ib. XLI 349 (s. Δαμοφῶν: sculptor); (9) f. ii BC ib. XXIII 219; XLI 325 A; XXXVIII 342; cf. XLI 350 (s. Φίλιππος, f. Δαμοφῶν); (10) s. ii BC *IG* v (2) 539-40 + *SEG* XLI 352 B (s. Δαμοφῶν: sculptor); (11) ~ ib. 352 A (s. Δαμοφῶν, Θεοφάνεια: sculptor)
TRIPHYLIA:
—LEPREON: (12) iv/iii BC ib. XXII 359

**Ξενόφρων**
SICILY: (1) ?v-iv BC Philostr., *VS* 511

**Ξενοφῶν**
ACHAIA:
—AIGION: (1) 380 BC *RE* (17); Moretti, *Olymp.* 400 (s. Μενέφυλος); (2) iii/ii BC *RE* (3); *IG* IX (1)² (1) 29, [26]; *Syll*³ 585, 28 (s. Εὐρυλέων, f. Ἄλκιθος)
—PHARAI: (3) ii/i BC *AE* 1973, p. 167 (f. Θρά-σων)
AITOLIA: (4) iii/ii BC Pantos, *Sphragismata* p. 153 no. 123; p. 447 f.
ARGOLIS:
—EPIDAUROS*: (5) c. 370 BC *IG* IV (1)² 102, 52
—TROIZEN: (6) iv BC ib. IV (1) 764, 4 (f. Τιμο-κλῆς)
ARKADIA:
—ALIPHEIRA: (7) ?273 BC *SEG* XXV 447, 11 (*IPArk* 24); *Chiron* 3 (1973) pp. 85-93 (date)
—KLEITOR: (8) i AD *IG* v (2) 379
—MAINALIOI: (9) 369-361 BC ib. 1, 19; Tod, *GHI* II 132 (date)
ELIS: (10) ?277 BC *FD* III (1) 126, 2 (s. Φιλῖνος)
KORINTHIA:
—KORINTH: (11) 464 BC Moretti, *Olymp.* 249-250; Pi., *O.* xiii, 28; cf. *Dionysiaca* pp. 1-16 (s. Θεσσαλός)
LAKONIA:
—KARYAI?: (12) ii-iii AD *IG* v (1) 922 (*GVI* 382)
—SPARTA: (13) hell.-imp. *IG* v (1) 195, 8 (Bradford (2)) (s. Ξ—); (14) f. ii AD *IG* v (1) 466, 2, 7; 1314, 30 (Bradford (1)) (s. Νυμφόδοτος, f. Νυμφόδοτος); (15) c. 105-110 AD *IG* v (1) 20 B, 4; *BSA* 26 (1923-5) p. 168 C 7, 5 (Bradford (3)) (f. Νυμφόδοτος)
S. ITALY (CAMPANIA):
—DIKAIARCHIA-PUTEOLI: (16) imp. *CIL* x 2711 (Lat. Marius Xenophon)
SICILY:
—KAMARINA: (17) f. v BC Cordano, *Tessere Pub-bliche* 58 (Arena, *Iscr. Sic.* II 137 A) (Ξε-νοφ[ō]ν: f. [..]ρο[..]ς)

**Ξενοχάρης**
ACHAIA:
—DYME*: (1) c. 219 BC *SGDI* 1612, 63 (*Tyche* 5 (1990) p. 124) (s. Ξενάρης)
LAKONIA:
—SPARTA: (2) c. 25-1 BC *IG* v (1) 212, 44 (Brad-ford (-)) (f. Ἀριστόδαμος)
MESSENIA:
—MESSENE: (3) f. iii BC *PAE* 1991, p. 99 no. 7, 17; (4) c. 146-32 BC *BMC Pelop.* p. 110 nos. 18-19 (coin)

**Ξενόχαρις**
S. ITALY (BRUTTIUM):
—LOKROI EPIZEPHYRIOI:
——(Πυρ.): (1) iv/iii BC De Franciscis 33, 5 (s. Φάλακρος)

**Ξενυλλίς**
DALMATIA:
—ISSA: (1) ii BC *SEG* XXXI 600 (d. Φιλύας)

**Ξένυλλος**
ILLYRIA:
—OLYMPE: (1) s. iii BC ib. XXXV 697 (s. Δαμάρ-μενος)
KORINTHIA:
—KORINTH: (2) c. 480 BC *Corinth* VIII (1) 28

**Ξένυς**
EPIROS: (1) c. 330 BC Cabanes, *L'Épire* p. 580 no. 55, 4; (2) iii BC ib. p. 587 no. 73, 7
—DODONA: (3) iii BC Antoniou, *Dodone* Ab, 35
—IKADOTOI: (4) m. iv BC Cabanes, *L'Épire* p. 576 no. 49, 5 (*SEG* XXVI 717) (s. Νικάνωρ)
—POLICAN (MOD.): (5) hell.? ib. XXIV 473 (s. Ἀρχέλαος)

**Ξενύτας**
ACHAIA:
—AIGION: (1) s. iii BC *IG* IV (1) 727 A, 9 (Perl-man H.1) (f. —κος)

**Ξενώ**

ACHAIA:
—TRITAIA: (1) hell.-imp. Neratzoulis p. 22 no. 8 (*Achaïe* II 318) (d. *Αἰσχρίων*)

ARGOLIS:
—HERMIONE: (2) iii BC *IG* IV (1) 728, 34

DALMATIA:
—ISSA: (3) iii BC *SEG* XXXV 691, 7 (*VAHD* 84 (1991) p. 256 no. 6) (d. *Ζωΐλος*)

EPIROS:
—AMBRAKIA: (4) iii-ii BC *Op. Ath.* 10 (1971) p. 64 no. 12, 3; cf. *VAHD* 84 (1991) p. 262 (d. *Νίκων*)
—BOUTHROTOS (PRASAIBOI): (5) a. 163 BC *IBouthrot* 50, 3 ?= (*Ξένα* (1))

ILLYRIA:
—EPIDAMNOS-DYRRHACHION: (6) hell.-imp. *IDyrrh* 336

KERKYRA: (7) f. iii BC *IG* IX (1)² (2) 470

LAKONIA:
—SPARTA: (8) f. iii AD ib. V (1) 535, 18 (Bradford (-)) (*Αὐρ. Ξ.*: d. *Εὔτυχος*)

**Ξένων**

ACHAIA: (1) 316-309 BC *IG* II² 1956, 194, 197; *Ancient Macedonia* 5 p. 445 with n. 10 (date) (?s. *Μεγακλῆς*); (2) iii/ii BC *IG* XII (9) 836 (f. *Φιλόστρατος*: date—Knoepfler); (3) 146 BC ib. IV (1)² 28, 99 (s. *Σωτηρίδας*: synoikos)
—AIGION: (4) m. ii BC *RE* (7)
—DYME: (5) s. iii BC *SEG* XIII 278, 29 (s. *Νίκανδρος*)
—PATRAI: (6) ?iii BC ib. XXXIV 472; (7) f. ii BC *RE* (6)
—PHARAI: (8) c. 210-207 BC *IG* IV (1)² 73, 22; *SEG* XXXV 303 (date) (s. *Σάτυρος*)

AIGINA: (9) ii/i BC *Alt-Ägina* I (2) p. 43 no. 3, 2 (s. *Δημήτριος*)

AITOLIA:
—PHISTYON: (10) 163 BC *IG* IX (1)² (1) 101, 11; 102, 2; 103, 3 ?= (*11*); (11) ~ ib. 102, 9-10; 103, 10 ?= (*10*)
—THERMOS*: (12) s. iii BC ib. 60 VII, 11

AKARNANIA:
—OINIADAI: (13) iii/ii BC ib. IX (1)² (2) 419. 10
—PALAIROS: (14) iii/ii BC ib. 550 ([*Ξ*]*ένων*); (15) ?ii BC ib. 559 ((*Ξ*)*ένων*)
—STRATOS: (16) ii BC ib. 394, 15 (f. *Ἀπολλώνιος*, *Λάμιος*); (17) a. 167 BC ib. IX (2) 6 a, 3; cf. Stählin p. 220 (date) (s. *Λάμιος*)
—THYRREION: (18) ii BC *GVI* 1822, 5 (*IG* IX (1)² (2) 313) (f. *Νίκαρχος*); (19) ~ ib. 252, 6 (s. *Σαμιάδας*)

ARGOLIS:
—ARGOS: (20) ii/i BC ib. IV (1) 694 (*Ξένω*[*ν*]: f. *Δαμαρέτα*); (21) ?114 BC ib. 558, 35 (Stephanis 1917); (22) c. 100-90 BC *SEG* XXXIII 290 A, 12; *BSA* 70 (1975) pp. 129-31 (date); cf. Stephanis 1922 (I f. *Ξένων* II); (23) ~ *SEG* XXXIII 290 A, 12; *BSA* 70 (1975) pp. 129-31 (date) (Stephanis 1922) (II s. *Ξένων* I)
—EPIDAUROS*: (24) c. 370 BC *IG* IV (1)² 102, 237, 283, 302
—HERMIONE: (25) iii BC ib. IV (1) 728, 10 (f. *Μενεκράτης*); (26) ~ *RE* (3) (tyrant); (27) 256-250 BC *IG* XI (2) 161 A, 35; 161 D, 85; 162 A, 26, 35; 203 D, 80; 204, 85; 226 A, 26; 287 A, 191; *ID* 291 d, 27; 317 a, 11; (28) ii-i BC *IG* IV (1) 732 I, 11 (s. *Ἀριστόλα*); (29) ~ ib. 732 III, 21 (f. *Ἀφροδισία*); (30) ~ ib. l. 26 (f. *Καλλισθένης*)
—ARKADIA: (31) ?253 BC Nachtergael, *Les Galates* 10, 27 (Stephanis 1923) (s. *Σάτυρος*)
—MEGALOPOLIS: (32) iii BC *Coll. Alex.* p. 203 no. 4, 5; (33) ?145 BC *IG* V (2) 439, 57 (f. *Ξενοκλῆς*, *Νικανδρία*); (34) ~ ib. l. 61 (s. *Ξενοκλῆς*, *Νικανδρία*); (35) ii/i BC ib. 442, 10 (s. *Καλλιγένης*, f. *Καλλιγένης*)
—PHIGALEIA: (36) ii/i BC ib. 426
—STYMPHALOS: (37) iii BC ib. 356, 8

—TEGEA: (38) ii AD ib. 55, 49 (s. *Εὐτυχίων*); (39) 165 AD ib. 50, 31 (s. *Χρυσέρως*); (40) 191 AD ib. 52, 7 (I f. *Ξένων* II); (41) ~ ib. l. 7 (II s. *Ξένων* I)
——(Krariotai): (42) f. iii BC ib. 36, 47 (f. *Χαρμίων*: metic)

EPIROS:
—AMBRAKIA: (43) ii BC *SEG* XLII 543 (f. *Ἀριστόδαμος*); (44) ?ii BC Unp. (Arta Mus.); (45) 153-144 BC *FD* III (4) 31, 3, 5 (s. *Φίλιππος*)
—BOUTHROTOS (PRASAIBOI): (46) a. 163 BC *IBouthrot* 33, 7 (*SEG* XXXVIII 492)
——Prochtheioi: (47) a. 163 BC *IBouthrot* 168, 12 (*SEG* XXXVIII 469) (s. *Εὐφράνωρ*)
—KASSOPE: (48) iv/iii BC *Thess. Mnem.* 72; 74 (f. *Ξέναρχος*, *Γάλαιθος*); (49) ?c. 215-195 BC *BMC Thessaly* p. 98 nos. 10-11; Franke, *Münz. v. Epirus* p. 77 V ser. 4 (coin) (*Ζήνων*—*BMC*)
—TEPELENE (MOD.): (50) i BC-i AD? *SEG* XXIV 474, 2; cf. Hammond, *Epirus* p. 738 (locn.) (s. *Λυκίσκος*)

ILLYRIA:
—APOLLONIA: (51) c. 250-50 BC Maier 32 + Münsterberg Nachtr. p. 12 (coin) (Ceka 92) (money.); (52) i BC Maier 136; 153 (coin) (s. *Φίλλος*: money.); (53) ii AD *IApoll* 207 (f. *Ἡρακλείδας*)
—EPIDAMNOS-DYRRHACHION: (54) c. 250-50 BC Maier 92-4; 103; 179; 351; 376; 388; 405; Münsterberg p. 39; p. 260 = Nachtr. pp. 14-16 (Ceka 353-63); cf. *IApoll Ref. Bibl.* n. 11 (coin) (money.)

KORINTHIA:
—KORINTH: (55) 362-359 BC *CID* II 1 II, 33; 5 II, 4; cf. 31, 29; (56) iii BC *IG* II² 9053 (f. *Ἀμύντωρ*); (57) ?254 BC Nachtergael, *Les Galates* 9, 14 (Stephanis 1918)
—SIKYON: (58) ?iv-iii BC Plin., *NH* XXXV 146 (Skalet 243) (Lat. Xenon: painter); (59) ?255 BC Nachtergael, *Les Galates* 8, 24 (Skalet 244; Stephanis 1921) (s. *Λύσανδρος*)

LAKONIA:
—SPARTA: (60) s. i BC *IG* V (1) 135, 9 (Bradford (4)) (f. *Τιμόκριτος*); (61) c. 30-20 BC *IG* V (1) 141, 28; *SEG* XXXV 329 (date) (Bradford (1)) (s. *Ἀν*—); (62) ~ *IG* V (1) 142, 6 (Bradford (5)); (63) c. 70-100 AD *IG* V (1) 676, 3 (Bradford (2)) (s. *Ξενόστρατος*); (64) a. 212 AD *IG* V (1) 600, 3, 11 (Bradford (3)) (*Αὐρ. Ξ.*: f. *Αὐρ. Φορτουνᾶτα*)

MESSENIA:
—ASINE: (65) hell.-imp. *IG* V (1) 1407 (f. *Τίμαιος*)
—THOURIA: (66) s. iii BC ib. 1386, 10 (s. *Ἐπιτέλης*); (67) ~ ib. l. 15 (s. *Ξένιππος*); (68) f. ii BC *SEG* XI 972, 87 (f. *Χαρίδαμος*); (69) ~ ib. l. 99 (s. *Θεόδοτος*); (70) ii/i BC *IG* V (1) 1384, 17 (s. *Σωσίνικος*); (71) ~ ib. l. 20 (s. *Πασίων*)
—PELOPONNESE: (72) c. 192 BC *SEG* XIII 327, 13 (*Ξέν*[*ω*]*ν*: f. *Αἰνησίων*)

S. ITALY (APULIA): (73) v BC *Mél. Nicole* p. 163 (vase)

S. ITALY (BRUTTIUM):
—LOKROI EPIZEPHYRIOI: (74) iv BC Iamb., *VP* 267 (*FVS* 1 p. 447)
——(Ἀλχ.): (75) iv/iii BC De Franciscis 15, 3; 26, 5 (s. *Σώσιππος*)
——(Μνα.): (76) 277 BC ib. 8, 2; 31, 2 (f. *Εὔφραστος*)

S. ITALY (CAMPANIA):
—MISENUM*: (77) imp. *CIL* X 3488 (Lat. L. Atilius Xeno)
—PANDATERIA: (78) imp. *Storia di Napoli* 1 p. 252 (Lat. Xenon)

S. ITALY (LUCANIA):
—METAPONTION: (79) m. v BC *FD* III (4) 453, 2 (-*νōν*: s. *Φάϋλλος*)

SICILY: (80) iii-ii BC Vandermersch p. 172 (amph.) (or S. Italy) ?= (*81*); (81) ~ ib. p. 173 (amph.) (or S. Italy) ?= (*80*)

—AKRAGAS: (82) v BC *Suda* A 1026 (*FSA* p. 108 F 1) (f. *Ἄκρων*)
—AKRAI: (83) ?iii BC *SGDI* 3240, 8 (*Akrai* p. 156 no. 7) (s. *Ἀριστέας*); (84) ii BC ib. p. 156 no. 6, 12 (f. *Ἀριστέας*)
—IAITON: (85) hell. *Sic. Arch.* 28 (1995) p. 29 (tile)
—KAMARINA: (86) f. v BC Cordano, *Tessere Pubbliche* 79 (-*νōν*: s. *Κορκυραῖος*)
—MENAI: (87) f. i BC Cic., *In Verr.* II iii 55 (Lat. Xeno)
—MORGANTINA: (88) ?iv/iii BC *SEG* XXXIX 1009, 6 ((*Ξ*)*ένωνος*: f. *Τίμων*); (89) iv/iii BC ib. 1013, 8 (s. *Ἵππαρχος*)
—NEAITON: (90) i AD *IG* II² 10292 (s. *Νεμήνιος*)
—SELINOUS: (91) vi/v BC Manganaro, *PdelP* forthcoming no. 18, 6 (-*νōν*: f. *Θωπύλος*); (92) ~ ib. l. 11 (-*νōν*: s. *Ἴνυκος*); (93) m. v BC *SEG* XXXIV 971 (Dubois, *IGDS* 35; Arena, *Iscr. Sic.* I 38; Lazzarini 955) (-*νōν*, *Μένōν*—Dubois: f. *Ἀλεξίας*); (94) ~ Dubois, *IGDS* 36, 7 (Arena, *Iscr. Sic.* I 69) (-*νōν*: f. *Σύνετος*)
—TAUROMENION: (95) c. 224 BC *IG* XIV 421 an. 17 (*SGDI* 5219) (f. *Φιλιστίων*); (96) c. 212 BC *IG* XIV 421 an. 29 (*SGDI* 5219) (f. *Τιμόλας*); (97) c. 206 BC *IG* XIV 421 an. 35 (*SGDI* 5219); (98) c. 197 BC *IG* XIV 421 an. 44 (*SGDI* 5219); (99) c. 186 BC *IG* XIV 421 an. 55 (*SGDI* 5219) (s. *Φιλιστίων*); (100) c. 166 BC *IG* XIV 421 an. 75 (*SGDI* 5219) (f. *Τιμῶναξ*); (101) c. 153-143 BC *IG* XIV 421 an. 98 (*SGDI* 5219); *IGSI* 4 III (IV), 17 an. 88 (f. *Τιμόλας*); (102) c. 148 BC ib. l. 57 an. 93 (f. *Ἀλέξανδρος*)
—TYNDARIS: (103) ?ii AD *IGUR* 823 (s. *Ἀρχιάδας*)

TRIPHYLIA:
—LEPREON: (104) a. 369 BC Moretti, *Olymp.* 426 (s. *Καλλιτέλης*)

**Ξηναγόρα**

ARGOLIS:
—ARGOS: (1) 105 BC *JÖAI* 14 (1911) Beibl. p. 146 no. 4, 23 (d. *Θάλλινος*)

**Ξηνέας**

ARGOLIS:
—ARGOS: (1) c. 245-236 BC *IG* IX (1)² (1) 25, 9 (f. *Τεισικράτης*)

**Ξηνιάδας**

SICILY:
—AKRAGAS: (1) s. ii BC *Acragas Graeca* 1 p. 34 no. 5, 12 (*IGUR* 2; Dubois, *IGDS* 185) (f. *Θεόδωρος*)

**Ξήνιππος**

SICILY:
—KAMARINA: (1) s. v BC ib. 121, 25 (Arena, *Iscr. Sic.* II 143; *SEG* XXXVIII 940; Cordano, 'Camarina VII' 45)

**Ξῆνις**

SICILY:
—TAUROMENION: (1) c. 215 BC *IG* XIV 421 an. 26 (*SGDI* 5219) (f. *Φίλιστος*)

**Ξηνοφάνης**

ARGOLIS:
—ARGOS: (1) iv-iii BC Unp. (Ch. Kritzas)

**Ξιγας**

SICILY:
—HERBESSOS: (1) vi/v BC Dubois, *IGDS* 168 b (vase) (Arena, *Iscr. Sic.* II 121) (*Ξιγᾶς* (n. pr.?)—Arena)

**Ξιϝάρας**

LAKONIA:
—LEUKAI*: (1) vi BC *SEG* XXXV 318; *AE* 1974, pl. 81 a (name) (n. pr.?)

**Ξοανικός**

MESSENIA:
—PYLOS: (1) imp.? *Harmonia* 2 (1901) p. 202 (s. *Ἀντιπᾶς*)

**Ξουθίας**
ARKADIA:
—TEGEA*: (1) m. v BC *IG* v (2) 159 (*IPArk* 1); *LSAG*² p. 216 no. 27 (or Lakonia: s. Φιλάχαιος)

**Ξοῦθος**
ZAKYNTHOS: (1) c. 230-200 BC *BCH* 45 (1921) p. 15 II, 144 (s. Ἀμφάρης)

**Ξύλλα**
S. ITALY (CAMPANIA):
—FRATTE DI SALERNO (MOD.): (1) f. v BC *SEG* XXXVII 817 A (vase) (Arena, *Iscr. Sic.* IV 33)

**Ξύστος**
LAKONIA:
—TAINARON-KAINEPOLIS: (1) ii-iii AD *IG* v (1) 1249 (*GVI* 2028) (f. Καλλίνικος)

S. ITALY (CAMPANIA):
—KYME: (2) s. ii AD *CIL* x 3695; 3695 a (Lat. C. Pomponius Xystus)
—NOLA: (3) byz. *ICUR* 2 p. 192 no. 7 (Lat. Syxtus)
—POMPEII: (4) i BC-i AD *CIL* IV 1458; 1459 a (Lat. Xustus); (5) ~ ib. 4440 (Lat. Xystus); (6) ~ ib. 5235 (Lat. Xystus); (7) ~ ib. 6785 (Lat. Xustus)

# O

**Ὀάτα**
ELIS:
—PALAIOPOLIS: (1) hell.? *Copenhagen NM Guides* p. 62 no. 5 F (bronze)

**Ὄβαλος**
ARKADIA: (1) 360 BC *CID* II 4 III, 5

**Ὄβριμος**
ILLYRIA:
—EPIDAMNOS-DYRRHACHION: (1) c. 250-50 BC Ceka, *Probleme* p. 151 no. 54 (coin) (pryt.) ?= (2); (2) ~ Maier 331-45; 486-7; *Jubice Hoard* p. 97 nos. 36-7 (coin) (Ceka 88; 118; 137; 207; 213; 218) + *IApoll Ref. Bibl.* n. 63 (227; 338; 382) (pryt.) ?= (1)

**Ὀβριμώ**
LAKONIA:
—SPARTA: (1) ?ii BC *IG* v (1) 229 (Bradford (-))

**Ὀδαῖος**
ARKADIA:
—TEGEA:
——(Krariotai): (1) m. iii BC *IG* v (2) 36, 92 (s. Ἐργόνικος)

**Ὀδυσσεύς**
S. ITALY (CAMPANIA):
—NOLA: (1) imp. *Atti Acc. Pontan.* 21 (1971-2) pp. 392-7 (Lat. Odysseus)

**Ὀέρδιος**
ILLYRIA:
—EPIDAMNOS-DYRRHACHION: (1) hell.-imp. *IDyrrh* 362 (f. Πράϋλα)

**Ὀθρυάδας**
LAKONIA:
—SPARTA: (1) f. vi BC *RE* (-); *IPr* 316, 11 (Poralla² 573) (-δης)

**Ὄθων**
SICILY: (1) b. i AD Gal. xii p. 403 (Ὀ(ρ)θων?: Diller: doctor)

**Οἴβαλος**
LAKONIA:
—SPARTA: (1) s. viii BC Paus. iv 12. 9 (Poralla² 574) (dub.?)
S. ITALY (APULIA):
—CANUSIUM: (2) i/ii AD *Epig. Rom. di Canosa* 63 (Lat. Oebalus: f. Νάρδις)

**Οἰβώτας**
ACHAIA:
—DYME: (1) 756 BC Moretti, *Olymp.* 6; cf. Ebert, *Gr. Sieg.* 22 (s. Οἰνίας)

**Οἰκιάδας**
AITOLIA: (1) ?262 BC *FD* III (4) 358, 3; *SGDI* 2514, 2; *IG* IX (1)² (1) 15, 11

**Οἴκιος**
ARKADIA:
—TEGEA: (1) c. 240-229 BC ib. v (2) 11, 15
S. ITALY (BRUTTIUM):
—KROTON*: (2) 98-105 AD *PdelP* 45 (1990) p. 307 no. 8 (Lat. Oecius: freed.)

**Οἴκις**
ACHAIA:
—DYME: (1) ii-i BC *SEG* XIV 373 d (f. Φιλίστα)
ARGOLIS:
—ARGOS: (2) c. 315 BC ib. XXXII 370, 10; (3) ?273 BC *FD* III (2) 205, 15
—HERMIONE: (4) ?iii-ii BC *IG* IV (1) 735, 1 (f. Καλλικράτις)

**Οἰκλῆς**
ACHAIA:
—PELLENE: (1) c. 338-300 BC *SEG* XXXII 476, 3; Roesch, *Ét. Béot.* pp. 271-2 (date); cf. *SEG* XXXVIII 385 (s. Ἀντιφάτας)

**Οἰκοδεσποινιανός**
ARKADIA:
—MANTINEIA-ANTIGONEIA: (1) ii-iii AD *IG* v (2) 275, 8 (s. Σόλων)

**Οἰκονόμος**
KORINTHIA:
—KORINTH: (1) ii AD *Corinth* IV (2) p. 209 no. 751; *Lampes antiques BN* II 324 (lamps)
S. ITALY (APULIA):
—LUCERIA*: (2) imp. *Rend. Linc.* 24 (1969) p. 29 no. 11 (Lat. Oeconomus: freed.)

**Οἰκοτέλης**
ARKADIA:
—TEGEA: (1) iv/iii BC *IG* v (2) 38, 65 (Οἰκοτέλ[ης])

**Οἰκουμένη**
S. ITALY (CALABRIA):
—BRENTESION-BRUNDISIUM*: (1) imp. *NScav* 1893, p. 122 (Lat. Antonia Eucumene: freed.); (2) ii-iii AD ib. 1897, p. 327 no. 9 (Lat. Erycia Oecumene: freed.)
S. ITALY (CAMPANIA):
—DIKAIARCHIA-PUTEOLI*: (3) imp. *IG* XIV 856 (Ὀκτ. Ὀ.: freed.)
—POMPEII: (4) i BC-i AD *CIL* x 1072 (Lat. Vettia Eucumene)

**Οἰναγῆς**
PELOPONNESE?: (1) s. iii BC *SEG* XXV 449, 34 (*IPArk* 26)

**Οἰνάνθιος**
KEPHALLENIA: (1) c. 200 BC *FD* III (4) 163, 7

**Οἰνάντιος**
ILLYRIA: (1) f. iii BC *Thess. Mnem.* 121 (f. Στρατονίκη)

**Οἰνάς**
S. ITALY (CAMPANIA):
—DIKAIARCHIA-PUTEOLI: (1) imp. *CIL* x 2807 (Lat. Oinas)

**Οἰνάτας**
EPIROS:
—TOSKESI (MOD.): (1) iv BC *AD* 23 (1968) Chron. p. 292 (Οἰν[ά]τας: f. Μναῖος)

**Οἴνεια**
KORINTHIA:
—KORINTH: (1) v BC *SEG* XXV 339 (Lazzarini 350 (bronze)); cf. *SEG* XXVIII 379

**Οἰνεύς**
ACHAIA?: (1) 193 BC *IG* v (2) 293, 25 (Ο[ἰ]νεύς: f. Σαραπόφιλος)
ELIS:
—OLYMPIA*: (2) 237-241 AD *IvOl* 117, 20 (Κάσσιος Ὀ.: ?s. Πολυκράτης: slave?)
MESSENIA:
—THOURIA: (3) ii-i BC *IG* v (1) 1385, 25 (f. Δάμων)

**Οἰνιάδας**
AITOLIA: (1) c. 271 BC ib. IX (1)² (1) 12, 40
S. ITALY (BRUTTIUM):
—LOKROI EPIZEPHYRIOI: (2) ?c. 475-450 BC Guarducci, *Ep. Gr.* 1 p. 303 no. 6 (Lazzarini 197; Landi, *DISMG* 61); *LSAG*² p. 286 no. 6 (date)

**Οἰνίας**
ACHAIA:
—DYME: (1) 756 BC Paus. vii 17. 6; cf. Ebert, *Gr. Sieg.* 22 (f. Οἰβώτας)
ILLYRIA:
—APOLLONIA: (2) i BC Maier 147 (coin) (money.)

**Οἰνίλος**
ARGOLIS:
—EPIDAUROS*: (1) c. 370 BC *IG* IV (1)² 102, 244

**Οἶνις**
MESSENIA:
—MESSENE: (1) 219 BC Plb. iv 31. 2

**Οἴνιχος**
ZAKYNTHOS: (1) ?iii/ii BC *IG* IX (1)² (2) 231 ([Ο]ἴνιχος: f. Χαιρίππα)

**Οἰνίων**
S. ITALY (CAMPANIA): (1) m. iv BC *LCS* p. 261 no. 235 (vase)

**Οἰνόβιος**
ACHAIA:
—KALLISTAI: (1) 198 BC *SGDI* 2073, 5 (Ο<ο>ἰνόβιος)

**Οἰνόθεος**
SICILY:
—SELINOUS: (1) s. vi BC Dubois, *IGDS* 31, 10 (Arena, *Iscr. Sic.* I 60); cf. *SEG* XXXVIII 962 (Ὀ[ἰ]νό[θ]εος?)

**Οἰνοκλέας**
AITOLIA: (1) ?228-215 BC *SGDI* 2525, 4

**Οἰνοκλῆς**
ARGOLIS:
—ARGOS: (1) 105 BC *JÖAI* 14 (1911) Beibl. p. 146 no. 4, 22 (s. Ἱεροκλῆς)

**Οἰνοκλίων**
S. ITALY (CAMPANIA):
—POMPEII: (1) i BC-i AD *CIL* IV 7384 (Lat. Oenoclion: fict.?)

**Οἰνώνη**
S. ITALY (CAMPANIA):
—DIKAIARCHIA-PUTEOLI: (1) imp. ib. x 2464 (Lat. Plautia Oenone: m. Fuficia Felicissima)

**Οἰνώπας**
S. ITALY: (1) iv BC *RE* (-) (Stephanis 1933) (Οἰνώνας—ms.)

**Οἴτας**
ARGOLIS:
—EPIDAUROS: (1) iii/ii BC Peek, *NIEpid* 15, 14 (s. Παγασίδας)
ELIS:
—OLYMPIA*: (2) f. iv BC *Ol. Forsch.* 5 p. 151 no. 8

**Οἰτύλος**
MESSENIA:
—KORONE: (1) ii-i BC *BMC Pelop.* p. 114 no. 6 (coin) (Οἰτ[ύλος])

**Οἴφιλος**
LAKONIA:
—SPARTA: (1) iii BC *SEG* XL 348 B, 3

**Οἰωνίδας**
PELOPONNESE: (1) ?c. 230-200 BC *BCH* 45 (1921) p. 11 II, 36

**Οἰώνιχος**
ARGOLIS:
—ARGOS: (1) 105 BC *JÖAI* 14 (1911) Beibl. p. 146 no. 4, 24 (Οἰ[ών]ιχο[ς]: f. Ζώπυρος)

**Ὄκκελος**
S. ITALY (LUCANIA):
—LEUKANOI: (1) iv BC *RE* (-); *FVS* 48

**Ὀκκελώ**
S. ITALY (LUCANIA):
—LEUKANOI: (1) iv BC Iamb., *VP* 267 (*FVS* 1 p. 448)

**Ὄκκιλος**
S. ITALY (LUCANIA):
—LEUKANOI: (1) iv BC Iamb., *VP* 267 (*FVS* 1 p. 447)

**Ὀκτάβιος**
ARKADIA:
—TEGEA: (1) 165 AD *IG* V (2) 50, 16 (s. Παπύλος)
KORINTHIA:
—KORINTH: (2) ii AD *Corinth* IV (2) pp. 210 no. 752; 282 no. 1433; *SEG* XXX 348; XL 306 (lamps) (Ὀκτάβειος—*SEG* XL, Ὀ(κ)τάβιος—*SEG* XXX, Ὀτράβιος—*SEG* XXX)

**Ὄλαπος**
ILLYRIA:
—EPIDAMNOS-DYRRHACHION (NR.)?: (1) ii BC ib. XXXVIII 572, 6; cf. *CRAI* 1991, p. 197 ff.; *L'Illyrie mérid.* 2 p. 206 (s. Βάτων)

**Ὀλβιάδας**
LAKONIA:
—SPARTA: (1) iv BC *IG* V (1) 1591 (Bradford (-))

**Ὀλβίστη**
ILLYRIA:
—LYCHNIDOS: (1) ii-iii AD *Sp.* 75 (1933) p. 59 no. 179 (Ἀννία Ὀ.: m. Δημόκριτος)

**Ὀλίγαιθος**
KORINTHIA:
—KORINTH: (1) her. Pi., *O.* xiii, 97 (Ὀλιγαιθίδαι (n. gent.))

**Ὄλίγος**
ELIS?: (1) c. 525-500 BC *Ol. Forsch.* 20 p. 224 Le 446 (s. Ὀλπριχίδας)

**Ὀλίδας**
ELIS: (1) ?iii BC Paus. vi 15. 2

**Ὀλιπίδας**
ARGOLIS:
—EPIDAUROS: (1) c. 370 BC *IG* IV (1)² 102, 86

**Ὀλκιάδας**
MESSENIA:
—THOURIA: (1) f. ii BC *SEG* XI 972, 109 (Ὀλβιάδας—ed.: f. Εὐμαρίδας)

**Ὀλκίας**
ILLYRIA: (1) s. iv BC *RE* Supplbd. 3 (-); Heckel, *Last Days* pp. 79 ff. (ident.) (fict.?)

**Ὀλόκαλος**
S. ITALY (CAMPANIA):
—DIKAIARCHIA-PUTEOLI: (1) imp. *CIL* X 2759 (Lat. Holocalus: s. Μυρωνίδης, Ἱπποδάμεια)

**Ὀλόμμνιος**
ILLYRIA:
—EPIDAMNOS-DYRRHACHION: (1) hell.-imp. *IDyrrh* 284 (f. Λαϊδάν)

**Ὀλονθεύς**
LAKONIA:
—SPARTA: (1) 370 BC X., *HG* vi 5. 33 (Poralla² 576)

**Ὀλπριχίδας**
ELIS?: (1) c. 525-500 BC *Ol. Forsch.* 20 p. 224 Le 446 (f. Ὄλίγος)

**Ὄλτιος**
DALMATIA:
—ISSA: (1) iii/ii BC Brunšmid p. 24 no. 12 (s. Ἔγκτ—)

**Ὀλτίσκος**
SICILY:
—ABAKAINON: (1) hell. *IGLMP* 124 (s. Ἀριστέας)

**Ὀλτίων**
DALMATIA:
—ISSA: (1) iv/iii BC *SEG* XXXV 685 (f. Ζώπυρος)
—ISSA?: (2) iii/ii BC Brunšmid p. 31 no. 27; *Istros* 2 (1935-6) pp. 18 ff. (or Dalmatia Tragurion)

**Ὄλτος**
SICILY:
—MORGANTINA (NR.): (1) ?iii BC Manganaro, *PdelP* forthcoming no. 8 (s. Κοιάτωρ)
—MORGANTINA: (2) ii BC *SEG* XXVII 655, 8 (Dubois, *IGDS* 194); cf. *PdelP* 44 (1989) p. 205 (f. Αἰσχρίων)

**Ὀλυμπᾶς**
EPIROS:
—NIKOPOLIS: (1) i AD *SEG* XXVII 240 b

**Ὀλυμπία**
ARGOLIS:
—ARGOS: (1) ii/iii AD *IG* IV (1) 593 (Κλ. Ὀλυμπία: d. Κλ. Τυχικός)
ILLYRIA:
—BYLLIONES (CAKRAN (MOD.)): (2) imp.? *SEG* XXXVIII 547 (-λυν-)
—EPIDAMNOS-DYRRHACHION: (3) iii-iv AD *IDyrrh* 60 (m. Στέφανος)
LAKONIA: (4) iv/iii BC *Bion of Borysthenes* p. 106 T1 (and South Russia Olbia-Borysthenes?: m. Βίων (Olbia-Borysthenes): het.)

**Ὀλυμπιάδας**
ACHAIA: (1) 146 BC *IG* IV (1)² 28, 157 (I f. Ὀλυμπιάδας II: synoikos); (2) ~ ib. l. 157 (II s. Ὀλυμπιάδας I: synoikos)
ARGOLIS:
—ARGOS: (3) ?274 BC *CID* II 120 A, 14; 122 II, 11 (s. Θρασυκλῆς)
——(Hyrnathioi): (4) iv/iii BC *SEG* XI 293, 4
—PHLEIOUS: (5) s. iii BC *IG* IV (1) 727 A, 5 (Perlman H.1) (Ὀλυμπ[ι]άδας)
ARKADIA:
—GORTYS: (6) ii-i BC *SEG* XXXV 348 (f. Λέων); (7) ~ ib. (s. Λέων)
—PHENEOS: (8) iii/ii BC *IG* VII 2387, 3 (Ὀλυμπιάδ[ας]); (9) i BC *SEG* XXXIII 291, 13; cf. Stephanis 2840 ([Ὀλ]υμπιάδας)
KORINTHIA:
—SIKYON: (10) c. 146-32 BC *BMC Pelop.* p. 52 nos. 197-8; *NC* 1984, p. 14 Group 10 no. 1 (coins)
LAKONIA:
—SPARTA: (11) s. i BC *IG* V (1) 124, 12 (Bradford (2)) (s. Ὀλύμπιχος); (12) c. 30-20 BC *IG* V (1) 211, 39 (Bradford (3)) (I f. Ὀλυμπιάδας II); (13) ~ *IG* V (1) 211, 39 (Bradford (1)) (II s. Ὀλυμπιάδας I)
LEUKAS: (14) 368 BC Tod, *GHI* II 134, 4

**Ὀλυμπιακός**
MESSENIA:
—KORONE: (1) 246 AD *IG* V (1) 1398, 87 (Ἰγν(άτιος) Ὀ.)
S. ITALY (CAMPANIA):
—SALERNUM: (2) imp. *IItal* 1 (1) 141 (*CIL* X 668) (Lat. Olympiacus); (3) byz. *IG* XIV 695 (Lat. Olympiacus)

**Ὀλυμπιανός**
KORINTHIA:
—KORINTH: (1) s. iii AD *Corinth* IV (2) p. 210 no. 753; XVIII (2) p. 31 no. 34; *SEG* XXVII 35. 20; XXXIX 337 a (lamps)
S. ITALY (CAMPANIA):
—DIKAIARCHIA-PUTEOLI: (2) ?ii AD *CIL* X 1583-5 (Lat. T. Flavius Olympianus)

**Ὀλυμπιάς**
ARGOLIS:
—HERMIONE: (1) ii/i BC *IG* IV (1) 721 (d. Νίκις); (2) ~ ib. IV (1)² 229, 1 (d. Νικάτας)
EPIROS:
—DODONA*: (3) ?iii BC *SEG* XIX 431 (Ὀλυνπ-: d. Κλεμήδης)
—MOLOSSOI: (4) c. 380-316 BC *RE* (5); Berve 581; Gal. xix p. 180; *CID* II 97, 6 with comm.; cf. *Chiron* 11 (1981) pp. 79 ff. (name) (d. Νεοπτόλεμος, m. Ἀλέξανδρος, Κλεοπάτρα (Makedonia): queen); (5) iii BC *RE* (6) (d. Πύρρος, m. Φθία)
—NIKOPOLIS: (6) imp. *SEG* XXIV 427 (Sarikakis 85) (Κλ. Ὀ.)
KEPHALLENIA:
—SAME: (7) iii AD *IG* IX (1) 643 (-λυν-)
S. ITALY (BRUTTIUM):
—KROTON: (8) imp. *NScav* 1912, Suppl. p. 60 (Lat. Olimpias)
S. ITALY (CAMPANIA):
—DIKAIARCHIA-PUTEOLI: (9) imp. *AJA* 2 (1898) p. 387 no. 36 (Lat. Sela Olymp[ias]); (10) ~ *CIL* X 2236 (Lat. Olympias); (11)

~ *NScav* 1913, p. 25 no. 4 (Lat. Crittia Olympias: m. Ἔρως)
—HERCULANEUM: **(12)** m. i AD *PdelP* 9 (1954) p. 57 no. 62 (Lat. Olympias)
—KYME*: **(13)** ?iii AD *CIL* x 2838; cf. *Puteoli* 12-13 (1988-9) p. 216 no. 5 (Lat. Aurelia Olympias: freed.)
—MISENUM*: **(14)** ii/iii AD *Forma Italiae* 14 p. 160 no. 18 (Lat. O[lym]pias)
S. ITALY (LUCANIA):
—ATINA LUCANA*: **(15)** imp. *IItal* III (1) 165 (*CIL* x 357) (Lat. Luxsilia Olympias: d. Χρυσίς: freed.)
—BLANDA IULIA: **(16)** imp. ib. 456 (*NScav* 1921, p. 468) (Lat. Cominia Olympias)
—POSEIDONIA-PAESTUM: **(17)** ii-iii AD *CIL* x 489 (Mello–Voza 200) (Lat. Aurelia Olympias)
SICILY:
—SYRACUSE: **(18)** iii-v AD Strazzulla 246 (Wessel 656); cf. Ferrua, *NG* 298 (Ὀλυμπία— Strazzulla)

### Ὀλυμπικός
ELIS:
—OLYMPIA*: **(1)** c. 177-185 AD *IvOl* 103, 26-7 (?s. Διογένης: slave?)
S. ITALY: **(2)** ?ii AD *CIL* x 8059. 169 (seal) (Lat. T. Flavius Olympicus)
S. ITALY (CAMPANIA):
—DIKAIARCHIA-PUTEOLI: **(3)** imp. ib. 2209 (Lat. L. Calpurnius Olympicus); **(4)** ~ ib. 3045 (Lat. M. Valerius [Ol]umpic(us): f. M. Valerius Felicissimus)

### Ὀλυμπῖνος
S. ITALY (CALABRIA):
—HYRIA: **(1)** imp. *Studi di Antichità* 1 p. 207 (Lat. Olympinus)

### Ὀλυμπιόδωρος
AKARNANIA:
—PHOITIAI: **(1)** iv BC *IG* IX (1)² (2) 602, 8
ARGOLIS:
—HERMIONE: **(2)** ii/i BC ib. IV (1) 721 (f. Κλεοφάντα); **(3)** ~ ib. IV (1)² 229, 2 (s. Νικάτας); **(4)** i BC-i AD? iii (1) 730 I, 7 (f. Ἱεροκλῆς)
—PHLEIOUS: **(5)** f. ii BC *FD* III (4) 435 + *SEG* XXVII 98 (Ὀλυ[μπι]όδωρος: f. Δάμων)
—TROIZEN: **(6)** iii AD *IG* IV (1) 796, 2 (*M. Αὐρ. Ὀ.*)
ARKADIA:
—MEGALOPOLIS: **(7)** ?ii AD ib. v (2) 122 (s. Κάλλων: sculptor)
—TEGEA:
——(Athaneatai): **(8)** s. iii BC ib. 36, 112 (-λυν-: s. Ὀλυ—: metic)
ELIS: **(9)** f. i AD *IvOl* 75, 12; 76, [2]; 77, 7; 80, 2 (f. Φιλίκων ὁ καὶ Θεότιμος: mantis/Iamidai)
—PISA: **(10)** 365-363 BC ib. 31, 10 (Ὀλυμπιόδω[ρος])
ILLYRIA:
—APOLLONIA: **(11)** i BC Maier 127 (coin) (f. Ἀρχήν)
—EPIDAMNOS-DYRRHACHION: **(12)** c. 250-50 BC Münsterberg p. 260; Nachtr. p. 16 (coin) (pryt.)
KORINTHIA:
—SIKYON: **(13)** ?254 BC Nachtergael, *Les Galates* 9, 35 (Skalet 246); cf. Stephanis 1327 (f. Καλλίας)
PELOPONNESE?: **(14)** s. iii BC *IG* v (1) 1426, 26 (s. Κάλλιππος)
SICILY:
—ZANKLE-MESSANA: **(15)** iv BC ib. IV (1)² 95, 79 (f. Ὀνάσιμος)
TRIPHYLIA: **(16)** c. 400-369 BC *SEG* XL 392

### Ὀλύμπιος
ARKADIA:
—THELPHOUSA: **(1)** c. 250-180 BC *IG* IV (1) 727 A, 13 (Perlman H.1) (Ὀλύμπ[—])

---

DALMATIA:
—ISSA: **(2)** iii BC Brunšmid p. 9 fr. G, 11 + *VAMZ* 1970, p. 37 frr. G and M (f. Καλλισθένης)
KORINTHIA:
—KORINTH: **(3)** s. v AD Cyr. S., *V. Cyriac.* 4
S. ITALY (CAMPANIA):
—POMPEII: **(4)** i BC-i AD *CIL* IV 3989 (Lat. Olumpius)
—SURRENTUM: **(5)** imp. ib. x 716 (Lat. M. Antonius Olympius)

### Ὄλυμπις
ARGOLIS:
—EPIDAUROS: **(1)** s. iii BC Peek, *NIEpid* 45 (s. Πολυκλῆς)
ARKADIA:
—PHIGALEIA: **(2)** v BC *IG* v (2) 425, 6 (Ὀλυ(μ)πις, Ὀλυπίς—ed.)
ITHAKE: **(3)** hell. *BCH* 29 (1905) p. 164 no. 6 (Ὀλύμπιος (gen.): f. Παντιμίας)
S. ITALY (BRUTTIUM):
—LOKROI EPIZEPHYRIOI:
——(Πυρ.): **(4)** iv/iii BC De Franciscis 14, 2 (Ὀλύμπις—ed.)
S. ITALY (CALABRIA):
—TARAS-TARENTUM: **(5)** c. 235-228 BC Vlasto 942-6; 1103 (coins) (Evans, *Horsemen* p. 194 IX C.1; p. 195 D.1; p. 196 nos. 1-2)
S. ITALY (CAMPANIA):
—NEAPOLIS: **(6)** iv/iii BC Sambon 451 (coins) (*SNG ANS Etruria–Calabria* 325) (Ὀ.?, Ὀλύμπιος?)
SICILY:
—KAMARINA: **(7)** hell. *SEG* XXXIX 1001, 7 (f. Κρήτων)
—LIPARA: **(8)** ii-i BC *Meligunis-Lipara* 5 p. 148 no. 2141; cf. *SEG* XLI 800 (Ὀλύμπιος (nom./gen.))
—SELINOUS?: **(9)** v BC ib. XXXIX 1021 I, 2 (Ὀλύ(μ)πις)
SYRACUSE?:
——(Ὑπα.): **(10)** hell. Manganaro, *PdelP* forthcoming no. 4 II, 4 (f. Γοργίας)
—TAUROMENION: **(11)** hell.? *SGDI* 5232 (I f. Ὄλυμπις II Μειστος); **(12)** ~ ib. (Ὀ. Μέστος: II s. Ὄλυμπις I); **(13)** c. 235 BC *IG* XIV 421 an. 6 (*SGDI* 5219) (s. Σωκράτης); **(14)** c. 222 BC *IG* XIV 421 an. 19 (*SGDI* 5219) (f. Ζώπυρος); **(15)** c. 211 BC *IG* XIV 421 an. 30 (*SGDI* 5219); **(16)** c. 204 BC *IG* XIV 421 an. 37 (*SGDI* 5219); **(17)** c. 202-163 BC *IG* XIV 421 an. 39; 421 an. 55; 421 an. 78 (*SGDI* 5219) (s. Δαμάρετος, f. Δαμάρετος); **(18)** c. 198 BC *IG* XIV 421 an. 43 (*SGDI* 5219) (s. Φρῦνις); **(19)** c. 170 BC *IGSI* 4 II (III), 17 an. 71 (f. Ἡρακλείδης); **(20)** c. 161 BC *IG* XIV 421 an. 80 (*SGDI* 5219); **(21)** c. 145-143 BC *IG* XIV 421 an. 98 (*SGDI* 5219); *IGSI* 4 III (IV), 81 an. 96 (s. Θεόδωρος); **(22)** ?ii/i BC *IG* XIV 421 D an. 2 (*SGDI* 5219) (I f. Ὄλυμπις II); **(23)** ~ *IG* XIV 421 D an. 2 (*SGDI* 5219) (II s. Ὄλυμπις I); **(24)** ~ *IG* XIV 421 [D] an. 2 (*SGDI* 5219) (f. Θεόκριτος); **(25)** ii/i BC *IGSI* 11 I, 3 (f. Θεόδωρος); **(26)** c. 40 BC *Cron. Arch.* 3 (1964) p. 56 I, 9, 13, 34, 38 (s. Θεόφιλος, f. Θεόκριτος)
——(Ἀσσιτ.): **(27)** ?ii/i BC *IGSI* 4 III (IV), 102 D an. 6 (f. Φρῦνις)
——(Ἀχαιο.): **(28)** ?ii/i BC *IG* XIV 421 D an. 4; 421 [D] an. 1 (*SGDI* 5219) (f. Γλαῦκος)
——(Οἰτ.): **(29)** ii/i BC *IGSI* 5 III, 23; 7 II, 18 (s. Ἡράκλητος)
——(Ταυ.): **(30)** ii/i BC ib. 8 II, 1 ([Ὀ]λυμπις)
—ZANKLE-MESSANA: **(31)** ?ii BC *IG* XIV 401, 2 (s. Ὑπέρβολος)

---

### Ὀλυμπίς
LAKONIA:
—SPARTA: **(1)** f. ii AD ib. v (1) 470, 4; *BSA* 80 (1985) pp. 215; 222 (ident., stemma) (Bradford (-)) (Οὐολοσσηνὴ Ὀ.: ?d. Λ. Οὐολοσσηνὸς Δαμάρης, Μεμμία Δαμοκρατία)

### Ὀλυμπίχα
LAKONIA:
—SPARTA: **(1)** ?i BC *IG* v (1) 755 (Bradford (1)) (d. Λευκτριάδας); **(2)** f. ii AD *IG* v (1) 233; *BSA* 80 (1985) pp. 203-4; 215; 222 (ident., stemma) (Bradford (2)) (Οὐολοσσηνὴ Ὀ.: ?d. Λ. Οὐολοσσηνὸς Δαμάρης, Μεμμία Δαμοκρατία)

### Ὀλύμπιχος
ACHAIA: **(1)** 316-309 BC *IG* II² 1956, 193; *Ancient Macedonia* 5 p. 445 with n. 10 (date)
—DYME: **(2)** iii-ii BC *Syll*³ 530, 16; cf. *Achaia und Elis* p. 115
AITOLIA:
—THERMOS?: **(3)** c. 500 BC *IG* IX (1)² (1) 91. 1; *LSAG*² p. 227 no. 7 (date) (Ὀλύνπ[ι]χος); **(4)** hell. *IG* IX (1)² (1) 91. 2, 5 ([Ὀλύ]μπιχος)
AKARNANIA:
—ECHINOS: **(5)** c. 325-315 BC *Hesp.* 57 (1988) p. 148 A, 25 (*SEG* XXXVI 331); cf. *Hesp.* 48 (1979) pp. 78 f. with pl. 22 c (f. Στίλπων)
ARKADIA:
—STYMPHALOS: **(6)** iii-ii BC *SEG* XLII 361
ELIS: **(7)** 36-24 BC *IvOl* 62, 12, 23 (I f. Ὀλύμπιχος II, Ζώπυρος); **(8)** ~ ib. l. 12 (II s. Ὀλύμπιχος I)
ILLYRIA:
—EPIDAMNOS-DYRRHACHION: **(9)** c. 250-50 BC *BMC Thessaly* p. 76 no. 164; Unp. (Paris, BN) 272 (coin) (pryt.); **(10)** ii-i BC *IDyrrh* 552 (tiles); **(11)** hell.-imp. ib. 283 (f. Λαήν)
KORINTHIA:
—KORINTH: **(12)** s. v BC *SEG* XXII 251 d (-λύν-); **(13)** c. 221 BC *IG* IV (1)² 42, 24 (s. Ἀπολλόδωρος)
LAKONIA:
—SPARTA: **(14)** s. i BC ib. v (1) 124, 12 (Bradford (-)) (Ὀλ[ύμ]πιχος: f. Ὀλυμπιάδας)
SICILY:
—MENAI: **(15)** inc. *Riv. Stor. Antica* 5 (1900-1) p. 57 (s. Πυρρίας)

### Ὀλυμπιώ
LAKONIA:
—SPARTA: **(1)** 170 BC *SEG* XLI 115 I, 34 ([Ὀ]λυμπιώ: d. Ἀγήτωρ)

### Ὀλυμπίων
ACHAIA:
—PATRAI: **(1)** m. ii BC *IG* IX (1)² (2) 208, 9 (f. Ἀγασίας)
ELIS:
—OLYMPIA*: **(2)** s. i BC *IvOl* 66, 5 (?s. Πρέπων)
ILLYRIA: **(3)** 168 BC Plb. xxix 3. 6; 4. 6

### Ὄλυμπος
ARGOLIS:
—EPIDAUROS*: **(1)** c. 365-335 BC *IG* IV (1)² 103, 34 (Ὀλυμ[πος])
ELIS: **(2)** c. 113-145 AD *IvOl* 90, 13; 91, 12; 92, 13-14; 95, [10] (II s. Ὄλυμπος I, f. Διόνικος); **(3)** ~ ib. 90, [13]; 91, 12; 92, 13 (I f. Ὄλυμπος II: mantis/Klytiadai); **(4)** c. 181-189 AD ib. 100, 12; 104, 15 (s. Τεισαμενός: mantis/Iamidai); **(5)** 181-213 AD ib. 102, 11; 103, 14; 106, 11; 107, 7; 110, 13; 112, [2] (Κλ. Ὄ.—103, 106 and 110, [Τιβ.] Κλ. Ὄλυνπος—102, [Τιβ.] Κλ. Ὄ.—107: mantis/Iamidai/N.) ?= (7); **(6)** 197-213 AD ib. 106, 12; 107, [9]; 108, [3]; 110, 15; 112, 4 (Αὐ(ρ). Ὀ.: s. Διόνικος: mantis/Klytiadai); **(7)** iii AD *SEG* XV 259, 12 ([Ὀλυ]μπος: mantis/Iamidai) ?= (5); **(8)** m. iii AD *IvOl* 120, 7 ([Ὀλ]υμπος)
EPIROS:
—NIKOPOLIS: **(9)** imp. *Ep. Chron.* 31 (1994) p. 42 no. 8 (*AD* 45 (1990) Chron. p. 257 no. 5)

ILLYRIA:
—EPIDAMNOS-DYRRHACHION: (**10**) i BC-i AD *AEp* 1978, no. 755 (Lat. D. Granius Olympus)
KORINTHIA:
—KORINTH: (**11**) imp. *Corinth* VIII (3) 350 (Lat. Fla. Olumpus)
—SIKYON: (**12**) iv BC Paus. vi 3. 13 (Skalet 247) (sculptor)
LAKONIA:
—SPARTA: (**13**) c. 220 AD *IG* V (1) 544, 11 (*Artemis Orthia* pp. 358-9 no. 145; Bradford (-)) (f. *M. Αὐρ. Πανθήρας*)
S. ITALY (APULIA):
—LUCERIA*: (**14**) imp. *Rend. Linc.* 24 (1969) p. 29 no. 11 (Lat. Olynpus: freed.)
S. ITALY (CAMPANIA):
—DIKAIARCHIA-PUTEOLI: (**15**) imp. *CIL* X 2467 (Lat. Olympus)
—POMPEII: (**16**) i BC-i AD ib. IV 8950 (Lat. Olympus)

**Ὀλυνθεύς**
LAKONIA:
—SPARTA: (**1**) 628-620 BC Moretti, *Olymp.* 62; 67 (Poralla² 577)

**Ὄλυνθος**
S. ITALY (CAMPANIA):
—POMPEII: (**1**) i BC-i AD *CIL* IV 4051 (Castrèn 124. 4) (Lat. Ti. Com(i)ni(u)s Olithus); (**2**) c. 51-62 AD *CIL* IV 3340. 80, 8 (Castrèn 318. 26) (Lat. N. Popidius Olynthus)

**Ὀλυττώι**
KORINTHIA:
—KORINTH: (**1**) c. 570-550 BC Amyx 81. 4 (vase) (Lorber 130) (-τōι: her.?)

**Ὀλώϊχος**
EPIROS:
—BOUTHROTOS: (**1**) ii-i BC *IBouthrot* 196 (f. *Νικόλαος*)

**Ὄμαρος**
AITOLIA: (**1**) ?263-261 BC *FD* III (3) 184, 2; 190, 1; *Syll*³ 498, 2; Nachtergael, *Les Galates* 3, [2]

**Ὄμηρος**
S. ITALY (APULIA):
—VENUSIA: (**1**) ii/iii AD *Rend. Linc.* 29 (1974) p. 610 no. 7 (Lat. M. Anniolenus Homerus)
S. ITALY (LUCANIA):
—GRUMENTUM*: (**2**) imp. *NScav* 1897, p. 182 (Lat. M. Servilius Homer(us): freed.)

**Ὀμιλεύς**
LAKONIA?: (**1**) vi/v BC *SEG* XXXIX 400 (bronze) (ḥο-)

**Ὀμιλία**
ARGOLIS:
—HERMIONE: (**1**) ii-i BC *IG* IV (1) 732 IV, 16 (m. *Ψαμάθα*)
S. ITALY (CALABRIA):
—BRENTESION-BRUNDISIUM: (**2**) imp. *CIL* IX 177 (Lat. Rutilia Homilia)

**Ὄμιλος**
ACHAIA:
—PATRAI*: (**1**) i BC/i AD *SEG* XXXII 421
AKARNANIA:
—OINIADAI: (**2**) ?iv-iii BC *IG* IX (1)² (2) 426. 1 (tile)
S. ITALY (CAMPANIA):
—POMPEII: (**3**) i BC-i AD *CIL* IV 2002 (Lat. Homilus)

**Ὀμολώ**
ARKADIA:
—TEGEA: (**1**) ii AD *SEG* XI 1081

**Ὁμόνοια**
ILLYRIA:
—APOLLONIA: (**1**) ii-i BC *IApoll* 136
KORINTHIA:
—KORINTH: (**2**) f. iii AD *Corinth* VIII (3) 302, 4 (Lat. Grania Homonoia: I m. *Κλώδιος Εὔφημος*, Clodius Granianus, *Κλωδία Ὁμόνοια* II); (**3**) ~ ib. l. 6 (Lat. Clodia Homonoia: II d. *Γρανία Ὁμόνοια* I)
LAKONIA:
—TAINARON-KAINEPOLIS: (**4**) ?ii BC *IG* V (1) 1252 (m. *Ἀκτή*)
S. ITALY (CAMPANIA):
—DIKAIARCHIA-PUTEOLI: (**5**) imp. *CIL* X 2378 (Lat. Ducennia Homonoia)
SICILY:
—LIPARA: (**6**) imp. *BTCGI* 9 p. 97 (*Κλωδία Ὀ.*)

**Ὁμοστάκιος**
EPIROS:
—MOLOSSOI:
——Kyestoi?: (**1**) ?c. 370-344 BC Cabanes, *L'Épire* p. 536 no. 2, 14

**Ὄμρικος**
KORINTHIA:
—KORINTH: (**1**) c. 590-570 BC Amyx 40. 2 (vase) (Lorber 42) (-ϙος: fict.?)

**Ὀμφάλη**
S. ITALY (CAMPANIA):
—DIKAIARCHIA-PUTEOLI: (**1**) imp. *CIL* X 2391 (Lat. Escionia Ompale)

**Ὀμφαλίων**
ACHAIA:
—DYME: (**1**) s. iii BC *SEG* XIII 278, 25
ELIS:
—PISA: (**2**) vii BC *FGrH* 244 F 334; Paus. vi 21. 1; 22. 2 (f. *Πανταλέων*)

**Ὀναῖος**
S. ITALY (BRUTTIUM):
—LOKROI EPIZEPHYRIOI: (**1**) iv/iii BC De Franciscis 36, 3 (s. *Χαιρέδαμος*)
——(Ἀγκ.): (**2**) iv/iii BC ib. 3, 3 (s. *Ζωΐλος*)
——(Ἀγφ.): (**3**) 277 BC ib. 8, 3; 31, 3 (s. *Φρασίλας*)
——(Ἀνξ.): (**4**) iv/iii BC ib. 24, 6 (f. *Εὔθυμος*)
——(Κοβ.): (**5**) iv/iii BC ib. 6, 5; 38, 2 (f. *Χαρίξενος*)
——(Μνα.): (**6**) iv/iii BC ib. 15, 4 (s. *Ζώϊππος*)
——(Πυρ.): (**7**) iv/iii BC ib. 12, 3 (f. *Ἀρχιππος*)
——(Σωτ.): (**8**) 277 BC ib. 8, 1; 31, 1
——(Τυν.): (**9**) iv/iii BC ib. 19, 2 (s. *Ζωΐλος*)
——(Φαω.): (**10**) iv/iii BC ib. 18, 6; 27, 8 (s. *Χαρίλας*)

**Ὀναίτελης**
LAKONIA:
—THALAMAI*: (**1**) hell.? *IG* V (1) 1320

**Ὀνασάδας**
EPIROS:
—AMBRAKIA: (**1**) f. ii BC *IC* 2 p. 25 no. 8 C (f. *Μνασήν*)

**Ὀνάσανδρος**
KORINTHIA:
—KORINTH: (**1**) m. iii BC *Corinth* VIII (3) 33 d, 7; *Deutsch. Lit.* 89 (1968) p. 540 (name) (*Ὀνάσανδ[ρος]*)
LAKONIA:
—AKRIAI: (**2**) ii/i BC *IG* V (1) 1189 (s. *Κλέαρετος*, f. *Κλέαρετος*)
—SPARTA: (**3**) c. 25-1 BC ib. 212, 39 (Bradford (-)) (s. *Τιμογένης*)

**Ὀνασιγένης**
SICILY:
—SYRACUSE: (**1**) 214 BC Plb. vii 4. 1 (-νη-)

**Ὀνασίδας**
SICILY:
—MORGANTINA: (**1**) ?iv/iii BC *SEG* XXXIX 1011, 7 ([Ὀν]ασίδας: s. *Λ*—)

**Ὀνασίκλεια**
ARKADIA:
—TEGEA: (**1**) ?i BC *IG* V (2) 198

**Ὀνασικλείδας**
LAKONIA:
—SPARTA: (**1**) c. 25-1 BC ib. V (1) 212, 24 (Bradford (2)) (f. *Δεξίνικος*); (**2**) c. 100-150 AD *IG* V (1) 60, 1; 279, 1; *SEG* XI 490, 6; 494, 5; 496, 5; 583, [1]; XXXVI 361, 4 (Bradford (1)) (s. *Φιλόστρατος*)

**Ὀνασικλῆς**
ACHAIA: (**1**) 146 BC *IG* IV (1)² 28, 109-10 (f. *Νικοκλῆς, Παιώνιος*: synoikos)
AIGINA: (**2**) ?ii-i BC *Alt-Ägina* I (2) p. 45 no. 16 (f. —*ένης*)
ARKADIA:
—TEGEA: (**3**) ii-iii AD *IG* V (2) 179, 7, 10 (*GVI* 130)
ILLYRIA:
—APOLLONIA: (**4**) hell. *IApoll* 28 (f. *Καλλίπολις*)
LAKONIA:
—SPARTA: (**5**) c. 10-20 AD *IG* V (1) 206, 2; *SEG* XXXV 330 (date) (Bradford (1)) (Ὀνασι[κλ]ῆς: s. *Πρατόνικος*); (**6**) c. 100 AD *SEG* XI 626, 4 (Bradford (2)) (f. *Φιλοκλείδας*)
MESSENIA:
—KORONE: (**7**) 246 AD *IG* V (1) 1398, 77 (*Αὐρ. Ὀ.*)
—MESSENE:
——(Hylleis): (**8**) 11 AD *PAE* 1992, p. 71 A, 15 (f. *Νίκιππος*)
——THOURIA: (**9**) ii-i BC *IG* V (1) 1385, 35 (Ὀν[α]σικλῆς: s. *Νικίας*); (**10**) f. ii BC *SEG* XI 972, 96 (s. *Δαμίων*)

**Ὀνασικράτης**
ARGOLIS:
—HERMIONE: (**1**) c. 100-90 BC ib. XXXIII 290 A, 28; *BSA* 70 (1975) pp. 129-31 (date) (Stephanis 1946) (s. *Σωφρονίων*)
ARKADIA:
—LYKOSOURA*: (**2**) imp. *IG* V (2) 523 (f. *Ξέναρχος*)
—MEGALOPOLIS: (**3**) i BC/i AD ib. 515 A, 21 (Ὀνασικ[ράτης]: f. *Ξέναρχος*)
—MEGALOPOLIS?: (**4**) 42 AD ib. 516, 7, 25 (f. *Τιμασιστράτα*)
LAKONIA:
—SPARTA: (**5**) ii/iii AD ib. V (1) 129, 3; 306, 5 (*Artemis Orthia* p. 328 no. 59); *IG* V (1) 557, 11; 558, 5; 559, 4; 653 b, 7; *BSA* 79 (1984) pp. 278 no. 4; 281-3 (date, stemma) (Bradford (2)) (*Σέξ. Πομπ. Ὀ.*, Ὀνασικράτηρ—306: I f. *Σέξ. Πομπ. Ὀνασικράτης* II, *Σέξ. Πομπ. Εὔδαμος, Σέξ. Πομπ. Γόργιππος*); (**6**) f. iii AD *IG* V (1) 558, 4; *BSA* 79 (1984) p. 282 (stemma) (Bradford (1)) (*Σέξ. Πομπ. Ὀ.*: II s. *Σέξ. Πομπ. Ὀνασικράτης* I)
MESSENIA:
—MESSENE: (**7**) 99 AD *SEG* XLI 336, 1
——(Kleolaidai): (**8**) 11 AD *PAE* 1992, p. 71 A, 27 (s. *Καλλισθένης*)
SICILY:
—HELOROS: (**9**) ii-i BC Dubois, *IGDS* 100, 1 (I f. *Ὀνασικράτης* II); (**10**) ~ ib. l. 1 (II s. *Ὀνασικράτης* I)
—TAUROMENION: (**11**) c. 208 BC *IG* XIV 421 an. 33 (*SGDI* 5219) (f. *Ὑπέρβολος*)
——(Ἀσιν.): (**12**) c. 180-145 BC *IG* XIV 421 an. 61 (*SGDI* 5219); *IGSI* 4 III (IV), 87 an. 97 (s. *Ὑπέρβολος*, f. *Ὑπέρβολος*)

**Ὀνασικράτιν**
ARKADIA:
—TEGEA: (**1**) i-ii AD *IG* V (2) 85

## Ὀνασικράτις
ARGOLIS:
—HERMIONE: (1) ii-i BC ib. IV (1) 732 IV, 21; (2) i BC-i AD? ib. 730 I, 2 (d. Κλεοπάτρα)

## Ὀνασίκριτος
AIGINA: (1) iv BC D.L. vi 75; FGrH 134 T 1-3 with Comm. (ident.) (-νη-: f. Ἀνδροσθένης, Φιλίσκος)
MESSENIA:
—MESSENE: (2) ii/i BC IG v (1) 1437, 16

## Ὀνασίλας
DALMATIA:
—ISSA:
——(Pamphyloi): (1) iv/iii BC Brunšmid p. 8, 30 (s. Διόφαντος)

## Ὀνάσιλος
ARKADIA: (1) 308 BC IG v (2) 550, 6

## Ὀνασιμίδας
ARKADIA?: (1) c. 200 BC SEG XVII 829, 4, 10, 17

## Ὀνάσιμος
ACHAIA: (1) 146 BC IG IV (1)² 28, 71 (s. Πρωτόμαχος: synoikos); (2) ~ ib. l. 129 (s. Τηρεύς: synoikos); (3) ~ ib. l. 147 (I f. Ὀνάσιμος II: synoikos); (4) ~ ib. l. 147 (II s. Ὀνάσιμος I: synoikos); (5) ~ ib. l. 150 (s. Θεόδωρος: synoikos); (6) ~ ib. l. 153 (I f. Ὀνάσιμος II: synoikos); (7) ~ ib. l. 153 (II s. Ὀνάσιμος I: synoikos); (8) ~ ib. l. 159 (f. Δαμάτριος: synoikos)
ARGOLIS:
—EPIDAUROS*: (9) c. 370-365 BC Peek, IAEpid 52 B, 3 ([Ὀν]άσιμος) ?= (10); (10) c. 365-335 BC IG IV (1)² 103, 167 ?= (9); (11) c. 290-270 BC ib. 109 II, 149
—HERMIONE: (12) ii-i BC ib. IV (1) 732 II, 19 (s. Ἀριστοκλῆς); (13) ~ ib. 732 III, 7 (f. Εὔπλους); (14) ~ ib. 732 IV, 13; (15) i BC-i AD? ib. 730 IV, 1 (f. Κύδων)
—TROIZEN: (16) ii BC ib. 806
ARKADIA:
—TEGEA: (17) iv BC ib. v (2) 31, 12 (f. Νικόστρατος); (18) m. iv BC ib. 6, 81 ([Ὀ]νάσιμος)
——(Krariotai): (19) f. iii BC ib. 36, 46 (s. Καλλίας: metic)
DALMATIA:
—ISSA: (20) iii BC SEG XXXV 691, 9 (VAHD 84 (1991) p. 256 no. 6) (s. Ξενοκλῆς)
——(Pamphyloi): (21) iv/iii BC Brunšmid p. 7, 19 (s. Κέφαλος); (22) ~ ib. l. 24 (f. Καλλιμαχίδας)
EPIROS:
—DODONA*: (23) v BC Ep. Chron. 10 (1935) p. 255 no. 14
—ORIKOS: (24) hell.-imp. Klio 40 (1962) p. 290
KORINTHIA:
—SIKYON: (25) 423 BC Th. iv 119. 2 (Skalet 248) (s. Μεγακλῆς)
LAKONIA:
—SPARTA: (26) c. 140-150 AD IG v (1) 68, 20 (Bradford (1)) (s. Ἔλενος); (27) c. 140-160 AD IG v (1) 74, 8 (Bradford (3)) (f. Ἀμίμητος); (28) f. iii AD IG v (1) 170, 21; BSA 80 (1985) p. 245 (date) (Bradford (4)) (I f. Αὐρ. Ὀνάσιμος II); (29) ~ IG v (1) 170, 21; BSA 80 (1985) p. 245 (date) (Bradford (2)) (Αὐρ. Ὀ.: II s. Ὀνάσιμος I); (30) iii/iv AD PLRE I s.v. Onesimus (2); Cartledge-Spawforth p. 182 (ident.); cf. LGPN I (7) (Bradford s.v. Onesimus) (s. Ἀφίνης, f. Ἀφίνης)
PELOPONNESE: (31) c. 192 BC SEG XIII 327, 20 (f. Βοΐσκος)
S. ITALY (BRUTTIUM):
—LOKROI EPIZEPHYRIOI:
——(Ἀγκ.): (32) iv/iii BC De Franciscis 22, 24 (f. Φιλόστρατος)
——(Ἀλα.): (33) iv/iii BC ib. 21, 5

——(Βοω.): (34) iv/iii BC ib. l. 5
——(Γαγ.): (35) 275 BC ib. 25, 2 (s. Σωσικράτης)
——(Κοβ.): (36) iv/iii BC ib. 21, 1
——(Πυρ.): (37) iv/iii BC ib. 39, 3 (Ὀνάσι[μος]: f. Πειθίας)
——(Στρ.): (38) iv/iii BC ib. 20, 1 (s. Νέαρχος); (39) ~ ib. 22, 20 (s. Ἀρκείδας)
——(Σωτ.): (40) iv/iii BC ib. 14, 2
——(Τιω.): (41) iv/iii BC ib. 11, 6 (f. Σαμίων)
——(Ψαθ.): (42) iv/iii BC ib. l. 7 (f. Ζωΐλος)
S. ITALY (CALABRIA):
—TARAS-TARENTUM?: (43) iv BC Guarducci, Ep. Gr. 3 p. 489 n. 3 (Landi, DISMG 209) (Ὀνάσιμ[ος])
SICILY:
—KAMARINA: (44) s. v BC Dubois, IGDS 121, 13 (Arena, Iscr. Sic. II 143; SEG XXXVIII 940; Cordano, 'Camarina VII' 46) (s. Ἀθανις)
—SYRACUSE: (45) hell. IG XIV Add. 9 a
—ZANKLE-MESSANA: (46) s. iv BC ib. IV (1)² 95, 79 (s. Ὀλυμπιόδωρος)

## Ὀνασίνικος
MESSENIA:
—MESSENE: (1) iv/iii BC ib. v (1) 1435, 7

## Ὀνασίπολις
LAKONIA:
—KYTHERA: (1) iii BC ib. 938

## Ὀνάσιππος
LAKONIA:
—HYPERTELEATON*: (1) imp. SEG XI 906 (bronze)
—SPARTA: (2) c. 125-150 AD IG v (1) 488, 2 (Bradford (-)) (s. Τιβ. Κλ. Δαμονίκης, Ἑτυμοκλήδεια)

## Ὀνασιφορίς
LAKONIA:
—SPARTA: (1) c. 239-244 AD IG v (1) 572, 12 (Bradford (-)) (Αὐρ. Ὀ.: d. Μ. Αὐρ. Δαμοκράτης)

## Ὀνασιφόρον
ARKADIA:
—KLEITOR: (1) i AD IG v (2) 374
—THELPHOUSA: (2) i BC SEG XI 1126; BCH 88 (1964) pp. 175-6 (date)
KEPHALLENIA:
—KRANIOI: (3) imp. IG IX (1) 613 (Κλαυδί[α] Ὀνασ[ιφ]ό(ρ)ον: m. Ἔρως)

## Ὀνασιφόρος
ARKADIA:
—TEGEA: (1) i AD SEG XXXVI 384 (date—LGPN)

## Ὀνασίχα
SICILY:
—THERMAI HIMERAIAI: (1) imp. IG XIV 335 (Σερβιλία Ὀ. (fem.nom./masc.gen.?))

## Ὀνασίων
ACHAIA: (1) 146 BC ib. IV (1)² 28, 96 (I f. Ὀνασίων II: synoikos); (2) ~ ib. l. 96 (II s. Ὀνασίων I: synoikos)
ARGOLIS:
—ARGOS: (3) ii AD Corinth VIII (1) 15 a, 4; cf. SEG XI 62
LAKONIA:
—SPARTA: (4) c. 90-100 AD ib. 560, 4; 609, 2 (Bradford (2)) (Ὀ[νασίων]—560: f. Ἀγησίππος); (5) c. 105-124 AD SEG XI 569, 19; 630, 1 (Bradford (2)); Bradford s.v. Ὀνησίων (2) (Ὀνησίων—569: I f. Ὀνασίων II); (6) ~ SEG XI 569, 19; 630, 1 (Bradford (2)); Bradford s.v. Ὀνησίων (1) (Ὀνησίων—569, [Ὀν]ασίων—630: II s. Ὀνασίων I); (7) m. ii AD IG v (1) 502, 10 (Bradford (2)) (f. Ἀγησιππία); (8) f. iii AD SEG XLII 320, 6 ([Ὀνα]σίων: f. Αὐρ. Εὐτυχιανός)

MESSENIA:
—ASINE (NR.): (9) ii/i BC IG v (1) 1403 = AD 25 (1970) Chron. p. 174

## Ὄνασος
LAKONIA:
—KYTHERA: (1) ?f. iv BC IG II² 9111 (f. Ἐπίκτησις)
S. ITALY: (2) ?i BC ib. XIV 2400. 8 (tiles)
S. ITALY (BRUTTIUM):
—RHEGION: (3) imp.? ib. 2400. 12 (tile)
SICILY:
—CASTEL DI IUDICA (MOD.): (4) ?iii BC Manganaro, PdelP forthcoming no. 6, 3 (s. Ἄλκιππος)
—LIPARA: (5) hell.? IG II² 9215 (s. Πύρρων)
—PARTHENIKON: (6) i BC SEG XXXII 927; Kokalos 36-7 (1990-1) pp. 139 ff.; cf. Wilson, Sicily p. 269 (tiles)
—SEGESTA: (7) f. i BC Cic., In Verr. II v 120 (Lat. Onasus)
—TAUROMENION: (8) c. 168 BC IG XIV 421 an. 73 (SGDI 5219) (f. Ἀρίστων)
——(Οἰτ.): (9) ?ii/i BC IG XIV 421 D an. 8 (SGDI 5219) (f. Ἀρτεμίδωρος)

## Ὀνασύλις
SICILY:
—TYNDARIS: (1) hell.? IG XIV 380; cf. Chiron 22 (1992) p. 386 (name) (Ὀνασύλιος (gen.))

## Ὀνασώ
ACHAIA:
—AIGEIRA: (1) ii-iii AD JÖAI 19-20 (1919) Beibl. p. 40 (m. Σεβῆρος)
LAKONIA: (2) 197 BC SGDI 2044, 2, 3 (slave/freed.)
—GERONTHRAI: (3) hell. IG v (1) 1128 (Ὀνασ[ώ])

## Ὀνάσων
ARGOLIS:
—EPIDAUROS: (1) ?iii AD Peek, IAEpid 232, 1 (s. Ἀρτίπους)
—HERMIONE: (2) i BC-i AD? IG IV (1) 730 II, 3 (Ὀνάσων: f. Ἀπολλώνιος)
MESSENIA:
—MESSENE:
——(Kresphontidai): (3) 11 AD PAE 1992, p. 71 A, 18 (f. Θέων)

## Ὀνάτας
AIGINA: (1) vi/v BC IG I³ 773; SEG XXXIII 412; RE (1); Overbeck 421-8; Alt-Ägina II (2) pp. 19-32; Page, FGE 1498; 1502; 1512 (s. Μίκων, ?f. Καλλιτέλης: sculptor)
ARKADIA:
—HERAIA: (2) iii BC IG v (2) 415, 9 (IPArk 23) (f. Φιλόξενος)
—PHIGALEIA: (3) s. i BC IvOl 402 (s. Πραξίας)
MESSENIA:
—MESSENE: (4) f. iii BC SEG XLI 342, 6; cf. PAE 1991, p. 100 no. 8; (5) c. 208 BC FD III (4) 135, 9 (s. Μνασισθένης)
—THOURIA: (6) ii-i BC IG v (1) 1385, 9 (s. Ἐπιτέλης)
S. ITALY (BRUTTIUM):
—KAULONIA?:
——(Πε.): (7) ?c. 475 BC IGSI 20, 1 (SEG IV 71; Landi, DISMG 168); LSAG² p. 261 no. 29 (date)
—KROTON: (8) ?iv BC Iamb., VP 267 (FVS I p. 446) (Ὀνατος—ms.: name—Nauck) ?= (9)
—KROTON?: (9) ?iv BC D.L. ii 46 ?= (8)
—PETELIA: (10) ?c. 475 BC IGSI 19, 7 (Landi, DISMG 171); LSAG² p. 259; p. 261 no. 28 (date)
S. ITALY (CAMPANIA):
—FRATTE DI SALERNO (MOD.): (11) f. v BC SEG XXXVII 817 B (vase) (Arena, Iscr. Sic. IV 33)
SICILY:
—ZANKLE-MESSANA: (12) c. 207 BC FD III (4) 135, 9 (s. Μνασισθένης)

**'Ονατίδας**
KORINTHIA:
—SIKYON: **(1)** ?253 BC Nachtergael, *Les Galates* 10, 39 (Skalet 249; Stephanis 1948) (s. *Χαρίδαμος*)

**'Ονάτιχος**
MESSENIA:
—ASINE: **(1)** hell.-imp. *IG* V (1) 1407 (*'Ονάσιμος?—IG*: f. *Δαμάτριος*)

**'Ονατορίδας**
ARKADIA:
—TEGEA: **(1)** s. iv BC ib. V (2) 41, 60 (*'Ονατορ[ίδας]*)

**'Ονατος**
LAKONIA:
—KOTYRTA: **(1)** imp. *SEG* II 174

**'Ονάτωρ**
SICILY:
—SYRACUSE?:
——(*'Ερμ.*): **(1)** hell. Manganaro, *PdelP* forthcoming no. 4 I, 7 (s. *Μνάμων*)

**'Ονειρος**
S. ITALY (BRUTTIUM):
—KROTON: **(1)** imp. *CIL* X 107-8 (Lat. C. Futius Onirus)
S. ITALY (CAMPANIA):
—ABELLA: **(2)** imp. ib. 1217 (Lat. N. Plaetorius Onirus)
—DIKAIARCHIA-PUTEOLI: **(3)** 61 AD Camodeca, *L'Archivio Puteolano* 1 p. 87 no. 18; Bove, *Documenti finanziarie* pp. 103-4 T.P. 21; pp. 104-5 T.P. 22 (Lat. C. Sulpicius Onirus)
—KYME: **(4)** imp. *Eph. Ep.* VIII 451 (Lat. Onirus: s. *'Ηρακλείδας, 'Αρμονία*)

**'Ονεστος**
KORINTHIA:
—KORINTH: **(1)** f. i AD *RE* s.v. Onestes (-); *IG* VII 1797-1805; *GP* 2400 ff. (or Thrace Byzantion)

**'Ονήρων**
SICILY:
—SELINOUS: **(1)** v BC Dubois, *IGDS* 35, 2 (Arena, *Iscr. Sic.* I 64) (*'Ονέρōν*)

**'Ονησᾶς**
AIGINA?: **(1)** imp. *EAD* XXX p. 357 no. 26 (s. *'Επαφρόδιτος*)
ARGOLIS:
—ARGOS: **(2)** ii AD *SEG* XLI 285 I, 17
ARKADIA:
—TEGEA: **(3)** ii AD *IG* V (2) 54, 12 (f. *Νάρκισσος*); **(4)** ~ ib. 55, 48 (I f. *'Ονησᾶς* II); **(5)** ~ ib. l. 48 (II s. *'Ονησᾶς* I); **(6)** ~ ib. l. 90 (f. *'Αφροδᾶς*); **(7)** m. ii AD ib. 48, 6; **(8)** ~ ib. l. 12 (*'Ονησᾶ[ς]*); **(9)** 165 AD ib. 50, 7 (f. *Πολύευκτος*)
ELIS: **(10)** m. iii AD *IvOl* 119, 2 (*['Ον]ησᾶς?*)
LAKONIA:
—SPARTA: **(11)** ii AD *IG* V (1) 159, 17 (Bradford (-)); **(12)** c. 202-205 AD *SEG* XXXVI 360, 6
MESSENIA:
—KORONE: **(13)** 246 AD *IG* V (1) 1398, 57 (*Αὐρ. 'Ο.*)
SICILY:
—KENTORIPA: **(14)** imp. *CIL* X 7008 (Lat. Onesas)

**'Ονησιμαία**
S. ITALY (CALABRIA):
—HYRIA?: **(1)** imp. *Epigraphica* 32 (1970) pp. 157-8 (Lat. O[ne]simaia)

**'Ονησίμη**
ARGOLIS:
—ARGOS: **(1)** byz. *SEG* XXXII 375
ILLYRIA:
—AULON (NR.): **(2)** iv AD ib. XXXIX 552
S. ITALY (APULIA):
—LUCERIA: **(3)** imp. *ASP* 34 (1981) p. 32 no. 41 (Lat. [One]sime)
—VENUSIA: **(4)** ii-iii AD *Epigraphica* 35 (1973) p. 151 no. 17 (*Museo di Venosa* p. 237 no. 8) (Lat. Vettia Onesime)
—VIBINUM: **(5)** iii AD *Bovino* p. 148 no. 200 (Lat. Onesime: slave?)
S. ITALY (CALABRIA):
—BRENTESION-BRUNDISIUM: **(6)** ii AD *Epigraphica* 32 (1970) p. 158 (Lat. On(e)sime)
S. ITALY (CAMPANIA):
—DIKAIARCHIA-PUTEOLI: **(7)** imp. *CIL* X 2115 (Lat. Onesime); **(8)** ~ ib. 2191 (Lat. Caepia Onesime); **(9)** ~ ib. 3108 (Lat. Vibia Onesime); **(10)** ~ *RAAN* 42 (1967) pp. 4-6 (Lat. Caecilia Onesime); **(11)** i-ii AD *CIL* X 2295 (Lat. Claudia Onesime: d. *Ζωσίμη*)
—DIKAIARCHIA-PUTEOLI*: **(12)** imp. ib. 8182 (Lat. Aplania Onesime: d. M. Aplanius Marcellus: freed.)
—MISENUM*: **(13)** imp. ib. 3628 (Lat. Silia Onesime: freed.)
S. ITALY (LUCANIA):
—ATINA LUCANA: **(14)** imp. *IItal* III (1) 178 (Lat. Antonia Onesime)
SICILY:
—SYRACUSE: **(15)** iii-iv AD Ferrua, *NG* 195 (*-σήμη*); **(16)** iii-v AD *IG* XIV 154 (Strazzulla 95; Agnello 10; Wessel 798)

**'Ονησιμιανός**
S. ITALY (APULIA):
—CANUSIUM: **(1)** 223 AD *Epig. Rom. di Canosa* 35 II, 33 (*CIL* IX 338) (Lat. Ti. Claudius Onesimianus); **(2)** ~ *Epig. Rom. di Canosa* 35 III, 47 (*CIL* IX 338) (Lat. A. Kanuleius Onesimianus); **(3)** ~ *Epig. Rom. di Canosa* 35 IV, 10 (*CIL* IX 338) (Lat. Ti. Claudius Onesimianus iun(ior))
S. ITALY (CAMPANIA):
—DIKAIARCHIA-PUTEOLI: **(4)** imp. ib. X 2851 (Lat. A. Plautius Onesimianus)
—NOLA: **(5)** imp. *NScav* 1900, p. 102 no. 3 (Lat. T. Marius Onesimianus: f. T. Marius Iulianus)

**'Ονήσιμος**
AIGINA: **(1)** iii AD *SEG* XI 15
ARKADIA:
—TEGEA: **(2)** ii AD *IG* V (2) 55, 50 (s. *Διόφαντος*); **(3)** 165 AD ib. 50, 78 (*M. 'Αντ. 'Ο.*); **(4)** a. 212 AD ib. 132. 2 (f. *'Αγαθοκλῆς*)
EPIROS: **(5)** ii/i BC Ugolini, *Alb. Ant.* I p. 193 no. 14 (*'Ονή[σιμος]*: f. *Σωτίχη*); **(6)** imp. *CIG* 1828 (*Κούρτ. 'Ο.*)
—NIKOPOLIS: **(7)** i AD *PAE* 1913, p. 97 no. 1 (Sarikakis 79) (*Τιβ. Κλ. 'Ο.*: f. *Σῖμος*)
ILLYRIA:
—APOLLONIA: **(8)** imp. *IApoll* 293 (*['Ον]ήσιμο[ς]*)
—APOLLONIA*: **(9)** imp. ib. 195 (freed.)
KORINTHIA:
—KORINTH: **(10)** ii/iii AD *Ag.* VII p. 97 no. 308; *Corinth* IV (2) p. 210 no. 754; *SEG* XXXIX 337 b (lamps); **(11)** ~ *Corinth* VIII (3) 299, 2
—KORINTH*: **(12)** i BC/i AD *SEG* XI 214 e
LAKONIA:
—ASOPOS: **(13)** imp. *IG* V (1) 1001 (f. *—δας*)
—EPIDAUROS LIMERA: **(14)** ii AD *SEG* XI 894 a, 4 = XLI 311 (*'Ονήσιμ[ο]ς*: f. *'Αλέξανδρος*)
—SPARTA: **(15)** imp. ib. XI 883 c (tile) (Bradford (1)) (*['Ον]ήσιμος*); **(16)** c. 90-100 AD *IG* V (1) 31, 12 (Bradford (2)) (f. *Κάρπος*)
S. ITALY (APULIA):
—CANUSIUM*: **(17)** ii-iii AD *Epig. Rom. di Canosa* 53 (Lat. Onesimus: freed.)
—LARINUM: **(18)** imp. *CIL* IX 758 (Lat. L. Moecius Onesimus)
—LUCERIA: **(19)** imp. ib. 857 (Lat. C. Gavius Honesimus: freed.); **(20)** ~ ib. 900 (Lat. Vitorius Onesimus); **(21)** ~ *ASP* 34 (1981) p. 32 no. 41 (Lat. Onesim[us])
—VENUSIA: **(22)** ii/iii AD *Rend. Linc.* 29 (1974) p. 626 no. 34 (Lat. Onesimus)
—VENUSIA*: **(23)** imp. *CIL* IX 600 (Lat. L. Vibius Onesimus: freed.)
S. ITALY (BRUTTIUM):
—TAURIANA: **(24)** i/ii AD *Epigraphica* 26 (1964) p. 79 = *Rend. Linc.* 19 (1964) p. 133 no. 1 (Lat. Sex. Arellius Onesimus)
S. ITALY (CALABRIA):
—BRENTESION-BRUNDISIUM: **(25)** imp. *CIL* IX 6132 (Lat. D. Pactumeius Onesimus); **(26)** iii AD *Studi Ribezzo* p. 88 no. 27 (Lat. Onesimus: s. Balentina)
S. ITALY (CAMPANIA):
—DIKAIARCHIA-PUTEOLI: **(27)** imp. *CIL* X 2562 (Lat. Iulius Onesimus); **(28)** ~ ib. 2574 (Lat. P. Iulius Onesimus: f. *Τρύφων*); **(29)** ~ ib. 2782 (Lat. C. Novius Onesimus); **(30)** ~ ib. 2889 (Lat. Olius Onesimus); **(31)** ~ *NScav* 1902, p. 398 (Lat. Marcius Onesimus: f. *'Αλεξάνδρεια*); **(32)** 35 AD Bove, *Documenti processuali* pp. 79-80 T.P. 14 (Lat. A. Castricius Onesimus); **(33)** ?ii AD *CIL* X 2437 (Lat. T. Flavius Onesimus); **(34)** ~ ib. 2702 (Lat. T. Flavius Onesimus); **(35)** s. ii AD *Puteoli* 6 (1982) p. 145 no. 2 (Lat. Aurelius Onesimus)
—DIKAIARCHIA-PUTEOLI*: **(36)** imp. *CIL* X 1913 (Lat. Onesimus: f. *'Ονησιφόρος*: slave?); **(37)** ~ ib. 1925 (Lat. L. Sattius Onesimus: freed.); **(38)** ?i-ii AD ib. 2557, 7 (Lat. Iulius Onesimus: freed.)
—HERCULANEUM: **(39)** i BC-i AD ib. IV 10561 (Lat. Onesimus); **(40)** ~ ib. 10598 (*-νέ-*); **(41)** m. i AD *PdelP* 3 (1948) p. 170 no. 15 (Lat. Sex. Cloelius Onesimus)
—HERCULANEUM*: **(42)** i BC-i AD *CIL* X 1403 f III, 13 (Lat. C. Calvisius Onesimus: freed.); **(43)** ~ ib. 1403 g I, 36 (Lat. C. Olius Onesimus: freed.); **(44)** ~ ib. 1403 g II, 15 (Lat. C. Iulius Onesimus: freed.)
—NEAPOLIS*: **(45)** i-ii AD ib. 1509; cf. Leiwo p. 88 (Lat. [M.] [Iuni]us Onesi[mus]: freed.)
—POMPEII: **(46)** i BC-i AD *CIL* IV 1330; 1332 (Lat. Onesimus); **(47)** ~ ib. 2477 a (Lat. Onesimus); **(48)** ~ ib. 3163 (Lat. Onesimus); **(49)** ~ ib. 3911 (Lat. Onesimus); **(50)** ~ ib. 4069 (Lat. Onesimus); **(51)** ~ ib. 4445 (Lat. Onesimus); **(52)** ~ ib. 4554 (Lat. Onesimus); **(53)** ~ ib. 5033 (Lat. Onesimus); **(54)** ~ ib. 5175 (Lat. Onesimus); **(55)** ~ ib. 6612 (Lat. Onesimus); **(56)** ~ ib. 6706 (Lat. Onesimus); **(57)** ~ ib. 8380 (Lat. Onesimus); **(58)** ~ ib. 8462 (Lat. Honesimus); **(59)** ~ ib. 8951 (Lat. Onesimus); **(60)** ~ *Neue Forsch. in Pompeji* p. 263 nos. 9-10 (Lat. Onesimus); **(61)** 54 AD *CIL* IV 3340. 5, 2, 4 (Castrèn 205. 18) (Lat. C. Iulius Onesimus); **(62)** 74 AD *CIL* IV 222; Franklin p. 67 (date) (Lat. Onesimus)
—SURRENTUM*: **(63)** imp. *NScav* 1928, p. 213 no. 6 (Lat. Onesimus: freed.)
S. ITALY (LUCANIA):
—MURO LUCANO (MOD.): **(64)** imp. *CIL* X 442 (Lat. M. Utianus Onesimus)
S. ITALY?: **(65)** imp.? *IG* XIV 2405. 26 (lamp)
SICILY:
—KAMARINA: **(66)** imp.? Manganaro, *PdelP* forthcoming no. 13
—KATANE: **(67)** imp. *Helikon* 2 (1962) pp. 490-1 (Lat. Onesimus: slave?)
—MEGARA HYBLAIA: **(68)** hell. *Mon. Ant.* 1 (1890) p. 763 (tile)
—MORGANTINA: **(69)** imp. *Epigrafia del Villaggio* p. 548 (Lat. M. Lucceius Onesimus)
—SYRACUSE: **(70)** imp. *IG* XIV 38 (*Λούκις Κορνήλις 'Ο.*); **(71)** iii-v AD Strazzulla 207 (Wessel 1343); **(72)** ~ Strazzulla 357 (Wessel 657)

(-ση-); (73) ~ Strazzulla 412; cf. Ferrua, *NG* 321
—TAUROMENION: (74) imp. *Rend. Linc.* 19 (1964) p. 133 no. 1 (Lat. Sex. Arellius Onesimus)

## Ὄνησίς
S. ITALY (CAMPANIA):
—DIKAIARCHIA-PUTEOLI*: (1) imp. *CIL* x 2637 (Lat. Laecania Onesis: freed.)

## Ὀνησιφόρος
ACHAIA:
—PATRAI: (1) imp. ib. III 519 (Lat. L. Curtius Onesiphorus)
ARGOLIS:
—ARGOS: (2) i/ii AD *IG* IV (1) 597, 1 (I f. Ὀνησιφόρος II); (3) ~ ib. l. 1 (II s. Ὀνησιφόρος I)
—EPIDAUROS: (4) imp. Peek, *NIEpid* 61, 6 (II s. Ὀνησιφόρος I); (5) ~ ib. l. 7 (I f. Ὀνησιφόρος II); (6) f. ii AD *IG* IV (1)² 381, 3; 382, 5 (s. Ἀφροδίσιος)
ARKADIA:
—KLEITOR: (7) imp. ib. v (2) 380; (8) a. 212 AD ib. 369, 13; *SEG* XXXI 347, 5
—TEGEA: (9) ii AD *IG* v (2) 55, 70 (Ὀφίλιος Ὀ.); (10) ~ ib. l. 74 (s. Πανέρως); (11) ~ ib. l. 76 (f. Σωτήριχος); (12) ~ ib. l. 83 (f. Ἱέρων); (13) ~ ib. l. 86 (f. Εὐήμερος); (14) 165 AD ib. 50, 30 (I f. Ὀνησιφόρος II); (15) ~ ib. l. 30 (II s. Ὀνησιφόρος I); (16) ~ ib. l. 60 (f. Παράμονος)
ELIS: (17) c. 5 AD *IvOl* 69, 26 ([Ὀν]ησιφόρος); (18) m. i AD ib. 78, 7; (19) 209-213 AD ib. 110, 10, 25 (Αὐ(ρ). Ὀ.: s. Κλεόμαχος, ?f. Διονύσιος)
KORINTHIA:
—KORINTH: (20) m. ii AD *Corinth* VIII (3) 287, 2 (Lat. M. Aenius Onesiphorus: I f. M. Αἴνιος Ὀνησιφόρος II); (21) ~ ib. l. 5 (Lat. M. Aenius Onesiphorus: II s. M. Αἴνιος Ὀνησιφόρος I, Καλλιάνα Ἱλάρα)
LAKONIA:
—SPARTA: (22) ?i AD *IG* v (1) 916 a (Bradford (5)); (23) i-ii AD *SEG* XI 884 c (tile); *BSA* 30 (1928-30) p. 238 no. 73 (Bradford (6)) (Ὀνησιφόρο[s]); (24) c. 100 AD *IG* v (1) 80, 6 (Bradford (13)) (f. Θέων); (25) c. 100-120 AD *SEG* XI 607, 7 ?= (26); (26) c. 105-110 AD *IG* v (1) 20 B, 2; *BSA* 26 (1923-5) p. 168 C 6/7, 5 (Bradford (1)) (s. Χρυσέρως) ?= (25); (27) ~ *SEG* XI 569, 20 (Bradford (4)) (s. Θέων); (28) c. 105-115 AD *IG* v (1) 103, 11 (Bradford (2)) ([Ὀ]νησιφόρος: s. Εὐδαμίδας); (29) c. 115-150 AD *SEG* XI 481, 3 (Bradford (12)) (f. Φιλοκράτης); (30) c. 125-150 AD *IG* v (1) 64, 2; *SEG* XI 575, [5] (Bradford (10)) (f. Ἐπιτυγχάνων); (31) ~ *IG* v (1) 484, 3 (Bradford (3)) (II s. Ὀνησιφόρος I); (32) ~ *IG* v (1) 484, 4 (Bradford (11)) (I f. Ὀνησιφόρος II); (33) c. 140-145 AD *IG* v (1) 63, 21 (Bradford (8)) (Π. Αἴλ. Ὀ.); (34) ~ *SEG* XI 583, 5 (Bradford (7)) ([Ὀνη]σιφόρος); (35) c. 140-160 AD *IG* v (1) 71 II, 4; 74, 5 (Bradford (3); (9)) (Τιβ. Κλ. Ὀ.: II s. Ὀνησιφόρος I); (36) c. 150-160 AD *IG* v (1) 71 II, 4 (Bradford (11)) (I f. Τιβ. Κλ. Ὀνησιφόρος II)
MESSENIA:
—KORONE: (37) 246 AD *IG* v (1) 1398, 70 (Αὐρ. Ὀ.)
—MESSENE: (38) 192 AD *PAE* 1969, p. 104, 12 (f. Συνέρως)
PELOPONNESE?: (39) 11 AD ib. 1992, p. 72 B, 20 (s. Ἀριστοκράτης)
S. ITALY (APULIA):
—CANUSIUM: (40) 223 AD *Epig. Rom. di Canosa* 35 II, 35 (*CIL* IX 338) (Lat. Q. Iunius Onesiphorus)
—VENUSIA*: (41) i-ii AD *Museo di Venosa* p. 210 no. 10 (*CIL* IX 541) (Lat. L. Messius Onesiphorus: freed.)

S. ITALY (CALABRIA):
—BRENTESION-BRUNDISIUM: (42) imp. *NScav* 1900, p. 245 no. 2 (*Rend. Linc.* 24 (1969) p. 172 no. 4)
—RUDIAE: (43) i BC-i AD *NScav* 1897, p. 405 no. 9 = Bernardini, *Rudiae* p. 88 (Susini, *Fonti Salento* p. 130 no. 74) (Lat. Onesiphorus)
—TARAS-TARENTUM: (44) imp. *Misc. Gr. Rom.* 3 p. 176 (Lat. Publicius Onesiforus)
S. ITALY (CAMPANIA):
—DIKAIARCHIA-PUTEOLI: (45) imp. *CIL* x 2874 (Lat. [P]omp[onius] [O]nesiphorus)
—DIKAIARCHIA-PUTEOLI*: (46) imp. ib. 1913 (Lat. Onesiphorus: s. Ὀνήσιμος: slave?); (47) ~ *NScav* 1927, p. 333 no. 9 (Lat. Onesiphor[us]: freed.)
—POMPEII: (48) i BC-i AD *CIL* IV 3912 (Lat. Onesiphorus)

## Ὄνησος
S. ITALY (LUCANIA):
—HYELE-VELIA: (1) hell.? *PdelP* 21 (1966) p. 336 no. 3 (s. Ἀπολλόδωρος, Ἀρίστων); (2) ~ ib. p. 336 no. 5 (f. Εὐάγορος); (3) imp.? *IG* XIV 659 a (p. 689) (s. Δῆμων)

## Ὀνήσυλος
ARKADIA:
—TEGEA: (1) ii AD ib. v (2) 55, 56 (f. Ἀγαθοκλῆς)

## Ὀνίσανδρος
S. ITALY (BRUTTIUM):
—SYBARIS-THOURIOI-COPIAE: (1) c. 450 BC *AMSMG* NS 15-17 (1974-6) p. 164 no. 6 (vase) (Landi, *DISMG* 69); cf. *LSAG*² p. 456 no. D (Ὀνίσαν[δρος], Ὀνίσαλ[ος]?)

## Ὀνομακλῆς
LAKONIA: (1) ii/i BC *IG* v (1) 1143, 2
—SPARTA: (2) 425 BC X., *HG* ii 3. 10 (Poralla² 578)

## Ὀνόμανδρος
ARKADIA:
—PHIGALEIA: (1) c. 240 BC *IG* v (2) 419, 7 (*IPArk* 28)

## Ὀνομάντιος
LAKONIA:
—SPARTA: (1) 413 BC X., *HG* ii 3. 10 (Poralla² 579)

## Ὀνόμαντις
SICILY:
—SYRACUSE: (1) iii-v AD Ferrua, *NG* 251 (s. Πουλίων)

## Ὀνόμαντος
ARGOLIS:
—ARGOS: (1) ?308 BC *IG* v (2) 550, 10 (s. Ἐρύμανθος)
ARKADIA:
—ORCHOMENOS: (2) ?c. 378 BC *BCH* 102 (1978) p. 335, 96 (*IPArk* 15)

## Ὀνόμαρχος
SICILY:
—KATANE: (1) inc. Ael., *NA* v 39 (tyrant)

## Ὀνομάστη
S. ITALY (CAMPANIA):
—MISENUM*: (1) imp. *CIL* x 3362 (Lat. Stonicia Ansia Heliane Onomaste)
SICILY:
—TYNDARIS: (2) imp. *Epigraphica* 51 (1989) p. 165 no. 20 (Lat. Onomaste)

## Ὀνομαστιανός
S. ITALY (CAMPANIA):
—DIKAIARCHIA-PUTEOLI: (1) imp. *CIL* x 2563 (Lat. Iulius Onomastianus)

## Ὀνομαστορίδας
LAKONIA:
—SPARTA: (1) 330 BC Berve 584 (Poralla² 580)

## Ὀνόμαστος
ELIS: (1) c. 575 BC Hdt. vi 127. 3 (s. Ἀγαῖος)
S. ITALY (BRUTTIUM):
—RHEGION: (2) 84-80 BC *SEG* I 418, 3 (*Suppl. It.* 5 p. 59 no. 11) (-μασσ-: s. Ἀγήσιππος)
S. ITALY (CAMPANIA):
—HERCULANEUM*: (3) i BC-i AD *CIL* X 1403 g I, 14 (Lat. Cn. Octavius Onomastus: freed.)
—KYME: (4) ?c. 500 BC Dubois, *IGDGG* I 16 (bronze) (Arena, *Iscr. Sic.* III 27); *LSAG*² p. 240 no. 8 (date) (s. Φειδίλεως)
—POMPEII: (5) i BC-i AD *CIL* IV 504 (Lat. Onomastus); (6) ~ ib. x 8058. 61 (seal) (Castrèn 47. 1) (Lat. Onomastus); (7) 70-79 AD *CIL* IV 9885; Mouritsen p. 110 (date) (Lat. Onomastus)
—SURRENTUM: (8) imp. *CIL* x 747 (Lat. M. Sittius Onomastus)
SICILY:
—TAUROMENION: (9) c. 210 BC *IG* XIV 421 an. 31 (*SGDI* 5219); (10) c. 170 BC *IG* XIV 421 an. 71 (*SGDI* 5219) (f. Ἡρέας)

## Ὀνομάτιον
EPIROS: (1) hell.-imp. *IG* II² 8541

## Ὀνομοκλῆς
ILLYRIA:
—APOLLONIA: (1) i BC *BMC Thessaly* p. 60 no. 55 (coin) (pryt.)

## Ὀνομόστατος
SICILY:
—NAXOS: (1) s. v BC *SEG* XXXVIII 953. 2 (Arena, *Iscr. Sic.* III 77); cf. *L'Incidenza dell'Antico* pp. 418-9 (date) (Ὀνόμ(α)στ<ατ>ος?: s. Ἐπαμένης)

## Ὀνυμακλῆς
AIGINA: (1) ?268 BC *FD* III (3) 200 (s. Ἀναξίλας)
ARGOLIS:
—TROIZEN: (2) ?146 BC *IG* IV (1) 757 B, 40 (Ὀνυμ[ακ]λῆς: f. Ἀνθεύς)

## Ὀνυμάντιος
KORINTHIA:
—KORINTH: (1) hell. *SEG* XXII 210

## Ὀνύμαστος
EPIROS:
—AMBRAKIA: (1) f. ii BC *IC* 2 p. 25 no. 8 C (Ὀ[ν]ύ[μ]αστος: s. —τρατος)

## Ὀξύθεμις
MESSENIA:
—KORONE?: (1) 732 BC Moretti, *Olymp.* 12

## Ὄξυλος
ELIS: (1) her. *RE* (2); *IvOl* 456, 5; *SEG* XIII 277, 2 (Ὀξυλίδης—SEG: oikist); (2) c. 77 or 81 AD *IvOl* 85, 6 (s. Σάμιππος); (3) 96-103 AD *IG* II² 1072, 8; cf. *SEG* XXIX 126 (date) (Ἀντώνιος Ὀ.: s. Ἀντώνιος Σάμιππος)

## Ὀξύμαχος
ARGOLIS:
—ARGOS:
——(Dymanes-Arkoidai): (1) c. 400 BC ib. 361, 31

## Ὀξυμένης
ARGOLIS:
—EPIDAUROS: (1) iii BC *IG* IV (1)² 239 (s. Κλεαρίστα)

## Ὀξυτίων
ARKADIA:
—THELPHOUSA: (1) a. 228 BC ib. 72 B, 20 (s. Δίυλλος)

## Ὀπολέας
ARKADIA:
—MANTINEIA-ANTIGONEIA: (1) c. 370 BC Paus.
viii 27. 2 (and Arkadia Megalopolis: oikist)

## Ὄππιος
SICILY:
—ENTELLA: (1) f. iii BC SEG XXX 1121, 4
(Dubois, IGDS 208); SEG XXX 1123, 4
(Dubois, IGDS 211); SEG XXXV 999, 4
(Dubois, IGDS 212) (f. Γναῖος)

## Ὀπτᾶτα
ILLYRIA:
—APOLLONIA: (1) imp. IApoll 130

## Ὀπωρίς
LAKONIA:
—SPARTA?: (1) ?550-525 BC IG V (1) 1497 (Lazzarini 87 (bronze)); LSAG² p. 199 no. 18
(date) (Poralla² 581) (hοπō-)
S. ITALY (CAMPANIA):
—KYME: (2) ?c. 450-425 BC Dubois, IGDGG I
20 (Arena, Iscr. Sic. III 29); LSAG² p. 240
no. 16 (date) (-πō-)

## Ὀρβανός
ARKADIA:
—TEGEA: (1) ii AD IG V (2) 55, 71-3 (f. Διομή-
δης, Δαμάτριος, Ἐπίγονος); (2) ~ ib. l. 93-4 (f.
Ἐπίγονος, Ἐπάγαθος)

## Ὀρειβάτης
ARKADIA:
—KLEITOR: (1) a. 212 AD ib. 369, 23; SEG XXXI
347, 16 (Ἰούλ. Ὀρειβάτης)
—TEGEA: (2) 165 AD IG V (2) 50, 17 (-ρι-: f.
Ἄμυκος)

## Ὀρεστάδας
ARGOLIS:
—KLEONAI: (1) c. 315 BC SEG XXXII 370, 13
KORINTHIA:
—KORINTH: (2) iv-iii BC ib. XVII 134 (vase)
S. ITALY (LUCANIA):
—METAPONTION: (3) vi/v BC FGrH 577; Iamb.,
VP 267 (FVS I p. 446)

## Ὀρέστας
EPIROS: (1) iii/ii BC PP 15586
—BOUTHROTOS (PRASAIBOI): (2) a. 163 BC
IBouthrot 15, 15 (SEG XXXVIII 472)
ILLYRIA:
—APOLLONIA: (3) ii-i BC IApoll 138
SICILY:
—LIPARA: (4) i BC SEG XLII 855 ([Κλώ]διος Ὀ.)

## Ὀρέστης
DALMATIA:
—TRAGURION: (1) imp. CIL III 2693 (Lat. Ore-
stes)
EPIROS:
—MOLOSSOI: (2) ?164 BC Cabanes, L'Épire p.
586 no. 71, 6 (f. Φιλοξένα)
—PHOTIKE: (3) imp. AE 1914, p. 241 no. II
(CIL III Suppl. 2 12301) (Lat. Orestes)
KORINTHIA:
—KORINTH: (4) 40 BC Amandry pp. 128-30;
RPC I p. 250 nos. 1122-3 (coin) (Lat. M.
Ant. Orest(es))
MESSENIA:
—ABIA: (5) imp. SEG XXIX 392
S. ITALY (CAMPANIA):
—DIKAIARCHIA-PUTEOLI: (6) imp. CIL X 1580
(Lat. Orestes)
—POMPEII: (7) i BC-i AD ib. IV 1233, 3 (Lat.
Orestes)

## Ὀρέστιλλα
S. ITALY (CAMPANIA):
—SARNUM: (1) imp. ib. X 1112 (Lat. Felix
Orestilla)

## Ὀρθαγόρας
AITOLIA: (1) 224 or 221 BC SGDI 2524, 5;
Nachtergael, Les Galates 64, 4; (2) c. 20-45
AD FD III (6) 13, 3-4 (f. Στρατονίκα)
ARGOLIS:
—ARGOS: (3) 190 BC IG II² 2313, 58; SEG
XXXVI 227 (locn.) (PA 11488) (and Athens?:
f. Πυθίλας)
——Sticheleion (Kleodaidai): (4) s. iii BC
Mnem. NS 43 (1915) p. 366 A, 8 (Perlman
A.17); Mnem. NS 43 (1915) pp. 366-7 B, 7
(Perlman A.18); SEG XVII 144, 12 (Perlman
A.20) (s. Πυθίλας)
ARKADIA: (5) ?255 BC Nachtergael, Les Galates
8, 51; cf. Stephanis 239 (f. Ἀπολλογένης)
EPIROS:
—ATHAMANES: (6) 316-309 BC IG II² 1956,
157; Ancient Macedonia 5 p. 445 with n. 10
(date)
KEPHALLENIA:
—PALE: (7) c. 230-200 BC BCH 45 (1921) p. 14
II, 137 (f. Νικέας)
KORINTHIA:
—KORINTH?: (8) f. iv BC Plu., Tim. 4 (FGrH
70 F 221; 566 F 116) (mantis)
—SIKYON: (9) vii BC RE (1) (Skalet 250) (s. Ἀν-
δρέας: tyrant)

## Ὀρθαῖος
AITOLIA: (1) ?253 BC Nachtergael, Les Galates
10, 3
—POTANA: (2) 186-?161 BC FD III (3) 2, 2;
SGDI 1725, 1; 2034, 1 (f. Νεοπάτρα (Potana
& Delphi)) ?= (3); (3) ?161 BC FD III (3) 2, 4
?= (4) (2); (4) 153-144 BC ib. 47, 9 ?= (3)

## Ὀρθολαΐδας
ARKADIA:
—PHIGALEIA: (1) c. 240 BC IG V (2) 419, 8
(IPArk 28)

## Ὀρθρίς
SICILY:
—SYRACUSE: (1) iii-v AD NScav 1915, p. 206
(Lat. Orthris)

## Ὄρθων
DALMATIA:
—ISSA: (1) iii BC Brunšmid p. 9 fr. G, 7 +
VAMZ 1970, p. 37 frr. G and M (s. Διο-
νύσιος)
——(Pamphyloi): (2) iv/iii BC Brunšmid p. 7, 26
(s. Φιλίαρχος); (3) ~ ib. p. 8, 33 (s. Νίκων)
MESSENIA:
—THOURIA: (4) ii-i BC IG V (1) 1385, 21 (f. Δέ-
ξων)
S. ITALY (BRUTTIUM):
—LOKROI EPIZEPHYRIOI:
——(Τηλ.): (5) 275 BC De Franciscis 25, 5 (s.
Σιλανός)
—RHEGION: (6) hell. IG XIV 2400. 14; SEG
XXXIII 781 b-c (brick); (7) 190 BC Syll³ 585,
82 (s. Ζώπυρος)
——(Ἐργ.): (8) ii BC IG XIV 616, 5 with Add.
p. 688 (Mus. Naz. Reggio p. 159 no. 29) (f.
Διονύσιος)
SICILY: (9) hell.-imp. IG XIV 456
—HALOUNTION: (10) i BC-i AD? ib. 370 (IG-
LMP 42) (s. Φορμίων)
—KAMARINA: (11) ?ii BC SEG XXXIX 996, 11
(Dubois, IGDS 126; Cordano, 'Camarina
VII' 141) (s. Φ—μος)
—MORGANTINA: (12) ?iv/iii BC SEG XXXIX
1008, 1
—SYRACUSE: (13) 308 BC D.S. xx 40. 1; (14)
f. iii BC HE 3426 (GVI 1359); (15) 148 BC
Moretti, Olymp. 638
—SYRACUSE?:
——(Ριπ.): (16) hell. NScav 1961, p. 349 with
fig. 15 b (bullet); cf. BE 1965, no. 502 (s.
Ἐμμενίδας)

## Ὀρθαγόρας
—TAUROMENION: (17) c. 234 BC IG XIV 421
an. 7 (SGDI 5219); (18) c. 211-176 BC IG
XIV 421 an. 30; 421 an. 65 (SGDI 5219) (s.
Θεόκριτος, f. Θεόκριτος); (19) c. 142 BC IG XIV
421 an. 99 (SGDI 5219)

## Ὀρίκαδμος
SICILY?: (1) arch.? Ael., VH xi 1 (fict.?)

## Ὀρίντας
ARKADIA: (1) 370-367 BC IG V (2) 2, 5

## Ὀριπίων
ARKADIA:
—MANTINEIA-ANTIGONEIA:
——(Posoidaia): (1) m. iv BC ib. 271, 15 (f. Εὐ-
τέλης)

## Ὄρκιος
ARGOLIS:
—ARGOS: (1) ii AD SEG XLI 285 II, 35 (n. pr.?)

## Ὀρμασίλας
ARGOLIS:
—ARGOS: (1) 337-324 BC CID II 32, 34, 39; 74
I, 46; 77 I, [7]; 97, 34; 99 A, [6]; 102 II B,
31; 120 A, 3; 122 III, 1 (s. Ἐχεκράτης) ?= (2);
(2) f. iii BC ib. 122 I, 10 (f. Ἀδάμας) ?= (1)

## Ὄρμενος
ARKADIA: (1) iii AD Heliod., Aeth. iv 3. 3 (fict.)

## Ὁρμή
S. ITALY (APULIA):
—TEANUM APULUM*: (1) imp. Teanum Apu-
lum p. 119 no. 49 (CIL IX 715) (Lat. Sorgia
Horme: freed.)

## Ὅρμος
S. ITALY (CAMPANIA):
—POMPEII: (1) i BC-i AD ib. IV 4907 (Lat. Hor-
mus)

## Ὀρνιχᾶς
SICILY:
—SOLOUS: (1) s. ii BC SEG XLI 836 ([Ἄν]ταλλος
Ὀ[ρνιχᾶ]ς: s. Ἀσκλαπός); (2) ?i BC IGLMP 114,
5; cf. SEG XXXVIII 964 (Ἄνταλλος Ὀ. (n. pr.?):
s. Ἄνταλλος)

## Ὄρνυτος
S. ITALY (BRUTTIUM):
—SYBARIS-THOURIOI-COPIAE: (1) s. i BC Hor.,
Carm. iii 9. 14 (Lat. Ornytos: f. Κάλαϊς)

## Ὄροβις
KERKYRA?: (1) hell. IG IX (1) 842 (bullet)

## Ὄροιδος
EPIROS:
—PARAUAIOI: (1) c. 430 BC Th. ii 80. 5

## Ὄροικος
MESSENIA:
—MESSENE: (1) ?253 BC Nachtergael, Les
Galates 10, 12 (Stephanis 1958) (Ὄροικος,
Ὄροιβος—SGDI: s. Φιλίσκος)

## Ὀρόμαχος
KERKYRA: (1) iii BC Unp. (IG arch.)

## Ὀρόντης
S. ITALY (CAMPANIA):
—DIKAIARCHIA-PUTEOLI*: (1) i/ii AD Puteoli 7-
8 (1983-4) p. 295 no. 1 (CIL X 1740) (Lat.
Orontes: f. Ἀλέξανδρος: freed.)

## Ὄρος
ILLYRIA:
—EPIDAMNOS-DYRRHACHION: (1) imp. IDyrrh
132 ((Ω)ρος?: f. Ἀφροδισία)

**Ὀρριππίδας**
Lakonia:
—sparta: (**1**) s. i bc *IG* v (1) 96, 4 (Bradford
(-)) (Ὀρ(ρ)ιππίδας)

**Ὀρσίας**
Argolis:
—epidauros: (**1**) c. 370 bc *IG* iv (1)² 102, 6,
[8], 18 + *SEG* xxv 383
———(Dymanes): (**2**) 146 bc *IG* iv (1)² 28, 6 (s.
Λᾶκρις)
Korinthia:
—korinth: (**3**) vi bc *SEG* xi 225 (Lazzarini
68; *CEG* i 353) (Ὀρσίας)

**Ὀρσικῖνος**
Sicily:
—syracuse: (**1**) iii-v ad Strazzulla 364 (Barreca
270)

**Ὀρσικράτης**
Akarnania: (**1**) c. 250-167 bc *NZ* 10 (1878)
p. 29 no. 30; *BMC Thessaly* p. 169 no. 12
(coins); cf. *Stud. D. M. Robinson* 2 p. 218 ff.
(f. Λέων)
—thyrreion: (**2**) m. iii bc *SEG* xl 464 II side
1, 8 (Ὀρσι[κράτης?]: ?f. Ἀριστόλας)

**Ὀρσίφαντος**
Lakonia:
—sparta: (**1**) vi/v bc Hdt. vii 227 (Poralla²
583) (f. Ἀλφειός, Μάρων)

**Ὀρτείρας**
S. Italy (Apulia):
—canusium: (**1**) ?c. 241-232 bc *IG* xi (4) 642,
4 (f. Βοῦζος)

**Ὀρτυγία**
Sicily:
—syracuse: (**1**) s. viii bc Plu., *Mor.* 773 B (d.
Ἀρχίας (Korinth): fict.?)

**Ὄρτυξ**
Sicily:
—akrai: (**1**) imp. *SEG* xlii 827

**Ὀρύας**
Argolis:
—hermione: (**1**) iii bc *IG* iv (1) 729 I, 5 (s.
Μελάνδρυς)

**Ὀρφανίων**
Sicily:
—kamarina: (**1**) s. v bc Dubois, *IGDS* 119,
4 (Arena, *Iscr. Sic.* II 145) (Ὀ[ρ]φαν[ί]ōν,
Ὀ[ρ]φάνōν—Arena, Φάνōν?—Dubois)

**Ὀρφεύς**
Achaia:
—aigeira: (**1**) c. 100-90 bc *SEG* xxxiii 290
A, 15; *BSA* 70 (1975) pp. 129-31 (date); cf.
Stephanis 1963 (I f. Ὀρφεύς II); (**2**) ~ *SEG*
xxxiii 290 A, 15; *BSA* 70 (1975) pp. 129-31
(date) (Stephanis 1963) (II s. Ὀρφεύς I)
S. Italy (Bruttium):
—kroton: (**3**) vi bc *FGrH* 697 F 9 ?= (**4**); (**4**)
~ *CGF* p. 20 (dub.) ?= (**3**)
S. Italy (Campania):
—herculaneum*: (**5**) m. i ad *Cron. Erc.* 7
(1977) p. 118 D, 8 (Lat. L. Cornelius Orph-
eus: freed.)
Sicily?: (**6**) imp. *CIL* x 8059. 394 (seal) (Lat.
C. T. Orpheus)

**Ὀσία**
Kephallenia:
—panormos: (**1**) imp. ib. 7314 (Lat. Osia)

**Ὄσιος**
Argolis:
—argos: (**1**) 105 bc *JÖAI* 14 (1911) Beibl. p.
146 no. 4, 6

**Ὄστρεις**
Sicily:
—zankle-messana: (**1**) imp. *IGLMP* 28 (Ὀ.
Λοινας)

**Οὐαλέριος**
Illyria:
—apollonia: (**1**) imp. *IApoll* 223 (Ο[ὐ]αλέριος:
f. Παραμόνα)

**Οὐάλης**
Sicily:
—zankle-messana: (**1**) iii-v ad *Arch. Class.* 17
(1965) p. 206

**Οὐάρις**
Arkadia:
—tegea: (**1**) ii ad *IG* v (2) 54, 21

**Οὔενδα**
Illyria:
—epidamnos-dyrrhachion: (**1**) hell.-imp.
*IDyrrh* 338 (d. Φαρνάκης)

**Οὐεργιλία**
Epiros:
—bouthrotos: (**1**) ?i bc *IBouthrot* 197
(Ugolini, *Alb. Ant.* 3 p. 209 no. 4) (d. Λεύκιος)

**Οὐερηκοῦνδος**
S. Italy (Campania):
—neapolis: (**1**) iii-iv ad *IG* xiv 826. 34 and 51
(*INap* 241) (Οὐερ[η]κοῦνδος)

**Οὐέττιος**
Sicily:
—motyka: (**1**) ii-iii ad *MEFRA* 106 (1994) pp.
107-8 no. 20 (-τηιος: s. Βοῦς)

**Οὐῆρα**
Sicily: (**1**) imp. *IG* xiv 803, 1 (*GVI* 1039;
*INap* 150); cf. Leiwo p. 127 no. 115

**Οὐηστῖνα**
Sicily: (**1**) imp. *Epigraphica* 5-6 (1943-4) p. 94

**Οὐιβία**
Sicily:
—akrai?: (**1**) imp. Manganaro, *QUCC* forthcoming no. 32

**Οὐικτωρῖνος**
S. Italy (Campania):
—neapolis: (**1**) iii-iv ad *IG* xiv 826. 32 (*INap*
243) (-ρεῖ-)

**Οὐίλλιος**
S. Italy (Campania):
—neapolis: (**1**) iv/iii bc Sambon 459 (coin)

**Οὐινθεμία**
Sicily:
—syracuse: (**1**) iii-v ad Ferrua, *NG* 19
(Ο[ὐ]ινθεμία)

**Οὐιτᾶλις**
S. Italy (Campania):
—neapolis: (**1**) iii-iv ad *IG* xiv 826. 33 (*INap*
242) (Οὐει-)

**Οὔλαμος**
Epiros:
—bouthrotos (prasaiboi):
———Prochtheioi: (**1**) a. 163 bc *IBouthrot* 168, 13
(*SEG* xxxviii 469) (s. Εὐφράνωρ)

**Οὐλίας**
Argolis:
—argos: (**1**) ?444 bc Pi., *N.* x, 24 (f. Θεαῖος)
Arkadia:
—mantineia-antigoneia: (**2**) c. 300-221 bc
*IG* v (2) 323. 106 (tessera) (Ο[ὐλ]ίας: s. —ρο-
κλῆς)

**Οὖλις**
Sicily:
—lipara: (**1**) inc. *Chiron* 22 (1992) p. 386 n. 5

**Οὐλπία**
Sicily:
—syracuse: (**1**) iii-v ad *IG* xiv 124 (*GVI*
1203; Strazzulla 62; Agnello 101; Wessel 258)
(-πήα: m. Θεοκτίστη)
—tauromenion: (**2**) iii-v ad *IG* xiv 155
(Strazzulla 96; Wessel 976); Ferrua, *NG* 478
(locn.)

**Οὐλπιανή**
Sicily:
—syracuse: (**1**) iii-v ad *IG* xiv 38 + *Riv. Arch.
Crist.* 18 (1941) p. 175 no. 38 (Οὐλπια[νή]?)

**Οὐρανία**
S. Italy (Campania):
—pompeii: (**1**) i bc-i ad *CIL* iv 9223; *Gnomon*
45 (1973) p. 268 (Castrèn 82. 2) (Lat. Cae-
cinia Orania)
Sicily:
—katane: (**2**) iii-iv ad Libertini, *Museo Biscari*
p. 316 no. 1 (d. Οὐράνιος)
—syracuse: (**3**) iii-v ad *NScav* 1907, p. 775
no. 40 (Barreca 200); cf. Ferrua, *NG* 92 (Ἰου-)

**Οὐράνιος**
S. Italy (Campania):
—nola: (**1**) ?v-vi ad *CIL* x 1385 (Lat. Uranius)
Sicily:
—katane: (**2**) iii-iv ad Libertini, *Museo Biscari*
p. 316 no. 1 (f. Οὐρανία)

**Οὐρανίων**
Sicily?: (**1**) iii-v ad *IG* xiv 598; cf. Ferrua,
*NG* 528 ([Οὐ]ράνιον—lap., [Οὐ]ρανίων—*IG*)

**Οὐρβανίων**
Sicily:
—katane: (**1**) imp. *IG* xiv 510, 3 (Ὀ. Γόνγε
(voc.)—lap., (Λ)όνγε? (voc.)—*IG*)

**Οὔρβανος**
Arkadia:
—tegea: (**1**) imp. ib. v (2) 253, 3
Illyria:
—epidamnos-dyrrhachion: (**2**) hell.-imp.
*IDyrrh* 214 (f. Εὐτυχὶς Κάρνεια)

**Οὔρβικα**
Sicily:
—syracuse: (**1**) iii-v ad *IG* xiv 156 (Strazzulla
97; Wessel 1064) (d. Ἑσπεριανός)

**Οὐρσακία**
Sicily:
—syracuse: (**1**) iii-v ad Strazzulla 219

**Οὐρσιανός**
Sicily:
—syracuse: (**1**) iii-v ad *IG* xiv 157 (Strazzulla
98); cf. Ferrua, *NG* 317 (Οὐρσ(ι)ανούς)

**Οὔρσουλος**
Sicily:
—katane: (**1**) iii-v ad *IG* xiv 544 (Wessel
1374)

**Οὐτάλης**
S. Italy (Lucania):
—herakleia: (**1**) f. ii bc *BCH* 45 (1921) p. 24
IV, 85 (*SEG* xxii 455); cf. *Sic. Gymn.* 17
(1964) pp. 46 f.

**Ὀφάλλιος**
S. Italy (Bruttium):
—petelia: (**1**) f. ii bc *BCH* 45 (1921) p. 24
col. IV, 86 (*SEG* xxii 455); cf. *Sic. Gymn.*
17 (1964) pp. 46 f. (Ὀφάλ[λιος])

## 'Οφέλανδρος
AKARNANIA:
—PALAIROS: (1) ii BC *IG* IX (1)² (2) 451, 6 (f. *Ἀντίπατρος*)
KORINTHIA:
—KORINTH: (2) c. 590-570 BC Amyx 40. 3 (vase) (Lorber 42) (fict.?)

## 'Οφέλλας
KORINTHIA:
—KORINTH: (1) i BC *SEG* XXV 278 (f. *Σωσιβία*)

## 'Οφέλων
ACHAIA: (1) 146 BC *IG* IV (1)² 28, 142 (f. *Ἀλέξ-ανδρος*: synoikos)

## 'Οφίλλιος
ARKADIA:
—TEGEA: (1) 191 AD ib. V (2) 52, 8

## 'Οφιονεύς
MESSENIA: (1) viii BC *RE* (2) (dub.)

## 'Οφρυάδας
AKARNANIA:
—ASTAKOS: (1) c. 325-315 BC *Hesp.* 57 (1988) p. 148 A, 53 (*SEG* XXXVI 331); cf. *Hesp.* 48 (1979) pp. 78 f. with pl. 22 c (f. *Ἡρακλείδας*)

## 'Οχίππων
ARGOLIS:
—ARGOS?: (1) v BC *IG* IV (1) 552, 6 (-ιπὄν)

## Ὄψιμος
EPIROS:
—BOUTHROTOS (PRASAIBOI): (1) a. 163 BC *IBouthrot* 19, 9 (*SEG* XXXVIII 476)
LEUKAS: (2) c. 167-50 BC BM coin 1928 2-2-1; *Coll. McClean* 5363 (coins)
S. ITALY (BRUTTIUM):
—RHEGION: (3) v-iv BC *FVS* 46

## Ὄψινος
LEUKAS: (1) v/iv BC Unp. (*IG* arch.)

## Ὄψιος
S. ITALY (LUCANIA):
—MONTEGIORDANO (MOD.): (1) s. iv BC *Atti Conv. Taranto* 21 (1981) p. 222 (vases) (*Νούιος Ὄ.*)

# Π

## Παγασίδας
ARGOLIS:
—EPIDAUROS: (1) iii/ii BC Peek, *NIEpid* 15, 14 (*Παγασί[δας]*: f. *Οἴτας*)

## Πάγκαλος
LAKONIA:
—SPARTA: (1) 395 BC *Hell. Oxy.* xxii 4 (Poralla² 584)
S. ITALY (CAMPANIA):
—DIKAIARCHIA-PUTEOLI: (2) imp. *CIL* X 2201 (Lat. L. Genucius Pancalus)
S. ITALY (LUCANIA):
—EBURUM?: (3) imp. *IItal* III (1) 280; cf. Solin, *Lukan. Inschr.* p. 58 (Lat. L. Fulvius Pa[nc]alus)
SICILY:
—SYRACUSE*: (4) imp. *SEG* XXXVIII 972 (-καλλ-: imp. freed.?)

## Πάγκαρπος
KEPHALLENIA:
—SAME: (1) imp. *IG* IX (1) 640 (*Πάν-*)
SICILY:
—KATANE: (2) imp. *CIL* X 7072 (Lat. Iulius Pancarpus)

## Παγκᾶς
ARKADIA:
—EUTRESIA?: (1) ?c. 500-475 BC *SEG* XXXIV 321 a; *LSAG*² p. 206 no. 4 (date)
MESSENIA: (2) ?c. 500-475 BC *SEG* XXXIV 321 a; *LSAG*² p. 206 no. 4 (date); *SEG* XXXVII 332 (name) (n. pr.?)

## Πάγκιος
KERKYRA: (1) m. iv BC Fraser–Rönne, *BWGT* p. 113 no. 5 (*Miscellanea* p. 186 n. 5) (or Korinthia Korinth?: *Πάνκιος* (nom.?): ?s. *Κορίν-θιος*)

## Παγκλῆς
ACHAIA: (1) 146 BC *IG* IV (1)² 28, 156 (f. *Φί-λειος*: synoikos)
AITOLIA: (2) ?262-253 BC Nachtergael, *Les Galates* 5, 29; 10, 35; Stephanis 1974 (*Πανκλῆς*—no. 10: s. *Κορύμβιος*)
ILLYRIA:
—EPIDAMNOS-DYRRHACHION: (3) hell.-imp. *IDyrrh* 387 (f. *Σώστρατος*)

LAKONIA:
—SPARTA: (4) s. i BC *IG* V (1) 92, 7 (Bradford (-)) (*Παν-*: s. *Πολύξενος*)
MESSENIA:
—MESSENE: (5) f. iii BC *PAE* 1991, p. 99 no. 7, 1
S. ITALY (CAMPANIA):
—NEAPOLIS: (6) her. *IG* XIV 742 (*INap* 42, 5) (*Πανκλεῖδαι* (n. gent.))

## Παγκράτης
ACHAIA:
—PATRAI: (1) i BC/i AD *SEG* XXIX 426, 1 (*Παν-*: f. *Σάλβιος ὁ καὶ Πομπήιος*)
ARGOLIS:
—ARGOS: (2) c. 345-323 BC *CID* II 34 I, [46]; 46 B III, [3], 14; 47 A II, 7; 47 C I, 5, [7]; 47 D I, 5; 49 A I, 5; 49 D-E; 56 I A, 20; 58 I, 4, 10, 36, 39; 59 II, 64; 62 III A, 10, 17; cf. p. 90; 63, 21; 81 A, 13; 93, [24], 40, [54]; 107, 16
—EPIDAUROS: (3) 360 BC ib. 4 II, 46 (s. *Ἐπικρά-της*); (4) c. 340-320 BC Peek, *NIEpid* 19 C, 11 (*Πανκράτ[ης]*)
ARKADIA: (5) iii-ii BC *RE* (3); *Suppl. Hell.* pp. 286-8 ?= (7); (6) 284 BC *PEleph* 3, 7
ARKADIA?: (7) hell. *HE* 2847 ff. ?= (5)
ILLYRIA:
—EPIDAMNOS-DYRRHACHION: (8) c. 250-50 BC Maier 199; 248; 282; Münsterberg Nachtr. pp. 15 + 17 (Ceka 365-9); *IApoll Ref. Bibl.* n. 96 (coin) (*Παν-*: money.); (9) ~ Maier 418 (Münsterberg Nachtr. p. 16); *Bakërr Hoard* p. 66 no. 15; p. 67 no. 100 (coin) (Ceka 89; 344; 401) (pryt.)
MESSENIA:
—THOURIA: (10) c. 315-280 BC *FD* III (4) 5, 2 (*Παμ-*: s. *Πασιτέλης*); (11) f. ii BC *SEG* XI 972, 20 (f. *Λυσίας*); (12) ~ ib. l. 89 (s. *Νικίας*)
S. ITALY (CAMPANIA):
—SURRENTUM: (13) imp. *CIL* X 744 (Lat. Pancratis)

## Παγκρατίδας
LAKONIA:
—HIPPOLA: (1) ?ii-i BC *IG* V (1) 1277 g (*Παν-*)
—KYTHERA?: (2) ii BC *SEG* XLI 326, 4 (s. *Λα-σθένης*)
—SPARTA: (3) iii AD *IG* V (1) 759 (Papaefthimiou p. 139 no. 13; Bradford (3)) (*Παν-*: I f. *Παγκρατίδας* II); (4) ~ *IG* V (1) 759 (Papaefthimiou p. 139 no. 13; Bradford (2)) (*Παν-*: II s. *Παγκρατίδας* I)
—TAINARON-KAINEPOLIS: (5) c. 212-225 AD *IG* V (1) 530, 2; *BSA* 79 (1984) pp. 265-7; 282 (ident., date, stemma) (Bradford (1)) (and Lakonia Sparta: *M. Αὐρ. Παγκρατίδας*: s. *Ἑλ-λάνικος*)

## Παγκρετέας
ARKADIA:
—MANTINEIA-ANTIGONEIA: (1) f. iii BC *IG* V (2) 272, 1 (*Παγκρετέ[ας]*)

## Παγχαρῖνος
ARGOLIS:
—TROIZEN: (1) iv BC ib. IV (1) 764, 5 (f. *Πασι-χάρης*)

## Παγχάριος
KORINTHIA:
—KORINTH: (1) iii-iv AD *SEG* XIII 228, 2; cf. XXII 223 (*Παν-*)

## Παγχαρίων
LAKONIA?: (1) ?i AD *IG* V (1) 930
SICILY:
—SYRACUSE?:
——(*Λαβ.*): (2) hell. Manganaro, *PdelP* forth-coming no. 4 I, 4 (*Παν-*: s. *Ἁρμάτης*)

## Παζαλία
S. ITALY (CALABRIA):
—TARAS-TARENTUM: (1) iv-iii BC Becatti, *Oreficerie Antiche* pp. 189-90 no. 339

## Παιάδας
LAKONIA: (1) s. iv BC *IG* II² 9151 (Bradford (-)) (-δης)

## Παιάνιος
ELIS: (1) 212 BC *IvOl* 179 (Moretti, *Olymp.* 583) (s. *Δαμάτριος*)
SICILY:
—SYRACUSE: (2) iv BC Manganaro, *PdelP* forth-coming no. 3, 2 (s. *Θέολλος*)
—TAUROMENION: (3) c. 234 BC *IG* XIV 421 an. 7 (*SGDI* 5219) (f. *Νικόδαμος*); (4) c. 194 BC *IG* XIV 421 an. 47 (*SGDI* 5219) (s. *Νικόδαμος*)

## Παιανόδωρος
ELIS: (1) s. iii BC *IvOl* 182 (*Παια[ν]όδωρος*: f. *Θρασωνίδης*)

## Παιδέρως
S. ITALY (LUCANIA):
—GRUMENTUM\*: (1) imp. *CIL* X 275 (Lat. C. Avidius Paideros: freed.)
—TRICARICO (MOD.): (2) imp. ib. 128 (Lat. C. Caevius Paider(os))
SICILY:
—LIPARA: (3) imp.? *Meligunis-Lipara* 5 p. 149 no. 2153; cf. *SEG* XLI 805 (Παιδείων?—ed.: s. Ἐλπίς)
—TAUROMENION?: (4) imp. *CIL* X 8059. 111 (seal) (Lat. Cl. Pederos)

## Παιδερωτιανός
S. ITALY (APULIA):
—CANUSIUM: (1) imp. *Epig. Rom. di Canosa* 120 (Lat. L. Dasimius Paederotianus)

## Παιδικός
SICILY:
—KAMARINA: (1) f. v BC Cordano, *Tessere Pubbliche* 109 (s. Θυ—)

## Παίδων
EPIROS:
—NIKOPOLIS: (1) imp. *Hellenika* 22 (1969) p. 69 no. 5 (Sarikakis 128) (f. Χρυσέα)

## Παίζουσα
S. ITALY (BRUTTIUM):
—RHEGION: (1) f. i AD *Suppl. It.* 5 p. 68 no. 23 (Lat. Paezusa)
S. ITALY (CALABRIA):
—TARAS-TARENTUM: (2) imp. *NScav* 1894, p. 69 no. 49 (Lat. Paezusa)
S. ITALY (CAMPANIA):
—DIKAIARCHIA-PUTEOLI: (3) imp. *CIL* X 2363 (Lat. Claudia Paezusa)
—NEAPOLIS: (4) ?i AD ib. 1501; cf. Leiwo p. 110 (Lat. Caninia Paezusa: m. M. Caninius Severus)
SICILY:
—KATANE: (5) imp. *CIL* X 7040 (Lat. Claudia Paezusa)

## Παΐλοκρος
LAKONIA:
—SPARTA: (1) v BC *IG* V (1) 1589

## Παίνικίδας
LAKONIA:
—OITYLOS: (1) iii/ii BC ib. 1295, 1 (Bradford (-))

## Παίπαλος
AITOLIA: (1) 217 BC Nachtergael, *Les Galates* 65, 3 ([Π]αίπαλος—Bosquet, [Ἀντ]ίπαλος—*SGDI* and *FD*)

## Πάϊς
SICILY:
—SYRACUSE: (1) byz. *SEG* IV 24 (-εις: slave?)

## Παίσος
KORINTHIA:
—KORINTH: (1) c. 570-550 BC Amyx 94 (vase) (Παίσōν?—*LGPN*: her.?)

## Παίτιάδας
LAKONIA:
—SPARTA: (1) c. 500-475 BC *SEG* XI 655 (Lazzarini 830); *LSAG*² p. 191 (date) (Poralla² 584b)

## Παίχνιος
KORINTHIA:
—KORINTH: (1) c. 590-570 BC Amyx 19 B. 7 (vase) (Lorber 37) (fict.?)

## Παίων
LAKONIA:
—SPARTA: (1) ii AD *IG* V (1) 730, 3 (*GVI* 1932; Bradford (-))

## Παιώνιος
ACHAIA: (1) 146 BC *IG* IV (1)² 28, 110 (s. Ὀνασικλῆς: synoikos)
ARGOLIS:
—EPIDAUROS: (2) ?iv BC Peek, *IAEpid* 72, 3 (Παιώ[νιος])

## Πακέα
S. ITALY (CAMPANIA):
—NEAPOLIS: (1) i BC/i AD *SEG* IV 96 (*INap* 152) (d. Ἐπίλυτος)

## Πακία
S. ITALY (LUCANIA):
—HYELE-VELIA: (1) imp.? *IG* XIV 660 (Landi, *DISMG* 47) (Τερτί[α] Π.: ?d. Διονύσιος)

## Πάκκιος
S. ITALY (BRUTTIUM):
—CATANZARO (MOD.): (1) hell. *SEG* IV 76 (terracotta) (Πάκιος Καλόνιος)
S. ITALY (CAMPANIA):
—NEAPOLIS: (2) imp. *Mon. Ant.* 8 (1898) p. 228
—PITHEKOUSSAI-AENARIA: (3) ?s. iii BC *IG* XIV 894; *BE* 1951, no. 252 (date) (Πάκι-: s. Νύμψιος); (4) hell.-imp.? *IG* XIV 2406. 64 (loomweight) (Πάκι-)
SICILY:
—ENTELLA: (5) iv/iii BC *SEG* XXX 1117, 2 (Dubois, *IGDS* 204); *SEG* XXX 1118, 2 (Dubois, *IGDS* 205) (f. Λεύκιος)

## Πακτίων
S. ITALY (CALABRIA):
—TARAS-TARENTUM: (1) vi BC Iamb., *VP* 267 (*FVS* 1 p. 446)

## Πάκυλλος
S. ITALY (CAMPANIA):
—PITHEKOUSSAI-AENARIA: (1) ?s. iii BC *IG* XIV 894; *BE* 1951, no. 252 (date) (f. Μάιος)

## Πακώνιος
LAKONIA:
—SPARTA: (1) f. i AD *IG* V (1) 270, 1; *Artemis Orthia* pp. 306-7 no. 20 (date) (Bradford (-)) (f. Ἡρακλείδας)

## Παλάθα
ELIS:
—KOILE (DAPHNIOTISSA (MOD.)): (1) hell. *SEG* XXXVIII 363 (n. pr.?)
SICILY:
—LIPARA: (2) iii BC *Meligunis-Lipara* 5 p. 151 no. 2164; cf. *SEG* XLI 809

## Παλαίμαχος
ARGOLIS:
—ARGOS?: (1) c. 315-280 BC *CID* II 115, 5

## Παλαιστέας
LAKONIA:
—KOTYRTA: (1) ii BC *IG* V (1) 961, 20

## Παλαιστρείτης
LAKONIA:
—SPARTA:
——Konosoura: (1) c. 212 AD ib. 566, 2 (Bradford (-)) (Μ. Αὐρ. Π.)

## Παλαίφατος
S. ITALY (CAMPANIA):
—POMPEII: (1) c. 51-62 AD *CIL* IV 3340. 92, 6 (Castrèn 457. 13) (Lat. C. Vibius Palepatus)

## Πάλακος
SICILY:
—LIPARA: (1) i BC/i AD *IG* XIV 395-6 + *Kokalos* 13 (1967) pp. 200-1 (Σέξ. Πομπ. Ἄπρος Π.: ?f. Πομπηΐα)

## Παλαμήδης
S. ITALY (LUCANIA):
—HYELE-VELIA?: (1) ?ii AD *RE* (3)

## Παλάμων
LAKONIA:
—SPARTA: (1) v BC *IG* V (1) 1590 (f. Δεσπόσιος)

## Παλάξιος
S. ITALY (CAMPANIA):
—DIKAIARCHIA-PUTEOLI: (1) imp. *CIL* X 1795 (Lat. M. Bassaeus Palaxius)

## Παλικίων
SICILY:
—HYBLA: (1) f. ii BC *BCH* 45 (1921) p. 25 IV, 105 (*SEG* XXII 455); cf. *Sic. Gymn.* 17 (1964) pp. 47 f.

## Πάλις
LAKONIA:
—SPARTA: (1) iii BC *SEG* XL 348 B, 9

## Παλλάδιος
MESSENIA:
—METHONE: (1) f. iv AD *Suda* Π 35 (I f. Παλλάδιος II); (2) ~ *RE* (1); *FGrH* 837 (II s. Παλλάδιος I)
SICILY:
—KATANE: (3) iii-v AD *IG* XIV 530 b (Wessel 1041 b) + Ferrua, *NG* 433

## Παλλάς
S. ITALY (CALABRIA):
—BRENTESION-BRUNDISIUM: (1) i AD *Epigraphica* 25 (1963) p. 74 no. 75; cf. *Scritti Degrassi* 3 pp. 70 ff. (Lat. Caninia Pallas); (2) ?i-ii AD *NScav* 1891, p. 172 (Lat. Iulia Pallas: m. L. Iulius Brundisinus)
S. ITALY (CAMPANIA):
—HERCULANEUM: (3) m. i AD Camodeca, *L'Archivio Puteolano* 1 p. 203 n. 7 (Lat. Herennia Pallas)
—POMPEII: (4) i BC-i AD *CIL* IV 7307 (Lat. Pallas)

## Παλλιάτης
LAKONIA:
—SPARTA: (1) ii-iii AD *IG* V (1) 757 (Bradford (-)) (Μ. Γέλλιος Θεσσαλιανὸς Π. (n. pr.?))

## Πάλλιχος
EPIROS:
—ARGOS (AMPHILOCH.): (1) ?270 BC *FD* III (2) 179, 1 (s. Λεύκαρχος)

## Παλμίων
ILLYRIA:
—EPIDAMNOS-DYRRHACHION: (1) hell.-imp. *IDyrrh* 124 (f. Ἀριστώ)

## Πάμιλλος
SICILY:
—MEGARA HYBLAIA: (1) m. vii BC Th. vi 4. 2 (and Sicily Selinous: Πάμμιλος—Hdn.: oikist)

## Πάμμαχος
SICILY:
—SYRACUSE?:
——(Μακ.): (1) hell. Manganaro, *PdelP* forthcoming no. 4 III, 1 (f. Θεόδωρος)

## Παμμένης
AIGINA: (1) imp. *GVI* 605 (f. Θεμίσων)

## Πάμμουσος
S. ITALY (CAMPANIA):
—DIKAIARCHIA-PUTEOLI: (1) imp. *NScav* 1889, p. 228 (Lat. Hilarion Pammusus)

## Πάμπειρος
ILLYRIA:
—APOLLONIA: (1) c. 250-50 BC Maier 80 (coin) (Ceka 40) (pryt.)

**Παμφάης**

ACHAIA?: (**1**) 193 BC *IG* V (2) 293, 23 (f. Ἀρχέδαμος)
ARGOLIS:
—ARGOS: (**2**) 228-146 BC *BMC Pelop.* p. 147 nos. 140-1 (coin)
——(Lykophronidai): (**3**) 105 BC *JÖAI* 14 (1911) Beibl. p. 146 no. 4, 3; *Mnem.* NS 44 (1916) p. 58 (locn.) (f. Λαχίας)
—EPIDAUROS: (**4**) s. iv BC *IG* IV (1)² 123, 134 (Πα[μ]φάης)

**Παμφαΐδας**

AITOLIA: (**1**) ?262 or 258 BC Nachtergael, *Les Galates* 5, 4

**Παμφίλα**

ACHAIA:
—PATRAI: (**1**) ii BC *Achaean Grave Stelai* 34 (d. Ἀριστώνυμος)
EPIROS:
—AVARICE (MOD.): (**2**) ii BC *SEG* XXIV 468 (d. Λυκώτας)
—BOUTHROTOS (PRASAIBOI): (**3**) a. 163 BC *IBouthrot* 14, 38 (*SEG* XXXVIII 471); (**4**) ~ *IBouthrot* 15, 9 (*SEG* XXXVIII 472); *IBouthrot* 45, 11 ?= (*15*); (**5**) ~ ib. 21, 5 (*SEG* XXXVIII 478); (**6**) ~ *IBouthrot* 22, 29 (*SEG* XXXVIII 479); (**7**) ~ *IBouthrot* 26, 18 (*SEG* XXXVIII 484); *IBouthrot* 137, 9; (**8**) ~ ib. 30, 4 (*SEG* XXXVIII 488); (**9**) ~ *IBouthrot* 31, 38 (*SEG* XXXVIII 490) (II d. Φίλιππος, Παμφίλα I); (**10**) ~ *IBouthrot* 31, 39 (*SEG* XXXVIII 490) (I m. Λυκώτας, Μελιτέα, Παμφίλα II); (**11**) ~ *IBouthrot* 32, 4 (*SEG* XXXVIII 491); (**12**) ~ *IBouthrot* 39, 5 (*SEG* XXXVIII 498); (**13**) ~ *IBouthrot* 41, 4 (*SEG* XXXVIII 500) ?= (*14*); (**14**) ~ *IBouthrot* 47, 5 ([Παμφ?]ίλα: d. Κεφαλῖνος) ?= (*13*); (**15**) ~ ib. l. 8 ?= (*4*); (**16**) ~ ib. 92, 5
—PHOINIKE: (**17**) iii/ii BC Cabanes, *L'Épire* pp. 569 ff. no. 47, 7 (*SEG* XXVI 720)
ILLYRIA:
—BYLLIONES BYLLIS: (**18**) ?f. ii BC ib. XXXVIII 538 (Παμφ(ί)λα)
S. ITALY (APULIA):
—VENUSIA*: (**19**) imp. *CIL* IX 590 (Lat. Tulliana Pamphila: freed.)
S. ITALY (CAMPANIA):
—DIKAIARCHIA-PUTEOLI*: (**20**) imp. ib. X 2821 (Lat. Paccia Pamphila: freed.)
—POMPEII: (**21**) i BC-i AD ib. IV 8475 (Lat. Pamphila—Solin)
—POMPEII*: (**22**) imp. *NScav* 1961, p. 200 no. 5 (Lat. Caesia Pamphila: freed.)
SICILY:
—LIPARA: (**23**) i BC *SEG* XLII 854 b (Παν-: m. Διογένης)

**Παμφίλη**

ARGOLIS:
—EPIDAUROS: (**1**) i AD *RE* (1) (?d. Σωτηρίδας)
EPIROS:
—NIKOPOLIS: (**2**) imp. *CIG* 1811 (Sarikakis 129) (Παν-: d. Πάμφιλος)

**Πάμφιλος**

ACHAIA:
—DYME*: (**1**) c. 50 BC *ILGR* 44, 1 (Lat. C. Antonius Pamphilus: freed.)
AIGINA: (**2**) ?iii AD *Alt-Ägina* I (2) p. 50 no. 47 (f. Αὐρ. Εὐφρόσυνος)
AITOLIA:
—THERMOS*: (**3**) s. iii BC *IG* IX (1)² (1) 60 II, 1
ARGOLIS:
—EPIDAUROS: (**4**) ii-iii AD ib. IV (1)² 468
—EPIDAUROS*: (**5**) c. 370-365 BC Peek, *IAEpid* 52 B, 61
ARKADIA:
—ORCHOMENOS: (**6**) 369-361 BC *IG* V (2) 1, 49; Tod, *GHI* II 132 (date)

DALMATIA:
—ISSA: (**7**) iii BC *SEG* XXXV 691, 2 (*VAHD* 84 (1991) p. 256 no. 6) (f. Ξενοκλῆς); (**8**) ~ *SEG* XXXV 691, 4 (*VAHD* 84 (1991) p. 256 no. 6) (s. Ξενοκλῆς); (**9**) iii/ii BC *SEG* XXXI 601 (*VAHD* 84 (1991) p. 258 no. 8) (Πάν-: s. Ἀπολλώνιος); (**10**) ii BC *SEG* XXXI 602, 7 (*VAHD* 84 (1991) p. 257 no. 7) (f. Νικασώ); (**11**) ~ Brunšmid p. 25 no. 14, 4 + *VAHD* 84 (1991) p. 248 no. 1 (s. Διονύσιος); (**12**) f. ii BC Brunšmid p. 23 no. 10, 2 (f. Σωσύλος)
—TRAGURION: (**13**) 56 BC Sherk 24 A, 7 (Π[άμ]φιλος: I f. Πάμφιλος II); (**14**) ~ ib. l. 7 (II s. Πάμφιλος I)
EPIROS:
—BOUTHROTOS (PRASAIBOI): (**15**) iii-ii BC *IBouthrot* 167 (Cabanes, *L'Épire* p. 568 no. 46) (s. Τροχιλλᾶς)
—NIKOPOLIS: (**16**) imp. *CIG* 1811 (Sarikakis 130) (Πάν-: f. Παμφίλη)
—NIKOPOLIS?: (**17**) imp. *RE* (24); Sarikakis 131 (or Korinthia Sikyon or Macedonia Amphipolis: ὁ ἐπικληθεὶς Φιλοπράγματος)
ILLYRIA:
—EPIDAMNOS-DYRRHACHION: (**18**) hell.-imp. *IDyrrh* 419 (Τρεβέλλιος Π.)
KORINTHIA:
—KORINTH: (**19**) c. 42 BC-14 AD Amandry pp. 133-8; pp. 140-2; *RPC* I p. 251 nos. 1127-8; p. 251 nos. 1132-3 (coins); *NC* 1989, p. 204 (date) (Lat. C. Heius Pamphilus); (**20**) i AD *Corinth* VIII (3) 150 (Lat. [C.] [Hei]us [P]amphilus) ?= (*21*); (**21**) f. i AD ib. 240 (Lat. Pam[philus]) ?= (*20*)
—SIKYON: (**22**) c. 365-340 BC *IG* II² 10305 (Skalet 252) (s. Καλλίας)
LAKONIA:
—SPARTA: (**23**) c. 100-105 AD *SEG* XI 537 b, 6 (Bradford (2)) (Πάμ[φ]ιλος: f. Λ—κράτης); (**24**) c. 100-125 AD *IG* V (1) 152, 4 (Bradford (1)) (f. Εὔδαμος)
MESSENIA:
—MESSENE: (**25**) ii-iii AD *SEG* XLI 366 C (Πάν-)
S. ITALY (APULIA):
—CANUSIUM: (**26**) i AD *Epig. Rom. di Canosa* 196 (*CIL* IX 379) (Lat. [Tu]ssidius Pamphilus)
—VENUSIA*: (**27**) imp. ib. 601 (Lat. M. Vibius Pamphi[lus]: freed.)
S. ITALY (BRUTTIUM):
—HIPPONION-VIBO VALENTIA*: (**28**) imp. ib. X 8041. 31 (tile) (Lat. Pamphilus)
S. ITALY (CAMPANIA):
—ABELLA*: (**29**) inc. *NScav* 1928, p. 385 no. 4 (Lat. Pamphilus: freed.)
—ATELLA*: (**30**) ?i AD *Puteoli* 12-13 (1988-9) p. 227 no. 12 (brick) (Lat. Q. Aufistius Pamp(hilus))
—DIKAIARCHIA-PUTEOLI*: (**31**) imp. *Eph. Ep.* VIII 387 (Lat. M. Modius Pamphilus: freed.)
—POMPEII: (**32**) i BC-i AD *CIL* IV 1579; cf. p. 208 (Lat. Pamph[ilus]); (**33**) ~ ib. 2310 h (Lat. Pamphilus); (**34**) ~ ib. 4705 (Lat. Pamph[ilus]); (**35**) ~ ib. X 8058. 19 (seal) (Castrèn 114. 2) (Lat. Cipius Pamphilus)
—POMPEII*: (**36**) m. i AD *CIL* X 1046 (Castrèn 92. 2); Kockel p. 165 (date) (Lat. L. Caltilius [P]amphilus: freed.)
SICILY: (**37**) hell.? *RE* (22); *Suppl. Hell.* 597
—LILYBAION: (**38**) f. i BC Cic., *In Verr.* II iv 32 (Lat. Pamphilus)
—TAUROMENION: (**39**) c. 189 BC *IG* XIV 421 an. 52 (*SGDI* 5219) (Πάν-)

**Πάμφις**

ARKADIA: (**1**) hell.? *SEG* XXXVIII 375

**Παναγίς**

PELOPONNESE?: (**1**) m. v BC Boardman, *Gems* pl. 562

**Παναίτιος**

ARGOLIS:
—ARGOS: (**1**) a. 316 BC *SEG* XIII 240, 2 (Perlman A.4) (s. Βράχας)
ILLYRIA:
—LYCHNIDOS: (**2**) ii-iii AD *Sp.* 77 (1934) p. 51 no. 45 (-νέ-)
SICILY:
—LEONTINOI: (**3**) s. vii BC *RE* (3) (tyrant)

**Παναίτωλος**

AITOLIA:
—PHYTAION: (**1**) ii BC *SEG* XXV 616 (f. Φιλόδαμος) ?= (*2*); (**2**) 167 BC *IG* IX (1)² (1) p. LII, s.a. 167 BC ?= (*1*)
AITOLIA?: (**3**) c. 220-200 BC *RE* (-); *PP* 15232

**Πανάνδριος**

ARKADIA:
—ORCHOMENOS: (**1**) c. 230-200 BC *BCH* 45 (1921) p. 13 II, 115 (f. Θρασυμένης)
ILLYRIA:
—EPIDAMNOS-DYRRHACHION: (**2**) hell. *IDyrrh* 87 (f. Αἴνυτος); (**3**) c. 250-50 BC Maier 336 (coin) (Ceka 236) (pryt.)

**Πανάρετος**

ARKADIA:
—MEGALOPOLIS: (**1**) c. 272 BC *IG* IX (1)² (1) 13, 11 (II s. Πανάρετος I); (**2**) ~ ib. l. 12 (Πανάρετος: I f. Πανάρετος II)
MESSENIA:
—MESSENE: (**3**) ii/iii AD ib. V (1) 1490 ([Π]ανά[ρ]ετος)

**Πάνδαρος**

S. ITALY (CAMPANIA):
—DIKAIARCHIA-PUTEOLI*: (**1**) imp. *AJA* 2 (1898) p. 378 no. 10 (Lat. Cossinius Pandarus: freed.)
—POMPEII: (**2**) i BC-i AD *CIL* IV 4522 (Lat. Pandarus)

**Πανδοσία**

SICILY: (**1**) ?f. iii BC *ZPE* 111 (1996) p. 136 no. 4

**Πανδοσῖνος**

S. ITALY (BRUTTIUM):
—PANDOSIA?: (**1**) 170 BC *RE* (-); Sherk 2, 54 (Γνάιος Π.: I ?f. Γάιος Πανδοσῖνος II); (**2**) ii/i BC *IG* XII (5) 917; cf. *RE* (-) (Γάιος Πανδυ-: II ?s. Γνάιος Πανδοσῖνος I)

**Πανέρως**

ARKADIA:
—KLEITOR: (**1**) iii AD *SEG* XXXI 347, 12
—TEGEA: (**2**) ii AD *IG* V (2) 55, 74 (f. Ὀνησιφόρος)

**Πανηγύριος**

S. ITALY: (**1**) imp. *CIL* X 8059. 304 (seal) (Lat. Panegyrius)

**Πανησίας**

KERKYRA: (**1**) ?ii-i BC *IG* IX (1) 795 (tile) (Πανησ[ίας])

**Πανθάλης**

ARGOLIS:
—ARGOS?: (**1**) v BC ib. IV (1) 552, 9 (-λε͂ς)
LAKONIA:
—BOIAI: (**2**) ii AD ib. V (1) 956; 957 b (Γ. Ἰούλ. Π.: s. Εὐήνωρ, f. Ἰουλ. Κλεανέτα)
—SPARTA: (**3**) c. 140-160 AD *SEG* XI 600, 8 (Bradford (5)) (— [ὁ] καὶ Πανθά[λης]); (**4**) c. 160-175 AD *IG* V (1) 45, 5, 14; 46, 5; *BSA* 80 (1985) p. 226 (date) (Bradford (3)) (Ἰουλ. Π.); (**5**) ii/iii AD *IG* V (1) 546, 5; 547, 2; 684, 2; *BSA* 79 (1984) pp. 281-3 (date); 80 (1985) pp. 241-2 (ident., stemma) (Bradford (2)) (Γ. Πομπώνιος Π. Διογένης Ἀριστέας: II f. Πομπώνιος Πανθάλης I ὁ καὶ Ἀριστοκλῆς, Πομπωνία

*Καλλιστονίκη ἡ καὶ Ἀρέτη*); (**6**) ~ *IG* v (1) 547,
7; *SEG* xxxv 337, 9; *BSA* 80 (1985) pp. 241-
2 (ident., stemma) (Bradford (1)) (*Πομπώνιος
Π. ὁ καὶ Ἀριστοκλῆς*: II s. *Πομπώνιος Πανθάλης* I *Διογένης Ἀριστέας, Μεμμία Λογγῖνα*, ?f.
*Γ. Πομπώνιος Ἀριστέας ὁ καὶ Περικλῆς*); (**7**) 359
AD *SEG* XI 464, 4 (Bradford (4))

**Πάνθαρις**
ARGOLIS:
—EPIDAUROS: (**1**) ii-iii AD Peek, *IAEpid* 236, 8
(*Πάνθαρις*)

**Πάνθεια**
LAKONIA:
—SPARTA: (**1**) imp. *IG* v (1) 799 (-*θηα*, *Πανθην*—
apogr.)
MESSENIA:
—KYPARISSIA: (**2**) ?i AD ib. 1422 (-*θι*-)
S. ITALY (APULIA):
—TURENUM: (**3**) ii AD *Epig. Rom. di Canosa* 113
(*CIL* IX 310) (Lat. Claudia Panthia: m. *Διο-
νύσιος*)
SICILY:
—AKRAGAS: (**4**) v BC D.L. viii 69

**Πανθείδας**
DALMATIA:
—ISSA:
——(Pamphyloi): (**1**) iv/iii BC Brunšmid p. 7, 23
(s. *Ἡρακλείδας*)

**Πάνθηρ**
LAKONIA:
—SPARTA: (**1**) c. 217-230 AD *SEG* XI 616 a, 4
(Bradford (-)) (*Π(ο)μ(π). Π.*)
S. ITALY (CAMPANIA):
—POMPEII: (**2**) m. i AD *CIL* IV 3340. 101, 11;
x 8058. 29 (seal) (Castrèn 152. 6) (Lat. T.
Dentatius Panther)

**Πανθήρα**
DALMATIA:
—TRAGURION: (**1**) imp. *CIL* III 2692 (Lat. Iul.
Panthera)
EPIROS:
—NIKOPOLIS: (**2**) iii AD *SEG* XXVII 232 (*Φουλ-
βεινία Π.*)
S. ITALY (APULIA):
—KAILIA*: (**3**) imp. *CIL* IX 277 (Lat. Lautinia
[Pa]nthera: freed.)
—VENUSIA: (**4**) imp. ib. 483 (Lat. Appuleia Pan-
thera)

**Πανθήρας**
ARKADIA:
—TEGEA: (**1**) ii AD *IG* v (2) 236 ([*Π*]*ανθήρας*); (**2**)
m. ii AD ib. 48, 13 (*Πανθή[ρας]*); (**3**) ~ ib. l. 18
(*Πανθήρ[ας]*); (**4**) 165 AD ib. 50, 67 (f. *Λεωνᾶς*)
LAKONIA:
—SPARTA: (**5**) ii AD ib. v (1) 159, 12 (Bradford
(2)); (**6**) c. 220 AD *IG* v (1) 544, 11 (*Artemis
Orthia* pp. 358-9 no. 145; Bradford (1)) (*M.
Αὐρ. Π.*: s. *Ὄλυμπος*)

**Πανθηρίς**
LAKONIA:
—GYTHEION: (**1**) ?i AD *IG* v (1) 1197 (d. *Πρω-
τογένης*)
S. ITALY (CAMPANIA):
—SALERNUM: (**2**) imp. *IItal* I (1) 212 (*CIL* x
615) (Lat. Mallia Pantheris)

**Πανθηρίσκος**
LAKONIA:
—SPARTA: (**1**) c. 140-160 AD *IG* v (1) 154, 16
(Bradford (2)) (I f. *Πανθηρίσκος* II); (**2**) ~ *IG*
v (1) 154, 16 (Bradford (1)) (II s. *Πανθηρίσκος*
I)

**Πάνθηρος**
ARKADIA:
—TEGEA: (**1**) 165 AD *IG* v (2) 50, 63 (I f. *Πάν-
θηρος* II); (**2**) ~ ib. l. 63 (II s. *Πάνθηρος* I)
LAKONIA:
—SPARTA: (**3**) i-ii AD ib. v (1) 196 (Bradford
(1)) ([*Πά*]*νθηρος*); (**4**) ii AD *IG* v (1) 159, 18
(Bradford (2))
MESSENIA:
—MESSENE: (**5**) s. ii BC *SEG* XLI 341, 10 (s.
*Ἀγαθοκλῆς*)

**Πάνθις**
ARKADIA:
—MANTINEIA-ANTIGONEIA: (**1**) c. 425-385 BC
*IG* v (2) 323. 21 (tessera) (f. *Ϝισϝόδαμος*)

**Πανθοίδας**
LAKONIA:
—SPARTA: (**1**) v/iv BC D.S. xiv 12. 4, 6; Plu.,
*Pel.* 15 (Poralla² 585)

**Πανική**
AIGINA: (**1**) ?i BC *IG* II² 7964 (d. *Μηνόδοτος*)

**Πανικώ**
DALMATIA:
—EPETION: (**1**) imp. *CIL* III 8551 (Lat. Panico)

**Πανίσκος**
S. ITALY (CAMPANIA):
—MISENUM*: (**1**) ?i-ii AD ib. X 3480 (Lat. C.
Iulius Paniscus)

**Πανίτας**
MESSENIA:
—MESSENE: (**1**) c. 240-220 BC *IG* VII 359, 3
(*IOrop* 166) (*Γανίτας*—*IG*: s. *Θαλησικλῆς*)

**Παννικίας**
SICILY:
—SYRACUSE: (**1**) iii-v AD Strazzulla 402 (Wessel
285); cf. Ferrua, *NG* 342 ([*Πα*]*ννικίας*)

**Πάννικος**
ACHAIA:
—PHARAI: (**1**) ii BC *Achaean Grave Stelai* 67
(-*ννει*-)
MESSENIA:
—MESSENE: (**2**) ?i BC *PAE* 1969, p. 100 a, 2
(*Πά[ν]νικ[ος]*—*LGPN*)

**Πάννις**
ARGOLIS:
—ARGOS: (**1**) iii BC *BCH* 38 (1914) p. 467 no.
9, 2 (s. *Αἰγύπιος*)

**Παννυχίς**
S. ITALY (CALABRIA):
—TARAS-TARENTUM?: (**1**) ?iv BC *NScav* 1881,
p. 435 (vase)
SICILY:
—AIGATES ISLANDS: (**2**) imp. *CIL* X 7493 (Lat.
Pannychis: m. *Νάρκισσος*)

**Πάννυχος**
LAKONIA:
—SPARTA: (**1**) c. 175-205 AD *IG* v (1) 150, 2;
*SEG* XXXVI 360, 7; *BSA* 81 (1986) p. 324 no.
5 (ident.) (Bradford (2)) (I f. *Πάννυχος* II); (**2**)
~ *IG* v (1) 150, 2; *SEG* XXXVI 360, 7; *BSA*
81 (1986) p. 324 no. 5 (ident.) (Bradford (1))
(II s. *Πάννυχος* I)
S. ITALY (APULIA):
—VENUSIA: (**3**) imp. *CIL* IX 496 (Lat. L. Cas-
sius Panny[chus])
S. ITALY (CAMPANIA):
—DIKAIARCHIA-PUTEOLI: (**4**) imp. ib. X 1929
(Lat. Pannychus: doctor)
—KYME: (**5**) 289 AD ib. 3698, 8-9 (Lat. Caelius
Pannychus)

**Πανόπιος**
S. ITALY (CAMPANIA):
—POMPEII: (**1**) i BC-i AD ib. IV 2165 b (Lat.
Panopius)

**Πάνορμος**
MESSENIA:
—ANDANIA: (**1**) ?viii BC Paus. iv 27. 1-2 (dub.)

**Πανσιτίμας**
ARKADIA:
—TEGEA: (**1**) her. *IG* v (2) 113 (*Πανσιτιμίδαι* (n.
gent.))

**Πάνσοφος**
MESSENIA:
—MESSENE?: (**1**) ii/i BC *SEG* XI 979, 33

**Πανταγάπη**
S. ITALY (CAMPANIA):
—NEAPOLIS: (**1**) iii-iv AD *IG* XIV 826. 35 (*INap*
222)

**Παντάδας**
ARGOLIS:
—PHLEIOUS?: (**1**) s. iv BC Peek, *NIEpid* 16, 23
(Perlman E.6) (*Παντάδ[ας]*: f. *Πάντων*)

**Πανταίνετος**
AITOLIA: (**1**) ?247 BC *Syll³* 444 A, 3; *CID* II
139, 3
ARGOLIS:
—ARGOS: (**2**) c. 458 BC *IG* I³ 1149, 56 (*Παν-
ταί[νετος]*, *Πάνται[νος]*?)
——(Dymanes-Doriadai): (**3**) c. 400 BC *SEG*
XXIX 361, 34
ARKADIA:
—PHENEOS: (**4**) c. 210-207 BC *IG* IV (1)² 73, 14;
*SEG* XXXV 303 (date) (s. *Διοφάνης*)
KORINTHIA:
—KORINTH: (**5**) s. iii BC *IG* IX (1)² (1) 24, 3 (f.
—*ιάδας*); (**6**) ~ *Corinth* VIII (3) 38, 3; (**7**) 207
BC *IMM* 42, 17 (s. *Μνασικλείδας*)

**Πάνταινος**
SICILY?: (**1**) s. ii AD *RE* (3); *DCB* (-)

**Παντακαρίδας**
KORINTHIA:
—KORINTH: (**1**) ?iii-ii BC *IG* IV (1) 200

**Παντακλείδας**
KORINTHIA:
—SIKYON: (**1**) ?269 BC *CID* II 120 A, 48; 122 I,
13 (f. *Δαϊάλκης*)

**Παντακλῆς**
ARGOLIS:
—ARGOS: (**1**) 105 BC *JÖAI* 14 (1911) Beibl. p.
146 no. 4, 7 (s. *Παντιάδας*)
—EPIDAUROS: (**2**) c. 365-335 BC *IG* IV (1)² 103,
142, 158
—HERMIONE: (**3**) ?263-255 BC Nachtergael, *Les
Galates* 2 bis, [5]; 3, [15]; 8, 31; 15 bis, 1
(Stephanis 1993) (s. *Ἀρίσταρχος*)
—TROIZEN: (**4**) iii BC *IG* IV (1) 774, 3 (*Παντα-
κλ[ῆς]*: f. *Ζωπυρίων*)
ARKADIA:
—TEGEA: (**5**) iv BC *SEG* XXXVI 382, 1
(*Παντακλ[ῆς]*?: f. —*ις*)
KORINTHIA:
—SIKYON: (**6**) ?257-255 BC Nachtergael, *Les
Galates* 7, 45 (s.p.); 8, 69 (Skalet 253;
Stephanis 1994) (s. *Δαάλκης*)
LAKONIA:
—SPARTA: (**7**) 407 BC X., *HG* i 3. 1; ii 3. 10;
Ael., *NA* xi 19 (Poralla² 586)

**Πανταλέων**
ACHAIA:
—DYME: (**1**) iii-ii BC *Syll³* 530, 10; cf. *Achaia
und Elis* p. 115 ([*Κυλλ*]*άνιος ἢ εἰ Π.*)
AITOLIA: (**2**) 206 BC *REG* 101 (1988) p. 15, 79
(*SEG* XXXVIII 1476)
—AGRINION: (**3**) c. 220-210 BC *SBBerlAk* 1936,
p. 359, 5

—KALYDON: (4) m. ii BC *IG* IX (1)² (1) 35, 2;
137, 38 (f. Φύλαξ) ?= (5)
—KALYDON?: (5) c. 225-200 BC *Corinth* VIII (3)
37, 7 + *SEG* XXV 325 ([Παντα[λέων]) ?= (4)
—KONOPE-ARSINOE: (6) c. 200 BC *BCH* 50
(1926) p. 125 no. 2 b, 4, 10 (s. Λέων)
—PLEURON: (7) 242-214 BC *RE* (5); *IG* IX (1)²
(1) p. L, s.a. 242 BC, 235 BC, 228 BC, 224 BC,
214 BC (s. Πέταλος, f. Ἀρχίδαμος); (8) c. 210
BC ib. 31, 81, 87 (f. Φύλαξ); (9) 186-174 BC
*RE* (6); *IG* IX (1)² (1) p. LI, s.a. 186 BC, 180
BC, 174 BC; IX (1)² (3) 626, 1; *IPerg* 164 (?s.
Ἀρχίδαμος)
AKARNANIA:
—STRATOS: (10) ii BC *IG* IX (1)² (2) 408 (*Gr.
Gr.* 213) (s. Ἄγεμος)
ELIS:
—PISA: (11) vii BC *RE* (1) (s. Ὀμφαλίων, f. Δα-
μοφῶν, Πύρρος: king)
EPIROS:
—DODONA: (12) iii BC Antoniou, *Dodone* Ab,
52; (13) f. ii BC *BCH* 45 (1921) p. 22 IV, 31
KORINTHIA:
—SIKYON: (14) 320 BC *IG* II² 3055 (Skalet 254;
Stephanis 1997); (15) 263 BC *IG* IX (1)² (1)
17, 85 (s. Σιλανίων)
PELOPONNESE?: (16) s. iii BC ib. V (1) 1426, 25
(f. Ἐχεφυλίδας)
S. ITALY (CALABRIA):
—TARAS-TARENTUM: (17) c. 266 BC ib. XII (9)
1187, 19; Robert, *Ét. Num. Gr.* pp. 179 ff.
(date) (f. Λέων)

**Πανταμιανός**
KORINTHIA:
—KORINTH: (1) byz. *Corinth* VIII (3) 547;
cf. *TMByz* 9 (1985) p. 363 no. 44
([Παν]ταμιανός)

**Πανταρέτα**
KORINTHIA:
—KORINTH: (1) c. 570-550 BC Amyx 110. 1
(vase) ([Π]ανταρέτα: fict.?)

**Παντάρης**
ACHAIA:
—PATRAI: (1) c. 247-199 BC *FD* III (1) p. 204
n. 1, 2 (f. Σώστρατος)
S. ITALY (BRUTTIUM):
—LOKROI EPIZEPHYRIOI: (2) v BC *PdelP* 45
(1990) pp. 62-4 (Παντά[ρης]?)
SICILY:
—GELA-PHINTIAS: (3) s. vi BC Hdt. vii 154. 1
(f. Κλέανδρος, Ἱπποκράτης); (4) c. 530-520 BC
*CEG* I 398 (Dubois, *IGDS* 132; Arena, *Iscr.
Sic.* I 4; Lazzarini 854; Ebert, *Gr. Sieg.* 5);
Moretti, *Olymp.* 151; cf. *Ol. Forsch.* I pp.
83 ff. (-ρες: s. Μενεκράτης); (5) c. 500-475 BC
Dubois, *IGDS* 147 (vase) (Arena, *Iscr. Sic.* I
10) (Παντάρης—Dubois, Παγχάρης—Lazzarini
and Arena)

**Παντάρκης**
AITOLIA:
—PELLOTIOI: (1) c. 272-271 BC *IG* IX (1)² (1)
12, [13], 23, 34; 13, 3 etc.
ARGOLIS:
—ARGOS: (2) v BC Schol. D. xviii 38
ARKADIA: (3) 284 BC *PEleph* 4, 2
—TEGEA: (4) c. 225 BC *SEG* XI 414, 3 (Perlman
E.5) (f. —κράτης)
ELIS: (5) 436 BC Moretti, *Olymp.* 318; (6) s. iii
BC *RE* (-); Moretti, *Olymp.* 577
KORINTHIA:
—KORINTH: (7) m. iii BC *Corinth* VIII (3) 33 f,
8 ([Παν]τάρκης: I f. Παντάρκης II); (8) ~ ib. l.
8 (II s. Παντάρκης I)

**Πανταῦχος**
AITOLIA:
—PELEIOI: (1) 163 BC *IG* IX (1)² (1) 102, 9, 11

**Πάνταχος**
ILLYRIA:
—AMANTIA: (1) s. ii BC *Iliria* 1977-8, p. 99 no.
35 (coin) (Παντα(ύ)χος?)

**Παντέας**
ARKADIA: (1) 370-367 BC *IG* V (2) 2, 7
—TEGEA: (2) i BC-i AD ib. 204 (Παντέας)

**Παντεύς**
LAKONIA:
—SPARTA: (1) 223-219 BC Plb. v 37. 8; Plu.,
*Cleom.* 23; 37-8 (Bradford (-))

**Παντιάδας**
ARGOLIS:
—ARGOS: (1) 105 BC *JÖAI* 14 (1911) Beibl. p.
146 no. 4, 8 (Παντ[ιάδ]ας: f. Πανтακλῆς)
ARKADIA:
—TEGEA:
——(Apolloniatai): (2) m. iii BC *IG* V (2) 36, 102
(Παντιάδας: s. Φιλοκλῆς)
LAKONIA:
—SPARTA: (3) c. 30-20 BC ib. V (1) 142, 25
(Bradford (-))

**Παντίας**
ACHAIA:
—TRITAIA?: (1) m. iii BC *IG* V (2) 368, 80 with
index (s. Πασιτέλης); (2) ~ ib. l. 81 with index
([Πα]ντίας: s. Λέων)
ARGOLIS:
—ARGOS*: (3) ii BC *SEG* XLII 279, 21
(slave/freed.?)
ARKADIA:
—TEGEA: (4) f. iv BC ib. XXXVII 676; (5) ii BC
*IG* V (2) 43, 9 ([Π]αντίας: s. Πειθίας)
LAKONIA: (6) c. 250-230 BC ib. VII 337, 2
(*IOrop* 113; Bradford (3)) (I f. Παντίας II,
Γοργίας); (7) ~ *IG* VII 337, 2 (*IOrop* 113;
Bradford (2)) (II s. Παντίας I)
—SPARTA: (8) c. 50-25 BC *IG* V (1) 208, 2 (Brad-
ford (1)) (s. Ἀντικλῆς)
SICILY:
—MORGANTINA: (9) ?iv/iii BC *SEG* XXXIX 1011,
4 (s. Λυκίσκος)

**Παντικλῆς**
DALMATIA:
—ISSA:
——(Dymanes): (1) iv/iii BC Brunšmid p. 8, 48

**Παντιμία**
LAKONIA:
—SPARTA: (1) ?i AD *IG* V (1) 588 (Bradford (-))
(Ἰουλ. Παν[τι]μία]?: d. Ἄγις, m. Γ. Ἰούλ. Σιμή-
δης); (2) c. 1-10 AD *IG* V (1) 209, 26; *SEG*
XXXV 331 (date) (Bradford (2)) (-τει-); (3) f. i
AD *IG* V (2) 542 (Bradford (1)) (Ἰουλ. Π.: d.
Γ. Ἰούλ. Λάκων)

**Παντιμίας**
ITHAKE: (1) hell. *BCH* 29 (1905) p. 164 no. 6
(s. Ὄλυμπις)

**Παντίνας**
ARKADIA:
—MANTINEIA-ANTIGONEIA: (1) c. 425-385 BC
*IG* V (2) 323. 7 (tessera) (s. Ἐρετριάδας)

**Παντῖνος**
ARKADIA:
—TEGEA: (1) iv BC ib. 31, 10 (s. Παντοκλῆς)

**Πάντιππος**
KORINTHIA:
—KORINTH: (1) c. 570-550 BC Amyx 104 B. 5
(vase) (Lorber 92) (her.?)

**Πάντις**
ARGOLIS:
—EPIDAUROS: (1) ii AD *IG* IV (1)² 488 (s. Καλ-
λίστρατος)

—TROIZEN: (2) ?146 BC ib. IV (1) 757 B, 22, 32
(or Arkadia: Παντιάδαι (koin.)—l. 32: s. Καλλιμαχίδας)

**Παντισθένης**
ARKADIA:
—MEGALOPOLIS: (1) 191-146 BC *BMC Pelop.*
p. 14 no. 166 (coin)
—TEGEA:
——(Apolloniatai): (2) iv/iii BC *IG* V (2) 38, 36
(s. Ἐπισθένης)

**Παντίτης**
LAKONIA:
—SPARTA: (1) 480 BC Hdt. vii 232 (Poralla² 587)

**Πάντιχος**
ARKADIA: (1) 320 BC *IG* V (2) 549, 21 (s. Λέον-
τις)
—TEGEA: (2) iii BC ib. 30, 14

**Παντόδαμος**
ARKADIA:
—KAPHYAI: (1) m. iii BC *BCH* 38 (1914) p. 462
no. 6, 3 (f. Τυτέας)

**Παντοῖος**
KORINTHIA:
—SIKYON: (1) ?255-254 BC Nachtergael, *Les
Galates* 8, 42; 9, 15; cf. Stephanis 600 (Skalet
255) (f. Δεξίνικος)

**Παντοκλείδας**
ARKADIA:
—MEGALOPOLIS: (1) 359 BC *CID* II 5 I, 32

**Παντοκλῆς**
ARKADIA:
—TEGEA: (1) iv BC *IG* V (2) 31, 10 (f. Παντῖνος);
(2) m. iv BC ib. 6, 102; (3) ~ ib. l. 113; (4)
iv/iii BC ib. 32, 1
KORINTHIA:
—SIKYON?: (5) iii-ii BC ib. IV (1) 429, 10; cf.
Stephanis 2569 (f. Φιλωνίδης)
LAKONIA:
—SPARTA: (6) c. 30-20 BC *IG* V (1) 211, 20
(Bradford (-)) (f. Νίκανδρος)

**Παντόνικος**
MESSENIA:
—MESSENE?: (1) ii/i BC *SEG* XI 979, 13; cf.
*JÖAI* 17 (1914) p. 88 ([Π]αντόνικος—*SEG*,
Ἀντ(ό)νικος—*JÖAI*)

**Παντώ**
LAKONIA: (1) imp. *IG* V (1) 1349 (Bradford (-))
(d. Μαρώνιος: Jew)

**Πάντων**
ARGOLIS:
—PHLEIOUS?: (1) s. iv BC Peek, *NIEpid* 16, 23
(Perlman E.6) (s. Παντιάδας)

**Πάπας**
ACHAIA: (1) 146 BC *IG* IV (1)² 28, 143 (f. Εὐτυ-
χίδας: synoikos)
S. ITALY (CALABRIA):
—TARAS-TARENTUM: (2) imp. *Misc. Gr. Rom.* 3
p. 201 no. T20 (Lat. Papas)
S. ITALY (CAMPANIA):
—DIKAIARCHIA-PUTEOLI: (3) imp. *CIL* X 2823
(*Eph. Ep.* VIII 415) (Lat. Papas)

**Πάπελος**
SICILY:
—PATERNO (MOD.): (1) iv-iii BC *Silver for the
Gods* pp. 58-61 nos. 25-7 (Π. Κασύννιος)

**Παπίας**
S. ITALY (CALABRIA):
—BRENTESION-BRUNDISIUM*: (1) imp. *CIL* IX
78 (Lat. L. Aruntius Papia: freed.)

S. Italy (Campania):
—dikaiarchia-puteoli*: (2) imp. ib. x 1550 (Lat. Cn. Com. Papias: freed.)

**Πάπος**
S. Italy (Campania):
—pompeii: (1) imp. *NScav* 1961, p. 200 no. 4 (Lat. Papus: f. Heia)
Sicily:
—lipara: (2) imp.? Libertini, *Isole Eolie* p. 227 no. 59 (*Πομπ. Π.*)

**Παπύλος**
Arkadia:
—tegea: (1) 165 AD *IG* v (2) 50, 16 (f. Ὀκτά-βιος)

**Παραβάλλων**
Elis: (1) iii BC Moretti, *Olymp.* 536 (f. Λαστρα-τίδας)

**Παραγόρας**
S. Italy (Bruttium):
—petelia: (1) ?c. 475 BC *IGSI* 19, 4 (Landi, *DISMG* 171); *LSAG*² p. 261 no. 28 (date)
Sicily:
—morgantina: (2) iv/iii BC *SEG* xxxix 1012, 5 (*Παραγ[όρας]*?)

**Παράδοξος**
Aigina: (1) iii AD *FD* iii (1) 469 (*Παράδο[ξος]*: f. Αὐρ. Νίκων)

**Παραιβάτας**
Lakonia:
—sparta: (1) s. vi BC Hdt. v 46. 1 (Poralla² 588) (-της)

**Παραλία**
S. Italy (Campania):
—neapolis: (1) iii-iv AD *IG* xiv 826. 36 (*INap* 244)

**Παραμόνα**
Illyria:
—apollonia: (1) imp. *IApoll* 223 (d. Οὐαλέ-ριος)

**Παραμόνη**
Argolis:
—epidauros: (1) 184 AD *IG* iv (1)² 393, 4 (d. Ἀβάσκαντος)
S. Italy (Campania):
—pompeii: (2) i BC-i AD ib. xiv 702 (Τερεντία Π.)

**Παράμονος**
Argolis:
—epidauros: (1) i BC Peek, *IAEpid* 19, 5 (*Παρ[άμονος]*?: f. Κωμάστας); (2) 135 AD Peek, *NIEpid* 8, 2 (f. Ἀσκληπᾶς)
Arkadia:
—tegea: (3) ii AD *IG* v (2) 55, 80 (f. Εὐτύχης); (4) 165 AD ib. 50, 60 (s. Ὀνησίφορος)
Elis:
—olympia*: (5) 185-189 AD *IvOl* 104, 26 (?s. Καλλίστρατος: slave?)
Illyria:
—apollonia: (6) hell. *IApoll* 28 (s. Φίλιππος)
—epidamnos-dyrrhachion: (7) c. 250-50 BC Maier 389; Münsterberg p. 260 = Nachtr. p. 15 (coin) (Ceka 370-1) (money.)
Kephallenia:
—pale: (8) hell. *IG* ix (1) 646
Lakonia:
—sparta: (9) f. iii AD ib. v (1) 170, 20; *BSA* 80 (1985) p. 245 (date) (Bradford (2)) (f. Αὐρ. Ποτάμων) ?= (10); (10) c. 221 AD *IG* v (1) 541, 8; *BSA* 79 (1984) pp. 270-3 (date) (Bradford (1)) (*M. Αὐρ. Π.*: s. Ἥδιστος) ?= (9)

**Παραμύθιος**
S. Italy (Campania):
—dikaiarchia-puteoli: (1) imp. *CIL* x 3091 (Lat. A. Vesonius Paramythius); (2) ~ *Eph. Ep.* viii 393 (Lat. Cattius Paramythius)
—dikaiarchia-puteoli*: (3) imp. *CIL* x 2112 (Lat. C. Asinius Paramythius Festianus: imp. freed.)

**Παράμυθος**
S. Italy (Campania):
—dikaiarchia-puteoli: (1) imp. *NScav* 1888, p. 197 no. 3 (Lat. Paramythus)

**Πάρας**
Lakonia:
—sparta: (1) iii/ii BC *IG* v (1) 717 (Papaefthimiou p. 151 no. 25); *Sculpture from Arcadia and Laconia* p. 241 (date) (Bradford (-)) (*Πάρα* (voc.))

**Παρασκευή**
S. Italy (Campania):
—nuceria alfaterna: (1) imp. *CIL* x 1101 (Lat. Baria Parasceue)

**Παρβόλας**
Sicily:
—kamarina: (1) f. v BC Cordano, *Tessere Pubbliche* 14 (-βό-?: f. Ἱπποκράτης)

**Παρδαλᾶς**
Arkadia:
—kleitor: (1) a. 212 AD *SEG* xxxi 347, 9
—tegea: (2) 165 AD *IG* v (2) 50, 36 (Ὀφίλλιος Π.)
Illyria:
—apollonia: (3) imp. *IApoll* 263
Lakonia:
—sparta: (4) c. 105-110 AD *IG* v (1) 20 B, 2; *BSA* 26 (1923-5) p. 168 C 7, 6 (Bradford (1)) (s. Θεοκλῆς)
——Limnai: (5) a. 212 AD *IG* v (1) 564, 3 (Bradford (2)) (f. M. Αὐρ. Δάμαρχος)
S. Italy (Calabria):
—taras-tarentum: (6) imp. *CIL* ix 240 (Lat. Pardalas)
S. Italy (Campania):
—pompeii: (7) i BC-i AD ib. iv 10218; *Gnomon* 45 (1973) p. 271 (Lat. [P]ardalas)

**Πάρδαλις**
S. Italy (Campania):
—pompeii: (1) i BC-i AD *CIL* iv 10063 (Lat. Pardalis: f. Otarius)

**Παρδαλίς**
Epiros:
—bouthrotos (prasaiboi): (1) a. 163 BC *IBouthrot* 106
Illyria:
—apollonia: (2) imp. *IApoll* 177 ([Παρ]δαλίς)
Lakonia:
—sparta: (3) ii-iii AD *IG* v (1) 732, 2 (*GVI* 986; Bradford (-))
—leukas: (4) iv/iii BC *AD* 26 (1971) Chron. p. 353 no. 10 with n. 13 (Παρδαλ[ίς], Πάρ-δαλ[ος]?)
S. Italy (Calabria):
—hydrous-hydruntum: (5) imp. *Ann. Univ. Lecce* 8-9 (1977-80) p. 231 d (Lat. Pardalis)

**Πάρδαλος**
S. Italy (Campania):
—pompeii: (1) i BC-i AD *CIL* iv 4998 (Lat. Pardalus)

**Παρδαλώ**
Lakonia:
—sparta: (1) i AD *SEG* xlii 327 (Παρδαλοῦ (voc.))

**Πάρδος**
Korinthia:
—korinth: (1) ii/iii AD *BM Lamps* 3 p. 405 no. Q3235; *Corinth* iv (2) p. 192 no. 590 (lamps) (*Πάρχος—BM Lamps*)
S. Italy (Campania):
—pompeii: (2) i BC-i AD *CIL* iv 3030 (Lat. Pardus)
S. Italy (Lucania):
—atina lucana: (3) imp. *IItal* iii (1) 142 (Lat. Pardus: f. Helvia Priva)

**Πάρευνος**
Korinthia:
—korinth: (1) c. 610-590 BC Amyx 5. 1 (vase) (Lorber 21) (fict.?)

**Παρεύτακτος**
Elis: (1) 141-145 AD *IvOl* 95, 6 (I f. Παρεύτα-κτος II); (2) ~ ib. l. 6 (II s. Παρεύτακτος I: X.)

**Παρθεμίδας**
Argolis:
—hermione: (1) iii BC *IG* iv (1) 729 I, 12 (s. Σῶσος)

**Παρθένα**
Aitolia:
—kastraki (mod.): (1) hell.-imp. *L'Illyrie mérid.* 1 p. 113 fig. 13 (*SEG* xxxvii 431)

**Παρθενικός**
Sicily:
—katane: (1) iii-v AD *NScav* 1931, p. 369 (Lat. Parthenicus)

**Παρθένιν**
Aigina?: (1) i-ii AD *EAD* xxx p. 357 no. 25 (d. Κέρδων)
Sicily:
—katane: (2) ?iv-v AD *NScav* 1931, p. 369 no. 2 + *Arctos* 21 (1987) p. 137 (Lat. L. Arria Parteenin)

**Παρθένιον**
Lakonia: (1) iii BC *IG* ii² 9152 = *AM* 67 (1942) p. 109 no. 210 (Bradford (-)) (d. Ἀρι-στείδας)

**Παρθένιος**
Lakonia:
—sparta: (1) c. 500 BC *SEG* xi 638, 5; *LSAG*² p. 201 no. 44 (date) (Παρθ[ένιος]?); (2) f. iv BC Paus. ix 13. 5 (Poralla² 589); (3) 116 or 117 AD *IG* v (1) 380, 8 (Bradford s.v. Ἀβάσκαντος (2)) (Ἀβάσκαντος Π.)
Messenia:
—messene: (4) m. iv BC *IG* ii² 9347, 7 (s. Φι-λόξενος)
S. Italy (Campania):
—neapolis: (5) imp. *CIL* x 8170; cf. Leiwo p. 92 (Lat. M. Octavius Parthenius)

**Παρθένις**
Sicily:
—syracuse: (1) iii-v AD *SEG* iv 3 (Agnello 39; Wessel 1244); cf. Ferrua, *NG* 269; (2) ~ Strazzulla 317 (Wessel 1361)

**Παρθενίς**
Argolis:
—argos: (1) iii BC *Mnem.* NS 47 (1919) p. 168 no. 19
Leukas: (2) hell. *IG* ix (1) 579
S. Italy (Campania):
—dikaiarchia-puteoli: (3) imp. *CIL* x 2825 (Lat. Parthenis); (4) ?i-ii AD ib. 2287 (Lat. Iulia Parthenis)

**Παρθενοπαῖος**
S. Italy (Bruttium):
—hipponion-vibo valentia: (1) imp. ib. 65; cf. *NScav* 1921, p. 489 (Lat. L. Atilius Partenop[aeu]s)

## Παρθενόπη

S. ITALY (CAMPANIA):
—DIKAIARCHIA-PUTEOLI: (2) imp. *CIL* x 2565 (Lat. Ti. Iulius Parthenopaeus)
—NEAPOLIS*: (3) ii-iii AD *NScav* 1891, p. 374; cf. Leiwo p. 98 no. 49 (Lat. Iulius Partenopeus: freed.)
SICILY:
—VICARI (MOD.): (4) imp. *CIL* x 7198; cf. *Eph. Ep.* VIII 695 (Lat. Parthenopaeus)

## Παρθενόπη

S. ITALY (CAMPANIA):
—DIKAIARCHIA-PUTEOLI: (1) imp. *CIL* x 2372 (Lat. Domitia Parthenope); (2) ~ ib. 2479 (Lat. Minicia Parthenope)
—NEAPOLIS: (3) imp. *NScav* 1892, p. 317; cf. Leiwo p. 99 no. 50 (Lat. Brinnia Parthenope: m. Ἡλιάς)

## Παρθενοπηνός

S. ITALY (CAMPANIA):
—DIKAIARCHIA-PUTEOLI: (1) imp. *CIL* x 2044 (Lat. Parthenopenus: f. Ambibia Fructosa)

## Πάρθενος

S. ITALY (CAMPANIA):
—SALERNUM: (1) s. i AD *IItal* I (1) 211 (*CIL* x 617) (Lat. C. Maeclonius Parthenus: s. Ἐφεσία)

## Πάρθης

S. ITALY (BRUTTIUM):
—RHEGION?: (1) ?iv BC *FGrH* 554 F 64

## Παρθῖνος

ILLYRIA:
—SKAMPIS: (1) imp. *AEp* 1955, no. 77 (Lat. Parthinus (n. pr.?))

## Παριανός

S. ITALY (CAMPANIA):
—NOLA: (1) 30 AD *CIL* x 1233 (Lat. T. Salvius Parianus); (2) 31 AD ib. (Lat. Sex. Parianus Serenus)

## Πάριος

KORINTHIA:
—KORINTH: (1) 358 AD Athan., *Fest. Ind.* 39 (Παρνάσιος?)

## Πάρις

LAKONIA:
—SPARTA: (1) c. 100 AD *SEG* XI 626, 5 (Bradford (-)) (s. Φιλόκαλος)
S. ITALY (CAMPANIA):
—DIKAIARCHIA-PUTEOLI: (2) imp. *AJA* 2 (1898) p. 386 no. 31 (Lat. Paris); (3) ?ii AD *CIL* x 2438 (Lat. T. Flavius Paris)
—HERCULANEUM: (4) i BC-i AD ib. IV 10607 (Lat. Paris)
—POMPEII: (5) i BC-i AD ib. 148; 1085; 1294; 1305; 2133; 2179 (Lat. Paris); (6) ~ ib. 330 (Lat. Paris); (7) ~ ib. 821; 7051 (Lat. Paris); (8) ~ ib. 1179 (Lat. Paris); (9) ~ ib. 2370; 2376 (Lat. Paris); (10) ~ ib. 3609 (Lat. Paris) ?= (18); (11) ~ ib. 3770 (Castrèn 221. 8) (Lat. Q. Lollius Paris); (12) ~ *CIL* IV 3867; 3866 (Lat. Paris); (13) ~ ib. 4338 (Castrèn 326. 2) (Lat. P. Umidius Paris); (14) ~ *CIL* IV 4585 (Lat. Paris); (15) ~ ib. 4978; 4981 (Lat. Paris); (16) ~ ib. 7056 (Lat. Paris); (17) ~ ib. 7367 (Lat. Paris); (18) ~ ib. 8484 (Lat. Paris) ?= (10); (19) ~ ib. 8501 (Lat. Paris); (20) ~ ib. 8746 (Lat. Paris); (21) ~ ib. 8856 (Lat. Paris); (22) ~ ib. 9216 (Lat. Paris); (23) ~ ib. 10215 (Lat. Paris); (24) ~ *RAAN* 49 (1974) p. 26 no. 10 (Lat. Paris)

## Παρμένεια

LEUKAS: (1) iv/iii BC Unp. (*IG* arch.)

## Παρμενείδας

SICILY:
—KAMARINA: (1) f. v BC Cordano, *Tessere Pubbliche* 82a (f. Νικόδαμος)

## Παρμενίδας

EPIROS:
—DODONA*: (1) v/iv BC *Ep. Chron.* 10 (1935) p. 255 no. 13
S. ITALY (LUCANIA):
—POSEIDONIA-PAESTUM: (2) 468 BC Moretti, *Olymp.* 235-6 (-δης)
SICILY:
—KAMARINA: (3) 528 BC ib. 125; Cordano, 'Camarina VII' 7

## Παρμενίδης

S. ITALY (LUCANIA):
—HYELE-VELIA: (1) vi/v BC *RE* (-); *FVS* 28; *SEG* XXXVIII 1020. 4; *PdelP* 25 (1970) p. 262 (Π. Οὐλιάδης—*SEG*: s. Πύρης, ?f. (ad.) Ζήνων)

## Παρμενίσκος

EPIROS: (1) m. ii BC *Thess. Mnem.* 46 (s. Ἀλέξανδρος)
—BOUTHROTOS (PRASAIBOI): (2) a. 163 BC *IBouthrot* 30, 4 (*SEG* XXXVIII 488); *IBouthrot* 48, 11; (3) ~ ib. 47, 7 ([Παρμ]ενίσκος); (4) ~ ib. 130, 2 ([Παρ]μενί[σκ]ος); (5) ~ ib. 131, 2 (?s. Σατυρῖνος)
—ORRAITAI?: (6) a. 163 BC ib. 10, 16 (*SEG* XXXVIII 464)
—PHOINIKE: (7) iii BC Ugolini, *Alb. Ant.* 2 p. 154 no. 7 (f. Πελειχίνας)
ILLYRIA:
—APOLLONIA: (8) c. 250-50 BC Maier 81; Münsterberg p. 37 (coin) (Ceka 112; 120) (pryt.); (9) ~ Maier 87 (coin) (Ceka 94) (money.); (10) iii/ii BC *IApoll* 22 bis; cf. *Le Arti* 5 (1943) p. 116 no. 1; Fraser–Rönne, *BWGT* p. 161; p. 174 n. 5 (date) (s. Δαμήν); (11) imp. *IApoll* 55 (f. Ἀριστήν)
—BYLLIONES (MARGELLIC (MOD.)): (12) hell. *SEG* XXXVIII 549 ([Παρμε?]νίσκως—lap.)
—EPIDAMNOS-DYRRHACHION: (13) c. 250-50 BC Ceka, *Probleme* p. 152 no. 57 (coin) (pryt.) ?= (14); (14) ~ Maier 337-345a; 489; Münsterberg Nachtr. p. 16 (Ceka 43; 61; 103; 107; 119; 138; 214; 246; 281; 312; 377; 383; 394; 419; 440 (coin)) (pryt.) ?= (13); (15) hell.-imp. *IDyrrh* 319 (Παρμενί(σ)κος: f. Μυρτίων); (16) ~ ib. 356 (f. Πλάτωρ)
KERKYRA: (17) ii-i BC *BCH* 19 (1895) pp. 369 ff. no. 19, 7; p. 372 no. 22 (I f. Παρμένισκος II); (18) ~ ib. pp. 369 ff. no. 19, 7; p. 372 no. [22] (II s. Παρμένισκος I); (19) i BC-i AD *IG* IX (1) 922; (20) ~ ib. 923; (21) 96-88 BC Moretti, *Olymp.* 659; 668; cf. s.v. 655-7 (s.p.) ?= (22); (22) c. 76 BC *IG* VII 417, 8, 18 (*IOrop* 525, 8)*IOrop* 525, 18 (s. Φιλίσκος) ?= (21); (23) s. ii AD *IG* IX (1) 730-1 (s. Λάκριτος)

## Παρμενίτας

ARGOLIS:
—HERMIONE: (1) iii BC ib. IV (1) 729 I, 9 (s. Λαχάρης)

## Παρμενίων

ARGOLIS:
—EPIDAUROS: (1) c. 340-320 BC Peek, *NIEpid* 19 C, 23
EPIROS:
—BOUTHROTOS (PRASAIBOI):
——Prochtheioi: (2) a. 163 BC *IBouthrot* 168, 14 (*SEG* XXXVIII 469) (f. Φιλίσκος)
ILLYRIA: (3) 168 BC Plb. xxix 3. 9; 11. 1; Liv. xliv 23. 4
—EPIDAMNOS-DYRRHACHION: (4) ?ii-i BC *IG* XII (8) 196, 5; cf. *IDyrrh* 515 (f. Σωσίλαος)

MESSENIA:
—MESSENE: (5) i BC/i AD *IG* V (1) 1438 a, 15 ([Παρ]μενίων)
S. ITALY (CALABRIA):
—TARAS-TARENTUM: (6) 156 BC *ID* 1416 B II, 114 (s. Δάζιμος)

## Παρμένων

ARGOLIS:
—ARGOS?: (1) ?i BC Bernand, *El-Kanaïs* 79
EPIROS:
—ARGETHIA (NR.): (2) hell. *SEG* XIII 387
ILLYRIA:
—EPIDAMNOS-DYRRHACHION: (3) iii BC *IDyrrh* 12 (s. Καλλιππίδας)
KERKYRA: (4) i BC-i AD *IG* IX (1) 924 (Παρμέν(ω)ν)
LAKONIA:
—SPARTA:
——Konosoura: (5) c. 212-230 AD ib. V (1) 684, 16 (Bradford (-)) (Μέμμιος Π.)
LAKONIA?: (6) ?v-iv BC *CGFP* 236, 19, 22 (fict.?)
LEUKAS: (7) hell.? *IG* IX (1) 568 ([Π]αρμένων)
S. ITALY (CAMPANIA):
—PONTECAGNANO (MOD.): (8) c. 520-510 BC *SEG* XXXIV 1019 (vase); cf. *LSAG*² p. 457 no. H (date)
SICILY:
—KAMARINA: (9) f. v BC Cordano, *Tessere Pubbliche* 1b (Arena, *Iscr. Sic.* II 126 A) (Πα[ρ]μένōν: f. Ἀντισθένης); (10) s. v BC Dubois, *IGDS* 121, 11 (Arena, *Iscr. Sic.* II 143; *SEG* XXXVIII 940; Cordano, 'Camarina VII' 47) (Π[αρμέ]νōν?: f. Δίων)
—LIPARA: (11) hell.? Libertini, *Isole Eolie* p. 225 no. 47

## Παρμήν

ILLYRIA:
—APOLLONIA: (1) hell. *IApoll* 23; cf. *Le Arti* 5 (1943) p. 118 no. 4; Fraser–Rönne, *BWGT* p. 174 n. 5 (date) (s. Πεντικός); (2) ~ *IApoll* 363 (tile); (3) ~ ib. 364 (tile); (4) c. 250-50 BC Münsterberg p. 36; Maier 30 (coin) (Ceka 93; 95-6) (money.); (5) ~ Maier 82 (coin) (Ceka 80) (pryt.); (6) ii-i BC *IApoll* 123 (f. Μνασώ); (7) ~ ib. 139 ([Π]αρμήν); (8) ~ ib. 140 (s. Ἀριστοκλῆς); (9) i BC Maier 128 (coin) (money.); (10) ~ ib. 129 (coin) (f. Ἀγήν)
——(Polo.): (11) iii/ii BC *IApoll* 7; cf. *L'Illyrie mérid.* 2 p. 207 (s. Σώστρατος)
—BALAIITAI*: (12) ii BC *SEG* XXXVIII 521, 10, 13; cf. *CRAI* 1991, pp. 197 ff.; *L'Illyrie mérid.* 2 p. 204 f. (s. Ἀριστήν); (13) ~ *SEG* XXXVIII 521, 25; cf. *CRAI* 1991, pp. 197 ff.; *L'Illyrie mérid.* 2 p. 204 f. (s. Τείσαρχος)
—EPIDAMNOS-DYRRHACHION: (14) c. 250-50 BC Maier 346 (coin) (Ceka 44) (pryt.); (15) hell.-imp. *IDyrrh* 170 (f. Διοκλῆς)

## Παρμίσκος

S. ITALY (LUCANIA):
—METAPONTION: (1) vi/v BC *RE* s.v. Parmeniskos (1); *FVS* 20; *ID* Index I s.v. Παρμενίσκος (Π.—Iamb. and *ID*, Παρμενίσκος—D.L. and Ath.)

## Παρμονίδας

SICILY:
—HALOUNTION: (1) iii/ii BC *Arch. Class.* 17 (1965) p. 202 a (Παρμον[ίδας]: s. Ἀρ—)

## Παρμόνιμος

SICILY:
—MORGANTINA: (1) iv/iii BC *SEG* XXXIX 1012, 7 (Παρμόν[ι]μος: f. Γοργίας)

## Παρμονίσκος

DALMATIA:
—ISSA: (1) hell. Brunšmid p. 30 no. 25 (s. Ζωΐλος)
ILLYRIA:
—APOLLONIA: (2) iii BC *IApoll* 5 (s. Δαμάγης)

**Πάρμονος**
EPIROS:
—BOUTHROTOS (PRASAIBOI): (**1**) a. 163 BC
*IBouthrot* 29, 46 (*SEG* XXXVIII 487)

**Παρμυνίς**
S. ITALY (CAMPANIA):
—FRATTE DI SALERNO (MOD.): (**1**) f. v BC ib.
XXXVII 817 B (vase) (Arena, *Iscr. Sic.* IV 33)

**Παρμώ**
ILLYRIA:
—APOLLONIA: (**1**) ii-i BC *IApoll* 141
—EPIDAMNOS-DYRRHACHION: (**2**) hell.-imp.
*IDyrrh* 340 (d. *Τρίτος*)

**Παρνάσσιος**
ACHAIA:
—PATRAI: (**1**) iv AD *PLRE* I (1)
KORINTHIA:
—KORINTH: (**2**) m. iv AD Seeck, *Libanius* pp.
231-2
—KORINTH*: (**3**) ii-iii AD *Corinth* VIII (3) 502, 3
(*TMByz* 9 (1985) pp. 291-2 no. 31) (*Μέμμιος
Πόντιος Πτολεμέος ὁ καὶ Παρνάσιος*)

**Πάρος**
AIGINA: (**1**) imp. *IG* IV (1) 131 (?f. *Μᾶρκος*)

**Πάρπαρος**
KYNOURIA:
—THYREATIS*: (**1**) vi/v BC *SEG* XXXV 302
(bronze); cf. XXXIX 368; XLII 290 (n. pr.?: f.
*Ἑλικίς*)

**Παρράσιος**
ARKADIA:
—ORCHOMENOS: (**1**) ?c. 369-361 BC *BCH* 102
(1978) p. 347, 3 (*IPArk* 14) .
ARKADIA?: (**2**) 369 BC *BCH* 39 (1915) p. 55 no.
III, 3

**Παρρησία**
ARGOLIS:
—HERMIONE: (**1**) ?ii-i BC *IG* IV (1) 733, 2
(*Παρρησία*)
KEPHALLENIA:
—KRANIOI: (**2**) imp.? ib. IX (1) 612 ([*Π*]*αρρησία*)

**Πασαγάθη**
LAKONIA:
—KARYAI?: (**1**) i AD ib. v (1) 924

**Πασάκων**
LAKONIA:
—SPARTA: (**1**) imp. ib. 805 (Bradford (1)); (**2**) c.
100-125 AD *IG* v (1) 153, 29 (Bradford (2))

**Πασάρατος**
SICILY:
—MEGARA HYBLAIA: (**1**) f. vi BC Dubois, *IGDS*
20, 1 (Arena, *Iscr. Sic.* I 13; *SEG* XXXVIII
945) (her.)

**Πασάριον**
LAKONIA:
—SPARTA: (**1**) c. 30-20 BC *IG* v (1) 142, 23
(Bradford (-)) (d. *Δα*—)

**Πάσαρχος**
KORINTHIA:
—KORINTH: (**1**) ?274 BC *CID* II 120 A, 33 (s.
*Κλεανδρίδας*)

**Πασέας**
ARGOLIS:
—EPIDAUROS*: (**1**) c. 370 BC *IG* IV (1)² 102,
265
ARKADIA:
—MANTINEIA-ANTIGONEIA: (**2**) ?s. i BC Paus.
viii 9. 6 (f. *Νικίππα*) ?= (*Πασίας* (2))
—MEGALOPOLIS: (**3**) ?131 BC *IG* v (2) 440, 8 (s.
*Φιλοκλῆς*, f. *Φιλοκλῆς*)

KORINTHIA:
—SIKYON: (**4**) c. 300-251 BC *RE* (1) (Skalet 256)
(f. *Ἀβαντίδας, Σωσώ*: tyrant)

**Πασέδας**
KORINTHIA:
—SIKYON: (**1**) f. v BC *SEG* XXIV 271 + *Hesp.*
41 (1972) p. 205 no. 7; *LSAG*² p. 442 no 14b
(date) (s. *Κορμίνας*)

**Πασιάδας**
ACHAIA: (**1**) 169 BC Plb. xxviii 12. 9; 19. 3
SICILY:
—GELA-PHINTIAS: (**2**) s. vi BC Guarducci, *Ep.
Gr.* I p. 252 no. 2 (Dubois, *IGDS* 128;
Arena, *Iscr. Sic.* II 3; *IGLMP* 15) (*Πασιάδαϝο*
(gen.))

**Πασιάδης**
LAKONIA:
—SPARTA: (**1**) c. 120 AD *IG* v (1) 1315, 22
(Bradford (-))

**Πασιάναξ**
ARKADIA: (**1**) iii BC *SEG* XXXVII 351; 352

**Πασίας**
ARKADIA:
—MANTINEIA-ANTIGONEIA: (**1**) ?iii BC *IG* v (2)
318, 9; (**2**) 64 or 62 BC ib. 265, 2 (f. *Νικίππα*)
?= (*Πασέας* (2))
EPIROS:
—DODONA*: (**3**) iv-iii BC *SGDI* 1569; cf. *Arch.
Pap.* 15 (1953) p. 78 (name) (*Π.* (n. pr.?),
[*παν*]*πασίας*?—Wilhelm)
KORINTHIA:
—SIKYON: (**4**) iii/ii BC Plin., *NH* xxxv 145
(Skalet 257) (Lat. Pasias: painter)

**Πασιγένης**
ACHAIA: (**1**) 146 BC *IG* IV (1)² 28, 148 (f. *Σωσίβιος*: synoikos)

**Πασίθεμις**
ARGOLIS:
—EPIDAUROS*: (**1**) c. 370-360 BC ib. 102, 94,
107, 283, 301; *SEG* XXV 383, 168; *BSA* 61
(1966) p. 271 no. 4 A, 16

**Πασίκλεια**
LAKONIA:
—GERONTHRAI: (**1**) ?ii AD *Mél. Daux* p. 225 no.
4; p. 226 no. 5 ([*Πασίκλει*]*ᾳ*—5)

**Πασικλείδας**
LAKONIA:
—SPARTA: (**1**) c. 90-100 AD *SEG* XI 558, 2
(Bradford (1)) (-*κλί*-: s. *Βιόδαμος*); (**2**) ~ *SEG*
XI 609, 7 (Bradford (2)) (s. *Ἐπ*—)

**Πασικλῆς**
ARGOLIS:
—EPIDAUROS: (**1**) ii/i BC Peek, *IAEpid* 151 (?s.
*Καλλικλῆς*)
ARKADIA:
—TEGEA: (**2**) i AD *IG* v (2) 47, 1 ([*Π*]*ασικλῆς*)
LAKONIA:
—SPARTA: (**3**) s. i BC ib. v (1) 93, 26; 210,
6 (Bradford (19)) (f. *Πασίξενος*); (**4**) ~ *IG* v
(1) 95, 17 (Bradford (2)) (s. *Ἀριστόδαμος*); (**5**)
c. 30-20 BC *IG* v (1) 142, 11 (Bradford (4))
(*Πασικλῆς*: s. *Εὐκλείδας*); (**6**) ~ *IG* v (1) 142,
16 (Bradford (10)) (s. *Σωκρατίδας*); (**7**) ~ *IG*
v (1) 211, 33 (Bradford (15)) (f. *Ἀριστόμαχος*); (**8**) c. 25-1 BC *IG* v (1) 50, 24 (Bradford
(1)) (*Πασικ(λ)ῆς*—maj., *Πασικ(λέους*) (gen.)—
ed.: f. *Εὔδαμ*—); (**9**) i AD *IG* v (1) 272; *Artemis
Orthia* pp. 307-8 no. 22 (date) (Bradford (21))
(f. *Φιλόστρατος*); (**10**) c. 80-100 AD *SEG* XI
608, 5 (Bradford (5)) (s. *Γοργώπας*); (**11**) c. 90-
100 AD *IG* v (1) 667, 10; *SEG* XI 534, 4; 570,
4 (Bradford (17)) (f. *Μνάσων*); (**12**) c. 95-110
AD *IG* v (1) 51, 10; 52, [2]; *SEG* XI 506, [1];

562, [6] (Bradford (9)) (s. *Φιλοκράτης*); (**13**) c.
100-125 AD *IG* v (1) 51, 20; 52, 5; 482, 4;
*SEG* XI 506, [4] (Bradford (20)) (f. *Κ. Οὐίβιος
Φιλοκλῆς*); (**14**) ~ *IG* v (1) 137, 2 (Bradford
(14)) (f. *Ἀπολλωνίδας*); (**15**) ii AD *IG* v (1) 159,
3 (Bradford (13)); (**16**) ?ii AD *IG* v (1) 731, 3
(*GVI* 1341; Bradford (7)) (s. *Λυσίμαχος*); (**17**)
f. ii AD *SEG* XLII 328; (**18**) c. 105-110 AD ib.
XI 569, 17 (Bradford (8)) (s. *Μνάσων*); (**19**) m.
ii AD *SEG* XI 643, 1 (Bradford (11)) (s. *Τύχιππος*); (**20**) c. 130-140 AD *IG* v (1) 66, 11
(Bradford (16)) (f. *Καλλικράτης*); (**21**) c. 140-
145 AD *IG* v (1) 63, 22 (Bradford (22)) (f.
*Τύχιππος*); (**22**) c. 150-160 AD *IG* v (1) 69, 32;
71 III, 32; *SEG* XI 554, [5] (Bradford (6))
(s. *Καλλικράτης*); (**23**) c. 230-260 AD *SEG* XI
633, 6 (Bradford (12)) (*Αὐ*[*ρ.*] [*Πα*]*σικλῆς*?: s.
*Ζωσιμᾶς*)
—Amyklai: (**24**) ii/i BC *IG* v (1) 26, 2 (Brad-
ford (18)) (f. *Πασικράτης*)
—SPARTA?: (**25**) 316 BC *IG* v (2) 549, 36 (Brad-
ford (3)) (s. *Ἄσιντος*)
MESSENIA:
—MESSENE?: (**26**) ii/i BC *SEG* XI 979, 46
S. ITALY (CALABRIA):
—TARAS-TARENTUM*: (**27**) s. i BC *RE* s.v.
Crassicius (2) (Lat. L. Crassicius Pasicles qui
et Pansa: freed.)
S. ITALY (LUCANIA):
—METAPONTION: (**28**) c. 262 BC *IG* IX (1)² (1)
17 A, 74 (f. *Θεόδωρος*)

**Πασικράτης**
ARKADIA:
—MEGALOPOLIS: (**1**) ?145 BC ib. v (2) 439, 43,
48 (s. *Ἱέρων*, f. *Ἱέρων, Κλεοννώ*)
LAKONIA:
—SPARTA: (**2**) ?i BC *SEG* II 60, 1-2 (Brad-
ford (3)) (freed.); (**3**) c. 10-20 AD *IG* v (1)
206, 4; *SEG* XXXV 330 (date) (Bradford (11))
(*Πα*[*σ*]*ικρ*[*ά*]*τ*[*ης*]); (**4**) i/ii AD *IG* v (1) 32 A, 2;
*SEG* XI 488, 6 (Bradford (5)); (**5**) c. 100 AD
*SEG* XI 536, 4 (Bradford (2)) (s. *Φιλόστρατος*);
(**6**) c. 100-120 AD *IG* v (1) 1315, 21 (Bradford
(6)); (**7**) c. 120 AD *IG* v (1) 40, 18; *SEG* XI
483, 3 (Bradford (5)) (*νεώτ.*); (**8**) ?c. 120 AD
*SEG* XI 680 (Bradford (9)) (*Πασι*[*κράτ*]*ης*: f.
—*της*); (**9**) m. ii AD *SEG* XI 622, 8 (Bradford
(7)) ([*Π*]*ασικρ*[*άτης*]); (**10**) c. 175-200 AD *SEG*
XI 503, 21 (Bradford (10)) (*Πασ*[*ι*]*κράτης*: f.
*Μένιππος*); (**11**) f. iii AD *IG* v (1) 300 (*Artemis
Orthia* p. 328 no. 58) (*Μ. Αὐρ.* [*Πασι*]*κράτης*)
—Amyklai: (**12**) ii/i BC *IG* v (1) 26, 2 (Brad-
ford (1)) (s. *Πασικλῆς*)
MESSENIA:
—MESSENE: (**13**) i BC/i AD *IG* v (1) 1438 a, 6
PELOPONNESE?: (**14**) 11 AD *PAE* 1992, p. 71 A,
35 (f. *Εὔδοξος*)
SICILY:
—GELA-PHINTIAS?: (**15**) v/iv BC Manganaro,
*PdelP* forthcoming no. 12 (f. *Φερσέφασσα*)

**Πάσιλλος**
SICILY:
—KAMARINA: (**1**) f. v BC Cordano, *Tessere Pubbliche* 80 (Arena, *Iscr. Sic.* II 141 A) (f. *Αἰνησίδαμος*)

**Πασίμαχος**
LAKONIA:
—SPARTA: (**1**) 393 BC X., *HG* iv 4. 10 (Poralla²
590); (**2**) i BC *IG* v (1) 126, 1 (Bradford (1));
(**3**) s. i BC *IG* v (1) 92, 5 (Bradford (3)) (f.
*Ἀριστόδαμος*); (**4**) ~ *IG* v (1) 93, 20 (Bradford
(2)) (f. *Ἀντίμαχος*)

**Πασίμηλος**
ARGOLIS:
—HERMIONE: (**1**) iii BC *IG* IV (1) 729 I, 4 (s.
*Σῶσος*); (**2**) ~ ib. l. 21 (f. *Σῶσος*)

## Πασινίκα

KORINTHIA:
—KORINTH: (3) 392-366 BC X., *HG* iv 4. 4; iv 4. 7; vii 3. 2

## Πασινίκα

LAKONIA: (1) i BC *IG* II² p. 884 no. 9152 a (d. Δαμόφιλος)

## Πασίνικος

S. ITALY (CAMPANIA):
—HERCULANEUM*: (1) i BC-i AD *CIL* X 1403 g III, 10 (Lat. Pasinicus: freed.)

## Πασινόα

ARKADIA:
—TEGEA: (1) ii AD *IG* v (2) 237

## Πασίνομος

ARGOLIS:
—HERMIONE: (1) iii BC ib. IV (1) 729 I, 18 (s. Τρεύθος)

## Πασῖνος

ARGOLIS:
—EPIDAUROS*: (1) c. 370-365 BC Peek, *IAEpid* 52 A, 54
LAKONIA:
—SPARTA: (2) c. 225-250 AD *SEG* XXXIV 308, 17 (Bradford (-)) (*M. Aὐρ. Πασεῖνος*: s. Πολύνικος)

## Πασιξένα

ARKADIA:
—GORTYS: (1) ii-i BC *SEG* XXXV 348 (Πασι[.]ένας τᾶς—*SEG*, Πασι[ξ]ένα—*LGPN*: d. Ξενόφιλος)

## Πασίξενος

ACHAIA: (1) iii BC Robert, *EEP* 114, 9
ARGOLIS:
—ARGOS: (2) ?320 BC *CID* II 42, 4
—EPIDAUROS*: (3) c. 370-360 BC *BSA* 61 (1966) p. 271 no. 4 A, 11-12
LAKONIA:
—SPARTA: (4) s. i BC *IG* v (1) 93, [26]; 210, 6 (Bradford (-)) (s. Πασικλῆς)

## Πασιππίδας

LAKONIA:
—SPARTA: (1) 410-409 BC X., *HG* i 1. 32; i 3. 13; i 3. 17 (Poralla² 591)

## Πάσιππος

ARKADIA: (1) m. ii BC Unp. (Tripolis Mus.) ([Π]άσιππος: f. Ἀσπασίς)
—MEGALOPOLIS: (2) 182 BC *IvOl* 46, 7 (*IPArk* 31 IIB)
DALMATIA:
—ISSA: (3) iii BC Brunšmid p. 9 fr. H, 4 (Πάσιππ[ος]: f. —s)

## Πασιτέλης

ACHAIA:
—TRITAIA?: (1) m. iii BC *IG* v (2) 368, 80 with index (Πασιτ[έλης]: f. Παντίας)
ARGOLIS:
—EPIDAUROS*: (2) c. 370-365 BC Peek, *IAEpid* 52 A, 47
—HERMIONE: (3) m. iv BC Unp. (Ch. Kritzas)
ARKADIA:
—TEGEA: (4) ii AD *IG* v (2) 43, 7 (s. Ἀγναγόρας)
——(Krariotai): (5) ?s. iv BC ib. 39, 15
LAKONIA:
—SPARTA: (6) s. i BC ib. v (1) 93, 19 (Bradford (1)) (s. Ἀνδρόνικος); (7) ~ *IG* v (1) 94, 14 (Bradford (2)) (s. Ἡρίδας); (8) ~ *IG* v (1) 910 (tiles) (Bradford (5)); (9) i BC/i AD *IG* v (1) 48, 16 (Bradford (3)) (s. Κλεάνωρ)
——Amyklai: (10) ii/i BC *IG* v (1) 26, 4, 9 (Bradford (4)) (s. Τέταρτος)
MESSENIA:
—THOURIA: (11) c. 315-280 BC *FD* III (4) 5, 3 (f. Παγκράτης)

## Πασιτελίδας

LAKONIA:
—SPARTA: (1) 422 BC Th. iv 132. 3; v 3. 2 (Poralla² 592) (Ἐπιτελίδας—Th. iv 132 mss.: s. Ἀγήσανδρος)

## Πασιφάνης

MESSENIA:
—MESSENE: (1) c. 255 BC *SEG* XI 414, 17 (Perlman E.5) ([Πα]σιφ[ά]νης: f. Ἀντιφῶν)

## Πασίφιλος

S. ITALY (APULIA):
—CANUSIUM: (1) iii BC *Epig. Rom. di Canosa* Instr. 58 (vase) (Πασίφιλ[ος]: ?s. Ἀνδρω—)
S. ITALY (CAMPANIA):
—DIKAIARCHIA-PUTEOLI: (2) 394 AD *CIL* X 1692 (Lat. Fabius Pasiphilus)
SICILY:
—SYRACUSE?: (3) 312-305 BC *RE* (1)

## Πασίφυγος

SICILY:
—KAMARINA: (1) f. v BC Cordano, *Tessere Pubbliche* 71 (Π(α)σίφυγος: s. Φιντίας)

## Πασιχάρεια

ARGOLIS:
—EPIDAUROS: (1) m. i AD *IG* IV (1)² 85, 4; 86, 23-4, 31 + Peek, *IAEpid* 36; *IG* v (1) 580; *BSA* 80 (1985) p. 194; pp. 198-201 (ident., stemma) (Bradford (-)) (and Lakonia Sparta: Μεμμία Π.: d. Τ. Στατίλιος Τιμοκράτης, Στατιλία Τιμοσθενίς (Sparta), m. Π. Μέμμιος Δεξίμαχος (Sparta), Μεμμία Τιμοσθενίς (Sparta), ?m. Μεμμία Δαμοκρατία (Sparta), Τ. Στατίλιος Λαμπρίας Μεμμιανός (Sparta?))
LAKONIA:
—SPARTA*: (2) s. vii BC *PMGF* I 107 (-ρηα: fict.)

## Πασιχάρης

ARGOLIS:
—EPIDAUROS: (1) c. 220-200 BC *SEG* XI 414, 4 (Perlman E.5) ([Π]ασιχάρης)
—TROIZEN: (2) iv BC *IG* IV (1) 764, 5 (s. Παγχαρῖνος)

## Πασίων

AIGINA: (1) s. iii BC *SEG* XI 413, 29 (Perlman E.4) (f. Ἀρίστανδρος)
AITOLIA: (2) c. 220 BC *ILind* 130, 4 (I s. Ἀλεξῆς, f. Ἀλεξῆς (Rhodes and Aitolia), Πασίων II (Rhodes and Aitolia))
ARGOLIS:
—EPIDAUROS: (3) i BC Peek, *IAEpid* 19, 5
EPIROS:
—AMBRAKIA: (4) ii-i BC *CIG* 1800, 5 (f. Ἀντίπατρος)
ILLYRIA:
—EPIDAMNOS-DYRRHACHION: (5) c. 250-50 BC *Bakërr Hoard* p. 67 no. 93 (Ceka 339); cf. *IApoll Ref. Bibl.* n. 98 (coin) (pryt.)
KERKYRA: (6) m. ii BC *IG* IX (1)² (2) 209, 20 (f. Ἐπιγένης)
LAKONIA:
—SPARTA: (7) i/ii AD ib. v (1) 190, 2 (Bradford (-))
MESSENIA:
—THOURIA: (8) ii/i BC *IG* v (1) 1384, 20 (f. Ξένων)
PELOPONNESE?: (9) 11 AD *PAE* 1992, p. 72 B, 3 (II s. Πασίων I); (10) ~ ib. l. 3-4 (I f. Πασίων II, Σωτᾶς)
SICILY: (11) iii-ii BC Vandermersch p. 174 (amph.) (or S. Italy)
—AKRAGAS: (12) s. ii BC *Acragas Graeca* I p. 34 no. 5, 11 (*IGUR* 2; Dubois, *IGDS* 185) (II s. Πασίων I); (13) ~ *Acragas Graeca* I p. 34 no. 5, 12 (*IGUR* 2; Dubois, *IGDS* 185) (I s. Κότης, f. Πασίων II)
—IAITON: (14) ii-i BC *SEG* XXVI 1070. 9 (tiles)

—KAMARINA: (15) iv/iii BC Dubois, *IGDS* 122, 4 (Cordano, 'Camarina VII' 142); (16) f. ii BC *BCH* 45 (1921) p. 25 IV, 104 (*SEG* XXII 455); cf. *Sic. Gymn.* 17 (1964) pp. 47 f. (Πασίω[ν])
—SEGESTA: (17) 49 BC *IG* XIV 282 (Π. Σισυρίων: s. Δέκιος)

## Πασκάλας

ARGOLIS:
—HERMIONE: (1) iii BC ib. IV (1) 729 II, 22 (f. Ἀμφιμήδης)

## Πασκεντία

SICILY:
—SYRACUSE: (1) iii-v AD Strazzulla 190 (Wessel 661); cf. Ferrua, *NG* 341

## Παστάς

S. ITALY (CALABRIA):
—BRENTESION-BRUNDISIUM: (1) imp. *CIL* IX 117 (Lat. Laenia Pastas: m. Q. Fufius Deceberilius)

## Πάστωρ

S. ITALY (CAMPANIA):
—NEAPOLIS: (1) 536 AD *RE* (3); *PLRE* III (2)

## Πασχασία

KORINTHIA:
—KORINTH: (1) byz. *Corinth* VIII (3) 545; cf. *TMByz* 9 (1985) p. 365 no. 61 (-κα-)
SICILY:
—KATANE: (2) 401/2 AD Wessel 261 (*Rend. Pont.* 22 (1946-7) p. 230 n. 3) (-κα-)
—SYRACUSE: (3) iii-v AD Strazzulla 297 (Wessel 847)

## Πασχάσιος

ARGOLIS:
—ARGOS: (1) vi AD *SEG* XXX 373 (-κα-)
SICILY:
—SYRACUSE: (2) iii-v AD *IG* XIV 158 (Strazzulla 99; Wessel 501); *BCH* 105 (1981) p. 489 f. (name); cf. *BZ* 8 (1899) p. 108 (Φασ-)

## Πασχάσις

SICILY:
—SYRACUSE: (1) iii-v AD Strazzulla 185 (Wessel 1319); cf. Ferrua, *NG* 21 (-κά-)

## Πάσχασος

S. ITALY (CAMPANIA):
—NEAPOLIS: (1) v AD *JIWE* I 34 (Lat. Pascasus: Jew) ?= (2); (2) ~ ib. 35 (Lat. Pascasus: f. Criscentia: Jew) ?= (1)

## Πάσχουσα

S. ITALY (CAMPANIA):
—SALERNUM*: (1) ?i-ii AD *IItal* I (1) 207 (*CIL* X 609) (Lat. Iulia Pascusa: freed.)

## Πάσων

ARGOLIS:
—HERMIONE: (1) iii BC *IG* IV (1) 729 II, 21 (f. Τιμάνωρ)
—PHLEIOUS: (2) 191-146 BC *BMC Pelop.* pp. 12-13 nos. 145-6 (coin)
ARKADIA:
—MEGALOPOLIS: (3) s. ii BC *IG* v (2) 437, 21; 443, 25; 444, 6; 445, 1, 11 (*IPArk* 32) (f. Ἀριστώνυμος)

## Πάταικος

ACHAIA:
—DYME: (1) 496 BC Moretti, *Olymp.* 171
KORINTHIA:
—KORINTH: (2) iv/iii BC Men., *Pk.* 469 f. (f. Μοσχίων, Γλυκέρα: fict.)
SICILY:
—GELA-PHINTIAS: (3) vi BC Hdt. vii 154. 1 (f. Αἰνησίδαμος)

**Πατανιτος?**
S. ITALY (LUCANIA):
—METAPONTION: (**1**) iv BC Landi, *DISMG* 150
(*Πε. Πατανιτος*)

**Πατᾶς**
AIGINA: (**1**) i BC-i AD? *IG* IV (1) 112 (f. *Δυλύπορις*)

**Πατερήν**
ILLYRIA:
—EPIDAMNOS-DYRRHACHION: (**1**) c. 250-50 BC
Maier 347-8 (coin) (Ceka 90; 237) (pryt.); (**2**)
ii-i BC *IDyrrh* 553 (tile); (**3**) hell.-imp. ib. 341
(-αρήν: s. *Φιλώτας*)

**Πατερώ**
S. ITALY (CAMPANIA):
—SALERNUM: (**1**) imp. *IItal* 1 (1) 225 (*CIL* x
655) (Lat. Patero)

**Πατησιάδας**
LAKONIA:
—SPARTA: (**1**) 417 BC X., *HG* ii 3. 10 (Poralla²
593)

**Πατούλκιος**
ILLYRIA:
—EPIDAMNOS-DYRRHACHION: (**1**) hell.-imp.
*IDyrrh* 179 (*Πατύλ-*: f. *Ἰταλία*)
S. ITALY (CAMPANIA):
—NEAPOLIS: (**2**) imp. *INap* 210 (*Πατούλκ[ιος]*)

**Πατρέας**
ARGOLIS:
—TROIZEN: (**1**) iv BC *IG* IV (1) 764, 6 (f. *Δαμο-
τέλης*)

**Πατρεύς**
LAKONIA:
—AMYKLAI: (**1**) her. *RE* (-) (and Achaia Patrai:
s. *Πρευγένης*: oikist/dub.)

**Πατρίας**
ELIS: (**1**) ?c. 475-450 BC *IvOl* 2, 1, 8; *LSAG*²
p. 220 no. 15 (date) (n. pr.?)

**Πατρικία**
AIGINA: (**1**) v-vi AD *IG* IV (1) 54 (*Μαρία ἡ καὶ
Π.*)

**Πατρίς**
S. ITALY (APULIA):
—LUCERIA: (**1**) imp. *ASP* 34 (1981) p. 12 no.
12 (Lat. Terentia Patris)

**Πατρόβιος**
KORINTHIA:
—KORINTH: (**1**) f. iii AD *Corinth* VIII (3) 302, 2
(Lat. L. Coranus Patrobius)

**Πατροκλέα**
EPIROS:
—BOUTHROTOS (PRASAIBOI): (**1**) a. 163 BC
*IBouthrot* 39, 5 (*SEG* XXXVIII 498)

**Πατροκλέας**
ARKADIA:
—ORESTHASION?: (**1**) v BC *IG* IX (2) 1098 (Laz-
zarini 740) (s. *Μάλλος*)

**Πατρόκλεια**
EPIROS:
—BOUTHROTOS (PRASAIBOI): (**1**) a. 163 BC
*IBouthrot* 59, 5 (*SEG* XXXVIII 510)

**Πατροκλείδας**
ARGOLIS:
—EPIDAUROS: (**1**) ii/i BC *IG* IV (1)² 234, 4 (s.
*Ἀστυλαΐδας*)
——(Hysminatai): (**2**) 146 BC ib. 28, 24 (s. *Σώ-
στρατος*)
——(Hysminatai?): (**3**) iii/ii BC ib. 335, 1 (f. *Νι-
κόλοχος*); (**4**) ~ ib. l. 3 (s. *Νικόλοχος*); (**5**) ii BC

ib. 99, 22 (Peek, *IAEpid* 44); *IG* IV (1)² 335,
4 (f. *Σώστρατος*)
——Lower Teichias: (**6**) c. 220-200 BC *SEG* XI
414, 28 (Perlman E.5)
——TROIZEN: (**7**) c. 220-200 BC *SEG* XI 414, 36
(Perlman E.5) (s. *Πάτρων*)
ARKADIA:
—TEGEA:
——(Apolloniatai): (**8**) m. iii BC *IG* V (2) 36, 98
(s. *Ξενοφάνης*)

**Πατροκλῆς**
AITOLIA:
—KALLION/KALLIPOLIS: (**1**) hell. ib. IX (1)² (1)
158
ARGOLIS:
—ARGOS: (**2**) m. v BC *IvOl* 159, 2 (f. *Ναυκύδης*,
?f. *Πολύκλειτος*)
—TROIZEN: (**3**) iv BC *IG* IV (1) 764, 2 (f. *Πά-
τρων*); (**4**) ~ ib. l. 8 (*Πατρ[ο]κλῆ[s]*)
ARKADIA:
—TEGEA: (**5**) ii BC *SEG* XI 1058, 5
EPIROS: (**6**) ?iii/ii BC *IG* VII 468 (*IOrop* 586) (f.
*Ἐλάφιον*)
—BOUTHROTOS (PRASAIBOI): (**7**) a. 163 BC
*IBouthrot* 52, 7 (*SEG* XXXVIII 517) (s. *Ἀν-
δρόνικος*)
KORINTHIA:
—KROMMYON: (**8**) c. 525-500 BC *Corinth* VIII
(3) 1
—SIKYON: (**9**) v/iv BC *RE* (8); Marcadé 1 22 ff.
s.v. Daidalos; *FD* III (4) 202 (Skalet 258) (f.
*Δαίδαλος*: sculptor)
LAKONIA:
—SPARTA: (**10**) 424 BC Th. iv 57. 3 (Poralla²
594) (f. *Τάνταλος*)
S. ITALY (BRUTTIUM):
—KROTON: (**11**) arch. *RE* (7) (s. *Κάτιλλος*:
sculptor)
—SYBARIS-THOURIOI-COPIAE: (**12**) inc. Clem.
Al., *Protr.* ii 30. 4
S. ITALY (CAMPANIA):
—SALERNUM: (**13**) imp. *IItal* 1 (1) 59 (*CIL* x
585) (Lat. M. Antonius Patrocles)

**Πάτροκλος**
AITOLIA:
—KALYDON: (**1**) s. ii BC *SEG* XXV 621, 12

**Πατρονίκα**
EPIROS:
—BOUTHROTOS (PRASAIBOI): (**1**) a. 163 BC
*IBouthrot* 92, 5

**Πατρόφιλος**
LAKONIA:
—SPARTA: (**1**) c. 10-20 AD *IG* V (1) 206, 3; *SEG*
XXXV 330 (date) (Bradford (-)) (*Πατρόφιλος*: f.
*Σωσίνικος*)
S. ITALY (CAMPANIA):
—POMPEII: (**2**) c. 51-62 AD *CIL* IV 3340. 47, 4,
8, [21] (Castrèn 314. 11) (Lat. Q. Pompeius
Patrophilus)

**Πατρώ**
EPIROS:
—BOUTHROTOS (PRASAIBOI): (**1**) a. 163 BC
*IBouthrot* 22, 23 (*SEG* XXXVIII 479); (**2**) ~
*IBouthrot* 25, 6; 28, 7 (*SEG* XXXVIII 483;
486); (**3**) ~ *IBouthrot* 32, 2 (*SEG* XXXVIII 491)
——Eschatioi?: (**4**) a. 163 BC *IBouthrot* 129, 5
ILLYRIA:
—EPIDAMNOS-DYRRHACHION: (**5**) hell.-imp.
*IDyrrh* 342 (d. *Ὑβριμος*)

**Πάτρων**
ACHAIA:
—AIGEIRA: (**1**) ?161 BC *FD* III (1) 49, 2 (f. *Θρά-
σων*, *Σωκράτης*)
ARGOLIS:
—HERMIONE: (**2**) ?ii-i BC *IG* IV (1) 731 I, 16 (f.
*Φιλοξένα*)

—TROIZEN: (**3**) iv BC ib. 764, 2 (s. *Πατροκλῆς*);
(**4**) c. 220-200 BC *SEG* XI 414, 37 (Perlman
E.5) ([*Π*]*άτρων*: f. *Πατροκλείδας*)
DALMATIA:
—ISSA: (**5**) ii/i BC Brunšmid p. 27 no. 19 (*SEG*
XL 515) + *VAHD* 84 (1991) p. 254 no. 4 (s.
*Δροσσος*, f. *Σωσίπολις*, *Σαβάθυρος*)
ELIS: (**6**) 141-145 AD *IvOl* 95, 8 (*Πάτρω[ν]*)
EPIROS:
—AMBRAKIA: (**7**) f. ii BC *IC* 2 p. 25 no. 8 C
ILLYRIA:
—APOLLONIA: (**8**) ii BC Cabanes, *L'Épire* p. 562
no. 37 (*IApoll* 6) (s. *Εὐκλείδας*)
—SKODRAI: (**9**) a. 168 BC *Iliria* 1972, p. 402
(coin)
KEPHALLENIA: (**10**) iii BC *AD* 29 (1974) Mel.
p. 103 no. 19
LAKONIA:
—OITYLOS: (**11**) iii/ii BC *IG* V (1) 1295, 4; cf.
*BSA* 10 (1903-4) p. 168 no. 5 (Bradford (1))
(*Πάτρων*); (**12**) ~ *IG* V (1) 1295, 6; cf. *BSA* 10
(1903-4) p. 168 no. 5 (Bradford (2)) (*Πάτρων*)

**Πατρῶος**
ARGOLIS:
—NAUPLIA: (**1**) iii-iv AD *SEG* I 72 (*Λικίνιος Ἰου-
κοῦνδος Π.*)

**Πατώ**
ILLYRIA:
—APOLLONIA: (**1**) ii-i BC *IApoll* 142 (d. *Γλαυ-
κίας*)

**Πάτων**
ILLYRIA:
—BYLLIONES: (**1**) c. 200-198 BC *SEG* XXXV 680,
3; cf. XXXVIII 541 (*Π[ά]των*: s. *Ἀνθρωπίσκος*)

**Παῦλα**
ARGOLIS:
—ARGOS: (**1**) v-vi AD Unp. (Oikonomou-
Laniado)
ILLYRIA:
—EPIDAMNOS-DYRRHACHION: (**2**) iii-iv AD
*IDyrrh* 60 (m. *Περπέτουα*)
KORINTHIA:
—KORINTH: (**3**) byz. *Corinth* VIII (3) 560, 8; cf.
*TMByz* 9 (1985) p. 366 no. 65 (d. *Λαυρέντιος*)
S. ITALY (CALABRIA):
—TARAS-TARENTUM: (**4**) i BC/i AD *GP* 2153
S. ITALY (CAMPANIA):
—NEAPOLIS: (**5**) iii-iv AD *IG* XIV 826. 37 (*INap*
246); (**6**) vi AD *IG* XIV 823 (*INap* 245); cf.
Leiwo p. 109 no. 77 (d. *Παῦλος*)
SICILY:
—SYRACUSE: (**7**) iii-v AD *SEG* XXXIX 1024; (**8**)
427 AD *IG* XIV 159 (Strazzulla 100; Wessel
675; Ferrua, *NG* 171)

**Παύλη**
SICILY:
—SYRACUSE: (**1**) iii-v AD Strazzulla 240 (Barreca
292)

**Παυλῖνα**
KORINTHIA:
—KORINTH: (**1**) byz. *PAE* 1962, p. 53; cf.
*TMByz* 9 (1985) p. 367 no. 85
SICILY:
—SYRACUSE: (**2**) iii-v AD *ASSiracusano* 1956, p.
54; (**3**) ~ Strazzulla 339 (Wessel 226)

**Παυλῖνος**
MESSENIA:
—MESSENE: (**1**) ii/i BC *IG* V (1) 1446 (f. *Θεότι-
μος*)
SICILY:
—ADRANON: (**2**) ?ii-iii AD *PdelP* 16 (1961) p.
132 (Ferrua, *NG* 472); cf. *Rupes loquentes* p.
497 no. 8

**Παῦλος**
AIGINA: (**1**) vii AD *RE* (23) (doctor)
ARGOLIS:
—ARGOS: (**2**) byz. *SEG* XXXII 375
—EPIDAUROS: (**3**) ?i AD Peek, *NIEpid* 48, 5 (*Πα[ῦλος]*)
KORINTHIA:
—KORINTH: (**4**) byz. *Hesp.* 41 (1972) p. 41 no. 33, 1 (*Παῦλ(ο)ς*: ?f. *Σωτηρίς*); (**5**) ~ *Corinth* VIII (3) 559, 3; cf. *TMByz* 9 (1985) p. 365 no. 54 (*Π. ἐπίκλην μ[α]κρόχειρ]*); (**6**) v AD *Corinth* VIII (3) 542, 2, 4; cf. *TMByz* 9 (1985) p. 365 no. 59 (f. *Ἀνίας*)
—KORINTH?: (**7**) v-vi AD *CIG* 8824 (*TMByz* 9 (1985) p. 294 no. 34 A); *Corinth* VIII (3) 509 (*TMByz* 9 (1985) p. 294 no. 34 B)
S. ITALY (CAMPANIA):
—NEAPOLIS: (**8**) vi AD *IG* XIV 823 (*INap* 245); cf. Leiwo p. 109 no. 77 (f. *Παῦλα*)
SICILY:
—COMISO (MOD.): (**9**) byz. *SEG* XXXIV 944-5
—SYRACUSE: (**10**) iii-v AD Strazzulla 301 (Wessel 617); cf. Ferrua, *NG* 62; (**11**) ~ Strazzulla 397 (Barreca 298); (**12**) ~ Ferrua, *NG* 201; (**13**) ~ ib. 337; (**14**) ?399 AD *IG* XIV 160 (Strazzulla 325; Wessel 1069); cf. Ferrua, *NG* 172

**Παυσανίας**
ACHAIA:
—PELLENE: (**1**) m. iii BC Peek, *IAEpid* 42, 60, 64 (Perlman E.3); Perlman p. 63 f. (date) (s. *Ἀνδρίων*)
AITOLIA: (**2**) c. 280-275 BC Flacelière p. 414 no. 47; *SEG* XV 338; (**3**) ?253 BC Nachtergael, *Les Galates* 10, 4
AKARNANIA:
—ASTAKOS: (**4**) ii BC *IG* IX (1)² (2) 435, 20 (f. *Νεοπτόλεμος*)
—KORONTA: (**5**) c. 325-315 BC *Hesp.* 57 (1988) p. 148 A, 50 (*SEG* XXXVI 331); cf. *Hesp.* 48 (1979) pp. 78 f. with pl. 22 c (s. *Θεοπροπίδας*)
ARGOLIS:
—ARGOS: (**6**) c. 322-320 BC *CID* II 109 A, 20; 113, 9-10
—EPIDAUROS: (**7**) f. iii BC *IG* IV (1)² 107, 15; (**8**) iii AD ib. 451
——Dexelis: (**9**) c. 220-200 BC Peek, *IAEpid* 331, 21 (Perlman E.5) (*[Πα]υσ[αν]ίας*)
ARKADIA:
—ORCHOMENOS: (**10**) 369-361 BC *IG* V (2) 1, 50; Tod, *GHI* II 132 (date)
—THELPHOUSA: (**11**) 369-361 BC *IG* V (2) 1, 68; Tod, *GHI* II 132 (date); (**12**) a. 228 BC *IG* IV (1)² 72 B, 21 (s. *Τρο—*)
ELIS: (**13**) 28-24 BC *IvOl* 64, 15; 65, [18] (f. *Καλλίας*); (**14**) c. 28 BC-5 AD ib. 64, 13, 17; 65, 14, [22]; 69, 14 (s. *Διογένης*: mantis/Iamidai/N.); (**15**) c. 5 AD ib. l. 21 (s. *Μ—*)
EPIROS:
—AMBRAKIA: (**16**) iii/ii BC *IG* IX (1) 686, 2, 17 (s. *Ἄτταλος*); (**17**) ii BC *SEG* XVII 308 (f. *Καρμόννη*)
—BOUTHROTOS (PRASAIBOI): (**18**) a. 163 BC *IBouthrot* 110, 9; (**19**) ~ ib. 128, 8 (s. *Ζώπυρος*)
—DODONA: (**20**) iii BC Antoniou, *Dodone* Ab, 29
—KASSOPE: (**21**) iii BC Helly, *Gonnoi* 10, 2 (s. *Μενεκράτης*); (**22**) ii BC *SEG* XXXIV 590 (f. *Νικομήδης, Φιλωτέρα*); (**23**) ~ ib.; cf. XXXV 672 (s. *Νικομήδης*)
—KODRION: (**24**) iii-ii BC *Iliria* 1972, p. 38 (pithos) (*Παο-*)
—OMPHALES CHIMOLIOI: (**25**) c. 330-310 BC Cabanes, *L'Épire* p. 578 no. 51, 10
—TRIPOLITAI: (**26**) ?c. 370-344 BC ib. p. 536 no. 2, 3 (*Παυ[σανίας]*?)
ILLYRIA:
—APOLLONIA: (**27**) iv BC *RE* (23); Marcadé I 86 (sculptor)

—EPIDAMNOS-DYRRHACHION: (**28**) c. 250-50 BC Maier 349 (coin) (Ceka 10; 238) (pryt.)
KORINTHIA:
—KORINTH?: (**29**) 79-96 AD *Epigraphica* 55 (1993) pp. 199 ff. (Lat. L. A[ure]lius [Paus]anias)
LAKONIA: (**30**) ?iii BC *IG* II² 9153 (Bradford (2)) (s. *Ναυκλῆς*); (**31**) imp.? *FGrH* 592
—SPARTA: (**32**) c. 510-469 BC *RE* (25) (Poralla² 595) (s. *Κλεόμβροτος*, ?s. *Ἀγχιθέα, Ἀλκαθόα, Θεανώ*, f. *Πλειστοάναξ, Κλεομένης, Ἀριστοκλῆς*: regent); (**33**) c. 445-375 BC *RE* (26); *FD* III (1) 509 (Poralla² 596) (s. *Πλειστοάναξ*, f. *Ἀγησίπολις, Κλεόμβροτος*: king); (**34**) s. i BC *IG* V (1) 94, 6 (Bradford (1)) (s. *Λαμέδων*); (**35**) ~ *IG* V (1) 124, 1 (Bradford (3)) (*[Πα]υσ[α]νίας*)
S. ITALY (CAMPANIA):
—DIKAIARCHIA-PUTEOLI: (**36**) 174 AD *OGIS* 595, 21
—HERCULANEUM*: (**37**) i BC-i AD *CIL* IV 10863 (terracotta)
SICILY:
—AKRAI: (**38**) ?iii BC *SGDI* 3239, 6 (*Akrai* p. 157 no. 9) (f. *Ἀριστόγειτος, Ἀρτέμων*); (**39**) ~ *SGDI* 3240, 6 (*Akrai* p. 156 no. 7) (s. *Σῶσις*); (**40**) iii-ii BC *SGDI* 3242, 8 (*Akrai* p. 157 no. 8) (f. *Σῶσις*); (**41**) ii-i BC *SGDI* 3246, 21 (*Akrai* pp. 152-3 no. 2; Dubois, *IGDS* 109) (*Παυσ[α]νίας*: f. *Ἀριστόγειτος*)
—GELA-PHINTIAS: (**42**) s. v BC *RE* Supplbd. 14 (28) (s. *Ἀγχίτας*: doctor); (**43**) iv/iii BC *BM Lamps* 1 pp. 310-11 no. Q666 (Dubois, *IGDS* 151 (lamp))
—KAMARINA: (**44**) ?iv/iii BC *SEG* XXXIV 940, 6 (Dubois, *IGDS* 124; *PdelP* 44 (1989) p. 192 no. 3; Cordano, 'Camarina VII' 143) (f. *Φίλιππος*); (**45**) ~ *SEG* XXXIV 940, 7 (Dubois, *IGDS* 124; *PdelP* 44 (1989) p. 192 no. 3; Cordano, 'Camarina VII' 144) (s. *Σωσικράτης*); (**46**) hell. *SEG* XXXIX 1001, 1 (s. —*ων*)
—MORGANTINA: (**47**) iv/iii BC ib. 1012, 8 (s. *Ἀρίστων*)
—TAUROMENION:
——*(Ἀρεθ.)*: (**48**) ii/i BC *IGSI* 11 I, 2, [23]; 12 I, 6, 10, 16, 21 etc.; 12 II, 9, 13, 18, 30 (II s. *Παυσανίας* I); (**49**) ~ ib. 12 I, 6, 10, 16, 21 etc.; 12 II, 10, 14, 18, 31 (I f. *Παυσανίας* II)

**Παυσέας**
MESSENIA:
—MESSENE: (**1**) m. iii BC *IG* V (2) 368, 84 (*Παυσέας*: f. *Λυσίνικος*)

**Παυσήν**
ILLYRIA:
—APOLLONIA: (**1**) hell. *IApoll* 342 (tile) (f. *Καλλήν*)

**Παυσίας**
AITOLIA:
—KALYDON: (**1**) iii/ii BC *IG* IX (1)² (1) 136, 12 (*Παυσίου* (gen.))
ARKADIA:
—KAPHYAI?: (**2**) c. 225 BC *SEG* XI 414, 7 (Perlman E.5) (s. *Τελέστας*)
—TEGEA: (**3**) f. ii BC *IG* V (2) 44, 24 (*Παυσία[ς]*)
KORINTHIA:
—SIKYON: (**4**) iv BC *RE* (-) (Skalet 259) (s. *Βρύας*, f. *Ἀριστόλαος*: painter)

**Παυσίμαχος**
ACHAIA:
—PATRAI: (**1**) 160-150 BC *IG* V (2) 367, 10, 34 (*IPArk* 19) (f. *Κρατησίλοχος*)

**Παύσιππος**
LAKONIA:
—SPARTA: (**1**) 330 BC Berve 617 (Poralla² 598)

**Παυσίων**
ARKADIA:
—THELPHOUSA: (**1**) iii/ii BC *IG* V (2) 511 (f. *Θύμων*)

**Παύσων**
AKARNANIA:
—THYRREION: (**1**) iii-ii BC *SEG* XXVII 159, 2; cf. *PAE* 1977, pl. 244 a (f. *Λύκος*)
EPIROS:
—AMBRAKIA: (**2**) s. ii BC Cabanes, *L'Épire* p. 548 no. 19 (*SEG* XXVI 694) (f. *Σιλανός*)
S. ITALY (CALABRIA):
—TARAS-TARENTUM: (**3**) iv/iii BC *IG* XIV 668 I, 7 (Landi, *DISMG* 194)

**Πάχων**
ARKADIA:
—TEGEA: (**1**) ii BC *IG* V (2) 43, 1 (Athaneatai): (**2**) s. iv BC ib. 41, 36 (f. *Κλεόδαμος*)
——(Krariotai): (**3**) m. iii BC ib. 36, 91 (f. *Τελέστας*)

**Πεδάκριτος**
ARGOLIS:
—ARGOS:
——(Pamphyloi): (**1**) iv/iii BC *SEG* XI 293, 3

**Πεδάνιος**
S. ITALY (BRUTTIUM):
—LOKROI EPIZEPHYRIOI: (**1**) i BC De Franciscis p. 144 n. 8 (tile)

**Πεδάρετος**
ARKADIA: (**1**) 316 BC *IG* V (2) 549, 35 (f. *Ἀμφαίνετος*)

**Πεδάριτος**
ARKADIA:
—TEGEA: (**1**) c. 369-362 BC ib. 173, 6; cf. *CEG* II 657; (**2**) f. iii BC *IG* V (2) 35, 35 (s. *Στιλπίων*)
——(Hippothoitai): (**3**) iii BC ib. 40, 21 (*Π[ε]δάριτος*: f. *Ἰμπεδόκριτος*)
LAKONIA:
—SPARTA: (**4**) v/iv BC *RE* (-) (Poralla² 599) (*Π.—Th., Παιδάρητος*—Plu.: s. *Λέων, Τελευτία*)

**Πεδέστρατος**
LAKONIA:
—SPARTA: (**1**) f. ii BC *IC* 4 p. 284 no. 208 A, 5 (Bradford (-)) (s. *Ἀγήτωρ*)

**Πεδία**
S. ITALY (CAMPANIA):
—AMALFI (MOD.): (**1**) iii-iv AD *IG* XIV 694 a (p. 689)

**Πεδίαρχος**
ARKADIA:
—MANTINEIA-ANTIGONEIA: (**1**) c. 300-221 BC ib. V (2) 323. 104 (tessera) (s. *Πεδιόστρατος*)
LAKONIA:
—ALAGONIA?: (**2**) iii BC ib. V (1) 1339
SICILY: (**3**) 480 BC Polyaen. i 27. 2
—SELINOUS: (**4**) vi/v BC Dubois, *IGDS* 50 (Arena, *Iscr. Sic.* I 50; Lazzarini 880 a); cf. *SEG* XL 806

**Πεδιόστρατος**
ARKADIA:
—MANTINEIA-ANTIGONEIA: (**1**) c. 300-221 BC *IG* V (2) 323. 104 (tessera) (*Πεδιόστρατ[ος]*: f. *Πεδίαρχος*)

**Πεδώνιος**
S. ITALY (CAMPANIA):
—S. CLEMENTE (MOD.): (**1**) imp. *Atti Conv. Taranto* 28 (1988) pp. 518-19 (-*νει*-: Jew)

**Πεδώνυμος**
ARGOLIS:
—ARGOS:
——(Hyrnathioi-Temenidai): (**1**) c. 400 BC *SEG* XXIX 361, 23 (-*δό*-)

**Πείανδρος**
EPIROS:
—ELEA: (1) c. 330 BC Cabanes, *L'Épire* p. 580 no. 55, 9

**Πειθαγόρας**
ARGOLIS:
—ARGOS: (1) f. i BC Unp. (Ch. Kritzas) (s. Σώ-δαμος)
——Kerkas (Sphyreidai): (2) a. 316 BC *SEG* XI 1084, 3 (Perlman A.3)
—EPIDAUROS: (3) iii BC *IG* IV (1)² 167, 3
SICILY:
—LIPARA: (4) vi BC Bernabò Brea–Cavalier, *Castello di Lipari* p. 90 (vase); cf. *SEG* XLII 863 (Πειθαγόρ(ας))
—SELINOUS: (5) s. vi BC Hdt. v 46. 2 (-ρης)
—TAUROMENION: (6) c. 175 BC *IG* XIV 421 an. 66 (*SGDI* 5219) (f. Φιλόξενος)

**Πείθανδρος**
ARGOLIS:
—TROIZEN*: (1) iv BC *IG* IV (1) 823, 10, 18

**Πειθανορίδας**
ARGOLIS:
—PHLEIOUS: (1) m. iii BC ib. VII 10, 6 (s. Νί-καιθος)

**Πειθάνωρ**
KORINTHIA:
—SIKYON: (1) ?255 BC Nachtergael, *Les Galates* 8, 55 (Skalet 260; Stephanis 2032)

**Πείθαρχος**
MESSENIA:
—MESSENE: (1) iii BC *SEG* XXIII 209, 13
SICILY:
—ZANKLE-MESSANA: (2) ?ii BC *IG* XIV 401, 8 (Πειθιαρχος (apogr.): f. —χος)

**Πειθέας**
LEUKAS: (1) c. 330 BC *SEG* XXIII 189 I, 8 (s. Πειθωνίδας)

**Πειθέρως**
S. ITALY (CALABRIA):
—RUDIAE: (1) i AD *Eph. Ep.* VIII 1 (Susini, *Fonti Salento* p. 116 no. 55) (Lat. C. Iulius Pitheros)

**Πειθιάδας**
ARKADIA:
—TEGEA: (1) f. iii BC *IG* V (2) 35, 13 ([Πει]θιάδας: s. Πείσανδρος)

**Πειθίας**
ARKADIA:
—MANTINEIA-ANTIGONEIA: (1) ?253 BC ib. II² 9282; Nachtergael, *Les Galates* 10, 54 (Stephanis 2033) (s. Ἐξαίνετος)
—MEGALOPOLIS: (2) 134 or 130 BC *FD* III (3) 120, 9, 15 (Πι-: s. Ἐρασίδαμος)
—TEGEA: (3) iv/iii BC *IG* V (2) 32, 7; (4) ii BC ib. 43, 8, 9 (f. Νικασίας, Παντίας)
KERKYRA: (5) 427 BC Th. iii 70. 3-6; (6) hell.? *IG* IX (1) 891 (-θεί-: ?s. Λυσίστρατος)
S. ITALY (BRUTTIUM):
—LOKROI EPIZEPHYRIOI:
——(Πυρ.): (7) iv/iii BC De Franciscis 39, 3 (s. Ὀνάσιμος)

**Πειθίδαμος**
KORINTHIA:
—KORINTH: (1) a. 191 BC *SEG* XXVI 392, 10 (f. Ἀρχέμαχος)
LAKONIA:
—GERONTHRAI: (2) v BC *IG* V (1) 1136 (Poralla² 600)

**Πειθίλας**
ARGOLIS:
—ARGOS: (1) iv/iii BC Peek, *IAEpid* 24, 7

——EPIDAUROS: (2) iv BC *IG* IV (1)² 186

**Πειθιμένης**
AITOLIA:
—THESTIEIS: (1) 225-205 BC *FD* III (3) 220, 4

**Πειθόι**
EPIROS:
—AMBRAKIA: (1) f. iii BC Unp. (Arta Mus., inscr.) (d. Κλείδαμος)

**Πειθόλαος**
AITOLIA:
—SPATTIOI: (1) c. 213 BC *IG* IX (1)² (1) 188, 33 ([Πει]θόλαος)

**Πειθόλας**
EPIROS:
—NIKOPOLIS: (1) imp. *SEG* XXVII 233 (s. Λυ-κίσκος)

**Πεῖθυς**
S. ITALY (BRUTTIUM):
—KROTON: (1) c. 356-355 BC *IG* IV (1)² 95, 42 (Perlman E.2); Perlman p. 40 f. (date) (f. Σώ-νικος)

**Πείθων**
KORINTHIA:
—SIKYON: (1) vi/v BC *SEG* XI 244, 4 (-θōν)

**Πειθωνίδας**
LEUKAS: (1) c. 330 BC ib. XXIII 189 I, 8 (f. Πει-θέας, Δαϊμένης)

**Πεϊκλείδας**
LAKONIA:
—SPARTA: (1) i BC-i AD? *IG* V (1) 690 (Bradford (-)) (f. Κλέων)

**Πεϊκράτης**
LAKONIA:
—HYPERTELEATON*: (1) iii BC *IG* V (1) 977, 13 (Bradford (-)) (f. Κρατηϊδάμεια)

**Πεϊκρατίδας**
LAKONIA:
—OITYLOS: (1) iii/ii BC *IG* V (1) 1295, 3 (Bradford (1)); (2) ~ *IG* V (1) 1295, 4 (Bradford (2))

**Πεϊππίς**
LAKONIA:
—PLEIAI*: (1) v BC *IG* V (1) 1107 a (Lazzarini 99; Poralla² 603) (-hιπίς)

**Πεϊτας**
LAKONIA:
—ASOPOS: (1) ii BC *IG* V (1) 962, 1, [14] (s. Κρατησαίνικος)
—SPARTA: (2) ii AD ib. 159, 30 (Bradford s.v. Πείτας (-)) (Πε(ί)ίτας, Πει[σέ]ας—*IG*)

**Πείραος**
AKARNANIA:
—THYRREION: (1) ii BC *IG* IX (1)² (2) 252, 11 (f. Φίλλυρος, Φατνιάδας)

**Πείρας**
ARGOLIS:
—ARGOS: (1) arch. Plu. fr. 158 (f. Καλλίθυια: dub.)

**Πειρίθος**
S. ITALY (BRUTTIUM):
—KROTON: (1) vi BC D.L. viii 83; *FVS* 1 p. 214 B1 (f. Ἀλκμαίων)

**Πεισαγόρα**
ARGOLIS:
—EPIDAUROS: (1) iv BC *IG* IV (1)² 199

**Πείσανδρος**
ARKADIA:
—TEGEA: (1) f. iii BC ib. V (2) 35, 13 (f. Πειθιά-δας)
—SPARTA: (2) 394 BC *RE* (10) (Poralla² 601) (?s. Ἀριστομενίδας)
SICILY:
—LIPARA: (3) v BC *SEG* XLII 861 (f. Μάτερις)
—ZANKLE-MESSANA: (4) ?ii BC *IG* XIV 401, 9 (Πειχ..ανδρος? (apogr.): s. Ἀγάθων)

**Πεισανορίδας**
KEPHALLENIA:
—PALE: (1) ?iv BC ib. I² 1070. 2

**Πείσαρχος**
SICILY:
—SYRACUSE: (1) 317 BC D.S. xix 6. 4; Polyaen. v 3. 8; cf. *RE* s.v. Tisarchos (-) (Τίσαρχος—Polyaen.)

**Πεισιάναξ**
SICILY:
—AKRAGAS: (1) v BC Wehrli, *Schule Arist.* vii fr. 83; *FGrH* 566 F 6

**Πεισίας**
ACHAIA:
—DYME*: (1) c. 219 BC *SGDI* 1612, 80 (*Tyche* 5 (1990) p. 124) (f. Ἀμμώνιος)
—PELLENE: (2) s. iii BC *IG* IV (1) 727 A, 7 + Perlman H.1; cf. *Chiron* 2 (1972) p. 115 n. 66 (Θερσίας—*IG*, Πε[ι]σίας—Perlman, (Π)ε[ι]σίας?—Habicht: s. Μέμνων) ?= (3); (3) 198 BC Liv. xxxii 22. 5 (Lat. Pisias: f. Μέ-μνων) ?= (2)
ARGOLIS:
—ARGOS: (4) 367 BC X., *HG* vii 1. 41
ARKADIA:
—KLEITOR: (5) i BC-i AD? *Achaean Grave Stelai* 4
—LOUSOI: (6) c. 230-200 BC *BCH* 45 (1921) p. 12 II, 68 (s. Νικέας)
—TEGEA: (7) ii BC *IG* V (2) 43, 10 (Πεισίας: s. Ἰσόδαμος)
——(Athaneatai): (8) iv/iii BC ib. 38, 16 ([Π]εισίας?: s. Φάϋλλος)
LAKONIA:
—SPARTA: (9) c. 140-160 AD ib. V (1) 113, 3 (Bradford (-)) (f. Τιμοσθενίδας)
S. ITALY (LUCANIA):
—HERAKLEIA:
——(Fε. γυῖον): (10) iv/iii BC *IGSI* 1 I, 183 (*DGE* 62; Uguzzoni–Ghinatti I) (s. Λεοντί-σκος)

**Πεισίδαμος**
LAKONIA:
—SPARTA: (1) f. ii BC *IC* 2 p. 23 no. 6 D (Bradford (1)) (s. Θαλίαρχος); (2) c. 133 AD *SEG* XI 580, 4 (Bradford (2)) (s. Τιμοσθενίδας)

**Πεισιδίκα**
ARGOLIS:
—HERMIONE: (1) ii-i BC *IG* IV (1) 732 III, 18 (m. Ἰσιάς); (2) ~ ib. l. 29 (m. Σώσιππος)

**Πεισίθεος**
AKARNANIA:
—ASTAKOS: (1) ii BC ib. IX (1)² (2) 435, 2, 7 (f. Θεογένης, Πράϋχος)

**Πεισικράτης**
ARGOLIS:
—TROIZEN: (1) ?146 BC ib. IV (1) 757 B, 22 (or Arkadia: f. Νίκανδρος)
S. ITALY (CALABRIA):
—TARAS-TARENTUM: (2) vi BC Iamb., *VP* 267 (*FVS* 1 p. 446)

**Πεισίλαος**
ARGOLIS:
—EPIDAUROS: (1) c. 370 BC *IG* IV (1)² 102, 82

LEUKAS: (2) c. 167-50 BC *BMC Thessaly* p. 180 no. 99; *Coll. de Luynes* 1940 (coins)

**Πεισίνοος**
ARGOLIS:
—HERMIONE: (1) iii BC *IG* IV (1) 729 II, 4 (s. Κλέων); (2) ~ ib. l. 12 (f. Θεαρίων)

**Πείσιππος**
LAKONIA:
—SPARTA: (1) c. 146-32 BC *Münzpr. der Laked.* p. 25 fig. 3 no. 17; p. 123 Group 8 series 17 (coin) (Πείσιπ(πος)); (2) s. i BC *IG* V (1) 92, 12 (Bradford (2)) (f. Νικοκράτης)

**Πεισιρρόδη**
S. ITALY (CALABRIA):
—TARAS-TARENTUM: (1) vi BC Iamb., *VP* 267 (*FVS* 1 p. 448) (πισιρρονδη—ms.: name—Westermann)

**Πεισίρροδος**
S. ITALY (CALABRIA):
—TARAS-TARENTUM: (1) vi BC Iamb., *VP* 267 (*FVS* 1 p. 446) (Πισίρροδος—ms.: name—Westermann)

**Πεῖσις**
SICILY:
—MEGARA HYBLAIA: (1) c. 500 BC *IvOl* 22 ab, 18 (Dubois, *IGDS* 28; Arena, *Iscr. Sic.* I 52) (or Sicily Selinous)

**Πεισις**
KEPHALLENIA:
—SAME: (1) ?iv-iii BC *SEG* XXXIX 486 (?s./d. Λύκων)

**Πεισίστρατος**
LAKONIA:
—SPARTA: (1) arch. Ps.-Plu., *de Fluv.* 10. 2 (Poralla² 605) (dub.); (2) iv/iii BC *CID* II 120 A, 26 (Poralla² 606) (f. —λαΐδας); (3) i BC *IG* V (1) 126, 6 (Bradford (-)) (s. Ἀρίστιππος)
SICILY:
—LIPARA: (4) ?iv BC *RE* (7); *FGrH* 574

**Πεισιτέλης**
AIGINA: (1) ?f. i BC *Alt-Ägina* I (2) p. 43 no. 4, 1 (f. Κυδιμένης)
ITHAKE: (2) hell. *Rev. Épig.* 1 (1913) p. 47 no. 8
LEUKAS: (3) hell. *IG* IX (1) 569

**Πεισίων**
KORINTHIA:
—SIKYON (NR.): (1) iii BC *SEG* XI 272

**Πεισόι**
MESSENIA:
—MESSENE: (1) i BC *IG* V (1) 1476

**Πεισώ**
AIGINA: (1) vi/v BC *SEG* XXXIX 332

**Πεκουλιάρις**
S. ITALY (CAMPANIA):
—NEAPOLIS: (1) imp. *INap* 191

**Πελαγία**
S. ITALY (CAMPANIA):
—BAIAI: (1) imp. *NScav* 1887, p. 154 (*Eph. Ep.* VIII 408) (Lat. Insteia Pelagia)
—DIKAIARCHIA-PUTEOLI: (2) ?i-ii AD *CIL* X 2604; cf. *Puteoli* 11 (1987) pp. 40-1 (Lat. Iulia Pelagia)
—POMPEII: (3) i BC-i AD *CIL* IV 2321 (Lat. Pelagia); (4) ~ *NScav* 1916, p. 303 no. 104 (Castrèn 457. 14) (Lat. Vibia Pelagia)
—SALERNUM: (5) imp. *IItal* I (1) 233 (Lat. Pelagia)

SICILY:
—KATANE: (6) iii-v AD *IG* XIV 530 + Ferrua, *NG* 433
—SYRACUSE: (7) iii-v AD *ASSiracusano* 1956, p. 57 (Πελα[γία])

**Πελαγιανή**
S. ITALY (LUCANIA):
—ATINA LUCANA: (1) ii AD *IItal* III (1) 137 (*CIL* X 339) (Lat. Antonia Pelagiane: d. Πελαγιανός)

**Πελαγιανός**
S. ITALY (BRUTTIUM):
—RHEGION: (1) iii AD *Suppl. It.* 5 p. 76 no. 37 (*SEG* XL 858 (lead)) ([Π]ελαγιανός)
S. ITALY (LUCANIA):
—ATINA LUCANA: (2) ii AD *IItal* III (1) 133; 137 (*CIL* X 338-9) (Lat. A. Antonius Pelagianus: I f. Πελαγιανός II, Πελαγιανή); (3) ~ *IItal* III (1) 137 (*CIL* X 339) (Lat. Antonius Pelagianus: II s. Πελαγιανός I)

**Πελάγιος**
S. ITALY (CAMPANIA):
—DIKAIARCHIA-PUTEOLI: (1) imp. ib. 2038 (Lat. Pelagius: f. Ἀλεξάνδρεια)
—POMPEII: (2) i BC-i AD ib. IV 8836 (Lat. Pelagius—Solin)
—SALERNUM: (3) imp. *IItal* I (1) 113 (*CIL* X 670) (Lat. Pelagius)
SICILY:
—HALAISA: (4) ii BC *IGSI* 2 A II, 80 (Dubois, *IGDS* 196)

**Πελάγις**
SICILY:
—SYRACUSE: (1) iii-v AD Barreca 403; cf. *Rend. Pont.* 22 (1946-7) p. 236 no. 40

**Πελασγος**
ARGOLIS:
—ARGOS: (1) c. 146-32 BC *BMC Pelop.* p. 145 nos. 119-20 (coin)
S. ITALY (APULIA):
—LARINUM: (2) imp. *CIL* IX 741 (Lat. Pelasgus)

**Πελεγρῖνα**
SICILY:
—AKRILLAI: (1) iii-v AD *Epigraphica* 12 (1950) p. 97 no. 3

**Πελεγρῖνος**
SICILY:
—SYRACUSE: (1) iii-v AD Strazzulla 163 (Agnello 18; Wessel 184); cf. Robert, *EEP* p. 196 + *Rend. Pont.* 22 (1946-7) p. 236 no. 41; (2) ~ Strazzulla 266 (Wessel 934); cf. Ferrua, *NG* 37 (Πελεγρί[νος], Πελεγρί[να]?)

**Πέλεια**
LEUKAS: (1) ii BC Unp. (Leukas Mus., inscr.) inv. 9 (Πέλειας—lap., Πελειάς?)

**Πελειχίνας**
EPIROS:
—PHOINIKE: (1) iii BC Ugolini, *Alb. Ant.* 2 p. 154 no. 7 (s. Παρμενίσκος)

**Πελεύων**
EPIROS:
—DODONA: (1) iii BC Antoniou, *Dodone* Aa, 8; (2) ~ ib. Ab, 43

**Πελέων**
EPIROS:
—CHERADROI: (1) hell. Cabanes, *L'Épire* p. 581 no. 56, 9

**Πέλλας**
S. ITALY (CAMPANIA):
—HERCULANEUM: (1) 41-79 AD *Cron. Erc.* 7 (1977) p. 115 A b, 14 (Lat. Pella)

**Πελλέας**
LAKONIA:
—SPARTA: (1) 394 BC X., *HG* iv 3. 23; *REG* 99 (1986) p. 137 (name) (Poralla² 607) (Πελλῆς—X.)

**Πέλλις**
ILLYRIA:
—APOLLONIA: (1) c. 250-50 BC Maier 84 (coin) (Ceka 66) (pryt.)
S. ITALY (BRUTTIUM):
—LOKROI EPIZEPHYRIOI:
——(Λογ.): (2) iv/iii BC De Franciscis 30, 5 (s. Ἐπαίνετος)

**Πέλλιχος**
KORINTHIA:
—KORINTH: (1) m. v BC *RE* (-) (f. Ἀριστεύς)

**Πελοπίδας**
ARKADIA:
—KYNAITHA: (1) c. 230-200 BC *BCH* 45 (1921) p. 12 II, 66 (f. Ἀριστομέδα, Δαμαγίδας, Εὐατέας, Σάτυρος)

**Πέλοψ**
ELIS: (1) i/ii AD *IvOl* 429, 6-7; 430, 3 (Τιβ. Κλ. Π.: s. Τιβ. Κλ. Ἀριστέας, Ἀντ. Κλεοδίκη)
LAKONIA:
—SPARTA: (2) c. 220-207 BC D.S. xxvii 1. 1; Liv. xxxiv 32. 1 (Bradford (1)) (s. Λυκοῦργος: king); (3) ii-i BC *IG* V (1) 1113, 2 (Bradford (2)) (s. Λαοδάμας)
S. ITALY (CAMPANIA):
—DIKAIARCHIA-PUTEOLI: (4) imp. *CIL* X 3092 (Lat. T. Vestorius Pelops)
—HERCULANEUM*: (5) i BC-i AD ib. 1403 g I, 22 (Lat. L. Quintilius Pelops: freed.)
—NEAPOLIS: (6) c. 240-225 BC *IG* VII 342, 1 (*IOrop* 111); *IG* VII 505, 4 (s. Δεξίας)
—POMPEII: (7) c. 51-62 AD *CIL* IV 3340. 83, 1, 6 (Castrèn 158. 22) (Lat. M. Epidius Pelops)

**Πελωρίς**
S. ITALY (CALABRIA):
—BRENTESION-BRUNDISIUM: (1) i AD *Taras* 6 (1986) p. 125 + *Arctos* 23 (1989) p. 215 (name) (Lat. Peloris)
S. ITALY (CAMPANIA):
—DIKAIARCHIA-PUTEOLI: (2) imp. *CIL* X 2413 (Lat. Peloris: d. Fausta)

**Πέμπαιος**
ARKADIA:
—TEGEA: (1) 191-146 BC Lindgren, *AGBC* 1646; Unp. (Oxford, AM) (coins)

**Πενίχων?**
MESSENIA:
—MESSENE: (1) m. iii BC *IG* V (2) 368, 86

**Πενπύλος**
ARGOLIS:
—MYKENAI: (1) ?c. 475 BC ib. IV (1) 494; *LSAG²* p. 173 (name, date) (Περίπυλος—IG)

**Πέντακλος**
S. ITALY (BRUTTIUM):
—KROTON: (1) inc. Apostol. xvii 62; Arsen. li 51

**Πεντίας**
KORINTHIA:
—SIKYON: (1) vi/v BC *SEG* XI 244, 5

**Πεντικός**
ILLYRIA:
—APOLLONIA: (1) hell. *IApoll* 23; cf. *Le Arti* 5 (1943) p. 118 no. 4; Fraser–Rönne, *BWGT* p. 174 n. 5 (date) (f. Παρμήν); (2) ?iii BC *IApoll* 378 ([Π]εντικός: s. Ἀρίστυλλος)

**Πέπλος**
S. ITALY (CAMPANIA):
—PITHEKOUSSAI-AENARIA: (**1**) s. ii AD *CIL* x 6801; cf. *Epigraphica* 34 (1972) p. 131 (date) (Lat. L. Funisulanus Peplus)

**Περάντας**
KORINTHIA:
—KORINTH: (**1**) viii BC Paus. ii 4. 4

**Περγαμίς**
MESSENIA:
—ANDANIA*: (**1**) iii AD Peek, *AG* 2 p. 58 no. 204 (Πε[ρ]γαμίς)

**Πέργαμος**
S. ITALY (CAMPANIA):
—POMPEII: (**1**) i BC-i AD *CIL* IV 4074 (Lat. Pergamus); (**2**) ~ ib. 8906 (Lat. Pergamus)

**Περδικίας**
KYNOURIA:
—TYROS*: (**1**) vi/v BC *IG* v (1) 1520 (bronze) (Lazzarini 287)

**Περεγρῖνα**
SICILY:
—SYRACUSE: (**1**) 452 AD Strazzulla 394 (Agnello 97; Wessel 127); cf. Ferrua, *NG* 146

**Περίαλος**
S. ITALY (BRUTTIUM):
—SYBARIS-THOURIOI-COPIAE: (**1**) v/iv BC Iamb., *VP* 74 (Πέριλλος—Wilamowitz, Περίλαος—Keil)

**Περίανδρος**
AKARNANIA: (**1**) 316 BC *IG* v (2) 549, 29 (*Syll*³ 314) (f. Ἀμύνανδρος)
—ANAKTORION: (**2**) 356-354 BC *IG* IV (1)² 95, 22 (Perlman E.2); Perlman pp. 46-9 (date) (f. Ἀριστίων); (**3**) c. 330 BC *SEG* XXIII 189 I, 3
ARKADIA: (**4**) s. iv BC *Thess. Mnem.* 176 (f. Κλευγένης)
—MANTINEIA-ANTIGONEIA: (**5**) c. 425-385 BC *IG* v (2) 323. 1 (tessera) ([Π]ερίανδρο[ς]: f. Γράδων); (**6**) c. 316-222 BC *SEG* XVII 143, 3 (Perlman A.15) (f. Θεαίνετος)
EPIROS:
—AMBRAKIA: (**7**) vii/vi BC Arist. *Pol.* 1304 a 32; 1311 a 39 (D.L. i 98) (tyrant)
KORINTHIA:
—KORINTH: (**8**) vii/vi BC *RE* (1) (s. Κύψελος, Κράτεια, f. Κύψελος, Λυκόφρων, Εὐαγόρας, Γόργος, Νικόλαος: tyrant)
S. ITALY (CAMPANIA):
—POMPEII*: (**9**) i AD *CIL* x 8048. 20 (vase) (Lat. Ti. Iulius Periander)

**Περιγένης**
ACHAIA:
—PHARAI: (**1**) iii-ii BC *Achaean Grave Stelai* 44 (f. Στολίς)
ARGOLIS:
—ARGOS: (**2**) c. 100-90 BC *SEG* XXXIII 290 A, 9; *BSA* 70 (1975) pp. 129-31 (date) (Stephanis 2043) (s. Διονύσιος)
—EPIDAUROS: (**3**) 133-134 AD *IG* IV (1)² 383, 6; 384, 7 (f. Λεωνίδας)
EPIROS:
—NIKOPOLIS: (**4**) imp. *AE* 1950-1, Chron. p. 39 no. 14 (Sarikakis 132) (s. Δικαῖος)
ILLYRIA:
—EPIDAMNOS-DYRRHACHION: (**5**) c. 250-50 BC Maier 181; 266; 369 (coin) (Ceka 372-4) (money.); (**6**) hell.-imp. *IDyrrh* 216 (f. Εὔφραΐς); (**7**) ~ ib. 275 (f. Κόνων); (**8**) ~ ib. 343; (**9**) ~ ib. 344 (s. Ἐπίκαδος); (**10**) ~ ib. 345 (s. Πραΰλος); (**11**) ~ ib. 363 (f. Πραΰλος)
KORINTHIA:
—KORINTH: (**12**) ii/i BC *EAD* xxx 25; (**13**) iv-v AD *RE* (4) (bp.)

**Περάντας** / next:

LAKONIA:
—KARDAMYLE: (**14**) i AD *SEG* XI 948, 18 (s. Φιλογένης)
S. ITALY (CAMPANIA):
—POMPEII: (**15**) m. i AD *CIL* IV 4057 (Lat. Cl. Perigenes)
SICILY:
—SYRACUSE: (**16**) iii-v AD Strazzulla 186 (Wessel 875); cf. Ferrua, *NG* 22

**Περιγενίς**
ILLYRIA:
—AMANTIA: (**1**) imp. Patsch, *Sandschak Berat* p. 46 no. 1 ([Π]εριγενίς)

**Περιήρης**
S. ITALY (CAMPANIA):
—KYME: (**1**) s. viii BC Th. vi 4. 5; Call. fr. 43, 58, 76; Paus. iv 23. 7 (and Sicily Zankle-Messana: oikist)

**Περίκαλος**
ILLYRIA:
—EPIDAMNOS-DYRRHACHION: (**1**) arch. *IDyrrh* 1

**Περικλείδας**
AKARNANIA:
—PALAIROS: (**1**) iv/iii BC *IG* IX (1)² (2) 464
LAKONIA:
—SPARTA: (**2**) f. v BC Th. iv 119. 2; Ar., *Lys.* 1138; Plu., *Cim.* 16 (Poralla² 608) (f. Ἀθάναιος)

**Περικλείδης**
ARGOLIS:
—HERMIONE: (**1**) ?i AD *IG* IV (1) 690, 2 (f. Ἀριστοξένα)

**Περικλῆς**
AKARNANIA:
—ASTAKOS: (**1**) m. iii BC ib. VII 12, 7 (f. Ἱππίας)
—OINIADAI: (**2**) 263-262 BC ib. IX (1)² (1) 3 A, 25
—STRATOS: (**3**) iv/iii BC ib. IX (1)² (2) 395, 10 (f. Λέων, Φρύνων, Σίμαιθος)
ARGOLIS:
—ARGOS: (**4**) ?m. v BC ib. IV (1) 615, 3 (Περίκλε[ος] (gen.): f. —ρος)
—EPIDAUROS: (**5**) c. 340-320 BC Peek, *NIEpid* 19 C, 8 ([Π]ερικ[λ]ῆς)
ARKADIA:
—MANTINEIA-ANTIGONEIA: (**6**) ?272 BC *FD* III (1) 33, 1 (f. Κλεύκριτος)
—TEGEA:
——(Krariotai): (**7**) iii BC *IG* v (2) 40, 27 (f. Ἀριστοτέλης)
KORINTHIA:
—KORINTH: (**8**) ii/iii AD ib. VII 4152 (Stephanis 2048) (and Boiotia Thespiai: Λαβέριος Π.)
LAKONIA:
—SPARTA: (**9**) s. i BC *IG* v (1) 93, 25; 211, 41 (Bradford (5)) (f. Ἀγήμων); (**10**) c. 30-20 BC *IG* v (1) 141, 29; *SEG* XXXV 329 (date) (Bradford (2)) (Περικ[λ]ῆ[ς]); (**11**) c. 100 AD *SEG* XI 510, 6 (Bradford (6)) (I f. Περικλῆς II); (**12**) ~ *SEG* XI 510, 6 (Bradford (1)) (II s. Περικλῆς I); (**13**) c. 100-115 AD *IG* v (1) 42, 20; *SEG* XI 483; 489, 2; 540, 1; 611, 3; XXXVI 361, 34 (Bradford (3)) (Κλ. Π.); (**14**) ii AD *IG* v (1) 608, 15 (Bradford (7)); (**15**) c. 150-160 AD *IG* v (1) 69, 33; 71 III, 37; *SEG* XI 554, 6 (Bradford (4)) (Πομπ. Π.); (**16**) c. 175-200 AD *SEG* XI 503, 19 (Bradford (8)); (**17**) m. iii AD *SEG* XXXV 337, 8; *BSA* 80 (1985) pp. 225; 239-43 (ident., stemma) (Γ. Πομπώνιος Ἀριστέας ὁ καὶ Π.: s. Πομπώνιος Πανθάλης ὁ καὶ Ἀριστοκλῆς, f. Πομπωνία Καλλιστονίκη)
SICILY:
—TAUROMENION: (**18**) c. 196 BC *IG* XIV 421 an. 45 (*SGDI* 5219) (s. Ἀριστόπολις); (**19**) c. 175 BC *IG* XIV 421 an. 66 (*SGDI* 5219)

**Περίκλυτος**
ARGOLIS:
—EPIDAUROS: (**1**) ?iv-iii BC Peek, *IAEpid* 127 (Περίκλυτ[ος]); (**2**) iv/iii BC ib. 142. 2

**Περίλα**
LAKONIA:
—HIPPOLA: (**1**) ?ii-i BC *IG* v (1) 1277 b

**Περίλαος**
ARGOLIS:
—ARGOS: (**1**) arch.? Paus. ii 23. 7 (tyrant/fict.?); (**2**) m. vi BC *RE* (4) (s. Ἀλκάνωρ)
ARKADIA:
—TEGEA:
——(Hippothoitai): (**3**) m. iii BC *IG* v (2) 36, 80 (s. Σίμων)
EPIROS: (**4**) 231 BC *CPR* XVIII 6
MESSENIA: (**5**) vi BC D.L. i 116
SICILY:
—AKRAGAS: (**6**) f. vi BC *RE* (9); cf. Call. fr. 47 (Πέριλλος?: fict.?)

**Περίλας**
ARGOLIS:
—ARGOS: (**1**) ?320 BC *IG* v (2) 549, 14 (f. Λυσίλοχος) ?= (2); (**2**) ~ ib. l. 17 (f. Ἀγησίστρατος) ?= (1)
—EPIDAUROS*: (**3**) c. 340-320 BC Peek, *NIEpid* 19 C, 14 (Πε[ρ]ίλ[ας])
ARKADIA:
—TEGEA:
——(Hippothoitai): (**4**) f. iii BC *IG* v (2) 36, 20 (Π[ε]ρίλα[ς])
KORINTHIA:
—SIKYON: (**5**) 479 BC Hdt. ix 103. 1 (Skalet 261)

**Περιλιπώι**
KORINTHIA:
—KORINTH: (**1**) c. 590-570 BC Amyx 76. 4 (vase) (Lorber 65) (-πόι: her.)

**Πέριλλος**
ARGOLIS:
—ARGOS:
——Pedion: (**1**) a. 338 BC *IG* XII (3) 1259, 16; cf. *Mnem.* NS 44 (1916) pp. 61-4
—EPIDAUROS: (**2**) m. iv BC *SEG* XLI 308
KORINTHIA:
—SIKYON: (**3**) vi/v BC ib. XI 244, 36

**Περίλος**
AIGINA: (**1**) s. v BC *IG* IV (1) 1590 (f. Αἰσχύλος)
KORINTHIA:
—KORINTH: (**2**) vi BC ib. 237 a (pinax) (Lazzarini 66) ([Π]ερίλος)

**Περιμήδα**
ARKADIA:
—TEGEA: (**1**) her. *FGrH* 306 F 4 (Π. ἡ καὶ Χοίρα: queen/fict.?)

**Περιμήδης**
ARKADIA:
—TEGEA: (**1**) s. iv BC *IG* v (2) 41, 62 (Περιμή[δης])

**Περίξενος**
AKARNANIA:
—PALAIROS: (**1**) iii BC ib. IX (1)² (2) 500

**Περισθένης**
SICILY:
—AKRAGAS: (**1**) f. vi BC *FGrH* 577 F 3 (fict.?)

**Περιστέρα**
S. ITALY (APULIA):
—VENUSIA*: (**1**) i AD *Museo di Venosa* p. 209 no. 8 (Lat. Creperia Peristera: freed.)

**Περιστέριος**
SICILY:
—LILYBAION: (1) imp. *ILS* 8982; *PLRE* I s.v. Pompeianus (7) (Lat. Iul. Cl. Peristerius Pompeianus)

**Περίτας**
MESSENIA:
—MESSENE: (1) ii BC *PAE* 1969, p. 116 no. 3 (f. Λυσιμάχα)

**Πέρκαλον**
LAKONIA:
—SPARTA: (1) vi/v BC Hdt. vi 65. 2 (Poralla² 609) (Πέρκαλος—Poralla: d. Χίλων)

**Περκέννιος**
S. ITALY (BRUTTIUM):
—AGER TEURANUS: (1) iii-ii BC *IG* XIV 2402. 3; *SEG* I 420; cf. Costabile, *Ist. Bruzio* p. 94 (tiles)

**Περκλείδας**
LAKONIA:
—GERONTHRAI: (1) hell.? *IG* V (1) 1126 a (Περκλεί[δας])

**Περκλῆς**
LAKONIA:
—OITYLOS: (1) iii/ii BC ib. 1295, 6 (Bradford (-))

**Πέρκων**
S. ITALY (CALABRIA):
—TARAS-TARENTUM: (1) 213-209 BC *RE* s.v. Nikon (10) (Νίκων ὁ ἐπικαλ. Π., Lat. Perco)

**Περκωνίων**
S. ITALY (BRUTTIUM): (1) i BC *IG* XIV 2400. 13; *Mon. Ant.* 24 (1916) p. 196; *Kokalos* 32 (1986) p. 236 nos. 64-5 (tiles) (nom., n. pr.?)

**Περπέτουα**
ILLYRIA:
—EPIDAMNOS-DYRRHACHION: (1) iii-iv AD *IDyrrh* 60 (d. Ἀντίοχος, Παῦλα)
S. ITALY (CAMPANIA):
—NEAPOLIS: (2) ii AD *IG* XIV 802 (*INap* 147); cf. Leiwo p. 105 no. 66 (m. Νοουία Ἑρμιόνη)

**Πέρσας**
KERKYRA: (1) imp. *AM* 27 (1902) p. 371 no. 55 (Κλ. Π.)
SICILY:
—SYRACUSE: (2) 183 BC *FD* III (3) 240, 9, 30 (*IG* IX (1)² (1) 179) (s. Διονύσιος)

**Περσεύς**
S. ITALY (LUCANIA):
—HYELE-VELIA: (1) imp. *CIL* X 8342 a (Lat. -ius Perseus)

**Πέρσιος**
SICILY:
—THERMAI HIMERAIAI: (1) ?ii-i BC *IG* XIV 316, 1 (Dubois, *IGDS* 203) (Ἀριστόδημος Π.: s. Νεμηνίδας)

**Πέρσις**
EPIROS:
—BOUTHROTOS (PRASAIBOI): (1) a. 163 BC *IBouthrot* 158

**Περφαντώ**
LAKONIA:
—SPARTA: (1) ?ii BC *SEG* XI 677 a; cf. Masson, *OGS* 2 p. 515 (Bradford s.v. Περφαντώ (-)) (Πέρφαντος (gen.)—ed. pr., Περφαντ(ῶ)ς? (gen.)—Tod: m. —δρα)

**Περφίλα**
LAKONIA:
—SPARTA: (1) c. 1-10 AD *IG* V (1) 209, 22; *SEG* XXXV 331 (date) (Bradford (-))

**Πετάλας**
KORINTHIA:
—KORINTH: (1) f. vi BC Amyx 47 (vase) (Lorber 77); cf. *SEG* XXIX 333 (Πετάλα (masc. gen., fem. nom.?): ?f. Ἀεσχυλῖνος)

**Πετάλη**
S. ITALY (CAMPANIA):
—NEAPOLIS: (1) imp. *CIL* X 8172; cf. Leiwo p. 92 (Lat. Octavia Petale)

**Πεταλίας**
AITOLIA: (1) ?265-264 BC *FD* III (3) 202, 2; III (4) 359, [35]; *SEG* XVIII 242, 2; *CID* II 130, [2] (or Thessaly?)

**Πετάλιος**
ARKADIA:
—TEGEA: (1) f. i BC *IG* V (2) 20, 22

**Πεταλλίς?**
S. ITALY (LUCANIA):
—HERAKLEIA*: (1) iv/iii BC *SEG* XXX 1163; cf. XXXVI 914 ([Πε]ταλλίς—*SEG*, Ἀνταλλίς—ed. pr.: slave?)

**Πέταλος**
ACHAIA:
—DYME: (1) s. iii BC ib. XIII 278, 22 (f. Σώσιμος)
AITOLIA:
—KALLION/KALLIPOLIS: (2) a. 170 BC *IG* IX (1) 226, 14 ([Π]έταλος); (3) 153-144 BC *SGDI* 2279, 10
—PLEURON: (4) c. 242-213 BC *IG* IX (1)² (1) 188, 35; *Syll*³ 621; Flacelière p. 275 n. 1 (date) (f. Πανταλέων)
AITOLIA?: (5) hell. *SBBerlAk* 1936, p. 386 no. 3 a (bullet)
AKARNANIA:
—STRATOS: (6) iv/iii BC *IG* IX (1)² (2) 395, 6 (f. Σῖμος)

**Πέτηλος**
ARKADIA:
—THISOA?: (1) f. iv BC *SEG* XIV 455, 4 (?f. Ἑταίριχος)

**Πετόας**
EPIROS:
—THESPROTOI: (1) 356-354 BC *IG* IV (1)² 95, 26 (Perlman E.2); Perlman p. 40 f. (date)

**Πετραῖος**
AITOLIA: (1) ?262 BC *FD* III (4) 357, 2 (Πετρα[ῖος])
EPIROS: (2) 189 BC Plb. xxi 26. 7 (f. Σίβυρτος)
KORINTHIA:
—SIKYON: (3) c. 100-90 BC *SEG* XXXIII 290 A, 18; *BSA* 70 (1975) pp. 129-31 (date) (Stephanis 2057) (s. Μενίσκος)

**Πετρᾶς**
S. ITALY (CAMPANIA):
—MISENUM*: (1) imp. *CIL* X 3387 (Lat. M. Musidius Petra)

**Πέτρος**
ARGOLIS:
—ARGOS: (1) v-vi AD Unp. (Oikonomou-Laniado) (s. Κοσμᾶς, Βρισηΐς)
KORINTHIA:
—KORINTH: (2) byz. *Corinth* VIII (1) 153; cf. *TMByz* 9 (1985) p. 360 no. 14; (3) ~ *Corinth* VIII (3) 595 (Πέτρ[ος]); (4) v AD *SEG* XXIX 318, 1 (s. Σέργιος)
S. ITALY (BRUTTIUM):
—HIPPONION-VIBO VALENTIA: (5) byz.? *IG* XIV 2412. 36 (*ICI* V 47) (ring))

**S. ITALY (CAMPANIA):**
—SALERNUM: (6) iv AD *IItal* I (1) 168 (*CIL* X 664) (Lat. Petrus: f. Petronia)
SICILY:
—SYRACUSE: (7) iii-v AD *IG* XIV 162 (Strazzulla 103); (8) ~ ib. 262 (Agnello 21; Wessel 857); (9) ~ Strazzulla 275 (Wessel 1161); (10) ~ Strazzulla 306 (Wessel 694); (11) ?iii-v AD Strazzulla 459 (Lat. Peterus); (12) iii-v AD Ferrua, *NG* 339 a; (13) 416 AD Strazzulla 327 (Barreca 304) ([Πέ]τρος); (14) ?433 AD *IG* XIV 195 (Strazzulla 153); cf. *SEG* XXXVI 877 (date)

**Πετροσέλινος**
S. ITALY (CAMPANIA):
—POMPEII*: (1) i BC-i AD *CIL* IV 10246 c, j (Lat. Petroselinus)

**Πέτρων**
AIGINA: (1) v-iv BC *RE* s.v. Petronas (-); *Anon. Med. Lond.* XX, 2 with index p. 115; Cels. iii 9. 2 (Πετρωνᾶς, Πετρωνᾶς—Gal.: doctor)
SICILY:
—HIMERA: (2) vi BC *RE* (-); *FVS* 16

**Πετρωνία**
KORINTHIA:
—KORINTH: (1) byz. *Corinth* VIII (1) 215, 10 (-ρου-)

**Πετρώνιος**
ILLYRIA:
—EPIDAMNOS-DYRRHACHION: (1) imp. *IDyrrh* 15 (f. Σαλούϊα)
S. ITALY (BRUTTIUM):
—HIPPONION-VIBO VALENTIA: (2) imp. *IG* XIV 2412. 37 (-τρό-)
SICILY:
—KATANE: (3) iii-v AD ib. 545 (Wessel 748)

**Πευθέας**
PELOPONNESE: (1) c. 192 BC *SEG* XIII 327, 18 (f. Ἀρέας)

**Πεύκετος**
LAKONIA: (1) imp.? *Syringes* 216 (Bradford (-)) (n. pr.?: ?f. Ἀσκλαπιάδας)

**Πευκόλαος**
EPIROS:
—PHOINIKE: (1) ?iii BC *SEG* XXXII 628 (s. Εὐμένης)
ILLYRIA:
—BYLLIONES: (2) c. 200 BC ib. XXXV 680, 9; cf. XXXVIII 541 (f. Νικόλαος)
—BYLLIONES BYLLIS: (3) iii-ii BC ib. 525 ([Πε]υκόλαος)

**Πεφιλημενός**
S. ITALY (CALABRIA):
—BRENTESION-BRUNDISIUM: (1) imp. *NScav* 1892, p. 353 aa = *Epigraphica* 25 (1963) p. 88 no. 108 (Lat. Pephilemenus)

**Πήγη**
ARGOLIS:
—MYKENAI: (1) ii/i BC *IG* IV (1) 505

**Πηνειός**
LAKONIA:
—SPARTA: (1) m. ii AD ib. V (1) 71 II, 5-6 (Bradford (-)) (f. Χρυσόγονος)

**Πίακις**
SICILY:
—SELINOUS: (1) m. v BC Dubois, *IGDS* 36, 6 (Arena, *Iscr. Sic.* I 69) (Πιάκιος—Arena: f. Δίων)

**Πιερία**
S. ITALY (CALABRIA):
—TARAS-TARENTUM: (1) ii BC *IG* II² 10414 (d. Πύθων)

## Πιερίς

S. ITALY (APULIA):
—CANUSIUM*: (1) imp. *Epig. Rom. di Canosa* 128 (*CIL* IX 376) (Lat. Egnatia Pieris: freed.)
S. ITALY (CAMPANIA):
—DIKAIARCHIA-PUTEOLI: (2) imp. ib. X 2666 (Lat. Pieris); (3) ~ ib. 3005 (Lat. Cosmia Pieris)
—POMPEII: (4) i BC-i AD ib. IV 5338 (Lat. Pieris)
S. ITALY (LUCANIA):
—VOLCEI: (5) imp. *IItal* III (1) 63 (*CIL* X 393) (Lat. Manilia Pieris: m. Πίερος, Silvina)

## Πίερος

S. ITALY (CAMPANIA):
—HERCULANEUM*: (1) i BC-i AD ib. 1403 g III, 47 (Lat. M. Calatorius Pierus: freed.)
—POMPEII: (2) i BC-i AD ib. IV 1901 (Castrèn 306. 1) (Lat. M. Pileus Pierus) ?= (3); (3) ~ *CIL* IV 2078; 2103; 2310 d; 2366; 2452; 3108; 3357; 3883; 4577; 7061; 7062; 7063; 8923; 8928 (Lat. Pierus) ?= (2); (4) ~ ib. 3921 (Castrèn 114. 3) (Lat. Cipius Pier(us))
S. ITALY (CAMPANIA)*: (5) i AD *CIL* X 8048. 22; *RAAN* 33 (1958) p. 295 no. 734 (vases) (Lat. L. Marcius Pierus)
S. ITALY (LUCANIA):
—VOLCEI: (6) imp. *IItal* III (1) 63 (*CIL* X 393) (Lat. Pierus: s. Πιερίς)

## Πιθάκα

KEPHALLENIA: (1) ?f. iv BC *Op. Ath.* 10 (1971) p. 75 n. 59 b + *REG* 85 (1972) p. 75 f.
LEUKAS: (2) m. iv BC *AD* 26 (1971) Chron. p. 354

## Πίθακος

AITOLIA:
—LITHOVOUNI (MOD.) (AKRAI?): (1) v/iv BC *SEG* XXXIV 466 (vase)
AKARNANIA:
—STRATOS: (2) f. iii BC *IG* IX (1)² (2) 391, 10
ILLYRIA:
—EPIDAMNOS-DYRRHACHION: (3) hell.-imp. *IDyrrh* 7 (f. Φιλόστρατος)
SICILY:
—SELINOUS: (4) s. vi BC Arena, *Iscr. Sic.* I 57 (vase) (Dubois, *IGDS* 81) (-ϙος); (5) vi/v BC Manganaro, *PdelP* forthcoming no. 18, 1 (Πίθα[κος])
—SELINOUS?: (6) vi/v BC *SEG* XXXIX 1020 A, 6 (-ϙος: s. Λ—)

## Πιθάνα

EPIROS:
—AMBRAKIA: (1) iii BC *BCH* 17 (1893) p. 633 (d. Μενοίτιος)

## Πιθάνη

S. ITALY (CALABRIA):
—BRENTESION-BRUNDISIUM: (1) imp. *CIL* IX 164 (Lat. Pithane)
S. ITALY (CAMPANIA):
—POMPEII: (2) i BC-i AD ib. IV 4439 (Lat. Pitane)
SICILY:
—TAUROMENION: (3) iii-v AD *IG* XIV 161 (Strazzulla 102); Ferrua, *NG* 479 (locn.) (Πει-)

## Πιθειός

ILLYRIA:
—EPIDAMNOS-DYRRHACHION (NR.)?: (1) ii BC *SEG* XXXVIII 572, 9; cf. *CRAI* 1991, p. 197 ff.; *L'Illyrie mérid.* 2 p. 206 (f. Τρίτος)

## Πιθθίας

SICILY:
—SELINOUS: (1) m. v BC Dubois, *IGDS* 36, 6 (Arena, *Iscr. Sic.* I 69)

## Πίθων

ELIS:
—OLYMPIA*: (1) v/iv BC *IvOl* 157 (Ebert, *Gr. Sieg.* 29); cf. Moretti, *Olymp.* 361 (f. —κράτης)
SICILY:
—CASTEL DI IUDICA (MOD.): (2) ?iii BC Manganaro, *PdelP* forthcoming no. 6, 1
—SELINOUS: (3) m. v BC Dubois, *IGDS* 34 (Arena, *Iscr. Sic.* I 70) (-ōν)

## Πίμφαλος

TRIPHYLIA:
—TYPANEAI: (1) c. 230-200 BC *BCH* 45 (1921) p. 12 II, 78 + *AJPh* 101 (1980) p. 320 (s. Σάκυλλος)

## Πίμφις

AKARNANIA:
—KORONTA: (1) 356-354 BC *IG* IV (1)² 95, 12 (Perlman E.2); Perlman p. 40 f. (date)

## Πίμφων

AKARNANIA:
—THYRREION: (1) ii BC *IG* IX (1)² (2) 250, 3 (f. Νικόμαχος); (2) ~ ib. l. 15 (s. Νικόμαχος)
LEUKAS: (3) ?256 BC *SGDI* 2659, 3 (*ZPE* 101 (1994) pp. 223 f.) (s. Τίμων)

## Πίννης

ILLYRIA:
—ARDIAIOI: (1) s. iii BC *RE* (1) (s. Ἄγρων, Τρίτευτα (Illyria): king)

## Πῖος

ARKADIA:
—MANTINEIA-ANTIGONEIA: (1) i/ii AD *IG* V (2) 287 (Πεῖ-: f. Ἱερώνυμος)
S. ITALY (CAMPANIA):
—DIKAIARCHIA-PUTEOLI: (2) imp. ib. XIV 851 (Πεῖ-)

## Πῖπα

SICILY:
—SYRACUSE: (1) f. i BC Cic., *In Verr.* II iii 77-8; *In Verr.* II v 81 (Lat. Pipa)

## Πίρειθος

KORINTHIA:
—KORINTH: (1) imp. *SEG* XXVII 36, 12 (lamp)

## Πισανός

ELIS: (1) 17-50 AD *IvOl* 221, 4; 426, 1 (*M. Ἀντ. Πεισανός*—221: f. *M. Ἀντ. Ἀλεξίων*); (2) m. i AD Moretti, *Olymp.* 782 (*Κάλλιππος Πεισανός*: s. *Κλ. Κλεοδίκη*) ?= (3); (3) i/ii AD *IvOl* 283, 4 (*Πεισ[ανός]*: f. *Γ. Ἀντ. Ἀλεξίων*) ?= (2)

## Πισθυῖος

KORINTHIA:
—SIKYON: (1) f. v BC *SEG* XI 259 (Πίσθυῖ[ος])

## Πίστα

ARGOLIS:
—ARGOS*: (1) iii BC *IG* IV (1) 528, 4 (slave/freed.?); (2) f. iii BC ib. 529, 13 (slave/freed.?)
—HERMIONE: (3) i BC-i AD? ib. 734, 4 (d. Διονυσία)

## Πισταγόρας

ARKADIA: (1) 312 BC ib. V (2) 549, 39 (s. Δαΐλοχος)

## Πιστάρα

SICILY:
—SYRACUSE (NESOS): (1) iii-v AD *SEG* IV 18 (Wessel 3)

## Πιστέας

AITOLIA:
—KALLION/KALLIPOLIS: (1) c. 20-45 AD *FD* III (6) 13, 53; cf. *BCH* 63 (1939) p. 173 (name) (f. Λέων: reading—Mulliez)

## Πίστη

S. ITALY (CAMPANIA):
—BAIAI: (1) imp. *NScav* 1897, p. 12 (Lat. Caecilia Piste)

## Πιστιανός

SICILY:
—KENTORIPA: (1) i-ii AD *CIL* X 7006 (*ILat. Palermo* 5) (Lat. M. Avianius Pistianus: f. Εὐτυχιανός)

## Πιστίας

ACHAIA:
—DYME: (1) iii BC *AJPh* 31 (1910) p. 399 no. 74 a, 9 (f. Λεωνίδας); (2) ~ ib. p. 399 no. 74 b, 3 (s. Φίντων)

## Πιστική

S. ITALY (LUCANIA):
—POTENTIA: (1) i AD *ZPE* 106 (1995) p. 289 no. 8 (Lat. Seia Pistica: m. Campuleia Caesonia)

## Πίστις

EPIROS:
—AMBRAKIA: (1) inc. Hammond, *Epirus* index
ILLYRIA:
—APOLLONIA: (2) imp. *IApoll* 212 (Κλαυδία Π.)
S. ITALY (CAMPANIA):
—DIKAIARCHIA-PUTEOLI: (3) imp. *CIL* X 2486 (Lat. Grania Pistis)
—SURRENTUM*: (4) imp. ib. 747 (Lat. Pistis: freed.)
SICILY:
—ZANKLE-MESSANA: (5) imp. *Epigraphica* 3 (1941) p. 256 no. 8 (Lat. Didia Pistis)

## Πιστόδαμος

ARKADIA:
—MT. KYLLENE*: (1) ?iv-iii BC *IG* V (2) 366 (Πιστόδαμ[ος])

## Πιστοκλῆς

ARKADIA:
—TEGEA:
——(Krariotai): (1) f. iii BC ib. 36, 44 (s. Φιλλίας: metic)

## Πιστοκράτης

ELIS: (1) iv BC Paus. vi 24. 5 (?f. Πύρρων)

## Πιστόλαος

KORINTHIA:
—KORINTH: (1) s. iii BC *IG* VII 513, 4; *Horos* 2 (1984) p. 119 f. (date) (s. Δαμάτριος)

## Πιστόξενος

ARKADIA:
—MANTINEIA-ANTIGONEIA:
——(Vanakisia): (1) m. iv BC *IG* V (2) 271, 20 (f. Εὐχαρίδας)
ILLYRIA:
—EPIDAMNOS-DYRRHACHION: (2) c. 250-50 BC Ceka, *Probleme* p. 152 no. 58 (coin) (pryt.) ?= (3); (3) ~ Maier 490; Münsterberg Nachtr. p. 16 (coin) (Ceka 313; 316; 326) (pryt.) ?= (2); (4) ii-i BC *IDyrrh* 554 (tile) (Πισ[τόξενος?]); (5) hell.-imp. ib. 346 (s. Ἐπιγένης)

## Πίστος

ELIS: (1) 197-201 AD *IvOl* 106, 4
ILLYRIA:
—APOLLONIA: (2) imp. *IApoll* 143 (s. Σελήνιον)
KERKYRA?: (3) i BC-i AD *IG* IX (1) 925
KORINTHIA:
—SIKYON: (4) i BC-i AD? Unp. (Sikyon Mus.)
LAKONIA:
—SPARTA: (5) s. i BC *IG* V (1) 133, 4 (Bradford (4)) (f. Σωκλείδας); (6) c. 125 AD *IG* V (1) 1314, 13 (Bradford (2)) (s. Κόλαξ); (7) c. 140-160 AD *IG* V (1) 154, 4 (Bradford (1)) (s. Βαθύλος); (8) 197 or 198 AD *IG* V (1) 448, 12 (Bradford (3)) (s. Φιλονικίδας)

S. Italy (Apulia):
—canusium: (9) imp. *Epig. Rom. di Canosa* 138 (Lat. C. Galbius Pistus)
S. Italy (Calabria):
—brentesion-brundisium: (10) imp. *CIL* ix 131 (Lat. Iulius Pistus); (11) ~ *NScav* 1892, p. 171 = *Epigraphica* 25 (1963) p. 38 no. 11; cf. *Scritti Degrassi* 3 p. 67 (Lat. T. Clodius Pistus)
S. Italy (Campania):
—dikaiarchia-puteoli: (12) imp. *NScav* 1897, p. 531 (Audollent, *Defix. Tab.* 204 (terracotta)); (13) 187 AD *CIL* x 1784 (Lat. Calp. Pistus)
—salernum*: (14) 117-137 AD *IItal* I (1) 191 (*CIL* x 549) (Lat. Pistus: imp. freed.)
S. Italy (Lucania):
—hyele-velia: (15) iii-v AD *IG* xiv 657 (Wessel 352) (f. Σίμων)
Sicily:
—syracuse: (16) iii-v AD ib. 714 + Ferrua, *NG* 79

**Πίστων**
Argolis:
—argos: (1) f. i BC Unp. (Ch. Kritzas) (s. Ἀριστόμαχος)
Sicily:
—halountion: (2) iii/ii BC *Arch. Class.* 17 (1965) p. 202; cf. *SEG* xxvi 1060
—segesta: (3) iv/iii BC ib. xxx 1119, 7 (Dubois, *IGDS* 206) (f. Ἀττικός)

**Πίσων**
Argolis:
—kalauria: (1) v/iv BC *RE* (-) (sculptor)

**Πίτα**
Illyria:
—epidamnos-dyrrhachion: (1) imp. *IDyrrh* 347

**Πιτθις**
Kephallenia:
—pale: (1) f. iii BC *BCH* 68-9 (1944-5) p. 121 no. 32, 2 ([Π]ιτθις)

**Πιτθώ**
Elis:
—olympia*: (1) ?c. 475-450 BC *IvOl* 12, 5 (*DGE* 416); *LSAG*² p. 220 no. 13 (date) (-θό: d. Ἀγεδᾶς)

**Πίτθων**
Elis: (1) m. iii BC *IG* v (2) 368, 58 (Πίτθω[ν]: f. Θεόδωρος)

**Πίτος**
Epiros:
—kodrion: (1) iii-ii BC *Iliria* 1972, p. 38 (pithos)

**Πιττίας**
Aitolia: (1) 290-280 BC *FD* iii (1) 150, 1 (s. Βαβύρτας)

**Πίττων**
Arkadia:
—mantineia-antigoneia: (1) iii-ii BC *IG* v (2) 319, 30 (Πίττων)

**Πιτύας**
Aigina: (1) hell.? ib. iv (1) 148
Lakonia:
—sparta: (2) 423 BC X., *HG* ii 3. 10 (Poralla² 610) ?= (3); (3) 406 BC X., *HG* i 6. 1 (Poralla² 610) ?= (2)

**Πιτύλος**
Argolis:
—argos: (1) i AD *IG* ii² 8366 (f. Ἐρωτίς)

Arkadia:
—mantineia-antigoneia: (2) ?15-16 AD ib. v (2) 274, 9, 21 (s. Ποσείδιππος)
Kerkyra: (3) i BC-i AD ib. ix (1) 938

**Πίτων**
Argolis:
—argos: (1) f. i BC Unp. (Ch. Kritzas) (f. Φιλιστίδας)

**Πλαγγών**
Aigina: (1) iv BC *Ag.* xvii 519, 8 (d. Λακλείδας)
Elis: (2) inc. Polem. fr. 64
Lakonia: (3) c. 350-320 BC *SEG* xii 193, 1, 4 (*CEG* ii 587; *GVI* 1820; Poralla² 610a) (d. Πρόμαχος: date—M.J.O.)

**Πλαδωμενός**
Illyria:
—epidamnos-dyrrhachion: (1) hell.-imp. *BUST* 1962 (2), p. 132 (*Stud. Alb.* 1965, p. 98) (Lat. Pladomenus)

**Πλαθώ**
S. Italy (Calabria):
—brentesion-brundisium: (1) iii BC *IG* ii² 8433

**Πλάθων**
Aigina: (1) c. 470 BC *SEG* iii 310 (bronze) (Guarducci, *Ep. Gr.* 1 pp. 198-9 no. 3; Lazzarini 56); *LSAG*² p. 113 no. 16 (date) (-θōν, Πλάτων—Lazzarini per err.: s. Προκλῆς)

**Πλαῖος**
Illyria:
—apollonia: (1) imp. *IApoll* 264 (s. Ἄψφος, f. Σεκούνδα)
—epidamnos-dyrrhachion: (2) hell.-imp. *IDyrrh* 348 (s. Τρίτος)

**Πλακίτας**
Sicily:
—selinous: (1) f. v BC Dubois, *IGDS* 38, 10 (Arena, *Iscr. Sic.* I 63) (s. Νανελαῖος)

**Πλάκιτος**
Sicily:
—syracuse: (1) iii-v AD *SEG* iv 20 (Wessel 364) (-κει-)

**Πλάνων**
S. Italy (Lucania): (1) v/iv BC *LCS* p. 68 no. 341 (vase) (-νōν, Γλάνον—ed.)

**Πλαρίας**
S. Italy (Calabria):
—hyria?: (1) c. 293-168 BC *Polemon* 4 (1949-50) p. 163 no. 300; cf. *SEG* xxxiii 455; *Synedrio Archaia Thessalia* pl. 79 e (f. Δάζος)

**Πλάσος**
S. Italy (Lucania):
—poseidonia-paestum: (1) iv BC *St. Etr.* 49 (1981) p. 343 no. 6 (*Atti Conv. Taranto* 13 (1973) pp. 364-5) (Γλάσος—ed.)

**Πλάστη**
Lakonia:
—tainaron-kainepolis: (1) imp. *IG* v (1) 1270

**Πλάτανος**
S. Italy (Campania):
—pompeii: (1) i BC-i AD *CIL* iv 2508, 15 (Lat. Platanus)

**Πλάτη**
S. Italy (Campania):
—dikaiarchia-puteoli*: (1) ?i-ii AD ib. x 1953 (Lat. Iulia Plate: freed.?)

**Πλάτθις**
Aigina: (1) 401 BC *IG* ii² 1386, 9; 1388, 39

**Πλατίας**
Arkadia:
—tegea: (1) m. iv BC ib. v (2) 6, 57, 85 (Πλατίας)

**Πλάτιος**
S. Italy (Bruttium):
—lokroi epizephyrioi:
——(Ἀνα.): (1) iv/iii BC De Franciscis 19, 4 (f. Εὐφραίνετος)

**Πλατούρα**
Illyria:
—epidamnos-dyrrhachion: (1) hell.-imp. *IDyrrh* 349; (2) ~ ib. 350; (3) ~ ib. 351; (4) ~ ib. 352 (d. Πλάτωρ)

**Πλατούριος**
Illyria:
—epidamnos-dyrrhachion (nr.)?: (1) ii BC *SEG* xxxviii 572, 8; cf. *CRAI* 1991, p. 197 ff.; *L'Illyrie mérid.* 2 p. 206 (f. Μέδεστις)

**Πλάτωρ**
Illyria:
—alinioi: (1) c. 215-200 BC *SEG* xv 273, 6 (*IOrop* 135); *AE* 1967, Chron. p. 9 no. 4 (locn.); cf. *L'Illyrie mérid.* 2 p. 165 (s. Δάζος)
S. Italy (Apulia):
—rubi: (2) hell.? *RA* 1932 (1), p. 40 no. 35 (loomweight) (*Bull. Mus. Hongr.* 53 (1979) pp. 30-1); cf. *SEG* xxx 1222 (name) (Fυναδεύς Π.)
S. Italy (Lucania):
—montescaglioso (mod.): (3) c. 375-350 BC *NScav* 1988-9, p. 340 no. 3 and fig. 45 (vase) (Πλάτυ(ρ)?—*LGPN*)

**Πλάτων**
Argolis:
—epidauros: (1) i-ii AD Peek, *NIEpid* 49, 2 (I f. Πλάτων II); (2) ~ ib. l. 2 (II s. Πλάτων I)
Epiros:
—dodona*: (3) ?iv BC *BCH* 80 (1956) p. 303 (s. Στέφανος)
Illyria:
—epidamnos-dyrrhachion: (4) c. 210-172 BC *IDyrrh* 517 (s. Γραῖος)
—skampis: (5) imp. *BUST* 1961 (1), p. 123 no. 23 (Lat. Plato)
S. Italy (Bruttium):
—lokroi epizephyrioi:
——(Δυσ.): (6) iv/iii BC De Franciscis 8, 4; 31, 4 (f. Χαιρεσίλας)
——(Ψαθ.): (7) iv/iii BC ib. 15, 6 (f. Εὔφρων)
—sybaris-thourioi-copiae: (8) f. i AD *NScav* 1970, Suppl. 3 p. 551 (Lat. C. Iulius Plato)
S. Italy (Calabria):
—brentesion-brundisium: (9) imp. ib. 1882, p. 423 b (Lat. -ius Plato)
Sicily:
—apollonia: (10) hell. *Mon. Ant.* 20 (1910) pp. 29-30 (vase) (*Ausonia* 8 (1913) p. 27; *Arch. Class.* 10 (1958) p. 223) (Πλάτω(ρ)?: potter)

**Πλάτωρ**
Dalmatia:
—solentia: (1) imp. Šašel, *IL* 2942 (Lat. Plator)
Epiros:
—ambrakia: (2) ii-i BC *CIG* 1800 + Leake, *Northern Greece* 4 plate xxxv no. 170, 25 (f. Διονύσιος)
Illyria: (3) 220 BC Plb. iv 55. 2; cf. *RE* (1) ?= (25); (4) f. ii BC Plb. xxix 13. 2; Liv. xliv 30. 2-3 (Πλευρᾶτος—Ath. [Plb.]: s. Πλευρᾶτος, Εὐρυδίκα)
—apollonia: (5) ii-i BC *IApoll* 159 (f. Τρίτος); (6) hell.-imp. ib. 65 (f. Γέτος)
—dimale: (7) c. 240-230 BC *IG* vii 282, 1-2 (*IOrop* 51) (s. Ἐπίκαδος)

—EPIDAMNOS-DYRRHACHION: (8) ii-i BC
*IDyrrh* 276 (f. Κορέτα); (9) hell.-imp. ib.
256 (f. Γενθήνα); (10) ~ ib. 352 (f. Πλατούρα);
(11) ~ ib. 353 (s. Ἐπίκαδος); (12) ~ ib. 354 (s.
Κέρδων); (13) ~ ib. 355 (s. Κλέβετος); (14) ~ ib.
356 (s. Παρμενίσκος); (15) ~ ib. 357 (Πλάτ[ωρ],
Πλατ[ούρα]?: s./d. Φαλακρίων); (16) ~ ib. 375
(f. Στρατονίκα); (17) ~ ib. 429 (f. Φίλα); (18)
imp. ib. 229 (f. Ζώπυρος)
—EPIDAMNOS-DYRRHACHION (NR.)?: (19) ii BC
*SEG* XXXVIII 572, 7; cf. *CRAI* 1991, p. 197
ff.; *L'Illyrie mérid.* 2 p. 206 (s. Σαλλήν)
—KORCA (MOD.): (20) hell. *Iliria* 1972, p. 18;
*SEG* XXXIII 487 (pithoi)
—LYCHNIDOS: (21) ii-iii AD *Sp.* 71 (1931) p.
110 no. 266 (*SEG* XXXIX 603) (f. Ἀννία)
—POGRADEC (MOD.): (22) imp. *Stud. Alb.* 1969
(2), p. 170 (1972 (1), p. 84) (f. Γενθιανός)
—SKAMPIS: (23) imp. Praschniker–Schober p.
58 no. 68 (Sestieri, *ILat. Albania* 89) (Lat.
M. Licinius Plator: freed.)
ILLYRIA?:
—THRINKA: (24) iii/ii BC *Philolakon* p. 239, 2;
p. 243 (locn.) (and Lakonia Sparta?: s. Σακό-
λας) (25) 207 BC Liv. xxviii 6. 1, 4, 7; 7. 1; cf.
*RE* (1) (Lat. Plator) ?= (3); (26) 163-159 BC
*PP* 15597; cf. Robert, *Noms indigènes* p. 414
S. ITALY: (27) 174 BC *SGDI* 1800, 2, 4-6
(slave/freed.)
S. ITALY (APULIA): (28) iv/iii BC Pagenstecher,
*Calen. Reliefkeramik* p. 120

**Πλατωρία**
ILLYRIA:
—POGRADEC (MOD.): (1) imp. *Iliria* 1976, p.
349 with pl. 17

**Πλειάς**
S. ITALY (APULIA):
—VENUSIA: (1) imp. *CIL* IX 587 (Lat. Titiolaeia
Plias: m. Ἰσιάς)

**Πλείσταινος**
AITOLIA: (1) iii BC *RE* (2); *BCH* 64-5 (1940-
1) p. 65 no. 4, 1; p. 66; Paus. vi 16. 1
([Πλε]ίσταινος—*BCH*: s. Εὐρύδαμος, f. —ονία);
(2) ?269 BC *SGDI* 2595, 2 (s. Ῥυσιάδας)
—KALLION/KALLIPOLIS: (3) 194 BC ib. 2075, 7;
(4) ?165 BC ib. 1818, 5; (5) ?153-144 BC ib.
2279, 2 (f. Λάδικος)
—PHOLANTIOI: (6) 263 BC *IG* IX (1)² (1) 17, 27
ELIS: (7) ?c. 450-425 BC *IvOl* 16, [2], 10, [16],
22; *LSAG*² p. 220 no. 17 (date); (8) iv BC
D.L. ii 105; *RE* (3)

**Πλειστάρχεια**
MESSENIA:
—MESSENE: (1) 31 BC-14 AD *SEG* XXIII 207, 27
(-χια: m. Διονύσιος)

**Πλείσταρχος**
ELIS: (1) iv BC D.L. ix 61 (?f. Πύρρων, Φιλίστα)
LAKONIA:
—SPARTA: (2) c. 485-458 BC *RE* (1) (Poralla²
611) (s. Λεωνίδας, Γοργώ: king)

**Πλειστέας**
ACHAIA:
—AIGEIRA?: (1) c. 252-248 BC *FD* III (4) 419, 1
(s. Πραξίων)
ARKADIA:
—PHENEOS: (2) c. 230-200 BC *BCH* 45 (1921) p.
13 II, 119 (Πλεισ[τ]έ[ας]—Oulhen: f. Φίλαιος)
—TEGEA: (3) m. iv BC *IG* V (2) 6, 87
([Πλ]ειστέας)

**Πλειστίας**
ARGOLIS:
—ARGOS: (1) hell.? *SEG* XXXV 169 A, 2
(Πλειστ[ί]ας: f. Ἀριστονίκα)

ARKADIA:
—MANTINEIA-ANTIGONEIA: (2) c. 300-221 BC
*IG* V (2) 323. 88 (tessera) (f. Αἰσχύλος)
—TEGEA: (3) f. iii BC ib. 35, 51 (s. Φιλόμβροτος)
—THELPHOUSA: (4) ii-i BC ib. 411 (Πλειστ[ίας]:
f. Χέλις)
KORINTHIA:
—SIKYON: (5) vi/v BC *SEG* XI 244, 34
LAKONIA:
—SPARTA: (6) ?c. 500-475 BC *IG* XII (9) 286
(*CEG* I 77; *GVI* 862; *Gr. Gr.* 37); *LSAG*² p.
88 no. 17 (date) (Poralla² 612)
MESSENIA:
—THOURIA: (7) f. ii BC *SEG* XI 972, 100 (s.
Καλλικράτης)

**Πλειστιάς**
ACHAIA:
—DYME: (1) iii BC *AJPh* 31 (1910) p. 399 no.
74 a, 4 (d. Ἀλεξίμαχος, m. Ἄλκα)

**Πλειστίερος**
ARKADIA:
—MEGALOPOLIS: (1) 369-361 BC *IG* V (2) 1, 30;
Tod, *GHI* II 132 (date)

**Πλειστοάναξ**
LAKONIA:
—SPARTA: (1) c. 475-408 BC *RE* (-) (Poralla²
613) (s. Παυσανίας, f. Παυσανίας: king)

**Πλειστόλας**
LAKONIA:
—SPARTA: (1) 422-421 BC Th. v 19. 1; 24. 1;
25. 1; X., *HG* ii 3. 10 (Poralla² 614)

**Πλειστόνικος**
MESSENIA:
—MESSENE: (1) f. iii BC *PAE* 1991, p. 99 no. 7,
6

**Πλειστόξενος**
LAKONIA:
—SPARTA: (1) c. 100-135 AD *IG* V (1) 79, 16;
485, 3; *SEG* XI 565, 3; XXXI 340, 4 (Bradford
(1); (2)) (Πρατόνικος—*SEG* XI per err. lap.: s.
Τιβ. Κλ. Ἁρμόνικος, f. Τιβ. Κλ. Ἁρμόνικος)

**Πλειστώ**
MESSENIA:
—PHARAI: (1) ii BC *IG* V (1) 1366 (-στοῖ (voc.))
S. ITALY (CALABRIA):
—TARAS-TARENTUM: (2) hell.? ib. XIV 2406. 66
(*RA* 1932 (1), p. 40 no. 36 (loomweight))
(Πλι-)

**Πλειστώι**
S. ITALY (CALABRIA):
—TARAS-TARENTUM: (1) iv/iii BC *IG* XIV 668
II, 20 (Landi, *DISMG* 194)

**Πλειστῶναξ**
ARKADIA:
—TEUTHIS: (1) hell.? *IG* V (2) 502

**Πλέκουσα**
S. ITALY (APULIA):
—VIBINUM*: (1) imp. *CIL* IX 6252 (Lat.
Octavia Plecusa: freed.)

**Πλευρᾶτος**
ILLYRIA: (1) c. 345 BC Did., *in D.* 12, 65-6
(Πλευρίας—Diod. xvi 93. 6); (2) iii/ii BC *RE*
(2) (s. Σκερδιλαΐδας, f. Γένθιος, Πλάτωρ: king
II); (3) ii BC ib. (5); (4) 168 BC ib. (4) (s.
Γένθιος, Ἔτλευνα)
—ARDIAIOI: (5) f. iii BC ib. (1) (f. Ἄγρων, ?f.
Σκερδιλαΐδας: king I)

**Πληροῦσα**
S. ITALY (CAMPANIA):
—POMPEII: (1) i BC-i AD *CIL* IV 7749 (Lat.
Plerousa)

**Πλήσμων**
ARGOLIS:
—EPIDAUROS: (1) 212-217 AD *IG* IV (1)² 610,
[6]; 611, 4 (Αὐρ. Π.)

**Πλήσταρχος**
ARKADIA:
—TEGEA: (1) iv/iii BC ib. V (2) 32, 5
([Π]λήσταρχος)

**Πληστιάδας**
LAKONIA:
—SELLASIA*: (1) c. 525 BC ib. V (1) 919 (*CEG*
I 373; Lazzarini 722); *LSAG*² p. 200 no.
24 (date) (Poralla² 615) (Πλε̄-, Πλειστιάδας—
Roehl)

**Πληστίερος**
ARKADIA:
—TEGEA: (1) iv/iii BC *IG* V (2) 32, 11

**Πληστονίκα**
LAKONIA:
—SPARTA: (1) hell.? ib. V (1) 800 (Bradford (-))
(-νεί-: d. Δαμόστρατος)

**Πλοκαμία**
S. ITALY (CAMPANIA):
—DIKAIARCHIA-PUTEOLI: (1) imp. *CIL* X 2755
(Lat. Munia Plocamia)

**Πλοκαμίς**
S. ITALY (CALABRIA):
—BRENTESION-BRUNDISIUM: (1) imp. *NScav*
1892, p. 243 = *Epigraphica* 25 (1963) p. 41
no. 14; p. 92 no. 122; p. 94 no. 129 (Lat.
Pomponia Plocamis)

**Πλοκαμίων**
S. ITALY (CALABRIA):
—BRENTESION-BRUNDISIUM: (1) imp. *NScav*
1892, p. 243 = *Epigraphica* 25 (1963) p. 41
no. 14; p. 92 no. 122; p. 94 no. 129 (Lat. Cn.
Pomponius Plocamio)

**Πλόκαμος**
ARKADIA:
—TEGEA: (1) ?i AD *IG* V (2) 213 ([Π]λόκαμος);
(2) 78 AD ib. 49, 7 (f. Σωτηρίων); (3) m. ii
AD ib. 48, 4 (Πλόκ[αμος]); (4) 165 AD ib. 50,
75 (s. Μουσαῖος); (5) iii AD ib. 152 (f. Π. Αἴλ.
Λεωνίδης)
EPIROS:
—NIKOPOLIS: (6) imp. *SEG* XXXIX 534 (s. Ἑρ-
μεία)
LAKONIA:
—HYPERTELEATON*: (7) imp. *IG* V (1) 1036
—LEUKTRA: (8) hell.-imp. ib. 1330 a
S. ITALY (APULIA):
—CANUSIUM*: (9) ii AD *Epig. Rom. di Canosa*
Add. 21 (Lat. A. Dastidius Plocamus: freed.)
S. ITALY (CAMPANIA):
—DIKAIARCHIA-PUTEOLI: (10) imp. *CIL* X
2389 = *ZPE* 71 (1988) p. 195 no. 3 (Lat.
Plocamus); (11) s. ii AD *Puteoli* 6 (1982) p.
153 no. 7 (Lat. Plocamus: f. Τόπυρος)
—HERCULANEUM: (12) i BC-i AD *CIL* IV 10545
(Lat. P(l)ocamus)
—HERCULANEUM*: (13) m. i AD ib. X 1403 g
III, 20 (Lat. [P]lo[c]amus: freed.)
—POMPEII: (14) i BC-i AD ib. IV 10093 a (Lat.
Proc[a]mus); (15) ?i AD *NScav* 1894, p. 383
(Lat. Plocamus: f. Τόπυρος); (16) ~ *Atti Acc.
Pontan.* 39 (1990) p. 287 no. 55 (Lat. L.
Melissaeus Plocamus) ?= (17)
—POMPEII*: (17) 39-40 AD *CIL* X 827 (Castrèn
246. 17) (Lat. L. Melissaeus Plocamus:
freed.) ?= (16)
—SURRENTUM: (18) imp. *St. Rom.* 2 (1914) p.
346 no. 1 = *NScav* 1928, p. 210 no. 18 (Lat.
Plocamus: I f. Πλόκαμος II); (19) ~ *St. Rom.*
2 (1914) p. 346 no. 1 = *NScav* 1928, p. 210
no. 18 (Lat. Plocamus: II s. Πλόκαμος I); (20)
~ *St. Rom.* 2 (1914) p. 346 no. 7 = *NScav*
1928, p. 207 no. 1 (Lat. Plocamus); (21) ~ *St.*

*Rom.* 2 (1914) p. 346 no. 9 = *NScav* 1928, p. 211 no. 19 (Lat. Plocamus: f. Ἵλαρος)

**Πλόκη**
S. ITALY (CAMPANIA):
—POMPEII: (**1**) i BC-i AD *CIL* IV 4784-5 (Lat. Ploce)

**Πλουσία**
S. ITALY (APULIA):
—CANUSIUM*: (**1**) i AD *Epig. Rom. di Canosa* 70 (Lat. Mettia Plusia: freed.)
S. ITALY (CAMPANIA):
—MISENUM*: (**2**) ?i-ii AD *CIL* X 3357 (Lat. Iulia Plusia: freed.)

**Πλούταρχος**
AIGINA: (**1**) 103 BC *IG* II² 1335, 48

**Πλουτίας**
ARGOLIS:
—EPIDAUROS: (**1**) ?iii BC Peek, *NIEpid* 120 ([Π]λουτίας)

**Πλουτίχα**
S. ITALY (BRUTTIUM):
—LOKROI EPIZEPHYRIOI: (**1**) i BC-i AD *NS* 604 (m. Δημώ (Zankle-Messana))

**Πλουτίων**
LAKONIA:
—HYPERTELEATON*: (**1**) imp. *IG* V (1) 1058 ([Πλ]ουτίων)

**Πλουτογένεια**
S. ITALY (CAMPANIA):
—NEAPOLIS: (**1**) s. ii AD ib. XIV 756 a, 2 (*INap* 34); cf. Leiwo p. 142 no. 118 (Κομινία Π.: m. Πάκκιος Καληδιανός)

**Πλοῦτος**
LAKONIA:
—SPARTA: (**1**) 359 BC *CID* II 5 I, 16 (Π[λοῦ]τος?); (**2**) c. 25-1 BC *IG* V (1) 212, 58 (Bradford (-)) (freed.)
S. ITALY (CAMPANIA):
—POMPEII: (**3**) 46 BC *CIL* I² 777, 16 (IV 60; Castrèn 296. 3) (Lat. M. [Tit]ius Plutus)

**Πλούτων**
ARGOLIS:
—EPIDAUROS: (**1**) iii AD *SEG* XXX 399

**Πλώτιος**
KORINTHIA:
—KORINTH: (**1**) i AD *Corinth* X 138; cf. *SEG* XI 219 b

**Ποδάνεμος**
ARGOLIS:
—PHLEIOUS: (**1**) v BC X., *HG* V 3. 13
LAKONIA:
—SPARTA: (**2**) 394 BC ib. iv 8. 10 (Poralla² 616)

**Ποδάρης**
ARKADIA:
—MANTINEIA-ANTIGONEIA: (**1**) 362 BC Paus. viii 9. 9-10; (**2**) 331 BC ib. 9. 9; 10. 5; (**3**) ?iii BC *IG* V (2) 318, 3 (Ποδ[ά]ρης); (**4**) ii-i BC ib. 321 (2a) (tile); (**5**) i BC ib. 309 (f. Πολυκράτεια); (**6**) s. i AD Paus. viii 9. 9

**Ποδᾶς**
ILLYRIA:
—APOLLONIA: (**1**) imp.? *IApoll* 190; cf. *SEG* XXXVII 533 (f. Ἀνδρίων, Γοργίας, Ἵππαρχος)

**Πόη?**
S. ITALY (CAMPANIA):
—MISENUM*: (**1**) ?i-ii AD *CIL* X 3430 (Lat. Claudia Poe: d. Διοκλῆς)

**Πόθαιος**
SICILY:
—SYRACUSE?: (**1**) s. vi BC *RE* (-)

**Ποθείνη**
EPIROS:
—BOUTHROTOS (PRASAIBOI): (**1**) ii AD Ugolini, *Alb. Ant.* 3 p. 223 c (Sestieri, *ILat. Albania* 4) (Lat. Pothine: d. Γ. Κλ. Ζώσιμος, Ἰουλ. Εὐτέρπη)
KERKYRA: (**2**) ii-iii AD *IG* IX (1) 964, 1 (Μεμμία Ποθίνη)
S. ITALY (CAMPANIA):
—DIKAIARCHIA-PUTEOLI*: (**3**) imp. *CIL* X 2182 (Lat. Caecilia Pothine: freed.)
—POMPEII: (**4**) ?i AD *NScav* 1916, p. 303 no. 49 (Castrèn 428. 13) (Lat. Valeria Pothine)
SICILY:
—LIPARA: (**5**) imp. Libertini, *Isole Eolie* p. 229 no. 6 (*ILat. Palermo* 8) (Lat. Vibia Erothine—ed., Vibia Pothine—Solin: m. Εὐφροσύνη)

**Ποθεινιανός**
S. ITALY (CAMPANIA):
—DIKAIARCHIA-PUTEOLI: (**1**) imp. *CIL* X 2998, 6 (Lat. C. Terentius Pothinianus: s. Ποθεινός, Marcia)

**Ποθεινίς**
ACHAIA:
—PATRAI: (**1**) i AD *ILGR* 71, 3 (Lat. Mamilia Potheinis)

**Ποθεινός**
S. ITALY (CAMPANIA):
—DIKAIARCHIA-PUTEOLI: (**1**) imp. *CIL* X 2998, 4 (Lat. C. Terentius Pothinus: II s. Ποθεινός I, Marcia); (**2**) ~ ib. l. 8 (Lat. C. Terentius Pothinus: III s. Ποθεινός I, Marcia); (**3**) ~ ib. l. 10 (Lat. C. Terentius Pothinus: I f. Πόθος, Ποθεινός II, Ποθεινιανός, Ποθεινός III)
—POMPEII: (**4**) i BC-i AD ib. IV 1718 (Lat. Pothinus); (**5**) ~ *Riv. Stud. Pomp.* 6 (1993-4) p. 219 (Lat. C. Iulius Pothinus); (**6**) 70-79 AD *CIL* IV 1165; Mouritsen p. 111 (date) (Lat. Pothinus)
S. ITALY (LUCANIA):
—GRUMENTUM: (**7**) imp. *Eph. Ep.* VIII 270 (Lat. –nius Pothi[n]us)

**Πόθος**
ARGOLIS:
—ARGOS: (**1**) i BC *SEG* XI 344, 1
ILLYRIA:
—APOLLONIA: (**2**) ?iii AD *IApoll* 273
S. ITALY (APULIA):
—CANUSIUM*: (**3**) imp. *Epig. Rom. di Canosa* 124 (Lat. [Sex.] [Deccia]nus Pothus: freed.)
S. ITALY (CALABRIA):
—BRENTESION-BRUNDISIUM: (**4**) ii/iii AD *Museo Ribezzo* 6 (1972) p. 57 (Lat. Pothus)
S. ITALY (CAMPANIA):
—DIKAIARCHIA-PUTEOLI: (**5**) imp. *CIL* X 2998, 2 (Lat. C. Terentius Pothus: s. Ποθεινός, Marcia)
—DIKAIARCHIA-PUTEOLI*: (**6**) imp. *AJA* 2 (1898) p. 385 no. 29 (Lat. M. Marius Pothus: freed.)
—POMPEII: (**7**) i BC-i AD *CIL* IV 1521 (Lat. Pothus)

**Ποθουμενός**
LAKONIA:
—HYPERTELEATON*: (**1**) imp. *IG* V (1) 1059

**Ποθοῦσα**
ARKADIA:
—THELPHOUSA: (**1**) ii-iii AD ib. V (2) 413 (*GVI* 1677) (Ἰουλ. Π.)

S. ITALY (APULIA):
—LARINUM: (**2**) imp. *Contr. Ist. Fil. Class.* 1 (1963) p. 250 no. 9 (Lat. Lappia Pothusa)
S. ITALY (CAMPANIA):
—DIKAIARCHIA-PUTEOLI: (**3**) imp. *CIL* X 2885 (Lat. Pothusa)

**Ποιανός**
DALMATIA:
—PHAROS: (**1**) 221 BC *PTeb* 815 fr. 3 v II, 21 (Ποιανός, Παρανός?: f. Δημήτριος)

**Ποιγένης**
S. ITALY (BRUTTIUM):
—LOKROI EPIZEPHYRIOI:
——(Γαψ.): (**1**) iv/iii BC De Franciscis 7, 5 (f. Κάλλιππος)

**Ποίκλιος**
KORINTHIA:
—KORINTH: (**1**) ?ii-iii AD *Kenchreai* V p. 46 no. 216 (*SEG* XXXI 296) (Ποικ(ίλ)ος?)

**Ποίμανδρος**
MESSENIA:
—MESSENE: (**1**) ?iii BC *FD* III (1) 517, 1 (f. Ἀρίστιππος)

**Ποίμαρχος**
ARGOLIS:
—METHANA-ARSINOE: (**1**) i BC *IG* IV (1) 853, 6 (f. Σωσικλείδας)
—TROIZEN: (**2**) ?146 BC ib. 757 B, 32

**Ποίμαχος**
EPIROS: (**1**) iii/ii BC *PP* 15598; *PPC* Π 29
—DODONA: (**2**) iii BC Antoniou, *Dodone* Ba, 5; (**3**) ~ ib. l. 23 (Π[οί]μαχος)

**Ποιμενία**
S. ITALY (CAMPANIA):
—DIKAIARCHIA-PUTEOLI: (**1**) imp. *CIL* X 2521 (Lat. Pimenia: m. Ἵλαρος)

**Ποιμενίδας**
ARKADIA:
—MEGALOPOLIS: (**1**) m. iv BC *IG* II² 161 a, 1; 161 b, 3

**Ποιμήν**
EPIROS: (**1**) iv-iii BC Cabanes, *L'Épire* p. 585 no. 68, 6 ([Πο]ιμήν)

**Ποίμνη**
S. ITALY (CALABRIA):
—BRENTESION-BRUNDISIUM*: (**1**) imp. *CIL* IX 195 (Lat. Patronia Poemne: freed.)

**Πολέας**
ARGOLIS:
—ARGOS: (**1**) f. i BC Unp. (Ch. Kritzas) (s. Λυσικράτης)
—EPIDAUROS: (**2**) c. 370 BC *IG* IV (1)² 102, 78
ARKADIA: (**3**) iii BC ib. V (2) 415, 12 (*IPArk* 23) (Πολέας)
—MANTINEIA-ANTIGONEIA: (**4**) f. iii BC *IG* V (2) 278, 6; *EILakArk* 17 (date)
—MEGALOPOLIS: (**5**) ii BC *IG* V (2) 447, 4
—TEGEA: (**6**) ?s. v BC ib. 107 (bronze)
——(Hippothoitai): (**7**) f. iii BC ib. 36, 59 (f. Εὐρυκρέτης)
—THELPHOUSA: (**8**) 369-361 BC ib. 1, 65; Tod, *GHI* II 132 (date)
KORINTHIA:
—SIKYON: (**9**) vi/v BC *SEG* XI 244, 23
SICILY:
—GELA-PHINTIAS: (**10**) vi/v BC Dubois, *IGDS* 139 (vase) (Arena, *Iscr. Sic.* II 19)
—TYNDARIS: (**11**) f. i BC Cic., *In Verr.* II iv 92 (Lat. Poleas)

**Πόλειος**
ARKADIA:
—MANTINEIA-ANTIGONEIA: (**1**) i BC *IG* V (2) 309 (s. Φιλόνικος)

## Πολεμαίνετος

SICILY:

—KAMARINA: (1) m. v BC Dubois, *IGDS* 120, 8 (Arena, *Iscr. Sic.* II 142 A; *SEG* XXXVIII 939; Cordano, 'Camarina VII' 49) (s. Πρόδοξος)

## Πολεμαῖος

AITOLIA: (1) ?257 BC Nachtergael, *Les Galates* 7, 6; (2) c. 141 BC *IG* IX (1)² (1) 34, 17
—APERANTOI: (3) iii BC *AD* 22 (1967) Chron. p. 322 (f. Ἀμύνανδρος, Λόχαγος)
—KALYDON: (4) c. 213 BC *IG* IX (1)² (1) 188, 2; (5) c. 117 BC *BCH* 74 (1950) p. 34 no. 1, 14, 20 (s. Ἁρπαγίων)
—OPHIONEIS: (6) imp.? *IG* IX (1)² (1) 161

AKARNANIA:

—STRATOS: (7) c. 169 BC ib. 69 (f. Ἀλέξανδρος)

AKARNANIA?: (8) iii BC Unp. (Agrinion Mus.)

EPIROS: (9) iii BC *AD* 11 (1927-8) Parart. p. 33 no. 10 (s. Νικάνωρ)

S. ITALY (BRUTTIUM):

—SYBARIS-THOURIOI-COPIAE: (10) iv BC Iamb., *VP* 267 (*FVS* 1 p. 447)

## Πολεμαρχίδας

ARKADIA:

—MEGALOPOLIS: (1) iv/iii BC *IG* v (2) 468 (terracotta) (f. Ἀπέλλιχος)

## Πολεμαρχίς

TRIPHYLIA:

—MAKISTOS (NR.): (1) ?500-475 BC *SEG* XXXI 356 B; *LSAG²* p. 450 no. B (date)

## Πολέμαρχος

ACHAIA: (1) iii BC *IG* XII (9) 827 (s. Διονύσιος: date—Knoepfler); (2) ?ii BC *Memnonion* 188 (f. Ἡράκλειτος)

AIGINA: (3) ?f. i BC *Alt-Ägina* I (2) p. 43 no. 4, 5 (s. Φίλων)

AITOLIA: (4) b. 262 BC *IG* IX (1)² (1) 16, 8; (5) ?278-277 BC *FD* III (1) 87, 2; 88, 2; (6) 263 BC *IG* IX (1)² (1) 17, 49 (Πολέμαρ[χος]); (7) c. 260 BC *FD* III (4) 178, 2; (8) ~ ib. l. 3; (9) ?257 BC Nachtergael, *Les Galates* 7, 6; (10) ?a. 246 BC *SGDI* 2509, 2; (11) c. 232-228 BC *Syll³* 499, 3; Nachtergael, *Les Galates* 62, [2]; (12) ii BC *IG* IX (1)² (1) 75 bis
—AGRINION: (13) 200 BC *FD* III (1) 451, 4, 11 (f. Σάτυρος)
—APERANTOI: (14) ?iii BC *SEG* XVII 276 (*L'Illyrie mérid.* 1 p. 111 fig. 10)
—EIDAIOI: (15) 225-205 BC *FD* III (3) 220, 3
—HYPOSIRIA: (16) f. iii BC *IG* IX (1)² (1) 6, 13 (Πολέ[μαρ]χος)
—KALYDON: (17) s. iv BC ib. IV (1)² 95, 7 (Perlman E.2); Perlman p. 40 f. (date) (f. Θέων); (18) s. ii BC *IG* IX (1)² (1) 72, 13 (f. Λύκωπος)
—KONOPE-ARSINOE: (19) c. 200 BC Plb. xviii 10. 9
—OPHIEIS: (20) 176 BC *SGDI* 1862, 2 (s. Τείσανδρος)
—POTIDANIA: (21) m. ii BC *SBBerlAk* 1936, p. 371 b, 15 (*SEG* XLI 528 B) (s. Νικίας)
—THYRISKAIOI: (22) c. 210 BC *IG* IX (1)² (1) 4, 7; cf. *REG* 101 (1988) pp. 25 ff. (date)
—TRICHONION: (23) s. iii BC *IG* IX (1)² (1) 117, 7; (24) c. 225-200 BC ib. 31, 4 (Πολέ[μαρχ]ος: I f. Πολέμαρχος II); (25) ~ ib. l. 4 (II s. Πολέμαρχος I)

AKARNANIA:

—KORONTA: (26) iii/ii BC ib. IX (1)² (2) 603 (s. Αἰσχρίων, f. Μύννος)
—PALAIROS: (27) hell.? ib. 569, 3
—STRATOS: (28) a. 167 BC ib. IX (2) 6 a, 3; cf. Stählin p. 220 (date) (f. Ἀλέξων)

ARGOLIS:

—KLEONAI: (29) ?c. 229 BC *SEG* XXIII 178, 26 (or Argolis Argos: f. Θεάσων)

ARKADIA:

—STYMPHALOS: (30) c. 370 BC *IG* IV (1)² 102, 23

KORINTHIA:

—KORINTH?: (31) i/ii AD Plu. fr. 215

LAKONIA:

—SPARTA: (32) f. vii BC Paus. iii 3. 3 (Poralla² 617); (33) c. 105-110 AD *IG* v (1) 20 B, 7; *SEG* XI 569, 10 (Bradford (-)) (f. Τ. Τρεβελληνὸς Ἀρεύς, Τ. Τρεβελληνὸς Φιλόστρατος)

LEUKAS: (34) hell. *IG* v (1) 6, 1 (f. Φίλιστος); (35) c. 167-50 BC *NZ* 10 (1878) p. 136 no. 31 (de Cadalvène, *Recueil* pp. 147-8 (coin)); (36) f. i BC *IG* IX (1) 534, 7 (*Iscr. Gr. Verona* p. 24) (I f. Πολέμαρχος II); (37) ~ *IG* IX (1) 534, 7 (*Iscr. Gr. Verona* p. 24) (II s. Πολέμαρχος I)

S. ITALY (CALABRIA):

—TARAS-TARENTUM: (38) vi BC Iamb., *VP* 267 (*FVS* 1 p. 446); (39) iv/iii BC *IG* XIV 668 I, 1 (Landi, *DISMG* 194)

S. ITALY (CAMPANIA):

—NEAPOLIS: (40) ii/i BC *EAD* XXX 49 (*IG* II² 9992) (f. Καλλινίκη)

SICILY:

—KAMARINA: (41) f. v BC Cordano, *Tessere Pubbliche* 65 (Arena, *Iscr. Sic.* II 139 A) (Πολέμα[ρ]χος: f. Ζωΐλος)
—MORGANTINA: (42) f. i BC Cic., *In Verr.* II iii 56 (Lat. Polemarchus)
—SYRACUSE: (43) c. 455-404 BC *RE* (1); cf. *APF* C 9 (s. Κέφαλος)
—TAUROMENION: (44) c. 207 BC *IG* XIV 421 an. 34 (*SGDI* 5219); (45) c. 192 BC *IG* XIV 421 an. 49 (*SGDI* 5219) (s. Ἀπολλόδωρος)

## Πολεμίτας

AITOLIA:

—DEXIEIS: (1) 191 BC ib. 1985, 9

LAKONIA:

—SPARTA: (2) iii BC *SEG* XL 348 B, 7-8 (Πολεμί[τ]ας)

## Πολεμοκράτης

ACHAIA: (1) 221 BC *Milet* 1 (3) 42, 3 (and Caria Miletos: s. Δαμοκράτης)

AITOLIA:

—THESTIEIS: (2) 213 BC *IG* IX (1)² (1) 96, 14

EPIROS:

—AMBRAKIA: (3) ?iii/ii BC Unp. (Arta Mus., inscr.) (Πολεμοκρά[της]: ?f. [Πο]λυκρ[άτης])

## Πολεμώ

MESSENIA:

—KYPARISSIA: (1) m. ii BC *IG* IX (1)² (3) 622, 6, 8 (slave/freed.)

## Πολέμων

AITOLIA:

—KALYDON: (1) 129 BC ib. IX (1)² (1) 137, 99 (f. Κλεόμαχος, —αγρος)
—KONOPE-ARSINOE: (2) 184 BC ib. 131, 8 (f. Νικόβουλος)
—THERMOS*: (3) s. iii BC ib. 60 V, 7

AKARNANIA:

—ASTAKOS: (4) hell.? ib. IX (1)² (2) 440
—KORONTA: (5) s. iii BC ib. 428 (s. Φασείδας)
—PALAIROS: (6) iii BC ib. 501

AKARNANIA?: (7) ii BC Unp. (Agrinion Mus.)

EPIROS:

—BOUTHROTOS (PRASAIBOI): (8) a. 163 BC *IBouthrot* 14, 17; 18, 4; 20, 3; 26, 10; 29, 4; 31, 81; 33, 20; 38, 8; 41, 14; 43, 17 (*SEG* XXXVIII 471; 475; 477; 484; 487; 490; 492; 497); *IBouthrot* 48, 6 (f. Βόϊσκος, Ἀργεία) ?= (11); (9) ~ ib. 18, 4; 26, 10; 29, 51; 30, 12, 28; 43, 18, 21-2 (*SEG* XXXVIII 475; 484; 487-8; 502); *IBouthrot* 48, 6; 51, 18 (s. Βόϊσκος, f. Βόϊσκος) ?= (13); (10) ~ ib. 28, 41 (*SEG* XXXVIII 478) (f. Κόρριθος); (11) ~ *IBouthrot* 37, 6 (*SEG* XXXVIII 496) ?= (8); (12) ~ *IBouthrot* 50, 6; (13) ~ ib. 54, 6 (*SEG* XXXVIII 505); *IBouthrot* 145, 12; 152, 6 (s. Βόϊσκος) ?= (9)
——Messaneoi: (14) a. 163 BC ib. 66, 5; 67, 3; 98, 1; 153, 3

——Messaneoi?: (15) a. 163 BC ib. 38, 12 (*SEG* XXXVIII 497) (f. Δεινομάχα)
——Tharioi (16) a. 163 BC *IBouthrot* 100, 7 (f. Νικόμαχος)
—DODONA: (17) iii BC Antoniou, *Dodone* Ba, 21
—OPADEIOI: (18) c. 200 BC Cabanes, *L'Épire* p. 558 no. 34, 3 (*SEG* XXVI 701)

ILLYRIA:

—BYLLIONES: (19) c. 200 BC ib. XXXV 680, 5; cf. XXXVIII 541 (f. Φίλιος)
—EPIDAMNOS-DYRRHACHION: (20) hell.-imp. *IDyrrh* 358 (Πολέμ[ων]: s. Φιλονείδας)

KORINTHIA:

—KORINTH: (21) iv/iii BC Men., *Pk.* 472 f. (fict.)

MESSENIA:

—MESSENE: (22) hell.? *PAE* 1993, p. 65

## Πολήν

S. ITALY (CALABRIA):

—TARAS-TARENTUM: (1) v BC *SEG* XXXIV 1026 (vase) (Πολένος (gen.))

## Πολιάδας

KORINTHIA:

—SIKYON: (1) vi-v BC Iamb., *VP* 267 (*FVS* 58 A)

LAKONIA:

—SPARTA:

——Pitana: (2) vi/v BC Hdt. ix 53. 2 (Poralla² 618) (-δης: f. Ἀμομφάρετος)

## Πολίαρχος

TRIPHYLIA:

—HYPANA: (1) c. 230-200 BC *BCH* 45 (1921) p. 12 II, 77 (s. Φαινέας)

## Πολίας

ARKADIA:

—MANTINEIA-ANTIGONEIA: (1) hell.? *IG* v (2) 320 (Πολί[ας]: I f. Πολίας II); (2) ~ ib. (Πολί[ας]: II s. Πολίας I)
—MEGALOPOLIS: (3) m. iii BC Peek, *IAEpid* 42, 3 (Perlman E.3); Perlman p. 63 f. (date) (Πολίας: f. Ἀξιόπιστος)
—TEGEA: (4) m. iii BC Peek, *IAEpid* 42, 22 (Perlman E.3); Perlman p. 63 f. (date) (f. Θέων); (5) ii BC *IG* IV (1)² 226 (s. Θέων, f. Στασίλας, Ἀγασώ); (6) ~ ib. v (2) 143 (s. Θέων) ?= (9); (7) ~ ib. 144 (Π[ο]λίας: ?s. Σώστρατος, f. Θέων); (8) ~ ib. 145 (s. Τιμοκρέτης); (9) f. ii BC ib. 44, 5 (s. Θέων) ?= (6); (10) ~ ib. l. 12 (Πο[λίας]: f. Τελέστας)

## Πολίταρχος

ARGOLIS:

—ARGOS: (1) ii-iii AD ib. IV (1) 649, 4 (Stephanis 2082) (Πολείταρ[χος])

## Πολίτας

AIGINA: (1) m. ii BC *Alt-Ägina* I (2) p. 43 no. 2

KERKYRA: (2) f. iii BC *IG* IX (1) 691, 8 (*Iscr. Gr. Verona* p. 22 A)

KORINTHIA:

—KORINTH: (3) 575-550 BC *AA* 1970, p. 34, fig. 3 (pinax)

LAKONIA:

—GERONTHRAI: (4) inc. *IG* v (1) 1137

SICILY:

—SYRACUSE?:

——(Ἐκγ.): (5) hell. *Mem. Linc.* 8 (1938) p. 127 no. 35. 1 (bullet) (*NScav* 1961, p. 349); cf. *BE* 1965, no. 502; cf. *L'Incidenza dell'Antico* pp. 420 ff. (f. Νικίας)

## Πολίτης

S. ITALY (CAMPANIA):

—POMPEII: (1) 70-79 AD *CIL* IV 7502-3; 7516; 7682; 7685; 7702-3; Mouritsen pp. 109-12 (date) (Lat. Polites)

## Πολιτική
S. ITALY (APULIA):
—LUCERIA*: (1) imp. *CIL* IX 878 (Lat. Plautia Politice: freed.)

## Πολιτικός
S. ITALY (CAMPANIA):
—POMPEII: (1) i BC-i AD ib. IV 1832; 1915; 1930 (Lat. Politicus)

## Πόλλα
SICILY:
—SYRACUSE: (1) iii-v AD Ferrua, *NG* 209

## Πολλαίτιος
AITOLIA: (1) ?c. 230 BC *FD* III (3) 219 bis, 3

## Πολλέας
SICILY:
—GELA-PHINTIAS: (1) vi/v BC *SEG* XVI 551 (sherd) (Πολ(λ)έας)
—TAUROMENION: (2) c. 232 BC *IG* XIV 421 an. 9 (*SGDI* 5219)

## Πολλείων
LAKONIA: (1) v BC *IG* V (1) 825 (Poralla² 619) (-ōν)

## Πολλήν
ILLYRIA:
—EPIDAMNOS-DYRRHACHION: (1) c. 250-50 BC Ceka 375; cf. *Bakërr Hoard* p. 67 no. 96; cf. *IApoll Ref. Bibl.* n. 100 (coin) (money.)

## Πολλία
ILLYRIA:
—EPIDAMNOS-DYRRHACHION: (1) hell.-imp. *IDyrrh* 359 (d. Μάαρκος)

## Πολλιάδας
ARGOLIS:
—ARGOS: (1) f. iii BC Moretti, *ISE* 41, 28 (Perlman A.24)
KORINTHIA:
—SIKYON: (2) vi/v BC *SEG* XI 244, 58

## Πολλίας
ARKADIA:
—MANTINEIA-ANTIGONEIA: (1) ?272 BC *FD* III (1) 30, 1 (f. Ἀναξίλας)
KORINTHIA:
—SIKYON: (2) vi/v BC *SEG* XI 244, 11
LAKONIA:
—SPARTA: (3) c. 25-1 BC *IG* V (1) 212, 14 (Bradford (2)) (f. Πολύνικος); (4) c. 110-127 AD *SEG* XI 489, 1 (Bradford (1)) (Γν(αῖος) Κανίνιος Π.)
SICILY:
—KAMARINA?: (5) ?v/iv BC Manganaro, *PdelP* forthcoming no. 14
—SYRACUSE: (6) ii-i BC *NScav* 1913, p. 279 (?f. Λεύκιος)

## Πόλλις
ARGOLIS:
—ARGOS: (1) 430 BC Th. ii 67. 1
—HERMIONE: (2) iii BC *IG* IV (1) 728, 5 (s. Ἀνθεμίων)
ARKADIA:
—MANTINEIA-ANTIGONEIA: (3) c. 300-221 BC ib. V (2) 323. 93 (tessera) (s. Πρόκριτος)
—MEGALOPOLIS: (4) ii BC ib. 447, 2
—ORCHOMENOS: (5) ?ii BC ib. 345, 12 ([Π]όλλις: s. Διονύσιος: date—*LGPN*)
—TEGEA: (6) m. iv BC ib. 6, 95
KYNOURIA:
—TYROS*: (7) vi BC ib. V (1) 1522 (vase) (Lazzarini 408) (Πόλις)
LAKONIA:
—SPARTA: (8) her. *FGrH* 26 F 1 xxxvi 2; 26 F 1 xlvii 1; Plu., *Mor.* 247 D; 296 C (Poralla² 620) (and Crete: Πόλις—xxxvi: oikist/dub.);

(9) c. 430-372 BC *RE* (1) (Poralla² 621); (10) hell.? *IG* V (1) 808 (Bradford (-))
MESSENIA:
—MESSENE: (11) ii/i BC *IG* V (1) 1437, 12
SICILY:
—NAXOS: (12) f. v BC *SEG* XXXVIII 953. 1 (Arena, *Iscr. Sic.* III 76); cf. *L'Incidenza dell'Antico* pp. 418-19 (Πολλίδαι (n. gent.))
—SYRACUSE: (13) vi BC *RE* s.v. Syrakusai (-) col. 1481; *ILind* 2 C, [60], 62; *FGrH* 554 F 4 with Comm. (s. Σωσίλας: tyrant/dub.)

## Πολλίς
KORINTHIA:
—KORINTH?: (1) imp. *CIL* III 544, 5 (Lat. Pollis)

## Πόλλιχος
ARGOLIS:
—ARGOS:
——(Hylleis): (1) c. 458 BC *IG* I³ 1149, 4 ([Π]όλλιχος)
ARKADIA:
—TEGEA:
——(Krariotai): (2) s. iv BC ib. V (2) 41, 45 (s. Ζώσιμος)
SICILY:
—SYRACUSE: (3) 413 BC Plu., *Nic.* 24
TRIPHYLIA:
—PTELEA: (4) ii BC *SEG* XVI 282, 5 ([Π]όλλιχο[ς])

## Πολλίων
ARKADIA:
—TEGEA: (1) ?iii BC *IG* V (2) 238
ILLYRIA:
—EPIDAMNOS-DYRRHACHION: (2) c. 250-50 BC *SNG Cop. Thessaly–Illyricum* 508; 520 (coin) (pryt.)
LAKONIA:
—SPARTA: (3) s. i BC *IG* V (1) 95, 20 (Bradford (2)) (f. Λύσιππος)

## Πόλλυς
AKARNANIA:
—ALYZIA: (1) ?f. iv BC *SEG* XLII 1041 (s. Θρασύκριτος)

## Πολύαινα
KORINTHIA:
—KORINTH: (1) m. ii AD *Corinth* VIII (3) 199, 2 (Lat. [Poly]aena)

## Πολυαίνετος
ARKADIA:
—MEGALOPOLIS: (1) 319 BC D.S. xviii 56. 5

## Πολυαινίδας
LAKONIA:
—SPARTA: (1) 364 BC X., *HG* vii 4. 23; Plu., *Mor.* 225 E (Poralla² 622) (s. Λόχαγος); (2) s. i BC *IG* V (1) 124, 11; 212, 37 (Bradford (1); (2)) (-νεί-: s. Ἀρίστανδρος, f. Ἀρίστανδρος)

## Πολύαινος
ARKADIA:
—MEGALOPOLIS: (1) 207 BC Plb. xi 15. 5 (Πολύβιος—ms., Π.—ed.)
—PHIGALEIA: (2) c. 230-200 BC *BCH* 45 (1921) p. 12 II, 83 (f. Δεινόβιος)
KORINTHIA:
—KORINTH: (3) imp. *Corinth* VIII (2) 180 (Lat. Polyaenus); (4) i/ii AD ib. VIII (3) 165 (Lat. Tib. Polyaenus); (5) s. ii AD ib. VIII (1) 15, 4 ([Γ.] [Τ]ούλ. Π.)
—SIKYON: (6) 54-68 AD Amandry pp. 209-15; p. 26 (ident.); *RPC* 1 p. 255 nos. 1201-2; p. 258 nos. 1238-44; BM coins 1872 7-9-281; 1895 7-3-9 (coins) (Γ. Ἰούλ. Π., Lat. G. Iulius Polyaenus)
MESSENIA:
—KYPARISSIA: (7) 206 BC *RE* (4)

PELOPONNESE: (8) 340 BC *CID* II 43, 44
SICILY:
—SYRACUSE: (9) 214 BC Liv. xxiv 22. 1 (Lat. Polyaenus)

## Πολυάλκης
AKARNANIA:
—EURIPOS: (1) c. 325-315 BC *Hesp.* 57 (1988) p. 148 A, 29 (*SEG* XXXVI 331); cf. *Hesp.* 48 (1979) pp. 78 f. with pl. 22 c (s. Χαιριμένης)
LAKONIA:
—SPARTA: (2) 431 BC Plu., *Per.* 30 (Poralla² 623)

## Πολύανδρος
MESSENIA:
—MESSENE: (1) ii BC *Ergon* 1995, p. 29

## Πολυάνθης
KORINTHIA:
—KORINTH: (1) 413-395 BC *RE* (-)
LAKONIA:
—SPARTA: (2) ?s. i AD *IG* V (1) 678, 5 (Bradford (-)) (Πολυά(ν)θης?)

## Πολυάρατος
LAKONIA:
—SPARTA: (1) iii BC *SEG* XL 348 B, 9 (Πολυάρατος)

## Πολυαρχίς
S. ITALY (BRUTTIUM):
—LOKROI EPIZEPHYRIOI?: (1) iv/iii BC *HE* 2805

## Πολύαρχος
ACHAIA: (1) hell. *IG* II² 8403 (IV (1) 125) (f. Κηφισόδωρος)
AITOLIA: (2) 280 BC Paus. x 20. 4
LAKONIA:
—SPARTA: (3) ii-i BC *IG* V (1) 858 (tiles) (Bradford (2)) (Πολύαρχ(ος)); (4) s. i BC *IG* V (1) 92, 9 (Bradford (1)) (s. Φίλιππος)
SICILY:
—AKRAI: (5) ii BC *IGLMP* 30, 5 (*Akrai* p. 155 no. 4) ([Πο]λύαρχος)
—NEAITON: (6) iii BC *RQ* 1904, p. 257 (Dubois, *IGDS* 101) (f. Ἀγέμαχος)
—SYRACUSE: (7) f. iv BC Wehrli, *Schule Arist.* ii fr. 50

## Πολυβιάδας
LAKONIA:
—SPARTA: (1) s. v BC X., *HG* ii 4. 35; *FGrH* 86 F 11 (Poralla² 624) (-δης: f. Ναυκλείδας); (2) f. iv BC X., *HG* v 3. 20; v 3. 26; D.S. xv 23. 2 (Poralla² 625) (-δης: s. Ναυκλείδας)

## Πολυβιανός
S. ITALY (CAMPANIA):
—STABIAE: (1) ?i-ii AD *RAAN* 19 (1938-9) p. 98 (Lat. Q. Voconius Polybianus: I f. Πολυβιανός II); (2) ~ ib. (Lat. M. Voconius Polybianus: II s. Πολυβιανός I, Συνωρίς)

## Πολύβιος
ARKADIA:
—MEGALOPOLIS: (1) hell. *IG* V (2) 469 (22) (tile); (2) c. 200-120 BC *RE* (1) (s. Λυκόρτας)
ELIS: (3) c. 177-189 AD *IvOl* 102, 12; 103, 13; 104, [14] (f. Κλεόμαχος: Klytiadai/A.)
LAKONIA:
—SPARTA: (4) ?134 AD *IG* V (1) 62, 18 (Bradford (1)) (s. Χαρίδοτος); (5) c. 170 AD *SEG* XI 530, 3 (Bradford (2)) (s. Μενίσκος)
MESSENIA:
—MESSENE: (6) ii AD *IvOl* 449, 2, 7; 450, 3, 12 (Τ. Φλ. Π.: s. Λυκόρτας) ?= (7); (7) ii-iii AD *IG* V (1) 1456 ([Τ.] [Φλ.] Π.) ?= (6); (8) m. iii AD *IvOl* 486, 4; 487, 5 (Bradford (3)) (and Lakonia Sparta: Τ. Φλ. Π.)
S. ITALY (CAMPANIA):
—DIKAIARCHIA-PUTEOLI: (9) imp. *IG* XIV 859, 12 (Audollent, *Defix. Tab.* 208); (10) ~ *CIL* X 1932 (Lat. Voconius Polybius)

**Πόλυβος**
—DIKAIARCHIA-PUTEOLI*: (**11**) imp. ib. 2690 (Lat. M. Maecius Polybius: freed.); (**12**) m. i AD ib. 2857; cf. *RAAN* 38 (1963) p. 20 (Lat. Polybius: imp. freed.)
—KYME: (**13**) 251 AD *CIL* x 3699 I, 4 (Lat. A. Firmius Polybius)
—NEAPOLIS: (**14**) ii-iii AD Smutny, *Gk. Lat. Inscr. at Berkeley* 8; cf. Leiwo p. 111 no. 79 (Lat. C. Amatius Polybius)
—POMPEII: (**15**) i BC-i AD *CIL* IV 2025; (**16**) ~ ib. 3083 (Lat. Polubius); (**17**) 70-79 AD ib. 98; 99; 113; 121; 132; 134; 258; 271; 316; 429; 699; 875; 886; 973; 1034; 1050; 1053; 1060; 1226; 2935 etc; *RAAN* 49 (1974) p. 27 no. 12; p. 28 no. 14 (Castrèn 205. 2) (Lat. C. Iulius Polybius); (**18**) ~ *CIL* IV 3379; Mouritsen pp. 109-12 (date) (Lat. Polybius)

**Πόλυβος**
KORINTHIA:
—KORINTH: (**1**) c. 570-550 BC Amyx 67. 4 (vase) (Lorber 123) (her.?)

**Πολύβουλος**
SICILY:
—AKRAI?: (**1**) iii-v AD Ferrua, *NG* 378 (or Sicily Syracuse?: *Πολύβο[υλος]?*—ed.)

**Πολυγένεια**
S. ITALY (CAMPANIA):
—DIKAIARCHIA-PUTEOLI: (**1**) imp. *CIL* x 2968 (Lat. Sossia Polygenia)

**Πολύγηρος**
AITOLIA:
—KLAUSEION (MOD.): (**1**) byz. *PAE* 1958, p. 61 β; cf. *BCH* 83 (1959) p. 664

**Πολύγνωτος**
ACHAIA:
—PELLENE?: (**1**) ?263-261 BC *FD* III (3) 190, 6
ARGOLIS:
—ARGOS: (**2**) ii-i BC *IG* IV (1) 544 (tiles) (*Πολύγνω(τος)*)
—ARGOS?: (**3**) m. iii BC Plu., *Arat*. 6-7
EPIROS:
—ARGOS (AMPHILOCH.): (**4**) ?272 BC *BCH* 94 (1970) p. 675 no. 1 B, 1 (*Π[ο]λύγν[ω]τος*)
KEPHALLENIA:
—PALE: (**5**) iii/ii BC Unp. (*IG* arch.)
LAKONIA:
—SPARTA: (**6**) c. 105-110 AD *SEG* XI 569, 7 (Bradford (-)) (f. *Ἀνδρόνικος*)

**Πολύγονος**
KORINTHIA:
—KORINTH: (**1**) f. vii BC Amyx Gr 3 (vase) (*SEG* XI 229) ([*Πο*]*λύγονος*)

**Πολυδαίτας**
AITOLIA:
—BOMIEIS: (**1**) 153-144 BC *BCH* 66-7 (1942-3) p. 78 no. 7, 6 (f. *Πυρρίας*)

**Πολυδάμας**
LAKONIA:
—SPARTA: (**1**) ?i BC *SEG* XI 846 (Bradford (1)) (s. *Φοιβίδας*); (**2**) ?s. i BC *IG* v (1) 262 (Bradford (3)) (*Πολυδ[άμαν]τος* (gen.)); (**3**) c. 30-20 BC *IG* v (1) 211, 4 (Bradford (2)) (s. *Πολύστρατος*)

**Πολυδαμίδας**
LAKONIA: (**1**) 423 BC Th. iv 123. 4; 129. 3; 130. 3 (Poralla² 626)

**Πολύδαμος**
S. ITALY (CAMPANIA):
—DIKAIARCHIA-PUTEOLI: (**1**) 26 AD Camodeca, *L'Archivio Puteolano* 1 p. 156 (Lat. C. [I]ulius Polydamus)

**Πολύδας**
KORINTHIA:
—KORINTH: (**1**) c. 570-550 BC Amyx 104 A. 1 (vase) (Lorber 92) (her.?)

**Πολυδέκτας**
LAKONIA:
—SPARTA: (**1**) her. *RE* s.v. Polydektes (3) (Poralla² 627) (-της: s. *Πρύτανις*, ?s. *Εὔνομος*, f. *Χάριλλος*: king/dub.)

**Πολυδεύκης**
ARKADIA:
—LYKOSOURA*: (**1**) ii/i BC *IG* v (2) 522 (*Πολυ[δεύ]κης*: f. *Κλεόδαμος*)
S. ITALY (BRUTTIUM):
—RHEGION: (**2**) ?f. v BC *SEG* IV 66 (n. pr.?: her.?)
SICILY:
—SYRACUSE: (**3**) iii-v AD *RQ* 1904, p. 257 (Wessel 1146) (*Πολυδε[ύ]κη[s]*)

**Πόλυδος**
KORINTHIA:
—KORINTH: (**1**) c. 570-550 BC Amyx 62 (vase) (Lorber 86) (her.?)
S. ITALY (BRUTTIUM):
—RHEGION*: (**2**) m. vi BC Rumpf, *Chalkid. Vas*. p. 46 no. 4 (vase) (Arena, *Iscr. Sic*. III p. 102-3 no. 7) (her.?)

**Πολυδώρα**
S. ITALY (CAMPANIA):
—DIKAIARCHIA-PUTEOLI: (**1**) imp. *CIL* x 2928 (Lat. Salvidiena Polydora: d. *Πολύδωρος*)

**Πολυδωρίδας**
KORINTHIA:
—KORINTH: (**1**) c. 570-550 BC Amyx 64. 1 (vase) (Lorber 97) (*Πολυδōρίδ(α)s*: her.?)

**Πολύδωρος**
AKARNANIA:
—THYRREION: (**1**) iii BC *IG* IX (1)² (2) 274 (*Πολύδω[ρος]*, *Πολυδώ[ρα?]*); (**2**) ii BC ib. 248, 7 (s. *Εὐπόλεμος*)
KORINTHIA:
—KORINTH: (**3**) c. 570-550 BC Amyx 104 B. 6 (vase) (Lorber 92) (her.?)
LAKONIA:
—SPARTA: (**4**) viii/vii BC *RE* (5) (Poralla² 628) (s. *Ἀλκαμένης*, f. *Εὐρυκράτης*: king); (**5**) s. vii BC *PMGF* 1 5 fr. 2, 18, 21; *ZPE* 91 (1992) pp. 1 ff. (ident.) (s. *Εὐρυκράτ—*)
S. ITALY (CAMPANIA):
—DIKAIARCHIA-PUTEOLI: (**6**) imp. *CIL* x 2928 (Lat. Salvidienus Polydorus: f. *Πολυδώρα*, Salvidiena Marcella)

**Πολύευκτος**
ACHAIA: (**1**) ?f. iv BC Aristox. fr. 136
AKARNANIA:
—THYRREION: (**2**) ii BC *IG* IX (1)² (2) 247, 2, 16, 19 (s. *Θεόδοτος*, f. *Φίλιππος*, *Κάλλιππος*)
ARKADIA:
—TEGEA: (**3**) i/ii AD ib. v (2) 81; (**4**) 165 AD ib. 50, 7 (s. *Ὀνησᾶς*)
LAKONIA:
—SPARTA: (**5**) s. i BC ib. v (1) 127, 1 (Bradford (3)) (*Πολύευκ[τος]*); (**6**) i/ii AD *IG* v (1) 40, 13; 507, 3; 607, 26; *SEG* XI 489, 3; 490, 3; 517, 2; 558, 14; 609, 5; *BSA* 75 (1980) pp. 214-19 (ident., date, stemma) (Bradford (2); (5); (6); (7)) (*Γ. Ἰούλ. Π*.: s. *Σιμήδης*, f. *Γ. Ἰούλ. Σιμήδης*, *Γ. Ἰούλ. Ἀγαθοκλῆς*); (**7**) c. 140-160 AD *IG* v (1) 112, 6 (Bradford (1)) (s. *Διονύσιος*); (**8**) c. 145-150 AD *IG* v (1) 283, 2 (*Artemis Orthia* p. 316 no. 36); *BSA* 75 (1980) p. 219 (date, stemma) (Bradford (8)) (?s. *Τιβ. Κλ. Δαμοκράτης*, f. *Τιβ. Κλ. Σωσικράτης*); (**9**) iii AD *IG* v (1) 752 (Papaefthimiou p. 132 no. 3; Bradford (4))

**Πολυεύχης**
AKARNANIA:
—PALAIROS: (**1**) iv BC *IG* IX (1)² (2) 453

**Πολύζαλος**
SICILY:
—GELA-PHINTIAS: (**1**) c. 530-473 BC *CEG* I 397 (Ebert, *Gr. Sieg*. 13 II); Page, *FGE* 818 (Lazzarini 858); *FGrH* 566 F 93; D.S. xi 48. 3 ff.; Schol. Pi., *O*. i Inscr. a; *O*. ii Inscr.; *O*. ii 29 b-d, 117k; cf. Beloch, *GG* II (2) pp. 168-9 (*Πολύζηλος*—lit. test.: s. *Δεινομένης*)
—SYRACUSE (NR.): (**2**) v BC Plu., *Nic*. 27 (*Πολυζήλειον*—estate)

**Πολύζηλος**
SICILY:
—ZANKLE-MESSANA: (**1**) vi BC *Suda* I 80 (?f. *Ἴβυκος* (Rhegion))

**Πολυξίς**
S. ITALY (CALABRIA):
—TARAS-TARENTUM: (**1**) iv/iii BC *IG* XIV 668 II, 6 (Landi, *DISMG* 194) + *SEG* XXX 1223 (*Πολυ(δ)ίς?*—*IG*, *Πόλυλις*—Landi, *Π*.—*SEG*)

**Πολυήρατος**
ARKADIA:
—MANTINEIA-ANTIGONEIA: (**1**) c. 300-221 BC *IG* v (2) 323. 45 (tessera) (f. *Λεόντιος*)
—MEGALOPOLIS: (**2**) s. ii BC ib. 439, 70 (s. *Καλλίβιος*)

**Πολυήρης**
ARKADIA:
—THISOA: (**1**) 191-146 BC Unp. (New York, ANS) (*ZfN* 9 (1882) p. 266 no. 2 (coin))

**Πολυκαρπία**
SICILY:
—SYRACUSE: (**1**) iii-v AD *NScav* 1893, p. 313 no. 144 + Ferrua, *NG* 301 ([*Πολ*]*υκαρπία*)

**Πολύκαρπος**
AITOLIA:
—KLAUSEION (MOD.): (**1**) byz. *PAE* 1958, p. 61 [a]; cf. *BCH* 83 (1959) p. 664
ELIS: (**2**) 141-145 AD *IvOl* 95, 15 ([*Πολ*]*ύκαρπος*: s. *Z*—)
—OLYMPIA*: (**3**) 113-117 AD ib. 91, 19 ([*Πο*]*λύκαρπος*: ?s. *Γάϊος*: slave?)
KORINTHIA:
—KORINTH: (**4**) byz. *Corinth* VIII (3) 618; cf. *TMByz* 9 (1985) p. 366 no. 74 (*Πολύκα[ρπος]*)
S. ITALY (CALABRIA):
—BRENTESION-BRUNDISIUM: (**5**) imp. *CIL* IX 92 (Lat. Cerell. Polycarpus)
S. ITALY (CAMPANIA):
—DIKAIARCHIA-PUTEOLI*: (**6**) imp. ib. x 2973 (Lat. T. Statilius Polycarpus: freed.); (**7**) ii AD *NScav* 1927, p. 332 no. 5; cf. *Puteoli* 3 (1979) p. 156 no. 2 (Lat. Polycarpus: freed.)
—POMPEII: (**8**) i BC-i AD *CIL* IV 2351 (Lat. Polycarpus); (**9**) ~ ib. 2470; cf. p. 223 (Lat. Polucarpus)

**Πολύκαστος**
ACHAIA:
—AIGEIRA?: (**1**) ii BC *SEG* XXIV 337, 1 (s. *Λακλείδας*)

**Πολύκλεια**
EPIROS:
—BOUTHROTOS (PRASAIBOI):
——Prakeleoi: (**1**) a. 163 BC *IBouthrot* 94, 8 (m. *Μενέφυλος*)

**Πολυκλείδας**
LAKONIA:
—SPARTA: (**1**) c. 25-1 BC *IG* v (1) 212, 28 (Bradford (1)) (s. *Ἀνδρίας*)

**Πολυκλείτα**

S. ITALY (APULIA):
—VENUSIA: (**1**) ii-iii AD *Rend. Linc.* 29 (1974) p. 617 no. 17 (Lat. Creperia Polyclita)

**Πολύκλειτος**

AITOLIA: (**1**) ?262 or 258 BC Nachtergael, *Les Galates* 5, 3; (**2**) ?247 BC *Syll*³ 444 A, 3; *CID* II 139, 3; 137, 3?

ARGOLIS:
—ARGOS: (**3**) v BC *RE* (10) (?s. Μόθων, Πατροκλῆς: sculptor); (**4**) iv BC ib. (11) (sculptor); (**5**) m. iii BC ib. (13); *TCam* 29, 15 (*ILind* 52 no. 23) (sculptor)
—ARGOS?: (**6**) f. iv BC *RE* (15)

ELIS: (**7**) s. i BC *IvOl* 337, 2; 338, 2-3; 339; [340]; [341]; [344] (s. Προξενίδης); (**8**) c. 177-185 AD ib. 103, 9 (Μ. Ἀντ. [Πο]λύκλειτος) ?= (*9*); (**9**) c. 177-201 AD ib. 102, 14; 103, 19; 104, 17; 106, [16] (Μ. Ἀντ. Π.: Π.) ?= (*8*)

EPIROS:
—OSSONIOI: (**10**) f. ii BC Cabanes, *L'Épire* p. 589 no. 75, 5 (*SEG* XXXVII 510)

S. ITALY (APULIA):
—VENUSIA: (**11**) imp. *CIL* IX 554 (Lat. Polyclitus)

S. ITALY (CAMPANIA):
—DIKAIARCHIA-PUTEOLI: (**12**) imp. ib. X 2251 (Lat. Cepius Polyclitus)

SICILY:
—AKRAI: (**13**) ?iii BC *SGDI* 3245, 6 (*Akrai* p. 158 no. 10; *IGLMP* 31) (Πολύκλε[ιτος])
—LIPARA: (**14**) iii-v AD Libertini, *Isole Eolie* p. 230 no. 9 (Lat. Polyclet[us])
—ZANKLE-MESSANA: (**15**) vi BC Schol. Ar., *Plut.* 407

**Πολυκλῆς**

ACHAIA: (**1**) 146 BC *IG* IV (1)² 28, 67 (s. Ἀριστοπάμων: synoikos)

ARGOLIS:
—ARGOS: (**2**) c. 370 BC *SEG* XI 379 b, 3 (sculptor)
—EPIDAUROS: (**3**) c. 365-335 BC *IG* IV (1)² 103, 16, 28, 33, 42, 69, 79, 87-9, 116; (**4**) s. iii BC Peek, *NIEpid* 45 (f. Γόργασος, Ὄλυμπις)
——(Dymanes): (**5**) 146 BC *IG* IV (1)² 28, 4 (s. Γόργασος)
—EPIDAUROS*: (**6**) c. 315-300 BC Peek, *IAEpid* 49, 11
—HERMIONE: (**7**) ii-i BC *IG* IV (1) 692 (f. Ξενότιμος)

ARKADIA:
—MANTINEIA-ANTIGONEIA: (**8**) hell.? ib. v (2) 340

EPIROS:
—DODONA: (**9**) ?164 BC Cabanes, *L'Épire* p. 586 no. 71, 9 (f. Σιμίας)

LAKONIA:
—SPARTA: (**10**) s. v BC Moretti, *Olymp.* 315 (Poralla² 629) (Π. ἐπίκλησιν λαβὼν Πολύχαλκος); (**11**) ii-i BC *IG* v (1) 859 (tiles) (Bradford (4)); (**12**) s. i BC *IG* v (1) 135, 5 (Bradford (1)) (s. Γόργιππος); (**13**) c. 25-1 BC *IG* v (1) 212, 11 (Bradford (3)) (s. Τεταρτίων); (**14**) ?s. i AD *IG* v (1) 661 (Bradford (6)) (f. Μένιππος); (**15**) c. 90-100 AD *SEG* XI 512, 3 (Bradford (5)) (s. Φιλοκράτης); (**16**) c. 100 AD *SEG* XI 510, 3 (Bradford (5)) (f. Καλλικράτης); (**17**) f. ii AD *SEG* XXXI 340, 8 (s. —εν—)

LEUKAS: (**18**) 263 BC *IG* IX (1)² (1) 3 A, 24; (**19**) iii/ii BC Unp. (*IG* arch.)

MESSENIA:
—KORONE: (**20**) ?ii BC *IG* v (1) 1395, 2 (s. Ἐπιχάρης)
—MESSENE: (**21**) ii BC *SEG* XLI 345 (f. Ἐπιχαρίς); (**22**) c. 146-32 BC *SNG Cop. Phliasia-Laconia* 507 (coin)
—THOURIA: (**23**) f. ii BC *SEG* XI 972, 104 (s. Τεταρτίδας)

SICILY:
—KAMARINA: (**24**) f. v BC Cordano, *Tessere Pubbliche* 41 (-κλές: f. Σάκις)
—SELINOUS: (**25**) v BC Dubois, *IGDS* 35, 1 (Arena, *Iscr. Sic.* I 64) (-κλές)

**Πολυκράτεια**

ARKADIA:
—MANTINEIA-ANTIGONEIA: (**1**) i BC *IG* v (2) 309 (d. Ποδάρης)

KORINTHIA:
—SIKYON: (**2**) ?iii BC ib. IV (1) 435 (Skalet 266) (I m. Πολυκράτεια II); (**3**) ~ *IG* IV (1) 435 (II d. Πολυκράτεια I); (**4**) iii/ii BC *RE* (-) (Skalet 267) (m. Δημήτριος (Macedon), Περσεύς (Macedon)); (**5**) m. ii AD *Syll*³ 846, 2 (Τιβ. Κλ. Π. Ναυσικάα: d. Τιβ. Κλ. Πολυκράτης, Τιβ. Κλ. Διογένεια)

LAKONIA:
—TEUTHRONE: (**6**) m. ii BC *SEG* XXII 306 (-τια: date—*LGPN*)

LEUKAS: (**7**) hell.? *IG* IX (1) 573

**Πολυκράτης**

ACHAIA: (**1**) 146 BC ib. IV (1)² 28, 120 (f. Σωτήριχος: synoikos)

AITOLIA:
—KALYDON: (**2**) s. ii BC *SEG* XXV 621, 4 (I f. Πολυκράτης II); (**3**) ~ ib. l. 4 (II s. Πολυκράτης I)

ARGOLIS:
—ARGOS: (**4**) c. 590-570 BC *IG* IV (1) 565 (Lazzarini 276); *LSAG*² p. 168 no. 5 (date) (-τēς); (**5**) 336-324 BC *CID* II 32, 34; 76 II, 22; 79 A I, 17; 95, [12]; 97, 22; 102 II B, 27; 120 A, 1; 121 III, 14; 122 I, 9 (s. Ἀντίων, f. Ἀντίων) ?= (*6*); (**6**) 333 BC ib. 82, 21 ?= (*5*); (**7**) a. 303 BC *CEG* II 816, 16; (**8**) ~ ib. l. 23; (**9**) f. iii BC Moretti, *ISE* 41, 27 (Perlman A.24) (f. —τας); (**10**) iii/ii BC *RE* (4); *PP* 2172; 15065 (*PPC* Π 34); *SEG* XXXI 1359 (I s. Μνασιάδας, f. Πολυκράτης II, Πτολεμαῖος, Ζευξώ, Εὐκράτεια, Ἑρμιόνη)); (**11**) ~ *PP* 15233 (*PPC* Π 35); *BE* 1949, no. 202 (family) (II s. Πολυκράτης I, Ζευξώ (Cyrene), f. Πολυκράτης III); (**12**) ii BC *PP* 4312 (III s. Πολυκράτης II); (**13**) c. 60 BC *IG* VII 420, 52 (*IOrop* 528) (s. Ἀγέμαχος)
——(Naupliadai): (**14**) ii/i BC *BCH* 33 (1909) p. 176 no. 2, 9 (f. Ἀντιγένης)
—EPIDAUROS: (**15**) iv BC *IG* IV (1)² 326 (s. Πολύκριτος); (**16**) i BC/i AD ib. 647; 654 (s. Εὐάνθης); (**17**) i AD Peek, *IAEpid* 274 (s. Καλλικλῆς); (**18**) f. ii AD *IG* IV (1)² 685; 686, 2 (Τιβ. Κλ. Π.: f. Κλ. Δαμαρώ)
——(Dymanes): (**19**) 146 BC ib. 28, 7 (s. Βαθυκλῆς)

ARKADIA: (**20**) 285 BC *PEleph* 2, 17 (*MChr* 311) (s. Ἡρακλείδης)
—MEGALOPOLIS: (**21**) ?145 BC *IG* v (2) 439, 49 (Πολυκρ[άτ]ης: s. Λέων)
—ORCHOMENOS: (**22**) m. iii BC *BCH* 38 (1914) p. 462 no. 6, 12

ELIS: (**23**) 221-249 AD *IvOl* 113, [1]; 114, [8]; 116, 11; 117, 12; 121, 14; *SEG* XV 258, 7 (Κλ. Π.: mantis/Iamidai); (**24**) 237-241 AD *IvOl* 117, 20 (?f. Κάσσιος Οἰνεύς)
—OLYMPIA*: (**25**) 237-241 AD ib. l. 21 (Πολυκ[ράτ]ης: ?s. Ἡλιόδωρος: slave?)

EPIROS:
—AMBRAKIA: (**26**) ?iii/ii BC Unp. (Arta Mus., inscr.) (?s. Πολεμοκράτης)

ITHAKE: (**27**) hell. *Rev. Épig.* 1 (1913) p. 47 no. 7

KORINTHIA:
—KORINTH: (**28**) ?iii BC *Corinth* VIII (1) 63 ([Πο]λυκράτης)
—SIKYON: (**29**) c. 146-32 BC *BMC Pelop.* p. 52 no. 199 (coin) (Πολυκρά[της]); (**30**) i/ii AD Plu., *Arat.* 1 (Skalet 269) (II s. Πολυκράτης I); (**31**) ~ *RE* (5); s.v. Plutarchos col. 683 (Skalet 268) (I f. Πολυκράτης II, Πυθοκλῆς); (**32**) m. ii

AD *Syll*³ 846, 4 (Τιβ. Κλ. Π.: II s. Πολυκράτης I, f. Τιβ. Κλ. Πολυκράτεια Ναυσικάα)

KYNOURIA:
—GLYMPEIS?: (**33**) ?i AD *SEG* XXXV 281 (f. Δαμόστρατος)

LAKONIA:
—OITYLOS: (**34**) f. ii BC *IG* v (1) 1296, 3 (f. Ἀριστοφάνης)
—LAKONIA?: (**35**) ?ii-i BC *FGrH* 118 (Bradford (-))

MESSENIA:
—MESSENE: (**36**) ii BC *Ergon* 1995, p. 29; (**37**) s. ii BC *SEG* XLI 341, 14 (s. Ξενοκράτης)
—THOURIA: (**38**) ii-i BC *IG* v (1) 1385, 23 (s. Τιμογένης); (**39**) f. ii BC *SEG* XI 972, 105 (s. Κλήτων)

PELOPONNESE: (**40**) 112 BC *FD* III (2) 70 A, 31 ([Π]ολυκράτης)

PELOPONNESE?: (**41**) a. 164 BC *IvOl* 47, 4 (s. Πολυ—)

SICILY:
—AKRAGAS: (**42**) c. 413-406 BC *NC* 1948, p. 3 no. 4 (coin) (Πολυκρά(της): coin engraver)

**Πολυκράτις**

LAKONIA:
—HIPPOLA: (**1**) s. ii BC *SEG* XLII 304

**Πολυκρέτεια**

ARKADIA:
—TEGEA: (**1**) ?iii-ii BC *IG* v (2) 250 (d. Ἀριστω—)

**Πολυκρέτης**

ARKADIA:
—TEGEA: (**1**) m. iv BC ib. 6, 78

**Πολυκρίνης**

LAKONIA:
—SPARTA: (**1**) iv BC *SEG* XI 639, 4

**Πολυκρίτα**

ITHAKE: (**1**) hell. *IG* IX (1) 675

**Πολύκριτος**

AIGINA: (**1**) vi/v BC Hdt. vi 50; 73 (f. Κριός); (**2**) 480 BC ib. viii 92-3 (s. Κριός)

AITOLIA: (**3**) 243 BC *RE* (5) ?= (*4*)
—KALLION/KALLIPOLIS: (**4**) c. 271-247 BC *IG* IX (1)² (1) p. XLIX, s.a. 271 BC, 263 BC, 254 BC, 247 BC ?= (*3*)

ARGOLIS:
—EPIDAUROS: (**5**) iv BC ib. IV (1)² 326 (f. Πολυκράτης)

KEPHALLENIA: (**6**) ?ii-i BC Unp. (*IG* arch.) ([Πο]λύκριτος)

KORINTHIA:
—KORINTH: (**7**) ?269 BC *CID* II 120 A, 35; 121 II, 11 (f. Σαμίων)

MESSENIA:
—MESSENE: (**8**) s. ii BC *SEG* XLI 341, 19 (f. —s)

**Πολύκτωρ**

ARGOLIS:
—ARGOS: (**1**) ?c. 575-550 BC ib. XI 314, 7; *LSAG*² p. 168 no. 8 (date) (-ϙτōρ); (**2**) v-iv BC Iamb., *VP* 267 (*FVS* I p. 447)

ELIS: (**3**) 12 BC Moretti, *Olymp.* 733 (s. Δαμόνικος)

**Πολυλαΐδας**

KORINTHIA:
—KORINTH: (**1**) c. 570-550 BC Amyx 54. 1 (vase) (Lorber 139) (fict.?)

**Πολύλας**

LEUKAS: (**1**) ?iii BC Unp. (*IG* arch.)

**Πόλυλλος**

SICILY:
—SYRACUSE?:
——(Ὑπα.): (**1**) hell. Manganaro, *PdelP* forthcoming no. 4 III, 6 (f. Νικαῖος)

**Πολύλος**
S. ITALY (CALABRIA):
—TARAS-TARENTUM: (**1**) ?c. 500-490 BC Landi, *DISMG* 178 (Lazzarini 343); *LSAG*² p. 284 no. 4 (date)

**Πολυμαθίδας**
KERKYRA: (**1**) f. iii BC *IG* IX (1) 691, 5 (*Iscr. Gr. Verona* p. 22 A) (*Πολυ[μα]θίδας*)

**Πολυμήδης**
ACHAIA:
—AIGION: (**1**) s. iii BC *RE* (6)
EPIROS:
—AMBRAKIA: (**2**) 360 BC *CID* II 4 III, 27 (s. *Τέλλυς*)
ILLYRIA:
—APOLLONIA: (**3**) hell.-imp. *IApoll* 103 (f. *Κλέα*)
—EPIDAMNOS-DYRRHACHION: (**4**) c. 250-50 BC Münsterberg p. 40 (coin) (pryt.); (**5**) ii-i BC *IDyrrh* 555 (tiles); (**6**) hell.-imp. ib. 394 (f. *Τάτα*)
S. ITALY (CAMPANIA):
—DIKAIARCHIA-PUTEOLI: (**7**) imp. *Puteoli* 4-5 (1980-1) p. 271 no. 6 (*Πολυμ[ήδης]*)

**Πολυμήστωρ**
ARKADIA: (**1**) her. Paus. viii 5. 9 (s. *Αἰγινήτης*: king)

**Πολύμναστος**
AKARNANIA:
—ASTAKOS: (**1**) ii BC *IG* IX (1)² (2) 434, 10 (f. *Λύκιος*)
ARGOLIS:
—PHLEIOUS: (**2**) iv BC Iamb., *VP* 251; 267 (*FVS* I p. 447)
—TROIZEN: (**3**) ?146 BC *IG* IV (1) 757 B, 6 (*Πο[λύμ]ναστος*)
ARKADIA: (**4**) ?257 BC Nachtergael, *Les Galates* 7, 10 (Stephanis 2106) (-*μνη*-: s. *Ἀλέξανδρος*)
—MEGALOPOLIS: (**5**) ?268 BC *FD* III (1) 27, 1 (*Π[ολύμ]ναστος*: f. *Λυσικλῆς*)

**Πολυμνία**
S. ITALY (CAMPANIA):
—DIKAIARCHIA-PUTEOLI: (**1**) c. 165-172 AD *Puteoli* 7-8 (1983-4) p. 81 (Lat. Flavia Polymnia Marciana: d. *Κλεωναῖος*, Iulia Valeria Marciane Crispinilla)

**Πόλυμνις**
ARGOLIS:
—ARGOS: (**1**) c. 315 BC *SEG* XXXII 370, 16 (*Πόλυμ[νις]*)

**Πολυνίκα**
ARGOLIS:
—ARGOS: (**1**) ?i AD *NS* 160

**Πολυνίκης**
ELIS: (**1**) 632 BC Moretti, *Olymp.* 60
ILLYRIA:
—SHKOZE (MOD.): (**2**) imp. Ugolini, *Alb. Ant.* I p. 192 no. 12 (-*νεί*-: f. *Εὐφράντα*, *Λοῦπος*)
LAKONIA:
—SPARTA: (**3**) c. 25-1 BC *IG* V (1) 212, 20 (Bradford (-)) (s. *Ἀγήσιππος*)

**Πολύνικος**
ARKADIA:
—MT. KYLLENE*: (**1**) ?iv-iii BC *IG* V (2) 365
ELIS: (**2**) ii-iii AD *IvOl* 471, 3 (*Κλ. Πολύνεικος*)
EPIROS:
—MOLOSSOI:
——Kyestoi: (**3**) a. 163 BC *IBouthrot* 69, 15; 70, 11; 71, 9 (*BCH* 118 (1994) pp. 129 f. B 1-3) (s. *Μυρτίλος*)
—VOTONOSI (MOD.): (**4**) ?f. iii BC *SEG* XXIV 459 (f. *Ἀσανδρος*)

LAKONIA:
—HYPERTELEATON*: (**5**) imp. *IG* V (1) 1060 (Bradford (1)) (s. *Ἀριστώνυμος*)
—SPARTA: (**6**) 400 BC X., *An.* vii 6. 1; vii 6. 39 ff.; vii 7. 13; vii 7. 56 (Poralla² 630); (**7**) c. 25-1 BC *IG* V (1) 212, 14 (Bradford (2)) (s. *Πολλίας*); (**8**) c. 225-250 AD *SEG* XXXIV 308, 17 (Bradford (3)) (-*νει*-: f. *M. Αὐρ. Πασῖνος*)

**Πολυνόα**
KERKYRA: (**1**) s. vii BC *CEG* I 144

**Πολύξεινος**
AKARNANIA:
—STRATOS: (**1**) ii BC *IG* IX (1)² (2) 394, 15 (s. *Λόχαγος*)

**Πολυξένα**
AKARNANIA:
—PALAIROS: (**1**) ?iii BC ib. 543
ARKADIA:
—HERAIA: (**2**) ?ii BC ib. V (2) 418
—PHIGALEIA: (**3**) iii BC ib. 427
—TEGEA: (**4**) ?c. 475-450 BC ib. 108 (Lazzarini 294); *LSAG*² p. 215 no. 24 (-*ξξέ*-)
EPIROS:
—DODONA*: (**5**) v-iv BC Carapanos, *Dodone* p. 45 no. 15
—MOLOSSOI: (**6**) c. 380-316 BC Plu., *Mor.* 401 A; cf. *Chiron* 11 (1981) pp. 79 ff. (name)

**Πολυξενίδας**
ACHAIA:
—DYME*: (**1**) c. 219 BC *SGDI* 1612, 55 (*Tyche* 5 (1990) p. 124) (s. *Μνασιππίδας*)
SICILY:
—SYRACUSE: (**2**) 208 BC *IMM* 72, 1 (Dubois, *IGDS* 97) (*Πολυξενί[δ]ας*: s. *Φιλόξενος*)

**Πολύξενος**
ACHAIA:
—PELLENE: (**1**) ?257-253 BC Nachtergael, *Les Galates* 7, 13; 10, 11 (f. *Καλλίας*) ?= (*2*); (**2**) ?255-253 BC ib. 8, 16; 10, 15 (f. *Ἄνδρων*) ?= (*1*)
AITOLIA: (**3**) 210 BC *IG* IX (1)² (1) 29, 12
—KALYDON: (**4**) a. 142 BC ib. 137, 60
AKARNANIA:
—THYRREION: (**5**) iii BC ib. IX (1)² (2) 270 (f. *Μενέπολις*)
ARGOLIS:
—ARGOS: (**6**) c. 365-335 BC ib. IV (1)² 103, 12, 14, 53, 73, 85, 88 (f. *Λυσιάδας*, ?f. *Δόρκων*)
—HERMIONE: (**7**) i BC-i AD? ib. IV (1) 734, 3
ARKADIA: (**8**) 168 BC Phld., *Acad. Ind.* 28, 7 (f. *Ἀγαμήστωρ*)
—MANTINEIA-ANTIGONEIA: (**9**) ii BC *IG* V (2) 319, 3, 8
—MEGALOPOLIS: (**10**) ii/i BC ib. 443, 24; 444, 5; 445, 10 (*IPArk* 32) (s. *Ἀρίστανδρος*); (**11**) ii AD *IG* V (2) 464 ([*Τιβ.*] *Κλ. Πο[λύξ]ενος*)
—ORCHOMENOS: (**12**) iii BC *BCH* 38 (1914) p. 471 no. 13 (*Πολύξ[ενος]*)
—TEGEA:
——(Krariotai): (**13**) s. iv BC *IG* V (2) 41, 48 (*Πολύξε[νος]*: f. *Τιλείας*)
EPIROS:
—ANTIGONEIA: (**14**) hell. *Iliria* 1972, p. 375 (tile) (*Πολύξε(νος)*)
—KASSOPE: (**15**) c. 130 BC Dakaris, *Kassope* p. 25 (*SEG* XXXVI 555); cf. *SEG* XLI 541 (f. *Κύλισος*)
—MOLOSSOI: (**16**) hell. Cabanes, *L'Épire* p. 581 no. 56, 12
KORINTHIA:
—KORINTH: (**17**) a. 191 BC *SEG* XXVI 392, 7 (s. *Νίκανδρος*)
LAKONIA:
—GYTHEION: (**18**) i-ii AD *IG* V (1) 1168 (f. *Τιβ. Κλ. Ἀκυλεῖνος*)

—SPARTA: (**19**) s. i BC ib. 92, 7 (Bradford (4)) (f. *Παγκλῆς*); (**20**) ?i AD *IG* V (1) 327 (Bradford (3)) (f. *Ἀλεξικράτης*); (**21**) c. 125-150 AD *IG* V (1) 62, 6; *SEG* XI 578, 4 (Bradford (5)) (*Πολύ(ξ)ενος*—*SEG*: I f. *Πολύξενος* II); (**22**) ~ *IG* V (1) 62, 6; *SEG* XI 578, 4 (Bradford (2)) (*Πολύ(ξ)ενος*—*SEG*: II s. *Πολύξενος* I)
—SPARTA?: (**23**) ?ii BC *SEG* II 160 (Bradford (1)) ([*Πολ*]*ύξενος*: s. *N—*)
S. ITALY (CALABRIA):
—TARAS-TARENTUM (NR.): (**24**) c. 575-550 BC *Taras* 10 (1990) p. 71 no. 6; pl. 37 (*SEG* XL 899)
SICILY:
—AKRAI: (**25**) ii-i BC *SGDI* 3246, 13 (*Akrai* pp. 152-3 no. 2; Dubois, *IGDS* 109) (f. *Ἀρτεμίδωρος*)
—GELA-PHINTIAS: (**26**) f. ii BC *IG* XIV 256, 40 (Dubois, *IGDS* 161); cf. *SEG* XL 804 (s. *Ἀγάθαρχος*)
—KEPHALOIDION: (**27**) hell.-imp. *IG* XIV 349 (*Πολύ[ξε]νος*)
—LIPARA: (**28**) hell. ib. 394 (Libertini, *Isole Eolie* p. 219 no. 12)
—MORGANTINA: (**29**) ?iv/iii BC *SEG* XXXIX 1008, 11 (s. *Ἐμμενίδας*)
—SYRACUSE: (**30**) v/iv BC *RE* (7); (**31**) f. iv BC [Pl.], *Ep.* 310 C; 314 C; cf. *RE* (7)
—SYRACUSE?:
——(*Και.*): (**32**) hell. *Mem. Linc.* 8 (1938) p. 128 no. 35. 8 (bullet) (s. *Ἀρκεσίλας*)
——(*Μακ.*): (**33**) hell. Manganaro, *PdelP* forthcoming no. 4 V, 8 (s. *Θράσυς*)
—TAUROMENION: (**34**) s. iv BC *FGrH* 566 F 33
ZAKYNTHOS: (**35**) i BC/i AD Moretti, *Olymp.* 737 (s. *Ἀπολλοφάνης*)

**Πολυξένων**
EPIROS:
—KASSOPE: (**1**) iv/iii BC *SEG* XXXIV 589 (f. *Φιλόξενος*)

**Πολυοῦχος**
AITOLIA:
—PHISTYON?: (**1**) f. ii BC *IG* IX (1)² (1) 111, 7 (f. *Σώτων*)

**Πολυπείθης**
AKARNANIA:
—STRATOS: (**1**) 154 BC *SGDI* 1908, 11, 15, 19 (f. *Ἁρμόξενος*, *Πολύφρων*)
LAKONIA:
—SPARTA: (**2**) vi/v BC Moretti, *Olymp.* 195 (Poralla² 631) (s. *Καλλιτέλης*); (**3**) 352 BC *CID* II 31, 60 (Poralla² 632)
LEUKAS: (**4**) i BC-i AD? *IG* IX (1) 570

**Πολυπέρχων**
AITOLIA: (**1**) c. 245 BC *RE* (3) (*Πολυσπέρχων*—mss.)
EPIROS:
—HOPLAINOI: (**2**) hell. Cabanes, *L'Épire* p. 584 no. 63, 10 (*SEG* XXVI 705) (*Πολυπ[έρχων]*)

**Πόλυς**
KORINTHIA:
—KORINTH: (**1**) c. 570-550 BC Amyx 100. 3 (vase) (Lorber 90) (her.)
SICILY:
—GELA-PHINTIAS: (**2**) f. v BC Dubois, *IGDS* 142 c (vase) (Arena, *Iscr. Sic.* II 23)
—LEONTINOI: (**3**) m. v BC *JNG* 33 (1983) p. 14 (coin graffito) (*Πολυ*—?: f. *Ἱέρων*)

**Πολυσθένης**
ARGOLIS:
—EPIDAUROS: (**1**) imp. Peek, *IAEpid* 153. 30 (*Π[ολ]υσθένης*)
ARKADIA:
—MANTINEIA-ANTIGONEIA: (**2**) iv/iii BC *SEG* XXXVI 378, 2 (*Πολυσθ[ένης]*)

**Πολυστράτα**
AKARNANIA:
—PALAIROS: (**1**) f. iii BC *IG* IX (1)² (2) 471

**Πολυστράτη**
ARGOLIS:
—ARGOS: (2) ?c. 415-400 BC ib. IV (1) 567 (Lazzarini 278); *LSAG²* p. 170 no. 49 (date); (3) a. 303 BC *CEG* II 816, 24
EPIROS:
—AMBRAKIA: (4) iii-ii BC *Op. Ath.* 10 (1971) p. 64 no. 12, 5; cf. *VAHD* 84 (1991) p. 262 (Π[ολυστ]ράτα: d. Ἐχεκλείδας)

**Πολυστράτη**
ACHAIA:
—PATRAI: (1) ii-i BC *Achaean Grave Stelai* 16 (Πο[λυστρ]άτη?)

**Πολυστρατίδας**
LAKONIA:
—SPARTA: (1) ?v-iv BC Plu., *Lyc.* 25; *Mor.* 231 F (Poralla² 604) (Πολυκράτίδας—231 F, Πεισιστρατίδας—Poralla); (2) c. 25-1 BC *IG* V (1) 212, 36 (Bradford (-)) (f. Ἀριστοκλῆς)

**Πολύστρατος**
ACHAIA:
—DYME*: (1) ii AD *Griech. Epigr. Kreta* p. 21 no. 24, 1; cf. *SEG* XXX 432
AITOLIA: (2) ?240-228 BC *FD* III (3) 218 A, 2
—THESTIEIS: (3) s. iii BC *SBBerlAk* 1936, p. 386 no. 2 a (f. Λυκέας)
ARGOLIS:
—ARGOS: (4) a. 303 BC *CEG* II 816, 17; (5) f. iii BC *CID* II 120 A, 15 (f. Ἀντικράτης); (6) f. i BC Unp. (Ch. Kritzas) (Πο[λύσ]τρατος: s. Φίλων)
——(Polatheis): (7) ?iv-iii BC *SEG* XXXIII 286 (Πολύσ[τρατος])
—PHLEIOUS: (8) 421 BC *IG* I³ 80, 15; 81, 15, 20
ARKADIA:
—THELPHOUSA: (9) a. 228 BC ib. IV (1)² 72 B, 26
EPIROS:
—AMBRAKIA: (10) arch.? *RE* (9) (sculptor); (11) ii-i BC *CIG* 1798 (f. Ἀπολλώνιος)
KORINTHIA:
—KORINTH: (12) c. 570-550 BC Amyx 102. 8 (vase) (Lorber 91) (Πο[λ]ύστρατος: her.?); (13) ?iii-ii BC *IG* IV (1) 198
LAKONIA:
—SPARTA: (14) c. 30-20 BC ib. V (1) 211, 4 (Bradford (-)) (f. Πολυδάμας)
MESSENIA:
—MESSENE: (15) iii/ii BC *SEG* XXIII 228 (f. Ἀντισθένης); (16) ii BC *Ergon* 1995, p. 29; (17) i AD *IG* V (1) 1439, 3
S. ITALY (BRUTTIUM):
—LOKROI EPIZEPHYRIOI:
——(Τω.): (18) 279 BC De Franciscis 13, 2 (s. Φιλωνίδας)
—SYBARIS-THOURIOI-COPIAE?: (19) f. iv BC *SEG* XXIX 1022 ([Πο]λύστρατος)
S. ITALY (LUCANIA):
—HYELE-VELIA: (20) ii/i BC ib. XIX 400, 3 (Π[ο]λύστρατο[ς]: f. Ἕρμων)
SICILY: (21) i/ii AD *IG* XIV 2395. 4; *Kokalos* 32 (1986) p. 236 no. 66 (tiles)

**Πολύτερπος**
KORINTHIA:
—KORINTH: (1) c. 590-570 BC Amyx 17. 1 (vase) (*SEG* XIV 303 a; Lorber 39; *CEG* I 452 i); cf. *SEG* XXIX 336 (n. pr.?: fict.?)

**Πολυτιμίδας**
AIGINA: (1) ?465 BC Pi., *N.* vi, 62

**Πολύτιμος**
KERKYRA: (1) ?iii BC *IG* IX (1) 695, 3, 6

**Πολύτροπος**
LAKONIA:
—SPARTA: (1) 369 BC X., *HG* vi 5. 11-13; D.S. xv 62. 1 (Poralla² 633)

**Πολύφαμος**
KORINTHIA:
—KORINTH: (1) c. 570-550 BC Amyx 102. 5 (vase) (Lorber 91) (her.?)

**Πολύφαντος**
LAKONIA:
—SPARTA: (1) m. iii BC Peek, *IAEpid* 42, 63 (Perlman E.3); Perlman p. 63 f. (date) (Bradford (-)) (s. Ἀρκεσίλας)

**Πολύφας**
KORINTHIA:
—KORINTH: (1) c. 570-550 BC Amyx 104 A. 3 (vase) (Lorber 92) (her.?)

**Πολυφόντας**
LAKONIA:
—SPARTA: (1) 220 BC Plb. iv 22. 12 (Bradford (-))

**Πολύφραστος**
ARKADIA:
—ORCHOMENOS: (1) 322 BC *SGDI* 2661, 2; cf. *IG* V (2) p. 146 s.v. Orchomenus (f. Ἀριστίων)

**Πολύφρων**
AITOLIA: (1) 280 BC Paus. x 20. 4; (2) ?273-272 BC *FD* III (1) 298, 2; 473, 2; III (3) 185, 2; 203, 2; (3) ?257 BC Nachtergael, *Les Galates* 7, 4; (4) hell.-imp. *IG* IX (1)² (1) 82 (s. Λύκος)
—KALLION/KALLIPOLIS: (5) 153-144 BC *SGDI* 2279, 11, 13 (f. Φάλανθος)
AKARNANIA:
—STRATOS: (6) 154 BC ib. 1908, 15, 18 (s. Πολυπείθης)

**Πολύχαλκος**
LAKONIA:
—SPARTA: (1) s. v BC Moretti, *Olymp.* 315 (Poralla² 629) (Πολυκλῆς ἐπίκλησιν λαβὼν Π.)

**Πολυχάρης**
ARGOLIS:
—ARGOS:
——Kolouris (Heraieis): (1) c. 330-300 BC *SEG* XXXIV 282, 3 (Πο[λυ]χάρης)
—EPIDAUROS: (2) c. 350-200 BC ib. XXVI 452. 3
—PHLEIOUS: (3) s. iv BC Peek, *NIEpid* 16, 26 (Perlman E.6) (f. Σάων)
—TROIZEN: (4) iii BC *IG* IV (1) 753, 2, 4, 6 with Add. (f. Φιλόξενος)
ARKADIA:
—MANTINEIA-ANTIGONEIA: (5) c. 300-221 BC ib. V (2) 323. 83 (tessera) (s. Λεόντιος); (6) f. iii BC ib. 272, 2 (Πολυχάρ[ης])
—MEGALOPOLIS: (7) 369-361 BC ib. 1, 33; Tod, *GHI* II 132 (date)
—TEGEA: (8) iv/iii BC *IG* V (2) 32, 3; (9) ~ ib. l. 9
ELIS: (10) 36-24 BC *IvOl* 59, 23; 62, 16; 64, 21; 66, 3 (s. Ἀριστοκράτης: M.)
MESSENIA: (11) 764 BC Moretti, *Olymp.* 4
—MESSENE: (12) ii-i BC *SEG* XLI 343, 12 ([Πο]λυχάρης)

**Πολύχαρμος**
AITOLIA: (1) ?273-272 BC *FD* III (1) 298, 2; 473, 3; III (3) 185, 2; 203, 2
—THERMOS: (2) 214 BC *IG* IX (1)² (1) 177, 19 (f. Δίκων)
ARKADIA:
—MANTINEIA-ANTIGONEIA: (3) c. 300-221 BC ib. V (2) 323. 47 (tessera) (s. Πυθέας)
—MEGALOPOLIS: (4) ii/iii AD ib. 517, 2 etc. (f. Σάων)
—PHIGALEIA: (5) ?iii AD *IvOl* 481
DALMATIA:
—PHAROS: (6) iii/ii BC *SEG* XXIII 489, [21], 32; cf. XLI 545 (f. —τυλος)

**Λακωνία:** [LAKONIA:]
—SPARTA: (7) 382 BC X., *HG* v 2. 41 (Poralla² 634); (8) ii AD *IG* V (1) 159, 37 (Bradford (-))
MESSENIA:
—METHONE: (9) ?ii AD *IG* V (1) 1417, 8 (Ἰουβέντιος Καικίλιος Π.: s. Ἰουβέντιος Καικίλιος Μουσαῖος)
SICILY:
—SYRACUSE: (10) i-ii AD Charito i 5. 2 etc. (fict.)

**Πολυχρονία**
SICILY:
—SYRACUSE: (1) iii-v AD Strazzulla 293; 295 (Wessel 880) (-νεία)

**Πολυχρόνιν**
SICILY:
—SYRACUSE: (1) iii-v AD Ferrua, *NG* 374 ([Πο]λυχρό[ν]ιν)

**Πολυχρόνιος**
KORINTHIA:
—KORINTH: (1) byz. *Corinth* VIII (1) 183 (Πολυχρ[όνιος]); (2) ?581 AD *SEG* XXIX 319, 2
SICILY:
—SYRACUSE: (3) iii-v AD Agnello 32 (Wessel 854)

**Πολυχρόνις**
ARGOLIS:
—ARGOS: (1) iii AD Unp. (Argos, Kavvadias)

**Πολφέννιος**
S. ITALY (CALABRIA):
—BRENTESION-BRUNDISIUM: (1) c. 175-170 BC Cabanes, *L'Épire* p. 554 f. no. 33, 6, 10 (*SEG* XXXVII 511) (Γάϊος Π.: s. Δάζος)

**Πόλων**
MESSENIA:
—KORONE: (1) ii BC *IG* V (1) 1397, 5
—MESSENE: (2) c. 146-32 BC *Coll. Rhousopoulos* 2626 (coin)

**Πομπαῖος**
ELIS:
—LASION: (1) c. 230-200 BC *BCH* 45 (1921) p. 14 II, 127 (f. Σφαῖρος)

**Πομπήϊα**
SICILY:
—LIPARA: (1) i BC/i AD *IG* XIV 395-6 + *Kokalos* 13 (1967) pp. 200-1 (?d. Σέξ. Πομπ. Ἄπρος Πάλακος)
—SYRACUSE: (2) 403 AD Strazzulla 166 (Wessel 778); Ferrua, *NG* 8 (name) ([Πο]μπήϊα: d. Διονυσία)

**Πομπήϊανός**
KORINTHIA:
—KORINTH: (1) ii/iii AD *SEG* XXIII 168 a (lamp) (Πον-)

**Πομπήϊος**
ACHAIA:
—PATRAI: (1) i BC/i AD ib. XXIX 426, 3 (Σάλβιος ὁ καὶ Π.: s. Παγκράτης)
MESSENIA:
—MESSENE: (2) i BC/i AD *IG* V (1) 1501

**Πομπίας**
ACHAIA:
—PELLENE: (1) m. iii BC ib. V (2) 368, 110 (f. Κλέων)

**Πόμπις**
KORINTHIA:
—KORINTH: (1) c. 221 BC ib. IV (1)² 42, 23 (s. Τιμολέων)

**Πομπίσκος**
ARKADIA: (1) ?iv BC Polyaen. v 33

**Πόμπων**
ARGOLIS:
—EPIDAUROS: (1) 152 AD IG IV (1)² 389, 3 (s. Ἐπαφροδίτᾶς)

**Πομπώνιος**
PELOPONNESE?: (1) 11 AD PAE 1992, p. 72 B, 17 (s. Ἀγαθοκλῆς)

**Πόνος**
S. ITALY (APULIA):
—VENUSIA: (1) imp. CIL IX 493 (Lat. [Cal]vius Ponus)

**Ποντήία**
S. ITALY (CAMPANIA):
—NEAPOLIS: (1) i BC/i AD INap 168, 7; cf. Leiwo p. 78 n. 89

**Ποντική**
S. ITALY (BRUTTIUM):
—LOKROI EPIZEPHYRIOI: (1) ii AD Costabile, Municipium Locrensium 6 (CIL x 20) (Lat. Sestia Pontice: m. Τρωίλος)
S. ITALY (CAMPANIA):
—DIKAIARCHIA-PUTEOLI: (2) ii AD ib. 2009 (Lat. Pontice: m. P. Aelius Puteolanus)

**Ποντικός**
S. ITALY (APULIA):
—CANUSIUM: (1) 223 AD Epig. Rom. di Canosa 35 IV, 33 (CIL IX 338) (Lat. L. Timinius Ponticus)
S. ITALY (CAMPANIA):
—DIKAIARCHIA-PUTEOLI: (2) imp. ib. X 2072 (Lat. Ponticus); (3) ~ ib. 2191 (Lat. Ti. Caepius Ponticus); (4) ~ ib. 2397 (Lat. Ponticus f. Εὔτυχος)
—MISENUM*: (5) imp. ib. 3425 (Lat. Iulius Ponticus: s. Ποντικός (Pontos), Καλλιτύχη); (6) ~ ib. 3603 (Lat. M. Timinius Ponticus)
—POMPEII: (7) c. 50-54 AD ib. 827, 7 (Castrèn 205. 21); Mouritsen p. 108 (date) (Lat. L. Iulius Ponticus)

**Πόντιος**
S. ITALY (BRUTTIUM):
—HIPPONION-VIBO VALENTIA: (1) hell.? IG XIV 2402. 2 (tile)

**Πόντις**
ILLYRIA:
—EPIDAMNOS-DYRRHACHION: (1) 516 BC Paus. vi 10. 7 (Ebert, Gr. Sieg. 4) (f. Κλεοσθένης)

**Ποντομέδοισα**
KORINTHIA:
—KORINTH: (1) c. 570-550 BC Amyx 96 (vase) (Πνοτομέδοισα: her.?)

**Πόντος**
S. ITALY (CAMPANIA):
—POMPEII: (1) i BC-i AD CIL IV 6830 (Lat. Pon[t]us)

**Ποπίλος**
SICILY: (1) hell. Vandermersch p. 175 (amph.) (Ποπίλ(ι)ος?)

**Πόπλιος**
ARGOLIS:
—EPIDAUROS: (1) i AD IG IV (1)² 501 (Πόπλιος: s. Ἐπαφρόδιτος); (2) 147 AD ib. 385
KERKYRA: (3) i BC ib. IX (1) 709 (s. Λεύκιος)
MESSENIA:
—MESSENE: (4) i BC-i AD? ib. V (1) 1474 (Πόπλ[ιος])
PELOPONNESE?: (5) 11 AD PAE 1992, p. 72 B, 8 (f. Γάιος)

SICILY:
—KATANE: (6) ii-i BC ISmyrna 689 III, 32 (f. Ἀπολλώνιος)
—LILYBAION: (7) s. iii BC SEG XXVI 1075; Lilibeo p. 178 no. 193 (-λει-: f. Δαμάτρις)

**Πόρις**
KORINTHIA:
—KORINTH: (1) c. 570-550 BC Amyx 105 A. 1 (vase) (Lorber 93) (Πόρις: fict.?)

**Πορισμός**
S. ITALY (CAMPANIA):
—DIKAIARCHIA-PUTEOLI*: (1) imp. CIL x 1951 (Lat. Lollianus Porresmus: freed.?)

**Πόρκος**
SICILY:
—HERBESSOS: (1) f. v BC Dubois, IGDS 167 (vase) (Arena, Iscr. Sic. II 119) (-ρος)

**Πόρος**
ARGOLIS:
—ARGOS: (1) iii-ii BC IG IV (1) 687; Peek, IA-Epid 306 (f. Θεόδωρος)

**Πορροίτας**
AITOLIA:
—BOUKATION: (1) c. 164 BC IG IX (1)² (1) 99, 4

**Πόρταξ**
SICILY:
—IAITON*: (1) ?iii BC SEG XXXI 827 ?= (2)
—PARTHENIKON: (2) ?iii BC ib. XXXII 927; XXXV 1016; Kokalos 36-7 (1990-1) pp. 139 ff. (tiles) ?= (1)

**Πορτία**
ILLYRIA:
—EPIDAMNOS-DYRRHACHION: (1) hell.-imp. IDyrrh 360 (d. Βαρναῖος); (2) ~ ib. 361 (d. Ἡρακλείδας)

**Πορτῖνος**
ILLYRIA:
—APOLLONIA: (1) c. 250-50 BC Maier 88 (coin) (Ceka 44) (pryt.)

**Πόρτις**
KORINTHIA:
—KORINTH: (1) f. iv BC BMC Corinth p. 13 no. 131 (coin graffito); JNG 33 (1983) p. 16 (name)

**Πορφύρα**
AKARNANIA:
—ECHINOS: (1) iv/iii BC SEG XXIX 472

**Πορφύριος**
SICILY:
—KATANE: (1) imp. CIL X 7014 (Lat. Porfyrius Mynatidius)
—SYRACUSE: (2) iii-v AD Strazzulla 371 (Agnello 28; Wessel 511)

**Πορφυρίς**
LEUKAS: (1) ?ii BC SEG XXVII 176 (Πορφυρ[ίς], Πορφύρ[α?])

**Πορφυρίων**
AKARNANIA:
—OINIADAI: (1) c. 325-315 BC Hesp. 57 (1988) p. 148 A, 36 (SEG XXXVI 331); cf. Hesp. 48 (1979) pp. 78 f. with pl. 22 c (s. Δαμοθάρσης)

**Ποσειδαῖος**
ARGOLIS:
—EPIDAUROS: (1) iii BC Peek, IAEpid 43, 34 ([Π]οσειδαῖος: s. Βίων); (2) i AD ib. 333, 1 (Ποσειδα[ῖος])

—HERMIONE: (3) c. 100-90 BC SEG XXXIII 290 A, 29; BSA 70 (1975) pp. 129-31 (date) (Stephanis 2125) (s. Σωφρονίων)
DALMATIA:
—ISSA:
——(Dymanes): (4) iv/iii BC Brunšmid p. 9, 59 (Ποσει[δ]αῖος: f. Ἀνθεύς)
——(Hylleis): (5) iv/iii BC ib. p. 8, 38 (Ποσε[ι]δαῖος: f. Ἀπολλόδωρος)

**Ποσείδης**
ARGOLIS:
—ARGOS: (1) v-iv BC Iamb., VP 128 (-σίδ-)
SICILY:
—SOLOUS: (2) f. i BC Cic., In Verr. II ii 102 (Lat. Posides Macro)
—SYRACUSE: (3) imp. IG XIV 37 (N. Κλώδιος Ποσαίδης)
—TAUROMENION: (4) inc. IOrop 675 (-σίδ-: s. Γλαῦκος)

**Ποσείδιππος**
ARKADIA:
—MANTINEIA-ANTIGONEIA: (1) ?15-16 AD IG V (2) 274, 10, 21 (Ποσείδιπ(π)ος—l. 10: f. Πιτύλος)
—MEGALOPOLIS: (2) 182 BC IvOl 46, 7 (IPArk 31 IIB)
ELIS: (3) f. ii AD IvOl 92, 11, 23 (s. Νίγερ, ?f. Ἀριστόνικος)
LAKONIA:
—KARDAMYLE: (4) i AD SEG XI 948, 4 (s. Ἄτ-ταλος)
—SPARTA: (5) c. 25-1 BC IG V (1) 212, 12 (Brad-ford (-)) (-σί-: s. Γάιος)
S. ITALY (LUCANIA):
—HERAKLEIA: (6) c. 100 BC ID 1713, 8 (-σί-: s. Τίτος, Θεοδώρα (Teos))

**Πόσειδις**
SICILY: (1) s. iii BC Kokalos 32 (1986) p. 237 nos. 67-8 (tiles)
—AKRAI: (2) ?iii BC SGDI 3240, 1 (Akrai p. 156 no. 7) (f. Ἡράκλειος); (3) ii-i BC SGDI 3246, 17 (Akrai pp. 152-3 no. 2; Dubois, IGDS 109) (s. Φίλων)

**Ποσειδωνία**
SICILY:
—SYRACUSE: (1) iii-v AD NScav 1907, p. 758 no. 12 (Wessel 193); cf. Ferrua, NG 82 (Ποσιδο[νία])
—TYNDARIS?: (2) ?iii AD Epigraphica 11 (1949) p. 60 (-σι-)

**Ποσειδώνιος**
AIGINA: (1) ?i BC Alt-Ägina I (2) p. 44 no. 10 (f. Μενέδημος); (2) imp. IG IV (1) 83, 2 (f. Ἀριστονόη)
AITOLIA?:
—TRAGAS?: (3) 205 BC ib. IX (1)² (3) 613, 10 ([Π]οσειδώνιος)
AKARNANIA: (4) iii/ii BC ib. XII (3) 304 (IX (1)² (2) 577) (s. Φιλήμων)
ARGOLIS:
—EPIDAUROS: (5) 138 AD Peek, IAEpid 230, 2 ([Π]οσ[ε]ιδ[ών]ιος: I f. Ποσειδώνιος II); (6) ~ ib. l. [2] (II s. Ποσειδώνιος I); (7) 308 AD IG IV (1)² 434
—METHANA-ARSINOE: (8) i BC ib. IV (1) 853, 8 (-σι-: s. Παρμ—)
ARKADIA:
—KLEITOR: (9) a. 212 AD ib. V (2) 369, 3 (Αὐρ. Ποσιδώνιος)
—TEGEA: (10) i AD ib. 46, 14 ([Π]οσειδώνιο[ς])
ELIS: (11) 20-16 BC IvOl 65, 5 (f. Θεοδόσιος)
ILLYRIA:
—APOLLONIA: (12) ii AD IApoll 205
KEPHALLENIA:
—SAME: (13) imp. IG IX (1) 639
KORINTHIA:
—KORINTH: (14) hell.? RE (5)
—KORINTH?: (15) s. ii AD Corinth VIII (3) 307, 4 (-νει-)

**Ποσειδῶνις**

LAKONIA:
—SPARTA: (16) c. 505-479 BC Hdt. ix 71. 2; 85.
1 (Poralla² 635); (17) c. 239-244 AD *IG* v (1)
572, 2 (Bradford (-)) (f. *M. Aὐρ. Δαμοκράτης*)

**Ποσειδῶνις**

SICILY:
—SYRACUSE: (1) iii-v AD *SEG* XXXIX 1026 =
Ferrua, *NG* 211 (-σιδό-—*SEG*, Ποσιδόν(ι)ος—
Ferrua)

**Ποσείδωρος**

SICILY:
—THERMAI HIMERAIAI: (1) f. i BC Cic., *In Verr.*
II iii 99 (Lat. Posidorus)

**Ποσθαλίων**

ARKADIA?: (1) c. 200 BC *SEG* XVII 829, 3

**Πόσθων**

DALMATIA:
—ISSA: (1) hell. Brunšmid p. 28 no. 22 (s. *Ξάνθιππος*)

**Πόσιλλα**

AIGINA: (1) imp. *GVI* 605 (m. *Θεμίσων*)

**Πόσιππος**

MESSENIA:
—MESSENE: (1) f. iii BC *SEG* XLI 342, 16; cf.
*PAE* 1991, p. 100 no. 8 (*Κόσιππος*—ed. pr.,
*Π.*—*SEG*)

**Πόσις**

S. ITALY (LUCANIA):
—HYELE-VELIA: (1) imp. *PdelP* 21 (1966) p.
336 no. 11 (f. *Ζωΐλος*)

**Ποσσικράτης**

ARKADIA:
—PARRHASIOI: (1) c. 369 BC Paus. viii 27. 2
(and Arkadia Megalopolis: oikist)

**Πόσσιτος**

AIGINA: (1) ii/i BC *Alt-Ägina* 1 (2) p. 43 no. 3,
1 (*Πόσιττος*: s. *Ἀλέξανδρος*)

**Ποτάμιλλα**

S. ITALY (CAMPANIA):
—MISENUM: (1) ?ii AD *NScav* 1928, p. 196 no.
4 + *Puteoli* 11 (1987) p. 139 no. 6 (Lat. Flavia
Potamilla: d. *Βίθυς* (Thrace, Bessoi))

**Πόταμις**

SICILY:
—SYRACUSE: (1) 410 BC *RE* (-) (s. *Γνῶσις*)

**Πόταμος**

ARGOLIS:
—ARGOS: (1) ?c. 575-550 BC *SEG* XI 336, 3;
*LSAG*² p. 168 no. 7 (date)

**Ποτάμων**

AITOLIA:
—THERMOS*: (1) s. iii BC *IG* IX (1)² (1) 60 VI,
15
—TRICHONION: (2) 154 BC *SGDI* 1908, 17 (f.
*Ξενόκριτος*)

EPIROS:
—PHILIPPIAS (MOD.): (3) ii BC *SEG* XXIV 425
(*Ποτάμω[ν]* (n. pr.?))

LAKONIA:
—SPARTA: (4) f. iii AD *IG* v (1) 170, 19; *BSA*
80 (1985) p. 245 (date) (Bradford (-)) (*Aὐρ.
Π.*: s. *Παράμονος*)

S. ITALY (CALABRIA):
—TARAS-TARENTUM: (5) imp. *NScav* 1896, p.
376 no. 3 (Lat. Cn. Pompeius Secundus Potamo)

SICILY: (6) f. i BC *RE* s.v. Papirius (71) (Lat.
L. Papirius Potamo)

**Ποτανέας**

MESSENIA: (1) ?c. 440 BC Richter, *Engraved
Gems* 421

**Ποτειδωνίδας**

KORINTHIA:
—KORINTH: (1) f. vi BC Amyx p. 607 no. 30
(pinax) ([*Π*]οτε͂δο̄νίδας)

**Ποτθίκα**

ILLYRIA:
—EPIDAMNOS-DYRRHACHION: (1) v/iv BC
*IDyrrh* 5

**Ποτῖνος**

LEUKAS: (1) ?iii BC *SBBerlAk* 1935, p. 709

**Ποτίσκος**

S. ITALY (CAMPANIA)*: (1) imp. *CIL* x 8042.
36; 8043. 76; *BM Terracottas* E 142 (tiles)
(Lat. Potiscus: imp. freed.)

**Ποτιωλανός**

DALMATIA:
—RIZON (NR.): (1) imp. *IGR* I 553 (n. pr.)

**Πούβλιος**

S. ITALY (CAMPANIA):
—DIKAIARCHIA-PUTEOLI: (1) imp. *IG* XIV 856

**Πουβλίωι**

EPIROS:
—AMBRAKIA: (1) i BC-i AD *CIG* 1806 + Fraser-
Rönne, *BWGT* p. 169 no. 71 (*Πουβλίωι*
(dat.)—ed.: d. *Ἀριστίων*)

**Πούδης**

ARGOLIS:
—EPIDAUROS: (1) imp. Peek, *IAEpid* 341

**Πουλάδας**

EPIROS:
—TOSKESI (MOD.): (1) iv BC *AD* 23 (1968)
Chron. p. 292 (s. *Ἀνδρόμαχος*)

**Πούλιος**

DALMATIA:
—ISSA: (1) iii/ii BC Brunšmid p. 24 no. 12 +
*BCH* 114 (1990) p. 506 fig. 4; p. 509 (*Πούλιος*:
s. *Γναῖος*)

**Πουλίων**

SICILY:
—SYRACUSE: (1) iii-v AD Ferrua, *NG* 251 (f.
*Ὀνόμαντις*)

**Πούλος**

SICILY:
—SYRACUSE: (1) iii-v AD *Rend. Pont.* 22 (1946-
7) p. 234 no. 29

**Πούλχρα**

LAKONIA:
—SPARTA: (1) ?s. ii AD *IG* v (1) 259, 5; *Artemis
Orthia* p. 299 no. 6 (date) (Bradford s.v.
*Πούρχλα*) (*Πούρχλα*—lap.: m. *Καλλικράτης*)

**Πούλχρος**

S. ITALY (BRUTTIUM):
—LOKROI EPIZEPHYRIOI: (1) i BC De Franciscis
p. 144 (brick)

**Πούπλιος**

KORINTHIA:
—KORINTH: (1) ii AD *Lampes d'Argos* 669; *Corinth* IV (2) p. 187 no. 552; *SEG* XXVII 35. 21
(lamps)

**Πράγορος**

ARKADIA:
—MEGALOPOLIS: (1) ?268 BC *FD* III (1) 17, 1
(f. *Ξενίας*)

**Πράθος**

AITOLIA:
—KALYDON: (1) f. iv BC *IG* IX (1)² (1) 138, 7

**Πρακτική**

KORINTHIA:
—KORINTH: (1) imp. *Corinth* VIII (2) 138 (Lat.
Clodia Bractice)

**Πρακτικός**

ILLYRIA:
—APOLLONIA: (1) ii AD *IApoll* 224 (*Οὔλπιος Π.*)

S. ITALY (CAMPANIA):
—DIKAIARCHIA-PUTEOLI: (2) imp. *CIL* x 2812
(Lat. Practicus)

SICILY:
—ZANKLE-MESSANA: (3) ?ii-iii AD *NScav* 1942,
p. 82 (*Σέλλιος Π.*)

**Πράμιος**

AITOLIA: (1) ?228-215 BC *SGDI* 2525, 2; cf.
*FD* III (4) 364 n.

**Πραξαγόρα**

EPIROS:
—DODONA*: (1) v BC *PAE* 1968, p. 56

**Πραξαγόρας**

AIGINA?: (1) ?f. v BC Page, *FGE* 510 (s. *Λυκαῖος*)

ELIS: (2) f. i BC *IvOl* 200; Moretti, *Olymp.* 672
([*Πραξ*]αγόρας: s. *Λέων*)

KORINTHIA:
—SIKYON: (3) ?253 BC Nachtergael, *Les Gala-
tes* 10, 45 (Skalet 271); cf. Stephanis 2139 (f.
*Πραξίων*)

S. ITALY (CAMPANIA):
—NEAPOLIS: (4) m. i BC *RE* (2)

SICILY:
—SYRACUSE: (5) s. iv BC *AP* ix 434, 3; *Suda
Θ* 166; cf. Gow, *Theocritus* I pp. xv-xvi (f.
*Θεόκριτος*)

**Πράξανδρος**

LAKONIA:
—SPARTA: (1) her. *RE* (-) (Poralla² 636) (and
Cyprus Lapethos: oikist/dub.)

SICILY:
—AKRAGAS: (2) vi/v BC Schol. Pi., *O.* ii 89 e (?s.
*Aἰνησίδαμος*)

**Πραξίας**

ACHAIA: (1) 146 BC *IG* IV (1)² 28, 69 (s. *Διονύσιος*: synoikos); (2) ~ ib. l. 111 (f. *Κεφαλίων*:
synoikos)

ARGOLIS:
—HERMIONE: (3) iii-ii BC ib. IV (1) 679, 37
(Perlman H.3) (f. *Ἀγόραιος*)
—TROIZEN: (4) ?146 BC *IG* IV (1) 757 B, 12 (f.
*Φιλόμηλος*)

ARKADIA: (5) iii BC Breccia, *Iscriz.* 307 (f. *Κρατίδας*)
—PHIGALEIA: (6) i BC/i AD *IvOl* 402 (f. *Ὀνάτας*)
—TEGEA: (7) f. iii BC *IG* v (2) 35, 20 (f. *Μένανδρος*); (8) ?255-253 BC Nachtergael, *Les Galates* 8, 38; 10, 70 (Stephanis 2136) (s. *Κρατέας*)

MESSENIA: (9) ?c. 425 BC *AD* 2 (1916) p. 115
no. 81, 6; *LSAG*² p. 206 no. 11 (date)

SICILY:
—TERRAVECCHIA DI CUTI (MOD.): (10) vi/v BC
Arena, *Iscr. Sic.* II 117 A (Dubois, *IGDS* 176
a 1)

**Πραξίβιος**

LAKONIA:
—GERONTHRAI: (1) v BC *IG* v (1) 1135 (Poralla²
s.v. *Πραξίβιος* 637) (*Π.*—*IG*, *Ἐραξίβιος*—lap.)

**Πραξιδάμας**

AIGINA: (1) m. vi BC *RE* (1); Moretti, *Olymp.*
112 (s. *Σαοκλείδας*)

ARGOLIS:
—METHANA-ARSINOE: (2) i BC *IG* IV (1) 853, 5
(f. *Ἐλπίας*)
—TROIZEN: (3) iii BC ib. 825, 4

**Πραξίδαμος**
ARGOLIS:
—HERMIONE: (1) ?ii-i BC ib. 731 III, 13 (f. Φιλία)
ARKADIA: (2) s. iv BC ib. 11² 8380 (f. Πραξίτας: date—M.J.O.)
—MEGALOPOLIS: (3) ?145 BC ib. v (2) 439, 33 (s. Διονύσιος)
—TEGEA:
——(Krariotai): (4) m. iii BC ib. 36, 94 (f. Θεόδωρος: metic)
DALMATIA:
—ISSA: (5) iv/iii BC Brunšmid p. 7, 1

**Πραξικράτης**
ARKADIA:
—TEGEA: (1) i BC IG v (2) 45, 10

**Πραξίλας**
EPIROS:
—BOUTHROTOS (PRASAIBOI): (1) a. 163 BC IBouthrot 45, 17 (s. Διογένης)

**Πράξιλλα**
KORINTHIA:
—SIKYON: (1) m. v BC RE (-); PMG 747-54 (Skalet 272)

**Πραξιμένης**
ARGOLIS:
—EPIDAUROS*: (1) c. 290-270 BC SEG XXV 402, 124 (Πραξ(ι)μέ[νης])
LAKONIA:
—SPARTA: (2) s. i BC IG v (1) 96, 11 (Bradford (-)) (Γά(ϊος) Π.); (3) c. 100 AD SEG XI 559, 6 (Bradford s.v. Πρασιμένης (2)) (Πρασιμένης—lap.: I f. Λ. Ἀπρώνιος Πραξιμένης II); (4) ~ SEG XI 559, 6 (Bradford s.v. Πρασιμένης (1)) (Λ. Ἀπρώνιος Πρασιμένης—lap.: II s. Πραξιμένης I)

**Πραξιμίας**
ARGOLIS:
—METHANA-ARSINOE: (1) hell.? SEG XXXIX 363 (-ξει-: f. Εὐκλείδας)

**Πράξιμος**
ARGOLIS:
—EPIDAUROS*: (1) c. 370 BC IG IV (1)² 102, 284 (Πράξιμ[ος])

**Πραξινίκα**
MESSENIA:
—MESSENE: (1) i BC ib. v (1) 1476

**Πραξινόα**
SICILY:
—SYRACUSE: (1) c. 272 BC Theoc., Id. xv passim (m. Ζωπυρίων: fict.)

**Πραξίνοος**
ARKADIA:
—MANTINEIA-ANTIGONEIA: (1) c. 425-385 BC IG v (2) 323. 17 (tessera) (s. Ἐγρετίων)

**Πράξινος**
AIGINA: (1) f. iv BC CEG II 532 (s. Τερείας)
ARGOLIS:
—TROIZEN: (2) 480 BC Hdt. vii 180
ARKADIA:
—MANTINEIA-ANTIGONEIA: (3) c. 300-221 BC IG v (2) 323. 84 (tessera) (Πραξίν[ος]: s. Σελίνιος)
LAKONIA:
—SPARTA: (4) f. vi BC SEG II 75-6 (Lazzarini 403c-d); LSAG² p. 198 no. 6 (date) (Poralla² 637a; Bradford (-)) (Π<π>ραξίνος—75, [Π]ραξῖνος—76)

**Πραξίτας**
ACHAIA:
—DYME: (1) ii BC Achaean Grave Stelai 18 (f. Σωτηρίχα)

ARKADIA: (2) s. iv BC IG 11² 8380 (s. Πραξίδαμος: date—M.J.O.)
LAKONIA:
—SPARTA: (3) 393 BC X., HG iv 4. 7-8; iv 4. 13; iv 5. 19 (Poralla² 638)

**Πραξιτέλης**
ARGOLIS:
—HERMIONE: (1) iv BC IG IV (1) 742, 7
—TROIZEN: (2) ?c. 500 BC CEG I 139; cf. Guarducci, Ep. Gr. 1 p. 364; (3) ?146 BC IG IV (1) 757 B, 17
ARKADIA:
—MANTINEIA-ANTIGONEIA: (4) c. 480-460 BC CEG I 380 i (and Sicily Syracuse and Sicily Kamarina: s. Κρῖνις)
—TEGEA: (5) iii BC IG v (2) 30, 7 (s. Σιμίας)
KORINTHIA:
—KORINTH?: (6) c. 335 BC CID II 62 I B I, 80

**Πραξιτίμα**
ARGOLIS:
—PHLEIOUS: (1) iv BC IG IV (1) 468

**Πραξιώ**
ARGOLIS:
—PHLEIOUS: (1) iv/iii BC ib. IV (1)² 620 + Peek, IAEpid 145 (d. Ἐρίτιμος)

**Πραξίων**
ACHAIA: (1) 146 BC IG IV (1)² 28, 61 (I f. Πραξίων II: synoikos); (2) ~ ib. l. 61 (II s. Πραξίων I: synoikos)
—AIGEIRA?: (3) c. 252-248 BC FD III (4) 419, 1 (f. Πλειστέας, Ἀργεῖος)
ARKADIA:
—TEGEA: (4) 356-345 BC CID II 31, 14; 34 I, 40; SEG XXXI 560, 2
KORINTHIA:
—SIKYON: (5) ?253 BC Nachtergael, Les Galates 10, 45 (Skalet 273; Stephanis 2139) (s. Πραξαγόρας)
LAKONIA:
—HIPPOLA: (6) i BC-i AD? IG v (1) 1277 c

**Πραξωνίδας**
ARKADIA:
—STYMPHALOS?: (1) iii BC ib. v (2) 354, 3

**Πρασίων**
MESSENIA:
—ASINE: (1) ii AD ib. v (1) 1408 (s. Πτολλαρίων)

**Πράσων**
LAKONIA:
—SPARTA: (1) 43-31 BC Münzpr. der Laked. p. 155 Group 17 series 16 (coin monogram); p. 161 Group 22 series 4 (coins) (Bradford (-)) (Πράσω[ν])

**Πράτα**
SICILY: (1) f. v BC Dubois, IGDS 218 (vase)

**Πρατακῶν**
ELIS: (1) 36-24 BC IvOl 62, 15 (I f. Πρατακῶν II); (2) ~ ib. l. 15 (II s. Πρατακῶν I: Μέ.)

**Πρατέας**
ARGOLIS:
—ARGOS: (1) ?c. 494-468 BC SEG XI 329 a, 2 (Lazzarini 747); cf. SEG XIII 246; LSAG² p. 169 no. 25 (date) (f. Βᾶλος); (2) iii BC SEG XVII 150, 1, 8 (s. Αἰσχύλος, f. Αἰσχύλος)
LAKONIA:
—SPARTA: (3) ii-i BC IG v (1) 860 (tiles) (Bradford (3)) (Πρατέ(ας)); (4) f. iii AD IG v (1) 794 (Papaefthimiou p. 143 no. 17; Bradford (2)); (5) c. 230-250 AD IG v (1) 314, 3 (Artemis Orthia p. 335 no. 71; BSA 79 (1984) p. 285 no. 17 (date) (Bradford (1)) (M. Αὐρ. [Πρ]ατέας: s. Τύραννος)

**Πρατεόνικος**
LAKONIA:
—KARDAMYLE: (1) ii AD SEG XI 966, 1, 6, 9 (GVI 1931) (II s. Πρατεόνικος I, Δαμώ); (2) ~ SEG XI 966, 7 (GVI 1931) (I f. Πρατεόνικος II)

**Πρατιάδας**
LAKONIA:
—SPARTA: (1) f. i AD IG v (1) 268; Artemis Orthia pp. 305-6 no. 18 (date) (Bradford (-)) (s. Ἀρίστων)

**Πρατίας**
ACHAIA:
—AIGION: (1) 170 BC SGDI 1774, 2 (s. Τελεσίας)
ARGOLIS:
—EPIDAUROS: (2) iv BC IG IV (1)² 172; (3) c. 220-200 BC SEG XI 414, 4 (Perlman E.5) (Πρ[α]τίας)

**Πρατίνας**
ARGOLIS:
—PHLEIOUS: (1) c. 540-470 BC RE (-) (?s. Πυρρωνίδας, Εὐκώμιος, f. Ἀριστίας)

**Πρᾶτις**
ACHAIA:
—PELLENE: (1) m. iii BC IG v (2) 368, 99 (s. Σιμ—)
MESSENIA:
—THOURIA: (2) f. ii BC SEG XI 972, 78 (f. Στέφανος)

**Πρατίων**
LAKONIA: (1) i BC ib. XLII 330
—SPARTA: (2) s. i BC IG v (1) 913; SEG XI 876; 881 b (tiles) (Bradford (1); (2)) (Πρασίων—IG)

**Πρατόδαμος**
LAKONIA:
—SPARTA: (1) 430 BC Th. ii 67. 1 (Poralla² 639)

**Πρατοκλῆς**
ARGOLIS:
—ARGOS: (1) c. 80-70 BC BCH 19 (1895) pp. 338-9 no. 12, 16 + AE 1936, Chron. p. 41 no. 217; BSA 70 (1975) p. 122 (date) (Stephanis 2140) (s. Τιμογένης)

**Πρατόλαος**
ARKADIA:
—TEGEA: (1) f. iii BC IG v (2) 35, 32 (Πρατ[όλαο]ς: f. Εὐρύτιμος)
LAKONIA:
—SPARTA: (2) m. i AD ib. IV (1)² 86, 24 (Peek, IAEpid 36); IG v (1) 580; 644; 605, 1; [847]?; BSA 80 (1985) pp. 194; 198-201 (stemma) (Bradford (6); (7)) (Π. Μέμμιος Π., Πρατόλας—IG 580 and SEG: ?s. Δεξίμαχος, ?f. (nat.) T. Στατίλιος Λαμπρίας Μεμμιανός, f. Π. Μέμμιος Δεξίμαχος, Μεμμία Λογγῖνα, ?f. Μεμμία Δαμοκρατία); (3) i/ii AD IG v (1) 117, 3; SEG XI 518, 3; BSA 80 (1985) pp. 194; 203 (ident., stemma) (Bradford (8)) (Π. Μέμμιος Π. Δέξτρος, Πρατόλας—117: ?s. Π. Μέμμιος Δεξίμαχος); (4) c. 150-225 AD IG v (1) 311, 3; 541, 10; 542, 5 (Artemis Orthia pp. 360-1 no. 146); IG v (1) 543, 7; 544, 15 (Artemis Orthia pp. 358-9 no. 145); IG v (1) 547, 10; 592, 9; BSA 79 (1984) pp. 270-3 (date); 80 (1985) pp. 194; 209-11 (ident., stemma) (Bradford (4)) (Π. Μέμμιος Π. ὁ καὶ Ἀριστοκλῆς: s. Π. Μέμμιος Δαμάρης, f. Π. Μέμμιος Δαμάρης, Μεμμία Λογγῖνα); (5) ~ IG v (1) 472, 8; 497, 2; 498, 3; 526, 9; 589, 4; SEG XI 683 a; 811, 8; BSA 80 (1985) pp. 225; 228-32 (ident., stemma) (Bradford (1); (3)) (Τιβ. Κλ. Π., Πρατόλας—SEG XI 811: I s. Τιβ. Κλ. Βρασίδας, Μεμμία Ἀγήτα, f. (ad.) Τιβ. Κλ. Ἀτλ. Πρατόλαος II ὁ καὶ Δαμοκρατίδας, f. Κλ. Δαμοσθένεια); (6) s. ii AD IG v (1) 537, 15; BSA 80

## Πρατόλας (cont.)

(1985) pp. 194; 205-6 (ident., stemma) (Bradford (9)) (Μέμμιος Π.: s. Π. Μέμμιος Δεξίμαχος); **(7)** f. iii AD *IG* v (1) 497, 10; 587, 11; *BSA* 80 (1985) pp. 225; 232-4; 246-8 (ident., stemma) (Bradford (11)) (Τιβ. Κλ. Αἴλ. Π. ὁ καὶ Δαμοκρατίδας: II ?s. (nat.) Π. Αἴλ. Δαμοκρατίδας, ?s. (ad.) Τιβ. Κλ. Πρατόλαος I); **(8)** ~ *IG* v (1) 589, 20; *BSA* 80 (1985) pp. 225; 238-9 (ident., stemma) (Bradford (10)) (Τιβ. Κλ. Π. ὁ καὶ Δαμοκρατίδας: s. Τιβ. Κλ. Εὔδαμος, Κλ. Δαμοσθένεια, f. Κλ. Ἀλκανδρίδας, Κλ. Ἐλπίς ἡ καὶ Καλλιστονίκη)

## Πρατόλας

Lakonia:
—sparta: **(1)** s. i BC *IG* v (1) 93, 23; 211, 25 (Bradford (2)) ([Π]ρατ[όλ]ας: s. Ἀριστότιμος); **(2)** ~ *IG* v (1) 141, 19, [21]; 142, 3; 209, 4-5; 374, 10; *BSA* 80 (1985) pp. 193-6 (ident., stemma) (Bradford (2); (13)) (f. Γ. Ἰούλ. Δεξίμαχος, Σιδέκτας); **(3)** i BC/i AD *IG* v (1) 143, 1; 263, 3 (*Artemis Orthia* p. 305 no. 17 (date) Bradford)); **(4)** i AD *IG* v (1) 580 (Bradford (7)) (Πό(πλιος) Π.: f. Μεμμία Τιμοσθενίς); **(5)** c. 1-10 AD *IG* v (1) 209, 11; *BSA* 80 (1985) pp. 194; 197 (ident., stemma) (Bradford (5)) (s. Γ. Ἰούλ. Δεξίμαχος); **(6)** c. 70-150 AD *IG* v (1) 53, 10; 54, [12]; 101, 3; 233, 1; 537, 3; *SEG* XI 572, 7; *BSA* 80 (1985) pp. 194; 202-4 (ident., stemma) (Bradford (7); (8)) (Π. Μέμμιος Π., Μέμμιος Δεξίμαχος—101: s. Π. Μέμμιος Δεξίμαχος, f. Π. Μέμμιος Δεξίμαχος, Μεμμία Ἀγήτα); **(7)** c. 110 AD *IG* v (1) 32 B, 10; **(8)** s. ii AD *SEG* XI 811, 3; *BSA* 80 (1985) pp. 225; 228-9 (stemma) (Bradford (12)) (f. Ἀγήτα)

Messenia:
—messene: **(9)** f. iii BC *SEG* XLI 342, 9; cf. *PAE* 1991, p. 100 no. 8 (Πρατόλας, Γασπόλας—*SEG*: name—*LGPN*)

Sicily:
—kamarina: **(10)** f. v BC Cordano, *Tessere Pubbliche* 33 (Πρατόλ[ας]: s. Ἀνδρόσκυλος)

## Πρατομάρης

Sicily:
—terravecchia di cuti (mod.): **(1)** vi/v BC Arena, *Iscr. Sic.* II 117 A (Dubois, *IGDS* 176); Manganaro, *PdelP* forthcoming no. 15 (Πρατομάρε̄ς—PdelP, Πρατομάκε̄ς—Dubois)

## Πρατόμαχος

Epiros:
—votonosi (mod.): **(1)** f. iii BC *SEG* XXIV 457 a ([Π]ρατόμαχος—LGPN, [Κ]ατόμαχος—ed.)

## Πρατομήδης

Arkadia:
—megalopolis: **(1)** ii BC *IG* v (2) 447, 9 (Πρατομ[ήδης]?)

## Πρατομηλίδας

Lakonia:
—sparta: **(1)** i AD Moretti, *Olymp.* 809 (Bradford (1)) ([Πρατο]μηλίδα[s]); **(2)** c. 100-110 AD *SEG* XI 563, 6 (Bradford (3)) (f. Εὐδόκιμος); **(3)** ?f. ii AD *SEG* XI 775 ([Τιβ.] [Κλ.] Πρατομηλίδαρ); **(4)** c. 105-110 AD *BSA* 26 (1923-5) p. 168 no. C 7, 9 (Bradford (2)) (f. Τιβ. Κλ. Νεόλαος)

## Πρατονικία

Lakonia:
—sparta: **(1)** ?ii-i BC *IG* v (1) 227 (Bradford (2)) ([Π]ρατονικία); **(2)** i BC/i AD *IG* v (1) 751 (Bradford (1))

## Πρατόνικος

Argolis:
—epidauros: **(1)** i-ii AD *IG* IV (1)² 38, 5
Lakonia:
—geronthrai: **(2)** ?ii AD *Mél. Daux* p. 225 no. 4; p. 226 no. 5 (-νει-)

—kardamyle: **(3)** i AD *SEG* XI 948, 18 (s. Ἄγιππος)
—leukai: **(4)** imp. *IG* v (1) 1107 II (Πρατόνικος)
—sparta: **(5)** 336-327 BC *CID* II 76 II, [32]; 79 A I, 21; 95, [16]; 97, 26-7; 120 A, 25; 121 III, 19? (Poralla² 640; Bradford (16)); **(6)** i BC-i AD *IG* v (1) 750 (Bradford (8)) (-νει-: s. Εὐκλείδας); **(7)** s. i BC *IG* v (1) 93, 22; 212, 52 (Bradford (11)) (s. Λυσίμαχος); **(8)** ~ *IG* v (1) 94, 3 (Bradford (4)) (s. Διο—); **(9)** ~ *IG* v (1) 133, 3 (Bradford (2)) (s. Ἀρχιτέλης); **(10)** c. 30-20 BC *IG* v (1) 142, 14 (Bradford (23)) (I f. Πρατόνικος II); **(11)** ~ *IG* v (1) 142, 14 (Bradford (12)) (II s. Πρατόνικος I); **(12)** ~ *IG* v (1) 211, 26 (Bradford (9)) (s. Καλλικράτης); **(13)** c. 25-1 BC *IG* v (1) 212, 23 (Bradford (17)); **(14)** ~ *IG* v (1) 212, 38 (Bradford (3)) (s. Δαμονικίδας); **(15)** i BC/i AD *BSA* 89 (1994) pp. 433-4 no. 2, 5 (s. Στρατόνικος); **(16)** ~ *IG* v (1) 48, 4; 212, 48 (Bradford (6)) (s. Ἐπίστρατος); **(17)** c. 10-20 AD *IG* v (1) 206, 2; *SEG* XXXV 330 (date) (Bradford (22)) (f. Ὀνασικλῆς); **(18)** c. 90-100 AD *SEG* XI 512, 6 (Bradford (14)) (-νει-: s. Σίτιμος) ?= (20); **(19)** ~ *SEG* XI 560, 7 (Bradford (19)) (Πρ[α]τόν[ικος]); **(20)** c. 90-125 AD *IG* v (1) 153, 24; *SEG* XI 514, 2?; 558, 3; 559, 2; 560, 2; 593, 1 (Bradford (26)) (Πρατόνεικος—*IG* 153 and *SEG* 559, Πρατ[όνικος]—*SEG* 560: f. Σίτιμος) ?= (18); **(21)** c. 100-110 AD *SEG* XI 611, 2 (Bradford (24)) (I f. Πρατόνικος II); **(22)** ~ *SEG* XI 611, 2 (Bradford (13)) (II s. Πρατόνικος I); **(23)** c. 100-120 AD *SEG* XI 537 a, 2; 637, [2] (Bradford (5)) (Π[ρ]ατόνεικος—537 a: s. Ἔννυχος); **(24)** c. 100-125 AD *IG* v (1) 40, 9; 42, 15, 22 + *SEG* XI 484 (name); *IG* v (1) 66, [5]; 298, 7 (*Artemis Orthia* pp. 315-16 no. 35); *SEG* XI 490, 2 (Bradford (20)) (Γ. Ἰούλ. Π., Πρατόνεικος—*IG* 42) ?= (25); **(25)** ii AD *IG* v (1) 123, 1 ?= (24); **(26)** c. 105-110 AD ib. 20 B, 11 (Bradford (7)) (-νει-: s. Εὔδαμος); **(27)** c. 130 AD *IG* v (1) 60, 3 (Bradford (10)) (Πρατό<υ>νικος: s. Λυσιάδας); **(28)** c. 140 AD *IG* v (1) 128, 6 (Bradford (27)) (Πρατόνε[ικος]); **(29)** c. 140-160 AD *SEG* XI 592 (Bradford (21)) ([Πρ]ατόνεικ[ος]); **(30)** c. 170 AD *SEG* XI 487; 530, 2 (Bradford (25)) ([Πρα]τόνικος: f. Πρατύλος)
——Limnai: **(31)** c. 70-100 AD *IG* v (1) 676, 10 (Bradford (15)) (s. —οφῶν)
Messenia:
—abia: **(32)** ?i/ii AD *IG* v (1) 1358, 2 (II s. Πρατόνικος I); **(33)** ~ ib. l. 3 (I f. Πρατόνικος II)
—messene: **(34)** iii BC *SEG* XXIII 210, 6; **(35)** s. ii BC ib. XLI 341, 17 (f. —ης)
—thouria: **(36)** s. iii BC *IG* v (1) 1386, 13 (f. Ἀντίας); **(37)** f. ii BC *SEG* XI 972, 101 (s. Ἀριστοκλῆς)

## Πρᾶτος

Akarnania: **(1)** hell. *Syringes* 593
Sicily:
—kamarina: **(2)** v-iv BC *ASSiciliano* 1966, p. 139 (Cordano, 'Camarina VII' 145)

## Πρατότας

Sicily:
—selinous?: **(1)** v BC *SEG* XXXIX 1021 I, 1

## Πράτουσα

Lakonia:
—sparta: **(1)** ii-iii AD *Laconia Survey* 2 p. 219 no. 12

## Πρατυΐδης?

Sicily:
—himera: **(1)** s. vi BC *Himera* 2 p. 691 no. 179 (sherd) (Dubois, *IGDS* 7) ([Πρ]ατυΐδης)

## Πρατύλος

Lakonia:
—hyperteleaton*: **(1)** imp. *IG* v (1) 1020
—sparta: **(2)** c. 170 AD *SEG* XI 487; 530, 1 (Bradford (1)) ([Πρα]τύλος: s. Πρατόνικος)
——Konosoura: **(3)** c. 212-230 AD *IG* v (1) 684, 12 (Bradford (2)) (Αὐρ. Π.)

## Πράτυρ

S. Italy (Apulia):
—canusium: **(1)** imp.? *Epig. Rom. di Canosa* 193 (*CIL* IX 401 (biling.)) ([Π]ράτυρ: s. Τίτουρος)

## Πράτων

Argolis:
—argos: **(1)** iv/iii BC *IG* IV (1) 572
Sicily:
—morgantina: **(2)** ?iv/iii BC *SEG* XXXIX 1009, 8 (f. Ἱπποσθένης)
—petra:
——(Σάννειος): **(3)** f. iii BC ib. XXX 1121, 24 (Dubois, *IGDS* 208); cf. *SEG* XL 785 (f. Θεόδωρος, Αἰσχύλις)
—selinous: **(4)** ?c. 425-400 BC Marcadé 1 2 (Dubois, *IGDS* 83); *LSAG*² p. 277 no. 44 (date) (f. Ἄκρων)

## Πραυγαῖος

Illyria:
—bylliones (rabije (mod.)): **(1)** ?s. ii BC *SEG* XXXII 626, 2; cf. XXXVIII 520; cf. *CRAI* 1991, p. 197 ff. ([Πρ]αυγαῖος: s. Πραυγισσός)

## Πραυγίμμας

Illyria:
—bylliones (rabije (mod.)): **(1)** ?s. ii BC *SEG* XXXII 626, 4; cf. XXXVIII 520; cf. *CRAI* 1991, p. 197 ff. ([Πρα]υγίμμας: s. Νικα—); **(2)** ~ *SEG* XXXII 626, 6; cf. XXXVIII 520; cf. *CRAI* 1991, p. 197 ff. ([Πρα]υγίμμας: s. Βοΐσκος)

## Πραυγισσός

Illyria:
—bylliones: **(1)** iii BC *SEG* XXXVIII 565
—bylliones (rabije (mod.)): **(2)** ?s. ii BC ib. XXXII 626, 2; cf. XXXVIII 520; cf. *CRAI* 1991, p. 197 ff. (Πραυγισ[σός]: f. Πραυγαῖος); **(3)** ~ *SEG* XXXII 626, 7 + XXXVIII 520; cf. *CRAI* 1991, p. 197 ff. ([Πρα]υγισσός: s. Διτ—)
—lissos: **(4)** imp. *Op. Ath.* 10 (1971) p. 81 n. 19 (s. Νικόδαμος)

## Πράϋλα

Epiros: **(1)** c. 240-220 BC *JHS* 57 (1937) p. 35 no. 9; cf. *IKourion* 60 comm. (Πρά[ϋλ]α: d. Μνασίμαχος, m. Ἀντίοχος)
Illyria:
—epidamnos-dyrrhachion: **(2)** hell.-imp. *IDyrrh* 362 (d. Ὀέρδιος)

## Πραϋλίς

Akarnania:
—stratos: **(1)** ii BC *SEG* XXIX 477
—thyrreion: **(2)** ?iii BC ib. XL 463
Sicily:
—syracuse (nesos): **(3)** iii-v AD ib. IV 18 (Wessel 3)

## Πράϋλλας

Illyria:
—bylliones nikaia (kljos (mod.)): **(1)** iii/ii BC *SEG* XXXV 696; cf. XXXVIII 569 (Πρα[ϋλ]λας: s. Ἀρτεμίδωρος)

## Πραϋλλίς

Epiros: **(1)** ?iv BC *IG* II² 8542

## Πράϋλλος

Illyria:
—olympe: **(1)** s. iii BC *SEG* XXXV 697 (s. Στράβιος)

## Πραΰλος
ARGOLIS:
—EPIDAUROS: (1) ii BC *IG* IV (1)² 355
EPIROS:
—ANTIGONEIA: (2) imp. *AE* 1914, p. 238 no. 15; Cabanes, *L'Épire* p. 234 n. 96 (locn.) (s. Σωστρίων)
—BOUTHROTOS (PRASAIBOI): (3) a. 163 BC *IBouthrot* 32, 16 (*SEG* XXXVIII 491)
ILLYRIA:
—BYLLIONES: (4) i BC Cabanes, *L'Épire* p. 562 no. 36 (*SEG* XXXVIII 570) (Πραΰ[λος]: f. Ἀσπίμμας)
—BYLLIONES BYLLIS: (5) ?ii BC ib. 522 (Π[ρα]ΰλος)
—EPIDAMNOS-DYRRHACHION: (6) ii-i BC *IDyrrh* 410 (f. Τευταία); (7) hell.-imp. ib. 345 (f. Περιγένης); (8) ~ ib. 363 (s. Περιγένης)
—SKODRAI: (9) a. 168 BC *Iliria* 1972, p. 402 (coin)
ITHAKE: (10) hell. *PAE* 1992, p. 210; (11) 208 BC *IMM* 36, 23 (f. Ἱγέρτας)
KORINTHIA:
—SIKYON: (12) vi/v BC *SEG* XI 244, 18

## Πραϋχίων
AKARNANIA:
—ASTAKOS: (1) m. iii BC ib. XXVII 153, 2-3; cf. *PAE* 1977, pl. 244 b (f. Ῥυσιάδας, —σων)

## Πράϋχος
AKARNANIA:
—ASTAKOS: (1) ii BC *IG* IX (1)² (2) 435, 7 (s. Πεισίθεος)
—STRATOS: (2) hell.? ib. 414 a (f. Κέφαλος)
ITHAKE: (3) inc. *AM* 27 (1902) p. 375

## Πρεπίς
S. ITALY (BRUTTIUM):
—KROTON: (1) ?i AD *CIL* X 109 (Lat. Iulia Prepis: d. Πρέπουσα, ?m. Γλάγος)
S. ITALY (CAMPANIA):
—DIKAIARCHIA-PUTEOLI: (2) i/ii AD ib. 2917 (Sinn, *Stadtröm. Marmorurnen* 457) (Lat. Roscia Prepis)
—SALERNUM*: (3) imp. *CIL* X 556 (Lat. Antonia Prepis: freed.)

## Πρεποντίων
ARKADIA:
—TEGEA: (1) imp.? *IG* V (2) 258
SICILY:
—SYRACUSE: (2) iii-v AD Ferrua, *NG* 309 (Πρεπόντι[ος] - ed.)

## Πρέπουσα
ACHAIA:
—DYME: (1) ii-i BC *SEG* XIV 373 b
S. ITALY (BRUTTIUM):
—KROTON: (2) ?i AD *CIL* X 109 (Lat. Prepusa: m. Πρεπίς)
S. ITALY (CAMPANIA):
—DIKAIARCHIA-PUTEOLI: (3) imp. ib. 2617; 2626 (Lat. Iunia Prepusa: m. Ἵλαρος, Ἀττίκιλλα, Iunia Sperata); (4) ~ ib. 2625 (Lat. Iunia Prepusa); (5) ~ *NScav* 1897, p. 531 fig. 5 (Audollent, *Defix. Tab.* 203 (terracotta))
—DIKAIARCHIA-PUTEOLI*: (6) imp. *CIL* X 2826, 7 (Lat. [Patulci]a Prepusa: freed.)
—POMPEII: (7) i BC-i AD ib. 1062 (Castrèn 405. 2) (Lat. Tettia Prepusa)
S. ITALY (LUCANIA):
—ATINA LUCANA: (8) imp. *IItal* III (1) 186 (*CIL* X 366) (Lat. Tatia Prepusa: d. M. Tatius Fructianus)
—VOLCEI: (9) imp. *IItal* III (1) 97 (Lat. Praepusa: m. M. Insteius Pulcher)
SICILY:
—SYRACUSE: (10) iii-v AD *IG* XIV 46 (Strazzulla 131; Wessel 233); cf. *Riv. Arch. Crist.* 18 (1941) p. 185 no. 51

## Πρέπων
DALMATIA:
—ISSA: (1) imp. *CIL* III 14333. 2 (Lat. Prepon)
ELIS: (2) s. i BC *IvOl* 66, 5, 7, 9 (?f. Ὀλυμπίων, Ἐπιμέλης, Ἡρακλείδης)
KERKYRA: (3) i AD *IG* IX (1) 712 (Λ. Σαίνιος Π.: s. Φίλιππος)
S. ITALY (CAMPANIA):
—DIKAIARCHIA-PUTEOLI: (4) i/ii AD *CIL* X 2917 (Sinn, *Stadtröm. Marmorurnen* 457) (Lat. L. Roscius Prepon)
—POMPEII: (5) i BC-i AD *CIL* IV 1399 (Lat. Iulius Prepo)
SICILY:
—SYRACUSE: (6) iii-v AD *SEG* XVIII 403

## Πρεσβύλος
ILLYRIA:
—APOLLONIA: (1) i BC Maier 125 (coin); Münsterberg Nachtr. p. 12 (s. Τιμόξενος: money.)
—BYLLIONES BYLLIS (NR.): (2) hell. *Iliria* 1982 (1), p. 108 no. 23 = p. 121 no. 47 (tile)

## Πρετιῶσα
S. ITALY (APULIA):
—VENUSIA: (1) v AD *JIWE* I 66 (*CIJ* I 591) (d. Φαυστῖνος: Jew)
SICILY:
—SYRACUSE: (2) imp. *SEG* XVI 539 i

## Πρευγένης
LAKONIA:
—AMYKLAI: (1) her. *RE* (-) (and Achaia Patrai: f. Πατρεύς, Ἀθερίων: oikist/dub.)

## Πρευκλητία
LAKONIA:
—SPARTA: (1) c. 170 AD *IG* V (1) 116, 11; *SEG* XI 590 (name) (Bradford (-))

## Πρεύραδος
ILLYRIA:
—APOLLONIA: (1) c. 250-50 BC Maier 87 (coin) (Ceka 94) (money.)

## Πρεύρατος
ILLYRIA:
—EPIDAMNOS-DYRRHACHION: (1) hell.-imp. *IDyrrh* 48 (s. Κλεον—); (2) ~ ib. 106 (f. Ἀννίκα); (3) ~ ib. 364 (s. Κλέων)

## Πρίαμος
S. ITALY (APULIA):
—GNATHIA-EGNATIA: (1) ii AD *Suppl. It.* 11 p. 43 no. 25 (Lat. C. Nevius Priamus)
S. ITALY (BRUTTIUM):
—SYBARIS-THOURIOI-COPIAE: (2) s. i BC *Epigraphica* 38 (1976) pp. 133-5; cf. *Atti Conv. Taranto* 32 (1992) p. 405 (date) (Lat. P. Paquius Priamus)

## Πριανθίς
LAKONIA:
—SPARTA?: (1) vi BC *IG* V (1) 226 (bronze) (Lazzarini 86); *LSAG*² p. 200 no. 39 (date) (Poralla² 641) (Πριανθίς)

## Πρίβατος
SICILY:
—SYRACUSE: (1) iii-v AD *IG* XIV 181 (Strazzulla 119; Agnello 14; Wessel 248); cf. Ferrua, *NG* 179 (Πρέ-)

## Πρικιπῖνα
ILLYRIA:
—BYLLIONES (GRESHICE (MOD.)): (1) iii AD *SEG* XXXVIII 543 (-κειπεῖ-)

## Πρίμα
ARGOLIS:
—ARGOS: (1) imp. *BCH* 33 (1909) p. 460 no. 24 (Πρεῖ-)

## Πρῖμος (col 3 top — Illyria continuation)
ILLYRIA:
—APOLLONIA: (2) i-ii AD *IApoll* 225; (3) ~ ib. 266; (4) ii AD ib. 216 (Πρεῖ-: slave?/freed.?)
SICILY:
—LIPARA: (5) imp. *BTCGI* 9 p. 96 (Πρεῖ-); (6) ~ ib.

## Πρίμερος
ARGOLIS:
—ARGOS: (1) ii AD *SEG* XLI 285 II, 35 (Πρεί-)

## Πριμιτῖβα
S. ITALY (CAMPANIA):
—NEAPOLIS: (1) iii-iv AD *INap* 247 (-τεῖ-)

## Πριμιτῖβος
SICILY:
—KATANE: (1) imp. *IG* XIV 497 a (Π[ρ]ειμιτεῖβος)

## Πριμίων
ELIS: (1) c. 221-230 AD *IvOl* 113, 13 ([Πρ]ειμίων)
—OLYMPIA*: (2) i BC/i AD ib. 74, 9 (Πρει-: ?s. Ἁρμόδιος: slave?)
ILLYRIA:
—APOLLONIA: (3) i BC-i AD *IApoll* 170 (Πρει-: s. Λυκόφρων)
KORINTHIA:
—KORINTH: (4) ii-iii AD *SEG* XXVII 35. 23 (lamp) (Πρειμιώνου (gen.))
S. ITALY (BRUTTIUM):
—RHEGION: (5) i BC/i AD ib. XXXIX 1062 A (Ἀλφιος Π.)
SICILY:
—SELINOUS: (6) i BC-i AD *IGLMP* 101

## Πριμογένεια
SICILY:
—COMISO (MOD.): (1) iii-v AD Pace, *Camarina* p. 163 no. 16 (*Riv. Arch. Crist.* 18 (1941) p. 201 no. 73); cf. Cordano, 'Camarina VII' 146 (Πριγομένια)
—THERMAI HIMERAIAI: (2) iii-v AD *SEG* XXXVI 832 (Πρειγομενία)

## Πριμογένης
EPIROS:
—NIKOPOLIS: (1) imp. ib. XXXIX 529 (Πρειμι-)
S. ITALY (BRUTTIUM):
—RHEGION*: (2) i BC/i AD ib. 1062 B-C (Πριμιγένης—C: slave?)
SICILY:
—KATANE: (3) iii-v AD *IG* XIV 546 (Wessel 752) (Πριγο-)
—SYRACUSE: (4) iii-v AD Strazzulla 342 (Wessel 1339); cf. Ferrua, *NG* 125 (Πριγόνης—lap., Πριγο(μέ)νης—Ferrua)

## Πριμογενιανός
KORINTHIA:
—KORINTH: (1) ii AD *JÖAI* 15 (1912) p. 54 no. 27, 7 (Μ. Αἰφίκιος Πριμιγενιανός)

## Πριμογένις
SICILY:
—KATANE: (1) imp. *IG* XIV 467 (Πριμι-: s. Γαλάτης)

## Πρῖμος
ARKADIA:
—MANTINEIA-ANTIGONEIA: (1) ?ii AD *IG* V (2) 327, 2, 11 (*GVI* 1066) (Πρεῖ-: s. Φίλα, f. Ἰόλη)
—TEGEA: (2) ii AD *IG* V (2) 55, 54 (Πρεῖ-: s. Δάφνος); (3) ~ ib. l. 81 (I f. Πρῖμος II); (4) ~ ib. l. 81 (II s. Πρῖμος I); (5) m. ii AD ib. 48, 14 (Πρεῖμο[ς])
ELIS: (6) 245-249 AD *IvOl* 121, 6 (Πρεῖ-: f. Αὐρ. Ἰουλιανός)
—OLYMPIA*: (7) imp. ib. 660; (8) c. 177-189 AD ib. 103, 28-9; 104, 25 (Πρεῖμος—104: ?s. Εὔτυχος: slave?)

KORINTHIA:
—KORINTH: (9) ii/iii AD *Corinth* IV (2) pp. 189
no. 566; 204 no. 692; 210 nos. 755-7; XVIII
(2) p. 30 no. 31; *SEG* XXVII 35. 22 (lamps)
(Πρεῖ-)
LAKONIA:
—SPARTA: (10) c. 50-80 AD *IG* V (1) 277, 2, 6;
*Artemis Orthia* pp. 308-9 no. 25 (date) (Brad-
ford (-)) (s. Νηρεύς)
S. ITALY (BRUTTIUM):
—HIPPONION-VIBO VALENTIA: (11) i BC-i AD
*SEG* 11 635
S. ITALY (CAMPANIA):
—NEAPOLIS: (12) iii-iv AD *IG* XIV 826. 38
(*INap* 226) (Πρεῖ-)
SICILY:
—AKRAI: (13) iii-v AD *Akrai* p. 168 no. 45
—KATANE: (14) imp. *IG* XIV 498; cf. *MEFRA*
106 (1994) p. 94 no. 7 (Πρεῖ-); (15) iii-v AD
Agnello 61 (f. Ἰανουάριος)
—SYRACUSE: (16) iii-v AD Strazzulla 406
(Wessel 139) (Πρεῖ-)

### Πρινητάδας
LAKONIA:
—SPARTA: (1) m. vi BC Hdt. v 41. 3 (Poralla²
642) (-δης: s. Δαμάρμενος)

### Πρίσκος
EPIROS:
—THESPROTOI: (1) iv AD *RE* (28); Seeck,
*Libanius* Priscus 1 (or Epiros Molossoi)
LAKONIA:
—HYPERTELEATON*: (2) imp. *IG* V (1) 1066
(Πρεί-: f. Χρυσάωρ)
SICILY:
—SYRACUSE: (3) iii-v AD *SEG* XXVII 662

### Προαγόρας
ARKADIA:
—MEGALOPOLIS: (1) 204 BC Plb. xiii 8. 7

### Προαγορίδας
ARKADIA:
—MANTINEIA-ANTIGONEIA: (1) m. iii BC *IG* V
(2) 368, 115 (f. —ίας)

### Προάγορος
ARKADIA:
—MEGALOPOLIS: (1) s. ii BC ib. 460 (and Lako-
nia Sparta: s. Δίαιος)

### Πρόαινος
KORINTHIA:
—KORINTH: (1) 393 BC X., *HG* iv 8. 10

### Πρόανδρος
AITOLIA:
—PHOLAI: (1) 178 BC *Syll*³ 636, 16 (I f. Πρόαν-
δρος II); (2) c. 178-171 BC *RE* (-); *IG* IX (1)²
(1) p. LII, s.a. 171 BC; *Syll*³ 636, 16 (II s.
Πρόανδρος I)
AKARNANIA:
—STRATOS: (3) c. 225-200 BC *IG* IX (1)² (1) 31,
8

### Πρόαρχος
ARKADIA?: (1) iv/iii BC *HE* 676 (?s. Φειδίας)

### Προαύγα?
LAKONIA:
—SPARTA: (1) f. iv BC Plu., *Ages*. 19; *RE* (-)
(Poralla² 648 s.v. Προλύτα) (Π.—ms. S, Προ-
λύτα—ms. Y, Ἱππολύτα—Keil and Ziegler: d.
Ἀγησίλαος, Κλεόρα)

### Πρόβα
SICILY:
—LIPARA: (1) iii-v AD Bernabò Brea, *Isole Eolie*
pp. 165 ff.; cf. Ferrua, *NG* 533

### Πρόγαμος
S. ITALY (CAMPANIA):
—POMPEII: (1) i BC-i AD *CIL* IV 8976 (Lat. Pro-
gamus)

### Πρόδαμος
S. ITALY (CAMPANIA):
—POMPEII*: (1) i AD ib. X 8042. 91; *Riv. Ist.
Naz. Arch. Stor. d'Arte* 10 (1987) p. 83 no.
204 (tiles) (Lat. L. Saginius Prodamus)

### Πρόδικος
ARGOLIS:
—EPIDAUROS: (1) c. 335-325 BC *IG* IV (1)² 106
I, 60, [62]; *SEG* XXV 389, 19, [37]

### Πρόδοξος
SICILY:
—KAMARINA: (1) m. v BC Dubois, *IGDS* 120,
8 (Arena, *Iscr. Sic.* II 142 A; *SEG* XXXVIII
939; Cordano, 'Camarina VII' 51) (f. Πολε-
μαίνετος); (2) ?iv/iii BC *SEG* XXXIX 1001, 8
(s. Λυκίσκος); (3) ?ii BC ib. 996, 10 (Dubois,
*IGDS* 126; Cordano, 'Camarina VII' 147) (s.
Σωσίας)

### Πρόθοος
LAKONIA:
—SPARTA: (1) 371 BC X., *HG* vi 4. 2; Plu., *Ages*.
28 (Poralla² 643)

### Προθυμία
S. ITALY (CAMPANIA):
—POMPEII: (1) i BC-i AD *CIL* IV 8497 (Lat. Pro-
thymia)

### Προθύμιος
AIGINA: (1) ?v BC *IG* IV (1) 183

### Πρόθυμος
ILLYRIA:
—EPIDAMNOS-DYRRHACHION: (1) hell.-imp.
*IDyrrh* 365; (2) ~ ib. 366
S. ITALY (APULIA):
—VENUSIA: (3) ii AD *Rend. Linc.* 29 (1974) p.
610 no. 6 (*Museo di Venosa* p. 147 no. 3) (Lat.
P. Tullius Prothymus)
SICILY:
—LILYBAION: (4) ?ii-i BC *SEG* XXXIV 955; cf.
XXXIX 1005 (f. Ἀχιλλεύς)

### Προῖτος
AKARNANIA:
—MATROPOLIS: (1) m. ii BC *IG* IX (1)² (2) 208,
5, [34] (s. Διοπείθης)
ELIS:
—OLYMPIA*: (2) v BC *IvOl* 658 (Προῖτ(ος): f.
Λεύκασπις)

### Πρόκλα
ARKADIA:
—KLEITOR: (1) hell.? *IG* V (2) 382
ELIS: (2) ii/iii AD *IvOl* 467, 3 (Βαιβία Π.: d.
Καικίλιος Πρόκλος, Ἀντ. Πῶλλα)
S. ITALY (CALABRIA):
—BRENTESION-BRUNDISIUM: (3) imp. *CIL* IX
163 (Lat. Cerelliana Procla)
S. ITALY (CAMPANIA):
—HERCULANEUM: (4) i BC-i AD ib. IV 10577

### Προκλείδας
AKARNANIA:
—ANAKTORION?: (1) ?c. 475-450 BC *CEG* I 142;
cf. *IG* IX (1)² (2) 214 (locn.) (Προκλείδα<ς>?)
ARGOLIS:
—ARGOS: (2) ii/i BC ib. IV (1) 635
ARKADIA:
—PHIGALEIA: (3) s. iv BC *SEG* XXIII 240; (4) ii
BC *IG* V (2) 420 (s. Ἀρίστων)

### Πρόκλη
S. ITALY (CAMPANIA):
—NEAPOLIS: (1) ii-iii AD ib. XIV 806 (*INap* 155)

### Προκλῆς
AIGINA: (1) c. 470 BC *SEG* III 310 (bronze)
(Guarducci, *Ep. Gr.* I pp. 198-9 no. 3; Laz-
zarini 56); *LSAG*² p. 113 no. 16 (date) (f.
Πλάθων, Ἐκεσθένης)
ARGOLIS:
—EPIDAUROS: (2) her. Paus. vii 4. 2 (and
Samos: s. Πιτυρεύς, f. Λεώγορος (Samos): oi-
kist); (3) s. vii BC *RE* (3) (f. Λυσιδίκα ἡ καὶ
Μέλισσα: tyrant)
—PHLEIOUS: (4) f. iv BC ib. (8) (s. Ἱππόνικος)
LAKONIA:
—SPARTA: (5) her. ib. (1) (Poralla² 644)
(s. Ἀριστόδαμος, Ἀργεία, ?f. Σόος, Εὐρυφῶν:
king/dub.); (6) 400-399 BC *RE* (7) (Poralla²
645) (and Mysia Teuthrania); (7) iv/iii BC
S.E., *M.* i 258 (Poralla² 646) (I f. Δαμάρατος,
Προκλῆς II); (8) ~ S.E., *M.* i 258 (Poralla²
647) (II s. Προκλῆς I, Πυθιάς (Stageiros))
S. ITALY (LUCANIA):
—HYELE-VELIA: (9) hell.? *PdelP* 25 (1970) p.
264 no. 8 (-κλέης: f. Κοκκύς)
—METAPONTION: (10) iv BC Iamb., *VP* 267
(*FVS* I p. 446)
SICILY:
—NAXOS: (11) 413-406 BC *HN*² pp. 160-1;
*Samml. Ludwig* (coin engraver); (12) 403 BC
*PCG* 5 p. 205 fr. 27; D.S. xiv 15. 2

### Προκλιανός
ARGOLIS:
—TROIZEN: (1) imp. *IG* IV (1) 835 A, 9; 835 B,
8 (Κλ. Π.)

### Πρόκλος
ELIS: (1) ii/iii AD *IvOl* 467, 5 (Καικίλιος Π.: f.
Βαιβία Πρόκλα)
ILLYRIA:
—APOLLONIA: (2) imp. *IApoll* 226 ([Π]ρόκλος)
KORINTHIA:
—KORINTH: (3) 3 AD *Corinth* VIII (1) 14, 76 (Γ.
Οὐιβούλλιος Π.); (4) ?39 AD ib. VIII (3) 156, 2
(Lat. A. Arrius Procl[us])
—KORINTH?: (5) c. 45 AD *FD* III (1) 534, 6-7
(Ἰουβέντιος Π.)
LAKONIA:
—SPARTA: (6) c. 150-160 AD *SEG* XI 585, 13;
XXX 410, [23] (Bradford (-)) (Γ. Ἰούλ. Π.)
MESSENIA:
—MESSENE: (7) 31 BC-14 AD *SEG* XXIII 207, 21;
*IvOl* 428, 3 (Μ. Ἀντ. Π.)
S. ITALY (CALABRIA):
—BRENTESION-BRUNDISIUM: (8) imp. *Rend.
Linc.* 24 (1969) p. 169 no. 1 (threptos)
S. ITALY (CAMPANIA):
—NEAPOLIS: (9) 71 AD *INap* 84 col. I, 6 (Ἰούλ.
Π. Ἀρτ.)
—POMPEII: (10) i BC-i AD *CIL* IV 1281 (Lat.
Proclus)
SICILY:
—AGYRION: (11) f. ii AD *IG* XIV 2405. 34; *BM
Lamps* 3 pp. 209-10 nos. Q1861, Q1866-7
(lamps)
—SYRACUSE: (12) iii-v AD Strazzulla 206; (13) ~
Ferrua, *NG* 365

### Πρόκνη
S. ITALY (APULIA):
—CANUSIUM*: (1) imp. *Epig. Rom. di Canosa*
201 (*CIL* IX 405) (Lat. Tagullia Procne:
freed.)
—LAVELLO (MOD.): (2) imp. ib. 649 (Lat. Oppia Prochne)

### Προκόπη
ILLYRIA:
—EPIDAMNOS-DYRRHACHION: (1) ?i AD *BUST*
1961 (1), p. 113 no. 11 (Lat. Sentia Procope)

### Πρόκριτος
ACHAIA:
—DYME*: (1) c. 219 BC *SGDI* 1612, 48, 52
(*Tyche* 5 (1990) p. 124) (f. Βουθύων)

**Πρόλαος**
ARKADIA:
—MANTINEIA-ANTIGONEIA: (2) c. 300-221 BC *IG* v (2) 323. 93 (tessera) (f. Πόλλις)
—TEGEA: (3) iii BC ib. 12

**Πρόλαος**
ELIS: (1) inc. Paus. v 2. 4 (f. Φίλανθος, Λάμπος)

**Πρόλοχος**
KEPHALLENIA?: (1) c. 330 BC *SEG* XXIII 189 I, 24 (f. —ος)

**Πρόμαθος**
AITOLIA:
—VLACHOMANDRA (MOD.): (1) s. vii BC *CEG* I 140

**Προμαχίδας**
KERKYRA: (1) ii BC *IG* IX (1) 694, 38 (*RIJG* XXV B); cf. *SEG* XXV 609 (s. Μυρτίλος); (2) ?ii BC *IG* IX (1) 796-7 (tiles)
KORINTHIA:
—SIKYON: (3) iv-iii BC Unp. (Sikyon Mus.); (4) c. 146-32 BC *BMC Pelop.* p. 52 no. 200; *NC* 1984, p. 14 Group 10 no. 2 (coin)

**Πρόμαχος**
ACHAIA:
—PELLENE: (1) v/iv BC Moretti, *Olymp.* 355 (s. Δρύων)
ARGOLIS:
—ARGOS: (2) f. ii BC *IG* XI (4) 1236 (Πρόμα[χος]: s. Ἀπολλώνιος)
KORINTHIA:
—KORINTH: (3) c. 570-550 BC Amyx 53. 3 (vase) (Lorber 138) (her.); (4) m. ii AD *Corinth* VIII (3) 265, 3 (*M. Ἀντ. Π.*)
LAKONIA: (5) c. 350-320 BC *SEG* XII 193, 2 (*CEG* II 587; *GVI* 1820; Poralla² 648a) (f. Πλαγγών: date—M.J.O.)

**Προμένεια**
EPIROS:
—DODONA: (1) m. v BC Hdt. ii 55 (fict.?)

**Πρόμνησος**
KEPHALLENIA: (1) her. Arist. fr. 611. 64 (Heraclid. Lemb. 64) (fict.)

**Πρόμουτος**
SICILY:
—SYRACUSE: (1) iii AD *NScav* 1907, p. 755 no. 1 (Barreca 288)

**Προνόα**
TRIPHYLIA:
—MAKISTOS: (1) 399-369 BC *SEG* XXXV 389, 12; cf. *Tyche* 2 (1987) p. 275 f. (masc./fem.?)

**Πρόνοια**
ILLYRIA:
—APOLLONIA: (1) ii-i BC *IApoll* 144
LAKONIA:
—BOIAI: (2) ii AD *IG* v (1) 958, 5; 959, 5 (d. Μελίχρως, Ἡρακλέα)

**Πρόνομος**
ARGOLIS:
—MYKENAI*: (1) iv-iii BC ib. IV (1) 500 (s. Εὐβωλίδας)

**Πρόνοος**
ARGOLIS:
—TROIZEN: (1) iii BC ib. 825, 7

**Προξένα**
TRIPHYLIA:
—LEPREON: (1) iii/ii BC *SEG* XXII 360, 1

**Προξενίδας**
ACHAIA:
—PHARAI: (1) iii-ii BC *Achaean Grave Stelai* 61 (s. Ξεναῖος)

**Προξενίδης**
ELIS: (1) 20-16 BC *IvOl* 65, 3 (f. Ἀλεξίων: N.); (2) m. i AD ib. 337, 2; 338, 3; [339]; cf. 340-4 (f. Πολύκλειτος)

**Πρόξενος**
AIGINA: (1) ?iii BC *IG* IV (1) 150 (or Boiotia?: s. Καλλίγειτος)
AITOLIA: (2) f. iii BC *SEG* XVI 373, 2 (f. Δαμασίας)
—TRICHONION: (3) 224 or 221 BC Nachtergael, *Les Galates* 64, 1; cf. *BCH* 53 (1929) p. 26 no. 4, [2]; *FD* III (4) [230] (f. Χαρίξενος); (4) f. ii BC *RE* Supplbd. 11 (10a); *IG* IX (1)² (1) p. LI, s.a. 183 BC
AITOLIA?: (5) 288 BC ib. II² 652, 21; Flacelière p. 90 n. 2 (locn.) (f. Αἴσχρων); (6) 204 BC *IG* II² 845, 12 (f. Αἴσχρων)
AKARNANIA:
—TYRBEION/TORYBEIA: (7) 356-354 BC ib. IV (1)² 95, 18 (Perlman E.2); Perlman p. 40 f. (date); cf. *BCH* 90 (1966) pp. 174 f. (locn.) (πρόξενος—ed.)
ARKADIA:
—KLEITOR: (8) 369-361 BC *IG* v (2) 1, 57; Tod, *GHI* II 132 (date)
—MEGALOPOLIS: (9) 360 BC *CID* II 4 III, 54 (f. Νικόλοχος); (10) 208 BC *IMM* 38, 26; (11) s. ii BC *IG* v (2) 439, 82 (Πρόξ[ενος]); (12) ii/i BC ib. 443, 8; 444, 6; 445, 11 (*IPArk* 32) (s. Ἀριστόδαμος)
—PHENEOS: (13) f. iv BC Paus. vi 1. 3 (f. Νεολαΐδας)
—TEGEA: (14) m. iv BC *IG* v (2) 6, 76; (15) c. 369 BC *RE* (7) (and Arkadia Megalopolis: oikist); (16) iii BC *SEG* XXII 317
——(Athaneatai): (17) s. iv BC *IG* v (2) 41, 35 (s. Μύλλων)
DALMATIA:
—ISSA: (18) iv/iii BC Brunšmid p. 9 fr. G, 16 + *VAMZ* 1970, p. 37 frr. G (Πρόξ[ενος]—LGPN, Πρώ[ταρχος]—edd.: f. Διονύσιος)
EPIROS:
—AMBRAKIA: (19) f. ii BC *AD* 39 (1984) Chron. p. 190 + pl. 77 γ (f. —στρατος)
EPIROS?: (20) iii BC *RE* (13); *FGrH* 703
ILLYRIA:
—EPIDAMNOS-DYRRHACHION: (21) ii-i BC *IDyrrh* 556 (tile) ([Π]ρόξενος)
LAKONIA: (22) ii BC *IG* v (1) 1111, 16
PELOPONNESE?: (23) s. iii BC ib. 1426, 7, 11
S. ITALY (BRUTTIUM):
—LOKROI EPIZEPHYRIOI: (24) ?c. 450-425 BC Th. iii 103. 3; Lazzarini 342 (Landi, *DISMG* 62); *LSAG*² p. 286 no. 7; *SEG* XXIX 952 (name) (s. Καπάρων)
——(Κρα.): (25) 276 BC De Franciscis 23, 5 (s. Σαθύων)
—SYBARIS-THOURIOI-COPIAE: (26) iv BC Iamb., *VP* 267 (*FVS* 1 p. 446)
S. ITALY (LUCANIA):
—HYELE-VELIA: (27) ?iv BC *SNG Oxford Italy-Sicily-Carthage* 1240; cf. *JNG* 33 (1983) p. 12 (coin graffito)
—POSEIDONIA-PAESTUM: (28) iv BC Iamb., *VP* 267 (*FVS* 1 p. 448)
SICILY:
—SYRACUSE: (29) 408 BC X., *HG* i 3. 13 (s. Ἕρμων)

**Πρόπας**
KORINTHIA:
—KORINTH: (1) i BC/i AD *IvOl* 453, 1 (Λού. Πετικ. Π.: s. Ὀκκία Πρίσκα)

**Πρόπολις**
S. ITALY (CAMPANIA):
—POMPEII: (1) i BC-i AD *Römische Gräberstrassen* p. 223 b (Lat. Calidia Propolis)

**Προσαιβίς**
EPIROS:
—NIKOPOLIS: (1) imp. *Hellenika* 22 (1969) p. 71 no. 9 (Sarikakis 138)

**Προσδέκτη**
SICILY:
—SYRACUSE: (1) imp. *NScav* 1920, p. 317 (Lat. Prosdecte)

**Πρόσδεκτος**
LAKONIA:
—OITYLOS: (1) 238-240 AD *IG* v (1) 1294, 8-9 (f. *M. Αὐρ. Νικηφόρος*)
SICILY:
—SYRACUSE: (2) ?iii AD *ASSicilia* 1938-9, p. 23 (Lat. Prosdectus)

**Πρόσδεξις**
S. ITALY (CALABRIA):
—TARAS-TARENTUM: (1) imp. *Eph. Ep.* VIII 67 (Lat. Venno[nia] Prosde[xis])
—VALETIUM: (2) i-ii AD *CIL* IX 6095 (Susini, *Fonti Salento* p. 167 no. 133) (Lat. Prosdexis)

**Προσδοκία**
SICILY:
—SYRACUSE: (1) iii-v AD *NScav* 1947, p. 189 no. 3 (Lat. Prosdocia)

**Προσδόκιμος**
S. ITALY (CAMPANIA):
—DIKAIARCHIA-PUTEOLI: (1) imp. *AJA* 2 (1898) p. 387 no. 37 (Lat. Prosdocimus)
—MISENUM: (2) imp. *Eph. Ep.* VIII 436 (Lat. C. Ascellius P(r)osdocimus)

**Πρόσδοξος**
S. ITALY (CAMPANIA):
—NUCERIA ALFATERNA: (1) imp. *CIL* x 1099 (Lat. M—icius Prosdoxus)

**Πρόσλαος**
KORINTHIA:
—SIKYON: (1) 218 BC Plb. iv 72. 9 (Skalet 275)

**Πρόσοδος**
S. ITALY (CAMPANIA):
—POMPEII: (1) c. 51-62 AD *CIL* IV 3340. 99, 10; 100, 13 (Castrèn 102. 15) (Lat. P. Terentius Prosodus)
—SALERNUM: (2) imp. *IItal* I (1) 159 (*CIL* x 636) (Lat. [Ser]torius Prosod[us]: s. Τύχη)

**Προσσάρας**
AIGINA: (1) ?s. vi BC *SEG* XI 6 (Προσσαρίδαι (n. gent.))

**Πρόσσων**
LAKONIA:
—SPARTA: (1) iv BC ib. 639, 8 (Πρόσσων: ?s. Ἄνδρ—)

**Προτέριος**
KEPHALLENIA: (1) s. iv AD *RE* (1)
SICILY:
—SYRACUSE: (2) iii-v AD Ferrua, *NG* 151

**Πρότιμος**
S. ITALY (BRUTTIUM):
—NICOTERA*: (1) imp. *NScav* 1882, p. 282 (brick)

**Προυνίκις**
SICILY:
—SYRACUSE: (1) iii-v AD *IG* XIV 163 (Strazzulla 104; Wessel 1316); cf. Ferrua, *NG* 318

**Πρόφαντος**
ARGOLIS:
—ARGOS: (1) ii AD *SEG* XXVIII 223, 3 (Βήδιος Π.: f. Βηδία Ἰώ)
KORINTHIA:
—SIKYON: (2) f. iii BC Plu., *Arat.* 2 (Skalet 276)

**Προφήτης**
S. Italy (Campania):
—herculaneum*: (1) m. i ad *Cron. Erc.* 7 (1977) p. 118 D, 5 (Lat. C. Proculeius Prophetes: freed.)

**Πρυαῖος**
Lakonia:
—sparta: (1) 427 bc *IG* v (1) 1231, 9 (Poralla² 649)
—tainaron-kainepolis: (2) imp.? *IG* v (1) 1236 (s. Ἀριστοτέλης)

**Πρύμνις**
Korinthia:
—korinth: (1) her. *RE* (-) (s. Ἀγέλας, f. Βάκχις: king)

**Πρύτανις**
Lakonia:
—sparta: (1) her. ib. (2) (Poralla² 650) (s. Εὐρυφῶν, f. Πολυδέκτας, ?f. Εὔνομος: king/dub.)

**Πρωῖας**
Akarnania:
—stratos: (1) iv/iii bc *IG* ix (1)² (2) 395, 3

**Πρώπινκος**
Sicily:
—panormos?: (1) imp. ib. xiv 2412. 28 (seal) (f. Λελία)

**Πρωτάγαθος**
Illyria:
—apollonia: (1) ?iii ad *IApoll* 279

**Πρωταγόρας**
Argolis:
—epidauros*: (1) c. 370 bc *IG* iv (1)² 102, 52, 57, 59, 109, 274
Dalmatia:
—issa:
——(Hylleis): (2) iv/iii bc Brunšmid p. 8, 32 (s. Φίντων)

**Πρώταρχος**
Dalmatia:
—issa: (1) iii/ii bc *SEG* xxxv 684 (*VAHD* 84 (1991) p. 254 no. 5) (s. Εὐχηρίδας); (2) ~ *SEG* xxxv 684 (*VAHD* 84 (1991) p. 254 no. 5) (ş. Εὐχηρίδας, f. Φιλισκώ, Εὐχηρίδας)
——(Hylleis): (3) iv/iii bc Brunšmid p. 8, 33 (s. Ζ—ος); (4) ~ ib. l. 39 (s. Αἰσχρίων); (5) ~ ib. l. 43 (f. Καλλίας)
S. Italy (Bruttium):
—lokroi epizephyrioi:
——(Τω.): (6) iv/iii bc De Franciscis 7, 7 (s. Δείναρχος)
Sicily:
—gela-phintias: (7) f. ii bc *IG* xiv 256, 41 (Dubois, *IGDS* 161); cf. *SEG* xl 804 (Πρώ(τ)αρχος: i f. Πρώταρχος II); (8) ~ *IG* xiv 256, 41 (Dubois, *IGDS* 161); cf. *SEG* xl 804 (II s. Πρώταρχος I)
—naxos: (9) f. v bc ib. xxxviii 953. 1 (Arena, *Iscr. Sic.* III 76); cf. *L'Incidenza dell'Antico* pp. 418-9 (Πρό-: s. Ἐπικράτης)
—tauromenion: (10) iii/ii bc PH 45 a, 12 (Stephanis 2152)
—thermai himeraiai: (11) imp. *IG* xiv 334
Sicily?: (12) s. iii bc *HE* 3528 (f. Διονύσιος: fict.?)

**Πρωτᾶς**
S. Italy (Bruttium):
—rhegion: (1) imp. *IG* xiv 624

**Πρωταύλης**
S. Italy (Apulia):
—venusia: (1) imp. *CIL* ix 468 (Lat. Protaules)

**Πρωτέας**
Dalmatia:
—issa:
——(Hylleis): (1) iv/iii bc Brunšmid p. 8, 45 (f. Ζωῖλος)

**Πρώτη**
S. Italy (Calabria):
—brentesion-brundisium: (1) s. i ad *Necropoli via Cappuccini* p. 286 no. E42 (Lat. Baebia Prote)
S. Italy (Campania):
—baiai: (2) imp. *AJA* 2 (1898) p. 393 no. 50 (Lat. Vibia Prote)
—dikaiarchia-puteoli*: (3) imp. *CIL* x 2162 (Lat. Barbia Prota: freed.)
—pompeii: (4) i bc-i ad ib. iv 4226 (Lat. Prote)
S. Italy (Lucania):
—grumentum: (5) imp. ib. x 254 (Lat. Prote)

**Πρώτιλα**
S. Italy (Apulia):
—teanum apulum: (1) imp. ib. ix 713 (701; *Museo Ribezzo* 10 (1977) p. 154 no. b) (Lat. Sestlia Protila: m. Titla)

**Πρωτίων**
Argolis:
—argos: (1) ii/i bc *IG* iv (1) 577
—methana-arsinoe: (2) i bc ib. 853, 8 (Πρωτίων: s. Ἑρμογένης)
Arkadia:
—tegea: (3) imp. ib. v (2) 240 (Προ-)
Lakonia:
—sparta: (4) ii ad ib. v (1) 159, 41 (Bradford (2)) (Πρωτ(ί)ων, Πρότων (n. pr.?)—apogr.); (5) c. 140-160 ad *IG* v (1) 149, 8 (Bradford (1))
S. Italy (Campania):
—dikaiarchia-puteoli*: (6) imp. *CIL* x 2700 (Lat. Q. Marcius Protio: freed.)
Sicily:
—katane: (7) imp. ib. 7047 (Lat. Arr. Protio, Erotio?—ed.)

**Πρωτόβιος**
Aitolia:
—konope-arsinoe: (1) hell. *SEG* xxxiv 469 (brick)

**Πρωτογένης**
Arkadia: (1) c. 247-199 bc *SGDI* 2609, 4 (f. Μαντίας)
Lakonia:
—gytheion: (2) ?i ad *IG* v (1) 1197 (f. Πανθηρίς); (3) m. ii ad ib. 1174, 14 (Σεπτούμμιος Π.)
S. Italy (Apulia):
—canusium*: (4) s. i bc *Epig. Rom. di Canosa* 197 (*CIL* ix 402) (Lat. L. Tutorius Protogen(es): freed.)
S. Italy (Bruttium):
—lokroi epizephyrioi:
——(Κοβ.): (5) iv/iii bc De Franciscis 39, 8 (f. Δαμαίνετος)
——(Τω.): (6) iv/iii bc ib. 2, 2 (s. Ἀμεινόκριτος); (7) ~ ib. 3, 3 (f. Ἀμεινόκριτος); (8) ~ ib. 6, 1; 19, 2 (s. Καλλικράτης); (9) ~ ib. 24, 4; 26, 5; 39, 8 (f. Καλλικράτης)
S. Italy (Campania):
—dikaiarchia-puteoli: (10) imp. *CIL* x 1552 (Lat. T. Aurelius Protogenes); (11) ~ *Eph. Ep.* viii 406 (Lat. C. Hostius Protogenes); (12) ?ii ad *IG* xiv 832
—pompeii: (13) 50-79 ad *CIL* iv 2975 (Lat. Protog[enes])
S. Italy (Lucania):
—herakleia: (14) 74 bc *ID* 1758, 1 (f. Διογένης)

**Πρωτόλαος**
Arkadia:
—mantineia-antigoneia: (1) 464 or 460 bc Moretti, *Olymp.* 256 (s. Διάλκης)

**Πρωτόμαχος**
Achaia: (1) 146 bc *IG* iv (1)² 28, 71 (f. Ὀνάσιμος: synoikos)
Aigina: (2) i bc-i ad? ib. iv (1) 151 (I f. Πρωτόμαχος II); (3) ~ ib. (II s. Πρωτόμαχος I)
Akarnania:
—stratos: (4) ii bc ib. ix (1)² (2) 394, 16 ([Πρω]τόμαχος: s. Λάφριος)
Dalmatia:
—issa: (5) ii/i bc Brunšmid p. 27 no. 19 (*SEG* xl 515) + *VAHD* 84 (1991) p. 254 no. 4 ([Π]ρωτόμ[αχος])
Elis: (6) ii bc Siebert, *Ateliers* pp. 109; 175 (date) (potter)
Epiros:
—bouthrotos (prasaiboi): (7) a. 163 bc *IBouthrot* 14, 7 (*SEG* xxxviii 471) (s. Νικάνωρ, Ἀττέα) ?= (11); (8) ~ *IBouthrot* 21, 4 (*SEG* xxxviii 478); (9) ~ *IBouthrot* 42, 14 (*SEG* xxxviii 501)
——Kapystioi: (10) a. 163 bc *IBouthrot* 166 (*SEG* xxxviii 465)
—prasaiboi: (11) a. 163 bc *IBouthrot* 92, 8 (f. Νικάνωρ) ?= (7)

**Πρῶτος**
Akarnania:
—thyrreion: (1) ii bc *IG* ix (1)² (2) 247, 18 (s. Δημήτριος)
Argolis:
—hermione: (2) i bc-i ad? ib. iv (1) 730 IV, 3 (s. Διογένης)
Arkadia:
—tegea: (3) 78 ad ib. v (2) 49, 5 (Τιβ. Κλ. Π.)
Elis: (4) f. i bc *IvOl* 214, [1]; 215, 1 (f. Μενέδημος)
Epiros:
—ambrakia: (5) ?ii bc *AD* 10 (1926) p. 66 (s. Νικασίλας)
S. Italy (Apulia):
—canusium: (6) i ad *Epig. Rom. di Canosa* Add. 30 (Lat. Prothus)
—daunioi: (7) i bc-i ad *IG* ii² 8477 + *SEG* xxviii 284
S. Italy (Campania):
—dikaiarchia-puteoli: (8) imp. *CIL* x 2225 (Lat. M. Kanius Protus)
—misenum*: (9) imp. ib. 3661 (Lat. Firmius Protus)
—nola: (10) imp. ib. 1291 (Lat. C. Bruttius Varius Protus)
—pompeii: (11) i bc-i ad ib. iv 2498 (Lat. Protus); (12) imp. ib. x 8357 (Lat. Protus)
Sicily:
—tyndaris: (13) ?ii bc *IG* xiv 375

**Πρωτοφάνης**
Sicily:
—syracuse: (1) s. iii bc *Arch. Class.* 17 (1965) p. 186 no. 1

**Πρώτων**
S. Italy (Apulia):
—vibinum: (1) imp. *Bovino* p. 146 no. 197 (Lat. Flavius Proto)

**Πτελλᾶς**
Messenia:
—korone: (1) 246 ad *IG* v (1) 1398, 94 (Αὐρ. Π.)

**Πτολεμαῖος**
Akarnania:
—anaktorion: (1) 216 bc ib. ix (1)² (2) 583, 65
—astakos: (2) ii bc ib. 434, 5 (f. Ἀντίγονος)
—stratos: (3) c. 215-200 bc *FD* III (2) 86, 5 + *Syll*³ 539 A, 5; cf. Nachtergael, *Les Galates* p. 291 (date) (Πτολε[μαῖος])
Argolis:
—argos: (4) iii/ii bc *PP* 15770 (*PPC* Π 64); *BE* 1949, no. 202 (family) (s. Πολυκράτης,

Ζευξώ (Cyrene)); (**5**) ii BC Le Rider, *Monnaies crétoises* p. 258 II, 1 (s. *Δημήτριος*); (**6**) iii AD *FD* III (1) 89, 1 (Stephanis 2164) (and Athens: *M. Αὐρ. (Πτ)ο(λ)εμαῖος*)

ARKADIA:
—MEGALOPOLIS: (**7**) iii BC *RE* (43); *FGrH* 161; *PP* 15068 (s. *Ἀγήσαρχος*)

EPIROS:
—MOLOSSOI: (**8**) c. 295-272 BC *RE* (16) (s. *Πύρρος, Ἀντιγόνη*); (**9**) c. 234 BC ib. (17) (s. *Ἀλέξανδρος, Ὀλυμπιάς*)
—NIKOPOLIS: (**10**) imp. *SEG* XXIV 433 (Sarikakis 163) (*Γ. Τέρτι[ο]ς Π.*)

ILLYRIA:
—APOLLONIA: (**11**) imp. *IApoll* 276 ([*Σ*]επτίμ[ιο]ς [*Πτ*]ολεμαῖος)
—DASSARETIOI: (**12**) ii-iii AD *Sp.* 75 (1933) p. 58 no. 177 ([— *Πτολε*]μαῖος); (**13**) iii AD *ZA* 20 (1970) p. 160 (f. *Αὐρ. Κράτης*)
—EPIDAMNOS-DYRRHACHION: (**14**) hell.-imp. *IDyrrh* 367 (f. *Πτολεμαῖς*); (**15**) imp. ib. 196 (f. *Ἐργασίων*)

KORINTHIA:
—KORINTH: (**16**) ii-iii AD *Corinth* VIII (1) 131
—KORINTH*: (**17**) ii-iii AD ib. VIII (3) 502, 2 (*TMByz* 9 (1985) pp. 291-2 no. 31) (*Μέμμιος Πόντιος Πτολεμέος ὁ καὶ Παρνάσιος*)

LAKONIA:
—KYTHERA: (**18**) inc. *Suda* Π 3032; *RE* (68)
—SPARTA: (**19**) i BC/i AD *BSA* 89 (1994) pp. 433-4 no. 2, 8 (f. *Νικοκράτης*)
LEUKAS: (**20**) ii-iii AD *Suda* A 4106 (or Egypt Alexandria: f. *Ἀρχίβιος*)

MESSENIA:
—THOURIA: (**21**) s. iii BC *IG* v (1) 1386, 7 (f. *Λεωνίδας*)

S. ITALY (CALABRIA):
—BRENTESION-BRUNDISIUM: (**22**) imp. *NScav* 1901, p. 306 no. 1 (Lat. P. Octavius Ptolemaeus)

S. ITALY (CAMPANIA):
—DIKAIARCHIA-PUTEOLI: (**23**) imp. *IG* XIV 2414. 125 (tessera); (**24**) ii-iii AD *AJA* 2 (1898) p. 377 no. 8 (Lat. M. Aurelius Ptolemaeus)
—NEAPOLIS: (**25**) imp.? *NScav* 1890, p. 127 (*INap* 181) (f. *Πύρρος*); (**26**) ~ *NScav* 1890, p. 127 (*INap* 181) (s. *Πύρρος*)
—NEAPOLIS*: (**27**) s. ii AD *IG* XIV 791 (*INap* 129) (*Τιβ. Κλ. Αὐρηλιανὸς Π.*)
—POMPEII: (**28**) i BC-i AD *CIL* IV 5278 (Lat. Ptolemaeus)

SICILY:
—SYRACUSE: (**29**) 227 BC *PPetr* III 21 (d), 5, 13-14 (s. *Ἑρμογένης*: t.e.)

## Πτολεμαῖς
ILLYRIA:
—EPIDAMNOS-DYRRHACHION: (**1**) hell.-imp. *IDyrrh* 367 (d. *Πτολεμαῖος*)

S. ITALY (BRUTTIUM):
—RHEGION: (**2**) 79 AD *CIL* X 7, 11 (Lat. Claudia Ptolemais)

S. ITALY (CAMPANIA):
—DIKAIARCHIA-PUTEOLI: (**3**) imp. ib. 1568 (Lat. Ptolemais: d. *Κυπρογένεια*); (**4**) ~ ib. 3018 (Lat. Tolemais)

## Πτόλιχος
AIGINA: (**1**) f. v BC *RE* (1); *Alt-Ägina* II (2) pp. 45-6 (s. *Συννοῶν*: sculptor)
KERKYRA: (**2**) m. v BC *RE* (2)

## Πτολλαρίων
MESSENIA:
—ASINE: (**1**) ii AD *IG* v (1) 1408 (f. *Πρασίων*)

## Πτωϊόδωρος
KORINTHIA:
—KORINTH: (**1**) vi BC Pi., *O.* xiii, 41; cf. *Dionysiaca* pp. 1-16 (f. *Θεσσαλός*)

## Πυγμαρίων
SICILY: (**1**) hell. *CGF* p. 104 fr. 76 (n. pr.?)

## Πυθάγγελος
ARKADIA:
—TEGEA:
——(Krariotai): (**1**) f. iii BC *IG* v (2) 36, 37 (f. *Ἀπολλᾶς*)
KORINTHIA:
—KORINTH: (**2**) c. 400-375 BC ib. II² 9080 (f. *Χρυσίς*)
LAKONIA:
—SPARTA: (**3**) c. 175-210 AD *SEG* XI 555, 8 (Bradford (-)) ([*Πυ*]θάγγελος: s. *Δαμοκράτης*)

## Πυθαγόρας
ARGOLIS:
—ARGOS: (**1**) iii/ii BC *RE* (7) (Lat. Pythagoras: s. *Ἀρίστιππος*)
—PHLEIOUS: (**2**) vi BC ib. (2b)
ELIS: (**3**) s. iii BC Paus. vi 15. 10 (f. *Κάπρος*)
LAKONIA:
—SPARTA: (**4**) 716 BC Moretti, *Olymp.* 18 (Poralla² 651); (**5**) 402-401 BC X., *An.* i 4. 2; *HG* iii 1. 1 (Poralla² 652) (*Σάμιος*—X., *Π. ὁ καὶ Σάμιος*?—Poralla² 659) ?= (*Σάμιος* (3))
S. ITALY (BRUTTIUM):
—RHEGION: (**6**) v BC *RE* (14); Overbeck 489 ff. (sculptor)
ZAKYNTHOS: (**7**) hell.? *RE* (2c)

## Πυθαίνετος
AIGINA: (**1**) hell.? ib. (-); *FGrH* 299

## Πυθάρατος
MESSENIA: (**1**) viii BC *RE* (1)

## Πύθαρχος
ARKADIA:
—MANTINEIA-ANTIGONEIA: (**1**) ?v BC Moretti, *Olymp.* 254

## Πυθᾶς
SICILY:
—SYRACUSE: (**1**) iii-v AD *IG* XIV 153 (Strazzulla 94; Agnello 9; Wessel 874)

## Πυθέας
ACHAIA:
—BOURA: (**1**) ii BC St. Byz. s.v. *Βοῦρα*; Overbeck 2109 (painter)
AIGINA: (**2**) vi/v BC *RE* (7) (f. *Λάμπων*); (**3**) f. v BC ib. (8); cf. Klee p. 91 no. 50; p. 100 no. 29 (s. *Λάμπων*); (**4**) 480 BC *RE* (9) (s. *Ἰσχένοος*); (**5**) 411-408 BC *ILind* 16, 3; *Athenaeum* 66 (1988) pp. 543 ff. (locn.) (or Egypt Naukratis: f. —*ας*); (**6**) 345-341 BC *CID* II 12 II, 15; 31, 78, 93
ARGOLIS:
—ARGOS: (**7**) ii/i BC Loewy 264 (sculptor)
—EPIDAUROS: (**8**) iv BC *IG* IV (1)² 2
—EPIDAUROS*: (**9**) c. 370-365 BC Peek, *IAEpid* 52 B, 68
—KLEONAI: (**10**) ?c. 229 BC *SEG* XXIII 178, 27 (or Argolis Argos)
ARKADIA:
—MANTINEIA-ANTIGONEIA: (**11**) c. 300-221 BC *IG* v (2) 323. 47 (tessera) (f. *Πολύχαρμος*)
—PHIGALEIA: (**12**) ?iv-iii BC *FGrH* 319 F 3; cf. Page, *FGE* p. 85
ITHAKE: (**13**) hell. *Rev. Épig.* 1 (1913) p. 47 no. 10
S. ITALY (CALABRIA):
—TARAS-TARENTUM: (**14**) c. 80-70 BC *IG* VII 3195, 22; *AE* 1925-6, pp. 35-6 no. 149, 17, [21] (*IOrop* 522); *BSA* 70 (1975) pp. 121-2 (date); cf. Stephanis 462 (*Πουθέας*—3195: f. *Ἀσκλαπιόδωρος*)
S. ITALY (CAMPANIA):
—DIKAIARCHIA-PUTEOLI: (**15**) 180-190 AD *CIL* X 1648 (Lat. Fl. Pytheas)

## Πυθέος
SICILY:
—SELINOUS: (**16**) ?c. 525-500 BC Dubois, *IGDS* 67 (Arena, *Iscr. Sic.* I 33; *GVI* 1670); *LSAG*² p. 277 no. 33 (date) (f. *Ἀρχέδαμος*)

## Πύθεος
DALMATIA:
—PHAROS: (**1**) iv BC Brunšmid p. 20 no. 5 (f. *Μαθις*)

## Πυθήν
DALMATIA:
—ISSA: (**1**) iii/ii BC *SEG* XXXI 601 (*VAHD* 84 (1991) p. 258 no. 8) (f. *Δαμώ*)
KORINTHIA:
—KORINTH: (**2**) 414-413 BC *RE* (-) (*Πύθης*—D.S.)

## Πυθία
AIGINA: (**1**) iv/iii BC *Ag.* XVII 394 (d. *Τιμόδοτος*)

## Πυθιάδας
KORINTHIA:
—SIKYON: (**1**) hell.? *IG* IX (1) 593 ([*Πυ*]θιάδας, [*Εὐ*]θιάδας: s. *Εὔθυμος*)

## Πυθίας
ACHAIA:
—PELLENE: (**1**) s. iii BC *RE* (1)
ARGOLIS:
—ARGOS: (**2**) i BC *AD* 26 (1971) Mel. pp. 34 ff., 17

## Πυθιάς
AKARNANIA:
—PALAIROS: (**1**) iii/ii BC *IG* IX (1)² (2) 538 ([*Π*]υθιάς)
KORINTHIA:
—SIKYON: (**2**) s. iv BC ib. II² 10302 (Skalet 277)

## Πυθικός
LAKONIA:
—SPARTA: (**1**) m. ii AD *IG* v (1) 73, 3; *SEG* XI 524, 23 (Bradford (-)) (f. —*της*)

## Πυθίλας
ARGOLIS:
—ARGOS: (**1**) 190 BC *IG* II² 2313, 58; *SEG* XXXVI 227 (locn.) (*PA* 12358) (and Athens: s. *Ὀρθαγόρας*)
——Sticheleion (Kleodaidai): (**2**) s. iii BC *Mnem.* NS 43 (1915) p. 366 A, 8 (Perlman A.17); *Mnem.* NS 43 (1915) pp. 366-7 B, 7 (Perlman A.18); *SEG* XVII 144, 12 (Perlman A.20) (f. *Ὀρθαγόρας*)

## Πυθιόνικος
S. ITALY (CALABRIA):
—TARAS-TARENTUM: (**1**) b. 212 BC Plb. viii 28. 9

## Πύθιος
MESSENIA:
—MESSENE?: (**1**) ii/i BC *SEG* XI 979, 63
SICILY:
—SYRACUSE: (**2**) f. i BC *RE* (5) (Lat. Pythius)

## Πύθις
KORINTHIA:
—KORINTH?: (**1**) c. 335 BC *CID* II 62 II A, 1
SICILY:
—KAMARINA: (**2**) v BC *QUCC* 78 (1995) p. 127 no. 2 (bronze) (f. *Ἄντανδρος*)

## Πυθίων
ACHAIA: (**1**) iv/iii BC *Ét. Thas.* 3 p. 321 no. 116 (s. *Ἀθανάδας*)
—DYME: (**2**) ?s. ii BC *Achaean Grave Stelai* 33 (s. *Διοκλῆς*)
—DYME*: (**3**) c. 219 BC *SGDI* 1612, 34 (*Tyche* 5 (1990) p. 124) (s. *Εὔξενος*)
AITOLIA:
—TRICHONION: (**4**) s. iii BC *IG* IX (1)² (1) 117, 2

**Πυθογένης**

AKARNANIA:
—THYRREION: (5) hell.-imp. ib. IX (1)² (2) 360 (Πειθίων—apogr.: f. Τελλίας)
ARGOLIS:
—HERMIONE: (6) i BC-i AD? ib. IV (1) 730 I, 9 (Πύχνων—apogr., Πυ[θί]ων—ed.: s. Μύρτα)
DALMATIA:
—ISSA: (7) imp. SEG XXXV 693
ELIS: (8) ?257 BC FD III (3) 196, 1 (f. Αἰχμύλος); (9) 113-165 AD IvOl 90, 12; 91, 13; 93, 7; 95, 11; 99, [12] (I f. Πυθίων II: Iamidai); (10) ~ ib. 90, 12; 91, 13; 93, [7]; 95, 11; 99, 12 (II s. Πυθίων I: mantis/Iamidai); (11) c. 201-209 AD ib. 107, 15 (f. —δρος); (12) m. iii AD ib. 119, 8; SEG XV 259, 10 ([Αὐρ.] Π.: mantis/Iamidai); (13) 233 AD IvOl 116, 9 (f. Ἰσίδωρος)
LAKONIA:
—SPARTA: (14) c. 120 AD IG V (1) 1315, 25 (Bradford (-)) (f. Φιλόστρατος)
SICILY:
—LILYBAION: (15) s. i BC HN² p. 150; Holm, Gesch. Sic. 3 p. 721; BMC Italy p. 95, 4-6; RPC 1 p. 655 (coin)
TRIPHYLIA:
—MAKISTOS: (16) 399-369 BC SEG XXXV 389, 13

**Πυθογένης**

ARKADIA:
—TEGEA: (1) ?i BC IG V (2) 168 (Πυθογέν[ης]?—IG, Πυθογε[ί]των]?—LGPN)
SICILY:
—ZANKLE-MESSANA: (2) vi/v BC Hdt. vi 23. 4

**Πυθοδίκη**

ARGOLIS:
—ARGOS: (1) i/ii AD IG IV (1) 643 (d. Τάλαος)

**Πυθόδοτος**

KORINTHIA:
—KORINTH: (1) c. 405 BC Paus. x 9. 10; cf. CEG II 819

**Πυθόδωρος**

ARGOLIS:
—ARGOS: (1) s. iv BC SEG I 355, 1, 4 (f. Πυθοκλῆς, Ἑλλάνικος); (2) iii/ii BC ib. XLII 278 (Πυθόδω[ρος])
—EPIDAUROS: (3) 225 AD IG IV (1)² 127, 15 (M. Αὐρ. Πυ[θόδωρ]ος)
——(Dymanes): (4) 146 BC ib. 28, 5 (s. Λαχάρης)
——Alekmeis: (5) c. 335-325 BC ib. 106 I, 11
—HERMIONE: (6) iii BC ib. IV (1) 728, 11 (s. Αἰσχένας) ?= (8); (7) ~ ib. l. 21 (s. Αἰσχίνας); (8) ~ ib. l. 22 (s. Αἰσχένας) ?= (6)
—TROIZEN: (9) iv BC ib. 823, 33
ARKADIA:
—TEGEA: (10) ?s. iv BC ib. V (2) 39, 7 (f. —λης)
EPIROS:
—AMBRAKIA: (11) f. iii BC Unp. (Arta Mus., inscr.) (f. Θεδώρα); (12) m. iii BC IG V (2) 368, 21 (s. Ἀγόρατος); (13) f. ii BC AD 39 (1984) Chron. p. 190 + pl. 77 γ (Πυθόδωρος, Εὐθύδωρος?: s. Ἀκήρατος); (14) a. 167 BC SEG XXXV 665 A, 8 (f. Ἀκήρατος)
KERKYRA: (15) a. 196 BC IG IX (2) 526, 13 (s. Σωσθένης)
KORINTHIA:
—SIKYON: (16) m. iv BC FGrH 115 F 248 (Skalet 278); (17) c. 210-207 BC IG IV (1)² 73, 12; SEG XXXV 303 (date) (Skalet 279) (f. Πυθοκλῆς)
MESSENIA: (18) ?c. 550 BC Lazzarini 357 (-δōρος)
—THOURIA: (19) f. ii BC SEG XI 972, 80 (s. Αὐτοκλῆς)
SICILY:
—SELINOUS: (20) m. v BC Dubois, IGDS 34 (Arena, Iscr. Sic. I 70) (Πυθόδ(ō)ρος)

—TAUROMENION: (21) c. 225-215 BC IG XIV 421 an. 16; 421 an. 26 (SGDI 5219) (f. Εὔφορος)

**Πυθοκλῆς**

AKARNANIA:
—STRATOS: (1) c. 200 BC IG IX (1)² (1) 31, 128 (f. Ξέναρχος)
ARGOLIS:
—ARGOS: (2) s. iv BC SEG I 355, 1, 4, 17 ([Π]υθοκλῆς: s. Πυθόδωρος)
—EPIDAUROS: (3) c. 370 BC IG IV (1)² 102, 37, 47, 84, 91, 110; (4) i-ii AD ib. 460 (s. Διονύσιος)
—HERMIONE: (5) ?268-255 BC Nachtergael, Les Galates 2 bis, [4]; 3, 3, 14; 4, 7; 5, [9]; 8, 30; 15, 1; 15 bis, 2 (Stephanis 2174) (s. Ἀρίσταρχος)
—METHANA-ARSINOE: (6) v BC IG IV (1) 860
ELIS: (7) 452 BC Moretti, Olymp. 284
KORINTHIA:
—KORINTH: (8) imp. IG IV (1) 399; (9) m. i AD Corinth VIII (1) 70, 3 ([Πυ]θοκλῆς)
—SIKYON: (10) hell.? Paus. ii 7. 9 (Skalet 283); (11) 263 BC IG IX (1)² (1) 17, 14 (s. Εὐφορίων); (12) 236 BC Moretti, Olymp. 571 (Skalet 282); (13) c. 210-207 BC IG IV (1)² 73, 12; SEG XXXV 303 (date) (Skalet 280) (s. Πυθόδωρος); (14) 116 BC IG II² 1009 col. IV, 106 + SEG XXXVIII 116 (f. Μνασέας); (15) i-ii AD Unp. (Sikyon Mus.) (Τ.β. Κλ. Π.); (16) i/ii AD Plu., Arat. 1 (Skalet 284) (s. Πολυκράτης)

**Πυθοκράτης**

DALMATIA:
—ISSA: (1) ii BC SEG XXXI 602, 4 (VAHD 84 (1991) p. 257 no. 7) (f. Δαμοκλέα)

**Πυθόκριτος**

ACHAIA: (1) 146 BC IG IV (1)² 28, 74 (f. Ματροχάρης: synoikos)
KORINTHIA:
—SIKYON: (2) f. vi BC Paus. vi 14. 10 (Skalet 285) (s. Καλλίνικος)

**Πυθόλαος**

AKARNANIA:
—LEKKA (MOD.): (1) iii BC IG IX (1)² (2) 224 with Add.

**Πυθόνικος**

ACHAIA:
—PELLENE: (1) iv BC SEG XI 1275
ARGOLIS:
—ARGOS*: (2) imp. BCH 27 (1903) p. 269 no. 22 (amph.) (s. Μοσχίων)
—HERMIONE: (3) ?265-259 BC Nachtergael, Les Galates 4, 17 (Stephanis 2177) (s. Νίκις)
ARKADIA:
—TEGEA: (4) ?i BC IG V (2) 168 ([Π]υθόν[ικος]?)

**Πύθων**

AIGINA: (1) iv BC Ag. XVII 393 (f. Νικαγόρα)
AKARNANIA:
—OINIADAI: (2) iii/ii BC IG IX (1)² (2) 419. 4
ARGOLIS:
—EPIDAUROS: (3) c. 365-335 BC ib. IV (1)² 103, 29, 31-2, 36, 38-9, 43, 48-51
ARKADIA: (4) 231 BC CPR XVIII 18, 372
—STYMPHALOS: (5) 191-146 BC BMC Pelop. p. 15 no. 170 (coin)
—TEGEA: (6) f. iii BC IG V (2) 35, 15 (f. Μελισσίων)
DALMATIA:
—ISSA:
——(Hylleis): (7) iv/iii BC Brunšmid p. 9, 51 ([Π]ύθων: s. Φιλόστρατος)
S. ITALY (CALABRIA):
—TARAS-TARENTUM: (8) ii BC IG II² 10414 (f. Πιερία)

S. ITALY (CAMPANIA):
—NEAPOLIS: (9) s. i BC ib. XIV 741 (INap 30); cf. Leiwo p. 152 (f. Λ. Ἐρέννιος Ἄριστος)
S. ITALY (LUCANIA):
—POSEIDONIA-PAESTUM: (10) m. iv BC RVP p. 136 f.
SICILY:
—HENNA: (11) c. 135 BC D.S. xxxiv-v 2. 15 (?f. Ἀντιγένης)
—KAMARINA: (12) s. v BC Dubois, IGDS 121, 5 (Arena, Iscr. Sic. II 143; SEG XXXVIII 940; Cordano, 'Camarina VII' 52) (-ōν, Πύθος—Cordano per err.: ?s. Διοκλῆς)
—KATANE: (13) s. iv BC RE (5); Berve 677 (or Thrace Byzantion)

**Πυκέλειος**

SICILY:
—SELINOUS: (1) f. v BC Dubois, IGDS 38, 11, 17 (Arena, Iscr. Sic. I 63) (f. Ἅλος)

**Πυκίνα**

S. ITALY (CALABRIA):
—MESSAPIOI: (1) 197 BC SGDI 2043, 2-3 (slave/freed.)

**Πυκισσός**

S. ITALY (CAMPANIA):
—POMPEII: (1) i BC-i AD CIL IV 3994 (Castrèn 85. 12) (Lat. Caesius Pycissus)

**Πυλάδας**

ARGOLIS:
—EPIDAUROS: (1) iv BC IG IV (1)² 198 ([Πυ]λάδας: f. Χαρμαντίδας)
ARKADIA:
—MANTINEIA-ANTIGONEIA: (2) ?iii BC ib. V (2) 318, 28 (Πυ[λ]ά[δ]ας)
EPIROS:
—PHOINIKE: (3) c. 330 BC SEG XXIII 189 I, 12
KORINTHIA:
—KORINTH: (4) s. vii BC FGrH 90 F 57. 7 (and Leukas: -δης: s. Κύψελος: oikist)

**Πυλάδης**

ARGOLIS:
—EPIDAUROS: (1) f. ii AD IG IV (1)² 382, 3 (Λ. Μάριος Π.)
ARKADIA:
—MEGALOPOLIS: (2) iii/ii BC Paus. viii 50. 3; Plu., Phil. 11 (Stephanis 2181)
—MEGALOPOLIS?: (3) iii/ii BC HE 82
KORINTHIA:
—KORINTH: (4) imp. Corinth VIII (3) 316 a (Lat. —arius Pyladis)
S. ITALY (APULIA):
—HERDONIA*: (5) imp. Ordona 2 p. 139 no. 15 (Lat. Cn. Axsius Pylades: freed.)
—VENUSIA: (6) imp. CIL IX 597 (Lat. Pylaes, Pyla(d)es?)
S. ITALY (CAMPANIA): (7) imp. IG XIV 2406. 70
—DIKAIARCHIA-PUTEOLI: (8) imp. CIL X 8042. 87 (tile) (Lat. Pylades); (9) ?i-ii AD ib. 2895 (Lat. C. Proculeius Pylades)
—DIKAIARCHIA-PUTEOLI*: (10) ?ii/iii AD Eph. Ep. VIII 369 (Lat. L. Aurelius Pylades: imp. freed.)
—POMPEII: (11) i BC-i AD CIL IV 10233 (Lat. Pilades); (12) ~ ib. 8058. 72 (seal) (Castrèn 324. 3) (Lat. C. Pro. Pylades)
SICILY: (13) hell.-imp. IG XIV 2411, 4 (bronze)

**Πυλαδίων**

S. ITALY (CAMPANIA):
—POMPEII*: (1) i BC-i AD CIL IV 7991 (Lat. Pyladion)

**Πύλιος**

KORINTHIA:
—KORINTH: (1) c. 570-550 BC Amyx 117. 3 (vase) (Lorber 102) (her.)

**Πύλλος**

DALMATIA:
—KERKYRA MELAINA?: (1) iv/iii BC Brunšmid p. 7, 2 (f. Δάζος)

—SOLENTIA: (2) imp. *CIL* III 3111 (Lat. M. Octavius Pullus)

ILLYRIA:

—ALINIOI: (3) c. 215-200 BC *SEG* XV 272, 7 (*IOrop* 134); *AE* 1967, Chron. p. 9 no. 4 (locn.); cf. *L'Illyrie mérid.* 2 p. 165 (s. *Δάζος*)

S. ITALY (APULIA):

—ARGYRIPPA-ARPI: (4) iii BC *HN*² p. 45; *SNG Cop. Apulia–Lucania* 607-8 (coins) (*Samml. Ludwig* 58)

—GRAVINA (MOD.): (5) s. v BC Santoro, *NSM* 1 p. 169 no. IM 0.322 (vase)

—SALAPIA: (6) iii BC *HN*² p. 49 (coins) (*SNG ANS Etruria–Calabria* 738)

### Πυνοδότα

S. ITALY (APULIA):

—MONTE SANNACE (MOD.): (1) v/iv BC *Mon. Ant.* 45 (1961) p. 325

### Πύρα

S. ITALY (CAMPANIA):

—AEQUANA: (1) imp. *NScav* 1897, p. 200 (Lat. Geminia Pyre)

### Πύραγρος

SICILY:

—AGYRION: (1) f. i BC Cic., *In Verr.* II iii 74 (Lat. Apollodorus Pyragrus)

### Πύραιθος

KEPHALLENIA:

—SAME: (1) hell. *IG* IX (1) 633 ([*Π*]ύ(ρ)αιθος)

### Πυραιμένης

ARGOLIS:

—ARGOS: (1) c. 235 BC ib. II² 1299, 110

### Πύραϊς

SICILY:

—SABUCINA (MOD.): (1) f. v BC Dubois, *IGDS* 174 (vase) (Arena, *Iscr. Sic.* II 109) (*Πυραΐ(ο)ς?*—ed.: potter)

### Πυραλλίς

S. ITALY (APULIA):

—LUCERIA*: (1) imp. *ASP* 34 (1981) p. 19 no. 20 (Lat. Caecilia Pyrallis: freed.)

—VENUSIA: (2) imp. *CIL* IX 548 (Lat. Ovia Pyrallis: d. *Ἀπολλώνιος*); (3) f. i AD *Rend. Linc.* 29 (1974) p. 622 no. 25 (Lat. Norbana Pyrallis)

S. ITALY (CALABRIA):

—RUDIAE: (4) i-ii AD Susini, *Fonti Salento* p. 115 no. 54 (Lat. Helvia Piralis)

S. ITALY (CAMPANIA):

—POMPEII: (5) i BC-i AD *CIL* IV 8959 (Lat. Pyralis)

—SALERNUM: (6) m. i BC *IItal* 1 (1) 126 (*CIL* X 598) (Lat. Helmonia Pyrallis)

### Πυραμίς

S. ITALY (CAMPANIA):

—DIKAIARCHIA-PUTEOLI: (1) imp. ib. 2189 (Lat. Caecilia Pyramis)

—POMPEII: (2) i BC-i AD ib. IV 1382 a (Lat. Pyramis)

### Πύραμος

ARGOLIS:

—ARGOS:

——(Dymanes-Amphiareteidai): (1) c. 400 BC *SEG* XXIX 361, 37

—MYKENAI: (2) i BC/i AD ib. XVII 140 (*Πύρραμος, Τύρρανος?*)

ILLYRIA:

—AULON (NR.): (3) imp. *BUST* 1961 (1), p. 121 no. 20 (Lat. Pyramus)

S. ITALY (APULIA):

—VENUSIA: (4) imp. *CIL* IX 537 (Lat. Pyramus)

S. ITALY (BRUTTIUM):

—LOKROI EPIZEPHYRIOI:

——(Ἀστ.): (5) iv/iii BC De Franciscis 20, 19 (f. *Θεόδωρος*)

S. ITALY (CALABRIA):

—BRENTESION-BRUNDISIUM: (6) imp. *CIL* IX 173; cf. *Epigraphica* 42 (1980) p. 156 (Lat. Pyramus: f. Secunda)

S. ITALY (CAMPANIA):

—HERCULANEUM: (7) m. i AD *PdelP* 3 (1948) p. 173 no. 18; p. 176 no. 21 (Lat. M. Antonius Pyramus)

—HERCULANEUM*: (8) m. i AD *CIL* X 1403 b + *Cron. Erc.* 7 (1977) p. 117 C b, 7 (Lat. M. Velleius Pyramus: freed.)

—POMPEII: (9) i BC-i AD *CIL* IV 1213 (Lat. Pyramus); (10) ~ ib. 10041; 10090 (Lat. Piramus); (11) ~ ib. 10159 (Lat. Pyramus); (12) 70-79 AD ib. 7581; Mouritsen p. 130 (name) (Lat. Puramus); (13) 78-79 AD *CIL* IV 3674; 3703 (Lat. Pyramus)

### Πυρβαλίων

ACHAIA: (1) 146 BC *IG* IV (1)² 28, 158 (s. *Δαμαίνετος*: synoikos)

ARGOLIS:

—ARGOS: (2) ?205 BC *AE* 1936, Chron. p. 39 no. 211, 6 (*Πουρ-*: s. *Στάσιππος*)

### Πύρβας

ILLYRIA:

—EPIDAMNOS-DYRRHACHION: (1) c. 250-50 BC Maier 350-1 (coin) (Ceka 203; 360) (pryt.)

### Πύργων

S. ITALY (CAMPANIA):

—KYME*: (1) v BC *REG* 23 (1910) p. 344 (bronze)

### Πυργαλίων

ARGOLIS:

—ARGOS:

——(Dymanes): (1) ?c. 460-450 BC *IG* IV (1) 517, 4 (Lazzarini 937); *LSAG*² p. 170 no. 32 (date)

—NEMEA*: (2) iv BC *SEG* XXVI 421. 2

### Πυργίας

ARGOLIS:

—MYKENAI: (1) ?c. 500-480 BC *IG* IV (1) 492, 5; *LSAG*² p. 174 no. 2 (date)

KORINTHIA:

—KORINTH: (2) ?c. 600-575 BC Amyx 29. 1 (vase) (Lorber 58) ([*Π*]υργίας: fict.?); (3) c. 590-570 BC Amyx 17. 2 (vase) (*SEG* XIV 303 b; Lorber 39; *CEG* I 452 ii); cf. *SEG* XXIX 336

—SIKYON: (4) vi/v BC ib. XI 244, 47

### Πύρης

S. ITALY (LUCANIA):

—HYELE-VELIA: (1) vi/v BC *FVS* I pp. 217-18 no. 28 A 1-2; *SEG* XXXVIII 1020. 4 (f. *Παρμενίδης*)

### Πυρίας

SICILY:

—GELA-PHINTIAS?: (1) f. v BC Dubois, *IGDS* 134 b, 9 (Arena, *Iscr. Sic.* II 47)

—SELINOUS: (2) ?v BC Manganaro, *PdelP* forthcoming no. 16 (*Πυρία[ς]?*)

### Πυριλάμπης

ELIS: (1) m. ii BC *BGU* 1939 A, 9 (s. *Ἐργόφιλος*, f. *Λιμναῖος*)

MESSENIA:

—MESSENE: (2) ?ii BC *RE* s.v. Pyrilampos (-); cf. Moretti, *Olymp.* 426 and 431; *SEG* XL 388 (ident.) (sculptor) ?= (*Πυρίλαμπος (1)*)

### Πυρίλαμπος

MESSENIA:

—MESSENE: (1) i BC *IvOl* 400, 4; cf. *SEG* XL 388 (s. *Ἀγίας*: sculptor) ?= (*Πυριλάμπης (2)*); (2) i BC/i AD *IG* V (1) 1438 a, 4

### Πυρῖνος

S. ITALY (CAMPANIA):

—NOLA?: (1) ?vii BC UP (Berlin Mus.) F 2563 (vase)

SICILY:

—SELINOUS: (2) f. v BC Dubois, *IGDS* 38, 7 (Arena, *Iscr. Sic.* I 63) (*Πυρ(ρ)ῖνος*—Dubois and Arena: f. *Σάρις*)

### Πύριχος

EPIROS:

—NIKOPOLIS: (1) imp. *PAE* 1913, p. 98 no. 13 (Sarikakis 139) (f. *Λεοντίς*)

### Πυροῖος

ARGOLIS:

—EPIDAUROS: (1) iii AD *IG* IV (1)² 527

### Πυρόμαλλος

KORINTHIA:

—KORINTH: (1) byz. *Corinth* VIII (1) 154; cf. *TMByz* 9 (1985) p. 360 no. 15 (f. *Ἀνδρέας*)

### Πυρόμαχος

ARGOLIS:

—EPIDAUROS*: (1) c. 370 BC *IG* IV (1)² 102, 275

### Πῦρος

SICILY:

—SELINOUS: (1) f. v BC Dubois, *IGDS* 38, 7 (Arena, *Iscr. Sic.* I 63) (*Πύρ(ρ)ος*—Dubois and Arena); (2) ~ Dubois, *IGDS* 38, 8 (Arena, *Iscr. Sic.* I 63) ?= (3); (3) ~ Dubois, *IGDS* 38, 9 (Arena, *Iscr. Sic.* I 63) (*Πύρ(ρ)ος*—Dubois and Arena: f. *Ῥοτύλος*) ?= (2); (4) ~ Dubois, *IGDS* 38, 16 (Arena, *Iscr. Sic.* I 63) (*Πύρ(ρ)ος*—Dubois and Arena: f. *Λυκῖνος*)

### Πύρραιθος

AITOLIA: (1) 217 BC Nachtergael, *Les Galates* 65, 3

### Πυρραλίων

ARKADIA:

—TEGEA: (1) iii BC *SEG* XXXIII 283 (f. *Μνασιάδας*)

### Πυρρανθίδας

AITOLIA?: (1) 217-207 BC *FD* III (3) 221, 4 + *BCH* 73 (1949) p. 268 no. 19 (or Thessaly?: *Πυρρανθίδ[ας]*—Daux, *Πυρραν(ο)ίδ[ας]?*)

### Πύρρανθος

ARKADIA:

—MEGALOPOLIS: (1) ?274 BC *FD* III (1) 46, 1 (s. *Ἀρίστων*); (2) c. 210-207 BC *IG* IV (1)² 73, 25; *SEG* XXXV 303 (date) (s. *Ἱερώνυμος*)

### Πυρρανοίδας

AITOLIA:

—AGRAIOI: (1) ii-i BC *IG* IX (1)² (1) 198; cf. IX (1)² (3) 634 n. on l. 9 (f. *Ἀντίγονος*)

### Πυρρᾶς

ARGOLIS:

—EPIDAUROS: (1) c. 370 BC ib. IV (1)² 102, 101

### Πυρρήν

ARGOLIS:

—EPIDAUROS: (1) c. 370-335 BC ib. 103, 31, 37, 70; Peek, *IAEpid* 52 A, 17 (*Πυ[ρρ]ήν*)

### Πυρρίας

AITOLIA: (1) c. 220-200 BC *RE* (4) col. 1420

—BOMIEIS: (2) 153-144 BC *BCH* 66-7 (1942-3) p. 78 no. 7, 6 (s. *Πολυδαίτας*)

—KALYDON: (3) m. ii BC *IG* IX (1)² (1) 137, 23

—THERMOS: (4) 163 BC ib. 102, 3

ARGOLIS:

—EPIDAUROS: (5) c. 370 BC ib. IV (1)² 102, 16

ARKADIA: (6) 400 BC X., *An.* vi 5. 11
—ALIPHEIRA*: (7) ?iii BC *SEG* XXV 453 ([*Π*]υρρία[s])
—HERAIA: (8) v/iv BC *Ét. Thas.* 3 p. 136 no. 16
—TEGEA: (9) arch.? Paus. viii 48. 1
EPIROS:
—AMBRAKIA: (10) ii BC *SEG* XLII 542 (f. Ἀγέλαος)
—DODONA: (11) iii BC Antoniou, *Dodone* Aa, 20
ITHAKE: (12) arch. *RE* (5) col. 1421; Arist. fr. 611. 71 (Heraclid. Lemb. 71) (fict.?)
KEPHALLENIA:
—PALE: (13) iii/ii BC Unp. (*IG* arch.) (Πυρριαδ—apogr., Πυρρία(s), Πυρριάδ(as)?)
S. ITALY (APULIA): (14) f. iv BC *Second Suppl. RVAp* 1 p. 7 no. 124 (vase) (fict.)
S. ITALY (CAMPANIA):
—CAPREAE: (15) iii/ii BC *IG* II² 8959
SICILY:
—AKRAGAS (NR.)?: (16) ?iv BC Manganaro, *QUCC* forthcoming no. 39
—GELA-PHINTIAS: (17) m. v BC Arena, *Iscr. Sic.* II 56 (vase) (Πυρρί[as])
—HERBESSOS: (18) s. v BC ib. 122 a (vase)
—KAMARINA: (19) f. v BC Cordano, *Tessere Pubbliche* 118 a (Πυρ[ρί]as); (20) ~ ib. 127 (f. —ις)
—MENAI: (21) inc. *Riv. Stor. Antica* 5 (1900-1) p. 57 (f. Ὀλύμπιχος)
—MORGANTINA: (22) c. 460 BC *SEG* XXXVIII 949 (vase) (Πυρ(ρ)ίας); (23) ?iv/iii BC ib. XXXIX 1008, 12 (s. Καράϊκος)
—SELINOUS: (24) vi/v BC Dubois, *IGDS* 50 (Arena, *Iscr. Sic.* I 50; Lazzarini 880 a); cf. *SEG* XL 806 (*Π*(ν)ρρία (gen.)—Lazzarini and Dubois, πρōτα—Arena); (25) f. v BC Dubois, *IGDS* 54 (Arena, *Iscr. Sic.* I 39; Lazzarini 744); *IGLMP* 56 (name) (f. Θεΰλλος)
—SYRACUSE?:
——(Λακυν.): (26) hell. *Mem. Linc.* 8 (1938) p. 127 no. 35. 4 (bullet); cf. *L'Incidenza dell'Antico* pp. 420 ff. (f. Ἀγέλαος)

**Πυρρίνα**
KORINTHIA:
—KORINTH: (1) f. iv BC Schol. Ar., *Pl.* 149 (-νη: het.)

**Πυρρῖνος**
AITOLIA: (1) 217 BC Nachtergael, *Les Galates* 65, 4
AKARNANIA:
—STRATOS: (2) ?153 BC *IG* IX (1)² (1) 109, 7

**Πυρρίς**
S. ITALY (BRUTTIUM):
—KRIMISA: (1) vi-v BC Landi, *DISMG* 174
S. ITALY (CAMPANIA):
—POMPEII: (2) i BC-i AD *CIL* IV 4158 (Lat. Pyris)

**Πυρρίσας**
AITOLIA:
—KONOPE-ARSINOE: (1) 250-150 BC Fraser-Rönne, *BWGT* p. 143 no. 1

**Πύρριχος**
AKARNANIA:
—PHOITIAI: (1) iv BC *IG* IX (1)² (2) 602, 11
—THYRREION: (2) 216 BC ib. 583, 18 (f. Ἀγαπάνωρ)
EPIROS:
—AMBRAKIA: (3) iii BC ib. IV (1)² 97, 37 + Peek, *IAEpid* 43 (f. —νος)
ILLYRIA:
—EPIDAMNOS-DYRRHACHION: (4) c. 250-50 BC Münsterberg Nachtr. p. 17; *Jubice Hoard* p. 97 nos. 46-7 (coin) (Ceka 405; 409) (pryt.) ?= (5); (5) ~ Ceka, *Probleme* p. 152 no. 61 (coin) (pryt.) ?= (4)
KORINTHIA:
—KORINTH: (6) s. v BC Th. vii 39. 2 (f. Ἀρίστων)

LAKONIA: (7) her. Wehrli, *Schule Arist.* ii fr. 103 (*RE* (2); Poralla² 652) (dub.)
S. ITALY (CAMPANIA):
—POMPEII: (8) i BC-i AD *CIL* IV 1944; 1868; 1920 (Lat. Pyrrhicus); (9) ~ ib. 2154 (Lat. Pyrrichus) ?= (10); (10) ~ ib. 2155 (Castrèn 124. 5) (Lat. C. Cominius Pyrrichus) ?= (9); (11) ~ *CIL* IV 4130 (Lat. Puricos); (12) ~ ib. 4492 (Lat. Pyrrhicus); (13) ~ ib. 5008 (Lat. Pyrrhichus); (14) ~ ib. 10104 e (Castrèn 375. 9) (Lat. Sextilius Pyrricus)
SICILY:
—AKRAI: (15) ii BC *Akrai* p. 156 no. 6, 17 (s. Ἀριστόγειτος)
—CASTEL DI IUDICA (MOD.): (16) ?iii BC Manganaro, *PdelP* forthcoming no. 6, 2 (f. Ἀλκιππος)
—KAMARINA: (17) f. v BC Cordano, *Tessere Pubbliche* 43 (Arena, *Iscr. Sic.* II 136 A) (Πύρριχο[s]: s. Νικοφάνης)
TRIPHYLIA:
—PHRIXA: (18) c. 230-200 BC *BCH* 45 (1921) p. 13 II, 86 (s. Ἀγυλλος)

**Πυρροίτας**
AKARNANIA:
—STRATOS: (1) 362 BC *CID* II 1 II, 22

**Πυρρόλοχος**
ARGOLIS:
—ARGOS: (1) 408 BC X., *HG* i 3. 13; *RE* (-)

**Πύρρος**
ACHAIA:
—PELLENE: (1) 263 BC *IG* IX (1)² (1) 17, 52 (s. Φ[ι]λ-)
AIGINA: (2) hell.-imp. ib. IV (1) 43 (f. Δημῶναξ)
AKARNANIA: (3) 221-204 BC *OGIS* 82; cf. *SB* 7306 (f. Λίχας)
—STRATOS: (4) 154 BC *SGDI* 1908, 15, 19 (f. Ἀρίστων)
—THYRREION: (5) iii BC *IG* IX (1)² (2) 275
ARGOLIS:
—TROIZEN: (6) ii BC ib. II² 10463 (f. Εὐφράνωρ); (7) f. ii BC ib. IV (1) 752, 9 + IV (1)² 77, 15
ELIS: (8) f. iv BC Paus. vi 1. 4 (f. Δεινόλοχος)
—PISA: (9) vii/vi BC ib. 22. 4 (s. Πανταλέων: king)
—THRAISTOS: (10) f. iv BC *IG* IX (1)² (1) 138, 2
EPIROS: (11) ii BC ib. II² 8543
—AMBRAKIA: (12) iii BC Unp. (Arta Mus., inscr.) ([*Π*ύ]ρρος)
—ANTIGONEIA: (13) ?iv BC *Iliria* 1972, p. 298 (Πύρρο (gen.))
—BOUTHROTOS (PRASAIBOI): (14) a. 163 BC *IBouthrot* 45, 8 (f. Ἀλέξανδρος)
——Delioi: (15) a. 163 BC ib. 67, 5 (f. Ἀλκιμος)
—MOLOSSOI: (16) 319-272 BC *RE* (13); *SEG* XXIII 186; XXXVII 513; *PAE* 1966, p. 77 no. 7 (armour) (s. Αἰακίδης, Φθία, f. Πτολεμαῖος, Ἑλενος, Ἀλέξανδρος, Ὀλυμπιάς: king I); (17) iii BC *RE* (14) (s. Ἀλέξανδρος, Ὀλυμπιάς: king II)
ILLYRIA:
—EPIDAMNOS-DYRRHACHION?: (18) vi BC ib. (17) (f. Ἑρμων, Λακράτης)
LAKONIA:
—SPARTA: (19) f. iii AD *IG* V (1) 503; 504, 10 and add.; *BSA* 79 (1984) pp. 279-83 (date) (Bradford (1)) (*Π.* Οὔ(λπ). *Π.*: s. Καλλικράτης); (20) a. 212 AD *SEG* XI 806, 4 (Bradford (2)) (Πύρρ[ος]: f. *Μ.* Αὐρ. Ξεναρχίδας)
MESSENIA: (21) viii/vii BC Paus. iv 14. 8 (?f. Ἀριστομένης, Ἀγναγόρα)
S. ITALY (CAMPANIA):
—KYME?: (22) c. 650 BC Dubois, *IGDGG* 1 22 (vase) (Arena, *Iscr. Sic.* III A 3); *LSAG²* p. 83 (Πύρ(ρ)ος: s. Ἀγασίλεϝος: potter)
—NEAPOLIS: (23) i BC-i AD? *INap* 156 (I f. Πύρρος II); (24) ~ ib. (II s. Πύρρος I); (25) imp. *Anc. Soc.* 19 (1988) p. 27 no. 149

—POMPEII: (26) i BC-i AD *CIL* IV 1852 (Lat. Pyrrhus); (27) ~ ib. 1934 (Lat. Pyrrhus)
S. ITALY (LUCANIA):
—HERAKLEIA:
——(Αἰ. πέλτα): (28) iv/iii BC *IGSI* 1 I, 5, 9, 97 (*DGE* 62; Uguzzoni–Ghinatti I); *IGSI* 1 II, 5, 8 (*DGE* 63; Uguzzoni–Ghinatti II) (f. Δάζιμος)
—SIRIS (NR.): (29) f. vii BC Dubois, *IGDGG* 1 47 (vase) (*SEG* XLI 858) (Πύρρō (gen.))
SICILY:
—GELA-PHINTIAS: (30) f. ii BC *IG* XIV 256, 45 (Dubois, *IGDS* 16); *SEG* XL 804 (name) (Πύρρος—*SEG*, Πυρρων(ί)δας]—*IG*, Πυρρόμμ[ις]—Dubois: f. Νίκαρος)
—KATANE: (31) imp. *CIL* X 7117 (Lat. Ineas Pyrrus)
—SYRACUSE: (32) iii-v AD Ferrua, *NG* 375 (Πύρρος—lap., Πύρ(ρ)ος—Ferrua)
—SYRACUSE?:
——(Μακ.): (33) hell. Manganaro, *PdelP* forthcoming no. 4 I, 12 (s. Σώπατρος)

**Πύρρων**
ARGOLIS:
—PHLEIOUS: (1) iv/iii BC *RE* (3) (s. Τίμαρχος)
ELIS: (2) ?c. 475 BC *SEG* XXXI 358, 1; *LSAG²* p. 450 no. E (date) (Πύρρō(ν)); (3) iv BC *DGE* 424, 8; (4) c. 360-270 BC *RE* (1) (?s. Πλείσταρχος, Πιστοκράτης)
S. ITALY (BRUTTIUM):
—LOKROI EPIZEPHYRIOI:
——(Προ.): (5) iv/iii BC De Franciscis 32, 5 (f. Νικίας)
S. ITALY (LUCANIA):
—METAPONTION: (6) iv BC Iamb., *VP* 267 (*FVS* 1 p. 446)
SICILY:
—LIPARA: (7) hell.? *IG* II² 9215 (Πύρρων: f. Ὀνασος); (8) ?i BC *Meligunis-Lipara* 5 p. 149 no. 2150; cf. *SEG* XLI 804; (9) hell.-imp.? *RE* (4); *FGrH* 836

**Πυρρωνίδας**
ARGOLIS:
—PHLEIOUS: (1) vi BC *Suda Π* 2230 (-δης: ?f. Πρατίνας)

**Πύρων**
ACHAIA:
—DYME*: (1) c. 219 BC *SGDI* 1612, 40 (*Tyche* 5 (1990) p. 124) (I f. Πύρων II); (2) ~ *SGDI* 1612, 40 (*Tyche* 5 (1990) p. 124) (II s. Πύρων I)
ARGOLIS:
—HERMIONE: (3) ?ii-i BC *IG* IV (1) 731 III, 3 (s. Δέξιος)
ILLYRIA:
—EPIDAMNOS-DYRRHACHION: (4) c. 250-50 BC Maier 352 (coin) (Ceka 239) (pryt.); (5) hell.-imp. *IDyrrh* 120 (f. Ἀριστομέδων)

**Πυρωνίδης**
S. ITALY (LUCANIA):
—POSEIDONIA-PAESTUM: (1) m. iv BC *RVP* p. 65 no. 19 (vase) (fict.)

**Πυστάκα**
AKARNANIA:
—ANAKTORION: (1) hell. *AD* 44 (1989) Chron. p. 145 (masc./fem. voc.?: d. Ἀλέξανδρος)
—ECHINOS?: (2) iii BC *IG* IX (1)² (2) 369 (masc./fem. voc.?)

**Πυστακίς**
ITHAKE: (1) i BC *PAE* 1992, p. 210
KEPHALLENIA:
—SAME: (2) hell. Fraser-Rönne, *BWGT* p. 118 no. 6, 5

**Πυστακίων**
EPIROS:
—DODONA*: (1) iv-iii BC *SGDI* 1580, 8

ITHAKE: (2) ?iii BC *BCH* 29 (1905) p. 163 no. 1
LEUKAS: (3) iii BC *IG* IV (1)² 350 ([Πυστ]ακίων: s. Καλλιλαΐδας: name—*LGPN*)

**Πυστίλος**
SICILY:
—GELA-PHINTIAS: (1) c. 580 BC Th. vi 4. 4 (and Sicily Akragas: oikist)

**Πυτίαρχος**
ARKADIA:
—TEGEA: (1) ?s. iv BC *IG* v (2) 39, 8 (f. —ων)

**Πύτταλος**
ELIS: (1) iv/iii BC Moretti, *Olymp.* 476 (s. Λάμπις)

**Πωϊνος**
ARGOLIS:
—KOILADA (MOD.): (1) imp. *SEG* XI 385 h

**Πῶλλα**
ARGOLIS:
—ARGOS: (1) i BC-i AD Unp. (Argos, Kavvadias); (2) imp. *IG* IV (1) 622, 4; (3) ~ ib. 646

—NAUPLIA: (4) imp. *SEG* I 72 (Οὐεσπικία Π.)
ELIS: (5) c. 67-105 AD *IvOl* 433, 3 (Γιγανία Π.: m. Τιβ. Κλ. Λύσων Κοσμόπολις); (6) ii/iii AD ib. 467, 6 (Ἀντ. Π.: m. Βαιβία Πρόκλα)
LAKONIA:
—SPARTA: (7) s. ii AD *IG* v (1) 587, 2 (Bradford (2)) (Πομπ. Π.: d. Θεόξενος); (8) f. iii AD *IG* v (1) 464, 14; *BSA* 80 (1985) pp. 244-5 (ident., stemma) (Πομπ. Π.: d. Σέξ. Πομπ. Θεόξενος); (9) ~ *IG* v (1) 602, 18; *BSA* 80 (1985) pp. 225; 239; 242 (ident., stemma) (Bradford (1)) (Κλ. Π.: d. Τιβ. Κλ. Εὔδαμος, Κλ. Δαμοσθένεια, m. Πομπωνία Καλλιστονίκη)

**Πωλλίων**
AKARNANIA:
—ALYZIA: (1) imp. *IG* IX (1)² (2) 447
ARGOLIS:
—EPIDAUROS: (2) 187 AD ib. IV (1)² 394 a; Peek, *IAEpid* 262 (Τιβ. Κλ. Π.)
LAKONIA:
—SPARTA: (3) c. 100-120 AD *IG* v (1) 97, 25; *SEG* XI 510, 4; 535, 2; 564, 25 (Bradford (2)) (Πολλίων—*SEG* XI 564: s. Ῥοῦφος); (4) f. ii

AD *IG* v (1) 62, 3; 107, [3]; *SEG* XI 606, [5] (Bradford (1)) (s. Ἰσόχρυσος); (5) c. 110-150 AD *IG* v (1) 114, 10; *SEG* XI 516, 2?; 543, 4 (Bradford (3)) (Π[ωλλ]ίων—*SEG* XI 516: f. Ἄγιππος)

**Πῶλος**
AIGINA: (1) s. iv BC *RE* (6); *SEG* I 362, 1, 3, 14, 28 (Stephanis 2187) (s. Σωσιγένης)
ARGOLIS:
—EPIDAUROS: (2) 712 BC Moretti, *Olymp.* 19
ARKADIA:
—MEGALOPOLIS: (3) ?iv-iii BC Paus. viii 31. 7; (4) 134 or 130 BC *FD* III (3) 120, 8, 15 (f. Σωσιγένης)
LAKONIA:
—SPARTA: (5) 400 BC X., *An.* vii 2. 5 (Poralla² 653)
MESSENIA:
—ITHOME: (6) hell.? Furtwängler, *Gemmen* 2 p. 315 LXI 39
SICILY:
—AKRAGAS: (7) s. v BC *RE* (3)

# P

**Ῥαδάμανθυς**
LAKONIA:
—SPARTA: (1) c. 30-20 BC *IG* v (1) 141, 17; *SEG* XXXV 329 (date) (Bradford (-)) (s. Γ. Ἰούλ. Εὐρυκλῆς)

**Ῥάδων**
SICILY:
—SYRACUSE:
——(Κραταιμείος): (1) iv BC Manganaro, *PdelP* forthcoming no. 3, 7 (f. Γοργύλος)

**Ῥαμία**
S. ITALY (APULIA):
—VALENZANO (MOD.): (1) ?c. 450 BC Troisi, *Epigrafi mobili* 113 (*LSAG*² p. 284 no. 11)

**Ῥαμφίας**
LAKONIA:
—SPARTA: (1) c. 475-415 BC *RE* (-) (Poralla² 654) (f. Κλέαρχος)

**Ῥάπα?**
SICILY: (1) ?f. iii BC *ZPE* 111 (1996) p. 136 no. 4

**Ῥασφαρμαυα?**
SICILY:
—SELINOUS: (1) m. v BC Dubois, *IGDS* 36, 4 (Arena, *Iscr. Sic.* I 69) (Ῥασφαρμαυκα?—Arena)

**Ῥατορᾶς**
SICILY:
—HERBESSOS: (1) ?s. vi BC *Kokalos* 14-15 (1968-9) p. 200 (vase)

**Ῥατορώ**
SICILY:
—TERRAVECCHIA DI CUTI (MOD.): (1) vi/v BC Arena, *Iscr. Sic.* II 117 A (Dubois, *IGDS* 176) (-ρỏ)

**Ῥάτωρ**
SICILY:
—ADRANON: (1) i BC-i AD? *IG* XIV 570 ([Κ]ράτωρ?: f. Καλλίστρατος)

**Ῥαύδιος**
KORINTHIA:
—SIKYON: (1) vi/v BC *SEG* XI 244, 30

**Ῥάχας**
AKARNANIA?: (1) s. iii BC *IG* XI (4) 519, 11 (s. Ἀντίοχος)

**Ῥεδόρας**
SICILY:
—CASTIGLIONE DI RAGUSA (MOD.): (1) m. vi BC *BdA* 80-1 (1993) pp. 155-6 (vase)

**Ῥῆγα**
S. ITALY (BRUTTIUM):
—SYBARIS-THOURIOI-COPIAE: (1) ?c. 550 BC Landi, *DISMG* 250; *LSAG*² p. 456 no. B (date) (Ῥε̄-)

**Ῥηγῖνος**
S. ITALY (BRUTTIUM):
—RHEGION: (1) imp. *SEG* XXIX 989 (Ῥη[γῖνος]); (2) i AD *IG* XIV 617, 6 (Γ. Ἰούλιος Ῥ.); (3) ~ ib. l. 8 (Κ. Καικίλιος Ῥ.)
SICILY:
—ENTELLA: (4) ii-i BC *Entella* I pp. 175-7 nos. 16-25 (tiles)

**Ῥῆγλος**
KORINTHIA:
—KORINTH: (1) imp. *SEG* XXX 348 (lamp)

**Ῥήδων**
ILLYRIA:
—DARDANIOI: (1) s. ii AD *ZA* 24 (1974) p. 255, 5 (s. Γέτας, Γενθιανή)
—LISSOS: (2) hell. *Stud. Alb.* 1972 (1), p. 70 no. 2 (coin); cf. *ZA* 24 (1974) p. 258 f. (name)

**Ῥηξίβιος**
S. ITALY (LUCANIA):
—METAPONTION: (1) iv BC Iamb., *VP* 267 (*FVS* I p. 446)

**Ῥηξίμαχος**
ARKADIA:
—TEGEA: (1) her.? *FGrH* 42 F 5 (f. Κριτόλαος, Δαμοδίκα: fict.)

**Ῥῆσος**
ARGOLIS:
—ARGOS*: (1) ii BC *SEG* XLII 279, 4 (slave/freed.?)
ARKADIA:
—KLEITOR: (2) ?274 BC *FD* III (1) 83, 16 (Κήσου (gen.)—lap., (Ῥ)ῆσος?)
—MEGALOPOLIS: (3) imp. *IG* v (2) 488 (-σσος)
S. ITALY (CAMPANIA):
—DIKAIARCHIA-PUTEOLI: (4) imp. *CIL* X 2122 (Lat. Q. Attius Resus)
—POMPEII: (5) i BC-i AD ib. IV 10118 (Lat. Resus)

**Ῥητορικός**
ARGOLIS:
—KALAURIA: (1) imp. *IG* IV (1) 847 (Κλ. Ῥ.)
LAKONIA:
—SPARTA: (2) a. 212 AD *BSA* 89 (1994) p. 435 no. 6, 7 (Μέμ(μιος) Ῥ.)

**Ῥῆτος**
S. ITALY (CAMPANIA):
—HERCULANEUM*: (1) i BC-i AD *CIL* X 1403 f II, 10 (Lat. Q. Marius Rhetus: freed.)

**Ῥίνθων**
SICILY:
—SYRACUSE: (1) iv/iii BC *RE* (-); *CGF* I pp. 183 ff.; *HE* 2830 with comm. (locn.) (or S. Italy (Calabria) Taras-Tarentum)

**Ῥίνων**
AIGINA: (1) hell.? *SB* 4043
ARGOLIS:
—ARGOS:
——(Pamphyloi): (2) ?c. 475 BC *SEG* XIII 239, 6; *LSAG*² p. 169 no. 22 (date) (f. Ἐπικράτης)

**Ῥινώτας**
ARGOLIS:
—EPIDAUROS*: (1) c. 370 BC *IG* IV (1)² 102, 212 (Ῥ[ιν]ώτας)

**Ῥίπιρ**
ELIS:
—PISATIS (KOSKINA (MOD.)): (1) ?c. 475-450
BC IvOl 718, 1; LSAG² p. 220 no. 16 (date)
(n. pr.?: s. Ξενϝάρηρ)

**Ῥιποτελίδας**
MESSENIA:
—PHARAI: (1) vi BC IG v (1) 1362 a; Lazza-
rini 409 (date) ([Ῥι]ποτελίδας, [Ῥαρ]οτελίδας—
Skias)

**Ῥίττων**
ELIS:
—OLYMPIA*: (1) f. iv BC Ol. Forsch. 23 pp. 97-
8 no. KFS 78 (vase)

**Ῥιψόλαος**
LAKONIA:
—SPARTA: (1) 624 BC Moretti, Olymp. 65 (Po-
ralla² 655)

**Ῥόγκα**
SICILY?: (1) ?v BC CGF p. 154 fr. 2 (ῥωγκα—
cod.)

**Ῥόδα**
ARGOLIS:
—HERMIONE: (1) i BC-i AD? IG IV (1) 734, 11
(d. Εὐπάμων)
MESSENIA:
—KORONE: (2) ii AD SEG XI 990 (d. Νεμέριος)
S. ITALY (CALABRIA):
—TARAS-TARENTUM: (3) imp. CIL IX 248 (Lat.
Messia Roda)

**Ῥόδη**
ARGOLIS:
—ARGOS: (1) byz. SEG XXVI 434, 2; cf. TMByz
9 (1985) p. 370 no. 119 (m. Κυριακή)
S. ITALY (CAMPANIA):
—DIKAIARCHIA-PUTEOLI: (2) imp. CIL X 2916
(Lat. Rhode: d. Λάκων)

**Ῥοδία**
ELIS:
—PISATIS (KLADEOS (MOD.)): (1) hell.-imp.
SEG XXV 469
SICILY:
—THERMAI HIMERAIAI: (2) i-ii AD CIL X 7429
(ILat. Term. Imer. 129) (Lat. Pompeia Rodia)

**Ῥοδίνη**
LAKONIA:
—SPARTA: (1) imp. IG v (1) 1592 b (Bradford
(-)) (d. Στράτιος)
S. ITALY (APULIA):
—LUCERIA: (2) imp. CIL IX 883 (Lat. Rodene)
S. ITALY (CALABRIA):
—BRENTESION-BRUNDISIUM*: (3) imp. NScav
1900, p. 153 no. 5 (Lat. Besia Rodini: freed.)
S. ITALY (CAMPANIA):
—DIKAIARCHIA-PUTEOLI: (4) imp. CIL X 2155
(Lat. Autronia Rhodine: d. Εὐτυχία)
—DIKAIARCHIA-PUTEOLI*: (5) imp. AJA 2
(1898) p. 387 no. 37 (Lat. Rodine: freed.); (6)
~ CIL X 2407 (Lat. Fabia Rhodine: freed.)
—NOLA: (7) imp. ib. 1309 (Lat. [I]ulia
Rhodi[ne])
SICILY:
—KATANE: (8) iii-v AD IG XIV 548 (IGLMP 8;
Wessel 1377; Ferrua, NG 444)

**Ῥόδινος**
S. ITALY (CAMPANIA):
—POMPEII: (1) i BC-i AD CIL IV 3443 (Lat.
Rodinus)
SICILY: (2) ?iv AD IGUR 60, 13 (IG XIV 1078
a)

**Ῥόδιον**
EPIROS: (1) ii/i BC ib. II² 8544 (d. Ῥόδιππος)
KERKYRA: (2) ii BC ib. IX (1) 940
KORINTHIA:
—SIKYON: (3) i BC ib. II² 10310 (Skalet 286) (d.
Ἀριστόδαμος)
S. ITALY (CALABRIA):
—TARAS-TARENTUM: (4) hell.? RA 1932 (1), p.
40 no. 39 (Ῥοδείω (gen.?))

**Ῥόδιππος**
ARGOLIS:
—ARGOS: (1) c. 70-60 BC IG VII 3197, 14, 45;
AE 1917, p. 166, 14; BCH 44 (1920) pp. 251-
2 no. 10, 20; BSA 70 (1975) pp. 121-3 (date);
cf. Stephanis 2191 (I f. Ῥόδιππος II); (2) ~
IG VII 3197, 14, 45; AE 1917, p. 166, 14;
BCH 44 (1920) pp. 251-2 no. 10, 20; BSA
70 (1975) pp. 121-3 (date) (Stephanis 2191)
(II s. Ῥόδιππος I)
EPIROS: (3) ii/i BC IG II² 8544 (f. Ῥόδιον)
S. ITALY (BRUTTIUM):
—KROTON: (4) iv BC Iamb., VP 267 (FVS 1 p.
446)

**Ῥοδογούνη**
SICILY:
—KATANE: (1) imp. GVI 1936 (MEFRA 106
(1994) p. 94 no. 6); cf. BE 1980, no. 593 (Ῥ.
τὸ πρὶν Ἐπαγαθώ)
—SYRACUSE: (2) iii-v AD Ferrua, NG 336 ([Ῥο-
δο]γύνη (n. pr.?))

**Ῥοδοκλέα**
AIGINA: (1) hell. IG IV (1) 152 (d. Ἀπολλόθεμις)

**Ῥοδοκλῆς**
AIGINA: (1) 284 BC PEleph 4, 8

**Ῥοδόπα**
KORINTHIA:
—KORINTH: (1) 146 BC HE 656 (d. Βοΐσκα)

**Ῥοδόπη**
EPIROS:
—PHOTIKE: (1) imp. Hammond, Epirus p. 744
no. 48 (Lat. Rhodope)
S. ITALY (APULIA):
—LUCERIA: (2) ?s. ii AD Rend. Linc. 24 (1969)
p. 28 no. 10 (Lat. Valeria Rhodope)
S. ITALY (CAMPANIA):
—NEAPOLIS: (3) ?i AD NScav 1892, p. 99; cf.
Leiwo p. 112 no. 87 (Lat. Iulia Rodope: d.
Ἑρμῆς)
—NOLA: (4) ?i-ii AD CIL X 1307 (Lat. Iulia
Rodhope: m. Ἀτίμητος)
—SURRENTUM*: (5) imp. ib. 749 (Lat. Plotia
Rhodope: freed.)
SICILY:
—SYRACUSE: (6) iii-v AD Strazzulla 305 (Agnello
24; Wessel 860)

**Ῥόδος**
SICILY:
—AKRAGAS: (1) 406 BC D.S. xiii 84. 1 (Ἀντισθέ-
νης ὁ ἐπικαλ. Ῥ.)

**Ῥόδων**
AIGINA?: (1) i-ii AD EAD XXX p. 357 no. 25 (f.
Κέρδων)
ARGOLIS:
—EPIDAUROS: (2) ?iv-iii BC SEG XXXIX 356 ter
ILLYRIA: (3) m. iii BC Thess. Mnem. 170 (s. Ἄρ-
χος)
LAKONIA:
—GYTHEION: (4) ii AD SEG 11 176
—SPARTA: (5) m. ii AD IG v (1) 108, 6 (Brad-
ford (2)) (I f. Ῥόδων II); (6) ~ IG v (1) 108, 6
(Bradford (1)) (II s. Ῥόδων I)
S. ITALY (CAMPANIA):
—MISENUM*: (7) ?ii-iii AD CIL X 3536 (Lat.
Aurelius Rodo)

SICILY:
—TAUROMENION: (8) iii-v AD IG XIV 165
(Strazzulla 106; Wessel 1044); Ferrua, NG
480 (locn.)

**Ῥοτύλος**
SICILY:
—SELINOUS: (1) f. v BC Dubois, IGDS 38, 5
(Arena, Iscr. Sic. I 63) ([Ῥ]οτύλος?: s. Ταμί-
ρας); (2) ~ Dubois, IGDS 38, 8 (Arena, Iscr.
Sic. I 63) (s. Πῦρος)

**Ῥούβριος**
LAKONIA:
—HYPERTELEATON*: (1) imp. IG v (1) 991 (I f.
Ῥούβριος II); (2) ~ ib. (II s. Ῥούβριος I)

**Ῥοῦφα**
ILLYRIA:
—EPIDAMNOS-DYRRHACHION: (1) imp. IDyrrh
368
S. ITALY (LUCANIA):
—HYELE-VELIA: (2) imp. PdelP 21 (1966) p.
341 no. 28

**Ῥουφίλιος?**
S. ITALY (CALABRIA):
—TARAS-TARENTUM: (1) i BC/i AD GP 2151
(Ῥουφῖνος—contra metr., Ῥ.?—Page, Ῥουφια-
νός—lemma)

**Ῥούφιλλα**
SICILY:
—SYRACUSE: (1) iii-v AD Führer p. 816 n.

**Ῥουφῖνα**
S. ITALY (CAMPANIA):
—NEAPOLIS: (1) iii-iv AD IG XIV 826. 39 (INap
248) (-φεῖ-)
SICILY:
—SYRACUSE: (2) iii-v AD IG XIV 164 (Strazzulla
105; Wessel 873); (3) ~ Rend. Pont. 22 (1946-
7) p. 238 no. 9; (4) ~ Strazzulla 284

**Ῥουφῖνος**
ILLYRIA:
—EPIDAMNOS-DYRRHACHION: (1) hell.-imp.
IDyrrh 13 (Ῥ(ο)υφῖνος)
KORINTHIA:
—KORINTH: (2) ii AD Ag. VII p. 91 nos. 231-
32; SEG XXVII 36. 15 (lamps) (Ῥο[υ]φεῖνος—
Ag., Ῥοῦ[φος]—SEG); (3) byz. Corinth VIII
(3) 564, 3; cf. TMByz 9 (1985) p. 366 no.
68
LAKONIA:
—SPARTA: (4) c. 225-250 AD SEG XI 806 a, 4
(Bradford (-)) (Τιβ. Κλ. Ῥουφεῖνος: s. Ὑγῖνος)
SICILY:
—SYRACUSE: (5) iii-v AD Strazzulla 238; (6) ~
ib. 349 (Wessel 658) ([Ῥου]φῖνος)

**Ῥουφίων**
AKARNANIA:
—ANAKTORION (NR.): (1) ?iii-iv AD AAA 4
(1971) p. 193 (f. Ἄνθος)
LAKONIA:
—SPARTA: (2) c. 170-190 AD SEG XI 627, 8
(Bradford (-)) (f. Ἀρτεμᾶς)

**Ῥοῦφος**
ARGOLIS:
—ARGOS: (1) imp. IG IV (1) 613; (2) iii AD ib.
672, 1 (I f. Αὐρ. Ῥοῦφος II)
—HERMIONE: (3) iii AD ib. 720, 1 ([Ῥ]οῦφος: I f.
Μ. Αὐρ. Ῥοῦφος II)
ARKADIA:
—TEGEA: (4) 165 AD ib. v (2) 50, 10 (f. Ἐπικτᾶς)
EPIROS:
—AMBRAKIA: (5) imp. BCH 17 (1893) p. 632
no. 2
ILLYRIA:
—EPIDAMNOS-DYRRHACHION: (6) imp. IDyrrh
369 (s. Δωσίθεος)
LAKONIA:
—GYTHEION: (7) f. i AD IG v (1) 1167, 3 (f.
Δαμονικίδας)

**—SPARTA: (8)** c. 100-120 AD ib. 97, 25; *SEG*
XI 510, 4; 535, 2; 564, 25 (Bradford (6)) (f.
*Πωλλίων*); **(9)** c. 150-160 AD *IG* v (1) 53, 4;
54, [3]; 64, 11; 276, 2; *SEG* XI 495, 2 (Brad-
ford (4)) (f. *Καλλικράτης*); **(10)** c. 170 AD *SEG*
XI 530, 4 (Bradford (1)) (*Ρο̣*[*ύφ*]*ο̣ς*: s. *Εὔδα-
μος*); **(11)** f. iii AD *IG* v (1) 563, 9 (Bradford
(5)) (f. *M. Αὐρ. Κλεάνωρ*); **(12)** c. 217-230 AD
*SEG* XI 616 a, 6 (Bradford (3)) (*Ῥοῦφ*[*ος*]: ?f.
*Αὐρ. Δαμάριστος*)
**—TAINARON-KAINEPOLIS: (13)** 198-211 AD
*SEG* XXIII 199, 22 (I f. *Ῥοῦφος* II); **(14)** ~
ib. l. 22 (II s. *Ῥοῦφος* I); **(15)** 213-217 AD *IG*
v (1) 1240, 14 (f. *Αὐρ. Ἄλκι—*)
S. ITALY (CAMPANIA):
**—DIKAIARCHIA-PUTEOLI: (16)** imp. ib. XIV
859, 10 (Audollent, *Defix. Tab.* 208)
SICILY:
**—ADRANON: (17)** ?ii-iii AD *PdelP* 16 (1961) p.
132 (Ferrua, *NG* 472); cf. *Rupes loquentes* p.
497 no. 8
**—MORGANTINA: (18)** i BC-i AD *SEG* XXIX 931-2

**Ρυσιάδας**
AITOLIA: **(1)** ?269 BC *SGDI* 2595, 2 (f. *Πλείσταινος*)

AKARNANIA: **(2)** 375 BC Tod, *GHI* II 126, 27
(*Ῥυσιάδ*[*ας*])
**—ASTAKOS: (3)** m. iii BC *SEG* XXVII 153, 3 +
*BE* 1978, no. 240; cf. *PAE* 1977, pl. 244 b
([*Τ*]*υσιάδας*—ed.: s. *Πραῦχίων*)

**Ρωμαία**
ARGOLIS:
**—ARGOS\*: (1)** ii-i BC *IG* IV (1) 530, 14; cf. *BCH*
33 (1909) p. 183 n. 2 (slave/freed.?)

**Ρωμανός**
KORINTHIA:
**—KORINTH: (1)** f. iv AD *Corinth* VIII (3) 657; cf.
*TMByz* 9 (1985) p. 366 no. 79
LAKONIA:
**—SPARTA: (2)** c. 230-260 AD *SEG* XI 633, 6
(Bradford (-)) (f. *Αὐρ. Εὐτυχίων*)

**Ρώμη**
S. ITALY (CAMPANIA):
**—NEAPOLIS: (1)** ii-iii AD *NScav* 1891, p. 374;
cf. Leiwo p. 98 no. 48 (Lat. Flavia Rome)
**—POMPEII: (2)** i BC-i AD *CIL* IV 2125 (Lat.
Rome)
SICILY:
**—KATANE: (3)** iii-v AD *Oikoumene* p. 605 no. 2

**Ρῶμις**
SICILY:
**—KAMARINA: (1)** f. v BC Dubois, *IGDS* 114
(vase) (Arena, *Iscr. Sic.* II 123; Cordano, 'Ca-
marina VII' 53) (*Ῥō̄μι* (dat.?))
**—SELINOUS: (2)** f. v BC Dubois, *IGDS* 38, 6, 17
(Arena, *Iscr. Sic.* I 63) (*Ῥō̄-*: s. *Καίλιος*); **(3)** ~
Dubois, *IGDS* 38, 19 (Arena, *Iscr. Sic.* I 63)
(*Ῥō̄-*: f. *Σάρις*)

**Ρῶμος**
S. ITALY (CAMPANIA):
**—POMPEII: (1)** i BC-i AD *CIL* IV 5239 (Lat. Ro-
mus)

**Ρωμύλος**
S. ITALY (APULIA):
**—VENUSIA: (1)** iv-v AD *JIWE* I 96 (*CIJ* I 592)
(*-μώ-*: Jew)

**Ρωξάνη**
S. ITALY (CAMPANIA):
**—POMPEII: (1)** i BC-i AD *CIL* IV 9235; *Gnomon*
45 (1973) p. 268 (Lat. Roxane)

# Σ

**Σάαιθος**
ARKADIA:
**—ORCHOMENOS: (1)** ?c. 369-361 BC *BCH* 102
(1978) p. 348, 31 (*IPArk* 14)

**Σάανδρος**
ARKADIA:
**—TEGEA:**
——(Apolloniatai): **(1)** s. iv BC *IG* v (2) 41, 14
(*Σ̣άανδρος*)

**Σαβάθυρος**
DALMATIA:
**—ISSA: (1)** f. ii BC Brunšmid p. 23 no. 10, 6
(*-θιρος*: s. *Δάμαρχος*); **(2)** i BC-i AD? ib. p. 27
no. 19 (*SEG* XL 515) + *VAHD* 84 (1991) p.
254 no. 4 (s. *Πάτρων*)

**Σαβαιθίς**
S. ITALY (BRUTTIUM):
**—LOKROI EPIZEPHYRIOI: (1)** iv/iii BC *HE* 2823

**Σαβάνας**
SICILY:
**—PHILOSOPHIANA: (1)** byz. *Riv. Arch. Crist.* 40
(1964) p. 177 (*Ἰούδας Σ.*)

**Σαβᾶς**
SICILY:
**—SYRACUSE: (1)** iii-v AD *Nuovo Didask.* 6 (1956)
p. 64 no. 30; cf. Ferrua, *NG* 102 (*Σαβᾶνος*
(gen.))

**Σαββάτιος**
S. ITALY (LUCANIA):
**—COSILINUM: (1)** s. iii AD *Epigraphica* 57
(1995) p. 203 no. 3 (Lat. Sabbatius: f. Triarius Pacatianus: Jew?)

**Σαββάτις**
SICILY:
**—SYRACUSE: (1)** iii-v AD Ferrua, *NG* 210 (*-βά-*);
**(2)** ~ ib. 264

**Σάββος**
KERKYRA?: **(1)** imp. *IG* IX (1) 974 (f. *Μιρᾶς*)

**Σαβίνα**
S. ITALY (CAMPANIA):
**—NEAPOLIS: (1)** iii-iv AD ib. XIV 826. 40 (*INap*
224-5) (*-βεῖ-*); **(2)** ~ *IG* XIV 826. 50 (*INap*
225) (*Σα̣*[*β*]*εῖνα*)
SICILY:
**—AKRAGAS: (3)** imp. *IG* XIV 264 (*-βεῖ-*: m. *Θεα-
νώ*)
**—KATANE: (4)** iii-v AD ib. 549 (Agnello 55;
Wessel 384) (*-βεῖ-*)
**—SYRACUSE: (5)** iii-v AD *NScav* 1905, p. 397
no. 3; cf. *Riv. Arch. Crist.* 18 (1941) p. 233
no. 127 (*-βεῖ-*)

**Σαβῖνος**
KEPHALLENIA: **(1)** ?ii AD *IG* IX (1) 651 (*-βεῖ-*: I
f. *Σαβῖνος* II); **(2)** ~ ib. (*-βεῖ-*: II s. *Σαβῖνος* I)
KERKYRA: **(3)** imp. ib. 965
KORINTHIA:
**—KORINTH: (4)** imp. *AP* vii 346 (*GVI* 1432);
**(5)** ii-iii AD *SEG* XXIX 340, 7 (Stephanis
2206) (*Λ. Κορνήλιος Σαβεῖνος*: s. *Λ. Κορνήλιος
Κόρινθος*)
S. ITALY (CALABRIA):
**—HYDROUS-HYDRUNTUM: (6)** iii-iv AD *JIWE*
I 134 (*CIJ* I 632); cf. *Puglia Paleocrist.
Altomed.* 3 p. 108 (f. *Γλύκα*: Jew)
S. ITALY (CAMPANIA):
**—NEAPOLIS: (7)** iii-iv AD *IG* XIV 826. 41 (*INap*
246) (*-βεῖ-*)
SICILY:
**—TAUROMENION: (8)** iii-v AD *IG* XIV 166
(Strazzulla 107); Ferrua, *NG* 480 (locn.) (f.
*Αὐξάνων*)

**Σαβοκλῆς**
MESSENIA:
**—MESSENE: (1)** f. iii BC *PAE* 1991, p. 99 no. 7,
25

**Σαβύλινθος**
EPIROS:
**—MOLOSSOI: (1)** c. 430 BC Th. ii 80. 6

**Σάβυλλος**
SICILY:
**—GELA-PHINTIAS: (1)** c. 498 BC Hdt. vii 154. 1

**Σαβύρτιος**
EPIROS:
**—BOUTHROTOS (PRASAIBOI): (1)** a. 163 BC
*IBouthrot* 42, 10-11 (*SEG* XXXVIII 501)
**—DODONA: (2)** iii BC Antoniou, *Dodone* Aa, 9
**—MOLOSSOI:**
——Kyestoi: **(3)** c. 230-219 BC Cabanes,
*L'Épire* p. 546 no. 14 (f. *Κρίσων*)
**—ONOPERNOI KARTATOI: (4)** ?c. 343-331 BC ib.
p. 577 no. 50, 2 (*Σαβύρ*[*τιος*]—Cabanes)

**Σάβων**
EPIROS:
**—GENOAIOI: (1)** 370-368 BC ib. p. 534 no. 1,
15, 31

**Σάγαρις**
KORINTHIA:
**—KORINTH\*: (1)** imp. *CIL* III 7268 (Lat.
Sagaris: slave/freed.)
S. ITALY (APULIA):
**—VENUSIA\*: (2)** imp. *IG* XIV 688, 6 (*CIL* IX
425 (biling.)) (freed.?)

**Σάγων**
S. ITALY (LUCANIA):
**—POSEIDONIA-PAESTUM: (1)** c. 300 BC *RVP* p.
360 no. 706 (vase)

**Σάδαμος**
ARKADIA:
**—MANTINEIA-ANTIGONEIA: (1)** c. 300-221 BC
*IG* v (2) 323. 67-8 (tesserae) (s. *Φιλέας*, f. *Φι-
λέας*)

**Σαέας**
ARKADIA:
—PYLAI?: (1) vi-v BC *SEG* XVIII 157 (s. Θρασύβουλος)

**Σαϝάναξ**
LAKONIA:
—GERONTHRAI: (1) c. 500 BC *IG* v (1) 1133, 6; *LSAG*² p. 201 no. 46 (date) (Poralla² 656)

**Σαθύων**
S. ITALY (BRUTTIUM):
—LOKROI EPIZEPHYRIOI:
——(Κρα.): (1) iv/iii BC De Franciscis 38, 5 (s. Φαικύλος) ?= (2); (2) 276 BC ib. 23, 5 (f. Πρόξενος) ?= (1)

**Σάθων**
LEUKAS: (1) f. i BC *IG* IX (1) 534, 6 (*Iscr. Gr. Verona* p. 24) (f. Διάκριτος)

**Σαϊάδας**
ELIS:
—OLYMPIA*: (1) ?v BC *IvOl* 725

**Σαίγαλος**
KORINTHIA:
—KORINTH: (1) 336-324 BC *CID* II 76 II, [31]; 95, 13; 97, 24; 102 II B, [33]; 120 A, 36 (f. Καλλισθένης)

**Σαϊθίδας**
MESSENIA:
—ASINE: (1) 193-195 AD *IG* v (1) 1412, 7 (Φλ. Σ.)
—MESSENE: (2) hell. *SEG* XXXIX 383; (3) c. 214 BC Paus. iv 32. 2 (Αἰθίδας—mss., Σ.—Hitzig); (4) i AD *IG* v (1) 1436, 10; (5) 57-68 AD *SEG* XLI 353, 7 ([Τιβ.] Κλ. Σ. [Καλιανός]?); (6) i/ii AD *PIR*² C 1004 (Τιβ. Κλ. Σ. Καλιανός: s. Κλ. Ὀστίλιος, f. Τιβ. Κλ. Φροντῖνος); (7) s. ii AD ib. C 1004a (Τιβ. Κλ. Σ. Καλιανός: s. Τιβ. Κλ. Φροντῖνος); (8) ii/iii AD ib. C 1005 (Τιβ. Κλ. Σ. Φροντῖνος: s. Τιβ. Κλ. Φροντῖνος Νικήρατος)

**Σαϊθίων**
ARKADIA:
—TEGEA: (1) f. iii BC *IG* v (2) 35, 19 (f. Καλλίστρατος)

**Σαίκλαρος**
ELIS: (1) c. 95-150 AD *IvOl* 431, 4; 439, 2; 440, 5; *ZPE* 99 (1993) p. 232 (stemma) (Κλ. Λουκηνὸς Σ.: s. Κλ. Ἀριστόμαντις, f. Λουκηνὴ Κλ. Μνασιθέα) ?= (2); (2) ?f. ii AD *IvOl* 126, [4] ([Κλ]. [Λ]ουκηνὸς [Σαίκλαρος]) ?= (1)

**Σαῖνις**
SICILY:
—GELA-PHINTIAS: (1) vi/v BC Dubois, *IGDS* 143 a (vase) (Arena, *Iscr. Sic.* II 18)

**Σάϊς**
ARKADIA:
—KYNOURIOI: (1) 369-361 BC *IG* v (2) 1, 44; Tod, *GHI* II 132 (date); (2) ~ *IG* v (2) 1, 45; Tod, *GHI* II 132 (date)
—MANTINEIA-ANTIGONEIA: (3) ?iii BC *IG* v (2) 318, 1

**Σαῖσκος**
ARKADIA:
—TEGEA: (1) m. iv BC ib. 6, 94

**Σαισώ**
SICILY:
—TERRAVECCHIA DI CUTI (MOD.): (1) s. v BC *SEG* XXVII 657, 9 (Dubois, *IGDS* 177; Arena, *Iscr. Sic.* II 118) (-σό: ?d. Ἄρχων)

**Σαίτιος**
ARKADIA:
—TEGEA: (1) m. iv BC *IG* v (2) 6, 59, 72

**Σάϊττος**
ARKADIA:
—TEGEA: (1) iv/iii BC ib. 38, 70 (Σαίτιος?: s. Λυ—)

**Σακάδας**
ARGOLIS:
—ARGOS: (1) ?vi BC *RE* (-)

**Σακίντας**
LAKONIA:
—AMYKLAI*: (1) ?iii BC *SEG* XVII 188 a (Bradford (-)) (Σ[α]κίντας: f. Καλλικράτης)

**Σάκις**
SICILY:
—KAMARINA: (1) f. v BC Cordano, *Tessere Pubbliche* 41 (s. Πολυκλῆς)

**Σακίς**
KORINTHIA:
—KORINTH: (1) c. 590-570 BC Amyx 33. 4 (vase) (Lorber 52) (her.?)

**Σακλέα**
ARKADIA:
—MEGALOPOLIS: (1) ii/iii AD *IG* v (2) 517, 2 etc. (m. Σάων)

**Σακλείδας**
ARKADIA:
—TEGEA: (1) m. iv BC ib. 6, 58

**Σακλῆς**
ARKADIA:
—MANTINEIA-ANTIGONEIA:
——(Posoidaia): (1) m. iv BC ib. 271, 16 ([Σ]ακλῆς: s. Ἐπίστρατος)
——TEGEA: (2) m. iv BC ib. 6, 109; (3) s. iii BC ib. 116, 7 (f. Εὐάρετος)
——(Krariotai): (4) s. iv BC ib. 41, 46 (s. Δίων)

**Σακόλας**
ILLYRIA?:
—THRINKA: (1) iii/ii BC *Philolakon* p. 239, 5; p. 243 (locn.) (f. Πλάτωρ)

**Σακρέτης**
ARKADIA:
—LOUSOI: (1) iv/iii BC *IG* v (2) 389, 14 (Perlman L.1)

**Σάκυλλος**
TRIPHYLIA:
—TYPANEAI: (1) c. 230-200 BC *BCH* 45 (1921) p. 12 II, 78 (f. Πίμφαλος)

**Σάκων**
ARKADIA:
—MEGALOPOLIS: (1) ?268 BC *FD* III (1) 19, 1 (s. Ν—)
SICILY:
—MONTE SARACENO (MOD.): (2) vi/v BC Dubois, *IGDS* 165 (Arena, *Iscr. Sic.* II 103) (-ϙōν: f. Μύλος); (3) ~ Dubois, *IGDS* 165 (Arena, *Iscr. Sic.* II 103) (-ϙōν: s. Μύλος)
—SELINOUS: (4) s. vi BC *SEG* XXXIV 969 (Arena, *Iscr. Sic.* I 47; Lazzarini 880 b; *IGLMP* 65) (-ϙōν)
—ZANKLE-MESSANA: (5) c. 650 BC Th. vi 5. 1 (and Sicily Himera: oikist)

**Σάλαιθος**
LAKONIA:
—SPARTA: (1) 428-427 BC ib. iii 25. 1; 27. 2; 35. 1; 36. 1 (Poralla² 657)
S. ITALY (BRUTTIUM):
—KROTON: (2) arch.? Luc., *Apol.* 4

**Σαλαμίς**
LEUKAS: (1) hell.? *IG* IX (1) 580; cf. *AM* 27 (1902) p. 360

**Σαλασσός**
SICILY:
—AKRAGAS: (1) 2 BC-14 AD *RPC* I p. 660 (Lat. Salassus)

**Σαλβία**
ILLYRIA:
—APOLLONIA: (1) ii-iii AD *IApoll* 374
SICILY:
—SYRACUSE: (2) iii-v AD *IG* XIV 139, 1 (Strazzulla 79; Agnello 44; Wessel 557) (m. Κυριακός, Κυριακή)
—SYRACUSE?: (3) iii-v AD *Riv. Arch. Crist.* 18 (1941) p. 236 no. 130
—TYNDARIS: (4) imp. *NScav* 1880, p. 199 no. 23

**Σάλβιος**
ACHAIA:
—PATRAI: (1) i BC/i AD *SEG* XXIX 426, 1 (Σ. ὁ καὶ Πομπήϊος: s. Παγκράτης)
ILLYRIA:
—APOLLONIA: (2) imp. *IApoll* 201
SICILY:
—RAGUSA (MOD.) (NR.): (3) ?ii-i BC *SEG* XLII 873. 2 (ΔΙΑΣΑΛΒΙΟ—lap., Σάλβιο[ς]?, Ἀλβιο[ς]—ed.: ?f. —λία)

**Σάλβις**
ARKADIA:
—TEGEA: (1) ii AD *IG* v (2) 54, 7

**Σαλιάρετος**
LAKONIA:
—SPARTA: (1) iv/iii BC *SEG* XI 668 (vase); *BSA* 30 (1928-30) pp. 245-6 fig. 3 no. 19 (Poralla² 657a) (Σαλιάρε[τος]?)

**Σαλίαρχος**
LAKONIA:
—SPARTA: (1) c. 25-1 BC *IG* v (1) 210, 23 (Bradford (-)) (Σα[λ]ίαρχος: f. Ἀριστόδαμος)

**Σαλίσκα**
LAKONIA:
—GERONTHRAI: (1) hell.? *IG* v (1) 1129

**Σάλλας**
DALMATIA:
—ISSA: (1) iii BC Brunšmid p. 9 fr. H, 8 ([Σάλ]λας: s. Αἰσχίνας); (2) ~ ib. l. 11 (Σαλ[λας]: f. —ος); (3) f. ii BC ib. p. 22 no. 9, 7 (f. Ξενότιμος)
——(Dymanes): (4) iv/iii BC ib. p. 8, 40 + Wilhelm, *Neue Beitr.* 3 p. 17 ([Σάλ]λας?: s. Σθένων)
——(Pamphyloi): (5) iv/iii BC Brunšmid p. 7, 21 (s. Φίλων); (6) ~ ib. l. 22 (f. Αἰσχίνας) ?= (7); (7) ~ ib. l. 25 (f. Ἀντίπατρος) ?= (6)
—ISSA?: (8) iii/ii BC ib. p. 31 no. 27; *Istros* 2 (1935-6) pp. 18 ff. (or Dalmatia Tragurion)
ILLYRIA:
—EPIDAMNOS-DYRRHACHION (NR.)?: (9) ii BC *SEG* XXXVIII 572, 13; cf. *CRAI* 1991, p. 197 ff.; *L'Illyrie mérid.* 2 p. 206

**Σαλλήν**
ILLYRIA:
—EPIDAMNOS-DYRRHACHION (NR.)?: (1) ii BC *SEG* XXXVIII 572, 7; cf. *CRAI* 1991, p. 197 ff.; *L'Illyrie mérid.* 2 p. 206 (f. Πλάτωρ)

**Σαλούϊα**
ILLYRIA:
—EPIDAMNOS-DYRRHACHION: (1) imp. *IDyrrh* 15 (d. Πετρώνιος)

**Σάλπις**
S. ITALY (BRUTTIUM):
—RHEGION: (1) ?i AD *IG* XIV 2406. 72 (vase) (Γ. Σ.)

**Σαλύνθιος**
AITOLIA:
—AGRAIOI: (**1**) v BC *RE* (-) (king)

**Σαμαγόρας**
ARGOLIS:
—TROIZEN: (**1**) iv BC *IG* IV (1) 764, 3 (s. Σάμος)

**Σάμανδρος**
KERKYRA: (**1**) i BC-i AD ib. IX (1) 938 (Σ(κ)άμανδρος?)

**Σαμβατεύς**
ARGOLIS:
—HERMIONE: (**1**) ii-i BC ib. IV (1) 732 I, 15 (Σαμβατεύς: s. Ἀλέξανδρος)

**Σάμβικος**
ELIS: (**1**) inc. Plu., *Mor.* 302 C

**Σαμιάδας**
AKARNANIA:
—KORONTA: (**1**) c. 325-315 BC *Hesp.* 57 (1988) p. 148 A, 51 (*SEG* XXXVI 331); cf. *Hesp.* 48 (1979) pp. 78 f. with pl. 22 c (s. Σαμίας)
—THYRREION: (**2**) ii BC *IG* IX (1)² (2) 252, 6 (f. Ξένων)

**Σαμίας**
ACHAIA:
—DYME*: (**1**) c. 219 BC *SGDI* 1612, 61 (*Tyche* 5 (1990) p. 124) (s. Εὔαρχος)
AKARNANIA:
—KORONTA: (**2**) c. 325-315 BC *Hesp.* 57 (1988) p. 148 A, 51 (*SEG* XXXVI 331); cf. *Hesp.* 48 (1979) pp. 78 f. with pl. 22 c (f. Σαμιάδας)
—PALAIROS: (**3**) iii BC *IG* IX (1)² (2) 502 (Σ. (masc. nom., fem. gen.?))
EPIROS:
—BOUTHROTOS (PRASAIBOI):
——Tharioi: (**4**) a. 163 BC *IBouthrot* 91, 14 (*SEG* XXXII 623) (f. Δόκιμος)

**Σαμίδας**
ACHAIA:
—DYME*: (**1**) c. 219 BC *SGDI* 1612, 20 (*Tyche* 5 (1990) p. 124) (s. Τιμέας)
ARKADIA:
—MANTINEIA-ANTIGONEIA: (**2**) 64 or 62 BC *IG* V (2) 265, 49 (f. Φιλήσιος)
ILLYRIA:
—APOLLONIA: (**3**) ?ii BC *IApoll* 146 (s. Νικάνωρ)

**Σάμιος**
ARKADIA:
—MANTINEIA-ANTIGONEIA: (**1**) c. 425-385 BC *IG* V (2) 323. 19 (tessera) (s. —ερετος)
LAKONIA:
—SPARTA:
——Pitana: (**2**) vi/v BC Hdt. iii 55. 2 (Poralla² 658) (s. Ἀρχίας, f. Ἀρχίας)
—SPARTA (PITANA?): (**3**) 402-401 BC X., *HG* iii 1. 1; D.S. xiv 19. 4-5 (Poralla² 659) (Σάμος—D.S.: ?s. Ἀρχίας) ?= (Πυθαγόρας (5))
MESSENIA:
—MESSENE: (**4**) 340 BC *FD* III (4) 4, 1 (s. Τορέας)
S. ITALY (CAMPANIA):
—POMPEII: (**5**) i BC-i AD *CIL* IV 1864 (Lat. Samius)
SICILY:
—KATANE (NR.): (**6**) ii-iii AD *SEG* XXXIV 948 (biling.); cf. *MEFRA* 106 (1994) p. 111 no. 21 ([Σ]άμ[ιος], Lat. Samius: f. Ruber)

**Σάμιππος**
ARKADIA:
—MANTINEIA-ANTIGONEIA: (**1**) ii AD Luc., *Nav.* 1; 27ff. (fict.)
ELIS: (**2**) m. iv BC *IG* II² 3827, 2 (s. Μολοσσός); (**3**) f. i BC *SEG* XVII 199, 2 (Θεότιμος ὁ καὶ Σ.: s. Ἑλλάνικος); (**4**) c. 77 or 81 AD *IvOl* 85, 2,

[6] (I f. Ὀξύλος, ?f. Σάμιππος II); (**5**) ~ ib. l. 8 (II ?s. Ἀντ. Σάμιππος I); (**6**) 96-103 AD *IG* II² 1072, 9; cf. *SEG* XXIX 126 (date) (Ἀντώνιος Σ.: f. Ἀντώνιος Ὀξύλος); (**7**) 157 AD *IvOl* 456, 3 (Μ. Ἀντ. Σ.: f. Ἀντ. Βαιβία)
S. ITALY (BRUTTIUM):
—LOKROI EPIZEPHYRIOI:
——(Γαψ.): (**8**) 276 BC De Franciscis 23, 3; 32, 3 (f. Σάμων)

**Σαμίτας**
LAKONIA:
—GERONTHRAI: (**1**) c. 500 BC *IG* V (1) 1133, 4; *LSAG²* p. 201 no. 46 (date) (Poralla² 660)

**Σαμίων**
ARGOLIS:
—EPIDAUROS*: (**1**) c. 370 BC *IG* IV (1)² 102, 39
KORINTHIA:
—KORINTH: (**2**) hell. ib. II² 9073 (s. Τελέστας); (**3**) ?269 BC *CID* II 120 A, 35; 121 II, 11 (s. Πολύκριτος)
S. ITALY (BRUTTIUM):
—LOKROI EPIZEPHYRIOI:
——(Γαυ.): (**4**) iv/iii BC De Franciscis 3, 10; 33, 2 (s. Ἱέρων)
——(Προ.): (**5**) iv/iii BC ib. 16, 4 (s. Σωσικράτης)
——(Τιω.): (**6**) iv/iii BC ib. 11, 5 (s. Ὀνάσιμος)

**Σαμοκλῆς**
ARGOLIS:
—EPIDAUROS*: (**1**) c. 370-365 BC Peek, *IAEpid* 52 A, 30 (Σαμοκλ[ῆς])
KORINTHIA:
—KORINTH: (**2**) f. iii BC Peek, *NIEpid* 39, 2 (Σαμο[κ]λῆ[s]: f. Θεαίσιος)

**Σαμόλας**
ACHAIA: (**1**) 400 BC *RE* (1)
ARKADIA: (**2**) a. 369 BC ib. (2); Marcadé 1 92 ([Σαμ]όλας—Marcadé: sculptor)
—MANTINEIA-ANTIGONEIA: (**3**) ?iii BC *IG* V (2) 318, 6 ([Σ]αμόλας)
LAKONIA:
—SPARTA: (**4**) c. 500 BC *SEG* XI 638, 3; *LSAG²* p. 201 no. 44 (date) (Σαμόλ[ας]?)

**Σάμος**
ACHAIA: (**1**) f. ii BC *IC* 2 p. 23 no. 6 F, 1 (f. Ἰάσων)
ARGOLIS:
—EPIDAUROS: (**2**) iv/iii BC Peek, *NIEpid* 20, 4, 10 (*SEG* XXV 404, 1, 7)
—TROIZEN: (**3**) iv BC *IG* IV (1) 764, 3 (f. Σαμαγόρας); (**4**) ?146 BC ib. 757 B, 39 (Σάμο[s])
DALMATIA:
—ISSA:
——(Hylleis): (**5**) iv/iii BC Brunšmid p. 9, 56 (f. Φιλοκράτης)
EPIROS:
—AMBRAKIA: (**6**) ii BC *SEG* XLII 543 (f. Νίκαρχος)
S. ITALY (CAMPANIA):
—MISENUM*: (**7**) ?ii-iii AD *CIL* X 3537/8 (Lat. Aurelius Samus)
—POMPEII: (**8**) i BC-i AD ib. IV 4340; 4377; 4383; 4395; 4420 (Lat. Samus)

**Σαμοφάνης**
ACHAIA:
—DYME: (**1**) c. 210-207 BC *IG* IV (1)² 73, 21; *SEG* XXXV 303 (date) (s. Θεύξενος)

**Σαμύθα**
EPIROS: (**1**) c. 330 BC Cabanes, *L'Épire* p. 580 no. 55, 3 (Σα[μ]ύθα)
S. ITALY (BRUTTIUM):
—LOKROI EPIZEPHYRIOI: (**2**) iv/iii BC *HE* 2808
S. ITALY (CALABRIA):
—TARAS-TARENTUM: (**3**) iv/iii BC *IG* XIV 668 I, 10 (Landi, *DISMG* 194)

**Σαμύλος**
LAKONIA:
—GERONTHRAI: (**1**) c. 500 BC *IG* V (1) 1133, 5; *LSAG²* p. 201 no. 46 (date) (Poralla² 661)

**Σαμψαῖος**
S. ITALY (CALABRIA):
—BRENTESION-BRUNDISIUM*: (**1**) imp. *CIL* IX 6104 (Lat. M(anius) Albinius Sampsaeus: freed.)

**Σάμων**
EPIROS:
—MOLOSSOI: (**1**) iv/iii BC Plu., *Pyrr.* 5. 10
S. ITALY (BRUTTIUM):
—LOKROI EPIZEPHYRIOI:
——(Γαψ.): (**2**) 276 BC De Franciscis 23, 3; 32, 3 (s. Σάμιππος)

**Σαμωνίδας**
ARKADIA:
—MANTINEIA-ANTIGONEIA: (**1**) c. 300-221 BC *IG* V (2) 323. 33 (tessera) (s. Καλλίμαχος)
SICILY:
—MORGANTINA: (**2**) c. 460 BC *SEG* XXXVIII 949 (vase)

**Σανδάλας**
AKARNANIA:
—PALAIROS: (**1**) iii BC *IG* IX (1)² (2) 503

**Σαννίων**
SICILY:
—HALOUNTION: (**1**) iii/ii BC *Arch. Class.* 17 (1965) p. 202 (Σαννίων)

**Σάννων**
S. ITALY (BRUTTIUM):
—RHEGION: (**1**) hell. *SEG* XXXIII 781 e (brick)
SICILY:
—KAMARINA: (**2**) ?iv/iii BC ib. XXXIV 940, 8 (Dubois, *IGDS* 124; *PdelP* 44 (1989) p. 192 no. 3; Cordano, 'Camarina VII' 148) (s. Ζώπυρος); (**3**) hell. *SEG* XXXIX 1001, 10 (s. Φίλων)
—TAUROMENION: (**4**) c. 231 BC *IG* XIV 421 an. 10 (*SGDI* 5219) (Σάνων)

**Σάνοννος**
ARKADIA:
—MEGALOPOLIS: (**1**) c. 272 BC *IG* IX (1)² (1) 13, 8 (Σανόννωι (dat.), Σάννων?: s. Δαμόφιλος)

**Σάνος**
PELOPONNESE?: (**1**) s. iii BC *SEG* XXV 449, 43 (*IPArk* 26) (s. Ν—)

**Σαοκλείδας**
AIGINA: (**1**) vii/vi BC Pi., *N.* vi, 21 (Σωκλῆς—Did. Schol. ad loc., Σωκλείδας—Wilamowitz: s. Ἀγησίμαχος, f. Πραξιδάμας)

**Σαοκλῆς**
ARKADIA:
—ORCHOMENOS: (**1**) ?c. 378 BC *BCH* 102 (1978) p. 335, 99 (*IPArk* 15)

**Σάος**
ARKADIA:
—TEGEA:
——(Apolloniatai): (**1**) s. iv BC *IG* V (2) 41, 15 (f. —ων)
LAKONIA:
—PYRRHICHOS: (**2**) iii-ii BC ib. V (1) 1284

**Σαοσίας**
ARKADIA:
—MANTINEIA-ANTIGONEIA: (**1**) ?272 BC *FD* III (1) 35, 1 (Σάθεος—ed.: f. Ἀλ—ει (dat.))

**Σαοσών**
ARKADIA:
—MANTINEIA-ANTIGONEIA: (**1**) c. 425-385 BC *IG* V (2) 323. 13 (tessera) (Σαοσώ[ν])

## Σαπρίκιος
SICILY:
—HALIKYAI: (1) s. vi AD SEG XXXVI 829 (mosaic) (Wessel 508 b) (Σ[απ]ρίκιος, Σατιρίκιος—Wessel)

## Σαπφίων
LAKONIA:
—SPARTA: (1) c. 90-150 AD IG V (1) 162, 3; 163, 2, 5; 189, 2; SEG XI 570, 5 (Bradford s.v. Καλλικράτης (17)) (Κλούβιος Καλλικράτης ὁ καὶ Σ., Σαφφίων—163: s. Καλλικράτης)

## Σαπφώ
ILLYRIA:
—EPIDAMNOS-DYRRHACHION: (1) hell.-imp. IDyrrh 372 (-φφώ: d. Κέρδων)

## Σάρα
KORINTHIA:
—KORINTH: (1) iii-iv AD Corinth VIII (3) 304, 3
S. ITALY (APULIA):
—VENUSIA: (2) iv-v AD JIWE I 111 (CIJ I 593) (Σάρρα: d. Βίτος: Jew)

## Σαραπιάς
ARGOLIS:
—ARGOS: (1) 105 BC JÖAI 14 (1911) Beibl. p. 146 no. 4, 27 ([Σα]ραπιάς: d. Σώστρατος)
KORINTHIA:
—KORINTH: (2) imp. Corinth VIII (3) 361

## Σαραπιόδωρος
SICILY:
—KAMARINA: (1) hell.? Manganaro, QUCC forthcoming no. 25 (Σαραπιόδ[ωρος]: f. Σώσιος)

## Σαραπίς
ILLYRIA:
—EPIDAMNOS-DYRRHACHION: (1) imp. IDyrrh 370 (Σαραπι[ς]? (n. pr.?))

## Σαραπίων
ACHAIA:
—PATRAI: (1) ?ii-i BC Achaean Grave Stelai 37
AIGINA: (2) ?i BC Alt-Ägina I (2) p. 44 no. 11, 3 (f. Ἡρακλείδης)
ARGOLIS:
—EPIDAUROS: (3) ?iv-iii BC SEG XXXIX 356 (f. Ἰσιάς)
EPIROS:
—AMBRAKIA: (4) 238-168 BC BMC Thessaly p. 96 no. 34 (coin)
LAKONIA:
—SPARTA: (5) c. 80-100 AD SEG XI 632, 4 ([Σαρα]πίων)
S. ITALY (CAMPANIA):
—NEAPOLIS: (6) c. 100 BC ID 1755, 4; 1931, 2 (s. Ἀλέξανδρος); (7) 94 BC ib. 1763, 7
—POMPEII: (8) i BC-i AD IG XIV 704
S. ITALY (LUCANIA):
—HYELE-VELIA: (9) ii/i BC CIG 6986 (Noll, Inschr. Wien. p. 44 no. 97) (s. Ζέφυρος, f. Νουμήνιος)
SICILY:
—ERYX: (10) imp. ASSiciliano 1887, p. 288 no. 722 (stamp) (Lat. Sarapi.)
—TAUROMENION:
——(Ἀρεθ.): (11) ii/i BC IGSI 8 II 9 (f. Ἀμμώνιος)

## Σαραπόφιλος
ACHAIA?: (1) 193 BC IG V (2) 293, 25 (Σα[ραπό]φιλος?: s. Οἰνεύς)

## Σάραυκος
ARKADIA: (1) 361 BC CID II 4 I, 42

## Σαργεύς
KORINTHIA:
—SIKYON: (1) 413 BC Th. vii 19. 4 (Skalet 287)

## Σαρέας
AIGINA: (1) imp.? IG IV (1) 139 (Σαρέας)

## Σάρις
SICILY:
—SELINOUS: (1) f. v BC Dubois, IGDS 38, 5 (Arena, Iscr. Sic. I 63); (2) ~ Dubois, IGDS 38, 7 (Arena, Iscr. Sic. I 63) (s. Πυρῖνος); (3) ~ Dubois, IGDS 38, 19 (Arena, Iscr. Sic. I 63) (s. Ῥῶμις)

## Σαρπηδών
AKARNANIA:
—STRATOS: (1) ?ii/i BC IG IX (1)² (2) 412, 1 (Σαρπ[ηδών])

## Σασάμας
AKARNANIA:
—PALAIROS: (1) iii BC ib. 504; Fraser–Rönne, BWGT p. 167 with pl. 26 (Σασάμα (voc.))

## Σάσαμος
SICILY:
—SELINOUS: (1) f. v BC Dubois, IGDS 39, 15 (Arena, Iscr. Sic. I 71) (Σάσα(μος))

## Σαστράτα
ARKADIA:
—TEGEA: (1) i BC IG V (2) 70

## Σάστρατος
ARKADIA:
—MANTINEIA-ANTIGONEIA: (1) c. 300-221 BC ib. 323. 65 (tessera) (f. Μαντίας)
—TEGEA: (2) iv BC ib. 31, 11 (f. Ἀριστομήδης); (3) s. iv BC SEG XXXVI 383, 4 (f. Καλλίας)

## Σατορνίλα
AIGINA?: (1) imp. EAD XXX p. 356 no. 18 (-νεῖ-)

## Σατορνίλος
SICILY:
—AKRAI (NR.): (1) iii-v AD NScav 1907, p. 495; cf. Riv. Arch. Crist. 18 (1941) p. 233 n. 1
—KATANE: (2) iii-v AD IG XIV 528 (Wessel 1212) (-τουρ-)
—KENTORIPA: (3) imp. IG XIV 583 (Σατορ[νῖ]λος)
—SYRACUSE: (4) iii-v AD ib. 167 (Strazzulla 108; Wessel 1150); ASSicilia 1938-9, p. 27 (name) (-τρο-: ?f. Μονίκα)

## Σατορνῖνα
ILLYRIA:
—BYLLIONES (CAKRAN (MOD.)): (1) iii AD SEG XXXVIII 545 (-νεῖ-)

## Σατορνῖνος
EPIROS:
—NIKOPOLIS: (1) imp. ib. XXXIX 546 (-νεῖ-: s. Σεκοῦνδος)

## Σατταρᾶς
SICILY:
—ZANKLE-MESSANA: (1) iii-v AD Epigraphica 3 (1941) p. 252 no. 1 (Αἰσάρις Σ.)

## Σάττιος
S. ITALY (LUCANIA):
—METAPONTION*: (1) iv BC Atti Conv. Taranto 13 (1973) p. 128 (terracotta) (Οὔϊος Σ.)

## Σάττων
S. ITALY (CALABRIA):
—TARAS-TARENTUM: (1) s. iv BC Guarducci, Ep. Gr. 1 p. 290 no. 10 (Landi, DISMG 189)

## Σατύρα
ACHAIA:
—DYME: (1) iii BC AJPh 31 (1910) p. 399 no. 74 c, 7 (m. Αἰσχρίων)

## AKARNANIA:
—ECHINOS?: (2) ii BC IG IX (1)² (2) 377
ARKADIA:
—KLEITOR: (3) iv/iii BC ib. XII (9) 1141; BCH 90 (1966) p. 230 n. 5 (date) (d. Σάτυρος)
EPIROS:
—AMBRAKIA: (4) f. iii BC Unp. (Arta Mus., inscr.) (d. Φρύνων)
—BOUTHROTOS (PRASAIBOI): (5) a. 163 BC IBouthrot 17, 33 (SEG XXXVIII 474) (d. Φρύνιχος) ?= (7); (6) ~ IBouthrot 30, 16 (SEG XXXVIII 488); (7) ~ IBouthrot 33, 11 (SEG XXXVIII 492); IBouthrot 134, 12 ?= (5); (8) ~ ib. 58, 9 (SEG XXXVIII 509); IBouthrot 105, 5
ILLYRIA:
—AMANTIA: (9) hell. Thess. Hemerol. 6 (1984) p. 216 no. 95
KERKYRA: (10) s. v BC PAE 1964, p. 58
KORINTHIA:
—SIKYON: (11) ii BC IG II² 10311 (Skalet 288)
S. ITALY (APULIA):
—LUCERIA: (12) imp. CIL IX 858 (Lat. Gavia Satyra)
S. ITALY (CAMPANIA):
—DIKAIARCHIA-PUTEOLI: (13) i BC-i AD ib. IV 10528 (Lat. Satura); (14) ?ii-iii AD ib. X 2691 (Lat. Aurelia Satura: m. Maecia Sperata)

## Σατυρήν
ILLYRIA:
—EPIDAMNOS-DYRRHACHION: (1) c. 250-50 BC Bakërr Hoard p. 67 nos. 108-9; Münsterberg Nachtr. p. 17 (coin) (Ceka 156; 158) (pryt.)

## Σατυρία
S. ITALY (CAMPANIA):
—HERCULANEUM: (1) 55 AD PdelP 1 (1946) p. 379 no. 1 (Lat. Satyria)
S. ITALY (LUCANIA):
—VOLCEI: (2) imp. CIL X 428 (Lat. Iuventia Saturia)

## Σατυρῖνος
AIGINA?: (1) 210-197 BC AE 1913, p. 91 no. 3
EPIROS:
—BOUTHROTOS (PRASAIBOI): (2) a. 163 BC IBouthrot 21, 43 (SEG XXXVIII 478); (3) ~ IBouthrot 41, 4 (SEG XXXVIII 500) (s. Κεφαλῖνος, f. Κεφαλῖνος) ?= (7); (4) ~ IBouthrot 43, 29 (SEG XXXVIII 502); (5) ~ IBouthrot 131, 2 (?f. Παρμενίσκος); (6) ~ ib. 143, 9 (s. Κρίσων)
——Kolonoi: (7) a. 163 BC ib. 141, 11 (?f. Κεφαλῖνος) ?= (3)
—PHOINIKE: (8) c. 330 BC SEG XXIII 189 I, 12

## Σατυρίων
ACHAIA: (1) iii-ii BC Achaean Grave Stelai 62 (s. Ἀριστότιμος)
—DYME: (2) s. iii BC SEG XIII 278, 20 (f. Ἀρχῖνος); (3) ~ ib. l. 23 ([Σ]ατυρίων: s. Φύλλαρος)
KEPHALLENIA:
—KRANIOI: (4) c. 230-200 BC BCH 45 (1921) p. 14 II, 138 (s. Δαμοφῶν)
S. ITALY (CALABRIA):
—TARAS-TARENTUM: (5) ii-i BC NS 198
S. ITALY (LUCANIA):
—HERAKLEIA: (6) ii/i BC ID 1967 a, 1 (f. Τίτος)
SICILY:
—LILYBAION: (7) imp. CIL X 7246 (Lat. –us Satyrio)

## Σάτυρος
ACHAIA: (1) hell. Suppl. Cir. 92, 2 (f. Φιλόδαμος); (2) 165 BC Plb. xxx 30. 1
—DYME*: (3) c. 219 BC SGDI 1612, 26 (Tyche 5 (1990) p. 124) (s. Ἀρίστων)
—PATRAI: (4) hell.? SGDI 1627 (s. Αἰσχίνας)
—PHARAI: (5) iii-ii BC Achaean Grave Stelai 59 (f. Δαμαρέτα); (6) c. 210-207 BC IG IV (1)² 73, 22; SEG XXXV 303 (date) (f. Ξένων)
AITOLIA: (7) ?269-268 BC FD III (4) 415, 7; CID II 128, 12; (8) c. 220-150 BC BMC Thessaly p. 199 no. 63 (coin) (Σάτυ[ρος])

—AGRINION: (9) 200 BC *FD* III (1) 451, 4, 11 (s. Πολέμαρχος); (10) 143-129 BC *IG* IX (1)² (1) p. LII, s.a. 143 BC, 136 BC, 129 BC; *FD* III (6) 83, 2 (s. Ἀνδρόνικος)

—ATTALEIA: (11) 204 BC *IG* IX (1)² (1) 95, 11

—PLEURON: (12) iv/iii BC *Suda* s.v. A 1127 (f. Ἀλέξανδρος)

AKARNANIA:

—STRATOS: (13) s. ii BC *IG* IX (1)² (1) 36, 15

—TYRBEION/TORYBEIA: (14) ?273 BC *FD* III (3) 203, 5, 11; cf. *BCH* 90 (1966) pp. 174 f. (locn.) (s. Νικόμαχος)

ARGOLIS:

—ARGOS: (15) ?257 BC Nachtergael, *Les Galates* 7, 36 (Stephanis 2242) (s. Σίμακος) ?= (16); (16) c. 232-228 BC Nachtergael, *Les Galates* 62, 5; cf. Stephanis 2273 (f. —ος) ?= (15)

—EPIDAUROS: (17) ii/i BC *IG* IV (1)² 64, 2 (Σάτ[υρος]: f. Ἀπολλώνιος)

—EPIDAUROS*: (18) c. 370-365 BC Peek, *IA-Epid* 52 B, 63-4

—TROIZEN: (19) iii BC *IG* IV (1) 824, 9

ARKADIA: (20) ?253 BC Nachtergael, *Les Galates* 10, 27; cf. Stephanis 1923 (f. Ξένων)

—KLEITOR: (21) iv/iii BC *IG* XII (9) 1141; *BCH* 90 (1966) p. 230 n. 5 (date) (f. Σατύρα)

—KYNAITHA: (22) c. 230-200 BC ib. 45 (1921) p. 12 II, 66 (s. Πελοπίδας); (23) ~ ib. l. 67 (s. Θεύξενος)

—LOUSOI: (24) iii BC *IG* V (2) 395, 4

—MANTINEIA-ANTIGONEIA: (25) c. 300-221 BC ib. 323. 48-9 (tesserae) (s. Ζευξίας)

—PHENEOS: (26) c. 315-280 BC *FD* III (1) 42, 2 (f. Δάολκος)

—THELPHOUSA: (27) ?ii BC *SEG* XI 1128; *BCH* 88 (1964) pp. 179-80 (date)

ELIS: (28) m. iv BC Moretti, *Olymp.* 462; 466; Petrakos, *Oropos* pp. 196-7 no. 47, 23, 26 (*IOrop* 520) (s. Λυσιάναξ: mantis/Iamidai)

EPIROS:

—AMBRAKIA: (29) s. iv BC *AD* 19 (1964) Chron. pp. 311-12 (moulds); (30) iii BC *SEG* XXV 701; (31) ?273 BC *IG* IX (1)² (1) 11, 19 (f. Δι—); (32) ii-i BC *CIG* 1799 (s. Νίκαρχος)

—AMBRAKIA*: (33) iv BC Unp. (Arta Mus., terracotta)

—BOUTHROTOS (PRASAIBOI): (34) a. 163 BC *IBouthrot* 15, 5 (*SEG* XXXVIII 472); (35) ~ *IBouthrot* 50, 8; (36) ~ ib. 110, 9 ([Σά]τυρος)

——Thoinaioi?: (37) a. 163 BC ib. 131, 2

——Thymaioi: (38) a. 163 BC ib. 111, 4, 9; 112, 4, 10; 113, 6 (s. Νίκανδρος)

—DODONA*: (39) hell. *SEG* XIX 428

—KASSOPE: (40) f. ii BC Cabanes, *L'Épire* p. 564 no. 41, 5 (s. Θεόδωρος)

—NIKOPOLIS: (41) s. ii AD Sarikakis 150; Stephanis 2234 (Σπέ(δ)ιος Σ.); (42) c. 200 AD *FD* III (6) 96, 4 (Sarikakis 141) (f. M. Αὐρ. Νικιάδης)

ILLYRIA:

—EPIDAMNOS-DYRRHACHION: (43) iii-ii BC *IDyrrh* 371

KERKYRA: (44) b. 227 BC *GVI* 922, 8 (*Gr. Gr.* 140) (f. Ἀλέξανδρος)

KORINTHIA:

—KORINTH: (45) f. iv BC Plu., *Tim.* 4 (*FGrH* 115 F 334) (mantis)

—SIKYON: (46) 344 BC *IG* II² 3068, 3 (Skalet 289; Stephanis 2237)

LAKONIA:

—SPARTA: (47) iii AD *IG* V (1) 251 (Bradford (3)) (f. Αὐρ. Κάλλουσα); (48) c. 225-250 AD *IG* V (1) 529, 15 (Bradford (1)) (Ἀβίδιος Σά[τ]υ[ρ]ος: s. Εὐτυχᾶς)

MESSENIA:

—MESSENE: (49) m. iv BC *AM* 67 (1942) p. 111 no. 216 (f. Ἀρκεσίλας); (50) 263 BC *IG* IX (1)² (1) 17, 62 (f. Δεινῆς)

—THOURIA: (51) f. ii BC *SEG* XI 972, 97 (f. Ἀπολλόδωρος)

---

PELOPONNESE: (52) c. 192 BC ib. XIII 327, 20 (f. —τίδας)

S. ITALY (APULIA):

—CANUSIUM: (53) 223 AD *Epig. Rom. di Canosa* 35 II, 22 (*CIL* IX 338) (Lat. C. Fulvius Satyrus)

S. ITALY (BRUTTIUM):

—LOKROI EPIZEPHYRIOI:

——(Σκα.): (54) 278 BC De Franciscis 30, 4 (f. Φίλιππος)

——(Ψαθ.): (55) iv/iii BC ib. 3, 2; 28, 5 (s. Ἀριστόκριτος)

S. ITALY (CALABRIA):

—BRENTESION-BRUNDISIUM: (56) i BC Desy, *Timbres amphoriques* 734 (amph.) (Lat. L. Marcius Saturus); (57) ~ ib. 735 (amph.) (Lat. P. Marcius Saturus)

S. ITALY (CAMPANIA):

—DIKAIARCHIA-PUTEOLI: (58) imp. *CIL* X 2193 (Lat. L. Caesellius Satyrus)

—HERCULANEUM: (59) 62 AD *Ostraka* 2 (1993) pp. 203-7 (Lat. M. [Nonius] Saty[rus])

—POMPEII: (60) i BC-i AD *CIL* IV 2046 (Lat. Satyr(us)); (61) ~ ib. 4985 (Lat. Saturus)

S. ITALY (LUCANIA):

—HERAKLEIA: (62) ii/i BC *ID* 1967 a, 2 (s. Τίτος, Θεοδώρα (Teos))

SICILY:

—GELA-PHINTIAS: (63) f. ii BC *IG* XIV 256, 46 (Dubois, *IGDS* 161); cf. *SEG* XL 804 (Σάτ(υ)ρος: f. Ἀπολλώνιος)

—MORGANTINA: (64) ?iv/iii BC ib. XXXIX 1008, 6 (s. Δάμων); (65) ~ ib. 1010, 4 ([Σά]τυρος: s. Ἀρίστων)

—SELINOUS: (66) m. vi BC Arena, *Iscr. Sic.* I 27 (*IGLMP* 79)

## Σατυρώ

AITOLIA:

—MESARISTA (MOD.): (1) iv/iii BC *SEG* XXXIV 470 (masc. dat.—*SEG* per err.)

## Σαύλαος

SICILY:

—TAUROMENION: (1) c. 231 BC *IG* XIV 421 an. 10 (*SGDI* 5219) (Σάϋλ(λ)ος?: s. Νυμφόδωρος)

## Σάϋλλος

ARKADIA:

—MEGALOPOLIS: (1) ?145 BC *IG* V (2) 439, 45 (f. Ζευξώ)

## Σαυνίδας

ELIS: (1) 209-241 AD *IvOl* 110, 7; 117, 5; 118, [5] (M. Βυψ(άνιος) Σ.: M.)

## Σαῦρις

SICILY:

—SELINOUS: (1) f. v BC Dubois, *IGDS* 44 (Arena, *Iscr. Sic.* I 49; *IGLMP* 67); (2) m. v BC Dubois, *IGDS* 36, 3 (Arena, *Iscr. Sic.* I 69)

## Σαύρων

S. ITALY (BRUTTIUM):

—LOKROI EPIZEPHYRIOI:

——(Θρα.): (1) iv/iii BC De Franciscis 4, 4; 22, 5 (f. Εὔφρων)

## Σάφις

ARGOLIS:

—HERMIONE: (1) ii-i BC *IG* IV (1) 732 II, 4 (f. Ἄριστον)

## Σάων

ARGOLIS:

—EPIDAUROS*: (1) c. 370-365 BC Peek, *IAEpid* 52 B, 74

—PHLEIOUS: (2) s. iv BC Peek, *NIEpid* 16, 26 (Perlman E.6) (s. Πολυχάρης)

ARKADIA:

—MANTINEIA-ANTIGONEIA:

---

——(Enyalia): (3) m. iv BC *IG* V (2) 271, 6 (I f. Σάων II); (4) ~ ib. l. 6 (II s. Σάων I)

—MEGALOPOLIS: (5) imp. ib. 517, 1 etc. (s. Πολύχαρμος, Σακλέα); (6) ~ ib. l. 24 (f. Ἀριστόκλεια)

—TEGEA: (7) m. iv BC ib. 6, 115; (8) f. iii BC ib. 35, 18 (f. Σαωνίδας)

EPIROS:

—AMBRAKIA: (9) i BC *GP* 2224

LAKONIA:

—SPARTA: (10) iii BC *SEG* XL 348 B, 3

MESSENIA:

—THOURIA: (11) f. ii BC ib. XI 972, 34 (f. Ἐπικράτης)

PELOPONNESE: (12) s. iii BC ib. XIII 278, 14 (f. Ἀγέμαχος)

## Σαωνίδας

ARGOLIS:

—ARGOS: (1) i AD ib. XXVI 429, 6, 8 (f. Εὔδικος, Δαμοκρίνης)

ARKADIA:

—TEGEA: (2) f. iii BC *IG* V (2) 35, 18 (s. Σάων)

——(Hippothoitai): (3) iv/iii BC ib. 38, 41 (f. Σαώτας)

## Σαώτας

ARKADIA:

—MANTINEIA-ANTIGONEIA: (1) f. iv BC ib. II² 9281 + *ZPE* 29 (1978) p. 68, 1, 2 (f. Κλεοφαντίς); (2) c. 300-221 BC *IG* V (2) 323. 34 (tessera) (s. Τελέσιππος)

—TEGEA: (3) ii BC ib. 43, 15; (4) f. ii BC ib. 44, 13 (Σα[ώ]τας: f. Ἀσκλάπων)

——(Hippothoitai): (5) iv/iii BC ib. 38, 41 (s. Σαωνίδας)

EPIROS:

—BOUTHROTOS (PRASAIBOI): (6) a. 163 BC *IBouthrot* 13, 18; cf. Ugolini, *Alb. Ant.* 3 p. 120 ([Σα?]ώτας: s. Λυσανίας); (7) ~ *IBouthrot* 14, 36; 22, 5 (*SEG* XXXVIII 471; 479) (s. Νικάνωρ); (8) ~ *IBouthrot* 17, 7, 9; 29, 7; 32, 29 (*SEG* XXXVIII 474; 487; 491) (s. Μυρτίλος) ?= (10); (9) ~ *IBouthrot* 29, 7 (*SEG* XXXVIII 487) (f. Μυρτίλος) ?= (12); (10) ~ *IBouthrot* 42, 16 (*SEG* XXXVIII 501) ?= (8); (11) ~ *IBouthrot* 43, 15 (*SEG* XXXVIII 502) (f. Λυσιμάχα); (12) ~ *IBouthrot* 103, 7 (f. Μυρτίλος) ?= (9); (13) ~ ib. 145, 11 (s. Κλεόμαχος)

——Anemotioi: (14) a. 163 BC ib. 114, 4, 8; 115, 13 (f. Μυρτίλος)

—CHAONES: (15) f. ii BC ib. 6, 17 (*SEG* XXXVIII 468) (s. Νίκανδρος)

—PRASAIBOI: (16) f. ii BC *IBouthrot* 1, 4; cf. *L'Illyrie mérid.* 1 p. 134

## Σάωτις

S. ITALY (BRUTTIUM):

—PETELIA: (1) ?c. 475 BC *IGSI* 19, 1 (Landi, *DISMG* 171; *LSAG*² p. 261 no. 28 (date)) (Σάō-, Σαωτίς?)

## Σεάμβυς

EPIROS:

—KELAITHOI: (1) ?iii BC *SGDI* 1355, 4; cf. Cabanes, *L'Épire* p. 582 no. 59

## Σέανθος

ARKADIA:

—STYMPHALOS: (1) c. 230-200 BC *BCH* 45 (1921) p. 13 II, 116 (?s. Ἀλεξίων)

## Σεβῆρα

S. ITALY (APULIA):

—VENUSIA: (1) v AD *JIWE* I 48 (*CIJ* I 594) (d. Ἰακώβ: Jew)

SICILY:

—KATANE: (2) iii-v AD *NScav* 1931, p. 369 (Wessel 870; *Riv. Arch. Crist.* 18 (1941) p. 239 no. 135)

**Σεβηρῖνος**
ILLYRIA:
—LYCHNIDOS: (1) ii/iii AD *ZA* 6 (1956) p. 167 no. 2
SICILY:
—AKRILLAI: (2) iii-v AD *Epigraphica* 12 (1950) p. 98 no. 4

**Σεβῆρος**
ACHAIA:
—AIGEIRA: (1) ii-iii AD *JÖAI* 19-20 (1919) Beibl. p. 40 (s. Ἀκίνδυνος, Ὀνασώ)
KORINTHIA:
—KORINTH: (2) imp. *Corinth* IV (2) p. 189 no. 572; *SEG* XXX 348 (lamps) ([Σεβ]ῆρος— *Corinth*)
LAKONIA:
—SPARTA: (3) 127 AD *IG* V (1) 1314, 29 (Bradford (3)) (f. Δαμαρχίας)
SICILY:
—CASTIGLIONE DI SICILIA (MOD.): (4) ii-iii AD *MEFRA* 106 (1994) p. 91 no. 8
—KATANE: (5) imp. *IG* XIV 502 (*ASSicilia-Orientale* 1958-9, pp. 15 ff.); cf. *MEFRA* 106 (1994) p. 97 no. 11 (Ζωσιμιανίδης Σ.)
—SYRACUSE: (6) iii-v AD Strazzulla 337 (Wessel 991)

**Σειλίας**
ILLYRIA:
—EPIDAMNOS-DYRRHACHION: (1) ii-i BC *IDyrrh* 405 (f. Τεμίτευτα)

**Σείρακος**
AITOLIA:
—MESATA: (1) f. iii BC *IG* XII (8) 151, 9 (s.p.), 12 (s. Ἰσχόμαχος)

**Σειράνιος**
S. ITALY (LUCANIA):
—LEUKANOI: (1) c. 208 BC *FD* III (4) 135, 14 (f. Διονύσιος)

**Σείρων**
LAKONIA:
—SPARTA: (1) ?f. iv BC Plu., *Mor.* 225 E (Poralla² 662) (s. Λόχαγος)

**Σεκονδία**
SICILY:
—SYRACUSE: (1) ii-i BC *NScav* 1913, p. 279 (m. Νικόλαος)

**Σέκονδος**
SICILY:
—LILYBAION: (1) ?i BC *Kokalos* 18-19 (1972-3) p. 195 (brick)

**Σεκοῦνδα**
ILLYRIA:
—APOLLONIA: (1) imp. *IApoll* 148 (-κῶ-); (2) ~ ib. 264 (Σεκοῦ(ν)δα: d. Πλαῖος)
LAKONIA:
—GYTHEION: (3) ii AD *SEG* II 178 (-κοῦντα)
S. ITALY (BRUTTIUM):
—RHEGION: (4) iii-v AD *IG* XIV 1997 (Wessel 1)
SICILY:
—KENTORIPA: (5) iii AD *NScav* 1907, p. 495
—LIPARA: (6) imp. *BTCGI* 9 p. 96
—PHILOSOPHIANA: (7) byz. *Riv. Arch. Crist.* 40 (1964) p. 206
—SYRACUSE: (8) iii-v AD *NScav* 1907, p. 755 no. 2 (Barreca 335); (9) ~ Strazzulla 258 (Wessel 1325)

**Σεκούνδιλλα**
ARGOLIS:
—PHLEIOUS: (1) imp. *IG* IV (1) 447

**Σεκουνδῖνα**
SICILY:
—KATANE: (1) iii-v AD *NScav* 1918, p. 63 no. 5 (Wessel 507) (Σεκουνδῖν[α], Σεκουνδῖν[ος])

**Σεκουνδῖνος**
KORINTHIA:
—KORINTH: (1) ii AD *SEG* XXVII 35. 25 (lamp)
—TENEA: (2) byz. ib. XXVIII 390

**Σεκουνδίων**
KERKYRA: (1) ?iii AD Unp. (*IG* arch.)
S. ITALY (BRUTTIUM):
—LOKROI EPIZEPHYRIOI: (2) s. iv AD *IG* XIV 625, 1 (*ICI* v 6); cf. Costabile, *Municipium Locrensium* p. 74 (locn., date) (f. Λεωντίς)

**Σεκοῦνδος**
ARKADIA:
—KLEITOR: (1) a. 212 AD *IG* V (2) 369, 8
—TEGEA: (2) i/ii AD ib. 81 (f. Κλεοπάτρα); (3) 165 AD ib. 50, 22 (s. Σωτήριχος)
ARKADIA?: (4) imp. ib. 504 (Τιβ. Κλ. Σ.)
EPIROS:
—NIKOPOLIS: (5) imp. *SEG* XXXIX 546 (s. Σατορνῖνος)
KORINTHIA:
—KORINTH: (6) ii/iii AD *Ag.* VII pp. 92 no. 239; 98 no. 309; *Corinth* IV (2) pp. 185 no. 537; 204 no. 693; 210 nos. 759-777; *Lampes antiques BN* I 30; *SEG* XXVII 36. 6 (lamps)
S. ITALY (CALABRIA):
—TARAS-TARENTUM: (7) i BC-i AD *RE* (18); *GP* 3380 ff.
S. ITALY (CAMPANIA):
—NEAPOLIS: (8) iii-iv AD *INap* 249 (Σεκο[ῦν]δος)
SICILY:
—SYRACUSE: (9) iii-v AD Strazzulla 409 (Barreca 336) ([Σεκ]οῦνδος)

**Σεκύνδιλλα**
EPIROS:
—NIKOPOLIS: (1) imp. Unp. (Nikopolis Mus.) (Φαδία Σ.)

**Σελείδας**
LAKONIA:
—SPARTA: (1) s. iv BC Moretti, *Olymp.* 487; Paus. vi 16. 6; *IG* V (2) 549, 31 (Poralla² 663; Bradford (-)) (Σελεάδας—Paus., Σ.—*IG*: s. Ἀλεξανδρίδας)

**Σέλευκος**
ACHAIA:
—PATRAI: (1) c. 185 BC *Milet* I (3) 148, 21; *Chiron* 19 (1989) pp. 279 ff. (date)
—TRITAIA: (2) imp.? *Achaean Grave Stelai* 63 (f. Φίλα)
AITOLIA: (3) iii/ii BC Pantos, *Sphragismata* p. 155 no. 126; p. 447 f. (-λυκχος)
ARGOLIS:
—EPIDAUROS: (4) m. ii AD *IG* IV (1)² 529; *ZPE* 103 (1994) pp. 103-4
ARKADIA:
—KLEITOR: (5) ii AD *IG* V (2) 383
EPIROS:
—AMBRAKIA: (6) ii-i BC *CIG* 1799 (s. Φιλιστίων)
—NIKOPOLIS?: (7) imp. *FD* III (4) p. 92 n. 3 to no. 60 (Sarikakis 62) (Ἰούλιος Σ.: f. Ἰουλία Χρυσέα)
KEPHALLENIA:
—KRANIOI?: (8) imp. *SEG* III 448
KORINTHIA:
—KORINTH: (9) ?iii AD *Hesp.* 63 (1994) pp. 116 ff. no. 5 col. III, 6 (lead)
S. ITALY (APULIA):
—ARGYRIPPA-ARPI*: (10) imp. *CIL* IX 935 (Lat. L. Plotius Seleucus: freed.)
S. ITALY (CALABRIA):
—BRENTESION-BRUNDISIUM: (11) imp. *NScav* 1889, p. 167 b (*Eph. Ep.* VIII 9) = *Epigraphica* 25 (1963) p. 96 no. 137 (Lat. Seleucus)
—TARAS-TARENTUM*: (12) i-ii AD *SEG* XXXIV 1020; cf. *Mus. Arch. Taranto* IV (1) p. 208
S. ITALY (CAMPANIA):
—DIKAIARCHIA-PUTEOLI: (13) imp. *AJA* 2 (1898) p. 388 no. 39 (Lat. Seleucus); (14) ~

*CIL* X 2275 (Lat. L. C. Seleucus); (15) ~ ib. 2667 (Lat. C. Longinius Seleucus: s. Valerius Longus); (16) 40 AD Bove, *Documenti finanziarie* pp. 64-6 T.P. 46 + 44 pag. 5, 3-4 (Lat. P. Annius Seleucus); (17) ?ii AD *CIL* X 3140 (Lat. Seleucus: f. Ulpia Vitalis)
—KYME: (18) 251 AD ib. 3699 II, 25 (Lat. C. Rufus Seleucus)
—NEAPOLIS: (19) f. i BC *IG* XIV 745 (*INap* 33); cf. Leiwo p. 145 no. 119 (I f. Σέλευκος II); (20) ~ *IG* XIV 745 (*INap* 33); cf. Leiwo p. 145 no. 119 (II s. Σέλευκος I)
SICILY:
—KATANE: (21) imp. *CIL* X 7088, 2 (Lat. -nte(i)us Seleucus); (22) ~ ib. l. 4 (Lat. -nte(i)us Seleucus)

**Σελήνη**
KORINTHIA:
—KORINTH: (1) 446 AD *SEG* XXXI 286, 3 (Σελή[νη])
S. ITALY (APULIA):
—CANUSIUM: (2) i-ii AD *Epig. Rom. di Canosa* 111 (*CIL* IX 368 with Add.) (Lat. Clatia Selene: d. Φυλλῖνος, Εὐτυχία)
—VIBINUM: (3) i AD *Bovino* p. 144 no. 195 (Lat. Selene)

**Σελήνιον**
ILLYRIA:
—APOLLONIA: (1) imp. *IApoll* 143 (m. Πίστος)
S. ITALY (BRUTTIUM):
—LOKROI EPIZEPHYRIOI: (2) i AD Costabile, *Municipium Locrensium* 3 (*CIL* X 19) (Lat. Acerronia Selenium: ?m. N. Calvius Rufus)

**Σεληνίς**
S. ITALY (APULIA):
—LUCERIA*: (1) imp. ib. IX 877 (Lat. Pilia Selenis: freed.)

**Σελίνιος**
ARKADIA:
—MANTINEIA-ANTIGONEIA: (1) c. 300-221 BC *IG* V (2) 323. 84 (tessera) (f. Πραξῖνος)

**Σέλινις**
SICILY:
—AKRAGAS: (1) iv/iii BC *Acragas Graeca* 1 p. 41 no. 11, 5 (Cabanes, *L'Épire* p. 543 no. 8; Dubois, *IGDS* 184)
—SELINOUS: (2) vi/v BC ib. 69 (Arena, *Iscr. Sic.* I 30; *IGLMP* 87) (Σέλ[ινις]: s. Λασοΐδας); (3) m. v BC Dubois, *IGDS* 65 (Arena, *Iscr. Sic.* I 31; *IGLMP* 92); (4) ~ Dubois, *IGDS* 77 (Arena, *Iscr. Sic.* I 23; *IGLMP* 94) (Σέλιν[ις]: f. Διονύσις); (5) s. v BC Dubois, *IGDS* 61 (*IGLMP* 99) (s. Δίων)
—TAUROMENION:
—(Ά-): (6) ii/i BC *IGSI* 6 IV, 32 (Σέαινις—ed.: s. Διόδοτος: name—*LGPN*)

**Σελινούντιος**
S. ITALY (BRUTTIUM):
—RHEGION: (1) iv BC Iamb., *VP* 267 (*FVS* 1 p. 447)
SICILY:
—SELINOUS: (2) vi/v BC Dubois, *IGDS* 37 a (Arena, *Iscr. Sic.* I 61 A); cf. *LSAG*² p. 277 no. 38 (Σελινῶντιος—ethn.?)

**Σελινώ**
DALMATIA:
—PHAROS: (1) iii BC *SEG* XXXI 606 (Šašcl, *IL* 2928) (d. Ἱπποκλῆς)
SICILY:
—SELINOUS: (2) s. v BC Dubois, *IGDS* 40, 8

**Σελινῶι**
KORINTHIA:
—KORINTH: (1) c. 570-550 BC Amyx 92 A. 4 (vase) (Lorber 120) (-νόι: het.?/fict.?)

Σελίξενος?
SICILY:
—SELINOUS: (2) m. v BC Dubois, *IGDS* 34
(Arena, *Iscr. Sic.* I 70) (-νόι)

Σελίξενος?
EPIROS:
—DODONA: (1) iii BC Antoniou, *Dodone* Aa, 28

Σελλαφῆς
SICILY:
—AKRAI: (1) imp. *SGDI* 5257 (*PdelP* 6 (1951)
p. 70 no. 4)

Σέλουρος
SICILY: (1) i BC/i AD *RE* (-)

Σεμέλα
SICILY:
—SYRACUSE?: (1) v BC *CGF* p. 111 fr. 109
(fict.?)

Σεμνη
KORINTHIA:
—KORINTH: (1) imp. *Corinth* VIII (3) 283, 2
(Lat. [Cor]nelia Semne: II d. Σέμνη I); (2)
~ ib. l. 3 (Lat. Semne: I m. Κορν. Σέμνη II)
S. ITALY (APULIA):
—CANUSIUM*: (3) imp. *Epig. Rom. di Canosa*
94 (*CIL* IX 363) (Lat. Semne: slave?)
S. ITALY (CAMPANIA):
—MISENUM*: (4) ?i-ii AD ib. x 3470 (Lat. Iulia
Semne)
SICILY:
—SYRACUSE: (5) iii-v AD *Rend. Pont.* 22 (1946-
7) p. 237 no. 42 (n. pr.?); (6) ~ *NScav* 1895,
p. 482 no. 158 ([Σ]έμνη); (7) ~ Ferrua, *NG*
330 c (Σέμν[η])

Σέμνος
ARKADIA:
—KLEITOR: (1) a. 212 AD *IG* v (2) 369, 26; *SEG*
XXXI 347, 19 (Αὐρ. Σ.)
S. ITALY (CAMPANIA):
—POMPEII: (2) i BC-i AD *CIL* IV 1302 (Lat.
Semnus)

Σεμπρώνιος
LAKONIA:
—GYTHEION: (1) i-ii AD *IG* v (1) 1178, 9 (s.
Σιμηλίδας)

Σέξτος
KORINTHIA:
—KORINTH: (1) ?i-ii AD *GVI* 1611 (*Gr. Gr.* 385)
S. ITALY: (2) c. 150 BC *ID* 1520, 6, 21, 29, 39,
41, 45, 52 (f. Μ. Μινάτιος)
SICILY:
—MORGANTINA: (3) i BC-i AD *SEG* XXIX 933
(Σέξ[τος])

Σεουῆρος
S. ITALY (CAMPANIA):
—NEAPOLIS: (1) iii-iv AD *IG* XIV 826. 43 (*INap*
251)

Σέπτουμος
ITHAKE: (1) imp. *IG* IX (1) 678

Σεραπᾶς
S. ITALY (CAMPANIA):
—POMPEII: (1) 14 BC *CIL* x 886 (Castrèn 381.
9) (Lat. M. Sittius Serapas: freed.)

Σεραπία
S. ITALY (CAMPANIA):
—DIKAIARCHIA-PUTEOLI: (1) imp. *CIL* x 2511
(Lat. Herennia Serapia)
SICILY:
—SYRACUSE: (2) iii-v AD Agnello 32 (Wessel
854)

Σεραπιάς
S. ITALY (CAMPANIA):
—MISENUM*: (1) ?i-ii AD *CIL* x 3596 (Lat. Iulia
Serapias: d. Ἀπολλινάρις)

Σεραπίς
S. ITALY (CAMPANIA):
—DIKAIARCHIA-PUTEOLI: (1) imp. ib. 2107
(Lat. Ascla Serapis)
—MISENUM*: (2) imp. ib. 3507 (Lat. Sentia
Serapis)

Σεραπίων
ARGOLIS:
—ARGOS: (1) i-ii AD *IG* IV (1) 587, 8 (f. Νικίας)
DALMATIA:
—PHAROS: (2) imp. *CIL* III 3103 (Lat. Pom-
ponius Serapio)
S. ITALY (CAMPANIA):
—DIKAIARCHIA-PUTEOLI: (3) imp. ib. x 2237
(Lat. L. Cassius Serapion); (4) ~ ib. 3018
(Lat. Memmius Se[r]apio); (5) ?ii/iii AD *AJA*
77 (1973) p. 159 no. 9 (Lat. Iunius Serapio)
—MISENUM*: (6) imp. *CIL* x 3638 (Lat. Ser-
apion: s. Annius Bassus, Τεσνεύς Σεραπιάς
(Egypt)); (7) ii/iii AD *NScav* 1909, p. 210
(Lat. Aur. Serapio)
—POMPEII: (8) i BC-i AD *CIL* IV 5260; 5262;
5277 (Lat. Serapion)
—POMPEII*: (9) s. i BC *Impegno per Pompeii* 3
OS (Castrèn 109. 17) (Lat. L. Ceius Serapio:
freed.)
S. ITALY (CAMPANIA)*: (10) imp. *NScav*
1902, p. 383 no. 4 (tile) (Lat. Serapio)

Σερᾶς
LAKONIA:
—SPARTA: (1) ii AD *IG* v (1) 159, 39 (Bradford
(1))
—SPARTA?: (2) ?iii AD *IG* v (1) 569; cf.
Cartledge–Spawforth p. 210 (Bradford (2)) (f.
Γ. Ρούβριος Βιάνωρ)

Σερβιλία
SICILY:
—SYRACUSE: (1) iii-v AD *ASSiracusano* 1956, p.
48

Σέργιος
ARGOLIS:
—HERMIONE: (1) byz. *SEG* XVII 171; cf.
*TMByz* 9 (1985) p. 371 no. 129 (Σέρ(γ)ιος)
KORINTHIA:
—KORINTH: (2) v AD *SEG* XXIX 318, 1 (f. Πέ-
τρος)
S. ITALY (BRUTTIUM):
—RHEGION: (3) iii-v AD *IG* XIV 629 (Wessel
129)

Σερδελαΐδας
ILLYRIA: (1) hell.-imp. *L'Illyrie mérid.* I p. 117
(Masson, *OGS* 2 p. 581) (f. Ἀμμάλα)

Σέρδων
S. ITALY?: (1) 259 BC *IG* XI (2) 115

Σέστος
DALMATIA:
—ISSA:
——(Dymanes): (1) iv/iii BC Brunšmid p. 9, 55;
cf. Wilhelm, *Neue Beitr.* 3 p. 17 (s. [.]λε[.]ας)

Σεύθας
ARKADIA:
—MEGALOPOLIS: (1) ?iv-iii BC *IG* v (2) 489
—TEGEA:
——(Krariotai): (2) f. iii BC ib. 36, 67 (s. Σώ-
σανδρος: metic)
KORINTHIA:
—SIKYON?: (3) 251 BC Plu., *Arat.* 5 (Skalet 290)
(slave?)

Σεύθης
EPIROS:
—NIKOPOLIS: (1) s. i AD *FD* III (6) 132, 4, 8,
9, 15 (Sarikakis 144) (s. Ἀπολλώνιος)

Σήϊα
S. ITALY (CAMPANIA):
—NEAPOLIS: (1) i BC/i AD *INap* 171; cf. Leiwo
p. 72 no. 13

Σηϊανός
SICILY:
—SYRACUSE: (1) iii-iv AD *SEG* XXXIX 1028

Σήμακος
KORINTHIA:
—KORINTH: (1) imp. ib. XXXII 364 + *Hesp.* 63
(1994) p. 112 no. 1

Σήραμβος
AIGINA: (1) f. v BC *RE* (2); *Alt-Ägina* II (2) p.
45 (sculptor)
ARGOLIS:
—HERMIONE: (2) iii BC *IG* IV (1) 729 I, 15, 16
(f. Λίβυς, Ἀριστόμαχος); (3) ~ ib. l. 23 (Σή-
ρα[μβ]ος)
S. ITALY (CALABRIA):
—TARAS-TARENTUM: (4) c. 212-209 BC Vlasto
971-4 (Evans, *Horsemen* p. 210 X A.1 (coin))

Σηρανδρίδας
LAKONIA:
—SPARTA: (1) c. 30-20 BC *IG* v (1) 211, 2 (Brad-
ford (-)) (f. Κλεόμαχος)

Σήριππος
LAKONIA:
—SPARTA: (1) 183 BC Plb. xxiii 4. 4; 9. 11
(Bradford (2)); (2) s. i BC *IG* v (1) 93, 13
(Bradford (3)); (3) ~ *IG* v (1) 124, 4 (Brad-
ford (5)) (Σήρ[ιπ]πος: f. Σικλείδας); (4) c. 30-20
BC *IG* v (1) 211, 5 (Bradford (6)) (f. Στέφα-
νος); (5) ~ *IG* v (1) 211, 23 (Bradford (1))
(s. Εὔξενος); (6) c. 25-1 BC *IG* v (1) 210, 34
(Bradford (4)) (f. Ἄλκιππος)
—THALAMAI: (7) i BC-i AD *IG* v (1) 1321 c

Σθενέδαμος
ILLYRIA:
—EPIDAMNOS-DYRRHACHION: (1) c. 250-50 BC
Münsterberg p. 40 (coin) (Ceka 11) (pryt.)

Σθενείδας
ARGOLIS:
—EPIDAUROS: (1) c. 340-320 BC Peek, *NIEpid*
19 B, 21; C, 7
——(Hysminatai): (2) 146 BC *IG* IV (1)² 28, 17
(s. Δαμαίνετος); (3) ~ ib. l. 19 (s. Ἀρίσταρχος)

Σθενελαΐδας
LAKONIA:
—SPARTA: (1) m. v BC *RE* (-) (Poralla² 664) (f.
Ἀλκαμένης)

Σθενέλαος
LAKONIA: (1) 405 BC X., *HG* ii 2. 2 (Poralla²
665)
—SPARTA: (2) 220 BC Plb. iv 22. 11 (Bradford
(-))

Σθένελας
ARGOLIS:
—ARGOS: (1) ?c. 575-550 BC *SEG* XI 336, 4;
*LSAG²* p. 168 no. 7 (date) (s. Ἐχεδαμίδας)

Σθένελος
S. ITALY (CAMPANIA):
—POMPEII: (1) i BC-i AD *CIL* IV 8534 (Lat.
Stenelus)

Σθενίδας
S. ITALY (BRUTTIUM):
—LOKROI EPIZEPHYRIOI?: (1) hell. *RE* (-)

**Σθένιος**
ARGOLIS:
—HERMIONE: (1) i BC-i AD? *IG* IV (1) 734, 1 (*Σθέν*[*ι*]*ος*: s. *Θεόπομπος*)
ARKADIA:
—MANTINEIA-ANTIGONEIA: (2) c. 300-221 BC ib. v (2) 323. 85 (tessera) (f. *Στράτυλλος*)
——(Posoidaia): (3) c. 425-400 BC *SEG* XXXI 348, 7 ([*Σ*]*θένιος*)
KERKYRA: (4) ?i BC *IG* IX (1) 798-800; 821; *Korkyra* I p. 169 no. 21 (tiles)
SICILY:
—THERMAI HIMERAIAI: (5) f. i BC Cic., *In Verr.* II ii 83 ff.; 147; *In Verr.* II iii 18; 41; *In Verr.* II iv; *In Verr.* II v 109; 128; cf. *RE* s.v. Stenius (2) (Lat. Sthenius)

**Σθένιππος**
ARKADIA:
—THELPHOUSA: (1) c. 210 BC *IG* IX (1)² (1) 31, 89 (s. *Θρασέας*)
KERKYRA: (2) iv/iii BC ib. IX (1) 976, 1 (s. *Ἀγαθοκλῆς*)
LAKONIA:
—SPARTA?: (3) ?f. iv BC Polyaen. ii 26 (Poralla² 666)

**Σθενίων**
ILLYRIA:
—EPIDAMNOS-DYRRHACHION: (1) hell.-imp. *IDyrrh* 67 (f. Ἄβα)

**Σθεννεύς**
AITOLIA: (1) ?a. 246 BC *SGDI* 2509, 2

**Σθενόλαος**
ARKADIA:
—ORCHOMENOS: (1) f. iii BC *BCH* 38 (1914) p. 461 no. 5, 8
—PSOPHIS: (2) c. 230-200 BC ib. 45 (1921) p. 14 II, 125 ([*Σ*]*θενόλαος*: f. *Δειολέων*, *Τεισαμενός*)

**Σθενόλας**
ARKADIA:
—MEGALOPOLIS: (1) 208 BC *IMM* 38, 40

**Σθένων**
AITOLIA:
—TRICHONION: (1) s. iii BC *IG* IX (1)² (1) 117, 6
DALMATIA:
—ISSA:
——(Dymanes): (2) iv/iii BC Brunšmid p. 8, 40 (f. *Σάλλας*)
PELOPONNESE: (3) s. iii BC *SEG* XIII 278, 15; (4) c. 192 BC ib. 327, 22 (f. —*νων*)

**Σθενωνίδας**
S. ITALY (BRUTTIUM):
—LOKROI EPIZEPHYRIOI: (1) vi-v BC *RE* (-)

**Σιάνθης**
ARGOLIS:
—EPIDAUROS: (1) i AD *IG* IV (1)² 659; 660; Peek, *IAEpid* 287 (*Τιβ. Ἰούλ. Σ.*, (*Εὐ*)*άνθης*—Peek: f. *Τιβ. Ἰούλ. Κλαυδιανός*)

**Σίβαλις**
DALMATIA:
—ISSA: (1) f. ii BC Brunšmid p. 23 no. 10, 8 (s. *Σωνύλος*)
——(Pamphyloi): (2) iv/iii BC ib. p. 8, 37 (f. *Ναύτωρ*)

**Σιβαυκός**
ARKADIA: (1) 362 BC *CID* II 1 II, 31

**Σιβοίτης**
AIGINA?: (1) i AD *EAD* XXX p. 357 no. 22 (s. *Δαϊμένης*)

**Σίβυλλα**
EPIROS:
—BOUTHROTOS (PRASAIBOI): (1) a. 163 BC *IBouthrot* 25, 30 (*SEG* XXXVIII 483); (2) ~ *IBouthrot* 27, 4 (*SEG* XXXVIII 485); (3) ~ *IBouthrot* 68, 9

**Σίβυλλος**
SICILY:
—GELA-PHINTIAS: (1) f. v BC Dubois, *IGDS* 149 g (vase) (Arena, *Iscr. Sic.* II 40) (*Σίβυλλος*)

**Σιβύρτας**
S. ITALY (BRUTTIUM):
—SYBARIS-THOURIOI-COPIAE: (1) iii BC Theoc., *Id.* v 5, 72 (fict.)

**Σιβύρτιος**
KORINTHIA:
—SIKYON: (1) c. 365-330 BC BM coin 1890 7-2-26; *Coll. Rhousopoulos* p. 147 no. 2474 (coin); *NC* 1983, pp. 32-3 (date)

**Σίβυρτος**
EPIROS: (1) 189 BC Plb. xxi 26. 7 (s. *Πετραῖος*)
KORINTHIA:
—KORINTH: (2) v AD *SEG* XXIX 322, 2 (*Σίβυ*[*ρτος*])

**Σίγη**
ARKADIA:
—TEGEA: (1) imp. ib. XXIII 234 (*Σεί-*)
SICILY:
—LIPARA: (2) imp. *IG* XIV 397 (Libertini, *Isole Eolie* p. 219 no. 15) (*Σεί-*)

**Σίγνα**
KEPHALLENIA:
—SAME: (1) imp. *SEG* XXXIV 475

**Σίδαμος**
LAKONIA:
—SPARTA: (1) m. i BC *IG* v (1) 260, 2; *Artemis Orthia* pp. 302-3 no. 11 (date) (Bradford (-))

**Σιδέκτας**
LAKONIA:
—SPARTA: (1) c. 25 BC-10 AD *IG* v (1) 209, 2-3; 212, 29 (Bradford (3); (6)) (s. *Λακιππίδας*, f. *Εὐρυβάνασσα*, *Τυνδάρης*); (2) i BC/i AD *IG* v (1) 141, 21; 142, 2; 209, 5; *BSA* 80 (1985) pp. 194; 197 (ident., stemma) (Bradford (4)) (*Σει-*: s. *Πρατόλας*, ?s. *Εὐρυβάνασσα*) ?= (3); (3) f. i AD *IG* v (1) 206, 1 (f. *Δεξίμαχος*) ?= (2); (4) i/ii AD ib. 32 A, 3; 34, [7]; 57, 6; 66, 16; 67, [6]; 114, 6; 470, 2; 536, 4; *SEG* XI 494, 1; 508, 6; 524, 16; 542, 3; 548, 14-15; 630, [3]; XIII 256, 6; *BSA* 80 (1985) pp. 194; 202-3 (ident., stemma) (Bradford (2)) (*Π. Μέμμιος Σ.*, *Σειδέκτας*—*IG* 57 & *SEG* 524 and 542: s. *Π. Μέμμιος Δεξίμαχος*, f. *Π. Μέμμιος Δαμάρης*); (5) ii/iii AD *SEG* XI 807, 3; Cartledge-Spawforth p. 180 (name) (*Σει-*: f. *Κύιντος Αὐφιδηνὸς Κόιντος*)

**Σίδεκτος**
KORINTHIA:
—KORINTH: (1) vii BC Paus. iv 19. 2

**Σιδηρᾶς**
LAKONIA:
—SPARTA: (1) c. 140-150 AD *SEG* XI 497, 1 (Bradford (-)) (s. *Ἀνίκητος*)

**Σίδιμος**
EPIROS:
—DODONA: (1) iii BC Antoniou, *Dodone* Aa, 30

**Σιδώνη**
S. ITALY (CAMPANIA):
—DIKAIARCHIA-PUTEOLI: (1) ?i-ii AD *CIL* X 2612 (Lat. Iulia Sidone)

**Σιδωνίη**
S. ITALY (CAMPANIA):
—DIKAIARCHIA-PUTEOLI: (1) imp. ib. 2107 (Lat. Ammia Sidonie: ?d. Ἡλιόδωρος)

**Σιδώνιος**
S. ITALY (CAMPANIA):
—HERCULANEUM*: (1) m. i AD ib. 1403 b + *Cron. Erc.* 7 (1977) p. 117 C b, 5 (Lat. M. Acc– Sidonius: freed.)

**Σικαινίας**
S. ITALY (BRUTTIUM):
—PETELIA: (1) ?c. 475 BC *IGSI* 19, 2 (Landi, *DISMG* 171); *LSAG²* p. 261 no. 28 (date) (*Σικαιν*<*ί*>*α*—*IGSI*)

**Σικάνα**
SICILY:
—KAMARINA: (1) m. v BC Dubois, *IGDS* 120, 6 (Arena, *Iscr. Sic.* II 142 A; *SEG* XXXVIII 939; Cordano, 'Camarina VII' 54) (m. *Συμαρία*)
—SELINOUS: (2) s. vi BC Dubois, *IGDS* 29, 3 (Arena, *Iscr. Sic.* I 59); cf. *SEG* XXXV 1021; cf. XXXVI 855

**Σικανός**
LAKONIA:
—SPARTA: (1) iii BC ib. XL 348 B, 3
SICILY:
—KAMARINA: (2) f. v BC Cordano, *Tessere Pubbliche* 23 (Arena, *Iscr. Sic.* II 131 A) (s. *Ἀρχωνίδας*); (3) ~ Cordano, *Tessere Pubbliche* 55 ([*Σι*]*κανός*: s. *Ἀπελλίων*); (4) ~ ib. 4a (*Σικα*[*νός*])
—SYRACUSE: (5) 415-413 BC *RE* (1) (s. *Ἐξάκεστος*)

**Σίκκις**
KEPHALLENIA:
—SAME: (1) iv BC *SEG* XXVII 179

**Σικλείδας**
ARKADIA:
—MEGALOPOLIS: (1) ?145 BC *IG* v (2) 439, 29 (f. *Φιλῖνος*)
LAKONIA:
—SPARTA: (2) s. i BC ib. v (1) 124, 4 (Bradford (1)) (s. *Σήριππος*); (3) c. 30-20 BC *IG* v (1) 142, 24 (Bradford (3)) (*Σικ*[*λείδας*]?: f. *Ἁρμονικία*); (4) c. 70-90 AD *IG* v (1) 275 (*Artemis Orthia* pp. 312-13 no. 30; Bradford (2))

**Σικλῆς**
LAKONIA:
—SPARTA: (1) c. 30-20 BC *IG* v (1) 211, 27 (Bradford (-)) (s. *Σωτηρίδας*)

**Σικουλία**
SICILY:
—KATANE: (1) imp. *Helikon* 2 (1962) p. 488

**Σικυώνη**
KORINTHIA:
—KORINTH: (1) ?iv BC Schol. Ar., *Pl.* 149; *Suda* E 3266 (het.)

**Σικυώνιος**
AITOLIA: (1) ?225 BC Nachtergael, *Les Galates* 63, 2 (*Σικυώ*[*νιος*], *Σικύω*[*ν*]—edd. pr.)
ARGOLIS:
—TROIZEN: (2) iii BC *SEG* XXXVII 310 (f. *Δαμαρέτα*)

**Σίκων**
ARKADIA:
—TEGEA: (1) iv BC *IG* v (2) 31, 7 (f. Ἴερων)
KEPHALLENIA:
—PALE: (2) iii/ii BC Unp. (*IG* arch.)
S. ITALY (CAMPANIA): (3) f. iv BC *LCS* p. 213 no. 72 (vase)

**Σιλάνα**
EPIROS:
—BOUTHROTOS (PRASAIBOI): (1) a. 163 BC *IBouthrot* 38, 15 (*SEG* XXXVIII 497)

—UZDINA (MOD.): (2) hell.? ib. XVI 387 (d. *Σί-μακος*)

**Σιλανίων**
KORINTHIA:
—SIKYON: (1) 263 BC *IG* IX (1)² (1) 17, 85 (f. *Πανταλέων*)

**Σιλανός**
DALMATIA:
—ISSA: (1) f. ii BC Brunšmid p. 22 no. 9, 10 + Wilhelm, *Neue Beitr.* 3 p. 18 ([*Σι*]λανός)
EPIROS:
—AMBRAKIA: (2) v/iv BC X., *An.* i 7. 18; cf. Ael., *NA* viii 5 (Philostr., *VA* viii 7) (mantis); (3) 238-168 BC *BMC Thessaly* p. 96 no. 35; *AD* 22 (1967) Chron. p. 342 (coins); (4) s. ii BC Cabanes, *L'Épire* p. 548 no. 19 (*SEG* XXVI 694) (s. *Παύσων*)
—BOUTHROTOS (PRASAIBOI): (5) a. 163 BC *IBouthrot* 39, 5 (*SEG* XXXVIII 498)
ILLYRIA:
—EPIDAMNOS-DYRRHACHION: (6) c. 250-50 BC Maier 129 (coin); Ceka 376 (money.)
KEPHALLENIA:
—SAME: (7) hell. Fraser–Rönne, *BWGT* p. 118 no. 6, 3
KERKYRA: (8) hell. *Syll*³ 1174, 1
PELOPONNESE?: (9) s. iii BC *IG* v (1) 1426, 21 (f. *Κόρυμβος*)
S. ITALY (BRUTTIUM):
—LOKROI EPIZEPHYRIOI:
——(*Κρα.*): (10) iv/iii BC De Franciscis 20, 13 (f. *Εὐκλείδας*)
——(*Τηλ.*): (11) iv/iii BC ib. 17, 1 ?= (*12*); (12) 275 BC ib. 25, 5 (f. *Ὄρθων*) ?= (*11*)
S. ITALY (CALABRIA):
—TARAS-TARENTUM: (13) imp. *CIL* IX 6402 (Lat. Silanus: s. Samouel: Jew)
SICILY:
—AGYRION: (14) i BC Manganaro, *PdelP* forthcoming no. 5, 3 (?f. *Φιλόξενος*)
—AKRAGAS: (15) c. 413-406 BC Jenkins, *Coins of Greek Sicily* pl. xvi, 14, 16 (coin)
—KALE AKTE?: (16) s. iii BC *RE* s.v. Silenos (1); *FGrH* 175 (or Scythia Minor Kallatis: -λη-)
—KAMARINA: (17) f. v BC Cordano, *Tessere Pubbliche* 10 (Arena, *Iscr. Sic.* II 129 A) (s. *Ἰθαιγένης*); (18) ~ Cordano, *Tessere Pubbliche* 115 (s. *Φάων*)
—SCIACCA (MOD.): (19) iii BC *SEG* XXXVI 854 (*Rupes loquentes* p. 500 no. 9) (I ?f. *Σιλανός* II); (20) ~ *SEG* XXXVI 854 (*Rupes loquentes* p. 500 no. 9) (II ?s. *Σιλανός* I)
—SELINOUS: (21) vi/v BC Manganaro, *PdelP* forthcoming no. 18, 9 (s. *Ἀγίας*); (22) m. v BC Dubois, *IGDS* 59 (Arena, *Iscr. Sic.* I 22; *IGLMP* 93) (s. *Εὐθυμίδας*)
—SYRACUSE: (23) iii-v AD Strazzulla 330 (Wessel 939)
—TAUROMENION: (24) c. 214-200 BC *IG* XIV 421 an. 27; 421 an. 41 (*SGDI* 5219) (f. *Σωσίστρατος*)
TRIPHYLIA:
—MAKISTOS: (25) 401 BC X., *An.* vii 4. 16

**Σίλας**
AITOLIA: (1) ?209 or 205 BC Flacelière p. 407 no. 38 b, [4]; Nachtergael, *Les Galates* 68, 4

**Σιλάσιμος?**
ARGOLIS:
—ARGOS: (1) imp. *IG* IV (1) 641 (*M. Ἀνταλίνιος Σιλάσιμος*)

**Σιλβανίων**
EPIROS:
—BOUTHROTOS: (1) iii AD *IBouthrot* 193 (*Γάλλιος Σ.*)


**Σιλβανός**
EPIROS:
—NIKOPOLIS: (1) imp. *CIG* 1816 (*SEG* XXXIV 593) (s. *Σώσος*)
SICILY:
—SYRACUSE: (2) iii-v AD ib. XXXIX 1022

**Σιλέας**
ELIS: (1) s. ii AD *IvOl* 461, 2 (*Γ. Φουφείκιος Σειλέα*[ς]) ?= (*3*); (2) ~ ib. l. 4 (*M. Οὐψάνιος Σειλέας*); (3) 185-189 AD ib. 104, 7 ([*Φουφ*]είκιος *Σειλέας*) ?= (*1*)

**Σιληνός**
AITOLIA:
—TRICHONION: (1) iii-ii BC *IG* IX (1)² (1) 120
ELIS: (2) v/iv BC Paus. vi 1. 4 (f. *Κλεογένης*)
S. ITALY (BRUTTIUM):
—RHEGION: (3) 433 BC *IG* I³ 53, 3; 1178, 3 (s. *Φῶκος*)
S. ITALY (CAMPANIA):
—POMPEII: (4) 3 AD *CIL* X 892 (Castrèn 42. 20) (Lat. Messius Arrius Silenus)
SICILY:
—KAMARINA: (5) ?264 BC *FD* III (3) 202, 3 (f. *Ἀρίσταρχος*)

**Σιληστρος**
EPIROS:
—SELIPIANA (MOD.): (1) inc. *AE* 1915, p. 77 no. 8, 1; Stählin p. 150 n. 5 (locn.) (*Σιλβεστρος*?—ed.)

**Σιλίς**
S. ITALY (CAMPANIA):
—POMPEII: (1) i BC-i AD *Atti Acc. Pontan.* 39 (1990) p. 287 no. 54 (Lat. Valeria Silis)

**Σίλλαξ**
S. ITALY (BRUTTIUM):
—RHEGION: (1) vi/v BC *RE* (-) (painter)
SICILY:
—GELA-PHINTIAS: (2) s. iv BC *IG* IV (1)² 95, 89 (Perlman E.2); Perlman pp. 46-9 (date)

**Σίλλων**
AKARNANIA:
—THYRREION: (1) ii BC *IG* IX (1)² (2) 252, 15 ((*Σ*)ίλλων)

**Σίλων**
PELOPONNESE: (1) s. iii BC *SEG* XIII 278, 7
S. ITALY (BRUTTIUM):
—LOKROI EPIZEPHYRIOI:
——(*Πυρ.*): (2) iv/iii BC De Franciscis 26, 3 (f. *Μένιππος*)
——(*Σκι.*): (3) iv/iii BC ib. 34, 10
——(*Σωτ.*): (4) iv/iii BC ib. 17, 3 (s. *Χαρμόνδας*)

**Σίμα**
AIGINA: (1) vi/v BC *SEG* XXXIX 333 A
AITOLIA:
—APERANTOI: (2) ?iv/iii BC *IG* IX (1)² (1) 166, 1 (*L'Illyrie mérid.* 1 p. 109 fig. 6)
AKARNANIA:
—ECHINOS?: (3) ii BC *IG* IX (1)² (2) 378
ARKADIA:
—TEGEA: (4) imp. ib. v (2) 239 (*Π. Σείμα* (masc./fem.?), *Πρεῖμα*?)
ILLYRIA?:
—APOLLONIA: (5) iv-iii BC ib. IX (2) 1174 (*IApoll* 312) (d. *Ἀλέξανδρος*)
KEPHALLENIA:
—SAME: (6) hell. *IG* IX (1) 629 + Unp. (*IG* arch.) ([*Αἱ*]σίμα—*IG*)
KORINTHIA:
—KORINTH: (7) f. vi BC Amyx 52 (vase) (Lorber 68) (*Σίμα*: fict.?); (8) c. 570-550 BC Amyx 105 A. 3 (vase) (Lorber 93) (fict.?)
SICILY:
—GELA-PHINTIAS: (9) f. v BC Arena, *Iscr. Sic.* II 25 (loomweight)


**Σίμαιθος**
AKARNANIA:
—PALAIROS: (1) s. iii BC *IG* IX (1)² (2) 528
—STRATOS: (2) iv/iii BC ib. 395, 12 (s. *Περικλῆς*)

**Σιμάκα**
AKARNANIA:
—PALAIROS: (1) iii/ii BC ib. 531
—THYRREION: (2) ii BC ib. 330
EPIROS: (3) imp. Ugolini, *Alb. Ant.* 1 p. 196 no. 18 (*Κλ. Σει*[μ]άκα)
—ARGOS (AMPHILOCH.): (4) iii BC *SEG* XXXII 561 (*Σιμάκας*—ed.: d. *Τρωϊάς*)
—BOUTHROTOS (PRASAIBOI): (5) a. 163 BC *IBouthrot* 117, 7
ILLYRIA:
—EPIDAMNOS-DYRRHACHION: (6) hell.-imp. *IDyrrh* 399 B (*Κλ. Σειμάκα*)

**Σίμακος**
ARGOLIS:
—ARGOS: (1) ?257 BC Nachtergael, *Les Galates* 7, 36; cf. Stephanis 2242 (f. *Σάτυρος*); (2) ?255-254 BC Nachtergael, *Les Galates* 8, 68; 9, 70 (Stephanis 2272) (s. *Μενεκράτης*)
EPIROS: (3) iii BC Cabanes, *L'Épire* p. 587 no. 73, 10 (*Σίμα*[κος]: f. *Σίμων*)
—BOUTHROTOS (PRASAIBOI): (4) a. 163 BC *IBouthrot* 14, 22; 21, 41; 31, 27; 39, 5 (*SEG* XXXVIII 471; 478; 490; 498); *IBouthrot* 135, 5; cf. Cabanes, *L'Épire* p. 406 (s. *Ἀντίγονος*); (5) ~ *IBouthrot* 21, 43 (*SEG* XXXVIII 478); (6) ~ *IBouthrot* 24, 4; 25, 5 (*SEG* XXXVIII 482-3); (7) ~ *IBouthrot* 28, 33; 33, 1 (*SEG* XXXVIII 486; 492); *IBouthrot* 48, 7 (f. *Ἀλεξίμαχος*); (8) ~ ib. 32, 21; 42, 9 (*SEG* XXXVIII 491; 501); (9) ~ *IBouthrot* 50, 4, 10 ?= (*11*); (10) ~ ib. 51, 27 (s. *Λυκίσκος*); (11) ~ ib. 106 (s. *Σώσανδρος*) ?= (*9*) (*15*); (12) ~ ib. 152, 4 (s. *Νικάσιος*)
——Naritioi: (13) a. 163 BC ib. 94, 10 (s. *Νέστωρ*)
——Phonidatoi: (14) a. 163 BC ib. 120, 6 (f. *Νικάνωρ*)
——Porronoi: (15) a. 163 BC ib. 69, 7-8, 14; 70, 6-7, 11; 71, 5, 9 (*BCH* 118 (1994) pp. 129 f. B 1-3) (s. *Σώσανδρος*, f. *Λέαινα*) ?= (*11*)
——Sakaronoi: (16) a. 163 BC *IBouthrot* 114, 9
——Telaioi: (17) a. 163 BC ib. 104, 15 (f. *Ἀγήσανδρος*)
——Tharioi: (18) a. 163 BC ib. 91, 14 (*SEG* XXXII 623) ([*Σί*]μακος: s. *Λύκων*) ?= (*23*)
——DODONA: (19) iii BC Antoniou, *Dodone* Ba, 22
——KAMMANOI BOUTHROTIOI: (20) a. 163 BC *IBouthrot* 60, 6 (*SEG* XXXVIII 511) (s. *Φάλακρος*)
—KEROPAT-?: (21) ?192 BC *Ténos* 2 pp. 102 f. B, 2 (*SEG* XL 690)
—NIKOPOLIS: (22) imp. *PAE* 1913, p. 97 no. 5 (Sarikakis 146) (Lat. Simacus: f. *Μουσαῖος*)
—PRASAIBOI: (23) a. 165 BC *IBouthrot* 60, 5; 62 (*SEG* XXXVIII 511; 513) (s. *Λύκων*) ?= (*18*)
—THESPROTOI: (24) 356-354 BC *IG* IV (1)² 95, 26 (Perlman E.2); Perlman p. 40 f. (date); (25) ii BC *IG* IV (1)² 99, 19 (s. *Φαλακρίων*)
—UZDINA (MOD.): (26) hell.? *SEG* XVI 387 (f. *Σιλάνα*)
ILLYRIA:
—APOLLONIA: (27) ii-i BC *IApoll* 147 (*Σεί-*)
KEPHALLENIA:
—KRANIOI: (28) i BC-i AD *IG* IX (1) 614
—SAME: (29) 208 BC *IMM* 35, 34 (f. *Κλευφάνης*)
KERKYRA: (30) ?ii BC *IG* IX (1) 708 (*Σ*[ίμα]κος: s. *Ἀγέλαος*)

**Σιμάλη**
ARKADIA: (1) 232 BC *CPR* XVIII 12, 238-39 (d. *Εὐήνωρ*)

**Σίμαλος**
S. ITALY (CALABRIA):
—TARAS-TARENTUM: (1) 103-101 BC *PPC* Σ 12 (II s. *Σίμαλος* I (Salamis)); (2) i BC *ID* 2619 II, 10 (f. *Εἰρήνη*)

## Σίμαργος
Aitolia?: (1) s. iii BC SEG XIX 379, 1

## Σιμάς
Akarnania:
—palairos: (1) s. iii BC IG IX (1)² (2) 527

## Σίμη
S. Italy (Campania):
—pompeii: (1) i BC-i AD CIL IV 4481 (Lat. Sime)
Sicily:
—terravecchia di cuti (mod.): (2) vi/v BC Arena, Iscr. Sic. II 117 A (Dubois, IGDS 176) (-μέ)

## Σιμήδης
Lakonia:
—sparta: (1) i/ii AD IG V (1) 152, 1; SEG XXX 407, 2; BSA 75 (1980) pp. 210-20 (ident., stemma) (Bradford (3)) (Τιβ. Κλ. Σ.: ?s. Τιβ. Κλ. Ἀριστοκράτης, Ἰουλ. Ἀπατάριον, f. Τιβ. Κλ. Ἀριστοκράτης); (2) ~ IG V (1) 507, 2; 588, 1; SEG XI 517, 2; BSA 75 (1980) p. 219 (stemma) (Bradford (2)) (Γ. Ἰουλ. Σειμήδης: s. Γ. Ἰουλ. Πολύευκτος, Ἰουλ. Νικιππία) ?= (6); (3) c. 90-100 AD SEG XI 558, 14; BSA 75 (1980) p. 219 (stemma) (Bradford (5)) (f. Γ. Ἰουλ. Πολύευκτος); (4) f. ii AD IG V (1) 163, 3 (Bradford (1)) (Σει-); (5) c. 105-110 AD SEG XI 569, 12, 14 (Bradford (4)) ?= (6); (6) c. 110-120 AD IG V (1) 101, 4; SEG XI 610, [7] (Bradford (4)) (Σει-) ?= (5) (2); (7) c. 150-175 AD SEG XXX 407, 2; BSA 75 (1980) pp. 210-20 (ident., stemma) (Bradford (3)) (Κλ. Σειμήδης: s. Κλ. Ἀριστοκράτης, Κλ. Τεισαμενίς (Athens and Sparta)); (8) a. 212 AD BSA 89 (1994) p. 435 no. 6, 9 (Σεμμή[δης])

## Σιμηλίδας
Lakonia:
—gytheion: (1) i-ii AD IG V (1) 1178, 3 (s. Θησεύς, f. Σεμπρώνιος, Νικίας)

## Σιμία
Argolis:
—hermione: (1) ii-i BC ib. IV (1) 732 III, 5
S. Italy (Calabria):
—brentesion-brundisium: (2) imp. CIL IX 210 + Epigraphica 42 (1980) p. 155 (Lat. Simia)

## Σιμιάδας
Aitolia:
—potidania: (1) m. ii BC SBBerlAk 1936, p. 371 a, 11 (SEG XLI 528 A); SBBerlAk 1936, p. 371 b, 12 (SEG XLI 528 B) (f. Ἀριστόδαμος)

## Σιμίας
Achaia:
—dyme: (1) iii BC AJPh 31 (1910) p. 399 no. 74 a, 19 (s. Θευδίων)
Achaia?: (2) c. 300 BC SEG XIV 375, 8; (3) 206 BC Plb. xi 18. 2, 6; Plu., Phil. 10 ?= (4); (4) 193 BC IG V (2) 293, 2, 19 (s. Καλλικράτης) ?= (3)
Aitolia:
—kalydon: (5) a. 142 BC ib. IX (1)² (1) 137, 81
—phistyon: (6) ii BC ib. 110 a, 5 (f. Τυρταῖος)
—prosch(e)ion: (7) 192 BC ib. 31, 27 (s. Ἡράκλειτος)
—thermos: (8) 163 BC ib. 102, 3
Akarnania:
—astakos: (9) ii BC ib. IX (1)² (2) 434, 6 (f. Νέαρχος)
Arkadia:
—heraia: (10) 369-361 BC ib. V (2) 1, 60; Tod, GHI II 132 (date)
—mantineia-antigoneia: (11) iv/iii BC SEG XXXVI 378, 1 (f. —αμος); (12) 64 or 62 BC IG V (2) 265, 48 (s. Ἀνθεμόκριτος)

—tegea: (13) iii BC ib. 30, 7 (f. Πραξιτέλης); (14) c. 240-229 BC ib. 12
Dalmatia:
—issa:
——(Hylleis): (15) iv/iii BC Brunšmid p. 8, 42 (s. Καλλήν)
Epiros:
—argos (amphiloch.): (16) ?272 BC FD III (1) 123, 2 (s. Λεωνίδας)
—bouthrotos (prasaiboi): (17) a. 163 BC IBouthrot 27, 2 (SEG XXXVIII 485) (f. Φαινώ); (18) ~ IBouthrot 152, 3
——Opatai: (19) a. 163 BC ib. 99, 7 (BCH 118 (1994) p. 121 B)
—dodona: (20) ?164 BC Cabanes, L'Épire p. 586 no. 71, 9 (Σει-: s. Πολυκλῆς)
—ioannina (mod.) (nr.): (21) iii/ii BC BCH 118 (1994) p. 727 (f. Ἀμμιλώ)
—kassope: (22) hell.? SEG XXIV 439 (f. Φιλία)
—kelaithoi: (23) hell. Cabanes, L'Épire p. 584 no. 63, 11 (SEG XXVI 705)
—orestoi: (24) ?164 BC Cabanes, L'Épire p. 586 no. 71, 7 (s. Λυκώτας)
Illyria:
—apollonia: (25) ?342-326 BC ib. p. 540 no. 4 (IApoll 308); (26) iii-ii BC ib. 42 (s. Λυκίσκος); (27) c. 250-50 BC Maier 33 (coin) (Ceka 98) (money.); (28) s. iii BC IApoll 176; cf. SEG XXXIX 550 (s. Ἀντίδωρος)
—aulon: (29) hell. Iliria 1977-8, p. 292 pl. IV.5 (SEG XXXII 621 (tile))
—olympe: (30) s. iii BC ib. XXXV 697 (f. Αἰσχίνας)
Kerkyra: (31) f. iii BC IG IX (1) 691, 6 (Iscr. Gr. Verona p. 22 A)
Lakonia:
—oitylos: (32) iii/ii BC IG V (1) 1295, 7 (Bradford (-))
Leukas: (33) ?iii BC Unp. (IG arch.)
Messenia:
—messene?: (34) ii/i BC SEG XI 979, 16 ([Σ]ιμίας)
S. Italy (Bruttium):
—lokroi epizephyrioi:
——(Κυλ.): (35) iv/iii BC De Franciscis 16, 2 (s. Σιμίσκος)
——(Λογ.): (36) iv/iii BC ib. 26, 7 (f. Ἐπαίνετος)
——(Σκα.): (37) iv/iii BC ib. 16, 5; 19, 7 (f. Σωσίλας); (38) ~ ib. 28, 4 (s. Λέων)
——(Τιω.): (39) 278 BC ib. 30, 2 (s. Ἀντίοχος)
Sicily:
—kamarina: (40) f. v BC Cordano, Tessere Pubbliche 11 (f. Λυκῖνος); (41) iv/iii BC SEG XXXIV 942, 4 (Dubois, IGDS 123; Cordano, 'Camarina VII' 149)
—selinous?: (42) vi/v BC SEG XXXIX 1020 A, 4 (s. Μίκυθος)
—syracuse?:
——(Ὑπα.): (43) hell. Manganaro, PdelP forthcoming no. 4 V, 9 (f. Δείνων)
—thermai himeraiai: (44) ?ii-i BC IG XIV 316, 3 (Dubois, IGDS 203) (f. Ἀριστόδαμος)

## Σιμίδας
Arkadia:
—tegea: (1) iii BC IG V (2) 30, 26 ([Σ]ιμ[ί]δας?); (2) ?218 BC ib. 16, 13
——(Apolloniatai): (3) f. iii BC ib. 36, 50 (s. Θίβρων)
Lakonia: (4) iii-ii BC ib. V (1) 1341, 7 (Bradford (-))

## Σιμίσκος
S. Italy (Bruttium):
—lokroi epizephyrioi:
——(Κυλ.): (1) iv/iii BC De Franciscis 16, 2 (f. Σιμίας)
Sicily:
—tauromenion: (2) c. 240 BC IG XIV 421 an. 1 (SGDI 5219) (f. Νυμφόδωρος)

## Σιμιχίας
S. Italy (Calabria):
—taras-tarentum: (1) vi BC Iamb., VP 267 (FVS 1 p. 446) (Σμιχίας—mss.: name—Schweigh.)

## Σιμιχίδας
Sicily:
—syracuse?: (1) f. iii BC Theoc., Id. vii, 21; Gow, Theocritus 2 pp. 127-9 (ident.) (or Kos)

## Σίμιχος
S. Italy (Bruttium):
—kaulonia?: (1) ?c. 475 BC IGSI 20, 3 (SEG IV 71; Landi, DISMG 168); LSAG² p. 261 no. 29 (date)
Sicily:
—kentoripa: (2) vi BC Porph., VP 21 (tyrant)

## Σιμίων
Korinthia:
—korinth: (1) c. 650-625 BC IG IV (1) 211 (pinax) (Lazzarini 58; CEG 1 357); LSAG² p. 131 no. 8 (date) (-ōν)

## Σιμμίας
Sicily:
—syracuse: (1) s. iv BC D.L. ii 114

## Σίμμος
Arkadia:
—orchomenos: (1) 265 BC SEG XXV 443, 9

## Σίμον
Aigina: (1) hell. IG II² 7966 (d. Ἑρμαῖος)
Korinthia:
—korinth: (2) ?iv BC ib. IV (1) 1553 (fals.?)

## Σῖμος
Achaia: (1) 146 BC ib. IV (1)² 28, 119 (s. Νικήρατος: synoikos)
—aigion: (2) ii/i BC Achaean Grave Stelai 22 (Σεί-: s. Δαμό—)
—patrai: (3) 191-146 BC BM coin 1920 8-5-1220 (coin)
—pharai: (4) iii-ii BC Achaean Grave Stelai 60 (f. Αἴσχυτος)
Aigina: (5) c. 225 BC SEG XI 414, 36 (Perlman E.5) (s. Ἐπικράτης)
Aitolia: (6) ?228-215 BC SGDI 2525, 4 ?= (8); (7) c. 220-217 BC FD III (4) 239 ([Σῖμ]ος: I? f. Σῖμος II?); (8) ~ ib. (II? s. Σῖμος I?) ?= (6)
—phistyon: (9) f. ii BC IG IX (1)² (1) 98, 9 (Σεί-)
—pholai: (10) s. ii BC SBBerlAk 1936, p. 364 no. 1, 1 ([Σ]ῖμος: s. Νίκων)
—phytaion: (11) 263-262 BC IG IX (1)² (1) 3 A, 19
—pleuron: (12) 196 BC ib. 30, 12 (f. Νίκαρχος)
Akarnania:
—stratos: (13) iv/iii BC ib. IX (1)² (2) 395, 6 (s. Πέταλος)
Argolis:
—argos*: (14) 105 BC JÖAI 14 (1911) Beibl. p. 146 no. 4, 8 (slave/freed.?)
—hermione: (15) ?iii-ii BC IG IV (1) 735, 3 (f. Τιμαία)
Arkadia:
—mantineia-antigoneia: (16) c. 300-221 BC ib. V (2) 323. 96 (tessera) (s. Διοφάνης)
—megalopolis: (17) c. 315-280 BC Nachtergael, Les Galates 6, [4]; 12, 2 (s. Καλλισθένης)
—pheneos: (18) c. 431-370 BC Coll. Philipsen 1419; Coll. Photiades 1183 (coin)
—tegea: (19) hell.? IG V (2) 170. 16 (tile); (20) f. iii BC ib. 35, 25 (s. Κλεοφάνης); (21) f. ii BC ib. 44, 9 (s. Ἰναίσιμος)
Epiros:
—arktanes?: (22) m. iv BC Cabanes, L'Épire p. 539 no. 3, 10
—dodona: (23) iii BC Antoniou, Dodone Ab, 34
—nikopolis: (24) i AD PAE 1913, p. 97 no. 1 ([Ὀνή]σιμος?: s. Τιβ. Κλ. Ὀνήσιμος)
Korinthia:
—sikyon: (25) vi/v BC SEG XI 244, 12

LAKONIA:
—SPARTA: (26) c. 30-20 BC *IG* V (1) 211, 10 (Bradford (-)) (f. *Σίπομπος*); (27) f. ii AD *SEG* XXXI 340, 9 (s. *Ἀρίστων*)
MESSENIA:
—THOURIA: (28) f. ii BC ib. XI 972, 70 (f. *Ξενόδαμος*); (29) ~ ib. l. 83 (s. *Σιμωνίδας*); (30) ii/i BC *IG* V (1) 1384, 2 (s. *Σώσανδρος*)
S. ITALY (BRUTTIUM):
—LOKROI EPIZEPHYRIOI:
——(*Θρα.*): (31) iv/iii BC De Franciscis 17, 2 (f. *Φιλοκλῆς*)
——(*Σωτ.*): (32) iv/iii BC ib. 7, 3 (f. *Σώσιππος*) ?= (33); (33) ~ ib. 34, 5 ?= (32)
S. ITALY (LUCANIA):
—POSEIDONIA-PAESTUM: (34) vi BC Iamb., *VP* 267 (*FVS* I p. 448)
S. ITALY?: (35) ii-i BC *Summa Gall. Auction* I 46 (s. *Δάμαστος*)
SICILY:
—GELA-PHINTIAS: (36) s. vi BC Arena, *Iscr. Sic.* II 7 (vase)
—KAMARINA: (37) f. v BC Cordano, *Tessere Pubbliche* 25 (Arena, *Iscr. Sic.* II 133 A) (f. *Εὐάγγελος*); (38) ~ Cordano, *Tessere Pubbliche* 27 (Arena, *Iscr. Sic.* II 134 A) (f. *Νικόμαχος*); (39) ~ Cordano, *Tessere Pubbliche* 46 (f. *Πυρι*—); (40) ~ ib. 78 (f. *Χειλῖνος*); (41) ?iv/iii BC *SEG* XXXIV 940, 9 (Dubois, *IGDS* 124; *PdelP* 44 (1989) p. 192 no. 3; Cordano, 'Camarina VII' 150) (s. *Γελώϊος*)
—LIPARA: (42) ?iii BC *NScav* 1929, p. 83 no. 11
—PETRA: (43) f. iii BC *SEG* XXX 1121, 26 (Dubois, *IGDS* 208) (f. *Ἀρίμναστος*)
—SYRACUSE: (44) iv BC *CIRB* 203 (f. *Μέλας*); (45) iii/ii BC *SEG* XXXIV 988
—SYRACUSE?:
——(*Λαβ.*): (46) hell. Manganaro, *PdelP* forthcoming no. 4 IV, 5 (f. *Ἰάρων*)
—TAUROMENION: (47) c. 202 BC *IG* XIV 421 an. 39 (*SGDI* 5219); (48) c. 189 BC *IG* XIV 421 an. 52 (*SGDI* 5219) (s. *Ἐπίξενος*)
——(*Μαν.*): (49) ii/i BC *IGSI* 9 II, 21 (f. *Ἡρακλείδας*)
—ZANKLE-MESSANA: (50) c. 650 BC Th. vi 5. 1 (and Sicily Himera: oikist)

**Σιμυλίς**
AKARNANIA:
—ASTAKOS (NR.): (1) iv/iii BC *SEG* XXXII 564 (*Σιμύλιος* (gen.))
S. ITALY (CALABRIA):
—TARAS-TARENTUM: (2) iv/iii BC *IG* XIV 668 II, 9 (Landi, *DISMG* 194)

**Σιμυλίων**
S. ITALY (LUCANIA):
—METAPONTION: (1) m. iii BC *SEG* XXX 1175, 13 (doctor)

**Σιμύλος**
AITOLIA: (1) ?a. 246 BC *SGDI* 2509, 3
ARGOLIS:
—ARGOS: (2) m. iii BC *IG* IV (1)² 96, 54 (Perlman E.3); Perlman p. 63 f. (date) (s. *Νικόστρατος*)
—EPIDAUROS: (3) iv BC *IG* IV (1)² 154
—EPIDAUROS*: (4) c. 370 BC *SEG* XXV 383, 198 (*Σιμ[ύλος]*) ?= (5); (5) c. 370-360 BC *BSA* 61 (1966) p. 271 no. 4 A, 16 ?= (4)
—HERMIONE*: (6) iv BC *IG* IV (1) 742, 17
KERKYRA?: (7) ?s. v BC *CEG* II 469
MESSENIA:
—MESSENE: (8) inc. Paus. vii 22. 2
S. ITALY (BRUTTIUM):
—LOKROI EPIZEPHYRIOI:
——(*Φαω.*): (9) 279 BC De Franciscis 13, 8 (s. *Μενοίτιος*)
SICILY:
—AKRAI:

——(*Νητ.*): (10) ii-i BC *SGDI* 3246, 19 (*Akrai* pp. 152-3 no. 2; Dubois, *IGDS* 109) (s. *Εὐκλῆς*)
—HALOUNTION: (11) hell.? Manganaro, *QUCC* forthcoming no. 23 (s. *Καλλιππίδας*)
—TAUROMENION: (12) c. 193 BC *IG* XIV 421 an. 48 (*SGDI* 5219)

**Σίμων**
ACHAIA:
—DYME*: (1) c. 219 BC ib. 1612, 39 (*Tyche* 5 (1990) p. 124) (f. *Θεοκλῆς*)
AIGINA: (2) f. v BC *RE* (12); cf. *Alt-Ägina* II (2) pp. 39-43 (sculptor)
AKARNANIA:
—PHOKREAI: (3) 216 BC *IG* IX (1)² (2) 583, 4, 64 (s. *Εὔαρχος*)
ARGOLIS:
—EPIDAUROS*: (4) c. 335-325 BC Peek, *IAEpid* 50, 18 (*Σί[μ]ων*) ?= (5); (5) c. 290-270 BC *BSA* 61 (1966) p. 307 no. 20, 125 ?= (4)
ARKADIA:
—MANTINEIA-ANTIGONEIA: (6) c. 425-385 BC *IG* V (2) 323. 4 (tessera) (s. *Ἀγασίας*); (7) ii AD ib. 325 (*GVI* 954)
—TEGEA:
——(Hippothoitai): (8) m. iii BC *IG* V (2) 36, 80 (f. *Περίλαος*)
EPIROS: (9) iii BC Cabanes, *L'Épire* p. 587 no. 73, 10 (s. *Σίμακος*)
S. ITALY (BRUTTIUM):
—LOKROI EPIZEPHYRIOI:
——(*Σκι.*): (10) iv/iii BC De Franciscis 20, 18 (f. *Ἀριστεύς*)
S. ITALY (CALABRIA):
—TARAS-TARENTUM: (11) iv/iii BC *IG* XIV 668 I, 16 (Landi, *DISMG* 194)
S. ITALY (CAMPANIA):
—DIKAIARCHIA-PUTEOLI*: (12) imp. *Röm. Mitt.* 19 (1904) p. 186 no. 1 (Lat. M. Heius Simo: freed.)
—POMPEII: (13) i BC-i AD *CIL* IV 6808 (Lat. Simo)
—SALERNUM: (14) imp. *IItal* I (1) 71 (Lat. Simo: f. Maxima)
S. ITALY (LUCANIA):
—HYELE-VELIA: (15) iii-v AD *IG* XIV 657 (Wessel 352) (*Ειμωνοσ*—apogr.: s. *Πίστος*)
SICILY:
—AKRAGAS: (16) iii-iv AD Manganaro, *QUCC* forthcoming no. 9 (Jew)

**Σιμώνδας**
EPIROS:
—DODONA: (1) iii BC Antoniou, *Dodone* Ab, 41

**Σιμωνίδας**
ARGOLIS:
—ARGOS:
——Asaminthos?: (1) ?iv-iii BC *SEG* XXXIII 286
KORINTHIA:
—KORINTH: (2) m. iv BC ib. XX 716, 28; cf. XXVII 1194
MESSENIA:
—THOURIA: (3) f. ii BC ib. XI 972, 83 (f. *Σῖμος*)
SICILY:
—SYRACUSE: (4) 207 BC *IMM* 72, 10 (Dubois, *IGDS* 97)

**Σιμωνίδης**
ZAKYNTHOS: (1) ?iv BC Wehrli, *Schule Arist.* iii fr. 92 (Stephanis 2281)

**Σίναβρος**
AKARNANIA:
—KORONTA: (1) inc. *IG* IX (1)² (2) 604 (s. *Ὑβρίας*)

**Σινάρας**
SICILY:
—ECHETLA: (1) vi/v BC Manganaro, *PdelP* forthcoming no. 8

**Σίναρος**
SICILY:
—TERRAVECCHIA DI CUTI (MOD.): (1) f. v BC *Di Terra in Terra* p. 56 no. 73 (loomweight); cf. *SEG* XLII 878

**Σίναυρος**
AKARNANIA:
—PALAIROS: (1) iii BC *L'Illyrie mérid.* 1984 p. 106 no. 1 (*SEG* XXXVII 435)

**Σίνδης**
ARGOLIS:
—HERMIONE: (1) ?ii-i BC *IG* IV (1) 731 II, 7 (s. *Ζεύξιλα*)

**Σίννας**
EPIROS:
—AMPHILOCHOI: (1) iii BC *GVI* 2017

**Σιννέας**
AITOLIA: (1) ?255 BC Nachtergael, *Les Galates* 8, 4; 19, 2; Flacelière p. 398 no. 21 c, 2

**Σίννος**
AKARNANIA:
—STRATOS: (1) f. iii BC *IG* IX (1)² (2) 400 (f. *Ἀνταῖος*)

**Σινώπη**
KORINTHIA:
—KORINTH: (1) ?iv BC Schol. Ar., *Pl.* 149 (het.)

**Σίξας**
SICILY:
—HIMERA: (1) s. vi BC *Himera* 2 p. 696 no. 238 (Dubois, *IGDS* 6; Arena, *Iscr. Sic.* III 50)

**Σίπομπος**
ARKADIA:
—TEGEA: (1) ii BC *IG* V (2) 43, 13 (s. *Ἀριστ*—)
LAKONIA:
—SPARTA: (2) imp. ib. V (1) 354 (*Artemis Orthia* p. 358 no. 81; Bradford (5)) (*Σείπ[ομπος]*); (3) c. 30-20 BC *IG* V (1) 211, 10 (Bradford (4)) (s. *Σῖμος*); (4) ~ *IG* V (1) 211, 24 (Bradford (1)) (s. *Ἀριστόδαμος*); (5) c. 25-1 BC *IG* V (1) 210, 7 (Bradford (7)) (*Σίπο[μπος]*: f. *Νικοκράτης*); (6) c. 100-120 AD *SEG* XI 545, [2]; 561, 1?; 562, 1; 637, [4] (Bradford (3)) (*Σεί*-, [*Σί*]*πομ[πος]*—561: s. *Κλεόνικος*); (7) c. 110-134 AD *IG* V (1) 32 B, 26; 34, 8; 62, 13; *SEG* XI 494, 2; 542, 6; 575, [1]; 613, 2? (Bradford (2)) (*Σεί*-: s. *Κλέων*, f. *Κλέων*)

**Σιργεύς**
PELOPONNESE?: (1) s. iii BC *IG* V (1) 1426, 22 (s. *Ἱερώνυμος*)

**Σίρων**
AKARNANIA:
—STRATOS: (1) iv/iii BC ib. IX (1)² (2) 395, 13 (f. *Ξέννυς*)
S. ITALY (CAMPANIA):
—NEAPOLIS: (2) i BC *RE* (-)

**Σισίνιος**
LAKONIA:
—ASOPOS: (1) byz. *IG* V (1) 974 (f. *Θεόδουλος*)

**Σισσινίων**
EPIROS:
—NIKOPOLIS: (1) imp. Unp. (Nikopolis Mus.) (*Σισσιν[ί]ων*)

**Σισύμβρινος**
ARGOLIS:
—HERMIONE: (1) v BC Wehrli, *Schule Arist.* Suppl. i fr. 6 (?f. *Λάσος*: dub.)

**Σισυρίων**
SICILY:
—SEGESTA: (1) 49 BC *IG* XIV 282 (*Πασίων Σ.*: s. *Δέκιος*)

**Σίσυρνος**
Akarnania:
—phoitiai: (1) 356-354 BC ib. IV (1)² 95, 11 (Perlman E.2); Perlman p. 40 f. (date)
Arkadia:
—mantineia-antigoneia: (2) c. 475-450 BC IG v (2) 262, 2 (IPArk 8); LSAG² p. 216 no. 29 (date) ([Σί]συρνος)

**Σίσυφος**
Illyria:
—epidamnos-dyrrhachion: (1) hell.-imp. IDyrrh 373 (Σεί-)
Korinthia:
—korinth: (2) ii AD SEG XVII 129 (Σεί-: her.?)
Lakonia:
—sparta: (3) v/iv BC X., HG iii 1. 8; FGrH 70 F 71 (Δερκυλίδας ὁ ἐπικαλ. Σ.)

**Σιτάλκας**
Elis: (1) c. 365 BC X., HG vii 4. 15 (Σταλκας—mss., Σ.—Mehler, Εὐάλκας—Keil)

**Σιτάλκης**
Dalmatia:
—issa:
——(Pamphyloi): (1) iv/iii BC Brunšmid p. 8, 48 (s. Ἀρι—)

**Σιτηρίς**
Messenia:
—messene: (1) ii/iii AD SEG XXIII 217, 3 (Κλ. Σιτηρίς)

**Σίτιμος**
Lakonia:
—sparta: (1) s. i BC IG v (1) 134, 7 (Bradford (1)) (Σεί-: s. Εὔδαμος); (2) c. 90-100 AD SEG XI 512, 6 (Bradford (6)) (Σείτει-: f. Πρατόνικος); (3) c. 90-125 AD IG v (1) 153, 23; SEG XI 514, [2]?; 558, 3; 559, 2; 560, 2; 593, 1 (Bradford (3)) (Σείτιμος—IG 153 and SEG 559, [Σίτι]μος—SEG 560: s. Πρατόνικος); (4) c. 100-105 AD SEG XI 537 b, 8 (Bradford (2)) ([Σί]τιμος: s. Εὐτυχίδας); (5) c. 125-150 AD IG v (1) 114, 1 (Bradford (5)) (Σε[ί]τε[ιμ]ος); (6) c. 127-145 AD IG v (1) 32 A, 6; 32 B, 29; 60, 4; SEG XI 494, 2; 583, 2 (Bradford (4)) (Σείτιμος—IG 32 A-B and 60 and SEG XI 583: II s. Σίτιμος I); (7) ~ IG v (1) 32 B, 30; 60, 4; SEG XI 583, [2] (Bradford (7)) (I f. Σίτιμος II)

**Σίττα**
S. Italy (Apulia):
—monte sannace (mod.): (1) hell. Atti Conv. Taranto 18 (1978) pp. 461-2

**Σίττιος**
Sicily:
—katane: (1) hell.? IG XIV 2405. 39 (tile)

**Σίττυρος**
Argolis:
—epidauros*: (1) c. 370-365 BC Peek, IAEpid 52 A, 24

**Σιτύλος**
Akarnania:
—phoitiai: (1) c. 425-400 BC IG IX (1)² (2) 390, 10 (f. Σπίνθαρος)

**Σιχάρης**
Lakonia:
—sparta: (1) c. 25-1 BC ib. v (1) 210, 43; 212, 54 (Bradford (-)) (s. Τεισαμενός: mantis)

**Σίχιος**
Lakonia:
—sparta: (1) f. vi BC SEG II 74 (Lazzarini 403b); LSAG² p. 198 no. 6 (date) (Poralla² 668b) (Σοίχις?—SEG)

**Σίων**
Arkadia:
—tegea: (1) s. iv BC SEG XXXVI 383, 2 (f. —ις)
Lakonia:
—sparta: (2) ?s. i BC IG v (1) 262 (Artemis Orthia pp. 303-4 no. 13; Bradford (2)) (s. Δάμιππος); (3) c. 25-1 BC IG v (1) 212, 13 (Bradford (1)) ([Σ]ίων: s. Ἀλκιππος)
Messenia:
—thouria: (4) f. ii BC SEG XI 972, 73 (f. Φιλόδαμος)
Sicily:
—kamarina: (5) f. v BC Cordano, Tessere Pubbliche 73 (-ōν: f. —λις)

**Σιωνίδας**
Lakonia:
—sparta: (1) c. 25-1 BC IG v (1) 212, 16 (Bradford (-)) (f. Δαμοκλῆς)

**Σκάδας**
Illyria:
—skodrai: (1) a. 168 BC God. Balk. Isp. 13. 11 (1976) p. 228 no. 11 (coin)

**Σκαλδας?**
Illyria:
—skodrai: (1) a. 168 BC ib. p. 228 no. 12 (coin) (Σκαλδ(ας))

**Σκάμανδρος**
Achaia:
—pellene: (1) 263 BC IG IX (1)² (1) 17, 98
Argolis:
—troizen: (2) iii BC ib. IV (1) 774, 8
S. Italy (Campania):
—pompeii: (3) i BC-i AD CIL IV 1647; 1649 a (Lat. Scamander); (4) ~ ib. 4159 (Lat. Scamander); (5) c. 51-62 AD ib. 3340. 92, 4 (Castrèn 190. 21) (Lat. Sex. Helvius Scaman[der]); (6) ~ CIL IV 3340. 111, 2 (Castrèn 278. 8) (Lat. [Nu]minius Sca[ma]nder); (7) 55 AD CIL IV 3340. 17, [16]; 56, 6; 103, 4 (Castrèn 273. 5) (Lat. Sex. Nonius Scamander)

**Σκάριφος**
S. Italy (Campania):
—pompeii: (1) i BC-i AD CIL IV 1892 (Lat. Scaripus)

**Σκαφίς**
S. Italy (Campania):
—pompeii: (1) f. i AD ib. x 1029 (Castrèn 204. 18); Kockel p. 99 (date) (Lat. Istacidia Scapis)

**Σκελεβρεύς?**
Korinthia:
—korinth: (1) iv BC Hp., Epid. iv 40; Index Hipp. s.v. (Κελεύρεος (gen.)—codd. al., (τὸ) σκαλεύειν—Littré)

**Σκενέτα**
Illyria: (1) ?iii/ii BC SEG XXX 529 (d. Τόρος)

**Σκέπας**
Epiros:
—kassope: (1) 356-354 BC IG IV (1)² 95, 25 (Perlman E.2); Perlman p. 40 f. (date)

**Σκερδιλαΐδας**
Illyria: (1) iii BC RE Supplbd. 5 (-) (?s. Πλευρᾶτος (Ardiaioi), f. Πλευρᾶτος); (2) ii BC ib. (s. Γένθιος, Ἔτλευα)

**Σκέψιμος**
S. Italy (Campania):
—pompeii: (1) i BC-i AD CIL IV 10246 h (Lat. Scepsimus)

**Σκέψις**
S. Italy (Campania):
—pompeii: (1) i BC-i AD ib. 2201 (Lat. Scepsini (dat.))
Sicily:
—thermai himeraiai: (2) i-ii AD ILat. Term. Imer. 84 (Lat. Cornelia Scepsis)

**Σκιάπων**
S. Italy (Bruttium):
—kaulonia: (1) i-ii AD SEG IV 72 (tile)

**Σκινδάλαμος**
S. Italy (Lucania):
—grumentum*: (1) imp. CIL x 245 (Lat. M. Artorius Scindalamus: freed.)

**Σκιούριος**
Dalmatia:
—pharos: (1) iii/ii BC SEG XXIII 489, 2; cf. XLI 545

**Σκίπας**
Elis:
—olympia*: (1) 245-249 AD IvOl 121, 21 (Σκεί-: ?s. Τ. Φλ. Ἀρχέλαος: slave?)

**Σκίρας**
S. Italy (Calabria):
—taras-tarentum: (1) ?iii BC RE (3); CGF I p. 190

**Σκιραφίδας**
Lakonia:
—sparta: (1) 405 BC FGrH 115 F 332 (Poralla² 667)

**Σκίρτος**
S. Italy (Campania):
—dikaiarchia-puteoli*: (1) ?i-ii AD CIL x 1739 (Lat. Ti. Claud. Scirtus: imp. freed.)

**Σκιώνη**
Korinthia:
—korinth: (1) ?iv BC Schol. Ar., Pl. 149; Suda E 3266 (het.)

**Σκοδρίνα**
Illyria:
—epidamnos-dyrrhachion: (1) imp. AEp 1978, no. 749 (Lat. Novia Scodrina (ethn.?))

**Σκόμβρος**
S. Italy (Bruttium):
—taisia: (1) f. ii BC BCH 45 (1921) p. 24 col. IV, 88 with p. 66 n. 3 (SEG XXII 466); cf. Sic. Gymn. 17 (1964) pp. 46 f. (Σκόμβ[ρος]?)

**Σκόμφος**
Akarnania:
—oiniadai: (1) v/iv BC Hp., Epid. v 3; Abh-MainzAk 1982 (9) p. 35 (locn.) (or Thessaly?)

**Σκόπαιος**
Epiros:
—molossoi: (1) iii/ii BC Syll³ 1206, 6; cf. Cabanes, L'Épire p. 583 no. 60 ([Σκ]όπαιος)

**Σκόπας**
Achaia: (1) 146 BC IG IV (1)² 28, 118 (s. Ἀριστάναξ: synoikos)
Aitolia:
—philotaieis: (2) m. ii BC ib. IX (1)² (1) 107, 2
—trichonion: (3) f. iii BC RE Supplbd. 7 (5); IG IX (1)² (1) p. XLIX, s.a. 272 BC (f. Σώσανδρος); (4) c. 225-205 BC RE Supplbd. 7 (6); PP 15241; IG IX (1)² (1) p. L, s.a. 220 BC, 212 BC, 205 BC; 4, 3; Ergon 1990, p. 47; cf. REG 101 (1988) pp. 25 ff.; IG IX (1)² (1) 31, 46, 48, 68; IX (1)² (3) 613, [2] (s. Σώσανδρος)
Messenia: (5) c. 475-440 BC ib. I³ 1355 (Σκόπας)
Sicily:
—agyrion: (6) i BC Manganaro, PdelP forthcoming no. 5, 1 (f. Σώσιππος)

**Σκοπίνας**
SICILY:
—SYRACUSE: (1) hell.? Vitruv. i 1. 17

**Σκόπιος**
S. ITALY (CAMPANIA):
—NOLA*: (1) imp. CIL x 1253 (Lat. Naeratius Scopius)

**Σκορδίας**
LAKONIA:
—SPARTA: (1) c. 140-150 AD IG v (1) 64, 3 (Bradford s.v. Ξενοκλῆς (7)) (Ξενοκλῆς Σ.: s. Φιλοξενίδας)

**Σκορπίος**
KORINTHIA:
—KORINTH: (1) imp. Mon. Ant. 24 (1916) p. 162; Riv. Arch. Crist. 18 (1941) p. 220 no. 104; cf. Arch. Class. 17 (1965) p. 207 n. 104; SEG XXXVIII 919 (M. Ἀντ. Σ.)

**Σκορπίων**
AITOLIA: (1) iii BC ib. XVIII 244, 3; (2) c. 285 BC IG ix (1)² (1) 51 (s. Δράκων)
—DAIANES: (3) 161 BC ib. 100, 8
—KALYDON: (4) iii/ii BC ib. 136, 10
—KONOPE-ARSINOE: (5) 213 BC ib. 96, 2, 10 (s. Κλεαρχίς)
—PHISTYON: (6) f. ii BC ib. 111, 3 (s. Ἀγήσων)
—THERMOS: (7) 214 BC ib. 177, 18 (f. Λυκίσκος)

**Σκόρπος**
S. ITALY (CAMPANIA):
—NEAPOLIS: (1) imp. CIL x 8171; cf. Leiwo p. 92 (Lat. M. Octavius Scorpus)

**Σκοτάδις**
SICILY:
—SYRACUSE: (1) iii-v AD Riv. Arch. Crist. 36 (1960) p. 27 no. 19

**Σκριβώνις**
S. ITALY (BRUTTIUM):
—RHEGION: (1) iii AD Suppl. It. 5 p. 76 no. 37 (SEG XL 858 (lead)) ([Σ]κρειβώνις)

**Σκύθας**
LAKONIA:
—SPARTA: (1) v/iv BC X., HG iii 4. 20; Plu., Ages. 16 (Poralla² 668) (-ης)
SICILY:
—KAMARINA: (2) s. v BC Dubois, IGDS 119, 7 (Arena, Iscr. Sic. II 145; Cordano, 'Camarina VII' 55) ([Σ]κύθας)

**Σκυθῖνος**
AIGINA: (1) ?iv BC IG iv (1) 155; (2) ii BC SEG XI 17
AITOLIA:
—THERMOS*: (3) s. iii BC IG ix (1)² (1) 60 II, 20
ARGOLIS:
—EPIDAUROS*: (4) c. 370-365 BC Peek, IAEpid 52 A, 44; (5) c. 290-270 BC IG iv (1)² 109 III, 144
LAKONIA:
—TAINARON-KAINEPOLIS: (6) 198-211 AD SEG XXIII 199, 19 (Γ. Ἰούλ. Σκυθεῖνος)

**Σκύθος**
EPIROS:
—DODONA*: (1) hell. PAE 1955, p. 171 no. a (SEG XIX 428) (n. pr.?)

**Σκυλακίδας**
ARGOLIS:
—EPIDAUROS:
——Alamais: (1) c. 310-300 BC IG iv (1)² 114, 14 ([Σ]κυλακίδας)


**Σκύλαξ**
ARGOLIS:
—EPIDAUROS*: (1) c. 370-365 BC Peek, IAEpid 52 A, 11 (Σκύλα[ξ])
KERKYRA: (2) ?ii-i BC IG IX (1) 801 (tile)
S. ITALY: (3) m. i AD CIG 7258; Vollenweider, Steinschneidekunst p. 79; p. 123 pl. 92
S. ITALY (CAMPANIA):
—POMPEII: (4) i BC-i AD CIL x 926 (Castrèn 222. 11) (Lat. Q. Lollius Scylax: s. Ἀντιοχίς)

**Σκύλλα**
AITOLIA:
—KALYDON?: (1) c. 250 BC FD III (3) 149, 1 (d. Διοκλῆς)

**Σκύλων**
ACHAIA:
—PATRAI: (1) m. iii BC IG v (2) 368, 60 (f. Λάκων)

**Σκυμνίς**
S. ITALY (CAMPANIA):
—POMPEII: (1) i BC-i AD CIL IV 10182 b; Gnomon 45 (1973) p. 276 (Lat. Scymnis); (2) 70-79 AD CIL IV 7658; Mouritsen p. 109 (date) (Lat. Scymnis)

**Σκύμνος**
ARGOLIS:
—EPIDAUROS: (1) iii/ii BC Peek, NIEpid 15, 13 ([Σκ]ύμνος?: f. Εὔαρχος)
S. ITALY (CALABRIA):
—TARAS-TARENTUM: (2) 324 BC Berve 713 (Stephanis 2285)
S. ITALY (CAMPANIA):
—DIKAIARCHIA-PUTEOLI: (3) ?i-ii AD CIL x 2274 (Lat. Ti. Claudius Scymnus: s. Καλλιγένης)
—NEAPOLIS: (4) i BC/i AD INap 161 (sculptor)
S. ITALY (LUCANIA):
—HYELE-VELIA: (5) imp. PdelP 25 (1970) p. 266 no. 12 (Lat. Terentius Scymnus)
SICILY:
—SYRACUSE: (6) i BC-i AD? IG XIV 12

**Σκυρθάνας**
ILLYRIA:
—EPIDAMNOS-DYRRHACHION: (1) c. 250-50 BC BMC Thessaly p. 76 no. 166; Unp. (Paris, BN) 267 (coin) (pryt.); (2) ii-i BC IDyrrh 557 (tiles); (3) hell.-imp. ib. 118 (f. Ἀριστήν)

**Σκύρων**
MESSENIA:
—MESSENE: (1) 221 BC Plb. iv 4. 3-4; 7

**Σκύτας**
AITOLIA?: (1) s. iv BC Ét. Thas. 3 p. 136 no. 17 (f. Λύκων)
SICILY:
—GELA-PHINTIAS: (2) f. v BC Dubois, IGDS 148 (vase) (Arena, Iscr. Sic. II 22)

**Σμαραγδίς**
S. ITALY (CALABRIA):
—RUDIAE: (1) ii AD CIL IX 29 (Susini, Fonti Salento p. 117 no. 57) (Lat. Marcia Zmaragdis)
S. ITALY (CAMPANIA):
—DIKAIARCHIA-PUTEOLI: (2) imp. CIL x 2410 (Lat. Fadia Zmaragdis)
—MISENUM: (3) imp. AJPh 30 (1909) p. 168 no. 19 (Lat. Novellia Ismaragdis)

**Σμάραγδος**
ARGOLIS:
—EPIDAUROS: (1) i-ii AD IG iv (1)² 487 (I f. Σμάραγδος II); (2) ~ ib. (Ζμά-: II s. Σμάραγδος I)
ILLYRIA:
—APOLLONIA: (3) imp. IApoll 243


S. ITALY (CAMPANIA):
—DIKAIARCHIA-PUTEOLI: (4) imp. CIL x 1959 (Lat. M. Perpernius Zmaragdus); (5) ~ ib. 3026 (Lat. Truttedius Zmaracdus); (6) ?ii AD ib. 2442 (Lat. T. Flavius Smaragdus)
—POMPEII: (7) i BC-i AD ib. IV 9153 (Lat. Zmaragdus)
SICILY:
—THERMAI HIMERAIAI: (8) imp. Eph. Ep. VIII 707 (ILat. Term. Imer. 152) (Lat. C. Trebonius Zmaragdus: f. Trebonia Modia)

**Σμίκρης**
ARKADIA: (1) 401 BC X., An. vi 3. 4-5

**Σμικρίνας**
S. ITALY (CALABRIA):
—TARAS-TARENTUM: (1) 352 BC Moretti, Olymp. 436 (Σμικρίνας, Μικρίνας—Afric.)

**Σμίκρος**
AIGINA: (1) v BC BMI 947 (SEG XLI 1708 (fals.?))

**Σμικυθίων**
KORINTHIA:
—KORINTH: (1) f. v BC Corinth XVIII (1) p. 102 no. 159 (vase) (-ōν)

**Σμίκων**
AIGINA: (1) iv-iii BC IG IV (1) 158

**Σμῖλις**
AIGINA: (1) f. vi BC RE (-); Overbeck 340-4; Alt-Ägina II (2) pp. 12-13 (Σκέλμις—Call. fr. 100: s. Εὐκλείδας: sculptor)

**Σμινδυρίδας**
S. ITALY (BRUTTIUM):
—SYBARIS-THOURIOI-COPIAE: (1) f. vi BC RE Supplbd. 10 (-) (s. Ἱπποκράτης)

**Σμίνθις**
ARKADIA:
—MEGALOPOLIS: (1) 369-361 BC IG v (2) 1, 29; Tod, GHI II 132 (date)

**Σμύρνα**
ARGOLIS:
—ARGOS: (1) imp. IG IV (1) 620, 3, 8 (Μαινία Σ.: d. Τίτος)

**Σμυρναία**
ARGOLIS:
—HERMIONE: (1) imp. ib. 723 ([Σμ]υρναία: d. Λεοντίδας)

**Σμύρναος**
ARGOLIS:
—EPIDAUROS: (1) ii-iii AD Peek, IAEpid 187 (s. Μυσ—)

**Σμύρνη**
S. ITALY (BRUTTIUM):
—HIPPONION-VIBO VALENTIA: (1) imp. CIL x 89 (Lat. Zmyrne); (2) ~ Rend. Pont. 60 (1987-8) p. 273 no. 16 (Lat. Stabia Zmyrne)
S. ITALY (CAMPANIA):
—DIKAIARCHIA-PUTEOLI: (3) imp. CIL x 3094 (Lat. Vettena Zmyrna)
—POMPEII: (4) i BC-i AD ib. IV 7221 (Lat. Ismurna); (5) 70-79 AD ib. 7863; 7864; Mouritsen pp. 109-12 (date) (Lat. Zmurina)

**Σοαίνας**
ARGOLIS:
—ARGOS: (1) 337-328 BC CID II 74 I, 72; 76 II, 21; 121 III, 12 (f. Σώδαμος)

**Σοΐδας**
LAKONIA:
—SPARTA: (1) c. 30-20 BC IG v (1) 211, 37 (Bradford (-)) (f. Φιλόφρων)
MESSENIA:
—KORONE: (2) 246 AD IG v (1) 1398, 56 (Αὐρ. Σο[ΐδ]ας)

**Σοϊκράτης**
ARGOLIS:
—ARGOS: (1) ii-i BC *Mnem.* NS 47 (1919) p. 165 no. 10, 1 (s. *Μένανδρος*)

**Σοΐλος**
ARKADIA:
—TEGEA: (1) ?s. iv BC *IG* v (2) 39, 3

**Σοϊξιάδας**
LAKONIA:
—SPARTA: (1) c. 50-25 BC ib. v (1) 254 (*Artemis Orthia* p. 355 no. 141; Bradford (1)) (s. *Ἀρικράτης*) ?= (2); (2) s. i BC *IG* v (1) 133, 2 (Bradford (2)) ?= (3) (1); (3) c. 25-1 BC *IG* v (1) 212, 34 (Bradford (3)) (f. *Στράτιος*) ?= (2)

**Σοϊξίας**
PELOPONNESE?: (1) 11 AD *PAE* 1992, p. 72 B, 9 (s. *Εὔβουλος*)

**Σοϊξίνικος**
MESSENIA:
—THOURIA: (1) f. ii BC *SEG* XI 972, 31 (s. *Δαμίσκος*)

**Σοΐξιππος**
MESSENIA:
—ABIA: (1) i BC/i AD *IG* v (1) 1353 (f. *Λυσαρχίς*)
—MESSENE: (2) f. iii BC *PAE* 1991, p. 99 no. 7, 27 ?= (3); (3) ~ ib. p. 100 no. 8, 1 (*Σωΐξιππος*—ed.) ?= (2)

**Σόϊξις**
MESSENE: (1) s. ii BC *SEG* XLI 341, 12 (f. *Αἰνησίας*)

**Σοϊξιτέλης**
LAKONIA:
—SPARTA: (1) c. 100-125 AD *IG* v (1) 137, 13, 17 (Bradford (1)) (s. *Εὔδαμος*) ?= (2); (2) c. 110 AD *IG* v (1) 99, 4 (Bradford (2)) ?= (1); (3) c. 125-150 AD *IG* v (1) 488, 6 (Bradford (3)) (f. *Ἐτυμοκλήδεια*)
MESSENIA:
—MESSENE: (4) iii BC *SEG* XXIII 209, 11

**Σοΐων**
LAKONIA:
—SPARTA: (1) iii BC ib. XL 348 B, 2

**Σόλειος**
AIGINA?: (1) f. v BC Schöne, *Mus. Bocchi* 513; *Riv. Stor. Antichità* 4 (1974) p. 4 pl. 1d (*Σολείδ* (gen.))

**Σολόγας**
LAKONIA:
—SPARTA: (1) 403-399 BC *ID* 87 b, 13 (Poralla² 669)

**Σολομῶν**
ARGOLIS:
—ARGOS: (1) byz. *BCH* 31 (1907) p. 184; cf. *TMByz* 9 (1985) p. 370 no. 113 (Jew)
KORINTHIA:
—KORINTH: (2) byz. *Corinth* VIII (3) 618; cf. *TMByz* 9 (1985) p. 366 no. 74 (*Σολομῶ[ν]*)

**Σόλων**
ARKADIA:
—MANTINEIA-ANTIGONEIA: (1) ii-iii AD *IG* v (2) 275, 9 (f. *Οἰκοδεσποινιανός*)
EPIROS:
—AMBRAKIA: (2) ii-i BC *AE* 1910, p. 397; cf. *AAA* 4 (1971) pp. 337 f.; cf. *SEG* XLII 543 (f. *Νίκανδρος*)
MESSENIA:
—THOURIA: (3) ii/i BC *IG* v (1) 1384, 9 (s. *Νικώνυμος*)

S. ITALY (CALABRIA):
—TARAS-TARENTUM: (4) hell.? ib. XIV 2406. 73 (*RA* 1932 (1), p. 40 no. 40 (loomweight))
S. ITALY (CAMPANIA):
—POMPEII: (5) i BC-i AD Siviero, *Ori e Ambre* 378 (ring)
SICILY:
—KENTORIPA: (6) iii AD *NScav* 1907, p. 494

**Σόος**
ARGOLIS:
—EPIDAUROS*: (1) c. 370-365 BC Peek, *IAEpid* 52 B, 24
LAKONIA:
—SPARTA: (2) her. *RE* (-) (Poralla² 670) (s. *Προκλῆς*, f. *Εὐρυφῶν*: king/dub.)

**Σόρδις**
KORINTHIA:
—KORINTH: (1) ?vi BC *IG* IV (1) 318 (pinax)

**Σόσαννα**
S. ITALY (CALABRIA):
—TARAS-TARENTUM*: (1) byz. *JIWE* I 118 (*CIJ* I 627) (Jew)

**Σοσμήνις**
SICILY:
—SYRACUSE: (1) iii-v AD Strazzulla 208

**Σόσσα**
SICILY: (1) iii-v AD *Riv. Arch. Crist.* 17 (1940) p. 50

**Σοσσία**
SICILY:
—KATANE: (1) imp. *IG* XIV 503 (*Πετρωνία Σ.*: m. *Χία*)

**Σόσσις**
SICILY:
—KATANE: (1) imp. ib. (*Κοΰντος Σ.*: f. *Χία*)

**Σουκκεσσός**
EPIROS:
—NIKOPOLIS: (1) imp. *Wiss. Mitth. Bosn.* 4 (1896) p. 390 no. 9 (Sarikakis 149) (*Σουκεσός*)
S. ITALY (CAMPANIA):
—NEAPOLIS: (2) imp. *IG* XIV 810 (*INap* 163); cf. Leiwo p. 106 no. 71
SICILY:
—TAUROMENION: (3) iii-v AD Ferrua, *NG* 488 ([*Σο*]*υκεσ*[*σός*])

**Σουσᾶς**
MESSENIA:
—MESSENE: (1) i BC-i AD *IG* v (1) 1434, 7 (*Κόϊντος Αὐφίδιος Σ.*: s. *Σπόριος*)

**Σόφα**
KORINTHIA:
—KORINTH: (1) iv/iii BC *SEG* XXII 209 (Lazzarini 351)

**Σοφαίνετος**
ARKADIA:
—STYMPHALOS: (1) 401 BC *RE* (-)

**Σοφαρχίς**
MESSENIA:
—MESSENE: (1) i/ii AD *SEG* XXIII 221 (m. *Τιμαρέτα*)

**Σόφας**
SICILY:
—AKRAGAS: (1) v BC Manganaro, *QUCC* forthcoming no. 3 (*Σόφα, Σοφᾶς* (n. pr.?))

**Σόφη**
ILLYRIA:
—EPIDAMNOS-DYRRHACHION: (1) ii AD *AEp* 1978, no. 760 (Lat. Aelia Sope: m. Sentius Restitutus)

S. ITALY (APULIA):
—CANUSIUM: (2) imp. *Epig. Rom. di Canosa* 46 (Lat. Sophe)
—LUCERIA: (3) imp. *Rend. Linc.* 24 (1969) p. 27 no. 9 a (Lat. Aemilia Sope)
S. ITALY (CAMPANIA):
—DIKAIARCHIA-PUTEOLI*: (4) imp. *CIL* x 2826, 10 (Lat. -nia Sophe: freed.)
—POMPEII: (5) i BC-i AD ib. IV 5095; 10013 (Lat. Sope)

**Σοφία**
ACHAIA:
—PATRAI: (1) ii-i BC *Achaean Grave Stelai* 19 (d. *Εὐθυκράτης*)
S. ITALY (CAMPANIA):
—MISENUM*: (2) imp. *CIL* x 3674 (Lat. Aemilia Sofia); (3) f. i AD *Epigraphica* 34 (1972) p. 141 (Lat. Iulia Sophia: freed.)
SICILY:
—KATANE: (4) iii-v AD *IG* XIV 552 (Agnello 56; Wessel 861); cf. *Riv. Arch. Crist.* 18 (1941) p. 239 no. 134
—KENTORIPA: (5) imp. *Riv. Stor. Antica* 5 (1900-1) p. 49 no. 16 (Lat. Sophia)
—SYRACUSE: (6) iii-v AD *IG* XIV 19; cf. Ferrua, *NG* 356

**Σοφιδόι**
LAKONIA:
—PYRRHICHOS: (1) iv-iii BC *IG* v (1) 1283

**Σόφιος**
ILLYRIA:
—EPIDAMNOS-DYRRHACHION: (1) c. 250-50 BC Ceka, *Probleme* p. 152 no. 63 (coin) (pryt.) ?= (2); (2) ~ Maier 354 (coin) (Ceka 327; 375) (pryt.) ?= (1)
KERKYRA: (3) hell. *IG* IX (1) 895 (s. *Σοφοκλῆς*, f. *Λαμία*)
MESSENIA:
—MESSENE: (4) s. iv BC Moretti, *Olymp.* 496; cf. Ebert, *Gr. Sieg.* 51; *CEG* II 823
—THOURIA: (5) f. ii BC *SEG* XI 972, 32 (s. *Ἐχέδαμος*)
SICILY: (6) hell.-imp. Manganaro, *QUCC* forthcoming no. 69

**Σοφοκλῆς**
ELIS:
—OLYMPIA*: (1) s. iv BC *IvOl* 229; 639; 640; *RE* (7) (sculptor)
EPIROS:
—AMBRAKIA: (2) ii-i BC *CIG* 1798
—BOUTHROTOS (PRASAIBOI):
——Bouthrotioi: (3) a. 163 BC *IBouthrot* 59, 7-8 (*SEG* XXXVIII 510) (s. *Θεμιστοκλῆς*)
——PRASAIBOI: (4) a. 163 BC *IBouthrot* 92, 6 (s. *Θεμίσων*)
KERKYRA: (5) hell. *IG* IX (1) 895 (f. *Σόφιος*)
MESSENIA:
—MESSENE: (6) c. 223 BC ib. IX (1)² (1) 31, 36 (s. *Ἀριστοκράτης*)

**Σοφόνικος**
MESSENIA:
—MESSENE: (1) f. iii BC *SEG* XLI 342, 11; cf. *PAE* 1991, p. 100 no. 8

**Σόφος**
MESSENIA:
—MESSENE: (1) 126 AD *IG* v (1) 1469, 6; cf. *SEG* XL 366
S. ITALY (CAMPANIA):
—POMPEII: (2) i BC-i AD *CIL* IV 1244 (Lat. Sophus)

**Σόφων**
ACHAIA:
—TRITAIA: (1) iii-ii BC *Achaean Grave Stelai* 6 (*Σόφων*—lap.: s. *Θρασύβουλος*)
AKARNANIA: (2) iv/iii BC *RE* (-); *CAF* 3 p. 296 fr. 1, 1; p. 327 fr. 4
ELIS: (3) i BC *SEG* XV 255 (f. *Λασθένης*); (4) 28-24 BC *IvOl* 64, 5, 27 (s. *Λύκος*, ?f. *Ἀλεξᾶς*: N.); (5) 57-61 AD ib. 79, 3 (I f. *Σόφων* II ὁ

καὶ Λυκίσκος); **(6)** ~ ib. l. 3, [7] ([Σόφω]ν ὁ καὶ
Λυκίσκος: II s. Σόφων I, ?f. Σόφων III); **(7)** ~
ib. l. 7 (III ?s. Σόφων II ὁ καὶ Λυκίσκος) ?=
*(8)*; **(8)** 85 AD *EA* 1905, p. 255 no. 1, 11 (s.
Λυκίσκος) ?= *(7)*; **(9)** f. ii AD *IvOl* 92, 10 (s.
Νίγερ) ?= *(10)*; **(10)** ~ ib. l. 22 (?f. Σύντροφος)
?= *(9)*; **(11)** 113-117 AD ib. 91, 10, 20 (s. Λυ-
κάων, ?f. Ἐπαφρόδιτος); **(12)** c. 201-213 AD ib.
107, [13]; 110, 21 (f. Αὐρ. Ἀλφειός)
MESSENIA:
—KYPARISSIA: **(13)** m. iii BC *IG* IV (1)² 96,
68 (Perlman E.3); Perlman p. 63 f. (date)
(Σό[φ]ων, Σό[λ]ων?: f. Ἀριστόνικος)
S. ITALY (LUCANIA): **(14)** f. iv BC *LCS* p. 72
no. 365 (vase) (n. pr.?)
—ATINA LUCANA: **(15)** imp. *IItal* III (1) 179
(Lat. Allidius Sopo: s. Σοφωνιανός, Κλαδίσκη)

**Σοφωνιανός**
S. ITALY (LUCANIA):
—ATINA LUCANA: **(1)** imp. ib. (Lat. Sopo-
nianus: f. Σόφων, Allidius Epulianus, Καλύβη)

**Σπάρτη**
KORINTHIA:
—KORINTH: **(1)** byz. *Corinth* VIII (1) 151
([Σπ]άρτη?)

**Σπαρτιάτης**
LAKONIA:
—SPARTA: **(1)** c. 105-115 AD *IG* V (1) 42, 18;
*SEG* XI 540, 3 (Bradford (1)) (s. Δαμάριστος);
**(2)** c. 140-145 AD *IG* V (1) 1314, 37 (n. pr.?);
**(3)** c. 140-160 AD ib. 112, 7; *SEG* XI 585, 1;
XXX 410, 9; XXXIV 307, [5] (Bradford (2)) (s.
Σωσίδαμος); **(4)** c. 230-250 AD *IG* V (1) 539, 4
(Bradford (4)) (I f. Μ. Αὐρ. Σπαρτιάτης II); **(5)**
~ *IG* V (1) 539, 4; *BSA* 79 (1984) pp. 276 n.
75 (ident.); 285 no. 16 (date) (Bradford (3))
(Μ. Αὐρ. Σ.: II s. Σπαρτιάτης I, ?f. Συμφώ)

**Σπαρτιατικός**
LAKONIA:
—SPARTA: **(1)** m. i AD *RE* (-) (Poralla² 671;
Bradford (4)) (Γ. Ἰούλ. Σ.: s. Γ. Ἰούλ. Λάκων); **(2)** i/ii AD *IG* V (1) 471, 2; *SEG* XI
510, 1; *BSA* 80 (1985) pp. 194; 200-1; 211-
12 (Bradford (5); (6)) (Π. Μέμμιος Σ.: I ?f.
Π. Μέμμιος Σπαρτιατικός II, Π. Μέμμιος Λάκων); **(3)** c. 100 AD *SEG* XI 510, 1 (Bradford
(5)); **(4)** ii AD *IG* V (1) 165 (Bradford (6))
(Σπαρτιατι[κός]); **(5)** f. ii AD *IG* V (1) 65, 18;
71 III, 1; 85, 3; 484, 2; *BSA* 80 (1985) pp.
194; 212 (ident., stemma); cf. Bradford (6)
(Π. Μέμμιος Σ.: II ?s. Π. Μέμμιος Σπαρτιατικός I, ?f. Π. Μέμμιος Εὔδαμος); **(6)** c. 150-220
AD *FD* III (1) 543; *IG* V (1) 500; 525, 9; 527,
13; 590, 11; *BSA* 80 (1985) pp. 225; 235-8
(ident., stemma) (Bradford (1); (8); (10)) (Τιβ.
Κλ. Σ.: s. Τιβ. Κλ. Βρασίδας, f. Τιβ. Κλ. Ἀριστοτέλης, Τιβ. Κλ. Εὔδαμος); **(7)** c. 212-235 AD
*IG* V (1) 554, 13; *BSA* 79 (1984) pp. 283-4
no. 6 (date); 80 (1985) pp. 194; 213 (ident.,
stemma) (Bradford (3)) (s. Π. Μέμμιος Εὔδαμος); **(8)** c. 225-250 AD *IG* V (1) 540; *BSA*
79 (1984) pp. 276-7 (date) (Bradford (9)) (f.
Χαρίσιον) ?= *(9)*; **(9)** c. 230-240 AD *IG* V (1)
312, 3 (*Artemis Orthia* p. 333 no. 68); *BSA*
79 (1984) pp. 284-5 no. 15 (date); 80 (1985)
pp. 194; 211 (ident., date) (Bradford (2)) (Π.
Μέμμιος Σπαρτιατικός: s. Π. Μέμμιος Δαμάρης)
?= *(8)*

**Σπατάλη**
S. ITALY (CAMPANIA):
—STABIAE: **(1)** imp. *Eph. Ep.* VIII 310 (Lat.
Volcasia S[p]a[t]ale: m. L. Cassius Kapito-
nianus)

**Σπάταλος**
LAKONIA:
—SPARTA: **(1)** f. iii AD *IG* V (1) 535, 2; *BSA*
79 (1984) p. 285 no. 19 (Bradford (-)) (Σέξ.
Πομπ. Σ.: s. Ἀγαθοκλῆς)
MESSENIA:
—MESSENE: **(2)** 192 AD *PAE* 1969, p. 104, 8 (s.
Νυμφόδοτος)
S. ITALY (CAMPANIA):
—POMPEII: **(3)** i BC-i AD *CIL* IV 1104 (Lat.
Spatalus); **(4)** ~ ib. 4742 (Lat. Spatalus)

**Σπεδιανός**
ARKADIA:
—MEGALOPOLIS: **(1)** ii AD *IG* V (2) 463 (Μ. Τά-
διος Σ.: s. Μ. Τάδιος Τιμοκράτης, f. Μ. Τάδιος
Τιμοκράτης, Μ. Τάδιος Σωτήριχος)

**Σπείρων**
S. ITALY (CAMPANIA):
—POMPEII: **(1)** i BC *Impegno per Pompeii* 7 OS
(Lat. Spiron)

**Σπένδιος**
S. ITALY (CAMPANIA)*: **(1)** m. iii BC *RE* (-)
(slave)

**Σπένδουσα**
EPIROS:
—NIKOPOLIS: **(1)** imp. *AD* 26 (1971) Chron. p.
335
S. ITALY (CAMPANIA):
—POMPEII: **(2)** i BC-i AD *CIL* IV 1403 (Lat.
Spendusa); **(3)** ~ ib. 4184; 7086 (Lat. Spen-
dusa); **(4)** ~ ib. 4639 (Lat. Spendusa)

**Σπένδων**
ARGOLIS:
—ARGOS: **(1)** ii/iii AD *IG* IV (1) 594, 2 (s. Ζώπυ-
ρος)
ARKADIA:
—TEGEA: **(2)** ii AD ib. v (2) 55, 27 (s. Ἐπικτᾶς)
ELIS: **(3)** m. i AD *IvOl* 78, 3 (s. Θηβ—)
LAKONIA: **(4)** arch.? Plu., *Lyc.* 28 (Poralla² 672)
—SPARTA: **(5)** f. ii AD *SEG* XI 491, 1 (Bradford
(3)) (f. Δαμοκράτης); **(6)** ?m. ii AD *IG* V (1) 47,
1 (Bradford (5)) (I f. Σπένδων II); **(7)** ~ *IG* V
(1) 47, 1 (Bradford (2)) (II s. Σπένδων I); **(8)**
c. 175-200 AD *IG* V (1) 129, 2 (Bradford (1))
(s. Σωσίνικος)
——Neopolitai: **(9)** c. 175 AD *IG* V (1) 680, 13
(Bradford (4)) (f. Γαληνός)
S. ITALY (CAMPANIA):
—DIKAIARCHIA-PUTEOLI: **(10)** imp. *CIL* X
2721 (Lat. C. Cartonius Spendon)
—HERCULANEUM: **(11)** i BC-i AD ib. 1403 c I, 6
(Lat. Ti. Acutius Spendon); **(12)** 69 AD *PdelP*
8 (1953) p. 461 no. 52 (*Cron. Erc.* 23 (1993)
pp. 115-9) (Lat. C. Iulius Spendon); **(13)** ~
ib. p. 116 no. 2 II 4 (Lat. C. Iulius Spendo)
—HERCULANEUM*: **(14)** m. i AD ib. 7 (1977) p.
117 C b, 16 (Lat. M. Ofillius Spendo: freed.)

**Σπεράντιος**
SICILY:
—SYRACUSE: **(1)** iii-v AD Strazzulla 214 (Barreca
337) (Σπη-)

**Σπερθίας**
LAKONIA:
—SPARTA: **(1)** f. v BC Hdt. vii 134. 2; 137; Plu.,
*Mor.* 235 F; 815 E; Stob. vii 70 (Poralla²
673) (Σπερθίης—Hdt., Σπέρτις, Σπέρχις—Plu.,
Σπέρχης—Stob.: s. Ἀνήριστος, f. Ἀνήριστος)

**Σπερχειός**
ELIS?: **(1)** 233 AD *IvOl* 482

**Σπεύδων**
S. ITALY (CAMPANIA):
—HERCULANEUM: **(1)** m. i AD *PdelP* 3 (1948) p.
170 no. 15 (Lat. M. Calatorius Speudon)

**Σπίνθαρος**
ACHAIA:
—PATRAI: **(1)** imp. *CIL* III 6096 (Lat. T. Lol-
lius Spintharus)
AKARNANIA:
—PHOITIAI: **(2)** c. 425-400 BC *IG* IX (1)² (2)
390, 9 (s. Σιτύλος)
KORINTHIA:
—KORINTH: **(3)** ?iv BC *RE* (2)
S. ITALY (CALABRIA):
—TARAS-TARENTUM: **(4)** v/iv BC *Suda* A 3927;
Ael., *NA* ii 11; Iamb., *VP* 197; Wehrli,
*Schule Arist.* ii fr. 54 a; fr. 59 (Μνασίας ὁ καὶ
Σ.: f. Ἀριστόξενος) ?= *(5)*; **(5)** iv BC Plu., *Mor.*
39 B; 592 F ?= *(4)*

**Σπινθήρ**
ARGOLIS:
—EPIDAUROS*: **(1)** c. 370-365 BC Peek, *IAEpid*
52 B, 56 (Σπι(ν)θ[ήρ]); **(2)** c. 335-325 BC *IG*
IV (1)² 106 I, 69

**Σπινθήρας**
ARGOLIS:
—ARGOS: **(1)** c. 458 BC ib. I³ 1149, 92
([Σ]πινθέρας)

**Σπόνδη**
ACHAIA:
—PATRAI: **(1)** iii-iv AD *SEG* XXIV 330

**Σπόνδος?**
ARGOLIS:
—EPIDAUROS: **(1)** 149 AD Peek, *IAEpid* 157
([Σπ]όνδος: s. Διοπείθης)

**Σπορίδας**
SICILY:
—KATANE: **(1)** imp. *CIL* X 7093 (Lat. Sporidas)

**Σπόριος**
MESSENIA:
—MESSENE: **(1)** i BC-i AD *IG* V (1) 1434, 7 (f.
Κόϊντος Αὐφίδιος Σουσᾶς)

**Σπόρος**
ARGOLIS:
—EPIDAUROS: **(1)** III AD *SEG* XXXIX 358, 6 (s.
Ἀλεξᾶς)
—HERMIONE: **(2)** i BC-i AD? *IG* IV (1) 734, 9 (f.
Στρατονίκα)
ARKADIA:
—TEGEA: **(3)** ii AD ib. v (2) 54, 9
LAKONIA:
—SPARTA: **(4)** imp. ib. v (1) 771 (Bradford (-))
S. ITALY (CAMPANIA):
—DIKAIARCHIA-PUTEOLI: **(5)** 48 AD Camodeca,
*L'Archivio Puteolano* I p. 106 no. 2 (Lat. Ti.
Iulius Sporus)
—POMPEII: **(6)** i BC-i AD *CIL* IV 5310; **(7)** ~ ib.
7355 (Lat. Sporus)
SICILY:
—SYRACUSE: **(8)** 356 AD ib. X 7167 (Strazzulla
419; Agnello 90); cf. *Riv. Arch. Crist.* 18
(1941) p. 190 no. 58 (Lat. Sporus)

**Σπούδη**
S. ITALY (CAMPANIA):
—POMPEII: **(1)** m. i AD *Impegno per Pompeii* 11
ES no. 5 (Castrèn 42. 21) (Lat. Arria Spude)

**Σπούδις**
ARGOLIS:
—EPIDAUROS?: **(1)** m. v BC *SEG* XXIV 274 (Laz-
zarini 941)

**Σπρίθιος**
ARGOLIS:
—EPIDAUROS:
——Dorimachis: **(1)** c. 220-200 BC *SEG* XI 414,
26 (Perlman E.5)

**Σπύριος**
S. ITALY (CAMPANIA):
—NEAPOLIS: **(1)** i BC/i AD *INap* 164, 1 ?= *(2)*;
**(2)** ~ ib. l. 2 ?= *(1)*

## Σπωσιανός
ACHAIA:
—PATRAI: (1) imp. *SEG* XXIX 424, 1, 6 (*Σπω-σιαῖος*—ed.)
KORINTHIA:
—KORINTH: (2) ii/iii AD *Ag.* VII pp. 92 no. 244; 94 no. 271; 98 nos. 313-4; *BM Lamps* 3 pp. 403 no. Q3241; 405 no. Q3256; *Corinth* IV (2) pp. 193 no. 599; 211 nos. 778-9; XVIII (2) pp. 28-32 nos. 20, 26, 30, 33, 37; *SEG* XXVII 35. 26 (lamps)

## Στάθμιος
ARKADIA:
—MANTINEIA-ANTIGONEIA: (1) c. 300-221 BC *IG* V (2) 323. 35 (tessera) (*Στάθμι*[*ος*]: f. *Τιμ*—)

## Στάϊος
S. ITALY (CAMPANIA):
—CAPREAE: (1) i BC-i AD? ib. XIV 901 (f. *Ταυρί-σκος*)

## Στάκτη
S. ITALY (CAMPANIA):
—DIKAIARCHIA-PUTEOLI: (1) imp. *CIL* X 3071 (Lat. Stacte)
—DIKAIARCHIA-PUTEOLI*: (2) imp. ib. 2648 (Lat. Larcia Stacte: d. *Χρήστη*: freed.); (3) ~ ib. 3071 (Lat. Valeria Stacte: freed.)
—PRETURO (MOD.): (4) imp. *NScav* 1928, p. 228 (Lat. Vibiedia Stacte: freed.)

## Στασέας
S. ITALY (CAMPANIA):
—NEAPOLIS: (1) ii/i BC *RE* (-)

## Στασίας
ARGOLIS:
—ARGOS: (1) c. 276 BC *TCam* 54, 8 (sculptor)
ARKADIA:
—TEGEA: (2) m. iv BC *IG* V (2) 6, 58; (3) iii BC ib. 109
SICILY:
—KAMARINA: (4) f. v BC Cordano, *Tessere Pubbliche* 39 (f. —*ας*)

## Στασικλῆς
ARGOLIS:
—TROIZEN: (1) iv BC *IG* IV (1) 749, 3 (*Σ*[*τα*]*σικλῆς*: f. *Χάρμος*)

## Στασίλας
ARKADIA:
—TEGEA: (1) ii BC ib. IV (1)² 226 (*Στ*[*α*]*σί*[*λ*]*ας*: s. *Πολίας*)

## Στασιμένης
ARGOLIS:
—EPIDAUROS*: (1) c. 335-325 BC ib. 108, 151, 157, 164, 168; 111, 8

## Στασίμη
SICILY:
—SYRACUSE: (1) iii-v AD Ferrua, *NG* 192

## Στάσιμος
S. ITALY (CAMPANIA):
—POMPEII: (1) c. 51-62 AD *CIL* IV 3340. 54, 15 (Castrèn 390. 6) (Lat. Statius Stasimus)
SICILY:
—SYRACUSE: (2) iii-v AD *Rend. Pont.* 22 (1946-7) p. 233 no. 23

## Στάσιππος
ARGOLIS:
—ARGOS: (1) ?205 BC *AE* 1936, Chron. p. 39 no. 211, 6 (f. *Πυρβαλίων*)
ARKADIA:
—TEGEA: (2) c. 370 BC *RE* (-)

## Στασίχορος
SICILY:
—LIPARA: (1) hell. *Meligunis-Lipara* 5 p. 69 T. 1994; cf. *SEG* XLI 796

## Στατία
ARKADIA:
—KLEITOR: (1) i-ii AD *IG* V (2) 372 (d. *Ἀριστό-πολις*)
S. ITALY (CAMPANIA):
—NEAPOLIS: (2) i BC *INap* 165; cf. Leiwo p. 83 no. 26 (d. *Μάμαρχος*)

## Στατιλία
SICILY:
—SYRACUSE: (1) iii-v AD Strazzulla 109 (Barreca 338)

## Στάτιος
KERKYRA: (1) imp. *IG* IX (1) 939
S. ITALY (CAMPANIA):
—NEAPOLIS: (2) ?i BC ib. XIV 812 (*INap* 169) (f. *Σωσιπάτρα*)
—NUCERIA ALFATERNA: (3) f. iii BC Unp. (Berlin, Staatl. Mus.); cf. Garrucci, *Monete dell'Italia Antica* 2 p. 168 pl. 116, 33 (coins)
S. ITALY (CAMPANIA)?: (4) iv-iii BC *CIG* 8493

## Σταυράκιος
S. ITALY (CAMPANIA):
—NOLA: (1) v-vi AD *CIL* X 1367 (Lat. Stauracius: f. Bonitus)

## Σταφίς
S. ITALY (CAMPANIA):
—POMPEII: (1) i BC-i AD ib. IV 1873; cf. p. 704 (Lat. Staphis)

## Σταφύλη
S. ITALY (APULIA):
—LARINUM*: (1) imp. ib. IX 6245 with Add. p. 695 (Lat. Gabbia Staphyle: freed.)
S. ITALY (CAMPANIA):
—DIKAIARCHIA-PUTEOLI: (2) imp. ib. X 2060 (Lat. Annia Stafyle); (3) ~ ib. 3143 (Lat. Staphile)
SICILY:
—SYRACUSE: (4) iii-v AD *NScav* 1907, p. 762 no. 23 (Barreca 318)

## Στάφυλος
S. ITALY (CAMPANIA):
—DIKAIARCHIA-PUTEOLI: (1) imp. *CIL* X 2803 (Lat. A. Ofillius Staphylus)
—HERCULANEUM: (2) m. i AD *PdelP* 3 (1948) p. 182 no. 30; 10 (1955) p. 453 no. 79; 83 (Lat. L. Opsius Staphylus)
—HERCULANEUM*: (3) m. i AD *Cron. Erc.* 7 (1977) p. 118 D, 10 (Lat. –llius Staphylus: freed.)
—POMPEII: (4) i BC-i AD *CIL* IV 2060 (Lat. Staphylus); (5) ~ ib. 4087; 4088 (Lat. Staphilus); (6) ~ ib. 4274 (Lat. Staphylus); (7) ~ *Römische Gräberstrassen* p. 216 f (Lat. L. Calventius Staphylus)
S. ITALY (LUCANIA):
—VOLCEI: (8) i AD *IItal* III (1) 112 (Lat. M. Iulius Staphylus)

## Στάχυς
ELIS: (1) 233 AD *IvOl* 116, 7, 11; cf. *ZPE* 99 (1993) p. 232 (stemma) (*Λ. Βετληνὸς Σ.*: f. *Νή-φων*: *Φ.*)
KORINTHIA:
—KORINTH: (2) 215 BC *PP* 4101; *SB* 6303, 6 etc. (s. *Θεοκλῆς*)
S. ITALY (APULIA):
—CANUSIUM: (3) 223 AD *Epig. Rom. di Canosa* 35 IV, 4 (*CIL* IX 338) (Lat. C. Iulius Stachys)

## S. ITALY (CAMPANIA):
—POMPEII: (4) i BC-i AD ib. IV 1936; cf. p. 213 (Lat. Stacus)

## Στερτίνιος
S. ITALY (CAMPANIA):
—BAIAI: (1) ii AD *RE* (1)

## Στεφανᾶς
KORINTHIA:
—KORINTH: (1) c. 50 AD *1 Ep. Cor.* 1. 16; 16. 15-17

## Στεφάνη
SICILY:
—SYRACUSE: (1) iii-v AD *IG* XIV 145 (Strazzulla 86)

## Στεφανηφόρος
SICILY:
—SYRACUSE: (1) iii AD *IGLMP* 108 (*Κ. Κορνι-φίκι*(*ος*) *Σ.*)

## Στεφανικός
S. ITALY (CAMPANIA):
—POMPEII: (1) c. 51-62 AD *CIL* IV 3340. 90, 1; 107, 8 (Castrèn 227. 13) (Lat. Lucretius Stephanicus)

## Στεφάνιος
SICILY:
—KATANE: (1) imp. *IG* XIV 506

## Στεφανίς
ARGOLIS:
—ARGOS: (1) 536 AD Unp. (Oikonomou-Laniado) (d. *Δημήτριος*, *Μυρωνίς*)
KORINTHIA:
—KORINTH: (2) byz. *Corinth* VIII (1) 147, 5; cf. *TMByz* 9 (1985) p. 360 no. 11
MESSENIA:
—PHARAI: (3) 30 AD *IG* V (1) 1359, 4 (d. *Ἀγα-θίας*)
S. ITALY (APULIA):
—HERDONIA: (4) f. iii *ZPE* 103 (1994) p. 162 no. 4 (Lat. Asinia Stephanis)
S. ITALY (CAMPANIA):
—DIKAIARCHIA-PUTEOLI: (5) ?i-ii AD *CIL* X 2613 (Lat. Iulia Stephanis: m. Ti. Iulius Felicissimus); (6) ?ii-iii AD ib. 3119 (Lat. Aurelia Stephan(i)s: d. *Στέφανος*)
—DIKAIARCHIA-PUTEOLI*: (7) ?i-ii AD ib. 2552 (Lat. Iulia Stephanis: freed.)

## Στεφανίων
ILLYRIA:
—EPIDAMNOS-DYRRHACHION: (1) ?i AD *AEp* 1978, no. 741 (Lat. L?. Caesius Stephanio)
S. ITALY (CAMPANIA):
—HERCULANEUM: (2) i BC-i AD *CIL* X 1403 d I, 16 (Lat. M. Nonius Stephanio)
—POMPEII: (3) i BC-i AD ib. IV 1114 (Lat. Stephanion)
SICILY:
—KATANE: (4) imp. ib. X 7089 (Lat. P. Sextilius Stephanio: s. Sextilius Severus)
—SYRACUSE: (5) imp.? *IG* XIV 2406. 76

## Στεφανοκλῆς
LAKONIA:
—SPARTA: (1) c. 30-20 BC ib. V (1) 211, 19 (Bradford (-)) (f. *Στέφανος*)

## Στέφανος
ACHAIA: (1) 159 BC Plb. XXXII 7. 1
ARGOLIS:
—EPIDAUROS: (2) 134 AD *IG* IV (1)² 384, 7 (s. *Εὔτυχος*)
ARKADIA:
—MANTINEIA-ANTIGONEIA: (3) c. 300-221 BC ib. V (2) 323. 100 (tessera) ([*Σ*]*τέφανος*: f. *Ἀγά-θαρχος*)
—TEGEA: (4) c. 365-335 BC ib. IV (1)² 103, 54
ELIS: (5) 245-249 AD *IvOl* 121, 12 (*Σόσσ*(*ιος*) *Σ.*: mantis/Klytiadai)

EPIROS: (6) iv/iii BC *IG* II² 8545
—BOUTHROTOS (PRASAIBOI): (7) a. 163 BC *IBouthrot* 39, 3 (*SEG* XXXVIII 498); *IBouthrot* 51, 28 (f. Ἀδυλώ)
—DODONA*: (8) ?iv BC *BCH* 80 (1956) p. 303 (f. Πλάτων)
ILLYRIA:
—APOLLONIA: (9) c. 250-50 BC Maier 48 (coin) (Ceka 99) (money.); (10) i BC Ceka, *Probleme* p. 139 no. 26 (coin) (pryt.)
—EPIDAMNOS-DYRRHACHION: (11) c. 250-50 BC Maier 196; 207; 318; 335; 343 (coin) (Ceka 377-83) (money.); (12) hell.-imp. *IDyrrh* 431 (f. Φιλέρως); (13) iii-iv AD ib. 60 (s. Εὐγένιος, Ὀλυμπία); (14) vi AD Agath. i 17
KERKYRA: (15) byz. *IG* IX (1) 717
KORINTHIA:
—KORINTH: (16) inc. *SEG* XXXI 297 (vase); (17) imp. *CIL* III 6099, 2 (Lat. Ti. Cl. Stephanus)
LAKONIA:
—SPARTA: (18) s. i BC *IG* V (1) 95, 11; 134, 5 (Bradford (15)) (I f. Στέφανος II); (19) ~ *IG* V (1) 95, 11; 134, 5 (Bradford (7)) (II s. Στέφανος I); (20) ~ *IG* V (1) 136, 4 (Bradford (2)) ([Σ]τέφανος: s. Ἀτ—); (21) c. 30-20 BC *IG* V (1) 211, 3 (Bradford (17)) (f. Τίμων); (22) ~ *IG* V (1) 211, 5 (Bradford (5)) (s. Σήριππος); (23) ~ *IG* V (1) 211, 19 (Bradford (6)) (s. Στεφανοκλῆς); (24) i BC/i AD *BSA* 89 (1994) pp. 433-4 no. 2, 4 (f. Νικοκράτης); (25) ?i AD *IG* V (1) 180, 9 (Στέφαν[ος]); (26) i-ii AD ib. 782 (Bradford (10)); (27) c. 1-10 AD *IG* V (1) 209, 28; *SEG* XXXV 331 (date) (Bradford (4)) (s. Φοιβίδας); (28) ?i/ii AD *IG* V (1) 187 (Στέφ[ανος]?); (29) c. 100 AD *SEG* XI 534, 2 (Bradford (12)) (f. Ἀγαθοκλῆς) ?= (31) (32); (30) c. 100-120 AD *SEG* XI 610, 4 (Bradford (3)) (s. Π—); (31) f. ii AD *SEG* XXXI 340, 2 (f. —κλῆς) ?= (29); (32) c. 115-140 AD *IG* V (1) 32 A, 1; 62, 5; *SEG* XI 547 a, [9]; 547 b, 5; 547 c, 2; 579, [8] (Bradford (13)) (f. Ἀγαθοκλῆς) ?= (29); (33) c. 150-160 AD *IG* V (1) 53, 22 (Bradford (1)) (s. Ἀνέγκλητος); (34) c. 175-200 AD *SEG* XI 503, 27 (Bradford (9)); (35) f. iii AD *IG* V (1) 303, 3 (*Artemis Orthia* pp. 327-8 no. 57); *BSA* 79 (1984) p. 283 no. 3 (Bradford (14)) (f. Νικηφόρος); (36) a. 212 AD *IG* V (1) 596, 11 (Bradford (16)) (I f. M. Αὐρ. Στέφανος II); (37) ~ *IG* V (1) 596, 11 (Bradford (8)) (M. Αὐρ. Σ.: II s. Στέφανος I); (38) c. 325-329 AD *SEG* XI 810, 6; *BSA* 79 (1984) p. 280 no. 15 (date) (Bradford (11)) (M. Αὐρ. Σ.)
MESSENIA:
—MESSENE: (39) c. 223 BC *IG* IX (1)² (1) 31, 35 (s. Κλεόστρατος); (40) ?f. i AD *PAE* 1992, p. 79, 9
—THOURIA: (41) ii-i BC *IG* V (1) 1385, 28 (s. Στράτων); (42) f. ii BC *SEG* XI 972, 78 (s. Πρᾶτις)
S. ITALY (BRUTTIUM):
—MONTALTO UFFUGO (MOD.): (43) ii-iii AD *NScav* 1939, p. 367 fig. 2 (Lat. L. Aurelius Stephanus)
S. ITALY (CAMPANIA):
—DIKAIARCHIA-PUTEOLI: (44) ?i-ii AD *CIL* X 2277 (Lat. Ti. Cl. Stephanus: f. Ἡράκλεια); (45) ?ii-iii AD ib. 3119 (Lat. L. Vitorius Stephanus: s. Vitoria Ianuaria, f. Στεφανίς)
—DIKAIARCHIA-PUTEOLI*: (46) imp. ib. 1921 (Lat. Stefanus: slave?); (47) ?i-ii AD ib. 2557, 6 (Lat. Iulius Stephanus: freed.)
—HERCULANEUM: (48) m. i AD *PdelP* 3 (1948) p. 171 no. 16; p. 182 no. 30; 8 (1953) p. 461 no. 50, 5; 16 (1961) p. 72 no. 102, 5 (Lat. C. Petronius Stephanus: II s. Στέφανος I); (49) ~ ib. 3 (1948) p. 182 no. 30 (Lat. C. Petronius Stephanus: I f. Στέφανος II); (50) ~ ib. 6 (1951) p. 224 no. 1 (Lat. C. Vibius Stephanus); (51) ~ *Cron. Erc.* 7 (1977) p. 116 B a, 6 (Lat. C. Petronius Steph[anus])

—HERCULANEUM*: (52) i BC-i AD *CIL* X 1403 g II, 38 (Lat. C. Petronius Stephanus: freed.)
—KYME: (53) 251 AD ib. 3699 (Lat. L. Ampius Stephanus)
—MISENUM: (54) imp. *AJA* 2 (1898) p. 395 no. 57 (Lat. M. Verius Stephanus); (55) ~ *Eph. Ep.* VIII 437 (Lat. C. Cascellius Stephanus)
—MISENUM*: (56) ?ii AD *CIL* X 3356 (Lat. M. Cocceius Stephanus)
—NEAPOLIS: (57) 535 AD Procop. v 8. 7 f.
—NOLA: (58) imp. *CIL* X 1332 (Lat. M. Valerius Stephanus); (59) byz. ib. 1381 (Lat. Stephanus); (60) ~ ib. 1382 (Lat. Stephanus)
—POMPEII: (61) i BC-i AD ib. IV 4804; (62) ~ ib. 6732 (Lat. Stephanus); (63) imp. *NScav* 1898, p. 500 (Castrèn 380. 1 (bronze)) (Lat. T. Siminius Stepanus); (64) ?55 AD *CIL* IV 3340. 18, 6 (Castrèn 158. 25) (Lat. M. Epidius Stephanus); (65) 70-79 AD *CIL* IV 7172; 7174; 7267; Mouritsen p. 111 (date) (Lat. Stephanus)
—POMPEII*: (66) ?i AD *NScav* 1939, p. 318 no. 465; 1946, p. 128 no. 409; 1948, (Castrèn 23. 18) (Lat. C. Alleius Stephanus: freed.)
—SURRENTUM: (67) imp. *St. Rom.* 2 (1914) p. 346 no. 4 = *NScav* 1928, p. 209 no. 10 (Lat. Stephanus: imp. freed.); (68) ?i-ii AD *St. Rom.* 2 (1914) p. 346 no. 17 = *NScav* 1928, p. 210 no. 16 (Lat. Ti. Claudius Stephanus)
S. ITALY (LUCANIA):
—METAPONTION: (69) byz.? ib. 1977, Suppl. p. 463 (vase)
—TEGIANUM: (70) imp. *IItal* III (1) 264 (*CIL* X 376) (Lat. Pompeius Stephanus)
SICILY:
—AKRAI: (71) 419 AD *IG* XIV 315 (Agnello 95; *Akrai* p. 169 no. 46)
—KATANE: (72) ?vi AD *Epigraphica* 51 (1989) pp. 174-5 no. 48 (Lat. Stephanus)
—SYRACUSE: (73) imp. *NScav* 1913, p. 268 (Lat. Stephan[us] Hostili[us]); (74) iii-v AD Strazzulla 175 (Στέφαν[ος], Στεφάν[η]); (75) ~ Ferrua, *NG* 212 (Lat. Istaefanus); (76) byz. *Epigraphica* 5-6 (1943-4) p. 93
—THERMAI HIMERAIAI*: (77) imp. *CIL* X 7433 (*ILat. Term. Imer.* 137) (Lat. Sex. Raecius Stephanus: freed.)

## Στησίχορος
S. ITALY (CAMPANIA)?: (1) imp. *IG* XIV 2414. 53 (tessera) ([Στ]ησίχορος)
SICILY:
—HIMERA?: (2) vii/vi BC *RE* (1); *PMGF* I testim. (or Sicily Matauros: Τεισίας Σ.?: ?s. Εὔφημος, Εὔφορβος, Εὐκλείδης, Εὐέτης); (3) f. iv BC *RE* (2)

## Στίαξ
ARGOLIS:
—EPIDAUROS: (1) c. 365-335 BC *IG* IV (1)² 103, 116, 118

## Στιβαδίων
SICILY:
—SYRACUSE: (1) iii-v AD ib. XIV 169 (Strazzulla 110; Wessel 1208)

## Στιβάς
S. ITALY (APULIA):
—LUCERIA: (1) imp. *CIL* IX 891 (Lat. Terentia Stibas)

## Στίβων
S. ITALY (CAMPANIA):
—STABIAE: (1) i AD *INap* 166

## Στίλπα
S. ITALY (CALABRIA):
—TARAS-TARENTUM: (1) iv/iii BC *IG* XIV 668 I, 8 (Landi, *DISMG* 194)

S. ITALY (LUCANIA):
—HERAKLEIA: (2) m. iv BC *Basilicata Antica* p. 99 (vase)

## Στίλπας
AKARNANIA:
—ANAKTORION: (1) ?ii/i BC *IG* IX (1)² (2) 232
ARKADIA:
—MANTINEIA-ANTIGONEIA: (2) c. 475-450 BC ib. V (2) 262, 8 (*IPArk* 8); *LSAG*² p. 216 no. 29 (date) (Στίλπας)
KORINTHIA:
—SIKYON: (3) 337-336 BC *CID* II 74 I, 75; 76 II, 24 (Skalet 291) (Στίλπου (gen.): f. Εὐάρμοστος)

## Στιλπίων
ARKADIA:
—TEGEA: (1) f. iii BC *IG* V (2) 35, 35 (f. Πεδάριτος)

## Στίλπυρος
ARKADIA:
—TEGEA:
——(Athaneatai): (1) iv/iii BC ib. 38, 18 (f. Καλλίας)

## Στίλπων
AKARNANIA:
—ECHINOS: (1) c. 325-315 BC *Hesp.* 57 (1988) p. 148 A, 25 (*SEG* XXXVI 331; cf. *Hesp.* 48 (1979) pp. 78 f. with pl. 22 c (s. Ὀλύμπιχος)
—PALAIROS: (2) ?iii BC *IG* IX (1)² (2) 542 ([Σ]τίλπων: ?f. Κλευμένης)
ARGOLIS:
—ARGOS: (3) c. 458 BC ib. I³ 1149, 15 (-πōν); (4) ii-i BC *Mnem.* NS 47 (1919) p. 164 no. 9, 6
—LEUKAS: (5) iii/ii BC *AD* 26 (1971) Chron. p. 353 no. 9
SICILY:
—KAMARINA?: (6) v/iv BC Manganaro, *PdelP* forthcoming no. 14 (Στί(λ)πων)

## Στίπακος
ARKADIA:
—TEGEA: (1) f. iii BC *SEG* XXXIII 319, 7 (f. Λάρχιππος)

## Στίπων
KORINTHIA:
—KORINTH: (1) vi BC *IG* IV (1) 319 (pinax) (-πōν)

## Στίχιος
S. ITALY (CAMPANIA):
—DIKAIARCHIA-PUTEOLI: (1) i AD *CIL* X 1735 (Lat. M. Annius Stichius)

## Στίχος
ARGOLIS:
—HERMIONE: (1) iii BC *IG* IV (1) 729 II, 18, 19 (f. Γηρίων, Σωσίων)

## Στοιχαῖς
S. ITALY (CALABRIA):
—RUDIAE: (1) imp. Susini, *Fonti Salento* p. 134 no. 80 (Lat. Stoichais)

## Στολιάδας
LEUKAS: (1) iii BC *AD* 26 (1971) Chron. p. 353 no. 4

## Στολίς
ACHAIA:
—PHARAI: (1) iii-ii BC *Achaean Grave Stelai* 44 (d. Περιγένης)

## Στόλος
ARKADIA:
—TEGEA: (1) ii AD *IG* V (2) 55, 33 (s. Γερμανός)
S. ITALY (APULIA):
—VENUSIA*: (2) i AD *Epigraphica* 35 (1973) p. 150 no. 12 (Lat. Q. Ovius Stolus: freed.)

## Στόλων

S. Italy (Campania):
—misenum*: (1) imp. CIL x 3547 (Lat. Sex. Bebius Stolo)
Sicily:
—panormos: (2) f. i ad RPC 1 p. 166 (Lat. P. Stolo)

## Στόμας

Aitolia: (1) ?a. 246 bc SGDI 2509, 2
—numenaieis: (2) iii bc L'Illyrie mérid. 1 p. 106 no. 1; cf. p. 97 (SEG xxxvii 435)
—philotaieis: (3) f. ii bc IG ix (1)² (1) 96, 22 (s. Ἀγήσων)
Argolis:
—troizen: (4) iv bc ib. iv (1) 764, 3 (f. Δέρκας)

## Στόμιος

Aitolia:
—konope-arsinoe: (1) ii bc SBBerlAk 1936, p. 360 no. 1, 10
Akarnania:
—alyzia: (2) m. iii bc IG v (2) 368, 18 (f. —λίας)
Elis: (3) f. iv bc Moretti, Olymp. 404
Epiros:
—argethia: (4) iv/iii bc Cabanes, L'Épire p. 544 no. 9, 2 (f. Θεόδωρος)

## Στόργη

S. Italy (Campania):
—neapolis: (1) i ad IG xiv 811 (INap 167) (Στλακκία Σ.)

## Στουδιῶσος

Sicily:
—kentoripa: (1) imp. Sic. Gymn. 16 (1963) p. 63; cf. MEFRA 106 (1994) p. 103

## Στόχασμος

S. Italy (Calabria):
—rudiae: (1) i bc-i ad Bernardini, Rudiae p. 107 (Susini, Fonti Salento p. 126 no. 70) (Lat. Stocasmus: f. Felix)

## Στράβαινος

Illyria:
—epidamnos-dyrrhachion: (1) hell.-imp. IDyrrh 411 (f. Τευταία)

## Στράβιος

Illyria:
—olympe: (1) s. iii bc SEG xxxv 697 (f. Πράϋλλος)

## Στράβων

S. Italy (Apulia):
—barion: (1) i-ii ad Suppl. It. 8 p. 36 no. 4 (CIL ix 283) (Lat. Pe[tr]onius Strab[o])
—canusium: (2) f. i ad Epig. Rom. di Canosa 29 (Lat. [L.] Baebius Strabo)
S. Italy (Campania):
—baiai: (3) s. i ad Puteoli 3 (1979) p. 160 no. 4 (Lat. Strabo)
Sicily: (4) m. iii bc RE (2) (Lat. Strabo)

## Στραμμενός

Argolis:
—argos: (1) f. iv bc D. lii 10

## Στραταγίς

Epiros:
—bouthrotos (prasaiboi): (1) a. 163 bc IBouthrot 29, 48 (SEG xxxviii 487) (d. Μάαρκος)

## Στράταγος

Aitolia: (1) iii bc AD 23 (1968) Mel. p. 109 no. 64 (s. Δορκίνας: locn.—Knoepfler); (2) ?262 bc FD iii (4) 358, 4; SGDI 2514, 2; (3) ?254 bc Syll³ 436, 3; Nachtergael, Les Galates 9, 4; (4) ?a. 246 bc SGDI 2509, 3

—kalydon: (5) c. 208-196 bc IG ix (1)² (1) 30, 22, 26, 31; 31, 131, 135; IMM 28, 6 (IG ix (1)² (1) 186) (f. Δαμόκριτος)
—konope-arsinoe: (6) 184 bc ib. 131, 7 (f. Ἀλέξων) ?= (7); (7) ~ ib. l. 11 ?= (6)
—phytaion: (8) f. iii bc ib. 6, 11
—pleuron: (9) c. 271 bc ib. 12, 24
Arkadia: (10) iii bc PP 15628 (s. Ἀντέας)
Epiros:
—argethia (nr.): (11) hell. SEG xiii 387
—bouthrotos (prasaiboi):
——Opatai: (12) a. 163 bc IBouthrot 93, 7 (f. Ἀγιάδας)

## Στρατέας

Arkadia:
—tegea: (1) ?218 bc IG v (2) 16, 8; (2) 165 ad ib. 50, 28 (f. Ζώσιμος)

## Στράτεια

Arkadia:
—tegea: (1) i bc-i ad? ib. 241 (Στράτ[ει]α)

## Στρατήγιος

Argolis:
—kalauria: (1) iii/iv ad ib. iv (1) 849, 3 (s. Σώστρατος)

## Στρατήν

Aitolia:
—kyparissos (mod.): (1) ?ii bc L'Illyrie mérid. 1 p. 108 no. 3 (SEG xxxvii 433) (Στρατῆλις—ed.)

## Στρατιλία

Sicily:
—syracuse: (1) iii-v ad IG xiv 168 (Strazzulla 109)

## Στράτιος

Achaia:
—patrai: (1) ii bc Achaean Grave Stelai 31 (Στράτιος: s. Μούτιος)
—tritaia: (2) 170-146 bc RE Supplbd. 11 (5a)
Aitolia: (3) iii/ii bc IG ii² 7990 + 7991 (s. Νικόβουλος); (4) ii bc ib. 7987 + SEG xviii 114
—kallion/kallipolis: (5) 173 bc SGDI 1856, 23
Akarnania:
—palairos: (6) iii/ii bc IG ix (1)² (2) 532
Argolis:
—argos: (7) ?253 bc Nachtergael, Les Galates 10, 72 (Stephanis 2305) (s. Κόμων)
—epidauros*: (8) c. 335-325 bc Peek, IAEpid 50, 19-20 (Σ[τ]ράτ[ι]ος) ?= (9); (9) c. 320-300 bc SEG xxv 397, 7; Peek, IAEpid 53, 17 ?= (8)
Elis: (10) s. i bc IG ii² 8529 (Σ(τ)ράτιος: f. Φιλῖνος)
Epiros:
—ambrakia: (11) c. 320 bc SEG xxxi 535 (Στρά[τ]ιος: f. Λαοδάμας)
Kerkyra: (12) ?ii-i bc IG ix (1) 803-4; AAA 13 (1980) pp. 290 f. (SEG xxxviii 434 (tiles)); (13) s. ii bc IG ix (2) 5 b, 5 ([Στρ]άτιος: s. Γνάθιος)
Korinthia:
—sikyon: (14) vi-v bc Iamb., VP 267 (FVS 58 A)
Lakonia:
—sparta: (15) imp. IG v (1) 1592 b (Bradford (4)) (Στράτιος: f. Ῥοδίνη); (16) c. 30-20 bc IG v (1) 211, 29 (Bradford (3)) (f. Ἆγις); (17) c. 25-1 bc IG v (1) 212, 34 (Bradford (1)) (s. Σοϊξιάδας); (18) c. 90-100 ad SEG xi 558, 15 (Bradford (2)); (19) a. 212 ad BSA 89 (1994) p. 435 no. 6, 5 (Στράτιο[ς]: f. Αὐρ. Δίδυμος)
Peloponnese: (20) c. 192 bc SEG xiii 327, 18 (s. Λ—)

S. Italy (Bruttium):
—brettioi: (21) ii-i bc ASAA 2 (1916) p. 157 no. 58; cf. ASCL 17 (1948) p. 1 n. 2 (date)
Sicily:
—morgantina: (22) ii bc SEG xxvii 655, 4 (Dubois, IGDS 194) (f. Αἰσχρίων); (23) ~ SEG xxvii 655, 4, 7 (Dubois, IGDS 194) (s. Αἰσχρίων)

## Στρατίππα

Lakonia:
—thalamai: (1) i bc-i ad IG v (1) 1321 b

## Στράτιππος

Arkadia:
—thelphousa: (1) a. 228 bc ib. iv (1)² 72 B, 24 (s. Ἀν—)
Dalmatia:
—issa:
——(Dymanes): (2) iv/iii bc Brunšmid p. 8, 38 (f. —ν)
Epiros:
—ambrakia: (3) f. ii bc IC 2 p. 25 no. 8 C
Sicily:
—syracuse: (4) hell.? IG xiv 6 ([Σ]τράτιππος, Κράτιππος?—IG); (5) c. 220 bc PP 2822 (s. Ἡρακλείδας)

## Στράτις

Messenia:
—thouria: (1) c. 182 bc SEG xi 972, 107 (Στράτιος?—lap.: s. Δείνων) ?= (2); (2) ii/i bc IG v (1) 1384, 12 (f. Δείνων) ?= (1)

## Στρατόβουλος

Akarnania:
—palairos: (1) ii bc ib. ix (1)² (2) 557

## Στρατόκλεια

Aitolia:
—pleuron: (1) iv/iii bc Suda s.v. A 1127 (m. Ἀλέξανδρος)

## Στρατοκλῆς

Achaia:
—dyme: (1) ?145 bc Sherk 43, 2; SEG xxxviii 372 (date)
—patrai: (2) hell.? SGDI 1628 (s. Ἀρχιτέλης)
Arkadia:
—tegea:
——(Krariotai): (3) iii bc IG v (2) 40, 13 (Στ[ρατ]οκλῆς: f. —ανδρος)
Lakonia:
—kythera: (4) ?255-254 bc Nachtergael, Les Galates 8, 33; 9, 45 (Stephanis 2308) (s. Κλεόστρατος)
Messenia:
—messene: (5) i bc/i ad IG v (1) 1438 a, 14 ([Στ]ρατοκλῆς)
Zakynthos: (6) f. iii bc SEG xiv 481 (f. Φιλῖνος)

## Στρατοκύδης

Epiros:
—bouthrotos (prasaiboi): (1) a. 163 bc IBouthrot 46, 5

## Στρατόλαος

Achaia:
—dyme: (1) s. iii bc SEG xiii 278, 18
Aitolia: (2) ?269 bc FD iii (4) 415, 7
—boukation: (3) 163 bc IG ix (1)² (1) 103, 9

## Στρατόλας

Argolis:
—argos: (1) iii bc BCH 27 (1903) p. 265 no. 13 (f. Ζηλουμενός)
Arkadia:
—orchomenos: (2) i bc/i ad IG v (2) 350 (Στρ(α)τόλας)
Elis: (3) 365-364 bc X., HG vii 4. 15, 31

## Στρατονίκα

Achaia:
—dyme: (1) ii-i bc SGDI 1617 c (d. Ἀγάθων)

AITOLIA: (**2**) c. 20-45 AD *FD* III (6) 13, 3, 14, 17 (d. Ὀρθαγόρας)

AKARNANIA:

—KORONTA: (**3**) f. iii BC *SEG* XXIX 473

ARGOLIS:

—EPIDAUROS: (**4**) iii BC *IG* IV (1)² 325 ([Στρ]ατονίκ[α])

—HERMIONE: (**5**) i BC-i AD? ib. IV (1) 734, 9 ([Στ]ρατονίκα, [Π]ρατονίκα?: d. Σπόρος)

EPIROS:

—BOUTHROTOS (PRASAIBOI): (**6**) a. 163 BC *IBouthrot* 14, 17; 22, 17; 26, 11; 29, 51; 30, 12, 28; 31, 82; 33, 20; 41, 14 (*SEG* XXXVIII 471; 479; 484; 487-8; 492; 500); *IBouthrot* 51, 18 (Στρατώ—no. 33: m. Πολέμων, Φιλίστα, Ἀργεία); (**7**) ~ ib. 14, 32 (*SEG* XXXVIII 471) (d. Νικόμαχος) ?= (**10**); (**8**) ~ *IBouthrot* 18, 12 (*SEG* XXXVIII 475) (Στρατο[νίκ]α—Cabanes, Στρατώ—Morricone) ?= (**13**); (**9**) ~ *IBouthrot* 19, 6 (*SEG* XXXVIII 476); (**10**) ~ *IBouthrot* 24, 4; 25, 4 (*SEG* XXXVIII 482-3) (Στρατώ—no. 25) ?= (**7**); (**11**) ~ *IBouthrot* 36, 10; 43, 39 (*SEG* XXXVIII 495; 502); *IBouthrot* 48, 5; (**12**) ~ ib. 116, 6 (*BCH* 118 (1994) p. 121 A); (**13**) ~ *IBouthrot* 160, 5, 7 ?= (**8**)

—MOLOSSOI: (**14**) c. 380-316 BC Plu., *Mor.* 401 A; cf. *Chiron* 11 (1981) pp. 79 ff. (name)

ILLYRIA:

—EPIDAMNOS-DYRRHACHION: (**15**) hell.-imp. *IDyrrh* 374 (-νεί-: d. Ἀντίοχος); (**16**) ~ ib. 375 (Στρα[τ]ονείκα: d. Πλάτωρ); (**17**) ~ ib. 376 (d. Ἀγαθίων)

KERKYRA: (**18**) hell.-imp. *AD* 45 (1990) Chron. p. 293 (d. Δαμάρετος)

**Στρατονίκη**

ARGOLIS:

—EPIDAUROS: (**1**) ii BC Peek, *IAEpid* 130 ([Σ]τρατονίκη: d. Νίκαιος)

ILLYRIA: (**2**) f. iii BC *Thess. Mnem.* 121 (d. Οἰνάντιος)

—APOLLONIA: (**3**) ii-i BC *IApoll* 150 (-τω-: d. Ἀνδρόνικος)

—EPIDAMNOS-DYRRHACHION: (**4**) ii AD *AEp* 1978, no. 745 (Lat. Fulvia Stratonice: m. M. Aelius Ursinianus)

S. ITALY (APULIA):

—BARION: (**5**) f. ii AD *Suppl. It.* 8 p. 39 no. 7 (Lat. Fabia Stratonice)

S. ITALY (CAMPANIA):

—DIKAIARCHIA-PUTEOLI: (**6**) imp. *CIL* X 2296 (Lat. Stratonice)

**Στρατόνικος**

ACHAIA:

—DYME: (**1**) ii BC *SEG* XIV 371 (s. Τιμοκράτης)

AITOLIA: (**2**) c. 266 BC *IG* XII (9) 1187, 21; cf. Robert, *Ét. Num. Gr.* p. 179 ff. (date) (f. Εὐρύας)

—HYPOSIRIA: (**3**) 263 BC *IG* IX (1)² (1) 17, 6

—TRICHONION: (**4**) s. iii BC ib. 117, 8; (**5**) ~ ib. l. 9

—TRICHONION?: (**6**) c. 200 BC *SBBerlAk* 1936, p. 387 no. 1 (Στρατόνικ[ος], Στρατονίκ[α]?)

AITOLIA?: (**7**) 165 BC *ZPE* 101 (1994) p. 128, 18

AKARNANIA:

—LYKONIKO (MOD.): (**8**) ii BC *IG* IX (1)² (2) 382

—THYRREION: (**9**) ii BC ib. 331

ARGOLIS:

—ARGOS: (**10**) 105 BC *JÖAI* 14 (1911) Beibl. p. 146 no. 4, 24 (Στρατό[νι]κος: s. Στρ—)

ARKADIA:

—HERAIA: (**11**) ?ii BC *IG* V (2) 418

—PHIGALEIA: (**12**) ?iii BC ib. 423 ([Στρ]ατονί[κος]?)

—TEGEA: (**13**) i AD ib. 46, 2 (Στρατόνικο[s]: s. Ζήνων)

EPIROS:

—AMBRAKIA: (**14**) a. 167 BC *SEG* XXXV 665 A, 7

ILLYRIA:

—EPIDAMNOS-DYRRHACHION: (**15**) c. 250-50 BC Maier 136; 154; 182; 211; 249; 344; 478; Münsterberg p. 260 = Nachtr. p. 14 (coin) (Ceka 384-94) (money.)

LAKONIA:

—SPARTA: (**16**) i BC/i AD *BSA* 89 (1994) pp. 433-4 no. 2, 6 (f. Πρατόνικος); (**17**) c. 150-160 AD *SEG* XI 585, 12; XXX 410, [21] (Bradford (-)) (-νει-: f. Ἰσιγένης)

MESSENIA:

—MESSENE: (**18**) iii BC *SEG* XXIII 209, 18

S. ITALY (CAMPANIA):

—DIKAIARCHIA-PUTEOLI: (**19**) imp. *CIL* X 2977 (Lat. Stratonicus: f. Στράτων)

**Στράτυλλα**

AKARNANIA:

—ANAKTORION: (**1**) s. iii BC *IG* IX (1)² (2) 225

**Στράτυλλος**

ARGOLIS:

—ARGOS:

——(Hyrnathioi-Temenidai): (**1**) c. 400 BC *SEG* XXIX 361, 26

ARKADIA:

—MANTINEIA-ANTIGONEIA: (**2**) c. 300-221 BC *IG* V (2) 323. 85 (tessera) (s. Σθένιος)

—TEGEA: (**3**) ii AD ib. 55, 53 (s. Ἄμυκος); (**4**) 165 AD ib. 50, 53 (s. Ἴλαρος)

**Στρατώ**

AITOLIA:

—PHISTYON: (**1**) imp. ib. IX (1)² (1) 113, 4 (d. Καλλίστρατος)

EPIROS:

—BOUTHROTOS (PRASAIBOI): (**2**) a. 163 BC *IBouthrot* 25, 8 (*SEG* XXXVIII 483); (**3**) ~ *IBouthrot* 28, 26; (**4**) ~ ib. 29, 42 (*SEG* XXXVIII 487) ([Σ]τρατώ); (**5**) ~ *IBouthrot* 33, 20; cf. 14, 17; 22, 17; 26, 11 etc. (Στρατονίκα—no. 14 etc.); (**6**) ~ ib. 47, 17 (d. Θεόδοτος, ?m. Θεόδοτος); (**7**) ~ ib. 50, 4, 10; (**8**) ~ ib. 77, 6; (**9**) ~ ib. 110, 5

ILLYRIA:

—EPIDAMNOS-DYRRHACHION: (**10**) ii-i BC *IDyrrh* 379 (d. Φιλόξενος); (**11**) hell.-imp. ib. 377; (**12**) ~ ib. 378

**Στράτων**

ACHAIA: (**1**) 146 BC *IG* IV (1)² 28, 116 (I f. Στράτων II: synoikos); (**2**) ~ ib. l. 116 (II s. Στράτων I: synoikos)

—PATRAI: (**3**) 185 BC ib. IX (1)² (1) 32, 44 (s. Ἀλέξανδρος)

AITOLIA: (**4**) 279-278 BC ib. XI (2) 161 B, 25; 162 B, 19

—ATTALEIA: (**5**) m. ii BC ib. IX (1)² (1) 107, 6

—KONOPE-ARSINOE: (**6**) 213-206 BC ib. p. L, s.a. 213 BC, 206 BC ?= (**7**); (**7**) f. ii BC ib. 96, 1, 17 with n. (f. Δωρίμαχος) ?= (**6**); (**8**) c. 166-159 BC ib. p. LI, s.a. 166 BC, 159 BC; 36, 1, 6; *FD* III (3) 54, 1 (s. Νικόβουλος)

—THERMOS*: (**9**) s. iii BC *IG* IX (1)² (1) 60 V, 10 ([Σ]τ[ρ]άτων); (**10**) ~ ib. 60 VI, 4; (**11**) ~ ib. l. 6

—TRICHONION?: (**12**) c. 200 BC *SBBerlAk* 1936, p. 387 no. 1

AKARNANIA:

—STRATOS: (**13**) i BC *IG* IX (1)² (1) 110, 10 (f. Ἑρμαῖος)

ARGOLIS:

—ARGOS: (**14**) hell.? *SEG* XI 356; (**15**) iii BC *IG* IV (1) 527, 10; cf. *SEG* XI 311 ([Σ]τράτω[ν]); (**16**) ~ ib. 313 d (?f. —στρατείδας); (**17**) iii/ii BC *IG* IV (1)² 208, 1; (**18**) s. ii BC Marcadé I 109 (f. Ξενόφιλος) ?= (**20**); (**19**) ii/i BC ib. 110-11 + *SEG* XIX 400; cf. *Corinth* VIII (3) 47; p. 20 with n. 10; *SEG* XVII 153 (s. Ξενόφιλος: sculptor); (**20**) 105 BC *JÖAI* 14 (1911) Beibl. p. 146 no. 4, 16 (Στράτω[ν]: f. Ξενόφιλος) ?= (**18**)

—ARGOS?: (**21**) f. ii BC *Hesp.* 40 (1971) pp. 197-8 no. 51, 11 (s. Τίμων)

—EPIDAUROS*: (**22**) c. 340-330 BC *IG* IV (1)² 112, 5, 10; *SEG* XXV 387 C, 3 (Στράτ[ων])

—HERMIONE: (**23**) iii BC *IG* IV (1) 729 I, 20 (f. Ἀστυάναξ); (**24**) ?ii-i BC ib. 731 I, 13 (f. Ἀμμία)

—TROIZEN: (**25**) ?273 BC *FD* III (2) 205, 5

ARKADIA:

—MANTINEIA-ANTIGONEIA: (**26**) iii BC *IG* V (2) 319, 11

EPIROS:

—AMBRAKIA: (**27**) ?254 BC Nachtergael, *Les Galates* 9, 60 (f. Φίλων); (**28**) ii-i BC *CIG* 1797 (*SGDI* 3183)

—BOUTHROTOS (PRASAIBOI): (**29**) a. 163 BC *IBouthrot* 28, 26; 143, 5 (*SEG* XXXVIII 486) ?= (**30**); (**30**) ~ *IBouthrot* 160, 10; 161, 5 (f. Λυκώτας) ?= (**29**); (**31**) ~ ib. 160, [9]; 161, 6 (s. Δόκιμος)

——Chrausinoi: (**32**) a. 163 BC ib. 139, 9 (f. Λαφύργας)

—DODONA: (**33**) iii BC Antoniou, *Dodone* Aa, 39 (Στράτων); (**34**) ~ ib. Ab, 53 (Στράτων); (**35**) ~ ib. Ba, 14

—HORRAION: (**36**) iv BC Cabanes, *L'Épire* p. 586 no. 70, 5; cf. *BCH* 109 (1985) p. 520 f. (locn.) (Σ[τ]ράτων)

—NIKOPOLIS: (**37**) imp. *Wiss. Mitth. Bosn.* 4 (1896) p. 387 no. 4 (Sarikakis 153) (f. Ἐπιγόνη)

ILLYRIA:

—EPIDAMNOS-DYRRHACHION: (**38**) c. 250-50 BC Schlosser p. 64 no. 335 (coin) (pryt.) ?= (**39**); (**39**) ~ Maier 355 (coin) (Ceka 45; 146) (pryt.) ?= (**38**)

KERKYRA: (**40**) iv/iii BC *IG* IX (1) 976, 2 (f. Τίμων); (**41**) ?iii BC ib. 682, 1; cf. Fraser-Rönne, *BWGT* p. 181; (**42**) c. 229-48 BC *BMC Thessaly* p. 149 nos. 525-6 (coins); (**43**) 208 BC *IMM* 44, 3 (f. Μνάσων); (**44**) ?168 BC Klee p. 16 II C, 90 (s. Ἀριστοκράτης)

KORINTHIA:

—KORINTH: (**45**) ?v BC *Hesp.* 41 (1972) p. 210 no. 9

LAKONIA:

—OITYLOS: (**46**) iii/ii BC *IG* V (1) 1295, 7 (Bradford (4))

—SPARTA: (**47**) c. 25-1 BC *IG* V (1) 210, 18 (Bradford (8)) (I f. Στράτων II); (**48**) ~ *IG* V (1) 210, 18 (Bradford (1)) (II s. Στράτων I); (**49**) c. 90-100 AD *SEG* XI 488, 5 (Bradford (6)); (**50**) c. 100 AD *IG* V (1) 273 (Bradford (7)) (I f. Κρατησικλῆς ὁ καὶ Στράτων II); (**51**) ~ *IG* V (1) 273 (Bradford s.v. Κρατησικλῆς (-)) (Κρατησικλῆς ὁ καὶ Σ.: II s. Στράτων I); (**52**) c. 100-125 AD *IG* V (1) 137, 5 (Bradford (5)) (Στ(ρ)άτων); (**53**) c. 132 AD *SEG* XI 579, 5 (Bradford (3)) (s. Ξενομένης)

——Limnai: (**54**) c. 70-100 AD *IG* V (1) 676, 9 (Bradford (2)) (freed.)

LEUKAS: (**55**) c. 167-50 BC *BMC Thessaly* p. 185 nos. 161-2; p. 186 no. 185; *SNG Cop. Epirus–Acarnania* 395 (coins)

MESSENIA:

—MESSENE: (**56**) ?i AD *IG* V (1) 1374 (I f. Στράτων II); (**57**) i AD ib. (II s. Στράτων I) ?= (**58**); (**58**) 42 AD *SEG* XXIII 208, 4 ?= (**57**)

—MESSENE?: (**59**) ii/i BC ib. XI 979, 57

—THOURIA: (**60**) ii-i BC *IG* V (1) 1385, 28 (f. Στέφανος)

S. ITALY (APULIA):

—LUCERIA: (**61**) imp. *CIL* IX 808 (Lat. P. Didiolenus Strato)

S. ITALY (CALABRIA):

—TARAS-TARENTUM: (**62**) iv BC *RE* (17); *FGrH* 48 (Stephanis 2316)

S. ITALY (CAMPANIA):
—DIKAIARCHIA-PUTEOLI: (63) imp. *CIL* x 2785 (Lat. Licinius Strato); (64) ~ ib. 2977 (Lat. Strato: s. *Στρατόνικος*)
—POMPEII: (65) i BC-i AD ib. IV 5276 (Lat. Strato)
SICILY:
—AKRAGAS: (66) c. 413-406 BC Jenkins, *Coins of Greek Sicily* pl. xvi, 16 (coins)
—BUTERA (MOD.): (67) f. v BC Dubois, *IGDS* 163 (vase) (Arena, *Iscr. Sic.* II 101) (-τōν)
—KAMARINA: (68) f. v BC Cordano, *Tessere Pubbliche* 72 (-τōν: f. *Ἐράτων*); (69) iv/iii BC *SEG* XXXIX 999, 3 (Dubois, *IGDS* 125) ([Σ]τράτων: f. *Νῑκις*)
—SYRACUSE: (70) s. iv BC *IG* II² 10398 (f. *Φιλίστα*); (71) iii/ii BC *EAD* XXX 445 ([Σ]τράτων); (72) iii-v AD *SEG* XVIII 404
——(*Κραταιμεῖος*): (73) iv BC Manganaro, *PdelP* forthcoming no. 3, 9 (*Σ(τ)ράτων*: f. *Ἀριστέας*)
—SYRACUSE?:
——(*Κατηλ.*): (74) hell. *Mem. Linc.* 8 (1938) p. 127 no. 35. 3 (bullet); cf. *L'Incidenza dell'Antico* pp. 420 ff. (f. *Κέντος*)
—TAUROMENION: (75) c. 206-196 BC *IG* XIV 421 an. 35; 421 an. 45 (*SGDI* 5219) (s. *Κλεόδωρος*); (76) c. 171 BC *IG* XIV 421 an. 70 (*SGDI* 5219) (f. *Ἱστιεῖός*)

### Στρατωνίδας
ARGOLIS:
—EPIDAUROS: (1) iv BC *IG* IV (1)² 185

### Στρίμπων
S. ITALY (CAMPANIA):
—PONTECAGNANO (MOD.): (1) c. 520-510 BC *SEG* XXXIV 1019 (vase); cf. *LSAG*² p. 457 no. H (date); *BE* 1995, no. 687 (date) (*Στρίν-πōν*)

### Στρίμφακος
SICILY:
—AKRAI: (1) imp. *Akrai* p. 164 no. 26 (*Κ. Σ.*)

### Στροβίλος
AITOLIA:
—PHISTYON: (1) 163 BC *IG* IX (1)² (1) 102, 9 (-βεί-)
ARKADIA:
—MANTINEIA-ANTIGONEIA: (2) i AD ib. V (2) 269; 270 (*Γ. Ἰούλ. Στροβεῖλος*)
S. ITALY (CAMPANIA):
—DIKAIARCHIA-PUTEOLI: (3) imp. *CIL* x 2766 (Lat. Strobilus)
—POMPEII: (4) c. 51-62 AD ib. IV 3340. 88, 8 (Castrèn 168. 2) (Lat. L. Flaminius Strobilus)
SICILY:
—SYRACUSE: (5) ii-i BC *IG* XIV 8, 5 (*IGLMP* 105) (f. —ρίδας)

### Στρογγυλίων
AITOLIA: (1) c. 334 BC *FD* III (1) 147, 1 (*Στρογγυλίω[ν]*: f. *Λεοντομένης*)

### Στρογιήν
ELIS: (1) f. i BC Moretti, *Olymp.* 670; *IvOl* 198, 1; 204, [1] (s. *Φίλιστος*, *Θεοδότα*)

### Στρομβιχίδας
ACHAIA:
—DYME*: (1) c. 219 BC *SGDI* 1612, 31 (*Tyche* 5 (1990) p. 124) (f. *Εὐκράτης*)

### Στρόμβιχος
AITOLIA: (1) c. 334 BC *FD* III (1) 148, 1 (*Στρόν-βι[χος]*: s. *Λάτταβος*)
—KALYDON: (2) m. ii BC *IG* IX (1)² (1) 137, 21, 45 (f. *Ἀλεξίμαχος*)
ILLYRIA:
—APOLLONIA: (3) 190 BC *Syll*³ 585, 95 (*IApoll* 316) (s. *Διονυσόδοτος*)

### Στροῦθος
ARGOLIS:
—EPIDAUROS*: (1) c. 370-365 BC Peek, *IAEpid* 52 A, 24, 31, 34, 40
SICILY:
—TAUROMENION: (2) c. 215 BC *IG* XIV 421 an. 26 (*SGDI* 5219); (3) c. 165 BC *IG* XIV 421 an. 76 (*SGDI* 5219) (f. *Ζώπυρος*)

### Στρυμόδωρος
AIGINA: (1) m. iv BC D. XXXVI 28-9

### Στύμφαλος
ACHAIA?: (1) 193 BC *IG* v (2) 293, 15 (f. *Δόρκων*)
SICILY:
—PANORMOS*: (2) imp. *CIL* x 7318 + *Eph. Ep.* VIII 697 (Lat. M. Scribonius Stymphalus: freed.)

### Στύραξ
ACHAIA:
—AIGION: (1) ii-iii AD *EA* 1884, p. 89, 2 (f. *Ἀλκαινέτη*)
ARGOLIS:
—ARGOS: (2) 255 BC *PCZ* 59182, 11, 25 (s. *Ἀπολλώνιος*)
LAKONIA:
—SPARTA: (3) c. 105-110 AD *SEG* XI 569, 13 (Bradford (-)) ([Στ]ύραξ: s. *Μνασίστρατος*)

### Στύφων
LAKONIA:
—SPARTA: (1) 425 BC Th. iv 38. 1 (Poralla² 675) (s. *Φάραξ*)

### Συάγρας
LAKONIA:
—SPARTA: (1) ?vi BC Paus. vi 4. 4 (Poralla² 676) (*Σνάδρας*—mss., *Σ.*—Studniczka: sculptor)

### Σύαγρος
AITOLIA: (1) c. 220 BC *IG* IX (1)² (1) p. L, s.a. 226 BC; Flacelière p. 416 no. 51, 2
LAKONIA:
—SPARTA: (2) 480 BC Hdt. vii 153. 1; 159; 160. 1 (Poralla² 677)

### Συαίτας
EPIROS:
—VOTONOSI (MOD.): (1) f. iii BC *SEG* XXIV 456, 1; (2) ~ ib. l. 6

### Συβότας
MESSENIA: (1) viii BC Paus. iv 3. 10; 4. 1 (f. *Φίντας*)

### Σύγγνωμος
S. ITALY (CALABRIA):
—TARAS-TARENTUM: (1) imp. *NScav* 1893, p. 252 (Lat. M. Plotius Sygnomus)

### Σύγγραφος
S. ITALY (APULIA):
—LUCERIA: (1) imp. *ASP* 34 (1981) p. 12 no. 12 (Lat. C. Calidius Syngraphus)

### Συγκάμων
SICILY:
—TYNDARIS: (1) ii-iii AD *IGUR* 456 (*Συνκάμων* (n. pr.?))

### Σύγκλητος
S. ITALY (CAMPANIA):
—POMPEII: (1) i BC-i AD *CIL* IV 3406 (Lat. A. Syncletus)

### Συγχαίρων
ELIS:
—OLYMPIA*: (1) 209-213 AD *IvOl* 110, 26 (*Συν-*: ?s. *Αὐρ. Μητρόβιος*: slave?)

### Συκᾶς
ILLYRIA:
—APOLLONIA: (1) imp. *IApoll* 151 (*Συκα*—lap.)

### Συκώι
SICILY:
—AKRAGAS: (1) c. 430-420 BC Dubois, *IGDS* 181 (coin graffito) (-κōι: kala)
—AKRAI: (2) vi BC *Akrai* p. 161 no. 21 (Dubois, *IGDS* 105) (-ϙōι)

### Συλακίς
LAKONIA:
—SPARTA: (1) s. vii BC *PMGF* I I, 72 with Schol. ad. loc. (Poralla² 678) (*Θυλακίς*—Schol.)

### Συλεύς
ARGOLIS:
—ARGOS: (1) ?c. 575-550 BC *SEG* XI 314, 5; *LSAG*² p. 168 no. 8 (date)
TRIPHYLIA:
—MAKISTOS: (2) 399-369 BC *SEG* XXXV 389, 11 (n. pr.?)

### Σύλιχος
ARGOLIS:
—ARGOS: (1) ?c. 460-450 BC ib. XVI 244, 4 (Lazzarini 939); *LSAG*² p. 170 no. 36 (date) (*Σύλιχ[ος]*); (2) c. 458 BC *IG* I³ 1149, 74
ELIS: (3) 191-146 BC *Corinth* VI p. 56 no. 349; *ZfN* 9 (1882) p. 270 no. 25 (coins)

### Σύλλος
S. ITALY (BRUTTIUM):
—KROTON: (1) ?vi BC Iamb., *VP* 150; 267 (*FVS* I p. 446); cf. *RE* (2) (*Σίλιος*—Iamb. 267)

### Συμάδας
ARGOLIS:
—PHLEIOUS: (1) ?s. v BC *IG* IV (1) 451 (s. *Ἀρχέλοχος*)

### Συμαρία
SICILY:
—KAMARINA: (1) m. v BC Dubois, *IGDS* 120, 6 (Arena, *Iscr. Sic.* II 142 A; *SEG* XXXVIII 939; Cordano, 'Camarina VII' 56) ((*Ε*)*ὐμαρία*?—Dubois: d. *Σικάνα*)

### Συμβίωσις
SICILY:
—TYNDARIS: (1) ?i AD *Epigraphica* 51 (1989) p. 165 no. 21 (Lat. Tullia Symbiosis)

### Συμβολικός
SICILY:
—KATANE: (1) imp. *CIL* x 7088 (Lat. Simbolicus)

### Συμμάχα
S. ITALY (CALABRIA):
—TARAS-TARENTUM: (1) iii BC *RA* 1932 (1), p. 40 no. 41 (*SEG* XXX 1222 C (loomweight)) (*Συμμά(χα)*—*SEG*)

### Συμμαχίδας
EPIROS:
—BOUTHROTOS (PRASAIBOI): (1) a. 163 BC *IBouthrot* 30, 35 (*SEG* XXXVIII 488) (f. *Νικάνωρ*)

### Συμμαχίς
EPIROS:
—ANTIGONEIA: (1) hell. ib. XXIV 470; Cabanes, *L'Épire* p. 234 n. 96 (locn.)
—BOUTHROTOS (PRASAIBOI): (2) a. 163 BC *IBouthrot* 14, 13 (*SEG* XXXVIII 471)

### Σύμμαχος
ACHAIA: (1) hell. *IEph* 2287 A, 3, 5 (*Σύν-*: f. *Δαμάτριος*, *Διονύσιος*)
—PELLENE: (2) f. iv BC *CEG* II 888, 18 (s. *Εὐμήδης*: mantis)

—PHARAI: (3) ii-i BC *Achaean Grave Stelai* 68 (I f. *Σύμμαχος* II); (4) ~ ib. (II s. *Σύμμαχος* I)
AITOLIA:
—DARDEOI: (5) f. ii BC *IG* IX (1)² (1) 96, 20 (s. *Εὐρύδαμος*)
—DEXIEIS: (6) 191 BC *SGDI* 1985, 9
ARKADIA:
—MANTINEIA-ANTIGONEIA*: (7) ii AD *IG* V (2) 277 (s. *Εὐοδία*)
DALMATIA:
—ISSA: (8) hell. Novak, *Vis* fig. 24 (*Σύμα-*: f. *Διονύσιος*)
ELIS: (9) v/iv BC Moretti, *Olymp.* 353 (s. *Αἰσχύλος*)
EPIROS:
—BOUTHROTOS (PRASAIBOI): (10) a. 163 BC *IBouthrot* 18, 17 (*SEG* XXXVIII 475) ?= (11); (11) ~ *IBouthrot* 22, 31 (*SEG* XXXVIII 479) ?= (10)
——Cheilioi: (12) a. 163 BC *IBouthrot* 98, 7 (f. *Ταυρίσκος*)
—DODONA: (13) iii BC Antoniou, *Dodone* Ba, 13
—MOLOSSOI: (14) iv-iii BC Cabanes, *L'Épire* p. 592 no. 77
—NIKOPOLIS: (15) i AD Plu., *Mor.* 667 D (Sarikakis 154); cf. *RE* s.v. Plutarchos (2) col. 686
KORINTHIA:
—KORINTH: (16) ii BC *IG* II² 9054 (f. *Ἀρέτα*)
LEUKAS: (17) c. 167-50 BC *BMC Thessaly* p. 185 nos. 163-4; p. 187 no. 186 (coins)
S. ITALY: (18) s. iv BC *IG* XIV 2408. 9 (*BM Bronzes* 325; *Roma Medio Repubblicana* p. 284 no. 8; *Misc. Etrusco-Italica* 1 p. 196 no. A7); *Laos* 2 p. 31 no. 10; (19) imp. *CIL* X 8059. 389 (seal) (Lat. Symmachus)
S. ITALY (BRUTTIUM):
—RHEGION: (20) s. ii BC *IG* XIV 615, 3; *Klearchos* 21 (1979) pp. 83-96 (date) (s. *Ἡράκλητος*)
S. ITALY (CALABRIA):
—TARAS-TARENTUM: (21) ?iv BC *IG* XIV 2406. 77; *SEG* XXXVI 900; Troisi, *Epigrafi mobili* 82 (loomweight) (*Συμμάχω* (gen.?))
S. ITALY (CAMPANIA):
—DIKAIARCHIA-PUTEOLI*: (22) imp. *CIL* X 2409 (Lat. Q. Fadius Symmachus: freed.)
—POMPEII: (23) i BC-i AD ib. IV 8631 (Lat. Summachus)
S. ITALY(LUCANIA):
—HERAKLEIA:
——(Fϵ. γυῖον): (24) iv/iii BC *IGSI* 1 I, 187 (*DGE* 62; Uguzzoni–Ghinatti I) (f. *Ἀριστόδαμος*)
SICILY: (25) hell. *SEG* XXXIII 455 (s. *Τίτταλος*)
—IAITON: (26) iii-ii BC ib. XXVI 1070. 1 (tiles)
—ZANKLE-MESSANA: (27) 428-424 BC *RE* (9); Moretti, *Olymp.* 325; 328

**Συμωνᾶς**
S. ITALY (CALABRIA):
—LUPIAE: (1) 521 AD *JIWE* I 107 (Lat. Symonas: ?f. Isa: Jew)

**Συμπάσχουσα**
S. ITALY (CAMPANIA):
—POMPEII: (1) i BC-i AD *CIL* IV 9172 (Lat. Symphascusa)

**Συμπότης**
SICILY:
—SYRACUSE: (1) iii-v AD *IG* XIV 170 (Strazzulla 111)

**Συμφέρουσα**
EPIROS:
—NIKOPOLIS: (1) imp. *AE* 1950-1, Chron. p. 37 (Sarikakis 155) (*Συν-*)
S. ITALY (APULIA):
—CANUSIUM: (2) imp. *Epig. Rom. di Canosa* 142 (*CIL* IX 383) (Lat. Mallia Symferusa)

—LARINUM: (3) s. i BC ib. 755; cf. *Forma Italiae* 36 p. 62 no. 2 (Lat. Itia Sunpherusa)
—TEANUM APULUM?: (4) imp. *Teanum Apulum* p. 151 no. 2a (or S. Italy (Apulia) Luceria: Lat. Symferusa)
S. ITALY (CALABRIA):
—BRENTESION-BRUNDISIUM: (5) imp. *CIL* IX 151 (Lat. [Sy]mpherusa); (6) ~ ib. 194 = *Epigraphica* 25 (1963) p. 81 no. 88; cf. 42 (1980) p. 158 (Lat. –cia Su[mph]erusa)
S. ITALY (CAMPANIA):
—ACERRAE*: (7) ?ii AD Unp. (Solin) (Lat. Flavia Sympherusa: freed.)
—DIKAIARCHIA-PUTEOLI: (8) imp. *CIL* X 2316 (Lat. Coelia Symferusa); (9) ?i-ii AD ib. 2541 (Lat. Lucilia Sympher(usa)); (10) ?ii AD ib. 2019 (Lat. Aelia Synforosa)
—MISENUM*: (11) imp. ib. 3641 (Lat. Symphae[rusa]: freed.)
—SALERNUM: (12) m. i BC *IItal* I (1) 127 (*CIL* X 599) (Lat. Helmonia Sympherusa); (13) imp. *IItal* I (1) 138 (*CIL* X 588) (Lat. Flaminia Sympherusa: freed.)
SICILY:
—KATANE: (14) imp. ib. 7066 (Lat. Antonia Sym[pheru]sa)
—SYRACUSE: (15) iii-v AD Ferrua, *NG* 379 ([*Συμφ*]*έρουσα*)

**Συμφέρων**
KORINTHIA:
—KORINTH*: (1) vi AD *Corinth* VIII (3) 541, 4; cf. *TMByz* 9 (1985) p. 365 no. 58
S. ITALY (CAMPANIA):
—DIKAIARCHIA-PUTEOLI*: (2) imp. *CIL* X 3060 (Lat. Sympheron: imp. freed.?)

**Συμφορίς**
ARKADIA:
—MEGALOPOLIS: (1) ii-iii AD *GVI* 1091, 3 (Raffeiner, *Sklaven* 19) (d. *Καρνεάδας*: slave?)

**Σύμφορον**
ARGOLIS:
—HERMIONE: (1) ?ii-i BC *IG* IV (1) 731 II, 15 (d. *Κλεομήδης*)

**Σύμφορος**
ARKADIA:
—KLEITOR: (1) a. 212 AD ib. V (2) 369, 16; *SEG* XXXI 347, 8 (s. *Εὐτύχης*); (2) ~ ib. l. 10 (*Πρῖμος Σ.*); (3) m. iii AD ib. XXXV 350 I, 4 (*Αὐρ. Σύμ*[*φ*]*ορος*)
—TEGEA: (4) 165 AD *IG* V (2) 50, 81 (*Κλ. Σ.*)
DALMATIA:
—KERKYRA MELAINA: (5) imp. *CIL* III 10083 (*ILS* 3179) (Lat. Signius Symphorus)
ELIS:
—OLYMPIA*: (6) b. 165 AD *IvOl* 99, 17 (*Σύμφο*[*ρος*]: slave?)
KERKYRA: (7) ii-iii AD *IG* IX (1) 964, 4 (*Μέμμιος Σ.*)
KORINTHIA:
—KORINTH: (8) f. iii AD *Ag.* VII p. 98 no. 310; *Corinth* IV (2) p. 190 nos. 575-6 (lamps) (*Σύν-*)
MESSENIA:
—MESSENE: (9) 80 AD *IG* V (1) 1468, 10; cf. *SEG* XL 366 (*Αὐφ. Σ.*); (10) 192 AD *PAE* 1969, p. 104, 11 (f. *Ἑδασηνός*)
S. ITALY (BRUTTIUM):
—HIPPONION-VIBO VALENTIA: (11) imp. *CIL* X 8059. 390 (seal) (Lat. Symphorus)
S. ITALY (CALABRIA):
—BRENTESION-BRUNDISIUM: (12) imp. ib. IX 56 (Lat. C. Pomponius Symphorus); (13) ~ ib. 100 (Lat. Clodius Symphorus); (14) ~ *NScav* 1889, p. 168 i (*Eph. Ep.* VIII 41) (Lat. N. Pomponius Sumphorus)
—TARAS-TARENTUM: (15) ?ii AD *SEG* XXXIV 1021

S. ITALY (CAMPANIA):
—DIKAIARCHIA-PUTEOLI*: (16) imp. *CIL* X 1727 (Lat. Aurelius Symphorus: imp. freed.); (17) ~ ib. 1944 (Lat. Symphorus: freed.?)
—HERCULANEUM: (18) i BC-i AD ib. IV 10680 (Lat. Sympo(rus))
—HERCULANEUM*: (19) c. 50-75 AD ib. X 1403 a I, 3 (Lat. C. Iulius Symphorus)
—NEAPOLIS: (20) imp. *NScav* 1895, p. 108 (Lat. Symphor(us): I f. *Σύμφορος* II); (21) ~ ib. (Lat. L. Iulius Symphorus: II s. *Σύμφορος* I, *Φυλλίς*)
—POMPEII: (22) i BC-i AD *CIL* IV 4430 (Lat. Symporus); (23) ~ ib. 10054; 10056 (Castrèn 463. 4); cf. *Gnomon* 45 (1973) p. 262 (Lat. T. Vinius Symphorus)
SICILY:
—AKRAI (NR.): (24) iii-v AD *NScav* 1907, p. 488; cf. *Riv. Arch. Crist.* 18 (1941) p. 233 n. 1
—PANORMOS: (25) ?iii-v AD Wessel 8
—ZANKLE-MESSANA?: (26) ?i AD *Epigraphica* 3 (1941) p. 258 no. 13 (Lat. C. Terentius Symphorus: s. *Σύντροφος*: doctor)

**Συμφώ**
LAKONIA:
—SPARTA: (1) c. 230-250 AD *IG* V (1) 539, 15; *Griech. Epigr. Kreta* p. 12 (name); *BSA* 79 (1984) p. 276 n. 75 (ident.) (Bradford s.v. *Συμφωνία* (-)) (*Αὐρ. Σ.*, *Συμφω*[*νία*]—*IG*: ?d. M. *Αὐρ. Σπαρτιάτης*)

**Συμφωνιακός**
S. ITALY (CALABRIA):
—BRENTESION-BRUNDISIUM: (1) imp. *CIL* IX 43 (Lat. Symphoniacus)

**Σύναρχος**
AKARNANIA:
—MEDION: (1) m. ii BC *IG* IX (1)² (2) 209, 5

**Συνέκδημος**
LAKONIA:
—HYPERTELEATON*: (1) imp. ib. V (1) 1061 (-*έγ*-: s. *Φιλόδημος*)
MESSENIA:
—KORONE: (2) 246 AD ib. 1398, 63 (*Αὐρ. Σ.*)
S. ITALY (CAMPANIA):
—DIKAIARCHIA-PUTEOLI: (3) imp. *CIL* X 1929 (Lat. Synecdemus); (4) ~ *RAAN* 42 (1967) pp. 4-6 (Lat. P. Minucius Synecdemus)

**Σύνεργος**
S. ITALY (CAMPANIA):
—DIKAIARCHIA-PUTEOLI: (1) imp. *AJA* 77 (1973) p. 156 no. 5 (Lat. Herennius Synergus)

**Συνεροῦσα**
S. ITALY (APULIA):
—TEANUM APULUM: (1) imp. *CIL* IX 719 (Lat. Sinerusa)
S. ITALY (CALABRIA):
—BRENTESION-BRUNDISIUM: (2) imp. *Eph. Ep.* VIII 31 (Lat. Licinia Synerusa)

**Συνέρως**
ARKADIA:
—TEGEA: (1) i AD *IG* V (2) 46, 13 (*Συνέρως*)
EPIROS:
—NIKOPOLIS: (2) imp. *SEG* XXVII 236 (*Αὐλ. Λουτάτιος Σ.*)
MESSENIA:
—KORONE: (3) 246 AD *IG* V (1) 1398, 25 (*Αὐρ. Σ.*)
—MESSENE: (4) 192 AD *PAE* 1969, p. 104, 12 (s. *Ὀνησιφόρος*)
S. ITALY (CAMPANIA):
—DIKAIARCHIA-PUTEOLI: (5) imp. *CIL* X 2929 (Lat. Cossinius Syneros: f. Salvillus, Faustus)
—DIKAIARCHIA-PUTEOLI*: (6) i AD *Puteoli* 7-8 (1983-4) p. 303 no. 5 (*CIL* X 2492) (Lat.

C. Gratilius Syneros: freed.); **(7)** ~ Puteoli 7-8 (1983-4) p. 303 no. 5 (*CIL* x 2492) (Lat. Mari[us] [S]yneros: freed.)
—POMPEII: **(8)** i BC-i AD ib. IV 1700 (Lat. Sineros); **(9)** ~ ib. 2252-3 (Lat. Syneros); **(10)** m. i AD *Impegno per Pompeii* 22 EN (Castrèn 325. 1) (Lat. L. Publicius Syneros); **(11)** 55 AD *CIL* IV 3340. 12, 21 (Lat. Syneros)
——(Boscoreale)*: **(12)** 26 AD *NScav* 1895, p. 215 (Castrèn 381. 11) (Lat. P. Sittius Syneros: freed.)
S. ITALY (LUCANIA):
—TEGIANUM: **(13)** imp. *IItal* III (1) 260 (*CIL* x 316) (Lat. C. Tegeanesis Syneros)

**Συνερωτίς**
S. ITALY (CAMPANIA):
—DIKAIARCHIA-PUTEOLI*: **(1)** imp. ib. 2492 (Lat. Gratilia Syneroti[s]: freed.)

**Συνέτα**
ARGOLIS:
—ARGOS*: **(1)** f. iii BC *IG* IV (1) 529, 8 (slave/freed.?)

**Σύνετος**
ARKADIA:
—STYMPHALOS: **(1)** ii BC *SEG* XLII 364 (Συνέτη—ed.)
LAKONIA:
—SPARTA: **(2)** ii-iv AD Robert, *Gladiateurs* p. 79 no. 12, 2 (Bradford (-)) (f. Νικηφόρος ὁ καὶ Νάρκισσος)
MESSENIA:
—KORONE: **(3)** 246 AD *IG* V (1) 1398, 97 (Αὐρ. Σ.)
S. ITALY (CAMPANIA):
—DIKAIARCHIA-PUTEOLI: **(4)** imp. *CIL* x 1834 (Lat. Synetu[s])
—HERCULANEUM*: **(5)** i BC-i AD ib. 1403 g III, 41 (Lat. L. Mammius Synetus: freed.)
—POMPEII: **(6)** i BC-i AD ib. IV 2285; 2287; 2288 (Lat. Synethus)
SICILY:
—SELINOUS: **(7)** m. v BC Dubois, *IGDS* 36, 6 (Arena, *Iscr. Sic.* I 69) (s. Ξένων)

**Συνέχη**
S. ITALY (CAMPANIA):
—DIKAIARCHIA-PUTEOLI: **(1)** imp. *CIL* x 2828 (Lat. Patulcia Syneche)

**Συνήθεια**
LEUKAS: **(1)** hell. *IG* IX (1) 581 (-θεα)
S. ITALY (APULIA):
—TEANUM APULUM: **(2)** imp. *Teanum Apulum* p. 121 no. 51 (Lat. Synethia)
S. ITALY (CALABRIA):
—BRENTESION-BRUNDISIUM: **(3)** imp. *Epigraphica* 25 (1963) p. 64 no. 57 (Lat. Accia Synethea)
S. ITALY (CAMPANIA):
—DIKAIARCHIA-PUTEOLI*: **(4)** imp. *CIL* x 2833 (Lat. Pavillia Synethea: freed.)
—NEAPOLIS: **(5)** i BC/i AD *INap* 168, 1; cf. Leiwo p. 78 no. 23 (-θια)

**Συνήθειος**
S. ITALY (CAMPANIA):
—POMPEII: **(1)** i BC-i AD *CIL* IV 2155 with Add. p. 465 (Lat. Synethaeus)

**Σύνις**
LAKONIA: **(1)** c. 550 BC *Cl. Rh.* 8 p. 86; *LSAG*² pp. 190 n. 2; 199 no. 16 (name) (Σίνυς—ed. pr.)

**Συννοῶν**
AIGINA: **(1)** vi/v BC *RE* (-); *Alt-Ägina* II (2) pp. 45-6 (f. Πτόλιχος: sculptor)

**Σύνοδος**
S. ITALY (CAMPANIA):
—NOLA: **(1)** imp. *CIL* x 1294 (Lat. Synodus)
—POMPEII: **(2)** 70-79 AD ib. IV 7418 (Castrèn 221. 12); Mouritsen p. 109 (date) (Lat. Lollius Synhodus)

**Σύνταξις**
S. ITALY (LUCANIA):
—VOLCEI: **(1)** imp. *Suppl. It.* 3 p. 73 no. 1 (Lat. Erenia Syntaxis: m. Erenia Successa)

**Συντρόφη**
S. ITALY (APULIA):
—CANNAE: **(1)** ii AD *Epig. Rom. di Canosa* 83 (*CIL* IX 320) (Lat. Syntrofe: m. Aurelia Ianuaria)

**Συντροφιανός**
S. ITALY (BRUTTIUM):
—RHEGION: **(1)** imp. *IG* XIV 618, 4 (Γ. Ἰούλ. Σ.)

**Σύντροφορ**
ELIS:
—OLYMPIA*: **(1)** i/ii AD *IvOl* 87, 4 ([Σ]ύντροφορ: ?s. Θεόφραστος: slave?)

**Σύντροφος**
ELIS:
—OLYMPIA*: **(1)** f. ii AD ib. 92, 22 (Σύ[ντ]ροφος: ?s. Σόφων: slave?)
KORINTHIA:
—SIKYON: **(2)** hell. *SEG* XXXIV 217 (f. Χρωτάριον)
LAKONIA:
—HYPERTELEATON*: **(3)** imp. *IG* V (1) 1083 (s. Φίλων)
—SPARTA: **(4)** ii AD ib. 159, 11 (Bradford (2)); **(5)** c. 150-160 AD *IG* V (1) 71 II, 21 (Bradford (1)) (s. Νίκανδρος)
S. ITALY (CAMPANIA):
—DIKAIARCHIA-PUTEOLI: **(6)** imp. *CIL* x 2713 (Lat. L. Marius Syntrophus: f. Εὐτυχιανός); **(7)** m. i AD Camodeca, *L'Archivio Puteolano* I p. 125 no. 5 (Lat. M. Amullius Syntrophus)
—KYME: **(8)** 251 AD *CIL* x 3699 I, 32 (Lat. C. Cautius (S)yntropus); **(9)** ~ ib. 3699 II, 5 (Lat. M. Valerius Syntropus)
—POMPEII: **(10)** i BC-i AD ib. IV 8711 (Lat. Verrius Syntrophus)
SICILY:
—LIPARA: **(11)** ?iii AD *NScav* 1947, p. 218 no. 5 + *Epigraphica* 11 (1949) pp. 54-5 (Κλώδις Σ.)
—SYRACUSE: **(12)** iii-v AD *IG* XIV 171 (Strazzulla 112; Wessel 1200)
—ZANKLE-MESSANA?: **(13)** ?i AD *Epigraphica* 3 (1941) p. 258 no. 13 (Lat. C. Terentius Syntrophus: f. Σύμφορος)

**Συντύχη**
S. ITALY (APULIA):
—CANUSIUM: **(1)** ?i-ii AD *Epig. Rom. di Canosa* 112 (*CIL* IX 369) (Lat. Syntyche)
S. ITALY (CALABRIA):
—BRENTESION-BRUNDISIUM: **(2)** ?ii AD ib. 116 (Lat. Flavia Synty[ch]e); **(3)** iii AD *NScav* 1892, p. 353 t (*Epigraphica* 25 (1963) p. 61 no. 50) (Lat. Octavia Suntuche)
—BRENTESION-BRUNDISIUM*: **(4)** imp. *CIL* IX 102 (Lat. Corfidia Syntyche: freed.); **(5)** ~ ib. 156 (Lat. Octavia Sy(n)tyche: freed.); **(6)** ~ ib. 6100 (Lat. Marcia Syntyche: freed.)
S. ITALY (CAMPANIA):
—BAIAI*: **(7)** imp. ib. x 1762 (Lat. Aviania Syntyche: freed.?)
—DIKAIARCHIA-PUTEOLI*: **(8)** imp. ib. 3014 (Lat. Titinia Syntyche: freed.)
—MISENUM*: **(9)** ?ii-iii AD *AJA* 2 (1898) p. 393 no. 51 (Lat. Aurelia Syntyche)
—SURRENTUM: **(10)** imp. *CIL* x 751 (Lat. Proba Syntyca)

**Συνωρίς**
S. ITALY (CAMPANIA):
—POMPEII: **(1)** i BC-i AD ib. IV 1397-8; 1408 (Lat. Synoris)
—STABIAE: **(2)** ?i-ii AD *RAAN* 19 (1938-9) p. 98 (Lat. Claudia Synoris: m. Πολυβιανός)

**Σύρα**
ARGOLIS:
—ARGOS:
——(Paionidai): **(1)** f. iii BC *IG* IV (1) 529, 22
ILLYRIA:
—APOLLONIA: **(2)** iii-ii BC *IApoll* 33
—EPIDAMNOS-DYRRHACHION: **(3)** ii-i BC *IDyrrh* 381 (d. Κέρδων); **(4)** hell.-imp. ib. 380; **(5)** imp. ib. 382 (Σ. Φρονίκα—lap.: ?d. Φρονίκας); **(6)** ?i AD *BUST* 1961 (1), p. 111 no. 9 (Lat. Sura)
ITHAKE: **(7)** iv/iii BC Unp. (Stavros Mus., Ithaka) (d. Σώτων)
S. ITALY (CAMPANIA):
—HERCULANEUM: **(8)** i BC-i AD *CIL* IV 10648 (Lat. Sira)
S. ITALY (LUCANIA):
—POSEIDONIA-PAESTUM*: **(9)** i AD Mello–Voza Add. p. 329 a (Lat. Titidia Sura: freed.)
SICILY:
—SYRACUSE*: **(10)** iii-v AD Strazzulla 216 (Wessel 177) (slave?)

**Συρακοσία**
SICILY:
—SYRACUSE: **(1)** iii-v AD *Riv. Arch. Crist.* 17 (1940) p. 48 no. 2

**Συρακόσιος**
SICILY:
—SYRACUSE: **(1)** iii-v AD *IG* XIV 172 (Strazzulla 72; Agnello 11; Wessel 872); cf. Ferrua, *NG* 174; **(2)** ~ Strazzulla 404 (Wessel 379); **(3)** ~ Agnello 32 (Wessel 854) (bp.)

**Συρακόσις**
SICILY:
—SYRACUSE (NESOS): **(1)** iii-v AD *SEG* IV 18 (Wessel 3)

**Συράκουσα**
SICILY:
—SYRACUSE: **(1)** s. viii BC Plu., *Mor.* 773 B (d. Ἀρχίας (Korinth): fict.?); **(2)** iii-v AD *IG* XIV 132 (Strazzulla 71; Wessel 1145) (Σε-)

**Συρία**
ARGOLIS:
—HERMIONE: **(1)** ?ii-i BC *IG* IV (1) 731 III, 15 (d. Σωκλῆς)

**Συριακός**
S. ITALY: **(1)** imp. *CIL* x 8059. 251 (seal) (Lat. M. Maius Syriacus)
SICILY:
—KATANE: **(2)** imp. ib. 7045 (Lat. M. Antonius Syriacus)

**Συριανός**
KORINTHIA:
—KORINTH: **(1)** imp. *Corinth* VIII (1) 74; **(2)** byz. ib. XII p. 336, 2884
S. ITALY (APULIA):
—VENUSIA: **(3)** v AD *JIWE* I 47 (*CIJ* I 579) (f. Ἀσθήρ: Jew)

**Σύριλλα**
AKARNANIA:
—ANAKTORION: **(1)** iii BC *IG* IX (1)² (2) 593 (Σύρι(λ)λα)
S. ITALY (APULIA):
—CANUSIUM*: **(2)** imp. *Epig. Rom. di Canosa* 123 (*CIL* IX 374) (Lat. Dasimia Syri[lla]: m. A. Dasimius Primigenius: freed.)

**Σύριον**
EPIROS:
—PHOINIKE: (1) iii BC Ugolini, *Alb. Ant.* 2 p. 155 no. 12

**Συρίσκα**
DALMATIA:
—TRAGURION: (1) imp. *CIL* III 2675 (Lat. Surisca)
SICILY:
—SYRACUSE: (2) imp. *IG* XIV 24 (*Δεκομία Σ.*)

**Συρίων**
S. ITALY (CAMPANIA):
—MISENUM*: (1) imp. *CIL* X 3486 (Lat. M. Plarentius Syrio)

**Σύρμας**
ILLYRIA:
—EPIDAMNOS-DYRRHACHION: (1) hell.-imp. *IDyrrh* 383 (*Σύρρας?*—ed.)

**Σύρος**
ARKADIA:
—TEGEA: (1) s. iv BC *SEG* XXXVI 383, 7 (s. *Μικυθίων*)
ELIS: (2) imp. *PAE* 1983, p. 165 with pl. 143 γ
—OLYMPIA*: (3) i BC/i AD *IvOl* 74, 10 (?s. *Πλειστ*—: slave?)
KORINTHIA:
—KORINTH: (4) i AD *Hesp.* 55 (1986) p. 278 no. 9 with fig. 3
S. ITALY (APULIA):
—CANUSIUM*: (5) ?i AD *Epig. Rom. di Canosa* 92 (*CIL* IX 361) (Lat. A. Baebius Surus: freed.)
S. ITALY (BRUTTIUM):
—RHEGION: (6) imp.? *IG* XIV 2400. 16 (tile)
S. ITALY (CAMPANIA):
—HERCULANEUM: (7) i BC-i AD *CIL* IV 10513 (Lat. Syrus)
—POMPEII: (8) i BC-i AD ib. 4770 (Lat. Syrus) ?= (9)
—POMPEII*: (9) i BC-i AD ib. 8732 (Lat. Syrus: slave?) ?= (8)
S. ITALY (LUCANIA):
—ATINA LUCANA: (10) imp. *IItal* III (1) 150 (*CIL* X 368) (Lat. Tullius Syrus); (11) ~ *IItal* III (1) 199 (Lat. Surus)
SICILY:
—SYRACUSE: (12) iii-v AD Strazzulla 320

**Συρτικός**
S. ITALY (CAMPANIA):
—POMPEII: (1) i BC-i AD *CIL* IV 568; 935 g; 9936 (Castrèn 454. 21) (Lat. P. Vettius Syrticus); (2) ~ *CIL* IV 799; 7762 (Castrèn 375. 12) (Lat. L. Sextius Syrticus)

**Συρτίς**
S. ITALY (CAMPANIA):
—NUCERIA ALFATERNA*: (1) i AD *SEG* XXXII 1023 (biling.) (Lat. Syrtis: freed.)

**Συρτόνικος?**
ARGOLIS:
—HERMIONE: (1) i BC-i AD? *IG* IV (1) 730 II, 5 (*Στρ[α]τόνικος?*—*LGPN*, *Εὐ(φρ)ονίσ(κ)ου*—Keil: f. *Ἀπολλώνιος*)

**Σύχαιος**
SICILY:
—KAMARINA: (1) f. v BC Cordano, *Tessere Pubbliche* 38

**Σφαῖρος**
ELIS:
—LASION: (1) c. 230-200 BC *BCH* 45 (1921) p. 14 II, 127 (s. *Πομπαῖος*)
LAKONIA:
—SPARTA: (2) 640 BC Moretti, *Olymp.* 55 (Poralla² 679)

S. ITALY (CAMPANIA):
—HERCULANEUM: (3) 62 AD *PdelP* 8 (1953) p. 460 no. 47 (Lat. L. Marcius Sphaerus)
—HERCULANEUM*: (4) i BC-i AD *CIL* X 1403 g I, 4 (Lat. Sphaerus: freed.)

**Σφακίας**
AITOLIA:
—THESTIEIS: (1) c. 202 BC *IG* IX (1)² (1) 30, 5

**Σφενδονίων**
ARGOLIS:
—ARGOS: (1) c. 458 BC ib. I³ 1149, 19 ([*Σ*]*φενδονίōν*)

**Σφένδων**
S. ITALY (CALABRIA):
—TARAS-TARENTUM: (1) iv/iii BC ib. XIV 668 I, 18 (Landi, *DISMG* 194)

**Σφογγεύς**
SICILY:
—AKRAI: (1) 35 AD *SEG* XLII 833, 12 (-*γεύς*: f. *Φαβία*)

**Σφοδρίας**
KORINTHIA:
—SIKYON: (1) 72 BC Moretti, *Olymp.* 688 (Skalet 292)
LAKONIA:
—SPARTA: (2) c. 420-371 BC *RE* (1); cf. D.S. xv 29. 5 (Poralla² 680) (*Σφοδριάδης*—D.S.: f. *Κλεώνυμος*)

**Σφοδρίων**
AKARNANIA:
—THYRREION: (1) iii BC *IG* IX (1)² (2) 596, 4 (s. *Ἡρακλε*—, f. *Να*—)
ARKADIA:
—TEGEA:
——(Krariotai): (2) iv/iii BC ib. v (2) 38, 26 (f. *Σφοδροκλῆς*)

**Σφοδροκλῆς**
ARKADIA:
—TEGEA:
——(Krariotai): (1) iv/iii BC ib. l. 26 (s. *Σφοδρίων*)

**Σφόρτος**
KORINTHIA:
—KORINTH: (1) c. 570-550 BC Amyx 92 A. 7 (vase) (Lorber 120) (fict.?)

**Σφύρας**
SICILY:
—SELINOUS: (1) vi/v BC Manganaro, *PdelP* forthcoming no. 18 (f. *Δεινίας*)

**Σφυρίδας**
ARGOLIS:
—EPIDAUROS*: (1) c. 370-365 BC Peek, *IAEpid* 52 B, 18

**Σχίδας**
EPIROS:
—ARTICHIA: (1) 356-354 BC *IG* IV (1)² 95, 30 (Perlman E.2); Perlman p. 40 f. (date); Hammond, *Epirus* pp. 518-19 (locn.)

**Σχῦρος**
ARGOLIS:
—HERMIONE: (1) iii BC *IG* IV (1) 729 II, 2 (s. *Εὐθυμήδης*)

**Σώανδρος**
ARGOLIS:
—ARGOS: (1) ii/i BC *SEG* XXVIII 1246, 31 (*Σώ[α]νδρος*: f. *Ἰναχίδας*)
KERKYRA: (2) ?ii-i BC *IG* IX (1) 807; cf. 806 (tiles) (*Σώ[σ]ανδρος?*—no. 807)

LAKONIA:
—SPARTA: (3) c. 80-110 AD ib. v (1) 97, 8; 674, 9; *SEG* XI 513, 2; 564, 15; 569, 3; 626, 1 (Bradford (2)) (s. *Τρύφων*); (4) c. 100-125 AD *IG* v (1) 57, 10 (Bradford (1)) (II s. *Σώανδρος* I); (5) ~ *IG* v (1) 57, [10] (Bradford (3)) (I f. *Σώανδρος* II)

**Σωγένης**
AIGINA: (1) f. v BC Pi., *N.* vii, 8, 70, 91; cf. Klee pp. 99-100 no. 26 (s. *Θεαρίων*)
ARGOLIS:
—EPIDAUROS*: (2) c. 370-365 BC Peek, *IAEpid* 52 B, 69
—TROIZEN: (3) iii BC *IG* IV (1) 824, 8 (s. *Νικόστρατος*)
KORINTHIA:
—KORINTH: (4) ii-iii AD *Corinth* VIII (1) 87 (*Πόντιος Σ.*)
S. ITALY: (5) s. iv BC *Neapolis* 2 (1914) p. 117; *Misc. Etrusco-Italica* 1 p. 196 no. A4 (bronze) (-*νēς*)
S. ITALY (CALABRIA):
—TARAS-TARENTUM: (6) c. 212-209 BC Vlasto 975-7; 987-8 (coins) (Evans, *Horsemen* p. 210 X B.1)

**Σωδάμας**
ARGOLIS:
—ARGOS: (1) 395 BC Paus. iii 9. 8

**Σώδαμος**
AKARNANIA:
—THYRREION: (1) m. iii BC *SEG* XL 464 II side 2, 4 ([*Σ*]*ώδαμος*)
ARGOLIS:
—ARGOS: (2) ?v BC *Argive Heraeum* 2 p. 332 nos. 1824-5 (*Σόδα[μος]*); (3) 337-328 BC *CID* II 74 I, 72; 76 II, 21; 79 A I, 18; 121 III, 12 (s. *Σοαίνας*); (4) iii BC *IG* IV (1)² 321 (f. *Κλεύδαμος*); (5) f. i BC Unp. (Ch. Kritzas) (f. *Πειθαγόρας*)
—EPIDAUROS: (6) ii/i BC *IG* IV (1)² 214; 216; 217; 219; Peek, *IAEpid* [96] (s. *Εὔκλιππος*, f. *Εὔκλιππος*, *Χαρικώ*); (7) i BC ib. 281 ([*Σ*]*ώδαμ[ος]*); (8) s. i BC *IG* IV (1)² 101, 4; 650; 651; 652, 2 (s. *Δαμοφάνης*, f. *Γν. Κορν. Νικάτας*, *Ἀρχέλοχος*)
—EPIDAUROS*: (9) c. 335-325 BC ib. 106 III, 116 (*Σώδ[αμος]*)
—HERMIONE: (10) ii BC ib. IV (1) 689 (s. *Ἑρμίας*); (11) ii-i BC ib. 732 IV, 25 (f. *Κέρδων*)
—HERMIONE*: (12) iv BC ib. 742, 2
—METHANA-ARSINOE: (13) i BC ib. 853, 8 (f. *Ἴάρων*)
ARKADIA:
—TEGEA: (14) ?vi BC Schol. E., *Hipp.* 264; Clem. Al., *Strom.* i 61. 1 (*Στρατόδημος*—Clem. Al.: s. *Ἐπήρατος*); (15) m. iv BC *IG* v (2) 6, 111
DALMATIA:
—ISSA: (16) hell. Brunšmid p. 26 no. 16 (f. *Εὔβουλος*)
EPIROS:
—AMBRAKIA: (17) iii/ii BC Unp. (Arta Mus., inscr.) (f. *Σώστρατος*); (18) a. 167 BC *SEG* XXXV 665 A, 7 (f. *Σωκράτης*)
—KASSOPE: (19) ?c. 215-195 BC *BMC Thessaly* p. 98 no. 9; Franke, *Münz. v. Epirus* p. 78 V ser. 5 (coin)
ILLYRIA:
—EPIDAMNOS-DYRRHACHION: (20) hell.-imp. *IDyrrh* 406 (f. *Τελλώ*)
MESSENIA:
—KOLONIDES: (21) 191-146 BC Unp. (Athens, NM) Empedocles Coll. 5017 (coin)
S. ITALY (CALABRIA):
—TARAS-TARENTUM: (22) c. 280-272 BC Vlasto 773-80; 782-8 (Evans, *Horsemen* p. 159 VII D.1; p. 159 VII E.1 (coins); *Samml. Ludwig* 101) (*Σάλωνος*—Evans)
S. ITALY (LUCANIA):
—HERAKLEIA: (23) iv/iii BC *NC* 1917, p. 174; 1918, p. 142; *Coll. McClean* 854 (coins) (van

Keuren, *Coinage of Heraclea* p. 84 no. 109); **(24)** ~ *SEG* xxx 1152 (Landi, *DISMG* 261)

**Σωζᾶς**
LAKONIA:
—SPARTA: **(1)** ii AD *IG* v (1) 159, 36 (Bradford (3)); **(2)** c. 110 AD *SEG* xi 516, 5 (Bradford (2)) (*Γ. Ἰούλ. Σ.*); **(3)** c. 170 AD *IG* v (1) 116, 12 (Bradford (1)) (II s. *Σωζᾶς* I); **(4)** ~ *IG* v (1) 116, [12] (Bradford (5)) (I f. *Σωζᾶς* II); **(5)** c. 230-260 AD *SEG* xi 633, 2 (Bradford (4)) ([*Σω*]*ζᾶς*: f. [*M*.] *Πόρκιο*[*s*] [*Λογ*]*γεῖνος*)

**Σωζομένη**
MESSENIA:
—MESSENE: **(1)** ii/iii AD *IG* v (1) 1483
S. ITALY (CAMPANIA):
—DIKAIARCHIA-PUTEOLI: **(2)** imp. *CIL* x 2730 (Lat. Sozomenes (gen.): m. Mercurius)
SICILY:
—LIPARA: **(3)** imp. *Epigraphica* 51 (1989) p. 192 no. 85 (Lat. Claudia Sozomene)
—SYRACUSE: **(4)** iii-v AD *Nuovo Didask.* 3 (1949) p. 33 no. 1

**Σωζομενός**
KORINTHIA:
—KORINTH: **(1)** ii AD *Ag.* VII p. 98 no. 311; *SEG* XXVII 35. 27 (lamps) ([*Σ*]*ωζωμενός*—*Ag.*)
LAKONIA:
—SPARTA: **(2)** m. iv AD Seeck, *Libanius* p. 281; *PLRE* I (-) (Bradford (-))
MESSENIA:
—MESSENE: **(3)** 80 AD *IG* v (1) 1468, 12; *SEG* XLI 340; cf. XL 366 (*Γ. Κάσιος Σ.*)
S. ITALY (CAMPANIA):
—POMPEII: **(4)** i BC-i AD *CIL* IV 343 (Lat. [S]ozomenus)
SICILY:
—SYRACUSE (NR.): **(5)** iii-v AD *NScav* 1912, p. 307

**Σώζουσα**
LAKONIA:
—SPARTA: **(1)** imp. *SEG* xi 686 (Bradford (-)) (m. *Σωσθένα*)
S. ITALY (CAMPANIA):
—DIKAIARCHIA-PUTEOLI: **(2)** imp. *CIL* x 2424 (Lat. Fisia Sozusa)
—MISENUM*: **(3)** imp. ib. 3397 (Lat. Pestania Sozusa)
SICILY:
—SYRACUSE: **(4)** imp. *IG* XIV 49
—THERMAI HIMERAIAI: **(5)** imp. *Eph. Ep.* VIII 701 (*ILat. Term. Imer.* 57) (Lat. Caecin[ia] Sozus[a])

**Σωϊάδας**
KORINTHIA:
—KORINTH: **(1)** 337-324 BC *CID* II 32, 33; 74 I, 74; 75 II, 48; 76 II, 23; 79 A I, 16; 95, 13; 97, 23; 102 II B, [32]; 120 A, 37; 121 III, 16 (*Σοϊάδας*—nos. 75-6, 121, *Σωϊδας*—nos. 74, 79, 95, 97: s. *Σωμήστωρ*)

**Σωΐβιος**
ARGOLIS:
—ARGOS:
——(Naupliadai): **(1)** ii/i BC *BCH* 33 (1909) p. 176 no. 2, 7 (II s. *Σωΐβιος* I); **(2)** ~ ib. l. 8 (I f. *Σωΐβιος* II)
—ARGOS*: **(3)** f. iii BC *IG* IV (1) 529, 9 (slave/freed.?)

**Σωΐδαμος**
LAKONIA:
—SPARTA: **(1)** f. ii BC *IC* 2 p. 244 no. 4 B, 1-2 (Bradford (-)) (f. *Ἀλεξίμαχος*)

**Σωϊκράτης**
ARGOLIS:
—ARGOS: **(1)** ii BC *SEG* XLII 279, 24 (f. *Δαμοκρίτα*); **(2)** ii-i BC *Mnem.* NS 47 (1919) p. 164 no. 9, 11 (s. *Ἀ*—); **(3)** 105 BC *JÖAI* 14 (1911) Beibl. p. 146 no. 4, 23 (*Σωϊκράτ*[*ης*]: f. —*αρία*)
——(A-): **(4)** ii-i BC *Mnem.* NS 47 (1919) p. 164 no. 9, 13

**Σωΐνικος**
LAKONIA:
—ASOPOS: **(1)** imp. *IG* v (1) 998
—HYPERTELEATON*: **(2)** imp. ib. 1062 (-*νει*-)

**Σωϊξίων**
LAKONIA:
—OITYLOS: **(1)** iii/ii BC ib. 1295, 8 (Bradford (-))

**Σώϊος**
SICILY:
—ENTELLA: **(1)** iv/iii BC *SEG* XXX 1120, 1 (Dubois, *IGDS* 207) (f. *Κίπος*)

**Σωϊπάτρα**
KORINTHIA:
—KORINTH: **(1)** i BC *IG* II² 9074 (*Σωιπάτρ*(*α*))

**Σῶϊσις**
MESSENIA:
—MESSENE: **(1)** 84 AD *SEG* XLI 334, 1 (s. *Ἐπίνικος*)

**Σώϊτιος**
LAKONIA:
—GYTHEION: **(1)** v BC ib. XI 926 (bronze) (Lazzarini 356; Poralla² 668a) (*Σō*-)

**Σώκα**
SICILY:
—KAMARINA: **(1)** v BC *SEG* XXXVIII 937 bis (Arena, *Iscr. Sic.* II 148) (*Σό*-)

**Σωκάννας**
S. ITALY (CALABRIA):
—TARAS-TARENTUM: **(1)** c. 212-209 BC Vlasto 984-6; 989-90 (coins) (Evans, *Horsemen* p. 211 X E.1; p. 211 X F.1)

**Σωκεύς**
SICILY:
—HERBESSOS: **(1)** ?v/iv BC *JNG* 33 (1983) p. 19 (gem)
—KAMARINA?: **(2)** ?v/iv BC Manganaro, *PdelP* forthcoming no. 14 (*Σō*-)

**Σωκλείδας**
AITOLIA: **(1)** c. 220-150 BC Thompson, *Agrinion* p. 74 no. 669 (coin) (*Σωκλεί*(*δας*))
ARGOLIS:
—ARGOS?: **(2)** v BC *IG* IV (1) 552, 9 (*Σ*[*ω*]*κλείδας*)
—EPIDAUROS*: **(3)** c. 320-300 BC ib. IV (1)² 110 A, 16
ARKADIA:
—TEGEA:
——(Athaneatai): **(4)** iv/iii BC ib. v (2) 38, 6 (f. *Διονύσιος*)
EPIROS:
—AMBRAKIA: **(5)** 238-168 BC Mionnet 2 p. 51 no. 41; *JIAN* 12 (1909-10) p. 45 no. 17 (coins) ([*Σ*]*ωκλείδα*(*s*)—*JIAN*); **(6)** iii/ii BC *SEG* XL 506 ([*Σ*]*ωκλείδ*[*ας*]: f. *Σώστρατος*)
KORINTHIA:
—SIKYON: **(7)** ?212-210 BC ib. XII 223, 1 (s. *Διονύσιος*)
LAKONIA:
—SPARTA: **(8)** 364 BC X., *HG* vii 4. 19 (Poralla² 681) (-*δης*); **(9)** m. iii BC *IG* IV (1)² 96, 30 (Perlman E.3); Perlman p. 63 f. (date) (Bradford (8)) (f. *Δαΐμαχος*); **(10)** i BC *IG* v (1) 125, 3 (Bradford (4)); **(11)** s. i BC *IG* v (1) 95, 10; 135, 1; *SEG* XI 505, 2 (Bradford (5)) (-*κλί*-: f.

*Ἁγησίνικος*); **(12)** ~ *IG* v (1) 133, 4 (Bradford (3)) (s. *Πίστος*); **(13)** ~ *IG* v (1) 141, 25 (*SEG* XXXV 329 (date)); *IG* v (1) 299; *FD* III (2) 160, 1 (Bradford (7)) (*Σωκ*[*λείδας*]—141, [*Σωκλεί*]*δας*—299: f. *Ἄλκιμος*); **(14)** c. 100-125 AD *IG* v (1) 152, 5; 153, 25 (Bradford (1)) (*Σωκλίδας*—152: s. *Εὔδαμος*); **(15)** c. 105-110 AD *IG* v (1) 20 B, 10; 75 B, [8] (Bradford (9)) (f. *Εὔδαμος*); **(16)** c. 105-122 AD *IG* v (1) 20 B, 1; 97, 19; *SEG* XI 564, 13; 574, [9] (Bradford (2)) (-*κλί*-: s. *Κλεώνυμος*)

**Σωκλήδεια**
LAKONIA:
—SPARTA: **(1)** a. 212 AD *IG* v (1) 597, 2 (Bradford (-)) (*Αὐρ. Σ.*: d. *Ἵλαρος*, m. *Αὐρ. Νικαφορίς*)

**Σωκλῆς**
ARGOLIS:
—ARGOS: **(1)** iii BC *IG* IV (1) 541 (tiles) ?= **(8)**
—EPIDAUROS:
——(Hylleis): **(2)** 146 BC ib. IV (1)² 28, 49 (f. *Λυσίστρατος*)
——(Hysminatai): **(3)** c. 335-325 BC ib. 106 III, 38; 108, 159; **(4)** 146 BC ib. 28, 14 (f. *Σώπολις*)
——Bounoia (Hylleis): **(5)** c. 365-335 BC ib. 103, 101
—EPIDAUROS*: **(6)** c. 335-325 BC ib. 106 I, [34], 67
—HERMIONE: **(7)** ?ii-i BC ib. IV (1) 731 III, 15 (f. *Συρία*)
—NEMEA*: **(8)** hell.? *AD* 45 (1990) Chron. p. 78 (tile) ?= **(1)**
ARKADIA:
—MANTINEIA-ANTIGONEIA: **(9)** c. 475-450 BC *IG* v (2) 262, 3 (*IPArk* 8); *LSAG*² p. 216 no. 29 (date) ([*Σ*]*ō*[*κλ*]*ῆς*)
—MEGALOPOLIS: **(10)** ii BC *IG* v (2) 447, 7
—TEGEA:
——(Hippothoitai): **(11)** iii BC ib. 40, 23 ([*Σ*]*ωκλῆς*: f. *Θεοκλῆς*)
EPIROS:
—BOUTHROTOS (PRASAIBOI): **(12)** a. 163 BC *IBouthrot* 117, 10 ?= **(14)**
——Essyrioi: **(13)** f. ii BC ib. 2, 6; 3, 6; 4, 5; 9, 2; 54, 6; 59, 7 (*SEG* XXXVIII 489; 505; 510); *IBouthrot* 69, 15; 70, 12; 71, 10 (*BCH* 118 (1994) p. 129 B 1-3); *IBouthrot* 75, 9; 76, 6; 93, 2; 94, [2]; 102, 4; 106, 5; 108, 5 (s. *Γλαυκίας*) ?= **(14)**
——Essyrioi?: **(14)** a. 163 BC ib. 105, 2?; 134, 8, 14 (f. *Γλαυκίας*) ?= **(12)** **(13)**
KORINTHIA:
—KORINTH: **(15)** vii/vi BC Amyx Gr 5 a. 4 (vase) (Lorber 2 a) (*Σόκλ ̄ες*); **(16)** c. 503 BC Hdt. v 92-3; Plu., *Mor.* 861 A (*Σωκλέης*—Hdt.)
—SIKYON: **(17)** 364 BC *Syll*³ 171 (Skalet 293) (*Σωκ*[*λῆς*])

**Σωκρατέα**
ARGOLIS:
—HERMIONE?: **(1)** i BC/i AD *IG* IV (1) 740; cf. *EAD* XXX 28
LEUKAS: **(2)** inc. *Alt-Ithaka* p. 329 β (*Σōκρατέą*—Klaffenbach)

**Σωκράτεια**
AITOLIA:
—KALLION/KALLIPOLIS: **(1)** ?160 BC *SGDI* 2280, 1, 3 (d. *Εὐαρμίδας*)
AKARNANIA:
—THYRREION: **(2)** s. iii BC *IG* IX (1)² (2) 287
ARGOLIS:
—ARGOS*: **(3)** f. iii BC ib. IV (1) 529, 14 (slave/freed.?)
—EPIDAUROS: **(4)** iii BC ib. IV (1)² 241 (d. *Σωκράτης*, ?m. *Τηλεφάνης*)
—HERMIONE: **(5)** i BC-i AD? ib. IV (1) 730 IV, 5 (-*τια*: m. *Θεοξένα*)
ILLYRIA: **(6)** 139-122 BC *FD* III (2) 222, 4, 5, 7, 9 (d. *Τιμώ*: slave/freed.)
LAKONIA:
—HYPERTELEATON: **(7)** iv AD *SEG* II 172 (-*τηα*)

## Σωκράτης

ACHAIA: (1) 401 BC D.S. xiv 19, 8; 25, 6; X., *An.* i 1. 11; i 2. 3 etc.; (2) 146 BC *IG* IV (1)² 28, 63 (s. Σωσᾶς: synoikos); (3) ~ ib. l. 68 (f. Σωτέλης: synoikos); (4) ~ ib. l. 102 (s. Δαμόκριτος: synoikos)
—AIGEIRA: (5) ?161 BC *FD* III (1) 49, 2, 7 (s. Πάτρων)
—PELLENE: (6) v BC Paus. vi 8. 1; cf. Moretti, *Olymp.* 263
—TRITAIA?: (7) m. iii BC *IG* v (2) 368, 78 with index (s. Ἀριστ—)
AIGINA: (8) ii/iii AD *Alt-Ägina* I (2) p. 47 no. 30 (*SEG* XXXVII 251) (s. Σωκ—)
AKARNANIA:
—STRATOS: (9) ii BC *IG* IX (1)² (2) 394, 10 (s. Σωτέλης, f. Σωτέλης)
—THYRREION: (10) ii BC ib. 247, 17; 251, 13 (f. Νίκανδρος); (11) ?ii BC ib. 338; (12) ii BC *SEG* XXVII 165
ARGOLIS:
—ARGOS: (13) s. iv BC ib. XXIX 364 (Σωκρά[της]: s. Ἀρν—); (14) hell. *IG* IV (1) 636; (15) 105 BC *JÖAI* 14 (1911) Beibl. p. 146 no. 4, 7 (f. Φιλίστα); (16) hell.-imp. *Suppl. Rod.* 81a, 1
—EPIDAUROS: (17) iv BC Peek, *IAEpid* 162; (18) ~ *IG* IV (1)² 181; 182; Peek, *NIEpid* 36; 37; (19) c. 365-335 BC *IG* IV (1)² 103, 147 ?= (27); (20) iii BC ib. 241 (f. Σωκράτεια); (21) c. 280 BC ib. 128, 1 (f. Ἰσυλλος); (22) ii/i BC ib. 346 (s. Τιμοκράτης); (23) ~ ib. 629, 1 (II s. Σωκράτης I); (24) ~ ib. l. 2 (I s. Ἀπολλώνιος, f. Σωκράτης II)
——(Hylleis): (25) 146 BC ib. 28, 57 (s. Νίκανδρος)
——Anaia: (26) c. 335-325 BC ib. 106 I, 91
——Mysias: (27) c. 365-335 BC ib. 103, 154 ?= (19)
—EPIDAUROS*: (28) c. 370-365 BC Peek, *IAEpid* 52 A, 7, 36
—HERMIONE: (29) iii BC *IG* IV (1) 728, 2 (f. Λέων); (30) ?ii-i BC ib. 731 I, 6 (f. Νῦσα); (31) ii-i BC ib. 732 IV, 6 (f. Σωσαρέτη); (32) iii AD ib. 713, 4 (Μ. Αὐρ. Σ.); (33) ~ *SEG* XVII 165, 1 (Μ. Αὐρ. Λικιννιανός)
—TROIZEN: (34) ?146 BC *IG* IV (1) 757 B, 8
ARKADIA:
—TEGEA:
——(Athaneatai): (35) s. iv BC ib. v (2) 41, 25 (f. —άτης)
ELIS: (36) i BC *IvOl* 68, 5 (Σωκράτ[ης])
EPIROS:
—AMBRAKIA: (37) ii-i BC *CIG* 1799 (f. Μαχάτας); (38) a. 167 BC *SEG* XXXV 665 A, 7 (s. Σώδαμος)
—BOUTHROTOS (PRASAIBOI): (39) a. 163 BC *IBouthrot* 31, 78 (*SEG* XXXVIII 490) (s. Κρίσων); (40) ~ *IBouthrot* 50, 2; (41) ~ ib. 108 (f. Νικόλαος)
——Asteatoi: (42) a. 163 BC ib. 144, 7 (s. Νικάνωρ)
—DODONA*: (43) iv-iii BC *SGDI* 1575 A
—KASSOPE: (44) ?c. 215-195 BC Franke, *Münz. v. Epirus* pp. 79-80 IX ser. 1-2 (coin)
ILLYRIA:
—AMANTIA: (45) hell.? *BUST* 1958 (2), p. 107 (*BE* 1967, no. 338)
—EPIDAMNOS-DYRRHACHION: (46) hell.-imp. *BCH* 19 (1895) pp. 369 ff. no. 19, 5; cf. *IDyrrh* 522 (s. Διονύσιος)
KEPHALLENIA:
—PRONNOI: (47) c. 210 BC *IG* IX (1)² (1) 31, 94 (s. Τιμοκράτης)
KERKYRA: (48) hell.? ib. IX (1) 889; (49) ?iii BC ib. 682, 4; cf. Fraser–Rönne, *BWGT* p. 181 (f. Γνάθιος); (50) i BC-i AD *IG* IX (1) 926
KORINTHIA:
—KORINTH: (51) iii BC *SEG* XXIII 583; (52) f. vi AD *Hesp.* 44 (1975) p. 205 no. 40 (lamp)
—SIKYON: (53) vi/v BC *SEG* XI 244, 38 (Σōκράτēς); (54) ~ ib. l. 52 (Σōκράτēς); (55) s. iv BC

*RE* (8) (Skalet 294); (56) iii BC *IG* II² 10298 (f. Διονύσιος); (57) ii BC ib. 10309 (f. Μούσιον); (58) c. 146-95 BC Roesch, *Ét. Béot.* p. 190 no. 35 (Skalet 295); cf. Stephanis 1184 (f. Θεόπομπος); (59) i BC *IG* II² 10312 (Σωκράτ[ης]: s. Φιλίσκος)
LAKONIA:
—SPARTA: (60) c. 80 BC ib. VII 416, 60 (*IOrop* 523; Bradford (8)) (f. Ἀριστοκλείδας); (61) s. i BC *IG* v (1) 95, 13 (Bradford (3)) (s. Ἱππαρχος); (62) c. 1-10 AD *IG* v (1) 209, 9; *SEG* XXXV 331 (date) (Bradford (11)) (f. Φιλόστρατος); (63) c. 100 AD *SEG* XI 510, 5 (Bradford (10)) (f. Φίλιππος); (64) c. 125 AD *IG* v (1) 1314, 5 (Bradford (2)) (Ἰούλ. Σ.: s. Εὐμένης); (65) s. ii AD *IG* v (1) 768 (Papaefthimiou p. 133 no. 4; Bradford (7)); (66) c. 170 AD *SEG* XI 530, 3 (Bradford (4)) (Κλ. Σ.); (67) c. 175-205 AD *IG* v (1) 473, 1; *SEG* XXXVI 360, 5; *BSA* 81 (1986) p. 324 no. 2 (ident., date) (Bradford (1)) (s. Ἀρίων); (68) c. 180 AD *IG* v (1) 144 a; *SEG* XI 501, 8 (Bradford (5))
——Limnai: (69) c. 70-100 AD *IG* v (1) 676, 8; *SEG* XI 488, 1 (Bradford (9)) (f. Ἐπάγαθος)
—LEUKAS: (70) c. 167-50 BC *BMC Thessaly* p. 185 nos. 165-6; p. 187 no. 187 (coins)
MESSENIA:
—THOURIA: (71) 182 BC *IvOl* 46, 9 (*IPArk* 31 IIB) (s. Ἀγαθίας)
S. ITALY (BRUTTIUM):
—LOKROI EPIZEPHYRIOI:
——(Ἀλχ.): (72) iv/iii BC De Franciscis 4, 3; 5, 3; 22, 3 (s. Φίλιππος)
S. ITALY (CALABRIA):
—BRENTESION-BRUNDISIUM: (73) imp. *CIL* IX 85 (Lat. Socratu (gen.?): ?f. Βίτων)
—TARAS-TARENTUM: (74) hell.? *IG* XIV 2406. 78 (*RA* 1932 (1), p. 40 no. 42 (loomweight)) (Σωκρά(της)); (75) c. 302-280 BC Vlasto 668-70 (Evans, *Horsemen* pp. 132-3 VI A.2 and 5 (coins)); (76) 146 or 145 BC *ID* 1442 A, 73; 1450 A, 113
S. ITALY (CAMPANIA):
—DIKAIARCHIA-PUTEOLI: (77) ?i-ii AD *CIL* X 1953 (Lat. C. Iulius Socr[ates])
—SALERNUM: (78) 497 AD *Apollo* 7 (1991) p. 41 (Lat. Socrates)
S. ITALY (LUCANIA):
—METAPONTION: (79) ?272 BC *FD* III (2) 178, 1 (s. Μόλων)
—POSEIDONIA-PAESTUM?: (80) ?i AD *IItal* I (1) 27* (*CIL* X 471) (or S. Italy (Lucania) Hyele-Velia: Lat. C. Iul. Socrates)
SICILY:
—KAMARINA: (81) iv/iii BC *SEG* XXXIX 999, 4 (Dubois, *IGDS* 125; Cordano, 'Camarina VII' 152) (Σωκρ[ά]της: s. Σωσικράτης)
—KATANE: (82) iii-v AD Agnello 58 (Wessel 1022)
—LIPARA: (83) hell.? Libertini, *Isole Eolie* p. 226 no. 53 (Σ[ω]κράτ[ης])
—TAUROMENION: (84) c. 235 BC *IG* XIV 421 an. 6 (*SGDI* 5219) (f. Ὀλυμπις); (85) c. 225 BC *IG* XIV 421 an. 16 (*SGDI* 5219); (86) c. 222 BC *IG* XIV 421 an. 19 (*SGDI* 5219)
—ZANKLE-MESSANA: (87) imp. *IG* XIV 410 (Βαλέριος Σ.)

## Σωκρατίδας

ARGOLIS:
—EPIDAUROS: (1) iv BC ib. IV (1)² 155
——(Azantioi): (2) 146 BC ib. 28, 28 (f. Νικόμαχος)
—EPIDAUROS?: (3) i AD *Suda* Π 139
LAKONIA:
—GYTHEION: (4) f. ii AD *IG* v (1) 1170, 7; 1171, 7 (II² 3596) (s. Δάμιππος); (5) 211 AD ib. v (1) 1163, 9 (s. Δάμιππος)
—SPARTA: (6) i BC-i AD ib. 744 (Bradford (2)) (?s. Δαμ—); (7) s. i BC *IG* v (1) 94, 4 (Bradford (1)) (s. Δαμ—); (8) c. 30-20 BC *IG* v

(1) 142, 16 (Bradford (4)) (f. Πασικλῆς); (9) c. 100-120 AD *IG* v (1) 99, 5; *SEG* XI 569, 11 (Bradford (3)) (s. Εὐδαμίδας) ?= (10); (10) c. 140 AD *IG* v (1) 128, 1 (Σω[κρατίδας]?: f. Εὐδαμίδας) ?= (9)
LEUKAS: (11) c. 167-50 BC *BMC Thessaly* p. 185 no. 167 (coin)

## Σωκράτις

EPIROS:
—BOUCHETION: (1) f. iii BC *Thess. Mnem.* 103 (d. Σωτίων)

## Σωκρέτης

ARKADIA:
—TEGEA: (1) m. iii BC *IG* v (2) 36, 78

## Σωμένης

KORINTHIA:
—SIKYON: (1) 176 BC *Syll*³ 585, 272 (Skalet 296) (I f. Σωμένης II); (2) ~ *Syll*³ 585, 272 (Skalet 297) (II s. Σωμένης I)

## Σωμήδης

AIGINA: (1) f. v BC *IG* IV (1) 63; *LSAG*² p. 113 no. 10 (date) (Σōμέδεος (gen.))
SICILY:
—SYRACUSE?:
——(Πλη.): (2) hell. Manganaro, *PdelP* forthcoming no. 4 IV, 1 (s. Σώταιρος)

## Σωμήστωρ

KORINTHIA:
—KORINTH: (1) 337-324 BC *CID* II 74 I, 74; 76 II, 24; 95, 13; 97, 23; 102 II B, 32; 120 A, 37; 121 III, 16 (f. Σωϊάδας)

## Σῶμος

S. ITALY (APULIA):
—KAILIA*: (1) imp. *CIL* IX 276 (Lat. P. Gellius Somus: freed.)

## Σωμροτίδας

SICILY:
—MEGARA HYBLAIA: (1) m. vi BC Guarducci, *Ep. Gr.* 1 p. 314 no. 5 (Dubois, *IGDS* 22; Arena, *Iscr. Sic.* I 3) (Σōμ-: s. Μανδροκλῆς: doctor)

## Σωναύτας

ARGOLIS:
—EPIDAUROS*: (1) c. 365-335 BC *IG* IV (1)² 103, 12 ([Σων]αύτας)

## Σώνικος

AITOLIA: (1) c. 240 BC Marcadé I 97, 2 (s. Ἀναξίων: sculptor)
—TNIMAIOI: (2) c. 225-200 BC *BCH* 50 (1926) p. 125 no. 2 a, 2 (f. Φαλακρίων)
ELIS: (3) 57-61 AD *IvOl* 79, 5 (-νει-)
—OLYMPIA*: (4) i BC ib. 423 (Σώ[ν]ικο[ς]: f. —νης)
S. ITALY (BRUTTIUM):
—KROTON: (5) c. 356-355 BC *IG* IV (1)² 95, 42 (Perlman E.2); Perlman p. 40 f. (date) (s. Πείθυς)

## Σώνοος

KORINTHIA:
—KORINTH?: (1) m. v BC *IG* IV (1) 357 (bronze) (Lazzarini 348) (Σō-: f. Ἀμων)

## Σωνύλος

DALMATIA:
—ISSA: (1) f. ii BC Brunšmid p. 23 no. 10, 8 (f. Σίβαλις)
——(Pamphyloi): (2) iv/iii BC ib. p. 8, 38 (s. Μένυλλος)

## Σώξενος

ARGOLIS:
—EPIDAUROS: (1) ?s. iv BC *IG* IV (1)² 191 + Peek, *NIEpid* 6; *IG* IV (1)² 192; *SEG* XXXVIII 319

## Σωπάτρα

ARGOLIS:
—ARGOS: (1) ii BC ib. XLII 279, 22 (d. Ἀγαλίδας)
—ARGOS*: (2) 105 BC JÖAI 14 (1911) Beibl. p. 146 no. 4, 15 ([Σω]πάτρα: slave/freed.?)
—HERMIONE: (3) ?ii-i BC IG IV (1) 731 II, 5 (m. Σωσώ)

## Σώπατρος

ACHAIA: (1) iii BC PPetr III 111, 6 (f. Φιλόθηρος)
AKARNANIA: (2) 200 BC Liv. xxxi 23. 8 (Lat. Sopater)
—ANAKTORION: (3) m. ii BC Syll3 669, 5, 6 (s. Σωτίων)
ARGOLIS:
—ARGOS: (4) f. iii BC IG IV (1) 529, 11 (Σώπατ[ρος], Σωπάτ[ρα]?); (5) 28 BC Moretti, Olymp. 723
—EPIDAUROS*: (6) c. 370-365 BC Peek, IAEpid 52 A, 29; 52 B, 76
ARKADIA:
—MANTINEIA-ANTIGONEIA: (7) c. 300-221 BC IG V (2) 323. 50 (tessera) (s. Φίλων); (8) c. 188-180 BC Thompson, Agrinion p. 42 nos. 393-4 (coins) (Σώπα[τρος])
—TEGEA: (9) f. iii BC IG V (2) 35, 40 (Σώπ[ατρος])
DALMATIA:
—ISSA: (10) hell. Brunšmid p. 26 no. 17 (SEG XL 513) + VAHD 84 (1991) p. 252 no. 2 (s. Ἀριστήν)
——(Dymanes): (11) iv/iii BC Brunšmid p. 7, 26 (f. Ἄνταλλος); (12) ~ ib. p. 9, 56 (f. Ζωΐλος)
EPIROS:
—AMBRAKIA: (13) hell.? CIG 1804 (f. Σωστρά-τα)
—BOUTHROTOS: (14) ?i BC IBouthrot 181 (Ugolini, Alb. Ant. 3 p. 211 no. 9) (Σώ-πατ[ρος])
—BOUTHROTOS (PRASAIBOI): (15) a. 163 BC IBouthrot 25, 8 (SEG XXXVIII 483) ?= (17); (16) ~ IBouthrot 31, 59 (SEG XXXVIII 490); IBouthrot 51, 20 (s. Νίκανδρος) ?= (18); (17) ~ ib. 45, 13 (s. Σωσίπατρος) ?= (15); (18) ~ ib. 122, 8 (s. Νίκανδρος) ?= (16)
ILLYRIA:
—APOLLONIA*: (19) ii AD IApoll 260 (M. Πό[ρκ(ιος)] [Σ]ώπατρος)
—EPIDAMNOS-DYRRHACHION: (20) hell.-imp. IDyrrh 289 (Λεύκι Κάτι Σώπατρε (voc.))
—SKODRAI: (21) a. 168 BC Iliria 1972, p. 400; God. Balk. Isp. 13. 11 (1976) p. 225 no. 4 (coin)
SICILY:
—AGYRION: (22) s. iii BC Holm, Gesch. Sic. 3 p. 716 no. 636 (coin)
—AKRAGAS: (23) c. 331-324 BC Hesp. 43 (1974) pp. 322 ff. no. 3, 5, 27 (s. Φιλιστίων)
—HALIKYAI: (24) f. i BC RE (5) (Lat. Sopater)
—LIPARA: (25) hell. Meligunis-Lipara 5 p. 69 T. 1994; cf. SEG XLI 799
—SELINOUS: (26) f. v BC Dubois, IGDS 33, 1-2 (Arena, Iscr. Sic. I 67)
—SYRACUSE: (27) 214 BC Liv. xxiv 23. 2; 24. 10 (Lat. Sopater); (28) c. 155 BC ID 1421 Acd II, 7; 1432 Bb II, 28; 1449 Aa I, 23
—SYRACUSE?: (29) ?s. i BC Sic. Gymn. 16 (1963) p. 61 (Ἀτείλιος Σαρρανὸς Σ.)
——(Ἑρμ.): (30) hell. Manganaro, PdelP forthcoming no. 4 I, 11 (f. Ἄνταλλος)
——(Μακ.): (31) hell. ib. l. 12 (Σώπατ[ρος]: f. Πύρρος)
——(Περ.): (32) hell. ib. l. 1 (s. Φίλων)
——(Πλη.): (33) hell. ib. no. 4 III, 3 (s. Σωσί-βιος)
—TAUROMENION: (34) c. 230 BC IG XIV 421 an. 11 (SGDI 5219) (35) c. 163 BC IG XIV 421 an. 78 (SGDI 5219) (s. Ἀπολλόδωρος)
—TYNDARIS: (36) f. i BC RE (6) (Lat. Sopater)

## Σωπολιανός

SICILY:
—SEGESTA: (1) iv/iii BC IG XIV 290, 2 (Dubois, IGDS 215); SEG XLI 825 (date) (Φάων Σ.: s. Νύμφων)

## Σώπολις

AKARNANIA:
—THYRREION: (1) ii BC IG IX (1)² (2) 314, 3 (?s. Λέων)
ARGOLIS:
—ARGOS?: (2) m. v BC Diehl, Hydria p. 217 B 97 (n. pr.?)
—EPIDAUROS: (3) i BC-i AD? Peek, NIEpid 56 a (Σώ[πο]λις: f. Εἰρήνη)
——(Hysminatai): (4) 146 BC IG IV (1)² 28, 14 (s. Σωκλῆς)
ARKADIA:
—TEGEA: (5) m. iv BC ib. V (2) 6, 109
ILLYRIA:
—APOLLONIA: (6) i BC Maier 129-30 (coin) (f. Ἀμφίας)
S. ITALY (LUCANIA):
—HERAKLEIA: (7) iv/iii BC SEG XXX 1166 (Landi, DISMG 217)
SICILY:
—SEGESTA: (8) ?ii-i BC IG XIV 288 (Dubois, IGDS 214 b; IGLMP 47) (s. Φάλακρος Ἐρύσ-σιος)
—SYRACUSE?: (9) 213 or 205 BC Nachtergael, Les Galates 66, 8, 10 (Stephanis 2339) (s. Νουμήνιος)
—TAUROMENION: (10) c. 191 BC IG XIV 421 an. 50 (SGDI 5219) (I f. Σώπολις II); (11) ~ IG XIV 421 an. 50 (SGDI 5219) (II s. Σώπολις II)

## Σῶς

AIGINA?: (1) f. v BC Riv. Stor. Antichità 4 (1974) p. 5 (vase) (Σωσ—?)

## Σωσανδρίδας

SICILY:
—SYRACUSE: (1) 208 BC IMM 72, 10 (Dubois, IGDS 97)

## Σώσανδρος

ACHAIA:
—PELLENE: (1) i BC-i AD SEG XI 1270 (f. Δά-μων)
AIGINA: (2) m. ii BC Alt-Ägina I (2) p. 43 no. 2; (3) i-ii AD ib. p. 46 no. 23 ([Σ]ώσανδρος)
AITOLIA: (4) iii BC PP 2046 + CE 26 (1951) p. 163 (IFayoum 16)
—PLEURON: (5) ?iii BC IG IX (2) 202 (RÉnip 124) (s. Εὔβουλος)
—TRICHONION: (6) s. iii BC IG IX (1)² (1) 24, [11]; 31, 84 (f. Δωρίμαχος); (7) c. 210-204 BC ib. 29, [8], 20; 31, 68, 125; cf. 13, 3 n. (ident.) (s. Σκόπας, f. Σκόπας)
AITOLIA?: (8) m. iii BC ib. 38, 8 (Σώσανδρ[ος])
AKARNANIA:
—MEDION: (9) c. 325-315 BC Hesp. 57 (1988) p. 148 A, 46 (SEG XXXVI 331); cf. Hesp. 48 (1979) pp. 78 f. with pl. 22 c (f. Νικόλαος, Σωτήριος)
—STRATOS: (10) ii BC IG IX (1)² (2) 394, 13 (s. —ίων); (11) ~ ib. 408 (Gr. Gr. 213)
—THYRREION: (12) iii-ii BC SEG XXVII 159, 5; cf. PAE 1977, pl. 244 a (s. Φρῦνος); (13) ii BC IG IX (1)² (2) 249, 7; (14) hell.-imp. ib. 359
ARGOLIS:
—EPIDAUROS:
——(Hysminatai): (15) 146 BC ib. IV (1)² 28, 164 (s. Νικόλοχος)
—METHANA-ARSINOE: (16) i BC ib. IV (1) 853, 9 (s. Διονύσιος)
ARKADIA: (17) i BC/i AD GP 2029 (fict.?)
—TEGEA:
——(Krariotai): (18) f. iii BC IG V (2) 36, 67 (Σώσαν[δρος]: f. Σεύθας: metic)

DALMATIA:
—ISSA: (19) f. ii BC Brunšmid p. 23 no. 10, 4 (s. Νίκαρχος)
——(Dymanes): (20) iv/iii BC ib. p. 9, 63 (Σώ[σ]ανδρος: s. Ἀριστόξενος)
——(Pamphyloi): (21) iv/iii BC ib. p. 8, 28 (s. Μικύλος)
EPIROS: (22) 263 BC IG IX (1)² (1) 17, 63 (s. Νικόμαχος); (23) 234-168 BC Franke, Münz. v. Epirus pp. 173-4 II ser. 19 (coin) (Σώ-σαν(δρος))
—AMBRAKIA: (24) hell.? SEG XVII 305 (s. Φιλο-κράτης); (25) iii-ii BC Op. Ath. 10 (1971) p. 65 no. 13; (26) ii-i BC CIG 1797 (SGDI 3183)
—BOUTHROTOS: (27) a. 163 BC IBouthrot 198 (Σώσαν[δρος]: s. Λυσι—)
—BOUTHROTOS (PRASAIBOI): (28) a. 163 BC ib. 14, 32 (SEG XXXVIII 471) ?= (32); (29) ~ IBouthrot 18, 7; 26, 13 (SEG XXXVIII 475; 484) (f. Ἀρκολέων); (30) ~ IBouthrot 18, 7; 26, 13; 30, 6 (SEG XXXVIII 475; 484; 488) (s. Ἀρκολέων); (31) ~ IBouthrot 22, 7 (SEG XXXVIII 479); (32) ~ IBouthrot 24, 3; 25, 4 (SEG XXXVIII 482-3) ?= (28); (33) ~ IBouth-rot 25, 25 (SEG XXXVIII 483) (Σώ[σα]νδρος); (34) ~ IBouthrot 26, [1], 20; (35) ~ ib. 50, 4, 10 ?= (46); (36) ~ ib. 106 (f. Σίμακος) ?= (46); (37) ~ ib. 130, 5; (38) ~ ib. 134, 16 (f. Θεό-τιμος); (39) ~ ib. 135, 13 (s. —νος); (40) ~ ib. 149, 8; (41) ~ ib. 152, 4
——Cheilioi: (42) a. 163 BC ib. 98, 7 (f. Κρατέας)
——Drymioi: (43) a. 163 BC ib. 8, 2 (SEG XXXVIII 480); IBouthrot 131, 4
——Opatai: (44) a. 163 BC ib. 99, 7 (BCH 118 (1994) p. 121 B)
——Pelmatioi: (45) a. 163 BC IBouthrot 69, 9; 70, 7; 71, 6 (BCH 118 (1994) pp. 129 f. B 1-3) (s. Μενέξιος)
——Porronoi: (46) a. 163 BC IBouthrot 69, 8; 71, 6; 80, 5 (BCH 118 (1994) pp. 129 f. B 1-3) (f. Σίμακος) ?= (36) (35)
——Tharioi: (47) a. 163 BC IBouthrot 126, 7 (s. Θεότιμος)
—KASSOPE: (48) f. ii BC Cabanes, L'Épire p. 564 no. 41, 7 (f. Φίλανδρος)
—THESPROTOI: (49) s. iii BC ib. p. 547 no. 17 (f. Μίλων)
KERKYRA: (50) hell. SEG XXV 613; (51) ii BC IG IX (1) 694, 38 (RIJG XXV B); cf. SEG XXV 609 (s. Θεύδωρος)
KORINTHIA:
—SIKYON: (52) m. iii BC Syll3 458 (Skalet 298) (f. Ἀριστόμαχος)
LAKONIA: (53) c. 100-90 BC SEG XXXIII 290 A, 30; BSA 70 (1975) pp. 129-31 (date); cf. Stephanis 2341 (I f. Σώσανδρος II); (54) ~ SEG XXXIII 290 A, 30; BSA 70 (1975) pp. 129-31 (date) (Stephanis 2341) (II s. Σώσαν-δρος I)
LEUKAS: (55) ii-i BC Ep. Chron. 31 (1994) p. 49 no. 5 (AD 45 (1990) Chron. p. 254 no. 5); (56) 167 BC Klio 75 (1993) p. 132, 2-3 (f. Ἄλ-κιμος); (57) c. 167-50 BC Unp. (Oxford, AM) 10. 11. 1947; Postolakas p. 85 no. 859 (NZ 10 (1878) p. 136 no. 35 (coins))
MESSENIA:
—THOURIA: (58) ii/i BC IG V (1) 1384, 2 (f. Σί-μος)
S. ITALY (BRUTTIUM):
—LOKROI EPIZEPHYRIOI:
——(Ψαθ.): (59) iv/iii BC De Franciscis 17, 5 (f. Δάμων); (60) ~ ib. 29, 4
S. ITALY (LUCANIA):
—HYELE-VELIA: (61) hell.? IG XIV 661 (Landi, DISMG 49) (?s. Ἀριστώνυμος, ?f. Φιλωνίδης); (62) imp. PdelP 21 (1966) p. 336 no. 8 (f. Ἱκεσίη)
SICILY:
—KAMARINA: (63) iii BC Manganaro, PdelP forthcoming no. 1, 7 (s. Θαρρύδαμος); (64) ~

ib. l. 8 (f. Ἀπολλωνίδας); **(65)** ~ ib. l. 9 (s. Σῶσις)
—PETRA: **(66)** f. iii BC *SEG* XXX 1121, 27 (Dubois, *IGDS* 208) (s. Ἀρίστων)
—SYRACUSE?:
——(Πλη.): **(67)** hell. Manganaro, *PdelP* forthcoming no. 4 II, 2 (s. Ἀρταμίδωρος)
—TAUROMENION: **(68)** c. 193 BC *IG* XIV 421 an. 48 (*SGDI* 5219) (f. Κλέων); **(69)** c. 40 BC *Cron. Arch.* 3 (1964) p. 54, I, 10

**Σωσαρέτα**
ARGOLIS:
—HERMIONE: **(1)** ii-i BC *IG* IV (1) 732 IV, 5 (d. Σωκράτης)

**Σώσαρχος**
MESSENIA:
—MESSENE: **(1)** iii BC *SEG* XXIII 210, 16 (Σό[σ]αρχος?)

**Σωσάρων**
LAKONIA:
—EPIDAUROS LIMERA: **(1)** imp. *IG* V (1) 1012 (s. Νικέρως)
—HYPERTELEATON*: **(2)** imp. ib. 1063 (s. Φιλόστρατος)

**Σωσᾶς**
ACHAIA: **(1)** 146 BC ib. IV (1)² 28, 63 (f. Σωκράτης: synoikos); **(2)** ~ ib. l. 122 (I f. Σωσᾶς II: synoikos); **(3)** ~ ib. l. 122 (II s. Σωσᾶς I: synoikos)
ARKADIA:
—TEGEA: **(4)** ii-iii AD *SEG* XXXIV 329

**Σωσήν**
S. ITALY: **(1)** hell. *IG* XIV 2395. 6 a-b; 2400. 17; *Kokalos* 20 (1974) p. 252 no. 23; 32 (1986) p. 239 no. 73 with n. 4; *SEG* XXXIV 957 (tiles) (or Sicily: Σωσῆνος (gen.))

**Σωσθένα**
LAKONIA:
—SPARTA: **(1)** imp. ib. XI 686 (Bradford (-)) ([Σωσ]θένα?: d. Σώζουσα, m. Εὐπορία)

**Σωσθένης**
AKARNANIA:
—THYRREION: **(1)** iii/ii BC *IG* IX (1)² (2) 308 (Σωσθέν[ης]: s. Σώστρατος)
ARGOLIS:
—EPIDAUROS (TRACHEIA (MOD.)): **(2)** 400-375 BC *SEG* XXIX 382 (Σωσθέ(νης)?: ?f. Εὐκλῆς)
—EPIDAUROS*: **(3)** c. 365-335 BC *IG* IV (1)² 103, 60
—HERMIONE: **(4)** ii-i BC ib. IV (1) 732 II, 15 (f. Ἰσίδωρος); **(5)** ~ ib. 732 III, 16 (Σωσ[θέν]ης: f. Ἀρτεμισία); **(6)** c. 135-130 BC *FD* III (4) 169, 2, 9 (Σ[ωσ]θένης: s. Ἀγαθοκλῆς)
—HERMIONE?: **(7)** iv BC *IG* IV (1) 747 A, 5 (s. Σωτελίδας)
DALMATIA:
—ISSA: **(8)** iii BC Brunšmid p. 9 fr. G, 13
——(Hylleis): **(9)** iv/iii BC ib. p. 9, 55 (f. Φίντων)
KERKYRA: **(10)** ?ii-i BC *IG* IX (1) 808 (tile); **(11)** a. 196 BC ib. IX (2) 526, 13 (f. Πυθόδωρος)
KORINTHIA:
—KORINTH: **(12)** i/ii AD *Corinth* VIII (3) 165 (Lat. Sosthe[nes])
—KORINTH?: **(13)** m. i AD *Act. Ap.* 18. 17; *1 Ep. Cor.* 1. 1 (Jew)
—SIKYON: **(14)** vi-v BC Iamb., *VP* 267 (*FVS* 58 A; Skalet 300)
LAKONIA:
—SPARTA: **(15)** c. 230-260 AD *SEG* XI 633, 9 (Bradford (1)) (Αὐρ. Σωσθ[ένη]s: II s. Σωσθένης I); **(16)** ~ *SEG* XI 633, 10 (Bradford (2)) (I f. Αὐρ. Σωσθένης II)

**Σωσιάδας**
LEUKAS: **(1)** ?iii BC Unp. (*IG* arch.)

**Σωσιάναξ**
ELIS: **(1)** 188-180 BC Thompson, *Agrinion* p. 38 nos. 333-5 (coin) (Σωσιάν[αξ])

**Σωσίας**
ACHAIA: **(1)** 146 BC *IG* IV (1)² 28, 62 (f. Νικόστρατος: synoikos); **(2)** ~ ib. l. 86 (f. Σωσικράτης: synoikos)
AKARNANIA:
—THYRREION: **(3)** ii BC ib. IX (1)² (2) 252, 14 (f. Σωτίων)
ARGOLIS:
—EPIDAUROS: **(4)** ii BC ib. IV (1)² 368 (Peek, *IAEpid* 153. 15)
—EPIDAUROS*: **(5)** c. 290-270 BC *IG* IV (1)² 109 III, 84
—TROIZEN: **(6)** iii BC ib. IV (1) 773 (s. Θέωρις)
ARKADIA:
—TEGEA: **(7)** s. v BC ib. V (2) 175, 5
DALMATIA:
—TRAGURION: **(8)** hell.? *SEG* XXXI 613 (f. Λυσώ)
ILLYRIA:
—EPIDAMNOS-DYRRHACHION: **(9)** hell.-imp. *IDyrrh* 384
KORINTHIA:
—KORINTH: **(10)** m. iii BC *Corinth* VIII (3) 33 f, 9
LAKONIA:
—HYPERTELEATON*: **(11)** imp. *IG* V (1) 1041 (Σωσ[ί]ας)
SICILY:
—AKRAGAS: **(12)** v BC Manganaro, *QUCC* forthcoming no. 2 ([Σ]ōσίας)
—GELA-PHINTIAS: **(13)** f. v BC Dubois, *IGDS* 131. 5 (Arena, *Iscr. Sic.* II 45) (Σο-)
—GELA-PHINTIAS?: **(14)** f. v BC Dubois, *IGDS* 134 b, 8 (Arena, *Iscr. Sic.* II 47) (Σō-)
—KAMARINA: **(15)** f. v BC Cordano, *Tessere Pubbliche* 18 (Σō-: f. Μαζάν); **(16)** ~ ib. 56 (Σ[ō]σία[ς]); **(17)** ~ ib. 132 (Σōσί[α]s: s. Ἱμεραῖος); **(18)** m. v BC Dubois, *IGDS* 120, 4 (Arena, *Iscr. Sic.* II 142 A; *SEG* XXXIX 939; Cordano, 'Camarina VII' 59) (Σō-: s. Ἀρχωνίδας); **(19)** ~ Dubois, *IGDS* 120, 5 (Arena, *Iscr. Sic.* II 142 A; *SEG* XXXVIII 939; Cordano, 'Camarina VII' 58) (Σō-: s. Ἀρχίας); **(20)** ?ii BC *SEG* XXXIX 996, 10 (Dubois, *IGDS* 126; Cordano, 'Camarina VII' 153) (Σωσ[ί]ας: f. Πρόδοξος)
—MORGANTINA: **(21)** ?iv/iii BC *SEG* XXXIX 1012, 4; **(22)** iv/iii BC ib. 1013, 5 (Σωσ[ία]s: s. Ξενοκλῆς)
—SELINOUS: **(23)** ?vi BC Manganaro, *PdelP* forthcoming no. 17 (Σō-)
—SYRACUSE: **(24)** c. 247-199 BC *SGDI* 2609, 3 (f. Σωσικλῆς)
—SYRACUSE?:
——(Υπα.): **(25)** hell. Manganaro, *PdelP* forthcoming no. 4 IV, 3 (f. Φιλόξενος)

**Σωσιβία**
ACHAIA:
—PELLENE: **(1)** ii-i BC *SEG* XI 1278
KEPHALLENIA:
—SAME: **(2)** imp. ib. XXXIV 475 (-συ-)
KORINTHIA:
—KORINTH: **(3)** i BC ib. XXV 278 (d. Ὀφέλλας)

**Σωσίβιος**
ACHAIA: **(1)** 220 BC *PPetr* III 112 g, 11 (s. Ξενόφαντος); **(2)** 146 BC *IG* IV (1)² 28, 148 (s. Πασιγένης: synoikos)
—PATRAI?: **(3)** i BC-i AD *Achaean Grave Stelai* 27
AKARNANIA:
—THYRREION: **(4)** ii BC *IG* IX (1)² (2) 251, 14 (Σωσικιος-lap., Σωσί(β)ιος, Σώσικος?-ed.: s. Διόφαντος)

ARGOLIS:
—EPIDAUROS: **(5)** i-ii AD Peek, *NIEpid* 49, 1 (f. Χάρης); **(6)** iii AD *IG* IV (1)² 528 (I f. Σωσίβιος II); **(7)** ~ ib. (II s. Σωσίβιος I)
—EPIDAUROS*: **(8)** c. 335-325 BC Peek, *IAEpid* 50, 19
—HERMIONE: **(9)** iii BC *IG* IV (1) 729 II, 7
—TROIZEN: **(10)** f. ii AD ib. 758, 17 (f. Ἀπελλῆς)
KORINTHIA:
—TENEA: **(11)** i AD ib. II² 10437 (f. Ζωπυρίς)
LAKONIA: **(12)** iii/ii BC *RE* (2); *FGrH* 595 (Bradford (4))
—SPARTA: **(13)** i-ii AD *IG* XIV 1691, 3 (Bradford (2)) (Γ. Ἰούλ. Σ.: s. Σερῆνος); **(14)** c. 110-135 AD *IG* V (1) 103, 12; *SEG* XI 579, 3 (Bradford (5)) (I f. Σωσίβιος II); **(15)** ~ *IG* V (1) 103, 12; *SEG* XI 579, 3 (Bradford (3)) (II s. Σωσίβιος I); **(16)** c. 140 AD *SEG* XI 522, 8 (Bradford (1)) ([Γ.] [Ἰούλ.] [Σωσί]βιος?: s. Κλεόδαμος)
S. ITALY (BRUTTIUM):
—LOKROI EPIZEPHYRIOI:
——(Θρα.): **(17)** 278 BC De Franciscis 12, 7; 27, 2; 30, 6 (f. Γλαυκίας)
S. ITALY (CALABRIA):
—TARAS-TARENTUM: **(18)** ?285-247 BC *RE* Supplbd. 7 (2a) (*PP* 4320a)
S. ITALY (LUCANIA):
—HERAKLEIA: **(19)** c. 280 BC *SNG ANS Etruria-Calabria* 83 (coin) (van Keuren, *Coinage of Heraclea* p. 79 no. 95)
SICILY:
—AKRAI: **(20)** hell.? *SGDI* 3244 (*Akrai* p. 158 no. 12) (f. Ἀριστόδαμος)
—SYRACUSE?:
——(Πλη.): **(21)** hell. Manganaro, *PdelP* forthcoming no. 4 III, 3 (f. Σώπατρος)

**Σωσιγένης**
AIGINA: **(1)** s. iv BC *SEG* I 362, 1, 4; cf. Stephanis 2187 (f. Πῶλος)
AKARNANIA:
—OINIADAI: **(2)** iii/ii BC *IG* IX (1)² (2) 419. 6
ARGOLIS:
—ARGOS: **(3)** hell. ib. VII 1563 (s. Ἀρίστανδρος)
—METHANA-ARSINOE: **(4)** ii-i BC ib. II² 9328 (f. Ἀριστοβούλα)
ARKADIA:
—MEGALOPOLIS: **(5)** ?iv-iii BC Paus. viii 31. 7 ?= (7); **(6)** 134 or 130 BC *FD* III (3) 120, 8, 15 (s. Πῶλος); **(7)** ii/i BC *IG* V (2) 443, 29 (*IPArk* 32); cf. *SEG* XLII 352 ?= (5)
—STYMPHALOS?: **(8)** iii BC *IG* V (2) 352, 9 ([Σω]σιγένης?: s. Φιλ—)
KERKYRA: **(9)** c. 229-48 BC *BMC Thessaly* p. 149 nos. 527-8 (coins)
LEUKAS: **(10)** hell.-imp. *AD* 44 (1989) Chron. p. 266 (*Ep. Chron.* 31 (1994) p. 43)
S. ITALY (CAMPANIA):
—NEAPOLIS: **(11)** 98 BC *ID* 1761, 5 (s. Θεόδωρος)
—POMPEII: **(12)** i BC-i AD *CIL* IV 8943 (Lat. Sosigenes)
SICILY:
—KAMARINA: **(13)** hell. *SEG* XXXIX 1001, 4, 6 (s. Ἀπολλωνίδας)

**Σωσίδαμος**
ARGOLIS:
—HERMIONE: **(1)** ?ii-i BC *IG* IV (1) 731 III, 8 (f. Ἐπίκτησις)
EPIROS:
—AMBRAKIA: **(2)** 128 BC *BCH* 49 (1925) p. 90 no. 19, 5, 10 (Σωσί[δ]αμος: I f. Σωσίδαμος II); **(3)** ~ ib. l. 5, 10 (II s. Σωσίδαμος I)
LAKONIA:
—SPARTA: **(4)** ?s. i AD *SEG* XI 485 (Bradford (3)) (Σωσίδαμ[ος]); **(5)** c. 100-110 AD *SEG* XI 517, 7; 537 a, 8; 537 b, 4; 563, 5; 564, 26; 569, 26 (Bradford (7)); (8)) (I f. Σωσίδαμος II); **(6)** ~ *SEG* XI 517, 7; 537 a, 8; 537 b, 4; 563, 5; 564,

26; 569, 26 (Bradford (1); (2)) (II s. Σωσίδα-
μος I); (7) ?f. ii AD IG v (1) 296, 2; Artemis
Orthia pp. 318-19 no. 41 (date) (Bradford (6))
(f. Νικάγορος); (8) c. 105-110 AD IG v (1) 20
B, 3; BSA 26 (1923-5) p. 168 C 6/7, 8 (Brad-
ford (4)) (f. Ἀγαθοκλῆς); (9) c. 140-145 AD IG
v (1) 1314, 40 (Bradford (5)) (f. Ἀριστέας);
(10) c. 140-160 AD IG v (1) 112, 7; SEG XI
585, 8; XXX 410, 9; XXXIV 307, 5 (Bradford
(9)) (f. Σπαρτιάτης)
MESSENIA:
—THOURIA: (11) ii-i BC IG v (1) 1385, 14 (f.
Νέων)
S. ITALY (BRUTTIUM):
—LOKROI EPIZEPHYRIOI:
——(Λακ.): (12) iv/iii BC De Franciscis 22, 6

Σωσίδας
ARGOLIS:
—HERMIONE: (1) ii-i BC IG IV (1) 732 IV, 24
(f. Ἀφροδίσιος)

Σωσίθεος
SICILY:
—ENTELLA: (1) f. i BC Cic., In Verr. II iii 200
(Lat. Sosítheus)
—SYRACUSE: (2) ?m. iii BC Suda Σ 860; RE (5);
cf. Fraser, Ptol. Alex. 2 pp. 851 nn. 356-7;
871 n. 6

Σωσικλέα
KORINTHIA:
—KORINTH: (1) i BC IG II² 9076

Σωσίκλεια
ARGOLIS:
—EPIDAUROS: (1) iii BC ib. IX (2) 362 (d. Ἀρι-
στοκλῆς)

Σωσικλείδας
ARGOLIS:
—METHANA-ARSINOE: (1) i BC ib. IV (1) 853, 6
(s. Ποίμαρχος)
KORINTHIA:
—SIKYON: (2) ?255-254 BC Nachtergael, Les
Galates 8, 72; 9, 77; cf. Stephanis 1750 (Σω-
σικλείδης—no. 8, Σωσικλέους (gen.)—no. 9: f.
Μόσχος)
PELOPONNESE: (3) 112 BC FD III (2) 70 A, 30
(s. Φιλοκράτης)

Σωσικλείδης
AIGINA: (1) 132 AD IG II² 3291, 8

Σωσικλῆς
AIGINA: (1) ?ii AD Alt-Ägina I (2) p. 49 no. 45
(M. Αὐρ. Σωσικλ[ῆς])
ARGOLIS:
—EPIDAUROS: (2) iii/ii BC IG IV (1)² 281 (s.
Ἀριστοκλῆς)
—NEMEA*: (3) hell.? SEG XXXIV 288 A; AD 45
(1990) Chron. p. 78 (tiles)
—PHLEIOUS: (4) iii BC SEG XI 278; (5) iii-ii BC
IG IV (1) 469
ARKADIA:
—MANTINEIA-ANTIGONEIA: (6) ?iii BC ib. v (2)
318, 8
—TEGEA: (7) ?ii BC ib. 242
——(Krariotai): (8) f. iii BC ib. 36, 45 (s. Μό-
σχος: metic)
ELIS:
—OLYMPIA*: (9) 245-249 AD IvOl 121, 22 (?s.
Αὐρ. Ἰουλιανός: slave?)
KORINTHIA:
—SIKYON: (10) ?273 BC FD III (1) 473, 6; III
(3) 203, 4 (Skalet 302)
LAKONIA:
—KARDAMYLE: (11) i AD SEG XI 948, 19 (f.
Ἐράτων)
MESSENIA:
—THOURIA: (12) ii-i BC IG v (1) 1385, 8 (s.
Ἐπιτέλης)

SICILY:
—SYRACUSE: (13) iv BC Suda Σ 863 (f. Σωσιφάνης); (14) hell. Plaut., Men. passim (Lat. Sos-
icles: fict.); (15) c. 247-199 BC SGDI 2609, 3
(s. Σωσίας)

Σωσικράτεια
ARGOLIS:
—ARGOS: (1) ii BC IG II² 8374, 1 (d. Ἀλέξανδρος)
—KLEONAI: (2) i BC-i AD SEG XXV 277, 1 (d.
Ἡρωίδης)
—TROIZEN: (3) i BC/i AD IG IV (1) 816 (-τηα)
LAKONIA:
—SPARTA: (4) c. 100-125 AD ib. v (1) 483, 9
(Bradford (-)) (d. Κλεώδαμος)
—TEUTHRONE: (5) ii-iii AD IG v (1) 1222 (GVI
991)
LEUKAS: (6) hell. IG IX (1) 582 (Fraser–Rönne,
BWGT p. 116 no. 4) (Σωσικράτει[α])

Σωσικράτη
ARGOLIS:
—EPIDAUROS: (1) imp. SEG XXX 400
(masc./fem.?)

Σωσικράτης
ACHAIA: (1) 146 BC Plb. xxxviii 18. 2-4; (2)
~ IG IV (1)² 28, 60 (I f. Σωσικράτης II:
synoikos); (3) ~ ib. l. 60 (II s. Σωσικράτης I:
synoikos); (4) ~ ib. l. 86 (s. Σωσίας: synoikos);
(5) ~ ib. l. 130 (f. Εὐκράτης: synoikos)
—DYME*: (6) c. 219 BC SGDI 1612, 30 (Tyche
5 (1990) p. 124) (f. Σωτίων)
AITOLIA: (7) ii/i BC IG II² 7992
AKARNANIA:
—PALAIROS: (8) ii-i BC SEG XXVII 156-7
ARGOLIS:
—EPIDAUROS: (9) ii BC IG IV (1)² 371 (Peek,
IAEpid 153. 18) (f. Σωτήριχος); (10) ii/i BC
IG IV (1)² 231 + Peek, IAEpid 99 (Σω-
σι[κράτης]—Peek, Σωσι[κλῆς]—IG: f. Ἀριστο-
κλῆς)
——(Azantioi): (11) 146 BC IG IV (1)² 28, 26 (s.
Ἀριστείδας)
—HERMIONE: (12) ?ii-i BC ib. IV (1) 731 I, 10
(f. Ἀμμία)
ARKADIA:
—KLEITOR: (13) a. 212 AD SEG XXXI 347, 7;
(14) m. iii AD ib. XXXV 350 I, 3 (Αὐρ. Σω-
σι[κ]ράτης: s. Εὐτύχης)
—TEGEA: (15) ?ii-i BC IG v (2) 243; (16) i/ii AD
ib. 87 (Σωσικράτης: f. Φλάβιος); (17) ii AD ib.
55, 34 (f. Εὐφρόσυνος); (18) ~ ib. l. 42 (f. Καλ-
λᾶς); (19) 165 AD ib. 50, 19 (f. Μᾶρκος)
——(Krariotai): (20) s. iii BC ib. 36, 126 (s. Καλ-
λίας: metic)
ARKADIA?: (21) c. 200 BC SEG XVII 829, 7, 16
ILLYRIA:
—APOLLONIA: (22) c. 250-50 BC Jubice Hoard
p. 98 no. 1 (coin) (Ceka 33) (pryt.); (23) ~
Maier 34; 78 (coin) (Ceka 103-4) (money.);
(24) imp. IApoll 152 ([Σω]σικράτης: s. ——ήν)
——(Ar.): (25) iii/ii BC ib. 7; cf. L'Illyrie mérid.
2 p. 207 (f. Νουμήνιος)
KEPHALLENIA:
—PRONNOI: (26) c. 210 BC IG IX (1)² (1) 31, 94
(s. Τιμοκράτης)
KORINTHIA:
—SIKYON: (27) ?257-255 BC Nachtergael, Les
Galates 7, 73; 8, 75 (Skalet 304; Stephanis
2350) (s. Λεπτίνας); (28) ?255 BC Nachtergael,
Les Galates 8, 29 (Skalet 304); cf. Stephanis
1466 (f. Κλέων); (29) ?253 BC Nachtergael, Les
Galates 10, 67 (Skalet 305; Stephanis 2351)
(s. Μνασίων); (30) s. iii BC IG IX (1)² (1) 24,
4 (s. Ἀλκαμένης); (31) c. 146-32 BC Coll. Mc-
Clean 6300 (coin); (32) ii-iii AD SEG XI 256,
1, 12 (s. Ἀρκαδίων, f. Ἀφροδισία, ?f. Ἡρᾶς)
LAKONIA:
—GYTHEION: (33) ii BC IG v (1) 1152
([Σ]ωσικράτ[ης]: f. Ἀγαθόκλεια)

—SPARTA: (34) c. 25-1 BC ib. 210, 36 (Bradford (20)) (f. Φίλιππος); (35) c. 1-10 AD IG
v (1) 209, 18; SEG XXXV 331 (date) (Bradford (17)) (f. Μαντικλῆς); (36) i/ii AD BSA 89
(1994) p. 434 no. 4, 3 (Σωσικρ[άτης]); (37) c.
90-100 AD SEG XI 609, 4; 626, 4 (Bradford
(19)) (f. Φιλήτωρ); (38) c. 100-105 AD SEG XI
561, 2 (Bradford (7)) ([Σω]σικράτης: s. Θεόδωρος); (39) c. 100-125 AD IG v (1) 137, 19
(Bradford (3)) (s. Φιλάκων); (40) ii AD IG v
(1) 159, 14 (Bradford (8)); (41) f. ii AD IG v
(1) 20 B, 7; 51, 35; 52, 8; 660, 2; SEG XI 537
a, 7; 537 b, 3; 538, 4; 594, 4 (Bradford (16))
(f. Κλέων); (42) c. 105-110 AD SEG XI 569, 6
(Bradford (6)) (s. Τάνταλος); (43) c. 105-140
AD SEG XI 482; 543, 1; 582, [3]? (Bradford
(10)) (M. Οὔλπ. Σ.); (44) c. 110 AD SEG XI
516, 3 (Bradford (14)) (f. Εὐδαμίδας); (45) c.
110-160 AD IG v (1) 65, 17; SEG XI 549,
7; 585, 4; 586, 3 (Bradford (1)) (s. Ἐπαφρόδιτος) ?= (50); (46) c. 120-130 AD IG v (1) 40,
21; SEG XI 575, [14] (Bradford (2)) (Σ. ὁ καὶ
Σώστρατος: s. Φιλουμενός); (47) 144 AD SEG
XLI 317, 1 (s. Ἀφθόνητος); (48) c. 145-150 AD
IG v (1) 283, 1 (Artemis Orthia p. 316 no.
36); BSA 75 (1980) p. 219 (date, stemma)
(Bradford (4)) (Τιβ. Κλ. Σ.: s. Πολύευκτος);
(49) c. 150-160 AD SEG XI 585, 7; XXX 410,
7; BSA 43 (1948) p. 236 (ident.) (Bradford
(15)) (f. Ἰούλ. Νέας, Καλλικράτης); (50) 150-
160 AD SEG XXX 410, 6; Chiron 10 (1980) p.
419 (ident.) ?= (45); (51) s. ii AD IG v (1) 323
(Artemis Orthia p. 336 no. 72; Bradford (13))
(Σωσικράτης: f. M. Οὐαλέριος Οὐλπιανὸς Ἀφθό-
νητος); (52) ~ SEG XI 598, 4 (Bradford (12))
(Σέξ. Πομπ. Οὐλπιανὸς Σ.); (53) c. 160-165 AD
SEG XI 498, 6 (Bradford (10)) (Οὐλ(π.) Σ.,
(Ἰ)ούλ. Σ.—ed.); (54) c. 175-200 AD SEG XI
503, 20 (Bradford (18)) (f. Ὀ—); (55) c. 220
AD IG v (1) 544, 12 (Artemis Orthia pp. 358-9
no. 145; Bradford (5)) (M. Αὐρ. Σ.: II s. Σω-
σικράτης I); (56) ~ IG v (1) 544, 13 (Artemis
Orthia pp. 358-9 no. 145; Bradford (21)) (I f.
M. Αὐρ. Σωσικράτης II)
MESSENIA:
—MESSENE: (57) hell. BMC Pelop. p. 110 no.
11 (coin) (Σωσικρά[της], Σωσικρα[τίδας]?); (58)
?ii BC IG v (1) 1477; (59) i BC/i AD ib.
1438 a, 2 (Σωσικρ[άτης]); (60) i AD ib. 1438
b ([Σ]ωσικράτ[ης])
——(Kresphontidai): (61) 11 AD PAE 1992, p.
71 A, 19 (I f. Σωσικράτης II); (62) ~ ib. l. 19
(II s. Σωσικράτης I)
S. ITALY (BRUTTIUM):
—LOKROI EPIZEPHYRIOI:
——(Ἀγκ.): (63) iv/iii BC De Franciscis 34, 5
——(Γαυ.): (64) iv/iii BC ib. 39, 5 (Σω-
σι(κ)ρά(της): s. Κληνίας) ?= (65); (65) 275 BC
ib. 25, 2 (f. Ὀνάσιμος) ?= (64)
——(Κοβ.): (66) iv/iii BC ib. 27, 3 (s. Σώσιππος)
——(Λακ.): (67) inc. ib. 39, 1 ?= (68); (68) iv/iii
BC ib. 27, 7 (s. Ἀπήμαντος) ?= (67)
——(Ὀμβ.): (69) iv/iii BC ib. 6, 3 (f. Θήρων)
——(Προ.): (70) iv/iii BC ib. 16, 4 (f. Σαμίων);
(71) ~ ib. 24, 3 (f. Σώσιππος)
SICILY:
—AKRAGAS: (72) 190 BC Syll³ 585, 92 (f. Λέον-
τις)
—KAMARINA: (73) ?iv/iii BC SEG XXXIV 940,
7 (Dubois, IGDS 124; PdelF 44 (1989) p.
192 no. 3; Cordano, 'Camarina VII' 154) (f.
Παυσανίας); (74) iv/iii BC SEG XXXIX 999,
4 (Dubois, IGDS 125; Cordano, 'Camarina
VII' 155) (f. Σωκράτης)
—SYRACUSE: (75) hell. IG XII (7) 43

Σωσίλαϝος
ARKADIA:
—PALLANTION: (1) f. vi BC ASAA NS 51-2
(1990-1) p. 227 no. 196 (bronze) (Dubois,
RDA 2 pp. 314-5) (Σō-, Σōϝίλαϝος—Dubois)

**Σωσίλαος**
ILLYRIA:
—EPIDAMNOS-DYRRHACHION: (1) ?ii-i BC *IG* XII (8) 196, 5; cf. *IDyrrh* 515 (Σωσιαλος—lap., Σωσί(λα)ος—ed.: s. Παρμενίων)

**Σωσίλας**
S. ITALY (BRUTTIUM):
—LOKROI EPIZEPHYRIOI:
——(Mνα.): (1) iv/iii BC De Franciscis 28, 6 (s. Ἀθάνιππος)
——(Σκα.): (2) iv/iii BC ib. 16, 5; 19, 7 (s. Σιμίας)
SICILY:
—SYRACUSE: (3) vi BC *ILind* 2 C, 62 (f. Πόλλις: dub.)

**Σωσιλήν**
ILLYRIA:
—EPIDAMNOS-DYRRHACHION: (1) hell.-imp. *IDyrrh* 448 (f. Φίλων)

**Σώσιλλα**
AKARNANIA:
—STRATOS: (1) ?ii/i BC *IG* IX (1)² (2) 412, 3 (*SGDI* 1382, 3) (ΣΩΙΣΙΑΛΛ—apogr., Σώσιλλ[α?]—*IG*, Σωσιάδ[ας]?—Heuzey, Σωσίλα[ς]—Bursian)

**Σωσίλοχος**
ILLYRIA:
—APOLLONIA: (1) c. 250-50 BC Münsterberg p. 37; *Bakërr Hoard* p. 64 nos. 98-102 (coin) (Ceka 105) (money.); (2) i BC Maier 159 (coin) (f. Ἀμίαντος)

**Σωσίμαχος**
DALMATIA:
—ISSA:
——(Pamphyloi): (1) iv/iii BC Brunšmid p. 8, 29 (s. Βουλαγόρας)
KEPHALLENIA:
—KRANIOI: (2) hell.-imp. *IG* IX (1) 615 (Σωζέμα[χ]ος)

**Σωσιμένης**
ELIS: (1) i BC/i AD *IvOl* 74, 3, 5; 78, 5; 80, 7 (s. Ἀγίας, f. Τυχηρίδης, Ἀσκληπιάδης)
ILLYRIA:
—EPIDAMNOS-DYRRHACHION: (2) i BC *IG* II² 8486 (f. Εὔτυχος)

**Σωσίμιος**
ITHAKE: (1) hell. ib. IX (1) 676 (Σωσί(β)ιος?)

**Σώσιμος**
ACHAIA:
—DYME: (1) s. iii BC *SEG* XIII 278, 22 (s. Πέταλος)
LAKONIA:
—SPARTA: (2) m. ii BC *IG* V (1) 1576 = *SEG* XI 861 b-c (vase); Siebert, *Ateliers* pp. 172-3 (date) (Bradford (2)) (potter); (3) c. 120 AD *IG* V (1) 1315, 26 (Bradford (1)) (Γ. Σ.: Νικαρετίδας)
SICILY: (4) iii-ii BC *ASSiciliaOrientale* 1919-20, p. 197 (bullet)
—ECHETLA: (5) vi/v BC Manganaro, *PdelP* forthcoming 11 (Σό-)

**Σωσινίκα**
AKARNANIA:
—THYRREION: (1) hell. *SEG* XXXII 566

**Σωσίνικος**
AKARNANIA:
—ALYZIA: (1) ii BC *IG* IX (1)² (2) 449
ELIS:
—OLYMPIA*: (2) 36-24 BC *IvOl* 62, 21 (?s. Ἡρακλείδης: Δου.)
LAKONIA:
—GYTHEION: (3) 211 AD *IG* V (1) 1163, 12 (s. Ἀριστοκλῆς)

—SPARTA: (4) c. 10-20 AD ib. 206, 3; *SEG* XXXV 330 (date) (Bradford (2)) (Σ[ω]σύνι[κ]ος: s. Πατρόφιλος); (5) c. 50-80 AD *IG* V (1) 277, 1; *Artemis Orthia* pp. 308-9 no. 25 (date) (Bradford (5)) (Σω<ι>σίνικος); (6) c. 134-138 AD *SEG* XI 533 b, 2; *BSA* 75 (1980) p. 208 (date) (Bradford (4)) (-νει-); (7) c. 140-160 AD *IG* V (1) 156 a, 3 (Bradford (6)) (Σωσίνικ[ος]: f. Ἀγαθίας); (8) c. 175-200 AD *IG* V (1) 129, 2 (Bradford (7)) (-νει-: f. Σπένδων); (9) f. iii AD *IG* V (1) 301, 7 (*Artemis Orthia* pp. 326-7 no. 55); *BSA* 79 (1984) p. 285 no. 18 (date) (Bradford (1)) (M. Αὐρ. Σωσίνεικος: s. Νικάρων)
—SPARTA?: (10) imp.? *SEG* I 89 (Bradford (3))
MESSENIA:
—THOURIA: (11) ii/i BC *IG* V (1) 1384, 17 (f. Ξένων)

**Σώσινος**
S. ITALY (BRUTTIUM):
—LOKROI EPIZEPHYRIOI:
——(Σκι.): (1) inc. De Franciscis 33, 3 (s. Ζώιππος) ?= (2); (2) iv/iii BC ib. 16, 1 ?= (1)

**Σώσιος**
SICILY:
—AKRAGAS: (1) ii/i BC *HN*² p. 124; *RPC* I p. 176 (coin)
—KAMARINA: (2) hell.? Manganaro, *QUCC* forthcoming no. 25 ([Σ]ώσιος: s. Σαραπιόδωρος)

**Σωσιπάτρα**
ARGOLIS:
—ARGOS: (1) ii/iii AD *IG* IV (1) 627
EPIROS: (2) iv-iii BC Cabanes, *L'Épire* p. 585 no. 68, 2 ([Σωσιπ]άτρα: d. Σωσίπατρος)
—BOUTHROTOS (PRASAIBOI): (3) a. 163 BC *IBouthrot* 48, 10
—PHOTIKE: (4) imp. *BCH* 79 (1955) p. 267 (Lat. Sosipatra)
ILLYRIA:
—APOLLONIA: (5) imp. *IApoll* 247 (m. Βυβλώ)
—BYLLIONES BYLLIS: (6) iii AD *SEG* XXXVIII 554 (m. Μακέτα)
KORINTHIA:
—KORINTH: (7) ii-iii AD *Corinth* VIII (1) 131 (Τυρανία Σ.); (8) m. ii AD ib. VIII (3) 170, [10]; 226, 8 (Ἀντ. Σ.: d. M. Ἀντ. Σῶσπις, m. Π. Αἴλ. Σώσπις)
S. ITALY (CAMPANIA):
—NEAPOLIS: (9) ?i BC *IG* XIV 812 (*INap* 169) (d. Στάτιος)

**Σωσίπατρος**
AIGINA: (1) m. ii BC *Alt-Ägina* I (2) p. 43 no. 2
ARGOLIS:
—ARGOS: (2) ii AD *SEG* XXXV 270-1
—HERMIONE: (3) iv BC ib. XI 382, 3 (Σωσίπα[τρος])
EPIROS: (4) iv-iii BC Cabanes, *L'Épire* p. 585 no. 68, 2 (Σω[σίπατ]ρος: f. Σωσιπάτρα)
—BOUTHROTOS (PRASAIBOI): (5) a. 163 BC *IBouthrot* 14, 40; 31, 55; 33, 23 (*SEG* XXXVIII 471; 490; 492); Ugolini, *Alb. Ant.* 3 p. 120, [12] (s. Χαβρίας, f. Λέων, ?f. Φαινώ); (6) ~ *IBouthrot* 15, 8; 21, 1; 22, 10; 41, 17 (*SEG* XXXVIII 472; 478-9; 500); *IBouthrot* 45, 10; 47, 6-7 (s. Φίλιππος, f. Φίλιππος, Σωσίπατρος II, Κλεόμητις, Νικίας); (7) ~ ib. 17, 19 (*SEG* XXXVIII 474); (8) ~ *IBouthrot* 21, 34; 28, 21; 29, 32; 36, 4 (*SEG* XXXVIII 478; 486-7; 495) (s. Φαλακρίων, f. Λύκος, Ἀρίστα, Μελισσός) ?= (18); (9) ~ *IBouthrot* 25, 8 (*SEG* XXXVIII 483) ?= (15); (10) ~ *IBouthrot* 30, 48; cf. *SEG* XXXVIII 499, 28; (11) ~ *IBouthrot* 31, 2 (*SEG* XXXVIII 490); (12) ~ *IBouthrot* 37, 5 (*SEG* XXXVIII 496); (13) ~ *IBouthrot* 42, 8 (*SEG* XXXVIII 501); (14) ~ ib. 45, 11 (II s. Σωσίπατρος I); (15) ~ ib. l. 13 (f. Σώπατρος) ?= (9); (16) ~ ib. 54, 5 (*SEG* XXXVIII 505)

(Σω[σίπα]τρος: s. Μενεστράτα); (17) ~ *IBouthrot* 93, 5; (18) ~ ib. 103, 9 (s. Φαλακρίων) ?= (8); (19) ~ ib. 121, 11; (20) ~ ib. 122, 6; (21) ~ ib. 130, 7 (f. Φρύνιχος) ?= (23); (22) ~ ib. 131, 9
—Ancheropaioi: (23) a. 163 BC ib. 30, 1; 32, 1 (*SEG* XXXVIII 488; 491) (f. Φρύνιχος) ?= (21)
—Bouthrotioi: (24) a. 163 BC *IBouthrot* 114, 10; 126, 8 (s. Γόργος)
—Kotylaioi: (25) a. 163 BC ib. 152, 2
—Loigyphioi: (26) a. 163 BC ib. 52, 10 (*SEG* XXXVIII 517)
—Opatai: (27) a. 163 BC *IBouthrot* 99, 7 (*BCH* 118 (1994) p. 121 B)
KORINTHIA:
—KORINTH: (28) inc. *SEG* XXXI 297 (vase)
LAKONIA:
—MESSA?: (29) imp. *IG* V (1) 1280, 12 (f. Ξεναρία)
—SPARTA: (30) ii AD ib. 159, 44 (Bradford (-))
MESSENIA:
—MESSENE: (31) i BC/i AD *IG* V (1) 1438 a, 7
S. ITALY (CAMPANIA):
—NEAPOLIS: (32) ?275 BC *FD* III (2) 177, 1 (f. Μεγακλῆς)
SICILY:
—SYRACUSE: (33) 208 BC *IMM* 72, 9 (Dubois, *IGDS* 97) (Σωσίπατρ[ος])
—SYRACUSE?:
——(Μακ.): (34) hell. Manganaro, *PdelP* forthcoming no. 4 III, 4 (Σωσίπατ(ρ)ος: f. Εὔδαμος)
—TAUROMENION: (35) c. 216-194 BC *IG* XIV 421 an. 25; 421 an. 47 (*SGDI* 5219) (f. Θεόδωρος); (36) c. 179 BC *IG* XIV 421 an. 62 (*SGDI* 5219) (s. Θεόδωρος)

**Σωσίπολις**
DALMATIA:
—ISSA: (1) ii/i BC Brunšmid p. 27 no. 19 (*SEG* XL 515) + *VAHD* 84 (1991) p. 254 no. 4 (s. Πάτρων)
LAKONIA:
—HYPERTELEATON*: (2) imp. *IG* V (1) 1021 (-πω-: I f. Σωσίπολις II); (3) ~ ib. (-πω-: II s. Σωσίπολις I)
—SPARTA: (4) c. 132 AD *SEG* XI 579, 3 (Bradford (2)) ([Σωσίπ]ολις?: s. Τήρης); (5) c. 133 AD *SEG* XI 580, 3 (Bradford (1)) (s. Εὔδαμος); (6) c. 212-220 AD *IG* V (1) 527, 3 (Bradford (3)) (f. M. Αὐρ. Ἀφροδίσιος)
S. ITALY (BRUTTIUM):
—LOKROI EPIZEPHYRIOI:
——(Λακ.): (7) iv/iii BC De Franciscis 16, 2; 24, 4 (f. Εὔφραστος)
—RHEGION:
——(Χιω.): (8) s. ii BC *IG* XIV 612, 1 (*Syll*³ 715; Dubois, *IGDGG* I 40) (s. Δαμάτριος)
SICILY:
—APOLLONIA: (9) hell.? *IG* XIV 364
—GELA-PHINTIAS: (10) f. ii BC ib. 256, 44 (Dubois, *IGDS* 161); cf. *SEG* XL 804 (s. Ἰσίδωρος)
—SYRACUSE: (11) ii-i BC *IG* XIV 8, 8 (*IGLMP* 105) (Σωσίπο[λις]: f. —ρος)

**Σώσιππος**
ACHAIA:
—DYME: (1) iii BC *AJPh* 31 (1910) p. 399 no. 74 a, 6 (f. Νικίας)
—DYME*: (2) c. 219 BC *SGDI* 1612, 65 (*Tyche* 5 (1990) p. 124) ([Σ]ώσιππος: s. Ἡρακλείδας)
AITOLIA: (3) ?246-221 BC *FD* III (4) 234
—THESTIEIS: (4) 213 BC *IG* IX (1)² (1) 96, 14
AKARNANIA:
—THYRREION: (5) c. 200 BC ib. IX (1)² (2) 296
ARGOLIS:
—HERMIONE: (6) ii-i BC ib. IV (1) 732 III, 29 (s. Πεισιδίκα)
ARKADIA:
—MEGALOPOLIS: (7) ii BC ib. V (2) 447, 6 ([Σ]ώσιππος)

EPIROS:
—BOUTHROTOS (PRASAIBOI): (8) a. 163 BC
   *IBouthrot* 17, 19 (*SEG* XXXVIII 474) ?= (*10*);
   (9) ~ *IBouthrot* 36, 8; 43, 42 (*SEG* XXXVIII
   495; 502) (s. *Λάμιος*); (10) ~ *IBouthrot* 43, 46
   (*SEG* XXXVIII 502) (f. *Εὐθωλίς*) ?= (*8*)
——Opatai: (11) a. 163 BC *IBouthrot* III, 9;
   112, 10 (f. *Λέων*)
KEPHALLENIA:
—PALE: (12) iii/ii BC Unp. (*IG* arch.)
S. ITALY (BRUTTIUM):
—LOKROI EPIZEPHYRIOI:
——(Ἀγκ.): (13) iv/iii BC De Franciscis 20, 14
   (s. *Ἀριστοφάνης*)
——(Ἀλχ.): (14) iv/iii BC ib. 15, 3; 26, 5 (f. *Ξέ-
   νων*)
——(Βοω.): (15) iv/iii BC ib. l. 3 (s. *Φίλυκος*)
——(Δυσ.): (16) iv/iii BC ib. 6, 5; 11, 3 (f. *Ζωΐ-
   λος*); (17) ~ ib. 24, 7 (f. *Εὐφρονίσκος*)
——(Κοβ.): (18) iv/iii BC ib. 27, 4 (f. *Σωσικρά-
   της*)
——(Λακ.): (19) iv/iii BC ib. 12, 5 (f. *Φιλιστίων*)
——(Ὀμβ.): (20) iv/iii BC ib. 29, 1
——(Προ.): (21) iv/iii BC ib. 24, 3 (s. *Σωσικρά-
   της*)
——(Πυρ.): (22) 276 BC ib. 23, 4 (f. *Ἀρκείδας*)
——(Σκι.): (23) iv/iii BC ib. 10, 3
——(Στρ.): (24) iv/iii BC ib. 29, 4
——(Σωτ.): (25) iv/iii BC ib. 7, 3 (s. *Σῖμος*); (26)
   ~ ib. 10, 6
SICILY:
—AGYRION: (27) ?i BC Manganaro, *PdelP* forth-
   coming no. 5, 1 (s. *Σκόπας*); (28) f. i BC Cic.,
   *In Verr.* II ii 25 (Lat. Sosippus)
—AKRAGAS: (29) f. i BC ib. *In Verr.* II iii 204
   (Lat. Sosippus)
—SYRACUSE: (30) 341 BC *CID* II 12 II, 24
—TYNDARIS: (31) f. i BC Cic., *In Verr.* II iv 92
   (Lat. Zosippus)

**Σῶσις**
DALMATIA:
—ISSA:
——(Dymanes): (1) iv/iii BC Brunšmid p. 8, 27
   (f. *Εὐκλῆς*)
S. ITALY (LUCANIA):
—HYELE-VELIA: (2) 157 BC *ID* 1416 B I, 106
SICILY:
—AKRAI: (3) iv-iii BC *Antiken Terracotten* 2 p.
   30; (4) ?iii BC *SGDI* 3239, 9 (*Akrai* p. 157
   no. 9) (f. *Φιλιστίων*) ?= (7); (5) ~ *SGDI* 3240,
   6 (*Akrai* p. 156 no. 7) (f. *Παυσανίας*) ?= (6);
   (6) ~ *SGDI* 3240, 6 (*Akrai* p. 156 no. 7) (f.
   *Ὕβριμος*) ?= (5); (7) ~ *SGDI* 3240, 9 (*Akrai*
   p. 156 no. 7) (f. *Φιλιστίων*) ?= (4); (8) ~ *SGDI*
   3243, 7 (*Akrai* p. 155 no. 5) (s. *Ἀριστοκλῆς*);
   (9) iii-ii BC *SGDI* 3242, 8 (*Akrai* p. 157 no.
   8) (s. *Παυσανίας*); (10) ii BC ib. p. 156 no. 6,
   22 (f. *Μενεκράτης*); (11) ii-i BC *SGDI* 3246, 46
   (*Akrai* pp. 152-3 no. 2; Dubois, *IGDS* 109)
   (f. *Ἀριστόδαμος*)
—GELA-PHINTIAS: (12) f. ii BC *IG* XIV 256, 3
   (Dubois, *IGDS* 161); cf. *SEG* XL 804 (s. *Νυμ-
   φόδωρος*)
—GELA-PHINTIAS?: (13) ?v/iv BC Manganaro,
   *PdelP* forthcoming no. 12 (Σδ-: f. *Φειδίας*)
—KAMARINA: (14) f. v BC Cordano, *Tessere Pub-
   bliche* 101 (Σδ-: f. *Ξενοκλῆς*); (15) iii BC Man-
   ganaro, *PdelP* forthcoming no. 1, 9 (f. *Σώσαν-
   δρος*)
—KATANE: (16) 46 BC Cic., *Ad Fam.* xiii 30. 1
   (and S. Italy (Campania) Neapolis: Lat. L.
   Manlius Sosis)
—KEPHALOIDION: (17) i BC-i AD *IG* XIV 351 +
   *SEG* XXXVII 763 (Σ. Κράφαγος: ?s. *Νύμφων*)
—LEONTINOI: (18) 433 BC *IG* I³ 54, 5 (Σδ-: s.
   *Γλαυκίας*)
—NOAI: (19) f. ii BC *BCH* 45 (1921) p. 25 col.
   IV, 108 + *SEG* XXII 455; cf. *Sic. Gymn.* 17
   (1964) pp. 47 f. (Σωσίστρατος—*BCH*: ?s. *Με-
   νεκράτης*)

—SYRACUSE: (20) 401 BC X., *An.* i 2. 9; (21)
   357 BC Plu., *Dio* 34-5; (22) 214-211 BC *RE*
   Supplbd. 15 (3) (Lat. Sosis); (23) ii-i BC *IG*
   XIV 8, 1 (*IGLMP* 105) ([Σ]ῶσις); (24) ~ *SEG*
   XXXIV 974, 7 (*IGLMP* 106) (s. *Ἀρισ*—)
—SYRACUSE?:
——(Ῥιπε.): (25) hell. *NScav* 1961, p. 349 (bul-
   let); cf. *BE* 1965, no. 502 (s. *Καράϊκος*)
——(Πλη.): (26) hell. Manganaro, *PdelP* forth-
   coming no. 4 III, 8 (s. *Ἕρμων*)
—TAUROMENION: (27) c. 158 BC *IG* XIV 421 an.
   83 (*SGDI* 5219) ?= (*29*); (28) ?ii/i BC *IG* XIV
   421 D an. 8 (*SGDI* 5219); *IGSI* 4 III (IV),
   136 D an. 8 (f. *Εὔδοξος*)
——(Ὀμ.): (29) c. 153-150 BC *IG* XIV 421 an. 91
   (*SGDI* 5219); *IGSI* 4 III (IV), 12 an. 87 (s.
   *Νυμφόδωρος*) ?= (*27*)

**Σῶσις**
AKARNANIA:
—ASTAKOS: (1) ?iii-ii BC *AD* 26 (1971) Chron.
   p. 321 (s./d. *Ἴων*)
S. ITALY (CAMPANIA):
—NEAPOLIS: (2) i BC/i AD *INap* 170, 2 (s./d.
   *Κράτιππος*)

**Σωσίστρατος**
ACHAIA:
—DYME: (1) ii/i BC *Achaean Grave Stelai* 55 (f.
   *Ἀρχέλαος*)
—DYME*: (2) c. 219 BC *SGDI* 1612, 57 (*Tyche*
   5 (1990) p. 124) (s. *Δεινίας*)
—PATRAI: (3) c. 146-32 BC Mionnet 2 p. 191
   no. 319 (coin) (f. *Ξενόφαντος*)
ARGOLIS:
—HERMIONE: (4) iv BC *SEG* XI 382, 17 (*Σω-
   σίσ[τρ]ατος*: f. *Θεώνιχος*); (5) ii-i BC *IG* IV (1)
   732 I, 1 (s. *Κλεοφάντα*); (6) i BC-i AD? ib. 730
   I, 13 (*Σωσίστ[ρ]ατος*)
ARKADIA:
—MANTINEIA-ANTIGONEIA: (7) ii BC ib. v (2)
   305 (I f. *Σωσίστρατος* II); (8) ~ ib. (II s. *Σω-
   σίστρατος* I)
—MEGALOPOLIS: (9) ?130 BC ib. 441, 9 (f. *Δα-
   μάλκης*, *Ζευξίας*)
EPIROS:
—AMBRAKIA: (10) ii-i BC *CIG* 1800, 10 (f. *Τι-
   μόδαμος*)
KORINTHIA:
—SIKYON: (11) 364-356 BC *CEG* II 811 (Skalet
   307) (f. *Σώστρατος*)
S. ITALY (BRUTTIUM):
—HIPPONION-VIBO VALENTIA: (12) hell.? *IG*
   XIV 2405. 41 (lamp) (*Σωσίστ(ρατος*))
—LOKROI EPIZEPHYRIOI: (13) vi/v BC Iamb.,
   *VP* 267 (*FVS* 1 p. 447)
——(Ἀγκ.): (14) iv/iii BC De Franciscis 20, 6 (f.
   *Φίντων*)
——(Ψαθ.): (15) iv/iii BC ib. 26, 2 (s. *Φιλοκράτης*)
SICILY:
—KAMARINA: (16) ?iv/iii BC *SEG* XXXIV 940,
   2 (Dubois, *IGDS* 124; *PdelP* 44 (1989) p.
   192 no. 3; Cordano, 'Camarina VII' 156)
   (*Σω[σί]στρατος*: s. *Θέων*) ?= (*17*); (17) iv/iii BC
   Manganaro, *PdelP* forthcoming no. 2, 7 (s.
   *Θέων*) ?= (*16*)
—SELINOUS: (18) s. v BC Dubois, *IGDS* 40, 2
—SYRACUSE: (19) hell. *NScav* 1892, p. 357 (f.
   *Μεγαλλίς*); (20) c. 320-314 BC *RE* (4); (21) c.
   280-276 BC ib. (5); (22) ?263-261 BC Nachter-
   gael, *Les Galates* 3, 18; cf. Stephanis 2551 (f.
   *Φιλόστρατος*)
——(Περηκυαταῖος): (23) iv BC Manganaro,
   *PdelP* forthcoming no. 3, 10 (s. *Γέλων*)
—TAUROMENION: (24) c. 214-200 BC *IG* XIV
   421 an. 27; 421 an. 41 (*SGDI* 5219) (s. *Σι-
   λανός*)

**Σωσιτέλης**
KORINTHIA:
—SIKYON: (1) 187 BC Plb. xxii 3. 6 (*Ρωσιτέλης*
   ms.: name—Reiske)

**Σωσιφάνης**
ARGOLIS:
—EPIDAUROS:
——(Hylleis): (1) 146 BC *IG* IV (1)² 28, 50 (f.
   *Λακλῆς*)
—KALAURIA: (2) iii BC ib. IV (1) 840, 4 (s. *Σω-
   φάνης*, *Ἀγασιγράτις*); (3) imp. ib. 846 (f. *Ἀγα-
   σικλῆς*)
SICILY:
—SYRACUSE: (4) iv BC *TrGF* 1 pp. 261-2 no.
   92; *PP* 16716 (s. *Σωσικλῆς*)
—TAUROMENION: (5) 207 BC *IG* XIV 421 an. 34
   (f. *Ἀπολλόδωρος*) ?= (*6*); (6) c. 200-?190 BC ib.
   421 an. 41; 421 an. 51; 421 an. 62 (*SGDI*
   5219) (f. *Διονύσιος*) ?= (*5*); (7) c. 149 BC *IG*
   XIV 421 an. 92 (*SGDI* 5219) (s. *Διονύσιος*)

**Σωσίχα**
AKARNANIA:
—THYRREION: (1) s. iii BC *IG* IX (1)² (2) 293
   (d. *Ὑβρίστας*)
MESSENIA:
—MESSENE: (2) hell. ib. II² 9343 (d. *Λύκων*); (3)
   iii BC ib. 9342 (-χη)

**Σωσιχάρης**
S. ITALY (BRUTTIUM):
—LOKROI EPIZEPHYRIOI:
——(Κυλ.): (1) iv/iii BC De Franciscis 5, 5 (f.
   *Σώτων*)

**Σωσίων**
ARGOLIS:
—ARGOS: (1) ii-i BC *Mnem.* NS 47 (1919) p. 164
   no. 9, 7 (f. *Δεξίας*)
—HERMIONE: (2) iii BC *IG* IV (1) 729 I, 8 (s.
   *Ἀρίστων*); (3) ~ ib. l. 19 (f. *Ξενόδοκος*); (4) ~
   ib. 729 II, 19 (s. *Στίχος*)
SICILY:
—SYRACUSE?: (5) s. v BC *RE* (-); *Samml. Ludwig*
   455 (coin) (coin engraver)

**Σῶσος**
ACHAIA: (1) 146 BC *IG* IV (1)² 28, 136 (s. *Φιλο-
   κράτης*: synoikos)
—DYME: (2) ?145 BC Sherk 43, 8, 17, 23; *SEG*
   XXXVIII 372 (date) (s. *Ταυρομένης*)
ARGOLIS:
—ARGOS: (3) iv-iii BC Unp. (Ch. Kritzas); (4)
   ii/i BC *IG* IV (1) 608 (f. *Δαμόστρατος*); (5) i-ii
   AD ib. 587, 10 (s. *Νικηφόρος*)
—ARGOS*: (6) ii BC *SEG* XLII 279, 25 ([Σ]ῶσος:
   f. *Σωτηρίς*: katoikos); (7) 105 BC *JÖAI* 14
   (1911) Beibl. p. 146 no. 4, 19 (slave/freed.?)
—HERMIONE: (8) iii BC *IG* IV (1) 729 I, 2 (s.
   *Μενήτιος*); (9) ~ ib. l. 4 (f. *Πασίμηλος*); (10) ~
   ib. l. 12 (f. *Παρθεμίδας*); (11) ~ ib. l. 21 (s.
   *Πασίμηλος*); (12) ~ ib. 729 II, 8 (s. *Ἀχαιός*)
ARKADIA:
—TEGEA: (13) ii AD ib. v (2) 55, 96 (s. *Μάρων*)
EPIROS:
—NIKOPOLIS: (14) imp. *CIG* 1816 (*SEG* XXXIV
   593); cf. *BE* 1990, no. 177
ILLYRIA:
—APOLLONIA: (15) c. 250-50 BC Münsterberg
   Nachtr. p. 13 (coin) (Ceka 132) (pryt.); (16)
   ~ Maier 119; 46; cf. *Jubice Hoard* p. 99 nos.
   59-63; Maier 55; 62; 105 (Ceka 100; 106-110);
   *IApoll Ref. Bibl.* n. 106 (coin) (money.)
—EPIDAMNOS-DYRRHACHION: (17) c. 250-50
   BC Maier 415 (coin) (Ceka 406); (18) ii-i BC
   *IDyrrh* 385
LAKONIA:
—SPARTA: (19) c. 140-160 AD *IG* V (1) 154, 15
   (Bradford s.v. *Σωσᾶς* (-)) (f. *Κάλλιστος*)
S. ITALY (CAMPANIA):
—DIKAIARCHIA-PUTEOLI: (20) imp. *CIL* x
   2046 (Lat. L. Accilius Sosus: f. *Ἐπινίκιος*)
SICILY:
—SYRACUSE: (21) 231 BC *CPR* XVIII 1 (I f. *Σῶ-
   σος* II); (22) ~ ib. (II s. *Σῶσος* I: t.e.)

**Σώσοτος**
S. ITALY (CAMPANIA):
—NEAPOLIS*: (1) i BC/i AD *INap* 171; cf. Leiwo p. 72 no. 13 (freed.)

**Σώσπις**
ILLYRIA:
—AMANTIA*: (1) hell.? Ugolini, *Alb. Ant.* 1 p. 197 no. 19 (Βαριανὸς Σ.)
KORINTHIA:
—KORINTH: (2) m. ii AD *Corinth* VIII (3) 226, 2 + *Mnem.* 4th Ser. 22 (1969) pp. 80-2 (name, ident.) (Π. Αἰλ. Σ., Σώσπιν[ος]—*Corinth*: s. Π. Αἰλ. Ἀπολλόδοτος, Ἀντ. Σωσιπάτρα)
—KORINTH?: (3) f. ii AD *Corinth* VIII (3) 170, [2], 10; 226, 4 (*Mnem.* 4th Ser. 22 (1969) pp. 80-2); Plu., *Mor.* 723 A etc. (Ἀντ. Σ., Lat. Antonius Sospes: s. Antonia Sedata, f. Ἀντ. Σωσιπάτρα)

**Σωστράτα**
ACHAIA:
—DYME: (1) iii BC *AJPh* 31 (1910) p. 399 no. 74 a, 18 (d. Φίλιππος, Μόσχιον); (2) ~ ib. l. 20
AKARNANIA:
—KORONTA: (3) iii-ii BC *IG* IX (1)² (2) 432, 4
—THYRREION: (4) iii BC ib. 276
ARGOLIS:
—ARGOS: (5) hell.? ib. II² 8375, 1 (-τη: d. Μέννυλλος); (6) hell.-imp.? *SEG* XXV 371; (7) i BC-i AD Unp. (Argos, Kavvadias)
—ARGOS*: (8) ii BC *SEG* XLII 279, 11 (slave/freed.?)
EPIROS:
—AMBRAKIA: (9) hell.? *CIG* 1804 (d. Σώπατρος)
—BOUTHROTOS (PRASAIBOI): (10) a. 163 BC *IBouthrot* 26, 7 (*SEG* XXXVIII 484); (11) ~ *IBouthrot* 29, 18 (*SEG* XXXVIII 487)
LEUKAS: (12) iii BC Unp. (Leukas Mus., inscr.) inv. 20

**Σωστρατίδας**
LAKONIA:
—SPARTA: (1) 429 BC X., *HG* ii 3. 10 (Poralla² 682)

**Σωστρατίων**
EPIROS:
—AMBRAKIA: (1) f. ii BC Unp. (Arta Mus., inscr.) (s. Φιντέρα?)

**Σώστρατος**
ACHAIA: (1) 146 BC *IG* IV (1)² 28, 101 (s. Σωτηρίδας: synoikos); (2) ~ ib. l. 132 (f. Βώτων: synoikos)
—DYME: (3) iii BC *AJPh* 31 (1910) p. 399 no. 74 a, 21 (s. Θράσων)
—KARYNEIA: (4) 215 BC *SEG* XV 113, 33 (*IRhamnous* 41) (f. Νικόμαχος)
—PATRAI: (5) c. 247-199 BC *FD* III (1) p. 204 n. 1, 2 (s. Πανταρης)
—PELLENE: (6) 460 BC Moretti, *Olymp.* 263
AIGINA: (7) s. vi BC *RE* (1); Landi, *DISMG* 9 (*LSAG*² p. 439 no. E); *Alt-Ägina* 11 (2) pp. 104-5 (s. Λαοδάμας); (8) ?f. iii AD ib. 1 (2) p. 48 no. 35 (I f. Αὐρ. Σώστρατος II); (9) ~ ib. (Αὐρ. Σ.: II s. Σώστρατος I)
AKARNANIA:
—ANAKTORION: (10) iii BC *IG* IX (1)² (2) 226
—THYRREION: (11) iii/ii BC ib. 308 (Σώστρα[τος]: f. Σωσθένης); (12) ii BC ib. 251, 12 (s. Μενοίτιος); (13) ~ ib. 252, 10 (f. Λυσικλῆς); (14) f. ii BC ib. 297
ARGOLIS:
—ARGOS: (15) ?c. 460-450 BC *Mnem.* NS 47 (1919) p. 161 no. 6, 9; *LSAG*² p. 170 no. 13 (date) (Σόστρα[τος]); (16) iv-iii BC Unp. (Ch. Kritzas); (17) ?325 BC *CID* II 101 I, 5; (18) 105 BC *JÖAI* 14 (1911) Beibl. p. 146 no. 4, 27 (Σώστρα[τος]: f. Σαραπιάς)
—ARGOS*: (19) 105 BC ib. l. 8 (slave/freed.?)

—EPIDAUROS: (20) 212-217 AD *IG* IV (1)² 612 I, 5 (M. Αὐρ. Σ.)
——(Hysminatai): (21) ii BC ib. 28, 24; 99, 22 (Peek, *IAEpid* 44); *IG* IV (1)² 335, 4 (s. Πατροκλείδας, f. Πατροκλείδας)
—HERMIONE: (22) ii-i BC ib. IV (1) 732 III, 20 (s. Μέγαλλα); (23) iii AD ib. 726, 2 (Αὐρ. Σ.: f. Λουκία, Αὐρ. Ἀντίγονος, Αὐρ. Νίκη)
—KALAURIA: (24) iii/iv AD ib. 849, 3 (Σώστρ[ατος]: f. Στρατήγιος)
ARKADIA:
—ORCHOMENOS*: (25) ?ii BC ib. V (2) 345, 13 (s. Ἀρι—: date—*LGPN*)
—STYMPHALOS: (26) ii BC *SEG* XLII 362 (Σώστρατο[ς], Σόστρατος—ed.)
—TEGEA: (27) c. 240-229 BC *IG* V (2) 10, 2; (28) ii BC ib. 144 (Σώστρατος: ?f. Πολίας); (29) ii-i BC ib. 165, 8
—THELPHOUSA: (30) a. 228 BC ib. IV (1)² 72 B, 27 (s. Ἀν—)
ELIS: (31) f. i AD *IvOl* 77, 14 (Σώστ[ρατος]); (32) c. 50-54 AD ib. 373, 5 ([Γ.] Ἰούλ. Σώστρα[τος]) ?= (33); (33) i/ii AD ib. 470, 7 (Γ. Ἰούλ. Σ.: ?f. Ἰούλ. Ἄπλα) ?= (32)
EPIROS:
—AMBRAKIA: (34) 238-168 BC Mionnet 2 p. 51 no. 42 (coin); (35) iii/ii BC *SEG* XL 506 (s. Σωκλείδας); (36) ~ Unp. (Arta Mus., inscr.) (s. Θεόδοτος); (37) ~ ib. (s. Σώδαμος); (38) ii BC *SEG* XLII 543
—BOUTHROTOS (PRASAIBOI): (39) iii-ii BC *IBouthrot* 167 (Cabanes, *L'Épire* p. 568 no. 46) (f. Λαμίσκος); (40) a. 163 BC *IBouthrot* 32, 12 (*SEG* XXXVIII 491)
—DODONA*: (41) ?iv BC Ep. Chron. 10 (1935) p. 260 no. 42 ([Σώ?]στρατος)
ILLYRIA:
—APOLLONIA: (42) c. 250-50 BC Maier 88 (coin) (Ceka 133); cf. Ceka p. 63 (pryt.)
——(Po.): (43) iii/ii BC *IApoll* 7; cf. *L'Illyrie mérid.* 2 p. 207 (s. Ἀγαθίων)
——(Polo.): (44) iii/ii BC *IApoll* 7; cf. *L'Illyrie mérid.* 2 p. 207 (f. Παρμήν)
—BYLLIONES NIKAIA: (45) f. i BC *AE* 1925-6, p. 26 no. 140, 11 ([Σώ]στρατος)
—EPIDAMNOS-DYRRHACHION: (46) iii BC *IDyrrh* 19 (f. Ἀριστίας); (47) ~ ib. (Σώσ(τ)ρατος: s. Εὐτυχίδας); (48) c. 250-50 BC Ceka, *Probleme* p. 152 no. 65 (coin) (pryt.); (49) hell.-imp. *IDyrrh* 386; (50) ~ ib. 387 (s. Παγκλῆς)
KEPHALLENIA:
—PALE: (51) iii/ii BC Unp. (*IG* arch.)
KERKYRA: (52) c. 229-48 BC *BMC Thessaly* p. 150 nos. 529-30; Naville sale 6 (28. 1. 1924) 1010; cf. Postolakas p. 34 nos. 422-3 (coins) (Σώστρα(τος)); (53) ?ii-i BC *IG* IX (1) 810 (tile); (54) i BC-i AD ib. 927
KORINTHIA:
—KORINTH: (55) iv BC D.H., *Din.* 2; Plu., *Mor.* 850 B (Σωκράτης)—Plu.: f. Δείναρχος); (56) f. ii BC *Corinth* VIII (1) 66 (s. Ἀγάθων)
—KORINTH?: (57) 273 BC *IG* IX (1)² (1) 11, 2 (s. Τι—)
—SIKYON: (58) 364-356 BC Moretti, *Olymp.* 420; 425; 433; *CEG* II 811 (Skalet 308) (Σ. ὁ ἀκροχερσίτης: s. Σωσίστρατος); (59) ?315 BC *BCH* 62 (1938) pp. 343-4 no. 8, 3 (s. Ἀρχέστρατος); (60) 119 BC *IG* II² 1008 col. IV, 113 (Skalet 309) (f. —στρατος)
LAKONIA:
—SPARTA: (61) c. 80-90 AD *IG* V (1) 674, 15 (Bradford (1)) (s. Θεόδωρος); (62) c. 80-100 AD *SEG* XI 608, 4 (Bradford (4)) (f. Καλλικράτης); (63) c. 100-125 AD *IG* V (1) 40, 23 (Bradford s.v. Σωσικράτης (2)) (Σωσικράτης ὁ καὶ Σ.: s. Φιλουμενός); (64) c. 225-250 AD *SEG* XXXIV 308, 10 (Bradford (3)) (M. Αὐρ. Σ.)
LEUKAS: (65) c. 167-50 BC Postolakas p. 67 no. 687 (*NZ* 10 (1878) p. 136 no. 36 (coin)); (66)

f. i BC *IG* IX (1) 534, 5, 12 (*Iscr. Gr. Verona* p. 24) (s. Λαμίσκος)
MESSENIA:
—MESSENE: (67) ?iv-ii BC *IG* V (1) 1492 (Σώστρα[τος]); (68) s. ii BC *SEG* XLI 341, 6 (s. Νικόξενος)
—THOURIA: (69) f. ii BC ib. XI 972, 111 (f. Καλλικράτης); (70) ii/i BC *IG* V (1) 1384, 23 (s. Φιλόξενος)
S. ITALY (CALABRIA):
—TARAS-TARENTUM: (71) c. 280-272 BC Vlasto 713-19; 1064 (coin) (Evans, *Horsemen* p. 157 VII A.2-3; p. 162 no. 3)
SICILY:
—ECHETLA: (72) vi/v BC Manganaro, *PdelP* forthcoming 3 (Σόστ(ρ)ατος)
—KAMARINA: (73) f. v BC Cordano, *Tessere Pubbliche* 32 (Σό-: s. Ξ—); (74) ~ ib. 60 (Arena, *Iscr. Sic.* II 138 A) (Σό-: s. Σω—)
—KENTORIPA: (75) f. i BC Cic., *In Verr.* II iii 57 (Lat. Sostratus)
—SYRACUSE: (76) 472 or 468 BC Pi., *O.* vi 9, 80 (f. Ἀγησίας); (77) ii-i BC *IG* XIV 8, 7 (*IGLMP* 105) (Σώστρα[τος]: I f. Σώστρατος II); (78) ~ *IG* XIV 8, 7 (*IGLMP* 105) ([Σώ]στρατος: II s. Σώστρατος I)

**Σωστρήν**
ILLYRIA:
—EPIDAMNOS-DYRRHACHION: (1) c. 250-50 BC Münsterberg p. 261; *Jubice Hoard* p. 97 nos. 44 ff. (coin) (Ceka 405; 407-10) (Σω(στρήν)—405: money.)

**Σωστρίων**
EPIROS:
—ANTIGONEIA: (1) imp. *AE* 1914, p. 238 no. 15; Cabanes, *L'Épire* p. 234 n. 96 (locn.) (f. Πραΰλος, Φιλίστα)
ILLYRIA:
—AMANTIA: (2) ii/i BC Ceka pp. 129-30; *Iliria* 1977-8, p. 99 no. 32; p. 99 no. 37 (coin)
—APOLLONIA: (3) ii BC Cabanes, *L'Épire* p. 562 no. 37 (*IApoll* 6) (f. Λυσήν)
—EPIDAMNOS-DYRRHACHION: (4) c. 250-50 BC *SNG Cop. Thessaly–Illyricum* 510; 517; Unp. (Paris, BN) 273; *IApoll* n. 107 (coin) (pryt.) ?= (6); (5) ~ Maier 109; 183; 267; 370 (coin) (Ceka 411-14) (money.); (6) ~ Maier 356-7 (coin) (Ceka 46; 130) (pryt.) ?= (4); (7) ii-i BC *IDyrrh* 558 (tiles); (8) hell.-imp. ib. 189 (f. Ἐπικαρπία); (9) ~ ib. 234 (Σω(σ)τρίων: f. Ἡγησίας); (10) ~ ib. 257 (f. Κάλα); (11) ~ ib. 388 ([Σω]στρίων)

**Σωσύλος**
ARGOLIS:
—ARGOS*: (1) 105 BC *JÖAI* 14 (1911) Beibl. p. 146 no. 4, 18 (slave/freed.?)
DALMATIA:
—ISSA: (2) f. ii BC Brunšmid p. 23 no. 10, 2 ([Σω]σύλος: s. Πάμφιλος); (3) ~ ib. l. 5 (s. Θεάγης)
ITHAKE: (4) hell. *IG* IX (1) 671 (Σωσύ[λος])
KEPHALLENIA: (5) 177 BC *SGDI* 1834, 2, 8
LAKONIA: (6) s. iii BC *RE* (-); *FGrH* 176 (Bradford (-))

**Σωσώ**
ACHAIA:
—PELLENE: (1) imp. *SEG* XI 1279
AITOLIA:
—PHANA?: (2) ii BC ib. XXIX 474 b
ARGOLIS:
—HERMIONE: (3) ?ii-i BC *IG* IV (1) 731 II, 5 (d. Σωπάτρα)
EPIROS:
—AMBRAKIA?: (4) ?s. ii BC *SEG* XXIX 474
—NIKOPOLIS: (5) imp. ib. XXXVII 527 (Sarikakis 87) (Κλαυδία Σ.: locn.—Cabanes)
KORINTHIA:
—SIKYON: (6) 264 BC Plu., *Arat.* 2 (Skalet 310) (d. Πασέας)

**Σωτάδας**

ARGOLIS:
—ARGOS: (1) c. 370 BC *IG* IV (1)² 102, 13; cf. *SEG* XXV 383, [22]
—EPIDAUROS*: (2) c. 370 BC *IG* IV (1)² 102, 162
—HERMIONE: (3) iii BC ib. IV (1) 729 II, 20 (I f. Σωτάδας II); (4) ~ ib. l. 20 (II s. Σωτάδας I)
—METHANA-ARSINOE: (5) ii-i BC ib. 869

KORINTHIA:
—KORINTH: (6) ?vi BC *Corinth* XV (3) p. 359 no. 3 (vase) (Σōτάδ[ας]?)

MESSENIA:
—THOURIA: (7) f. ii BC *SEG* XI 972, 16 (f. Καλλισθένης)

SICILY:
—SYRACUSE?:
——(Ὑπα.): (8) hell. Manganaro, *PdelP* forthcoming no. 4 V, 1 (f. Ἀρταμίδωρος)

**Σωτάδης**

ARKADIA:
—ALIPHEIRA: (1) i BC-i AD *IG* II² 8046 (f. Λαμίσκα)
—KLEITOR: (2) a. 212 AD ib. V (2) 369, 20 + *SEG* XXXI 347, 13-14 (I f. Αὐρ. Ἀρκαδίων, Αὐρ. Σωτάδης II); (3) ~ *IG* V (2) 369, 21 + *SEG* XXXI 347, 14 (Αὐρ. Σ.: II s. Σωτάδης I)

**Σώταιρις**

AKARNANIA:
—PALAIROS: (1) iii BC *IG* IX (1)² (2) 505

**Σώταιρος**

AIGINA: (1) ?i BC *Alt-Ägina* I (2) p. 46 no. 19 ([Σ]ώταιρος)

ARGOLIS:
—EPIDAUROS: (2) c. 370 BC *IG* IV (1)² 102, 43-4, 64, 256, 260, 268-9, 273

EPIROS:
—DODONA*: (3) iv BC Carapanos, *Dodone* p. 41 no. 5 (Lazzarini 143)

KORINTHIA:
—KORINTH: (4) c. 450-425 BC *Syll³* 55, 2 (*LSAG²* p. 99 no. 10)
—SIKYON: (5) hell.? *IG* II² 10313

MESSENIA:
—THOURIA: (6) ii-i BC ib. V (1) 1385, 26 (s. Ἄσανδρος)

S. ITALY (CAMPANIA):
—POMPEII*: (7) i BC-i AD *CIL* IV 8052 (Lat. Soterus: freed.)

SICILY:
—SELINOUS: (8) ?m. vi BC Dubois, *IGDS* 48 (Arena, *Iscr. Sic.* I 44; *IGLMP* 62) (Σό-)
—SYRACUSE?:
——(Πλη.): (9) hell. Manganaro, *PdelP* forthcoming no. 4 IV, 1 (f. Σωμήδης)

**Σωτακλῆς**

ILLYRIA:
—APOLLONIA:
——(Litai): (1) iii/ii BC *IApoll* 7; *L'Illyrie mérid.* 2 p. 207 (locn.) (Σωτεακλῆς—lap., Σωτ<ε>ακλῆς: s. Εὔδαμος)

**Σώτακος**

AITOLIA:
—KALYDON: (1) 129 BC *IG* IX (1)² (1) 137, 96 (f. Θράσων)

AKARNANIA:
—STRATOS: (2) ii BC ib. IX (1)² (2) 394, 12 (s. Σωτέας)

ILLYRIA:
—EPIDAMNOS-DYRRHACHION: (3) c. 250-50 BC *Coll. Hunter* 2 p. 7 no. 54 (coin) (pryt.)

ITHAKE: (4) hell. *Rev. Épig.* 1 (1913) p. 47 no. 5

KEPHALLENIA:
—SAME: (5) 208 BC *IMM* 35, 2 (f. Τίμων) ?= (6)
—SAME?: (6) ?205-203 BC *FD* III (2) 134 b, 7 (s.p.) (*Syll³* 564) (Σωτάκ[ου] (gen.)) ?= (5)

LEUKAS: (7) hell. *IG* IX (1) 584

**Σωτάκων**

ARGOLIS:
—EPIDAUROS: (1) i BC *SEG* XI 451 (f. Ἀριστέας)

**Σωτᾶρ**

ELIS:
—OLYMPIA*: (1) i/ii AD *IvOl* 88, 3

**Σωτᾶς**

ARGOLIS:
—EPIDAUROS: (1) ?iii BC Peek, *IAEpid* 123 (Σωτᾶς: f. Τίμων)

ARKADIA:
—TEGEA: (2) ii AD *IG* V (2) 55, 45 (I f. Σωτᾶς II); (3) ~ ib. l. 45 (Σωτᾶς: II s. Σωτᾶς I); (4) 165 AD ib. 50, 9 (I f. Σωτᾶς II); (5) ~ ib. l. 9 (II s. Σωτᾶς I)

DALMATIA:
—ISSA: (6) iii BC *VAMZ* 1970, p. 36 fr. K

EPIROS:
—BOUTHROTOS (PRASAIBOI): (7) hell.? *IBouthrot* 199 (*RAAN* 21 (1941) p. 281) (s. Σωτήριχος)

ILLYRIA:
—APOLLONIA: (8) ?ii BC *IApoll* 11 (f. Ταρούλας)

MESSENIA:
—ASINE: (9) ii AD *IG* V (1) 1408 (I f. Σωτᾶς II); (10) ~ ib. (II s. Σωτᾶς I)
—MESSENE:
——(Daiphontidai): (11) 11 AD *PAE* 1992, p. 71 A, 22 (s. Τίμων)

PELOPONNESE?: (12) 11 AD ib. p. 72 B, 4 (s. Πασίων)

S. ITALY (CAMPANIA):
—POMPEII: (13) i BC-i AD *CIL* IV 1466; (14) ~ ib. 7590 (Lat. Sotas—Solin, T(h)yasotas—*CIL*)

**Σωτέας**

AKARNANIA:
—STRATOS: (1) ii BC *IG* IX (1)² (2) 394, 12 (Σωτέ[ας]: f. Σώτακος)

LAKONIA:
—SPARTA: (2) ii AD ib. V (1) 159, 23 (Bradford (-))

TRIPHYLIA:
—PYRGOI: (3) 205 BC *IG* IX (1)² (1) 31, 111 (s. Κτήσιππος)

**Σώτειρα**

LAKONIA:
—SPARTA:
——Konosoura: (1) c. 212 AD ib. V (1) 566, 8 (Bradford (-)) (Αὐρ. Σ.)

S. ITALY (LUCANIA):
—POSEIDONIA-PAESTUM: (2) imp. Mello–Voza 182 (Lat. Sotera)

SICILY:
—SYRACUSE: (3) iii-v AD Strazzulla 197 (Wessel 783) (-τι-); (4) ~ Ferrua, *NG* 199 (-τι-)

**Σωτέλης**

ACHAIA: (1) 146 BC *IG* IV (1)² 28, 68 (s. Σωκράτης: synoikos)

AKARNANIA:
—STRATOS: (2) ii BC ib. IX (1)² (2) 394, 10 (f. Σωκράτης); (3) ~ ib. l. 11 (s. Σωκράτης)
—THYRREION: (4) iii-ii BC *SEG* XXVII 159, 6; cf. *PAE* 1977, pl. 244 a (f. Σωτίων); (5) ii BC *IG* IX (1)² (2) 247, 10 (s. Ἐπιτέλης)

ARGOLIS:
—ARGOS: (6) 31 BC-14 AD *IvOl* 420, 2 (f. (ad.) Κλεογένης)
—EPIDAUROS: (7) iv BC *SEG* XXXVIII 323 (vase); (8) iii BC *IG* IV (1)² 337 (f. Εὐρύκλεια)
—EPIDAUROS*: (9) c. 370-360 BC *BSA* 61 (1966) p. 271 no. 4 A, 13

ARKADIA:
—MANTINEIA-ANTIGONEIA: (10) i-ii AD *IG* V (2) 326 (*GVI* 1241) (s. Ὠφέλιμος)

—ORCHOMENOS*: (11) ?ii BC *IG* V (2) 345, 10 (s. Λεπτίνας)
—TEGEA: (12) f. iii BC ib. 35, 29 (I f. Σωτέλης II); (13) ~ ib. l. 29 (II s. Σωτέλης I); (14) ~ ib. 36, 34
——(Apolloniatai): (15) f. iii BC ib. l. 69 (f. Δεξίας)
——(Krariotai): (16) s. iv BC ib. 41, 49 (Σωτέλ[ης]?: f. Σωτελίδας)

DALMATIA:
—ISSA: (17) ii BC *SEG* XXXI 600 (f. Καλλήν, Μομψίδας)

ILLYRIA:
—APOLLONIA: (18) c. 250-50 BC Maier 79 (coin) (Ceka 111) (money.)

KORINTHIA:
—KORINTH: (19) ?iii BC *IG* II² 9060 (f. Ἀρχίδαμος)
—SIKYON: (20) ?263-258 BC Nachtergael, *Les Galates* 3, 17; 5, 30; cf. Stephanis 2411 (f. Τίμανδρος)

MESSENIA:
—MESSENE: (21) iii/ii BC *IG* V (1) 1442
—THOURIA: (22) f. ii BC *SEG* XI 972, 94 (s. Δεξιάδας)

S. ITALY (LUCANIA):
—METAPONTION: (23) hell. *IG* XIV 2406. 79 (vase)

SICILY:
—TAUROMENION:
——(Σπαρ.): (24) ii/i BC *IGSI* 10 I, 26 (I f. Σωτέλης II); (25) ~ ib. l. 26 (II s. Σωτέλης I)
——(Σπαρτ.): (26) ?ii/i BC *IG* XIV 421 D an. 4 (*SGDI* 5219) (s. Ἀγάθων)

**Σωτελίδας**

ARGOLIS:
—HERMIONE?: (1) iv BC *IG* IV (1) 747 A, 6 (f. Σωσθένης)

ARKADIA:
—TEGEA:
——(Krariotai): (2) s. iv BC ib. V (2) 41, 49 (s. Σωτέλης)

**Σωτήρ**

ARGOLIS:
—HERMIONE: (1) ii-i BC ib. IV (1) 732 V, 5 (Σ[ω]τήρ: f. Δαμάτριος)

S. ITALY (BRUTTIUM):
—SYBARIS-THOURIOI-COPIAE: (2) ii-i BC *NScav* 1972, Suppl. p. 196 (amph.)

S. ITALY (CAMPANIA):
—DIKAIARCHIA-PUTEOLI: (3) imp. *CIL* X 1585 (Lat. T. Stlaccius Soter); (4) ~ *NScav* 1901, p. 20 (Lat. C. Belleus Soter); (5) ?ii AD *CIL* X 2598 (Lat. C. Vicirrius Soter)
—DIKAIARCHIA-PUTEOLI*: (6) imp. *NScav* 1885, p. 371 a (*Eph. Ep.* VIII 386) (Lat. Soter: doctor/imp. freed.)
—HERCULANEUM*: (7) c. 50-75 AD *CIL* X 1403 a I, 4 (Lat. Q. Allius Soter)
—POMPEII: (8) i BC-i AD ib. IV 8166 (Lat. Soter); (9) ~ ib. 10245; *Gnomon* 45 (1973) p. 271 (Lat. Soter); (10) c. 51-62 AD *CIL* IV 3340. 91, [6] (Castrèn 397. 5) (Lat. Q. Sulpicius Soter)

SICILY: (11) ?vi/v BC Manganaro, *QUCC* forthcoming no. 71 (ring) (Σōτέρ)
—AKRILLAI: (12) iii-v AD *Epigraphica* 12 (1950) p. 94 no. 1; cf. Ferrua, *NG* 508
—KATANE: (13) imp. *Epigraphica* 51 (1989) p. 171 no. 38 (Lat. L. Vib. Sot[er]: s. Legata, Νίκερως); (14) ~ *CIL* X 7091 (Lat. Soter); (15) 427 AD *SEG* XVII 441; cf. Ferrua, *NG* 405 a
—SYRACUSE: (16) iii-v AD *Rend. Pont.* 22 (1946-7) p. 232 no. 13; (17) ~ *SEG* XV 586; (18) ~ *NScav* 1947, p. 211 no. 2; (19) ~ Ferrua, *NG* 265
—THERMAI HIMERAIAI: (20) ii-i AD *CIL* X 7371 (*ILat. Term. Imer.* 40) (Lat. Soter)
—ZANKLE-MESSANA: (21) imp. *CIL* X 6984 (Lat. C. Iulius Soter)

## Σωτηρᾶς

ARGOLIS:
—HERMIONE: (1) iii AD IG IV (1) 718, 1 (M. Αὐρ. Σ.: II s. M. Αὐρ. Σωτηρᾶς I); (2) ~ ib. l. 4 (M. Αὐρ. Σ.: I f. M. Αὐρ. Σωτηρᾶς II)
ARKADIA:
—TEGEA: (3) imp. ib. v (2) 244; (4) ii AD ib. 55, 84 (I f. Σωτηρᾶς II); (5) ~ ib. l. 84 (II s. Σωτηρᾶς I); (6) 165 AD ib. 50, 2 (s. Μᾶρκος); (7) ~ ib. l. 35 (Βάριος Σ.); (8) ~ ib. l. 45 (s. Ἀφροδᾶς)
LAKONIA:
—SPARTA: (9) ii AD ib. v (1) 159, 28 (Bradford (-))

## Σωτηρία

ARGOLIS:
—ARGOS: (1) v-vi AD Unp. (Oikonomou-Laniado)
—EPIDAUROS: (2) i-ii AD Peek, IAEpid 319 ([Σω]τηρία)
LAKONIA:
—GYTHEION: (3) ii-iii AD IG v (1) 1200
—KYTHERA: (4) hell.? ib. 943 (Σωτηρ(ί)α)
—SPARTA: (5) ii-iii AD ib. 245 (Bradford (-))
S. ITALY (APULIA):
—CANNAE*: (6) i-ii AD Epig. Rom. di Canosa 57 (CIL IX 319) (Lat. Iulia Soteria: freed.)
S. ITALY (CALABRIA):
—BRENTESION-BRUNDISIUM: (7) imp. ib. 91 (Lat. Aninia Soteria)
S. ITALY (CAMPANIA):
—DIKAIARCHIA-PUTEOLI: (8) imp. NScav 1901, p. 20 (Lat. Bellea Soteria)
SICILY:
—SYRACUSE: (9) iii-v AD IG XIV 173 (Strazzulla 113; Wessel 1344)

## Σωτηριανός

S. ITALY (APULIA):
—CANUSIUM: (1) 223 AD Epig. Rom. di Canosa 35 I, 38; II, 10 (CIL IX 338) (Lat. C. Galbius Soterianus)

## Σωτηρίδας

ACHAIA: (1) 146 BC IG IV (1)² 28, 99 (f. Ξέ-νων: synoikos); (2) ~ ib. l. 101 (f. Σώστρατος: synoikos); (3) ~ ib. l. 127 (s. Ἀριστοκράτης: synoikos); (4) ~ ib. l. 135 (s. Ἀριστοκράτης)
AIGINA: (5) ?f. i AD Alt-Ägina I (2) p. 46 no. 20, 4 (s. Ἑρμ—)
AITOLIA:
—KASILIOI: (6) s. ii BC SEG XXV 621, 7 (f. Βε-ρενίκα)
AKARNANIA:
—PALAIROS: (7) ii BC IG IX (1)² (2) 451, 22
ARGOLIS:
—EPIDAUROS: (8) i AD RE (1) (?f. Παμφίλη); (9) 149 AD Peek, IAEpid 162, 2 (-τεί- Σωτηρίδας)
—EPIDAUROS*: (10) c. 370-365 BC ib. 52 Á, 47
—HERMIONE: (11) iv BC SEG XI 382, 19 (s. Τέ-λεσις)
ARKADIA:
—TEGEA:
——(Athaneatai): (12) iv/iii BC IG v (2) 38, 12 ([Σωτ]ηρίδα[ς]?)
ELIS:
—OLYMPIA*: (13) 265 AD IvOl 122, 18 (?s. Ἀρ-χέλαος: slave?)
EPIROS:
—NIKOPOLIS: (14) imp. PAE 1913, p. 97 no. 3 (Sarikakis 158) (f. Σωτηρίχα)
KORINTHIA:
—KORINTH: (15) ii/iii AD Ag. VII pp. 95 no. 278; 98 no. 312; BM Lamps 3 p. 404 nos. Q3244, Q3250; Corinth IV (2) p. 212 nos. 781-4; SEG XXVII 35. 28 (lamps)
—SIKYON: (16) 401 BC X., An. iii 4. 47 ff. (Skalet 311)
LAKONIA:
—SPARTA: (17) i BC SEG XIII 248, 14; cf. Stephanis 2780 (Bradford (16)); (18) s. i BC

IG v (1) 906 (tiles) (Bradford (5)) (Σωτη-ρίδ[ας]); (19) c. 30-20 BC IG v (1) 211, 27 (Bradford (15)) (f. Σικλῆς); (20) i BC/i AD IG v (1) 48, 17 (Bradford (1)) (s. Ἀγαθοκλῆς); (21) ~ SEG XI 679, 4 (Bradford (12)) ([Σω-τη]ρίδας: f. Λυσίνικος); (22) ii AD IG v (1) 159, 15 (Bradford (7)); (23) ii-iii AD IG v (1) 765 (Bradford (6)); (24) m. ii AD IG v (1) 71 II, 21; 561, 2 (Bradford (10)) (f. M. Αὐρ. Χρυσό-γονος); (25) ?134 AD IG v (1) 62, 11 (Bradford (4)) (s. Φιλήμων); (26) c. 140-145 AD IG v (1) 1314, 42 (Bradford (9)); (27) c. 140-150 AD IG v (1) 85, 11 (Bradford (3)) (s. Εὐδίαιτος); (28) c. 140-160 AD IG v (1) 68, 18; SEG XI 587, 2 (Bradford (11)) (f. Ἔλενος); (29) ~ IG v (1) 112, 3; 113, 2; 128, 9; SEG XI 585, 3; 586, [1]; XXX 410, 4 (Bradford (14)) (f. Φι-λουμενός); (30) c. 212-220 AD IG v (1) 560, 8 (Bradford (2)) (s. M. Αὐρ. Χρυσόγονος); (31) a. 212 AD IG v (1) 600, 5 (Bradford (13)) (f. Αὐρ. Νικηφόρος)
——Amyklai: (32) ii/i BC IG v (1) 26, 1 (Brad-ford (12)) (f. Λυσίνικος)
MESSENIA:
—MESSENE: (33) 31 BC-14 AD SEG XXIII 207, 32 (f. Νικηφόρος); (34) ~ ib. l. 32 (s. Νικηφόρος)
SICILY:
—SEGESTA: (35) imp.? IG XIV 289

## Σωτηρίδης

ARGOLIS:
—EPIDAUROS: (1) i-ii AD Peek, NIEpid 86 (f. —ις)

## Σωτηρίδιον

SICILY:
—SYRACUSE: (1) iii-v AD Oikoumene p. 605 no. 3 (Guarducci, Ep. Gr. 4 p. 522 no. 1); cf. Ferrua, NG 425 b

## Σωτηρικιανός

S. ITALY (CAMPANIA):
—DIKAIARCHIA-PUTEOLI: (1) imp. CIL X 2508 (Lat. Pompeius Sotericianus)

## Σωτηρικλῆς

LAKONIA:
—ASOPOS: (1) imp. IG v (1) 996 (f. Ἁγησίδαμος)

## Σωτήριος

AKARNANIA:
—MEDION: (1) c. 325-315 BC Hesp. 57 (1988) p. 148 A, 46 (SEG XXXVI 331); cf. Hesp. 48 (1979) pp. 78 f. with pl. 22 c (s. Σώσανδρος)
SICILY:
—SYRACUSE: (2) s. iv BC IG II² 10395

## Σωτηρίς

AIGINA?: (1) imp. EAD XXX p. 356 no. 17 with n. 1 (d. Φιλουμένη)
AKARNANIA: (2) 183 BC IG II² 2332 I, 97
ARGOLIS:
—ARGOS*: (3) f. iii BC ib. IV (1) 529, 7 (slave/freed.?); (4) ii BC SEG XLII 279, 25 (Σωτηρίς: d. Σῶσος: katoikos)
—HERMIONE: (5) ii-i BC IG IV (1) 732 III, 14 (d. Ἀγαπᾶτις)
—METHANA-ARSINOE: (6) i BC ib. II² 9329 ([Σω]τηρίς: d. Ἀσκλαπιάδας)
ITHAKE: (7) hell. Unp. (IG arch.) (Σωτηρ[ίς])
KORINTHIA:
—KORINTH: (8) hell. IG II² 9077; (9) byz. Hesp. 41 (1972) p. 41 no. 33, 3 (?d. Παῦλος)
LAKONIA:
—GYTHEION: (10) i-ii AD IG v (1) 1176, 3 (m. Εὐδαμία)
MESSENIA:
—MESSENE: (11) iii-ii BC ib. II² 9344
S. ITALY (CALABRIA):
—BRENTESION-BRUNDISIUM: (12) imp. CIL IX 101 (Lat. Clodia So(t)eris)

S. ITALY (CAMPANIA):
—DIKAIARCHIA-PUTEOLI: (13) imp. ib. X 2303 (Lat. Clodia Soteris: m. Κλεοπάτρα); (14) ~ NScav 1885, p. 371 b (Lat. Sulpicia Soteris)
—POMPEII: (15) i BC-i AD Römische Gräberstrassen p. 223 c (Lat. Callidia So-teris)
—SURRENTUM: (16) imp. St. Rom. 2 (1914) p. 346 = NScav 1928, p. 211 no. 23 (Lat. Gellia Soteris)
S. ITALY (LUCANIA):
—VOLCEI: (17) s. ii AD Suppl. It. 3 p. 77 no. 6 (Lat. Acilia Soteris)
SICILY: (18) v/iv BC Unp. (BM) GR 1982.12-14.1
—ACATE (MOD.): (19) iii-v AD Rend. Pont. 45 (1972-3) p. 191 no. 2
—CINISI (MOD.): (20) imp. IG XIV 289; IG-LMP 14 (locn.) (Σωτηρίδ[ας]?)
—KATANE: (21) iii-v AD IG XIV 550 (Wessel 332)
—LIPARA: (22) ?ii-i BC Meligunìs-Lipára 5 p. 183 T. 2179; cf. SEG XLI 816
—SYRACUSE: (23) imp. IG XIV 21 (Ἀλφία Σω[τη]ρίς); (24) ~ ib. 36 + Riv. Arch. Crist. 18 (1941) p. 198 no. 68 (K. Σ.); (25) iii-v AD Ferrua, NG 207 (-ρής)
—THERMAI HIMERAIAI: (26) ii-iii AD ILat. Term. Imer. 85 (Lat. Cor. Soteris)

## Σωτηρις

ARKADIA:
—TEGEA: (1) imp. IG v (2) 243; (2) ~ ib. p. 146 no. 244
ILLYRIA:
—APOLLONIA: (3) ii-i BC IApoll 153
—EPIDAMNOS-DYRRHACHION: (4) hell.-imp. IDyrrh 389 (?s./d. Εὔπορος)
LAKONIA:
—SPARTA: (5) ii-iii AD IG v (1) 777 (Bradford s.v. Σωτηρείς (-)) (Σωτηρει (voc.))
LEUKAS: (6) hell. IG IX (1) 583 + Fraser-Rönne, BWGT p. 116 no. 2

## Σωτηρίσκος

LAKONIA:
—KYTHERA: (1) c. 250 BC IG XI (4) 636, 9 (f. Ἀριστάγορος)

## Σωτηρίχα

ACHAIA:
—BOURA: (1) imp. SGDI 1610, 3
—DYME: (2) ii BC Achaean Grave Stelai 18 (d. Πραξίτας)
—TRITAIA: (3) ii-i BC ib. 72 (d. Ἀπολλᾶς)
EPIROS:
—KASSOPE: (4) hell. SEG XVII 311 (m. Ἐμναύ-τα)
—NIKOPOLIS: (5) imp. PAE 1913, p. 97 no. 3 (Sarikakis 159) (d. Σωτηρίδας, Μέθη)
ILLYRIA:
—APOLLONIA: (6) ?i BC IApoll 154 (-ρίκα: d. Ἀθανίων)

## Σωτήριχος

ACHAIA: (1) 146 BC IG IV (1)² 28, 120 (s. Πο-λυκράτης: synoikos)
AKARNANIA:
—THYRREION: (2) ii BC ib. IX (1)² (2) 248, 14
ARGOLIS:
—EPIDAUROS: (3) ii BC ib. IV (1)² 371 (Peek, IAEpid 153. 18) (s. Σωσικράτης); (4) III AD SEG XXXIX 358, 9 (s. Ἀπολλοφάνης)
—HERMIONE: (5) imp. IG IV (1) 698 (K. Καικί-λιος Σ.)
—METHANA-ARSINOE: (6) ii-i BC ib. 865 + SEG XXXVII 319
—TROIZEN: (7) f. iii BC IG II² 1273, 2, 10, 16
ARKADIA:
—KLEITOR: (8) m. iii AD SEG XXXV 350 II, 9 (Αὐρ. Σωτήριχος: s. Χρύσιππος)
—LYKOSOURA*: (9) 38-72 AD IG v (2) 524
—MEGALOPOLIS: (10) ii AD ib. 463 (Τάδιος Σ.: s. M. Τάδιος Σπεδιανός, Κλ. Ἰούλιττα)

—TEGEA: (11) ?i AD ib. 245; (12) ii AD ib. 54, 10; (13) ~ ib. 55, 25 (s. Διονύσιος); (14) ~ ib. l. 76 (s. Ὀνησιφόρος); (15) ~ ib. l. 85 (s. Κάλλιστος); (16) ?ii AD ib. 214 (Σωτήριχος); (17) 165 AD ib. 50, 21 (I f. Σωτήριχος II); (18) ~ ib. l. 21 (II s. Σωτήριχος I); (19) ~ ib. l. 22 (f. Σεκοῦνδος); (20) ~ ib. l. 27 (f. Νίκων); (21) ~ ib. l. 40 (I f. Σωτήριχος II); (22) ~ ib. l. 40 (II s. Σωτήριχος I); (23) ~ ib. l. 66 (I f. Σωτήριχος II); (24) ~ ib. l. 66 (II s. Σωτήριχος I)

ELIS: (25) 72 BC Moretti, Olymp. 691 ?= (26); (26) s. i BC IvOl 213 (f. Θαλίαρχος) ?= (25); (27) imp. ib. 740 (tile) ([Σω]τήριχος); (28) ?i AD EA 1905, p. 259 no. 2, 11 (f. Εὐθυκλῆς); (29) 209-213 AD IvOl 110, 11 (f. Αὐρ. Μητρόβιος); (30) c. 221-230 AD ib. 113, 15 ([Σω]τήριχος)

EPIROS:
—BOUTHROTOS (PRASAIBOI): (31) hell.? IBouthrot 199 (RAAN 21 (1941) p. 281) ([Σ]ωτήριχος: f. Σωτᾶς); (32) a. 163 BC IBouthrot 45, 7 (s. Ἀπολλοφάνης); (33) ~ ib. 46, 3; (34) ~ ib. l. 4; (35) ~ ib. l. 4; (36) ~ ib. 61 (SEG XXXVIII 512)
—KASSOPE: (37) hell. Ep. Chron. 29 (1988-9) pp. 89 ff.; cf. BE 1991, no. 360
—NIKOPOLIS: (38) imp. Unp. (Nikopolis Mus.) (Βιλλιηνὸς Σ.)

ILLYRIA:
—EPIDAMNOS-DYRRHACHION: (39) hell.-imp. IDyrrh 390 (s. Ἀλέξανδρος)

KORINTHIA:
—KORINTH: (40) ii-i BC IG II² 9078 (s. Θεόδοτος)

LAKONIA:
—SPARTA: (41) c. 100-120 AD ib. v (1) 97, 16; SEG XI 564, 10; 565, 5; 642, 1 (Bradford (6)) (f. Ἀλεξίμαχος); (42) ii AD IG v (1) 159, 19 (Bradford (4)); (43) ii-iii AD IG v (1) 732, 3 (GVI 986; Bradford (7)); (44) ~ IG v (1) 762 (Bradford (3)); (45) c. 125 AD IG v (1) 1314, 12 (Bradford (1)) (s. X—); (46) c. 140-160 AD SEG XI 600, 3 (Bradford (5)) (Μέμμιος Σ.)
——Limnai: (47) c. 70-100 AD IG v (1) 676, 19 (Bradford (2)) (Σωτήρ[ιχο]ς: s. Καθήκων)
—LEUKAS: (48) c. 167-50 BC NZ 10 (1878) p. 136 no. 37 (coin)

MESSENIA:
—MESSENE: (49) m. iii BC Peek, IAEpid 42, 61, 64 (Perlman E.3); Perlman p. 63 f. (date) (f. Φίλων)

S. ITALY (BRUTTIUM):
—LOKROI EPIZEPHYRIOI:
——(Κρα.): (50) iv/iii BC De Franciscis 22, 22 (s. Εὐφρονίσκος)
—RHEGION*: (51) i BC/i AD SEG XXXIX 1062 B (slave?)

S. ITALY (CALABRIA):
—BRENTESION-BRUNDISIUM: (52) imp. CIL IX 112 (Lat. [L.] [F]aenius So[t]erichus); (53) ~ ib. 123 (Lat. P. Gifinius Sotericus)
—BRENTESION-BRUNDISIUM*: (54) ii-iii AD NScav 1893, p. 121; cf. Epigraphica 32 (1970) p. 168 (Lat. Soterichus: freed.)

S. ITALY (CAMPANIA):
—DIKAIARCHIA-PUTEOLI: (55) imp. CIL x 2969 (Lat. [So]terichus); (56) ~ ib. 2970 (Lat. Sotericus)
—DIKAIARCHIA-PUTEOLI*: (57) ?ii AD ib. 2959 (Lat. M. Ulpius Soterichus: imp. freed.)
—NEAPOLIS: (58) i BC/i AD INap 172, 2; cf. Leiwo p. 77 no. 20 (II s. Σωτήριχος I); (59) ~ INap 172, 3; cf. Leiwo p. 77 no. 20 (I f. Σωτήριχος II)
—POMPEII: (60) i BC-i AD CIL IV 3165 (Lat. Sotericus); (61) 70-79 AD ib. 7432; 7632; 7635; Mouritsen p. 110 (date) (Lat. Sotericus)
—S. ANASTASIA (MOD.): (62) s. i AD RAAN 49 (1974) p. 231 (Lat. Soterichus: freed.?)

SICILY:
—KATANE: (63) imp. CIL x 7054 (Lat. M. Caeparius Soterichus)
—TAUROMENION*: (64) imp. ib. 8059. 376 (seal) (Lat. Soterichus)

## Σωτηρίων

ACHAIA: (1) 146 BC IG IV (1)² 28, 123 (f. Ζώπυρος: synoikos)
AIGINA: (2) ?f. i AD Alt-Ägina I (2) p. 45 no. 17, 2 (s. Μᾶρκος)
AIGINA?: (3) imp. EAD XXX p. 356 no. 17 with n. 1 (f. Ἀφθόνητος)
ARGOLIS:
—EPIDAUROS: (4) i BC-i AD IG IV (1)² 35; (5) ii-iii AD ib. 39 (s. Εὐκρατέα); (6) iii-iv AD ib. 539; (7) 250 AD ib. 413 (I f. Σωτηρίων II); (8) ~ ib. (II s. Σωτηρίων I)
——(Hylleis): (9) c. 335-325 BC ib. 106 III, 38; 108, 159
—EPIDAUROS?: (10) ?i BC SEG I 71
—HERMIONE: (11) iii BC IG IV (1) 728, 18; (12) ?ii-i BC ib. 731 I, 8 (f. Μένανδρος); (13) ~ ib. 731 II, 4 (s. Δαμοκλέα); (14) ii-i BC ib. 732 II, 16 (s. Φιλοκλῆς); (15) ~ ib. 732 III, 23 (s. Ἀφροδισία); (16) ~ ib. 732 IV, 8 (f. Σωτιδώ); (17) i BC-i AD? ib. 730 V, 2 (f. Νικοκλέα); (18) i BC-i AD SEG XVII 161 ([Σ]ωτηρίων)
ARKADIA:
—TEGEA: (19) 78 AD IG v (2) 49, 7 (s. Πλόκαμος)
KEPHALLENIA: (20) imp.? SEG XXX 516
KERKYRA: (21) ii BC IG IX (1) 692, 8 (Iscr. Gr. Verona p. 22 B) ([Σω]τηρίων)
LAKONIA:
—SPARTA: (22) imp. IG v (1) 1016 (Bradford (-)) (Σωτηρί<ι>[ω]ν, Σωτηρίων—IG index)

## Σώτηρος

ARKADIA:
—TEGEA: (1) ii AD IG v (2) 55, 47 (s. Ἑλενιανός)
ELIS: (2) iv-v AD SEG XXII 332, 2; cf. TMByz 9 (1985) p. 373 no. 152 (πρεσβύτ.)
KERKYRA: (3) iii-ii BC AE 1914, p. 235 no. 4 (f. Τιμαρχίς)

## Σωτηρώ

ARGOLIS:
—EPIDAUROS: (1) iv/iii BC Peek, NIEpid 75
EPIROS:
—NIKOPOLIS: (2) imp. AE 1950-1, Chron. p. 36 (Sarikakis 119) (Νοβία Σ.)

## Σωτηρῶι

ARKADIA:
—PHIGALEIA: (1) imp. SEG XXIII 250
—TEGEA: (2) ii-iii AD IG v (2) 178 (GVI 960) (m. Ἀπολλώνις)

## Σωτία

EPIROS:
—AMBRAKIA: (1) ?ii BC AD 10 (1926) p. 67 fig. 4

## Σωτίας

ARKADIA:
—MANTINEIA-ANTIGONEIA: (1) c. 300-221 BC IG v (2) 323. 71 (tessera) ([Σ]ωτίας: f. Δαμέας)

## Σωτιδώ

ARGOLIS:
—HERMIONE: (1) ii-i BC ib. IV (1) 732 IV, 7 (d. Σωτηρίων)

## Σωτίμεια

ARGOLIS:
—EPIDAUROS: (1) iv BC Peek, IAEpid 138 (Σωτ[ί]μεια?)

## Σωτιμίδας

ARGOLIS:
—EPIDAUROS: (1) iii-ii BC Le Rider, Monnaies crétoises p. 258 I, 6 (f. Ἀφθόνητος); (2) ~ ib. l. 7 (s. Ἀφθόνητος)

EPIROS:
—KASSOPE: (3) iii BC IG IX (1)² (2) 243, 3 (Σωτι[μίδας?]: s. Ξενίας)
LAKONIA:
—MESSA?: (4) imp. ib. v (1) 1280, 1, 2 (-τει-: f. Δαμόχαρις, Φιλιππίς); (5) ~ ib. l. 4, 6 (s. Ἐπίχαρις, f. Φιλοκλῆς); (6) ~ ib. l. 7 (s. Φίλιππος)
—TEUTHRONE: (7) i BC/i AD ib. v (2) 538 (Σωτιμίδας: f. Δαμόχαρις); (8) ~ ib. (Σωτιμίδας: s. Δαμόχαρις, Ἀριστήδεια)
S. ITALY (BRUTTIUM):
—LOKROI EPIZEPHYRIOI: (9) hell.? Landi, DISMG 245 (Σωτιμί(δας))

## Σώτιμος

ARGOLIS:
—EPIDAUROS: (1) c. 370 BC IG IV (1)² 102, 60
EPIROS?: (2) s. iv BC Liv. viii 24. 12
KORINTHIA:
—SIKYON: (3) 192 BC SEG XIII 327, 24 (f. —ξενος)
LAKONIA: (4) ii BC IG II² 9154 (Σώτι<ι>μος)
PELOPONNESE: (5) c. 230-200 BC BCH 45 (1921) p. 13 II, 106 (f. Φίλων)

## Σώτιον

ILLYRIA:
—BYLLIONES BYLLIS: (1) ?f. ii BC SEG XXXVIII 538

## Σωτίχη

EPIROS: (1) ii/i BC Ugolini, Alb. Ant. I p. 193 no. 14 (d. Ὀνήσιμος)

## Σωτίων

ACHAIA:
—DYME: (1) ii-i BC SEG XI 1262 (s. Ἀλεξικλῆς); (2) c. 219 BC SGDI 1612, 30 (Tyche 5 (1990) p. 124) (s. Σωσικράτης)
—PELLENE: (3) ?ii AD IG II² 10056 (f. Φιλώτας)
ACHAIA?: (4) 193 AD ib. v (2) 293, 5 (f. Ἀρίστων)
AITOLIA: (5) 217 BC Nachtergael, Les Galates 65, 4
—KALYDON: (6) a. 142 BC IG IX (1)² (1) 137, 61 (Σωτ[ίω]ν)
—TRICHONION: (7) s. iii BC ib. 117, 4
AKARNANIA: (8) 259 BC ib. XI (2) 115, 21 (Stephanis 2372) ?= (9); (9) ?254 BC Nachtergael, Les Galates 9, 54; cf. Stephanis 350 (f. Ἀριστοκράτης) ?= (8)
—ANAKTORION: (10) 216 BC IG IX (1)² (2) 583, 66; (11) m. ii BC Syll³ 669, 6 (f. Σώπατρος)
—ASTAKOS: (12) hell. IG IX (1)² (2) 441; (13) ii BC ib. 434, 11 (s. Ἑσπερίων); (14) ~ ib. l. 12, 16 (s. Λέων, f. Λέων); (15) ~ ib. 435, 9 (s. Ταύρων); (16) ~ ib. l. 11 (I f. Σωτίων II); (17) ~ ib. l. 11 (II s. Σωτίων I); (18) ~ ib. l. 14 (s. Κλέων); (19) ~ ib. l. 18 (s. Λεύκιος); (20) ~ ib. l. 5-6 (f. Φόξος, Φίλων)
—LEKKA (MOD.): (21) iii BC ib. 595 ([Σ]ωτίω[ν]: s. Δυστρίων?)
—OINIADAI: (22) s. iii BC ib. 422; Fraser-Rönne, BWGT pl. 25 (s. Δαμόνικος)
—THYRREION: (23) iii BC IG IX (1)² (2) 277; (24) ~ ib. 278; (25) ~ SEG XXV 627 (s. Κριτ—); (26) iii-ii BC ib. XXVII 159, 1; cf. PAE 1977, pl. 244 a (f. Τιμόλαος); (27) ~ SEG XXVII 159, 6; cf. PAE 1977, pl. 244 a (s. Σωτέλης); (28) iii-i BC IG IX (1)² (2) 348; (29) f. iii BC SEG XXVII 164 (s. Φιλόνικος); (30) m. iii BC ib. XL 464 II side 1, 5 (?s. Εὔθυμος); (31) 216 BC IG IX (1)² (2) 583, 18, 64 (s. Ἀλέξανδρος); (32) ii BC ib. 248, 11 (f. Φαινέας); (33) ~ ib. 249, 1 (f. —των); (34) ~ ib. l. 4 (s. Δωρίμαχος); (35) ~ ib. l. 5 (s. Ἀνδ—); (36) ~ ib. 250, [5], 16 (s. Διόφαντος, f. Διόφαντος); (37) ~ ib. 252, 14 (s. Σωσίας); (38) ii/i BC ib. 256, 5; (39) hell.-imp. ib. 361
ARGOLIS:
—ARGOS: (40) ii BC SEG XLII 279, 13
ARKADIA:
—MEGALOPOLIS: (41) ii BC IG v (2) 453 (f. Νίκιππος)

ELIS: (42) 36-24 BC *IvOl* 62, 13 (I f. *Σωτίων* II); (43) ~ ib. l. 13 (II s. *Σωτίων* I); (44) 28-24 BC ib. 64, 32 (f. *Εὔθυμος*)
EPIROS:
—AMBRAKIA: (45) ii-i BC *BCH* 79 (1955) p. 267
—BOUCHETION: (46) f. iii BC *Thess. Mnem.* 103 (f. *Σωκράτις*)
—BOUTHROTOS (PRASAIBOI): (47) a. 163 BC *IBouthrot* 38, 11 (*SEG* XXXVIII 497) (s. *Νίκανδρος*, f. *Νίκανδρος*)
—KASSOPE: (48) f. ii BC Cabanes, *L'Épire* p. 564 no. 41, 8 (s. *Λύκωπος*)
—NIKOPOLIS: (49) c. 75-100 AD *FD* III (4) 114, 5 (Sarikakis 21) ([*Κλ*.? *Ἀ*]*φείνιος Σ.*)
ILLYRIA:
—APOLLONIA: (50) c. 250-50 BC Maier 81 (coin) (Ceka 112) (*Σωτί*(*ων*): money.); (51) ?ii-i BC *IApoll* 96 (f. *Θευόδοτος*)
—EPIDAMNOS-DYRRHACHION: (52) c. 250-50 BC Ceka 91 (coin) (pryt.) ?= (53); (53) ~ Ceka, *Probleme* p. 152 no. 68 (coin) (pryt.) ?= (52); (54) ~ Maier 472; Münsterberg Nachtr. p. 16 (Ceka 404; 415-16); *IApoll Ref. Bibl.* n. 109 (coin) (*Σω*(*τίων*)—404: money.); (55) ii-i BC *IDyrrh* 559 (tiles); (56) f. ii BC *SEG* XXXVIII 558
ITHAKE: (57) hell.? *IG* IX (1) 680; (58) 208 BC *IMM* 36, 30
KEPHALLENIA:
—PRONNOI: (59) hell. *IG* IX (1) 647 (Fraser-Rönne, *BWGT* p. 116 no. 1); (60) f. iii BC *Op. Ath.* 10 (1971) p. 67 no. 16; (61) c. 210 BC *IG* IX (1)² (1) 31, 95 (s. *Τιμοκράτης*, f. *Αἰακίδας*)
—SAME: (62) f. iii BC *Op. Ath.* 10 (1971) p. 66 no. 12 (*BCH* 83 (1959) p. 658)
KERKYRA: (63) ?ii-i BC *IG* IX (1) 811 (tile)
LAKONIA:
—SPARTA:
——Limnai: (64) c. 70-100 AD ib. V (1) 676, 12 (Bradford (-)) (f. *Τιμοκράτης*)
LEUKAS: (65) c. 167-50 BC *BMC Thessaly* p. 187 nos. 188-9 (coins); (66) f. i BC *IG* IX (1) 534, 7, 11 (*Iscr. Gr. Verona* p. 24) (f. *Ἄνδρων*)
S. ITALY: (67) c. 200-175 BC *IG* XI (4) 808 (s. *Θεόδωρος*)

**Σωτύλος**
AITOLIA: (1) ?257-255 BC Nachtergael, *Les Galates* 7, 43; 8, 46; Stephanis 2373 (s. *Φιλόξενος*); (2) 224 or 221 BC *SGDI* 2524, 5; Nachtergael, *Les Galates* 64, 4
AKARNANIA:
—ASTAKOS: (3) ii BC *IG* IX (1)² (2) 435, 8 (f. *Λάμιος*)

**Σωτώ**
EPIROS:
—AMBRAKIA: (1) ?ii BC Unp. (Arta Mus., inscr.)
KEPHALLENIA:
—PRONNOI: (2) f. iii BC *Op. Ath.* 10 (1971) p. 67 no. 16

**Σώτων**
AITOLIA:
—PHISTYON?: (1) f. ii BC *IG* IX (1)² (1) 111, 6 (*Σωτ*(*ί*)*ων?*—ed.: s. *Πολυοῦχος*: sculptor)
AKARNANIA:
—ANAKTORION: (2) m. ii BC *Syll*³ 669, 2 (f. *Θεύδοτος*)
—ASTAKOS: (3) ii BC *IG* IX (1)² (2) 435, 4 (s. *Φαιδρίας*); (4) ~ ib. l. 10 (I f. *Σώτων* II); (5) ~ ib. l. 10 (II s. *Σώτων* I); (6) ~ ib. l. 16 (s. *Ἀγήσαρχος*)
—THYRREION: (7) ii BC ib. 248, 3 (s. *Τε*—)

EPIROS:
—AMBRAKIA: (8) v/iv BC *BCH* 79 (1955) p. 267 (f. *Κωνώπα*); (9) hell. *SEG* XXIV 421 (I f. *Σώτων* II); (10) ~ ib. (II s. *Σώτων* I); (11) iii BC *BCH* 17 (1893) p. 633 (f. *Λαμίσκος*); (12) ii-i BC *CIG* 1800, 3 (*Σωτων*—apogr., *Σωτ*(*ί*)*ων*—*CIG*: s. *Καλλίστρατος*); (13) a. 167 BC *SEG* XXXV 665 A, 10; (14) ~ ib. l. 11 (s. *Λαμίσκος*); (15) s. ii BC Unp. (Arta Mus., inscr.) (s. *Μένανδρος*)
—NIKOPOLIS: (16) i AD *AAA* 4 (1971) p. 337 (*AD* 26 (1971) Chron. p. 337) (freed.)
ITHAKE: (17) iv/iii BC Unp. (Stavros Mus., Ithaka) (f. *Σύρα*)
MESSENIA:
—MESSENE: (18) ii/i BC *IG* V (1) 1437, 18
—THOURIA: (19) 102-114 AD ib. 1381, 8 (f. *Μάρκος*)
S. ITALY (BRUTTIUM):
—LOKROI EPIZEPHYRIOI:
——(*Κυλ*.): (20) iv/iii BC De Franciscis 5, 5 (s. *Σωσιχάρης*)

**Σωφάνης**
ACHAIA: (1) m. ii BC *PP* 15246; *PPC* Σ 53
ARGOLIS:
—ARGOS:
——Keramis: (2) iii BC *SEG* XIII 241, 9 (f. *Ἀρχέμαχος*)
—EPIDAUROS: (3) 191-146 BC *BMC Pelop.* p. 8 no. 94 (coin) (*Σωφά*(*νης*)?, *Σώφα*(*ντος*)?)
——(Hysminatai): (4) c. 370 BC *IG* IV (1)² 102, 10
—KALAURIA: (5) iii BC ib. IV (1) 840, 4, 8 (f. *Σωσιφάνης*, *Νικαγόρα*, *Ἀριστόκλεια*); (6) ~ ib. 841, 11 (s. *Πολι*—)
—METHANA-ARSINOE: (7) iii BC *SEG* XXXVII 320
—TROIZEN: (8) 327-324 BC *CID* II 97, 31; 99 A, [2]; 102 II B, 37 (f. *Εὐφάνης*)

**Σώφαντος**
ARGOLIS:
—EPIDAUROS: (1) iv/iii BC *IG* IV (1)² 202 + Peek, *IAEpid* 91 (name)

**Σώφιλος**
ARGOLIS:
—ARGOS: (1) iii BC *IG* IV (1) 527, 4; cf. *BCH* 37 (1913) p. 308 + *SEG* XI 311 ([*Σ*]*ώφιλ*[*ος*], *Σωΐφιλ*[*ος*]—Vollgraff)
DALMATIA:
—ISSA: (2) iii/ii BC Brunšmid p. 21 no. 8; *Istros* 2 (1935-6) pp. 18 ff. (date)
ILLYRIA:
—APOLLONIA: (3) ii-i BC *IApoll* 149 (*Σό*-: f. *Ἀ*—*α*)
KORINTHIA:
—SIKYON?: (4) iv BC *RE* (1); *PCG* 7 pp. 594-9 (Skalet 313) (or Thessaly Thebes)

**Σωφρόνα**
AKARNANIA:
—PALAIROS: (1) iii/ii BC *IG* IX (1)² (2) 533
ARGOLIS:
—HERMIONE: (2) iii BC ib. IV (1) 728, 35
S. ITALY (LUCANIA):
—HYELE-VELIA: (3) imp. *PdelP* 21 (1966) p. 336 no. 4 (d. *Ἀγαθῖνος*)

**Σωφρονία**
SICILY:
—SYRACUSE: (1) iii-v AD Strazzulla 184 (Wessel 684); cf. Ferrua, *NG* 20 (-*φρω*-); (2) ~ Strazzulla 297 (Wessel 847)

**Σωφρονίδας**
SICILY:
—KAMARINA: (1) hell. *SEG* XXXIX 1001, 8 (f. *Τιμοκράτης*)
—TAUROMENION: (2) c. 193 BC *IG* XIV 421 an. 48 (*SGDI* 5219) (s. *Φιλιστίων*)

**Σωφρόνιος**
ARGOLIS:
—HERMIONE: (1) ii-i BC *IG* IV (1) 732 III, 22
ILLYRIA:
—SKAMPIS: (2) iii-iv AD *SEG* XXIII 482 (brick)

**Σωφρονίσκος**
S. ITALY (BRUTTIUM):
—LOKROI EPIZEPHYRIOI:
——(*Σκι*.): (1) iv/iii BC De Franciscis 11, 2; 18, 5 (s. *Καλλίδαμος*)

**Σωφρονίων**
ARGOLIS:
—HERMIONE: (1) c. 100-90 BC *SEG* XXXIII 290 A, 28-9; *BSA* 70 (1975) pp. 129-31 (date); cf. Stephanis 1946; 2125 (f. *Ὀνασικράτης*, *Ποσειδαῖος*)

**Σωφροσύνα**
EPIROS:
—BOUTHROTOS (PRASAIBOI): (1) a. 163 BC *IBouthrot* 28, 19 (*SEG* XXXVIII 486); *IBouthrot* 144, 5; (2) ~ ib. 102, 2
LAKONIA:
—SPARTA: (3) c. 212-220 AD *IG* V (1) 560, 7 (Bradford (-)) (d. *M. Αὐρ. Χρυσόγονος*)
SICILY:
—SYRACUSE: (4) f. iv BC Plu., *Dio* 6; cf. Beloch, *GG* III (2) pp. 102-7 (d. *Διονύσιος*, *Ἀριστομάχα*, m. *Ἀπολλοκράτης*)

**Σωφροσύνη**
SICILY:
—SYRACUSE: (1) iii-v AD *IG* XIV 174 (Strazzulla 142); cf. Ferrua, *NG* 175

**Σώφρων**
AIGINA: (1) hell.? *IG* IV (1) 149 (*Σώφρω*[*ν*])
ARGOLIS:
—EPIDAUROS: (2) iii AD ib. IV (1)² 401, 2
—HERMIONE: (3) ii-i BC ib. IV (1) 732 IV, 23 (f. *Ἄτταλος*)
EPIROS:
—AMBRAKIA: (4) v BC Moretti, *Olymp.* 321
—NIKOPOLIS: (5) imp. *Hellenika* 22 (1969) p. 68 no. 3 (Sarikakis 160) (s. *Φιλάργυρος*); (6) ~ Epict., *Ench.* iii 4. 9 (Sarikakis 161)
LAKONIA:
—SPARTA: (7) imp. *IG* V (1) 799 (Bradford (1)); (8) c. 212-235 AD *IG* V (1) 554, 1 (Bradford (3)) (*Τιβ. Κλ. Σ.*)
S. ITALY (CAMPANIA):
—DIKAIARCHIA-PUTEOLI*: (9) imp. *CIL* X 2826, 9 (Lat. Sophron: freed.)
SICILY:
—SYRACUSE: (10) s. v BC *RE* (1); *CGF* 1 pp. 152 ff.; cf. *SP* III 73 (s. *Ἀγαθοκλῆς*, *Δαμνασυλλίς*, f. *Ξέναρχος*)

**Σωχαρίδας**
KORINTHIA:
—SIKYON: (1) s. iii BC *SEG* III 346, 2 (Skalet 37) (f. *Ἀντιμένης*)

**Σωχεύς**
SICILY:
—HERBESSOS: (1) ?vi BC *SEG* XXXV 1010 (gem) (gen.?)

# T

**Τάγης**
S. ITALY (CAMPANIA):
—POMPEII: (1) c. 51-62 AD *CIL* IV 3340. 67, 21; 76, 12; 101, 10; 113, 9; 115, 6 (Castrèn 129. 41) (Lat. P. Cornelius Tages)

**Ταγίλος**
S. ITALY (APULIA):
—ARGYRIPPA-ARPI: (1) 191 BC *Syll³* 585, 65 (f. Σάλσιος Ταγύλλιος)

**Ταγύλλιος**
S. ITALY (APULIA):
—ARGYRIPPA-ARPI: (1) 191 BC ib. l. 64 (Σάλσιος Τ.: s. Ταγίλος)

**Ταῖς**
ARGOLIS:
—EPIDAUROS: (1) iv BC *IG* IV (1)² 329 (d. Ἀντ-αλλίδας)

**Τάλαος**
ARGOLIS:
—ARGOS: (1) i/ii AD ib. IV (1) 643 (f. Πυθοδίκη)

**Ταλθύβιος**
ACHAIA:
—PELLENE: (1) c. 279-247 BC *FD* III (4) 403 II, 1 (f. Ἀχαιός)

**Τάλιος**
AIGINA?: (1) m. vii BC *Anfore da trasporto* p. 49 no. 1 (or Athens?: locn.—A.W.J)

**Ταλούρας**
AITOLIA:
—PHISTYON?: (1) i BC *IG* IX (1)² (1) 110 b, 12 (f. Νικίας)

**Ταμαχρίδας**
ELIS:
—THRAISTOS: (1) f. iv BC ib. 138, 13 (Ταμαχρίδας)

**Ταμίρας**
SICILY:
—SELINOUS: (1) f. v BC Dubois, *IGDS* 38, 5 (Arena, *Iscr. Sic.* I 63) (f. Ῥοτύλος)

**Τάμμαρος**
SICILY:
—IAITON: (1) ii-i BC *SEG* XXVI 1070. 2 (tiles)
—SELINOUS:
——(Ἡρακλείδας): (2) m. v BC Dubois, *IGDS* 36, 4 (Arena, *Iscr. Sic.* I 69) (f. Ἄθανις)

**Τάναγρος**
LAKONIA:
—TAINARON-KAINEPOLIS: (1) imp. *IG* V (1) 1247, 3 (Ὥλος Ὀφίλλιος Τ.)

**Τάνταλος**
LAKONIA:
—SPARTA: (1) 424 BC Th. iv 57. 3-4 (Poralla² 684) (s. Πατροκλῆς); (2) ?i-ii AD *IG* V (1) 671 (Bradford (2)); (3) c. 105-110 AD *SEG* XI 569, 6 (Bradford (1)) (f. Σωσικράτης)
—SPARTA?: (4) ?iv BC *CGFP* i p. 196 Sopatr. F 19 (?f. Θίβρων)

**Ταραντῖνος**
ILLYRIA:
—DIMALE: (1) iii BC *Iliria* 1986 (1), p. 102 no. 1 (ethn.?: sculptor)

**Τάρας**
KORINTHIA:
—KORINTH: (1) c. 570-550 BC Amyx 117. 4 (vase) (Τάρας: her.)

---

LAKONIA:
—SPARTA: (2) ii/i BC *IG* V (1) 966, 2 (Bradford (3)) (f. Μελησιππίδας); (3) s. i BC *IG* V (1) 874 (Bradford (2)); (4) c. 30-1 BC *IG* V (1) 211, 43; 212, 41 (Bradford (1); (2)) (s. Τιμόλας, f. Τιμόλας)

**Ταρεντῖνα**
S. ITALY (CALABRIA):
—LUPIAE: (1) imp. Susini, *Fonti Salento* p. 152 no. 104 (Lat. Procilia Tarentina)

**Ταρούλας**
ILLYRIA:
—APOLLONIA: (1) ?ii BC *IApoll* 11 (s. Σωτᾶς)

**Ταρουτῖνος**
AIGINA?: (1) imp. *EAD* XXX p. 356 no. 20 (I f. Ταρουτῖνος II); (2) ~ ib. (II s. Ταρουτῖνος I)

**Τάρσα**
S. ITALY (CAMPANIA):
—MISENUM*: (1) imp. *CIL* X 3527 (Lat. Babu. Tarsa)

**Τάρσος**
S. ITALY (CAMPANIA):
—NEAPOLIS: (1) 14-37 AD *IG* XIV 714 (*INap* 1); cf. Leiwo p. 162 no. 136 (Τιβ. Ἰούλ. Τ.)

**Τάρχιος**
S. ITALY (CAMPANIA):
—NEAPOLIS: (1) i AD *SEG* IV 96 (*INap* 152, 4) (s. Ἐπίλυτος)

**Τάσκος**
LAKONIA:
—SPARTA: (1) iii BC *IG* V (1) 145, 3 (Bradford (2)) (f. Ἀντίμαχος); (2) ~ *IG* V (1) 708 (Bradford (1))

**Τάτα**
ILLYRIA:
—EPIDAMNOS-DYRRHACHION: (1) hell.-imp. *IDyrrh* 391; (2) ~ ib. 392 (d. Ἀριστίων); (3) ~ ib. 393 (d. Λαῦδος); (4) ~ ib. 394 (d. Πολυμήδης); (5) ~ ib. 395 (d. Χάκας); (6) imp. ib. 49 (d. Λαιδίας)
—KUKES (MOD.): (7) imp. *BUST* 1961 (1), p. 120 no. 19 (Lat. Tata)

**Ταταία**
ILLYRIA:
—EPIDAMNOS-DYRRHACHION: (1) ?i-ii AD *IDyrrh* 396 (Τ. Γράνια)

**Ταταίη**
S. ITALY (CAMPANIA):
—KYME: (1) ?c. 675-650 BC Dubois, *IGDGG* I 12 (vase) (Arena, *Iscr. Sic.* III 16); *LSAG²* p. 238 no. 3 (date) (-ταίε̄)

**Τατιανός**
ARKADIA:
—TEGEA: (1) ii AD *IG* V (2) 55, 39 (f. Ζώσιμος)

**Τατιάς**
S. ITALY (CAMPANIA):
—MISENUM*: (1) imp. *Epigraphica* 34 (1972) p. 140 (Lat. Tatias)

**Τάτιον**
EPIROS:
—BOUTHROTOS (PRASAIBOI): (1) a. 163 BC *IBouthrot* 45, 17 (d. Διογένης)

---

**Τατίς**
S. ITALY (CAMPANIA):
—DIKAIARCHIA-PUTEOLI: (1) imp. *CIL* X 2368 (Lat. Licinia Tatis)

**Τατώ**
ILLYRIA:
—APOLLONIA: (1) ii-i BC *IApoll* 155
—EPIDAMNOS-DYRRHACHION: (2) hell.-imp. *IDyrrh* 398 (d. Ἀμμίκα)

**Ταύρα**
ILLYRIA:
—APOLLONIA: (1) ii-i BC *IApoll* 156

**Ταυριανή**
S. ITALY (BRUTTIUM):
—LOKROI EPIZEPHYRIOI: (1) ii AD *Suppl. It.* 3 p. 25 no. 7 (Lat. Tauriane)

**Ταυριανός**
SICILY:
—SYRACUSE: (1) iii-v AD Strazzulla 187 (Barreca 348) (Ταυριαν(ό)ς)

**Ταυρίας**
ACHAIA:
—DYME: (1) s. iii BC *SEG* XIII 278, 24 (s. Φίλων)

**Ταύριννα**
EPIROS:
—BOUTHROTOS (PRASAIBOI): (1) a. 163 BC *IBouthrot* 77, 6

**Ταυρῖνος**
ELIS: (1) iii BC *IvOl* 180; cf. Moretti, *Olymp.* 563 (f. —ς)
S. ITALY (CAMPANIA):
—DIKAIARCHIA-PUTEOLI: (2) imp. *IG* XIV 849

**Ταυρίσκος**
AITOLIA:
—ARAKYNEIS: (1) 263 BC ib. IX (1)² (1) 17, 81 (f. Ἄστυδος)
—PROSCH(E)ION: (2) c. 245 BC ib. 11, 49 (s. Ἀλέξων)
AKARNANIA:
—THYRREION: (3) 356-354 BC ib. IV (1)² 95, 16 (Perlman E.2); Perlman p. 40 f. (date)
ARKADIA:
—MEGALOPOLIS: (4) imp. *CIL* III 496, 3; cf. 7250 ([Ταυ]ρίσκος, Lat. Tauriscus); (5) i BC/i AD *IG* V (2) 456 (Τ. Ἀρμ[ίνιο]ς Τ.)
EPIROS:
—ANTIGONEIA: (6) i BC *AE* 1914, p. 238 no. 14; Cabanes, *L'Épire* p. 234 n. 96 (locn.) (s. Σ—, f. —νωρ)
—BOUTHROTOS (PRASAIBOI): (7) a. 163 BC *IBouthrot* 14, 22; 31, 25 (*SEG* XXXVIII 471; 490) (f. Ἀνδρόνικος); (8) ~ *IBouthrot* 17, 27 (*SEG* XXXVIII 474); (9) ~ *IBouthrot* 17, 31; 25, 29; 29, 63 (*SEG* XXXVIII 474; 483; 487) ?= (12); (10) ~ *IBouthrot* 40, 11 (*SEG* XXXVIII 499)
——Cheilioi: (11) a. 163 BC *IBouthrot* 98, 7 (s. Σύμμαχος); (12) ~ ib. 116, 3, 8 (*BCH* 118 (1994) p. 121 A) (s. Εὐρύμμας) ?= (9)
——Cherrioi: (13) a. 163 BC *IBouthrot* 8, 1 (*SEG* XXXVIII 480); (14) ~ *IBouthrot* 111, 12; 112, 13 (f. Ἀνδρόνικος)
——Optasinoi: (15) a. 163 BC ib. 141, 7 (Τ[αυρ]ίσ[κ]ος: f. Ἀνδρόνικος)
——Phonidatoi: (16) a. 163 BC ib. 75, 2; 76, 1; 77, 1; 99, [1], 5 (*BCH* 118 (1994) p. 121 B)
ILLYRIA:
—EPIDAMNOS-DYRRHACHION: (17) ?iii BC *IDyrrh* 35 (f. Ἱερήν)
KERKYRA: (18) ii BC Unp. (*IG* arch.)
S. ITALY (CAMPANIA):
—CAPREAE: (19) i BC-i AD? *IG* XIV 901 (s. Στά-ιος)

**Ταυρίων**

—DIKAIARCHIA-PUTEOLI: **(20)** imp. *CIL* x 2621 (Lat. M. Iunius Tauriscus); **(21)** ~ ib. 2995 (Lat. Tauriscus)
—HERCULANEUM: **(22)** m. i AD *PdelP* 9 (1954) p. 55 no. 60, 1 (Lat. L. Caninius Tauriscus)
SICILY:
—KAMARINA: **(23)** f. v BC Cordano, *Tessere Pubbliche* 8 (Τα(υ)ρίσκος: s. Χαροπίας)
—LEONTINOI: **(24)** 433 BC *IG* I³ 54, 7 (f. Θεότιμος)

**Ταυρίων**
ARGOLIS:
—EPIDAUROS: **(1)** i-ii AD ib. IV (1)² 486 (f. Ἀπολλόδωρος)
—HERMIONE: **(2)** i AD ib. II² 8497 (f. Ἅβρον)
—PHLEIOUS: **(3)** m. iii BC ib. VII 10, 6 (f. Τελεσίας)
MESSENIA:
—THOURIA: **(4)** ii-i BC ib. V (1) 1385, 6 (f. Τελίσκος)
S. ITALY (CALABRIA):
—BRENTESION-BRUNDISIUM*: **(5)** imp. *NScav* 1891, p. 172 = *Epigraphica* 25 (1963) p. 85 no. 97 (Lat. P. Gerellanus Taurio: freed.)

**Ταυρομένης**
ACHAIA:
—DYME: **(1)** ?145 BC Sherk 43, 8; *SEG* XXXVIII 372 (date) (f. Σῶσος)

**Ταῦρος**
ARGOLIS:
—EPIDAUROS: **(1)** c. 335-325 BC *IG* IV (1)² 106 I, [17], 23 (Τα[ῦρος]?)
KORINTHIA:
—KORINTH: **(2)** ii AD *FD* III (3) 247, 2 (Βαρβάτιος *T.*)
LAKONIA:
—SPARTA: **(3)** 423 BC Th. iv 119. 2 (Poralla² 685) (s. Ἐχετιμίδας)
S. ITALY (CALABRIA):
—BRENTESION-BRUNDISIUM*: **(4)** i/ii AD *Museo Ribezzo* 12 (1980-87) p. 177 (*CIL* IX 6099); cf. *Epigraphica* 51 (1989) p. 77 (Lat. L. Pacilius Taurus: s. L. Publilius Auctus, Νίκη)
S. ITALY (CAMPANIA):
—DIKAIARCHIA-PUTEOLI: **(5)** imp. *CIL* X 2190 (Lat. M. Fabius Taurus); **(6)** ~ ib. 2955 (Lat. L. Sextilius Taurus: s. Μηνόθεμις); **(7)** ?ii AD *Puteoli* 3 (1979) p. 154 no. 1 (*CIL* X 1884) (Lat. T. Marcius Taur(us))
—POMPEII: **(8)** i BC-i AD ib. IV 5228 (Lat. Taurus)
—SALERNUM: **(9)** imp. *IItal* 1 (1) 148 (*CIL* X 537) (Lat. C. Titinius Taurus: f. Titinius Pulcher)
SICILY:
—KATANE: **(10)** imp. *NScav* 1918, p. 59 (Lat. Taurus)

**Ταυροσθένης**
AIGINA: **(1)** 448-444 BC Moretti, *Olymp.* 308

**Ταύρων**
AKARNANIA: **(1)** iv/iii BC *SB* 6831, 2
—ASTAKOS: **(2)** ii BC *IG* IX (1)² (2) 435, 9 (f. Σωτίων)
—THYRREION: **(3)** hell. *SEG* XXXII 565 (s. Φιλικός)

**Ταυρώπη**
SICILY:
—COMISO (MOD.): **(1)** iii-v AD *IG* XIV 255 (*SEG* IV 32; Wessel 643); cf. *Riv. Arch. Crist.* 18 (1941) p. 198 no. 69; cf. Cordano, 'Camarina VII' 158 (Ταυρώπα—*IG*)

**Ταφιάδας**
AKARNANIA:
—PALAIROS: **(1)** ?iii BC *IG* IX (1)² (2) 456

**Τάχινος**
S. ITALY (CAMPANIA):
—DIKAIARCHIA-PUTEOLI*: **(1)** imp. *CIL* X 3110 (Lat. [P]ulcrius Tachinus: freed.)

**Ταχιστόλαϝος**
LAKONIA:
—AIGIAI*: **(1)** c. 525-500 BC *AAA* 18 (1985) pp. 246-53

**Ταχυκλῆς**
LAKONIA:
—SPARTA: **(1)** s. i BC *IG* V (1) 94, 24 (Bradford (-)) (s. Καλλ—)

**Τεβύκιος**
LAKONIA:
—GERONTHRAI: **(1)** c. 500 BC *IG* V (1) 1133, 3; cf. *SEG* XI 918; *LSAG*² p. 201 no. 46 (date) (Poralla² 686) (Τεβύκ(ρ)ος—*SEG*)

**Τεῖϊς**
LAKONIA:
—SPARTA: **(1)** vi/v BC *SEG* XI 656 (Lazzarini 407; Poralla² 686a) (-hις)

**Τεισαμενός**
ACHAIA:
—DYME?: **(1)** s. iii BC *SEG* XIII 278, 26
ARGOLIS:
—EPIDAUROS: **(2)** iii BC *IG* IV (1)² 160
ARKADIA:
—PSOPHIS: **(3)** c. 230-200 BC *BCH* 45 (1921) p. 14 II, 124 (Τ[ει]σαμενός—Oulhen: s. Σθενόλαος)
ELIS: **(4)** f. v BC *RE* (4); cf. *SEG* XXIX 450, 3 (and Lakonia Sparta: s. Ἀντίοχος, f. Ἀγέλοχος (Sparta): mantis/Iamidai); **(5)** c. 181-189 AD *IvOl* 100, [12]; 104, 15 (Τεισ[αμενός]—104: f. Ὄλυμπος: mantis/Iamidai); **(6)** 221-265 AD ib. 113, [2]; 114, 8; 116, 12; 117, 13; 121, 15; 122, 12; *SEG* XV 258, 8 (Κλ. *T.*, Τισαμενός—114: mantis/Iamidai)
ILLYRIA:
—APOLLONIA: **(7)** ?iii BC *IApoll* 383 (Τισαμενοῦ (gen.): f. Τιμοσθένης)
LAKONIA:
—SPARTA: **(8)** 399 BC X., *HG* iii 3. 11 (Poralla² 704) (Τι-: ?s. Ἀγέλοχος: mantis?); **(9)** s. i BC *IG* V (1) 141, 5; 210, 43; 212, 54; 465, 6; 578, 2 (Bradford (6); (7)) (f. Σιχάρης, Ἀλκιβία); **(10)** ~ *IG* V (1) 465, 2 (Bradford (2)) (s. Δάμιππος, Ἀλκιβία); **(11)** c. 100-120 AD *IG* V (1) 99, 6; 103, 12; *BSA* 26 (1923-5) p. 168 C 7, 1 (Bradford (5)); **(12)** c. 110-120 AD *IG* V (1) 298, 4; *Artemis Orthia* pp. 315-16 no. 35 (date) (Bradford (3)) (s. Ἴαμος, f. Κριτόδαμος); **(13)** ?s. ii AD *IG* V (1) 258, 8; *Artemis Orthia* pp. 301-2 no. 8 (date) (Bradford (1)); **(14)** m. iii AD *IG* V (1) 598, 7; 599, 5, 17 (Bradford (4)) (M. Αὐρ. *T.*: s. Στρατα—, f. Ἡράκλεια)
TRIPHYLIA:
—MAKISTOS: **(15)** iv/iii BC *SEG* XXXIX 628 (f. Νικόμαχος)

**Τεισάνδριχος**
KORINTHIA:
—KORINTH: **(1)** iii BC *IG* IV (1) 201 (Τεισάν[δρι]χος)

**Τείσανδρος**
AITOLIA:
—APODOTOI: **(1)** 426 BC Th. iii 100. 1
—OPHIEIS: **(2)** 176 BC *SGDI* 1862, 2 (f. Πολέμαρχος)
AKARNANIA:
—HYPOREIAI: **(3)** 356-354 BC *IG* IV (1)² 95, 35 (Perlman E.2); Perlman p. 40 f. (date); Robert, *Hell.* 1 pp. 106 ff. (locn.)
—PALAIROS: **(4)** s. iii BC *IG* IX (1)² (2) 529
—STRATOS: **(5)** c. 425-400 BC ib. 390, 8; **(6)** iv/iii BC ib. 395, 8 (s. Μενεκράτης)

**Τεισίας** (see below column 3)

ARGOLIS:
—TROIZEN: **(7)** 342 BC *CID* II 11 [A-B]; 31, 78
ARKADIA:
—TEGEA: **(8)** c. 240-229 BC *IG* V (2) 11, 18
SICILY:
—MORGANTINA: **(9)** iv/iii BC *PdelP* 44 (1989) p. 214 ([*T*]είσα[νδρος]); **(10)** ~ *SEG* XXXIX 1013, 7
—NAXOS: **(11)** f. vi BC Moretti, *Olymp.* 94; 98; 101; 105 (s. Κλεόκριτος)
—ZANKLE-MESSANA: **(12)** ?ii BC *IG* XIV 401, 4, 10 (f. Φρυνίδας, —κλείδας)

**Τεισανδρωίας**
KERKYRA: **(1)** c. 500 BC *SEG* XXX 524 (-δρō-)

**Τείσαρχος**
AITOLIA: **(1)** ?273-272 BC *FD* III (1) 298, [3]; 473, [3]; III (3) 185, 2; 203, 2; **(2)** 224 or 221 BC *SGDI* 2524, 4; Nachtergael, *Les Galates* 64, 3
EPIROS:
—BOUTHROTOS (PRASAIBOI):
—Kestrinoi Asantoi: **(3)** a. 163 BC *IBouthrot* 91, 12 (*SEG* XXXII 623) (f. Δαμόκριτος)
ILLYRIA:
—BALAIITAI*: **(4)** ii BC ib. XXXVIII 521, 25; cf. *CRAI* 1991, pp. 197 ff.; *L'Illyrie mérid.* 2 p. 204 f. (f. Παρμήν)
MESSENIA:
—MESSENE: **(5)** i BC *IG* V (1) 1457; **(6)** 31 BC-14 AD *SEG* XXIII 207, 10 (s. Διονύσιος)
SICILY:
—SYRACUSE: **(7)** 317 BC *RE* s.v. Tisarchos (-)

**Τεισέας**
LEUKAS: **(1)** iv/iii BC *AD* 26 (1971) Chron. p. 353 no. 1

**Τεισήν**
ARGOLIS:
—EPIDAUROS: **(1)** iv BC *IG* IV (1)² 249 = *SEG* XXXII 386; Peek, *IAEpid* 85; 324; cf. *PdelP* 48 (1993) pp. 394-5

**Τεισίας**
ACHAIA:
—AIGION: **(1)** c. 210-207 BC *IG* IV (1)² 73, 17; *SEG* XXXV 303 (date) (s. Ἐχεκράτης)
AIGINA: **(2)** f. v BC B. xii; cf. Klee p. 104 no. 147
AITOLIA: **(3)** c. 232-228 BC *Syll*³ 499, 3; Nachtergael, *Les Galates* 62, [2]
—KALLION/KALLIPOLIS: **(4)** 195 BC *SGDI* 2119, 6
ARGOLIS:
—ARGOS: **(5)** i AD *SEG* XXVI 429, 5, 7 (s. Διάκτωρ, f. Διάκτωρ)
—KALAURIA: **(6)** iii BC *IG* IV (1) 840, 2 ([*T*ε]ισίας: f. Ἀγασιγράτις)
ARKADIA:
—ALIPHEIRA: **(7)** s. iii BC Orlandos, *Alipheira* p. 219 no. 4
—TEGEA: **(8)** f. ii BC *IG* V (2) 44, 26 ([*T*ε]ισίας?, [*Π*ε]ισίας?)
ILLYRIA:
—EPIDAMNOS-DYRRHACHION: **(9)** hell.-imp. *IDyrrh* 404 (s. Λυκῖνος)
LAKONIA:
—KYTHERA: **(10)** hell.-imp. *IG* V (1) 942, 1
SICILY:
—GELA-PHINTIAS: **(11)** f. iv BC *Ag.* XVII 445 (*IG* II² 8460) (s. Ἡρακλείδας)
—HIMERA?: **(12)** vii/vi BC *RE* s.v. Stesichoros (1); *PMG* p. 95 f. (or Sicily Matauros: *T.* Στησίχορος?: ?s. Εὔφημος, Εὔφορβος, Εὐκλείδης, Εὐέτης)
—KAMARINA: **(13)** m. v BC Orsi, *Le necropoli di Passo Marinaro* p. 139
—SYRACUSE: **(14)** v BC *RE* (6)

**Τεισίδαμος**
ILLYRIA:
—APOLLONIA: (1) hell. *IApoll* 24; cf. *Le Arti* 5 (1943) p. 117 no. 2; Fraser–Rönne, *BWGT* p. 174 n. 5 (date) (f. Νεαγένης)

**Τεισικλῆς**
MESSENIA:
—THOURIA: (1) f. ii BC *SEG* XI 972, 85 (s. Καλλικράτης)

**Τεισικράτης**
ARGOLIS:
—ARGOS: (1) c. 245-236 BC *IG* IX (1)² (1) 25, 9 (s. Ξηνέας)
—HERMIONE: (2) ii-i BC ib. IV (1) 732 III, 11, 13 (f. Εὐτύχα, Ἱεροκλέα)
ARKADIA:
—MANTINEIA-ANTIGONEIA: (3) ?iii BC ib. v (2) 319, 14, 37
KORINTHIA:
—SIKYON: (4) c. 325-270 BC *RE* (-); *IG* VII 267 (*IOrop* 385); *IG* VII 384 (*IOrop* 415); *IG* VII 431, 5 (*IOrop* 416); *AD* 25 (1970) Mel. p. 139 no. 2; *Chiron* 19 (1989) pp. 518-19 (date) (Skalet 315) (s. Θοινίας, f. Θοινίας, Ἀρκεσίλαος: sculptor)
S. ITALY (BRUTTIUM):
—KROTON: (5) 496-492 BC Moretti, *Olymp.* 166; 172

**Τεισιλαΐδας**
ILLYRIA:
—APOLLONIA: (1) c. 250-50 BC *Bakërr Hoard* p. 63 nos. 39-42 (Ceka 45); Maier 107 (coin) (Ceka 71 (name)) (pryt.)

**Τεισίμαχος**
AKARNANIA: (1) iii BC Pagenstecher, *Nekrop.* p. 51 no. 44 (Τι-: f. Νικοκράτης)
ARKADIA:
—ALIPHEIRA: (2) 191-146 BC *BMC Pelop.* p. 14 no. 159; Unp. (Oxford, AM) (coins) ([Λυ]σίμαχος—*BMC*)
—TEGEA:
——(Hippothoitai): (3) iii BC *IG* v (2) 40, 40 (f. Τείσιμος)

**Τείσιμος**
ARKADIA:
—TEGEA:
——(Hippothoitai): (1) iii BC ib. l. 40 (s. Τεισίμαχος)

**Τεισίππα**
AKARNANIA:
—PALAIROS: (1) iii/ii BC ib. IX (1)² (2) 534 (d. Νίκων)

**Τείσιππος**
AITOLIA:
—TRICHONION: (1) 163-156 BC ib. IX (1)² (1) p. LII, s.a. 163 BC, 156 BC; p. XLV, 74 ff.; cf. *BCH* 56 (1932) pp. 314 ff.; *IG* IX (1)² (3) 631, 1 (Τίσιππος—*IG* no. 102)

**Τεῖσις**
AIGINA?: (1) iv-iii BC ib. IV (1) 115 (f. Εὐρυβίοτος)
AITOLIA:
—PHYTAION: (2) ii/i BC *SEG* XVII 273, 4 (Τι-: s. Νίκανδρος)
ARGOLIS:
—EPIDAUROS: (3) iii BC *IG* IV (1)² 348 (Τει[σ]ις: s. Ἀρχιλέων)
ARKADIA:
—TEGEA:
——(Athaneatai): (4) s. iv BC ib. v (2) 41, 37 (f. Δαμέας)
MESSENIA: (5) viii BC Paus. iv 9. 3-4 (Τι-: s. Ἄλκις)

**Τεισίδαμος** *(SICILY column)*
SICILY:
—AKRAGAS: (6) iv/iii BC *Acragas Graeca* 1 p. 41 no. 11, 4 (Cabanes, *L'Épire* p. 543 no. 8; Dubois, *IGDS* 184) (Τεί[σι]ς)

**Τεισίς**
ELIS: (1) c. 95-105 AD *IvOl* 438, 2; *ZPE* 99 (1993) p. 232 (stemma) (Νουμισία Τ.: d. Λ. Βετληνὸς Λαῖτος, Φλ. Γοργώ)

**Τεισίων**
ILLYRIA:
—APOLLONIA: (1) i BC Ceka, *Probleme* p. 139 no. 26 (coin)

**Τεισύας**
ITHAKE: (1) ?i BC *IG* IX (1) 679 (Fraser–Rönne, *BWGT* p. 119 no. 6)

**Τείσων**
ACHAIA:
—PATRAI: (1) f. ii BC *IC* 2 p. 23 no. 6 E, 1; (2) 192 BC Liv. xxxv 26. 7 (Lat. Tiso)
AITOLIA: (3) iii BC *IG* II² 7993 (Τεί[σ]ων)
MESSENIA:
—MESSENE: (4) iv/iii BC ib. v (1) 1425, 1 (Τί-: s. Ἱκαδεύς); (5) i BC/i AD ib. 1438 a, 10 (Τί-)
S. ITALY (CAMPANIA):
—PITHEKOUSSAI-AENARIA: (6) c. 700 BC Dubois, *IGDGG* 1 6 a-b (vase) (Arena, *Iscr. Sic.* III 3; *LSAG*² p. 453 no. 1 b) (-σōν)
SICILY:
—SYRACUSE: (7) f. iv BC [Pl.], *Ep.* 363 C

**Τελεάρχος**
ARGOLIS:
—ARGOS: (1) iv-iii BC Unp. (Ch. Kritzas)

**Τελέας**
AITOLIA:
—KALYDON: (1) a. 142 BC *IG* IX (1)² (1) 137, 77 ([Τ]ελέας)
ARGOLIS:
—EPIDAUROS: (2) iii BC ib. IV (1)² 165, 5; (3) ii BC ib. 213 (f. Εὔδαμος); (4) ~ ib. (s. Εὔδαμος, Τιμοκράτις)
ARKADIA:
—ALIPHEIRA: (5) iii BC *EILakArk* 11 (Orlandos, *Alipheira* p. 218 no. 3) (f. Ἀπέλλιχος)
—TEGEA: (6) s. ii BC *BMI* 1154 a, 3; *BE* 1972, no. 37 (date) (s. Δαμόκριτος)
KORINTHIA:
—KORINTH: (7) v BC *FGrH* 268 F 6 (f. Χρύσιλλα)

**Τελέδαμος**
ARGOLIS:
—ARGOS: (1) m. iv BC *RE* (3)
S. ITALY (BRUTTIUM):
—LOKROI EPIZEPHYRIOI:
——(Κυλ.): (2) iv/iii BC De Franciscis 6, 7 (s. Αἰσχύλος)

**Τελέδας**
AITOLIA:
—AGRAIOI: (1) hell.? *IG* IX (1)² (1) 168
AKARNANIA:
—MALESADHA (MOD.): (2) i BC/i AD? Heuzey, *Le Mont Olympe* p. 490 no. 61

**Τελέιππος**
ARGOLIS:
—ARGOS: (1) iii BC *IG* IV (1) 618 I, 3, 4; II, 8 (f. Τελέστας)
——(Arkeidai): (2) iii BC *SEG* XXXI 306, 4 (Perlman A.25)

**Τέλεμμος**
AITOLIA:
—APERANTOI: (1) ?ii BC *IG* IX (1)² (1) 163 (f. Κλεότας)

**Τελένικος**
AITOLIA:
—APERANTOI: (1) ?ii BC ib. 164 (s. Ἀγοραῖος)
AKARNANIA:
—DERION: (2) c. 325-315 BC *Hesp.* 57 (1988) p. 148 A, 42 (*SEG* XXXVI 331); cf. *Hesp.* 48 (1979) pp. 78 f. with pl. 22 c (s. Ἀγήσανδρος)
ARGOLIS:
—EPIDAUROS: (3) iv/iii BC Peek, *IAEpid* 51, 9; *BSA* 61 (1966) p. 319 no. 26 (date) (Τελ[έ]νικο[ς]) ?= (6); (4) ?262 BC *CID* II 120 A, 52 (s. Τελεσέας)
——Naupheis: (5) c. 335-325 BC *IG* IV (1)² 106 I, 92; (6) c. 290-270 BC ib. 109 III, 134 ?= (3)
KERKYRA?: (7) hell. ib. IX (1) 841; *Korkyra* 1 p. 171 no. 9 (bullet) (Τελένι[κος] (n. pr.?))

**Τελέσαρχος**
ACHAIA:
—PHARAI: (1) iii BC *Achaean Grave Stelai* 3 (s. Ἀλκίας)
AIGINA: (2) 478 BC Pi., *I.* viii, 2 (f. Κλέανδρος)
AITOLIA:
—APEIRIKOI: (3) c. 200 BC *FD* III (4) 163, 3; (4) 178 BC *Syll*³ 636, 17 (f. Ἀνάξανδρος)
AKARNANIA:
—THYRREION: (5) s. iii BC *IG* IX (1)² (2) 288
ARGOLIS:
—ARGOS?: (6) ?iv BC *RE* (1); *FGrH* 309
ARKADIA:
—(7) c. 208 BC *FD* III (4) 135, 10 (f. Μνασικλῆς)
—MANTINEIA-ANTIGONEIA: (8) iii BC *IG* v (2) 319, 12
ILLYRIA:
—APOLLONIA: (9) c. 250-50 BC Maier 37 (Ceka 113); Maier 51 (coin) (Ceka 114) (money.)
MESSENIA:
—MESSENE: (10) 208 or 207 BC *FD* III (4) 23, 4; 24, 3 (f. Ξενάρετος)

**Τελέσας**
ARGOLIS:
—EPIDAUROS: (1) iv BC *IG* IV (1)² 183
ARKADIA:
—TEGEA:
——(Athaneatai): (2) s. iv BC ib. v (2) 41, 32 (f. Καλλίστρατος)

**Τελεσέας**
ARGOLIS:
—EPIDAUROS: (1) ?262 BC *CID* II 120 A, 52 (f. Τελένικος)

**Τελεσίας**
ACHAIA:
—AIGION: (1) 170 BC *SGDI* 1774, 3 (f. Πρατίας)
AKARNANIA:
—PALAIROS: (2) iii BC *IG* IX (1)² (2) 506
ARGOLIS:
—EPIDAUROS: (3) c. 365-335 BC ib. IV (1)² 103, 52, 57, 62, 64, 66, 68, 70-1, 75-6
—PHLEIOUS: (4) m. iii BC ib. VII 10, 6 (s. Ταυρίων)
—TROIZEN: (5) 140 BC ib. II² 971, 16; cf. Osborne, *Naturalization* D102 (and Athens)
MESSENIA:
—MESSENE: (6) iii BC *SEG* XXIII 209, 17

**Τελεσιβόλα**
S. ITALY (LUCANIA):
—MIGLIONICO (MOD.): (1) f. v BC *PdelP* 23 (1968) pp. 449-51 (Lo Porto, *Civ. indig. nella Lucania orientale* p. 202 (bronze)); cf. *LSAG*² p. 463 no. C (date)

**Τελεσίδας**
EPIROS:
—BOUTHROTOS (PRASAIBOI): (1) a. 163 BC *IBouthrot* 50, 1; 152, 5 (f. Λυσανίας)
SICILY: (2) 356 BC Plu., *Dio* 42 (-δης)

**Τελεσικράτης**
ARGOLIS:
—TROIZEN*: (1) iv BC *IG* IV (1) 823, 65

**Τελέσιλλα**
ARGOLIS:
—ARGOS: (**1**) vi/v BC *RE* (-); *PMG* 717-26

**Τελεσῖνα**
S. ITALY (APULIA):
—VENUSIA: (**1**) imp. *CIL* IX 582 (Lat. Thelesina)
S. ITALY (CAMPANIA):
—DIKAIARCHIA-PUTEOLI: (**2**) imp. ib. X 3123 (Lat. Telesina)

**Τελεσίνικος**
KORINTHIA:
—KORINTH: (**1**) 413 BC Polyaen. v 32

**Τελεσῖνος**
ARKADIA:
—MANTINEIA-ANTIGONEIA: (**1**) c. 300-221 BC *IG* v (2) 323. 54 (tessera) (f. Ἀντίφας)

**Τελέσιος**
S. ITALY (CAMPANIA):
—POMPEII: (**1**) i BC-i AD *CIL* IV 4021 (Lat. Telesius)

**Τελέσιππος**
ARKADIA:
—MANTINEIA-ANTIGONEIA: (**1**) c. 300-221 BC *IG* v (2) 323. 34 (tessera) (f. Σαώτας)
—MEGALOPOLIS: (**2**) iii BC ib. 490 ([T]ελέσιππος)

**Τέλεσις**
ARGOLIS:
—HERMIONE: (**1**) iv BC *SEG* XI 382, 20 (s. Εὐφάνης, f. Σωτηρίδας)

**Τέλεσος**
KORINTHIA:
—KORINTH?: (**1**) c. 540-525 BC ib. XXIII 264 c ([T]έλεσος)

**Τελεσταῖορ**
ELIS: (**1**) ?i AD *IvOl* 419 (I f. Τελεσταῖορ II); (**2**) ~ ib. (II s. Τελεσταῖορ I)

**Τελέστας**
AIGINA: (**1**) f. v BC *IG* IV (1) 60
AITOLIA: (**2**) ?257 BC Nachtergael, *Les Galates* 7, 4
AKARNANIA:
—MEDION: (**3**) 216 BC *IG* IX (1)² (2) 583, 21 (f. Αἰσχίνας)
ARGOLIS:
—ARGOS: (**4**) c. 458 BC ib. I³ 1149, 12; (**5**) ~ ib. l. 70 (-σστας); (**6**) ?c. 450-425 BC *SEG* XI 295 (Lazzarini 399; *Nemea* I p. 278 no. 27); *LSAG*² p. 170 no. 44 (date); (**7**) iv BC *IG* IV (1) 568 (f. Ἀστυόχεια); (**8**) iii BC ib. 618 I, 3 ([Τε]λέστας: s. Τελέσιππος)
—EPIDAUROS: (**9**) f. iii BC ib. IV (1)² 201 (f. Τιμόδωρος); (**10**) ~ ib. (s. Τιμόδωρος)
—NEMEA*: (**11**) inc. *SEG* XXIX 349 d; *Nemea Guide* p. 36 (ident.) (Τ[ε]λέστας) ?= (27)
ARKADIA:
—KAPHYAI?: (**12**) c. 225 BC *SEG* XI 414, 7 (Perlman E.5) ([T]ε[λέσ]τας: f. Παυσίας)
—TEGEA: (**13**) m. iv BC *IG* v (2) 6, 91 (I f. Τελέστας II); (**14**) ~ ib. l. 91 (Τελέσ[τα]ς: II s. Τελέστας I); (**15**) ~ ib. l. 92; (**16**) ~ ib. l. 92; (**17**) c. 225 BC *SEG* XI 414, 23 (Perlman E.5) (f. Θεόδωρος); (**18**) f. ii BC *IG* v (2) 44, 12 (s. Πολίας); (**19**) ?i BC ib. 246
——(Krariotai): (**20**) m. iii BC ib. 36, 91 (s. Πάχων)`
ARKADIA?: (**21**) ii BC *IvOl* 48, 3 ([T]ελέστας)
ELIS: (**22**) ?i AD ib. 413 ([T]ελέστας: f. Θεοξένα)
KORINTHIA:
—KORINTH: (**23**) viii BC *RE* (4) (s. Ἀριστόδαμος: king); (**24**) hell. *IG* II² 9073 (f. Σαμίων)

**LAKONIA**: (**25**) c. 600-575 BC *LSAG*² p. 199 no. 7 (-σστας) ?= (**26**); (**26**) ?vi/v BC Paus. v 23. 7 (Poralla² 687) (sculptor) ?= (25)
MESSENIA:
—MESSENE: (**27**) iv BC Moretti, *Olymp.* 453 ?= (11)
SICILY:
—SELINOUS: (**28**) v/iv BC *RE* s.v. Telestes (6); *PMG* 805 ff. (-της)

**Τελέστροφος**
KORINTHIA:
—KORINTH: (**1**) m. vii BC Amyx 1. 5 (vase) (Lorber 1) (Τελέ[σ]τροφος: her.?)

**Τελέστωρ**
LAKONIA:
—SELLASIA*: (**1**) iii BC *IG* v (1) 921 (Bradford (-))

**Τελεσφοριανός**
SICILY:
—SYRACUSE: (**1**) imp. *CIL* x 7130. 19 (Lat. Telesporianus)

**Τελεσφόρος**
LAKONIA:
—SPARTA: (**1**) c. 140 AD *IG* v (1) 65, 1; *SEG* XI 523, 3; 636? (Bradford (-)) (s. Ἀνθεσφόρος)
LEUKAS: (**2**) ii-iii AD *GVI* 880; cf. *AD* 28 (1973) Chron. pl. 420 στ.
S. ITALY (APULIA):
—RUBI: (**3**) iii AD *Suppl. It.* 5 p. 21 no. 3 (Lat. [Tele]sfhorus)
S. ITALY (CAMPANIA):
—DIKAIARCHIA-PUTEOLI: (**4**) imp. *CIL* x 2812 (Lat. L. Orenius Telesphorus); (**5**) ~ ib. 2996 (Lat. Telesph[orus]); (**6**) ~ ib. 3207; cf. *Puteoli* 11 (1987) p. 61 (Lat. [T]elespho[rus])
—DIKAIARCHIA-PUTEOLI*: (**7**) imp. *CIL* x 2386 (Lat. M. Epidius Telesphorus: freed.); (**8**) ~ *Eph. Ep.* VIII 387 (Lat. M. Modius Telesphorus: freed.)
—HERCULANEUM: (**9**) m. i AD *PdelP* 3 (1948) p. 168 no. 13; p. 169 no. 14; p. 171 no. 16 (Lat. C. Petronius Thelesphorus)
SICILY:
—SYRACUSE: (**10**) iii-v AD *IG* XIV 50 (Strazzulla 128); *ASSicilia* 1938-9, p. 25; cf. *Riv. Arch. Crist.* 18 (1941) p. 189 no. 55
—THERMAI HIMERAIAI: (**11**) imp. *CIL* x 7439 (*ILat. Term. Imer.* 148) (Lat. [-]ius Telesphorus)

**Τελέσων**
AITOLIA: (**1**) ?263-261 BC *FD* III (3) 184, 1; [190]; *Syll*³ 498, 2; Nachtergael, *Les Galates* 3, 1; *SGDI* 2590, 2 (s. Καρίων)
ARKADIA:
—TEGEA: (**2**) c. 400-375 BC *IG* II² 10435 (*GVI* 1653) (f. Θεοίτας)
LEUKAS: (**3**) f. i BC *IG* IX (1) 534, 10 (*Iscr. Gr. Verona* p. 24) (f. Ἀγήμων)

**Τελέτας**
SICILY:
—SELINOUS?: (**1**) v BC *SEG* XXXIX 1021 II, 6; cf. *BE* 1990, no. 863 (Τελέ(σ)τας?)

**Τελέτη**
S. ITALY (APULIA):
—VENUSIA: (**1**) imp. *CIL* IX 481 (Lat. Antonia Telete)
S. ITALY (CALABRIA):
—BRENTESION-BRUNDISIUM: (**2**) imp. *NScav* 1897, p. 326 no. 4 (Lat. [V]ibia Tele[te])

**Τελευταγόρας**
S. ITALY (LUCANIA):
—HYELE-VELIA: (**1**) v BC *FVS* I pp. 247-8 no. 29 A 1-2 (f. Ζήνων)

**Τελευτία**
LAKONIA:
—SPARTA: (**1**) s. v BC Plu., *Mor.* 241 E (Poralla² 688); Cartledge, *Agesilaos* pp. 145-6 (stemma) (m. Πεδάριτος, ?m. Ἀνταλκίδας)

**Τελευτίας**
LAKONIA:
—SPARTA: (**1**) c. 425-381 BC *RE* (-); Cartledge, *Agesilaos* pp. 145-6 (stemma) (Poralla² 689) (s. Θεόδωρος, Εὐπωλία)

**Τελεφάνης**
LAKONIA:
—GERONTHRAI: (**1**) s. v BC *IG* v (1) 1125; *LSAG*² p. 201 no. 58 (date) (Poralla² 694) (-νēς)

**Τέλη**
S. ITALY (CAMPANIA):
—PITHEKOUSSAI-AENARIA: (**1**) ?vii BC Landi, *DISMG* 2 (Τέλē (n. pr.?))

**Τέλης**
ARGOLIS:
—EPIDAUROS*: (**1**) c. 370-360 BC Peek, *IAEpid* 52 B, 73-4; *BSA* 61 (1966) p. 272 no. 4 B II, 5

**Τελητίας**
ARGOLIS:
—KLEONAI: (**1**) ?vi-v BC Plu., *Mor.* 553 A

**Τελίσκος**
MESSENIA:
—THOURIA: (**1**) ii-i BC *IG* v (1) 1385, 6 (s. Ταυρίων)

**Τελλεύς**
ARGOLIS:
—ARGOS: (**1**) v BC *SEG* XXXII 365 b——(Melanippidai): (**1**) v BC *SEG* XXXII 365 b
—ARGOS*: (**2**) f. iii BC *IG* IV (1) 529, 5; cf. *BCH* 37 (1913) p. 309 (slave/freed.?)

**Τελλέων**
S. ITALY (LUCANIA):
—HERAKLEIA: (**1**) ?v/iv BC *SEG* XXX 1150 (-ōν)

**Τελλήν**
KORINTHIA:
—KORINTH: (**1**) ?vi BC *Corinth* XV (3) p. 361 no. 20 (Τε<ν>λλέν)
S. ITALY (CALABRIA):
—TARAS-TARENTUM: (**2**) iv-iii BC *Bull. Mus. Hongr.* 53 (1979) p. 37 (terracotta) (Τελλή[ν])

**Τελλίας**
AKARNANIA:
—THYRREION: (**1**) hell.-imp. *IG* IX (1)² (2) 360 (s. Πυθίων)
ARGOLIS:
—TROIZEN: (**2**) iv BC ib. IV (1) 763 (f. Ἀριστονίκα); (**3**) iii BC ib. 774, 8
ARKADIA: (**4**) 304 BC ib. v (2) 550, 16
—MANTINEIA-ANTIGONEIA: (**5**) f. iii BC ib. 272, 7 (Τελλί[ας])
ELIS: (**6**) vi/v BC Paus. x 1. 8, 10, 11; 13. 7; Hdt. viii 27. 3 (Τελλίης—Hdt.: mantis)
EPIROS:
—DODONA*: (**7**) ?iv BC *Ep. Chron.* 10 (1935) p. 257 no. 20
SICILY:
—SYRACUSE: (**8**) 414 BC Th. vi 103. 4

**Τέλλις**
KORINTHIA:
—SIKYON: (**1**) 708 BC Moretti, *Olymp.* 20 (Skalet 316)
LAKONIA:
—SPARTA: (**2**) c. 490-420 BC Th. ii 25. 2; iii 69. 1; iv 70. 1; Paus. iii 14. 1 (Poralla² 690) (f. Βρασίδας) ?= (**3**); (**3**) 421 BC Th. v 19. 2; 24 ?= (2)

**Τέλλυς**
EPIROS:
—AMBRAKIA: (1) 360 BC *CID* II 4 III, 27 (f. Πολυμήδης)

**Τελλώ**
ILLYRIA:
—EPIDAMNOS-DYRRHACHION: (1) hell.-imp. *IDyrrh* 406 (d. Σώδαμος)

**Τέλλων**
ARKADIA:
—ORESTHASION: (1) 472 BC Moretti, *Olymp.* 231; Lazzarini 851; cf. Ebert, *Gr. Sieg.* 14 (s. Δαήμων)
SICILY:
—KAMARINA: (2) s. v BC Dubois, *IGDS* 121, 16 (Arena, *Iscr. Sic.* II 143; *SEG* XXXVIII 940) ([T]έλλōν—Dubois, [Ἐντ]έλλōν—Arena)

**Τέλων**
AKARNANIA:
—STRATOS: (1) hell.? *IG* IX (1)² (2) 414 b (f. Ἀνδρόνικος)
ARGOLIS:
—ARGOS:
——(Hyrnathioi-Temenidai): (2) c. 400 BC *SEG* XXIX 361, 19 (-λōν)
—EPIDAUROS: (3) iv BC *IG* IV (1)² 186
EPIROS:
—ARGOS (AMPHILOCH.): (4) hell.? ib. IX (1) 532 (f. Ἀνδρόνικος)

**Τεμίτευτα**
ILLYRIA:
—EPIDAMNOS-DYRRHACHION: (1) ii-i BC *IDyrrh* 405 (d. Σειλίας)

**Τέμμανδρος**
EPIROS:
—VOTONOSI (MOD.): (1) hell.? *SEG* XXIV 466 (Τέμμανδ[ρος])

**Τερείας**
AIGINA: (1) f. iv BC *CEG* II 532 (f. Πραξῖνος)

**Τερμόνιος**
ACHAIA: (1) 281 BC *Hesp.* 65 (1996) p. 252 (f. Καλλίστρατος)
—DYME: (2) ii-i BC *SGDI* 1617 a (f. Καλλώ)

**Τερπαίνετος**
ARKADIA:
—ALIPHEIRA: (1) iii BC Orlandos, *Alipheira* p. 225 (Τερ[π]αίνετος)

**Τερπέφιλος**
SICILY:
—SELINOUS: (1) vi/v BC Manganaro, *PdelP* forthcoming no. 18, 3 (f. Ἡρίφιλος)

**Τέρπνος**
S. ITALY: (1) imp. *CIL* X 8059. 370 (seal) (Lat. L. Sexsaeus Terpnus)
S. ITALY (CAMPANIA):
—HERCULANEUM: (2) m. i AD *Cron. Erc.* 7 (1977) p. 116 B a, 10 (Lat. M. Nonius Terpnus)
—NEAPOLIS: (3) i BC-i AD? *IG* XIV 828, 2 (*INap* 265; Wessel 1025)
—POMPEII: (4) i BC-i AD *CIL* IV 6804 (Lat. Terpnus); (5) ?i AD *NScav* 1916, p. 302 no. 1 (Lat. Terpnos)
SICILY:
—ACATE (MOD.): (6) iii-v AD *Rend. Pont.* 45 (1972-3) p. 192 no. 3 + Ferrua, *NG* 511 ([Τέρ]πνος—Ferrua, [Εὔ]πλιος—ed.)

**Τέρπουσα**
S. ITALY (CALABRIA):
—HYRIA*: (1) imp. *CIL* IX 231 (Lat. Sextia Terpusa: freed.)

**Τέρπων**
EPIROS: (1) iv-iii BC Cabanes, *L'Épire* p. 585 no. 68, 5 ([T]έρπων)

**Τερτία**
ARKADIA:
—TEGEA: (1) a. 212 AD *IG* V (2) 132. 2 (Αὐρ. T.)
EPIROS:
—KHOSEPSI (MOD.): (2) imp. *SEG* XXIV 415 (Τηερ-: d. Ἀρχίας)
ILLYRIA:
—APOLLONIA: (3) imp. *IApoll* 206
—EPIDAMNOS-DYRRHACHION: (4) imp. *Stud. Alb.* 1965, p. 74 no. 49 (Lat. Tertia)
MESSENIA:
—MESSENE: (5) ii AD *SEG* XXII 355
S. ITALY (CALABRIA):
—BRENTESION-BRUNDISIUM: (6) imp. *IG* XII (5) 86 (d. Ἰάσων)

**Τέρτιος**
ARKADIA:
—TEGEA: (1) 165 AD ib. V (2) 50, 44 (s. Ἀφροδᾶς)
KORINTHIA:
—KORINTH: (2) f. ii AD *Ag.* VII p. 90 no. 223; *SEG* XXVII 35. 29 (lamps)
S. ITALY (CAMPANIA):
—NEAPOLIS: (3) i AD *IG* XIV 726 (*INap* 14); cf. Leiwo p. 163 no. 139

**Τέρτις**
SICILY:
—HYKKARA?: (1) iii-iv AD *Kokalos* 17 (1971) p. 184 (I f. Τέρτις II); (2) ~ ib. (II s. Τέρτις I, Φοίβη)

**Τερτυλλιανός**
SICILY:
—SYRACUSE: (1) iii-v AD *IG* XIV 175 + Führer p. 815 n. (Strazzulla 151; Wessel 313) (Τερτουλλ(ι)αν[ός])

**Τέρτυλλος**
ARKADIA:
—KLEITOR: (1) 212 AD *IvOl* 473 (Τιβ. Κλ. T.: f. Κλ. Τύχη)
S. ITALY (CAMPANIA):
—NEAPOLIS: (2) iii-iv AD *IG* XIV 826. 44 (*INap* 252)

**Τερψίας**
KORINTHIA:
—KORINTH: (1) vi BC Pi., *O.* xiii, 42 with Schol.; *Dionysiaca* pp. 1-16 (ident.) (?f. Ἐρίτιμος, Ναμερτίδας)

**Τερψικλῆς**
EPIROS:
—DODONA*: (1) v BC Carapanos, *Dodone* p. 40 no. 3 (Lazzarini 142)

**Τεταρτίδας**
LAKONIA:
—GYTHEION?: (1) ?ii BC *RA* 1904, p. 8 no. 5 (Bradford (-))
MESSENIA:
—THOURIA: (2) f. ii BC *SEG* XI 972, 38 (f. Αἰνέας) ?= (3); (3) c. 182 BC ib. l. 104 (f. Πολυκλῆς) ?= (2)

**Τεταρτίων**
LAKONIA:
—SPARTA: (1) c. 25-1 BC *IG* V (1) 212, 11 (Bradford (2)) (f. Πολυκλῆς); (2) c. 105-135 AD *IG* V (1) 97, 22; 99, 3; *SEG* XI 564, 22; 580, 5 (Bradford (1)) (Τετα(ρ)τίων—*SEG* XI 580: f. Νικίας)

**Τέταρτος**
AIGINA: (1) ?ii-i BC *Alt-Ägina* I (2) p. 45 no. 16 (f. —ος) ?= (2); (2) ?i BC ib. p. 44 no. 7 ([Τέ]ταρτος: f. Ἀρισ—) ?= (1)

ARKADIA:
—MEGALOPOLIS: (3) hell.-imp. *IG* V (2) 469 (24) (tile) (n. pr.?)
—TEGEA: (4) iv/iii BC ib. 32, 6
LAKONIA:
—SPARTA: (5) iv BC ib. V (1) 1233, 6 (Poralla² 691)
——Amyklai: (6) ii/i BC *IG* V (1) 26, 5 (Bradford (-)) (f. Πασιτέλης)
SICILY:
—KAMARINA: (7) f. v BC Cordano, *Tessere Pubbliche* 18 (f. Τίμων)

**Τετιμαμένα**
LAKONIA:
—SPARTA: (1) ?i AD *IG* V (1) 520 (Bradford (-)) (Ἰουλ. Τετειμαμένα)

**Τετραΐτης**
S. ITALY (CAMPANIA):
—POMPEII*: (1) i BC-i AD *CIL* IV 538 (Lat. Tetraites: freed.)

**Τέτρατος**
LAKONIA:
—PYRRHICHOS: (1) imp. *IG* V (1) 1594

**Τεύθιος**
LAKONIA:
—HYPERTELEATON*: (1) imp. ib. 1064 (T(ι)β. T.?)

**Τεύθρας**
KERKYRA: (1) c. 330-315 BC *SEG* XXIII 189 I, 13; *Hesp.* 57 (1988) p. 148 B, 7 (*SEG* XXXVI 331); cf. *Hesp.* 48 (1979) pp. 78 f. with pl. 22 (f. Αἰσχρίων, —ίδας)

**Τευκρία**
ARGOLIS:
—TROIZEN: (1) v BC *IG* IV (1) 803 ([T]ευκρία)

**Τεῦκρος**
EPIROS:
—MOLOSSOI: (1) iv BC *RE* (3) (s. Ἀλκέτας)
S. ITALY: (2) hell. Vandermersch p. 175 (amph.) (Lat. Teucr(os))

**Τεύπαλος**
ELIS:
—ANDRIA?: (1) inc. *FGrH* 408

**Τεύτα**
ILLYRIA: (1) iii BC *RE* (-)

**Τευταία**
ILLYRIA:
—APOLLONIA*: (1) imp. *IApoll* 29 (-τέα: d. Ἐπίκαδος, m. Ἰουκοῦνδα: freed.)
—BERAT (MOD.): (2) imp. *Stud. Alb.* 1969 (2), p. 176 (1972 (1), p. 83) (-τέα)
—EPIDAMNOS-DYRRHACHION: (3) ii-i BC *IDyrrh* 410 (d. Πραῦλος); (4) ~ ib. 412 (d. Τεύτιος); (5) hell.-imp. ib. 407 (d. Ἀλεξήν); (6) ~ ib. 408 (d. Βρῦγος); (7) ~ ib. 409 ([T]ευταία: d. Νικόμαχος); (8) ~ ib. 411 (d. Στράβαινος)

**Τευτίαπλος**
ELIS: (1) 427 BC Th. iii 29. 2

**Τεύτικος**
ILLYRIA: (1) c. 168 BC Liv. xliv 31. 9 (Lat. Teuticus)

**Τεύτιος**
ILLYRIA:
—EPIDAMNOS-DYRRHACHION: (1) ii-i BC *IDyrrh* 412 (f. Τευταία)

**Τεῦτος**
SICILY:
—INESSA-AITNA?: (1) f. vi BC Polyaen. v 1. 4

**Τέφαντος**
ILLYRIA:
—EPIDAMNOS-DYRRHACHION: (**1**) c. 250-50 BC
Maier 358 (coin) (Ceka 159) (pryt.)

**Τέφιλος**
ILLYRIA:
—EPIDAMNOS-DYRRHACHION: (**1**) c. 250-50 BC
Ceka, *Probleme* p. 152 no. 69 (coin); cf. *Iliria*
1992, p. 161 no. 32 (tile) (pryt.) ?= (**2**); (**2**) ~
Maier 359; Münsterberg *Nachtr.* p. 17 (coin)
(Ceka 92; 273) (pryt.) ?= (**1**); (**3**) ii-i BC *Iliria*
1992, p. 161 no. 32 (tile); (**4**) imp. *IDyrrh* 45
(*Τέφ*[*ιλος*?], *Τέφ*[*αντος*?]: f. *Μυρώ*)

**Τέχναρχος**
LAKONIA:
—AMYKLAI*: (**1**) c. 510-500 BC *IG* V (1) 823;
*LSAG*² p. 200 no. 32 (date) (Poralla² 692)

**Τέχνη**
SICILY:
—THERMAI HIMERAIAI: (**1**) i-ii AD *CIL* X 7428
(*ILat. Term. Imer.* 127) (Lat. Pacilia Techne:
d. *Ἀπολαύστη*, Veteranus)

**Τέχνων**
ARGOLIS:
—EPIDAUROS*: (**1**) c. 335-325 BC *IG* IV (1)² 106
I, 4, [41], 45, [56] + *SEG* XXV 389, [8], [14],
[43], [47], [53]; *IG* IV (1)² 108, 147, 153-4 ?=
(**2**); (**2**) c. 290-270 BC ib. 109 I, [115]; II, 116,
126, 151; III, 96 ?= (**1**)
KORINTHIA:
—SIKYON?: (**3**) 251 BC Plu., *Arat.* 5; 7; 20
(Skalet 317) (slave?)

**Τῆθυς**
S. ITALY (CAMPANIA):
—SALERNUM*: (**1**) ?i AD *IItal* I (1) 238 III,
14 (*CIL* X 557) (Lat. L. Appuleius Tethus:
freed.)

**Τήλαιθος**
ARGOLIS:
—EPIDAUROS: (**1**) iii BC *IG* IV (1)² 167, 2 (f.
*Τύρβις*)

**Τηλαμίδας**
DALMATIA:
—ISSA:
——(Pamphyloi): (**1**) iv/iii BC Brunšmid p. 8, 44
(*Τηλαμί*[*δας*])

**Τηλάριον**
LAKONIA:
—ASOPOS: (**1**) imp. *IG* V (1) 973

**Τηλέας**
AITOLIA: (**1**) 217 BC Nachtergael, *Les Galates*
65, 2 (*Τηλέᾳ* (gen.), *Τελ*[*έ*]*δ*[*α*]? (gen.)—*FD*)
ARGOLIS:
—EPIDAUROS: (**2**) iii BC Peek, *IAEpid* 43, 35 (f.
*Διονύσιος*)
MESSENIA:
—MESSENE: (**3**) iv/iii BC *IG* V (1) 1435, 16

**Τηλέγονος**
SICILY:
—SYRACUSE?:
——(*Λογ.*): (**1**) hell. Manganaro, *PdelP* forth-
coming no. 4 V, 5 (f. *Ἄλεξις*)

**Τηλεκλείδας**
KORINTHIA:
—KORINTH: (**1**) 345 BC Plu., *Tim.* 7 (-*δης*)

**Τηλεκλῆς**
ACHAIA:
—AIGEIRA: (**1**) 160-153 BC Plb. xxxii 3. 14;
xxxiii 1. 3; 3. 2 ?= (**2**); (**2**) 156 BC *IG* VII
411, 2, 31 (Petrakos, *Oropos* pp. 187-8 no.
44; *IOrop* 307) (f. *Ἱέρων*) ?= (**1**)

S. ITALY (LUCANIA):
—METAPONTION: (**3**) s. iii BC *RE* (2)

**Τήλεκλος**
LAKONIA:
—SPARTA: (**1**) viii BC ib. (-) (Poralla² 693) (s.
*Ἀρχέλαος*, f. *Ἀλκαμένης*: king)

**Τηλέμαχος**
AITOLIA:
—POTIDANIA: (**1**) m. ii BC *SBBerlAk* 1936, p.
371 a, 8 (*SEG* XLI 528 A) (s. *Λαδάμης*)
ARGOLIS:
—EPIDAUROS: (**2**) iii BC *IG* IV (1)² 241 (f. *Τη-
λεφάνης*); (**3**) ii BC ib. 214; 216-19; 223; Peek,
*IAEpid* 96 (s. *Τηλεφάνης*, f. *Λαφάντα*)
ELIS: (**4**) iv/iii BC *IvOl* 177, 1 (I f. *Τηλέμαχος*
II); (**5**) ~ Moretti, *Olymp.* 531 (II s. *Τηλέμα-
χος* I); (**6**) f. i BC *IvOl* 199; 406, 3; 408, 3;
Moretti, *Olymp.* 671 (s. *Λέων*, ?f. (ad.) —*νις*)
?= (**8**); (**7**) m. i BC *IvOl* 207 (f. *Χάροψ*); (**8**) 36
BC ib. 59, 9 (I f. (ad.) —*ων ὁ καὶ Τηλέμαχος*
II) ?= (**6**); (**9**) ~ ib. l. 10 (—*ων* [*ὁ*] [*καὶ*] *Τηλέ-
μα*[*χος*]: II s. (ad.) *Τηλέμαχος* I, s. *Κάλλιππος*)
?= (**11**); (**10**) i BC/i AD ib. 242, 2 (*Κάλλιπ*[*πος*]
[*Τηλέμα*]*χος*: III s. *Τηλέμαχος* II); (**11**) ~ ib. l.
3 (*Τηλ*[*έμαχος*]: II f. *Κάλλιππος Τηλέμαχος* III)
?= (**9**)
KORINTHIA:
—KORINTH: (**12**) 344 BC Plu., *Tim.* 13
S. ITALY (CAMPANIA):
—POMPEII: (**13**) ?i AD *NScav* 1946, p. 120 no.
326 a-b (Lat. L. Gavius Thelemachus)
SICILY:
—AKRAGAS: (**14**) f. vi BC *FGrH* 568 F 2; Schol.
Pi., *O.* iii 38 (f. *Ἐμμενίδας*, *Ξενόδικος*)

**Τηλεστράτα**
LEUKAS: (**1**) ii BC *AM* 27 (1902) p. 371 no. 53

**Τηλεφάνης**
AITOLIA: (**1**) c. 315-280 BC *FD* III (1) 143, 1 (s.
*Καλλέας*)
ARGOLIS:
—EPIDAUROS: (**2**) iv-iii BC *IG* IV (1)² 10
([*Τ*]*ηλεφάνης*); (**3**) f. ii BC ib. 218; 241 (s. *Τη-
λέμαχος*, ?s. *Σωκράτεια*, f. *Τηλέμαχος*)
——Tantalis: (**4**) c. 290-270 BC ib. 109 II, 153
—EPIDAUROS*: (**5**) c. 370-365 BC Peek, *IAEpid*
52 A, 27 (*Τηλε*[*φάνης*])
ARKADIA:
—STYMPHALOS: (**6**) c. 230-200 BC *BCH* 45
(1921) p. 13 II, 116 (?s. *Ἀλεξίων*)
KORINTHIA:
—SIKYON: (**7**) arch. *RE* (3) (Skalet 318) (Lat.
Telephanes: painter); (**8**) 343 BC *CID* II 31,
97

**Τήλεφος**
AITOLIA: (**1**) m. iii BC Pantos, *Sphragismata* p.
154 no. 125; p. 447 f.
KORINTHIA:
—KORINTH: (**2**) s. viii BC Plu., *Mor.* 773 B (and
Sicily Syracuse: fict.?)
S. ITALY (CAMPANIA):
—DIKAIARCHIA-PUTEOLI: (**3**) ?ii AD *CIL* X 3128
(Lat. M. Ulpius Telephus)

**Τηλίμαχος**
ARKADIA:
—KLEITOR: (**1**) 369-361 BC *IG* V (2) 1, 53; Tod,
*GHI* II 132 (date)

**Τηλίνης**
SICILY:
—GELA-PHINTIAS: (**1**) ?vii BC Hdt. vii 153-4;
(**2**) ?i BC *IG* XIV 258 (*Τελινε* (gen.)—apogr.)

**Τηλοκλῆς**
S. ITALY (BRUTTIUM):
—LOKROI EPIZEPHYRIOI:
——(*Ὀμβ.*): (**1**) iv/iii BC De Franciscis 34, 3

**Τηλόκριτος**
ACHAIA: (**1**) 169 BC Plb. xxviii 12. 7

**Τηλυκράτης**
LEUKAS: (**1**) c. 405 BC Paus. x 9. 10; cf. *CEG* II
819

**Τῆλυς**
S. ITALY (BRUTTIUM):
—SYBARIS-THOURIOI-COPIAE: (**1**) s. vi BC *RE*
(-) (tyrant)

**Τήλων**
ACHAIA:
—AIGEIRA: (**1**) ii BC Wilhelm, *Beitr.* p. 109 no.
94 (f. —*αστος*)

**Τημένης**
LAKONIA:
—SPARTA: (**1**) s. i BC *IG* V (1) 124, 10 (Bradford
(-)) (*Τη*[*μ*]*ένου* (gen.): f. *Νικάσιππος*)

**Τηρεύς**
ACHAIA: (**1**) 146 BC *IG* IV (1)² 28, 128, 129 (f.
*Ἀγάθων*, *Ὀνάσιμος*: synoikos)
AKARNANIA:
—ANAKTORION: (**2**) ?354 BC Tod, *GHI* II 160,
8 (*Τερêος* (gen.): f. *Ἄρκος*)
ELIS: (**3**) m. iii BC *IG* V (2) 368, 55 (f. *Θράσων*);
(**4**) c. 230-200 BC *BCH* 45 (1921) p. 15 II,
145 (s. *Θράσων*)
ILLYRIA:
—APOLLONIA: (**5**) ?ii BC *IApoll* 157; (**6**) imp. ib.
258 (*Λ. Λικίνιος Τηρε*[*ύς*])
—EPIDAMNOS-DYRRHACHION: (**7**) hell.-imp.
*IDyrrh* 414 (s. *Τρεβέλλιος*)
S. ITALY (CAMPANIA):
—POMPEII: (**8**) i BC-i AD *CIL* IV 3377 (Lat.
Thereus)

**Τήρης**
LAKONIA:
—SPARTA: (**1**) c. 132 AD *SEG* XI 579, 3 (Brad-
ford (-)) (f. *Σωσίπολις*)
S. ITALY (APULIA):
—LARINUM: (**2**) imp. *CIL* IX 750 (Lat. Teres: I
f. *Τήρης* II); (**3**) ~ ib. (Lat. M. Colius Teres:
II s. *Τήρης* I, Gavia Libertas)
S. ITALY (CAMPANIA):
—POMPEII: (**4**) i BC-i AD ib. IV 1959 (Castrèn
205. 30) (Lat. Ti. Iulius Teres)

**Τήριλλος**
SICILY:
—HIMERA: (**1**) vi/v BC *RE* (-) (s. *Κρίνιππος*, f.
*Κυδίππη*: tyrant)

**Τηρίων**
S. ITALY (CAMPANIA):
—NOLA*: (**1**) ?ii AD *CIL* X 1302 (Lat. T. Flavius
Terio: freed.)

**Τιβέριος**
ARGOLIS:
—ARGOS: (**1**) imp. *IG* IV (1) 625, 1, 4

**Τίγρις**
ILLYRIA:
—EPIDAMNOS-DYRRHACHION: (**1**) imp. *AEp*
1978, no. 747 (Lat. Crastina Tigris)
LEUKAS: (**2**) iii BC *RE* (2)
S. ITALY (CALABRIA):
—RUDIAE: (**3**) i-ii AD *NScav* 1897, p. 404 no.
6 = Bernardini, *Rudiae* p. 89 (Susini, *Fonti
Salento* p. 127 no. 71) (Lat. Iren(e) Tigris)

**Τίθασος**
S. ITALY (CAMPANIA):
—HERCULANEUM*: (**1**) i BC-i AD *CIL* X 1403 g
III, 4 (Lat. -us Tithasus: freed.)

**Τίθθη**
EPIROS:
—NIKOPOLIS: (1) imp. *SEG* XXVII 238 (n. pr.?:
?d. Λοῦπος)

**Τίκιος**
SICILY:
—PATERNO (MOD.): (1) iv-iii BC *Silver for the
Gods* pp. 58-61 nos. 25; 28

**Τίλδυος?**
S. ITALY (APULIA):
—AECAE: (1) ii AD *Scritti Zambelli* p. 337 (Lat.
Ti. Claudius Tildyus)

**Τιλείας**
ARKADIA:
—TEGEA: (1) m. iv BC *IG* V (2) 6, 103
——(Krariotai): (2) s. iv BC ib. 41, 48 (Τιλεί[α]ς:
s. Πολύξενος)

**Τιλιώ**
S. ITALY (BRUTTIUM):
—LOKROI EPIZEPHYRIOI: (1) iv BC *Locri Epize-
firi* 2 pl. 10 no. 7 (vase)

**Τίμα**
ARGOLIS:
—EPIDAUROS: (1) hell.? *SEG* XXXIX 357 a

**Τιμάγαθος**
ARGOLIS:
—EPIDAUROS: (1) c. 290-270 BC *IG* IV (1)² 109
II, 134, 145, 159
—TROIZEN: (2) hell.-imp. ib. IV (1) 815

**Τιμάγγελος**
ARGOLIS:
—ARGOS: (1) c. 365-335 BC ib. IV (1)² 103, 168

**Τιμαγένης**
ARGOLIS:
—EPIDAUROS*: (1) c. 370-360 BC *BSA* 61
(1966) p. 272 no. 4 B II, 6, 10-11
LAKONIA:
—AIGIAI*: (2) c. 525-500 BC *AAA* 18 (1985)
pp. 246-53 (Τιμαγένε<νε>ι (dat.): her.?)

**Τιμάγητος**
ARGOLIS:
—ARGOS: (1) iii BC *IG* IV (1) 618 II, 1
(Τι[μάγ]ητος: f. Καλλίδαμος)

**Τιμαγόρα**
ARGOLIS:
—EPIDAUROS (KARATZIA (MOD.)): (1) ?iii BC
Peek, *NIEpid* 121
EPIROS:
—BOUTHROTOS (PRASAIBOI): (2) a. 163 BC
*IBouthrot* 31, 71 (*SEG* XXXVIII 490)
—OPHYLLEIS: (3) f. ii BC *IBouthrot* 6, 7, 13-14
(*SEG* XXXVIII 468) (Τει-: d. Νικόλαος)
S. ITALY?: (4) vi/v BC *Mél. Vatin* p. 183
(bronze) (Τιμαγόραι (dat.), Τιμαγόρας—ed.)

**Τιμαγόρας**
ARGOLIS:
—ARGOS: (1) ii-i BC *IG* IV (1) 530, 2; cf. *BCH*
33 (1909) p. 183 n. 2 (f. Ἀριστοκράτης)
——(Kleodaidai): (2) ii/i BC ib. p. 176 no. 2, 13
(s. Χαρίτιμος)
ARKADIA:
—TEGEA: (3) 430 BC Th. ii 67. 1
EPIROS:
—MOLOSSOI: (4) ?164 BC Cabanes, *L'Épire* p.
586 no. 71, 5 (f. Φιλοξένα)
SICILY:
—GELA-PHINTIAS: (5) s. iv BC *RE* (4); (6) ?277
BC *FD* III (1) 125, 2 (s. Ζωΐλος)

**Τιμάγορος**
AITOLIA: (1) ?253 BC Nachtergael, *Les Galates*
10, 5

—APERANTOI: (2) iii-ii BC *IG* IX (1)² (1) 162 (f.
Εὐρυνόμη)
—DEXEIES: (3) 191 BC *SGDI* 1985, 9; (4) ?165
BC ib. 1818, 1, 3
ARGOLIS:
—ARGOS:
——(Pamphyloi-Aischiadai): (5) c. 400 BC *SEG*
XXIX 361, 12
—EPIDAUROS*: (6) hell.-imp.? ib. XI 443 b
LAKONIA:
—SPARTA: (7) c. 25-1 BC *IG* V (1) 212, 21 (Brad-
ford (1)) (s. Λααστρατίδας) ?= (8); (8) ~ *IG* V (1)
212, 25 (Bradford (2)) (f. Κρατέας) ?= (7)

**Τιμαία**
ARGOLIS:
—HERMIONE: (1) ?iii-ii BC *IG* IV (1) 735, 3 (Τι-
μεία—maj.: d. Σίμος)
LAKONIA:
—SPARTA: (2) s. v BC Plu., *Ages.* 3; *Alc.* 23 (Po-
ralla² 695) (m. Λατυχίδας)

**Τιμαΐδας**
ARGOLIS:
—EPIDAUROS: (1) c. 210-207 BC *IG* IV (1)² 73,
4; *SEG* XXXV 303 (date) (f. Ἀρχέλοχος)

**Τιμαίνετος**
ARGOLIS:
—EPIDAUROS: (1) iv BC *IG* IV (1)² 2; (2) m. iv
BC *SEG* XXVI 451; (3) f. ii BC *REG* 62 (1949)
p. 28 face B, 9 (f. Καλλικῶν); (4) c. 150 BC
*SEG* XI 377, 9; Peek, *IAEpid* 30, 7 (s. Καλλι-
κῶν) ?= (5)
——(Azantioi): (5) 146 BC *IG* IV (1)² 28, 43 (f.
Φιλοκλῆς) ?= (4)
—EPIDAUROS*: (6) c. 370-360 BC *BSA* 61
(1966) p. 272 no. 4 B II, 10 (Τιμαίνε[τος])
—PHLEIOUS: (7) 498 BC Paus. x 7. 7
ARKADIA:
—MANTINEIA-ANTIGONEIA: (8) c. 300-221 BC
*IG* V (2) 323. 80 (tessera) (f. Κλεώνομος)
ELIS: (9) m. iv BC *IvOl* 44, 7; (10) ii/i BC ib.
398, 2 ([Τι]μαίν[ετ]ος: f. Δαμάριστος)

**Τίμαιον**
MESSENIA:
—MESSENE: (1) iii BC *SEG* XXXIX 382 (XLI 360)
(Τίμεον (n. pr.?))

**Τίμαιος**
ACHAIA:
—DYME: (1) s. iii BC ib. XIII 278, 25 (f. Ἀριστέας)
—PATRAI: (2) hell.? *SGDI* 1628
AITOLIA: (3) m. iii BC *IG* V (2) 419, 2 (*IPArk*
28) ?= (4); (4) 244 or 240 BC *SGDI* 2511, 2
(Flacelière p. 402 no. 29) ?= (3) (5); (5) c. 240
BC *RE* (1); *IG* IX (1)² (1) p. L, s.a. 240 BC;
cf. 174, 1 with n.; cf. Flacelière p. 224 n. 5
(date) ?= (4)
—KONOPE-ARSINOE: (6) 185 BC *IG* IX (1)² (1)
71, 8; Sherk 37 B, 53; cf. *SEG* XXVII 123; (7)
173 BC *SGDI* 1853, 2 (f. Εὔδαμος)
—PHISTYON: (8) f. ii BC *IG* IX (1)² (1) 111, 5
(f. Ἐχέλαος) ?= (10); (9) 190 BC ib. 97, 4, 12;
(10) c. 164 BC ib. 99, 3 ?= (8); (11) s. ii BC
*SBBerlAk* 1936, p. 364 no. 1, 9
ARGOLIS:
—ARGOS:
——(Eualkidai): (12) iv/iii BC *SEG* XXX 356, 4
—EPIDAUROS: (13) hell.? ib. XL 224 (s.
Ἀριστίων); (14) ?ii BC Peek, *NIEpid* 30
([Τί]μαιο[ς]); (15) i AD *IG* IV (1)² 500
(Τί[μαιο]ς)
—METHANA-ARSINOE: (16) i BC ib. IV (1) 853,
7 (f. Ἀπολλώνιος)
—NEMEA*: (17) f. iv BC *SEG* XXX 352
ELIS: (18) 396 BC Moretti, *Olymp.* 374
(Stephanis 2410)
EPIROS:
—VOTONOSI (MOD.): (19) ?s. iii BC *SEG* XXIV
458 (Τεί-: f. Κάμανδρος)

ILLYRIA:
—APOLLONIA: (20) c. 210 BC *IG* IX (1)² (1) 31,
79; *SGDI* 2026, 8 (s. Μένανδρος, f. Μένανδρος)
KEPHALLENIA:
—SAME: (21) c. 230-200 BC *BCH* 45 (1921) p.
14 II, 140 (s. Τιμόμαχος)
MESSENIA:
—ASINE: (22) hell.-imp. *IG* V (1) 1407 (s. Ξένων)
S. ITALY (APULIA):
—CANUSIUM: (23) v/iv BC *Atti Conv. Taranto*
15 (1975) p. 641 (vase)
S. ITALY (BRUTTIUM):
—LOKROI EPIZEPHYRIOI: (24) vi/v BC *RE* (4);
*FVS* 49 (dub.)
——(Προ.): (25) 279 BC De Franciscis 13, 6; 33,
4 (f. Δαμάσιππος)
S. ITALY (CAMPANIA):
—POMPEII: (26) i BC-i AD *CIL* IV 1859 (Lat.
Timaeus)
SICILY:
—SYRACUSE: (27) i BC *SEG* XIV 580
—TAUROMENION: (28) iv/iii BC *RE* (3); *FGrH*
566 (s. Ἀνδρόμαχος)

**Τιμακλείδας**
ARGOLIS:
—EPIDAUROS*: (1) c. 290-270 BC *IG* IV (1)² 109
III, 36 ([Τι]μακλείδας)

**Τιμάκων**
LAKONIA:
—SPARTA: (1) f. iii AD ib. V (1) 541, 5; 545, 2;
*SEG* XI 825, 4, 7 (Bradford (2)) (M. Αὐρ. Τ.,
Τειμάκων—541 and *SEG*: I s. Ξενοκλῆς, f. M.
Αὐρ. Φίλητος, M. Αὐρ. Τιμάκων II); (2) ~ *SEG*
XI 825, 6 (Bradford (1)) (M. Αὐρ. Τειμάκων: II
s. M. Αὐρ. Τιμάκων I)

**Τίμαλλος**
EPIROS:
—BOUTHROTOS (PRASAIBOI): (1) a. 163 BC
*IBouthrot* 140, 4

**Τιμαμένα**
LAKONIA:
—SPARTA: (1) ii-iii AD *IG* V (1) 806 (Bradford
(-)) (Τει-)

**Τιμάνδρα**
ITHAKE: (1) hell. *SEG* XVII 258 (d. Φεῖδις)
SICILY:
—HYKKARA: (2) v/iv BC *RE* (3) (Δαμασάνδρα—
Ath., Ἐπιμάνδρα—Schol. Arist. and *Plu.* 179:
m. Λαΐς: het.)

**Τιμανδρίδας**
ACHAIA?: (1) 37 AD *IG* VII 2711, 37 (Τειμαν-
δρ[ίδας]: f. —δαμος)
ARKADIA: (2) iii BC *SEG* XXXVII 352
KORINTHIA:
—SIKYON: (3) vi/v BC ib. XI 244, 69
LAKONIA:
—SPARTA: (4) inc. Ael., *VH* xiv 3. 2 (Poralla²
696)

**Τίμανδρος**
ACHAIA:
—PATRAI?: (1) iii BC *Achaean Grave Stelai* 5 (f.
Θέων)
ARKADIA:
—MEGALOPOLIS: (2) s. ii BC *IG* V (2) 439, 74 (f.
Βοιωτός)
—PHIGALEIA: (3) i/ii AD *IvOl* 441; 442 (and
Messenia Kyparissia: Τιβ. Ὅππιος Τείμανδρος:
s. Ἀριστόδαμος)
—TEGEA: (4) ii AD *IG* V (2) 55, 66 (Τείμαν(δρος)?:
f. Νίκων)
ELIS: (5) imp. *IvOl* 741-742 (tiles) (Τεί-)
EPIROS:
—AMBRAKIA: (6) iii-ii BC *Op. Ath.* 10 (1971) p.
64 no. 12, 4; cf. *VAHD* 84 (1991) p. 262 (f.
Ξεναρέτα)

KORINTHIA:
—SIKYON: (7) vi/v BC *SEG* XI 244, 28; (8) ?263-258 BC Nachtergael, *Les Galates* 3, 17; 5, [30] (Stephanis 2411) ([Τί]μανδρος: s. Σωτέλης)
LAKONIA:
—SPARTA: (9) 43-31 BC *Münzpr. der Laked.* p. 147 Group 16 series 15; pp. 156-7 Group 19 series 2 (coin) (Bradford (-))
MESSENIA:
—KORONE: (10) 246 AD *IG* V (1) 1398, 98 (Αὐρ. Τείμ[ανδρ]ος)
S. ITALY (BRUTTIUM):
—RHEGION: (11) inc. ib. XIV 622 (terracotta) (Ῥύμανδρος—apogr., (Τί)μανδρος—ed.: s. Μοσχίων)
SICILY:
—HALOUNTION: (12) ii-i BC ib. 366 (*IGLMP* 43) (f. Βίωτος)

### Τιμάνθας
SICILY:
—GELA-PHINTIAS: (1) s. iv BC *IG* IV (1)² 95, 87 + Peek, *IAEpid* 41 (Τ[ιμ]άνθας)

### Τιμάνθης
ACHAIA:
—AIGEIRA: (1) iv BC *SEG* XI 1268
ARGOLIS:
—ARGOS?: (2) iii BC *BCH* 96 (1972) p. 138; cf. *BE* 1973, no. 181 (f. Τιμανθίς)
—EPIDAUROS: (3) iv/iii BC *IG* IV (1)² 161
—KLEONAI: (4) 456 BC Paus. vi 8. 4; Moretti, *Olymp.* 273
KORINTHIA:
—KORINTH: (5) 435 BC Th. i 29. 2 (f. Τιμάνωρ)
—SIKYON: (6) m. iii BC Plu., *Arat.* 32 (Skalet 321) (painter) ?= (7); (7) c. 250 BC Plu., *Arat.* 12 (Skalet 321) ?= (6)
SICILY:
—GELA-PHINTIAS: (8) f. v BC Dubois, *IGDS* 149 e (vase) (Arena, *Iscr. Sic.* II 32)

### Τιμανθίς
ARGOLIS:
—ARGOS?: (1) iii BC *BCH* 96 (1972) p. 138; cf. *BE* 1973, no. 181 (d. Τιμάνθης)

### Τιμανορίδας
ACHAIA:
—PATRAI: (1) 246 BC *IG* IX (1)² (1) 17, 132 (Τιμανορίδας: f. Θεόδωρος) ?= (2); (2) c. 210-207 BC ib. IV (1)² 73, 19 (f. Ἀγανορίδας) ?= (1); (3) ii/i BC *SEG* XIX 400, 1 (s. Ἀγίας)
ARKADIA:
—MEGALOPOLIS: (4) f. iii BC *EILakArk* 20 (s. Ἀριστείας)
KORINTHIA:
—KORINTH: (5) f. iv BC D. lix 29-32; 36

### Τιμάνωρ
ARGOLIS:
—HERMIONE: (1) iii BC *IG* IV (1) 729 II, 21 (s. Πάσων)
ARKADIA:
—HERAIA: (2) iii BC ib. v (2) 415, 11 (*IPArk* 23) (f. Ἀρχίδαμος)
EPIROS:
—BOUTHROTOS (PRASAIBOI): (3) a. 163 BC *IBouthrot* 14, 34; 31, 40 (*SEG* XXXVIII 471; 490) (I s. Λύκος, f. Τιμάνωρ II, ?f. Φιλίστιον) ?= (6); (4) ~ *IBouthrot* 14, 34; 31, 41 (*SEG* XXXVIII 471; 490) (II s. Τιμάνωρ I); (5) ~ *IBouthrot* 77, 5; (6) ~ ib. 152, 2 (s. Λύκος) ?= (3)
——Opatai: (7) a. 163 BC ib. 104, 13; 160, [9]; 161, 5 (s. Κέφαλος)
——Thymaioi: (8) a. 163 BC ib. 144, 5 (f. Λύκος)
ITHAKE: (9) 208 BC *IMM* 36, 1 ([Τ]ιμάνωρ)
KORINTHIA:
—KORINTH: (10) 435 BC Th. i 29. 2 (s. Τιμάνθης)

---

—SIKYON: (11) c. 230-200 BC *BCH* 45 (1921) p. 11 II, 35 ([Τι]μάνωρ)

### Τιμάρατος
S. ITALY (BRUTTIUM):
—LOKROI EPIZEPHYRIOI: (1) vii BC *RE* (-) ?= (Τιμάρης (1))

### Τιμαρέτα
AIGINA: (1) vi/v BC *IG* XII (9) 285, 9-10, 14-15 (*CEG* I 108) (-τε̄: m. Μνασίθεος)
ARKADIA: (2) hell.? *AMGR* 1935-9, p. 121 no. 7 ([Τ]ιμαρέτ[α]: d. —οχος)
—ALIPHEIRA: (3) s. iii BC Orlandos, *Alipheira* p. 218 no. 1
ELIS: (4) f. i BC *IvOl* 201; 204, [2]; Moretti, *Olymp.* 673 (d. Φίλιστος, Θεοδότα)
EPIROS:
—DODONA: (5) m. v BC Hdt. ii 55 (fict.?)
KERKYRA: (6) hell. *Syll*³ 1174, 8; (7) ~ Unp. (*IG* arch.) (m. Τίμων)
MESSENIA:
—MESSENE: (8) i/ii AD *SEG* XXIII 221 (d. Θιώτας, Σοφαρχίς)
PELOPONNESE: (9) hell. *HE* 3826, 3830

### Τιμαρέτη
ARGOLIS:
—HERMIONE: (1) iii AD *IG* IV (1) 717, 8-9 (Αὐρ. Τειμαρέτη)
KORINTHIA:
—KORINTH: (2) v/iv BC *SEG* XXX 579

### Τιμάρετος
ARGOLIS:
—EPIDAUROS: (1) c. 365-335 BC *IG* IV (1)² 103, 9

### Τιμάρης
S. ITALY (BRUTTIUM):
—LOKROI EPIZEPHYRIOI: (1) vii/vi BC Iamb., *VP* 130; 267 (*FVS* I p. 447) ?= (Τιμάρατος (1)); (2) iii BC Landi, *DISMG* 113 (f. —ία)

### Τιμάριν
LAKONIA:
—MESSA?: (1) imp. *IG* V (1) 1279 (Τειμάρειν)

### Τιμαρίστα
AKARNANIA:
—PALAIROS: (1) f. iii BC ib. IX (1)² (2) 472
ARGOLIS:
—EPIDAUROS: (2) iv BC ib. IV (1)² 195
KORINTHIA:
—KORINTH: (3) ?vi BC *Hesp.* 41 (1972) p. 211 no. 10 (-σστα)
MESSENIA:
—MESSENE: (4) iii-ii BC *SEG* XXXVIII 346 a + XLI 370; cf. *PAE* 1987, pl. 80 a

### Τιμάριστος
LAKONIA:
—SPARTA: (1) 43-31 BC *Münzpr. der Laked.* p. 147 Group 16 series 16; p. 154 Group 17 series 11 and 13; p. 157 Group 19 series 3 (coins) (Bradford (2)); (2) i BC/i AD *IG* V (1) 48, 13 (Bradford (11)) (s. Δάμων)

### Τιμάρχη
ARGOLIS:
—HERMIONE: (1) imp. *IG* IV (1) 724, 2 (Τει-: d. Τίμαρχος)

### Τιμαρχίδας
LAKONIA:
—SPARTA: (1) ?134 AD ib. V (1) 62, 12 (Bradford (2)) (Τει-: I f. Τιμαρχίδας II); (2) ~ *IG* V (1) 62, 12 (Bradford (1)) (Τει-: II s. Τιμαρχίδας I)
MESSENIA:
—MESSENE: (3) m. iii BC *IG* V (2) 368, 85 (s. Λυσα—)

---

SICILY:
—SYRACUSE: (4) 70 BC Cic., *In Verr.* II iv 138 (Lat. Timarchides: f. Διόδωρος)

### Τιμαρχίς
ACHAIA:
—PATRAI: (1) iv/iii BC *Achaean Grave Stelai* 15 (d. Τιμόδαμος)
ARKADIA:
—HERAIA: (2) f. iii BC *IG* V (2) 416
KERKYRA: (3) iii-ii BC *AE* 1914, p. 235 no. 4 (d. Σώτηρος)
MESSENIA:
—MESSENE: (4) c. 220 BC *SEG* XXXVIII 339; cf. *PAE* 1971, p. 166 no. 7 ([Τιμα]ρχίς: d. Λέων); (5) i AD *SEG* XXIII 220 a, 1; 220 b, 3 (d. Δαμαρχίδας, m. Μεγώ)

### Τίμαρχος
ACHAIA: (1) 146 BC *IG* IV (1)² 28, 90 (f. Φίλων: synoikos)
AITOLIA: (2) iii BC Polyaen. v 25; Front., *Strat.* iii 2. 11; cf. *RE* (4)
—KONOPE-ARSINOE?: (3) 184 BC *IG* IX (1)² (1) 131, 21
—POTIDANIA: (4) m. ii BC *SBBerlAk* 1936, p. 371 a, 12 (*SEG* XLI 528 A) (s. Εὐβουλίδας)
—PTOLEMAIS: (5) 225-205 BC *FD* III (3) 220, 6; Flacelière p. 258 n. 6 (locn.)
ARGOLIS:
—ARGOS: (6) c. 365-335 BC *IG* IV (1)² 103, 53; (7) iii/ii BC *SEG* XLII 278
—ARGOS*: (8) iii BC ib. XXX 364, 2 (s. Δημαίνετος)
—EPIDAUROS:
——(Azantioi): (9) 146 BC *IG* IV (1)² 28, 33 (s. Ἀριστοκράτης)
——Miltias (Azantioi): (10) m. iii BC ib. 96, 72 (Perlman E.3); Perlman p. 63 f. (date)
—EPIDAUROS?: (11) s. vii BC Plu., *Mor.* 403 C-D
—HERMIONE: (12) imp. *IG* IV (1) 724, 3 (Τεί-: f. Τιμάρχη); (13) i BC/i AD ib. 722, 4 (Τεί-: I f. Ἀρίσταινος, Τίμαρχος II); (14) ~ ib. l. 4 (Τεί-: II s. Τίμαρχος I)
—PHLEIOUS: (15) iv BC D.L. ix 109 (f. Τίμων); (16) s. iv BC *Suda* Π 3239 (f. Πύρρων)
ARKADIA:
—KLEITOR: (17) ?253 BC Nachtergael, *Les Galates* 10, 33 (Stephanis 2412) (s. Ἀνδροίτας)
—MANTINEIA-ANTIGONEIA: (18) c. 300-221 BC *IG* V (2) 323. 94 (tessera) (s. Ἐπηρατίδας); (19) 296 BC Moretti, *Olymp.* 514
KORINTHIA:
—KORINTH: (20) imp. *Corinth* VIII (3) 300, 1 (*GVI* 2020) (f. Φιλίστα)
—SIKYON: (21) ?221 BC *PUG* III 101 (s. Κράτης)
LAKONIA:
—SPARTA: (22) iii BC *SEG* XL 348 B, 4; (23) s. i BC *IG* V (1) 95, 12; 96, 8; 133, 1 (Bradford (1)) (s. Νικίας); (24) ?s. i BC *IG* V (1) 262 (Bradford (2)); (25) ?i-ii AD *IG* V (1) 668 (Bradford (3)) (f. Κλέων)
MESSENIA:
—MESSENE: (26) iv BC *IG* V (1) 1471; (27) f. i AD *SEG* XXIII 207, 17 (Τεί-: s. Θέων)
S. ITALY (LUCANIA):
—HERAKLEIA:
——(Ἀσ. βότρυς): (28) iv/iii BC *IGSI* 1 I, 95 (*DGE* 62; Uguzzoni–Ghinatti I) (s. Νίκων)

### Τιμᾶς
LAKONIA:
—SPARTA: (1) ii AD *IG* V (1) 1369, 9 (Bradford (-)) (d. Ἰούνιος, m. Χαριτέλης, Ἰούνιος)

### Τιμᾶς
EPIROS: (1) imp. Ugolini, *Alb. Ant.* 1 p. 196 no. 18 (Τει-)
ILLYRIA:
—EPIDAMNOS-DYRRHACHION: (2) ii-i BC *IDyrrh* 401 (Τει-: s. Θερσίας); (3) hell.-imp. ib. 399 A (Τει-); (4) ~ ib. 400 (Τει-: s. Ἀμφικλῆς); (5) ~ ib. 402 (Τει-: s. Μενέας)

**Τιμας**
ARGOLIS:
—EPIDAUROS: (1) hell.? SEG XXIX 381 (masc./fem.)

**Τιμασαγόρα**
ILLYRIA:
—EPIDAMNOS-DYRRHACHION: (1) ii-i BC IDyrrh 403 (Τει-)

**Τιμάσαρχος**
AIGINA: (1) ?473 BC Pi., N. iv, 10, 78; cf. Klee p. 101 no. 53 (s. Τιμόκριτος)

**Τιμασίας**
AKARNANIA:
—ECHINOS: (1) c. 266 BC IG XII (9) 1187, 9; Robert, Ét. Num. Gr. pp. 179 ff. (date) (f. Φαίαξ)

**Τιμασίδας**
ARKADIA:
—HELISSON: (1) c. 221 BC IG IV (1)² 42, 4

**Τιμασίθεος**
ARGOLIS:
—EPIDAUROS*: (1) c. 370 BC ib. 102, 55, 238
S. ITALY (BRUTTIUM):
—KROTON: (2) 512 BC Moretti, Olymp. 145
SICILY:
—LIPARA: (3) 393 BC RE (-)
—LIPARA*: (4) ii/i BC Meligunis-Lipara 5 p. 183 T. 2181; cf. Kokalos 32 (1986) pp. 240-1 nos. 76-7 (tiles)

**Τιμασικράτης**
AKARNANIA:
—PALAIROS: (1) ii BC AD 22 (1967) Chron. p. 324 (f. Λυσάνωρ)
ARGOLIS:
—ARGOS: (2) ii BC SEG XLII 279, 9
—METHANA-ARSINOE: (3) ii BC IG IV (1) 855, 2 (f. Ξενοφάντα)
MESSENIA:
—MESSENE: (4) s. ii BC SEG XLI 341, 3 (f. Λυσίμαχος)

**Τιμασιμβρότα**
LAKONIA:
—SPARTA: (1) s. vii BC PMGF 1 5 fr. 2, 16, 21; ZPE 91 (1992) pp. 1 ff. (ident., stemma) (d. Εὐρυκράτ—)

**Τιμάσιος**
S. ITALY (BRUTTIUM):
—SYBARIS-THOURIOI-COPIAE: (1) ?v BC Iamb., VP 267 (FVS 1 p. 447)

**Τιμασίπολις**
S. ITALY (BRUTTIUM):
—LOKROI EPIZEPHYRIOI:
——(Ἀλχ.): (1) iv/iii BC De Franciscis 20, 20 (I f. Τιμασίπολις II); (2) ~ ib. l. 20 (II s. Τιμασίπολις I)
——(Προ.): (3) iv/iii BC ib. 6, 5 (f. Κλεοσθένης); (4) 277 BC ib. 8, 4; 31, [4] (s. Κλεοσθένης)

**Τιμασίς**
ILLYRIA:
—EPIDAMNOS-DYRRHACHION: (1) hell.-imp. IDyrrh 415

**Τιμασιστράτα**
ARKADIA:
—MEGALOPOLIS?: (1) 42 AD IG V (2) 516, 6, 18 etc. (d. Ὀνασικράτης)

**Τιμασίων**
ACHAIA: (1) 146 BC ib. IV (1)² 28, 105 (f. Τίμασος: synoikos)
DALMATIA:
—ISSA: (2) iii BC SEG XXXV 686 (f. Νικώ); (3) ii BC Brunšmid p. 25 no. 14, 2 + VAHD 84

(1991) p. 248 no. 1 (Τει-: s. Διονύσιος) ?= (4); (4) ~ Brunšmid p. 25 no. 14, 6 + VAHD 84 (1991) p. 248 no. 1 (Τει-: f. Γλυκύρα) ?= (3); (5) f. ii BC Brunšmid p. 23 no. 10, 9 (Τει-: s. Ἀπολλωνίδας)
—ISSA?: (6) iii/ii ib. p. 31 no. 27; Istros 2 (1935-6) pp. 18 ff. (or Dalmatia Tragurion: Τει-: f. Εὐάρης)
—TRAGURION: (7) 56 BC Sherk 24 A, 8 (Τιμα[σίω]ν: f. Κλεέμπορος)
KORINTHIA:
—KORINTH: (8) f. ii BC Corinth VIII (1) 73, 2 (s. Κρίτων, Νικα—)
MESSENIA:
—MESSENE: (9) iv/iii BC IG V (1) 1435, 2
SICILY:
—SYRACUSE?:
——(Πλη.): (10) hell. Manganaro, PdelP forthcoming no. 4 II, 9 (s. Ἀριστοκλῆς)

**Τίμασος**
ACHAIA: (1) 146 BC IG IV (1)² 28, 105 (s. Τιμασίων: synoikos)

**Τιμασώ**
SICILY:
—LIPARA: (1) hell. SEG XXXIV 958

**Τιμασώι**
SICILY:
—SELINOUS: (1) vi/v BC Dubois, IGDS 37 b (Arena, Iscr. Sic. 1 61 B); cf. LSAG² p. 277 no. 38 (-σόι)

**Τιμέας**
ACHAIA:
—DYME*: (1) c. 219 BC SGDI 1612, 20-1 (Tyche 5 (1990) p. 124) (f. Σαμίδας, Ξέναρχος)
AIGINA: (2) hell.? IG VII 162 (s. Ἀβίαντος); (3) c. 225 BC SEG XI 414, 36 (Perlman E.5) (f. Κάλλιππος)
ARGOLIS:
—HERMIONE: (4) ?146 BC IG IV (1) 757 B, 5 (s. Λ—)
ARKADIA:
—HERAIA: (5) iii BC ib. v (2) 415, 8 (IPArk 23) (s. Μιθυλῖνος)
EPIROS:
—NIKOPOLIS: (6) imp. Hellenika 22 (1969) p. 69 no. 5 (Sarikakis 162) (Τει-: f. Διοδότα)
ILLYRIA:
—APOLLONIA: (7) 361 BC CID II 4 I, 76; cf. IApoll 305
—EPIDAMNOS-DYRRHACHION: (8) c. 250-50 BC Ceka, Probleme p. 152 no. 70 (coin) (pryt.) ?= (9); (9) ~ Maier 360; Münsterberg p. 261 = Nachtr. p. 17 (coin) (Ceka 47; 139?; 160; 410) (pryt.) ?= (8)
—ITHAKE: (10) iii-ii BC GVI 102 (Gr. Gr. 224) (s. Εὐθύδαμος)
KORINTHIA:
—KORINTH: (11) 500-475 BC Amyx Gr 22 (vase) (IG IV (1) 351); LSAG² p. 132 no. 33 (date)
LAKONIA:
—SPARTA: (12) 336 BC CID II 24 II, 10 (Poralla² 697)
S. ITALY (BRUTTIUM):
—RHEGION: (13) ii BC Mus. Naz. Reggio p. 159 no. 28 (s. T—)

**Τιμείας**
AIGINA: (1) iii BC SEG XXVI 919, 22 (f. Καλλιγ—)
ARGOLIS:
—TROIZEN: (2) iii BC ib. XXXVII 310 (Τ[ι]μεί[ας], Τ[ι]μει[ός]?)
ARKADIA:
—ALIPHEIRA: (3) iii BC EILakArk 11, 5 (GVI 1505; Gr. Gr. 196) (f. Θέων)

**Τιμειός**
ARGOLIS:
—TROIZEN: (1) iii BC IG IV (1) 807

**Τιμέλας**
AKARNANIA:
—THYRREION: (1) ii/i BC GVI 1122, 11 (IG IX (1)² (2) 340) (s. Φιλίσκος)

**Τίμη**
SICILY:
—KATANE: (1) imp. ib. XIV 508 (Τιμη—?)

**Τιμήν**
ILLYRIA:
—APOLLONIA: (1) c. 250-50 BC Maier 36 (Ceka 115 (coin)); (2) ii-i BC IApoll 164 (f. Φίλων); (3) i BC Maier 131; 163 (coin) (s. Ἀνδρο—: money.)
—EPIDAMNOS-DYRRHACHION: (4) imp. IDyrrh 17 (Τει-: f. Τίτος)

**Τιμήνωρ**
SICILY:
—LEONTINOI: (1) 433 BC IG 1³ 54, 4 (-μένōρ: s. Ἀγαθοκλῆς)

**Τιμήσιος**
ARGOLIS:
—ARGOS: (1) iv BC FGrH 390 F 1, 32

**Τιμησίων**
AIGINA: (1) ii/i BC Alt-Ägina I (2) p. 43 no. 3, 5 (s. Νικοκλῆς) ?= (2); (2) ?i BC ib. p. 44 no. 11 (f. Νικοκλῆς) ?= (1)

**Τιμιάδας**
ARGOLIS:
—EPIDAUROS: (1) ?iii BC Peek, IAEpid 226, 2 ([Τιμ]ιάδᾱς: f. Τιμόκριτος)

**Τιμίας**
ARKADIA:
—KLEITOR: (1) m. iii BC IG IV (1)² 96, 46 (Perlman E.3); Perlman p. 63 f. (date) (s. Ἀθανίων)

**Τιμίων**
ARKADIA:
—TEGEA:
——(Apolloniatai): (1) s. iv BC IG V (2) 174 a, 4
——(Krariotai): (2) iv/iii BC ib. 38, 24 (s. Καλλικρέτης)
LAKONIA:
—OITYLOS: (3) iii/ii BC ib. V (1) 1295, 5 (Bradford (-))

**Τιμογένης**
ARGOLIS:
—ARGOS: (1) c. 80-70 BC BCH 19 (1895) pp. 338-9 no. 12, 16 + AE 1936, Chron. p. 41 no. 217; BSA 70 (1975) p. 122 (date); cf. Stephanis 2140 (f. Πρατοκλῆς)
ARKADIA:
—THELPHOUSA: (2) c. 230-200 BC BCH 45 (1921) p. 12 II, 75 (s. Λάμπος)
ELIS: (3) 69-73 AD IvOl 84, 24 (Τει-)
EPIROS:
—AMBRAKIA: (4) s. iv BC IG IV (1)² 95, 82 (Perlman E.2); Perlman pp. 46-9 (date)
LAKONIA:
—SPARTA: (5) hell.? IG V (1) 617 (Τιμογ[ένης]?: f. Τιμοκράτεια); (6) s. i BC ib. 92, 10 (Bradford (1)) (s. Διοκλῆς); (7) c. 25-1 BC IG V (1) 212, 39 (Bradford (2)) (Τιμογένη[s]: f. Ὀνάσανδρος)
MESSENIA:
—MESSENE: (8) f. ii BC SEG XLI 331, 2 (f. Ἀριστις)
—THOURIA: (9) s. iii BC IG V (1) 1386, 8 (f. Τιμόξενος); (10) ii-i BC ib. 1385, 23 (f. Πολυκράτης)

**Τιμόδαμος**
ACHAIA:
—PATRAI: (1) iv/iii BC Achaean Grave Stelai 15 (f. Τιμαρχίς)

AIGINA: (2) c. 230-200 BC *BCH* 45 (1921) p. 14 II, 143 (s. *Τιμόλαος*)
AITOLIA: (3) hell. *IEph* 2511 (s. *Μέγων*)
ARGOLIS:
—EPIDAUROS: (4) c. 370 BC *IG* IV (1)² 102, 33
ARKADIA:
—ORCHOMENOS: (5) c. 230-200 BC *BCH* 45 (1921) p. 13 II, 114 (f. *Κλεόμαντις*)
EPIROS:
—AMBRAKIA: (6) hell. *IG* IX (1) 537; cf. *AM* 27 (1902) p. 354 (*Τι[μόδαμος]*: I f. *Τιμόδαμος* II); (7) ~ *IG* IX (1) 537; cf. *AM* 27 (1902) p. 354 (II s. *Τιμόδαμος* I: sculptor); (8) hell.? *SEG* XXIV 419 (f. *Ἀγησίας*); (9) ii-i BC *CIG* 1800, 10 (s. *Σωσίστρατος*)
—DODONA*: (10) iv BC *PAE* 1968, p. 54 a; cf. *L'Illyrie mérid.* 2 pp. 61 f.
KORINTHIA:
—KORINTH: (11) iv BC Plu., *Tim.* 3; D.S. xvi 65. 2; 90. 1 (*Τιμαίνετος*—D.S.: f. *Τιμολέων*, *Τιμοφάνης*)
—SIKYON: (12) vi/v BC *SEG* XI 244, 68; (13) 217 BC Nachtergael, *Les Galates* 65, 11 (Skalet 322); cf. Stephanis 1840 (f. *Νικοκλῆς*)
—SIKYON?: (14) ?265-259 BC Nachtergael, *Les Galates* 4, 20 (f. *Νικοκλῆς*)
LAKONIA:
—GERONTHRAI: (15) c. 500 BC *IG* V (1) 1134, 7; *LSAG*² p. 201 no. 45 (date) (Poralla² 698)
—SPARTA: (16) c. 1-10 AD *IG* V (1) 209, 7; *SEG* XXXV 331 (date) (Bradford (-)) (s. *Δαμόστρατος*)
—SPARTA?: (17) m. v BC *RA* 1971, p. 202 fig. 11 (gem) (-δη-)
S. ITALY (BRUTTIUM):
—LOKROI EPIZEPHYRIOI:
——(*Ἀστ.*): (18) iv/iii BC De Franciscis 12, 1
SICILY:
—GELA-PHINTIAS: (19) ?i BC *IG* XIV 259 (*Τιμόδ[αμος]*)

**Τιμοδίκα**
ILLYRIA:
—LISSOS: (1) imp. *Op. Ath.* 10 (1971) p. 81 n. 19

**Τιμόδοτος**
AIGINA: (1) iv/iii BC *Ag.* XVII 394 ([*Τι*]*μόδοτ[ος]*: f. *Πυθία*)

**Τιμόδωρος**
ARGOLIS:
—EPIDAUROS: (1) f. iii BC *IG* IV (1)² 201 (s. *Τελέστας*, f. *Τελέστας*)
ARKADIA: (2) 304 BC ib. V (2) 550, 24

**Τιμοθέα**
AKARNANIA:
—PALAIROS: (1) iii BC ib. IX (1)² (2) 507
ITHAKE: (2) hell. *Rev. Épig.* 1 (1913) p. 47 no. 6
KERKYRA: (3) imp. *IG* IX (1) 866
S. ITALY (APULIA):
—LUCERIA: (4) vi AD *CIL* IX 933; cf. *Puglia Paleocrist. Altomed.* 5 pp. 7-8 (Lat. Timotea)
SICILY:
—SYRACUSE: (5) iii-v AD *IG* XIV 176 (Strazzulla 114)

**Τιμόθεος**
ACHAIA:
—DYME: (1) ?145 BC Sherk 43, 23; *SEG* XXXVIII 372 (date) (s. *Νικίας*)
AITOLIA: (2) 217 BC Nachtergael, *Les Galates* 65, 3
AKARNANIA:
—STRATOS: (3) 154 BC *SGDI* 1908, 16 (f. *Τίμων*)
ARGOLIS:
—EPIDAUROS: (4) iii-iv AD *IG* IV (1)² 541 (*Τει*-: I f. *Τιμόθεος* II); (5) ~ ib. ([*Τειμό*]*θεος*: II s. *Τιμόθεος* I)

—TROIZEN: (6) f. ii AD ib. IV (1) 758, 2, 29 (*Τει*-: f. *Ἰσίων*)
ARKADIA:
—MEGALOPOLIS: (7) 359 BC *CID* II 5 I, 35 (*Τι[μ]όθεος*)
—MEGALOPOLIS*: (8) 457 AD *IG* V (2) p. XXXIII, 36 (bp.)
EPIROS:
—NIKOPOLIS: (9) s. ii AD *AEp* 1901, no. 126, 52 (Lat. M. Aur. Timotheus)
KORINTHIA:
—KORINTH: (10) imp. *CIL* III 7272, 3 (Lat. Antonius Timotheus: f. *Ἀντ. Ἀλέξανδρος*)
LAKONIA:
—SPARTA: (11) c. 130-140 AD *IG* V (1) 66, 8 (Bradford (-)) ([*Τι*]*μόθεο[ς]*)
LEUKAS: (12) c. 167-50 BC BM coin 1909 5-4-21; Unp. (Oxford, AM) Sept. 1975 (coins)
PELOPONNESE: (13) s. iii BC *SEG* XIII 278, 15 (f. *Ξενοκλῆς*)
S. ITALY: (14) imp. *CIL* X 8059. 403 (seal) (Lat. Timotheus)
S. ITALY (APULIA):
—BARION: (15) vi AD *Puglia Paleocrist. Altomed.* 4 p. 145 (mosaic) (Lat. Timotheus)
S. ITALY (CAMPANIA):
—DIKAIARCHIA-PUTEOLI: (16) imp. *CIL* X 1834 (Lat. Timotheu[s]); (17) ~ ib. 3095 (Lat. C. Vettenius Timotheus: s. *Ἔρως*)
S. ITALY (LUCANIA):
—METAPONTION: (18) vi/v BC *Anon. Med. Lond.* VIII 11 (doctor)
SICILY: (19) ?iii AD *IEph* 2223, [4]
—SYRACUSE: (20) iii-v AD *IG* XIV 177 (Strazzulla 115; Agnello 12; Wessel 1108); cf. Ferrua, *NG* 176 (-*θης*: f. *Κρισκωνία*); (21) ~ *NScav* 1907, p. 768 no. 34 + Ferrua, *NG* 89 (Barreca 340) (*Τιμό[θεος]*); (22) ~ Strazzulla 392 (Wessel 162); cf. Ferrua, *NG* 131
ZAKYNTHOS: (23) v-iv BC *TrGF* 4 p. 52 T48 (Stephanis 2416)

**Τιμόι**
EPIROS:
—AMBRAKIA: (1) m. iii BC Unp. (Arta Mus.)

**Τιμοκάδης**
ACHAIA:
—DYME: (1) c. 210-180 BC *FD* III (3) 122, 2; *SEG* XXII 214, [2] (f. *Ἀρίσταινος*) ?= (*Δαμοκάδης* (1))

**Τιμόκλεια**
ARGOLIS:
—ARGOS*: (1) 105 BC *JÖAI* 14 (1911) Beibl. p. 146 no. 4, 6 (slave/freed.?)
MESSENIA:
—KYPARISSIA: (2) i BC *SEG* XI 1027 (*Τιμόκλε[ια]*)

**Τιμοκλείδας**
ARGOLIS:
—EPIDAUROS: (1) c. 370 BC *IG* IV (1)² 102, 90
——(Hysminatai): (2) 146 BC ib. 28, 15 (s. *Δαμέας*)
KORINTHIA:
—SIKYON: (3) c. 275-265 BC ib. XI (4) 704, 4, 9-10; Vial p. 98 (ident., date) (s. *Θεύτιμος*) ?= (4); (4) c. 265 BC *RE* (-) (Skalet 323) ?= (3)

**Τιμοκλῆς**
ACHAIA:
—DYME*: (1) c. 219 BC *SGDI* 1612, 37 (*Tyche* 5 (1990) p. 124) (s. *Χαιρέας*)
—PELLENE: (2) ?c. 315-280 BC *FD* III (4) 403 VI, 1 (s. *Δαρεῖος*)
AKARNANIA:
—THYRREION: (3) iii-ii BC *SEG* XXVII 159, 3; cf. *PAE* 1977, pl. 244 a (f. *Λέων*)

ARGOLIS:
—ARGOS: (4) ?c. 525-500 BC *IG* IV (1) 510 b (Ebert, *Gr. Sieg.* 10; Lazzarini 865); *LSAG*² p. 169 no. 16 (date) (-*κλῆς*)
——Prosymna (Pholygadai): (5) iv/iii BC Moretti, *ISE* 40, 4
—EPIDAUROS: (6) c. 365-335 BC *IG* IV (1)² 103, 33, 69, 79; (7) c. 335-325 BC ib. 106 I, 75; III, 43, 116; 108, 150; (8) ?iii BC Peek, *IAEpid* 226, 3 ([*T*]*ιμο[κ]λῆς*: s. *Ἀνδροκλῆς*); (9) i BC-i AD? Peek, *NIEpid* 60 (*Τιμοκ[λῆς]*: s. *Νικόστρατος*); (10) i-ii AD *IG* IV (1)² 37; (11) 135 AD Peek, *IAEpid* 154, 2 (*Τει*-: s. *Ἀριστοκράτης*); (12) iii-iv AD ib. 227 (*Τει*-: f. *Ἀντέρως*)
—TROIZEN: (13) iv BC *IG* IV (1) 764, 4 (s. *Ξενοφῶν*); (14) 360 BC *CID* II 4 II, 42 (f. *Θεσσαλός*)
ARKADIA:
—MEGALOPOLIS: (15) f. ii BC *IG* V (2) 19 (s. *Ἀπολλώνιος*)
—TEGEA: (16) 191-146 BC *BMC Pelop.* p. 15 no. 172; *Coll. Weber* 2 p. 503 no. 4351 (coin) (*TIMNΑΣ*—*BMC* per err.)
——(Apolloniatai): (17) s. iv BC *IG* V (2) 174 a, 3; (18) m. iii BC ib. 36, 100 (s. *Τιμοκρῆς*)
ELIS:
—OLYMPIA*: (19) s. v BC *Ol. Forsch.* 5 p. 151 no. 10
KERKYRA: (20) ?ii-i BC *IG* IX (1) 812 (tile)
KORINTHIA:
—SIKYON: (21) 166 BC ib. II² 2316, 5, 9 (s. *Χαρικλῆς*)
LAKONIA:
—GYTHEION: (22) hell. ib. V (1) 1193
—SPARTA: (23) s. i BC ib. 92, 3 (Bradford (3)) (s. *Μεναλκίδας*); (24) ~ *IG* V (1) 94, 8 (Bradford (1)) (s. *Δεξίδαμος*); (25) ~ *IG* V (1) 95, 3; 211, 7 (Bradford (9)) (f. *Τίμων*); (26) imp. *IG* V (1) 747 (Bradford (6)); (27) c. 30-20 BC *IG* V (1) 211, 28 (Bradford (2)) (s. *Κλέων*); (28) i-ii AD *IG* V (1) 654, 8 (Bradford (10)) (*Τε[ι]μο[κ]λῆς*: f. *Τιμοσθενίς*); (29) c. 100-110 AD *IG* V (1) 97, 18; *SEG* XI 534, 3; 564, 12 (Bradford (4)) (*Τειμοκλῆς*—*SEG*: s. *Θεόδωρος*); (30) f. ii AD *IG* V (1) 162, 15 (Bradford (12)) (*Τει*-); (31) c. 122 AD *SEG* XI 574, 5 (Bradford (11)) ([*Τ*]*ειμοκλῆ[ς]*); (32) c. 217-230 AD *SEG* XI 616 a, 3 (Bradford (5)) (I f. M. Αὐρ. *Τιμοκλῆς* II ὁ καὶ *Κλεοίτας*) ?= (34); (33) ~ *SEG* XI 616 a, 3; *BSA* 79 (1984) p. 284 no. 12 (ident., date) (Bradford (8)) (M. Αὐρ. *Τειμοκλῆς* ὁ καὶ *Κλεο[ί]τας*: II s. *Τιμοκλῆς* I); (34) c. 220 AD *SEG* XXXIV 311, 2; *BSA* 79 (1984) pp. 267-9 (date) (Bradford (7)) (*Τει*-: f. M. Αὐρ. *Κλεάρετος*) ?= (32)
S. ITALY (BRUTTIUM):
—LOKROI EPIZEPHYRIOI:
——(*Στρ.*): (35) 276 BC De Franciscis 23, 2; 25, 4 (f. *Τίμων*)
SICILY:
—GELA-PHINTIAS: (36) f. v BC Arena, *Iscr. Sic.* II 26 (vase) (*Τ[ι]μοκλ̣ε̄́ς*)

**Τιμοκρατέα**
ARKADIA:
—LYKOSOURA*: (1) f. ii AD *IG* V (2) 520 ([*Τι*]*μοκρατέα*?: d. *Ἀγίας*)

**Τιμοκράτεια**
AITOLIA:
—KYPARISSOS (MOD.): (1) ?f. iii BC *L'Illyrie mérid.* 1 p. 106 no. 2 (*SEG* XXXVII 432) (*Τιμοκρατηας*—lap.)
LAKONIA:
—SPARTA: (2) hell.? *IG* V (1) 617 (Bradford (2)) (d. *Τιμογένης*); (3) ?a. 212 AD *IG* V (1) 606, 2; *SEG* XI 818 (Bradford (1)) (Αὐρ. *Τειμοκράτεια*: d. *Ἀσκληπιάδης*)
SICILY:
—KAMARINA: (4) m. v BC Dubois, *IGDS* 120, 7 (Arena, *Iscr. Sic.* II 142 A; *SEG* XXXVIII 935; Cordano, 'Camarina VII' 60)

**Τιμοκράτης**

ACHAIA:
—AIGION: (1) 157 BC FD III (3) 126, 4, 5 (f. Δαμοκλῆς)
—DYME: (2) c. 219 BC SGDI 1612, 2 (Tyche 5 (1990) p. 124); (3) ii BC SEG XIV 371 (f. Στρατόνικος)
—PELLENE: (4) m. iii BC IG V (2) 368, 111 (s. Λυ—)
AITOLIA: (5) ?209 or 205 BC Flacelière p. 407 no. 38 b, [5]; Nachtergael, Les Galates 68, 4
—KALYDON: (6) 129 BC IG IX (1)² (1) 137, 94 (f. Μνάσιππος)
AKARNANIA:
—ECHINOS: (7) hell.? SEG XLII 485 (s. Τιμόστρατος)
—THYRREION: (8) ii BC IG IX (1)² (2) 247, 21 (f. Καλλικράτης)
ARGOLIS:
—ARGOS: (9) v BC RE (10); (10) a. 303 BC CEG II 816, 8; (11) iii BC IG II² 8364 (Τιμοκρ[άτης]: f. Δαμοσθένης); (12) c. 210-207 BC ib. IV (1)² 73, 7; SEG XXXV 303 (date) (s. Τίμων)
—EPIDAUROS: (13) iv BC ZPE 103 (1994) p. 106 no. 1 (s. Ἱππίας); (14) c. 365-335 BC IG IV (1)² 103, 113, 115 ?= (28); (15) iii BC ib. 165, 3 (Τιμοκρ[άτη]ς); (16) iii/ii BC ib. 306 A, 2 + Peek, IAEpid 129; (17) c. 221 BC IG IV (1)² 42, 8; (18) ii/i BC Peek, IAEpid 151 (f. Καλλικλῆς); (19) ~ IG IV (1)² 346 (f. Σωκράτης); (20) imp. Peek, IAEpid 98 (Τιμοκρά[της]: s. ..όδωρος); (21) i-ii AD IG IV (1)² 545 (s. Δάμιππος); (22) c. 1-70 AD ib. 80, 4; 81, 7, 17 (Peek, IAEpid 34); IG IV (1)² 82, 5; 83, 17; 84, 26, 38, 40; 85, 3; 86, 30 + Peek, IAEpid 36, 3, 19; IG IV (1)² 670, 4; 671, 2; 675, 2; 676, 2; 677, 2; 679, 4; 681, 1; v (1) 478, 7; Peek, IAEpid 34, 7, 17; 289, 5; Peek, NIEpid 68, 5; BSA 80 (1985) pp. 249-55 (ident., date, stemma) (T. Στατίλιος Τειμοκράτης: s. T. Στατίλιος Λαμπρίας, ?f. (ad.) T. Στατίλιος Λαμπρίας Μεμμιανός (Sparta?), f. T. Στατίλιος Λαμπρίας, Μεμμία Πασιχάρεια); (23) ii AD IG IV (1)² 673 (Τει[μ]οκράτης: s. Λαμπρίας) ?= (24); (24) f. ii AD ib. 678, 3; Peek, NIEpid 87, 2; BSA 80 (1985) pp. 249; 255-6 (ident., date, stemma) (T. Στατίλιος Τειμοκράτης: ?s. T. Στατίλιος Λαμπρίας Μεμμιανός (Sparta?), ?f. Λαμπρίας) ?= (23); (25) s. ii AD IG IV (1) 590, 3; Peek, NIEpid 66, 2; BSA 80 (1985) pp. 249; 256-8 (ident., date, stemma) (and Argolis Argos: T. Στατίλιος Τειμοκράτης Μεμμιανός: s. Λαμπρίας)
——Miltias (Azantioi): (26) m. iii BC IG IV (1)² 96, 72 (Perlman E.3); Perlman p. 63 f. (date)
——Pagasina (Azantioi): (27) iv/iii BC IG IV (1)² 58, 5, 13
——Phragias: (28) c. 365-335 BC ib. 103, 135 ?= (14)
——Pleiatios (Hylleis): (29) c. 335-325 BC ib. 106 II, 135 (Τιμοκρά[της]); (30) m. iii BC Peek, IAEpid 42, 2 (Perlman E.3); Perlman p. 63 f. (date) (Τ[ιμοκ]ρ[άτ]ης)
—EPIDAUROS*: (31) c. 335-325 BC IG IV (1)² 106 I, 60, 62; SEG XXV 389, [19], 36
—TROIZEN: (32) iv BC IG IV (1) 764, 4 (s. Ἀριστοκράτης)
ARKADIA:
—KYNOURIOI: (33) 369-361 BC ib. v (2) 1, 41; Tod, GHI II 132 (date)
—MANTINEIA-ANTIGONEIA: (34) c. 230-200 BC BCH 45 (1921) p. 13 II, 113
—MEGALOPOLIS: (35) ii AD IG V (2) 463 (M. Τάδιος Σπεδιανός) ?= (75); (36) ~ ib. (Τάδιος Τειμοκράτης: s. M. Τάδιος Σπεδιανός, Κλ. Ἰούλιττα)

ELIS: (37) iv BC Hp., Epid. v 2
ELIS?: (38) v BC IvOl 13, 1, 9 (s. Μάληξ)
EPIROS:
—AMBRAKIA: (39) f. ii BC AD 39 (1984) Chron. p. 190 + pl. 77 γ (f. Καλλικλῆς)
—BOUTHROTOS (PRASAIBOI):
——Netidioi: (40) a. 163 BC IBouthrot 91, 8 (SEG XXXII 623)
—NIKOPOLIS: (41) imp. ILS 8865 (Sarikakis 175)
ILLYRIA:
—AMANTIA: (42) ii BC Ugolini, Alb. Ant. 1 p. 195 no. 16
—APOLLONIA: (43) c. 250-50 BC Maier 89 (coin) (Ceka 121) (pryt.); (44) ~ Maier 95 (coin) (Ceka 116) (money.)
KEPHALLENIA:
—PRONNOI: (45) c. 210 BC IG IX (1)² (1) 31, 95 (f. Σωσικράτης, Ἰσόδαμος, Σωκράτης, Σωτίων)
KORINTHIA:
—KORINTH: (46) ?s. v BC Hesp. 41 (1972) p. 153 no. 16; (47) 431 BC Th. ii 33. 1 (f. Τιμόξενος); (48) 70 BC Breccia, Monum. 1 p. 126 c, 14 (f. Φίλιππος)
—SIKYON: (49) 327-326 BC CID II 97, 30; 99 A, [1]; 120 A, 43 (Skalet 324) (f. Κράτης); (50) ii AD SEG XVIII 139 a, 2 (Ἰούλ. Τειμοκράτης)
LAKONIA: (51) inc. Ath. 15c (Poralla² 701; Bradford (9)); (52) 72 BC IG V (1) 1114, 3 + p. 306 add.; 1146, 32 ([Τι]μοκράτης—1114)
—ASINE: (53) 266 BC PSorb 14, 7; (54) 191-146 BC BMC Pelop. p. 13 no. 152; BCH 75 (1951) p. 134 no. 2 (coin)
—PELLANA: (55) 195 BC Plb. xviii 17. 1; Liv. xxxiv 29. 14; 40. 7 (Bradford (8)) (or Achaia Pellene)
—SPARTA: (56) 429 BC Th. ii 85. 1; 92. 3 (Poralla² 699); (57) 369 BC X., HG vii 1. 13 (Poralla² 700); (58) iii-ii BC SEG XXXVI 364; (59) s. i BC IG V (1) 94, 10 (Bradford (1)) (s. Ἀγη—); (60) imp. IG V (1) 609, 1 (Τιμοκρά[της]?); (61) c. 30-20 BC ib. 211, 35 (Bradford (13)) (f. Δαμάγητος); (62) c. 25-1 BC IG V (1) 210, 2 (Bradford (2)) (s. Δαμοκράτης); (63) ~ IG V (1) 210, 24 (Bradford (3)) (s. Διονυσόδωρος); (64) i BC/i AD? IG V (1) 264 (Artemis Orthia p. 298 no. 4; Bradford (4)) (s. Ἐπινικίδας); (65) c. 80-90 AD IG V (1) 674, 12 (Bradford (14)) (f. Δάμιππος); (66) c. 80-100 AD SEG XI 608, 3 (Bradford (12)) (f. Ἀριστοκράτης); (67) c. 100-110 AD SEG XI 611, 5 (Bradford (15)) (f. Καλλίστρατος); (68) 137 AD IG V (1) 59, 7; SEG XI 521 b, [6] (Bradford (5)) (Τει-: s. Καλλίστρατος); (69) c. 140-145 AD IG V (1) 1314, 41 (Bradford (16)) (I f. Τιμοκράτης II); (70) ~ IG V (1) 1314, 41 (Bradford (7)) (II s. Τιμοκράτης I)
——Limnai: (71) c. 70-100 AD IG V (1) 676, 12 (Bradford (6)) ([Τι]μοκράτης: s. Σωτίων)
—THALAMAI: (72) iii/ii BC IG V (1) 1322
MESSENIA:
—ASINE: (73) 191-146 BC BMC Pelop. p. 13 no. 152; BM coin 1920 5-15-121 (coin)
—MESSENE: (74) 31 BC-14 AD SEG XXIII 207, 31 (f. Ἀσκλάπων, Ξενοκράτης); (75) s. ii AD AR 1983-84, p. 30 with fig. 42 (M. Τάδιος Τειμοκράτης: f. M. Τάδιος Λυκόρτας) ?= (35)
—THOURIA: (76) f. ii BC SEG XI 972, 41 (f. Ἀριστοφάνης); (77) ~ ib. l. 119 (f. Δαμάτριος)
S. ITALY (CALABRIA):
—TARAS-TARENTUM: (78) iv/iii BC IG XIV 668 I, 3 (Landi, DISMG 194)
S. ITALY (LUCANIA):
—HERAKLEIA:
——(ha. ἔμβολος): (79) iv/iii BC IGSI 1 I, 166 (DGE 62; Uguzzoni–Ghinatti I) (f. Ἡρακλείδας)
SICILY:
—AKRAGAS: (80) vi BC Luc., Phal. 1 9 (fict.)
—KAMARINA: (81) hell. SEG XXXIX 1001, 8 (s. Σωφρονίδας)

—SYRACUSE: (82) c. 365 BC X., HG vii 4. 12 ?= (83); (83) 361 BC Plu., Dio 21; Ael., VH xii 47 ?= (82); (84) c. 264 BC IG XII (5) 1061, 2 (f. Ἱάρων)
ZAKYNTHOS: (85) c. 245-236 BC ib. IX (1)² (1) 25, 67 (s. Ἄγιππος)

**Τιμοκράτις**

ARGOLIS:
—EPIDAUROS: (1) ii BC ib. IV (1)² 213 (d. Τίμων, m. Τελέας); (2) ~ SEG XV 211 (d. Ἱππίας)
MESSENIA: (3) ii AD AD 2 (1916) p. 117 no. 82 (d. Ἀγαθίας)

**Τιμοκρέτης**

ARKADIA:
—TEGEA: (1) m. iv BC IG V (2) 6, 98 (f. Εὔδαμος); (2) s. iii BC ib. 36, 127; (3) ii BC ib. 145 (f. Πολίας)
——(Hippothoitai): (4) iv/iii BC ib. 38, 48 (s. Ἀρισταῖος)
KEPHALLENIA:
—PRONNOI: (5) v BC SBBerlAk 1935, p. 713 (AD 24 (1969) Chron. p. 273) (Τιμοκρέτος (gen.))

**Τιμοκρῆς**

ARKADIA:
—TEGEA:
——(Apolloniatai): (1) m. iii BC IG V (2) 36, 100 (Τιμόκρεος (gen.): f. Τιμοκλῆς)

**Τιμοκρίτα**

ARGOLIS:
—PHLEIOUS: (1) iii BC ib. IV (1) 471 (Τιμοκρίτ[α])

**Τιμόκριτος**

AIGINA: (1) ?473 BC Pi., N. iv, 13 (f. Τιμάσαρχος)
AKARNANIA:
—THYRREION: (2) ?s. iii BC GVI 749, 2 (IG IX (1)² (2) 298)
ARGOLIS:
—ARGOS:
——Mykenai (Daiphonteis): (3) 195 BC ib. IV (1) 497, 5 ([Τι]μόκριτος: f. Δελφίων)
——EPIDAUROS: (4) ?iii BC Peek, IAEpid 226, 1 ([Τιμ]όκρ[ρ]ιτος: s. Τιμιάδας)
EPIROS:
—ARGETHIA: (5) f. ii BC BCH 45 (1921) p. 30 V D b, 5
LAKONIA:
—SPARTA: (6) s. i BC IG V (1) 135, 9 (Bradford (1)) (s. Ξένων); (7) c. 105-110 AD IG V (1) 97, 17; SEG XI 564, 11 (Bradford (3)) (Τειμόκριτος—SEG: f. Ἄλκαστος); (8) m. ii AD IG V (1) 160, 3 (Bradford (2))

**Τιμόλα**

AITOLIA:
—KALLION/KALLIPOLIS: (1) imp. IG IX (1)² (1) 159 (fem. nom./masc. gen.?)

**Τιμόλαος**

AIGINA: (1) c. 230-200 BC BCH 45 (1921) p. 14 II, 143 (f. Τιμόδαμος)
AITOLIA:
—APERANTOI: (2) iii BC SBBerlAk 1936, p. 388 no. 2, 6 (L'Illyrie mérid. 1 p. 110 fig. 7) (f. Κρατῖνος)
AITOLIA?: (3) iii BC FD III (4) 131, 3 (Τιμ[όλαος?]: s. Ἀρισταινέτα); (4) ~ ib. 130-1 (f. Ἀρισταινέτα)
AKARNANIA:
—THYRREION: (5) iii-ii BC SEG XXVII 159, 1; cf. PAE 1977, pl. 244 a (s. Σωτίων)
ELIS: (6) m. ii BC IvOl 411; (7) 20-16 BC ib. 65, 9 (s. Ἀλεξίων)
KORINTHIA:
—KORINTH: (8) 411-394 BC RE (2)
LAKONIA:
—SPARTA: (9) 192 BC Plb. xx 12. 2-3; Plu., Phil. 15 (Bradford (1))
MESSENIA:
—MESSENE: (10) ii/i BC IG V (1) 1437, 17

**Τιμόλας**

SICILY:
—HIMERA: (11) s. vi BC *Himera* 2 p. 692 no. 191 (vase) (Τιμόλα[ος])

**Τιμόλας**

ELIS: (1) i BC-i AD *IvOl* 218 (s. Ἀρχιάδας, f. Ἀρχιάδας)
KORINTHIA:
—KORINTH: (2) 337 BC *CID* II 74 I, 75 (f. Εὐπειθίδας)
LAKONIA:
—SPARTA: (3) c. 30-20 BC *IG* V (1) 211, 43 (Bradford (3)) (f. Τάρας); (4) c. 25-1 BC *IG* V (1) 212, 41 (Bradford (2)) (s. Τάρας); (5) i/ii AD *BSA* 89 (1994) p. 434 no. 3 (Τιμόλας: s. Νικοκράτης)
SICILY:
—TAUROMENION: (6) c. 212 BC *IG* XIV 421 an. 29 (*SGDI* 5219) (s. Ξένων); (7) c. 153-143 BC *IG* XIV 421 an. 88; 421 an. 98 (*SGDI* 5219); *IGSI* 4 III (IV), 17 an. 88 (s. Ξένων); (8) c. 148 BC ib. l. 58 an. 93 + *Comptes et Inventaires* p. 178 (*SEG* XXXVIII 975 n. on. l. 58) ([Τι]μόλας: s. Φιλόξενος)

**Τιμολέων**

AKARNANIA:
—KORONTA: (1) iv/iii BC ib. XXIX 476 (s. Ἀντιλέων)
ELIS: (2) 272 BC Plu., *Mor.* 252 B
KORINTHIA:
—KORINTH: (3) c. 400-334 BC *RE* (-) (s. Τιμόδαμος, Δαμαρίστα); (4) c. 221 BC *IG* IV (1)² 42, 23 (f. Πόμπις)
MESSENIA:
—MESSENE: (5) iii BC *SEG* XXIII 209, 10

**Τιμόλοχος**

ACHAIA:
—AIGION: (1) ?228-215 BC *SGDI* 2525, 6 (f. Θευκλῆς)
AITOLIA: (2) m. iii BC *IG* XII (5) 857, 11 + IX (1)² (1) 191 ?= (5); (3) ?254 BC *Syll*³ 436, 2; Nachtergael, *Les Galates* 9, 3
—KALYDON: (4) c. 142 BC *IG* IX (1)² (1) 137, 47 (s. Μενέστρατος)
—POTIDANIA: (5) 263-262 BC ib. 3 A, 19 ?= (2)

**Τιμόμαχος**

ACHAIA:
—DYME: (1) s. iii BC *SEG* XIII 278, 17 (Τιμόμα[χος])
AIGINA: (2) ?275 BC *FD* III (1) 195, 2 (s. Εὐσθένης)
ARGOLIS:
—ARGOS: (3) ii-i BC *SEG* XXXIV 815 (s. Τιμόπολις)
ARKADIA:
—MEGALOPOLIS: (4) hell. *IG* V (2) 469. 25 (tile) (Τιμόμα.) ?= (5); (5) hell.? ib. p. 146 no. 553. 11 (tile) ([Τι]μόμα[χος]) ?= (4)
EPIROS:
—BOUTHROTOS (PRASAIBOI): (6) a. 163 BC *IBouthrot* 19, 3 (*SEG* XXXVIII 476)
KEPHALLENIA:
—SAME: (7) c. 230-200 BC *BCH* 45 (1921) p. 14 II, 141 (f. Τίμαιος, Ξενόλαος, Φρυνίων)

**Τιμομένης**

LAKONIA:
—SPARTA: (1) ii/i BC *IG* V (1) 966, 1 (Bradford (2)) (Τιμομέ[νη]ς: f. Ἐπηρατίδας); (2) c. 140-160 AD *IG* V (1) 109, 1, 9; 295, 2 (*Artemis Orthia* p. 322 no. 48; Bradford (1)) ([Τιμο]μένης—295)

**Τιμόνικος**

ARGOLIS:
—EPIDAUROS: (1) c. 340-330 BC *IG* IV (1)² 112, 23
ARKADIA: (2) hell. *Memnonion* 549 ([Τι]μόνικος—ed., [Δα]μόνικος?—*LGPN*)

**Τιμονόη**

ILLYRIA:
—AULON: (1) imp. *CIG* 1829 (Ἰουν. Τιμνην—apogr., Τιμ(ο)ν(ό)η—*CIG*: d. Ἰούν. Καστελλανός, Σαυφηΐα Χρύση)

**Τιμοξένα**

ACHAIA:
—PELLENE: (1) 341 BC *CID* II 12 I, 63 (d. Θεάρκης)

**Τιμόξενος**

ACHAIA: (1) s. iii BC *RE* (1); (2) 146 BC *IG* IV (1)² 28, 121 (s. Τίμων: synoikos)
ACHAIA?: (3) 37 AD ib. VII 2711, 36 (II s. Τιμόξενος I); (4) ~ ib. l. 37 ([Τ]ειμόξενος: I f. Τιμόξενος II)
AIGINA: (5) ?i AD *Alt-Ägina* I (2) p. 45 no. 14 (Τιμόξε[νος])
AITOLIA:
—KALLION/KALLIPOLIS: (6) 173 BC *SGDI* 1856, 23 ?= (7); (7) 153-144 BC ib. 2279, 10 ?= (6)
AKARNANIA?: (8) ii BC Unp. (Agrinion Mus.) (s. Ἵππαρχος)
ARGOLIS:
—PHLEIOUS: (9) v BC B. ix 102 (Τιμόξ[ενος]: f. Αὐτομήδης)
ARKADIA:
—STYMPHALOS: (10) ?303-301 BC *IG* V (2) 351, 11; *SEG* XXXI 351 (date)
—TEGEA: (11) iv/iii BC *IG* V (2) 38, 10
——(Athaneatai): (11) iv/iii BC *IG* V (2) 38, 10
ILLYRIA:
—APOLLONIA: (12) c. 250-50 BC Maier 90; Münsterberg p. 37 (Ceka 23); Bakërr Hoard p. 64 nos. 98-102 (coin) (Ceka 105) (pryt.); (13) i BC Maier 125 (coin) (f. Πρεσβύλος)
KERKYRA: (14) ii/iii AD Clem. Al., *Strom.* i 132. 3 (dub.)
KORINTHIA:
—KORINTH: (15) 431 BC Th. ii 33. 1 (s. Τιμοκράτης)
LAKONIA:
—SPARTA: (16) s. i BC *IG* V (1) 93, 35; 211, 42 (Bradford (4)) (f. Φιλοκλῆς); (17) i BC/i AD *IG* V (1) 48, 6 (Bradford (3)) (f. Καλλικρατίδας); (18) ~ *IG* V (1) 48, 7 (Bradford (1)) (s. Φιλοκλῆς); (19) ~ *IG* V (1) 48, 9; *SEG* XI 974, 1, 27 (Bradford (2)) (f. Δαμόχαρις)
MESSENIA:
—THOURIA: (20) s. iii BC *IG* V (1) 1386, 8 (s. Τιμογένης); (21) ~ ib. l. 11 (s. Τίμων)
S. ITALY (CALABRIA):
—TARAS-TARENTUM?: (22) f. v BC *CVA Adolphseck* 1 pl. 41
S. ITALY (CAMPANIA): (23) iv BC *Mon. Ant.* 22 (1913) p. 703 (potter)

**Τιμόπολις**

ARGOLIS:
—ARGOS: (1) ii-i BC *SEG* XXXIV 815 (f. Τιμόμαχος)

**Τιμόπτολις**

ELIS: (1) inc. Paus. vi 15. 7 (s. Λάμπις)

**Τιμοσθένης**

ACHAIA:
—DYME: (1) iii BC *AJPh* 31 (1910) p. 399 no. 74 b, 1 (I f. Τιμοσθένης II); (2) ~ ib. l. 1 (II s. Τιμοσθένης I)
AIGINA: (3) f. v BC Pi., *O.* viii, 15; cf. Klee p. 102 no. 119 (s. Ἰφίων)
AKARNANIA:
—OINIADAI: (4) c. 325-315 BC *Hesp.* 57 (1988) p. 148 A, 37 (*SEG* XXXVI 331); cf. *Hesp.* 48 (1979) pp. 78 f. with pl. 22 c (f. Φίλων)
ARGOLIS:
—ARGOS: (5) v-iv BC Iamb., *VP* 267 (*FVS* 1 p. 447)

—EPIDAUROS: (6) ii-i BC Peek, *IAEpid* 153. 14 (s. Τίμων)
——(Dymanes): (7) 146 BC *IG* IV (1)² 28, 8 (f. Φιλάγαθος)
—EPIDAUROS*: (8) ii AD Peek, *IAEpid* 296 (Τιμοσθέ[νης]: f. —α)
ARKADIA: (9) iii BC *IG* V (2) 415, 5 (*IPArk* 23) (Τιμοσθ[έ]νης: s. Ἀρίσαμος)
ELIS: (10) iv/iii BC Moretti, *Olymp.* 505
ILLYRIA:
—APOLLONIA: (11) ?iii BC *IApoll* 383 (s. Τεισαμενός)
KORINTHIA:
—KORINTH: (12) m. iii BC *Corinth* VIII (1) 60 (f. Καφισοτέλης); (13) c. 221 BC *IG* IV (1)² 42, 25 (s. Τίμυλλος); (14) a. 191 BC *SEG* XXVI 392, 9 (s. Ἀγαθανδρίδας)
MESSENIA:
—THOURIA: (15) f. ii BC ib. XI 972, 88 (s. Κλέων)

**Τιμοσθενίδας**

LAKONIA:
—SPARTA: (1) c. 133 AD ib. 580, 4 (Bradford (-)) (Τειμοσθε[νίδας]: f. Πεισίδαμος) ?= (2); (2) c. 140-160 AD *IG* V (1) 113, 3; *SEG* XI 618 (name) (Bradford (-)) ([Δαμ]οσθενίδας?—*IG*, [Τιμ]οσθενίδας?—*SEG*: s. Πεισίας) ?= (1)

**Τιμοσθενίς**

LAKONIA:
—SPARTA: (1) i-ii AD *IG* V (1) 654, 7 (Bradford (3)) (Τει-: d. Τιμοκλῆς); (2) c. 10-70 AD *IG* IV (1)² 84, 40; 85, 3; 86, 9, 20, 30 + Peek, *IAEpid* 36; *IG* IV (1)² 604, 5; 670, 2; 681, 2; V (1) 478, 4; Peek, *NIEpid* 51; *BSA* 80 (1985) pp. 215-9; 249-53 (ident., stemma) (Bradford (1)) (and Argolis Epidauros: Στατιλία Τειμοσθενίς: d. Δαμάρης, m. Τ. Στατίλιος Λαμπρίας (Epidauros), Μεμμία Πασιχάρεια (Epidauros)); (3) m. i AD *IG* V (1) 580 (Bradford (2)) (Μεμμία Τειμοσθενίς: d. Π. Μέμμιος Πρατόλας, Μεμμία Πασιχάρεια (Epidauros))

**Τιμοστράτα**

ARGOLIS:
—EPIDAUROS*: (1) ii-i BC Peek, *IAEpid* 318, 2 (Τιμοστ[ράτα])

**Τιμοστρατίδας**

ARKADIA:
—ORCHOMENOS: (1) ?c. 369-361 BC *BCH* 102 (1978) p. 348, 33 (*IPArk* 14)

**Τιμοστρατίς**

ARGOLIS:
—EPIDAUROS: (1) hell.? *SEG* XXIX 381

**Τιμόστρατος**

AKARNANIA:
—ECHINOS: (1) hell.? ib. XLII 485 (f. Τιμοκράτης)
—THYRREION: (2) ii BC *IG* IX (1)² (2) 332
ARGOLIS:
—ARGOS: (3) 146 BC Unp. (Ch. Kritzas)
—EPIDAUROS: (4) c. 221 BC *IG* IV (1)² 42, 12; (5) ii-i BC Peek, *IAEpid* 318, 6 (Τιμόστ[ρατος]: f. Καλλιφάης)
—HERMIONE: (6) iii BC *IG* IV (1) 728, 6 (s. Λακρατεύς); (7) ~ ib. l. 27
ARKADIA:
—PALLANTION: (8) a. 316 BC *SEG* XI 1084, 35 (Perlman A.3) (s. Ἀλκίας)
—TEGEA: (9) ii BC *IG* V (2) 43, 6 (s. Ἀριστ—)
——(Apolloniatai): (10) iv/iii BC ib. 38, 33 (Τιμόσ[τρατος]: s. Ξενοκλῆς)
——(Athaneatai): (11) iv/iii BC ib. l. 2 (f. —σθένης)
——(Hippothoitai): (12) f. iii BC ib. 36, 71 (f. Ἀρισταῖος)
KORINTHIA:
—KORINTH: (13) iii BC *CIA* III App. 73

**Τιμοτέλης**
LAKONIA:
—SPARTA: (**14**) s. i BC *IG* v (1) 254 (*Artemis Orthia* p. 355 no. 141; Bradford (1)); (**15**) c. 100-125 AD *IG* v (1) 137, 21 (Bradford (3)) (f. Καλλικράτης); (**16**) m. ii AD *IG* v (1) 160, 4 (Bradford (2))

**Τιμοτέλης**
ARKADIA:
—MANTINEIA-ANTIGONEIA: (**1**) c. 300-221 BC *IG* v (2) 323. 46 (tessera) (f. Λεύκιππος)
LAKONIA:
—SPARTA: (**2**) c. 150-160 AD ib. v (1) 71 II, 9 (Bradford (2)) (I f. Τιμοτέλης II); (**3**) ~ *IG* v (1) 71 II, 9 (Bradford (1)) (II s. Τιμοτέλης I)

**Τιμοῦχος**
ARKADIA:
—MANTINEIA-ANTIGONEIA: (**1**) c. 225 BC *SEG* XI 414, 37 (Perlman E.5) (f. Λεότιμος)

**Τιμοφάνης**
ACHAIA:
—DYME*: (**1**) c. 219 BC *SGDI* 1612, 14-15 (*Tyche* 5 (1990) p. 124) (f. Κλεαφάνης, Νικομένης)
KORINTHIA:
—KORINTH: (**2**) c. 400-345 BC *RE* (-) (s. Τιμόδαμος, Δαμαρίστα)
LAKONIA:
—SPARTA: (**3**) s. i BC *IG* v (1) 133, 5 (Bradford (-)) (f. Δίων)

**Τιμόφαντος**
ARKADIA:
—MANTINEIA-ANTIGONEIA:
——(Hoplodmia): (**1**) m. iv BC *IG* v (2) 271, 13 (s. Ἄλκιππος)

**Τιμοφράδης**
LEUKAS: (**1**) 356-354 BC ib. IV (1)² 95, 20 (Perlman E.2); Perlman p. 40 f. (date)

**Τιμοχάρης**
S. ITALY (BRUTTIUM):
—KROTON?: (**1**) m. iii BC *IG* XII Suppl. p. 138 no. 313, 5 (Τιμοχά[ρης])

**Τίμυλλος**
KORINTHIA:
—KORINTH: (**1**) c. 221 BC ib. IV (1)² 42, 25 (f. Τιμοσθένης)

**Τιμύλος**
ARGOLIS:
—EPIDAUROS: (**1**) 336 BC *CID* II 75 II, 51; 76 II, 29 (s. Λαγόρας); (**2**) iii BC *IG* IV (1)² 165, 7 (Τιμύλ[ος])
LAKONIA:
—OITYLOS: (**3**) iii/ii BC ib. v (1) 1295, 10 (Bradford (-))

**Τιμύχα**
LAKONIA:
—SPARTA?: (**1**) f. iv BC Iamb., *VP* 189; 192-4; 267 (*FVS* 1 p. 448; Poralla² 702) (and S. Italy (Bruttium) Kroton)

**Τιμώ**
AKARNANIA:
—AKTION?: (**1**) iii BC *SBBerlAk* 1936, p. 363 no. 4 (Τιμοῖ (voc.))
ARGOLIS:
—EPIDAUROS: (**2**) iii BC *IG* IV (1)² 349 (d. Δαμόφιλος)
ARKADIA?: (**3**) iii/ii BC ib. v (1) 724, 6 (Bradford (-))
ILLYRIA: (**4**) 139-122 BC *FD* III (2) 222, 4, 5, 7, 9 (m. Σωκράτεια: slave/freed.)
—EPIDAMNOS-DYRRHACHION: (**5**) hell. *IDyrrh* 24 (d. Ἑορταῖος)

ITHAKE: (**6**) iv BC *SEG* XXIX 484 (Τιμῶς (fem. gen.)—Masson and *IG* arch., Τῖμος—*Op. Ath.*)
S. ITALY (BRUTTIUM):
—SYBARIS-THOURIOI-COPIAE: (**7**) ?c. 550 BC Landi, *DISMG* 253 (loomweight); *LSAG*² p. 456 no. F (date); cf. *SEG* XLI 853 (-μό)
SICILY:
—SYRACUSE: (**8**) hell.-imp. *IG* XII (1) 472

**Τίμων**
ACHAIA: (**1**) 146 BC ib. IV (1)² 28, 83 (s. Εὐθύδαμος: synoikos); (**2**) ~ ib. l. 121 (f. Τιμόξενος: synoikos)
—DYME: (**3**) c. 270 BC ib. IX (1)² (1) 13, 35 (s. Ἀθηνάδας)
—DYME*: (**4**) c. 219 BC *SGDI* 1612, 38 (*Tyche* 5 (1990) p. 124) (s. Εὔανδρος)
AIGINA: (**5**) ii-i BC *ASAA* 2 (1916) p. 169 no. 130
AITOLIA:
—KALYDON: (**6**) s. ii BC *SEG* XXV 621, 4 (f. Λυσικλῆς)
—THERMOS*: (**7**) s. iii BC *IG* IX (1)² (1) 60 V, 3; (**8**) ~ ib. 60 VII, 15
AKARNANIA:
—ANAKTORION: (**9**) iii BC ib. IX (1)² (2) 227 ([T]ίμων)
—PALAIROS: (**10**) iii/ii BC ib. 551
—STRATOS: (**11**) 154 BC *SGDI* 1908, 15 (s. Τιμόθεος)
ARGOLIS:
—ARGOS: (**12**) f. iv BC *SEG* XIV 320; (**13**) c. 210-207 BC *IG* IV (1)² 73, 8; *SEG* XXXV 303 (date) (f. Τιμοκράτης); (**14**) ?170 BC *IG* II² 2315, 18; Habicht, *Athen hell. Zeit* pp. 118-19 (date); p. 133 (ethn.) (f. Νίκανδρος)
—ARGOS?: (**15**) f. ii BC *Hesp.* 40 (1971) pp. 197-8 no. 51, 11 (f. Στράτων)
—EPIDAUROS: (**16**) ?iii BC Peek, *IAEpid* 123 (s. Σωτᾶς); (**17**) ii BC *IG* IV (1)² 213 (f. Τιμοκράτις); (**18**) ii-i BC Peek, *IAEpid* 153. 14 (Τί[μ]ω[ν]: f. Τιμοσθένης)
—PHLEIOUS: (**19**) c. 320-230 BC *RE* (13) (s. Τίμαρχος); (**20**) iii BC *IG* IV (1) 472 (Τιμων—?)
ARKADIA:
—PALLANTION: (**21**) a. 316 BC *SEG* XI 1084, 34 (Perlman A.3) (f. Μίλων)
—TEGEA: (**22**) 369 BC *RE* (1) (and Arkadia Megalopolis: oikist)
ELIS: (**23**) c. 400-365 BC ib. (3-4); Moretti, *Olymp.* 364 (s. Αἴγυπτος, f. Αἴγυπτος); (**24**) ?320 BC *IG* v (2) 549, 3 (f. Δαμέας); (**25**) iii/ii BC *RE* (2); Moretti, *Olymp.* 601; (**26**) 36-24 BC *IvOl* 59, [18]; 62, 5 (f. Μικκίας: mantis/Klytiadai)
EPIROS:
—AMBRAKIA: (**27**) ?253 BC Nachtergael, *Les Galates* 10, 62 (f. Δαμότιμος); (**28**) f. ii BC *IC* 2 p. 25 no. 8 C (f. —όδωρος); (**29**) ~ ib. (s. Δαμίων)
KEPHALLENIA:
—SAME: (**30**) 208 BC *IMM* 35, 2 (s. Σώτακος)
KERKYRA: (**31**) iv/iii BC *IG* IX (1) 976, 2 (s. Στράτων); (**32**) hell.? Unp. (*IG* arch.) (s. Θεκλῆς, Τιμαρέτα)
KORINTHIA:
—SIKYON: (**33**) vi/v BC *SEG* XI 244, 10 (-μōν)
LAKONIA:
—SPARTA: (**34**) iii-ii BC ib. XXXVI 364; (**35**) i BC *IG* v (1) 338; *Artemis Orthia* p. 342 no. 91 (date) (Bradford (3)) (f. —[κ]λῆς); (**36**) s. i BC *IG* v (1) 95, 3; 211, 7 (Bradford (2)) (s. Τιμοκλῆς); (**37**) c. 30-20 BC *IG* v (1) 211, 3 (Bradford (1)) (s. Στέφανος)
LEUKAS: (**38**) ?256 BC *SGDI* 2659, 2 (*ZPE* 101 (1994) pp. 223 f.) (s. Γάτιμος, f. Βιάνωρ, Πίμφων)
MESSENIA:
—MESSENE:
——(Daiphontidai): (**39**) 11 AD *PAE* 1992, p. 71 A, 22 (f. Σωτᾶς)

—THOURIA: (**40**) s. iii BC *IG* v (1) 1386, 11 (f. Τιμόξενος); (**41**) ii-i BC ib. 1385, 11-12 (f. Νίκιππος, Λεοντεύς); (**42**) f. ii BC *SEG* XI 972, 115 (s. Ἀριστέας)
PELOPONNESE: (**43**) s. iii BC ib. XIII 278, 11 (f. Φαῖδρος)
PELOPONNESE?: (**44**) 11 AD *PAE* 1992, p. 72 B, 6 (f. Ἀλεξᾶς)
S. ITALY (BRUTTIUM):
—LOKROI EPIZEPHYRIOI:
——(Κρα.): (**45**) iv/iii BC De Franciscis 22, 9 (f. Εὔδαμος)
——(Στρ.): (**46**) 276 BC ib. 23, 2; 25, 3 (s. Τιμοκλῆς)
——(Σωτ.): (**47**) 275 BC ib. 12, 6; 25, 3 (f. Νικόδαμος)
——(Τιω.): (**48**) iv/iii BC ib. 20, 16 (s. Καλλικράτης)
——(Τνν.): (**49**) iv/iii BC ib. 14, 6
S. ITALY (LUCANIA):
—METAPONTION: (**50**) inc. Münsterberg p. 12 (coin)
SICILY:
—KAMARINA: (**51**) f. v BC Cordano, *Tessere Pubbliche* 15 ([T]ίμōν: s. Φιλῖνος); (**52**) ~ ib. 18 (-μōν: s. Τέταρτος)
—MORGANTINA: (**53**) ?iv/iii BC *SEG* XXXIX 1009, 6 (s. Ξένων)
—SYRACUSE: (**54**) iii/ii BC *RE* (7); *ID* 399 A passim; 405, 30 f.; 442 B, 74; *IG* XI (4) 759; XII (5) 816-17 (s. Νυμφόδωρος, f. Νυμφόδωρος); (**55**) i BC *SEG* XIV 580

**Τιμῶναξ**
AIGINA: (**1**) 337-324 BC *CID* II 74 I, 78; 76 II, [29]; 97, 32; 99 A, [3]; 102 II B, 36 (Τιμῶναξ—97: f. Νικήρατος)
SICILY:
—TAUROMENION: (**2**) c. 166 BC *IG* XIV 421 an. 75 (*SGDI* 5219) (s. Ξένων)

**Τιμώνασσα**
ARGOLIS:
—ARGOS: (**1**) vi BC *RE* (-) (d. Γοργίλος, m. Ἰοφῶν (Athens), Ἡγησίστρατος (Athens))

**Τιμωνίδας**
EPIROS:
—AMBRAKIA: (**1**) hell.? *SEG* XXXIX 523 (f. Εὐαρέτα)
KORINTHIA:
—KORINTH: (**2**) c. 590-570 BC Amyx 27. 6 (vase) (Lorber 40); Amyx 28. 1 (pinax) (Lorber 41) (-μō-: s. Βίας: potter/painter)
LEUKAS: (**3**) m. iv BC *RE* (-); *FGrH* 561

**Τιναξίνοος**
SICILY:
—GELA-PHINTIAS: (**1**) f. v BC Dubois, *IGDS* 131. 1 (Arena, *Iscr. Sic.* II 45) (-ξοί-)

**Τίνθωρ**
S. ITALY (CAMPANIA):
—NEAPOLIS: (**1**) s. i BC *INap* 141; cf. Leiwo p. 83 no. 27 (f. Μάμαρκος)
SICILY?: (**2**) f. iii BC Vandermersch pp. 175-6 (amph.) (or S. Italy: Τίνθ(ωρ)?)

**Τίππακος**
ILLYRIA:
—KORCA (MOD.): (**1**) hell. *Iliria* 1971, p. 44 fig. 8; *SEG* XXXIII 487 (pithoi)

**Τιτάνιος**
LAKONIA:
—SPARTA: (**1**) ii AD *IG* v (1) 730, 2 (*GVI* 1932; Bradford (-)) (Τει-)

**Τίταρος**
LAKONIA:
—SPARTA:
——Mesoa: (**1**) s. vii BC *Suda* A 1289 (Poralla² 704) (?f. Ἀλκμάν: dub.)

**Τίτας**
SICILY:
—KAMARINA: (1) s. v BC Dubois, *IGDS* 121, 6 (Arena, *Iscr. Sic.* II 143; *SEG* XXXVIII 940; Cordano, 'Camarina VII' 61) (?f. *Διοκλῆς*)
—SABUCINA (MOD.): (2) m. v BC Dubois, *IGDS* 171 (vase) (Arena, *Iscr. Sic.* II 108)

**Τίτελος**
SICILY:
—SELINOUS: (1) f. v BC Dubois, *IGDS* 38, 18 (Arena, *Iscr. Sic.* I 63) (s. *Φοῖνιξ*); (2) ~ Dubois, *IGDS* 38, 19 (Arena, *Iscr. Sic.* I 63) (s. *Νανελαῖος*)

**Τιτιανή**
SICILY:
—SYRACUSE: (1) iii-v AD Strazzulla 378 + Ferrua, *NG* 140 (Wessel 544)

**Τιτίγελλα?**
SICILY:
—SYRACUSE (CHRYSARION): (1) iii-v AD *SEG* XVIII 400 (*Τί<τι>γελλα*—ed.)

**Τίτορμος**
AITOLIA: (1) f. vi BC Hdt. vi 127

**Τίτος**
ARGOLIS:
—ARGOS: (1) imp. *IG* IV (1) 620, 8 (f. *Μαινία Σμύρνα*); (2) ~ *Mnem.* NS 47 (1919) p. 167 no. 17 (*Τίτος*); (3) ~ *SEG* XI 346 (*GVI* 615)
ARKADIA:
—MANTINEIA-ANTIGONEIA: (4) 27 BC-15 AD *IG* V (2) 268, 7; 307 (f. *Εὐφρόσυνος*) ?= (5); (5) ?16 AD ib. 274, 5 (f. *Μᾶρκος*) ?= (4)
—TEGEA: (6) ii-iii AD *SEG* XXXVI 384 (date—*LGPN*)
EPIROS:
—NIKOPOLIS: (7) imp. *IBouthrot* 179 (Ugolini, *Alb. Ant.* 3 p. 123); (8) ?i AD *Ep. Chron.* 31 (1994) p. 42 no. 12 (*AD* 45 (1990) Chron. p. 257 no. 8) (f. *Νικάνωρ*)
ILLYRIA:
—EPIDAMNOS-DYRRHACHION: (9) ii-i BC *IDyrrh* 436 (f. *Φιλιστίδας*); (10) imp. ib. 17 (*Τεί-*: s. *Τιμήν*)
—TAULANTIOI: (11) iv/iii BC Polyaen. viii 19; cf. Beloch, *GG* IV (2) p. 382 n. 1 (?s. *Γλαυκίας*)
LAKONIA:
—SPARTA: (12) c. 175-200 AD *SEG* XI 503, 22 (Bradford (-)) (s. *Λούκιος*)
S. ITALY (BRUTTIUM):
—KROTON: (13) 63 BC Plu., *Cic.* 18
S. ITALY (LUCANIA):
—HERAKLEIA: (14) ii/i BC *ID* 1967 a, 1; 1967 b, 2; 1713, 8; *EAD* XXX 502 (I s. *Σατυρίων*, f. *Σάτυρος*, *Τίτος* II, *Θεοδώρα*, *Ποσείδιππος*); (15) ~ *ID* 1967 b, 2 (II s. *Τίτος* I, *Θεοδώρα* (Teos))
SICILY:
—AKRAI: (16) 35 AD *SEG* XLII 833, 11 (f. *Αὐλία*)
—IAITON: (17) iii-ii BC ib. XXVI 1070. 7 (tiles)

**Τιτταβώ**
SICILY:
—NAXOS: (1) s. v BC Dubois, *IGDS* 1 (vase) (Arena, *Iscr. Sic.* III 75); cf. *SEG* XXXV 1015 (-βό, *Τίτταβος?*—*SEG*)

**Τίτταλος**
SICILY: (1) hell. ib. XXXIII 455 (f. *Σύμμαχος*)

**Τίττελος**
SICILY:
—SEGESTA: (1) f. iii BC *IG* XIV 291 (Dubois, *IGDS* 216); *SEG* XLI 825 (date) (s. *Ἀρτεμίδωρος*); (2) ?ii BC *IG* XIV 287 (Dubois, *IGDS* 213) (f. *Διόδωρος Ἀππειραῖος*); (3) ~ *SEG* XLI 829 ([*Τίττ*]ελος: ?s. *Ἀγ*—)

**Τίττη**
EPIROS:
—NIKOPOLIS: (1) imp. *AE* 1914, p. 254 no. 3

**Τίτυρμος**
AITOLIA:
—PHOLAI: (1) iv BC *IG* II² 10482 = 10036

**Τίτυρος**
MESSENIA:
—PHARAI: (1) ?c. 500-475 BC ib. v (1) 1362 e (Poralla² 705); *LSAG²* p. 206 no. 5 (*Τίτυρ*[ος], *Τίτυλ*[λος]—Skias)

**Τλαμονίδας**
LAKONIA?: (1) 381 BC X., *HG* v 3. 3-4 (Poralla² 706) (*Τλη-*)

**Τλανώ**
ARGOLIS:
—HERMIONE: (1) ?ii-i BC *IG* IV (1) 731 II, 1 (d. *Ἀφροδισία*)

**Τλασίμαχος**
EPIROS:
—AMBRAKIA: (1) 296-292 BC Moretti, *Olymp.* 524-5 (*FGrH* 257 a F4)

**Τλασωνίδας**
ACHAIA:
—PELLENE: (1) c. 400 BC *IG* II² 1386, 6; 1388, 33; 1407, 33 (*Τλησωνίδης*: f. *Γέλων*)

**Τληπόλεμος**
ARGOLIS:
—HERMIONE: (1) ?ii-i BC ib. IV (1) 731 II, 6 (f. *Χαρίτα*)

**Τολμίδας**
ARKADIA:
—TEGEA: (1) f. iii BC ib. v (2) 35, 31 (*Τολμ*[ίδας]: f. *Ἀριστίων*)
ELIS: (2) 401 BC X., *An.* ii 2. 20; iii 1. 46 (-δης); (3) i BC *IvOl* 68, 2 (*Τολ*[μίδας]?)

**Τόλοφος**
AITOLIA:
—OPHIONEIS: (1) 426 BC Th. iii 100. 1

**Τονίος**
KORINTHIA:
—KORINTH: (1) s. vii BC Amyx 21. 1 (vase) (Lorber 57) (her.?)

**Τοξότας**
ARKADIA:
—TEGEA:
——(Krariotai): (1) iii BC *IG* v (2) 40, 19 (*Τοξό*[τ]ας: f. *Δεξίλαος*)

**Τόπερκος**
SICILY:
—KAMARINA: (1) s. v BC Dubois, *IGDS* 121, 4 (Arena, *Iscr. Sic.* II 143; *SEG* XXXVIII 940; Cordano, 'Camarina VII' 48) (τō *Πέρκō*—Arena: f. —*ιξ*)

**Τόπυρος**
S. ITALY (CAMPANIA):
—POMPEII: (1) ?i AD *NScav* 1894, p. 383 (Lat. Topyrus: s. *Πλόκαμος*)

**Τορέας**
MESSENIA:
—MESSENE: (1) 340 BC *FD* III (4) 4, 1 (f. *Σάμιος*)

**Τόρος**
ILLYRIA: (1) ?iii/ii BC *SEG* XXX 529 (f. *Σκενέτα*)

**Τόρων**
ARGOLIS:
—ARGOS: (1) iii BC *IG* IV (1) 772, 3; IV (1)² 228, 1; 698 (s. *Ἀπελλίων*: sculptor)

**Τραγήλιος**
ARGOLIS:
—EPIDAUROS*: (1) c. 370-365 BC Peek, *IAEpid* 52 A, 44

**Τραγίσκος**
S. ITALY (CALABRIA):
—TARAS-TARENTUM: (1) 212 BC *RE* (-)

**Τραγοξίδας**
SICILY:
—GELA-PHINTIAS: (1) ii/i BC *SEG* XXXI 837, 2 (*T. Κοσσούτις*)

**Τράγων**
SICILY: (1) iii-ii BC Vandermersch p. 176 (or S. Italy: *Σ̣τ̣άϊο*[ς] *T.*)

**Τράσιος**
DALMATIA:
—ISSA: (1) iii/ii BC Brunšmid p. 24 no. 12; cf. *BCH* 114 (1990) p. 506 fig. 4 (*Τράσιος*—ed. and Masson, *Ὄλτιος?*: s. *Τρίτος*)

**Τράσος**
ILLYRIA:
—BYLLIONES: (1) ii BC *SEG* XXXVIII 534 (s. *Ἱέρων*)

**Τραύζινα**
ILLYRIA:
—EPIDAMNOS-DYRRHACHION: (1) hell.-imp. *IDyrrh* 416 (d. *Γάϊος*); (2) ~ ib. 417 (d. *Γάϊος*)

**Τραῦζος**
ILLYRIA:
—EPIDAMNOS-DYRRHACHION: (1) hell.-imp. ib. 152 (f. *Γενθίς*); (2) ~ ib. 418 (s. *Ἐπιγένης*); (3) ~ ib. 421 (f. *Τρίτος*)

**Τραῦσος**
ILLYRIA:
—APOLLONIA: (1) imp. *IApoll* 158
S. ITALY (CALABRIA): (2) hell.-imp. *IG* XIV 2406. 83; cf. Susini, *Fonti Salento* p. 176 no. 164 bis (*Τραῖσος*—Susini)

**Τράχαλος**
LAKONIA:
—SPARTA: (1) 328-324 BC *CID* II 32, 36; 95, [15]; 97, 26; 102 II B, 34; 120 A, 24 (Poralla² 707); (2) c. 200 BC *IG* XI (4) 718, 3-4 (*Τρά*[χαλος]?, (*Σ*)*τρα*——ed.: f. *Ξένιππος*: name—*LGPN*)
S. ITALY (APULIA):
—CANNAE: (3) ii-iii AD *Epig. Rom. di Canosa* 33 (Lat. C. Aemilius Trachalus: f. *Μικκίων*, Aemilius Fronto)

**Τρεβέλλιος**
ILLYRIA:
—EPIDAMNOS-DYRRHACHION: (1) hell.-imp. *IDyrrh* 414 (f. *Τηρεύς*)

**Τρέβιος**
S. ITALY (CAMPANIA):
—FRATTE DI SALERNO (MOD.): (1) f. v BC *St. Etr.* 49 (1981) p. 338 no. 28; cf. *LSAG²* p. 457 no. I (vase) (date)
—NEAPOLIS: (2) i BC/i AD *SEG* IV 96 (*INap* 116) (s. *Ἐπίλυτος*); (3) ~ *SEG* IV 98 (*INap* 152) (f. *Ἐπίλυτος*); (4) ~ ib. 109, 2; cf. Leiwo p. 77 no. 21 (f. *Δίκα*); (5) ~ *INap* 173, 2; cf. Leiwo p. 60 no. 1 ([*Τρ*]*έβιο*[ς]: s. *Ζωΐλος*); (6) ~ *INap* 174, 1; cf. Leiwo p. 60 no. 1 (I f. *Τρέβιος* II); (7) ~ *INap* 174, 1; cf. Leiwo p. 60 no. 1 (II s. *Τρέβιος* I); (8) ~ *INap* 174, 6; cf. Leiwo p. 60 no. 1; (9) ~ *INap* 174 bis (*Τρέ*[βιος]: f. *Νυμψία*); (10) ~ ib.
S. ITALY (CAMPANIA)?: (11) s. iii BC *HN²* p. 47; cf. *SNG ANS Etruria–Calabria* 776-7 (locn.) (coins)

## Τρεβώνις

S. ITALY?: **(12)** hell.? *Italic Dialects* 6 (*Τρέβις Σεστιες*); **(13)** c. 179 BC *ID* 442 B, 130 (*Βίβιος Τ.*)

## Τρεβῶνις

SICILY:
—GELA-PHINTIAS: **(1)** ii/i BC *SEG* XXXI 837, 5

## Τρέλλων

SICILY:
—SYRACUSE?: **(1)** v/iv BC *CGF* p. 175 fr. 132 (n. pr.?)

## Τρεῦθος

ARGOLIS:
—HERMIONE: **(1)** iii BC *IG* IV (1) 729 I, 18 (f. *Πασίνομος*); **(2)** ~ ib. 729 II, 11 (f. *Άνανθος*)

## Τριανός

SICILY:
—SYRACUSE*: **(1)** iii-v AD ib. XIV 19; cf. Ferrua, *NG* 356 (*Πρίαμος?*, *Τριάριος?*—*IG*: slave?)

## Τρίβων

ELIS:
—OLYMPIA*: **(1)** vi BC *SEG* XI 1256

## Τριεσπέριος

ARGOLIS:
—ARGOS: **(1)** iv AD ib. XVI 264 (tiles)

## Τρίτα

ARGOLIS:
—EPIDAUROS: **(1)** iv/iii BC *IG* IV (1)² 202

## Τριταῖος

ARKADIA:
—MEGALOPOLIS: **(1)** f. iii BC Paus. viii 27. 11 (f. (ad.) *Άριστόδαμος*)

## Τριτέας

ARKADIA:
—MEGALOPOLIS: **(1)** ?145 BC *IG* v (2) 439, 39 (f. *Κάλλιππος*)
—ORCHOMENOS: **(2)** iv BC *BCH* 63 (1939) p. 145 inv. 2382 (f. *Φίλων*)

## Τρίτευτα

ILLYRIA: **(1)** s. iii BC *RE* (-) (m. *Πίννης* (Ardiaioi))

## Τριτεύτας

ILLYRIA:
—BYLLIONES: **(1)** ?f. ii BC *SEG* XXXVIII 538

## Τριτία

ACHAIA:
—PELLENE: **(1)** ?ii-iii AD ib. XI 1274, 8

## Τρίτιος

ARKADIA:
—MANTINEIA-ANTIGONEIA:
——(Enyalia): **(1)** m. iv BC *IG* v (2) 271, 8 (s. *Ϝικάδιος*)
MESSENIA:
—ABIA: **(2)** i BC/i AD ib. v (1) 1353 (s. *Έργῖνος*)
—THOURIA: **(3)** f. ii BC *SEG* XI 972, 82 (s. *Έπικρατίδας*)

## Τρίτος

DALMATIA:
—ISSA: **(1)** iii/ii BC Brunšmid p. 24 no. 12 (f. *Τράσιος*)
—ISSA?: **(2)** iii-ii BC ib. p. 32 no. 30, [1], 2-3 (*Τρίτο[s]*: s. *Δαμάτριος*, f. *Δαμάτριος*, *Δάμων*)
EPIROS:
—NIKOPOLIS: **(3)** imp. *Ep. Chron.* 31 (1994) p. 41 no. 4 (*AD* 45 (1990) Chron. p. 257 no. 1) (f. *Εὔφρω*)
ILLYRIA: **(4)** hell. *Iliria* 1982 (1), p. 121 no. 48 (tile); cf. p. 123; **(5)** f. ii BC *RE* Supplbd. 3 s.v. Ettritus (-) (Liv. xliv 30. 3) (Lat. et

Tritus/Ettritus?); **(6)** 170 BC Plb. xxviii 8. 9 (n. pr.?)
—APOLLONIA: **(7)** ii-i BC *IApoll* 159 (s. *Πλάτωρ*); **(8)** hell.-imp. ib. 335-6 (s. *Μουσαῖος*); **(9)** imp. ib. 326 (f. *Άγαθίων*); **(10)** ~ ib. 334
—EPIDAMNOS-DYRRHACHION: **(11)** hell. *IDyrrh* 204 (f. *Εὐκλείδας*); **(12)** c. 250-50 BC Maier 345; 390 (coin) (Ceka 419-20) (money.); **(13)** hell.-imp. *IDyrrh* 140 (f. *Βέρσας*); **(14)** ~ ib. 192 (f. *Έπίκτησις*); **(15)** ~ ib. 211 (f. *Εὔστρατος*); **(16)** ~ ib. 340 (f. *Παρμώ*); **(17)** ~ ib. 348 (f. *Πλαῖος*); **(18)** ~ ib. 420; **(19)** ~ ib. 421 (s. *Τραῦζος*)
—EPIDAMNOS-DYRRHACHION (NR.)?: **(20)** ii BC *SEG* XXXVIII 572, 5; cf. *CRAI* 1991, p. 197 ff.; *L'Illyrie mérid.* 2 p. 206 (I f. *Τρίτος* II); **(21)** ~ *SEG* XXXVIII 572, 5; cf. *CRAI* 1991, p. 197 ff.; *L'Illyrie mérid.* 2 p. 206 (II s. *Τρίτος* I); **(22)** ~ *SEG* XXXVIII 572, 9; cf. *CRAI* 1991, p. 197 ff.; *L'Illyrie mérid.* 2 p. 206 (s. *Πιθειός*)
SICILY:
—IAITON: **(23)** hell. *Sic. Arch.* 27 (1994) pp. 34-5 (tile)

## Τρίτυλλα

ARGOLIS:
—EPIDAUROS: **(1)** f. iii BC *IG* IV (1)² 201

## Τρίτυλλος

ARGOLIS:
—EPIDAUROS: **(1)** iii BC ib. 98, 5
—TROIZEN: **(2)** iii BC ib. IV (1) 774, 9; **(3)** 153-144 BC *SGDI* 2295, 16 (s. *Φιλοκράτης*)

## Τριτύμαλλος

MESSENIA: **(1)** 224 BC *RE* (-) (*Τριπύλος*—Plu. *Arat.* 41)

## Τριτώ

ILLYRIA: **(1)** ?iii/ii BC *SEG* XXX 529

## Τρίτων

KEPHALLENIA?: **(1)** i BC-i AD ib. 516; cf. *BE* 1981, no. 68 (locn.) (or Messenia?)
LAKONIA:
—OITYLOS: **(2)** iii/ii BC *IG* v (1) 1295, 5 (Bradford (2))
—SPARTA:
——Limnai: **(3)** c. 70-100 AD *IG* v (1) 676, 14 (Bradford (4)) (I f. *Τρίτων* II); **(4)** ~ *IG* v (1) 676, 14 (Bradford (1)) (II s. *Τρίτων* I)
LAKONIA?: **(5)** i BC-i AD *SEG* XXX 516; *BE* 1981, no. 68 (locn.)
MESSENIA:
—MESSENE: **(6)** iv/iii BC *IG* v (1) 1425, 18 ?= **(7)**; **(7)** f. iii BC *PAE* 1991, p. 99 no. 7, 4 ?= **(6)**; **(8)** s. ii BC *BCH* 95 (1971) p. 544, [3], 12, 17 (f. *Νικομήδης*)
S. ITALY (CALABRIA):
—BRENTESION-BRUNDISIUM*: **(9)** f. i AD *Studi di Antichità* 6 pp. 311-18 (Lat. Verzus Trito: s. *Θῆμος*)

## Τριτωνίς

AIGINA: **(1)** iii-iv AD Alciphr. i 4 (fict.)

## Τριφυλλίων

ARGOLIS:
—METHANA-ARSINOE: **(1)** ?v-iv BC *SEG* XXXIX 364 ([*Τ*]*ριφυλλίων*)

## Τριχᾶς

AITOLIA: **(1)** 244 or 240 BC *SGDI* 2512, 2 + Flacelière p. 402 no. 28 a; Nachtergael, *Les Galates* 59, [3]
—DAIANES: **(2)** 161 BC *IG* IX (1)² (1) 100, 8
—EOITANES: **(3)** 263 BC ib. 17, 54, 62, 70, 76 etc.
—PLEURON: **(4)** f. iii BC *Das Heroon von Kalydon* p. 293, 9

AKARNANIA:
—STRATOS: **(5)** 169 BC *IG* IX (1)² (1) 69 (f. *Άγέλοχος*); **(6)** 161-153 BC ib. p. LII, s.a. 161 BC, 153 BC; IX (1)² (3) 638 12, 1 (?s. *Άγέλοχος*)

## Τροπιανός

S. ITALY (CAMPANIA):
—CAPREAE: **(1)** imp.? ib. XIV 896 (*Κόρινθος Τ.*?—*IG*)

## Τρόπος

ARGOLIS:
—HERMIONE: **(1)** imp. ib. IV (1) 715, 4 (f. *Λουκία*)

## Τροῦθος

LAKONIA:
—SPARTA: **(1)** f. vi BC *SEG* II 70-1 (*Artemis Orthia* p. 368 no. 169. 7-8; Lazzarini 403h-i); *LSAG*² p. 198 no. 6 (Poralla² 707a; Bradford (-))

## Τροφιμᾶς

S. ITALY (APULIA):
—SIPONTUM*: **(1)** ii AD *Epigraphica* 34 (1972) p. 135 (Serricchio, *Iscrizioni di Siponto* 11) (Lat. Laetorius Trophimas: freed.)
S. ITALY (CAMPANIA):
—SALERNUM*: **(2)** imp. *IItal* 1 (1) 210 (*CIL* x 614) (Lat. L. Lartius Trophimas: freed.)

## Τροφίμη

EPIROS:
—NIKOPOLIS: **(1)** i/ii AD *Hellenika* 22 (1969) p. 69 no. 6 (Sarikakis 178) (*Φλ. Τ.*: I m. *Φλ. Τροφίμη* II); **(2)** ~ *Hellenika* 22 (1969) p. 69 no. 6 (Sarikakis 179) (*Φλ. Τ.*: II d. *Φλ. Τροφίμη* I)
ILLYRIA:
—EPIDAMNOS-DYRRHACHION: **(3)** imp. *AEp* 1978, no. 749 (Lat. Novellia Trophime)
S. ITALY (APULIA):
—GNATHIA-EGNATIA: **(4)** imp. *CIL* IX 269 (Lat. Grittia Trophim[e])
—LUCERIA: **(5)** imp. *ASP* 34 (1981) p. 6 no. 4 (Lat. Iunia Trophime)
S. ITALY (CALABRIA):
—BRENTESION-BRUNDISIUM: **(6)** imp. *CIL* IX 64 (Lat. Acceratia Trophime)
S. ITALY (CAMPANIA):
—DIKAIARCHIA-PUTEOLI: **(7)** imp. ib. X 1757 (Lat. Patulcia Trophime); **(8)** ~ ib. 2496 (Lat. Clodia Trophime: m. Harmonia Rufina); **(9)** ~ ib. 2889 (Lat. [P]rastinia Trhofime); **(10)** ~ ib. 2985 (Lat. Sulpicia Trophime); **(11)** ~ ib. 3084 (Lat. Verania Trophime); **(12)** ?i-ii AD ib. 2142 (Lat. Iulia Trofime)
—MISENUM*: **(13)** imp. ib. 3447 (Lat. Titia Trofime)
—POMPEII: **(14)** i BC-i AD ib. IV 2039 (Lat. Trofime)
SICILY:
—NEAITON: **(15)** imp. *Helikon* 2 (1962) p. 497 n. 65
—SYRACUSE: **(16)** iii-v AD *Riv. Arch. Crist.* 36 (1960) p. 41 no. 41; **(17)** ~ *SEG* IV 19 (Wessel 171) + Ferrua, *NG* 275 (*Ματιδία Τ.*)

## Τροφιμιανός

ELIS: **(1)** iii AD *SEG* XV 259, 18
S. ITALY (APULIA):
—CANUSIUM: **(2)** 223 AD *Epig. Rom. di Canosa* 35 IV, 39 (*CIL* IX 338) (Lat. Q. Iunius Trophimianus)
S. ITALY (CAMPANIA):
—DIKAIARCHIA-PUTEOLI: **(3)** imp. *Mem. Accad. Arch. Napoli* 3 (1955) p. 45 (Lat. C. Stonicius Trophimianus)

## Τροφιμίων

S. ITALY (CAMPANIA):
—DIKAIARCHIA-PUTEOLI: **(1)** imp. *AJA* 77 (1973) p. 160 no. 10 (Lat. Sex. Patulcius Trophimion)
SICILY:
—SYRACUSE: **(2)** iii-v AD Ferrua, *NG* 329 (-*μεί*-)

—SYRACUSE (PALATION)?: **(3)** iii-v AD Wessel 6; cf. Ferrua, *NG* 93b

**Τρόφιμος**
ARGOLIS:
—ARGOS: **(1)** iii AD *BCH* 27 (1903) p. 268 no. 20 I-II ([Αὐ]ρ. Τρόφ[ι]μος)
—METHANA-ARSINOE: **(2)** iii AD *IG* IV (1) 856 (Αὐρ. Τ.)
ILLYRIA:
—APOLLONIA: **(3)** ii AD *IApoll* 229
KORINTHIA:
—KORINTH: **(4)** iii AD *PAE* 1965, p. 163 n. 2 (doctor)
—KORINTH?: **(5)** imp.? *IG* IV (1) 365 (doctor)
LAKONIA:
—HYPERTELEATON: **(6)** iv AD *SEG* 11 172
MESSENIA:
—KORONE: **(7)** 246 AD *IG* V (1) 1398, 73 (Ὀπ(πιος) Τ.)
S. ITALY (APULIA):
—CANUSIUM*: **(8)** ii AD *Epig. Rom. di Canosa* 86 (Lat. C. Galbius Trophimus: freed.)
—VENUSIA: **(9)** imp. *CIL* IX 518 (Lat. L. Livius Trophimus)
S. ITALY (CAMPANIA):
—DIKAIARCHIA-PUTEOLI: **(10)** imp. *AJA* 2 (1898) p. 387 no. 37 (Lat. P. Trofymus); **(11)** ~ *CIL* X 2379 (Lat. A. Ducennius Trophimus); **(12)** ~ ib. 2923 (Lat. P. Sabidius Trophimus: f. Sabidia Secunda); **(13)** ~ ib. 3025 (Lat. -cceius Trophim[us]); **(14)** ?i-ii AD ib. 1872 (Lat. M. Antonius Trophimus: f. Antonia Iucunda); **(15)** ?ii AD ib. 2280 (Lat. Ti. Claudius Trophimus)
—DIKAIARCHIA-PUTEOLI*: **(16)** imp. ib. 2523 (Lat. M. Horatius Trophimus: freed.)
—HERCULANEUM: **(17)** i BC-i AD ib. 1403 d I, 27 (Lat. C. Novius Trophimus)
—POMPEII: **(18)** i BC-i AD ib. IV 1630 (Lat. Trophimus); **(19)** ~ ib. 1803 (Lat. Trophimus); **(20)** ~ ib. 4706 (Lat. Trophimus); **(21)** ~ ib. 7309 b (Castrèn 205. 33) (Lat. C. Iulius Trophimus); **(22)** c. 51-62 AD *CIL* IV 3340. 84, 1 (Castrèn 158. 27) (Lat. Epidius Trophimus); **(23)** ~ *CIL* IV 3340. 108, 6 (Castrèn 372. 5) (Lat. L. Sestius Trophimus); **(24)** 55 AD *CIL* IV 3340. 13, 17; 61, 8; 66, 17; 76, 5; 108, [5]; 8957 (Castrèn 210. 4) (Lat. L. Laelius Trophimus)
—POMPEII*: **(25)** i BC-i AD *CIL* IV 8944 (Lat. Trophimus: slave?)
—SALERNUM: **(26)** imp. *IItal* I (1) 143 (*CIL* X 8345) (Lat. T. Litucius Trophimus)
—SALERNUM*: **(27)** i BC/i AD *IItal* I (1) 190 (*CIL* X 1753) (Lat. L. Atilius Trophimus: freed.)
—STABIAE: **(28)** i AD ib. 784 (Lat. C. Pomponius Trophimus)
S. ITALY (LUCANIA):
—POTENTIA: **(29)** ?ii AD *Misc. Gr. Rom.* 8 p. 436 no. 2 (Lat. P. Petronius Trophimus: s. Χρήστη)
SICILY:
—KATANE: **(30)** imp. *NScav* 1956, pp. 181-2 (Lat. Trophimus)
—SYRACUSE: **(31)** imp. ib. 1913, p. 268 (Lat. Trophimus)
—TAUROMENION: **(32)** imp. *IG* XIV 438 (Ῥώσκις Τρόφ[ιμος])

**Τροχιλλᾶς**
EPIROS:
—BOUTHROTOS (PRASAIBOI): **(1)** iii-ii BC *IBouthrot* 167 (Cabanes, *L'Épire* p. 568 no. 46) (f. Πάμφιλος)

**Τροχιμμᾶς**
EPIROS:
—BOUTHROTOS (PRASAIBOI): **(1)** a. 163 BC *IBouthrot* 52, 5 (*SEG* XXXVIII 517) (f. Φιλόξενος)

**Τρυγῆς**
ARGOLIS:
—ARGOS:
——(Aithonidai): **(1)** m. iv BC ib. XVII 146, 5

**Τρυγήτη**
SICILY:
—KAMARINA (NR.): **(1)** iii-v AD *IG* XIV 255 a p. 686 (Pace, *Camarina* p. 165 no. 30); cf. *Riv. Arch. Crist.* 18 (1941) p. 199 no. 71 (Τρυχή-τη—Pace)
—SYRACUSE: **(2)** iii-v AD Strazzulla 237 (Wessel 1333); cf. Ferrua, *NG* 292

**Τρύγητος**
EPIROS:
—ANTIGONEIA: **(1)** v-vi AD *Iliria* 1977-8, p. 234 pl. V b (mosaic)
ILLYRIA:
—EPIDAMNOS-DYRRHACHION: **(2)** i BC-i AD *CIL* III 619 (Sestieri, *ILat. Albania* 36) (Lat. C. Iulius Tryget(us))
S. ITALY (BRUTTIUM):
—HIPPONION-VIBO VALENTIA: **(3)** imp. *Rend. Pont.* 60 (1987-8) p. 273 no. 15 (*CIL* X 84) (Lat. Trygetus)
S. ITALY (CAMPANIA):
—DIKAIARCHIA-PUTEOLI: **(4)** imp. ib. 8059. 156 (seal) (Lat. Trygetus)
SICILY:
—MOTYKA (HORTENSIANA): **(5)** iii-v AD *SEG* XXVII 662 (f. Εὐτυχία)
—SYRACUSE: **(6)** iii-v AD ib. IV 14; cf. Ferrua, *NG* 273 a

**Τρύγων**
SICILY:
—HIMERA?: **(1)** v BC *IG* XIV 597; cf. *ASNP* 20 (1990) p. 425 (-γῶν, Τρυγόν—Manganaro)
—ZANKLE-MESSANA: **(2)** imp. *IG* XIV 412 (Τρυγόνι[ος]?)

**Τρῦπις**
ARGOLIS:
—ARGOS: **(1)** c. 146-32 BC *BMC Pelop.* pp. 145-6 nos. 121-2 (coin)

**Τρύφαινα**
ARGOLIS:
—HERMIONE: **(1)** ?ii-i BC *IG* IV (1) 731 III, 10 (d. Ἀρχῖνος)
S. ITALY (CALABRIA):
—BRENTESION-BRUNDISIUM: **(2)** ii-i AD *CIL* IX 129 (Susini, *Fonti Salento* p. 182 no. 1 a) (Lat. Kaninia Tryphaena)
S. ITALY (CAMPANIA):
—DIKAIARCHIA-PUTEOLI: **(3)** imp. *CIL* X 2190 (Lat. Caecilia Tryphena)
—SURRENTUM: **(4)** imp. ib. 690 (Lat. Valeria Tryfena)
SICILY:
—SYRACUSE: **(5)** hell.-imp. *NS* 594 (d. Φιλίαρχος)

**Τρυφέρα**
ILLYRIA:
—EPIDAMNOS-DYRRHACHION: **(1)** hell.-imp. *IDyrrh* 422; **(2)** ~ ib. 423; **(3)** ~ ib. 424 (d. Γέτας); **(4)** ~ ib. 425 (d. Νίκων)
S. ITALY (APULIA):
—CANUSIUM: **(5)** i-ii AD *Epig. Rom. di Canosa* 58, 5 (*CIL* IX 348) (Lat. Maria Tryphera)
—CANUSIUM*: **(6)** ii/iii AD *Epig. Rom. di Canosa* 65 (Lat. Romania Tryphera: freed.)
S. ITALY (CALABRIA):
—BRENTESION-BRUNDISIUM*: **(7)** imp. *Epigraphica* 25 (1963) p. 37 no. 10 (Lat. [Ce]cilia Truphera: freed.)
S. ITALY (CAMPANIA):
—DIKAIARCHIA-PUTEOLI*: **(8)** imp. *CIL* X 3073 (Lat. Valeria Truphera: freed.)

SICILY:
—PACHINO (MOD.): **(9)** ii-iii AD *Arch. Class.* 17 (1965) p. 199, 5 (d. Ἐλπιδηφόρος, Νίκη)

**Τρύφερος**
ARKADIA:
—TEGEA: **(1)** 165 AD *IG* V (2) 50, 58 (s. Ὠφέλιμος)
LAKONIA:
—SPARTA: **(2)** i-ii AD ib. V (1) 228 (Bradford (3)) (Τρύφε[ρος]: f. —ίμα); **(3)** c. 105-110 AD *IG* V (1) 20 B, 3; *BSA* 26 (1923-5) p. 168 C 7, 3 (Bradford (1)) (s. Ἐπαφρόδιτος)
S. ITALY (CAMPANIA):
—DIKAIARCHIA-PUTEOLI: **(4)** imp. *CIL* X 3022 (Lat. Trifer(us))

**Τρυφηνία**
S. ITALY (CAMPANIA):
—DIKAIARCHIA-PUTEOLI: **(1)** imp. ib. 2982 (Lat. Tryphenia: m. Suettia Victoria)

**Τρύφων**
ACHAIA:
—PATRAI: **(1)** ii BC *Achaean Grave Stelai* 64 (f. Κλεόπολις)
ARGOLIS:
—ARGOS: **(2)** ii/i BC *IG* IV (1) 626; **(3)** c. 160 AD *SEG* III 334, 27; cf. Stephanis 1046 (f. Ζώσιμος)
—EPIDAUROS: **(4)** 216 AD *IG* IV (1)² 404 (M. Αὐρ. Τ.: s. Διόφαντος)
KEPHALLENIA: **(5)** imp.? *Miscellanea* p. 187 no. 7
KORINTHIA:
—KORINTH: **(6)** byz. *Corinth* VIII (3) 556, 5; cf. *TMByz* 9 (1985) p. 363 no. 40
LAKONIA:
—SPARTA: **(7)** c. 80-110 AD *IG* V (1) 97, 8; 674, 9; *SEG* XI 513, 2; 564, 15; 569, 3; 626, 1 (Bradford (-)) (f. Σώανδρος)
S. ITALY (CAMPANIA):
—DIKAIARCHIA-PUTEOLI: **(8)** imp. *CIL* X 2574 (Lat. P. Iulius Tryfo: s. Ὀνήσιμος); **(9)** ii-iii AD *IG* XIV 834 (f. Νιγρῖνος, Ἀγαθοκλῆς)
—HERCULANEUM: **(10)** m. i AD *PdelP* 16 (1961) p. 72 no. 101, 1 (Lat. M. Nonius Tryp(h)o[n])
S. ITALY (CAMPANIA)?: **(11)** imp. *IG* XIV 2414. 54 (tessera)
S. ITALY (LUCANIA):
—ATINA LUCANA: **(12)** imp. *IItal* III (1) 154 (*CIL* X 349) (Lat. Sex. Cellius Tripho)
SICILY:
—KAMARINA (NR.): **(13)** imp. *IG* XIV 255 b (Pace, *Camarina* p. 165 no. 31; Wessel 311)
SICILY?: **(14)** ii-i BC *IGLMP* 33 (s. Ἰκάδιος)

**Τρύφωνα**
S. ITALY (CAMPANIA):
—DIKAIARCHIA-PUTEOLI: **(1)** imp. *CIL* X 2184 (Lat. Caecilia Triphona)

**Τρυφωνιανός**
MESSENIA:
—KORONE: **(1)** 246 AD *IG* V (1) 1398, 41 (Ἀττ. Τ.)
—MESSENE: **(2)** ii-iii AD *SEG* XLI 366 B (Κλ. Δῶρος Τ.) ?= (3); **(3)** 174 AD ib. 337, 3 (s. Εὐχάριστος) ?= (2)

**Τρυφῶσα**
ILLYRIA:
—EPIDAMNOS-DYRRHACHION: **(1)** hell.-imp. *IDyrrh* 426
S. ITALY (CAMPANIA):
—DIKAIARCHIA-PUTEOLI: **(2)** ?i-ii AD *CIL* X 2551 (Lat. Claudia Tryfosa); **(3)** ?ii AD ib. 3138 (Lat. Ulpia Tryphosa)
—DIKAIARCHIA-PUTEOLI*: **(4)** imp. ib. 2523 (Lat. Horatia Tryphosa: freed.)

**Τρωδάντιος**
SICILY:
—LIPARA: (5) imp. ib. 7492 (Libertini, *Isole Eolie* p. 228 no. 5) (Lat. Valeria Tryphosa)

**Τρωδάντιος**
S. ITALY (APULIA):
—SALAPIA: (1) 300-225 BC *SNG ANS Etruria–Calabria* 739 (coins) (*HN²* p. 49)

**Τρωϊάς**
AITOLIA:
—TRICHONION: (1) iii BC *IG* IX (1)² (1) 118
EPIROS:
—ARGOS (AMPHILOCH.): (2) iii BC *SEG* XXXII 561 (m. Σιμάκα)
—MOLOSSOI: (3) iv BC Plu., *Pyrr.* 1. 5 (d. Νεοπτόλεμος, m. Αἰακίδης); (4) iv/iii ib. (d. Αἰακίδης, Φθία (Thessaly))

**Τρωΐλος**
ACHAIA:
—DYME: (1) hell.? *SEG* XIV 373 a (f. Λέαινα)
ARKADIA:
—PHENEOS: (2) 191-146 BC *SNG Cop. Phliasia-Laconia* 344 (coin)
ELIS: (3) 372-368 BC Moretti, *Olymp.* 412-13; cf. *CEG* II 828 (s. Ἀλκίνοος)
LAKONIA:
—SPARTA: (4) ?iii AD *IG* V (1) 728, 1 (*GVI* 1406; Bradford (-))
MESSENIA:
—MESSENE: (5) 126 AD *IG* V (1) 1469, 6; cf. *SEG* XL 366 (Κλ. Τ.)
S. ITALY (BRUTTIUM):
—LOKROI EPIZEPHYRIOI: (6) ii AD Costabile, *Municipium Locrensium* 6 (*CIL* X 20) (Lat. C. Cornelius Troilus: s. Ποντική)

**Τυβροίτας**
AITOLIA:
—BOUKATION: (1) f. ii BC *IG* IX (1)² (1) 98, 5

**Τυδεύς**
ELIS: (1) iv/iii BC Paus. vi 16. 2

**Τύλος**
S. ITALY (CAMPANIA):
—HERCULANEUM*: (1) i BC-i AD *CIL* X 1403 g I, 28 (Lat. C. Livius Tylus: freed.)

**Τυνδαρεύς**
LAKONIA:
—SPARTA: (1) i AD Ap. Ty., *Ep.* 62 (fict.?)

**Τυνδάρης**
LAKONIA:
—SPARTA: (1) c. 50 BC-20 AD *IG* V (1) 209, 3, 24; *SEG* XXXV 331 (date) (Bradford (1)) (s. Σιδέκτας); (2) ?i AD *IG* V (1) 180, 14 + *SEG* XI 635 (Bradford s.v. Τυνδαρεύς (1)) ([Τυν]δάρη[s]); (3) c. 75-150 AD Plu., *Mor.* 717-19; 728 E; *IG* V (1) 74, 4; 87, 5; 446, 6; *SEG* XI 585, 10; XXX 410, 13; Cartledge–Spawforth pp. 178-80 (ident.) (Bradford (4)) (?s. Ζεύξιππος, f. Ζεύξιππος); (4) c. 130 AD *IG* V (1) 60, 4 (Bradford (2)) (Τυνδάρι (dat.))

**Τυνδαρίδας**
SICILY:
—SYRACUSE: (1) 454 BC D.S. xi 86. 4-5 (-δης)

**Τυνδαρίς**
S. ITALY (CAMPANIA):
—POMPEII: (1) i BC-i AD *CIL* IV 5190 (Lat. Tyndaris)
SICILY:
—PANORMOS: (2) imp. ib. X 7321 (Lat. Suetia Tyndaris)

**Τυνδάριχος**
KORINTHIA:
—SIKYON: (1) f. iii BC *RE* (-); *PCG* 4 p. 32 (Skalet 325)

**Τυνδαρίων**
SICILY:
—SYRACUSE?: (1) hell. *IG* XIV 2407. 16; cf. *L'Incidenza dell'Antico* pp. 420 ff. (bullet) (s. Καλλίδαμος)
—TAUROMENION: (2) iv/iii BC *RE* (-)

**Τυννίχας**
AKARNANIA:
—PHOITIAI (NR.): (1) f. iv BC *AD* 25 (1970) Chron. p. 297 β

**Τύννιχος**
LAKONIA:
—SPARTA:
——Pitana: (1) ?vi BC *HE* 1654; Plu., *Mor.* 234 F (Poralla² 708) (f. Θρασύβουλος)

**Τυραννίς**
LAKONIA:
—SPARTA: (1) m. iii AD *SEG* XXXV 337, 3; *BSA* 80 (1985) pp. 225; 239-43 (ident., stemma) (Κλ. Τ.: d. Τιβ. Κλ. Εὔδαμος, Κλ. Δαμοσθένεια)
S. ITALY (CALABRIA):
—BRENTESION-BRUNDISIUM: (2) ii AD *Epigraphica* 27 (1965) p. 164 (Lat. Marcia Tyrannis)
S. ITALY (CAMPANIA):
—DIKAIARCHIA-PUTEOLI: (3) imp. *CIL* X 2360 (Lat. Tyrannis: d. Δανάη)
—NOLA: (4) imp. *NScav* 1900, p. 101 no. 1 (Lat. Papia Tyrannis)

**Τύραννος**
KORINTHIA:
—KORINTH: (1) imp. *SEG* XXXII 364 + *Hesp.* 63 (1994) p. 112 no. 1 (Μάριος Τ.); (2) m. i AD *Corinth* VIII (3) 324 b (Lat. [Pu]blilius Tyrannu[s]); (3) s. ii AD ib. VIII (1) 15, 76 + *SEG* XI 62, 28 (Π. Ὠκλάτιος Τ.)
LAKONIA:
—SPARTA: (4) c. 230-250 AD *IG* V (1) 314, 3 (*Artemis Orthia* p. 335 no. 71); *BSA* 79 (1984) p. 285 no. 17 (date) (Bradford (-)) (Τύραν[νος]: f. Μ. Αὐρ. Πρατέας)
S. ITALY (APULIA):
—CANUSIUM: (5) ?i/ii AD *Epig. Rom. di Canosa* 60 (*CIL* IX 349) (Lat. Tyrannus: slave?)
—LARINUM: (6) imp. ib. 745 (Lat. Tyrannus)
S. ITALY (CAMPANIA):
—CAPREAE: (7) imp. *ZPE* 71 (1988) p. 198 no. 12 (Lat. Tyrann[us])
—DIKAIARCHIA-PUTEOLI*: (8) imp. *CIL* X 2382 (Lat. Cn. Egnatius Tyrannus: freed.)
—POMPEII: (9) i BC-i AD ib. IV 221; 224; Mouritsen p. 109 (date) (Lat. Tyrannus); (10) ~ *CIL* IV 543 (Lat. Tyranus); (11) ~ ib. 8045 (Lat. Tyrannus); (12) ~ ib. 10219 (Lat. Tyrannus); (13) 57 AD ib. 3340. 34, 11 (Lat. Fabius Tyrannus)
—SALERNUM: (14) imp. *IItal* I (1) 197 (*CIL* X 577) (Lat. Ser. Anicius Turannus)
SICILY:
—SYRACUSE: (15) iii-v AD Strazzulla 369 (Wessel 710)

**Τύρβις**
ARGOLIS:
—EPIDAUROS: (1) c. 350-200 BC *SEG* XXVI 452. 3 (Τύρ[β]ις); (2) iii BC *IG* IV (1)² 167, 2 (s. Τήλαιθος)

**Τυρία**
S. ITALY (CAMPANIA):
—POMPEII: (1) i BC-i AD *CIL* IV 2319 e, l; 3119 (Lat. Tyria)

**Τυρίχα**
S. ITALY (CALABRIA):
—TARAS-TARENTUM: (1) iv/iii BC *IG* XIV 668 II, 15 (Landi, *DISMG* 194)

**Τύρος**
DALMATIA:
—ISSA:
——(Dymanes): (1) iv/iii BC Brunšmid p. 8, 31 (f. ...ιος)
SICILY:
—LEONTINOI: (2) v BC *JNG* 33 (1983) p. 12 (coin graffito)

**Τυρρακῖνος**
SICILY:
—HELOROS: (1) f. i BC Cic., *In Verr.* II iii 129 (Lat. Tyracinus)

**Τυρρανά**
SICILY:
—SELINOUS: (1) vi/v BC Dubois, *IGDS* 37 b (Arena, *Iscr. Sic.* I 61 B); cf. *LSAG²* p. 277 no. 38 (ethn.?)

**Τυρρηνός**
S. ITALY (CAMPANIA):
—POMPEII: (1) 56 AD *CIL* IV 3340. 19, 6, 9, 18 (Castrèn 175. 19) (Lat. C. Fulvius Thyrrenus)
ZAKYNTHOS: (2) iii AD Hld. v 18. 5-46 (fict.)

**Τυρσηνίς**
S. ITALY (BRUTTIUM):
—SYBARIS-THOURIOI-COPIAE: (1) ?v BC Iamb., *VP* 267 (*FVS* 1 p. 448)

**Τυρσηνός**
S. ITALY (BRUTTIUM):
—SYBARIS-THOURIOI-COPIAE: (1) ?v BC Iamb., *VP* 267 (*FVS* 1 p. 447)

**Τυρταῖος**
AITOLIA:
—PHISTYON: (1) ii BC *IG* IX (1)² (1) 110 a, 4 (s. Σιμίας)
ARKADIA:
—MANTINEIA-ANTIGONEIA: (2) iv BC Ps.-Plu., *Mor.* 1138 A (fict.?)
LAKONIA:
—SPARTA: (3) m. vii BC *RE* (1); *IEG* 2 pp. 149-63; *IPr* 316, 4 (Poralla² 709; Stephanis 2443) (s. Ἀρχέμβροτος)

**Τυρωνίδας**
ARKADIA:
—TEGEA: (1) arch.? Paus. viii 48. 1

**Τυτέας**
ARKADIA:
—KAPHYAI: (1) m. iii BC *BCH* 38 (1914) p. 462 no. 6, 3 (s. Παντόδαμος)

**Τύφων**
ACHAIA:
—AIGION: (1) vii BC Paus. vi 3. 12 (and S. Italy (Bruttium) Kaulonia: oikist)

**Τυχαῖος**
KORINTHIA:
—SIKYON: (1) vi/v BC *SEG* XI 244, 16
LAKONIA:
—SPARTA: (2) c. 105-110 AD *IG* V (1) 51, 39; 52, 9 (Bradford (1)) (II s. Τυχαῖος I); (3) ~ *IG* V (1) 51, [39]; 52, [9] (Bradford (2)) (I f. Τυχαῖος II)

**Τυχαμένης**
MESSENIA:
—KYPARISSIA: (1) c. 100-90 BC *SEG* XXXIII 290 A, 19; *BSA* 70 (1975) pp. 129-31 (date) (Stephanis 2444) (s. Δεξίθεος)
—MESSENE: (2) 31 BC-14 AD *SEG* XXIII 207, 15 (s. Δορκωνίδας)

## Τύχανδρος
LAKONIA:
—SPARTA: (**1**) ?ii BC *IG* V (1) 912 (tiles) (Brad-
ford (-)) ([*T*]ύχανδρος)

## Τυχανίδας
ARKADIA:
—PHENEOS: (**1**) m. iii BC *IG* IV (1)² 96, 48 (Perlman E.3); Perlman p. 63 f. (date) (f. Γόργιππος)

## Τυχάρετος
LAKONIA:
—SPARTA: (**1**) i-ii AD *IG* V (1) 579 (Bradford (-))
(f. Ἀράτα)

## Τυχέας
ARKADIA:
—TEGEA: (**1**) ii AD *IG* V (2) 55, 82 (f. Ἀντέρως)

## Τύχη
ARKADIA:
—KLEITOR: (**1**) 212 AD *IvOl* 473 (and Elis: Κλ.
Τ.: d. Τιβ. Κλ. Τέρτυλλος, Αἰμιλία Φιλοξένα)
DALMATIA:
—ISSA: (**2**) i/ii AD Unp. (Split Museum) (Τιετι-
μία? Τ.); (**3**) ~ ib. (Τίτια Τ.)
EPIROS: (**4**) i AD *CIL* III 12300, 5 (Lat. Tyce:
d. Φλ. Εὔνους)
KORINTHIA:
—KORINTH: (**5**) imp. *Corinth* VIII (3) 288 (Lat.
Tyche); (**6**) vi AD *Hesp.* 36 (1967) p. 423, 5;
cf. *TMByz* 9 (1985) p. 367 no. 88
LAKONIA:
—GYTHEION: (**7**) f. i BC *IG* V (1) 1186, 2, 20
(*GVI* 2003) (m. Ἄτταλος)
—SPARTA: (**8**) ii AD *SEG* 11 159 (Bradford (-))
S. ITALY (APULIA):
—BARION: (**9**) ?ii AD *CIL* IX 302 (Lat. Ulpia
Tyc(i)he)
—CANUSIUM*: (**10**) imp. *Epig. Rom. di Canosa*
94 (*CIL* IX 363) (Lat. Baebia Tyche: freed.);
(**11**) i/ii AD *Epig. Rom. di Canosa* 80 (Lat. Raia
Tyche: freed.)
—LARINUM*: (**12**) imp. *CIL* IX 6249 (Lat.
Papia Tyche: freed.)
S. ITALY (BRUTTIUM):
—LOKROI EPIZEPHYRIOI: (**13**) ?ii AD Costabile,
*Municipium Locrensium* 20 (*CIL* X 32) (Lat.
Octavia T[y]c[h]e); (**14**) iii AD *Suppl. It.* 3 p.
32 no. 18 (Lat. Vagellia Tyche)
S. ITALY (CALABRIA):
—BRENTESION-BRUNDISIUM: (**15**) imp. *CIL* IX
157 (Lat. Octavia Tyche)
—BRENTESION-BRUNDISIUM*: (**16**) imp. ib. 141
= *NScav* 1880, p. 501 (Lat. Maria Tyche:
freed.)
—RUDIAE: (**17**) inc. ib. 1897, p. 405 no. 13 (Lat.
Tyche); (**18**) i-ii AD Bernardini, *Rudiae* p. 86
(Susini, *Fonti Salento* p. 108 no. 44) (Lat.
Antonia Tyche)
—TARAS-TARENTUM: (**19**) ii AD *Misc. Gr. Rom.*
3 p. 202 no. T23 (Lat. Castricia Tyche)
S. ITALY (CAMPANIA):
—DIKAIARCHIA-PUTEOLI: (**20**) imp. *AJA* 2
(1898) p. 379 no. 13 (Lat. Cincia Tyche); (**21**)
~ ib. 77 (1973) p. 156 no. 5 (Lat. Herennia
Tyche); (**22**) ~ *CIL* X 1592 (Lat. Ducennia
Tyche); (**23**) ~ ib. 2119 (Lat. Atilia Tyche);
(**24**) ~ ib. 2252 (Lat. Pollia Tyche); (**25**) ~
ib. 2835 (Lat. Perelia Tyche: m. P. Anteius

Quadratus); (**26**) ~ ib. 2886 (Lat. Potiolana
Tyche); (**27**) ~ ib. 2937 (Lat. Scalia Tyche: m.
Scalia Magna); (**28**) ~ ib. 3033 (Lat. Tyche);
(**29**) ?i-ii AD ib. 1739 (Lat. Vettia Tyche);
(**30**) ~ ib. 2606 (Lat. Tyche: m. Iulia Primi-
genia); (**31**) ~ ib. 2614 (Lat. Iulia Tyche: m.
Ἀφροδίσιος); (**32**) ?ii AD ib. 2438 (Lat. Tyche);
(**33**) ~ ib. 3106 (Lat. Aelia Tyche: m. Vibia
Faustina)
—DIKAIARCHIA-PUTEOLI*: (**34**) imp. ib. 2869
(Lat. Pompeia Tyche: freed.); (**35**) 52 AD Ca-
modeca, *L'Archivio Puteolano* I pp. 120-1 no.
4 (Lat. Tyche: slave?)
—KYME: (**36**) f. i AD *AJPh* 30 (1909) p. 68 no. 5
(*Eph. Ep.* VIII 445) (Lat. Ovia Tyche: m. C.
Ovius Sollemnis)
—LITERNUM*: (**37**) imp. *CIL* X 3715 (Lat.
Saenia Tyche: freed.)
—MISENUM*: (**38**) imp. ib. 3405 (Lat. Publicia
Tyche: freed.); (**39**) ~ ib. 3420 (Lat. Plotia
Tyche: freed.); (**40**) ~ ib. 3455 (Lat. Tyche:
slave?); (**41**) ~ ib. 3557 (Lat. Tyche: freed.);
(**42**) ?i-ii AD ib. 3522 (Lat. Iulia Tyche)
—NEAPOLIS: (**43**) imp. *IG* XIV 813 (*INap* 175);
cf. Leiwo p. 107 no. 72 (d. Ἑλενίων); (**44**) iii-iv
AD *INap* 253
—NUCERIA ALFATERNA: (**45**) imp. *NScav* 1883,
p. 418 (*Eph. Ep.* VIII 333) (Lat. Pomponia
Tyche)
—PITHEKOUSSAI-AENARIA*: (**46**) imp. *CIL* X
6802 (Lat. Tyche: freed.)
—POMPEII: (**47**) 3 BC ib. IV 2450 (Lat. Tyche);
(**48**) c. 40-60 AD ib. X 1023; Kockel p. 75
(date) (Lat. Tyche); (**49**) c. 51-62 AD *CIL* IV
3340. 88, 1 (Lat. Lidine Tyche)
—POMPEII*: (**50**) m. i AD *Impegno per Pompeii*
9 ES; *CIL* X 1030 (Castrèn 265. 4); Kockel
p. 106 (date) (Lat. Naevoleia Tyche: freed.)
—SALERNUM: (**51**) imp. *IItal* 1 (1) 159 (*CIL* X
636) (Lat. –ra Tyche: m. Πρόσοδος)
—STABIAE: (**52**) imp. *RAAN* 19 (1938-9) p. 98
(Lat. Hostilia Tyche)
—SURRENTUM: (**53**) ?i-ii AD *St. Rom.* 2 (1914)
p. 346 no. 15 = *NScav* 1928, p. 210 no. 17
(Lat. Claudia Tyche)
S. ITALY (LUCANIA):
—CALLE (MOD.): (**54**) imp. *BdA* 52 (1967) p. 44
(Lat. Cor(nelia) Tyche: m. Ἥλιος)
SICILY:
—KATANE: (**55**) imp. *CIL* X 7090 (Lat. Silia
Tyche: m. Δῖος); (**56**) ~ ib. 7096 (Lat. Tyche)
—KATANE*: (**57**) imp. ib. 7097 + *Epigraphica* 3
(1941) p. 268 no. 39 (*ILat. Palermo* 3) (Lat.
Tyche: slave?)
—SYRACUSE: (**58**) imp. *CIL* X 7150 (Lat. Tyche:
m. Εὐάγγελος, Τυχικός); (**59**) iii-v AD *IG* XIV
178 (Strazzulla 116; Wessel 196); cf. Ferrua,
*NG* 177; (**60**) ~ ib. 335 a
—ZANKLE-MESSANA?: (**61**) imp. *CIL* X 6987
(Lat. –ulcia Tyche)
—ZANKLE-MESSANA*: (**62**) imp. ib. 6985 (Lat.
Magullia Tyche: freed.)

## Τυχηρίδης
ELIS: (**1**) m. i AD *IvOl* 78, 5 ([Τυ]χηρίδης: s. Σωσιμένης)

## Τυχίη
S. ITALY (LUCANIA):
—ATINA LUCANA: (**1**) imp. *IItal* III (1) 145
(*CIL* X 347) (Lat. Tucieni (dat.))

## Τυχική
S. ITALY (CAMPANIA):
—POMPEII: (**1**) i BC-i AD ib. IV 7249 (Lat.
Tychice)

## Τυχικός
ARGOLIS:
—ARGOS: (**1**) ii AD *IG* IV (1) 593; *SEG* XVI 253,
13 (Τι(β). Κλ. Τ.: f. Κλ. Ὀλυμπία); (**2**) ~ ib.
XXXV 270-1 (Τιβ. Κλ. Τ.: I f. Γ. Κλ. Τυχικός
II); (**3**) ~ ib. (Γ. Κλ. Τ.: II s. Τιβ. Κλ. Τυχικός
I); (**4**) iii AD *BCH* 27 (1903) p. 268 no. 20
VII (Αὐρ. Τυχ[ικός])
ARKADIA:
—TEGEA: (**5**) 165 AD *IG* V (2) 50, 11, 12 (f. Εὔ-
τυχος, Εὐφρόσυνος)
LAKONIA:
—SPARTA: (**6**) ii AD ib. V (1) 491, 3 (Bradford
(-)) (f. Κλ. Κάσιος)
S. ITALY (CALABRIA):
—BRENTESION-BRUNDISIUM: (**7**) imp. *CIL* IX
6122 (Lat. A. Gabinius Thychicus)
SICILY:
—SYRACUSE: (**8**) imp. ib. X 7150 (Lat. Tychicus:
s. Τύχη); (**9**) iii-v AD Strazzulla 346 (Wessel
1320)

## Τύχιος
S. ITALY (CAMPANIA):
—DIKAIARCHIA-PUTEOLI: (**1**) imp. *CIL* X 2678
(Lat. Tychius: s. Εὐτυχιανός)

## Τύχιππος
ARKADIA:
—MEGALOPOLIS?: (**1**) i BC *IG* V (2) 545
LAKONIA:
—HYPERTELEATON*: (**2**) imp. ib. V (1) 1047 (f.
Δαμάρης)
—SPARTA: (**3**) c. 140-145 AD ib. 63, 22; *SEG* XI
643, 1 (Bradford (1)) (Τύ[χιππος]?—*SEG*: s.
Πασικλῆς, f. Πασικλῆς)

## Τυχίς
ILLYRIA:
—APOLLONIA: (**1**) ii-iii AD *IApoll* 230 + *SEG*
XXIII 485

## Τύχων
AIGINA?: (**1**) f. v BC *Riv. Stor. Antichità* 4
(1974) p. 5 (sherd)
ARGOLIS:
—EPIDAUROS: (**2**) c. 365-335 BC *IG* IV (1)² 103,
41
S. ITALY: (**3**) iii-ii AD *Epig. Rom. di Canosa* In-
str. 18 (amph.) (Vandermersch p. 176)
SICILY:
—HIMERA: (**4**) ?vi BC *JNG* 33 (1983) p. 16 (coin
graffito) (-ōν)
—SYRACUSE: (**5**) ii BC *IG* II² 10396 (s. Ἀσκλα-
πιάδας)

## Τυχώς
SICILY:
—GELA-PHINTIAS: (**1**) f. v BC Arena, *Iscr. Sic.*
II 41 (vase) (Τυχõτος (gen.))

## Τωβίας
SICILY:
—HALAISA*: (**1**) byz. *SEG* XLI 776 (bp.)

# Y

Ὑακινθίς
ARKADIA:
—PHENEOS: (1) iv AD Alciphr. iii 12. 3 (fict.)

Ὑάκινθος
ACHAIA:
—PATRAI: (1) imp. CIL III 7262 (Lat. Hyacinthus: freed.)
S. ITALY (APULIA):
—AECAE*: (2) imp. ib. IX 951 (Lat. Caesonianus Hyacinthus: freed.)
—CANUSIUM*: (3) imp. Epig. Rom. di Canosa 175 (CIL IX 6190) (Lat. [H]yacinthus: freed.)
S. ITALY (CAMPANIA):
—DIKAIARCHIA-PUTEOLI: (4) ?ii AD ib. X 2434 (Lat. Fl. Yachintus)
—DIKAIARCHIA-PUTEOLI (NR.): (5) ii-iii AD BdA 48 (1963) p. 27 (Lat. Aurelius [H]yacinthus)
—HERCULANEUM: (6) i BC-i AD CIL IV 10525 (Lat. Hyacinthus); (7) ~ ib. X 1403 d II, 6 (Lat. L. Cominius Hyacinthus)
—HERCULANEUM*: (8) i BC-i AD ib. 1403 l II, 13; cf. Cron. Erc. 7 (1977) p. 116 c, 13 (Lat. L. Appuleius Hyacinthus: freed.)
—KYME: (9) ?iii AD IG XIV 870 (GVI 629)
—NOLA*: (10) imp. CIL X 1262 (Lat. Hyacinthus: freed.)
—POMPEII: (11) i BC-i AD ib. IV 1400 (Lat. Iacintus); (12) ~ ib. 4327 (Lat. Herachinthus, H(y)acinthus—Solin); (13) ~ ib. 10225 (Lat. Yacinthus)
S. ITALY (CAMPANIA)*: (14) i BC/i AD ib. X 8042. 60 (tiles) (Lat. Hyacinthus: imp. freed.)
SICILY:
—SYRACUSE: (15) iii-v AD NScav 1947, p. 210 (Ἰάκην-)
SICILY?: (16) iii-v AD IGLMP 142

Ὑάλισος
S. ITALY (APULIA):
—LUCERIA: (1) i AD ASP 34 (1981) p. 14 no. 14 (Lat. Hyalissus)
S. ITALY (CAMPANIA):
—POMPEII*: (2) i BC-i AD CIL X 920 (Lat. Hyalissus: slave?)

Ὑάς
S. ITALY (CAMPANIA):
—DIKAIARCHIA-PUTEOLI: (1) imp. ib. 2137 (Lat. Aul. Hya); (2) ~ ib. 3016 (Lat. Aulia Hya)

Ὕβλων
SICILY: (1) s. viii BC Th. vi 4. 1 (king)

Ὑβρίας
AKARNANIA:
—KORONTA: (1) inc. IG IX (1)² (2) 604 (f. Σίναβρος)

Ὑβρίλαος
AITOLIA: (1) ?252-248 BC Syll³ 422, 3 + Flacelière p. 399 no. 24 with n.
—BOUKATION: (2) 164 BC IG IX (1)² (1) 99, 8, 10 ?= (3) (4); (3) 163 BC ib. 103, 8 ?= (2); (4) c. 162 BC ib. 106, 3 ?= (2); (5) ~ ib. l. 4 (s. Φιλίστας)

Ὑβρίλας
AKARNANIA:
—ECHINOS: (1) c. 266 BC ib. XII (9) 1187, 10; Robert, Ét. Num. Gr. pp. 179 ff. (date) (s. Ἰδρόμας)
ARGOLIS:
—ARGOS: (2) ?c. 450-425 BC IG IV (1) 514 (Lazzarini 277); LSAG² p. 170 no. 46 (date) (hυβ-)

Ὑβρίμμας
EPIROS:
—BOUTHROTOS (PRASAIBOI): (1) a. 163 BC IBouthrot 19, 3 (SEG XXXVIII 476); (2) ~ IBouthrot 25, 6 (SEG XXXVIII 483); (3) ~ IBouthrot 30, 4 (SEG XXXVIII 488); IBouthrot 48, 12; (4) ~ ib. 36, 16 (SEG XXXVIII 495) (f. Μάχα)
—DODONA: (5) iii BC Antoniou, Dodone Ab, 30

Ὕβριμος
EPIROS:
—BOUTHROTOS (PRASAIBOI): (1) a. 163 BC IBouthrot 40, 7 (SEG XXXVIII 499); (2) ~ IBouthrot 131, 8?; 156, 9 (BCH 118 (1994) p. 127 no. 12, 9) (s. Νικάνωρ); (3) ~ IBouthrot 143, 6 (Ὕβρι[μος]); (4) ~ ib. l. 10 (f. Βοῖσκος)
——Kestrinoi: (5) a. 163 BC ib. 68, 10
——OPHYLLIOI: (6) a. 163 BC ib. 116, 10 (BCH 118 (1994) p. 121 A)
ILLYRIA:
—EPIDAMNOS-DYRRHACHION: (7) hell.-imp. IDyrrh 342 (f. Πατρώ)
SICILY:
—AKRAI: (8) ?iii BC SGDI 3240, 8 (Akrai p. 156 no. 7) (s. Σῶσις)
—SYRACUSE?: (9) f. ii BC IG XI (4) 758; cf. Durrbach, Choix p. 87 (ident.) (f. Φίλων)

Ὑβρίστας
AITOLIA: (1) 217 BC Nachtergael, Les Galates 65, 5
—AGRINION: (2) 165-143 BC IG IX (1)² (1) p. LII, s.a. 165 BC; IX (1)² (3) 639. 8, 1; ZPE 101 (1994) p. 128, 5 (s. Βούλαρχος)
AKARNANIA:
—STRATOS: (3) s. ii BC IG IX (1)² (1) 36, 14 (s. Ἀγέμαχος)
—THYRREION: (4) s. iii BC ib. IX (1)² (2) 293 (f. Σωσίχα)
ARKADIA?: (5) ?c. 480-470 BC ib. IV (1)² 703 (bronze); LSAG² p. 216 no. 39 (locn., date) (hυβρίσστας)
LAKONIA: (6) 190 BC Liv. xxxvii 13. 12 (Bradford (-)) (Lat. Hybristas)

Ὕβριχος
S. ITALY (CAMPANIA):
—FRATTE DI SALERNO (MOD.): (1) f. v BC SEG XXXVII 817 B (vase) (Arena, Iscr. Sic. IV 33)

Ὑβρίων
LAKONIA:
—SELLASIA: (1) iv-iii BC Laconia Survey 2 p. 214 no. 2

Ὑγιαρώ
ARKADIA:
—TEGEA: (1) ii AD SEG XI 1077 (GVI 1400)

Ὑγίεια
LAKONIA:
—SPARTA: (1) ii AD IG V (1) 726, 4 (GVI 646; Bradford (-))
S. ITALY (APULIA):
—CANUSIUM: (2) i AD Epig. Rom. di Canosa 71 (Lat. Allia Hygia: m. Fortunata, Ὑγῖνος); (3) ii-iii AD ib. 133 (CIL IX 381) (Lat. Flabia Hycia)
—VENUSIA: (4) imp. Epigraphica 35 (1973) p. 151 no. 15 (Lat. [Sexti]lia Hygia); (5) ?ii AD CIL IX 519 (Lat. Flavia Hycia)
S. ITALY (BRUTTIUM):
—HIPPONION-VIBO VALENTIA: (6) imp. ib. X 66 (Lat. Atilia Hygia)
S. ITALY (CALABRIA):
—BRENTESION-BRUNDISIUM*: (7) ?i-ii AD NScav 1891, p. 172 (Lat. Iulia Hygia: freed.)

S. ITALY (CAMPANIA):
—ATELLA: (8) imp. CIL X 3734 (Lat. Verria Hygia)
—DIKAIARCHIA-PUTEOLI: (9) imp. ib. 1911 (Lat. Hygia); (10) ~ ib. 2712 (Lat. Cosconia Hygia: m. M. Marius Proculus); (11) ~ ib. 3143 (Lat. Hygia); (12) ~ ib. 8194 (Lat. Hygia: m. Ἰσιάς); (13) ?ii-iii AD ib. 2148 (Lat. Aurelia Hygia)
—HERCULANEUM: (14) i BC-i AD ib. 929 (Castrèn 205. 15); cf. Cron. Erc. 8 (1978) p. 155 no. 66 (locn.) (Lat. Iulia Hygia)
—MISENUM*: (15) imp. CIL X 3375 (Lat. Iunia Hygia: ?m. L. Valerius Ispanus (Sirmium))
—POMPEII: (16) i BC-i AD ib. IV 4595 (Lat. Hygia); (17) ~ Römische Gräberstrassen p. 216 c (Lat. Hygia)
—SALERNUM*: (18) s. i AD IItal I (1) 133 (CIL X 582; Sinn, Stadtröm. Marmorurnen 194) (Lat. Cornelia Hygia: freed.)
—STABIAE: (19) b. 79 AD IG XIV 700 (m. Θεότιμος)
SICILY:
—KATANE: (20) imp. ib. 509 (-γία)
—LIPARA: (21) imp. Epigraphica 51 (1989) p. 195 no. 90 (Lat. Hygia: d. Γαμική)
—SYRACUSE: (22) imp. IG XIV 38 (-γία); (23) iii-v AD ib. 180 (Strazzulla 118; Wessel 933); cf. Ferrua, NG 178 (-γία); (24) byz. SEG IV 16 (-γία)
—SYRACUSE?: (25) iii-v AD Nuovo Didask. 4 (1950) p. 63 no. 23 (Σοσία Ὑγία)
—ZANKLE-MESSANA*: (26) imp. CIL X 6982 (Lat. Coelia Hygia: freed.)

Ὑγινιανός
SICILY:
—LILYBAION*: (1) imp. ib. 7235 (Lat. –sius Hyginianus)

Ὑγῖνος
ARGOLIS:
—EPIDAUROS: (1) 194 AD IG IV (1)² 555, 6 + Peek, IAEpid 231 (-γεῖ-: II s. Ὑγῖνος I); (2) ~ IG IV (1)² 555, 7 + Peek, IAEpid 231 (-γεῖ-: I f. Ὑγῖνος II)
—TROIZEN: (3) f. ii AD IG IV (1) 758, 18 (-γεῖ-)
ARKADIA:
—LYKOSOURA*: (4) imp. ib. V (2) 547. 2 (terracotta) (-γέ-)
—TEGEA: (5) 165 AD ib. 50, 39 (-γεῖ-: I f. Ὑγῖνος II); (6) ~ ib. l. 39 (-γεῖ-: II s. Ὑγῖνος I)
ELIS: (7) ?f. i AD IvOl 127, 4 with comm. ([—o]s Ὑγεῖνος); (8) c. 201-249 AD ib. 107, 13; 110, 21; 121, 24 (M. Αὐρ. Ὑγεῖνος)
EPIROS:
—NIKOPOLIS: (9) imp. SEG XLII 545 (s. Κομμοῦνος)
ILLYRIA:
—APOLLONIA: (10) imp. IApoll 160 (-ιῆνος)
KYNOURIA:
—EUA?: (11) ii AD SEG XXXV 293
LAKONIA:
—KYTHERA: (12) hell.? IG V (1) 943
—SPARTA: (13) c. 170-190 AD SEG XI 627, 1 (Bradford (3)) (-γεῖ-: I f. Ὑγῖνος II); (14) ~ SEG XI 627, 1 (Bradford (1)) (-γεῖ-: II s. Ὑγῖνος I); (15) f. iii AD IG V (1) 653 a, 7 (Artemis Orthia p. 356 no. 142); SEG XI 806 a, 4 (Bradford (2)) (-γεῖ-: f. Τιβ. Κλ. Ῥουφῖνος, Τι. Κλ. Εἰρανίων)
S. ITALY (APULIA):
—CANUSIUM: (16) i AD Epig. Rom. di Canosa 71 (Lat. Hyginus: s. Ὑγίεια)
—VENUSIA*: (17) imp. Epigraphica 35 (1973) p. 151 no. 15 (Lat. [P.] [S]extilius Hyginus: freed.)

**Ὑδδιηῖς**

S. ITALY (BRUTTIUM):
—RHEGION: (**18**) imp. *NScav* 1886, p. 139 (*Eph. Ep.* VIII 249) (Lat. Hyginus)

S. ITALY (CALABRIA):
—BRENTESION-BRUNDISIUM: (**19**) imp. *CIL* IX 119 (Lat. A. Gabinius Hyginus)

S. ITALY (CAMPANIA):
—DIKAIARCHIA-PUTEOLI: (**20**) imp. ib. x 2075 (Lat. M. Antonius Hyginus); (**21**) 47 AD *Puteoli* 6 (1982) p. 51 (Lat. Hyginus)
—DIKAIARCHIA-PUTEOLI*: (**22**) ?i-ii AD *Eph. Ep.* VIII 396 (Lat. Ti. Claudius Hyginus: s. Φιλουμένη: freed.)
—KYME: (**23**) imp. ib. 451 (Lat. C. Sulpicius Hyginus); (**24**) ~ ib. (Lat. Hyginus: s. Ἡρακλείδας, Ἁρμονία)
—POMPEII: (**25**) i BC-i AD *CIL* IV 2249 (Lat. Hyginus); (**26**) ~ ib. 10233 (Lat. Hyginus); (**27**) c. 51-62 AD ib. 3340. 128 (Castrèn 154. 1) (Lat. Q. Didius Hyginus); (**28**) 56 AD *CIL* IV 3340. 46, 5, [9], [24] (Castrèn 23. 10) (Lat. M. All. Hyginus); (**29**) 57 AD *CIL* IV 3340. 28, 16; 54, 14; 57, 12; 66, 18; 74, 8; 78, 5; 81, 6 (Castrèn 267. 2) (Lat. N. Nerius Hyginus)
—SALERNUM*: (**30**) imp. *IItal* I (1) 78 (Lat. L. Plautius Hyginus: freed.)

SICILY:
—LIPARA: (**31**) hell.-imp. Libertini, *Isole Eolie* p. 222 no. 33 (-γεί-)
—MOTYKA (NR.): (**32**) iii-v AD *IG* XIV 251 (Wessel 1046)
—SYRACUSE: (**33**) iii-v AD ib. 1370 (Barreca 350); cf. Ferrua, *NG* 97; (**34**) iv AD *IG* XIV 179 (Strazzulla 117; Agnello 13; Wessel 626); cf. *Riv. Arch. Crist.* 18 (1941) p. 166 no. 26 (Ὑγεῖνος (ὁ)? καὶ Γεννάδις)

**Ὑδδιηῖς**

S. ITALY (BRUTTIUM):
—KRIMISA: (**1**) ?iii BC *AMSMG* 1932, p. 130 (n. pr.?)

**Ὑκώ**

SICILY: (**1**) ?f. iii BC *ZPE* 111 (1996) p. 136 no. 4 (Ὑκώ)

**Ὑλαῖος**

AITOLIA:
—LYSIMACHEIA: (**1**) c. 215-200 BC *FD* III (2) 86, 9 (*Syll*³ 539 A); cf. Nachtergael, *Les Galates* p. 291 (date)

ARGOLIS:
—HERMIONE: (**2**) ii-i BC *IG* IV (1) 732 II, 29 (s. Ἡρακλείδας)

ARKADIA:
—TEGEA: (**3**) c. 240-229 BC ib. V (2) 11, 17

**Ὑλας**

DALMATIA:
—EPETION: (**1**) imp. *CIL* III 8553 (Lat. Vivius Hyla)

KORINTHIA:
—KORINTH: (**2**) iv AD *AP* xiv 137, 8 (dub.)

S. ITALY (CAMPANIA):
—DIKAIARCHIA-PUTEOLI*: (**3**) 56 AD *CIL* x 1574 (Lat. C. Tantilius Hyla: freed.)
—HERCULANEUM*: (**4**) i BC-i AD ib. 1403 g III, 6 (Lat. -us Hyla: freed.)
—NEAPOLIS: (**5**) iii-iv AD *IG* XIV 826. 10 (*INap* 254)
—POMPEII: (**6**) i BC-i AD *CIL* IV 4582 (Lat. Hyla); (**7**) ~ ib. 4625 (Castrèn 278. 4) (Lat. P. Numisius Hyla); (**8**) ~ *CIL* IV 4810 (Lat. Hyla); (**9**) c. 51-62 AD ib. 3340. 81, 1, 10 (Castrèn 56. 1) (Lat. Audasius Hyla)

**Ὑλη**

ARKADIA:
—HERAIA: (**1**) ?iii-ii BC *SEG* XXII 326

S. ITALY (BRUTTIUM):
—SYBARIS-THOURIOI-COPIAE*: (**2**) f. i AD *NScav* 1970, Suppl. 3 p. 551 (Lat. Domitia Hyle: freed.)

**Ὑλίτας**

S. ITALY (CAMPANIA):
—SALERNUM: (**1**) m. i AD *IItal* I (1) 158 (Sinn, *Stadtröm. Marmorurnen* 146) (Lat. Cn. Pomponius Hylitas)

**Ὑλλος**

S. ITALY (CAMPANIA):
—HERCULANEUM: (**1**) m. i AD *PdelP* 16 (1961) p. 69 no. 91 (Lat. Hyllus)

**Ὑμεναῖος**

ARGOLIS:
—EPIDAUROS*: (**1**) c. 335-325 BC Peek, *IAEpid* 50, 16, 22

S. ITALY (BRUTTIUM):
—HIPPONION-VIBO VALENTIA: (**2**) imp. *CIL* x 69 (Lat. Q. Caesius Hymenaeus)

S. ITALY (CAMPANIA):
—HERCULANEUM*: (**3**) i BC-i AD ib. 1403 l I, 3 + *Cron. Erc.* 7 (1977) p. 116 b, 9 (Lat. M. Claudius Hymenaeus: freed.) ?= (**4**); (**4**) i AD *CIL* x 1448 (Lat. M. Claudius Hymenaeus: imp. freed.) ?= (**3**)
—POMPEII: (**5**) i BC-i AD *NScav* 1916, p. 303 no. 38 (Castrèn 182. 2) (Lat. L. Geganius Hymenaeus); (**6**) 56 AD *CIL* IV 3340. 25, 20; 77, 8; 7509; 7692; 9518-19 (Castrèn 158. 17) (Lat. M. Epidius Hymenaeus)

**Ὑμένιος**

EPIROS: (**1**) hell. *SGDI* 1360; cf. Cabanes, *L'Épire* p. 584 no. 64 (?f. Ἕρμων)

**Ὑμηττός**

S. ITALY (CAMPANIA):
—POMPEII: (**1**) i BC-i AD *CIL* IV 4781 (-μητό-)

S. ITALY (LUCANIA):
—POSEIDONIA-PAESTUM: (**2**) imp. Mello-Voza 31 (Lat. L. Caelius Hymetus)

**Ὑμνίς**

ARGOLIS:
—ARGOS: (**1**) ii-i BC *IG* II² 8376 (d. Καλλιτέλης)

S. ITALY (BRUTTIUM):
—LOKROI EPIZEPHYRIOI: (**2**) imp. Costabile, *Municipium Locrensium* 41 (*CIL* x 28) (Lat. Cantinia Hymnis)

**Ὑμνος**

ACHAIA:
—PELLENE: (**1**) ?ii-iii AD *SEG* XI 1274, 1

ARGOLIS:
—ARGOS: (**2**) ?i BC *ILGR* 89 (biling.) (Μ. Περπέρνας Υ.)

ARKADIA: (**3**) ?254 BC Nachtergael, *Les Galates* 9, 33 (Stephanis 2445) (s. Δεινοκράτης)

LAKONIA:
—SPARTA: (**4**) c. 220 AD *IG* V (1) 653, 6; 653 b, 3 (*Artemis Orthia* pp. 356-8 no. 143; Bradford s.v. Κλεώνυμος (3)) (Μ. Αὐρ. Κλεώνυμος ὁ καὶ Υ.: II s. Ὑμνος I); (**5**) ~ *IG* V (1) 653 b, 3 (*Artemis Orthia* pp. 356-8 no. 143; Bradford (-)) (I f. Μ. Αὐρ. Κλεώνυμος ὁ καὶ Ὑμνος II)

S. ITALY (APULIA):
—CERIGNOLA (MOD.): (**6**) i AD *Epig. Rom. di Canosa* 106 (*CIL* IX 685) (Lat. A. Canuleius Hymnus: freed.)

S. ITALY (CAMPANIA):
—AEQUANA: (**7**) imp. ib. x 765 (Lat. Ymnus)
—DIKAIARCHIA-PUTEOLI: (**8**) imp. ib. 2111 (Lat. M. Asinius Hymnus); (**9**) ~ ib. 2908 (Lat. P. Rabirius Hymnus: s. Φοίβη); (**10**) ~ ib. 3048 (Lat. M. Valerius Hymnus: f. Valeria Sabina)
—SALERNUM: (**11**) imp. *IItal* I (1) 38 (Lat. P. Baberius Hymnus: s. Φοίβη); (**12**) ~ ib. 42

(*CIL* x 567) (Lat. T. Annianus Hymnus: f. Ἅγιος)

**Ὑπατιανός**

ELIS: (**1**) ?f. iii AD *IvOl* 127, 3 ([Κλ]. Ὑπατια[νός]); (**2**) c. 201-265 AD ib. 107, [12]; 110, 19; 115, [11]; 117, 17; 118, [17]; 120, 11; 121, 18; 122, 15; [138]; [139] (Κλ. Υ.); (**3**) 209-213 AD ib. 110, 5 (Τιβ. Κλ. Υ.: Φ.)

**Ὑπατος**

S. ITALY (CAMPANIA):
—CAPREAE: (**1**) imp. *IG* XIV 902, 9 (*GVI* 1576)
—POMPEII: (**2**) i BC-i AD *CIL* IV 9996 (Lat. Hypatus)

**Ὑπεράνθης**

ARKADIA:
—TEGEA: (Krariotai): (**1**) m. iii BC *IG* V (2) 36, 95 (f. Λάμιχος: metic)

**Ὑπεράνωρ**

ARGOLIS:
—HERMIONE: (**1**) iii BC ib. IV (1) 729 I, 11 (f. Ἐτέοκλος)

**Ὑπερβάλλων**

EPIROS:
—NIKOPOLIS: (**1**) a. 30 BC *SEG* XXIV 434 (Sarikakis 165) (f. Θεόδοτος)

LEUKAS: (**2**) c. 167-50 BC *BMC Thessaly* p. 180 no. 100; *SNG Cop. Epirus–Acarnania* 384 (coin)

**Ὑπερβάτας**

ACHAIA: (**1**) s. iii BC *RE* (1); (**2**) ii BC ib. s.v. Hyperbatas (2)

**Ὑπέρβιος**

KORINTHIA:
—KORINTH: (**1**) arch. Plin., *NH* vii 198 (Lat. Hyperbius: potter)

SICILY:
—SYRACUSE: (**2**) 420 BC Moretti, *Olymp.* 334

**Ὑπερβόλη**

ARGOLIS:
—ARGOS: (**1**) i BC *SEG* XI 345, 1

S. ITALY (CAMPANIA):
—DIKAIARCHIA-PUTEOLI: (**2**) ?i-ii AD *CIL* x 2946 (Lat. Sextilia Hyperbole)
—POMPEII: (**3**) i BC-i AD ib. IV 3197 (Lat. Hyperbole)

**Ὑπέρβολος**

SICILY:
—KAMARINA: (**1**) f. v BC Cordano, *Tessere Pubbliche* o (Arena, *Iscr. Sic.* II 124 A) (hυπέρβολō (gen.): f. —ύτας)
—TAUROMENION: (**2**) c. 208-180 BC *IG* XIV 421 an. 33; 421 an. 61 (*SGDI* 5219) (s. Ὀνασικράτης, f. Ὀνασικράτης); (**3**) c. 146 BC *IGSI* 4 III (IV), 80 an. 96 ([Ὑπ]έρ[βο]λος: s. Νυμφόδωρος) (—Ἀσιν.); (**4**) c. 145 BC ib. l. 87 an. 97 (s. Ὀνασικράτης)
—ZANKLE-MESSANA: (**5**) ?ii BC *IG* XIV 401, 2, 13 (f. Ὄλυμπις)

**Ὑπερίων**

SICILY:
—SYRACUSE: (**1**) iii-v AD Strazzulla 305 (Agnello 24; Wessel 860); cf. Ferrua, *NG* 63 (Χεπερίων—Strazzulla and Agnello, Οὐεσπερίων?—Wessel and Ferrua: bp.)

**Ὑπερμένης**

LAKONIA:
—SPARTA: (**1**) 372 BC X., *HG* vi 2. 25 (Poralla² 711)

SICILY:
—KAMARINA: (**2**) f. v BC Cordano, *Tessere Pubbliche* 12 (hυπ[ερμέν]ēs: f. —στρατος)

**Ὑπερμενίδας**

KORINTHIA:
—KORINTH: (**1**) vii BC Paus. iv 19. 2 (-δης)

## Ὑπέρνικος
ARGOLIS:
—ARGOS: (1) iii BC *IG* IV (1) 527, 22; cf. *BCH* 37 (1913) p. 309 (Ἰπ[πό] νικος?)

## Ὑπέροχος
S. ITALY (CAMPANIA):
—KYME: (1) hell. *RE* (-); *FGrH* 576

## Ὕπηνος
ELIS:
—PISA: (1) 724 BC Moretti, *Olymp.* 15

## Ὑπόδικος
KORINTHIA:
—KORINTH: (1) c. 575 BC *AJA* 30 (1926) p. 448 ([h]υπόδιφος)

## Ὑπομονή
SICILY:
—SYRACUSE: (1) iii-v AD *SEG* XXXIX 1023

## Ὕποπτος
S. ITALY (CAMPANIA):
—DIKAIARCHIA-PUTEOLI*: (1) ?i-ii AD *CIL* X 2558 (Lat. C. Iulius Hypoptus: freed.)

## Ὑράδιος
ILLYRIA:
—LYCHNIDOS: (1) ii-iii AD *Sp.* 77 (1934) p. 51 no. 45

## Ὑραῖος
LAKONIA:
—SPARTA: (1) her. Paus. iii 15. 8 (s. Αἰγεύς, f. Μαῖσις, Λαίας, Εὐρώπας: dub.)

## Ὕρκος
ELIS: (1) ?vi BC *SEG* XXIV 301 (ʰύρρος)

## Ὑρμινία
LAKONIA: (1) c. 500 BC *IG* V (1) 824 (Poralla² 712) (Ὑρμι[ν]αί[α]—*IG*: name—*LGPN*)

## Ὕσμων
ELIS: (1) f. iv BC Moretti, *Olymp.* 391

## Ὕσπληξ
SICILY:
—SYRACUSE: (1) imp. *NScav* 1947, p. 178

## Ὑσσεμάτας
ARGOLIS:
—ARGOS: (1) ?c. 525-500 BC *SEG* XI 305, 1; *LSAG*² p. 168 no. 15 (date) (ʰυσ(σ)εμάτας)

## Ὑψαῖος
S. ITALY (CAMPANIA):
—POMPEII: (1) i BC-i AD *CIL* IV 181; 270 (Lat. Hypsaeus) ?= (3); (2) 3 AD *Eph. Ep.* VIII 316; *CIL* X 907-8 (Castrèn 21. 1) (Lat. D. Alfidius Hypsaeus); (3) 58 AD *CIL* IV 170; 187; 200; 3340. 142, 1, 28; 143, 11; 147, 1, 16, 20; 150, 1 (Castrèn 442. 1) (Lat. L. Verannius Hypsaeus) ?= (1)

## Ὑψηχίδας
LAKONIA:
—SPARTA: (1) c. 600 BC Plu., *Sol.* 10 (Poralla² 713)

## Ὑψικλῆς
KORINTHIA:
—SIKYON: (1) 72 BC Moretti, *Olymp.* 684 (Skalet 326)

## Ὗψις
SICILY:
—SELINOUS: (1) vi/v BC Dubois, *IGDS* 66 (Arena, *Iscr. Sic.* I 34; *IGLMP* 97) (ʰύ-); (2) f. v BC Dubois, *IGDS* 39, 3 (Arena, *Iscr. Sic.* I 71) (ʰύψ(ις)?); (3) ~ Dubois, *IGDS* 39, 7 (Arena, *Iscr. Sic.* I 71) (ʰύψ(ις)?)

# Φ

## Φάβεννος
LAKONIA:
—SPARTA: (1) ?c. 252-248 BC *Syll*³ 422, 7 (Bradford (-)) (Φάβ(ϝ)εννος)

## Φαβία
SICILY:
—AKRAI: (1) 35 AD *SEG* XLII 833, 11 (d. Σφογγεύς, m. Αὐλία)

## Φάβιλλα
SICILY:
—AKRAI: (1) 35 AD ib. l. 12 (Φά[βιλ]λα?: d. Αὐλία)

## Φάβουλλος
ARGOLIS:
—EPIDAUROS: (1) i-ii AD *IG* IV (1)² 499; 561, 2

## Φάδις
SICILY:
—SOLOUS: (1) iii-ii BC *SEG* XXXIV 973 (loom-weight) (dub.—A.W.J.)

## Φαέθων
S. ITALY (CAMPANIA):
—HERCULANEUM: (1) m. i AD *PdelP* 9 (1954) p. 55 no. 59, 6 (Lat. M. Antonius Phaeto)

## Φαεινίς
ARGOLIS:
—ARGOS: (1) s. v BC Th. iv 133. 3

## Φαενίκης
ARGOLIS:
—HERMIONE: (1) ?ii-i BC *IG* IV (1) 731 I, 18 (s. Κλειναγόρας)

## Φαένιππος
ARGOLIS:
—ARGOS: (1) f. v BC *SEG* XXXVIII 310 (-ιπος)

## Φαεννίς
EPIROS:
—CHAONES: (1) iv/iii BC *RE* (-)

## Φαηνά
ARGOLIS:
—ARGOS:
——(Damoitadai): (1) ii-i BC *IG* IV (1) 530, 6-7; cf. *BCH* 33 (1909) p. 183 n. 2
ARKADIA:
—MANTINEIA-ANTIGONEIA: (2) 46 or 44 BC *IG* V (2) 266, 21 (d. Δαμασίλας, Θεοδώρα); (3) ~ ib. l. [1], 32, 38 (d. Δαμάτριος, m. Θεοδώρα)

## Φαηνός
ARGOLIS:
—ARGOS: (1) a. 303 BC *CEG* II 816, 18; (2) c. 250-146 BC BM coin 1920 5-15-134; *SNG Cop. Argolis–Aegean Islands* 53 (coin) ?= (4); (3) iii/ii BC *BCH* 27 (1903) p. 260 no. 1 (s. Ἀριστοκράτης); (4) 191-146 BC *BMC Pelop.* p. 13 nos. 155-6 (coin) ?= (2)
—ARGOS?: (5) f. i BC *SEG* XXIII 180, 3 (s. Θιοδέκτας: date—Kritzas)
LAKONIA: (6) 76 BC *IG* V (1) 1146, 9 (Φαη(ι)νός)

## Φαιανίδης
MESSENIA:
—ASINE: (1) 193-195 AD ib. 1412, 9 (Αἰλ. Φ[α]ιανίδης, Φ[α]ιωνίδης?—index)

## Φαίαξ
AKARNANIA:
—ECHINOS: (1) c. 266 BC ib. XII (9) 1187, 9; Robert, *Ét. Num. Gr.* pp. 179 ff. (date) (s. Τιμασίας)
—KERKYRA: (2) i BC-i AD *IG* IX (1) 718
—LEUKAS: (3) 216 BC ib. IX (1)² (2) 583, 4, 63 (s. Ἐχεμένης)
SICILY:
—AKRAGAS: (4) f. v BC *RE* (5)

## Φαιδιμίδας
ARGOLIS:
—ARGOS: (1) i BC *IG* II² 8369, 2 (f. Καλλιστώ)
ARKADIA:
—TEGEA: (2) iv/iii BC ib. V (2) 38, 30 (f. Λάαρχος)

## Φαίδιμος
ARGOLIS:
—EPIDAUROS: (1) c. 370-360 BC *BSA* 61 (1966) p. 271 no. 4 A, 22
ARKADIA: (2) hell. *Syringes* 29 (f. Ἱπποκράτης)
—MANTINEIA-ANTIGONEIA: (3) iii BC *IG* V (2) 319. 20; 27; 33 (Φαίδιμ[ος]—319. 27)
—STYMPHALOS: (4) iii BC ib. 356, 6
LAKONIA:
—SPARTA: (5) 420 BC Th. v 42. 1 (Poralla² 714)

## Φαιδρέας
ARKADIA:
—TEGEA: (1) 369-361 BC *IG* V (2) 1, 11; Tod, *GHI* II 132 (date)

## Φαιδρίας
AKARNANIA:
—ASTAKOS: (1) ii BC *IG* IX (1)² (2) 435, 4 (f. Σώτων)
ARGOLIS:
—EPIDAUROS: (2) f. ii AD ib. IV (1)² 678, 5 (f. Τιβ. Κλ. Ξενοκλῆς); (3) a. 130 AD Peek, *IA-Epid* 199, 2 ?= (4); (4) c. 150-175 AD *IG* IV (1)² 686, 4 (Τιβ. Κλ. Φ.: s. Τιβ. Κλ. Ξενοκλῆς, Κλ. Δαμαρώ) ?= (3)

## Φαῖδρος
ARGOLIS:
—PHLEIOUS?: (1) c. 220-200 BC *SEG* XI 414, 10 (Perlman E.5) (s. Κλεάνωρ)
ARKADIA:
—MANTINEIA-ANTIGONEIA: (2) 369-361 BC *IG* V (2) 1, 35; Tod, *GHI* II 132 (date); (3) 117-138 AD *IG* V (2) 302 (Ἀ. Μαίκιος Φ.)

—TEGEA:
——(Hippothoitai): (4) iii BC ib. 40, 22 (f. Φιλο-
κλῆς)
ILLYRIA:
—EPIDAMNOS-DYRRHACHION: (5) hell.-imp.
IDyrrh 445 (f. Φιλώ)
PELOPONNESE: (6) s. iii BC SEG XIII 278, 11 (s.
Τίμων)

**Φαίδων**
ELIS: (1) v/iv BC RE (3)
KORINTHIA:
—KORINTH: (2) imp. AE 1977, p. 80 no. 28, 4
(Lat. Phaedon)
S. ITALY (CAMPANIA):
—DIKAIARCHIA-PUTEOLI: (3) imp. CIL X 2210
(Lat. L. Calpur. Phaedo) ?= (4)
—DIKAIARCHIA-PUTEOLI*: (4) imp. ib. 1943
(Lat. L. Calpurnius Phaedon: freed.?) ?= (3)
S. ITALY (LUCANIA):
—POSEIDONIA-PAESTUM: (5) ?v-iv BC Iamb.,
VP 267 (FVS 1 p. 448)

**Φαικίων**
S. ITALY (BRUTTIUM):
—LOKROI EPIZEPHYRIOI:
——(Ἀλχ.): (1) iv/iii BC De Franciscis 6, 4 (f.
Εὔπολις) ?= (3); (2) ~ ib. 12, 9 (s. Εὔπολις); (3)
~ ib. 26, 1 ?= (1)

**Φαικύλος**
ACHAIA:
—PHARAI: (1) v/iv BC Achaean Grave Stelai 11
(Φαικύλος)
KERKYRA: (2) ii BC Fraser–Rönne, BWGT p.
112 no. 4
S. ITALY (BRUTTIUM):
—LOKROI EPIZEPHYRIOI:
——(Ἀνα.): (3) 278 BC De Franciscis 30, 2 (f.
Χαιρέδαμος)
——(Κρα.): (4) iv/iii BC ib. 38, 5 (f. Σαθύων)
——(Κυλ.): (5) iv/iii BC ib. 10, 8

**Φαίκων**
S. ITALY (BRUTTIUM):
—LOKROI EPIZEPHYRIOI:
——(Κρα.): (1) iv/iii BC ib. 6, 3 (s. Χαρμόνδας)
SICILY:
—PALIKE: (2) iv/iii BC Röm. Mitt. 69 (1962) pp.
14-20

**Φαιναγόρας**
ARGOLIS:
—HERMIONE: (1) ?ii-i BC IG IV (1) 731 I, 2 (f.
Διονύσιον)

**Φαίνανδρος**
ARGOLIS:
—ARGOS?: (1) f. i BC SEG XXIII 180, 5
([Φ]αίνανδρος: s. Χάρμις: date—Kritzas)

**Φαιναρέτα**
AKARNANIA:
—PALAIROS: (1) ?iii/ii BC IG IX (1)² (2) 554
([Φαι]ναρέ[τα])
EPIROS:
—BOUTHROTOS (PRASAIBOI): (2) a. 163 BC
IBouthrot 15, 7 (SEG XXXVIII 472); (3) ~
IBouthrot 68, 9; (4) ~ ib. 122, 6
—MOLOSSOI: (5) iv/iii BC Plu., Pyrr. 5. 10 (-τη)

**Φαιναρέτη**
S. ITALY (CAMPANIA):
—NEAPOLIS: (1) i BC/i AD INap 177, 4 (d. Νύμ-
ψιος)

**Φαινέας**
AITOLIA: (1) c. 262 BC IG IX (1)² (1) 18, 11
—ANDREATAI: (2) 163 BC ib. 101, 8
—BOUKATION: (3) c. 162 BC ib. 106, 11, 13


—KONOPE-ARSINOE: (4) 198-190 BC RE (-); IG
IX (1)² (1) p. LI, s.a. 198 BC, 192 BC; Sherk
37 B, 8; cf. SEG XXVII 123
AKARNANIA:
—THYRREION: (5) ii BC IG IX (1)² (2) 248, 11
(Φαινέ<λ>ας: s. Σωτίων)
ARKADIA: (6) 370-367 BC ib. v (2) 2, 8 (Φαινέας)
TRIPHYLIA:
—HYPANA: (7) c. 230-200 BC BCH 45 (1921) p.
12 II, 77 (f. Πολίαρχος)

**Φαινέμαχος**
AIGINA: (1) hell.-imp. IG IV (1) 44

**Φαινίας**
ARGOLIS:
—EPIDAUROS*: (1) c. 335-325 BC ib. IV (1)² 106
I, 111
ILLYRIA:
—EPIDAMNOS-DYRRHACHION: (2) imp. IDyrrh
230 (Ζώπυρος Φ.—lap.: ?f. Ζώπυρος)

**Φαίνιππος**
ARGOLIS:
—ARGOS: (1) 105 BC JÖAI 14 (1911) Beibl. p.
146 no 4, 3 (Φαίνιπ[πος])
——(Dymmadai): (2) iii BC SEG XXX 371
([Φ]αίνιππος)
—EPIDAUROS: (3) iv/iii BC IG IV (1)² 258 (s.
Ἀντιφάνης: sculptor)
ILLYRIA:
—EPIDAMNOS-DYRRHACHION: (4) c. 250-50 BC
Maier 362 (coin) (Ceka 240; 402) (pryt.)

**Φαινίς**
S. ITALY (CAMPANIA):
—NOLA: (1) imp. Atti Acc. Pontan. 21 (1971-2)
pp. 392-7 (Lat. –ia Phaenis)

**Φαινοκλείδας**
MESSENIA:
—THOURIA: (1) s. iii BC IG V (1) 1386, 5 (f.
Κτησικλῆς)

**Φαῖνος**
S. ITALY (CAMPANIA):
—DIKAIARCHIA-PUTEOLI*: (1) imp. CIL X
2844 (Lat. Phainus: slave?)

**Φαίνουσα**
S. ITALY (CALABRIA):
—LUPIAE*: (1) i-ii AD NScav 1957, pp. 191-
3 (Susini, Fonti Salento p. 149 no. 98) (Lat.
Caesia Phaenusa: freed.)
S. ITALY (CAMPANIA):
—DIKAIARCHIA-PUTEOLI: (2) ?i-ii AD CIL X
2895 (Lat. Iulia Phaenusa)

**Φαινύλις**
SICILY:
—LIPARA: (1) inc. Chiron 22 (1992) p. 386

**Φαινύλος**
EPIROS:
—DODONA*: (1) iv BC PAE 1932, p. 52 no. 2

**Φαινώ**
EPIROS:
—BOUTHROTOS (PRASAIBOI): (1) a. 163 BC
IBouthrot 14, 40; 31, 57; 33, 23 (SEG XXXVIII
471; 490; 492) (?d. Σωσίπατρος); (2) ~ IBouthrot 18, 14 (SEG XXXVIII 475); (3) ~ IBouthrot 23, 3 (SEG XXXVIII 481); (4) ~ IBouthrot
27, 2 (SEG XXXVIII 485) (d. Σιμίας); (5) ~
IBouthrot 28, 36; 36, 17 (SEG XXXVIII 486;
495); IBouthrot 139, 6 (Φ[αινώ—no. 28) ?=
(10); (6) ~ ib. 32, 31; 34, 2 (SEG XXXVIII
491; 493); (7) ~ IBouthrot 45, 18; (8) ~ ib. 66,
8; 75, 7; (9) ~ ib. 93, 5; (10) ~ ib. 114, 6; 116,
6 (BCH 118 (1994) p. 121 no. A) ?= (5)
SICILY:
—LIPARA: (11) inc. Chiron 22 (1992) p. 386


—THERMAI HIMERAIAI: (12) ?i BC IG XIV 340
(?d. Ζώπυρος Ὠκιδίας)

**Φαίνων**
AITOLIA:
—LYSIMACHEIA: (1) c. 245-236 BC ib. IX (1)²
(1) 25, 13

**Φαῖσκος**
S. ITALY (BRUTTIUM):
—LOKROI EPIZEPHYRIOI:
——(Τηλ.): (1) 279 BC De Franciscis 13, 7; 17,
5 (s. Φάων)
S. ITALY (LUCANIA):
—METAPONTION: (2) ?m. v BC B. xi 14 (f. Ἀλεξί-
δαμος)

**Φαίων**
S. ITALY (BRUTTIUM):
—LOKROI EPIZEPHYRIOI:
——(Βοω.): (1) iv/iii BC De Franciscis 14, 5 ?=
(Φάων (3))

**Φαιωνίδας**
LAKONIA:
—AIGILIA*: (1) ?ii-i BC IG V (1) 951 c (bullet)
([Φ]αιωνίδας)

**Φάλαικος**
EPIROS:
—AMBRAKIA: (1) ii AD RE (1); cf. Ael., NA xii
40 (Φαῦλος—Ael.: fict.)

**Φαλαίνιος**
SICILY:
—SYRACUSE: (1) c. 310 BC POxy 2399, 34 (Διό-
γνητος ὁ Φ. ἐπικαλούμενος)

**Φάλακρα**
AITOLIA:
—KALLION/KALLIPOLIS: (1) 166 BC SGDI
1747, 4 etc. (slave/freed.)
—KONOPE-ARSINOE: (2) ii BC SEG XL 457
—PHISTYON: (3) ii BC IG IX (1)² (1) 110 a, 7
ILLYRIA:
—APOLLONIA: (4) hell. IApoll 24; cf. Le Arti 5
(1943) p. 117 no. 2; Fraser–Rönne, BWGT
p. 174 n. 5 (date) (d. Λυσίμαχος)
—BYLLIONES (MARGELLIC (MOD.)): (5) hell.
SEG XXXVIII 549 (Φαλάκ[ρα?])
SICILY:
—LIPARA: (6) hell. Meligunis-Lipara 5 p. 69 T.
1994; cf. SEG XLI 797

**Φαλάκριος**
ARGOLIS:
—TROIZEN: (1) iv BC IG IV (1) 823, 17, 21, 31
EPIROS:
—BOUTHROTOS (PRASAIBOI): (2) a. 163 BC
IBouthrot 73

**Φαλακρίων**
AITOLIA:
—KALYDON: (1) a. 142 BC IG IX (1)² (1) 137,
62
—PAMPHIA: (2) c. 162 BC ib. 105, 11
—PHISTYON: (3) 190 BC ib. 97, 11 (f. Ἀγήσων)
—THERMOS: (4) 163 BC ib. 102, 7-8 (s. Ἀλέξαν-
δρος)
—THESTIEIS: (5) 213 BC ib. 96, 13
—TNIMAIOI: (6) c. 225-200 BC BCH 50 (1926)
p. 125 no. 2 a, 2 (s. Σώνικος)
—TRICHONION: (7) s. iii BC IG IX (1)² (1) 117,
10
AKARNANIA:
—ASTAKOS: (8) ii BC ib. IX (1)² (2) 435, 21 (f.
—στρατος)
—MATROPOLIS: (9) 190 BC SEG XXVII 123, 11;
cf. Sherk 37 B; BCH Suppl. 4 (1977) p. 131
(locn.) (or Thessaly?)
—THYRREION: (10) iii BC IG IX (1)² (2) 246, 14
(s. Εὐδ—); (11) hell.-imp. ib. 356 (f. Λυκίσκος)
EPIROS: (12) ii BC Cabanes, L'Épire p. 590 no.
76, 16 (SEG XXVI 704)
—BOUTHROTOS (PRASAIBOI): (13) a. 163 BC
IBouthrot 21, 5 (SEG XXXVIII 478); (14) ~
IBouthrot 21, 34; 28, 21; 36, 4 (SEG XXXVIII

478; 486; 495) (f. Σωσίπατρος) ?= (19); (15)
~ IBouthrot 23, 3 (SEG XXXVIII 481); (16)
~ IBouthrot 43, 6 (SEG XXXVIII 502); (17) ~
IBouthrot 67, 6 (f. Βοΐσκος); (18) ~ ib. 103, 8;
156, 10; 157, 7 (BCH 118 (1994) p. 127 nos.
12-13 7) (s. Βοΐσκος); (19) ~ IBouthrot 103,
10 (f. Σωσίπατρος) ?= (14); (20) ~ ib. 140, 10;
(21) ~ ib. 148; (22) ~ ib. 164
——Asteatoi: (23) a. 163 BC ib. 122, 7
(Φαλ[ακρίων], Φάλ[ακρος]?: s. Λυκίσκος)
——Opatai: (24) a. 163 BC ib. 97, 8 (s. Νίκων)
—THESPROTOI: (25) ii BC IG IV (1)² 99, 19 (f.
Σίμακος)

ILLYRIA:
—EPIDAMNOS-DYRRHACHION: (26) c. 250-50
BC Ceka, Probleme p. 152 no. 71 (coin)
(pryt.) ?= (27); (27) ~ Maier 363-4; 491;
Münsterberg p. 261; Nachtr. p. 17 (coin)
(Ceka 108; 120; 228; 260) (pryt.) ?= (26);
(28) 208 BC IMM 46, 2 (IDyrrh 514)
([Φα]λακρ[ίων]?]: s. —φῶν); (29) hell.-imp. ib.
357 (Φαλα[κρί]ων: f. Πλάτωρ); (30) ~ ib. 453
(f. Ὡραῖς)
—GUREZEZE (MOD.): (31) hell. Iliria 1982 (1),
p. 112 no. 59 = p. 121 no. 50 (tile)
KEPHALLENIA:
—SAME: (32) 208 BC IMM 35, 1

**Φάλακρος**
AITOLIA: (1) ?240-228 BC FD III (3) 218 A, 2
—LYSIMACHEIA: (2) imp. IG IX (1)² (1) 129
—PHISTYON: (3) iii/ii BC ib. 95, 9; 97, 12; 98, 2
—TRICHONION: (4) s. iii BC ib. 117, 9
AKARNANIA:
—PALAIROS: (5) s. iii BC ib. IX (1)² (2) 525
ARGOLIS:
—ARGOS: (6) s. iv BC Peek, NIEpid 16, 30 (Perlman E.6) (s. Ἀνδροσθένης)
ARKADIA:
—ASEA: (7) 191-146 BC Unp. (Paris, BN)
Coll. Delepierre; Unp. (Oxford, AM) (coins)
(Φά[λα]κρος?—Paris BN, [—]αλα[—]ρο(ς)?—
Oxford AM)
EPIROS:
—BOUTHROTOS (PRASAIBOI): (8) a. 163 BC
IBouthrot 17, 13; 31, 68 (SEG XXXVIII 474;
490) (s. Θύρμαξ) ?= (12); (9) ~ IBouthrot 22,
34 (SEG XXXVIII 479); (10) ~ IBouthrot 26,
3?; 28, 4; 29, 25 (SEG XXXVIII 486-7); (11) ~
IBouthrot 31, 67 (SEG XXXVIII 490) (f. Θύρμαξ); (12) ~ IBouthrot 43, 7 (SEG XXXVIII
502) ?= (8); (13) ~ IBouthrot 76, 4, 6?; cf.
L'Illyrie mérid. 2 p. 220 n. 6 (f. Λύκος) ?=
(14) (16); (14) ~ IBouthrot 76, 4; cf. L'Illyrie
mérid. 2 p. 220 n. 6 (s. Γέρων) ?= (13); (15) ~
IBouthrot 76, 5; cf. L'Illyrie mérid. 2 p. 220
n. 6 (s. Λύκος)
—KAMMANOI BOUTHROTIOI: (16) a. 163 BC
IBouthrot 60, 6 (SEG XXXVIII 511) (f. Λύκος)
?= (13); (17) ~ IBouthrot 60, 7 (SEG XXXVIII
511) (f. Σίμακος)
ILLYRIA:
—APOLLONIA: (18) iv BC IApoll 385; (19)
hell. ib. 365 (tile); (20) c. 250-50 BC Maier
42; Münsterberg p. 36 (coin) (Ceka 117-18)
(money.)
—EPIDAMNOS-DYRRHACHION: (21) hell.-imp.
IDyrrh 484 ([Φάλα?]κρος)
ILLYRIA?: (22) m. iv BC Cabanes, L'Épire p.
576 no. 49, 6 (SEG XXVI 717) (slave/freed.)
KERKYRA: (23) c. 229-48 BC BMC Thessaly p.
150 nos. 531-5; SNG Cop. Epirus–Acarnania
235 (coins); (24) ?ii-i BC IG IX (1) 822 (tile)
S. ITALY (BRUTTIUM):
—LOKROI EPIZEPHYRIOI: (25) hell.? De Franciscis p. 103 (Φάλ<λ>ακρος: f. Κ[—]ιππος)
——(Πυρ.): (26) iv/iii BC ib. 33, 5 (f. Ξενόχαρις)
—RHEGION*: (27) i BC/i AD SEG XXXIX 1062 B
(slave?)

---

SICILY:
—AKRAGAS: (28) iv/iii BC Acragas Graeca 1 p.
32 no. 3 (Dubois, IGDS 183) (s. Θεύδωρος)
—KENTORIPA: (29) ?s. iii BC Sic. Gymn. 2
(1949) p. 91 no. 1, 8 + 16 (1963) p. 54
(Φά[λακρος]?: f. Ἡρακλείδας) ?= (30); (30) ~ ib.
2 (1949) p. 91 no. 1, 9 (Φά[λακρος]?: f. Νικίας)
?= (29); (31) ~ ib. l. 10 + 16 (1963) p. 54 (s.
Εὔβ—); (32) ~ ib. 2 (1949) p. 91 no. 1, 11 +
16 (1963) p. 54 (s. Ζ—); (33) 72-70 BC RE (3)
(Lat. Phalacrus)
—SEGESTA: (34) ?ii-i BC IG XIV 288 (Dubois,
IGDS 214 a-b; IGLMP 46-7) (Φάλακ[ρος]
Ἐρύσσιος: s. Διόδωρος, f. Σώπολις)
—TAUROMENION: (35) c. 192 BC IG XIV 421 an.
49 (SGDI 5219); (36) c. 174-160 BC IG XIV
421 an. 67; 421 an. 81 (SGDI 5219) (s. Ἄνταλλος)
——(Ταν.): (37) c. 145 BC IGSI 4 III (IV), 88
an. 97 (Φάλακ[ρος]: s. Ἀριστοκράτης)
—THERMAI HIMERAIAI: (38) ?ii/i BC SGDI
3248 (Kokalos 20 (1974) p. 219 no. 1) (f.
Ἀπολλόδωρος)

**Φαλανέας**
EPIROS:
—DODONA: (1) iii BC Antoniou, Dodone Ab, 23

**Φάλανθος**
AITOLIA:
—KALLION/KALLIPOLIS: (1) 194 BC SGDI
2075, 6; (2) 153-144 BC ib. 2279, 10, 13 (s.
Πολύφρων)
LAKONIA:
—SPARTA: (3) viii/vii BC RE s.v. Phalantos (-)
(Poralla² 715) (and S. Italy (Calabria) Taras-
Tarentum: s. Ἄρατος: oikist/dub.)

**Φαλάρειτος?**
ILLYRIA:
—BYLLIONES BYLLIS: (1) ?ii BC SEG XXXVIII
522 (Φαλαρείτης? (ethn.?))

**Φάλαρις**
AKARNANIA:
—STRATOS: (1) hell. IG IX (1) 594 (s. Αἰσχρίων)
S. ITALY (CALABRIA):
—TARAS-TARENTUM: (2) imp. NScav 1894, p.
68 no. 46 (Lat. Phaleres)
SICILY:
—AKRAGAS: (3) f. vi BC RE (-) (s. Λεωδάμας
(Astypalaia): tyrant)

**Φάλαρος**
ARKADIA:
—TEGEA:
——(Hippothoitai): (1) iii BC IG V (2) 40, 39 (f.
Ξενότιμος)

**Φαλαυσίας**
AITOLIA:
—ETHANIOI: (1) b. 238 BC ib. IX (1)² (1) 31,
185 ?= (2); (2) c. 232-228 BC Syll³ 499, 2;
Nachtergael, Les Galates 62, [2] ?= (1)

**Φαλέας**
SICILY:
—SYRACUSE: (1) ?iii BC IG II² 10397 (s. Δαμάτριος)

**Φαλείας**
EPIROS:
—DODONA: (1) iii BC Antoniou, Dodone Aa, 35
([Φ]αλείας); (2) ~ ib. Ab, 37

**Φαλῖνος**
EPIROS:
—DODONA: (1) iii BC ib. l. 6
ZAKYNTHOS: (2) v/iv BC RE (-); FGrH 688
F23 (Φ.—Xen., Φάλλυνος, Φάυλλος—Plu., Φά-
λυνος—Diod.)

---

**Φαλίος**
ILLYRIA:
—EPIDAMNOS-DYRRHACHION: (1) hell. IDyrrh
293 (f. Λεῦκος); (2) hell.-imp. ib. 97 (f. Ἀναξι-
κλέα)
KORINTHIA:
—KORINTH: (3) vii BC RE (1) (and Illyria
Epidamnos-Dyrrhachion: s. Ἐρατοκλείδας: oi-
kist)

**Φαναῖος**
DALMATIA:
—ISSA: (1) iii BC VAMZ 1970, p. 36 fr. K
(Φαν[αῖος])
——(Dymanes): (2) iv/iii BC Brunšmid p. 7, 22;
p. 8, 29 ([Φαναῖ]ος—l. 22: s. Ζώιλος, f. Ζώιλος)

**Φανάκτης**
ARGOLIS:
—NAUPLIA: (1) ?i AD IG IV (1) 671

**Φάνας**
ACHAIA:
—PELLENE: (1) 512 BC RE (-); Moretti, Olymp.
142-144
MESSENIA: (2) viii BC ib. 31

**Φανέας**
AITOLIA:
—PHISTYON: (1) ii BC IG IX (1)² (1) 110 a, 4 (f.
Νικόλαος)

**Φάνης**
LAKONIA:
—SPARTA: (1) s. i BC ib. V (1) 93, 15 (Bradford
(-)) (Φάν[ητ]ος (gen.): f. Ἀντιαλκίδας)

**Φανιάδας**
AKARNANIA:
—PALAIROS: (1) iii BC IG IX (1)² (2) 508

**Φανίας**
ARKADIA:
—MEGALOPOLIS: (1) ?265-259 BC Nachtergael,
Les Galates 2, 8; 4, 16; 6, 5; cf. Stephanis
2561 (f. Φίλων)
EPIROS:
—BOUTHROTOS (PRASAIBOI): (2) a. 163 BC
IBouthrot 21, 32 (SEG XXXVIII 478)
——Bouthrotioi: (3) a. 163 BC IBouthrot 116, 9
(BCH 118 (1994) p. 121 A); IBouthrot 120,
10 (I f. Φανίας II); (4) ~ ib. 116, 9 (BCH 118
(1994) p. 121 A); IBouthrot 120, 9 (II s. Φα-
νίας I)
SICILY:
—SYRACUSE?:
——(Ἀσια.): (5) hell. IG XIV 2407. 18; Mem.
Linc. 8 (1938) p. 127 no. 35. 7 (locn.); cf.
L'Incidenza dell'Antico pp. 420 ff. (bullet)
([Φ]ανίας)

**Φανίδης**
S. ITALY (LUCANIA):
—LEUKANOI: (1) c. 208 BC FD III (4) 135, 10
(f. Μενέδαμος)

**Φάνιον**
KORINTHIA:
—KORINTH: (1) ii-i BC IG II² 9079

**Φᾶνις**
ARKADIA:
—MANTINEIA-ANTIGONEIA: (1) c. 475-450 BC
ib. V (2) 262, 9 (IPArk 8); LSAG² p. 216 no.
29 (date) (Φᾶνις)

**Φανίς**
AIGINA: (1) f. iv BC IG II² 7963

**Φανίσκος**
ILLYRIA:
—EPIDAMNOS-DYRRHACHION: (1) c. 250-50 BC
Münsterberg p. 40; cf. IApoll Ref. Bibl. n.
111 (coin) (pryt.) ?= (2); (2) ~ Maier 365-
72; Münsterberg p. 40 (coin) (Ceka 167; 177;
282; 295; 374; 414; 441; 443; 458) (pryt.) ?=
(1); (3) ii-i BC IDyrrh 560 (tiles)

**Φανίτας**
EPIROS:
—DODONA: (**1**) iii BC Antoniou, *Dodone* Ab, 54

**Φαννιανός**
S. ITALY (CAMPANIA):
—NEAPOLIS: (**1**) i AD *IG* XIV 795, 9 (*INap* 133);
cf. Leiwo p. 124 no. 111

**Φανόδωρος**
S. ITALY (LUCANIA):
—TEGIANUM (NR.): (**1**) ?iii AD *Rupes loquentes*
p. 438 (Lat. Aur. Fanodorus)

**Φανόκλεια**
ARGOLIS:
—ARGOS: (**1**) i-ii AD *IG* IV (1) 610 (Στατειλία
[Φα]νόκλεια, [Ξε]νόκλεια?)

**Φανοκλῆς**
ACHAIA:
—ASCHEION?: (**1**) c. 315-280 BC *FD* III (1) 413,
1 ([Φ]ανοκ[λῆς]: s. Κάφις)

**Φᾶνος**
S. ITALY (BRUTTIUM):
—RHEGION: (**1**) imp.? *IG* XIV 2400. 26 + *SEG*
IV 68 (tiles)
S. ITALY (CAMPANIA):
—POMPEII: (**2**) i BC-i AD *CIL* IV 2936 (Lat.
P[h]anus)

**Φανόστρατος**
ARKADIA: (**1**) iii BC *IEph* 1412 (s. Εὐκλέων)

**Φάντα**
ARGOLIS:
—HERMIONE?: (**1**) iii BC *IG* IV (1) 746

**Φαντίας**
ARGOLIS:
—ARGOS?: (**1**) m. iii BC Peek, *IAEpid* 42, 61
(Perlman E.3); Perlman p. 63 f. (date) (Φάν-
τας—Perlman: s. Ἀντίπατρος)

**Φάντος**
ARGOLIS:
—TROIZEN: (**1**) 337-336 BC *CID* II 74 I, 76; 75
II, 50; 76 I, 19; 76 II, 25 (s. Θυρρειάδας)

**Φαντώ**
DALMATIA:
—ISSA: (**1**) iii-ii BC Brunšmid p. 28 no. 21
([Φα]ντώ: d. Νέζος); (**2**) s. iii BC *SEG* XXXV
682; cf. *BCH* 114 (1990) p. 507-8 (d. Ἐ—);
(**3**) ~ *SEG* XXXV 682; cf. *BCH* 114 (1990) p.
507-8 (d. Πυ—); (**4**) ii BC Brunšmid p. 25 no.
14, 5 + *VAHD* 84 (1991) p. 248 no. 1 (d. Φι-
λοκράτης); (**5**) ~ Brunšmid p. 25 no. 14, 7 +
*VAHD* 84 (1991) p. 248 no. 1 (d. Φιλοκράτης)
—TRAGURION: (**6**) imp. Šašel, *IL* 731 (Lat.
I(ulia) Panto)

**Φάντων**
ARGOLIS:
—PHLEIOUS: (**1**) iv BC *RE* (-)

**Φάραξ**
LAKONIA:
—SPARTA: (**1**) m. v BC Th. iv 38. 1 (Poralla²
716) (f. Στύφων); (**2**) c. 430-360 BC X., *HG* iii
2. 12; iv 5. 6; vi 5. 33; *Hell. Oxy.* ii 1; D.S.
xiv 63. 4; 79. 4-5 (Poralla² 717) (Φαρακίδας—
D.S. xiv 63: I ?s. Στύφων, ?f. Φάραξ II) ?=
(**5**); (**3**) f. iv BC *RE* (5) (Poralla² 718) (II ?s.
Φάραξ I); (**4**) m. iv BC *FGrH* 115 F 192; Plu.,
*Dio* 48; *Tim.* 11 (Poralla² 718); (**5**) b. 280 BC
*IG* XI (2) 161 B, 87 ?= (**2**)

**Φάρας**
EPIROS: (**1**) iv BC *Ag.* XVII 457 (Φάρα(ξ)?)

**Φαρνάκης**
ILLYRIA:
—EPIDAMNOS-DYRRHACHION: (**1**) hell.-imp.
*IDyrrh* 338 (f. Οὔενδα)
KORINTHIA:
—KORINTH: (**2**) imp. *JÖAI* 15 (1912) p. 54 no.
27, 9 (Κ. Κορν. Φ.)
S. ITALY (APULIA):
—CANUSIUM: (**3**) imp. *Epig. Rom. di Canosa* 9
(*CIL* IX 328) (Lat. Pharnaces: slave?)
—CANUSIUM*: (**4**) imp. *Epig. Rom. di Canosa*
162 (*CIL* IX 393) (Lat. Murdius Pharnaces:
freed.)
S. ITALY (CALABRIA):
—BRENTESION-BRUNDISIUM: (**5**) imp. *NScav*
1888, p. 751 (*Eph. Ep.* VIII 10) (Lat. L. Ben-
nonius Pharna(c)es: freed.)
S. ITALY (CAMPANIA):
—NEAPOLIS: (**6**) iii-iv AD *IG* XIV 826. 45 (*INap*
255)

**Φάρος**
ARKADIA:
—TEGEA: (**1**) iv/iii BC *IG* v (2) 38, 63 (s. Φα—)
S. ITALY (BRUTTIUM):
—LOKROI EPIZEPHYRIOI: (**2**) imp. *Suppl. It.* 3
p. 28 no. 11 (Lat. Pharus)

**Φαρσάλιος**
MESSENIA:
—MESSENE: (**1**) ?272 BC *SEG* XII 220 (s. Εὐτρό-
φιμος)

**Φάρυκος**
AITOLIA: (**1**) c. 240 BC Plb. ix 34. 10 (Φαρύλος?)

**Φασείδας**
AKARNANIA:
—KORONTA: (**1**) s. iii BC *IG* IX (1)² (2) 428 (f.
Πολέμων)

**Φασηλίς**
S. ITALY (APULIA):
—VENUSIA: (**1**) f. i AD *Rend. Linc.* 29 (1974) p.
622 no. 26 (*Museo di Venosa* p. 237 no. 9)
(Lat. Magia Phaselis)

**Φασικλῆς**
ARKADIA:
—PHIGALEIA: (**1**) v BC *IG* v (2) 425, 1 (-κλ̃ς)

**Φάσις**
S. ITALY (CALABRIA):
—TARAS-TARENTUM: (**1**) i-ii AD *Misc. Gr. Rom.*
3 p. 160 (Lat. D. Lucretius Phasis)

**Φατνιάδας**
AKARNANIA:
—THYRREION: (**1**) ii BC *IG* IX (1)² (2) 252, 12 (s.
Πείραος); (**2**) ?94 BC *Phegos* pp. 267 f. (coins)
(f. Λέων)

**Φαυΐδας**
ARKADIA:
—TEGEA:
——(Hippothoitai): (**1**) iv/iii BC *IG* v (2) 38, 53
(s. Εὔνοστος)

**Φαυλέας**
ARKADIA:
—MELPEIA*: (**1**) ?c. 510-500 BC ib. 555 (bronze)
(Lazzarini 108); *LSAG*² p. 215 no. 7 (date)

**Φάυλλος**
ARGOLIS:
—ARGOS: (**1**) iv BC *IG* IV (1)² 330 (f. —σίμαχος);
(**2**) a. 316 BC *SEG* XIII 240, 10 (Perlman
A.4) (I f. Φάυλλος II); (**3**) ~ *SEG* XIII 240,
10 (Perlman A.4) (II s. Φάυλλος I); (**4**) s. iii

BC Plu., *Mor.* 760 A-B; *RE* (4); (**5**) 196 BC
*IG* IX (1)² (1) 30, 25 (Φάϋλος: f. Λυσίμαχος)
—EPIDAUROS:
——(Hysminatai): (**6**) 146 BC ib. IV (1)² 28, 13
(s. Καλλισθένης)
—EPIDAUROS*: (**7**) c. 370 BC ib. 102, 35
ARKADIA:
—TEGEA:
——(Athaneatai): (**8**) iv/iii BC ib. v (2) 38, 16 (f.
Πεισίας)
S. ITALY (BRUTTIUM):
—KROTON: (**9**) c. 500-470 BC *RE* (2); *IG* I³
823 (Lazzarini 844); *SEG* XVII 442 (Landi,
*DISMG* 163; Lazzarini 879; *LSAG*² p. 261
no. 22 (date)) (Φάϝλλος—*SEG* XVII etc)
—SYBARIS-THOURIOI-COPIAE: (**10**) c. 356-355
BC *IG* IV (1)² 95, 43 (Perlman E.2); Perlman
p. 40 f. (date) (f. Φρασίδας)
S. ITALY (LUCANIA):
—HYELE-VELIA: (**11**) ii-i BC *SEG* XXXII 922; cf.
XXXIV 957. 5
—METAPONTION: (**12**) m. v BC *FD* III (4) 453,
3 (f. Ξένων)
SICILY:
—KAMARINA: (**13**) f. v BC Cordano, *Tessere
Pubbliche* 70 (Φάϋλλο[ς]); (**14**) s. v BC *SEG*
XXXVIII 935, 3 (Arena, *Iscr. Sic.* II 147) (f.
Ἐπιείκης, ?f. Ἀριστώι); (**15**) ~ Dubois, *IGDS*
119, 3 (Arena, *Iscr. Sic.* II 145) ([Φ]άϋλλος)
—SYRACUSE: (**16**) 453 BC D.S. xi 88. 4

**Φαυσίων**
ARKADIA:
—TEGEA: (**1**) ii AD *IG* v (2) 55, 63 (f. Εὐτύχης)

**Φαῦστα**
LAKONIA:
—SPARTA: (**1**) iii AD ib. v (1) 733, 4 (*GVI* 1054;
Bradford (-))

**Φαυστῖνα**
S. ITALY (APULIA):
—VENUSIA: (**1**) iv-v AD *JIWE* I 116 (-στεῖ-:
Jew); (**2**) v AD ib. 65 (*CIJ* I 598) (Φα(υ)στῖνα:
d. Ἀνασ—: Jew); (**3**) ~ *JIWE* I 71 (*CIJ* I 597)
(Φαο-: Jew)

**Φαυστῖνος**
S. ITALY (APULIA):
—VENUSIA: (**1**) iv-v AD *JIWE* I 111 (*CIJ* I 593)
(s. Βινκόμαλος: Jew); (**2**) v AD *JIWE* I 61 (*CIJ*
I 599) (Φαο-: Jew); (**3**) ~ *JIWE* I 62 (*CIJ* I
590) (Φαοστίνι (gen.): f. Λογγῖνος: Jew); (**4**) ~
*JIWE* I 66 (*CIJ* I 591) (Φαυστῖ[νος]: f. Πρε-
τιῶσα: Jew); (**5**) ~ *JIWE* I 76 (*CIJ* I 600) (s.
Ἰσά: doctor/Jew); (**6**) ~ *JIWE* I 77 (*CIJ* I 578)
(Jew); (**7**) ~ *JIWE* I 78 (*CIJ* I 601) (Jew)

**Φαῦστος**
ARGOLIS:
—TROIZEN: (**1**) imp. *IG* IV (1) 777 (I f. Φαῦστος
II); (**2**) ~ ib. (II s. Φαῦστος I); (**3**) ~ ib. 798
(I f. Φαῦστος II); (**4**) ~ ib. (II s. Φαῦστος I,
Λύκα)
ELIS: (**5**) 113 AD *IvOl* 90, 4; 94, [4] (f. Μᾶρ-
κος); (**6**) 197-201 AD ib. 106, 7 ([Φ]αῦστ[ος]: s.
Φίλιππος)
EPIROS:
—NIKOPOLIS: (**7**) imp. *SEG* XXXIX 547
LAKONIA:
—GYTHEION: (**8**) imp. *IG* v (1) 1205 (Φῶ-)
—SPARTA: (**9**) iii AD ib. 733, 1, 5 (*GVI* 1054;
Bradford (-)) (s. Ἄγνη)
S. ITALY (CAMPANIA):
—KYME: (**10**) imp. *Eph. Ep.* VIII 451 (Lat.
Faustus: s. Ἡρακλείδας, Ἁρμονία)
SICILY:
—SYRACUSE: (**11**) iii-v AD *Nuovo Didask.* 6
(1956) p. 65 no. 35 (Φαῦ[στος])
—SYRACUSE (NESOS): (**12**) iii-v AD Strazzulla
217 (Wessel 4); cf. Ferrua, *NG* 284

**Φάφιλος**
ILLYRIA:
—EPIDAMNOS-DYRRHACHION: (**1**) hell.-imp.
*IDyrrh* 428 (s. Ἐπιγένης)

**Φάων**

ARGOLIS:
—EPIDAUROS: (**1**) iv/iii BC *IG* IV (1)² 328
KORINTHIA:
—KORINTH: (**2**) ?ii AD ib. IV (1) 442 (*Λ. Σερ[β]ί[λ]ιος Φ.*: s. *Λ. Σερβίλιος Μάξιμος*)
S. ITALY (BRUTTIUM):
—LOKROI EPIZEPHYRIOI:
——(*Βοω.*): (**3**) iv/iii BC De Franciscis 34, 3 ?= (*Φαίων (1)*)
——(*Τηλ.*): (**4**) 279 BC ib. 13, 8; 17, 5 (f. *Φαΐσκος*)
S. ITALY (LUCANIA):
—VOLCEI?: (**5**) s. i AD *IItal* III (1) 7 (*CIL* x 444) (or Italy (Hirpini) Compsa: Lat. L. Domitius Phaon)
SICILY:
—KAMARINA: (**6**) f. v BC Cordano, *Tessere Pubbliche* 115 (-ōν: f. *Σιλανός*)
—SEGESTA: (**7**) iv/iii BC *IG* XIV 290, 1 (Dubois, *IGDS* 215); *SEG* XLI 825 (date) (*Φ. Σωπολιανός*: s. *Νύμφων*)

**Φεβρονία**

SICILY:
—ZANKLE-MESSANA: (**1**) iii-v AD Ferrua, *NG* 529

**Φειδάλιος**

KORINTHIA:
—KORINTH: (**1**) inc. *FGrH* 30 (*Φ., Φειδίας, Φιλάδιος*—mss.: dub.)

**Φείδας**

ARGOLIS:
—METHANA-ARSINOE: (**1**) iii BC *SEG* XXXVII 320 ([*Φ*]*είδαντο*[ς] (gen.))

**Φειδέτα**

EPIROS:
—BOUTHROTOS (PRASAIBOI): (**1**) a. 163 BC *IBouthrot* 19, 6 (*SEG* XXXVIII 476); (**2**) ~ *IBouthrot* 21, 5 (*SEG* XXXVIII 478); (**3**) ~ *IBouthrot* 31, 52, 64 (*SEG* XXXVIII 490); (**4**) ~ *IBouthrot* 38, 7 (*SEG* XXXVIII 497); (**5**) ~ *IBouthrot* 45, 6
——Cherrioi?: (**6**) a. 163 BC ib. 49, 3; 111, 7; 112, 9
—MOLOSSOI: (**7**) c. 343-330 BC Cabanes, *L'Épire* p. 588 no. 74, 5 (*SEG* XXVI 700) (d. *Ίνων*)

**Φειδιάδας**

AIGINA: (**1**) s. v BC Favorin. fr. 64 (s. *Θαλῆς*: dub.)

**Φειδίας**

AITOLIA: (**1**) iii BC *Eretria* VI 164 (*SEG* XXVIII 725. 1); (**2**) ~ Robert, *EEP* p. 114, 13
ARKADIA:
—MANTINEIA-ANTIGONEIA: (**3**) ?iii BC *IG* v (2) 318, 15, 20, 22
ARKADIA?: (**4**) iv/iii BC *HE* 677 (?f. *Πρόαρχος*)
ILLYRIA:
—APOLLONIA: (**5**) hell. *IApoll* 366 (tile) (*Φι-*)
—EPIDAMNOS-DYRRHACHION: (**6**) hell.-imp. *IDyrrh* 452 (*Φι-*: f. *Χρήσιμος*)
KORINTHIA:
—KORINTH: (**7**) c. 570-550 BC Amyx 49 (vase) (Lorber 80) (*Φι-*: fict.?); (**8**) imp. *JÖAI* 15 (1912) p. 54 no. 27, 9 (*Κ. Κορν. Φ.*)
LAKONIA:
—LEUKTRA: (**9**) imp. *SEG* XXII 312 (*Φι-*: s. *Ἀφροδίσιος*)
—SPARTA: (**10**) 35-31 BC *Münzpr. der Laked.* p. 161 Group 22 series 3 (coin) (Bradford (-))
—SPARTA?: (**11**) f. iii BC *CID* II 122 I, 7
—TEUTHRONE: (**12**) iii/ii BC *SEG* XXII 304, 3 (s. *Φίλων*: date—*LGPN*)
MESSENIA:
—MESSENE: (**13**) ii/i BC *IG* v (1) 1437, 15

S. ITALY (CALABRIA):
—TARAS-TARENTUM: (**14**) hell.? ib. XIV 2406. 86 (*Φε(ι)δί(ας), Φε(ι)δί(ς)*? (n. pr.?): ?s. *Ἀρχίνικος*)
SICILY:
—GELA-PHINTIAS?: (**15**) ?v/iv BC Manganaro, *PdelP* forthcoming no. 12 (*Φιδ-*: ?f. *Σῶσις, Ἐπίδαμος*)
—SYRACUSE: (**16**) iv/iii BC *RE* (1) (f. *Ἀρχιμήδης*)
—ZANKLE-MESSANA: (**17**) iv BC *Suda* Δ 1062 (Wehrli, *Schule Arist.* i fr. 1) (f. *Δικαίαρχος*)

**Φειδίλας**

LAKONIA:
—SPARTA: (**1**) 403-399 BC *ID* 87 b, 14 (Poralla² 719) (*Φε̄-*)
S. ITALY (BRUTTIUM):
—LOKROI EPIZEPHYRIOI:
——(*Προ.*): (**2**) iv/iii BC De Franciscis 38, 7 (s. *Δεινομένης*)

**Φειδίλεως**

S. ITALY (CAMPANIA):
—KYME: (**1**) ?c. 500 BC Dubois, *IGDGG* i 28 (bronze) (Arena, *Iscr. Sic.* III 27); *LSAG²* p. 240 no. 8 (date) (*Φειδίλεō* (gen.), *Φειδίλεōς*—Arena, *Φειδίλεōς*—Dubois: f. *Ὀνόμαστος*)

**Φείδιον**

LEUKAS: (**1**) iii BC *AD* 26 (1971) Chron. p. 351

**Φείδιππος**

ARGOLIS:
—ARGOS: (**1**) c. 220-200 BC *SEG* XI 414, 11 (Perlman E.5) ([*Φ*]*είδι*[*π*]*πος*: f. *Λύσιππος*)
KORINTHIA:
—KORINTH: (**2**) s. iii BC *IG* VII 513, 3; *Horos* 2 (1984) p. 119 f. (date) (*Φίδι*[*μ*]*ος*—ed., *Φίδι*[*ππ*]*ος*—*LGPN*: f. *Δαμάτριος*)
LAKONIA:
—SPARTA: (**3**) s. i BC *IG* v (1) 93, 34 (Bradford (-)) ([*Φε*]*ίδιππος*)

**Φεῖδις**

AKARNANIA:
—PALAIROS: (**1**) iii/ii BC *IG* IX (1)² (2) 552 (*Φείδιος* (gen.))
ITHAKE: (**2**) hell. *SEG* XVII 258 (f. *Τιμάνδρα*)

**Φειδιστώ**

EPIROS:
—OMPHALES CHIMOLIOI: (**1**) c. 330-310 BC Cabanes, *L'Épire* p. 578 no. 51, 12 (*Φι-, Φι(λ)ιστώ?*)

**Φείδιχος**

LAKONIA:
—GERONTHRAI: (**1**) c. 500 BC *IG* v (1) 1134, 6; *LSAG²* p. 201 no. 45 (date) (Poralla² 720) ([*Φ*]*είδιχος*)

**Φειδοκλῆς**

ARGOLIS:
—EPIDAUROS*: (**1**) c. 370-365 BC Peek, *IAEpid* 52 A, 14

**Φειδοκράτης**

ARGOLIS:
—EPIDAUROS*: (**1**) c. 370-360 BC *IG* IV (1)² 102, 290; *BSA* 61 (1966) p. 272 no. 4 B II, 22; cf. Peek, *IAEpid* 48

**Φειδόλαος**

AITOLIA:
—THERMOS*: (**1**) s. iii BC *IG* IX (1)² (1) 60 VI, 12
EPIROS:
—MOLOSSOI: (**2**) ?iv/iii BC *SGDI* 1354, 5; cf. Cabanes, *L'Épire* p. 582 no. 58 (f. *Πολιτ—*)
PELOPONNESE: (**3**) c. 192 BC *SEG* XIII 327, 17 (s. *Δαιτίφαντος*)

**Φειδόλας**

ARGOLIS:
—EPIDAUROS*: (**1**) c. 370-365 BC *IG* IV (1)² 102, 277; Peek, *IAEpid* 52 A, 10
KORINTHIA:
—KORINTH: (**2**) 512 BC Moretti, *Olymp.* 147; 152; Ebert, *Gr. Sieg.* 6; 7; Page, *FGE* 502; cf. pp. 401-2

**Φειδόστρατος**

ARGOLIS:
—METHANA-ARSINOE: (**1**) iii BC *SEG* XXXVII 320 ([*Φ*]*ειδόστ*[*ρα*]*τος*); (**2**) c. 163-146 BC *IG* IV (1)² 76, 2

**Φείδυλα**

EPIROS:
—KOILOPOI: (**1**) ?iv/iii BC *SGDI* 1354, 8; cf. Cabanes, *L'Épire* p. 582 no. 58

**Φείδυλλα**

EPIROS:
—BOUTHROTOS (PRASAIBOI): (**1**) a. 163 BC *IBouthrot* 52, 6 (*SEG* XXXVIII 517) (?d. *Λύκος*)

**Φειδῦς**

EPIROS:
—BOUTHROTOS (PRASAIBOI):
——Cheilioi: (**1**) a. 163 BC *IBouthrot* 75, 3; 76, 2; 77, 2 (*Φιδῦς*—nos. 75-6)
—DODONA: (**2**) iii BC Antoniou, *Dodone* Ab, 13; (**3**) ~ ib. l. 47; (**4**) ~ ib. l. 50

**Φειδώ**

AKARNANIA:
—KECHRINIA (MOD.): (**1**) ?s. iv BC *AD* 26 (1971) Chron. p. 325; cf. *L'Illyrie mérid.* 1984 p. 111 fig. 12

**Φείδων**

AKARNANIA:
—OINIADAI: (**1**) c. 325-315 BC *Hesp.* 57 (1988) p. 148 A, 35 (*SEG* XXXVI 331); cf. *Hesp.* 48 (1979) pp. 78 f. with pl. 22 c (?s. *Δαμοθάρσης*)
ARGOLIS:
—ARGOS: (**2**) vii/vi BC *RE* (3) (s. *Ἀριστοδαμίδας*, f. *Λακάδης*: tyrant)
—KLEONAI: (**3**) ?c. 560 BC *SEG* XI 290, 5 (Ebert, *Gr. Sieg.* 2; Lazzarini 847; *Nemea* I p. 277 no. 25); *LSAG²* p. 150 no. 5 (date) (-δōν: f. *Ἀριστις*)
EPIROS: (**4**) v/iv BC Unp. (Ioannina Mus.) (*Φέδ-*)
—DODONA*: (**5**) iv BC *SEG* XV 401
KORINTHIA:
—KORINTH: (**6**) viii BC Arist., *Pol.* 1265b 12
LAKONIA:
—SPARTA: (**7**) hell. *SEG* XI 884 e (tile) (Bradford (-)) (*Φι-*)

**Φειδωνίδας**

ARGOLIS:
—TROIZEN: (**1**) ?146 BC *IG* IV (1) 757 B, 24 (*Φι-*: s. *Νειλόδωρος*)

**Φέλινος**

EPIROS:
—DODONA: (**1**) iii BC Antoniou, *Dodone* Ba, 38

**Φερέας**

ARKADIA:
—TEGEA:
——(Hippothoitai): (**1**) iv/iii BC *IG* v (2) 38, 47 (s. *Φιλοκλῆς*)

**Φερεκλῆς**

KORINTHIA:
—KORINTH: (**1**) ?269 BC *CID* II 120 A, 39; 121 II, 16 (f. *Γοργίας*)

**Φερεκράτης**

ILLYRIA:
—APOLLONIA: (**1**) v/iv BC D.S. xiv 13. 4

**Φερεκύδης**

MESSENIA:
—MESSENE: (2) c. 225 BC *SEG* XI 414, 15 + Peek, *IAEpid* 331 (Perlman E.5) ([Φ]ερεκράτης)

**Φερεκύδης**

LAKONIA:
—SPARTA: (1) her. Plu., *Pelop.* 21; *RE* (2) (dub.)

**Φερέλαος**

AKARNANIA: (1) c. 250-167 BC *NZ* 10 (1878) p. 29 nos. 27-8 (coin) (*BMC Thessaly* p. 168 no. 8) (Φ. [..]ερικαλ[ος?])

**Φερέμβροτος**

ACHAIA:
—DYME: (1) ?iii-ii BC *SGDI* 1619 (s. Κληνίς)

**Φερενίκα**

EPIROS:
—BOUTHROTOS (PRASAIBOI): (1) a. 163 BC *IBouthrot* 22, 20 (*SEG* XXXVIII 479); (2) ~ *IBouthrot* 30, 30 (*SEG* XXXVIII 488); (3) ~ *IBouthrot* 50, 8
——Drymioi: (4) a. 163 BC ib. 15, 4; 21, 49 (*SEG* XXXVIII 472; 478); *IBouthrot* 156, 4; 157, 3 (*BCH* 118 (1994) p. 127 nos. 12-13) (d. Μυρτίλος)

**Φερένικος**

AITOLIA:
—DARDEOI: (1) c. 164 BC *IG* IX (1)² (1) 99, 12
—DEXIEIS: (2) 185 BC ib. 32, 30
—KALYDON: (3) s. ii BC *SEG* XXV 621, 12
ARGOLIS:
—EPIDAUROS:
——Selegeis: (4) c. 365-335 BC *IG* IV (1)² 103, 32; cf. *SEG* XXV 386
ELIS: (5) hell.? Moretti, *Olymp.* 974
EPIROS:
—MOLOSSOI: (6) ?164 BC Cabanes, *L'Épire* p. 586 no. 71, 5 (s. Δεξίλαος)
—VOTONOSI (MOD.): (7) f. iii BC *SEG* XXIV 461 (s. Ἄρχιννυς)
ILLYRIA:
—EPIDAMNOS-DYRRHACHION: (8) c. 250-50 BC Maier 185; Münsterberg Nachtr. p. 14 (coin) (Ceka 421-2) (-νει-: money.)

**Φέρης**

KORINTHIA:
—KORINTH: (1) c. 570-550 BC Amyx 66. 12 (vase) (Lorber 122) (-ρês: her.)

**Φερίας**

AIGINA: (1) 468-464 BC Moretti, *Olymp.* 255; *CEG* I 350; cf. Ebert, *Gr. Sieg.* 19 (s. Χάρης)

**Φέρις**

ARKADIA:
—THELPHOUSA: (1) a. 228 BC *IG* IV (1)² 72 B, 31 ([Φ]έρις, [Χ]έρις?: s. Κρίθων)

**Φέριστος**

S. ITALY (LUCANIA):
—HYELE-VELIA: (1) c. 340 BC Plu., *Tim.* 35

**Φέρουσα**

S. ITALY (BRUTTIUM):
—PETELIA: (1) ?i/ii AD *Klearchos* 23 (1981) p. 37 no. 1 (Lat. Flavia Pher(usa))

**Φερσέφασσα**

SICILY:
—GELA-PHINTIAS?: (1) ?v/iv BC Manganaro, *PdelP* forthcoming no. 12 (d. Πασικράτης)

**Φέρτων**

ARKADIA:
—MANTINEIA-ANTIGONEIA:
——(Posoidaia): (1) c. 425-400 BC *SEG* XXXI 348, 4

**Φηγεύς**

S. ITALY (CAMPANIA):
—DIKAIARCHIA-PUTEOLI: (1) imp. *CIL* X 2878 (Lat. L. Pontius Phegeus)

**Φηλικᾶς**

EPIROS:
—NIKOPOLIS: (1) imp. *AD* 26 (1971) Chron. p. 335

**Φηλικιανός**

SICILY:
—THERMAI HIMERAIAI: (1) iii-v AD Ferrua, *NG* 266

**Φηλικίων**

SICILY:
—SYRACUSE: (1) iii-v AD *SEG* XVI 536 (-λη-?)

**Φήλικλα**

S. ITALY (BRUTTIUM):
—LOKROI EPIZEPHYRIOI: (1) s. iv AD *IG* XIV 625, 2 (*ICI* v 6); cf. Costabile, *Municipium Locrensium* p. 74 (locn., date) (m. Λεοντίς)
S. ITALY (CAMPANIA):
—NEAPOLIS: (2) iii-iv AD *INap* 258 (-λει-)

**Φηλίκων**

ARKADIA:
—TEGEA: (1) ii AD *IG* v (2) 54, 23

**Φῆλιξ**

ARGOLIS:
—ARGOS: (1) ii AD *SEG* XVI 253, 11 (s. Φιλοκτήτης)
EPIROS:
—NIKOPOLIS: (2) imp. *CIG* 1820 (Sarikakis 166) (f. Ἐπαφρᾶς)
LAKONIA:
—SPARTA: (3) c. 140-145 AD *SEG* XI 550, 6 (Bradford (-)) (Φήλι[ξ]: s. Ἀνδρόνικος); (4) ~ *SEG* XI 550, 14; *BSA* 29 (1927-8) pp. 23-4 (name) (Bradford (-)) ([Φ]ήλι]κος? (gen.): ?f. Νίκανδρος)
SICILY:
—LIPARA: (5) imp. *BTCGI* 9 p. 96 (Φέλειξ)
—SYRACUSE: (6) iii-v AD Strazzulla 159 ([Φῆ]λιξ); (7) ~ ib. 262 (Agnello 21; Wessel 857) (doctor)

**Φήμη**

SICILY:
—HERBITA: (1) ii-iii AD *Arch. Class.* 17 (1965) p. 200 (Φ. Αἰμιλία)

**Φήμιος**

ITHAKE: (1) her. Wehrli, *Schule Arist.* iv fr. 192

**Φηρῆς**

ACHAIA:
—PELLENE: (1) ?274 BC *FD* III (4) 403 I, 1 (f. Θόας)

**Φησῖνος**

SICILY:
—ADRANON: (1) ?ii-iii AD *PdelP* 16 (1961) p. 132 (Ferrua, *NG* 472); cf. *Rupes loquentes* p. 497 no. 8 (-σεῖ-)

**Φῆσος**

PELOPONNESE?: (1) ii AD *PAE* 1992, p. 72 B, 13 (f. Λεύκιος)

**Φῆστος**

ELIS:
—OLYMPIA*: (1) imp. *IvOl* 659

**Φθία**

EPIROS:
—MOLOSSOI: (1) f. v BC *RE* (9) (d. Ἄδματος); (2) s. iii BC *RE* (8); *HSCP* Suppl. 1 (1940) pp. 483 ff.; cf. *REG* 94 (1981) pp. 34. f. (ident.)

(also called Χρυσηΐς?: d. Ἀλέξανδρος II, Ὀλυμπιάς, m. Φίλιππος (king V Macedon))

**Φθιώτης**

ARKADIA:
—TEGEA: (1) 334 BC *CID* II 79 A I, 34

**Φθόγγος**

KORINTHIA:
—KORINTH: (1) ii/iii AD *Ag.* VII p. 92 no. 243; *Corinth* IV (2) p. 188 no. 562; *Lampes antiques BN* 1 24; *SEG* XXVII 35. 30 (lamps) (Φ[θό]νγος)

**Φιάλη**

ILLYRIA:
—APOLLONIA: (1) i/ii AD *IApoll* 189 (Φλ.? Φ.: d. T. Φλ. Φιλωνίδης)
S. ITALY (CALABRIA):
—TARAS-TARENTUM: (2) imp. *CIL* IX 6168 (Lat. Phiale)

**Φίαλος**

S. ITALY (CAMPANIA):
—NUCERIA ALFATERNA*: (1) imp. ib. X 1090 (Lat. -us Phialus: freed.)

**Φῖδα**

SICILY:
—SYRACUSE: (1) iii-v AD Ferrua, *NG* 267 (Lat. Fidae (gen./dat.))

**Φικέλη?**

S. ITALY (APULIA):
—CERIGNOLA (MOD.): (1) i AD *Epig. Rom. di Canosa* 106 (*CIL* IX 685) (Lat. Canuleia Ficele: freed.?)

**Φικούλης?**

KORINTHIA:
—KORINTH: (1) inc. Tz., *ad Lyc.* 177 (fict.)

**Φίλα**

ACHAIA:
—DYME: (1) iii BC *AJPh* 31 (1910) p. 399 no. 74 a, 15; (2) ~ ib. p. 399 no. 74 c, 3; (3) ~ ib. l. 9 (m. Θευγένης); (4) ii-i BC *SEG* XIV 373 c (d. Λέων)
—TRITAIA: (5) hell. Neratzoulis p. 19 no. 1 (*Achaïe* II 315) ([Φ]ίλα: d. Διονύσιος); (6) imp.? *Achaean Grave Stelai* 63 (d. Σέλευκος)
AIGINA: (7) imp. *IG* IV (1) 76 (d. Ἐπικράτεια)
ARGOLIS:
—METHANA-ARSINOE: (8) ii-i BC ib. 868
ARKADIA:
—MANTINEIA-ANTIGONEIA: (9) ?ii AD ib. v (2) 327, 1 (*GVI* 1066) (m. Πρῖμος)
ELIS: (10) f. iii BC D.L. iv 40 (het.); (11) ii BC *SEG* XLI 387 (d. Λεοντομένης)
—PISATIS (GOUMERO (MOD.)): (12) ii-i BC ib. XXVI 474
EPIROS:
—ATHAMANES: (13) iii/ii BC *ID* 338 Bb, [29]; 385 a, 24 (d. Θεόδωρος)
—BOUTHROTOS (PRASAIBOI): (14) a. 163 BC *IBouthrot* 18, 14 (*SEG* XXXVIII 475); (15) ~ *IBouthrot* 39, 6 (*SEG* XXXVIII 498)
—NIKOPOLIS: (16) iii AD ib. XXVII 232 (Μεμ(μία) Φ.)
ILLYRIA:
—EPIDAMNOS-DYRRHACHION: (17) hell.-imp. *IDyrrh* 429 (d. Πλάτωρ)
ITHAKE: (18) hell. *Rev. Épig.* 1 (1913) p. 47 no. 1
KEPHALLENIA:
—PRONNOI: (19) imp. Unp. (*IG* arch.)
MESSENIA:
—MESSENE: (20) hell. *IG* II² 9346 (d. Φίλων); (21) i BC-i AD ib. 9345 (*Ag.* XVII 546, 1)
S. ITALY (CALABRIA):
—TARAS-TARENTUM (NR.): (22) iii BC *SEG* XLI 885. 3 (loomweight)
S. ITALY (CAMPANIA):
—DIKAIARCHIA-PUTEOLI: (23) imp. *CIL* X 3066 (Lat. Valeria Phila)

**Φιλάγαθος**
ARGOLIS:
—EPIDAUROS:
——(Dymanes): (1) 146 BC *IG* IV (1)² 28, 8 (s. Τιμοσθένης)

**Φιλαγόρας**
ACHAIA:
—DYME: (1) iii BC *AJPh* 31 (1910) p. 399 no. 74 a, 14 (s. Φιλοκλῆς)
ARGOLIS:
—ARGOS: (2) 105 BC *JÖAI* 14 (1911) Beibl. p. 146 no. 4, 9 (Φιλαγό[ρας], Φιλαγό[ρα]?: s. Ἀπολλόδωρος)

**Φιλάγριος**
EPIROS: (1) iii-iv AD *RE* (2); cf. *PLRE* I (1) (s. Φιλοστόργιος: doctor)
SICILY:
—SYRACUSE: (2) f. vi AD ib. II (3) (Lat. Philagrius)

**Φίλαγρος**
ACHAIA:
—PATRAI: (1) ?ii-i BC *Achaean Grave Stelai* 37
ARGOLIS:
—HERMIONE: (2) f. iii BC *IG* XII (7) 16, 3 (f. Νικίας)
EPIROS:
—BOUTHROTOS (PRASAIBOI): (3) a. 163 BC *IBouthrot* 21, 16 (*SEG* XXXVIII 478)
SICILY:
—KAMARINA: (4) ?iv/iii BC ib. XXXIX 1000

**Φιλαδέλφα**
S. ITALY (CAMPANIA):
—HERCULANEUM: (1) i BC-i AD Maiuri, *Nuovi Scavi* p. 418; cf. *Cron. Erc.* 8 (1978) p. 152 no. 51 (Lat. Philad[e]lp[h]a)

**Φιλαδέλφεια**
SICILY:
—SYRACUSE: (1) iii-v AD Strazzulla 160 (Wessel 1038)

**Φιλάδελφος**
EPIROS:
—NIKOPOLIS: (1) imp. *Hellenika* 22 (1969) p. 71 no. 10 (Sarikakis 168) (I f. Φιλάδελφος II); (2) ~ *Hellenika* 22 (1969) p. 71 no. 10 (Sarikakis 167) (II s. Φιλάδελφος I)
KORINTHIA:
—KORINTH: (3) ?i AD *Corinth* VIII (3) 421 (Lat. Philadel[phus]); (4) 99 AD *Hesp.* 44 (1975) p. 397, 11
LAKONIA:
—SPARTA: (5) m. i AD *IG* V (1) 509, 2 (Bradford s.v. Λυσίνεικος (1)) (Π. Μέμμιος Λυσίνικος Φ.: s. Λυσίνικος); (6) ~ *IG* V (1) 509, 5 (Bradford s.v. Γοργιππίδας (1)) (Π. Μέμμιος Γοργιππίδας Φ.: s. Λυσίνικος)
S. ITALY (APULIA):
—VENUSIA*: (7) i BC/i AD *Museo di Venosa* p. 212 no. 15 (*CIL* IX 571) (Lat. P. Servius Philadelpus: freed.)
S. ITALY (CAMPANIA):
—CUBULTERIA*: (8) iii AD *Iscr. Trebula Caiatia Cubulteria* 102 (*CIL* X 4624) (Lat. Q. Fabius Filadel[fus]: freed.)
—DIKAIARCHIA-PUTEOLI: (9) imp. *IG* XIV 843 (*CIL* X 2597) (Lat. Philadelphus); (10) ~ ib. 2104 (Lat. C. Arrius Philadelphus); (11) ~ ib. 2245 (Lat. A. Caucius Philadelphus); (12) ~ ib. 2597 (Lat. Philadelphus); (13) ~ ib. 2845 (Lat. Philadelphus); (14) 38 AD Camodeca, *L'Archivio Puteolano* I p. 143 no. 1 (Lat. L. Pontius Philadelphus)
—DIKAIARCHIA-PUTEOLI*: (15) imp. *CIL* X 1920 (Lat. Philadelphus: slave?)
—HERCULANEUM: (16) i BC-i AD *RAAN* 33 (1958) p. 244 no. 18; cf. *Cron. Erc.* 8 (1978) p. 152 no. 51 (Lat. Philadelp[hus])

—POMPEII: (17) i BC *SEG* XXX 1180; (18) i BC-i AD *CIL* IV 3990 (Castrèn 390. 4) (Lat. L. Statius Philodelpus: freed.)
—POMPEII*: (19) i BC-i AD *Atti Acc. Pontan.* 39 (1990) p. 289 no. 64 (Lat. P. Ancarsulenus Philadelphus: freed.)
—SALERNUM: (20) imp. *IItal* I (1) 80 (Lat. Cn. Pom(peius) Philadelph(us): f. Iucundus)
SICILY:
—SYRACUSE: (21) imp. *IG* XIV 51; cf. *Riv. Arch. Crist.* 18 (1941) p. 193 n. 2 and fig. 30 ?= (22); (22) ~ *Rend. Pont.* 22 (1946-7) p. 232 no. 10 ?= (21); (23) iii-v AD ib. p. 237 no. 41

**Φιλαθήναιος**
LAKONIA:
—SPARTA: (1) m. ii AD *SEG* XI 622, 2 (Bradford (-)) (Φ[ι]λαθήναιος: f. Ἀρέτων)

**Φιλαίθα**
S. ITALY (CALABRIA):
—TARAS-TARENTUM: (1) imp.? *IG* XIV 2405. 43 (lamp)

**Φίλαιθος**
KORINTHIA:
—KORINTH: (1) a. 191 BC *SEG* XXVI 392, 8 (f. Ἀρχεμαχίδας)
MESSENIA:
—THOURIA: (2) ii-i BC *IG* V (1) 1385, 2 (f. Ἐπίνικος)

**Φιλαίνετος**
SICILY:
—TAUROMENION:
——(Σπαρ.): (1) f. i BC *Cron. Arch.* 3 (1964) p. 46 IV, 24 (f. Ἀριστοκλείδας)

**Φιλαινίς**
AKARNANIA:
—THYRREION: (1) ii BC *IG* IX (1)² (2) 333
ARGOLIS:
—ARGOS: (2) ii/i BC ib. IV (1) 658 (d. Εὐ—)
ARKADIA?: (3) ?iv/iii BC *HE* 682 (d. Κλείνα)
EPIROS:
—NIKOPOLIS: (4) imp. *PAE* 1913, p. 97 no. 4 (Sarikakis 169)
ILLYRIA:
—EPIDAMNOS-DYRRHACHION: (5) hell.-imp. *IDyrrh* 430 (d. Νικοτέλης)
S. ITALY (APULIA):
—CANUSIUM*: (6) i-ii AD *Epig. Rom. di Canosa* 79 (Lat. Livia Pilaenis: freed.)
S. ITALY (CALABRIA):
—BRENTESION-BRUNDISIUM: (7) imp. *CIL* IX 59 (Lat. L. Nemestronia Philaenis)
S. ITALY (CAMPANIA):
—DIKAIARCHIA-PUTEOLI: (8) imp. *Röm. Mitt.* 19 (1904) p. 187 no. 5 (Lat. Philaenis: m. Ἰωνία)
SICILY:
—THERMAI HIMERAIAI: (9) imp. *CIL* X 7406 (*ILat. Term. Imer.* 99) (Lat. [Ul]pia Filenis)

**Φίλαινος**
KERKYRA: (1) imp.? *IG* IX (1) 931
LEUKAS: (2) ?iii BC Unp. (*IG* arch.)
SICILY:
—SELINOUS?: (3) v BC *SEG* XXXIX 1021 III, 2

**Φιλαίνων**
S. ITALY (CAMPANIA):
—NEAPOLIS: (1) i BC/i AD *INap* 177, 1 (Φιμίνων—apogr., Φι(λα)ίνων—ed.)

**Φίλαιος**
AIGINA: (1) imp. *IG* IV (1) 82 ([Φ]ίλαιος: f. Νικόλαος)
ARKADIA:
—PHENEOS: (2) c. 230-200 BC *BCH* 45 (1921) p. 13 II, 119 ([Φ]ίλαιος: s. Πλειστέας)

MESSENIA:
—THOURIA: (3) f. ii BC *SEG* XI 972, 81 (s. Γλαῦκος)
SICILY:
—TAUROMENION: (4) c. 205 BC *IG* XIV 421 an. 36 (*SGDI* 5219)

**Φίλακος**
S. ITALY (BRUTTIUM):
—LOKROI EPIZEPHYRIOI:
——(Λακ.): (1) iv/iii BC De Franciscis 3, 9 (f. Φίλιππος)
—RHEGION: (2) s. ii BC *IG* XIV 615, 4; *Klearchos* 21 (1979) pp. 83-96 (date) (Φ(ύ)λακος—*IG*: s. Φιλιστίων)

**Φιλάκριος**
ILLYRIA:
—BYLLIONES BYLLIS: (1) ?f. ii BC *SEG* XXXVIII 538

**Φιλάκων**
LAKONIA:
—SPARTA: (1) c. 90-100 AD *IG* V (1) 79, 2; *SEG* XI 539, 2 (Bradford (1)) (s. Δαμοκράτης) ?= (3); (2) c. 100-125 AD *IG* V (1) 137, 19; *SEG* XI 612 (name) (Bradford s.v. Πλάκων (-)) (Πλάκων—apogr.: f. Σωσικράτης); (3) c. 115-125 AD *SEG* XI 543, 2; 575, 13 (Bradford (2)) (f. Δαμοκράτης) ?= (1)

**Φιλάνβροτος**
AITOLIA:
—POTIDANIA: (1) m. ii BC *SBBerlAk* 1936, p. 371 b, 3, 10, 12 (*SEG* XLI 528 B) (f. Κλέων, Κριτόδαμος)

**Φιλανδρίδας**
AKARNANIA: (1) ?f. iv BC Paus. vi 2. 1
ARGOLIS:
—ARGOS: (2) ii BC *BCH* 33 (1909) pp. 456-7 no. 23, 15 (Φιλανδρ[ίδας], Φίλανδρ[ος]?)
——(Hylleis): (3) iv/iii BC *SEG* XI 293, 2 (Φιλ[αν]δρί(δ)ας)
KERKYRA: (4) iv/iii BC *IG* IX (1) 976, 4 (f. Δαμαίνετος)

**Φίλανδρος**
ACHAIA:
—PHELLOA: (1) c. 350 BC *FD* III (4) 386, 2; cf. *BCH* 101 (1977) p. 46 ([Φί]λανδρος?, [Ὀφέ]λανδρος?)
AKARNANIA: (2) c. 250-167 BC *NZ* 10 (1878) p. 28 no. 26 (coin)
EPIROS:
—AMBRAKIA: (3) a. 167 BC *SEG* XXXV 665 A, 10 (Φίλαν[δρος?])
—DODONA: (4) iii BC Antoniou, *Dodone* Aa, 16 (Φίλανδρος)
—KASSOPE: (5) f. ii BC Cabanes, *L'Épire* p. 564 no. 41, 6 (s. Σώσανδρος); (6) i BC ib. p. 564 no. 42, 11 (*SEG* XXVI 718) (s. Ἀλκάνωρ)
LEUKAS: (7) c. 167-50 BC *BMC Thessaly* p. 180 nos. 101 and 103 (coins)

**Φίλανθος**
ELIS: (1) inc. Paus. v 2. 4 (s. Πρόλαος, Λυσίππα: dub.) ?= (Φιλάνθρωπος (1))

**Φιλάνθρωπος**
ELIS: (1) inc. Giannini, *Parad. Gr.* p. 221 (dub.) ?= (Φίλανθος (1))

**Φίλαος**
ARGOLIS:
—HERMIONE: (1) ii-i BC *IG* IV (1) 732 II, 8

**Φίλαργος**
ARGOLIS:
—EPIDAUROS*: (1) c. 370 BC ib. IV (1)² 102, 81

**Φιλάργυρος**
ARKADIA:
—KLEITOR: (1) i-ii AD ib. V (2) 384
—ORCHOMENOS: (2) 192 AD ib. 346 (Τ. Φλ. Φ.)

**Epiros:**

—BOUTHROTOS (PRASAIBOI): (3) imp. Ugolini, *Alb. Ant.* 3 p. 232 (tile) (Lat. Philargirus Atianus)

—NIKOPOLIS: (4) imp. *Hellenika* 22 (1969) p. 68 no. 3 (Sarikakis 170) (f. Σώφρων)

**Illyria:**

—BYLLIONES BYLLIS: (5) imp. *Iliria* 1987 (2), p. 108 no. 70 (Lat. P. Gavius Philargyrus)

**S. Italy (Apulia):**

—CANUSIUM*: (6) imp. *Epig. Rom. di Canosa* 207 (*CIL* IX 408) (Lat. Ti. Vettius Philargyrus: freed.)

—LARINUM: (7) imp. ib. 759 (Lat. Philargyrus)

—LUCERIA*: (8) imp. *Teanum Apulum* p. 153 no. 4 a (Lat. Cn. Trebius Philargyrus: freed.)

—VENUSIA: (9) imp. *CIL* IX 435 (Lat. Philargyrus); (10) i BC/i AD *Museo di Venosa* p. 212 no. 14 (*CIL* IX 557) (Lat. Aufidius Philargyrus)

—VENUSIA*: (11) i BC ib. I² 1703 (IX 471) (Lat. Philargyrus: freed.); (12) i BC/i AD *Museo di Venosa* p. 212 no. 15 (*CIL* IX 571) (Lat. P. Servius Philargyrus: freed.)

**S. Italy (Calabria):**

—BRENTESION-BRUNDISIUM: (13) imp. ib. 54 = *Epigraphica* 25 (1963) p. 48 no. 32 (Lat. C. Oc[tavius] Phila[rgyrus]); (14) ~ *NScav* 1889, p. 167 h (*Eph. Ep.* VIII 38) (Lat. D. Patronius Phil[a]rg[y]rus)

**S. Italy (Campania):**

—DIKAIARCHIA-PUTEOLI: (15) imp. *CIL* X 1960 (Lat. Philarcyrus); (16) ~ ib. 2846 (VI 9086) (Lat. Philargyrus); (17) ~ ib. X 3024 (Lat. C. Trolius Philargurus); (18) ~ ib. 3266 (Lat. [Phi]largyr[us])

—DIKAIARCHIA-PUTEOLI*: (19) imp. ib. 2774 (Lat. C. Munius Philargurus: freed.)

—POMPEII: (20) i BC-i AD *NScav* 1893, p. 335 no. 12 (Castrèn 386. 3) (Lat. L. Spurius Philargyrus); (21) c. 51-62 AD *CIL* IV 3340. 82, 4 (Castrèn 226. 2) (Lat. L. Lucilius Philargyrus)

—SALERNUM*: (22) ?i AD *IItal* I (1) 238 I, 16 (*CIL* X 557) (Lat. L. Appuleius Philargyrus: freed.)

—SUESSULA*: (23) imp. ib. 3769 (Lat. P. Rutedius Philargyrus: freed.)

**S. Italy (Lucania):**

—GRUMENTUM: (24) imp. ib. 205; *Eph. Ep.* VIII 269 (Lat. Q. Vibiedius Philargyrus)

—GRUMENTUM*: (25) imp. *NScav* 1901, p. 25 (Lat. M. Picacilius Philargyrus: freed.)

**Sicily:**

—LIPARA: (26) imp. *Epigraphica* 51 (1989) p. 191 no. 81 (Lat. C. Publilius [Phil]argurus)

—PANORMOS: (27) imp. *CIL* X 7312 (Lat. L. Mallius Philargyrus)

—THERMAI HIMERAIAI*: (28) i-ii AD *ILat. Term. Imer.* 86 (Lat. [L. Cor]nificius [Phila]rgyrus: freed.?)

**Φιλάριν**

**Lakonia:**

—HIPPOLA: (1) ?ii-i BC *IG* V (1) 1277 i (Φιχά-ριν—lap.); (2) i BC-i AD? ib. 1277 f

—HYPERTELEATON: (3) imp. *SEG* II 171

—TEUTHRONE: (4) hell.-imp. *IG* V (1) 1221 (Φι-λάρ[ιν])

**S. Italy (Campania):**

—DIKAIARCHIA-PUTEOLI: (5) imp. *CIL* X 2610 (Lat. Philar(i)n: m. Iul. Secunda)

**Φιλάριστος**

**Arkadia:**

—KLEITOR: (1) a. 212 AD *IG* V (2) 369, 5 (Κλ. Φ.)

**Lakonia:**

—OITYLOS: (2) a. 212 AD ib. V (1) 1301 a (f. Αὐρ. Δαμοσθένεια)

---

**Φιλαρχίδας**

**Achaia?:** (1) 193 BC ib. V (2) 293, 16 (f. Λαγέ-νης)

**Argolis:**

—PHLEIOUS: (2) iv BC ib. IV (1) 452 (f. Μελιθή-ριος)

**Lakonia:** (3) 185 BC *SGDI* 1950, 5, 6, 9 (slave/freed.)

**Messenia:**

—MESSENE: (4) f. iii BC *PAE* 1991, p. 99 no. 7, 16

**Φίλαρχος**

**Argolis:**

—ARGOS: (1) c. 210-207 BC *IG* IV (1)² 73, 9; *SEG* XXXV 303 (date) (f. Φιλόδαμος)

**Arkadia:**

—MEGALOPOLIS: (2) ?131 BC *IG* V (2) 440, 13 (f. Θεόδωρος); (3) ~ ib. l. 14 (s. Θεόδωρος)

**Korinthia:**

—SIKYON: (4) vi/v BC *SEG* XI 244, 24

**Sicily:**

—AKRAI: (5) iii-ii BC *SGDI* 3242, 12 (*Akrai* p. 157 no. 8) (f. Εὐκλῆς)

**Φίλας**

**S. Italy (Calabria):**

—GROTTAGLIE (MOD.): (1) iii BC *ASP* 22 (1969) pp. 93-4 (Φ. (gen.?))

**Φιλαστείρα**

**S. Italy (Campania):**

—DIKAIARCHIA-PUTEOLI: (1) imp. *NScav* 1897, p. 531 (Audollent, *Defix. Tab.* 205 (terracotta)) (Φιλ(α)στείρα)

**Φιλατάδας**

**Messenia:**

—MESSENE: (1) 99 AD *SEG* XLI 336, 6 (f. Ἐπι-κουρίδας); (2) ~ ib. l. 8 (s. Ἐπικουρίδας)

**Φιλάχαιος**

**Arkadia:**

—TEGEA*: (1) m. v BC *IG* V (2) 159 (*IPArk* 1); *LSAG*² p. 216 no. 27 (or Lakonia: f. Ξουθίας)

**Φιλέα**

**Sicily:**

—SYRACUSE: (1) hell. *NS* 197 (Φιλέα)

**Φιλέας**

**Achaia:**

—DYME: (1) iii-ii BC *Syll*³ 530, 15; cf. *Achaia und Elis* p. 115

**Argolis:**

—ARGOS: (2) v BC *SEG* XI 339, 8 ([Φ]ιλέας: s. Ἀλεξίμαχος); (3) ?c. 480-475 BC *JÖAI* 14 (1911) Beibl. p. 142 no. 2, 3 (Lazzarini 938); *LSAG*² p. 169 no. 21 (date); (4) c. 458 BC *IG* I³ 1149, 68 ([Φ]ιλέας); (5) 326-324 BC *CID* II 120 A, 4; 122 III, [3] (f. Δεινίας)

—(Hyrnathioi): (6) iv/iii BC *SEG* XI 293, 4

—HERMIONE*: (7) ii-i BC *IG* IV (1) 745 (II s. Φιλέας I: sculptor); (8) ii/i BC ib. (I f. Φιλέας II, Ζεύξιππος)

**Arkadia:** (9) iii BC ib. V (2) 415, 3 (*IPArk* 23) (Φιλέα[ς]: s. Κλεόμβροτος)

—MANTINEIA-ANTIGONEIA: (10) c. 300-221 BC *IG* V (2) 323. 67 (tessera) (f. Σάδαμος); (11) ~ ib. 323. 68 (tessera) (s. Σάδαμος)

—MEGALOPOLIS: (12) ii BC ib. 143 ([Φιλέ]ας: s. Ζεύξιππος: sculptor)

—MEGALOPOLIS?: (13) ?i AD ib. IV (1) 745 (Loewy 141) (I f. Φιλέας II, Ζεύξιππος); (14) ~ *IG* IV (1) 745 (Loewy 141) (II s. Φιλέας I: sculptor)

—PALLANTION: (15) a. 316 BC *SEG* XI 1084, 34 (Perlman A.3) (s. Φιλήμων)

—STYMPHALOS: (16) iv-iii BC *SEG* XLII 358 ([Φ]ιλέας)

—TEGEA: (17) c. 240-229 BC *IG* V (2) 11, 16

---

—(Hippothoitai): (18) iv/iii BC ib. 38, 40 (s. Δαμοκλῆς)

—THELPHOUSA: (19) s. iii BC *FD* III (4) 20 + *SEG* XXXI 540 (Ἀγιφιλέας—*FD*: f. Ἆγις)

**Dalmatia:**

—ISSA: (20) iii BC Brunšmid p. 9 fr. G, 2 (Φι-λέ[ας])

—(Pamphyloi): (21) iv/iii BC ib. p. 7, 20 (f. Βουλαγόρας)

**Lakonia:**

—OITYLOS: (22) iii/ii BC *IG* V (1) 1295, 10 (Bradford (2))

—SPARTA: (23) imp.? *IG* V (1) 247 (Bradford (4)) (f. Νικίας); (24) c. 30-20 BC *IG* V (1) 211, 22 (Bradford (3)) (f. Ἀριστοκλῆς); (25) ii AD *IG* V (1) 159, 25 (Bradford (1))

**Messenia:**

—MESSENE: (26) s. ii BC *BCH* 95 (1971) p. 544, 3, 11, 17 (s. Φιλοκράτης)

—(Kleolaidai): (27) 11 AD *PAE* 1992, p. 71 A, 28 (s. Δημήτριος)

—MESSENE?: (28) ii/i BC *SEG* XI 979, 28

**S. Italy (Calabria):**

—TARAS-TARENTUM: (29) 212 BC *RE* (3) (Lat. Phileas) ?= (30); (30) c. 210 BC Liv. XXV 7. 11 (Lat. Phileas) ?= (29); (31) 189 BC *Syll*³ 585, 125 (f. Λύκος)

**Sicily:**

—TAUROMENION: (32) s. iii BC *FGrH* 575 F 5; (33) c. 229-212 BC *IG* XIV 421 an. 12; 421 an. 29 (*SGDI* 5219) (f. Ἕρμων)

**Φίλεια**

**Argolis:**

—ARGOS: (1) iii BC *IG* IV (1) 527, 4; cf. *BCH* 37 (1913) p. 309

**Arkadia:**

—ALIPHEIRA: (2) s. iii BC Orlandos, *Alipheira* p. 218 no. 2

—KYNAITHA: (3) ii BC *Achaean Grave Stelai* 48

—TEGEA: (4) i AD *IG* V (2) 247

**Epiros:**

—BOUTHROTOS (PRASAIBOI): (5) a. 163 BC *IBouthrot* 18, 20 (*SEG* XXXVIII 475) (Φί-λε[ι]α)

**Leukas:** (6) hell. Fraser-Rönne, *BWGT* p. 115 no. 1

**S. Italy (Calabria):**

—TARAS-TARENTUM: (7) iv-iii BC *SEG* XXXVI 904 (Troisi, *Epigrafi mobili* 86 (loomweight)) (Φιλείας (nom./gen.?))

**Φιλείας**

**Sicily:**

—SELINOUS?: (1) v BC *SEG* XXXIX 1021 II, 5; cf. *BE* 1990, no. 863 (Φιλέ(τ)ας?—*BE*)

**Φίλειος**

**Achaia:** (1) 146 BC *IG* IV (1)² 28, 156 (s. Παγ-κλῆς: synoikos)

**Φιλέρως**

**Achaia:**

—PATRAI: (1) imp. *EA* 1855, p. 1270 no. 2580 (Σερβίλιος Φ.)

**Argolis:**

—ARGOS: (2) ?119 AD *FD* III (4) 82, 2 (f. Μού-τατος)

**Arkadia:**

—TEGEA: (3) ii AD *IG* V (2) 55, 60 (I f. Φιλέρως II); (4) ~ ib. l. 60 (II s. Φιλέρως I)

**Elis:** (5) 36 BC *IvOl* 59, 6 (f. —ων); (6) imp. ib. 139, 5 ([Φιλ]έρως: s. —φῶν)

**Epiros:**

—NIKOPOLIS: (7) imp. *SEG* XXXIX 532 (Αἰφλά-του? Φιλέρωτος (gen.)—ed., Γάϊ. Φλάβιος Φ.: f. Ἀντέρως)

**Illyria:**

—APOLLONIA: (8) imp. *IApoll* 97 (f. Θηραμένης)

—EPIDAMNOS-DYRRHACHION: (9) hell.-imp. *IDyrrh* 50; (10) ~ ib. 431 (s. Στέφανος); (11) ?ii AD *Stud. Alb.* 1965, p. 72 no. 46 (Lat. Q. Dyrracinus Phileros)

KORINTHIA:
—KORINTH: (12) ii-iii AD SEG XI 138 c (Lat. [P]hilero(s))
LAKONIA:
—SPARTA: (13) c. 80-160 AD IG v (1) 68, 15; 112, 2, 15; 676, 5 (Bradford (1); (2)) (Γ. Ἰούλ. Φ.: s. Θεόξενος, f. Θεόξενος); (14) c. 100-110 AD IG v (1) 97, 6; SEG XI 511, 5; 564, 6 (Bradford (4)) (f. Δαμοκράτης); (15) c. 140-160 AD IG v (1) 65, 11; 115, 3 (Bradford (3))
S. ITALY (APULIA):
—CANUSIUM: (16) i-ii AD Epig. Rom. di Canosa 64 (Lat. Phileros)
—LARINUM*: (17) s. i BC Frenz p. 153 no. 139 (Lat. C. Mevius Phileros: freed.)
—VENUSIA: (18) s. i BC Museo di Venosa p. 148 no. 5 (CIL IX 465) (Lat. Phileros)
—VENUSIA*: (19) imp. ib. 556 (Lat. L. Pontius Phileros: freed.)
S. ITALY (CALABRIA):
—HYDROUS-HYDRUNTUM: (20) imp. NScav 1957, p. 191 (Susini, Fonti Salento p. 100 no. 34) (Lat. C. Atilius Phileros)
—RUDIAE: (21) inc. NScav 1897, p. 407 no. 15 (Lat. Philerus)
S. ITALY (CAMPANIA):
—DIKAIARCHIA-PUTEOLI: (22) ?i-ii AD CIL x 1728 (Lat. Ti. Claudius Phileros)
—DIKAIARCHIA-PUTEOLI*: (23) imp. ib. 1887 (Lat. Phileros: freed.)
—NOLA*: (24) imp. ib. 1272 (Lat. L. Sattius Phileros: freed.)
—POMPEII: (25) i BC-i AD ib. IV 1826 (Lat. Phileros); (26) ~ ib. 4896 (Lat. Phileros); (27) ~ ib. 5420 (Lat. Phileros); (28) ~ ib. x 8058. 84 (seal) (Castrèn 391. 1) (Lat. M. Statilius Phileros)
—POMPEII*: (29) i BC Impegno per Pompeii Add. II (Lat. M. Artorius Phileros: freed.); (30) i BC-i AD ib. 23 OS (PdelP 40 (1985) p. 431 f.; Castrèn 450. 6) (Lat. P. Vesonius Phileros: freed.)
—RUFRAE*: (31) imp. CIL x 4832 (Lat. C. Satilius Pileros: freed.)
—SALERNUM*: (32) imp. IItal I (1) 70 (Lat. N. Mari. Phileros: freed.); (33) ?i AD ib. 238 III, 13 (CIL x 557) (Lat. L. Appuleius Phileros: freed.)
S. ITALY (LUCANIA):
—POSEIDONIA-PAESTUM*: (34) m. i BC ib. I² 3149 (Mello–Voza 9) (Lat. C. Iulius Phileros: freed.)
SICILY: (35) imp. ASSiciliano 1887, p. 302 no. 843 (amph.) (Lat. Philero)
—THERMAI HIMERAIAI: (36) i AD ILat. Term. Imer. 128 (Lat. Cn. Patulcius Phileros)

## Φιλέστα
AKARNANIA:
—THYRREION: (1) ii BC IG IX (1)² (2) 334 (Φ. (masc./fem. voc.))

## Φιλέταιρος
ILLYRIA:
—EPIDAMNOS-DYRRHACHION: (1) hell.-imp. IDyrrh 51
S. ITALY (APULIA):
—CANUSIUM*: (2) imp. Epig. Rom. di Canosa 100 (CIL IX 364 and Add.) (Lat. P. Barbatius Philotaerus: freed.)
S. ITALY (CAMPANIA):
—POMPEII: (3) i BC-i AD ib. IV 653 (Lat. Phyloterus); (4) ~ ib. 2192 (Lat. Phileterus)

## Φιλέτας
EPIROS:
—DODONA*: (1) ?iii BC SEG XIX 430 a

## Φιλέτις
LAKONIA: (1) iii-ii BC IG v (1) 1341, 6 (Bradford (-))

## Φιλεύς
ARKADIA:
—TEGEA?: (1) m. iii BC IG v (2) 368, 3

## Φίλημα
S. ITALY (LUCANIA):
—GRUMENTUM*: (1) imp. CIL x 274 (Lat. Vettia Philelma: freed.)

## Φιλημάτιν
S. ITALY (CALABRIA):
—TARAS-TARENTUM: (1) ?i-ii AD ib. IX 243 (Lat. Iulia Filematin)

## Φιλημάτιον
ARKADIA:
—MANTINEIA-ANTIGONEIA: (1) ?ii-i BC IG v (2) 336
S. ITALY (APULIA):
—VENUSIA*: (2) m. i AD Rend. Linc. 29 (1974) p. 618 no. 19 (Lat. Flavia Philematio: freed.)
S. ITALY (BRUTTIUM):
—LOKROI EPIZEPHYRIOI*: (3) i AD Costabile, Municipium Locrensium 31 (CIL x 25) (Lat. Philematium)
S. ITALY (CAMPANIA):
—DIKAIARCHIA-PUTEOLI: (4) imp. ib. 2847 (Lat. Philematio)
—DIKAIARCHIA-PUTEOLI*: (5) imp. ib. 2821 (Lat. Philematio: freed.?)
—NOLA: (6) imp. ib. 1320 (Lat. [Ph]ilematio)
—POMPEII*: (7) i AD ib. IV 9251; cf. Gnomon 49 (1973) p. 275 (Lat. P(i)lematio: slave?)
S. ITALY (LUCANIA):
—GRUMENTUM*: (8) imp. NScav 1901, p. 25 (Lat. Titia Philematio: m. Νικηφόρος: freed.)

## Φιλημένα
S. ITALY (LUCANIA):
—HERAKLEIA: (1) iii-ii BC SEG XXXIII 765 (d. Νίκων)

## Φιλήμενος
S. ITALY (CALABRIA):
—TARAS-TARENTUM: (1) iv/iii BC IG XIV 668 II, 1 (Landi, DISMG 194) (Φιλή[μενος], Φιλή[μων]?); (2) c. 272-235 BC Vlasto 884-7 (Evans, Horsemen p. 179 VIII E.1 (coin)); (3) 212-209 BC RE (-); Liv. xxvii 16. 3 (Lat. Philemenus)
S. ITALY (LUCANIA):
—METAPONTION: (4) c. 356-355 BC IG IV (1)² 95, 50 (Perlman E.2); Perlman pp. 46-9 (date)

## Φιλήμων
AKARNANIA: (1) iii/ii BC IG XII (3) 304 (IX (1)² (2) 577) (f. Ποσειδώνιος); (2) m. ii BC ib. 208, 1, [31]
—ASTAKOS: (3) ii BC ib. 434, 14 (f. Ἄνδρων)
—THYRREION: (4) iii BC ib. 245, 17 ([Φι]λήμων)
ARGOLIS:
—ARGOS: (5) 105 BC JÖAI 14 (1911) Beibl. p. 146 no. 4, 22 (f. Δαμοκλῆς)
ARKADIA:
—PALLANTION: (6) a. 316 BC SEG XI 1084, 34 (Perlman A.3) (f. Φιλέας)
ELIS:
—PYLOS: (7) hell.? SEG XXV 457; cf. AD 20 (1965) Chron. p. 219 n. 10
ILLYRIA:
—APOLLONIA: (8) c. 250-50 BC Münsterberg Nachtr. p. 13 (coin) (Ceka 123) (money.)
—EPIDAMNOS-DYRRHACHION: (9) c. 250-50 BC Maier 130; 228-9; 327; Münsterberg Nachtr. p. 15 (coin) (Ceka 424-8) (money.)
LAKONIA:
—GYTHEION: (10) c. 100-75 BC IG v (1) 1144, 22, 23; 1181 (s. Θεόξενος, f. Θεόξενος)
—SPARTA: (11) ii-iii AD ib. 246 (Bradford (1)); (12) ?134 AD IG v (1) 62, 11 (Bradford (3)) (f. Σωτηρίδας)

LEUKAS: (13) c. 167-50 BC BMC Thessaly p. 185 no. 168; p. 187 nos. 190-1; Coll. Hunter 2 p. 25 no. 9 (coins) (II s. Φιλήμων I); (14) ~ ib. (coin) (I f. Φιλήμων II)
S. ITALY (APULIA):
—CANUSIUM: (15) imp. Epig. Rom. di Canosa Instr. 159 (loomweight) (Lat. Philemo); (16) ~ ib. Instr. 160 (loomweight) (Lat. Pilem(o))
—CANUSIUM*: (17) m. i BC ib. 75 (CIL I² 1707; IX 352) (Lat. A. Arrius Philemo: freed.)
S. ITALY (CAMPANIA):
—DIKAIARCHIA-PUTEOLI: (18) imp. ib. x 2842 (Lat. L. Petronius Philemo: s. Ἡδόνη)
—HERCULANEUM: (19) i BC-i AD ib. 1404 (Lat. Philemo)
—NEAPOLIS: (20) i BC-i AD? IG XIV 800 (INap 145) (f. Μηνόφιλος)
SICILY:
—SYRACUSE: (21) hell. IG XIV Add. 9 a ([Φιλ]ήμων)
—SYRACUSE?: (22) c. 368-263 BC RE (7) (PP 16723); PCG 7 pp. 318 ff.; Osborne, Naturalization T85 (and Athens Diomeia or Cilicia Soloi)
—TYNDARIS: (23) imp. IG XIV 378 (Ἰούνιος Φ.)

## Φιληρατίδας
LAKONIA:
—SPARTA: (1) c. 170 AD ib. v (1) 116, 14 + SEG XI 590; Cartledge–Spawforth p. 180 n. 6 (name) (Bradford (5)) (Ἰούλ. Φ., Φιλ(οκ)ρατίδας—SEG: s. Ἱππόδαμος)

## Φιληρατίς
LAKONIA:
—KYTHERA: (1) hell.-imp. IG v (1) 942, 4

## Φιλήρατος
EPIROS:
—BOUTHROTOS (PRASAIBOI): (1) imp. Ugolini, Alb. Ant. 3 p. 218 (Lat. Fil[e]ratus)
KORINTHIA:
—KORINTH: (2) iii-ii BC IG XII (3) 832 (s. Ἀγυλίδας)

## Φιλησία
ELIS:
—LETRINOI?: (1) ii BC SEG XI 1174 b (Φιλησίαρ (fem. gen.))

## Φιλήσιος
ACHAIA: (1) 401-400 BC RE (2)
AKARNANIA:
—ALYZIA: (2) m. ii BC IG IX (1)² (2) 209, 18 (s. Θράσων)
ARGOLIS:
—TROIZEN: (3) ?369 BC ib. IV (1) 748, 22
ARKADIA:
—MANTINEIA-ANTIGONEIA: (4) 64 or 62 BC ib. v (2) 265, 49 (s. Σαμίδας)
DALMATIA:
—ISSA: (5) hell.? Brunšmid p. 24 no. 13 (VAHD 84 (1991) p. 258 no. 9) (f. Ἀγησίδαμος); (6) ii BC SEG XXXI 602, 1 (VAHD 84 (1991) p. 257 no. 7) (f. Κλεέμπορος); (7) ~ SEG XXXI 602, 5 (VAHD 84 (1991) p. 257 no. 7) (s. Κλεέμπορος)
KORINTHIA:
—KORINTH: (8) f. i AD Corinth VIII (2) 110 (ILGR 116) (Lat. Philesius: f. Καλλικράτεια)

## Φιλητάδας
ARGOLIS:
—HERMIONE: (1) iii BC IG IV (1) 729 I, 6 (f. Θαρσύτας)

## Φιλήτας
SICILY:
—GELA-PHINTIAS?: (1) f. v BC Dubois, IGDS 134 b, 3 (Arena, Iscr. Sic. II 47) (-λέ-)

**Φιλήτη**
S. ITALY (APULIA):
—MONTEMILONE (MOD.): (1) s. ii AD *Epig. Rom. di Canosa* 211 (*Museo di Venosa* p. 239 no. 13); *Epig. Rom. di Canosa* 213 (Lat. Aelia Philete: d. Φίλητος, Κωμική: imp. freed.)
S. ITALY (CAMPANIA):
—DIKAIARCHIA-PUTEOLI: (2) imp. *CIL* x 2091 (Lat. Cl. Philete); (3) ~ *NScav* 1885, p. 145 (*Eph. Ep.* VIII 411) (Lat. Marcia Philete)
—MISENUM*: (4) ?i-ii AD *CIL* x 3451 (Lat. Iulia Filete: freed.)
SICILY:
—SYRACUSE: (5) iii-v AD Strazzulla 382 (Wessel 750); cf. Ferrua, *NG* 141 a

**Φιλήτιος**
KORINTHIA:
—KORINTH: (1) ii/i BC *Corinth* VIII (3) 47 a (Φιλητίων?)

**Φιλητίς**
LAKONIA:
—HIPPOLA: (1) ii-iii AD *SEG* XXVI 456, 1; XXXI 335 (name) (Φιλητί (voc.))

**Φίλητος**
EPIROS:
—NIKOPOLIS: (1) imp. *PAE* 1913, p. 97 no. 12 (Sarikakis 171) (f. Φιλιτίων)
KERKYRA: (2) imp. *IG* IX (1) 967 (Δομίτιος Φ.)
KORINTHIA:
—KORINTH: (3) imp. *JÖAI* 15 (1912) p. 55 no. 27, 12 (Ἰούλ. Φ.)
LAKONIA:
—SPARTA: (4) c. 150 AD *IG* v (1) 71 II, 12 (Bradford (3)) (s. Δαμακίων); (5) c. 175-210 AD *IG* v (1) 309, 2 (*Artemis Orthia* p. 329 no. 62); *SEG* XI 740, [2]; *BSA* 79 (1984) p. 283 no. 1 (date) (Bradford (4)) (Φιλητορ—*IG*: II s. Φίλητος I); (6) ~ *IG* v (1) 309, 3 (*Artemis Orthia* p. 329 no. 62); *SEG* XI 740, 2; *BSA* 79 (1984) p. 283 no. 1 (date) (Bradford (6)) (Φί[λητος]—*SEG*: I f. Φίλητος II); (7) f. iii AD *SEG* XI 825, 3 (Bradford (5)) (*M*. Αὐρ. Φ.: s. *M*. Αὐρ. Τιμάκων); (8) m. iii AD *IG* v (1) 565, 2; *SEG* XI 633, 9 (Bradford (1); (2)) (*M*. Αὐρ. Φ.: s. Ἀγαθόπους)
S. ITALY (APULIA):
—CANUSIUM*: (9) imp. *Epig. Rom. di Canosa* 94 (*CIL* IX 363) (Lat. Philetus: slave?)
S. ITALY (CALABRIA):
—BRENTESION-BRUNDISIUM: (10) i/ii AD *Necropoli via Cappuccini* p. 269 no. E14 (Lat. Ti. Claud[ius] Philetu[s])
S. ITALY (CAMPANIA):
—DIKAIARCHIA-PUTEOLI: (11) imp. *CIL* x 2200 (Lat. P. Caesonius Philetus); (12) ~ ib. 2331 (Lat. P. Cornelius Philetus)
—HERCULANEUM: (13) i BC-i AD ib. 1403 d I, 26 (Lat. L. Annius Philetus); (14) m. i AD *PdelP* 3 (1948) p. 177 no. 23 (Lat. Q. Iunius Philetus) ?= (15)
—HERCULANEUM*: (15) i AD *CIL* IV 10779 (amph.) (Lat. Iunius Philetus) ?= (14)
—NUCERIA ALFATERNA: (16) imp. *NScav* 1932, pp. 317-18 (Lat. Philetus)
—POMPEII: (17) i BC-i AD *CIL* IV 2402 (Lat. Filetus); (18) ~ ib. 4433 (Lat. Philetus); (19) ~ ib. 5106 (Lat. Philetus); (20) ~ ib. 8403 (Lat. Philetus); (21) ?i AD *NScav* 1916, p. 302 no. 7 a (Lat. Philethus); (22) 55 AD *CIL* IV 3340. 12, 15; 17, 14; 54, 12; 75, 12 (Castrèn 42. 16) (Lat. Q. Arrius Philetus)
—POMPEII*: (23) i AD *CIL* x 8042. 100 (tile) (Lat. A. Tatius Philetus)
—SALERNUM: (24) ?i AD *IItal* I (1) 61 (Lat. Philetus)

**Φιλήτωρ**
ELIS:
—PISA: (1) ii BC *GVI* 453 (f. Ἄστεια)

LAKONIA:
—SPARTA: (2) c. 90-100 AD *SEG* XI 609, 4; 626, 4 (Bradford (-)) (Γ. Ἰούλ. Φ.: s. Σωσικράτης)
S. ITALY (CAMPANIA):
—POMPEII: (3) i BC-i AD *CIL* IV 9015 (Lat. Filetor)

**Φιλία**
AKARNANIA:
—KORONTA: (1) iii BC *IG* IX (1)² (2) 429 (d. Χρέμας)
—THYRREION: (2) iii/ii BC ib. 309
ARGOLIS:
—EPIDAUROS: (3) iii BC ib. IV (1)² 242 (Φιλί[α])
—HERMIONE: (4) ?ii-i BC ib. IV (1) 731 III, 13 (d. Πραξίδαμος)
EPIROS:
—AMBRAKIA: (5) hell.? *CIG* 1805 (d. Κλέων)
—KASSOPE: (6) hell.? *SEG* XXIV 439 (d. Σιμίας)
—KONTATES (MOD.): (7) iii BC ib. XXXIV 591
S. ITALY (LUCANIA):
—HERAKLEIA: (8) ?iv BC *BdA* 54 (1969) p. 139 (terracotta) ?= (9); (9) iii BC Landi, *DISMG* 216. 1 (loomweight) ?= (8)

**Φιλιάδας**
MESSENIA:
—MESSENE: (1) iv BC D. xvii 4; 7; xviii 295; Plb. xviii 14. 3, 12 (f. Νέων, Θρασύλοχος)

**Φιλίαρχος**
DALMATIA:
—ISSA:
——(Hylleis): (1) iv/iii BC Brunšmid p. 8, 36 (s. Διωνδας)
——(Pamphyloi): (2) iv/iii BC ib. p. 7, 26 (f. Ὀρθων)
EPIROS:
—BOUTHROTOS: (3) ?ii BC *IBouthrot* 173 (Ugolini, *Alb. Ant.* 3 p. 121) (s. Νικοκράτης)
—BOUTHROTOS (PRASAIBOI): (4) a. 163 BC *IBouthrot* 28, 6 (*SEG* XXXVIII 486)
S. ITALY (BRUTTIUM):
—LOKROI EPIZEPHYRIOI:
——(Θρα.): (5) iv/iii BC De Franciscis 24, 2 (f. Φίλιππος)
——(Προ.): (6) iv/iii BC ib. 19, 5 (s. Ἡράκλητος)
——(Τιω.): (7) iv/iii BC ib. 32, 7 (s. Φιλόδαμος)
S. ITALY (CALABRIA):
—TARAS-TARENTUM: (8) c. 302-280 BC Vlasto 673-5 (Evans, *Horsemen* p. 132 VI A.3 (coins)); (9) c. 212-209 BC Vlasto 981-3 (Evans, *Horsemen* p. 211 X D.1 (coins))
SICILY: (10) ii/i BC *Kokalos* 32 (1986) pp. 242-3 nos. 80-90 (tiles)
—KENTORIPA: (11) ?s. iii BC *Sic. Gymn.* 2 (1949) p. 91 no. 1, 7 + 16 (1963) p. 54 (s. Εὐ—); (12) ii-i BC Dubois, *IGDS* 189, 2 (*SEG* XLII 837) (I f. Φιλίαρχος II); (13) ~ Dubois, *IGDS* 189, 2 (*SEG* XLII 837) (II s. Φιλίαρχος I)
—MORGANTINA: (14) iv/iii BC ib. XXXIX 1008, 9 (f. Ἰάρων); (15) ~ ib. l. 10 (s. Ἀπολλωνίδας)
—SYRACUSE: (16) hell.-imp. *NS* 594 (f. Τρύφαινα)
—TAUROMENION: (17) ?ii/i BC *IG* XIV 421 III (*SGDI* 5219) ([Φι]λ[ί]αρχος)
——(Σακ.): (18) ?ii/i BC *IG* XIV 421 D an. 11 (*SGDI* 5219) (f. Εὔανδρος)

**Φιλιάστρα**
S. ITALY (CAMPANIA):
—DIKAIARCHIA-PUTEOLI: (1) imp. *CIL* x 2201 (Lat. Filiastra)

**Φιλίαστρος**
S. ITALY (CAMPANIA):
—SALERNUM: (1) imp. *IItal* I (1) 175 (*CIL* x 590) (Lat. Anthio Filiastrus)

**Φιλίδας**
MESSENIA:
—ASINE: (1) ?316 BC *SEG* XII 219 (s. Νεοκλῆς)
—MESSENE: (2) ii/iii AD *IG* v (1) 1472

**Φιλικά**
ITHAKE: (1) hell. Unp. (*IG* arch.) (Φιλικ[ά], Φίλικ[έ]? (voc.))
KERKYRA: (2) iii/ii BC *SEG* XXVII 172
LEUKAS: (3) hell.-imp. *IG* IX (1) 585

**Φιλικίων**
S. ITALY (CAMPANIA):
—POMPEII: (1) i BC-i AD *CIL* IV 3163-4 (Lat. Filicio)

**Φιλικός**
AKARNANIA: (1) c. 250-167 BC *NZ* 10 (1878) p. 30 no. 33; *Coll. de Luynes* 1918 (coins)
—THYRREION: (2) hell. *SEG* XXXII 565 (f. Ταύρων)
ARGOLIS:
—EPIDAUROS: (3) iv/iii BC ib. XIV 328 (s. Ἀρχίδαμος)
——Dorimachis: (4) c. 220-200 BC ib. XI 414, 26 (Perlman E.5)
DALMATIA:
—ISSA: (5) iii BC *SEG* XXXI 598 (f. Θεύδωρος)
——(Hylleis): (6) iv/iii BC Brunšmid p. 8, 46 (s. Ζωΐλος)
KERKYRA: (7) iii BC *RE* s.v. Philiskos (4); Fraser, *Ptol. Alex.* 2 p. 859 n. 407 (ident.) (s. Φιλώτας)
LAKONIA:
—SPARTA: (8) c. 25-1 BC *SEG* XI 875 (brick) (Bradford (-))
S. ITALY (LUCANIA):
—HYELE-VELIA: (9) hell.? *PdelP* 25 (1970) p. 263 no. 4 (f. Ἀρίστα)
SICILY:
—SYRACUSE: (10) iv/iii BC *Ag.* XVII 669 (*SEG* XIV 227) (f. Λυσίς)

**Φιλικώ**
SICILY:
—LIPARA: (1) ?iii BC *Meligunis-Lipara* 5 p. 150 no. 2161; cf. *SEG* XLI 807 (Φιλικκώ)

**Φιλίκων**
ELIS: (1) i AD *IvOl* 75, [12]; 76, 2; 77, [7]; 80, 2, 4; 81, [12]; 84, [13]; 85, [10]; 86, 8; *EA* 1905, p. 255 no. 1, 8 (Φ. ὁ καὶ Θεότιμος—75-7 and 80: s. Ὀλυμπιόδωρος, f. Ἴαμος: mantis/Iamidai)

**Φίλινα**
ELIS:
—LASION: (1) vi BC *SEG* XI 1173 b
—PISATIS (KAVKANIA (MOD.)): (2) f. iii BC ib. XXV 470

**Φιλίνθα**
KEPHALLENIA:
—SAME: (1) hell. Fraser-Rönne, *BWGT* p. 118 no. 6, 2

**Φιλινίων**
ARKADIA: (1) ?253 BC Nachtergael, *Les Galates* 10, 28 (Stephanis 2493) (s. Γόργος)

**Φίλιννα**
S. ITALY (CAMPANIA):
—DIKAIARCHIA-PUTEOLI*: (1) imp. *CIL* x 2409 (Lat. Cameria Philinna: freed.)
SICILY:
—SYRACUSE: (2) s. iv BC *AP* ix 434, 3; *Suda* Θ 166; cf. Gow, *Theocritus* I pp. xv-xvi (m. Θεόκριτος)

**Φιλῖνος**
AKARNANIA:
—ANAKTORION: (1) iv/iii BC *IG* IX (1)² (2) 212, 2 (s. Πλ..αρχος)
—PALAIROS: (2) iii BC ib. 509

ARGOLIS:
—EPIDAUROS*: (3) c. 370-365 BC Peek, *IAEpid*
52 A, 26; (4) c. 290-270 BC *IG* IV (1)² 109 I,
125; *BSA* 61 (1966) p. 306 no. 20, 116
ARKADIA:
—MEGALOPOLIS: (5) ii BC *IG* V (2) 447, 8; (6)
?145 BC ib. 439, 29 (s. Σικλείδας); (7) ii-iii AD
ib. 491 (-λεί-)
ELIS: (8) ?277 BC *FD* III (1) 126, 3 (f. Ξενοφῶν);
(9) s. i BC *IG* II² 8529 (s. Στράτιος)
EPIROS:
—ARGOS (AMPHILOCH.): (10) iv/iii BC *SEG*
XXXII 560
KORINTHIA:
—KORINTH: (11) iv/iii BC Men., *Pk.* 1026 (fict.);
(12) ?148 BC Plb. xxxviii 18. 6; (13) s. i BC *Co-
rinth* VIII (2) 2; 3; 101; 131; 132; VIII (3) 155,
1; 241, 2 (Lat. Cn. Babbius Philinus)
—KORINTH?: (14) s. ii AD ib. VIII (1) 15, 74 +
*SEG* XI 62, 26 (Λ. Ἐρέννιος Φιλεῖνος)
MESSENIA:
—MESSENE: (15) iii BC ib. XXIII 210, 10; (16) i
BC/i AD *IG* V (1) 1438 a, 5
S. ITALY (CALABRIA):
—TARAS-TARENTUM: (17) ?iv AD *CIG* 4705 q
(*SB* 8576) (f. Φίλιππος)
S. ITALY (CAMPANIA):
—DIKAIARCHIA-PUTEOLI: (18) imp. *NScav*
1887, p. 450 (*Eph. Ep.* VIII 390) (Lat. Apisius
Philinus: f. Apisia Vitalis)
—NEAPOLIS*: (19) ii-iii AD *IG* XIV 815 (*INap*
178); cf. Leiwo p. 126 no. 113 (-λεί-: slave?)
SICILY:
—AKRAGAS: (20) s. iii BC *RE* (8); *FGrH* 174
—HERBITA: (21) f. i BC Cic., *In Verr.* II iii 80
(Lat. Philinus)
—KAMARINA: (22) f. v BC Cordano, *Tessere Pub-
bliche* 15 (Φ(ι)λῖνος: f. Τίμων); (23) iv/iii BC
*SEG* XXXIV 942, 1 (Dubois, *IGDS* 123; Cor-
dano, 'Camarina VII' 159) (f. Διονύσιος); (24)
hell. *SEG* XXXIX 1001, 1
—MORGANTINA: (25) ?iv/iii BC ib. 1009, 7 (f.
Διονύσιος); (26) iv/iii BC ib. 1012, 6 (s. Διονύ-
σιος)
—SELINOUS: (27) s. v BC Dubois, *IGDS* 62 (*IG-
LMP* 100) (s. Δίων)
—SYRACUSE: (28) iv/iii BC Ugolini, *Alb. Ant.* 2
p. 154 no. 6 (f. Αἰσχρίων)
ZAKYNTHOS: (29) f. iii BC *SEG* XIV 481
([Φ]ιλῖνος: s. Στρατοκλῆς)

**Φιλιξώ**
SICILY:
—SYRACUSE: (1) hell. *NScav* 1892, p. 359

**Φίλιος**
ARKADIA:
—TEGEA: (1) s. iii BC *IG* V (2) 116, 3 (s. Φίλων)
DALMATIA:
—ISSA: (2) ii BC *SEG* XXXI 602, 8 (*VAHD* 84
(1991) p. 257 no. 7) (f. Θεμιστόλα)
ILLYRIA:
—BYLLIONES: (3) c. 200 BC *SEG* XXXV 680, 5;
cf. XXXVIII 541 ([Φ]ίλιος: s. Πολέμων)
LAKONIA:
—OITYLOS: (4) iii/ii BC *IG* V (1) 1295, 5 (Brad-
ford (-))
LEUKAS: (5) c. 167-50 BC *SNG Delepierre* 1245
(coin)
S. ITALY (CAMPANIA):
—NEAPOLIS: (6) i BC *IG* XIV 817 (*INap* 181);
cf. Leiwo p. 118 no. 104 (f. Χάρμης)
S. ITALY (LUCANIA):
—METAPONTION: (7) inc. *SEG* XXX 1176 F. 15;
(8) iii BC ib. XXXVII 780
SICILY:
—AKRAI: (9) ii BC *Akrai* p. 156 no. 6, 19 (f. Δα-
μοκράτης); (10) ii-i BC *SGDI* 3246, 26 (*Akrai*
pp. 152-3 no. 2; Dubois, *IGDS* 109) ([Φ]ίλιος:
f. Δαμοκράτης)

—IAITON*: (11) hell. *AA* 1994, p. 241 (bullet)
(f. Μαρσ—); (12) ~ ib. p. 241 no. 5 a-b (bullet)
(?f. Ἀνδρέας)
—SYRACUSE?:
——(Πλε.): (13) hell. *Mem. Linc.* 8 (1938) p.
127 no. 35. 5 (bullet); cf. *BE* 1965, no. 502;
cf. *L'Incidenza dell'Antico* p. 422 and fig. 3
(f. Φιντύλος: name—Guarducci)

**Φιλίππα**
ARGOLIS:
—HERMIONE: (1) ii-i BC *IG* IV (1) 732 V, 7
ARKADIA:
—KLEITOR: (2) iii BC *Achaean Grave Stelai* 4
KORINTHIA:
—KORINTH: (3) ii-iii AD *Corinth* VIII (1) 134, 1
(-ίπα: m. Δομετία Σατορνῖλα Ἀπολλωνίς)
MESSENIA:
—MESSENE: (4) iii/ii BC *PAE* 1991, p. 91 (d.
Φιλόμηλος, m. Χαιρήμων)

**Φιλίππη**
ARKADIA:
—KLEITOR: (1) i-ii AD *IG* V (2) 375 (Fraser-
Rönne, *BWGT* p. 202 no. 1)

**Φιλιππιανός**
SICILY:
—SABUCINA (MOD.): (1) iii-iv AD *BdA* 48 (1963)
p. 260 and fig. 28 (Wilson, *Sicily* p. 216 fig.
21 (tile)) (Lat. Filippianus)

**Φιλιππίδας**
EPIROS:
—BOUTHROTOS (PRASAIBOI): (1) a. 163 BC
*IBouthrot* 18, 14 (*SEG* XXXVIII 475); (2) ~
*IBouthrot* 48, 9; (3) ~ ib. 113, 12; (4) ~ ib.
135, 15 (Φι[λι]π[π]ίδας); (5) ~ ib. 142, 9; (6) ~
ib. 166 (*SEG* XXXVIII 465) (Φιλλιπί-: f. Φιλ-
ιππος)
——Aigorrioi: (7) a. 163 BC *IBouthrot* 90, 7 (f.
Λάμιος) ?= (11)
——Dranoi: (8) a. 163 BC ib. 132, 6-7 (f. Λυκώ-
τας)
——Euryoi: (9) a. 163 BC ib. 97, 4 (-λιπί-: f.
Λέων) ?= (10); (10) ~ ib. l. 8 (-λιπί-: f. Λάμιος)
?= (9)
——PRASAIBOI: (11) a. 163 BC ib. 56, 9 (*SEG*
XXXVIII 507) (-λιπί-: f. Λάμιος) ?= (7)
LAKONIA:
—ASOPOS: (12) ii/i BC *IG* V (1) 1143, 3
(Φιλ[ιπ]πίδας: f. Φιλόμηλος)
MESSENIA:
—MESSENE: (13) m. iii BC *IC* 2 p. 29 no. 13 B,
2 (s. Κλεόδαμος)

**Φιλιππίδης**
ILLYRIA:
—APOLLONIA: (1) imp. *IApoll* 238 (?f. Ἡρωΐς);
(2) i AD ib. 180 (Κλαύδιος Φ.: f. Τιβ. Κλαύδιος
Ἀκύλας)
—LYCHNIDOS: (3) ii-iii AD *Sp.* 71 (1931) p. 222
no. 592 (-λιπεί-)

**Φιλιππίς**
LAKONIA:
—MESSA?: (1) imp. *IG* V (1) 1280, 2 (d. Σωτιμί-
δας)
S. ITALY (CALABRIA):
—TARAS-TARENTUM: (2) ?205-203 BC *FD* III (4)
427 III, 2 (d. Ἀνδρόνικος)

**Φιλιππίων**
MESSENIA:
—MESSENE: (1) 31 BC-14 AD *SEG* XXIII 207, 30
(Τ. Νίννιος Φ.)

**Φίλιππος**
ACHAIA: (1) c. 250 BC *IG* XII Suppl. p. 134 no.
304, 12 (s. Λεω—); (2) 168 BC *RE* (24); Plb.
xxx 13. 3; (3) 146 BC *IG* IV (1)² 28, 85 (f.
Ζώπυρος: synoikos)

—DYME: (4) iii BC *AJPh* 31 (1910) p. 399 no.
74 a, 16 (f. Σωστράτα)
—PELLENE (AZANES): (5) ?436 BC Moretti,
*Olymp.* 319
AITOLIA:
—POTIDANIA: (6) m. ii BC *SBBerlAk* 1936, p.
371 b, 13 (*SEG* XLI 528 B) (s. Ἀλέξανδρος)
AKARNANIA: (7) s. iv BC *RE* (63); Berve 788
(doctor); (8) iii/ii BC *RE* (64); *Syll*³ 585, 33
(s. Ἀλέξανδρος)
—OINIADAI: (9) ?iv-iii BC *IG* IX (1)² (2) 426. 2
(tile)
—THYRREION: (10) ii BC ib. 247, 16 (s. Πολύευ-
κτος); (11) ~ ib. 251, 9 (f. Ἀδάμαστος)
ARGOLIS:
—ARGOS: (12) iii BC *SEG* XXXI 306, 6 (Perlman
A.25) (I f. Φίλιππος II); (13) ~ *SEG* XXXI 306,
6 (Perlman A.25) (II s. Φίλιππος I); (14) ?272
BC *FD* III (1) 82 (I f. Φίλιππος II, Ἀγησίστρα-
τος, Ἰσομέντωρ); (15) ~ ib. (II s. Φίλιππος I)
—EPIDAUROS: (16) i-ii AD *IG* IV (1)² 469
—EPIDAUROS*: (17) c. 370-360 BC *BSA* 61
(1966) p. 271 no. 4 A, 12, 17
—HERMIONE: (18) ?ii-i BC *IG* IV (1) 731 II, 14
ARKADIA: (19) iv/iii BC Moretti, *Olymp.* 529; cf.
Ebert, *Gr. Sieg.* 55
—KLEITOR: (20) imp. *IG* V (2) 371 (f. Ἀρχίας)
—MANTINEIA-ANTIGONEIA: (21) c. 300-221 BC
ib. 323. 86 (tessera) (s. Εὐθύδαμος); (22) ?ii BC
ib. 318, 24
—MEGALOPOLIS: (23) iii/ii BC *RE* (12) (s. Ἀλέξ-
ανδρος (Macedon))
—MEGALOPOLIS?: (24) 42 AD *IG* V (2) 516, 2
etc. (f. Νικάσιππος)
—TEGEA: (25) m. iii BC ib. IV (1)² 96, 70 (Perl-
man E.3); Perlman p. 63 f. (date) (f. Ἀριστεύς);
(26) s. iii BC *IG* V (2) 116, 5 (s. Ἀγαθοκλῆς);
(27) f. ii BC ib. 44, 30 (Φιλίππ[ος])
ELIS: (28) 197-201 AD *IvOl* 106, 7 (f. Φαῦστος)
—PISATIS (PHRANGONESI (MOD.)): (29) imp.
*SEG* XXXI 366, 3
EPIROS: (30) c. 250 BC *IG* XI (4) 635, 11 (f.
Δείνων, —μαχος); (31) s. iii BC *RE* (54) (Lat.
Philippus)
—AMBRAKIA: (32) iv/iii BC *SEG* XXV 693; (33)
153-144 BC *FD* III (4) 31, 3, 5 (f. Ξένων); (34)
s. ii BC Cabanes, *L'Épire* p. 548 no. 19 (*SEG*
XXVI 694)
—ANTIGONEIA: (35) imp. *AE* 1914, p. 238 no.
15; Cabanes, *L'Épire* p. 234 n. 96 (locn.) (f.
Λυσίμαχος)
—BOUTHROTOS (PRASAIBOI): (36) a. 163 BC
*IBouthrot* 14, 11, 21; 17, 15; 21, 7, 15; 31, 32;
40, 1, 15; 44, 4 (*SEG* XXXVIII 471; 474; 478;
490; 499) (s. Φωτεύς, f. Φωτεύς, Ἀρίστων, Φι-
λότας) ?= (44); (37) ~ *IBouthrot* 14, 30 (*SEG*
XXXVIII 471); (38) ~ *IBouth-
rot* 14, 30; 21, 22 (*SEG* XXXVIII 471; 478)
(s. Ἀνδρόνικος); (39) ~ *IBouthrot* 15, 8; 22,
11; 41, 18 (*SEG* XXXVIII 472; 479; 500) (s.
Σωσίπατρος); (40) ~ *IBouthrot* 15, 10 (*SEG*
XXXVIII 472); (41) ~ *IBouthrot* 17, 27 (*SEG*
XXXVIII 474); (42) ~ *IBouthrot* 18, 5 (*SEG*
XXXVIII 475); (43) ~ *IBouthrot* 21, 1; 41, 17
(*SEG* XXXVIII 478; 500); *IBouthrot* 45, 10;
47, 6 (f. Σωσίπατρος); (44) ~ ib. 22, 16 (*SEG*
XXXVIII 479) ?= (84) (36); (45) ~ *IBouthrot*
25, 23 (*SEG* XXXVIII 483) ([Φί]λιππος); (46)
~ *IBouthrot* 26, 3 (*SEG* XXXVIII 484); (47) ~
*IBouthrot* 26, 3; 28, 4; 29, 25 (*SEG* XXXVIII
484; 486-7); (48) ~ *IBouthrot* 28, 19 (*SEG*
XXXVIII 486); *IBouthrot* 144, 3 (s. Μαχάτας)
?= (56); (49) ~ ib. 29, 16 (*SEG* XXXVIII 487)
(s. Κέφαλος); (50) ~ *IBouthrot* 29, 21 (*SEG*
XXXVIII 487); (51) ~ *IBouthrot* 29, 36 (*SEG*
XXXVIII 487); (52) ~ *IBouthrot* 31, 36 (*SEG*
XXXVIII 490) (s. Λυκώτας, f. Λυκώτας, Μελι-
τέα, Παμφίλα); (53) ~ *IBouthrot* 32, 2 (*SEG*
XXXVIII 491) ?= (55); (54) ~ *IBouthrot* 33, 5
(*SEG* XXXVIII 492); (55) ~
ib. 37, 1 (*SEG* XXXVIII 496) (s. Νικάδας) ?=

*(53)*; **(56)** ~ *IBouthrot* 40, 4 (*SEG* XXXVIII 499); *IBouthrot* 149, 7 ?= *(48)*; **(57)** ~ ib. 43, 11; cf. *SEG* XXXVIII 502 (s. Φιλόξενος); **(58)** ~ *IBouthrot* 44, 2 (f. Φιλόξενος); **(59)** ~ ib. 51, 14 (s. Φιλόξενος); **(60)** ~ ib. l. 21; **(61)** ~ ib. 77, 9 (s. *N*—); **(62)** ~ ib. 92, 5; **(63)** ~ ib. 93, 6; **(64)** ~ ib. 102, 2; **(65)** ~ ib. 103, 6; **(66)** ~ ib. 115, 5 (f. Γέλων); **(67)** ~ ib. 121, 13, 14? (s. Λέων) ?= *(73)*; **(68)** ~ ib. 129, 8 (f. Νικάδας); **(69)** ~ ib. 130, 3; **(70)** ~ ib. 166 (*SEG* XXXVIII 465) (s. Φιλιππίδας)

——Bouthrotioi: **(71)** a. 163 BC *IBouthrot* 108 (f. Δείνων)

——Dranoi: **(72)** a. 163 BC ib. 132, 6 (?s. Λυκώτας)

——Euryoi: **(73)** a. 163 BC ib. 97, 5 (s. Λέων) ?= *(67)*

——Hermiatoi: **(74)** a. 163 BC ib. 68, 2; 72, 3, 8; 74; 116, 9 (*BCH* 118 (1994) p. 121 A); *IBouthrot* 138, 3; 166, 1 ?= *(75)*; **(75)** ~ ib. 77, 6; 94, 9 (s. Λυκόφρων) ?= *(74)*

——Hypoppaioi: **(76)** a. 163 BC ib. 78, 3; 79, 3; 80, 3; 81, 3; 82, 2; 83, 3; 84, 3; 85, 2; 86, 3; 87, 2; 88, 2 (*BCH* 118 (1994) pp. 122 f. nos. 1-11); *IBouthrot* 110, 3

——Hypoppaioi?: **(77)** ?192 BC *Ténos* 2 pp. 102 f. B, 1 (*SEG* XL 690) ([Φί]λιππος)

——Kammeoi: **(78)** a. 163 BC *IBouthrot* 118, 4; 119 (f. Κραινώ)

——Kartonoi: **(79)** a. 163 BC ib. 66, 3; 67, 1; 75, 4; 76, 2, 6; 77, 3; **(80)** ~ ib. 144, 8 (f. Νικάδας)

——Loigyphioi: **(81)** a. 163 BC ib. 107

——Metoreis: **(82)** a. 163 BC ib. 158

——Opatai: **(83)** a. 163 BC ib. 152, 2

——Parthaioi: **(84)** a. 163 BC ib. 139, 2; 140, 3 (s.p.) (s. Φωτεύς) ?= *(44)*

——Porronoi: **(85)** a. 163 BC ib. 126, 2 ?= *(93)*

——Sarpingioi: **(86)** a. 163 BC ib. 139, 8 (s. Λυκώτας)

——Tykonioi: **(87)** a. 163 BC ib. 52, 2; 54, 2; 60, 2 (*SEG* XXXVIII 517; 505; 511)

—CHAONES:

——Myonoi: **(88)** iii/ii BC *IBouthrot* 7 (*SEG* XXXVIII 470) (Φιλι[ππος?]: f. Ἀνδρόνικος)

—DODONA: **(89)** c. 330 BC Cabanes, *L'Épire* p. 580 no. 55, 5 (-λιπος); **(90)** iii BC Antoniou, *Dodone* Aa, 2; **(91)** ?164 BC Cabanes, *L'Épire* p. 586 no. 71, 9 (s. Ἱερός)

—GENOAIOI: **(92)** c. 330 BC ib. p. 539 no. 3, 9

—HYPORRONIOI: **(93)** a. 163 BC *IBouthrot* 127, 2 (*BCH* 118 (1994) p. 128 A) ?= *(85)*

—KAMMANOI BOUTHROTIOI: **(94)** a. 163 BC *IBouthrot* 60, 6 (*SEG* XXXVIII 511) (f. Νικάνωρ)

—NIKOPOLIS: **(95)** imp. *ILGR* 163 (Sarikakis 172) (Lat. Philippu[s])

—THESPROTOI: **(96)** c. 330 BC Cabanes, *L'Épire* p. 580 no. 55, 10

ILLYRIA:

—APOLLONIA: **(97)** hell. *IApoll* 28 (f. Παράμονος); **(98)** ii-i BC ib. 162 (Φιλ<λ>ιππος: s. Ἀντίλοχος); **(99)** i BC Maier 148 (coin) (money.); **(100)** imp. *IApoll* 43 (?s. Ἀμύντας); **(101)** ~ ib. 267 (Φιλιππ(π)ος); **(102)** ~ ib. 373 (Φιλιππ[ος])

—EPIDAMNOS-DYRRHACHION: **(103)** hell. *IDyrrh* 24 (f. Ἑορταῖος); **(104)** c. 250-50 BC *BMC Thessaly* p. 77 nos. 183-4 (coin) (pryt.) ?= *(105)*; **(105)** ~ Maier 374; 492; Münsterberg Nachtr. p. 17; *Jubice Hoard* p. 96 no. 13; Münsterberg p. 40 (coin) (Ceka 12; 93; 263; 333; 340) (pryt.) ?= *(104)*; **(106)** ii-i BC *IDyrrh* 561 (tiles); **(107)** hell.-imp. ib. 193 (f. Ἐπίκτησις); **(108)** ~ ib. 315 (Μόμμιος Φ.); **(109)** ~ ib. 329 (f. Νικήν); **(110)** ~ ib. 432; **(111)** ~ ib. 433 (s. Μενοίτας); **(112)** ~ ib. 434 (s. Φίλων); **(113)** ~ ib. 435 (Φιλιππ[ος]); **(114)** imp. ib. 52 (Φιλιππ[πος]); **(115)** ~ ib. 57 (Φιλ<λ>ιππος: f. Δημοσθένης)

—KORCA (MOD.): **(116)** hell. *SEG* XXXIII 487 (pithoi)

—LYCHNIDOS?: **(117)** ii-i BC ib. I 254 (s. Μουντανός)

KEPHALLENIA:

—PALE: **(118)** iii/ii BC Unp. (*IG* arch.)

KERKYRA: **(119)** i AD *IG* IX (1) 712 (f. Λ. Σαίνιος Πρέπων)

KERKYRA?: **(120)** imp. ib. 854 (vase)

KORINTHIA:

—KORINTH: **(121)** m. iii BC *Corinth* VIII (3) 33 a, 3 (Φίλιπ[πος]); **(122)** 70 BC *PP* 4342 (s. Τιμοκράτης); **(123)** ii-iii AD *SEG* XI 140 c

—SIKYON: **(124)** f. iii BC *IG* II² 3078, 4 (Skalet 327; Stephanis 2503)

LAKONIA:

—HYPERTELEATON*: **(125)** imp. *IG* V (1) 1067

—MESSA?: **(126)** imp. ib. 1280, 7-8 (s. Φιλοκλῆς, f. Σωτιμίδας)

—SPARTA: **(127)** 412-411 BC Th. viii 28. 5; 87. 6; 99 (Poralla² 725); **(128)** s. i BC *IG* V (1) 92, 9 (Bradford (20)) (f. Πολύαρχος); **(129)** 46 BC Cic., *Fam.* xiii 28 a. 1 (Bradford (9)) (Lat. Philippus); **(130)** c. 25-1 BC *IG* V (1) 210, 14 (Bradford (3)) (s. Καλλίστρατος); **(131)** ~ *IG* V (1) 210, 35 (Bradford (8)) (s. Σωσικράτης); **(132)** i BC/i AD? *IG* V (1) 177, 4 (Bradford (15)) (I f. Φίλιππος II); **(133)** ~ *IG* V (1) 177, 4 (Bradford (4)) (II s. Φίλιππος I: mantis?); **(134)** ?i AD *IG* V (1) 180, 5 (Bradford (11)); **(135)** ~ *IG* V (1) 328 (Bradford (10)); **(136)** c. 90-110 AD *SEG* XI 513, 7; 560, 3 (Bradford (16)) (Φιλιπ[πος]—560: I f. Φίλιππος II); **(137)** ~ *SEG* XI 513, 7; 560, 3 (Bradford (5)) ([Φιλιπ]πος—560: II s. Φίλιππος I); **(138)** c. 100 AD *SEG* XI 510, 5 (Bradford (7)) (s. Σωκράτης); **(139)** c. 105-122 AD *SEG* XI 569, 21; 574, [3] (Bradford (2)) (s. Δαμόνικος); **(140)** c. 110-115 AD *SEG* XI 540, 5 (Bradford (1)) (s. Ἄνθιππος); **(141)** c. 125-137 AD *IG* V (1) 114, 6; *SEG* XI 548, [14] (Bradford (17)) (I f. Φίλιππος II); **(142)** ~ *IG* V (1) 114, 6; *SEG* XI 548, [14] (Bradford (6)) (II s. Φίλιππος I); **(143)** m. ii AD *IG* V (1) 87, 3; 113, 5; 160, [7]; 446, 4 (Bradford (14)) (f. Ἀγαθοκλῆς); **(144)** c. 140-150 AD *IG* V (1) 71 II, 8, 18-19; *SEG* XI 550, 8; cf. 526 (Bradford (12)) (Γ. Ἰούλ. Φ.: f. Ἐπαφρόδιτος); **(145)** c. 160-170 AD *IG* V (1) 109, 8 (Bradford (19)) (f. Φιλονικίδας); **(146)** f. iii AD *IG* V (1) 170, 13 (Bradford (18)) (f. Αὐρ. Φίλων) ?= *(147)*; **(147)** a. 217 AD *IG* V (1) 551, 11; *SEG* XI 800, 2? (Bradford (13)) (Μ. Αὐρ. Φ.) ?= *(146)*

—TEUTHRONE: **(148)** imp. *IG* V (1) 1220 a (s. Κλέων); **(149)** ii AD *SEG* XXII 308 (f. Δάμαρχος)

MESSENIA:

—ANDANIA*: **(150)** ?ii/iii AD *IG* V (1) 1391, 3

—MESSENE: **(151)** iii/ii BC *SEG* XXXVIII 342; cf. XLI 350; *Sculpture from Arcadia and Laconia* p. 102, 1 (*SEG* XLI 333) (f. Δαμοφῶν, Ξενόφιλος); **(152)** 192 BC *IG* IX (1)² (1) 31, 23 (s. Ἀριστόμαχος); **(153)** s. ii BC *SEG* XLI 352 A (s. Δαμοφῶν: sculptor?); **(154)** 80 AD *IG* V (1) 1468, 7; cf. *SEG* XL 366 (f. Ἀπελλίων)

—METHONE: **(155)** ?ii AD *IG* V (1) 1417, 2 (Γ. Ἰούλ. Φ.)

—THOURIA: **(156)** ii-i BC ib. 1385, 3 (f. Φιλόκλειτος); **(157)** f. ii BC *SEG* XI 972, 128 (s. Νικιάδας)

PELOPONNESE: **(158)** 112 BC *FD* III (2) 70 A, 31 ([Φί]λιππος: s. Ἡρωίδης)

S. ITALY: **(159)** imp. *CIL* X 8059. 95 (seal) (Lat. Q. Cal. Philippus)

S. ITALY (APULIA):

—HERDONIA: **(160)** ?ii/i BC *Taras* 9 (1989) p. 224 (Lat. Pilipus Cepalo Faber Alexsander)

S. ITALY (BRUTTIUM):

—KAULONIA?: **(161)** ?c. 475 BC *IGSI* 20, 7 (*SEG* IV 71; Landi, *DISMG* 168); *LSAG*² p. 261 no. 29 (date)

—KROTON: **(162)** s. vi BC Moretti, *Olymp.* 135 (s. Βουτακίδας)

—LOKROI EPIZEPHYRIOI:

——(Ἀλχ.): **(163)** iv/iii BC De Franciscis 4, 3; 5, 3; 22, 4 (f. Σωκράτης)

——(Λακ.): **(164)** iv/iii BC ib. 3, 9 (s. Φίλακος)

——(Θρα.): **(165)** iv/iii BC ib. 24, 2 (s. Φιλίαρχος)

——(Σκα.): **(166)** 278 BC ib. 30, 4 (s. Σάτυρος)

—MEDMA: **(167)** iv BC *RE* (42); *FD* III (1) 578 I, 18; III (4) 39, 4 (and Lokris (Opuntian) Opous)

S. ITALY (CALABRIA):

—TARAS-TARENTUM: **(168)** ?205-203 BC ib. 427 III, 1 (f. Ἀνδρόνικος); **(169)** ~ ib. l. 2 (s. Ἀνδρόνικος); **(170)** ?iv AD *CIG* 4705 q (*SB* 8576) (Φιλ<λ>ιππος: s. Φιλῖνος)

S. ITALY (CAMPANIA):

—DIKAIARCHIA-PUTEOLI: **(171)** imp. *CIL* X 2848 (Lat. [Phi]lippus); **(172)** ?i-ii AD ib. 1893 (*JIWE* I 23) (Lat. Ti. Claudius Philippus: Jew?); **(173)** m. i AD Bove, *Documenti processuali* p. 115 T.P. 24 pag. 2, 3 (Lat. Q. Laberius Philippus); **(174)** 45-48 AD Camodeca, *L'Archivio Puteolano* I p. 189; p. 249 (Lat. M. Lollius Philippus)

—HERCULANEUM: **(175)** i BC-i AD *CIL* IV 10588 b; **(176)** ~ *RAAN* 33 (1958) p. 278 no. 484 (Lat. Marcius Phi[lippus])

—MISENUM: **(177)** 113 AD De Franciscis, *Sacello Augustali* p. 25 no. 6; p. 27 (Lat. L. Laninius Philippus: f. Ἑρμῆς)

—MISENUM*: **(178)** imp. *CIL* X 3524 (Lat. Iunius Philippus)

—POMPEII: **(179)** i BC-i AD ib. IV 5080 (Lat. Pilipus); **(180)** ~ ib. 7316 (Castrèn 205. 20) (Lat. Iulius Philippus) ?= *(183)*; **(181)** ~ *CIL* IV 9178; **(182)** ~ ib. 4280-1; 4301; 4369 (Lat. Philippus); **(183)** m. i AD *RAAN* 49 (1974) p. 25 no. 6; p. 26 no. 8 (Lat. C. Iulius Philippus) ?= *(180)*; **(184)** 70-79 AD *CIL* IV 304; Mouritsen p. 110 (date) (Lat. Philippus); **(185)** ~ *CIL* IV 567; Mouritsen p. 112 (date) (Lat. Piliphus)

—POMPEII*: **(186)** 32 AD *CIL* X 899, 1 (Lat. Philippus: freed.?)

S. ITALY (LUCANIA):

—HERAKLEIA:

——(Ἀλ. λωτήριον): **(187)** iv/iii BC *IGSI* 1 I, 185 (*DGE* 62; Uguzzoni–Ghinatti I) (I f. Φίλιππος II); **(188)** ~ *IGSI* 1 I, 185 (*DGE* 62; Uguzzoni–Ghinatti I) (II s. Φίλιππος I)

—POSEIDONIA-PAESTUM*: **(189)** m. i BC *CIL* I² 3149 (Mello–Voza 9) (Lat. M. Avianius Philippus: freed.)

S. ITALY?: **(190)** hell. *CIG* 7274; King, *Engraved Gems* p. 278 (dub.)

SICILY:

—AKRAGAS: **(191)** f. v BC Dubois, *IGDS* 180 b, 2 (Arena, *Iscr. Sic.* II 90) (-ιπος)

—HALOUNTION: **(192)** imp.? *IG* XIV 374

—KAMARINA: **(193)** ?iv/iii BC *SEG* XXXIV 940, 6 (Dubois, *IGDS* 124; *PdelP* 44 (1989) p. 192 no. 3; Cordano, 'Camarina VII' 160) (s. Παυσανίας)

—LIPARA: **(194)** hell.? Libertini, *Isole Eolie* p. 225 no. 49

—SYRACUSE: **(195)** ?137 BC *SGDI* 2098, 4 (f. Ἀπολλόδωρος); **(196)** iii-v AD *IG* XIV 183 (Strazzulla 120) (Φιλ<λ>ιπ(π)ος)

—THERMAI HIMERAIAI: **(197)** i-ii AD *IGLMP* 120; cf. *SEG* XXVI 1064 (M. Μουνάτιος Φ.)

TRIPHYLIA:

—MAKISTOS: **(198)** 399-369 BC ib. XXXV 389, 11

Φίλις

MESSENIA:

—THOURIA: **(1)** f. ii BC ib. XI 972, 36 (s. Φιλόστρατος)

Φιλίς

EPIROS:

—BOUTHROTOS (PRASAIBOI): **(1)** a. 163 BC *IBouthrot* 18, 8; 26, 13 (*SEG* XXXVIII 475; 484); **(2)** ~ *IBouthrot* 99, 4 (*BCH* 118 (1994)

**Φιλις**

p. 121 B); (3) ~ IBouthrot 126, 6; cf. L'Illyrie
mérid. 2 p. 221 n. 11 (d. Κέφαλος)

**Φιλις**

ITHAKE: (1) hell. Rev. Épig. 1 (1913) p. 47 no.
13
KEPHALLENIA:
—SAME: (2) hell. Op. Ath. 10 (1971) p. 66 no.
11 (.φιλις?)

**Φιλίσκος**

AIGINA: (1) iv BC RE (6); TrGF 1 pp. 258-9;
FGrH 134 T3 with Comm. (s. Ὀνασίκριτος)
AKARNANIA:
—THYRREION: (2) iii BC IG IX (1)² (2) 279; (3)
ii/i BC GVI 1122, 1 (IG IX (1)² (2) 340) (f.
Τιμέλας)
ARGOLIS:
—EPIDAUROS*: (4) c. 370-360 BC BSA 61
(1966) p. 272 no. 4 B II, 5 ([Φιλί]σκος)
—KALAURIA: (5) iii BC IG IV (1) 850, 3
—TROIZEN: (6) iv BC ib. 823, 12 (Φιλίσκ[ος]); (7)
s. ii BC BMI 1154 a, 4; BE 1972, no. 37 (date)
(s. Κυδίμαχος); (8) i/ii AD IG IV (1) 835 C, 4
(Κλώδιος Φ.); (9) 103-114 AD ib. 795, 14 (Γν.
Κορν. Φ.)
ARKADIA: (10) iii BC ib. v (2) 415, 2 (IPArk 23)
(Φιλίσκ[ος]: f. Θέαρος)
—MEGALOPOLIS: (11) ii/i BC IG v (2) 443, 5
(IPArk 32) (s. Ἁλιόδωρος)
—THELPHOUSA: (12) s. iii BC FD III (4) 15 (s.
Ἁγίας)
DALMATIA:
—ISSA?: (13) hell.? Brunšmid p. 32 no. 28 (s.
Δρωπίων)
EPIROS:
—BOUTHROTOS (PRASAIBOI): (14) a. 163
BC IBouthrot 19, 1 (SEG XXXVIII 476)
(Φιλίσκ[ος]: s. Ἀλ—); (15) ~ IBouthrot 24, 1
(f. Νικόμαχος)
——Prochtheioi: (16) a. 163 BC ib. 168, 14
(SEG XXXVIII 469) (s. Παρμενίων)
ILLYRIA:
—APOLLONIA: (17) iv/iii BC IApoll 387
KEPHALLENIA:
—SAME: (18) 208 BC IMM 35, 2 (s. Ἀνδρομήδης)
KERKYRA: (19) c. 76 BC IG VII 417, 8, 18
(IOrop 525, 8) (f. Παρμενίσκος)
KORINTHIA:
—KORINTH: (20) 97 BC IG II² 1337, 5; SEG
XVI 111 (date) (f. Νικασίς)
—SIKYON: (21) hell. IG IV (1) 433 (Skalet 328);
(22) i BC IG II² 10312 (Φιλίσκ[ος]: f. Σωκρά-
της)
LAKONIA:
—HORMIAI?: (23) c. 475-450 BC ib. IV (1)² 146;
LSAG² p. 182 no. 14 (date)
MESSENIA:
—MESSENE: (24) ?253 BC Nachtergael, Les Ga-
lates 10, 12; cf. Stephanis 1958 (f. Ὅροικος)
S. ITALY (BRUTTIUM):
—LOKROI EPIZEPHYRIOI:
——(Ψαθ.): (25) 277 BC De Franciscis 8, 4; 31,
4 (f. Φιλιστίων)
S. ITALY (CALABRIA):
—TARAS-TARENTUM: (26) c. 272-235 BC Vlasto
888-9 (Evans, Horsemen p. 179 VIII F.1
(coins))
S. ITALY (LUCANIA):
—HYELE-VELIA: (27) hell. Op. Ath. 10 (1971) p.
65 no. 8 (s. Ἡρόδοτος)
SICILY:
—SYRACUSE: (28) hell. NScav 1892, p. 357 (f.
Χρύσιον)
—TAUROMENION: (29) c. 222-205 BC IG XIV
421 an. 19; 421 an. 36 (SGDI 5219) (f. Θεό-
δωρος)

**Φιλισκώ**

DALMATIA:
—ISSA: (1) iii/ii BC SEG XXXV 684 (VAHD 84
(1991) p. 254 no. 5) (d. Πρώταρχος)

**Φιλίστα**

ACHAIA:
—DYME: (1) ii-i BC SEG XIV 373 d (d. Οἶκις)
AKARNANIA:
—PALAIROS: (2) iii BC IG IX (1)² (2) 510 (Φιλί-
στας (fem. gen./masc. nom.?))
—THYRREION: (3) ?iii BC ib. 301 (Φ.
(masc./fem. voc.?))
ARGOLIS:
—ARGOS: (4) ii BC ib. II² 8377, 1 (d. Φίλλις); (5)
105 BC JÖAI 14 (1911) Beibl. p. 146 no. 4,
6 (d. Σωκράτης); (6) i BC-i AD Unp. (Argos,
Kavvadias)
—ARGOS?: (7) ?iii BC IDyrrh 53 (or Epiros Ar-
gos (Amphiloch.))
ARKADIA:
—THELPHOUSA: (8) ?i AD SEG XI 1133; BCH
88 (1964) pp. 176-8 (date)
DALMATIA:
—ISSA: (9) iii BC SEG XXXV 691, 3 (VAHD 84
(1991) p. 256 no. 6) (d. Ξενοκλῆς)
ELIS: (10) c. 400 BC IG II² 8530 (-στη); (11)
iv/iii BC D.L. ix 66 (?d. Πλείσταρχος)
EPIROS:
—AMBRAKIA: (12) iii/ii BC Unp. (Arta Mus., in-
scr.) (d. Ἰσίδωρος)
—ANTIGONEIA: (13) imp. AE 1914, p. 238 no.
15; Cabanes, L'Épire p. 234 n. 96 (locn.) (d.
Σωστρίων)
—BOUTHROTOS (PRASAIBOI): (14) a. 163
BC IBouthrot 14, 18; 22, 17; 23, 5; 31, 82; 38, 8;
41, 14 (SEG XXXVIII 471; 479; 481, 1; 490;
497; 500); IBouthrot 51, 18; (15) ~ ib. 14, 33
(SEG XXXVIII 471) ?= (24); (16) ~ IBouth-
rot 17, 7, 9; 29, 7 (SEG XXXVIII 474; 487)
?= (34); (17) ~ IBouthrot 17, 13; 31, 69 (SEG
XXXVIII 474; 490) (?d. Θύρμαξ) ?= (36); (18)
~ IBouthrot 19, 5 (SEG XXXVIII 476); (19)
~ IBouthrot 19, 5 (SEG XXXVIII 476); (20)
~ IBouthrot 22, 8 (SEG XXXVIII 479) (Φιλ-
ίσ[τα]); (21) ~ IBouthrot 22, 10 (SEG XXXVIII
479); (22) ~ IBouthrot 22, 32 (SEG XXXVIII
479); (23) ~ IBouthrot 22, 35 (SEG XXXVIII
479); (24) ~ IBouthrot 24, 4 (SEG XXXVIII
482) ?= (15); (25) ~ IBouthrot 25, 11; 31, 90
(SEG XXXVIII 483; 490); (26) ~ IBouthrot 29,
13 (SEG XXXVIII 487); IBouthrot 136, 8 ?=
(37); (27) ~ ib. 29, 14; (28) ~ ib. l. 56 (SEG
XXXVIII 487); (29) ~ IBouthrot 31, 72 (SEG
XXXVIII 490); (30) ~ IBouthrot 31, 79 (SEG
XXXVIII 490); (31) ~ IBouthrot 32, 7 (SEG
XXXVIII 491); (32) ~ IBouthrot 32, 21; 42, 9
(SEG XXXVIII 491; 501); (33) ~ IBouthrot 39,
2; 42, 18 (SEG XXXVIII 498; 501) (?d. Δέξιππος, Ἀρσινόα); (34) ~ IBouthrot 42, 16 (SEG
XXXVIII 501) ?= (16); (35) ~ IBouthrot 42,
10-11; (36) ~ ib. 43, 6 (SEG XXXVIII 502) ?=
(17); (37) ~ IBouthrot 47, 9 ?= (26); (38) ~ ib.
51, 21; (39) ~ ib. 68, 9; (40) ~ ib. 102, 2; (41)
~ ib. 103, 5; (42) ~ ib. 137, 10; (43) ~ ib. 148;
(44) ~ ib. 149, 8; (45) ~ ib. 152, 4
—DODONA*: (46) iv-iii BC PAE 1956, p. 155 no.
12
EPIROS?:
—ARRONOS: (47) 370-368 BC Cabanes, L'Épire
p. 534 no. 1, 3
KERKYRA: (48) i-ii AD Unp. (IG arch.); (49) ~
ib.
KORINTHIA:
—KORINTH: (50) hell.-imp. Corinth VIII (3)
300, 1 (GVI 2020) (d. Τίμαρχος); (51) i BC/i
AD AE 1977, p. 78 no. 24, 2 (Lat. Licinia
Philista: m. Ἥιος Ἀγάθων)
LEUKAS: (52) hell.? Unp. (IG arch.)
S. ITALY (APULIA):
—KAILIA: (53) s. iv BC RVAp p. 528 no. 255
(vase)
S. ITALY (CALABRIA):
—TARAS-TARENTUM: (54) iv/iii BC IG XIV 668
II, 12 (Landi, DISMG 194)

SICILY:
—KAMARINA?: (55) v/iv BC Manganaro, PdelP
forthcoming no. 14
—LIPARA: (56) hell.-imp. IG XIV 398 (Libertini,
Isole Eolie p. 219 no. 16)
—SYRACUSE: (57) s. iv BC IG II² 10398
((Φ)ιλίστα: d. Στράτων); (58) ?ii BC Milet 1 (3)
79, 9 (and Caria Miletos: d. Ματροφάνης, m.
Ματροφάνης); (59) imp. IG XIV 23 (m. Ἀφρο-
δισιάς)

**Φιλίστας**

AITOLIA:
—BOUKATION: (1) c. 162 BC ib. IX (1)² (1) 106,
4 (f. Ὑβρίλαος)
ARGOLIS:
—NEMEA*: (2) hell. SEG XXXVIII 301 (Φιλίστα
(masc. gen.)—vase)
ILLYRIA:
—BYLLIONES BYLLIS: (3) ?ii BC ib. 522 (masc.
nom./fem. gen.?)

**Φιλιστέας**

ELIS: (1) m. iii BC IG v (2) 368, 57 (s. Νικόδρομος)

**Φιλιστίδας**

AIGINA: (1) ii BC ib. II² 7954 (-δης: f. Διονύσιος)
ARGOLIS:
—ARGOS: (2) ?304 BC ib. v (2) 550, 19; (3) iii-ii
BC Memnonion 425-6 (-δης); (4) ii BC SEG XIV
323; (5) f. i BC Unp. (Ch. Kritzas) (s. Πίτων);
(6) i BC/i AD? SEG XI 313 a, 1, 4
—EPIDAUROS:
——(Hysminatai): (7) 146 BC IG IV (1)² 28, 20
(s. Εὐκράτων)
——Upper Oiseia: (8) m. iii BC ib. 96, 41 (Perl-
man E.3); Perlman p. 63 f. (date)
ARKADIA:
—TEGEA:
——(Krariotai): (9) s. iii BC IG v (2) 36, 125 (s.
Εὐφράνωρ: metic)
ILLYRIA:
—BYLLIONES: (10) c. 200 BC SEG XXXV 680,
10; cf. XXXVIII 541 (s. Φιλιστίων)
—BYLLIONES BYLLIS: (11) hell. Iliria 1982 (1),
p. 121 no. 53 (tile) ([Φ]ιλιστίδας)
—EPIDAMNOS-DYRRHACHION: (12) c. 250-50
BC Münsterberg p. 40 (coin) (Ceka 153)
(pryt.); (13) ii-i BC IDyrrh 295 (f. Λύκος); (14)
~ ib. 436 (s. Τίτος)
LAKONIA: (15) iii-ii BC IG v (1) 1341, 4 (Brad-
ford 2)
—SPARTA: (16) i BC-i AD IG v (1) 916 b (Brad-
ford (1)) (-τει-)
S. ITALY (CALABRIA):
—TARAS-TARENTUM: (17) iv BC Röm. Mitt. 68
(1961) p. 163 with n. 57 (terracotta)
S. ITALY (LUCANIA):
—METAPONTION: (18) f. iv BC IG XIV 648
(Landi, DISMG 152) (f. Εὔξενος)
SICILY:
—GELA-PHINTIAS: (19) f. v BC Dubois, IGDS
130 (Arena, Iscr. Sic. II 37) (s. Εὔξενος)
—SYRACUSE: (20) f. iv BC [Pl.], Ep. 315 E; (21)
324 BC Berve 791 (Stephanis 2508)

**Φιλίστιον**

EPIROS:
—BOUTHROTOS (PRASAIBOI): (1) a. 163 BC
IBouthrot 14, 34; 31, 41 (SEG XXXVIII 471;
490) (?d. Τιμάνωρ I); (2) ~ IBouthrot 21,
13 (SEG XXXVIII 478) (d. Αἴσχρων); (3) ~
IBouthrot 29, 2 (SEG XXXVIII 487)
KERKYRA: (4) iii/ii BC GVI 1511, 3; cf. Fraser-
Rönne, BWGT p. 112 no. 3 (d. Ἀγήν, Ἁρπα-
λίς)

**Φιλιστίς**

AKARNANIA:
—PALAIROS: (1) iii BC IG IX (1)² (2) 511 (Φιλί-
στιος (gen.?))

Φιλιστίχα

KERKYRA: (2) hell. ib. IX (1) 589, 1 (d. Ἀριστομέδων)
SICILY:
—SYRACUSE: (3) f. iii BC RE (-); Rupes loquentes
p. 448 (d. Λεπτίνας, m. Γέλων: queen)

Φιλιστίχα
EPIROS:
—BOUTHROTOS (PRASAIBOI): (1) a. 163 BC
IBouthrot 72, 5

Φιλιστίων
AKARNANIA:
—MATROPOLIS: (1) m. ii BC IG IX (1)² (2) 588
(s. Δέξανδρος)
ARGOLIS:
—ARGOS: (2) 218 BC Pouilloux, Forteresse p. 134
no. 18, 8 + SEG XLI 92, 20 (IRhamnous 38)
—ARGOS*: (3) ii-i BC IG IV (1) 530, 18; cf. BCH
33 (1909) p. 183 n. 2 (slave/freed.?)
ELIS:
—OPHIOUS: (4) c. 230-200 BC ib. 45 (1921) p.
14 II, 128 (f. Φ—ρος: name—Oulhen)
EPIROS:
—AMBRAKIA: (5) ?iii/ii BC SEG XXV 700 (f. Νί-
κανδρος); (6) ii-i BC CIG 1798 (f. Ἀμίτιος?); (7)
~ ib. 1799 (f. Σέλευκος)
—BOUTHROTOS (PRASAIBOI): (8) a. 163 BC
IBouthrot 17, 29 (SEG XXXVIII 474) (f. Ἡρά-
κλειτος)
ILLYRIA:
—APOLLONIA: (9) c. 250-50 BC Maier 54; 69;
93 (coin) (Ceka 125-7) (money.); (10) ~ Maier
91-3 (coin) (Ceka 31; 42; 127) (pryt.)
—BYLLIONES: (11) c. 200 BC SEG XXXV 680,
10; cf. XXXVIII 541 (f. Φιλιστίδας); (12) ~ ib.
XXXV 680, 12; cf. XXXVIII 541 ([Φιλι]στίων: s.
Νικόμαχος: name—Cabanes)
—BYLLIONES BYLLIS: (13) iii BC ib. 529 (s.
Νικόλαος)
—EPIDAMNOS-DYRRHACHION: (14) c. 250-50
BC Münsterberg Nachtr. p. 17 (coin) (Ceka
429) (money.); (15) 84-60 BC BCH 63 (1939)
p. 169, 3 (IDyrrh 525) (s. Φιλ—)
MESSENIA:
—MESSENE: (16) iii BC SEG XXIII 209, 20
S. ITALY (BRUTTIUM):
—LOKROI EPIZEPHYRIOI: (17) iv BC RE (4);
FSA pp. 109 ff. (doctor); (18) iii BC IG IX
(1) 685, 4, 21 (s. Θεύδωρος)
——(Ἀνα.): (19) iv/iii BC De Franciscis 22, 14
(s. Δεξίας)
——(Δυσ.): (20) iv/iii BC ib. 17, 7 (s. Ἀρκείδας)
——(Θρα.): (21) iv/iii BC ib. 32, 7 (f. Φρασίλας)
——(Λακ.): (22) iv/iii BC ib. 12, 5 (s. Σώσιππος)
——(Λογ.): (23) 275 BC ib. 25, 6 (f. Νίκιππος)
——(Ψαθ.): (24) 277 BC ib. 8, 4; 31, 4 (s. Φιλίσ-
κος)
—RHEGION: (25) s. ii BC IG XIV 615, 4;
Klearchos 21 (1979) pp. 83-96 (date) (f. Φί-
λακος)
—TERINA: (26) iv/iii BC RE (6); Regling, Terina
passim ?= (27) (28)
S. ITALY (CALABRIA):
—TARAS-TARENTUM: (27) iv/iii BC Evans,
Horsemen p. 109 f. (coin) (Φιλισ(τίων)) ?= (26)
S. ITALY (LUCANIA):
—HYELE-VELIA: (28) iv/iii BC RE (5); Silver
Coinage of Velia pp. 93-123 (ident.) (coins)
?= (26)
SICILY:
—AKRAGAS: (29) c. 331-324 BC Hesp. 43 (1974)
pp. 322 ff. no. 3, 5 etc. (Φιλιστ[ίω]ν: f. Σώπα-
τρος)
—AKRAI: (30) ?iii BC SGDI 3239, 8 (Akrai p.
157 no. 9) (f. Διονυσόδωρος, Κρίθων); (31) ~
SGDI 3239, 9 (Akrai p. 157 no. 9) (s. Σῶσις)
?= (33); (32) ~ SGDI 3239, 12 (Akrai p. 157
no. 9); (33) ~ SGDI 3240, 9 (Akrai p. 156
no. 7) (s. Σῶσις) ?= (31); (34) iii-ii BC SGDI
3242, 6 (Akrai p. 157 no. 8)

—MORGANTINA: (35) ii BC SEG XXVII 655, 6, 9
(Dubois, IGDS 194) (?f. Ἀρίσταρχος)
—NEAITON: (36) iii/ii BC SGDI 5260 (Sic.
Gymn. 16 (1963) p. 55); cf. Rupes loquentes
p. 454 (s. Ἐπικράτης)
—SYRACUSE: (37) 212 BC Liv. xxv 28. 5 (Lat.
Philistio); (38) ?ii-i BC NScav 1920, p. 325 (f.
Ἀναξώ)
—SYRACUSE?:
——(Λαβ.): (39) hell. Manganaro, PdelP forthcoming no. 4 I, 2 (s. Φιλωνίδας)
—TAUROMENION: (40) c. 240-226 BC IG XIV
421 an. 1; 421 an. 15 (SGDI 5219) (s. Θαρρίας); (41) c. 224-186 BC IG XIV 421 an. 17;
421 an. 55 (SGDI 5219) (s. Ξένων, f. Ξένων);
(42) c. 223-213 BC IG XIV 421 an. 8; 421 an.
14; 421 an. 28 (SGDI 5219) (s. Ἀθανις); (43)
c. 208 BC IG XIV 421 an. 33 (SGDI 5219);
(44) c. 199-187 BC IG XIV 421 an. 42; 421 an.
51; 421 an. 54 (SGDI 5219) (I f. Φιλιστίων
II); (45) ~ IG XIV 421 an. 42; 421 an. 51; 421
an. 54 (SGDI 5219) (II s. Φιλιστίων I); (46) c.
195 BC IG XIV 421 an. 46 (SGDI 5219); (47)
c. 193 BC IG XIV 421 an. 48 (SGDI 5219) (f.
Σωφρονίδας); (48) c. 191 BC IG XIV 421 an. 50
(SGDI 5219); (49) c. 177-167 BC IG XIV 421
an. 64; 421 an. 74 (SGDI 5219) (s. Ἀγέας);
(50) c. 174 BC IG XIV 421 an. 67 (SGDI 5219)
(f. Ζώπυρος); (51) c. 160 BC IG XIV 421 an.
81 (SGDI 5219) (f. Ἀνδρίσκος); (52) c. 40 BC
Cron. Arch. 3 (1964) p. 54 I, 24 (f. Νεμήνιος)
——(Δαμ.): (53) c. 169-157 BC IG XIV 421 an.
72; 421 an. 84 (SGDI 5219) (I f. Φιλιστίων
II); (54) ~ IG XIV 421 an. 72; 421 an. 84
(SGDI 5219) (II s. Φιλιστίων I)
——(Ἴδομ.?): (55) c. 166 BC IG XIV 421 an. 75
(SGDI 5219) (I f. Φιλιστίων II); (56) ~ IG XIV
421 an. 75 (SGDI 5219) (II s. Φιλιστίων I)
——(Σπαρ.): (57) s. ii BC SEG XXXII 936 (f.
Νυμφόδωρος); (58) c. 147 BC IG XIV 421 an.
94 (SGDI 5219) (I f. Φιλιστίων II); (59) ~ IG
XIV 421 an. 94 (SGDI 5219) (II s. Φιλιστίων
I); (60) ?ii/i BC IGSI 4 III (IV), 138 D an. 8
(f. Φρῦνις); (61) ii/i BC ib. 8 I, 3 ([Φιλι]στίων)
——(Σπαρτ.): (62) ?ii/i BC IG XIV 421 D an. 3
(SGDI 5219) (f. Ἀγέας); (63) ~ IG XIV 421
D an. 13 (SGDI 5219); IGSI 10 II, 26 (s.
Ἀγέας)
——(Χαλκ.): (64) ii/i BC ib. 7 II, 33 (s. Ἀπολλώ-
νιος)

Φίλιστος
ACHAIA:
—DYME*: (1) c. 219 BC SGDI 1612, 73 (Tyche
5 (1990) p. 124) (s. Ἡρακλείδας)
AKARNANIA:
—KORONTA: (2) iii-ii BC IG IX (1)² (2) 432, 3;
(3) ~ ib. l. 5
—LIMNAIA: (4) c. 325-315 BC Hesp. 57 (1988)
p. 148 A, 32 (SEG XXXVI 331); cf. Hesp. 48
(1979) pp. 78 f. with pl. 22 c (s. Ἀριστόμαχος)
ARGOLIS:
—ARGOS: (5) ii BC IG IV (1)² 99, 18 (s. Καλλι-
σθένης)
ELIS: (6) f. i BC IvOl 198; 201; 204 (f. Στρογγῖν,
Τιμαρέτα); (7) ~ ib. 206; cf. Moretti, Olymp.
679 ([Φιλί]στος); (8) ~ ib. 674 (s. Ἀντιφάνης);
(9) m. i BC IvOl 411 (f. —άμιον); (10) 36 BC
ib. 59, 11 (s. Δι—)
—OLYMPIA*: (11) i BC ib. 205 (Φίλισ[τος]: f.
Φιλόνικος)
EPIROS:
—BOUTHROTOS: (12) iii BC IBouthrot 187
(Ugolini, Alb. Ant. 3 p. 96)
—BOUTHROTOS (PRASAIBOI): (13) a. 163
BC IBouthrot 26, 9 (SEG XXXVIII 484)
([Φί]λιστος: s. Δαμόκριτος); (14) ~ IBouthrot
29, 54
—TEPELENE (MOD.): (15) i BC-i AD? SEG XXIV
474, 3; cf. Hammond, Epirus p. 738 (locn.)

([Φί]λιστος: s. Λυκώτας) ?= (16); (16) ~ SEG
XXIV 474, 5 (-σστος: f. Νίκανος) ?= (15)
ILLYRIA:
—EPIDAMNOS-DYRRHACHION: (17) c. 250-50
BC SNG Fitz. Macedonia–Acarnania p. 46
no. 2544 (coin) (pryt.)
LAKONIA:
—SPARTA: (18) iii BC SEG XL 348 B, 5
LEUKAS: (19) hell. IG V (1) 6, 1 (s. Πολέμαρ-
χος); (20) 216 BC ib. IX (1)² (2) 583, 20 (f.
Ἐπίστρατος); (21) c. 167-50 BC BMC Thessaly
p. 185 nos. 169-70 (coins); (22) hell.-imp. AD
44 (1989) Chron. p. 266 (Ep. Chron. 31 (1994)
p. 43)
S. ITALY (BRUTTIUM):
—LOKROI EPIZEPHYRIOI:
——(Δυσ.): (23) iv/iii BC De Franciscis 4, 3; 5,
3; 22, 3; 39, 5 (f. Εὔθυμος)
S. ITALY (CALABRIA):
—TARAS-TARENTUM: (24) hell.? IG XIV 2406.
84 (RA 1932 (1), p. 41 no. 50 (loomweight))
(Φίλισ(τος)?)
SICILY:
—AKRAI: (25) ?iii BC SGDI 3240, 9 (Akrai p.
156 no. 7) (f. Νικασίων); (26) ~ ib. SGDI
3246, 30 (Akrai pp. 152-3 no. 2; Dubois,
IGDS 109) (f. Φίλων); (27) ~ SGDI 3246, 32
(Akrai pp. 152-3 no. 2; Dubois, IGDS 109)
(s. Φίλων)
—SYRACUSE: (28) c. 430-356 BC RE (3) + SEG
XXVI 1123 III B, 1; FGrH 556 (s. Ἀρχομενί-
δας)
—TAUROMENION: (29) c. 215 BC IG XIV 421
an. 26 (SGDI 5219) (s. Ξῆνις); (30) c. 168 BC
IG XIV 421 an. 73 (SGDI 5219) (s. Θεόφι-
λος); (31) c. 152 BC IG XIV 421 an. 89 (SGDI
5219) (f. Ἡρακλείδας); (32) ?ii/i BC IG XIV 421
D [an. 7] (SGDI 5219); IGSI 4 III (IV), 117
D an. 7 (s. Ἵππων); (33) ~ IG XIV 421 III
(SGDI 5219) ([Φίλ]ιστος?)

Φιλιστώ
ARGOLIS:
—ARGOS*: (1) ii-i BC IG IV (1) 530, 11; cf. BCH
33 (1909) p. 183 n. 2 (slave/freed.?)
—MYKENAI: (2) hell.? SEG III 315 c (loom-
weight) (Φιλιστ(o)ῦς (gen.), Φιλιστῦς (nom.?))
S. ITALY (LUCANIA):
—HYELE-VELIA: (3) inc. ib. XXVIII 819 (d. Θρά-
συς)
SICILY:
—ABAKAINON: (4) ii-i BC IGLMP 123
—TAUROMENION: (5) hell.-imp. SGDI 5233

Φιλίτας
ACHAIA:
—TRITAIA: (1) hell.-imp. Neratzoulis p. 21 no.
6 with fig. 16 (Achaïe II 316)

Φιλιτίων
EPIROS:
—NIKOPOLIS: (1) imp. PAE 1913, p. 97 no. 12
(Sarikakis 173) (s. Φίλητος)

Φίλλα
ARKADIA:
—PHIGALEIA: (1) i BC/i AD SEG XXIII 248
S. ITALY (CALABRIA):
—S. PANCRAZIO SALENTINO (MOD.): (2) imp.
NScav 1884, p. 378 (Eph. Ep. VIII 18); cf.
Epigraphica 25 (1963) p. 70 no. 69 (Lat. Filla:
d. Λαμίσκα)

Φίλλακος
AITOLIA: (1) iv BC IG II² 7994; (2) c. 200 BC
ib. 4931
—POTIDANIA: (3) m. ii BC SBBerlAk 1936, p.
371 b, 15 (SEG XLI 528 B) (Φί[λλ]ακος: s.
Εὐβουλίδας)

Φιλλέας
AITOLIA: (1) ?273 BC FD III (2) 205; (2) 217
BC Nachtergael, Les Galates 65, 3 (Φιλλ[έας],
Φιλλ[ίδας]?—FD)

Φιλλῆς

Akarnania:
—stratos: (3) 208 bc *IG* ix (1)² (1) p. L, s.a.
208 bc; 31, 60, 66 (s. Ἐπίνικος)
Illyria:
—apollonia: (4) ii-i bc *IApoll* 161

Φιλλῆς
Elis: (1) ?vi-v bc Moretti, *Olymp.* 975

Φιλλιάδας
Argolis:
—epidauros*: (1) c. 290-270 bc *IG* iv (1)² 109
II, 108, 156; *SEG* xxv 400, 121; 401 B, [68];
402, 134 (Φιλλ(ι)άδας—*SEG* xxv 402)
Messenia:
—messene: (2) s. iv bc ib. xli 362 (s. Νέων)

Φιλλίας
Akarnania:
—anaktorion: (1) iii/ii bc *IG* ix (1)² (2) 230
—stratos: (2) iv/iii bc ib. 395, 4 (s. Τηλα—)
Arkadia:
—tegea:
——(Krariotai): (3) f. iii bc ib. v (2) 36, 44 (f.
Πιστοκλῆς: metic)
Elis: (4) m. iii bc ib. 368, 133 with Index s.v
(f. Ἀρχίας)
Illyria:
—epidamnos-dyrrhachion: (5) c. 250-50 bc
*BMC Thessaly* p. 77 nos. 174-5; cf. *IApoll
Ref. Bibl.* n. 112 (coin) (pryt.) ?= (6); (6)
~ Maier 375-6 (coin) (Ceka 48; 139?; 361)
(pryt.) ?= (5)
Messenia:
—kyparissia: (7) ?iv/iii bc *IG* v (2) 390 (Perlman L.3)
—messene: (8) 208 or 207 bc *FD* iii (4) 23, 4;
24, 4 (f. Ἐπιχάρης)

Φιλλίδας
Aitolia: (1) c. 243-229 bc *SEG* xxxiii 317 ?=
(2); (2) 219 bc *RE* Supplbd. 7 (2) ?= (1)

Φίλλιος
Epiros:
—molossoi: (1) ii bc *SGDI* 1358, 8; cf.
Cabanes, *L'Épire* p. 583 no. 62
S. Italy (Campania):
—kyme: (2) imp. *CIL* x 3700, 2 (Lat. Varius
Phillius)

Φίλλις
Achaia:
—pellene: (1) c. 315-280 bc *FD* iii (1) 426, 3
([Φίλ]λις: s. Ἀγέας)
Argolis:
—argos: (2) ?v bc *Argive Heraeum* 2 p. 332
nos. 1824-5 (Φίλλι[ς], Φιλλί[ας]—ed.); (3) 345-
324 bc *CID* ii 31, 77; 32, 35; 75 II, 44; 79 A
I, 19; 95, [12]; 97, 22; 102 II B, 27; 121 III,
13 (Φίλις—no. 97: s. Δείναρχος); (4) 327-324
bc ib. 32, 35; 97, 27; 102 II B, 29 (s. Ἀλκίας);
(5) a. 324 bc ib. 120 A, 8 ([Φί]λλις); (6) ?274
bc ib. l. 15; 122 II, 12 (f. Φιλοκλῆς); (7) ii bc
*IG* ii² 8377, 2 (f. Φιλίστα)
Arkadia:
—megalopolis: (8) ii bc ib. v (2) 447, 12
([Φ]ίλλις)
Elis: (9) 69-73 ad *IvOl* 84, 20 (f. Ἐπέραστος)
Messenia:
—messene: (10) 361 bc *CID* ii 4 I, 29

Φιλλίχα
Argolis:
—phleious: (1) iv bc *SEG* xli 272 A

Φίλλος
Akarnania:
—stratos: (1) s. iv bc *IG* iv (1)² 95, 59 (Perlman E.2); Perlman pp. 46-9 (date)

Illyria:
—apollonia: (2) i bc Maier 136; cf. 153 (coin)
(f. Ξένων)
S. Italy (Campania):
—kyme: (3) imp. *CIL* x 3697 (Lat. Cn. Lucceius Fillus)

Φιλλύρας
Arkadia:
—mantineia-antigoneia: (1) ?iii bc *IG* v (2)
319, 35 (Φιλλύρα[ς])

Φίλλυρος
Achaia?: (1) 193 bc ib. 293, 21 (s. Ξενίας)
Akarnania:
—thyrreion: (2) ii bc ib. ix (1)² (2) 252, 11
(s. Πείραος)

Φίλλυς
Arkadia:
—tegea: (1) ii ad ib. v (2) 55, 37 (f. Κάλλιστος)
Elis: (2) c. 400 bc Seltman, *Temple Coins of
Olympia* 262a (*JNG* 33 (1983) p. 12 (coin
graffito)); (3) ?i ad *EA* 1905, p. 259 no. 2,
7, 8 (I f. Φίλλυς II, Νυμφόδοτος); (4) ~ ib. l. 8
([Φί]λλυς: II s. Φίλλυς I)

Φιλλώ
Lakonia: (1) imp. *IG* v (1) 1343 (Bradford (-))
(d. Δάμων)
S. Italy (Calabria):
—taras-tarentum: (2) iv/iii bc *NScav* 1940,
p. 434 (lamp)
S. Italy (Lucania):
—poseidonia-paestum: (3) c. 470 bc Lazzarini 702 (Landi, *DISMG* 128; *CEG* I 395);
*LSAG*² p. 260 no. 7 (date) (-λό: d. Χαρμυλί-
δας)

Φιλογένης
Arkadia:
—megalopolis: (1) ?145 bc *IG* v (2) 439, 30
(f. Ἀριστίων)
—kerkyra: (2) f. iii bc ib. ix (1) 691, 6 (*Iscr. Gr.
Verona* p. 22 A)
Lakonia:
—kardamyle: (3) i ad *SEG* xi 948, 18 (f. Περιγένης)
S. Italy (Calabria):
—brentesion-brundisium*: (4) imp. *CIL* ix
217 (Lat. L. Audius Philogenes: freed.)
S. Italy (Campania):
—pompeii: (5) i bc-i ad ib. iv 9916 (Lat. Philogenes)

Φιλόδαμος
Achaia: (1) hell. *Suppl. Cir.* 92, 1 (s. Σάτυρος);
(2) 146 bc *IG* iv (1)² 28, 78 (s. Ἀριστογένης:
synoikos)
—dyme*: (3) c. 219 bc *SGDI* 1612, 27 (*Tyche*
5 (1990) p. 124) (f. Εὔφαμος)
Aitolia: (4) ?a. 246 bc *SGDI* 2509, 2; (5) f. ii
bc *OGIS* 134 (f. Μελαγκόμας)
—philotaieis: (6) c. 157 bc *IG* ix (1)² (1) 108,
9
—phytaion: (7) ii bc *SEG* xxv 616 (s. Παναίτωλος)
—potana: (8) ?161 bc *FD* iii (3) 2, 4
Argolis:
—argos: (9) iv-iii bc Unp. (Ch. Kritzas); (10)
212 bc *RE* (4); (11) c. 210-207 bc *IG* iv (1)²
73, 8; *SEG* xxxv 303 (date) (s. Φίλαρχος); (12)
?ii bc ib. xxxviii 312, 1 (I f. Φιλόδαμος II);
(13) ~ ib. l. 1 (II s. Φιλόδαμος I)
—hermione: (14) ?ii-i bc *IG* iv (1) 731 III, 12
(s. Κλεοπάτρα)
Arkadia:
—orchomenos: (15) ?c. 369-361 bc *BCH* 102
(1978) p. 348, 32 (*IPArk* 14)
—phigaleia: (16) v bc *IG* v (2) 425, 2; (17) iii
bc ib. 427
—tegea: (18) s. iii bc ib. 36, 106

Elis: (19) 272 bc Plu., *Mor.* 251 A (-δη-: f. Μίκκα); (20) f. ii ad *IvOl* 470, 5 (Π. Μέμμιος Φ.:
s. Γ. Μέμμιος Εὔδαμος, Ἰουλ. Ἅπλα)
Epiros:
—bouthrotos (prasaiboi): (21) a. 163 bc
*IBouthrot* 101, 3 (f. Ἄρχιλλος); (22) ~ ib. l.
3 (s. Ἄρχιλλος)
Illyria:
—apollonia: (23) c. 250-50 bc Maier 94 (coin)
(Ceka 28) (pryt.); (24) i bc Maier 154-6 (coin)
(pryt.)
—epidamnos-dyrrhachion: (25) c. 250-50
bc Ceka, *Probleme* p. 152 no. 75 (coin) (pryt.)
?= (26); (26) ~ Maier 377-84; 386; 388-9;
Münsterberg p. 40; Nachtr. p. 17 (Ceka 49;
62; 97; 104; 121; 126; 128; 215; 229; 247; 261;
283; 314; 328; 362; 371; 429); Maier 385; 387
(coin) (pryt.) ?= (25); (27) ii-i bc *IDyrrh* 562
(tile)
Korinthia:
—korinth: (28) s. iii bc *Corinth* viii (3) 38, 5
(f. —μος)
Lakonia:
—oitylos: (29) iii/ii bc *IG* v (1) 1295, 9 (Bradford (3))
—sparta: (30) s. i bc *IG* v (1) 907 (tile) (Bradford (2))
—tainaron-kainepolis: (31) imp. *IG* v (1)
1245 (f. Ζεύξιππος)
Messenia:
—kyparissia: (32) m. iii bc ib. iv (1)² 96, 68
(Perlman E.3); Perlman p. 63 f. (date) (f. Διονυσόδωρος)
—messene?: (33) ii/i bc *SEG* xi 979, 27
(Φιλόδαμ[ος])
—thouria: (34) f. ii bc ib. 972, 54 (f. Ἄκρων);
(35) ~ ib. l. 73 (s. Σίων); (36) ~ ib. l. 113 (f.
Κλεαιθίδας)
S. Italy (Apulia):
—larinum*: (37) i bc *CIL* I² 1712 (ix 752)
(Lat. M. Drusius Philodamus: freed.)
S. Italy (Bruttium):
—lokroi epizephyrioi: (38) iv bc Iamb., *VP*
267 (*FVS* I p. 447)
——(Θρα.): (39) iv/iii bc De Franciscis 9, 2
——(Ὀμβ.): (40) iv/iii bc ib. l. 17
——(Τω.): (41) iv/iii bc ib. 32, 7 (f. Φιλίαρχος)
S. Italy (Calabria):
—taras-tarentum: (42) f. iv bc *IG* ii² 248, 1
([Φι]λόδαμος: f. Δαμόξενος)
S. Italy (Campania):
—pompeii: (43) i bc-i ad *CIL* iv 9934 b;
*Gnomon* 45 (1973) p. 268 (Lat. Philoda[mus])
Sicily: (44) hell. *Kokalos* 32 (1986) p. 244 no.
91 (tiles)
—gela-phintias: (45) ?i bc *IG* xiv 257 (Φιλό-
δα[μος])
—heloros: (46) f. ii bc *BCH* 45 (1921) p. 25
IV, 100 (*SEG* xxii 455); cf. *Sic. Gymn.* 17
(1964) pp. 47 f. (Φιλόδαμ[ος])
—selinous: (47) vi/v bc Manganaro, *PdelP*
forthcoming no. 18, 12 (f. Ἀγίας)
—tauromenion: (48) c. 228 bc *IG* xiv 421 an.
13 (*SGDI* 5219) (s. Ἀπολλωνίδας); (49) c. 156
bc *IG* xiv 421 an. 85 (*SGDI* 5219); (50) c.
151 bc *IGSI* 4 III (IV), 36 an. 90 (s. Ἀριστόπολις) ?= (51)
——(Ἀλκ.): (51) ii/i bc *IG* xiv 421 D an. 9; 421
[D] an. 1 (*SGDI* 5219); *IGSI* 4 III (IV), 157
D an. 9 (f. Ἀριστόπολις) ?= (50)
——(Ταν.): (52) ?ii/i bc *IG* xiv 421 D an. 7
(*SGDI* 5219) ([Φι]λόδαμος: s. Θεόφιλος)
—tyndaris: (53) ?iii bc *SEG* xxxvii 765

Φιλοδεσποτίς
S. Italy (Campania):
—surrentum: (1) imp. *St. Rom.* 2 (1914) p.
346 no. 18 = *NScav* 1928, p. 209 no. 11 (Lat.
Philodespotis)

Φιλοδέσποτος
Arkadia:
—tegea: (1) i ad *IG* v (2) 208 (Φει-: slave?)

S. ITALY (CALABRIA):
—BRENTESION-BRUNDISIUM: (2) imp. *Epigraphica* 25 (1963) p. 62 no. 56; cf. *Scritti Degrassi* 3 p. 68 (Lat. Philodespotos)
—BRENTESION-BRUNDISIUM*: (3) imp. *NScav* 1892, p. 352 r = *Epigraphica* 25 (1963) p. 84 no. 94 (Lat. M. Octavius Philodespotus: freed.)
S. ITALY (CAMPANIA):
—DIKAIARCHIA-PUTEOLI: (4) imp. *CIL* x 2847 (Lat. Philedespotus); (5) ~ ib. 3104 (Lat. C. Vibbius Philadespotus: freed.)
—DIKAIARCHIA-PUTEOLI*: (6) imp. ib. 2386 (Lat. M. Epidius Philodespotus: freed.); (7) 62 AD ib. 1549 (Lat. Claudius Philodespotus: imp. freed.)
—HERCULANEUM: (8) i BC-i AD *RAAN* 33 (1958) p. 289 no. 691; cf. *Cron. Erc.* 8 (1978) p. 155 no. 62 (Lat. Q. Iunius Phil(o)desp(otus): freed.)
—POMPEII: (9) c. 51-62 AD *CIL* IV 3340. 75, 11; 114, 6 (Castrèn 297. 8) (Lat. A. Paccius Philodespotus: freed.); (10) 56 AD *CIL* IV 3340. 22, 19; 34, 12; 43, 18; 101, 8 (Castrèn 112. 2) (Lat. M. Cestilius Philod(espotus): freed.)
—POMPEII*: (11) i BC-i AD *Römische Gräberstrassen* p. 227 (Lat. T. Vibius Philodespotus: freed.)
—SALERNUM*: (12) ?i AD *IItal* I (1) 238 I, 14 (*CIL* x 557) (Lat. L. Appuleius Philodespotus: freed.)

**Φιλόδηλος**
AITOLIA:
—VLACHOMANDRA (MOD.): (1) vii BC *AD* 22 (1967) Chron. p. 318 (Φιλοδήλō (gen.))

**Φιλόδημος**
LAKONIA:
—HYPERTELEATON*: (1) imp. *IG* v (1) 1061 (f. Συνέγδημος)
S. ITALY (CAMPANIA):
—POMPEII: (2) c. 55-60 AD *CIL* IV 3340. 43, 18 (Lat. M. Cestillius Philode[m]us)

**Φιλόδοκος**
LAKONIA:
—SPARTA: (1) 391 BC D.S. xiv 97. 3 (Poralla² 726) (Φιλόδικος—mss. inf.)

**Φιλόδρομος**
LAKONIA:
—SPARTA: (1) iii BC *SEG* XL 348 B, 3 (Φιλόδρομ[ος])

**Φιλόδωρος**
ACHAIA:
—PELLENE: (1) v/iv BC *Milet* I (1) 13, 10 f. (Φι[λό]δωρος: f. Ἐπίφρων)
SICILY:
—MORGANTINA: (2) ?iv/iii BC *SEG* XXXIX 1010, 8 ([Φι]λόδωρος—ed., [Ἀπολ]λόδωρος?: s. Κρίθων)

**Φιλοθάλης**
KORINTHIA:
—SIKYON: (1) s. iii BC *IG* IV (1) 428, 1 (Skalet 329) (f. Καλλίστρατος)

**Φιλοθέα**
S. ITALY (CAMPANIA):
—POMPEII: (1) i BC-i AD *CIL* IV 3710 (Lat. Philoth[ea])

**Φιλόθεος**
LAKONIA:
—SPARTA: (1) c. 140 AD *IG* v (1) 65, 9 (Bradford (1)) (s. Φιλοκλῆς); (2) c. 140-145 AD *IG* v (1) 1314, 33 (Bradford (2)); (3) c. 150-160 AD *IG* v (1) 53, 16 (Bradford (3)) (f. Κλέων)


**Φιλοθέρσης**
ARGOLIS:
—EPIDAUROS: (1) c. 365-335 BC *IG* IV (1)² 103, 119

**Φιλόθηρος**
ACHAIA: (1) iii BC *PPetr* III 111, 6 (s. Σώπατρος)
ARKADIA:
—PHIGALEIA: (2) ii BC *IG* v (2) 428; (3) s. i BC *IvOl* 402 (s. Ἄρχιππος)

**Φιλόθιν**
EPIROS: (1) hell. *SGDI* 1361; cf. Cabanes, *L'Épire* p. 584 no. 65

**Φιλοίτιος**
AKARNANIA?:
—PHYLEIA: (1) 356-354 BC *IG* IV (1)² 95, 37 (Perlman E.2); Perlman p. 40 f. (date)

**Φίλοιτος**
MESSENIA:
—MESSENE: (1) c. 140 BC *IvOl* 52, 32 (s. Κράτιος)

**Φιλόκαλον**
ARGOLIS:
—TROIZEN: (1) i BC/i AD *IG* IV (1) 819

**Φιλόκαλος**
LAKONIA:
—HYPERTELEATON*: (1) imp. ib. v (1) 1042 (s. Ἀσκληπιάδης)
—SPARTA: (2) c. 100 AD *SEG* XI 626, 5 (Bradford (2)) (f. Πάρις); (3) c. 100-125 AD *IG* v (1) 153, 27; *SEG* XI 569, 22 (Bradford (1)) (f. Νήδυμος)
S. ITALY (APULIA):
—CANUSIUM*: (4) imp. *Epig. Rom. di Canosa* 61 (*CIL* IX 350) (Lat. P. Valerius Philocalus: freed.)
—HERDONIA*: (5) ii AD *Ordona* 6 p. 131 no. 47 (Lat. N. Granius Philocalus: freed.)
—LUCERIA: (6) imp. *CIL* IX 823 (Lat. M. Luccius Philocalus: freed.)
S. ITALY (CAMPANIA):
—DIKAIARCHIA-PUTEOLI: (7) imp. ib. x 3033 (Lat. Philocalus)
—DIKAIARCHIA-PUTEOLI*: (8) imp. ib. 2404 (Lat. M. Fabius Philocalus: freed.)
—POMPEII: (9) i BC-i AD ib. IV 882 (Lat. Pilo[ca]lus); (10) ~ ib. 1775-6; 3079 (Lat. Pilocalus); (11) c. 51-62 AD ib. 3340. 80, 4 (Castrèn 161. 13) (Lat. M. Fabius Philocalus)
—SALERNUM: (12) imp. *IItal* I (1) 34 (*CIL* x 559) (Lat. L. Asinius Philo[ca]lus: f. Asinia Venusta)
SICILY:
—THERMAI HIMERAIAI: (13) i-ii AD ib. 7374 (*ILat. Term. Imer.* 44) (Lat. M. Philocalus: f. Ἀσιατικός)

**Φιλόκας**
ARKADIA:
—TEGEA: (1) iii BC *IG* v (2) 40, 20

**Φιλοκλέα**
EPIROS:
—BOUTHROTOS (PRASAIBOI): (1) a. 163 BC *IBouthrot* 31, 95 (*SEG* XXXVIII 490); *IBouthrot* 51, 24; (2) ~ ib. 32, 25 (*SEG* XXXVIII 491) (Φιλοκλέ[α])

**Φιλόκλεια**
ARKADIA:
—MEGALOPOLIS: (1) iv/iii BC *IG* v (2) 479, 5; (2) ~ ib. l. 8 (Φιλόκλεια)
—THELPHOUSA: (3) i BC/i AD *SEG* XI 1132; *BCH* 88 (1964) pp. 178-9 (date)

**Φιλοκλείδα**
LEUKAS: (1) iv/iii BC Carapanos, *Dodone* p. 40 no. 2 (*IGA* 339); cf. *SEG* XXXII 1651 no.


11 (name) (Φιλοκλέδα (masc. nom.), Φιλοκλέδα(ς)?: s. Δαμόφιλος)

**Φιλοκλείδας**
ACHAIA:
—DYME: (1) s. iii BC ib. XIII 278, 21
ARGOLIS:
—EPIDAUROS: (2) c. 370 BC *IG* IV (1)² 102, 90 (-κλί-)
LAKONIA:
—GYTHEION: (3) i BC-i AD ib. v (1) 1194 ([Φ]ιλοκλείδας)
—SPARTA: (4) ?ii BC ib. 908 a (tiles) (Bradford (5)) (Φιλοκλείδ(ας)); (5) ii/i BC *IG* v (1) 966, 3 + p. 306 add. ([Φιλο]κλείδας?: f. Ἀγαθοκλῆς); (6) c. 25-1 BC ib. 210, 25 (Bradford (1)) (s. Κάρπος); (7) ?i AD *IG* v (1) 180, 4 (Bradford (4)) (Φιλοκλεί[δας]); (8) c. 100 AD *SEG* XI 626, 4 (Bradford (2)) (-κλί-: s. Ὀνασικλῆς); (9) c. 105-110 AD *IG* v (1) 51, 4, 26; 52, [1]; 97, 1; *SEG* XI 538, 1; 564, 1 (Bradford (3)) (Γ. Ἰούλ. Φ., Φιλοκλίδας—97); (10) m. ii AD *IG* v (1) 71 III, 46; 86, 24; 108, 3 (Bradford (6)) (f. Ἀγαθοκλῆς)
LEUKAS: (11) iv-iii BC *AM* 27 (1902) p. 366 no. 27 ([Φ]ιλοκλείδας)
MESSENIA:
—THOURIA: (12) ii-i BC *IG* v (1) 1385, 33 (f. Φίλων)

**Φιλοκλείδης**
LAKONIA:
—SPARTA: (1) c. 140-160 AD ib. 154, 8; *SEG* XI 600, 2 (Bradford (-)) (s. Δημήτριος)

**Φιλόκλειτος**
MESSENIA:
—THOURIA: (1) ii-i BC *IG* v (1) 1385, 3 (s. Φίλιππος)

**Φιλοκλῆς**
ACHAIA: (1) 146 BC ib. IV (1)² 28, 114 (s. Φίλων: synoikos)
—AIGEIRA: (2) ?182 BC ib. 625 (f. Ἄρχων)
—DYME: (3) iii BC *AJPh* 31 (1910) p. 399 no. 74 a, 14 (f. Φιλαγόρας); (4) iii-ii BC *Syll*³ 530, 1; cf. *Achaia und Elis* p. 115
AKARNANIA: (5) iii BC Robert, *EEP* p. 114, 3
—THYRREION: (6) ii BC *IG* IX (1)² (2) 251, 5
ARGOLIS:
—ARGOS: (7) f. iii BC *HE* 760; (8) ?274 BC *CID* II 120 A, 15; 122 II, 12 (s. Φίλλις); (9) ii BC *IG* IV (1)² 627 (s. Ἁρμόδιος); (10) ~ *SEG* XLII 279, 5; (11) ~ ib. l. 12 (Φιλοκ(λ)ῆς); (12) ~ ib. l. 14 (Φιλοκ(λ)ῆς); (13) ?165 BC *Syll*³ 585, 309; cf. Stephanis 2562 (f. Φίλων); (14) c. 146-32 BC *BMC Pelop.* p. 146 nos. 123-4 (coin); (15) i BC *SEG* XXXIII 291, 6; cf. Stephanis 2524 (Φιλοκ[λ]ῆς: f. Φιλοκλῆς II); (16) ~ *SEG* XXXIII 291, 6 (Stephanis 2524) (Φιλ[οκλ]ῆς: II s. Φιλοκλῆς I)
——(Dmaihippidai): (17) ii/i BC *BCH* 33 (1909) p. 176 no. 2, 11 (s. Ξενόφαντος)
——EPIDAUROS: (18) iii BC *IG* IV (1)² 337 + Peek, *IAEpid* 146 (Φιλοκλ[ῆς]: s. Δαμοκύδης)
——(Azantioi): (19) 146 BC *IG* IV (1)² 28, 43 (s. Τιμαίνετος)
—HERMIONE: (20) ii-i BC ib. IV (1) 732 II, 17 (f. Σωτηρίων)
—KALAURIA: (21) m. iii BC ib. IV (1)² 96, 43 (Perlman E.3); Perlman p. 63 f. (date) (f. Μένανδρος)
—TROIZEN: (22) ?200 BC *PP* 4126 (s. Ἱεροκλῆς); (23) f. ii BC *IG* IV (1) 752, 8 + IV (1)² 77, 14
ARKADIA:
—MANTINEIA-ANTIGONEIA: (24) ii BC ib. v (2) 292 (Φιλοκλῆ[ς])
—MEGALOPOLIS: (25) ?131 BC ib. 440, 8 (f. Πασέας); (26) ~ ib. l. 11 (s. Πασέας, Ἀρχενίκα); (27) i BC-i AD ib. IV (1)² 656, 7; *SEG* XI 382 a (Loewy 271a) (s. Καλλικράτης: sculptor)
—TEGEA:

——(Apolloniatai): (28) iv/iii BC *IG* v (2) 38, 29 (s. Ἀριστίων); (29) m. iii BC ib. 36, 102 (f. Παντιάδας)

——(Hippothoitai): (30) iv/iii BC ib. 38, 47 (f. Φερέας); (31) iii BC ib. 40, 22 (s. Φαῖδρος)

——(Krariotai): (32) iii BC ib. l. 18 (s. Κλεόδωρος)

EPIROS:

—AMBRAKIA: (33) iii-ii BC *Op. Ath.* 10 (1971) p. 64 no. 12, 1; cf. *VAHD* 84 (1991) p. 262 (f. Χαιρήν)

—ANTIGONEIA: (34) ?ii BC *AE* 1914, p. 237 no. 13; Cabanes, *L'Épire* p. 234 n. 96 (locn.) ([Φ]ιλοκλῆς)

ILLYRIA:

—APOLLONIA: (35) c. 250-50 BC Maier 95 (coin) (Ceka 116) (pryt.); (36) i BC Maier 132 (coin) (s. Γεν–: money.); (37) ~ ib. 156 (coin) (money.); (38) hell.-imp. *IApoll* 79 (f. Ἐρωτίς)

KORINTHIA:

—KORINTH: (39) 244 BC *SEG* XXXII 118 I, 65

LAKONIA:

—GERONTHRAI: (40) hell. *IG* v (1) 1128

—GYTHEION: (41) 211 AD ib. 1163, 13 (Τερέντιος Φ. νέος)

—MESSA?: (42) imp. ib. 1280, 5 (f. Λαβίππα); (43) ~ ib. l. 6 (s. Σωτιμίδας); (44) ~ ib. l. 8 (f. Φίλιππος)

—SPARTA: (45) ii-i BC ib. 862 (tiles) (Bradford (9)); (46) f. ii BC *SEG* XI 861 a (vase); Siebert, *Ateliers* pp. 172-3 (date) (Bradford (7)) (potter); (47) s. i BC *IG* v (1) 92, 2 (Bradford (2)) (s. Ἀσκλάπων); (48) c. 30-20 BC *IG* v (1) 211, 42 (Bradford (6)) (s. Τιμόξενος) ?= (50); (49) c. 25-1 BC *IG* v (1) 212, 8 (Bradford (3)); (50) i BC/i AD *IG* v (1) 48, 8 (Bradford (14)) (f. Τιμόξενος) ?= (48); (51) i-ii AD *IG* v (1) 654, 2, 10 (Bradford (15)) ([Φιλο]κλῆς–l. 2, Φιλοκ[λῆς]–l. 10); (52) ?i-ii AD *IG* v (1) 1575 (Bradford (8)); (53) s. i AD *IG* v (1) 278, 3; *SEG* XI 558, 9; 559, 4 (Bradford (12)) (f. Μ. Ἀνθέστιος Φιλοκράτης); (54) c. 80-90 AD *IG* v (1) 674, 7 (Bradford (10)) ([Φιλ]οκλῆς); (55) c. 100-125 AD *IG* v (1) 51, 19; 52, 5; 482, 2; *SEG* XI 506, [4] (Bradford (4)) (Κ. Οὐίβιος Φ., Κ. Βείβιος Φ.–52: s. Πασικλῆς); (56) ~ *IG* v (1) 152, 8 (Bradford (1)) (s. Ἀριστόξενος); (57) c. 125-150 AD *IG* v (1) 107, 5 (Bradford (17)) (Φιλοκλῆς); (58) c. 140 AD *IG* v (1) 65, 9 (Bradford (13)) (f. Φιλόθεος); (59) c. 140-160 AD *IG* v (1) 68, [26]; 69, 25; 70, 3; 71 III, 8; *SEG* XI 585, 12; XXX 410, [20] (Bradford (11)) (I f. Φιλοκλῆς II); (60) ~ *IG* v (1) 69, 25; 70, 3; 71 III, 8; *SEG* XI 585, 12; XXX 410, [20] (Bradford (5)) (II s. Φιλοκλῆς I)

MESSENIA:

—KORONE: (61) 246 AD *IG* v (1) 1398, 60 (Αὐρ. Φ.)

—MESSENE: (62) f. iii BC *SEG* XLI 342, 3; cf. *PAE* 1991, p. 100 no. 8; (63) 243 BC *SEG* XII 371, 18 (f. —λ[.]ος)

—THOURIA: (64) f. ii BC ib. XI 972, 108 (f. Κράτων)

S. ITALY (BRUTTIUM):

—LOKROI EPIZEPHYRIOI:

——(Γαγ.): (65) 278 BC De Franciscis 30, 3 (s. Φιλώνδας)

——(Θρα.): (66) iv/iii BC ib. 17, 2 (s. Σῖμος)

S. ITALY (CALABRIA):

—TARAS-TARENTUM: (67) c. 302-280 BC Vlasto 687-90 (Evans, *Horsemen* p. 134 VI C.3 (coin)); (68) c. 235-228 BC Vlasto 950-4 (coin) (Evans, *Horsemen* p. 195 IX F.1)

S. ITALY (CAMPANIA):

—DIKAIARCHIA-PUTEOLI: (69) imp. *CIL* x 2310 (Lat. C. Valerius Philocles)

S. ITALY (LUCANIA):

—METAPONTION: (70) m. iii BC *SEG* XXX 1175, 15 (doctor)

SICILY:

—AKRAGAS: (71) s. iv BC *IG* IV (1)² 95, 91 (Perlman E.2); Perlman pp. 46-9 (date) (Φιλ[ο]κλῆ[ς]: f. Θεστίας)

—AKRAI: (72) ii-i BC *SGDI* 3246, 15 (*Akrai* pp. 152-3 no. 2; Dubois, *IGDS* 109) (s. Φίλων)

—APOLLONIA: (73) ii-i BC *IG* XIV 364 a (*IGLMP* 39)

## Φιλοκόμψα

S. ITALY (CAMPANIA):

—NOLA*: (1) imp. *CIL* x 1327 (Lat. Alfia Philocompsa: freed.)

## Φιλοκρατέα

ARGOLIS:

—HERMIONE: (1) i BC-i AD? *IG* IV (1) 730 III, 7 (d. Ἀπολλωνία)

## Φιλοκράτεια

ARGOLIS:

—ARGOS:

——(Aithaleis): (1) ii/i BC *BCH* 33 (1909) p. 176 no. 2, 15 (d. Λυσίων)

——Pa–: (2) f. iii BC *IG* IV (1) 529, 19

LAKONIA:

—SPARTA: (3) ?i AD ib. v (1) 514, 1 (Bradford (1)) (–τι–: d. Καλλικλείδας); (4) c. 200-225 AD *IG* v (1) 591, 2; *BSA* 80 (1985) pp. 224; 238 (ident., stemma) (Bradford (2)) (Κλ. Φιλοκράτ[ια]: d. Τιβ. Κλ. Ἀριστοτέλης, Ἰουλ. Ἐτυμοκλήδεια)

MESSENIA:

—MESSENE: (5) hell.? *SEG* XXIII 213 (d. Ἵππαρχος)

## Φιλοκράτης

ACHAIA: (1) 146 BC *IG* IV (1)² 28, 65 (f. Δαμοκλῆς: synoikos); (2) ~ ib. l. 131 (f. Ἀσκλαπιάδας: synoikos); (3) ~ ib. l. 136 (f. Σῶσος: synoikos)

—DYME: (4) c. 270 BC ib. IX (1)² (1) 13, 35 (s. Ἀριστοφάνης)

—PHARAI: (5) hell. *SEG* XIV 373 f

AKARNANIA:

—PALAIROS: (6) hell.? *IG* IX (1)² (2) 569, 4

ARGOLIS:

—ARGOS: (7) c. 458 BC ib. I³ 1149, 14 (-τ̄ες); (8) 213 or 205 BC Nachtergael, *Les Galates* 66, 7 (Stephanis 2530) (s. Λύσιππος); (9) ii BC *SEG* XLII 279, 15 (Φιλοκρά[της], Φιλοκρά[τεια]?)

——(Naupliadai): (10) m. iv BC ib. XVII 146, 3

—TROIZEN: (11) 153-144 BC *SGDI* 2295, 16 (f. Τρίτυλλος)

ARKADIA:

—TEGEA: (12) i BC/i AD *IG* v (2) 83 (s. Δαμόνικος, f. Δαμόνικος); (13) 165 AD ib. 50, 43 (s. Δίδυμος)

——(Apolloniatai): (14) iv/iii BC ib. 38, 32 (Φιλ[οκ]ράτης: f. Θεοκλῆς)

DALMATIA:

—ISSA: (15) ii BC Brunšmid. p. 25 no. 14, 5 + *VAHD* 84 (1991) p. 248 no. 1 (f. Φαντώ); (16) ~ Brunšmid p. 25 no. 14, 7 + *VAHD* 84 (1991) p. 248 no. 1 (f. Φαντώ)

——(Hylleis): (17) iv/iii BC Brunšmid p. 9, 56 ([Φι]λοκράτης: s. Σάμος)

ELIS: (18) hell. Plaut., *Capt.* passim (Lat. Philocrates: fict.)

EPIROS: (19) 154 BC *SGDI* 1901, 4, 6 (slave/freed.)

—AMBRAKIA: (20) hell.? *SEG* XVII 305 (f. Σώσανδρος); (21) ii BC *NS* 547 (s. Νύσιος)

—BOUTHROTOS (PRASAIBOI): (22) a. 163 BC *IBouthrot* 45, 8 (s. Ὠφελίων)

ILLYRIA:

—APOLLONIA: (23) c. 250-50 BC *NZ* 20 (1927) p. 54 (coin) (Ceka 41) (pryt.); (24) ~ Maier 96 (coin) (Ceka 11) (pryt.)

—EPIDAMNOS-DYRRHACHION: (25) iii BC *IGB* I² 37; cf. *IDyrrh* 516 (s. Λεωνίδας); (26) c. 250-50 BC Ceka, *Probleme* p. 152 no. 76 (coin)

(pryt.) ?= (27); (27) ~ *Jubice Hoard* p. 97 nos. 39/40 (coin) (Ceka 341) (pryt.) ?= (26)

KORINTHIA:

—SIKYON: (28) s. iii BC *IG* II² 9052, 3 (*GVI* 1699; *Gr. Gr.* 215); Osborne, *Naturalization* T 97 (f. Φίλων: date—M.J.O.); (29) iii/ii BC *IG* II² 9052, 6, 8 (*GVI* 1699; *Gr. Gr.* 215); Osborne, *Naturalization* T 97 (and Athens Hamaxanteia: s. Φίλων, Ἀριστόκλεια (Korinth): date—M.J.O.)

LAKONIA:

—KYTHERA: (30) ii BC *IG* II² 9113 (f. Φιλοξενίδας)

—SPARTA: (31) c. 50-120 AD ib. v (1) 278, 2; 281, 4 (*Artemis Orthia* pp. 314-15 no. 34); *SEG* XI 558, 9; 559, 4 (Bradford (6)) (Μ. Ἀνθέστιος Φ.: s. Φιλοκλῆς, f. Δαμίων); (32) c. 80-100 AD *SEG* XI 609, 3; XXXVI 361, 32 (Bradford s.v. Δαμοκλῆς (2)) (f. Δαμοκλῆς: ident.—*LGPN*); (33) c. 90-100 AD *SEG* XI 512, 3 (Bradford (15)) (f. Πολυκλῆς); (34) c. 95-105 AD *SEG* XI 562, 3 (Bradford (13)) (Φιλοκράτ[ης]: f. Καλλικρατίδας); (35) c. 95-110 AD *IG* v (1) 51, 8; 52, 2; *SEG* XI 562, 5 (Bradford (10)) (f. Ἄλεξις); (36) ~ *IG* v (1) 51, 11; 52, 3; *SEG* XI 506, [1]; 562, 6 (Bradford (14)) (f. Πασικλῆς); (37) c. 100-120 AD *IG* v (1) 32 B, 1; 51, 33; 52, 7; 60, 1-2; 103, 10; 138, 2; 492, 3-4; *SEG* XI 538, 3; 545, [4]; 548, [19]; 582, 2 (Bradford s.v. Δαμοκλῆς (2)) (Δαμοκλῆς ὁ καὶ Φ.: s. Δαμοκλῆς, f. Δαμοκλῆς, Δαμονίκης); (38) ii AD *IG* v (1) 583, 11 (Bradford (17)); (39) c. 105-110 AD *IG* v (1) 51, 16; 52, 4; *SEG* XI 506, 3 (Bradford (2)) (s. Διογένης); (40) c. 105-115 AD *IG* v (1) 42, 16 (Bradford (7)) (II s. Φιλοκράτης I); (41) ~ *IG* v (1) 42, 17 (Bradford (16)) (I f. Φιλοκράτης II); (42) ~ *IG* v (1) 103, 14 (Bradford (8)) ([Φι]λοκράτης: s. Θεόδωρος, ?s. Καλλικράτεια); (43) c. 115-150 AD *SEG* XI 481, 3 (Bradford (5)) (s. Ὀνησιφόρος); (44) c. 125 AD *SEG* XI 575, 11 (Bradford (9)); (45) c. 125-150 AD *IG* v (1) 73, 6; 87, 6; 160, 6; 446, 7 (Bradford (4)) (s. Κλέανδρος); (46) m. ii AD *IG* v (1) 71 II, 16; 113, 6; 161, 5 (Bradford (1)) (s. Ἀγαθοκλῆς); (47) f. iii AD *IG* v (1) 170, 15; *BSA* 80 (1985) p. 245 (date) (Bradford (11)) (f. Αὐρ. Χαρίτων); (48) c. 220 AD *IG* v (1) 544, 9 (*Artemis Orthia* pp. 358-9 no. 145; Bradford (3)) (Μ. Αὐρ. Φ.: s. Ἐλπίνικος); (49) c. 230-260 AD *IG* v (1) 556, 11 (Bradford (12)) (f. Αὐρ. Εὐτυχίων)

MESSENIA: (50) ii AD *AD* 2 (1916) p. 117 no. 82 (s. Φιλωνίδας)

—KOLONIDES: (51) ii BC *IG* v (1) 1402, 3 (s. Ξενιάδας)

—KORONE: (52) i AD ib. 1394, 8

—MESSENE: (53) iv/iii BC ib. 1435, 13; (54) s. ii BC *BCH* 95 (1971) p. 544, 3, 11, [17] + *SEG* XXXVII 447 (name) (f. Φιλέας); (55) ~ *BCH* 95 (1971) p. 544, [3], 12, [17] (s. Ἵππων); (56) ii/i BC *SEG* XXXVIII 341, 2 (f. Καλλικράτις); (57) 31 BC-14 AD ib. XXIII 207, 22 (f. Εὐάμερος)

——(Aristomachidai): (58) 11 AD *PAE* 1992, p. 71 A, 8 (s. Νίκαιος)

—THOURIA: (59) f. ii BC *SEG* XI 972, 75 (f. Λύσανδρος); (60) ~ ib. l. 122 (f. Νικάριστος)

PELOPONNESE: (61) 112 BC *FD* III (2) 70 A, 30 (f. Σωσικλείδας); (62) ~ ib. l. 35

PELOPONNESE?: (63) 11 AD *PAE* 1992, p. 72 B, 10 (I f. Φιλοκράτης II); (64) ~ ib. l. 10 (II s. Φιλοκράτης I)

S. ITALY (BRUTTIUM):

—LOKROI EPIZEPHYRIOI:

——(Γαγ.): (65) iv/iii BC De Franciscis 16, 2 (s. Ἀρίσταρχος)

——(Ὀμβ.): (66) iv/iii BC ib. 5, 5 (f. Εὐγενίδας)

——(Ψαθ.): (67) iv/iii BC ib. 26, 2 (f. Σωσίστρατος)

S. ITALY (CALABRIA):

—TARAS-TARENTUM: (68) c. 272-235 BC Vlasto 825-33; 867-76 (Evans, *Horsemen* p. 177

VIII A.6-7; p. 178 VIII C.2-3 (coin)) (Φι-
λοκρά(της)) ?= (69); (69) ~ Vlasto 850-1 (coin)
?= (68); (70) s. iii BC IG IX (1)² (1) 24, 12 (f.
K—)
S. Italy (Campania):
—DIKAIARCHIA-PUTEOLI: (71) ii-i BC CIL III
574, 1 (biling.) (Κοσσίνιος Φ., Lat. A. Cossi-
nius Philocrates)
—POMPEII: (72) i BC-i AD ib. IV 1952 (fals.?)
(Lat. Philocratis)
SICILY:
—AGYRION: (73) f. i BC Cic., In Verr. II ii 25
(Lat. Philocrates)
—AKRAGAS: (74) f. v BC Schol. Pi., O. iii 68 a
(s. Θήρων)
—AKRAI: (75) ii BC Akrai p. 156 no. 6, 1; (76)
ii-i BC SGDI 3246, 34 (Akrai pp. 152-3 no.
2; Dubois, IGDS 109) (Φιλ[οκράτ]ης?: f. Ἀ—)
——(Ἀναυ.): (77) ii BC Akrai p. 154 no. 3, 1 (Φ.)
—GELA-PHINTIAS: (78) ?i BC IG XIV 257
—KENTORIPA: (79) ?s. iii BC Sic. Gymn. 2
(1949) p. 91 no. 1, 12 + 16 (1963) p. 54
—PATERNO (MOD.): (80) ii BC IG XIV 12*; cf.
Sic. Gymn. 16 (1963) p. 57 n. 42; PdelP 20
(1965) p. 176
—SYRACUSE: (81) ?304 BC IG V (2) 550, 20, 26;
(82) 208 BC IMM 72, 9 (Dubois, IGDS 97)
—SYRACUSE?:
——(Πλη.): (83) hell. Manganaro, PdelP forth-
coming no. 4 IV, 2 (s. Φίλων)

**Φιλοκρατίδας**
LAKONIA:
—OITYLOS: (1) ?ii-i BC IG V (1) 1298
—SPARTA: (2) iii BC SEG XL 348 B, 4; (3) c.
90-125 AD IG V (1) 80, 2; 481, 1-2 (Brad-
ford (4)) (s. Καλλικράτης, f. Καλλικράτεια); (4)
c. 150-175 AD IG V (1) 116, 3; SEG XI 530,
4 (Bradford (1)) (s. Ἀγαθοκλῆς); (5) c. 170
AD IG V (1) 116, 13; SEG XI 590 (name)
(Bradford (3)) (Ἰούλ. Φιλ(ο)κρατίδα[s]—SEG,
Φιλ[η]ρατίδα[s]—IG); (6) c. 221 AD IG V (1)
541, 4; BSA 79 (1984) pp. 270-3 (date)
(Bradford (2)) (Μ. Αὐρ. Φ.: s. Εὐδαμίδας)

**Φιλοκράτις**
ARKADIA:
—PHIGALEIA: (1) s. iii BC SEG XXIII 244
LAKONIA:
—BOIAI: (2) ii AD IG V (1) 957 a (Ἰουλ. Φ.: d. Γ.
Ἰούλ. Θρασέας, Ἰουλ. Κλεαινέτα)

**Φιλοκρατίων**
ARGOLIS:
—METHANA-ARSINOE: (1) imp. SEG XXXVIII
327

**Φιλοκτήτης**
ARGOLIS:
—ARGOS: (1) ii AD ib. XVI 253, 6 (I f. Φιλοκτήτης
II); (2) ~ ib. l. 6 (II s. Φιλοκτήτης I); (3) ~ ib.
l. 11 (Φιλοκτ[ήτ]ης: f. Φήλιξ)

**Φιλοκύρις**
SICILY:
—SYRACUSE: (1) iii-v AD Riv. Arch. Crist. 18
(1941) p. 228 no. 118; cf. Ferrua, NG 141 b
([Φιλ]οκύρις)

**Φιλόκυρος**
S. Italy (Campania):
—DIKAIARCHIA-PUTEOLI: (1) ?i-ii AD CIL X
2541 (Lat. Lucilius Philocyrus)

**Φιλοκύων**
LAKONIA:
—SPARTA: (1) c. 505-479 BC Hdt. ix 71. 2; 85
(Poralla² 727)

**Φιλόκωμος**
S. Italy (Calabria):
—TARAS-TARENTUM: (1) ?iv BC NScav 1881, p.
435 (vase)

**Φιλόλαος**
AITOLIA:
—PHISTYON: (1) c. 162-161 BC IG IX (1)² (1)
100, 2; 106, 5, 8
KORINTHIA:
—KORINTH: (2) s. viii BC RE (3)
LAKONIA:
—SPARTA: (3) 360-354 BC CID II 4 II, 53; 31,
6, 35 (Poralla² 728)
S. Italy (Calabria):
—TARAS-TARENTUM: (4) v BC RE Supplbd. 13
(-); FVS 44 (or S. Italy (Bruttium) Kroton)

**Φιλολέως**
SICILY:
—SELINOUS: (1) m. v BC Dubois, IGDS 34
(Arena, Iscr. Sic. I 70) (-ōs)

**Φιλολόγιος**
SICILY:
—SYRACUSE: (1) iii-v AD Strazzulla 270 (Wessel
186 a)

**Φιλόλογος**
ARKADIA:
—TEGEA: (1) imp. IG V (2) 253, 1
ILLYRIA:
—EPIDAMNOS-DYRRHACHION: (2) i BC-i AD
CIL III 614 (Sestieri, ILat. Albania 31) (Lat.
Philo[log]us: eye doctor)
S. Italy (Campania):
—HERCULANEUM: (3) m. i AD PdelP 3 (1948) p.
171 no. 16 (Lat. Messenius Philologus)
—HERCULANEUM*: (4) c. 50-75 AD CIL X 1403
a I, 23 (Lat. C. Messenius Philologus: freed.)
—POMPEII: (5) i BC/i AD ib. 958; Mouritsen p.
102 (date) (Lat. M-us Philologus); (6) 57 AD
CIL IV 3340. 40, 15 (Castrèn 81. 21) (Lat. A.
Caecilius Philologus)

**Φιλομάθεια**
ARGOLIS:
—ARGOS: (1) ii AD SEG XVI 259, 4 (Κλ. Φιλομά-
θια: ?m. Γν. Πομπ. Διόδοτος, Γν. Πομπ. Κλεο-
σθένης, Γν. Πομπ. Καλλέας); (2) ~ ib. XLI 285
II, 32 (-θια)

**Φιλόμαχος**
LAKONIA:
—SPARTA: (1) c. 208 BC FD III (4) 135, 8 (Brad-
ford (-)) (s. Νεόδαμος)

**Φιλόμβροτος**
ARKADIA:
—TEGEA: (1) f. iii BC IG V (2) 35, 52 (f. Πλει-
στίας)
—THELPHOUSA: (2) s. iii BC FD III (4) 19 (f.
—ων)
LAKONIA:
—SPARTA: (3) ?676-668 BC Moretti, Olymp. 35;
37; 41 (Poralla² 729)

**Φιλομένης**
KORINTHIA:
—SIKYON: (1) ?255 BC Nachtergael, Les Galates
8, 57; cf. Stephanis 40 (f. Ἀγιμένης)

**Φιλομήλα**
AITOLIA:
—KALLION/KALLIPOLIS: (1) 143 BC IG IX (1)²
(3) 639. 8, 3 (d. Γλαυκέας)

**Φιλομηλίδας**
ARKADIA:
—MANTINEIA-ANTIGONEIA: (1) c. 475-450 BC
ib. V (2) 262, 4 (IPArk 8); LSAG² p. 216 no.
29 (date) ([Φ]ιλομέλίδας)
LAKONIA:
—OITYLOS: (2) iii/ii BC IG V (1) 1295, 6 (Brad-
ford (-))

**Φιλόμηλος**
ACHAIA:
—DYME*: (1) c. 219 BC SGDI 1612, 28 (Tyche
5 (1990) p. 124) (s. Εὔδικος)
AITOLIA: (2) 280 BC Paus. x 22. 13
AKARNANIA:
—THYRREION: (3) iii BC IG IX (1)² (2) 245, 3
ARGOLIS:
—EPIDAUROS: (4) ?c. 475-450 BC ib. IV (1)² 143
(Lazzarini 353); LSAG² p. 182 no. 15 (date)
(-μέ-: s. Μιλτεύς); (5) iv BC Peek, NIEpid 31
—EPIDAUROS*: (6) c. 370-365 BC Peek, IAEpid
52 A, 43
—HERMIONE: (7) iii BC IG IV (1) 728, 8
—TROIZEN: (8) ?146 BC ib. 757 B, 12 (s. Πρα-
ξίας)
EPIROS:
—AMBRAKIA: (9) hell. SEG XXIV 421 (Φιλόμη-
δος—edd.: s. Λυσίας); (10) a. 167 BC ib. XXXV
665 A, 8
LAKONIA:
—ASOPOS: (11) ii/i BC IG V (1) 1143, 3 (s. Φιλ-
ιππίδας)
—SPARTA: (12) c. 125 AD ib. 1314, 11 (Bradford
(-)) (s. Ἡρέας)
MESSENIA:
—MESSENE: (13) iii/ii BC PAE 1991, p. 91 (f.
Φιλίππα)
—THOURIA: (14) f. ii BC SEG XI 972, 86 (f. Δά-
μων)
S. Italy (Bruttium):
—LOKROI EPIZEPHYRIOI:
——(Τηλ.): (15) iv/iii BC De Franciscis 32, 6 (f.
Ἀμάνιτος)

**Φιλόμμα**
EPIROS:
—BOUCHETION: (1) iii BC IG IX (1)² (2) 512

**Φιλόμουσος**
ARKADIA:
—TEGEA: (1) 165 AD ib. V (2) 50, 48 (f. Ἵππων)
ELIS: (2) 213-232 AD IvOl 111, 4; SEG XV 258,
6 (Τ. Φλ. Φ.)
EPIROS: (3) s. i BC CIL III 7259 (Lat.
Philomusus: freed.)
ILLYRIA:
—EPIDAMNOS-DYRRHACHION: (4) hell.-imp.
IDyrrh 437
LAKONIA:
—SPARTA: (5) s. i BC IG V (1) 135, 13 (Brad-
ford (-)) (s. Ἱέραρχος); (6) c. 115-120 AD SEG
XI 543, 3 (Bradford (3)) (f. Ξενοκράτης); (7) c.
212-235 AD IG V (1) 305, 4 (Artemis Orthia
pp. 333-4 no. 69); BSA 79 (1984) p. 283 no.
5 (date) (Bradford (4)) (f. Μ. Αὐρ. Ζεύξιππος ὁ
καὶ Κλέανδρος)
MESSENIA:
—KORONE: (8) imp. SEG XXXVIII 336; (9) 246
AD IG V (1) 1398, 36 (Αὐρ. Φ.)
S. Italy (Apulia):
—BARION*: (10) i BC-i AD Mus. Arch. di Bari
p. 151 no. 5 (CIL IX 301) (Lat. C. Tarutius
Philomusus: freed.)
S. Italy (Bruttium):
—HIPPONION-VIBO VALENTIA*: (11) imp. ib. X
8041. 32 (tile) (Lat. Pilomus)
S. Italy (Campania):
—DIKAIARCHIA-PUTEOLI: (12) m. i AD Camo-
deca, L'Archivio Puteolano I p. 125 no. 5
(Lat. C. Passennius Philomusus: freed.)
—DIKAIARCHIA-PUTEOLI*: (13) imp. AJA 2
(1898) p. 380 no. 16 (Lat. L. Faenius
Philomusus: freed.)
—POMPEII*: (14) i BC-i AD Eph. Ep. VIII 317
(Lat. Philomus(us): freed.)
—SALERNUM*: (15) ?i AD IItal I (1) 238 II, 3
(CIL X 557) (Lat. L. Appuleius Philomusus:
freed.); (16) ~ IItal I (1) 238 II, 16 (CIL X
557) (Lat. L. Appuleius Philomusus: freed.)

**Φιλομύστης**
S. Italy (Apulia):
—celenza valfortore (mod.): (1) imp. *AEp*
1973, no. 223 (Lat. C. Calvius Philomust(es))

**Φιλοναύτα**
Akarnania:
—thyrreion: (1) iii bc *IG* ix (1)² (2) 280;
cf. *Philol.* 108 (1964) pp. 295 f. (name)
([Φι]λ[ο]ναύτα)

**Φιλοναύτης**
Achaia: (1) 231 bc *CPR* xviii 25, 47 (s. Καλλικράτης: t.e.)

**Φιλονείδας**
Illyria:
—epidamnos-dyrrhachion: (1) hell.-imp.
*IDyrrh* 358 (Φιλονείδ[ας]: f. Πολέμων)

**Φιλονίδας**
S. Italy (Bruttium):
—rhegion: (1) 84-80 bc *SEG* i 418, 2 (*Suppl.
It.* 5 p. 59 no. 11) (I f. Φιλονίδας II); (2) ~
*SEG* i 418, 2 (*Suppl. It.* 5 p. 59 no. 11) (II
s. Φιλονίδας I)

**Φιλονίκα**
Argolis:
—argos:
——(Smireidai): (1) ii-i bc *IG* iv (1) 530, 13;
cf. *BCH* 33 (1909) p. 183 n. 2
S. Italy (Campania):
—capreae*: (2) ?iii ad *Epigraphica* 34 (1972)
p. 142 (Lat. [Cor]nelia [P]hilonica: freed.?)

**Φιλονικίδας**
Lakonia:
—sparta: (1) c. 25-1 bc *IG* v (1) 210, 46 (Bradford (3)) (f. Ἀριστοκλῆς); (2) c. 80-100 ad *IG* v
(1) 147, 4 (Bradford (1)) (-νει-: s. Νικοκράτης);
(3) c. 160-170 ad *IG* v (1) 109, 8 (Bradford
(2)) (-νει-: s. Φίλιππος); (4) 197 or 198 ad *IG*
v (1) 448, 12 (Bradford (4)) (-νει-: f. Πίστος)

**Φιλόνικος**
Aitolia: (1) 244 or 240 bc *SGDI* 2511, 2
(Flacelière p. 402 no. 29)
Akarnania:
—thyrreion: (2) f. iii bc *SEG* xxvii 164 (f.
Σωτίων)
Argolis:
—argos: (3) c. 366-338 bc Petrakos, *Oropos* pp.
196-7 no. 47, 20 (*IOrop* 520); (4) ?320 bc *IG*
v (2) 549, 7 (I f. Φιλόνικος II); (5) ~ ib. l. 7
(II s. Φιλόνικος I)
—epidauros: (6) i-ii ad Peek, *IAEpid* 214 (s.
Λεύκιος); (7) ii-iii ad ib. 247 ([Φι]λόνικος)
Arkadia:
—mantineia-antigoneia: (8) i bc *IG* v (2)
309 (Φιλόνικος: f. Πόλειος)
—megalopolis: (9) 320 bc ib. 549, 7 (I f. Φιλόνικος II); (10) ~ ib. l. 7 (II s. Φιλόνικος I);
(11) ii/i bc ib. 442, 19 (s. Αἰσχρίων)
—mt. kyllene*: (12) iv-iii bc ib. 362
—tegea: (13) ii-i bc ib. 165, 1
Elis: (14) c. 140 bc *IvOl* 52, 25 (*Syll*³ 683)
—olympia*: (15) i bc *IvOl* 205 (Moretti,
*Olymp.* 678) (s. Φίλιστος)
Epiros:
—dodona: (16) iii bc Antoniou, *Dodone* Ba, 9;
(17) ~ ib. Bb, 1
—orestoi: (18) ?164 bc Cabanes, *L'Épire* p.
586 no. 71, 7 (s. Εὐρύμμας)
Illyria:
—epidamnos-dyrrhachion: (19) hell.-imp.
*IDyrrh* 268 (f. Κλεβέτα)
Lakonia:
—sparta: (20) f. i ad *IG* v (1) 271; *Artemis Orthia* p. 307 no. 21 (date) (Bradford (3)) (I f.
Φιλόνικος II); (21) ~ *IG* v (1) 271; *Artemis Orthia* p. 307 no. 21 (date) (Bradford (1)) (II s.

Φιλόνικος I); (22) s. ii ad *SEG* xi 739 (Brad-
ford (2)) (-νει-)
Leukas: (23) iii-ii bc *IG* ix (1) 571 (f. Μυρτίλος)
S. Italy (Bruttium):
—lokroi epizephyrioi:
——(Ἀλχ.): (24) iv/iii bc De Franciscis 11, 8 (s.
Φιλωνίδας)
S. Italy (Campania):
—salernum*: (25) ?i ad *IItal* i (1) 238 I,
12 (*CIL* x 557) (Lat. L. Appuleius Pilonico:
freed.)
Zakynthos: (26) ?278 bc *FD* iii (2) 185 (f.
Μοσχίων)

**Φιλόνομος**
Lakonia:
—amyklai: (1) her. *RE* (-) (king/dub.)
Sicily:
—katane: (2) f. v bc Ael. fr. 2 (dub.)

**Φιλοξένα**
Argolis:
—hermione: (1) ?ii-i bc *IG* iv (1) 731 I, 16 (d.
Πάτρων)
Arkadia:
—kleitor: (2) 212 ad *IvOl* 473 (Αἰμιλία Φ.: m.
Κλ. Τύχη)
Epiros:
—molossoi: (3) ?164 bc Cabanes, *L'Épire* p.
586 no. 71, 5 (d. Τιμαγόρας); (4) ~ ib. l. 6 (d.
Ὀρέστης)
—nikopolis: (5) imp. Unp. (Nikopolis Mus.)
Kerkyra: (6) ii bc *IG* ix (1) 934 (d. Λυσίμαχος)
Korinthia:
—korinth: (7) vi ad *Hesp.* 36 (1967) p. 423, 6;
cf. *TMByz* 9 (1985) p. 367 no. 88
S. Italy (Lucania):
—herakleia*: (8) iv/iii bc *SEG* xxx 1166
(Landi, *DISMG* 217); cf. *SEG* xxxvi 914
(slave?)

**Φιλοξενίδας**
Arkadia:
—heraia: (1) imp. ib. xi 1138 (Φιλοξενί[δας])
—megalopolis: (2) 336 bc *FD* iii (4) 380 (f.
Φιλόξενος)
—tegea: (3) hell.? *IG* v (2) 170. 17 (tile) (Φιλο-
ξενίδ[ας])
Lakonia:
—kythera: (4) ii bc ib. II² 9113 (-δης: s. Φιλοκράτης)
—sparta: (5) c. 80-120 ad ib. v (1) 99, 2; 147,
1; *SEG* xi 562, 4; 569, 8 (Bradford (1)) (s.
Ἀριστοδάμας); (6) c. 140-150 ad *IG* v (1) 64,
3 (Bradford (4)) (f. Ξενοκλῆς Σκορδίας); (7) c.
160 ad *IG* v (1) 71 III, 56; 86, 34 (Bradford
(2)) (s. Ἀριστοκλῆς); (8) c. 212-235 ad *IG* v (1)
144 c (Bradford (3)) (Αὐρ. Φ.: s. Χαρμόσυνος)
Leukas: (9) iii/ii bc Unp. (*IG* arch.)
Messenia:
—messene: (10) f. i ad *SEG* xxiii 206, 1; 208,
6 etc.; *Ergon* 1995, p. 31 (f. Μνασίστρατος)

**Φιλοξενίδης**
Dalmatia:
—pharos: (1) iv/iii bc *SEG* xxxi 605 (f. Κόμων)
Lakonia:
—sparta: (2) 197 or 198 ad *IG* v (1) 448, 8, 10
(Bradford (5)) (M. Τάδιος Φ.)

**Φιλόξενος**
Achaia:
—dyme: (1) iii bc *AJPh* 31 (1910) p. 399 no.
74 c, 8 (s. Εὐγείτων, f. Θευγένης)
—helike: (2) f. v bc *SEG* xxxvi 718 (s. Κέλων)
Aigina: (3) ?i bc *Alt-Ägina* i (2) p. 44 no. 10
(s. Εὔδαμος)
Aitolia: (4) ?265-264 bc *FD* iii (3) 202, 2; III
(4) 359, 34; *SEG* xviii 242, [3]; *CID* II 130,
[1]; (5) ?255 bc Nachtergael, *Les Galates* 8,
46; cf. Stephanis 2373 (f. Σωτύλος)

—boukation: (6) f. ii bc *IG* ix (1)² (1) 98, 6
?= (7); (7) 190 bc ib. 97, 13 ?= (6); (8) c. 162
bc ib. 106, 10 ?= (9); (9) 161 bc ib. 100, 5 ?=
(8)
—kallion/kallipolis: (10) c. 225 bc *SEG* xi
414, 38 (Perlman E.5) (s. Λυκόρτας)
—kalydon: (11) 129 bc *IG* ix (1)² (1) 137, 97
(s. Νικόβουλος)
—konope-arsinoe: (12) 213 bc ib. 96, 2, 10
(s. Κλεαρχίς)
—pleuron: (13) c. 208 bc *FD* iii (4) 134, 11
—thermos*: (14) s. iii bc *IG* ix (1)² (1) 60 IV,
11
Akarnania:
—palairos: (15) ii bc ib. ix (1)² (2) 451, 1
([Φι]λόξεν[ος]: s. Κλέων)
—phoitiai: (16) m. ii bc ib. 208, 4, [33] (s.
Ἡράκλειτος)
—stratos: (17) iv/iii bc ib. 395, 14-16 (f. Θρασύμαχος, Νέαιθος, Ἀρνίοπος)
—stratos (nr.): (18) ii/i bc Unp. (Lazaros
Kolonos–E.L. Schwandner) (tile)
Argolis:
—argos: (19) m. v bc Peek, *NIEpid* 10 (s. Φυλακίδας)
—epidauros:
——Erilais: (20) c. 365-335 bc *IG* iv (1)² 103,
129, 148
—hermione: (21) iii bc ib. iv (1) 729 II, 15 (s.
Ἀνδροκλῆς)
—methana-arsinoe: (22) ii-i bc ib. 864
—troizen: (23) iii bc ib. 753, [2], 4, 6 with
Add. (s. Πολυχάρης); (24) ~ ib. 774, 7 (Φι-
λόξ[ενος])
Arkadia:
—heraia: (25) iii bc ib. v (2) 415, 9 (*IPArk* 23)
([Φι]λόξενος: s. Ὀνάτας)
—megalopolis: (26) 336 bc *FD* iii (4) 380 (s.
Φιλοξενίδας); (27) s. ii bc *IG* v (2) 439, 81
—phigaleia: (28) c. 272 bc ib. ix (1)² (1) 13,
19 (f. Εὐάγαθος)
—tegea: (29) iv bc ib. v (2) 31, 6 (I f. Φιλόξενος
II); (30) ~ ib. l. 6 (II s. Φιλόξενος I); (31) ?253
bc Nachtergael, *Les Galates* 10, 63 (Stephanis
2544) (s. Ἕλλαν)
——(Hippothoitai): (32) iv/iii bc *IG* v (2) 38,
49 (s. Φιλωνίδας)
—thelphousa: (33) a. 228 bc ib. iv (1)² 72 B,
23 (s. Δαϊ—)
Dalmatia:
—tragurion: (34) 56 bc Sherk 24 A, 9 (s. Διονύσιος)
Elis:
—olympia*: (35) imp. *SEG* xxii 357
Epiros: (36) iii bc Cabanes, *L'Épire* p. 587 no.
73, 8
—ambrakia: (37) iv/iii bc *SEG* xxxix 523 (f.
Μοσχίων); (38) iii-ii bc *Op. Ath.* 10 (1971) p.
64 no. 9 (Φιλόξε[νος]: s. Θεο—)
—amphilochoi: (39) c. 153 bc *IG* ix (1)² (3)
638 12, 6 (slave)
—bouthrotos (prasaiboi): (40) a. 163 bc
*IBouthrot* 29, 27 ?= (51); (41) ~ ib. 39, 2;
42, 17 (*SEG* xxxviii 498; 501) (?s. Δέξιππος,
Ἀρσινόα); (42) ~ *IBouthrot* 43, 10-12; cf. *SEG*
xxxviii 502 (s. Εὐρύμμας, f. Φίλιππος, Λυκίσκα) ?= (51); (43) ~ *IBouthrot* 44, 2 (s. Φίλιππος); (44) ~ ib. 47, 19 ([Φ]ιλ[όξ]ενος); (45) ~ ib.
51, 14 (f. Φίλιππος); (46) ~ ib. 52, 5-6 (*SEG*
xxxviii 517) (s. Τροχιμμάς); (47) ~ *IBouthrot*
100, 7 (s. Λυσίμαχος); (48) ~ ib. 128, 9; 131, 7
(s. Λέων); (49) ~ ib. 128, 10; 131, 8; 147, [11];
156, 11; 157, 6 (*BCH* 118 (1994) p. 127 nos.
12-13) (f. Δέξιππος); (50) ~ *IBouthrot* 156, 11
(*BCH* 118 (1994) p. 127 no. 12) (s. Φιλώτας)
——Phorrioi: (51) a. 163 bc *IBouthrot* 48, 1; 49,
1 (s. Εὐρύμμας) ?= (40) (42); (52) ~ ib. 136, 2
—chaones: (53) f. ii bc ib. 6, 16 (*SEG* xxxviii
468) (s. Νικάδας)
—dodona: (54) c. 330 bc Cabanes, *L'Épire* p.
580 no. 55, 5

—KASSOPE: (55) iv/iii BC *SEG* XXXIV 589 (s. *Πολυξένων*); (56) c. 130 BC Dakaris, *Kassope* p. 25 (*SEG* XXXVI 555); cf. *SEG* XLI 541 (f. *Ἵππαρχος*)
—ONOPERNOI: (57) c. 330 BC Cabanes, *L'Épire* p. 580 no. 55, 11

ILLYRIA:
—EPIDAMNOS-DYRRHACHION: (58) ii-i BC *IDyrrh* 379 (f. *Στρατώ*)

KERKYRA: (59) c. 500 BC *SEG* XXX 519 (*Φιλόξε*[*νος*], *Φιλοξέ*[*να*?]); (60) iv/iii BC *IG* IX (1) 706 (*Korkyra* 1 p. 163 no. 1) (s. *Αἰσχρίων*); (61) hell. *IG* IX (1) 707 ([*Φιλό*]*ξενος*: s. *Μολώτας*); (62) ?ii-i BC ib. 814 (tile); (63) c. 166 BC ib. II² 2316, 7-8 (f. *Ἀγασίλαος*)

KORINTHIA:
—KORINTH: (64) c. 315-280 BC *SEG* I 192, 1 ([*Φι*]*λόξενος*); (65) f. iii BC *Das Heroon von Kalydon* p. 294, 2 (f. *Μικίων*); (66) 217 BC Nachtergael, *Les Galates* 65, 8 (Stephanis 2545) (s. *Ξεννιάδας*)

LAKONIA:
—GERONTHRAI: (67) ?iii BC *Mél. Daux* p. 226 no. 6
—KYTHERA: (68) c. 435-380 BC *RE* (23); *PMG* 814-35 (Poralla² 729a) (s. *Εὐλυτίδας*)
—SPARTA: (69) iii BC *SEG* XL 348 B, 7; (70) s. i BC *IG* V (1) 94, 19 (Bradford (6)) (*Φι*[*λό*]*ξενος*]?: I f. *Φιλόξενος* II); (71) ~ *IG* V (1) 94, 19 (Bradford (3)) ([*Φιλό*]*ξενος*?: II s. *Φιλόξενος* I); (72) c. 25-1 BC *IG* V (1) 210, 4 (Bradford (2)) (s. *Εὐαμερίων*); (73) ~ *IG* V (1) 212, 32 (Bradford (5)) (f. *Δαμόλας*); (74) i BC/i AD *IG* V (1) 48, 15 (Bradford (1)) (s. *Δαμόλας*); (75) c. 90-100 AD *SEG* XI 558, 8 (Bradford (7)) (f. *Θαλίαρχος*); (76) ii-iii AD *IG* V (1) 801 (Bradford (4))
—LEUKAS: (77) c. 350-250 BC Postolakas p. 70 no. 718; *NZ* 10 (1878) p. 22 n. 22; *Coll. Philipsen* 793; Sambon sale (Florence 25. 3. 1889) p. 53 no. 442 (coins)
—LEUKAS?: (78) v/iv BC *RE* (24) (?s. *Λευκάδιος*)

MESSENIA:
—MESSENE: (79) m. iv BC *IG* II² 9347, 1, 5, 8 (s. *Δίων*, f. *Δίων*, *Παρθένιος*); (80) iii BC *SEG* XXIII 209, 15; (81) 31 BC-14 AD ib. 207, 29 (s. *Διογένης*)
—MESSENE?: (82) ii/i BC ib. XI 979, 39
—THOURIA: (83) f. ii BC ib. 972, 22, 24 (*Φίλων*—l. 24 ed.: f. *Φίλων*, *Ἀριστοφάνης*); (84) ~ ib. l. 55 (s. *Φίλων*); (85) ~ ib. l. 103 (s. *Ἀριστοφάνης*); (86) ii/i BC *IG* V (1) 1384, 6 (s. *Ἀγαθάμερος*); (87) ~ ib. l. 23 (f. *Σώστρατος*)

S. ITALY (CALABRIA):
—TARAS-TARENTUM: (88) ?c. 500-475 BC Landi, *DISMG* 179 (Troisi, *Epigrafi mobili* 94 (terracotta)); *LSAG*² p. 285 no. 5 (date); cf. *Getty Mus. Journ.* 9 (1981) p. 42 (date)

S. ITALY (CAMPANIA):
—DIKAIARCHIA-PUTEOLI: (89) imp. *CIL* X 2920 (Lat. Q. Rutilius Filoxenus)
—KYME*: (90) imp. *NScav* 1888, p. 197 (*Eph. Ep.* VIII 450) (Lat. P. Sextilius Philoxenus: freed.)
—POMPEII*: (91) i BC *Impegno per Pompeii* 7 OS (Castrèn 169. 6) (Lat. P. Flavius Philoxsenus: freed.)

SICILY: (92) m. i BC Cic., *ad Fam.* xiii 35. 1 (Lat. C. Avianius Philoxenus)
—AGYRION: (93) i BC Manganaro, *PdelP* forthcoming no. 5, 2 (?s. *Σιλανός*)
—HALAISA: (94) ii BC *IGSI* 2 A II, 74 (Dubois, *IGDS* 196) (s. *Μενίσκος*)
—KALE AKTE: (95) m. i BC Cic., *ad Fam.* xiii 37 (Lat. Philoxenus: f. *Ἱππίας*)
—KAMARINA: (96) ?iv/iii BC *SEG* XXXIV 940, 4 (Dubois, *IGDS* 124; *PdelP* 44 (1989) p. 192 no. III; Cordano, 'Camarina VII' 161)
—NEAITON: (97) ii BC *IG* II² 9993

—SYRACUSE: (98) 208 BC *IMM* 72, 1 (Dubois, *IGDS* 97) (f. *Πολυξενίδας*); (99) imp. *NScav* 1912, p. 299
—SYRACUSE?:
—(*Ὑπα*.): (100) hell. Manganaro, *PdelP* forthcoming no. 4 IV, 3 (s. *Σωσίας*)
—TAUROMENION: (101) c. 218-204 BC *IG* XIV 421 an. 23; 421 an. 37 (*SGDI* 5219) (s. *Φιλωνίδας*); (102) c. 175 BC *IG* XIV 421 an. 66 (*SGDI* 5219) (s. *Πειθαγόρας*); (103) c. 148 BC *IGSI* 4 III (IV), 58 an. 93 + *Comptes et Inventaires* p. 178 (*SEG* XXXVIII 975 n. on l. 58) (*Φι*[*λό*]*ξενος*: f. *Τιμόλας*)

## Φιλοπάτρα

EPIROS:
—BOUTHROTOS (PRASAIBOI): (1) a. 163 BC *IBouthrot* 18, 9 (*SEG* XXXVIII 475)

ILLYRIA:
—LYCHNIDOS: (2) ii-iii AD *Sp.* 71 (1931) p. 107 no. 256

## Φιλοπάτωρ

ILLYRIA:
—EPIDAMNOS-DYRRHACHION: (1) hell.-imp. *IDyrrh* 438 (n. pr.?)

S. ITALY (CAMPANIA):
—POMPEII: (2) i BC-i AD *CIL* IV 3122 (Castrèn 35. 7) (Lat. Antonius Philopater)

## Φιλοπείθης

KEPHALLENIA:
—SAME: (1) ?iv-iii BC *SEG* XXXIX 486 (s. *Λύκων*)

## Φιλοποίμην

ARGOLIS:
—METHANA-ARSINOE: (1) i BC *IG* IV (1) 853, 4 (*Φιλοποί*[*μ*]*ην*)

ARKADIA:
—GORTYS: (2) ii BC *SEG* XXXV 349 (f. *Κράτεια*)
—MEGALOPOLIS: (3) hell. *IG* V (2) 469 (7) (tile); (4) c. 253-183 BC *RE* (-); *IG* V (2) 461 (s. *Κραῦγις*, f. *Θεαρίδας*, ?f. *Δαμοκράτης*); (5) m. ii BC ib. 535 (s. *Θεαρίδας*, f. *Θεαρίδας*) ?= (6); (6) ii/i BC ib. 442, 8 (*Φιλ*[*οποίμην*]?: f. *Θεαρίδας*) ?= (5); (7) ~ ib. 445, 10 (*IPArk* 32)

## Φιλόποινος

AITOLIA: (1) 244 or 240 BC *SGDI* 2512, 3 (Flacelière p. 402 no. 28 a); Nachtergael, *Les Galates* 59, 4
—KALLION/KALLIPOLIS: (2) c. 300 BC *FD* III (1) 422, 1 ([*Φιλό*]*ποι*[*νος*])

## Φιλορώμη

SICILY:
—SYRACUSE: (1) iii-v AD Strazzulla 188 (Wessel 1345); cf. *Riv. Arch. Crist.* 18 (1941) p. 220 no. 104 (locn.)

## Φιλοσθένης

ARGOLIS:
—EPIDAUROS: (1) c. 365-335 BC *IG* IV (1)² 103, 128, 133, 139

ARKADIA:
—MANTINEIA-ANTIGONEIA: (2) 64 or 62 BC ib. V (2) 265, 50 (f. *Αἴθων*)

KORINTHIA:
—KORINTH: (3) s. iv BC *Corinth* VIII (1) 11, 3 (*Φιλοσθέ*[*νης*]: f. *Φιλοχάρης*)

## Φιλοστέφανος

KORINTHIA:
—KORINTH: (1) v BC [Themist.], *Ep.* 6-7 with Doenges edn. p. 105 (fict.?)

## Φιλόστοργος

S. ITALY (CAMPANIA):
—DIKAIARCHIA-PUTEOLI: (1) ?i-ii AD *CIL* X 2566 (Lat. C. Iulius Philostorgus)

—POMPEII: (2) c. 51-62 AD ib. IV 3340. 48, 5, 10, 16 (Castrèn 198. 1) (Lat. A. Hordionius Philostorgus); (3) ~ *CIL* IV 3340. 114, 5 (Castrèn 198. 2) (Lat. M. Hordionius Philostorgus)

## Φιλοστράτα

ACHAIA:
—DYME: (1) ii BC *Achaean Grave Stelai* 32 (d. *Κάνωπος*)

KORINTHIA:
—KROMMYON: (2) ii-iii AD *Corinth* VIII (1) 46 (*GVI* 989; *Gr. Gr.* 418)

MESSENIA:
—MESSENE: (3) iii-ii BC *SEG* XXXVIII 346 a + XLI 370; cf. *PAE* 1987, pl. 80 a

## Φιλοστράτη

KORINTHIA:
—KORINTH: (1) iv AD *Corinth* VIII (3) 658, 6 (*GVI* 1939); cf. *TMByz* 9 (1985) p. 367 no. 80

## Φιλοστράτις

LAKONIA:
—SPARTA: (1) 361 BC *CID* II 4 I, 55 (Poralla² 730)

## Φιλόστρατος

ACHAIA: (1) c. 235-225 BC *SEG* XV 276, 2 (*IOrop* 65) (f. *Λέων*); (2) iii/ii BC *IG* XII (9) 836 (s. *Ξένων*: date—Knoepfler)

AIGINA: (3) ?c. 480-470 BC ib. IV (1) 7 (Lazzarini 719; *CEG* I 349); *LSAG*² p. 113 no. 15 (date) (s. *Δαμοφόων*)

AITOLIA:
—KALYDON: (4) m. ii BC *IG* IX (1)² (1) 137, 25

DALMATIA:
—ISSA:
—(Hylleis): (5) iv/iii BC Brunšmid p. 9, 51 (f. *Πύθων*)

EPIROS:
—BOUTHROTOS (PRASAIBOI): (6) a. 163 BC *IBouthrot* 31, 47 (*SEG* XXXVIII 490) (II s. *Φιλόστρατος* I); (7) ~ *IBouthrot* 31, 48 (*SEG* XXXVIII 490) (I f. *Φιλόστρατος* II); (8) ~ *IBouthrot* 32, 33 (*SEG* XXXVIII 491); (9) ~ *IBouthrot* 38, 9 (*SEG* XXXVIII 497); (10) ~ *IBouthrot* 38, 16 (*SEG* XXXVIII 497); (11) ~ *IBouthrot* 40, 3 (*SEG* XXXVIII 499); (12) ~ *IBouthrot* 77, 8; (13) ~ ib. 123-4; [125] (*BCH* 118 (1994) p. 120 nos. 3-5) (*Φιλόσστρατος*—no. 124)
—Aigidorioi?: (14) f. ii BC *IBouthrot* 5, 3 ?= (17)
—Hypoppaioi: (15) a. 163 BC ib. 67, 7
—Kathraioi: (16) iii-ii BC ib. 167 (Cabanes, *L'Épire* p. 568 no. 46)
—MOLOSSOI: (17) ii BC *RE* (3) ?= (14)

ILLYRIA:
—APOLLONIA:
—(Le.): (18) iii/ii BC *IApoll* 7; cf. *L'Illyrie mérid.* 2 p. 207 (s. *Φίλων*)
—EPIDAMNOS-DYRRHACHION: (19) c. 250-50 BC Maier 186; 268 (coin) (Ceka 430-1) (money.); (20) hell.-imp. *IDyrrh* 7 (s. *Πίθακος*)

KERKYRA: (21) c. 229-48 BC Welzl 3502 (coin)

LAKONIA:
—HYPERTELEATON*: (22) imp. *IG* V (1) 1063 (f. *Σωσάρων*)
—SPARTA: (23) iii-ii BC *SEG* XXXVI 364 (*Φιλόσ*[*τρατος*]?); (24) i BC-i AD *IG* V (1) 652, 2 (Bradford (15)) (f. *Ἐπίγονος*, *Ἐπίκτητος*, *Φοιβίων*); (25) ~ *SEG* XI 883 d (tile) (Bradford (10)) (*Φιλόστρ*[*ατος*]?); (26) s. i BC *IG* V (1) 95, 14 (Bradford (1)) (s. *Δαμόστρατος*); (27) ~ *IG* V (1) 136, 2 (Bradford (9)); (28) ~ *IG* V (1) 136, 7 (Bradford (8)); (29) c. 30-20 BC *IG* V (1) 142, 15 (Bradford (14)) (f. *Ἐπιχάρεια*); (30) c. 25-1 BC *IG* V (1) 212, 5 (Bradford (3)) (s. *Φιλωνίδας*); (31) i AD *IG* V (1)

272; *Artemis Orthia* pp. 307-8 no. 22 (date)
(Bradford (2)) (s. *Πασικλῆς*); (**32**) c. 1-10 AD
*IG* v (1) 209, 9; *SEG* XXXV 331 (date) (Bradford (6)) (s. *Σωκράτης*); (**33**) c. 80-90 AD *IG* v
(1) 674, 4 (Bradford (20)) (f. —*κίδας*); (**34**) ~
*IG* v (1) 674, 11 (Bradford (17)) (f. *Καλλικράτης*); (**35**) c. 100 AD *SEG* XI 536, 4 (Bradford
(19)) (f. *Πασικράτης*); (**36**) c. 100-150 AD *IG*
v (1) 60, 1; 279, 1; *SEG* XXXVI 361, 5 (Bradford (18)) (f. *Ὀνασικλείδας*); (**37**) c. 105-110 AD
*SEG* XI 569, 10 (Bradford (4)) ([*T.*] *Τρεβελληνὸς Φ.*: s. *Πολέμαρχος*); (**38**) c. 110 AD *SEG*
XI 542, 5 (Bradford (13)) (f. *Δαμάριστος*); (**39**)
c. 120 AD *IG* v (1) 1315, 25 (Bradford (5)) (s.
*Πυθίων*); (**40**) c. 140 AD *IG* v (1) 138, 6 (Bradford (7)) (s. —*ιππος*); (**41**) c. 140-160 AD *IG*
v (1) 154, 11 (Bradford (16)) (f. *Εὐδαιμοκλῆς*);
(**42**) s. ii AD *IG* v (1) 171, 1 (Bradford (12))
(*Φιλόστρα[τος]*); (**43**) c. 170 AD *IG* v (1) 116,
5 (Bradford (11)) (*Τιβ. Κλ. Φ.*)
MESSENIA:
—MESSENE: (**44**) iii BC *SEG* XXIII 210, 15; (**45**)
31 BC-14 AD ib. 207, 13
—THOURIA: (**46**) f. ii BC ib. XI 972, 36 (f. *Φίλις*);
(**47**) ~ ib. l. 93 (s. *Ἀριστώνυμος*)
S. ITALY (APULIA):
—VENUSIA*: (**48**) imp. *CIL* IX 590 (Lat. L.
Tullianus Philostratus: freed.)
S. ITALY (BRUTTIUM):
—LOKROI EPIZEPHYRIOI:
——(*Ἀγκ.*): (**49**) iv/iii BC De Franciscis 22, 24
(s. *Ὀνάσιμος*)
——(*Λογ.*): (**50**) iv/iii BC ib. 2, 6; 7, 3 (s. *Φίντων*)
SICILY:
—SYRACUSE: (**51**) ?263-261 BC Nachtergael, *Les
Galates* 3, 18 (Stephanis 2549) ([*Φιλ*]*όστρατος*:
s. *Σωσίστρατος*)

**Φιλόσων**
KERKYRA: (**1**) iv BC *SEG* XXV 610 + *BCH* 91
(1967) p. 671 n. 1 (*Φιλόσωνος* (gen.)—*BCH*,
*Ἀρβλόσωνος*—*SEG*)

**Φιλότας**
EPIROS:
—BOUTHROTOS (PRASAIBOI): (**1**) a. 163 BC
*IBouthrot* 17, 15; 21, 7, 15; 40, 15 (*SEG*
XXXVIII 474; 478; 499) (s. *Φίλιππος*); (**2**) ~
*IBouthrot* 21, 24 (*SEG* XXXVIII 478); (**3**) ~
*IBouthrot* 21, 45 (*SEG* XXXVIII 478); (**4**) ~
*IBouthrot* 21, 46 (*SEG* XXXVIII 478); (**5**) ~
*IBouthrot* 22, 9 (*SEG* XXXVIII 479) ?= (*9*); (**6**)
~ *IBouthrot* 27, 9 (*SEG* XXXVIII 485); (**7**) ~
*IBouthrot* 30, 23; 40, 10 (*SEG* XXXVIII 488;
499); (**8**) ~ *IBouthrot* 36, 22 (*SEG* XXXVIII
495); (**9**) ~ *IBouthrot* 45, 5 (s. *Ἀρίστων*) ?=
(*5*); (**10**) ~ ib. 50, 9
—DODONA*: (**11**) iv-iii BC *SGDI* 1579
S. ITALY (BRUTTIUM):
—TERINA: (**12**) c. 325-300 BC *IGSI* 21, 5 (*SEG*
IV 73; Landi, *DISMG* 170) (*Φιλότατι* (dat.):
s. *Ἱστιαῖος*)

**Φιλοτέλης**
ARGOLIS:
—EPIDAUROS*: (**1**) c. 370-365 BC Peek, *IAEpid*
52 B, 54

**Φιλοτιμίδης**
S. ITALY (APULIA): (**1**) f. iv BC *Phlyax Vases*
p. 38 (fict.)

**Φιλότιμος**
ACHAIA:
—DYME*: (**1**) c. 50 BC *ILGR* 44, 4 (Lat. M.
Fulvius Philotimus: freed.)
AIGINA: (**2**) s. v BC *RE* (4); Moretti, *IAG* 30;
*Alt-Ägina* II (2) p. 46 (sculptor)
AITOLIA:
—THERMOS*: (**3**) s. iii BC *IG* IX (1)² (1) 60 V, 1
(*Φιλότιμος*?)

AKARNANIA:
—THYRREION: (**4**) ii BC ib. IX (1)² (2) 248, 1
(*Φι*[*λ*]*ότ*[*ιμος*])
ARGOLIS:
—ARGOS: (**5**) 337 BC *CID* II 74 II, 24
(*Φι*[*λό*]*τι*[*μ*]*ος*)
ILLYRIA:
—APOLLONIA: (**6**) imp. *IApoll* 337
S. ITALY (APULIA):
—LARINUM: (**7**) ii-iii AD *Contr. Ist. Fil. Class.*
1 (1963) p. 249 no. 7 (Lat. P. Didius
[P]hilotimus)
S. ITALY (CALABRIA):
—BRENTESION-BRUNDISIUM*: (**8**) imp. *CIL* IX
6104, 2 (Lat. M(anius) Albinius Philotimus:
freed.); (**9**) ~ ib. l. 3 (Lat. M(anius) Albinius
Philotimus: freed.)

**Φιλότονος**
S. ITALY (CAMPANIA):
—POMPEII: (**1**) i BC-i AD ib. IV 5436 (Lat. Philo-
tonus)

**Φιλουμένα**
AITOLIA:
—KALYDON: (**1**) hell. *IG* IX (1)² (1) 146
ARGOLIS:
—EPIDAUROS: (**2**) hell.? Peek, *NIEpid* 57 B
EPIROS:
—BOUTHROTOS (PRASAIBOI): (**3**) a. 163 BC
*IBouthrot* 26, 18 (*SEG* XXXVIII 484); (**4**) ~
*IBouthrot* 31, 88 (*SEG* XXXVIII 490); (**5**) ~
*IBouthrot* 32, 12 (*SEG* XXXVIII 491); (**6**) ~
*IBouthrot* 43, 8 (*SEG* XXXVIII 502); (**7**) ~
*IBouthrot* 51, 6 ([*Φι*]*λουμένα*); (**8**) ~ ib. 151,
7
ILLYRIA:
—EPIDAMNOS-DYRRHACHION: (**9**) ii-i BC
*IDyrrh* 440 (d. *Λαίδων*); (**10**) hell.-imp. ib.
439 (d. *Εὐτυχίδας*)
MESSENIA:
—ASINE: (**11**) ?i/ii AD *IG* v (1) 1416 (*Σωφηέα Φ.*)
S. ITALY (CALABRIA):
—BRENTESION-BRUNDISIUM*: (**12**) imp. *CIL*
IX 6130 (Lat. Octavia Philumina: freed.)
S. ITALY (CAMPANIA):
—DIKAIARCHIA-PUTEOLI*: (**13**) imp. ib. X 2246
(Lat. Caudia Philumina: freed.); (**14**) ?i-ii AD
*Eph. Ep.* VIII 396 (Lat. Philumena: m. *Ὑγῖ-
νος*: freed.)
—POMPEII*: (**15**) m. i BC *CIL* I² 3133 (*Impegno
per Pompeii* 13 OS; Castrèn 448. 1) (Lat. Ver-
tia Philumina: freed.)
S. ITALY (LUCANIA):
—POSEIDONIA-PAESTUM*: (**16**) imp. Mello–
Voza 174 (Lat. Venedia Philum[ena]: freed.)

**Φιλουμένη**
AIGINA?: (**1**) imp. *EAD* XXX p. 356 no. 17 with
n. 1 (m. *Σωτηρίς*)
ARGOLIS:
—ARGOS: (**2**) imp. *IG* II² 8378 (d. *Αὖλος*)
ILLYRIA:
—EPIDAMNOS-DYRRHACHION: (**3**) hell.-imp.
*IDyrrh* 441 (d. *Ἀπολλωνίδης*)
KERKYRA?: (**4**) imp. *IG* IX (1) 973; cf. Fraser–
Rönne, *BWGT* p. 98 n. 53
LAKONIA:
—SPARTA: (**5**) imp. *SEG* XI 865 (Bradford (-))
S. ITALY (CAMPANIA):
—DIKAIARCHIA-PUTEOLI: (**6**) imp. *CIL* X 2309
(Lat. Iunia Philumene); (**7**) i/ii AD *AJA* 77
(1973) p. 155 no. 4 (Lat. Cl. Philumene)
SICILY:
—SYRACUSE: (**8**) iii-v AD *IG* XIV 187 (Strazzulla
125; Agnello 15; Wessel 616); cf. Ferrua, *NG*
180; (**9**) ~ *Rend. Pont.* 22 (1946-7) p. 238 no.
47 (-*μή*-)

**Φιλουμενός**
ARGOLIS:
—ARGOS: (**1**) iii AD *BCH* 27 (1903) p. 268 no.
20 I-II ([*A*]*ὐρ. Φιλο*[*υ*]*μενός*)
ARKADIA:
—KLEITOR: (**2**) a. 212 AD *IG* v (2) 369, 4 (*Αὐρ.
Φ.*)
ELIS: (**3**) 141-145 AD *IvOl* 95, 8 (s. *Ἀργεῖος*) ?=
(*4*); (**4**) ~ ib. l. 18 ([*Φι*]*λουμε*[*νός*] ?= (*3*); (**5**)
241 AD ib. 118, 10 (*Φιλουμ*[*ενός*])
EPIROS:
—NIKOPOLIS: (**6**) imp. *Hellenika* 22 (1969) p.
72 no. 13 (Sarikakis 174) (*Φιλουμ*[*ενός*])
KORINTHIA:
—KORINTH: (**7**) byz. *Corinth* VIII (3) 628; cf.
*TMByz* 9 (1985) p. 366 no. 76 (*Φιλουμε*[*νός*],
*Φιλουμέ*[*νη*]?)
LAKONIA:
—SPARTA: (**8**) c. 100-125 AD *IG* v (1) 40, 22;
*SEG* XI 575, 14 (Bradford (8)) (f. *Σωσικράτης
ὁ καὶ Σώστρατος*); (**9**) ii AD *IG* v (1) 159, 27
(Bradford (5)); (**10**) c. 132 AD *SEG* XI 579,
7 (Bradford (4)) (—*ς Βαλεριανός Φ.*); (**11**) c.
140-160 AD *IG* v (1) 112, 3; 113, 2; 128, 9;
*SEG* XI 585, 3; 586, 1; XXX 410, 4 (Bradford
(2)) (s. *Σωτηρίδας*); (**12**) ~ *IG* v (1) 154, 14
(Bradford (6)) (f. *Λεοντᾶς*); (**13**) s. ii AD *IG* v
(1) 493, 14 (Bradford (3)); (**14**) c. 170-190 AD
*SEG* XI 627, 7 (Bradford (7)) (I f. *Φιλουμενός*
II); (**15**) ~ *SEG* XI 627, 7 (Bradford (1)) (II
s. *Φιλουμενός* I)
S. ITALY (APULIA):
—LUCERIA: (**16**) ii-iii AD *CIL* IX 836 (Lat. Aur.
Philumenus)
S. ITALY (CALABRIA):
—BRENTESION-BRUNDISIUM: (**17**) imp. ib. 66
(Lat. L. Aemilius Philumenus)
S. ITALY (CAMPANIA):
—DIKAIARCHIA-PUTEOLI: (**18**) imp. *NScav*
1902, p. 381 no. 1 (Lat. C. Laecanius Phi-
lumenus)
—NEAPOLIS: (**19**) i AD *CIL* X 1507; cf. Leiwo p.
90 (Lat. M. Geminius Philumenus)
—POMPEII: (**20**) i BC-i AD *CIL* IV 3185 (Lat.
Philumenus)
—STABIAE*: (**21**) imp. *RAAN* 19 (1938-9) p.
124 (Lat. Clodius Filumenus: freed.)
SICILY:
—KATANE: (**22**) imp. *Helikon* 2 (1962) p. 490
(Lat. Filumenus: slave?)
—SYRACUSE: (**23**) iii-v AD Strazzulla 181 + Fer-
rua, *NG* 18
—THERMAI HIMERAIAI: (**24**) imp. *Epigraphica* 3
(1941) p. 263 no. 25 (*ILat. Term. Imer.* 89)
(Lat. Filum[enus])

**Φιλοῦσα**
ARGOLIS:
—ARGOS: (**1**) imp. *IG* IV (1) 613 (d. *Εὐκράτης*)
LAKONIA:
—SPARTA: (**2**) imp. ib. v (1) 776 (Bradford (2));
(**3**) i-ii AD *IG* v (1) 764 (Bradford (1))

**Φιλοῦσις**
SICILY:
—SYRACUSE: (**1**) iii-v AD Strazzulla 249 a
(Wessel 1063); cf. *Riv. Arch. Crist.* 18 (1941)
p. 168 no. 29 (masc./fem.?)

**Φιλοφάνης**
ARKADIA?: (**1**) c. 200 BC *SEG* XVII 829, 6, 12,
15

**Φιλοφαντώ**
SICILY:
—LIPARA: (**1**) inc. *BTCGI* 9 p. 93

**Φιλόφρων**
AITOLIA:
—KALYDON: (**1**) a. 142 BC *IG* IX (1)² (1) 137,
61 (*Φιλ*[*όφρ*]*ων*)
LAKONIA:
—SPARTA: (**2**) c. 30-20 BC ib. v (1) 211, 37
(Bradford (-)) (s. *Σοΐδας*)

**Φιλοχάρης**
KERKYRA: (**1**) hell. *IG* IX (1) 932 (f. *Λύκος*: reading—*IG* arch.)
KORINTHIA:
—KORINTH: (**2**) s. iv BC *Corinth* VIII (1) 11, 3 (s. *Φιλοσθένης*)
S. ITALY (BRUTTIUM):
—LOKROI EPIZEPHYRIOI:
——(*Γαγ.*): (**3**) 279 BC De Franciscis 13, 3 (f. *Θράσυλλος*)

**Φιλοχαρίδας**
LAKONIA:
—SPARTA: (**1**) 422-420 BC *RE* (-) (Poralla² 731) (s. *Ἐρυξιλαΐδας*)

**Φιλοχαρῖνος**
LAKONIA: (**1**) 96-98 AD *IG* V (1) 1161, 8 (f. *Ἐπινικίδας*)
—SPARTA: (**2**) c. 105-160 AD ib. 32 B, 20; 65, 20; 85, 16; 114, 3; 128, 11; *SEG* XI 546 a, 5; 546 b, 5; XXXVI 361, [13] (Bradford (2)) (-ρεῖνορ: f. *Λύσιππος*); (**3**) c. 150-160 AD *IG* V (1) 292, 3 (*Artemis Orthia* pp. 323-4 no. 50; Bradford (1)) (-ρεῖνορ: s. *Λύσιππος*); (**4**) ~ *IG* V (1) 294 (*Artemis Orthia* p. 325 no. 52; Bradford (1)) (*Γ. Ἰούλ. Φιλοχαρεῖνορ*)

**Φιλόχαρις**
S. ITALY (CALABRIA):
—TARAS-TARENTUM: (**1**) 281 BC *RE* (-) (*Φ. ὁ ἐπικαλ. Θαΐς*)

**Φιλόχορος**
AITOLIA:
—POTIDANIA: (**1**) m. ii BC *SBBerlAk* 1936, p. 371 a, 13 (*SEG* XLI 528 A) (-χωρος: s. *Μίκος*)
KEPHALLENIA:
—SAME: (**2**) iv/iii BC Fraser–Rönne, *BWGT* p. 117 no. 2. 5 ([*Φ*]ιλόχωρος)
S. ITALY (CAMPANIA):
—SALERNUM: (**3**) s. i AD *IItal* I (1) 151 (*CIL* X 555) (Lat. Philochorus: f. *Ἀνθοῦσα*)

**Φιλτέρα**
ILLYRIA:
—APOLLONIA: (**1**) ii-i BC *IApoll* 165 (*Φι*(λ)*τέρα*: d. *Διογένης*)

**Φίλτυς**
S. ITALY (BRUTTIUM):
—KROTON: (**1**) iv BC Iamb., *VP* 267 (*FVS* I p. 448) (d. *Θέοφρις*)

**Φίλτων**
ARKADIA:
—TEGEA: (**1**) hell.? *IG* V (2) 170. 18 (tile) (*Φίλτων*)
MESSENIA:
—MESSENE: (**2**) m. iii BC ib. 368, 49

**Φιλύας**
DALMATIA:
—ISSA: (**1**) ii BC *SEG* XXXI 600 (f. *Ξενυλλίς*)

**Φίλυκος**
S. ITALY (BRUTTIUM):
—LOKROI EPIZEPHYRIOI: (**1**) m. vi BC Unp. (A.W.J.) (*Φίλυρος*—A.W.J.)
——(*Ἀγκ.*): (**2**) iv/iii BC De Franciscis 27, 3 (s. *Ζωΐλος*)
——(*Βοω.*): (**3**) iv/iii BC ib. 26, 3 (f. *Σώσιππος*)
TRIPHYLIA:
—MAKISTOS: (**4**) 399-369 BC *SEG* XXXV 389, 12

**Φίλυλλα**
LAKONIA:
—SPARTA: (**1**) s. vii BC *PMGF* I 1, 75 (Poralla² 732)
S. ITALY (BRUTTIUM):
—TERINA:
——(*Πο.*): (**2**) c. 325-300 BC *IGSI* 21, 1 (*SEG* IV 73; Landi, *DISMG* 170) (*Φίλυλλα*?: d. *Κ*—)

**Φιλυλλίς**
ILLYRIA:
—EPIDAMNOS-DYRRHACHION: (**1**) hell.-imp. *IDyrrh* 442 (d. *Λύσιππος*)

**Φίλυλλος**
S. ITALY (BRUTTIUM):
—TERINA: (**1**) c. 325-300 BC *IGSI* 21, 14 (*SEG* IV 73; Landi, *DISMG* 170) (*Φίλυλλος*)

**Φιλύρα**
S. ITALY (BRUTTIUM):
—TORANO CASTELLO (MOD.): (**1**) iv BC *GRBS* 26 (1985) p. 181 no. 127 (*Φιλίρα*—ed.: d. —λα)

**Φίλυρος**
SICILY:
—MEGARA HYBLAIA: (**1**) c. 525-500 BC *IvOl* 22 a, 18 (Dubois, *IGDS* 28; Arena, *Iscr. Sic.* I 52) (or Sicily Selinous: [*Φ*]ίλυρο[ς])

**Φίλυς**
ELIS: (**1**) hell.? Paus. vi 14. 11 (f. *Ἀναυχίδας*)
PELOPONNESE: (**2**) s. iii BC *SEG* XIII 278, 10 (s. *Μεθίκων*)

**Φιλύτας**
S. ITALY (BRUTTIUM):
—SYBARIS-THOURIOI-COPIAE: (**1**) 616 BC Moretti, *Olymp.* 71 (*Φιλήτας*—Paus., *Φιλώτας*—Afric.)

**Φιλώ**
EPIROS:
—BOUTHROTOS (PRASAIBOI): (**1**) a. 163 BC *IBouthrot* 17, 19 (*SEG* XXXVIII 474) ([*Φ*]ιλώ); (**2**) ~ *IBouthrot* 29, 54 (*SEG* XXXVIII 487); (**3**) ~ *IBouthrot* 148
ILLYRIA:
—EPIDAMNOS-DYRRHACHION: (**4**) hell.-imp. *IDyrrh* 443 (d. *Ἀρχήν*); (**5**) ~ ib. 444 (d. *Εὐκλείδας*); (**6**) ~ ib. 445 (d. *Φαῖδρος*)

**Φιλώι**
KORINTHIA:
—KORINTH: (**1**) c. 570-550 BC Amyx 71. 2 (vase) (Lorber 127) (-λόι: her.?)

**Φίλωμα**
S. ITALY (APULIA):
—CONVERSANO (MOD.): (**1**) i/ii AD *CIL* IX 274 (Lat. Flavia Philoma: d. *Δάφνος*: imp. freed.)

**Φιλωμένα**
SICILY:
—LIPARA: (**1**) imp. *IG* XIV 399 (Libertini, *Isole Eolie* p. 219 no. 17)

**Φιλώμενος**
S. ITALY (CALABRIA):
—BRENTESION-BRUNDISIUM: (**1**) imp. *ASP* 22 (1969) pp. 94-5 (terracotta) (*Φιλώμενος*, *Φιλώνυμος*?)

**Φίλων**
ACHAIA: (**1**) hell. *IDidyma* II 138 (s. *Διόδωρος*) ?= (*2*); (**2**) ?c. 250 BC *IG* XI (4) 1191 (s. *Διόδωρος*, f. *Ἡραΐς*) ?= (*1*); (**3**) 146 BC ib. IV (1)² 28, 90 (s. *Τίμαρχος*: synoikos); (**4**) ~ ib. l. 114 (f. *Φιλοκλῆς*: synoikos); (**5**) ~ ib. l. 154 (f. *Εὔμαιος*: synoikos)
—AIGION: (**6**) hell. *SEG* XLI 401 B
—DYME: (**7**) s. iii BC ib. XIII 278, 21 (f. *Αἰσχρίων*); (**8**) ~ ib. l. 24 (f. *Ταυρίας*)
—DYME*: (**9**) c. 219 BC *SGDI* 1612, 12 (*Tyche* 5 (1990) p. 124) (s. *Θράσων*)
—PATRAI: (**10**) iii-iv AD *CIL* III 522 (Lat. Philon)
AIGINA: (**11**) ?f. i BC *Alt-Ägina* I (2) p. 43 no. 4, 5 (f. *Πολέμαρχος*)
AITOLIA: (**12**) ?253 BC Nachtergael, *Les Galates* 10, 3; (**13**) f. ii BC *IG* IX (1)² (1) 178, 4 (s. *Ἀπ*—)
—KALYDON: (**14**) iii BC ib. 144 (f. *Λυκόφρων*); (**15**) c. 142 BC ib. 137, 46 (s. *Ἀγέλαος*)
—PHISTYON: (**16**) ii BC ib. 110 a, 2
—PLEURON: (**17**) 271-263 BC ib. 3 A, 17; 13, 38; 18, 3, 7
—TRICHONION: (**18**) 187 BC *Syll*³ 585, 158 (s. *Εὔδαμος*)
AKARNANIA:
—ANAKTORION: (**19**) hell.? *IG* IX (1)² (2) 236
—ASTAKOS: (**20**) ii BC ib. 435, 6 (s. *Σωτίων*)
—MEDION: (**21**) m. ii BC ib. 209, 3 (s. *Ἄρκος*)
—OINIADAI: (**22**) ?iv-iii BC ib. 426. 4; *SEG* XLII 486 (tile); (**23**) c. 325-315 BC *Hesp.* 57 (1988) p. 148 A, 37 (*SEG* XXXVI 331); cf. *Hesp.* 48 (1979) pp. 78 f. with pl. 22 c (s. *Τιμοσθένης*)
—PALAIROS: (**24**) f. iii BC *IG* IX (1)² (2) 473
ARGOLIS:
—ARGOS: (**25**) ?165 BC *Syll*³ 585, 309 (Stephanis 2562) (s. *Φιλοκλῆς*); (**26**) f. i BC Unp. (Ch. Kritsas) (*Φί*[*λω*]*ν*: f. *Πολύστρατος*); (**27**) imp. *IG* IV (1) 582
—EPIDAUROS: (**28**) c. 365-335 BC ib. IV (1)² 103, 158; (**29**) imp. ib. 445 (f. *Ἀντίοχος*)
—EPIDAUROS*: (**30**) c. 370 BC ib. 102, 184, 245, 280; (**31**) c. 370-360 BC Peek, *IAEpid* 52 B, 66, 70-1, 75; *BSA* 61 (1966) p. 272 no. 4 B II, 2
—HERMIONE: (**32**) iv BC *IG* IV (1) 741, 4; (**33**) ii-i BC ib. 732 IV, 9 (s. *Ἀγαθοκλῆς*); (**34**) m. ii BC *SEG* XI 377, 7; XXXI 328, 6; Peek, *IAEpid* 30, 6 (s. *Καλλίστρατος*)
—TROIZEN*: (**35**) iv BC *IG* IV (1) 823, 40
ARKADIA:
—MANTINEIA-ANTIGONEIA: (**36**) c. 300-221 BC ib. V (2) 323. 50 (tessera) (f. *Σώπατρος*)
—MEGALOPOLIS: (**37**) ?265-259 BC Nachtergael, *Les Galates* 2, 8; 4, 16; 6, 5 (Stephanis 2561) (s. *Φανίας*)
—ORCHOMENOS: (**38**) iv BC *BCH* 63 (1939) p. 145 inv. 2382 (s. *Τριτέας*)
—PHENEOS: (**39**) iv/iii BC *SEG* XXX 356, 4 (I f. *Φίλων* II); (**40**) ~ ib. l. 4 (II s. *Φίλων* I)
—TEGEA: (**41**) f. iii BC *IG* V (2) 36, 32; (**42**) s. iii BC ib. 116, 3 (f. *Φίλιος*); (**43**) m. ii AD ib. 48, 19
——(Apolloniatai): (**44**) m. iii BC ib. 36, 97 (f. *Θρασέας*)
——(Athaneatai): (**45**) s. iii BC ib. l. 109 (s. *Ἀριστοτέλης*)
——(Hippothoitai): (**46**) iii BC ib. 40, 42 (f. *Κλέας*)
—THELPHOUSA: (**47**) 242 BC *SEG* XII 371, 31 (s. —ος); (**48**) c. 230-200 BC *BCH* 45 (1921) p. 12 II, 73 + *SEG* XXX 494 (s. *Μοισέας*)
DALMATIA:
—ISSA: (**49**) f. ii BC Brunšmid p. 23 no. 10, 11 ([*Φί*]*λων*: s. *Αἰσχίνας*)
——(Dymanes): (**50**) iv/iii BC ib. p. 8, 36 (f. *Εὔξενος*)
——(Pamphyloi): (**51**) iv/iii BC ib. p. 7, 21 (f. *Σάλλας*)
ELIS: (**52**) s. iv BC *SEG* XX 716, 25 + XXVII 1194
—PISA: (**53**) 365-363 BC *IvOl* 36, 6 (Perlman O.1) (*Φίλ*[*ων*]: s. *Λυκομήδης*)
EPIROS: (**54**) hell. *IG* XII (8) 594 (*SEG* XXXI 770 a)
—AMBRAKIA: (**55**) v/iv BC *BCH* 79 (1955) p. 267 (f. *Φιλωτίς*); (**56**) ?254 BC Nachtergael, *Les Galates* 9, 60 (s. *Στράτων*)
—BOUTHROTOS (PRASAIBOI): (**57**) a. 163 BC *IBouthrot* 14, 31 (*SEG* XXXVIII 471); (**58**) ~ *IBouthrot* 29, 21; (**59**) ~ ib. 76, 7 (s. *Μηλοφῶν*)
—DODONA*: (**60**) ?iv-iii BC *PAE* 1929, p. 127
—ONOPERNOI: (**61**) s. c. 330 BC Cabanes, *L'Épire* p. 580 no. 55, 11
—THESPROTOI: (**62**) i BC *SEG* XIII 248, 8 (s. *Αἰνέας*)

ILLYRIA:
—APOLLONIA: (63) c. 250-50 BC Maier 98 (coin) (Ceka 18) (pryt.); (64) ii-i BC IApoll 105 (f. Κλεινώ); (65) ~ ib. 131 (f. Νικαρέτα); (66) ?ii-i BC ib. 163; (67) ii-i BC ib. 164 (s. Τιμήν); (68) ?ii-i BC ib. 367 (tile) (Φίλω[ν]); (69) i BC Maier 161 (coin) (s. Ζώπυρος: pryt.); (70) ~ ib. 157-9 (coin) (pryt.); (71) imp. IApoll 90 (f. Ζωΐλα); (72) ~ ib. 137 (f. Ὀππία Ζωΐλα)
——(Le.): (73) iii/ii BC ib. 7; cf. L'Illyrie mérid. 2 p. 207 (f. Φιλόστρατος)
—BYLLIONES (BALISH (MOD.)): (74) imp. JÖAI 21-2 (1922) Beibl. p. 200 no. 15 (Lat. Philo/Philo-?)
—EPIDAMNOS-DYRRHACHION: (75) c. 250-50 BC Münsterberg p. 41 (coin) (pryt.) ?= (77); (76) ~ Maier 110; 131; 168; 187; 300; 306 + 485; 328; 345a; 371; 468/9; Münsterberg p. 39 (coin) (Ceka 423; 432-41) (money.); (77) ~ Maier 391-3; 482; Münsterberg p. 15 (coin) (Ceka 50; 122; 154; 178; 216; 230; 330) (pryt.) ?= (75); (78) ?ii-i BC IG XII (8) 196, 3; cf. IDyrrh 515 (s. —αστ—); (79) ii-i BC ib. 571 (tile) ([Φ]ιλωνο[ς] (gen.)); (80) hell.-imp. ib. 96 (Λάων—Toci: f. Ἄμμινα); (81) ~ ib. 180 (f. Ἐλευθέριν); (82) ~ ib. 259 (f. Καλλήν); (83) ~ ib. 269 (f. Κλειτία); (84) ~ ib. 318 (f. Μυρτιώ); (85) ~ ib. 434 (f. Φίλιππος); (86) ~ ib. 446 (s. Ἀρχήν); (87) ~ ib. 447 (s. Νικήν); (88) ~ ib. 448 (s. Σωσιλήν); (89) imp. ib. 54
—GUREZEZE (MOD.): (90) hell. Iliria 1982 (1), p. 105 no. 11 = p. 121 no. 54; cf. p. 123; cf. SEG II 382 (tile)

KEPHALLENIA:
—KRANIOI: (91) i BC-i AD IG IX (1) 614
—SAME: (92) hell. ib. 629; (93) hell.-imp. ib. 624 (I f. Φίλων II); (94) ~ ib. (II s. Φίλων I)
KERKYRA: (95) 504 BC Moretti, Olymp. 155 ?= (96); (96) 500 BC RE (12); Moretti, Olymp. 161; 168; cf. Ebert, Gr. Sieg. 11; cf. Page, FGE 802 (s. Γλαῦκος) ?= (95); (97) c. 229-48 BC BMC Thessaly p. 150 nos. 536-48; SNG Cop. Epirus-Acarnania 236-8; SNG Evelpidis II 1976-84 (coins)

KORINTHIA:
—KORINTH: (98) c. 590-570 BC Amyx 33. 7 (vase) (Lorber 52) (-λōν: her.?); (99) iii BC IG IV (1)² 98, 3; (100) s. ii AD Corinth VIII (1) 15, 31 (Γ. Κλώδιος Φ.)
—KORINTH*: (101) ?iv BC ib. XIV p. 136 no. 90
—SIKYON: (102) c. 370-365 BC Peek, IAEpid 52 B, 41, 44, [45]; (103) ?iii/ii BC IOrop 521, 21 (f. Φιλωνίδας); (104) c. 200-175 BC IG II² 9052, 3, 5, 6 (GVI 1699; Gr. Gr. 215) (s. Φιλοκράτης, f. Φιλοκράτης (and Hamaxanteia): doctor)
LAKONIA: (105) iii BC IG V (1) 1340, 1 (Bradford (6))
—GYTHEION: (106) 282 AD IG V (1) 1164, 6 ([Φ]ίλων)
—HIPPOLA: (107) iii/ii BC ib. 1336, 3, 12 (s. Δα—)
—HYPERTELEATON*: (108) imp. ib. 1043; (109) ~ ib. 1083 (f. Σύντροφος)
—SPARTA: (110) ii-i BC ib. 1226, [1], 8 (Bradford (2)) (s. Ἀντι—); (111) c. 25-1 BC IG V (1) 212, 27 (Bradford (1)) ([Φ]ίλων: s. Ἀνδρίας); (112) c. 100-110 AD SEG XI 611, 5 (Bradford (5)) (I f. Φίλων II); (113) ~ SEG XI 611, 5 (Bradford (4)) (II s. Φίλων I); (114) f. iii AD IG V (1) 170, 13; BSA 80 (1985) p. 245 (date) (Bradford (3)) (Αὐρ. Φ.: s. Μ. Αὐρ. Φίλιππος)
—TEUTHRONE: (115) iii/ii BC SEG XXII 304, 3 (f. Φειδίας: date—LGPN)
LEUKAS: (116) hell. IG IX (1) 586
MESSENIA:
—KOLONIDES: (117) ii BC ib. V (1) 1402, 7
—MESSENE: (118) hell. ib. II² 9346 (f. Φίλα); (119) f. iii BC PAE 1991, p. 99 no. 7, 12; (120) m. iii BC Peek, IAEpid 42, 60, 64 (Perlman E.3); Perlman p. 63 f. (date) (s. Σωτήριχος);

(121) ii BC SEG XLI 347 (f. Ἀμύντας I); (122) ?i AD Ergon 1995, p. 31 (f. Χαρικλῆς)
—MESSENE?: (123) ii/i BC SEG XI 979, 20
—THOURIA: (124) ii-i BC IG V (1) 1385, 33 (s. Φιλοκλείδας); (125) f. ii BC SEG XI 972, 22 (s. Φιλόξενος, f. Φιλόξενος); (126) ~ ib. l. 102 (f. Εὐχάρης); (127) ~ ib. l. 118 (f. Ἀγαθοκλῆς)
PELOPONNESE: (128) c. 230-200 BC BCH 45 (1921) p. 13 II, 106 ([Φ]ίλων: s. Σώτιμος)
S. ITALY (APULIA):
—LARINUM: (129) i AD Forma Italiae 36 p. 152 (Lat. [Ma]rcius Philo)
—VENUSIA: (130) f. i AD Rend. Linc. 29 (1974) p. 621 no. 24 (Lat. P. Magius Philo)
S. ITALY (BRUTTIUM):
—KRIMISA: (131) ?c. 475 BC IGSI 18, 3 (SEG IV 75; Landi, DISMG 173); LSAG² p. 261 no. 30 (date) (-λōν)
—LOKROI EPIZEPHYRIOI: (132) iv BC SEG XXXV 1030 A-B; cf. XXXVIII 996
——(Βω.): (133) iv/iii BC De Franciscis 27, 8 (f. Ἀρίστων)
——(Δυσ.): (134) iv/iii BC ib. 20, 5 (s. Εὐκλείδας)
——(Μνα.): (135) iv/iii BC ib. 39, 3 (s. Χάριππος)
——(Φαω.): (136) iv/iii BC ib. 22, 9 (s. Γνάθις)
S. ITALY (CALABRIA):
—BRENTESION-BRUNDISIUM: (137) imp. CIL IX 6100 (Lat. Philo)
—BRENTESION-BRUNDISIUM*: (138) ii-i BC Museo Ribezzo 10 (1977) p. 113 no. 2 (vase) (potter)
—TARAS-TARENTUM: (139) c. 302-280 BC Vlasto 683-6 (coin) (Evans, Horsemen p. 133 VI C.1-2); (140) c. 100-90 BC SEG XIX 335, 9, 43; cf. BSA 70 (1975) pp. 127 ff. (date); cf. Stephanis 2564 (I f. Φίλων II); (141) ~ SEG XIX 335, 9, 29-30, 43; cf. BSA 70 (1975) pp. 127 ff. (date) (Stephanis 2564) (II s. Φίλων I)
S. ITALY (CAMPANIA):
—DIKAIARCHIA-PUTEOLI*: (142) imp. CIL X 2367 (Lat. C. Octavius Philo: freed.)
—KYME: (143) ?i-ii AD Eph. Ep. VIII 444 (Lat. C. Iulius Philo)
—POMPEII: (144) i BC-i AD CIL IV 1984 (Lat. Philo); (145) ~ ib. 5431 (Lat. Philo)
S. ITALY (CAMPANIA)*: (146) imp. ib. X 8042. 85 (tile) (Lat. Philo: slave?)
S. ITALY (LUCANIA):
—HERAKLEIA: (147) f. iii BC NC 1918, p. 141 no. 75 (coin) (van Keuren, Coinage of Heraclea pp. 80-1 nos. 98-100, 102)
—METAPONTION: (148) inc. St. Byz. s.v. Μεταπόντιον; (149) m. iii BC SEG XXX 1175, 11 (Φίλω[ν]: doctor)
SICILY: (150) f. iii BC Vandermersch p. 177 (amph.) (or S. Italy: Φίλω(ν))
—ADRANON: (151) iii-ii BC PdelP 16 (1961) p. 127
—AKRAGAS: (152) c. 430-420 BC Dubois, IGDS 181 (coin graffito) (-λōν); (153) s. ii BC Acragas Graeca I p. 34 no. 5, 2 (IGUR 2; Dubois, IGDS 185) (f. Νυμφόδωρος)
—AKRAI: (154) iii-ii BC Akrai p. 162 no. 22. 13; (155) ii-i BC SGDI 3246, 15, 17 (Akrai pp. 152-3 no. 2; Dubois, IGDS 109) (f. Φιλοκλῆς, Πόσειδις); (156) ~ SGDI 3246, 30, 32 (Akrai pp. 152-3 no. 2; Dubois, IGDS 109) (s. Φίλιστος, f. Φίλιστος); (157) ~ SGDI 3246, 36, 38 (Akrai pp. 152-3 no. 2; Dubois, IGDS 109) (f. Ἀρχέδαμος, Ἱέρων)
—HALAISA: (158) m. i BC Cic., ad Fam. xiii 32. 1 (Lat. C. Clodius Philo)
—IAITON: (159) ii-i BC SEG XXVI 1070. 6; XXXIII 746 (tiles)
—KAMARINA: (160) hell. ib. XXXIX 1001, 10 (f. Σάννων)
—LILYBAION*: (161) imp. CIL X 7215 (Lat. C. Cornelius Philo: freed.)
—MORGANTINA: (162) ?iv/iii BC SEG XXXIX 1008, 11 (s. Ἐμμενίδας); (163) ii BC ib. XXVII

655, 5, 8 (Dubois, IGDS 194); cf. PdelP 44 (1989) p. 205 (?s. Ἀρίσταρχος)
—SELINOUS: (164) vi/v BC Manganaro, PdelP forthcoming no. 18 (-λōν: f. Νακώι)
—SOLOUS: (165) iii/ii BC Kokalos 9 (1963) pp. 186-7 (s. Ἀπολλώνιος); (166) ~ ib. (s. Ἄριστων)
—SYRACUSE: (167) 402 AD Strazzulla 168 (Φίλω(ν))
—SYRACUSE?: (168) hell. Manganaro, PdelP forthcoming no. 4 II, 1 (s. Κόγχων); (169) f. ii BC IG XI (4) 758; cf. Durrbach, Choix p. 87 (ident.) (s. Ὕβριμος)
——(Μακ.): (170) hell. Manganaro, PdelP forthcoming no. 4 II, 3 (s. Βλόσων); (171) ~ ib. no. 4 III, 2 (f. Ἡρακλείδας)
——(Περ.): (172) hell. ib. no. 4 I, 1 (f. Σώπατρος)
——(Πλη.): (173) hell. ib. no. 4 IV, 2 (f. Φιλοκράτης)
—TAUROMENION: (174) c. 152 BC IGSI 4 III (IV), 28 an. 89 (s. Δαμάτριος); (175) ?ii/i BC IG XIV 421 D an. 4 (f. Δαμάτριος) ?= (178); (176) ~ ib. 421 D an. 6 (SGDI 5219); IGSI 4 III (IV), 100 D an. 6 (f. Νικόστρατος) ?= (179)
——(Πεα.): (177) c. 154-149 BC IG XIV 421 an. 92 (SGDI 5219); IGSI 4 III (IV), 13 an. 87 (f. Καλλίμαχος); (178) ?ii/i BC IG XIV 421 D an. 7; 421 D an. 13 (SGDI 5219); IGSI 4 III (IV), 118 D an. 7 (f. Δαμάτριος) ?= (175); (179) ~ IG XIV 421 III (SGDI 5219) (f. Νικόστρατος) ?= (176)
—TYNDARIS: (180) ?i BC Arch. Class. 17 (1965) p. 203 (f. Ἀντίμαχος); (181) f. i BC Cic., In Verr. II iv 48 (Lat. Cn. Pompeius Philo)
ZAKYNTHOS: (182) hell. Syringes 213

## Φιλωνᾶς

KORINTHIA:
—KORINTH: (1) ii-iii AD SEG XI 132, 4; 133 (s. Διονύσιος); (2) ~ ib. 138 e, 1

## Φιλώνδας

S. ITALY (BRUTTIUM):
—LOKROI EPIZEPHYRIOI:
——(Γαυ.): (1) 278 BC De Franciscis 30, 3 (f. Φιλοκλῆς)
——(Λακ.): (2) 278 BC ib. l. 1, 16
——(Πυρ.): (3) iv/iii BC ib. 14, 7
—SYBARIS-THOURIOI-COPIAE: (4) iii BC Theoc., Id. v 112 (fict.)
SICILY:
—SELINOUS?: (5) vi/v BC SEG XXXIX 1020 A, 12 (-δōν-: s. Χοιρίνας)

## Φιλωνίδας

ARGOLIS:
—ARGOS*: (1) iii BC IG IV (1) 528, 3 (slave/freed.?)
—EPIDAUROS: (2) i-ii AD ib. IV (1)² 523 (s. Ἱερώνυμος)
—EPIDAUROS*: (3) c. 370 BC ib. 102, 172 ?= (4); (4) c. 365-335 BC ib. 103, 164-5, 170, 172, 176-7 ?= (3)
—TROIZEN: (5) iv BC ib. IV (1) 764, 8 (s. Λυκέας); (6) iii BC SEG XXXVII 312
ARKADIA:
—TEGEA: (7) f. ii BC IG V (2) 44, 25 (Φιλωνίδα[ς])
——(Hippothoitai): (8) iv/iii BC ib. 38, 49 (f. Φιλόξενος); (9) f. iii BC ib. 36, 21 ([Φι]λωνίδας?, [Ἀπολ]λωνίδας?)
ELIS: (10) ?272-271 BC FD III (3) 185, 5; 187, 2; cf. SEG XL 419 (f. Ἀλεξεινίδας)
EPIROS:
—BOUTHROTOS: (11) f. ii BC IBouthrot 2, 5; 3, 5; 4, 4 (f. Λύκων) ?= (12)
—BOUTHROTOS (PRASAIBOI): (12) a. 163 BC ib. 101, 4 (f. Λύκων) ?= (11)
ILLYRIA:
—APOLLONIA: (13) c. 250-50 BC Maier 97; Bakërr Hoard p. 64 no. 90 (coin) (Ceka 87) (pryt.); (14) i BC Ceka, Probleme p. 139 no. 28 (coin); (15) ~ Maier 162; 164-5 (coin) (pryt.)

——(Amphineis): **(16)** iii BC Robert, *Hell.* 10 p. 283 ff.; cf. *CRAI* 1991, p. 197 ff.; *L'Illyrie mérid.* 2 p. 204 f. (f. *Μαίσων*)

—EPIDAMNOS-DYRRHACHION: **(17)** c. 250-50 BC Münsterberg 41 (coin) (Ceka 329) (pryt.) ?= *(18)*; **(18)** ~ Ceka, *Probleme* p. 152 no. 78 (coin) (pryt.) ?= *(17)*; **(19)** ~ Maier 123; Münsterberg p. 40 (coin) (Ceka 442-3) (money.); **(20)** s. i BC *RE* (6) (doctor) ?= *(65)*

KERKYRA: **(21)** ?iii BC *IG* IX (1) 695, 6 ([Φι]λωνίδας: s. *Αἰσχύλος*); **(22)** iii-ii BC ib. 815-18; *Korkyra* 1 p. 169 nos. 23-5; Ugolini, *Alb. Ant.* 3 p. 231 no. 2 (tiles); **(23)** c. 229-48 BC *BMC Thessaly* p. 151 f. nos. 549-56; *SNG Cop. Epirus–Acarnania* 239 (coins)

KORINTHIA:

—KORINTH: **(24)** v/iv BC Ar., *Pl.* 179, 303; Schol. Ar., *Pl.* 179 (-δης); **(25)** iii-ii BC *SEG* XXVII 34 (f. *Φιλωτίς*)

—SIKYON: **(26)** ?iii/ii BC *IOrop* 521, 21 (-δης: s. *Φίλων*)

LAKONIA:

—GERENIA: **(27)** iii/ii BC *IG* V (1) 1336, 18

—SPARTA: **(28)** c. 25-1 BC ib. 212, 5 (Bradford (12)) (f. *Φιλόστρατος*); **(29)** c. 1-10 AD *IG* V (1) 209, 20; *SEG* XXXV 331 (date) (Bradford (10)) (I f. *Φιλωνίδας* II); **(30)** ~ *IG* V (1) 209, 20; *SEG* XXXV 331 (date) (Bradford (3)) (II s. *Φιλωνίδας* I); **(31)** c. 70-90 AD *IG* V (1) 480, 13 (Bradford (13)) (f. *Ξενοκράτης*); **(32)** f. ii AD *SEG* XXXI 340, 5 (f. —*νικίδας*); **(33)** m. ii AD ib. XI 623, 5 (Bradford (11)) (I f. *Φιλωνίδας* II); **(34)** ~ *SEG* XI 623, 5 (Bradford (4)) ([Φιλ]ωνίδας: II s. *Φιλωνίδας* I); **(35)** c. 130-140 AD *IG* V (1) 66, 6 (Bradford (8)) ([Φι]λωνίδας: f. *Γ. Ἰούλ. Νικηφόρος*); **(36)** c. 140-160 AD *SEG* XI 600, 4 (Bradford (7)) (Φ[ι]λωνίδας: f. *Εὐκρίνης*); **(37)** c. 150-160 AD *SEG* XI 525, 26; 533 a, 2; 585, 12; XXX 410, [19] (Bradford (11)) (I f. *Φιλωνίδας* II); **(38)** ~ *SEG* XI 525, 26; 533 a, 2; 585, 12; XXX 410, 19 (Bradford (4)) (II s. *Φιλωνίδας* I); **(39)** ~ *SEG* XI 585, 4; 586, 2; 600, 4-5; XXX 410, 5 (Bradford (2)) (Φιλωνί[δας]—586: s. *Εὐκρίνης*); **(40)** ~ *SEG* XI 585, 12; XXX 410, 18 (Bradford (1)) (Φιλ[ωνίδας]—*SEG* XXX: s. *Ἁγίων*); **(41)** c. 175-200 AD *SEG* XI 503, 23 (Bradford (6)) (f. *Γ. Ἰούλ. Ἁγίων*); **(42)** f. iii AD *IG* V (1) 310, 5 (*Artemis Orthia* pp. 332-3 no. 67); *IG* V (1) 544, 3 (*Artemis Orthia* pp. 358-9 no. 145); *IG* V (1) 547, 15; 549, 3; *SEG* XI 799, 2; *BSA* 79 (1984) p. 284 no. 11 (date) (Bradford (9)) ([Φιλωνί]δας—*SEG*: f. *Μ. Αὐρ. Νικηφόρος*)

MESSENIA: **(43)** ii AD *AD* 2 (1916) p. 117 no. 82 (f. *Φιλοκράτης*)

—MESSENE: **(44)** iv BC *IG* V (1) 1471; **(45)** i BC *SEG* XIII 248, 10; cf. Stephanis 2570 (f. *Φιλώνιχος*); **(46)** 31 BC-14 AD *SEG* XXIII 207, 29 (s. *Διογένης*); **(47)** f. ii AD *IvOl* 445, 2, 5 (s. *Διογένης*)

—MESSENE?: **(48)** ?f. ii BC *SEG* XXIII 219 (f. *Θεοφάνεια*)

S. ITALY: **(49)** ?315 BC *FD* III (4) 388, 1

S. ITALY (BRUTTIUM):

—LOKROI EPIZEPHYRIOI: **(50)** 280 BC De Franciscis 35, 3 (f. —*χος*)

——(Ἀλχ.): **(51)** iv/iii BC ib. 11, 9 (f. *Φιλόνικος*)

——(Βοω.): **(52)** iv/iii BC ib. 29, 3

——(Πυρ.): **(53)** iv/iii BC ib. 3, 8 (f. *Εὐκαμίδας*) ?= *(54)*; **(54)** ~ ib. 9, 3 ?= *(53)*

——(Τω.): **(55)** iv/iii BC ib. 34, 8 ?= *(56)*; **(56)** 279 BC ib. 13, 3 (f. *Πολύστρατος*) ?= *(55)*

—TERINA:

——(Κι.): **(57)** c. 325-300 BC *IGSI* 21, 14 (*SEG* IV 73; Landi, *DISMG* 170)

S. ITALY (CALABRIA):

—TARAS-TARENTUM: **(58)** iv BC Iamb., *VP* 267 (*FVS* 1 p. 446) (-δης); **(59)** f. iv BC Pl., *Ep.* 357 D (-δης); **(60)** 281 BC *RE* (2) (Φιλωνίδης ἡ κοτύλη)

S. ITALY (LUCANIA):

—METAPONTION: **(61)** iii/ii BC Landi, *DISMG* 154

SICILY:

—AKRAI: **(62)** ii-i BC *SGDI* 3246, 3 (*Akrai* pp. 152-3 no. 2; Dubois, *IGDS* 109) (I f. *Φιλωνίδας* II); **(63)** ~ *SGDI* 3246, 3 (*Akrai* pp. 152-3 no. 2; Dubois, *IGDS* 109) (*Μορφιανός* (dem.?): II s. *Φιλωνίδας* I)

—ENTELLA: **(64)** iv/iii BC *SEG* XXX 1119, 1 (Dubois, *IGDS* 206); cf. *SEG* XXXIX 1014 (s. *Φιλ*—)

—KATANE: **(65)** f. i AD Scrib. 97; cf. *RE* s.v. Philonides (6) (doctor) ?= *(20)*

—MORGANTINA: **(66)** ?iv/iii BC *SEG* XXXIX 1008, 9 (-λο-: s. *Ἡρακλείδας*); **(67)** ~ ib. 1011, 6; **(68)** iv/iii BC ib. 1012, 5 (f. *Ἡράκλειος*); **(69)** ~ ib. 1013, 4 (s. *Δράκων*); **(70)** ~ ib. l. 4 (s. *Ἡρακλείδας*)

—SYRACUSE: **(71)** ii BC *IG* II² 10399 (Φ[ι]λωνίδης: s. *Ἀλκαῖος*)

——(Περηκυναταῖος): **(72)** iv BC Manganaro, *PdelP* forthcoming no. 3, 3 (s. *Νεμήνιος*)

—SYRACUSE?:

——(Ἀλτρι.): **(73)** hell. *Mem. Linc.* 8 (1938) p. 127 no. 35. 2 (bullet); cf. *L'Incidenza dell'Antico* pp. 420 ff. (s. *Εὐπόλεμος*)

——(Λαβ.): **(74)** hell. Manganaro, *PdelP* forthcoming no. 4 I, 2 (f. *Φιλιστίων*)

——(Μακ.): **(75)** hell. ib. no. 4 V, 2 (f. *Ἀρταμίδωρος*)

——(Ὑπα.): **(76)** hell. ib. l. 4 (f. *Φιντίας*)

—TAUROMENION: **(77)** c. 219 BC *IG* XIV 421 an. 22 (*SGDI* 5219); **(78)** c. 218-204 BC *IG* XIV 421 an. 23; 421 an. 37 (*SGDI* 5219) (f. *Φιλόξενος*); **(79)** c. 211-199 BC *IG* XIV 421 an. 30; 421 an. 42 (*SGDI* 5219) (s. *Καλλίμαχος*); **(80)** c. 204 BC *IG* XIV 421 an. 37 (*SGDI* 5219) (f. *Νυμφόδωρος*); **(81)** c. 176 BC *IG* XIV 421 an. 65 (*SGDI* 5219); **(82)** c. 166 BC *IG* XIV 421 an. 75 (*SGDI* 5219); *IGSI* 4 II (III), [46] an. 75; **(83)** c. 157 BC *IG* XIV 421 an. 84 (*SGDI* 5219); **(84)** c. 149 BC *IGSI* 4 III (IV), 50 an. 92 (f. *Ἀρτεμίδωρος*); **(85)** ii/i BC ib. 5 IV, 14 (I f. *Φιλωνίδας* II); **(86)** ~ ib. l. 14 (II s. *Φιλωνίδας* I)

——(Ἀσσι.): **(87)** c. 146-142 BC *IG* XIV 421 an. 99 (*SGDI* 5219); *IGSI* 4 III (IV), 73 an. 95 + *Comptes et Inventaires* p. 178 (*SEG* XXXVIII 975 n. on l. 72) (s. *Κρίθων*)

ZAKYNTHOS: **(88)** BC. 263-253 BC *IG* XI (2) 113, 25; Nachtergael, *Les Galates* 7, 2, 48; 8, 1; 9, 1; 10, 1; cf. p. 274 n. 240 (Stephanis 2568); cf. Stephanis 2567 (-δης: s. *Ἀριστόμαχος*, ?f. *Ἀριστόμαχος* (Athens))

## Φιλωνίδης

ELIS:

—OLYMPIA*: **(1)** iv/iii BC *IvOl* 177, 3; *RE* (8) (sculptor)

ILLYRIA:

—APOLLONIA: **(2)** i/ii AD *IApoll* 189 (Τ. Φλ. Φ.: f. Φλ. *Γενθίς*, Φλ.? *Φιάλη*)

KORINTHIA:

—SIKYON?: **(3)** iii-ii BC *IG* IV (1) 429, 10 (Stephanis 2569) (s. *Παντοκλῆς*)

S. ITALY (CAMPANIA):

—KYME?: **(4)** 321-307 BC *FD* III (4) 388, 1; cf. *SEG* XXVII 85 (locn.) (or S. Italy (Bruttium) Sybaris-Thourioi-Copiae)

S. ITALY (LUCANIA):

—HYELE-VELIA: **(5)** hell.? *IG* XIV 661 (Landi, *DISMG* 49) (?s. *Σώσανδρος*)

SICILY:

—HENNA: **(6)** i BC *RE* (6) (or Sicily Katane: doctor)

## Φιλωνίς

AITOLIA:

—KALLION/KALLIPOLIS: **(1)** iii/ii BC *AD* 26 (1971) Chron. p. 283

## Φιλώνιχος

MESSENIA:

—MESSENE: **(1)** i BC ib. XIII 248, 10; Stephanis 2570 (s. *Φιλωνίδας*)

## Φιλωνυμία

LAKONIA:

—OITYLOS: **(1)** f. ii BC *IG* V (1) 1296, 5, 8 (m. *Ἀριστοφάνης*)

## Φιλωνυμίδας

LAKONIA:

—OITYLOS: **(1)** f. ii BC ib. l. 7

—SPARTA: **(2)** c. 25-1 BC ib. 50, 26; 95, 19; 127, [7] (Bradford (-)) (f. *Ἄρχιππος*); **(3)** i AD *SEG* XXVI 462, 1 ([Φιλω]νυμίδας)

## Φιλώνυμος

LAKONIA:

—OITYLOS: **(1)** iii/ii BC *IG* V (1) 1295, 7 (Bradford (-))

MESSENIA:

—ASINE: **(2)** ii-i BC *IG* V (1) 1416

S. ITALY (LUCANIA):

—HERAKLEIA:

——(Ϝε. τρίπους): **(3)** iv/iii BC *IGSI* 1 I, 3, 9, 97 (*DGE* 62; Uguzzoni–Ghinatti I); *IGSI* 1 II, 2, 7 (*DGE* 63; Uguzzoni–Ghinatti II) (s. *Ζωπυρίσκος*)

——(ha. ἄνθεμα): **(4)** iv/iii BC *IGSI* 1 I, 166 (*DGE* 62; Uguzzoni–Ghinatti I) (I f. *Φιλώνυμος* II); **(5)** ~ *IGSI* 1 I, 166 (*DGE* 62; Uguzzoni–Ghinatti I) (II s. *Φιλώνυμος* I)

——(ha. ἔμβολος): **(6)** iv/iii BC *IGSI* 1 I, 182 (*DGE* 62; Uguzzoni–Ghinatti I) (f. *Δάμαρχος*)

## Φιλώτας

ACHAIA:

—PELLENE: **(1)** ?ii AD *IG* II² 10056 (s. *Σωτίων*)

AITOLIA:

—APERANTOI: **(2)** ?iv/iii BC ib. IX (1)² (1) 166, 3 + *AbhBerlAk* 1958 (2), p. 9 (*L'Illyrie mérid.* 1 p. 109 fig. 6)

—TRICHONION: **(3)** 185 BC *IG* IX (1)² (1) 32, 12

ARKADIA:

—GORTYS: **(4)** iii AD *SEG* XI 1165, 2 (*Μ. Τουρπίλιος Φ.*)

ARKADIA?: **(5)** 365 BC ib. XXII 339, 12 (Φιλ[ώτας]?) ?= *(6)*; **(6)** c. 365 BC ib. 340, 8 (Φιλώτα[s]) ?= *(5)*

DALMATIA:

—ISSA:

——(Hylleis): **(7)** iv/iii BC Brunšmid p. 9, 50 (f. *Εὔβουλος*)

ELIS:

—OLYMPIA*: **(8)** 365 BC *SEG* XXII 340, 8

EPIROS:

—BOUTHROTOS (PRASAIBOI): **(9)** a. 163 BC *IBouthrot* 18, 14 (*SEG* XXXVIII 475) (s. *Καλλικράτης*) ?= *(18)*; **(10)** ~ *IBouthrot* 19, 3 (*SEG* XXXVIII 476); **(11)** ~ *IBouthrot* 32, 7 (*SEG* XXXVIII 491) ?= *(13)*; **(12)** ~ *IBouthrot* 35, 4 (*SEG* XXXVIII 494); *IBouthrot* 133, 6 (f. *Διογένης, Καλλικράτης*) ?= *(17) (16)*; **(13)** ~ ib. 35, 6 (*SEG* XXXVIII 494) ?= *(11)*; **(14)** ~ *IBouthrot* 36, 22 (*SEG* XXXVIII 495); **(15)** ~ *IBouthrot* 156, 11 (*BCH* 118 (1994) p. 127 no. 12) (f. *Φιλόξενος*)

——Bouthrotioi: **(16)** a. 163 BC *IBouthrot* 8, 3 (*SEG* XXXVIII 480) (f. *Διογένης*) ?= *(12)*; **(17)** ~ *IBouthrot* 67, 6; 95, 5 (f. *Καλλικράτης*) ?= *(12)*; **(18)** ~ ib. 67, 6; 95, 4 (s. *Καλλικράτης*) ?= *(9)*; **(19)** ~ ib. 113, 18

—KASSOPE: **(20)** c. 130 BC Dakaris, *Kassope* p. 25 (*SEG* XXXVI 555); cf. *SEG* XLI 541 (s. *Φρύνων*); **(21)** i BC Cabanes, *L'Épire* p. 564 no. 42, 4 (*SEG* XXVI 71) (s. —*μων*)

LAKONIA:

—HIPPOLA: **(2)** i BC-i AD? *IG* V (1) 1278

MESSENIA:

—MESSENE: **(3)** i BC-i AD *SEG* XLI 371 (?d. *Ἀφρο*—)

ILLYRIA:
—APOLLONIA: (22) c. 250-50 BC Maier 9; 49; 75 + Münsterberg Nachtr. p. 13; Maier 88; *Jubice Hoard* p. 89 no. 83 (coin) (Ceka 128-33) (money.)
—EPIDAMNOS-DYRRHACHION: (23) hell.? *IDyrrh* 18; (24) c. 250-50 BC *SNG Cop. Thessaly–Illyricum* 511; 522; Unp. (Paris, BN) 274; 277 (coin) (pryt.) ?= (26); (25) ~ Maier 111; 113; 147; 189; 200; 221; 250; 258; 269; 329; 372; 402; Münsterberg p. 38; p. 40; Nachtr. p. 16 (coin) (Ceka 444-59) (money.); (26) ~ Maier 394-6; Münsterberg Nachtr. p. 17 (coin) (Ceka 13; 51; 98; 105; 274; 331) (pryt.) ?= (24); (27) ii-i BC *IDyrrh* 449; (28) ~ ib. 563 (tiles); (29) f. ii BC *PP* 15130; *IC* 3 p. 112 no. 14; *SEG* XXXI 1521, [8] (*IDyrrh* 518-19) (s. Γένθιος); (30) hell.-imp. ib. 320 (f. Μυρώ); (31) ~ ib. 341 (f. Πατερήν); (32) ~ ib. 450 (s. Θεομήδης); (33) ~ ib. 451 (s. Λαιδίας)
KEPHALLENIA:
—PRONNOI: (34) hell.? *IG* IX (1) 648
KERKYRA: (35) iii BC *Suda* Φ 358; *RE* s.v. Philiskos (4) (f. Φιλικός); (36) c. 229-48 BC *BMC Thessaly* p. 152 nos. 557-62; *SNG Cop. Epirus-Acarnania* 240-3 (coins); (37) ?ii BC *IG* IX (1) 708 (s. Ἴακχος); (38) ?ii-i BC ib. 819; *BM Terracottas* E 132 (tiles)
KORINTHIA:
—SIKYON: (39) b. 364 BC *IG* II² 1643, 20; *ID* 104, 92; *IG* XI (2) 161 B, 13 (Skalet 331-2)
—LEUKAS: (40) c. 167-50 BC *BMC Thessaly* p. 183 nos. 130-1 (coins)
MESSENIA:
—MESSENE: (41) iii BC *SEG* XXIII 210, 23; (42) i AD *IG* V (1) 1436, 7
S. ITALY (BRUTTIUM):
—HIPPONION-VIBO VALENTIA: (43) c. 315-280 BC *FD* III (1) 176, 1; cf. *SEG* XL 421 (s. Δήμαρχος)
S. ITALY (CALABRIA):
—TARAS-TARENTUM: (44) iv/iii BC *IG* XIV 668 I, 11 (Landi, *DISMG* 194); (45) c. 302-280 BC Vlasto 708 (coin); *Riv. It. Num.* 62 (1960) p. 49 and fig. 25. 10 (name); (46) ?c. 300 BC *BCH* 68-9 (1944-5) p. 98 no. 5, 2 ([Φ]ιλώτας: f. Ἐπι—); (47) ?iii BC *NScav* 1940, p. 322 (lamp); (48) c. 272-235 BC Vlasto 823-4; 846-9 (coins) (Evans, *Horsemen* p. 177 VIII A.5; p. 177 VIII A.11)
S. ITALY (LUCANIA):
—HERAKLEIA:
——(Κυ. θρῖναξ): (49) iv/iii BC *IGSI* 1 I, 6, 9, 98 (*DGE* 62; Uguzzoni–Ghinatti I) (s. Ἰστιειός)
——(Με. κιβώτιον): (50) iv/iii BC *IGSI* 1 I, 180-1 (*DGE* 62; Uguzzoni–Ghinatti I) (f. Βορμίων, Ἀρκάς)
SICILY:
—AGYRION: (51) i BC Manganaro, *PdelP* forthcoming no. 5, 7 ([Φιλ]ώτας?: f. Ἀσσῖνος)
—SABUCINA (MOD.): (52) vi/v BC Arena, *Iscr. Sic.* II 105 (vase) (-λό-)

Φιλωτέρα
EPIROS: (1) m. iii BC Polyaen. viii 52 (m. Μίλων)
—BOUTHROTOS (PRASAIBOI): (2) a. 163 BC *IBouthrot* 14, 23; 18, 3; 21, 41; 31, 25 (*SEG* XXXVIII 471; 475; 478; 490); cf. Cabanes, *L'Épire* p. 406 (?m. Μεγανίκα); (3) ~ *IBouthrot* 14, 31 (*SEG* XXXVIII 471); (4) ~ *IBouthrot* 14, 37; 22, 5; 28, 13 (*SEG* XXXVIII 471; 479; 486) (?d. Νικάνωρ); (5) ~ *IBouthrot* 15, 4 (*SEG* XXXVIII 472); (6) ~ *IBouthrot* 18, 18 (*SEG* XXXVIII 475); (7) ~ *IBouthrot* 21, 3 (*SEG* XXXVIII 478); (8) ~ *IBouthrot* 24, 3; 25, 4 (*SEG* XXXVIII 482-3); (9) ~ *IBouthrot* 25, 27 (*SEG* XXXVIII 483); (10) ~ *IBouthrot* 29, 42 (*SEG* XXXVIII 487); (11) ~ *IBouthrot* 29, 54 (*SEG* XXXVIII 487); (12) ~ *IBouthrot* 30, 23; 40, 9 (*SEG* XXXVIII 488; 499); (13) ~ *IBouthrot* 30, 30 (*SEG* XXXVIII 488); (14) ~ *IBouthrot* 38, 5 (*SEG* XXXVIII 497); (15) ~ *IBouthrot* 42, 12 (*SEG* XXXVIII 501); (16) ~ *IBouthrot* 42, 5-6 (*SEG* XXXVIII 501); (17) ~ *IBouthrot* 50, 6, 11; (18) ~ ib. 99, 3 (*BCH* 118 (1994) p. 121 B)
—KASSOPE: (19) ii BC *AE* 1914, p. 238 no. 16 (d. Ἀνδρομένης); (20) ~ *SEG* XXXIV 590 (d. Παυσανίας)
LAKONIA:
—OITYLOS: (21) imp. *IG* V (1) 1305

Φιλωτία
ILLYRIA:
—EPIDAMNOS-DYRRHACHION: (1) iii BC *IDyrrh* 19 (d. Ἀρχέδαμος)
KERKYRA: (2) ii BC Unp. (*IG* arch.)

Φιλώτιον
EPIROS:
—BOUTHROTOS (PRASAIBOI): (1) a. 163 BC *IBouthrot* 21, 16 (*SEG* XXXVIII 478); (2) ~ *IBouthrot* 31, 95 (*SEG* XXXVIII 490); *IBouthrot* 51, 24

Φιλωτίς
AKARNANIA:
—PALAIROS: (1) f. iii BC *IG* IX (1)² (2) 474
ARGOLIS:
—ARGOS:
——Po-: (2) f. iii BC ib. IV (1) 529, 13-14
—EPIDAUROS: (3) m. iv BC *SEG* XXXV 310
EPIROS: (4) iii/ii BC Plb. xxxii 5. 13 (m. Χάροψ)
—AMBRAKIA: (5) v/iv BC *BCH* 79 (1955) p. 267 (d. Φίλων)
—BOUTHROTOS (PRASAIBOI): (6) a. 163 BC *IBouthrot* 19, 3 (*SEG* XXXVIII 476)
ILLYRIA:
—APOLLONIA: (7) imp. *IApoll* 196
ITHAKE: (8) hell. *IG* IX (1) 664
KERKYRA: (9) s. iv BC ib. II² 9015; (10) hell.? Fraser–Rönne, *BWGT* p. 111 no. 1
KORINTHIA:
—KORINTH: (11) iii-ii BC *SEG* XXVII 34 (d. Φιλωνίδας)
LEUKAS: (12) ii BC *AM* 27 (1902) p. 370 no. 48 a; (13) ~ ib. p. 371 no. 51; (14) ~ Unp. (*IG* arch.)

Φίμης
SICILY:
—PANORMOS: (1) f. i BC Cic., *In Verr.* II iii 93 (Lat. Diocles Phimes)

Φίνγρης
KORINTHIA:
—KORINTH: (1) c. 570-550 BC Amyx 88. 4 (vase) (Lorber 109) (-ρε̄ς: her.)

Φινέτα
EPIROS:
—AMBRAKIA: (1) hell. *SEG* XXXIX 523

Φίντας
MESSENIA: (1) viii BC *RE* (-) (s. Συβότας, f. Ἀντίοχος, Ἀνδροκλῆς)

Φιντέας
SICILY:
—KAMARINA: (1) ?ii BC *SEG* XXXIX 997, 7 (Cordano, 'Camarina VII' 162) ([Φι]ντέας: s. Μάχανος)

Φίντεια
ILLYRIA:
—BERAT (MOD.): (1) imp. Ugolini, *Alb. Ant.* 1 p. 192 no. 11 + *SEG* XXIII 488 (Φίνγε[ια]—Ugolini)

Φιντέρα
EPIROS:
—AMBRAKIA: (1) f. ii BC Unp. (Arta Mus., inscr.) (Φιντέρα?: d. Σωστρατίων)

LEUKAS: (2) inc. *JNG* 33 (1983) p. 14 n. 45 (coin graffito)

Φιντίας
EPIROS:
—TATARNA (MOD.): (1) hell.? Hammond, *Epirus* p. 738 no. 22
S. ITALY (BRUTTIUM):
—RHEGION: (2) hell.? *IG* XIV 2400. 19 (Landi, *DISMG* 33. 4 (tiles))
S. ITALY (CALABRIA):
—SATYRION*: (3) v/iv BC *LCS* p. 694 (vase) (Φιντ[ίας]—ed., Φιντ[ύλος]?, Φίντ[ων]?)
S. ITALY (LUCANIA):
—HERAKLEIA: (4) iv/iii BC *IGSI* 1 I, 168 (*DGE* 62; Uguzzoni–Ghinatti I) (s. Κρατῖνος)
SICILY:
—AKRAGAS: (5) iv/iii BC *RE* (2); Imhoof-Blümer, *MGr* pl. A. 16 (tyrant)
—KAMARINA: (6) f. v BC Cordano, *Tessere Pubbliche* 71 (f. Πασίφυγος); (7) hell. *SEG* XXXIX 1001, 7 (f. Ἀπολλώνιος)
—MORGANTINA: (8) ?iv/iii BC ib. 1008, 10 (f. Δείνων)
—SYRACUSE: (9) v/iv BC Dubois, *IGDS* 91 (vase); (10) f. iv BC *RE* (3); *FVS* 55
—SYRACUSE?:
——(Νητ.): (11) hell. Manganaro, *PdelP* forthcoming no. 4 II, 8 (s. Ἀγάθαρχος)
——(Ὑπα.): (12) hell. ib. V, 4 (s. Φιλωνίδας)
—TAUROMENION: (13) c. 184 BC *IG* XIV 421 an. 57 (*SGDI* 5219)

Φίντις
LEUKAS: (1) iv-iii BC *AM* 27 (1902) p. 366 no. 26
SICILY:
—SYRACUSE: (2) 468 BC Pi., *O.* vi 22

Φιντύλος
ILLYRIA:
—APOLLONIA: (1) a. 179 BC *Syll*³ 638 (*IDyrrh* 520); Kramolisch p. 54 A, 18 (date) (f. Λυσάνωρ)
S. ITALY (CALABRIA):
—TARAS-TARENTUM: (2) c. 280-272 BC Vlasto 720-31 (Evans, *Horsemen* p. 157 VII A.4 (coins))
SICILY:
—MEGARA HYBLAIA: (3) f. v BC Dubois, *IGDS* 25 (Arena, *Iscr. Sic.* I 12) (s. Εὔκριτος)
—SYRACUSE?:
——(Πλε.): (4) hell. *Mem. Linc.* 8 (1938) p. 127 no. 35. 5 (bullet) (*NScav* 1961, p. 349); cf. *BE* 1965, no. 502; cf. *L'Incidenza dell'Antico* p. 422 fig. 3 (s. Φίλιος)

Φιντώ
EPIROS?:
—ARRONOS: (1) 370-368 BC Cabanes, *L'Épire* p. 534 no. 1, 22

Φίντων
ACHAIA:
—DYME: (1) iii BC *AJPh* 31 (1910) p. 399 no. 74 b, 3 (s. Ἀφαιστίων, f. Ἀρίστων, Πιστίας)
ARGOLIS:
—HERMIONE: (2) iv/iii BC *HE* 2357 (s. Βαθυκλῆς)
ARKADIA:
—TEGEA: (3) s. iii BC *IG* V (2) 116, 2 (f. Δαμέας)
DALMATIA:
—ISSA:
——(Dymanes): (4) iv/iii BC Brunšmid p. 7, 23 (f. —τιμος)
——(Hylleis): (5) iv/iii BC ib. p. 8, 32 (Φ[ίντω]ν?, Φ[ίλω]ν—edd.: f. Πρωταγόρας); (6) ~ ib. p. 9, 55 (Φ[ί]ντων: s. Σωσθένης); (7) ~ ib. l. 63 (s. Δ—)
ILLYRIA:
—AMANTIA: (8) ii BC Ugolini, *Alb. Ant.* 1 p. 191 no. 9 (s. Ἀλέξανδρος)
—BYLLIONES BYLLIS: (9) hell. *Iliria* 1982 (1), p. 107 no. 20 = p. 121 no. 55 (tile); cf. p. 122

S. Italy (Bruttium):
—lokroi epizephyrioi: (10) i bc-i ad? Landi, DISMG 244, 2
——(Άγκ.): (11) iv/iii bc De Franciscis 20, 6 (s. Σωσίστρατος)
——(Θρα.): (12) iv/iii bc ib. 3, 7 (s. Ἡράκλητος)
——(Λογ.): (13) iv/iii bc ib. 2, 6; 7, 3 (f. Φιλόστρατος)
Sicily:
—akrai: (14) ?iii bc SGDI 3243 (Akrai p. 155 no. 5) (s. Φίλι—)
—gela-phintias?: (15) f. v bc Dubois, IGDS 134 b, 2 (Arena, Iscr. Sic. II 47) (-τōν)
—halountion: (16) i bc-i ad IG xiv 371 (Φ. Εὔμαχος)
—morgantina: (17) ?iv/iii bc SEG xxxix 1011, 5 (s. Λυκίσκος)

**Φιρμῖνος**
Sicily:
—syracuse: (1) iii-v ad Strazzulla 212 (Φυρμῖν[ος])

**Φίρμος**
Illyria:
—apollonia: (1) imp. IApoll 231 (Φύρ-)
Lakonia:
—sparta: (2) s. ii ad IG v (1) 46, 11 (Bradford (-)) (f. Μ. Ἀριστοκράτης)

**Φλαβιανή**
Korinthia:
—korinth: (1) ii ad SEG xli 273 B, 4 (d. Ξειναγόρης, m. Ἀριστομένης)

**Φλαβιανός**
Korinthia:
—korinth: (1) ii ad ib. 273 A, 3; 273 B, 1 (I f. Φλαβιανός II, Ξειναγόρης); (2) ~ ib. l. 2-3 (II s. Φλαβιανός I, Σαλβία (Thessaly), f. Μένανδρος)
S. Italy (Campania):
—neapolis: (3) iii-iv ad INap 259
Sicily:
—katane: (4) iii-v ad NScav 1915, p. 216

**Φλάβιος**
Arkadia:
—tegea: (1) i/ii ad IG v (2) 87 (s. Σωσικράτης)
Korinthia:
—korinth: (2) imp. SEG xxx 348 (lamp)
Sicily:
—syracuse: (3) iii-v ad Rend. Pont. 22 (1946-7) p. 234 no. 30 + Nuovo Didask. 6 (1956) p. 57 no. 12 (Φλάβι[ος])

**Φλαμινία**
Sicily:
—lipara: (1) ?iii ad Epigraphica 3 (1941) p. 270 no. 46 (-με-)

**Φλέβων**
Korinthia:
—korinth: (1) c. 600-575 bc IG iv (1) 234-6 (pinakes) (Lazzarini 62 and 270); LSAG² p. 131 no. 15 (date) (-βōν)

**Φλέγουσα**
S. Italy (Calabria):
—manduria*: (1) i ad Atti Conv. Taranto 12 (1972) p. 369 (Ann. Univ. Lecce 6 (1971-3) p. 69 no. 1) (Lat. Annia Flegusa: freed.)
S. Italy (Campania):
—dikaiarchia-puteoli*: (2) imp. CIL x 2649 (Lat. Phlegusa: freed.)

**Φλέγων**
Arkadia:
—tegea: (1) f. iii bc IG v (2) 42, 4 (s. Εὐ—); (2) f. ii bc ib. 44, 11 (Φλέγ[ων]: f. Εὔιδος)


Lakonia:
—sparta: (3) c. 220 ad SEG xxxiv 311, 8; BSA 79 (1984) pp. 267-9 (date) (Bradford (-)) (Ἀβί(διος) Φ.)
S. Italy (Campania):
—dikaiarchia-puteoli: (4) imp. CIL x 2892 (Lat. Phlegon)
—pompeii: (5) c. 51-62 ad ib. iv 3340. 92, 8 (Castrèn 365. 6) (Lat. L. Septumius Ph[leg]on)

**Φλογίδας**
Lakonia:
—sparta: (1) 405 bc FGrH 70 F 205 (Poralla² 733)

**Φλῶρα**
Sicily: (1) imp. Epigraphica 5-6 (1943-4) p. 93 (Φλôρα)

**Φλωρεντία**
Lakonia:
—asopos: (1) byz. IG v (1) 974 (Φλωρεντ(ί)α: m. Θεόδουλος)

**Φλωρέντιος**
Sicily: (1) imp. Epigraphica 5-6 (1943-4) p. 94

**Φοίβη**
Arkadia:
—mantineia-antigoneia: (1) imp. IG v (2) 283 (terracotta)
Dalmatia:
—tragurion: (2) imp. CIL iii 2696 (Lat. Pomp. Phyeba)
Illyria:
—apollonia: (3) ii ad IApoll 209 (Ἰουλία Φ.: d. Ἄκτη)
Korinthia:
—korinth kenchreai: (4) m. i ad Ep. Rom. 16. 1
S. Italy (Apulia):
—barion: (5) imp. CIL ix 292 (Lat. Caec. Phoebe)
—rubi: (6) i/ii ad Suppl. It. 5 p. 22 no. 4 (Lat. Phoebe: d. Crispia Ampliata)
S. Italy (Bruttium):
—rhegion: (7) ?f. v bc SEG iv 66 (Φοίβε̄ (n. pr.?): her.?)
S. Italy (Calabria):
—brentesion-brundisium*: (8) ?i-ii ad CIL ix 132 (Lat. Iulia Phoebe: freed.)
—taras-tarentum: (9) imp. NScav 1893, p. 254 no. 2 (Lat. Nemetoria Phoebe)
S. Italy (Campania):
—aequana*: (10) imp. ib. 1896, p. 332 (Lat. Phoebe: freed.)
—dikaiarchia-puteoli: (11) imp. CIL x 2467 (Lat. —abia Fybe); (12) ~ ib. 2908 (Lat. Rabiria Phoebe: m. Ὕμνος); (13) ?i-ii ad ib. 2202 (Lat. Claudia Phoebe)
—pompeii: (14) i bc-i ad ib. iv 5347-8 (Lat. Phoebe)
—salernum: (15) imp. IItal i (1) 38 (Lat. Baberia Phoebe(be): m. Ὕμνος)
Sicily:
—hykkara?: (16) iii-iv ad Kokalos 17 (1971) p. 184 (m. Τέρτις)

**Φοιβιανή**
S. Italy (Campania):
—dikaiarchia-puteoli: (1) imp. CIL x 3136 (Lat. Ulpia Phoe(b)iane)

**Φοιβιανός**
S. Italy (Apulia):
—luceria (nr.): (1) imp. ib. ix 938 (Lat. Phoebianus)
S. Italy (Campania):
—dikaiarchia-puteoli: (2) imp. ib. x 3029 (Lat. Cn. Saenius Phoebianus)


**Φοιβίας**
Sicily:
—syracuse: (1) imp. IG xiv 52

**Φοιβίδας**
Lakonia:
—sparta: (1) c. 420-378 bc RE (-) (Poralla² 734) (f. Ἰσάδας); (2) ?i bc SEG xi 846 (Bradford (2)) (f. Πολυδάμας); (3) c. 1-10 ad IG v (1) 209, 28; SEG xxxv 331 (date) (Bradford (3)) (f. Στέφανος); (4) c. 140 ad IG v (1) 128, 12 (Bradford (1)) (Δεκούμιος Φ.)

**Φοῖβις**
Lakonia:
—sparta: (1) 227 bc Plu., Cleom. 8 (Bradford (-))

**Φοιβίων**
Lakonia:
—sparta: (1) i bc-i ad IG v (1) 652, 5 (Bradford (-)) (s. Φιλόστρατος)
Messenia:
—korone: (2) 246 ad IG v (1) 1398, 53 (Αὐρ. Φ.)
S. Italy (Campania):
—dikaiarchia-puteoli: (3) imp. CIL x 2967 (Lat. Q. Sosius Foebio); (4) ?i-ii ad ib. 2587 (Lat. Iunius Phoebion)

**Φοῖβος**
Arkadia:
—tegea: (1) 165 ad IG v (2) 50, 23 (s. Μόσχος)
Elis: (2) 141-145 ad IvOl 95, 5 (Λ. Καικίλιος Φ. [ὁ] καὶ Ἔφηβος: T.)
Lakonia:
—sparta: (3) c. 120-135 ad IG v (1) 34, 2; SEG xi 579, 8; 582, [7] (Bradford (2)) (Φο(ί)βος—IG: f. Σέξ. Οὔλπ. Σεβῆρος); (4) c. 221 ad IG v (1) 541, 7; BSA 79 (1984) pp. 270-3 (date) (Bradford (1)) (Μ. Αὐρ. Φ.: s. Νικα—)
S. Italy (Apulia):
—barion: (5) imp. CIL ix 290 (Lat. M. Appale(nus) Phoebus: s. Ἀπφιάς)
—canusium: (6) i ad Epig. Rom. di Canosa Add. 24 (Lat. [Ph]oebus)
—luceria: (7) imp. CIL ix 875 (Lat. Petronius Phoebus)
S. Italy (Calabria):
—brentesion-brundisium: (8) imp. ib. 146 (Lat. M. Mussienius Phoebus)
S. Italy (Campania):
—dikaiarchia-puteoli: (9) imp. ib. x 1948 (Lat. Phoebus); (10) ~ ib. 2849 (Lat. Phoebus); (11) ?i-ii ad ib. 3036, 5 (Lat. L. Octavius Phoebus); (12) 112 ad ib. 1633 (NScav 1896, p. 296) (Lat. L. Plutius Phoebus)
—herculaneum: (13) i bc-i ad CIL iv 10676 (Lat. Phoebus); (14) m. i ad PdelP 3 (1948) p. 173 no. 17 (Lat. Q. Festus Phoebus); (15) ~ ib. 6 (1951) p. 227 no. 9, 12 (9 (1954) p. 55 no. 60) (Lat. C. Iulius Phoebus)
—herculaneum*: (16) c. 50-75 ad CIL x 1403 a III, 6 (Lat. L. Venuleius Phoebus: freed.)
—kyme: (17) imp. NScav 1891, p. 235 (Lat. Hosidius Phoebus)
—misenum: (18) ?i-ii ad De Franciscis, Sacello Augustali p. 47 (Lat. C. Iulius Phoebus)
—neapolis: (19) imp. NScav 1894, p. 173 (Lat. Phoebus)
—pompeii: (20) i bc-i ad CIL iv 1701 (Castrèn 184. 1) (Lat. M. Geminius Phoebus); (21) ~ CIL iv 1850 (Lat. Phoebus); (22) ~ ib. 2182 (Lat. Phoeb[us] ?= (23); (23) ~ ib. 2184 (Lat. Phoebus) ?= (22); (24) ~ ib.; 2194; 2207; 2248 (Lat. Phoebus); (25) ~ ib. 2194 (Lat. Phoebus); (26) ~ ib. 2949; 2310 a; 2141; 2949 (Lat. Phoebus); (27) ~ ib. 4514, 4 (Lat. Phoebus); (28) ~ ib. 4774 (Lat. Phoebus); (29) ~ ib. 4856 (Lat. Phoebus); (30) ~ ib. 4923 (Lat.

Phoebus); **(31)** ~ ib. 4940 (Lat. Phoebus); **(32)** ~ ib. 10143 (Lat. Phoebus); **(33)** ~ ib. x 8058. 66 (seal) (Lat. Phoebus); **(34)** ?55 AD ib. IV 3340. 18, 7 (Castrèn 190. 16) (Lat. M. Helvius Phoebus); **(35)** 70-79 AD *CIL* IV 103; Mouritsen p. 110 (date) (Lat. Phoebus); **(36)** ~ *CIL* IV 785; x 849 (Castrèn 81. 20) (Lat. L. Caecilius Phoebus)

—STABIAE: **(37)** imp. *RAAN* 19 (1938-9) p. 86 (Lat. Phoebus)

SICILY: **(38)** imp. *CIL* x 8045. 20 (tile) (Lat. C. Satrius Phoebus)

**Φοινίκη**
S. ITALY (CAMPANIA):
—DIKAIARCHIA-PUTEOLI: **(1)** imp. ib. 2343 (Lat. Lucceia Finice)

**Φοινικίδας**
ACHAIA: **(1)** 146 BC *IG* IV (1)² 28, 82 (f. Δαμοχάρης: synoikos)

**Φοινικίδης**
AKARNANIA:
—OINIADAI: **(1)** iii/ii BC ib. IX (1)² (2) 419. 5 (Οἰνικίδης—ed., Φ.—*LGPN*); **(2)** ~ ib. 419. 11

**Φοῖνιξ**
AIGINA: **(1)** f. v BC ib. IV (1) 55-6; *LSAG²* p. 113 no. 10 (date) (n. pr.?: ?f. Εὐρύμαχος, Μενεκράτης)
AKARNANIA:
—OINIADAI: **(2)** v/iv BC Hp., *Epid.* v 4; *Abh-MainzAk* 1982 (9) p. 35 (locn.) (or Thessaly?)
ARGOLIS:
—ARGOS: **(3)** c. 458 BC *IG* I³ 1149, 67
——kaion (Lykotadai): **(4)** a. 316 BC *Mnem.* NS 43 (1915) pp. 375-6 F, 3 (Perlman A.7); *Hesp.* 21 (1952) p. 217 (locn.) (Φοῖν[ι]ξ)
S. ITALY (CAMPANIA):
—DIKAIARCHIA-PUTEOLI: **(5)** 38 AD Camodeca, *L'Archivio Puteolano* 1 p. 143 no. 1 (Lat. T. Vestorius Phoenix)
—POMPEII: **(6)** i BC-i AD *CIL* IV 9850; cf. *Epigraphica* 30 (1968) p. 123 (Lat. Phoenix)
SICILY:
—AKRAGAS: **(7)** ?v BC Call. fr. 64, 6
—KATANE: **(8)** imp. *CIL* x 7065 (Lat. Foenix)
—SELINOUS: **(9)** f. v BC Dubois, *IGDS* 38, 15 (Arena, *Iscr. Sic.* I 63) (s. Καίλιος) ?= (10); **(10)** ~ Dubois, *IGDS* 38, 18 (Arena, *Iscr. Sic.* I 63) (f. Ἄπελος, Τίτελος) ?= (9)

**Φοίνισσα**
AIGINA: **(1)** ii BC *IG* IV (1) 13 (d. Ἐρίτιμος)
ARGOLIS:
—PHLEIOUS: **(2)** i BC/i AD ib. 453

**Φοῖσκος**
EPIROS:
—DODONA: **(1)** iii BC Antoniou, *Dodone* Ba, 40

**Φολύνδας**
EPIROS:
—DODONA: **(1)** iii BC ib. Aa, 10

**Φονδάνιος**
ILLYRIA:
—APOLLONIA: **(1)** i BC Maier 158 (coin) (money.)

**Φοντειανός**
S. ITALY (CAMPANIA):
—NEAPOLIS: **(1)** iii-iv AD *INap* 235

**Φόξος**
AKARNANIA:
—ASTAKOS: **(1)** ii BC *IG* IX (1)² (2) 435, 5 (s. Σωτίων)

**Φορβάδας**
EPIROS:
—AMBRAKIA: **(1)** s. iv BC ib. IV (1)² 95, 81 (Perlman E.2; *REG* 84 (1971) p. 355); *SEG* XXIII 189 I, 10; Perlman pp. 46-9 (date) (Κορράδας—*IG* per err.)

**Φόρμις**
ARKADIA:
—MAINALIOI: **(1)** f. v BC Paus. v 27. 1-2, 7 (and Sicily Syracuse)
SICILY:
—SYRACUSE: **(2)** f. v BC *RE* (-); *CGF* I p. 148 (Φόρμος—*Suda*)

**Φορμίσκος**
ACHAIA:
—DYME: **(1)** ?145 BC Sherk 43, 21; *SEG* XXXVIII 372 (date) ([Φορ]μίσκος?, [Δα]μίσκος?: s. Ἐχεσθένης)
EPIROS:
—ANTIGONEIA: **(2)** f. ii BC Cabanes, *L'Épire* p. 552 no. 29 (s. Φι—)
—DODONA: **(3)** iii BC Antoniou, *Dodone* Ab, 19 (Φορμίσκος); **(4)** ~ ib. Ba, 8; **(5)** ii BC *SEG* XXXIII 477 (tile) ([Φορ]μίσκος, [Λα]μίσκος?)
—MOLOSSOI: **(6)** hell. Cabanes, *L'Épire* p. 584 no. 63, 2, 7 (*SEG* XXVI 705) (s. Βοῖσκος, Δαμναγόρα)

**Φορμίων**
AKARNANIA: **(1)** 338 BC Osborne, *Naturalization* D 16, 8; **(2)** ~ ib. l. 15-16, 20
—OINIADAI: **(3)** ?iii BC *IG* IX (1)² (2) 423 (s. Θυΐων)
ARGOLIS:
—ARGOS: **(4)** 243-240 BC *PP* 2547 (Ἑρμίων—ed. pr.)
ELIS: **(5)** m. iv BC *RE* (7)
EPIROS:
—BOUTHROTOS (PRASAIBOI): **(6)** a. 163 BC *IBouthrot* 29, 29 (*SEG* XXXVIII 487) (f. Λυκίσκα)
LAKONIA: **(7)** arch.? Clem. Al., *Strom.* i 133. 2 (Poralla² 735) (dub.)
LEUKAS: **(8)** c. 350-250 BC Postolakas p. 70 no. 717; *NZ* 10 (1878) p. 22 n. 22 (coins)
S. ITALY (BRUTTIUM):
—LOKROI EPIZEPHYRIOI:
——(Λακ.): **(9)** iv/iii BC De Franciscis 39, 2 (s. Μένων)
——(Σωτ.): **(10)** iv/iii BC ib. 2, 5 (s. Ζώιππος)
SICILY:
—HALOUNTION: **(11)** i BC-i AD? *IG* XIV 370 (*IGLMP* 42) (f. Ὄρθων)

**Φόρμος**
AKARNANIA:
—ANAKTORION: **(1)** ?354 BC Tod, *GHI* II 160, 8
ARGOLIS:
—EPIDAUROS*: **(2)** c. 370-365 BC Peek, *IAEpid* 52 B, 59

**Φόρνιος**
S. ITALY (CAMPANIA):
—NEAPOLIS: **(1)** imp. *IG* XIV 816 (*INap* 179) (s. Ἀπολλοφάνης)

**Φορτουνᾶτα**
KEPHALLENIA:
—SAME: **(1)** imp. Fraser–Rönne, *BWGT* p. 117 no. 5 ([Φορτ]ουνᾶτα)
SICILY:
—SYRACUSE: **(2)** iii-v AD *IG* XIV 184 (Strazzulla 121; Wessel 1371); cf. *Riv. Arch. Crist.* 18 (1941) p. 165 no. 25

**Φορτουνατίων**
SICILY:
—AKRILLAI: **(1)** iii/iv AD *Journ. Glass Stud.* 2 (1960) p. 74 (Libertini, *Mus. Arch. Sirac.* p. 48 (glass)) (Φουρ-)

**Φορτουνᾶτος**
ARKADIA:
—TEGEA: **(1)** 165 AD *IG* v (2) 50, 6 (f. Ἀφροδίσιος)
KORINTHIA:
—KORINTH?: **(2)** m. i AD *1 Ep. Cor.* 16. 17
KYNOURIA:
—EUA?: **(3)** m. ii AD *SEG* XXXV 292 (f. Ἀντιοχίς)
SICILY:
—SYRACUSE: **(4)** iii-v AD *IG* XIV 185 (Strazzulla 143; Wessel 836) (Φουρτων[ᾶ]τος)

**Φορτούνις**
SICILY:
—SYRACUSE: **(1)** iii-v AD Strazzulla 396 (Wessel 1337); cf. Ferrua, *NG* 147 (Φροτούνης)

**Φόρυς**
ELIS:
—OLYMPIA*: **(1)** vi BC *IvOl* 717; cf. *Syll³* 1070; cf. *Riv. Fil.* NS 16 (1938) p. 166 f. (Φό[λ]α—*IvOl*, Φόρυ[ος]—*Syll*, Φωκίω[ν]ο[ς]—*Riv. Fil.*: f. Βύβων)

**Φόσυρος**
ELIS: **(1)** c. 50 BC *SEG* XXXVII 388, 7 (f. Λεόντιχος)

**Φουλακίων**
LAKONIA:
—SPARTA: **(1)** c. 125 AD ib. XI 575, 12 (Bradford (2)) (I f. Φουλακίων II); **(2)** ~ *SEG* XI 575, 12 (Bradford (1)) (II s. Φουλακίων I)

**Φουνδανία**
ILLYRIA:
—APOLLONIA: **(1)** imp. *IApoll* 166 (d. Ὠφελίων)

**Φουρία**
SICILY:
—AKRAI: **(1)** imp. *Akrai* p. 165 no. 32
—SYRACUSE: **(2)** imp. *IG* XIV 53

**Φοῦσκος**
SICILY:
—SYRACUSE: **(1)** iii-v AD Strazzulla 285 (Wessel 722); cf. Ferrua, *NG* 52

**Φραάτης**
S. ITALY (CALABRIA):
—HYRIA: **(1)** i/ii AD *Misc. Gr. Rom.* 3 p. 220 (Lat. T. Flavius Phrates: f. C. Avius Rufus)

**Φράδιος**
SICILY:
—SYRACUSE: **(1)** iii-v AD Strazzulla 298; cf. Ferrua, *NG* 60 (Φρά(σ)ιος?, (Ἀ)ράδιος?—Ferrua)

**Φράδμων**
ARGOLIS:
—ARGOS: **(1)** m. v BC *RE* (-); *SEG* XXIV 387, 6 (sculptor); **(2)** iv-iii BC Unp. (Ch. Kritzas) (Φ(ρ)άδμων)

**Φραιαρίδας**
ARGOLIS:
—MYKENAI: **(1)** ?c. 500-480 BC *IG* IV (1) 492, 1; *LSAG²* p. 174 no. 2 (date) (Φραhι-)

**Φρασιάδας**
S. ITALY (BRUTTIUM):
—LOKROI EPIZEPHYRIOI: **(1)** ?c. 500-480 BC Lazzarini 195 (Landi, *DISMG* 59); *LSAG²* p. 286 no. 4 (date)

**Φρασιαρίδας**
ARKADIA:
—MEGALOPOLIS: **(1)** c. 185 BC *Milet* I (3) 148, 19; *Chiron* 19 (1989) pp. 279 ff. (date)

**Φρασίδαμος**
MESSENIA:
—MESSENE?: **(1)** ii/i BC *SEG* XI 979, 32

**Φρασίδας**
Argolis:
—epidauros*: (1) c. 315-300 bc Peek, *IAEpid*
49, 1 (Φρασί[δ]ας)
S. Italy (Bruttium):
—sybaris-thourioi-copiae: (2) c. 356-355
bc *IG* iv (1)² 95, 43 (Perlman E.2); Perlman
p. 40 f. (date) (s. Φάϋλλος)

**Φρασίλας**
S. Italy (Bruttium):
—lokroi epizephyrioi:
——(Ἀγφ.): (1) 277 bc De Franciscis 8, 3; 31, 3
(f. Ὀναῖος)
——(Θρα.): (2) iv/iii bc ib. 32, 7 (s. Φιλιστίων)

**Φράσιλλος**
S. Italy (Lucania):
—herakleia: (1) s. iv bc *FD* iii (4) 390, 1

**Φρασισθένης**
Aigina: (1) imp. *IG* iv (1) 46
Argolis:
—troizen: (2) iii bc ib. 824, 3 (f. Μενεκράτης);
(3) ?146 bc ib. 757 A, 43

**Φράστης**
S. Italy (Campania):
—pompeii: (1) i bc-i ad *CIL* iv 4909 (Lat.
Phrastes)

**Φραστορίδας**
Achaia:
—pellene: (1) iv bc *Eretria* vi 180 (s. Ἀκήρατος)

**Φράστος**
S. Italy (Campania):
—pompeii: (1) i bc-i ad *CIL* iv 5393; 5414
(Lat. Phrastos)

**Φράστωρ**
Sicily:
—syracuse:
——(Ἑριμεῖος): (1) iv bc Manganaro, *PdelP*
forthcoming no. 3, 8 (s. Θεύπομπος)

**Φράσων**
Epiros:
—embesos (mod.): (1) ii bc *AD* 22 (1967)
Chron. p. 321 (f. Ἐχεκράτης)

**Φρίκινα**
Illyria:
—bylliones (cakran (mod.)): (1) iii-ii. bc
*SEG* xxxviii 547

**Φρικίνας**
Akarnania:
—medion: (1) c. 325-315 bc *Hesp.* 57 (1988)
p. 148 A, 45 (*SEG* xxxvi 331); cf. *Hesp.* 48
(1979) pp. 78 f. with pl. 22 c (s. Νικήρατος)

**Φρῖκος**
Aitolia:
—kalydon: (1) iii/ii bc *IG* ix (1)² (1) 136, 9
Argolis:
—epidauros:
——Mysias: (2) c. 365-335 bc ib. iv (1)² 103,
129

**Φρικύλος**
Illyria:
—gurezeze (mod.): (1) hell. *Iliria* 1982 (1), p.
104 no. 4 = p. 121 no. 56 (tile)

**Φρίκων**
Aitolia: (1) ?271 bc *Syll*³ 419, 2
—pleuron: (2) i bc-i ad *IG* ix (2) 401 (*RÉnip*
100) (s. Καλλίστρατος)

Argolis:
—epidauros*: (3) c. 370-365 bc *IG* iv (1)²
102, 60, 224, 236, 298 + *SEG* xxv 383, 81,
207; Peek, *IAEpid* 52 A, 16-17, 77

**Φρίξος**
Lakonia:
—sparta: (1) 369 bc Plu., *Ages.* 32 (Poralla²
736)
Sicily:
—lipara: (2) hell.? *IG* xiv 385 + *SEG* xxxiv
958 ([Φ]ρίξ[ος]: f. Ἀδείμαντος)

**Φρονήσιον**
Argolis:
—epidauros: (1) iii ad Peek, *NIEpid* 88, 3
([Φρο]νήσιον?)

**Φρόνησις**
Epiros:
—bouthrotos: (1) iii-ii bc *IBouthrot* 172
(Ugolini, *Alb. Ant.* 3 p. 118)
S. Italy (Apulia):
—canusium*: (2) i ad *Epig. Rom. di Canosa*
Add. 10 (*Mus. Arch. di Bari* p. 165 no. 14)
(Lat. Tutoria Phronesis: freed.)

**Φρονίκας**
Illyria:
—epidamnos-dyrrhachion: (1) imp. *IDyrrh*
382 (Φρονίκα (gen.?): ?f. Σύρα)

**Φρονιμᾶς**
Arkadia:
—tegea: (1) ii ad *IG* v (2) 55, 92 (f. Ἰσᾶς)

**Φρόνιμος**
S. Italy (Campania):
—dikaiarchia-puteoli: (1) imp. *CIL* x 3014
(Lat. T. Hordion. Phronim(us): freed.)
—pompeii: (2) i bc-i ad ib. iv 1484; cf. p. 208
(Lat. Phronim[u]s); (3) ~ ib. 3092 (Lat. Pro-
nimus); (4) ~ ib. 8337 (Lat. Phronimus); (5)
34 ad ib. x 901, 1; 902, 1 (Lat. [Phroni]mus,
Phr[onimus]); (6) 55 ad ib. iv 3340. 14, 18;
24, 13; 43, 17; 50, 8 etc (Castrèn 251. 8) (Lat.
A. Messius Phronimus: freed.)

**Φροντίδας**
S. Italy (Calabria):
—taras-tarentum: (1) f. iv bc Iamb., *VP* 267
(*FVS* 1 p. 446); *RE* s.v. Photidas (-) ?= (Φωτίδας (1))

**Φροντίς**
S. Italy (Campania):
—dikaiarchia-puteoli: (1) imp. *CIL* x 2882
(Lat. Pontia Frontis)

**Φρουκτῶσος**
S. Italy (Campania):
—neapolis: (1) iii-iv ad *IG* xiv 826. 48 (*INap*
260)

**Φρουνίλος?**
Illyria:
—epidamnos-dyrrhachion: (1) hell.-imp.
*IDyrrh* 243 (Φ[ρο?]υνίλος?: f. Θεοδωρίδας)

**Φρουραρχίδας**
Lakonia:
—sparta: (1) f. iv bc Paus. ix 13. 5 (Poralla²
737)

**Φρουρίδας**
Argolis:
—troizen: (1) ?146 bc *IG* iv (1) 757 B, 37 (s.
Ἀρίσταιχμος)

**Φρυγία**
Argolis:
—argos: (1) iii bc *SEG* xiv 318

**Φρύγιλλος**
Korinthia:
—korinth: (1) hell.? *BMC Corinth* p. 22 no.
226 (coin graffito); *JNG* 33 (1983) p. 14
(name); *Essays S. Robinson* pp. 127; 139
(date) (Φρύγι(λλος)?, Φρυγί(ας)?)
S. Italy (Bruttium):
—sybaris-thourioi-copiae: (2) 425-400 bc
*SNG Oxford* 903 (coin) (Φρύ(γιλλος)?) ?= (4)
Sicily:
—syracuse?: (3) v bc *HN*² p. 175; *Samml.
Ludwig* 460; Boardman, *Gems* p. 200 fig. 529
(coin); (4) ~ *RE* (-) ?= (2)

**Φρύγιος**
S. Italy (Campania):
—pompeii: (1) i bc-i ad *CIL* iv 1975 a (Lat.
Phrygius)

**Φρύνα**
Sicily:
—herbessos: (1) f. v bc Dubois, *IGDS* 167
(vase) (Arena, *Iscr. Sic.* ii 119)

**Φρύνεος**
Epiros:
—ambrakia: (1) s. iv bc Unp. (Arta Mus., inscr.) (Φ. (nom.?): s. Εὔστρατος)

**Φρύνη**
S. Italy (Campania):
—abella*: (1) inc. *NScav* 1928, p. 383 no. 2
(Lat. Orfia Phryne: freed.)

**Φρυνίδας**
Sicily:
—zankle-messana: (1) ?ii bc *IG* xiv 401, 4
(-νεί-: s. Τείσανδρος)

**Φρυνίκα**
Illyria:
—epidamnos-dyrrhachion: (1) hell. *IDyrrh*
55 (nom./gen.?)

**Φρῦνις**
Lakonia: (1) 413 bc Th. viii 6. 4 (Poralla² 738)
S. Italy (Lucania):
—poseidonia-paestum: (2) f. iv bc *RVP* p.
65 no. 19 (vase) (fict.)
Sicily:
—selinous: (3) f. v bc Dubois, *IGDS* 33, 3
(Arena, *Iscr. Sic.* i 67)
—tauromenion: (4) c. 237 bc *IG* xiv 421 an.
4 (*SGDI* 5219); (5) c. 231 bc *IG* xiv 421 an.
10 (*SGDI* 5219) (s. Διονύσιος); (6) c. 198 bc
*IG* xiv 421 an. 43 (*SGDI* 5219) (f. Ὄλυμπις);
(7) c. 191 bc *IG* xiv 421 an. 50 (*SGDI* 5219);
(8) c. 181-149 bc *IG* xiv 421 an. 60; 421
an. 80; 421 an. 90 (*SGDI* 5219); *IGSI* 4 III
(IV), 52 an. 92 (s. Ἀπολλόδωρος, f. Ἀπολλόδωρος); (9) c. 171 bc *IG* xiv 421 an. 70 (*SGDI*
5219) (I f. Φρῦνις II); (10) ~ *IG* xiv 421 an. 70
(*SGDI* 5219) (II s. Φρῦνις I); (11) c. 155-148
bc *IG* xiv 421 an. 93 (*SGDI* 5219); *IGSI*
4 III (IV), 5 an. 86 (I f. Φρῦνις II); (12) ~
*IG* xiv 421 an. 93 (*SGDI* 5219); *IGSI* 4 III
(IV), 5 an. 86 (II s. Φρῦνις I); (13) f. i bc ib.
5 II, 5; 6 III, 6, [19], 30; 5 IV, 10; 6 I, 2; 6
II, 1; 6 III, 6, 24; 6 IV, 5, 25; 7 I, 1, 16, 31;
7 II 11, 26; 8 I, 17; 8 II, 7, 20; 9 I, [2]; 9 II,
14; 10 I, 7, 15, 24, 32; 10 II, 23; 11 II, 19;
12 I, 37; 12 II, 36; 12 III, 31; *SEG* xxxviii
973 A; *Cron. Arch.* 3 (1964) pp. 42 ff. I, 10;
II, 11; III, 9, 39; IV, 18, 34; (14) c. 40 bc ib.
p. 54 I, 21 (I f. Φρῦνις II); (15) ~ ib. l. 21 (II
s. Φρῦνις I)
——(Ἀσσιπ.): (16) ?ii/i bc *IGSI* 4 III (IV), 102
D an. 6 (s. Ὄλυμπις)
——(Δαμ.): (17) ?ii/i bc *IG* xiv 421 D an. 1
(*SGDI* 5219) (I f. Φρῦνις II); (18) ~ *IG* xiv
421 D an. 1 (*SGDI* 5219) (Φρῦ(ν)ις: II s. Φρῦνις I); (19) ~ *IGSI* 4 III (IV), 139 D an. 8 (f.
Ἀπολλόδωρος); (20) ii/i bc ib. 7 I 22 (I f. Φρῦνις
II); (21) ~ ib. (II s. Φρῦνις I)
——(Σπαρ.): (22) ?ii/i bc ib. 4 III (IV), 139 D
an. 8 (s. Φιλιστίων)

**Φρυνίσκα**
EPIROS:
—BOUTHROTOS (PRASAIBOI):
——Cherrioi: (1) a. 163 BC IBouthrot 98, 5

**Φρυνίσκος**
ACHAIA: (1) 400 BC X., An. vii 2. 1; vii 2. 29 etc.
ELIS: (2) iv BC SEG XV 241, 5
S. ITALY (BRUTTIUM):
—LOKROI EPIZEPHYRIOI:
——(Ἀλχ.): (3) iv/iii BC De Franciscis 12, 6 (f. Νικασικράτης)

**Φρύνιχος**
AKARNANIA:
—ALYZIA: (1) imp. IG IX (1)² (2) 448 (Φρύνιχ[ος?], Φρυνιχ[ίδης?]—ed.)
EPIROS:
—BOUTHROTOS (PRASAIBOI): (2) a. 163 BC IBouthrot 17, 33 (SEG XXXVIII 474) (f. Σατύρα); (3) ~ IBouthrot 25, 15 (SEG XXXVIII 483); IBouthrot 30, 48; cf. SEG XXXVIII 499, 27; (4) ~ IBouthrot 130, 7 (s. Σωσίπατρος) ?= (6)
——Ancheropaioi: (5) a. 163 BC ib. 30, 1; 32, 1 (SEG XXXVIII 488; 491) (s. Σωσίπατρος) ?= (6); (6) ~ IBouthrot 116, 11 (BCH 118 (1994) p. 121 A) ?= (4) (5)
KEPHALLENIA:
—PALE: (7) iii/ii BC Unp. (IG arch.) (Φρύνι[χ]ο[ς])
S. ITALY (CALABRIA):
—TARAS-TARENTUM: (8) iv BC Iamb., VP 267 (FVS 1 p. 446); (9) iv-iii BC Wuilleumier, Tarente p. 723 s.v. (terracotta) (Φρύνιχ[ος])
S. ITALY (CAMPANIA):
—POMPEII: (10) i BC-i AD CIL IV 7941; 9112 (Lat. Prunicus)

**Φρυνίων**
AKARNANIA:
—THYRREION: (1) ii/i BC IG IX (1)² (2) 256, 8
ARGOLIS:
—PHLEIOUS: (2) f. iv BC Pl., Ep. ix 358b (f. Ἐχεκράτης)
EPIROS:
—AMBRAKIA: (3) hell. SEG XXXIX 523 (s. Ἀγήσανδρος)
—BOUTHROTOS (PRASAIBOI): (4) a. 163 BC IBouthrot 43, 32 (SEG XXXVIII 502) (f. Διονύσιος)
ILLYRIA:
—APOLLONIA: (5) ii-i BC IApoll 167
—EPIDAMNOS-DYRRHACHION: (6) c. 250-50 BC Maier 95; 397-8 (Ceka 149?; 151; 241; 403); IApoll Ref. Bibl. n. 109 (coin) ((Φρυ)νίωνος (gen.)—403; pryt.)
KEPHALLENIA:
—SAME: (7) c. 230-200 BC BCH 45 (1921) p. 14 II, 141 (s. Τιμόμαχος)
LEUKAS: (8) ii BC AM 27 (1902) p. 370 no. 46
S. ITALY (BRUTTIUM):
—LOKROI EPIZEPHYRIOI:
——(Ψαθ.): (9) iv/iii BC De Franciscis 32, 4 (f. Γνάθις)

**Φρῦνος**
AKARNANIA:
—THYRREION: (1) iii-ii BC SEG XXVII 159, 5; cf. PAE 1977, pl. 244 a (f. Σώσανδρος)
EPIROS:
—ORESTOI: (2) ?c. 370-344 BC Cabanes, L'Épire p. 536 no. 2, 13
ILLYRIA:
—EPIDAMNOS-DYRRHACHION: (3) c. 250-50 BC Maier 399 (coin) (Ceka 242; 345) (pryt.)
S. ITALY (BRUTTIUM):
—LOKROI EPIZEPHYRIOI: (4) v BC IG XIV 632 (bronze) (Landi, DISMG 65)

SICILY:
—KAMARINA: (5) iv/iii BC Dubois, IGDS 122, 3 (Φ(ρ)ῦνος: f. Ἀπολλωνίδας)
—MORGANTINA: (6) iv/iii BC SEG XXXIX 1013, 5 (s. Εὐκλείδας)

**Φρύνων**
AKARNANIA:
—STRATOS: (1) iv/iii BC IG IX (1)² (2) 395, 11 (s. Περικλῆς)
EPIROS:
—AMBRAKIA: (2) f. iii BC Unp. (Arta Mus., inscr.) (f. Σατύρα)
—KASSOPE: (3) c. 130 BC Dakaris, Kassope p. 25 (SEG XXXVI 555); cf. SEG XLI 541 (f. Φιλώτας)
ITHAKE: (4) hell.-imp. AM 27 (1902) p. 376 no. 59 (f. Κλεομήδης)
SICILY:
—LEONTINOI: (5) ?f. v BC Paus. v 22. 7

**Φρύξ**
KORINTHIA:
—KORINTH: (1) c. 610-590 BC Amyx 18. 10 (vase) (Lorber 28); LSAG² p. 131 no. 9 (date); (2) c. 570-550 BC Amyx 102. 9 (vase) (Lorber 91) (her.?)
S. ITALY (CAMPANIA):
—POMPEII: (3) i BC-i AD CIL IV 8902 (Lat. Pryx)

**Φρύσκανος**
EPIROS:
—DODONA: (1) iii BC Antoniou, Dodone Aa, 18

**Φύγων**
ARGOLIS:
—TROIZEN: (1) 362-361 BC CID II 1 I, 32; 4 I, 11

**Φυκιάδας**
S. ITALY (BRUTTIUM):
—KROTON: (1) iv BC Iamb., VP 267 (FVS 1 p. 446)

**Φυλακίδας**
AIGINA: (1) f. v BC Pi., I. v, 18, 60; vi, 7, 57; cf. Klee p. 90 nos. 45 and 48; p. 100 no. 39 (s. Λάμπων)
ARGOLIS:
—ARGOS: (2) m. v BC Peek, NIEpid 10 (f. Φιλόξενος)
—EPIDAUROS*: (3) c. 370-360 BC BSA 61 (1966) p. 272 no. 4 B II, 4; (4) c. 365-335 BC IG IV (1)² 103, 50
KORINTHIA:
—KORINTH: (5) a. 324 BC CID II 120 A, 38; 122 I, 12 (s. Λέων)

**Φύλακος**
ARKADIA:
—ORCHOMENOS: (1) ?c. 369-361 BC BCH 102 (1978) p. 347, 16 (IPArk 14) (her.?)
LAKONIA:
—SPARTA: (2) c. 560 BC Stibbe, Lakonische Vasenmaler p. 117 (or Cyrenaica Cyrene?: n. pr.?: dub.)
SICILY:
—MORGANTINA: (3) ?iv/iii BC SEG XXXIX 1011, 5 (Φύλαϙ[ος])

**Φύλαξ**
AITOLIA:
—KALYDON: (1) 162-135 BC IG IX (1)² (1) p. LII, s.a. 162 BC, 155 BC, 149 BC, 142 BC; 137, 37; IX (1)² (3) 639. 7, 2 (s. Πανταλέων)
—KALYDON?: (2) c. 225-200 BC Corinth VIII (3) 37, 7 (SEG XXV 325)
—PLEURON: (3) c. 210 BC IG IX (1)² (1) 31, 81, 87 (s. Πανταλέων)

S. ITALY (APULIA):
—TEANUM APULUM*: (4) imp. Teanum Apulum p. 57 no. 6 (CIL IX 704) (Lat. Q. Muttienus Phylax)
S. ITALY (CAMPANIA):
—POMPEII: (5) 2 BC ib. X 890, 1 (Castrèn 434. 15) (Lat. A. Veius Phylax)

**Φύλαρχος**
SICILY:
—HALOUNTION: (1) 72-70 BC RE (2) (Lat. Phylarchus)
—KAMARINA: (2) ?iv/iii BC SEG XXXIX 1001, 9 (Φ[ί]λ[α]ρχος—ed., Φ[ύ]λ[α]ρχος—LGPN: s. Ἄνταλλος)
—KENTORIPA: (3) 70 BC Cic., In Verr. II iv 50 (Lat. Phylarchus)

**Φυλεύς**
MESSENIA: (1) viii BC Paus. iv 13, 5; RE (5)

**Φύλλαρος**
ACHAIA:
—DYME: (1) s. iii BC SEG XIII 278, 23 (f. Σατυρίων)

**Φυλλεύς**
EPIROS:
—DODONA*: (1) v-iv BC Carapanos, Dodone p. 44 no. 13 (f. Βηναῖος)

**Φυλλίδας**
EPIROS:
—AMPHILOCHOI: (1) c. 208 BC FD III (4) 135, 21 (f. Ἀντίοχος, —οχος)

**Φυλλῖνος**
S. ITALY (APULIA):
—CANUSIUM: (1) i-ii AD Epig. Rom. di Canosa 111 (CIL IX 368 with Add.) (Lat. L. Clatius Phyllinus: f. Σελήνη)

**Φύλλιος**
LAKONIA:
—SPARTA: (1) 272 BC Plu., Pyrrh. 28 (Bradford (-))

**Φυλλίς**
S. ITALY (APULIA):
—LARINUM: (1) f. i AD Forma Italiae 36 p. 131 no. 2 (Lat. Pyllis)
S. ITALY (CAMPANIA):
—NEAPOLIS: (2) imp. NScav 1895, p. 108 (Lat. Phyllis: m. Σύμφορος); (3) i AD CIL X 1507; cf. Leiwo p. 90 (Lat. Salaria Phyllis)
—POMPEII: (4) i BC-i AD CIL IV 1265 a (Lat. Fyllis); (5) ~ ib. 7057 (Lat. Fyllis)

**Φυλοπίδας**
LAKONIA:
—SPARTA: (1) c. 394-371 BC D.L. ii 53 (Poralla² 739)

**Φυρταῖος**
AITOLIA: (1) ?316 BC FD III (4) 387, 3 (f. Λέων, Νικόστρατος, Ἀλέξανδρος)

**Φυσάλα**
AKARNANIA:
—PALAIROS: (1) ii BC IG IX (1)² (2) 558

**Φυσαλίων**
PELOPONNESE?: (1) s. iii BC ib. V (1) 1426, 14 (s. Ἀνδρόνικος)

**Φύσαλος**
ELIS: (1) c. 295-288 BC BSA 19 (1912-13) p. 85 no. 3, 9 (f. Λυκίσκος)

**Φύσκα**
SICILY:
—SYRACUSE?: (1) v/iv BC CGF p. 158 fr. *23 (n. pr.?)

**Φυσκίδας**
AITOLIA:
—TRICHONION: (1) iv BC FGrH 115 F 248 (s. Λυκόλας)

**Φυσκίων**
AITOLIA: (**1**) iii BC *PP* 4132 with Add. (Φυ(σ)κίων); (**2**) ?a. 246 BC *SGDI* 2509, 2
—KALLION/KALLIPOLIS: (**3**) 153-144 BC ib. 2279, 11
—KASILIOI: (**4**) 263 BC *IG* IX (1)² (1) 17, 92 (f. .α..θανίας)
—PHISTYON: (**5**) ii BC ib. 110 a, 5
DALMATIA:
—EPETION: (**6**) imp. *CIL* III 8534 (Lat. Fuscio: s. Ἱλαρώ)
EPIROS:
—BOUTHROTOS (PRASAIBOI): (**7**) a. 163 BC *IBouthrot* 26, 18 (*SEG* XXXVIII 484); *IBouthrot* 137, 9 (s. Λυσανίας, ?f. Λυσανίας); (**8**) ~ ib. 89, 1, 10
——Aixonioi: (**9**) a. 163 BC ib. 127, 3 (*BCH* 118 (1994) p. 128 A) (?f. Λυσανίας)
——Amorgioi: (**10**) a. 163 BC *IBouthrot* 66, 2; 68, 4; 69, 4; 70, 3; 71, 2 (*BCH* 118 (1994) p. 129 nos. B 1-3); *IBouthrot* 98, 3
——Parthaioi: (**11**) a. 163 BC ib. 149, 9 ([Φυσκ]ίων?: s. Λυσανίας)

**Φύσκος**
AITOLIA: (**1**) ?c. 275-250 BC *Syll³* 411; 412, 3, 9, 12 (*IEK* 35); *IvOl* 295 (f. Νεοπτόλεμος); (**2**) 244 or 240 BC *SGDI* 2512, 3 + Flacelière p. 402 no. 28 a; Nachtergael, *Les Galates* 59, 4; (**3**) c. 232-228 BC *Syll³* 499, 2; Nachtergael, *Les Galates* 62, [2]
AKARNANIA:
—THYRREION: (**4**) c. 330 BC *SEG* XXIII 189 I, 4

**Φύσκων**
KORINTHIA:
—KORINTH: (**1**) c. 550-525 BC *IG* IV (1) 322 (pinax) (-ϙὸν)
SICILY:
—AKRAI: (**2**) hell.? ib. XIV 225 (*Akrai* p. 163 no. 24) ([Φ]ύσκων)

**Φυσσία**
KORINTHIA:
—KORINTH: (**1**) ?iii-ii BC *IG* IV (1) 362

**Φυσσίας**
ELIS: (**1**) f. iii BC *IvOl* 175 (Moretti, *Olymp.* 540) (Φυσσί[ας]: f. Νίκαρχος); (**2**) 217 BC Plb. v 94. 6; cf. Moretti, *Olymp.* 540; (**3**) c. 100-90 BC *SEG* XXXIII 290 A, 16; *BSA* 70 (1975) pp. 129-31 (date); cf. Stephanis 653 (f. Δημοσθένης)

**Φυσταῖος**
EPIROS:
—THESPROTOI: (**1**) m. iv BC Cabanes, *L'Épire* p. 576 no. 49, 3 (*SEG* XXVI 717)

**Φύτιος**
ARKADIA:
—TEGEA:
——(Athaneatai): (**1**) s. iii BC *IG* v (2) 36, 108 (f. Δαμέας)
S. ITALY (BRUTTIUM):
—RHEGION: (**2**) vii-vi BC *RE* (2) ?= (*3*); (**3**) vi BC *Suda* I 80 (?f. Ἴβυκος) ?= (*2*)

**Φύτων**
S. ITALY (BRUTTIUM):
—RHEGION: (**1**) 387 BC *RE* (-) (Φοίτων—Aristipp. fr. 35)

**Φωκίων**
KORINTHIA:
—KORINTH: (**1**) v BC *SEG* XXII 251 a
MESSENIA:
—KYPARISSIA: (**2**) ii BC ib. XXV 436 = *AD* 25 (1970) Chron. p. 174 (Φωκίων)

**Φῶκος**
S. ITALY (BRUTTIUM):
—RHEGION: (**1**) 433 BC *IG* I³ 53, 3; 1178, 3 (f. Σιληνός)

**Φωκύλος**
ARGOLIS:
—HERMIONE: (**1**) iii BC ib. IV (1) 729 II, 13 (s. Κλήσιππος)

**Φώλων**
SICILY:
—SYRACUSE: (**1**) iii-v AD Strazzulla 163 (Agnello 18; Wessel 184); cf. Robert, *EEP* p. 196 + *Rend. Pont.* 22 (1946-7) p. 236 no. 41

**Φωσέας**
KORINTHIA:
—SIKYON: (**1**) vi/v BC *SEG* XI 244, 25 (Φὅ-)

**Φωσφόρος**
KORINTHIA:
—KORINTH: (**1**) iii AD *BM Lamps* 3 p. 405 no. Q3260; *Corinth* IV (2) pp. 190 nos. 573-4; 195 no. 616; 204 nos. 695-7; XVIII (2) p. 29 no. 24; *SEG* XXVII 35. 24; 151; XXX 348 (lamps) (Πωσ-, Πρωσφόρος—*SEG* XXX)
LAKONIA:
—SPARTA: (**2**) c. 140-160 AD ib. XI 500 (Bradford (-)) ([Ο]ὐάριος Φ.)
S. ITALY (CAMPANIA):
—BAIAI: (**3**) imp. *NScav* 1887, p. 154 (*Eph. Ep.* VIII 408) (Lat. C. Insteius Posphorus)
—HERCULANEUM*: (**4**) m. i AD *CIL* x 1403 b + *Cron. Erc.* 7 (1977) p. 117 C b, 8 (Lat. L. Luscius Phosphor: freed.)
—POMPEII: (**5**) i BC-i AD *CIL* IV 2241 (Lat. Posphorus); (**6**) ~ ib. 1336-7 (Lat. Phosphor); (**7**)

i AD ib. x 8058. 67 (seal) (Lat. Phosphorus); (**8**) m. i AD ib. IV 3340. 93, 4 (Castrèn 397. 2) (Lat. Q. Sulpicius Phosphorus); (**9**) c. 51-62 AD *CIL* IV 3340. 98, 3 (Castrèn 397. 1) (Lat. C. Sulpicius Phosporus)
—SALERNUM: (**10**) imp. *CIL* x 646 (Lat. Posphorus: f. Veratia Regina)

**Φωτεύς**
EPIROS:
—BOUTHROTOS (PRASAIBOI): (**1**) a. 163 BC *IBouthrot* 14, 11, 28; 19, 4; 21, 15; 31, 33; 40, 1; 44, 5 (*SEG* XXXVIII 471; 476; 478; 490; 499) (f. Φίλιππος, Μαχάτας) ?= (*4*); (**2**) ~ *IBouthrot* 14, 21; 17, 15; 21, 7, 15; 31, 34; 40, 15 (*SEG* XXXVIII 471; 474; 478; 490; 499) (s. Φίλιππος); (**3**) ~ *IBouthrot* 28, 18 (*SEG* XXXVIII 486); *IBouthrot* 144, 4 (s. Μαχάτας) ?= (*5*); (**4**) ~ ib. 137, 5 (f. Μαχάτας) ?= (*6*) (*1*)
——Parthaioi: (**5**) a. 163 BC ib. 111, 11; 112, 11; 120, 2 (s.p.) (s. Μαχάτας) ?= (*3*); (**6**) ~ ib. 139, 2 (f. Φίλιππος) ?= (*4*)

**Φωτίδας**
S. ITALY (CALABRIA):
—TARAS-TARENTUM?: (**1**) 360 BC D.L. iii 15. 22; *RE* (-) ?= (Φροντίδας (*1*))

**Φωτίνη**
KORINTHIA:
—KORINTH: (**1**) v-vi AD Bees 41; cf. *TMByz* 9 (1985) p. 359 no. 6
SICILY:
—SYRACUSE: (**2**) iii-v AD *IG* XIV 187 (Strazzulla 125; Agnello 15; Wessel 616); cf. Ferrua, *NG* 180

**Φωτῖνος**
SICILY:
—SYRACUSE: (**1**) iii-v AD Wessel 885 + Ferrua, *NG* 90 a

**Φώτιος**
KORINTHIA:
—KORINTH: (**1**) 536-553 AD *SEG* XXIX 302 (bp.)

**Φῶτος**
S. ITALY (CAMPANIA):
—POMPEII: (**1**) i BC-i AD *CIL* IV 9001 (Lat. Photus)

**Φώτυος**
EPIROS:
—CHAONES: (**1**) c. 430 BC Th. ii 80. 5 (Φώτιος—edd.)

**Χαβρίας**
EPIROS:
—BOUTHROTOS (PRASAIBOI): (**1**) a. 163 BC *IBouthrot* 31, 56 (*SEG* XXXVIII 490); Ugolini, *Alb. Ant.* 3 p. 120, 12 (f. Σωσίπατρος)
——Cherrioi: (**2**) a. 163 BC *IBouthrot* 98, 5

**Χαβρῖνος**
ARGOLIS:
—HERMIONE: (**1**) v BC Wehrli, *Schule Arist.* Suppl. i fr. 6 (?f. Λάσος: dub.)

**Χαιρᾶς**
LAKONIA:
—HYPERTELEATON*: (**1**) imp. *IG* v (1) 1065 (s. Ἀρτεμᾶς)

**Χαιρέας**
ACHAIA:
—DYME*: (**1**) c. 219 BC *SGDI* 1612, 37 (*Tyche* 5 (1990) p. 124) (f. Τιμοκλῆς)
AITOLIA?: (**2**) c. 220-216 BC *IG* IV (1)² 44, 6
AKARNANIA:
—ASTAKOS: (**3**) hell.? ib. IX (1)² (2) 442 ([Χα]ιρέα[ς])
EPIROS:
—AMBRAKIA: (**4**) 238-168 BC *JIAN* 12 (1909-10) p. 45 no. 18 (coin); (**5**) ii BC *SEG* XLII 542 (Χαιρέα (gen.), χαίρετ[ε]—ed.: f. Μενέλαος); (**6**) a. 167 BC ib. XXXV 665 A, 10 (s. Αἰσωπίδας)
KEPHALLENIA:
—KRANIOI: (**7**) hell.-imp. *IG* IX (1) 615
KORINTHIA:
—KORINTH: (**8**) 191-146 BC *BMC Pelop.* p. 12 nos. 141-2 (coin)
—SIKYON: (**9**) ?iv BC Moretti, *Olymp.* 954 (Skalet 334) (s. Χαιρήμων)
S. ITALY (CAMPANIA):
—MISENUM*: (**10**) ii AD *Puteoli* 11 (1987) p. 146 no. 10 (Lat. Q. Sabidius Chaer(eas))
—NEAPOLIS: (**11**) iv/iii BC *IGSI* 1 I, 187 (*DGE* 62; Uguzzoni–Ghinatti I) (s. Δάμων); (**12**) i BC/i AD *INap* 94; cf. Leiwo p. 77 no. 22 (f. Ἀρισταγόρη); (**13**) ~ *INap* 109, 7; cf. Leiwo p. 77 no. 21 (s. Μαραῖος)
SICILY:
—SYRACUSE: (**14**) i-ii AD Charito i 1. 3 (s. Ἀρίστων: fict.)

**Χαιρέδαμος**
KORINTHIA:
—SIKYON: (**1**) vii/vi BC *FGrH* 90 F 61 (Skalet 335) (-δη-)
S. ITALY (BRUTTIUM):
—LOKROI EPIZEPHYRIOI: (**2**) iv/iii BC De Franciscis 36, 3 ([Χα]ιρέδαμος: f. Ὀναῖος)
——(Ἀνα.): (**3**) 278 BC ib. 30, 2 (s. Φαικύλος)
——(Ἀνξ.): (**4**) iv/iii BC ib. 15, 1
——(Κρα.): (**5**) iv/iii BC ib. 3, 5 (f. Χαιρέλας)
SICILY:
—TAUROMENION: (**6**) c. 151 BC *IGSI* 4 III (IV), 33 an. 90 (f. Ζώπυρος)

**Χαιρέλας**
S. ITALY (BRUTTIUM):
—LOKROI EPIZEPHYRIOI:
——(Γαυ.): (**1**) iv/iii BC De Franciscis 19, 7 (s. Δαμοφάων)
——(Κρα.): (**2**) iv/iii BC ib. 3, 5 (s. Χαιρέδαμος)

**Χαιρέμαχος**
ARGOLIS:
—PHLEIOUS: (**1**) iii BC *IG* IV (1) 463 (Χαιρέμαχος: f. Καλλικράτεια)

**Χαιρεσίας**
AITOLIA?: (**1**) c. 340-335 BC *CID* II 20, 9

**Χαιρεσίλαος**
KORINTHIA:
—KORINTH: (**1**) f. ii BC *Corinth* VIII (1) 3 + *HSCP* 53 (1942) p. 110 (ΧΛΙΡΕΣΙΛΛΟΝ—lap., Χ(α)ιρεσίλλος—*Corinth*, Χ(α)ιρεσίλ(α)ος—*HSCP*)

**Χαιρεσίλας**
S. ITALY (BRUTTIUM):
—LOKROI EPIZEPHYRIOI:
——(Δυσ.): (**1**) 277 BC De Franciscis 8, 4; 31, 4 (s. Πλάτων)
——(Πυρ.): (**2**) iv/iii BC ib. 24, 7; 38, 5 (f. Ἀμεινοκλῆς)

**Χαιρεστράτα**
ACHAIA:
—AIGION?: (**1**) c. 400 BC *IG* II² 7946 (-τη)

**Χαιρήμων**
AKARNANIA:
—ECHINOS: (**1**) c. 80 BC ib. VII 416, 16 (*IOrop* 523); *IG* VII 542, 5 (f. Ἀμεινίας)
ARKADIA:
—MANTINEIA-ANTIGONEIA: (**2**) c. 300-221 BC ib. v (2) 323. 66 (tessera) (Χαιρήμων: f. Μνασίων)
EPIROS:
—AMBRAKIA: (**3**) ?ii BC Unp. (Arta Mus.) ([Χ]αιρήμων)
ILLYRIA?:
—APOLLONIA: (**4**) f. ii BC *Thess. Mnem.* 130 (f. Ἀνδρόνικος)
KORINTHIA:
—SIKYON: (**5**) ?iv BC Paus. vi 3. 1 (Skalet 336) (f. Χαιρέας)
LAKONIA:
—SPARTA: (**6**) c. 30-20 BC *IG* v (1) 211, 15 (Bradford (-)) (s. Καλλινίκης)
MESSENIA:
—MESSENE: (**7**) s. iii BC *IG* IV (1) 727 B, 2 (Perlman H.2) (s. Εὐαίνετος); (**8**) iii/ii BC *PAE* 1991, p. 91 (s. Δαμοκράτης, Φιλίππα) ?= (12) (11)
—MESSENE?: (**9**) ii/i BC *SEG* XI 979, 34
—THOURIA: (**10**) ii-i BC *IG* v (1) 1385, 10 (f. Νίκιππος); (**11**) f. ii BC *SEG* XI 972, 57 (s. Δαμοκράτης) ?= (8); (**12**) c. 175-150 BC *IG* v (1) 1384, 8 (f. Δαμοκράτης) ?= (8)
SICILY:
—SYRACUSE?:
——(Μακ.): (**13**) hell. Manganaro, *PdelP* forthcoming no. 4 III, 9 (f. Καλλίστρατος)
TRIPHYLIA:
—LEPREON: (**14**) iii BC *SEG* XXIII 239 (s. Χαιρέας)

**Χαιρήν**
EPIROS:
—AMBRAKIA: (**1**) iii-ii BC *Op. Ath.* 10 (1971) p. 64 no. 12, 1-2; cf. *VAHD* 84 (1991) p. 262 (s. Φιλοκλῆς, f. Ἐχεκλείδας)
ILLYRIA:
—APOLLONIA: (**2**) c. 250-50 BC Maier 120; 99 (coin) (Ceka 8; 91) (pryt.); (**3**) i BC *BMC Thessaly* p. 60 no. 56 (coin)
—GUREZEZE (MOD.): (**4**) hell. *Iliria* 1982 (1), p. 104 nos. 1-2 = p. 121 no. 57 (tile); cf. p. 122; cf. *SEG* II 383

**Χαιρησίλεως**
SICILY:
—GELA-PHINTIAS: (**1**) vi/v BC Lazzarini 393; *SEG* XII 410; cf. XXXVII 756 (Χαιρεσίλεοι (dat.): her.?)

**Χαιρήτιος**
SICILY:
—AVOLA (MOD.): (**1**) i BC ib. XXXIV 981 (I f. Χαιρήτιος II); (**2**) ~ ib. (II s. Χαιρήτιος I)

**Χαιριάδας**
ARKADIA:
—ORCHOMENOS: (**1**) ?c. 378 BC *BCH* 102 (1978) p. 334, 19, 35 (*IPArk* 15)
LAKONIA:
—OITYLOS: (**2**) iii/ii BC *IG* v (1) 1295, 4 (Bradford (-))
MESSENIA:
—MESSENE: (**3**) f. iii BC *PAE* 1991, p. 99 no. 7, 19

**Χαιρίας**
KORINTHIA:
—KORINTH: (**1**) vii/vi BC Amyx Gr 5 b. 6 (vase) (Lorber 2 b) (Χαιρία[s], Χαιριά[δας]—Amyx)
S. ITALY (APULIA):
—CANUSIUM*: (**2**) imp. *Epig. Rom. di Canosa* 187 (Lat. C. Tampius Chaeria: freed.)
S. ITALY (CAMPANIA):
—KYME: (**3**) ?c. 450 BC Dubois, *IGDGG* I 21 c (vase) (Arena, *Iscr. Sic.* III 21); *LSAG*² p. 240 no. 13 (date) (Χαιρίō (gen.), Χ.—Dubois, Χαιρής—Arena)

**Χαιριγένης**
ARKADIA:
—MANTINEIA-ANTIGONEIA: (**1**) ?iii BC *IG* v (2) 318, 11

**Χαιρίθεος**
KORINTHIA:
—SIKYON: (**1**) 224 or 221 BC Nachtergael, *Les Galates* 64, 7 (Skalet 337); cf. Stephanis 2595 (f. Χαῖρις)

**Χαιρίλας**
LAKONIA:
—SPARTA: (**1**) 418 BC X., *HG* ii 3. 10 (Poralla² 740)

**Χαίριλλος**
ILLYRIA:
—EPIDAMNOS-DYRRHACHION: (**1**) c. 250-50 BC Maier 400-2 (coin) (Ceka 179; 198; 459) (pryt.) ?= (1)

**Χαιριμένης**
AKARNANIA:
—EURIPOS: (**1**) c. 325-315 BC *Hesp.* 57 (1988) p. 148 A, 29-30 (*SEG* XXXVI 331); cf. *Hesp.* 48 (1979) pp. 78 f. with pl. 22 c (f. Εὔαλκος, Πολυάλκης)

**Χαιρίππα**
ZAKYNTHOS: (**1**) ?iii/ii BC *IG* IX (1)² (2) 231 ([Χ]αιρίππα: d. Οὔνιχος)

**Χαίριππος**
ARKADIA:
—MANTINEIA-ANTIGONEIA: (**1**) c. 425-385 BC ib. v (2) 323. 11 (tessera) ([Χ]αίριπο[s]: s. Ποσι—)
SICILY:
—KAMARINA: (**2**) m. v BC Dubois, *IGDS* 120, 2 (Arena, *Iscr. Sic.* II 142 A; *SEG* XXXVIII 939; Cordano, 'Camarina VII' 62) (Χαίριπος—Arena, Χαίριτος—Dubois: f. Ἀριστόδαμος)

**Χαῖρις**
ARGOLIS:
—EPIDAUROS*: (**1**) c. 370 BC *IG* IV (1)² 102, 87
KERKYRA: (**2**) her. Wehrli, *Schule Arist.* iv fr. 192

**Χαιρίων**

KORINTHIA:
—SIKYON: (3) 224 or 221 BC Nachtergael, *Les Galates* 64, 7 (Skalet 338; Stephanis 2595) (s. *Χαιρίθεος*)
LAKONIA:
—SPARTA: (4) ?viii-vii BC *HE* 2717 (Poralla² 741) (s. *Ἰφικρατίδας, Ἀλεξίππα*: fict.?)
MESSENIA:
—THOURIA: (5) ii-i BC *IG* v (1) 1385, 32 (f. *Καλλιππίδας*)
SICILY:
—KAMARINA: (6) s. v BC Dubois, *IGDS* 121, 23 (Arena, *Iscr. Sic.* II 143; *SEG* XXXVIII 940; Cordano, 'Camarina VII' 63) (s. *Διο—*)

**Χαιρίων**

ARKADIA:
—MANTINEIA-ANTIGONEIA: (1) c. 300-221 BC *IG* v (2) 323. 69 (tessera) (s. *Εὐάγης*)
KORINTHIA:
—KORINTH: (2) 263 BC ib. IX (1)² (1) 17, 84 (s. *Νέων*)

**Χαιρόλας**

ELIS: (1) f. i BC *IvOl* 399, 2 (f. *Μαλιάδας*)
KORINTHIA:
—KORINTH: (2) 343 BC *CID* II 31, 98; cf. ll. 26, 28, 29

**Χαίρουσα**

S. ITALY (CAMPANIA):
—DIKAIARCHIA-PUTEOLI: (1) imp. *CIL* X 2340 (Lat. Cornelia Caerusa); (2) ~ ib. 2907 (Lat. Quintilia Chaerusa)
SICILY:
—SYRACUSE: (3) iii-v AD *RQ* 1904, p. 257 (Wessel 1146) (*Χέ-*)
—TAUROMENION: (4) imp. *IG* XIV 441

**Χαιρύλος**

S. ITALY (BRUTTIUM):
—LOKROI EPIZEPHYRIOI:
——(*Πετ.*): (1) iv/iii BC De Franciscis 20, 10 (f. *Χαρίξενος*)
SICILY:
—SYRACUSE: (2) iii BC *NScav* 1905, p. 387 (f. *Μινύρα*)

**Χαίρων**

ACHAIA:
—PELLENE: (1) iv BC *RE* (4); Moretti, *Olymp.* 432, 437, 443, 447
ARKADIA:
—MEGALOPOLIS: (2) m. iv BC Plu., *Alex.* 3
LAKONIA:
—BOIAI: (4) ii AD *IG* v (1) 958, 1 (f. *Π. Μέμμιος Κλεάρετος*)
—OITYLOS: (5) imp. ib. 1300
—SPARTA: (6) 403 BC X., *HG* ii 4. 33 (Poralla² 742); (7) hell.? Plb. xxiii 4. 5; 18. 4; xxiv 7. 1, 6-8 (Bradford (2)); (8) b. 140 BC *ID* 1439 Abc II, 24; 1449 Aab II, 28; 1450 A, 104 (Bradford (3)) (*Χ[αίρων]—ID* 1439); (9) ?i BC *IG* v (1) 811 (Bradford (4)); (10) c. 25-1 BC *IG* v (1) 210, 38 (Bradford (1)) (s. *Ἀγαθοκλῆς*)
MESSENIA:
—THOURIA: (11) f. ii BC *SEG* XI 972, 98 (s. *Εὐδαιμονίδας*)
S. ITALY (CAMPANIA):
—DIKAIARCHIA-PUTEOLI: (12) imp. *CIL* X 2323 (Lat. L. Consius Chaero)

**Χαιρωνίδας**

ARKADIA:
—STYMPHALOS: (1) iii BC *IG* v (2) 356, 7
ELIS: (2) s. iii BC *HE* 1399 (-δης)

**Χάκας**

ILLYRIA:
—EPIDAMNOS-DYRRHACHION: (1) hell.-imp. *IDyrrh* 395 (f. *Τάτα*)

**Χαλέας**

LAKONIA:
—SPARTA: (1) ?s. i AD *IG* v (1) 282; *Artemis Orthia* pp. 313-14 no. 31 (date) (Bradford (2)) (f. *Δαμοκλείδας*)

**Χαλίδιος**

S. ITALY (BRUTTIUM):
—VARAPODIO (MOD.): (1) f. iii BC *Klearchos* 8 (1966) p. 65 (tile)

**Χάλινος**

LAKONIA:
—SPARTA: (1) c. 105-110 AD *IG* v (1) 20 B, 2; 97, 20; 184, [3]; *SEG* XI 564, 14; *BSA* 26 (1923-5) p. 168 C 7, 4 (Bradford (2)) (*Χαλεῖνος—20 B and SEG*: I f. *Χαλῖνος* II); (2) ~ *IG* v (1) 20 B, 2; 97, 20; 184, 3?; *SEG* XI 564, 14; *BSA* 26 (1923-5) p. 168 C 7, 4 (Bradford (1)) (-λεῖ-: II s. *Χαλῖνος* I)

**Χαλκίδας**

ILLYRIA:
—EPIDAMNOS-DYRRHACHION: (1) c. 250-50 BC Maier 403-4; Münsterberg Nachtr. p. 17 (coin) (Ceka 52; 284; 296) (pryt.)

**Χαλκιδεύς**

LAKONIA:
—SPARTA: (1) 412 BC *RE* (-) (Poralla² 743)

**Χαλκις**

ITHAKE: (1) hell. *Rev. Épig.* 1 (1913) p. 47 no. 4 (*Χαλχις—*apogr.)

**Χαλκοδάμανς**

ARGOLIS:
—ARGOS?: (1) c. 625-600 BC *IG* v (1) 231 (bronze) (Lazzarini 720); cf. *LSAG²* p. 156 (-ϙο-)

**Χαμαιλίς**

ARKADIA:
—LOUSOI*: (1) ?iv BC *IG* v (2) 397 (*Χαμ[αι]λίς?*)

**Χάμυνος**

ELIS:
—PISA: (1) vii BC Paus. vi 21. 1 (fict.?)

**Χαρά**

KORINTHIA:
—KORINTH: (1) ?ii/iii AD *SEG* XL 303 (*νεωτ.*)
SICILY:
—SYRACUSE: (2) iii-v AD Strazzulla 253; cf. Ferrua, *NG* 28
—THERMAI HIMERAIAI: (3) imp. *CIL* X 7450 (*ILat. Term. Imer.* 171) (Lat. Chara)

**Χάραττα**

EPIROS:
—AMBRAKIA: (1) her. *FGrH* 69 F 1, 7

**Χαρέας**

ARKADIA:
—TEGEA: (1) f. ii BC *IG* v (2) 44, 8 (s. *Κλέων*)
KEPHALLENIA:
—PALE: (2) c. 450-430 BC ib. I³ 1359
LAKONIA:
—SPARTA: (3) iii BC *SEG* XL 348 B, 10
TRIPHYLIA:
—LEPREON: (4) iii BC ib. XXIII 239 (f. *Χαιρήμων*)

**Χάρεια**

S. ITALY (APULIA):
—BARION: (1) imp. *CIL* IX 286 (Lat. Aemilia Charia)

**Χαρείδας**

ARKADIA:
—MANTINEIA-ANTIGONEIA: (1) 369-361 BC *IG* v (2) 1, 39; Tod, *GHI* II 132 (date)

**Χάρης**

ACHAIA?: (1) 193 BC *IG* v (2) 293, 13 (s. *Ἀπολλώνιος*)
AIGINA: (2) f. v BC Paus. vi 14. 1; *CEG* 1 350; cf. Ebert, *Gr. Sieg.* 19 (-ρῆς: f. *Φερίας*)
ARGOLIS:
—EPIDAUROS: (3) i-ii AD Peek, *NIEpid* 49, 1, 3 (s. *Σωσίβιος*, f. *Ἀσκλαπιάς*)
ILLYRIA:
—DARDANIOI: (4) s. ii AD *ZA* 24 (1974) p. 255, 5 (s. *Γέτας, Γενθιανή*)
—EPIDAMNOS-DYRRHACHION: (5) c. 250-50 BC Maier 132; 208 (coin) (Ceka 460-1) (money.)
KORINTHIA:
—KORINTH: (6) c. 570-550 BC Amyx 57. 13 (vase) (Lorber 83) (-ρῆς: potter/painter)
LAKONIA:
—SPARTA: (7) c. 125-160 AD *IG* v (1) 62, 4; *SEG* XI 495, 1; 585, 2; XXX 410, 3 (Bradford (2)) (I f. *Χάρης* II); (8) ~ *IG* v (1) 62, 4; *SEG* XI 495, 1; 585, 2; 587, 6; XXX 410, 3 (Bradford (1)) (II s. *Χάρης* I)
SICILY?: (9) f. iii BC Vandermersch p. 177 (amph.) (or S. Italy)

**Χαρησίδαμος**

MESSENIA:
—THOURIA: (1) f. ii BC *SEG* XI 972, 76 (f. *Δαμοθάλης*)

**Χαρητίδας**

LAKONIA:
—SPARTA: (1) hell.-imp. *IG* v (1) 195, 4 (Bradford (-)) ([Χ]αρητίδας?)
MESSENIA:
—MESSENE: (2) c. 140 BC *IvOl* 52, 5 (s. *Δορκωνίδας*)

**Χαρίας**

AIGINA: (1) her. Pi., *N.* viii, 46 (*Χαριάδαι* (n. gent.))
ARGOLIS:
—EPIDAUROS*: (2) c. 370-365 BC Peek, *IAEpid* 52 B, 54

**Χαρίγνητος**

AKARNANIA:
—PALAIROS: (1) iii/ii BC *IG* IX (1)² (2) 553

**Χαρίδαμος**

ARKADIA:
—HERAIA: (1) ?ii BC ib. v (2) 418
—KLEITOR: (2) 331-328 BC *Syll³* 291 (s. *Ἀγίας*)
ILLYRIA:
—APOLLONIA: (3) c. 250-50 BC Maier 50 (coin) (Ceka 134) (money.)
KORINTHIA:
—SIKYON: (4) ?253 BC Nachtergael, *Les Galates* 10, 39 (Skalet 339); cf. Stephanis 1948 (-δη-: f. *Ὀνατίδας*)
MESSENIA:
—MESSENE: (5) f. iii BC *PAE* 1991, p. 99 no. 7, 13; (6) i AD *IG* v (1) 1436, 21 (*Χαρίδα[μος]*)
—THOURIA: (7) f. ii BC *SEG* XI 972, 87 (s. *Ξένων*)
S. ITALY (BRUTTIUM):
—LOKROI EPIZEPHYRIOI:
——(*Γαυ.*): (8) iv/iii BC De Franciscis 19, 3 (s. *Καικινιάδας*)
——(*Τηλ.*): (9) 277 BC ib. 8, 3; 31, 3 (s. *Χαρίλας*)
TRIPHYLIA:
—PTELEA: (10) ii BC *SEG* XVI 282, 3 (*Χαρίδαμο[s]*)

**Χαρίδημος**

S. ITALY (CAMPANIA):
—POMPEII: (1) i BC-i AD *CIL* IV 3106 (Lat. Charidem[us])

**Χαρίδοτος**

LAKONIA:
—SPARTA: (1) ?134 AD *IG* v (1) 62, 18 (Bradford (-)) (*Χαρίδο[τος]*: f. *Πολύβιος*)

**Χαρίκλεια**
AIGINA: (1) ii BC *IG* IV (1) 13 (d. Ἀριστοκλείδης)
ARGOLIS:
—ARGOS: (2) 470-450 BC ib. I³ 858 (d. Γλαυκίνος)
LEUKAS: (3) iii BC *AD* 25 (1970) Chron. p. 332; (4) iii/ii BC *SEG* XXVII 173 (Χαρίκλε[ια])

**Χαρικλείδας**
ARGOLIS:
—EPIDAUROS: (1) c. 365-335 BC *IG* IV (1)² 103, 34, 45, 66, 81, 92 + *SEG* XXV 386, 8c
KORINTHIA:
—KORINTH: (2) c. 610-590 BC Amyx 18. 7 (vase) (Lorber 28); *LSAG*² p. 131 no. 9 (date) (-κλί-)

**Χαρικλείδης**
ARGOLIS:
—EPIDAUROS: (1) iii BC Peek, *IAEpid* 308

**Χαρικλῆς**
AIGINA: (1) ?270 BC *FD* III (4) 149, 1 (s. Λαοφῶν)
ARGOLIS:
—EPIDAUROS: (2) i-ii AD *IG* IV (1)² 484, 3, 6 (s. Μένανδρος, f. Ἱεροκλῆς)
ARKADIA:
—TEGEA:
——(Krariotai): (3) iv/iii BC ib. v (2) 38, 25 (Χαρ[ι]κλῆς: f. Δάμων)
EPIROS:
—AMBRAKIA: (4) c. 210 BC ib. IX (1)² (1) 31, 83
—BOUTHROTOS (PRASAIBOI): (5) a. 163 BC *IBouthrot* 37, 4 (*SEG* XXXVIII 496) ?= (6); (6) ~ *IBouthrot* 43, 49 (*SEG* XXXVIII 502) ?= (5)
ILLYRIA:
—APOLLONIA: (7) c. 250-50 BC Maier 100 (coin) (Ceka 60) (pryt.)
KORINTHIA:
—KORINTH: (8) ii AD Luc., *Am.* 9; 18 (fict.)
—SIKYON: (9) 166 BC *IG* II² 2316, 5, 10 (f. Τιμοκλῆς)
MESSENIA:
—MESSENE: (10) ?i AD *Ergon* 1995, p. 31 (s. Φίλων)
S. ITALY (BRUTTIUM):
—LOKROI EPIZEPHYRIOI:
——(Ὀμβ.): (11) iv/iii BC De Franciscis 20, 8 (s. Χάριππος)

**Χαρικράτης**
ARGOLIS:
—EPIDAUROS*: (1) c. 370-365 BC Peek, *IAEpid* 52 A, 7 (Χαρικρ[άτη]ς)
KORINTHIA:
—KORINTH: (2) s. viii BC Plu., *Mor.* 293 A

**Χαρικώ**
ARGOLIS:
—ARGOS: (1) imp. *IG* IV (1) 639
—EPIDAUROS: (2) s. ii BC ib. IV (1)² 218 (d. Νικάρετος, m. Λαφάντα); (3) f. i BC ib. 217 (d. Σώδαμος, Λαφάντα, ?m. Εὔνομος, Λαφάντα); (4) m. i BC ib. 220 (d. Κλεαιχμίδας, ?d. Λαφάντα, m. Λαφάντα)

**Χαρίλαος**
ARKADIA:
—MANTINEIA-ANTIGONEIA: (1) ?v/iv BC ib. v (2) 284 (bronze)
S. ITALY (APULIA)?: (2) v-iv BC Parlangèli, *Studi Messapici* p. 245 O. 44; Mayer, *Apulien* p. 287 and pl. 33. 10 (Χαριλ(α)ος)
S. ITALY (BRUTTIUM):
—LOKROI EPIZEPHYRIOI?: (3) 328 BC *IG* II² 3052
S. ITALY (CAMPANIA):
—NEAPOLIS: (4) 326 BC Liv. viii 25. 9 (Lat. Charilaus)

**Χαρίλας**
S. ITALY (BRUTTIUM):
—LOKROI EPIZEPHYRIOI:
——(Πυρ.): (1) iv/iii BC De Franciscis 28, 4 (f. Εὔφραιος)
——(Τηλ.): (2) 277 BC ib. 8, 3; 31, 3 (f. Χαρίδαμος)
——(Τιω.): (3) iv/iii BC ib. 27, 3 (f. Νέαιθος)
——(Φαω.): (4) iv/iii BC ib. 18, 6; 27, 9 (f. Ὀναῖος) ?= (5); (5) ~ ib. 38, 1 ?= (4)
SICILY: (6) iii-ii BC Vandermersch p. 177 (amph.) (or S. Italy)

**Χαρίλεως**
ARGOLIS:
—EPIDAUROS*: (1) c. 340-320 BC Peek, *NIEpid* 19 A, 13 (Χαρίλεως)
S. ITALY (CAMPANIA):
—KYME?: (2) m. v BC Arena, *Iscr. Sic.* III 23 (vase)
—NEAPOLIS: (3) iv/iii BC Sambon 469 (coins) (*SNG ANS Etruria–Calabria* 359)
SICILY: (4) m. v BC *IGA* 526 (vase) (or S. Italy: Χαρίλεῶς (gen.))

**Χαρίλης**
S. ITALY (CAMPANIA):
—NEAPOLIS: (1) i BC/i AD *INap* 151, 1; cf. Leiwo p. 104 no. 61 (f. Ἄστος); (2) ~ *INap* 180 (I f. Χαρίλης II); (3) ~ ib. (II s. Χαρίλης I)

**Χάριλλος**
LAKONIA:
—SPARTA: (1) her. *RE* (-) (Poralla² 747); cf. Hdt. viii 131. 2; Plu., *Lyc.* 3; cf. *FGrH* 244 F 62 (Armenian) (Χάριλλος, Χαρίλος—Hdt. mss., Χαρίλευς—Hdt. edd., Χαρίλαος—Plu.: s. Πολυδέκτας, ?s. Εὔνομος, f. Νίκανδρος: king/dub.)

**Χαρίλος**
LAKONIA:
—KOSMAS (MOD.): (1) c. 525 BC *IG* V (1) 927 (bronze) (Lazzarini 84); *LSAG*² p. 200 no. 37 (date) (Poralla² 746)
SICILY:
—SELINOUS?: (2) v BC *SEG* XXXIX 1021 II, 1

**Χαριμένης**
ARGOLIS:
—ARGOS: (1) 242 BC Plu., *Arat.* 25 (mantis)

**Χαρίμορτος**
AITOLIA?: (1) iii/ii BC *PP* 4428

**Χαρῖνος**
ARGOLIS:
—ARGOS: (1) imp. *IG* IV (1) 601 (Μ. Πομπ. Χαρεῖνος)
—EPIDAUROS: (2) ii-iii AD ib. IV (1)² 530 (-ρεῖ-: I f. Χαρῖνος II); (3) ~ ib. (-ρεῖ-: II s. Χαρῖνος I)
ELIS: (4) inc. Moretti, *Olymp.* 955-956
LAKONIA:
—OITYLOS: (5) iii/ii BC *IG* V (1) 1295, 2 (Bradford (2))
—SPARTA: (6) c. 25-1 BC *IG* V (1) 210, 30 (Bradford (1)) (s. Γοργιάδας)
MESSENIA:
—THOURIA: (7) ii-i BC *IG* V (1) 1385, 31 (f. Δαμοκλείδας)
S. ITALY (LUCANIA):
—POSEIDONIA-PAESTUM: (8) m. iv BC *RVP* p. 84 no. 125 (vase) (fict.)
SICILY:
—HIMERA: (9) c. 500-475 BC *Himera* 2 p. 680 no. 40 (vase) (Dubois, *IGDS* 10; Arena, *Iscr. Sic.* III 47)

**Χαρίξενος**
ACHAIA: (1) 257 BC *PKöln* 314 (f. Νίκαιος: t.e.)
AITOLIA: (2) m. iii BC *IG* IX (1)² (1) pp. XLIX ff., s.a. 255 BC, 248 BC, 241 BC, 234 BC; 18, 18; 181; *BCH* 51 (1927) pp. 349 ff.; Pantos, *Sphragismata* p. 146 no. 117; p. 447 f.; Nachtergael, *Les Galates* 21-3; 24 (s.p.); [25] (date); cf. p. 330 n. 131 (s. Κυδρίων)
—ATTALEIA: (3) 204 BC *IG* IX (1)² (1) 95, 11
—KALYDON: (4) m. ii BC ib. 137, 24
—PAMPHIA: (5) c. 162 BC ib. 105, 10
—PLEURON: (6) m. iii BC ib. 22, 6, 7
—TRICHONION: (7) hell.? ib. 122; (8) c. 288-270 BC ib. p. XLIX, s.a. 288 BC, 281 BC, 270 BC; *SEG* XXX 512; (9) s. iii BC *FD* III (4) 230; *BCH* 53 (1929) p. 26 no. 4, 1 ?= (11); (10) ~ *IG* IX (1)² (1) 117, 6; (11) 224 or 221 BC Nachtergael, *Les Galates* 64, 1 (s. Πρόξενος) ?= (9)
ARGOLIS:
—ARGOS: (12) ii/i BC *SEG* XXVIII 1246, 24-5 (f. Ἀριστόκριτος)
—HERMIONE: (13) imp. *IG* IV (1) 714, 4; (14) ii AD *SEG* XVII 163, 4 (f. Θεοδώρα); (15) iii AD *IG* IV (1) 716, 1 (Αὐρ. Χ.: II s. Χαρίξενος I); (16) ~ ib. l. 2 (I s. Κέλαδος, f. Αὐρ. Χαρίξενος II)
ELIS: (17) ?c. 475 BC *SEG* XXXI 358, 2; *LSAG*² p. 450 no. E (date)
KORINTHIA:
—SIKYON: (18) ii AD Luc., *Tox.* 22 (fict.)
LAKONIA:
—SPARTA: (19) s. i BC *IG* V (1) 95, 9 (Bradford (12)) (f. Ξενοκλῆς); (20) c. 25-1 BC *IG* V (1) 212, 18 (Bradford (5)); (21) i AD *IG* V (1) 274, 1 (*Artemis Orthia* pp. 309-10 no. 26) (f. Λυσικράτης); (22) c. 50-110 AD *IG* V (1) 508; *SEG* XI 488, 3; 537 a, 1; 538; 776, 4 (Bradford (1); (7)) (Γ. Ἰούλ. Χ.: s. Ἰούλ. Ἀριστόδαμος, Ἰούλ. Νίκιον); (23) i/ii AD *IG* V (1) 18 A, 3; 19, 16; 34, 6; 467, 2; 476, 2; 667, 5; cf. *SEG* XI 479 (Bradford (6)) (Τ. Φλαούϊος Χ., Φλάβιος Χ.—34) (24) ~ *IG* V (1) 32 A, 5; 83?; 275, 2 (*Artemis Orthia* pp. 312-13 no. 30); *IG* V (1) 1314, 2; *SEG* XI 548, 13 (Bradford (4); (8)) (Γ. Ἰούλ. Χ.: s. Γ. Ἰούλ. Λυσικράτης) ?= (29); (25) ii AD *IG* V (1) 176, 4 (Bradford (10)) (I f. Χαρίξενος II); (26) ~ *IG* V (1) 176, 4 (Bradford (2)) (II s. Χαρίξενος I); (27) c. 110-120 AD *IG* V (1) 298, 1; *Artemis Orthia* pp. 315-16 no. 35 (date) (Bradford (3)) (s. Δαμοκρατίδας); (28) c. 125-150 AD *SEG* XI 578, 2 (Bradford (9)) (Χαρίξε(ν)ος: f. Ἀγαπητός); (29) c. 150-160 AD *IG* V (1) 53, 8 (f. Γ. Ἰούλ. Λυσικράτης) ?= (24)
MESSENIA:
—THOURIA: (30) f. ii BC *SEG* XI 972, 116 (I f. Χαρίξενος II); (31) ~ ib. l. 116 (II s. Χαρίξενος I)
S. ITALY (BRUTTIUM):
—LOKROI EPIZEPHYRIOI:
——(Εὐρ.): (32) 277 BC De Franciscis 8, 1; 31, [1] (f. Νέαιθος)
——(Κοβ.): (33) iv/iii BC ib. 2, 1 ?= (34); (34) ~ ib. 6, 4 (s. Ὀναῖος) ?= (33); (35) ~ ib. 32, 6 (f. Ἁγίων)
——(Λακ.): (36) iv/iii BC ib. 17, 7 (s. Εὐφίλιστος)
——(Μνα.): (37) iv/iii BC ib. 19, 4 (s. Εὔφρων)
——(Πετ.): (38) iv/iii BC ib. 20, 10 (s. Χαιρύλος)

**Χάριππος**
ARGOLIS:
—EPIDAUROS:
——(Azantioi): (1) 146 BC *IG* IV (1)² 28, 36 (s. Ἁγησίας)
MESSENIA:
—MESSENE: (2) s. ii BC *SEG* XLI 341, 5 (s. Ἐπιθάλης)
S. ITALY (BRUTTIUM):
—LOKROI EPIZEPHYRIOI:
——(Ἀγκ.): (3) iv/iii BC De Franciscis 5, 6 (f. Δείναρχος)

——(Μνα.): (4) iv/iii bc ib. 39, 3 (Χάρ(ι)ππος: f. Φίλων)

——(Ὀμβ.): (5) iv/iii bc ib. 20, 8 (f. Χαρικλῆς)

**Χάρις**
Achaia:
—patrai: (1) hell.-imp. CIG 1552 (Χαριτος (gen.)—apogr.)
S. Italy (Apulia): (2) f. iv bc NScav 1883, p. 566 (vase) (fict.)
S. Italy (Bruttium):
—hipponion-vibo valentia: (3) ?i ad Rend. Pont. 60 (1987-8) p. 273 no. 11; CIL x 75 (Lat. Raia Charis: m. Μυρρίνη)
—hipponion-vibo valentia*: (4) imp. ib. 88 (Lat. Pullia Charis: freed.)
S. Italy (Campania):
—dikaiarchia-puteoli: (5) imp. AJA 2 (1898) p. 377 no. 9 (Lat. Bennia Charis); (6) ~ CIL x 2106 (Lat. Clodia Charis); (7) ~ ib. 2526 (Lat. Cassia Charis: m. P. Ortensius Severus); (8) ~ Eph. Ep. viii 395 (Lat. Charis)
—dikaiarchia-puteoli*: (9) imp. CIL x 3098, 5 (Lat. Veturia Charis: m. Ἀνίκητος, Κιτιάς I, Κιτιάς II, Veturia Severa: freed.)
Sicily:
—panormos: (10) imp. Epigraphica 3 (1941) p. 267 no. 35 (Lat. Charis); (11) ~ CIL x 7308 (Lat. Charis: slave?)
—terravecchia di cuti (mod.): (12) f. v bc Di Terra in Terra pp. 56-7 nos. 74-8; cf. SEG xlii 879 (Χάρι[ς])

**Χαρίσιον**
Lakonia:
—sparta: (1) c. 225-250 ad IG v (1) 540 (Bradford (-)) (-ρεί-: d. Σπαρτιατικός)

**Χαρίσιος**
Elis: (1) m. iv bc D. lix 18; cf. Ath. 593 f.
S. Italy (Campania):
—herculaneum: (2) c. 59 ad PdelP 9 (1954) p. 64 no. 66, 3 (Lat. M. Calatorius Charisius)
—kyme: (3) imp. Mon. Ant. 22 (1913) p. 764 (mosaic) (Lat. M. Papirius Carisius)
—pompeii: (4) i bc-i ad CIL iv 4322 (Lat. Carisius)

**Χάρισος**
Korinthia:
—korinth: (1) s. iv bc Corinth viii (1) 11, 12 (Χαρίσ(ι)ος?: s. Δε—)

**Χαρίτα**
Argolis:
—argos: (1) iii bc IG iv (1) 527, 13; cf. BCH 37 (1913) p. 309 ([X]αρίτα)
—hermione: (2) ?ii-i bc IG iv (1) 731 II, 6 (d. Τληπόλεμος)
Elis: (3) ii bc ib. II² 8531
Korinthia:
—korinth: (4) c. 610-590 bc Corinth xiii p. 321 no. X-141 (vase) (Χαρίτα); (5) c. 550 bc Amyx Gr 15. 3 (vase) (Lorber 153) (het.?/fict.?)

**Χαριτέλης**
Lakonia:
—sparta: (1) ii ad IG v (1) 1369, 2, 8, 11 (Bradford (2)) (I s. Λάδικος, f. Χαριτέλης II, Ἰούνιος); (2) ~ IG v (1) 1369, 10 (Bradford (1)) (II s. Χαριτέλης I, Τιμάς)
Messenia:
—kyparissia: (3) s. iii bc Liv. xxxii 21. 23 (Lat. Chariteles)

**Χαρίτη**
S. Italy (Apulia):
—rubi: (1) i/ii ad Suppl. It. 5 p. 22 no. 4 (Lat. [C]arita: d. Crispia Ampliata); (2) ii ad Epigrafia e Territorio 2 pp. 77 ff. no. 16 (CIL ix

6185) (Lat. Licinia Charite: m. M. Licinius M–ilus)
S. Italy (Bruttium):
—lokroi epizephyrioi: (3) iii-iv ad Costabile, Municipium Locrensium 36 (Lat. Charite: d. Μαργαρίς)
S. Italy (Campania):
—dikaiarchia-puteoli: (4) imp. AJA 2 (1898) p. 378 no. 10 (Lat. Caecilia Charite: freed.); (5) ~ CIL x 2253 (Lat. Charite)

**Χαρίτιμος**
Argolis:
—argos:
——(Kleodaidai): (1) ii/i bc BCH 33 (1909) p. 176 no. 2, 13 (f. Τιμαγόρας)
Korinthia:
—sikyon: (2) ?255 bc Nachtergael, Les Galates 8, 41 (Skalet 340); cf. Stephanis 1616 (f. Μαρσύας)

**Χαρίτιν**
Sicily:
—syracuse: (1) iii-v ad ASSiracusano 1956, p. 47 ([Χα]ρίτιν)

**Χαριτώ**
Argolis:
—hermione: (1) ii-i bc IG iv (1) 732 II, 25 (m. Δωρίς)

**Χαρίτων**
Arkadia:
—tegea: (1) i ad ib. v (2) 47, 4
Illyria:
—apollonia: (2) imp. IApoll 233 (f. Δρείγαλος?)
Lakonia:
—sparta: (3) ii ad IG v (1) 159, 2 (Bradford (3)); (4) 127 ad IG v (1) 1314, 27 (Bradford (1)) (s. Καλλικράτης); (5) f. iii ad IG v (1) 170, 15; BSA 80 (1985) p. 245 (date) (Bradford (2)) (Αὐρ. Χ.: s. Φιλοκράτης)
S. Italy (Calabria):
—brentesion-brundisium: (6) imp. Epigraphica 25 (1963) p. 74 no. 76; cf. 42 (1980) p. 155 (Lat. Appalius Cha(r)ito); (7) ~ NScav 1889, p. 167 a (Eph. Ep. viii 8) (Lat. A. Allienus Charito)
S. Italy (Campania):
—dikaiarchia-puteoli: (8) imp. CIL x 2139 (Lat. Aurelius Charito); (9) m. iv ad PLRE I (-); Puteoli 4-5 (1980-1) p. 119 no. 4 (Lat. Sept(imius) Carito)
—dikaiarchia-puteoli?: (10) imp. CIL x 1833; cf. Puteoli 11 (1987) p. 42 (Lat. –uleius Charito)
—kyme: (11) 251 ad CIL x 3699 II, 8 (Lat. C. Iulius Carito)
—neapolis: (12) ?i ad NScav 1892, p. 56 (Lat. Aelius Charito)
—pompeii: (13) i bc-i ad CIL iv 3976 (Castrèn 129. 12) (Lat. Cornelius Carito); (14) ~ Atti Acc. Pontan. 39 (1990) p. 293 no. 72 (Lat. Poppaeus Chariton)
—stabiae: (15) i ad CIL x 783 (Lat. M. Perpenna Charito)
—surrentum: (16) imp. ib. 737 (Lat. C. Iulius Charito); (17) ~ Cinquant' Anni Lic. Class. p. 281 no. 4 (Lat. M. Livius Charito)
—surrentum*: (18) imp. CIL x 696 (Lat. Charito: imp. freed.)
Sicily:
—akragas: (19) f. vi bc Wehrli, Schule Arist. vii fr. 65
—apollonia: (20) iii-v ad IG xiv 361
—lilybaion: (21) hell.-imp. Mon. Ant. 33 (1929) p. 58 ([X]αρίτων)
—neaiton: (22) ii-iii ad Helikon 2 (1962) p. 498
—panormos: (23) imp. CIL x 7307 (Lat. Assyrius Charito)

—syracuse: (24) iii-v ad Strazzulla 244 (Barreca 370)

**Χαριτῶσα**
S. Italy (Campania):
—dikaiarchia-puteoli: (1) imp. CIL x 2240 (Lat. Octavia Charitus(a)—ed.)
—neapolis: (2) ?iv ad IG xiv 824 (INap 261; Wessel 696); cf. Leiwo p. 109 no. 78

**Χαριφῶν**
Messenia:
—pharai: (1) ?c. 500-475 bc IG v (1) 1362 b (Poralla² 748); LSAG² p. 206 no. 5 (date) (-φο̄ν, Χαρίφο[ενος]—Skias)

**Χαρμανδρίδας**
Aigina: (1) m. iv bc D.L. iii 14 (Favorin. fr. 65) (f. Χάρμανδρος)

**Χάρμανδρος**
Aigina: (1) m. iv bc RE (1); D.L. iii 14 (Favorin. fr. 65) (s. Χαρμανδρίδας)

**Χαρμαντίδας**
Argolis:
—epidauros: (1) iv bc IG iv (1)² 198 (s. Πυλάδας)
—epidauros*: (2) c. 370-365 bc Peek, IAEpid 52 A, 27 (Χαρμα[ντ]ίδας)
—hermione: (3) v bc Wehrli, Schule Arist. Suppl. i fr. 6 (-δης: ?f. Λάσος: dub.)

**Χαρμαντίδης**
Sicily:
—leontinoi: (1) v bc Paus. vi 17. 8; IvOl 293, 1 (CEG ii 830) (f. Γοργίας, Ἡρόδικος)

**Χάρμας**
S. Italy (Campania):
—neapolis: (1) i bc/i ad INap 103; cf. Leiwo p. 104 no. 60 (f. Βίβιος)

**Χαρμενίων**
Korinthia:
—korinth: (1) i ad Mart. x 65 (Lat. Charmenion)

**Χάρμης**
S. Italy (Campania):
—neapolis: (1) i bc IG xiv 817 (INap 181); cf. Leiwo p. 118 no. 104 (s. Φίλιος)
Sicily: (2) iv bc Vandermersch p. 178 (amph.) (or S. Italy)

**Χαρμιάδας**
Arkadia:
—mantineia-antigoneia: (1) ii bc IG v (2) 297

**Χαρμίδας**
Achaia:
—pellene: (1) 340 bc FD iii (1) 398, 2 (f. Ἐκέφυλος)
Elis: (2) ?444 bc Moretti, Olymp. 310 (Ebert, Gr. Sieg. 24)
Lakonia:
—sparta: (3) ?s. viii bc Paus. iii 2. 7 (Poralla² 749) (s. Εὔθυς: fict.?)
S. Italy (Bruttium):
—lokroi epizephyrioi:
——(Φαω.): (4) iv/iii bc De Franciscis 32, 8 (f. Εὔφραστος)
Sicily:
—sampieri (mod.): (5) iii-v ad Riv. Arch. Crist. 18 (1941) p. 215 no. 93 (Καρμίδας?)

**Χαρμίδης**
Sicily:
—katane: (1) imp. IG xiv 552 (Agnello 56; Wessel 861); cf. Riv. Arch. Crist. 18 (1941) p. 239 no. 134 (Χαρμ[—]—IG and Wessel, Χαρμ[ίδης]—Agnello and Ferrua)

## Χαρμῖνος

LAKONIA:
—SPARTA: (1) 400-399 BC X., *An.* vii 6. 1; vii 6. 39; vii 7. 13 ff; vii 7. 56 (Poralla² 750)
MESSENIA:
—MESSENE: (2) iii BC *SEG* XXIII 209, 6; (3) ~ ib. l. 13; (4) s. ii BC ib. XLI 341, 7 (Χαρμένος—ed. pr. per err.: s. Εὐφρονῖνος)
—THOURIA: (5) s. iii BC *IG* v (1) 1386, 14 (f. Θεοκλῆς)

## Χάρμιος

AITOLIA: (1) ?228-215 BC *FD* III (4) 364, 2 with n.; cf. *SGDI* 2525

## Χάρμις

ARGOLIS:
—ARGOS?: (1) f. i BC *SEG* XXIII 180, 5 (f. Φαίνανδρος: date—Kritzas)
LAKONIA:
—SPARTA: (2) 668 BC Moretti, *Olymp.* 40 (Poralla² 751); (3) ~ Moretti, *Olymp.* 40 (Poralla² 751 (ident.)) ?= (Χίονις (2))

## Χαρμίων

ARKADIA:
—TEGEA:
——(Krariotai): (1) f. iii BC *IG* v (2) 36, 47 (s. Ξένων: metic)

## Χαρμόνδας

S. ITALY (BRUTTIUM):
—LOKROI EPIZEPHYRIOI:
——(Κρα.): (1) iv/iii BC De Franciscis 6, 3 (f. Φαίκων)
——(Σωτ.): (2) iv/iii BC ib. 17, 3 (f. Σίλων)

## Χαρμονικίς

ARKADIA:
—HERAIA: (1) ?ii BC *IG* v (2) 418; *BCH* 89 (1965) p. 586 (name, date) (Χαρμονικί (voc.))

## Χάρμος

ARGOLIS:
—EPIDAUROS*: (1) c. 370-360 BC *BSA* 61 (1966) p. 271 no. 4 A, 17
—TROIZEN: (2) ?iv BC *IG* IV (1) 749, 2 (s. Στασικλῆς)
DALMATIA:
—PHAROS: (3) iv/iii BC *GVI* 1532 (*CEG* II 662) (s. Καλλίας)
KORINTHIA:
—KORINTH: (4) inc. *Syringes* 705; 711 (f. Ἀρίστερμις)
—SIKYON: (5) vi/v BC *SEG* XI 244, 8
LAKONIA:
—SPARTA: (6) 336 BC *CID* II 24 II, 3 (Poralla² 754)
—SPARTA?: (7) i BC/i AD *GP* 1388 (s. Λυκῖνος)
SICILY:
—SYRACUSE: (8) 4 or iii BC Wehrli, *Schule Arist.* iii fr. 90 (Stephanis 2621)

## Χαρμοσύνη

SICILY:
—TYNDARIS: (1) imp. *Epigraphica* 51 (1989) p. 165 nos. 20-22 (Lat. Asinia Charmosyne)

## Χαρμόσυνος

LAKONIA:
—SPARTA: (1) ii/iii AD *IG* v (1) 144 a-c (Bradford (1)) (s. Αὐγουστιανός, f. Αὐρ. Αὐγουστιανός, Αὐρ. Φιλοξενίδας); (2) f. iii AD *IG* v (1) 333 (*Artemis Orthia* p. 337 no. 77; Bradford (2)) (Αὐρ. [Χαρμ]]όσυν[ος]?)
MESSENIA:
—KORONE: (3) 246 AD *IG* v (1) 1398, 66 (Αὐρ. Χαρμόσυνος)
SICILY:
—SYRACUSE: (4) iii-v AD *Riv. Arch. Crist.* 36 (1960) p. 25 no. 11; cf. Ferrua, *NG* 104

## Χαρμυλίδας

S. ITALY (LUCANIA):
—POSEIDONIA-PAESTUM: (1) c. 470 BC Lazzarini 702 (Landi, *DISMG* 128; *CEG* 1 395); *LSAG*² p. 260 no. 7 (date) (f. Φιλλώ)

## Χαρμύλος

AIGINA: (1) ii/i BC *Alt-Ägina* 1 (2) p. 43 no. 3, 3 (s. Κόπρις); (2) ?i AD ib. p. 45 no. 14 (Χαρμύλ[ος])

## Χαρμωνίδας

MESSENIA:
—MESSENE: (1) s. ii BC *SEG* XLI 341, 4 (s. Δαμιππίδας)

## Χαροπίας

SICILY:
—KAMARINA: (1) f. v BC Cordano, *Tessere Pubbliche* 8 (f. Ταυρίσκος)

## Χαροπίδας

AKARNANIA:
—THYRREION: (1) 216 BC *IG* IX (1)² (2) 583, 19 (s. Νίκανδρος)
EPIROS: (2) 208 BC *IMM* 32, 38, 48

## Χαροπῖνος

ILLYRIA:
—EPIDAMNOS-DYRRHACHION: (1) c. 250-50 BC Maier 405; Münsterberg Nachtr. p. 17 (coin) (Ceka 285; 363) (pryt.)
MESSENIA:
—ABIA: (2) ?c. 500-475 BC *IG* v (1) 1356 (Poralla² 753); *LSAG*² p. 206 no. 6 (date)
S. ITALY (LUCANIA):
—HYELE-VELIA: (3) 188 BC *Syll*³ 585, 129 (s. Ἄνταλλος)

## Χάροπος

ACHAIA:
—DYME: (1) s. iii BC *SEG* XIII 278, 27
ELIS: (2) c. 365 BC X., *HG* vii 4. 15-16
KORINTHIA:
—SIKYON: (3) c. 545-530 BC *ABV* p. 146 no. 20 (Skalet 341)

## Χάροψ

AIGINA: (1) arch.? Luc., *JConf.* 16
AKARNANIA:
—ALYZIA: (2) ?354 BC Tod, *GHI* II 160, 6 (s. Δάδων)
ARGOLIS:
—PHLEIOUS: (3) s. iv BC Peek, *NIEpid* 16, 25 (Perlman E.6) (f. Καρνεάδας)
ELIS: (4) ?257 BC *FD* III (3) 195, 1 (s. Ἀστυοχίδας); (5) m. i BC *IvOl* 207 (Moretti, *Olymp.* 707) (s. Τηλέμαχος) ?= (6); (6) 36-24 BC *IvOl* 62, 10; 64, 16; 65, [20] (f. Ἱππίας) ?= (5)
EPIROS: (7) ?198 BC *IG* II² 2313, 24; *SEG* XLI 113; Habicht, *Athen hell. Zeit* p. 130 (ident.); p. 134 (date) (f. Ἀλκέμαχος) ?= (9)
—CHARADROS: (8) a. 167 BC *SEG* XXXV 665 A, 14 (f. Βοΐσκος)
—OPATOI: (9) iii/ii BC *RE* Supplbd. 1 (11); *Ténos* 2 pp. 102 f. A, 2 (*SEG* XL 690) (s. Μαχάτας, f. Μαχάτας) ?= (7); (10) f. ii BC *RE* Supplbd. 1 (12); Cabanes, *L'Épire* index s.v. (s. Μαχάτας, Φιλωτίς)
TRIPHYLIA:
—MAKISTOS: (11) 399-369 BC *SEG* XXXV 389, 12

## Χάρτας

AITOLIA:
—TRICHONION: (1) s. iii BC *IG* IX (1)² (1) 117, 10
LAKONIA:
—SPARTA: (2) ?vi BC Paus. vi 4. 4 (Poralla² 755) (sculptor)

## Χαρτέλης

MESSENIA:
—PYLOS: (1) v/iv BC *IG* v (1) 1419 (Poralla² 756) (-λε̄ς)

## Χαρτηρίς

LAKONIA:
—TAINARON-KAINEPOLIS: (1) ii/iii AD *IG* v (1) 601, 6; *BSA* 79 (1984) p. 265 (ident., date); p. 284 (stemma) (Bradford (1)) (m. Αὐρ. Ἀριστόκλεια); (2) c. 220-240 AD *IG* v (1) 601, 2; *BSA* 79 (1984) p. 265 (ident., date); p. 284 (stemma) (Bradford (2)) (and Lakonia Sparta: Αὐρ. Χ.: d. Αὐρ. Ἀριστοτέλης, Αὐρ. Ἀριστόκλεια, m. M. Αὐρ. Εὔπορος)

## Χαρτίας

MESSENIA:
—MESSENE: (1) m. iii BC *IG* v (2) 368, 48

## Χάρτις

MESSENIA:
—MESSENE: (1) 87 AD *SEG* XLI 335, 10 (f. Ἐχέδαμος)

## Χαρτίων

MESSENIA:
—MESSENE: (1) iii BC ib. XXIII 210, 5 ?= (2)
—MESSENE?: (2) f. iii BC *IG* XII (9) 217, 2, 9 (f. Κρατησικλῆς: locn.—Knoepfler) ?= (1)

## Χάρτος

ARGOLIS:
—EPIDAUROS:
——Melkidon: (1) c. 365-335 BC ib. IV (1)² 103, 127
MESSENIA: (2) ?i AD ib. v (1) 1374 (s. Εὐθυκλῆς)

## Χαρτύλος

LAKONIA:
—SPARTA: (1) f. vi BC *SEG* II 77 (Lazzarini 403e); *LSAG*² p. 198 no. 6 (date) (Poralla² 756a; Bradford (-)) (Χαρτύλο[ς])

## Χάρτων

LAKONIA:
—TAINARON-KAINEPOLIS: (1) imp. *IG* v (1) 1246 (Τιβ. Κλ. Χ.)

## Χάρυλλος

MESSENIA:
—MESSENE: (1) s. ii BC *SEG* XLI 341, 9 (Χάριλλος—ed., Χαρύαλος—*SEG*: s. Καλλῖνος)

## Χάρων

ARGOLIS:
—ARGOS: (1) ?c. 575-550 BC ib. XI 336, 6; *LSAG*² p. 168 no. 7 (date) (-ρō̄ν: s. Ἀρχεσίλας)
ELIS:
—OLYMPIA*: (2) c. 550 BC *SEG* XXXI 375 (vase) (-ρō̄ν)
KORINTHIA:
—KORINTH: (3) c. 570-550 BC Amyx 59. 1; 78. 4; 102. 7; 112. 1 (vases) (Lorber 94); Lorber 110; 91; 104 (her.?)
LAKONIA:
—SPARTA: (4) v/iv BC Plu., *Mor.* 233 E (Poralla² 757)
SICILY:
—MORGANTINA: (5) iv/iii BC *SEG* XXXIX 1013, 5 (f. Ἄνταλλος)
—SELINOUS: (6) vi/v BC Manganaro, *PdelP* forthcoming no. 18, 8 (-ρō̄ν: s. Ἀγάσαρχος)

## Χαρώνδας

ARGOLIS:
—EPIDAUROS*: (1) c. 370-365 BC Peek, *IAEpid* 52 A, 26; 52 B, 69
SICILY:
—KATANE: (2) vi BC *RE* (1)

**Χειλᾶς**
S. Italy (Lucania):
—METAPONTION: (1) iv bc Iamb., *VP* 267 (*FVS* 1 p. 446) (*Χιλᾶς*—ms.: name— Schweigh.)

**Χειλέων**
Lakonia:
—SPARTA: (1) inc. *CAG* XVIII (1) p. 126, 9

**Χείλεως**
Arkadia:
—TEGEA: (1) 481-479 bc *RE* (-)

**Χειλῖνος**
Sicily:
—KAMARINA: (1) f. v bc Cordano, *Tessere Pubbliche* 78 (*Χ[ει]λῖνος*—ed., *Φ[ι]λῖνος?*—*LGPN*: s. *Σῖμος*)

**Χείλων**
Achaia:
—PATRAI: (1) s. iv bc Paus. vi 4. 6; cf. Ebert, *Gr. Sieg.* 50 (I f. *Χείλων* II); (2) ~ Moretti, *Olymp.* 461, 465; cf. Ebert, *Gr. Sieg.* 50 (II s. *Χείλων* I)

**Χείμαρος**
S. Italy (Bruttium):
—LOKROI EPIZEPHYRIOI: (1) ?c. 475-450 bc Guarducci, *Ep. Gr.* 1 p. 303 no. 6 (Lazzarini 197; Landi, *DISMG* 61); *LSAG²* p. 286 no. 6 (date)

**Χείμων**
Argolis:
—ARGOS: (1) 448 bc Moretti, *Olymp.* 298 (*Κίμων*—*FGrH* 415: f. *Ἀριστεύς*)

**Χειρικράτης**
Lakonia:
—SPARTA: (1) 395 bc *Hell. Oxy.* xix 1; xxii 4 (Poralla² 758)

**Χειρίσοφος**
Lakonia:
—SPARTA: (1) 401-400 bc *RE* (1) (Poralla² 759)

**Χελίας**
Argolis:
—TROIZEN: (1) ?146 bc *IG* IV (1) 757 A, 22 (f. —*τιμος*)

**Χελιδών**
S. Italy (Apulia):
—CANUSIUM: (1) ii-iii ad *Epig. Rom. di Canosa* 152 (*CIL* IX 387) (Lat. Chelido: m. P. Libuscidius Faustinus)
S. Italy (Campania):
—DIKAIARCHIA-PUTEOLI: (2) imp. *IG* XIV 2414. 55 (tessera) (*[Χ]ελιδών*)
—KYME*: (3) imp. *NScav* 1887, p. 410 (*Eph. Ep.* VIII 449) (Lat. Furia Chelido: freed.)
—MISENUM*: (4) imp. *CIL* X 3488 (Lat. Atilia Chelido: freed.)
—NOLA: (5) imp. ib. 1320 (Lat. Chelido)
—POMPEII: (6) i bc-i ad *IG* XIV 706 (*Λολλία Χειλειδών*)

**Χέλις**
Arkadia:
—THELPHOUSA: (1) ii-i bc ib. v (2) 411 (*[Χ]έλις?*: s. *Πλειστίας*)

**Χερρίας**
Argolis:
—TROIZEN*: (1) iv bc ib. IV (1) 823, 60

**Χερσίας**
Arkadia:
—ORCHOMENOS: (1) her. *RE* (-) (fict.?)

**Χερσικλείδας**
Argolis:
—TROIZEN: (1) ?146 bc *IG* IV (1) 757 B, 25 (*Χε[ρ]σικλείδας*)

**Χερσικράτης**
Korinthia:
—KORINTH: (1) s. viii bc *RE* (-); *Korkyra* 1 p. 164 no. 3 (and Kerkyra: *Χερσικρατίδαι* (n. gent.)—*Korkyra*: oikist)

**Χέρσυς**
Akarnania:
—MEDION: (1) 208 bc *IMM* 31, 3 (*IG* IX (1)² (2) 582)
—THYRREION: (2) ii bc *SEG* XXV 628, 4 (f. —*ν*) ?= (3); (3) a. 167 bc *NZ* 10 (1878) p. 178 no. 34; *BMC Thessaly* p. 193 no. 14 (coin) ?= (2)

**Χηρίας**
Aitolia: (1) ?263-261 bc *FD* III (3) 184, 2; 190, [1]; *Syll³* 498, 3; Nachtergael, *Les Galates* 3, [2]

**Χηρικράτης**
Messenia:
—THOURIA: (1) ii-i bc *IG* v (1) 1385, 18 (f. *Ἀγαθοκλῆς*); (2) f. ii bc *SEG* XI 972, 84 (s. *Ἀγιτέλης*)

**Χία**
S. Italy (Apulia):
—VENUSIA*: (1) ii bc *Museo di Venosa* p. 112 no. 2 (Lat. Blaia Chia: freed.)
S. Italy (Campania):
—NEAPOLIS: (2) i bc-i ad *IG* XIV 796 a (*INap* 140); cf. Leiwo p. 125 no. 112 (*Λικινία Χεία*)
—POMPEII*: (3) i bc-i ad *NScav* 1894, p. 15 no. 1 (Castrèn 151. 2) (Lat. Dellia Chia: freed.)
Sicily:
—KATANE: (4) imp. *IG* XIV 503 (*Χεία*: d. *Κοΰντος Σόσσις, Πετρονία Σοσσία*)

**Χιακός**
S. Italy: (1) iv-iii bc *Misc. Etrusco-Italica* 1 p. 194 no. A1 (bronze) (*Χηακ(ό)ς?*)

**Χίλα**
S. Italy (Apulia):
—VENUSIA: (1) imp. *Rend. Linc.* 31 (1976) p. 287 no. 7 (Lat. Statia Chila)
S. Italy (Campania):
—SURRENTUM*: (2) imp. *NScav* 1928, p. 212 no. 1 (Lat. Chila: imp. freed.)

**Χίλιος**
Arkadia:
—KLEITOR: (1) c. 140-120 bc *BCH* 60 (1936) p. 12 no. 1, 8, 16 (f. *Ἱππέας*)
—TEGEA: (2) 479 bc Hdt. ix 9. 1; Polyaen. v 30 (*Χ.*—Polyaen., *Χίλεος*—Hdt.)

**Χίλων**
Elis: (1) 272 bc Paus. v 5. 1
Korinthia:
—KORINTH: (2) 43 or 42 bc Amandry pp. 123-4; *RPC* 1 p. 250 no. 1117 (coin) (Lat. P. Tadi(us) Chilo)
Lakonia:
—SPARTA: (3) f. vi bc *RE* (1) (Poralla² 760) (s. *Δαμάγητος*, f. *Χιλωνίς*, ?f. *Δαμάρμενος*); (4) s. vi bc Hdt. vi 65. 2 (Poralla² 761) (s. *Δαμάρμενος*, f. *Πέρκαλον*); (5) 364 bc *X.*, *HG* vii 4. 23 (Poralla² 762); (6) s. iii bc Plb. iv 81. 1 (Bradford (1)) (*Χείλων*—Plb.)
S. Italy (Apulia):
—CANUSIUM: (7) i ad *Epig. Rom. di Canosa* 43 (Lat. D. Marius Cilo)
S. Italy (Calabria):
—BRENTESION-BRUNDISIUM: (8) s. i bc *CIL* I² 3173 (Lat. L. Servilius C[il]o)

S. Italy (Campania):
—ABELLA: (9) imp. ib. X 1204; 1210 (Lat. T. Antistius Cilo)
—DIKAIARCHIA-PUTEOLI: (10) imp. ib. 8185 (Lat. C. Artorius Cilo); (11) f. ii ad ib. 2133 (*Puteoli* 9-10 (1985-6) p. 57 no. 4); *CIL* X 6791 (Lat. A. Avianius Cilo)
—KYME: (12) imp. ib. 2930; 8042. 92 (tiles) (Lat. C. Satrius Cilo); (13) ?iii ad ib. 2838; cf. *Puteoli* 12-13 (1988-9) p. 216 no. 5 (Lat. L. Pescennius Cilo)
—POMPEII: (14) 14 bc *CIL* X 885; 886 (Castrèn 297. 4) (Lat. N. Paccius Chilo)

**Χιλωνίδας**
Aigina: (1) hell. *IG* IV (1) 101 (*Χιλωνίδ[ας]*, *Φιλωνίδ[ας]?*)
Lakonia:
—SPARTA: (2) iii bc *SEG* XL 348 B, 6

**Χιλωνίς**
Lakonia:
—SPARTA: (1) s. viii bc Polyaen. viii 34; Quint., *Inst.* ii 17. 20 (Poralla² 763) (*Χειλωνίς*—Polyaen.: d. *Κλεάδας*); (2) m. vi bc Iamb., *VP* 267 (*FVS* 1 p. 447; Poralla² 764) (d. *Χίλων*); (3) f. iii bc Plu., *Pyrrh.* 26-8; Parthen. xxiii; *FD* III (4) 418 (Bradford (1)) (*Χειλωνίς*—Parth.: d. *Λατυχίδας*, m. *Ἀρεύς*: queen); (4) m. iii bc Plu., *Agis* 17-18 (Bradford (2)) (d. *Λεωνίδας, Κρατησίκλεια*, m. *Ἀγησίπολις, Κλεομένης*); (5) ~ *SEG* 11 117-19; 121 (vases) (*Artemis Orthia* pp. 372-4 nos. 61-5 and 142; Bradford (3)) (date—*LGPN*)

**Χιμαρίδας**
Lakonia?: (1) ?c. 550-525 bc *SEG* XVI 284 (bronze) (Lazzarini 358); *LSAG²* p. 202 no. 67 (locn., date) (or Triphylia Skillous)

**Χίμαρος**
Sicily:
—AKRAI: (1) s. vi bc *Akrai* p. 161 no. 20 (Dubois, *IGDS* 107) (*Τίμαρος*—apogr., *Χίμαρος*—*IG* XIV 227 et al., *(Χ)ίμαρος*—*LGPN*, *Τίμαδος*—al., *Τίμαρος*—Dubois: f. *Λύσις*)
—SELINOUS: (2) m. v bc ib. 34 (Arena, *Iscr. Sic.* I 70) (*Χίμ(α)ρος*)

**Χίμεννα**
Sicily:
—THERMAI HIMERAIAI: (1) imp. *CIL* X 7394 (*ILat. Term. Imer.* 79) (Lat. Coponia Chimenn(a): freed.)

**Χιόνη**
S. Italy (Bruttium):
—PETELIA: (1) ii-iii ad *Klearchos* 5 (1963) p. 81 no. 8 (Lat. Sallustia Chione)
S. Italy (Calabria):
—TARAS-TARENTUM: (2) imp. *NScav* 1896, p. 375 no. 1 (Lat. Chione)
S. Italy (Campania):
—SALERNUM: (3) m. i ad *IItal* 1 (1) 172 (*CIL* X 527) (Lat. Valeria Chione)
Sicily:
—THERMAI HIMERAIAI: (4) i ad *Epigraphica* 3 (1941) p. 261 no. 20 (*ILat. Term. Imer.* 162) (Lat. [V]olumnia Chione)

**Χιονίδας**
Arkadia: (1) 320 bc *IG* V (2) 549, 4 (s. *Εὐαίνετος*)

**Χίονις**
Korinthia:
—KORINTH: (1) vi/v bc Paus. x 13. 7; *RE* (3); Overbeck 480-1; 2053 (sculptor)
Lakonia:
—SPARTA: (2) 664-656 bc *RE* (1); Moretti, *Olymp.* 42-7 (Poralla² 765) ?= (*Χάρμις (3)*); (3) 421 bc Th. v 19. 1; 24 (Poralla² 766)

**Χιόνισσα**
S. ITALY (LUCANIA):
—GRUMENTUM*: (1) imp. *CIL* x 273 (Lat. Titia Chionissa: freed.)

**Χῖος**
ILLYRIA:
—EPIDAMNOS-DYRRHACHION: (1) imp. ib. III 12308 (Lat. [L.] Brexius Chius)
S. ITALY (APULIA):
—LUCERIA: (2) ii AD *Lucera Romana* p. 33 (Lat. Chius)
S. ITALY (CALABRIA):
—BRENTESION-BRUNDISIUM: (3) 31 AD *Athenaeum* 42 (1964) pp. 299-306 (Lat. Chius)
S. ITALY (CAMPANIA):
—DIKAIARCHIA-PUTEOLI: (4) imp. *CIL* x 2367 (Lat. Cn. Pitius Chius)
—HERCULANEUM*: (5) i BC-i AD ib. 1403 f III, 10 (Lat. L. Quintilius Chius: freed.)
—POMPEII (6) i BC-i AD ib. IV 1397 (Lat. Cius); (7) ~ ib. 1820 (Lat. Chius) ?= (8); (8) ~ ib. 1852 ?= (7); (9) ~ ib. 7096 (Lat. Cius); (10) ~ ib. 7425 (Lat. Chius)

**Χίρων**
KORINTHIA:
—KORINTH: (1) f. vi BC Amyx p. 608 no. 45 (pinax) (-ρōν)
S. ITALY (LUCANIA):
—POSEIDONIA-PAESTUM: (2) ?c. 550-500 BC Landi, *DISMG* 122; *LSAG*² p. 259 no. 2 (date) (her.?)
SICILY:
—KAMARINA: (3) m. v BC Dubois, *IGDS* 120, 2 (Arena, *Iscr. Sic.* II 142 A; *SEG* XXXVIII 939; Cordano, 'Camarina VII' 64) (-ρōν: f. Ἀρχεθάλης)

**Χισμίδας**
LAKONIA:
—SPARTA: (1) f. vi BC *SEG* II 72 (Lazzarini 403g); *LSAG*² p. 198 no. 6 (date) (Poralla² 766b; Bradford (-))

**Χιώ**
S. ITALY (BRUTTIUM):
—SYBARIS-THOURIOI-COPIAE: (1) ?c. 550 BC Landi, *DISMG* 253 (loomweight); *LSAG*² p. 456 no. F (date); cf. *SEG* XLI 853 (Χιō̄ (n. pr.?))

**Χίων**
ARGOLIS:
—ARGOS: (1) i BC-i AD Unp. (Argos, Kavvadias)

**Χιωνίδας**
KORINTHIA:
—KORINTH: (1) a. 191 BC *SEG* XXVI 392, 7 ([Χ]ιωνίδας: f. Νικάτας)

**Χλαινέας**
AITOLIA: (1) 211 BC Plb. ix 31. 7; 32. 6 + 10; 33. 2 + 10 ?= (2)
—KALYDON: (2) 217-207 BC *FD* III (3) 221, 3 ?= (1)

**Χλεμύτας**
KERKYRA: (1) c. 315-280 BC ib. III (4) 406, 3 (s. Ἀλύπητος); (2) ~ ib. l. 3 (f. Λυσήν)

**Χλευώ**
SICILY:
—TERRAVECCHIA DI CUTI (MOD.): (1) f. v BC *Di Terra in Terra* p. 57 no. 79 (loomweight); cf. *SEG* XLII 880 (Χλευō̄)

**Χλίδανον**
EPIROS: (1) ii/i BC *IG* II² 8546 (d. Καλλίας)

**Χλίδων**
ARGOLIS:
—TROIZEN: (1) iii BC ib. IV (1) 824, 6 (slave?)

**Χλόη**
S. ITALY (APULIA):
—VENUSIA: (1) imp. *CIL* IX 586 (Lat. Bivellia Cloe)
S. ITALY (CAMPANIA):
—DIKAIARCHIA-PUTEOLI: (2) imp. ib. x 2988 (Lat. Sulpicia Chloe)
—DIKAIARCHIA-PUTEOLI*: (3) imp. ib. 2741 (Lat. Mindia Chloe: freed.)
—POMPEII: (4) i BC-i AD ib. IV 1646 (Lat. Chloe); (5) ~ ib. 4430 (Lat. Cloe); (6) ~ ib. 8321 a (Lat. Chloe); (7) ~ ib. 8608 (Lat. Chole); (8) ~ ib. 8618; 8626; 8635 (Lat. Chloe); (9) ~ *Römische Gräberstrassen* p. 216 c (Lat. Calventia Cloe: d. Numisius Auctus)
—SURRENTUM: (10) imp. *CIL* x 741 (Lat. Choe, Ch(l)oe?)
SICILY:
—SYRACUSE: (11) iii-v AD Strazzulla 354; cf. Ferrua, *NG* 130 (Κλωις (gen.)—lap., Κάλης?—Ferrua)

**Χλῶρος**
S. ITALY (CAMPANIA):
—POMPEII: (1) i BC-i AD *CIL* IV 921 (Lat. Chlorus)
SICILY:
—HALAISA?: (2) f. i BC Cic., *In Verr.* II ii 23; 102 (Lat. Sextus Pompeius Chlorus)
—LILYBAION: (3) ii BC *IG* XIV 279; *Semitica* 26 (1976) pp. 93 ff. (name) (Ἰμύλχ Ἰνίβαλος Χ.: s. Ἰμίλχων)

**Χνοάδας**
MESSENIA:
—ABIA: (1) ?c. 450 BC *IG* V (1) 1357; *LSAG*² p. 206 no. 9 (date)

**Χοίρα**
ARKADIA:
—TEGEA: (1) her. Paus. viii 47. 2; 48. 5 (Μάρπησσα ἡ Χ. ἐπονομαζομένη: fict.?)

**Χοίρασος**
KORINTHIA:
—KORINTH: (1) ?m. vii BC Amyx Gr 2 (vase) (*SEG* XXV 343)

**Χοιρίδιον**
TRIPHYLIA:
—PTELEA: (1) ii BC ib. XVI 282, 4; cf. *BE* 1958, no. 246 ([Χ]οιρίδ[ιον], [Μ]οιρίδ[ιον]?)

**Χοιρίλος**
DALMATIA:
—ISSA:
——(Pamphyloi): (1) iv/iii BC Brunšmid p. 8, 45 (s. Κ—)
ELIS: (2) iv/iii BC Moretti, *Olymp.* 480

**Χοιρίνα**
LEUKAS: (1) iv BC *AM* 27 (1902) p. 369 no. 36

**Χοιρίνας**
SICILY:
—SELINOUS?: (1) vi/v BC *SEG* XXXIX 1020 A, 12 (f. Φιλώνδας)

**Χοιρίων**
SICILY:
—KATANE: (1) c. 410-400 BC *HN*² 133; *Samml. Ludwig* 33 (coin)

**Χοῖρος**
AIGINA: (1) v/iv BC *IG* IV (1) 71
S. ITALY (BRUTTIUM):
—RHEGION: (2) vi/v BC Hdt. vii 170. 3; Paus. v 26. 5; *IvOl* [267] (Dubois, *IGDGG* I 35; Arena, *Iscr. Sic.* III 64); *LSAG*² p. 247 nos. 8-10 (date) (f. Μίκυθος)

**Χοραγικλῆς**
ARKADIA:
—MEGALOPOLIS: (1) ii/i BC *IG* V (2) 443, 3 (*IPArk* 32)

**Χοραγίς**
KEPHALLENIA:
—SAME: (1) hell. *IG* IX (1) 637

**Χοραγίων**
ARGOLIS:
—TROIZEN: (1) iii BC ib. IV (1) 825, 1

**Χορέας**
ARKADIA:
—PHENEOS: (1) c. 315-280 BC *FD* III (1) 39, 1 ([Χ]ορέας?: f. Νικόλαος)

**Χορηβίς**
LAKONIA:
—GERONTHRAI: (1) iii/ii BC *IG* V (1) 1118

**Χοροιθίς**
ARGOLIS:
—EPIDAUROS: (1) ii-iii AD Peek, *IAEpid* 204 (Χοροιθ[ίς])

**Χοροκλῆς**
ARGOLIS:
—EPIDAUROS: (1) iii BC ib. 102 ([Χ]ορο[κλ]ῆς: s. Ξενόδοκος)

**Χόρος**
S. ITALY (CAMPANIA):
—POMPEII: (1) i BC-i AD *CIL* IV 4735 (Lat. Chorus)

**Χορτᾶς**
ILLYRIA:
—APOLLONIA: (1) imp. *IApoll* 47 (f. Ἀλεξίων)

**Χόρτων**
SICILY:
—LILYBAION: (1) ii BC *IG* XIV 273; 277 (M. Οὐαλέριος Χ.: s. Διόγνητος Μήγας)

**Χορώι**
KORINTHIA:
—KORINTH: (1) c. 570-550 BC Amyx 85. 1 (vase) (Lorber 145) (-ρōι: her.?)
SICILY:
—COMISO (MOD.): (2) f. v BC *CEG* I 147 (Dubois, *IGDS* 127; Arena, *Iscr. Sic.* II 150; Cordano, 'Camarina VII' 8); cf. *SEG* XLII 847 (-ρōι)

**Χόσης**
ARGOLIS:
—ARGOS: (1) m. vii BC ib. XI 306 (Χοσē̄ (gen.))

**Χρέμας**
AKARNANIA: (1) c. 167 BC *RE* Supplbd. I (-); *IG* II² 951, 5 with Add. p. 669
—KORONTA: (2) iii BC ib. IX (1)² (2) 429 (f. Φιλία)
—MEDION: (3) 216 BC ib. 583, 21 (s. Δράκων)

**Χρέμης**
ARGOLIS:
—ARGOS: (1) ?325 BC *CID* II 101 II, 14

**Χρέμων**
ARGOLIS:
—ARGOS: (1) c. 365-335 BC *IG* IV (1)² 103, 12, 44, 54-5, 88, 116; (2) c. 335-334 BC *CID* II 62 I A I, 2, 12, 24 (s.e.); 79 A I, 35
ARKADIA:
—TEGEA: (3) c. 240-229 BC *IG* V (2) 10, 8

**Χρηίμίδας**
LAKONIA:
—OITYLOS: (1) iii/ii BC ib. V (1) 1295, 6 (Bradford (-))

**Χρηματίνη**
ARGOLIS:
—HERMIONE: (**1**) iii AD *SEG* XVII 165, 5 (Αὐρ. Χρηματίνη: m. *M. Αὐρ. Λικιννιανός*)

**Χρησιλεοῦς**
SICILY:
—SYRACUSE: (**1**) imp. *NScav* 1913, p. 265 (vase)

**Χρησίμη**
ILLYRIA:
—APOLLONIA: (**1**) imp. *IApoll* 268
S. ITALY (CALABRIA):
—BRENTESION-BRUNDISIUM: (**2**) imp. *CIL* IX 6392 (Lat. Camurtia Chresime)
S. ITALY (CAMPANIA):
—CAPREAE: (**3**) imp. *ZPE* 71 (1988) p. 197 no. 8, 2, 8 (Lat. Nonia Crhesime)
—POMPEII: (**4**) i BC-i AD *CIL* IV 8261 (Lat. Chresime)
—SALERNUM: (**5**) imp. *IItal* I (1) 210 (*CIL* X 614) (Lat. Lartia Chresime)

**Χρησιμίδας**
MESSENIA:
—KOLONIDES: (**1**) ii BC *IG* V (1) 1402, 6

**Χρησίμιον**
S. ITALY (BRUTTIUM):
—RHEGION: (**1**) imp. *CIL* X 8339 c (Lat. Crhesimion)

**Χρήσιμος**
ACHAIA: (**1**) 146 BC *IG* IV (1)² 28, 146 (I f. Χρήσιμος II: synoikos); (**2**) ~ ib. l. 146 (II s. Χρήσιμος I: synoikos)
ARKADIA:
—TEGEA: (**3**) iii BC ib. V (2) 30, 5 ([Χρ]ήσιμος: s. Ὠφελίων)
DALMATIA:
—RIZON: (**4**) imp. Šašel, *IL* 633 (Lat. Calpurnius Chresimus)
EPIROS:
—BOUTHROTOS: (**5**) ii BC *IBouthrot* 190 (f. Ἀλύπητος)
ILLYRIA:
—EPIDAMNOS-DYRRHACHION: (**6**) hell.-imp. *IDyrrh* 452 (s. Φειδίας)
KEPHALLENIA?: (**7**) imp.? *Miscellanea* p. 187 no. 7
S. ITALY: (**8**) iv-iii BC *IG* XIV 2408. 13 (*Roma Medio Repubblicana* 423. 1; *Misc. Etrusco-Italica* I p. 194 no. A2); (**9**) ?iii BC *SEG* XXXII 562 (*L'Illyrie mérid.* I p. 112 fig. 11)
S. ITALY (APULIA):
—CANUSIUM*: (**10**) imp. *Epig. Rom. di Canosa* 114 (*CIL* IX 370) (Lat. C. Cocius Chresimus: freed.)
—LARINUM: (**11**) imp. ib. 740 (Lat. Sex. Cerrinius Chresimus: freed./doctor?)
S. ITALY (CAMPANIA):
—HERCULANEUM*: (**12**) i BC-i AD ib. X 1403 g II, 30 (Lat. L. Aelius Chresimus: freed.)
—POMPEII: (**13**) i BC-i AD ib. IV 3964; 3965 (Lat. Cresimus); (**14**) ~ ib. 4243 (Lat. Cresimus); (**15**) ~ ib. 4726 (Lat. Cresimus); (**16**) 56 AD ib. 3340. 26, 22; X 8058. 91 (seal) (Castrèn 457. 7) (Lat. C. Vibius Cresimus)
—SALERNUM: (**17**) imp. *IItal* I (1) 132 (*CIL* X 571) (Lat. Chresimus)
S. ITALY (LUCANIA):
—POSEIDONIA-PAESTUM: (**18**) imp. Mello–Voza 186 (Lat. Chres[imus]?)
SICILY:
—SYRACUSE: (**19**) iii-v AD *IG* XIV 188 (Strazzulla 126; Wessel 697); cf. *Nuovo Didask.* 6 (1956) p. 52 no. 1; (**20**) ~ *Rend. Pont.* 22 (1946-7) p. 234 no. 31
—THERMAI HIMERAIAI: (**21**) imp. *CIL* X 7388 (*ILat. Term. Imer.* 68) (Lat. Chresimus)

**Χρήστη**
S. ITALY (APULIA):
—CANUSIUM: (**1**) imp. *Epig. Rom. di Canosa* 182 (*CIL* IX 398) (Lat. Sulpicia Crheste)
—CANUSIUM*: (**2**) i AD *Epig. Rom. di Canosa* 89 (Lat. Antonia Chreste: freed.)
—SPINAZZOLA (MOD.): (**3**) imp. *Epigrafia e Territorio* I p. 33 no. 7 (Lat. Cresta)
S. ITALY (CALABRIA):
—LUPIAE: (**4**) i-ii AD *NScav* 1957, p. 193 (Susini, *Fonti Salento* p. 148 no. 97) (Lat. Caesia Creste)
S. ITALY (CAMPANIA):
—DIKAIARCHIA-PUTEOLI: (**5**) imp. *CIL* X 2135 (Lat. Avivania Chreste: m. D. Avianius Rufus); (**6**) ~ ib. 2728 (Lat. Memia Creste); (**7**) ~ ib. 3021 (Lat. Chreste); (**8**) ~ ib. 8370 (Lat. Pupidia Chreste); (**9**) ?i-ii AD ib. 2587 (Lat. Iulia Chreste); (**10**) ?ii AD ib. 3149 (Lat. Criste)
—DIKAIARCHIA-PUTEOLI*: (**11**) imp. ib. 2648 (Lat. Carisia Chreste: m. Στάκτη: freed.); (**12**) ~ ib. 2738 (Lat. Naevia Chreste: freed.)
—SALERNUM: (**13**) imp. *IItal* I (1) 37 (*CIL* X 2153) (Lat. Elvia Chresta); (**14**) ?i AD *IItal* I (1) 46 (Lat. Chreste)
S. ITALY (LUCANIA):
—POTENTIA: (**15**) ?ii AD *Misc. Gr. Rom.* 8 p. 436 no. 2 (Lat. Petronia Chreste: m. Τρόφιμος)
SICILY:
—SYRACUSE: (**16**) byz. *SEG* IV 25 (Κρίστη)

**Χρηστία**
S. ITALY (CALABRIA):
—BRENTESION-BRUNDISIUM: (**1**) imp. *Epigraphica* 25 (1963) p. 76 no. 78 (Lat. Octabia Chrestya)

**Χρήστιλλος**
S. ITALY (LUCANIA):
—GRUMENTUM: (**1**) imp. *CIL* X 277 (Lat. Praetumeus Chrestillus)

**Χρηστίων**
MESSENIA:
—KORONE: (**1**) 246 AD *IG* V (1) 1398, 83 (Αἰλ. Χρησ[τί]ων)
S. ITALY (CALABRIA):
—LUPIAE: (**2**) imp. Susini, *Fonti Salento* p. 154 no. 108 (Lat. Chrestio)

**Χρηστιώνιος**
S. ITALY (LUCANIA):
—VOLCEI*: (**1**) imp. *IItal* III (1) 288 (Lat. Q. Poppaedius Chrestionius: freed.)

**Χρῆστος**
LAKONIA:
—SPARTA: (**1**) imp. *IG* V (1) 474 (Bradford (2)) (Παπείριος X.)
S. ITALY (APULIA):
—VENUSIA: (**2**) i AD *Rend. Linc.* 24 (1969) p. 14 no. 7 (*Museo di Venosa* p. 217 no. 26) (Lat. Q. Baebius [Chr]estus)
S. ITALY (CALABRIA):
—BRENTESION-BRUNDISIUM*: (**3**) imp. *CIL* IX 207 (Lat. L. Volumnius Chrestus: freed.)
S. ITALY (CAMPANIA):
—DIKAIARCHIA-PUTEOLI: (**4**) imp. ib. X 2356, 2 (Lat. C. Cupiennius Chrestus: II s. Χρῆστος I, Κυπρογένεια); (**5**) ~ ib. l. 4 (Lat. C. Cupiennius Chrestus: I f. Χρῆστος II, C. Cupiennius Primitibus)
—DIKAIARCHIA-PUTEOLI*: (**6**) imp. ib. 3117 (Lat. A. Vitellius Chrestus: s. Ἀνθέμιον: freed.)
—HERCULANEUM: (**7**) i BC-i AD *Riv. Stud. Pomp.* 3 (1989) p. 291 (tile) (Lat. Chrest(us))
—POMPEII: (**8**) i BC-i AD *CIL* IV 2457 (Lat. Chrestus); (**9**) ~ ib. 3987 (Lat. Crestus); (**10**) ~ ib. 5023 (Lat. Crestus)

—SALERNUM*: (**11**) ?i AD *IItal* I (1) 238 I, 15 (*CIL* X 557) (Lat. L. Appuleius Chrestus: freed.)
SICILY:
—SYRACUSE: (**12**) iii-v AD *SEG* XV 582; cf. Ferrua, *NG* 303
—SYRACUSE*: (**13**) 314 AD Eus., *HE* x 5, 21-4 (bp.)

**Χριθύλος**
KORINTHIA:
—SIKYON: (**1**) vi/v BC *SEG* XI 244, 33

**Χριστῖνα**
SICILY:
—SYRACUSE: (**1**) iii-v AD *Rend. Pont.* 22 (1946-7) p. 234 no. 31 (Χρη-)

**Χριστόδουλος**
ARGOLIS:
—ARGOS: (**1**) v-vi AD Unp. (Oikonomou-Laniado) (Χρη-)

**Χριστοφόρος**
S. ITALY (BRUTTIUM):
—RHEGION: (**1**) byz. *Bull. Arch. Crist.* 6 (1888-9) p. 90 (Lat. Christophorus: bp.)

**Χρόμιος**
ARGOLIS:
—ARGOS: (**1**) c. 550 BC Hdt. i 82; Plu., *Mor.* 306 B; *FGrH* 287 F 2a-b
S. ITALY (CAMPANIA):
—POMPEII: (**2**) i BC-i AD *CIL* IV 4319; 4410 (Lat. Chromius)
SICILY:
—GELA-PHINTIAS: (**3**) c. 530-470 BC *RE* (8) (and Sicily Syracuse: s. Ἁγησίδαμος)
—KAMARINA: (**4**) f. v BC Cordano, *Tessere Pubbliche* 98 (s. Γύγας)

**Χρόμων**
MESSENIA: (**1**) 426 BC Th. iii 98. 1

**Χρονία**
S. ITALY (CAMPANIA):
—SALERNUM: (**1**) imp. *IItal* I (1) 78 (Lat. Plautia Cronie)

**Χρόνιος**
ARKADIA:
—TEGEA: (**1**) ?m. iii BC Paus. viii 45. 6
S. ITALY (CAMPANIA):
—HERCULANEUM*: (**2**) i BC-i AD *CIL* X 1403 g I, 31 (Lat. L. Venidius Chronius: freed.); (**3**) c. 50-75 AD ib. 1403 a II, 4 (Lat. M. Nonius Chronius: freed.)

**Χρόνις**
ILLYRIA:
—LYCHNIDOS: (**1**) ii-iii AD *Sp.* 77 (1934) p. 50 no. 44 (I f. Χρόνις II); (**2**) ~ ib. (II s. Χρόνις I: imp. freed.)

**Χρύσα**
S. ITALY (CAMPANIA):
—POMPEII: (**1**) i BC-i AD *SIRIS* p. 486 (Castrèn 239. 2) (Lat. Manilia Chrysa)

**Χρυσάγγελος**
SICILY:
—SYRACUSE: (**1**) iii-v AD Strazzulla 374 (Wessel 1365) (-σάνγε-)

**Χρύσαλλος**
S. ITALY (CAMPANIA):
—HERCULANEUM: (**1**) i BC-i AD *CIL* IV 10604 a (Lat. Crysalus)

**Χρυσάμαξος**
LAKONIA:
—SPARTA: (**1**) 596 BC Moretti, *Olymp.* 78 (Poralla² 768) (n. pr.?)

**Χρυσανθᾶς**
SICILY:
—ZANKLE-MESSANA: (**1**) imp. *CIL* x 6983 (Lat. Annius Chrysanta)

**Χρυσάνθιος**
S. ITALY (CAMPANIA):
—ATELLA*: (**1**) iv AD *PLRE* I (3); *Atti Acc. Arch. Napoli* 25 (1908) pp. 80-1 (Lat. Tannonius Chrysantius) ?= (**3**)
—DIKAIARCHIA-PUTEOLI*: (**2**) s. iv AD *PLRE* I (1); *CIL* x 1815; *Puteoli* 4-5 (1980-1) p. 119 no. 5 (Lat. Tannonius Boionius Chrysantius: II s. *Χρυσάνθιος* I); (**3**) ~ *PLRE* I (2); *CIL* x 1813; 3714; *AEp* 1976, no. 141; *Puteoli* 4-5 (1980-1) p. 119 no. 5 (Lat. Tannonius Chrysantius: I f. *Χρυσάνθιος* II) ?= (**1**)

**Χρυσανθίς**
KORINTHIA:
—KORINTH: (**1**) ?c. 500-475 BC *SEG* XXII 234 (Lazzarini 71); *LSAG*² p. 132 no. 34 (*Χρυσ-ανθ*[ίς])
S. ITALY (APULIA):
—CANUSIUM*: (**2**) i AD *Epig. Rom. di Canosa* 146 (Lat. Servilia Chrysanthis: freed.)

**Χρύσανθος**
ILLYRIA:
—AULON?: (**1**) imp. *SEG* I 264 (*Miscellanea* p. 190 no. 15) (I f. *Χρύσανθος* II); (**2**) ~ *SEG* I 264 (*Miscellanea* p. 190 no. 15) (II s. *Χρύσαν-θος* I)
S. ITALY (APULIA):
—AECAE: (**3**) imp. *AEp* 1972, no. 140 (Lat. Chrysanthus)
—CANUSIUM*: (**4**) i-ii AD *Epig. Rom. di Canosa* 79 (Lat. L. Artorius Crysanthus: freed.)
—VENUSIA: (**5**) imp. *CIL* IX 468 (Lat. Chrysantus)
S. ITALY (BRUTTIUM):
—HIPPONION-VIBO VALENTIA*: (**6**) imp. ib. x 62 (Lat. C. Alfidius Chrysantus: freed.)
—LOKROI EPIZEPHYRIOI*: (**7**) imp. *Eph. Ep.* VIII 843; cf. *Suppl. It.* 3 p. 20 (Lat. Vagellius Crisantus: freed.)
S. ITALY (CALABRIA):
—BRENTESION-BRUNDISIUM: (**8**) i AD *Epigraphica* 25 (1963) p. 34 no. 3; cf. 42 (1980) p. 154 (name) (Lat. C. Pinnius Chrysanthus)
S. ITALY (CAMPANIA):
—DIKAIARCHIA-PUTEOLI: (**9**) imp. *CIL* x 1738 (Lat. Cn. Domitius Chrysanthus); (**10**) ~ ib. 1873 (Lat. A. Arrius Chrysanthus); (**11**) ?i-ii AD ib. 2262 (Lat. Ti. Claudius Chrysant[hus])
—DIKAIARCHIA-PUTEOLI*: (**12**) imp. ib. 1562 (Lat. Chrysanthus: imp. freed.); (**13**) ?ii-iii AD ib. 2140 (Lat. M. Aurelius Chrysanthus: imp. freed.)
—HERCULANEUM*: (**14**) i BC-i AD ib. 1403 g II, 23 (Lat. Q. Iunius Chrysanthus: freed.)
—POMPEII: (**15**) i BC-i AD ib. IV 2392 (Castrèn 251. 4) (Lat. A. Messius Crysanthus); (**16**) ~ *CIL* IV 2508, 8 (Lat. Crysantus); (**17**) ~ ib. 4384; 4361 (Castrèn 402. 5) (Lat. M. Terentius Crysanthus); (**18**) ~ *CIL* IV 7986 b (Lat. Crysan(thus)) ?= (**19**); (**19**) ~ ib. 8176 (Castrèn 235. 1) (Lat. Magulnius Chrysanthus) ?= (**18**); (**20**) ~ *CIL* IV 9934 a (Castrèn 129. 13) (Lat. Corn. Chrysanthus; (**21**) 54 AD *CIL* IV 3340. 7, 21; 12, 20; 15, 17; 79, 1; 85, 6; 89, 7; 103, 5; 110, 7 (Castrèn 10. 1) (Lat. P. Aefulanus Chrysanthus)
SICILY:
—SYRACUSE: (**22**) iii-v AD Ferrua, *NG* 49 (Lat. [Ch]risantus)

**Χρυσαρέτα**
ELIS: (**1**) 53 AD *IvOl* 435, 5; *ZPE* 99 (1993) p. 232 (stemma) (*Ἰουλ. Χ.*: m. *Κλ. Ἀλκινόα*); (**2**) f. ii AD *IvOl* 439, 4; 440, 7; *ZPE* 99 (1993) p.

232 (stemma) (*Βετληνὴ Κασσία Χ.*: m. *Λουκηνὴ Κλ. Μνασιθέα*)

**Χρυσάριον**
S. ITALY (APULIA):
—VENUSA*: (**1**) i BC/i AD *Museo di Venosa* p. 212 no. 15 (*CIL* IX 571) (Lat. Servia Crysario: freed.)
S. ITALY (CALABRIA):
—BRENTESION-BRUNDISIUM*: (**2**) imp. ib. 6131 (Lat. Pacilia Chrysarium: freed.)
S. ITALY (CAMPANIA):
—DIKAIARCHIA-PUTEOLI*: (**3**) imp. ib. x 2816 (Lat. Trebia Crysario: freed.)

**Χρυσᾶς**
LAKONIA:
—SPARTA: (**1**) s. ii AD *SEG* XLII 331; (**2**) c. 175-200 AD *IG* v (1) 89, 15 (Bradford (-)) (*Ἰούλ. Χ.*)

**Χρύσασπις**
S. ITALY (APULIA):
—LUCERIA: (**1**) imp. *ASP* 34 (1981) p. 24 no. 28; cf. *ZPE* 76 (1989) p. 149 no. 2 + 103 (1994) p. 159 no. 1 (Lat. Chrysaspis: I f. *Χρύσασπις* II); (**2**) ~ *ASP* 34 (1981) p. 24 no. 28; cf. *ZPE* 76 (1989) p. 149 no. 2 + 103 (1994) p. 159 no. 1 (Lat. Chrysaspis: II s. *Χρύσασπις* I)
S. ITALY (CAMPANIA):
—POMPEII: (**3**) i BC-i AD *CIL* IV 1661 (Lat. Chrysaspis)

**Χρυσάων**
S. ITALY (CAMPANIA):
—DIKAIARCHIA-PUTEOLI: (**1**) imp. ib. x 2751 (Lat. T. Munatius Chrysaon)

**Χρυσάωρ**
LAKONIA:
—HYPERTELEATON*: (**1**) imp. *IG* v (1) 1066 (s. *Πρῖσκος*)

**Χρυσέα**
EPIROS:
—NIKOPOLIS: (**1**) imp. *Hellenika* 22 (1969) p. 69 no. 5 (Sarikakis 180) (d. *Παίδων*, m. *Διοδότα*)
—NIKOPOLIS?: (**2**) imp. *FD* III (4) p. 92 n. 3 to no. 60 (Sarikakis 65) (*Ἰουλία Χ.*: d. *Ἰούλιος Σέλευκος*)

**Χρύσερμος**
KORINTHIA:
—KORINTH: (**1**) i AD *FGrH* 287 (dub.)

**Χρυσέρως**
ARKADIA:
—TEGEA: (**1**) 165 AD *IG* v (2) 50, 32 (II s. *Χρυσ-έρως* I); (**2**) ~ ib. l. 31-2 (I f. *Χρυσέρως* II, *Ξένων*)
KORINTHIA:
—KORINTH: (**3**) byz. *Corinth* VIII (1) 160 (f. *Εὐ-τύχη*)
LAKONIA:
—SPARTA: (**4**) c. 105-110 AD *IG* v (1) 20 B, 2; *BSA* 26 (1923-5) p. 168 C 7, 5 (Bradford (4)) (f. *Ὀνησιφόρος*) ?= (**7**); (**5**) c. 160-170 AD *IG* v (1) 109, 9 (Bradford (3)) (I f. *Χρυσέρως* II); (**6**) ~ *IG* v (1) 109, 9 (Bradford (1)) (II s. *Χρυσέρως* I)
—Pitana: (**7**) c. 105 AD *IG* v (1) 675, 6 (Bradford (2)) (f. *Ἀλεξᾶς*) ?= (**4**)
S. ITALY (APULIA):
—CANUSIUM*: (**8**) imp. *Epig. Rom. di Canosa* Add. 9 (Lat. L. Numellius Chrysero[s]: freed.)
S. ITALY (CALABRIA):
—BRENTESION-BRUNDISIUM: (**9**) imp. *Epigraphica* 25 (1963) p. 86 no. 100; cf. 42 (1980) p. 156 (Lat. [Chr]yseros)

S. ITALY (CAMPANIA):
—DIKAIARCHIA-PUTEOLI*: (**10**) imp. *AJA* 2 (1898) p. 385 no. 29 (Lat. Chryseros: freed.)
—HERCULANEUM: (**11**) m. i AD *PdelP* 3 (1948) p. 182 no. 30; 10 (1955) p. 470 no. 87 (Lat. Marius Chryseros)
—POMPEII: (**12**) i BC-i AD *CIL* IV 4601 (Lat. Chryseros); (**13**) ~ ib. 4816 (Lat. Chryseros); (**14**) ~ ib. 8347 (Lat. Chryseros); (**15**) ~ ib. 8854 b (Lat. Cryseros); (**16**) ~ *NScav* 1916, p. 303 no. 81 (*Apollo* 6 (1985-88) p. 247) (Lat. Chryseros: f. *Ἀτίμητος*); (**17**) f. i AD *CIL* x 1006 (Castrèn 204. 9); Kockel p. 67 (date) (Lat. Istacidius Crisyrus); (**18**) c. 51-62 AD *CIL* IV 3340. 48, 6, 11, 22; 131, 5 (Castrèn 161. 5) (Lat. M. Fab. Chryseros); (**19**) ~ *CIL* IV 3340. 111, 8 (Castrèn 81. 11) (Lat. Caecilius Chryseros); (**20**) 57 AD *CIL* IV 3340. 35, 6, 10, 23, 27 (Castrèn 23. 7) (Lat. Cn. Alleius Chryseros); (**21**) ~ *CIL* IV 3340. 40, 17; x 8058. 76 (seal) (Castrèn 387. 1) (Lat. M. Stabius Chryseros)
SICILY: (**22**) imp. *IG* XIV 2405. 44; *Riv. Stor. Antica* 5 (1900-1) p. 49; *BM Lamps* 3 p. 208

**Χρύση**
ILLYRIA:
—AULON: (**1**) imp. *CIG* 1829 (*Σαυφηία Χ.*: m. *Ἰουν. Τιμονόη*)
LAKONIA:
—SPARTA: (**2**) v/iv BC *FGrH* 115 F 240 (Poralla² 769)

**Χρυσηΐς**
EPIROS: (**1**) s. iii BC Plb. v 89. 7; *HSCP* Suppl. 1 (1940) pp. 483 ff.; cf. *REG* 94 (1981) pp. 34 f. (ident.) (also called *Φθία*?)
S. ITALY (CAMPANIA):
—MISENUM*: (**2**) ?ii AD *CIL* x 3356 (Lat. Aelia Chryseis)
—NEAPOLIS: (**3**) ii-iii AD *IG* XIV 806 (*INap* 155)

**Χρύσης**
SICILY:
—SYRACUSE: (**1**) imp. *IG* XIV 55 (X.?, *Χρυση-ῖς*?); (**2**) iii-v AD Strazzulla 304 (Barreca 376) (*Χρυσ(ί)ς*?); (**3**) ~ Wessel 495 + Ferrua, *NG* 88

**Χρυσῆς**
ARKADIA:
—TEGEA: (**1**) ii AD *IG* v (2) 55, 91 (s. *Ἀρτεμᾶς*)

**Χρύσιλλα**
ARGOLIS:
—PHLEIOUS: (**1**) iv BC *SEG* XXVI 416, 3
KORINTHIA:
—KORINTH: (**2**) v BC *FGrH* 268 F 6 (-λλη: d. *Τελέας*)

**Χρύσιον**
SICILY:
—SYRACUSE: (**1**) hell. *NScav* 1892, p. 357 (d. *Φιλίσκος*); (**2**) ~ ib. p. 360

**Χρύσιππος**
ARGOLIS:
—ARGOS*: (**1**) iii BC *IG* IV (1) 528, 5 ([X]ρύσιππος: slave/freed.?)
ARKADIA:
—KLEITOR: (**2**) m. iii AD *SEG* XXXV 350 II, 9 (*Χρύσιππ[ος]*: f. *Αὐρ. Σωτήριχος*)
ILLYRIA:
—EPIDAMNOS-DYRRHACHION*: (**3**) imp. *Stud. Alb.* 1965, p. 74 no. 49 (Lat. Catiedius Chrussippus: freed.)
KORINTHIA:
—KORINTH: (**4**) inc. Artem. iv 31; (**5**) ?vi/v BC Iamb., *VP* 267 (*FVS* 1 p. 448)
MESSENIA:
—ASINE: (**6**) ii AD *IG* v (1) 1414 (f. *Ἀρχιδώ*)
—MESSENE: (**7**) f. iii BC *PAE* 1991, p. 99 no. 7,

——(Hylleis): (8) 11 AD ib. 1992, p. 71 A, 14 (s. *Κάλλων*)

S. ITALY (CAMPANIA):

—DIKAIARCHIA-PUTEOLI: (9) imp. *CIL* x 2379 (Lat. Ducenius Crhysippus)

SICILY:

—AKRAGAS: (10) f. v BC *Acragas Graeca* 1 p. 32 no. 2 (Dubois, *IGDS* 179; Arena, *Iscr. Sic.* II 91) (-*ιπος*)

## Χρύσις

KORINTHIA:

—KORINTH: (1) 431 BC Th. ii 33. 1 (f. *Εὔμαχος*); (2) f. iii BC *CID* II 122 I, 4 (f. Ἐοι[—]ρεύς)

## Χρυσίς

ARGOLIS:

—ARGOS: (1) v BC Th. ii 2. 1; iv 133; Paus. ii 17. 7; iii 5. 6

DALMATIA:

—PHAROS: (2) imp. *CIL* III 3088; cf. Šašel, *IL* 2936 (Lat. Laelia Crisis: slave/freed.?)

—TRAGURION: (3) imp. *CIL* III 2698 (Lat. Servilia Crysis: slave/freed.?)

ILLYRIA:

—EPIDAMNOS-DYRRHACHION*: (4) imp. *AEp* 1978, no. 761 (Lat. Chrysis: m. Ἀρέθουσα)

KORINTHIA:

—KORINTH: (5) c. 400-375 BC *IG* II² 9080 (d. *Πυθάγγελος*)

S. ITALY (APULIA):

—CANUSIUM: (6) imp. *Epig. Rom. di Canosa* 200 (*CIL* IX 403) (Lat. Vavidia Chrysis)

—VENUSIA: (7) imp. *Epigraphica* 35 (1973) p. 145 no. 4 (Lat. Helvia Chry[sis])

S. ITALY (BRUTTIUM):

—LOKROI EPIZEPHYRIOI: (8) iv BC *Locri Epizefiri* 2 pl. 10 no. 11 (vase)

S. ITALY (CALABRIA):

—BRENTESION-BRUNDISIUM: (9) imp. *Epigraphica* 25 (1963) p. 68 no. 65 (Lat. Maecia Crysis)

—PORTO CESAREO (MOD.): (10) imp. *CIL* IX 12 (Susini, *Fonti Salento* p. 92 no. 25) (Lat. Lucilia Chrysis)

—TARAS-TARENTUM: (11) imp. *CIL* IX 240 (Lat. Crusis)

S. ITALY (CAMPANIA):

—DIKAIARCHIA-PUTEOLI: (12) imp. ib. x 1886 (Lat. Pomponia Chrysis); (13) ~ ib. 2057 (Lat. Annia Chrysis: m. M. Annius Fortunatus); (14) ~ *RAAN* 42 (1967) pp. 4-6 (Lat. Aemilia Chrysis); (15) ?ii AD *CIL* x 2012 (Lat. Aelia Chrysis)

—NEAPOLIS: (16) iii-iv AD *IG* XIV 826. 49 (*INap* 239)

—SALERNUM: (17) imp. *IItal* I (1) 175 (*CIL* x 590) (Lat. Fl. Chrysis)

—SURRENTUM: (18) imp. *St. Rom.* 2 (1914) p. 346 no. 19 = *NScav* 1928, p. 211 no. 20 (Lat. Chrysis)

S. ITALY (LUCANIA):

—ATINA LUCANA*: (19) imp. *IItal* III (1) 165 (*CIL* x 357) (Lat. Luxsilia [Ch]rysis: m. Ὀλυμπιάς: freed.)

—HYELE-VELIA: (20) hell.? *PdelP* 21 (1966) p. 337 no. 12

SICILY:

—SYRACUSE: (21) imp. *CIL* x 7147 (Lat. Chrysi[s]); (22) iii-v AD *IG* XIV 190 (Strazzulla 133; Wessel 1317) (*Χρύσις?*—Strazzulla); (23) ~ *NScav* 1892, p. 357; (24) ~ Agnello 34; (25) 435 AD *IG* XIV 189 (Strazzulla 124; Agnello 16; Wessel 475); Ferrua, *NG* 181 (date)

—TAUROMENION: (26) iii-v AD *IG* XIV 447 (*IGLMP* 116); cf. Ferrua, *NG* 486

## Χρυσιφόρος

SICILY:

—MOTYKA: (1) iii-v AD Agnello 69

## Χρυσογόνη

LAKONIA: (1) inc. Thphyl., *Ep.* 12 (Stephanis 2636) (het./fict.)

S. ITALY (CAMPANIA):

—DIKAIARCHIA-PUTEOLI: (2) iii AD *Puteoli* 11 (1987) p. 132 no. 4 (Lat. Lucilia Crysogone)

## Χρυσόγονος

ACHAIA:

—DYME: (1) iii BC Wilhelm, *Beitr.* p. 69 no. 57

KORINTHIA:

—KORINTH: (2) f. iii AD *Ag.* VII p. 201 no. A (lamp); (3) byz. *Corinth* VIII (3) 612; cf. *TMByz* 9 (1985) p. 366 no. 73 ([*Χ*]ρυσόγο[*νος*])

LAKONIA:

—SPARTA: (4) c. 150-160 AD *IG* v (1) 69, 34; *SEG* XI 554, 7 (Bradford (5)) (I f. *Πακτούμειος Χρυσόγονος* II); (5) ~ *IG* v (1) 69, 34; 71 III, 38; *SEG* XI 554, 7 (Bradford (1)) (*Πακ(τούμειος) X. νεώτ.*: II s. *Χρυσόγονος* I); (6) ~ *IG* v (1) 71 II, 5 (Bradford (3)) (s. *Πηνειός*); (7) c. 150-220 AD *IG* v (1) 71 II, 20; 560, 2; 561, 2 (Bradford (4)) (*M. Αὐρ. X.*: s. *Σωτηρίδας*, f. *Σωτηρίδας, Σωφροσύνα*); (8) ii/iii AD *IG* v (1) 89, 9; 561, 11 (Bradford (2)) (*M. Αὐρ. X.*: s. *Δίων*)

S. ITALY (BRUTTIUM):

—RHEGION: (9) imp. *NScav* 1888, p. 67 (*Eph. Ep.* VIII 248) (Lat. Crysogonus)

—TAURIANA: (10) imp. *NScav* 1889, p. 283 (*Eph. Ep.* VIII 250) (Lat. [C]hrysogonus: s. Lartianus)

S. ITALY (CALABRIA):

—BRENTESION-BRUNDISIUM*: (11) imp. *CIL* IX 94 (Lat. Chrysogonus: freed.)

S. ITALY (CAMPANIA):

—DIKAIARCHIA-PUTEOLI: (12) imp. ib. x 2984 (Lat. M. Aeclanius Chrysogonus: f. T. Sullius Albanus)

## Χρυσοδίκη

S. ITALY (APULIA):

—VENUSIA: (1) i-ii AD *Rend. Linc.* 31 (1976) p. 286 no. 5 (*Museo di Venosa* p. 238 no. 11) (Lat. Cornelia Chrysodice)

## Χρυσόθεμις

ARGOLIS:

—ARGOS: (1) f. v BC *RE* (6) (sculptor)

LAKONIA:

—GYTHEION: (2) hell. *IG* v (1) *1202

## Χρυσοθόη

S. ITALY (CAMPANIA):

—DIKAIARCHIA-PUTEOLI*: (1) ?ii AD *CIL* x 2005 (Lat. Aelia Chrysothoe: freed.)

## Χρυσόμαλλος

S. ITALY (APULIA):

—CANUSIUM: (1) 223 AD *Epig. Rom. di Canosa* 35 III, 42 (*CIL* IX 338) (Lat. P. Pacilius Chrysomallus)

S. ITALY (CAMPANIA):

—MISENUM*: (2) ?iii AD *Epigraphica* 34 (1972) p. 142 (Lat. M. Antonius Chrysomallus: freed.)

## Χρυσόπολις

ILLYRIA:

—EPIDAMNOS-DYRRHACHION: (1) imp. *AEp* 1978, no. 756 (Lat. Terentia Chrysopolis)

S. ITALY (APULIA):

—VENUSIA*: (2) i BC/i AD *Museo di Venosa* p. 212 no. 15 (*CIL* IX 571) (Lat. Servia Crysopolis: freed.)

S. ITALY (CAMPANIA):

—DIKAIARCHIA-PUTEOLI: (3) imp. ib. x 2560 (Lat. Marcia Chrysopolis)

—POMPEII: (4) i BC-i AD ib. IV 4128 (Lat. Chrysopolis)

SICILY:

—SYRACUSE: (5) imp. *Epigraphica* 3 (1941) p. 269 no. 43 (Lat. Chrysopolis)

## Χρῦσος

LAKONIA:

—HYPERTELEATON*: (1) imp. *IG* v (1) 1044

S. ITALY (BRUTTIUM):

—LOKROI EPIZEPHYRIOI: (2) iii-iv AD Costabile, *Municipium Locrensium* 35 (Lat. Duc. Chrysus)

## Χρυσώι

ARGOLIS:

—NEMEA*: (1) f. v BC *SEG* XXIX 353 b (-*σόι*)

## Χρύσων

SICILY:

—ADRANON: (1) i BC-i AD? *IG* XIV 567 (*Χρύσων*: f. *Αἰσχύλος*)

## Χρῶμις

ARKADIA:

—STYMPHALOS: (1) iii BC ib. v (2) 356, 6

## Χρωτάριον

KORINTHIA:

—SIKYON: (1) hell. *SEG* XXXIV 217 (d. *Σύντροφος*)

## Χρωτώ

ARKADIA:

—TEGEA: (1) hell.-imp.? *IG* v (2) 259

## Χύρων

MESSENIA: (1) iii BC Plb. iv 4. 1; *RE* (-)

## Χυτρίς

AKARNANIA:

—PALAIROS: (1) ?iii/ii BC *IG* IX (1)² (2) 555

—THYRREION: (2) iii BC ib. 281

## Χύτρων

EPIROS:

—CHARADROS: (1) a. 167 BC *SEG* XXXV 665 A, 15 (f. *Νικάνωρ*)

# Ψ

**Ψακᾶς**
ELIS:
—OLYMPIA?: (1) inc. Schol. Ar., *Ach.* 1150a
(Ὀλυμπιακὸς καλούμενος Ψ.)
S. ITALY (CAMPANIA):
—POMPEII: (2) i BC-i AD *CIL* IV 3905, 1
(Castrèn 195. 5) (Lat. Histius Psacas)

**Ψαλυχίας**
AIGINA: (1) her. Pi., *I.* vi, 63 (Ψαλυχιάδαι (n.
gent.))

**Ψαμάθα**
ARGOLIS:
—HERMIONE: (1) ii-i BC *IG* IV (1) 732 IV, 16
(d. Ὁμιλία)

**Ψαμάθη**
S. ITALY (CAMPANIA):
—POMPEII: (1) i BC-i AD *CIL* IV 6860 (Lat.
Psamathe); (2) c. 55-60 AD ib. 3340. 43, 6,
10 (Castrèn 159. 1) (Lat. Equitia Psamathe)

**Ψαμέας**
PELOPONNESE?: (1) s. iii BC *SEG* XXV 449, 47
(*IPArk* 26)

**Ψαμμήτιχος**
KORINTHIA:
—KORINTH: (1) vii/vi BC *RE* Supplbd. 9 (5) (s.
Γόργος: tyrant)

**Ψαμώνιος**
ACHAIA:
—BOURA: (1) ?s. iv BC *Achaean Grave Stelai* 2
(s. Θρασύμαχος)

**Ψαῦμις**
SICILY:
—KAMARINA: (1) 456-452 BC *RE* (-); Moretti,
*Olymp.* 280; 292 (s. Ἄκρων)

**Ψαῦος**
SICILY:
—SYRACUSE: (1) iii-v AD Ferrua, *NG* 17

**Ψεκάς**
S. ITALY (CAMPANIA):
—BAIAI: (1) imp. *NScav* 1897, p. 13 (Lat.
Psechas)
—DIKAIARCHIA-PUTEOLI: (2) imp. *CIL* X 2485;
*Puteoli* 11 (1987) p. 51 (name) (Lat. Pseca[s]);
(3) ~ *CIL* X 2698 (Lat. Marcia Psechas: m. T.
Marcius Maximianus); (4) ?i-ii AD ib. 2946
(Lat. Sempronia Psechas)
—DIKAIARCHIA-PUTEOLI*: (5) imp. ib. 2837
(Lat. Perpernia Psechas: freed.)
—SALERNUM: (6) i AD *IItal* 1 (1) 64 (Lat.
Octavia Psecas: m. Fronto)

**Ψύλλα**
KERKYRA:
—(Hylleis): (1) ii BC *IG* IX (1) 694, 5, 36-7,
39 etc. (*RIJG* XXV B); cf. *SEG* XXV 609 (d.
Ἄλκιμος)

**Ψυλλίων**
AITOLIA:
—BOUKATION: (1) 190 BC *IG* IX (1)² (1) 97, 11
(f. Ἀγήτας)
ILLYRIA:
—APOLLONIA: (2) c. 250-50 BC Maier 105
(Ceka 110); *IApoll Ref. Bibl.* n. 106 (coin)
(pryt.); (3) i BC Maier 152; cf. 126; cf. *Grecs
et Illyriens* p. 106 n. 27 (coin) (Ψυχλίων—126
err.: money.)

**Ψύλλος**
DALMATIA:
—ISSA:

—(Hylleis): (1) iv/iii BC Brunšmid p. 7, 20
(Ψύλλ[ος], Ψύλλ[ας?], Ψυλλ[ίων]?: s. —ίσκος)
ILLYRIA:
—APOLLONIA: (2) c. 250-50 BC *Bakërr Hoard*
p. 65 no. 131; Maier 104; Münsterberg p. 37
(coin) (Ceka 135-6) (Ψύλ(λος)—135: money.);
(3) ~ Maier 101; Münsterberg p. 37 (coin)
(Ceka 22; 29; 74; 122) (pryt.); (4) iii/ii BC
*IApoll* 7; cf. *L'Illyrie mérid.* 2 p. 207 (s. Ἀρι-
στήν)

**Ψυχάριον**
S. ITALY (CAMPANIA):
—DIKAIARCHIA-PUTEOLI*: (1) imp. *CIL* X
2134 (Lat. Ofillia Psychario: freed.)
S. ITALY (LUCANIA):
—GRUMENTUM: (2) imp. ib. 226 (Lat. Helvia
Psychario)

**Ψύχη**
S. ITALY (CAMPANIA):
—DIKAIARCHIA-PUTEOLI: (1) imp. ib. 2718
(Lat. Maria Psyche)
—DIKAIARCHIA-PUTEOLI*: (2) imp. *AJA* 2
(1898) p. 385 no. 29 (Lat. Psyche: freed.)
—POMPEII: (3) i BC-i AD *CIL* IV 1362 (Lat.
Psyce); (4) m. i AD *Impegno per Pompeii* 9 ES
no. 7 (Lat. Psiche)
SICILY:
—SYRACUSE: (5) iii-v AD *Rend. Pont.* 22 (1946-
7) p. 233 no. 22

**Ψωρίων**
SICILY:
—THERMAI HIMERAIAI: (1) i-ii AD *CIL* X 7363
(*ILat. Term. Imer.* 32) (Lat. P. Antonius
Psorio)

# Ω

**Ὤγυγος**
ACHAIA: (1) her. *RE* (2)

**Ὠκεανός**
S. ITALY (APULIA): (1) imp. *Mus. Arch. di
Bari* p. 181 no. 27 (Lat. [O]ceanus)
S. ITALY (CAMPANIA):
—CAPREAE: (2) imp. *Eph. Ep.* VIII 673/4 (Lat.
Oceanus)
—DIKAIARCHIA-PUTEOLI*: (3) imp. *CIL* X
2389 = *ZPE* 71 (1988) p. 195 no. 3 (Lat. C.
Erucius Oceanus: freed.)
—HERCULANEUM: (4) i BC-i AD *CIL* IV 10578
(Lat. Ocaeanus)
—POMPEII: (5) i BC-i AD ib. 3494 d (Lat.
Oceanus)

**Ὠκιδίας**
SICILY:
—THERMAI HIMERAIAI: (1) ?i BC *IG* XIV 340
(*Ζώπυρος* Ὠ.: s. Ἀρτέμων, ?f. Φαινώ)

**Ὤκιμον**
KORINTHIA:
—KORINTH: (1) ?iv BC *RE* s.v. Okimon col.
2383; *PCG* 2 p. 242; 7 p. 85; Hyp. fr. 13
(het.)

**Ὤκυλλος**
LAKONIA:
—SPARTA: (1) f. iv BC X., *HG* v 4. 22; vi 5. 33
(Poralla² 770)

**Ὤκυτος**
KORINTHIA:
—KORINTH: (1) 480 BC Hdt. viii 5. 1 (f. Ἀδεί-
μαντος); (2) 423 BC Th. iv 119. 2 (f. Αἰνέας)

**Ὠλένιος**
S. ITALY (CAMPANIA):
—DIKAIARCHIA-PUTEOLI: (1) imp. *CIL* X 2248
(Lat. L. Ceionius Olenius)

**Ὠμίας**
LAKONIA:
—SPARTA: (1) 220 BC Plb. iv 23. 5; 24. 8 (Brad-
ford (-))

**Ὠνύμων**
KORINTHIA:
—KORINTH: (1) vi BC *IG* IV (1) 316 (pinax)
(Ὀνύμōν)

**Ὦπις**
S. ITALY (CALABRIA):
—IAPYGES: (1) vi/v BC Paus. x 13. 10 (king)

**Ὥρα**
S. ITALY (APULIA):
—LARINUM: (1) imp. *Forma Italiae* 36 p. 100
no. 5 (Lat. [Me]ssia Hora)

**Ὡραία**
ARGOLIS:
—ARGOS: (1) byz. *IG* IV (1) 628, 7 (-ρέα)
S. ITALY (CAMPANIA):
—DIKAIARCHIA-PUTEOLI: (2) imp. *CIL* X 2651
(Lat. Licinia Horaea: d. Ἀτίμητος, Μένουσα)
SICILY:
—KATANE: (3) imp. *IG* XIV 510, 1

**Ὡραΐς**
EPIROS:
—BOUTHROTOS (PRASAIBOI): (1) a. 163 BC
*IBouthrot* 31, 24 (*SEG* XXXVIII 490)
ILLYRIA:
—EPIDAMNOS-DYRRHACHION: (2) hell.-imp.
*IDyrrh* 453 (d. Φαλακρίων); (3) ~ ib. 454
(-ρεῖς)
SICILY:
—KATANE: (4) i-ii AD *MEFRA* 106 (1994) p. 86
no. 4 (Σεπτίκις Ὡραΐς)

**Ὡρίων**
LAKONIA:
—SPARTA: (1) a. 212 AD *IG* V (1) 685, 7 (Brad-
ford (-)) (Ἰούλ. Ὡρείων)

Ὧρος

S. Italy (Campania):
—pompeii: (2) i bc-i ad *CIL* iv 3340. 85, 9 (Castrèn 204. 6) (Lat. M. Istacidius Orion)
Sicily:
—syracuse: (3) imp. *NScav* 1912, pp. 293-4 + Ferrua, *NG* 241 (Lat. Sex. Alfius Orion)

Ὧρος

Arkadia:
—tegea: (1) 165 ad *IG* v (2) 50, 70 (f. Ἰσίδωρος)
S. Italy (Campania):
—pompeii: (2) i bc-i ad *CIL* iv 5183 (Lat. Horus); (3) c. 51-62 ad ib. 3340. 48, 19; 74, 11; 116, 5; 133, 4 (Castrèn 338. 2) (Lat. M. Rufellius Horus); (4) 56 ad *CIL* iv 3340. 19, 19 (Castrèn 340. 1) (Lat. C. Ruleius Horus)

Ὠρότυχος

Aigina: (1) ii-iii ad *AE* 1913, p. 95 no. 6 β (s. Ζώσιμος)

Ὠφέλας

Arkadia:
—teuthis?: (1) hell.? *IG* v (2) 503

Ὠφελία

Lakonia:
—hippola: (1) ii-i bc ib. v (1) 1334 a + *AAA* 1 (1968) p. 119 no. 1 (locn.) (date—*LGPN*)
Lakonia?: (2) ii-i bc *SEG* xxxii 401

Ὠφελίμα

Arkadia:
—tegea: (1) ii ad ib. xi 1080

Messenia:
—messene: (2) hell.? *PAE* 1993, p. 63

Ὠφέλιμος

Akarnania:
—astakos: (1) s. iii bc *IG* ix (1)² (2) 438 om. *IG*
Arkadia:
—mantineia-antigoneia: (2) i-ii ad ib. v (2) 326 (*GVI* 1241) (f. Σωτέλης)
—tegea: (3) 165 ad *IG* v (2) 50, 58 (f. Τρύφερος)
—tegea*: (4) m. v ad *SEG* xxxiv 330 (bp.)
Korinthia:
—korinth: (5) byz. *IG* iv (1) 408, 2; cf. *TMByz* 9 (1985) p. 359 no. 4

Ὠφελίς

S. Italy (Calabria):
—rudiae: (1) i-ii ad *NScav* 1957, p. 197 (Susini, *Fonti Salento* p. 131 no. 75) (Lat. Ophelis)

Ὠφελίων

Achaia: (1) 146 bc *IG* iv (1)² 28, 112 (f. Διονύσιος: synoikos); (2) ~ ib. l. 149 (s. Δάμων: synoikos)
Aitolia:
—trichonion: (3) iii bc ib. ix (1)² (1) 119
Akarnania:
—palairos: (4) iii bc ib. ix (1)² (2) 513
Argolis:
—argos: (5) a. 303 bc *CEG* ii 816, 22
—argos?: (6) v bc *IG* iv (1) 552, 10 (Ὀφελίōν)

—argos*: (7) f. iii bc ib. 529, 2 (Ὠφελίω[ν]: slave/freed.?)
—epidauros*: (8) c. 310-300 bc ib. iv (1)² 114, 20, 28
—hermione: (9) ?ii-i bc ib. iv (1) 731 III, 5 (s. Ἑρμαῖος)
—troizen: (10) iii bc ib. 774, 10
Arkadia:
—tegea: (11) iii bc ib. v (2) 30, 5 (Ὠφ[ε]λίων: f. Χρήσιμος)
——(Hippothoitai): (12) iv/iii bc ib. 38, 51 (f. Δαμόξενος)
Epiros:
—ambrakia: (13) ii bc Unp. (Arta Mus., inscr.) ([Ὠ]φελίων)
—bouthrotos (prasaiboi): (14) a. 163 bc *IBouthrot* 45, 926, 20 (f. Φιλοκράτης)
—dodona*: (15) ?iv-iii bc Carapanos, *Dodone* p. 47 no. 19 (Lazzarini 144)
Illyria:
—apollonia: (16) imp. *IApoll* 166 (f. Φουνδανία)
Korinthia:
—korinth: (17) s. iii bc *Corinth* viii (3) 38, 2
Lakonia:
—sparta: (18) c. 105 ad *SEG* xi 546 a, 6; 546 b, 6; 585, [10] (Bradford (1)); (3)) (Γ. Ἀντ. Ὠ.: I s. Ἄγλαος, f. Ἀντ. Ὠφελίων II); (19) c. 147-160 ad *IG* v (1) 87, 4; 114, 5; 446, 5; *SEG* xi 585, 10; xxx 410, 11 (Bradford (2)) (Ἀντ. Ὠ.: II s. Γ. Ἀντ. Ὠφελίων I)
S. Italy (Campania):
—kyme: (20) ii-iii ad *Puteoli* 3 (1979) p. 165 no. 7 (*CIL* x 2221) (Lat. M. Calvius Offelio)
—neapolis: (21) 570 ad ib. 1535 (Lat. Opilio)

# REVERSE INDEX OF NAMES IN VOLUME IIIA

| | | | | |
|---|---|---|---|---|
| Ναυσικάα | Δαμοκλέα | Εὐτυχαία | Πέλεια | Εὐγένεια |
| Ἀρχελάα | Ἀρτεμοκλέα | Λαβία | Ἐργοτέλεια | Πολυγένεια |
| Μάα | Ξενοκλέα | Φαβία | Νικοτέλεια | Λασθένεια |
| Δανάα | Ἀνδροκλέα | Βιβία | Ἀβροτέλεια | Καλλισθένεια |
| Ἄβα | Ἱεροκλέα | Ἀλκιβία | Ἀνδροτέλεια | Ἐρισθένεια |
| Θήβα | Πατροκλέα | Ἀλεξιβία | Ἀφέλεια | Δαμοσθένεια |
| Εὔλιβα | Ἐρατοκλέα | Σωσιβία | Αἰγίλεια | Εὐρυσθένεια |
| Πριμιτῖβα | Εὐκλέα | Ἀντιβία | Βασίλεια | Μένεια |
| Πρόβα | Μενέα | Οὐιβία | Φίλεια | Ἀλκιμένεια |
| Γᾶ | Ἀρσινέα | Σαλβία | Μεγάκλεια | Προμένεια |
| Λαμάγα | Ἀνδρέα | Ζηνοβία | Ἡράκλεια | Ἀριστομένεια |
| Ἀπῆγα | Χρυσέα | Ματροβία | Θέκλεια | Παρμένεια |
| Ῥῆγα | Κρατέα | Ἀφοβία | Καλλίκλεια | Εὐμένεια |
| Προαύγα | Νικοκρατέα | Λεσβία | Χαρίκλεια | Ξένεια |
| Λάβδα | Φιλοκρατέα | Ἀκουβία | Νικασίκλεια | Οἴνεια |
| Ἀνδρομέδα | Τιμοκρατέα | Πελαγία | Ὀνασίκλεια | Κάρνεια |
| Ἀριστομέδα | Εὐκρατέα | Εὐλογία | Πασίκλεια | Εἰρώνεια |
| Αὐτομέδα | Σωκρατέα | Γεωργία | Κρατησίκλεια | Ἀριστώνεια |
| Λήδα | Μελιτέα | Φρυγία | Σωσίκλεια | Θεοπρέπεια |
| Περιμήδα | Ἀγιστέα | Ὀρτυγία | Ἀγαθόκλεια | Εὐπρέπεια |
| Ἀριστομήδα | Ἀττέα | Δῖα | Διόκλεια | Ἵππεια |
| Λυταΐδα | Γναῖϝα | Ἀρκαδία | Φιλόκλεια | Καισάρεια |
| Κάνδιδα | Ἀλκινόϝα | Θωμαδία | Δαμόκλεια | Χάρεια |
| Φιλοκλείδα | Πολυνόϝα | Πεδία | Δημόκλεια | Ἐπιχάρεια |
| Ἐξοίδα | Γάζα | Ἐλπιδία | Εὐδαιμόκλεια | Πασιχάρεια |
| Λέπιδα | Δάζα | Βρασιδία | Τιμόκλεια | Ἄνδρεια |
| Φῖδα | Παλάθα | Νυμφιδία | Φανόκλεια | Ἀλεξάνδρεια |
| Οὔενδα | Ψαμάθα | Σεκονδία | Ἱερόκλεια | Ἱέρεια |
| Σεκοῦνδα | Φιλαίθα | Ῥοδία | Ἰατρόκλεια | Ἑταιρεία |
| Ἰουκοῦνδα | Ϝοινάνθα | Εὐοδία | Πατρόκλεια | Θράσεια |
| Ῥόδα | Εὐάνθα | Κονκορδία | Στρατόκλεια | Γαλάτεια |
| Ἀκρίβεα | Φιλίνθα | Εὐδία | Ἀριστόκλεια | Ἐράτεια |
| Μεδέα | Κορίνθα | Λυδία | Εὔκλεια | Κράτεια |
| Μνασιθέα | Μάρθα | Κλωδία | Θεύκλεια | Μενεκράτεια |
| Δωσιθέα | Μικύθα | Θεοσέβεια | Πολύκλεια | Ἐχεκράτεια |
| Ἀγχιθέα | Σαμύθα | Εὐσέβεια | Εὐρύκλεια | Δαϊκράτεια |
| Ἀξιοθέα | Κρωμύθα | Αἰγεία | Λαδάμεια | Καλικράτεια |
| Φιλοθέα | Ἴα | Ἀργεία | Δηϊδάμεια | Καλλικράτεια |
| Τιμοθέα | Ἀβαία | Κυμβάδεια | Κρατηΐδάμεια | Δεξικράτεια |
| Δωροθέα | Γάϊα | Ἡδεῖα | Ἀρχιδάμεια | Ἐπικράτεια |
| Κυματοθέα | Ἰδαία | Ἐτυμοκλήδεια | Λαοδάμεια | Λυσικράτεια |
| Πακέα | Ἱστιαία | Σωκλήδεια | Ἱπποδάμεια | Σωσικράτεια |
| Ἀλικέα | Δικαία | Νικομήδεια | Κάδμεια | Ἀντικράτεια |
| Φιλέα | Νικαία | Ἀριστήδεια | Λαθέμεια | Λεοκράτεια |
| Κλέα | Μαῖα | Ἀγάθεια | Σωτίμεια | Κλεοκράτεια |
| Ἡρακλέα | Ὀνησιμαία | Φιλομάθεια | Αὐτόμεια | Νεοκράτεια |
| Σακλέα | Τιμαία | Ἀλήθεια | Ἐπιφάνεια | Νικοκράτεια |
| Ἀναξικλέα | Ῥωμαία | Συνήθεια | Θεοφάνεια | Φιλοκράτεια |
| Δεξικλέα | Ἀνναία | Ξενοπείθεια | Ἐπιγένεια | Δαμοκράτεια |
| Κρατησικλέα | Σμυρναία | Ἄνθεια | Ἰσιγένεια | Τιμοκράτεια |
| Σωσικλέα | Γραῖα | Πάνθεια | Ἰφιγένεια | Ξενοκράτεια |
| Ῥοδοκλέα | Θηραία | Ἀγίεια | Κλεογένεια | Δεινοκράτεια |
| Θεοκλέα | Ὡραία | Ὑγίεια | Διογένεια | Ἀριστοκράτεια |
| Ἀγαθοκλέα | Νισαία | Γλύκεια | Πριμογένεια | Εὐκράτεια |
| Διοκλέα | Ταταία | Θάλεια | Ἑρμογένεια | Πολυκράτεια |
| Νικοκλέα | Κρεταία | Κάλεια | Κυπρογένεια | Σωκράτεια |
| Φιλοκλέα | Τευταία | Ἐπιμέλεια | Πλουτογένεια | Στράτεια |

| | | | | |
|---|---|---|---|---|
| Κρέτεια | Στατιλία | Δοξία | Ἀσία | Βηρυτία |
| Καλλικρέτεια | Φιλία | Εὐδοξία | Καλβασία | Φιλωτία |
| Εὐθυκρέτεια | Διφιλία | Μελίβοια | Ἀγασία | Σωτία |
| Πολυκρέτεια | Θαλλία | Δοία | Κασία | Καλλίθυια |
| Ἄντεια | Πολλία | Κοΐα | Ἀρκασία | Μυῖα |
| Φίντεια | Αὐλία | Εὔπλοια | Βοσκασία | Σαλούϊα |
| Ἄστεια | Εὐβουλία | Διάνοια | Δαμασία | Νουΐα |
| Ἀρίστεια | Ἰουλία | Ξένοια | Θαυμασία | Ἀδελφία |
| Φιλαδέλφεια | Σικουλία | Ἐπίνοια | Ἀθανασία | Ἀμφία |
| Βάκχεια | Εὐπωλία | Ὁμόνοια | Ἀσπασία | Νυμφία |
| Ἀντιόχεια | Καπιτωλία | Πρόνοια | Εὐφρασία | Σοφία |
| Ἀγελόχεια | Νικοδαμία | Εὔνοια | Ἀναστασία | Εὐμορφία |
| Ἀστυόχεια | Εὐδαμία | Ἀπία | Πασχασία | Εὐφία |
| Πλειστάρχεια | Πλοκαμία | Ἀραπία | Ἐφεσία | Χία |
| Δαζία | Λαμία | Σεραπία | Φιλησία | Εὐμαχία |
| Ἰστληΐα | Ῥαμία | Ἠπία | Μαγνησία | Ἐλεγχία |
| Μαννήϊα | Οὐινθεμία | Ἀσκληπία | Παρρησία | Νεαρχία |
| Πομπήϊα | Νοημία | Οὐλπία | Εὐπραισία | Δικαρχία |
| Σήϊα | Εὐφημία | Ὀλυμπία | Ἀφροδισία | Δημαρχία |
| Ποντήϊα | Σιμία | Ἀγιππία | Ἀρτεμισία | Ἱππαρχία |
| Ἀγαθία | Παντιμία | Ἀγηίππία | Ὁσία | Ἀσχία |
| Εὐσταθία | Ἀμμία | Νικιππία | Πανδοσία | Ἡσυχία |
| Κορινθία | Μαμμία | Ἀγησιππία | Θεοδοσία | Ἐπιτυχία |
| Πυθία | Νομία | Καρπία | Θευδοσία | Εὐτυχία |
| Φθία | Εὐνομία | Ἐπικαρπία | Συρακοσία | Νυμφία |
| Πακία | Ἑρμία | Εὔκαρπία | Εὐποσία | Ἄκα |
| Οὐρσακία | Κοσμία | Πολυκαρπία | Ἀμβροσία | Πιθάκα |
| Λανικία | Προθυμία | Ἀνθρωπία | Κληρισσία | Σιμάκα |
| Ἁρμονικία | Εὐθυμία | Θεαρία | Σοσσία | Πυστάκα |
| Πρατονικία | Φιλωνυμία | Ἀζαρία | Φυσσία | Ῥόγκα |
| Πατρικία | Φουνδανία | Μακαρία | Διονυσία | Οὔρβικα |
| Μουσικία | Δαρδανία | Ἰλαρία | Ἀγουσία | Δίκα |
| Μικκία | Μανία | Μαρία | Πλουσία | Λαδίκα |
| Ἀλκία | Οὐρανία | Συμαρία | Ἰγνατία | Κλειδίκα |
| Προσδοκία | Ποιμενία | Ξεναρία | Γονατία | Καλλιδίκα |
| Μαρκία | Ξενία | Ἰανουαρία | Δαμοκρατία | Πεισιδίκα |
| Εὐσκία | Εὐθηνία | Νικανδρία | Στατία | Λυσιδίκα |
| Λευκία | Τρυφηνία | Λυσανδρία | Βονιφατία | Λαοδίκα |
| Λυκία | Ἐπαινία | Ἐλευθερία | Πρευκλητία | Κλεοδίκα |
| Καλυκία | Δινία | Πιερία | Ἀφροδιτία | Νικοδίκα |
| Λουκία | Φλαμινία | Νοκερία | Κλειτία | Δαμοδίκα |
| Μινουκία | Ὑρμινία | Βαλερία | Τριτία | Τιμοδίκα |
| Παζαλία | Πολυμνία | Δευτερία | Ἀβουνδαντία | Ξενοδίκα |
| Καλία | Ἀννία | Κυθηρία | Βυζαντία | Ἀριστοδίκα |
| Εὐλαλία | Ἐπιγονία | Σωτηρία | Βιγιλαντία | Λαυδίκα |
| Μαλία | Μακεδονία | Αἰθρία | Ἀκαμαντία | Εὐθυδίκα |
| Παραλία | Ἁρμονία | Τευκρία | Κωνσταντία | Εὐρυδίκα |
| Ἰταλία | Φεβρονία | Γρηγορία | Γαυδεντία | Ματυδίκα |
| Κασταλία | Σωφρονία | Εὐπορία | Πασκεντία | Ἀβοζίκα |
| Μασχαλία | Χρονία | Κοπρία | Βαλεντία | Ποτθίκα |
| Λελία | Πολυχρονία | Δαματρία | Φλωρεντία | Μαλίκα |
| Ὠφελία | Ποσειδωνία | Δημητρία | Λεοντία | Φιλικά |
| Ἡλία | Ἰωνία | Μηστρία | Αἰγυπτία | Μαλλίκα |
| Κορνηλία | Κρισκωνία | Μναιστρία | Τερτία | Ἀμμίκα |
| Γενεθλία | Ἀπολλωνία | Φουρία | Πορτία | Νίκα |
| Αἰλία | Νομωνία | Συρία | Μυρτία | Μεγανίκα |
| Σερβιλία | Πετρωνία | Τυρία | Ἀνθεστία | Λανίκα |
| Οὐεργιλία | Ἀντωνία | Σατυρία | Χρηστία | Καλλενίκα |
| Καικιλία | Εὐπραξία | Αἰσχρία | Νοστία | Βερενίκα |
| Ὁμιλία | Εὐταξία | Πλατωρία | Ἀττία | Φερενίκα |
| Στρατιλία | Ἀλεξία | Βικτωρία | Τελευτία | Ἐχενίκα |

| | | | | |
|---|---|---|---|---|
| Ἀρχενίκα | Λάλα | Νεπώτιλλα | Δαζίμα | Θερμοξένα |
| Κληίνίκα | Ἀμμάλα | Φίλλα | Ὠφελίμα | Κλεινοξένα |
| Πραξινίκα | Φυσάλα | Ῥούφιλλα | Μάξιμα | Προξένα |
| Πασινίκα | Βιτάλα | Βάρχιλλα | Πρῖμα | Ἀριστοξένα |
| Ναυσινίκα | Σεμέλα | Πόλλα | Σίμα | Εὐξένα |
| Σωσινίκα | Φιλομήλα | Κόπρολλα | Δασίμα | Θευξένα |
| Ἀννίκα | Μέγιλα | Σίβυλλα | Ζωσίμα | Πολυξένα |
| Θεονίκα | Κρηῖλα | Φείδυλλα | Τίμα | Φαηνά |
| Κλεονίκα | Ἄμμιλα | Κύλλα | Καλλιτίμα | Μαδήνα |
| Ἀγαθονίκα | Σατορνίλα | Νίκυλλα | Πραξιτίμα | Ἀνδήνα |
| Καλονίκα | Ἀλέξιλα | Σκύλλα | Διοτίμα | Γενθήνα |
| Φιλονίκα | Ζεύξιλα | Φίλυλλα | Ξενοτίμα | Λήνα |
| Μονίκα | Περίλα | Ξύλλα | Ἱεροτίμα | Κλήνα |
| Δαμονίκα | Βασίλα | Μάρυλλα | Γράμμα | Εἰρήνα |
| Ἰθμονίκα | Βάσσιλα | Ἄπρυλλα | Φιλόμμα | Εὐήνα |
| Ἱππονίκα | Πρώτιλα | Στράτυλλα | Γλύμμα | Αἴνα |
| Πατρονίκα | Φίλα | Κρίτυλλα | Διζομα | Λέαινα |
| Στρατονίκα | Μνασιφίλα | Τρίτυλλα | Διανόμα | Γνάθαινα |
| Πληστονίκα | Παμφίλα | Ψύλλα | Ἀνάπαυμα | Λάκαινα |
| Καλλιστονίκα | Θεοφίλα | Πῶλλα | Διδύμα | Δάμαινα |
| Ἀριστονίκα | Μηνοφίλα | Τελεσιβόλα | Γεῦμα | Κοπαίνα |
| Κλευνίκα | Ἡροφίλα | Κλεόλα | Ἀριστωνύμα | Πολύαινα |
| Πολυνίκα | Περφίλα | Βιόλα | Εὐωνύμα | Τρύφαινα |
| Φρυνίκα | Χίλα | Νικόλα | Κλεαίχμα | Σαβῖνα |
| Κλεωνίκα | Ζωῖλα | Δαμόλα | Ἀξίωμα | Ἀργῖνα |
| Ἀσίκα | Φήλικλα | Τιμόλα | Φίλωμα | Σεκουνδῖνα |
| Νεσσίκα | Πρόκλα | Κριτόλα | Ἄνα | Κλείνα |
| Ζωτικά | Λεπούσκλα | Θεμιστόλα | Δαρδάνα | Τραύζινα |
| Ἄκκα | Ἀμύκλα | Ἀριστόλα | Πιθάνα | Ἀνθῖνα |
| Μίκκα | Μέγαλλα | Ἄπλα | Λολλιάνα | Φρίκινα |
| Ἄλκα | Τιτίγελλα | Παῦλα | Θενιανα | Λυκίνα |
| Ξενοδόκα | Μάρκελλα | Πράϋλα | Λεϝκάνα | Πυκίνα |
| Θεοπρόκα | Γέμελλα | Ἄδυλα | Σικάνα | Φίλινα |
| Κέρκα | Ἄσελλα | Βάδυλα | Σιλάνα | Μαρκελλῖνα |
| Μίρκα | Κάτελλα | Φείδυλα | Νᾶνα | Γεμελλῖνα |
| Βουδόρκα | Φάβιλλα | Δίνδυλα | Ἰράνα | Παυλῖνα |
| Λυκίσκα | Σεκύνδιλλα | Μικύλα | Εἰράνα | Ἀσκυλῖνα |
| Σαλίσκα | Σεκούνδιλλα | Δάμμυλα | Φειράνα | Καπιτωλῖνα |
| Λαμίσκα | Ἀττίκιλλα | Ἄννυλα | Τυρρανά | Ζαίμινα |
| Μενίσκα | Ἄμιλλα | Ἀρχεβούλα | Κυράνα | Ἄμμινα |
| Ξενίσκα | Ποτάμιλλα | Καλλιβούλα | Βένιγνα | Δομνῖνα |
| Εὐφρονίσκα | Κόσμιλλα | Νικασιβούλα | Σίγνα | Μαννῖνα |
| Κυνίσκα | Ἀνθιάνιλλα | Ἀγησιβούλα | Κλεογένα | Σατορνῖνα |
| Φρυνίσκα | Κατιάνιλλα | Νικοβούλα | Παρθένα | Κοίνα |
| Βοΐσκα | Κριτόνιλλα | Κριτοβούλα | Σωσθένα | Πρικιπῖνα |
| Ἱππίσκα | Πράξιλλα | Ἀριστοβούλα | Ἑλένα | Κρισπῖνα |
| Ματερίσκα | Βόϊλλα | Εὐβούλα | Μένα | Δρωπῖνα |
| Ζωπυρίσκα | Νόϊλλα | Θεοδούλα | Τιμαμένα | Πελεγρῖνα |
| Συρίσκα | Μάπιλλα | Μαξιμούλα | Τετιμαμένα | Περεγρῖνα |
| Φύσκα | Κόπριλλα | Ἄννουλα | Ἐρεμένα | Σκοδρῖνα |
| Γλαύκα | Κύριλλα | Κριτοβώλα | Φιλημένα | Ματερῖνα |
| Λεύκα | Μύριλλα | Λαδάμα | Φιλουμένα | Χοιρῖνα |
| Λύκα | Σύριλλα | Ἀλκιδάμα | Φιλωμένα | Μακρῖνα |
| Καλύκα | Τελέσιλλα | Καλλιδάμα | Ξένα | Πυρρῖνα |
| Γλύκα | Ἀγήσιλλα | Ἀμφιδάμα | Πασιξένα | Μυρῖνα |
| Βαβελύκα | Πόσιλλα | Ἀριστοδάμα | Θεοξένα | Αὐγουρῖνα |
| Κλύκα | Χρύσιλλα | Εὐρυδάμα | Κλεοξένα | Ζωπυρῖνα |
| Ἀρκολύκα | Σώσιλλα | Ἀπάμα | Φιλοξένα | Τελεσῖνα |
| Σώκα | Κοδράτιλλα | Ἄνθεμα | Δαμοξένα | Καιλεσῖνα |
| Μεγάλα | Ἀβασκάντιλλα | Φίλημα | Τιμοξένα | Κοσῖνα |
| Κάλα | Ὀρέστιλλα | Εὔρημα | Ἑρμοξένα | Βάτινα |

| | | | | |
|---|---|---|---|---|
| Κωνσταντῖνα | Ἀριστονόα | Εὐάνδρα | Νεοπάτρα | Δημώνασσα |
| Κλημεντῖνα | Εὐνόα | Κλευάνδρα | Φιλοπάτρα | Τιμώνασσα |
| Ταρεντῖνα | Εὐρυνόα | Λύδρα | Κλευπάτρα | Φερσέφασσα |
| Καστῖνα | Ῥάπα | Μύδρα | Σωπάτρα | Μάρπησσα |
| Κελεστῖνα | Κρέπα | Λίβερα | Φιλιάστρα | Κρῆσσα |
| Οὐηστῖνα | Πῖπα | Ἐλευθέρα | Αὔρα | Ἴσσα |
| Χριστῖνα | Στίλπα | Ἱέρα | Ταύρα | Κίσσα |
| Φαυστῖνα | Κάμπα | Καλλιέρα | Κύρα | Μέλισσα |
| Κόττινα | Ῥοδόπα | Γλυκέρα | Γλυκύρα | Κίλισσα |
| Ἐλάφινα | Fιόπα | Καλημέρα | Λύρα | Φοίνισσα |
| Δέλφινα | Καλιόπα | Ἱμέρα | Φιλύρα | Χιόνισσα |
| Ῥουφῖνα | Καλλιόπα | Ἀμετέρα | Κολλύρα | Γαλάτισσα |
| Δυραχῖνα | Ἀρνιόπα | Φιλτέρα | Ἀμύρα | Κόσσα |
| Μόσχινα | Ἀστερόπα | Φιντέρα | Λαμύρα | Σόσσα |
| Θεότεκνα | Λαβίππα | Περιστέρα | Κινύρα | Λίβυσσα |
| Δόμνα | Γοργίππα | Δευτέρα | Μινύρα | Νῦσα |
| Ἄννα | Κυδίππα | Φιλοτέρα | Ἀρούρα | Διόνυσα |
| Ἀράβαννα | Ἀγηΐππα | Λουκιφέρα | Πλατούρα | Φλέγουσα |
| Σόσαννα | Ἀνθίππα | Τρυφέρα | Πύρα | Θεάδουσα |
| Ἰώαννα | Ξανθίππα | Σεβήρα | Κυπύρα | Μέδουσα |
| Γέννα | Νικίππα | Πανθήρα | Ζωπύρα | Αὐτομέδουσα |
| Βίρκεννα | Ἀλκίππα | Κύθηρα | Σύρα | Σπένδουσα |
| Χίμεννα | Φιλίππα | Κλεησισήρα | Σατύρα | Παίζουσα |
| Γλύκιννα | Καλλίππα | Οὐήρα | Γλαφύρα | Μελίζουσα |
| Μέλιννα | Δαμίππα | Αἴθρα | Ἐφύρα | Σώζουσα |
| Φίλιννα | Μενίππα | Ἵρα | Πορφύρα | Ἀρέθουσα |
| Κόριννα | Δηνίππα | Νέαιρα | Πούλχρα | Ἀνθοῦσα |
| Ταύριννα | Κληνίππα | Μαχαίρα | Αἴσχρα | Ποθοῦσα |
| Ἀντιγόνα | Αἰνίππα | Φιλαστείρα | Ὤρα | Ἀρίουσα |
| Ἑρμιόνα | Ἀγωνίππα | Σώτειρα | Θεδώρα | Συράκουσα |
| Κόνα | Ἀλεξίππα | Χοίρα | Ἀρτεμιδώρα | Πλέκουσα |
| Παραμόνα | Ἐλξίππα | Φαλάκρα | Ἰσιδώρα | Ἀρέσκουσα |
| Ἀγεμόνα | Χαιρίππα | Κλεαγόρα | Θεοδώρα | Μέλουσα |
| Σωφρόνα | Ἐρασίππα | Δικαιαγόρα | Διοδώρα | Φιλοῦσα |
| Θάρνα | Τεισίππα | Νικαγόρα | Διονυσιοδώρα | Θάλλουσα |
| Σμύρνα | Θερσίππα | Τιμαγόρα | Ξενοδώρα | Κάλλουσα |
| Νεῦνα | Λυσίππα | Ἀγναγόρα | Ζηνοδώρα | Μέλλουσα |
| Ἀμύνα | Στρατίππα | Κληναγόρα | Ἀθηνοδώρα | Μοῦσα |
| Βάτουννα | Ἀριστίππα | Ξηναγόρα | Μηνοδώρα | Δάμουσα |
| Φρύνα | Εὐίππα | Δαμναγόρα | Ἱεροδώρα | Βρέμουσα |
| Δικαιοσύνα | Ἀρχίππα | Ἀναξαγόρα | Διονυσοδώρα | Λανθάνουσα |
| Ἀβροσύνα | Κωνώπα | Πραξαγόρα | Νυμφοδώρα | Μένουσα |
| Εὐφροσύνα | Εὐρώπα | Ζευξαγόρα | Θευδώρα | Εὐφραίνουσα |
| Σωφροσύνα | Μετώπα | Τιμασαγόρα | Πολυδώρα | Φαίνουσα |
| Ἱερωσύνα | Μεγάρα | Ἀγησαγόρα | Φλῶρα | Κρίνουσα |
| Ματρώνα | Ἱλάρα | Πεισαγόρα | Ἄμμασα | Εὐνοῦσα |
| Τρύφωνα | Κλάρα | Κληταγόρα | Ἄρκεσα | Πρέπουσα |
| Ἄλεξα | Μάρα | Κλειταγόρα | Αἶσα | Θέλπουσα |
| Νίξα | Μιμάρα | Ἀρισταγόρα | Γρίθισα | Τέρπουσα |
| Δόξα | Σάρα | Κληγόρα | Ἄρκισα | Ἐροῦσα |
| Κλεοδόξα | Ζωσάρα | Εὐπόρα | Ποντομέδοισα | Συνεροῦσα |
| Ἀγαθόα | Πιστάρα | Ἀγησιχόρα | Ἀστυμέλοισα | Φέρουσα |
| Ἀλκαθόα | Χαρά | Εὐχόρα | Λάρισα | Συμφέρουσα |
| Κοικόα | Ἄβρα | Ἄπρα | Τάρσα | Πληροῦσα |
| Ἀλκινόα | Νικάνδρα | Λάμπρα | Βάσσα | Χαίρουσα |
| Πραξινόα | Τιμάνδρα | Μάτρα | Λαάνασσα | Πράτουσα |
| Θελξινόα | Ἀναξάνδρα | Κλεπάτρα | Εὐρυβάνασσα | Βρύουσα |
| Πασινόα | Ἀλεξάνδρα | Σωσιπάτρα | Ἰφιάνασσα | Καθήχουσα |
| Ἀρσινόα | Κασσάνδρα | Ἀντιπάτρα | Λάνασσα | Πάσχουσα |
| Ἀρμονόα | Κλειτάνδρα | Σωιπάτρα | Μίνασσα | Συμπάσχουσα |
| Προνόα | Ἀντάνδρα | Κλεοπάτρα | Διώνασσα | Χρύσα |

| | | | | |
|---|---|---|---|---|
| Πρετιῶσα | Ἀρχαρέτα | Κλεαρίστα | Μύχα | Γαμική |
| Ἐρῶσα | Κληρέτα | Νικαρίστα | Τιμύχα | Κωμική |
| Χαριτῶσα | Κορέτα | Δαμαρίστα | Βοστρύχα | Νίκη |
| Τρυφῶσα | Δυσπσετα | Τιμαρίστα | Ζαοτύχα | Πανική |
| Αὐδᾶτα | Ἀγήτα | Ξεναρίστα | Εὐτύχα | Γενική |
| Φειλάτα | Μιλήτα | Εὐχαρίστα | Φιλοκόμψα | Βερενίκη |
| Ἀδμάτα | Κλήτα | Φαῦστα | Ἰακώβ | Ἐχενίκη |
| Φορτουνᾶτα | Ἀγαπήτα | Μύστα | Ἀδάη | Καλλινίκη |
| Ὀάτα | Ἀφροδίτα | Ἰοῦστα | Δανάη | Φοινίκη |
| Ἀράτα | Ἐπαφροδίτα | Βενοῦστα | Θήβη | Ἐπινίκη |
| Ἐράτα | Κλείτα | Ἄττα | Φοίβη | Ἐλπινίκη |
| Πράτα | Πολυκλείτα | Χάραττα | Θίσβη | Λυσινίκη |
| Σαστράτα | Μελίτα | Μέλιττα | Καλύβη | Κλεονίκη |
| Τηλεστράτα | Πίτα | Ἰούλιττα | Λαλάγη | Ἀγαθονίκη |
| Μενεστράτα | Μαργαρίτα | Σίττα | Πήγη | Ἱππονίκη |
| Χαιρεστράτα | Χαρίτα | Ἐμαῦτα | Σίγη | Ἱερονίκη |
| Ἀρχεστράτα | Μέριτα | Ἐμιναῦτα | Ἐκλόγη | Στρατονίκη |
| Καλλιστράτα | Δαμοκρίτα | Φιλοναῦτα | Στόργη | Καλλιστονίκη |
| Τιμασιστράτα | Τιμοκρίτα | Τεύτα | Αὔγη | Ἀριστονίκη |
| Μνασιστράτα | Ἀριστοκρίτα | Ἔτευτα | Ἰλιάδη | Κλευνίκη |
| Ἀγησιστράτα | Εὔκρίτα | Τεμίτευτα | Λάδη | Δαφνική |
| Νικοστράτα | Πολυκρίτα | Τρίτευτα | Κλάδη | Ἰωνική |
| Μεγαλοστράτα | Τρίτα | Ἱππολύτα | Ἴδη | Καρική |
| Φιλοστράτα | Ἀτίτα | Ρασφαρμαυα | Λυσίδη | Μουσική |
| Δαμοστράτα | Ζωΐτα | Ἔτλευα | Ἀρουάνδη | Ἀσιατική |
| Τιμοστράτα | Ἀθίκτα | Περπέτουα | Σπόνδη | Πολιτική |
| Ξενοστράτα | Κέλτα | Φιλαδέλφα | Ρόδη | Πρακτική |
| Πολυστράτα | Θωμάντα | Σόφα | Κλειορόδη | Ποντική |
| Σωστράτα | Εὐφράντα | Ροῦφα | Πεισιρρόδη | Πιστική |
| Τάτα | Φάντα | Κοσσύφα | Λύδη | Μυστική |
| Ὀπτᾶτα | Λαφάντα | Μάχα | Σπούδη | Ἀττική |
| Κλεβέτα | Κλεοφάντα | Ἀγεμάχα | Κλέη | Ζωτική |
| Φειδέτα | Ξενοφάντα | Καλλιμάχα | Ἀγάθη | Βιωτική |
| Δαζέτα | Μηνοφάντα | Δεξιμάχα | Πασαγάθη | Ἐρωτική |
| Μακέτα | Ἀμέντα | Νικασιμάχα | Ψαμάθη | Γραφική |
| Ἰκέτα | Κούϊντα | Λυσιμάχα | Μέθη | Δελφική |
| Σκενέτα | Δότα | Συμμάχα | Τίθθη | Τυχική |
| Αἰνέτα | Δεαδότα | Κρεομάχα | Ἄνθη | Ἄλκη |
| Κλεαινέτα | Θεοδότα | Ἀντιομάχα | Εὐάνθη | Πλόκη |
| Δαμαινέτα | Διοδότα | Νικομάχα | Κολοκύνθη | Κλαδίσκη |
| Ἀρισταινέτα | Πυννοδότα | Δεινομάχα | Νόθη | Μενίσκη |
| Φινέτα | Θευδότα | Ἀνδρομάχα | Ταταίη | Γλαύκη |
| Συνέτα | Εὐβιότα | Κλειτομάχα | Μελίη | Καλύκη |
| Ἀρέτα | Τιμασιμβρότα | Ἀριστομάχα | Σιδωνίη | Γλύκη |
| Λεαρέτα | Κλησιμβρότα | Πρωτομάχα | Ἱκεσίη | Ἀμύκη |
| Κλεαρέτα | Αἰνησιμβρότα | Μαλίχα | Ἱστίη | Μεγάλη |
| Νεαρέτα | Κούαρτα | Φιλλίχα | Τυχίη | Αἰγιάλη |
| Νικαρέτα | Μύρτα | Κυλίχα | Ἰθάκη | Φιάλη |
| Λαρέτα | Δάστα | Λαμίχα | Κυριακή | Κάλη |
| Δαμαρέτα | Κάστα | Δεινίχα | Ἀκτιακή | Σιμάλη |
| Τιμαρέτα | Θέστα | Ὀλυμπίχα | Ἀχαϊκή | Ἀπάλη |
| Θαυμαρέτα | Φιλέστα | Ἱππίχα | Λυσιδίκη | Σπατάλη |
| Ξεναρέτα | Ἀδίστα | Σωτηρίχα | Λαοδίκη | Πετάλη |
| Φαιναρέτα | Ἡδίστα | Τυρίχα | Κλεοδίκη | Μυρτάλη |
| Μνασαρέτα | Φιλίστα | Ὀνασίχα | Πυθοδίκη | Ὀμφάλη |
| Ἀγησαρέτα | Καλλίστα | Σωσίχα | Ἰσοδίκη | Αἴγλη |
| Χρυσαρέτα | Πίστα | Μυρτίχα | Χρυσοδίκη | Γέλη |
| Σωσαρέτα | Ἀρίστα | Φιλιστίχα | Αὐτοδίκη | Ἀγέλη |
| Πανταρέτα | Νικαάρίστα | Πλουτίχα | Λαυδίκη | Φικέλη |
| Ἀρισταρέτα | Ἀγαρίστα | Κλεόχα | Εὐρυδίκη | Θυμέλη |
| Εὐαρέτα | Μεγαρίστα | Μόσχα | Ἑλίκη | Τέλη |

| | | | | |
|---|---|---|---|---|
| Νεφέλη | Ταυριανή | Ἠπιόνη | Ἐλάτη | Ἡδίστη |
| Μνησιφίλη | Νασσιανή | Ἡσιόνη | Πλάτη | Καλλίστη |
| Παμφίλη | Τιτιανή | Χιόνη | Δυνάτη | Πίστη |
| Δαμοφίλη | Κουϊντιανή | Καλλόνη | Ἀπάτη | Ἀρίστη |
| Πρόκλη | Ἀντιοχιανή | Παραμόνη | Νικηράτη | Κλεαρίστη |
| Ἔλλη | Εὐτυχιανή | Ὑπομονή | Σωσικράτη | Κρατίστη |
| Ἰόλλη | Ῥωξάνη | Ἀλκυόνη | Δαμοκράτη | Θεοκτίστη |
| Ὑπερβόλη | Καμπάνη | Σμύρνη | Νικοστράτη | Ἀπολαύστη |
| Ἰόλη | Κυάνη | Ῥοδογούνη | Φιλοστράτη | Γνωστή |
| Αἰόλη | Στεφάνη | Φρύνη | Δαμοστράτη | Τίττη |
| Νικοπόλη | Καλλιφάνη | Δικαιοσύνη | Πολυστράτη | Αὐτή |
| Ἀνατολή | Ἄγνη | Χαρμοσύνη | Μελέτη | Κλύτη |
| Ἐπιστόλη | Ἀριάγνη | Εὐφροσύνη | Τελέτη | Ἱππολύτη |
| Ἀριστόλη | Ἀριάδνη | Σωφροσύνη | Ἀλκαινέτη | Ἀνύτη |
| Ὕλη | Ἑλένη | Δάφνη | Κλεισταινέτη | Ζώτη |
| Αὔλη | Καμένη | Τέχνη | Εὐνέτη | Πρώτη |
| Παύλη | Λιμένη | Μεδώνη | Ἀρέτη | Παρασκευή |
| Ἀρκύλη | Σωζομένη | Σιδώνη | Τιμαρέτη | Νύμφη |
| Κριτοβούλη | Ἀγαλλομένη | Λεώνη | Φαιναρέτη | Συντρόφη |
| Θεοδούλη | Μελπομένη | Διώνη | Τρυγήτη | Σόφη |
| Σταφύλη | Κλυμένη | Σκιώνη | Φιλήτη | Ἄπφη |
| Ἄμη | Οἰκουμένη | Οἰνώνη | Γαμήτη | Ἰάχη |
| Θαλάμη | Φιλουμένη | Σικυώνη | Ἐπιθυμήτη | Νικομάχη |
| Νέμη | Ἀγαπωμένη | Χρυσοθόη | Νοήτη | Κλευμάχη |
| Ἐπιστήμη | Εὐξένη | Χλόη | Ἀφροδίτη | Συνέχη |
| Φήμη | Κομμαγηνή | Ἀρσινόη | Ἐπαφροδίτη | Σωτίχη |
| Μονίμη | Γαλήνη | Θεονόη | Κλείτη | Ἐκδόχη |
| Καρπίμη | Σελήνη | Τιμονόη | Λίτη | Ἄρχη |
| Σίμη | Μυτιλήνη | Ἀριστονόη | Μελίτη | Τιμάρχη |
| Στασίμη | Ἀβουλήνη | Αὐτονόη | Χαρίτη | Ἀριστάρχη |
| Ὀνησίμη | Κρωταμήνη | Πόη | Ἀσυγκρίτη | Εὔχη |
| Χρησίμη | Νήνη | Βερόη | Ξενοκρίτη | Τύχη |
| Ζωσίμη | Εἰρήνη | Μερόη | Ἐλαφίτη | Ἀγαθητύχη |
| Δρωσίμη | Κρήνη | Καλλιρρόη | Ἀκτή | Καλλιτύχη |
| Τίμη | Ῥοδίνη | Ἀγάπη | Στάκτη | Ἰσιτύχη |
| Τροφίμη | Ποθείνη | Πανταγάπη | Προσδέκτη | Συντύχη |
| Ἄμμη | Κροκίνη | Νάπη | Ἐκλέκτη | Λαμπροτύχη |
| Νόμη | Ἀλίνη | Ἰωτάπη | Εὔκτη | Εὐτύχη |
| Εὐρυνόμη | Ἀκυλίνη | Εὐμόλπη | Ἀβασκάντη | Ψύχη |
| Ἱπποδρόμη | Κυπαρίνη | Ῥοδόπη | Ἀταλάντη | Κόμψη |
| Ὁρμή | Θερινή | Καλλιόπη | Θεοδότη | Ζώη |
| Ἡδύμη | Ἐλευθερίνη | Προκόπη | Διοδότη | Γοργόι |
| Διδύμη | Μυρρίνη | Παρθενόπη | Ἀσκληπιοδότη | Σοφιδόι |
| Κώμη | Μυρσίνη | Μερόπη | Μηνοδότη | Πειθόι |
| Γνώμη | Χρηματίνη | Ἐντρόπη | Νυμφοδότη | Κλιόι |
| Ῥώμη | Μελιτίνη | Κυδίππη | Βιότη | Καλλιόι |
| Φιλορώμη | Μαρτίνη | Φιλίππη | Γράπτη | Δαμιόι |
| Πιθάνη | Ἀττίνη | Ἀθανίππη | Θρέπτη | Νικόι |
| Γαιανή | Φωτίνη | Μενίππη | Γλύπτη | Τιμόι |
| Φλαβιανή | Ἄκνη | Εὐίππη | Κρύπτη | Ξενόι |
| Φοιβιανή | Πρόκνη | Εὐκάρπη | Σπάρτη | Ἀγησόι |
| Πελαγιανή | Σέμνη | Εὐτέρπη | Ἑόρτη | Πεισόι |
| Γενθιανή | Ποίμνη | Σινώπη | Ἄστη | Ἀριστόι |
| Μαρκιανή | Ἀργέννη | Ταυρώπη | Βλάστη | Ἀρχόι |
| Αἰλιανή | Ἡρέννη | Εὐρώπη | Γελάστη | Γοργώι |
| Ἰουλιανή | Καρμόννη | Κυπάρη | Πλάστη | Λυσιδώι |
| Δαμιάνη | Ἐπιγόνη | Ἀφάρη | Ὀνομάστη | Ἀμαθώι |
| Ἀμμιανή | Ἀντιγόνη | Ἡμετέρη | Ἀγοράστη | Ἀρχαιώι |
| Ἀρρηνιανή | Χρυσογόνη | Ἀρισταγόρη | Χρήστη | Διώι |
| Οὐλπιανή | Ἡδόνη | Χρύση | Ὀλβίστη | Φιώι |
| Ἀγριππιανή | Ἑρμιόνη | Ἰσοχρύση | Μεγίστη | Πουβλιώι |

| | | | | |
|---|---|---|---|---|
| Νακώι | Τιμήν | Μέθιον | Ὤκιμον | Κινάδων |
| Νικώι | Παρμήν | Νίκιον | Σῖμον | Ῥάδων |
| Ἀκριοκώι | Μενήν | Βομβύκιον | Χλίδανον | Ϝράδων |
| Συκώι | Ξενήν | Βουβάλιον | Καπρόγονον | Μύγδων |
| Μαλώι | Ἀλεξήν | Ἀμπέλιον | Ἀβρότονον | Μακεδών |
| Γελώι | Ἱππήν | Κάλλιον | Μναμόσυνον | Μέδων |
| Φιλώι | Ἱερήν | Ἡδύλιον | Εὐφρόσυνον | Λαμέδων |
| Αἰνώι | Πατερήν | Δάμιον | Ἐπίδοξον | Ἀλκιμέδων |
| Σελινώι | Χαιρήν | Ἀνθέμιον | Ἔπιδοον | Καλλιμέδων |
| Περιλιπώι | Πυρρήν | Χρησίμιον | Ἵλαρον | Ἀντιμέδων |
| Ἱππώι | Σωστρήν | Φάνιον | Ἄβρον | Ἀμφιμέδων |
| Ἱμερώι | Σατυρήν | Παρθένιον | Ὀνασιφόρον | Λαομέδων |
| Σωτηρώι | Μνασήν | Ξένιον | Σύμφορον | Διομέδων |
| Χορώι | Τεισήν | Σελήνιον | Λάμπρον | Ἱππομέδων |
| Δυρώι | Θερσήν | Ἀκροθίνιον | Μύρον | Ἀριστομέδων |
| Εὐφρώι | Ναυσήν | Κρίνιον | Δῶρον | Αὐτομέδων |
| Δωρώι | Παυσήν | Νίννιον | Ἐπαφρόδιτον | Εὐρυμέδων |
| Τιμασώι | Λυσήν | Εἰκόνιον | Ἄμεμπτον | Ἐμπέδων |
| Ἀρκεσώι | Σωσήν | Λευκόϊον | Ἄριστον | Ἀνθήδων |
| Λυσώι | Στρατήν | Κέπιον | Κάλλιχον | Σαρπηδών |
| Χρυσώι | Ἀριστήν | Κάρπιον | Δάων | Ῥήδων |
| Ἐρατώι | Ἀρχήν | Τηλάριον | Ἑλικάων | Καρχηδών |
| Πλειστώι | Ἀγάθιν | Δαμάριον | Λυκάων | Λαΐδων |
| Ἀριστώι | Μελάνθιν | Ζηνάριον | Ἀγλάων | Παΐδων |
| Ὀλυττώι | Φιλόθιν | Πασάριον | Σάων | Φαΐδων |
| Κυκυώι | Νίκιν | Χρυσάριον | Χρυσάων | Φεΐδων |
| Ϝαχώι | Ἀρτέμιν | Ἀπατάριον | Ἑκατάων | Χελιδών |
| Λεχώι | Παρθένιν | Χρωτάριον | Φάων | Χλίδων |
| Λαιδάν | Πολυχρόνιν | Εὐχάριον | Λαφάων | Μυρμιδών |
| Μαζάν | Ἐγκάρπιν | Ψυχάριον | Καλλιφάων | Δάνδων |
| Ϝερζάν | Ἀγάριν | Νεμέριον | Δαμοφάων | Σπένδων |
| Ζιλιαν | Ἀγαθάριν | Σύριον | Ξενοφάων | Σφένδων |
| Θερσιάν | Νικάριν | Ἀγάσιον | Εὐρυφάων | Κόνδων |
| Ἔλλαν | Φιλάριν | Νικάσιον | Μαχάων | Ῥόδων |
| Ἀλκμάν | Δαμάριν | Γυμνάσιον | Γράβων | Κέρδων |
| Ἀκαρνάν | Τιμάριν | Εὐκλήσιον | Στράβων | Σέρδων |
| Ἀμεντάν | Ἐρωτάριν | Ἀθηνήσιον | Σάβων | Σπεύδων |
| Ἀρτάφαν | Ἐλευθέριν | Φρονήσιον | Φλέβων | Κύδων |
| Λαήν | Ἀστέριν | Χαρίσιον | Λίβων | Καμύδων |
| Ἀγήν | Λευκόσιν | Διονύσιον | Τρίβων | Κορύδων |
| Γοργήν | Φιλημάτιν | Μούσιον | Στίβων | Δέων |
| Πυθήν | Ὀνασικράτιν | Χρύσιον | Λόβων | Ϝικαδέων |
| Στρογιήν | Χαρίτιν | Φιλημάτιον | Βύβων | Θέων |
| Νικήν | Ἀμαράντιν | Ὀνομάτιον | Ἄγων | Ἡμιθέων |
| Βοικήν | Καλλίστιν | Ἀρωμάτιον | Μάγων | Λέων |
| Ἀλκήν | Βύττιν | Τάτιον | Δαμάγων | Πανταλέων |
| Λυκήν | Μόσχιν | Λεόντιον | Τράγων | Πελέων |
| Καλήν | Νίκεον | Φιλίστιον | Σάγων | Δαϊλέων |
| Ἐθελήν | Κάλλεον | Καλλίστιον | Πλαγγών | Χειλέων |
| Σωσιλήν | Δάμεον | Ἀρίστιον | Φλέγων | Ἀντιλέων |
| Καλλήν | Λένεον | Φιλώτιον | Μέγων | Ἀρχιλέων |
| Σαλλήν | Ἀρίστεον | Σώτιον | Ἀρήγων | Κλέων |
| Κεφαλλήν | Τίμαιον | Ἐλάφιον | Αἴγων | Ἡρακλέων |
| Ἕλλην | Ἄγιον | Ἄρχιον | Θέλγων | Εὐκλέων |
| Τελλήν | Δῖον | Μόσχιον | Γόργων | Τελλέων |
| Πολλήν | Ἀρκάδιον | Ἡσύχιον | Πύργων | Γοργολέων |
| Πολήν | Φείδιον | Ἐπιλώϊον | Λύγων | Νικολέων |
| Δαμήν | Σωτηρίδιον | Ξενικόν | Τρύγων | Ἀρκολέων |
| Λιμήν | Ἐγχειρίδιον | Γλαῦκον | Φύγων | Λυκολέων |
| Ποιμήν | Χοιρίδιον | Φιλόκαλον | Δάδων | Βουκολέων |
| Φιλοποίμην | Ῥόδιον | Πέρκαλον | Ϝάδων | Δαμολέων |

| | | | | |
|---|---|---|---|---|
| Τιμολέων | Ἐργίων | Δευκαλίων | Σιλανίων | Μαρίων |
| Δεινολέων | Γοργίων | Πυρραλίων | Ἀδρανίων | Πυγμαρίων |
| Ἱππολέων | Δίων | Θεσσαλίων | Εἰρανίων | Ζωναρίων |
| Ἀγρολέων | Στιβαδίων | Φυσαλίων | Οὐρανίων | Λιπαρίων |
| Εὐρυλέων | Ἰκαδίων | Κεφαλίων | Στεφανίων | Λουπαρίων |
| Θρασυλέων | Ἀρκαδίων | Ὀμφαλίων | Ὀρφανίων | Ἐρωταρίων |
| Νέων | Πυλαδίων | Ἀβλίων | Σθενίων | Παγχαρίων |
| Ἐννέων | Ἑρμαδίων | Εὐτραπελίων | Ἐλενίων | Ὑβρίων |
| Ἐρατέων | Ἐμπεδίων | Εὐτελίων | Παρμενίων | Ἀνδρίων |
| Ξένϝων | Βαυκιδίων | Ὠφελίων | Χαρμενίων | Σφοδρίων |
| Αὐγάζων | Νυμφιδίων | Ἡλίων | Ξενίων | Κυδρίων |
| Ἀμαζών | Κωμωιδίων | Οἰνοκλίων | Ἀθηνίων | Ἀθερίων |
| Ἀκμάζων | Καλανδίων | Θαλλίων | Εὐηνίων | Ἐλευθερίων |
| Ἀγάθων | Κενδίων | Καλλίων | Φιλινίων | Εὐαμερίων |
| Πλάθων | Σεκουνδίων | Ἀπελλίων | Οἰνίων | Ἑσπερίων |
| Γνάθων | Ἀφροδίων | Κολλίων | Ϝοινίων | Ὑπερίων |
| Σάθων | Εὐοδίων | Πολλίων | Σισσινίων | Γηρίων |
| Φαέθων | Θευδίων | Τριφυλλίων | Ἐρυμνίων | Τηρίων |
| Ἀρέθων | Λυδίων | Ψυλλίων | Σαννίων | Σωτηρίων |
| Αἴθων | Βουδίων | Πωλλίων | Μυννίων | Χαιρίων |
| Νεαίθων | Ἡρακλείων | Βουκολίων | Σφενδονίων | Μαχαιρίων |
| Διαίθων | Ἀνδροκλείων | Στρογγυλίων | Κρονίων | Γιρίων |
| Κιναίθων | Εὐκλείων | Ἡδυλίων | Σωφρονίων | Χοιρίων |
| Πείθων | Πολλείων | Μικυλίων | Εὐθυνίων | Φαλακρίων |
| Μίθων | Ξενείων | Σιμυλίων | Φρυνίων | Λοκρίων |
| Νίθων | Ϝίων | Κορβουλίων | Περκωνίων | Θορίων |
| Πίθων | Μεληΐων | Εὐβουλίων | Ἀναξίων | Κορίων |
| Κρίθων | Θίων | Ἰουλίων | Πραξίων | Εὐπορίων |
| Εὐέλθων | Ἀγαθίων | Πουλίων | Δεξίων | Ἀλεκτορίων |
| Ῥίνθων | Ἀλαθίων | Αἰσχυλίων | Ἀλεξίων | Εὐφορίων |
| Ὄθων | Ἀραθθίων | Εὐμωλίων | Ἀρηξίων | Λαμπρίων |
| Κόθων | Σαϊθίων | Αἰτωλίων | Ἰξίων | Κοπρίων |
| Μόθων | Ἀνθίων | Μίων | Σωιξίων | Κερρίων |
| Ὄρθων | Γοργυθίων | Γαμίων | Νοίων | Δυστρίων |
| Πόσθων | Μικυθίων | Δαμίων | Σοΐων | Σωστρίων |
| Πίτθων | Σμικυθίων | Καρδαμίων | Ἀπίων | Ταυρίων |
| Κρεύθων | Πυθίων | Πλοκαμίων | Ἀσκλαπίων | Θυρίων |
| Πύθων | Κωθίων | Ἐπαμίων | Σαραπίων | Κυρίων |
| Ἴων | Κίων | Σαμίων | Σεραπίων | Λαμπυρίων |
| Ἀγλαΐων | Φουλακίων | Ἀνθεμίων | Ἀσκληπίων | Εὐπυρίων |
| Μαίων | Δαμακίων | Ἀρτεμίων | Καιπίων | Ζωπυρίων |
| Δαμαίων | Πυστακίων | Εὐφημίων | Ὀριπίων | Συρίων |
| Ἀλκμαίων | Θραϊκίων | Ἰμίων | Στιλπίων | Σισυρίων |
| Ἑρμαίων | Φαικίων | Εὐδαιμίων | Ὀλυμπίων | Σατυρίων |
| Παίων | Παλικίων | Ἀλκιμίων | Ἱππίων | Πορφυρίων |
| Ἡραίων | Φηλικίων | Πριμίων | Φιλιππίων | Ἐπαφρίων |
| Ἀκταίων | Φιλικίων | Σιμίων | Καρπίων | Αἰσχρίων |
| Φαίων | Μικίων | Ζωσιμίων | Εὐκαρπίων | Ὠρίων |
| Ἰχαίων | Νικίων | Τιμίων | Σκορπίων | Δωρίων |
| Βίων | Μικκίων | Τροφιμίων | Θωπίων | Ψωρίων |
| Λαβίων | Ἀλκίων | Παλμίων | Δρωπίων | Σίων |
| Ἀρεταβίων | Ἀρκίων | Ἀρμίων | Ἀνθρωπίων | Ἀγασίων |
| Φοιβίων | Μαρκίων | Χαρμίων | Ἀρίων | Ἐργασίων |
| Κολομβίων | Κερκίων | Ἑρμίων | Τυνδαρίων | Νικασίων |
| Ἀγίων | Δορκίων | Βορμίων | Θεαρίων | Τιμασίων |
| Μαγίων | Φυσκίων | Φορμίων | Κανθαρίων | Μνασίων |
| Ἀρπαγίων | Γλαυκίων | Ἐνδυμίων | Καρίων | Ὀνασίων |
| Κοραγίων | Φωκίων | Σιλβανίων | Μαρκαρίων | Πασίων |
| Χοραγίων | Πυρβαλίων | Οὐρβανίων | Λυκαρίων | Πρασίων |
| Ἡγίων | Πυργαλίων | Ἀθανίων | Ἱλαρίων | Νεσίων |
| Αἰγίων | Ποσθαλίων | Μελανίων | Πτολλαρίων | Αὐτεσίων |

| | | | | |
|---|---|---|---|---|
| Ἀγησίων | Ἐφωτίων | Μόκων | Παλάμων | Ἐπιτυγχάνων |
| Τιμησίων | Θυΐων | Δέρκων | Μνάμων | Ἄγνων |
| Αἰνησίων | Λυΐων | Κέρκων | Κλεοπάμων | Σθένων |
| Ἰσίων | Ἀρεφίων | Πέρκων | Ἀριστοπάμων | Μένων |
| Πεισίων | Ἰφίων | Δόρκων | Εὐπάμων | Παρμένων |
| Τεισίων | Δελφίων | Δάσκων | Εὐδράμων | Εὐμένων |
| Εὐθοσίων | Ἀμφίων | Ἀρέσκων | Σάμων | Κρευμένων |
| Θερσίων | Νουνφίων | Μύσκων | Ἀσάμων | Ξένων |
| Κρασσίων | Σαπφίων | Φύσκων | Ποτάμων | Πολυξένων |
| Μελισσίων | Μορφίων | Γλαύκων | Φράδμων | Ζήνων |
| Παυσίων | Ῥουφίων | Λεύκων | Ἀγέμων | Ἴνων |
| Φαυσίων | Χίων | Λύκων | Ἡγέμων | Αἴνων |
| Λυσίων | Ἀρραχίων | Γλύκων | Ἀνθέμων | Φιλαίνων |
| Σωσίων | Ἐχίων | Ἄλων | Πολέμων | Εὐφραίνων |
| Φορτουνατίων | Βακχίων | Θάλων | Βρέμων | Φαίνων |
| Ἀρατίων | Μαλχίων | Κάλων | Χρέμων | Δείνων |
| Φιλοκρατίων | Ἀρχίων | Μιτάλων | Ἀρτέμων | Μείνων |
| Ἀρποκρατίων | Αἰσχίων | Κεφάλων | Δαήμων | Ἀμείνων |
| Πρατίων | Μοσχίων | Ὕβλων | Ἀγήμων | Ἐπαμείνων |
| Σωστρατίων | Πραϋχίων | Γέλων | Ἡγήμων | Ἀλκίνων |
| Ἀετίων | Ἐπιτυχίων | Θέλων | Δήμων | Νίνων |
| Λαιετίων | Εὐτυχίων | Κέλων | Αἰδήμων | Θοίνων |
| Ἐγρετίων | Λάκων | Μέλων | Φιλήμων | Ῥίνων |
| Κλητίων | Μαλάκων | Τέλων | Μνήμων | Μέμνων |
| Ἐπαφροδιτίων | Φιλάκων | Ὀφέλων | Νοήμων | Ἀγαμέμνων |
| Φιλιτίων | Ἀπελλάκων | Τήλων | Ἀπήμων | Ἐρύμνων |
| Καλλιτίων | Εὐδαιμάκων | Χείλων | Χαιρήμων | Σάννων |
| Πακτίων | Τιμάκων | Κίλων | Εὐρήμων | Θαρσύννων |
| Ὀλτίων | Ξενάκων | Μίλων | Εὐκτήμων | Κόνων |
| Ἀντίων | Δεινακῶν | Σίλων | Εὐσχήμων | Κύνων |
| Κρησκεντίων | Ἐξάκων | Φίλων | Αἵμων | Θαρρύνων |
| Λεοντίων | Δράκων | Χίλων | Εὐδαίμων | Φρύνων |
| Πρεποντίων | Σάκων | Παραβάλλων | Χείμων | Θαρσύνων |
| Κοτίων | Πασάκων | Ὑπερβάλλων | Κίμων | Τέχνων |
| Δαμοτίων | Πρατακῶν | Κάλλων | Μίμων | Δαμώνων |
| Ἱπποτίων | Σωτάκων | Βέλλων | Εὐκαρίμων | Δέξων |
| Τεταρτίων | Μίγκων | Ἀπέλλων | Δρίμων | Ἀλέξων |
| Χαρτίων | Κρέκων | Τρέλλων | Σίμων | Συννοῶν |
| Μυρτίων | Καθήκων | Τέλλων | Τίμων | Δαμοφόων |
| Εὐφραστίων | Φαίκων | Κίλλων | Κόμων | Σκιάπων |
| Ἀνθεστίων | Δίκων | Σίλλων | Σολομῶν | Ἀσκλάπων |
| Νεστίων | Εἰκών | Κύλλων | Δρόμων | Θεράπων |
| Ἀρεστίων | Μεθίκων | Μύλλων | Χρόμων | Βλέπων |
| Χρηστίων | Κίκων | Βόλων | Κάρμων | Πρέπων |
| Ἀφαιστίων | Ἑλικών | Κόλων | Ἕρμων | Ἐπιτρέπων |
| Ἡφαιστίων | Φηλίκων | Μόλων | Θέρμων | Ἀσκλήπων |
| Μεγιστίων | Φιλίκων | Πόλων | Ἐχετέρμων | Λίπων |
| Ἀλιστίων | Καλλικῶν | Σόλων | Δάσμων | Ἀλίπων |
| Καλιστίων | Μίκων | Στόλων | Πλήσμων | Στίπων |
| Φιλιστίων | Σμίκων | Εὐστόλων | Ὕσμων | Θάλπων |
| Καλλιστίων | Νίκων | Αὐλών | Θύμων | Στίλπων |
| Ἀριστίων | Γνίκων | Γύλων | Ἀμύμων | Λάμπων |
| Βενουστίων | Δαμονίκων | Κύλων | Κνύμων | Στρίμπων |
| Ἐμαυτίων | Ἀλεξίκων | Σκύλων | Ὠνύμων | Πόμπων |
| Ὀξυτίων | Μητρικῶν | Φώλων | Δρύμων | Ἵππων |
| Πλουτίων | Φρίκων | Ἄμων | Ἐτύμων | Ὀχίππων |
| Εὐρυτίων | Σίκων | Δάμων | Ἀριώμων | Κάρπων |
| Ζωτίων | Ἀττίκων | Εὐδάμων | Γνώμων | Τέρπων |
| Ἐρωτίων | Ἄλκων | Εὐρυδάμων | Κανών | Ἴαρων |
| Πρωτίων | Βόλκων | Κάμων | Πλάνων | Κάρων |
| Σωτίων | Δόκων | Συγκάμων | Αὐξάνων | Νικάρων |

| | | | | |
|---|---|---|---|---|
| Λάρων | Ξενόφρων | Γείτων | Ἀλκιφῶν | Σωσιάναξ |
| Μάρων | Δαιτόφρων | Θεογείτων | Καλλιφῶν | Ἀμφιάναξ |
| Νάρων | Ἀριστόφρων | Ἀριστογείτων | Γνίφων | Ἀρχιάναξ |
| Καπάρων | Εὔφρων | Εὐγείτων | Κολοιφῶν | Πλειστοάναξ |
| Σωσάρων | Εὐθύφρων | Κλείτων | Χαριφῶν | Ἀριστάναξ |
| Χάρων | Πολύφρων | Μελίτων | Ἀρριφῶν | Εὐρυάναξ |
| Εὐχάρων | Λεώφρων | Μίτων | Μνασιφῶν | Ἀστυάναξ |
| Ἄβρων | Σώφρων | Πίτων | Ἀγησιφῶν | Δόναξ |
| Θίβρων | Αἴσχρων | Καπίτων | Κτησιφῶν | Δαμῶναξ |
| Ἄγρων | Δώρων | Χαρίτων | Ἀντιφῶν | Δημῶναξ |
| Ἴγρων | Θεάσων | Κρίτων | Πίμφων | Τιμῶναξ |
| Ἄνδρων | Ἰάσων | Τρίτων | Νύμφων | Ἑρμῶναξ |
| Γέρων | Μνάσων | Φίλτων | Λαοφῶν | Ἡρῶναξ |
| Ἱέρων | Ὀνάσων | Πάντων | Κλεοφῶν | Μητρῶναξ |
| Συμφέρων | Πάσων | Φάντων | Ἡλιοφῶν | Πλειστῶναξ |
| Γάϝρων | Ἐράσων | Μίντων | Νικοφῶν | Ἅρπαξ |
| Ἤρων | Θράσων | Φίντων | Μηλοφῶν | Φάραξ |
| Θήρων | Πράσων | Κρότων | Δαμοφῶν | Ἱέραξ |
| Ὀνήρων | Φράσων | Λέπτων | Δημοφῶν | Ζῆραξ |
| Ἔχθρων | Τελέσων | Χάρτων | Ξενοφῶν | Ἄνθραξ |
| Κιθαιρών | Ἀγήσων | Φέρτων | Σόφων | Κόραξ |
| Χαίρων | Νήσων | Χόρτων | Καφισοφῶν | Στύραξ |
| Συγχαίρων | Κτήσων | Μύρτων | Κλειτοφῶν | Θώραξ |
| Θείρων | Αἴσων | Ἄστων | Ἀριστοφῶν | Πόρταξ |
| Σπείρων | Μαίσων | Θέστων | Τρύφων | Κάρχαξ |
| Σείρων | Τείσων | Ἴστων | Εὐρυφῶν | Μάληξ |
| Κίρων | Ϝίσων | Καλλίστων | Τύφων | Ὕσπληξ |
| Μίρων | Ἀρκίσων | Πίστων | Στύφων | Βάρηξ |
| Λαπίρων | Λίσων | Ἄριστων | Μάχων | Θρᾷξ |
| Σίρων | Θεμίσων | Νόστων | Πάχων | Ἕλιξ |
| Βαιστίρων | Πίσων | Σάττων | Κόγχων | Φῆλιξ |
| Χίρων | Κρίσων | Πίττων | Ἐμπεδίχων | Κίλιξ |
| Ἄκρων | Σαοσών | Ῥίττων | Μειλίχων | Φοῖνιξ |
| Μάκρων | Κόσων | Κύτων | Πενίχων | Λάριξ |
| Κόρων | Βλόσων | Πλούτων | Ἰμίλχων | Γλαῦξ |
| Τόρων | Φιλόσων | Κρύτων | Ἄρχων | Ἴᾱπυξ |
| Ἄσπρων | Δαμόσων | Φύτων | Πολυπέρχων | Θάρυξ |
| Θάρρων | Μόρσων | Βώτων | Μύχων | Βέβρυξ |
| Πύρρων | Βέσσων | Πρώτων | Τύχων | Ἔρυξ |
| Μάτρων | Πρόσσων | Σώτων | Γάψων | Φρύξ |
| Πάτρων | Παύσων | Δύων | Λάβαξ | Ὄρτυξ |
| Πέτρων | Ἀλκύσων | Μουδύων | Φαίαξ | Εὐανορίδαρ |
| Γάστρων | Λύσων | Πελεύων | Στίαξ | Νικίαρ |
| Μύστρων | Βρύσων | Θύων | Μέλλαξ | Καλλίαρ |
| Χύτρων | Χρύσων | Σαθύων | Σίλλαξ | Ἀρχέλαρ |
| Σαύρων | Βάτων | Βουθύων | Κόλαξ | Αἰσχίναρ |
| Ταύρων | Ἑκάτων | Θηρικύων | Γύλαξ | Ἄσπαρ |
| Σκύρων | Πλάτων | Ἀλκύων | Σκύλαξ | Σωτᾶρ |
| Μύρων | Πάτων | Φιλοκύων | Φύλαξ | Νίγερ |
| Πύρων | Ἐράτων | Λύων | Θύρμαξ | Κέλερ |
| Χύρων | Κράτων | Βρύων | Μύρμαξ | Δέξτερ |
| Ἐχέφρων | Εὐκράτων | Δρύων | Λεάναξ | Ἀσκληπιάδηρ |
| Ἀλκίφρων | Πράτων | Θηρύων | Κλεᾶναξ | Αἰθήρ |
| Καλλίφρων | Στράτων | Ἀμφιτρύων | Λαϝάναξ | Ξενοπείθηρ |
| Ἐπίφρων | Μέτων | Ἀλεκτρύων | Σαϝάναξ | Πάνθηρ |
| Ἀρίφρων | Ἀρέτων | Βοτρύων | Ἡλιάναξ | Σπινθήρ |
| Λεόφρων | Θειογήτων | Ἐριχύων | Ἐπιάναξ | Ἔσθηρ |
| Κλεόφρων | Κήτων | Ἀρκεφῶν | Πασιάναξ | Νικοκλῆρ |
| Νεόφρων | Κλήτων | Ἀρχεφῶν | Ἀγησιάναξ | Ξενϝάρηρ |
| Λυκόφρων | Κρήτων | Νήφων | Πεισιάναξ | Ἀμφικράτηρ |
| Φιλόφρων | Βίτων | Δαΐφων | Λυσιάναξ | Ἀστήρ |

| | | | | |
|---|---|---|---|---|
| Μνάστηρ | Μέντωρ | Νειάδας | Ναυσιάδας | Ἀγεδᾶς |
| Μνήστηρ | Ἰσομέντωρ | Ἀρειάδας | Λυσιάδας | Τελέδας |
| Σωτήρ | Ἀμύντωρ | Θυρρειάδας | Ῥυσιάδας | Πασέδας |
| Ῥίπιρ | Κάστωρ | Ἀγαθιάδας | Σωσιάδας | Ἀντιρήδας |
| Τελεσταῖορ | Ἀλάστωρ | Πειθιάδας | Κρατιάδας | Ἴδας |
| Νικόδρομορ | Μνάστωρ | Ἀνθιάδας | Πρατιάδας | Διϝαίδας |
| Σύντροφορ | Πάστωρ | Πυθιάδας | Παϊτιάδας | Ἀγκαίδας |
| Πλάτυρ | Φράστωρ | Μικιάδας | Γειτιάδας | Λαΐδας |
| Πράτυρ | Θέστωρ | Νικιάδας | Μιτιάδας | Ἀγελαΐδας |
| Ἀρίσταρχυρ | Ἀκέστωρ | Οἰκιάδας | Μιλτιάδας | Σερδελαΐδας |
| Χρυσάωρ | Τελέστωρ | Ἀλκιάδας | Μαντιάδας | Σθενελαΐδας |
| Ἄγβωρ | Νέστωρ | Ὀλκιάδας | Ἐννυμαντιάδας | Μενελαΐδας |
| Τίνθωρ | Μενέστωρ | Φυκιάδας | Παντιάδας | Ἐχελαΐδας |
| Μαῖωρ | Μήστωρ | Μαλιάδας | Βοτιάδας | Ἀρχελαΐδας |
| Εὐβάνωρ | Ἀγαμήστωρ | Φιλιάδας | Πληστιάδας | Σκερδιλαΐδας |
| Ἀγάνωρ | Πολυμήστωρ | Κυκλιάδας | Λουϊάδας | Καλλιλαΐδας |
| Θεάνωρ | Σωμήστωρ | Καλλιάδας | Γραφιάδας | Ἀναξιλαΐδας |
| Κλεάνωρ | Ἴστωρ | Φιλλιάδας | Ταφιάδας | Ἀρξιλαΐδας |
| Εὐϝάνωρ | Ναύτωρ | Πολλιάδας | Ἐχιάδας | Ἐρυξιλαΐδας |
| Ἀγαθάνωρ | Κάβας | Πολιάδας | Βακχιάδας | Μνασιλαΐδας |
| Πειθάνωρ | Σαβᾶς | Στολιάδας | Ἀρχιάδας | Τεισιλαΐδας |
| Βιάνωρ | Κέββας | Βουλιάδας | Κυλωϊάδας | Ἀντιλαΐδας |
| Νικάνωρ | Ἀρύββας | Φουλιάδας | Σωϊάδας | Ἀμφιλαΐδας |
| Ἀλκάνωρ | Κολήβας | Ἀμιάδας | Σακάδας | Μισγολαΐδας |
| Τιμάνωρ | Κισκιβᾶς | Δαμιάδας | Νικάδας | Νεολαΐδας |
| Αἰχμάνωρ | Λιβάς | Λαμιάδας | Ἀλκάδας | Ὀρθολαΐδας |
| Ἀλεξάνωρ | Στιβάς | Σαμιάδας | Σκάδας | Ἰολαΐδας |
| Ἀγαπάνωρ | Κύμβας | Ἀρθμιάδας | Λυκάδας | Νικολαΐδας |
| Γεράνωρ | Πύρβας | Σιμιάδας | Λάδας | Ξενολαΐδας |
| Ὑπεράνωρ | Ἀγᾶς | Τιμιάδας | Γελάδας | Κριτολαΐδας |
| Εὐφράνωρ | Ἀκράγας | Χαρμιάδας | Ἀγελάδας | Ἀριστολαΐδας |
| Ἰσάνωρ | Μέγας | Αἰχμιάδας | Ἀκουσιλάδας | Αὐτολαΐδας |
| Αἰσάνωρ | Γίγας | Φανιάδας | Πουλάδας | Εὐλαΐδας |
| Θερσάνωρ | Ξιγας | Ξενιάδας | Πυλάδας | Πολυλαΐδας |
| Λυσάνωρ | Λογάς | Ξηνιάδας | Ἀμάδας | Ἀστυλαΐδας |
| Ἀντάνωρ | Σολόγας | Δεινιάδας | Ἐπιτιμάδας | Τιμαΐδας |
| Ἀριστάνωρ | Λαφύργας | Καικινιάδας | Κομάδας | Εὐμαΐδας |
| Εὐάνωρ | Αὐγᾶς | Οἰνιάδας | Συμάδας | Κραταΐδας |
| Εὐχάνωρ | Γύγας | Κομνιάδας | Ἀθανάδας | Ἱκεταΐδας |
| Ἀγήνωρ | Κρεύγας | Ξεννιάδας | Ἀλκινάδας | Παμφαΐδας |
| Τιμήνωρ | Ἀλύγας | Ἀρνιάδας | Γεννάδας | Φοιβίδας |
| Ἀντήνωρ | Φορβάδας | Φατνιάδας | Χνοάδας | Νικαγίδας |
| Εὐήνωρ | Κλεάδας | Δεξιάδας | Γεράδας | Δαμαγίδας |
| Κλέπωρ | Νεάδας | Ἀλεξιάδας | Ἀθηράδας | Φλογίδας |
| Ἐννεάτωρ | Καρνεάδας | Σοϊξιάδας | Λαφυράδας | Εὐεργίδας |
| Κοιάτωρ | Λαϊάδας | Ἀρξιάδας | Ὀνασάδας | Γοργίδας |
| Πλάτωρ | Παιάδας | Ἀπιάδας | Ἰσάδας | Ἐπικυδίδας |
| Ὀνάτωρ | Σαϊάδας | Ἀσκλαπιάδας | Φιλατάδας | Πανθείδας |
| Φιλοπάτωρ | Βιάδας | Ὀλυμπιάδας | Φιλητάδας | Κνιδιείδας |
| Ῥάτωρ | Λαβιάδας | Ἱππιάδας | Πρινητάδας | Ἀρκείδας |
| Ἀγήτωρ | Ἀλκιβιάδας | Ναυεριάδας | Ἀρητάδας | Ἀλείδας |
| Φιλήτωρ | Ὀλβιάδας | Χαιριάδας | Ἐπιτάδας | Σελείδας |
| Κλήτωρ | Πολυβιάδας | Ἐρετριάδας | Παντάδας | Βασιλείδας |
| Ἀγαμήτωρ | Εὐρυβιάδας | Λευκτριάδας | Ὀρεστάδας | Ἀγακλείδας |
| Κλείτωρ | Ἀγιάδας | Ἀσιάδας | Βουτάδας | Μεγακλείδας |
| Διάκτωρ | Ϝαγιάδας | Δαμασιάδας | Δωτάδας | Λακλείδας |
| Ἀνάκτωρ | Γοργιάδας | Μνασιάδας | Λυκωτάδας | Τιμακλείδας |
| Ἕκτωρ | Φειδιάδας | Πασιάδας | Σωτάδας | Ἡρακλείδας |
| Βίκτωρ | Λυδιάδας | Φρασιάδας | Ὀθρυάδας | Σακλείδας |
| Εὔκτωρ | Ἀργειάδας | Πατησιάδας | Ὀφρυάδας | Παντακλείδας |
| Πολύκτωρ | Δυμειάδας | Θυρσιάδας | Ἀρχάδας | Τηλεκλείδας |

| | | | | |
|---|---|---|---|---|
| Μενεκλείδας | Ἡρακληΐδας | Καλλιτελίδας | Θεοτιμίδας | Φρικνίδας |
| Ἐχεκλείδας | Εὐκληΐδας | Ἐπιτελίδας | Εὐτιμίδας | Ἐρυμνίδας |
| Πειικλείδας | Αἰνηΐδας | Πασιτελίδας | Πολυτιμίδας | Κοννίδας |
| Καλλικλείδας | Ἀριστηΐδας | Ῥιποτελίδας | Σωτιμίδας | Χιονίδας |
| Ἐπικλείδας | Ἀγαθίδας | Εὐτελίδας | Τολμίδας | Φιλονίδας |
| Χαρικλείδας | Αὐταγαθίδας | Σωτελίδας | Εὐνομίδας | Δαμονίδας |
| Περικλείδας | Εὐμαθίδας | Σιμηλίδας | Εὐαρμίδας | Τλαμονίδας |
| Σικλείδας | Πολυμαθίδας | Θεομηλίδας | Χαρμίδας | Μναμονίδας |
| Ἀγασικλείδας | Εὐηθίδας | Φιλομηλίδας | Θεοχαρμίδας | Ἀγημονίδας |
| Μνασικλείδας | Αἰθίδας | Πρατομηλίδας | Θιοκορμίδας | Αἱμονίδας |
| Ὀνασικλείδας | Κλεαιθίδας | Ἀριστομηλίδας | Μυρμίδας | Εὐδαιμονίδας |
| Πασικλείδας | Δαμαιθίδας | Εὐμηλίδας | Εὐθυμίδας | Ἀκμονίδας |
| Ἀγησικλείδας | Σαϊθίδας | Θρασυμηλίδας | Φιλωνυμίδας | Παρμονίδας |
| Χερσικλείδας | Λυσαιθίδας | Φιλίδας | Κλεαιχμίδας | Ἀλκιφρονίδας |
| Ναυσικλείδας | Εὐπειθίδας | Θεοφιλίδας | Μανίδας | Λυκοφρονίδας |
| Λυσικλείδας | Πυρρανθίδας | Ἀριστοφιλίδας | Ἀλκμανίδας | Εὐφρονίδας |
| Σωσικλείδας | Εὐανθίδας | Δορκωϊλίδας | Ἐπανίδας | Σωφρονίδας |
| Ἀντικλείδας | Μενεσθίδας | Ἀγαλλίδας | Ἀντιφανίδας | Εὐγειτονίδας |
| Ἀρχικλείδας | Εὐπαιΐδας | Ἀνταλλίδας | Μαχανίδας | Σαυνίδας |
| Σαοκλείδας | Αἰακίδας | Φιλλίδας | Τυχανίδας | Φρυνίδας |
| Θεοκλείδας | Σκυλακίδας | Φυλλίδας | Ἀγγενίδας | Ναραωνίδας |
| Ἀγαθοκλείδας | Φυλακίδας | Ὀλίδας | Ἀριστογενίδας | Σαωνίδας |
| Διοκλείδας | Ἐξακίδας | Ἀβολίδας | Εὐγενίδας | Καβωνίδας |
| Θιοκλείδας | Θωρακίδας | Ἐπιβολίδας | Κλευγενίδας | Θιγγωνίδας |
| Νικοκλείδας | Βουτακίδας | Ἀγυλίδας | Σθενίδας | Ποτειδωνίδας |
| Φιλοκλείδας | Μανδρηκίδας | Δερκυλίδας | Γοργοσθενίδας | Φειδωνίδας |
| Δαμοκλείδας | Θραϊκίδας | Χαρμυλίδας | Νικοσθενίδας | Θεωνίδας |
| Τιμοκλείδας | Νικίδας | Εὔβουλίδας | Τιμοσθενίδας | Λεωνίδας |
| Ἐτυμοκλείδας | Κληνικίδας | Θρασυβουλίδας | Ἀνδροσθενίδας | Κλεωνίδας |
| Ξενοκλείδας | Παίνικίδας | Ἐρπυλίδας | Αὐτοσθενίδας | Νεωνίδας |
| Φαινοκλείδας | Καλλινικίδας | Ἐχεφυλίδας | Ποιμενίδας | Πειθωνίδας |
| Ἱπποκλείδας | Φοινικίδας | Αἰσχυλίδας | Ἐπιμενίδας | Φαιωνίδας |
| Ἀνδροκλείδας | Ἐπινικίδας | Εὐβωλίδας | Ἀντιμενίδας | Βιωνίδας |
| Μανδροκλείδας | Κλεονικίδας | Μίδας | Ἀμφιμενίδας | Διωνίδας |
| Προκλείδας | Φιλονικίδας | Λαδαμίδας | Ἐμμενίδας | Φιωνίδας |
| Ἰατροκλείδας | Δαμονικίδας | Ἐχεδαμίδας | Νικομενίδας | Οἰωνίδας |
| Πατροκλείδας | Ἀριστονικίδας | Ἀλκιδαμίδας | Ἀριστομενίδας | Σιωνίδας |
| Ἐρατοκλείδας | Εὐνικίδας | Καλλιδαμίδας | Ἀρχομενίδας | Θυϊωνίδας |
| Παντοκλείδας | Νεοικίδας | Ἀναξιδαμίδας | Δαμαρμενίδας | Χιωνίδας |
| Ἀριστοκλείδας | Ἀλκίδας | Ἀρχιδαμίδας | Παρμενίδας | Νικωνίδας |
| Αὐτοκλείδας | Δααλκίδας | Λαοδαμίδας | Ὑπερμενίδας | Δορκωνίδας |
| Περκλείδας | Ἀντιαλκίδας | Ἀριστοδαμίδας | Εὐμενίδας | Μιλωνίδας |
| Ναυκλείδας | Μεναλκίδας | Εὐδαμίδας | Λυσιξενίδας | Φιλωνίδας |
| Εὐκλείδας | Μνασαλκίδας | Πολυδαμίδας | Λυίξενίδας | Χιλωνίδας |
| Πολυκλείδας | Ἀνταλκίδας | Εὐρυδαμίδας | Θεοξενίδας | Ἀπολλωνίδας |
| Δορυκλείδας | Εὔαλκίδας | Εὔκαμίδας | Φιλοξενίδας | Δαμωνίδας |
| Εὔρυκλείδας | Ἀμφαλκίδας | Τηλαμίδας | Δαμοξενίδας | Σαμωνίδας |
| Σωκλείδας | Χαλκίδας | Σαμίδας | Προξενίδας | Σιμωνίδας |
| Καλλείδας | Θεοπροκίδας | Ἀρισαμίδας | Ἀριστοξενίδας | Τιμωνίδας |
| Σθενείδας | Δερκίδας | Εὐφαμίδας | Εὔξενίδας | Χαρμωνίδας |
| Παρμενείδας | Κερκίδας | Παρθεμίδας | Πολυξενίδας | Σθενωνίδας |
| Αἰνείδας | Φυσκίδας | Φαιδιμίδας | Ἀρσενίδας | Πραξωνίδας |
| Φιλονείδας | Γλαυκίδας | Χρήμίδας | Κληνίδας | Ἀνδρωνίδας |
| Εὐαρείδας | Λευκίδας | Ἀλκιμίδας | Νεμηνίδας | Χαιρωνίδας |
| Ἀμφαρείδας | Λυκίδας | Σιμίδας | Πολυαινίδας | Ἀκρωνίδας |
| Χαρείδας | Θαρυκίδας | Ὀνασιμίδας | Δεινίδας | Πυρρωνίδας |
| Κορείδας | Ναρυκίδας | Χρησιμίδας | Ἀλεξεινίδας | Μυρωνίδας |
| Φασείδας | Ἀγαλίδας | Αἰσιμίδας | Ἀρμινίδας | Τυρωνίδας |
| Ἀριστείδας | Θιοπαλίδας | Χισιμίδας | Φοινίδας | Ἀσωνίδας |
| Ἰφιστείδας | Κεφαλίδας | Ἐχετιμίδας | Ἐρασινίδας | Τλασωνίδας |
| Φείδας | Ἀμπελίδας | Ἐπιτιμίδας | Ἀρχινίδας | Θρασωνίδας |

| | | | | |
|---|---|---|---|---|
| Στρατωνίδας | Αἰσωπίδας | Φραστορίδας | Τιμοστρατίδας | Ἀνοχίδας |
| Γειτωνίδας | Εὐωπίδας | Θεστορίδας | Πολυστρατίδας | Ἀστυοχίδας |
| Ἀριστωνίδας | Τυνδαρίδας | Ἀκεστορίδας | Εὐρυστρατίδας | Λααρχίδας |
| Θυωνίδας | Θεαρίδας | Μυρρίδας | Σωστρατίδας | Νααρχίδας |
| Ἰχωνίδας | Κλεαρίδας | Γυρίδας | Εὐεργετίδας | Ἀγαθαρχίδας |
| Ἀρχωνίδας | Φραίαρίδας | Σμινδυρίδας | Λαμπετίδας | Θαλιαρχίδας |
| Δαρχωνίδας | Φρασιαρίδας | Ἐπικουρίδας | Νικαρετίδας | Νικαρχίδας |
| Ἀλεξίδας | Παντακαρίδας | Διοσκουρίδας | Μενητίδας | Λαρχίδας |
| Τραγοξίδας | Ἑτοιμαρίδας | Φρουρίδας | Αἰνητίδας | Φιλαρχίδας |
| Εὐδοξίδας | Χιμαρίδας | Λαμπυρίδας | Χαρητίδας | Δαμαρχίδας |
| Ζευξίδας | Εὐμαρίδας | Σφυρίδας | Εὐδαιτίδας | Πολεμαρχίδας |
| Ματτυξίδας | Θυμαρίδας | Διφρίδας | Ἀβαντίδας | Τιμαρχίδας |
| Βοΐδας | Εὐαρίδας | Ταμαχρίδας | Κλεαντίδας | Ξεναρχίδας |
| Εὐβοΐδας | Μενεχαρίδας | Μελαγχρίδας | Ἀκμαντίδας | Ἱππαρχίδας |
| Ἀλκιθοΐδας | Φιλοχαρίδας | Θεοδωρίδας | Χαρμαντίδας | Φρουραρχίδας |
| Πανθοΐδας | Αὐτοχαρίδας | Εὐδωρίδας | Εὐαντίδας | Ἰσαρχίδας |
| Δαμοθοΐδας | Εὐχαρίδας | Θευδωρίδας | Ἐκφαντίδας | Λυσαρχίδας |
| Πυρρανοΐδας | Σωχαρίδας | Πολυδωρίδας | Ξενοφαντίδας | Ἀρισταρχίδας |
| Ἱππονοΐδας | Νεβρίδας | Παγασίδας | Καροφαντίδας | Εὐαρχίδας |
| Εὐνοΐδας | Κλεανδρίδας | Θεασίδας | Ἐσφαντίδας | Λωρχίδας |
| Σοΐδας | Ἀγαθανδρίδας | Τιμασίδας | Λεοντίδας | Σχίδας |
| Λασοΐδας | Νικανδρίδας | Ὀνασίδας | Κρεοντίδας | Μοσχίδας |
| Ἀλκισοΐδας | Ἀλκανδρίδας | Βρασίδας | Φροντίδας | Ἀναυχίδας |
| Εὐσοΐδας | Λανδρίδας | Φρασίδας | Σωμροτίδας | Δαμουχίδας |
| Ὀλιπίδας | Φιλανδρίδας | Τελεσίδας | Ἀκρυπτίδας | Λατυχίδας |
| Εὐριπίδας | Τιμανδρίδας | Ἀγησίδας | Τεταρτίδας | Εὐτυχίδας |
| Εὐκαμπίδας | Χαρμανδρίδας | Δαμαισίδας | Ναμερτίδας | Γριψίδας |
| Λαπομπίδας | Μενανδρίδας | Κισσίδας | Ἀστίδας | Μομψίδας |
| Θεοπομπίδας | Ἀναξανδρίδας | Λισσίδας | Εὐμναστίδας | Κυλωΐδας |
| Πελοπίδας | Ἀλεξανδρίδας | Λυσίδας | Ἐξακεστίδας | Ἡρωΐδας |
| Ἑλλοπίδας | Ἐπανδρίδας | Σωσίδας | Ἀτρεστίδας | Σκαλδας |
| Φυλοπίδας | Σηρανδρίδας | Εὐβατίδας | Ἀδειστίδας | Δένδας |
| Χαροπίδας | Μνασανδρίδας | Ἀτλατίδας | Φιλιστίδας | Νένδας |
| Θεοπροπίδας | Ἀγησανδρίδας | Ἀκματίδας | Εὐνοστίδας | Χαρμόνδας |
| Θευπροπίδας | Λυσανδρίδας | Ἁρματίδας | Φαττίδας | Φολύνδας |
| Θωροπίδας | Σωσανδρίδας | Ὀνατίδας | Εὐλυτίδας | Εὐρύνδας |
| Ἀγιππίδας | Ἀριστανδρίδας | Φιληρατίδας | Εὐρυτίδας | Θεώνδας |
| Γοργιππίδας | Εὐανδρίδας | Ἐπηρατίδας | Θεογνωτίδας | Διώνδας |
| Μεληΐππίδας | Εὐαμερίδας | Κρατίδας | Φωτίδας | Νικώνδας |
| Κρατηΐππίδας | Ἀστερίδας | Ἀκρατίδας | Μαλαυίδας | Φιλώνδας |
| Λακιππίδας | Ἡρίδας | Λακρατίδας | Φαυΐδας | Σιμώνδας |
| Νικιππίδας | Σωτηρίδας | Ἐννυμακρατίδας | Κουΐδας | Χαρώνδας |
| Φιλιππίδας | Εὐχηρίδας | Παγκρατίδας | Σκιραφίδας | Ἡρώνδας |
| Καλλιππίδας | Λακρίδας | Δαϊκρατίδας | Ἀρχεμαχίδας | Δαιτώνδας |
| Δαμιππίδας | Λαγορίδας | Πειΐκρατίδας | Καλλιμαχίδας | Ποδᾶς |
| Δεινιππίδας | Δεξαγορίδας | Καλλικρατίδας | Μνασιμαχίδας | Ἀφροδᾶς |
| Δεξιππίδας | Προαγορίδας | Ἐπικρατίδας | Λυσιμαχίδας | Δέρδας |
| Ἀλεξιππίδας | Ἀγανορίδας | Ἀντικρατίδας | Ἀντιμαχίδας | Κέρδας |
| Ἡριππίδας | Πειθανορίδας | Ἰφικρατίδας | Συμμαχίδας | Θευδᾶς |
| Θηριππίδας | Τιμανορίδας | Κλεοκρατίδας | Προμαχίδας | Κύδας |
| Ὀρριππίδας | Αἰσανορίδας | Φιλοκρατίδας | Ἀριστομαχίδας | Λακύδας |
| Μνασιππίδας | Πεισανορίδας | Δαμοκρατίδας | Εὐμαχίδας | Πολύδας |
| Πασιππίδας | Λυσανορίδας | Δεινοκρατίδας | Εὐρυμαχίδας | Βουδᾶς |
| Ἀγησιππίδας | Εὐανορίδας | Ἱπποκρατίδας | Ἰναχίδας | Ἰούδας |
| Μελησιππίδας | Σπορίδας | Ἀριστοκρατίδας | Βραχίδας | Εὐνούδας |
| Κρατησιππίδας | Ὀνατορίδας | Αὐτοκρατίδας | Ὑψηχίδας | Γαρτύδας |
| Κρατιππίδας | Ἀγητορίδας | Εὐκρατίδας | Στρομβιχίδας | Ἀτόφδας |
| Εὐτερπίδας | Διακτορίδας | Εὐρυκρατίδας | Σιμιχίδας | Εὐρυώδας |
| Ἐριασπίδας | Ἑκτορίδας | Ἀστυκρατίδας | Ὀλπριχίδας | Λαέας |
| Εὐπίδας | Ὀνομαστορίδας | Σωκρατίδας | Ἀνιοχίδας | Σαέας |
| Ἀνθρωπίδας | Μναστορίδας | Λαστρατίδας | Ἀρχιλοχίδας | Ἀγέας |

| | | | | |
|---|---|---|---|---|
| Ϝαγέας | Ξενέας | Ἀντέας | Αὐγείας | Γελλίας |
| Ἡγέας | Ξηνέας | Παντέας | Ἀνθείας | Ἀπελλίας |
| Γοργέας | Αἰνέας | Φιντέας | Φαλείας | Τελλίας |
| Αὐγέας | Χλαινέας | Θαρτέας | Ἡλείας | Φιλλίας |
| Ἀδέας | Φαινέας | Ἀστέας | Τιλείας | Πολλίας |
| Ἰμπεδέας | Κινέας | Παλαιστέας | Φιλείας | Γυλλίας |
| Βαθέας | Βοινέας | Μεγιστέας | Πλειάς | Μεγυλλίας |
| Ἀγαθέας | Μιμνέας | Πλειστέας | Τιμείας | Κυλλίας |
| Μαθθέας | Μεννέας | Φιλιστέας | Ἑρμείας | Μυλλίας |
| Πειθέας | Ξεννέας | Θεμιστέας | Ἀγνείας | Πολίας |
| Κριθέας | Σιννέας | Πιστέας | Αἰνείας | Οὐλίας |
| Ἀνθέας | Ἀρνέας | Ἀριστέας | Μεννείας | Δαμίας |
| Γενθέας | Κωνέας | Αὐτέας | Ἀρείας | Λαμίας |
| Εὐθέας | Δεξέας | Τυτέας | Ἀνδρείας | Λαμιάς |
| Πευθέας | Ἱππέας | Μωτέας | Ἀνερείας | Σαμίας |
| Πυθέας | Ἑρπέας | Πρωτέας | Τερείας | Θεμίας |
| Νικέας | Ἀρέας | Σωτέας | Μνασείας | Πραξιμίας |
| Μικκέας | Γαρέας | Δερφέας | Ἀριστείας | Βριμίας |
| Ἀρκέας | Σαρέας | Ἀρχέας | Πυρϝίας | Σιμίας |
| Ἀπαρκέας | Χαρέας | Εὐχέας | Βαδῆας | Τιμίας |
| Δορκέας | Λαβρέας | Τυχέας | Αἰνηῖας | Παντιμίας |
| Γλαυκέας | Ἀγρέας | Αἴϝας | Ἀγαθίας | Ἀμμιάς |
| Λυκέας | Φαιδρέας | Δάζας | Πιθθίας | Σιμμίας |
| Φαλέας | Ἀνδρέας | Δίζας | Πειθίας | Ἑρμίας |
| Χαλέας | Φερέας | Σωζᾶς | Κανθίας | Αἰχμίας |
| Κελέας | Ἡρέας | Θηρήας | Ξανθίας | Ὠμίας |
| Μελέας | Γηρέας | Ἄθας | Κορινθιάς | Ἀνίας |
| Τελέας | Χαιρέας | Ἀγαθᾶς | Σπερθίας | Νεανίας |
| Τηλέας | Τορέας | Ἰωναθᾶς | Βωρθίας | Ἑλλανίας |
| Σιλέας | Χορέας | Ἀνθᾶς | Εὐθίας | Ἀνανίας |
| Φιλέας | Λαμπρέας | Τιμάνθας | Ξουθίας | Παυσανίας |
| Κλέας | Ζαρρέας | Χρυσανθᾶς | Πυθίας | Λυσανίας |
| Καλικλέας | Πατρέας | Κορινθᾶς | Πυθιάς | Φανίας |
| Διοκλέας | Εὐρέας | Σεύθας | Μακίας | Ἀγνίας |
| Ξενοκλέας | Ἀσέας | Σκύθας | Ἀμβρακίας | Ξενίας |
| Οἰνοκλέας | Ἀγασέας | Πυθᾶς | Σφακίας | Ζηνίας |
| Πατροκλέας | Μνασέας | Ἰάς | Ἐξηκίας | Κληνίας |
| Ἀριστοκλέας | Πασέας | Νικαίας | Περδικίας | Μηνιάς |
| Εὔκλέας | Θρασέας | Λαίας | Νικίας | Ἰσμηνίας |
| Θαλλέας | Στασέας | Βίας | Παννικίας | Αἰνίας |
| Καλλέας | Τελεσέας | Φοιβίας | Μικκίας | Καινίας |
| Πελλέας | Ἰσέας | Λοβίας | Ἀλκίας | Σικαινίας |
| Ἀπελλέας | Τεισέας | Τωβίας | Ὀλκίας | Φαινίας |
| Φιλλέας | Κοισέας | Ἀγίας | Ἀποκίας | Δεινίας |
| Πολλέας | Μοισέας | Μεγίας | Δορκίας | Δϝεινίας |
| Πολέας | Θερσέας | Ἡγίας | Γλαυκίας | Κλεινίας |
| Ὀπολέας | Παυσέας | Αἰγίας | Λευκίας | Ἀμεινίας |
| Φαυλέας | Λυσέας | Ἐργίας | Λυκίας | Οἰνίας |
| Δαμέας | Γνωσέας | Γοργίας | Ἀλίας | Θοινίας |
| Ψαμέας | Φωσέας | Γεωργίας | Μεγαλίας | Κικνίας |
| Δημέας | Ζατέας | Δίας | Καλίας | Ξεννίας |
| Τιμέας | Κρατέας | Λαμπαδίας | Πεταλίας | Κυδωνίας |
| Δρομέας | Ξενοκρατέας | Καλεδίας | Χελίας | Εὐωνίας |
| Θαυμέας | Πρατέας | Ἐμπεδίας | Ἡλιάς | Πραξίας |
| Λιχμέας | Στρατέας | Λαιδίας | Ἡλίας | Δεξίας |
| Νέας | Εὐατέας | Μειδίας | Ζηλίας | Ἀλεξίας |
| Φαλανέας | Παγκρετέας | Φειδίας | Σειλίας | Σοϊξίας |
| Ποτανέας | Κλητέας | Ὠκιδίας | Μυσσκλίας | Ζευξίας |
| Φανέας | Κλειτέας | Σκορδίας | Κυκλίας | Δρωξίας |
| Ἐπιφανέας | Τριτέας | Κυδίας | Ἀγαλλίας | Ἀρκοίας |
| Μενέας | Ἐπικτέας | Λυδίας | Καλλίας | Κυλοίας |

| | | | | |
|---|---|---|---|---|
| Κροίας | Πανησίας | Αὐτίας | Κάλας | Παλλάς |
| Ἀσκλαπιάς | Αἰνησίας | Τελευτίας | Πασκάλας | Σάλλας |
| Ἀναπίας | Κτησίας | Πλουτίας | Πετάλας | Πέλλας |
| Παπίας | Ἰσίας | Σωτίας | Μυτάλας | Ἀπελλᾶς |
| Σαραπιάς | Ἰσιάς | Γυίας | Εὐάλας | Πτελλᾶς |
| Σεραπιάς | Ἴσιας | Δελφιάς | Ἀγέλας | Ὀφέλλας |
| Ἀσκληπιάς | Ἀφροδισιάς | Ἀμφίας | Μέλας | Ἀχιλλᾶς |
| Ἐλπίας | Κλεισίας | Ῥαμφίας | Τιμέλας | Τροχιλλᾶς |
| Εὐελπίας | Πεισίας | Καμοφίας | Σθενέλας | Ἀπολλᾶς |
| Πομπίας | Τεισίας | Ἀπφιάς | Χαιρέλας | Πραΰλλας |
| Ὀλυμπιάς | Δαμισίας | Λαχίας | Ὠφέλας | Παρβόλας |
| Χαροπίας | Καφισίας | Κλιμαχίας | Ἀρχέλας | Φειδόλας |
| Θευπροπίας | Σαοσίας | Ἐχίας | Εὔχελας | Κλεόλας |
| Ἱππίας | Θαρσίας | Σιμιχίας | Ἧλας | Νεόλας |
| Καρπίας | Θερσίας | Λοχιάς | Ἴλας | Ἀγαθόλας |
| Κυπίας | Χερσίας | Ἀρχίας | Νικαΐλας | Πειθόλας |
| Ἀλυπιάς | Ὀρσίας | Δαμαρχίας | Φειδίλας | Αἰόλας |
| Θωπίας | Λισσίας | Ψαλυχίας | Ἀρκεΐλας | Βιόλας |
| Καρίας | Μελισσίας | Γαψίας | Νειλᾶς | Σακόλας |
| Πλαρίας | Φυσσίας | Καγψίας | Χειλᾶς | Νικόλας |
| Χαρίας | Φαλαυσίας | Βλεψίας | Ἀγηΐλας | Λυκόλας |
| Ἀβρίας | Παυσίας | Κλεψίας | Πειθίλας | Δαμόλας |
| Χαβρίας | Λυσίας | Καμψίας | Πυθίλας | Σαμόλας |
| Ὑβρίας | Διονυσιάς | Τερψίας | Καλλίλας | Τιμόλας |
| Φαιδρίας | Μουσιάς | Τεισανδρῶας | Ἀναξίλας | Σθενόλας |
| Ἀνδρίας | Σωσίας | Πρῶας | Ϝαναξίλας | Ξενόλας |
| Λαανδρίας | Γλαυκατίας | Τρωϊάς | Πραξίλας | Δεινόλας |
| Σφοδρίας | Γαλατίας | Ἀκᾶς | Δεξίλας | Χαιρόλας |
| Φερίας | Πλατίας | Βριάκας | Ἀλεξίλας | Πρατόλας |
| Ἰηρίας | Ἐρατίας | Ἐπάκας | Ἀρξίλας | Στρατόλας |
| Χηρίας | Κρατίας | Δράκας | Χαρίλας | Κλειτόλας |
| Χαιρίας | Πρατίας | Ἡρακᾶς | Ὑβρίλας | Κριτόλας |
| Καβιρίας | Τατιάς | Χάκας | Περίλας | Πλειστόλας |
| Λαμπρίας | Τελητίας | Ψακᾶς | Χαιρίλας | Καλιστόλας |
| Θαρρίας | Κλητίας | Παγκᾶς | Θερρίλας | Ἀριστόλας |
| Χερρίας | Κλειτίας | Ἔκας | Σίλας | Κρατιστόλας |
| Πυρρίας | Κιτιάς | Ψεκάς | Νικασίλας | Ὕλας |
| Πατρίας | Κριτίας | Δικᾶς | Δαμασίλας | Ἀκύλας |
| Δημητριάς | Ἀκτιάς | Εὐδίκας | Ὀρμασίλας | Πολύλας |
| Ταυρίας | Ἀντίας | Φηλικᾶς | Μνασίλας | Ταρούλας |
| Εὐρίας | Μαντίας | Κιλικᾶς | Ὀνασίλας | Θρασύλας |
| Πυρίας | Παντίας | Νικᾶς | Φρασίλας | Ἀρτύλας |
| Αἰσχρίας | Φαντίας | Φρονίκας | Στασίλας | Δάμας |
| Βασίας | Πεντίας | Μενεκκᾶς | Ἀγεσίλας | Δαμᾶς |
| Ἀγασίας | Φιντίας | Ἀρίκκας | Ἀνθεσίλας | Ἀδάμας |
| Ϝασίας | Λεοντίας | Ἀντίκκας | Ἀρκεσίλας | Λαδάμας |
| Νικασίας | Χαρτίας | Ἀνδρόκκας | Χαιρεσίλας | Ἀρχεδάμας |
| Λασίας | Γυρτιάς | Λύκκας | Ἀρχεσίλας | Πραξιδάμας |
| Δαμασίας | Ἀστίας | Σιτάλκας | Ἀγησίλας | Ἀμφιδάμας |
| Τιμασίας | Βαστίας | Φιλόκας | Θερσίλας | Λαοδάμας |
| Μνασίας | Ἑστίας | Ἀρκάς | Ἀκουσίλας | Κλεοδάμας |
| Πασίας | Θεστίας | Δέρκας | Σωσίλας | Λαϝοδάμας |
| Θρασίας | Ἀκεστίας | Δορκάς | Ἀντίλας | Δαϊοδάμας |
| Στασίας | Μεγιστίας | Λυκοδόρκας | Ἀννίλας | Ἀνδροδάμας |
| Τελεσίας | Πλειστίας | Λευκάς | Φίλας | Ἀριστοδάμας |
| Χαιρεσίας | Πλειστιάς | Γλυκᾶς | Γνωΐλας | Εὐδάμας |
| Ἀγησίας | Ϝιστίας | Λουκᾶς | Ἡρακλᾶς | Κλευδάμας |
| Ἡγησίας | Θεμιστίας | Συκᾶς | Ἀσκλᾶς | Πολυδάμας |
| Λησίας | Πιστίας | Ἀταιτυκας | Κυκλάς | Εὐρυδάμας |
| Μελησίας | Ἀριστίας | Σανδάλας | Ἀμύκλας | Σωδάμας |
| Νησιας | Πιττίας | Παρδαλᾶς | Καλλᾶς | Ἀθάμας |

| | | | | |
|---|---|---|---|---|
| Ἀκάμας | Σοαίνας | Σκόπας | Ἀθηναγόρας | Χρυσᾶς |
| Σασάμας | Καλοκλείνας | Πρόπας | Κληναγόρας | Ζωσᾶς |
| Ἀρυτάμας | Μικίνας | Αὐτόπας | Φαιναγόρας | Σωσᾶς |
| Εὐαμᾶς | Φρικίνας | Ἀγρίππας | Δειναγόρας | Παραιβάτας |
| Χρέμας | Μικκίνας | Γοργώπας | Κλειναγόρας | Ἱπποβάτας |
| Ἀρτεμᾶς | Δορκίνας | Θώπας | Ἀναξαγόρας | Ὑπερβάτας |
| Φρονιμᾶς | Δαμίνας | Λυκώπας | Πραξαγόρας | Ναυβάτας |
| Σιμάς | Καμινᾶς | Οἰνώπας | Θελξαγόρας | Εὐρυβάτας |
| Ζωσιμᾶς | Κορμίνας | Εὐρώπας | Προαγόρας | Ἀγάτας |
| Τιμάς | Οἰνάς | Κασώπας | Ἱππαγόρας | Λεξειάτας |
| Τιμᾶς | Ἐλπίνας | Ξιϝάρας | Παραγόρας | Νικάτας |
| Τιμας | Σκοπίνας | Καρᾶς | Θαρραγόρας | Γαλάτας |
| Πανσιτίμας | Θωπίνας | Εὐμάρας | Εὐφραγόρας | Αἰγλάτας |
| Τροφιμᾶς | Δρωπίνας | Σινάρας | Μνασαγόρας | Ἀδαμάτας |
| Ἰκμάς | Θηρίνας | Πάρας | Ἀγησαγόρας | Ὑσσεμάτας |
| Ἐχέμμας | Χοιρίνας | Προσσάρας | Ἰσαγόρας | Δελμάτας |
| Πραυγίμμας | Σμικρίνας | Τάρας | Θαρσαγόρας | Κομάτας |
| Ἀσπίμμας | Εὐκρίνας | Σατταρᾶς | Θερσαγόρας | Οἰνάτας |
| Ὑβρίμμας | Πρατίνας | Φάρας | Λυσαγόρας | Ὀνάτας |
| Τροχιμμᾶς | Παντίνας | Συάγρας | Κλειταγόρας | Δροάτας |
| Λαόμμας | Λεπτίνας | Ἐλευθερᾶς | Πισταγόρας | Πατᾶς |
| Κλεόμμας | Μαμερτίνας | Κέρας | Ἀρισταγόρας | Καλλιπάτας |
| Ἀλεξόμμας | Ἀττινᾶς | Σερᾶς | Τελευταγόρας | Εὐπάτας |
| Ἀδύμμας | Καρφίνας | Ἥρᾶς | Πρωταγόρας | Εὐφράτας |
| Εἰδύμμας | Λεσφίνας | Σιδηρᾶς | Εὐαγόρας | Ἐστάτας |
| Εὐρύμμας | Λισφίνας | Πανθήρας | Ἀρχαγόρας | Ἀντιφάτας |
| Κομᾶς | Διχίνας | Σπινθήρας | Ἰσχαγόρας | Εὐφάτας |
| Μελαγκόμας | Πελειχίνας | Βουθήρας | Κληγόρας | Μαχάτας |
| Νικομᾶς | Αἰσχίνας | Σωτηρᾶς | Ρεδόρας | Γέτας |
| Ἐριοκόμας | Γυμνάς | Τεύθρας | Διοσκορᾶς | Ἀγέτας |
| Νόμας | Σωκάννας | Χαιρᾶς | Εὐπορᾶς | Ἀρχαγέτας |
| Νομάς | Μέννας | Κορδίρας | Ρατορᾶς | Εὐεργέτας |
| Καλινόμας | Σίννας | Πείρας | Πυρρᾶς | Δέτας |
| Δρόμας | Λεονᾶς | Ὀρτείρας | Πετρᾶς | Ἱκέτας |
| Ἰδρόμας | Μονᾶς | Σκίρας | Μητρᾶς | Ἀλκέτας |
| Νικοδρόμας | Συμονᾶς | Μιρᾶς | Ἀριστρᾶς | Γλαυκέτας |
| Στόμας | Βαρνᾶς | Ταμίρας | Γύρας | Τελέτας |
| Χάρμας | Λιβύρνας | Μοιρᾶς | Αἰθύρας | Φιλέτας |
| Ἑρμᾶς | Εὐθύνας | Δαμοκρᾶς | Φιλλύρας | Κλεαρέτας |
| Σύρμας | Ἀμύνας | Ἀρποκρᾶς | Κινύρας | Ἱππαγρέτας |
| Κοσμᾶς | Λεωνᾶς | Καρποκρᾶς | Ταλούρας | Ἀγήτας |
| Δύμας | Ἰωνᾶς | Κλεαγόρας | Σφύρας | Νικήτας |
| Εὐμᾶς | Καλωνᾶς | Πειθαγόρας | Ἐπαφρᾶς | Φιλήτας |
| Εὐθύμας | Φιλωνᾶς | Ὀρθαγόρας | Εὐφρᾶς | Εὐκλήτας |
| Βούμας | Ἱερωνᾶς | Ϝορθαγόρας | Δωρᾶς | Αἰγινήτας |
| Σαβάνας | Ἀλεξᾶς | Πυθαγόρας | Ἀρκέσας | Δαίτας |
| Ἀθάνας | Σίξας | Διαγόρας | Τελέσας | Πολυδαίτας |
| Σκυρθάνας | Θόας | Νικαγόρας | Νικησας | Συαίτας |
| Μελάνας | Πετόας | Λαγόρας | Κλησᾶς | Ἐπαφροδιτᾶς |
| Φάνας | Ἀγαπᾶς | Ἐσθλαγόρας | Ὀνησᾶς | Πειῖτας |
| Στεφανᾶς | Πάπας | Φιλαγόρας | Ἰσᾶς | Πλακίτας |
| Λαχανᾶς | Σεραπᾶς | Βουλαγόρας | Ἀρκίσας | Φιλίτας |
| Ἀλμένας | Σκέπας | Βωλαγόρας | Λίσας | Καλλίτας |
| Ἀρμένας | Ἀσκληπᾶς | Δαμαγόρας | Πυρρίσας | Πολίτας |
| Αἰσχένας | Αἰγιπᾶς | Σαμαγόρας | Βέρσας | Ὑλίτας |
| Ζηνάς | Σκίπας | Τιμαγόρας | Θέρσας | Σαμίτας |
| Ἀθηνᾶς | Ἀντιπᾶς | Ἑρμαγόρας | Πέρσας | Πολεμίτας |
| Μυκηνᾶς | Στίλπας | Αἰχμαγόρας | Κόσσας | Πανίτας |
| Ληνᾶς | Κάμπας | Ἀθαναγόρας | Λύσας | Φανίτας |
| Μήνας | Λαμπάς | Ἀγναγόρας | Διονυσᾶς | Παρμενίτας |
| Μηνᾶς | Ὀλυμπᾶς | Ξεναγόρας | Σουσᾶς | Πραξίτας |

| | | | | |
|---|---|---|---|---|
| Οἴτας | Χορτᾶς | Ὀρύας | Ἀπολλωνιάδης | Ἀριστοκλείδης |
| Ἐργοίτας | Βαβύρτας | Εὐρύας | Δεξιάδης | Εὐκλείδης |
| Θεοίτας | Σιβύρτας | Θρασύας | Ἀλεξιάδης | Ποσείδης |
| Κλεοίτας | Λασύρτας | Τεισύας | Ἀσκληπιάδης | Ἀριστείδης |
| Ἐτεοίτας | Δαμάστας | Μοισύας | Βοριάδης | Λαφείδης |
| Διοίτας | Κωμάστας | Θαρσύας | Πασιάδης | Θεοφείδης |
| Δαμοίτας | Νάστας | Μαρσύας | Λυσιάδης | Θευφείδης |
| Μενοίτας | Παστάς | Εὐφρατύας | Διονυσιάδης | Εὐανθίδης |
| Ξενοίτας | Ἐξακέστας | Πιτύας | Μιλτιάδης | Φοινικίδης |
| Ἀπποίτας | Τελέστας | Ἀρτύας | Λακάδης | Λυκκίδης |
| Τυβροίτας | Μενέστας | Ἐλέφας | Ἀλκάδης | Ἀλκίδης |
| Ἀγροίτας | Ὀρέστας | Νικηφᾶς | Ἰοκάδης | Βακχυλίδης |
| Ἀνδροίτας | Θυέστας | Νιφάς | Δαμοκάδης | Εὐφαμίδης |
| Ἀνεροίτας | Λαΐστας | Βονιφᾶς | Τιμοκάδης | Ἀνθεμίδης |
| Πορροίτας | Γαλαίστας | Ἀντίφας | Ξενοκάδης | Φιλοτιμίδης |
| Πυρροίτας | Λογίστας | Νυμφᾶς | Ἀνδροκάδης | Χαρμίδης |
| Ἱππίτας | Φιλίστας | Σόφας | Εὐκάδης | Φαιανίδης |
| Ἀγρίτας | Ἀρίστας | Πολύφας | Λάδης | Ζωσιμιανίδης |
| Περίτας | Ὑβρίστας | Ϝάχας | Πυλάδης | Φανίδης |
| Τίτας | Δαφίστας | Ῥάχας | Τιμοφράδης | Ἐμμενίδης |
| Ἀγχίτας | Ἀρχίστας | Βράχας | Σωτάδης | Παρμενίδης |
| Λοχίτας | Ἀρύστας | Νιράχας | Εὐρυάδης | Φιλοξενίδης |
| Ἀρχίτας | Γνώστας | Λίχας | Ἀνδρομέδης | Προξενίδης |
| Εὐπράκτας | Ἀττᾶς | Τυννίχας | Δαμοκήδης | Λεωνίδης |
| Λαδέκτας | Νικώττας | Ὀρνιχᾶς | Δημοκήδης | Φιλωνίδης |
| Σιδέκτας | Ἀρχεναύτας | Τριχᾶς | Ἀγαμήδης | Ἀπολλωνίδης |
| Θιοδέκτας | Σωναύτας | Εὐδωρίχας | Παλαμήδης | Σιμωνίδης |
| Πολυδέκτας | Θευτᾶς | Ϝόλχας | Κλεμήδης | Μυρωνίδης |
| Ἐπικτᾶς | Τριτεύτας | Ἄρχας | Ἐχεμήδης | Πυρωνίδης |
| Θεοκτᾶς | Θύτας | Ἀρχάς | Ἁλιμήδης | Θρασωνίδης |
| Ἐπιτευκτᾶς | Σκύτας | Μοσχᾶς | Καλλιμήδης | Νικιππίδης |
| Μέλτας | Φιλύτας | Εὐτυχᾶς | Περιμήδης | Φιλιππίδης |
| Θεάντας | Χλεμύτας | Μώχας | Σιμήδης | Σωτηρίδης |
| Μελάντας | Ξενύτας | Ἱπποθράης | Ἀμφιμήδης | Τυχηρίδης |
| Περάντας | Δινύτας | Λαφάης | Ἀρχιμήδης | Ἀστορίδης |
| Εὐάντας | Βούτας | Καλλιφάης | Θεομήδης | Καστορίδης |
| Μέντας | Κλεούτας | Ἀντιφάης | Κλεομήδης | Διοσκουρίδης |
| Σακίντας | Ἀνδρύτας | Ἀρχιφάης | Διομήδης | Εὐπυρίδης |
| Ὀρίντας | Θαρσύτας | Παμφάης | Νικομήδης | Χαρμαντίδης |
| Φίντας | Ἀρχύτας | Κλεοφάης | Λυκομήδης | Πρατυΐδης |
| Δόντας | Σαώτας | Νικοφάης | Ἀνδρομήδης | Βακχίδης |
| Λεοντᾶς | Λαβώτας | Ξενοφάης | Πρατομήδης | Δημαρχίδης |
| Πολυφόντας | Οἰβώτας | Εὐφάης | Ἀριστομήδης | Ἱππαρχίδης |
| Ἀμύντας | Ἀντιδώτας | Εὐσέβης | Αὐτομήδης | Εὐτυχίδης |
| Ἐχύντας | Θεώτας | Θεάγης | Εὐμήδης | Ἡρωΐδης |
| Συβότας | Θιώτας | Μάγης | Κλευμήδης | Σίνδης |
| Θεοδότας | Λυκώτας | Δαμάγης | Εὐθυμήδης | Φερεκύδης |
| Κλεότας | Φιλώτας | Οἰναγῆς | Πολυμήδης | Ἐπικύδης |
| Κότας | Μολώτας | Τάγης | Εὐρυμήδης | Λυσικύδης |
| Φιλότας | Ῥινώτας | Διατάγης | Θρασυμήδης | Θιοκύδης |
| Δαμότας | Πρωτᾶς | Λιτάγης | Λεωμήδης | Δαμοκύδης |
| Τοξότας | Εὐρώτας | Δαμοτάγης | Σωμήδης | Ἀνδροκύδης |
| Ἱππότας | Μυρώτας | Εὐάγης | Βασιλείδης | Στρατοκύδης |
| Πρατότας | Σωτᾶς | Μέγης | Κλείδης | Ναυκύδης |
| Ἄρτας | Ὕας | Αὐγῆς | Ἡρακλείδης | Θευκύδης |
| Μεγάρτας | Κλέας | Ζύγης | Χαρικλείδης | Λεωκύδης |
| Χάρτας | Θύας | Τρυγῆς | Περικλείδης | Πούδης |
| Ἰγέρτας | Βλύας | Ἀργεάδης | Λυσικλείδης | Εὐμάθης |
| Ἀμέρτας | Φιλύας | Ἀλκιβιάδης | Σωσικλείδης | Ἐπιγήθης |
| Ναμέρτας | Βρύας | Νικιάδης | Φιλοκλείδης | Εὐήθης |
| Λυκόρτας | Δρύας | Ἀλκιάδης | Ἱεροκλείδης | Καλλιπείθης |

| | | | | |
|---|---|---|---|---|
| Θεοπείθης | Ἐπιθάλης | Ὀνομακλῆς | Θεοκλῆς | Εὐκλῆς |
| Κλεοπείθης | Μνασιθάλης | Ὀνυμακλῆς | Νεοκλῆς | Θευκλῆς |
| Διοπείθης | Ἀμφιθάλης | Ἡρακλῆς | Ἐτεοκλῆς | Νευκλῆς |
| Φιλοπείθης | Πανθάλης | Σακλῆς | Ξενϝοκλῆς | Βαθυκλῆς |
| Δαμοπείθης | Φιλοθάλης | Ἀρετακλῆς | Ἀγαθοκλῆς | Εὐθυκλῆς |
| Ξενοπείθης | Δαμοθάλης | Παντακλῆς | Πυθοκλῆς | Πολυκλῆς |
| Ἀνδροπείθης | Μάλης | Σωτακλῆς | Διοκλῆς | Εὐρυκλῆς |
| Ἀριστοπείθης | Νικοσάλης | Παγκλῆς | Θιοκλῆς | Θρασυκλῆς |
| Πολυπείθης | Οὐτάλης | Θεκλῆς | Βρομιοκλῆς | Ἀρτυκλῆς |
| Ἄνθης | Οὐάλης | Τηλεκλῆς | Νικοκλῆς | Ἀστυκλῆς |
| Κλεάνθης | Ἀγγελῆς | Μενεκλῆς | Μεγαλοκλῆς | Ταχυκλῆς |
| Ἀριάνθης | Ἐπιμέλης | Φερεκλῆς | Καλοκλῆς | Σωκλῆς |
| Σιάνθης | Αἰσιμέλης | Ἐχεκλῆς | Τηλοκλῆς | Ἀγαλλῆς |
| Τιμάνθης | Ἰσομέλης | Νηκλῆς | Φιλοκλῆς | Μεγαλλῆς |
| Ὑπεράνθης | Εὐμέλης | Δαϊκλῆς | Δαμοκλῆς | Κάλλης |
| Εὐάνθης | Τέλης | Διαικλῆς | Σαμοκλῆς | Ἀπελλῆς |
| Πολυάνθης | Ἀτέλης | Νικαίκλῆς | Δημοκλῆς | Φιλλῆς |
| Πάρθης | Ἐχετέλης | Χοραγικλῆς | Εὐδαιμοκλῆς | Ἀχιλλῆς |
| Σεύθης | Ὀναίτέλης | Αἰγικλῆς | Κυδοιμοκλῆς | Ἀνατόλης |
| Θρασυκλείης | Ἀγιτέλης | Ξανθικλῆς | Ἐτοιμοκλῆς | Ἀσκαύλης |
| Κοττείης | Κλειτέλης | Καλλικλῆς | Τιμοκλῆς | Πρωταύλης |
| Γλαυκίης | Καλλιτέλης | Δεξικλῆς | Νομοκλῆς | Λύλης |
| Μελησίης | Πραξιτέλης | Ἀλεξικλῆς | Ὀνομοκλῆς | Φικούλης |
| Κυκυίης | Σοϊξιτέλης | Οἰκλῆς | Ἑρμοκλῆς | Λαδάμης |
| Φαρνάκης | Ἐπιτέλης | Ἐπικλῆς | Εὐθυμοκλῆς | Χρέμης |
| Ἐξάκης | Χαριτέλης | Χαρικλῆς | Ἐτυμοκλῆς | Κλήμης |
| Εὐάκης | Μνασιτέλης | Περικλῆς | Ἀθανοκλῆς | Φίμης |
| Διηνέκης | Πασιτέλης | Θηρικλῆς | Φανοκλῆς | Χάρμης |
| Ἀριδείκης | Πεισιτέλης | Σωτηρικλῆς | Στεφανοκλῆς | Ἑρμῆς |
| Ἐπιείκης | Σωσιτέλης | Δωρικλῆς | Ξενοκλῆς | Μαγγάνης |
| Νικῆς | Ἀρχιτέλης | Σικλῆς | Μηνοκλῆς | Μάνης |
| Φαενίκης | Ἀγλαοτέλης | Ἀγασικλῆς | Δεινοκλῆς | Φάνης |
| Κληνίκης | Ἐργοτέλης | Μνασικλῆς | Ἀμεινοκλῆς | Κλεαφάνης |
| Καλλινίκης | Θεοτέλης | Ὀνασικλῆς | Οἰνοκλῆς | Διαφάνης |
| Κλεονίκης | Δικαιοτέλης | Πασικλῆς | Ἀσσινοκλῆς | Λαφάνης |
| Δαμονίκης | Θιοτέλης | Στασικλῆς | Ἱπποκλῆς | Τελεφάνης |
| Πολυνίκης | Νικοτέλης | Φασικλῆς | Ἰαροκλῆς | Τηλεφάνης |
| Διοκκῆς | Οἰκοτέλης | Ἀγησικλῆς | Ἰλαροκλῆς | Κλειφάνης |
| Δαάλκης | Φιλοτέλης | Θαλησικλῆς | Ἀνδροκλῆς | Καλλιφάνης |
| Εὐβάλκης | Δαμοτέλης | Κρατησικλῆς | Μανδροκλῆς | Δεξιφάνης |
| Νεάλκης | Εὐδαιμοτέλης | Κτησικλῆς | Σφοδροκλῆς | Ἐπιφάνης |
| Δαϊάλκης | Τιμοτέλης | Τεισικλῆς | Ἱεροκλῆς | Μνασιφάνης |
| Διάλκης | Θυμοτέλης | Θερσικλῆς | Χοροκλῆς | Πασιφάνης |
| Ἀντιάλκης | Ξενοτέλης | Ναυσικλῆς | Προκλῆς | Λυσιφάνης |
| Δαμάλκης | Κρινοτέλης | Λυσικλῆς | Ἰατροκλῆς | Σωσιφάνης |
| Μενάλκης | Ἀβροτέλης | Σωσικλῆς | Πατροκλῆς | Ἀντιφάνης |
| Ἐπάλκης | Ἀνδροτέλης | Ἀντικλῆς | Καφισοκλῆς | Ἐκφάνης |
| Μνασάλκης | Καφισοτέλης | Μαντικλῆς | Διονυσοκλῆς | Θεοφάνης |
| Σιτάλκης | Ἀριστοτέλης | Παντικλῆς | Ἐρατοκλῆς | Κλεοφάνης |
| Ἀντάλκης | Δυοτέλης | Μενεστικλῆς | Πρατοκλῆς | Νεοφάνης |
| Εὐάλκης | Χαρτέλης | Ἰφικλῆς | Στρατοκλῆς | Διοφάνης |
| Πολυάλκης | Εὐτέλης | Ἀμφικλῆς | Παντοκλῆς | Θιοφάνης |
| Ἀμφάλκης | Ἀγλωτέλης | Ἀρχικλῆς | Καλλιστοκλῆς | Νικοφάνης |
| Θεάρκης | Σωτέλης | Τερψικλῆς | Θεμιστοκλῆς | Μεγαλοφάνης |
| Ξενάρκης | Ἀνδρωφέλης | Ὑψικλῆς | Πιστοκλῆς | Φιλοφάνης |
| Παντάρκης | Χαρίλης | Σαοκλῆς | Ἀριστοκλῆς | Ἀπολλοφάνης |
| Κρήσκης | Κασίλης | Σαβοκλῆς | Αὐτοκλῆς | Δαμοφάνης |
| Πολυδεύκης | Θεοφίλης | Ἐμπεδοκλῆς | Δυοκλῆς | Σαμοφάνης |
| Θαλῆς | Ἀγακλῆς | Ἰμπεδοκλῆς | Σοφοκλῆς | Δημοφάνης |
| Ἀρχεθάλης | Μεγακλῆς | Φειδοκλῆς | Περκλῆς | Τιμοφάνης |
| Αἰθάλης | Λακλῆς | Ῥοδοκλῆς | Ναυκλῆς | Ξενοφάνης |

| | | | | |
|---|---|---|---|---|
| Ζηνοφάνης | Κλευγένης | Πειθιμένης | Ἐκπρέπης | Ἱπποθράσης |
| Ἀθηνοφάνης | Πρευγένης | Ἀλκιμένης | Εὐπρέπης | Εὐθράσης |
| Μηνοφάνης | Σωγένης | Καλλιμένης | Πυριλάμπης | Χόσης |
| Ξηνοφάνης | Λασθένης | Εὐλιμένης | Ἰσπῆς | Δάρσης |
| Κλεινοφάνης | Ἐκεσθένης | Ἀναξιμένης | Ἀλύπης | Δαμοθάρσης |
| Ἡροφάνης | Κλεσθένης | Πραξιμένης | Ἄρης | Φιλοθέρσης |
| Ματροφάνης | Ἐχεσθένης | Δεξιμένης | Τυνδάρης | Δαμοθέρσης |
| Μητροφάνης | Κλεισθένης | Ἀλεξιμένης | Ποδάρης | Κισσῆς |
| Διονυσοφάνης | Λακισθένης | Ἐπιμένης | Θέαρης | Χρύσης |
| Ἀστοφάνης | Αἰκισθένης | Χαριμένης | Κλέαρης | Χρυσῆς |
| Ἀριστοφάνης | Ἀλκισθένης | Θηριμένης | Ξενϝάρης | Ἰωσῆς |
| Πρωτοφάνης | Καλλισθένης | Χαιριμένης | Διάρης | Φραάτης |
| Εὐφάνης | Ἐπισθένης | Ἀγασιμένης | Θιάρης | Ὀρειβάτης |
| Θευφάνης | Περισθένης | Στασιμένης | Ἀμφιάρης | Ἐπιβάτης |
| Κλευφάνης | Ἀγασισθένης | Κλεοσιμένης | Δαμάρης | Εὐβάτης |
| Ἀστυφάνης | Μνασισθένης | Θερσιμένης | Τιμάρης | Παλλιάτης |
| Ἀγλωφάνης | Φρασισθένης | Λυσιμένης | Πρατομάρης | Σπαρτιάτης |
| Σωφάνης | Ἀγησισθένης | Σωσιμένης | Εὐμάρης | Γαλάτης |
| Μάγνης | Κρατισθένης | Ἀντιμένης | Θυμάρης | Ἀρμάτης |
| Θεαγένης | Ἀντισθένης | Παμμένης | Μενάρης | Κοδράτης |
| Κλεαγένης | Παντισθένης | Θεομένης | Ξενάρης | Κράτης |
| Νεαγένης | Ἀμφισθένης | Λεομένης | Παντάρης | Λακράτης |
| Νικαγένης | Ἐμπεδοσθένης | Κλεομένης | Εὐάρης | Παγκράτης |
| Λαγένης | Κλεοσθένης | Νικομένης | Ἀμφάρης | Μενεκράτης |
| Τιμαγένης | Νικοσθένης | Φιλομένης | Χάρης | Φερεκράτης |
| Αἰσαγένης | Φιλοσθένης | Τιμομένης | Λαχάρης | Ἐχεκράτης |
| Μεταγένης | Δαμοσθένης | Ξενομένης | Καλλιχάρης | Ἀρχεκράτης |
| Ἰθαιγένης | Δημοσθένης | Δεινομένης | Ἐπιχάρης | Δαϊκράτης |
| Κλειγένης | Τιμοσθένης | Ἀνδρομένης | Σιχάρης | Ἀγηικράτης |
| Καλλιγένης | Δεινοσθένης | Ταυρομένης | Πασιχάρης | Δηϊκράτης |
| Ποιγένης | Ἱπποσθένης | Λεοντομένης | Σωσιχάρης | Πειικράτης |
| Ἐπιγένης | Ἀνδροσθένης | Ἀριστομένης | Θεοχάρης | Καλικράτης |
| Περιγένης | Ταυροσθένης | Αὐτομένης | Λεοχάρης | Μελικράτης |
| Χαιριγένης | Ἐρατοσθένης | Ὑπερμένης | Κλεοχάρης | Καλλικράτης |
| Ὀνασιγένης | Αὐτοσθένης | Εὐμένης | Διοχάρης | Ξενικράτης |
| Πασιγένης | Εὐσθένης | Κλευμένης | Θιοχάρης | Ἀναξικράτης |
| Ἰσιγένης | Κλευσθένης | Εὐθυμένης | Φιλοχάρης | Πραξικράτης |
| Ναυσιγένης | Πολυσθένης | Κλυμένης | Δαμοχάρης | Δεξικράτης |
| Σωσιγένης | Βορυσθένης | Ὀξυμένης | Τιμοχάρης | Ἀλεξικράτης |
| Ἀντιγένης | Εὐρυσθένης | Δορυμένης | Ξενοχάρης | Σοϊκράτης |
| Λυίγένης | Λεωσθένης | Εὐρυμένης | Ματροχάρης | Ἐπικράτης |
| Θεογένης | Σωσθένης | Θρασυμένης | Εὐχάρης | Ἀρικράτης |
| Κλεογένης | Μένης | Σωμένης | Πολυχάρης | Χαρικράτης |
| Πυθογένης | Ἀλκαμένης | Ἐπαίνης | Φίνγρης | Χηρικράτης |
| Δικαιογένης | Δεξαμένης | Δεινῆς | Φέρης | Χειρικράτης |
| Διογένης | Ἐπαμένης | Τηλίνης | Περιήρης | Νικασικράτης |
| Φιλογένης | Θηραμένης | Λακρίνης | Τήρης | Δαμασικράτης |
| Ἀπολλογένης | Εἰραμένης | Δαμοκρίνης | Εὐήρης | Τιμασικράτης |
| Πριμογένης | Θεκταμένης | Εὐκρίνης | Πολυήρης | Μνασικράτης |
| Τιμογένης | Ἀνταμένης | Εὐθυκρίνης | Φηρῆς | Ὀνασικράτης |
| Ἑρμογένης | Τυχαμένης | Πολυκρίνης | Μίθρης | Πασικράτης |
| Ἀθηνογένης | Ἐχεμένης | Κρητίνης | Κρής | Τελεσικράτης |
| Μηνογένης | Ἀρχεμένης | Αἰσχίνης | Σμίκρης | Ἀγησικράτης |
| Ναιρογένης | Τημένης | Ἀψίνης | Τιμοκρής | Πεισικράτης |
| Διονυσογένης | Δαϊμένης | Ἰωάννης | Ξειναγόρης | Τεισικράτης |
| Μουσογένης | Ἀλθαιμένης | Πίννης | Ἡραγόρης | Χερσικράτης |
| Ἐρατογένης | Πυραιμένης | Κύνης | Εὐαγόρης | Ὀρσικράτης |
| Θεμιστογένης | Κραταιμένης | Δάφνης | Λαμπρής | Ποσσικράτης |
| Ἀριστογένης | Ἀγιμένης | Θειναμάξης | Δαμοθέρρης | Ναυσικράτης |
| Πρωτογένης | Κυδιμένης | Ἀλεξῆς | Πύρης | Λυσικράτης |
| Θευγένης | Κλειμένης | Λαπρέπης | Δαϊθράσης | Σωσικράτης |

| | | | | |
|---|---|---|---|---|
| Ἀντικράτης | Ἀλήτης | Δαναΐς | Ὄστρεις | Οἶκις |
| Μαντικράτης | Φιλοκτήτης | Ἀθαναΐς | Παναϝίς | Σικκις |
| Ἀμφικράτης | Προφήτης | Ζηναΐς | Δαξίς | Ἄλκις |
| Ἀρχικράτης | Διαίτης | Ἀθηναΐς | Πολυζίς | Χαλκις |
| Σωΐκράτης | Τετραΐτης | Ληναΐς | Θαηΐς | Δόρκις |
| Φειδοκράτης | Παλαιστρείτης | Μναΐς | Ἀγηΐς | Δορκις |
| Λεοκράτης | Πολίτης | Γενναΐς | Ὑδδιηΐς | Εὔσκις |
| Κλεοκράτης | Σιβοίτης | Πάϊς | Ἐριῆις | Βαύκις |
| Νεοκράτης | Ἀγροίτης | Ἡραΐς | Ἡρακληΐς | Λυκίς |
| Πυθοκράτης | Παντίτης | Πύραϊς | Νηρηΐς | Σίβαλις |
| Ἰοκράτης | Φανάκτης | Εὐφραΐς | Βρισηΐς | Βουβαλίς |
| Νικοκράτης | Θεοδέκτης | Σάϊς | Χρυσηΐς | Πάρδαλις |
| Φιλοκράτης | Διοφάντης | Ταΐς | Ἀριστηϝίς | Παρδαλίς |
| Ἀπολλοκράτης | Ξενοφάντης | Νυμφαΐς | Ἄγαθις | Μαρτίαλις |
| Δαμοκράτης | Ὀρόντης | Στοιχαΐς | Μαθις | Εὔκαλις |
| Πολεμοκράτης | Δαϊφόντης | Βάβις | Γνάθις | Δαμαλίς |
| Δημοκράτης | Κρεσφόντης | Νάβις | Εὐστάθις | Πάλις |
| Τιμοκράτης | Ἀραότης | Εὐσέβις | Σαβαιθίς | Ἀρπαλίς |
| Ἑρμοκράτης | Κότης | Χορηβίς | Χοροιθίς | Νατάλις |
| Ἑλλανοκράτης | Συμπότης | Προσαιβίς | Ἀνθίς | Οὐϊτάλις |
| Μενοκράτης | Ἀνόπτης | Φοίβις | Νεανθίς | Μυρταλίς |
| Ξενοκράτης | Μελικέρτης | Κτησίβις | Ϝιανθίς | Κεφαλίς |
| Ἑλληνοκράτης | Μύρτης | Σάλβις | Πριανθίς | Εὐαγγελίς |
| Δεινοκράτης | Φράστης | Κλέοβις | Ἀκανθίς | Μέλις |
| Ἱπποκράτης | Μέστης | Νιοβίς | Τιμανθίς | Μελίς |
| Ἰσοκράτης | Ὀρέστης | Ὄροβις | Πάνθις | Ἀμπελίς |
| Πιστοκράτης | Μύστης | Τύρβις | Ἀμαρανθίς | Ὠφελίς |
| Ἀριστοκράτης | Φιλομύστης | Ἄγις | Χρυσανθίς | Χέλις |
| Αὐτοκράτης | Ναύτης | Ἀγίς | Εὐανθίς | Φασηλίς |
| Ναυκράτης | Φιλοναύτης | Πελάγις | Γενθίς | Χαμαιλίς |
| Εὐκράτης | Θύτης | Ξεναγίς | Ὑακινθίς | Ἄγγειλις |
| Κλευκράτης | Αἰσχύτης | Χοραγίς | Σμίνθις | Σμίλις |
| Εὐθυκράτης | Φθιώτης | Στραταγίς | Κορινθίς | Δαμαριλίς |
| Τηλυκράτης | Θηριώτης | Κυνηγίς | Κόρυνθις | Σιλίς |
| Πολυκράτης | Θεοσχώτης | Γόργις | Νοθίς | Βασιλίς |
| Εὐρυκράτης | Μύης | Γοργίς | Ἀθίς | Φίλις |
| Ἀστυκράτης | Ἀκούης | Γοργις | Πλάθις | Φιλίς |
| Ἀγλωκράτης | Σελλαφῆς | Αὖγις | Πιτθις | Φιλις |
| Σωκράτης | Ἀψέφης | Κραῦγις | Εὔθις | Μηνοφιλίς |
| Εὐφράτης | Ἀγλωτρόφης | Εἰκάδις | Εὔμυθις | Θευφιλίς |
| Ληγέτης | Λάχης | Γεννάδις | Πύθις | Ἡράκλις |
| Καλλιέτης | Κυριάρχης | Λαμπάδις | Βῶθις | Διοκλίς |
| Ἱκέτης | Ξενάρχης | Σκοτάδις | Ὡραΐς | Ἀνδροκλίς |
| Δρυπέτης | Εὐτύχης | Φάδις | Ἀχαΐς | Ἀγαλλίς |
| Ἀρέτης | Διεύχης | Σμαραγδίς | Τεΐΐς | Ἀναγαλλίς |
| Σακρέτης | Δαμεύχης | Ἴμπεδις | Πίακις | Μεγαλλίς |
| Μενεκρέτης | Πολυεύχης | Πόσειδις | Συλακίς | Ἰαλλίς |
| Δαϊκρέτης | Εὐτύχης | Φεῖδις | Κάνακις | Κάλλις |
| Καλλικρέτης | Βαΐς | Κνίδις | Κοννακίς | Καλλίς |
| Ἐπικρέτης | Θηβαΐς | Ἐλπίδις | Ἔξακις | Καλλις |
| Μαντικρέτης | Θαΐς | Δάνδις | Ἀμβρακίς | Μιμαλλίς |
| Νεοκρέτης | Δικάϊς | Βενδίς | Ἀνθρακίς | Μυραλλίς |
| Τιμοκρέτης | Λαΐς | Εὐοδίς | Θωρακίς | Πυραλλίς |
| Ϝισοκρέτης | Κάλαϊς | Ναρδίς | Σάκις | Πεταλλίς |
| Ἀριστοκρέτης | Ἀγλαΐς | Σόρδις | Σακίς | Ἀνταλλίς |
| Αὐτοκρέτης | Ἀρχελαΐς | Σπούδις | Μαστακίς | Μέλλις |
| Πολυκρέτης | Κλεολαΐς | Κλώδις | Πυστακίς | Πέλλις |
| Εὐρυκρέτης | Νικολαΐς | Μαίεις | Ἑλικίς | Ἄπελλις |
| Σωκρέτης | Πτολεμαΐς | Καλεῖς | Νίκις | Τέλλις |
| Εὐέτης | Ἑρμαΐς | Κλέϊς | Χαρμονικίς | Μυρτιλλίς |
| Νικήτης | Ναΐς | Νηρεῖς | Προυνίκις | Φίλλις |

| | | | | |
|---|---|---|---|---|
| Νεολλίς | Ὀνασύλις | Πριμογένις | Λυχνίς | Πειίππίς |
| Πόλλις | Ἀγησύλις | Παρθένις | Τρεβώνις | Φιλιππίς |
| Πολλίς | Θεστυλίς | Παρθενίς | Σκριβώνις | Ἐρπίς |
| Πραΰλλίς | Ἀριστύλις | Τιμοσθένις | Ἀγωνίς | Θέρπις |
| Βάρδυλλις | Ἀρχύλις | Ἑλενίς | Ποσειδώνις | Ἀσπίς |
| Κλεΰλλίς | Ἀρχυλίς | Ξένις | Κερδωνίς | Ἴασπις |
| Βαθυλλίς | Ἀρχυλις | Ξενις | Θεωνίς | Λεύκασπις |
| Κύλλις | Αἰσχύλις | Ζῆνις | Λεωνίς | Χρύσασπις |
| Φιλυλλίς | Αἰσχυλίς | Ζηνίς | Ἀργιλεωνίς | Θέσπις |
| Ξενυλλίς | Εὐθωλίς | Σεληνίς | Κλεωνίς | Σῶσπις |
| Ἑρπυλλίς | Περγαμίς | Κλῆνις | Εὐρυλεωνίς | Ἀλυπίς |
| Ἀμαρυλλίς | Δᾶμις | Κληνίς | Ἀγαθωνίς | Ἄλυπις |
| Ἄσυλλις | Λύγδαμις | Μῆνις | Θιωνίς | Τρῦπις |
| Δαμνασυλλίς | Ἰσοδαμίς | Σοσμήνις | Λακωνίς | Ὦπις |
| Φυλλίς | Πλοκαμίς | Νουμήνις | Κρησκώνις | Εὐῶπις |
| Εὐκολίς | Λάμις | Νουμηνίς | Γλυκωνίς | Βάρις |
| Μόλις | Σαλαμίς | Ξῆνις | Φιλωνίς | Βαρίς |
| Νεάπολις | Κινναμίς | Τυρσηνίς | Χιλωνίς | Σάγαρις |
| Ἀγέπολις | Δύναμις | Καινίς | Ἀπολλώνις | Μαργαρίς |
| Μενέπολις | Πυραμίς | Μελαινίς | Ἀπολλωνίς | Τυνδαρίς |
| Ἀρχέπολις | Πόταμις | Φιλαινίς | Ἀρτεμωνίς | Θεαρίς |
| Εὐήπολις | Θέμις | Ἔπαινις | Ζηνωνίς | Θεαρις |
| Ἀγηΐπολις | Πασίθεμις | Σαῖνις | Ἱερωνίς | Κλέαρις |
| Καλλίπολις | Ἀνθεμίς | Φαινίς | Μυρωνίς | Φάρις |
| Ἀναξίπολις | Ϝιανθεμίς | Φαεινίς | Κοιτωνίς | Νεθαρίς |
| Ἀλεξίπολις | Ἀπολλόθεμις | Δεῖνις | Τριτωνίς | Πάνθαρις |
| Ἐπίπολις | Ἀγνόθεμις | Ποθεινίς | Ἀντώνις | Πεκουλιάρις |
| Τιμασίπολις | Μηνόθεμις | Κλείνις | Κροτωνίς | Λᾶρις |
| Ὀνασίπολις | Χρυσόθεμις | Σέλινις | Ἄναξις | Φάλαρις |
| Ἀγησίπολις | Ἀριστόθεμις | Οἶνις | Ἀναξίς | Μάρις |
| Μνησίπολις | Ὀξύθεμις | Κρῖνις | Εὔπραξις | Δαμαρίς |
| Σωσίπολις | Ἄρτεμις | Ἄσινις | Σύνταξις | Ξεναρις |
| Κλεόπολις | Κλῆμις | Μυρτινίς | Δέξις | Ἀπολλινάρις |
| Νεόπολις | Ἀρμίς | Ἀττίνις | Πρόσδεξις | Πάρις |
| Δικαιόπολις | Χάρμις | Ὑμνίς | Λέξις | Σάρις |
| Νικόπολις | Ἑρμίς | Σκυμνίς | Ἄλεξις | Ἑταρις |
| Τιμόπολις | Ἀρίστερμις | Λυκυμνίς | Μεῖξις | Οὐάρις |
| Κοσμόπολις | Φόρμις | Πόλυμνις | Σόϊξις | Χάρις |
| Ἀκρόπολις | Θαῦμις | Πρύμνις | Θέοξις | Ἐπιχαρίς |
| Πρόπολις | Ψαῦμις | Πάννις | Εὖξις | Θεόχαρις |
| Θερσόπολις | Αἶχμις | Τυραννίς | Ζεῦξις | Φιλόχαρις |
| Χρυσόπολις | Ἀμωμίς | Φαεννίς | Ἐπίτευξις | Δαμόχαρις |
| Ἀριστόπολις | Ῥῶμις | Ξεννίς | Ἔρυξις | Δημόχαρις |
| Ἰσχόπολις | Χρῶμις | Κορwνίς | Καλοΐς | Ξενόχαρις |
| Εὔπολις | Λιβανίς | Κλέοννις | Δαμονοΐς | Νεβρίς |
| Σώπολις | Ἀγανίς | Κυννίς | Εὐνοΐς | Τίγρις |
| Τιμόπτολις | Δαρδανίς | Ἀμαζονίς | Σαραπίς | Λεανδρίς |
| Στολίς | Ἄθανις | Χίονις | Σεραπίς | Εὐανδρίς |
| Ἄμπλις | Μέλανις | Εἰκονίς | Ϝέπις | Καλλιτίβερις |
| Πραΰλίς | Καστάνις | Μονίς | Πρεπίς | Ἐλευθερίς |
| Γύλις | Πρύτανις | Ἡγεμονίς | Θάλπις | Ϝερις |
| Ἄγυλις | Φᾶνις | Εὐφρονίς | Σάλπις | Πιερίς |
| Δικαιΰλις | Φανίς | Χρόνις | Ἐλπίς | Βαλέρις |
| Νίκυλις | Στεφανίς | Πολυχρόνις | Μόλπις | Μερίς |
| Δαμυλίς | Θέογνις | Εὖνις | Λάμπις | Εὐαμερίς |
| Σιμυλίς | Θεογνίς | Παρμυνίς | Πόμπις | Ἀγαθημερίς |
| Φαινύλις | Θεῦγνις | Φορτούνις | Ὄλυμπις | Εὐημερίς |
| Οὖλις | Θεαγενίς | Φρῦνις | Ὀλυμπίς | Μονέρις |
| Βοῦλις | Περιγενίς | Σύνις | Αὔτοπις | Ἑσπερίς |
| Ἰούλις | Θεογενίς | Δάφνις | Ἴππις | Μάτερις |
| Νικασύλις | Διογενίς | Δαφνίς | Γοργιππίς | Ἀστέρις |

| | | | | |
|---|---|---|---|---|
| Ἀστερίς | Λυκωρίς | Λῦσις | Μάντις | Ἐπιμαχίς |
| Φέρις | Ἔλωρις | Λυσίς | Θεόμαντις | Συμμαχίς |
| Γῆρις | Πελωρίς | Μυσίς | Κλεόμαντις | Ἀστομάχις |
| Δῆρις | Συνωρίς | Διονύσις | Ὀνόμαντις | Εὔσταχις |
| Θῆρις | Ὀπωρίς | Διονυσίς | Ἀριστόμαντις | Βάκχις |
| Πανθηρίς | Θασίς | Φιλουσις | Πάντις | Βακχίς |
| Κυθηρίς | Ἴασις | Μουσίς | Εὐφραντίς | Μαλχίς |
| Εὐετηρίς | Νικασίς | Χρύσις | Κωνστάντις | Ἀντιοχίς |
| Σιτηρίς | Γελάσις | Χρυσίς | Κλειφαντίς | Ἄνοχις |
| Χαρτηρίς | Κλάσις | Συμβίωσις | Κλεοφαντίς | Ἀρχίς |
| Σωτηρίς | Ἄμασις | Μωσίς | Ἀργέντις | Κλεαρχίς |
| Σώτηρις | Δαμασίς | Γνῶσις | Φίντις | Νεαρχίς |
| Ὀρθρίς | Δήμασις | Fρωσις | Λέοντις | Ἐτεαρχίς |
| Ἶρις | Τιμασίς | Σῶσις | Λεοντίς | Ἀγαθαρχίς |
| Σωταιρίς | Ἀθανάσις | Σωσις | Λεοντις | Θαλιαρχίς |
| Χαῖρις | Μνᾶσις | Ἄτις | Δρακοντίς | Δεκαρχίς |
| Κοῖρις | Μνασις | Σαββάτις | Πόντις | Δαμαρχίς |
| Μοῖρις | Ἀσπασίς | Εὐσαμβάτις | Ἄποντις | Πολεμαρχίς |
| Βούσιρις | Ἔρασις | Ἀλεᾶτις | Φροντίς | Τιμαρχίς |
| Ἀκρίς | Ἀναστάσις | Ἀγιᾶτις | Ἄμυντις | Ξεναρχίς |
| Λᾶκρις | Ἐπίστασις | Ἀρκάτις | Ἔκοτις | Λυσαρχίς |
| Λόκρις | Φάσις | Ἀγαλματίς | Φιλοδεσποτίς | Ἀρισταρχίς |
| Δαμαγορίς | Πασχάσις | Ἰγνάτις | Κροτίς | Πολυαρχίς |
| Ἐξαγορίς | Τέλεσις | Ἀγαπάτις | Βαπτίς | Σοφαρχίς |
| Μαρμορίς | Νέμεσις | Ἀγασιγράτις | Χάρτις | Αἶσχις |
| Πόρις | Γένεσις | Φιληρατίς | Τέρτις | Μοσχίς |
| Δυλύπορις | Ἦσις | Κράτις | Πόρτις | Παννυχίς |
| Νικαφορίς | Ἄγησις | Κρατις | Μύρτις | Ἡσύχις |
| Νικηφορίς | Νίκησις | Καλλικράτις | Μυρτίς | Τυχίς |
| Ὀνασιφορίς | Κλησις | Ἐπικράτις | Μυρτις | Εὐτύχις |
| Συμφορίς | Αἴνησις | Ὀνασικράτις | Συρτίς | Εὐτυχίς |
| Δορυφορίς | Μνῆσις | Λυσικράτις | Μέδεστις | Σκέψις |
| Κόπρις | Ὀνησίς | Νικοκράτις | Ἄλκηστις | Νῆψις |
| Κύπρις | Φρόνησις | Φιλοκράτις | Φιλιστίς | Νεμψίς |
| Κυπρίς | Αὔξησις | Δαμοκράτις | Πίστις | Κόμψις |
| Πυρρίς | Ἄδρησις | Τιμοκράτις | Ἄριστις | Καλίοψις |
| Δαμάτρις | Εὔρησις | Εὔκράτις | Ἀριστίς | Ὕψις |
| Πατρίς | Εὕρησίς | Πολυκράτις | Ἄνυστις | Ζηνωῖς |
| Δημήτρις | Ἐπίκτησις | Σωκράτις | Μέττις | Ἡρωῖς |
| Χυτρίς | Μαΐσις | Πρᾶτις | Βυττίς | Νικοδάμανς |
| Σαῦρις | Κόργισις | Στράτις | Βύτις | Χαλκοδάμανς |
| Ἄγυρις | Ἀφροδίσις | Φιλοστράτις | Σάωτις | Κρήσκενς |
| Διήγυρις | Πείσις | Τιμοστρατίς | Νεωτίς | Δᾶος |
| Ἀργύρις | Πεισις | Τατίς | Φιλωτίς | Αὐδαός |
| Εὖρις | Τείσις | Θέτις | Μολωτίς | Λᾶος |
| Φιλοκύρις | Τεισίς | Ἱκέτις | Ἐρωτίς | Τάλαος |
| Λυρίς | Νῖσις | Ἀλκέτις | Ἑρμερωτίς | Ἄγλαος |
| Μύρις | Σῶισις | Φιλέτις | Συνερωτίς | Ἀγέλαος |
| Ἄμυρις | Κάδοσις | Ἄρετις | Κάφις | Σθενέλαος |
| Θάμυρις | Συρακόσις | Νικαρετίς | Σκαφίς | Μενέλαος |
| Λάπυρις | Πόσις | Φιλητίς | Ἐλαφίς | Αἰνέλαος |
| Λαμπυρίς | Δροσίς | Κλῆτις | Σάφις | Φερέλαος |
| Ζωπυρίς | Θέρσις | Κλητις | Σταφίς | Ἐχέλαος |
| Ἀπτυρίς | Θερσίς | Ἀδμητίς | Ἀσταφίς | Ἀρχέλαος |
| Πορφυρίς | Πέρσις | Κλεόμητις | Ἰφίς | Ἐρχέλαος |
| Ἄχυρις | Θύρσις | Δαῖτις | Fῖφις | Καιίλαος |
| Θέοφρις | Κασσίς | Βίτις | Ἄλφις | Ἀναξίλαος |
| Αἰσχρίς | Μελισσίς | Μελίτις | Δέλφις | Δεξίλαος |
| Δωρίς | Δόσσις | Βελτίς | Πάμφις | Ἀλεξίλαος |
| Θέωρις | Νοσσίς | Ἄντις | Μέμφις | Ἐπίλαος |
| Θεωρίς | Σόσσις | Ἀμιαντίς | Πίμφις | Χαρίλαος |

| | | | | |
|---|---|---|---|---|
| Ὑβρίλαος | Κότταβος | Πρεύραδος | Ἀρίβαζος | Εὔανθος |
| Περίλαος | Σάββος | Σμάραγδος | Δάζος | Βρύανθος |
| Θηρίλαος | Ἔφηβος | Αὐτόμεδος | Νέζος | Μουκάκενθος |
| Δωρίλαος | Λασκίβος | Ἔμπεδος | Τραῦζος | Λέβινθος |
| Ἀγασίλαος | Κόροιβος | Λῆδος | Βοῦζος | Ὑάκινθος |
| Νικασίλαος | Φοῖβος | Κίναιδος | Ἄγαθος | Σαβύλινθος |
| Μνασίλαος | Δατῖβος | Κνίδος | Νικάγαθος | Κήρινθος |
| Ἀγεσίλαος | Πριμιτῖβος | Ὄροιδος | Φιλάγαθος | Κόρινθος |
| Ἀνθεσίλαος | Ἴαμβος | Εὔιδος | Τιμάγαθος | Ζάκυνθος |
| Ἀρκεσίλαος | Κέραμβος | Σέκονδος | Ἐπάγαθος | Ὄλυνθος |
| Χαιρεσίλαος | Σήραμβος | Σπόνδος | Ἀνδράγαθος | Νόθος |
| Ἀγησίλαος | Διθύραμβος | Ἄσπονδος | Αὐτάγαθος | Ἀριστόνοθος |
| Πεισίλαος | Κάσαμβος | Σεκοῦνδος | Πρωτάγαθος | Πόθος |
| Λυσίλαος | Λύσιμβος | Οὐερηκοῦνδος | Εὐάγαθος | Δέκαρθος |
| Ἀκουσίλαος | Εὐκόλυμβος | Ἡσίοδος | Ἀρχάγαθος | Γόργυθος |
| Σωσίλαος | Κόρυμβος | Ἔνοδος | Πρόμαθος | Τρεῦθος |
| Φίλαος | Κόλοβος | Σύνοδος | Πράθος | Μίκυθος |
| Φειδόλαος | Ἄφοβος | Ῥόδος | Ζῆθος | Μιρίκυθος |
| Κλεόλαος | Ἄταρβος | Πεισίρροδος | Βόηθος | Σκύθος |
| Νεόλαος | Ἴρβος | Πρόσοδος | Σάαιθος | Μῦθος |
| Πειθόλαος | Εὔφορβος | Εὔοδος | Ὀλίγαιθος | Παράμυθος |
| Πυθόλαος | Πόλυβος | Νάρδος | Δάϊθος | Ἀρχίμυθος |
| Ἰόλαος | Γλάγος | Πάρδος | Λέαιθος | Βοῦθος |
| Αἰόλαος | Ξέναγος | Κέρδος | Νέαιθος | Διόσκουθος |
| Νικόλαος | Κύναγος | Λαῦδος | Ἀρίαιθος | Ξοῦθος |
| Πευκόλαος | Κόρραγος | Λυδός | Νίκαιθος | Τροῦθος |
| Λυκόλαος | Στράταγος | Πόλυδος | Λύκαιθος | Στροῦθος |
| Φιλόλαος | Κράφαγος | Ἄστυδος | Γάλαιθος | Ἀβαῖος |
| Δαμόλαος | Λόχαγος | Ἀρίωδος | Σάλαιθος | Βεβαῖος |
| Τιμόλαος | Γόγγος | Δεξίθεος | Τήλαιθος | Λοβαῖος |
| Ἑρμόλαος | Φθόγγος | Εὐξίθεος | Φίλαιθος | Γάϊος |
| Σθενόλαος | Μελίφθογγος | Χαιρίθεος | Σίμαιθος | Ἀγαῖος |
| Ξενόλαος | Λόγγος | Τιμασίθεος | Κόμαιθος | Ἀργαῖος |
| Κρινόλαος | Βέγος | Μνασίθεος | Ξέναιθος | Ἐργαῖος |
| Ἱππόλαος | Ναύπηγος | Μνησίθεος | Κύναιθος | Πραυγαῖος |
| Ἀνδρόλαος | Ὀλίγος | Πεισίθεος | Πύρραιθος | Γαδαῖος |
| Πρόλαος | Λόγος | Λυσίθεος | Πύραιθος | Ἀχλαδαῖος |
| Πρατόλαος | Φιλόλογος | Δωσίθεος | Πίρειθος | Μενεδαῖος |
| Στρατόλαος | Μρόγος | Σωσίθεος | Ἄλκιθος | Ἰδαῖος |
| Κριτόλαος | Ἄργος | Ἀμφίθεος | Κνοίθος | Ποσειδαῖος |
| Πιστόλαος | Βάργος | Νικόθεος | Πειρίθος | Ἀρριδαῖος |
| Ἀριστόλαος | Φίλαργος | Φιλόθεος | Κόρριθος | Ὀδαῖος |
| Πρωτόλαος | Μάργος | Δαμόθεος | Ἄνθος | Θρασυδαῖος |
| Ἰσχόλαος | Σίμαργος | Τιμόθεος | Κλέανθος | Θεαῖος |
| Μοσχόλαος | Νάργος | Οἰνόθεος | Σέανθος | Κλεαῖος |
| Ῥιψόλαος | Σύνεργος | Δωρόθεος | Μελίανθος | Δαζαῖος |
| Πρόσλαος | Γόργος | Ἀριστόθεος | Ἀρίανθος | Μαθαῖος |
| Σαύλαος | Φιλόστοργος | Πύθεος | Ἐρίανθος | Ἐκεθαῖος |
| Εὐθύλαος | Λυκοῦργος | Κέος | Κάνθος | Πόθαιος |
| Κύλαός | Γεώργος | Ἄλεος | Ἄκανθος | Ὀρθαῖος |
| Θρασύλαος | Πέλασγος | Γαλεός | Φάλανθος | Βιαῖος |
| Εὔμαος | Ὤγυγος | Μέλεος | Μέλανθος | Δίαιος |
| Δαναός | Λάζυγος | Κλέος | Φίλανθος | Θιαῖος |
| Κραναός | Βρῦγος | Νέος | Ἐρίμανθος | Ἑστιαῖος |
| Σμύρναος | Πασίφυγος | Φρύνεος | Ἐρύμανθος | Ἰστιαῖος |
| Πείραος | Δάρωγος | Δεξίλαϝος | Ἄνανθος | Ἀγκαῖος |
| Σάος | Λέκαδος | Ἀρκεσίλαϝος | Ξάνθος | Δικαῖος |
| Μάχαος | Ἐπίκαδος | Σωσίλαϝος | Ἵππανθος | Νίκαιος |
| Βάβος | Κέλαδος | Ταχιστόλαϝος | Ἀμάρανθος | Ἀλκαῖος |
| Γράβος | Εὐκέλαδος | Λαδάμαϝος | Πύρρανθος | Βαρκαῖος |
| Λάτταβος | Κλάδος | Ἀγασίληϝος | Χρύσανθος | Λυκαῖος |

| | | | | |
|---|---|---|---|---|
| Λάϊος | Ἀππειραῖος | Κορύμβιος | Ἀργεῖος | Ἀκάκιος |
| Αἰγλαῖος | Ἀγοραῖος | Δεινόβιος | Μήδειος | Ἐξάκιος |
| Ἔλαῖος | Πετραῖος | Οἰνόβιος | Ἀφρόδειος | Σταυράκιος |
| Ἀγέλαιος | Ὑραῖος | Ἀνδρόβιος | Συνήθειος | Ὁμοστάκιος |
| Νανελαῖος | Κορκυραῖος | Πατρόβιος | Πιθειός | Πάγκιος |
| Φίλαιος | Εὔφραῖος | Μητρόβιος | Κοκκαίειος | Δέκιος |
| Ἀμυκλαῖος | Κορσαῖος | Δωρόβιος | Ἀλιειός | Ἀλέκιος |
| Βαλλαῖος | Κοσσαῖος | Ἀριστόβιος | Ἱστιειός | Μαίκιος |
| Ἀπελλαῖος | Νυσαῖος | Αὐτόβιος | Λυκειός | Μινίκιος |
| Πλαῖος | Μουσαῖος | Πρωτόβιος | Ἀλειός | Ἐπινίκιος |
| Ὑλαῖος | Ἑκαταῖος | Ἀφόβιος | Πυκέλειος | Οἴκιος |
| Ἀγυλαῖος | Ἀπεταῖος | Ὑπέρβιος | Ἠλεῖος | Σαπρίκιος |
| Ματυλαῖος | Ἀρεταῖος | Λέσβιος | Βασίλειος | Μαυρίκιος |
| Μάιος | Κληταῖος | Εὔβιος | Φίλειος | Τίκιος |
| Πολεμαῖος | Τριταῖος | Ζύβιος | Ἡράκλειος | Πάκκιος |
| Πτολεμαῖος | Ἀκταῖος | Ταλθύβιος | Πόλειος | Πατούλκιος |
| Βημαῖος | Εὔκταῖος | Εὐθύβιος | Σόλειος | Ὄρκιος |
| Τίμαιος | Ἀνταῖος | Πολύβιος | Τιμειός | Ἀρέσκιος |
| Ἀμμαῖος | Ἑορταῖος | Ζανούβιος | Μελανειός | Εὔσκιος |
| Κομαῖος | Τυρταῖος | Εὐρύβιος | Πηνειός | Τεβύκιος |
| Ἑρμαῖος | Φυρταῖος | Ζώβιος | Εὐφρόνειος | Λεύκιος |
| Εὔμαῖος | Στάϊος | Κώβιος | Ἄφνειος | Λύκιος |
| Κυμαῖος | Ἀρισταῖος | Ἄγιος | Ἐπειός | Λούκιος |
| Αἰχμαῖος | Φυσταῖος | Λάγιος | Ἄρειος | Ἰδάλιος |
| Ἀθάναιος | Δυαῖος | Πελάγιος | Δαρεῖος | Φειδάλιος |
| Κυραναῖος | Λύαιος | Εὐπράγιος | Μαμμάρειος | Θάλιος |
| Ἰταναῖος | Πρυαῖος | Κυνήγιος | Θερειός | Εὐλάλιος |
| Φαναῖος | Ἀχαιός | Στρατήγιος | Κόρειος | Μάλιος |
| Γναῖος | Φιλάχαιος | Φιλολόγιος | Ἀστειός | Εἰνάλιος |
| Μέναιος | Λοχαῖος | Σέργιος | Ἀλφειός | Φαρσάλιος |
| Δεξαμεναῖος | Σύχαιος | Γεώργιος | Βακχεῖος | Τάλιος |
| Ὑμεναῖος | Τυχαῖος | Φρύγιος | Σπερχειός | Πετάλιος |
| Ξεναῖος | Σαμψαῖος | Δῖος | Φίος | Βιτάλιος |
| Ἀθήναιος | Ὑψαῖος | Ἰκάδιος | Δάζιος | Φαλίος |
| Φιλαθήναιος | Βίος | Φικάδιος | Λάζιος | Ἀσφάλιος |
| Ἐπιλήναιος | Ἀβλάβιος | Λευκάδιος | Θρασυδήϊος | Πούβλιος |
| Εἰρηναῖος | Φλάβιος | Παλλάδιος | Κοκκήϊος | Ἀμπέλιος |
| Μναῖος | Στράβιος | Ἑλλάδιος | Πομπήϊος | Ἥλιος |
| Λιμναῖος | Ὀκτάβιος | Γεννάδιος | Ἀγάθιος | Τραγήλιος |
| Ἀνναῖος | Τρέβιος | Λαμπάδιος | Γνάθιος | Δήλιος |
| Γενναῖος | Εὔσέβιος | Ἐπικράδιος | Εὐστάθιος | Κορνήλιος |
| Ὄναιος | Ἀρχέβιος | Ὑράδιος | Ἀέθιος | Αὐρήλιος |
| Νεμονάϊος | Βίβιος | Φράδιος | Κίθιος | Γενέθλιος |
| Βαρναῖος | Ἀλκίβιος | Χαλίδιος | Εὐξίθιος | Καίλιος |
| Δαφναῖος | Λίβιος | Γενεθλίδιος | Σπρίθιος | Αἰμίλιος |
| Κλεωναῖος | Καλλίβιος | Λεωνίδιος | Μελάνθιος | Ἀτίλιος |
| Πέμπαιος | Ἀναξίβιος | Ἐλπίδιος | Οἰνάνθιος | Φίλιος |
| Πομπαῖος | Φαναξίβιος | Αὐφίδιος | Χρυσάνθιος | Ῥουφίλιος |
| Σκόπαιος | Πραξίβιος | Ἔνδιος | Εὐάνθιος | Χίλιος |
| Παρθενοπαῖος | Ἀλεξίβιος | Καλένδιος | Γένθιος | Ποίκλιος |
| Ἀστεροπαῖος | Ῥηξίβιος | Σπένδιος | Κορίνθιος | Μάλλιος |
| Ἱππαῖος | Νικασίβιος | Κοθόδιος | Κύνθιος | Ὀφάλλιος |
| Καραῖος | Αἰνησίβιος | Ἁρμόδιος | Ζακύνθιος | Τρεβέλλιος |
| Μαραῖος | Λυσίβιος | Εὐόδιος | Σαλύνθιος | Γέλλιος |
| Ἀπταραῖος | Σωσίβιος | Ὀέρδιος | Βιύσθιος | Οὐίλλιος |
| Γραῖος | Ἀντίβιος | Λόρδιος | Εὔθιος | Φίλλιος |
| Εὔδραῖος | Ἀγχίβιος | Κλαύδιος | Τεύθιος | Ὀφίλλιος |
| Ἱεραῖος | Ἀρχίβιος | Ῥαύδιος | Παραμύθιος | Ταγύλλιος |
| Ἱμεραῖος | Σωίβιος | Εὔδιος | Πύθιος | Ἀσύλλιος |
| Κρατεραῖος | Ἄλβιος | Βούδιος | Ἐρατυΐος | Φύλλιος |
| Ἥραιος | Σάλβιος | Κλώδιος | Δάκιος | Ἀνατόλιος |

| | | | | |
|---|---|---|---|---|
| Πόπλιος | Ἀρμένιος | Πομπώνιος | Εὐαμέριος | Φιλήσιος |
| Ναύπλιος | Ὑμένιος | Μαρώνιος | Νεμέριος | Εὐκλήσιος |
| Πούπλιος | Εὐμένιος | Σεμπρώνιος | Νουμέριος | Τιμήσιος |
| Ἀκύλιος | Ξένιος | Πετρώνιος | Τριεσπέριος | Μαγνήσιος |
| Ἰούλιος | Ἀρσένιος | Αἰσώνιος | Προτέριος | Ἀρνήσιος |
| Πούλιος | Ἀθήνιος | Ἀντώνιος | Περιστέριος | Εὐτρήσιος |
| Πύλιος | Μήνιος | Σικυώνιος | Μελιθήριος | Εὔρήσιος |
| Αἰσχύλιος | Νεμήνιος | Ἄξιος | Εὐετήριος | Θεαίσιος |
| Δάμιος | Νεομήνιος | Παλάξιος | Σωτήριος | Καίσιος |
| Λάμιος | Νευμήνιος | Δέξιος | Ἐγκαίριος | Ἀφροδίσιος |
| Πράμιος | Νουμήνιος | Ἀλέξιος | Ἀτείριος | Ἀρτεμίσιος |
| Σάμιος | Εὐήνιος | Μενέξιος | Κριός | Χαρίσιος |
| Ἀρτέμιος | Φαλαίνιος | Εὐδόξιος | Φαλάκριος | Ἀκρίσιος |
| Φήμιος | Σελίνιος | Λόξιος | Φιλάκριος | Καφίσιος |
| Εὐφήμιος | Ἐντελλίνιος | Μελίβοιος | Γρηγόριος | Ὅσιος |
| Στάθμιος | Νίνιος | Κοῖος | Ἀμφικόριος | Θεοδόσιος |
| Αἰγίμιος | Ἐρασίνιος | Κολοῖος | Σπόριος | Θευδόσιος |
| Δασίμιος | Σισίνιος | Εὔπλοιος | Εὐπόριος | Συρακόσιος |
| Σωσίμιος | Στερτίνιος | Νοῖος | Κλειτόριος | Λευκόσιος |
| Μέμμιος | Λήμνιος | Ἐννόϊος | Διακτόριος | Δεσπόσιος |
| Μόμμιος | Ὀλόμμνιος | Πυροῖος | Νεστόριος | Ἀμβρόσιος |
| Κόμιος | Βάννιος | Παντοῖος | Δαμάτριος | Πέρσιος |
| Νόμιος | Κριάννιος | Πῖος | Μήτριος | Κάσσιος |
| Εὐνόμιος | Ἰωάννιος | Ἄπιος | Δημήτριος | Θαλάσσιος |
| Βρόμιος | Ἔννιος | Ἀγάπιος | Πανηγύριος | Παρνάσσιος |
| Χρόμιος | Γέννιος | Αἰγλαπιός | Ἀβεύριος | Μύσσιος |
| Στόμιος | Περκέννιος | Ἀσκληπιός | Κύριος | Ἐρύσσιος |
| Χάρμιος | Πολφέννιος | Εὐήπιος | Μύριος | Ἠλύσιος |
| Ἕρμιος | Κοσπίννιος | Ὀλύμπιος | Ἀμύριος | Νύσιος |
| Ἐράσμιος | Κασίννιος | Σκόπιος | Σκιούριος | Διονύσιος |
| Προθύμιος | Ἐπιγόνιος | Πανόπιος | Πλατούριος | Μαλούσιος |
| Εὐθύμιος | Μακεδόνιος | Μερόπιος | Βετούριος | Σώσιος |
| Δινύμιος | Καλχηδόνιος | Θεοπρόπιος | Σπύριος | Σαββάτιος |
| Εὐκώμιος | Μαρδόνιος | Ὄππιος | Μαρτύριος | Αἰβάτιος |
| Πεδάνιος | Ἰόνιος | Σκορπίος | Πορφύριος | Βιζάτιος |
| Φονδάνιος | Καλόνιος | Αἰγύπιος | Λάφριος | Πλάτιος |
| Δαρδάνιος | Τερμόνιος | Ἀγγάριος | Μολύσχριος | Κλιμάτιος |
| Εὐϝάνιος | Εὐφρόνιος | Λογάριος | Δώριος | Δελμάτιος |
| Βυζάνιος | Σωφρόνιος | Μακάριος | Ἄσιος | Μινάτιος |
| Παιάνιος | Χρόνιος | Λυκάριος | Δάσιος | Ἀράτιος |
| Ἀβιάνιος | Πολυχρόνιος | Μάριος | Κάσιος | Κράτιος |
| Λουκάνιος | Αὐσόνιος | Ἀπολλινάριος | Νικάσιος | Στράτιος |
| Κυλλάνιος | Τονίος | Πάριος | Λάσιος | Στάτιος |
| Νάνιος | Φόρνιος | Καισάριος | Ἰλάσιος | Βονιφάτιος |
| Αὐξάνιος | Ἰούνιος | Ἰανουάριος | Τιμάσιος | Ἀέτιος |
| Καράνιος | Διούνιος | Παγχάριος | Κωμάσιος | Λαέτιος |
| Γράνιος | Μονούνιος | Ῥούβριος | Ἀθανάσιος | Δουκέτιος |
| Σειράνιος | Νεπτούνιος | Ἄγριος | Ἀσπάσιος | Δομέτιος |
| Οὐράνιος | Παίχνιος | Φιλάγριος | Θράσιος | Δουμέτιος |
| Τιτάνιος | Ἀδώνιος | Εὐάγριος | Ἀγοράσιος | Ἀρχέτιος |
| Εὐάνιος | Πεδώνιος | Γάνγριος | Παρράσιος | Δοκήτιος |
| Στεφάνιος | Ποσειδώνιος | Ζώγριος | Τράσιος | Φιλήτιος |
| Ἐπιφάνιος | Σιδώνιος | Ἄνδριος | Ἐορτάσιος | Μενήτιος |
| Εὐγένιος | Κριθώνιος | Πανάνδριος | Ἀναστάσιος | Χαιρήτιος |
| Παρθένιος | Παιώνιος | Εὐάνδριος | Πασχάσιος | Πολλαίτιος |
| Σθένιος | Χρηστιώνιος | Ἀέριος | Ἱκέσιος | Παναίτιος |
| Κλεοσθένιος | Πακώνιος | Κλεβέριος | Τελέσιος | Σαίτιος |
| Δεκένιος | Ἀπολλώνιος | Τιβέριος | Ἐφέσιος | Δουλκίτιος |
| Ὠλένιος | Ψαμώνιος | Ἐλευθέριος | Ϝάδήσιος | Ἀμίτιος |
| Μένιος | Ἀμμώνιος | Βαλέριος | Μελήσιος | Φιλοίτιος |
| Λιμένιος | Ἀπώνιος | Οὐαλέριος | Μιλήσιος | Μενοίτιος |

| | | | | |
|---|---|---|---|---|
| Τρίτιος | Σόφιος | Κάλαικος | Δεξίνικος | Καρικός |
| Σωίτιος | Χῖος | Φάλαικος | Ἀλεξίνικος | Ἀνδρικός |
| Ἄκτιος | Ἀμάχιος | Ἰλαϊκός | Σοϊξίνικος | Δευτερικός |
| Ὄλτιος | Ναυμάχιος | Καράϊκος | Ἐπίνικος | Κλήρικός |
| Βάντιος | Σίχιος | Πάταικος | Ἐλπίνικος | Λοκρικός |
| Καραβάντιος | Στίχιος | Ἀχαϊκός | Ὀνασίνικος | Ὄμρικος |
| Τρωδάντιος | Βάκχιος | Ἐφηβικός | Πασίνικος | Ῥητορικός |
| Ἀδαμάντιος | Μωλόχιος | Σάμβικος | Τελεσίνικος | Θεατρικός |
| Ὀνομάντιος | Εὐστόχιος | Γεωργικός | Ἀγησίνικος | Λυρικός |
| Ὀνυμάντιος | Τάρχιος | Λάδικος | Κρατησίνικος | Φρῖκος |
| Οἰνάντιος | Ἡσύχιος | Παιδικός | Ναυσίνικος | Δωρικός |
| Σπεράντιος | Τύχιος | Κλείδικος | Λυσίνικος | Μουσικός |
| Ϝαιράντιος | Εὐτύχιος | Καλλίδικος | Σωσίνικος | Ἀσιατικός |
| Μέντιος | Ἀρχέψιος | Ἐπίδικος | Ἀρχίνικος | Σπαρτιατικός |
| Αὐξέντιος | Νύμψιος | Λυσίδικος | Σωῖνικος | Ἱερατικός |
| Λαυρέντιος | Ὄψιος | Ἀντίδικος | Γυμνικός | Κρητικός |
| Φλωρέντιος | Γελώϊος | Ἔκδικος | Μάννικος | Πολιτικός |
| Λεόντιος | Ἀχελώϊος | Κλεόδικος | Πάννικος | Πρακτικός |
| Ἀκόντιος | Σώϊος | Μεθοδικός | Γεννικός | Ἔκτικος |
| Δρακόντιος | Ἀστράβακος | Νικόδικος | Λαόνικος | Ἐπιτευκτικός |
| Πόντιος | Λάβδακος | Δαμόδικος | Ἐργόνικος | Πεντικός |
| Γερόντιος | Βύνδακος | Ἁρμόδικος | Μακεδονικός | Ποντικός |
| Σελινούντιος | Ἴθακος | Ξενόδικος | Κυδόνικος | Συρτικός |
| Ἑλλότιος | Πίθακος | Ἱππόδικος | Λεόνικος | Ἀστικός |
| Κλέπτιος | Αἰακός | Ὑπόδικος | Κλεόνικος | Δομεστικός |
| Αἰγύπτιος | Ἰλιακός | Ἡρόδικος | Πρατεόνικος | Μυστικός |
| Λαέρτιος | Συμφωνιακός | Πρόδικος | Ἐτεόνικος | Ἀττικός |
| Τέρτιος | Ὀλυμπιακός | Ἰσόδικος | Ἀγαθόνικος | Τεύτικος |
| Σαβύρτιος | Κυριακός | Ἀριστόδικος | Πυθόνικος | Ζωτικός |
| Σιβύρτιος | Συριακός | Εὔδικος | Διόνικος | Ἐρωτικός |
| Βλάστιος | Ἀκτιακός | Κλεύδικος | Πυθιόνικος | Ἠπειρωτικός |
| Θέστιος | Χιακός | Εὐθύδικος | Ἀξιόνικος | Γραφικός |
| Εὐέστιος | Λάκος | Εὐρύδικος | Εἰκονικός | Δελφικός |
| Ἁφαίστιος | Μαλακός | Κύζικος | Φιλόνικος | Νυμφικός |
| Θεμίστιος | Πάλακος | Ἀτθικός | Δαμόνικος | Τυχικός |
| Εὐελπίστιος | Φίλακος | Πυθικός | Δημόνικος | Ἵκκος |
| Ἀντίστιος | Φίλλακος | Κῖκος | Τιμόνικος | Μίκκος |
| Λαφύστιος | Φύλακος | Ἁλικός | Ἁρμόνικος | Κόκκος |
| Σάττιος | Σήμακος | Ἰταλικός | Ἑρμόνικος | Βύκκος |
| Οὐέττιος | Δρίμακος | Φιλικός | Ἱππόνικος | Λάαλκος |
| Σίττιος | Σίμακος | Ἀπέλλικος | Ἀνδρόνικος | Δαΐαλκος |
| Γύττιος | Ἄνακος | Συμβολικός | Ἱερόνικος | Δάμαλκος |
| Βρύττιος | Στίπακος | Ἀργολικός | Πρατόνικος | Μέναλκος |
| Βύτιος | Ἵππακος | Ἀνατολικός | Στρατόνικος | Εὔαλκος |
| Τεύτιος | Τίππακος | Μίκος | Κριτόνικος | Πολύχαλκος |
| Κλύτιος | Δρώπακος | Κωμικός | Παντόνικος | Δάολκος |
| Μούτιος | Ἄρακος | Γνωμικός | Συρτόνικος | Πρώπινκος |
| Βηρύτιος | Μαρακός | Λάνικος | Πλειστόνικος | Λάδοκος |
| Φύτιος | Ἄβρακος | Ἑλλάνικος | Ἀριστόνικος | Μήδοκος |
| Βοιώτιος | Σείρακος | Ξοανικός | Σοφόνικος | Λίδοκος |
| Γλώτιος | Γύρακος | Κατάνικος | Ὑπέρνικος | Ἄνδοκος |
| Πλώτιος | Λύρακος | Στεφανικός | Εὔνικος | Φιλόδοκος |
| Φώτιος | Ἀρίστακος | Παρθενικός | Βιθυνικός | Δαμόδοκος |
| Εὔιος | Βώτακος | Τελένικος | Πολύνικος | Δημόδοκος |
| Πισθυῖος | Σώτακος | Ξενικός | Δαφνικός | Ξενόδοκος |
| Νούϊος | Στρίμφακος | Φερένικος | Ἰωνικός | Ἀριστόδοκος |
| Κρατύϊος | Μέλαγκος | Ἐχένικος | Λακωνικός | Ἄνδροκος |
| Κνέφιος | Ἀλώπεκος | Κλήνικος | Σώνικος | Κρόκος |
| Ἀκρίφιος | Μάληκος | Εἰρηνικός | Μένοικος | Ἄρκος |
| Νύμφιος | Μίθαικος | Κληΐνικος | Ὄροικος | Μάαρκος |
| Λόφιος | Κάϊκος | Καλλίνικος | Ὀλυμπικός | Μᾶρκος |

| | | | | |
|---|---|---|---|---|
| Μάμαρκος | Ἀνδρίσκος | Ἀγχίαλος | Ἀρίζηλος | Ἡρόφιλος |
| Μάμερκος | Εὐβαβερίσκος | Κάλος | Πολύζηλος | Πατρόφιλος |
| Τόπερκος | Πανθηρίσκος | Πάγκαλος | Θυῖηλος | Ἀριστόφιλος |
| Λούπερκος | Σωτηρίσκος | Καίκαλος | Πασίμηλος | Αὐτόφιλος |
| Δόρκος | Εἰρίσκος | Περίκαλος | Κλεόμηλος | Θεύφιλος |
| Μόρκος | Δορίσκος | Κόκκαλος | Φιλόμηλος | Ἀρνούφιλος |
| Πόρκος | Κορίσκος | Φιλόκαλος | Εὔμηλος | Ἀστύφιλος |
| Ὕρκος | Πρίσκος | Ὁλόκαλος | Βραχύμηλος | Σώφιλος |
| Μένασκος | Ταυρίσκος | Κώκαλος | Πέτηλος | Ἀρχίλος |
| Τάσκος | Ζωπυρίσκος | Λάλος | Ἄθλος | Μοσχίλος |
| Ἄρεσκος | Κρατίσκος | Εὔλαλος | Εὔαθλος | Ζωΐλος |
| Γόλτεσκος | Ὀλτίσκος | Μάλος | Στροβίλος | Τρωΐλος |
| Ἑρμαῖσκος | Λεοντίσκος | Σίμαλος | Ταγίλος | Πένταχλος |
| Σαῖσκος | Ποτίσκος | Βινκόμαλος | Ἐργίλος | Τήλεκλος |
| Φαῖσκος | Μυΐσκος | Παίπαλος | Γοργίλος | Μάντικλος |
| Λαγίσκος | Λοχίσκος | Τεύπαλος | Δενδίλος | Θέοκλος |
| Τραγίσκος | Μύσκος | Θεσσαλός | Νεῖλος | Ἐτέοκλος |
| Δίσκος | Ἐτροῦσκος | Μέσσαλος | Ὀκκίλος | Ἄνδροκλος |
| Ἁρμοδίσκος | Φοῦσκος | Φύσαλος | Ὄμιλος | Πρόκλος |
| Κλείσκος | Φύσκος | Μάταλος | Οἰνίλος | Πάτροκλος |
| Εὐκλείσκος | Σιβαυκός | Σπάταλος | Γυμνίλος | Θράσυκλος |
| Νείσκος | Γλαῦκος | Πέταλος | Σατορνίλος | Κάβαλλος |
| Δαζίσκος | Σάραυκος | Ἰταλός | Φρουνίλος | Μέγαλλος |
| Ἀνθίσκος | Δραῦκος | Τάνταλος | Δρωνίλος | Θάλλος |
| Ἀλεξικίσκος | Ἴβυκος | Κάσταλος | Δεξίλος | Κάλλος |
| Ἀνκίσκος | Λεῦκος | Ἄτταλος | Σοΐλος | Μύσκαλλος |
| Λυκίσκος | Ζάλευκος | Τίτταλος | Ποπίλος | Μάλλος |
| Τελίσκος | Σέλευκος | Πύτταλος | Χαρίλος | Τίμαλλος |
| Βασιλίσκος | Βρεῦκος | Εὐρύαλος | Περίλος | Πυρόμαλλος |
| Φιλίσκος | Λύκος | Κέφαλος | Χοιρίλος | Χρυσόμαλλος |
| Θαλλίσκος | Γάλυκος | Πίμφαλος | Ὀνάσιλος | Τριτύμαλλος |
| Αὐλίσκος | Γλύκος | Στύμφαλος | Κωσίλος | Χρύσαλλος |
| Αἰσχυλίσκος | Φίλυκος | Τράχαλος | Μυρτίλος | Ἄνταλλος |
| Ἀμίσκος | Αὐτόλυκος | Ῥῆγλος | Πυστίλος | Βέλλος |
| Δαμίσκος | Ἄμυκος | Ἕλος | Μυτίλος | Μάρκελλος |
| Λαμίσκος | Ἴνυκος | Ἄγγελος | Λάφιλος | Μύσκελλος |
| Ἀρτεμίσκος | Φάρυκος | Θεάγγελος | Ἑρμάφιλος | Γέμελλος |
| Σιμίσκος | Μῶκος | Ἀγαθάγγελος | Ἀρετάφιλος | Ἔντελλος |
| Παρμίσκος | Φῶκος | Πυθάγγελος | Φάφιλος | Ἔχελλος |
| Ἑρμίσκος | Ἆλος | Τιμάγγελος | Τερπέφιλος | Γίλλος |
| Φορμίσκος | Βᾶλος | Χρυσάγγελος | Τέφιλος | Ἄγιλλος |
| Εὐθυμίσκος | Ἰνίβαλος | Εὐάγγελος | Δίφιλος | Μέγιλλος |
| Πανίσκος | Οἴβαλος | Εἴελος | Καλλίφιλος | Φρύγιλλος |
| Φανίσκος | Κάμβαλος | Ἴκελος | Οἴφιλος | Κίλλος |
| Θεοφανίσκος | Κύμβαλος | Φίκελος | Ἀρίφιλος | Μίκιλλος |
| Μενίσκος | Ὄβαλος | Ὄκκελος | Ἡρίφιλος | Ἄμιλλος |
| Παρμενίσκος | Βούβαλος | Μύσκελος | Μνασίφιλος | Κάμιλλος |
| Ξενίσκος | Ἀστράγαλος | Βύκελος | Πασίφιλος | Πάμιλλος |
| Παρμονίσκος | Μέγαλος | Νύμμελος | Ἀντίφιλος | Δέξιλλος |
| Εὐφρονίσκος | Σαίγαλος | Σθένελος | Πάμφιλος | Χάριλλος |
| Σωφρονίσκος | Δρείγαλος | Ἄπελος | Ἀργόφιλος | Πέριλλος |
| Ἀρνίσκος | Δαίδαλος | Πάπελος | Ἐργόφιλος | Τήριλλος |
| Εὐνίσκος | Ἄρδαλος | Εὐτράπελος | Θεόφιλος | Χαίριλλος |
| Κυνίσκος | Πάρδαλος | Ἄμπελος | Νικόφιλος | Μνάσιλλος |
| Φρυνίσκος | Ζᾶλος | Τίτελος | Δαμόφιλος | Πάσιλλος |
| Βοΐσκος | Πολύζαλος | Τίττελος | Θαμόφιλος | Φράσιλλος |
| Φοΐσκος | Αἰγιαλός | Κύψελος | Δημόφιλος | Ἀρκέσιλλος |
| Πομπίσκος | Κείαλος | Ἀρίδηλος | Ξενόφιλος | Κάτιλλος |
| Ἀνθρωπίσκος | Περίαλος | Ἔκδηλος | Ζηνόφιλος | Κράτιλλος |
| Νεβρίσκος | Φίαλος | Φιλόδηλος | Μηνόφιλος | Ἄλτιλλος |
| Ἀδρίσκος | Ἀμφίαλος | Ζῆλος | Σαραπόφιλος | Χρήστιλλος |

| | | | | |
|---|---|---|---|---|
| Μυΐλλος | Αἴπολος | Κλεόβουλος | Εὔχυλος | Ϝισϝόδαμος |
| Φίλλος | Εὐέμπολος | Νικόβουλος | Βυχχύλος | Βιόδαμος |
| Ἄρχιλλος | Στόλος | Ἀνδρόβουλος | Εὔβωλος | Νικόδαμος |
| Θέολλος | Κρατίστολος | Στρατόβουλος | Μενέκωλος | Φιλόδαμος |
| Λόλλος | Αὐτόστολος | Κριτόβουλος | Πῶλος | Τιμόδαμος |
| Ὕλλος | Ἄπλος | Ἀριστόβουλος | Παναίτωλος | Ξενόδαμος |
| Θράϋλλος | Τευτίαπλος | Αὐτόβουλος | Γάμος | Ἱππόδαμος |
| Πράϋλλος | Πέπλος | Εὔβουλος | Πρόγαμος | Πρόδαμος |
| Σάϋλλος | Ἔνοπλος | Κλεύβουλος | Πέργαμος | Μεσόδαμος |
| Φάϋλλος | Αὖλος | Εὐθύβουλος | Εὔγαμος | Ἰσόδαμος |
| Σάβυλλος | Καῦλος | Πολύβουλος | Δᾶμος | Ϝισόδαμος |
| Σίβυλλος | Ζεύξαυλος | Θρασύβουλος | Σάδαμος | Πρατόδαμος |
| Ἄγυλλος | Παῦλος | Θεόδουλος | Λύγδαμος | Κριτόδαμος |
| Μέγυλλος | Πραῦλος | Χριστόδουλος | Ἀγέδαμος | Παντόδαμος |
| Θέϋλλος | Πρεσβῦλος | Πούλος | Τελέδαμος | Μεγιστόδαμος |
| Βάθυλλος | Κρωβύλος | Οὔρσουλος | Σθενέδαμος | Πιστόδαμος |
| Ἀγάθυλλος | Ἄγυλος | Πάπυλος | Μενέδαμος | Ἀριστόδαμος |
| Δίυλλος | Γογγύλος | Δαΐπυλος | Ἐρέδαμος | Αὐτόδαμος |
| Κύλλος | Ἀργύλος | Θριπύλος | Χαιρέδαμος | Εὔδαμος |
| Πάκυλλος | Γοργύλος | Ἀγχίπυλος | Θαρρέδαμος | Θεύδαμος |
| Σάκυλλος | Ἀδύλος | Ἔμπυλος | Ἐχέδαμος | Κλεύδαμος |
| Μίκυλλος | Ἡδύλος | Πενπύλος | Ἀρχέδαμος | Εὐθύδαμος |
| Νίκυλλος | Μειδύλος | Θωπύλος | Ἀγίδαμος | Πολύδαμος |
| Ὤκυλλος | Κλεῦλος | Δρωπύλος | Κλείδαμος | Θαρρύδαμος |
| Φίλυλλος | Βαθύλος | Μαρύλος | Ἀγηΐδαμος | Εὐρύδαμος |
| Πόλυλλος | Κριθύλος | Ἡρύλος | Πειθίδαμος | Θρασύδαμος |
| Μύλλος | Χριθύλος | Θηρύλος | Ἀλκίδαμος | Σώδαμος |
| Δάμυλλος | Γαιῦλος | Χαιρύλος | Θαλίδαμος | Ἴαμος |
| Τίμυλλος | Φαικύλος | Θρασύλος | Καλλίδαμος | Πρίαμος |
| Μένυλλος | Μικύλος | Ὀνήσυλος | Ἀναξίδαμος | Πλόκαμος |
| Ξένυλλος | Νικύλος | Γαισύλος | Πραξίδαμος | Δαμόκαμος |
| Φάβουλλος | Φρικύλος | Ϝισύλος | Δεξίδαμος | Σκινδάλαμος |
| Πύλλος | Μικκύλος | Ἐπίσυλος | Ἀλεξίδαμος | Θάλαμος |
| Χάρυλλος | Κροκύλος | Νεσσύλος | Ἀρηξίδαμος | Κάλαμος |
| Γέρυλλος | Δερκύλος | Σωσύλος | Ἀρμοξίδαμος | Κύλαμος |
| Βήρυλλος | Δορκύλος | Τύλος | Εὐξίδαμος | Οὔλαμος |
| Εὔρυλλος | Κυνίσκυλος | Κρατύλος | Ζευξίδαμος | Μᾶμος |
| Σύλλος | Ἀνδρόσκυλος | Πρατύλος | Ἐπίδαμος | Κίνναμος |
| Θράσυλλος | Φωκύλος | Νοήτυλος | Χαρίδαμος | Κέραμος |
| Ἴσυλλος | Πολύλος | Μιτύλος | Σίδαμος | Ἐμπέραμος |
| Στράτυλλος | Μύλος | Οἴτυλος | Ἀγασίδαμος | Πύραμος |
| Τρίτυλλος | Δαμύλος | Πιτύλος | Ἰασίδαμος | Σάμος |
| Τέρτυλλος | Σαμύλος | Σιτύλος | Μνασίδαμος | Σάσαμος |
| Ἄστυλλος | Δημύλος | Φιντύλος | Ἀρασίδαμος | Ἀρίσαμος |
| Ἀρίστυλλος | Αἰμύλος | Ῥοτύλος | Ἐρασίδαμος | Θεόσαμος |
| Βράχυλλος | Δριμύλος | Θρεπτύλος | Φρασίδαμος | Εὔσαμος |
| Ἔχυλλος | Σιμύλος | Χαρτύλος | Ἀγησίδαμος | Πόταμος |
| Βάκχυλλος | Τιμύλος | Ἄστυλος | Αἰνησίδαμος | Λάτταμος |
| Ἄρχυλλος | Χαρμύλος | Ἀρίστυλος | Χαρησίδαμος | Καλλίφαμος |
| Ψύλλος | Ἑρμύλος | Σωτύλος | Πεισίδαμος | Ἀγλαόφαμος |
| Ἐκηβόλος | Αἰχμύλος | Στάφυλος | Τεισίδαμος | Θιόφαμος |
| Ἐπήβολος | Κωμύλος | Ἐκέφυλος | Θερσίδαμος | Ἀριστόφαμος |
| Ἀντίβολος | Ῥωμύλος | Μενέφυλος | Λυσίδαμος | Εὔφαμος |
| Ἀνδρόβολος | Φαινύλος | Βρεφύλος | Σωσίδαμος | Πολύφαμος |
| Ὑπέρβολος | Δεινύλος | Ἐχέφυλος | Ἀμφίδαμος | Εὐρύφαμος |
| Δόλος | Σωνύλος | Ἐρίφυλος | Ἀρχίδαμος | Κάδμος |
| Αἴολος | Δεξύλος | Ἀριστόφυλος | Εὐαρχίδαμος | Ὀρίκαδμος |
| Νίκολος | Ὀξύλος | Μειχύλος | Σωΐδαμος | Ἄγεμος |
| Βουκόλος | Βοῦλος | Βακχύλος | Ἔκδαμος | Τληπόλεμος |
| Ἀγχίμολος | Μνησίβουλος | Ἀρχύλος | Κλεόδαμος | Εὐπόλεμος |
| Αὐτόμολος | Ἀντίβουλος | Αἰσχύλος | Νεόδαμος | Μενεπτόλεμος |

| | | | | |
|---|---|---|---|---|
| Κλεοπτόλεμος | Σώσιμος | Εὐρύνομος | Ἀρίσταιχμος | Κοσμιανός |
| Νεοπτόλεμος | Γάτιμος | Κλεώνομος | Κῶμος | Διογενιανός |
| Λαϝοπτόλεμος | Μενέτιμος | Ἐρατώνομος | Φιλόκωμος | Πριμογενιανός |
| Ποδάνεμος | Ἐχέτιμος | Λάδρομος | Ἄμωμος | Εὐγενιανός |
| Μένεμος | Ἀρχέτιμος | Καλλίδρομος | Σύγγνωμος | Ἑλενιανός |
| Μενέδημος | Μναΐτιμος | Ἐπίδρομος | Ῥῶμος | Ἰωβινιανός |
| Ἀλκίδημος | Καλλίτιμος | Νικόδρομος | Σῶμος | Ὑγινιανός |
| Χαρίδημος | Ἐπίτιμος | Φιλόδρομος | Λίβανος | Ποθεινιανός |
| Αἰνεσίδημος | Χαρίτιμος | Εὔδρομος | Σιλβανός | Οἰκοδεσποινιανός |
| Λυσίδημος | Ἐρίτιμος | Κάρτομος | Ὀρβανός | Κωνσταντινιανός |
| Συνέκδημος | Σίτιμος | Ἄρμος | Οὐρβᾶνος | Φαννιανός |
| Νικόδημος | Μνασίτιμος | Ἵππαρμος | Ἠριδανός | Ἐρεννιανός |
| Φιλόδημος | Ἀμφίτιμος | Ἐχέταρμος | Δάρδανος | Ἀμμωνιανός |
| Ἀριστόδημος | Ἔντιμος | Χάρμος | Ὠκεανός | Μυρωνιανός |
| Εὔδημος | Ἐμπεδότιμος | Μενέχαρμος | Ἐπιλάνθανος | Σοφωνιανός |
| Θῆμος | Θεότιμος | Ἐπίχαρμος | Γαβιανός | Τρυφωνιανός |
| Κνῆμος | Λεότιμος | Κλεόχαρμος | Φλαβιανός | Ἀξιανός |
| Εὔφημος | Κλεότιμος | Εὔχαρμος | Φοιβιανός | Ἀλεξιανός |
| Εὔσχημος | Διότιμος | Πολύχαρμος | Λεσβιανός | Ποιανός |
| Εὐτύχημος | Θιότιμος | Χρύσερμος | Πολυβιανός | Ὀλυμπιανός |
| Ἰσθμός | Φιλότιμος | Φίρμος | Πελαγιανός | Ἐπισκοπιανός |
| Αἷμος | Δαμότιμος | Ὅρμος | Κελαδιανός | Τροπιανός |
| Αἴγιμος | Ἑρμότιμος | Πάνορμος | Σπεδιανός | Φιλιππιανός |
| Βάδιμος | Ξενότιμος | Ἔνορμος | Ἐλπιδιανός | Ἱλαριανός |
| Φαίδιμος | Ἀνδρότιμος | Τίτορμος | Νυμφιδιανός | Μαριανός |
| Σίδιμος | Ἱερότιμος | Εὔορμος | Εὐοδιανός | Ἰσμαριανός |
| Κύδιμος | Πρότιμος | Φόρμος | Κλαυδιανός | Παριανός |
| Δάζιμος | Ἀριστότιμος | Τίτυρμος | Κλωδιανός | Ἰανουαριανός |
| Ἄνθιμος | Θεύτιμος | Δάσμος | Ἡρακλειανός | Ἀδριανός |
| Κίμος | Πολύτιμος | Στόχασμος | Φοντειανός | Βαλεριανός |
| Ἄλκιμος | Εὐρύτιμος | Θέσμος | Βουληϊανός | Ἑσπεριανός |
| Ἱππάλκιμος | Ἀστύτιμος | Λόγισμος | Πομπηϊανός | Σωτηριανός |
| Δόκιμος | Σώτιμος | Πορισμός | Σηϊανός | Δεκριανός |
| Προσδόκιμος | Τρόφιμος | Μύρισμος | Ἀγαθιανός | Εὐποριανός |
| Εὐδόκιμος | Εὐτρόφιμος | Κόσμος | Ἀνδραγαθιανός | Καρποφοριανός |
| Ὠφέλιμος | Εὐτύχιμος | Θεόκοσμος | Ἀνθιανός | Τελεσφοριανός |
| Μόνιμος | Σκέψιμος | Εὔκοσμος | Γενθιανός | Εὐφοριανός |
| Παρμόνιμος | Ὄψιμος | Νήδυμος | Φηλικιανός | Κοπριανός |
| Φρόνιμος | Δέκμος | Δίδυμος | Μινικιανός | Ἀσπριανός |
| Μάξιμος | Εὔγραμμος | Ἀγάθυμος | Βερνικιανός | Κυπριανός |
| Πράξιμος | Τέλεμμος | Πρόθυμος | Σωτηρικιανός | Τριανός |
| Αὔξιμος | Σίμμος | Εὔθυμος | Ἀττικιανός | Δεξτριανός |
| Κάρπιμος | Δίομος | Ἀγώνυμος | Μαρκιανός | Ταυριανός |
| Ὄβριμος | Δέκομος | Πεδώνυμος | Λυκιανός | Συριανός |
| Ὕβριμος | Λάνομος | Θεώνυμος | Λουκιανός | Νεστωριανός |
| Πρῖμος | Ἀγένομος | Λεώνυμος | Αὐρηλιανός | Οὐρσιανός |
| Γνώριμος | Δένομος | Κλεώνυμος | Αἰλιανός | Κασσιανός |
| Σῖμος | Δεξίνομος | Ἀγαθώνυμος | Καικιλιανός | Διονυσιανός |
| Ἄσιμος | Ἐπίνομος | Νικώνυμος | Αἰμιλιανός | Ἀρεσκουσιανός |
| Ἐργάσιμος | Πασίνομος | Φιλώνυμος | Ἀτιλιανός | Σπωσιανός |
| Δάσιμος | Ἀντίνομος | Ἰαρώνυμος | Δαψιλιανός | Ὑπατιανός |
| Σιλάσιμος | Ἀμφίνομος | Ἱερώνυμος | Προκλιανός | Γρατιανός |
| Ὀνάσιμος | Ἀρχίνομος | Ἀριστώνυμος | Ἀχιλλιανός | Εὐκρατιανός |
| Γεράσιμος | Θεόνομος | Εὐώνυμος | Τερτυλλιανός | Τατιανός |
| Στάσιμος | Νικόνομος | Ἀμφώνυμος | Σωπολιανός | Νικητιανός |
| Ὀνήσιμος | Οἰκονόμος | Σέπτουμος | Ἰουλιανός | Διοκλητιανός |
| Χρήσιμος | Φιλόνομος | Δρύμος | Πανταμιανός | Ἀτιμητιανός |
| Αἴσιμος | Δαμόνομος | Ἔτυμος | Ὀνησιμιανός | Ἑρμητιανός |
| Ἰναίσιμος | Ἱερόνομος | Κλέαιχμος | Ζωσιμιανός | Ἐπαφροδιτιανός |
| Τείσιμος | Πρόνομος | Μέναιχμος | Τροφιμιανός | Ἐκλεκτιανός |
| Ζώσιμος | Εὔνομος | Μίναιχμος | Ἑρμιανός | Ἰουβεντιανός |

| | | | | |
|---|---|---|---|---|
| Γεντιανός | Κεχαρισμενός | Φίλαινος | Μιθυλῖνος | Ἐπικρατῖνος |
| Ἑλλησποντιανός | Κλύμενος | Δάμαινος | Ἀεσχυλῖνος | Κλεοκρατῖνος |
| Θεοδοτιανός | Θεοκλύμενος | Πρόαινος | Αἰσχυλῖνος | Ἰκετῖνος |
| Ἀσκληπιοδοτιανός | Διαδουμενός | Ἔπαινος | Δαμῖνος | Ἐπέτινος |
| Ὀνομαστιανός | Ποθουμενός | Θρίπαινος | Μαξιμῖνος | Παντῖνος |
| Καλλιστιανός | Ζηλουμενός | Ἵππαινος | Χαρμῖνος | Ταραντῖνος |
| Πιστιανός | Φιλουμενός | Ἄραινος | Φιρμῖνος | Κωνσταντῖνος |
| Αὐγουστιανός | Μενεδημερούμενος | Πάνταινος | Νῖνος | Λεντῖνος |
| Βοιωτιανός | Ζητουμενός | Πλείσταινος | Εὐφρονῖνος | Βαλεντῖνος |
| Ἐρωτιανός | Πλαδωμενός | Ἀρίσταινος | Σατορνῖνος | Λεοντῖνος |
| Παιδερωτιανός | Φιλώμενος | Εὔαινος | Ἀντωνῖνος | Βροντῖνος |
| Νυμφιανός | Ἀγαπωμενός | Πολύαινος | Πραξῖνος | Ἀμυντῖνος |
| Συντροφιανός | Ξένος | Φαῖνος | Ἀλεξῖνος | Ποτῖνος |
| Εὐμορφιανός | Μενέξενος | Σαβῖνος | Θοῖνος | Μαμερτῖνος |
| Εὐτυχιανός | Κλείξενος | Ἰουβῖνος | Κλεόθοινος | Πορτῖνος |
| Νικανός | Ἀγηΐξενος | Λογγῖνος | Εὔθοινος | Καλλιστῖνος |
| Ἀφρικανός | Σελίξενος | Ῥηγῖνος | Κοῖνος | Ἀριστῖνος |
| Σικανός | Καλλίξενος | Αἴγινος | Φιλόποινος | Φαυστῖνος |
| Εὔσκανος | Ἐπίξενος | Ἐργῖνος | Ὀλυμπῖνος | Ἰουστῖνος |
| Φρύσκανος | Χαρίξενος | Ὑγῖνος | Χαροπῖνος | Ταρουτῖνος |
| Σιλανός | Περίξενος | Κελαδῖνος | Καλλιππῖνος | Φωτῖνος |
| Ἡρακλανός | Πασίξενος | Σεκουνδῖνος | Ἀγριππῖνος | Θυϊνός |
| Κιλλανός | Λυσίξενος | Ῥόδινος | Κρισπῖνος | Ῥουφῖνος |
| Ποτιωλανός | Θεόξενος | Δεῖνος | Ἀνθρώπινος | Τάχινος |
| Δεκόμανος | Κλεόξενος | Ποθεινός | Ἔαρινος | Ἐχῖνος |
| Γερμανός | Ἀγαθόξενος | Κλεῖνος | Ἱλαρῖνος | Ἀρχῖνος |
| Ῥωμανός | Νικόξενος | Εὔκλεινος | Μαρῖνος | Ὄψινος |
| Κάρανος | Φιλόξενος | Εὔξεινος | Ἱππαρῖνος | Λώϊνος |
| Ἔρανος | Δαμόξενος | Πολύξεινος | Χαρῖνος | Πωινος |
| Κοίρανος | Τιμόξενος | Εὔσεινος | Παγχαρῖνος | Θεότεκνος |
| Ἀγύρανος | Ἁρμόξενος | Βριζῖνος | Φιλοχαρῖνος | Κύκνος |
| Σάνος | Κλεινόξενος | Ἀγαθῖνος | Χαβρῖνος | Σέμνος |
| Πισανός | Πρόξενος | Ἄνθινος | Σισύμβρινος | Λῆμνος |
| Πλάτανος | Πλειστόξενος | Παρθῖνος | Πελεγρῖνος | Μέριμνος |
| Νεοπολιτανός | Πιστόξενος | Σκυθῖνος | Νιγρῖνος | Ἀμέριμνος |
| Μοντανός | Ἀριστόξενος | Τυρρακῖνος | Ἀνδρῖνος | Ὕμνος |
| Μουντανός | Εὔξενος | Ὀρσικῖνος | Ἀστερῖνος | Σκύμνος |
| Βάττανος | Θεύξενος | Ἀλκῖνος | Ἀριστερῖνος | Ἄννος |
| Φᾶνος | Πολύξενος | Καρκῖνος | Σεβηρῖνος | Τύραννος |
| Στέφανος | Θρασύξενος | Κερκῖνος | Μακρῖνος | Ἰώαννος |
| Φιλοστέφανος | Σώξενος | Γλαυκῖνος | Πυρρῖνος | Φάβεννος |
| Μάχανος | Φαηνός | Λυκῖνος | Ταυρῖνος | Ἄργεννος |
| Ἐπιτύγχανος | Δαμασκηνός | Γλυκῖνος | Κυρῖνος | Ξέννος |
| Ἄγνος | Λῆνος | Ἄλινος | Μύρινος | Δόσσεννος |
| Μάγνος | Γαληνός | Θάλινος | Πυρῖνος | Σίννος |
| Πάρθενος | Σιληνός | Φαλῖνος | Σατυρῖνος | Νόννος |
| Καλλιπάρθενος | Κλῆνος | Κεφαλῖνος | Ἰεσωρῖνος | Σάνοννος |
| Ἔλενος | Μῆνος | Χαλῖνος | Βικτωρῖνος | Μύννος |
| Ἀλεξαμενός | Ἰσμηνός | Πετροσέλινος | Οὐικτωρῖνος | Γόνος |
| Τεισαμενός | Εὔμηνος | Εὐτέλινος | Γελασῖνος | Τηλέγονος |
| Φιλήμενος | Λυΐξηνος | Φέλινος | Πασῖνος | Ἀρχέγονος |
| Πεφιλημενός | Παρθενοπηνός | Χειλῖνος | Ἐρασῖνος | Ἐπίγονος |
| Εὐλίμενος | Ὕπηνος | Φιλῖνος | Τελεσῖνος | Ἠρίγονος |
| Στραμμενός | Τυρρηνός | Ἀμφιλῖνος | Φησῖνος | Ἀντίγονος |
| Σωζομενός | Ἀπύρηνος | Θάλλινος | Πανδοσῖνος | Θεόγονος |
| Ἀλεξομενός | Ἐδασηνός | Καλλῖνος | Ἄσσινος | Χρυσόγονος |
| Μελπομενός | Τυρσηνός | Μαρκελλῖνος | Ἐλευσῖνος | Πολύγονος |
| Ἄρμενος | Εὔηνος | Κατυλλῖνος | Λυσῖνος | Διάκονος |
| Δαμάρμενος | Στράβαινος | Φυλλῖνος | Σωσῖνος | Εὐδιάκονος |
| Ὄρμενος | Εὔραινος | Παυλῖνος | Εὐπατινός | Παράμονος |
| Ἄσμενος | Ἐλάινος | Βομβυλῖνος | Κρατῖνος | Πάρμονος |

| | | | | |
|---|---|---|---|---|
| Πόνος | Ὄλαπος | Λεύκιππος | Κτήσιππος | Λύκαρος |
| Ἄπονος | Πάπος | Θάλιππος | Πείσιππος | Φάλαρος |
| Λυσίπονος | Θαλλίεπος | Κάλιππος | Τείσιππος | Ἴλαρος |
| Φιλότονος | Κίπος | Ἐθέλιππος | Γίσιππος | Κλᾶρος |
| Δαΐφονος | Ἔγκολπος | Φίλιππος | Πόσιππος | Σαίκλαρος |
| Δηΐφονος | Μόλπος | Εὔκλιππος | Παύσιππος | Φέσκλαρος |
| Τέρπνος | Εὔμολπος | Κάλλιππος | Λύσιππος | Φύλλαρος |
| Λιβυρνός | Κάμπος | Γύλιππος | Χρύσιππος | Χείμαρος |
| Κύρνος | Λάμπος | Δάμιππος | Γνώσιππος | Χίμαρος |
| Σίσυρνος | Πυρίλαμπος | Σάμιππος | Σώσιππος | Τάμμαρος |
| Κέραυνος | Σίπομπος | Νόμιππος | Κράτιππος | Ὄμαρος |
| Ἀκίνδυνος | Θεόπομπος | Ἕρμιππος | Στράτιππος | Ἴσμαρος |
| Πάρευνος | Διόπομπος | Ἄνιππος | Ἀρέτιππος | Νάρος |
| Βιθυνός | Εὔπομπος | Ἀθάνιππος | Ἄντιππος | Κίναρος |
| Εὔθυνος | Θεύπομπος | Μελάνιππος | Πάντιππος | Σίναρος |
| Χάμυνος | Ὄλυμπος | Κυάνιππος | Ἀρίστιππος | Πάρος |
| Κομμοῦνος | Δίοπος | Φαένιππος | Εὔιππος | Λίπαρος |
| Φρῦνος | Καλλίοπος | Σθένιππος | Ἀμεύιππος | Πάρπαρος |
| Χαρμόσυνος | Ἀρνίοπος | Μένιππος | Ἔχιππος | Κύπαρος |
| Εὐφρόσυνος | Εὐρίοπος | Ξένιππος | Ἄρχιππος | Ἄσαρος |
| Δάφνος | Δαμόκοπος | Κλήνιππος | Λάρχιππος | Τίταρος |
| Εὔαιφνος | Ἐπίσκοπος | Ξήνιππος | Εὐάρχιππος | Φάρος |
| Ἡδωνός | Χάροπος | Αἴνιππος | Τύχιππος | Κάρχαρος |
| Δαζίωνος | Ἀέροπος | Φαίνιππος | Ἄψιππος | Θοξούχαρος |
| Ἄμαξος | Αἴροπος | Δείνιππος | Ζώιππος | Ἄβρος |
| Χρυσάμαξος | Θεόπροπος | Κλείνιππος | Κάρπος | Σίναβρος |
| Ἄλεξος | Ἄρροπος | Ἀμείνιππος | Πάγκαρπος | Ἔβρος |
| Ἐπίτεξος | Τρόπος | Κρίνιππος | Εὔκαρπος | Νέβρος |
| Φρίξος | Λάτροπος | Γώνιππος | Πολύκαρπος | Σκόμβρος |
| Δόξξος | Εὔτροπος | Ἀγώνιππος | Πολύτερπος | Μόλοβρος |
| Παράδοξος | Πολύτροπος | Ἀνάξιππος | Ἄδορπος | Μελέαγρος |
| Ἐπίδοξος | Ἵππος | Δέξιππος | Σκόρπος | Βάλαγρος |
| Ἔνδοξος | Δάιππος | Ἀλέξιππος | Κρίσπος | Φίλαγρος |
| Πρόδοξος | Νικάιππος | Ἀρήξιππος | Ἄλυπος | Τάναγρος |
| Πρόσδοξος | Λάιππος | Σοΐξιππος | Λοῦπος | Πύραγρος |
| Εὔδοξος | Δαμάιππος | Ζεύξιππος | Λάττυπος | Ἄνταγρος |
| Φόξος | Δράιππος | Διώξιππος | Λύκωπος | Εὔαγρος |
| Βοάθοος | Βίππος | Χάριππος | Κάνωπος | Σύαγρος |
| Ἀλκίθοος | Ἄγιππος | Νικάνδριππος | Μελάνωπος | Νίγρος |
| Πρόθοος | Μέγιππος | Θήριππος | Ἰνωπός | Κέδρος |
| Κατάκοος | Ἔργιππος | Σήριππος | Ἀστερωπός | Φαίδρος |
| Ἀρχένοος | Γόργιππος | Χαίριππος | Ἄνθρωπος | Λάανδρος |
| Ἰσχένοος | Βείδιππος | Θάρριππος | Ἀκάνθρωπος | Σάανδρος |
| Ἀλκίνοος | Ποσείδιππος | Ἀγάσιππος | Φιλάνθρωπος | Θέανδρος |
| Τιναξίνοος | Φείδιππος | Νικάσιππος | Ἄσωπος | Λέανδρος |
| Πραξίνοος | Ῥόδιππος | Ἐλάσιππος | Αἴσωπος | Κλέανδρος |
| Θελξίνοος | Κέρδιππος | Δαμάσιππος | Δύσωπος | Νέανδρος |
| Ἀγησίνοος | Κύδιππος | Μνάσιππος | Μέτωπος | Ἀγήανδρος |
| Πεισίνοος | Τελέιππος | Ὀνάσιππος | Βάρβαρος | Πείθανδρος |
| Ἀντίνοος | Κλέιππος | Πάσιππος | Λόγγαρος | Λαΐανδρος |
| Θιόνοος | Αἰρήιππος | Ἐράσιππος | Πάνδαρος | Πείανδρος |
| Δαμόνοος | Κρατήιππος | Θράσιππος | Μίνδαρος | Περίανδρος |
| Πρόνοος | Ἀγάθιππος | Στάσιππος | Θέαρος | Νίκανδρος |
| Ἀριστόνοος | Ἄνθιππος | Ἀλκέσιππος | Κάνθαρος | Ἄλκανδρος |
| Αὐτόνοος | Ξάνθιππος | Τελέσιππος | Σπίνθαρος | Λάνδρος |
| Εὔνοος | Εὔθιππος | Ἀγήσιππος | Βύνθαρος | Κάλανδρος |
| Εὐθύνοος | Βΐιππος | Κλεήσιππος | Κάρος | Ἔλανδρος |
| Σώνοος | Νίκιππος | Μελήσιππος | Ἴκαρος | Ὀφέλανδρος |
| Ἑρμάξοος | Ἄλκιππος | Κλήσιππος | Μίκαρος | Φίλανδρος |
| Σόος | Δόρκιππος | Ἀρήσιππος | Νίκαρος | Δάμανδρος |
| Ἄσκλαπος | Γλαύκιππος | Κρατήσιππος | Λεύκαρος | Κάμανδρος |

| | | | | |
|---|---|---|---|---|
| Σκάμανδρος | Καλήμερος | Σπόρος | Πῦρος | Ἀθηνόδωρος |
| Σάμανδρος | Εὐήμερος | Γλυκύσπορος | Διάπυρος | Μηνόδωρος |
| Θέμανδρος | Ἵμερος | Εὔπορος | Στίλπυρος | Καρπόδωρος |
| Ἀρχέμανδρος | Πρίμερος | Τόρος | Τόπυρος | Ἀσωπόδωρος |
| Ποίμανδρος | Ἕσπερος | Ἐλπιδηφόρος | Ζώπυρος | Ἡρόδωρος |
| Τίμανδρος | Κράτερος | Νικηφόρος | Σύρος | Ματρόδωρος |
| Τέμμανδρος | Ἀμετερός | Στεφανηφόρος | Φόσυρος | Μητρόδωρος |
| Ὀνόμανδρος | Ἡμέτερος | Ὀνασιφόρος | Τύρος | Καφισόδωρος |
| Χάρμανδρος | Δεύτερος | Ὀνησιφόρος | Σάτυρος | Κηφισόδωρος |
| Θαύμανδρος | Ναύερος | Χρυσιφόρος | Τίτυρος | Διονυσόδωρος |
| Μένανδρος | Τρύφερος | Σύμφορος | Βότυρος | Ἑκατόδωρος |
| Ξένανδρος | Ἧρος | Κερδοφόρος | Ἱππότυρος | Ἀκεστόδωρος |
| Φαίνανδρος | Σεβῆρος | Καρποφόρος | Σίττυρος | Ἀριστόδωρος |
| Ἀμύνανδρος | Πολύγηρος | Δωροφόρος | Γλάφυρος | Νυμφόδωρος |
| Ἀνάξανδρος | Πάνθηρος | Χριστοφόρος | Ζέφυρος | Εὔδωρος |
| Πράξανδρος | Φιλόθηρος | Ἀνθεσφόρος | Σχῦρος | Θεύδωρος |
| Δέξανδρος | Εὔθηρος | Τελεσφόρος | Ἰσχυρός | Κλεύδωρος |
| Ἀλέξανδρος | Κλεύθηρος | Φωσφόρος | Πούλχρος | Κύδωρος |
| Πρόανδρος | Κύθηρος | Εὔφορος | Κάλλαισχρος | Πολύδωρος |
| Ἔπανδρος | Κλῆρος | Δορυφόρος | Ὧρος | Θέωρος |
| Ἄσανδρος | Ὅμηρος | Χόρος | Γῶρος | Ἀντίωρος |
| Ὀνάσανδρος | Σώτηρος | Στασίχορος | Δῶρος | Χλῶρος |
| Μενέσανδρος | Σεουῆρος | Στησίχορος | Θέδωρος | Κύρβασος |
| Ἀρέσανδρος | Καλόκαιρος | Φιλόχορος | Κλέδωρος | Γόργασος |
| Ἀγήσανδρος | Εὔκαιρος | Εὔχορος | Ποσείδωρος | Τίθασος |
| Ἡγήσανδρος | Ἑταῖρος | Κάπρος | Ἀρταμίδωρος | Ἴασος |
| Ἑρμήσανδρος | Φιλέταιρος | Πύρρος | Ἀρτεμίδωρος | Θίασος |
| Αἰνήσανδρος | Σώταιρος | Σωσίπατρος | Ἀναξίδωρος | Λάσος |
| Πείσανδρος | Σφαῖρος | Ἀντίπατρος | Ἐπίδωρος | Πλάσος |
| Τείσανδρος | Ὄνειρος | Κλεόπατρος | Ἡσίδωρος | Δάμασος |
| Ὀνίσανδρος | Ἤπειρος | Νεόπατρος | Ἰσίδωρος | Τίμασος |
| Θέρσανδρος | Πάμπειρος | Κλεύπατρος | Ἀντίδωρος | Ὄνασος |
| Κάσσανδρος | Κύπειρος | Σώπατρος | Θεόδωρος | Ἵππασος |
| Λύσανδρος | Εὔχειρος | Πέτρος | Κλεόδωρος | Χοίρασος |
| Σώσανδρος | Μίρος | Δέξτρος | Ἡρακλεόδωρος | Τράσος |
| Κλείτανδρος | Ἐρύκοιρος | Γάστρος | Πυθόδωρος | Πάσχασος |
| Ἄντανδρος | Χοῖρος | Φιλίαστρος | Διόδωρος | Ἄρκεσος |
| Ἀρίστανδρος | Ἄκρος | Σίληστρος | Ἡρακλειόδωρος | Τέλεσος |
| Εὔανδρος | Βάλακρος | Ἴστρος | Ἀλφειόδωρος | Ἔφεσος |
| Λύανδρος | Φάλακρος | Μήζωτρος | Ἁλιόδωρος | Πρόμνησος |
| Πόλυανδρος | Εὔακρος | Γάλαυρος | Ἡλιόδωρος | Ὄνησος |
| Μάχανδρος | Σμίκρος | Μαῦρος | Ἀσκλαπιόδωρος | Ῥῆσος |
| Ἄρχανδρος | Παΐλοκρος | Σίναυρος | Σαραπιόδωρος | Φῆσος |
| Ἴσχανδρος | Τεῦκρος | Ταῦρος | Ἀσκληπιόδωρος | Κάβαισος |
| Τύχανδρος | Ὄρος | Ἀρθέταυρος | Ὀλυμπιόδωρος | Γάλαισος |
| Σώανδρος | Νικάγορος | Βύρος | Διονυσιόδωρος | Κάλαισος |
| Κύλινδρος | Λάγορος | Ἄργυρος | Ἑστιόδωρος | Βλαῖσος |
| Εὐβάβερος | Τιμάγορος | Φιλάργυρος | Ἰστιόδωρος | Παῖσος |
| Ἐλεύθερος | Ἑρμάγορος | Ἰσάργυρος | Πτωΐόδωρος | Ἀγόραισος |
| Ἱερός | Κλενάγορος | Εὖρος | Νικόδωρος | Ὑάλισος |
| Καλλίερος | Προάγορος | Σαβάθυρος | Νειλόδωρος | Κύλισος |
| Δαμίερος | Πράγορος | Κῦρος | Φιλόδωρος | Νῖσος |
| Κοσμίερος | Μνασάγορος | Φιλόκυρος | Ἀπελλόδωρος | Κοῖσος |
| Πίερος | Ἀντάγορος | Φίλυρος | Ἀπολλόδωρος | Χάρισος |
| Πληστίερος | Ἀριστάγορος | Φίλλυρος | Τιμόδωρος | Κρῖσος |
| Πλειστίερος | Εὐάγορος | Μύρος | Ἑρμόδωρος | Κύτισος |
| Γλυκερός | Ἐπίκορος | Θάμυρος | Στρυμόδωρος | Καφισός |
| Εὐβάμερος | Διόσκορος | Λάμυρος | Ἀθανόδωρος | Ἄλγαλσος |
| Ἀγαθάμερος | Πόρος | Ἐπίκουρος | Παιανόδωρος | Κάλσος |
| Εὐάμερος | Ἔμπορος | Σέλουρος | Ἀδρανόδωρος | Κέλσος |
| Ἀγαθήμερος | Κλεέμπορος | Ματοῦρος | Φανόδωρος | Νόσος |

| | | | | |
|---|---|---|---|---|
| Κόνοσος | Ἀχενατος | Λυσίστρατος | Ξεναίνετος | Θεοδώρητος |
| Κάποσος | Μίνατος | Σωσίστρατος | Ἐξαίνετος | Ἀχώρητος |
| Δρόσος | Λεόννατος | Ἀμφίστρατος | Ἐπαίνετος | Ἀκράτητος |
| Θάρσος | Ὄνατος | Ἀρχίστρατος | Τερπαίνετος | Θεαίτητος |
| Τάρσος | Φορτουνᾶτος | Φειδόστρατος | Εὐφραίνετος | Κτῆτος |
| Θύρσος | Δωνᾶτος | Κλεόστρατος | Πανταίνετος | Ἐπίκτητος |
| Ἀγάθυρσος | Ὕπατος | Νεόστρατος | Ἀρισταίνετος | Εὐδίαιτος |
| Μεγάθυρσος | Ἄρατος | Πεδιόστρατος | Εὐαίνετος | Λάϊτος |
| Βάσσος | Κλεάρατος | Νικόστρατος | Πολυαίνετος | Λαῖτος |
| Σαλασσός | Πυθάρατος | Φιλόστρατος | Ἀμφαίνετος | Βίτος |
| Σουκκεσσός | Νικάρατος | Δαμόστρατος | Σοφαίνετος | Ἑρμαφρόδιτος |
| Ἴσσος | Δαμάρατος | Δημόστρατος | Σύνετος | Ἐπαφρόδιτος |
| Ναϊσσός | Τιμάρατος | Αἰμόστρατος | Ἰαπετός | Καλλίγειτος |
| Πραυγισσός | Ἐπάρατος | Τιμόστρατος | Πεδάρετος | Ἀριστόγειτος |
| Κισσός | Πασάρατος | Φανόστρατος | Κλεάρετος | Λειτός |
| Νάρκισσος | Πολυάρατος | Μενόστρατος | Νεάρετος | Κλεῖτος |
| Πυκισσός | Γρᾶτος | Ξενόστρατος | Σαλιάρετος | Ἡράκλειτος |
| Λίσσος | Κουαδρᾶτος | Ἱππόστρατος | Νικάρετος | Φιλόκλειτος |
| Μέλισσος | Κοδρᾶτος | Εὔστρατος | Δαμάρετος | Εὔκλειτος |
| Ἀμισσός | Ἔρατος | Κλεύστρατος | Δημάρετος | Πολύκλειτος |
| Νεοσσός | Νεμέρατος | Πολύστρατος | Τιμάρετος | Φαλάρειτος |
| Μολοσσός | Ἑσπερᾶτος | Σώστρατος | Πανάρετος | Κίτος |
| Δαμοσσός | Κλεήρατος | Πλευρᾶτος | Ξενάρετος | Πλάκιτος |
| Δροσσος | Ἀκήρατος | Πρεύρατος | Αὐτάρετος | Κάλλιτος |
| Δορυσσός | Νικήρατος | Ἀκρότατος | Εὐάρετος | Ἀμάνιτος |
| Γαῦσος | Φιλήρατος | Ἐπίστατος | Ἀμομφάρετος | Πατανιτος |
| Τραῦσος | Ἐπήρατος | Ὀνομόστατος | Τυχάρετος | Φίλοιτος |
| Λῦσος | Πολυήρατος | Εὔστατος | Ξεναίρετος | Προῖτος |
| Μυσός | Ἄκρατος | Μούτατος | Ἄγητος | Πίτος |
| Γέννσος | Εὔκρατος | Παλαίφατος | Δαμάγητος | Πεδάριτος |
| Μοῦσος | Ἀγόρατος | Κλεόφατος | Τιμάγητος | Κλεάριτος |
| Πάμμουσος | Πρᾶτος | Ἀετός | Εὐάγητος | Εὐχάριτος |
| Φιλόμουσος | Τέτρατος | Κλέβετος | Τρύγητος | Κρίτος |
| Χρῦσος | Λάστρατος | Κόβετος | Ἀνίκητος | Πεδάκριτος |
| Ἐλίχρυσος | Σάστρατος | Γέτος | Μέλητος | Διάκριτος |
| Ἰσόχρυσος | Ἀγέστρατος | Βέγετος | Φίλητος | Λάκριτος |
| Ἀλογίωσος | Πεδέστρατος | Δέτος | Εὐφίλητος | Ἀσύγκριτος |
| Στουδιῶσος | Κλέστρατος | Θεύδετος | Ἀνάκλητος | Βουλήκριτος |
| Μέλλωσος | Μενέστρατος | Εὔϝετος | Ἡράκλητος | Καλλίκριτος |
| Σῶσος | Αἰνέστρατος | Ἄθετος | Ἀνέγκλητος | Ὀνασίκριτος |
| Φρουκτῶσος | Ἐχέστρατος | Αἰετός | Σύγκλητος | Ἀντίκριτος |
| Ἄτος | Ἀρχέστρατος | Ἄλκετος | Εὔκλητος | Ἀμφίκριτος |
| Πρίβατος | Δαΐστρατος | Ἄρκετος | Ἀβόλητος | Ἔκκριτος |
| Εὔβατος | Λαΐστρατος | Δέρκετος | Ἄδμητος | Ἰμπεδόκριτος |
| Εὐρύβατος | Δαμαΐστρατος | Πεύκετος | Ἀμίμητος | Μηδόκριτος |
| Ξενάγατος | Μναΐστρατος | Βένετος | Ἀτίμητος | Θεόκριτος |
| Κραύγατος | Ἀγηΐστρατος | Μένετος | Κλεόμητος | Κλεόκριτος |
| Δάτος | Ἀλκίστρατος | Ξένετος | Ἀμώμητος | Πυθόκριτος |
| Δαυδᾶτος | Καλίστρατος | Κλήνετος | Ἐπίγνητος | Θιόκριτος |
| Κλόϝατος | Καλλίστρατος | Αἴνετος | Χαρίγνητος | Τηλόκριτος |
| Γαΐζατος | Δεξίστρατος | Θεαίνετος | Θεόγνητος | Δαμόκριτος |
| Ἀμπλιᾶτος | Ἐπίστρατος | Κλεαίνετος | Διόγνητος | Ἀνθεμόκριτος |
| Ἀπτοίατος | Ἀρίστρατος | Εὐϝαίνετος | Καλογένητος | Δημόκριτος |
| Ἀνίκατος | Δαμασίστρατος | Πυθαίνετος | Αἴνητος | Τιμόκριτος |
| Ἐπίκατος | Μνασίστρατος | Διαίνετος | Ἀφθόνητος | Ἑρμόκριτος |
| Ἀσάλατος | Ἐρασίστρατος | Ἀλκαίνετος | Αὔξητος | Ξενόκριτος |
| Ἔλατος | Ἀγησίστρατος | Φιλαίνετος | Νόητος | Ἀμεινόκριτος |
| Μίλατος | Ἡγησίστρατος | Δαμαίνετος | Ἀγαπητός | Ἀνδρόκριτος |
| Ἀδάματος | Μνησίστρατος | Πολεμαίνετος | Ἀλύπητος | Πρόκριτος |
| Ἄδματος | Πεισίστρατος | Δημαίνετος | Ῥήτος | Ἀριστόκριτος |
| Αὐτόματος | Ναυσίστρατος | Τιμαίνετος | Εὔρητος | Εὔκριτος |

| | | | | |
|---|---|---|---|---|
| Κλεύκριτος | Σώφαντος | Ἐπίχαρτος | Ἄνοιστος | Πρόμουτος |
| Πολύκριτος | Κέντος | Δαμόχαρτος | Πίστος | Αἴπυτος |
| Θρασύκριτος | Κίντος | Λίβερτος | Ἔλπιστος | Ἤρυτος |
| Τρίτος | Κόϊντος | Σκίρτος | Εὐέλπιστος | Εὔρυτος |
| Πόσσιτος | Ἄσιντος | Ἔορτος | Ἀξιόπιστος | Καλλίφυτος |
| Τίτος | Κούϊντος | Χαρίμορτος | Ἄριστος | Νεόφυτος |
| Ἴφιτος | Πόντος | Κύνορτος | Κλεάριστος | Αἴσχυτος |
| Γίφιτος | Σέξτος | Σφόρτος | Νικάριστος | Βῶτος |
| Εὐκατάλλακτος | Κλεύβοτος | Σίβυρτος | Φιλάριστος | Βίωτος |
| Θεοφύλακτος | Ἀρτεμίδοτος | Κύρτος | Δαμάριστος | Βοιωτός |
| Εὔπρακτος | Εὐμενίδοτος | Ἄψυρτος | Τιμάριστος | Λωτός |
| Ἀγγίφρακτος | Χαρίδοτος | Ἄστος | Ἀνάριστος | Ζηλωτός |
| Εὔτακτος | Θεόδοτος | Ἄκαστος | Αὐτάριστος | Καλλίγνωτος |
| Παρεύτακτος | Πυθόδοτος | Ἄλκαστος | Εὐάριστος | Ἀρίγνωτος |
| Σίδεκτος | Διόδοτος | Πολύκαστος | Εὐχάριστος | Εὔγνωτος |
| Πρόσδεκτος | Θιόδοτος | Βλάστος | Ἔριστος | Πολύγνωτος |
| Ἔκλεκτος | Ἀσκληπιόδοτος | Δάμαστος | Φέριστος | Πρῶτος |
| Ἄστεκτος | Ἀπολλόδοτος | Ἀδάμαστος | Ἀνήριστος | Θεσπρωτός |
| Ἄθικτος | Τιμόδοτος | Δέμαστος | Εὐπόριστος | Ἄτωτος |
| Αὔκτος | Ζηνόδοτος | Ὀνόμαστος | Ἀχώριστος | Φῶτος |
| Εὔκτος | Ἀθηνόδοτος | Θαύμαστος | Κράτιστος | Ψαῦος |
| Ἔπευκτος | Μηνόδοτος | Ὀνύμαστος | Θεόκτιστος | Τίλδυος |
| Πολύευκτος | Ἀμμωνόδοτος | Ἀείμναστος | Ἄρμοστος | Βάθυος |
| Ἄσφαλτος | Ἡρόδοτος | Ἀρίμναστος | Εὐάρμοστος | Εὐνσιβίνος |
| Ὄλτος | Κηφισόδοτος | Ἐρίμναστος | Θεόνοστος | Λῦος |
| Θέαντος | Διονυσόδοτος | Ἡρίμναστος | Εὔνοστος | Φώτυος |
| Ἀβίαντος | Θευόδοτος | Ἀμφίμναστος | Θεύνοστος | Κόρδαφος |
| Ἀμίαντος | Νυμφόδοτος | Θεόμναστος | Ἀπόλαυστος | Κόλαφος |
| Ἀβάσκαντος | Εὔδοτος | Κλεόμναστος | Φαῦστος | Ἔπαφος |
| Ἀπήμαντος | Θεύδοτος | Εὔμναστος | Ἀμέθυστος | Κατάγραφος |
| Ἀδείμαντος | Διόζοτος | Θεύμναστος | Ξύστος | Σύγγραφος |
| Ὀνόμαντος | Βίοτος | Κλεύμναστος | Ἰοῦστος | Τήλεφος |
| Ἀθαύμαντος | Εὐβίοτος | Πολύμναστος | Βενοῦστος | Εὔψηφος |
| Ἐνύμαντος | Εὐρυβίοτος | Εὔπαστος | Γνωστός | Ἄρειφος |
| Ἀμάραντος | Ἀδέσποτος | Ἄδραστος | Ἄττος | Σκάριφος |
| Ἄκραντος | Φιλοδέσποτος | Ἔραστος | Βάττος | Ἔριφος |
| Εὔφραντος | Φερέμβροτος | Ἐπέραστος | Βλάττος | Δελφός |
| Βέρσαντος | Ἐχέμβροτος | Φράστος | Ὑμηττός | Φιλάδελφος |
| Εὔαντος | Ἀρχέμβροτος | Θεόφραστος | Σάιττος | Σκόμφος |
| Φάντος | Καλλίμβροτος | Εὔφραστος | Βίττος | Νύμφος |
| Τέφαντος | Κλεόμβροτος | Θεύφραστος | Βόττος | Λόφος |
| Δαΐφαντος | Φιλόμβροτος | Πολύφραστος | Γρόττος | Τόλοφος |
| Ἀρίφαντος | Φιλάνβροτος | Ἄσβεστος | Ἐμαυτός | Σύντροφος |
| Ὀρσίφαντος | Κρότος | Ἄγεστος | Ἐμίναυτος | Τελέστροφος |
| Δαιτίφαντος | Σώσοτος | Ἐξάκεστος | Εὐπαίδευτος | Ἐπίστροφος |
| Ἔκφαντος | Ἄτοτος | Ἐξήκεστος | Τεῦτος | Ἱππόστροφος |
| Θεόφαντος | Γράπτος | Ὄνεστος | Ὤκυτος | Εὔστροφος |
| Κλεόφαντος | Ἄγραπτος | Ἄρεστος | Θέλυτος | Σόφος |
| Διόφαντος | Εὔαπτος | Εὐάρεστος | Ἐπίλυτος | Χειρίσοφος |
| Δαμόφαντος | Λέπτος | Σέστος | Ἀμφίλυτος | Πάνσοφος |
| Δημόφαντος | Θρέπτος | Θεόμνηστος | Κλύτος | Καλλίμορφος |
| Τιμόφαντος | Ἄγναμπτος | Χρῆστος | Ἀγακλυτός | Εὔμορφος |
| Ἑρμόφαντος | Ἄμεμπτος | Θεόχρηστος | Περίκλυτος | Θηλύμορφος |
| Ξενόφαντος | Ὕποπτος | Εὔχρηστος | Θεόλυτος | Γρόσφος |
| Μηνόφαντος | Αἴγυπτος | Φῆστος | Δαμόλυτος | Ῥοῦφος |
| Ξεινόφαντος | Γλύπτος | Ἄφαιστος | Ξενόλυτος | Σίσυφος |
| Πρόφαντος | Ἄρτος | Ἤδιστος | Ἱππόλυτος | Κόσσυφος |
| Ἀριστόφαντος | Ἀτέκμαρτος | Φίλιστος | Εὔλυτος | Γᾶχος |
| Ἔσφαντος | Τέταρτος | Εὐφίλιστος | Ὄρνυτος | Δίαχος |
| Εὔφαντος | Χάρτος | Κάλλιστος | Πλοῦτος | Λάμαχος |
| Πολύφαντος | Λάχαρτος | Θέμιστος | Εὔπλουτος | Μνάμαχος |

| | | | | |
|---|---|---|---|---|
| Ἀγέμαχος | Ὀρόμαχος | Πύριχος | Φαστύοχος | Κλείταρχος |
| Ἡγέμαχος | Πρόμαχος | Ὀνάτιχος | Ἄρχος | Πολίταρχος |
| Ἀλκέμαχος | Πυρόμαχος | Ψαμμήτιχος | Λάαρχος | Ἄνταρχος |
| Τηλέμαχος | Πρατόμαχος | Πάντιχος | Λέαρχος | Πλήσταρχος |
| Μενέμαχος | Κλειτόμαχος | Λεόντιχος | Τελέαρχος | Πλείσταρχος |
| Φαινέμαχος | Ἀριστόμαχος | Βότιχος | Κλέαρχος | Ἀρίσταρχος |
| Χαιρέμαχος | Πρωτόμαχος | Μύρτιχος | Νέαρχος | Πλούταρχος |
| Ἀγχέμαχος | Ἰσχόμαχος | Στίχος | Ἐτέαρχος | Πρώταρχος |
| Ἀρχέμαχος | Ναύμαχος | Δαμάστιχος | Φίσϝαρχος | Ναύαρχος |
| Ἰσχέμαχος | Εὔμαχος | Δομέστιχος | Εὔϝαρχος | Εὔαρχος |
| Ἀγήμαχος | Κλεύμαχος | Ἀρίστιχος | Ἀγάθαρχος | Πολύαρχος |
| Δαΐμαχος | Εὐθύμαχος | Ζώτιχος | Πείθαρχος | Ζώαρχος |
| Παλαίμαχος | Ὀξύμαχος | Ὀλώϊχος | Πύθαρχος | Μόσχος |
| Μναΐμαχος | Δορύμαχος | Βάκχος | Δικαίαρχος | Πράϋχος |
| Κυδίμαχος | Θαρρύμαχος | Ἰόβακχος | Λαΐαρχος | Πανταὔχος |
| Κλείμαχος | Εὐρύμαχος | Ἴακχος | Πεδίαρχος | Εὔχος |
| Ἀλκίμαχος | Θρασύμαχος | Βρόκχος | Ἁλίαρχος | Πάννυχος |
| Τηλίμαχος | Λεώμαχος | Μάλχος | Θαλίαρχος | Ἔννυχος |
| Καλλίμαχος | Ἀγλώμαχος | Κόλχος | Σαλίαρχος | Δαδοῦχος |
| Δεξίμαχος | Κάναχος | Δάϊοχος | Φιλίαρχος | Τιμοῦχος |
| Ἀλεξίμαχος | Θίβραχος | Ἄνίοχος | Πολίαρχος | Ἀριστοῦχος |
| Ῥηξίμαχος | Βάτραχος | Ἡνίοχος | Διονυσίαρχος | Πολυοῦχος |
| Ζευξίμαχος | Πάνταχος | Ἀξίοχος | Ἱστίαρχος | Ἥσυχος |
| Ποίμαχος | Ἔλεγχος | Μητίοχος | Πυτίαρχος | Εὐβήσυχος |
| Ἐπίμαχος | Ἦχος | Ἀντίοχος | Νίκαρχος | Καλάτυχος |
| Θηρίμαχος | Στρόμβιχος | Ἀγέλοχος | Λεύκαρχος | Καλλίτυχος |
| Δωρίμαχος | Φείδιχος | Ἀρχέλοχος | Κάλαρχος | Ἐπίτυχος |
| Θηβασίμαχος | Πάλλιχος | Δαΐλοχος | Ὕλαρχος | Καλότυχος |
| Νικασίμαχος | Πέλλιχος | Ἀγίλοχος | Φίλαρχος | Ὡρότυχος |
| Τλασίμαχος | Ἀπέλλιχος | Ληΐλοχος | Βούλαρχος | Εὔτυχος |
| Μνασίμαχος | Πόλλιχος | Δεξίλοχος | Φύλαρχος | Ἀστώχος |
| Πασίμαχος | Βόλιχος | Ἀλεξίλοχος | Δάμαρχος | Μόψος |
| Ἀγησίμαχος | Δόλιχος | Μνασίλοχος | Μάμαρχος | Δόρωψος |
| Τεισίμαχος | Πτόλιχος | Ἀγησίλοχος | Πολέμαρχος | Ἄψψος |
| Ναυσίμαχος | Σύλιχος | Κρατησίλοχος | Δήμαρχος | Πατρῶος |
| Παυσίμαχος | Δάμιχος | Θερσίλοχος | Ποίμαρχος | Λίβυς |
| Λυσίμαχος | Λάμιχος | Ναυσίλοχος | Τίμαρχος | Σεάμβυς |
| Σωσίμαχος | Σίμιχος | Λυσίλοχος | Ὀνόμαρχος | Ἄγυς |
| Ἀντίμαχος | Ἰσμήνιχος | Σωσίλοχος | Ἔρμαρχος | Ἡδύς |
| Ἀμφίμαχος | Αἴνιχος | Ἀντίλοχος | Κώμαρχος | Ϝεῖδυς |
| Ἀγχίμαχος | Οἴνιχος | Ἀμφίλοχος | Μέναρχος | Φειδῦς |
| Πάμμαχος | Τύννιχος | Ἀρχίλοχος | Ξέναρχος | Ἐλπιδῦς |
| Σύμμαχος | Φρύνιχος | Νικόλοχος | Δείναρχος | Κλεολαεύς |
| Κλεόμαχος | Θεώνιχος | Τιμόλοχος | Σύναρχος | Ἀγεύς |
| Γαιόμαχος | Οἰώνιχος | Δεινόλοχος | Τέχναρχος | Σφογγεύς |
| Διόμαχος | Φιλώνιχος | Ἱππόλοχος | Ἔξαρχος | Φηγεύς |
| Νικόμαχος | Ἀσκλάπιχος | Ἀνδρόλοχος | Ἀλέξαρχος | Αἰγεύς |
| Φιλόμαχος | Λάμπιχος | Πρόλοχος | Πρόαρχος | Σαργεύς |
| Δαμόμαχος | Ὀλύμπιχος | Πυρρόλοχος | Ἵππαρχος | Σιργεύς |
| Τιμόμαχος | Ἵππιχος | Ἀριστόλοχος | Ἱέραρχος | Ἰκαδεύς |
| Μενόμαχος | Τυνδάριχος | Αὐτόλοχος | Ἀγάσαρχος | Ϝινναδεύς |
| Κληνόμαχος | Θεάριχος | Εὐρύλοχος | Τιμάσαρχος | Ἐπιτάδευς |
| Δεινόμαχος | Φάριχος | Θρασύλοχος | Μνάσαρχος | Βιδεύς |
| Κλεινόμαχος | Εὐμάριχος | Θορσύλοχος | Πάσαρχος | Χαλκιδεύς |
| Μιμνόμαχος | Ὕβριχος | Ἄνοχος | Τελέσαρχος | Τυδεύς |
| Ἀμυννόμαχος | Τεισάνδριχος | Ἔποχος | Ἀγήσαρχος | Κρηθεύς |
| Ἱππόμαχος | Σωτήριχος | Ὑπέροχος | Κλήσαρχος | Ἀνθεύς |
| Ἀνδρόμαχος | Ἑταίριχος | Ἄντοχος | Ἴσαρχος | Ὀλονθεύς |
| Θηρόμαχος | Μοίριχος | Εὔοχος | Πείσαρχος | Ὀλυνθεύς |
| Ἱρόμαχος | Πύρριχος | Μύοχος | Τείσαρχος | Μενεσθεύς |
| Κοιρόμαχος | Βότριχος | Ἀστύοχος | Σώσαρχος | Ἀγιεύς |

| | | | | |
|---|---|---|---|---|
| Αἰγιεύς | Ἀρχεύς | Μελάνδρυς | Γοργώ | Φιλώ |
| Λαμιεύς | Σωχεύς | Καλόδρυς | Ἀνθηδώ | Θαλλώ |
| Ἀριεύς | Βάθυς | Γῆρυς | Βιδώ | Καλλώ |
| Δωριεύς | Τῆθυς | Κορύς | Ἀγιδώ | Τελλώ |
| Λυγκεύς | Βίθυς | Φόρυς | Φειδώ | Φιλλώ |
| Ἁλικεύς | Πείθυς | Βότρυς | Νικιδώ | Ὁμολώ |
| Νικεύς | Ῥαδάμανθυς | Ἔπαφρῦς | Ἀλκιδώ | Ἀδυλώ |
| Δορκεύς | Εὔθυς | Θράσυς | Γλαυκιδώ | Δαμώ |
| Μυρκεύς | Νικῦς | Χέρσυς | Ἀλφησιδώ | Καμώ |
| Σωκεύς | Κοκκύς | Δερκέτυς | Σωτιδώ | Ἀγεμώ |
| Αἰγιαλεύς | Βῶκυς | Μίτυς | Ἀρχιδώ | Ἀνθεμώ |
| Καλεύς | Ἄλυς | Φίλτυς | Ἀφροδώ | Πολεμώ |
| Νειλεύς | Θῆλυς | Κότυς | Θεώ | Ἀρτεμώ |
| Ὁμιλεύς | Τῆλυς | Μάρτυς | Κλεώ | Δημώ |
| Βασιλεύς | Φίλυς | Ἄριστυς | Νεώ | Ὀβριμώ |
| Φιλεύς | Μιραλλύς | Ἀπφῦς | Βραζώ | Τιμώ |
| Τελλεύς | Ἀγέλλυς | Γᾶχυς | Ἐπαγαθώ | Ἀντιμώ |
| Ἀχιλλεύς | Τέλλυς | Στάχυς | Πλαθώ | Παρμώ |
| Εὐβολλεύς | Φίλλυς | Βρόχυς | Μυρθώ | Ἀγανώ |
| Φυλλεύς | Πόλλυς | Βῶχυς | Πιτθώ | Θεανώ |
| Συλεύς | Πόλυς | Γόργως | Ἰώ | Κλεανώ |
| Φυλεύς | Μῦς | Ἀλέως | Δικαιώ | Ἀθανώ |
| Μαμεύς | Δᾶμυς | Φειδίλεως | Βιώ | Τλανώ |
| Νομεύς | Γένυς | Χείλεως | Κλειώ | Ἀγνώ |
| Δρομεύς | Ξένυς | Χαρίλεως | Δαζιώ | Ξενώ |
| Καλανεύς | Κραῖνυς | Χαιρησίλεως | Δηλιώ | Κραινώ |
| Οἰνεύς | Δεινῦς | Νικόλεως | Τιλιώ | Φαινώ |
| Φοινεύς | Ξέννυς | Φιλολέως | Καλλιώ | Δεινώ |
| Σθεννεύς | Ἄρχιννυς | Γέλως | Κληνιώ | Κλεινώ |
| Ἠϊονεύς | Διονῦς | Ἀπολλώς | Πραξιώ | Σελινώ |
| Ὀφιονεύς | Ἄλεξυς | Ἔρως | Βοιώ | Καλλινώ |
| Ἀγεμονεύς | Βοῦς | Παιδέρως | Ὀλυμπιώ | Κρινώ |
| Κονωνεύς | Χρησιλεοῦς | Πειθέρως | Ἀριώ | Ἀννώ |
| Αὐσωνεύς | Ἀλκάθους | Νικέρως | Ἐλευθεριώ | Ναννώ |
| Βαναξεύς | Ἀπολλοῦς | Φιλέρως | Λαμηριώ | Μεννώ |
| Δεξεύς | Κατάπλους | Ἑρμέρως | Εὐποσιώ | Ξεννώ |
| Ἀλεξεύς | Εὔπλους | Πανέρως | Λυσιώ | Κλεοννώ |
| Ἀρεύς | Δαμοῦς | Συνέρως | Ματιώ | Κονώ |
| Τυνδαρεύς | Ἀρχένους | Λυσέρως | Μυρτιώ | Ἀναξώ |
| Νεκταρεύς | Εἰρηνοῦς | Χρυσέρως | Χιώ | Ἀλεξώ |
| Σκελεβρεύς | Ἀλκίνους | Ἀντέρως | Βακχιώ | Ἐλιξώ |
| Ἀνδρεύς | Θερσίνους | Νυμφέρως | Λακώ | Φιλιξώ |
| Νηρεύς | Ἀντίνους | Νηρως | Ἡρακώ | Νιξώ |
| Τηρεύς | Ἀμφίνους | Μελίχρως | Θευτακώ | Ζευξώ |
| Πατρεύς | Μεγιστόνους | Σῶς | Θραϊκώ | Ἀσκληπώ |
| Δωρεύς | Ἀριστόνους | Τυχώς | Φιλικώ | Ἱππώ |
| Θησεύς | Εὔνους | Ἰωσήφ | Καλλικώ | Ἀλυπώ |
| Περσεύς | Εὐθύνους | Ἰμύλχ | Νικώ | Κλεαρώ |
| Ὀδυσσεύς | Εὐρύνους | Θίοψ | Πανικώ | Ὑγιαρώ |
| Σαμβατεύς | Ἀρτίπους | Αἰθίοψ | Ἰθμονικώ | Νικαρώ |
| Λακρατεύς | Μελάμπους | Πέλοψ | Χαρικώ | Ἱλαρώ |
| Μελητεύς | Ἀγαθόπους | Χάροψ | Δικκώ | Δαμαρώ |
| Μιλτεύς | Νικαροῦς | Μέροψ | Κικκώ | Μενναρώ |
| Παντεύς | Μελίχρους | Δεινόροψ | Φιλισκώ | Λυσαρώ |
| Λεοντεύς | Εὔχρους | Κίνυψ | Ὑκώ | Κλειταρώ |
| Κοντεύς | Κάπυς | Θάρυψ | Παρδαλώ | Ἱερώ |
| Καλιστεύς | Ἵππυς | Κώνωψ | Βυβλώ | Εὐαμερώ |
| Ἀριστεύς | Καρπῦς | Λαώ | Ἐκκελώ | Ἡμερώ |
| Φωτεύς | Ἴαρυς | Τιτταβώ | Ὀκκελώ | Ματερώ |
| Ἐλαφεύς | Θράρυς | Ἀγώ | Γοργιλώ | Πατερώ |
| Ὀρφεύς | Ἄνδρυς | Μεγώ | Ἀμμιλώ | Ἡρώ |

| | | | | |
|---|---|---|---|---|
| Σωτηρώ | Τιμασώ | Πατώ | Φαντώ | Κλυτώ |
| Ϝατορώ | Μνασώ | Ἐρατώ | Φιλοφαντώ | Δωτώ |
| Πατρώ | Ὀνασώ | Καλικρατώ | Περφαντώ | Βιωτώ |
| Βοστρώ | Ἀναστασώ | Στρατώ | Φιντώ | Χρωτώ |
| Μυρώ | Ἀγησώ | Τατώ | Βαρτώ | Σωτώ |
| Ζωπυρώ | Νικησώ | Ἀρετώ | Μυρτώ | Χλευώ |
| Σατυρώ | Αἰνησώ | Λητώ | Ἀστώ | Ἐννώ |
| Ἀφρώ | Κρατησώ | Ἀφροδιτώ | Δαστώ | Μυρτιφώ |
| Ἐπαφρώ | Σαισώ | Κλειτώ | Μεγιστώ | Συμφώ |
| Εὔφρώ | Πεισώ | Βοιτώ | Φειδιστώ | Σαπφώ |
| Ἡδυχρώ | Κλινοσώ | Λαμπιτώ | Πλειστώ | Καλλιμορφώ |
| Δωρώ | Θερσώ | Χαριτώ | Φιλιστώ | Ἀρχώ |
| Ἀγασώ | Κισσώ | Τριτώ | Καλλιστώ | Εὐτυχώ |
| Νικασώ | Λυσώ | Ἐπικτώ | Θεμιστώ | |
| Μυλασώ | Σωσώ | Παντώ | Ἀριστώ | |